Stanley Gibbo
SIMPLIFIED CATALOGUE

Stamps of the World

2007 Edition

IN COLOUR

An illustrated and priced four-volume guide to the postage stamps of the whole world, excluding changes of paper, perforation, shade and watermark

VOLUME 4

COUNTRIES N–R

STANLEY GIBBONS LTD
London and Ringwood

By Appointment to
Her Majesty the Queen
Stanley Gibbons Limited
London
Philatelists

72nd Edition

Published in Great Britain by
Stanley Gibbons Ltd
Publications Editorial, Sales Offices and Distribution Centre
Parkside, Christchurch Road,
Ringwood, Hampshire BH24 3SH
Telephone 01425 472363

ISBN: 085259-633-2

Published as Stanley Gibbons Simplified Stamp Catalogue from 1934 to 1970, renamed Stamps of the World in 1971, and produced in two (1982-88), three (1989-2001), four (2002-2005) or five (from 2006) volumes as Stanley Gibbons Simplified Catalogue of Stamps of the World. This volume published October 2006

S.G. Item No. 2884 (07)

Printed in Great Britain by CPI Bath Press, Somerset

Stanley Gibbons
SIMPLIFIED CATALOGUE
Stamps of the **World**

This popular catalogue is a straightforward listing of the stamps that have been issued everywhere in the world since the very first–Great Britain's famous Penny Black in 1840.

This edition, in which both the text and the illustrations have been captured electronically, is arranged completely alphabetically in a five-volume format. Volume 1 (Countries A–C), Volume 2 (Countries D–H), Volume 3 (Countries I–M), Volume 4 (Countries N–R) and Volume 5 (Countries S-Z).

Readers are reminded that the Catalogue Supplements, published in each issue of **Gibbons Stamp Monthly**, can be used to update the listings in **Stamps of the World** as well as our 22-part standard catalogue. To make the supplement even more useful the Type numbers given to the illustrations are the same in the Stamps of the World as in the standard catalogues. The first Catalogue Supplement to this Volume appeared in the September 2006 issue of **Gibbons Stamp Monthly**.

Gibbons Stamp Monthly can be obtained through newsagents or on postal subscription from Stanley Gibbons Publications, Parkside, Christchurch Road, Ringwood, Hants BH24 3SH.

The catalogue has many important features:

- The vast majority of illustrations are now in full colour to aid stamp identification.
- All Commonwealth and all Europe, America and Asia miniature sheets are now included.
- As an indication of current values virtually every stamp is priced. Thousands of alterations have been made since the last edition.
- By being set out on a simplified basis that excludes changes of paper, perforation, shade, watermark, gum or printer's and date imprints it is particularly easy to use. (For its exact scope see "Information for users" pages following.)
- The thousands of colour illustrations and helpful descriptions of stamp designs make it of maximum appeal to collectors with thematic interests.
- Its catalogue numbers are the world-recognised Stanley Gibbons numbers throughout.
- Helpful introductory notes for the collector are included, backed by much historical, geographical and currency information.
- A very detailed index gives instant location of countries in this volume, and a cross-reference to those included in the other volumes.

Over 1,900 stamps and miniature sheets and 500 new illustrations have been added to the listings in this volume.

The listings in this edition are based on the standard catalogues: Part 1, Commonwealth & British Empire Stamps 1840–1952, Part 2 (Austria & Hungary) (6th edition), Part 3 (Balkans) (4th edition), Part 4 (Benelux) (5th edition), Part 5 (Czechoslovakia & Poland) (6th edition), Part 6 (France) (6th edition), Part 7 (Germany) (7th edition), Part 8 (Italy & Switzerland) (6th edition), Part 9 (Portugal & Spain) (5th edition), Part 10 (Russia) (5th edition), Part 11 (Scandinavia) (5th edition), Part 12 (Africa since Independence A-E) (2nd edition), Part 13 (Africa since Independence F-M) (1st edition), Part 14 (Africa since Independence N-Z) (1st edition), Part 15 (Central America) (2nd edition), Part 16 (Central Asia) (4th edition), Part 17 (China) (6th edition), Part 18 (Japan & Korea) (4th edition), Part 19 (Middle East) (6th edition), Part 20 (South America) (3rd edition), Part 21 (South-East Asia) (4th edition) and Part 22 (United States) (5th edition).

This edition includes major repricing for France Part 6 and United States Part 22.

Acknowledgements

A wide-ranging revision of prices for European countries has been undertaken for this edition with the intention that the catalogue should be more accurate to reflect the market for foreign issues.

Many dealers in both Great Britain and overseas have participated in this scheme by supplying copies of their retail price lists on which the research has been based.

We would like to acknowledge the assistance of the following for this edition:

J BAREFOOT LTD
of York, England

Sir CHARLES BLOMEFIELD
of Chipping Camden, England

T. BRAY
of Shipley, West Yorks, England

HOLMGREN STAMPS
of Bollnas, Sweden

INDIGO
of Orewa, New Zealand

ALEC JACQUES
of Selby, England

D.J.M. KERR
of Earlston, England

MICHAEL ROGERS INC
of Winter Park, U.S.A.

NORAYR AGOPIAN
of Lymassol, Cyprus

PHIL-INDEX
of Eastbourne, England

ROBSTINE STAMPS
of Hampshire, England

ROWAN S BAKER
of London, England

Where foreign countries have been repriced this year in Stamps of the World and where there is no up-to-date specialised foreign volume in a country these will be the new Stanley Gibbons prices.

It is hoped that this improved pricing scheme will be extended to other foreign countries and thematic issues as information is consolidated.

Information for users

Aim

The aim of this catalogue is to provide a straightforward illustrated and priced guide to the postage stamps of the whole world to help you to enjoy the greatest hobby of the present day.

Arrangement

The catalogue lists countries in alphabetical order and there is a complete index at the end of each volume. For ease of reference country names are also printed at the head of each page.

Within each country, postage stamps are listed first. They are followed by separate sections for such other categories as postage due stamps, parcel post stamps, express stamps, official stamps, etc.

All catalogue lists are set out according to dates of issue of the stamps, starting from the earliest and working through to the most recent.

Scope of the Catalogue

The *Simplified Catalogue of Stamps of the World* contains listings of postage stamps only. Apart from the ordinary definitive, commemorative and air-mail stamps of each country – which appear first in each list – there are sections for the following where appropriate:

- postage due stamps
- parcel post stamps
- official stamps
- express and special delivery stamps
- charity and compulsory tax stamps
- newspaper and journal stamps
- printed matter stamps
- registration stamps
- acknowledgement of receipt stamps
- late fee and too late stamps
- military post stamps
- recorded message stamps
- personal delivery stamps

We receive numerous enquiries from collectors about other items which do not fall within the categories set out above and which consequently do not appear in the catalogue lists. It may be helpful, therefore, to summarise the other kinds of stamp that exist but which we deliberately exclude from this postage stamp catalogue.

We do *not* list the following:

Fiscal or revenue stamps: stamps used solely in collecting taxes or fees for non-postal purposes. Examples would be stamps which pay a tax on a receipt, represent the stamp duty on a contract or frank a customs document. Common inscriptions found include: Documentary, Proprietary, Inter. Revenue, Contract Note.

Local stamps: postage stamps whose validity and use are limited in area, say to a single town or city, though in some cases they provided, with official sanction, services in parts of countries not covered by the respective government.

Local carriage labels and Private local issues: many labels exist ostensibly to cover the cost of ferrying mail from one of Great Britain's offshore islands to the nearest mainland post office. They are not recognised as valid for national or international mail. Examples: Calf of Man, Davaar, Herm, Lundy, Pabay, Stroma. Items from some other places have only the status of tourist souvenir labels.

Telegraph stamps: stamps intended solely for the prepayment of telegraphic communication.

Bogus or "phantom" stamps: labels from mythical places or non-existent administrations. Examples in the classical period were Sedang, Counani, Clipperton Island and in modern times Thomond and Monte Bello Islands. Numerous labels have also appeared since the War from dissident groups as propaganda for their claims and without authority from the home governments. Common examples are labels for "Free Albania", "Free Rumania" and "Free Croatia" and numerous issues for Nagaland, Indonesia and the South Moluccas ("Republik Maluku Selatan").

Railway letter fee stamps: special stamps issued by railway companies for the conveyance of letters by rail. Example: Talyllyn Railway. Similar services are now offered by some bus companies and the labels they issue likewise do not qualify for inclusion in the catalogue.

Perfins ("perforated initials"): numerous postage stamps may be found with initial letters or designs punctured through them by tiny holes. These are applied by private and public concerns as a precaution against theft and do not qualify for separate mention.

Information for users

Labels: innumerable items exist resembling stamps but – as they do not prepay postage – they are classified as labels. The commonest categories are:

- propaganda and publicity labels: designed to further a cause or campaign;
- exhibition labels: particularly souvenirs from philatelic events;
- testing labels: stamp-size labels used in testing stamp-vending machines;
- Post Office training school stamps: British stamps overprinted with two thick vertical bars or SCHOOL SPECIMEN are produced by the Post Office for training purposes;
- seals and stickers: numerous charities produce stamp-like labels, particularly at Christmas and Easter, as a means of raising funds and these have no postal validity.

Cut-outs: items of postal stationery, such as envelopes, cards and wrappers, often have stamps impressed or imprinted on them. They may usually be cut out and affixed to envelopes, etc., for postal use if desired, but such items are not listed in this catalogue.

Collectors wanting further information about exact definitions are referred to *Philatelic Terms Illustrated,* published by Stanley Gibbons and containing many illustrations in colour.

There is also a priced listing of the postal fiscals of Great Britain in our *Commonwealth & British Empire Stamps 1840–1952* Catalogue and in Volume 1 of the *Great Britain Specialised* Catalogue (5th and later editions).

Catalogue Numbers

Stanley Gibbons catalogue numbers are recognised universally and any individual stamp can be identified by quoting the catalogue number (the one at the left of the column) prefixed by the name of the country and the letters "S.G.". Do not confuse the catalogue number with the type numbers which refer to illustrations.

Prices

Prices in the left-hand column are for unused stamps and those in the right-hand column for used. Prices are given in pence and pounds:

100 pence (p) 1 pound (£1).

Prices are shown as follows:

10 means 10p (10 pence);
1.50 means £1.50 (1 pound and 50 pence);
For £100 and above, prices are in whole pounds.

Our prices are for stamps in fine condition, and in issues where condition varies we may ask more for the superb and less for the sub-standard.

The minimum catalogue price quoted is 10p. For individual stamps prices between 10p and 95p are provided as a guide for catalogue users. The lowest price charged for individual stamps purchased from Stanley Gibbons is £1.00.

The prices quoted are generally for the cheapest variety of stamps but it is worth noting that differences of watermark, perforation, or other details, outside the scope of this catalogue, may often increase the value of the stamp.

Prices quoted for mint issues are for single examples. Those in se-tenant pairs, strips, blocks or sheets may be worth more.

Where prices are not given in either column it is either because the stamps are not known to exist in that particular condition, or, more usually, because there is no reliable information as to value.

All prices are subject to change without prior notice and we give no guarantee to supply all stamps priced. Prices quoted for albums, publications, etc. advertised in this catalogue are also subject to change without prior notice.

Due to different production methods it is sometimes possible for new editions of Parts 2 to 22 to appear showing revised prices which are not included in that year's *Stamps of the World.*

Unused Stamps

In the case of stamps from *Great Britain* and the *Commonwealth,* prices for unused stamps of Queen Victoria to King George V are for lightly hinged examples; unused prices of King Edward VIII to Queen Elizabeth II issues are for unmounted mint. The prices of unused Foreign stamps are for lightly hinged examples for those issued before 1946, thereafter for examples unmounted mint.

Used Stamps

Prices for used stamps generally refer to fine postally used examples, though for certain issues they are for cancelled-to-order.

Information for users

Guarantee

All stamps supplied by us are guaranteed originals in the following terms:

If not as described, and returned by the purchaser, we undertake to refund the price paid to us in the original transaction. If any stamp is certified as genuine by the Expert Committee of the Royal Philatelic Society, London, or by B.P.A. Expertising Ltd., the purchaser shall not be entitled to make any claim against us for any error, omission or mistake in such certificate.

Consumers' statutory rights are not affected by the above guarantee.

Currency

At the beginning of each country brief details give the currencies in which the values of the stamps are expressed. The dates, where given, are those of the earliest stamp issues in the particular currency. Where the currency is obvious, e.g. where the colony has the same currency as the mother country, no details are given.

Illustrations

Illustrations of any surcharges and overprints which are shown and not described are actual size; stamp illustrations are reduced to $\frac{3}{4}$ linear, *unless otherwise stated.*

"Key-Types"

A number of standard designs occur so frequently in the stamps of the French, German, Portuguese and Spanish colonies that it would be a waste of space to repeat them. Instead these are all illustrated on page xiv together with the descriptive names and letters by which they are referred to in the lists.

Type Numbers

These are the bold figures found below each illustration. References to "Type **6**", for example, in the lists of a country should therefore be understood to refer to the illustration below which the number **"6"** appears. These type numbers are also given in the second column of figures alongside each list of stamps, thus indicating clearly the design of each stamp. In the case of Key-Types – see above – letters take the place of the type numbers.

Where an issue comprises stamps of similar design, represented in this catalogue by one illustration, the corresponding type numbers should be taken as indicating this general design.

Where there are blanks in the type number column it means that the type of the corresponding stamps is that shown by the last number above in the type column of the same issue.

A dash (–) in the type column means that no illustration of the stamp is shown.

Where type numbers refer to stamps of another country, e.g. where stamps of one country are overprinted for use in another, this is always made clear in the text.

Stamp Designs

Brief descriptions of the subjects of the stamp designs are given either below or beside the illustrations, at the foot of the list of the issue concerned, or in the actual lists. Where a particular subject, e.g. the portrait of a well-known monarch, recurs frequently the description is not repeated, nor are obvious designs described.

Generally, the unillustrated designs are in the same shape and size as the one illustrated, except where otherwise indicated.

Surcharges and Overprints

Surcharges and overprints are usually described in the headings to the issues concerned. Where the actual wording of a surcharge or overprint is given it is shown in bold type.

Some stamps are described as being "Surcharged in words", e.g. **TWO CENTS**, and others "Surcharged in figures and words", e.g. **20 CENTS**, although of course many surcharges are in foreign languages and combinations of words and figures are numerous. There are often bars, etc., obliterating old values or inscriptions but in general these are only mentioned where it is necessary to avoid confusion.

No attention is paid in this catalogue to colours of overprints and surcharges so that stamps with the same overprints in different colours are not listed separately.

Numbers in brackets after the descriptions of overprinted or surcharged stamps are the catalogue numbers of the unoverprinted stamps.

Note – the words "inscribed" or "inscription" always refer to wording incorporated in the design of a stamp and not surcharges or overprints.

Coloured Papers

Where stamps are printed on coloured paper the description is given as e.g. "4 c. black on blue" – a stamp printed in black on blue paper. No attention is paid in this catalogue to difference in the texture of paper, e.g. laid, wove.

Information for users

Watermarks

Stamps having different watermarks, but otherwise the same, are not listed separately. No reference is therefore made to watermarks in this volume.

Stamp Colours

Colour names are only required for the identification of stamps, therefore they have been made as simple as possible. Thus "scarlet", "vermilion", "carmine" are all usually called red. Qualifying colour names have been introduced only where necessary for the sake of clearness.

Where stamps are printed in two or more colours the central portion of the design is in the first colour given, unless otherwise stated.

Perforations

All stamps are perforated unless otherwise stated. No distinction is made between the various gauges of perforation but early stamp issues which exist both imperforate and perforated are usually listed separately.

Where a heading states "Imperf. or perf". or "Perf. or rouletted" this does not necessarily mean that all values of the issue are found in both conditions.

Dates of Issue

The date given at the head of each issue is that of the appearance of the earliest stamp in the series. As stamps of the same design or issue are usually grouped together a list of King George VI stamps, for example, headed "1938" may include stamps issued from 1938 to the end of the reign.

Se-tenant Pairs

Many modern issues are printed in sheets containing different designs or face values. Such pairs, blocks, strips or sheets are described as being "se-tenant" and they are outside the scope of this catalogue, although reference to them may occur in instances where they form a composite design.

Miniature Sheets

As an increasing number of stamps are now only found in miniature sheets, Stamps of the World will, in future, list these items. This edition lists all Commonwealth, European and Asian countries' miniature sheets, plus those of all other countries which have appeared in the catalogue supplement during the past three years. Earlier miniature sheets of non-Commonwealth countries will be listed in future editions.

"Appendix" Countries

We regret that, since 1968, it has been necessary to establish an Appendix (at the end of each country as appropriate) to which numerous stamps have had to be consigned. Several countries imagine that by issuing huge quantities of unnecessary stamps they will have a ready source of income from stamp collectors – and particularly from the less-experienced ones. Stanley Gibbons refuse to encourage this exploitation of the hobby and we do not stock the stamps concerned.

Two kinds of stamp are therefore given the briefest of mentions in the Appendix, purely for the sake of record. Administrations issuing stamps greatly in excess of true postal needs have the offending issues placed there. Likewise it contains stamps which have not fulfilled all the normal conditions for full catalogue listing.

These conditions are that the stamps must be issued by a legitimate postal authority, recognised by the government concerned, and are adhesives, valid for proper postal use in the class of service for which they are inscribed. Stamps, with the exception of such categories as postage dues and officials, must be available to the general public at face value with no artificial restrictions being imposed on their distribution.

The publishers of this catalogue have observed, with concern, the proliferation of 'artificial' stamp-issuing territories. On several occasions this has resulted in separately inscribed issues for various component parts of otherwise united states or territories.

Stanley Gibbons Publications have decided that where such circumstances occur, they will not, in the future, list these items in the SG catalogue without first satisfying themselves that the stamps represent a genuine political, historical or postal division within the country concerned. Any such issues which do not fulfil this stipulation will be recorded in the Catalogue Appendix only.

Stamps in the Appendix are kept under review in the light of any newly acquired information about them. If we are satisfied that a stamp qualifies for proper listing in the body of the catalogue it is moved there.

Information for users

"Undesirable Issues"

The rules governing many competitive exhibitions are set by the Federation Internationale de Philatelie and stipulate a downgrading of marks for stamps classed as "undesirable issues".

This catalogue can be taken as a guide to status. All stamps in the main listings and Addenda are acceptable. Stamps in the Appendix should not be entered for competition as these are the "undesirable issues".

Particular care is advised with Aden Protectorate States, Ajman, Bhutan, Chad, Fujeira, Khor Fakkan, Manama, Ras al Khaima, Sharjah, Umm al Qiwain and Yemen. Totally bogus stamps exist (as explained in Appendix notes) and these are to be avoided also for competition. As distinct from "undesirable stamps" certain categories are not covered in this catalogue purely by reason of its scope (see page viii). Consult the particular competition rules to see if such are admissable even though not listed by us.

Where to Look for More Detailed Listings

The present work deliberately omits details of paper, perforation, shade and watermark. But as you become more absorbed in stamp collecting and wish to get greater enjoyment from the hobby you may well want to study these matters.

All the information you require about any particular postage stamp will be found in the main Stanley Gibbons Catalogues.

Commonwealth countries before 1952 are covered by the Commonwealth & British Empire Stamps 1840–1952 published annually. Post-1952 Commonwealth Stamps are listed in the growing range of Commonwealth Country Catalogues.

For foreign countries you can easily find which catalogue to consult by looking at the country headings in the present book.

To the right of each country name are code letters specifying which volume of our main catalogues contains that country's listing.

The code letters are as follows:

Pt. 2 Part 2

Pt. 3 Part 3 etc.

(See page xiii for complete list of Parts.)

So, for example, if you want to know more about Chinese stamps than is contained in the *Simplified Catalogue of Stamps of the World* the reference to

CHINA Pt. 17

guides you to the Gibbons Part 17 *(China)* Catalogue listing for the details you require.

New editions of Parts 2 to 22 appear at irregular intervals.

Correspondence

Whilst we welcome information and suggestions we must ask correspondents to include the cost of postage for the return of any stamps submitted plus registration where appropriate. Letters should be addressed to The Catalogue Editor at Ringwood.

Where information is solicited purely for the benefit of the enquirer we regret we cannot undertake to reply.

Identification of Stamps

We regret we do not give opinions as to the genuineness of stamps, nor do we identify stamps or number them by our Catalogue.

Users of this catalogue are referred to our companion booklet entitled *Stamp Collecting – How to Identify Stamps.* It explains how to look up stamps in this catalogue, contains a full checklist of stamp inscriptions and gives help in dealing with unfamiliar scripts.

Stanley Gibbons would like to complement your collection

At Stanley Gibbons we offer a range of services which are designed to complement your collection.

Our modern stamp shop, the largest in Europe, together with our rare stamp department has one of the most comprehensive stocks of Great Britain in the world, so whether you are a beginner or an experienced philatelist you are certain to find something to suit your special requirements.

Alternatively, through our Mail Order services you can control the growth of your collection from the comfort of your own home. Our Postal Sales Department regularly sends out mailings of Special Offers. We can also help with your wants list—so why not ask us for those elusive items?

Why not take advantage of the many services we have to offer? Visit our premises in the Strand or, for more information, write to the appropriate address on page x.

The Stanley Gibbons Group Addresses

Stanley Gibbons Limited,
Stanley Gibbons Auctions

399 Strand, London WC2R 0LX
Telephone 020 7836 8444, Fax 020 7836 7342,
E-mail: enquiries@stanleygibbons.co.uk
Website: www.stanleygibbons.com for all departments.

Auction Room and Specialist Stamp Departments.
Open Monday–Friday 9.30 a.m. to 5 p.m.

Shop. Open Monday–Friday 9 a.m. to 5.30 p.m. and Saturday 9.30 a.m. to 5.30 p.m.

Stanley Gibbons Publications

Parkside, Christchurch Road, Ringwood, Hants BH24 3SH.
Telephone 01425 472363 (24 hour answer phone service), Fax 01425 470247,
E-mail: info@stanleygibbons.co.uk
Website: www.stanleygibbons.com

Publications Mail Order. FREEPHONE 0800 611622
Monday–Friday 8.30 a.m. to 5 p.m.

Fraser's Autographs, photographs, letters, documents

399 Strand, London WC2R 0LX
Autographs, photographs, letters and documents

Telephone 020 7836 8444, Fax 020 7836 7342,
E-mail: info@frasersautographs.co.uk
Website: www.frasersautographs.com

Monday–Friday 9 a.m. to 5.30 p.m. and Saturday 10 a.m. to 4 p.m.

Stanley Gibbons Publications Overseas Representation

Stanley Gibbons Publications are represented overseas by the following sole distributors (*) or licensees (**).

Australia*
Lighthouse Philatelic (Aust.) Pty. Ltd.
Locked Bag 5900 Botany DC, New South Wales, 2019 Australia.

Stanley Gibbons (Australia) Pty. Ltd.**
Level 6, 36 Clarence Street, Sydney, New South Wales 2000, Australia.

Belgium and Luxembourg*
Davo c/o Philac, Rue du Midi 48, Bruxelles, 1000 Belgium.

Canada*
Unitrade, 99 Floral Parkway,
Toronto, Ontario,
Canada M6L 2C4.

Denmark*
Samlerforum/Davo,
Ostergade 3,
DK 7470 Karup, Denmark.

Finland*
Davo c/o Kapylan Merkkiky Pohjolankatu 1
00610 Helsinki, Finland.

France*
Davo France (Casteilla), 10, Rue Leon Foucault, 78184 St. Quentin Yvelines Cesex, France.

Hong Kong*
Po-on Stamp Service, GPO Box 2498, Hong Kong.

Israel*
Capital Stamps, P.O. Box 3769, Jerusalem 91036, Israel.

Italy*
Ernesto Marini Srl,
Via Struppa 300, I-16165,
Genova GE, Italy.

Japan*
Japan Philatelic Co. Ltd.,
P.O. Box 2, Suginami-Minami, Tokyo, Japan.

Netherlands*
Davo Publications, P.O. Box 411, 7400 AK Deventer, Netherlands.

New Zealand**
Mowbray Collectables.
P.O. Box 80, Wellington, New Zealand.

Norway*
Davo Norge A/S, P.O. Box 738 Sentrum, N-0105, Oslo, Norway.

Saudi Arabia*
Arabian Stamps Centre,
P.O. Box 54645, Riyadh 11524,
Saudi Arabia.

Singapore*
Stamp Inc Collectibles Pte Ltd.,
10 Ubi Cresent, #01-43 Ubi Tech Park,
Singapore 408564.

Sweden*
Chr Winther Soerensen AB, Box 43,
S-310 Knaered, Sweden.

U.S.A.*
Filatco Inc
P.O. Box 520 McLean
VA22101-0520
U.S.A.

Abbreviations

Anniv.	denotes	Anniversary
Assn.	,,	Association
Bis.	,,	Bistre
Bl.	,,	Blue
Bldg.	,,	Building
Blk.	,,	Black
Br.	,,	British or Bridge
Brn.	,,	Brown
B.W.I.	,,	British West Indies
C.A.R.I.F.T.A.	,,	Caribbean Free Trade Area
Cent.	,,	Centenary
Chest.	,,	Chestnut
Choc.	,,	Chocolate
Clar.	,,	Claret
Coll.	,,	College
Commem.	,,	Commemoration
Conf.	,,	Conference
Diag.	,,	Diagonally
E.C.A.F.E.	,,	Economic Commission for Asia and Far East
Emer.	,,	Emerald
E.P.T. Conference	,,	European Postal and Telecommunications Conference
Exn.		Exhibition
F.A.O.	,,	Food and Agriculture Organization
Fig.	,,	Figure
G.A.T.T.	,,	General Agreement on Tariffs and Trade
G.B.	,,	Great Britain
Gen.	,,	General
Govt.	,,	Government
Grn.	,,	Green
Horiz.	,,	Horizontal
H.Q.	,,	Headquarters
Imperf.	,,	Imperforate
Inaug.	,,	Inauguration
Ind.	,,	Indigo
Inscr.	,,	Inscribed or inscription
Int.	,,	International
I.A.T.A.	,,	International Air Transport Association
I.C.A.O.	,,	International Civil Aviation Organization
I.C.Y.	,,	International Co-operation Year
I.G.Y.	,,	International Geophysical Year
I.L.O.	,,	International Labour Office (or later, Organization)
I.M.C.O.	,,	Inter-Governmental Maritime Consultative Organization
I.T.U.	,,	International Telecommunication Union
Is.	,,	Islands
Lav.	,,	Lavender
Mar.	,,	Maroon
mm.	,,	Millimetres
Mult.	,,	Multicoloured
Mve.	denotes	Mauve
Nat.	,,	National
N.A.T.O.	,,	North Atlantic Treaty Organization
O.D.E.C.A.	,,	Organization of Central American States
Ol.	,,	Olive
Optd.	,,	Overprinted
Orge. or oran.	,,	Orange
P.A.T.A.	,,	Pacific Area Travel Association
Perf.	,,	Perforated
Post.	,,	Postage
Pres.	,,	President
P.U.	,,	Postal Union
Pur.	,,	Purple
R.	,,	River
R.S.A.	,,	Republic of South Africa
Roul.	,,	Rouletted
Sep.	,,	Sepia
S.E.A.T.O.	,,	South East Asia Treaty Organization
Surch.	,,	Surcharged
T.	,,	Type
T.U.C.	,,	Trades Union Congress
Turq.	,,	Turquoise
Ultram.	,,	Ultramarine
U.N.E.S.C.O.	,,	United Nations Educational, Scientific Cultural Organization
U.N.I.C.E.F.	,,	United Nations Children's Fund
U.N.O.	,,	United Nations Organization
U.N.R.W.A.	,,	United Nations Relief and Works Agency for Palestine Refugees in the Near East
U.N.T.E.A.	,,	United Nations Temporary Executive Authority
U.N.R.R.A.	,,	United Nations Relief and Rehabilitation Administration
U.P.U.	,,	Universal Postal Union
Verm.	,,	Vermilion
Vert.	,,	Vertical
Vio.	,,	Violet
W.F.T.U.	,,	World Federation of Trade Unions
W.H.O.	,,	World Health Organization
Yell.	,,	Yellow

Arabic Numerals

As in the case of European figures, the details of the Arabic numerals vary in different stamp designs, but they should be readily recognised with the aid of this illustration:

٠	١	٢	٣	٤
0	1	2	3	4
٥	٦	٧	٨	٩
5	6	7	8	9

Stanley Gibbons Stamp Catalogue
Complete List of Parts

1 Commonwealth & British Empire Stamps 1840–1952 (Annual)

Foreign Countries

2 Austria & Hungary (6th edition, 2002)
Austria · U.N. (Vienna) · Hungary

3 Balkans (4th edition, 1998)
Albania · Bosnia & Herzegovina · Bulgaria · Croatia · Greece & Islands · Macedonia · Rumania · Slovenia · Yugoslavia

4 Benelux (5th edition, 2003)
Belgium & Colonies · Luxembourg · Netherlands & Colonies

5 Czechoslovakia & Poland (6th edition, 2002)
Czechoslovakia · Czech Republic · Slovakia · Poland

6 France (6th edition, 2006)
France · Colonies · Post Offices · Andorra · Monaco

7 Germany (7th edition, 2005)
Germany · States · Colonies · Post Offices

8 Italy & Switzerland (6th edition, 2003)
Italy & Colonies · Liechtenstein · San Marino · Switzerland · U.N. (Geneva) · Vatican City

9 Portugal & Spain (5th edition, 2004)
Andorra · Portugal & Colonies · Spain & Colonies

10 Russia (5th edition, 1999)
Russia · Armenia · Azerbaijan · Belarus · Estonia · Georgia · Kazakhstan · Kyrgyzstan · Latvia · Lithuania · Moldova · Tajikistan · Turkmenistan · Ukraine · Uzbekistan · Mongolia

11 Scandinavia (5th edition, 2001)
Aland Islands · Denmark · Faroe Islands · Finland · Greenland · Iceland · Norway · Sweden

12 Africa since Independence A-E (2nd edition, 1983)
Algeria · Angola · Benin · Burundi · Cameroun · Cape Verdi · Central African Republic · Chad · Comoro Islands · Congo · Djibouti · Equatorial Guinea · Ethiopia

13 Africa since Independence F-M (1st edition, 1981)
Gabon · Guinea · Guinea-Bissau · Ivory Coast · Liberia · Libya · Malagasy Republic · Mali · Mauritania · Morocco · Mozambique

14 Africa since Independence N-Z (1st edition, 1981)
Niger Republic · Rwanda · St. Thomas & Prince · Senegal · Somalia · Sudan · Togo · Tunisia · Upper Volta · Zaire

15 Central America (2nd edition, 1984)
Costa Rica · Cuba · Dominican Republic · El Salvador · Guatemala · Haiti · Honduras · Mexico · Nicaragua · Panama

16 Central Asia (4th edition, 2006)
Afghanistan · Iran · Turkey

17 China (6th edition,1998)
China · Taiwan · Tibet · Foreign P.O.s · Hong Kong · Macao

18 Japan & Korea (4th edition, 1997)
Japan · Korean Empire · South Korea · North Korea

19 Middle East (6th edition, 2005)
Bahrain · Egypt · Iraq · Israel · Jordan · Kuwait · Lebanon · Oman · Qatar · Saudi Arabia · Syria · U.A.E. · Yemen

20 South America (3rd edition, 1989)
Argentina · Bolivia · Brazil · Chile · Colombia · Ecuador · Paraguay · Peru · Surinam · Uruguay · Venezuela

21 South-East Asia (4th edition, 2004)
Bhutan · Burma · Indonesia · Kampuchea · Laos · Nepal · Philippines · Thailand · Vietnam

22 United States (6th edition, 2005)
U.S. & Possessions · Marshall Islands · Micronesia · Palau · U.N. (New York, Geneva, Vienna)

Thematic Catalogues

Stanley Gibbons Catalogues for use with **Stamps of the World.**
Collect Aircraft on Stamps (out of print)
Collect Birds on Stamps (5th edition, 2003)
Collect Chess on Stamps (2nd edition, 1999)
Collect Fish on Stamps (1st edition, 1999)
Collect Fungi on Stamps (2nd edition, 1997)
Collect Motor Vehicles on Stamps (1st edition, 2004)
Collect Railways on Stamps (3rd edition, 1999)
Collect Ships on Stamps (3rd edition, 2001)

Key-Types

(see note on page vii)

French Group

A. "Blanc."

B. "Mouchon."

C "Merson."

D. "Tablet."

E.

F.

G.

H.

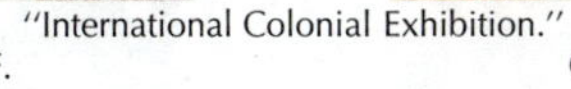
"International Colonial Exhibition."

I. "Faidherbe."

J. "Palms."

K. "Balay."

L. "Natives."

M. "Figure."

German Group

N. "Yacht."

O. "Yacht."

Spanish Group

X. "Alfonso XII."

Y. "Baby."

Z. "Curly Head"

Portuguese Group

P. "Crown."

Q. "Embossed."

R. "Figures."

S. "Carlos."

T. "Manoel."

U. "Ceres."

V. "Newspaper."

W. "Due."

STANLEY GIBBONS SIMPLIFIED CATALOGUE OF STAMPS OF THE WORLD—VOLUME 4 COUNTRIES N–R

NABHA Pt. 1

A "Convention" state in the Punjab, India.

12 pies = 1 anna; 16 annas = 1 rupee.
Stamps of India optd **NABHA STATE.**

1885. Queen Victoria. Vert opt.
1 **23** ½a. turquoise . . . . 3·75 5·00
2 – 1a. purple . . . . 48·00 £170
3 – 2a. blue . . . . 20·00 55·00
4 – 4a. green (No. 96) . . . . 80·00 £200
5 – 8a. mauve £325
6 – 1r. grey (No. 79) £350

1885. Queen Victoria. Horiz opt.
36 **40** 3p. red 50 20
14 **23** ½a. turquoise 30 10
15 – 9p. red . . . . £175 3·25
17 – 1a. purple . . . . 2·25 90
18 – 1a.6p. brown . . . . 1·50 3·50
20 – 2a. blue . . . . 2·50 1·75
22 – 3a. orange . . . . 3·50 2·00
12 – 4a. green (No. 69) . . . . 38·00 £190
24 – 4a. green (No. 96) . . . . 5·50 2·25
26 – 6a. brown (No. 80) . . . . 3·25 3·50
27 – 8a. mauve . . . . 3·00 4·50
28 – 12a. purple on red . . . . 4·00 4·50
29 – 1r. grey (No. 101) . . . . 13·00 50·00
30 **37** 1r. green and red . . . . 12·00 5·50
31 **38** 2r. red and orange £130 £275
32 3r. brown and green £130 £350
33 5r. blue and violet £130 £475

1903. King Edward VII.
37 3p. grey 75 15
38 ½a. green (No. 122) . . . . 1·10 60
39 1a. red (No. 123) . . . . . 1·60 1·00
40a 2a. lilac . . . . 3·00 35
40b 2½a. blue . . . . 19·00 90·00
41 3a. orange . . . . 1·25 40
42 4a. olive . . . . 3·75 1·75
43 6a. bistre . . . . 3·25 17·00
44 8a. mauve . . . . 9·50 23·00
45 12a. purple on red . . . . 4·00 24·00
46 1r. green and red . . . . . 9·00 16·00

1907. As last, but inscr "INDIA POSTAGE & REVENUE".
47 ½a. green (No. 149) . . . . . 1·50 1·25
48 1a. red (No. 150) . . . . . . 1·25 70

1913. King George V. Optd in two lines.
49a **55** 3p. grey 25 35
50 **56** ½a. green 35 15
51 **57** 1a. red . . . . 1·25 10
59 1a. brown . . . . 5·50 3·00
52 **59** 2a. lilac 80 80
53 **62** 3a. orange 50 35
54 **63** 4a. olive . . . . 65 1·60
55 **64** 6a. bistre . . . . 1·00 5·50
56a **65** 8a. mauve . . . . 4·50 4·75
57 **66** 12a. red . . . . 2·25 22·00
58 **67** 1r. brown and green . . . 9·00 6·00

1928. King George V. Optd in one line.
60 **55** 3p. grey . . . . 1·75 15
61 **56** ½a. green 80 20
73 **79** ½a. green 50 40
61a **80** 9p. green . . . . 11·00 11·00
62 **57** 1a. brown . . . . 1·50 15
74 **81** 1a. brown 50 30
63 **82** 1¼a. mauve . . . . 2·25 6·50
64 **70** 2a. lilac . . . . 2·50 35
65 **61** 2½a. orange . . . . 1·00 8·50
66 **62** 3a. blue . . . . 2·75 1·40
75 **57** 3a. red . . . . 4·00 15·00
76 **63** 4a. olive . . . . 5·00 4·25
67 **71** 4a. green . . . . 3·75 2·00
71 **67** 2r. red and orange . . . . 28·00 £110
72 5r. blue and purple . . . . 70·00 £325

1938. King George VI. Nos. 247/63.
77 **91** 3p. slate . . . . 7·50 1·00
78 ½a. brown . . . . 7·00 1·25
79 9p. green . . . . 20·00 4·50
80 1a. red . . . . 3·00 80
81 **92** 2a. red . . . . 1·25 7·00
82 – 2a.6p. violet . . . . 1·25 10·00
83 – 3a. green . . . . 1·40 6·00
84 – 3a.6p. blue . . . . 1·40 22·00
85 – 4a. brown . . . . 7·00 7·00
86 – 6a. green . . . . 3·00 23·00
87 – 8a. violet . . . . 2·25 22·00
88 – 12a. red . . . . 2·50 22·00
89 **93** 1r. slate and brown . . . 11·00 28·00
90 2r. purple and brown . . . 28·00 £100
91 5r. green and blue . . . . 38·00 £180
92 10r. purple and red . . . . 55·00 £400
93 15r. brown and green . . . £170 £750
94 25r. slate and purple . . . £140 £750

1942. King George VI. Optd **NABHA** only.
95 **91** 3p. slate . . . . 35·00 4·50
105 **100a** 3p. slate . . . . 1·25 1·00
96 **91** ½a. brown . . . . 80·00 6·00
106 **100a** ½a. mauve . . . . . . 3·00 1·40
97 **91** 9p. green . . . . 11·00 14·00
107 **100a** 9p. green . . . . 2·50 1·40
98 **91** 1a. red . . . . 11·00 3·50
108 **100a** 1a. red . . . . 1·00 3·75
109 **101** 1a.3p. brown . . . . . . 1·00 3·25
110 1½a. violet . . . . 2·50 2·50
111 2a. red . . . . 1·10 4·25
112 3a. violet . . . . 6·50 4·50
113 3½a. blue . . . . 17·00 55·00
114 **102** 4a. brown . . . . 1·75 1·00
115 6a. green . . . . 12·00 50·00
116 8a. violet . . . . 11·00 38·00
117 12a. purple . . . . 9·00 55·00

OFFICIAL STAMPS
Stamps of Nabha optd **SERVICE.**

1885. Nos. 1/3 (Queen Victoria).
O1 ½a. turquoise . . . . 4·00 1·10
O2 1a. purple 70 20
O3 2a. blue . . . . 75·00 £150

1885. Nos. 14/30 (Queen Victoria).
O 6 ½a. turquoise 40 10
O 8 1a. purple . . . . 1·50 25
O 9 2a. blue . . . . 2·75 1·25
O11 3a. orange . . . . 25·00 85·00
O13 4a. green (No. 4) . . . . . 3·25 1·25
O15 6a. brown . . . . 20·00 30·00
O17 8a. mauve . . . . 2·75 1·25
O18 12a. purple on red . . . . 6·50 20·00
O19 1r. grey . . . . 38·00 £300
O20 1r. green and red . . . . . 30·00 80·00

1903. Nos. 37/46 (King Edward VII).
O25 3p. grey . . . . 2·00 16·00
O26 ½a. green 80 35
O27 1a. red 80 10
O29 2a. lilac . . . . 2·25 40
O30 4a. olive . . . . 1·60 50
O32 8a. mauve . . . . 1·60 1·50
O34 1r. green and red . . . . . 1·60 2·50

1907. Nos. 47/8 (King Edward VII inscr "INDIA POSTAGE & REVENUE").
O35 ½a. green . . . . 1·25 50
O36 1a. red 75 30

1913. Nos. 54 and 58 (King George V).
O37 **63** 4a. olive . . . . 10·00 60·00
O38 **67** 1r. brown and green . . . 55·00 £450

1913. Official stamps of India (King George V) optd **NABHA STATE.**
O39a **55** 3p. grey . . . . 1·00 9·00
O40 **56** ½a. green 60 15
O41 **57** 1a. red 50 10
O42 **59** 2a. purple 75 60
O43 **63** 4a. olive 75 50
O44 **65** 8a. mauve . . . . 1·50 2·00
O46 **67** 1r. brown and green . . 5·00 3·50

1932. Stamps of India (King George V) optd **NABHA STATE SERVICE.**
O47 **55** 3p. grey 10 15
O48 **81** 1a. brown 15 15
O49 **63** 4a. olive . . . . 21·00 2·50
O50 **65** 8a. mauve . . . . 1·00 2·25

1938. Stamps of India (King George VI) optd **NABHA STATE SERVICE.**
O53 **91** 9p. green . . . . 4·25 4·00
O54 1a. red . . . . 18·00 1·10

1943. Stamps of India (King George VI) optd **NABHA.**
O55 **O 20** 3p. slate . . . . 1·25 1·50
O56 ½a. brown . . . . 1·10 30
O57 ½a. purple . . . . 4·00 1·00
O58 9p. green . . . . 1·25 30
O59 1a. red 60 20
O61 1½a. violet 70 40
O62 2a. orange . . . . 2·25 1·50
O64 4a. brown . . . . 4·25 3·25
O65 8a. violet . . . . 5·50 18·00

1943. Stamps of India (King George VI) optd **NABHA SERVICE.**
O66 **93** 1r. slate and brown . . . 8·50 38·00
O67 2r. purple and brown . . 28·00 £170
O68 5r. green and blue £170 £500

NAGORNO-KARABAKH Pt. 10

The mountainous area of Nagorno-Karabakh, mainly populated by Armenians, was declared an Autonomous Region within the Azerbaijan Soviet Socialist Republic on 7 July 1923.

Following agitation for union with Armenia in 1988 Nagorno-Karabakh was placed under direct U.S.S.R. rule in 1989. On 2 September 1991 the Regional Soviet declared its independence and this was confirmed by popular vote on 10 December. By 1993 fighting between Azerbaijan forces and those of Nagorno-Karabakh, supported by Armenia, led to the occupation of all Azerbaijan territory separating Nagorno-Karabakh from the border with Armenia. A ceasefire under Russian auspices was signed on 18 February 1994.

1993. 100 kopeks = 1 rouble.
1995. 100 louma = 1 dram.

1 National Flag

1993. Inscr "REPUBLIC OF MOUNTAINOUS KARABAKH".
1 **1** 1r. multicoloured 20 20
2 – 3r. blue, purple and brown . . 60 60
3 – 15r. red and blue . . . . . . 3·00 3·00
MS4 80×80 mm. 20r. brown, ultramarine and red . . . . . 4·00 4·00
MS5 60×80 mm. 20r. brown, ultramarine and red (imperf) 4·00 4·00
DESIGNS: 3r. President Arthur Mkrtchian; 15r. "We are Our Mountains" (sculpture of man and woman); 20r. Gandzasar Monastery.

Ա (2 "A") Բ (2a "P") Գ (2b "K")

1995. Nos. 1 and 3 surch in Armenian script as T **2/2b**.
6 **2** (50d.) on 1r. multicoloured 1·25 1·25
7 **2a** (100d.) on 15r. red and blue 2·25 2·25
8 **2b** (200d.) on 15r. red and blue 4·75 4·75

3 Dadiwank Monastery

1996. 5th Anniv of Independence. Multicoloured.
9 50d. Type **3** 50 50
10 100d. Parliament Building, Stepanakert 90 90
11 200d. "We are Our Mountains" (sculpture of man and woman) . . . . . 1·60 1·60
MS12 110×82 mm. 50d. Map and flag; 100d. As No. 10; 200d. As No. 11; 500d. Republic coat-of-arms (colours of national flag extend diagonally across the miniature sheet from bottom left to top right with the order incorrectly shown as orange, blue and red) . . . . 2·75 2·75

4 Boy playing Drum and Fawn (Erna Arshakyan)

1997. Festivals. Multicoloured.
13 50d. Type **4** (New Year) . . . 35 35
14 200d. Madonna and Child with angels (Mihran Akopyan) (Christmas) (vert) 1·75 1·75

5 Eagle and Demonstrator with Flag

1998. 10th Anniv of Karabakh Movement.
15 **5** 250d. multicoloured 75 75

6 Parliament Summer Palace

1998. 5th Anniv of Liberation of Shushi. Mult.
16 100d. Type **6** 30 30
17 250d. Church of the Saviour (vert) 75 75
MS18 124×92 mm. 750d. Type **6** 2·25 2·25

NAKHICHEVAN Pt. 10

An autonomous province of Azerbaijan, separated from the remainder of the republic by Armenian territory. Nos. 1 and 2 were issued during a period when the administration of Nakhichevan was in dispute with the central government.

100 qopik = 1 manat.

1 President Aliev

1993. 70th Birthday of President H. Aliev of Nakhichevan.
1 **1** 5m. black and red . . . . . . 3·75 3·75
2 – 5m. multicoloured . . . . . . 3·75 3·75
MS3 110×90 mm. Nos. 1/2 . . . 8·00 8·00
DESIGN: No. 2, Map of Nakhichevan.

NAMIBIA Pt. 1

Formerly South West Africa, which became independent on 21 March 1990.

1990. 100 cents = 1 rand.
1993. 100 cents = 1 Namibia dollar.

141 Pres. Sam Nujoma, Map of Namibia and National Flag

1990. Independence. Multicoloured.
538 18c. Type **141** 20 15
539 45c. Hands releasing dove and map of Namibia (vert) 50 75
540 60c. National flag and map of Africa . . . . 1·00 1·50

142 Fish River Canyon

1990. Namibia Landscapes. Multicoloured.
541 18c. Type **142** 25 20
542 35c. Quiver-tree forest, Keetmanshoop 50 35
543 45c. Tsaris Mountains . . . 60 55
544 60c. Dolerite boulders, Keetmanshoop 70 65

143 Stores on Kaiser Street, c. 1899

1990. Centenary of Windhoek. Multicoloured.
545 18c. Type **143** 20 20
546 35c. Kaiser Street, 1990 . . . 30 35
547 45c. City Hall, 1914 . . . . 40 65
548 60c. City Hall, 1990 . . . . 50 1·00

144 Maizefields

145 Gypsum

1990. Farming. Multicoloured.
549 20c. Type **144** 15 20
550 35c. Sanga bull 30 35
551 50c. Damara ram 40 45
552 65c. Irrigation in Okavango 50 60

1991. Minerals. As Nos. 519/21 and 523/33 of South West Africa, some with values changed and new design (5r.), inscr "Namibia" as T **145**. Multicoloured.
553 1c. Type **145** 10 10
554 2c. Fluorite 15 10
555 5c. Mimetite 20 10
556 10c. Azurite 30 10
557 20c. Dioptase 35 10
558 25c. Type **139** 35 15
559 30c. Tsumeb lead and copper complex 50 20
560 35c. Rosh Pinah zinc mine 50 20
561 40c. Diamonds 65 25
562 50c. Uis tin mine 65 25
563 65c. Boltwoodite 65 35
564 1r. Rossing uranium mine . . 70 50
565 1r.50 Wulfenite . . . . . . 1·10 70
566 2r. Gold . . . . 1·50 1·10
567 5r. Willemite (vert as T **145**) 3·00 2·75

146 Radiosonde Weather Balloon

1991. Centenary of Weather Service. Mult.
568 20c. Type **146** 20 20
569 35c. Sunshine recorder . . . 35 30
570 50c. Measuring equipment . . 45 50
571 65c. Meteorological station, Gobabeb 50 60

147 Herd of Zebras

1991. Endangered Species. Mountain Zebra. Mult.
572 20c. Type **147** . . . . 1·10 60
573 25c. Mare and foal . . . . . 1·25 70
574 45c. Zebras and foal . . . . 2·00 1·75
575 60c. Two zebras . . . . . . 2·50 3·00

148 Karas Mountains

1991. Mountains of Namibia. Multicoloured.
576 20c. Type **148** 20 20
577 25c. Gamsberg Mountains . . 30 30
578 45c. Mount Brukkaros . . . 45 70
579 60c. Erongo Mountains . . . 65 1·00

149 Bernabe de la Bat Camp

1991. Tourist Camps. Multicoloured.
580 20c. Type **149** 45 30
581 25c. Von Bach Dam Recreation Resort 55 45
582 45c. Gross Barmen Hot Springs 85 65
583 60c. Namutoni Rest Camp 1·00 1·00

150 Artist's Pallet

1992. 21st Anniv of Windhoek Conservatoire. Multicoloured.
584 20c. Type **150** 20 15
585 25c. French horn and cello 25 20
586 45c. Theatrical masks 50 60
587 60c. Ballet dancers . . . . . 65 1·00

151 Mozambique Mouthbrooder

1992. Freshwater Angling. Multicoloured.
588 20c. Type **151** 40 20
589 25c. Large-mouthed yellowfish 45 20
590 45c. Common carp 85 50
591 60c. Sharp-toothed catfish . . 95 65

152 Old Jetty

1992. Centenary of Swakopmund. Mult.
592 20c. Type **152** 25 25
593 25c. Recreation centre . . . 25 25
594 45c. State House and lighthouse 80 60
595 60c. Sea front 85 75
MS596 118 × 93 mm. Nos. 592/5 1·90 1·60

153 Running

154 Wrapping English Cucumbers

1992. Olympic Games, Barcelona. Mult.
597 20c. Type **153** 25 20
598 25c. Map of Namibia, Namibian flag and Olympic rings 30 20
599 45c. Swimming 50 40
600 60c. Olympic Stadium, Barcelona 65 55
MS601 115 × 75 mm. Nos. 597/600 (sold at 2r.) . . . . 2·25 2·75

1992. Integration of the Disabled. Mult.
602 20c. Type **154** 20 15
603 25c. Weaving mats 20 15
604 45c. Spinning thread 40 30
605 60c. Preparing pot plants . . 55 50

155 Elephants in Desert

1993. Namibia Nature Foundation. Rare and Endangered Species. Multicoloured.
606 20c. Type **155** 40 20
607 25c. Sitatunga in swamp . . 30 20
608 45c. Black rhinoceros 65 50
609 60c. Hunting dogs 65 60
MS610 217 × 59 mm. Nos. 606/9 (sold at 2r.50) . . . . 3·75 3·50

156 Herd of Simmentaler Cattle

1993. Centenary of Simmentalar Cattle in Namibia. Multicoloured.
611 20c. Type **156** 30 10
612 25c. Cow and calf 30 15
613 45c. Bull 60 40
614 60c. Cattle on barge 85 75

157 Sand Dunes, Sossusvlei

1993. Namib Desert Scenery. Multicoloured.
615 30c. Type **157** 25 20
616 40c. Blutkuppe 25 20
617 65c. River Kuiseb, Homeb 40 45
618 85c. Desert landscape 60 65

158 Smiling Child

1993. S.O.S. Child Care in Namibia. Mult.
619 30c. Type **158** 20 20
620 40c. Family 25 20
621 65c. Modern house 45 55
622 85c. Young artist with mural 65 80

159 "Charaxes jasius"

160 White Seabream

1993. Butterflies. Multicoloured.
623 5c. Type **159** 20 20
624 10c. "Acraea anemosa" . . . 20 20
625 20c. "Papilio nireus" 30 10
626 30c. "Junonia octavia" . . . 30 10
627 40c. "Hypolimnus misippus" 30 10
628 50c. "Physcaeneura panda" 40 20
629 65c. "Charaxes candiope" . . 40 30
630 85c. "Junonia hierta" . . . 50 40
631 90c. "Colotis cellmene" . . . 50 40
632 $1 "Cacyreus dicksoni" . . . 55 35
633 $2 "Charaxes bohemani" . . 80 80
634 $2.50 "Stugeta bowkeri" . . 1·00 1·10
635 $5 "Byblia anvatara" . . . . 1·50 1·75
See also No. 648.

1994. Coastal Angling. Multicoloured.
636 30c. Type **160** 25 25
637 40c. Kob 25 25
638 65c. West coast steenbras . . 40 40
639 85c. Galjoen 60 60
MS640 134 × 89 mm. Nos. 636/9 (sold at $2.50) . . . . 2·00 2·50

161 Container Ship at Wharf

1994. Incorporation of Walvis Bay Territory into Namibia. Multicoloured.
641 30c. Type **161** 40 30
642 65c. Aerial view of Walvis Bay 60 80
643 85c. Map of Namibia . . . . 95 1·25

162 "Adenolobus pechuelii"

163 Yellow-billed Stork

1994. Flowers. Multicoloured.
644 35c. Type **162** 25 25
645 40c. "Hibiscus elliottiae" . . 25 25
646 65c. "Pelargonium cortusifolium" 40 40
647 85c. "Hoodia macrantha" . . 50 60

1994. Butterflies. As T **159**, but inscr "STANDARDISED MAIL". Multicoloured.
648 (–) "Graphium antheus" . . 15 20
No. 648 was initially sold at 35c., but this was subsequently increased to reflect changes in postal rates.

1994. Storks. Multicoloured.
649 35c. Type **163** 50 30
650 40c. Abdim's stork 50 30
651 80c. African open-bill stork 80 50
652 $1.10 White stork . . . . . 1·00 65

164 Steam Railcar, 1908

1994. Steam Locomotives. Multicoloured.
653 35c. Type **164** 45 30
654 70c. Krauss side-tank locomotive No. 106, 1904 70 50
655 80c. Class 24 locomotive, 1948 . . . . 75 55
656 $1.10 Class 7C locomotive, 1914 . . . . 1·10 80

165 Cape Cross Locomotive No. 84 "Prince Edward", 1895

1995. Cent of Railways in Namibia. Mult.
657 35c. Type **165** 45 25
658 70c. Steam locomotive, German South West Africa 70 35
659 80c. South African Railways Class 8 steam locomotive 75 40
660 $1.10 Trans-Namib Class 33-400 diesel-electric locomotive . . . . 1·10 55
MS661 101 × 94 mm. Nos. 657/60 2·75 2·50

166 National Arms

167 Living Tortoise and "Geochelone stromeri" (fossil)

1995. 5th Anniv of Independence.
662 **166** (–) multicoloured 40 30
No. 662 is inscribed "STANDARDISED MAIL" and was initially sold for 35c., but this was subsequently increased to reflect changes in postal rates.

1995. Fossils. Multicoloured.
663 40c. Type **167** 65 25
664 80c. Ward's diamond bird and "Diamantornis wardi" (fossil eggs) . . . . . . 1·00 70
665 90c. Hyraxes and "Prohyrax hendeyi" skull . . . . . . 1·10 80
666 $1.20 Crocodiles and "Crocodylus lloydi" skull 1·40 1·40

168 Martii Rautanen and Church

169 Ivory Buttons

1995. 125th Anniv of Finnish Missionaries in Namibia. Multicoloured.
667 40c. Type **168** 25 20
668 80c. Albin Savola and hand printing press 50 50
669 90c. Karl Weikkolin and wagon 60 65
670 $1.20 Dr. Selma Rainio and Onandjokwe Hospital . . . 85 95

1995. Personal Ornaments. Multicoloured.
671 40c. Type **169** 20 20
672 80c. Conus shell pendant . . 45 45
673 90c. Cowrie shell headdress 55 55
674 $1.20 Shell button pendant 85 95

169a Warthog

1995. "Singapore '95" International Stamp Exhibition. Sheet 110 × 52 mm, containing design as No. 359b of South West Africa.
MS675 **169a** $1.20 multicoloured 1·10 1·20

170 U.N. Flag

1995. 50th Anniv of the United Nations.
676 **170** 40c. blue and black . . . 20 20

171 Bogenfels Arch

1996. Tourism. Multicoloured.
677 (–) Type **171** 15 15
678 90c. Ruacana Falls 30 30
679 $1 Epupa Falls 30 30
680 $1.30 Herd of wild horses . . 35 50
No. 677 is inscribed "Standardised Mail" and was initially sold at 45c.

172 Sister Leoni Kreitmeier and Dobra Education and Training Centre

1996. Centenary of Catholic Missions in Namibia. Multicoloured.
681 50c. Type **172** 20 20
682 95c. Father Johann Malinowski and Heirachabis Mission . . . 30 40
683 $1 St. Mary's Cathedral, Windhoek 30 40
684 $1.30 Archbishop Joseph Gotthardt and early church, Ovamboland . . . 35 80

172a Caracal

1996. "CAPEX '96" International.Stamp Exhibition, Toronto. Sheet 105 × 45 mm, containing design as No. 358c of South West Africa.
MS685 **172a** $1.30 multicoloured 1·00 1·40

173 Children and UNICEF Volunteer

1996. 50th Anniv of UNICEF. Multicoloured.
686 (–) Type **173** 15 15
687 $1.30 Girls in school 60 60
No. 686 is inscribed "STANDARD POSTAGE" and was initially sold at 50c.

174 Boxing

1996. Centennial Olympic Games, Atlanta. Mult.
688 (–) Type **174** 15 15
689 90c. Cycling 50 40
690 $1 Swimming 30 40
691 $1.30 Running 30 55
No. 688 is inscribed "Standard Postage" and was initially sold at 50c.

175 Scorpius

1996. Stars in the Namibian Sky. Multicoloured.
692 (–) Type **175** 15 15
693 90c. Sagittarius 25 30
694 $1 Southern Cross 30 30
695 $1.30 Orion 40 50
MS696 100 × 80 mm. No. 694 . . 1·50 1·75
No. 692 is inscribed "Standard Postage" and was initially sold at 50c.
See also No. **MS**706.

176 Urn-shaped Pot

1996. Early Pottery. Multicoloured.
697 (–) Type **176** 15 15
698 90c. Decorated storage pot 30 40
699 $1 Reconstructed cooking pot 30 40
700 $1.30 Storage pot 35 70
No. 697 is inscribed "Standard Postage" and was initially sold at 50c.

177 Khauxa!nas Ruins

1997. Khaux!nas Ruins.
701 **177** (–) multicoloured 35 20
702 – $1 multicoloured 75 55
703 – $1.10 multicoloured . . . 85 75
704 – $1.50 multicoloured . . . 1·40 1·75
DESIGNS: $1 to $1.50, Different views.
No. 701 is inscribed "Standard postage" and was initially sold at 50c.

178 Ox

1997. "HONG KONG '97" International Stamp Exhibition and Chinese New Year ("Year of the Ox"). Sheet 103 × 67 mm.
MS705 **178** $1.30 multicoloured 1·10 1·40

1997. Support for Organised Philately. No. **MS**696 with margin additionally inscr "Reprint February 17 1997. Sold in aid of organised philately N$3.50".
MS706 $1 Southern Cross (sold at $3.50) . . . . 2·00 2·25

179 Heinrich von Stephan

180 Cinderella Waxbill

1997. Death Centenary of Heinrich von Stephan (founder of U.P.U.).
709 **179** $2 multicoloured . . . . 1·00 1·00

1997. Waxbills. Multicoloured.
710 50c. Type **180** 20 20
711 60c. Black-cheeked waxbill 20 20

181 Helmeted Guineafowl

1997. Greetings Stamp.
712 **181** $1.20 multicoloured . . . 1·00 1·00
For similar designs see Nos. 743/6.

182 Jackass Penguins Calling

1997. Endangered Species. Jackass Penguin. Mult.
713 (–) Type **182** 35 30
714 $1 Incubating egg 55 40
715 $1.10 Adult with chick . . . 60 50
716 $1.50 Penguins swimming . . 75 60
MS717 101 × 92 mm. As Nos. 713/16, but without WWF symbol (sold at $5) . . . . . 1·90 1·50
No. 713 is inscribed "STANDARD POSTAGE" and was initially sold at 50c.

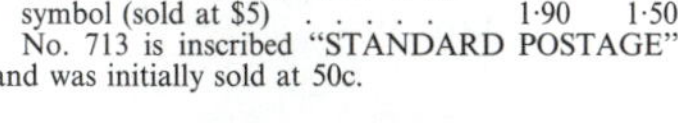

183 Caracal

1997. Wildcats. Multicoloured.
718 (–) Type **183** 20 20
719 $1 "Felis lybic" 40 30
720 $1.10 Serval 50 40
721 $1.50 Black-footed cat . . . 60 55
MS722 100 × 80 mm. $5 As No. 721 2·00 2·25
No. **MS**722 was sold in aid of organised philately in Southern Africa.
No. 718 is inscribed "STANDARD POSTAGE" and was initially sold at 50c.

184 "Catophractes alexandri"

1997. Greeting Stamps. Flowers and Helmeted Guineafowl. Multicoloured.
723 (–) Type **184** 10 15
724 (–) "Crinum paludosum" . . . 10 15
725 (–) "Gloriosa superba" . . . 10 15
726 (–) "Tribulus zeyheri" . . . 10 15
727 (–) "Aptosimum pubescens" 10 15
728 50c. Helmeted guineafowl raising hat 10 15
729 50c. Holding bouquet 10 15
730 50c. Ill in bed 10 15
731 $1 With heart round neck . . 20 25
732 $1 With suitcase and backpack 20 25
Nos. 723/7 are inscribed "Standard Postage" and were initially sold at 50c. each.

185 Collecting Bag

1997. Basket Work. Multicoloured.
733 50c. Type **185** 20 20
734 90c. Powder basket 30 30
735 $1.20 Fruit basket 35 35
736 $2 Grain basket 70 75

186 Veterinary Association Coat of Arms

1997. 50th Anniv of Namibian Veterinary Association.
737 **186** $1.50 multicoloured . . . 50 50

187 Head of Triceratops

1997. Youth Philately. Dinosaurs. Sheet 82 × 56 mm.
MS738 **187** $5 multicoloured . . 1·50 1·75

188 German South West Africa Postman

189 False Mopane

1997. World Post Day.
739 **188** (–) multicoloured 20 20
No. 739 is inscribed "STANDARD POSTAGE" and was initially sold at 50c.

1997. Trees. Multicoloured.
740 (–) Type **189** 15 20
741 $1 Ana tree 30 40
742 $1.10 Shepherd's tree 35 55
743 $1.50 Kiaat 50 70
No. 740 is inscribed "STANDARD POSTAGE" and was initially sold at 50c.

1997. Christmas. As T **181**, showing Helmeted Guineafowl, each with festive frame. Mult.
744 (–) Guineafowl facing right 20 20
745 $1 Guineafowl in grass . . . 35 30
746 $1.10 Guineafowl on rock . . 35 40
747 $1.50 Guineafowl in desert 50 55
MS748 110 × 80 mm. $5 Helmeted guineafowl (vert) . . . . . . 2·75 2·75
No. 744 is inscribed "standard postage" and was initially sold at 50c.

190 Flame Lily

191 John Muafangejo

1997. Flora and Fauna. Multicoloured.
749 5c. Type **190** 10 10
750 10c. Bushman poison . . . 10 10
751 20c. Camel's foot 10 10
752 30c. Western rhigozum . . . 15 10
753 40c. Blue-cheeked bee-eater 15 15
754 50c. Laughing dove 15 15
755a (–) Peach-faced lovebird ("Roseyfaced Lovebird") 10 10
756 60c. Lappet-faced vulture . . 20 10
757 90c. Southern yellow-billed hornbill ("Yellow-billed Hornbill") 25 20
758 $1 Lilac-breasted roller . . . 30 25
759 $1.10 Hippopotamus . . . 35 25
760 $1.20 Giraffe 40 25
761a (–) Leopard 20 25
762 $1.50 Elephant 40 30
763 $2 Lion 45 40
764 $4 Buffalo 80 70
765 $5 Black rhinoceros . . . . 1·10 1·00
766 $10 Cheetah . . . . 1·75 2·00
No. 755 is inscribed "standard postage" and was initially sold at 50c.; No. 761 is inscribed "postcard rate" and was initially sold at $1.20.
Nos. 755, 758 and 761 exist with ordinary or self-adhesive gum.

1997. 10th Death Anniv of John Muafangejo (artist).
770 **191** (50c.) multicoloured . . . 40 40
No. 770 is inscribed "STANDARD POSTAGE" and was initially sold at 50c.

192 Gabriel B. Taapopi

1998. Gabriel B. Taapopi (writer) Commemoration.
771 **192** (–) silver and brown . . . 40 40

No. 771 is inscribed "STANDARD POSTAGE" and was initially sold at 50c.

193 Year of the Tiger

1998. International Stamp and Coin Exhibition, 1997, Shanghai. Sheets 165 × 125 mm or 97 × 85 mm, containing multicoloured designs as T **193**. (a) Lunar New Year.

MS772 165 × 125 mm. $2.50 × 6. Type **193**; Light green tiger and circular symbol; Yellow tiger and head symbol; Blue tiger and square symbol; Emerald tiger and square symbol; Mauve tiger and triangular symbol (61 × 29 mm) 2·50 3·25

MS773 97 × 85 mm. $6 Symbolic tiger designs (71 × 40 mm) 1·25 1·40

(b) Chinese Calendar.

MS774 165 × 125 mm. $2.50 × 6. Various calendar symbols (24 × 80 mm) 2·50 3·25

MS775 97 × 85 mm. $6 Soft toy tigers (71 × 36 mm) 1·25 1·40

(c) 25th Anniv of Shanghai Communique.

MS776 165 × 125 mm. $3.50 × 4. Pres. Nixon's visit to China, 1972; Vice Premier Deng Xiaoping's visit to U.S.A., 1979; Pres. Reagan's visit to China, 1984; Pres. Bush's visit to China, 1989 (61 × 32 mm) 2·50 3·00

MS777 97 × 85 mm. $6 China–U.S.A. Communique, 1972 (69 × 36 mm) 1·25 1·40

(d) Pres. Deng Xiaoping's Project for Unification of China.

MS778 165 × 125 mm. $3.50 × 4. Beijing as national capital; Return of Hong Kong; Return of Macao; Links with Taiwan (37 × 65 mm) 2·50 3·00

MS779 97 × 85 mm. $6 Reunified China (71 × 41 mm) 1·25 1·40

(e) Return of Macao to China, 1999.

MS780 Two sheets, each 165 × 120 mm. (a) $4.50 × 3 Carnival dragon and modern Macao (44 × 33 mm). (b) $4.50 × 3 Ruins of St. Paul's Church, Macao (62 × 29 mm) Set of 2 sheets 4·00 5·50

MS781 Two sheets, each 97 × 85 mm. (a) $6 Carnival dragon and modern Macao (62 × 32 mm). (b) $6 Deng Xiaoping and ruins of St. Paul's Church, Macao (71 × 36 mm) Set of 2 sheets 2·00 2·75

194 Leopard

1998. Large Wild Cats. Multicoloured.

782 $1.20 Type **194** 50 25
783 $1.90 Lioness and cub 70 65
784 $2 Lion 70 80
785 $2.50 Cheetah 80 1·10
MS786 112 × 98 mm. Nos. 782/5 2·40 2·50

195 Narra Plant

196 Collecting Rain Water

1998. Narra Cultivation.

787 **195** $2.40 multicoloured 45 45

1998. World Water Day.

788 **196** (–) multicoloured 40 40

No. 788 is inscribed "STANDARD POSTAGE" and was initially sold at 50c. On 1 April 1998 the standard postage rate was increased to 55c.

1998. Diana, Princess of Wales Commemoration. Sheet 145 × 70 mm, containing vert designs as T **91** of Kiribati. Multicoloured.

MS789 $1 Princess Diana wearing protective mask; $1 Wearing Red Cross badge; $1 Wearing white shirt; $1 Comforting crippled child 1·60 1·75

197 White-faced Scops Owl ("Whitefaced Owl")

1998. Owls of Namibia. Multicoloured.

790 55c. Black-tailed tree rat (20 × 24 mm) 30 30
791 $1.50 Type **197** 50 55
792 $1.50 African barred owl ("Barred Owl") 50 55
793 $1.90 Spotted eagle owl 70 75
794 $1.90 Barn owl (61 × 24 mm) 70 75

See also No. **MS**850.

198 "Patella ganatina" (Limpet)

1998. Shells. Multicoloured.

795 (–) Type **198** 25 10
796 $1.10 "Cymatium cutaceum africanum" (Triton) 55 30
797 $1.50 "Conus mozambicus" (Cone) 75 65
798 $6 "Venus verrucosa" (Venus clam) 2·50 3·00
MS799 109 × 84 mm. Nos. 795/8 4·00 5·00

No. 795 is inscribed "Standard Postage" and was initially sold at 55c.

199 Underwater Diamond Excavator

1998. Marine Technology. Sheet 70 × 90 mm.

MS800 **199** $2.50 multicoloured 1·75 1·75

200 "Chinga" (cheetah)

1998. Wildlife Conservation. "Racing for Survival" (Olympic sprinter Frank Frederiks v cheetah). Sheet 108 × 80 mm.

MS801 **200** $5 multicoloured 1·75 2·00

201 Namibian Beach

1998. World Environment Day. Multicoloured.

802 (–) Type **201** 10 10
803 $1.10 Okavango sunset 25 25
804 $1.50 Sossusvlei 35 40
805 $1.90 African Moringo tree 40 50

No. 802 is inscribed "STANDARD POSTAGE" and was initially sold at 55c.

202 Two Footballers

203 Chacma Baboon

1998. World Cup Football Championship, France. Sheet 80 × 56 mm.

MS806 **202** $5 multicoloured 1·25 1·50

1998. Animals with their Young. Sheet 176 × 60 mm, containing T **203** and similar vert designs.

MS807 $1.50, Type **203**; $1.50, Blue Wildebeest; $1.50, Meercat (suricate); $1.50, African Elephant; $1.50, Burchell's Zebra 1·50 1·75

204 Carmine Bee Eater

1998. Wildlife of the Caprivi Strip. Multicoloured.

808 60c. Type **204** 50 50
809 60c. Sable antelope (40 × 40 mm) 50 50
810 60c. Lechwe (40 × 40 mm) 50 50
811 60c. Woodland waterberry 50 50
812 60c. Nile monitor (40 × 40 mm) 50 50
813 60c. African jacana 50 50
814 60c. African fish eagle 50 50
815 60c. Woodland kingfisher 50 50
816 60c. Nile crocodile (55 × 30 mm) 50 50
817 60c. Black mamba (32 × 30 mm) 50 50

Nos. 808/17 were printed together, se-tenant, with the backgrounds forming a composite design.

205 Black Rhinoceros and Calf

1998. "ILSAPEX '98" International Stamp Exhibition, Johannesburg. Sheet 103 × 68 mm.

MS818 **205** $5 multicoloured 1·50 1·75

206 Blue Whale

1998. Whales of the Southern Oceans (joint issue with Norfolk Island and South Africa). Sheet 103 × 70 mm.

MS819 **206** $5 multicoloured 1·75 2·00

207 Damara Dik-dik

208 Yoka perplexed

1999. "Fun Stamps for Children". Animals. Mult.

820 $1.80 Type **207** 1·25 1·25
821 $2.65 Striped tree squirrel (26 × 36 mm) 2·25 2·25

1999. "Yoka the Snake" (cartoon). Multicoloured. Self-adhesive.

822 $1.60 Type **208** 35 40
823 $1.60 Yoka under attack (33 × 27 mm) 35 40
824 $1.60 Yoka caught on branch 35 40
825 $1.60 Yoka and wasps (33 × 27 mm) 35 40
826 $1.60 Yoka and footprint 35 40
827 $1.60 Yoka and tail of red and white snake 35 40
828 $1.60 Mouse hunt (33 × 27 mm) 35 40
829 $1.60 Snakes entwined 35 40
830 $1.60 Red and white snake singing 35 40
831 $1.60 Yoka sulking (33 × 27 mm) 35 40

209 "Windhuk" (liner)

1999. "Windhuk" (liner) Commemoration. Sheet 110 × 90 mm.

MS832 **209** $5.50 multicoloured 1·25 1·50

210 Zogling Glider, 1928

1999. Gliding in Namibia. Multicoloured.

833 $1.60 Type **210** 40 50
834 $1.80 Schleicher glider, 1998 60 70

211 Yoka the Snake with Toy Zebra

1999. "iBRA '99" International Stamp Exhibition, Nuremberg. Sheet 110 × 84 mm.

MS835 **211** $5.50 multicoloured 1·25 1·50

212 Greater Kestrel

1999. Birds of Prey. Multicoloured.

836 60c. Type **212** 50 25
837 $1.60 Common kestrel ("Rock Kestrel") 1·00 70
838 $1.80 Red-headed falcon ("Red-necked Falcon") 1·00 85
839 $2.65 Lanner falcon 1·75 2·25

213 Wattled Crane

1999. Wetland Birds. Multicoloured.

840 $1.60 Type **213** 75 55
841 $1.80 Variegated sandgrouse ("Burchell's Sandgrouse") 85 70
842 $1.90 White-collared pratincole ("Rock Pratincole") 85 70
843 $2.65 Eastern white pelican 1·40 1·60

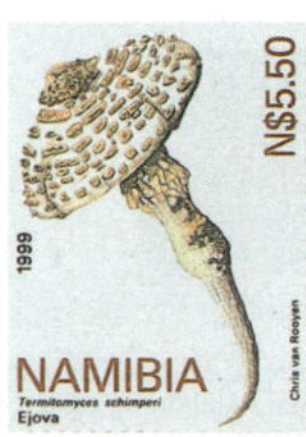

214 "Termitomyces schimperi" (fungus)

216 Johanna Gertze

215 "Eulophia hereroensis" (orchid)

1999. "PhilexFrance '99" International Stamp Exhibition, Paris. Sheet 79 × 54 mm.

MS844 **214** $5.50 multicoloured 1·50 1·60

1999. "China '99" International Philatelic Exhibition, Beijing. Orchids. Multicoloured.

845 $1.60 Type **215** 60 50
846 $1.80 "Ansellia africana" 70 60
847 $2.65 "Eulophia leachii" 95 95
848 $3.90 "Eulophia speciosa" 1·25 1·50
MS849 72 × 72 mm. $5.50 "Eulophia walleri" 1·75 2·00

1999. Winning entry in 5th Stamp World Cup, France. Sheet 120 × 67 mm, design as No. 794, but with changed face value. Multicoloured.

MS850 $11 Barn owl (61 × 24 mm) 4·50 4·50

1999. Johanna Gertze Commemoration.

851 **216** $20 red, pink and blue 4·00 4·50

217 Sunset over Namibia

1999. New Millennium. Multicoloured.

852 $2.20 Type **217** 70 80
853 $2.40 Sunrise over Namibia 90 1·10
MS854 77 × 54 mm. $9 Globe (hologram) (37 × 44 mm) . . . 2·75 3·00

218 South African Shelduck

2000. Ducks of Namibia. Multicoloured.

855 $2 Type **218** 70 55
856 $2.40 White-faced whistling duck 80 70
857 $3 Comb duck ("Knobbilled duck") 90 90
858 $7 Cape shoveler . . . . . . 2·00 2·50

No. 858 is inscribed "Cape shoveller" in error.

2000. Nos. 749/52 surch with **standard postage** (859) or new values (others).

859 (–) on 5c. Type **190** 30 15
860 $1.80 on 30c. Western rhigozum 60 40
861 $3 on 10c. Bushman poison 85 90
862 $6 on 20c. Camel's foot . . . 1·50 1·75

No. 859 was initially sold at 65c. The other surcharges show face values.

220 Namibian Children

2000. 10th Anniv of Independence. Multicoloured.

863 65c. Type **220** 40 15
864 $3 Namibian flag . . . . . 1·00 1·10

221 Actor playing Jesus wearing Crown of Thorns

2000. Easter Passion Play. Multicoloured.

865 $2.10 Type **221** 60 60
866 $2.40 On the way to Calvary 65 65

222 Tenebrionid Beetle

223 *Welwitschia mirabilis*

2000. "The Stamp Show 2000" International Stamp Exhibition, London. Wildlife of Namibian Dunes. Sheet 165 × 73 mm, containing T **222** and similar multicoloured designs.

MS867 $2 Type **222**; $2 Namib golden mole; $2 Brown hyena; $2 Shovel-snouted lizard (49 × 30 mm); $2 Dune lark (25 × 36 mm); $6 Namib side-winding adder (25 × 36 mm) . . 5·00 5·50

2000. *Welwitschia mirabilis* (prehistoric plant). Multicoloured.

868 (–) Type **223** 30 15
869 $2.20 *Welwitschia mirabilis* from above 70 50
870 $3 Seed pods 90 90
871 $4 Flats covered by *Welwitschia mirabilis* . . . 1·10 1·25

No. 868 is inscribed "Standard inland mail" and was originally sold for 65c.

224 High Energy Stereoscopic System Telescopes

2000. High Energy Stereoscopic System Telescopes Project. Namibian Khomas Highlands. Sheet 100 × 70 mm.

MS872 **224** $11 multicoloured . . 4·50 4·50

225 Jackal-berry Tree

2000. Trees with Nutritional Value. Multicoloured.

873 (–) Type **225** 35 25
874 $2 Sycamore fig 65 65
875 $2.20 Bird plum 70 70
876 $7 Marula . . . . 1·75 2·25

No. 873 is inscribed "Standard inland mail" and was originally sold for 65c.

226 Yoka and Nero the Elephant

2000. "Yoka the Snake" (cartoon) (2nd series). Sheet 103 × 68 mm.

MS877 **226** $11 multicoloured . . 4·00 4·25

227 Striped Anemone

229 Wood-burning Stove

228 Cessna 210 Turbo Aircraft

2001. Sea Anemone. Multicoloured.

878 (–) Type **227** 30 15
879 $2.45 Violet-spotted anemone 70 55
880 $3.50 Knobbly anemone . . 90 90
881 $6.60 False plum anemone 1·60 1·90

No. 878 is inscribed "Standard inland mail" and was originally sold for 70c.

2001. Civil Aviation. Multicoloured.

882 (–) Type **228** 40 15
883 $2.20 Douglas DC-6B airliner 70 50
884 $2.50 Pitts S2A bi-plane . . . 75 55
885 $13.20 Bell 407 helicopter . . 4·00 4·25

No. 882 is inscribed "Standard inland mail" and was originally sold for 70c.

2001. Renewable Energy Sources. Multicoloured.

886 (–) Type **229** 40 45
887 (–) Biogas digester 40 45
888 (–) Solar cooker 40 45
889 (–) Re-cycled tyre 40 45
890 (–) Solar water pump 40 45
891 $3.50 Solar panel above traditional hut . . . . . . 90 1·00
892 $3.50 Solar street light . . . 90 1·00
893 $3.50 Solar panels on hospital building . . . . . 90 1·00
894 $3.50 Solar telephone . . . . 90 1·00
895 $3.50 Wind pump . . . . . . 90 1·00

Nos. 886/95 were printed together, se-tenant, with the backgrounds forming a composite design.

Nos. 886/90 are inscribed "Standard Mail" and were originally sold for $1 each.

230 Ruppell's Parrot

231 Plaited Hair, Mbalantu

2001. Flora and Fauna from the Central Highlands. Multicoloured.

896 (–) Type **230** 40 45
897 (–) Flap-necked chameleon (40 × 30 mm) 40 45
898 (–) Klipspringer (40 × 30 mm) 40 45
899 (–) Rockrunner (40 × 30 mm) 40 45
900 (–) Pangolin (40 × 40 mm) . . 40 45
901 $3.50 Camel thorn (55 × 30 mm) . . . . . . 90 1·00
902 $3.50 Berg aloe (40 × 30 mm) 90 1·00
903 $3.50 Kudu (40 × 40 mm) . . 90 1·00
904 $3.50 Rock agama (40 × 40 mm) . . . . . . 90 1·00
905 $3.50 Armoured ground cricket (40 × 30 mm) . . . 90 1·00

Nos. 896/905 were printed together, se-tenant, with the backgrounds forming a composite design.

Nos. 896/900 are inscribed "Standard Mail" and were originally sold for $1 each.

2002. Traditional Women's Hairstyles and Headdresses. Multicoloured.

906 (–) Type **231** 30 35
907 (–) Cloth headdress, Damara 30 35
908 (–) Beaded hair ornaments, San 30 35
909 (–) Leather ekori headdress, Herero 30 35
910 (–) Bonnet, Baster 30 35
911 (–) Seed necklaces, Mafue . . 30 35
912 (–) Thihukeka hairstyle, Mbukushu 30 35
913 (–) Triangular cloth headdress, Herero 30 35
914 (–) Goat-skin headdress, Himba 30 35
915 (–) Horned headdress, Kwanyama 30 35
916 (–) Headscarf, Nama 30 35
917 (–) Plaits and oshikoma, Ngandjera/Kwaluudhi . . 30 35

Nos. 906/17 are inscribed "STANDARD MAIL" and were originally sold for $1 each.

232 African Hoopoe

2002. Birds. Multicoloured.

918 (–) Type **232** 45 25
919 $2.20 Paradise flycatcher . . 60 45
920 $2.60 Swallowtailed bee eater 75 75
921 $2.80 Malachite kingfisher . . 85 1·00

No. 918 is inscribed "Standard Mail" and was originally sold for $1.

233 The Regular Floods of Kuiseb River

2002. Ephemeral Rivers. Multicoloured.

922 $1.30 Type **233** 40 25
923 $2.20 Tsauchab River after heavy rainfall (39 × 31 mm) 60 45
924 $2.60 Elephants in the sandbed of the Hoarusib River (89 × 24 mm) 80 70
925 $2.80 Nossob River after heavy rainfall (39 × 32 mm) 80 80
926 $3.50 Fish River and birds (23 × 57 mm) . . . . . . 95 1·10

No. 922 is inscribed "Standard Mail" and was initially sold for $1.30.

234 Wall Mounted Telephone, 1958

2002. 10th Anniv of Nampost and Telecommunication. Multicoloured.

MS927 102 × 171 mm. ($1.30) Type **234**; ($1.30) Courier van; ($1.30) Black wall mounted phone; ($1.30) Pillar box and envelope; ($1.30) Black desk top phone; ($1.30) Computer; ($1.30) Unplugged phone; ($1.30) Dolphin carrying envelope; ($1.30) Modern multi-function phone; ($1.30) Plane and envelopes . . 3·00 3·50
MS928 102 × 171 mm. ($1.30) Type **234** × 2; ($1.30) Black wall mounted phone ; ($1.30) Black desk top phone × 2; ($1.30) Unplugged phone × 2; ($1.30) Modern multi-function phone × 2 3·00 3·50
MS929 102 × 171 mm. ($1.30) Courier van × 2; ($1.30) Pillar box and envelope × 2; ($1.30) Computer × 2; ($1.30) Dolphin carrying envelope × 2; ($1.30) Plane and envelopes × 2 . . . 3·00 3·50

The stamps in Nos. **MS**927/9 were all inscribed "Standard Mail" and were initially sold for $1.30.

2002. Nos. 749/50 optd **standard postage**.

930 ($1.30) Type **190** 40 40
931 ($1.30) Bushman poison . . . 40 40

Nos. 930/1 are inscribed "standard postage" and were initially sold for $1.30.

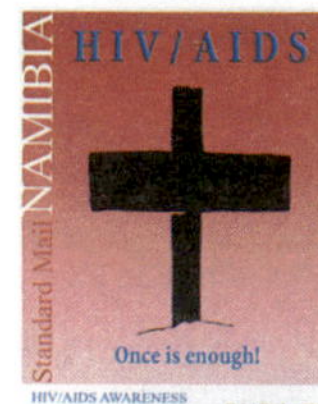

235 Black Cross

2002. Health Care. AIDS Awareness. Multicoloured.

932 ($1.30) Type **235** 30 20
933 $2.45 Blood cell 65 45
934 $2.85 Hand reaching to seated man 70 65
935 $11.50 Three test tubes . . . 3·00 3·50

No. 932 was inscribed "Standard Mail" was initially sold for $1.30.

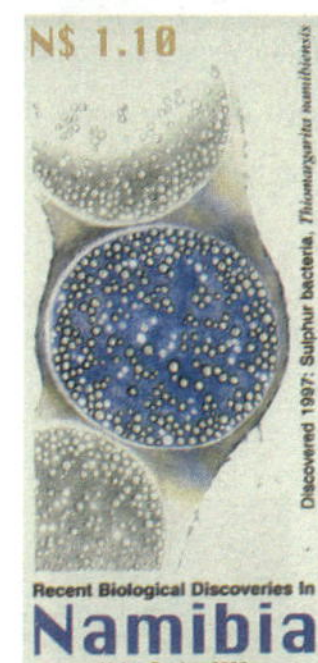

236 Sulphur Bacteria

2003. New Discoveries in Namibia. Multicoloured.

936 $1.10 Type **236** 30 20
937 $2.45 *Whiteheadia etesionamibensis* 65 45
938 $2.85 Cunene Flathead (horiz) 70 55
939 $3.85 Zebra Racer (horiz) . . 85 80
940 $20 Gladiator . . . . 4·25 4·75

237 Water and electricity supply

2003. Rural Development. Multicoloured.

941 $1.45 Type **237** 40 30
942 ($2.85) Conservancy formation and land use diversification 60 50
943 $4.40 Education and health services . . . . 1·25 1·10
944 ($11.50) Communication and road infrastructure . . . . 3·00 3·50

Nos. 942 and 944 were inscribed "Postcard Rate" (942) "Registered Mail" (944) were initially sold at $2.75 and $11.50 respectively.

238 Cattle Grazing and People Fishing at an Oshana

2003. Cuvelai Drainage System. Multicoloured.
945 $1.10 Type **238** 15 20
946 $2.85 Omadhiya Lakes . . . 50 55
947 ($3.85) Aerial view of Oshanas 65 70
No. 947 was inscribed "Non Standard Mail" and initially sold for $3.85.

239 Statue of Soldier and Obelisk

2003. National Monuments, Heroes Acre, Windhoek. Multicoloured.
948 ($1.45) Type **239** 50 50
949 ($2.75) Statue of woman . . 65 65
950 ($3.85) Stone monument . . 1·10 1·10
No. 948 was inscribed "Standard Mail" and sold for $1.45. No. 949 was inscribed "Postcard Rate" and sold for $2.75. No. 950 was inscribed "Non Standard Mail" and sold for $3.85.

240 Namibian Flag

2003. 25th Anniv of the Windhoek Philatelic Society. Sheet 67 × 57 mm.
MS951 **240** $10 multicoloured . . 2·25 2·50

241 Surveying Equipment

2003. Centenary of Geological Survey. Sheet 67 × 57 mm.
MS952 **241** $10 multicoloured . . 2·25 2·50

2003. Winning Stamp of the Eighth Stamp World Cup. Sheet 140 × 80 mm. Multicoloured.
MS953 $3.15 As No. 924 . . . . 2·50 2·50

242 Vervet Monkey

2004. Vervet Monkeys. Multicoloured.
954 $1.60 Type **242** 40 30
955 $3.15 Two monkeys in tree 80 90
956 $3.40 Adult monkey with offspring 80 90
957 ($14.25) Monkey chewing twig . . . . 3·50 4·00
MS958 80 × 60 mm. $4.85 As No. 957 . . . . 1·50 1·60
No. 957 was inscribed "Inland Registered Mail Paid" and was initially sold for $14.25.

243 Honey Bees on Sickle Bush

2004. Honey Bees. Multicoloured.
959 ($1.60) Type **243** 40 30
960 ($2.70) Bee on daisy . . . 70 75
961 ($3.05) Bee on aloe 75 80
962 ($3.15) Bee on cats claw . . . 80 85
963 ($14.25) Bees on edging senecio . . . . 3·50 4·00
MS964 75 × 55 mm. $4.85 Bee on pretty lady (flower) . . . . . 1·50 1·60
Nos. 959, 961 and 963 were each inscribed "standard mail" (959), "postcard rate" (961) "inland registered mail paid" (963) and were initially sold for $1.60, $3.05 and $14.25 respectively.

244 Dove

2004. Centenary of the War of Anti-Colonial Resistance.
965 ($1.69) Type **244** 40 40
MS966 105 × 70 mm. $5 As No. 965 1·50 1·60
No. 965 was inscribed "Standard Mail" and sold for $1.60 initially.

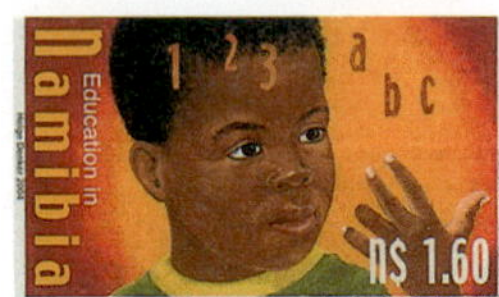

245 Boy and Pre-school Lessons

2004. Education. Multicoloured.
967 Type **245** 40 30
968 $2.75 Teacher and primary and secondary school lessons 70 75
969 $4.40 Teacher and vocational lessons 90 95
970 ($12.65) Teacher and life skill lessons . . . . 3·00 3·50
No. 970 was inscribed "Registered Mail" and sold for $12.65.

246 Loading Fish on Dockside

2004. Fishing Industry. Multicoloured.
971 $1.60 Type **246** 40 30
972 $2.75 Ship at dockside . . . 70 75
973 $4.85 Preparing fish . . . . 1·10 1·25

247 Joseph Fredericks House

2004. Historical Buildings of Bethanie. Multicoloured.
974 ($1.60) Type **247** 40 30
975 ($3.05) Schmelen House . . . 70 75
976 ($4.40) Rhenish Mission Church 90 95
977 ($12.65) Stone Church . . . 3·00 3·50
No. 974 was inscribed "Standard Mail" and sold for $1.60. No. 975 was inscribed "Postcard Rate" and sold for $3.05. No. 976 was inscribed "Non Standard Mail" and sold for $4.40. No 977 was inscribed "Registered Mail" and sold for $12.65.

248 Wrestling

2004. Olympic Games, Athens. Multicoloured.
978 ($1.60) Type **248** 40 30
979 $2.90 Boxing (vert) 75 80
980 $3.40 Shooting 90 95
981 $3.70 Mountain biking (vert) 95 1·00
No. 978 was inscribed "Standard Mail" and sold for $1.60.
No. 981 was also issued incorrectly inscribed "XVIII Olympiad".

248a African Fish Eagle (Namibia)

2004. 1st Joint Issue of Southern Africa Postal Operators Association Members. Sheet 170 × 95 mm containing T **248a** and similar hexagonal designs showing national birds of Association members. Multicoloured.
MS982 $3.40 Type **248a**; $3.40 Two African fish eagles perched (Zimbabwe); $3.40 Peregrine falcon (Angola); $3.40 Cattle egret (Botswana); $3.40 Purple-crested turaco ("Lourie") (Swaziland); $3.40 Stanley ("Blue") Crane (South Africa); $3.40 Bar-tailed trogon (Malawi) (inscribed "apaloderma vittatum"); $3.40 Two African fish eagles in flight (Zambia) . . . . 7·25 7·50
The stamp depicting the Bar-tailed trogon is not inscribed with the country of which the bird is a national symbol.
Miniature sheets of similar designs were also issued by Zimbabwe, Angola, Botswana, Swaziland, South Africa, Malawi and Zambia.

249 Gemsbok

2005. Centenary of Rotary International.
983 **249** $3.70 multicoloured . . . 85 85

250 President Hifikepunye Pohamba

251 Mariqua ("Marico") Sunbird

2005. Inauguration of Pres. Hifikepunye Pohamba.
984 **250** ($1.70) multicoloured . . 40 30
No. 984 was inscribed "Standard mail" and initially sold for $1.70.

2005. Sunbirds. Multicoloured.
985 $2.90 Type **251** 70 70
986 $3.40 Dusky sunbird 80 80
987 ($4.80) White-breasted ("bellied") sunbird . . . . 1·10 1·10
988 ($15.40) Scarlet-chested sunbird . . . . 3·50 3·75
MS989 100 × 70 mm. $10 Amethyst sunbird . . . . 2·40 2·75
No. 987 was inscribed "Non Standard Mail" and No. 988 "Registered Inland Postage Paid" and sold for $4.80 and $15.40 respectively.

2005. Nos. 751, 754, 757/8, 762 and 764/6 surch.
991 (–) on 20c. Camel's foot (flower) (surch **Standard Mail 90c.**) 40 30
993 (–) on 50c. Laughing dove (surch **Standard Mail 50c.**) 40 30
994 (–) on 90c. Yellow-billed hornbill (surch **Standard Mail 90c.**) 40 30
995 (–) on $1 Lilac-breasted roller (surch **Standard Mail 90c.**) 40 30
996 $2.90 on 20c. Camel's foot (surch **$2.90 on 20c.**) . . . 70 60
997 $2.90 on 20c. Camel's foot (surch **$2.90 on 20c.**) . . . 70 60
998 $2.90 on 90c. Yellow-billed hornbill (surch **$2.90 on 90c.**) 70 60
999 (–) on $1.50 Elephant as T **253** (surch in two lines **Standard Mail 90c.**) 1·10 90
1000 (–) on $4 Buffalo (surch **Standard Mail 50c.**) . . . 1·10 90
1001 $5.20 on 20c. Camel's foot (surch **$2.90 on 20c.**) . . . 1·25 1·00
1002 $5.20 on 90c. Yellow-billed hornbill (surch **$2.90 on 20c.**) . . . . 1·25 1·00
1003 (–) on $4 Buffalo (surch **Registered Standard Mail**) 4·25 4·00
1004 (–) on $10 Cheetah (surch **Registered Standard Mail**) 5·00 4·50
1005 $25 on $5 Black rhinoceros (surch **$2.90 on 20c.**) . . . 6·00 5·50
1006 $50 on $10 Cheetah (surch **$50 on $10**) . . . . . . 12·00 11·00
Nos. 990/5 are inscribed "Standard Mail" and were originally sold for $1.70. Nos. 999/1000 are inscribed "Non Standard Mail" and was originally sold for $4.80. No. 1003 is inscribed "Registered Standard Mail" and was originally sold for $15.40. No. 1004 is inscribed "Registered Non Standard Mail" and was originally sold for $18.50.

261 Nara (*Acanthosicyos horridus*)

2005. Plants with Medicinal Value. Multicoloured.
1013 (–) Type **261** 40 30
1014 $2.90 Devil's claw 70 60
1015 (–) *Hoodia gordonii* 75 65
1016 (–) *Tsamma* . . . . 1·00 90
No. 1013 is inscribed "Standard Mail", 1015 "Postcard Rate" and 1016 "Non Standard Mail" and they were originally sold for $1.70, $3.10 and $4.80 respectively.

262 Vegetables

2005. Crop Production in Namibia. Multicoloured.
1017 $2.90 Type **262** 70 60
1018 $3.40 Pearl millet 80 70
1019 (–) Maize . . . . 3·25 3·00
No. 1019 is inscribed "Registered Mail" and was originally sold for $13.70.

263 Cape Gull

2006. Seagulls of Namibia. Multicoloured.
1020 $3.10 Type **263** 75 65
1021 $4 Hartlaub's gull . . . . . 1·00 85
1022 $5.50 Sabine's gull . . . . 1·25 1·10
1023 (–) Grey-headed gull . . . . 4·00 3·75
No. 1023 is inscribed "Inland Registered Mail Paid" and was originally sold for $16.20.

NANDGAON Pt. 1

A state of central India. Now uses Indian stamps.

12 pies = 1 anna; 16 annas = 1 rupee.

1

2 (½a.)

1891. Imperf.
1 **1** ½a. blue . . . . 6·00 £170
2 2a. pink . . . . 24·00 £500

1893. Imperf.
5 **2** ½a. green . . . . 24·00 65·00
6 1a. red . . . . 55·00 £120
4 2a. red . . . . 11·00 85·00

OFFICIAL STAMPS

1893. Optd **M.B.D.** in oval.
O1 **1** ½a. blue £350
O4 **2** ½a. green . . . . 6·00 11·00
O5 1a. red . . . . 10·00 35·00
O6 2a. red . . . . 9·00 23·00

NAPLES — Pt. 8

A state on the S.W. coast of Central Italy, formerly part of the Kingdom of Sicily, but now part of Italy.

200 tornesi = 100 grano = 1 ducato.

1 Arms under Bourbon Dynasty

4 Cross of Savoy

1858. The frames differ in each value. Imperf.

8	**1**	½t. blue	£150000	£10000
1a		½g. red	£2250	£475
2		1g. red	£450	40·00
3		2g. red	£275	12·00
4a		5g. red	£4500	£9500
5a		10g. red	£5000	£32000
6a		20g. red	£6500	£1300
7a		50g. red	£10000	£3000

1860. Imperf.

9	**4**	½t. blue	£38000	£3750

NATAL — Pt. 1

On the east coast of S. Africa. Formerly a British Colony, later a province of the Union of S. Africa.

12 pence = 1 shilling;
20 shillings = 1 pound.

1

1857. Embossed stamps. Various designs.

1	**1**	1d. blue	—	£1100
2		1d. red	—	£1700
3		1d. buff	—	£1000
4	–	3d. red	—	£400
5	–	6d. green	—	£1100
6	–	9d. blue	—	£7000
7	–	1s. buff	—	£5500

The 3d., 6d., 9d. and 1s. are larger. Beware of reprints.

6

7

1859.

19	**6**	1d. red	90·00	27·00
12		3d. blue	£110	32·00
13		6d. grey	£190	50·00
24		6d. violet	55·00	28·00

1867.

25	**7**	1s. green	£160	30·00

1869. Variously optd **POSTAGE** or **Postage**.

50	**6**	1d. red	£100	42·00
82		1d. yellow	70·00	42·00
53		3d. blue	£160	48·00
83		6d. violet	60·00	7·50
84	**7**	1s. green	60·00	7·00

1870. Optd **POSTAGE** in a curve.

59	**7**	1s. green	85·00	10·00
108		1s. orange	4·25	1·25

1870. Optd **POSTAGE** twice, reading up and down.

60	**6**	1d. red	80·00	13·00
61		3d. blue	85·00	13·00
62		6d. violet	£160	27·00

1873. Optd **POSTAGE** once, reading up.

63	**7**	1s. brown	£200	21·00

23

28

16

1874. Queen Victoria. Various frames.

97a	**23**	½d. green	3·25	1·00
99	–	1d. red	3·75	30
107	–	2d. olive	3·25	1·40
113	**28**	2½d. blue	6·00	1·25
100	–	3d. blue	£100	17·00
101	–	3d. grey	4·50	2·00
102	–	4d. brown	6·00	1·25
103	–	6d. lilac	5·50	1·50
73	**16**	5s. red	75·00	30·00

1877. No. 99 surch ½ **HALF**.

85	½d. on 1d. red	29·00	65·00

POSTAGE

Half-penny

(21)

POSTAGE.

Half-Penny

(29)

1877. Surch as T **21**.

91	**6**	½d. on 1d. yellow	8·50	15·00
92		1d. on 6d. violet	50·00	15·00
93		1d. on 6d. red	£100	45·00

1885. Surch in words.

104	½d. on 1d. red (No. 99)	16·00	11·00
105	2d. on 3d. grey (No. 101)	19·00	5·50
109	2½d. on 4d. brown (No. 102)	10·00	13·00

1895. No. 23 surch with T **29**.

114	**6**	½d. on 6d. violet	2·00	4·25

1895. No. 99 surch **HALF**.

125	HALF on 1d. red	2·75	2·00

31

32

1902.

127	**31**	½d. green	3·00	30
147		1d. red	6·00	15
129		1½d. green and black	3·50	2·50
130		2d. red and olive	2·50	25
131		2½d. blue	1·50	3·25
132		3d. purple and grey	1·25	1·50
152		4d. red and brown	2·75	1·25
134		5d. black and orange	2·25	2·75
135		6d. green and purple	2·25	2·75
136		1s. red and blue	3·00	3·25
137		2s. green and violet	50·00	9·00
138		2s.6d. purple	40·00	12·00
139		4s. red and yellow	70·00	75·00
140	**32**	5s. blue and red	30·00	11·00
141		10s. red and purple	70·00	26·00
142		£1 black and blue	£180	55·00
143		£1.10s. green and violet	£400	£100
162		£1.10s. orange and purple	£1200	£2000
144		£5 mauve and black	£2750	£650
145		£10 green and orange	£7500	£3000
145b		£20 red and green	£15000	£7500

1908. As T **31/2** but inscr "POSTAGE POSTAGE".

165	**31**	6d. purple	4·50	2·75
166		1s. black on green	6·00	2·50
167		2s. purple and blue on blue	15·00	3·00
168		2s.6d. black and red on blue	25·00	3·00
169	**32**	5s. green and red on yellow	22·00	26·00
170		10s. green and red on green	75·00	80·00
171		£1 purple and black on red	£275	£250

OFFICIAL STAMPS

1904. Optd **OFFICIAL**.

O1	**31**	½d. green	3·00	35
O2		1d. red	4·50	70
O3		2d. red and olive	24·00	12·00
O4		3d. purple and grey	14·00	4·00
O5		6d. green and purple	48·00	65·00
O6		1s. red and blue	£150	£200

NAURU — Pt. 1

An island in the W. Pacific Ocean, formerly a German possession and then administered by Australia under trusteeship. Became a republic on 31 January 1968.

1916. 12 pence = 1 shilling;
20 shillings = 1 pound.
1966. 100 cents = 1 Australian dollar.

1916. Stamps of Gt. Britain (King George V) optd **NAURU**.

1	**105**	½d. green	2·25	8·00
2	**104**	1d. red	1·75	6·50
15	**105**	1½d. brown	25·00	42·00
4	**106**	2d. orange	2·00	13·00
6	**104**	2½d. blue	2·75	7·00
7	**106**	3d. violet	2·00	4·50
8		4d. green	2·00	8·50
9	**107**	5d. brown	2·25	10·00
10		6d. purple	5·00	10·00
11	**108**	9d. black	8·50	23·00
12		1s. brown	7·00	19·00
20	**109**	2s.6d. brown	65·00	£100
22		5s. red	£100	£140
23		10s. blue	£250	£325

4

6

1924.

26A	**4**	½d. brown	1·75	2·75
27B		1d. green	2·50	3·00
28B		1½d. red	1·00	1·50
29B		2d. orange	2·25	8·00
30B		2½d. blue	3·00	4·00
31A		3d. blue	4·00	13·00
32B		4d. green	4·25	13·00
33B		5d. brown	4·75	4·00
34B		6d. violet	4·50	5·00
35A		9d. olive	9·50	19·00
36B		1s. red	7·00	2·75
37B		2s.6d. green	29·00	35·00
38B		5s. purple	38·00	50·00
39B		10s. yellow	85·00	£100

1935. Silver Jubilee. Optd **HIS MAJESTY'S JUBILEE. 1910-1935.**

40	**4**	1½d. red	75	80
41		2d. orange	1·50	4·25
42		2½d. blue	1·50	1·50
43		1s. red	5·00	3·50

1937. Coronation.

44	**6**	1½d. red	45	1·75
45		2d. orange	45	2·75
46		2½d. blue	45	1·75
47		1s. purple	65	1·75

8 Anibare Bay

18 "Iyo" ("calophyllum")

21 White Tern

1954.

48	–	½d. violet	20	60
49a	**8**	1d. green	20	40
50	–	3½d. red	1·75	75
51	–	4d. blue	2·00	1·50
52	–	6d. orange	70	20
53	–	9d. red	60	20
54	–	1s. purple	30	30
55	–	2s.6d. green	2·50	1·00
56	–	5s. mauve	8·00	2·25

DESIGNS—HORIZ: ½d. Nauruan netting fish; 3½d. Loading phosphate from cantilever; 4d. Great frigate bird; 6d. Canoe; 9d. Domaneab (meeting house); 2s.6d. Buada Lagoon. VERT: 1s. Palm trees; 5s. Map of Nauru.

1963.

57	–	2d. multicoloured	75	2·25
58	–	3d. multicoloured	40	35
59	**18**	5d. multicoloured	40	75
60	–	8d. black and green	2·00	80
61	–	10d. black	40	30
62	**21**	1s.3d. blue, black and green	1·50	4·50
63	–	2s.3d. blue	2·75	55
64	–	3s.3d. multicoloured	1·50	2·75

DESIGNS—VERT (As Type **21**): 2d. Micronesian pigeon. (26 × 29 mm): 10d. Capparis (flower). HORIZ (As Type **18**): 3d. Poison nut (flower); 8d. Black lizard; 2s.3d. Coral pinnacles; 3s.3d. Nightingale reed warbler ("Red Warbler").

22 "Simpson and his Donkey"

1965. 50th Anniv of Gallipoli Landing.

65	**22**	5d. sepia, black and green	15	10

24 Anibare Bay

27 "Towards the Sunrise"

1966. Decimal Currency. As earlier issues but with values in cents and dollars as in T **24**. Some colours changed.

66	**24**	1c. blue	15	10
67	–	2c. purple (as No. 48)	15	40
68	–	3c. green (as No. 50)	30	2·00
69	–	4c. multicoloured (as T **18**)	20	10
70	–	5c. blue (as No. 54)	25	60
71	–	7c. black & brn (as No. 60)	30	10
72	–	8c. green (as No. 61)	20	10
73	–	10c. red (as No. 51)	40	10
74	–	15c. bl, blk and grn (as T **21**)	60	2·00
75	–	25c. brown (as No. 63)	30	1·00
76	–	30c. mult (as No. 58)	45	30
77	–	35c. mult (as No. 64)	75	35
78	–	50c. mult (as No. 57)	1·50	80
79	–	$1 mauve (as No. 56)	75	1·00

The 25c. is as No. 63 but larger, 27½ × 25 mm.

1968. Nos. 66/79 optd **REPUBLIC OF NAURU**.

80	**24**	1c. blue	10	30
81	–	2c. purple	10	10
82	–	3c. green	15	10
83	–	4c. multicoloured	15	10
84	–	5c. blue	10	10
85	–	7c. black and brown	25	10
86	–	8c. green	15	10
87	–	10c. red	60	15
88	–	15c. blue, black and green	1·25	2·50
89	–	25c. brown	20	15
90	–	30c. multicoloured	55	15
91	–	35c. multicoloured	1·25	30
92	–	50c. multicoloured	1·25	35
93	–	$1 purple	75	50

1968. Independence.

94	**27**	5c. multicoloured	10	10
95	–	10c. black, green and blue	10	10

DESIGN: 10c. Planting seedling, and map.

29 Flag of Independent Nauru

1969.

96	**29**	15c. yellow, orange and blue	50	15

30 Island, "C" and Stars

1972. 25th Anniv of South Pacific Commission.

97	**30**	25c. multicoloured	30	30

1973. 5th Anniv of Independence. No. 96 optd **Independence 1968-1973.**

98	**29**	15c. yellow, orange and blue	20	30

32 Denea

33 Artefacts and Map

1973. Multicoloured.

99	1c. Ekwenababae	40	20
100	2c. Kauwe iud	45	20
101	3c. Rimone	45	20
102	4c. Type **32**	45	40
103	5c. Erekogo	45	40
104	7c. Racoon butterflyfish ("Ikimago") (horiz)	50	80

105 8c. Catching flying fish (horiz) 30 20
106 10c. Itsibweb (ball game) (horiz) 30 20
107 15c. Nauruan wrestling . . . 35 20
108 20c. Snaring great frigate birds ("Frigate Birds") . . 70 70
109 25c. Nauruan girl 40 30
110 30c. Catching common noddy birds ("Noddy Birds") (horiz) 60 40
111 50c. Great frigate birds ("Frigate Birds") (horiz) 80 75
112 $1 Type **33** 80 75

34 Co-op Store

1973. 50th Anniv of Nauru Co-operative Society. Multicoloured.
113 5c. Type **34** 20 30
114 25c. Timothy Detudamo (founder) 20 15
115 50c. N.C.S. trademark (vert) 45 55

35 Phosphate Mining

1974. 175th Anniv of First Contact with the Outside World. Multicoloured.
116 7c. M.V. "Eigamoiya" (bulk carrier) 65 90
117 10c. Type **35** 50 25
118 15c. Fokker Fellowship "Nauru Chief" 65 30
119 25c. Nauruan chief in early times 50 35
120 35c. Capt. Fearn and 18th-century frigate (70 × 22 mm) . . . . . 2·25 2·50
121 50c. 18th-century frigate off Nauru (70 × 22 mm) . . . 1·25 1·40

The ship on the 35c. and 50c. is wrongly identified as the "Hunter" (snow).

36 Map of Nauru

37 Rev. P. A. Delaporte

1974. Centenary of U.P.U. Multicoloured.
122 5c. Type **36** 15 20
123 8c. Nauru Post Office 15 20
124 20c. Nauruan postman . . . 15 10
125 $1 U.P.U. Building and Nauruan flag 40 60
MS126 157 × 105 mm. Nos. 122/5. Imperf . . . . 2·00 5·50

1974. Christmas and 75th Anniv of Rev. Delaporte's Arrival.
127 **37** 15c. multicoloured 20 20
128 20c. multicoloured 30 30

38 Map of Nauru, Lump of Phosphate Rock and Albert Ellis

1975. Phosphate Mining Anniversaries. Mult.
129 5c. Type **38** 25 40
130 7c. Coolies and mine 35 40
131 15c. Electric phosphate train, barges and ship . . . . . 1·00 1·40
132 25c. Modern ore extraction 1·25 1·50

ANNIVERSARIES: 5c. 75th anniv of discovery; 7c. 70th anniv of Mining Agreement; 15c. 55th anniv of British Phosphate Commissioners; 25c. 5th anniv of Nauru Phosphate Corporation.

39 Micronesian Outrigger

41 "Our Lady" (Yaren Church)

40 New Civic Centre

1975. South Pacific Commission Conf, Nauru (1st issue). Multicoloured.
133 20c. Type **39** 75 40
134 20c. Polynesian double-hull 75 40
135 20c. Melanesian outrigger . . 75 40
136 20c. Polynesian outrigger . . 75 40

1975. South Pacific Commission Conf, Nauru (2nd issue). Multicoloured.
137 30c. Type **40** 15 15
138 50c. Domaneab (meeting-house) 30 30

1975. Christmas. Stained-glass Windows. Mult.
139 5c. Type **41** 15 30
140 7c. "Suffer little children" (Orro Church) 15 30
141 15c. As 7c. 20 60
142 25c. Type **41** 25 80

42 Flowers floating towards Nauru

1976. 30th Anniv of Islanders' Return from Truk. Multicoloured.
143 10c. Type **42** 10 10
144 14c. Nauru encircled by garland 15 10
145 25c. Nightingale reed warbler and maps 85 25
146 40c. Return of the islanders 45 35

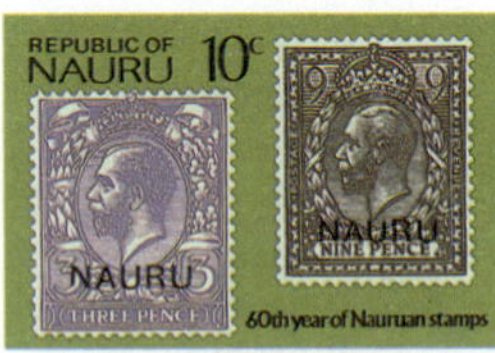

43 3d. and 9d. Stamps of 1916

1976. 60th Anniv of Nauruan Stamps. Mult.
147 10c. Type **43** 15 15
148 15c. 6d. and 1s. stamps . . . 15 15
149 25c. 2s.6d. stamp 20 25
150 50c. 5s. "Specimen" stamp 25 35

44 "Pandanus mei" and "Enna G" (cargo liner)

1976. South Pacific Forum, Nauru. Mult.
151 10c. Type **44** 25 20
152 20c. "Tournefortia argentea" with Boeing 737 and Fokker Fellowship aircraft 40 30
153 30c. "Thespesia populnea" and Nauru Tracking Station 40 30
154 40c. "Cordia subcordata" and produce 40 35

45 Nauruan Choir

46 Nauru House and Coral Pinnacles

1976. Christmas. Multicoloured.
155 15c. Type **45** 10 10
156 15c. Nauruan choir 10 10
157 20c. Angel in white dress . . 15 15
158 20c. Angel in red dress . . . 15 15

1977. Opening of Nauru House, Melbourne. Mult.
159 15c. Type **46** 15 15
160 30c. Nauru House and Melbourne skyline 25 25

47 Cable Ship "Anglia"

48 Father Kayser and First Catholic Church

1977. 75th Anniv of First Trans-Pacific Cable and 20th Anniv of First Artificial Earth Satellite.
161 **47** 7c. multicoloured 20 10
162 – 15c. blue, grey and black 30 15
163 – 20c. blue, grey and black 30 20
164 – 25c. multicoloured 30 20

DESIGNS: 15c. Tracking station, Nauru; 20c. Stern of "Anglia"; 25c. Dish aerial.

1977. Christmas. Multicoloured.
165 15c. Type **48** 10 10
166 25c. Congregational Church, Orro 15 15
167 30c. Catholic Church, Arubo 15 15

49 Arms of Nauru

1978. 10th Anniv of Independence.
168 **49** 15c. multicoloured 20 15
169 60c. multicoloured 35 30

1978. Nos. 159/60 surch.
170 **46** 4c. on 15c. multicoloured 45 1·50
171 5c. on 15c. multicoloured 45 1·50
172 – 8c. on 30c. multicoloured 45 1·50
173 – 10c. on 30c. multicoloured 45 1·50

51 Collecting Shellfish

1978.
174 **51** 1c. multicoloured 50 30
175 – 2c. multicoloured 50 30
176 – 3c. multicoloured . . . . . 2·00 1·00
177 – 4c. brown, blue and black 50 30
178 – 5c. multicoloured . . . . . 2·25 1·00
179 – 7c. multicoloured . . . . . 30 1·50
180 – 10c. multicoloured 30 20
181 – 15c. multicoloured 40 30
182 – 20c. grey, black and blue 30 30
183 – 25c. multicoloured 30 30
184 – 30c. multicoloured . . . . 1·75 45
185 – 32c. multicoloured . . . . 2·75 1·25
186 – 40c. multicoloured . . . . 1·75 2·25
187 – 50c. multicoloured . . . . 1·50 1·25
188 – $1 multicoloured . . . . . 55 1·00
189 – $2 multicoloured . . . . . 60 1·00
190 – $5 grey, black and blue . . 1·10 2·25

DESIGNS: 2c. Coral outcrop; 3c. Reef scene; 4c. Girl with fish; 5c. Reef heron; 7c. Catching fish, Buada Lagoon; 10c. Ijuw Lagoon; 15c. Girl framed by coral; 20c. Pinnacles, Anibare Bay reef; 25c. Pinnacle at Meneng; 30c. Head of great frigate bird; 32c. White-capped noddy birds in coconut palm; 40c. Wandering tattler; 50c. Great frigate birds on perch; $1 Old coral pinnacles at Topside; $2 New pinnacles at Topside; $5 Blackened pinnacles at Topside.

52 A.P.U. Emblem

53 Virgin and Child

1978. 14th General Assembly of Asian Parliamentarians' Union. Nauru.
191 **52** 15c. multicoloured 20 25
192 – 20c. black, blue and gold 20 25

DESIGN: 20c. As Type **52**, but with different background.

1978. Christmas. Multicoloured.
193 7c. Type **53** 10 10
194 15c. Angel in sunrise scene (horiz) 10 10
195 20c. As 15c. 15 15
196 30c. Type **53** 20 20

54 Baden-Powell and Cub Scout

1978. 70th Anniv of Boy Scout Movement. Mult.
197 20c. Type **54** 20 15
198 30c. Scout 25 20
199 50c. Rover Scout 35 30

55 Wright Flyer I over Nauru

1979. Flight Anniversaries. Multicoloured.
200 10c. Type **55** 25 15
201 15c. Fokker F.VIIa/3m "Southern Cross" superimposed on nose of Boeing 737 . . . . . . 35 20
202 15c. "Southern Cross" and Boeing 737 (front view) . . 35 20
203 30c. Wright Flyer I over Nauru airfield 60 30

ANNIVERSARIES: Nos. 200, 203, 75th anniv of powered flight; 201/2, 50th anniv of Kingsford-Smith's Pacific flight.

56 Sir Rowland Hill and Marshall Islands 10pf. stamp of 1901

1979. Death Cent of Sir Rowland Hill. Mult.
204 5c. Type **56** 15 10
205 15c. Sir Rowland Hill and "Nauru" opt on G.B. 10s. "Seahorse" stamp of 1916–23 . . . . 25 20
206 60c. Sir Rowland Hill and Nauru 60c. 10th anniv of Independence stamp, 1978 55 40
MS207 159 × 101 mm. Nos. 204/6 85 1·25

57 Dish Antenna, Transmitting Station and Radio Mast

1979. 50th Anniv of International Consultative Radio Committee. Multicoloured.
208 7c. Type **57** 15 10
209 32c. Telex operator 35 25
210 40c. Radio operator 40 25

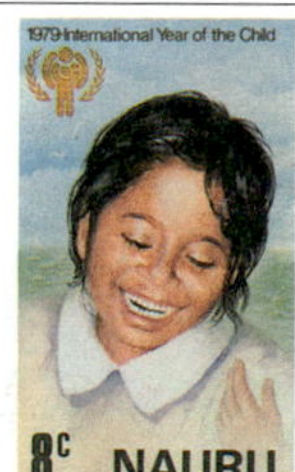

58 Smiling Child

1979. International Year of the Child.
211 **58** 8c. multicoloured 10 10
212 – 15c. multicoloured 15 15
213 – 25c. multicoloured 20 20
214 – 32c. multicoloured 20 20
215 – 50c. multicoloured 25 25
DESIGNS: 15c. to 50c. Smiling children.

59 Ekwenababae (flower), Scroll inscribed "Peace on Earth" and Star

1979. Christmas. Multicoloured.
216 7c. Type **59** 10 10
217 15c. "Thespia populnea" (flower), scroll inscribed "Goodwill towards Men" and star 10 10
218 20c. Denea (flower), scroll inscribed "Peace on Earth" and star 10 10
219 30c. Erekogo (flower), scroll inscribed "Goodwill toward Men" and star 20 20

60 Dassault Bregeut Mystere Falcon 50 over Melbourne

1980. 10th Anniv of Air Nauru. Multicoloured.
220 15c. Type **60** 35 15
221 20c. Fokker F.28 Fellowship over Tarawa 40 15
222 25c. Boeing 727-100 over Hong Kong 40 15
223 30c. Boeing 737 over Auckland 40 15

61 Steam Locomotive

1980. 10th Anniv of Nauru Phosphate Corporation. Multicoloured.
224 8c. Type **61** 10 10
225 32c. Electric locomotive . . . 20 20
226 60c. Diesel-hydraulic locomotive 35 35
MS227 168 × 118 mm. Nos. 224/6 1·00 2·50
No. **MS**227 also commemorates the "London 1980" International Stamp Exhibition.

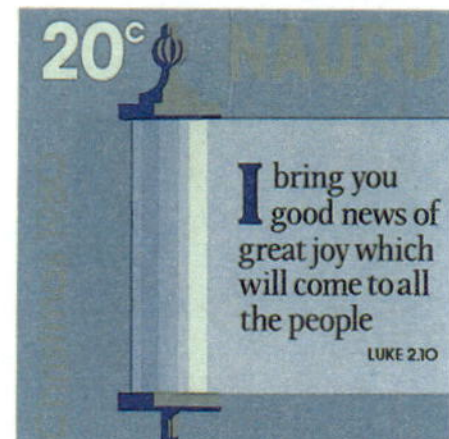

62 Verse 10 from Luke, Chapter 2 in English

1980. Christmas. Verses from Luke, Chapter 2. Multicoloured.
228 20c. Type **62** 10 10
229 20c. Verse 10 in Nauruan . . . 10 10
230 30c. Verse 14 in English . . . 15 15
231 30c. Verse 14 in Nauruan . . 15 15
See also Nos. 248/51.

63 Nauruan, Australia, Union and New Zealand Flags on Aerial View of Nauru

1980. 20th Anniv of U.N. Declaration on the Granting of Independence to Colonial Countries and Peoples. Multicoloured.
232 25c. Type **63** 15 15
233 50c. U.N. Trusteeship Council (72 × 23 mm) . . . 15 15
234 50c. Nauru independence ceremony, 1968 (72 × 23 mm) 25 25

64 Timothy Detudamo

1981. 30th Anniv of Nauru Local Government Council. Head Chiefs. Multicoloured.
235 20c. Type **64** 15 15
236 30c. Raymond Gadabu . . . 15 15
237 50c. Hammer DeRoburt . . 25 25

65 Casting Net by Hand

1981. Fishing. Multicoloured.
238 8c. Type **65** 15 10
239 20c. Outrigger canoe 25 15
240 32c. Outboard motor boat . . 35 20
241 40c. Trawler 35 25
MS242 167 × 116 mm. No. 241 × 4 2·25 2·00
No. **MS**242 was issued to commemorate the "WIPA 1981" International Stamp Exhibition, Vienna.

66 Bank of Nauru Emblem and Building

1981. 5th Anniv of Bank of Nauru.
243 **66** $1 multicoloured 60 60

67 Inaugural Speech

1981. U.N. Day. E.S.C.A.P. (United Nations Economic and Social Commission for Asia and the Pacific) Events. Multicoloured.
244 15c. Type **67** 15 15
245 20c. Presenting credentials . . 15 15
246 25c. Unveiling plaque 20 20
247 30c. Raising U.N. flag . . . 25 25

1981. Christmas. Bible Verses. Designs as T **62**. Multicoloured.
248 20c. Matthew 1, 23 in English 15 15
249 20c. Matthew 1, 23 in Nauruan 15 15
250 30c. Luke 2, 11 in English . . 20 20
251 30c. Luke 2, 11 in Nauruan 20 20

68 Earth Satellite Station

1981. 10th Anniv of South Pacific Forum. Mult.
252 10c. Type **68** 20 15
253 20c. "Enna G" (cargo liner) 25 20
254 30c. Boeing 737 airliner . . . 25 25
255 40c. Local produce 25 30

69 Nauru Scouts leaving for 1935 Frankston Scout Jamboree

1982. 75th Anniv of Boy Scout Movement. Mult.
256 7c. Type **69** 15 15
257 8c. Two Nauru scouts on "Nauru Chief", 1935 (vert) 15 15
258 15c. Nauru scouts making pottery, 1935 (vert) 15 20
259 20c. Lord Huntingfield addressing Nauru scouts, Frankston Jamboree, 1935 20 25
260 25c. Nauru cub and scout, 1982 . . . . 20 30
261 40c. Nauru cubs, scouts and scouters, 1982 . . . . . . 30 45
MS262 152 × 114 mm. Nos. 256/61. Imperf . . . . 1·25 2·25
No. **MS**262 also commemorates Nauru's participation in the "Stampex" National Stamp Exhibition, London.

70 100 kw Electricity Generating Plant under Construction (left side)

1982. Ocean Thermal Energy Conversion. Mult.
263 25c. Type **70** 60 30
264 25c. 100 kw Electricity Generating Plant under construction (right side) . . 60 30
265 40c. Completed plant (left) 80 40
266 40c. Completed plant (right) 80 40
Nos. 263/4 and 265/6 were each issued as horizontal se-tenant pairs, forming composite designs.

71 S.S. "Fido"

1982. 75th Anniv of Phosphate Shipments. Mult.
267 5c. Type **71** 40 10
268 10c. Steam locomotive "Nellie" 50 20
269 30c. Class "Clyde" diesel locomotive 60 50
270 60c. M.V. "Eigamoiya" (bulk carrier) 65 80
MS271 165 × 107 mm. $1 "Eigamoiya", "Rosie-D" and "Kolle-D" (bulk carriers) (67 × 27 mm) . . . . 1·50 2·25
No. **MS**271 was issued to commemorate "ANPEX 82" National Stamp Exhibition, Brisbane.

72 Queen Elizabeth II on Horseback

1982. Royal Visit. Multicoloured.
272 20c. Type **72** 30 20
273 50c. Prince Philip, Duke of Edinburgh 40 45
274 $1 Queen Elizabeth II and Prince Philip (horiz) . . . 45 1·00

73 Father Bernard Lahn

1982. Christmas. Multicoloured.
275 10c. Type **73** 20 35
276 30c. Reverend Itubwa Amram 20 50
277 40c. Pastor James Aingimen 25 80
278 50c. Bishop Paul Mea . . . 30 1·10

74 Speaker of the Nauruan Parliament
75 Nauru Satellite Earth Station

1983. 15th Anniv of Independence. Mult.
279 15c. Type **74** 20 20
280 20c. Family Court in session 25 25
281 30c. Law Courts building (horiz) 25 25
282 50c. Parliamentary chamber (horiz) 40 40

1983. World Communications Year. Mult.
283 5c. Type **75** 20 10
284 10c. Omni-directional range installation 20 15
285 20c. Emergency short-wave radio 25 25
286 25c. Radio Nauru control room 40 30
287 40c. Unloading air mail . . . 90 45

76 Return of Exiles from Truk on M.V. "Trienza", 1946

1983. Angam Day. Multicoloured.
288 15c. Type **76** 20 25
289 20c. Mrs. Elsie Agio (exile community leader) (vert) (25 × 41 mm) 20 25
290 30c. Child on scales (vert) (25 × 41 mm) 35 40
291 40c. Nauruan children (vert) (25 × 41 mm) 45 50

77 "The Holy Virgin, Holy Child and St. John" (School of Raphael)
78 S.S. "Ocean Queen"

1983. Christmas. Multicoloured.
292 5c. Type **77** 10 10
293 15c. "Madonna on the Throne, surrounded by Angels" (School of Sevilla) 20 15
294 50c. "The Mystical Betrothal of St. Catherine with Jesus" (School of Veronese) (horiz) 60 40

1984. 250th Anniv of "Lloyd's List" (newspaper). Multicoloured.
295 20c. Type **78** 30 20
296 25c. M.V "Enna G" 35 25
297 30c. M.V "Baron Minto" . . 40 30
298 40c. Sinking of M.V. "Triadic", 1940 . . . . . 50 45

79 1974 U.P.U. $1 Stamp

1984. Universal Postal Union Congress, Hamburg.
299 **79** $1 multicoloured . . . . . 70 1·25

80 "Hypolimnas bolina" (female)

1984. Butterflies. Multicoloured.

300	25c. Type **80**	35	40
301	30c. "Hypolimnas bolina" (male)	35	55
302	50c. "Danaus plexippus"	40	85

81 Coastal Scene

1984. Life in Nauru. Multicoloured.

303	1c. Type **81**	10	40
304	3c. Nauruan woman (vert)	15	40
305	5c. Modern trawler	40	50
306	10c. Golfer on the links	90	50
307	15c. Excavating phosphate (vert)	90	65
308	20c. Surveyor (vert)	65	55
309	25c. Air Nauru Boeing 727 airliner	80	55
310	30c. Elderly Nauruan (vert)	50	50
311	40c. Loading hospital patient onto Boeing 727 aircraft	90	55
312	50c. Skin-diver with fish (vert)	1·00	80
313	$1 Tennis player (vert)	2·50	3·25
314	$2 Anabar Lagoon	2·50	3·75

82 Buada Chapel

1984. Christmas. Multicoloured.

315	30c. Type **82**	40	50
316	40c. Detudamo Memorial Church	50	65
317	50c. Candle-light service, Kayser College (horiz)	60	70

83 Air Nauru Boeing 737 Jet on Tarmac

1985. 15th Anniv of Air Nauru. Multicoloured.

318	20c. Type **83**	50	35
319	30c. Stewardesses on Boeing 737 aircraft steps (vert)	60	60
320	40c. Fokker F.28 Fellowship over Nauru	75	75
321	50c. Freight being loaded onto Boeing 727 (vert)	85	85

84 Open Cut Mining

1985. 15th Anniv of Nauru Phosphate Corporation. Multicoloured.

322	20c. Type **84**	1·00	60
323	25c. Diesel locomotive hauling crushed ore	2·00	1·00
324	30c. Phosphate drying plant	1·75	1·00
325	50c. Early steam locomotive	2·50	1·75

85 Mother and Baby on Beach

86 Adult Common Noddy with Juvenile

1985. Christmas. Multicoloured.

326	50c. Beach scene	1·50	2·25
327	50c. Type **85**	1·50	2·25

Nos. 326/7 were printed together, se-tenant, forming a composite design.

1985. Birth Bicentenary of John J. Audubon (ornithologist). Common ("Brown") Noddy. Mult.

328	10c. Type **86**	35	35
329	20c. Adult and immature birds in flight	50	70
330	30c. Adults in flight	65	85
331	50c. "Brown Noddy" (John J. Audubon)	80	1·10

87 Douglas Motor Cycle

1986. Early Transport on Nauru. Multicoloured.

332	15c. Type **87**	80	70
333	20c. Primitive lorry	95	95
334	30c. German-built steam locomotive, 1910	1·50	1·50
335	40c. "Baby" Austin car	1·75	1·75

88 Island and Bank of Nauru

1986. 10th Anniv of Bank of Nauru. Children's Paintings. Multicoloured.

336	20c. Type **88**	20	30
337	25c. Borrower with notes and coins	25	35
338	30c. Savers	30	40
339	40c. Customers at bank counter	35	55

89 "Plumeria rubra"

1986. Flowers. Multicoloured.

340	20c. Type **89**	30	70
341	25c. "Tristellateia australis"	40	85
342	30c. "Bougainvillea cultivar"	50	1·00
343	40c. "Delonix regia"	60	1·25

90 Carol Singers

1986. Christmas. Multicoloured.

344	20c. Type **90**	40	30
345	$1 Carol singers and hospital patient	1·60	3·50

91 Young Girls Dancing

1987. Nauruan Dancers. Multicoloured.

346	20c. Type **91**	80	80
347	30c. Stick dance	1·00	1·25
348	50c. Boy doing war dance (vert)	1·75	2·50

92 Hibiscus Fibre Skirt

1987. Personal Artefacts. Multicoloured.

349	25c. Type **92**	75	75
350	30c. Headband and necklets	85	85
351	45c. Decorative necklets	1·10	1·10
352	60c. Pandanus leaf fan	1·60	1·60

93 U.P.U. Emblem and Air Mail Label

94 Open Bible

1987. World Post Day.

353	**93** 40c. multicoloured	1·50	1·25
MS354	122×82 mm. $1 U.P.U. emblem and map of Pacific showing mail routes (114×74 mm)	3·00	3·50

1987. Centenary of Nauru Congregational Church.

355	**94** 40c. multicoloured	1·50	1·75

95 Nauruan Children's Party

1987. Christmas. Multicoloured.

356	20c. Type **95**	75	50
357	$1 Nauruan Christmas dinner	2·75	3·25

96 Loading Phosphate on Ship

1988. 20th Anniv of Independence. Mult.

358	25c. Type **96**	1·00	1·00
359	40c. Tomano flower (vert)	1·50	1·50
360	55c. Great frigate bird (vert)	2·25	2·25
361	$1 Arms of Republic (35×35 mm)	2·50	3·50

97 Map of German Marshall Is. and 1901 5m. Yacht Definitive

1988. 80th Anniv of Nauru Post Office. Mult.

362	30c. Type **97**	75	75
363	50c. Letter and post office of 1908	1·00	1·25
364	70c. Nauru Post Office and airmail letter	1·25	1·50

98 "Itubwer" (mat)

1988. String Figures. Multicoloured.

365	25c. Type **98**	35	35
366	40c. "Etegerer – the Pursuer"	50	60
367	55c. "Holding up the Sky"	65	70
368	80c. "Manujie's Sword"	1·00	1·75

99 U.P.U. Emblem and National Flag

1988. Cent of Nauru's Membership of U.P.U.

369	**99** $1 multicoloured	1·25	1·25

100 "Hark the Herald Angels"

1988. Christmas. Designs showing words and music from "Hark the Herald Angels Sing".

370	**100** 20c. black, red and yellow	60	30
371	– 60c. black, red and mauve	1·40	1·25
372	– $1 black, red and green	2·25	2·25

101 Logo (15th anniv of Nauru Insurance Corporation)

102 Mother and Baby

1989. Anniversaries and Events. Multicoloured.

373	15c. Type **101**	30	30
374	50c. Logos (World Telecommunications Day and 10th anniv of Asian-Pacific Telecommunity)	75	85
375	$1 Photograph of island scene (150 years of photography)	1·75	2·00
376	$2 Capitol and U.P.U. emblem (20th U.P.U. Congress, Washington)	2·75	4·50

1989. Christmas. Multicoloured.

377	20c. Type **102**	50	30
378	$1 Children opening presents	2·25	3·25

103 Eigigu working while Sisters play

104 Early Mining by Hand

1989. 20th Anniv of First Manned Landing on Moon. Legend of "Eigigu, the Girl in the Moon". Multicoloured.

379	25c. Type **103**	3·00	2·75
380	30c. Eigigu climbing tree	3·25	3·00
381	50c. Eigigu stealing toddy from blind woman	6·00	5·50
382	$1 Eigigu on Moon	8·00	7·50

1990. 20th Anniv of Nauru Phosphate Corporation. Multicoloured.

383	50c. Type **104**	1·00	1·00
384	$1 Modern mining by excavator	1·50	2·00

105 Sunday School Class

106 Eoiyepiang laying Baby on Mat

1990. Christmas. Multicoloured.

385	25c. Type **105**	90	1·25
386	25c. Teacher telling Christmas story	90	1·25

Nos. 385/6 were printed together, se-tenant, forming a composite design.

1990. Legend of "Eoiyepiang, the Daughter of Thunder and Lightning". Multicoloured.

387	25c. Type **106**	1·50	60
388	30c. Eoiyepiang making floral decoration	1·75	70
389	50c. Eoiyepiang left on snow-covered mountain	2·25	2·00
390	$1 Eoiyepiang and warrior	3·25	3·50

107 Oleander

1991. Flowers. Multicoloured.

391	15c. Type **107**	15	20
392	20c. Lily	15	20
393	25c. Passion flower	20	25
394	30c. Lily (different)	25	30
395	35c. Caesalpinia	30	35
396	40c. Clerodendron	35	40
397	45c. "Baubina pinnata"	40	45
398	50c. Hibiscus (vert)	40	45
399	75c. Apocymaceae	65	70
400	$1 Bindweed (vert)	85	90

401 $2 Tristellateia (vert) . . . . 1·70 1·80

402 $3 Impala lily (vert) . . . . 2·50 2·75

108 Jesus Christ and Children (stained glass window)

1991. Christmas. Sheet 124 × 82 mm.

MS403 **108** $2 multicoloured . . 4·25 4·75

109 Star and Symbol of Asian Development Bank

1992. 25th Annual Meeting of Asian Development Bank.

404 **109** $1.50 multicoloured . . . 2·00 2·50

110 Gifts under Christmas Tree

1992. Christmas. Children's Paintings. Mult.

405 45c. Type **110** 75 75

406 60c. Father Christmas in sleigh . . . . 1·00 1·50

111 Hammer DeRoburt

112 Running, Constitution Day Sports

1993. 25th Anniv of Independence and Hammer DeRoburt (former President) Commemoration.

407 **111** $1 multicoloured . . . . 2·50 3·00

1993. 15th Anniv of Constitution Day. Mult.

408 70c. Type **112** . . . . 1·40 1·40

409 80c. Part of Independence Proclamation . . . . . . 1·40 1·40

113 Great Frigate Birds, Flying Fish and Island

1993. 24th South Pacific Forum Meeting, Nauru. Multicoloured.

410 60c. Type **113** . . . . 1·40 1·50

411 60c. Red-tailed tropic bird, great frigate bird, dolphin and island . . . . 1·40 1·50

412 60c. Racoon butterflyfish ("Ikimago"), coral and sea urchins . . . . 1·40 1·50

413 60c. Three different types of fish with corals . . . . . 1·40 1·50

MS414 140 × 130 mm. Nos. 410/13 7·00 8·00

Nos. 410/13 were printed together, se-tenant, forming a composite design.

114 "Peace on Earth, Goodwill to Men" and Star

1993. Christmas. Multicoloured.

415 55c. Type **114** 85 85

416 65c. "Hark the Herald Angels Sing" and star 90 90

115 Girls with Dogs

1994. "Hong Kong '94" International Stamp Exhibition. Chinese New Year ("Year of the Dog"). Multicoloured.

417 $1 Type **115** . . . . 1·50 2·00

418 $1 Boys with dogs . . . . . 1·50 2·00

MS419 100 × 75 mm. Nos. 417/18 3·00 3·75

1994. "Singpex '94" National Stamp Exhibition, Singapore. No. **MS**419 optd "SINGPEX '94" and emblem in gold on sheet margin.

MS420 100 × 75 mm. Nos. 417/18 3·00 3·75

116 Weightlifting

117 Peace Dove and Star over Island

1994. 15th Commonwealth Games, Victoria, Canada.

421 **116** $1.50 multicoloured . . . 1·40 2·00

1994. Christmas. Multicoloured.

422 65c. Type **117** 90 90

423 75c. Star over Bethlehem . . 1·00 1·00

118 Air Nauru Airliner and Emblems

1994. 50th Anniv of I.C.A.O. Multicoloured.

424 55c. Type **118** 50 55

425 65c. Control tower, Nauru International Airport . . . 60 65

426 80c. D.V.O.R. equipment . . 70 1·00

427 $1 Crash tenders . . . . . . 90 1·10

MS428 165 × 127 mm. Nos. 424/7 4·00 4·50

119 Emblem and Olympic Rings

1994. Nauru's Entry into Int Olympic Committee.

429 **119** 50c. multicoloured 50 50

120 Nauruan Flag

1995. 50th Anniv of United Nations (1st issue). Multicoloured.

430 75c. Type **120** . . . . 1·40 1·40

431 75c. Arms of Nauru . . . . 1·40 1·40

432 75c. Outrigger canoe on coastline . . . . 1·40 1·40

433 75c. Airliner over phosphate freighter . . . . 1·40 1·40

MS434 110 × 85 mm. Nos. 430/3 4·50 5·50

Nos. 430/3 were printed together, se-tenant, forming a composite design.

See also Nos. 444/5.

121 Signing Phosphate Agreement, 1967

1995. 25th Anniv of Nauru Phosphate Corporation. Multicoloured.

435 60c. Type **121** . . . . 80 1·00

436 60c. Pres. Bernard Dowiyogo and Prime Minister Keating of Australia shaking hands . . . . . . 80 1·00

MS437 120 × 80 mm. $2 Excavating phosphate . . . . 2·75 3·25

1995. International Stamp Exhibitions. No. 309 surch.

438 50c. on 25c. multicoloured (surch **at Beijing**) . . . . . 1·40 1·40

439 $1 on 25c. multicoloured (surch **at Jakarta**) . . . . 1·40 1·75

440 $1 on 25c. multicoloured (surch **at Singapore**) . . . 1·40 1·75

123 Sea Birds (face value at top right)

1995. Olympic Games, Atlanta. Sheet 140 × 121 mm, containing T **123** and similar vert designs. Multicoloured.

MS441 60c.+15c. Type **123**; 60c.+15c. Sea brids (face value at top left); 60c.+15c. Four dolphins; 60c.+15c. Pair of dolphins . . 4·50 5·00

The premiums on No. **MS**441 were for Nauru sport development.

124 Children playing on Gun

1995. 50th Anniv of Peace. Multicoloured.

442 75c. Type **124** . . . . 1·75 2·00

443 $1.50 Children making floral garlands . . . . 1·75 2·00

125 Nauru Crest, Coastline and U.N. Anniversary Emblem

126 Young Girl praying

1995. 50th Anniv of United Nations (2nd issue). Multicoloured.

444 75c. Type **125** . . . . 90 1·00

445 $1.50 Aerial view of Nauru and U.N. Headquarters, New York . . . . 1·60 2·00

1995. Christmas. Multicoloured.

446 60c. Type **126** . . . . 90 1·00

447 70c. Man praying . . . . . 90 1·00

127 Returning Refugees and Head Chief Timothy Detudamo

1996. 50th Anniv of Nauruans' Return from Truk.

448 **127** 75c. multicoloured . . . . 90 1·00

449 $1.25 multicoloured . . . 1·60 2·00

MS450 120 × 80 mm. Nos. 448/9 3·25 4·00

128 Nanjing Stone Lion

1996. "CHINA '96" 9th Asian International Stamp Exhibition, Peking. Sheet 130 × 110 mm.

MS451 **128** 45c. multicoloured 1·00 1·25

129 Symbolic Athlete

1996. Centenary of Modern Olympic Games. Mult.

452 40c. Type **129** 90 70

453 50c. Symbolic weightlifter . . 1·00 90

454 60c. Weightlifter (horiz) . . . 1·10 1·00

455 $1 Athlete (horiz) . . . . . 1·50 2·00

130 The Nativity and Angel

1996. Christmas. Multicoloured.

456 50c. Type **130** 60 60

457 70c. Angel, world map and wild animals . . . . 80 1·00

131 Dolphin (fish)

1997. Endangered Species. Fishes. Multicoloured.

458 20c. Type **131** 95 95

459 30c. Wahoo . . . . 1·10 1·10

460 40c. Sailfish . . . . 1·25 1·25

461 50c. Yellow-finned tuna . . . 1·40 1·40

132 Statue of Worshipper with Offering

133 Princess Elizabeth and Lieut. Philip Mountbatten, 1947

1997. "HONG KONG '97" International Stamp Exhibition. Statues of different worshippers (1c. to 15c.) or Giant Buddha of Hong Kong (25c.).

462 **132** 1c. multicoloured 20 20

463 – 2c. multicoloured 20 20

464 – 5c. multicoloured 25 25

465 – 10c. multicoloured 30 30

466 – 12c. multicoloured 30 30

467 – 15c. multicoloured 30 30
468 – 25c. multicoloured 40 40

1997. Golden Wedding of Queen Elizabeth and Prince Philip.
469 **133** 80c. black and gold . . . 90 1·00
470 – $1.20 multicoloured . . . 1·40 1·60
MS471 150 × 110 mm. Nos. 469/70 (sold at $3) . . . . 3·00 3·50
DESIGN: $1.20, Queen Elizabeth and Prince Philip, 1997.

134 Conference Building

1997. 28th Parliamentary Conference of Presiding Officers and Clerks. Sheet 150 × 100 mm.
MS472 **134** $2 multicoloured . . 1·75 2·00

135 Commemorative Pillar

1997. Christmas. 110th Anniv of Nauru Congregational Church. Multicoloured.
473 60c. Type **135** 60 55
474 80c. Congregational Church 80 90

136 Weightlifter

138 Diana, Princess of Wales

137 Juan Antonio Samaranch and Aerial View

1998. Commonwealth, Oceania and South Pacific Weightlifting Championships, Nauru. Sheet 180 × 100 mm, containing T **136** and similar vert designs showing weightlifters.
MS475 40c., 60c., 80c., $1.20 multicoloured . . . . 2·25 2·75

1998. Visit of International Olympic Committee President.
476 **137** $2 multicoloured . . . . 1·75 2·00

1998. Diana, Princess of Wales Commemoration. Multicoloured.
477 70c. Type **138** 55 60
478 70c. Wearing white shirt . . 55 60
479 70c. With tiara 55 60
480 70c. In white jacket 55 60
481 70c. Wearing pink hat . . . 55 60
482 70c. In white suit 55 60

139 Gymnastics

140 Sqn. Ldr. Hicks (Composer of Nauru's National Anthem) conducting

1998. 16th Commonwealth Games, Kuala Lumpur, Malaysia. Multicoloured.
483 40c. Type **139** 40 40
484 60c. Athletics 55 60
485 70c. Sprinting 65 70
486 80c. Weightlifting 70 80
MS487 153 × 130 mm. Nos. 483/6 1·90 2·40

1998. 30th Anniv of Independence. Multicoloured.
488 $1 Type **140** 85 80
489 $2 Sqn. Ldr. Hicks and score 1·75 2·25
MS490 175 × 110 mm. Nos. 488/9 2·50 3·25

141 Palm Trees, Fish, Festive Candle and Flower

1998. Christmas. Multicoloured.
491 85c. Type **141** . . . . 80 1·00
492 95c. Flower, present, fruit and island scene . . . . . 85 1·00

142 18th-century Frigate

1998. Bicentenary of First Contact with the Outside World. Multicoloured.
493 $1.50 Type **142** . . . . . . 1·50 1·75
494 $1.50 Capt. John Fearn . . . 1·50 1·75
MS495 173 × 131 mm. Nos. 493/4 3·00 3·75
No. 493 is wrongly identified as "Hunter" (snow).

143 H.M.A.S. "Melbourne" (cruiser)

1999. "Australia '99" World Stamp Exhibition, Melbourne. Ships. Sheet 101 × 120 mm, containing T **143** and similar multicoloured designs.
MS496 70c. Type **143**; 80c. H.M.A.S. "D'Amantina" (frigate); 90c. "Alcyone" (experimental ship); $1 "Rosie-D" (bulk carrier); $1.10 Outrigger canoe (80 × 30 mm) . . . . 4·25 4·75

1999. 30th Anniv of First Manned Landing on Moon. As T **98a** of Kiribati. Multicoloured.
497 70c. Neil Armstrong (astronaut) 65 70
498 80c. Service and lunar module on way to Moon 70 80
499 90c. Aldrin and "Apollo 11" on Moon's surface . . . . 85 1·00
500 $1 Command module entering Earth's atmosphere . . . . 90 1·25
MS501 90 × 80 mm. $2 Earth as seen from Moon (circular, 40 mm diam) . . . . 1·90 2·40

144 Emblem and Forms of Transport

1999. 125th Anniv of Universal Postal Union.
502 **144** $1 multicoloured . . . . 1·00 1·25

145 Killer Whale

146 Girl holding Candle

1999. "China '99" International Philatelic Exhibition, Beijing. Sheet 185 × 85 mm, containing T **145** and similar vert design. Multicoloured.
MS503 50c. Type **145**; 50c. Swordfish . . . . 1·00 1·40

1999. Christmas. Multicoloured.
504 65c. Type **146** 70 75
505 70c. Candle and Christmas tree 80 85

147 Nauruan Woman in Traditional Dress and Canoes

2000. New Millennium. Multicoloured.
506 70c. Type **147** . . . . 1·25 1·25
507 $1.10 Aspects of modern Nauru . . . . 2·00 2·00
508 $1.20 Woman holding globe and man at computer . . . 2·00 2·00
MS509 149 × 88 mm. Nos. 506/8 4·50 4·75

148 Power Plant

2000. Centenary of Phosphate Discovery. Mult.
510 $1.20 Type **148** . . . . . . 1·25 1·25
511 $1.80 Phosphate train . . . . 2·00 2·00
512 $2 Albert Ellis and phosphate sample . . . . 2·00 2·25
MS513 79 × 131 mm. Nos. 510/12 4·50 5·50

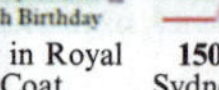

149 Queen Mother in Royal Blue Hat and Coat

150 Running and Sydney Opera House

2000. 100th Birthday of Queen Elizabeth the Queen Mother. Sheet 150 × 106 mm, containing T **149** and similar horiz designs, each including photograph of Queen Mother as a child. Multicoloured.
MS514 150 × 106 mm. $1 Type **149**; $1.10 In lilac hat and coat; $1.20 In turquoise hat and coat; $1.40 In greenish blue hat and coat with maple leaf brooch . . . . . . 4·50 5·00

2000. Olympic Games, Sydney. Multicoloured.
515 90c. Type **150** . . . . 1·25 1·00
516 $1 Basketball . . . . 1·50 1·25
517 $1.10 Weightlifting and cycling . . . . 1·50 1·50
518 $1.20 Running and Olympic Torch . . . . 1·50 1·60

151 Flower, Christmas Tree and Star

2000. Christmas. Multicoloured.
519 65c. Type **151** 60 70
520 75c. Decorations, toy engine and palm tree 65 75
MS521 134 × 95 mm. Nos. 519/20 2·00 2·50

152 Noddy and Part of Island

2001. 32nd Pacific Islands Forum, Nauru. Multicoloured.
522 90c. Type **152** . . . . 1·75 1·50
523 $1 Frigate bird in flight and part of island . . . . . . 1·90 1·75
524 $1.10 Two frigate birds and part of island . . . . . 2·00 1·90
525 $2 Frigate bird and Nauru airport . . . . 2·75 2·75
MS526 145 × 130 mm. Nos. 522/5 7·50 8·00
Nos. 522/5 were printed together, se-tenant, forming a composite view of Nauru.

153 Princess Elizabeth in A.T.S. Uniform, 1946

2002. Golden Jubilee.
527 **153** 70c. black, mauve and gold . . . . 1·40 1·50
528 – 80c. multicoloured . . . . 1·40 1·50
529 – 90c. black, mauve and gold . . . . 1·50 1·60
530 – $1 multicoloured . . . . 1·50 1·60
MS531 162 × 95 mm. Nos. 527/30 and $4 multicoloured . . . . 8·00 8·50
DESIGNS—HORIZ: 80c. Queen Elizabeth in multicoloured hat; 90c. Princess Elizabeth at Cheltenham Races, 1951; $1 Queen Elizabeth in evening dress, 1997. VERT (38 x 51 mm)—$4 Queen Elizabeth after Annigoni.
Designs as Nos. 527/30 in No. **MS**531 omit the gold frame around each stamp and the "Golden Jubilee 1952–2002" inscription.

154 Statue of Liberty with U.S. and Nauru Flags

2002. In Remembrance. Victims of Terrorist Attacks on U.S.A. (11 September 2001).
532 **154** 90c. multicoloured . . . . 1·00 1·10
533 $1 multicoloured . . . . 1·10 1·25
534 $1.10 multicoloured . . . 1·25 1·40
535 $2 multicoloured . . . . 2·00 2·25

155 *Parthenos sylvia*

2002. Butterflies of the Pacific. Multicoloured.
536 50c. Type **155** 85 85
537 50c. *Delias madetes* 85 85
538 50c. *Danaus philene* 85 85
539 50c. *Arhopala hercules* . . . 85 85
540 50c. *Papilio canopus* 85 85
541 50c. *Danaus schenkii* 85 85
542 50c. *Pairthenos tigrina* . . . 85 85
543 50c. *Mycalesis phidon* 85 85
544 50c. *Vindula sapor* 85 85
MS545 85 × 60 mm. $2 *Graphium agamemnon* . . . . 2·75 3·25
Nos. 536/44 were printed together, se-tenant, forming a composite design.

156 Queen Elizabeth in London, 1940

2002. Queen Elizabeth the Queen Mother Commemoration.
546 **156** $1.50 black, gold and purple . . . . 2·25 2·50
547 – $1.50 multicoloured . . . 2·25 2·50
MS548 145 × 70 mm. Nos. 546/7 4·50 5·00
DESIGNS: No. 547, Queen Mother in Norwich, 1990.
Designs as Nos. 546/7 in No. **MS**548 omit the "1900–2002" inscription and the coloured frame.

157 Turntable Ladder and Burning Building

2002. International Firefighters. Multicoloured.
549 20c. Type **157** 50 40
550 50c. Firefighting tug and burning ship . . . . 1·00 70
551 90c. Fighting a forest fire . . 1·40 1·10
552 $1 Old and new helmets . . . 1·50 1·25

553 $1.10 Steam-driven pump and modern fire engine . . . . 1·50 1·40
554 $2 19th-century and present day hose teams . . . . . 2·50 3·00
MS555 110 × 90 mm. $5 Airport fire engine . . . . 8·00 8·50

158 First Catholic Church, Arubo

2002. Centenary of Catholic Church on Nauru.
556 **158** $1.50 brown and black . . 1·40 1·60
557 – $1.50 violet and black . . 1·40 1·60
558 – $1.50 blue and black . . . 1·40 1·60
559 – $1.50 green and black . . 1·40 1·60
560 – $1.50 blue and black . . . 1·40 1·60
561 – $1.50 red and black . . . 1·40 1·60
DESIGNS: No. 557, Father Friedrich Gründl (first missionary); 558, Sister Stanisla; 559, Second Catholic church, Ibwenape; 560, Brother Kalixtus Bader (lay brother); 561, Father Alois Kayser (missionary).

159 "Holy Family with dancing Angels" (Van Dyck)

2002. Christmas. Religious Art. Multicoloured.
562 15c. Type **159** 40 25
563 $1 "Holy Virgin with Child" (Cornelis Bloemaert after Lucas Cangiasius) . . . . 1·25 75
564 $1.20 "Holy Family with Cat" (Rembrandt) . . . . 1·40 90
565 $3 "Holy Family with St. John" (Pierre Brebiette after Raphael) . . . . . . 3·25 4·00

160 Bubble Tentacle Sea Anemone and Fire Anemonefish ("Red-and-Black Anemone Fish")

2003. Endangered Species. Sea Anemones and Anemonefish. Multicoloured.
566 15c. Type **160** 45 30
567 $1 Leathery sea anemone and orange-finned anemonefish 1·50 80
568 $1.20 Magnificent sea anemone and pink anemonefish . . . . 1·60 1·10
569 $3 Merten's sea anemone and yellow-tailed anemonefish ("Clark's Anemone Fish") 3·50 4·00

161 Santos-Dumont's *Ballon No. 6* flying around Eiffel Tower, 1901

2003. Centenary of Powered Flight. Airships. Multicoloured.
570 50c. Type **161** 80 85
571 50c. USS *Shenandoah* 80 85
572 50c. Airship R101, 1929 . . . 80 85
573 50c. British Beardmore Airship R34, 1919 (first double crossing of North Atlantic) 80 85
574 50c. Zeppelin LZ-1 (first flight, 1900) 80 85
575 50c. Airship USS *Los Angeles* moored to airship tender USS *Patoka* 80 85
576 50c. Goodyear C-71 airship 80 85
577 50c. LZ-130 *Graf Zeppelin II* 80 85
578 50c. Zeppelin airship over Alps 80 85
MS579 150 × 100 mm. $2 LZ-127 *Graf Zeppelin* over Mount Fuji; $2 LZ-127 *Graf Zeppelin* over San Francisco; $2 LZ-127 *Graf Zeppelin* exchanging mail with Soviet ice breaker over Franz Josef Land . . . . 8·50 9·00

162 Nightingale Reed Warbler

2003. Bird Life International. Nightingale Reed Warbler ("Nauru Reed Warbler"). Multicoloured.
580 $1.50 Type **162** . . . . . 2·25 2·50
581 $1.50 Nightingale reed warbler on reeds (horiz) . . 2·25 2·50
MS582 175 × 80 mm. $1.50 Head (horiz); Type **162**; $1.50 Singing; $1.50 No. 581; $1.50 Adult and nestlings (horiz) . . . . 8·50 9·00

163 *The Aigle* and HMS *Defiance*

2005. Bicentenary of the Battle of Trafalgar (1st issue). Multicoloured.
583 25c. Type **163** 50 40
584 50c. French *Eprouvette* . . . 80 70
585 75c. *The Santissima Trinidad* and HMS *Africa* . . . . . 1·10 1·10
586 $1 Emperor Napoleon Bonaparte (vert) . . . . . 1·40 1·40
587 $1.50 HMS *Victory* . . . . . 2·00 2·25
588 $2.50 Vice-Admiral Sir Horatio Nelson (vert) . . . 3·00 3·25
MS589 120 × 79 mm. $2.50 Admiral Villeneuve (vert); $2.50 *Formidable* (vert) . . . . 5·50 6·00
No. 587 contains traces of powdered wood from HMS *Victory*.
See also Nos. 603/5.

164 *Komet* (German raider)

2005. 60th Anniv of the End of World War II. Pacific Explorer World Stamp Exhibition (**MS**600). Multicoloured.
590 75c. Type **164** . . . . 1·10 1·10
591 75c. *Le Triomphant* (French warship) . . . . 1·10 1·10
592 75c. Type 97 Te-Ke (Japanese tank) . . . . 1·10 1·10
593 75c. USAF B-24 Liberator aircraft . . . . 1·10 1·10
594 75c. USS *Paddle* (US submarine) . . . . 1·10 1·10
595 75c. *Coral Princess* (B-25G Mitchell aircraft) . . . . . 1·10 1·10
596 75c. Spitfires . . . . 1·10 1·10
597 75c. HMAS *Diamantina* (River Class Frigate) . . . 1·10 1·10
598 75c. D-Day Landings . . . . 1·10 1·10
599 75c. Crowds gathered and Union Jack flag . . . . . 1·10 1·10
MS600 90 × 60 mm. $5 HMAS *Manoora* (Australian troop ship) 5·50 6·00

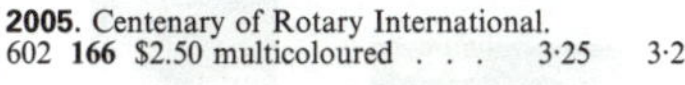

165 Pope John Paul II **166** Rotary Emblem

2005. Commemoration of Pope John Paul II.
601 **165** $1 multicoloured . . . . 1·40 1·40

2005. Centenary of Rotary International.
602 **166** $2.50 multicoloured . . . 3·25 3·25

167 Rota Bridled White-Eye

2005. Birdlife International. Multicoloured.
MS603 Three sheets each 170 × 85 mm. (a) 25c. × 6, Type **167**; Truk ("Faichuk") White-eye; Savaii ("Samoan") White-eye; Bridled white-eye; Ponape ("Long-billed") White-eye; Golden white-eye. (b) 50c. × 6, Kuhl's ("Lorikeet") Lory; Masked shining parrot; Kandavu ("Crimson") shining parrot; Tahitian lorikeet ("Blue Lory"); Stephen's lory ("Henderson Lorikeet"); Ultramarine ("Lorikeet") lory. (c) $1 × 6, Atoll fruit dove; Henderson Island fruit dove; Rarotongan ("Cook Islands") fruit dove; Rapa Island fruit dove; Whistling dove; Mariana fruit dove . . . . . 17·00 18·00
The backgrounds of Nos. **MS**603a/c form composite designs.

168 HMS *Victory* **169** *The Little Fir Tree*

2005. Bicentenary of the Battle of Trafalgar (2nd issue). Multicoloured.
604 50c. Type **168** 70 60
605 $1 Ships engaged in battle (horiz) . . . . 1·25 1·25
606 $5 Admiral Lord Nelson . . 5·00 5·50

2005. Christmas and Birth Bicentenary of Hans Christian Andersen (writer). Multicoloured.
607 25c. Type **169** 40 30
608 50c. *The Wild Swans* 70 60
609 75c. *The Farmyard Cock and the Weather Cock* . . . . 1·00 1·00
610 $1 *The Storks* . . . . 1·25 1·25
611 $2.50 *The Toad* . . . . . . 3·00 3·25
612 $5 *The Ice Maiden* . . . . . 5·00 5·50

NAWANAGAR Pt. 1

A state of India, Bombay District. Now uses Indian stamps.

6 docra = 1 anna.

1 (1 docra) **2** (2 docra)

1877. Imperf or perf.
1 **1** 1doc. blue . . . . 75 25·00

1880. Imperf.
6ab **2** 1doc. lilac . . . . 3·50 7·50
8 c 2doc. green . . . . 4·25 10·00
9 b 3doc. yellow . . . . 6·00 12·00

4 (1 docra)

1893. Imperf or perf.
13 **4** 1doc. black . . . . 1·75 6·00
14 2doc. green . . . . 1·75 6·50
15b 3doc. yellow . . . . 1·75 10·00

NEAPOLITAN PROVINCES Pt. 8

Temporary issues for Naples and other parts of S. Italy which adhered to the new Kingdom of Italy in 1860.

200 tornesi = 100 grano = 1 ducato.

1

1861. Embossed. Imperf.
2 **1** ½t. green . . . . 9·25 £140
5 ½g. brown £130 £150
9 1g. black . . . . £325 19·00
10 2g. blue . . . . 80·00 9·50
15 5g. red . . . . £140 90·00
18 10g. orange £100 £170
19 20g. yellow £425 £1600
23 50g. slate . . . . 23·00 £7000

NEGRI SEMBILAN Pt. 1

A state of the Federation of Malaya, incorporated in Malaysia in 1963.

100 cents = 1 dollar (Straits or Malayan).

1891. Stamp of Straits Settlements optd **Negri Sembilan**.
1 **5** 2c. red . . . . 3·00 6·00

2 Tiger

3

1891.
2 **2** 1c. green . . . . 3·00 1·00
3 2c. red . . . . 3·25 8·50
4 5c. blue . . . . 30·00 40·00

1896.
5 **3** 1c. purple and green . . . . 13·00 6·50
6 2c. purple and brown . . . . 35·00 £110
7 3c. purple and red . . . . . 14·00 1·25
8 5c. purple and yellow . . . . 8·50 9·50
9 8c. purple and blue . . . . . 29·00 17·00
10 10c. purple and orange . . . 27·00 14·00
11 15c. green and violet . . . . 42·00 75·00
12 20c. green and olive . . . . 65·00 38·00
13 25c. green and red . . . . . 70·00 90·00
14 50c. green and black . . . . 75·00 65·00

1898. Surch in words and bar.
15 **3** 1c. on 15c. green and violet £100 £300
16 **2** 4c. on 1c. green . . . . . . 2·50 16·00
17 **3** 4c. on 3c. purple and red . . 3·25 18·00
18 **2** 4c. on 5c. blue . . . . 1·25 15·00

1898. Surch in words only.
19 **3** 4c. on 8c. purple and blue . . 6·50 4·25

6 Arms of Negri Sembilan

7 Arms of Negri Sembilan

1935.
21 **6** 1c. black . . . . 1·00 20
22 2c. green . . . . 1·00 20
23 2c. orange . . . . 4·25 65·00
24 3c. green . . . . 8·00 8·00
25 4c. orange . . . . 1·25 10
26 5c. brown . . . . 1·75 10
27 6c. red . . . . 15·00 2·50
28 6c. grey . . . . 4·75 75·00
29 8c. grey . . . . 2·00 10
30 10c. purple . . . . 1·00 10
31 12c. blue . . . . 2·50 50
32 15c. blue . . . . 10·00 50·00
33 25c. purple and red . . . . . 1·25 70
34 30c. purple and orange . . . 3·50 2·00
35 40c. red and purple . . . . . 2·50 2·00
36 50c. black on green . . . . . 5·00 2·25
37 $1 black and red on blue . . 4·00 3·75
38 $2 green and red . . . . . . 32·00 17·00
39 $5 green and red on green . . 21·00 70·00

1948. Silver Wedding. As T **4b/c** of Pitcairn Islands.
40 10c. violet 15 50
41 $5 green . . . . 20·00 28·00

1949.
42 **7** 1c. black 30 10
43 2c. orange 30 10
44 3c. green 30 30
45 4c. brown 30 10
46a 5c. purple 30 45
47 6c. grey . . . . 1·25 10
48 8c. red 50 75
49 8c. green . . . . 2·25 1·60
50 10c. mauve 20 10
51 12c. red . . . . 2·25 2·75
52 15c. blue . . . . 3·00 10
53 20c. black and green 50 75
54 20c. blue . . . . 1·00 10
55 25c. purple and orange . . . 50 10
56 30c. red and purple . . . . . 1·25 2·50
57 35c. red and purple . . . . . 1·00 1·00
58 40c. red and purple . . . . . 1·75 4·75
59 50c. black and blue . . . . . 2·75 20
60 $1 blue and purple . . . . . 3·75 2·25
61 $2 green and red . . . . . . 12·00 18·00
62 $5 green and brown . . . . . 50·00 55·00

1949. U.P.U. As T **4d/g** of Pitcairn Islands.
63 10c. purple 20 10
64 15c. blue . . . . 1·40 2·75

65 25c. orange . . . . 30 2·25
66 50c. black . . . . 60 3·25

1953. Coronation. As T **4h** of Pitcairn Islands.
67 10c. black and purple . . . . 1·25 50

1957. As Nos. 92/102 of Kedah but inset Arms of Negri Sembilan.
68 1c. black 10 10
69 2c. red 10 10
70 4c. sepia 10 10
71 5c. lake 10 10
72 8c. green . . . . 1·00 1·40
73 10c. sepia . . . . 2·00 10
74 10c. purple . . . . 5·00 10
75 20c. blue . . . . 1·00 10
76a 50c. black and blue 75 10
77 $1 blue and purple . . . . . 1·50 2·00
78 $2 green and red . . . . . 7·50 16·00
79 $5 brown and green . . . . 11·00 18·00

8 Tuanku Munawir

1961. Installation of Tuanku Munawir as Yang di-Pertuan Besar of Negri Sembilan.
80 **8** 10c. multicoloured 30 70

9 "Vanda hookeriana"

1965. As Nos. 115/21 of Kedah but with Arms of Negri Sembilan inset and inscr "NEGERI SEMBILAN" as in T **6**.
81 **9** 1c. multicoloured . . . . . . 10 1·60
82 – 2c. multicoloured . . . . . . 10 1·60
83 – 5c. multicoloured 40 10
84 – 6c. multicoloured 40 60
85 – 10c. multicoloured 40 10
86 – 15c. multicoloured 80 10
87 – 20c. multicoloured . . . . . 1·25 1·00
The higher values used in Negri Sembilan were Nos. 20/7 of Malaysia (National Issues).

10 Negri Sembilan Crest and Tuanku Ja'afar

1968. Installation of Tuanku Ja'afar as Yang di-Pertuan Besar of Negri Sembilan.
88 **10** 15c. multicoloured 15 70
89 50c. multicoloured . . . . . 30 1·40

11 "Hebomoia glaucippe"

1971. Butterflies. As Nos. 124/30 of Kedah but with Arms of Negri Sembilan inset as T **11** and inscr "negeri sembilan".
91 – 1c. multicoloured . . . . . 40 2·00
92 – 2c. multicoloured . . . . . 70 2·00
93 – 5c. multicoloured . . . . . 1·00 20
94 – 6c. multicoloured . . . . . 1·00 2·00
95 **11** 10c. multicoloured . . . . . 1·00 10
96 – 15c. multicoloured . . . . . 1·40 10
97 – 20c. multicoloured . . . . . 1·40 50
The higher values in use with this issue were Nos. 64/71 of Malaysia (National Issues).

12 "Hibiscus rosa-sinensis"

13 Oil Palm

1979. Flowers. As Nos. 135/41 of Kedah but with Arms of Negri Sembilan and inscr "negeri sembilan" as in T **12**.
103 1c. "Rafflesia hasseltii" . . . 10 1·25
104 2c. "Pterocarpus indicus" . . 10 1·25
105 5c. "Lagerstroemia speciosa" 15 40
106 10c. "Durio zibethinus" . . . 20 10
107 15c. Type **12** 20 10
108 20c. "Rhododendron scortechinii" 25 10
109 25c. "Etlingera elatior" (inscr "Phaeomeria speciosa") . . 45 25

1986. As Nos. 152/8 of Kedah but with Arms of Negri Sembilan and inscr "NEGERI SEMBILAN" as T **13**.
117 1c. Coffee 10 20
118 2c. Coconuts 15 20
119 5c. Cocoa 20 20
120 10c. Black pepper 25 10
121 15c. Rubber 30 10
122 20c. Type **13** 35 10
123 30c. Rice 35 10

NEPAL Pt. 21

An independent kingdom in the Himalayas N. of India.

1861. 16 annas = 1 rupee.
1907. 64 pice = 1 rupee.
1954. 100 paisa = 1 rupee.

1 (1a.) Crown and Kukris

2 (½a.) Bow and Arrow and Kukris

3 Siva Mahadeva (2p.)

1881. Imperf or pin-perf.
34 **2** ½a. black . . . . 2·75 1·80
35 ½a. orange £375 £190
42 **1** 1a. blue . . . . 6·75 2·00
14 1a. green . . . . 48·00 48·00
16c 2a. violet . . . . 37·00 37·00
40 2a. brown . . . . 11·00 4·50
41 4a. green . . . . 7·50 7·50

1907. Various sizes.
57 **3** 2p. brown 35 35
58 4p. green . . . . 1·10 75
59 8p. red 75 50
60 16p. purple . . . . 11·00 2·75
61 24p. orange . . . . 11·00 1·80
62 32p. blue . . . . 15·00 2·20
63 1r. red . . . . 30·00 18·00
50 5r. black and brown . . . . 26·00 12·00

5 Swayambhunath Temple, Katmandu

7 Guheswari Temple, Patan

8 Sri Pashupati (Siva Mahadeva)

1949.
64 **5** 2p. brown 90 75
65 – 4p. green 90 75
66 – 6p. pink . . . . 1·80 75
67 – 8p. red . . . . 1·80 1·10
68 – 16p. purple . . . . 1·80 1·10
69 – 20p. blue . . . . 3·75 1·80
70 **7** 24p. red . . . . 3·00 1·10
71 – 32p. blue . . . . 5·50 1·80
72 **8** 1r. orange . . . . 30·00 18·00
DESIGNS—As Type **5**: 4p. Pashupatinath Temple, Katmandu; 6p. Tri-Chundra College; 8p. Mahabuddha Temple. 26 × 30 mm: 16p. Krishna Mandir Temple, Patan. As Type **7**: 20p. View of Katmandu; 32p. The twenty-two fountains, Balaju.

9 King Tribhuvana

10 Map of Nepal

1954. (a) Size 18 × 22 mm.
73 **9** 2p. brown . . . . 1·80 35
74 4p. green . . . . 6·00 1·10
75 6p. red . . . . 1·50 35
76 8p. lilac . . . . 1·10 35
77 12p. orange . . . . 11·00 1·80

(b) Size 25½ × 29½ mm.
78 **9** 16p. brown . . . . 1·50 35
79 20p. red . . . . 3·00 1·10
80 24p. purple . . . . 2·50 1·10
81 32p. blue . . . . 3·75 1·10
82 50p. mauve . . . . 30·00 5·50
83 1r. red . . . . 44·00 8·75
84 2r. orange . . . . 37·00 7·50

(c) Size 30 × 18 mm.
85 **10** 2p. brown . . . . 1·50 75
86 4p. green . . . . 6·00 1·10
87 6p. red . . . . 15·00 1·80
88 8p. lilac . . . . 1·10 75
89 12p. orange . . . . 15·00 1·80

(d) Size 38 × 21½ mm.
90 **10** 16p. brown . . . . 1·80 75
91 20p. red . . . . 3·00 75
92 24p. purple . . . . 2·20 75
93 32p. blue . . . . 5·50 1·50
94 50p. mauve . . . . 30·00 5·50
95 1r. red . . . . 48·00 7·50
96 2r. orange . . . . 37·00 7·50

11 Mechanization of Agriculture

13 Hanuman Dhoka, Katmandu

1956. Coronation.
97 **11** 4p. green . . . . 6·00 6·00
98 – 6p. red and yellow . . . . 3·75 3·00
99 – 8p. violet . . . . 3·00 1·50
100 **13** 24p. red . . . . 6·00 6·00
101 – 1r. red . . . . £110 95·00
DESIGNS—As Type **11**: 8p. Processional elephant. As Type **13**: 6p. Throne; 1r. King and Queen and mountains.

15 U.N. Emblem and Nepalese Landscape

16 Nepalese Crown

1956. 1st Anniv of Admission into U.N.O.
102 **15** 12p. blue and brown . . . 7·50 6·00

1957. (a) Size 18 × 22 mm.
103 **16** 2p. brown 75 75
104 4p. green . . . . 1·10 75
105 6p. red 75 75
106 8p. violet 75 75
107 12p. red . . . . 4·00 1·10

(b) Size 25½ × 29½ mm.
108 **16** 16p. brown . . . . 5·50 1·80
109 20p. red . . . . 8·75 2·50
110 24p. mauve . . . . 5·50 2·20
111 32p. blue . . . . 7·50 2·50
112 50p. pink . . . . 15·00 5·50
113 1r. salmon . . . . 37·00 11·00
114 2r. orange . . . . 22·00 7·50

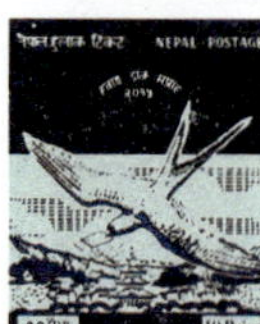
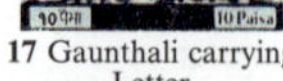
17 Gaunthali carrying Letter

18 Temple of Lumbini

1958. Air. Inauguration of Nepalese Internal Airmail Service.
115 **17** 10p. blue . . . . 1·90 1·90

1958. Human Rights Day.
116 **18** 6p. yellow . . . . 1·50 1·50

19 Nepalese Map and Flag

1959. 1st Nepalese Elections.
117 **19** 6p. red and green 50 45

20 Spinning Wheel

21 King Mahendra

1959. Cottage Industries.
118 **20** 2p. brown 45 45

1959. Admission of Nepal to U.P.U.
119 **21** 12p. blue 50 45

22 Vishnu

23 Nyatopol Temple, Bhaktapur

1959.
120 **22** 1p. brown 15 15
121 – 2p. violet 15 15
122 – 4p. blue 50 35
123 – 6p. pink 50 15
124 – 8p. brown 35 15
125 – 12p. grey 50 15
126 **23** 16p. violet and brown . . 50 15
127 20p. red and blue . . . . 1·80 75
128 **23** 24p. red and green . . . . 1·80 75
129 32p. blue and lilac . . . . 1·10 75
130 50p. green and red . . . . 1·80 75
131 – 1r. blue and brown . . . . 16·00 6·00
132 – 2r. blue and purple . . . . 15·00 6·25
133 – 5r. red and violet . . . . . 60·00 55·00
DESIGNS—As Type **22**. HORIZ: 2p. Krishna; 8p. Siberian musk deer; 12p. Indian rhinoceros. VERT: 4p. Himalayas; 6p. Gateway, Bhaktapur Palace. As Type **23**. VERT: 1r., 2r. Himalayan monal pheasant; 5r. Satyr tragopan.

24 King Mahendra opening Parliament

1959. Opening of 1st Nepalese Parliament.
134 **24** 6p. red . . . . 1·10 1·10

25 Sri Pashupatinath

26 Children, Pagoda and Mt. Everest

1959. Renovation of Sri Pashupatinath Temple, Katmandu.
135 **25** 4p. green (18 × 25 mm) . . 75 75
136 8p. red (21 × 28½ mm) . . . 1·50 75
137 1r. blue (24½ × 33½ mm) . . 8·75 6·00

1960. Children's Day.
137a **26** 6p. blue . . . . 15·00 11·00

27 King Mahendra

28 Mt. Everest

1960. King Mahendra's 41st Birthday.
138 **27** 1r. purple . . . . 1·60 1·10
See also Nos. 163/4a.

1960. Mountain Views.
139 – 5p. brown and purple . . . 35 15
140 **28** 10p. purple and blue . . . 50 20
141 – 40p. brown and violet . . 1·30 80
DESIGNS: 5p. Machha Puchhre; 40p. Manaslu (wrongly inscr "MANSALU").

29 King Tribhuvana

30 Prince Gyanendra cancelling Children's Day Stamps of 1960

1961. 10th Democracy Day.
142 **29** 10p. orange and brown . . 15 15

1961. Children's Day.
143 **30** 12p. orange . . . . 37·00 37·00

31 King Mahendra

32 Campaign Emblem and House

1961. King Mahendra's 42nd Birthday.

144	31	6p. green	35	35
145		12p. blue	50	50
146		50p. red	1·10	1·10
147		1r. brown	1·80	1·80

1962. Malaria Eradication.

148	32	12p. blue	35	35
149	–	1r. orange and red	1·10	1·10

DESIGN: 1r. Emblem and Nepalese flag.

33 King Mahendra on Horseback

34 Bhana Bhakta Acharya

1962. King Mahendra's 43rd Birthday.

150	33	10p. blue	20	20
151		15p. brown	35	35
152		45p. brown	75	75
153		1r. grey	1·10	1·10

1962. Nepalese Poets.

154	34	5p. brown	35	35
155	–	10p. turquoise	35	35
156	–	40p. green	50	50

PORTRAITS: 10p. Moti Ram Bhakta; 40p. Sambhu Prasad.

35 King Mahendra

36 King Mahendra

1962.

157	35	1p. red	15	10
158		2p. blue	15	10
158a		3p. grey	50	35
159		5p. brown	15	10
160	36	10p. purple	15	15
161		40p. brown	35	35
162		75p. green	11·00	11·00
162a	35	75p. green	1·50	75
163	27	2r. red	1·50	1·50
164		5r. green	3·00	3·00
164a		10r. violet	11·00	8·75

No. 162a is smaller, $17\frac{1}{2} \times 20$ mm.

37 Emblems of Learning

1963. UNESCO "Education for All" Campaign.

165	37	10p. black	35	15
166		15p. brown	50	35
167		50p. blue	90	75

38 Hands holding Lamps

1963. National Day.

168	38	5p. blue	15	15
169		10p. brown	15	15
170		50p. purple	75	50
171		1r. green	1·50	75

39 Campaign Symbols

40 Map of Nepal and Open Hand

1963. Freedom from Hunger.

172	39	10p. orange	35	15
173		15p. blue	50	35
174		50p. green	1·10	75
175		1r. brown	1·50	1·30

1963. Rastruya Panchayat.

176	40	10p. green	15	15
177		15p. purple	35	35
178		50p. grey	95	50
179		1r. blue	1·50	90

41 King Mahendra

42 King Mahendra and Highway Map

1963. King Mahendra's 44th Birthday.

180	41	5p. violet	15	15
181		10p. brown	35	15
182		15p. green	50	35

1964. Inauguration of East–West Highway.

183	42	10p. orange and blue	15	15
184		15p. orange and blue	35	20
185		50p. brown and green	60	35

43 King Mahendra at Microphone

44 Crown Prince Birendra

1964. King Mahendra's 45th Birthday.

186	43	1p. brown	15	15
187		2p. grey	20	20
188		2r. brown	1·10	1·10

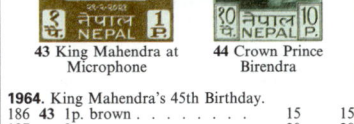

1964. Crown Prince's 19th Birthday.

189	44	10p. green	90	75
190		15p. brown	90	75

45 Flag, Kukris, Rings and Torch

46 Nepalese Family

1964. Olympic Games, Tokyo.

191	45	10p. blue, red and pink	95	75

1965. Land Reform.

192	–	2p. black and green	35	35
193	–	5p. brown and green	35	35
194	–	10p. purple and grey	35	35
195	46	15p. brown and yellow	50	50

DESIGNS: 2p. Farmer ploughing; 5p. Ears of wheat; 10p. Grain elevator.

47 Globe and Letters

48 King Mahendra

1965. Introduction of International Insured and Parcel Service.

196	47	15p. violet	35	35

1965. King Mahendra's 46th Birthday.

197	48	50p. purple	90	75

49 Four Martyrs

50 I.T.U. Emblem

1965. "Nepalese Martyrs".

198	49	15p. green	20	15

1965. I.T.U. Centenary.

199	50	15p. black and purple	50	35

51 I.C.Y. Emblem

52 Devkota (poet)

1965. International Co-operation Year.

200	51	1r. multicoloured	1·10	90

1965. Devkota Commemoration.

201	52	15p. brown	35	30

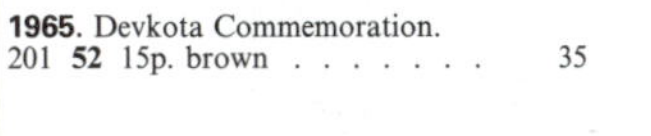

54 Flag and King Mahendra

1966. Democracy Day.

202	54	15p. red and blue	75	50

55 Siva Parvati and Pashuvati Temple

1966. Maha Siva-Ratri Festival.

203	55	15p. violet	45	35

56 "Stamp" Emblem

1966. Nepalese Philatelic Exhibition, Katmandu.

204	56	15p. orange and green	50	35

57 King Mahendra

58 Queen Mother

1966. King Mahendra's 47th Birthday.

205	57	15p. brown and yellow	45	30

1966. Queen Mother's 60th Birthday.

206	58	15p. brown	35	35

59 Queen Ratna

60 Flute-player and Dancer

1966. Children's Day.

207	59	15p. brown and yellow	45	35

1966. Krishna Anniv.

208	60	15p. violet and yellow	45	35

61 "To render service..."

1966. 1st Anniv of Nepalese Red Cross.

209	61	50p. red and green	4·50	1·50

62 W.H.O. Building on Flag

63 Paudyal

1966. Inaug of W.H.O. Headquarters, Geneva.

210	62	1r. violet	2·20	1·50

1966. Leknath Paudyal (poet) Commemoration.

211	63	15p. blue	45	35

64 Rama and Sita

65 Buddha

1967. Rama Navami, 2024, birthday of Rama.

212	64	15p. brown and yellow	45	35

1967. Buddha Jayanti, birthday of Buddha.

213	65	75p. purple and orange	35	35

66 King Mahendra addressing Nepalese

1967. King Mahendra's 48th Birthday.

214	66	15p. brown and blue	45	35

67 Queen Ratna and Children

68 Ama Dablam (mountain)

1967. Children's Day.

215	67	15p. brown and cream	45	35

1967. International Tourist Year.

216	68	5p. violet (postage)	35	35
217	–	65p. brown	75	75
218	–	1r.80 red and blue (air)	1·80	1·50

DESIGNS—38 × 20 mm: 65p. Bhaktapur Durbar Square. $35\frac{1}{2} \times 25\frac{1}{2}$ mm: 1r.80, Plane over Katmandu.

69 Open-air Class

1967. Constitution Day. "Go to the Village" Educational Campaign.

219	69	15p. multicoloured	45	35

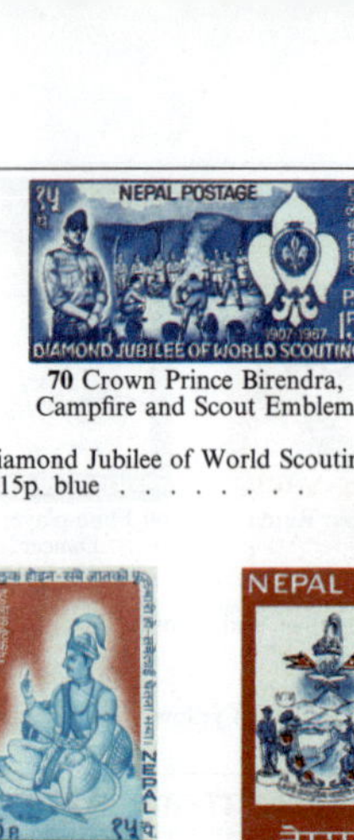

70 Crown Prince Birendra, Campfire and Scout Emblem

1967. Diamond Jubilee of World Scouting.
220 **70** 15p. blue 75 50

71 Prithvi Narayan Shah (founder of Kingdom)

72 Arms of Nepal

1968. Bicentenary of the Kingdom.
221 **71** 15p. blue and red 75 50

1968. National Day.
222 **72** 15p. blue and red 75 50

73 W.H.O. Emblem and Nepalese Flag

1968. 20th Anniv of W.H.O.
223 **73** 1r.20 blue, red and yellow 3·00 2·20

74 Sita and Janaki Temple

1968. Sita Jayanti.
224 **74** 15p. brown and violet . . 50 35

75 King Mahendra, Mountains and Himalayan Monal Pheasant

1968. King Mahendra's 49th Birthday.
225 **75** 15p. multicoloured 65 35

76 Garuda and Airline Emblem

1968. Air. 10th Anniv of Royal Nepalese Airlines.
226 **76** 15p. brown and blue . . . 35 35
227 – 65p. blue 75 75
228 – 2r.50 blue and orange . . . 2·50 2·20
DESIGNS—DIAMOND ($25\frac{1}{2} \times 25\frac{1}{2}$ mm): 65p. Route-map. As Type **76**: 2r.50, Convair Metropolitan airliner over Mount Dhaulagiri.

77 Flag, Queen Ratna and Children

78 Human Rights Emblem and Buddha

1968. Children's Day and Queen Ratna's 41st Birthday.
229 **77** 5p. red, yellow and green 35 30

1968. Human Rights Year.
230 **78** 1r. red and green . . . . . 3·00 2·20

79 Crown Prince Birendra and Dancers

1968. Crown Prince Birendra's 24th Birthday, and National Youth Festival.
231 **79** 25p. blue 75 50

80 King Mahendra, Flags and U.N. Building, New York

81 Amsu Varma (7th-century ruler)

1969. Nepal's Election to U.N. Security Council.
232 **80** 1r. multicoloured . . . . . 1·10 90

1969. Famous Nepalese.
233 **81** 15p. violet and green . . . 50 1·50
234 – 25p. turquoise 75 75
235 – 50p. brown 95 95
236 – 1r. purple and brown . . . 1·10 90
DESIGNS—VERT: 25p. Ram Shah (17th-century King of Gurkha); 50p. Bhimsen Thapa (19th-century Prime Minister). HORIZ: 1r. Bal Bhadra Kunwar (19th-century warrior).

82 I.L.O. Emblem

1969. 50th Anniv of I.L.O.
237 **82** 1r. brown and mauve . . . 5·50 3·75

83 King Mahendra

85 Queen Ratna, and Child with Toy

84 King Tribhuvana and Queens

1969. King Mahendra's 50th Birthday.
238 **83** 25p. multicoloured 45 45

1969. 64th Birth Anniv of King Tribhuvana.
239 **84** 25p. brown and yellow . . 45 45

1969. National Children's Day.
240 **85** 25p. mauve and brown . . 45 45

86 Rhododendron

87 Durga, Goddess of Victory

1969. Flowers. Multicoloured.
241 25p. Type **86** 60 50
242 25p. Narcissus 60 50
243 25p. Marigold 60 50
244 25p. Poinsettia 60 50

1969. Durga Pooja Festival.
245 **87** 15p. black and orange . . 35 35
246 50p. violet and brown . . 80 80

88 Crown Prince Birendra and Princess Aishwarya

1970. Royal Wedding.
247 **88** 25p. multicoloured 45 20

89 Produce, Cow and Landscape

1970. Agricultural Year.
248 **89** 25p. multicoloured 45 35

90 King Mahendra, Mt. Everest and Nepalese Crown

1970. King Mahendra's 51st Birthday.
249 **90** 50p. multicoloured 75 50

91 Lake Gosainkunda

1970. Nepalese Lakes. Multicoloured.
250 5p. Type **91** 35 35
251 25p. Lake Phewa Tal 50 50
252 1r. Lake Rara Daha 90 90

92 A.P.Y. Emblem

1970. Asian Productivity Year.
253 **92** 1r. blue 90 75

93 Queen Ratna and Children's Palace, Taulihawa

1970. National Children's Day.
254 **93** 25p. grey and brown . . . 45 35

94 New Headquarters Building

1970. New U.P.U. Headquarters, Berne.
255 **94** 2r.50 grey and brown . . . 1·00 80

95 U.N. Flag

1970. 25th Anniv of United Nations.
256 **95** 25p. blue and purple . . . 45 35

96 Durbar Square, Patan

1970. Tourism. Multicoloured.
257 15p. Type **96** 35 15
258 25p. Boudhanath Stupa (temple) (vert) 50 35
259 1r. Mt. Gauri Shankar . . . 90 75

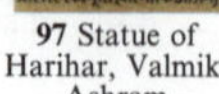

97 Statue of Harihar, Valmiki Ashram

98 Torch within Spiral

1971. Nepalese Religious Art.
260 **97** 25p. black and brown . . . 45 30

1971. Racial Equality Year.
261 **98** 1r. red and blue . . . . . 1·10 80

99 King Mahendra taking Salute

1971. King Mahendra's 52nd Birthday.
262 **99** 15p. purple and blue . . . 45 30

100 Sweta Bhairab

1971. Bhairab Statues of Shiva.
263 **100** 15p. brown and chestnut 35 35
264 – 25p. brown and green . . 35 35
265 – 50p. brown and blue . . . 75 75
DESIGNS: 25p. Mahankal Bhairab; 50p. Kal Bhairab.

101 Child presenting Queen Ratna with Garland

1971. National Children's Day.
266 **101** 25p. multicoloured . . . 45 30

102 Iranian and Nepalese Flags on Map of Iran

1971. 2,500th Anniv of Persian Empire.
267 **102** 1r. multicoloured . . . . 1·10 75

103 Mother and Child

1971. 25th Anniv of UNICEF.
268 **103** 1r. blue . . . . 1·10 75

104 Mt. Everest

1971. Tourism. Himalayan Peaks.
269 **104** 25p. dp brown, brn and bl 35 15
270 – 1r. black, brown and blue 75 50
271 – 1r.80 green, brown & blue 1·30 95
DESIGNS: 1r. Mt. Kanchenjunga; 1r.80, Mt. Annapurna I.

105 Royal Standard **106** Araniko and White Dagoba, Peking

1972. National Day.
272 **105** 25p. black and red . . . 45 30

1972. Araniko (13th-century architect) Commem.
273 **106** 15p. brown and blue . . . 20 20

107 Open Book

1972. International Book Year.
274 **107** 2p. brown and buff . . . 15 15
275 5p. black and brown . . . 15 15
276 1r. black and blue 90 75

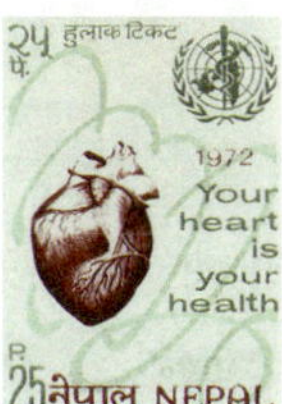

108 Human Heart

1972. World Heart Month.
277 **108** 25p. red and green . . . 45 35

109 King Mahendra **110** King Birendra

1972. 1st Death Anniv of King Mahendra.
278 **109** 25p. brown and black . . 45 30

1972. King Birendra's 28th Birthday.
279 **110** 50p. purple and brown . . 50 45

111 Northern Border Costumes **112** Sri Baburam Acharya

1973. National Costumes. Multicoloured.
280 25p. Type **111** 35 15
281 50p. Hill-dwellers 45 35
282 75p. Katmandu Valley . . . 60 45
283 1r. Inner Terai 90 60

1973. 85th Birth Anniv of Sri Baburam Acharya (historian).
284 **112** 25p. grey and red 15 10

113 Nepalese Family

1973. 25th Anniv of W.H.O.
285 **113** 1r. blue and orange . . . 90 75

114 Birthplace of Buddha, Lumbini

1973. Tourism. Multicoloured.
286 25p. Type **114** 35 15
287 75p. Mt. Makalu 50 35
288 1r. Castle, Gurkha 75 75

115 Transplanting Rice

1973. 10th Anniv of World Food Programme.
289 **115** 10p. brown and violet . . 15 15

116 Interpol H.Q., Paris

1973. 50th Anniv of International Criminal Police Organization (Interpol).
290 **116** 25p. blue and brown . . . 35 20

117 Shri Shom Nath Sigdyal **118** Cow

1973. 1st Death Anniv of Shri Shom Nath Sigdyal (scholar).
291 **117** 1r.25 violet 90 75

1973. Domestic Animals. Multicoloured.
292 2p. Type **118** 15 15
293 3r.25 Yak . . . . 1·60 1·10

119 King Birendra

1974. King Birendra's 29th Birthday.
294 **119** 5p. brown and black . . . 15 15
295 15p. brown and black . . 20 15
296 1r. brown and black . . 75 50

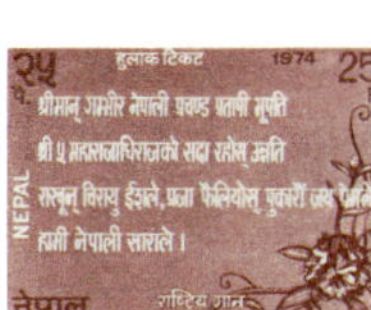

120 Text of National Anthem **121** King Janak seated on Throne

1974. National Day.
297 **120** 25p. purple 35 15
298 – 1r. green 50 45
DESIGN: 1r. Anthem musical score.

1974. King Janak Commemoration.
299 **121** 2r.50 multicoloured . . . 1·80 1·50

122 Emblem and Village

1974. 25th Anniv of SOS Children's Village International.
300 **122** 25p. blue and red 35 35

123 Football **124** W.P.Y. Emblem

1974. Nepalese Games. Multicoloured.
301 2p. Type **123** 15 15
302 2r.75 Baghchal (diagram) . . 1·10 90

1974. World Population Year.
303 **124** 5p. blue and brown . . . 20 15

125 U.P.U. Monument, Berne **126** Red Lacewing

1974. Centenary of U.P.U.
304 **125** 1r. black and green . . . 75 50

1974. Nepalese Butterflies. Multicoloured.
305 10p. Type **126** 15 15
306 15p. Leaf buttefly 45 20
307 1r.25 Leaf butterfly (underside) . . . . 1·10 75
308 1r.75 Red-breasted jezebel . . 1·30 1·10

127 King Birendra **128** Muktinath

1974. King Birendra's 30th Birthday.
309 **127** 25p. black and green . . 20 20

1974. "Visit Nepal" Tourism. Multicoloured.
310 25p. Type **128** 35 15
311 1r. Peacock window, Bhaktapur (horiz) 75 45

129 Guheswari Temple

1975. Coronation of King Birendra. Multicoloured.
312 25p. Type **129** 35 15
313 50p. Lake Rara (37 × 30 mm) 35 15
314 1r. Throne and sceptre (46 × 26 mm) 50 35
315 1r.25 Royal Palace, Katmandu (46 × 26 mm) 1·10 50
316 1r.75 Pashupatinath Temple (25 × 31 mm) 75 75
317 2r.75 King Birendra and Queen Aishwarya (46 × 25 mm) . . . . . . 1·10 90
MS318 143 × 105 mm. Nos. 314/15 and 317. Imperf . . . . 4·00 4·00

130 Tourism Year Emblem

1975. South Asia Tourism Year. Multicoloured.
319 2p. Type **130** 15 15
320 25p. Temple stupa (vert) . . 35 35

131 Tiger

1975. Wildlife Conservation. Multicoloured.
321 2p. Type **131** 35 35
322 5p. Swamp deer (vert) . . . 35 35
323 1r. Lesser panda 75 75

132 Queen Aishwarya and I.W.Y. Emblem

1975. International Women's Year.
324 **132** 1r. multicoloured 50 35

133 Rupse Falls **134** King Birendra

1975. Tourism. Multicoloured.
325 2p. Mt. Ganesh Himal (horiz) 15 15
326 25p. Type **133** 15 15
327 50p. Kumari ("Living Goddess") 50 35

1975. King Birendra's 31st Birthday.
328 **134** 25p. violet and mauve . . 20 15

136 Flag and Map **138** Flags of Nepal and Colombo Plan

137 Transplanting Rice

1976. Silver Jubilee of National Democracy Day.
330 **136** 2r.50 red and blue 90 75

1976. Agriculture Year.
331 **137** 25p. multicoloured . . . 20 15

1976. 25th Anniv of Colombo Plan.
332 **138** 1r. multicoloured 50 45

139 Running **140** "Dove of Peace"

1976. Olympic Games, Montreal.
333 **139** 3r.25 black and blue . . . 1·50 1·10

1976. 5th Non-aligned Countries' Summit Conf.
334 **140** 5r. blue, yellow and black 1·90 1·30

141 Lakhe Dance

1976. Nepalese Dances. Multicoloured.
335 10p. Type **141** 15 15
336 15p. Maruni dance 15 15
337 30p. Jhangad dance 35 20
338 1r. Sebru dance 50 35

142 Nepalese Lily **143** King Birendra

1976. Flowers. Multicoloured.
339 30p. Type **142** 50 15
340 30p. "Meconopsis grandis" 50 15

341 30p. "Cardiocrinum giganteum" (horiz) 50 15
342 30p. "Megacodon stylophorus" (horiz) . . . 50 15

1976. King Birendra's 32nd Birthday.
343 **143** 5p. green 15 10
344 30p. dp brown, brn & yell 20 15

144 Liberty Bell

1976. Bicentenary of American Revolution.
345 **144** 10r. multicoloured . . . . 2·75 2·40

145 Kaji Amarsingh Thapa

1977. Kaji Amarsingh Thapa (19th-century warrior) Commemoration.
346 **145** 10p. green and brown . . 15 15

146 Terracotta Figurine and Kapilavastu

1977. Tourism.
347 **146** 30p. violet 15 15
348 – 5r. green and brown . . . 1·50 1·10
DESIGN: 5r. Ashokan pillar, Lumbini.

147 Great Indian Hornbill

1977. Birds. Multicoloured.
349 5p. Type **147** 45 20
350 15p. Cheer pheasant (horiz) 80 20
351 1r. Green magpie (horiz) . . 1·30 50
352 2r.30 Spiny babbler . . . . 2·40 75

148 Tukuche Himal and Police Flag

1977. 1st Anniv of Ascent of Tukuche Himal by Police Team.
353 **148** 1r.25 multicoloured . . . 20 15

149 Map of Nepal and Scout Emblem

150 Dhanwantari, the Health-giver

1977. 25th Anniv of Scouting in Nepal.
354 **149** 3r.50 multicoloured . . . 45 30

1977. Health Day.
355 **150** 30p. green 20 15

151 Map of Nepal and Flags

152 King Birendra

1977. 26th Consultative Committee Meeting of Colombo Plan, Katmandu.
356 **151** 1r. multicoloured 35 20

1977. King Birendra's 33rd Birthday.
357 **152** 5p. brown 15 15
358 1r. brown 35 35

153 General Post Office, Katmandu, and Seal

1978. Centenary of Nepalese Post Office.
359 **153** 25p. brown and agate . . 15 15
360 – 75p. brown and agate . . 35 35
DESIGN: 75p. General Post Office, Katmandu, and early postmark.

154 South-west Face of Mt. Everest

1978. 25th Anniv of First Ascent of Mt. Everest.
361 **154** 2r.30 grey and brown . . 90 50
362 – 4r. blue and green . . . . 1·30 1·10
DESIGN: 4r. South face of Mt. Everest.

155 Sun, Ankh and Landscape

1978. World Environment Day.
363 **155** 1r. green and orange . . . 35 20

156 Queen Mother Ratna

157 Rapids, Tripsuli River

1978. Queen Mother's 50th Birthday.
364 **156** 2r.30 green 75 50

1978. Tourism. Multicoloured.
365 10p. Type **157** 15 10
366 50p. Window, Nara Devi, Katmandu 20 15
367 1r. Mahakali dance (vert) . . 45 35

158 Lapsi ("Choerospondias axillaris")

159 Lamp and U.N. Emblem

1978. Fruits. Multicoloured.
368 5p. Type **158** 20 10
369 1r. Katus (vert) 50 35
370 1r.25 Rudrakshya 75 45

1978. 30th Anniv of Human Rights Declaration.
371 **159** 25p. brown and red . . . 15 10
372 1r. blue and red 35 20

160 Wright Flyer I and Boeing 727-100

161 King Birendra

1978. Air. 75th Anniv of First Powered Flight.
373 **160** 2r.30 blue and brown . . 90 75

1978. King Birendra's 34th Birthday.
374 **161** 30p. blue and brown . . . 15 10
375 2r. brown and violet . . . 60 45

162 Red Machchhindranath and Kamroop and Patan Temples

1979. Red Machchhindranath (guardian deity) Festival.
376 **162** 75p. brown and green . . 35 20

163 "Buddha's Birth" (carving, Maya Devi Temple)

164 Planting a Sapling

1979. Lumbini Year.
377 **163** 1r. yellow and brown . . 35 20

1979. Tree Planting Festival.
378 **164** 2r.30 brown, green & yellow 90 75

165 Chariot of Red Machchhindranath

166 Nepalese Scouts and Guides

1979. Bhoto Jatra (Vest Exhibition) Festival.
379 **165** 1r.25 multicoloured . . . 45 35

1979. International Year of the Child.
380 **166** 1r. brown 45 35

167 Mount Pabil

168 Great Grey Shrike

1979. Tourism.
381 **167** 30p. green 15 15
382 – 50p. red and blue 15 15
383 – 1r.25 multicoloured . . . 45 45
DESIGNS: 50p. Yajnashala, Swargadwari. 1r.25, Shiva-Parbati (wood carving, Gaddi Baithak Temple).

1979. International World Pheasant Association Symposium, Katmandu. Multicoloured.
384 10p. Type **168** (postage) . . . 20 15
385 10r. Fire-tailed sunbird . . . 5·50 3·50
386 3r.50 Himalayan monal pheasant (horiz) (air) . . . 1·90 1·60

169 Lichchhavi Coin (obverse)

170 King Birendra

1979. Coins.
387 **169** 5p. orange and brown . . 15 15
388 – 5p. orange and brown . . 15 15
389 – 15p. blue and indigo . . . 15 15
390 – 15p. blue and indigo . . . 15 15
391 – 1r. blue and deep blue . . 45 45
392 – 1r. blue and deep blue . . 45 45
DESIGNS: No. 388, Lichchhavi coin (reverse); 389, Malla coin (obverse); 390, Malla coin (reverse); 391, Prithvi Narayan Shah coin (obverse); 392, Prithvi Narayan Shah coin (reverse).

1979. King Birendra's 35th Birthday. Mult.
393 25p. Type **170** 15 10
394 2r.30 Reservoir 75 50

171 Samyak Pooja Festival

1980. Samyak Pooja Festival, Katmandu.
395 **171** 30p. brown, grey & purple 15 15

172 Sacred Basil

1980. Herbs. Multicoloured.
396 5p. Type **172** 15 10
397 30p. Valerian 20 10
398 1r. Nepalese pepper 35 20
399 2r.30 Himalayan rhubarb . . 75 50

173 Gyandil Das

174 Everlasting Flame and Temple, Shirsasthan

1980. Nepalese Writers.
400 **173** 5p. lilac and brown . . . 10 10
401 – 30p. purple and brown . . 15 10
402 – 1r. green and blue 30 20
403 – 2r.30 blue and green . . . 60 50
DESIGNS: 30p. Siddhidas Amatya; 1r. Pahalman Singh Swanr; 2r.30, Jay Prithvi Bahadur Singh.

1980. Tourism. Multicoloured.
404 10p. Type **174** 10 10
405 1r. Godavari Pond 35 20
406 5r. Mount Dhaulagiri . . . . 1·20 90

175 Bhairab Dancer

176 King Birendra

1980. World Tourism Conf, Manila, Philippines.
407 **175** 25r. multicoloured . . . . 5·25 4·00

1980. King Birendra's 36th Birthday.
408 **176** 1r. multicoloured 35 20

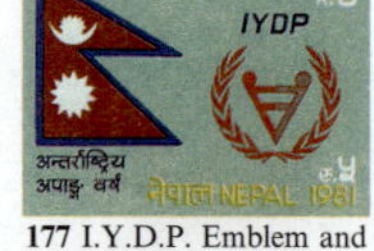

177 I.Y.D.P. Emblem and Nepalese Flag

1981. International Year of Disabled Persons.
409 **177** 5r. multicoloured . . . . 1·50 1·10

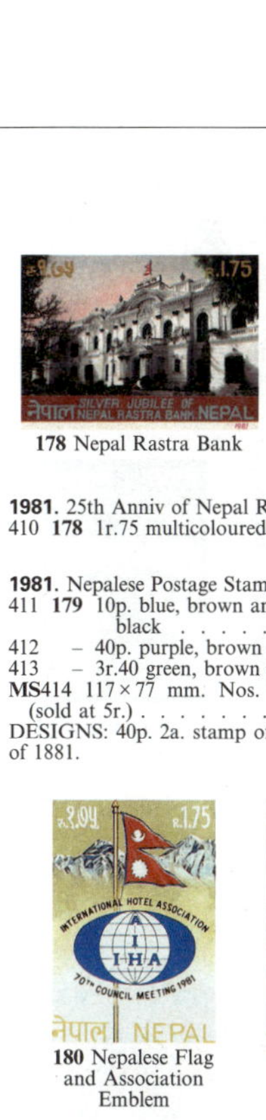

178 Nepal Rastra Bank

179 One Anna Stamp of 1881

1981. 25th Anniv of Nepal Rastra Bank.
410 **178** 1r.75 multicoloured . . . 45 35

1981. Nepalese Postage Stamp Centenary.
411 **179** 10p. blue, brown and black 15 10
412 – 40p. purple, brown & blk 15 10
413 – 3r.40 green, brown & blk 90 75
MS414 117 × 77 mm. Nos. 411/13 (sold at 5r.) . . . . 2·20 2·20
DESIGNS: 40p. 2a. stamp of 1881; 3r.40, 4a. stamp of 1881.

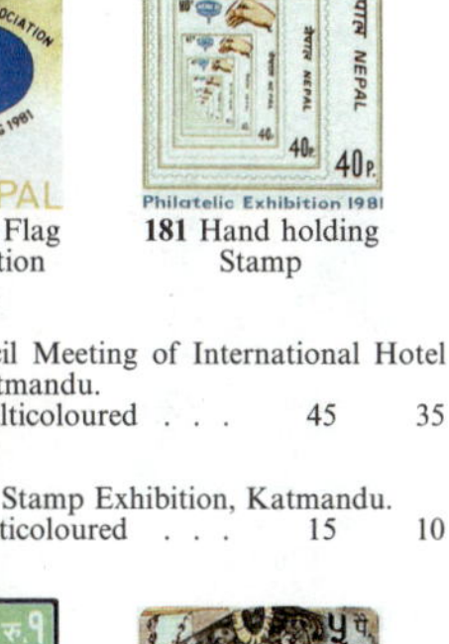

180 Nepalese Flag and Association Emblem

181 Hand holding Stamp

1981. 70th Council Meeting of International Hotel Association, Katmandu.
415 **180** 1r.75 multicoloured . . . 45 35

1981. "Nepal 81" Stamp Exhibition, Katmandu.
416 **181** 40p. multicoloured . . . 15 10

182 King Birendra

183 Image of Hrishikesh, Ridi

1981. King Birendra's 37th Birthday.
417 **182** 1r. multicoloured 30 20

1981. Tourism. Multicoloured.
418 5p. Type **183** 10 10
419 25p. Tripura Sundari Temple, Baitadi 10 10
420 2r. Mt. Langtang Lirung . . 45 20

184 Academy Building

185 Balakrishna Sama

1982. 25th Anniv of Royal Nepal Academy.
421 **184** 40p. multicoloured . . . 15 15

1982. 1st Death Anniv of Balakrishna Sama (writer).
422 **185** 1r. multicoloured 20 20

186 "Intelsat V" and Dish Aerial

187 Mount Nuptse

1982. Sagarmatha Satellite Earth Station, Balambu.
423 **186** 5r. multicoloured . . . . 1·30 75

1982. 50th Anniv of Union of International Alpinist Associations. Multicoloured.
424 25p. Type **187** 15 15
425 2r. Mount Lhotse (31 × 31 mm) 50 35
426 3r. Mount Everest (39 × 31 mm) . . . . . . 1·10 50
Nos. 424/6 were issued together, se-tenant, forming a composite design.

188 Games Emblem and Weights

189 Indra Sarobar Lake

1982. 9th Asian Games, New Delhi.
427 **188** 3r.40 multicoloured . . . 90 75

1982. Kulekhani Hydro-electric Project.
428 **189** 2r. multicoloured 50 35

190 King Birendra

191 N.I.D.C. Emblem

1982. King Birendra's 38th Birthday.
429 **190** 5p. multicoloured 15 15

1983. 25th Anniv (1984) of Nepal Industrial Development Corporation.
430 **191** 50p. multicoloured . . . 15 15

192 Boeing 727 over Himalayas

1983. 25th Anniv of Royal Nepal Airlines.
431 **192** 1r. multicoloured 45 20

193 W.C.Y. Emblem and Nepalese Flag

194 Sarangi

1983. World Communications Year.
432 **193** 10p. multicoloured . . . 15 15

1983. Musical Instruments. Multicoloured.
433 5p. Type **194** 10 10
434 10p. Kwota (drum) 10 10
435 50p. Narashinga (horn) . . . 20 20
436 1r. Murchunga 35 35

195 Chakrapani Chalise

196 King Birendra and Doves

1983. Birth Centenary of Chakrapani Chalise (poet).
437 **195** 4r.50 multicoloured . . . 45 35

1983. King Birendra's 39th Birthday.
438 **196** 5r. multicoloured 50 30

197 Barahkshetra Temple and Image of Barah

1983. Tourism. Multicoloured.
439 1r. Type **197** 10 10
440 2r.20 Temple, Triveni 20 15
441 6r. Mount Cho-oyu 50 35

198 Auditing Accounts

1984. 25th Anniv of Auditor General.
442 **198** 25p. multicoloured . . . 50 45

199 Antenna and Emblem

1984. 20th Anniv of Asia-Pacific Broadcasting Union.
443 **199** 5r. multicoloured . . . . 1·30 1·10

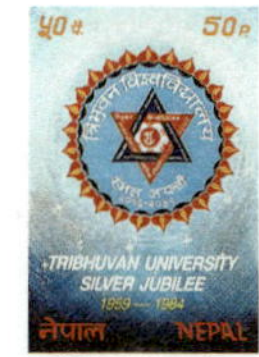

200 University Emblem

201 Boxing

1984. 25th Anniv of Tribhuvan University.
444 **200** 50p. multicoloured . . . 20 15

1984. Olympic Games, Los Angeles.
445 **201** 10r. multicoloured . . . . 2·20 1·50

202 Family and Emblem

203 National Flag and Emblem

1984. 25th Anniv of Nepal Family Planning Association.
446 **202** 1r. multicoloured 20 15

1984. Social Service Day.
447 **203** 5p. multicoloured 15 15

204 Gharial

205 "Vishnu as Giant" (stone carving)

1984. Wildlife. Multicoloured.
448 10p. Type **204** 15 15
449 25p. Snow leopard 20 20
450 50p. Blackbuck 35 35

1984. Tourism. Multicoloured.
451 10p. Type **205** 10 10
452 1r. Temple of Chhinna Masta Bhagavati and sculpture (horiz) 20 15
453 5r. Mount Api . . . . 1·30 80

206 King Birendra

1984. King Birendra's 40th Birthday.
454 **206** 1r. multicoloured 20 15

207 Animals and Mountains

208 Shiva

1985. Sagarmatha (Mt. Everest) National Park.
455 **207** 10r. multicoloured . . . . 4·00 1·50

1985. Traditional Paintings. Details of cover of "Shiva Dharma Purana". Multicoloured.
456 50p. Type **208** 20 20
457 50p. Multi-headed Shiva talking to woman 20 20
458 50p. Brahma and Vishnu making offering (15 × 22 mm) 20 20
459 50p. Shiva in single- and multi-headed forms 20 20
460 50p. Shiva talking to woman 20 20
Nos. 456/60 were printed together, se-tenant, forming a composite design.

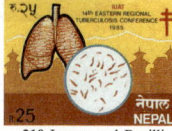

209 U.N. Flag

210 Lungs and Bacilli

1985. 40th Anniv of U.N.O.
461 **209** 5r. multicoloured . . . . 1·10 75

1985. 14th Eastern Regional Tuberculosis Conf, Katmandu.
462 **210** 25r. multicoloured . . . . 5·25 3·75

211 Flags of Member Countries

1985. 1st South Asian Association for Regional Co-operation Summit.
463 **211** 5r. multicoloured . . . . 1·10 75

212 Jaleshwar Temple

213 I.Y.Y. Emblem

1985. Tourism. Multicoloured.
464 10p. Type **212** 10 10
465 1r. Temple of Goddess Shaileshwari, Silgadi . . . 20 15
466 2r. Phoksundo Lake 45 20

1985. International Youth Year.
467 **213** 1r. multicoloured 20 15

214 King Birendra

215 Devi Ghat Hydro-electric Project

1985. King Birendra's 41st Birthday.
468 **214** 50p. multicoloured . . . 15 15

1985.
469 **215** 2r. multicoloured 50 35

216 Emblem

217 Royal Crown

1986. 25th Anniv of Panchayat System (partyless government).
470 **216** 4r. multicoloured 90 75

1986.
471 **217** 5p. brown and deep brown 10 10
472 – 10p. blue 15 15
474 – 50p. blue 20 20
476 – 1r. brown and ochre . . . 15 10
DESIGNS: 10p. Mayadevi Temple of Lumbini (Buddha's birthplace); 50p. Pashupati Temple; 1r. Royal Crown.

218 Pharping Hydro-electric Station

1986. 75th Anniv of Pharping Hydro-electric Power Station.
480 **218** 15p. multicoloured . . . 15 15

219 Emblem and Map

1986. 25th Anniv of Asian Productivity Organization.
481 **219** 1r. multicoloured 20 15

220 Mt. Pumori, Himalayas (35 × 22 mm)

221 King Birendra

1986. Tourism. Multicoloured.
482 60p. Type **220** 15 10
483 8r. "Budhanilkantha" (sculpture of reclining Vishnu), Katmandu Valley 1·50 1·10

1986. King Birendra's 42nd Birthday.
484 **221** 1r. multicoloured 20 15

222 I.P.Y. Emblem

223 National Flag and Council Emblem

1986. International Peace Year.
485 **222** 10r. multicoloured . . . . 1·60 1·30

1987. 10th Anniv of National Social Service Co-ordination Council.
486 **223** 1r. multicoloured 20 15

224 Emblem and Forest

1987. 1st Nepal Scout Jamboree, Katmandu.
487 **224** 1r. brown, orange and blue 45 15

225 Ashokan Pillar and Maya Devi

1987. Lumbini (Buddha's Birthplace) Development Project.
488 **225** 4r. multicoloured 75 50

226 Emblem

227 Emblem

1987. 3rd South Asian Association for Regional Co-operation Summit, Katmandu.
489 **226** 60p. gold and red 15 15

1987. 25th Anniv of Rastriya Samachar Samiti (news service).
490 **227** 4r. purple, blue and red 75 50

228 Kashthamandap, Katmandu

229 Gyawali

1987.
491 **228** 25p. multicoloured . . . 15 15

1987. 89th Birth Anniv of Surya Bikram Gyawali.
492 **229** 60p. multicoloured . . . 15 15

230 Emblem

231 King Birendra

1987. International Year of Shelter for the Homeless.
493 **230** 5r. multicoloured 90 75

1987. King Birendra's 43rd Birthday.
494 **231** 25p. multicoloured . . . 15 15

232 Mt. Kanjiroba

1987.
495 **232** 10r. multicoloured . . . . 1·60 1·10

233 Crown Prince Dipendra

1988. Crown Prince Dipendra's 17th Birthday.
496 **233** 1r. multicoloured 20 15

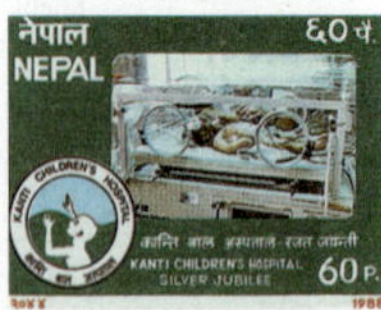

234 Baby in Incubator

1988. 25th Anniv of Kanti Children's Hospital, Katmandu.
497 **234** 60p. multicoloured . . . 15 15

235 Swamp Deer

236 Laxmi, Goddess of Wealth

1988. 12th Anniv of Royal Shukla Phanta Wildlife Reserve.
498 **235** 60p. multicoloured . . . 35 15

1988. 50th Anniv of Nepal Bank Ltd.
499 **236** 2r. multicoloured 35 20

237 Queen Mother

238 Hands protecting Blood Droplet

1988. 60th Birthday of Queen Mother.
500 **237** 5r. multicoloured 90 75

1988. 25th Anniv of Nepal Red Cross Society.
501 **238** 1r. red and brown 20 15

239 Temple and Statue

1988. Temple of Goddess Bindhyabasini, Pokhara.
502 **239** 15p. multicoloured . . . 15 15

240 King Birendra

241 Temple

1988. King Birendra's 44th Birthday.
503 **240** 4r. multicoloured 75 45

1989. Pashupati Area Development Trust.
504 **241** 1r. multicoloured 20 15

242 Emblem

243 S.A.A.R.C. Emblem

1989. 10th Anniv of Asia-Pacific Telecommunity.
505 **242** 4r. green, black and violet 45 30

1989. South Asian Association for Regional Co-operation Year against Drug Abuse and Trafficking.
506 **243** 60p. multicoloured . . . 15 15

244 King Birendra

245 Child Survival Measures

1989. King Birendra's 45th Birthday.
507 **244** 2r. multicoloured 35 15

1989. Child Survival Campaign.
508 **245** 1r. multicoloured 15 15

246 Lake Rara

1989. Rara National Park.
509 **246** 4r. multicoloured 45 30

247 Mt. Amadablam

1989.
510 **247** 5r. multicoloured 75 35

248 Crown Prince Dipendra

249 Temple of Manakamana, Gorkha

1989. Crown Prince Dipendra's Coming-of-Age.
511 **248** 1r. multicoloured 15 15

1990.
512 **249** 60p. black and violet . . 15 15

250 Emblem and Children

251 Emblem

1990. 25th Anniv of Nepal Children's Organization.
513 **250** 1r. multicoloured 15 15

1990. Centenary of Bir Hospital.
514 **251** 60p. red, blue and yellow 15 15

252 Emblem

253 Goddess and Bageshwori Temple, Nepalgunj

1990. 20th Anniv of Asian–Pacific Postal Training Centre, Bangkok.
515 **252** 4r. multicoloured 50 30

1990. Tourism. Multicoloured.
516 1r. Type **253** 15 15
517 5r. Mt. Saipal (36 × 27 mm) 60 35

254 Leisure Activities

1990. South Asian Association for Regional Co-operation Girls' Year.
518 **254** 4r.60 multicoloured . . . 25 15

255 King Birendra

256 Koirala

1990. King Birendra's 46th Birthday.
519 **255** 2r. multicoloured 20 15

1990. 76th Birth Anniv of Bisweswar Prasad Koirala (Prime Minister, 1959–60).
520 **256** 60p. black, orange and red 10 10

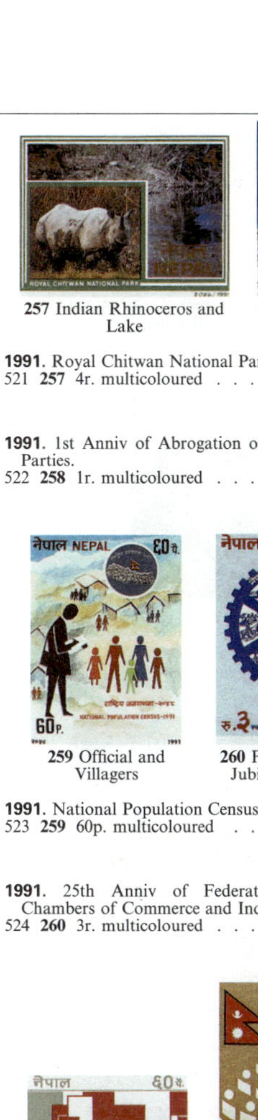

257 Indian Rhinoceros and Lake

258 Flower and Crowd

1991. Royal Chitwan National Park.
521 **257** 4r. multicoloured 75 35

1991. 1st Anniv of Abrogation of Ban on Political Parties.
522 **258** 1r. multicoloured 15 15

259 Official and Villagers

260 Federation and Jubilee Emblems

1991. National Population Census.
523 **259** 60p. multicoloured . . . 15 15

1991. 25th Anniv of Federation of Nepalese Chambers of Commerce and Industry.
524 **260** 3r. multicoloured 35 20

261 Crosses

262 Delegates

1991. 25th Anniv (1990) of Nepal Junior Red Cross.
525 **261** 60p. red and grey 10 10

1991. 1st Session of Revived Parliament.
526 **262** 1r. multicoloured 15 15

263 King Birendra making Speech

1991. Constitution Day.
527 **263** 50p. multicoloured . . . 10 10

264 Rama and Janaki (statues) and Vivaha Mandap

266 King Birendra

265 Mt. Kumbhakarna

1991. 5th Anniv of Rebuilt Vivaha Mandap Pavilion, Janaki Temple.
528 **264** 1r. multicoloured 15 15

1991. Tourism.
529 **265** 4r.60 multicoloured . . . 50 30

1991. King Birendra's 47th Birthday.
530 **266** 8r. multicoloured 90 50

267 Houses

268 Glass magnifying Society Emblem

1991. South Asian Association for Regional Co-operation Year of Shelter.
531 **267** 9r. multicoloured 90 60

1992. 25th Anniv (1991) of Nepal Philatelic Society.
532 **268** 4r. multicoloured 45 30

269 Rainbow over River and Trees

1992. Environmental Protection.
533 **269** 60p. multicoloured . . . 15 15

270 Nutrition, Education and Health Care

1992. Rights of the Child.
534 **270** 1r. multicoloured 15 15

271 Thakurdwara Temple, Bardiya

272 Bank Emblem

1992. Temples. Multicoloured.
535 75p. Type **271** (postage) . . . 10 10
536 1r. Namo Buddha Temple, Kavre 10 10
537 2r. Narijhowa Temple, Mustang 15 10
538 11r. Dantakali Temple, Bijayapur (air) . . . . . . 1·00 65

1992. 25th Anniv of Agricultural Development Bank.
539 **272** 40p. brown and green . . 15 15

273 Pin-tailed Green Pigeon

1992. Birds. Multicoloured.
540 1r. Type **273** 10 10
541 3r. Bohemian waxwing . . . 30 15
542 25r. Rufous-tailed desert (inscr "Finch") lark . . . 2·20 1·50

274 King Birendra exchanging Swords with Goddess Sree Bhadrakali

275 Pandit Kulchandra Gautam

1992. King Birendra's 48th Birthday.
543 **274** 7r. multicoloured 60 35

1992. Poets. Multicoloured, frame colour given in brackets.
544 1r. Type **275** 15 10
545 1r. Chittadhar Hridaya (drab) 15 10
546 1r. Vidyapati (stone) 15 10
547 1r. Teongsi Sirijunga (grey) 15 10

276 Shooting and Marathon

277 Golden Mahseer

1992. Olympic Games, Barcelona.
548 **276** 25r. multicoloured . . . . 2·20 1·50

1993. Fishes. Multicoloured.
549 25p. Type **277** 10 10
550 1r. Marinka 10 10
551 5r. Indian eel 20 10
552 10r. False loach 35 20
MS553 90 × 70 mm. Nos. 549/52 1·80 1·80

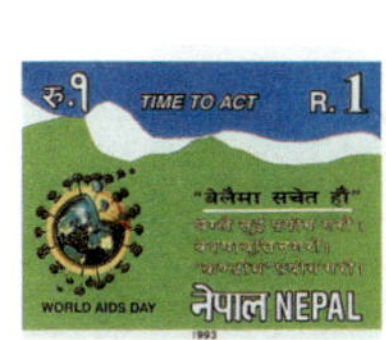

278 Antibodies attacking Globe

279 Tanka Prasad Acharya (Prime Minister, 1956–57)

1993. World AIDS Day.
554 **278** 1r. multicoloured 15 15

1993. Death Anniversaries. Multicoloured.
555 25p. Type **279** (1st anniv) . . 10 10
556 1r. Sungdare Sherpa (mountaineer) (4th anniv) 10 10
557 7r. Siddhi Charan Shrestha (poet) (1st anniv) 50 30
558 15r. Falgunanda (religious leader) (44th anniv) . . . . 1·10 75

280 Bagh Bairab Temple, Kirtipur

1993. Holy Places. Multicoloured.
559 1r.50 Type **280** 10 10
560 5r. Devghat (gods' bathing place), Tanahun 35 20
561 8r. Halesi Mahadev Cave (hiding place of Shiva), Khotang 60 35

281 Tushahiti Fountain, Sundari Chowk, Patan

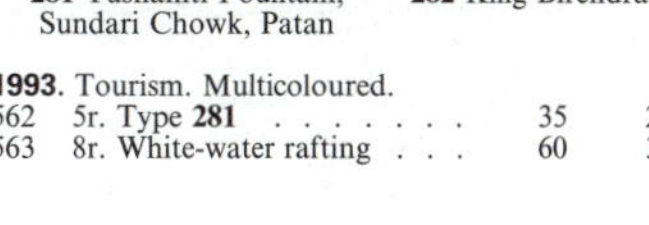

282 King Birendra

1993. Tourism. Multicoloured.
562 5r. Type **281** 35 20
563 8r. White-water rafting . . . 60 35

1993. King Birendra's 49th Birthday.
564 **282** 10r. multicoloured 75 45

283 Monument

284 Mt. Everest

1994.
565 **283** 20p. brown 10 10
566 – 25p. red 10 10
567 – 30p. green 10 10
568 **284** 1r. multicoloured 15 15
569 – 5r. multicoloured 35 20
DESIGNS—20 × 22 mm: 25p. State arms. 22 × 20 mm: 30p. Lumbini. 25 × 15 mm: 5r. Map of Nepal, crown and state arms and flag.

285 Pasang Sherpa

1994. 1st Death Anniv of Pasang Sherpa (mountaineer).
570 **285** 10r. multicoloured 75 45

286 Cigarette, Lungs and Crab's Claws

287 Postal Delivery

1994. Anti-smoking Campaign.
571 **286** 1r. multicoloured 15 15

1994.
572 **287** 1r.50 multicoloured . . . 15 15

288 Khuda

1994. Weapons. Multicoloured.
573 5r. Kukris (three swords and two scabbards) 35 20
574 5r. Type **288** 35 20
575 5r. Dhaal (swords and shield) 35 20
576 5r. Katari (two daggers) . . . 35 20

289 Workers and Emblem

1994. 75th Anniv of I.L.O.
577 **289** 15r. gold, blue & ultram 1·10 75

290 Landscape

1994. World Food Day.
578 **290** 25r. multicoloured . . . . 1·80 1·20

291 "Dendrobium densiflorum"

292 Family

1994. Orchids. Multicoloured.
579 10r. Type **291** 75 45
580 10r. "Coelogyne flaccida" . . 75 45
581 10r. "Cymbidium devonianum" 75 45
582 10r. "Coelogyne corymbosa" 75 45

1994. International Year of the Family.
583 **292** 9r. emerald, green and red 65 45

293 Emblem and Airplane

294 "Russula nepalensis"

1994. 50th Anniv of I.C.A.O.
584 **293** 11r. blue, gold and deep blue 80 50

1994. Fungi. Multicoloured.
585 7r. Type **294** 50 30
586 7r. Morels ("Morchella conica") 50 30
587 7r. Caesar's mushroom ("Amanita caesarea") . . . 50 30
588 7r. "Cordyceps sinensis" . . 50 30

295 Dharanidhar Koirala (poet)

1994. Celebrities. Multicoloured.
589 1r. Type **295** 10 10
590 2r. Narayan Gopal Guruwacharya (singer) . . 15 10
591 6r. Bahadur Shah (vert) . . . 45 30
592 7r. Balaguru Shadananda . . 50 30

296 King Birendra, Flag, Map and Crown

1994. King Birendra's 50th Birthday (1st issue).
593 **296** 9r. multicoloured 65 45
See also No. 621.

297 Lake Tilicho, Manang

1994. Tourism. Multicoloured.
594 9r. Type **297** 65 45
595 11r. Taleju Temple, Katmandu (vert) 80 50

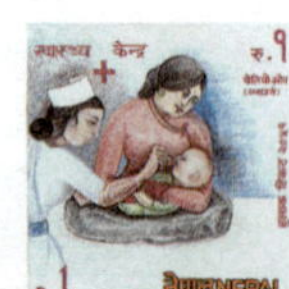
298 Health Care

1994. Children's Activities. Multicoloured.
596 1r. Type **298** 10 10
597 1r. Classroom 10 10
598 1r. Playground equipment . . 10 10
599 1r. Stamp collecting 10 10

299 Singhaduarbar

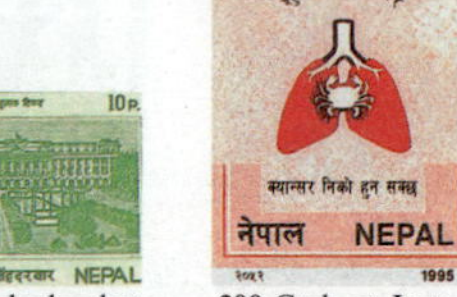
300 Crab on Lungs

1995.
600 **299** 10p. green 10 10
601 – 50p. blue 10 10
DESIGN—VERT: 50p. Pashupati.

1995. Anti-cancer Campaign.
602 **300** 2r. multicoloured 15 15

301 Chandra Man Singh Maskey (artist)

302 Bhakti Thapa (soldier)

1995. Celebrities. Multicoloured.
603 3r. Type **301** 20 15
604 3r. Parijat (writer) 20 15
605 3r. Bhim Nidhi Tiwari (writer) 20 15
606 3r. Yuddha Prasad Mishra (writer) 20 15

1995. Celebrities. Multicoloured.
607 15p. Type **302** 10 10
608 1r. Madan Bhandari (politician) 10 10
609 4r. Prakash Raj Kaphley (human rights activist) . . 10 15

303 Gaur ("Bos gaurus")

1995. "Singapore '95" International Stamp Exhibition. Mammals. Multicoloured.
610 10r. Type **303** 75 45
611 10r. Lynx ("Felis lynx") . . . 75 45
612 10r. Assam macaque ("Macaca assamensis") . . 75 45
613 10r. Striped hyena ("Hyaena hyaena") 75 45

304 Anniversary Emblem

1995. 50th Anniv of F.A.O.
614 **304** 7r. multicoloured 50 30

305 Figures around Emblem

306 Bhimeswor Temple, Dolakha

1995. 50th Anniv of U.N.O.
615 **305** 50r. multicoloured . . . . 3·75 2·40

1995. Tourism. Multicoloured.
616 1r. Type **306** 10 10
617 5r. Ugra Tara Temple, Dadeldhura (horiz) 35 20
618 7r. Mt. Nampa (horiz) . . . 50 30
619 18r. Nrity Aswora (traditional Pauba painting) (27 × 39 mm) . . . . . . 1·30 90
620 20r. Lumbini (Buddha's birthplace) (28 × 28 mm) 1·50 95

307 King Birendra

309 King Birendra

308 Anniversary Emblem

1995. King Birendra's 50th Birthday (1994) (2nd issue).
621 **307** 1r. multicoloured 15 15

1995. 10th Anniv of South Asian Association for Regional Co-operation.
622 **308** 10r. multicoloured 75 45

1995. King Birendra's 51st Birthday.
623 **309** 12r. multicoloured 90 60

310 Karnali Bridge

1996.
624 **310** 7r. multicoloured 50 30

311 State Arms

312 Kaji Kalu Pande (soldier and royal adviser)

1996.
625 **311** 25p. red 15 15

1996. Political Figures. Multicoloured.
626 75p. Type **312** 10 10
627 1r. Pushpa Lal Shrestha (Nepal Communist Party General-Secretary) 10 10
628 5r. Suvarna Shamsher Rana (founder of Nepal Democratic Congress Party) 35 20

313 Hem Raj Sharma (grammarian)

314 Runner and Track

1996. Writers. Multicoloured.
629 1r. Type **313** 10 10
630 3r. Padma Prasad Bhattarai (Sanskrit scholar) 20 15
631 5r. Bhawani Bhikshu (novelist) 35 20

1996. Olympic Games, Atlanta.
632 **314** 7r. multicoloured 50 30

315 Kasthamandap, Katmandu

316 Hindu Temple, Arjundhara

1996. Temples.
633 **315** 10p. red and black . . . 10 10
634 50p. black and red . . . 10 10
635 – 1r. red and blue 10 10
DESIGN—VERT: 1r. Nyata Pola temple, Bhaktapur.

1996. Tourism. Multicoloured.
636 1r. Type **316** 10 10
637 2r. Durbar, Nuwakot 15 10
638 8r. Gaijatra Festival, Bhaktapur 65 45
639 10r. Lake Beganas, Kaski . . 90 60

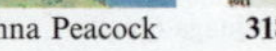
317 Krishna Peacock

318 Ashoka Pillar

1996. Butterflies and Birds. Multicoloured.
640 5r. Type **317** 45 30
641 5r. Great barbet ("Great Himalayan Barbet") . . . 45 30
642 5r. Sarus crane 45 30
643 5r. Northern jungle queen . . 45 30
Nos. 640/3 were issued together, se-tenant, forming a composite design.

1996. Centenary of Rediscovery of Ashoka Pillar, Lumbini (birthplace of Buddha).
644 **318** 12r. multicoloured . . . . 1·00 65

319 King Birendra

1996. King Birendra's 52nd Birthday.
645 **319** 10r. multicoloured 60 60

320 Mt. Annapurna South and Mt. Annapurna I

1996. The Himalayas.
646 18r. Type **320** . . . . 1·10 75
647 18r. Mt. Machhapuchhre and Mt. Annapurna III . . . . 1·10 75
648 18r. Mt. Annapurna IV and Mt. Annapurna II . . . . 1·10 75
Nos. 646/8 were issued together, se-tenant, forming a composite design.

321 King Birendra before Throne

1997. Silver Jubilee of King Birendra's Accession.
649 **321** 2r. multicoloured 15 15

322 Mountains and National Flags

323 Postal Emblem

1997. 40th Anniv of Nepal–Japan Diplomatic Relations.
650 **322** 18r. multicoloured . . . . 1·30 90

1997.
651 **323** 2r. red and brown 15 15

324 Campaign Emblem

1997. National Tourism Year.
652 **324** 2r. red and blue 15 10
653 – 10r. multicoloured 75 45
654 – 18r. multicoloured . . . . 1·30 90
655 – 20r. multicoloured . . . . 1·50 95
DESIGNS—HORIZ: 10r. Upper Mustang mountain peak; 18r. Rafting, River Sunkoshi. VERT: 20r. Changunarayan.

325 Chepang Couple

326 National Flags and Handshake

1997. Ethnic Groups. Multicoloured.
656 5r. Type **325** 35 20
657 5r. Gurung couple 35 20
658 5r. Rana Tharu couple 35 20

1997. 50th Anniv of Nepal United States Diplomatic Relations.
659 **326** 20r. multicoloured 1·50 95

327 Riddhi Bahadur Malla (writer)

328 "Jasminum gracile"

1997. Celebrities. Multicoloured.
660 2r. Type **327** 15 10
661 2r. Dr. K. I. Singh (politician) 15 10

1997. Flowers. Multicoloured.
662 40p. Type **328** 10 10
663 1r. China aster 10 10
664 2r. "Manglietia insignis" 15 10
665 15r. "Luculia gratissima" 1·20 75

329 Dhiki (corn crusher)

1997. Traditional Technology. Multicoloured.
666 5r. Type **329** 35 2·20
667 5r. Janto (mill stone) 35 2·20
668 5r. Kol (oil mill) (vert) 35 2·20
669 5r. Okhal (implement for pounding rice) (vert) 35 2·20

330 King Birendra

331 Sunrise, Shree Antudanda, Ilam

1997. King Birendra's 53rd Birthday.
670 **330** 10r. multicoloured 75 45

1998. Tourism. Multicoloured.
671 2r. Type **331** 15 10
672 10r. Maitidevi Temple, Katmandu 75 45
673 18r. Great Renunciation Gate, Kapilavastu 1·30 90
674 20r. Mt. Cholatse, Solukhumbu (vert) 1·50 95

332 Ram Prasad Rai (nationalist)

1998. Personalities.
675 **332** 75p. black and brown 10 10
676 – 1r. black and mauve 15 15
677 – 2r. black and green 20 15
678 – 2r. black and blue 20 15
679 – 5r.40 black and red 35 20
DESIGNS: No. 676, Imansing Chemjong (Kiranti language specialist); 677, Tulsi Meher Shrestha (social worker); 678, Maha Pundit Dadhi Ram Marasini (poet); 679, Mahananda Sapkota (educationalist and writer).

333 Match Scenes

1998. World Cup Football Championship, France.
680 **333** 12r. multicoloured 90 60

334 Ganesh Man Singh

1998. 1st Death Anniv of Ganesh Man Singh (politician).
681 **334** 5r. multicoloured 35 20

335 World Map and Nepalese Soldiers

1998. 40 Years of Nepalese Army Involvement in United Nations Peace Keeping Missions.
682 **335** 10r. multicoloured 75 45

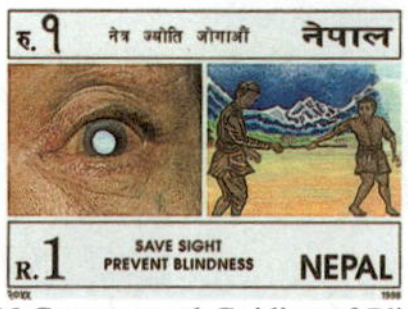

336 Cataract and Guiding of Blind Man

1998. Cataract Awareness Campaign.
683 **336** 1r. multicoloured 15 15

337 King Cobra

1998. Snakes. Multicoloured.
684 1r.70 Type **337** 10 10
685 2r. Golden tree snake 15 10
686 5r. Asiatic rock python 35 20
687 10r. Karan's pit viper 75 45

338 Dove and Profile

1998. 50th Anniv of Universal Declaration of Human Rights.
688 **338** 10r. multicoloured 75 45

339 Disabled Persons

340 King Birendra

1998. Asian and Pacific Decade of Disabled Persons.
689 **339** 10r. multicoloured 75 45

1998. King Birendra's 54th Birthday.
690 **340** 2r. multicoloured 15 15

341 Dam and Power House

1998. River Marsyangdi Hydro-electric Power Station.
691 **341** 12r. multicoloured 90 60

342 Hospital and Emblem

1999. 25th Anniv of Nepal Eye Hospital.
692 **342** 2r. multicoloured 15 15

343 Kalika Bhagawati Temple, Baglung

1999. Tourism. Multicoloured.
693 2r. Type **343** 15 10
694 2r. Chandan Nath Temple, Jumla (vert) 15 75
695 12r. Bajrayogini Temple, Sankhu (vert) 1·10 75
696 15r. Mt. Everest 1·30 90
697 15r. Ashokan Pillar, Lumbini, and English translation of its inscription (39 × 27 mm) 1·30 90

344 Four-horned Antelope

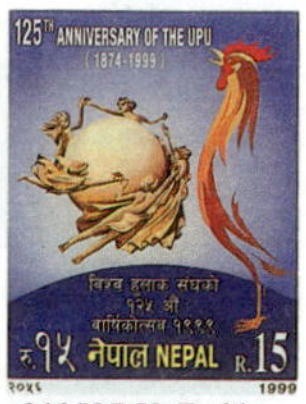

346 U.P.U. Emblem and Cockerel

345 Him Kanchha (mascot) and Games Emblem

1999. Mammals. Multicoloured.
698 10r. Type **344** 90 60
699 10r. Argali (Ovis ammon) 90 60

1999. 8th South Asian Sports Federation Games, Katmandu.
700 **345** 10r. multicoloured 90 60

1999. 125th Anniv of Universal Postal Union.
701 **346** 15r. multicoloured 1·30 15

347 Ramnarayan Mishra (revolutionary, 1922–67)

1999. Personalities.
702 **347** 1r. green and black 10 10
703 – 1r. brown and black 10 10
704 – 1r. blue and black 10 10
705 – 2r. red and black 15 10
706 – 2r. blue and black 15 10
707 – 2r. buff and black 15 10
DESIGNS: No. 703, Master Mitrasen (writer, 1895–1946); 704, Bhupi Sherchan (poet, 1935–89); 705, Rudraraj Pandey (writer, 1901–87); 706, Gopalprasad Rimal (writer, 1917–73); 707, Mangaladevi Singh (revolutionary, 1924–96).

348 Sorathi Dance

1999. Local Dances. Multicoloured.
708 5r. Type **348** 45 30
709 5r. Bhairav dance 45 30
710 5r. Jhijhiya dance 45 30

349 Children working and writing

1999. Nepal's involvement in International Programme on the Elimination of Child Labour.
711 **349** 12r. multicoloured 1·10 75

350 King Birendra

1999. King Birendra's 55th Birthday.
712 **350** 5r. multicoloured 45 30

351 Headquarters

2000. 60th Anniv of Radio Nepal.
713 **351** 2r. multicoloured 15 15

352 Queen Aishwarya

353 Front Page of Newspaper and Emblem

2000. Queen Aishwarya's 50th Birthday.
714 **352** 15r. multicoloured 1·30 1·30

2000. Centenary of *Gorkhapatra* (newspaper).
715 **353** 10r. multicoloured 80 80

354 Tchorolpa Glacial Lake, Dolakha

2000. Tourist Sights. Multicoloured.
716 12r. Type **354** 1·00 1·00
717 15r. Dakshinkali Temple, Kathmandu 1·30 1·30
718 18r. Mount Annapurna (50th anniv of first ascent) 1·50 1·50

355 Ranipokhari Pagoda, Kathmandu

2000.
719 **355** 50p. black and orange 10 10
720 1r. black and blue 10 10
721 2r. black and brown 15 15

356 Soldier and Child

2000. 50th Anniv of Geneva Convention.
725 **356** 5r. multicoloured 45 45

357 Runners

2000. Olympic Games, Sydney.
726 **357** 25r. multicoloured . . . . 2·20 2·20

358 Hridayachandra Singh Pradhan (writer)

359 Indian Rhinoceros (male)

2000. Personalities.
727 **358** 2r. black and yellow . . . 15 15
728 – 2r. black and brown . . . 15 15
729 – 5r. black and blue . . . 45 45
730 – 5r. black and red . . . 45 45
DESIGNS: No. 728, Thir Barn Malla (revolutionary); 729, Krishna Prasad Koirala (social reformer); 730, Manamohan Adhikari (politian).

2000. Wildlife. Multicoloured.
731 10r. Type **359** 90 90
732 10r. Indian rhinoceros (*Rhinoceros unicornis*) (female) 90 90
733 10r. Lesser adjutant stork (*Leptoptilos javanicus*) . . . 90 90
734 10r. Bengal florican (*Houbaropsis bengalensis*) 90 90

360 Orchid (*Dactylorhiza hatagirea*)

361 King Birendra

2000. Flowers. Multicoloured.
735 5r. Type **360** 45 45
736 5r. *Mahonia napaulensis* (horiz) 45 45
737 5r. *Talauma hodgsonii* (horiz) 45 45

2000. King Birendra's 56th Birthday.
738 **361** 5r. multicoloured 45 45

362 King Tribhuvana and Crowd

2001. 50th Anniv of Constitutional Monarchy.
739 **362** 5r. multicoloured 45 45

363 Crowd and Emblem

2001. Population Census.
740 **363** 2r. multicoloured 15 15

364 Khaptad Baba (religious leader)

365 Asiatic Coinwort (*Centella asiatica*)

2001. Personalities.
741 **364** 2r. pink and black 15 15
742 – 2r. mauve and black . . . 15 15
743 – 2r. magenta and black . . 15 15
744 – 2r. red and black 15 15
745 – 2r. blue and black 15 15
DESIGNS: No. 742, Bhikkhu Pragyananda Mahathera (Buddhist writer and teacher); 743, Guru Prasad Mainali (author); 744, Tulsi Lal Amatya Politician); 745, Madan Lal Agrawal (industrialist).

2001. Plants. Multicoloured.
746 5r. Type **365** 45 45
747 15r. *Bergenia ciliata* . . . . 1·50 1·50
748 30r. Himalayan yew (*Taxus baccata wallichania*) . . . 3·00 3·00

366 Pipal Tree (*Ficus religiosa*)

367 Tents

2001.
749 **366** 10r. multicoloured 90 90

2001. 50th Anniv of United Nations High Commissioner for Refugees.
750 **367** 20r. multicoloured . . . . 1·80 1·80

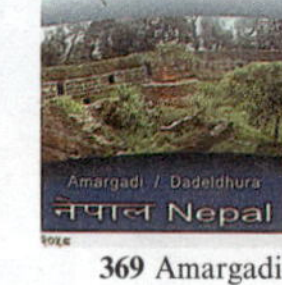

368 National Flag

369 Amargadi Fort

2001.
751 **368** 10p. red and blue 15 15

2001. Tourism. Multicoloured.
752 2r. Type **369** 15 15
753 5r. Hiranyavarna Mahavihar (Golden Temple) (vert) . . 45 45
754 15r. Jugal mountain range . . 1·30 1·30

370 King Birendra

2001. 57th Birth Anniv of King Birendra.
755 **370** 15r. multicoloured . . . . 1·30 1·30

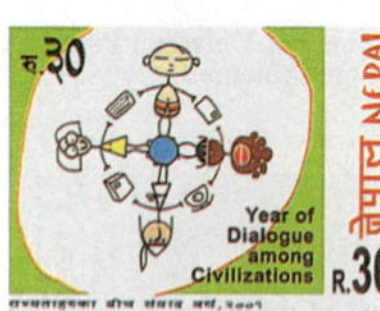

371 Children encircling Globe

2001. United Nations Year of Dialogue among Civilizations.
756 **371** 30r. multicoloured . . . . 2·50 2·50

372 Scout Emblem

2002. 50th Anniv of Nepalese Scouts.
757 **372** 2r. chestnut and olive . . 20 20

373 World Cup Emblem and Footballer

2002. World Cup Football Championships, Japan and South Korea.
758 **373** 15r. multicoloured . . . . 1·30 1·30

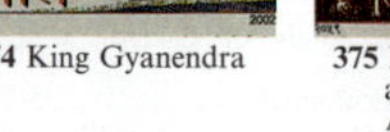

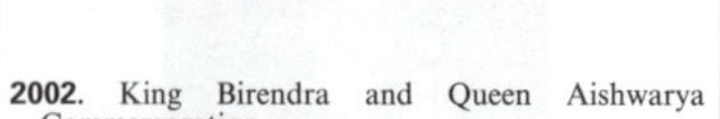

374 King Gyanendra

375 King Birendra and Queen Aishwarya

2002. 1st Anniv of Accession of King Gyanendra.
759 **374** 5r. multicoloured 45 45

2002. King Birendra and Queen Aishwarya Commemoration.
760 **375** 10r. multicoloured 45 45

376 "Aryabalokiteshwor"

377 Family encircled by Barbed Wire (Siddhimuni Shakya)

2002. Paintings. Multicoloured.
761 5r. Type **376** 45 45
762 5r. "Moti (pearl)" (King Birendra) (horiz) 45 45

2002. Social Awareness.
763 **377** 1r. black and brown . . . 10 10
764 – 2r. black and lilac 15 15
DESIGNS: Type **377** (integration of untouchables); 2r. Children leaving for school (treatment of girls).

378 Leaf Beetle

379 Valley and Mountains

2002. Insects. Multicoloured.
765 3r. Type **378** 30 30
766 5r. Short horn grasshopper 45 45

2002. International Year of Mountains.
767 **379** 5r. multicoloured 45 45

380 Pathibhara Devisthan, Taplejung

2002. Tourism. Multicoloured.
768 5r. Type **380** 45 45
769 5r. Galeshwor Mahadevsthan, Myagdi 45 45
770 5r. Ramgram Stupa, Nawalparasi 45 45
771 5r. Mt. Nilgiri, Mustang . . 45 45

381 Dayabor Singh Kansakar (philanthropist)

383 Anniversary Emblem

382 Members Flags and Organization Emblem

2002. Personalities. Multicoloured.
772 2r. Type **381** 15 15
773 25r. Ekai Kawaguchi (first Japanese to visit Nepal) . . 2·20 2·20

2002. South Asian Association for Regional Co-operation (SAARC) Charter Day.
774 **382** 15r. multicoloured . . . . 1·30 1·30

2003. 50th Anniv of Chamber of Commerce.
775 **383** 5r. multicoloured 10 10

384 FNCCI Emblem

2003. Industry and Commerce Day.
776 **384** 5r. multicoloured 10 10

385 Mt. Everest

2003. 50th Anniv of the First Ascent of Mount Everest.
777 **385** 25r. multicoloured 40 20

386 Babu Chiri Sherpa

2003. Babu Chiri Sherpa (mountaineer) Commemoration.
778 **386** 5r. multicoloured 10 10

387 King Gyanendra

2003. 57th Birth Anniv of King Gyanendra.
779 **387** 5r. multicoloured 10 10

388 Tea Garden

2003. Eastern Nepal Tea Gardens.
780 **388** 25r. multicoloured 40 20

389 Dilli Raman Regmi

2003. 2nd Death Anniv of Dilli Raman Regmi (politician and historian).
781 **389** 5r. brown and black . . . 10 10

390 Gopal Das Shrestha

2003. 5th Death Anniv of Gopal Das Shrestha (journalist).
782 **390** 5r. green and black . . . 10 10

391 Container, Crane and Emblem

2003. Export Year.
783 **391** 25r. multicoloured 40 20

392 Sankhadhar Sakhwaa (statue) and Celebrating Crowd

2003. Sankhadhar Sakhwaa (founder of Nepal calender).
784 **392** 5r. multicoloured 10 10

393 Ganesh (statue), Kageshwar

394 Lotus

2003. Tourist Sights. Multicoloured.
785 5r. Type **393** 10 10
786 5r. Hydroelectric dam on Kali Gandaki river (horiz) 10 10
787 30r. Buddha (statue), Swayambhu (horiz) 50 25

2003. Flowers. Multicoloured.
788 10r. Type **394** 20 10
789 10r. Picrorhiza 20 10
790 10r. Himalayan rhubarb . . 20 10
791 10r. Jasmine 20 10

395 Emblem and Symbols of Social Work

2004. 50th Anniv of Social Services of United Mission to Nepal.
792 **395** 5r. multicoloured 10 10

396 NNJS Emblem

2004. 25th Anniv of Nepal Netra Jyoti Sangh (NNJS) (eye care organization).
793 **396** 5r. multicoloured 10 10

397 Society Emblem

2004. 50th Anniv of Marwadi Sewa Samiti, Nepal (charitable organization).
794 **397** 5r. multicoloured 10 10

398 King Gyanendra

399 APT Emblem

2004. 58th Birth Anniv of King Gyanendra.
795 **398** 5r. multicoloured 10 10

2004. 25th Anniv of Asia—Pacific Tele-Community (APT).
796 **399** 5r. multicoloured 10 10

400 Anniversary Emblem

2004. 50th Anniv of Management Education.
797 **400** 5r. multicoloured 10 10

401 Anniversary Emblem

2004. Centenary of FIFA (Fedération Internationale de Football Association).
798 **401** 20r. multicoloured 30 15

402 Mt. Lhotse

2004. 50th Anniv of Assent Mt Cho Oyu. Multicoloured.
799 10r. Type **402** 20 10
800 10r. Makalu 20 10
801 10r. Manasalu 20 10
802 10r. Annapurna 20 10
803 10r. Everest 20 10
804 10r. Kanchenjunga main peak 20 10
805 10r. Cho Oyu 20 10
806 10r. Dhaulagiri 20 10

403 Narahari Nath

2004. Personalities. Multicoloured.
807 5r. Type **403** (religious scholar) 10 10
808 5r. Nayaraj Panta (historian) 10 10

404 *Sasia ochracea* Hodgson (inscr "Rufous piculet" woodpecker)

2004. Biodiversity. Multicoloured.
809 10r. Type **404** 20 10
810 10r. Atlas moth (*Attacus atlas*) 20 10
811 10r. *Swertia multicaulis* . . . 20 10
812 10r. High altitude rice (*Oryza sativa*) 20 10

405 Mayadevi Temple, Lumbini

2004. Tourism. Multicoloured.
813 10r. Type **405** 20 10
814 10r. Gadhimai, Bara 20 10

406 Writer and Emblem

407 Jayavarma

2004. 50th Anniv of Madan Puraskar (language and literature prize).
815 **406** 5r. multicoloured 10 10

2004. Sculpture. Multicoloured.
816 10r. Type **407** (National museum, Kathmandu) . . 20 10
817 10r. Umamaheswar (Kathmandu) 20 10
818 10r. Vishwarupa (Bhaktapur) 20 10
819 10r. Krishna playing flute (Makawanpur) 20 10

408 Building Facade

2005. 50th Anniv of Nepal Rasta Bank.
820 **408** 2r. multicoloured 10 10

409 Mt. Makalu

2005. 50th Anniv of First Ascent of Mt. Makalu.
821 **409** 10r. multicoloured 20 10

410 Mt. Kanchanjunga

2005. 50th Anniv of First Ascent of Mt. Kanchanjunga.
822 **410** 12r. multicoloured 20 10

411 King Gyanendra

2005. 59th Birth Anniv of King Gyanendra.
823 **411** 5r. multicoloured 10 10

412 Birth of Buddha

2005. Buddha. Showing the life of Buddha. Multicoloured border given.
824 10r. Type **412** 20 10
825 10r. Enlightenment 20 10
826 10r. First sermon 20 10
827 10r. Mahaparinirvana 20 10
828 10r. Type **412** (green) 20 10
829 10r. As No. 825 (green) . . . 20 10
830 10r. As No. 826 (green) . . . 20 10
831 10r. As No. 827 (green) . . . 20 10
832 10r. Type **412** (vermilion) . . 20 10
833 10r. As No. 825 (vermilion) 20 10
834 10r. As No. 826 (vermilion) 20 10
835 10r. As No. 827 (vermilion) 20 10
836 10r. Type **412** (violet) 20 10
837 10r. As No. 825 (violet) . . . 20 10
838 10r. As No. 826 (violet) . . . 20 10
839 10r. As No. 827 (violet) . . . 20 10

413 *Phyllanthus emblica*

2005. Fruit. Multicoloured.
840 10r. Type **413** 20 10
841 10r. *Juglans regia* 20 10
842 10r. *Aegle marmelos* 20 10
843 10r. *Rubus ellipticus* 20 10

414 Queen Mother Ratna Rajya Laxmi Devi Shah

2005. 77th Birth Anniv of Queen Mother Ratna Rajya Laxmi Devi Shah.
844 **414** 20r. multicoloured 30 15

415 Asian Elephant

2005. Endangered Species. Mammals. Multicoloured border colour given.
845 10r. Type **415** 20 10
846 10r. Clouded leopard 20 10
847 10r. Gangetic dolphin 20 10
848 10r. Indian pangolin 20 10
849 10r. Type **415** (green) 20 10
850 10r. As No. 846 (green) . . . 20 10
851 10r. As No. 847 (green) . . . 20 10
852 10r. As No. 848 (green) . . . 20 10
853 10r. Type **415** (vermilion) . . 20 10
854 10r. As No. 846 (vermilion) 20 10
855 10r. As No. 847 (vermilion) 20 10
856 10r. As No. 848 (vermilion) 20 10
857 10r. Type **415** (violet) 20 10
858 10r. As No. 846 (violet) . . . 20 10
859 10r. As No. 847 (violet) . . . 20 10
860 10r. As No. 848 (violet) . . . 20 10

416 Bhupalmansingh Karki

2005. Bhupalmansingh Karki (politician) Commemoration.
861 **416** 2r. multicoloured 10 10

417 Kalinchok Bhagawati, Dolakha

2005. Tourism. Multicoloured.
862 5r. Type **417** 10 10
863 5r. Panauti City, Kabhrepalanchok 10 10
864 5r. Ghodaghodi Lake, Kailali 10 10
865 5r. Budhasubba, Sunasari . . 10 10

418 Sherpa Jewellery

2005. Tribal Jewellery. Multicoloured.
866 25r. Type **418** 40 20
867 25r. Newar 40 20
868 25r. Tharu 40 20
869 25r. Limbu 40 20

419 Stupa and Chinese and Nepalese Flags

2005. 50th Anniv of Nepal–China Diplomatic Relations.
870 **419** 30r. multicoloured 50 25

420 Flags

2005. 50th Anniv of United Nations Membership.
871 **420** 50r. multicoloured 80 40

OFFICIAL STAMPS

O 25 Nepalese Arms and Soldiers

काज सरकारी
(**O 28**)

1960. (a) Size 30 × 18 mm.
O135 **O 25** 2p. brown 10 10
O136 4p. green 15 10
O137 6p. red 15 10
O138 8p. violet 15 15
O139 12p. orange 20 20

(b) Size 38 × 27 mm.
O140 **O 25** 16p. brown 35 30
O141 24p. red 50 45
O142 32p. purple 60 60
O143 50p. blue . . . . . 1·10 1·00
O144 1r. red . . . . . . 2·20 1·90
O145 2r. orange . . . . . 4·50 4·00

1960. Optd as Type **O 28**.
O146 **27** 1r. purple 90

1961. Optd with Type **O 28**.
O148 **35** 1p. red 15 15
O149 2p. blue 15 15
O150 5p. brown 20 20
O151 **36** 10p. purple 10 10
O152 40p. brown 15 15
O153 75p. green 20 20
O154 **27** 2r. red 60 60
O155 5r. green . . . . . . 1·60 1·60

NETHERLANDS Pt. 4

A kingdom in the N.W. of Europe on the North Sea.

1852. 100 cents = 1 gulden (florin).
2002. 100 cents = 1 euro.

1

3 King William III

4

1852. Imperf.
1 **1** 5c. blue . . . . £225 30·00
2 10c. red . . . . £225 27·00
3b 15c. orange £600 £100

1864. Perf.
8 **3** 5c. blue . . . . £200 16·00
9 10c. red . . . . £300 7·50
10 15c. orange . . . . £500 90·00

1867.
17d **4** 5c. blue . . . . 85·00 2·40
18c 10c. red . . . . £150 3·00
19c 15c. brown . . . . £650 30·00
20 20c. green . . . . £600 23·00
15 25c. purple £2250 £100
22 50c. gold £2750 £160

5

6

1869.
58 **5** ½c. brown . . . . 24·00 4·00
53 1c. black . . . . £190 70·00
59 1c. green . . . . 11·50 2·40
55a 1½c. red . . . . £130 80·00
56a 2c. yellow . . . . 42·00 12·00
62 2½c. mauve . . . . £500 70·00

1872.
80 **6** 5c. blue . . . . 9·00 30
81 7½c. brown . . . . 38·00 17·00
82 10c. red . . . . 60·00 1·60
83 12½c. grey . . . . 65·00 2·40
84 15c. brown . . . . £375 5·00
85 20c. green . . . . £450 5·00
86 22½c. green . . . . 80·00 45·00
87 25c. lilac . . . . £575 4·00
97 50c. bistre . . . . £750 10·00
90 1g. violet . . . . £500 40·00
75 – 2g.50 blue and red £950 £110
No. 75 is similar to Type **6** but larger and with value and country scrolls transposed.

8

9 Queen Wilhelmina

1876.
133 **8** ½c. red . . . . 3·00 10
134 1c. green . . . . 9·50 10
137 2c. yellow . . . . 38·00 2·75
139 2½c. mauve . . . . 15·00 30

1891.
147a **9** 3c. orange . . . . 8·75 2·00
148a 5c. blue . . . . 5·00 25
149b 7½c. brown . . . . 17·00 5·25
150b 10c. red . . . . 25·00 1·40
151b 12½c. grey . . . . 25·00 1·50
152a 15c. brown . . . . 50·00 4·00
153b 20c. green . . . . 65·00 3·00
154a 22½c. green . . . . 32·00 11·50
155 25c. mauve . . . . £110 5·25
156a 50c. bistre . . . . £500 16·00
159 – 50c. brown and green . . . 75·00 9·50
157 **9** 1g. violet . . . . £550 65·00
160 – 1g. green and brown . . . £190 19·00
161 – 2g.50 blue and red £450 £140
165 – 5g. red and green £700 £400
Nos. 159, 160, 161 and 165 are as Type **9** but larger and with value and country scrolls transposed.

11

12

13

14

1898. Nos. 174 and 176 also exist imperf.
167 **12** ½c. lilac 60 20
168 1c. red . . . . 1·10 15
170 1½c. blue . . . . 3·00 35
171 2c. brown . . . . 4·50 20
172 2½c. green . . . . 3·75 20
173 **13** 3c. orange . . . . 17·00 3·50
174 3c. green . . . . 1·50 15
175 4c. purple . . . . 1·50 90
176 4½c. mauve . . . . 3·75 3·75
177b 5c. red . . . . 1·75 15
178 7½c. brown 75 20
179 10c. grey . . . . 7·50 15
180 12½c. blue . . . . 4·00 25
181 15c. brown . . . . 95·00 3·50
182 15c. red and blue . . . . . 7·50 15
183 17½c. mauve . . . . 50·00 12·00
184 17½c. brown and blue . . . 18·00 90
185 20c. green £120 70
186 20c. grey and green . . . . 12·00 45
187 22½c. green and brown . . . 11·50 50
188 25c. blue and pink . . . . 11·50 30
189 30c. purple and mauve . . . 25·00 50
190 40c. orange and green . . . 38·00 90
191 50c. red and green £110 95
192 50c. violet and grey . . . . 65·00 90
193 60c. green and olive . . . . 38·00 1·10
194a **11** 1g. green . . . . 50·00 75
195b 2½g. lilac . . . . 95·00 3·50
196a 5g. red . . . . £225 5·50
197 10g. red £750 £700

1906. Society for the Prevention of Tuberculosis.
208 **14** 1c. (+1c.) red . . . . . . 18·00 10·00
209 3c. (+3c.) green . . . . . 32·00 22·00
210 5c. (+5c.) violet . . . . . 30·00 15·00

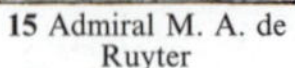
15 Admiral M. A. de Ruyter

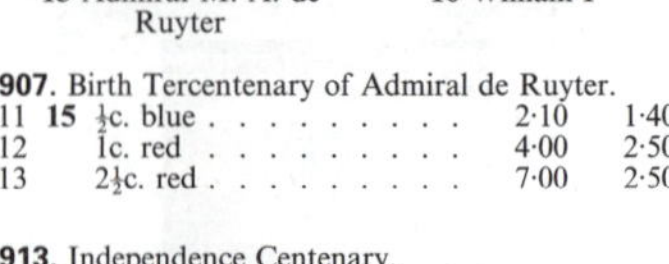
16 William I

1907. Birth Tercentenary of Admiral de Ruyter.
211 **15** ½c. blue . . . . 2·10 1·40
212 1c. red . . . . 4·00 2·50
213 2½c. red . . . . 7·00 2·50

1913. Independence Centenary.
214 **16** 2½c. green on green 90 85
215 – 3c. yellow on cream . . . 1·40 1·25
216 – 5c. red on buff . . . . . 1·40 90
217 – 10c. grey . . . . 4·25 2·40
218 **16** 12½c. blue on blue . . . . 3·25 2·25
219 – 20c. brown . . . . . . 12·50 10·00
220 – 25c. blue . . . . 15·00 8·75
221 – 50c. green . . . . 32·00 28·00
222 **16** 1g. red . . . . 48·00 20·00
223 – 2½g. lilac . . . . £120 48·00
224 – 5g. yellow on cream . . . £250 40·00
225 – 10g. orange £750 £750
DESIGNS: 3c., 20c., 2½g. William II; 5c., 25c., 5g. William III; 10c., 50c., 10g. Queen Wilhelmina.

1919. Surch **Veertig Cent** (40c.) or **Zestig Cent** (60c.).
234 **13** 40c. on 30c. purple & mve 32·00 3·75
235 60c. on 30c. purple & mve 32·00 3·50

1920. Surch in figures.
238 **13** 4c. on 4½c. mauve . . . . 5·25 1·75
236 **11** 2.50 on 10g. red £140 £120
237 – 2.50 on 10g. red (No. 225) £150 £110

23

24

1921. Air.
239 **23** 10c. red . . . . 1·75 1·40
240 15c. green . . . . 6·25 2·25
241 60c. blue . . . . 19·00 20

1921.
242 **24** 5c. green . . . . 8·75 20
243 12½c. red . . . . 20·00 3·25
244 20c. blue . . . . 26·00 25

25 Lion in Dutch Garden and Orange Tree (emblematical of Netherlands)

26

27

1923.
248 **25** 1c. violet 65 65
249 2c. orange . . . . 6·00 20
250 **26** 2½c. green . . . . 2·10 70
251 **27** 4c. blue . . . . 1·50 60

1923. Surch.
252 **12** 2c. on 1c. red 60 20
253 2c. on 1½c. blue 60 25
254 **13** 10c. on 3c. green . . . . 5·00 20
255 10c. on 5c. red . . . . . 10·00 55
256 10c. on 12½c. blue . . . . 8·25 60
257a 10c. on 17½c. brown & blue . . . . 4·50 4·00
258a 10c. on 22½c. olive & brown . . . . 4·50 4·00

30

31

1923. 25th Anniv of Queen's Accession.
259 **31** 2c. green 30 10
260 **30** 5c. green 40 25
261 **31** 7½c. red 50 25
262 10c. red 40 10
263 20c. blue . . . . 4·25 80
264 25c. yellow . . . . 7·50 1·60
265b 35c. orange . . . . 8·00 3·50
266a 50c. black . . . . 18·00 50
267 **30** 1g. red . . . . 35·00 7·25
268 2½g. black £250 £200
269 5g. blue £225 £170

1923. Surch **DIENST ZEGEL PORTEN AAN TEEKEN RECHT** and value.
270 **13** 10c. on 3c. green . . . . . 1·25 1·10
271 1g. on 17½c. brown & blue 80·00 17·00

33

1923. Culture Fund.
272 **33** 2c. (+5c.) blue on pink . . 20·00 17·00
273 – 10c. (+5c.) red on pink . . 20·00 17·00
DESIGN: 10c. Two women.

35 Carrier Pigeon

36 Queen Wilhelmina

1924.
304C **35** ½c. grey 45 30
305A 1c. red 20 10
306C 1½c. mauve 40 10
424a 1½c. grey 20 10
425 2c. orange 20 10
426a 2½c. green . . . . 1·60 20
427 3c. green 20 10
427a 4c. blue 20 10
428 **36** 5c. green 20 10
429 6c. brown 20 10
279A 7½c. yellow 60 10
313A 7½c. violet . . . . . . 4·00 10
314A 7½c. red 30 10
279cA 9c. red and black . . . 1·60 1·50
281A 10c. red . . . . 1·75 10
317A 10c. blue . . . . 2·75 10
282A 12½c. red . . . . 2·10 40
319A 12½c. blue 35 10
320A 15c. blue . . . . 7·25 20
321C 15c. yellow 85 60
322C 20c. blue . . . . 5·50 2·50
434 21c. brown . . . . . . 25·00 90
324B 22½c. brown . . . . . . 6·75 2·40
434a 22½c. orange . . . . . 15·00 18·00
435 25c. green . . . . . . 5·00 15
326A 27½c. grey . . . . . . 4·50 20
437 30c. violet . . . . . . 6·00 20
286cA 35c. brown . . . . . . 35·00 7·00
437a 40c. brown . . . . . . 9·50 20
330A 50c. green . . . . . . 5·50 20
289A 60c. violet . . . . . . 30·00 95
331A 60c. black . . . . . . 23·00 1·00
301 1g. blue (23 × 29 mm) 8·75 50
302 2½g. red (23 × 29 mm) 90·00 5·25
303 5g. black (23 × 29 mm) £180 2·75
For further stamps in Type **35**, see Nos. 546/57.

1924. International Philatelic Exn, The Hague.
290 **36** 10c. green . . . . 38·00 38·00
291 15c. black . . . . 42·00 42·00
292 35c. red . . . . 38·00 38·00

37

38

1924. Dutch Lifeboat Centenary.
293 **37** 2c. brown . . . . 4·00 3·00
294 **38** 10c. brown on yellow . . . 7·00 2·50

39

40 Arms of South Holland

1924. Child Welfare.
295 **39** 2c. (+2c.) green . . . . . 2·10 2·10
296 7½c. (+3½c.) brown . . . . 5·25 6·25
297 10c. (+2½c.) red . . . . . 4·50 1·75

1925. Child Welfare. Arms as T **40**.
298A – 2c. (+2c.) green and yellow 90 85
299A – 7½c. (+3½c.) violet and blue . . . . 4·50 4·75
300A **40** 10c. (+2½c.) red and yellow . . . . 3·50 60
ARMS: 2c. North Brabant; 7½c. Gelderland.
See also Nos. 350/3A and 359/62A.

1926. Child Welfare. Arms as T **40**.
350A 2c. (+2c.) red and silver . . 55 50
351A 5c. (+3c.) green and blue 1·60 1·40
352A 10c. (+3c.) red and green 2·40 30
353A 15c. (+3c.) yellow and blue 6·25 5·75
ARMS: 2c. Utrecht; 5c. Zeeland; 10c. North Holland; 15c. Friesland.

46 Queen Wilhelmina

47 Red Cross Allegory

1927. 60th Anniv of Dutch Red Cross Society.
354a **46** 2c. (+2c.) red . . . . . . 3·25 2·40
355 – 3c. (+2c.) green . . . . . 6·25 9·00
356 – 5c. (+3c.) blue . . . . . 1·10 1·10
357a – 7½c. (+3½c.) blue . . . . 5·50 2·25
358 **47** 15c. (+5c.) red and blue 9·75 10·00
PORTRAITS: 2c. King William III; 3c. Queen Emma; 5c. Henry, Prince Consort.

1927. Child Welfare. Arms as T **40**.
359A 2c. (+2c.) red and lilac . . 45 45
360A 5c. (+3c.) green and yellow 1·75 1·60
361A 7½c. (+3½c.) red and black 4·00 40
362A 15c. (+3c.) blue and brown 6·00 5·50
ARMS: 2c. Drente; 5c. Groningen; 7½c. Limburg; 15c. Overyssel.

48 Sculler

49 Footballer

1928. Olympic Games, Amsterdam.
363 **48** 1½c.+1c. green . . . . . . 2·25 1·60
364 – 2c.+1c. purple . . . . . . 3·00 2·00
365 **49** 3c.+1c. green . . . . . . 2·50 2·40
366 – 5c.+1c. blue . . . . 3·00 1·60
367 – 7½c.+2½c. orange . . . . . 3·00 1·90
368 – 10c.+2c. red . . . . 8·00 6·00
369 – 15c.+2c. blue . . . . . . 8·00 4·50
370 – 30c.+3c. sepia . . . . . . 25·00 24·00
DESIGNS—HORIZ: 2c. Fencing. VERT: 5c. Sailing; 7½c. Putting the shot; 10c. Running; 15c. Show-jumping; 30c. Boxing.

50 Lieut. Koppen

1928. Air.
371 **50** 40c. red 60 60
372 – 75c. green 60 60
DESIGN: 75c. Van der Hoop.

52 J. P. Minckelers

53 Mercury

1928. Child Welfare.
373 **52** 1½c.+1½c. violet 60 50
374 – 5c.+3c. green . . . . . . 1·90 70
375a – 7½c.+2½c. red . . . . . . 3·50 35
376a – 12½c.+3½c. blue . . . . . 10·00 7·50
PORTRAITS: 5c. Boerhaave; 7½c. H. A. Lorentz; 12½c. G. Huygens.

1929. Air.
377 **53** 1½g. black . . . . 2·75 1·60
378 4½g. red . . . . 1·60 3·00
379 7½g. green . . . . 25·00 4·00

1929. Surch **21**.
380 **36** 21c. on 22½c. brown . . . 21·00 1·40

55 "Friendship and Security"

56 Rembrandt and "De Staalmeesters"

1929. Child Welfare.
381A **55** 1½c. (+1½c.) grey . . . . 2·25 50
382C 5c. (+3c.) green . . . . . 3·75 80
383A 6c. (+4c.) red . . . . . 2·25 35
384A 12½c. (+3½c.) blue . . . . 15·00 13·00

1930. Rembrandt Society.
385 **56** 5c. (+5c.) green . . . . . 8·00 7·50
386 6c. (+5c.) black . . . . . 5·50 3·75
387 12½c. (+5c.) blue . . . . . 8·50 8·50

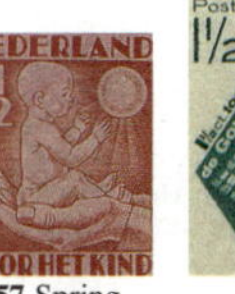
57 Spring

58

59 Queen Wilhelmina

1930. Child Welfare.
388A **57** 1½c. (+1½c.) red . . . . 1·60 50
389A – 5c. (+3c.) green . . . . . 2·75 65
390A – 6c. (+4c.) purple . . . . 2·40 40
391A – 12½c. (+3½c.) blue . . . . 19·00 9·50
DESIGNS (allegorical): 5c. Summer; 6c. Autumn; 12½c. Winter.

1931. Gouda Church Restoration Fund.
392 **58** 1½c.+1½c. green . . . . . 17·50 15·00
393 – 6c.+4c. red . . . . 21·00 18·00
DESIGN: No. 393, Church facade.

1931.
395 – 70c. blue and red (postage) . . . . 30·00 45
395b – 80c. green and red . . . . £110 3·25
394 **59** 36c. red and blue (air) . . 12·50 75
DESIGNS: 70c. Portrait and factory; 80c. Portrait and shipyard.

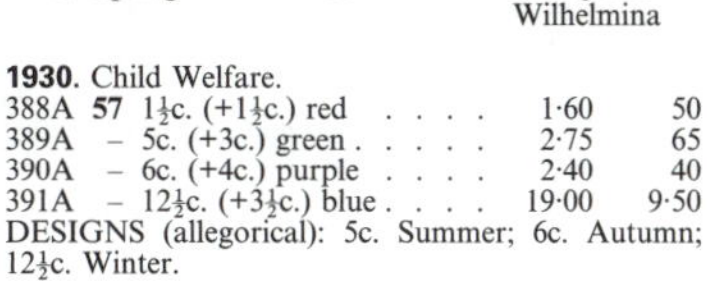
61 Mentally Deficient Child

62 Windmill and Dykes, Kinderdijk

63 Gorse (Spring)

1931. Child Welfare.
396A – 1½c. (+1½c.) red and blue 1·60 1·50
397A **61** 5c. (+3c.) green and purple . . . . 5·25 1·50
398A – 6c. (+4c.) purple and green . . . . 5·25 1·50
399A – 12½c. (+3½c.) blue and red . . . . 30·00 22·00
DESIGNS: 1½c. Deaf mute; 6c. Blind girl; 12½c. Sick child.

1932. Tourist Propaganda.
400 **62** 2½c.+1½c. green and black 7·75 4·75
401 – 6c.+4c. grey and black . . 10·75 4·75
402 – 7½c.+3½c. red and black . . 30·00 15·00
403 – 12½c.+2½c. blue and black 35·00 22·00
DESIGNS: 6c. Aerial view of Town Hall, Zierikzee; 7½c. Bridges at Schipluiden and Moerdijk; 12½c. Tulips.

1932. Child Welfare.
404A **63** 1½c. (+1½c.) brown & yell 2·50 45
405A – 5c. (+3c.) blue and red 3·25 80
406A – 6c. (+4c.) green and orange . . . . 2·50 40
407A – 12½c. (+3½c.) blue & orange . . . . 27·00 22·00
DESIGNS: Child and: 5c. Cornflower (Summer); 6c. Sunflower (Autumn); 12½c. Christmas rose (Winter).

64 Arms of House of Orange

65 Portrait by Goltzius

1933. 4th Birth Centenary of William I of Orange. T **64** and portraits of William I inscr "1533", as T **65**.
408 **64** 1½c. black 60 30
409 **65** 5c. green . . . . 1·75 30
410 – 6c. purple . . . . 2·75 15
411 – 12½c. blue . . . . 16·00 3·00
DESIGNS: 6c. Portrait by Key; 12½c. Portrait attributed to Moro.

68 Dove of Peace

69 Projected Monument at Den Helder

70 "De Hoop" (hospital ship)

1933. Peace Propaganda.
412 **68** 12½c. blue . . . . 8·75 35

1933. Seamen's Fund.
413 **69** 1½c. (+1½c.) red . . . . . 3·25 1·60
414 **70** 5c. (+3c.) green and red . . 10·25 3·00
415 – 6c. (+4c.) green . . . . . 16·00 2·40
416 – 12½c. (+3½c.) blue . . . . 23·00 17·00
DESIGNS: 6c. Lifeboat; 12½c. Seaman and Seamen's Home.

73 Pander S.4 Postjager

1933. Air. Special Flights.
417 **73** 30c. green 75 70

74 Child and Star of Epiphany

75 Princess Juliana

1933. Child Welfare.
418A **74** 1½c. (+1½c.) orange and grey . . . . 1·60 50
419A 5c. (+3c.) yellow and brown . . . . 2·25 65
420A 6c. (+4c.) gold and green 3·25 60
421A 12½c. (+3½c.) silver and blue . . . . 25·00 17·00

1934. Crisis stamps.
438 – 5c. (+4c.) purple . . . . . 12·50 3·00
439 **75** 6c. (+5c.) blue . . . . . . 10·50 4·25
DESIGN: 5c. Queen Wilhelmina.

76 Dutch Warship

77 Dowager Queen Emma

1934. Tercentenary of Curacao.
440 – 6c. black . . . . 3·25 15
441 **76** 12½c. blue . . . . 22·00 2·50
DESIGN: 6c. Willemstad Harbour.

1934. Anti-T.B. Fund.
442 **77** 6c. (+2c.) blue . . . . . . 12·50 1·50

78 Destitute child

79 H. D. Guyot

1934. Child Welfare.
443 **78** 1½c. (+1½c.) brown . . . . 1·60 50
444 5c. (+3c.) red . . . . . . 2·50 1·00
445 6c. (+4c.) green . . . . . 2·50 30
446 12½c. (+3½c.) blue . . . . 25·00 16·00

1935. Cultural and Social Relief Fund.
447 **79** 1½c. (+1½c.) red . . . . . 1·75 1·60
448 – 5c. (+3c.) brown . . . . . 4·50 5·00
449 – 6c. (+4c.) green . . . . . 5·50 85
450 – 12½c. (+3½c.) blue . . . . 27·00 5·75
PORTRAITS: 5c. A. J. M. Diepenbrock; 6c. F. C. Donders; 12½c. J. P. Sweelinck.
See also Nos. 456/9, 469/72, 478/82 and 492/6.

80 Aerial Map of Netherlands

81 Child picking Fruit

1935. Air Fund.
451 **80** 6c. (+4c.) brown . . . . . 27·00 9·25

1935. Child Welfare.
452 **81** 1½c. (+1½c.) red 65 45
453 5c. (+3c.) green . . . . . 1·60 1·40
454 6c. (+4c.) brown . . . . . 1·60 40
455 12½c. (+3½c.) blue . . . . 23·00 8·25

1936. Cultural and Social Relief Fund. As T **79**.
456 1½c. (+1½c.) sepia . . . . . 90 1·00
457 5c. (+3c.) green . . . . . . 4·25 3·50
458 6c. (+4c.) red . . . . 3·75 55
459 12½c. (+3½c.) blue . . . . . 14·00 3·25
PORTRAITS: 1½c. H. Kamerlingh Onnes; 5c. Dr. A. S. Talma; 6c. Mgr. Dr. H. J. A. M. Schaepman; 12½c. Desiderius Erasmus.

83 Pallas Athene

1936. Tercentenary of Utrecht University Foundation.
460 **83** 6c. red . . . . 1·75 25
461 – 12½c. blue . . . . 5·50 8·75
DESIGN: 12½c. Gisbertus Voetius.

84 Child Herald

85 Scout Movement

1936. Child Welfare.
462 **84** 1½c. (+1½c.) slate 60 35
463 5c. (+3c.) green . . . . . 2·25 75
464 6c. (+4c.) brown . . . . . 2·00 30
465 12½c. (+3½c.) blue . . . . 15·00 4·25

1937. Scout Jamboree.
466 – 1½c. black and green . . . 20 15
467 **85** 6c. brown and black . . . 1·50 15
468 – 12½c. black and blue . . . 4·50 1·25
DESIGNS: 1½c. Scout Tenderfoot Badge; 12½c. Hermes.

1937. Cultural and Social Relief Fund. Portraits as T **79**.
469 1½c.+1½c. sepia 60 60
470 5c.+3c. green . . . . 5·50 4·00
471 6c.+4c. purple . . . . 1·25 40
472 12½c.+3½c. blue . . . . . . 8·25 1·00
PORTRAITS: 1½c. Jacob Maris; 5c. F. de la B. Sylvius; 6c. J. van den Vondel; 12½c. A. van Leeuwenhoek.

86 "Laughing Child" by Frans Hals

87 Queen Wilhelmina

1937. Child Welfare.
473 **86** 1½c. (+1½c.) black 20 15
474 3c. (+2c.) green . . . . . 1·60 1·10
475 4c. (+2c.) red 65 50
476 5c. (+3c.) green 60 15
477 12½c. (+3½c.) blue . . . . 7·50 1·25

1938. Cultural and Social Relief Fund. As T **79**.
478 1½c.+1½c. sepia 40 50
479 3c.+2c. green 65 35
480 4c.+2c. red . . . . 2·00 2·10
481 5c.+3c. green . . . . 2·50 35
482 12½c.+3½c. blue . . . . . . 9·25 1·10
PORTRAITS: 1½c. M. van St. Aldegonde; 3c. O. G. Heldring; 4c. Maria Tesselschade; 5c. Rembrandt; 12½c. H. Boerhaave.

1938. 40th Anniv of Coronation.
483 **87** 1½c. black 20 15
484 5c. red 30 15
485 12½c. blue . . . . 3·75 1·50

88 Carrion Crow
89 Boy with Flute

1938. Air. Special Flights.
486 **88** 12½c. blue and grey . . . 65 65
790a 25c. blue and grey . . . . 4·00 1·75

1938. Child Welfare.
487 **89** 1½c.+1½c. black 20 30
488 3c.+2c. brown 50 40
489 4c.+2c. green 90 85
490 5c.+3c. red 45 20
491 12½c.+3½c. blue . . . . . 10·00 2·00

1939. Cultural and Social Relief Fund. As T **79**.
492 1½c.+1½c. brown 65 60
493 2½c.+2½c. green . . . . . 3·50 2·75
494 3c.+3c. red . . . . 90 1·25
495 5c.+3c. green . . . . . . 2·75 35
496 12½c.+3½c. blue . . . . . 6·75 1·10
PORTRAITS: 1½c. M. Maris; 2½c. Anton Mauve; 3c. Gerardus van Swieten; 5c. Nicolas Beets; 12½c. Pieter Stuyvesant.

91 St. Willibrord's landing in the Netherlands
92 Replica of Locomotive "De Arend"
93 Child and Cornucopia

1939. 12th Death Centenary of St. Willibrord.
497 **91** 5c. green 75 15
498 – 12½c. blue . . . . 5·50 3·00
DESIGN: 12½c. St. Willibrord as Bishop of Utrecht.

1939. Centenary of Netherlands Railway.
499 **92** 5c. green 80 15
500 – 12½c. blue . . . . 8·25 4·25
DESIGN: 12½c. Electric railcar.

1939. Child Welfare.
501 **93** 1½c.+1½c. black 20 25
502 2½c.+2½c. green . . . . . 5·50 3·00
503 3c.+3c. red 75 30
504 5c.+3c. green . . . . . . 1·10 25
505 12½c.+3½c. blue . . . . . 4·50 1·50

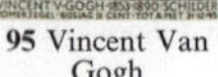
94 Queen Wilhelmina
95 Vincent Van Gogh
98 Girl with Dandelion

1940.
506 **94** 5c. green 30 10
506a 6c. brown 70 15
507 7½c. red 30 10
508 10c. purple 30 10
509 12½c. blue 30 10
510 15c. blue 30 10
510a 17½c. blue . . . . 1·25 85
511 20c. violet 65 15
512 22½c. olive . . . . 1·25 1·00
513 25c. red 50 15
514 30c. ochre . . . . 1·00 40
515 40c. green . . . . 2·00 85
515a 50c. orange . . . . 8·00 65
515b 60c. purple . . . . 8·00 2·50

1940. Cultural and Social Relief Fund.
516 **95** 1½c.+1½c. brown . . . . . 2·00 50
517 – 2½c.+2½c. green . . . . 6·00 1·10
518 – 3c.+3c. red . . . . . . 3·50 1·10
519 – 5c.+3c. green . . . . . 7·50 40
520 – 12½c.+3½c. blue . . . . 6·75 85
PORTRAITS: 1½c. E. J. Potgieter; 3c. Petrus Camper; 5c. Jan Steen; 12½c. Joseph Scaliger.
See also Nos. 558/62 and 656/60.

1940. As No. 519, colour changed. Surch.
521 7½c.+2½c. on 5c.+3c. red . . 65 40

1940. Surch with large figures and network.
522 **35** 2½ on 3c. red . . . . . . 3·00 40
523 5 on 3c. green 20 15
524 7½ on 3c. red 20 10
525 10 on 3c. green 20 15
526 12½ on 3c. blue 40 30
527 17½ on 3c. green 70 65
528 20 on 3c. green 50 15
529 22½ on 3c. green . . . . . 90 1·00
530 25 on 3c. green 55 35
531 30 on 3c. green 70 45
532 40 on 3c. green 85 65
533 50 on 3c. green . . . . . 1·00 65
534 60 on 3c. green . . . . . 1·90 1·40
535 70 on 3c. green . . . . . 4·00 2·40
536 80 on 3c. green . . . . . 6·00 5·25
537 100 on 3c. green . . . . . 35·00 35·00
538 250 on 3c. green . . . . . 42·00 40·00
539 500 on 3c. green . . . . . 40·00 38·00

1940. Child Welfare.
540 **98** 1½c.+1½c. violet 90 30
541 2½c.+2½c. olive . . . . . 2·50 85
542 4c.+3c. blue . . . . . . 3·00 95
543 5c.+3c. green . . . . . . 3·25 15
544 7½c.+3½c. red 95 15

1941.
546 **35** 5c. green 10 10
547 7½c. red 10 10
548 10c. violet 80 15
549 12½c. blue 30 30
550 15c. blue 80 35
551 17½c. red 15 15
552 20c. violet 85 15
553 22½c. olive 15 25
554 25c. lake 35 30
555 30c. brown . . . . 3·00 30
556 40c. green 15 30
557 50c. brown 15 15

1941. Cultural and Social Relief Fund. As T **95** but inscr "ZOMERZEGEL 31.12.46".
558 1½c.+1½c. brown 85 30
559 2½c.+2½c. green 85 30
560 4c.+3c. red 85 30
561 5c.+3c. green 85 30
562 7½c.+3½c. purple 85 30
PORTRAITS: 1½c. Dr. A. Mathijsen; 2½c. J. Ingenhousz; 4c. Aagje Deken; 5c. Johan Bosboom; 7½c. A. C. W. Staring.

100 "Titus Rembrandt"
101 Legionary

1941. Child Welfare.
563 **100** 1½c.+1½c. black 50 30
564 2½c.+2½c. olive 50 30
565 4c.+3c. blue 50 30
566 5c.+3c. green 50 30
567 7½c.+3½c. red 50 30

1942. Netherlands Legion Fund.
568 **101** 7½c.+2½c. red 75 60
569 – 12½c.+87½c. blue . . . . 6·25 6·00
MS569a 155×110 mm. No. 568 (block of ten) . . . . £110 70·00
MS569b 96×97 mm. No. 569 (block of ten) . . . . 90·00 80·00
DESIGN—HORIZ: 12½c. Legionary with similar inscription.

1943. 1st European Postal Congress. As T **26** but larger (21×27½ mm) surch **EUROPEESCHE P T T VEREENIGING 19 OCTOBER 1942 10 CENT**.
570 **26** 10c. on 2½c. yellow 20 25

103 Seahorse
104 Michiel A. de Ruyter

1943. Old Germanic Symbols.
571 **103** 1c. black 10 10
572 – 1½c. red 10 10
573 – 2c. blue 10 10
574 – 2½c. green 10 10
575 – 3c. red 10 10
576 – 4c. brown 10 10
577 – 5c. olive 10 10
DESIGNS—VERT: 1½c. Triple crowned tree; 2½c. Birds in ornamental tree; 4c. Horse and rider. HORIZ: 2c. Swans; 3c. Trees and serpentine roots; 5c. Prancing horses.

1943. Dutch Naval Heroes.
578 **104** 7½c. red 10 10
579 – 10c. green 15 10
580 – 12½c. blue 15 15
581 – 15c. violet 15 15
582 – 17½c. grey 15 15
583 – 20c. brown 15 15
584 – 22½c. red 15 20
585 – 25c. purple 45 55
586 – 30c. blue 15 20
587 – 40c. grey 15 15
PORTRAITS: 10c. Johan Evertsen; 12½c. Maarten H. Tromp; 15c. Piet Hein; 17½c. Wilhelm Joseph van Gent; 20c. Witte de With; 22½c. Cornelis Evertsen; 25c. Tjerk Hiddes de Fries; 30c. Cornelis Tromp; 40c. Cornelis Evertsen the younger.

105 Mail Cart
106 Child and Doll's House

1943. Stamp Day.
589 **105** 7½c.+7½c. red 15 15

1944. Child Welfare and Winter Help Funds. Inscr "WINTERHULP" (1½c. and 7½c.) or "VOLKSDIENST" (others).
590 **106** 1½c.+3½c. black 15 20
591 – 4c.+3½c. brown 15 20
592 – 5c.+5c. green 15 20
593 – 7½c.+7½c. red 15 20
594 – 10c.+40c. blue 15 20
DESIGNS: 4c. Mother and child; 5c., 10c. Mother and children; 7½c. Child and wheatsheaf.

107 Infantryman
111 Queen Wilhelmina

1944.
595 **107** 1½c. black 10 10
596 – 2½c. green 10 10
597 – 3c. brown 10 10
598 – 5c. blue 10 10
599 **111** 7½c. red 10 10
600 10c. orange 10 10
601 12½c. blue 10 10
602 15c. red . . . . 1·40 1·25
603 17½c. green . . . . 1·10 1·10
604 20c. violet 50 30
605 22½c. red . . . . 1·10 90
606 25c. brown . . . . 1·75 1·40
607 30c. green 30 20
608 40c. purple . . . . 2·10 1·90
609 50c. mauve . . . . 1·40 1·00
DESIGNS—HORIZ: 2½c. "Nieuw Amsterdam" (liner); 3c. Airman. VERT: 5c. "De Ruyter" (cruiser).
The above set was originally for use on Netherlands warships serving with the Allied Fleet, and was used after liberation in the Netherlands.

112 Lion and Dragon
113

1945. Liberation.
610 **112** 7½c. orange 20 15

1945. Child Welfare.
611 **113** 1½c.+2½c. grey 30 30
612 2½c.+3½c. green 30 30
613 5c.+5c. brown 30 30
614 7½c.+4½c. red 30 30
615 12½c.+5½c. blue 30 30

114 Queen Wilhelmina
115 Emblem of Abundance

1946.
616 **114** 1g. blue . . . . 1·75 50
617 2½g. red . . . . £130 10·50
618 5g. green . . . . £130 27·00
619 10g. violet . . . . £130 26·00

1946. War Victims' Relief Fund.
620 **115** 1½c.+3½c. black 50 30
621 2½c.+5c. green 60 55
622 5c.+10c. violet 60 55
623 7½c.+15c. red 50 30
624 12½c.+37½c. blue 95 55

116 Princess Irene
117 Boy on Roundabout

1946. Child Welfare.
625 **116** 1½c.+1½c. brown 60 55
626 – 2½c.+1½c. green 60 55
627 **116** 4c.+2c. red 70 55
628 – 5c.+2c. brown 70 55
629 – 7½c.+2½c. red 60 15
630 – 12½c.+7½c. blue 60 55
PORTRAITS: 2½c., 5c. Princess Margriet; 7½c., 12½c. Princess Beatrix.

1946. Child Welfare.
631 **117** 2c.+2c. violet 60 45
632 4c.+2c. green 60 45
633 7½c.+2½c. red 60 45
634 10c.+5c. purple 70 15
635 20c.+5c. blue 95 65

118 Numeral
119 Queen Wilhelmina
122 Children

1946.
636 **118** 1c. red 10 10
637 2c. blue 10 10
638 2½c. orange . . . . 7·50 1·60
638a 3c. brown 10 10
639 4c. green 35 10
639a 5c. orange 10 10
639c 6c. grey 35 15
639d 7c. red 15 10
639f 8c. mauve 15 10

1947.
640 **119** 5c. green . . . . 1·10 10
641 6c. black 40 10
642 6c. blue 60 10
643 7½c. red 40 20
644 10c. purple 70 10
645 12½c. red 70 40
646 15c. violet . . . . 8·25 10
647 20c. blue . . . . 8·75 10
648 22½c. green 70 65
649 25c. blue . . . . 16·00 10
650 30c. orange . . . . 16·00 25
651 35c. blue . . . . 16·00 55
652 40c. brown . . . . 19·00 55
653 – 45c. blue . . . . 22·00 12·00
654 – 50c. brown . . . . 14·50 30
655 – 60c. red . . . . 18·00 2·25
Nos. 653/5 are as Type **119** but have the inscriptions in colour on white ground.

1947. Cultural and Social Relief Fund. As T **95** but inscr "ZOMERZEGEL ... 13.12.48".
656 2c.+2c. red 85 45
657 4c.+2c. green . . . . . . 1·40 65
658 7½c.+2½c. violet . . . . . 1·90 85
659 10c.+5c. brown . . . . . 1·75 35
660 20c.+5c. blue . . . . . . 1·40 65
PORTRAITS: 2c. H. van Deventer; 4c. P. C. Hooft; 7½c. Johan de Witt; 10c. J. F. van Royen; 20c. Hugo Grotius.

1947. Child Welfare.
661 **122** 2c.+2c. brown 15 15
662 – 4c.+2c. green . . . . . 1·10 55
663 – 7½c.+2½c. brown . . . . 1·10 85
664 – 10c.+5c. lake . . . . . 1·25 15
665 **122** 20c.+5c. blue . . . . . . 1·40 85
DESIGN: 4c. to 10c. Baby.

124 Ridderzaal, The Hague
125 Queen Wilhelmina

1948. Cultural and Social Relief Fund.
666 **124** 2c.+2c. brown . . . . . 1·90 45
667 – 6c.+4c. green . . . . . 2·00 55
668 – 10c.+5c. red . . . . . . 1·40 30
669 – 20c.+5c. blue . . . . . . 2·00 85
BUILDINGS: 6c. Palace on the Dam; 10c. Kneuterdijk Palace; 20c. Nieuwe Kerk, Amsterdam.

1948. Queen Wilhelmina's Golden Jubilee.
670 **125** 10c. red 15 10
671 20c. blue . . . . 2·25 1·90

126 Queen Juliana 127 Boy in Canoe

1948. Coronation.
672 **126** 10c. brown . . . . 1·60 10
673 20c. blue . . . . 2·00 50

1948. Child Welfare.
674 **127** 2c.+2c. green 15 15
675 – 5c.+3c. green . . . . . . 2·25 70
676 – 6c.+4c. grey . . . . . . 1·25 15
677 – 10c.+5c. red 50 15
678 – 20c.+8c. blue . . . . . . 2·25 1·00
DESIGNS: 5c. Girl swimming; 6c. Boy on toboggan; 10c. Girl on swing; 20c. Boy skating.

128 Terrace near Beach

1949. Cultural and Social Relief Fund.
679 **128** 2c.+2c. yellow and blue 2·00 20
680 – 5c.+3c. yellow and blue 3·50 1·90
681 – 6c.+4c. green . . . . . . 3·00 45
682 – 10c.+5c. yellow and blue 3·75 10
683 – 20c.+5c. blue . . . . . . 3·50 1·90
DESIGNS: 5c. Hikers in cornfield; 6c. Campers by fire; 10c. Gathering wheat; 20c. Yachts.

129 Queen Juliana 130 Queen Juliana 131 Hands reaching for Sunflower

1949.
684 **129** 5c. green 65 10
685 6c. blue 40 10
686 10c. orange 40 10
687 12c. red . . . . 1·90 1·75
688 15c. green . . . . . . 5·75 10
689 20c. blue . . . . 4·25 10
690 25c. brown . . . . . . 12·50 10
691 30c. violet . . . . . . 8·75 10
692 35c. blue . . . . 23·00 15
693 40c. purple . . . . . . 40·00 30
694 45c. orange . . . . . . 1·90 80
695 45c. violet . . . . . . 55·00 55
696 50c. green . . . . . . 10·00 25
697 60c. brown . . . . . . 15·00 20
697a 75c. red . . . . 70·00 1·25
698 **130** 1g. red . . . . 4·00 15
699 2½g. brown . . . . . . £250 2·00
700a 5g. brown . . . . . . £450 3·50
701 10g. violet . . . . . . £300 15·00

1949. Red Cross and Indonesian Relief Fund.
702 **131** 2c.+3c. yellow and grey 95 30
703 6c.+4c. yellow and red . . 60 35
704 10c.+5c. yellow and blue 3·75 25
705 30c.+10c. yellow & brn 9·50 3·00

132 Posthorns and Globe 133 "Autumn"

1949. 75th Anniv of U.P.U.
706 **132** 10c. lake 95 10
707 20c. blue . . . . 9·50 2·25

1949. Child Welfare Fund. Inscr "VOOR HET KIND".
708 **133** 2c.+3c. brown 40 15
709 – 5c.+3c. red . . . . . . 6·50 1·90
710 – 6c.+4c. green . . . . . 3·50 40
711 – 10c.+5c. grey 40 15
712 – 20c.+7c. blue . . . . . 5·50 1·50
DESIGNS: 5c. "Summer"; 6c. "Spring"; 10c. "Winter"; 20c. "New Year".

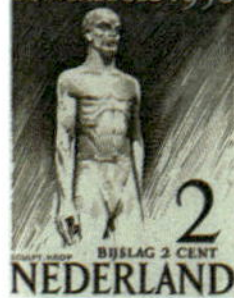

134 Resistance Monument 135 Section of Moerdijk Bridge

1950. Cultural and Social Relief Fund. Inscr "ZOMERZEGEL 1950".
713 **134** 2c.+2c. brown . . . . . 2·00 1·10
714 – 4c.+2c. green . . . . . 11·50 10·50
715 – 5c.+3c. grey . . . . . . 8·75 3·25
716 – 6c.+4c. violet . . . . . 4·50 65
717 **135** 10c.+5c. slate . . . . . 6·00 35
718 – 20c.+5c. blue . . . . . 17·00 14·00
DESIGNS—VERT: 4c. Sealing dykes; 5c. Rotterdam skyscraper. HORIZ: 6c. Harvesting; 20c. "Overijssel" (canal freighter).

1950. Surch with bold figure **6**.
719 **119** 6c. on 7½c. red . . . . . 2·25 15

137 Good Samaritan and Bombed Church 138 Janus Dousa

1950. Bombed Churches Rebuilding Fund.
720 **137** 2c.+2c. olive . . . . . . 7·25 1·75
721 5c.+3c. brown . . . . . 10·50 10·25
722 6c.+4c. green . . . . . 7·25 3·00
723 10c.+5c. red . . . . . . 17·50 65
724 20c.+5c. blue . . . . . 32·00 29·00

1950. 375th Anniv of Leyden University.
725 **138** 10c. olive . . . . 4·25 15
726 – 20c. blue . . . . 4·25 1·25
PORTRAIT: 20c. Jan van Hout.

139 Baby and Bees 140 Bergh Castle

1950. Child Welfare. Inscr "VOOR HET KIND".
727 **139** 2c.+3c. red 30 15
728 – 5c.+3c. olive . . . . . 10·00 3·75
729 – 6c.+4c. green . . . . . 3·50 65
730 – 10c.+5c. purple 40 15
731 – 20c.+7c. blue . . . . . 10·50 9·00
DESIGNS: 5c. Boy and fowl; 6c. Girl and birds; 10c. Boy and fish; 20c. Girl, butterfly and frog.

1951. Cultural and Social Relief Fund. Castles.
732 – 2c.+2c. violet . . . . . 2·50 1·25
733 **140** 5c.+3c. red . . . . . . 8·75 5·50
734 – 6c.+4c. sepia . . . . . 3·00 55
735 – 10c.+5c. green . . . . 6·00 30
736 – 20c.+5c. blue . . . . . 8·50 7·50
DESIGNS—HORIZ: 2c. Hillenraad; 6c. Hernen. VERT: 10c. Rechteren; 20c. Moermond.

141 Girl and Windmill 142 Gull

1951. Child Welfare.
737 **141** 2c.+3c. green 60 15
738 – 5c.+3c. blue . . . . . 7·50 4·25
739 – 6c.+4c. brown . . . . . 5·50 65
740 – 10c.+5c. lake 35 15
741 – 20c.+7c. blue . . . . . 7·50 6·50
DESIGNS: Each shows boy or girl: 5c. Crane; 6c. Fishing nets; 10c. Factory chimneys; 20c. Flats.

1951. Air.
742 **142** 15g. brown £275 £125
743 25g. black £275 £125

143 Jan van Riebeeck

1952. Tercentenary of Landing in South Africa and Van Riebeeck Monument Fund.
744 **143** 2c.+3c. violet . . . . . 5·50 3·75
745 6c.+4c. green . . . . . 6·25 4·50
746 10c.+5c. red . . . . . . 7·25 4·50
747 20c.+5c. blue . . . . . 5·50 3·50

144 Miner 145 Wild Rose

1952. 50th Anniv of State Mines, Limburg.
748 **144** 10c. blue . . . . 2·25 10

1952. Cultural and Social Relief Fund. Floral designs inscr "ZOMERZEGEL 1952".
749 **145** 2c.+2c. green and red . . 70 50
750 – 5c.+3c. yellow and green 2·50 2·75
751 – 6c.+4c. green and red . . 2·25 1·00
752 – 10c.+5c. green & orange 1·90 35
753 – 20c.+5c. green and blue 10·50 8·50
FLOWERS: 5c. Marsh marigold; 6c. Tulip; 10c. Marguerite; 20c. Cornflower.

146 Radio Masts 147 Boy feeding Goat

1952. Netherlands Stamp Centenary and Centenary of Telegraph Service.
754 – 2c. violet 50 10
755 **146** 6c. red 60 15
756 – 10c. green 50 10
757 – 20c. slate . . . . 7·50 1·90
DESIGNS: 2c. Telegraph poles and steam train; 10c. Postman delivering letters, 1852; 20c. Postman delivering letters, 1952.

1952. International Postage Stamp Exn, Utrecht ("ITEP"). Nos. 754/7 but colours changed.
757a – 2c. brown . . . . 20·00 15·00
757b **146** 6c. blue . . . . 20·00 15·00
757c – 10c. lake . . . . 20·00 15·00
757d – 20c. blue . . . . 20·00 15·00
Nos. 757a/d were sold only in sets at the Exhibition at face plus 1g. entrance fee.

1952. Child Welfare.
758 **147** 2c.+3c. black and olive 20 20
759 – 5c.+3c. black and pink . . 3·00 1·25
760 – 6c.+4c. black and green 2·50 45
761 – 10c.+5c. black & orange 15 15
762 – 20c.+7c. black and blue 7·50 6·00
DESIGNS: 5c. Girl riding donkey; 6c. Girl playing with dog; 10c. Boy and cat; 20c. Boy and rabbit.

1953. Flood Relief Fund. Surch **19 53 10c +10 WATERSNOOD**.
763 **129** 10c.+10c. orange 65 15

149 Hyacinth 150 Red Cross

1953. Cultural and Social Relief Fund.
764 **149** 2c.+2c. green and violet 70 40
765 – 5c.+3c. green & orange 2·10 1·75
766 – 6c.+4c. yellow and green 2·00 55
767 – 10c.+5c. green and red . . 3·25 15
768 – 20c.+5c. green and blue 13·15 12·00
FLOWERS: 5c. African marigold; 6c. Daffodil; 10c. Anemone; 20c. Dutch iris.

1953. Red Cross Fund. Inscr "RODE KRUIS".
769 **150** 2c.+3c. red and sepia . . 95 45
770 – 6c.+4c. red and brown . . 3·75 2·50
771 – 7c.+5c. red and olive . . 1·10 45
772 – 10c.+5c. red 65 15
773 – 25c.+8c. red and blue . . 8·25 5·00
DESIGNS: 6c. Man with lamp; 7c. Rescue worker in flooded area; 10c. Nurse giving blood transfusion; 25c. Red Cross flags.

151 Queen Juliana 152 Queen Juliana

1953.
775 **151** 10c. brown 15 10
776 12c. turquoise 15 10
777 15c. red 15 10
777b 18c. turquoise 15 10
778 20c. purple 15 10
778b 24c. olive 25 20
779 25c. blue 25 10
780a 30c. orange 40 10
781 35c. brown 70 10
781a 37c. turquoise 50 15
782 40c. slate 40 10
783 45c. red 40 10
784 50c. green 55 10
785 60c. brown 65 10
785a 62c. red . . . . 3·00 2·50
785b 70c. blue 65 10
786 75c. purple 65 15
786a 80c. violet 65 10
786b 85c. green . . . . . . 1·10 10
786c 95c. brown . . . . . . 1·40 25
787 **152** 1g. red . . . . 1·90 20
788 2½g. green . . . . . . 8·75 15
789 5g. black . . . . 3·75 30
790 10g. blue . . . . 17·50 1·75

153 Girl with Pigeon 154 M. Nijhoff (poet)

1953. Child Welfare. Inscr "VOOR HET KIND".
791 – 2c.+3c. blue and yellow 15 15
792 – 5c.+3c. lake and green . . 3·25 2·25
793 **153** 7c.+5c. brown and blue 3·75 85
794 – 10c.+5c. lilac and bistre 15 15
795 – 25c.+8c. turq & pink . . 11·00 10·00
DESIGNS: 2c. Girl, bucket and spade; 5c. Boy and apple; 10c. Boy and tjalk (sailing boat); 25c. Girl and tulip.

1954. Cultural and Social Relief Fund.
796 **154** 2c.+3c. blue . . . . . . 1·90 1·60
797 – 5c.+3c. brown . . . . . 2·75 1·75
798 – 7c.+5c. red . . . . . . 3·75 1·40
799 – 10c.+5c. green . . . . 7·25 60
800 – 25c.+8c. purple . . . . 10·50 11·00
PORTRAITS: 5c. W. Pijper (composer); 7c. H. P. Berlage (architect); 10c. J. Huizinga (historian); 25c. Vincent van Gogh (painter).

155 St. Boniface 156 Boy and Model Glider

1954. 1200th Anniv of Martyrdom of St. Boniface.
801 **155** 10c. blue . . . . 2·75 10

1954. National Aviation Fund.
802 **156** 2c.+2c. green . . . . . . 1·40 1·00
803 – 10c.+4c. blue . . . . . . 3·50 65
PORTRAIT: 10c. Dr. A. Plesman (aeronautical pioneer).

157 Making Paperchains 158 Queen Juliana

1954. Child Welfare.
804 **157** 2c.+3c. brown 15 15
805 – 5c.+3c. olive . . . . . . 1·75 1·50
806 – 7c.+5c. blue . . . . . . 1·60 55
807 – 10c.+5c. red 15 15
808 – 25c.+8c. blue . . . . . 9·25 5·75
DESIGNS—VERT: 5c. Girl brushing her teeth; 7c. Boy and toy boat; 10c. Nurse and child. HORIZ: 25c. Invalid boy drawing in bed.

1954. Ratification of Statute for the Kingdom.
809 **158** 10c. red . . . . 1·00 15

159 Factory, Rotterdam 160 "The Victory of Peace"

1955. Cultural and Social Relief Fund.
810 **159** 2c.+3c. brown . . . . . 1·25 1·10
811 – 5c.+3c. green . . . . . 1·40 95
812 – 7c.+5c. red . . . . . . 1·25 95
813 – 10c.+5c. blue . . . . . 2·10 20
814 – 25c.+8c. brown . . . . 11·50 9·50

DESIGNS—HORIZ: 5c. Post Office, The Hague; 10c. Town Hall, Hilversum; 25c. Office Building, The Hague. VERT: 7c. Stock Exchange, Amsterdam.

1955. 10th Anniv of Liberation.
815 **160** 10c. red . . . . 1·60 15

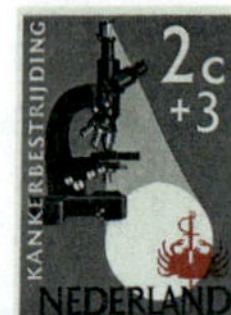

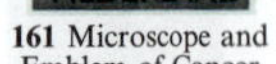

161 Microscope and Emblem of Cancer
162 "Willem van Loon" (D. Dircks)

1955. Queen Wilhelmina Anti-cancer Fund.
816 **161** 2c.+3c. black and red . . 60 55
817 5c.+3c. green and red . . 1·60 1·25
818 7c.+5c. purple and red . . 1·40 65
819 10c.+5c. blue and red . . 90 15
820 25c.+8c. olive and red . . 5·75 5·75

1955. Child Welfare Fund.
821 **162** 2c.+3c. green 45 15
822 – 5c.+3c. red . . . . . . 2·25 95
823 – 7c.+5c. brown . . . . . 4·00 80
824 – 10c.+5c. blue 40 15
825 – 25c.+8c. lilac . . . . . 9·25 7·75
PORTRAITS: 5c. "Portrait of a Boy" (J. A. Backer); 7c. "Portrait of a Girl" (unknown); 10c. "Philips Huygens" (A. Hanneman); 25c. "Constantin Huygens" (A. Hanneman).

163 "Farmer"

1956. Cultural and Social Relief Fund and 350th Birth Anniv of Rembrandt. Details from Rembrandt's paintings.
826 **163** 2c.+3c. slate . . . . . . 2·75 2·50
827 – 5c.+3c. olive . . . . . 1·75 1·40
828 – 7c.+5c. brown . . . . . 4·25 4·00
829 – 10c.+5c. green . . . . 12·50 65
830 – 25c.+8c. brown . . . . 18·00 16·00
PAINTINGS: 5c. "Young Tobias with Angel"; 7c. "Persian wearing Fur Cap"; 10c. "Old Blind Tobias"; 25c. Self-portrait, 1639.

164 Yacht
165 Amphora

1956. 16th Olympic Games, Melbourne.
831 **164** 2c.+3c. black and blue . . 75 65
832 – 5c.+3c. black and yellow 1·25 95
833 **165** 7c.+5c. black and brown 1·40 95
834 – 10c.+5c. black and grey 2·75 55
835 – 25c.+8c. black and green 6·50 5·75
DESIGNS: As Type **164**: 5c. Runner; 10c. Hockey player; 25c. Water polo player.

1956. Europa. As T **110** of Luxembourg.
836 10c. black and lake . . . . . 2·25 10
837 25c. black and blue . . . . . 50·00 1·60

167 "Portrait of a Boy" (Van Scorel)

1956. Child Welfare Fund. 16th-century Dutch Paintings.
838 **167** 2c.+3c. grey and cream 40 10
839 – 5c.+3c. olive and cream 1·25 1·10
840 – 7c.+5c. purple & cream 3·50 1·50
841 – 10c.+5c. red and cream 40 15
842 – 25c.+8c. blue and cream 7·25 3·75
PAINTINGS: 5c. "Portrait of a Boy"; 7c. "Portrait of a Girl"; 10c. "Portrait of a Girl"; 25c. "Portrait of Eechie Pieters".

168 "Curacao" (trawler) and Fish Barrels
169 Admiral M. A. de Ruyter

1957. Cultural and Social Relief Fund. Ships.
843 – 4c.+3c. blue . . . . . . 1·25 1·00
844 – 6c.+4c. lilac . . . . . . 2·25 1·90
845 – 7c.+5c. red . . . . . . 1·90 1·25
846 **168** 10c.+8c. green . . . . . 3·75 35
847 – 30c.+8c. brown . . . . 4·75 4·25
DESIGNS: 4c. "Gaasterland" (freighter); 6c. Coaster; 7c. "Willem Barendsz" (whale factory ship) and whale; 30c. "Nieuw Amsterdam" (liner).

1957. 350th Birth Anniv of M. A. de Ruyter.
848 **169** 10c. orange 70 15
849 – 30c. blue . . . . 4·75 1·90
DESIGN: 30c. De Ruyter's flagship, "De Zeven Provincien".

170 Blood Donors' Emblem
171 "Europa" Star

1957. 90th Anniv of Netherlands Red Cross Society and Red Cross Fund.
850 **170** 4c.+3c. blue and red . . . 1·10 1·10
851 – 6c.+4c. green and red . . 1·40 1·25
852 – 7c.+5c. red and green . . 1·40 1·25
853 – 10c.+8c. red and ochre . . 1·25 15
854 – 30c.+8c. red and blue . . 2·75 2·50
DESIGNS: 6c. "J. Henry Dunant" (hospital ship); 7c. Red Cross; 10c. Red Cross emblem; 30c. Red Cross on globe.

1957. Europa.
855 **171** 10c. black and blue . . . 60 10
856 30c. green and blue . . . 7·00 1·50

172 Portrait by B. J. Blommers
173 Walcheren Costume

1957. Child Fund Welfare. 19th- and 20th-Century Paintings by Dutch Masters.
857 **172** 4c.+4c. red 40 15
858 – 6c.+4c. green . . . . . 2·50 1·90
859 – 8c.+4c. sepia . . . . . 3·25 1·90
860 – 12c.+9c. purple 40 15
861 – 30c.+9c. blue . . . . . 8·25 6·75
PORTRAITS: Child paintings by: W. B. Tholen (6c.); J. Sluyters (8c.); M. Maris (12c.); C. Kruseman (30c.).

1958. Cultural and Social Relief Fund. Provincial Costumes.
862 **173** 4c.+4c. blue 70 55
863 – 6c.+4c. ochre . . . . . 1·60 1·00
864 – 8c.+4c. red . . . . . . 4·75 1·60
865 – 12c.+9c. brown . . . . 1·75 20
866 – 30c.+9c. lilac . . . . . 7·50 6·25
COSTUMES: 6c. Marken; 8c. Scheveningen; 12c. Friesland; 30c. Volendam.

1958. Surch **12 C**.
867 **151** 12c. on 10c. brown . . . 1·25 10

1958. Europa. As T **119a** of Luxembourg.
868 12c. blue and red 20 10
869 30c. red and blue . . . . . 1·00 65

176 Girl on Stilts and Boy on Tricycle
177 Cranes

1958. Child Welfare Fund. Children's Games.
870 **176** 4c.+4c. blue 20 15
871 – 6c.+4c. red . . . . . . 2·50 1·75
872 – 8c.+4c. green . . . . . 1·75 1·00
873 – 12c.+9c. red 20 15
874 – 30c.+9c. blue . . . . . 6·00 4·75

DESIGNS: 6c. Boy and girl on scooter; 8c. Boys playing leap-frog; 12c. Boys on roller-skates; 30c. Girl skipping and boy in toy car.

1959. 10th Anniv of N.A.T.O. As T **123** of Luxembourg (N.A.T.O. emblem).
875 12c. blue and yellow 20 10
876 30c. blue and red . . . . . 1·00 60

1959. Cultural and Social Relief Fund. Prevention of Sea Encroachment.
877 – 4c.+4c. blue on green . . 1·40 1·25
878 – 6c.+4c. brown on grey . . 95 90
879 – 8c.+4c. violet on blue . . 2·25 1·40
880 **177** 12c.+9c. green on yell . . 4·25 20
881 – 30c.+9c. black on red . . 6·50 6·00
DESIGNS: 4c. Tugs and caisson; 6c. Dredger; 8c. Labourers making fascine mattresses; 30c. Sand-spouter and scoop.

1959. Europa. As T **123a** of Luxembourg.
882 12c. red 20 10
883 30c. green . . . . 3·60 3·25

178 Silhouette of Douglas DC-8 Airliner and World Map
179 Child in Play-pen

1959. 40th Anniv of K.L.M. (Royal Dutch Airlines).
884 **178** 12c. blue and red 20 10
885 – 30c. blue and green . . . 1·60 1·25
DESIGN: 30c. Silhouette of Douglas DC-8 airliner.

1959. Child Welfare Fund.
886 **179** 4c.+4c. blue and brown 20 15
887 – 6c.+4c. brown and green 1·75 1·40
888 – 8c.+4c. blue and red . . . 2·75 1·75
889 – 12c.+9c. red, black and blue 20 10
890 – 30c.+9c. turquoise and yellow . . . . 4·25 3·50
DESIGNS: 6c. Boy as "Red Indian" with bow and arrow; 8c. Boy feeding geese; 12c. Traffic warden escorting children; 30c. Girl doing homework.

180 Refugee Woman
181 White Water-lily

1960. World Refugee Year.
891 **180** 12c.+8c. purple 35 15
892 30c.+10c. green . . . . . 3·50 2·25

1960. Cultural and Social Relief Fund. Flowers.
893 – 4c.+4c. red, green and grey 95 60
894 – 6c.+4c. yellow, green and salmon . . . . 1·40 1·25
895 **181** 8c.+4c. multicoloured . . 3·25 1·90
896 – 12c.+8c. red, green and buff . . . . 2·75 30
897 – 30c.+10c. blue, green and yellow . . . . 6·00 5·00
FLOWERS—VERT: 4c. "The Princess" tulip; 6c. Gorse; 12c. Poppy; 30c. Blue sea-holly.

182 J. van der Kolk
183 Marken Costume

1960. World Mental Health Year.
898 **182** 12c. red 85 15
899 – 30c. blue (J. Wier) . . . . 6·50 2·40

1960. Europa. As T **113a** of Norway.
900 12c. yellow and red 20 10
901 30c. yellow and blue . . . . 3·00 1·90

1960. Child Welfare Fund. Costumes. Mult portraits.
902 **183** 4c.+4c. slate 35 15
903 – 6c.+4c. ochre . . . . . 2·40 1·25
904 – 8c.+4c. turquoise . . . . 5·00 1·75
905 – 12c.+9c. violet 30 10
906 – 30c.+9c. grey . . . . . 7·25 5·75
DESIGNS: Costumes of: 6c. Volendam; 8c. Bunschoten; 12c. Hindeloopen; 30c. Huizen.

184 Herring Gull
185 Doves

1961. Cultural and Social Relief Fund. Beach and Meadow Birds.
907 **184** 4c.+4c. slate and yellow 1·25 1·25
908 – 6c.+4c. sepia and brown 1·40 1·40
909 – 8c.+4c. brown and olive 1·10 2·00
910 – 12c.+8c. black and blue 2·40 40
911 – 30c.+10c. black & green 3·00 2·75
BIRDS—HORIZ: 6c. Oystercatcher; 12c. Pied avocet. VERT: 8c. Curlew; 30c. Northern lapwing.

1961. Europa.
912 **185** 12c. brown 10 10
913 30c. turquoise 30 30

186 St. Nicholas
187 Queen Juliana and Prince Bernhard

1961. Child Welfare.
914 **186** 4c.+4c. red 20 15
915 – 6c.+4c. blue . . . . . . 1·25 90
916 – 8c.+4c. bistre . . . . . 1·25 1·00
917 – 12c.+9c. green 20 10
918 – 30c.+9c. orange . . . . 3·50 3·00
DESIGNS: 6c. Epiphany; 8c. Palm Sunday; 12c. Whitsuntide; 30c. Martinmas.

1962. Silver Wedding.
919 **187** 12c. red 20 10
920 30c. green . . . . 1·40 75

188 Detail of "The Repast of the Officers of the St. Jorisdoelen" after Frans Hals
189 Telephone Dial

1962. Cultural, Health and Social Welfare Funds.
921 – 4c.+4c. green . . . . . . 1·10 90
922 – 6c.+4c. black 90 90
923 – 8c.+4c. purple . . . . . 1·40 1·25
924 – 12c.+8c. bistre . . . . . 1·40 40
925 **188** 30c.+10c. blue . . . . . 1·60 1·40
DESIGNS—HORIZ: 4c. Roman cat (sculpture). VERT: 6c. "Pleuroceras spinatus" (ammonite); 8c. Pendulum clock (after principle of Huygens); 12c. Ship's figurehead.

1962. Completion of Netherlands Automatic Telephone System. Inscr "1962".
926 **189** 4c. red and black 20 10
927 – 12c. drab and black . . . 55 10
928 – 30c. ochre, blue and black 2·25 1·60
DESIGNS—VERT: 12c. Diagram of telephone network. HORIZ: 30c. Arch and telephone dial.

190 Europa "Tree"
191 "Polder" Landscape (reclaimed area)

1962. Europa.
929 **190** 12c. black, yellow & bistre 10 10
930 30c. black, yellow and blue . . . . 1·00 1·25

1962.
935 – 4c. deep blue and blue . . 10 10
937 **191** 6c. deep green and green 40 15
938 – 10c. deep purple and purple 10 10
DESIGNS: 4c. Cooling towers, State mines, Limburg; 10c. Delta excavation works.

192 Children cooking Meal

193 Ears of Wheat

1962. Child Welfare.
940 **192** 4c.+4c. red 20 15
941 – 6c.+4c. bistre 95 55
942 – 8c.+4c. blue . . . . . . 1·60 1·40
943 – 12c.+9c. green 20 10
944 – 30c.+9c. lake . . . . . . 2·75 2·50
DESIGNS—Children: 6c. Cycling; 8c. Watering flowers; 12c. Feeding poultry; 30c. Making music.

1963. Freedom from Hunger.
945 **193** 12c. ochre and blue . . . 20 10
946 30c. ochre and red . . . 1·25 1·00

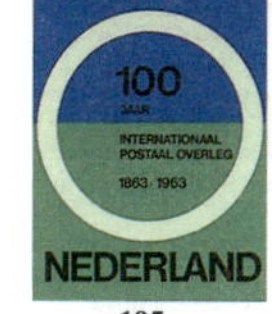

194 "Gallery" Windmill

195

1963. Cultural, Health and Social Welfare Funds. Windmill types.
947 **194** 4c.+4c. blue . . . . . . 1·10 1·00
948 – 6c.+4c. violet . . . . . . 1·10 1·00
949 – 8c.+4c. green . . . . . . 1·40 1·40
950 – 12c.+8c. brown . . . . . 1·40 30
951 – 30c.+10c. red . . . . . . 1·75 1·90
WINDMILLS—VERT: 6c. North Holland polder; 12c. "Post"; 30c. "Wip". HORIZ: 8c. South Holland polder.

1963. Paris Postal Conference Centenary.
952 **195** 30c. blue, green & blk . . 1·40 1·25

196 Wayside First Aid Post

1963. Red Cross Fund and Centenary (8c.).
953 **196** 4c.+4c. blue and red . . . 40 40
954 – 6c.+4c. violet and red . . 35 30
955 – 8c.+4c. red and black . . 1·10 80
956 – 12c.+9c. brown and red 20 10
957 – 30c.+9c. green and red . . 1·60 1·40
DESIGNS: 6c. "Books" collection-box; 8c. Crosses; 12c. "International Aid" (Negro children at meal); 30c. First aid party tending casualty.

197 "Co-operation"

198 "Auntie Luce sat on a goose ..."

1963. Europa.
958 **197** 12c. orange and brown . . 20 10
959 30c. orange and green . . 1·40 1·10

1963. Child Welfare.
960 **198** 4c.+4c. ultramarine & bl 20 15
961 – 6c.+4c. green and red . . 70 65
962 – 8c.+4c. brown & green . . 95 60
963 – 12c.+9c. violet & yellow 20 10
964 – 30c.+8c. blue and pink . . 1·60 1·40
DESIGNS (Nursery rhymes): 6c. "In the Hague there lives a count ..."; 8c. "One day I passed a puppet's fair ..."; 12c. "Storky, storky, Billy Spoon ..."; 30c. "Ride on a little pram ...".

199 William, Prince of Orange, landing at Scheveningen

200 Knights' Hall, The Hague

1963. 150th Anniv of Kingdom of the Netherlands.
965 **199** 4c. black, bistre and blue 10 10
966 5c. black, red and green 20 10
967 – 12c. bistre, blue and black 10 10
968 – 30c. red and black 75 60

DESIGNS: 12c. Triumvirate: Van Hogendorp, Van Limburg, and Van der Duyn van Maasdam; 30c. William I taking oath of allegiance.

1964. 500th Anniv of 1st States-General Meeting.
969 **200** 12c. black and olive . . . 20 10

201 Guide Dog for the Blind

1964. Cultural, Health and Social Welfare Funds. Animals.
970 **201** 5c.+5c. red, black and olive 60 45
971 – 8c.+5c. brown, black and red 40 30
972 – 12c.+9c. black, grey and bistre 60 20
973 – 30c.+9c. multicoloured . . 70 65
DESIGNS: 8c. Three red deer; 12c. Three kittens; 30c. European bison and calf.

202 University Arms

203 Signal No. 144, Amersfoort Station

1964. 350th Anniv of Groningen University.
974 **202** 12c. slate 10 10
975 – 30c. brown 25 25
DESIGN: 30c. "AG" monogram.

1964. 125th Anniv of Netherlands Railways.
976 **203** 15c. black and green . . . 20 10
977 – 40c. black and yellow . . 75 70
DESIGN: 40c. Class ELD-4 electric train.

204 Bible and Dove

1964. 150th Anniv of Netherlands Bible Society.
978 **204** 15c. brown 20 10

205 Europa "Flower"

206 Young Artist

1964. Europa.
979 **205** 15c. green 20 10
980 20c. brown 40 40

1964. 20th Anniv of "BENELUX". As T **150a** of Luxembourg, but smaller 35 × 22 mm.
981 15c. violet and flesh 20 10

1964. Child Welfare.
982 **206** 7c.+3c. blue and green . . 50 45
983 – 10c.+5c. red, pink and green 40 40
984 – 15c.+10c. yellow, black and bistre 20 10
985 – 20c.+10c. red, sepia and mauve 60 45
986 – 40c.+15c. green & blue . . 1·00 80
DESIGNS: 10c. Ballet-dancing; 15c. Playing the recorder; 20c. Masquerading; 40c. Toy-making.

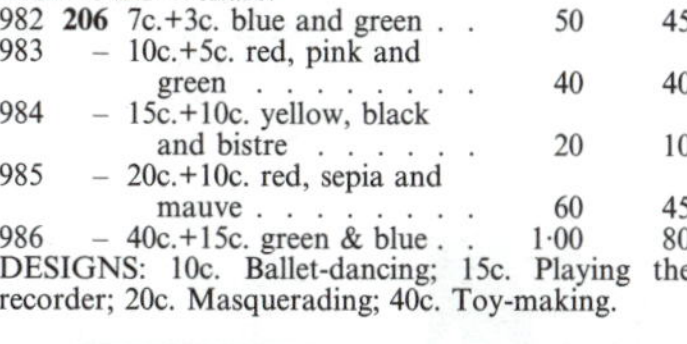

207 Queen Juliana

208 "Killed in Action" (Waalwijk) and "Destroyed Town" (Rotterdam) (monuments)

1964. 10th Anniv of Statute for the Kingdom.
987 **207** 15c. green 20 10

1965. "Resistance" Commemoration.
988 **208** 7c. black and red 20 10
989 – 15c. black and olive . . . 20 10
990 – 40c. black and red 95 85
MONUMENTS: 15c. "Docker" (Amsterdam) and "Killed in Action" (Waalwijk); 40c. "Destroyed Town" (Rotterdam) and "Docker" (Amsterdam).

209 Medal of Knight (Class IV)

210 I.T.U. Emblem and "Lines of Communication"

1965. 150th Anniv of Military William Order.
991 **209** 1g. grey . . . . 1·60 65

1965. Centenary of I.T.U.
992 **210** 20c. blue and drab . . . 20 25
993 40c. brown and blue . . . 60 45

211 Veere

1965. Cultural, Health and Social Welfare Funds.
994 **211** 8c.+6c. black and yellow 35 25
995 – 10c.+6c. black & turq . . 50 40
996 – 18c.+12c. black & brn . . 40 25
997 – 20c.+10c. black & blue . . 50 40
998 – 40c.+10c. black & green 55 45
DESIGNS: (Dutch towns): 10c. Thorn; 18c. Dordrecht; 20c. Staveren; 40c. Medemblik.

212 Europa "Sprig"

1965. Europa.
999 **212** 18c. black, red and brown 20 10
1000 20c. black, red and blue 30 30

213 Girl's Head

1965. Child Welfare. Multicoloured.
1001 8c.+6c. Type **213** 20 15
1002 10c.+6c. Ship 50 50
1003 18c.+12c. Boy (vert) 20 15
1004 20c.+10c. Duck-pond . . . 65 55
1005 40c.+10c. Tractor . . . . 1·90 75
MS1006 143 × 124 mm. Nos. 1001 (5) and 1003 (6) . . . . 26·00 21·00

214 Marines of 1665 and 1965

215 "Help them to a safe Haven" (Queen Juliana)

1965. Tercentenary of Marine Corps.
1007 **214** 18c. blue and red 20 10

1966. Intergovernmental Committee for European Migration (I.C.E.M.) Fund.
1008 **215** 10c.+7c. yellow & blk . . 50 35
1009 40c.+20c. red & black 40 25
MS1010 117 × 44 mm. Nos. 1008 and 1009 (2) . . . . 3·50 1·10

216 Writing Materials

217 Aircraft in Flight

1966. Cultural, Health and Social Welfare Funds. Gysbert Japicx Commem and 200th Anniv of Netherlands Literary Society. Multicoloured.
1011 10c.+5c. Type **216** 40 40
1012 12c.+8c. Part of MS, Japicx's poem "Wobbelke" 40 40
1013 20c.+10c. Part of miniature, "Knight Walewein" . . . 55 40
1014 25c.+10c. Initial "D" and part of MS, novel, "Ferguut" 70 55
1015 40c.+20c. 16th-century printery (woodcut) . . . 55 55

1966. Air (Special Flights).
1016 **217** 25c. multicoloured . . . 20 45

218 Europa "Ship"

219 Infant

1966. Europa.
1017 **218** 20c. green and yellow . . 20 10
1018 40c. deep blue and blue 35 25

1966. Child Welfare.
1019 **219** 10c.+5c. red and blue . . 20 15
1020 – 12c.+8c. green and red 20 15
1021 – 20c.+10c. blue and red 20 15
1022 – 25c.+10c. purple & bl . . 95 85
1023 – 40c.+20c. red & green 90 80
MS1024 132 × 125 mm. Nos. 1019 × 4, 1020 × 5, 1021 × 3 2·75 2·25
DESIGNS: 12c. Young girl; 20c. Boy in water; 25c. Girl with moped; 40c. Young man with horse.

220 Assembly Hall

1967. 125th Anniv of Delft Technological University.
1025 **220** 20c. sepia and yellow . . 20 10

221 Common Northern Whelk Eggs

1967. Cultural, Health and Social Welfare Funds. Marine Fauna.
1026 **221** 12c.+8c. brown & grn 30 30
1027 – 15c.+10c. blue, light blue and deep blue 30 30
1028 – 20c.+10c. mult 30 25
1029 – 25c.+10c. brown, purple and bistre 60 55
1030 – 45c.+20c. mult 80 65
DESIGNS: 15c. Common northern whelk; 20c. Common blue mussel; 25c. Jellyfish; 45c. Crab.

222 Cogwheels

223 Netherlands 5c. Stamp of 1852

1967. Europa.
1031 **222** 20c. blue and light blue 40 10
1032 45c. purple & light purple . . . . 1·10 80

1967. "Amphilex 67" Stamp Exn, Amsterdam.
1035 **223** 20c. blue and black . . . 2·25 1·90
1036 – 25c. red and black . . . 2·25 1·90
1037 – 75c. green and black . . 2·25 1·90
DESIGNS: 25c. Netherlands 10c. stamp of 1864; 75c. Netherlands 20c. stamp of 1867.

Nos. 1035/7 were sold at the exhibition and at post offices at 3g.70, which included entrance fee to the exhibition.

224 "1867–1967" **225** "Porcupine Lullaby"

1967. Centenary of Dutch Red Cross.

1038 12c.+8c. blue and red . . . 30 30
1039 15c.+10c. red 50 40
1040 20c.+10c. olive and red . . 30 20
1041 25c.+10c. green and red . . 50 50
1042 45c.+20c. grey and red . . . 70 65

DESIGNS: 12c. Type **224**; 15c. Red crosses; 20c. "NRK" ("Nederlandsche Rood Kruis") in the form of a cross; 25c. Maltese cross and "red" crosses; 45c. "100" in the form of a cross.

1967. Child Welfare. Multicoloured.

1043 12c.+8c. Type **225** 20 20
1044 15c.+10c. "The Whistling Kettle" 20 20
1045 20c.+10c. "Dikkertje Dap" (giraffe) 20 20
1046 25c.+10c. "The Flower-seller" . . . . 1·25 80
1047 45c.+20c. "Pippeloentje" (bear) . . . . 1·10 85
MS1048 150×108 mm. Nos. 1043 (3), 1044 (4), 1045 (3) . . . . 4·00 3·75

226 "Financial Automation"

1968. 50th Anniv of Netherlands Postal Cheque and Clearing Service.

1049 **226** 20c. red, black and yellow 20 10

227 St. Servatius' Bridge, Maastricht

1968. Cultural, Health and Social Welfare Funds. Dutch Bridges.

1050 **227** 12c.+8c. green . . . . . 1·40 95
1051 – 15c.+10c. brown 70 65
1052 – 20c.+10c. red 50 25
1053 – 25c.+10c. blue 55 55
1054 – 45c.+20c. blue 90 85

BRIDGES: 15c. Magere ("Narrow"), Amsterdam; 20c. Railway, Culemborg; 25c. Van Brienenoord, Rotterdam; 45c. Oosterschelde, Zeeland.

228 Europa "Key"

1968. Europa.

1055 **228** 20c. blue 30 10
1056 45c. red 95 80

229 "Wilhelmus van Nassouwe" **230** Wright Type A and Cessna 150F

1968. 400th Anniv of Dutch National Anthem, "Wilhelmus".

1057 **229** 20c. multicoloured . . . 20 10

1968. Dutch Aviation Anniversaries.

1058 12c. black, red and mauve 20 10
1059 20c. black, emerald and green 20 10
1060 45c. black, blue and green 1·25 1·10

DESIGNS AND EVENTS: 12c. T **230** (60th anniv (1967) of Royal Netherlands Aeronautical Assn); 20c. Fokker F.II and Fellowship aircraft (50th anniv (1969) of Royal Netherlands Aircraft Factories "Fokker"); 45c. De Havilland D.H.9B biplane and Douglas DC-9 airliner (50th anniv (1969) of Royal Dutch Airlines "KLM").

231 "Goblin"

1968. Child Welfare.

1061 **231** 12c.+8c. pink, black and green 20 15
1062 – 15c.+10c. pink, blue and black 20 15
1063 – 20c.+10c. blue, green and black 20 15
1064 – 25c.+10c. red, yellow and black . . . . . . 1·60 1·10
1065 – 45c.+20c. yellow, orange and black . . . . . . 1·60 1·25
MS1066 106½×151 mm. Nos. 1061 (3), 1062 (2), 1063 (3) . . . 9·00 9·00

DESIGNS: 15c. "Giant"; 20c. "Witch"; 25c. "Dragon"; 45c. "Sorcerer".

232 "I A O" (Internationale Arbeidsorganisatie)

1969. 50th Anniv of I.L.O.

1067 **232** 25c. red and black . . . 60 10
1068 45c. blue and black . . . 1·00 90

233 Queen Juliana **234** Villa, Huis ter Heide (1915)

1969. (a) Type **233**.

1069 **233** 25c. red . . . . 1·40 20
1069c 30c. brown 15 20
1070a 35c. blue 20 10
1071a 40c. red 30 10
1072a 45c. blue 30 10
1073a 50c. purple 25 10
1073c 55c. red 20 10
1074a 60c. blue 20 10
1075 70c. brown 50 10
1076 75c. green 60 10
1077 80c. red 65 10
1077a 90c. grey 65 10

(b) Size 22×33 mm.

1078 – 1g. green 70 10
1079 – 1g.25 lake 95 10
1080 – 1g.50 brown . . . . . . 1·10 10
1081 – 2g. mauve . . . . 1·40 10
1082 – 2g.50 blue . . . . 1·75 10
1083 – 5g. grey . . . . 3·50 10
1084 – 10g. blue . . . . 7·00 1·10

DESIGN: 1g.to 10g. similar to Type **233**.

1969. Cultural, Health and Social Welfare Funds. 20th-century Dutch Architecture.

1085 **234** 12c.+8c. black & brn . . 70 70
1086 – 15c.+10c. black, red and blue 70 70
1087 – 20c.+10c. black & vio . . 70 70
1088 – 25c.+10c. brown & grn 70 30
1089 – 45c.+20c. black, blue and yellow 70 70

DESIGNS: 15c. Private House, Utrecht (1924); 20c. Open-air School, Amsterdam (1930); 25c. Orphanage, Amsterdam (1960); 45c. Congress Building, The Hague (1969).

235 Colonnade **236** Stylized "Crab" (of Cancer)

1969. Europa.

1090 **235** 25c. blue 40 10
1091 45c. red . . . . 1·40 1·10

1969. 20th Anniv of Queen Wilhelmina Cancer Fund.

1092 **236** 12c.+8c. violet 65 60
1093 25c.+10c. orange 95 40
1094 45c.+20c. green . . . . 1·75 1·50

1969. 25th Anniv of "BENELUX" Customs Union. As T **186** of Luxembourg.

1095 25c. multicoloured 30 10

238 Erasmus **239** Child with Violin

1969. 500th Birth Anniv of Desiderius Erasmus.

1096 **238** 25c. purple on green . . 30 10

1969. Child Welfare.

1097 – 12c.+8c. black, yellow and blue 20 15
1098 **239** 15c.+10c. black and red 20 15
1099 – 20c.+10c. black, yellow and red . . . . 1·75 1·40
1100 – 25c.+10c. black, red and yellow 20 15
1101 – 45c.+20c. black, red and green . . . . 2·00 1·75
MS1102 150×99 mm. Nos. 1097 (4), 1098 (4), 1100 (2) . . . . . 10·00 9·00

DESIGNS—VERT: 12c. Child with recorder; 20c. Child with drum. HORIZ: 25c. Three choristers; 45c. Two dancers.

240 Queen Juliana and "Sunlit Road"

1969. 25th Anniv of Statute for the Kingdom.

1103 **240** 25c. multicoloured . . . 30 10

241 Prof. E. M. Meijers (author of "Burgerlijk Wetboek")

1970. Introduction of New Netherlands Civil Code ("Burgerlijk Wetboek").

1104 **241** 25c. ultramarine, green and blue 30 10

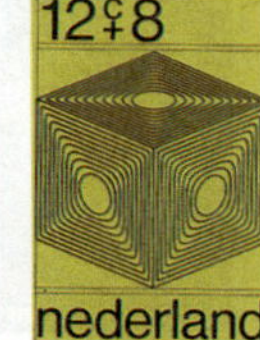

242 Netherlands Pavilion **243** "Circle to Square"

1970. Expo 70 World Fair, Osaka, Japan.

1105 **242** 25c. grey, blue and red 30 15

1970. Cultural, Health and Social Welfare Funds.

1106 **243** 12c.+8c. black on yell . . 1·10 1·25
1107 – 15c.+10c. black on silver 1·10 1·25
1108 – 20c.+10c. black . . . . 1·10 1·25
1109 – 25c.+10c. black on bl . . 1·10 75
1110 – 45c.+20c. white on grey 1·10 1·25

DESIGNS: 15c. Parallel planes in cube; 20c. Overlapping scales; 25c. Concentric circles in transition; 45c. Spirals.

244 "V" Symbol **245** "Flaming Sun"

1970. 25th Anniv of Liberation.

1111 **244** 12c. red, blue and brown 40 10

1970. Europa.

1112 **245** 25c. red 40 10
1113 45c. blue . . . . 1·60 1·00

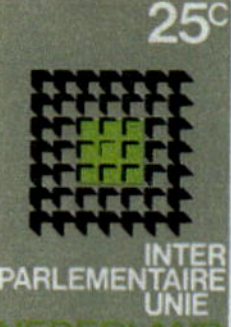

246 "Work and Co-operation" **247** Globe on Plinth

1970. Inter-Parliamentary Union Conference.

1114 **246** 25c. green, black and grey 60 10

1970. 25th Anniv of United Nations.

1115 **247** 45c. black, violet & blue 1·00 85

248 Human Heart **249** Toy Block

1970. Netherlands Heart Foundation.

1116 **248** 12c.+8c. red, black and yellow 70 75
1117 25c.+10c. red, black and mauve 70 65
1118 45c.+20c. red, black and green 70 60

1970. Child Welfare. "The Child and the Cube".

1119 **249** 12c.+8c. blue, violet and green 20 15
1120 – 15c.+10c. green, blue and yellow . . . . . 1·40 1·40
1121 **249** 20c.+10c. mauve, red and violet . . . . . . 1·40 1·40
1122 – 25c.+10c. red, yellow and mauve 20 15
1123 **249** 45c.+20c. grey, cream and black . . . . . . 1·75 1·60
MS1124 126×145 mm. Nos. 1119 (9), 1122 (2) . . . . 18·00 16·00

DESIGN: 15c., 25c. As Type **249**, but showing underside of block.

250 "Fourteenth Census 1971"

1971. 14th Netherlands Census.

1125 **250** 15c. purple 20 10

251 "50 years of Adult University Education" **252** Europa Chain

1971. Cultural, Health and Social Welfare Funds. Other designs show 15th-century wooden statues by unknown artists.

1126 **251** 15c.+10c. black, red and yellow . . . . 1·40 1·40
1127 – 20c.+10c. black and green on green . . . . 1·25 1·00
1128 – 25c.+10c. black and orange on orange . . 1·25 60
1129 – 30c.+15c. black and blue on blue . . . . . . 1·40 1·40
1130 – 45c.+20c. black and red on pink . . . . . . 1·40 1·40

STATUES: 20c. "Apostle Paul"; 25c. "Joachim and Ann"; 30c. "John the Baptist and Scribes"; 45c. "Ann, Mary and Christ-Child" (detail).

1971. Europa.

1131 **252** 25c. yellow, red and black 40 10
1132 45c. yellow, blue & black 1·40 1·25

253 Carnation Symbol of Prince Bernhard Fund **254** "The Good Earth"

1971. Prince Bernhard's 60th Birthday.
1133 **253** 15c. yellow, grey & black . . . 20 15
1134 – 20c. multicoloured . . . 65 40
1135 – 25c. multicoloured . . . 30 15
1136 – 45c.+20c. black, purple and yellow . . . . . 2·50 2·25
DESIGNS—HORIZ: 20c. Panda symbol of World Wildlife Fund. VERT: 25c. Prince Bernhard; 45c. Statue, Borobudur Temple, Indonesia.

1971. Child Welfare.
1137 **254** 15c.+10c. red, purple and black 20 15
1138 – 20c.+10c. mult 30 20
1139 – 25c.+10c. mult 20 20
1140 – 30c.+15c. blue, violet and black . . . . . . 1·10 65
1141 – 45c.+20c. blue, green and black . . . . . . 1·90 1·40
MS1142 100 × 145 mm. Nos. 1137 (6), 1138 and 1139 (2) . . . . 12·00 11·50
DESIGNS—VERT: 20c. Butterfly; 45c. Reflecting water. HORIZ: 25c. Sun waving; 30c. Moon winking.

255 Delta Map

256 "Fruits"

1972. Delta Sea-Defences Plan.
1143 **255** 20c. multicoloured . . . 20 10

1972. Cultural, Health and Social Welfare Funds. "Floriade Flower Show" (20c., 25c.) and "Holland Arts Festival" (30c., 45c.). Multicoloured.
1144 20c.+10c. Type **256** . . . . 1·10 90
1145 25c.+10c. "Flower" . . . . 1·10 90
1146 30c.+15c. "Sunlit Landscape" . . . . . . 1·10 65
1147 45c.+25c. "Music" . . . . 1·10 90

257 "Communications"

258 "There is more to be done in the world than ever before" (Thorbecke)

1972. Europa.
1148 **257** 30c. brown and blue . . 95 10
1149 45c. brown and orange . . 1·40 1·10

1972. Death Centenary of J. R. Thorbecke (statesman).
1150 **258** 30c. black and blue . . . 70 15

259 Netherlands Flag

260 Hurdling

1972. 400th Anniv of Netherlands Flag.
1151 **259** 20c. multicoloured . . . 50 20
1152 25c. multicoloured . . . 1·25 15

1972. Olympic Games, Munich. Multicoloured.
1153 20c. Type **260** 20 15
1154 30c. Diving 20 15
1155 45c. Cycling . . . . 1·10 1·10

261 Red Cross

262 Prince Willem-Alexander

1972. Netherlands Red Cross.
1156 **261** 5c. red 20 15
1157 – 20c.+10c. red and pink . . 55 55
1158 – 25c.+10c. red & orange . . 95 85
1159 – 30c.+15c. red & black . . 70 55
1160 – 45c.+25c. red and blue . . 1·00 90
DESIGNS: 20c. Accident services; 25c. Blood transfusion; 30c. Refugee relief; 45c. Child care.

1972. Child Welfare. Multicoloured.
1161 25c.+15c. Type **262** 20 15
1162 30c.+10c. Prince Johan Friso (horiz) 70 65
1163 35c.+15c. Prince Constantin (horiz) 70 15
1164 50c.+20c. The Three Princes (horiz) . . . . 2·40 2·00
MS1165 126 × 109 mm. Nos. 1161 × 4 and 1163 × 3 . . . . . . 8·00 7·00

263 Tulips in Bloom

264 "De Zeven Provincien" (De Ruyter's flagship)

1973. Tulip Exports.
1166 **263** 25c. multicoloured . . . 65 10

1973. Cultural, Health and Social Welfare Funds. Dutch Ships. Multicoloured.
1167 25c.+15c. Type **264** 95 90
1168 30c.+10c. "W.A. Scholten" (steamship) (horiz) . . . 95 90
1169 35c.+15c. "Veendam" (liner) (horiz) . . . . 1·10 75
1170 50c.+20c. Fishing boat (from etching by R. Nooms) . . . . 1·25 1·25

265 Europa "Posthorn"

266 Hockey-players

1973. Europa.
1171 **265** 35c. light blue and blue 55 10
1172 50c. blue and violet . . . 95 85

1973. Events and Anniversaries. Multicoloured.
1173 25c. Type **266** 40 25
1174 30c. Gymnastics . . . . . 2·00 60
1175 35c. Dish aerial (vert) . . . 50 15
1176 50c. Rainbow 85 75
EVENTS—VERT: 25c. 75th anniv of Royal Netherlands Hockey Association; 30c. World Gymnastics Championships, Rotterdam. HORIZ: 35c. Opening of Satellite Station, Burum; 50c. Centenary of World Meteorological Organization.

267 Queen Juliana

268 "Co-operation"

1973. Silver Jubilee of Queen Juliana's Accession.
1177 **267** 40c. multicoloured . . . 50 15

1973. International Development Co-operation.
1178 **268** 40c. multicoloured . . . 95 10

269 "Chess"

270 Northern Goshawk

1973. Child Welfare.
1179 **269** 25c.+15c. red, yellow and black 40 20
1180 – 30c.+10c. green, mauve and black . . . . . . 1·60 65
1181 – 40c.+20c. yellow, green and black 40 15
1182 – 50c.+20c. blue, yellow and black . . . . . . 1·60 2·00
MS1183 74 × 144 mm. Nos. 1179 × 2, 1180 and 1181 × 3 . . . . 11·50 11·00
DESIGNS: 30c. "Noughts and crosses"; 40c. "Maze"; 50c. "Dominoes".

1974. "Nature and Environment". Multicoloured.
1184 25c. Type **270** . . . . . . 1·10 55
1185 25c. Tree . . . . 1·10 55
1186 25c. Fisherman and frog . . 1·10 55
Nos. 1184/6 were issued together, se-tenant, forming a composite design.

271 Bandsmen (World Band Contest, Kerkrade)

272 Football on Pitch

1974. Cultural, Health and Social Welfare Funds.
1187 **271** 25c.+15c. mult 95 85
1188 – 30c.+10c. mult 95 85
1189 – 40c.+20c. brown, black and red 95 65
1190 – 50c.+20c. purple, black and red 95 85
DESIGNS: 30c. Dancers and traffic-lights ("Modern Ballet"); 40c. Herman Heijermans; 50c. "Kniertje" (character from Heijermans' play "Op hoop van zegan"). The 40c. and 50c. commemorate the 50th death anniv of the playwright.

1974. Sporting Events.
1191 **272** 25c. multicoloured . . . 20 15
1192 – 40c. yellow, red & mauve 35 15
DESIGNS AND EVENTS—HORIZ: 25c. (World Cup Football Championship, West Germany). VERT: 40c. Hand holding tennis ball (75th anniv of Royal Dutch Lawn Tennis Association).

273 Netherlands Cattle

274 "BENELUX" (30th Anniv of Benelux (Customs Union))

1974. Anniversaries. Multicoloured.
1193 25c. Type **273** . . . . . . 8·75 1·90
1194 25c. "Cancer" 95 20
1195 40c. "Suzanna" (lifeboat) seen through binoculars 70 20
EVENTS AND ANNIVERSARIES: No. 1193, Cent of Netherlands Cattle Herdbook Society; 1194, 25th anniv of Queen Wilhelmina Cancer Research Fund; 1195, 150th anniv of Dutch Lifeboat Service.

1974. International Anniversaries.
1196 **274** 30c. green, turquoise & blue 30 15
1197 – 45c. deep blue, silver & blue 50 15
1198 – 45c. yellow, blue & black 50 15
DESIGNS—VERT: No. 1197, NATO emblem (25th anniv); 1198, Council of Europe emblem (25th anniv).

275 Hands with Letters

276 Boy with Hoop

1974. Centenary of Universal Postal Union.
1199 **275** 60c. multicoloured . . . 55 45

1974. 50th Anniv of Child Welfare Issues. Early Photographs.
1200 **276** 30c.+15c. brown & blk 20 15
1201 – 35c.+20c. brown 55 55
1202 – 45c.+20c. black 55 25
1203 – 60c.+20c. black . . . . 1·25 1·40
MS1204 75 × 145 mm. Nos. 1200 × 4 and 1201/2 . . . . 4·75 4·50
DESIGNS: 35c. Child and baby; 45c. Two young girls; 60c. Girl sitting on balustrade.

277 Amsterdam

278 St. Hubertus Hunting Lodge, De Hoge Veluwe National Park

1975. Anniversaries. Multicoloured.
1205 30c. Type **277** 30 30
1206 30c. Synagogue and map . . 30 30
1207 35c. Type **277** 40 15
1208 45c. "Window" in human brain 35 45
ANNIVERSARIES: Nos. 1205, 1207, Amsterdam (700th anniv); 1206, Portuguese-Israelite Synagogue, Amsterdam (300th anniv); 1208, Leyden University and university education (400th anniv).

1975. Cultural, Health and Social Welfare Funds. National Monument Year. Preserved Monuments. Multicoloured.
1209 35c.+20c. Type **278** 55 55
1210 40c.+15c. Bergijnhof (Beguinage), Amsterdam (vert) 55 55
1211 50c.+20c. "Kuiperspoort" (Cooper's gate), Middelburg (vert) 70 55
1212 60c.+20c. Orvelte village, Drenthe 95 85

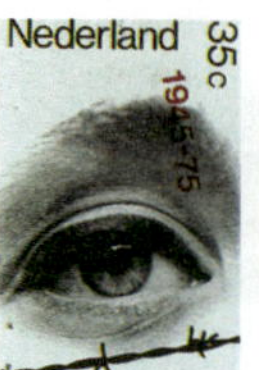
279 Eye and Barbed Wire

280 Company Emblem and "Stad Middelburg" (schooner)

1975. 30th Anniv of Liberation.
1213 **279** 35c. black and red . . . 35 10

1975. Centenary of Zeeland Shipping Company.
1214 **280** 35c. multicoloured . . . 35 15

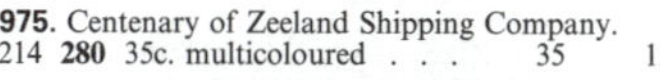

281 Dr. Albert Schweitzer crossing Lambarene River

1975. Birth Centenary of Dr. Schweitzer (medical missionary).
1215 **281** 50c. multicoloured . . . 40 10

282 Man and Woman on "Playing-card"

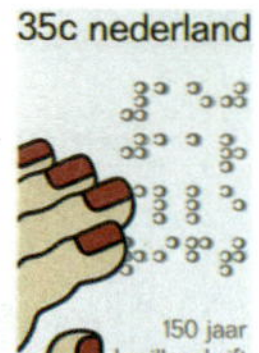
283 Braille Reading

1975. International Events. Multicoloured.
1216 35c. Type **282** (Int Women's Year) 35 15
1217 50c. Metric scale (Metre Convention cent) (horiz) 40 10

1975. 150th Anniv of Invention of Braille.
1218 **283** 35c. multicoloured . . . 35 15

284 Dutch 25c. Coins

285 "Four Orphans" (C. Simons), Torenstraat Orphanage, Medemblik

1975. Savings Campaign.
1219 **284** 50c. grey, green and blue 40 10

1975. Child Welfare. Historic Ornamental Stones. Multicoloured.
1220 35c.+15c. Type **285** 20 15
1221 40c.+15c. "Milkmaid" Kooltuin Alkmaar . . . 50 50

1222 50c.+25c. "Four Sons of Aymon seated on Beyaert", Herengracht . . 40 20
1223 60c.+25c. "Life at the Orphanage", Molenstraat Orphanage, Gorinchem 1·00 75
MS1224 145 × 75 mm. Nos. 1220 × 3 and 1222 × 2 . . . . 3·25 3·00

286 18th-century Lottery Ticket
287 Numeral

1976. 250th Anniv of National Lottery.
1225 **286** 35c. multicoloured . . . 35 15

1976. (a) Ordinary gum.
1226 **287** 5c. grey 10 10
1227 10c. blue 10 10
1228 25c. violet 20 10
1229 40c. brown 40 10
1230 45c. blue 40 10
1231 50c. mauve 40 10
1232 55c. green 65 10
1233 60c. yellow 70 10
1234 65c. brown . . . . . . 1·00 10
1235 70c. violet 85 10
1236 80c. mauve . . . . . . 1·50 10

(b) Self-adhesive gum.
1237 **287** 5c. grey 10 10
1238 10c. blue 10 10
1239 25c. violet 15 10

288 West European Hedgehog

1976. Cultural, Health and Social Welfare Funds. Nature Protection (40, 75c.) and Anniversaries. Multicoloured.
1241 40c.+20c. Type **288** 60 45
1242 45c.+20c. Open book (vert) 60 45
1243 55c.+20c. People and organization initials . . . 65 30
1244 75c.+25c. Frog and spawn (vert) 85 80
ANNIVERSARIES: No. 1242, 175th anniv of Primary education and centenary of Agricultural education; 1243, 75th anniv of Social Security Bank and legislation.

289 Admiral Michiel de Ruyter (statue)

1976. 300th Death Anniv of Admiral Michiel de Ruyter.
1245 **289** 55c. multicoloured . . . 40 15

290 Guillaume Groen van Prinsterer

1976. Death Centenary of Guillaume Groen van Prinsterer (statesman).
1246 **290** 55c. multicoloured . . . 40 15

291 Detail of 18th-century Calendar

1976. Bicentenary of American Revolution.
1247 **291** 75c. multicoloured . . . 55 35

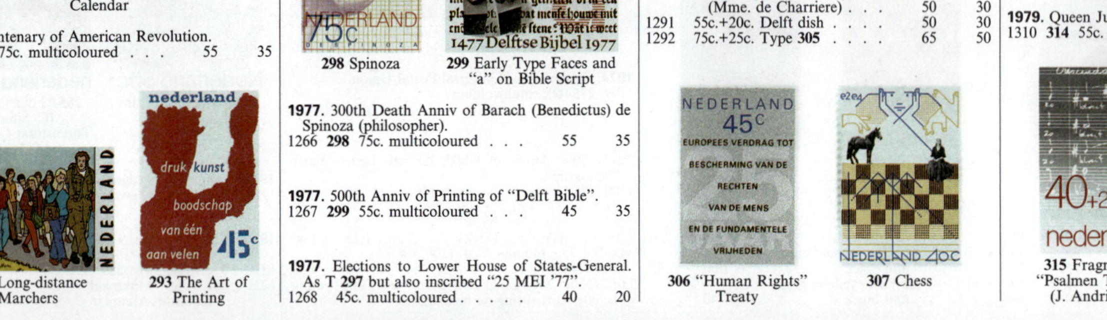

292 Long-distance Marchers
293 The Art of Printing

1976. Sport and Recreation Anniversaries. Mult.
1248 40c. Type **292** 30 25
1249 55c. Runners "photo-finish" 65 25
ANNIVERSARIES: 40c. 60th Nijmegen Long-distance March; 55c. Royal Dutch Athletics Society (75th anniv).

1976. Anniversaries.
1250 **293** 45c. red and blue 30 25
1251 – 55c.+25c. mult 50 45
DESIGNS AND EVENTS: 45c. Type **293** (75th anniv of Netherlands Printers' organization); 55c. Rheumatic patient "Within Care" (50th anniv of Dutch Anti-Rheumatism Association).

294 Dutch Tjalk and Reclaimed Land
295 Queen Wilhelmina 4½c. Stamp, 1919

1976. Zuider Zee Project—Reclamation and Urbanization. Multicoloured.
1252 **294** 40c. blue, olive and red 30 15
1253 – 75c. yellow, red and blue 55 45
DESIGN: 75c. Duck flying over reclaimed land.

1976. "Amphilex '77" International Stamp Exhibition, Amsterdam (1977) (1st series). Stamp Portraits of Queen Wilhelmina. Multicoloured.
1254 – 55c.+55c. blue, deep grey and grey 95 80
1255 **295** 55c.+55c. purple, deep grey and grey 95 80
1256 – 55c.+55c. brown, deep grey and grey 95 80
1257 – 75c.+75c. turquoise, deep grey and grey 95 80
1258 – 75c.+75c. blue, deep grey and grey 95 80
DESIGNS: No. 1254, 5c. stamp, 1891; 1256, 25c. stamp, 1924; 1257, 15c. stamp, 1940; 1258, 25c. stamp, 1947.
See also Nos. 1273/6.

296 "Football" (J. Raats)

1976. Child Welfare. Children's Paintings. Mult.
1259 40c.+20c. Type **296** 30 25
1260 45c.+20c. "Boat" (L. Jacobs) 30 30
1261 55c.+20c. "Elephant" (M. Lugtenburg) 40 15
1262 75c.+25c. "Caravan" (A. Seeleman) 70 85
MS1263 145 × 75 mm. Nos. 1259/61 × 2 . . . . 2·25 2·00

297 Ballot-paper and Pencil

1977. National Events. Multicoloured.
1264 40c. "Energy" (vert) 30 10
1265 45c. Type **297** 40 15
EVENTS: 40c. "Be wise with energy" campaign; 45c. Elections to Lower House of States-General.
See also No. 1268.

298 Spinoza
299 Early Type Faces and "a" on Bible Script

1977. 300th Death Anniv of Barach (Benedictus) de Spinoza (philosopher).
1266 **298** 75c. multicoloured . . . 55 35

1977. 500th Anniv of Printing of "Delft Bible".
1267 **299** 55c. multicoloured . . . 45 35

1977. Elections to Lower House of States-General. As T **297** but also inscribed "25 MEI '77".
1268 45c. multicoloured 40 20

300 Altar of Goddess Nehalennia
301 "Kaleidoscope"

1977. Cultural, Health and Social Welfare Funds. Roman Archaeological Discoveries.
1269 – 40c.+20c. mult 40 30
1270 **300** 45c.+20c. black, stone and green 50 30
1271 – 55c.+20c. black, blue and red 50 30
1272 – 75c.+25c. black, grey and yellow 65 50
DESIGNS: 40c. Baths, Heerlen; 55c. Remains of Zwammerdam ship; 75c. Parade helmet.

1977. "Amphilex 1977" International Stamp Exhibition, Amsterdam (2nd series). As T **295**.
1273 55c.+45c. grn, brn & grey 55 35
1274 55c.+45c. blue, brn & grey 55 45
1275 55c.+45c. blue, brn & grey 55 45
1276 55c.+45c. red, brn & grey 55 35
MS1277 100 × 72 mm. Nos. 1273 and 1276 . . . . 90 75
DESIGNS: No. 1273, Queen Wilhelmina 1g. stamp, 1898; 1274, Queen Wilhelmina 20c. stamp, 1923; 1275, Queen Wilhelmina 12½c. stamp, 1938; 1276, Queen Wilhelmina 10c. stamp, 1948.

1977. Bicentenary of Netherlands Society for Industry and Commerce.
1278 **301** 55c. multicoloured . . . 45 10

302 Man in Wheelchair and Maze of Steps
303 Risk of Drowning

1977. Anniversaries.
1279 **302** 40c. brown, green & blue 30 15
1280 – 45c. multicoloured . . . 30 20
1281 – 55c. multicoloured . . . 40 10
DESIGNS—HORIZ: 40c. Type **302** (50th anniv of A.V.O. Nederland); 45c. Diagram of water current (50th anniv of Delft Hydraulic Laboratory). VERT: 55c. Teeth (centenary of dentists' training in Netherlands).

1977. Child Welfare. Dangers to Children. Mult.
1282 40c.+20c. Type **303** 35 20
1283 45c.+20c. Medicine cabinet (poisons) 35 20
1284 55c.+20c. Balls in road (traffic) 35 20
1285 75c.+25c. Matches (fire) . . 65 65
MS1286 75 × 144 mm. Nos. 1282/4 × 2 . . . . 2·40 1·40

304 "Postcode"
305 Makkum Dish

1978. Introduction of Postcodes.
1287 **304** 40c. red and blue 30 10
1288 45c. red and blue 30 10

1978. Cultural, Health and Social Welfare Funds. Multicoloured.
1289 40c.+20c. Anna Maria van Schurman (writer) 40 30
1290 45c.+20c. Passage from letter by Belle de Zuylen (Mme. de Charriere) . . . 50 30
1291 55c.+20c. Delft dish 50 30
1292 75c.+25c. Type **305** 65 50

306 "Human Rights" Treaty
307 Chess

1978. European Series.
1293 **306** 45c. grey, black and blue 30 15
1294 – 55c. black, stone and orange 45 10
DESIGN: 55c. Haarlem Town Hall (Europa).

1978. Sports.
1295 **307** 40c. multicoloured . . . 30 15
1296 – 45c. red and blue 30 20
DESIGN: 45c. The word "Korfbal".

308 Kidney Donor
309 Epaulettes

1978. Health Care. Multicoloured.
1297 **308** 40c. black, blue and red 30 20
1298 – 45c. multicoloured . . . 30 20
1299 – 55c.+25c. red, grey and black 50 45
MS1300 144 × 50 mm. No. 1299 × 3 1·10 1·10
DESIGNS—VERT: 45c. Heart and torch. HORIZ: 55c. Red crosses on world map.

1978. 150th Anniv of Royal Military Academy, Breda.
1301 **309** 55c. multicoloured . . . 40 10

310 Verkade as Hamlet

1978. Birth Centenary of Eduard Rutger Verkade (actor and producer).
1302 **310** 45c. multicoloured . . . 30 20

311 Boy ringing Doorbell

1978. Child Welfare. Multicoloured.
1303 40c.+20c. Type **311** 40 20
1304 45c.+20c. Child reading . . 50 20
1305 55c.+20c. Boy writing (vert) 50 20
1306 75c.+25c. Girl and blackboard 65 65
MS1307 144 × 75 mm. Nos. 1303/5 × 2 . . . . 2·40 2·00

312 Clasped Hands and Arrows
313 Names of European Community Members

1979. 400th Anniv of Treaty of Utrecht.
1308 **312** 55c. blue 40 20

1979. First Direct Elections to European Assembly.
1309 **313** 45c. red, blue and black 30 15

314 Queen Juliana

1979. Queen Juliana's 70th Birthday.
1310 **314** 55c. multicoloured . . . 40 15

315 Fragment of "Psalmen Trilogie" (J. Andriessen)
316 Netherlands Stamps and Magnifying Glass

1979. Cultural, Health and Social Welfare Funds.
1311 **315** 40c.+20c. grey and red . . . 40 30
1312 – 45c.+20c. grey and red . . . 50 30
1313 – 55c.+20c. mult 50 25
1314 – 75c.+25c. mult 65 45
DESIGNS AND EVENTS: 150th anniv of Musical Society; 45c. Choir. Restoration of St. John's Church, Gouda (stained glass windows); 55c. Mary (detail, "Birth of Christ"); 75c. William of Orange (detail, "Relief of Leyden").

1979. Europa and 75th Anniv of Scheveningen Radio. Multicoloured.
1315 55c. Type **316** 40 15
1316 75c. Liner and Morse Key . . 55 40

317 Map of Chambers of Commerce
318 Action Shot of Football Match

1979. 175th Anniv of First Dutch Chamber of Commerce, Maastricht.
1317 **317** 45c. multicoloured . . . 30 20

1979. Anniversaries. Multicoloured.
1318 45c. Type **318** (centenary of organized football) . . . 30 20
1319 55c. Women's suffrage meeting (60th anniv of Women's suffrage) (vert) 40 15

319 Porch of Old Amsterdam Theatre

1979. 300th Death Annivs of Joost van den Vondel (poet) and Jan Steen (painter). Multicoloured.
1320 40c. Type **319** 30 20
1321 45c. "Gay Company" (detail) (Jan Steen) . . . 30 20

320 Hindustani Girl on Father's Shoulder (The Right to Love)

1979. Child Welfare. International Year of the Child.
1322 **320** 40c.+20c. grey, red and yellow 40 20
1323 – 45c.+20c. grey, red and black 50 20
1324 – 55c.+20c. grey, black and yellow 50 20
1325 – 75c.+25c. black, blue and red 65 65
MS1326 144 × 75 mm. Nos. 1322/4, each × 2 . . . . 2·40 2·00
DESIGNS—HORIZ: 45c. Chilean child from refugee camp (The Right to Medical Care). VERT: 55c. Senegalese boy from Sahel area (The Right to Food); 75c. Class from Albert Cuyp School, Amsterdam (The Right to Education).

321 A. F. de Savornin Lohman
322 Dunes

1980. Dutch Politicians. Multicoloured.
1327 45c. Type **321** (Christian Historical Union) 30 20
1328 50c. P. J. Troelstra (Socialist Party) 30 20
1329 60c. P. J. Oud (Liberal Party) 50 20

1980. Cultural, Health and Social Welfare Funds. Multicoloured.
1330 45c.+20c. Type **322** 50 30
1331 50c.+20c. Country estate (vert) 50 30
1332 60c.+25c. Lake District . . 55 30
1333 80c.+35c. Moorland 70 50

323 Avro Type 683 Lancaster dropping Food Parcels
324 Queen Beatrix and New Church, Amsterdam

1980. 35th Anniv of Liberation. Multicoloured.
1334 45c. Type **323** 40 20
1335 60c. Anne Frank (horiz) . . 50 10

1980. Installation of Queen Beatrix.
1336 **324** 60c. blue, red and yellow 1·00 30
1337 65c. blue, red and yellow 1·40 10

325 Young Stamp Collectors
326 "Flight"

1980. "Jupostex 1980" Stamp Exhibition, Eindhoven, and Dutch Society of Stamp Dealers Show, The Hague.
1338 **325** 50c. multicoloured . . . 40 30

1980. Air. (Special Flights).
1339 **326** 1g. blue and black . . . 80 65

327 Bridge Players and Cards
328 Road Haulage

1980. Sports Events. Multicoloured.
1340 50c. Type **327** (Bridge Olympiad, Valkenburg) 40 20
1341 60c.+25c. Sportswoman in wheelchair (Olympics for the Disabled, Arnhem and Veenendaal) 55 40

1980. Transport.
1342 **328** 50c. multicoloured . . . 40 15
1343 – 60c. blue, brown & black 50 15
1344 – 80c. multicoloured . . . 65 30
DESIGNS: 60c. Rail transport; 80c. Motorized canal barge.

329 Queen Wilhelmina

1980. Europa.
1345 **329** 60c. black, red and blue 50 10
1346 – 80c. black, red and blue 65 30
DESIGN: 80c. Sir Winston Churchill.

330 Abraham Kuyper (first rector) and University Seal

1980. Centenary of Amsterdam Free University.
1347 **330** 50c. multicoloured . . . 40 15

331 "Pop-up" Book
332 Saltmarsh

1980. Child Welfare. Multicoloured.
1348 45c.+20c. Type **331** 40 20
1349 50c.+20c. Child flying on a book (vert) 50 40
1350 60c.+30c. Boy reading "Kikkerkoning" (vert) . . 55 10
1351 80c.+30c. Dreaming in a book 65 65
MS1352 144 × 75 mm. Nos. 1348 × 2 and 1350 × 3 . . . . 2·40 1·00

1981. Cultural, Health and Social Welfare Funds. Multicoloured.
1353 45c.+20c. Type **332** 40 30
1354 55c.+25c. Dyke 50 30
1355 60c.+25c. Drain 55 30
1356 65c.+30c. Cultivated land 65 30

333 Parcel (Parcel Post)

1981. P.T.T. Centenaries. Multicoloured.
1357 45c. Type **333** 40 15
1358 55c. Telephone, dish aerial and telephone directory page (public telephone service) 45 15
1359 65c. Savings bank books, deposit transfer card and savings bank stamps (National Savings Bank) 50 10
MS1360 145 × 75 mm. Nos. 1357/9 1·25 90

334 Huis ten Bosch Royal Palace, The Hague

1981.
1361 **334** 55c. multicoloured . . . 45 15

335 Carillon

1981. Europa. Multicoloured.
1362 45c. Type **335** 40 20
1363 65c. Barrel organ 50 15

336 Council of State Emblem and Maps of 1531 and 1981

1981. 450th Anniv of Council of State.
1364 **336** 65c. orange, deep orange and red 50 10

337 Marshalling Yard, Excavator and Ship's Screw

1981. Industrial and Agricultural Exports. Mult.
1365 45c. Type **337** 40 15
1366 55c. Inner port, cast-iron component and weighing machine 45 20
1367 60c. Airport, tomato and lettuce 50 40
1368 65c. Motorway interchange, egg and cheese 50 10

338 "Integration in Society"

1981. Child Welfare. Integration of Handicapped Children. Multicoloured.
1369 45c.+25c. Type **338** 40 10
1370 55c.+20c. "Integration in the Family" (vert) 50 50
1371 60c.+25c. Child vaccinated against polio (Upper Volta project) (vert) . . . 55 50
1372 65c.+30c. "Integration among Friends" 65 10
MS1373 144 × 76 mm. Nos. 1369 × 3 and 1372 × 2 . . . . 2·40 1·75

339 Queen Beatrix
340 Agnieten Chapel and Banners

1981.
1374 **339** 65c. brown and black . . 55 10
1375 70c. lilac and black . . . 70 10
1376 75c. pink and black . . 70 10
1377 90c. green and black . . 1·10 10
1378 1g. lilac and black . . . 70 15
1379 1g.20 bistre and black 1·25 20
1380 1g.40 green and black . . 1·75 20
1381 1g.50 lilac and black . . 1·10 20
1382 2g. bistre and black . . 1·40 15
1383 2g.50 orange and black 1·75 30
1384 3g. blue and black . . 2·10 20
1385 4g. green and black . . 3·00 20
1386 5g. blue and black . . . 3·75 20
1387 6g.50 lilac and black . . 5·75 20
1388 7g. blue and black . . . 4·75 30
1389 7g.50 green and black . . 5·75 50
For this design but on uncoloured background see Nos. 1594/1605.

1982. 350th Anniv of University of Amsterdam.
1395 **340** 65c. multicoloured . . . 50 10

341 Skater
342 Apple Blossom

1982. Centenary of Royal Dutch Skating Association.
1396 **341** 45c. multicoloured . . . 40 20

1982. Cultural, Health and Social Welfare Funds. Multicoloured.
1397 50c.+20c. Type **342** 50 30
1398 60c.+25c. Anemones 55 30
1399 65c.+25c. Roses 55 30
1400 70c.+30c. African violets . . 65 55

343 Stripes in National Colours

1982. Bicentenary of Netherlands–United States Diplomatic Relations.
1401 **343** 50c. red, blue and black 40 20
1402 65c. red, blue and black 55 15

344 Sandwich Tern and Eider
345 Zebra Crossing

1982. Waddenzee. Multicoloured.
1403 50c. Type **344** 40 20
1404 70c. Barnacle Geese 55 10

1982. 50th Anniv of Dutch Road Safety Organization.
1405 **345** 60c. multicoloured . . . 50 30

346 Ground Plan of Enkhuizen Fortifications
347 Aerial view of Palace and Liberation Monument

1982. Europa. Multicoloured.
1406 50c. Type **346** 40 20
1407 70c. Part of ground plan of Coevorden fortifications 55 10

1982. Royal Palace, Dam Square, Amsterdam. Mult.
1408 50c. Facade, ground plan and cross-section of palace 40 10
1409 60c. Type **347** 50 10

348 Great Tits and Child **349** Touring Club Activities

1982. Child Welfare. Child and Animal. Mult.
1410 50c.+30c. Type **348** 40 15
1411 60c.+20c. Child arm-in-arm with cat 50 15
1412 65c.+20c. Child with drawing of rabbit 65 45
1413 70c.+30c. Child with palm cockatoo 70 70
MS1414 75 × 144 mm. Nos. 1410 × 4 and 1411 . . . . 2·50 2·10

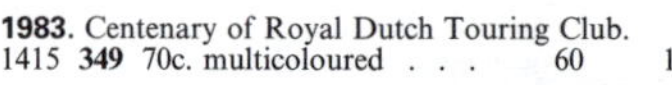

1983. Centenary of Royal Dutch Touring Club.
1415 **349** 70c. multicoloured . . . 60 10

350 Johan van Oldenbarnevelt (statesman) (after J. Houbraken) **351** Newspaper

1983. Cultural, Health and Social Welfare Funds.
1416 **350** 50c.+20c. pink, blue and black 50 40
1417 – 60c.+25c. mult 65 40
1418 – 65c.+25c. mult 70 55
1419 – 70c.+30c. grey, black and gold 70 55
DESIGNS: 60c. Willem Jansz Blaeu (cartographer) (after Thomas de Keijser); 65c. Hugo de Groot (statesman) (after J. van Ravesteyn); 70c. "Saskia van Uylenburch" (portrait of his wife by Rembrandt).

1983. Europa. Multicoloured.
1420 50c. Type **351** (75th anniv of Netherlands Newspaper Publishers Association) 40 20
1421 70c. European Communications Satellite and European Telecommunication Satellites Organization members' flags 55 10

352 "Composition 1922" (P. Mondriaan) **353** "Geneva Conventions"

1983. De Stijl Art Movement. Multicoloured.
1422 50c. Type **352** 40 15
1423 65c. Contra construction from "Maison Particuliere" (C. van Eesteren and T. van Doesburg) 50 30

1983. Red Cross.
1424 **353** 50c.+25c. mult 50 45
1425 – 60c.+20c. mult 55 45
1426 – 65c.+25c. mult 65 45
1427 – 70c.+30c. grey, black and red 70 65
DESIGNS: 60c. Red Cross and text "charity, independence, impartiality"; 65c. "Socio-medical work"; 70c. Red Cross and text "For Peace".

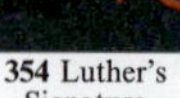

354 Luther's Signature **355** Child looking at Donkey and Ox through Window

1983. 500th Birth Anniv of Martin Luther (Protestant Reformer).
1428 **354** 70c. multicoloured . . . 55 10

1983. Child Welfare. Child and Christmas. Mult.
1429 50c.+10c. Type **355** 50 45
1430 50c.+25c. Child riding flying snowman 55 15
1431 60c.+30c. Child in bed and star 65 70
1432 70c.+30c. Children dressed as the three kings 70 15
MS1433 144 × 75 mm. Nos. 1430 × 4 and 1432 × 2 . . . . 3·00 3·00

356 Parliament

1984. Second Elections to European Parliament.
1434 **356** 70c. multicoloured . . . 50 10

357 Northern Lapwings **358** St. Servaas

1984. Cultural, Health and Social Welfare Funds. Pasture Birds. Multicoloured.
1435 50c.+20c. Type **357** 50 40
1436 60c.+25c. Ruffs 55 40
1437 65c.+25c. Redshanks (vert) 65 55
1438 70c.+30c. Black-tailed godwits (vert) 70 55

1984. 1600th Death Anniv of St. Servaas (Bishop of Tongeren and Maastricht).
1439 **358** 60c. multicoloured . . . 50 15

359 Bridge

1984. Europa. 25th Anniv of European Post and Telecommunications Conference.
1440 **359** 50c. deep blue and blue 40 15
1441 70c. green and light green 55 10

360 Eye and Magnifying Glass

1984. Centenary of Organized Philately in the Netherlands and "Filacento" International Stamp Exhibition, The Hague. Multicoloured.
1442 50c.+20c. Type **360** 55 45
1443 60c.+25c. 1909 cover . . . 65 55
1444 70c.+30c. Stamp club meeting, 1949 . . . . . . 65 65
MS1445 144 × 50 mm. Nos. 1442/4 2·50 2·00

361 William of Orange (after Adriaen Thomaszoon Key)

1984. 400th Death Anniv of William of Orange.
1446 **361** 70c. multicoloured . . . 55 15

362 Giant Pandas and Globe **363** Graph and Leaf

1984. World Wildlife Fund.
1447 **362** 70c. multicoloured . . . 70 15

1984. 11th International Small Business Congress, Amsterdam.
1448 **363** 60c. multicoloured . . . 50 20

364 Violin Lesson **365** Sunny, First Dutch Guide-Dog

1984. Child Welfare. Strip Cartoons. Mult.
1449 50c.+25c. Type **364** 40 30
1450 60c.+20c. At the dentist . . 70 55
1451 65c.+20c. The plumber . . . 85 75
1452 70c.+30c. The king and money chest 65 30
MS1453 75 × 144 mm. Nos. 1449 × 4 and 1452 × 2 . . . . 3·50 3·50

1985. 50th Anniv of Royal Dutch Guide-Dog Fund.
1454 **365** 60c. black, ochre and red 50 20

366 Plates and Cutlery on Place-mat **367** Saint Martin's Church, Zaltbommel

1985. Tourism. Multicoloured.
1455 50c. Type **366** (centenary of Travel and Holidays Association) 40 20
1456 70c. Kroller-Muller museum emblem, antlers and landscape (50th anniv of De Hoge Veluwe National Park) 55 10

1985. Cultural, Health and Social Welfare Funds. Religious Buildings. Multicoloured.
1457 50c.+20c. Type **367** 55 45
1458 60c.+25c. Winterswijk synagogue and Holy Ark (horiz) 65 55
1459 65c.+25c. Bolsward Baptist church 70 55
1460 70c.+30c. Saint John's Cathedral, 's-Hertogenbosch (horiz) 70 40

368 Star of David, Illegal Newspapers and Rifle Practice (Resistance Movement) **369** Piano Keyboard

1985. 40th Anniv of Liberation.
1461 **368** 50c. black, stone and red 45 20
1462 – 60c. black, stone and blue 50 15
1463 – 65c. black, stone & orge 55 45
1464 – 70c. black, stone & green 55 20
DESIGNS: 60c. Bombers over houses, "De Vliegende Hollander" (newspaper) and soldier (Allied Forces); 65c. Soldiers and civilians, "Parool" (newspaper) and American war cemetery, Margraten (Liberation); 70c. Women prisoners, prison money and Burma Railway (Dutch East Indies).

1985. Europa. Music Year. Multicoloured.
1465 50c. Type **369** 40 20
1466 70c. Organ 55 10

370 National Museum, Amsterdam (centenary)

1985. Anniversaries and Events. Multicoloured.
1467 50c. Type **370** 40 20
1468a 60c. Teacher with students (bicentenary of Amsterdam Nautical College) 50 25
1469 70c. Ship's mast and rigging ("Sail '85", Amsterdam) 55 10

371 Porpoise and Graph

1985. Endangered Animals.
1470 **371** 50c. black, blue and red 40 20
1471 – 70c. black, blue and red 55 15
DESIGN: 70c. Seal and PCB molecule structure.

372 Ignition Key and Framed Photograph ("Think of Me")

1985. Child Welfare. Road Safety. Multicoloured.
1472 50c.+25c. Type **372** 55 20
1473 60c.+20c. Child holding target showing speeds . . 55 65
1474 65c.+20c. Girl holding red warning triangle 65 75
1475 70c.+30c. Boy holding "Children Crossing" sign 90 20
MS1476 132 × 80 mm. Nos. 1472 × 4 and 1475 × 2 . . . . 3·50 3·50

373 Penal Code Extract

1986. Centenary of Penal Code.
1477 **373** 50c. black, yellow & purple 40 15

374 Surveyor with Pole and N.A.P. Water Gauge

1986. 300th Anniv of Height Gauging Marks at Amsterdam.
1478 **374** 60c. multicoloured . . . 45 15

375 Windmill, Graph and Cloudy Sky

1986. Inaug of Windmill Test Station, Sexbierum.
1479 **375** 70c. multicoloured . . . 55 10

376 Scales **377** Het Loo Palace Garden, Apeldoorn

1986. Cultural, Health and Social Welfare Funds. Antique Measuring Instruments. Multicoloured.
1480 50c.+20c. Type **376** 55 35
1481 60c.+25c. Clock (vert) . . . 55 35
1482 65c.+25c. Barometer (vert) 65 65
1483 70c.+30c. Jacob's staff . . . 70 85

1986. Europa. Multicoloured.
1484 50c. Type **377** 40 20
1485 70c. Tree with discoloured crown 50 10

378 Cathedral **379** Drees at Binnenhof, 1947

1986. Utrecht Events.
1486 **378** 50c. multicoloured . . . 50 30
1487 – 60c. blue, pink and black 55 30
1488 – 70c. multicoloured . . . 70 20
DESIGNS—VERT: 50c. Type **378** (completion of interior restoration); 60c. German House (75th anniv of Heemschut Conservation Society). HORIZ: 70c. Extract from foundation document (350th anniv of Utrecht University).

1986. Birth Centenary of Dr. Willem Drees (politician).
1489 **379** 55c. multicoloured . . . 55 20

380 Draughts as Biscuits in Saucer
381 Map of Flood Barrier

1986. 75th Anniversary of Royal Dutch Draughts Association (1490) and Royal Dutch Billiards Association (1491). Multicoloured.
1490 75c. Type **380** 65 65
1491 75c. Player in ball preparing to play 20 20

1986. Delta Project Completion. Multicoloured.
1492 65c. Type **381** 55 30
1493 75c. Flood barrier 65 20

382 Children listening to Music (experiencing)
383 Engagement Picture

1986. Child Welfare. Child and Culture.
1494 55c.+25c. Type **382** 70 65
1495 65c.+35c. Boy drawing (achieving) 75 45
1496 75c.+35c. Children at theatre (understanding) 85 20
MS1497 150 × 72 mm. Nos. 1494, 1495 × 2 and 1496 × 2 . . . . 3·50 3·00

1987. Golden Wedding of Princess Juliana and Prince Bernhard.
1498 **383** 75c. orange, black and gold 70 20

384 Block of Flats and Hut

1987. International Year of Shelter for the Homeless (65c.) and Centenary of Netherlands Salvation Army (75c.). Multicoloured.
1499 65c. Type **384** 55 30
1500 75c. Army officer, meeting and tramp 65 20

385 Eduard Douwes Dekker (Multatuli) and De Harmonie Club

1987. Writers' Death Annivs. Multicoloured.
1501 55c. Type **385** (centenary) 50 30
1502 75c. Constantijn Huygens and Scheveningseweg, The Hague (300th anniv) . . . 1·00 20

386 Steam Pumping Station, Nijerk

1987. Cultural Health and Social Welfare Funds. Industrial Buildings.
1503 **386** 55c.+30c. red, grey and black 90 80
1504 – 65c.+35c. grey, black and blue . . . . . . 1·00 80
1505 – 75c.+35c. grey, yellow and black . . . . . . 1·10 65

DESIGNS: 65c. Water tower, Deventer; 75c. Brass foundry, Joure.

387 Dance Theatre, Scheveningen (Rem Koolhaas)

1987. Europa. Architecture. Multicoloured.
1506 55c. Type **387** 50 30
1507 75c. Montessori School, Amsterdam (Herman Hertzberger) 65 20

388 Auction at Broek op Langedijk

1987. Centenary of Auction Sales (55, 75c.) and 150th Anniv of Groningen Agricultural Society (65c.). Multicoloured.
1508 55c. Type **388** 50 30
1509 65c. Groningen landscape and founders' signatures 70 30
1510 75c. Auction sale and clock 70 20

389 Telephone Care Circles
390 Map of Holland

1987. Dutch Red Cross. Multicoloured.
1511 55c.+30c. Type **389** 70 70
1512 65c.+35c. Red cross and hands (Welfare work) . . 80 60
1513 75c.+35c. Red cross and drip (Blood transfusion) 90 50

1987. 75th Anniv of Netherlands Municipalities Union.
1514 **390** 75c. multicoloured . . . 65 20

391 Noordeinde Palace, The Hague
392 Woodcutter

1987.
1515 **391** 65c. multicoloured . . . 55 10

1987. Child Welfare. Child and Profession. Mult.
1516 55c.+25c. Type **392** 65 70
1517 65c.+35c. Woman sailor . . 80 50
1518 75c.+35c. Woman pilot . . 90 30
MS1519 150 × 72 mm. Nos. 1516, 1517 × 2 and 1518 × 2 . . . . 3·50 3·25

393 Star
394 "Narcissus cyclamineus" "Peeping Tom" and Extract from "I Call You Flowers" (Jan Hanlo)

1987. Christmas.
1520 **393** 50c. red, blue and green 65 25
1521 50c. yellow, red and blue 65 25
1522 50c. red, blue and yellow 65 20
1523 50c. yellow, red and green 65 20
1524 50c. blue, green and red 65 20
The first colour described is that of the St. George's Cross.

1988. "Filacept" European Stamp Exhibition, The Hague (1st issue). Flowers. Multicoloured.
1525 55c.+55c. Type **394** 90 85
1526 75c.+70c. "Rosa gallica" "Versicolor" and "Roses" (Daan van Golden) . . . 1·10 1·10
1527 75c.+70c. Sea holly and 1270 map of The Hague 1·10 1·10
See also No. **MS**1542.

395 Quagga

1988. Cultural, Health and Social Welfare Funds. 150th Anniv of Natura Artis Magistra Zoological Society. Multicoloured.
1528 55c.+30c. Type **395** 65 70
1529 65c.+35c. American manatee 85 85
1530 75c.+35c. Orang-utan (vert) 90 50

396 Man's Shoulder
397 Traffic Scene with Lead Symbol crossed Through

1988. 75th Anniv of Netherlands Cancer Institute.
1531 **396** 75c. multicoloured . . . 60 20

1988. Europa. Transport. Multicoloured.
1532 55c. Type **397** (lead-free petrol) 50 20
1533 75c. Cyclists reflected in car wing mirror (horiz) . . . 85 20

398 Pendulum, Prism and Saturn

1988. 300th Anniv of England's Glorious Revolution. Multicoloured.
1534 65c. Type **398** 55 20
1535 75c. Queen Mary, King William III and 17th-century warship . . 70 20

399 "Cobra Cat" (Appel)
400 Sailing Ship and Map of Australia

1988. 40th Anniv of Founding of Cobra Painters Group. Multicoloured.
1536 55c. Type **399** 65 65
1537 65c. "Kite" (Corneille) . . . 65 65
1538 75c. "Stumbling Horse" (Constant) 70 35

1988. Bicentenary of Australian Settlement.
1539 **400** 75c. multicoloured . . . 70 20

401 Statue of Erasmus, Rotterdam
402 "Rain"

1988. 75th Anniv of Erasmus University, Rotterdam (1540) and Centenary of Concertgebouw Concert Hall and Orchestra (1541).
1540 **401** 75c. deep green and green 65 20
1541 – 75c. violet 65 20
DESIGN: No. 1541, Violin and Concertgebouw concert hall.

1988. "Filacept" European Stamp Exhibition, The Hague (2nd issue). Flowers. Sheet 144 × 62 mm.
MS1542 Nos. 1525/7 . . . . . . 3·50 3·25

1988. Child Welfare. Centenary of Royal Netherlands Swimming Federation. Children's drawings. Multicoloured.
1543 55c.+25c. Type **402** 65 55
1544 65c.+35c. "Getting Ready for the Race" 85 50
1545 75c.+35c. "Swimming Test" 85 35
MS1546 150 × 72 mm. Nos. 1543, 1544 × 2 and 1545 × 2 . . . . 3·50 3·50

403 Stars

1988. Christmas.
1547 **403** 50c. multicoloured . . . 55 10

404 Postal and Telecommunications Services

1989. Privatization of Netherlands PTT.
1548 **404** 75c. multicoloured . . . 70 20

405 "Solidarity"
406 Members' Flags

1989. Trade Unions. Multicoloured.
1549 55c. Type **405** 50 20
1550 75c. Talking mouths on hands 65 20

1989. 40th Anniv of NATO.
1551 **406** 75c. multicoloured . . . 65 20

407 Boier
408 Boy with Homemade Telephone

1989. Cultural, Health and Social Welfare Funds. Old Sailing Vessels.
1552 **407** 55c.+30c. green & blk 70 75
1553 – 65c.+35c. blue & black 85 75
1554 – 75c.+35c. brown & blk 1·00 75
DESIGNS: 65c. Fishing smack; 75c. Clipper.

1989. Europa. Children's Games. Multicoloured.
1555 55c. Type **408** 50 20
1556 75c. Girl with homemade telephone 75 20

409 Wheel on Rail
410 Boy with Ball and Diagram of Goal Scored in European Championship

1989. 150th Anniv of Netherlands' Railways. Mult.
1557 55c. Type **409** 50 30
1558 65c. Steam, electric and diesel locomotives 50 30
1559 75c. Diesel train, station clock and "The Kiss" (sculpture by Rodin) . . . 55 20

1989. Centenary of Royal Dutch Football Assn.
1560 **410** 75c. multicoloured . . . 55 20

411 Map
412 Right to Housing

1989. 150th Anniv of Division of Limburg between Netherlands and Belgium.
1561 **411** 75c. multicoloured . . . 55 20

1989. Child Welfare. 30th Anniv of Declaration of Rights of the Child. Multicoloured.
1562 55c.+25c. Type **412** 65 65
1563 65c.+35c. Right to food . . 70 55
1564 75c.+35c. Right to education 85 30
MS1565 150 × 72 mm. Nos. 1562, 1563 × 2 and 1564 × 2 . . . . 3·50 3·50

413 Candle

414 "Arms of Leiden" (tulip) and Plan of Gardens in 1601

1989. Christmas.
1566 **413** 50c. multicoloured . . . 55 10

1990. 400th Anniv of Hortus Botanicus (botanical gardens), Leiden.
1567 **414** 65c. multicoloured . . . 50 30

415 Pointer on Graduated Scale

416 "Self-portrait" (detail)

1990. Centenary of Labour Inspectorate.
1568 **415** 75c. multicoloured . . . 65 20

1990. Death Centenary of Vincent van Gogh (painter). Multicoloured.
1569 55c. Type **416** 60 20
1570 75c. "Green Vineyard" (detail) 70 20

417 Summer's Day

1990. Cultural, Health and Social Welfare Funds. The Weather. Multicoloured.
1571 55c.+30c. Type **417** 70 65
1572 65c.+35c. Clouds and isobars (vert) 90 75
1573 75c.+35c. Satellite weather picture (vert) . . . . . . 1·00 70

418 Zuiderkerk Ruins

1990. 50th Anniv of German Bombing of Rotterdam.
1574 **418** 55c. deep brown, brown and black 50 30
1575 – 65c. multicoloured . . . 60 20
1576 – 75c. multicoloured . . . 65 20
DESIGNS: 65c. City plan as stage; 75c. Girder and plans for future construction.

419 Postal Headquarters, Groningen, and Veere Post Office

420 Construction of Indiaman and Wreck of "Amsterdam"

1990. Europa. Post Office Buildings.
1577 – 55c. grey, mauve & brn 50 30
1578 **419** 75c. blue, green and grey 65 20
DESIGN: 55c. As Type **419** but inscr "Postkantoor Veere".

1990. 3rd Anniv of Dutch East India Company Ships Association (replica ship project) (1579) and "Sail 90", Amsterdam (1580). Multicoloured.
1579 65c. Type **420** 60 35
1580 75c. Crew manning yards on sailing ship 65 20

421 Queens Emma, Wilhelmina, Juliana and Beatrix

422 Flames, Telephone Handset and Number

1990. Netherlands Queens of the House of Orange.
1581 **421** 150c. multicoloured . . . 1·40 65

1990. Introduction of National Emergency Number.
1582 **422** 65c. multicoloured . . . 60 30

423 Girl riding Horse

424 Falling Snow

1990. Child Welfare. Hobbies. Multicoloured.
1583 55c.+25c. Type **423** 65 60
1584 65c.+35c. Girl at computer 85 50
1585 75c.+35c. Young philatelist 90 40
MS1586 150 × 71 mm. Nos. 1583, 1584 × 2 and 1585 × 2 . . . . 4·25 3·50

1990. Christmas.
1587 **424** 50c. multicoloured . . . 45 10

425 Industrial Chimneys, Exhaust Pipes and Aerosol Can (Air Pollution)

1991. Environmental Protection. Multicoloured.
1588 55c. Type **425** 60 30
1589 65c. Outfall pipes and chemicals (sea pollution) 65 30
1590 75c. Agricultural chemicals, leaking drums and household landfill waste (soil pollution) 70 20

426 German Raid on Amsterdam Jewish Quarter and Open Hand

1991. 50th Anniv of Amsterdam General Strike.
1591 **426** 75c. multicoloured . . . 65 20

427 Princess Beatrix and Prince Claus on Wedding Day

428 Queen Beatrix

1991. Royal Silver Wedding Anniversary. Mult.
1592 75c. Type **427** 70 20
1593 75c. Queen Beatrix and Prince Claus on horseback 70 20

1991. (a) Ordinary gum.
1594 **428** 75c. deep green & green 1·40 30
1595 80c. brown & lt brown 50 10
1597 90c. blue 65 20
1598 1g. violet 70 20
1599 1g.10 blue 85 20
1600 1g.30 blue and violet 90 20
1601 1g.40 green and olive 90 15
1601a 1g.50 green . . . . . . 5·50 1·60
1602 1g.60 purple and mauve 1·00 20
1603 2g. brown . . . . . . 1·10 20
1603a 2g.50 purple . . . . . 2·50 85
1604 3g. blue . . . . 2·00 20
1605 5g. red . . . . 1·75 20
1706 7g.50 violet . . . . . . 5·25 1·40
1708 10g. green . . . . . . 6·75 65

(b) Self-adhesive gum.
1606 **428** 1g. violet . . . . 1·00 80
1607 1g.10 blue . . . . . . 1·10 90
1608 1g.45 green . . . . . . 1·25 1·10
1609 2g.50 purple . . . . . 2·50 2·10
1609a 5g. red . . . . 5·25 4·50

429 "Meadow" Farm, Wartena, Friesland

430 Gerard Philips's Experiments with Carbon Filaments

1991. Cultural, Health and Social Welfare Funds. Traditional Farmhouses. Multicoloured.
1610 55c.+30c. Type **429** 85 80
1611 65c.+35c. "T-house" farm, Kesteren, Gelderland . . 90 80
1612 75c.+35c. "Courtyard" farm, Nuth, Limburg . . 1·00 80

1991. 75th Anniv of Netherlands Standards Institute (65c.) and Centenary of Philips Organization (others). Multicoloured.
1615 55c. Type **430** 60 35
1616 65c. Wiring to Standard NEN 1010 (horiz) 65 20
1617 75c. Laser beams reading video disc 70 20

431 Man raising Hat to Space

432 Sticking Plaster over Medal

1991. Europa. Europe in Space. Multicoloured.
1618 55c. Type **431** 55 40
1619 75c. Ladders stretching into space 70 20

1991. 75th Anniv of Nijmegen International Four Day Marches.
1620 **432** 80c. multicoloured . . . 65 20

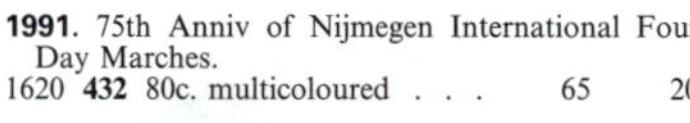

433 Jacobus Hendericus van't Hoff

1991. Dutch Nobel Prize Winners (1st series). Multicoloured.
1621 60c. Type **433** (chemistry, 1901) 60 35
1622 70c. Pieter Zeeman (physics, 1902) 65 30
1623 80c. Tobias Michael Carel Asser (peace, 1911) . . . 70 20
See also Nos. 1690/2 and 1773/5.

434 Children and Open Book

1991. Centenary (1992) of Public Libraries in the Netherlands.
1624 **434** 70c. drab, black & mauve 65 25
1625 – 80c. multicoloured . . . 70 20
DESIGN: 80c. Books on shelf.

435 Girls with Doll and Robot

436 "Greetings Cards keep People in Touch"

1991. Child Welfare. Outdoor Play. Multicoloured.
1626 60c.+30c. Type **435** 70 40
1627 70c.+35c. Bicycle race . . . 1·00 90
1628 80c.+40c. Hide and seek . . 90 40
MS1629 144 × 75 mm. Nos. 1626 × 4 and 1638 × 2 . . . . 5·00 4·50

1991. Christmas.
1630 **436** 55c. multicoloured . . . 45 10

437 Artificial Lightning, Microchip and Oscilloscope

1992. 150th Anniv of Delft University of Technology.
1631 **437** 60c. multicoloured . . . 55 30

438 Extract from Code

1992. Implementation of Property Provisions of New Civil Code.
1632 **438** 80c. multicoloured . . . 70 20

439 Volleyball

1992. Winter Olympic Games, Albertville and Summer Games, Barcelona. Sheet 125 × 72 mm containing T **439** and similar vert designs. Multicoloured.
MS1633 80c. Type **439**; 80c. Putting the shot and rowing; 80c. Speed skating and rowing; 80c. Hockey 3·25 2·75

440 Tulips ("Mondrian does not like Green")

1992. "Expo '92" World's Fair, Seville. Mult.
1634 70c. Type **440** 65 30
1635 80c. "Netherland Expo '92" 70 20

441 Tasman's Map of Staete Landt (New Zealand)

1992. 350th Anniv of Discovery of Tasmania and New Zealand by Abel Tasman.
1636 **441** 70c. multicoloured . . . 65 30

442 Yellow and Purple Flowers

443 Geometric Planes

1992. Cultural, Health and Social Welfare Funds. "Floriade" Flower Show, Zoetermeer. Mult.
1637 60c.+30c. Water lilies . . . 90 80
1638 70c.+35c. Orange and purple flowers . . . . . 1·10 90
1639 80c.+40c. Type **442** . . . 1·25 65

1992. 150th Anniv of Royal Association of Netherlands Architects (60c.) and Inauguration of New States General Lower House (80c.). Mult.
1643 60c. Type **443** 55 30
1644 80c. Atrium and blue sky (symbolizing sending of information into society) 70 20

444 Globe and Columbus

445 Moneta (Goddess of Money)

1992. Europa. 500th Anniv of Discovery of America by Columbus.
1645 **444** 60c. multicoloured . . . 65 30
1646 – 80c. black, mauve & yellow 85 20
DESIGN—VERT: 80c. Galleon.

1992. Centenary of Royal Netherlands Numismatics Society.
1647 **445** 70c. multicoloured . . . 65 25

446 Teddy Bear wearing Stethoscope

447 List of Relatives and Friends

1992. Centenary of Netherlands Paediatrics Society.
1648 **446** 80c. multicoloured . . . 70 20

1992. 50th Anniv of Departure of First Deportation Train from Westerbork Concentration Camp.
1649 **447** 70c. multicoloured . . . 65 25

448 Cross

1992. 125th Anniv of Netherlands Red Cross. Multicoloured.
1650 60c.+30c. Type **448** 90 80
1651 70c.+35c. Supporting injured person . . . . 1·10 90
1652 80c.+40c. Red cross on dirty bandage . . . . 1·25 65

449 "United Europe" and European Community Flag

450 Queen Beatrix on Official Birthday, 1992, and at Investiture

1992. European Single Market.
1656 **449** 80c. multicoloured . . . 70 20

1992. 12½ Years since Accession to the Throne of Queen Beatrix.
1657 **450** 80c. multicoloured . . . 70 20

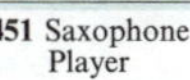

451 Saxophone Player

452 Poinsettia

1992. Child Welfare. Child and Music. Mult.
1658 60c.+30c. Type **451** 85 50
1659 70c.+35c. Piano player . . . 90 60
1660 80c.+40c. Double bass player . . . . 1·00 75
MS1661 144 × 75 mm. Nos. 1658 × 3, 1659 × 2 and 1660 . . . 4·50 4·25

1992. Christmas.
1662 **452** 55c. multicoloured (centre of flower silver) 45 10
1663 55c. multicoloured (centre red) 45 10

453 Cycling

1993. Centenary of Netherlands Cycle and Motor Industry Association.
1664 **453** 70c. multicoloured . . . 65 35
1665 – 80c. brown, grey & yell 70 20
DESIGN: 80c. Car.

454 Collages

455 Mouth to Mouth Resuscitation

1993. Greetings Stamps. Multicoloured.
1666 70c. Type **454** 60 20
1667 70c. Collages (different) . . 60 20

1993. Anniversaries. Multicoloured.
1668 70c. Type **455** (centenary of Royal Netherlands First Aid Association) 65 35
1669 80c. Pests on leaf (75th anniv of Wageningen University of Agriculture) 70 20
1670 80c. Lead driver and horses (bicentenary of Royal Horse Artillery) 70 20

456 Emblems

1993. 150th Anniv of Royal Dutch Notaries Association. Each red and violet.
1671 80c. Type **456** ("150 Jaar" reading up) 70 20
1672 80c. As Type **456** but emblems inverted and "150 Jaar" reading down 70 20
Nos. 1671/2 were issued together in horizontal tete-beche pairs, each pair forming a composite design.

457 Large White

458 Elderly Couple

1993. Butterflies. Multicoloured.
1673 70c. Pearl-bordered fritillary 70 35
1674 80c. Large tortoiseshell . . . 80 20
1675 90c. Type **457** 90 80
MS1676 104 × 71 mm. 160c. Common blue . . . . 1·90 1·90

1993. Cultural, Health and Social Welfare Funds. Senior Citizens' Independence.
1677 70c.+35c. Type **458** . . . . 1·10 1·10
1678 70c.+35c. Elderly man . . . 1·10 1·10
1679 80c.+40c. Elderly woman with dog . . . . 1·25 85

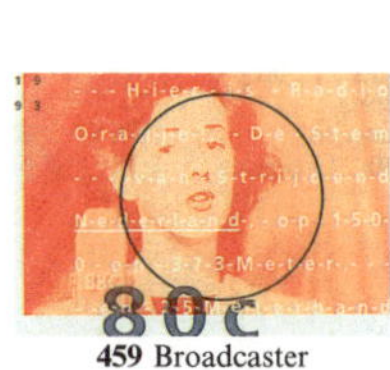

459 Broadcaster

460 Sports Pictograms

1993. Radio Orange (Dutch broadcasts from London during Second World War). Mult.
1683 80c. Type **459** 70 20
1684 80c. Man listening to radio in secret 70 20

1993. 2nd European Youth Olympic Days. Mult.
1685 70c. Type **460** 70 30
1686 80c. Sports pictograms (different) 80 20

461 "The Embodiment of Unity" (Wessel Couzijn)

462 Johannes Diderik van der Waals (Physics, 1910)

1993. Europa. Contemporary Art. Multicoloured.
1687 70c. Type **461** 70 35
1688 80c. Architectonic sculpture (Per Kirkeby) 80 20
1689 160c. Sculpture (Naum Gabo) (vert) . . . . . . 1·40 1·10

1993. Dutch Nobel Prize Winners (2nd series).
1690 **462** 70c. blue, black and red 65 30
1691 – 80c. mauve, black & red 70 20
1692 – 90c. multicoloured . . . 90 75
DESIGNS: 80c. Willem Einthoven (medicine, 1924); 90c. Christiaan Eijkman (medicine, 1929).

463 Pen and Pencils

1993. Letter Writing Campaign. Multicoloured.
1693 80c. Type **463** 65 20
1694 80c. Envelope 65 20

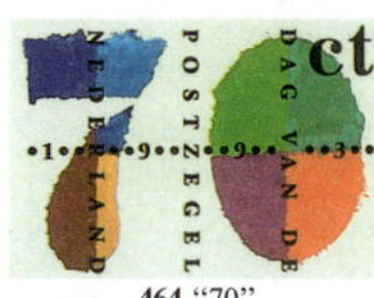

464 "70"

1993. Stamp Day (70c.) and Netherlands PTT (80c.). Multicoloured.
1695 70c. Type **464** 65 30
1696 80c. Dish aerial and dove carrying letter 70 20

465 Child in Newspaper Hat

1993. Child Welfare. Child and the Media. Mult.
1697 70c.+35c. Type **465** 90 65
1698 70c.+35c. Elephant using headphones 90 65
1699 80c.+40c. Television . . . . 1·10 50
MS1700 143 × 75 mm. Nos. 1697/99, each × 2 . . . . 5·75 4·00

466 Candle

1993. Christmas. Multicoloured.
1711 55c. Type **466** 45 10
1712 55c. Fireworks 45 10
Both designs have a number of punched holes.

467 "Composition"

1994. 50th Death Anniv of Piet Mondriaan (artist). Multicoloured.
1713 70c. "The Red Mill" (detail) 65 30
1714 80c. Type **467** 70 20
1715 90c. "Broadway Boogie Woogie" (detail) 90 60

468 Barnacle Goose

1994. "Fepapost 94" European Stamp Exhibition, The Hague. Multicoloured.
1716 70c.+60c. Type **468** . . . . 1·00 85
1717 80c.+70c. Bluethroat . . . . 1·10 1·25
1718 90c.+80c. Garganey . . . . 1·25 1·10

469 Downy Rose

1994. Wild Flowers. Multicoloured.
1719 70c. Type **469** 65 30
1720 80c. Daisies 70 20
1721 90c. Wood forgetmenot . . 90 75
MS1722 71 × 50 mm. 160c. Orange lily . . . . 1·90 1·75

470 Airplane

1994. 75th Aircraft Industry Anniversaries.
1723 **470** 80c. blue and black . . . 70 20
1724 – 80c. grey, red and black 70 20
1725 – 80c. multicoloured . . . 70 20
DESIGNS: No. 1723, Type **470** (KLM (Royal Dutch Airlines)); 1724, Plan and outline of aircraft and clouds (Royal Netherlands Fokker Aircraft Industries); 1725, Airplane and clouds (National Aerospace Laboratory).

471 Woman using Telephone

472 Eisinga's Planetarium

1994. Cultural, Health and Social Welfare Funds. Senior Citizens' Security. Multicoloured.
1726 70c.+35c. Type **471** 90 90
1727 80c.+40c. Man using telephone . . . . 1·10 1·10
1728 90c.+35c. Man using telephone (different) . . . 1·25 1·10

1994. Anniversaries. Multicoloured.
1732 80c. Type **472** (250th birth anniv of Eise Eisinga) . . 70 20
1733 90c. Astronaut and boot print on Moon surface (25th anniv of first manned Moon landing) 1·10 65

473 Players Celebrating

1994. World Cup Football Championship, U.S.A.
1734 **473** 80c. multicoloured . . . 70 30

474 Stock Exchange

1994. Quotation of Netherlands PTT (KPN) on Stock Exchange.
1735 **474** 80c. multicoloured . . . 70 20

475 Road Sign, Car and Bicycle

1994. Anniversaries and Events. Multicoloured.
1736 70c. Type **475** (centenary of provision of road signs by Netherlands Motoring Association) 65 40
1737 80c. Equestrian sports (World Equestrian Games, The Hague) . . . 70 20

476 Footprint and Sandal

1994. Second World War. Multicoloured.
1738 80c. Type **476** (war in Netherlands Indies, 1941–45) 70 20
1739 90c. Soldier, children and aircraft dropping paratroops (50th anniv of Operation Market Garden (Battle of Arnhem)) (vert) 90 60

477 Brandaris Lighthouse, Terschelling

1994. Lighthouses. Multicoloured.
1740 70c. Type **477** 65 40
1741 80c. Ameland (vert) 70 20
1742 90c. Vlieland (vert) 90 75

1994. "Fepapost '94" European Stamp Exhibition, The Hague (2nd issue). Sheet 144 × 62 mm.
MS1743 Nos. 1716/18 plus 3 labels 3·30 3·50

478 Decorating

479 Star and Christmas Tree

1994. Child Welfare. "Together". Multicoloured.
1744 70c.+35c. Type **478** 90 65
1745 80c.+40c. Girl on swing knocking fruit off tree (vert) . . . . 1·10 60
1746 90c.+35c. Girl helping boy onto playhouse roof (vert) 1·10 1·10
MS1747 144 × 75mm. No. 1744 × 2, 1745 × 3 and 1746 . . . . . . 6·25 5·25

1994. Christmas. Multicoloured.
1748 55c. Type **479** 45 10
1749 55c. Candle and star 45 10

480 Flying Cow

1995.
1750 **480** 100c. multicoloured . . . 1·10 30

481 "Prayer" (detail)

1995. Anniversary and Events.
1751 **481** 80c. multicoloured . . . 70 30
1752 – 80c. multicoloured . . . 70 30
1753 – 80c. black and red . . . 70 30
DESIGNS—VERT: No. 1751, Type **481** (50th death anniv of Hendrik Werkman (graphic designer); 1752, "Mesdag Panorama" (detail) (re-opening of Mesdag Museum). HORIZ: No. 1753, Mauritius 1847 2d. "POST OFFICE" stamp (purchase of remaining mint example in private hands by PTT Museum).

482 Joriz Ivens (documentary maker)

1995. Year of the Film (centenary of motion pictures). Multicoloured.
1754 70c. Type **482** 65 30
1755 80c. Scene from "Turkish Delight" 70 20

483 Mahler and Score of 7th Symphony

1995. Mahler Festival, Amsterdam.
1756 **483** 80c. black and blue . . . 70 30

484 Dates and Acronym

1995. Centenaries. Multicoloured.
1757 80c. Type **484** (Netherlands Institute of Chartered Accountants) 70 20
1758 80c. Builders, bricklayer's trowel and saw (Netherlands Association of Building Contractors) 70 20

485 Postcard from Indonesia

486 "40 45"

1995. Cultural, Health and Social Welfare Funds. Mobility of the Elderly. Multicoloured.
1759 70c.+35c. Type **485** 90 85
1760 80c.+40c. Couple reflected in mirror . . . . 1·10 85
1761 100c.+45c. Couple with granddaughter at zoo . . 1·25 1·25
MS1762 144 × 75 mm. Nos. 1759 × 2, 1760 × 3 and 1761 . . . 7·25 6·50

1995. 50th Anniversaries. Multicoloured.
1763 80c. Type **486** (end of Second World War) . . . 70 30
1764 80c. "45 95" (liberation) . . 70 30
1765 80c. "50" (U.N.O.) 70 30

487 Birthday Cake and Signs of the Zodiac

488 Scout

1995. Birthday Greetings.
1766 **487** 70c. multicoloured . . . 1·75 30

1995. Events. Multicoloured.
1767 70c. Type **488** (World Scout Jamboree, Dronten) . . . 70 30
1768 80c. Amsterdam harbour ("Sail '95" and finish of Tall Ships Race) (horiz) 70 20

489 Common Kestrel

490 Petrus Debye (Chemistry, 1936)

1995. Birds of Prey. Multicoloured.
1769 70c. Type **489** 65 30
1770 80c. Face of hen harrier (horiz) 70 20
1771 100c. Red kite (horiz) . . . 90 75
MS1772 72 × 50 mm. 160c. Honey buzzard . . . . 1·90 1·75

1995. Dutch Nobel Prize Winners (3rd series). Multicoloured.
1773 80c. Type **490** 70 20
1774 80c. Frederik Zernike (Physics, 1953) 70 20
1775 80c. Jan Tinbergen (Economics, 1969) 70 20

491 Eduard Jacobs and Jean-Louis Pisuisse

1995. Centenary of Dutch Cabaret. Multicoloured.
1776 70c. Type **491** 70 30
1777 80c. Wim Kan and Freek de Jonge . . . . 1·10 20

492 "The Schoolteacher" (Leonie Ensing)

493 Children with Stars

1995. Child Welfare. "Children and Fantasy". Children's Computer Drawings. Multicoloured.
1778 70c.+35c. "Dino" (Sjoerd Stegeman) (horiz) 85 85
1779 80c.+40c. Type **492** . . . . 1·00 85
1780 100c.+50c. "Children and Colours" (Marcel Jansen) (horiz) . . . . 1·25 1·40
MS1781 144 × 74 mm. Nos. 1778 × 2, 1779 × 3 and 1780 . . . 5·25 4·50

1995. Christmas. Self-adhesive.
1782 **493** 55c. red, yellow and black 60 10
1783 – 55c. blue, yellow and black 60 10
DESIGN: No. 1783, Children looking at star through window.

494 "Woman in Blue reading a Letter"

495 Trowel, Daffodil Bulb and Glove

1996. Johannes Vermeer Exhibition, Washington and The Hague. Details of his Paintings. Mult.
1784 70c. "Lady writing a Letter with her Maid" 65 40
1785 80c. "The Love Letter" . . 70 30
1786 100c. Type **494** . . . . . . 1·10 90
MS1787 144 × 75 mm. Nos. 1784/6 2·50 2·25

1996. Spring Flowers. Multicoloured.
1788 70c. Type **495** 65 40
1789 80c. Tulips "kissing" woman 70 20
1790 100c. Snake's-head fritillary (detail of painting, Charles Mackintosh) . . . 1·75 85
MS1791 72 × 50 mm. 160c. Crocuses 1·75 1·50

496 Putting up "MOVED" sign

497 Swimming

1996. Change of Address Stamp.
1792 **496** 70c. multicoloured . . . 1·00 40

For 80c. self-adhesive version of this design see No. 1826.

1996. Cultural, Health and Social Welfare Funds. The Elderly in the Community. Multicoloured.
1793 70c.+35c. Type **497** 85 80
1794 80c.+40c. Grandad bottle-feeding baby . . . . . . 1·00 90
1795 100c.+50c. Playing piano . . 1·40 1·25
MS1796 144 × 75 mm. Nos. 1793 × 2, 1794 × 3 and 1795 . . . 6·00 6·50

498 Beside Car

1996. Heer Bommel (cartoon character). Sheet 108 × 50 mm containing T **498** and similar horiz design. Multicoloured.
MS1797 70c. Type **498**; 80c. Reading letter . . . . 1·75 1·50

499 Cycling

1996. Tourism. Multicoloured.
1798 70c. Type **499** 65 10
1799 70c. Paddling in sea 65 20
1800 80c. Traditional architecture, Amsterdam 70 20
1801 100c. Windmills, Zaanse Schand Open-Air Museum 85 30

500 Parade in Traditional Costumes

1996. Bicentenary of Province of North Brabant.
1802 **500** 80c. multicoloured . . . 70 20

501 Lighting Olympic Torch

502 Erasmus Bridge

1996. Sporting Events. Multicoloured.
1803 70c. Type **501** (Olympic Games, Atlanta) 65 20
1804 80c. Flag and cyclists (Tour de France cycling championship) 70 20
1805 100c. Player, ball and Wembley Stadium (European Football Championship, England) 85 55
1806 160c. Olympic rings and athlete on starting block (Olympic Games, Atlanta) 1·25 55

1996. Bridges and Tunnels. Multicoloured.
1807 80c. Type **502** 65 20
1808 80c. Wijker Tunnel (horiz) . 65 20
1809 80c. Martinus Nijhoff Bridge (horiz) 65 20

503 Children in School Uniforms

504 Bert and Ernie

1996. 50th Anniv of UNICEF. Multicoloured.
1810 70c. Type **503** 65 20
1811 80c. Girl carrying platter on head 65 20

1996. Sesame Street (children's television programme). Multicoloured.
1812 70c. Type **504** 65 20
1813 80c. Bears holding Big Bird's foot 60 15

505 Petrus Plancius

506 Books and Baby

1996. 16th-century Voyages of Discovery.
1814 **505** 70c. black, yellow and red 60 40
1815 – 80c. multicoloured . . . 65 20
1816 – 80c. multicoloured . . . 65 20
1817 – 100c. multicoloured . . . 65 65
DESIGNS: No. 1815, Cornelis de Houtman; 1816, Willem Barentsz; 1817, Mahu en De Cordes.

1996. Child Welfare. Multicoloured.
1818 70c.+35c. Type **506** 65 75
1819 80c.+40c. Animals and boy 90 85
1820 80c.+40c. Tools and girl . . 90 60
MS1821 75 × 144 mm. Nos. 1818/20, each × 2 . . . . 5·25 4·50

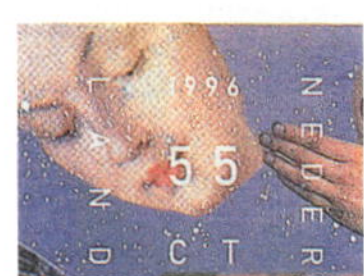
507 Woman's Face and Hand

1996. Christmas. Multicoloured. Self-adhesive.
1822 55c. Type **507** 50 20
1823 55c. Woman's eyes and man shouting 50 20
1824 55c. Bird's wing, hands and detail of man's face . . . 50 20
1825 55c. Men's faces and bird's wing 50 20
Nos. 1822/5 were issued together, se-tenant, forming a composite design.

1997. Change of Address Stamp. Self-adhesive.
1826 **496** 80c. multicoloured . . . 60 30
No. 1826 was intended for use by people moving house.

508 Numeral on Envelope with Top Flap

1997. Business Stamps. Multicoloured. Self-adhesive.
1827 80c. Type **508** 50 20
1828 160c. Numeral on envelope with side flap . . . . . . 1·00 40

509 Skaters

1997. 15th Eleven Cities Skating Race.
1829 **509** 80c. multicoloured . . . 65 20

510 Heart

1997. Greetings Stamps.
1830 **510** 80c. multicoloured . . . 50 30
The price quoted for No. 1830 is for an example with the heart intact. The heart can be scratched away to reveal different messages.

511 Pony

1997. Nature and the Environment. Multicoloured.
1831 80c. Type **511** 65 20
1832 100c. Cow 90 65
MS1833 72 × 50 mm. 160c. Sheep 1·60 1·40

512 Suske, Wiske, Lambik and Aunt Sidonia

1997. Suske and Wiske (cartoon by Willy Vandersteen). Multicoloured.
1834 80c. Type **512** 50 20
MS1835 108 × 50 mm. 80c. Wilbur; 80c. Type **512** . . . . 1·60 1·40

513 Rosebud

1997. Cultural, Health and Social Welfare Funds. The Elderly and their Image. Multicoloured.
1836 80c.+40c. Type **513** 90 80
1837 80c.+40c. Rose stem 90 80
1838 80c.+40c. Rose 90 80
MS1839 144 × 75 mm. Nos. 1836/8, each × 2 . . . . 5·50 5·00

514 Birthday Cake

1997. Greetings Stamps. Multicoloured.
1840 80c. Type **514** 50 20
1841 80c. Cup of coffee, glasses of wine, candles, writing letter, and amaryllis . . . 50 20
See also No. 1959.

515 "REKENKAMER ..." (550th anniv of Court of Audit)
516 Clasped Hands over Red Cross

1997. Anniversaries.
1842 **515** 80c. multicoloured . . . 65 25
1843 – 80c. red, yellow and black 65 25
1844 – 80c. red, black and blue 65 25
DESIGNS—50th anniv of Marshall Plan (post-war American aid for Europe): No. 1843, Map of Europe; 1844, Star and stripes.

1997. Red Cross.
1845 **516** 80c.+40c. mult . . . . . 1·10 1·10

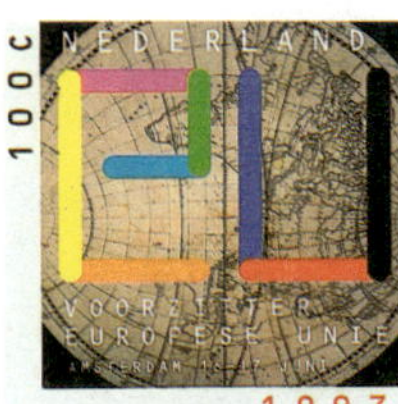

517 "eu" and Globe

1997. European Council of Ministers' Summit, Amsterdam.
1846 **517** 100c. multicoloured . . . 1·00 40

518 Children playing in Boat

1997. Water Activities. Multicoloured.
1847 80c. Type **518** 60 25
1848 1g. Skutsje (sailing barges) race, Friesland 80 40

519 "vernuft"

1997. Anniversaries. Multicoloured.
1849 **519** 80c. ultramarine and blue 60 25
1850 – 80c. ultramarine and blue 60 25
1851 – 80c. multicoloured . . . 60 30
1852 – 80c. multicoloured . . . 60 25
DESIGNS: No. 1849, Type **519** (150th anniv of Royal Institute of Engineers); 1850, "adem" (centenary of Netherlands Asthma Centre, Davos, Switzerland); 1851, Flower (centenary of Florens College (horticultural college) and 125th anniv of Royal Botanical and Horticultural Society); 1852, Pianist accompanying singer (birth bicentenary of Franz Schubert (composer)).

520 "Nederland80"

1997. Youth. Multicoloured.
1853 **520** 80c. red and blue 50 25
1854 – 80c. multicoloured . . . 50 25
DESIGN: No. 1854, "NEDERLAND80" in style of computer games giving appearance of three-dimensional block on race track.

521 Stork with Bundle

1997. New Baby Stamp. Self-adhesive gum.
1855 **521** 80c. multicoloured . . . 50 30
See also Nos. 1960, 2120 amd 2189.

522 "Little Red Riding Hood"
523 Heads and Star

1997. Child Welfare. Fairy Tales. Multicoloured.
1856 80c.+40c. Type **522** . . . . 1·00 65
1857 80c.+40c. Man laying loaves on ground ("Tom Thumb") . . . . 1·00 65
1858 80c.+40c. Woodman with bottle ("Genie in the Bottle") . . . . 1·00 65
MS1859 144 × 75 mm. Nos. 1856/8, each × 2 . . . . 6·00 4·75

1997. Christmas. Multicoloured, colour of background given.
1860 **523** 55c. yellow 50 25
1861 55c. blue 50 25
1862 – 55c. orange 50 25
1863 – 55c. red 50 25
1864 – 55c. green 50 25
1865 **523** 55c. green 50 25
DESIGN: Nos. 1862/4, Heads and heart.

524 Light across Darkness
525 Cow and "Ship" Tiles

1998. Bereavement Stamp.
1866 **524** 80c. blue 50 35

1998. Delft Faience.
1867 **525** 100c. multicoloured . . . 65 35
1868 – 160c. blue . . . . 1·00 90
DESIGN: 160c. Ceramic tile showing boy standing on head.

526 Strawberries in Bloom (Spring)
527 Handshake

1998. The Four Seasons. Multicoloured.
1869 80c. Type **526** 65 65
1870 80c. Strawberry, flan and strawberry plants (Summer) 65 65
1871 80c. Bare trees and pruning diagram (Winter) 65 65
1872 80c. Orchard and apple (Autumn) 65 65

1998. Anniversaries. Multicoloured.
1873 80c. Type **527** (350th anniv of Treaty of Munster) . . 60 40
1874 80c. Statue of Johan Thorbecke (politician) (150th anniv of Constitution) 60 40
1875 80c. Child on swing (50th anniv of Declaration of Human Rights) 60 40

528 Bride and Groom

529 Shopping List

1998. Wedding Stamp. Self-adhesive gum.
1876 **528** 80c. multicoloured . . . 50 35
See also No. 1961.

1998. Cultural, Health and Social Welfare Funds. Care and the Elderly.
1877 80c.+40c. Type **529** . . . . 1·00 95
1878 80c.+40c. Sweet . . . . . . 1·00 95
1879 80c.+40c. Training shoe . . 1·00 95
MS1880 144 × 75 mm. Nos. 1877/9, each × 2 . . . . 6·00 5·50

530 Letters blowing in Wind

1998. Letters to the Future.
1881 **530** 80c. multicoloured . . . 60 40

531 Customers

1998. Centenary of Rabobank.
1882 **531** 80c. yellow, green and blue 60 40

532 Goalkeeper catching Boot

1998. Sport. Multicoloured.
1883 80c. Type **532** (World Cup Football Championship, France) 50 40
1884 80c. Family hockey team (centenary of Royal Netherlands Hockey Federation) (35 × 24 mm) 60 30

533 Map of Friesland, c. 1600

1998. 500th Anniv of Central Administration of Friesland.
1885 **533** 80c. multicoloured . . . 60 40

534 River Defences

1998. Bicentenary of Directorate-General of Public Works and Water Management. Multicoloured.
1886 80c. Type **534** 60 40
1887 1g. Sea defences 80 55

535 "tnt post groep"

1998. Separation of Royal Netherlands PTT into TNT Post Groep and KPN NV (telecommunications).
1888 **535** 80c. black, blue and red . . . 60 45
1889 – 80c. black, blue and green 60 45
DESIGN: No. 1889, "kpn nv".
Nos. 1888/9 were issued together, se-tenant, forming a composite design of the complete "160".

536 Books and Keyboard

1998. Cultural Anniversaries. Multicoloured.
1890 80c. Type **536** (bicentenary of National Library) . . . 60 40
1891 80c. Maurits Escher (graphic artist, birth centenary) looking at his mural "Metamorphose" in The Hague Post Office (vert) 60 40
1892 80c. Simon Vestdijk (writer, birth centenary) and page from "Fantoches" (vert) 60 40

537 Queen Wilhelmina

1998. Royal Centenaries. Sheet 144 × 75 mm containing T **537** and similar vert design. Multicoloured.
MS1893 80c. Type **537** (coronation); 80c. Gilded Coach . . . . . . 1·60 1·40

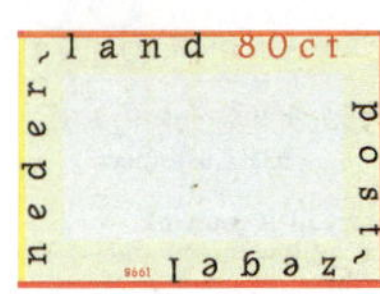

538 "land 80 ct"

1998. Greetings Stamps. Multicoloured. Self-adhesive.
1894 80c. Type **538** (top of frame red) 70 50
1895 80c. "80 ct post" (top of frame mauve) 70 50
1896 80c. Type **538** (top of frame orange) 70 50
1897 80c. "80 ct post" (top of frame orange) 70 50
1898 80c. Type **538** (top of frame yellow) 70 50
The part of the frame used for identification purposes is above the face value.
Nos. 1894/8 were only available in sheetlets of ten stamps and 20 labels (five stamps and ten labels on each side of the card). It was intended that the sender should insert the appropriate greetings label into the rectangular space on each stamp before use.

539 Rabbits

1998. Domestic Pets. Multicoloured.
1899 80c. Type **539** 60 45
1900 80c. Drent partridge dog . . 50 45
1901 80c. Kittens 50 40

540 Cathy and Jeremy writing a Letter

1998. 25th Anniv of Jack, Jacky and the Juniors (comic strip characters).
1902 80c. Type **540** 50 40
MS1903 108 × 50 mm. 80c. Type **540**; 80c. Posting letter 1·40 1·25

541 St. Nicholas on Horseback

1998. Child Welfare. Celebrations. Multicoloured.
1904 80c.+40c. Type **541** . . . . 1·00 70
1905 80c.+40c. Making birthday cake . . . . 1·00 70
1906 80c.+40c. Carnival parade 1·00 70
MS1907 144 × 75 mm. Nos. 1904/6, each × 2 . . . . 6·00 4·75

542 Hare and Snowball

543 House and Tree on Snowball

1998. Christmas. Self-adhesive.
1908 **542** 55c. blue, red and black 75 35
1909 – 55c. multicoloured . . . 75 35
1910 – 55c. blue, red and black 75 35
1911 – 55c. multicoloured . . . 75 35
1912 – 55c. blue, red and black 75 35
1913 – 55c. green, blue and red 75 35
1914 – 55c. green, blue and red 75 35
1915 – 55c. green, blue and red 75 35
1916 – 55c. green, blue and red 75 35
1917 – 55c. green, blue and red 75 35
1918 – 55c. blue, green and red 75 35
1919 – 55c. red, green and black 75 35
1920 – 55c. blue, green and red 75 35
1921 – 55c. green, red and black 75 35
1922 – 55c. blue, green and red 75 35
1923 – 55c. blue, green and red 75 35
1924 – 55c. blue, green and red 75 35
1925 – 55c. blue, green and red 75 35
1926 – 55c. blue, green and red 75 35
1927 – 55c. blue, green and red 75 35
DESIGNS: No. 1909, House and snowball; 1910, Dove and snowball; 1911, Christmas tree and snowball; 1912, Reindeer and snowball; 1913, Hare; 1914, House; 1915, Dove; 1916, Christmas tree; 1917, Reindeer; 1918, House and hare; 1919, House and heart; 1920, Dove and house; 1921, Christmas tree and house; 1922, House and reindeer; 1923, Christmas tree and hare; 1924, Christmas tree and house; 1925, Christmas tree and dove; 1926, Christmas tree and heart; 1927, Christmas tree and reindeer.

1999. Make-up Rate Stamp.
1928 **543** 25c. red and black . . . 25 20

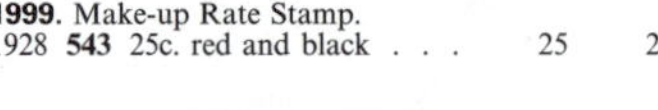

544 Euro Coin

1999. Introduction of the Euro (European currency).
1929 **544** 80c. multicoloured . . . 60 30

545 Pillar Box, 1850

1999. Bicentenary of Netherlands Postal Service.
1930 **545** 80c. multicoloured . . . 60 60

546 Richard Krajicek serving

547 White Spoonbill

1999. Centenary of Royal Dutch Lawn Tennis Federation.
1931 **546** 80c. multicoloured . . . 50 45

1999. Protection of Bird and Migrating Waterfowl. Multicoloured.
1932 80c. Type **547** (centenary of Dutch Bird Protection Society) 60 40
1933 80c. Section of globe and arctic terns (African–Eurasian Waterbird Agreement) 60 40

548 Haarlemmerhout in Autumn

549 Woman

1999. Parks during the Seasons. Multicoloured.
1934 80c. Type **548** 50 60
1935 80c. Sonsbeek in winter . . 50 60
1936 80c. Weerribben in summer 50 60
1937 80c. Keukenhof in spring . . 50 60

1999. Cultural, Health and Social Welfare Funds. International Year of the Elderly. Multicoloured.
1938 80c.+40c. Type **549** . . . . 1·00 95
1939 80c.+40c. Man (green background) . . . . . . 1·00 95
1940 80c.+40c. Man (blue background) . . . . . . 1·00 95
MS1941 144 × 75 mm. Nos. 1938/40, each × 2 . . . . 5·25 4·75

550 Lifeboats on Rough Sea

551 "I Love Stamps"

1999. Water Anniversaries. Multicoloured.
1942 80c. Type **550** (175th Anniv of Royal Netherlands Lifeboat Association) . . 60 45
1943 80c. Freighters in canal (150th Anniv of Royal Association of Ships' Masters "Schuttevaer") 60 45

1999.
1944 **551** 80c. blue and red 50 50
1945 – 80c. red and blue 50 50
DESIGN: No. 1945, "Stamps love Me".

552 "The Goldfinch" (Carel Fabritius)

1999. 17th-century Dutch Art. Multicoloured. Self-adhesive gum (1g.).
1946 80c. Type **552** 70 65
1947 80c. "Self-portrait" (Rembrandt) 70 65
1948 80c. "Self-portrait" (Judith Leyster) 70 65
1949 80c. "St. Sebastian" (Hendrick ter Brugghen) 70 65
1950 80c. "Beware of Luxury" (Jan Steen) 70 65
1951 80c. "The Sick Child" (Gabriel Metsu) 70 65
1952 80c. "Gooseberries" (Adriaen Coorte) 70 65
1953 80c. "View of Haarlem" (Jacob van Ruisdael) . . 70 65
1954 80c. "Mariaplaats, Utrecht" (Pieter Saenredam) . . . 70 65
1955 80c. "Danae" (Rembrandt) 70 65
1956 1g. "The Jewish Bride" (Rembrandt) 65 55

553 "80" on Computer Screen

1999. Ordinary or self-adhesive gum.
1957 **553** 80c. multicoloured . . . 50 40

554 Amaryllis, Coffee Cup, Candles, Letter Writing and Wine Glasses

1999. Greetings Stamp. Self-adhesive.
1959 **554** 80c. multicoloured . . . 50 40

1999. New Baby Stamp. As No. 1855 but ordinary gum.
1960 **521** 80c. multicoloured . . . 50 50

1999. Wedding Stamp. As No. 1876 but ordinary gum.
1961 **528** 80c. multicoloured . . . 50 50

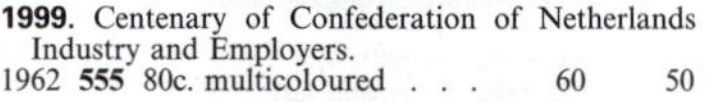
555 Victorian Heavy Machinery and Modern Computer

1999. Centenary of Confederation of Netherlands Industry and Employers.
1962 **555** 80c. multicoloured . . . 60 50

556 Tintin and Snowy wearing Space Suits

1999. 70th Anniv of Tintin (comic strip character by Herge). Scenes from "Explorers on the Moon". Multicoloured.
1963 80c. Type **556** 50 50
MS1964 108 × 50 mm. 80c. Tintin, Snowy and Captain Haddock in moon buggy; 80c. Type **556** . . 1·60 1·40

557 Pillar Box, 1850

1999. Bicentenary of Netherlands Postal Service (2nd issue). Sheet 144 × 75 mm.
MS1965 **557** 5g. red, black and blue 4·00 3·50

558 Digger (completion of Afsluitdijk, 1932)

1999. The Twentieth Century. Multicoloured.
1966 80c. Type **558** . . . . . . 1·10 80
1967 80c. Space satellite . . . . 1·10 80
1968 80c. Berlage Commodity Exchange, Amsterdam (inauguration, 1903) . . 1·10 80
1969 80c. Empty motorway (car-free Sundays during oil crisis, 1973–74) . . . . . 1·10 80
1970 80c. Old man (Old Age Pensions Act, 1947) . . . 1·10 80
1971 80c. Delta Flood Project, 1953–97 . . . . 1·10 80
1972 80c. Players celebrating (victory of Netherlands in European Cup Football Championship, 1998) . . 1·10 80
1973 80c. Four riders on one motor cycle (liberation and end of Second World War, 1945) . . . . 1·10 80
1974 80c. Woman posting vote (Women's Franchise, 1919) . . . . 1·10 80
1975 80c. Ice skaters (eleven cities race) . . . . 1·10 80

559 Pluk van de Pettevlet on Fire Engine

1999. Child Welfare. Characters created by Fiep Westendorp. Multicoloured.
1976 80c.+40c. Type **559** . . . . 1·00 75
1977 80c.+40c. Otje drinking through straw . . . . . 1·00 75
1978 80c.+40c. Jip and Janneke with cat . . . . 1·00 75
MS1979 144 × 75 mm. Nos. 1976/8, each × 2 . . . . 6·00 4·75

560 Father Christmas (Robin Knegt)

561 "25"

1999. Christmas. Winning entries in design competition. Multicoloured.

1980 55c. Type **560** 50 25
1981 55c. Angel singing (Davinia Bovenlander) (vert) . . . 50 25
1982 55c. Dutch doughnuts in box (Henk Drenth) . . . 50 25
1983 55c. Moon wearing Christmas hat (Lizet van den Berg) (vert) 50 25
1984 55c. Father Christmas carrying sacks (Noortje Kruse) 50 25
1985 55c. Clock striking midnight (Hucky de Haas) (vert) . . 50 25
1986 55c. Ice skater (Marleen Bos) 50 25
1987 55c. Human Christmas tree (Mariette Strik) (vert) . . 50 25
1988 55c. Woman wearing Christmas tree earrings (Saskia van Oversteeg) . . 50 25
1989 55c. Woman vacuuming pine needles (Frans Koenis) (vert) 50 25
1990 55c. Angel with harp and music score (Evelyn de Zeeuw) 50 25
1991 55c. Hand balancing candle, star, hot drink, hat and Christmas tree on fingers (Aafke van Ewijk) (vert) 50 25
1992 55c. Christmas tree (Daan Roepman) (vert) 50 25
1993 55c. Cat wearing crown (Sjoerd van der Zee) (vert) 50 25
1994 55c. Bird flying over house (Barbara Vollers) 50 25
1995 55c. Baby with angel wings (Rosmarijn Schmink) (vert) 50 25
1996 55c. Dog wearing Christmas hat (Casper Heijstek and Mirjam Cnosser) 50 25
1997 55c. Angel flying (Patricia van der Neut) (vert) . . . 50 25
1998 55c. Nativity (Marco Cockx) 50 25
1999 55c. Christmas tree with decorations (Matthias Meiling) (vert) 50 25

2000. Make-up Rate Stamp.

2000 **561** 25c. red, blue and yellow 20 25

562 1 Guilder Coin, Margaret of Austria (Regent of Netherlands) (after Bernard van Orley) and "Coronation of Charles V" (Juan de la Coate)

2000. 500th Birth Anniv of Charles V, Holy Roman Emperor. Multicoloured.

2001 80c. Type **562** 60 50
2002 80c. Map of the Seventeen Provinces, "Charles V after the Battle of Muehlberg" (Titian) and Margaret of Parma (Regent of Netherlands) (after Antonius Mohr) . . 60 50

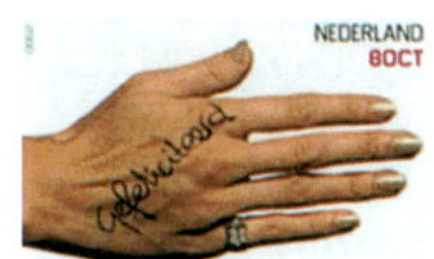

563 "Gefeliciteerd" ("Congratulations")

2000. Greetings stamps. Showing greetings messages on hands. Multicoloured.

2003 80c. Type **563** 60 55
2004 80c. "Succes met je nieuwe baan" ("Good luck with your new job") 60 55
2005 80c. "gefeliciteerd met je huis" ("Congratulations on your new home") . . 60 55
2006 80c. "PROFICIAT" ("Congratulations") . . . 60 55
2007 80c. "Succes" ("Hope you have success") 60 55
2008 80c. "Veel geluk samen" ("Good luck together") 60 55
2009 80c. "Proficiat met je diploma" ("Congratulations on passing your exam") . . . 60 55
2010 80c. "Geluk" ("Good luck") 60 55
2011 80c. "Van Harte" ("Cordially") 60 55
2012 80c. "GEFELICITEERD MET JE RUBEWIUS!" ("Congratulations on passing your driving test!") 60 55

564 Players celebrating

565 Man and Woman passing Ball

2000. European Football Championship, Netherlands and Belgium. Multicoloured.

2013 80c. Type **564** 50 30
2014 80c. Football 50 30

2000. Cultural, Health and Social Welfare Funds. Senior Citizens. Multicoloured.

2015 80c.+40c. Type **565** 90 60
2016 80c.+40c. Woman picking apples 90 60
2017 80c.+40c. Woman wearing swimming costume . . . 90 60
MS2018 144 × 74 mm. Nos. 2015/17, each × 2 . . . . 6·25 5·25

566 "Feigned Sadness" (C. Troost)

2000. Bicentenary of the Rijksmuseum, Amsterdam. Multicoloured. (a) Ordinary gum.

2019 80c. Type **566** 60 55
2020 80c. "Harlequin and Columbine" (porcelain figurine) (J. J. Kandler) 60 55
2021 80c. "Ichikawa Ebizo IV" (woodcut) (T. Sharaku) 60 55
2022 80c. "Heavenly Beauty" (sandstone sculpture) . . 60 55
2023 80c. "St. Vitus" (wood sculpture) 60 55
2024 80c. "Woman in Turkish Costume" (J. E. Liotard) 60 55
2025 80c. "J. van Speyk" (J. Schoemaker Doyer) . . 60 55
2026 80c. "King Saul" (engraving) (L. van Leyden) 60 55
2027 80c. "L'Amour Menacant" (marble sculpture) (E. M. Falconet) 60 55
2028 80c. "Sunday" (photograph) (C. Ariens) 60 55

(b) Self-adhesive.

2029 80c. "The Nightwatch" (Rembrandt) 60 55

567 "80" and "Doe Maar" Record Cover

2000. Doe Maar (Dutch pop group). Multicoloured.

2030 80c. Type **567** 50 45
2031 80c. "80" and song titles . . 50 45

568 "Dutch Landscape" (Jeroen Krabb)

2000. Priority Mail. Contemporary Art. Self-adhesive.

2033 **568** 110c. multicoloured . . . 60 50

569 "The Nightwatch" (Rembrandt)

2000. Priority Mail. Self-adhesive.

2034 **569** 110c. multicoloured . . . 65 65

570 *Libertad* (full-rigged cadet ship)

2000. "Sail Amsterdam 2000". Sailing Ships. Multicoloured.

2036 80c. Type **570** 45 20
2037 80c. *Amerigo Vespucci* (cadet ship) and figurehead . . . 45 20
2038 80c. *Dar Mlodziezy* (full-rigged cadet ship) and sail 45 20
2039 80c. *Europa* (cadet ship) and wheel 45 20
2040 80c. *Kruzenshtern* (cadet barque) and bell 45 20
2041 80c. *Sagres II* (cadet barque) and sail 45 20
2042 80c. *Alexander von Humboldt* (barque) and sail 45 20
2043 80c. *Sedov* (cadet barque) and sailors dropping sail 45 20
2044 80c. *Mir* (square-rigged training ship) 45 20
2045 80c. *Oosterschelde* (schooner) and rope . . . 45 20

571 Roller Skating

2000. Sjors and Sjimmie (comic strip characters by Frans Piet). Multicoloured.

2046 80c. Type **571** 45 20
2047 80c. In car 45 20
2049 80c. Listening to radio . . . 45 20
2050 80c. Swinging on rope . . . 45 20
MS2048 108 × 50 mm. 80c. As No. 2049; 80c. As No. 2047 . . 1·10 90

2000. Bereavement Stamp. As No. 1866 but self-adhesive.

2051 **524** 80c. blue 45 20

572 Green Dragonfly

2000. Endangered Species. Multicoloured.

2052 80c. Type **572** 45 20
2053 80c. Weather loach 45 20

573 Canal Boat

2000. 150th Anniv (2002) of Netherlands Stamps (1st issue). Sheet 108 × 50 mm containing T **573** and similar horiz design. Multicoloured.

MS2054 80c. Type **573**; 80c. Mail carriage . . . . 1·10 1·10

See also Nos. **MS**2138 and **MS**2250.

574 Children wearing Monster Hats

575 Couple with Christmas Tree

2000. Child Welfare. Multicoloured. (a) Self-adhesive gum.

2055 80c.+40c. Type **574** 65 40
2056 80c.+40c. Boy sailing bath-tub 65 40
2057 80c.+40c. Children brewing magical stew 65 40

(b) Ordinary gum.

MS2058 80c.+40c. Type **574**; 80c.+40c. Ghostly games; 80c.+40c. Girl riding crocodile; 80c.+40c. As No. 2056; 80c.+40c. As No. 2057; 80c.+40c. Children playing dragon . . . . 4·75 2·75

2000. Christmas. Multicoloured.

2059 60c. Type **575** 35 15
2060 60c. Children making snow balls 35 15
2061 60c. Couple dancing 35 15
2062 60c. Man playing French horn 35 15
2063 60c. Man carrying Christmas tree 35 15
2064 60c. Man carrying young child 35 15
2065 60c. Woman reading book 35 15
2066 60c. Couple kissing 35 15
2067 60c. Man playing piano . . 35 15
2068 60c. Woman watching from window 35 15
2069 60c. Woman sitting in chair 35 15
2070 60c. Man sitting beside fire 35 15
2071 60c. Snowman flying 35 15
2072 60c. Couple in street 35 15
2073 60c. Child playing violin . . 35 15
2074 60c. Children on sledge . . 35 15
2075 60c. Man writing letter . . . 35 15
2076 60c. Woman carrying plate of food 35 15
2077 60c. Family 35 15
2078 60c. Woman sleeping . . . 35 15

576 Moon

577 Whinchat

2001. Make-up Rate Stamp.

2079 **576** 20c. multicoloured . . . 15 10

2001. Centenary of Royal Dutch Nature Society. Multicoloured.

2080 80c. Type **577** 45 20
2081 80c. Family in rowing boat 45 20
2082 80c. Fox 45 20
2083 80c. Couple bird watching 45 20
2084 80c. Flowers 45 20

578 Poem (by E. du Perron)

2001. "Between Two Cultures". National Book Week. Multicoloured.

2085 80c. Type **578** 45 20
2086 80c. Men in street 45 20
2087 80c. Poem (by Hafid Bouazza) 45 20
2088 80c. Woman and young men 45 20
2089 80c. Poem (by Adriaan van Dis) 45 20
2090 80c. Profiles of two women 45 20
2091 80c. Poem (by Kader Abdolah) 45 20
2092 80c. Two young girls . . . 45 20
2093 80c. Poem (by Ellen Ombre) 45 20
2094 80c. Boy carrying map . . . 45 20

579 Rotterdam Bridge

2001. Priority Mail. Rotterdam, European City of Culture. Self-adhesive gum.

2095 **579** 110c. multicoloured . . . 65 25

580 Emergency Rescuers

2001. International Year of Volunteers. Sheet 108 × 50 mm. containing Type **580** and similar horiz design. Multicoloured.

MS2096 80c. Type 508, 80c. Animal rescuers . . . . 1·10 1·10

581 Chess Board

2001. Birth Centenary of Machgielis "Professor Max" Euwe (chess player). Sheet 108 × 50 mm containing T **581** and similar horiz design. Multicoloured.

MS2097 80c. Type **581**; 80c. Euwe and chess pieces . . . . 1·10 1·10

582 Helen's Flower (*Helenium rubinzwerg*)

2001. Flowers. Multicoloured. (a) Self-adhesive gum.
2098 80c.+40c. Type **582** 65 40
2099 80c.+40c. Russian hollyhock (*Alcea rugosa*) 65 40
2100 80c.+40c. Persian cornflower (*Centaurea dealbata*) . . . 65 40

(b) Ordinary gum.
MS2101 144 × 75 mm. 80c.+40c. *Caryopteris* "Heavenly Blue"; 80c.+40c. Type **582**; 80c.+40c. As No. 2099; 80c.+40c. Spurge (*Euphorbia schillingii*); 80c.+40c. As No. 2100; 80c.+40c. Hooker inula (*Inula hookeri*) . . . . . 4·75 4·00

583 "Autumn" (detail) (L. Gestel)

2001. Art Nouveau. Multicoloured.
2102 80c. Type **583** 45 20
2103 80c. Book cover by C. Lebeau for *De Stille Kracht* 45 20
2104 80c. Burcht Federal Council Hall, Amsterdam (R. N. Roland Holst and H. P. Berlage) 45 20
2105 80c. "O Grave Where is Thy Victory" (painting) (J. Throop) 45 20
2106 80c. Vases by C. J. van der Hoef from Amphora factory 45 20
2107 80c. Capital from staircase of Utrecht building (J. Mendes da Costa) . . 45 20
2108 80c. Illustration of common peafowl from *The Happy Owls* (T. van Hoytema) 45 20
2109 80c. "The Bride" (detail) (painting) (J. Thorn Prikker) 45 20
2110 80c. Factory-printed cotton fabric (M. Duco Crop) . . 45 20
2111 80c. Dentz van Schaik room (L. Zyl) 45 20

2001. As T **428** but with face value expressed in euros and cents. Self-adhesive gum.
2112 85c. blue 50 20

584 Sky and Landscape

2001. Self-adhesive gum.
2113 **584** 85c. multicoloured . . . 50 20

585 Arrows

2001. Business Coil Stamp. Self-adhesive gum.
2114 **585** 85c. purple and silver . . 50 20

586 Reclaimed Land

2001. Multicoloured. Self-adhesive gum.
2115 85c. Type **586** (postage) . . 50 20
2116 1g.20 Beach (priority mail) 65 25
2117 1g.65 Town and canal . . . 90 35

587 House carrying Suitcase

2001. Greetings Stamps. Self-adhesive gum.
2118 **587** 85c. black and yellow . . 50 20
2119 – 85c. red, yellow and gold 50 20
2120 – 85c. multicoloured . . . 50 20
2121 – 85c. multicoloured . . . 50 20

DESIGNS: No. 2118, Type **587** (change of address stamp); 2119, Couple (wedding stamp); 2120, As Type **521** (new baby); 2121, As Type **524** (bereavement stamp).

588 Tom and Jerry **589** "Veel Geluk" ("Good Luck")

2001. Cartoon Characters. Multicoloured.
2122 85c. Type **588** 50 20
2123 85c. Fred Flintstone and Barney Rubble 50 20
2124 85c. Johnny Bravo 50 20
2125 85c. Dexter posting letter . . 50 20
2126 85c. Powerpuff Girls 50 20

2001. Greetings Stamps. Multicoloured. Self-adhesive gum.
2127 85c. Type **589** 50 20
2128 85c. "Gefeliciteerd!" ("Congratulations!") . . . 50 20
2129 85c. "Veel Geluk" with envelope flap (horiz) . . . 50 20
2130 85c. "Gefeliciteerd!" with envelope flap (horiz) . . . 50 20
2131 85c. "Proficiat" ("Congratulations") . . . 50 20
2132 85c. "Succes !" ("Success") 50 20
2133 85c. "Van Harte ..." ("Cordially ...") 50 20
2134 85c. "Proficiat" with envelope flap (horiz) . . . 50 50
2135 85c. "Succes !" with envelope flap (horiz) . . . 50 20
2136 85c. "Van Harte ..." with envelope flap (horiz) . . . 50 20

590 Guilder Coins **591** Waaigat Canal and Williamstad, Curacao (J. E. Heemskerk after G. C. W. Voorduin)

2001. Replacement of the Guilder. Self-adhesive.
2137 **590** 12g.75 silver . . . . . . 7·00 3·00

2001. 150th Annivs of Netherlands Stamps (2002) (2nd issue) and of Royal Institute foe Linguistics and Anthropology. Sheet 108 × 50 mm containing T **591** and similar horiz design. Multicoloured.
MS2138 85c. Type **591**; 85c. Pangka sugar refinery, Java (J.C. Grieve after A. Salm) . . . . 1·40 1·40

592 Magnifier, Target Mark and Dots

2001. Centenary of Royal Dutch Printers' Association. Sheet 108 × 50 mm containing T **592** and similar horiz design. Multicoloured.
MS2139 85c. Type **592**; 85c. Magnifier, computer zoom symbol and colour palette . . . . 1·40 1·40

593 Computer Figure and River

2001. Child Welfare. Multicoloured. (a) Self-adhesive gum.
2140 85c.+40c. Type **593** . . . . 1·25 1·00

(b) Ordinary gum.
MS2141 146 × 76 mm. 85c.+40c. Figure and printer; 85c.+40c. Road, car and figure; 85c.+40c. Post box, blocks and droplets; 85c.+40c. Post box, figure and stairs; 85c.+40c. Type **593**; 85c.+40c. Figure swinging on rope and log in river . . . . 5·50 5·50

594 Clock and Grapes **595** "12"

2001. Christmas. Multicoloured. Self-adhesive gum.
2142 60c. Type **594** 35 15
2143 60c. Stars and bun 35 15
2144 60c. Steeple and buns . . . 35 15
2145 60c. Cherub and coins . . . 35 15
2146 60c. Champagne bottle . . . 35 15
2147 60c. Wreath around chimney 35 15
2148 60c. Tower 35 15
2149 60c. Christmas tree bauble 35 15
2150 60c. Playing card with Christmas tree as sign . . 35 15
2151 60c. Cake seen through window 35 15
2152 60c. Decorated Christmas tree 35 15
2153 60c. Father Christmas . . . 35 15
2154 60c. Sign displaying hot drink 35 15
2155 60c. Candles seen through window 35 15
2156 60c. Illuminated roof-tops 35 15
2157 60c. Reindeer 35 15
2158 60c. Snowman 35 15
2159 60c. Parcel 35 15
2160 60c. Bonfire 35 15
2161 60c. Children on toboggan 35 15

2002. Make-up Rate Stamp. (a) Self-adhesive gum.
2162 **595** 2c. red 15 10
2166 12c. green 15 10

(b) Ordinary gum.
2169 **595** 2c. red 15 10
2170 5c. mauve 10 10
2171 10c. blue 15 10

596 Queen Beatrix **597** Arrows

2002. Queen Beatrix. Self-adhesive gum.
2175 **596** 25c. brown and green 35 15
2176 39c. blue and pink . . 50 20
2177 40c. blue and brown . . 50 20
2178 50c. pink and green . . 65 25
2179 55c. mauve and brown 75 45
2180 57c. blue and purple . . 75 60
2180a 61c. violet and brown 80 40
2181 65c. green and violet . . 85 35
2182 70c. deep green and green 95 60
2183 72c. ochre and blue . . 80 1·00
2183a 76c. ochre and green . . 90 45
2184 78c. blue and brown . . 1·00 40
2185 €1 green and blue . . 1·25 50
2187 €3 mauve and green 3·75 1·50

2002. Business Coil Stamps. Self-adhesive gum.
2195 **597** 39c. purple and silver . . 50 20
2196 78c. blue and gold . . . 1·00 40

598 Prince Willem-Alexander and Máxima Zorreguieta

2002. Marriage of Prince Willem-Alexander and Maxima Zorreguieta. Sheet 145 × 75 mm, containing T **598** and similar horiz design.
MS2197 **598** 39c. black, silver and orange; 39c. multicoloured . . 1·25 1·25
DESIGN: 39c. "Willem-Alexander Maxima" and "222".

599 Sky and Landscape

2002. Self-adhesive gum.
2198 **599** 39c. multicoloured . . . 55 25

600 Couple **601** "Veel Geluk" ("Good Luck")

2002. Greetings Stamps. Face values in euros. Self-adhesive gum.
2199 – 39c. black and yellow . . 55 25
2200 **600** 39c. red, yelow and gold 55 25
2201 – 39c. multicoloured . . . 55 25
2202 – 39c. blue 55 25

DESIGNS: No. 2199, As Type **587** (change of address stamp); 2200, Type **600** (wedding stamp); 2201, As Type **521** (new baby); 2202, As Type **524** (bereavement stamp).

2001. Greetings Stamps. Face values in euros. Multicoloured. Self-adhesive gum.
2203 39c. Type **601** 55 25
2204 39c. "Gefeliciteerd!" ("Congratulations!") . . . 55 25
2205 39c. "Veel Geluk" ("Good Luck") (horiz) 55 25
2206 39c. "Gefeliciteerd!" with envelope flap (horiz) . . . 55 25
2207 39c. "Proficiat" ("Congratulations") . . . 55 25
2208 39c. "Succes !" ("Success") 55 25
2209 39c. "Van Harte..." ("Cordially ...") 55 25
2210 39c. "Proficiat" with envelope flap (horiz) . . . 55 25
2211 39c. "Succes !" with envelope flap (horiz) . . . 55 25
2212 39c. "Van Harte..." with envelope flap (horiz) . . . 55 25

602 Reclaimed Land

2002. Landscapes. Face values in euros. Multicoloured. Self-adhesive gum.
2213 39c. Type **603** (postage) . . 55 25
2214 54c. Beach (priority mail) 70 30
2215 75c. Town and canal . . . 1·00 40

603 Water Lily **604** Flowers and Red Crosses

2002. "Floriade 2002" International Horticultural Exhibition, Harlemmermeer. Flowers. Multicoloured.
2216 39c. + 19c. Type **603** . . . 80 50
2217 39c. + 19c. Dahlia 80 50
2218 39c. + 19c. Japanese cherry blossom 80 50
2219 39c. + 19c. Rose 80 50
2220 39c. + 19c. Orchid 80 50
2221 39c. + 19c. Tulip 80 50
Nos. 2216/21 were printed on paper impregnated with perfume which was released when the stamps were scratched.

2002. Red Cross. 10th Annual Blossom Walk.
2222 **604** 39c. + 19c. multicoloured 80 50

605 Langnek

2002. 50th Anniv of Efteling Theme Park. Multicoloured. Self-adhesive gum.
2223 39c. Type **605** 55 25
2224 39c. Pardoes de Tovernar . 55 25
2225 39c. Droomvlucht Elfje . . 55 25
2226 39c. Kleine Boodschap . . . 55 25
2227 39c. Holle Bolle Gijs 55 25

606 "West Indies Landscape" (Jan Mostaert)

2002. Landscape Paintings. Showing paintings and enlarged detail in foreground. Multicoloured.
2228 39c. Type **606** 55 25
2229 39c. "Riverbank with Cows" (Aelbert Cuyp) 55 25
2230 39c. "Cornfield" (Jacob van Ruisdael) 55 25
2231 39c. "Avenue at Middelharnis" (Meindert Hobbema) 55 25
2232 39c. "Italian Landscape with Umbrella Pines" (Hendrik Voogd) 55 25
2233 39c. "Landscape in Normandy" (Andreas Schelfhout) 55 25
2234 39c. "Landscape with Waterway" (Jan Toorop) 55 25
2235 39c. "Landscape" (Jan Sluijters) 55 25

2236 39c. "Kismet" (Michael Raedecker) 55 25
2237 39c. "Untitled" (Robert Zandvliet) 55 25

607 Circus Performers

608 Circles

2002. Priority Mail. Europa. Circus. Multicoloured.
2238 54c. Type **607** 70 30
2239 54c. Lions and Big Top . . 70 30

2002. Business Coil Stamp. Self-adhesive gum.
2240 **608** 39c. deep blue, blue and red 55 25
2241 78c. green, light green and red . . . . 1·10 45

609 Dutch East Indiaman and 1852 Stamps

2002. 150th Anniv of Netherlands Stamps. 400th Anniv of Dutch East India Company (V. O. C.). Sheet 108 × 50 mm, containing T **609** and similar horiz design. Multicoloured.
MS2250 39c. Type **609**; 39c. Two Dutch East Indiamen and and stamps of 1852 . . . . 1·10 45

610 Boatyard, Spakenburg

2002. Industrial Heritage. Multicoloured.
2251 39c. Type **610** 55 25
2252 39c. Limekiln, Dedemsvaart 55 25
2253 39c. Steam-driven pumping station, Cruquius 55 25
2254 39c. Mine-shaft winding gear, Heerlen 55 25
2255 39c. Salt drilling tower, Hengelo 55 25
2256 39c. Windmill, Weidum . . 55 25
2257 39c. Brick-works, Zevenaar 55 25
2258 39c. "Drie Hoefijzers" brewery, Breda 55 25
2259 39c. Water-treatment plant, Tilburg 55 25
2260 39c. "Nodding-donkey" oil pump, Schoonebeck . . . 55 25

611 Cat and Child

2002. Child Welfare. Sheet 147 × 76 mm, containing T **611** and similar horiz designs. Multicoloured.
MS2261 Type **611**, 39c.+19c. Blue figure and upper part of child with green head; 39c.+19c. Child and ball; 39c.+19c. Child with yellow head and raised arms; 39c.+19c. Child with brown head and left arm raised; 39c.+19c. Dog and child . . . . 4·00 2·20

612 Woman and Child

2002. Christmas. Multicoloured. Self-adhesive gum.
2262 29c. Type **612** 40 15
2263 29c. Seated man facing left 40 15
2264 29c. Profile with raised collar 40 15
2265 29c. Stream and figure wearing scarf 40 15
2266 29c. Woman, tree and snowflakes 40 15
2267 29c. Snowflakes and man wearing knee-length coat beside grasses 40 15
2268 29c. Snowflakes, man, and gate and stream 40 15
2269 29c. Snowflakes, windmill, stream and woman . . . 40 15
2270 29c. Seated man facing right 40 15
2271 29c. Willow tree and profile of child facing left 40 15
2272 29c. Man leaning against tree 40 15
2273 29c. Man with hands in pockets 40 15
2274 29c. Seated couple 40 15
2275 29c. Fir tree and man's profile facing left 40 15
2276 29c. Man carrying child on shoulders 40 15
2277 29c. Profile of boy facing right 40 15
2278 29c. Standing child facing left 40 15
2279 29c. Snowflakes, sea and upper part of man with raised collar 40 15
2280 29c. Sea behind man wearing hat and glasses 40 15
2281 29c. Figure with out-stretched arms 40 15

Nos. 2262/81 were issued together, se-tenant, the stamps arranged in strips of five, each strip forming a composite design.

613 "Landscape with Four Trees"

614 "Self-portrait with Straw Hat"

2003. 150th Birth Anniv of Vincent Van Gogh (artist). Multicoloured. (a) Ordinary gum.
2282 39c. Type **613** 55 25
2283 39c. "The Potato Eaters" . . 55 25
2284 39c. "Four Cut Sunflowers" 55 25
2285 39c. "Self-portrait with Grey Felt Hat" 55 25
2286 39c. "The Zouave" 55 25
2287 39c. "Place Du Forum Cafe Terrace by Night, Arles" 55 25
2288 39c. "Tree Trunks in Long Grass" 55 25
2289 39c. "Almond Blossom" . . . 55 25
2290 39c. "Auvers-sur-Oise" . . . 55 25
2291 39c. "Wheatfield with Crows, Auvers-sur-Oise" 55 25

(b) Self-adhesive gum.
2292 39c. Type **614** 55 25
2293 59c. "Vase with Sunflowers" 55 25
2294 75c. "The Sower" 55 25

615 North Pier, Ijmuiden

2003. 50th Anniv of Floods in Zeeland, North Brabant and South Holland. Designs showing photographs from national archives. Each grey and black.
2295 39c. Type **615** 55 25
2296 39c. Hansweert Lock 55 55
2297 39c. Building dam, Wieringermeer 55 25
2298 39c. Ijsselmeer Dam 55 25
2299 39c. Breached dyke, Willemstad 55 25
2300 39c. Repairing dyke, Stavenisse 55 25
2301 39c. Building dam, Zandkreek 55 25
2302 39c. Building dam, Grevelingen 55 25
2303 39c. Flood barrier, Oosterschelde 55 25
2304 39c. Floods, Roermond . . 55 25

616 See-through Register (security feature)

2003. 300th Anniv of Joh. Enschede (printers). Multicoloured.
2305 39c. Type **616** 55 25
2306 39c. Fleischman's musical notation 55 25

No. 2305 has the remaining symbols of the see-through register printed on the back over the gum. This forms a complete design when held up to the light.

No. 2305 was embossed with a notional barcode and No. 2306 with a security device.

617 Alstroemeria

2003. Flower Paintings. Multicoloured.
2307 39c.+19c. Type **617** 80 50
2308 39c.+19c. Sweet pea 80 50
2309 39c.+19c. Pansies 80 50
2310 39c.+19c. Trumpet vine . . 80 50
2311 39c.+19c. Lychnis 80 50
2312 39c.+19c. Irises 80 50

618 Oystercatcher

619 "39"

2003. Fauna of the Dutch Shallows. Winning Entry in Stamp Design Competition. Multicoloured.
MS2313 Two sheets, each 140 × 82 mm. (a) 39c. × 4, Type **618**; Spoonbill (horiz); Eider duck: Grey seal (horiz) (b) 59c. × 4, Herring gull; Curlew (horiz); Seals and gull; Crab (horiz) . . 5·25 5·25

MS2313 (b) were issued with "PRIORITY/ Prioritaire" label attached at either upper or lower edge.

2003. Greetings Stamps. Two sheets, each 122 × 170 mm, containing T **619** and similar vert designs. Multicoloured.
MS2314 (a) 39c. × 10, Type **619** (blue) (green) (purple) (pink) (orange) (yellow) (olive) (turquoise) (red) (brown); (b) 39c. × 10, Flowers; Flag; Present; Champagne glass; Medal; Guitar; Balloons; Cut-out figures; Slice of cake; Garland . . . . 10·50 10·50

Nos. **MS**2314a/b were each issued with a se-tenant label attached at left showing either Marjolein Bastin (artist); Paint tubes and splashes (painting, Marjolein Bastin); Humberto Tan (television presenter); Figures symbolising Red Cross; Daphne Deckers (presenter and actress); Fan-mail; Prime Minister Jan Balkenende; Palm top computer; Sien Diels (Sesame Street presenter); Tommie (character from Sesame Street) (**MS**2314a) or a girl (**MS**2314b). The labels could be personalised by the addition of a photograph for an inclusive fee of €12 for the first sheet and €5.95 for subsequent sheets bearing the same design.

620 Coffee Cup

2003. 250th Anniv of Douwe Egberts (coffee and tea retailers). Multicoloured.
2315 39c. Type **620** 55 10
2316 39c. As No. 2315 but with colours reversed 55 10

Nos. 2315/16 were impregnated with the scent of coffee which was released when the stamps were rubbed.

621 Airplane, Ship and Trucks

2003. Land, Air and Water. Winning Entry in Stamp Design Competition. Multicoloured.
2318 39c. Cat, bird, fish and envelope 55 10

622 Nelson Mandela and Child

2003. 85th Birth Anniv of Nelson Mandela (President of South Africa). Multicoloured.
2319 39c. Type **622** 55 10
2320 39c. Children (Nelson Mandela's Children's Fund) 55 10

623 "For You from Me"

2003. Self-adhesive gum.
2321 **623** 39c. multicoloured . . . 55 10

624 Children Kissing

625 "39"

2003. Winning Entries in Stamp Design Competition. Sheet 108 × 151 mm containing T **624** and similar horiz designs. Multicoloured.
MS2322 39c. × 10, Type **624**; Traditional costume; Cat; Puppies; Child; Bride and groom; 2CV cars; Motorcycle; Peacock butterfly; Flowers . . . . 5·50 5·50

2003. Company Stamp. Self adhesive.
2323 **626** 39c. multicoloured . . . 55 10

626 Coloured Squares

2003. Stamp Day. 75th Anniv of Netherlands Association of Stamp Dealers (NVPH).
2324 **626** 39c. multicoloured . . . 55 10

627 Notepad, Radio and Ballet Shoes

2003. Child Welfare. Sheet 147 × 76 mm containing T **627** and similar horiz designs. Multicoloured.
MS2325 39c.+19c. × 6, Type **627**; Masks and open book; Microphone, music notation and paint brush; Violin, pencil, football and television; Drum and light bulbs; Trumpet, light bulbs, hat and earphones . . . . . . 5·00 5·00

628 Star

629 Family

2003. Greetings Stamp.
2326 **628** 29c. multicoloured . . . 45 45

2003. Christmas. Multicoloured. Self-adhesive.
2327 29c. Type **629** 45 15
2328 29c. Parcel 45 15
2329 29c. Cat and dog 45 15
2330 29c. Tree 45 15
2331 29c. Hands holding glasses 45 15
2332 29c. Bell 45 15
2333 29c. Hand holding pen . . . 45 15
2334 29c. Stag's head 45 15
2335 29c. Hand holding toy windmill 45 15
2336 29c. Holly leaf 45 15
2337 29c. Candle flame 45 15
2338 29c. Star 45 10
2339 29c. Couple 45 15
2340 29c. Snowman 45 15
2341 29c. Fireplace and fire . . . 45 15
2342 29c. Angel 45 15
2343 29c. Couple dancing 45 15
2344 29c. Round bauble 45 15
2345 29c. Mother and child . . . 45 15
2346 29c. Pointed bauble 45 15

630 Queen Beatrix as Baby

2003. The Royal Family. Queen Beatrix. Sheet 123 × 168 mm containing T **630** and similar horiz designs. Multicoloured.
MS2347 39c. × 10, Type **630**; Sitting on swing as small child; As young girl leading pony; Reading magazine; With Claus von Amsberg on their engagement; Holding baby Prince Willem-Alexander; Royal family when young; Queen Beatrix and Prince Claus dancing; Prince Willem-Alexander, Prince Johan Friso, Prince Claus, Queen Beatrix and Prince Constantijn, Queen Beatrix viewing painting in art gallery . . . 5·50 4·25

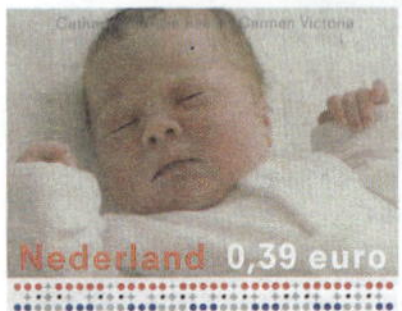

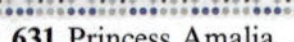

631 Princess Amalia **632** "Woman Reading a Letter" (Gabriel Metsu) (detail)

2003. Birth of Princess Amalia of Netherlands. Sheet 104 × 71 mm.
MS2348 **631** 39c. multicoloured . . . 55 60

2004. Art. Multicoloured. Self-adhesive.
2349 61c. Type **632** 85 45
2350 77c. "The Love Letter" (Jan Vermeer) (detail) . . . . 1·10 75

633 Water, Buildings and Rainbow

2004. 150th Anniv of Royal Netherlands Meteorological Institute (KNMI). Multicoloured.
2351 39c. Type **633** 55 45
2352 39c. Water, buildings and rainbow (different) . . . 55 45
Nos. 2351/2 were issued together, se-tenant, forming a composite design.

634 Patchwork **635** Iris

2004. Business Stamp. Self-adhesive.
2353 **634** 39c. multicoloured . . . 55 15
2354 78c. multicoloured . . . 1·10 20

2004. Flower Paintings. Multicoloured.
2355 39c.+19c. Type **635** 70 60
2356 39c.+19c. Lily 70 60
2357 39c.+19c. Poppy 70 60
2358 39c.+19c. Tulips 70 60
2359 39c.+19c. Orange flower . . 70 60
2360 39c.+19c. Thistle 70 60

636 Spiker C4 (1922)

2004. 50th Anniv of Dutch Youth Philately Association.
2361 **636** 39c. multicoloured . . . 55 15
2362 – 39c. orange and black . . . 55 15
DESIGNS: No. 2361, Type **636**; 2362, Spiker C8 Double12 R (2003).

637 Czech Republic Flag, Stamp, Map and Country Identification Code

2004. Enlargement of European Union. Sheet 108 × 150 mm containing T **637** and similar horiz designs showing the flag, stamp, map and country identification code of the new member states. Multicoloured.
MS2363 39c. × 10, Type **637**; Lithuania; Estonia; Poland; Malta; Hungary. Latvia; Slovakia; Cyprus; Slovenia . . . . . . 5·50 5·50

638 "39" and Rays

2004. Greetings Stamp.
2364 **689** 39c. multicoloured . . . 55 15

2004. Company Stamp. Self adhesive.
2365 **626** 39c. multicoloured . . . 55 15

639 Prince Willem-Alexander and Máxima Zorreguieta on their Engagement

2004. The Royal Family. Prince Willem-Alexander. Sheet 123 × 168 mm containing T **639** and similar horiz designs. Multicoloured.
MS2366 39c. × 10, Type **639**; Máxima Zorreguieta showing engagement ring; Facing each other on their wedding day; Facing left; Kissing; Princess Maxima leaning towards Prince Willem-Alexander; Royal couple with Princess Amalia; With Princess Amalia and reading book; Princess Maxima holding Princess Amalia at christening font; At font Princess Amalia looking upwards . . . 5·50 4·25

640 Red Squirrel

2004. Veluwe Nature Reserve. Two sheets, each 144 × 81 mm containing T **640** and similar horiz designs. Multicoloured.
MS2367 (a) 39c. × 4, Type **640**; Hoopoe; Deer; Wild boar (b) 61c. × 4, Fox; Woodpecker; Stag and hind; Mouflon sheep . . . . . 6·00 4·75

641 Pen Nib

2004. Greetings Stamps. Sheet 144 × 75 mm containing T **641** and similar square designs.
MS2368 39c. light orange and orange; 39c. multicoloured; 39c. blue and red . . . . 1·70 1·70
DESIGNS: 39c.Type **641**; 39c. Hand; 39c. Profiles.

642 "Mercury and Argus"

2004. 350th Death Anniv of Carel Fabritius (artist). Paintings. Multicoloured.
2369 39c. Type **642** 55 10
2370 39c. "Self Portrait" (wearing large hat) 55 10
2371 39c. "Mercury and Aglauros" 55 10
2372 39c. "Abraham de Potter" . . 55 10
2373 39c. "Hagar and the Angel" . 55 10
2374 39c. "The Sentry" 55 10
2375 39c. "Hera" 55 10
2376 39c. "Self Portrait" (wearing small-brimmed hat) . . . 55 10
2377 39c. "Self Portrait" (hatless) 55 10
2378 39c. "The Goldfinch" . . . 55 10

643 Pumpkin and Football

2004. Child Welfare. 80th Anniv of Foundation for Children's Welfare Stamps. Sheet 144 × 75 mm containing T **643** and similar horiz designs. Multicoloured.
MS2379 39c.+19c. × 6, Type **643**; Lemon skipping; Orange cycling; Pear skateboarding; Banana doing sit-ups; Strawberry weightlifting . . . 4·75 4·75

644 Snowman **645** Family as Shadows

2004. Greetings Stamp.
2380 **644** 29c. multicoloured . . . 20 10

2004. Christmas. Multicoloured. Self-adhesive.
2381 29c. Type **645** 20 10
2382 29c. Girls holding parcels . . 20 10
2383 29c. Girl and dog 20 10
2384 29c. Two children 20 10
2385 29c. Sheep 20 10
2386 29c. Two polar bears . . .
2387 29c. Children making snowman 20 10
2388 29c. Couple pulling tree . . 20 10
2389 29c. Couple swimming . . . 20 10
2390 29c. Three people wearing fur hats 20 10
2391 29c. Type **645** 20 10
2392 29c. As No. 2382 . . . . . 20 10
2393 29c. As No. 2383 . . . . . 20 10
2394 29c. As No. 2384 . . . . . 20 10
2395 29c. As No. 2385 . . . . . 20 10
2396 29c. As No. 2386 . . . . . 20 10
2397 29c. As No. 2387 . . . . . 20 10
2398 29c. As No. 2388 . . . . . 20 10
2399 29c. As No. 2389 . . . . . 20 10
2400 29c. As No. 2390 . . . . . 20 10

646 Woman (NOVIB) **647** Two Hearts

2004. Christmas. Charity Stamps. Multicoloured. Self-adhesive.
2401 29c.+10c. Type **646** 55 45
2402 29c.+10c. Children (Stop AIDS Now) 55 45
2403 29c.+10c. Deer (Natuurmonumenten) . . 55 45
2404 29c.+10c. Two boys (KWF Kankerbestrijding) . . . 55 45
2405 29c.+10c. Girl holding baby (UNICEF) 55 45
2406 29c.+10c. Two boys writing (Plan Nederland) 55 45
2407 29c.+10c. Bauble containing mother and child (Tros Helpt) 55 45
2408 29c.+10c. Canoeist and snow covered mountains (Greenpeace) 55 45
2409 29c.+10c. Woman and child (Artsen Zonder Grenzen) 55 45
2410 29c.+10c. Girl feeding toddler (World Food Programme) 55 45

2005. Greetings Stamp. Self-adhesive.
2411 **647** 39c. multicoloured . . . 55 10

648 Traditional and Modern Windmills **651** "Trying" (Liza May Post)

2005. Dutch Buildings. Multicoloured. Self-adhesive gum.
2412 39c. Type **648** 55 10
2413 65c. Canal-side house and modern housing 90 70
2414 81c. Farmhouse and greenhouse . . . . 1·10 90

2005. Art. Multicoloured.
2415 39c. Type **651** 55 10
2416 39c. "Emilie" (Sidi el Karchi) 55 10
2417 39c. "ZT" (Koen Vermeule) 55 10
2418 39c. "Het Bedrijf" (Atelier van Lieshout) 55 10
2419 39c. "Me kissing Vinoodh" (Inez van Lamsweerde) . . 55 10
2420 39c. "Lena" (Carla van de Puttelaar) 55 10
2421 39c. "NR. 13" (Tom Claassen) 55 10
2422 39c. "Zonder Titel" (Pieter Kusters) 55 10
2423 39c. "Witte Roos" (Ed van der Kooy) 55 10
2424 39c. "Portrait of a Boy" (Tiong Ang) 55 10

652 Symbols of Industry **654** "Who is the Wisest"

653 Cormorant

2005. Business Stamps. Entrepreneur Week. Self-adhesive.
2425 **652** 39c. multicoloured . . . 55 10

2005. Centenary of Vereniging Natuurmonumenten (Nature preservation society). Multicoloured.
2426 39c. Type **653** 55 10
2427 39c. Pike 55 10
2428 39c. Blue-tailed damsel fly 55 10
2429 39c. Water lily 55 10
2430 65c. Hawfinch 90 70
2431 65c. Sonebeeker sheep . . 90 70
2432 65c. Sand lizard 90 70
2433 65c. Common blue butterfly 90 70
MS2434 Two sheets, each 144 × 81 mm. (a) 39c. × 4, As Nos. 2426/9 (b) 65c. × 4, As Nos. 2430/3 . . . . 5·75 5·75
Nos. 2430/3 and the stamps of **MS**2434b, each have a Priority label attached at left.

2005. Birth Centenary of Cornelis Jetses (children's reading book illustrator). Showing illustrations from "Ot en Sien". Multicoloured.
2435 39c.+19c. Type **654** 80 65
2436 39c.+19c. "Two old chums" 80 65
2437 39c.+19c. "His own fault" 80 65
2438 39c.+19c. "What does Puss think?" 80 65
2439 39c.+19c. "Nothing forgotten" 80 65
2440 39c.+19c. "Two bright things" 80 65
Nos. 2435/7 and 2438/40, each had a se-tenant label at head and foot, the upper inscribed with text from the book, the lower showing a modern photograph on the same theme.

655 Queen Beatrix and Prince Claus (Coronation, 1980) **656** Circles

2005. 25th Anniv of Coronation of Queen Beatrix. Multicoloured.
2441 39c. Type **655** 55 10
2442 78c. Seated (Queen's speech, 1991) . . . . 1·10
2443 117c. With Nelson Mandela (state visit, 1999) . . . . 1·50
2444 156c. Wearing glasses (visit to Netherlands Antilles, 1999) . . . . 2·10
2445 225c. Wearing hat (speech to European Parliament, 2004) . . . . 3·10
MS2446 144 × 75 mm. 39c. Type **655**; 78c. As No. 2442; 117c. As No. 2443; 156c. As No. 2444; 225c. As No. 2445 . . . . . . 8·25 8·25

2005. Business Coil Stamps.
2447 **656** 39c. copper 55 10
2448 78c. silver . . . . 1·10

MARINE INSURANCE STAMPS

M 22

1921.
M238 **M 22** 15c. green . . . . . 9·25 45·00
M239 60c. red . . . . 11·00 55·00

M240 75c. brown . . . . . 12·50 65·00
M241 – 1g.50 blue . . . . . 65·00 £500
M242 – 2g.25 brown £110 £700
M243 – 4½g. black £180 £850
M244 – 7½g. red £250 £1200
DESIGNS (inscr "DRIJVENDE BRANDKAST"): 1g.50, 2g.25, "Explosion"; 4½g., 7½g. Lifebelt.

OFFICIAL STAMPS

1913. Stamps of 1898 optd **ARMENWET.**
O214 **12** 1c. red . . . . 3·50 3·00
O215 1½c. blue . . . . 95 2·25
O216 2c. brown . . . . 6·25 7·00
O217 2½c. green . . . . 16·00 12·50
O218 **13** 3c. green . . . . 3·50 1·25
O219 5c. red . . . . 3·50 4·75
O220 10c. grey . . . . 35·00 40·00

POSTAGE DUE STAMPS

D 8 D 9

1870.
D76 **D 8** 5c. brown on yellow . . 55·00 11·75
D77 10c. purple on blue . . . £110 15·00
For same stamps in other colours, see Netherlands Indies, Nos. D1/5.

1881.
D174 **D 9** ½c. black and blue . . . 40 40
D175 1c. black and blue . . . 1·25 40
D176 1½c. black and blue . . 65 50
D177 2½c. black and blue . . 1·75 40
D178 3c. black and blue . . . 1·60 1·00
D179 4c. black and blue . . . 1·60 1·60
D180 5c. black and blue . . . 9·75 40
D181 6½c. black and blue . . 35·00 32·00
D182 7½c. black and blue . . 1·75 60
D183 10c. black and blue . . 28·00 50
D184 12½c. black and blue . . 23·00 1·25
D185 15c. black and blue . . 28·00 95
D186 20c. black and blue . . 24·00 6·25
D187 25c. black and blue . . 35·00 60
D188 1g. red and blue . . . 90·00 29·00
No. D188 is inscribed "EEN GULDEN".

1906. Surch.
D213 **D 9** 3c. on 1g. red and blue 28·00 28·00
D215 4 on 6½c. black and blue . . . . 4·50 5·50
D216 6½ on 20c. black & blue 3·75 4·50
D214 50c. on 1g. red & blue £125 £125

1907. De Ruyter Commemoration. stamps surch **PORTZEGEL** and value.
D217A **15** ½c. on 1c. red . . . . . 1·25 1·25
D218A 1c. on 1c. red 70 70
D219A 1½c. on 1c. red 70 70
D220A 2½c. on 1c. red . . . . 1·60 1·60
D221A 5c. on 2½c. red . . . . 1·60 70
D222A 6½c. on 2½c. red . . . . 3·00 3·00
D223A 7½c. on ½c. blue . . . . 1·90 1·40
D224A 10c. on ½c. blue . . . . 1·90 95
D225A 12½c. on ½c. blue . . . 4·50 4·50
D226A 15c. on 2½c. red . . . . 6·25 3·75
D227A 25c. on ½c. blue . . . . 8·25 7·50
D228A 50c. on ½c. blue . . . . 40·00 35·00
D229A 1g. on ½c. blue . . . . 60·00 48·00

1912. Re-issue of Type D 9 in one colour.
D230 **D 9** ½c. blue 40 40
D231 1c. blue 40 40
D232 1½c. blue . . . . 2·00 1·75
D233 2½c. blue 60 40
D234 3c. blue . . . . 1·10 70
D235 4c. blue 55 55
D236 4½c. blue . . . . 5·00 4·75
D237 5c. blue 65 55
D238 5½c. blue . . . . 4·75 4·50
D239 7c. blue . . . . 2·25 2·25
D240 7½c. blue . . . . 3·25 1·60
D241 10c. blue . . . . 1·10 55
D242 12½c. blue 55 55
D453 15c. blue 55 55
D244 20c. blue 55 40
D245 25c. blue . . . . 65·00 95
D246 50c. blue 55 40

D 25 D 121

1921.
D442 **D 25** 3c. blue 75 20
D445 6c. blue 40 40
D446 7c. blue 55 55
D447 7½c. blue 55 50
D448 8c. blue 55 40
D449 9c. blue 65 65
D450 11c. blue 55 55
D247 12c. blue 50 40
D455 25c. blue 50 40
D456 30c. blue 50 40
D458 1g. red 70 40

1923. Surch in white figures in black circle.
D272 **D 9** 1c. on 3c. blue 70 70
D273 2½c. on 7c. blue . . . . 1·10 55
D274 25c. on 1½c. blue . . . 8·25 70
D275 25c. on 7½c. blue . . . 9·25 55

1924. Stamps of 1898 surch **TE BETALEN PORT** and value in white figures in black circle.
D295 **13** 4c. on 3c. green . . . . 1·40 1·25
D296 **12** 5c. on 1c. red 70 40
D297 10c. on 1½c. blue . . . . 1·10 50
D298 **13** 12½c. on 5c. red . . . . 1·25 50

1947.
D656 **D 121** 1c. blue 20 20
D657 3c. blue 20 25
D658 4c. blue . . . . 9·25 95
D659 5c. blue 20 20
D660 6c. blue 40 40
D661 7c. blue 25 25
D662 8c. blue 25 25
D663 10c. blue 25 20
D664 11c. blue 50 50
D665 12c. blue 95 85
D666 14c. blue 95 70
D667 15c. blue 40 20
D668 16c. blue 85 85
D669 20c. blue 35 25
D670 24c. blue . . . . 1·25 1·25
D671 25c. blue 40 25
D672 26c. blue . . . . 1·40 1·60
D673 30c. blue 60 20
D674 35c. blue 70 20
D675 40c. blue 70 20
D676 50c. blue 95 25
D677 60c. blue . . . . 1·00 50
D678 85c. blue . . . . 15·00 55
D679 90c. blue . . . . 3·00 65
D680 95c. blue . . . . 3·00 65
D681 1g. red . . . . 2·25 20
D682 1g.75 red . . . . 5·50 35
For stamps as Types D 121, but in violet, see under Surinam.

INTERNATIONAL COURT OF JUSTICE

Stamps specially issued for use by the Headquarters of the Court of International Justice. Nos. J1 to J36 were not sold to the public in unused condition.

1934. Optd **COUR PER- MANENTE DE JUSTICE INTER- NATIONALE.**
J1 **35** 1½c. mauve . . . . — 55
J2 2½c. green . . . . — 55
J3 **36** 7½c. red . . . . — 95
J4 **68** 12½c. blue . . . . — 25·00
J7 **36** 12½c. blue . . . . — 18·00
J5 15c. yellow . . . . — 1·25
J6 3c. purple . . . . — 2·25

1940. Optd **COUR PER- MANANTE DE JUSTICE INTER- NATIONALE.**
J 9 **94** 7½c. red . . . . — 9·25
J10 12½c. blue . . . . — 9·25
J11 15c. blue . . . . — 9·25
J12 30c. bistre . . . . — 9·25

1947. Optd **COUR INTERNATIONALE DE JUSTICE.**
J13 **94** 7½c. red . . . . — 1·10
J14 10c. purple . . . . — 1·10
J15 12½c. blue . . . . — 1·10
J16 20c. violet . . . . — 1·10
J17 25c. red . . . . — 1·10

J 3 — J 4 Peace Palace, The Hague — J 5 Queen Juliana

1950.
J18 **J 3** 2c. blue . . . . — 8·25
J19 4c. green . . . . — 8·25

1951.
J20 **J 4** 2c. lake . . . . — 60
J21 3c. blue . . . . — 60
J22 4c. green . . . . — 60
J23 5c. brown . . . . — 60
J24 **J 5** 6c. mauve . . . . — 2·10
J25 **J 4** 6c. green . . . . — 90
J26 7c. red . . . . — 90
J27 **J 5** 10c. green . . . . — 20
J28 12c. red . . . . — 1·75
J29 15c. red . . . . — 20
J30 20c. blue . . . . — 25
J31 25c. brown . . . . — 25
J32 30c. purple . . . . — 40
J33 **J 4** 40c. blue . . . . — 35
J34 45c. red . . . . — 50
J35 50c. mauve . . . . — 55
J36 **J 5** 1g. grey . . . . — 65

J 6 Olive Branch and Peace Palace, The Hague

1989.
J37 **J 6** 5c. black and yellow . . . 15 15
J38 10c. black and blue . . . 15 15
J39 25c. black and red 20 20
J41 50c. black and green . . . 35 40
J42 55c. black and mauve . . 40 35
J43 60c. black and bistre . . . 40 45
J44 65c. black and green . . . 40 45
J45 70c. black and blue . . . 45 50
J46 75c. black and yellow . . 45 60
J47 80c. black and green . . . 50 65
J49 1g. black and orange . . . 65 75
J50 1g.50 black and blue . . . 95 1·25
J51 1g.60 black and brown . . 1·00 1·25
J54 – 5g. multicoloured . . . . 3·50 3·75
J56 – 7g. multicoloured . . . . 4·25 5·00
DESIGNS: 5, 7g. Olive branch and column.

PROVINCIAL STAMPS

The following stamps, although valid for postage throughout Netherlands, were only available from Post Offices within the province depicted and from the Philatelic Bureau.

V 1 Freisland — V 2 Nijmegen

2002. Multicoloured.
V 1 39c. Type **V 1** 55 25
V 2 39c. Drenthe 55 25
V 3 39c. North Holland 55 25
V 4 39c. Gelderland 55 25
V 5 39c. North Brabant 55 25
V 6 39c. Groningen 55 25
V 7 39c. South Holland 55 25
V 8 39c. Utrecht 55 25
V 9 39c. Limburg 55 25
V10 39c. Zeeland 55 25
V11 39c. Flevoland 55 25
V12 39c. Overijssel 55 25

2005. Multicoloured.
V13 39c. Type **V 2** 55 10
V14 39c. Nederland, Overjissel . . 55 10
V15 39c. Rotterdam 55 10
V16 39c. Weesp 55 10
V17 39c. Rotterdam 55 10
V18 39c. Weesp 55 10

NETHERLANDS ANTILLES Pt. 4

Curacao and other Netherlands islands in the Caribbean Sea. In December 1954 these were placed on an equal footing with Netherlands under the Crown.

100 cents = 1 gulden.

48 Spanish Galleon — 49 Alonso de Ojeda

1949. 450th Anniv of Discovery of Curacao.
306 **48** 6c. green . . . . 3·25 2·00
307 **49** 12½c. red . . . . 4·00 3·25
308 **48** 15c. blue . . . . 4·00 2·50

50 Posthorns and Globe — 51 Leap-frog

1949. 75th Anniv of U.P.U.
309 **50** 6c. red . . . . 4·00 2·75
310 25c. blue . . . . 4·00 1·25

1950. As numeral and portrait types of Netherlands but inscr "NED. ANTILLEN".
325 **118** 1c. brown 10 10
326 1½c. blue 10 10
327 2c. orange 10 10
328 2½c. green 90 20
329 3c. violet 20 10
329a 4c. green 60 35
330 5c. red 10 10
310a **129** 5c. yellow 20 10
311 6c. purple . . . . 1·40 10
311a 7½c. brown . . . . 5·50 10
312a 10c. red . . . . 1·60 1·60
313 12½c. green . . . . . . 2·50 20
314a 15c. blue 30 10
315a 20c. orange 40 25
316 21c. black . . . . 2·50 1·60
316a 22½c. green . . . . . . 6·25 10

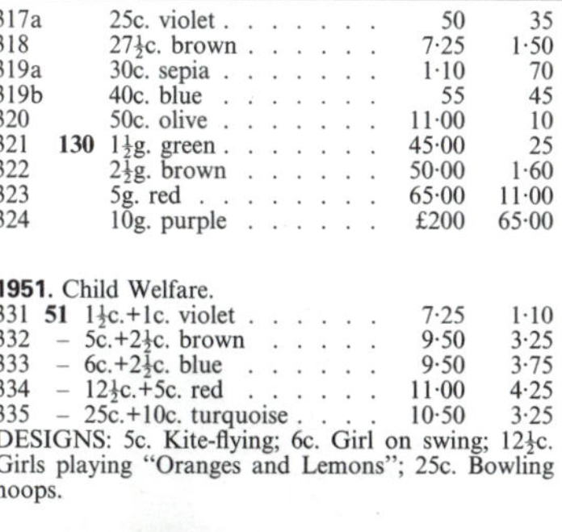

317a 25c. violet 50 35
318 27½c. brown . . . . . . 7·25 1·50
319a 30c. sepia . . . . 1·10 70
319b 40c. blue 55 45
320 50c. olive . . . . 11·00 10
321 **130** 1½g. green . . . . . . 45·00 25
322 2½g. brown . . . . . . 50·00 1·60
323 5g. red . . . . 65·00 11·00
324 10g. purple . . . . . . £200 65·00

1951. Child Welfare.
331 **51** 1½c.+1c. violet . . . . . 7·25 1·10
332 – 5c.+2½c. brown . . . . 9·50 3·25
333 – 6c.+2½c. blue . . . . . 9·50 3·75
334 – 12½c.+5c. red . . . . . 11·00 4·25
335 – 25c.+10c. turquoise . . . 10·50 3·25
DESIGNS: 5c. Kite-flying; 6c. Girl on swing; 12½c. Girls playing "Oranges and Lemons"; 25c. Bowling hoops.

52 Gull over Ship

54 Fort Beekenburg

1952. Seamen's Welfare Fund. Inscr "ZEEMANSWELVAREN".
336 **52** 1½c.+1c. green . . . . . 7·25 1·25
337 – 6c.+4c. brown . . . . . 9·00 3·25
338 – 12½c.+7c. mauve . . . . 9·00 3·50
339 – 15c.+10c. blue . . . . . 11·00 4·25
340 – 25c.+15c. red . . . . . . 10·50 4·25
DESIGNS: 6c. Sailor and lighthouse; 12½c. Sailor on ship's prow; 15c. Tanker in harbour; 25c. Anchor and compass.

1953. Netherlands Flood Relief Fund. No. 321 surch **22½ Ct. +7½ Ct. WATERSNOOD NEDERLAND 1953.**
341 **130** 22½c.+7½c. on 1½g. green 1·25 1·25

1953. 250th Anniv of Fort Beekenburg.
342 **54** 22½c. brown . . . . 5·00 50

55 Aruba Beach

1954. 3rd Caribbean Tourist Assn Meeting.
343 **55** 15c. blue and buff . . . . 5·00 2·75

1954. Ratification of Statute of the Kingdom. As No. 809 of Netherlands.
344 **158** 7½c. green 90 85

56 "Anglo" Flower

1955. Child Welfare.
345 **56** 1½c.+1c. bl, yell & turq . . 1·75 80
346 – 7½c.+5c. red, yellow & vio 3·75 2·25
347 – 15c.+5c. red, grn & olive 3·75 2·40
348 – 22½c.+7½c. red, yell & bl 3·75 2·25
349 – 25c.+10c. red, yell & grey 3·75 2·40
FLOWERS: 7½c. White Cayenne; 15c. "French" flower; 22½c. Cactus; 25c. Red Cayenne.

57 Prince Bernhard and Queen Juliana

1955. Royal Visit.
350 **57** 7½c.+2½c. red 20 20
351 22½c.+7½c. blue . . . . . 1·10 1·10

59 Oil Refinery

1955. 21st Meeting of Caribbean Commission.
352 – 15c. blue, green and brown 3·75 2·40
353 **59** 25c. blue, green and brown 4·50 2·75
DESIGN (rectangle, 36 × 25 mm): 15c. Aruba Beach.

60 St. Anne Bay

1956. 10th Anniv of Caribbean Commission.
354 **60** 15c. blue, red and black . . 35 35

61 Lord Baden-Powell

1957. 50th Anniv of Boy Scout Movement.
355 **61** 6c.+1½c. yellow 60 55
356 7½c.+2½c. green 60 55
357 15c.+5c. red 60 55

62 "Dawn of Health"

1957. 1st Caribbean Mental Health Congress, Aruba.
358 **62** 15c. black and yellow . . . 35 35

63 Saba

1957. Tourist Publicity. Multicoloured.
359 7½c. Type **63** 45 45
360 15c. St. Maarten 45 45
361 25c. St. Eustatius 45 45

64 Footballer

65 Curacao Intercontinental Hotel

1957. 8th Central American and Caribbean Football Championships.
362 **64** 6c.+2½c. orange 95 75
363 – 7½c.+5c. red . . . . 1·40 1·10
364 – 15c.+5c. green . . . . . . 1·40 1·10
365 – 22½c.+7½c. blue . . . . . 1·40 90
DESIGNS—HORIZ: 7½c. Caribbean map. VERT: 15c. Goalkeeper saving ball; 22½c. Footballers with ball.

1957. Opening of Curacao Intercontinental Hotel.
366 **65** 15c. blue 35 35

66 Map of Curacao
67 American Kestrel

1957. International Geophysical Year.
367 **66** 15c. deep blue and blue . . 75 75

1958. Child Welfare. Bird design inscr "VOOR HET KIND". Multicoloured.
368 2½c.+1c. Type **67** 50 30
369 7½c.+1½c. Yellow oriole . . . 95 80
370 15c.+2½c. Scaly-breasted ground doves . . . . . . 1·10 1·00
371 22½c.+2½c. Brown-throated conure . . . . 1·25 90

68 Greater Flamingoes (Bonaire)

1958. Size 33½ × 22 mm.
372 **68** 6c. pink and green . . . 1·90 15
373 A 7½c. yellow and brown . . 20 15
374 8c. yellow and blue . . . 20 15
375 B 10c. yellow and grey . . . 20 15
376 C 12c. grey and green . . . 20 15
377 D 15c. blue and green . . . 20 15
377a 15c. lilac and green . . . 15 10
378 E 20c. grey and red 20 15
379 A 25c. green and blue . . . 30 15
380 D 30c. green and brown . . 30 15
381 E 35c. pink and grey . . . 35 15
382 C 40c. green and mauve . . 50 15
383 B 45c. blue and violet . . . 50 15
384 **68** 50c. pink and brown . . . 50 15
385 E 55c. green and red 55 25
386 **68** 65c. pink and green . . . 65 30
387 D 70c. orange and purple . . 1·25 50
388 **68** 75c. pink and violet . . . 70 50
389 B 85c. green and brown . . 80 70
390 E 90c. orange and blue . . . 90 90
391 C 95c. yellow and orange . . 1·10 1·00
392 D 1g. grey and red . . . . 1·00 15
393 A 1½g. brown and violet . . 1·40 20
394 C 2½g. yellow and blue . . . 2·40 40
395 B 5g. mauve and brown . . 5·00 75
396 **68** 10g. pink and blue . . . 9·00 5·00
DESIGNS: A. Dutch Colonial houses (Curacao); B. Mountain and palms (Saba); C. Town Hall (St. Maarten); D. Church tower (Aruba); E. Memorial obelisk (St. Eustatius).
For larger versions of some values see Nos. 653/6.

69

1958. 50th Anniv of Netherlands Antilles Radio and Telegraph Administration.
397 **69** 7½c. lake and blue 20 20
398 15c. blue and red 35 35

70 Red Cross Flag and Antilles Map
71 Aruba Caribbean Hotel

1958. Neth. Antilles Red Cross Fund. Cross in red.
399 **70** 6c.+2c. brown 30 30
400 7½c.+2½c. green 55 55
401 15c.+5c. yellow 55 55
402 22½c.+7½c. blue 55 55

1959. Opening of Aruba Caribbean Hotel.
403 **71** 15c. multicoloured 35 35

72 Zeeland

1959. Curacao Monuments Preservation Fund. Multicoloured.
404 6c.+1½c. Type **72** . . . . . 1·25 90
405 7½c.+2½c. Saba Island . . . 1·25 90
406 15c.+5c. Molenplein (vert) . . 1·25 90
407 22½c.+7½c. Scharloobrug . . 1·25 90
408 25c.+7½c. Brievengat . . . . 1·25 90

73 Water-distillation Plant
74 Antilles Flag

1959. Inauguration of Aruba Water-distillation Plant.
409 **73** 20c. light blue and blue . . 50 50

1959. 5th Anniv of Ratification of Statute of the Kingdom.
410 **74** 10c. red, blue and light blue 50 35
411 20c. red, blue and yellow 50 35
412 25c. red, blue and green . . 50 35

75 Fokker F.XVIII "De Snip" over Caribbean
76 Mgr. Niewindt

1959. 25th Anniv of K.L.M. Netherlands–Curacao Air Service. Each yellow, deep blue and blue.
413 10c. Type **75** 50 35
414 20c. Fokker F.XVIII "De Snip" over globe 50 35
415 25c. Douglas DC-7C "Seven Seas" over Handelskade (bridge), Willemstad . . . 50 15
416 35c. Douglas DC-8 at Aruba Airport 50 55

1960. Death Centenary of Mgr. M. J. Niewindt.
417 **76** 10c. purple 55 45
418 20c. violet 55 55
419 25c. olive 55 55

77 Flag and Oil-worker
78 Frogman

1960. Labour Day.
420 **77** 20c. multicoloured 45 45

1960. Princess Wilhelmina Cancer Relief Fund. Inscr "KANKERBESTRIJDING".
421 **78** 10c.+2c. blue . . . . . . 1·40 1·10
422 – 20c.+3c. multicoloured . . 1·40 1·40
423 – 25c.+5c. red, blue & blk 1·40 1·40
DESIGNS—HORIZ: 20c. Queen angelfish; 25c. Big-scaled soldierfish.

79 Child on Bed

1961. Child Welfare. Inscr "voor het kind".
424 6c.+2c. black and green . . . 35 30
425 10c.+3c. black and red . . . 35 30
426 20c.+6c. black and yellow . . 35 30
427 25c.+8c. black and orange . . 35 30
DESIGNS: 6c. Type **79**; 10c. Girl with doll; 20c. Boy with bucket; 25c. Children in classroom.

80 Governor's Salute to the American Naval Brig "Andrew Doria" at St. Eustatius

1961. 185th Anniv of 1st Salute to the American Flag.
428 **80** 20c. multicoloured 65 65

1962. Royal Silver Wedding. As T **187** of Netherlands.
429 10c. orange 30 30
430 25c. blue 30 30

81 Jaja (nursemaid) and Child
82 Knight and World Map

1962. Cultural Series.
431 – 6c. brown and yellow . . . 35 30
432 – 10c. multicoloured 35 30
433 – 20c. multicoloured 35 35
434 **81** 25c. brown, green and black 35 35
MS435 108 × 134 mm. Nos. 431/4 1·90 1·90
DESIGNS: 6c. Corn-masher; 10c. Benta player; 20c. Petji kerchief.

1962. 5th International Candidates Chess Tournament, Curacao.
436 **82** 10c.+5c. green 95 70
437 20c.+10c. red 95 70
438 25c.+10c. blue 95 70

1963. Freedom from Hunger. No. 378 surch **TEGEN DE HONGER** wheat sprig and **+10c**.
439 20c.+10c. grey and red . . . 55 55

84 Family Group

1963. 4th Caribbean Mental Health Congress, Curacao.
440 **84** 20c. buff and blue 30 30
441 – 25c. red and blue 30 30
DESIGN: 25c. Egyptian Cross emblem.

85 "Freedom"

1963. Centenary of Abolition of Slavery in Dutch West Indies.
442 **85** 25c. brown and yellow . . 35 30

86 Hotel Bonaire

1963. Opening of Hotel Bonaire.
443 **86** 20c. brown 35 30

87 Child and Flowers
88 Test-tube and Flask

1963. Child Welfare. Child Art. Multicoloured.
444 5c.+2c. Type **87** 35 30
445 6c.+3c. Children and flowers (horiz) 35 30
446 10c.+5c. Girl with ball (horiz) 35 30
447 20c.+10c. Men with flags (horiz) 35 30
448 25c.+12c. Schoolboy 35 30

1963. 150th Anniv of Kingdom of the Netherlands. As No. 968 of Netherlands, but smaller, 26 × 27 mm.
449 25c. green, red and black . . 35 30

1963. Chemical Industry, Aruba.
450 **88** 20c. red, light green and green 45 45

89 Winged Letter

1964. 35th Anniv of 1st U.S.–Curacao Flight. Multicoloured.
451 20c. Type **89** 35 35
452 25c. Route map, Sikorsky S-38 flying boat and Boeing 707 . . . . 35 35

90 Trinitaria

1964. Child Welfare. Multicoloured.
453 6c.+3c. Type **90** 30 30
454 10c.+5c. Magdalena 30 30
455 20c.+10c. Yellow keiki . . . 30 30
456 25c.+11c. Bellisima 30 30

91 Caribbean Map

1964. 5th Caribbean Council Assembly.
457 **91** 20c. yellow, red and blue 35 30

92 "Six Islands" **93** Princess Beatrix

1964. 10th Anniv of Statute for the Kingdom.
458 **92** 25c. multicoloured 35 30

1965. Visit of Princess Beatrix.
459 **93** 25c. red 35 35

94 I.T.U. Emblem and Symbols

1965. Centenary of I.T.U.
460 **94** 10c. deep blue and blue 20 20

95 "Asperalla" (tanker) at Curacao

1965. 50th Anniv of Curacao's Oil Industry. Multicoloured.
461 10c. Catalytic cracking plant (vert) 30 20
462 20c. Type **95** 30 20
463 25c. Super fractionating plant (vert) 30 30

96 Flag and Fruit Market, Curacao

1965.
464 **96** 1c. blue, red and green 10 10
465 – 2c. blue, red and yellow 10 10
466 – 3c. blue, red and cobalt 10 10
467 – 4c. blue, red and orange 10 10
468 – 5c. blue, red and blue 20 10
469 – 6c. blue, red and pink 20 10
DESIGNS (Flag and): 2c. Divi-divi tree; 3c. Lace; 4c. Greater flamingoes; 5c. Church; 6c. Lobster.
Each is inscr with a different place-name.

97 Cup Sponges

1965. Child Welfare. Marine Life. Multicoloured.
470 6c.+3c. Type **97** 20 20
471 10c.+5c. Cup sponges (diff) 20 20
472 20c.+10c. Sea anemones on star coral 30 20
473 25c.+11c. Basket sponge, blue chromis and "Brain" coral 35 30

98 Marine and Seascape **99** Budgerigars and Wedding Rings

1965. Tercentenary of Marine Corps.
474 **98** 25c. multicoloured 20 20

1966. Intergovernmental Committee for European Migration (I.C.E.M.) Fund. As T **215** of Netherlands.
475 35c.+15c. bistre and brown 30 30

1966. Marriage of Crown Princess Beatrix and Herr Claus von Amsberg.
476 **99** 25c. multicoloured 30 20

100 Admiral de Ruyter and Map

1966. 300th Anniv of Admiral de Ruyter's Visit to St. Eustatius.
477 **100** 25c. ochre, violet and blue 20 20

101 "Grammar" **102** Cooking

1966. 25 Years of Secondary Education.
478 **101** 6c. black, blue and yellow 20 20
479 – 10c. black, red and green 20 20
480 – 20c. black, blue and yellow 30 20
481 – 25c. black, red and green 30 20
DESIGNS: The "Free Arts", figures representing: 10c. "Rhetoric" and "Dialect"; 20c. "Arithmetic" and "Geometry"; 25c. "Astronomy" and "Music".

1966. Child Welfare. Multicoloured.
482 6c.+3c. Type **102** 20 20
483 10c.+5c. Nursing 20 20
484 20c.+10c. Metal-work fitting 30 20
485 25c.+11c. Ironing 30 20

103 "Gelderland" (cruiser)

1967. 60th Anniv of Royal Netherlands Navy League.
486 **103** 6c. bronze and green 20 20
487 – 10c. ochre and yellow 20 20
488 – 20c. brown and sepia 30 20
489 – 25c. blue and indigo 30 20
SHIPS: 10c. "Pioneer" (schooner); 20c. "Oscilla" (tanker); 25c. "Santa Rosa" (liner).

104 M. C. Piar **105** "Heads in Hands"

1967. 150th Death Anniv of Manuel Piar (patriot).
490 **104** 20c. brown and red 30 20

1967. Cultural and Social Relief Funds.
491 **105** 6c.+3c. black and blue 20 20
492 10c.+5c. black & mauve 20 20
493 20c.+10c. purple 30 20
494 25c.+11c. blue 30 20

106 "The Turtle and the Monkey" **107** Olympic Flame and Rings

1967. Child Welfare. "Nanzi" Fairy Tales. Mult.
495 6c.+3c. "Princess Long Nose" (vert) 20 20
496 10c.+5c. Type **106** 20 20
497 20c.+10c. "Nanzi (spider) and the Tiger" 30 20
498 25c.+11c. "Shon Arey's Balloon" (vert) 90 70

1968. Olympic Games, Mexico. Multicoloured.
499 10c. Type **107** 30 30
500 20c. "Throwing the discus" (statue) 30 30
501 25c. Stadium and doves 30 30

108 "Dance of the Ribbons"

1968. Cultural and Social Relief Funds.
502 **108** 10c.+5c. multicoloured 20 20
503 15c.+5c. multicoloured 20 20
504 20c.+10c. multicoloured 30 20
505 25c.+10c. multicoloured 30 20

109 Boy with Goat

1968. Child Welfare Fund. Multicoloured.
506 6c.+3c. Type **109** 20 20
507 10c.+5c. Girl with dog 20 20
508 20c.+10c. Boy with cat 30 20
509 25c.+11c. Girl with duck 30 20

110 Fokker Friendship 500 **111** Radio Pylon, "Waves" and Map

1968. Dutch Antillean Airlines.
510 **110** 10c. blue, black and yellow 30 30
511 – 20c. blue, black and brown 30 30
512 – 25c. blue, black and pink 30 30
DESIGNS: 20c. Douglas DC-9; 25c. Fokker Friendship 500 in flight and Douglas DC-9 on ground.

1969. Opening of Broadcast Relay Station, Bonaire.
513 **111** 25c. green, dp blue & blue 30 30

112 "Code of Laws" **113** "Carnival"

1969. Centenary of Netherlands Antilles Court of Justice.
514 **112** 20c. green, gold & lt green 30 30
515 – 25c. multicoloured 30 30
DESIGN: 25c. "Scales of Justice".

1969. Cultural and Social Relief Funds. Antilles' Festivals. Multicoloured.
516 10c.+5c. Type **113** 35 35
517 15c.+5c. "Harvest Festival" 35 35
518 20c.+10c. "San Juan Day" 35 35
519 25c.+10c. "New Years' Day" 35 35

114 I.L.O. Emblem, "Koenoekoe" House and Cacti

1969. 50th Anniv of I.L.O.
520 **114** 10c. black and blue 20 20
521 25c. black and red 30 20

115 Boy playing Guitar **118** St. Anna Church, Otrabanda, Curacao

117 Radio Station, Bonaire

1969. Child Welfare.
522 **115** 6c.+3c. violet & orange 30 30
523 – 10c.+5c. green & yellow 35 35
524 – 20c.+10c. red and blue 35 35
525 – 25c.+11c. brown & pink 40 40
DESIGNS: 10c. Girl playing recorder; 20c. Boy playing "marimula"; 25c. Girl playing piano.

1969. 15th Anniv of Statute of the Kingdom. As T **240** of the Netherlands, but inscr "NEDERLANDSE ANTILLEN".
526 25c. multicoloured 30 30

1970. 5th Anniv of Trans-World Religious Radio Station, Bonaire. Multicoloured.
527 10c. Type **117** 20 20
528 15c. Trans-World Radio emblem 20 20

1970. Churches of the Netherlands Antilles. Mult.
529 10c. Type **118** 35 30
530 20c. "Mikve Israel-Emanuel" Synagogue, Punda, Curacao (horiz) 35 30
531 25c. Pulpit Fort Church Curacao 35 30

119 "The Press" **120** Mother and Child

1970. Cultural and Social Relief Funds. "Mass-media". Multicoloured.
532 10c.+5c. Type **119** 50 50
533 15c.+5c. "Films" 50 50
534 20c.+10c. "Radio" 50 50
535 25c.+10c. "Television" 50 50

1970. Child Welfare. Multicoloured.
536 6c.+3c. Type **120** 50 50
537 10c.+5c. Child with piggy-bank 50 50
538 20c.+10c. Children's Judo 50 50
539 25c.+11c. "Pick-a-back" 50 50

121 St. Theresia's Church, St. Nicolaas, Aruba **122** Lions Emblem

1971. 40th Anniv of St. Theresia Parish, Aruba.
540 **121** 20c. multicoloured 30 30

1971. 25th Anniv of Curacao Lions Club.
541 **122** 25c. multicoloured 35 35

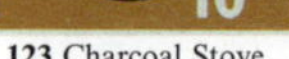

123 Charcoal Stove  **125** Admiral Brion

1971. Cultural and Social Relief Funds. Household Utensils. Multicoloured.

542 10c.+5c. Type **123** 55 55
543 15c.+5c. Earthenware water vessel 55 55
544 20c.+10c. Baking oven 55 55
545 25c.+10c. Kitchen implements 55 55

1971. Prince Bernhard's 60th Birthday. Design as No. 1135 of Netherlands.

546 45c. multicoloured 55 55

1971. 150th Death Anniv of Admiral Pedro Luis Brion.

547 **125** 40c. multicoloured 35 35

126 Bottle Doll **127** Queen Emma Bridge, Curacao

1971. Child Welfare. Home-made Toys. Mult.

548 15c.+5c. Type **126** 65 65
549 20c.+10c. Simple cart 65 65
550 30c.+15c. Spinning-tops 65 65

1971. Views of the Islands. Multicoloured.

551 1c. Type **127** 10 10
552 2c. The Bottom, Saba 10 10
553 3c. Greater flamingoes, Bonaire 10 10
554 4c. Distillation plant, Aruba 10 10
555 5c. Fort Amsterdam, St. Maarten 20 10
556 6c. Fort Oranje, St. Eustatius 20 10

128 Ship in Dock **129** Steel Band

1972. Inauguration of New Dry Dock Complex, Willemstad, Curacao.

557 **128** 30c. multicoloured 35 35

1972. Cultural and Social Relief Funds. Folklore. Multicoloured.

558 15c.+5c. Type **129** 70 70
559 20c.+10c. "Seu" festival 70 70
560 30c.+15c. "Tambu" dance 70 70

130 J. E. Irausquin **131** Dr. M. F. da Costa Gomez

1972. 10th Death Anniv of Juan Enrique Irausquin (Antilles statesman).

561 **130** 30c. red 35 35

1972. 65th Birth Anniv of Moises F. da Costa Gomez (statesman).

562 **131** 30c. black and green 35 35

132 Child playing with Earth **133** Pedestrian Crossing

1972. Child Welfare. Multicoloured.

563 15c.+5c. Type **132** 75 75
564 20c.+10c. Child playing in water 75 75
565 30c.+15c. Child throwing ball into the air 75 75

1973. Cultural and Social Relief Funds. Road Safety.

566 **133** 12c.+6c. multicoloured 80 80
567 – 15c.+7c. grn, orge & red 80 80
568 – 40c.+20c. multicoloured 80 80

DESIGNS: 15c. Road-crossing patrol; 40c. Traffic lights.

134 William III (portrait from stamp of 1873) **135** Map of Aruba, Curacao and Bonaire

1973. Stamp Centenary.

569 **134** 15c. violet, mauve and gold 35 25
570 – 20c. multicoloured 50 35
571 – 30c. multicoloured 50 35

DESIGNS: 20c. Antilles postman; 30c. Postal Service emblem.

1973. Inauguration of Submarine Cable and Microwave Telecommunications Link. Multicoloured.

572 15c. Type **135** 50 45
573 30c. Six stars ("The Antilles") 50 45
574 45c. Map of Saba, St. Maarten and St. Eustatius 50 45
MS575 145 × 50 mm. Nos. 572/4 2·25 1·75

136 Queen Juliana **137** Jan Eman

1973. Silver Jubilee of Queen Juliana's Reign.

576 **136** 15c. multicoloured 55 55

1973. 16th Death Anniv of Jan Eman (Aruba statesman).

577 **137** 30c. black and green 35 35

138 "1948–1973" **139** L. B. Scott

1973. Child Welfare Fund. 25th Anniv of 1st Child Welfare Stamps.

578 **138** 15c.+5c. light green, green and blue 70 70
579 – 20c.+10c. brown, green and blue 70 70
580 – 30c.+15c. violet, blue and light blue 70 70
MS581 108 × 75 mm. Nos. 578 × 2, 579 × 2 3·50 3·25

DESIGNS: No. 579, Three Children; 580, Mother and child.

1974. 8th Death Anniv of Lionel B. Scott (St. Maarten statesman).

582 **139** 30c. multicoloured 35 35

140 Family Meal **141** Girl combing Hair

1974. Family Planning Campaign. Multicoloured.

583 6c. Type **140** 20 20
584 12c. Family at home 30 30
585 15c. Family in garden 35 30

1974. Cultural and Social Relief Funds. "The Younger Generation". Multicoloured.

586 12c.+6c. Type **141** 1·00 90
587 15c.+7c. "Pop dancers" 1·00 90
588 40c.+20c. Group drummer 1·00 90

142 Desulphurisation Plant

1974. 50th Anniv of Lago Oil Co, Aruba. Mult.

589 15c. Type **142** 30 30
590 30c. Fractionating towers 35 35
591 45c. Lago refinery at night 55 55

143 U.P.U. Emblem **144** "A Carpenter outranks a King"

1974. Centenary of Universal Postal Union.

592 **143** 15c. gold, green and black 50 45
593 30c. gold, blue and black 50 45

1974. Child Welfare. Children's Songs. Mult.

594 15c.+5c. Type **144** 80 80
595 20c.+10c. Footprints ("Let's Do a Ring-dance") 80 80
596 30c.+15c. "Moon and Sun" 80 80

145 Queen Emma Bridge  **146** Ornamental Ventilation Grid

1975. Antillean Bridges. Multicoloured.

597 20c. Type **145** 45 45
598 30c. Queen Juliana Bridge 45 45
599 40c. Queen Wilhelmina Bridge 55 55

1975. Cultural and Social Welfare Funds.

600 **146** 12c.+6c. multicoloured 70 70
601 – 15c.+7c. brown & stone 70 70
602 – 40c.+20c. multicoloured 70 70

DESIGNS: 15c. Knight accompanied by buglers (tombstone detail); 40c. Foundation stone.

147 Sodium Chloride Molecules

1975. Bonaire Salt Industry. Multicoloured.

603 15c. Type **147** 50 35
604 20c. Salt incrustation and blocks 50 45
605 40c. Map of salt area (vert) 55 45

148 Fokker F.XVIII "De Snip" and Old Control Tower

1975. 40th Anniv of Aruba Airport. Mult.

606 15c. Type **148** 35 25
607 30c. Douglas DC-9-30 and modern control tower 50 35
608 40c. Tail of Boeing 727-200 and "Princess Beatrix" Airport buildings 50 45

149 I.W.Y. Emblem

1975. International Women's Year. Multicoloured.

609 6c. Type **149** 20 20
610 12c. "Social Development" 35 25
611 20c. "Equality of Sexes" 50 35

150 Children making Windmill

1975. Child Welfare. Multicoloured.

612 15c.+5c. Type **150** 70 70
613 20c.+10c. Child modelling clay 70 70
614 30c.+15c. Children drawing pictures 70 70

151 Beach, Aruba **152** J. A. Abraham (statesman)

1976. Tourism. Multicoloured.

615 40c. Type **151** 55 55
616 40c. Fish Kiosk, Bonaire 55 55
617 40c. "Table Mountain", Curacao 55 55

1976. Abraham Commemoration.

618 **152** 30c. purple on brown 45 45

153 Dyke Produce **154** Arm holding Child

1976. Agriculture, Animal Husbandry and Fisheries. Multicoloured.

619 15c. Type **153** 35 25
620 35c. Cattle 55 45
621 45c. Fishes 55 50

1976. Child Welfare. "Carrying the Child".

622 **154** 20c.+10c. multicoloured 70 65
623 – 25c.+12c. multicoloured 70 65
624 – 40c.+18c. multicoloured 70 65

DESIGNS—HORIZ: 25c. VERT: 40c. Both similar to Type **154** showing arm holding child.

155 "Andrew Doria" (naval brig) receiving Salute **156** Carnival Costume

1976. Bicentenary of American Revolution. Multicoloured.

625 25c. Flags and plaque, Fort Oranje 70 45
626 40c. Type **155** 70 45
627 55c. Johannes de Graaff, Governor of St. Eustatius 70 70

1977. Carnival.

628 – 25c. multicoloured 55 50
629 **156** 35c. multicoloured 55 50
630 – 40c. multicoloured 55 50

DESIGNS: 25c., 40c. Women in Carnival costumes.

157 Tortoise (Bonaire) **158** "Ace" Playing Card

1977. Rock Paintings. Multicoloured.
631 25c. Bird (Aruba) 50 35
632 35c. Abstract (Curaca) . . . 50 45
633 40c. Type **157** 55 45

1977. Sixth Central American and Caribbean Bridge Championships. Multicoloured.
634 **158** 20c.+10c. red and black 50 35
635 – 25c.+12c. multicoloured 50 50
636 – 40c.+18c. multicoloured 65 65
MS637 75 × 108 mm. Nos. 634/5 × 2
DESIGNS—VERT: 25c. "King" playing card. HORIZ: 40c. Bridge hand.

1977. "Amphilex 77" International Stamp Exhibition, Amsterdam. Sheet 175 × 105 mm.
MS638 Nos. 634/6 but with green backgrounds . . . . 3·50 3·25

159 "Cordia sebestena"

160 Bells outside Main Store

1977. Flowers. Multicoloured.
639 25c. Type **159** 50 35
640 40c. "Albizzia lebbeck" (vert) 55 40
641 55c. "Tamarindus indica" . . 65 65

1977. 50th Anniv of Spritzer and Fuhrmann (jewellers). Multicoloured.
642 20c. Type **160** 50 35
643 40c. Globe basking in sun . . 55 50
644 55c. Antillean flag and diamond ring 65 65

161 Children with Toy Animal

1977. Child Welfare. Multicoloured.
645 15c.+15c. Type **161** 25 20
646 20c.+10c. Children with toy rabbit 50 50
647 25c.+12c. Children with toy cat 55 55
648 40c.+18c. Children with toy beetle 65 55
MS649 108 × 75 mm. Nos. 646 × 2, 648 × 2 . . . . 2·40 2·10

162 "The Unspoiled Queen" (Saba)

1977. Tourism. Multicoloured.
650 25c. Type **162** 20 10
651 35c. "The Golden Rock" (St. Eustatius) 25 20
652 40c. "The Friendly Island" (St. Maarten) 25 25

1977. As Nos. 378, 381/2 and 385, but larger, (39 × 22 mm).
653 E 20c. grey and red . . . . . 1·60 65
654 35c. pink and brown . . . 3·50 3·00
655 C 40c. green and mauve . . . 55 35
656 E 55c. green and red 75 50

163 19th-century Chest

164 Water-skiing

1978. 150th Anniv of Netherlands Antilles' Bank. Multicoloured.
657 **163** 15c. blue and light blue 20 10
658 – 20c. orange and gold . . 20 20
659 – 40c. green and deep green 25 25
DESIGNS: 20c. Bank emblem; 40c. Strong-room door.

1978. Sports Funds. Multicoloured.
660 15c.+5c. Type **164** 20 20
661 20c.+10c. Yachting 20 20
662 25c.+12c. Football 20 20
663 40c.+18c. Baseball 35 30

165 "Erythrina velutina"

166 "Polythysana rubrescens"

1978. Flora of Netherlands Antilles. Multicoloured.
664 15c. "Delconix regia" 20 20
665 25c. Type **165** 25 20
666 50c. "Gualacum officinale" (horiz) 35 35
667 55c. "Gilricidia sepium" (horiz) 50 50

1978. Butterflies. Multicoloured.
668 15c. Type **166** 20 20
669 25c. "Caligo sp." 25 20
670 35c. "Prepona praeneste" . . 35 35
671 40c. "Morpho sp." 50 45

167 "Conserve Energy" (English)

168 Red Cross

1978. Energy Conservation.
672 **167** 15c. orange and black . . 20 20
673 – 20c. green and black . . . 25 20
674 – 40c. red and black 50 40
DESIGNS: As No. 672 but text in Dutch (20c.) or in Papiamento (40c.).

1978. 150th Birth Anniv of Henri Dunant (founder of Red Cross).
675 **168** 55c.+25c. red and blue . . 25 25
MS676 144 × 50 mm. No. 675 × 3 2·10 2·10

169 Curacao from Sea, and Punched Tape

170 Boy Rollerskating

1978. 70th Anniv of Antilles Telecommunications Corporation (Landsradio). Multicoloured.
677 20c. Type **169** 25 25
678 40c. Ship's bridge, punched tape and radio mast . . . 35 35
679 55c. Satellite and aerial (vert) 55 55

1978. Child Welfare. Multicoloured.
680 15c.+5c. Type **170** 50 35
681 20c.+10c. Boy and girl flying kite 55 45
682 25c.+12c. Boy and girl playing marbles 55 50
683 40c.+18c. Girl riding bicycle 65 55
MS684 75 × 108 mm. Nos. 680/1 × 2 1·60 1·40

171 Ca'i Awa (pumping station)

172 Aruba Coat of Arms (float)

1978. 80th Death Anniv of Leonard Burlington Smith (entrepreneur and U.S. Consul).
685 **171** 25c. multicoloured . . . 20 20
686 – 35c. black, greenish yellow and yellow 25 25
687 – 40c. multicoloured 50 25
DESIGNS—VERT: 35c. Leonard Burlington Smith. HORIZ: 40c. Opening ceremony of Queen Emma Bridge, 1888.

1979. 25th Aruba Carnival. Multicoloured.
688 40c.+10c. Float representing heraldic fantasy 50 35
689 75c.+20c. Type **172** 70 70

173 Goat and P.A.H.O. Emblem

174 Yacht and Sun

1979. 12th Inter-American Ministerial Meeting on Foot and Mouth Disease and Zoonosis Control, Curacao. Multicoloured.
690 50c. Type **173** 35 35
691 75c. Horse and conference emblem 45 45
692 150c. Cows, flag and Pan-American Health Organization (P.A.H.O.) and W.H.O. emblems . . . 1·00 1·00
MS693 143 × 50 mm. As Nos. 690/2 but background colours changed 2·00 2·00

1979. 12th International Sailing Regatta, Bonaire. Multicoloured.
694 15c.+5c. Type **174** 20 20
695 35c.+25c. Yachts 35 35
696 40c.+15c. Yacht and globe (horiz) 50 45
697 55c.+25c. Yacht, sun and flamingo 65 50
MS698 124 × 72 mm. Nos. 694/7 1·60 1·60

175 Corps Members

176 "Melochia tomentosa"

1979. 50th Anniv of Curacao Volunteer Corps.
699 **175** 15c.+10c. blue, red and ultramarine 20 20
700 – 40c.+20c. blue, violet and gold 55 55
701 – 1g. multicoloured 70 65
DESIGNS: 40c. Sentry in battle dress and emblem; 1g. Corps emblem, flag and soldier in ceremonial uniform.

1979. Flowers. Multicoloured.
702 25c. "Casearia tremula" . . . 30 20
703 40c. "Cordia cylindrostachya" 35 35
704 1g.50 Type **176** . . . . . . 1·10 1·10

177 Girls reading Book

178 Dove and Netherlands Flag

1979. International Year of the Child.
705 **177** 20c.+10c. multicoloured 25 25
706 – 25c.+12c. multicoloured 35 35
707 – 35c.+15c. violet, brown and black 55 45
708 – 50c.+20c. multicoloured 65 65
MS709 75 × 108 mm. Nos. 705 and 707, each × 2 . . . . 1·50 1·40
DESIGNS: 25c. Toddler and cat; 35c. Girls carrying basket; 50c. Boy and girl dressing-up.

1979. 25th Anniv of Statute of the Kingdom. Multicoloured.
710 65c. Type **178** 65 55
711 1g.50 Dove and Netherlands Antilles flag . . . . 1·10 1·10

179 Map of Aruba and Foundation Emblem

1979. 30th Anniv of Aruba Cultural Centre Foundation. Multicoloured.
712 95c. Type **179** 80 80
713 1g. Foundation headquarters 90 90

180 Brass Chandelier

1980. 210th Anniv of Fort Church, Curacao.
714 **180** 20c.+10c. yellow, black and brown 25 25
715 – 50c.+25c. multicoloured 55 55
716 – 100c. multicoloured . . . 80 80
DESIGNS: 50c. Pipe organ; 100c. Cupola tower, 1910.

181 Rotary Emblem and Cogwheel

1980. 75th Anniv of Rotary International. Multicoloured.
717 45c. Rotary emblem 35 35
718 50c. Globe and cogwheels . . 50 35
719 85c. Type **181** 70 70
MS720 120 × 75 mm. Nos. 717/19 1·50 1·50

182 Savings Box

1980. 75th Anniv of Post Office Savings Bank. Multicoloured.
721 25c. Type **182** 25 20
722 150c. Savings box (different) 1·25 1·25

183 Queen Juliana Accession Stamp

1980. Accession of Queen Beatrix.
723 **183** 25c. red, green and gold 20 20
724 – 60c. green, red and gold 50 45
DESIGN: 60c. 1965 Royal Visit stamp.

184 Sir Rowland Hill

185 Gymnastics (beam exercise)

1980. "London 1980" International Stamp Exhibition.
725 **184** 45c. black and green . . . 35 35
726 – 60c. black and red 50 50
727 – 1g. red, black and blue . . 90 90
MS728 160 × 90 mm. 45c. black and red; 60c. black and blue; 1g. red, black and green . . . . . . 1·90 1·90
DESIGNS: 60c. "London 1980" logo; 1g. Airmail label.

1980. Sports Funds.
729 **185** 25c.+10c. red and black 25 25
730 – 30c.+15c. yellow & blk . . 35 35
731 – 45c.+20c. light green, green and black 55 50
732 – 60c.+25c. pink, orange and black 70 65
MS733 75 × 144 mm. Nos. 729 and 732, each × 3 . . . . 2·75 2·50
DESIGNS: 30c. Gymnastics (horse vaulting); 45c. Volleyball; 60c. Basketball.

186 White-fronted Dove

1980. Birds. Multicoloured.
734 25c. Type **186** 25 25
735 60c. Tropical mockingbird . . 65 55
736 85c. Bananaquit 90 70

187 "St. Maarten Landscape"

188 Rudolf Theodorus Palm

1980. Child Welfare. Children's Drawings. Multicoloured.

737	25c.+10c. Type **187**	35	25
738	30c.+15c. "Bonaire House"	50	50
739	40c.+20c. "Child writing on Board"	55	55
740	60c.+25c. "Dancing Couple" (vert)	70	65
MS741	149 × 108 mm. Nos. 737 and 740, each × 3 plus four labels	3·00	2·75

1981. Birth Centenary (1980) of Rudolf Theodorus Palm (musician).

742 **188**	60c. brown and yellow	55	55
743 –	1g. buff and blue	1·00	90

DESIGN: 1g. Musical score and hands playing piano.

189 Map of Aruba and TEAM Emblem

190 Boy in Wheelchair

1981. 50th Anniv of Evangelical Alliance Mission (TEAM) in Antilles. Multicoloured.

744	30c. Type **189**	25	25
745	50c. Map of Curacao and emblem	55	45
746	1g. Map of Bonaire and emblem	1·00	90

1981. International Year of Disabled Persons. Multicoloured.

747	25c.+10c. Blind woman	35	35
748	30c.+15c. Type **190**	50	45
749	45c.+20c. Child in walking frame	70	70
750	60c.+25c. Deaf girl	80	80

191 Tennis

192 Gateway

1981. Sports Funds. Multicoloured.

751	30c.+15c. Type **191**	55	45
752	50c.+20c. Swimming	70	70
753	70c.+25c. Boxing	1·00	90
MS754	100 × 72 mm. Nos. 751/3	2·25	2·10

1981. 125th Anniv of St. Elisabeth's Hospital. Multicoloured.

755	60c. Type **192**	55	55
756	1g.50 St. Elisabeth's Hospital	1·40	1·40

193 Marinus van der Maarel (promoter)

194 Mother and Child

1981. 50th Anniv (1980) of Antillean Boy Scouts Association. Multicoloured.

757	45c.+20c. Wolf Cub and leader	80	80
758	70c.+25c. Type **193**	1·10	1·10
759	1g.+50c. Headquarters, Ronde Klip	1·60	1·60
MS760	144 × 50 mm. Nos. 757/9	3·50	3·50

1981. Child Welfare. Multicoloured.

761	35c.+15c. Type **194**	45	45
762	45c.+20c. Boy and girl	65	65
763	55c.+25c. Child with cat	80	80
764	85c.+40c. Girl with teddy bear	1·25	1·25
MS765	75 × 108 mm. Nos. 761 and 763, each × 2	2·50	2·50

195 "Jatropha gossypifolia"

196 Pilot Gig approaching Ship

1981. Flowers. Multicoloured.

766	45c. "Cordia globosa"	40	35
767	70c. Type **195**	75	70
768	100c. "Croton flavens"	90	90

1982. Centenary of Pilotage Service. Mult.

769	70c. Type **196**	90	90
770	85c. Modern liner and map of Antilles	1·10	1·00
771	1g. Pilot boarding ship	1·25	1·10

197 Fencing

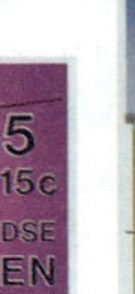

198 Holy Ark

1982. Sports Funds.

772 **197**	35c.+15c. mauve and violet	70	65
773 –	45c.+20c. blue and deep blue	90	80
774 –	70c.+35c. multicoloured	1·40	1·25
775 –	85c.+40c. brown and deep brown	1·60	1·40
MS776	144 × 50 mm. No. 774 × 2 plus label	3·25	3·75

DESIGNS: 45c. Judo; 70c. Football; 85c. Cycling.

1982. 250th Anniv of Dedication of Mikve Israel-Emanuel Synagogue, Curacao. Mult.

777	75c. Type **198**	1·00	80
778	85c. Synagogue facade	1·10	80
779	150c. Tebah (raised platform)	1·60	1·40

199 Peter Stuyvesant (Governor) and Flags of Netherlands, Netherlands Antilles and United States

200 Airport Control Tower

1982. Bicentenary of Netherlands–United States Diplomatic Relations.

780 **199**	75c. multicoloured	1·10	90
MS781	101 × 70 mm. No. 780	1·40	1·20

See also No. **MS**996.

1982. International Federation of Air Traffic Controllers.

782 –	35c. black, ultramarine and blue	55	35
783 **200**	75c. black, green and light green	1·00	80
784 –	150c. black, orange and salmon	1·60	1·40

DESIGNS: 35c. Radar plot trace; 150c. Radar aerials.

201 Mail Bag

202 Brown Chromis

1982. "Philexfrance 82" International Stamp Exhibition, Paris. Multicoloured.

785	45c. Exhibition emblem	65	50
786	85c. Type **201**	1·00	60
787	150c. Netherlands Antilles and French flags	1·60	1·40
MS788	125 × 64 mm. Nos. 785/7	3·25	2·75

1982. Fishes. Multicoloured.

789	35c. Type **202**	70	45
790	75c. Spotted trunkfish	1·25	90
791	85c. Blue tang	1·40	1·10
792	100c. French angelfish	1·50	1·10

203 Girl playing Accordion

1982. Child Welfare. Multicoloured.

793	35c.+15c. Type **203**	80	65
794	75c.+35c. Boy playing guitar	1·40	1·25
795	85c.+40c. Boy playing violin	1·60	1·40
MS796	144 × 50 mm. Nos. 793/5	4·00	3·50

204 Saba House

1982. Cultural and Social Relief Funds. Local Houses. Multicoloured.

797	35c.+15c. Type **204**	90	65
798	75c.+35c. Aruba House	1·50	1·25
799	85c.+40c. Curacao House	1·75	1·40
MS800	72 × 100 mm. Nos. 797/9	4·50	3·25

205 High Jumping

1983. Sports Funds. Multicoloured.

801	35c.+15c. Type **205**	70	55
802	45c.+20c. Weightlifting	1·10	90
803	85c.+40c. Wind-surfing	1·60	1·40

206 Natural Bridge, Aruba

207 W.C.Y. Emblem and Means of Communication

1983. Tourism. Multicoloured.

804	35c. Type **206**	65	55
805	45c. Lac Bay, Bonaire	70	65
806	100c. Willemstad, Curacao	1·40	1·25

1983. World Communications Year.

807 **207**	1g. multicoloured	1·40	1·25
MS808	100 × 72 mm. No. 807	1·50	1·25

208 "Curacao" (paddle-steamer) and Post Office Building

209 Mango ("Mangifera indica")

1983. "Brasiliana 83" International Stamp Exhibition, Rio de Janeiro. Multicoloured.

809	45c. Type **208**	80	70
810	55c. Brazil flag, exhibition emblem and Netherlands Antilles flag and postal service emblem	90	80
811	100c. Governor's Palace, Netherlands Antilles, and Sugarloaf Mountain, Rio de Janeiro	1·50	1·40
MS812	100 × 72 mm. Nos. 809/11	3·25	2·75

1983. Flowers. Multicoloured.

813	45c. Type **209**	90	70
814	55c. "Malpighia punicifolia"	1·00	80
815	100c. "Citrus aurantifolia"	1·60	1·40

210 Boy and Lizard

1983. Child Welfare. Multicoloured.

816	45c.+20c. Type **210**	1·10	90
817	55c.+25c. Girl watching ants	1·25	1·10
818	100c.+50c. Girl feeding donkey	2·10	1·90
MS819	100 × 72 mm. Nos. 816/18	4·50	4·00

211 Aruba Water Jar

212 Saba

1983. Cultural and Social Relief Funds. Pre-Columbian Pottery.

820 **211**	45c.+20c. light blue, blue and black	1·25	1·00
821 –	55c.+25c. pink, red and black	1·40	1·25
822 –	85c.+40c. stone, green and black	1·60	1·40
823 –	100c.+50c. light brown, brown and black	2·10	2·00

DESIGNS: 55c. Aruba decorated bowl; 85c. Curacao human figurine; 100c. Fragment of Curacao female figurine.

1983. Local Government Buildings. Multicoloured.

824	20c. Type **212**	25	25
825	25c. St. Eustatius	25	25
826	30c. St. Maarten	35	35
827	35c. Aruba	2·40	45
828	45c. Bonaire	55	55
829	55c. Curacao	70	65
830	60c. Type **212**	65	65
831	65c. As No. 825	70	70
832	70c. Type **212**	65	45
833	75c. As No. 826	90	90
834	85c. As No. 827	3·00	1·10
835	85c. As No. 828	80	55
836	90c. As No. 828	1·10	1·10
837	95c. As No. 829	1·25	1·25
838	1g. Type **212**	1·25	1·10
839	1g.50 As No. 825	1·50	1·40
841	2g.50 As No. 826	2·50	1·75
842	5g. As No. 828	5·50	3·50
843	10g. As No. 829	9·50	6·00
844	15g. Type **212**	14·00	9·50

213 Note-taking, Typesetting and Front Page of "Amigoe"

1984. Centenary of "Amigoe de Curacao" (newspaper). Multicoloured.

845	45c. Type **213**	70	65
846	55c. Printing press and newspapers	80	70
847	85c. Reading newspaper	1·40	1·25

214 W.I.A. and I.C.A.O. Emblems

1984. 40th Anniv of I.C.A.O.

848 **214**	25c. multicoloured	45	35
849 –	45c. violet, blue and black	90	65
850 –	55c. multicoloured	1·00	75
851 –	100c. multicoloured	1·60	1·25

DESIGNS: 45c. I.C.A.O. anniversary emblem; 55c. A.L.M. and I.C.A.O. emblems; 100c. Fokker F.XIII airplane "De Snip".

215 Fielder

1984. Sports Funds. 50th Anniv of Curacao Baseball Federation. Multicoloured.

852	25c.+10c. Type **215**	90	65
853	45c.+20c. Batter	1·40	1·10
854	55c.+25c. Pitcher	1·60	1·40
855	85c.+40c. Running for base	1·90	1·60
MS856	144 × 50 mm. Nos. 852/5	5·75	4·25

216 Microphones and Radio

1984. Cultural and Social Relief Funds. Radio and Gramophone. Multicoloured.

857 45c.+20c. Type **216** . . . . 1·40 1·10
858 55c.+25c. Gramophones and record . . . . 1·90 1·40
859 100c.+50c. Gramophone with horn . . . . 2·10 1·90

217 Bonnet-maker

1984. Centenary of Curacao Chamber of Commerce and Industry. Multicoloured.

860 45c. Type **217** . . . . 1·25 90
861 55c. Chamber emblem . . . 1·25 90
862 1g. "Southward" (liner) passing under bridge . . . 1·75 1·40

No. 861 is an inverted triangle.

218 Black-faced Grassquit

219 Eleanor Roosevelt and Val-Kill, Hyde Park, New York

1984. Birds. Multicoloured.

863 45c. Type **218** . . . . 1·00 80
864 55c. Rufous-collared sparrow 1·25 1·40
865 150c. Blue-tailed emerald . . 1·90 1·90

1984. Birth Centenary of Eleanor Roosevelt.

866 **219** 45c. multicoloured 80 65
867 – 85c. black, gold and bistre 1·25 1·10
868 – 100c. black, yellow and red . . . . 1·10 1·25

DESIGNS: 85c. Portrait in oval frame; 100c. Eleanor Roosevelt with children.

220 Child Reading

221 Adult Flamingo and Chicks

1984. Child Welfare. Multicoloured.

869 45c.+20c. Type **220** . . . . 1·10 1·00
870 55c.+25c. Family reading . . 1·40 1·40
871 100c.+50c. Family in church 1·90 1·90
MS872 100 × 72 mm. Nos. 869/71 4·50 4·50

1985. Greater Flamingoes. Multicoloured.

873 25c. Type **221** 70 55
874 45c. Young flamingoes . . . 1·10 75
875 55c. Adult flamingoes . . . . 1·10 90
876 100c. Flamingoes in various flight positions . . . . . . 1·90 1·40

222 Symbols of Entered Apprentice

223 Players with Ball

1985. Bicentenary of De Vergenoeging Masonic Lodge, Curacao. Multicoloured.

877 45c. Type **222** . . . . 1·00 70
878 55c. Symbols of the Fellow Craft . . . . 1·10 1·00
879 100c. Symbols of the Master Mason . . . . 1·90 1·60

1985. Sports Funds. Football. Multicoloured.

880 10c.+5c. Type **223** 55 35
881 15c.+5c. Dribbling ball . . . 55 45
882 45c.+20c. Running with ball 1·10 1·00
883 55c.+25c. Tackling . . . . 1·40 1·25
884 85c.+40c. Marking player with ball . . . . 1·90 1·75

224 Boy using Computer

1985. Cultural and Social Welfare Funds. International Youth Year. Multicoloured.

885 45c.+20c. Type **224** . . . . 1·25 1·10
886 55c.+25c. Girl listening to records . . . . 1·50 1·40
887 100c.+50c. Boy break-dancing . . . . 2·25 2·10

225 U.N. Emblem

1985. 40th Anniv of U.N.O.

888 **225** 55c. multicoloured . . . . 1·00 90
889 1g. multicoloured . . . . 1·50 1·40

226 Pierre Lauffer and Poem

227 Eskimo

1985. Papiamentu (Creole language). Multicoloured.

890 45c. Type **226** 55 55
891 55c. Wave inscribed "Papiamentu" 75 75

1985. Child Welfare. Multicoloured.

892 5c.+5c. Type **227** 35 20
893 10c.+5c. African child 50 25
894 25c.+10c. Chinese girl 70 50
895 45c.+20c. Dutch girl . . . . 1·10 90
896 55c.+25c. Red Indian girl . . 1·25 1·10
MS897 100 × 72 mm. Nos. 894/6 3·25 2·50

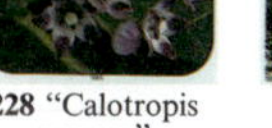

228 "Calotropis procera"

229 Courthouse

1985. Flowers. Multicoloured.

898 5c. Type **228** 35 20
899 10c. "Capparis flexuosa" . . 35 20
900 20c. "Mimosa distachya" . . 55 35
901 45c. "Ipomoea nil" 90 65
902 55c. "Heliotropium ternatum" . . . . 1·10 70
903 150c. "Ipomoea incarnata" 1·90 1·60

1986. 125th Anniv of Curacao Courthouse. Multicoloured.

904 5c. Type **229** 25 20
905 15c. States room (vert) . . . 35 20
906 25c. Court room 55 35
907 55c. Entrance (vert) 90 70

230 Sprinting

231 Girls watching Artist at work

1986. Sports Funds. Multicoloured.

908 15c.+5c. Type **230** 90 45
909 25c.+10c. Horse racing . . . 1·10 70
910 45c.+20c. Motor racing . . . 1·40 1·00
911 55c.+25c. Football . . . . . 1·50 1·25

1986. Curacao Youth Care Foundation. Multicoloured.

912 30c.+15c. Type **231** 90 65
913 45c.+20c. Children watching sculptor at work . . . . . 1·10 80
914 55c.+25c. Children watching potter at work . . . . . . 1·40 1·10

232 Chained Man

1986. 25th Anniv of Amnesty International. Multicoloured.

915 45c. Type **232** 80 55
916 55c. Dove behind bars . . . 90 65
917 100c. Man behind bars . . . 1·40 1·10

233 Post Office Mail Box

234 Boy playing Football

1986. Mail Boxes. Multicoloured.

918 10c. Type **233** 20 20
919 25c. Street mail box on pole 35 25
920 45c. Street mail box in brick column 65 55
921 55c. Street mail box 80 65

1986. Child Welfare. Multicoloured.

922 20c.+10c. Type **234** 55 50
923 25c.+15c. Girl playing tennis 70 55
924 45c.+20c. Boy practising judo 90 80
925 55c.+25c. Boy playing baseball . . . . 1·10 1·00
MS926 75 × 72 mm. Nos. 924/5 2·10 1·75

235 Brothers' First House and Mauritius Vliegendehond

236 Engagement Picture

1986. Centenary of Friars of Tilburg Mission. Multicoloured.

927 10c. Type **235** 30 20
928 45c. St. Thomas College and Mgr. Ferdinand E. C. Kieckens 75 55
929 55c. St. Thomas College courtyard and Fr. F.S. de Beer 85 70

1987. Golden Wedding of Princess Juliana and Prince Bernhard.

930 **236** 1g.35 orange, blk & gold 2·10 1·60
MS931 50 × 72 mm. No. 930 . . 3·00 1·40

237 Map

238 Girls playing Instruments

1987. 150th Anniv of Maduro Holding Inc. Multicoloured.

932 70c. Type **237** 70 65
933 85c. Group activities 90 80
934 1g.55 Saloman Elias Levy Maduro (founder) . . . . 1·60 1·60

1987. Cultural and Social Relief Funds.

935 **238** 35c.+15c. multicoloured 70 65
936 – 45c.+25c. light green, green and blue . . . . 1·10 80
937 – 85c.+40c. multicoloured 1·40 1·25

DESIGNS: 45c. Woman pushing man in wheelchair. 85c. Bandstand.

239 Map and Emblem

1987. 50th Anniv of Curacao Rotary Club. Multicoloured.

938 15c. Type **239** 20 20
939 50c. Zeelandia country house (meeting venue) 65 55
940 65c. Emblem on map of Curacao 75 70

240 Octagon (house where Bolivar's sisters lived)

1987. 175th Anniv of Simon Bolivar's Exile on Curacao (60, 80c.) and 50th Anniv of Bolivarian Society (70, 90c.). Multicoloured.

941 60c. Type **240** 70 65
942 70c. Society headquarters, Willemstad, Curacao . . . 80 70
943 80c. Room in Octagon . . . 1·00 90
944 90c. Portraits of Manuel Carlos Piar, Simon Bolivar and Pedro Luis Brion . . . 1·10 1·00

241 Baby

1987. Child Welfare. Multicoloured.

945 40c.+15c. Type **241** . . . . 1·00 70
946 55c.+25c. Child . . . . . . 1·25 1·00
947 115c.+50c. Youth . . . . . 1·75 1·50
MS948 144 × 50 mm. Nos. 945/7 4·25 1·40

242 White-tailed Tropic Birds

1987. 25th Anniv of Netherlands Antilles National Parks Foundation. Multicoloured.

949 70c. Type **242** 70 65
950 85c. White-tailed deer 90 80
951 155c. Iguana . . . . 1·60 1·50

243 Printing Press and Type

1987. 175th Anniv of "De Curacaosche Courant" (periodical and printing shop). Multicoloured.

952 55c. Type **243** 70 55
953 70c. Keyboard and modern printing press 85 65

244 William Godden (founder)

1988. 75th Anniv of Curacao Mining Company. Multicoloured.

954 40c. Type **244** 70 45
955 105c. Phosphate processing plant . . . . 1·50 1·10
956 155c. Tafelberg (source of phosphate) . . . . 2·25 1·60

245 Flags, Minutes and John Horris Sprockel (first President)

246 Bridge through "100"

1988. 50th Anniv of Netherlands Antilles Staten (legislative body). Multicoloured.

957 65c. Type **245** 70 70
958 70c. Ballot paper and schematic representation of extension of voting rights 90 70
959 155c. Antilles and Netherlands flags and birds representing five Antilles islands and Aruba . . . . 1·60 1·40

1988. Cultural and Social Relief Funds. Centenary of Queen Emma Bridge, Curacao. Mult.

960 55c.+25c. Type **246** . . . . 1·10 65
961 115c.+55c. Willemstad harbour (horiz) . . . . . . 1·75 1·40
962 190c.+60c. Leonard B. Smith (engineer) and flags (horiz) 2·75 2·50

247 Broken Chain

1988. 125th Anniv of Abolition of Slavery. Mult.

963 155c. Type **247** . . . . . . 1·50 1·40
964 190c. Breach in slave wall . . 1·75 1·40

248 Flags and Map

249 Charles Hellmund (Bonaire councillor)

1988. 3rd Inter-American Foundation of Cities "Let us Build Bridges" Conference, Curacao. Multicoloured.

965 80c. Type **248** . . . . 1·00 70
966 155c. Bridge and globe . . . 1·40 1·25

1988. Celebrities. Multicoloured.

967 55c. Type **249** 65 45
968 65c. Atthelo Maud Edwards-Jackson (founder of Saba Electric Company) 70 50
969 90c. Nicolaas Debrot (Governor of Antilles, 1962–69) . . . . 1·10 90
970 120c. William Charles de la Try Ellis (lawyer and politician) . . . . 1·25 1·10

250 Child watching Television

251 "Cereus hexagonus"

1988. Child Welfare. Multicoloured.

971 55c.+25c. Type **250** . . . . 1·00 65
972 65c.+30c. Boy with radio . . 1·10 90
973 115c.+55c. Girl using computer . . . . 1·60 1·40
MS974 118 × 67 mm. Nos. 971/3 3·25 2·50

1988. Cacti. Multicoloured.

975 55c. Type **251** 70 50
976 115c. Melocactus . . . . . . 1·25 90
977 125c. "Opuntia wentiana" . . 1·25 1·10

252 Magnifying Glass over 1936 and 1980 Stamps

253 Crested Bobwhite

1989. Cultural and Social Relief Funds. 50th Anniv of Curacao Stamp Association. Multicoloured.

978 30c.+10c. Type **252** 80 45
979 55c.+20c. Picking up stamp with tweezers (winning design by X. Rico in drawing competition) . . . 1·10 80
980 80c.+30c. Barn owl and stamp album . . . . . . 1·25 1·00

Nos. 978/80 were printed together, se-tenant, forming a composite design.

1989. 40th Anniv of Curacao Foundation for Prevention of Cruelty to Animals. Multicoloured.

981 65c. Type **253** 90 70
982 115c. Dogs and cats . . . . 1·25 1·10

254 "Sun Viking" in Great Bay Harbour, St. Maarten

255 Paula Clementina Dorner (teacher)

1989. Tourism. Cruise Liners. Multicoloured.

983 70c. Type **254** 90 70
984 155c. "Eugenio C" entering harbour, St. Annabay, Curacao . . . . 1·60 1·10

1989. Celebrities. Multicoloured.

985 40c. Type **255** 65 45
986 55c. John Aniseto de Jongh (pharmacist and politician) 70 50
987 90c. Jacobo Jesus Maria Palm (musician) . . . . . 1·00 80
988 120c. Abraham Mendes Chumaceiro (lawyer and social campaigner) . . . . 1·25 1·10

256 Boy and Girl under Tree

257 Hand holding "7"

1989. Child Welfare. Multicoloured.

989 40c.+15c. Type **256** 90 65
990 65c.+30c. Two children playing on shore . . . . . 1·10 90
991 115c.+35c. Adult carrying child . . . . 1·60 1·40
MS992 92 × 62 mm. 155c.+75c. Children playing on shore . . . 3·25 2·50

1989. 40th Anniv of Queen Wilhelmina Foundation for Cancer Care. Multicoloured.

993 30c. Type **257** 55 45
994 60c. Seated figure and figure receiving radiation treatment 80 70
995 80c. Figure exercising and Foundation emblem . . . 1·00 70

1989. "World Stamp Expo '89" International Stamp Exhibition, Washington, D.C. Sheet 112 × 65 mm containing multicoloured designs as previous issues but with changed values.

MS996 70c. As No. 625; 155c. Type **199**; 250c. Type **80** . . . 5·00 4·50

258 Fireworks

259 "Tephrosia cinerea"

1989. Christmas. Multicoloured.

997 30c. Type **258** 50 35
998 100c. Christmas tree decorations . . . . 1·10 90

1990. Flowers. Multicoloured.

999 30c. Type **259** 35 35
1000 55c. "Erithalis fruticosa" . . 65 55
1001 65c. "Evolvulus antillanus" 70 65
1002 70c. "Jacquinia arborea" . . 80 70
1003 125c. "Tournefortia onaphalodes" . . . . . . 1·40 1·40
1004 155c. "Sesuvium portulacastrum" . . . . 1·90 1·40

260 Girl Guides

261 Nun with Child, Flag and Map

1990. Cultural and Social Relief Funds. Mult.

1005 30c.+10c. Type **260** (60th anniv) 70 50
1006 40c.+15c. Totolika (care of mentally handicapped organization) (17th anniv) 90 70
1007 155c.+65c. Boy scout (60th anniv) . . . . 2·50 2·50

1990. Centenary of Arrival of Dominican Nuns in Netherlands Antilles. Multicoloured.

1008 10c. Type **261** 20 20
1009 55c. St. Rose Hospital and St. Martin's Home, St. Maarten 65 50
1010 60c. St. Joseph School, St. Maarten 70 65

262 Goal Net, Ball and Shield

263 Carlos Nicolaas-Perez (philologist and poet)

1990. Multicoloured.

1011 65c.+30c. Type **262** (65th anniv of Sport Unie Brion Trappers football club) . . 1·10 1·00
1012 115c.+55c. Guiding addict from darkness towards sun (anti-drugs campaign) 1·75 1·75

1990. Meritorious Antilleans. Multicoloured.

1013 40c. Type **263** 50 35
1014 60c. Evert Kruythoff (writer) 70 65
1015 80c. John de Pool (writer) 90 80
1016 150c. Joseph Sickman Corsen (poet and composer) . . . . 1·75 1·60

264 Queen Emma

265 Isla Refinery

1990. Dutch Queens of the House of Orange. Multicoloured.

1017 100c. Type **264** . . . . . . 1·40 1·10
1018 100c. Queen Wilhelmina . . 1·40 1·10
1019 100c. Queen Juliana . . . . 1·40 1·10
1020 100c. Queen Beatrix . . . . 1·40 1·10
MS1021 77 × 64 mm. 250c. Queens Emma, Wilhelmina, Juliana and Beatrix (35 × 24 mm) . . . . .

1990. 75th Anniv of Oil Refining on Curacao.

1022 **265** 100c. multicoloured . . . 1·25 1·25

266 Flower and Bees

267 Parcels

1990. Child Welfare. International Literacy Year. Designs illustrating letters of alphabet. Multicoloured.

1023 30c.+5c. Type **266** 65 45
1024 55c.+10c. Dolphins and sun 1·00 70
1025 65c.+15c. Donkey with bicycle . . . . 1·10 90
1026 100c.+20c. Goat dreaming of house . . . . 1·50 1·75
1027 115c.+25c. Rabbit carrying food on yoke . . . . . . 1·75 1·50
1028 155c.+55c. Lizard, moon and cactus . . . . 2·75 2·40

1990. Christmas. Multicoloured.

1029 30c. Type **267** (25th anniv of Curacao Lions Club's Good Neighbour project) 55 35
1030 100c. Mother and child . . 1·40 1·10

268 Flag, Map and Distribution of Mail

269 Scuba Diver and French Grunt

1991. 6th Anniv of Express Mail Service.

1031 **268** 20g. multicoloured . . . 23·00 22·00

1991. Fishes. Multicoloured.

1032 10c. Type **269** 35 20
1033 40c. Spotted trunkfish . . . 65 45
1034 55c. Copper sweepers . . . 85 70
1035 75c. Skindiver and yellow goatfishes . . . . 1·10 90
1036 100c. Black-barred soldier-fishes . . . . 1·50 1·25

270 Children and Stamps

1991. Cultural and Social Relief Funds. Mult.

1037 30c.+10c. Type **270** (12th anniv of Philatelic Club of Curacao) 70 55
1038 65c.+25c. St. Vincentius Brass Band (50th anniv) 1·25 1·10
1039 155c.+55c. Games and leisure pursuits (30th anniv of FESEBAKO) (Curacao community centres) . . . . 2·75 2·50

271 "Good Luck"

272 Westpoint Lighthouse, Curacao

1991. Greetings Stamps. Multicoloured.

1040 30c. Type **271** 35 35
1041 30c. "Thank You" 35 35
1042 30c. Couple and family ("Love You") 35 35
1043 30c. Song birds ("Happy Day") 35 35
1044 30c. Greater flamingo and medicines ("Get Well Soon") 35 35
1045 30c. Flowers and balloons ("Happy Birthday") . . . 35 35

1991. Lighthouses. Multicoloured.

1046 30c. Type **272** 50 45
1047 70c. Willems Toren, Bonaire 80 80
1048 115c. Klein Curacao lighthouse . . . . 1·60 1·60

273 Peter Stuyvesant College

1991. 50th Anniv of Secondary Education in Netherlands Antilles (65c.) and "Espamer '91" Spain–Latin America Stamp Exhibition, Buenos Aires (125c.). Multicoloured.

1049 65c. Type **273** 70 70
1050 125c. Dancers of Netherlands Antilles, Argentina and Portugal (vert) . . . . 1·40 1·40

274 Octopus with Letters and Numbers

275 Nativity

1991. Child Welfare. Multicoloured.

1051 40c.+15c. Type **274** 90 70
1052 65c.+30c. Parents teaching arithmetic . . . . . . 1·40 1·25
1053 155c.+65c. Bird and tortoise with clock . . . . . . 2·75 2·75
MS1054 118 × 67 mm. 55c.+25c. Owl with letters and national flag; 100c.+35c. Books and bookworms; 115c.+50c. Dragon, ice-cream cone and icicles. Imperf 4·50 4·00

1991. Christmas. Multicoloured.

1055 30c. Type **275** 35 35
1056 100c. Angel appearing to shepherds . . . . 1·10 1·10

276 Joseph Alvarez Correa (founder) and Headquarters of S.E.L. Maduro and Sons
277 Fawn

1991. 75th Anniv of Maduro and Curiel's Bank. Multicoloured.
1057 30c. Type **276** 65 50
1058 70c. Lion rampant (bank's emblem) and "75" . . . 1·10 90
1059 155c. Isaac Haim Capriles (Managing Director, 1954–74) and Scharloo bank branch . . . . . . 1·90 1·75

1992. The White-tailed Deer. Multicoloured.
1060 5c. Type **277** (postage) . . . 20 20
1061 10c. Young adults 25 20
1062 30c. Stag 50 35
1063 40c. Stag and hind in water 65 45
1064 200c. Stag drinking (air) . . 2·40 2·40
1065 355c. Stag calling . . . . . 4·25 4·00

278 Windsurfer
279 The Alhambra, Grenada

1992. Cultural and Social Relief Funds. Olympic Games, Barcelona. Multicoloured.
1066 30c.+10c. Type **278** (award of silver medal to Jan Boersma, 1988 Games) . . 75 55
1067 55c.+25c. Globe, national flag and Olympic rings . . 1·10 90
1068 115c.+55c. Emblem of National Olympic Committee (60th anniv) 2·10 2·00
Nos. 1066/8 were issued together, se-tenant, forming a composite design.

1992. "Granada '92" International Stamp Exhibition (250c.) and "Expo '92" World's Fair, Seville (500c.). Sheet 92 × 52 mm containing T **279** and similar horiz design. Multicoloured.
MS1069 250c. Type **279**; 500c. Carthusian Monastery, Seville, and Columbus . . . . 10·00 9·00

280 "Santa Maria"

1992. "World Columbian Stamp Expo '92", Chicago. Multicoloured.
1070 250c. Type **280** . . . . . . 3·00 2·75
1071 500c. Chart and Columbus 5·75 5·50

281 View of Dock and Town
282 Angela de Lannoy-Willems

1992. Curacao Port Container Terminal. Mult.
1072 80c. Type **281** 90 90
1073 125c. Crane and ship . . . 1·40 1·40

1992. Celebrities.
1074 **282** 30c. black, brown & grn 35 35
1075 – 40c. black, brown & blue 55 45
1076 – 55c. black, brown & orge 70 65
1077 – 70c. black, brown and red 80 70
1078 – 100c. black, brown & blue . . . . 1·10 1·10
DESIGNS: 30c. Type **282** (first woman Member of Parliament); 40c. Lodewijk Daniel Gerharts (entrepreneur on Bonaire); 55c. Cyrus Wilberforce Wathey (entrepreneur on St. Maarten); 70c. Christian Winkel (Deputy Governor of Antilles); 100c. Mother Joseph (founder of Roosendaal Congregation (Franciscan welfare sisterhood)).

283 Spaceship
284 Queen Beatrix and Prince Claus

1992. Child Welfare. Multicoloured.
1079 30c.+10c. Type **283** 55 45
1080 70c.+30c. Robot . . . . . 1·10 1·10
1081 100c.+40c. Extra-terrestrial being . . . . 1·60 1·50
MS1082 94 × 54 mm. 155c.+70c. Martian . . . . 3·25 2·75

1992. 12½ Years since Accession to the Throne of Queen Beatrix (100c.) and Royal Visit to Netherlands Antilles (others). Designs showing photos of previous visits to the Antilles. Multi.
1083 70c. Type **284** 80 80
1084 100c. Queen Beatrix signing book . . . . 1·10 1·10
1085 175c. Queen Beatrix and Prince Claus with girl . . 1·90 1·90

285 Crib
286 Hibiscus

1992. Christmas. Multicoloured.
1086 30c. Type **285** 50 35
1087 100c. Mary and Joseph searching for lodgings (vert) . . . . 1·40 1·10

1993. Flowers. Multicoloured.
1088 75c. Type **286** 80 80
1089 90c. Sunflower . . . . . . 1·00 1·00
1090 175c. Ixora . . . . 1·90 1·90
1091 195c. Rose . . . . 2·25 2·25

287 De Havilland Twin Otter and Flight Paths
288 Pekingese

1993. Anniversaries. Multicoloured.
1092 65c. Type **287** (50th anniv of Princess Juliana International Airport, St. Maarten) 70 70
1093 75c. Laboratory worker and National Health Laboratory (75th anniv) 80 80
1094 90c. De Havilland Twin Otter on runway at Princess Juliana International Airport . . 1·00 1·00
1095 175c. White and yellow cross (50th anniv of Princess Margriet White and Yellow Cross Foundation for District Nursing) . . . . 1·90 1·90

1993. Dogs. Multicoloured.
1096 65c. Type **288** 80 70
1097 90c. Standard poodle . . . 1·10 1·00
1098 100c. Pomeranian . . . . . 1·25 1·10
1099 175c. Papillon . . . . . . 2·00 1·90

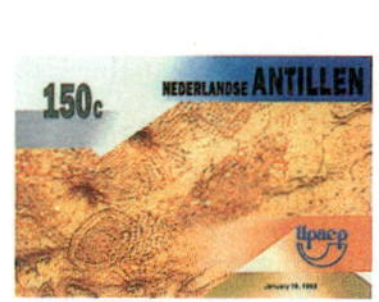

289 Cave Painting, Bonaire
290 "Sun and Sea"

1993. "Brasiliana '93" International Stamp Exhibition, Rio de Janeiro, and Admittance of Antilles to Postal Union of the Americas, Spain and Portugal. Multicoloured.
1100 150c. Type **289** . . . . . . 1·60 1·60
1101 200c. Exhibition emblem and Antilles flag . . . . 2·10 2·10
1102 250c. Globe and hand signing U.P.A.E.P. agreement . . . . 2·75 2·75

1993. "Carib-Art" Exhibition, Curacao. Multicoloured.
1103 90c. Type **290** . . . . . . 1·00 1·00
1104 150c. "Heaven and Earth" 1·60 1·60

291 "Safety in the Home"

1993. Child Welfare. Child and Danger. Mult.
1105 65c.+25c. Type **291** . . . . 1·10 1·00
1106 90c.+35c. Child using seat belt ("Safety in the Car") (vert) . . . . 1·40 1·40
1107 175c.+75c. Child wearing armbands ("Safety in the Water") . . . . 2·75 2·75
MS1108 168 × 79 mm. 35c.+15c. × 5, Child writing in exercise book ("Danger of Failing at School") 4·00 2·75

292 Consulate, Curacao
293 "Mother and Child" (mosaic)

1993. Bicentenary of United States Consul General to the Antilles. Multicoloured.
1109 65c. Type **292** 80 70
1110 90c. Arms of Netherlands Antilles and U.S.A . . . 1·10 1·00
1111 175c. American bald eagle 2·00 1·90

1993. Christmas. Works by Lucila Engels-Boskaljon. Multicoloured.
1112 30c. Type **293** 40 30
1113 115c. "Madonna and Christ" (painting) . . . . 1·25 1·25

294 Basset Hound
295 Common Caracara

1994. Dogs. Multicoloured.
1114 65c. Type **294** 95 75
1115 75c. Pit bull terrier . . . . 1·10 80
1116 90c. Cocker spaniel . . . . 1·25 1·00
1117 175c. Chow-chow . . . . . 2·10 1·90

1994. Birds. Multicoloured.
1118 50c. Type **295** 90 55
1119 95c. Green peafowl . . . . 1·50 1·25
1120 100c. Scarlet macaw . . . . 1·40 1·25
1121 125c. Troupial . . . . . . 1·75 1·40

296 Joseph Husurell Lake
297 Players' Legs

1994. Celebrities. Multicoloured.
1122 65c. Type **296** (founder of United People's Liberation Front) 70 70
1123 75c. Efrain Jonckheer (politician and diplomat) 90 80
1124 100c. Michiel Martinus Romer (teacher) . . . . . 1·10 1·10
1125 175c. Carel Nicolaas Winkel (social reformer) . . . . 2·00 1·90

1994. World Cup Football Championship, U.S.A. Multicoloured.
1126 90c. Type **297** . . . . . . 1·10 1·00
1127 150c. Foot and ball . . . . 1·75 1·60
1128 175c. Referee's whistle and cards . . . . 2·00 1·90

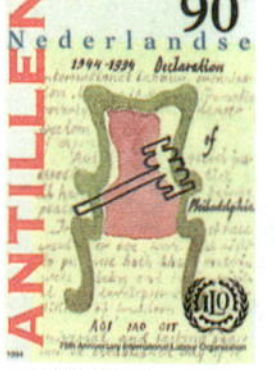

298 Chair and Hammer
299 Birds and Dolphin

1994. 75th Anniv of International Labour Organization. Multicoloured.
1129 90c. Type **298** . . . . . . 1·25 1·10
1130 110c. Heart and "75" . . . 1·40 1·25
1131 200c. Tree . . . . 2·50 2·50

1994. Nature Protection. Multicoloured.
1132 10c. Type **299** 30 30
1133 35c. Dolphin, magnificent frigate bird, brown pelican and troupial 50 50
1134 50c. Coral, iguana, lobster and fish 65 65
1135 125c. Fish, turtle, queen conch, greater flamingoes and American wigeons . . 1·60 1·60
MS1136 84 × 70 mm. Nos. 1132/5 3·50 3·25

300 1945 7½c. Netherlands Stamp
301 Mother and Child

1994. "Fepapost '94" European Stamp Exhibition, The Hague. Multicoloured.
1137 2g.50 Type **300** . . . . . . 2·75 2·50
1138 5g. Curacao 1933 6c. stamp 5·50 5·25
MS1139 96 × 55 mm. Nos. 1137/8 9·50 8·25

1994. Child Welfare. International Year of the Family. Multicoloured.
1140 35c.+15c. Type **301** 60 50
1141 65c.+25c. Father and daughter reading together 1·25 1·10
1142 90c.+35c. Grandparents . . 2·10 2·00
MS1143 86 × 51 mm. 175c.+75c. I.Y.F. emblem . . . . 3·50 2·75

302 Dove in Hands

1994. Christmas. Multicoloured.
1144 30c. Type **302** 50 35
1145 115c. Globe and planets in hands . . . . 1·50 1·25

303 Carnival and Houses
304 Handicapped and Able-bodied Children

1995. Carnival. Multicoloured.
1146 125c. Type **303** . . . . . . 1·50 1·40
1147 175c. Carnival and harbour 2·10 1·90
1148 250c. Carnival and rural house . . . . 3·00 2·75

1995. 50th Anniv of Mgr. Verriet Institute (for the physically handicapped). Multicoloured.
1149 65c. Type **304** 80 70
1150 90c. Cedric Virginie (wheelchair-bound bookbinder) . . . . . . 1·10 1·00

305 Dobermann

1995. Dogs. Multicoloured.
1151 75c. Type **305** . . . . . . 1·10 85
1152 85c. German shepherd . . . 1·25 1·00
1153 100c. Bouvier . . . . 1·40 1·10
1154 175c. St. Bernard . . . . . 2·40 1·90

306 Bonaire

1995. Flags and Arms of the Constituent Islands of the Netherlands Antilles. Multicoloured.
1155 10c. Type **306** 20 10
1156 35c. Curacao 50 35
1157 50c. St. Maarten 70 55
1158 65c. Saba 90 70
1159 75c. St. Eustatius (also state flag and arms) . . . . . 1·00 80
1160 90c. Island flags and state arms . . . . 1·10 1·00

307 Monument to Slave Revolt of 1795

309 Sealpoint Siamese

1995. Cultural and Social Relief Funds. Bicentenary of Abolition of Slavery in the Antilles (1161/2) and Children's Drawings on Philately (1163/4). Multicoloured.
1161 30c.+10c. Type **307** 55 50
1162 45c.+15c. Magnificent frigate bird and slave bell 70 65
1163 65c.+25c. "Stamps" from Curacao and Bonaire (Nicole Wever and Sabine Anthonio) . . . . 1·10 1·00
1164 75c.+35c. "Stamps" from St. Maarten, St. Eustatius and Saba (Chad Jacobs, Martha Hassell and Dion Humphreys) . . . . . . 1·25 1·10

1995. Hurricane Relief Fund. Nos. 831, 833 and 838 surch **ORKAAN LUIS** and premium.
1165 65c.+65c. multicoloured . . 1·60 1·50
1166 75c.+75c. multicoloured . . 1·75 1·60
1167 1g.+1g. multicoloured . . . 2·40 2·10

1995. Cats. Multicoloured.
1168 25c. Type **309** 50 30
1169 60c. Maine coon 90 65
1170 65c. Silver Egyptian mau . . 1·00 75
1171 90c. Angora . . . . 1·25 1·00
1172 150c. Blue smoke Persian . . 2·00 1·60

310 Helping Elderly Woman across Road

1995. Child Welfare. Children and Good Deeds. Multicoloured.
1173 35c.+15c. Type **310** 60 55
1174 65c.+25c. Reading newspaper to blind person 1·10 1·00
1175 90c.+35c. Helping younger brother . . . . 1·40 1·25
1176 175c.+75c. Giving flowers to the sick . . . . 2·75 2·50

311 Wise Men on Camels

312 Serving the Community

1995. Christmas. Multicoloured.
1177 30c. Type **311** 50 35
1178 115c. Fireworks over houses 1·40 1·25

1996. 50th Anniv of Curacao Lions Club. Multicoloured.
1179 75c. Type **312** . . . . . . 1·10 80
1180 105c. Anniversary emblem 1·40 1·25
1181 250c. Handshake . . . . . 3·25 2·75

313 Disease on Half of Leaf

314 Dish Aerial and Face

1996. 60th Anniv of Capriles Psychiatric Clinic, Otrabanda on Rif. Multicoloured.
1182 60c. Type **313** 70 65
1183 75c. Tornado and sun over house . . . . 1·10 80

1996. Centenary of Guglielmo Marconi's Patented Wireless Telegraph. Multicoloured.
1184 85c. Type **314** . . . . . . 1·00 90
1185 175c. Dish aerial and morse transmitter . . . . 2·10 1·90

315 Letters and Buildings

316 Gulf Fritillary

1996. Translation of Bible into Papiamentu (Creole language). Multicoloured.
1186 85c. Type **315** . . . . . . 1·00 90
1187 225c. Bible and alphabets 2·75 2·40

1996. "Capex '96" International Stamp Exhibition, Toronto, Canada. Butterflies. Multicoloured.
1188 5c. Type **316** 20 10
1189 110c. "Callithea philotima" 1·25 1·10
1190 300c. Clipper . . . . 3·50 3·25
1191 750c. "Euphaedra francina" 8·75 8·25
MS1192 132 × 75 mm. Nos. 1189/90 5·75 4·50

317 Mary Johnson-Hassell (introducer of drawn-thread work to Saba, 57th death)

1996. Anniversaries.
1193 **317** 40c. orange and black on grey 60 50
1194 – 50c. green and black on grey 70 55
1195 – 75c. red and black on grey . . . . 1·00 80
1196 – 80c. blue and black on grey . . . . 1·10 1·00

DESIGNS: 40c. Type **317** (introducer of drawn-thread work to Saba); 50c. Cornelius Marten (Papa Cornes) (pastor to Bonaire); 75c. Phelippi Chakutoe (union leader); 85c. Chris Engels (physician, artist, author and fencing champion).

318 Shire

1996. Horses. Multicoloured.
1197 110c. Type **318** . . . . . 1·50 1·25
1198 225c. Shetland ponies . . . 2·75 2·50
1199 275c. British thoroughbred 2·25 3·00
1200 350c. Przewalski mare and foal . . . . 4·50 4·00

319 Street Child and Shanty Town

320 Straw Hat with Poinsettias and Gifts

1996. Child Welfare. 50th Anniv of UNICEF. Multicoloured.
1201 40c.+15c. Type **319** 70 65
1202 75c.+25c. Asian child weaver . . . . 1·25 1·10
1203 110c.+45c. Child in war zone of former Yugoslavia (vert) . . . . 1·90 1·75
1204 225c.+100c. Impoverished Caribbean mother and child (vert) . . . . . . 3·75 3·50

1996. Christmas. Multicoloured. Self-adhesive.
1205 35c. Type **320** 60 35
1206 150c. Father Christmas . . 2·00 1·60

321 Emblem

322 Deadly Galerina

1997. Cultural and Social Relief Funds.
1207 **321** 40c.+15c. black and yellow 70 65
1208 – 75c.+30c. blue, mauve and black . . . . . 1·25 1·10
1209 – 85c.+40c. red and black 1·60 1·50
1210 – 110c.+50c. black, green and red . . . . 1·90 1·90

DESIGNS: 40c. Type **321** (50th anniv of Curacao Foundation for Care and Resettlement of Ex-prisoners); 75c. Emblem (60th anniv (1996) of General Union of Public Servants (ABVO)); 85c. Flag of Red Cross (65th anniv of Curacao division); 110c. National Red Cross emblem (65th anniv of Curacao division).

1997. Fungi. Multicoloured.
1211 40c. Type **322** 60 50
1212 50c. Destroying angel . . . 75 55
1213 75c. Cep . . . . 1·10 80
1214 175c. Fly agaric . . . . . 2·25 1·90

323 Budgerigars

1997. Birds. Multicoloured.
1215 5c. Type **323** 25 10
1216 25c. Sulphur-crested cockatoo 70 30
1217 50c. Yellow-shouldered Amazon 95 55
1218 75c. Purple heron . . . . . 1·10 80
1219 85c. Ruby topaz hummingbird . . . . . . 1·40 90
1220 100c. South African crowned crane . . . . . 1·60 1·10
1221 110c. Vermilion flycatcher 1·75 1·10
1222 125c. Greater flamingo . . 1·75 1·40
1223 200c. Osprey . . . . 2·50 2·25
1224 225c. Keel-billed toucan . . 3·00 2·50

324 Parrots ("Love")

325 "Correspondence"

1997. Greetings Stamps. Multicoloured. (a) As T **324**.
1225 40c. Type **324** 50 45
1226 75c. Waterfall ("Positivism") 95 80
1227 85c. Roses ("Mothers' Day") . . . . 1·10 1·00
1228 100c. Quill pen ("Correspondence") . . . 1·25 1·10
1229 110c. Leaves, rainbow and heart ("Success") . . . . 1·40 1·25
1230 225c. Ant on flower ("Congratulations") . . . 2·75 2·50

(b) As T **325**.
1231 40c. Motif as in Type **324** 80 80
1232 40c. Type **325** 80 80
1233 75c. Petals and moon ("Positivism") . . . . . 1·10 1·10
1234 75c. Motif as No. 1226 . . 1·10 1·10
1235 75c. Sun and moon ("Success") . . . . 1·10 1·10
1236 85c. Motif as No. 1227 . . 1·10 1·10
1237 100c. Motif as No. 1228 . . 1·60 1·40
1238 110c. Motif as No. 1229 . . 1·40 1·40
1239 110c. Heart between couple ("Love") . . . . 1·40 1·25
1240 225c. Motif as No. 1230 . . 3·25 3·25

326 Rat

327 2½ Cent Coin (Plaka)

1997. "Pacific '97" International Stamp Exhibition, San Francisco. Chinese Zodiac. Designs showing Tangram (puzzle) representations and Chinese symbols for each animal. Multicoloured.
1241 5c. Type **326** 15 10
1242 5c. Ox 15 10
1243 5c. Tiger 15 10
1244 40c. Rabbit 60 50
1245 40c. Dragon 60 50
1246 40c. Snake 60 50
1247 75c. Horse . . . . 1·00 80
1248 75c. Goat . . . . 1·00 80
1249 75c. Monkey . . . . 1·00 80
1250 100c. Rooster . . . . 1·25 1·10
1251 100c. Dog . . . . 1·25 1·10
1252 100c. Pig . . . . 1·25 1·10
MS1253 145 × 150 mm. Nos. 1241/52 10·50 10·50

1997. Coins. Obverse and reverse of coins. Multicoloured.
1254 85c. Type **327** . . . . . . 1·25 1·00
1255 175c. 5 cent (Stuiver) . . . 2·10 2·00
1256 225c. 2½ gulden (Fuerte) . . 3·25 2·50

328 Score of "Atras de Nos" and Salsa Drummer

1997. Child Welfare. The Child and Music. Multicoloured.
1257 40c.+15c. Type **328** 65 60
1258 75c.+25c. Score of "For Elise" and pianist . . . . 1·10 1·00
1259 110c.+45c. Score of "Blues for Alice" and flautist . . 1·90 1·75
1260 225c.+100c. Score of "Yesterday" and guitarist 2·75 2·50

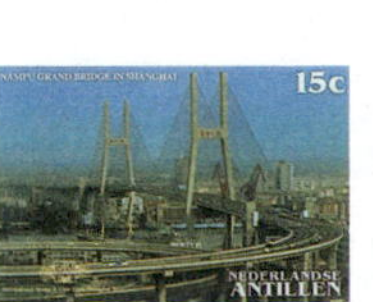

329 Nampu Grand Bridge, Shanghai

330 Worshippers (detail of mural by Marcolino Maas in Church of the Holy Family, Willemstad, Curacao)

1997. "Shanghai 1997" International Stamp and Coin Exhibition, China. Multicoloured.
1261 15c. Type **329** 20 20
1262 40c. Giant panda 70 55
1263 75c. Tiger (New Year) (vert) 1·10 90
MS1264 108 × 78 mm. 90c. The Bund, Shanghai . . . . 2·10 1·60

1997. Christmas and New Year. Multicoloured.
1265 35c. Type **330** 60 40
1266 150c. Popping champagne cork and calendar (New Year) . . . . 2·00 1·60

331 Partial Eclipse

332 Camera and Painting

1998. Total Solar Eclipse, Curacao. Multicoloured.
1267 85c. Type **331** . . . . . . 1·10 1·00
1268 110c. Close-up of sun in total eclipse . . . . . . 1·60 1·25
1269 225c. Total eclipse . . . . . 3·00 2·75
MS1270 85 × 52 mm. 750c. Hologram of stages of the eclipse 11·00 11·00

1998. Cultural and Social Relief Funds. Mult.
1271 40c.+15c. Type **332** (50th anniv of Curacao Museum) 70 65
1272 40c.+15c. Desalination plant and drinking water (70 years of seawater desalination) 70 65

1273 75c.+25c. Mangrove roots and shells (Lac Cai wetlands, Bonaire) (vert) . . . 1·40 1·10
1274 85c.+40c. Lake and underwater marine life (Little Bonaire wetlands) (vert) . . . . 1·75 1·60

333 Salt Deposit, Dead Sea

334 Superior, 1923, and Elias Moreno Brandao

1998. "Israel 98" International Stamp Exhibition, Tel Aviv. Multicoloured.
1275 40c. Type **333** 45 45
1276 75c. Zion Gate, Jerusalem 90 80
1277 110c. Masada . . . . . . 1·25 1·10
MS1278 58 × 91 mm. 225c. Mikve Israel-Emanuel Synagogue, Curacao . . . . 3·00 3·00

1998. 75th Anniv of E. Moreno Brandao and Sons (car dealers). Chevrolet Motor Cars. Multicoloured.
1279 40c. Type **334** . . . . . . 1·60 1·00
1280 55c. Roadster, 1934 . . . . 1·75 1·40
1281 75c. Styleline deluxe sedan, 1949 . . . . 2·10 1·75
1282 110c. Bel Air convertible, 1957 . . . . 3·25 2·50
1283 225c. Corvette Stingray coupe, 1963 . . . . . . 5·50 5·25
1284 500c. Chevelle SS-454 2-door hardtop, 1970 . . . 13·50 12·00

335 State Flag and Arms

336 Christina Flanders (philanthropic worker)

1998. 50th Anniv of Netherlands Antilles Advisory Council. Multicoloured.
1285 75c. Type **335** 90 80
1286 85c. Gavel . . . . 1·00 95

1998. Death Anniversaries. Multicoloured.
1287 40c. Type **336** (second anniv) 50 45
1288 75c. Abraham Jesurun (writer and first president of Curacao Chamber of Commerce, 80th anniv) 95 80
1289 85c. Capt. Gerrit Newton (seaman and shipyard manager, 50th anniv (1999)) . . . . 1·00 95
1290 110c. Eduardo Adriana (sportsman, first anniv) 1·40 1·10

337 Ireland Pillar Box

338 Globe and New Post Emblem

1998. Postboxes (1st series). Multicoloured.
1291 15c. Type **337** 25 15
1292 40c. Nepal postbox 60 45
1293 75c. Uruguay postbox . . . 1·00 80
1294 85c. Curacao postbox . . . 1·00 1·00
See also Nos. 1413/16.

1998. Privatization of Postal Services.
1295 **338** 75c. black, blue and red 90 80
1296 – 110c. multicoloured . . . 1·40 1·10
1297 – 225c. multicoloured . . . 2·50 2·40
DESIGNS—VERT: 110c. Tree and binary code. HORIZ: 225c. 1949 25c. U.P.U. stamp, reproduction of No. 1296 and binary code.

339 Black Rhinoceros

1998. Endangered Species. Multicoloured.
1298 5c. Type **339** 40 10
1299 75c. White-tailed hawk (vert) . . . . 1·10 80
1300 125c. White-tailed deer . . . 1·75 1·40
1301 250c. Tiger ("Tigris") (vert) 3·25 2·75

340 Short-finned Mako ("Mako Shark")

1998. Fishes. Multicoloured.
1302 275c. Type **340** . . . . . . 3·75 3·00
1303 350c. Manta ray . . . . . 4·50 3·75

341 1950 5c. Stamp

342 Child with Family Paper Chain

1998. "70th Anniv of Dutch Stamp Dealers Club" Stamp Exhibition, The Hague. Multicoloured.
1304 225c. Type **341** . . . . . . 2·50 60
1305 500c. 1950 Queen Juliana 15c. stamp . . . . 5·50 5·50
MS1306 72 × 50 mm. 500c. Curacao 1922 12½c. stamp . . . . . . 6·25 6·25

1998. Child Welfare. Universal Rights of the Child. Multicoloured.
1307 40c.+15c. Type **342** (right to name and nationality) . . 65 60
1308 75c.+25c. Children eating water melons (right to health care) . . . . . . 1·10 1·00
1309 110c.+45c. Children painting (right of handicapped children to special care) 1·90 1·75
1310 225c.+100c. Children playing with can telephones (right to freedom of expression) . . 3·75 3·50

343 Former Office, Curacao

1998. 60th Anniv of PriceWaterhouseCoopers (accountancy firm). Multicoloured.
1311 75c. Type **343** . . . . . . 1·50 85
1312 225c. Modern office, Curacao . . . . 3·00 2·40

344 "Christmas Tree" (Theodora van Ierland)

345 Avila Beach Hotel and Dr. Pieter Maal (founder)

1998. Christmas. Children's Paintings. Multicoloured.
1313 35c. Type **344** 40 50
1314 150c. "Post in mail box" (Anna Sordam) . . . . . 1·75 1·60

1999. 50th Anniv of Avila Beach Hotel. Mult.
1315 75c. Type **345** . . . . . . 1·00 80
1316 110c. Beach and flamboyant tree . . . . 1·40 1·25
1317 225c. Mesquite tree . . . . 2·75 2·40

346 Rabbit and Great Wall of China

347 Girls hugging and Wiri

1999. "China 1999" International Stamp Exhibition, Peking. Year of the Rabbit. Multicoloured.
1318 75c. Type **346** 60 80
1319 225c. Rabbit and Jade Pagoda (vert) . . . . . . 2·75 2·40
MS1320 88 × 53 mm. 225c. Rabbit (vert) . . . . 3·00 3·00

1999. 50th Anniv of Government Correctional Institute. Musical instruments. Multicoloured.
1321 40c. Type **347** 60 45
1322 75c. Institute building and bamba . . . . 1·00 80
1323 85c. Boy at lathe and triangle (horiz) . . . . . 1·00 90

348 Launch of Ship

349 Godett

1999. 500th Anniv of First Written Record (by Amerigo Vespucci) of Curacao. Multicoloured.
1324 75c. Type **348** . . . . . . 1·10 80
1325 110c. Otrobanda, 1906 . . . 1·50 1·25
1326 175c. Nos. 1324/5 and anniversary emblem . . . 2·25 2·00
1327 225c. Fort Beeckenburg, Caracasbaai . . . . . . 2·75 2·40
1328 500c. 1949 12½c. stamp and sailing ship . . . . 5·75 5·50

1999. Fourth Death Anniv of Wilson Godett (politician).
1329 **349** 75c. multicoloured . . . 1·10 80

350 Amerindians and Old Map

1999. The Millennium. Multicoloured. (a) Size 35½ × 35½ mm. Ordinary gum.
1330 5c. Type **350** (arrival of Alonso de Ojeda, Amerigo Vespucci and Juan de la Cosa, 1499) . . 40 40
1331 10c. Dutch ship, indian and soldier on horseback (Dutch conquest, 1634) 40 40
1332 40c. Flags of constituent islands of Netherlands Antilles, Autonomy Monument in Curacao and document granting autonomy, 1954 . . . . . 60 60
1333 75c. Telephone and Curacao 1873 25c. King William III stamp (installation of telephones on Curacao, 1892) . . . 1·00 1·00
1334 85c. Fokker F.XVIII airplane "De Snip" (first Amsterdam–Curacao flight, 1934) . . . . . . 1·10 1·10
1335 100c. Oil refinery, Curacao (inauguration, 1915) . . . 1·10 1·10
1336 110c. Dish aerial, undersea fibre optic cable and dolphins (telecommunications) . . 1·40 1·40
1337 125c. Curacao harbour, bridge and bow of cruise liner (tourism) . . . . . 1·75 1·75
1338 225c. Ka'i orgel (musical instrument) and couple in folk costume (culture) . . 2·75 2·75
1339 350c. Brown-throated conure, caracara, yellow-shouldered amazon and greater flamingoes (nature) . . . . 4·25 4·25

(b) Size 29 × 29 mm. Self-adhesive.
1340 5c. Type **350** 40 40
1341 10c. As No. 1331 . . . . 40 40
1342 40c. As No. 1332 . . . . 60 60
1343 75c. As No. 1333 . . . . 1·00 1·00
1344 85c. As No. 1334 . . . . 1·10 1·10
1345 100c. As No. 1335 . . . . 1·10 1·10
1346 110c. As No. 1336 . . . . 1·40 1·40
1347 125c. As No. 1337 . . . . 1·75 1·75
1348 225c. As No. 1338 . . . . 2·75 2·75
1349 350c. As No. 1339 . . . . 4·25 4·25

351 Ijzerstraat, Otrobanda

1999. Cultural and Social Relief Funds. Willemstad, World Heritage Site. Multicoloured.
1350 40c.+15c. Type **351** 70 65
1351 75c.+30c. Oldest house in Punda (now Postal Museum) (vert) . . . . . 1·40 1·10
1352 110c.+50c. "The Bridal Cake" (now Central National Archives), Scharloo . . . . 2·00 1·75

352 St. Paul's Roman Catholic Church, Saba

1999. Tourist Attractions. Multicoloured.
1357 150c. Type **352** . . . . . . 2·40 1·60
1359 250c. Greater flamingoes, Bonaire . . . . 3·25 2·75
1361 500c. Courthouse, St. Maarten . . . . . . 6·00 5·50

353 Basketball

1999. Child Welfare. Sports. Multicoloured.
1370 40c.+15c. Type **353** . . . . 1·00 65
1371 75c.+25c. Golf . . . . . . 1·60 1·10
1372 110c.+45c. Fencing . . . . 2·10 1·60
1373 225c.+100c. Tennis . . . . 4·25 3·50

354 *Saintpaulia ionantha*

1999. Flowers. Multicoloured.
1374 40c. Type **354** 80 80
1375 40c. *Gardenia jasminioides* 80 80
1376 40c. Allamanda 80 80
1377 40c. Bougainvillea 80 80
1378 75c. Strelitzia . . . . 1·00 1·00
1379 75c. Cymbidium . . . . . . 1·00 1·00
1380 75c. Phalaenopsis . . . . . 1·00 1·00
1381 75c. *Cassia fistula* . . . . . 1·00 1·00
1382 110c. Doritaenopsis . . . . 1·60 1·60
1383 110c. Guzmania . . . . . . 1·60 1·60
1384 225c. *Catharanthus roseus* 2·75 2·75
1385 225c. *Caralluma hexagona* 2·75 2·75

355 Children wearing Hats

356 Man, Baby and Building Blocks (Fathers' Day)

1999. Christmas. Multicoloured.
1386 35c. Type **355** 50 40
1387 150c. Clock face and islands 1·90 1·60

2000. Greetings Stamps. Multicoloured.
1388 40c. Type **356** 55 50
1389 40c. Women and globe (Mothers' Day) 55 50
1390 40c. Hearts and flowers (Valentine's Day) 55 50
1391 75c. Puppy and present ("Thank You") 95 90
1392 110c. Butterfly and vase of flowers (Special Occasions) . . . . 1·10 1·00
1393 150c. As No. 1389 . . . . 2·25 2·10
1394 150c. As No. 1390 . . . . 2·25 2·10
1395 225c. Hands and wedding rings (Anniversary) . . . 2·75 2·75

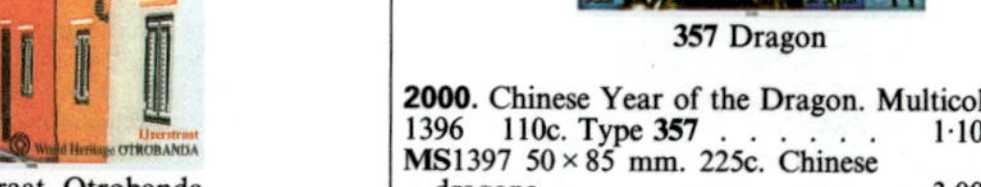

357 Dragon

2000. Chinese Year of the Dragon. Multicoloured.
1396 110c. Type **357** . . . . . . 1·10 1·00
MS1397 50 × 85 mm. 225c. Chinese dragons . . . . 3·00 3·00

358 Red Eyed Tree Frog

2000. Endangered Animals. Multicoloured.

1398 40c. Type **358** . . . . . . 1·00 1·00
1399 75c. King penguin (vert) . . 1·60 1·60
1400 85c. Killer whale (vert) . . . 1·60 1·60
1401 100c. African elephant (vert) 1·60 1·60
1402 110c. Chimpanzee (vert) . . 1·60 1·60
1403 225c. Tiger . . . . 3·00 3·00

359 Children playing **360** Space Shuttle Launch

2000. Cultural and Social Relief Funds. Mult.

1404 75c.+30c. Type **359** . . . . 1·00 95
1405 110c.+50c. Schoolchildren performing science experiments . . . . . . 2·10 2·00
1406 225c.+100c. Teacher giving lesson (vert) . . . . . . 3·75 3·75

2000. "World Stamp Expo 2000", Anaheim, California. Space Exploration. Multicoloured.

1407 75c. Type **360** . . . . . . 1·40 1·00
1408 225c. Astronaut, Moon and space station . . . . 3·00 3·00
MS1409 100 × 70 mm. 225c. Futuristic space station . . . . 3·25 3·25

361 Cycling **362** People

2000. Olympic Games, Sydney. Multicoloured.

1410 75c. Type **361** . . . . . . 1·10 1·10
1411 225c. Athletics . . . . . . 3·00 3·00
MS1412 50 × 72 mm. 225c. Swimming . . . . 2·75 2·75

2000. Postboxes (2nd series). As T **337**. Multicoloured.

1413 110c. Mexico postbox . . . 1·40 1·40
1414 175c. Dubai postbox . . . . 2·25 2·25
1415 350c. Great Britain postbox 4·25 4·25
1416 500c. United States of America postbox . . . . 6·00 6·00

2000. Social Insurance Bank. Multicoloured.

1417 75c. Type **362** . . . . . . 1·00 1·00
1418 110c. Adult holding child's hand (horiz) . . . . . . 1·40 1·40
1419 225c. Anniversary emblem 3·25 3·25

363 Child reaching towards Night Sky **364** Angels and Score of *Jingle Bells* (carol)

2000. Child Welfare. Multicoloured.

1420 40c.+15c. Type **363** . . . . 1·00 1·00
1421 75c.+25c. Children using Internet (horiz) . . . . . . 1·60 1·60
1422 110c.+45c. Children playing with toy boat (horiz) . . 2·40 2·40
1423 225c.+100c. Children consulting map . . . . . 4·00 4·00

2000. Christmas. Multicoloured.

1424 40c. Type **364** 70 70
1425 150c. Seasonal messages in different languages (horiz) 2·10 2·10

365 Red King Snake **366** Forest

2001. Chinese Year of the Snake. Multicoloured.

1426 110c. Type **365** . . . . . . 1·40 1·40
MS1427 87 × 53 mm. 225c. Indian cobra (*Naja naja*) (vert) . . . . 3·50 3·50

2001. "HONG KONG 2001" World Stamp Exhibition. Landscapes. Multicoloured.

1428 25c. Type **366** 55 55
1429 40c. Palm trees and waterfall 75 75
1430 110c. Spinner dolphins (*Stenella longirostris*) . . . 1·25 1·25

367 Persian Shaded Golden Cat **368** *Mars* (Dutch ship of the line)

2001. Cats and Dogs. Multicoloured.

1431 55c. Type **367** . . . . . . 1·10 1·10
1432 75c. Burmese bluepoint cat and kittens . . . . 1·40 1·40
1433 110c. American wirehair . . 1·75 1·75
1434 175c. Golden retriever dog 2·10 2·10
1435 225c. German shepherd dog 3·00 3·00
1436 750c. British shorthair silver tabby . . . . 9·00 9·00

2001. Ships. Multicoloured.

1437 110c. Type **368** . . . . . . 1·40 1·40
1438 275c. *Alphen* (frigate) . . . 3·50 3·50
1439 350c. *Curacao* (paddle-steamer) (horiz) . . . . . 4·50 4·50
1440 500c. *Pioneer* (schooner) (horiz) . . . . 6·25 6·25

369 Pen and Emblem **370** Fedjai riding Bicycle

2001. 5th Anniv of Caribbean Postal Union. Multicoloured.

1441 75c.+25c. Type **369** 75 75
1442 110c.+45c. Emblem . . . . 1·10 1·10
1443 225c. + 100c. Silhouettes encircling globe . . . . . 2·40 2·40

2001. Fedjai (cartoon postman) (1st series). Multicoloured.

1444 5c. Type **370** 10 10
1445 40c. Fedjai and children . . 30 25
1446 75c. Fedjai and post box containing bird's nest and chicks 55 45
1447 85c. Fedjai and elderly woman 60 50
1448 100c. Barking dog and Fedjai sitting on postbox 75 60
1449 110c. Fedjai and boy reading comic 80 65

See also Nos. 1487/90.

371 Cave Entrance and Area Map **372** Streamertail (*Trochilus polytmus*)

2001. Kueba Boza (Muzzle Cave). Multicoloured.

1450 85c. Type **371** 60 50
1451 110c. *Leptonycteris nivalis cursoae* (bat) 80 65
1452 225c. *Glosophaga elongata* (bat) . . . . 1·60 1·25

2001. Birds. Multicoloured.

1453 10c. Type **372** 10 10
1454 85c. Eastern white pelican (*Pelecanus onocrotalus*) . . 60 50
1455 110c. Gouldian finch (*Erythrura gouldiae*) . . . 80 65
1456 175c. Painted bunting (*Passerina ciris*) . . . . . 1·25 1·00
1457 250c. Atlantic puffin (*Fratercula artica*) . . . . 1·90 1·50
1458 350c. American darter (*Anhinga anhinga*) . . . . 2·50 2·00

373 Chapel Facade and Map of St. Maarten Island

2001. 150th Anniv of Philipsburg Methodist Chapel. Multicoloured.

1459 75c. Type **373** 55 45
1460 110c. Rainbow, open Bible and map of St. Maarten 80 65

374 Boy feeding Toddler

2001. Child Welfare. Youth Volunteers. Multicoloured.

1461 40c.+15c. Type **374** 40 35
1462 75c.+25c. Girls dancing (vert) 75 60
1463 110c.+45c. Boy and elderly woman (vert) . . . . . . 1·10 90

375 Children of Different Nations **376** Prince Willem-Alexander

2001. Christmas. Multicoloured.

1464 40c. Type **375** 30 25
1465 150c. Children and Infant Jesus (vert) . . . . 1·10 90

2002. Wedding of Crown Prince Willem-Alexander to Maxima Zorreguieta. Multicoloured.

1466 75c. Type **376** 55 45
1467 110c. Princess Maxima . . . 80 65
MS1468 75 × 72 mm. 2g.25, Prince Willem-Alexander facing left; 2g.75, Princess Maxima facing left 3·75 3·75

377 Horse **378** Blue-tailed Emerald (*Chlorostilbon mellisugus*) and Passion Flower (*Passiflora foetida*)

2002. Chinese New Year. Year of the Horse. Multicoloured.

1469 25c. Type **377** 20 15
MS1470 52 × 86 mm. 95c. Horse's head 75 75

2002. Flora and Fauna. Multicoloured.

1471 50c. Type **378** 35 30
1472 95c. Lineated anole (*Anolis lineatus*) and *Cordia sebestena* (flower) (horiz) 65 55
1473 120c. Dragonfly (*Odonata*) (horiz) 90 75
1474 145c. Hermit crab (*Coenobita clypeatus*) (horiz) . . . . 1·10 90
1475 285c. Paper wasp (*Polistes versicolor*) . . . . . . 2·10 1·75

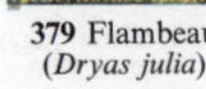

379 Flambeau (*Dryas julia*) **380** Flags as Football

2002. Butterflies. Multicoloured.

1480 25c. Type **379** 20 15
1481 145c. Monarch (*Danaus plexippus*) (horiz) . . . . 1·10 90
1482 400c. *Mechanitis polymnia* (horiz) . . . . 2·75 2·25
1483 500c. *Pyrrhopygopsis socrates* (wrongly inscr "Pyrrhapygopsis socrates") (horiz) . . . . 3·50 2·75

2002. World Cup Football Championship, Japan and South Korea. Multicoloured.

1484 95c.+35c. Type **380** 95 75
1485 145c.+55c. Player and globe as football . . . . 1·50 1·25
1486 240c.+110c. Player and ball 2·50 2·00

381 Fedjai skipping

2002. Fedjai (cartoon postman) (2nd series). Multicoloured.

1487 10c. Type **381** 10 10
1488 55c. Fedjai and dog in rubbish bin (vert) 40 35
1489 95c. Fedjai presenting envelope on tray (vert) . . 70 55
1490 240c. Fedjai helping elderly woman across road (vert) 90 70

382 Man **383** *Wingfieldara casseta*

2002. "The Potato Eaters" (Vincent Van Gogh). Amphilex 2002 International Stamp Exhibition, Amsterdam. Designs showing parts of painting. Multicoloured.

1491 70c. Type **382** 40 30
1492 95c. Man (different) 60 50
1493 145c. Woman facing front 90 70
1494 240c. Woman facing left . . 1·40 1·10
MS1495 98 × 75 mm. 500c. As No. 1494 but design enlarged (horiz) . . . . 3·00 3·00

2002. Orchids. Multicoloured.

1496 95c. Type **383** 60 50
1497 285c. *Cymbidium Magna Charta* . . . . 1·70 1·40
1498 380c. *Brassolaeliocattleya* 2·25 1·80
1499 750c. *Miltonia spectabilis* 4·50 3·50

384 Lion wearing Snorkel

2001. Child Welfare. Multicoloured.

1500 50c.+15c. Type **384** 40 40
1501 95c.+35c. Kangaroo 80 80
1502 145c.+55c. Goat and penguin . . . . 1·20 1·20
1503 240c.+100c. Lizard and toucan . . . . 3·40 3·40

385 Christmas Trees

2002. Christmas. T **385** and similar horiz design. Multicoloured.

1504 95c. Type **385** 60 50
1505 240c. Lanterns . . . . . . 1·40 1·10

386 Savanna Hawk (*Buteogallus meridionalis*) **387** Goat's Head

2002. Birds. Multicoloured.

1506 5c. Type **386** 10 10
1507 20c. Black-spotted barbet (*Capito niger*) 15 10

1508 30c. Scarlet macaw (*Ara macao*) 20 15
1509 35c. Great jacamar (*Jacamerops aurea*) . . . 20 15
1510 70c. White-necked jacobin (*Florisuga mellivora*) . . . 40 30
1511 85c. Crimson fruit-crow (*Haematoderis militaris*) (inscr "Heamatoderus") 55 45
1512 90c. Peach-fronted conure (*Aratinga aurea*) 55 45
1513 95c. Green oropendula (*Psarocolius viridis*) . . . 60 50
1514 100c. Eastern meadowlark (*Stumella magna*) (horiz) 60 50
1515 145c. Sun conure (*Aratinga solstitalis*) (horiz) 85 70
1516 240c. White-tailed toucan (*Trogon virdis*) . . . . . 1·40 1·10
1517 285c. Red-billed toucan (*Ramphastos tucanus*) . . 1·70 1·40

2003. New Year. Year of the Goat.
1518 **387** 25c. multicoloured . . . 15 10
MS1519 86 × 52 mm. 96c. black, red and grey 30 30
DESIGN: 95c. Rearing goat.

388 Leeward Islands

2003. Cultural and Social Relief Funds. Sheet 150 × 61 mm containing T **388** and similar multicoloured designs showing maps.
MS1520 25c.+10c. Type **388**; 30c.+15c. Windward Islands (vert); 55c.+25c. Curacao and Bonaire; 85c.+35c. St. Marten, Saba and St. Eustatius (vert); 95c +40c. Caribbean . . . . 2·25 2·25

389 *Rhetus arcius*

390 Trumpet

2003. Butterflies. Multicoloured.
1521 5c. Type **389** 10 10
1522 10c. *Evenus teresina* (horiz) 10 10
1523 25c. *Bhutanitis thaidina* (horiz) 15 10
1524 30c. *Semomesia capanea* (horiz) 20 15
1525 45c. *Papilio machaon* (horiz) 25 20
1526 55c. *Papilio multicaudata* 30 25
1527 65c. *Graphium weiskei* . . . 40 30
1528 95c. *Aneyluris formosissima venabalis* 60 50
1529 100c. *Euphaedra neophron* (horiz) 60 50
1530 145c. *Ornithoptera goliath Samson* (horiz) 85 70
1531 275c. *Aneyluris colubra* . . 1·60 1·30
1532 350c. *Papilio lorquinianus* 2·10 1·70

2003. Musical Instruments. Sheet 125 × 61 mm containing T **390** and similar vert designs. Multicoloured.
MS1533 20c. Type **390**; 75c. Drums; 145c. Tenor saxophone; 285c. Double bass . . . . 1·50 1·50

391 Early Banknote

392 10 Gilder Banknote

2003. 300th Anniv of Joh. Enschede (printers). Two sheets containing T **391** and similar vert designs. Multicoloured.
MS1534 (a) 120 × 61 mm. 70c. Type **391**; 95c. 1873 stamp; 145c. Revenue stamp; 240c. 1967 banknote (b) 85 × 52 mm. 550c. Johan Enschede building, Haarlem . . . . 6·50 6·50

2003. 175th Anniv of Central Bank. Multicoloured.
1535 95c. Type **392** . . . . . . 1·40 1·40
1536 145c. Street map and bank building . . . . 2·10 2·10
1537 285c. "First Instructions of the Bank of Curacao" (vert) . . . . 3·50 3·50

393 Fedjai proposing to Angelina

395 Bombay Cat

394 15th-century Egyptian Boat

2003. Fedjai (cartoon postman) (3rd series). Sheet 120 × 61 mm containing T **393** and similar multicoloured designs.
MS1538 30c. Type **393**; 95c. Married couple; 145c. Taking Angelina to maternity hospital (horiz); 240c. With baby in post bag . . . . 7·50 7·50

2003. Watercraft.
1539 **394** 5c. multicoloured 25 25
1540 – 5c. multicoloured 25 25
1541 – 35c. reddish orange and black 45 45
1542 – 35c. multicoloured . . . 45 45
1543 – 40c. multicoloured . . . 50 50
1544 – 40c. multicoloured . . . 50 50
1545 – 60c. multicoloured . . . 75 75
1546 – 60c. orange and black 75 75
1547 – 75c. multicoloured . . . 1·00 1·00
1548 – 75c. multicoloured . . . 1·00 1·00
1549 – 85c. multicoloured (horiz) . . . . 1·20 1·20
1550 – 85c. multicoloured (horiz) . . . . 1·20 1·20
DESIGNS: 5c. Type **394**; 5c. Model boat from Tutankhamen's tomb; 35c. Ulysseus and the Sirens (vase decoration); 35c .Egyptian river craft; 40c. Greek dromon (galley); 40c. Illustration from *Vergilius Aenes* (15th-century book); 60c. Javanese fusta (galley); 60c. Greek trading ship; 75c. 16th-century Venetian; 75c. Mora (Bayeux tapestry); 85c. Captain Cook's *Earl of Pembroke*; 85c. *Savannah* (transatlantic steamship).

2003. Cats. Multicoloured.
1551 5c. Type **395** 15 15
1552 20c. Persian seal point . . . 35 35
1553 25c. British shorthair . . . 45 45
1554 50c. British blue 60 60
1555 65c. Persian chinchilla . . . 85 85
1556 75c. Tonkinese red point . . 95 95
1557 85c. Balinese lilac tabby point . . . . 1·20 1·20
1558 95c. Persian shaded cameo 1·30 1·30
1559 100c. Burmilla . . . . . . 1·40 1·40
1560 145c. Chocolate tortie shaded silver eastern shorthair . . . . 1·90 1·90
1561 150c. Devon rex . . . . . . 2·00 2·00
1562 285c. Persian black tabby 3·75 3·75

396 Child under Shower

397 Cacti hung with Baubles

2003. Child Welfare. Sheet 125 × 61 mm containing T **396** and similar vert designs. Multicoloured.
MS1563 50c.+15c. Type **396**; 95c.+35c. Girl holding umbrella; 145c.+55c. Boy watering plants; 240c.+110c. Hands under water tap . . . . 9·50 9·50

2003. Christmas. Multicoloured.
1564 75c. Type **397** 85 85
1565 240c. Cacti as figures holding fairy lights and clock . . . . 2·50 2·50

398 "BON" (Bonaire)

2003. Tourism. Multicoloured.
1566 50c. Type **398** 60 60
1567 75c. "CUR" (Curaao) . . . 95 95
1568 95c. "SAB" (Saba) . . . . 1·10 1·10
1569 120c. "EUX" (St. Eustatius) 1·40 1·40
1570 145c. "SXM" (Saint Martin) 1·50 1·50
1571 240c. "CUR" (Curaao) . . 2·50 2·50
1572 285c. "SXM" (Saint Martin) 3·00 3·00
1573 380c. Emblem . . . . . . 3·75 3·75

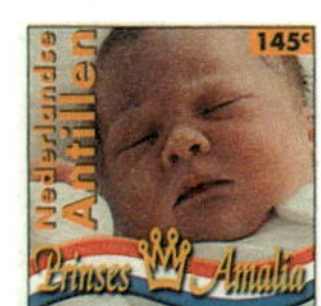

399 Princess Amalia

400 Monkey

2004. Birth of Princess Amalia of Netherlands. Two sheets containing T **399** and similar square design. Multicoloured.
MS1574 (a) 120 × 61 mm. 145c. Type **399**; 380c. Crown Prince Willem Alexander holding Princess Amalia (b) 90 × 120 mm. No. **MS**1574 × 2 . . . . 5·25 5·25

2004. New Year. Year of the Monkey. Multicoloured.
1575 95c. Type **400** 60 50
MS1576 100 × 72 mm. 145c. Monkey and fan 95 95

401 Belevedere (inscr "L.B. Smithplein 3)

2004. Houses. Multicoloured.
1577 10c. Type **401** 10 10
1578 25c. Hoogstraat 27 . . . . 15 10
1579 35c. Landhuis, Brievengat 20 15
1580 65c. Scharlooweg 102 . . . 40 30
1581 95c. Hoogstrat 21–25 . . . 60 50
1582 145c. Villa Maria 95 75
1583 275c. Werfstraat 6 . . . . . 1·75 1·40
1584 350c. Landhuis, Ronde Klip 2·25 1·80

402 Elephant

2004. Fauna. Multicoloured.
1585 5c. Type **402** 10 10
1586 10c. Elephant facing left . . 10 10
1587 25c. Elephant amongst trees 15 10
1588 35c. Chimpanzee 20 15
1589 45c. Chimpanzee holding stick 30 25
1590 55c. Head of chimpanzee . . 35 30
1591 65c. Polar bear and cub . . 40 30
1592 95c. Polar bear facing left 60 50
1593 100c. Polar bear and cub (different) 60 50
1594 145c. Lion facing right . . . 95 75
1595 275c. Lion facing left . . . 1·75 1·40
1596 350c. Head of lion . . . . 2·25 1·80

403 Diesel Locomotive (1977)

404 Harp

2004. Transport. Multicoloured.
1597 10c. Type **403** 10 10
1598 55c. Water-carrier (1900) . . 35 30
1599 75c. Ford Model A (1903) 45 35
1600 85c. Tanker (2004) 55 45
1601 95c. Wright Flyer (1903) . . 60 50
1602 145c. Penny Farthing bicycle (1871) 95 75

2004. Musical Instruments. Multicoloured.
1603 70c. Type **404** 45 35
1604 95c. Lute 60 50
1605 145c. Violin (horiz) 95 75
1606 240c. Zither (horiz) . . . . 1·50 1·20

405 Miniature Pinscher

2004. Dogs. Multicoloured.
1607 5c. Type **405** 10 10
1608 5c. Pomeranian 10 10
1609 35c. Longhaired Teckel (dachshund) 20 15
1610 35c. Shih Tzu 20 15
1611 40c. Boxer puppy 25 20
1612 40c. Jack Russell terrier . . 25 20
1613 60c. Basset hound 40 30
1614 60c. Braque de l'Ariege . . 40 30
1615 75c. Afghan hound 45 35
1616 75c. Old English sheepdog 45 35
1617 85c. Entlebucher Sennen . . 55 45
1618 85c. Mastiff 55 45

406 Dragon and Curacao Harbour

2004. International Stamp Exhibition, Singapore. Multicoloured.
1619 95c. Type **406** 60 50
1620 95c. Merlion and flags . . . 60 50
1621 145c. Dragon and Brion Plaza, Otrobanda 95 75
1622 145c. Dr. A. C. Wathey Cruise and Cargo Facility, St. Maarten 95 75
MS1623 106 × 72 mm. 500c. As No. 1620 . . . . 3·25 3·25

407 *Pomacanthus paru*

2004. Fish and Ducks. Multicoloured.
1624 30c. Type **407** 20 15
1625 65c. *Epinephelus guttatus* . . 40 30
1626 70c. *Mycteroperca interstitialis* 45 35
1627 75c. *Holacanthus isabelita* 45 35
1628 85c. *Epinephelus itajara* . . 55 45
1629 95c. *Holacanthus ciliaris* . . 60 50
1630 100c. American widgeon (*Anas Americana*) and *Sphyraena barracuda* (inscr "Sphyreana") . . . 60 50
1631 145c. Blue-winged teal (*Anas discors*) 95 75
1632 250c. Bahama pintail (*Anas bahamensis*) . . . . . . 1·60 1·30
1633 285c. Lesser scaup (*Aythya affinis*) . . . . 1·80 1·50

POSTAGE DUE STAMPS

1952. As Type D **121** of Netherlands but inscr "NEDERLANDSE ANTILLEN".
D336 1c. green 10 10
D337 2½c. green 65 65
D338 5c. green 20 10
D339 6c. green 55 50
D340 7c. green 55 50
D341 8c. green 55 50
D342 9c. green 55 50
D343 10c. green 30 20
D344 12½c. green 30 20
D345 15c. green 35 30
D346 20c. green 35 50
D347 25c. green 55 10
D348 30c. green . . . . 1·25 1·50
D349 35c. green . . . . 1·60 1·50
D350 40c. green . . . . 1·25 1·50
D351 45c. green . . . . 1·50 1·50
D352 50c. green . . . . 1·25 1·25

NETHERLANDS INDIES Pt. 4

A former Dutch colony, consisting of numerous settlements in the East Indies, of which the islands of Java and Sumatra and parts of Borneo and New Guinea are the most important. Renamed Indonesia in 1948, Independence was granted during 1949. Netherlands New Guinea remained a Dutch possession until 1962 when it was placed under U.N. control, being incorporated with Indonesia in 1963.

100 cents = 1 gulden.

1 King William III

2

1864. Imperf.
1 **1** 10c. red £325 £100

1868. Perf.
2 **1** 10c. red £1000 £180

1870. Perf.
27 **2** 1c. green . . . . 5·50 3·50
28 2c. purple . . . . £100 90·00
29 2c. brown . . . . 8·00 4·50
30 2½c. buff . . . . 45·00 23·00

12 5c. green 65·00 7·00
32 10c. brown 18·00 1·10
40 12½c. drab 5·25 2·50
34 15c. brown 23·00 2·50
5 20c. blue £110 3·50
36 25c. purple 24·00 1·40
44 30c. green 40·00 4·50
17 50c. red 27·00 3·25
38 2g.50 green and purple 90·00 16·00

5 6 Queen Wilhelmina

1883.

87 5 1c. green 1·40 20
88 2c. brown 1·40 20
89 2½c. buff 1·40 70
90 3c. purple 1·75 20
86 5c. green 45·00 26·00
91 5c. blue 14·00 20

1892.

94 6 10c. brown 7·00 40
95 12½c. grey 12·00 24·00
96 15c. brown 17·00 1·60
97 20c. blue 38·00 1·60
98 25c. purple 32·00 1·60
99 30c. green 48·00 2·00
100 50c. red 35·00 1·60
101 2g.50 blue and brown £130 38·00

1900. Netherlands stamps of 1898 surch **NED.-INDIE** and value.

111 13 10c. on 10c. lilac 2·40 40
112 12½c. on 12½c. blue 3·00 80
113 15c. on 15c. brown 4·00 80
114 20c. on 20c. green 20·00 80
115 25c. on 25c. blue and pink 17·00 80
116 50c. on 50c. red and green 32·00 1·10
117 11 2½g. on 2½g. lilac 50·00 19·00

1902. Surch.

118 5 ½ on 2c. brown 50 35
119 2½ on 3c. purple 55 50

11 12

13

1902.

120 11 ½c. lilac 60 30
121 1c. olive 60 30
122 2c. brown 4·00 35
123 2½c. green 2·40 20
124 3c. orange 2·75 1·25
125 4c. blue 17·00 9·00
126 5c. red 6·00 20
127 7½c. grey 4·00 35
128 12 10c. slate 1·60 20
129 12½c. blue 2·00 20
130 15c. brown 9·75 2·10
131 17½c. bistre 4·00 30
132 20c. grey 2·00 1·50
133 20c. olive 27·00 25
134 22½c. olive and brown 4·75 30
135 25c. mauve 11·50 30
136 30c. brown 32·00 30
137 50c. red 25·00 30
138 13 1g. lilac 60·00 40
206 1g. lilac on blue 42·00 4·75
139 2½g. grey 70·00 1·60
207 2½g. grey on blue 60·00 26·00

1902. No. 130 optd with horiz bars.

140 15c. brown 2·00 70

1905. No. 132 surch **10 cent.**

141 10c. on 20c. grey 2·75 1·25

1908. Stamps of 1902 optd **JAVA**.

142 ½c. lilac 35 20
143 1c. olive 60 30
144 2c. brown 2·50 2·50
145 2½c. green 1·50 20
146 3c. orange 1·10 1·00
147 5c. red 2·50 20
148 7½c. grey 2·00 1·75
149 10c. slate 1·00 20
150 12½c. blue 2·10 70
151 15c. brown 3·25 3·00
152 17½c. bistre 1·75 65
153 20c. olive 10·00 70
154 22½c. olive and brown 4·75 2·75
155 25c. mauve 4·75 30
156 30c. brown 28·00 2·50
157 50c. red 19·00 70
158 1g. lilac 45·00 3·00
159 2½g. grey 65·00 50·00

1908. Stamps of 1902 optd **BUITEN BEZIT**.

160 ½c. lilac 45 35
161 1c. olive 55 35
162 2c. brown 1·90 2·50
163 2½c. green 1·10 35
164 3c. orange 1·00 1·10
165 5c. red 3·10 50
166 7½c. grey 3·00 2·50
167 10c. slate 1·10 20
168 12½c. blue 9·75 2·25
169 15c. brown 4·50 2·50
170 17½c. bistre 2·10 1·75
171 20c. olive 8·75 2·10
172 22½c. olive and brown 6·25 4·50
173 25c. mauve 7·00 35
174 30c. brown 15·00 2·10
175 50c. red 7·00 80
176 1g. lilac 55·00 4·50
177 2½g. grey 85·00 55·00

19 20

1912.

208 19 ½c. lilac 30 20
209 1c. green 30 20
210 2c. brown 55 20
264 2c. grey 55 20
211 2½c. green 1·40 20
265 2½c. pink 70 20
212 3c. brown 55 20
266 3c. green 1·10 20
213 4c. blue 1·10 20
267 4c. green 1·10 20
268 4c. bistre 9·00 4·00
214 5c. pink 1·25 20
269 5c. green 1·10 20
270 5c. blue 70 20
215 7½c. brown 70 20
271 7½c. bistre 70 20
216 20 10c. red 1·10 20
272 19 10c. lilac 1·75 20
217 20 12½c. blue 1·25 20
273 12½c. red 1·25 35
274 15c. blue 7·00 30
218 17½c. brown 1·25 20
219 20c. green 2·10 20
275 20c. blue 2·10 20
276 20c. orange 12·50 20
220 22½c. orange 2·10 75
221 25c. mauve 2·10 20
222 30c. grey 2·10 20
277 32½c. violet and orange 2·10 30
278 35c. brown 7·25 55
279 40c. green 2·75 20

21

1913.

223 21 50c. green 4·75 20
280 60c. blue 6·00 20
281 80c. orange 4·75 35
224 1g. brown 4·00 20
283 1g.75 lilac 20·00 1·75
225 2½g. pink 16·00 1·25

1915. Red Cross. Stamps of 1912 surch **+5 cts.** and red cross.

243 1c.+5c. green 5·50 5·50
244 5c.+5c. pink 5·50 5·50
245 10c.+5c. red 7·00 7·00

1917. Stamps of 1902, 1912 and 1913 surch.

246 ½c. on 2½c. (No. 211) 35 35
247 1c. on 4c. (No. 213) 35 55
250 12½c. on 17½c. (No. 218) 30 20
251 12½c. on 22½c. (No. 220) 35 20
248 17½c. on 22½c. (No. 134) 1·75 70
252 20c. on 22½c. (No. 220) 35 20
249 30c. on 1g. (No. 138) 6·25 1·75
253 32½c. on 50c. (No. 223) 1·00 20
254 40c. on 50c. (No. 223) 3·50 50
255 60c. on 1g. (No. 224) 5·75 35
256 80c. on 1g. (No. 224) 6·25 80

1922. Bandoeng Industrial Fair. Stamps of 1912 and 1917 optd **3de N. I. JAARBEURS BANDOENG 1922.**

285 1c. green 7·00 7·00
286 2c. brown 7·00 7·00
287 2½c. pink 55·00 60·00
288 3c. yellow 7·00 8·00
289 4c. blue 35 35
290 5c. green 12·50 10·00
291 7½c. brown 9·50 8·00
292 10c. lilac 65·00 80·00
293 12½c. on 22½c. orge (No. 251) 8·00 9·00
294 17½c. brown 5·50 7·00
295 20c. blue 7·00 7·00

Nos. 285/95 were sold at a premium for 3, 4, 5, 6, 8, 9, 10, 12½, 15, 20 and 22c. respectively.

33 36 Fokker F.VIIa

1923. Queen's Silver Jubilee.

296 33 5c. green 35 35
297 12½c. red 35 35
298 20c. blue 70 35
299 50c. orange 2·50 90
300 1g. purple 4·25 60
301 2½g. grey 38·00 32·00
302 5g. brown £120 £110

1928. Air. Stamps of 1912 and 1913 surch **LUCHTPOST**, Fokker F.VII airplane and value.

303 10c. on 12½c. red 1·25 1·25
304 20c. on 25c. mauve 2·75 2·75
305 40c. on 80c. orange 2·10 2·10
306 75c. on 1g. sepia 1·10 1·10
307 1½g. on 2½g. red 7·25 7·25

1928. Air.

308 36 10c. purple 35 35
309 20c. brown 90 75
310 40c. red 1·10 75
311 75c. green 2·40 35
312 1g.50 orange 4·25 75

1930. Air. Surch **30** between bars.

313 36 30c. on 40c. red 1·10 40

38 Watch-tower 40 M. P. Pattist in Flight

1930. Child Welfare. Centres in brown.

315 – 2c. (+1c.) mauve 1·10 1·00
316 38 5c. (+2½c.) green 4·50 3·50
317 – 12½c. (+2½c.) red 3·50 70
318 – 15c. (+5c.) blue 5·00 5·25

DESIGNS—VERT: 2c. Bali Temple. HORIZ: 12½c. Minangkabau Compound; 15c. Buddhist Temple, Borobudur.

1930. No. 275 surch **12½**.

319 12½c. on 20c. blue 80 20

1931. Air. 1st Java–Australia Mail.

320 40 1g. brown and blue 15·00 12·50

41

1931. Air.

321 41 30c. red 2·75 35
322 4½g. blue 9·00 2·75
323 7½g. green 11·50 3·50

42 Ploughing

1931. Lepers' Colony.

324 42 2c. (+1c.) brown 2·50 2·00
325 – 5c. (+2½c.) green 4·00 4·00
326 – 12½c. (+2½c.) red 3·25 65
327 – 15c. (+5c.) blue 7·75 6·75

DESIGNS: 5c. Fishing; 12½c. Native actors; 15c. Native musicians.

1932. Air. Surch **50** on Fokker F.VIIa/3m airplane.

328 36 50c. on 1g.50 orange 3·25 55

44 Plaiting Rattan 45 William of Orange

1932. Salvation Army. Centres in brown.

329 – 2c. (+1c.) purple 55 55
330 44 5c. (+2½c.) green 3·00 2·25
331 – 12½c. (+2½c.) red 90 35
332 – 15c. (+5c.) blue 4·25 3·50

DESIGNS: 2c. Weaving; 12½c. Textile worker; 15c. Metal worker.

1933. 400th Birth Anniv of William I of Orange.

333 45 12½c. red 1·60 40

46 Rice Cultivation 47 Queen Wilhelmina

1933.

335 46 1c. violet 30 20
397 2c. purple 10 40
337 2½c. bistre 30 20
338 3c. green 30 20
339 3½c. grey 30 20
340 4c. green 90 20
401 5c. blue 10 10
342 7½c. violet 1·10 20
343 10c. red 2·00 20
403 47 10c. red 10 10
334 12½c. brown 8·00 35
345 12½c. red 55 20
404 15c. blue 10 10
405 20c. purple 35 10
348 25c. green 2·10 20
349 30c. blue 3·50 20
350 32½c. bistre 9·00 8·25
408 35c. violet 5·00 1·50
352 40c. green 2·75 20
353 42½c. yellow 2·75 35
354 50c. blue 5·00 35
355 60c. blue 5·50 70
356 80c. red 7·00 1·10
357 1g. violet 8·75 35
358 1g.75 green 18·00 10·00
414 2g. green 25·00 12·50
359 2g.50 purple 21·00 1·75
415 5g. bistre 24·00 6·25

The 50c. to 5g. are larger, 30 × 30 mm.

48 Pander S.4 Postjager

1933. Air. Special Flights.

360 48 30c. blue 1·50 1·50

49 Woman and Lotus Blossom 53 Cavalryman and Wounded Soldier

1933. Y.M.C.A. Charity.

361 49 2c. (+1c.) brown & purple 70 45
362 – 5c. (+2½c.) brown and green 2·40 2·00
363 – 12½c. (+2½c.) brown & orge 2·75 30
364 – 15c. (+5c.) brown and blue 3·25 2·75

DESIGNS: 5c. Symbolizing the sea of life; 12½c. Y.M.C.A. emblem; 15c. Unemployed man.

1934. Surch.

365 36 2c. on 10c. purple 35 50
366 2c. on 20c. brown 35 30
367 41 2c. on 30c. red 35 65
368 36 42½c. on 75c. green 4·75 35
369 42½c. on 1g.50 orange 4·75 50

1934. Anti-tuberculosis Fund. As T **77** of Netherlands.

370 12½c. (+2½c.) brown 1·75 55

1935. Christian Military Home.

371 – 2c. (+1c.) brown and purple 1·75 1·25
372 53 5c. (+2½c.) brown and green 3·50 3·50
373 – 12½c. (+2½c.) brown & orge 3·50 30
374 – 15c. (+5c.) brown and blue 5·25 5·25

DESIGNS: 2c. Engineer chopping wood; 12½c. Artilleryman and volcano victim; 15c. Infantry bugler.

54 Dinner-time

55 Boy Scouts

1936. Salvation Army.
375 **54** 2c. (+1c.) purple . . . . . 1·25 70
376 5c. (+2½c.) blue . . . . . 1·50 1·25
377 7½c. (+2½c.) violet . . . . 1·50 1·60
378 12½c. (+2½c.) orange . . . 1·50 40
379 15c. (+5c.) blue . . . . . 2·50 2·40
Nos. 376/9 are larger, 30 × 27 mm.

1937. Scouts' Jamboree.
380 **55** 7½c. (+2½c.) green . . . . 1·00 95
381 12½c. (+2½c.) red . . . . . 1·00 55

1937. Nos. 222 and 277 surch in figures.
382 10c. on 30c. slate . . . . . . 2·50 30
383 10c. on 32½c. violet and orange . . . . 2·75 35

59 Sifting Rice

62 Douglas DC-2 Airliner

1937. Relief Fund. Inscr "A.S.I.B.".
385 **59** 2c. (+1c.) sepia and orange 1·40 80
386 – 3½c. (+1½c.) grey . . . . . 1·40 90
387 – 7½c. (+2½c.) green & orange . . . . 1·50 1·10
388 – 10c. (+2½c.) red and orange 1·50 30
389 – 20c. (+5c.) blue . . . . . 1·40 1·40
DESIGNS: 3½c. Mother and children; 7½c. Ox-team ploughing rice-field; 10c. Ox-team and cart; 20c. Man and woman.

1938. 40th Anniv of Coronation. As T **87** of Netherlands.
390 2c. violet 10 10
391 10c. red 10 10
392 15c. blue . . . . 1·40 70
393 20c. red 70 35

1938. Air Service Fund. 10th Anniv of Royal Netherlands Indies Air Lines.
394 **62** 17½c. (+5c.) brown 90 90
395 – 20c. (+5c.) slate 90 90
DESIGN: 20c. As Type **62**, but reverse side of airliner.

63 Nurse and Child

1938. Child Welfare. Inscr "CENTRAAL MISSIE-BUREAU".
416 **63** 2c. (+1c.) violet 80 55
417 – 3½c. (+1½c.) green . . . . 1·25 1·10
418 – 7½c. (+2½c.) red 90 90
419 – 10c. (+2½c.) red . . . . . 1·00 30
420 – 20c. (+5c.) blue . . . . . 1·25 1·10
DESIGNS—(23 × 23 mm): Nurse with child suffering from injuries to eye (3½c.), arm (7½c.), head (20c.) and nurse bathing a baby (10c.).

63a Group of Natives

64 European Nurse and Patient

1939. Netherlands Indies Social Bureau and Protestant Church Funds.
421 – 2c. (+1c.) violet 30 30
422 – 3½c. (+1½c.) green 35 30
423 **63a** 7½c. (+2½c.) brown 30 30
424 – 10c. (+2½c.) red . . . . . 1·60 1·00
425 **64** 10c. (+2½c.) red . . . . . 1·60 90
426 – 20c. (+5c.) blue 55 50
DESIGNS—VERT: 2c. as Type **63a** but group in European clothes. HORIZ: 3½c., 10c. (No. 424) as Type **64**, but Native nurse and patient.

1940. Red Cross Fund. No. 345 surch **10+5 ct** and cross.
428 **47** 10c.+5c. on 12½c. red . . . 3·50 55

68 Queen Wilhelmina

69 Netherlands Coat of Arms

1941. As T **94** of Netherlands but inscr "NED. INDIE" and T **68**.
429 – 10c. red 55 35
430 – 15c. blue . . . . 2·50 1·75
431 – 17½c. orange . . . . 1·00 70
432 – 20c. mauve . . . . 30·00 32·00
433 – 25c. green . . . . 40·00 42·00
434 – 30c. brown . . . . 4·50 1·40
435 – 35c. purple £160 £350
436 – 40c. green . . . . 12·00 3·50
437 – 50c. red . . . . 3·50 75
438 – 60c. blue . . . . 3·00 75
439 – 80c. red . . . . 3·00 75
440 – 1g. violet . . . . 3·00 75
441 – 2g. green . . . . 16·00 1·75
442 – 5g. bistre £300 £600
443 – 10g. green . . . . 42·00 18·00
444 **68** 25g. orange £250 £140
Nos 429/36 measure 18 × 23 mm, Nos. 431/43 20½ × 26 mm.

1941. Prince Bernhard Fund for Dutch Forces.
453 **69** 5c.+5c. blue and orange . . 75 15
454 10c.+10c. blue and red . . 75 15
455 1g.+1g. blue and grey . . . 16·00 10·75

70 Doctor and Child

71 Wayangwong Dancer

1941. Indigent Mohammedans' Relief Fund.
456 **70** 2c. (+1c.) green . . . . . 1·10 55
457 – 3½c. (+1½c.) brown . . . . 5·25 2·75
458 – 7½c. (+2½c.) violet . . . . 4·50 3·50
459 – 10c. (+2½c.) red . . . . . 1·75 35
460 – 15c. (+5c.) blue . . . . . 13·00 7·00
DESIGNS: 3½c. Native eating rice; 7½c. Nurse and patient; 10c. Nurse and children; 15c. Basket-weaver.

1941.
461 – 2c. red 30 15
462 – 2½c. purple 55 15
463 – 3c. green 55 35
464 **71** 4c. green 50 35
465 – 5c. blue 10 10
466 – 7½c. violet 55 10
DESIGNS (dancers): 2c. Menari; 2½c. Nias; 3c. Legon; 5c. Padjoge; 7½c. Dyak.
See also Nos. 514/16.

72 Paddyfield

73 Queen Wilhelmina

1945.
467 **72** 1c. green 55 15
468 – 2c. mauve 55 30
469 – 2½c. purple 55 15
470 – 5c. blue 35 15
471 – 7½c. olive 75 15
472 **73** 10c. brown 35 15
473 15c. blue 35 15
474 17½c. red 35 15
475 20c. purple 35 15
476 30c. grey 35 15
477 – 60c. grey 75 15
478 – 1g. green . . . . 1·10 15
479 – 2½g. orange . . . . 3·50 70
DESIGNS: As Type **72**: 2c. Lake in W. Java; 2½c. Medical School, Batavia; 5c. Seashore; 7½c. Douglas DC-2 airplane over Bromo Volcano. (30 × 30 mm): 60c. to 2½g. Portrait as Type **73** but different frame.

76 Railway Viaduct near Soekaboemi

81 Queen Wilhelmina

1946.
484 **76** 1c. green 30 20
485 – 2c. brown 30 20
486 – 2½c. red 30 20
487 – 5c. blue 30 20
488 – 7½c. blue 30 20
DESIGNS: 2c. Power station; 3c. Minangkabau house; 5c. Tondano scene (Celebes); 7½c. Buddhist Stupas, Java.

1947. Surch in figures.
502 – 3c. on 2½c. red (No. 486) 30 20
503 – 3c. on 7½c. blue (No. 488) 30 20
504 **76** 4c. on 1c. green 30 20
505 – 45c. on 60c. blue (No. 355) 1·40 95
No. 505 has three bars.

1947. Optd **1947**.
506 **47** 12½c. red 35 20
507 25c. green 35 20
508 – 40c. green (No. 436) . . . 55 20
509 **47** 50c. blue 75 30
510 80c. red . . . . 1·10 65
511 – 2g. green (No. 441) . . . . 4·00 55
512 – 5g. brown (No. 442) . . . 10·75 6·75

1948. Relief for Victims of the Terror. Surch **PELITA 15+10 Ct.** and lamp.
513 **47** 15c.+10c. on 10c. red . . . 30 30

1948. Dancers. As T **71**.
514 3c. red (Menari) 35 20
515 4c. green (Legon) 35 20
516 7½c. brown (Dyak) 70 65

1948.
517 **81** 15c. orange 90 70
518 20c. blue 35 35
519 25c. green 35 35
520 40c. green 35 35
521 45c. mauve 55 70
522 50c. lake 50 35
523 80c. red 55 35
524 1g. violet 50 35
525 10g. green . . . . 30·00 12·50
526 25g. orange . . . . 60·00 50·00
Nos. 524/6 are larger, 21 × 26 mm.

1948. Queen Wilhelmina's Golden Jubilee. As T **81** but inscr "1898 1948".
528 15c. orange 40 30
529 20c. blue 40 30

1948. As T **126** of Netherlands.
530 15c. red 50 35
531 20c. blue 50 35

MARINE INSURANCE STAMPS

1921. As Type M **22** of the Netherlands, but inscribed "NED. INDIE".
M257 15c. green . . . . 9·00 28·00
M258 60c. red . . . . 9·00 45·00
M259 75c. brown . . . . 9·00 48·00
M260 1g.50 blue . . . . 27·00 £225
M261 2g.25 brown . . . . . . 32·00 £275
M262 4½g. black . . . . 60·00 £550
M263 7½g. red . . . . 75·00 £600

OFFICIAL STAMPS

1911. Stamps of 1892 optd **D** in white on a black circle.
O178 **6** 10c. brown . . . . 2·40 1·40
O179 12½c. grey . . . . 4·00 5·25
O180 15c. bistre . . . . 4·00 3·50
O181 20c. blue . . . . 3·50 2·10
O182 25c. mauve . . . . 13·00 9·75
O183 50c. red . . . . 3·00 2·00
O184 2g.50 blue and brown . . 55·00 55·00

1911. Stamps of 1902 (except No. O185) optd **DIENST**.
O186 ½c. lilac 35 70
O187 1c. olive 35 35
O188 2c. brown 35 35
O185 2½c. yellow (No. 91) . . . 90 1·90
O189 2½c. green . . . . 1·75 1·75
O190 3c. orange 55 50
O191 4c. blue 35 35
O192 5c. red . . . . 1·10 90
O193 7½c. grey . . . . 2·75 2·75
O194 10c. slate 35 35
O195 12½c. blue . . . . 2·50 2·50
O196 15c. brown 90 90
O197 15c. brown (No. 140) . . . 35·00
O198 17½c. bistre . . . . 3·50 2·75
O199 20c. olive 90 55
O200 22½c. olive and brown . . . 3·50 3·50
O201 25c. mauve . . . . 2·10 1·90
O202 30c. brown . . . . 1·10 65
O203 50c. red . . . . 14·00 9·00
O204 1g. lilac . . . . 3·50 1·60
O205 2½g. grey . . . . 32·00 35·00

POSTAGE DUE STAMPS

1874. As Postage Due stamps of Netherlands. Colours changed.
D56 **D 8** 5c. yellow £300 £250
D57 10c. green on yellow . . £110 90·00
D59 15c. orange on yellow . . 22·00 18·00
D60 20c. green on blue . . . 35·00 14·50

1882. As Type D **10** of Netherlands.
D63b 2½c. black and red . . . . 55 1·10
D64b 5c. black and red . . . . 55 1·10
D65 10c. black and red . . . . 4·50 5·00
D70 15c. black and red . . . . 4·50 4·50
D71c 20c. black and red . . . . 90·00 55
D76b 30c. black and red . . . . 3·50 4·50
D72b 40c. black and red . . . . 2·50 1·25
D73b 50c. black and pink . . . . 1·40 1·60
D67 75c. black and red . . . . 1·10 1·40

1892. As Type D **9** of Netherlands.
D102 2½c. black and pink . . . 1·10 35
D103 5c. black and pink . . . . 3·50 30
D104b 10c. black and pink . . . 4·50 2·50
D105 15c. black and pink . . . 15·00 2·50
D106b 20c. black and pink . . . 5·50 2·00
D107 30c. black and pink . . . 23·00 8·00
D108 40c. black and pink . . . 20·00 3·00
D109 50c. black and pink . . . 12·50 1·25
D110 75c. black and pink . . . 25·00 5·50

1913. As Type D **9** of Netherlands.
D226 1c. orange . . . . 10 1·75
D489 1c. violet 75 90
D227 2½c. orange 10 10
D527 2½c. brown . . . . 1·10 1·25
D228 3½c. orange . . . . 10 1·75
D491 3½c. blue 70 90
D229 5c. orange 10 10
D230 7½c. orange 10 10
D493 7½c. green 90 90
D231 10c. orange 10 10
D494 10c. mauve 90 90
D232 12½c. orange . . . . 2·75 10
D448 15c. orange . . . . 1·90 1·25
D234 20c. orange 20 10
D495 20c. blue . . . . 90 1·10
D235 25c. orange 20 10
D496 25c. yellow . . . . 90 1·10
D236 30c. orange 20 20
D497 30c. brown . . . . 1·10 1·10
D237 37½c. orange . . . . 18·00 14·50
D238 40c. orange 20 20
D498 40c. green . . . . 1·10 1·25
D239 50c. orange . . . . 2·10 10
D499 50c. yellow . . . . 1·50 1·50
D240 75c. orange . . . . 2·75 20
D500 75c. blue . . . . 1·50 1·50
D241 1g. orange . . . . 5·00 7·25
D452 1g. blue . . . . 1·40 90
D501 100c. green . . . . 1·50 1·50

1937. Surch **20**.
D384 **D 5** 20c. on 37½c. red . . . 90 50

1946. Optd **TE BETALEN PORT** or surch also.
D480 2½c. on 10c. red (No. 429) 90 90
D481 10c. red (No. 429) . . . . 2·00 2·00
D482 20c. mauve (No. 432) . . . 5·50 5·50
D483 40c. green (No. 436) . . . 45·00 45·00

For later issues see **INDONESIA**.

NETHERLANDS NEW GUINEA

Pt. 4

The Western half of the island of New Guinea was governed by the Netherlands until 1962, when control was transferred to the U.N. (see West New Guinea). The territory later became part of Indonesia as West Irian (q.v.).

100 cents = 1 gulden.

1950. As numeral and portrait types of Netherlands but inscr "NIEUW GUINEA".
1 **118** 1c. grey 25 20
2 2c. orange 25 20
3 2½c. olive 50 20
4 3c. mauve . . . . 1·90 1·40
5 4c. green . . . . 1·90 1·25
6 5c. blue . . . . 3·25 20
7 7½c. brown 50 20
8 10c. violet . . . . 1·90 20
9 12½c. red . . . . 1·90 1·60
10 **129** 15c. brown . . . . 2·25 75
11 20c. blue 90 20
12 25c. red 90 20
13 30c. blue . . . . 11·00 20
14 40c. green . . . . 1·50 20
15 45c. brown . . . . 5·00 75
16 50c. orange . . . . 1·10 20
17 55c. grey . . . . 10·00 55
18 80c. purple . . . . 10·50 3·25
19 **130** 1g. red . . . . 11·50 20
20 2g. brown . . . . 9·00 1·40
21 5g. green . . . . 12·50 1·25

1953. Netherlands Flood Relief Fund. Nos. 6, 10 and 12 surch **hulp nederland 1953** and premium.
22 **118** 5c.+5c. blue . . . . 9·00 9·00
23 **129** 15c.+10c. brown . . . . . 9·00 9·00
24 25c.+10c. red . . . . 9·00 9·00

5 Lesser Bird of Paradise

6 Queen Juliana

1954.
25 **5** 1c. yellow and red 15 15
26 5c. yellow and brown . . . 20 20
27 – 10c. brown and blue . . . 20 20
28 – 15c. brown and yellow . . 25 20
29 – 20c. brown and green . . . 1·10 65
DESIGN: 10, 15, 20c. Greater bird of paradise.

1954.
30 **6** 25c. red 25 25
31 30c. blue 25 25
32 40c. orange . . . . 2·25 2·25
33 45c. green . . . . 75 1·25
34 55c. turquoise 55 25
35 80c. grey 90 35

36   85c. brown . . . .   1·25   50
37   1g. purple . . . .   4·75   2·25

1955. Red Cross. Nos. 26/8 surch with cross and premium.
38 **5** 5c.+5c. yellow and sepia . .   1·25   1·10
39 – 10c.+10c. brown and blue . .   1·25   1·10
40 – 15c.+10c. brown and lemon   1·25   1·10

8 Child and Native Hut
10 Papuan Girl and Beach Scene

1956. Anti-leprosy Fund.
41 – 5c.+5c. green . . . .   1·10   1·00
42 **8** 10c.+5c. purple . . . . . .   1·10   1·00
43 – 25c.+10c. blue . . . .   1·10   1·00
44 **8** 30c.+10c. buff . . . . . .   1·10   1·00
DESIGN: 5c., 25c. Palm-trees and native hut.

1957. Child Welfare Fund.
51 **10** 5c.+5c. lake . . . .   1·10   1·00
52 – 10c.+5c. green . . . . . .   1·10   1·00
53 **10** 25c.+10c. brown . . . . .   1·10   1·00
54 – 30c.+10c. blue . . . . . .   1·10   1·00
DESIGN: 10c., 30c. Papuan child and native hut.

11 Red Cross and Idol
12 Papuan and Helicopter

1958. Red Cross Fund.
55 **11** 5c.+5c. multicoloured . . .   1·10   1·10
56 – 10c.+5c. multicoloured . . .   1·10   1·10
57 **11** 25c.+10c. multicoloured . .   1·10   1·10
58 – 30c.+10c. multicoloured . .   1·10   1·10
DESIGN: 10c., 30c. Red Cross and Asman-Papuan bowl in form of human figure.

1959. Stars Mountains Expedition, 1959.
59 **12** 55c. brown and blue . . . .   1·25   90

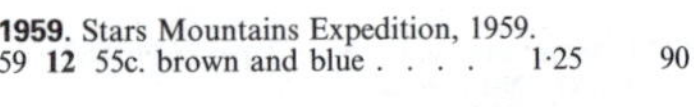

13 Blue-crowned Pigeon

14 "Tecomanthe dendrophila"

1959.
60 **13** 7c. purple, blue and brown   35   35
61   12c. purple, blue and green   35   35
62   17c. purple and blue   35   35

1959. Social Welfare. Inscr "SOCIALE ZORG".
63 **14** 5c.+5c. red and green . . .   75   65
64 – 10c.+5c. purple, yellow and olive   75   65
65 – 25c.+10c. yellow, green and red   75   65
66 – 30c.+10c. green and violet   75   65
DESIGNS: 10c. "Dendrobium attennatum Lindley"; 25c. "Rhododendron zoelleri Warburg"; 30c. "Boea cf. urvillei".

1960. World Refugee Year. As T **180** of Netherlands.
67   25c. blue   65   65
68   30c. ochre   65   65

16 Paradise Birdwing

1960. Social Welfare Funds. Butterflies.
69 **16** 5c.+5c. multicoloured . . .   90   90
70 – 10c.+5c. bl, blk & salmon   90   90
71 – 25c.+10c. red, sepia & yell   90   90
72 – 30c.+10c. multicoloured . .   90   90
BUTTERFLIES: 10c. Large green-banded blue; 25c. Red lacewing; 30c. Catops owl butterfly.

17 Council Building, Hollandia

1961. Opening of Netherlands New Guinea Council.
73 **17** 25c. turquoise   25   35
74   30c. red   25   35

18 "Scapanes australis"

19 Children's Road Crossing

1961. Social Welfare Funds. Beetles.
75 **18** 5c.+5c. multicoloured . . .   50   35
76 – 10c.+5c. multicoloured . . .   50   35
77 – 25c.+10c. multicoloured . .   50   35
78 – 30c.+10c. multicoloured . .   50   35
BEETLES: 10c. Brenthid weevil; 25c. "Neolamprima adolphinae" (stag beetle); 30c. "Aspidomorpha aurata" (leaf beetle).

1962. Road Safety Campaign. Triangle in red.
79 **19** 25c. blue   25   35
80 – 30c. green (Adults at road crossing)   25   35

1962. Silver Wedding of Queen Juliana and Prince Bernhard. As T **187** of Netherlands.
81   55c. brown   35   50

21 Shadow of Palm on Beach

1962. 5th South Pacific Conference, Pago Pago. Multicoloured.
82   25c. Type **21**   25   40
83   30c. Palms on beach   25   40

22 Lobster

1962. Social Welfare Funds. Shellfish. Multicoloured.
84   5c.+5c. Crab (horiz)   20   20
85   10c.+5c. Type **22**   20   20
86   25c.+10c. Spiny lobster . . .   25   25
87   30c.+10c. Shrimp (horiz) . . .   25   35

POSTAGE DUE STAMPS

1957. As Type D **121** of Netherlands but inscr "NEDERLANDS NIEUW GUINEA".
D45   1c. red   20   25
D46   5c. red   75   1·25
D47   10c. red . . . .   1·90   2·40
D48   25c. red . . . .   2·75   1·10
D49   40c. red . . . .   2·75   1·25
D50   1g. blue . . . .   3·50   4·50

For later issues see **WEST NEW GUINEA** and **WEST IRIAN**.

NEVIS   Pt. 1

One of the Leeward Islands, Br. W. Indies. Used stamps of St. Kitts–Nevis from 1903 until June 1980 when Nevis, although remaining part of St. Kitts–Nevis, had a separate postal administration.

1861. 12 pence = 1 shilling;
20 shillings = 1 pound.
1980. 100 cents = 1 dollar.

1

2

5

(The design on the stamps refers to a medicinal spring on the Island).

1861. Various frames.
15 **1** 1d. red . . . .   22·00   17·00
6 **2** 4d. red . . . .   £120   65·00
12   4d. orange . . . .   £120   23·00
7 – 6d. lilac . . . .   £120   55·00
20 – 1s. green . . . .   90·00   £110

1879.
25 **5** ½d. green . . . .   5·50   15·00
23   1d. mauve . . . .   75·00   38·00
27a   1d. red . . . .   11·00   11·00
28   2½d. brown . . . .   £120   50·00
29   2½d. blue . . . .   19·00   19·00
30   4d. blue . . . .   £325   50·00
31   4d. grey . . . .   12·00   4·00
32   6d. green £400   £350
33   6d. brown . . . .   24·00   60·00
34   1s. violet £110   £180

1883. Half of No. 23 surch **NEVIS. ½d.**
35 **5** ½d. on half 1d. mauve . . .   £850   48·00

1980. Nos. 394/406 of St. Christopher, Nevis and Anguilla with "St. Christopher" and "Anguilla" obliterated.
37   5c. Radio and T.V. station . .   10   10
38   10c. Technical college   10   10
39   12c. T.V. assembly plant . . .   10   30
40   15c. Sugar cane harvesting . .   10   10
41   25c. Crafthouse (craft centre)   10   10
42   30c. "Europa" (liner)   20   15
43   40c. Lobster and sea crab . .   15   40
44   45c. Royal St. Kitts Hotel and golf course   80   70
45   50c. Pinney's Beach, Nevis . .   15   30
46   55c. New runway at Golden Rock   60   15
47    $1 Picking cotton   15   30
48    $5 Brewery   30   75
49    $10 Pineapples and peanuts . .   40   1·00

7a Queen Elizabeth the Queen Mother

1980. 80th Birthday of Queen Elizabeth the Queen Mother.
50 **7a** $2 multicoloured   20   30

8 Nevis Lighter

9 Virgin and Child

1980. Boats. Multicoloured.
51   5c. Type **8**   10   10
52   30c. Local fishing boat   15   10
53   55c. "Caona" (catamaran) . .   15   10
54    $3 "Polynesia" (cruise schooner) (39 × 53 mm) . .   40   40

1980. Christmas. Multicoloured.
55   5c. Type **9**   10   10
56   30c. Angel   10   10
57    $2.50 The Wise Men   20   30

10 Charlestown Pier
11 New River Mill

1981. Multicoloured.
58A   5c. Type **10**   10   10
59A   10c. Court House and Library   10   10
60A   15c. Type **11**   10   10
61A   20c. Nelson Museum   10   10
62A   25c. St. James' Parish Church   15   15
63A   30c. Nevis Lane   15   15
64A   40c. Zetland Plantation . . .   20   20
65A   45c. Nisbet Plantation . . .   20   25
66A   50c. Pinney's Beach   25   25
67A   55c. Eva Wilkin's Studio . .   25   30
68A $1 Nevis at dawn   30   45
69A $2.50 Ruins of Fort Charles   35   80
70A $5 Old Bath House   40   1·00
71A $10 Beach at Nisbet's . . .   50   2·00

11a "Royal Caroline"

11b Prince Charles and Lady Diana Spencer

1981. Royal Wedding. Royal Yachts. Multicoloured.
72   55c. Type **11a**   15   15
73   55c. Type **11b**   40   40
74    $2 "Royal Sovereign"   30   30
75    $2 As No. 73   80   1·25
76    $5 "Britannia"   45   80
77    $5 As No. 73 . . . .   1·00   2·00
MS78 120 × 109 mm. $4.50 As No. 73 . . . .   1·10   1·25

12 "Heliconius charithonia"

1982. Butterflies (1st series). Multicoloured.
81   5c. Type **12**   10   10
82   30c. "Siproeta stelenes"   20   10
83   55c. "Marpesia petreus" . . .   25   15
84    $2 "Phoebis agarithe"   60   80
See also Nos. 105/8.

13 Caroline of Brunswick, Princess of Wales, 1793

1982. 21st Birthday of Princess of Wales. Mult.
85   30c. Type **13**   10   10
86   55c. Coat of arms of Caroline of Brunswick   15   15
87    $5 Diana, Princess of Wales   1·25   1·25

1982. Birth of Prince William of Wales. Nos. 85/7 optd **ROYAL BABY**.
88   30c. As Type **13**   10   10
89   55c. Coat of arms of Caroline of Brunswick   15   15
90    $5 Diana, Princess of Wales   60   1·00

14 Cyclist

1982. 75th Anniv of Boy Scout Movement. Multicoloured.
91   5c. Type **14**   20   10
92   30c. Athlete   25   10
93    $2.50 Camp cook   50   65

15 Santa Claus

1982. Christmas. Children's Paintings. Mult.
94   15c. Type **15**   10   10
95   30c. Carollers   10   10
96    $1.50 Decorated house and local band (horiz)   15   25
97    $2.50 Adoration of the Shepherds (horiz)   25   40

16 Tube Sponge

19 Montgolfier Balloon, 1783

17 H.M.S. "Boreas" off Nevis

1983. Corals (1st series). Multicoloured.
98 15c. Type **16** 10 10
99 30c. Stinging coral 15 10
100 55c. Flower coral 15 10
101 $3 Sea rod and red fire sponge 50 80
MS102 82 × 115 mm. Nos. 98/101 1·40 2·50
See also Nos. 423/6.

1983. Commonwealth Day. Multicoloured.
103 55c. Type **17** 15 10
104 $2 Capt. Horatio Nelson and H.M.S. "Boreas" at anchor 45 60

1983. Butterflies (2nd series). As T **12**. Mult.
105 30c. "Pyrgus oileus" 20 10
106 55c. "Junonia evarete" (vert) 20 10
107 $1.10 "Urbanus proteus" (vert) 30 40
108 $2 "Hypolimnas misippus" 40 75

1983. Nos. 58 and 60/71 optd **INDEPENDENCE 1983**.
109B 5c. Type **10** 10 10
110B 15c. Type **11** 10 10
111B 20c. Nelson Museum . . . 10 10
112B 25c. St. James' Parish Church 10 15
113B 30c. Nevis Lane 15 15
114B 40c. Zetland Plantation . . 15 20
115B 45c. Nisbet Plantation . . . 15 25
116B 50c. Pinney's Beach 15 25
117B 55c. Eva Wilkin's Studio . . 15 30
118B $1 Nevis at dawn 15 30
119B $2.50 Ruins of Fort Charles 25 45
120B $5 Old Bath House 30 55
121B $10 Beach at Nisbet's . . . 40 70

1983. Bicentenary of Manned Flight. Mult.
122 10c. Type **19** 10 10
123 45c. Sikorsky S-38 flying boat (horiz) 15 10
124 50c. Beech 50 Twin Bonanza (horiz) 15 10
125 $2.50 Hawker Siddeley Sea Harrier (horiz) . . . . . . 30 1·25
MS126 118 × 145 mm. Nos. 122/5 75 1·25

20 Mary praying over Holy Child

1983. Christmas. Multicoloured.
127 5c. Type **20** 10 10
128 30c. Shepherds with flock . . 10 10
129 55c. Three Angels 10 10
130 $3 Boy with two girls 30 60
MS131 135 × 149 mm. Nos. 127/30 85 2·00

21 "County of Oxford" (1945)

1983. Leaders of the World. Railway Locomotives (1st series). The first in each pair shows technical drawings and the second the locomotive at work.
132 **21** 55c. multicoloured 10 20
133 – 55c. multicoloured 10 20
134 – $1 red, blue and black . . 10 20
135 – $1 multicoloured 10 20
136 – $1 purple, blue and black 10 20
137 – $1 multicoloured 10 20
138 – $1 red, black and yellow 10 20
139 – $1 multicoloured 10 20
140 – $1 multicoloured 10 20
141 – $1 multicoloured 10 20
142 – $1 yellow, black and blue 10 20
143 – $1 multicoloured 10 20
144 – $1 yellow, black and purple 10 20
145 – $1 multicoloured 10 20
146 – $1 multicoloured 10 20
147 – $1 multicoloured 10 20
DESIGNS: Nos. 132/3, "County of Oxford", Great Britain (1945); 134/5, "Evening Star", Great Britain (1960); 136/7, Stanier Class 5 No. 44806, Great Britain (1934); 138/9, "Pendennis Castle", Great Britain (1924); 140/1, "Winston Churchill", Great Britain (1946); 142/3, "Mallard", Great Britain (1938) (inscr "1935" in error); 144/5, "Britannia", Great Britain (1951); 146/7, "King George V", Great Britain.
See also Nos. 219/26, 277/84, 297/308, 352/9 and 427/42.

22 Boer War

1984. Leaders of the World. British Monarchs (1st series). Multicoloured.
148 5c. Type **22** 10 10
149 5c. Queen Victoria 10 10
150 50c. Queen Victoria at Osborne House 10 30
151 50c. Osborne House 10 30
152 60c. Battle of Dettingen . . . 10 30
153 60c. George II 10 30
154 75c. George II at the Bank of England 10 30
155 75c. Bank of England 10 30
156 $1 Coat of Arms of George II 10 30
157 $1 George II (different) . . . 10 30
158 $3 Coat of Arms of Queen Victoria 20 50
159 $3 Queen Victoria (different) 20 50
See also Nos. 231/6.

23 Golden Rock Inn

1984. Tourism (1st series). Multicoloured.
160 55c. Type **23** 25 20
161 55c. Rest Haven Inn 25 20
162 55c. Cliffdwellers Hotel . . . 25 20
163 55c. Pinney's Beach Hotel . . 25 20
See also Nos. 245/8.

24 Early Seal of Colony

1984.
164 **24** $15 red . . . . 1·10 4·00

25 Cadillac

1984. Leaders of the World Automobiles (1st series). As T **25**. The first design in each pair shows technical drawings and the second paintings.
165 1c. yellow, black and mauve 10 10
166 1c. multicoloured 10 10
167 5c. blue, mauve and black . . 10 10
168 5c. multicoloured 10 10
169 15c. multicoloured 10 15
170 15c. multicoloured 10 15
171 35c. mauve, yellow and black 10 25
172 35c. multicoloured 10 25
173 45c. blue, mauve and black 10 25
174 45c. multicoloured 10 25
175 55c. multicoloured 10 25
176 55c. multicoloured 10 25
177 $2.50 mauve, black and yellow 20 40
178 $2.50 multicoloured 20 40
179 $3 blue, yellow and black . . 20 40
180 $3 multicoloured 20 40
DESIGNS: No. 165/6, Cadillac "V16 Fleetwood Convertible" (1932); 167/8, Packard "Twin Six Touring Car" (1916); 169/70, Daimler "2 Cylinder" (1886); 171/2, Porsche "911 S Targa" (1970); 173/4, Benz "Three Wheeler" (1885); 175/6, M.G. "TC" (1947); 177/8, Cobra "Roadster 289" (1966); 179/80, Aston Martin "DB6 Hardtop" (1966).
See also Nos. 203/10, 249/64, 326/37, 360/371 and 411/22.

26 Carpentry

1984. 10th Anniv of Culturama Celebrations. Multicoloured.
181 30c. Type **26** 10 10
182 55c. Grass mat and basket making 10 10
183 $1 Pottery firing 15 25
184 $3 Culturama Queen and dancers 40 55

27 Yellow Bell

29 C. P. Mead

28 Cotton-picking and Map

1984. Flowers. Multicoloured.
185A 5c. Type **27** 10 10
186A 10c. Plumbago 10 10
187A 15c. Flamboyant 10 10
188B 20c. Eyelash orchid 60 30
189A 30c. Bougainvillea 10 15
190B 40c. Hibiscus 30 30
191A 50c. Night-blooming cereus 15 20
192A 55c. Yellow mahoe 15 25
193A 60c. Spider-lily 15 25
194A 75c. Scarlet cordia 20 30
195A $1 Shell-ginger 20 40
196A $3 Blue petrea . . . . . . 30 1·10
197A $5 Coral hibiscus . . . . 50 2·00
198A $10 Passion flower . . . . 80 3·50

1984. 1st Anniv of Independence of St. Kitts–Nevis. Multicoloured.
199 15c. Type **28** 10 10
200 55c. Alexander Hamilton's birthplace 10 10
201 $1.10 Local agricultural produce 20 40
202 $3 Nevis Peak and Pinney's Beach . . . . 50 1·00

1984. Leaders of the World. Automobiles (2nd series). As T **25**. The first in each pair shows technical drawings and the second paintings.
203 5c. black, blue and brown . . 10 10
204 5c. multicoloured 10 10
205 30c. black, turquoise and brown 15 15
206 30c. multicoloured 15 15
207 50c. black, drab and brown 15 15
208 50c. multicoloured 15 15
209 $3 black, brown and green 30 45
210 $3 multicoloured 30 45
DESIGNS: Nos. 203/4, Lagonda "Speed Model" touring car (1929); 205/6, Jaguar "E-Type" 4.2 litre (1967); 207/8, Volkswagen "Beetle" (1947); 209/10, Pierce Arrow "V12" (1932).

1984. Leaders of the World. Cricketers (1st series). As T **29**. The first in each pair shows a head portrait and the second the cricketer in action. Multicoloured.
211 5c. Type **29** 10 10
212 5c. C. P. Mead 10 10
213 25c. J. B. Statham 20 30
214 25c. J. B. Statham 20 30
215 55c. Sir Learie Constantine 30 40
216 55c. Sir Learie Constantine 30 40
217 $2.50 Sir Leonard Hutton . . 50 1·25
218 $2.50 Sir Leonard Hutton . . 50 1·25
See also Nos. 237/4.

1984. Leaders of the World. Railway Locomotives (2nd series). As T **21**. The first in each pair shows technical drawings and the second the locomotive at work.
219 5c. multicoloured 10 10
220 5c. multicoloured 10 10
221 10c. multicoloured 10 10
222 10c. multicoloured 10 10
223 60c. multicoloured 15 25
224 60c. multicoloured 15 25
225 $2 multicoloured 50 70
226 $2 multicoloured 50 70
DESIGNS: Nos. 219/20, Class EF81 electric locomotive, Japan (1968); 221/22, Class 5500 electric locomotive, France (1927); 223/4, Class 240P, France (1940); 225/6, "Hikari" express train, Japan (1964).

30 Fifer and Drummer from Honeybees Band

1984. Christmas. Local Music. Multicoloured.
227 15c. Type **30** 15 10
228 40c. Guitar and "barhow" players from Canary Birds Band 25 10
229 60c. Shell All Stars steel band 30 10
230 $3 Organ and choir, St. John's Church, Fig Tree . . . . 1·25 1·00

1984. Leaders of the World. British Monarchs (2nd series). As T **22**. Multicoloured.
231 5c. King John and Magna Carta 10 10
232 5c. Barons and King John . . 10 10
233 55c. King John 10 15
234 55c. Newark Castle 10 15
235 $2 Coat of arms 25 40
236 $2 King John (different) . . 25 40

1984. Leaders of the World. Cricketers (2nd series). As T **29**. The first in each pair listed shows a head portrait and the second the cricketer in action. Multicoloured.
237 5c. J. D. Love 10 10
238 5c. J. D. Love 10 10
239 15c. S. J. Dennis 10 15
240 15c. S. J. Dennis 10 15
241 55c. B. W. Luckhurst 15 20
242 55c. B. W. Luckhurst 15 20
243 $2.50 B. L. D'Oliveira . . . 40 60
244 $2.50 B. L. D'Oliveira . . . 40 60

1984. Tourism (2nd series). As T **23**. Multicoloured.
245 $1.20 Croney's Old Manor Hotel 15 25
246 $1.20 Montpelier Plantation Inn 15 25
247 $1.20 Nisbet's Plantation Inn 15 25
248 $1.20 Zetland Plantation Inn 15 25

1985. Leaders of the World. Automobiles (3rd series). As T **25**. The first in each pair shows technical drawings and the second paintings.
249 1c. black, green and light green 10 10
250 1c. multicoloured 10 10
251 5c. black, blue and light blue 10 10
252 5c. multicoloured 10 10
253 10c. black, green and light green 10 10
254 10c. multicoloured 10 10
255 50c. black, green and brown 10 10
256 50c. multicoloured 10 10
257 60c. black, green and blue . . 10 10
258 60c. multicoloured 10 10
259 75c. black, red and orange 10 10
260 75c. multicoloured 10 10
261 $2.50 black, green and blue 20 30
262 $2.50 multicoloured 20 30
263 $3 black, green and light green 20 30
264 $3 multicoloured 20 30
DESIGNS: Nos. 249/50, Delahaye "Type 35 Cabriolet" (1935); 251/2, Ferrari "Testa Rossa" (1958); 253/4, Voisin "Aerodyne" (1934); 255/6, Buick "Riviera" (1963); 257/8, Cooper "Climax" (1960); 259/60, Ford "999" (1904); 261/2, MG "M-Type Midget" (1930); 263/4, Rolls- Royce "Corniche" (1971).

31 Broad-winged Hawk

1985. Local Hawks and Herons. Multicoloured.
265 20c. Type **31** . . . . 1·25 20
266 40c. Red-tailed hawk . . . . 1·40 30
267 60c. Little blue heron . . . . 1·40 40
268 $3 Great blue heron (white phase) . . . . 2·75 1·90

32 Eastern Bluebird

1985. Leaders of the World. Birth Bicentenary of John J. Audubon (ornithologist) (1st issue). Multicoloured.
269 5c. Type **32** 10 10
270 5c. Common cardinal 10 10
271 55c. Belted kingfisher 20 55
272 55c. Mangrove cuckoo . . . 20 55
273 60c. Yellow warbler 20 55
274 60c. Cerulean warbler 20 55

275 $2 Burrowing owl . . . . . 60 1·25
276 $2 Long-eared owl . . . . . 60 1·25
See also Nos. 285/92.

1985. Leaders of the World. Railway Locomotives (3rd series). As T **21**. The first in each pair showing technical drawings and the second the locomotive at work.
277 1c. multicoloured 10 10
278 1c. multicoloured 10 10
279 60c. multicoloured 20 20
280 60c. multicoloured 20 20
281 90c. multicoloured 25 25
282 90c. multicoloured 25 25
283 $2 multicoloured 40 60
284 $2 multicoloured 40 60
DESIGNS: Nos. 277/8, Class "Wee Bogie", Great Britain (1882); 279/80, "Comet", Great Britain (1851); 281/2, Class 8H No. 6173, Great Britain (1908); 283/4, Class A No. 23, Great Britain (1866).

1985. Leaders of the World. Birth Bicentenary of John J. Audubon (ornithologist) (2nd issue). As T **32**. Multicoloured.
285 1c. Painted bunting 10 10
286 1c. Golden-crowned kinglet 10 10
287 40c. Common flicker 25 40
288 40c. Western tanager 25 40
289 60c. Varied thrush 25 45
290 60c. Evening grosbeak . . . 25 45
291 $2.50 Blackburnian warbler 50 80
292 $2.50 Northern oriole 50 80

33 Guides and Guide Headquarters

1985. 75th Anniv of Girl Guide Movement. Multicoloured.
293 15c. Type **33** 10 10
294 60c. Girl Guide uniforms of 1910 and 1985 (vert) . . . 15 25
295 $1 Lord and Lady Baden-Powell (vert) 20 40
296 $3 Princess Margaret in Guide uniform (vert) . . . 50 1·25

1985. Leaders of the World. Railway Locomotives (4th series). As T **21**. The first in each pair shows technical drawings and the second the locomotive at work.
297 5c. multicoloured 10 10
298 5c. multicoloured 10 10
299 30c. multicoloured 10 15
300 30c. multicoloured 10 15
301 60c. multicoloured 10 20
302 60c. multicoloured 10 20
303 75c. multicoloured 10 25
304 75c. multicoloured 10 25
305 $1 multicoloured 10 25
306 $1 multicoloured 10 25
307 $2.50 multicoloured 20 60
308 $2.50 multicoloured 20 60
DESIGNS: Nos. 297/8, "Snowdon Ranger" (1878); 299/300, Large Belpaire locomotive, Great Britain (1904); 301/2, Class "County" No. 3821, Great Britain (1904); 303/4, "L'Outrance", France (1877); 305/6, Class PB-15, Australia (1899); 307/8, Class 64, Germany (1928).

34 The Queen Mother at Garter Ceremony

35 Isambard Kingdom Brunel

1985. Leaders of the World. Life and Times of Queen Elizabeth the Queen Mother. Various vertical portraits.
309 **34** 45c. multicoloured 10 15
310 – 45c. multicoloured 10 15
311 – 75c. multicoloured 10 20
312 – 75c. multicoloured 10 20
313 – $1.20 multicoloured . . . 15 35
314 – $1.20 multicoloured . . . 15 35
315 – $1.50 multicoloured . . . 20 40
316 – $1.50 multicoloured . . . 20 40
MS317 85×114 mm. $2 multicoloured; $2 multicoloured 50 1·40
Each value was issued in pairs showing a floral pattern across the bottom of the portraits which stops short of the left-hand edge on the first stamp and of the right-hand edge on the second.

1985. 150th Anniv of Great Western Railway. Designs showing railway engineers and their achievements. Multicoloured.
318 25c. Type **35** 15 35
319 25c. Royal Albert Bridge, 1859 . . . . 15 35
320 50c. William Dean 20 45
321 50c. Locomotive "Lord of the Isles", 1895 . . . . . . 20 45
322 $1 Locomotive "Lode Star", 1907 . . . . 25 65
323 $1 G. J. Churchward 25 65
324 $2.50 Locomotive "Pendennis Castle", 1924 . . . . . . 35 80
325 $2.50 C. B. Collett 35 80
Nos. 318/19, 320/1, 322/3 and 324/5 were printed together se-tenant, each pair forming a composite design.

1985. Leaders of the World. Automobiles (4th series). As T **25**. The first in each pair shows technical drawings and the second paintings.
326 10c. black, blue and red . . . 10 10
327 10c. multicoloured 10 10
328 35c. black, turquoise and blue 10 25
329 35c. multicoloured 10 25
330 75c. black, green and brown 10 40
331 75c. multicoloured 10 40
332 $1.15 black, brown and green 15 45
333 $1.15 multicoloured 15 45
334 $1.50 black, blue and red . . 15 50
335 $1.50 multicoloured 15 50
336 $2 black, lilac and violet . . 20 60
337 $2 multicoloured 20 60
DESIGNS: Nos. 326/7, Sunbeam "Coupe de l'Auto" (1912); 328/9, Cisitalia "Pininfarina Coupe" (1948); 330/1, Porsche "928S" (1980); 332/3, MG "K3 Magnette" (1933); 334/5, Lincoln "Zephyr" (1937); 336/7, Pontiac 2 Door (1926).

1985. Royal Visit. Nos. 76/7, 83, 86, 92/3, 98/9 and 309/10 optd **CARIBBEAN ROYAL VISIT 1985** or surch also.
338 **16** 15c. multicoloured . . . . 75 1·25
339 – 30c. multicoloured (No. 92) 1·75 1·75
340 – 30c. multicoloured (No. 99) 75 1·25
341 – 40c. on 55c. mult (No. 86) 1·75 2·00
342 **34** 45c. multicoloured . . . . 1·50 3·25
343 – 45c. multicoloured (No. 310) . . . . . . 1·50 3·25
344 – 55c. multicoloured (No. 83) 1·50 1·25
345 – $1.50 on $5 multicoloured (No. 76) . . . . 2·25 3·00
346 – $1.50 on $5 multicoloured (No. 77) . . . . 13·00 17·00
347 – $2.50 mult (No. 93) . . . 2·25 3·50

36 St. Paul's Anglican Church, Charlestown

1985. Christmas. Churches of Nevis (1st series). Multicoloured.
348 10c. Type **36** 15 10
349 40c. St. Theresa Catholic Church, Charlestown . . . 35 30
350 60c. Methodist Church, Gingerland 40 50
351 $3 St. Thomas Anglican Church, Lowland . . . . 80 2·75
See also Nos. 462/5.

1986. Leaders of the World. Railway Locomotives (5th series). As T **21**. The first in each pair shows technical drawings and the second the locomotive at work.
352 30c. multicoloured 15 25
353 30c. multicoloured 15 25
354 75c. multicoloured 25 50
355 75c. multicoloured 25 50
356 $1.50 multicoloured 40 70
357 $1.50 multicoloured 40 70
358 $2 multicoloured 50 80
359 $2 multicoloured 50 80
DESIGNS: Nos. 352/3, "Stourbridge Lion", U.S.A. (1829); 354/5, EP-2 Bi-Polar electric locomotive, U.S.A. (1919); 356/7, Gas turbine No. 59, U.S.A. (1953); 358/9 Class FL9 diesel locomotive No. 2039, U.S.A. (1955).

1986. Leaders of the World. Automobiles (5th series). As T **25**. The first in each pair showing technical drawings and the second paintings.
360 10c. black, brown and green 10 10
361 10c. multicoloured 10 10
362 60c. black, orange and red 15 25
363 60c. multicoloured 15 25
364 75c. black, light brown and brown 15 25
365 75c. multicoloured 15 25
366 $1 black, light grey and grey 15 30
367 $1 multicoloured 15 30
368 $1.50 black, yellow and green 20 35
369 $1.50 multicoloured 20 35
370 $3 black, light blue and blue 30 65
371 $3 multicoloured 30 65
DESIGNS: Nos. 360/1, Adler "Trumpf" (1936); 362/3, Maserati "Tipo 250F" (1957); 364/5, Oldsmobile "Limited" (1910); 366/7, Jaguar "C-Type" (1951); 368/9, ERA "1.5L B Type" (1937); 370/1, Chevrolet "Corvette" (1953).

37 Supermarine Spitfire Prototype, 1936

1986. 50th Anniv of Spitfire (fighter aircraft). Multicoloured.
372 $1 Type **37** 20 50
373 $2.50 Supermarine Spitfire Mk 1A in Battle of Britain, 1940 . . . . 30 75
374 $3 Supermarine Spitfire Mk XII over convoy, 1944 30 75
375 $4 Supermarine Spitfire Mk XXIV, 1948 . . . . . 30 1·25
MS376 114×86 mm. $6 Supermarine Seafire Mk III on escort carrier H.M.S. "Hunter" 1·10 3·75

38 Head of Amerindian

39 Brazilian Player

38a Queen Elizabeth in 1976

1986. 500th Anniv (1992) of Discovery of America by Columbus (1st issue). Multicoloured.
377 85c. Type **38** . . . . 85 1·00
378 85c. Exchanging gifts for food from Amerindians . . 85 1·00
379 $1.75 Columbus's coat of arms . . . . 1·40 2·00
380 $1.75 Breadfruit plant . . . 1·40 2·00
381 $2.50 Columbus's fleet . . . 1·40 2·25
382 $2.50 Christopher Columbus 1·40 2·25
MS383 95×84 mm. $6 Christopher Columbus (different) . . . . . 6·00 9·50
The two designs of each value were printed together, se-tenant, each pair forming a composite design showing charts of Columbus's route in the background.
See also Nos. 546/54, 592/600, 678/84 and 685/6.

1986. 60th Birthday of Queen Elizabeth II. Multicoloured.
384 5c. Type **38a** 10 10
385 75c. Queen Elizabeth in 1953 15 25
386 $2 In Australia 20 60
387 $8 In Canberra, 1982 (vert) 75 2·00
MS388 85×115 mm. $10 Queen Elizabeth II . . . . 4·50 7·50

1986. World Cup Football Championship, Mexico. Multicoloured.
389 1c. Official World Cup mascot (horiz) 10 10
390 2c. Type **39** 10 10
391 5c. Danish player 10 10
392 10c. Brazilian player (different) 10 10
393 20c. Denmark v Spain . . . 20 20
394 30c. Paraguay v Chile . . . 30 30
395 60c. Italy v West Germany 40 55
396 75c. Danish team (56×36 mm) 40 65
397 $1 Paraguayan team (56×36 mm) 50 70
398 $1.75 Brazilian team (56×36 mm) . . . . . . 60 1·25
399 $3 Italy v England . . . . . 75 1·90
400 $6 Italian team (56×36 mm) 1·10 3·00
MS401 Five sheets, each 85×115 mm. (a) $1.50 As No. 398. (b) $2 As No. 393. (c) $2 As No. 400. (d) $2.50 As No. 395. (e) $4 As No. 394 Set of 5 sheets 12·00 15·00

40 Clothing Machinist

1986. Local Industries. Multicoloured.
402 15c. Type **40** 20 15
403 40c. Carpentry/joinery workshop 45 30
404 $1.20 Agricultural produce market . . . . 1·25 1·50
405 $3 Fishing boats landing catch . . . . 2·50 3·25

40a Prince Andrew in Midshipman's Uniform

1986. Royal Wedding. Multicoloured.
406 60c. Type **40a** 15 25
407 60c. Miss Sarah Ferguson . . 15 25
408 $2 Prince Andrew on safari in Africa (horiz) 40 60
409 $2 Prince Andrew at the races (horiz) 40 60
MS410 115×85 mm. $10 Duke and Duchess of York on Palace balcony after wedding (horiz) 2·50 5·00
See also Nos. 454/7.

1986. Automobiles (6th series). As T **25**. The first in each pair showing technical drawings and the second paintings.
411 15c. multicoloured 10 10
412 15c. multicoloured 10 10
413 45c. black, light blue and blue 20 25
414 45c. multicoloured 20 25
415 60c. multicoloured 20 30
416 60c. multicoloured 20 30
417 $1 black, light green and green 25 40
418 $1 multicoloured 25 40
419 $1.75 black, lilac and deep lilac 30 50
420 $1.75 multicoloured 30 50
421 $3 multicoloured 50 90
422 $3 multicoloured 50 90
DESIGNS: Nos. 411/12, Riley "Brooklands Nine" (1930); 413/14, Alfa Romeo "GTA" (1966); 415/16, Pierce Arrow "Type 66" (1913); 417/18, Willys-Knight "66A" (1928); 419/20, Studebaker "Starliner" (1953); 421/2, Cunningham "V-8" (1919).

41 Gorgonia

41a Statue of Liberty and World Trade Centre, Manhattan

1986. Corals (2nd series). Multicoloured.
423 15c. Type **41** 25 15
424 60c. Fire coral 55 55
425 $2 Elkhorn coral . . . . . . 90 2·00
426 $3 Vase sponge and feather star . . . . 1·10 2·50

1986. Railway Locomotives (6th series). As T **21**. The first in each pair showing technical drawings and the second the locomotive at work.
427 15c. multicoloured 10 10
428 15c. multicoloured 10 10
429 45c. multicoloured 15 25
430 45c. multicoloured 15 25
431 60c. multicoloured 20 30
432 60c. multicoloured 20 30
433 75c. multicoloured 20 40
434 75c. multicoloured 20 40
435 $1 multicoloured 20 50
436 $1 multicoloured 20 50
437 $1.50 multicoloured 25 60
438 $1.50 multicoloured 25 60
439 $2 multicoloured 30 65
440 $2 multicoloured 30 65
441 $3 multicoloured 35 80
442 $3 multicoloured 35 80
DESIGNS: Nos. 427/8, Connor Single Class, Great Britain (1859); 429/30, Class P2 "Cock o' the North", Great Britain (1934); 431/2, Class 7000 electric locomotive, Japan (1926); 433/4, Class P3, Germany (1897); 435/6, "Dorchester", Canada (1836); 436/7, Class "Centennial" diesel locomotive, U.S.A. (1969); 439/40, "Lafayette", U.S.A. (1837); 441/2, Class C-16 No. 222, U.S.A. (1882).

1986. Centenary of Statue of Liberty. Multicoloured.
443 15c. Type **41a** 20 15
444 25c. Sailing ship passing statue 30 20
445 40c. Statue in scaffolding . . 30 25
446 60c. Statue (side view) and scaffolding 30 30
447 75c. Statue and regatta . . . 40 40
448 $1 Tall Ships parade passing statue (horiz) 40 45
449 $1.50 Head and arm of statue above scaffolding 40 60

450 $2 Ships with souvenir flags (horiz) 55 80

451 $2.50 Statue and New York waterfront 60 90

452 $3 Restoring statue 80 1·25

MS453 Four sheets, each 85 × 115 mm. (a) $3.50 Statue at dusk. (b) $4 Head of Statue. (c) $4.50 Statue and lightning. (d) $5 Head and torch at sunset Set of 4 sheets 3·50 11·00

1986. Royal Wedding (2nd issue). Nos. 406/9 optd **Congratulations to T.R.H. The Duke & Duchess of York.**

454 60c. Prince Andrew in midshipman's uniform 15 40

455 60c. Miss Sarah Ferguson 15 40

456 $2 Prince Andrew on safari in Africa (horiz) 40 1·00

457 $2 Prince Andrew at the races (horiz) 40 1·00

42 Dinghy sailing

1986. Sports. Multicoloured.

458 10c. Type **42** 20 10

459 25c. Netball 35 15

460 $2 Cricket 3·00 2·50

461 $3 Basketball 3·75 3·00

43 St. George's Anglican Church, Gingerland

44 Constitution Document, Quill and Inkwell

1986. Christmas. Churches of Nevis (2nd series). Multicoloured.

462 10c. Type **43** 15 10

463 40c. Trinity Methodist Church, Fountain 30 25

464 $1 Charlestown Methodist Church 60 65

465 $5 Wesleyan Holiness Church, Brown Hill 2·75 4·00

1987. Bicentenary of U.S. Constitution and 230th Birth Anniv of Alexander Hamilton (U.S. statesman). Multicoloured.

466 15c. Type **44** 10 10

467 40c. Alexander Hamilton and Hamilton House 20 25

468 60c. Alexander Hamilton 25 35

469 $2 Washington and his Cabinet 90 1·40

MS470 70 × 82 mm. $5 Model ship "Hamilton" on float, 1788 6·50 7·50

1987. Victory of "Stars and Stripes" in America's Cup Yachting Championship. No. 54 optd **America's Cup 1987 Winners 'Stars & Stripes'.**

471 $3 Windjammer S.V. "Polynesia" 1·10 1·60

46 Fig Tree Church

1987. Bicentenary of Marriage of Horatio Nelson and Frances Nisbet. Multicoloured.

472 15c. Type **46** 20 10

473 60c. Frances Nisbet 50 30

474 $1 H.M.S. "Boreas" (frigate) 1·50 1·25

475 $3 Captain Horatio Nelson 3·00 3·75

MS476 102 × 82 mm. $3 As No. 473; $3 No. 475 5·00 6·50

47 Queen Angelfish

1987. Coral Reef Fishes. Multicoloured.

477 60c. Type **47** 35 60

478 60c. Blue angelfish 35 60

479 $1 Stoplight parrotfish (male) 40 80

480 $1 Stoplight parrotfish (female) 40 80

481 $1.50 Red hind 45 90

482 $1.50 Rock hind 45 90

483 $2.50 Coney (bicoloured phase) 50 1·50

484 $2.50 Coney (red-brown phase) 50 1·50

Nos. 478, 480, 482 and 484 are inverted triangles.

48 "Panaeolus antillarum"

50 Hawk-wing Conch

49 Rag Doll

1987. Fungi (1st series). Multicoloured.

485 15c. Type **48** 80 30

486 50c. "Pycnoporus sanguineus" 1·50 80

487 $2 "Gymnopilus chrysopellus" 2·75 3·25

488 $3 "Cantharellus cinnabarinus" 3·25 4·50

See also Nos. 646/53.

1987. Christmas. Toys. Multicoloured.

489 10c. Type **49** 10 10

490 40c. Coconut boat 20 25

491 $1.20 Sandbox cart 55 60

492 $5 Two-wheeled cart 1·75 4·00

1988. Sea Shells and Pearls. Multicoloured.

493 15c. Type **50** 20 15

494 40c. Rooster-tail conch 30 20

495 60c. Emperor helmet 50 40

496 $2 Queen or pink conch 1·60 2·00

497 $3 King helmet 1·75 2·25

51 Visiting Pensioners at Christmas

52 Athlete on Starting Blocks

1988. 125th Anniv of International Red Cross. Multicoloured.

498 15c. Type **51** 10 10

499 40c. Teaching children first aid 15 20

500 60c. Providing wheelchairs for the disabled 25 35

501 $5 Helping cyclone victim 2·10 3·50

1988. Olympic Games, Seoul. Multicoloured.

502 10c. Type **52** 10 35

503 $1.20 At start 50 85

504 $2 During race 85 1·25

505 $3 At finish 1·25 1·50

MS506 137 × 80 mm. As Nos. 502/5, but each size 24 × 36 mm 2·75 3·75

Nos. 502/5 were printed together, se-tenant, each strip forming a composite design showing an athlete from start to finish of race.

53 Outline Map and Arms of St. Kitts–Nevis

53a House of Commons passing Lloyd's Bill, 1871

1988. 5th Anniv of Independence.

507 **53** $5 multicoloured 2·10 3·00

1988. 300th Anniv of Lloyd's of London. Multicoloured.

508 15c. Type **53a** 25 10

509 60c. "Cunard Countess" (liner) (horiz) 1·40 65

510 $2.50 Space shuttle deploying satellite (horiz) 2·50 3·00

511 $3 "Viking Princess" (cargo liner) on fire, 1966 2·75 3·00

54 Poinsettia

1988. Christmas. Flowers. Multicoloured.

512 15c. Type **54** 10 10

513 40c. Tiger claws 15 20

514 60c. Sorrel flower 25 30

515 $1 Christmas candle 40 60

516 $5 Snow bush 1·60 3·75

55 British Fleet off St. Kitts

56 Cicada

1989. "Philexfrance 89" International Stamp Exhibition, Paris. Battle of Frigate Bay, 1782. Multicoloured.

517 50c. Type **55** 1·40 1·50

518 $1.20 Battle off Nevis 1·60 1·90

519 $2 British and French fleets exchanging broadsides 2·00 2·25

520 $3 French map of Nevis, 1764 2·50 2·75

Nos. 517/19 were printed together, se-tenant, forming a composite design.

1989. "Sounds of the Night". Multicoloured.

521 10c. Type **56** 20 15

522 40c. Grasshopper 40 35

523 60c. Cricket 55 50

524 $5 Tree frog 3·75 5·50

MS525 135 × 81 mm. Nos. 521/4 5·50 7·00

56a Vehicle Assembly Building, Kennedy Space Centre

1989. 20th Anniv of First Manned Landing on Moon. Multicoloured.

526 15c. Type **56a** 15 10

527 40c. Crew of "Apollo 12" (30 × 30 mm) 20 20

528 $2 "Apollo 12" emblem (30 × 30 mm) 1·00 1·75

529 $3 "Apollo 12" astronaut on Moon 1·40 2·00

MS530 100 × 83 mm. $6 Aldrin undertaking lunar seismic experiment 2·50 3·50

57 Queen or Pink Conch feeding

1990. Queen or Pink Conch. Multicoloured.

531 10c. Type **57** 60 30

532 40c. Queen or pink conch from front 90 40

533 60c. Side view of shell 1·25 90

534 $1 Black and flare 1·60 2·00

MS535 72 × 103 mm. $5 Underwater habitat 3·50 4·50

58 Wyon Medal Portrait

59

1990. 150th Anniv of the Penny Black.

536 **58** 15c. black and brown 15 10

537 – 40c. black and green 30 25

538 – 60c. black 45 55

539 – $4 black and blue 2·50 3·75

MS540 114 × 84 mm. $5 black, red and brown 4·00 5·00

DESIGNS: 40c. Engine-turned background; 60c. Heath's engraving of portrait; $4 Essay with inscriptions; $5 Penny Black.

No. MS540 also commemorates "Stamp World London 90" International Stamp Exhibition.

1990. 500th Anniv of Regular European Postal Services.

541 **59** 15c. brown 20 15

542 – 40c. green 35 25

543 – 60c. violet 55 65

544 – $4 blue 2·75 3·75

MS545 110 × 82 mm. $5 red, brown and grey 4·00 5·00

Nos. 541/5 commemorate the Thurn and Taxis postal service and the designs are loosely based on those of the initial 1852–58 series.

60 Sand Fiddler

1990. 500th Anniv (1992) of Discovery of America by Columbus (2nd issue). New World Natural History—Crabs. Multicoloured.

546 5c. Type **60** 10 20

547 15c. Great land crab 15 15

548 20c. Blue crab 15 15

549 40c. Stone crab 30 30

550 60c. Mountain crab 45 45

551 $2 Sargassum crab 1·40 1·75

552 $3 Yellow box crab 1·75 2·25

553 $4 Spiny spider crab 2·25 3·00

MS554 Two sheets, each 101 × 70 mm. (a) $5 Sally Lightfoot. (b) $5 Wharf crab Set of 2 sheets 9·00 10·00

60a Duchess of York with Corgi

1990. 90th Birthday of Queen Elizabeth the Queen Mother.

555 **60a** $2 black, mauve and buff 1·40 1·60

556 – $2 black, mauve and buff 1·40 1·60

557 – $2 black, mauve and buff 1·40 1·60

MS558 90 × 75 mm. $6 brown, mauve and black 3·50 4·25

DESIGNS: No. 556, Queen Elizabeth in Coronation robes, 1937; 557, Duchess of York in garden; MS558, Queen Elizabeth in Coronation robes, 1937 (different).

61 MaKanaky, Cameroons

62 "Cattleya deckeri"

1990. World Cup Football Championship, Italy. Star Players. Multicoloured.

559 10c. Type **61** 40 10

560 25c. Chovanec, Czechoslovakia 45 15

561 $2.50 Robson, England . . . 2·75 3·25
562 $5 Voller, West Germany . . 3·75 5·50
MS563 Two sheets, each 90×75 mm. (a) $5 Maradona, Argentina. (b) $5 Gordillo, Spain Set of 2 sheets . . . . 6·75 8·00

1990. Christmas. Native Orchids. Mult.
564 10c. Type **62** 55 20
565 15c. "Epidendrum ciliare" . . 55 20
566 20c. "Epidendrum fragrans" 65 20
567 40c. "Epidendrum ibaguense" 85 25
568 60c. "Epidendrum latifolium" 1·10 50
569 $1.20 "Maxillaria conferta" 1·40 1·75
570 $2 "Epidendrum strobiliferum" . . . . . . 1·75 2·75
571 $3 "Brassavola cucullata" . . 2·00 3·00
MS572 102×71 mm. $5 "Rodriguezia lanceolata" . . . 7·00 8·00

62a Two Jugs

1991. 350th Death Anniv of Rubens. Details from "The Feast of Achelous". Multicoloured.
573 10c. Type **62a** 55 15
574 40c. Woman at table . . . . 1·00 30
575 60c. Two servants with fruit 1·25 45
576 $4 Achelous . . . . 3·25 5·50
MS577 101×71 mm. $5 "The Feast of Achelous" . . . . 4·50 5·50

63 "Agraulis vanillae"

1991. Butterflies. Multicoloured.
578B 5c. Type **63** 20 50
579A 10c. "Historis odius" . . . 40 50
580B 15c. "Marpesia corinna" . 20 20
581B 20c. "Anartia amathea" . . 30 30
582B 25c. "Junonia evarete" . . 30 30
583B 40c. "Heliconius charithonia" 40 30
584B 50c. "Marpesia petreus" . 70 35
585A 60c. "Dione juno" 75 50
586B 75c. "Heliconius doris" . . 80 60
586cB 80c. As 60c. 80 60
587A $1 "Hypolimnas misippus" . 90 80
588A $3 "Danaus plexippus" . . 2·00 2·75
589A $5 "Heliconius sara" . . . 2·75 4·00
590A $10 "Tithorea harmonia" . 5·00 8·00
591A $20 "Dryas julia" . . . . 9·50 13·00

64 "Viking Mars Lander", 1976

1991. 500th Anniv of Discovery of America by Columbus (1992) (3rd issue). History of Exploration. Multicoloured.
592 15c. Type **64** 20 20
593 40c. "Apollo 11", 1969 . . . 30 25
594 60c. "Skylab", 1973 . . . . 45 45
595 75c. "Salyut 6", 1977 . . . . 55 55
596 $1 "Voyager 1", 1977 . . . . 65 65
597 $2 "Venera 7", 1970 . . . . 1·25 1·60
598 $4 "Gemini 4", 1965 . . . . 2·50 3·25
599 $5 "Luna 3", 1959 . . . . . 2·75 3·25
MS600 Two sheets, each 105×76 mm. (a) $6 Bow of "Santa Maria" (vert). (b) $6 Christopher Columbus (vert) Set of 2 sheets . . . . 8·00 9·00

65 Magnificent Frigate Bird

1991. Island Birds. Multicoloured.
601 40c. Type **65** 85 65
602 40c. Roseate tern 85 65
603 40c. Red-tailed hawk 85 65
604 40c. Zenaida dove 85 65
605 40c. Bananaquit 85 65
606 40c. American kestrel 85 65
607 40c. Grey kingbird 85 65
608 40c. Prothonotary warbler . . 85 65
609 40c. Blue-hooded euphonia 85 65
610 40c. Antillean crested hummingbird 85 65
611 40c. White-tailed tropic bird 85 65
612 40c. Yellow-bellied sapsucker 85 65
613 40c. Green-throated carib . . 85 65
614 40c. Purple-throated carib . . 85 65
615 40c. Red-billed whistling duck ("Black-bellied tree-duck") 85 65
616 40c. Ringed kingfisher . . . 85 65
617 40c. Burrowing owl 85 65
618 40c. Ruddy turnstone 85 65
619 40c. Great blue heron 85 65
620 40c. Yellow-crowned night-heron 85 65
MS621 76×59 mm. $6 Great egret 10·00 11·00
Nos. 601/20 were printed together, se-tenant, forming a composite design.

65a Queen Elizabeth at Polo Match with Prince Charles

1991. 65th Birthday of Queen Elizabeth II. Multicoloured.
622 15c. Type **65a** 40 20
623 40c. Queen and Prince Philip on Buckingham Palace balcony 50 35
624 $2 In carriage at Ascot, 1986 1·75 1·75
625 $4 Queen Elizabeth II at Windsor polo match, 1989 3·00 3·75
MS626 68×90 mm. $5 Queen Elizabeth and Prince Philip . . 4·25 5·00

1991. 10th Wedding Anniv of Prince and Princess of Wales. As T **65a**. Multicoloured.
627 10c. Prince Charles and Princess Diana 85 20
628 50c. Prince of Wales and family 90 30
629 $1 Prince William and Prince Harry . . . . 1·40 1·00
630 $5 Prince and Princess of Wales . . . . 4·50 4·00
MS631 68×90 mm. $5 Prince and Princess of Wales in Hungary, and young princes at Christmas . . 6·00 6·00

65b Class C62 Steam Locomotive

1991. "Phila Nippon '91" International Stamp Exhibition, Tokyo. Japanese Railway Locomotives. Multicoloured.
632 10c. Type **65b** 90 30
633 15c. Class C56 steam locomotive (horiz) . . . . 1·00 30
634 40c. Class C55 streamlined steam locomotive (horiz) 1·50 50
635 60c. Class 1400 steam locomotive (horiz) . . . . 1·60 80
636 $1 Class 485 diesel rail car 1·90 1·00
637 $2 Class C61 steam locomotive . . . . 3·00 2·50
638 $3 Class 485 diesel train (horiz) . . . . 3·25 3·00
639 $4 Class 7000 electric train (horiz) . . . . 3·50 3·75
MS640 Two sheets, each 108×72 mm. (a) $5 Class D51 steam locomotive (horiz). (b) $5 "Hikari" express train (horiz) Set of 2 sheets . . . . 8·50 9·00

65c "Mary being Crownd by an Angel"

1991. Christmas. Drawings by Albrecht Durer.
641 **65c** 10c. black and green . . 15 10
642 – 40c. black and orange . . 30 25
643 – 60c. black and blue . . . 35 30
644 – $3 black and mauve . . . 1·40 2·75
MS645 Two sheets, each 96×124 mm. (a) $6 black. (b) $6 black Set of 2 sheets . . . . . 5·50 6·25
DESIGNS: 40c. "Mary with the Pear"; 60c. "Mary in a Halo"; $3 "Mary with Crown of Stars and Sceptre"; $6 (MS645a) "The Holy Family" (detail); $6 (MS645b) "Mary at the Yard Gate" (detail).

66 "Marasmius haemtocephalus"

67 Monique Knol (cycling), Netherlands

66a Charlestown from the Sea

1991. Fungi (2nd series). Multicoloured.
646 15c. Type **66** 30 20
647 40c. "Psilocybe cubensis" . . 40 30
648 60c. "Hygrocybe acutoconica" 50 40
649 75c. "Hygrocybe occidentalis" 60 60
650 $1 "Boletellus cubensis" . . . 70 70
651 $2 "Gymnopilus chrysopellus" . . . . . . 1·25 1·50
652 $4 "Cantharellus cinnabarinus" . . . . . . 2·25 2·75
653 $5 "Chlorophyllum molybdites" . . . . 2·25 2·75
MS654 Two sheets, each 70×58 mm. (a) $6 "Psilocybe cubensis", "Hygrocybe acutoconica" and "Boletellus cubensis" (horiz). (b) $6 "Hygrocybe occidentalis", "Marasmius haematocephalus" and "Gymnopilus chrysopellus" (horiz) Set of 2 sheets . . . . 9·00 9·50

1992. 40th Anniv of Queen Elizabeth II's Accession. Multicoloured.
655 10c. Type **66a** 50 10
656 40c. Charlestown square . . 70 25
657 $1 Mountain scenery . . . . 1·25 60
658 $5 Early cottage . . . . . . 3·25 3·75
MS659 Two sheets, each 74×97 mm. (a) $6 Queen or pink conch on beach. (b) $6 Nevis sunset Set of 2 sheets . . . . . 8·50 9·00

1992. Olympic Games, Barcelona. Gold Medal Winners of 1988. Multicoloured.
660 20c. Type **67** . . . . 1·25 50
661 25c. Roger Kingdom (hurdles), U.S.A. 60 40
662 50c. Yugoslavia (men's waterpolo) . . . . 1·00 50
663 80c. Anja Fichtel (foil), West Germany . . . . 1·10 70
664 $1 Said Aouita (mid-distance running), Morocco . . . . 1·25 80
665 $1.50 Yuri Sedykh (hammer throw), U.S.S.R. . . . . . 1·40 1·60
666 $3 Shushunova (women's gymnastics), U.S.S.R. . . . 2·50 3·00
667 $5 Valimir Artemov (men's gymnastics), U.S.S.R. . . . 2·75 3·50
MS668 Two sheets, each 103×73 mm. (a) $6 Niam Suleymanoglu (weightlifting), Turkey. (b) $6 Florence Griffith-Joyner (women's 100 metres), U.S.A. Set of 2 sheets . . . . 5·50 7·00
No. 660 is inscribed "France" in error.

68 "Landscape" (Mariano Fortuny i Marsal)
69 Early Compass and Ship

1992. "Granada '92" International Stamp Exhibition, Spain. Spanish Paintings. Multicoloured.
669 20c. Type **68** 40 30
670 25c. "Dona Juana la Loca" (Francisco Pradilla Ortiz) (horiz) 40 30
671 50c. "Idyll" (Fortuny i Marsal) 60 50
672 80c. "Old Man Naked in the Sun" (Fortuny i Marsal) 80 70
673 $1 "The Painter's Children in the Japanese Salon" (detail) (Fortuny i Marsal) 90 80
674 $2 "The Painter's Children in the Japanese Salon" (different detail) (Fortuny i Marsal) . . . . 1·40 1·40
675 $3 "Still Life: Sea Bream and Oranges" (Luis Eugenio Melendez) (horiz) . . . . 2·25 2·75
676 $5 "Still Life: Box of Sweets, Pastry and Other Objects" (Melendez) . . . . 2·75 3·50
MS677 Two sheets, each 121×95 mm. (a) $6 "Bullfight" (Fortuny i Marsal) (111×86 mm). (b) $6 "Moroccans" (Fortuny i Marsal) (111×86 mm). Imperf Set of 2 sheets . . . . 5·50 6·50

1992. 500th Anniv of Discovery of America by Columbus (4th issue) and "World Columbian Stamp Expo '92", Chicago. Multicoloured.
678 20c. Type **69** 75 25
679 50c. Manatee and fleet . . . 1·25 50
680 80c. Green turtle and "Santa Maria" . . . . 1·50 80
681 $1.50 "Santa Maria" and arms . . . . 2·25 1·75
682 $3 Queen Isabella of Spain and commission . . . . . 2·50 3·25
683 $5 Pineapple and colonists . . 3·00 4·50
MS684 Two sheets, each 101×70 mm. (a) $6 British storm petrel and town (horiz). (b) $6 Peppers and carib canoe (horiz) Set of 2 sheets . . . . 10·00 12·00

1992. 500th Anniv of Discovery of America by Columbus (5th issue). Organization of East Caribbean States. As Nos. 911/12 of Montserrat. Multicoloured.
685 $1 Columbus meeting Amerindians 50 50
686 $2 Ships approaching island 1·25 1·40

69a Empire state Building

1992. Postage Stamp Mega Event, New York. Sheet 100×70 mm.
MS687 **69a** $6 multicoloured . . . 4·50 5·00

70 Minnie Mouse

71 Care Bear and Butterfly

70a "The Virgin and Child between Two Saints" (Giovanni Bellini)

1992. Mickey's Portrait Gallery. Mult.
688 10c. Type **70** 50 20
689 15c. Mickey Mouse 50 20
690 40c. Donald Duck 70 30
691 80c. Mickey Mouse, 1930 . . 90 70
692 $1 Daisy Duck . . . . . . 1·00 80
693 $2 Pluto . . . . 1·75 1·50
694 $4 Goofy . . . . 2·75 3·00
695 $5 Goofy, 1932 . . . . . . 2·75 3·00
MS696 Two sheets. (a) 102 × 128 mm. $6 Mickey in armchair (horiz). (b) 128 × 102 mm. $6 Mickey and Minnie in airplane (horiz) Set of 2 sheets . . . . 10·00 11·00

1992. Christmas. Religious Paintings. Mult.
697 20c. Type **70a** 40 15
698 40c. "The Virgin and Child surrounded by Four Angels" (Master of the Castello Nativity) 55 25
699 50c. "Virgin and Child surrounded by Angels with St. Frediano and St. Augustine" (detail) (Filippo Lippi) 60 30
700 80c. "The Virgin and Child between St. Peter and St. Sebastian" (Bellini) . . 85 70
701 $1 "The Virgin and Child with St. Julian and St. Nicholas of Myra" (Lorenzo di Credi) . . . . 1·00 80
702 $2 "St. Bernadino and a Female Saint presenting a Donor to Virgin and Child" (Francesco Bissolo) 1·75 1·50
703 $4 "Madonna and Child with Four Cherubs" (ascr Barthel Bruyn) . . . . . . 2·75 3·50
704 $5 "The Virgin and Child" (Quentin Metsys) . . . . . 3·00 3·50
MS705 Two sheets, each 76 × 102 mm. (a) $6 "Virgin and Child surrounded by Two Angels" (detail) (Perugino). (b) $6 "Madonna and Child with the Infant, St. John and Archangel Gabriel" (Sandro Botticelli) Set of 2 sheets . . . . 7·00 8·00
No. 699 is inscribed "Fillipo Lippi" in error.

1993. Ecology. Multicoloured.
706 80c. Type **71** 60 60
MS707 71 × 101 mm. $2 Care Bear on beach . . . . 2·25 2·50

71a "The Card Cheat" (left detail) (La Tour)

1993. Bicentenary of the Louvre, Paris. Multicoloured.
708 $1 Type **71a** 85 85
709 $1 "The Card Cheat" (centre detail) (La Tour) 85 85
710 $1 "The Card Cheat" (right detail) (La Tour) 85 85
711 $1 "St. Joseph, the Carpenter" (La Tour) . . . 85 85
712 $1 "St. Thomas" (La Tour) . . 85 85
713 $1 "Adoration of the Shepherds" (left detail) (La Tour) 85 85
714 $1 "Adoration of the Shepherds" (right detail) (La Tour) 85 85
715 $1 "Mary Magdalene with a Candle" (La Tour) 85 85
MS716 70 × 100 mm. $6 "Archangel Raphael leaving the Family of Tobius" (Rembrandt) (52 × 85 mm) . . . . 4·25 4·75

71b Elvis Presley

1993. 15th Death Anniv of Elvis Presley (singer). Multicoloured.
717 $1 Type **71b** . . . . 1·40 1·00
718 $1 Elvis with guitar . . . . 1·40 1·00
719 $1 Elvis with microphone . . 1·40 1·00

72 Japanese Launch Vehicle H-11

73 "Plumeria rubra"

1993. Anniversaries and Events. Mult.
720 15c. Type **72** 60 30
721 50c. Airship "Hindenburg" on fire, 1937 (horiz) . . . 1·00 65
722 75c. Konrad Adenauer and Charles de Gaulle (horiz) 65 65
723 80c. Red Cross emblem and map of Nevis (horiz) . . . 1·25 80
724 80c. "Resolute" (yacht), 1920 1·25 80
725 80c. Nelson Museum and map of Nevis (horiz) . . . 1·25 80
726 80c. St. Thomas's Church (horiz) 70 80
727 $1 Blue whale (horiz) . . . . 2·00 1·25
728 $3 Mozart . . . . 3·00 2·75
729 $3 Graph and U.N. emblems (horiz) . . . . 1·75 2·25
730 $3 Lions Club emblem . . . 1·75 2·25
731 $5 Soviet "Energia" launch vehicle SL-17 . . . . . . 3·25 3·75
732 $5 Lebaudy-Juillot airship No. 1 "La Jaune" (horiz) 3·25 3·75
733 $5 Adenauer and Pres. Kennedy (horiz) . . . . . 3·25 3·75
MS734 Five sheets. (a) 104 × 71 mm. $6 Astronaut. (b) 104 × 71 mm. $6 Zeppelin LZ-5, 1909 (horiz). (c) 100 × 70 mm. $6 Konrad Adenauer (horiz). (d) 75 × 103 mm. $6 "America 3" (yacht), 1992 (horiz). (e) 98 × 66 mm. $6 Masked reveller from "Don Giovanni" (horiz) Set of 5 sheets . . . . . . 18·00 19·00
ANNIVERSARIES AND EVENTS—Nos. 720, 731, **MS**734a, International Space Year; 721, 732, **MS**734b, 75th death anniv of Count Ferdinand von Zeppelin (airship pioneer); 722, 733, **MS**734c, 25th death anniv of Konrad Adenauer (German statesman); 723, 50th anniv of St. Kitts–Nevis Red Cross; 724, **MS**734d, Americas Cup Yachting Championship; 725, Opening of Nelson Museum; 726, 150th anniv of Anglican Diocese of North-eastern Caribbean and Aruba; 727, Earth Summit '92, Rio; 728, **MS**734e, Death bicent of Mozart; 729, International Conference on Nutrition, Rome; 730, 75th anniv of International Association of Lions Clubs.

1993. West Indian Flowers. Multicoloured.
735 10c. Type **73** 75 30
736 25c. "Bougainvillea" 90 30
737 50c. "Allamanda cathartica" . 1·10 50
738 80c. "Anthurium andraeanum" . . . . . . 1·50 70
739 $1 "Ixora coccinea" . . . . 1·75 75
740 $2 "Hibiscus rosa-sinensis" . 2·75 2·25
741 $4 "Justicia brandegeeana" . 4·00 4·75
742 $5 "Antigonon leptopus" . . 4·00 4·75
MS743 Two sheets, each 100 × 70 mm. (a) $6 "Lantana camara". (b) $6 "Petrea volubilis" Set of 2 sheets . . . . 7·50 8·50

74 Antillean Blue (male)

1993. Butterflies. Multicoloured.
744 10c. Type **74** 60 40
745 25c. Cuban crescentspot (female) 75 40
746 50c. Ruddy daggerwing . . . 1·00 50
747 80c. Little yellow (male) . . . 1·25 75
748 $1 Atala . . . . 1·25 90
749 $1.50 Orange-barred giant sulphur . . . . 2·00 2·25
750 $4 Tropic queen (male) . . . 3·25 4·50
751 $5 Malachite . . . . 3·25 4·50
MS752 Two sheets, each 76 × 105 mm. (a) $6 Polydamas swallowtail (male). (b) $6 West Indian buckeye Set of 2 sheets 10·00 11·00

74a 10c. Queen Elizabeth II at Coronation (photograph by Cecil Beaton)

1993. 40th Anniv of Coronation.
753 **74a** 10c. multicoloured 15 20
754 – 80c. brown and black . . 45 55
755 – $2 multicoloured . . . . 1·10 1·40
756 – $4 multicoloured . . . . 2·00 2·25
MS757 71 × 101 mm. $6 multicoloured . . . . 3·00 3·50
DESIGNS—38 × 47 mm: 80c. Queen wearing Imperial State Crown; $2 Crowning of Queen Elizabeth II; $4 Queen and Prince Charles at polo match. 28½ × 42½ mm: $6 "Queen Elizabeth II, 1977" (detail) (Susan Crawford).

75 Flag and National Anthem

76 "Annunciation of Mary"

75a Imre Garaba (Hungary) and Michel Platini (France) (horiz)

1993. 10th Anniv of Independence of St. Kitts–Nevis. Multicoloured.
758 25c. Type **75** . . . . 1·40 35
759 80c. Brown pelican and map of St. Kitts–Nevis . . . . 1·60 1·25

1993. World Cup Football Championship 1994, U.S.A. Multicoloured.
760 10c. Type **75a** 70 30
761 25c. Diego Maradona (Argentina) and Giuseppe Bergomi (Italy) 85 30
762 50c. Luis Fernandez (France) and Vasily Rats (Russia) 1·10 45
763 80c. Victor Munez (Spain) . . 1·50 65
764 $1 Preben Elkjaer (Denmark) and Andoni Goicoechea (Spain) . . . . 1·75 85
765 $2 Elzo Coelho (Brazil) and Jean Tigana (France) . . . 2·75 2·25
766 $3 Pedro Troglio (Argentina) and Sergei Alejnikov (Russia) . . . . 3·00 3·25
767 $5 Jan Karas (Poland) and Antonio Luiz Costa (Brazil) . . . . 3·75 4·75
MS768 Two sheets. (a) 100 × 70 mm. $5 Belloumi (Algeria) (horiz). (b) 70 × 100 mm. $5 Trevor Steven (England) Set of 2 sheets . . . 11·00 11·00

1993. Christmas. Religious Paintings by Durer. Black, yellow and red (Nos. 769/73 and 776) or multicoloured (others).
769 20c. Type **76** 50 15
770 40c. "The Nativity" (drawing) 70 30
771 50c. "Holy Family on a Grassy Bank" 80 30
772 80c. "The Presentation of Christ in the Temple" . . . 1·00 55
773 $1 "Virgin in Glory on the Crescent" . . . . 1·25 70
774 $1.60 "The Nativity" (painting) . . . . 2·00 2·25
775 $3 "Madonna and Child" . . 2·50 3·25
776 $5 "The Presentation of Christ in the Temple" (detail) . . . . 3·25 4·75
MS777 Two sheets, each 105 × 130 mm. (a) $6 "Mary, Child and the Long-tailed Monkey" (detail) (Durer). (b) $6 "The Rest on the Flight into Egypt" (detail) (Jean-Honure Fragonard) (horiz) Set of 2 sheets 8·50 9·50

77 Mickey Mouse playing Basketball

1994. Sports and Pastimes. Walt Disney cartoon characters. Multicoloured (except No. **MS**786a).
778 10c. Type **77** 40 30
779 25c. Minnie Mouse sunbathing (vert) 50 20
780 50c. Mickey playing volleyball 70 40
781 80c. Minnie dancing (vert) . . 80 60
782 $1 Mickey playing football 1·00 70
783 $1.50 Minnie hula hooping (vert) . . . . 1·75 2·00
784 $4 Minnie skipping (vert) . . 2·75 3·50
785 $5 Mickey wrestling Big Pete 2·75 3·50
MS786 Two sheets. (a) 127 × 102 mm. $6 Mickey, Donald Duck and Goofy in tug of war (black, red and green). (b) 102 × 127 mm. $6 Mickey using Test your Strength machine Set of 2 sheets . . . . 9·00 10·00

1994. "Hong Kong '94" International Stamp Exhibition. No. **MS**752 optd with "HONG KONG '94" logo on sheet margins.
MS787 Two sheets, each 76 × 105 mm. (a) $6 Polydamas swallowtail (male). (b) $6 West Indian buckeye Set of 2 sheets 7·50 8·00

77a Girl with Umbrella

1994. Hummel Figurines. Multicoloured.
788 5c. Type **77a** 15 40
789 25c. Boy holding beer mug and parsnips 45 15
790 50c. Girl sitting in tree . . . 65 35
791 80c. Boy in hat and scarf . . 85 60
792 $1 Boy with umbrella . . . . 1·00 70
793 $1.60 Girl with bird . . . . 1·75 1·75
794 $2 Boy on sledge . . . . . . 2·00 2·00
795 $5 Boy sitting in apple tree 2·75 3·75
MS796 Two sheets, each 94 × 125 mm. (a) Nos. 788 and 792/4. (b) Nos. 789/91 and 795 Set of 2 sheets . . . . 6·50 7·50

79 Beekeeper collecting Wild Nest

1994. Beekeeping. Multicoloured.
797 50c. Type **79** 65 30
798 80c. Beekeeping club 90 40
799 $1.60 Extracting honey from frames . . . . 1·75 1·75
800 $3 Keepers placing queen in hive . . . . 2·75 3·75
MS801 100 × 70 mm. $6 Queen and workers in hive and mechanical honey extractor . . . . 5·00 5·50

80 Blue Point Himalayan

1994. Persian Cats. Multicoloured.
802 80c. Type **80** . . . . 1·10 90
803 80c. Black and white Persian 1·10 90
804 80c. Cream Persian . . . . . 1·10 90
805 80c. Red Persian . . . . . . 1·10 90
806 80c. Persian . . . . 1·10 90
807 80c. Persian black smoke . . 1·10 90
808 80c. Chocolate smoke Persian 1·10 90
809 80c. Black Persian . . . . . 1·10 90
MS810 Two sheets, each 100 × 70 mm. (a) $6 Silver tabby Persian. (B) $6 Brown tabby Persian Set of 2 sheets . . . . 10·00 11·00

81 Black Coral

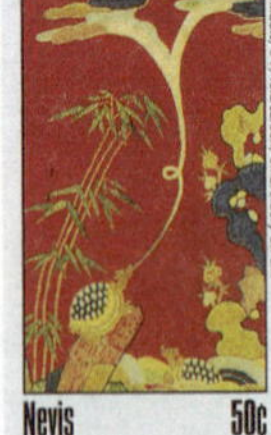

83 Symbol 1. Turtles and Cloud

82 Striped Burrfish

1994. Endangered Species. Black Coral.
811 **81** 25c. multicoloured 60 75
812 – 40c. multicoloured 70 80
813 – 50c. multicoloured 70 80
814 – 80c. multicoloured 80 90
DESIGNS: 40c. to 80c. Different forms of coral.

1994. Fishes. Multicoloured.
815 10c. Type **82** 50 50
816 50c. Flame-backed angelfish 55 55
817 50c. Reef bass 55 55
818 50c. Long-finned damselfish ("Honey Gregory") 55 55
819 50c. Saddle squirrelfish . . . 55 55
820 50c. Cobalt chromis 55 55
821 50c. Genie's neon goby . . . 55 55
822 50c. Slender-tailed cardinalfish 55 55
823 50c. Royal gramma 55 55
824 $1 Blue-striped grunt 75 75
825 $1.60 Blue angelfish . . . . 1·00 1·25
826 $3 Cocoa damselfish . . . . 1·50 1·75
MS827 Two sheets, each 100 × 70 mm. (a) $6 Blue marlin. (b) $6 Sailfish (vert) Set of 2 sheets 8·00 8·50
Nos. 816/23 were printed together, se-tenant, forming a composite design.
No. 824 is inscribed "BLUESRIPED GRUNT" in error.

1994. "Philakorea '94" International Stamp Exhibition, Seoul. Longevity symbols. Multicoloured.
828 50c. Type **83** 35 50
829 50c. Symbol 2. Manchurian cranes and bamboo 35 50
830 50c. Symbol 3. Deer and bamboo 35 50
831 50c. Symbol 4. Turtles and Sun 35 50
832 50c. Symbol 5. Manchurian cranes under tree 35 50
833 50c. Symbol 6. Deer and tree 35 50
834 50c. Symbol 7. Turtles and rock 35 50
835 50c. Symbol 8. Manchurian cranes above tree 35 50

84 Twin-roofed House with Veranda

1994. Island Architecture. Multicoloured.
836 25c. Type **84** 70 20
837 50c. Two-storey house with outside staircase 95 30
838 $1 Government Treasury . . 1·40 1·10
839 $5 Two-storey house with red roof . . . . 4·00 6·00
MS840 102 × 72 mm. $6 Raised bungalow with veranda . . . . 3·75 5·00

85 William Demas

1994. First Recipients of Order of Caribbean Community. Multicoloured.
841 25c. Type **85** 30 10
842 50c. Sir Shridath Ramphal 50 45
843 $1 Derek Walcott . . . . . 2·25 1·25

86 "The Virgin Mary as Queen of Heaven" (detail) (Jan Provost)

88 Rufous-breasted Hermit

87 Mickey and Minnie Mouse

1994. Christmas. Religious Paintings. Multicoloured.
844 20c. Type **86** 20 10
845 40c. "The Virgin Mary as Queen of Heaven" (different detail) (Provost) 35 25
846 50c. "The Virgin Mary as Queen of Heaven" (different detail) (Provost) 40 30
847 80c. "Adoration of the Magi" (detail) (Circle of Van der Goes) 60 40
848 $1 "Adoration of the Magi" (different detail) (Circle of Van der Goes) 70 50
849 $1.60 "Adoration of the Magi" (different detail) (Circle of Van der Goes) 1·25 1·50
850 $3 "Adoration of the Magi" (different detail) (Circle of Van der Goes) . . . . 2·00 2·50
851 $5 "The Virgin Mary as Queen of Heaven" (different detail) (Provost) 3·00 3·75
MS852 Two sheets, each 96 × 117 mm. (a) $5 "The Virgin Mary as Queen of Heaven" (different detail) (Provost). (b) $6 "Adoration of the Magi" (different detail) (Circle of Van der Goes) Set of 2 sheets . . . . . 8·00 8·50

1995. Disney Sweethearts (1st series). Walt Disney Cartoon Characters. Multicoloured.
853 10c. Type **87** 20 20
854 25c. Donald and Daisy Duck 35 20
855 50c. Pluto and Fifi 50 35
856 80c. Clarabelle Cow and Horace Horsecollar 70 50
857 $1 Pluto and Figaro 85 65
858 $1.50 Polly and Peter Penguin . . . . 1·25 1·50
859 $4 Prunella Pullet and Hick Rooster . . . . 2·50 3·25
860 $5 Jenny Wren and Cock Robin . . . . 2·50 3·25
MS861 Two sheets, each 133 × 107 mm. (a) $6 Daisy Duck (vert). (b) $6 Minnie Mouse (vert) Set of 2 sheets . . . . 8·50 9·00
See also Nos. 998/1007.

1995. Birds. Multicoloured.
862 50c. Type **88** 50 50
863 50c. Purple-throated carib . . 50 50
864 50c. Green mango 50 50
865 50c. Bahama woodstar . . . 50 50
866 50c. Hispaniolan emerald . . 50 50
867 50c. Antillean crested hummingbird 50 50
868 50c. Green-throated carib . . 50 50
869 50c. Antillean mango 50 50
870 50c. Vervain hummingbird 50 50
871 50c. Jamaican mango 50 50
872 50c. Cuban emerald 50 50
873 50c. Blue-headed hummingbird 50 50
874 50c. Hooded merganser . . . 50 50
875 80c. Green-backed heron . . 75 50
876 $2 Double-crested cormorant 1·25 1·40
877 $3 Ruddy duck . . . . . . 1·50 1·75
MS878 Two sheets, each 100 × 70 mm. (a) $6 Black skimmer. (b) $6 Snowy plover Set of 2 sheets . . . . 8·00 8·50
No. 870 is inscribed "VERVIAN" in error.

89 Pointer

1995. Dogs. Multicoloured.
879 25c. Type **89** 30 20
880 50c. Old Danish pointer . . . 50 50
881 80c. Irish setter 65 65
882 80c. Weimaraner 65 65
883 80c. Gordon setter 65 65
884 80c. Brittany spaniel 65 65
885 80c. American cocker spaniel 65 65
886 80c. English cocker spaniel 65 65
887 80c. Labrador retriever . . . 65 65
888 80c. Golden retriever 65 65
889 80c. Flat-coated retriever . . 65 65
890 $1 German short-haired pointer 75 75
891 $2 English setter . . . . . . 1·40 1·40
MS892 Two sheets, each 72 × 58 mm. (a) $6 German shepherds. (b) $6 Bloodhounds Set of 2 sheets . . . . 8·00 8·50
"POINTER" is omitted from the inscription on No. 890. No. **MS**892a is incorrectly inscribed "SHEPHARD".

90 "Schulumbergera truncata"

1995. Cacti. Multicoloured.
893 40c. Type **90** 30 20
894 50c. "Echinocereus pectinatus" 40 25
895 80c. "Mammillaria zeilmanniana alba" 65 40
896 $1.60 "Lobivia hertriehiana" 1·10 1·25
897 $2 "Hammatocactus setispinus" . . . . 1·40 1·50
898 $3 "Astrophytum myriostigma" . . . . . . 1·60 2·00
MS899 Two sheets, each 106 × 76 mm. (a) $6 "Opuntia robusta". (b) $6 "Rhipsalidopsis gaertneri" Set of 2 sheets . . . 7·00 7·50

91 Scouts backpacking

1995. 18th World Scout Jamboree, Netherlands. Multicoloured.
900 $1 Type **91** . . . . 1·00 1·10
901 $2 Scouts building aerial rope way . . . . 1·50 1·75
902 $4 Scout map reading . . . . 2·00 2·25
MS903 101 × 71 mm. $6 Scout in canoe (vert) . . . . 4·00 4·50
Nos. 900/2 were printed together, se-tenant, forming a composite design.

91a Clark Gable and Aircraft

1995. 50th Anniv of End of Second World War in Europe. Multicoloured.
904 $1.25 Type **91a** . . . . . . 1·00 1·00
905 $1.25 Audie Murphy and machine-gunner . . . . . 1·00 1·00
906 $1.25 Glenn Miller playing trombone . . . . 1·00 1·00
907 $1.25 Joe Louis and infantry 1·00 1·00
908 $1.25 Jimmy Doolittle and U.S.S. "Hornet" (aircraft carrier) . . . . 1·00 1·00
909 $1.25 John Hersey and jungle patrol . . . . 1·00 1·00
910 $1.25 John F. Kennedy in patrol boat . . . . 1·00 1·00
911 $1.25 James Stewart and bombers . . . . 1·00 1·00
MS912 101 × 71 mm. $6 Jimmy Doolittle (vert) . . . . 4·00 4·50

92 Oriental and African People

1995. 50th Anniv of United Nations. Each lilac and black.
913 $1.25 Type **92** 55 80
914 $1.60 Asian people . . . . . 75 1·10
915 $3 American and European people . . . . 1·40 1·60
MS916 105 × 75 mm. $6 Pres. Nelson Mandela of South Africa . . . . 3·00 3·50
Nos. 913/15 were printed together, se-tenant, forming a composite design.

1995. 50th Anniv of F.A.O. As T **92**. Multicoloured.
917 40c. Woman wearing yellow headdress 15 60
918 $2 Babies and emblem . . . 85 1·25
919 $3 Woman wearing blue headdress . . . . 1·25 1·60
MS920 105 × 80 mm. $6 Man carrying hoe . . . . 2·75 3·75
Nos. 917/19 were printed together, se-tenant, forming a composite design.
No. **MS**920 is inscribed "1945–1955" in error.

93 Rotary Emblem on Nevis Flag

1995. 90th Anniv of Rotary International. Multicoloured.
921 $5 Type **93** . . . . 2·50 3·25
MS922 95 × 66 mm. $6 Rotary emblem and beach . . . . . . 3·00 3·75

93a Queen Elizabeth the Queen Mother (pastel drawing)

1995. 95th Birthday of Queen Elizabeth the Queen Mother.
923 **93a** $1.50 brown, light brown and black . . . . . . 2·25 1·75
924 – $1.50 multicoloured . . . 2·25 1·75
925 – $1.50 multicoloured . . . 2·25 1·75
926 – $1.50 multicoloured . . . 2·25 1·75
MS927 102 × 127 mm. $6 multicoloured . . . . 6·00 6·00
DESIGNS: No. 924, Wearing pink hat; 925, At desk (oil painting); 926, Wearing blue hat; **MS**927, Wearing tiara.
No. **MS**927 was also issued additionally inscribed "IN MEMORIAM 1900–2002" on margin.

93b Grumman F4F Wildcat

1995. 50th Anniv of End of Second World War in the Pacific. United States Aircraft. Multicoloured.
928 $2 Type **93a** . . . . 1·40 1·40
929 $2 Chance Vought F4U-1A Corsair . . . . 1·40 1·40
930 $2 Vought SB2U Vindicator 1·40 1·40
931 $2 Grumman F6F Hellcat . . 1·40 1·40
932 $2 Douglas SDB Dauntless 1·40 1·40
933 $2 Grumman TBF-1 Avenger 1·40 1·40
MS934 108 × 76 mm. $6 Chance Vought F4U-1A Corsair on carrier flight deck . . . . . . 5·50 6·50

94 Emil von Behring (1901 Medicine)

1995. Centenary of Nobel Trust Fund. Past Prize Winners. Multicoloured.
935 $1.25 Type **94** 75 85
936 $1.25 Wilhelm Rontgen (1901 Physics) 75 85
937 $1.25 Paul Heyse (1910 Literature) 75 85
938 $1.25 Le Duc Tho (1973 Peace) 75 85
939 $1.25 Yasunari Kawabata (1968 Literature) 75 85
940 $1.25 Tsung-dao Lee (1957 Physics) 75 85

941 $1.25 Werner Heisenberg (1932 Physics) 75 85
942 $1.25 Johannes Stark (1919 Physics) 75 85
943 $1.25 Wilhelm Wien (1911 Physics) 75 85
MS944 101×71 mm. $6 Kenzaburo Oe (1994 Literature) . . . . . 3·25 3·75

95 American Eagle Presidents' Club Logo

1995. 10th Anniv of American Eagle Air Services to the Caribbean. Sheet 70×100 mm, containing T **95** and similar horiz design. Multicoloured.
MS945 80c. Type **95**; $3 Aircraft over Nevis beach . . . . . . 2·40 2·50

96 Great Egrets

1995. Marine Life. Multicoloured.
946 50c. Type **96** 55 55
947 50c. 17th-century galleon . . 55 55
948 50c. Galleon and marlin . . 55 55
949 50c. Herring gulls 55 55
950 50c. Nassau groupers 55 55
951 50c. Spotted eagleray 55 55
952 50c. Leopard shark and hammerhead 55 55
953 50c. Hourglass dolphins . . . 55 55
954 50c. Spanish hogfish 55 55
955 50c. Jellyfish and seahorses 55 55
956 50c. Angelfish and buried treasure 55 55
957 50c. Hawksbill turtle 55 55
958 50c. Common octopus . . . 55 55
959 50c. Moray eel 55 55
960 50c. Queen angelfish and butterflyfish 55 55
961 50c. Ghost crab and sea star 55 55
MS962 Two sheets. (a) 106×76 mm. $5 Nassau grouper. (b) 76×106 mm. $5 Queen angelfish (vert) Set of 2 sheeets . . . . 7·00 7·00

No. **MS**962 also commemorates the "Singapore '95" International Stamp Exhibition.

Nos. 946/61 were printed together, se-tenant, forming a composite design.

97 SKANTEL Engineer

1995. 10th Anniv of SKANTEL (telecommunications company). Multicoloured.
963 $1 Type **97** 60 50
964 $1.50 SKANTEL sign outside Nevis office . . . . 80 1·25
MS965 76×106 mm. $5 St. Kitts SKANTEL office (horiz) . . . 3·00 3·50

98 "Rucellai Madonna and Child" (detail) (Duccio)

1995. Christmas. Religious Paintings by Duccio di Buoninsegna. Multicoloured.
966 20c. Type **98** 20 15
967 50c. "Angel form the Rucellai Madonna" (detail) 40 25
968 80c. "Madonna and Child" (different) 60 40
969 $1 "Angel from the Annunciation" (detail) . . 75 60
970 $1.60 "Madonna and Child" (different) . . . . 1·25 1·50
971 $3 "Angel from the Rucellai Madonna" (different) . . . 1·90 2·75
MS972 Two sheets, each 102×127 mm. (a) $5 "Nativity with the Prophets Isaiah and Ezekiel" (detail). (b) $6 "The Crevole Madonna" (detail) Set of 2 sheets . . . . 6·50 7·50

99 View of Nevis Four Seasons Resort

1996. 5th Anniv of Four Seasons Resort, Nevis. Multicoloured.
973 25c. Type **99** 15 20
974 50c. Catamarans, Pinney's Beach 25 30
975 80c. Robert Trent Jones II Golf Course 40 45
976 $2 Prime Minister Simeon Daniel laying foundation stone . . . . 1·00 1·40
MS977 76×106 mm. $6 Sunset over resort . . . . 3·00 3·50

100 Rat, Plant and Butterfly

1996. Chinese New Year ("Year of the Rat"). Multicoloured.
978 $1 Type **100** 50 60
979 $1 Rat with prickly plant . . 50 60
980 $1 Rat and bee 50 60
981 $1 Rat and dragonfly 50 60
MS982 74×104 mm. Nos. 978/81 2·25 2·50
MS983 74×104 mm. $3 Rat eating 2·00 2·25

101 Ancient Greek Boxers

1996. Olympic Games, Atlanta. Previous Medal Winners. Multicoloured.
984 25c. Type **101** 25 20
985 50c. Mark Spitz (U.S.A.) (Gold – swimming, 1972) 35 30
986 80c. Siegbert Horn (East Germany) (Gold – single kayak slalom, 1972) . . . 50 45
987 $1 Jim Thorpe on medal (U.S.A.), 1912 (vert) . . . 60 70
988 $1 Glenn Morris on medal (U.S.A.), 1936 (vert) . . . 60 70
989 $1 Bob Mathias on medal (U.S.A.), 1948 and 1952 (vert) 60 70
990 $1 Rafer Johnson on medal (U.S.A.), 1960 (vert) . . . 60 70
991 $1 Bill Toomey (U.S.A.), 1968 (vert) 60 70
992 $1 Nikolay Avilov (Russia), 1972 (vert) 60 70
993 $1 Bruce Jenner (U.S.A.), 1976 (vert) 60 70
994 $1 Daley Thompson (Great Britain), 1980 and 1984 (vert) 60 70
995 $1 Christian Schenk (East Germany), 1988 (vert) . . 60 70
996 $3 Olympic Stadium and Siegestor Arch, Munich (vert) . . . . 1·60 2·00
MS997 Two sheets, each 105×75 mm. (a) $5 Willi Holdorf (West Germany) (Gold – decathlon, 1964) (vert). (b) $5 Hans-Joachim Walde (West Germany) (Silver – decathlon, 1968) (vert) Set of 2 sheets . . 6·50 7·00

1996. Disney Sweethearts (2nd series). As T **87**. Walt Disney Cartoon Characters. Multicoloured.
998 $2 Pocahontas and John Smith . . . . 2·00 1·50
999 $2 Mowgli and the Girl . . 2·00 1·50
1000 $2 Belle and the Beast . . . 2·00 1·50
1001 $2 Cinderella and Prince Charming . . . . 2·00 1·50
1002 $2 Pinocchio and the Dutch Girl . . . . 2·00 1·50
1003 $2 Grace Martin and Henry Coy . . . . 2·00 1·50
1004 $2 Snow White and the Prince . . . . 2·00 1·50
1005 $2 Aladdin and Jasmine . . 2·00 1·50
1006 $2 Pecos Bill and Slue Foot Sue . . . . 2·00 1·50
MS1007 Two sheets, each 110×130 mm. (a) $6 Sleeping Beauty and Prince Phillip (vert). (b) $6 Ariel and Eric Set of 2 sheets . . . . 10·00 11·00

102 Qian Qing Gong, Peking

1996. "CHINA '96" 9th Asian International Stamp Exhibition, Peking. Peking Pagodas. Multicoloured.
1008 $1 Type **102** 50 60
1009 $1 Temple of Heaven . . . 50 60
1010 $1 Zhongnanhai 50 60
1011 $1 Da Zing Hall, Shehyang Palace 50 60
1012 $1 Temple of the Sleeping Buddha 50 60
1013 $1 Huang Qiong Yu, Altar of Heaven 50 60
1014 $1 The Grand Bell Temple 50 60
1015 $1 Imperial Palace 50 60
1016 $1 Pu Tuo Temple 50 60
MS1017 104×74 mm. $6 Summer Palace of Emperor Wan Yan-liang (vert) . . . . 3·00 3·50

102a Queen Elizabeth II

1996. 70th Birthday of Queen Elizabeth II. Multicoloured.
1018 $2 Type **102a** . . . . 1·25 1·40
1019 $2 Wearing evening dress . 1·25 1·40
1020 $2 In purple hat and coat . 1·25 1·40
MS1021 125×103 mm. $6 Taking the salute at Tropping the Colour 4·00 4·25

103 Children reading Book

1996. 50th Anniv of UNICEF. Multicoloured.
1022 25c. Type **103** 30 20
1023 50c. Doctor and child . . . 60 30
1024 $4 Children . . . . 2·75 3·50
MS1025 75×105 mm. $6 Young girl (vert) . . . . 3·00 3·50

104 Cave Paintings, Tassili n'Ajjer, Algeria

1996. 50th Anniv of UNESCO. Multicoloured.
1026 25c. Type **104** 80 25
1027 $2 Temple, Tikai National Park, Guatemala (vert) . . 1·50 1·60
1028 $3 Temple of Hera, Samos, Greece . . . . 1·90 2·50
MS1029 106×76 mm. $6 Pueblo, Taos, U.S.A. . . . . 3·00 3·50

105 American Academy of Ophthalmology Logo

1996. Centenary of American Academy of Ophthalmology.
1030 **105** $5 multicoloured . . . . 3·25 3·50

106 "Rothmannia longiflora"

107 Western Meadowlark on Decoration

1996. Flowers. Multicoloured.
1031 25c. Type **106** 25 20
1032 50c. "Gloriosa simplex" . . 35 30
1033 $1 "Monodora myristica" . 60 70
1034 $1 Giraffe 60 70
1035 $1 "Adansonia digitata" . . 60 70
1036 $1 "Ansellia gigantea" . . . 60 70
1037 $1 "Geissorhiza rochensis" 60 70
1038 $1 "Arctotis venusta" . . . 60 70
1039 $1 "Gladiotus cardinalis" . 60 70
1040 $1 "Eucomis bicolor" . . . 60 70
1041 $1 "Protea obtusifolia" . . 60 70
1042 $2 "Catharanthus roseus" . 1·10 1·25
1043 $3 "Plumbago auriculata" . 1·60 1·90
MS1044 75×105 mm. $5 "Strelitzia reginae" . . . . 2·50 3·00

1996. Christmas. Birds. Multicoloured.
1045 25c. Type **107** 30 20
1046 50c. Bird (incorrectly inscr as "American goldfinch") with decorations (horiz) 45 30
1047 80c. Santa Claus, sleigh and reindeer (horiz) 60 45
1048 $1 American goldfinch on stocking 70 55
1049 $1.60 Northern mockingbird ("Mockingbird") with snowman decoration . . . 1·00 1·10
1050 $5 Yellow-rumped cacique and bauble . . . . 2·75 3·50
MS1051 Two sheets. (a) 106×76 mm. $6 Blue and yellow macaw ("Macaw") (horiz). (b) 76×106 mm. $6 Vermilion flycatcher (horiz) Set of 2 sheets 7·00 7·50

No. 1048 is inscribed "WESTERN MEADOWLARK" and No. 1050 "YELLOW-RUMPED CAIEQUE", both in error.

108 Ox (from "Five Oxen" by Han Huang)

1997. Chinese New Year ("Year of the Ox"). T **108** and similar oxen from the painting by Han Huang. Sheet 230×93 mm.
MS1052 50c., 80c., $1.60, $2 multicoloured . . . . 3·25 3·50

The fifth ox appears on a small central label.

109 Giant Panda eating Bamboo Shoots

110 Elquemedo Willett

1997. "HONG KONG '97" International Stamp Exhibition. Giant Pandas. Multicoloured.
1053 $1.60 Type **109** . . . . . 1·25 1·25
1054 $1.60 Head of panda . . . 1·25 1·25
1055 $1.60 Panda with new-born cub . . . . 1·25 1·25
1056 $1.60 Panda hanging from branch . . . . 1·25 1·25
1057 $1.60 Panda asleep on tree 1·25 1·25
1058 $1.60 Panda climbing trunk 1·25 1·25
MS1059 73×103 mm. $5 Panda with cub . . . . 2·50 3·00

1997. Nevis Cricketers. Multicoloured.
1060 25c. Type **110** 30 25
1061 80c. Stuart Williams 70 50
1062 $2 Keith Arthurton . . . . 1·25 1·50
MS1063 Two sheets, each 106×76 mm. (a) $5 Willett, Arthurton and Williams as part of the 1990 Nevis team (horiz). (b) $5 Williams and Arthurton as part of the 1994 West Indies team Set of 2 sheets . . . . 6·00 6·50

111 Crimson-speckled Moth

1997. Butterflies and Moths. Multicoloured.
1064 10c. Type **111** 20 30
1065 25c. Purple emperor 35 20
1066 50c. Regent skipper 45 30
1067 80c. Provence burnet moth 70 45
1068 $1 Common wall butterfly 70 80
1069 $1 Red-lined geometrid . . 70 80
1070 $1 Boisduval's autumnal moth 70 80
1071 $1 Blue pansy 70 80
1072 $1 Common clubtail 70 80
1073 $1 Tufted jungle king . . . 70 80
1074 $1 Lesser marbled fritillary 70 80
1075 $1 Peacock royal 70 80
1076 $1 Emperor gum moth . . . 70 80
1077 $1 Orange swallow-tailed moth 70 80
1078 $4 Cruiser butterfly . . . . 2·25 2·75
MS1079 Two sheets. (a) 103 × 73 mm. $5 Great purple. (b) 73 × 103 mm. $5 Jersey tiger moth Set of 2 sheets . . . . 5·50 6·50
No. 1073 is inscribed "TUFTED JUNGLE QUEEN" in error.

112 Boy with Two Pigeons

1997. 300th Anniv of Mother Goose Nursery Rhymes. Sheet 72 × 102 mm.
MS1080 **112** $5 multicoloured . . 2·75 3·50

113 Paul Harris and Literacy Class

1997. 50th Death Anniv of Paul Harris (founder of Rotary International). Multicoloured.
1081 $2 Type **113** . . . . . . 1·00 1·25
MS1082 78 × 108 mm. $5 Football coaching session, Chile . . . . 2·50 3·00

113a Queen Elizabeth II

1997. Golden Wedding of Queen Elizabeth and Prince Philip. Multicoloured.
1083 $1 Type **113a** 95 95
1084 $1 Royal Coat of Arms . . 95 95
1085 $1 Queen Elizabeth wearing red hat and coat with Prince Philip 95 95
1086 $1 Queen Elizabeth in blue coat and Prince Philip . . 95 95
1087 $1 Caernarvon Castle . . . 95 95
1088 $1 Prince Philip in R.A.F. uniform 95 95
MS1089 100 × 70 mm. $5 Queen Elizabeth at Coronation . . . 3·00 3·50

113b Russian reindeer post, 1859

1997. "Pacific '97" International Stamp Exhibition, San Francisco. Death Centenary of Heinrich von Stephan.
1090 **113b** $1.60 green . . . . . . 90 1·10
1091 – $1.60 brown . . . . . 90 1·10
1092 – $1.60 blue . . . . . . 90 1·10
MS1093 82 × 118 mm. $5 sepia 2·50 3·00
DESIGNS: No. 1091, Von Stephan and Mercury; 1092, "City of Cairo" (paddle-steamer), Mississippi, 1800s; **MS**1093, Von Stephan and Bavarian postal messenger, 1640.

113c "Scattered Pines, Tone River"

1997. Birth Bicentenary of Hiroshige (Japanese painter). "One Hundred Famous Views of Edo". Multicoloured.
1094 $1.60 Type **113c** . . . . . 1·25 1·25
1095 $1.60 "Mouth of Nakagawa River" . . . . 1·25 1·25
1096 $1.60 "Niijuku Ferry" . . . 1·25 1·25
1097 $1.60 "Horie and Nekozane" . . . . 1·25 1·25
1098 $1.60 "Konodai and the Tone River" . . . . . . 1·25 1·25
1099 $1.60 "Maple Trees, Tekona Shrine and Bridge, Mama" . . . . 1·25 1·25
MS1100 Two sheets, each 102 × 127 mm. (a) $6 "Mitsumata Wakarenofuchi". (b) $6 "Moto-Hachiman Shrine, Sunamura" Set of 2 sheets . . . . 7·00 7·50

114 Augusta National Course, U.S.A.

1997. Golf Courses of the World. Multicoloured.
1101 $1 Type **114** 80 80
1102 $1 Cabo del Sol, Mexico . . 80 80
1103 $1 Cypress Point, U.S.A. . . 80 80
1104 $1 Lost City, South Africa 80 80
1105 $1 Moscow Country Club, Russia 80 80
1106 $1 New South Wales, Australia 80 80
1107 $1 Royal Montreal, Canada 80 80
1108 $1 St. Andrews, Scotland . . 80 80
1109 $1 Four Seasons Resort, Nevis 80 80

115 "Cantharellus cibarius"

116 Diana, Princess of Wales

1997. Fungi. Multicoloured.
1110 25c. Type **115** 30 20
1111 50c. "Stropharia aeruginosa" 40 30
1112 80c. "Suillus hiteus" 60 65
1113 80c. "Amanita muscaria" . . 60 65
1114 80c. "Lactarius rufus" . . . 60 65
1115 80c. "Amanita rubescens" . . 60 65
1116 80c. "Armillaria mellea" . . 60 65
1117 80c. "Russula sardonia" . . 60 65
1118 $1 "Boletus edulis" 65 70
1119 $1 "Pholiota lenta" 65 70
1120 $1 "Cortinarius bolaris" . . 65 70
1121 $1 "Coprinus picaceus" . . 65 70
1122 $1 "Amanita phalloides" . . 65 70
1123 $1 "Cystolepiota aspera" . . 65 70
1124 $3 "Lactarius turpis" . . . 1·75 2·00
1125 $4 "Entoloma clypeatum" 2·25 2·50
MS1126 Two sheets, each 98 × 68 mm. (a) $5 "Galerina mutabilis". (b) $5 "Gymnopilus junonius" Set of 2 sheets . . . 6·00 6·50
Nos. 1112/17 and 1118/23 respectively were printed together, se-tenant, with the backgrounds forming composite designs.

1997. Diana, Princess of Wales Commemoration. Multicoloured.
1127 $1 Type **116** . . . . . . 1·00 90
1128 $1 Wearing white blouse . . 1·00 90
1129 $1 In wedding dress, 1981 1·00 90
1130 $1 Wearing turquoise blouse 1·00 90
1131 $1 Wearing tiara . . . . . 1·00 90
1132 $1 Wearing blue blouse . . 1·00 90
1133 $1 Wearing pearl necklace 1·00 90
1134 $1 Wearing diamond drop earrings . . . . 1·00 90
1135 $1 Wearing sapphire necklace and earrings . . 1·00 90

117 Victoria Govt Class S Pacific Locomotive, Australia

1997. Trains of the World. Multicoloured.
1136 10c. Type **117** 35 20
1137 50c. Express steam locomotive, Japan 55 30
1138 80c. L.M.S. steam-turbine locomotive, Great Britain 75 45
1139 $1 Electric locomotive, Switzerland 90 55
1140 $1.50 "Mikado" steam locomotive, Sudan . . . . 1·25 1·40
1141 $1.50 "Mohammed Ali el Kebir" steam locomotive, Egypt . . . . 1·25 1·40
1142 $1.50 Southern Region steam locomotive "Leatherhead" . . . . . 1·25 1·40
1143 $1.50 Great Southern Railway Drumm battery-powered railcar, Ireland 1·25 1·40
1144 $1.50 Pacific locomotive, Germany . . . . 1·25 1·40
1145 $1.50 Canton–Hankow Railway Pacific locomotive, China . . . . 1·25 1·40
1146 $2 L.M.S. high-pressure locomotive, Great Britain 1·60 1·75
1147 $3 Great Northern Railway "Kestrel", Ireland . . . . 2·00 2·25
MS1148 Two sheets, each 71 × 48 mm. (a) $5 L.M.S. high-pressure locomotive. (b) $5 G.W.R. "King George V" Set of 2 sheets . . . . 7·00 7·50

118 "Selection of Angels" (detail) (Durer)

1997. Christmas. Paintings. Multicoloured.
1149 20c. Type **118** 30 15
1150 25c. "Selection of Angels" (different detail) (Durer) 35 20
1151 50c. "Andromeda and Perseus" (Rubens) 55 30
1152 80c. "Harmony" (detail) (Raphael) 75 45
1153 $1.60 "Harmony" (different detail) (Raphael) . . . . 1·40 1·50
1154 $5 "Holy Trinity" (Raphael) 3·50 4·50
MS1155 Two sheets, each 114 × 104 mm. (a) $5 "Study Muse" (Raphael) (horiz). (b) $5 "Ezekiel's Vision" (Raphael) (horiz) Set of 2 sheets . . . . 6·50 7·00

119 Tiger (semi-circular character at top left)

1998. Chinese New Year ("Year of the Tiger"). Multicoloured.
1156 80c. Type **119** 60 60
1157 80c. Oblong character at bottom right 60 60
1158 80c. Circular character at top left 60 60
1159 80c. Square character at bottom right 60 60
MS1160 67 × 97 mm. $2 Tiger (vert) 1·40 1·60

120 Social Security Board Emblem

121 Soursop

1998. 20th Anniv of Social Security Board. Multicoloured.
1161 30c. Type **120** 20 15
1162 $1.20 Opening of Social Security building, Charlestown (horiz) . . . 80 1·00
MS1163 100 × 70 mm. $6 Social Security staff (59 × 39 mm) . . 3·50 4·00

1998. Fruits. Multicoloured.
1164A 5c. Type **121** 10 30
1165A 10c. Carambola 15 30
1166A 25c. Guava 25 15
1167A 30c. Papaya 25 15
1168A 50c. Mango 35 25
1169A 60c. Golden apple 40 30
1170A 80c. Pineapple 50 35
1171A 90c. Watermelon 60 40
1172A $1 Bananas 70 50
1173A $1.80 Orange . . . . . . 1·25 1·25
1174A $3 Honeydew . . . . . . 1·75 1·75
1175A $5 Canteloupe . . . . . . 3·00 3·25
1176A $10 Pomegranate . . . . 5·50 6·00
1177A $20 Cashew . . . . 9·50 11·00

122 African Fish Eagle ("Fish Eagle")

1998. Endangered Species. Multicoloured.
1178 30c. Type **122** 40 25
1179 80c. Summer tanager at nest 60 35
1180 90c. Orang-Utan and young 65 40
1181 $1 Young chimpanzee . . . 70 80
1182 $1 Keel-billed toucan . . . 70 80
1183 $1 Chaco peccary 70 80
1184 $1 Spadefoot toad and insect 70 80
1185 $1 Howler monkey 70 80
1186 $1 Alaskan brown bear . . 70 80
1187 $1 Koala bears 70 80
1188 $1 Brown pelican 70 80
1189 $1 Iguana 70 80
1190 $1.20 Tiger cub 80 80
1191 $2 Cape pangolin . . . . . 1·40 1·50
1192 $3 Hoatzin . . . . 1·75 1·90
MS1193 Two sheets, each 69 × 99 mm. (a) $5 Young mandrill. (b) $5 Polar bear cub Set of 2 sheets . . . . 6·50 7·00
No. 1185 is inscribed "MOWLER MONKEY" and No. 1192 "MOATZIN", both in error.

123 Chaim Topol (Israeli actor)

1998. "Israel 98" International Stamp Exn, Tel-Aviv.
1194 **123** $1.60 multicoloured . . 1·25 1·25

124 Boeing 747 200B (U.S.A.)

1998. Aircraft. Multicoloured.
1195 10c. Type **124** 30 30
1196 90c. Cessna 185 Skywagon (U.S.A.) 65 40
1197 $1 Northrop B-2 A (U.S.A.) 70 80
1198 $1 Lockheed SR-71A (U.S.A.) 70 80
1199 $1 Beechcraft T-44A (U.S.A.) 70 80
1200 $1 Sukhoi Su-27UB (U.S.S.R.) 70 80
1201 $1 Hawker Siddeley Harrier GR. Mk1 (Great Britain) 70 80
1202 $1 Boeing E-3A Sentry (U.S.A.) 70 80
1203 $1 Convair B-36H (U.S.A.) 70 80
1204 $1 IAI KFIR C2 (Israel) . . 70 80
1205 $1.80 McDonnell Douglas DC-9 SO (U.S.A.) . . . . 1·40 1·40
1206 $5 Airbus A-300 B4 (U.S.A.) . . . . 3·50 4·00
MS1207 Two sheets, each 76 × 106 mm. (a) $5 Lockheed F-117A (U.S.A.) (56 × 42 mm). (b) $5 Concorde (Great Britain) (56 × 42 mm) Set of 2 sheets . . 7·50 7·50

125 Anniversary Logo

127 Prime Minister Kennedy Simmonds receiving Constitutional Instruments from Princess Margaret, 1983

126 Butterflyfish

1998. 10th Anniv of "Voice of Nevis" Radio.

1208 **125** 20c. vio, lt vio & blk . . 30 25
1209 – 30c. multicoloured . . . 30 25
1210 – $1.20 multicoloured . . 1·00 1·25
MS1211 110 × 85 mm. $5 multicoloured . . . . 3·25 3·50

DESIGNS: 30c. Evered Herbert (Station Manager); $1.20, V.O.N. studio; $5 Merritt Herbert (Managing Director).

1998. International Year of the Ocean. Multicoloured.

1212 30c. Type **126** 30 15
1213 80c. Bicolor cherub 65 35
1214 90c. Copperbanded butterfly-fish (vert) . . . 70 80
1215 90c. Forcepsfish (vert) . . . 70 80
1216 90c. Double-saddled butterfly-fish (vert) . . . 70 80
1217 90c. Blue surgeonfish (vert) 70 80
1218 90c. Orbiculate batfish (vert) 70 80
1219 90c. Undulated triggerfish (vert) 70 80
1220 90c. Rock beauty (vert) . . 70 80
1221 90c. Flamefish (vert) 70 80
1222 90c. Queen angelfish (vert) 70 80
1223 $1 Pyjama cardinal fish . . 70 80
1224 $1 Wimplefish 70 80
1225 $1 Long-nosed filefish . . . 70 80
1226 $1 Oriental sweetlips 70 80
1227 $1 Blue-spotted boxfish . . 70 80
1228 $1 Blue-stripe angelfish . . . 70 80
1229 $1 Goldrim tang 70 80
1230 $1 Blue chromis 70 80
1231 $1 Common clownfish . . . 70 80
1232 $1.20 Silver badgerfish . . . 80 80
1233 $2 Asfur angelfish . . . . . 1·40 1·50
MS1234 Two sheets. (a) 76 × 106 mm. $5 Red-faced batfish (vert). (b) 106 × 76 mm. $5 Longhorned cowfish (vert) Set of 2 sheets . . . . 7·00 7·50

Nos. 1214/22 and 1223/31 respectively were printed together, se-tenant, with the backgrounds forming composite designs.

No. 1223 is inscribed "Pygama" in error.

1998. 15th Anniv of Independence.

1235 **127** $1 multicoloured 70 70

128 Stylized "50"

1998. 50th Anniv of Organization of American States.

1236 **128** $1 blue, light blue and black 70 70

129 365 "California"

1998. Birth Centenary of Enzo Ferrari (car manufacturer). Multicoloured.

1237 $2 Type **129** . . . . 1·60 1·60
1238 $2 Pininfarina's P6 . . . . 1·60 1·60
1239 $2 250 LM . . . . 1·60 1·60
MS1240 104 × 70 mm. $5 212 "Export Spyder" (91 × 34 mm) 4·50 4·75

130 Scouts of Different Nationalities

1998. 19th World Scout Jamboree, Chile. Multicoloured.

1241 $3 Type **130** . . . . 2·00 2·25
1242 $3 Scout and Gettysburg veterans, 1913 . . . . . 2·00 2·25
1243 $3 First black scout troop, Virginia, 1928 . . . . . 2·00 2·25

131 Gandhi in South Africa, 1914

133 Princess Diana

132 Panavia Tornado F3

1998. 50th Death Anniv of Mahatma Gandhi. Multicoloured.

1244 $1 Type **131** 80 80
1245 $1 Gandhi in Downing Street, London 80 80

1998. 80th Anniv of Royal Air Force. Multicoloured.

1246 $2 Type **132** . . . . 1·50 1·60
1247 $2 Panavia Tornado F3 firing Skyflash missile . . 1·50 1·60
1248 $2 Tristar Mk1 Tanker refuelling Tornado GR1 1·50 1·60
1249 $2 Panavia Tornado GR1 firing AIM-9L missile . . 1·50 1·60
MS1250 Two sheets, each 91 × 68 mm. (a) $5 Bristol F2B Fighter and two peregrine falcons (birds). (b) $5 Wessex helicopter and EF-2000 Eurofighter Set of 2 sheets . . . . 8·00 8·00

1998. 1st Death Anniv of Diana, Princess of Wales.

1251 **133** $1 multicoloured 75 75

134 Kitten and Santa Claus Decoration

1998. Christmas. Multicoloured.

1252 25c. Type **134** 25 15
1253 60c. Kitten playing with bauble 40 30
1254 80c. Kitten in Christmas stocking (vert) 50 35
1255 90c. Fox Terrier puppy and presents 60 40
1256 $1 Angel with swallows . . 70 45
1257 $3 Boy wearing Santa hat (vert) . . . . 2·00 2·50
MS1258 Two sheets. (a) 71 × 102 mm. $5 Two dogs. (b) 102 × 71 mm. $5 Family with dog (vert) Set of 2 sheets . . . . . 7·00 7·50

135 Mickey Mouse

1998. 70th Birthday of Mickey Mouse. Walt Disney cartoon characters playing basketball. Mult.

1259 $1 Type **135** 95 85
1260 $1 Donald Duck bouncing ball 95 85
1261 $1 Minnie Mouse in green kit 95 85
1262 $1 Goofy wearing purple . . 95 85
1263 $1 Huey in green baseball cap 95 85
1264 $1 Goofy and Mickey . . . 95 85
1265 $1 Mickey bouncing ball . . 95 85
1266 $1 Huey, Dewey and Louie 95 85
1267 $1 Mickey, in purple, shooting ball 95 85
1268 $1 Goofy in yellow shorts and vest 95 85
1269 $1 Minnie in purple 95 85
1270 $1 Mickey in yellow vest and blue shorts 95 85
1271 $1 Minnie in yellow 95 85
1272 $1 Donald spinning ball on finger 95 85
1273 $1 Donald and Mickey . . 95 85
1274 $1 Dewey shooting for goal 95 85
MS1275 Four sheets. (a) 127 × 105 mm. $5 Minnie wearing purple bow (horiz). (b) 105 × 127 mm. $5 Minnie wearing green bow (horiz). (c) 105 × 127 mm. $6 Mickey in yellow vest (horiz). (d) 105 × 127 mm. $6 Mickey in purple vest (horiz) Set of 4 sheets 15·00 15·00

136 Black Silver Fox Rabbits

1999. Chinese New Year ("Year of the Rabbit"). Multicoloured.

1276 $1.60 Type **136** . . . . . . 1·00 1·00
1277 $1.60 Dutch rabbits (brown with white "collar") . . . 1·00 1·00
1278 $1.60 Dwarf rabbits (brown) 1·00 1·00
1279 $1.60 Netherlands Dwarf rabbits (white with brown markings) . . . . 1·00 1·00
MS1280 106 × 76 mm. $5 Dwarf albino rabbit and young (57 × 46 mm) . . . . 3·00 3·50

137 Laurent Blanc (France)

1999. Leading Players of 1998 World Cup Football Championship, France. Multicoloured.

1281 $1 Type **137** 75 75
1282 $1 Dennis Bergkamp (Holland) 75 75
1283 $1 Davor Sukor (Croatia) 75 75
1284 $1 Ronaldo (Brazil) 75 75
1285 $1 Didier Deschamps (France) 75 75
1286 $1 Patrick Kluivert (Holland) 75 75
1287 $1 Rivaldo (Brazil) 75 75
1288 $1 Zinedine Zidane (France) 75 75
MS1289 121 × 96 mm. $5 Zinedine Zidane (France) . . . . 3·25 3·50

Nos. 1281/8 were printed together, se-tenant, with the backgrounds forming a composite design.

138 Kritosaurus

1999. "Australia '99" World Stamp Exhibition, Melbourne. Prehistoric Animals. Multicoloured.

1290 30c. Type **138** 40 20
1291 60c. Oviraptor 50 30
1292 80c. Eustreptospondylus . . 60 35
1293 $1.20 Tenontosaurus 80 85
1294 $1.20 Edmontosaurus . . . 80 85
1295 $1.20 Avimimus 80 85
1296 $1.20 Minmi 80 85
1297 $1.20 Segnosaurus 80 85
1298 $1.20 Kentrosaurus 80 85
1299 $1.20 Deinonychus 80 85
1300 $1.20 Saltasaurus 80 85
1301 $1.20 Compsoganthus . . . 80 85
1302 $1.20 Hadrosaurus 80 85
1303 $1.20 Tuojiangosaurus . . . 80 85
1304 $1.20 Euoplocephalus . . . 80 85
1305 $1.20 Anchisaurus 80 85
1306 $2 Ouranosaurus . . . . . 1·40 1·50
1307 $3 Muttaburrasaurus . . . 1·90 1·25
MS1308 Two sheets, each 110 × 85 mm. (a) $5 Triceratops. (b) $5 Stegosaurus Set of 2 sheets 7·00 7·50

Nos. 1294/9 and 1300/5 respectively were printed together, se-tenant, with the backgrounds forming composite designs.

139 Emperor Haile Selassie of Ethiopia

1999. Millennium Series. Famous People of the Twentieth Century. World Leaders. Multicoloured.

1309 90c. Type **139** 70 60
1310 90c. Haile Selassie and Ethiopian warriors (56 × 41 mm) 70 60
1311 90c. David Ben-Gurion, woman soldier and ancient Jewish prophet (56 × 41 mm) 70 60
1312 90c. David Ben-Gurion (Prime Minister of Israel) 70 60
1313 90c. President Franklin D. Roosevelt of U.S.A. and Mrs. Roosevelt . . . 70 60
1314 90c. Franklin and Eleanor Roosevelt campaigning (56 × 41 mm) 70 60
1315 90c. Mao Tse-tung and the Long March, 1934 (56 × 41 mm) 70 60
1316 90c. Poster of Mao Tse-tung (founder of People's Republic of China) . . . 70 60
MS1317 Two sheets. (a) 76 × 105 mm. $5 President Nelson Mandela of South Africa. (b) 105 × 76 mm. $5 Mahatma Gandhi (leader of Indian Independence movement) Set of 2 sheets . . . . 7·00 7·50

140 Malachite Kingfisher

1999. Birds. Multicoloured.

1318 $1.60 Type **140** . . . . . . 1·00 1·10
1319 $1.60 Lilac-breasted roller 1·00 1·10
1320 $1.60 Swallow-tailed bee eater . . . . 1·00 1·10
1321 $1.60 Jay ("Eurasian Jay") 1·00 1·10
1322 $1.60 Black-collared apalis 1·00 1·10
1323 $1.60 Grey-backed camaroptera . . . . . . 1·00 1·10
1324 $1.60 Yellow warbler . . . 1·00 1·10
1325 $1.60 Common yellowthroat 1·00 1·10
1326 $1.60 Painted bunting . . . 1·00 1·10
1327 $1.60 Belted kingfisher . . . 1·00 1·10
1328 $1.60 American kestrel . . . 1·00 1·10
1329 $1.60 Northern oriole . . . 1·00 1·10
MS1330 Two sheets, each 76 × 106 mm. (a) $5 Bananaquit. (b) $5 Groundscraper thrush (vert) Set of 2 sheets . . . . 7·00 7·50

141 "Phaius" hybrid

142 Miss Sophie Rhys-Jones and Prince Edward

1999. Orchids. Multicoloured.

1331 20c. Type **141** 30 20
1332 25c. "Cuitlauzina pendula" 30 20
1333 50c. "Bletilla striata" . . . 45 25
1334 80c. "Cymbidium" "Showgirl" 60 35
1335 $1 "Cattleya intermedia" . . 70 75
1336 $1 "Cattleya" "Sophia Martin" 70 75
1337 $1 "Phalaenopsis" "Little Hal" 70 75
1338 $1 "Laeliocattleya alisal" "Rodeo" 70 75
1339 $1 "Laelia lucasiana fournieri" 70 75
1340 $1 "Cymbidium" "Red Beauty" 70 75
1341 $1 "Sobralia" sp. 70 75
1342 $1 "Promenaea xanthina" 70 75
1343 $1 "Cattleya pumpernickel" 70 75
1344 $1 "Odontocidium artur elle" 70 75
1345 $1 "Neostylis lou sneary" 70 75
1346 $1 "Phalaenopsis aphrodite" 70 75
1347 $1 "Arkundina graminieolia" 70 75
1348 $1 "Cymbidium" "Hunter's Point" 70 75
1349 $1 "Rhynchostylis coelestis" 70 75

1350 $1 "Cymbidium" "Elf's Castle" 70 75
1351 $1.60 "Zygopetalum crinitium" (horiz) 1·00 1·00
1352 $3 "Dendrobium nobile" (horiz) 1·90 2·25
MS1353 Two sheets, each 106 × 81 mm. (a) $5 "Spathoglottis plicata" (horiz). (b) $5 "Arethusa bulbosa" Set of 2 sheets 7·00 7·50

1999. Royal Wedding. Multicoloured.
1354 $2 Type **142** 1·40 1·40
1355 $2 Miss Sophie Rhys-Jones at Ascot 1·40 1·40
1356 $2 Miss Sophie Rhys-Jones smiling 1·40 1·40
1357 $2 Prince Edward smiling 1·40 1·40
1358 $2 Miss Sophie Rhys-Jones wearing black and white checked jacket 1·40 1·40
1359 $2 Prince Edward and Miss Sophie Rhys-Jones wearing sunglasses 1·40 1·40
1360 $2 Miss Sophie Rhys-Jones wearing black hat and jacket 1·40 1·40
1361 $2 Prince Edward wearing red-striped tie 1·40 1·40
MS1362 Two sheets, each 83 × 66 mm. (a) $5 Prince Edward and Miss Sophie Rhys-Jones smiling (horiz). (b) $5 Prince Edward kissing Miss Sophie Rhys-Jones (horiz) Set of 2 sheets 7·00 7·50

142a "Beuth" (railway locomotive) and Baden 1851 1k. stamp

1999. "iBRA '99" International Stamp Exhibition, Nuremberg. Multicoloured.
1363 30c. Type **142a** 30 25
1364 80c. "Beuth" and Brunswick 1852 1sgr. stamp 50 45
1365 90c. "Kruzenshtern" (cadet barque) and Bergedorf 1861 ½s. and 1s. stamps 60 50
1366 $1 "Kruzenshtern" and Bremen 1855 3gr. stamp 70 70
MS1367 134 × 90 mm. $5 1912 First Bavarian air flight label 3·25 3·50

142b "Women returning Home at Sunset" (women by lake)

1999. 150th Death Anniv of Katsushika Hokusai (Japanese artist). Multicoloured.
1368 $1 Type 142a 70 80
1369 $1 "Blind Man" (without beard) 70 80
1370 $1 "Women returning Home at Sunset" (women descending hill) 70 80
1371 $1 "Young Man on a White Horse" 70 80
1372 $1 "Blind Man" (with beard) 70 80
1373 $1 "Peasant crossing a Bridge" 70 80
1374 $1.60 "Poppies" (one flower) 1·00 1·10
1375 $1.60 "Blind Man" (with beard) 1·00 1·10
1376 $1.60 "Poppies" (two flowers) 1·00 1·10
1377 $1.60 "Abe No Nakamaro gazing at the Moon from a Terrace" 1·00 1·10
1378 $1.60 "Blind Man" (without beard) 1·00 1·10
1379 $1.60 "Cranes on a Snowy Pine" 1·00 1·10
MS1380 Two sheets, each 74 × 103 mm. (a) $5 "Carp in a Waterfall". (b) $5 "Rider in the Snow" Set of 2 sheets 7·00 7·50

142c First Class carriage, 1837.

1999. "PhilexFrance '99" International Stamp Exhibition, Paris. Two sheets, each 106 × 81 mm, containing horiz designs. Multicoloured.
MS1381 (a) $5 Type 142c. (b) $5 "141.R" Mixed Traffic steam locomotive Set of 2 sheets 7·00 7·50

143 Steelband

1999. 25th Culturama Festival. Multicoloured.
1382 30c. Type **143** 30 15
1383 80c. Clowns 60 35
1384 $1.80 Masqueraders with band 1·40 1·10
1385 $5 Local string band 3·25 3·50
MS1386 91 × 105 mm. $5 Carnival dancers (50 × 37 mm) 3·25 3·50

143a Lady Elizabeth Bowes-Lyon on Wedding Day, 1923

1999. "Queen Elizabeth the Queen Mother's Century".
1387 **143a** $2 black and gold 1·50 1·50
1388 – $2 multicoloured 1·50 1·50
1389 – $2 black and gold 1·50 1·50
1390 – $2 multicoloured 1·50 1·50
MS1391 153 × 157 mm. $6 multicoloured 3·75 4·00
DESIGNS: No. 1388, Duchess of York with Princess Elizabeth, 1926; 1389, King George VI and Queen Elizabeth during Second World War; 1390, Queen Mother in 1983. 37 × 49 mm: No. **MS**1391, Queen Mother in 1957.

No. **MS**1391 was also issued with the embossed gold coat of arms at bottom left replaced by the inscription "Good Health and Happiness to Her Majesty the Queen Mother on her 101st Birthday".

144 "The Adoration of the Magi" (Durer)

146 Boris Yeltsin (President of Russian Federation, 1991)

145 Flowers forming Top of Head

1999. Christmas. Religious Paintings. Multicoloured.
1392 30c. Type **144** 25 15
1393 90c. "Canigiani Holy Family" (Raphael) 55 40
1394 $1.20 "The Nativity" (Durer) 95 55
1395 $1.80 "Madonna and Child surrounded by Angels" (Rubens) 1·25 1·10
1396 $3 "Madonna and Child surrounded by Saints" (Rubens) 1·90 2·25
MS1397 76 × 106 mm. $5 "Madonna and Child by a Window" (Durer) (horiz) 3·00 3·50

1999. Faces of the Millennium: Diana, Princess of Wales. Showing collage of miniature flower photographs. Multicoloured.
1398 $1 Type **145** (face value at left) 75 75
1399 $1 Top of head (face value at right) 75 75
1400 $1 Ear (face value at left) 75 75
1401 $1 Eye and temple (face value at right) 75 75
1402 $1 Cheek (face value at left) 75 75
1403 $1 Cheek (face value at right) 75 75
1404 $1 Blue background (face value at left) 75 75
1405 $1 Chin (face value at right) 75 75
Nos. 1398/1405 were printed together, se-tenant, and when viewed as a sheetlet, forms a portrait of Diana, Princess of Wales.

145a Jonathan Swift ("Gulliver's Travels", 1726)

2000. New Millennium. People and Events of Eighteenth Century (1700–49). Multicoloured.
1406 30c. Type **145a** 35 30
1407 30c. Emperor Kangxi of China 35 30
1408 30c. Bartolommeo Cristofori (invention of piano, 1709) 35 30
1409 30c. Captain William Kidd hanging on gibbet, 1701 35 30
1410 30c. William Herschel (astronomer) 35 30
1411 30c. King George I of Great Britain, 1714 35 30
1412 30c. Peter the Great of Russia (trade treaty with China, 1720) 35 30
1413 30c. "Death" (bubonic plague in Austria and Germany, 1711) 35 30
1414 30c. "Standing Woman" (Kaigetsudo Dohan (Japanese artist)) 35 30
1415 30c. Queen Anne of England, 1707 35 30
1416 30c. Anders Celcius (invention of centigrade thermometer, 1742) 35 30
1417 30c. Vitus Bering (discovery of Alaska and Aleutian Islands, 1741) 35 30
1418 30c. Edmund Halley (calculation of Halley's Comet, 1705) 35 30
1419 30c. John Wesley (founder of Methodist Church, 1729) 35 30
1420 30c. Sir Isaac Newton (publication of "Optick Treatise", 1704) 35 30
1421 30c. Queen Anne (Act of Union between England and Scotland, 1707) (59 × 39 mm) 35 30
1422 30c. Johann Sebastian Bach (composition of "The Well-tempered Klavier", 1722) 35 30
No. 1418 is inscribed "cometis" in error.

2000. New Millennium. People and Events of Twentieth Century (1990–99). Multicoloured.
1423 50c. Type **146** 45 40
1424 50c. American soldiers and burning oil wells (Gulf War, 1991) 45 40
1425 50c. Soldiers (Bosnian Civil War, 1992) 45 40
1426 50c. Pres. Clinton, Yitzchak Rabin and Yasser Arafat (Oslo Accords, 1993) 45 40
1427 50c. Prime Ministers John Major and Albert Reynolds (Joint Declaration on Northern Ireland, 1993) 45 40
1428 50c. Frederik de Klerk and Nelson Mandela (end of Apartheid, South Africa, 1994) 45 40
1429 50c. Cal Ripkin (record number of consecutive baseball games, 1995) 45 40
1430 50c. Kobe from air (earthquake, 1995) 45 40
1431 50c. Mummified Inca girl preserved in ice, 1995 45 40
1432 50c. NASA's "Sojourner" on Mars, 1997 45 40
1433 50c. Dr. Ian Wilmat and cloned sheep, 1997 45 40
1434 50c. Death of Princess Diana, 1997 45 40
1435 50c. Fireworks over Hong Kong on its return to China, 1997 45 40
1436 50c. Mother with septuplets, 1998 45 40
1437 50c. Guggenheim Museum, Bilbao, 1998 45 40
1438 50c. "2000" and solar eclipse, 1999 (59 × 39 mm) 45 40
1439 50c. Pres. Clinton (impeachment in 1999) 45 40
No. 1423 incorrectly identifies his office as "Prime Minister".

147 Dragon

2000. Chinese New Year ("Year of the Dragon"). Multicoloured.
1440 $1.60 Type **147** 1·10 1·10
1441 $1.60 Dragon with open claws (face value bottom left) 1·10 1·10
1442 $1.60 Dragon holding sphere (face value bottom right) 1·10 1·10
1443 $1.60 Dragon looking up (face value bottom left) 1·10 1·10
MS1444 76 × 106 mm. $5 Dragon (37 × 50 mm) 3·50 3·75

148 Spotted Scat

2000. Tropical Fish. Showing fish in spotlight. Multicoloured.
1445 30c. Type **148** 30 15
1446 80c. Delta topsail platy ("Platy Variatus") 55 35
1447 90c. Emerald betta 65 40
1448 $1 Sail-finned tang 75 80
1449 $1 Black-capped basslet ("Black-capped Gramma") 75 80
1450 $1 Sail-finned snapper ("Majestic Snapper") 75 80
1451 $1 Purple fire goby 75 80
1452 $1 Clown triggerfish 75 80
1453 $1 Forceps butterflyfish ("Yellow Long-nose") 75 80
1454 $1 Clown wrasse 75 80
1455 $1 Yellow-headed jawfish 75 80
1456 $1 Oriental sweetlips 75 80
1457 $1 Royal gramma 75 80
1458 $1 Thread-finned butterflyfish 75 80
1459 $1 Yellow tang 75 80
1460 $1 Bicoloured angelfish 75 80
1461 $1 Catalina goby 75 80
1462 $1 Striped mimic blenny ("False Cleanerfish") 75 80
1463 $1 Powder-blue surgeonfish 75 80
1464 $4 Long-horned cowfish 2·75 3·00
MS1465 Two sheets, each 97 × 68 mm. (a) $5 Clown killifish. (b) $5 Twin-spotted wrasse ("Clown Coris") Set of 2 sheets 7·00 7·50
Nos. 1448/55 and 1456/63 were each printed together, se-tenant, the backgrounds forming composite designs.

149 Miniature Pinscher

149a Prince William shaking hands

2000. Dogs of the World. Multicoloured.
1466 10c. Type **149** 20 30
1467 20c. Pyrenean mountain dog 25 30
1468 30c. Welsh springer spaniel 30 20
1469 80c. Alaskan malamute 65 40
1470 90c. Beagle (horiz) 75 80
1471 90c. Bassett hound (horiz) 75 80
1472 90c. St. Bernard (horiz) 75 80
1473 90c. Rough collie (horiz) 75 80
1474 90c. Shih tzu (horiz) 75 80
1475 90c. American bulldog (horiz) 75 80
1476 $1 Irish red and white setter (horiz) 75 80
1477 $1 Dalmatian (horiz) 75 80
1478 $1 Pomeranian (horiz) 75 80
1479 $1 Chihuahua (horiz) 75 80
1480 $1 English sheepdog (horiz) 75 80
1481 $1 Samoyed (horiz) 75 80

1482 $2 Bearded collie 1·40 1·50
1483 $3 American cocker spaniel 1·90 2·25
MS1484 Two sheets. (a) 76 × 106 mm. $5 Leonberger dog. (b) 106 × 76 mm. $5 Longhaired miniature dachshund (horiz) Set of 2 sheets 7·00 7·50

2000. 18th Birthday of Prince William. Mult.
1485 $1.60 Type **149a** 1·10 1·10
1486 $1.60 Wearing ski outfit 1·10 1·10
1487 $1.60 At airport 1·10 1·10
1488 $1.60 Wearing blue shirt and jumper 1·10 1·10
MS1489 100 × 80 mm. $5 At official engagement (38 × 50 mm) 3·50 3·75

150 "Mariner 9"

2000. "EXPO 2000" World Stamp Exhibition, Anaheim, U.S.A. Exploration of Mars. Multicoloured.
1490 $1.60 Type **150** 1·10 1·10
1491 $1.60 "Mars 3" 1·10 1·10
1492 $1.60 "Mariner 4" 1·10 1·10
1493 $1.60 "Planet B" 1·10 1·10
1494 $1.60 "Mars Express Lander" 1·10 1·10
1495 $1.60 "Mars Express" 1·10 1·10
1496 $1.60 "Mars 4" 1·10 1·10
1497 $1.60 "Mars Water" 1·10 1·10
1498 $1.60 "Mars 1" 1·10 1·10
1499 $1.60 "Viking" 1·10 1·10
1500 $1.60 "Mariner 7" 1·10 1·10
1501 $1.60 "Mars Surveyor" 1·10 1·10
MS1502 Two sheets, each 106 × 76 mm. (a) $5 "Mars Observer" (horiz). (b) $5 "Mars Climate Orbiter" Set of 2 sheets 7·00 7·50
Nos. 1490/5 and 1496/1501 were each printed together, se-tenant, with the backgrounds forming composite designs.

150b "Rani Radovi", 1969

2000. 50th Anniv of Berlin Film Festival. Showing actors, directors and film scenes with awards. Multicoloured.
1503 $1.60 Type **150b** 1·10 1·10
1504 $1.60 Salvatore Giuliano (director), 1962 1·10 1·10
1505 $1.60 "Schonzeit fur Fuches", 1966 1·10 1·10
1506 $1.60 Shirley Maclaine (actress), 1971 1·10 1·10
1507 $1.60 Simone Signoret (actress), 1971 1·10 1·10
1508 $1.60 Tabejad Bijad (director), 1974 1·10 1·10
MS1509 97 × 103 mm. $5 "Komissar", 1988 3·50 3·75

150c Locomotion No. 1, 1875, and George Stephenson

2000. 175th Anniv of Stockton and Darlington Line (first public railway). Multicoloured.
1510 $3 Type**150b** 2·25 2·25
1511 $3 Original drawing of Richard Trevithick's locomotive, 1804 2·25 2·25

150d Johann Sebastian Bach

2000. 250th Death Anniv of Johann Sebastian Bach (German composer). Sheet 76 × 88 mm, containing vert design.
MS1512 **150d** $5 multicoloured 3·50 3·75

151 Albert Einstein

2000. Election of Albert Einstein (mathematical physicist) as *Time Magazine* "Man of the Century". Showing portraits with photographs in background. Multicoloured.
1513 $2 Type **151** 1·60 1·60
1514 $2 Riding bicycle 1·60 1·60
1515 $2 Standing on beach 1·60 1·60

151a LZ-129 *Hindenburg*, 1929

2000. Centenary of First Zeppelin Flight.
1516 **151a** $3 green, purple and black 2·00 2·25
1517 – $3 green, purple and black 2·00 2·25
1518 – $3 green, purple and black 2·00 2·25
MS1519 116 × 76 mm. $5 green, mauve and black 3·50 3·75
DESIGNS: (38 × 24 mm)—No. 1517, LZ-1, 1900; 1518, LZ-11 *Viktoria Luise*. (50 × 37 mm)—No. **MS**1519, LZ-127 *Graf Zeppelin*, 1928.
No. 1516 is inscribed "Hindenberg" in error.

151b Gisela Mauermeyer (discus), Berlin (1936)

2000. Olympic Games, Sydney. Multicoloured.
1520 $2 Type **151b** 1·40 1·40
1521 $2 Gymnast on uneven bars 1·40 1·40
1522 $2 Wembley Stadium, London (1948) and Union Jack 1·40 1·40
1523 $2 Ancient Greek horseman 1·40 1·40

151c Elquemeda Willett

2000. West Indies Cricket Tour and 100th Test Match at Lord's. Multicoloured.
1524 $2 Type **151c** 1·50 1·25
1525 $3 Keith Arthurton 2·00 2·25
MS1526 121 × 104 mm. $5 Lord's Cricket Ground (horiz) 3·25 3·50

152 King Edward III of England

2000. Monarchs of the Millennium.
1527 **152** $1.60 black, stone and brown 1·25 1·25
1528 – $1.60 multicoloured 1·25 1·25
1529 – $1.60 multicoloured 1·25 1·25
1530 – $1.60 black, stone and brown 1·25 1·25
1531 – $1.60 black, stone and brown 1·25 1·25
1532 – $1.60 purple, stone and brown 1·25 1·25
MS1533 115 × 135 mm. $5 multicoloured 3·50 3·75
DESIGNS: No. 1528, Emperor Charles V (of Spain); 1529, King Joseph II of Hungary; 1530, Emperor Henry II of Germany; 1531, King Louis IV of France; 1532, King Ludwig II of Bavaria; **MS**1533, King Louis IX of France.

153 Member of The Angels

154 Bob Hope in Ranger Uniform, Vietnam

2000. Famous Girl Pop Groups. Multicoloured.
1534 90c. Type **153** 60 60
1535 90c. Member of The Angels with long hair 60 60
1536 90c. Member of The Angels with chin on hand 60 60
1537 90c. Member of The Dixie Cups (record at left) 60 60
1538 90c. Member of The Dixie Cups with shoulder-length hair 60 60
1539 90c. Member of The Dixie Cups with short hair and slide 60 60
1540 90c. Member of The Vandellas (record at left) 60 60
1541 90c. Member of The Vandellas ("Nevis" clear of hair) 60 60
1542 90c. Member of The Vandellas ("is" of "Nevis" on hair) 60 60
Each horizontal row depicts a different group with Nos. 1534/6 having green backgrounds, Nos. 1537/9 yellow and Nos. 1540/2 mauve.

2000. Bob Hope (American entertainer).
1543 **154** $1 black, grey and mauve 75 75
1544 – $1 Indian red, grey and mauve 75 75
1545 – $1 black, grey and mauve 75 75
1546 – $1 multicoloured 75 75
1547 – $1 black, grey and mauve 75 75
1548 – $1 multicoloured 75 75
DESIGNS: No. 1544, On stage with Sammy Davis Jnr.; 1545, With wife Dolores; 1546, Playing golf; 1547, Making radio broadcast; 1548, Visiting Great Wall of China.

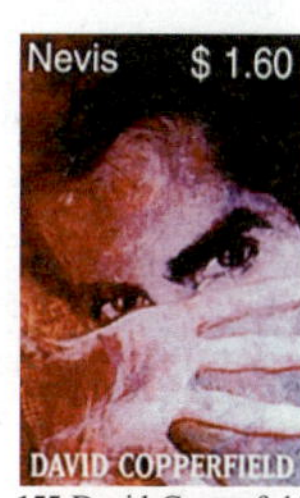

155 David Copperfield

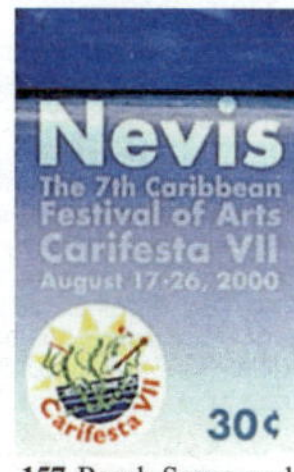

157 Beach Scene and Logo

156 Mike Wallace

2000. David Copperfield (conjurer).
1549 **155** $1.60 multicoloured 1·25 1·25

2000. Mike Wallace (television journalist). Sheet 120 × 112 mm.
MS1550 **156** $5 multicoloured 3·25 3·50

2000. 2nd Caribbean Beekeeping Congress. No. **MS**801 optd **2nd Caribbean Beekeeping Congress August 14–18, 2000** on top margin.
MS1551 100 × 70 mm. $6 Queen and workers in hive and mechanical honey extractor 3·75 4·00

2000. "Carifesta VII" Arts Festival. Multicoloured.
1552 30c. Type **157** 30 15
1553 90c. Carnival scenes 65 45
1554 $1.20 Stylized dancer with streamers 90 1·10

158 Golden Elegance Oriental Lily

2000. Caribbean Flowers. Multicoloured.
1555 30c. Type **158** 30 20
1556 80c. Frangipani 60 35
1557 90c. Star of the March 70 75
1558 90c. Tiger lily 70 75
1559 90c. Mont Blanc lily 70 75
1560 90c. Torch ginger 70 75
1561 90c. Cattleya orchid 70 75
1562 90c. St. John's wort 70 75
1563 $1 Culebra 70 75
1564 $1 Rubellum lily 70 75
1565 $1 Silver elegance oriental lily 70 75
1566 $1 Chinese hibiscus 70 75
1567 $1 Tiger lily (different) 70 75
1568 $1 Royal poincia 70 75
1569 $1.60 Epiphyte 1·00 1·10
1570 $1.60 Enchantment lily 1·00 1·10
1571 $1.60 Glory lily 1·00 1·10
1572 $1.60 Purple granadilla 1·00 1·10
1573 $1.60 Jacaranda 1·00 1·10
1574 $1.60 Shrimp plant 1·00 1·10
1575 $1.60 Garden zinnia 1·00 1·10
1576 $5 Rose elegance lily 3·25 3·50
MS1577 Two sheets. (a) 75 × 90 mm. $5 Bird of paradise (plant). (b) 90 × 75 mm. $5 Dahlia Set of 2 sheets 7·00 7·50
Nos. 1557/62, 1563/8 and 1569/74 were each printed together, se-tenant, with the backgrounds forming composite designs.

159 Aerial View of Resort

2000. Re-opening of Four Seasons Resort. Mult.
1578 30c. Type **159** 50 50
1579 30c. Palm trees on beach 50 50
1580 30c. Golf course 50 50
1581 30c. Couple at water's edge 50 50

160 "The Coronation of the Virgin" (Velazquez)

2000. Christmas. Religious Paintings. Multicoloured.
1582 30c. Type **160** 25 15
1583 80c. "The Immaculate Conception" (Velazquez) 55 35
1584 90c. "Madonna and Child" (Titian) (horiz) 60 40
1585 $1.20 "Madonna and Child with St. John the Baptist and St. Catherine" (Titian) (horiz) 90 1·10
MS1586 108 × 108 mm. $6 "Madonna and Child with St. Catherine" (Titian) (horiz) 3·75 4·00
Nos. 1584/5 are both inscribed "Titien" in error.

161 Snake coiled around Branch

2001. Chinese New Year. "Year of the Snake". Multicoloured.
1587 $1.60 Type **161** 1·10 1·10
1588 $1.60 Snake in tree 1·10 1·10
1589 $1.60 Snake on path 1·10 1·10
1590 $1.60 Snake by rocks 1·10 1·10
MS1591 70 × 100 mm. $5 Cobra at foot of cliff 3·25 3·50

162 Charlestown Methodist Church

2001. Leeward Islands District Methodist Church Conference. Multicoloured.
1592 50c. Type **162** 35 40
1593 50c. Jessups Methodist Church 35 40
1594 50c. Clifton Methodist Church 35 40
1595 50c. Trinity Methodist Church 35 40

1596 50c. Combermere Methodist Church 35 40
1597 50c. New River Methodist Church 35 40
1598 50c. Gingerland Methodist Church 35 40

163 Two Giraffes

2001. Wildlife from "The Garden of Eden". Multicoloured.
1599 $1.60 Type **163** . . . . . . 1·10 1·10
1600 $1.60 Rainbow boa constrictor . . . . 1·10 1·10
1601 $1.60 Suffolk sheep and mountain cottontail hare 1·10 1·10
1602 $1.60 Bluebuck antelope . . 1·10 1·10
1603 $1.60 Fox . . . . 1·10 1·10
1604 $1.60 Box turtle . . . . . . 1·10 1·10
1605 $1.60 Pileated woodpecker ("Red-crested Woodpecker") and unicorn . . . . 1·10 1·10
1606 $1.60 African elephant . . . 1·10 1·10
1607 $1.60 Siberian tiger . . . . 1·10 1·10
1608 $1.60 Greater flamingo and Adam and Eve . . . . . 1·10 1·10
1609 $1.60 Hippopotamus . . . 1·10 1·10
1610 $1.60 Harlequin frog . . . 1·10 1·10
MS1611 Four sheets, each 84 × 69 mm. (a) $5 Keel-billed toucan ("Toucan") (vert). (b) $5 American bald eagle. (c) $5 Koala bear (vert). (d) $5 Blue and yellow macaw (vert) Set of 4 sheets . . 13·00 14·00

Nos. 1599/1604 and 1605/10 were each printed together, se-tenant, with the backgrounds forming composite designs.

164 Zebra

2001. Butterflies of Nevis. Multicoloured.
1612 30c. Type **164** 35 20
1613 80c. Julia 65 40
1614 $1 Ruddy dagger 75 80
1615 $1 Common morpho . . . 75 80
1616 $1 Banded king shoemaker 75 80
1617 $1 Figure of eight 75 80
1618 $1 Grecian shoemaker . . . 75 80
1619 $1 Mosaic 75 80
1620 $1 White peacock 75 80
1621 $1 Hewitson's blue hairstreak 75 80
1622 $1 Tiger pierid 75 80
1623 $1 Gold drop helicopsis . . 75 80
1624 $1 Cramer's mesene 75 80
1625 $1 Red-banded pereute . . . 75 80
1626 $1.60 Small flambeau . . . 1·10 1·10
1627 $5 Purple mort bleu . . . 3·25 3·50
MS1628 Two sheets, each 72 × 100 mm. (a) $5 Common mechanitis. (b) $5 Hewitson's pierella Set of 2 sheets . . . . 7·00 7·50

165 *Clavulinopsis corniculata*

2001. Caribbean Fungi. Multicoloured.
1629 20c. Type **165** 25 20
1630 25c. *Cantharellus cibarius* . . 25 20
1631 50c. *Chlorociboria aeruginascens* 40 30
1632 80c. *Auricularia auricula-judae* 65 40
1633 $1 *Entoloma incanum* . . . 75 80
1634 $1 *Entoloma nitidum* 75 80
1635 $1 *Stropharia cyanea* 75 80
1636 $1 *Otidea onotica* 75 80
1637 $1 *Aleuria aurantia* 75 80
1638 $1 *Mitrula paludosa* 75 80
1639 $1 *Gyromitra esculenta* . . . 75 80
1640 $1 *Helvella crispa* 75 80
1641 $1 *Morcella semilibera* . . . 75 80
1642 $2 *Peziza vesiculosa* . . . . 1·40 1·50
1643 $3 *Mycena acicula* . . . . . 1·90 2·25
MS1644 Two sheets, each 110 × 85 mm. (a) $5 *Russula sardonia*. (b) $5 *Omphalotus olearius* Set of 2 sheets . . . . 7·00 7·50

166 Early Life of Prince Shotoku

2001. "Philanippon 01" International Stamp Exhibition, Tokyo. Prince Shotoku Pictorial Scroll. Multicoloured.
1645 $2 Type **166** . . . . 1·40 1·40
1646 $2 With priests and nuns, and preaching . . . . . 1·40 1·40
1647 $2 Subduing the Ezo . . . 1·40 1·40
1648 $2 Playing with children . . 1·40 1·40
1649 $2 Passing through gate . . 1·40 1·40
1650 $2 Battle against Mononobe-no-Moriya . . 1·40 1·40
1651 $2 Yumedono Hall . . . . 1·40 1·40
1652 $2 Watching dog and deer 1·40 1·40

167 Prince Albert
168 Queen Elizabeth II wearing Blue Hat

2001. Death Centenary of Queen Victoria. Multicoloured.
1653 $1.20 Type **167** 90 90
1654 $1.20 Queen Victoria at accession 90 90
1655 $1.20 Queen Victoria as a young girl 90 90
1656 $1.20 Victoria Mary Louisa, Duchess of Kent (Queen Victoria's mother) . . . 90 90
1657 $1.20 Queen Victoria in old age 90 90
1658 $1.20 Albert Edward, Prince of Wales as a boy 90 90
MS1659 97 × 70 mm. $5 Queen Victoria at accession . . . . . 3·25 3·50

2001. Queen Elizabeth II's 75th Birthday. Multicoloured.
1660 90c. Type **168** 65 65
1661 90c. Wearing tiara 65 65
1662 90c. Wearing yellow hat . . 65 65
1663 90c. Wearing grey hat . . . 65 65
1664 90c. Wearing red hat . . . 65 65
1665 90c. Bare-headed and wearing pearl necklace . . 65 65
MS1666 95 × 107 mm. $5 Wearing blue hat . . . . 3·50 3·75

169 Christmas Candle (flower)
171 Maracana Football Stadium, Brazil 1950

170 Flag of Antigua & Barbuda

2001. Christmas. Flowers. Multicoloured.
1667 30c. Type **169** 25 15
1668 90c. Poinsettia (horiz) . . . 60 40
1669 $1.20 Snowbush (horiz) . . . 85 65
1670 $3 Tiger claw . . . . 1·90 2·25

2001. Flags of the Caribbean Community. Multicoloured.
1671 90c. Type **170** 75 75
1672 90c. Bahamas 75 75
1673 90c. Barbados 75 75
1674 90c. Belize 75 75
1675 90c. Dominica 75 75
1676 90c. Grenada 75 75
1677 90c. Guyana 75 75
1678 90c. Jamaica 75 75
1679 90c. Montserrat 75 75
1680 90c. St. Kitts & Nevis . . . 75 75
1681 90c. St. Lucia 75 75
1682 90c. Surinam 75 75
1683 90c. St. Vincent and the Grenadines 75 75
1684 90c. Trinidad & Tobago . . 75 75

No. 1675 shows the former flag of Dominica, superseded in 1990.

2001. World Cup Football Championship, Japan and Korea (2002). Multicoloured.
1685 $1.60 Type **171** . . . . . . 1·10 1·10
1686 $1.60 Ferenc Puskas (Hungary), Switzerland 1954 . . . . 1·10 1·10
1687 $1.60 Luiz Bellini (Brazil), Sweden 1958 . . . . . . 1·10 1·10
1688 $1.60 Mauro (Brazil), Chile 1962 . . . . 1·10 1·10
1689 $1.60 West German cap, England 1966 . . . . . . 1·10 1·10
1690 $1.60 Pennant, Mexico 1970 1·10 1·10
1691 $1.60 Passarella (Argentina), Argentina 1978 . . . . . 1·10 1·10
1692 $1.60 Dino Zoff (Italy), Spain 1982 . . . . 1·10 1·10
1693 $1.60 Azteca Stadium, Mexico 1986 . . . . 1·10 1·10
1694 $1.60 San Siro Stadium, Italy 1990 . . . . 1·10 1·10
1695 $1.60 Dennis Bergkamp (Holland), U.S.A. 1994 1·10 1·10
1696 $1.60 Stade de France, France 1998 . . . . . . 1·10 1·10
MS1697 Two sheets, each 88 × 75 mm. (a) $5 Detail of Jules Rimet Trophy, Uruguay 1930. (b) $5 Detail of World Cup Trophy, Japan/Korea 2002 Set of 2 sheets 7·00 7·50

Nos. 1685 and 1687 are inscribed "Morocana" and "Luis" respectively, both in error.

172 Queen Elizabeth and Duke of Edinburgh in reviewing Car

2002. Golden Jubilee. Multicoloured.
1698 $2 Type **172** . . . . 1·40 1·40
1699 $2 Prince Philip . . . . . . 1·40 1·40
1700 $2 Queen Elizabeth wearing yellow coat and hat . . . 1·40 1·40
1701 $2 Queen Elizabeth and horse at polo match . . . 1·40 1·40
MS1702 76 × 108 mm. $5 Queen Elizabeth with Prince Philip in naval uniform . . . . 3·50 3·75

173 Chestnut and White Horse

2002. Chinese New Year ("Year of the Horse"). Paintings by Ren Renfa. Multicoloured.
1703 $1.60 Type **173** . . . . . . 1·10 1·10
1704 $1.60 Bay horse . . . . . . 1·10 1·10
1705 $1.60 Brown horse . . . . 1·10 1·10
1706 $1.60 Dappled grey horse . . 1·10 1·10

174 Beechey's Bee

2002. Fauna. Multicoloured.
1707 $1.20 Type **174** 90 90
1708 $1.20 Banded king shoemaker butterfly . . . 90 90
1709 $1.20 Streaked sphinx caterpillar 90 90
1710 $1.20 Hercules beetle 90 90
1711 $1.20 South American palm weevil 90 90
1712 $1.20 Giant katydid 90 90
1713 $1.60 Roseate spoonbill . . 1·10 1·10
1714 $1.60 White-tailed tropicbird 1·10 1·10
1715 $1.60 Ruby-throated tropicbird . . . . 1·10 1·10
1716 $1.60 Black skimmer . . . 1·10 1·10
1717 $1.60 Black-necked stilt . . 1·10 1·10
1718 $1.60 Mourning dove . . . 1·10 1·10
1719 $1.60 Sperm whale and calf 1·10 1·10
1720 $1.60 Killer whale . . . . . 1·10 1·10
1721 $1.60 Minke whales . . . . 1·10 1·10
1722 $1.60 Fin whale . . . . . . 1·10 1·10
1723 $1.60 Blaineville's beaked whale . . . . 1·10 1·10
1724 $1.60 Pygmy sperm whale 1·10 1·10
MS1725 Three sheets, each 105 × 78 mm. (a) $5 Click beetle. (b) $5 Royal tern. (c) $5 Humpback whale (vert) . . . . 9·50 10·50

Nos. 1707/12 (insects), 1713/18 (birds) and 1719/24 (whales) were each printed together, se-tenant, with the backgrounds forming composite designs.

175 Mount Assiniboine, Canada
177 Women's Figure Skating

176 Horse-riders on Beach

2002. International Year of Mountains. Multicoloured.
1726 $2 Type **175** . . . . 1·40 1·40
1727 $2 Mount Atitlan, Guatemala . . . . 1·40 1·40
1728 $2 Mount Adams, U.S.A. 1·40 1·40
1729 $2 The Matterhorn, Switzerland . . . . 1·40 1·40
1730 $2 Mount Dhaulagiri, Nepal 1·40 1·40
1731 $2 Mount Chamlang, Nepal 1·40 1·40
MS1732 106 × 125 mm. $5 Mount Kvaenangen, Norway . . . . 3·25 3·50

Nos. 1727 and 1729 are inscribed "ATAILAN" and "MATTHERORN", both in error.

2002. Year of Eco Tourism. Multicoloured.
1733 $1.60 Type **176** . . . . . . 1·10 1·10
1734 $1.60 Windsurfing . . . . . 1·10 1·10
1735 $1.60 Pinney's Beach . . . 1·10 1·10
1736 $1.60 Hikers by beach . . . 1·10 1·10
1737 $1.60 Robert T. Jones Golf Course . . . . 1·10 1·10
1738 $1.60 Scuba diver and fish 1·10 1·10
MS1739 115 × 90 mm. $5 Snorkel diver on reef . . . . 3·25 3·50

2002. Winter Olympic Games, Salt Lake City. Multicoloured.
1740 $2 Type **177** . . . . 1·40 1·50
1741 $2 Aerial skiing . . . . . . 1·40 1·50
MS1742 88 × 119 mm. Nos. 1740/1 2·75 3·00

178 Two Scout Canoes in Mist
179 U.S. Flag as Statue of Liberty with Nevis Flag

2002. 20th World Scout Jamboree, Thailand. Multicoloured.
1743 $2 Type **178** . . . . 1·40 1·40
1744 $2 Canoe in jungle . . . . 1·40 1·40
1745 $2 Scout on rope-ladder . . 1·40 1·40
1746 $2 Scouts with inflatable boats . . . . 1·40 1·40
MS1747 105 × 125 mm. $5 Scout painting . . . . 3·25 3·50

2002. "United We Stand". Support for Victims of 11 September 2001 Terrorist Attacks.
1748 **179** $2 multicoloured . . . . . 1·40 1·40

180 "Nevis Peak with Windmill" (Eva Wilkin)

2002. Art. Mmulticoloured (except Nos. 1750/1).
1749 $1.20 Type **180** 90 90
1750 $1.20 "Nevis Peak with ruined Windmill" (Eva Wilkin) (brown and black) 90 90
1751 $1.20 "Fig Tree Church" (Eva Wilkin) (brown and black) 90 90
1752 $1.20 "Nevis Peak with Blossom" (Eva Wilkin) 90 90
1753 $2 "Golden Pheasants and Loquat" (Kano Shoei) (30 × 80 mm) . . . . . 1·40 1·40
1754 $2 "Flowers and Birds of the Four Seasons" (Winter) (Ikeda Koson) (30 × 80 mm) . . . . . . 1·40 1·40

1755 $2 "Pheasants and Azaleas" (Kano Shoei) (30 × 80 mm) . . . . . . 1·40 1·40
1756 $2 "Flowers and Birds of the Four Seasons" (Spring) (Ikeda Koson) (different) (30 × 80 mm) 1·40 1·40
1757 $3 "White Blossom" (Shikibu Terutada) (38 × 62 mm) . . . . . . 1·75 1·90
1758 $3 "Bird and Flowers" (Shikibu Terutada) (38 × 62 mm) . . . . . . 1·75 1·90
1759 $3 "Bird and Leaves" (Shikibu Terutada) (38 × 62 mm) . . . . . . 1·75 1·90
1760 $3 "Red and White Flowers" (Shikibu Terutada) (38 × 62 mm) 1·75 1·90
1761 $3 "Bird on Willow Tree" (Yosa Buson) (62 × 38 mm) . . . . . . 1·75 1·90
1762 $3 "Bird on Peach Tree" (Yosa Buson) (62 × 38 mm) . . . . . . 1·75 1·90
MS1763 Two sheets, each 105 × 105 mm. (a) $5 "Golden Pheasants among Rhododendrons" (Yamamoto Baiitsu) (38 × 62 mm). (b) $5 "Musk Cat and Camellias" (Uto Gyoshi) (62 × 38 mm) . . . . 7·00 7·50

Nos. 1757/62 were printed together, se-tenant, with the backgrounds forming a composite design.

181 "Madonna and Child Enthroned with Saints" (Pietro Perugino)

182 Claudio Reyna (U.S.A.) and Torsten Frings (Germany)

2002. Christmas. Religious Art. Multicoloured.

1764 30c. Type **181** 25 15
1765 80c. "Adoration of the Magi" (Domenico Ghirlandaio) 50 35
1766 90c. "San Zaccaria Altarpiece" (Giovanni Bellini) 60 40
1767 $1.20 "Presentation at the Temple" (Bellini) 90 75
1768 $5 "Madonna and Child" (Simone Martini) . . . . 3·25 3·50
MS1769 102 × 76 mm. $6 "Maesa" (Martini) . . . . 3·50 4·00

2002. World Cup Football Championship, Japan and Korea. Multicoloured.

1770 $1.20 Type **182** 90 90
1771 $1.20 Michael Ballack (Germany) and Eddie Pope (U.S.A.) 90 90
1772 $1.20 Sebastian Kehl (Germany) and Brian McBride (U.S.A.) 90 90
1773 $1.20 Carlos Puyol (Spain) and Eul Yong Lee (South Korea) 90 90
1774 $1.20 Jin Cheul Choi (South Korea) and Gaizka Mendieta (Spain) 90 90
1775 $1.20 Juan Valeron (Spain) and Jin Cheul Choi (South Korea) 90 90
1776 $1.60 Emile Heskey (England) and Edmilson (Brazil) . . . . 1·10 1·10
1777 $1.60 Rivaldo (Brazil) and Sol Campbell (England) 1·10 1·10
1778 $1.60 Ronaldinho (Brazil) and Nicky Butt (England) 1·10 1·10
1779 $1.60 Ilhan Mansiz (Turkey) and Omar Daf (Senegal) 1·10 1·10
1780 $1.60 Hasan Sas (Turkey) and Pape Bouba Diop (Senegal) . . . . 1·10 1·10
1781 $1.60 Lamine Diata (Senegal) and Hakan Sukur (Turkey) . . . . . 1·10 1·10
MS1782 Four sheets, each 82 × 82 mm. (a) $3 Sebastian Kehl (Germany); $3 Frankie Hejduk (U.S.A.). (b) $3 Hong Myung Bo (South Korea); $3 Gaizka Mendieta (Spain). (c) $3 David Beckham (England) and Roque Junior (Brazil); $3 Paul Scholes (England) and Rivaldo (Brazil). (d) $3 Alpay Ozalan (Turkey); $3 Khalilou Fadiga (Senegal) . . . 13·00 15·00

No. 1780 is inscribed "Papa" in error.

183 Ram and Two Ewes

2003. Chinese New Year ("Year of the Ram").

1783 **183** $2 multicoloured . . . . 1·40 1·40

184 Marlene Dietrich

2003. Famous People of the 20th Century. (a) 10th Death Anniv of Marlene Dietrich. Multicoloured.

MS1784 127 × 165 mm. $1.60 × 2 Type **184**; $1.60 × 2 Wearing white coat and black hat; $1.60 × 2 Holding cigarette . . . . . . 5·50 6·00
MS1785 76 × 51 mm. $5 Marlene Dietrich . . . . 3·25 3·50

(b) 25th Death Anniv of Elvis Presley. Sheet 154 × 151 mm. Multicoloured.

MS1786 $1.60 × 6 Elvis Presley 6·00 6·50

(c) Life and Times of President John F. Kennedy. Two sheets, each 126 × 141 mm.

MS1787 $2 Taking Oath of Office, 1961 (black, brown and rose); $2 Watching swearing in of Cabinet Officers (black, brown and rose); $2 With Andrei Gromyko (Soviet Foreign Minister), 1963 (multicoloured); $2 Making speech during Cuban Missile Crisis, 1962 (black, violet and rose) . . . . 5·00 5·50
MS1788 $2 Robert and Ted Kennedy (brothers) (slate, violet and rose); $2 John F. Kennedy (slate, violet and rose); $2 John as boy with brother Joe Jnr (maroon, black and rose); $2 With Robert Kennedy in Rose Garden of White House (multicoloured) . . . . 5·00 5·50

(d) 75th Anniv of First Solo Transatlantic Flight. Two sheets, each 142 × 126 mm. Multicoloured.

MS1789 $2 Ryan Airlines crew attaching wing to fuselage of NYP Special *Spirit of St. Louis*; $2 Charles Lindbergh with Donald Hall and Mr. Mahoney (president of Ryan Airlines); $2 Lindbergh planning flight; $2 Donald Hall (chief engineer of Ryan Airlines) working on plans of aircraft . . 5·00 5·50
MS1790 $2 Donald Hall and drawing of *Spirit of St. Louis*; $2 Charles Lindbergh; $2 *Spirit of St. Louis* being towed from factory; $2 *Spirit of St. Louis* at Curtis Field before flight . . . 5·00 5·50

185 Princess Diana

2003. 5th Death Anniv of Diana, Princess of Wales. Multicoloured.

MS1791 203 × 150 mm. $2 Type **185**; $2 Wearing white dress and four strings of pearls; $2 Wearing black sleeveless dress; $2 Wearing black and white hat . . . . 5·00 5·50
MS1792 95 × 116 mm. $5 Wearing pearl and sapphire choker . . 3·25 3·50

186 Abraham Lincoln Bear

2003. Centenary of the Teddy Bear. Multicoloured.

MS1793 137 × 152 mm. $2 Type **186**; $2 Napolean bear; $2 Henry VIII bear; $2 Charlie Chaplin bear 3·75 4·00
MS1794 100 × 70 mm. $5 Baseball bear . . . . 3·25 3·50

186a Gustave Garrigou (1911)

2003. Centenary of Tour de France Cycle Race. Showing past winners. Multicoloured.

MS1795 160 × 100 mm. $2 Type **186a**; $2 Odile Defraye (1912); $2 Philippe Thys (1913); $2 Philippe Thys (1914) . . . . . 4·25 4·25
MS1796 100 × 70 mm. $5 Francois Faber . . . . 3·75 4·00

187 Cadillac 355-C V8 Sedan (1933)

2003. Centenary of General Motors Cadillac. Multicoloured.

MS1797 120 × 170 mm. $2 Type **187**; $2 Eldorado (1953); $2 Coupe Deville (1977); $2 Seville Elegante (1980) . . . . 5·00 5·50
MS1798 84 × 120 mm. $5 Cadillac (1954) . . . . 3·25 3·50

188 Corvette (1970)

2003. 50th Anniv of General Motors Chevrolet Corvette. Multicoloured.

MS1799 120 × 140 mm. $2 Type **188**; $2 Corvette (1974); $2 Corvette (1971); $2 Corvette (1973) . . 5·00 5·50
MS1800 120 × 85 mm. $5 C5 Corvette (1997) . . . . 3·25 3·50

189 Queen Elizabeth II on Coronation Day

190 Prince William

2003. 50th Anniv of Coronation. Multicoloured.

MS1801 156 × 93 mm. $3 Type **189**; $3 Queen wearing Imperial State Crown (red background); $3 Wearing Imperial State Crown (in recent years) . . . . 6·00 6·50
MS1802 106 × 76 mm. $5 Wearing tiara and blue sash . . . . . 3·50 3·75

2003. 21st Birthday of Prince William of Wales. Multicoloured.

MS1803 147 × 86 mm. $3 Type **190**; $3 Wearing jacket and blue and gold patterned tie; $3 Wearing fawn jumper . . . . 6·00 6·50
MS1804 98 × 68 mm. $5 Prince William . . . . 3·50 3·75

190a A. V. Roe's Triplane I, 1909

2003. Centenary of Powered Flight. A. V. Roe (aircraft designer) Commemoration. Multicoloured.

MS1805 177 × 96 mm. $1.80 Type **190a**; $1.80 Avro Type D biplane, 1911; $1.80 Avro Type F, 1912; $1.80 Avro 504 4·75 5·00
MS1806 106 × 76 mm. $5 Avro No. 561, 1924 . . . . 3·25 3·50

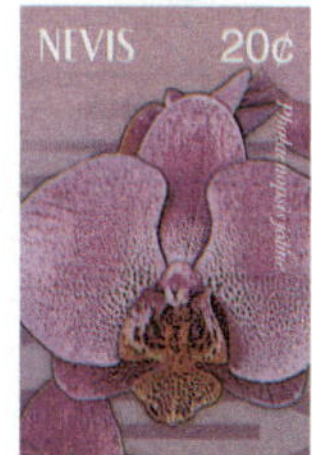

191 *Phalaenopsis joline*

2003. Orchids, Marine Life and Butterflies. Multicoloured.

1807 20c. Type **191** 30 20
1808 30c. Nassau grouper (fish) 35 30
1809 30c. *Perisama bonplandii* (butterfly) (horiz) 35 30
1810 80c. Acropora (coral) . . . 55 35
1811 90c. Doubletooth soldierfish (horiz) 65 55
1812 90c. *Danaus Formosa* (butterfly) (horiz) 65 55
1813 $1 *Amauris vasati* (butterfly) (horiz) 75 60
1814 $1.20 Vanda thonglor (orchid) 90 70
1815 $2 Potinara (orchid) (horiz) 1·40 1·40
1816 $3 *Lycaste aquila* (orchid) (horiz) . . . . 2·00 2·25
1817 $3 *Lycorea ceres* (butterfly) (horiz) . . . . 2·00 2·25
1818 $5 American manatee (horiz) . . . . 3·25 3·50
MS1819 136 × 116 mm. $2 *Brassolaelia cattleya*; $2 *Cymbidium claricon*; $2 *Calanthe restita*; $2 *Odontoglossum crispum* (orchids) (all horiz) . . . . . 5·50 6·00
MS1820 116 × 136 mm. $2 Lionfish; $2 Copper-banded butterflyfish; $2 Honeycomb grouper; $2 Blue tang (all horiz) . . . . 5·50 6·00
MS1821 136 × 116 mm. $2 *Kallima rumia*; $2 *Nessaea ancaeus*; $2 *Callicore cajetani*; $2 *Hamadryas guatemalena* (butterflies) (all horiz) 5·50 6·00
MS1822 Three sheets, each 96 × 66 mm. (a) $5 *Odontioda brocade* (orchid). (b) $5 Blue-striped grunt (fish). (c) $5 *Euphaedra medon* (butterfly) (all horiz) . . . . 9·75 10·50

192 "Madonna of the Magnificat" (Botticelli)

2003. Christmas. Multicoloured.

1823 30c. Type **192** 25 15
1824 90c. "Madonna with the Long Neck" (detail) (Parmigianino) 60 40
1825 $1.20 "Virgin and Child with St. Anne" (detail) (Da Vinci) 90 60
1826 $5 "Madonna and Child and Scenes from the Life of St. Anne" (detail) (Filippo Lippi) . . . . . 3·25 3·50
MS1827 96×113 mm. $6 "The Conestabile Madonna" (Raphael) 3·50 4·00

193 Two Stylised Men and AIDS Ribbon

2003. World AIDS Awareness Day. Multicoloured.

1828 90c. Type **193** 65 50
1829 $1.20 Nevis flag and map and ribbon . . . . 1·10 1·10

194 Monkey King

2004. Chinese New Year ("Year of the Monkey"). Grey, black and brown (**MS**1030) or multicoloured (**MS**1031).

MS1030 Sheet 102×130 mm. $1.60 Type **194**×4 . . . . 3·75 4·00
MS1031 Sheet 70×100 mm. $3 Monkey King (29×39 mm) . . 1·90 2·25

195 Guide Badges

2004. 50th Anniv of Nevis Girl Guides. Multicoloured.

1032 30c. Type **195** 25 15
1033 90c. Mrs Gwendolyn Douglas-Jones and Miss Bridget Hunkins (past and present Commissioners) (horiz) 60 40
1034 $1.20 Lady Olave Baden Powell 85 60
1035 $5 Photographs of Girl Guides . . . . 3·25 3·50

196 "The Morning After" (1945)

2004. 25th Death Anniv of Norman Rockwell (artist) (2003). Multicoloured.

MS1036 150×180 mm. $2 Type **196**; $2 "Solitaire" (1950); $2 "Easter Morning" (1959); $2 "Walking to Church" (1953) . . . . 5·50 6·00
MS1037 90×98 mm. $5 "The Graduate" (1959) (horiz) . . . 3·50 3·75

197 "Woman with a Hat" (1935)

2004. 30th Death Anniv of Pablo Picasso (2003) (artist). Multicoloured.

MS1838 Two sheets each 133×168 mm. (a) $2 Type **197**; $2 "Seated Woman" (1937); $2 "Portrait of Nusch Eluard" (1937); $2 "Woman in a Straw Hat" (1936). (b) $2 "L'Arlesienne" (1937); $2 "The Mirror" (1932); $2 "Repose" (1932); $2 "Portrait of Paul Eluard" (1937). Set of 2 sheets . . . . 9·50 10·50
MS1839 Two sheets. (a) 75×100 mm. $5 "Portrait of Nusch Eluard" (with green ribbon in hair) (1937). (b) 100×75 mm. $5 "Reclining Woman with a Book" (1939). Imperf. Set of 2 sheets . . . . 7·00 7·50

198 "Still Life with a Drapery" (1899)

2004. 300th Anniv of St. Petersburg. "Treasures of the Hermitage". Multicoloured.

1840 30c. Type **198** 25 15
1841 90c. "The Smoker" (1895) (vert) 60 40
1842 $2 "Girl with a Fan" (1881) (vert) . . . . 1·40 1·25
1843 $5 "Grove" (1912) (vert) . . 3·25 3·50
MS1844 94×74 mm. $5 "Lady in the Garden" (1867). Imperf . . 3·25 3·50

199 John Denver **200** Marilyn Monroe

2004. John Denver (musician) Commemoration. Sheet 127×107 mm containing T **199** and similar vert designs. Multicoloured.

MS1845 $1.20 Type **199**; $1.20 Wearing patterned shirt; $1.20 Wearing dark shirt; $1.20 Wearing white shirt . . . . 3·25 3·50

2004. Marilyn Monroe Commemoration. Multicoloured.

1846 60c. Type **200** 70 60
MS1847 175×125 mm. $2 Pouting; $2 Laughing and looking left; $2 Laughing with head tilted back; $2 Smiling wearing drop earrings (37×50 mm) . . . . 5·00 5·50

201 Brain

2004. Arthur the Aardvark and Friends. Multicoloured.

MS1848 Three sheets, each 152×185. (a) $1×6, Type **201**; Sue Ellen; Buster; Francine; Muffy; Binky. (b) $2×4, Binky inside heart; Sue Ellen inside heart; Brain inside heart; Francine inside heart wearing red top. (c) $2×4, Arthur inside heart; D.W. inside heart; Francine inside heart wearing pink top; Buster inside heart . . . . 12·00 13·00

202 HMCS *Penetang*

2004. 60th Anniv of D-Day Landings. Multicoloured.

MS1849 Two sheets. (a) 136×122 mm. $1.20×6 Type **202**; Infantry disembarking from landing craft; Landing craft tank from above; Two landing craft tanks; Landing barge kitchen; Battleship *Texas*. (b) 96×76 mm. $6 HMS *Scorpion* . . . . . . 9·00 9·50

203 Medal (Mexico City, 1968)

2004. Olympic Games, Athens. Multicoloured.

1850 30c. Type **203** 30 20
1851 90c. Pentathlon (Greek art) 65 50
1852 $1.80 Avery Brundage (International Olympic Committee, 1952–1972) 1·30 1·30
1853 $3 Tennis (Antwerp, 1920) (horiz) . . . . 1·75 1·90

204 Deng Xiaoping **206** Elvis Presley

205 Peace Dove carrying Olive Branch

2004. Birth Centenary of Deng Xiaoping (leader of China, 1978–89). Sheet 96×66 mm.

MS1854 **204** $5 multicoloured . . 3·25 3·00

2004. United Nations International Year of Peace. Sheet 142×82 mm containing horiz designs as T **205**. Multicoloured.

MS1855 $3×3, Type **205**; Dove from front; Dove angled left 5·25 5·50

2004. Elvis Presley (entertainer) Commemoration. Multicoloured.

MS1856 Two sheets, each 146×103 mm. (a) $1.20×6, Type **206**×3; magenta background×3. (b) $1.20×6, scarlet jumper; yellow jumper; blue jumper; turquoise jumper; purple jumper; green jumper . . . . 11·00 10·00

207 Nery Pumpido (Argentina)

2004. Centenary of FIFA (Federation Internationale de Football Association) (**MS**1857) and World Cup Football Championship (**MS**1858). Multicoloured.

MS1857 192×96 mm. $2×4, Type **207**; Gary Lineker (England); Thomas Hassler (Germany); Sol Campbell (England). (b) 107×86 mm. $5 Michael Owen (England) . . . 3·25 3·50
MS1858 90×115 mm. $5 Jason Berkley Joseph (Nevis) (38×50 mm) . . . . 3·25 3·50

208 "Santa's Good Boys"

2004. Christmas. Paintings by Norman Rockwell. Multicoloured.

1859 25c. Type **208** 25 15
1860 30c. "Ride 'em Cowboy" . . 30 20
1861 90c. "Christmas Sing Merrillie" 65 50
1862 $5 "The Christmas Newsstand" . . . . . . 3·25 3·50
MS1863 63×72 mm. $5 "Is He Coming". Imperf . . . . . . 3·25 3·50

209 Steam Idyll, Indonesia

2004. Bicentenary of Steam Trains. Multicoloured.

1864 $3 Type **209** . . . . 1·75 1·90
1865 $3 2-8-2, Syria . . . . . . 1·75 1·90
1866 $3 Narrow Gauge Mallet 0-4-4-0, Portugal . . . . 1·75 1·90
1867 $3 Western Pacific Bo Bo Road Switcher, USA . . 1·75 1·90
MS1868 100×70 mm. $5 LMS 5305, Great Britain . . . . 3·25 3·50

210 Gekko Gecko

2005. Reptiles and Amphibians. Multicoloured.

1869 $1.20 Type **210** 90 90
1870 $1.20 Eyelash viper 90 90
1871 $1.20 Green iguana 90 90
1872 $1.20 Whistling frog 90 90
MS1873 96×67 mm. $5 Hawksbill turtle . . . . 3·25 3·50

211 Rufous Hummingbird

2005. Hummingbirds. Multicoloured.

1874 $2 Type **211** . . . . 1·40 1·40
1875 $2 Green-crowned brilliant 1·40 1·40
1876 $2 Ruby-throated hummingbird . . . . . . 1·40 1·40
1877 $2 Purple-throated carib . . 1·40 1·40
MS1878 79×108 mm. $5 Rivoli's ("Magnificent") Hummingbird 3·25 3·50

212 *Xeromphalina campanella*

2005. Mushrooms. Multicoloured.
MS1879 137 × 127 mm. $2 × 4, Type **212**; *Calvatia sculpta*; *Mitrula elegans*; *Aleuria aurantia* 5·00 5·50
MS1880 97 × 68 mm. $5 *iSarcoscypha coccinea* 3·25 3·50

213 Hawksbill Turtle (Leon Silcott)

2005. Hawksbill Turtle. Children's Drawings. Multicoloured.
1881 30c. Type **213** 25 15
1882 90c. Hawksbill turtle on sand (Kris Liburd) 60 35
1883 $1.20 Spotted hawksbill turtle (Alice Webber) 95 75
1884 $5 Hawksbill turtle in water (Jeuaunito Huggins) 3·25 3·50

214 Zebra Shark

2005. Sharks. Multicoloured.
MS1885 99 × 137 mm. $2 × 4, Type **214**; Caribbean reef shark; Blue shark; Bronze whaler 5·00 5·50
MS1886 96 × 67 mm. $5 Blacktip reef shark 3·25 3·50

215 Rooster

2005. Chinese New Year ("Year of the Rooster"). Multicoloured.
1887 75c. Type **215** 50 55
1888 75c. Pink silhouette of rooster 50 55
1889 75c. Grey silhouette of rooster 50 55
1890 75c. Rooster on rose-lilac background 50 55

216 Enola Gay and Flight Crew

2005. 60th Anniv of Victory in Japan. Multicoloured.
1891 $2 Type **216** 1·40 1·40
1892 $2 Bomb exploding over Hiroshima 1·40 1·40
1893 $2 Souvenir of Japanese Surrender Ceremony 1·40 1·40
1894 $2 Japanese Delegation aboard USS *Missouri* 1·40 1·40
1895 $2 General Macarthur speaking 1·40 1·40

217 Brazil Team, 1958

2005. 75th Anniv of First World Cup Football Championship. Multicoloured.
1896 $2 Type **217** 1·40 1·40
1897 $2 Brazil and Sweden 1·40 1·40
1898 $2 Rasunda Stadium, Stockholm 1·40 1·40
1899 $2 Edson Arantes do Nascimento (Pele) 1·40 1·40
MS1900 115 × 89 mm. $5 Brazil celebrating with Swedish flag 3·25 3·50

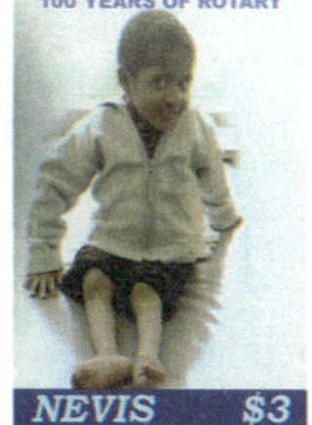

218 Friedrich von Schiller **219** Young Boy

2005. Death Bicentenary of Friedrich von Schiller (poet and dramatist). Multicoloured.
1901 $3 Type **218** 1·75 1·90
1902 $3 Friedrich von Schiller (black and white portrait) 1·75 1·90
1903 $3 Birthplace of Friedrich von Schiller 1·75 1·90
MS1904 100 × 70 mm. $5 Friedrich von Schiller statue, Chicago 3·25 3·50

2005. Centenary of Rotary International (humanitarian organisation). Multicoloured.
1905 $3 Type **219** 1·75 1·90
1906 $3 Immunising child 1·75 1·90
1907 $3 Boy with leg braces and crutches 1·75 1·90
MS1908 103 × 70 mm. $5 Two children and adult (horiz) 3·25 3·50

220 Admiral Sir William Cornwallis

2005. Bicentenary of the Battle of Trafalgar. Multicoloured.
1909 30c. Type **220** 30 20
1910 90c. Captain Maurice Suckling (Comptroller of the Navy) 65 35
1911 $1.20 Richard Earl Howe (First Lord of the Admiralty) 95 75
1912 $3 Sir John Jervis (First Earl of St Vincent) 2·00 2·25
MS1913 83 × 119 mm. $5 Richard Earl Howe on quarterdeck of *Queen Charlotte* 3·25 3·50

221 General Charles de Gaulle

2005. 60th Anniv of Victory in Europe.
1914 **221** $2 multicoloured 1·40 1·40
1915 $2 sepia and pink 1·40 1·40
1916 $2 black and yellow 1·40 1·40
1917 $2 brown, stone and blue 1·40 1·40
1918 $2 multicoloured 1·40 1·40
DESIGNS: No. 1914, Type **221**; 1915, General George S. Patton; 1916, Field Marshall Bernhard Montgomery; 1917, Prisoners of War; 1918, "Germany Defeated!".

222 "The Little Mermaid" (sculpture) **224** Captain Nemo ("20,000 Leagues under the Sea")

223 Tyrannosaurus Rex

2005. Birth Bicentenary of Hans Christian Andersen (writer). Multicoloured.
1919 $2 Type **222** 1·40 1·40
1920 $2 *Thumbelina* 1·40 1·40
1921 $2 *The Snow Queen* 1·40 1·40
1922 $2 *The Emperor's New Clothes* 1·40 1·40
MS1923 100 × 75 mm. $6 Hans Christian Andersen 3·50 3·75

2005. Prehistoric Animals. Multicoloured.
1924 30c. Type **223** 30 20
1925 $5 Hadrosaur 2·10 2·20
MS1926 Three sheets. (a) 104 × 128 mm. $1.20 × 6, Apatosaurus; Camarasaurus; Iguanodon; Edmontosaurus; Centrosaurus; Euoplocephalus. (b) 128 × 104 mm. $1.20 × 6 (vert), Deinotherium; Platybelodon; Palaeoloxodon; Arsinoitherium; Procoptodon; Macrauchenia; (c) 104 × 128 mm. $1.20 × 6, Ouranosaurus; Parasaurolophus; Psittacosaurus; Stegasaurus; Scelidosaurus; Hypsilophodon 12·00 13·00
MS1927 Three sheets. (a) 97 × 77 mm. $5 Brontotherium. (b) 98 × 87 mm. $5 Daspletosaurus; (c) 98 × 92 mm. $5 Pliosaur 9·75 10·50
The backgrounds of Nos. **MS**1926a/c form a composite design which bleeds onto the sheet margins.

2005. Death Centenary of Jules Verne (writer). Multicoloured.
1928 $2 Type **224** 1·40 1·40
1929 $2 Michael Strogoff 1·40 1·40
1930 $2 Phileas Fogg ("Around the World in 80 Days") 1·40 1·40
1931 $2 Captain Cyrus Smith ("Mysterious Island") 1·40 1·40
MS1932 78 × 100 mm. $5 Pat Boone ("Journey to the Centre of the Earth") 3·25 3·50
No. 1930 is inscribed "Phinias Fogg".

225 No. SG69 of Vatican City optd with Type **69**

2005. Pope John Paul II Commemoration. Multicoloured.
1933 90c. Type **225** 65 50
1934 $4 Pope John Paul II (28 × 42 mm) 2·75 3·00

226 Shareef Abdur-Rahim (Portland Trail Blazers) **227** Dr Sun Yat-Sen

2005. National Basketball Association. Multicoloured.
1935 $1 Type **226** 70 70
1936 $1 Vince Carter (New Jersey Nets) 70 70
1937 $1 Shaun Livingston (Los Angeles Clippers) 70 70
1938 $1 Theo Ratliff (Portland Trail Blazers) 70 70
1939 $1 Rasheed Wallace (Detroit Pistons) 70 70

2005. TAIPEI 2005 International Stamp Exhibition. 80th Death Anniv of Dr Sun Yat-Sen (Chinese revolutionary leader). Multicoloured.
1940 $2 Type **227** 1·40 1·40
1941 $2 Wearing jacket and tie 1·40 1·40
1942 $2 In front of statue 1·40 1·40
1943 $2 In front of building 1·40 1·40

228 "Madonna and the Angels" (detail) (Fra Angelico)

2005. Christmas. Multicoloured.
1944 25c. Type **228** 25 15
1945 30c. "Madonna and the Child" (detail) (Filippo Lippi) 30 20
1946 90c. "Madonna and Child" (detail) (Giotto) 65 50
1947 $4 "Madonna of the Chair" (detail) (Raphael) 2·75 3·00
MS1948 67 × 97 mm. $5 "Adoration of the Magi" (Giovanni Batista Tiepolo) (horiz) 3·25 3·00

229 "A Dog" (Ren Xun)

2006. Chinese New Year ("Year of the Dog").
1949 **229** 75c. multicoloured 70 60

230 Eldorado National Forest, California

2006. Centenary of United States Forest Service (2005). Multicoloured.
1950 $1.60 Type **230** 1·20 1·20
1951 $1.60 Pisgah National Forest, North Carolina 1·20 1·20
1952 $1.60 Chattahoochee-Oconee National Forests, Georgia 1·20 1·20
1953 $1.60 Nantahala National Forest, North Carolina 1·20 1·20
1954 $1.60 Bridger-Teton National Forest, Wyoming 1·20 1·20
1955 $1.60 Mount Hood National Forest, Oregon 1·20 1·20
MS1956 Two sheets, each 104 × 70 mm. (a) $6 Klamath National Forest, California (horiz). (b) $6 The Source Rain Forest Walk, Nevis 7·00 7·25

OFFICIAL STAMPS

1980. Nos. 40/49 optd **OFFICIAL**.
O 1 15c. Sugar cane being harvested 10 10
O 2 25c. Crafthouse (craft centre) 10 10
O 3 30c. "Europa" (liner) 10 10
O 4 40c. Lobster and sea crab 15 15
O 5 45c. Royal St. Kitts Hotel and golf course 20 20
O 6 50c. Pinney's Beach, Nevis 15 20
O 7 55c. New runway at Golden Rock 15 20
O 8 $1 Picking cotton 15 25
O 9 $5 Brewery 45 55
O10 $10 Pineapples and peanuts 70 90

1981. Nos. 60/71 optd **OFFICIAL**.
O11 15c. New River Mill 10 10
O12 20c. Nelson Museum 10 10
O13 25c. St. James' Parish Church 10 15
O14 30c. Nevis Lane 15 15
O15 40c. Zetland Plantation 15 20
O16 45c. Nisbet Plantation 20 25
O17 50c. Pinney's Beach 20 25
O18 55c. Eva Wilkin's Studio 25 30
O19 $1 Nevis at dawn 30 30
O20 $2.50 Ruins of Fort Charles 40 50
O21 $5 Old Bath House 50 65
O22 $10 Beach at Nisbet's 80 1·00

1983. Nos. 72/7 optd or surch **OFFICIAL**.
O23 45c. on $2 "Royal Sovereign" 10 15
O24 45c. on $2 Prince Charles and Lady Diana Spencer 20 25
O25 55c. "Royal Caroline" 10 15
O26 55c. Prince Charles and Lady Diana Spencer 25 25
O27 $1.10 on $5 "Britannia" 20 25
O28 $1.10 on $5 Prince Charles and Lady Diana Spencer 55 60

1985. Nos. 187/98 optd **OFFICIAL**.
O29 15c. Flamboyant 20 20
O30 20c. Eyelash orchid 30 30
O31 30c. Bougainvillea 30 40
O32 40c. Hibiscus sp 30 40
O33 50c. Night-blooming cereus 35 40
O34 55c. Yellow mahoe 35 45
O35 60c. Spider-lily 40 50
O36 75c. Scarlet cordia 45 55
O37 $1 Shell-ginger 60 60

O38 $3 Blue petrea . . . . . . 1·25 1·75
O39 $5 Coral hibiscus . . . . . 2·00 2·25
O40 $10 Passion flower . . . . . 3·00 2·50

1993. Nos. 578/91 optd **OFFICIAL**.
O41 5c. Type **63** 55 75
O42 10c. "Historis odius" 60 75
O43 15c. "Marpesia corinna" . . 70 60
O44 20c. "Anartia amathea" . . 70 40
O45 25c. "Junonia evarete" . . . 70 40
O46 40c. "Heliconius charithonia" 85 45
O47 50c. "Marpesia petreus" . . 85 45
O48 75c. "Heliconius doris" . . . 1·25 60
O49 80c. "Dione juno" . . . . . 1·25 50
O50 $1 "Hypolimnas misippus" . 1·25 80
O51 $3 "Danaus plexippus" . . . 2·50 2·75
O52 $5 "Heliconius sara" . . . . 3·50 4·00
O53 $10 "Tithorea harmonia" . . 6·50 7·00
O54 $20 "Dryas julia" . . . . . 12·00 13·00

1999. Nos. 1166/77 optd **OFFICIAL**.
O55 25c. Guava 25 15
O56 30c. Papaya 25 15
O57 50c. Mango 35 25
O58 60c. Golden apple 40 30
O59 80c. Pineapple 50 35
O60 90c. Watermelon 60 40
O61 $1 Bananas 70 50
O62 $1.80 Orange . . . . 1·25 1·25
O63 $3 Honeydew . . . . 1·75 1·90
O64 $5 Cantaloupe . . . . . . 3·00 3·25
O65 $10 Pomegranate . . . . . 5·50 6·00
O66 $20 Cashew . . . . 9·50 11·00

NEW BRUNSWICK Pt. 1

An eastern province of the Dominion of Canada, whose stamps are now used.

1851. 12 pence = 1 shilling;
20 shilling = 1 pound.
1860. 100 cents = 1 dollar.

1 Royal Crown and Heraldic Flowers of the United Kingdom

1851.
2 **1** 3d. red £2000 £325
4 6d. yellow £4500 £700
5 1s. mauve £13000 £4000

2 Locomotive

3 Queen Victoria

1860.
8 **2** 1c. purple . . . . 45·00 40·00
10 **3** 2c. orange . . . . 23·00 21·00
13 – 5c. brown £5500
14 – 5c. green . . . . 20·00 15·00
17 – 10c. red . . . . 42·00 45·00
18 – 12½c. blue . . . . 55·00 40·00
19 – 17c. black . . . . 38·00 50·00
DESIGNS—VERT: 5c. brown, Charles Connell; 5c. green, 10c. Queen Victoria; 17c. King Edward VII when Prince of Wales. HORIZ: 12½c. Steamship.

NEW CALEDONIA Pt. 6

A French Overseas Territory in the S. Pacific, E. of Australia, consisting of New Caledonia and a number of smaller islands.

100 centimes = 1 franc.

1 Napoleon III

1860. Imperf.
1 **1** 10c. black £225

Nos. 5/30 are stamps of French Colonies optd or surch.

1881. "Peace and Commerce" type surch **N C E** and new value. Imperf.
5 H 05 on 40c. red on yellow . . 16·00 13·50
8a 5 on 40c. red on yellow . . 11·50 11·00
9 5 on 75c. red . . . . 50·00 38·00
6 25 on 35c. black on orange £200 £200
7 25 on 75c. red £275 £275

1886. "Peace and Commerce" (imperf) and "Commerce" types surch **N.C.E. 5c.**
10 J 5c. on 1f. green . . . . . . 28·00 30·00
11 H 5c. on 1f. green £8000 £11000

1891. "Peace and Commerce" (imperf) and "Commerce" types surch **N.-C.E. 10 c.** in ornamental frame.
13 H 10c. on 40c. red on yellow 38·00 38·00
14 J 10c. on 40c. red on yellow 19·00 12·00

1892. "Commerce" type surch **N.-C.E. 10 centimes** in ornamental frame.
15 J 10c. on 30c. brown on drab 17·00 8·75

1892. Optd **NLLE CALEDONIE**. (a) "Peace and Commerce" type. Imperf.
16 H 20c. red on green £250 £275
17 35c. black on orange . . . . 75·00 70·00
19 1f. green £200 £200

(b) "Commerce" type.
20 J 5c. green on green . . . . . 25·00 12·00
21 10c. black on lilac . . . . £120 80·00
22 15c. blue . . . . £110 50·00
23 20c. red on green . . . . . £120 70·00
24 25c. brown on yellow . . . 34·00 5·00
25 25c. black on pink . . . . £120 10·50
26 30c. brown on drab . . . £100 80·00
27 35c. black on orange . . . £200 £140
29 75c. red on pink £150 £120
30 1f. green £120 £120

1892. "Tablet" key-type inscr "NLLE CALEDONIE ET DEPENDANCES".
31 D 1c. black and red on blue . . 1·10 10
32 2c. brown and blue on buff 35 35
33 4c. brown and blue on grey 1·30 4·50
55 5c. green and red . . . . . 3·25 15
34 10c. black and blue on lilac 3·75 30
56 10c. red and blue . . . . . 6·00 30
35 15c. blue and red . . . . . 5·75 2·50
57 15c. grey and red . . . . . 7·25 20
36 20c. red and blue on green 25·00 70
37 25c. black and red on pink 4·50 7·75
58 25c. blue and red . . . . . 9·75 3·25
38 30c. brown and blue on drab 11·50 1·20
39 40c. red and blue on yellow 9·25 11·50
40 50c. red and blue on pink 16·00 7·75
59 50c. brown and red on blue 48·00 90·00
60 50c. brown and blue on blue 50·00 34·00
41 75c. brown & red on orange 75·00 24·00
42 1f. green and red . . . . . 16·00 20·00

1892. Surch **N-C-E** in ornamental scroll and new value. (a) "Peace and Commerce" type. Imperf.
44 H 10 on 1f. green £4500 £3750

(b) "Commerce" type.
45 J 5 on 20c. red on green . . . 44·00 6·00
46 5 on 75c. red on pink . . . . 19·00 17·00
48 10 on 1f. green . . . . 15·00 8·25

1899. Stamps of 1892 surch (a) **N-C-E** in ornamental scroll and **5**.
50 D 5 on 2c. brown & bl on buff 8·50 17·00
51 5 on 4c. brown & bl on grey 1·10 3·25

(b) **N.C.E.** and **15** in circle.
52 D 15 on 30c. brown and blue on drab . . . . 3·50 6·75
53 15 on 75c. brown and red on orange . . . . 11·50 16·00
54 15 on 1f. green and red . . 50·00 30·00

1902. Surch **N.-C.E.** and value in figures.
61 D 5 on 30c. brown and blue on drab . . . . 2·50 8·75
62 15 on 40c. red and blue on yellow . . . . 3·50 7·50

1903. 50th Anniv of French Annexation. Optd **CINQUANTENAIRE 24 SEPTEMBRE 1853 1903** and eagle.
63 D 1c. black and red on blue . . 30 1·10
64 2c. brown and blue on buff 1·50 2·30
65 4c. brown and blue on grey 6·00 5·50
66 5c. green and red . . . . . 1·40 3·25
69 10c. black and blue on lilac 3·50 5·00
70 15c. grey and red . . . . . 7·25 1·50
71 20c. red and blue on green 10·00 19·00
72 25c. black and red on pink 11·50 17·00
73 30c. brown and blue on drab 19·00 22·00
74 40c. red and blue on yellow 44·00 16·00
75 50c. red and blue on pink 60·00 55·00
76 75c. brown & blue on orange . . . . 65·00 £120
77 1f. green and red £120 £120

1903. Nos. 64 etc further surch with value in figures within the jubilee opt.
78 D 1 on 2c. brown & bl on buff 65 65
79 2 on 4c. brown & bl on grey 3·00 3·75
80 4 on 5c. green and red . . . 70 2·75
82 10 on 15c. grey and red . . 45 2·00
83 15 on 20c. red and blue on green . . . . 1·10 3·75
84 20 on 25c. black and red on pink . . . . 2·75 4·25

15 Kagu

16

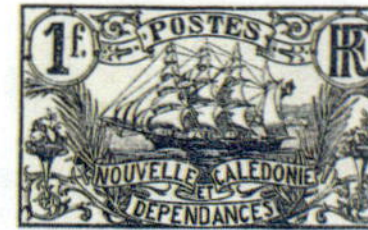

17 "President Felix Faure" (barque)

1905.
85 **15** 1c. black on green 10 25
86 2c. brown 10 10
87 4c. blue on orange 10 40
88 5c. green 80 10
112 5c. blue 10 25
113 10c. green . . . . 1·30 40
114 10c. red 45 45
90 15c. lilac 30 15
91 **16** 20c. brown 10 10
92 25c. blue on green . . . . 1·70 25
115 25c. red on yellow 20 10
93 30c. brown on orange . . . 65 1·50
116 30c. red . . . . 2·00 3·50
117 30c. orange 30 95
94 35c. black on yellow . . . 85 1·10
95 40c. red on green . . . . 1·70 1·70
96 45c. red . . . . 1·40 2·50
97 50c. red on orange . . . . 4·25 3·25
118 50c. blue . . . . 1·20 85
119 50c. grey 35 75
120 65c. blue . . . . 1·80 2·75
98 75c. olive . . . . 2·00 2·75
121 75c. blue . . . . 30 1·80
122 75c. violet . . . . 80 3·50
99 **17** 1f. blue on green . . . . 1·80 2·30
123 1f. blue . . . . 2·00 3·25
100 2f. red on blue . . . . . 3·25 4·50
101 5f. black on orange . . . . 11·00 12·00

1912. Stamps of 1892 surch.
102 D 05 on 15c. grey and red . . 85 1·20
103 05 on 20c. red and blue on green . . . . 30 1·40
104 05 on 30c. brown and blue on drab . . . . 55 2·75
105 10 on 40c. red and blue on yellow . . . . 90 1·80
106 10 on 50c. brown and blue on blue . . . . 1·20 2·50

1915. Surch **NCE 5** and red cross.
107 **15** 10c.+5c. red . . . . 1·20 1·10

1915. Surch **5c** and red cross.
109 **15** 10c.+5c. red . . . . . . 1·80 4·25
110 15c.+5c. lilac . . . . . . 15 3·25

1918. Surch **5 CENTIMES**.
111 **15** 5c. on 15c. lilac . . . . . 4·00 5·00

1922. Surch **0 05**.
124 **15** 0.05 on 15c. lilac 10 70

1924. Types **15/17** (some colours changed) surch.
125 **15** 25c. on 15c. lilac . . . . . 30 2·75
126 **17** 25c. on 2f. red on blue . . 1·10 3·25
127 25c. on 5f. black on orange 45 4·75
128 **16** 60 on 75c. green . . . . . 10 1·80
129 65 on 45c. purple . . . . . 50 3·25
130 85 on 45c. purple . . . . . 1·00 3·75
131 90 on 75c. red . . . . . . 25 2·50
132 **17** 1f.25 on 1f. blue . . . . . 55 4·75
133 1f.50 on 1f. blue on blue 1·30 3·00
134 3f. on 5f. mauve . . . . . 1·60 5·00
135 10f. on 5f. green on mauve 1·70 17·00
136 20f. on 5f. red on yellow 12·00 34·00

22 Pointe des Paletuviers

23 Chief's Hut

24 La Perouse, De Bougainville and "L'Astrolabe"

1928.
137 **22** 1c. blue and purple . . . . 20 1·60
138 2c. green and brown . . . 10 2·30
139 3c. blue and red . . . . . 15 4·00
140 4c. blue and orange . . . 15 2·50
141 5c. brown and blue . . . . 15 1·30
142 10c. brown and lilac . . . 15 45
143 15c. blue and brown . . . 15 45
144 20c. brown and red . . . . 60 1·40
145 25c. brown and green . . . 45 10
146 **23** 30c. deep green and green 15 75
147 35c. mauve and black . . . 65 10
148 40c. green and red . . . . 20 2·75
149 45c. red and blue . . . . 2·50 4·75
150 45c. green and deep green 3·00 3·75
151 50c. brown and mauve . . 20 10
152 55c. red and blue . . . . 3·50 1·50
153 60c. red and blue . . . . 25 4·75
154 65c. blue and brown . . . 70 85
155 70c. brown and mauve . . 2·30 4·75
156 75c. drab and blue . . . . 1·50 2·30
157 80c. green and purple . . . 2·00 4·50
158 85c. brown and green . . . 3·00 2·30
159 90c. pink and red . . . . 2·30 2·75
160 90c. red and brown . . . . 2·00 3·00
161 **24** 1f. pink and drab . . . . 5·75 1·90
162 1f. carmine and red . . . . 2·00 1·90
163 1f. green and red . . . . . 1·10 4·00
164 1f.10 brown and green . . 9·75 25·00
165 1f.25 green and brown . . 3·25 5·00
166 1f.25 carmine and red . . . 1·20 5·25
167 1f.40 red and blue . . . . 1·50 4·75
168 1f.50 light blue and blue 50 2·30
169 1f.60 brown and green . . 2·30 5·50
170 1f.75 orange and blue . . . 3·00 3·50
171 1f.75 blue and ultramarine 2·75 4·75
172 2f. brown and orange . . . 90 35
173 2f.25 blue and ultramarine 2·00 5·25
174 2f.50 brown . . . . 75 3·75
175 3f. brown and mauve . . . 90 5·25
176 5f. brown and blue . . . . 80 2·30
177 10f. brown & pur on pink 2·30 4·25
178 20f. brown & red on yellow 2·75 4·00

1931. "Colonial Exhibition" key-types.
179 E 40c. green and black . . . 5·25 10·00
180 F 50c. mauve and black . . . 5·25 4·50
181 G 90c. red and black . . . . 5·00 9·75
182 H 1f.50 blue and black . . . 5·00 5·00

1932. Paris–Noumea Flight. Optd with Couzinet 33 airplane and **PARIS-NOUMEA Verneilh-Deve-Munch 5 Avril 1932**.
183 **23** 40c. olive and red £350 £350
184 50c. brown and mauve . . £350 £325

1933. 1st Anniv of Paris–Noumea Flight. Optd **PARIS-NOUMEA Premiere liaison aerienne 5 Avril 1932** and Couzinet 33 airplane.
185 **22** 1c. blue and purple . . . . 8·00 20·00
186 2c. green and brown . . . 9·00 18·00
187 4c. blue and orange . . . 7·75 18·00
188 5c. brown and blue . . . . 8·50 19·00
189 10c. brown and lilac . . . 9·00 19·00
190 15c. blue and brown . . . 7·50 18·00
191 20c. brown and red . . . . 7·50 18·00
192 25c. brown and green . . . 10·50 20·00
193 **23** 30c. deep green and green 8·25 19·00
194 35c. mauve and black . . . 9·00 19·00
195 40c. green and red . . . . 8·50 12·50
196 45c. red and blue . . . . 9·00 19·00
197 50c. brown and mauve . . 6·75 19·00
198 70c. brown and mauve . . 8·50 21·00
199 75c. drab and blue . . . . 10·00 16·00
200 85c. brown and green . . . 8·50 16·00
201 90c. pink and red . . . . 8·50 16·00
202 **24** 1f. pink and drab . . . . 10·50 23·00
203 1f.25 green and brown . . 10·50 22·00
204 1f.50 light blue and blue 13·50 22·00
205 1f.75 orange and blue . . . 6·25 13·50
206 2f. brown and orange . . . 10·50 26·00
207 3f. brown and mauve . . . 10·50 25·00
208 5f. brown and blue . . . . 14·50 26·00
209 10f. brown & pur on pink 8·50 25·00
210 20f. brown & red on yellow 7·75 26·00

1937. International Exhibition, Paris. As T **4a** of Niger.
211 20c. violet . . . . 95 4·00
212 30c. green . . . . 65 5·25
213 40c. red . . . . 30 3·25
214 50c. brown and blue . . . . 40 2·50
215 90c. red . . . . 65 4·00
216 1f.50 blue . . . . 35 2·30
MS216a 120 × 100 mm. 3f. sepia 11·50 30·00
DESIGNS—HORIZ: 30c. Sailing ships; 40c. Berber, Negress and Annamite; 90c. France extends torch of civilization; 1f.50, Diane de Poitiers. VERT: 50c. Agriculture.

27 Breguet Saigon Flying Boat over Noumea

1938. Air.
217 **27** 65c. violet . . . . 85 4·75
218 4f.50 red . . . . 3·00 4·50
219 7f. green . . . . 50 4·00
220 9f. blue . . . . 4·25 5·25
221 20f. orange . . . . 3·25 3·25
222 50f. black . . . . 3·25 7·25

1938. Int Anti-cancer Fund. As T **17a** of Oceanic Settlement.
223 1f.75+50c. blue . . . . . . 3·50 30·00

1939. New York World's Fair. As T **17b** of Oceanic Settlement.
224 1f.25 red . . . . 45 5·75
225 2f.25 blue . . . . 50 3·50

1939. 150th Anniv of French Revolution. As T **17c** of Oceanic Settlement.
226 45c.+25c. green and black (postage) . . . . 11·00 23·00
227 70c.+30c. brown and black 10·00 16·00
228 90c.+35c. orange and black 9·75 23·00
229 1f.25+1f. red and black . . . 11·00 23·00
230 2f.25+2f. blue and black . . . 12·00 23·00

231 4f.50+4f. black and orange (air) . . . . 8·25 55·00

1941. Adherence to General de Gaulle. Optd **France Libre**.
232 **22** 1c. blue and purple . . . . 4·75 24·00
233 2c. green and brown . . . 6·25 23·00
234 3c. blue and red . . . . 5·00 38·00
235 4c. blue and orange . . . 4·75 23·00
236 5c. brown and blue . . . 4·00 23·00
237 10c. brown and lilac . . . 4·25 42·00
238 15c. blue and brown . . . 26·00 30·00
239 20c. brown and red . . . 20·00 23·00
240 25c. brown and green . . . 18·00 28·00
241 **23** 30c. deep green and green 17·00 23·00
242 35c. mauve and black . . . 19·00 23·00
243 40c. green and red . . . . 21·00 23·00
244 45c. green and deep green 22·00 25·00
245 50c. brown and mauve . . 17·00 25·00
246 55c. red and blue . . . . 24·00 30·00
247 60c. red and blue . . . . 14·00 25·00
248 65c. blue and brown . . . 29·00 30·00
249 70c. brown and mauve . . 13·00 30·00
250 75c. drab and blue . . . . 18·00 30·00
251 80c. green and purple . . . 19·00 25·00
252 85c. brown and green . . . 15·00 28·00
253 90c. pink and red . . . . 16·00 28·00
254 **24** 1f. carmine and red . . . . 16·00 42·00
255 1f.25 green and brown . . 11·00 28·00
256 1f.40 red and blue . . . . 15·00 28·00
257 1f.50 light blue and blue 13·50 28·00
258 1f.60 brown and green . . 16·00 28·00
259 1f.75 orange and blue . . . 20·00 28·00
260 2f. brown and orange . . . 20·00 28·00
261 2f.25 blue and ultramarine 19·00 28·00
262 2f.50 brown . . . . 22·00 32·00
263 3f. brown and mauve . . . 13·50 30·00
264 5f. brown and blue . . . . 13·50 30·00
265 10f. brown & pur on pink 16·00 46·00
266 20f. brown & red on yellow 16·00 55·00

29 Kagu

30 Fairey FC-1 Airliner

1942. Free French Issue. (a) Postage.
267 **29** 5c. brown . . . . 10 3·50
268 10c. blue . . . . 10 2·75
269 25c. green . . . . 10 2·50
270 30c. red . . . . 25 2·75
271 40c. green . . . . 60 2·00
272 80c. purple . . . . 65 1·50
273 1f. mauve . . . . 1·00 65
274 1f.50 red 90 25
275 2f. black . . . . 1·10 35
276 2f.50 blue . . . . 1·60 3·25
277 4f. violet . . . . 1·00 40
278 5f. yellow 85 60
279 10f. brown 85 40
280 20f. green . . . . 1·10 2·30

(b) Air.
281 **30** 1f. orange . . . . 15 4·50
282 1f.50 red . . . . 20 4·25
283 5f. purple . . . . 35 2·75
284 10f. black . . . . 40 3·75
285 25f. blue . . . . 40 1·90
286 50f. green 50 80
287 100f. red . . . . 85 1·50

1944. Mutual Aid and Red Cross Funds. As T **19b** of Oceanic Settlements.
288 5f.+20f. red . . . . 60 5·50

1945. Eboue. As T **20a** of Oceanic Settlements.
289 2f. black . . . . 25 4·25
290 25f. green . . . . 1·00 3·25

1945. Surch.
291 **29** 50c. on 5c. brown 45 35
292 60c. on 5c. brown . . . . 30 4·75
293 70c. on 5c. brown . . . . 40 5·00
294 1f.20 on 5c. brown . . . . 15 3·75
295 2f.40 on 25c. green . . . . 1·50 5·25
296 3f. on 25c. green . . . . . 1·50 1·70
297 4f.50 on 25c. green . . . . 90 4·50
298 15f. on 2f.50 blue . . . . 1·40 70

1946. Air. Victory. As T **20b** of Oceanic Settlements.
299 8f. blue . . . . 15 4·00

1946. Air. From Chad to the Rhine. As T **25a** of Madagascar.
300 **35** 5f. black . . . . 75 3·50
301 – 10f. red . . . . 45 2·50
302 – 15f. blue . . . . 50 5·50
303 – 20f. brown . . . . 80 5·00
304 – 25f. green . . . . 50 5·25
305 – 50f. purple . . . . 55 5·50
DESIGNS: 5f. Legionaries by Lake Chad; 10f. Battle of Koufra; 15f. Tank Battle, Mareth; 20f. Normandy Landings; 25f. Liberation of Paris; 50f. Liberation of Strasbourg.

36 Two Kagus
37 Sud Est Languedoc Airliners over Landscape

1948. (a) Postage.
306 **36** 10c. purple and yellow . . 10 3·25
307 30c. purple and green . . . 10 4·75
308 40c. purple and brown . . 10 3·00
309 – 50c. purple and pink . . . 70 20
310 – 60c. brown and yellow . . 65 2·75
311 – 80c. green and light green 55 3·00
312 – 1f. violet and orange . . . 95 15
313 – 1f.20 brown and blue . . . 65 3·50
314 – 1f.50 blue and yellow . . . 30 80
315 – 2f. brown and green . . . 75 10
316 – 2f.40 red and purple . . . 85 4·75
317 – 3f. violet and orange . . . 1·40 45
318 – 4f. indigo and blue 95 15
319 – 5f. violet and red . . . . . 1·00 20
320 – 6f. brown and yellow . . . 70 40
321 – 10f. blue and orange . . . 90 25
322 – 15f. red and blue . . . . . 1·00 40
323 – 20f. violet and yellow . . . 85 40
324 – 25f. blue and orange . . . 1·20 60

(b) Air.
325 – 50f. purple and orange . . 2·50 3·00
326 **37** 100f. blue and green . . . 6·50 2·50
327 – 200f. brown and yellow . . 4·25 4·25
DESIGNS—As T **36**: HORIZ: 50c. to 80c. Ducos Sanatorium; 1f.50, Porcupine Is; 2f. to 4f. Nickel foundry; 5f. to 10f. "The Towers of Notre Dame" Rocks. VERT: 15f. to 25f. Chief's hut. As T **37**: HORIZ: Sud Est Languedoc airliner over- 50f. St. Vincent Bay; 200f. Noumea.

38 People of Five Races, Bomber and Globe

1949. Air. 75th Anniv of U.P.U.
328 **38** 10f. multicoloured . . . . 1·50 8·50

39 Doctor and Patient
40

1950. Colonial Welfare Fund.
329 **39** 10f.+2f. purple & brown 1·40 11·00

1952. Military Medal Centenary.
330 **40** 2f. red, yellow and green 1·80 5·25

41 Admiral D'Entrecasteaux

1953. French Administration Centenary. Inscr "1853 1953".
331 **41** 1f.50 lake and brown . . . 1·70 1·70
332 – 2f. blue and turquoise . . 1·10 70
333 – 6f. brown, blue and red . . 2·30 1·80
334 – 13f. blue and green . . . . 2·50 1·90
DESIGNS: 2f. Mgr. Douarre and church; 6f. Admiral D'Urville and map; 13f. Admiral Despointes and view.

42 Normandy Landings, 1944

1954. Air. 10th Anniv of Liberation.
335 **42** 3f. blue and deep blue . . 8·50 8·75

43 Towers of Notre-Dame (rocks)

44 Coffee

45 Transporting Nickel

1955.
336 **43** 2f.50c. blue, green and sepia (postage) . . . . . 45 1·60
337 3f. blue, brown and green 1·80 2·75
338 **44** 9f. deep blue and blue . . 60 25
339 **45** 14f. blue and brown (air) 70 75

46 Dumbea Barrage

47 "Xanthostemon"

1956. Economic and Social Development Fund.
340 **46** 3f. green and blue 40 30

1958. Flowers.
341 **47** 4f. multicoloured . . . . . 80 1·10
342 – 15f. red, yellow and green 1·60 95
DESIGN: 15f. Hibiscus.

48 "Human Rights"
49 Zebra Lionfish

1958. 10th Anniv of Declaration of Human Rights.
343 **48** 7f. red and blue . . . . . 50 1·10

1959.
344 **49** 1f. brown and grey 30 20
345 – 2f. blue, purple and green 1·20 1·60
346 – 3f. red, blue and green . . 35 55
347 – 4f. purple, red and green 1·70 2·75
348 – 5f. bistre, blue and green 2·50 2·30
349 – 10f. multicoloured 70 25
350 – 26f. multicoloured . . . . 1·40 4·75
DESIGNS—HORIZ: 2f. Outrigger canoes racing; 3f. Harlequin tuskfish; 5f. Sail Rock, Noumea; 26f. Fluorescent corals. VERT: 4f. Fisherman with spear. 10f. Blue sea lizard and "Spirographe" (coral).

49a The Carved Rock, Bourail

1959. Air.
351 – 15f. green, brown and red 2·30 2·75
352 – 20f. brown and green . . 8·75 5·00
353 – 25f. black, blue and purple . . . . 8·50 3·75
354 – 50f. brown, green and blue . . . . 4·50 3·75
355 – 50f. brown, green and blue . . . . 5·50 4·00
356 – 100f. brown, green & blue 23·00 9·50
357 **49a** 200f. brown, green & blue 9·25 10·00
DESIGNS—HORIZ: 15f. Fisherman with net; 20f. New Caledonia nautilus; 25f. Underwater swimmer shooting bump-headed unicornfish; 50f. (No. 355), Isle of Pines; 100f. Corbeille de Yate. VERT: 50f. (No. 354), Yate barrage.

49b Napoleon III
49c Port-de-France, 1859

1960. Postal Centenary.
358 **15** 4f. red . . . . 25 1·00
359 – 5f. brown and lake . . . 35 1·60
360 – 9f. brown and turquoise 45 2·30
361 – 12f. black and blue . . . 40 2·75
362 **49b** 13f. blue . . . . 85 2·75
363 **49c** 19f. red, green & turquoise . . . . 1·00 1·90
364 – 33f. red, green and blue 1·30 3·25
MS364a 150 × 80 mm. Nos. 358, 362 and 364 . . . . 3·25 19·00
DESIGNS—As Type **49c**: HORIZ: 5f. Girl operating cheque-writing machine; 12f. Telephone receiver and exchange building; 33f. As Type **49c** but without stamps in upper corners. VERT: 9f. Letter-box on tree.

49d Map of Pacific and Palms

1962. 5th South Pacific Conference, Pago-Pago.
365 **49d** 15f. multicoloured . . . . 1·70 2·50

49e Map and Symbols of Meteorology

1962. 3rd Regional Assembly of World Meteorological Association, Noumea.
366 **49e** 50f. multicoloured . . . . 3·75 8·00

50 "Telstar" Satellite and part of Globe

1962. Air. 1st Transatlantic TV Satellite Link.
367 **50** 200f. turquoise, brown & bl . . . . 10·50 15·00

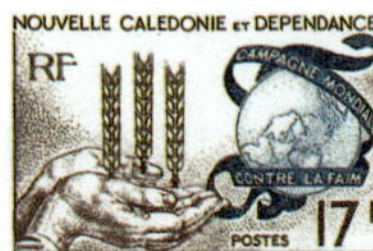

51 Emblem and Globe

1963. Freedom from Hunger.
368 **51** 17f. blue and purple . . . 1·40 3·00

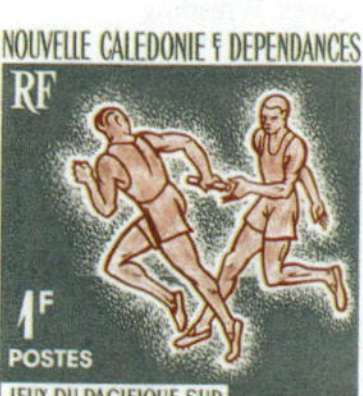

52 Relay-running

53 Centenary Emblem

1963. 1st South Pacific Games, Suva, Fiji.
369 **52** 1f. red and green . . . . . 40 2·30
370 – 7f. brown and blue . . . . 60 3·50
371 – 10f. brown and green . . . 1·20 2·50
372 – 27f. blue and deep purple 2·50 4·50
DESIGNS: 7f. Tennis; 10f. Football; 27f. Throwing the javelin.

1963. Red Cross Centenary.
373 **53** 37f. red, grey and blue . . 4·00 11·50

54 Globe and Scales of Justice

54a "Bikkia fritillarioides"

1963. 15th Anniv of Declaration of Human Rights.
374 **54** 50f. red and blue . . . . . 5·50 14·50

1964. Flowers. Multicoloured.
375 1f. "Freycinettia" . . . . . 40 4·00
376 2f. Type **54a** . . . . 35 1·90
377 3f. "Xanthostemon francii" 85 2·75
378 4f. "Psidiomyrtus locellatus" 1·70 2·00
379 5f. "Callistemon suberosum" 2·30 2·75
380 7f. "Montrouziera sphaeroidea" (horiz) . . . 3·25 3·25
381 10f. "Ixora collina" (horiz) 3·25 3·00
382 17f. "Deplanchea speciosa" 4·75 4·75

54b "Ascidies polycarpa"

54c "Philately"

1964. Corals and Marine Animals from Noumea Aquarium.
383 **54b** 7f. red, brown and blue (postage) . . . . 1·75 2·50
384 – 10f. red and blue . . . . 2·00 2·30
385 – 17f. red, green and blue 4·00 1·10
388 – 13f. bistre, black and orange (air) . . . . . 3·50 3·50
389 – 15f. green, olive and blue 4·75 3·25
390 – 25f. blue and green . . . 6·75 7·75
386 – 27f. multicoloured . . . . 3·50 5·50
387 – 37f. multicoloured . . . . 6·00 8·50
DESIGNS—As T **54b**: VERT: 10f. "Alcyonium catalai" (coral). HORIZ: 17f. "Hymenocera elegans" (crab). 48×28 mm: 27f. Palette surgeonfish; 37f. "Phyllobranchus" (sea slug). 48×27 mm: 13f. Twin-spotted wrasse (young); 15f. Twin-spotted wrasse (subadult); 25f. Twin-spotted wrasse (adult).

1964. "PHILATEC 1964" Int Stamp Exn, Paris.
391 **54c** 40f. brown, green & violet 4·00 9·25

54d Houailou Mine

1964. Air. Nickel Production at Houailou.
392 **54d** 30f. multicoloured . . . . 2·50 6·75

54e Ancient Greek Wrestling

1964. Air. Olympic Games, Tokyo.
393 **54e** 10f. sepia, mauve & green 11·50 21·00

55 Weather Satellite

56 "Syncom" Communications Satellite, Telegraph Poles and Morse Key

1965. Air. World Meteorological Day.
394 **55** 9f. multicoloured . . . . . 4·25 4·25

1965. Air. Centenary of I.T.U.
395 **56** 40f. purple, brown and blue . . . . 6·25 12·00

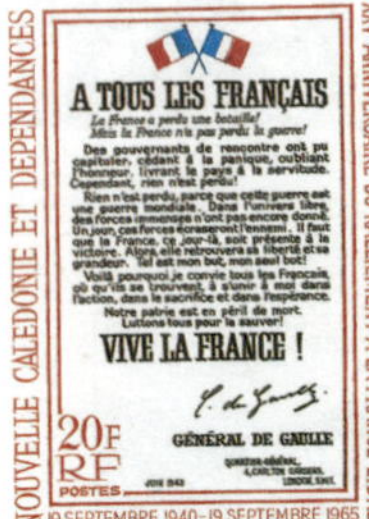

56a De Gaulle's Appeal of 18 June 1940

56b Amedee Lighthouse

1965. 25th Anniv of New Caledonia's Adherence to the Free French.
396 **56a** 20f. black, red and blue 6·00 11·00

1965. Inauguration of Amedee Lighthouse.
397 **56b** 8f. bistre, blue and green 1·80 2·50

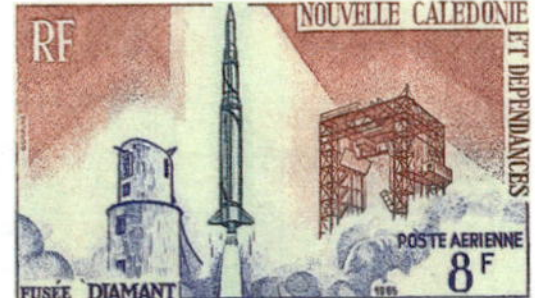

56c Rocket "Diamant"

1966. Air. Launching of 1st French Satellite.
398 **56c** 8f. lake, blue and turquoise . . . . 2·50 4·50
399 – 12f. lake, blue & turquoise 3·00 4·50
DESIGN: 12f. Satellite "A1".

56d Games Emblem

1966. Publicity for 2nd South Pacific Games, Noumea.
400 **56d** 8f. black, red and blue . . 1·00 2·30

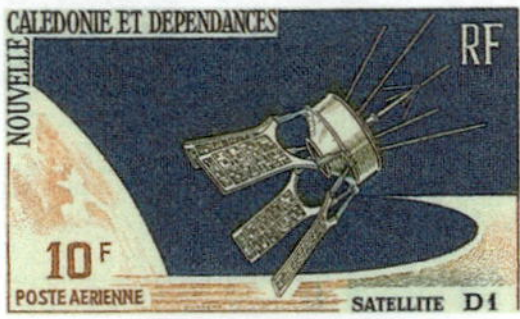

56e Satellite "D1"

1966. Air. Launching of Satellite "D1".
401 **56e** 10f. brown, blue and buff 1·20 3·00

57 Noumea, 1866 (after Lebreton)

1966. Air. Centenary of Renaming of Port-de-France as Noumea.
402 **57** 30f. slate, red and blue . . 3·00 8·25

58 Red-throated Parrot Finch

59 UNESCO Allegory

1966. Birds. Multicoloured.
403 1f. Type **58** (postage) . . . . 2·75 2·75
404 1f. New Caledonian grass warbler . . . . 1·70 1·70
405 2f. New Caledonian whistler 3·00 1·80
406 3f. New Caledonian pigeon ("Notou") . . . . 4·25 2·30
407 3f. White-throated pigeon ("Collier blanc") . . . . . 2·75 2·50
408 4f. Kagu . . . . 3·75 2·00
409 5f. Horned parakeet . . . . 6·25 3·00
410 10f. Red-faced honeyeater . . 9·50 4·50
411 15f. New Caledonian friarbird . . . . 8·25 3·75
412 30f. Sacred kingfisher . . . . 13·50 8·25
413 27f. Horned parakeet (diff) (air) . . . . 5·50 5·50
414 37f. Scarlet honeyeater . . . 8·25 12·50
415 39f. Emerald dove . . . . . 16·00 8·25
416 50f. Cloven-feathered dove 12·00 15·00
417 100f. Whistling kite . . . . . 40·00 22·00
Nos. 413/14 are 26×45½ mm; Nos. 415/17 are 27½×48 mm.

1966. 20th Anniv of UNESCO.
418 **59** 16f. purple, ochre and green . . . . 2·75 2·50

60 High Jumping

1966. South Pacific Games, Noumea.
419 **60** 17f. violet, green and lake 1·90 1·30
420 – 20f. green, purple and lake 3·00 2·75
421 – 40f. green, violet and lake 3·50 6·00
422 – 100f. purple, turq & lake 7·25 13·00
MS423 149×99 mm. Nos. 419/22 22·00 55·00
DESIGNS: 20f. Hurdling; 40f. Running; 100f. Swimming.

61 Lekine Cliffs

1967.
424 **61** 17f. grey, green and blue 1·50 1·20

62 Ocean Racing Yachts

1967. Air. 2nd Whangarei–Noumea Yacht Race.
425 **62** 25f. red, blue and green . . 4·25 5·00

63 Magenta Stadium

1967. Sport Centres. Multicoloured.
426 10f. Type **63** . . . . 2·75 2·50
427 20f. Ouen-Toro swimming pool . . . . 4·00 1·60

64 New Caledonian Scenery

1967. International Tourist Year.
428 **64** 30f. multicoloured . . . . 3·50 4·00

65 19th-century Postman

1967. Stamp Day.
429 **65** 7f. red, green and turquoise 2·30 2·50

66 "Papilio montrouzieri"

1967. Butterflies and Moths.
430 **66** 7f. blue, black and green (postage) . . . . 3·00 2·30
431 – 9f. blue, brown and mauve 3·00 2·00
432 – 13f. violet, purple & brown 4·25 5·25
433 – 15f. yellow, purple and blue . . . . 6·50 4·50
434 – 19f. orange, brown and green (air) . . . . 7·25 3·25
435 – 29f. purple, red and blue 8·50 11·00
436 – 85f. brown, red and yellow 19·00 20·00
BUTTERFLIES—As T **66**: 9f. "Polyura clitarchus"; 13f. Common eggfly (male), and 15f. (female). 48×27 mm: 19f. Orange tiger; 29f. Silver-striped hawk moth; 85f. "Dellas elipsis".

67 Garnierite (mineral), Factory and Jules Garnier

1967. Air. Centenary of Garnierite Industry.
437 **67** 70f. multicoloured . . . . 6·50 13·00

67a Lifou Island

1967. Air.
438 **67a** 200f. multicoloured . . . 11·50 12·50

67b Skier and Snow-crystal

1967. Air. Winter Olympic Games, Grenoble.
439 **67b** 100f. brown, blue & green 10·50 22·00

68 Bouquet, Sun and W.H.O. Emblem

69 Human Rights Emblem

1968. 20th Anniv of W.H.O.
440 **68** 20f. blue, red and violet . . 1·90 2·00

1968. Human Rights Year.
441 **69** 12f. red, green and yellow 1·20 2·50

70 Ferrying Mail Van across Tontouta River

1968. Stamp Day.
442 **70** 9f. brown, blue and green 2·75 2·00

71 Geography Cone

72 Dancers

1968. Sea Shells.
443 – 1f. brn, grey & grn (postage) . . . . 2·30 2·50
444 – 1f. purple and violet . . . 1·70 2·00
445 – 2f. purple, red and blue . . 3·00 2·50
446 – 3f. brown and green . . . 2·00 1·90
447 – 5f. red, brown and violet 3·00 95
448 **71** 10f. brown, grey and blue 2·00 2·00
449 – 10f. yellow, brown and red 3·25 3·25
450 – 10f. black, brown & orange 2·75 2·00
451 – 15f. red, grey and green . . 6·50 4·50

452 – 21f. brown, sepia and green 6·50 4·00
453 – 22f. red, brown & blue (air) . . . . 6·50 3·75
454 – 25f. brown and red . . . . 3·00 3·50
455 – 33f. brown and blue . . . 8·25 6·75
456 – 34f. violet, brown & orange 8·25 3·50
457 – 39f. brown, grey and green 7·25 6·50
458 – 40f. black, brown and red 7·00 5·75
459 – 50f. red, purple and green 4·50 7·25
460 – 60f. brown and green . . . 13·50 13·50
461 – 70f. brown, grey and violet 10·00 12·00
462 – 100f. brown, black and blue . . . . 20·00 26·00

DESIGNS—VERT: 1f. (No. 443) Swan conch ("Strombus epidromis"); 1f. (No. 444) Scorpion conch ("Lambis scorpius"); 3f. Common spider conch; 10f. (No. 450) Variable conch ("Strombus variabilis"). 27 × 48 mm: 22f. Laciniate cone; 25f. Orange spider conch; 34f. Vomer conch; 50f. Chiragra spider conch. 36 × 22 mm: 2f. Snipe's-bill murex; 5f. Troschel's murex; 10f. (No. 449) Sieve cowrie; 15f. "Murex sp."; 21f. Mole cowrie. 48 × 27 mm: 33f. Eyed cowrie; 39f. Lienardi's cone; 40f. Cabrit's cone; 60f. All-red map cowrie; 70f. Scarlet cone; 100f. Adusta murex.

1968. Air.
463 **72** 60f. red, blue and green . . 6·50 12·00

73 Rally Car

1968. 2nd New Caledonian Motor Safari.
464 **73** 25f. blue, red and green . . 3·00 3·50

74 Caudron C-60 "Aiglon" and Route Map

1969. Air. Stamp Day. 30th Anniv of 1st Noumea–Paris Flight by Martinet and Klein.
465 **74** 29f. red, blue and violet . . 3·50 2·75

75 Concorde in Flight

1969. Air. 1st Flight of Concorde.
466 **75** 100f. green and light green 16·00 32·00

76 Cattle-dip

1969. Cattle-breeding in New Caledonia.
467 **76** 9f. brown, green and blue (postage) . . . . 2·30 2·00
468 – 25f. violet, brown and green . . . . 3·25 3·75
469 – 50f. purple, red & grn (air) 5·75 5·50

DESIGNS: 25f. Branding. LARGER 48 × 27 mm; 50f. Stockman with herd.

77 Judo

1969. 3rd South Pacific Games, Port Moresby, Papua New Guinea.
470 **77** 19f. purple, bl & red (post) 2·00 1·50
471 – 20f. black, red and green 2·75 2·75
472 – 30f. black and blue (air) . . 4·75 5·75
473 – 39f. brown, green and black . . . . 7·50 7·50

DESIGNS—HORIZ: 20f. Boxing; 30f. Diving (38 × 27 mm). VERT: 39f. Putting the shot (27 × 48 mm).

1969. Air. Birth Bicentenary of Napoleon Bonaparte. As T **114b** of Mauritania. Multicoloured.
474 40f. "Napoleon in Coronation Robes" (Gerard) (vert) . . . . . . 17·00 18·00

78 Douglas DC-4 over Outrigger Canoe

1969. Air. 20th Anniv of Regular Noumea–Paris Air Service.
475 **78** 50f. green, brown and blue 13·00 8·25

79 I.L.O. Building Geneva

1969. 50th Anniv of I.L.O.
476 **79** 12f. brown, violet & salmon . . . . 2·30 3·75

80 "French Wings around the World"

1970. Air. 10th Anniv of French "Around the World" Air Service.
477 **80** 200f. brown, blue and violet . . . . 26·00 10·50

81 New U.P.U. Building, Berne

1970. Inauguration of New U.P.U. Headquarters Building, Berne.
478 **81** 12f. red, grey and brown 3·25 2·75

82 Packet Steamer "Natal", 1883

1970. Stamp Day.
479 **82** 9f. black, green and blue 5·25 2·75

83 Cyclists on Map

1970. Air. 4th "Tour de Nouvelle Caledonie" Cycle Race.
480 **83** 40f. brown, blue & lt blue 8·25 6·75

84 Mt. Fuji and Japanese "Hikari" Express Train

1970. Air. "EXPO 70" World Fair, Osaka, Japan. Multicoloured.
481 20f. Type **84** . . . . 5·00 4·00
482 45f. "EXPO" emblem, map and Buddha . . . . 6·50 3·00

85 Racing Yachts

1971. Air. One Ton Cup Yacht Race Auckland, New Zealand.
483 **85** 20f. green, red and black 5·00 2·30

86 Steam Mail Train, Dumbea

1971. Stamp Day.
484 **86** 10f. black, green and red 4·75 4·00

87 Ocean Racing Yachts

1971. 3rd Whangarei–Noumea Ocean Yacht Race.
485 **87** 16f. turquoise, green and blue . . . . 6·25 4·25

88 Lieut.-Col. Broche and Theatre Map

1971. 30th Anniv of French Pacific Battalion's Participation in Second World War Mediterranean Campaign.
486 **88** 60f. multicoloured . . . . 10·00 7·00

89 Early Tape Machine  **90** Weightlifting

1971. World Telecommunications Day.
487 **89** 19f. orange, purple and red 3·25 4·25

1971. 4th South Pacific Games, Papeete, French Polynesia.
488 **90** 11f. brown & red (postage) 3·00 3·00
489 – 23f. violet, red and blue . . 4·25 85
490 – 25f. green and red (air) . . 4·00 4·00
491 – 100f. blue, green and red 5·50 5·75

DESIGNS—VERT: 23f. Basketball. HORIZ: 48 × 27 mm: 25f. Pole-vaulting; 100f. Archery.

91 Port de Plaisance, Noumea

1971. Air.
492 **91** 200f. multicoloured . . . . 17·00 12·50

92 De Gaulle as President of French Republic, 1970

93 Publicity Leaflet showing De Havilland Gipsy Moth "Golden Eagle"

1971. 1st Death Anniv of General De Gaulle.
493 **92** 34f. black and purple . . . 6·50 3·75
494 – 100f. black and purple . . 10·50 12·50

DESIGN: 100f. De Gaulle in uniform, 1940.

1971. Air. 40th Anniv of 1st New Caledonia to Australia Flight.
495 **93** 90f. brown, blue and orange . . . . 10·00 11·50

94 Downhill Skiing

1972. Air. Winter Olympic Games, Sapporo, Japan.
496 **94** 50f. green, red and blue . . 9·75 6·50

95 St. Mark's Basilica, Venice

1972. Air. UNESCO "Save Venice" Campaign.
497 **95** 20f. brown, green and blue 5·00 4·75

96 Commission Headquarters, Noumea

1972. Air. 25th Anniv of South Pacific Commission.
498 **96** 18f. multicoloured . . . . 2·75 4·25

97 Couzinet 33 "Le Biarritz" and Noumea Monument

1972. Air. 40th Anniv of 1st Paris–Noumea Flight.
499 **97** 110f. black, purple & green 2·75 2·50

98 Pacific Island Dwelling 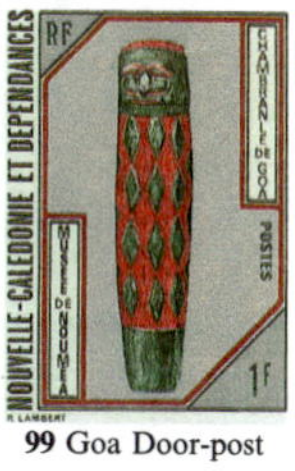 **99** Goa Door-post

1972. Air. South Pacific Arts Festival, Fiji.
500 **98** 24f. brown, blue and orange . . . . 5·00 2·00

1972. Exhibits from Noumea Museum.
501 **99** 1f. red, green & grey (post) 1·90 1·80
502 – 2f. black, green & deep grn 1·60 1·80
503 – 5f. multicoloured . . . . . 2·50 2·30
504 – 12f. multicoloured . . . . 4·00 2·75
505 – 16f. multicoloured (air) . . 3·75 2·75
506 – 40f. multicoloured . . . . 6·00 3·00

DESIGNS: 2f. Carved wooden pillow; 5f. Monstrance; 12f. Tchamba mask; 16f. Ornamental arrowheads; 40f. Portico, chief's house.

100 Hurdling over "H" of "MUNICH"

1972. Air. Olympic Games, Munich.
507 **100** 72f. violet, purple and blue . . . . 7·50 7·25

101 New Head Post Office Building, Noumea

1972. Air.

508 **101** 23f. brown, blue and green . . . . 4·25 2·50

102 J.C.I. Emblem

1972. 10th Anniv of New Caledonia Junior Chamber of Commerce.

509 **102** 12f. multicoloured . . . . 2·75 2·50

103 Forest Scene

1973. Air. Landscapes of the East Coast. Multicoloured.

510 11f. Type **103** . . . . 3·50 2·30
511 18f. Beach and palms (vert) 4·50 4·25
512 21f. Waterfall and inlet (vert) 6·50 5·00
See also Nos. 534/6.

104 Moliere and Characters

1973. Air. 300th Death Anniv of Moliere (playwright).

513 **104** 50f. multicoloured . . . . 4·50 4·50

105 Tchamba Mask

1973.

514 **105** 12f. purple (postage) . . . 5·25 3·75
515 – 23f. blue (air) . . . . . . 13·00 8·75
DESIGN: 23f. Concorde in flight.

106 Liner "El Kantara" in Panama Canal

1973. 50th Anniv of Marseilles–Noumea Shipping Service via Panama Canal.

516 **106** 60f. black, brown & green 12·00 7·75

107 Globe and Allegory of Weather

1973. Air. Centenary of World Meteorological Organization.

517 **107** 80f. multicoloured . . . . 8·25 5·50

108 DC-10 in Flight

1973. Air. Inauguration of Noumea–Paris DC-10 Air Service.

518 **108** 100f. green, brown & blue 16·00 7·75

109 Common Egg Cowrie

1973. Marine Fauna from Noumea Aquarium. Multicoloured.

519 8f. Black-wedged butterflyfish (daylight) . . . . 2·75 2·30
520 14f. Black-wedged butterflyfish (nocturnal) . . 3·50 2·75
521 3f. Type **109** (air) . . . . . 2·00 2·00
522 32f. Orange-spotted surgeonfish (adult and young) . . . . 7·50 3·50
523 32f. Green-lined paper bubble ("Hydatina") . . . . . . 3·50 4·25
524 37f. Pacific partridge tun ("Dolium perdix") . . . . 5·75 3·25

111 Office Emblem

1973. 10th Anniv of Central Schools Co-operation Office.

532 **111** 20f. blue, yellow and green . . . . 2·75 2·50

112 New Caledonia Mail Coach, 1880

1973. Air. Stamp Day.

533 **112** 15f. multicoloured . . . . 4·25 2·30

1974. Air. Landscapes of the West Coast. As T **103**. Multicoloured.

534 8f. Beach and palms (vert) . . 2·50 3·75
535 22f. Trees and mountain . . 3·25 3·50
536 26f. Trees growing in sea . . 2·75 2·75

113 Centre Building

1974. Air. Opening of Scientific Studies Centre, Anse-Vata, Noumea.

537 **113** 50f. multicoloured . . . . 5·00 4·50

114 "Bird" embracing Flora

1974. Nature Conservation.

538 **114** 7f. multicoloured . . . . 1·70 1·90

115 18th-century French Sailor

1974. Air. Discovery and Reconnaissance of New Caledonia and Loyalty Islands.

539 – 20f. violet, red and blue 3·75 4·25
540 – 25f. green, brown and red 3·25 4·50
541 **115** 28f. brown, blue and green . . . . 3·25 4·00
542 – 30f. blue, brown and red 4·75 4·75
543 – 36f. red, brown and blue 6·25 6·25
DESIGNS—HORIZ: 20f. Captain Cook, H.M.S. "Endeavour" and map of Grand Terre island; 25f. La Perouse, "L'Astrolabe" and map of Grand Terre island (reconnaissance of west coast); 30f. Entrecasteaux, ship and map of Grand Terre island (reconnaissance of west coast); 36f. Dumont d'Urville, "L'Astrolabe" and map of Loyalty Islands.

116 "Telecommunications"

1974. Air. Centenary of U.P.U.

544 **116** 95f. orange, purple & grey 5·00 7·25

117 "Art"

1974. Air. "Arphila 75" International Stamp Exhibition, Paris (1975) (1st issue).

545 **117** 80f. multicoloured . . . . 7·00 4·00
See also No. 554.

118 Hotel Chateau-Royal

1974. Air. Inauguration of Hotel Chateau Royal, Noumea.

546 **118** 22f. multicoloured . . . . 3·25 2·50

118a Animal Skull, Burnt Tree and Flaming Landscape

1975. "Stop Bush Fires".

547 **118a** 20f. multicoloured . . . 1·90 2·30

119 "Cricket"

1975. Air. Tourism. Multicoloured.

548 3f. Type **119** . . . . 3·25 2·50
549 25f. "Bougna" ceremony . . 3·50 3·75
550 31f. "Pilou" native dance . . 4·75 3·00

120 "Calanthe veratrifolia" **121** Global "Flower"

1975. New Caledonian Orchids. Multicoloured.

551 8f. Type **120** (postage) . . . 3·00 2·00
552 11f. "Lyperanthus gigas" . . 2·75 2·30
553 42f. "Eriaxis rigida" (air) . . 7·50 4·00

1975. Air. "Arphila 75" International Stamp Exhibition, Paris (2nd issue).

554 **121** 105f. purple, green & blue 8·75 5·00

122 Throwing the Discus

1975. Air. 5th South Pacific Games, Guam.

555 24f. Type **122** . . . . 4·75 4·25
556 50f. Volleyball . . . . 5·75 3·00

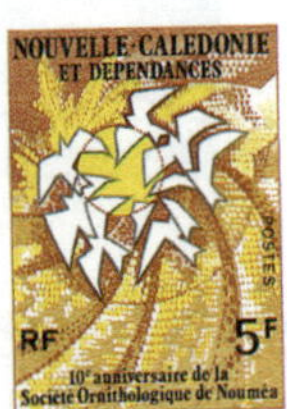

123 Festival Emblem **124** Birds in Flight

1975. "Melanesia 2000" Festival, Noumea.

557 **123** 12f. multicoloured . . . . 2·30 2·00

1975. 10th Anniv of Noumea Ornithological Society.

558 **124** 5f. multicoloured . . . . 1·80 1·90

125 Pres. Pompidou **127** Brown Booby

126 Concordes

1975. Pompidou Commemoration.

559 **125** 26f. grey and green . . . 3·00 2·75

1976. Air. First Commercial Flight of Concorde.

560 **126** 147f. blue and red . . . . 19·00 12·50

1976. Ocean Birds. Multicoloured.

561 1f. Type **127** . . . . 1·30 2·00
562 2f. Blue-faced booby . . . . 1·60 1·90
563 8f. Red-footed booby (vert) 3·50 2·50

128 Festival Emblem

1976. South Pacific Festival of Arts, Rotorua, New Zealand.
564 **128** 27f. multicoloured . . . . 3·50 4·00

129 Lion and Lions' Emblem

130 Early and Modern Telephones

1976. 15th Anniv of Lions Club, Noumea.
565 **129** 49f. multicoloured . . . . 5·00 6·00

1976. Air. Telephone Centenary.
566 **130** 36f. multicoloured . . . . 4·25 4·50

131 Capture of Penbosct

1976. Air. Bicent of American Revolution.
567 **131** 24f. purple and brown . . 3·50 3·00

132 Bandstand

1976. "Aspects of Old Noumea". Multicoloured.
568 25f. Type **132** . . . . 3·00 2·50
569 30f. Monumental fountain (vert) . . . . 3·75 2·75

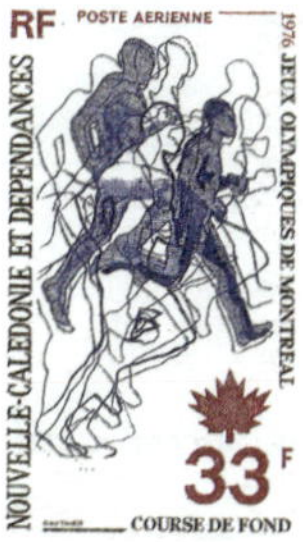

133 Athletes

1976. Air. Olympic Games, Montreal.
570 **133** 33f. violet, red and purple 4·25 3·00

134 "Chick" with Magnifier

1976. Air. "Philately in Schools", Stamp Exhibition, Noumea.
571 **134** 42f. multicoloured . . . . 5·25 4·75

135 Dead Bird and Trees

1976. Nature Protection.
572 **135** 20f. multicoloured . . . . 2·30 2·30

136 South Pacific Heads

1976. 16th South Pacific Commission Conference.
573 **136** 20f. multicoloured . . . . 3·00 2·50

137 Old Town Hall, Noumea

1976. Air. Old and New Town Halls, Noumea. Mult.
574 75f. Type **137** . . . . 7·50 4·50
575 125f. New Town Hall . . . . 11·00 5·00

138 Water Carnival

1977. Air. Summer Festival, Noumea.
576 **138** 11f. multicoloured . . . . 3·00 2·30

139 "Pseudophyllanax imperialis" (cricket)

1977. Insects.
577 **139** 26f. emerald, green & brn 4·00 4·50
578 – 31f. brown, sepia & green 4·50 4·00
DESIGN: 31f. "Agrianome fairmairei" (long-horn beetle).

140 Miniature Roadway

1977. Air. Road Safety.
579 **140** 50f. multicoloured . . . . 4·75 3·75

141 Earth Station

1977. Earth Satellite Station, Noumea.
580 **141** 29f. multicoloured . . . . 2·75 2·75

142 "Phajus daenikeri"

1977. Orchids. Multicoloured.
581 22f. Type **142** . . . . 3·00 4·00
582 44f. "Dendrobium finetianum" . . . . 4·75 5·00

143 Mask and Palms

1977. La Perouse School Philatelic Exn.
583 **143** 35f. multicoloured . . . . 2·75 2·75

144 Trees

1977. Nature Protection.
584 **144** 20f. multicoloured . . . . 1·80 2·30

145 Palm Tree and Emblem

1977. French Junior Chambers of Commerce Congress.
585 **145** 200f. multicoloured . . . 10·00 9·00

146 Young Bird

1977. Great Frigate Birds. Multicoloured.
586 16f. Type **146** (postage) . . . 2·30 3·00
587 42f. Adult male bird (horiz) (air) . . . . 6·50 5·50

147 Magenta Airport and Map of Internal Air Network

1977. Air. Airports. Multicoloured.
588 24f. Type **147** . . . . 4·00 4·00
589 57f. La Tontout International Airport, Noumea . . . . 6·75 5·50

1977. Air. 1st Commercial Flight of Concorde, Paris–New York. Optd **22.11.77 PARIS NEW-YORK**.
590 **126** 147f. blue and red . . . . 29·00 27·00

149 Horse and Foal

1977. 10th Anniv of S.E.C.C. (Horse-breeding Society).
591 **149** 5f. brown, green and blue 3·00 3·25

150 "Moselle Bay" (H. Didonna)

1977. Air. Views of Old Noumea (1st series).
592 **150** 41f. multicoloured . . . . 7·25 5·50
593 – 42f. purple and brown . . 5·25 4·00
DESIGN—49 × 27 mm: 42f. "Settlers Valley" (J. Kreber).

151 Black-naped Tern

1978. Ocean Birds. Multicoloured.
594 22f. Type **151** . . . . 2·50 4·00
595 40f. Sooty tern . . . . 4·50 3·25

152 "Araucaria montana"

153 "Halityle regularis"

1978. Flora. Multicoloured.
596 16f. Type **152** (postage) . . . 2·00 2·75
597 42f. "Amyema scandens" (horiz) (air) . . . . 3·75 2·50

1978. Noumea Aquarium.
598 **153** 10f. multicoloured . . . . 2·30 1·80

154 Turtle

1978. Protection of the Turtle.
599 **154** 30f. multicoloured . . . . 1·90 4·00

155 New Caledonian Flying Fox

1978. Nature Protection.
600 **155** 20f. multicoloured . . . . 3·00 2·30

156 "Underwater Carnival"

1978. Air. Aubusson Tapestry.
601 **156** 105f. multicoloured . . . 6·75 6·50

157 Pastor Maurice Leenhardt

1978. Birth Centenary of Pastor Maurice Leenhardt.
602 **157** 37f. sepia, green & orange 4·50 3·50

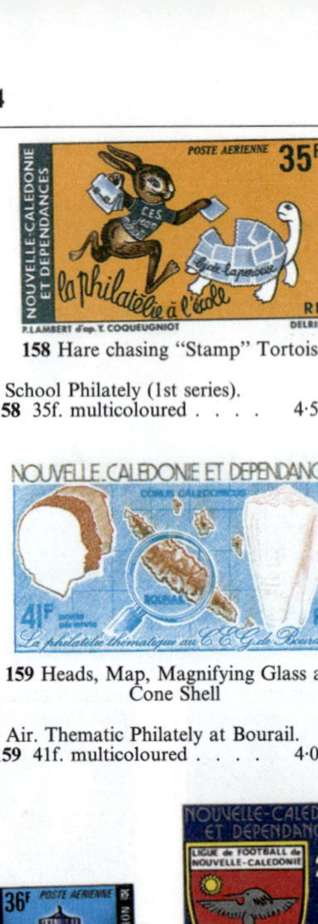

158 Hare chasing "Stamp" Tortoise

1978. School Philately (1st series).
603 **158** 35f. multicoloured . . . . 4·50 3·75

159 Heads, Map, Magnifying Glass and Cone Shell

1978. Air. Thematic Philately at Bourail.
604 **159** 41f. multicoloured . . . . 4·00 4·25

160 Candles

161 Footballer and League Badge

1978. 3rd New Caledonian Old People's Day.
605 **160** 36f. multicoloured . . . . 2·50 3·50

1978. 50th Anniv of New Caledonian Football League.
606 **161** 26f. multicoloured . . . . 2·75 3·00

162 "Fauberg Blanchot" (after Lacouture)

1978. Air. Views of Old Noumea.
607 **162** 24f. multicoloured . . . . 3·00 4·00

163 Map of Lifou, Solar Energy Panel and Transmitter Mast

1978. Telecommunications through Solar Energy.
608 **163** 33f. multicoloured . . . . 4·25 4·25

164 Petroglyph, Mere Region

165 Ouvea Island and Outrigger Canoe

1979. Archaeological Sites.
609 **164** 10f. red . . . . 2·50 1·00

1979. Islands. Multicoloured.
610 11f. Type **165** . . . . 2·50 3·50
611 31f. Mare Island and ornaments (horiz) . . . . 2·30 1·10
See also Nos. 629 and 649.

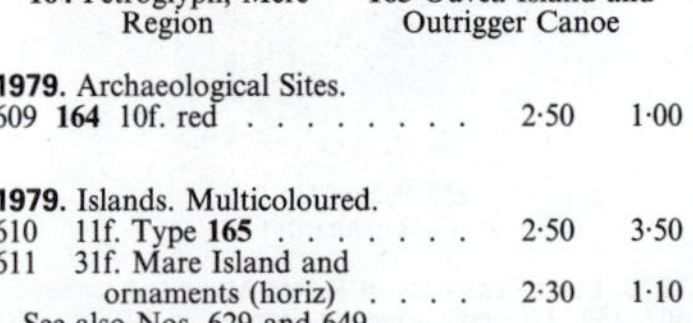

166 Satellite Orbit of Earth

167 19th-century Barque and Modern Container Ship

1979. Air. 1st World Survey of Global Atmosphere.
612 **166** 53f. multicoloured . . . . 3·75 4·50

1979. Air. Centenary of Chamber of Commerce and Industry.
613 **167** 49f. mauve, blue & brown 4·50 4·00

168 Child's Drawing

1979. Air. International Year of the Child.
614 **168** 35f. multicoloured . . . . 3·75 4·00

169 House at Artillery Point

1979. Views of Old Noumea.
615 **169** 20f. multicoloured . . . . 2·30 3·25

170 Skipjack Tuna

1979. Air. Sea Fishes (1st series). Multicoloured.
616 29f. Type **170** . . . . 3·50 3·50
617 30f. Black marlin . . . . 3·50 3·25
See also Nos. 632/3 and 647/8.

171 L. Tardy de Montravel (founder) and View of Port-de-France (Noumea)

1979. Air. 125th Anniv of Noumea.
618 **171** 75f. multicoloured . . . . 5·75 4·00

172 The Eel Queen (Kanaka legend)

173 Auguste Escoffier

1979. Air. Nature Protection.
619 **172** 42f. multicoloured . . . . 3·75 3·25

1979. Auguste Escoffier Hotel School.
620 **173** 24f. brown, green and turquoise . . . . 2·50 4·00

174 Games Emblem and Catamarans

1979. 6th South Pacific Games, Fiji.
621 **174** 16f. multicoloured . . . . 2·50 1·90

175 Children of Different Races, Map and Postmark

1979. Air. Youth Philately.
622 **175** 27f. multicoloured . . . . 2·50 2·75

176 Aerial View of Centre

1979. Air. Overseas Scientific and Technical Research Office (O.R.S.T.O.M.) Centre, Noumea.
623 **176** 25f. multicoloured . . . . 3·75 3·00

177 "Agathis ovata"

1979. Trees. Multicoloured.
624 5f. Type **177** . . . . 2·00 1·90
625 34f. "Cyathea intermedia" . . 2·75 2·30

178 Rodeo Riding

1979. Pouembout Rodeo.
626 **178** 12f. multicoloured . . . . 3·00 1·70

179 Hill, 1860 10c. Stamp and Post Office

1979. Air. Death Centenary of Sir Rowland Hill.
627 **179** 150f. black, brown & orge 9·75 7·25

180 "Bantamia merleti"

1980. Noumea Aquarium. Fluorescent Corals (1st issue).
628 **180** 23f. multicoloured . . . . 2·50 2·50
See also No. 646.

1980. Islands. As T **165**. Multicoloured.
629 23f. Map of Ile des Pins and ornaments (horiz) . . . . 2·30 1·90

181 Outrigger Canoe

1980. Air.
630 **181** 45f. blue, turq & indigo 3·25 2·30

182 Globe, Rotary Emblem, Map and Carving

1980. Air. 75th Anniv of Rotary International.
631 **182** 100f. multicoloured . . . 5·50 4·00

1980. Air. Sea Fishes (2nd series). As T **170**. Multicoloured.
632 34f. Angler holding dolphin (fish) . . . . 2·50 3·50
633 39f. Fishermen with sailfish (vert) . . . . 2·75 2·75

183 "Hibbertia virotii"

184 High Jumper, Magnifying Glass, Albums and Plimsoll

1980. Flowers. Multicoloured.
634 11f. Type **183** . . . . 1·60 85
635 12f. "Grevillea meisneri" . . 1·90 1·80

1980. School Philately.
636 **184** 30f. multicoloured . . . . 3·25 2·30

185 Scintex Super Emeraude Airplane and Map

1980. Air. Coral Sea Air Rally.
637 **185** 31f. blue, green and brown . . . . 3·00 3·50

186 Sailing Canoe

1980. Air. South Pacific Arts Festival, Port Moresby.
638 **186** 27f. multicoloured . . . . 2·50 3·25

187 Road Signs as Road-users

1980. Road Safety.
639 **187** 15f. multicoloured . . . . 1·60 1·90

188 "Parribacus caledonicus"

1980. Noumea Aquarium. Marine Animals (1st series). Multicoloured.
640 5f. Type **188** . . . . 1·00 1·80
641 8f. "Panulirus versicolor" . . 1·20 1·70
See also Nos. 668/9.

189 Kiwanis Emblem

1980. Air. 10th Anniv of Noumea Kiwanis Club.
642 **189** 50f. multicoloured . . . . 3·50 4·00

190 Sun, Tree and Solar Panel

1980. Nature Protection. Solar Energy.
643 **190** 23f. multicoloured . . . . 1·90 3·25

191 Old House, Poulou

1980. Air. Views of Old Noumea (4th series).
644 **191** 33f. multicoloured . . . . 2·00 2·75

192 Charles de Gaulle **193** Manta Ray

1980. Air. 10th Death Anniv of Charles de Gaulle (French statesman).
645 **192** 120f. green, olive and blue 6·00 5·00

1981. Air. Noumea Aquarium. Fluorescent Corals (2nd series). As T **180**. Multicoloured.
646 60f. "Trachyphyllia geoffroyi" . . . . 3·25 2·75

1981. Sea Fishes (3rd series). Multicoloured.
647 23f. Type **193** . . . . 2·00 3·00
648 25f. Grey reef shark . . . . 1·80 3·00

1981. Islands. As T **165**. Multicoloured.
649 26f. Map of Belep Archipelago and diver (horiz) . . . . 3·25 3·00

194 "Xeronema moorei"

1981. Air. Flowers. Multicoloured.
650 38f. Type **194** . . . . 2·30 1·60
651 51f. "Geissois pruinosa" . . 2·75 1·90

195 Yuri Gagarin and "Vostok 1"

1981. Air. 20th Anniv of First Men in Space. Multicoloured.
652 64f. Type **195** . . . . 3·25 4·50
653 155f. Alan Shepard and "Freedom 7" . . . . 6·50 5·00
MS654 149 × 119 mm. As Nos. 652/3 but colours changed (sold at 225f.) 21·00 23·00

196 Liberation Cross, "Zealandia" (troopship) and Badge

1981. Air. 40th Anniv of Departure of Pacific Battalion for Middle East.
655 **196** 29f. multicoloured . . . . 3·50 3·50

197 Rossini's Volute **198** Sail Corvette "Constantine"

1981. Shells. Multicoloured.
656 1f. Type **197** . . . . 1·00 1·60
657 2f. Clouded cone . . . . . . 80 1·70
658 13f. Stolid cowrie (horiz) . . 1·70 2·75

1981. Ships (1st series).
659 **198** 10f. blue, brown and red 2·00 2·00
660 – 25f. blue, brown and red 2·75 3·25
DESIGN: 25f. Paddle-gunboat "Le Phoque", 1853.
See also Nos. 680/1 and 725/6.

199 "Echinometra mathaei"

1981. Air. Water Plants. Multicoloured.
661 38f. Type **199** . . . . 1·60 3·25
662 51f. "Prionocidaris verticillata" . . . . 1·70 3·25

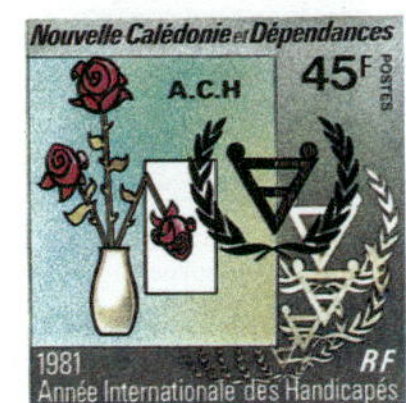
200 Broken-stemmed Rose and I.Y.D.P. Emblems

1981. International Year of Disabled Persons.
663 **200** 45f. multicoloured . . . . 2·75 2·75

201 25c. Surcharged Stamp of 1881 **202** Latin Quarter

1981. Air. Stamp Day.
664 **201** 41f. multicoloured . . . . 2·30 3·25

1981. Air. Views of Old Noumea.
665 **202** 43f. multicoloured . . . . 3·25 3·25

203 Trees and Unicornfish **204** Victor Roffey and "Golden Eagle"

1981. Nature Protection.
666 **203** 28f. blue, green and brown . . . . 1·30 3·25

1981. Air. 50th Anniv of First New Caledonia–Australia Airmail Flight.
667 **204** 37f. black, violet and blue 3·00 3·25

1982. Noumea Aquarium. Marine Animals (2nd series). As T **188**. Multicoloured.
668 13f. "Calappa calappa" . . . 80 3·00
669 25f. "Etisus splendidus" . . . 1·00 1·50

205 "La Rousette"

1982. Air. New Caledonian Aircraft (1st series).
670 **205** 38f. brown, red and green 3·00 3·00
671 – 51f. brown, orange & grn 3·00 3·25
DESIGN: 51f. "Le Cagou".
See also Nos. 712/13.

206 Chalcantite, Ouegoa

1982. Rocks and Minerals (1st series). Multicoloured.
672 15f. Type **206** . . . . 1·20 2·75
673 30f. Anorthosite, Blue River 1·60 3·25
See also Nos. 688/9.

207 De Verneilh, Deve and Munch (air crew), Couzinet 33 "Le Biarritz" and Route Map

1982. Air. 50th Anniv of First Flight from Paris to Noumea.
674 **207** 250f. mauve, blue and black . . . . 11·50 8·25

208 Scout and Guide Badges and Map

1982. Air. 50th Anniv of New Caledonian Scout Movement.
675 **208** 40f. multicoloured . . . . 2·00 2·50

209 "The Rat and the Octopus" (Canaque legend)

1982. "Philexfrance 82" International Stamp Exhibition, Paris.
676 **209** 150f. blue, mauve and deep blue . . . . . . 7·00 6·75

210 Footballer, Mascot and Badge

1982. Air. World Cup Football Championship, Spain.
677 **210** 74f. multicoloured . . . . 3·00 3·25

211 Savanna Trees at Niaoulis **212** Islanders, Map and Kagu

1982. Flora. Multicoloured.
678 20f. Type **211** . . . . 1·70 3·00
679 29f. "Melaleuca quinquenervia" (horiz) . . 2·00 2·75

1982. Ships (2nd series). As T **198**.
680 44f. blue, purple and brown 3·25 2·30
681 59f. blue, light brown and brown . . . . 3·75 3·25
DESIGNS: 44f. Naval transport barque "Le Cher"; 59f. Sloop "Kersaint", 1902.

1982. Air. Overseas Week.
682 **212** 100f. brown, green & blue 5·00 3·00

213 Ateou Tribal House **214** Grey's Fruit Dove

1982. Traditional Houses.
683 **213** 52f. multicoloured . . . . 2·30 3·75

1982. Birds. Multicoloured.
684 32f. Type **214** . . . . 2·75 3·00
685 35f. Rainbow lory . . . . . 2·75 3·50

215 Canoe

1982. Central Education Co-operation Office.
686 **215** 48f. multicoloured . . . . 2·30 3·25

216 Bernheim and Library

1982. Bernheim Library, Noumea.
687 **216** 36f. brown, purple & blk 1·80 2·50

1983. Air. Rocks and Minerals (2nd series). As T **206**. Multicoloured.
688 44f. Paya gypsum (vert) . . . 2·30 3·50
689 59f. Kone silica (vert) . . . . 2·75 3·50

217 "Dendrobium oppositifolium"

1983. Orchids. Multicoloured.
690 10f. Type **217** . . . . 1·10 1·70
691 15f. "Dendrobium munificum" . . . . 1·20 1·60
692 29f. "Dendrobium fractiflexum" . . . . . . 1·80 2·00

218 W.C.Y. Emblem, Map of New Caledonia and Globe

1983. Air. World Communications Year.
693 **218** 170f. multicoloured . . . 6·25 5·25

219 "Crinum asiaticum"

1983. Flowers. Multicoloured.
694 1f. Type **219** 45 70
695 2f. "Xanthostemon aurantiacum" . . . . . . 45 1·20
696 4f. "Metrosideros demonstrans" (vert) . . . 45 2·00

220 Wall Telephone and Noumea Post Office, 1890

1983. 25th Anniv of Post and Telecommunications Office. Multicoloured.
697 30f. Type **220** . . . . 1·90 2·30
698 40f. Telephone and Noumea Post Office, 1936 . . . . . 2·00 2·75
699 50f. Push-button telephone and Noumea Post Office, 1972 . . . . 2·50 3·00
MS700 114 × 94 mm. As Nos. 697/9 but colours changed . . . . . 10·00 20·00

221 "Laticaudata laticaudata"

224 Volleyball

223 Bangkok Temples

1983. Noumea Aquarium. Sea Snakes. Multicoloured.
701 31f. Type **221** . . . . 2·50 1·50
702 33f. "Laticauda colubrina" 2·75 2·75

1983. Air. New Caledonian Aircraft (2nd series). As T **205**. Each red, mauve & brown.
712 46f. Mignet HM14 "Pou du Ciel" . . . . 3·75 3·25
713 61f. Caudron C-600 "Aiglon" 4·00 3·50

1983. Air. "Bangkok 1983" International Stamp Exhibition.
714 **223** 47f. multicoloured . . . . 2·30 3·50

1983. 7th South Pacific Games, Western Samoa.
715 **224** 16f. purple, blue and red 1·70 3·00

225 Oueholle

1983. Air.
716 **225** 76f. multicoloured . . . . 2·75 3·25

226 Desert and Water Drop showing Fertile Land

227 Barn Owl

1983. Water Resources.
717 **226** 56f. multicoloured . . . . 2·50 3·00

1983. Birds of Prey. Multicoloured.
718 34f. Type **227** . . . . 3·00 3·50
719 37f. Osprey . . . . 3·00 3·75

228 "Young Man on Beach" (R. Mascart)

229 "Conus chenui"

1983. Air. Paintings. Multicoloured.
720 100f. Type **228** . . . . . . 3·75 4·50
721 350f. "Man with Guitar" (P. Nielly) . . . . 10·00 7·75

1984. Sea Shells (1st series). Multicoloured.
722 5f. Type **229** . . . . 1·70 1·80
723 15f. Molucca cone . . . . . 1·80 2·50
724 20f. "Conus optimus" . . . 2·30 3·00
See also Nos. 761/2 and 810/11.

230 "St. Joseph" (freighter)

1984. Ships (3rd series). Each black, red and blue.
725 18f. Type **230** . . . . 2·50 3·00
726 31f. "Saint Antoine" (freighter) . . . . 2·75 3·00

231 Yellow-tailed Anemonefish

1984. Air. Noumea Aquarium. Fishes. Multicoloured.
727 46f. Type **231** . . . . 2·30 2·50
728 61f. Bicoloured angelfish . . 3·00 4·00

232 Arms of Noumea

233 "Araucaria columnaris"

1984.
729 **232** 35f. multicoloured . . . . 2·75 3·00

1984. Air. Trees. Multicoloured.
730 51f. Type **233** . . . . 3·75 2·30
731 67f. "Pritchardiopsis jeanneneyi" . . . . 4·00 3·25

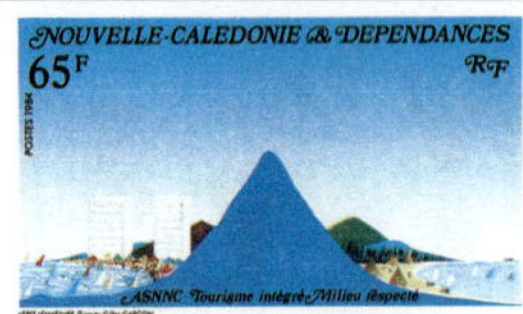

234 Tourist Centres

1984. Nature Protection.
732 **234** 65f. multicoloured . . . . 2·75 3·25

235 Swimming

1984. Air. Olympic Games, Los Angeles. Multicoloured.
733 50f. Type **235** . . . . 2·50 3·75
734 83f. Windsurfing . . . . . . 3·25 4·50
735 200f. Marathon . . . . . . 7·25 9·25

236 "Diplocaulobium ou-hinnae"

1984. Orchids. Multicoloured.
736 16f. Type **236** . . . . 1·50 3·00
737 38f. "Acianthus atepalus" . . 2·00 3·50

237 Royal Exhibition Hall, Melbourne

1984. Air. "Ausipex 84" International Stamp Exhibition, Melbourne.
738 **237** 150f. green, brown & mve 6·50 7·75
MS739 143 × 104 mm. **237** 150f. mauve and violet . . . . . . 11·00 13·50

238 School and Arrow Sign-post

239 Anchor, Rope and Stars

1984. Centenary of Public Education.
740 **238** 59f. multicoloured . . . . 2·30 2·50

1984. Air. Armed Forces Day.
741 **239** 51f. multicoloured . . . . 2·75 3·00

240 "Women looking for Crabs" (Mme. Bonnet de Larbogne)

1984. Air. Art. Multicoloured.
742 120f. Type **240** . . . . . . 4·25 3·75
743 300f. "Cook discovering New Caledonia" (tapestry by Pilioko) . . . . 10·00 12·50

241 Kagu

1985.
744 **241** 1f. blue . . . . 85 1·60
745 2f. green . . . . 85 1·40
746 3f. orange . . . . 90 2·50
747 4f. green . . . . 95 2·30
748 5f. mauve . . . . 90 1·50
749 35f. red . . . . 1·90 2·75
750 38f. red . . . . 1·80 2·50
751 40f. red . . . . 3·25 3·00
For similar design but with "& DEPENDANCES" omitted, see Nos. 837/43.

1985. Sea Shells (2nd series). As T **229**. Multicoloured.
761 55f. Bubble cone . . . . . . 2·50 2·75
762 72f. Lambert's cone . . . . 2·75 3·75

243 Weather Station transmitting Forecast to Boeing 737 and Trawler

1985. World Meteorology Day.
763 **243** 17f. multicoloured . . . . 2·30 2·75

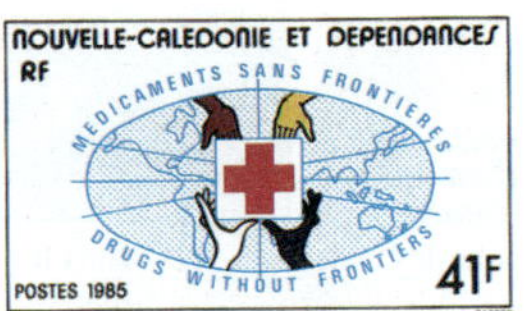

244 Map and Hands holding Red Cross

1985. International Medicines Campaign.
764 **244** 41f. multicoloured . . . . 2·75 3·00

245 Electronic Telephone Exchange

1985. Inaug of Electronic Telephone Equipment.
765 **245** 70f. multicoloured . . . . 2·75 3·25

246 Marguerite la Foa Suspension Bridge

1985. Protection of Heritage.
766 **246** 44f. brown, red and blue 2·50 3·25

247 Kagu with Magnifying Glass and Stamp

1985. "Le Cagou" Stamp Club.
767 **247** 220f. multicoloured . . . 7·25 7·50
MS768 120 × 100 mm. No. 767 (sold at 230f.) . . . . 9·50 14·00

248 Festival Emblem

1985. 4th Pacific Arts Festival, Papeete. Mult.
769 55f. Type **248** . . . . 2·00 3·50
770 75f. Girl blowing trumpet triton . . . . 2·50 4·00

249 Flowers, Barbed Wire and Starving Child

1985. International Youth Year.
771 **249** 59f. multicoloured . . . . 1·80 3·25

250 "Amedee Lighthouse" (M. Hosken) **251** Tree and Seedling

1985. Electrification of Amedee Lighthouse.
772 **250** 89f. multicoloured . . . . 3·25 3·00

1985. "Planting for the Future".
773 **251** 100f. multicoloured . . . 3·25 4·00

252 De Havilland Dragon Rapide and Route Map

1985. Air. 30th Anniv of First Regular Internal Air Service.
774 **252** 80f. multicoloured . . . . 4·25 4·00

253 Hands and U.N. Emblem

1985. 40th Anniv of U.N.O.
775 **253** 250f. multicoloured . . . 8·00 7·75

254 School, Map and "Nautilus"

1985. Air. Jules Garnier High School.
776 **254** 400f. multicoloured . . . 18·00 10·00

255 Purple Swamphen

1985. Birds. Multicoloured.
777 50f. Type **255** . . . . 2·30 3·50
778 60f. Island thrush . . . . . 2·50 3·75

256 Aircraft Tail Fins and Eiffel Tower

1986. Air. 30th Anniv of Scheduled Paris–Noumea Flights.
779 **256** 72f. multicoloured . . . . 3·50 3·75

257 Merlet Scorpionfish

1986. Noumea Aquarium. Multicoloured.
780 10f. Emperor angelfish . . . 55 1·70
781 17f. Type **257** . . . . 70 2·75

258 Kanumera Bay, Isle of Pines

1986. Landscapes (1st series). Multicoloured.
782 50f. Type **258** . . . . 1·80 3·25
783 55f. Inland village . . . . . 1·90 2·50
See also Nos. 795/6 and 864/5.

259 "Bavayia sauvagii"

1986. Geckos. Multicoloured.
784 20f. Type **259** . . . . 1·50 2·75
785 45f. "Rhacodactylus leachianus" . . . . 2·30 3·25

260 Players and Azteca Stadium

1986. World Cup Football Championship, Mexico.
786 **260** 60f. multicoloured . . . . 2·00 3·75

261 Vivarium, Nou Island

1986. Air. Protection of Heritage.
787 **261** 230f. deep brown, blue and brown . . . . . . 7·25 7·00

262 Pharmaceutical Equipment

1986. 120th Anniv of First Pharmacy.
788 **262** 80f. multicoloured . . . . 2·75 4·00

263 "Coelogynae licastioides"

1986. Orchids. Multicoloured.
789 44f. Type **263** . . . . 2·30 3·25
790 58f. "Calanthe langei" . . . 2·75 2·75

264 Black-backed Magpie

1986. "Stampex 86" National Stamp Exhibition, Adelaide.
791 **264** 110f. multicoloured . . . 4·50 6·25

265 Aerospatiale/Aeritalia ATR 42 over New Caledonia

1986. Air. Inaugural Flight of ATR 42.
792 **265** 18f. multicoloured . . . . 2·50 2·75

266 Emblem and 1860 Stamp **267** Arms of Mont Dore

1986. Air. "Stockholmia 86" International Stamp Exhibition.
793 **266** 108f. black, red and lilac 3·75 4·50

1986.
794 **267** 94f. multicoloured . . . . 3·25 4·00

1986. Landscapes (2nd series). As T **258**. Multicoloured.
795 40f. West coast (vert) . . . . 1·10 2·00
796 76f. South . . . . 1·70 2·30

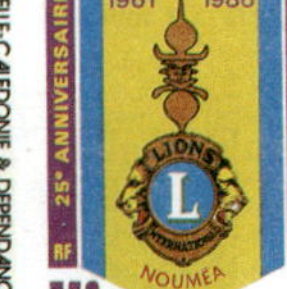

268 Wild Flowers **269** Club Banner

1986. Association for Nature Protection.
797 **268** 73f. multicoloured . . . . 3·75 3·75

1986. 25th Anniv of Noumea Lions Club.
798 **269** 350f. multicoloured . . . 8·75 14·00

270 "Moret Bridge" (Alfred Sisley)

1986. Paintings. Multicoloured.
799 74f. Type **270** . . . . 2·75 3·75
800 140f. "Hunting Butterflies" (Berthe Morisot) . . . . . 4·75 4·00

271 Emblem and Sound Waves **272** "Challenge France"

1987. Air. 25th Anniv of New Caledonia Amateur Radio Association.
801 **271** 64f. multicoloured . . . . 1·20 3·50

1987. America's Cup Yacht Race. Multicoloured.
802 30f. Type **272** . . . . 2·00 3·25
803 70f. "French Kiss" . . . . . 3·00 4·00

273 "Anona squamosa" and "Graphium gelon"

1987. Plants and Butterflies. Multicoloured.
804 46f. Type **273** . . . . 3·00 3·25
805 54f. "Abizzia granulosa" and "Polyura gamma" . . . . 3·50 3·50

274 Peaceful Landscape, Earphones and Noisy Equipment

1987. Air. Nature Protection. Campaign against Noise.
806 **274** 150f. multicoloured . . . 5·25 5·00

275 Isle of Pines Canoe

1987. Canoes. Each brown, green and blue.
807 72f. Type **275** . . . . 2·50 3·75
808 90f. Ouvea canoe . . . . . 3·00 3·00

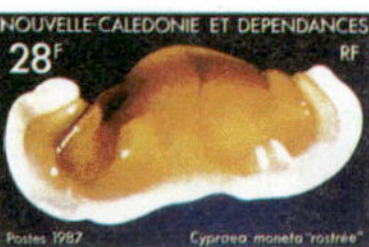

276 Town Hall

1987. New Town Hall, Mont Dore.
809 **276** 92f. multicoloured . . . . 3·25 4·00

277 Money Cowrie

1987. Sea Shells (3rd series). Multicoloured.
810 28f. Type **277** . . . . 1·50 2·00
811 36f. Martin's cone . . . . . 1·90 3·25

278 Games Emblem **279** Emblem

1987. 8th South Pacific Games. Noumea (1st issue).
812 **278** 40f. multicoloured . . . . 1·70 2·30
See also Nos. 819/21.

1987. 13th Soroptimists International Convention, Melbourne.
813 **279** 270f. multicoloured . . . 8·75 10·00

280 New Caledonia White-Eye

1987. Birds. Multicoloured.
814 18f. Type **280** . . . . 1·90 2·75
815 21f. Peregrine falcon (vert) . . . 1·90 2·75

281 Flags on Globe

1987. 40th Anniv of South Pacific Commission.
816 **281** 200f. multicoloured . . . 6·75 7·00

282 Globe and Magnifying Glass on Map of New Caledonia

1987. Schools Philately.
817 **282** 15f. multicoloured . . . . 1·20 2·75

283 Cricketers

1987. Air. French Cricket Federation.
818 **283** 94f. multicoloured . . . . 3·75 3·75

284 Golf

1987. 8th South Pacific Games, Noumea (2nd issue). Multicoloured.
819 20f. Type **284** . . . . 1·60 2·75
820 30f. Rugby football . . . . . 2·75 3·00
821 100f. Long jumping . . . . 3·25 4·00

285 Arms of Dumbea  **287** University

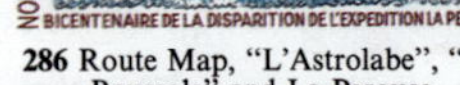

286 Route Map, "L'Astrolabe", "La Boussole" and La Perouse

1988. Air.
822 **285** 76f. multicoloured . . . . 3·75 2·75

1988. Bicentenary of Disappearance of La Perouse's Expedition.
823 **286** 36f. blue, brown and red 3·25 2·50

1988. French University of South Pacific, Noumea and Papeete.
824 **287** 400f. multicoloured . . . 11·50 12·50

288 Semicircle Angelfish  **289** Mwaringou House, Canala

1988. Noumea Aquarium. Fishes. Multicoloured.
825 30f. Type **288** . . . . 3·00 3·00
826 46f. Sapphire sergeant major 3·50 3·25

1988. Traditional Huts. Each brown, green and blue.
827 19f. Type **289** . . . . 1·40 2·75
828 21f. Nathalo house, Lifou (horiz) . . . . 1·40 1·90

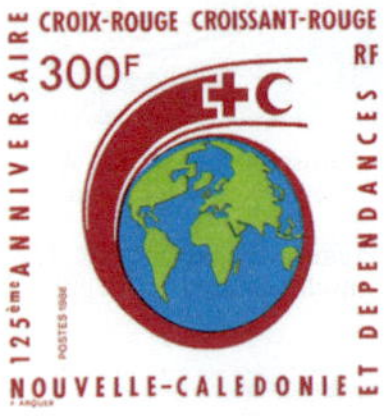

290 Anniversary Emblem

1988. 125th Anniv of International Red Cross.
829 **290** 300f. blue, green and red 10·00 7·75

291 "Ochrosia elliptica"

1988. Medicinal Plants. Multicoloured.
830 28f. Type **291** (postage) . . . 1·70 2·75
831 64f. "Rauvolfia sevenetii" (air) . . . . 2·50 3·25

292 "Gymnocrinus richeri"

1988.
832 **292** 51f. multicoloured . . . . 2·30 3·00

293 Furnished Room and Building Exterior

1988. Bourail Museum and Historical Association.
833 **293** 120f. multicoloured . . . 3·50 5·00

294 La Perouse sighting Phillip's Fleet in Botany Bay

1988. "Sydpex 88" Stamp Exhibition, Sydney. Multicoloured.
834 42f. Type **294** . . . . 3·00 3·25
835 42f. Phillip sighting "La Boussole" and "L'Astrolabe" . . . . . . 3·00 3·50
MS836 175×120 mm. Nos. 834/5 (sold at 120f.) . . . . 6·75 7·75

295 Kagu  **297** Laboratory Assistant, Noumea Institute and Pasteur

296 Table Tennis

1988.
837 **295** 1f. blue . . . . 2·30 1·50
838 2f. green . . . . 2·30 2·00
839 3f. orange . . . . 2·30 2·50
840 4f. green . . . . 2·30 1·50
841 5f. mauve . . . . 2·30 2·30
842 28f. orange . . . . 2·75 2·75
843 40f. red . . . . 3·00 2·50

1988. Olympic Games, Seoul.
846 **296** 150f. multicoloured . . . 5·50 4·25

1988. Centenary of Pasteur Institute, Paris.
847 **297** 100f. red, black and blue 4·25 3·75

298 Georges Baudoux

1988. Writers.
848 **298** 72f. brown, green and purple (postage) . . . . 3·00 3·50
849 – 73f. brown, bl & blk (air) 2·75 2·75
DESIGN: 73f. Jean Mariotti.

299 Map and Emblems

1988. Air. Rotary International Anti-Polio Campaign.
850 **299** 220f. multicoloured . . . 6·25 6·25

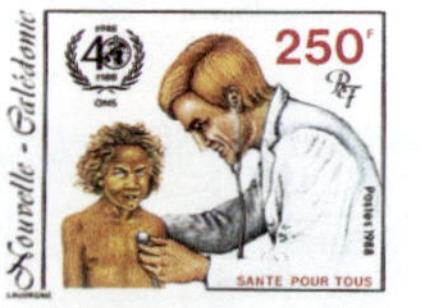

300 Doctor examining Child

1988. 40th Anniv of W.H.O.
851 **300** 250f. multicoloured . . . 8·00 6·50

301 "Terre des Hommes" (L. Bunckley)

1988. Paintings. Multicoloured.
852 54f. Type **301** . . . . 3·75 3·25
853 92f. "Latin Quarter" (Marik) 3·50 4·00

302 Arms of Koumac  **303** "Parasitaxus ustus"

1989.
854 **302** 200f. multicoloured . . . 7·75 7·00

1989. Flowers. Multicoloured.
855 80f. Type **303** . . . . 2·50 3·75
856 90f. "Tristaniopsis guillainii" (horiz) . . . . 2·75 4·00

304 "Plesionika sp."

1989. Marine Life. Multicoloured.
857 18f. Type **304** . . . . 2·75 2·30
858 66f. Sail-backed scorpionfish 3·00 3·50
859 110f. Cristiate latiaxis . . . . 4·75 3·50

305 "Liberty" **306** Canoe and Diamond Decoration

1989. Bicentenary of French Revolution and "Philexfrance 89" International Stamp Exhibition, Paris. Multicoloured.
860 40f. Type **305** (postage) . . . 1·80 2·30
861 58f. "Equality" (air) . . . . 2·30 1·60
862 76f. "Fraternity" . . . . . . 3·25 3·00
MS863 155×110 mm. 180f. "Liberty" "Equality" and "Fraternity" (92×51 mm) . . 8·00 8·50

1989. Landscapes (3rd series). As T **258**. Mult.
864 180f. Ouaieme ferry (post) . . 7·00 4·00
865 64f. "The Broody Hen" (rocky islet), Hienghene (air) . . . . 2·50 3·25

1989. Bamboo Decorations by C. Ohlen. Each black, bistre and orange.
866 70f. Type **306** (postage) . . . 3·00 2·50
867 44f. Animal design (air) . . . 1·80 3·25

307 "Hobie Cat 14" Yachts

1989. 10th World "Hobie Cat" Class Catamaran Championship, Noumea.
868 **307** 350f. multicoloured . . . 10·00 11·00

308 Book Title Pages and Society Members

1989. 20th Anniv of Historical Studies Society.
869 **308** 74f. black and brown . . 3·25 2·75

309 Fort Teremba

1989. Protection of Heritage.
870 **309** 100f. green, brown & blue . . . 3·25 4·00

310 "Rochefort's Escape" (Edouard Manet)

1989. Paintings. Multicoloured.
871 130f. Type **310** . . . . . . 5·25 3·50
872 270f. "Self-portrait" (Gustave Courbet) . . . . 8·25 9·25

311 Fr. Patrick O'Reilly

1990. Writers.
873 **311** 170f. black and mauve . . 5·25 5·50

312 Grass and Female Butterfly

1990. "Cyperacea costularia" (grass) and "Paratisiphone lyrnessa" (butterfly). Multicoloured.
874 50f. Type **312** (postage) . . . 3·00 3·25
875 18f. Grass and female butterfly (different) (air) . . 2·00 1·80
876 94f. Grass and male butterfly 4·00 4·00

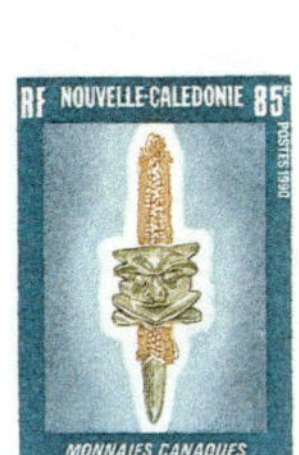

313 "Maize" Stem with Face

RF NOUVELLE-CALEDONIE 230 F
EXPOSITION DE JADE ET DE NACRE

314 Exhibit

1990. Kanaka Money.
877 **313** 85f. olive, orange & green 3·25 2·75
878 – 140f. orange, black & grn 4·75 4·75
DESIGN: 140f. "Rope" stem with decorative end.

1990. Jade and Mother-of-pearl Exhibition.
879 **314** 230f. multicoloured . . . 7·50 7·50

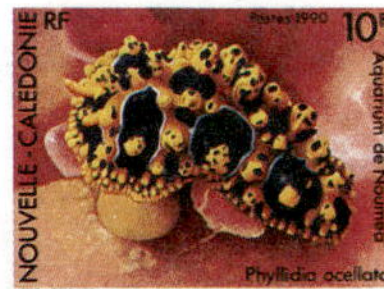

315 Ocellate Nudibranch

1990. Noumea Aquarium. Sea Slugs. Multicoloured.
880 10f. Type **315** . . . . 80 2·50
881 42f. "Chromodoris kuniei" (vert) . . . . 1·60 3·00

316 Head of "David" (Michelangelo) and Footballers

1990. World Cup Football Championship, Italy.
882 **316** 240f. multicoloured . . . 8·50 7·50

317 De Gaulle **318** Neounda Site

1990. Air. 50th Anniv of De Gaulle's Call to Resist.
883 **317** 160f. multicoloured . . . 5·00 6·00

1990. Petroglyphs.
884 **318** 40f. brown, green and red (postage) . . . . 1·50 3·00
885 – 58f. black, brown and blue (air) . . . . 2·50 2·50
DESIGN—HORIZ: 58f. Kassducou site.

319 Map and Pacific International Meeting Centre

1990.
886 **319** 320f. multicoloured . . . 8·00 7·50

320 New Zealand Cemetery, Bourail **321** Kagu

1990. Air. "New Zealand 1990" International Stamp Exhibition, Auckland. Multicoloured.
887 80f. Type **320** . . . . 2·75 3·00
888 80f. Brigadier William Walter Dove . . . . 2·75 4·00
MS889 140 × 100 mm. 150f. Kagu, brown kiwi and maps of New Caledonia and New Zealand 7·75 8·50

1990.
890 **321** 1f. blue . . . . 2·50 2·50
891 2f. green . . . . 2·50 1·80
892 3f. yellow . . . . 2·50 2·50
893 4f. green . . . . 2·50 2·50
894 5f. violet . . . . 2·50 1·50
895 9f. grey . . . . 2·50 2·50
896 12f. red . . . . 2·50 2·50
897 40f. mauve . . . . 1·20 2·75
898 50f. red . . . . 1·30 3·00
899 55f. red . . . . 3·25 3·00

The 5 and 55f. exist both perforated with ordinary gum and imperforate with self-adhesive gum.

For design with no value expressed see No. 994.

322 "Munidopsis sp"

324 "Gardenia aubryi"

323 Emblem

1990. Air. Deep Sea Animals. Multicoloured.
900 30f. Type **322** . . . . 1·10 3·00
901 60f. "Lyreidius tridentatus" 1·70 3·25

1990. Air. 30th South Pacific Conference, Noumea.
902 **323** 85f. multicoloured . . . . 2·30 3·75

1990. Flowers. Multicoloured.
903 105f. Type **324** . . . . . . 3·50 4·00
904 130f. "Hibbertia baudouinii" 4·25 4·75

325 De Gaulle

1990. Air. Birth Centenary of Charles de Gaulle (French statesman).
905 **325** 410f. blue . . . . 13·50 8·50

326 "Mont Dore, Mountain of Jade" (C. Degroiselle)

1990. Air. Pacific Painters. Multicoloured.
906 365f. Type **326** (postage) . . 11·00 10·00
907 110f. "The Celieres House" (M. Petron) (air) . . . . . 3·75 4·75

327 Fayawa-Ouvea Bay

1991. Air. Regional Landscapes. Multicoloured.
908 36f. Type **327** . . . . 2·50 3·00
909 90f. Coastline of Mare . . . 2·75 3·75

328 Louise Michel and Classroom

1991. Writers.
910 **328** 125f. mauve and blue . . 4·75 4·50
911 – 125f. blue and brown . . 4·75 4·50
DESIGN: No. 911, Charles B. Nething and photographer.

329 Houailou Hut

330 Northern Province

1991. Melanesian Huts. Multicoloured.
912 12f. Type **329** . . . . 2·30 2·50
913 35f. Hienghene hut . . . . . 2·75 3·00

1991. Provinces. Multicoloured.
914 45f. Type **330** . . . . 1·20 2·50
915 45f. Islands Province . . . . 1·20 2·50
916 45f. Southern Province . . . 1·20 2·50

331 "Dendrobium biflorum"

1991. Orchids. Multicoloured.
917 55f. Type **331** . . . . 3·50 3·25
918 70f. "Dendrobium closterium" . . . . 3·75 3·25

332 Japanese Pineconefish

1991. Fishes. Multicoloured.
919 60f. Type **332** . . . . 3·75 2·30
920 100f. Japanese bigeye . . . . 4·75 4·00

333 Research Equipment and Sites

1991. French Scientific Research Institute for Development and Co-operation.
921 **333** 170f. multicoloured . . . 8·25 4·75

334 Emblem **336** Emblems

335 Map and Dragon

1991. 9th South Pacific Games, Papua New Guinea.
922 **334** 170f. multicoloured . . . 8·00 4·75

1991. Centenary of Vietnamese Settlement in New Caledonia.
923 **335** 300f. multicoloured . . . 11·00 8·50

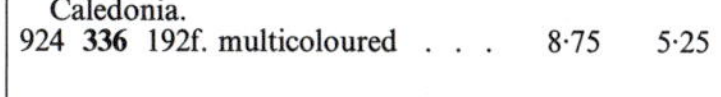

1991. 30th Anniv of Lions International in New Caledonia.
924 **336** 192f. multicoloured . . . 8·75 5·25

337 Map, "Camden" (missionary brig), Capt. Robert Clark Morgan and Trees

1991. 150th Anniv of Discovery of Sandalwood.
925 **337** 200f. blue, turquoise & grn . . . . 9·00 5·50

338 "Phillantus" and Common Grass Yellow

1991. "Phila Nippon '91" International Stamp Exhibition, Tokyo. Plants and Butterflies. Mult.
926 8f. Type **338** . . . . 1·70 2·30
927 15f. "Pipturus incanus" and "Hypolimnas octocula" . . 1·90 2·30
928 20f. "Stachytarpheta urticaefolia" and meadow argos . . . . 2·00 2·50
929 26f. "Malaisia scandens" and "Cyrestis telamon" . . . . 2·30 2·75
MS930 100 × 122 mm. 75f. *Cyrestis telamon*; 75f. *Hypolimnas octocula*; 75f. *Eurema hecabe*; 75f. *Precis villida* (all vert) . . . . 15·00 16·00

339 Nickel Processing Plant and Dam

1991. 50th Anniv of Central Economic Co-operation Bank. Multicoloured.
931 76f. Type **339** . . . . 3·00 3·50
932 76f. Housing and hotels . . . 3·00 3·50

340 "Caledonian Cricket" (Marcel Moutouh)

1991. Air. Pacific Painters. Multicoloured.
933 130f. Type **340** . . . . 6·25 4·00
934 435f. "Saint Louis" (Janine Goetz) . . . . 17·00 12·50

341 Blue River (½-size illustration)

1992. Air. Blue River National Park.
935 **341** 400f. multicoloured . . . 9·50 8·50
MS936 127 × 91 mm. No. 935 (sold at 450f.) . . . . 12·50 11·00

342 La Madeleine Falls

1992. Nature Protection.
937 **342** 15f. multicoloured . . . . 1·20 1·90
MS938 122 × 88 mm. No. 937 (sold at 150f.) . . . . 4·25 4·50

343 Lapita Pot

345 "Pinta"

344 Barqueta Bridge

1992. Air. Noumea Museum.
939 **343** 25f. black and orange . . 1·60 1·90

1992. Air. "Expo '92" World's Fair, Seville.
940 **344** 10f. multicoloured . . . . 1·40 1·80

1992. Air. "World Columbian Stamp Expo '92", Chicago. Multicoloured.
941 80f. Type **345** . . . . 2·30 1·90
942 80f. "Santa Maria" . . . . . 2·75 2·75
943 80f. "Nina" . . . . 2·75 2·75
MS944 160 × 70 mm. 110f. Eric the Red and longship; 110f. Christopher Columbus and arms; 110f. Amerigo Vespucci (sold at 360f.) . . . . 8·00 8·50

346 Manchurian Crane and Kagu within "100"

1992. Centenary of Arrival of First Japanese Immigrants. Multicoloured, background colours given.
945 **346** 95f. yellow . . . . 3·00 1·60
946 95f. grey . . . . 3·00 2·50

347 Synchronised Swimming

1992. Olympic Games, Barcelona.
947 **347** 260f. multicoloured . . . 4·75 4·25

348 Bell Airacobra, Grumman F4F Wildcat, Barrage Balloon, Harbour and Nissen Huts

1992. 50th Anniv of Arrival of American Forces in New Caledonia.
948 **348** 50f. multicoloured . . . . 2·30 2·30

349 "Wahpa" (Paul Mascart)

1992. Air. Pacific Painters.
949 **349** 205f. multicoloured . . . 4·75 3·50

350 Australian Cattle Dog

352 "Amalda fuscolingua"

351 Entrecasteaux and Fleet

1992. Air. Canine World Championships.
950 **350** 175f. multicoloured . . . 4·00 3·25

1992. Air. Navigators. Bicentenary of Landing of Admiral Bruni d'Entrecasteaux on West Coast of New Caledonia.
951 **351** 110f. orange, blue & green 2·75 2·75

1992. Air. Shells. Multicoloured.
952 30f. Type **352** . . . . 2·00 2·00
953 50f. "Cassis abbotti" . . . . 2·30 2·30

353 Deole

1992. Air. "La Brousse en Folie" (comic strip) by Bernard Berger. Multicoloured.
954 80f. Type **353** . . . . 2·50 2·50
955 80f. Tonton Marcel . . . . . 2·50 1·60
956 80f. Tathan . . . . 2·50 2·50
957 80f. Joinville . . . . 2·50 2·50

354 Lagoon

1993. Lagoon Protection.
958 **354** 120f. multicoloured . . . 3·25 2·75

355 Harbour (Gaston Roullet)

1993. Air. Pacific Painters.
959 **355** 150f. multicoloured . . . 3·75 3·00

356 Symbols of New Caledonia

1993. School Philately. "Tourism my Friend".
960 **356** 25f. multicoloured . . . . 1·90 1·90

357 Still and Plantation

1993. Air. Centenary of Production of Essence of Niaouli.
966 **357** 85f. multicoloured . . . . 1·30 2·50

358 Planets and Copernicus

1993. Air. "Polska '93" International Stamp Exhibition, Poznan. 450th Death Anniv of Nicolas Copernicus (astronomer).
967 **358** 110f. blue, turquoise & grey . . . . 2·00 2·50

359 Noumea Temple

1993. Air. Centenary of First Protestant Church in Noumea.
968 **359** 400f. multicoloured . . . 8·75 6·75

1993. No. 898 surch **55F**.
969 **321** 55f. on 50f. red . . . . . 2·30 2·30

361 Malabou

1993. Air. Regional Landscapes.
970 **361** 85f. multicoloured . . . . 2·75 2·50

362 Locomotive and Bridge

1993. Air. Centenary of Little Train of Thio.
971 **362** 115f. red, green and lilac 3·00 2·50

363 Rochefort

364 "Megastylis paradoxa"

1993. Air. 80th Death Anniv of Henri Rochefort (journalist).
972 **363** 100f. multicoloured . . . 2·00 2·50

1993. Air. "Bangkok 1993" International Stamp Exhibition, Thailand. Multicoloured.
973 30f. Type **364** . . . . 1·80 1·60
974 30f. "Vanda coerulea" . . . 1·80 1·60
MS975 120 × 90 mm. 140f. Exhibition centre (51 × 39 mm) 7·25 4·50

365 Route Map and Boeing 737-300/500

1993. Air. 10th Anniv of Air Cal (national airline).
976 **365** 85f. multicoloured . . . . 2·75 2·50

366 "Francois Arago" (cable ship)

1993. Air. Centenary of New Caledonia–Australia Telecommunications Cable.
977 **366** 200f. purple, blue & turq . . . 5·75 3·75

367 "Oxypleurodon orbiculatus"

1993. Air. Deep-sea Life.
978 **367** 250f. multicoloured . . . 6·50 4·00

368 Aircraft, Engine and Hangar

1993. Air. 25th Anniv of Chamber of Commerce and Industry's Management of La Tontouta Airport, Noumea.
979 **368** 90f. multicoloured . . . . 2·75 2·30

369 First Christmas Mass, 1843 (stained glass window, Balade church)

1993. Air. Christmas.
980 **369** 120f. multicoloured . . . 3·25 2·50

370 Bourail

1993. Town Arms. Multicoloured.
981 70f. Type **370** . . . . 2·75 2·50
982 70f. Noumea . . . . 2·75 2·50
983 70f. Canala . . . . 2·50 2·50
984 70f. Kone . . . . 2·50 2·50
985 70f. Paita . . . . 3·50 2·50
986 70f. Dumbea . . . . 2·50 2·50
987 70f. Koumac . . . . 2·50 2·50
988 70f. Ponerihouen . . . . . . 2·50 2·50
989 70f. Kaamoo Hyehen . . . . 2·50 2·50
990 70f. Mont Dore . . . . . . 3·75 2·50
991 70f. Thio . . . . 2·50 2·50
992 70f. Kaala-Gomen . . . . . 2·50 2·50
993 70f. Touho . . . . 2·50 2·50

1994. No value expressed.
994 **321** (60f.) red . . . . 2·00 1·60

371 Dog, Exhibition Emblem and Chinese Horoscope Signs (New Year)

1994. Air. "Hong Kong '94" International Stamp Exhibition. Multicoloured.
995 60f. Type **371** . . . . 2·00 2·00
MS996 161 × 120 mm. 105f. Giant panda (51 × 39 *mm*); 105f. Kagu (51 × 39 mm) . . . . 6·50 6·75

372 Airbus Industrie A340

1994. Air 1st Paris–Noumea Airbus Flight. Self-adhesive.
997 **372** 90f. multicoloured . . . . 3·25 2·50

1994. "Philexjeunes '94" Youth Stamp Exhibition, Grenoble. No. 960 optd **PHILEXJEUNES'94 GRENOBLE 22–24 AVRIL**.
998 **356** 25f. multicoloured . . . . 1·30 1·60

374 Photograph of Canala Post Office and Post Van

1994. 50th Anniv of Noumea–Canala Postal Service.
999 **374** 15f. brown, green and blue . . . . 1·40 1·60

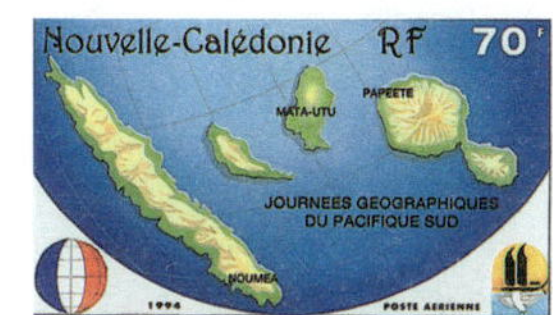

375 Pacific Islands on Globe

1994. Air. South Pacific Geographical Days.
1000 **375** 70f. multicoloured . . . 2·50 1·70

376 Post Office, 1859

1994. Postal Administration Head Offices. Mult.
1001 30f. Type **376** . . . . . . 1·80 1·70
1002 60f. Posts and Telecommunications Office, 1936 . . . . . . 2·50 2·00
1003 90f. Ministry of Posts and Telecommunications, 1967 3·00 2·50
1004 120f. Ministry of Posts and Telecommunications, 1993 3·75 3·00

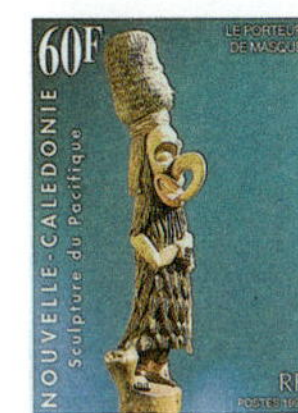

377 "The Mask Wearer"

1994. Pacific Sculpture.
1005 **377** 60f. multicoloured . . . 2·30 1·90

378 "Legend of the Devil Fish" (Micheline Neporon)

1994. Air. Pacific Painters.
1006 **378** 120f. multicoloured . . . 3·00 2·75

379 "Chambeyronia macrocarpa"

380 Podtanea Pot

1994.
1007 **379** 90f. multicoloured . . . 3·00 2·00

1994. Air. Noumea Museum.
1008 **380** 95f. multicoloured . . . 3·00 2·50

381 Trophy, U.S. Flag and Ball

1994. Air. World Cup Football Championship, U.S.A.
1009 **381** 105f. multicoloured . . . 3·00 2·75

1994. No. D707 with "Timbre Taxe" obliterated by black bar.
1010 D **222** 5f. multicoloured . . 14·50 3·75

382 Timor Deer

1994. Bourail Fair.
1011 **382** 150f. multicoloured . . . 4·25 3·00

383 Korean Family

1994. Air. "Philakorea 1994" International Stamp Exhibition, Seoul. Multicoloured.
1012 60f. Type **383** . . . . . . 2·00 1·90
MS1013 110 × 110 mm. 35f. Containers, peppers and emblem (36 × 37 mm); 35f. Carafe, celery, cannage and garlic (36 × 37 mm); 35f. Container and turnips (36 × 37 mm); 35f. Jug, seafood and lemon (36 × 37 mm) . . . 5·00 5·25

384 "L'Atalante" (oceanographic research vessel)

1994. Air. ZoNeCo (evaluation programme of Economic Zone).
1014 **384** 120f. multicoloured . . . 3·50 3·00

385 "Nivose"

1994. Attachment of the "Nivose" (French surveillance frigate) to New Caledonia. Multicoloured.
1015 30f. Type **385** . . . . . . 1·90 1·70
1016 30f. Aircraft over frigate . . 1·90 1·70
1017 30f. Frigate moored at quay 1·90 1·70
1018 60f. Frigate and map of New Caledonia on parchment . . . . . . 2·50 2·00
1019 60f. Ship's bell . . . . . . 2·50 2·00
1020 60f. Frigate and sailor . . . 2·50 2·00

386 Driving Cattle

1994. Air. 1st European Stamp Salon, Flower Gardens, Paris. Multicoloured.
1021 90f. Aerial view of island . . 2·50 2·50
1022 90f. Type **386** . . . . . . 2·50 2·50

387 Paper Darts around Girl

1994. School Philately.
1023 **387** 30f. multicoloured . . . 1·70 1·60

388 Jaques Nervat

1994. Writers.
1024 **388** 175f. multicoloured . . . 5·00 3·25

389 Satellite transmitting to Globe and Computer Terminal

1994. Air. 50th Anniv of Overseas Scientific and Technical Research Office.
1025 **389** 95f. multicoloured . . . 3·50 2·50

390 Emblem and Temple

1994. Air. 125th Anniv of Freemasonary in New Caledonia.
1026 **390** 350f. multicoloured . . . 10·00 5·25

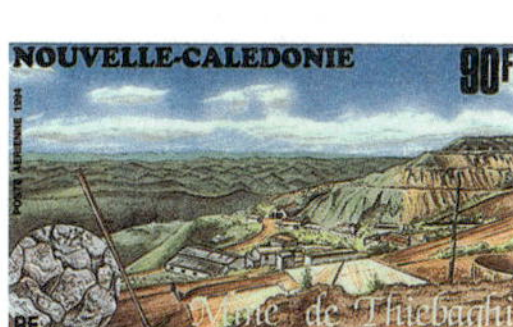

391 Thiebaghi Mine

1994. Air.
1027 **391** 90f. multicoloured . . . 2·75 2·50

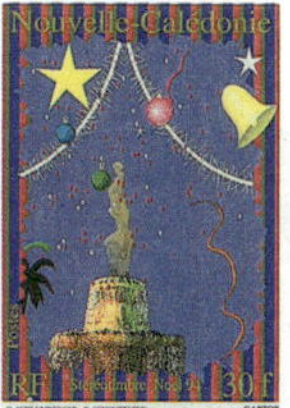

392 Place des Cocotiers, Noumea

1994. Christmas.
1028 **392** 30f. multicoloured . . . 1·80 1·80

No. 1028 covers any one of five stamps which were issued together in horizontal se-tenant strips, the position of the bell, tree and monument differing on each stamp. The strip is stated to produce a three-dimensional image without use of a special viewer.

393 Globe and Newspapers

1994. 50th Anniv of "Le Monde" (newspaper).
1029 **393** 90f. multicoloured . . . 3·50 2·50

394 1988 100f. Pasteur Institute Stamp

1995. Death Centenary of Louis Pasteur (chemist).
1030 **394** 120f. multicoloured . . . 3·00 2·75

395 Pictorial Map

1995. Air. Tourism.
1031 **395** 90f. multicoloured . . . 2·50 2·50

396 Profile of De Gaulle (Santucci) and Cross of Lorraine

1995. 25th Death Anniv of Charles de Gaulle (French President, 1959–69).
1032 **396** 1000f. deep blue, blue and gold . . . . . . 22·00 22·00

397 Emblem

1995. Pacific University Teachers' Training Institute.
1033 **397** 100f. multicoloured . . . 3·00 2·50

398 "Sylviornis neocaledoniae"

1995.
1034 **398** 60f. multicoloured . . . 2·50 1·90

399 Swimming, Cycling and Running

1995. Triathlon.
1035 **399** 60f. multicoloured . . . 2·00 2·00

400 Tent and Trees

1995. 50th Anniv of Pacific Franc.
1036 **400** 10f. multicoloured . . . 1·50 1·50
No. 1036 covers any one of four stamps which were issued together in horizontal se-tenant strips, the position of the central motif rotating slightly in a clockwise direction from the left to the right-hand stamp. The strip is stated to produce a three-dimensional image without use of a special viewer.

401 Bourbon Palace (Paris), Map of New Caledonia and Chamber

1995. 50th Anniversaries. Multicoloured.
1037 60f. Type **401** (first representation of New Caledonia at French National Assembly) 2·30 1·90
1038 90f. National emblems, De Gaulle and Allied flags (end of Second World War) . . . . 3·00 2·50
1039 90f. U.N. Headquarters, New York (U.N.O.) . . . 2·75 2·50

402 "Sebertia acuminata"

1995.
1040 **402** 60f. multicoloured . . . 2·50 2·00

403 Common Noddy

1995. "Singapore'95" International Stamp Exhibition. Sea Birds. Multicoloured.
1041 5f. Type **403** . . . . 1·30 1·40
1042 10f. Silver gull . . . . . . 1·30 1·40
1043 20f. Roseate tern . . . . . 1·50 1·60
1044 35f. Osprey . . . . 1·90 1·80
1045 65f. Red-footed booby . . . 2·30 2·50
1046 125f. Great frigate bird . . 3·50 3·00
MS1047 130 × 100 mm. Nos. 1041/6 5·50 6·00

404 Golf

1995. 10th South Pacific Games.
1048 **404** 90f. multicoloured . . . 2·75 2·50

405 "The Lizard Man" (Dick Bone)

1995. Pacific Sculpture.
1049 **405** 65f. multicoloured . . . 1·80 2·00

406 Venue

1995. Air. 35th South Pacific Conference.
1050 **406** 500f. multicoloured . . . 9·50 8·25

407 Silhouette of Francis Carco

1995. Writers.
1051 **407** 95f. multicoloured . . . 2·30 2·50

408 Ouare

1995. Air. Kanak Dances. Multicoloured.
1052 95f. Type **408** . . . . . . 2·30 2·50
1053 100f. Pothe . . . . 2·30 2·50

409 Saw-headed Crocodilefish

1995. World of the Deep.
1054 **409** 100f. multicoloured . . . 3·00 2·50

410 "Mekosuchus inexpectatus"

1996. Air.
1055 **410** 125f. multicoloured . . . 3·00 2·75

411 Vessel with decorated Rim

1996. Noumea Museum.
1056 **411** 65f. multicoloured . . . 2·00 2·00

412 "Captaincookia margaretae"

1996. Flowers. Multicoloured.
1057 65f. Type **412** . . . . . . 1·60 2·00
1058 95f. "Ixora cauliflora" . . . 2·30 2·50

413 Pirogue on Beach

1996. World Pirogue Championships, Noumea. Multicoloured.
1059 30f. Type **413** . . . . . . 1·80 1·60
1060 65f. Pirogue leaving shore 2·50 1·90
1061 95f. Double-hulled pirogue 3·00 2·30
1062 125f. Sports pirogue . . . . 3·50 3·00
Nos. 1059/62 were issued together, se-tenant, forming a composite design.

414 Red Batfish

1996. "China'96" International Stamp Exhibition, Peking. Deep Sea Life. Multicoloured.
1063 25f. Type **414** . . . . . . 1·60 1·60
1064 40f. "Perotrochus deforgesi" (slit shell) . . . . 1·80 1·70
1065 65f. "Mursia musorstomia" (crab) . . . . 2·30 2·00
1066 125f. Sea lily . . . . 3·50 2·75

415 "Sarcolchilus koghiensis"

1996. "Capex'96" International Stamp Exhibition, Toronto, Canada. Orchids. Multicoloured.
1067 5f. Type **415** . . . . 15 1·30
1068 10f. "Phaius robertsii" . . . 95 1·30
1069 25f. "Megastylis montana" 1·10 1·50
1070 65f. "Dendrobium macrophyllum" . . . . . 1·50 2·00
1071 95f. "Dendrobium virotii" 2·50 2·50
1072 125f. "Ephemerantha comata" . . . . 2·75 2·75

416 Indonesian Couple beneath Tree

417 Louis Brauquier

1996. Air. Centenary of Arrival of First Indonesian Immigrants.
1073 **416** 130f. multicoloured . . . 3·00 3·00

1996. Air. Writers.
1074 **417** 95f. multicoloured . . . 2·50 2·50

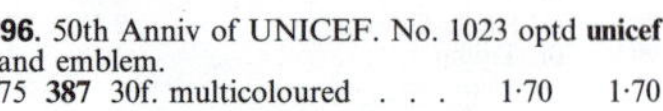
1996. 50th Anniv of UNICEF. No. 1023 optd **unicef** and emblem.
1075 **387** 30f. multicoloured . . . 1·70 1·70

419 Dish Aerial

1996. Air. Anniversaries. Multicoloured.
1076 95f. Type **419** (20th anniv of New Caledonia's first Earth Station) . . . . . 2·50 2·50
1077 125f. Guglielmo Marconi (inventor) and telegraph masts (centenary of radio-telegraphy) . . . . 3·00 3·00

420 Tribal Dance

1996. Air. 7th South Pacific Arts Festival.
1078 **420** 100f. multicoloured . . . 2·75 2·50

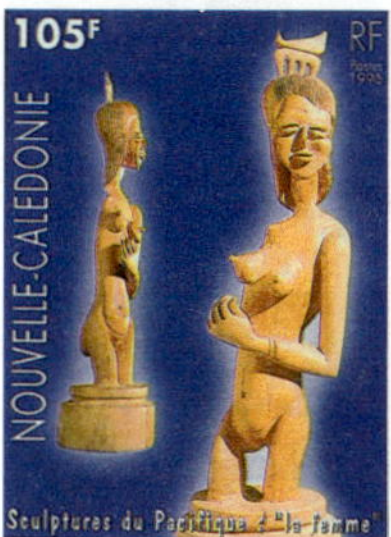
421 "The Woman" (Elija Trijikone)

1996. Sculptures of the Pacific.
1079 **421** 105f. multicoloured . . . 2·75 2·30

422 Ordination, St. Joseph's Cathedral, Noumea

1996. 50th Anniv of Ordination of First Priests in New Caledonia.
1080 **422** 160f. multicoloured . . . 4·25 3·25

423 "Man" (Paula Boi)

1996. Pacific Painters.
1081 **423** 200f. multicoloured . . . 4·50 3·75

424 Gaica Dance

1996.
1082 **424** 500f. multicoloured . . . 12·00 8·25

425 Great Reef

1996. Air. 50th Autumn Stamp Show, Paris. Multicoloured.
1083 95f. Type **425** . . . . . . 2·75 2·50
1084 95f. Mount Koghi . . . . . 2·75 2·50

426 Decorated Sandman

1996. Christmas.
1085 **426** 95f. multicoloured . . . 2·75 2·00

427 Horned Tortoises

1997. Air.
1086 **427** 95f. multicoloured . . . 2·50 2·50

428 Emblem

1997. Air. 50th Anniv of South Pacific Commission.
1087 **428** 100f. multicoloured . . . 3·00 2·50

429 Junk, Hong Kong, Ox and Flag

1997. Air. "Hong Kong '97" International stamp exhibiton. Year of the Ox. Multicoloured.
1088 95f. Type **429** . . . . 3·00 2·50
MS1089 121 × 91 mm. 75f. Farmer ploughing with ox (39 × 29 mm); 75f. Cattle grazing (39 × 29 mm) 5·25 5·25

430 Mitterrand

1997. 1st Death Anniv of Francois Mitterrand (French President, 1981–95).
1090 **430** 1000f. multicoloured . . 24·00 18·00

431 Windmill ("Letters from My Windmill")
432 Lapita Pot with Geometric Pattern

1997. Death Centenary of Alphonse Daudet (writer). Multicoloured.
1091 65f. Type **431** . . . . . . 2·50 2·00
1092 65f. Boy sitting by wall ("The Little Thing") . . . 2·50 2·00
1093 65f. Hunter in jungle ("Tartarinde Tarascon") 2·50 2·00
1094 65f. Daudet at work . . . . 2·50 2·00
MS1095 100 × 120 mm. Nos. 1091/4 7·25 7·50

1997. Air. Melanesian Pottery in Noumea Museum. Multicoloured.
1096 95f. Type **432** . . . . . . 3·00 2·50
1097 95f. Lapita pot with "face" design . . . . 3·00 2·50

433 French Parliament Building and Lafleur

1997. Appointment of Henri Lafleur as First New Caledonian Senator in French Parliament.
1098 **433** 105f. multicoloured . . . 3·25 2·75

434 Cotton Harlequin Bug

1997. Insects. Multicoloured.
1099 65f. Type **434** . . . . . . 2·75 2·50
1100 65f. "Kanakia gigas" . . . 2·75 2·50
1101 65f. "Aenetus cohici" (moth) 2·75 2·50

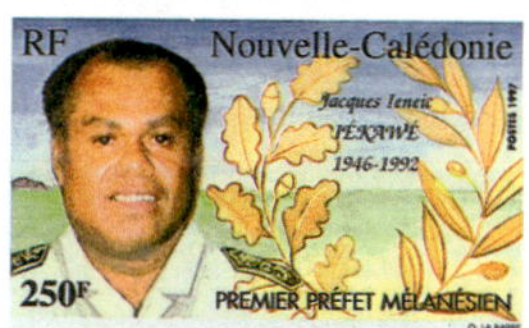
435 Iekawe

1997. 5th Death Anniv of Jacques Ieneic Iekawe (first Melanesian Prefect).
1102 **435** 250f. multicoloured . . . 6·00 4·50

436 Consolidated Catalina Flying Boat and South Pacific Routes Map

1997. Air. 50th Anniv of Establishment by TRAPAS of First Commercial Air Routes in South Pacific. Multicoloured.
1103 95f. Type **436** . . . . . . 2·30 2·50
1104 95f. TRAPAS emblem, seaplane and New Caledonia domestic flight routes . . . . 2·30 2·50

437 Kagu

438 Cup and Harness Racing

1997.
1105 **437** 5f. violet 10 10
1107 30f. orange 75 70
1113 95f. blue . . . . 2·30 2·30
1114 100f. blue . . . . 2·40 2·40
No. 1114 also comes self-adhesive.
See also No. 1128.

1997. Equestrian Sports. Multicoloured.
1118 65f. Type **438** . . . . . . 2·50 2·00
1119 65f. Cup and horse racing 2·50 2·00

439 Port de France (engraving)

1997.
1120 **439** 95f. multicoloured . . . 2·75 2·30

440 "Marianne", Voter and Tiki

441 Seahorses

1997. 50th Anniv of First Elections of Melanesian Representatives to French Parliament.
1121 **440** 150f. multicoloured . . . 3·50 3·00

1997. 5th Indo-Pacific Fishes Conference.
1122 **441** 100f. multicoloured . . . 2·75 2·30

442 Hammerhead Shark Dance Mask (Ken Thaiday)

1997. Pacific Art and Culture. Multicoloured.
1123 100f. Type **442** . . . . . . 2·75 2·30
1124 100f. Painting of traditional Melanesian images by Yvette Bouquet . . . . . 2·75 2·30
1125 100f. "Doka" (figurines by Frank Haikiu) . . . . . 2·75 2·30

443 Father Christmas surfing to Earth

1997. Christmas. Multicoloured.
1126 95f. Type **443** . . . . . . 2·50 2·30
1127 100f. Dolphin with "Meilleurs Voeux" banner 2·50 2·30

1998. As Nos. 1107/13 but with no value expressed. Ordinary or self-adhesive gum.
1128 **437** (70f.) red . . . . 2·30 1·60

444 "Lentinus tuber-regium"

445 Mask from Northern Region

1998. Edible Mushrooms. Multicoloured.
1130 70f. Type **444** . . . . . . 2·30 2·00
1131 70f. "Morchella anteridiformis" . . . . . 2·30 1·30
1132 70f. "Volvaria bombycina" 2·30 1·30

1998. Territorial Museum. Multicoloured.
1133 105f. Type **445** . . . . . . 2·75 1·50
1134 110f. Section of door frame from Central Region . . . 2·75 1·50

446 Painting by Gauguin

1998. 150th Birth Anniv of Paul Gauguin (painter).
1135 **446** 405f. multicoloured . . . 7·25 4·50

447 Player

1998. World Cup Football Championship, France.
1136 **447** 100f. multicoloured . . . 2·50 2·30

448 "Mitimitia"

1998. Tjibaou Cultural Centre. Multicoloured.
1137 30f. Type **448** . . . . . . 1·60 1·50
1138 70f. Jean-Marie Tjibaou (politician) and Centre . . 2·00 1·90
1139 70f. Detail of a Centre building (Renzo Piano) (vert) . . . . 2·00 1·90
1140 105f. "Man Bird" (Mathias Kauage) (vert) . . . . . 2·50 2·30

449 Broken Chains and Slaves

1998. 150th Anniv of Abolition of Slavery.
1141 **449** 130f. brown, blue and purple . . . . 2·75 1·80

450 Dogs watching Postman delivering Letter

1998. Stamp Day.
1142 **450** 70f. multicoloured . . . 2·00 1·60

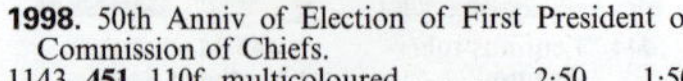

451 Vincent Bouquet

1998. 50th Anniv of Election of First President of Commission of Chiefs.
1143 **451** 110f. multicoloured . . . 2·50 1·50

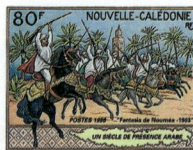

452 Noumea Fantasia, 1903

1998. 100 Years of Arab Presence.
1144 **452** 80f. multicoloured . . . 2·00 1·20

453 Departure

1998. "Portugal 98" International Stamp Exhibition, Lisbon. 500th Anniv of Vasco da Gama's Voyage to India via Cape of Good Hope. Multicoloured.
1145 100f. Type **453** . . . . . . 2·50 2·30
1146 100f. Fleet at Cape of Good Hope . . . . 2·50 1·50
1147 100f. Vasco da Gama meeting Indian king . . . 2·50 1·50
1148 100f. Vasco da Gama in armorial shield flanked by plants . . . . 2·50 2·30
MS1149 160 × 130 mm. 70f. Route map (39 × 51 mm); 70f. Vasco da Gama (39 × 51 mm); 70f. *Sao Gabriel* (flagship) and fleet (39 × 51 mm) . . . . 7·50 5·25

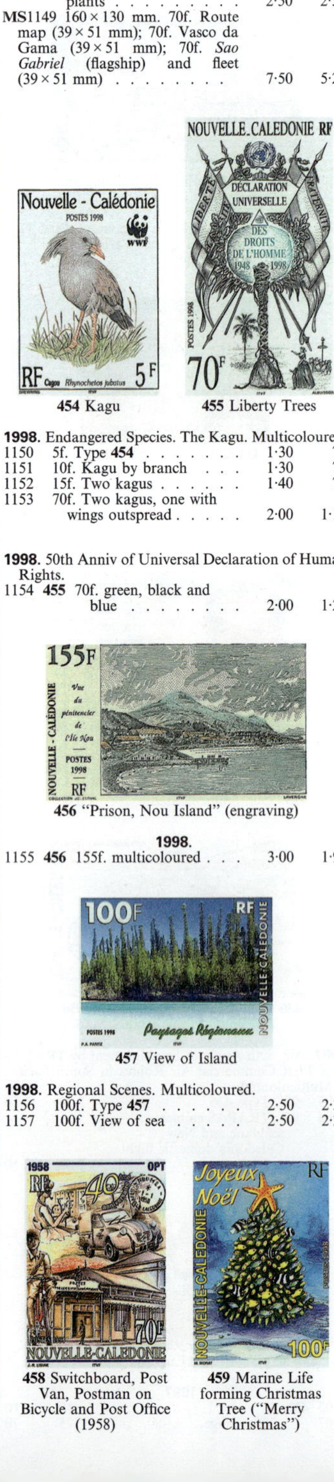

454 Kagu **455** Liberty Trees

1998. Endangered Species. The Kagu. Multicoloured.
1150 5f. Type **454** . . . . 1·30 70
1151 10f. Kagu by branch . . . 1·30 70
1152 15f. Two kagus . . . . . . 1·40 70
1153 70f. Two kagus, one with wings outspread . . . . . 2·00 1·10

1998. 50th Anniv of Universal Declaration of Human Rights.
1154 **455** 70f. green, black and blue . . . . 2·00 1·20

456 "Prison, Nou Island" (engraving)

1998.
1155 **456** 155f. multicoloured . . . 3·00 1·90

457 View of Island

1998. Regional Scenes. Multicoloured.
1156 100f. Type **457** . . . . . . 2·50 2·30
1157 100f. View of sea . . . . . 2·50 2·30

458 Switchboard, Post Van, Postman on Bicycle and Post Office (1958)

459 Marine Life forming Christmas Tree ("Merry Christmas")

1998. 40th Anniv of Posts and Telecommunications Office. Multicoloured.
1158 70f. Type **458** . . . . . . 1·50 1·10
1159 70f. Automatic service machine, woman with mobile phone, dish aerial, motor cycle courier and post office (1998) . . . . 1·50 1·10

1998. Greetings stamps. Multicoloured.
1160 100f. Type **459** . . . . . . 2·30 1·70
1161 100f. Treasure chest ("Best Wishes") . . . . 2·30 1·30
1162 100f. Fish ("Good Holiday") . . . . 2·30 2·00
1163 100f. Fishes and reefs ("Happy Birthday") . . . 2·30 2·00

460 Map, Memorial and "Monique"

1998. 20th Anniv of Erection of Memorial to the Victims of the "Monique" (inter-island freighter) Disaster.
1164 **460** 130f. multicoloured . . . 2·50 2·30

461 "Argiope aetherea"

1999. Spiders. Multicoloured.
1165 70f. Type **461** . . . . . . 1·90 1·10
1166 70f. "Latrodectus hasselti" 1·90 1·10
1167 70f. "Cyrtophora moluccensis" . . . . . . 1·90 1·10
1168 70f. "Barycheloides alluvviophilus" . . . . . 1·90 1·10

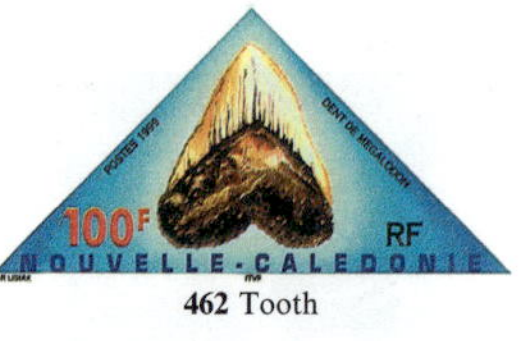

462 Tooth

1999. Giant-toothed Shark. (*Carcharodon megalodon*). Multicoloured.
1169 100f. Type **462** . . . . . . 2·30 1·30
MS1170 90 × 120 mm. 70f. Giant-toothed shark (29 × 39 mm); 70f. Diver, giant-toothed shark and great white shark (39 × 29 mm); 70f. Decaying tooth and section of jawbone (triangular, 55 × 28 mm) 4·50 3·25

463 Athletics

1999. 11th South Pacific Games. Multicoloured.
1171 5f. Type **463** . . . . 1·30 70
1172 10f. Tennis . . . . 1·30 70
1173 30f. Karate . . . . 1·50 1·40
1174 70f. Baseball . . . . 1·90 1·10

464 Bwanjep

466 School Building and Computer

465 Scene from "Les Filles de la Neama" and Bloc

1999. Traditional Musical Instruments. Mult.
1175 30f. Type **464** . . . . . . 1·50 80
1176 70f. Bells . . . . 1·90 1·10
1177 100f. Flutes . . . . 2·30 1·30

1999. 29th Death Anniv of Paul Bloc (writer).
1178 **465** 105f. blue, green & purple . . . . 2·30 1·30

1999. 20th Anniv of Auguste Escoffier Commercial and Hotelier Professional School. Multicoloured.
1179 70f. Type **466** . . . . . . 1·10 1·10
1180 70f. School building and chef's hat . . . . 1·10 1·10

467 Unloading Supplies, Helicopters and Map

1999. Humanitarian Aid.
1181 **467** 135f. multicoloured . . . 2·50 1·70

468 10c. Napoleon III Stamp, 1860

1999. 140th Anniv (2000) of First New Caledonian Stamp and "Philexfrance 99" International Stamp Exhibition, Paris.
1182 **468** 70f. multicoloured . . . 1·10 1·10
MS1183 155 × 110 mm. 100f. black (two 1860 10c. stamps) (recess) (36 × 29 mm); 100f. multicoloured (1860 10c. stamp) (thermography) (36 × 29 mm); 100f. Close-up of Napoleon's head (litho) (36 × 29 mm); 100f. gold and black (1860 10c. stamp) (embossing); 700f. 1997 Kagu design and hologram of Napoleon's head (44 × 35 mm) . . . . 19·00 19·00

469 Food Platter

1999. Hotels and Restaurants. Multicoloured.
1184 5f. Type **469** . . . . 1·30 70
1185 30f. Seafood platter . . . . 1·50 80
1186 70f. Hotel cabins by lake . . 1·90 1·10
1187 100f. Modern hotel and swimming pool . . . . . 2·30 2·00

470 Eiffel Tower, Lighthouse with 1949 and 1999 Aircraft

1999. Air. 50th Anniv of First Paris–Noumea Scheduled Flight.
1188 **470** 100f. multicoloured . . . 2·00 1·80

471 Paintings ($\frac{1}{2}$-size illustration)

1999.
1189 **471** 70f. multicoloured . . . 1·90 1·10

472 Aji Aboro (Kanak dance)

1999.
1190 **472** 70f. multicoloured . . . 1·90 1·10

473 Chateau Hagen

1999. Historic Monuments of South Province.
1191 **473** 155f. multicoloured . . . 2·75 1·60

474 Children protecting Tree

1999. Nature Protection: "Don't touch my Tree".
1192 **474** 30f. multicoloured . . . 1·50 75

475 Children around Tree

1999. Greetings Stamps. Multicoloured.
1193 100f. Type **475** ("Merry Christmas") . . . . . . 2·30 1·40
1194 100f. Children with flowers and star ("Best Wishes 2000") . . . . 2·30 1·40
1195 100f. Children and Year 2000 cake ("Happy Birthday") . . . . 2·30 1·40
1196 100f. Children looking in pram ("Congratulations") 2·30 1·40

476 Amedee Lighthouse

2000.
1197 **476** 100f. multicoloured . . . 2·30 1·70

477 *L'Emile Renouf* (four-masted steel barque)

2000. Centenary of Loss of *Emile Renouf* on Durand Reef, Insel Mare.
1198 **477** 135f. multicoloured . . . 2·50 1·50

478 Painted Shells (Gilles Subileau)

2000. Pacific Painters.
1199 **478** 155f. multicoloured . . . 2·75 1·60

479 Snake

2000. Chinese New Year. Year of the Dragon. Sheet 121 × 90 mm containing T **479** and similar horiz design. Multicoloured.
MS1200 105f. Type **479**; 105f. Dragon . . . . 3·50 3·75

480 Prawn

2000. Noumia Aquarium. Multicoloured.
1201 70f. Type **480** . . . . . . 1·90 1·10
1202 70f. Fluorescent corals . . . 1·90 1·10
1203 70f. Hump-headed wrasse (*Cheilinus undulatus*) . . . 1·90 1·10

481 Lockheed P-38 Lightning Fighter

2000. Air. Birth Centenary of Antoine de Saint-Exupery (writer and pilot).
1204 **481** 130f. multicoloured . . . 2·50 1·50

482 Aerial View

2000. Mangrove Swamp, Voh.
1205 **482** 100f. multicoloured . . . 2·30 1·30

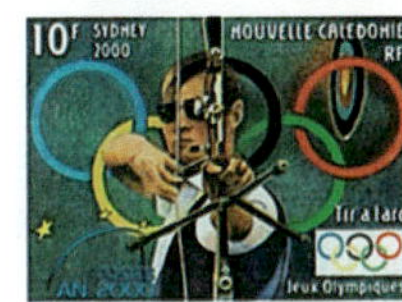
483 Archery

2000. Olympic Games, Sydney. Multicoloured.
1206 10f. Type **483** . . . . . . 1·30 70
1207 30f. Boxing . . . . 1·40 80
1208 80f. Cycling . . . . 2·00 1·20
1209 100f. Fencing . . . . 2·30 1·30

484 Museum Exhibit

2000. Museum of New Caledonia. Multicoloured.
1210 90f. Type **484** . . . . . . 2·00 1·30
1211 105f. Museum exhibit . . . 2·30 1·40

485 Library Building and Lucien Bernheim

2000. Bernheim Library, Noumea.
1212 **485** 500f. brown, blue and green . . . . 7·50 5·00

486 Painting

2000. Eighth Pacific Arts Festival, Kanaky, New Caledonia. Sheet 120 × 90 mm containing T **486** and similar horiz designs. Multicoloured.
MS1213 70f. Type **486**; 70f. Human figures; 70f. Stylized faces and fish; 70f. Stylized faces and fishes on coloured squares . . . . . . 4·50 4·50

487 Henri Dunant (founder), Baby and Patients with Volunteers

2000. Red Cross.
1214 **487** 100f. multicoloured . . . 2·30 1·30

488 Canoeist

2000. Regional Landscapes. Multicoloured.
1215 100f. Type **488** . . . . . . 2·30 1·30
1216 100f. Speedboat near island 2·30 1·30
1217 100f. Sunset and man on raft . . . . 2·30 1·30

489 Queen Hortense

490 Boy on Roller Skates (Kevyn Pamoiloun)

2000.
1218 **489** 110f. red, green and blue 2·30 1·40

2000. "Philately at School". Entries in Children's Painting Competition. Multicoloured.
1219 70f. Type **490** . . . . . . 1·90 1·10
1220 70f. People using airborne vehicles (Lise-Marie Samanich) . . . . 1·90 1·10
1221 70f. Aliens (Alexandre Mandin) . . . . 1·90 1·10

491 Kagu Parents ("Congratulations")

2000. Greetings Stamps. Multicoloured.
1222 100f. Type **491** . . . . . . 2·30 2·00
1223 100f. Kagu on deck chair ("Happy Holidays") . . . 2·30 1·30
1224 100f. Kagu with bunch of flowers ("Best Wishes") 2·30 1·30

492 The Nativity

2000. Christmas.
1225 **492** 100f. multicoloured . . . 2·30 1·30

493 Snakes

2001. Chinese New Year. Year of the Snake. Multicoloured.
1226 100f. Type **493** . . . . . . 2·30 1·30
MS1227 130 × 91 mm. 70f. Snake and Pacific island; 70f. Snake and Chinese symbols . . . . 2·75 2·75

494 *France II* (barque)

2001. Reconstruction of *France II* .
1228 **494** 110f. multicoloured . . . 1·40 1·40

495 Two Nautili

2001. Noumea Aquarium. The New Calendonia Nautilus. Multicoloured.
1229 100f. Type **495** . . . . . . 1·40 1·40
1230 100f. Section through nautilus . . . . 1·40 1·40
1231 100f. Two nautili (different) 1·40 1·40

496 New Caledonian Crow, Tools and Emblem

2001. Association for the Protection of New Caledonian Nature (ASNNC).
1232 **496** 70f. multicoloured . . . 90 90

497 Humpback Whale and Calf

2001. Operation Cetaces (marine mammal South Pacific study programme). Multicoloured.
1233 100f. Type **497** . . . . . . 1·40 1·40
1234 100f. Whales leaping . . . . 1·40 1·40

498 "Guards of Gaia" (statue) (I.Waia)

2001. Ko Neva 2000 Prize Winner.
1235 **498** 70f. multicoloured . . . 95 1·40

499 "Vision of Oceania" (J. Lebars)

2001.
1236 **499** 110f. multicoloured . . . 95 1·40

500 Profiles

2001. Year of Communication.
1237 **500** 265f. multicoloured . . . 2·75 2·00

501 Air International Caledonie Airbus A310-300

2001. Air. First Anniv of Noumea–Osaka Passenger Service.
1238 **501** 110f. multicoloured . . . 1·50 1·40

502 "The Solitary Boatman" (Marik)

2001. Pacific Painters.
1239 **502** 110f. multicoloured . . . 1·40 1·20

503 Observation Capsule on Coral Reef

2001.
1240 **503** 135f. multicoloured . . . 1·70 1·40

504 Qanono Church, Lifou

2001.
1241 **504** 500f. multicoloured . . . 5·75 3·75

505 Fernande Leriche (educator and author)

507 Kite Surfer

506 Cyclists

2001.
1242 **505** 155f. brown, red and blue . . . . 2·20 1·60

2001. 1st Olympic Gold Medal for New Caledonian Sportsman.
1243 **506** 265f. multicoloured . . . 3·75 1·70

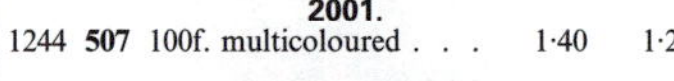

2001.
1244 **507** 100f. multicoloured . . . 1·40 1·20

508 Children on Book

2001. School Philately.
1245 **508** 70f. multicoloured . . . 95 95

509 Easo

2001. Lifou Island. Multicoloured.
1246 100f. Type **509** . . . . . . 1·40 1·20
1247 100f. Jokin . . . . 1·40 1·20

510 Father Christmas

2001. Christmas. Multicoloured.
1248 100f. Type **510** . . . . . . 1·40 1·10
1249 100f. Bat with spotted wings and "Meilleurs Voeux" 1·40 1·10
1250 100f. Bat with party hat and red nose and "Vive la Fete" . . . . 1·40 1·10

511 Horse and Sea Horse

2002. Chinese New Year. Year of the Horse. Multicoloured.
1251 100f. Type **511** . . . . . . 1·50 1·20
MS1252 190 × 30 mm. 70f. Horse's head; 70f. Sea horse . . . . . 2·75 2·75

512 Two Flying Foxes

2002. St. Valentine's Day.
1253 **512** 100f. multicoloured . . . 1·50 1·20

513 Cricketer in Traditional Dress

2002. Cricket.
1254 **513** 100f. multicoloured . . . 1·40 1·20

514 Ancient Axe

2002.
1255 **514** 505f. multicoloured . . . 6·00 4·75

515 Hobie 16 Catamaran

2002. Hobie 16 Catamaran World Championship.
1256 **515** 70f. multicoloured . . . 95 95

516 Loggerhead Turtle (*Caretta caretta*)

2002. Noumea Aquarium. Sheet 185 × 120 mm in shape of turtle containing T **516** and similar horiz designs. Multicoloured.
MS1257 30f. Type **516**; 30f. Green sea turtle (*Chelonia mydas*); 70f. Hawksbill turtle (*Eretmochelys imbricata*) (inscr "imbricat"); 70f. Leatherback sea turtle (*Dermochelys coriacea*) . . . . 3·75 3·75

517 Player

2002. World Cup Football Championship 2002, Japan and South Korea.
1258 **517** 100f. multicoloured . . . 1·50 1·20

518 Coffee Bean Plant

2002. Coffee Production. Multicoloured.
1259 70f. Type **518** . . . . 1·10 1·10
1260 70f. Coffee production process . . . . 1·10 1·10
1261 70f. Cafe and cup of coffee 1·10 1·10

519 *Alcmene* (French corvette)

2002. Exploration of Coast of New Caledonia by *Alcmene*.
1262 **519** 210f. multicoloured . . . 1·10 1·10

520 Emma Piffault (statue)

521 Circus School

2002. Emma Piffault Commemoration.
1263 **520** 10f. multicoloured . . . 25 25

2002.
1264 **521** 70f. multicoloured . . . 95 95

522 Telescope and Caillard

2002. 90th Birth Anniv of Edmond Caillard (astronomer).
1265 **522** 70f. multicoloured . . . 95 95

523 Face in Landscape, Couple, Ship and Birds

2002. Jean Mariotti (writer).
1266 **523** 70f. multicoloured . . . 95 95

524 Adult Sperm Whale and Calf

2002. New Caledonia–Norfolk Island Joint Issue. Operation Cetaces (marine mammal study). Multicoloured.
1267 100f. Type **524** . . . . . . 1·40 1·20
1268 100f. Sperm whale attacked by giant squid . . . . . 1·40 1·20
Stamps of similar designs were issued by Norfolk Islands.

525 Coral Snake Musicians

2002. Christmas.
1269 **525** 100f. multicoloured . . . 1·40 1·10

526 Central Mountain Chain

2002. International Year of Mountains. Litho.
1270 **526** 100f. multicoloured . . . 1·40 1·20

527 Powder Store, Bourail Military Post (½-size illustration)

2002.
1271 **527** 1000f. multicoloured . . 12·00 8·75

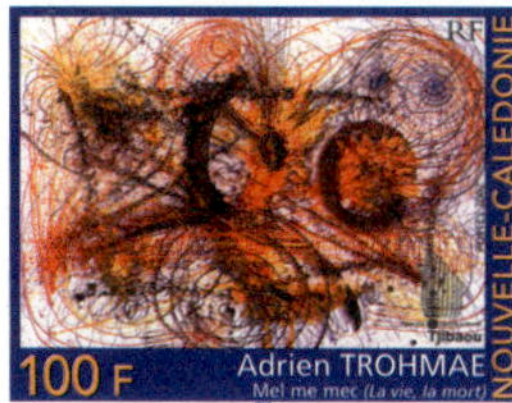

528 "Life and Death" (Adrian Trohmae)

2002. Pacific Painters.
1272 **528** 100f. multicoloured . . . 1·40 1·10

529 Couple enclosed in Heart

2003. St. Valentine's Day.
1273 **529** 100f. multicoloured . . . 1·40 1·10

530 Goat's Head

2003. Chinese New Year. Year of the Goat.
1274 **530** 100f. multicoloured . . . 1·40 1·10

531 Kagu

532 1903 Stamp

2003. (a) With face value.
1274a 1f. green 10 10
1274b **531** 3f. blue 10 10
1275 10f. green 20 20
1276 15f. agate 20 20
1277 30f. orange 75 70
1277a 100f. ultramarine . . . 2·40 2·40

(b) No value expressed. Ordinary or self-adhesive gum.
1278 (70f.) scarlet 90 20

2003. Centenary of First Kagu Stamp.
1290 **532** 70f. multicoloured . . . 95 95

533 High-finned Grouper (*Epinephelus maculates*)

2003. Noumea Aquarium. Groupers. Multicoloured.
1291 70f. Type **533** 95 95
1292 70f. Purple-spotted grouper (*Plectropomus leopardus*) 95 95
1293 70f. Hump-back grouper (*Cromileptes altivelis*) . . 95 95

534 School Building

2003. Grand Noumea High School.
1294 **534** 70f. multicoloured . . . 95 95

535 Shooting

2003. 12th South Pacific Games, Suva. Multicoloured.
1295 5f. Type **535** 15 15
1296 30f. Rugby 50 35
1297 70f. Tennis 95 95

536 Adult Sea Cow and Calf (½-size illustration)

2003. Sea Cow (*Dugong dugon*). Operation Cetaces (marine mammal study). Multicoloured.
1298 100f. Type **536** . . . . . . 1·40 1·20
1299 100f. Adult and calf grazing (40 × 30 mm) . . . . . . 1·40 1·20
Nos. 1298/9 were printed together, se-tenant, forming a composite design.

537 "The Harvest"

2003. Death Centenary of Paul Gauguin (artist) (1st issue).
1300 **537** 100f. multicoloured . . . 1·40 1·20
See also No. **MS**1303.

538 Governor Feillet

2003. Death Centenary of Governor Feillet (first governor).
1301 **538** 100f. black and green . . 1·40 1·20

539 Aircalin Airbus A330–200

2003. 20th Anniv of Aircalin.
1302 **539** 100f. multicoloured . . . 1·40 1·20

540 Tahitian Heads (sketch)

2003. Death Centenary of Paul Gauguin (artist) (2nd issue). Sheet 130 × 90 mm containing T **540** and similar vert design. Multicoloured.
MS1303 100f. Type **540**; 100f. Still-life with Maori statue . . . . 2·75 2·75
Stamps of a similar design were issued by Wallis et Futuna.

541 *Bavayia cyclura*

2003. Geckos. Sheet 140 × 110 mm containing T **541** and similar horiz designs. Multicoloured.
MS1304 30f. × 2, Type **541**; *Rhacodactylus chahoua*; 70f. × 2, *Rhacodactylus ciliatus*; *Eurydactylodes vieillardi* . . . 4·75 4·75

542 German Shepherd Dog

2003.
1305 **542** 105f. multicoloured . . . 1·40 1·20

543 Rade de Balade (1853)

2003.
1306 **543** 110f. brown, green and blue . . . . 1·40 1·20

544 Men and Women surrounding Port (painting) (Robert Tatin)

2003. Pacific Painters.
1307 **544** 135f. multicoloured . . . 1·70 1·50

2003. World Cup Football Championships, Japan and South Korea. As No. 1257 but with inscription added to sheet margin.
MS1308 185 × 120 mm 30f. Type **516**; 30f. Green sea turtle (*Chelonia mydas*); 70f. Hawksbill turtle (*Eretmochelys imbricate*) (inscr "imbricat"); 70f. Leatherback sea turtle (*Dermochelys coriacea*) . . . . 3·75 3·75

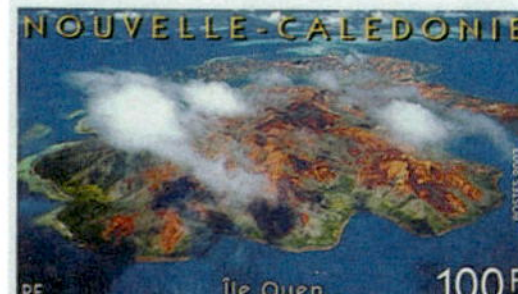

545 Ouen Island

2003.
1309 **545** 100f. multicoloured . . . 1·10 1·20

546 Characters from "Brousse en Folie"

2003. Christmas. "Brousse en Folie" (Bush in Madness) (comic strip created by Bernard Berger).
1310 **546** 100f. multicoloured . . . 1·40 1·20

547 Tiger King

2003. Year of the Monkey (1st issue). Sheet 130 × 100 mm containing T **547** and similar vert design. Multicoloured.
MS1311 100f. × 2 Type **547**; Monkey King on horseback . . . . . 2·75 2·75

548 Three Monkeys

2004. Year of the Monkey (2nd issue).
1312 **548** 70f. multicoloured . . . 1·00 70

549 Cupid enclosed in Heart

2004. St. Valentine's Day.
1313 **549** 100f. multicoloured . . . 1·40 1·20

550 Whale (½-size illustration)

2004. Blainville's Beaked Whales (*Mesoplodon densirostris*). Operation Cetaces (marine mammal study). Sheet 196 × 96 mm containing T **550** and similar horiz design. Multicoloured.
MS1314 100f. × 2 Type **550**; Head of whale (40 × 30 mm) . . . . . 3·00 3·00
The stamps and margin of **MS**1314 form a composite design.

551 Blue-spotted Stingray (*Dasyatis kuhlii*)

2004. Noumea Aquarium. Rays. Multicoloured.
1315 100f. Type **551** . . . . . . 1·40 1·20
1316 100f. Spotted eagle ray (*Aetobatus narinari*) . . . 1·40 1·20
1317 100f. Marbled stingray (*Taeniura meyrni*) . . . . 1·40 1·20

552 Postman on Horseback

2004. Postal Service.
1318 **552** 105f. multicoloured . . . 1·50 1·30

553 Decauville C/N 637 Locomotive (1905)

2004. Railways.
1319 **553** 155f. multicoloured . . . 2·20 1·90

554 *Oxera sulfurea*

2004. Endangered Species. Forest Flowers. Multicoloured.
1320 100f. Type **554** . . . . . . 1·40 1·20
1321 100f. *Turbina inopinata* . . . 1·40 1·20
1322 100f. *Gardenia urvillei* . . . 1·40 1·20

555 Carving, House and Tree

2004. Sandalwood. Multicoloured.
1323 200f. Type **555** . . . . . . 3·00 3·00
(b) Size 40 × 30 mm.
MS1324 141 × 110 mm. 100f. × 3, Fruit; Distillery; Sandalwood products . . . . 4·50 4·50

556 Early and Modern Noumea

2004. 150th Anniv of Noumea.
1325 **556** 70f. multicoloured . . . 1·00 85

557 Cat

2004. Cats. Multicoloured.
1326 100f. Type **557** . . . . . . 1·40 1·20
1327 100f. Oriental . . . . 1·40 1·20
1328 100f. White Persian . . . . 1·40 1·20
1329 100f. Birman . . . . 1·40 1·20
1330 100f. European shorthair . . 1·40 1·20
1331 100f. Abyssinian . . . . . 1·40 1·20

558 Gymnasts

2004. Olympic Games, Athens. Multicoloured.
1332 70f. Type **558** . . . . 1·00 1·00
1333 70f. Women's relay . . . . 1·00 1·00
1334 70f. Men's volleyball . . . 1·00 1·00

559 Face, Butterfly, Hut and Trees

2004. French Research in the Pacific. Multicoloured.
1335 100f. Type **559** . . . . . . 1·40 1·40
1336 100f. Palms, dolphin and woman . . . . 1·40 1·20

560 Walla Bay, Belep

2004. Tourism.
1337 **560** 100f. multicoloured . . . 1·40 1·20

561 "Tradimodernition" (Nat D.)

2004. Pacific Painters.
1338 **561** 505f. multicoloured . . . 7·00 7·00

562 Nativity

2004. Christmas.
1339 **562** 100f. multicoloured . . . 1·40 1·20

563 Rooster

2005. New Year. "Year of the Rooster".
1340 **563** 100f. multicoloured . . . 1·40 1·20

564 Anniversary Emblem

2005. Centenary of Rotary International.
1341 **564** 110f. multicoloured . . . 1·50 1·30

565 People from Many Nations

2005. French-speaking Culture.
1342 **565** 135f. multicoloured . . . 1·90 1·60
A stamp of similar design was issued by Wallis et Futuna.

566 Swimming, Cycling and Running

2005. International Triathlon Competition, Noumea.
1343 **566** 80f. multicoloured . . . 1·10 95

567 Passenger Ship

2005. Coastal Tour.
1344 **567** 75f. multicoloured . . . 1·10 90

568 Pan-tropical Spotted Dolphins (*Stenella attenuate*)

2005. Operation Cetaces (marine mammal study). Multicoloured.
1345 100f. Type **568** . . . . . . 1·40 1·20
1346 100f. Bottle-nose dolphin (*Tursiop truncates*) (inscr "Tiurciop") . . . . . . 1·40 1·20
1347 100f. Spinner dolphin (*Stenella longirostris*) . . . 1·40 1·00

569 Corpet et Louvet 0-6-OTs Locomotive

2005. Railways.
1348 **569** 745f. multicoloured . . . 11·00 11·00

570 Black-tip Reef Shark (*Carcharhinus melanopterus*)

2005. Noumea Aquarium. Sheet 140 × 90 mm containing T **570** and similar horiz design. Multicoloured.
MS1349 110f. × 2, Type **551**; Tawny nurse shark (*Nebrius ferrugineus*) 3·25 3·25
The stamps and margin of **MS**1349 form a composite design.

571 *Eunymphicus uvaeensis*

2005. Endangered Species. Birds. Multicoloured.
1350 75f. Type **571** . . . . 1·10 90
1351 75f. *Eunymphicus cornutus* 1·10 90
1352 75f. *Cyanoramphus saisseti* 1·10 90

572 Luengoni Beach, Lifou

2005. Tourism.
1353 **572** 85f. multicoloured . . . 1·20 1·00

573 Emblem and People of Many Nations ($\frac{1}{2}$-size illustration)

2005. East Pacific Region IOMS Conference, Noumea.
1354 **573** 150f. multicoloured . . . 2·00 1·70

574 "My Dream of Peace" (Mendoza)

2005. International Day of Peace.
1355 **574** 85f. multicoloured . . . 1·20 1·00

2005. Nos. 1114 and 1277a surch.
1356 10f. on 100f. blue (No. 1114) 15 10
1357 10f. on 100f. ultramarine (No. 1277a) 15 10

2005. Nos. 1345/7 surch.
1358 10f. on 100f. multicoloured 15 10
1359 10f. on 100f. multicoloured 15 10
1360 10f. on 100f. multicoloured 15 10

577 Ouare

2005. Petroglyphs (rock paintings).
1361 **577** 120f. violet and vermilion . . . . . . 1·30 1·10
1362 – 120f. chocolate and blue 1·30 1·10
1363 – 120f. green and scarlet vermilion . . . . . . 1·30 1·10
DESIGNS: 1361, Type **577**; 1362, Balade; 1363, Croix enveloppees (wrapped crosses).

578 Marquis du Bouzet

579 Santa sailing Yacht

2005. Birth Bicentenary of Marquis du Bouzet (governor).
1364 **578** 500f. black, blue and violet . . . . 5·75 4·50

2005. Christmas.
1365 **579** 110f. multicoloured . . . 1·30 1·10

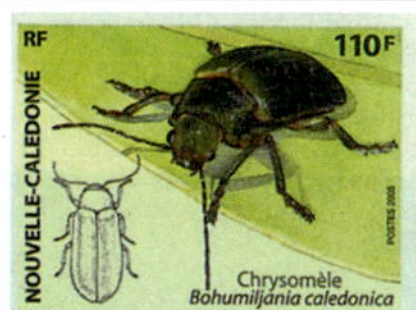

580 *Bohumiljania caledonica*

2005. Insects. Multicoloured.

1366 110f. Type **580** 1·30 1·10
1367 110f. *Bohumiljania humboldti* 1·30 1·10
1368 110f. *Cazeresia Montana* 1·30 1·10

581 Snakes and Twigs

2005. Kanak and Oceanic Art Fund.

1369 **581** 190f. multicoloured 2·20 1·75

OFFICIAL STAMPS

O 49 Ancestor Pole

O 110 Carved Wooden Pillow (Noumea Museum)

1958. Inscr "OFFICIEL".

O344 **O 49** 1f. yellow 40 85
O345 3f. green 55 90
O346 4f. purple 70 40
O347 5f. blue 45 1·10
O348 9f. black 90 1·30
O349 A 10f. violet 2·30 60
O350 13f. green 1·00 3·25
O351 15f. blue 2·00 1·60
O352 24f. mauve 3·00 2·00
O353 26f. orange 1·50 2·75
O354 B 50f. green 1·40 6·50
O355 100f. brown 6·00 17·00
O356 200f. red 5·50 38·00

DESIGNS: A, B, Different idols.

1973.

O525 **O 110** 1f. green, blk & yell 2·75 2·50
O526 2f. red, black & grn 2·75 3·50
O527 3f. green, blk & brn 2·75 3·25
O528 4f. green, black & bl 2·75 3·00
O529 5f. green, blk & mve 3·00 2·50
O530 9f. green, black & bl 3·00 3·75
O531 10f. green, blk & orge 3·25 2·50
O532 11f. grn, blk & mve 2·75 3·50
O533 12f. green, blk & turq 3·25 2·75
O534 15f. green, blk & lt grn 2·00 3·00
O535 20f. green, blk & red 2·75 3·50
O536 23f. green, blk & red 3·00 3·75
O537 24f. green, blk & bl 2·00 3·75
O538 25f. green, blk & grey 2·30 3·75
O539 26f. green, blk & yell 2·30 3·75
O540 29f. red, black & grn 2·30 3·50
O541 31f. red, black & yell 2·30 3·25
O542 35f. red, black & yell 2·30 3·25
O543 36f. green, blk & mve 2·30 3·75
O544 38f. red, black & brn 2·75 3·75
O545 40f. red, black & bl 2·75 3·75
O546 42f. green, blk & brn 2·30 3·75
O547 50f. green, blk & bl 2·50 4·00
O548 58f. blue, blk & grn 3·25 4·00
O549 65f. red, black & mve 2·75 4·00
O550 76f. red, black & yell 3·75 4·25
O551 100f. green, blk & red 3·50 4·50
O552 200f. green, blk & yell 6·25 7·00

PARCEL POST STAMPS

1926. Optd **Colis Postaux** or surch also.

P137 **17** 50c. on 5f. green on mauve 50 5·25
P138 1f. blue 50 6·00
P139 2f. red on blue 1·00 6·75

1930. Optd **Colis Postaux**.

P179 **23** 50c. brown and mauve 45 3·00
P180 **24** 1f. pink and drab 75 5·00
P181 2f. brown and orange 55 5·50

POSTAGE DUE STAMPS

1903. Postage Due stamps of French Colonies optd **CINQUANTENAIRE 24 SEPTEMBRE 1853 1903** and eagle. Imperf.

D78 U 5c. blue 1·50 1·10
D79 10c. brown 9·00 5·25
D80 15c. green 30·00 2·30
D81 30c. red 14·00 19·00
D82 50c. purple 80·00 8·75
D83 60c. brown on buff £200 44·00
D84 1f. pink 23·00 10·00
D85 2f. brown £750 £800

D 18 Outrigger Canoe

D 25 Sambar Stag

D 38

1906.

D102 **D 18** 5c. blue on blue 25 25
D103 10c. brown on buff 30 2·75
D104 15c. green 25 3·00
D105 20c. black on yellow 45 1·60
D106 30c. red 50 3·25
D107 50c. blue on cream 75 5·50
D108 60c. green on blue 50 2·75
D109 1f. green on cream 65 5·75

1926. Surch.

D137 **D 18** 2f. on 1f. mauve 60 8·25
D138 3f. on 1f. brown 1·30 8·25

1928.

D179 **D 25** 2c. brown and blue 10 2·30
D180 4c. green and red 10 2·30
D181 5c. grey and orange 45 2·75
D182 10c. blue and mauve 10 1·00
D183 15c. red and olive 15 2·75
D184 20c. olive and red 1·80 4·50
D185 25c. blue and brown 10 3·75
D186 30c. olive and green 20 4·25
D187 50c. red and brown 1·90 4·00
D188 60c. red and mauve 2·75 4·75
D189 1f. green and blue 2·75 4·75
D190 2f. olive and red 4·00 4·25
D191 3f. brown and violet 3·00 4·25

1948.

D328 **D 38** 10c. mauve 10 4·50
D329 30c. brown 10 5·00
D330 50c. green 15 5·00
D331 1f. brown 15 5·00
D332 2f. red 45 4·50
D333 3f. brown 25 4·50
D334 4f. blue 45 5·25
D335 5f. red 40 5·50
D336 10f. green 70 5·75
D337 20f. blue 70 4·75

D 222 New Caledonian Flying Fox

1983.

D703 **D 223** 1f. multicoloured 1·00 2·50
D704 2f. multicoloured 1·00 2·50
D705 3f. multicoloured 1·00 2·50
D706 4f. multicoloured 1·10 2·75
D707 5f. multicoloured 1·10 2·75
D708 10f. multicoloured 1·10 2·75
D709 20f. multicoloured 1·30 3·00
D710 40f. multicoloured 1·90 3·50
D711 50f. multicoloured 2·00 3·75

NEWFOUNDLAND Pt. 1

An island off the east coast of Canada. A British Dominion merged since 1949 with Canada, whose stamps it now uses.

1857. 12 pence = 1 shilling;
20 shillings = 1 pound.
1866. 100 cents = 1 dollar.

1

2

3 Royal Crown and Heraldic Flowers of the United Kingdom

1857. Imperf.

1 **1** 1d. purple £110 £180
10 **2** 2d. red £375 £500
11 **3** 3d. green 80·00 £160
12 **2** 4d. red £2500 £850
13 **1** 5d. brown £100 £350
14 **2** 6d. red £3000 £600
7 6½d. red £2750 £3000
8 8d. red £275 £500
9 1s. red £15000 £5500

The frame design of Type **2** differs for each value.

1861. Imperf.

16 **1** 1d. brown £200 £350
17 **2** 2d. lake £200 £450
18 4d. lake 38·00 £100
19a **1** 5d. brown 65·00 £200
20 **2** 6d. lake 25·00 £100
21 6½d. lake 80·00 £450
22 8d. lake 90·00 £600
23 1s. lake 42·00 £300

6 Codfish

7 Common Seal on Ice-floe

8 Prince Consort

9 Queen Victoria

10 Schooner

11 Queen Victoria

1866. Perf (2c. also roul).

31 **6** 2c. green 85·00 40·00
26 **7** 5c. brown £550 £170
32 **8** 10c. black £200 45·00
33 **9** 12c. brown 48·00 48·00
29 **10** 13c. orange £110 85·00
30 **11** 24c. blue 38·00 38·00

12 King Edward VII when Prince of Wales

14 Queen Victoria

1868. Perf or roul.

34 **12** 1c. purple 65·00 55·00
36 **14** 3c. orange £300 £100
37 3c. blue £275 22·00
38 **7** 5c. black £250 £110
43 5c. blue £180 3·50
39 **14** 6c. red 9·00 21·00

19 Newfoundland Dog

15 King Edward VII when Prince of Wales

16 Codfish

17

18 Common Seal on Ice-floe

20 Atlantic Brigantine

21 Queen Victoria

1880.

49 **19** ½c. red 14·00 7·50
59 ½c. black 9·50 5·00
44a **15** 1c. brown 30·00 11·00
50a 1c. green 6·00 3·50
46 **16** 2c. green 50·00 26·00
51 2c. orange 20·00 6·00
47a **17** 3c. blue 80·00 4·50
52 3c. brown 65·00 2·00
59a **18** 5c. blue 70·00 4·25
54 **20** 10c. black 60·00 55·00

1890.

55 **21** 3c. grey 35·00 2·25

This stamp on pink paper was stained by sea-water.

22 Queen Victoria

23 John Cabot

24 Cape Bonavista

25 Caribou-hunting

1897. 400th Anniv of Discovery of Newfoundland and 60th Year of Queen Victoria's Reign. Dated "1497 1897".

66 **22** 1c. green 2·75 7·50
67 **23** 2c. red 2·25 2·75
68 **24** 3c. blue 3·50 1·00
69 **25** 4c. olive 9·50 5·00
70 – 5c. violet 14·00 3·00
71 – 6c. brown 9·50 3·25
72 – 8c. orange 21·00 9·00
73 – 10c. brown 42·00 8·50
74 – 12c. blue 35·00 7·50
75 – 15c. red 20·00 18·00
76 – 24c. violet 25·00 23·00
77 – 30c. blue 48·00 75·00
78 – 35c. red 60·00 65·00
79 – 60c. black 19·00 13·00

DESIGNS—As Type **24**: 5c. Mining; 6c. Logging; 8c. Fishing; 10c. Cabot's ship, the "Matthew"; 15c. Seals; 24c. Salmon-fishing; 35c. Iceberg. As Type **23**: 12c. Willow/red grouse; 30c. Seal of the Colony; 60c. Henry VII.

1897. Surch **ONE CENT** and bar.

80 **21** 1c. on 3c. grey 55·00 24·00

39 Prince Edward, later Duke of Windsor

40 Queen Victoria

1897. Royal portraits.

83 **39** ½c. olive 2·25 1·50
84 **40** 1c. red 3·25 3·50
85a – 1c. green 11·00 20
86 – 2c. orange 5·00 5·50
87 – 2c. red 17·00 40
88 – 3c. orange 22·00 30
89 – 4c. violet 26·00 4·75
90 – 5c. blue 42·00 3·00

DESIGNS: 2c. King Edward VII when Prince of Wales; 3c. Queen Alexandra when Princess of Wales; 4c. Queen Mary when Duchess of York; 5c. King George V when Duke of York.

45 Map of Newfoundland

46 King James I

47 Arms of Colonisation Co.

49 "Endeavour" (immigrant ship), 1610

1908.

94 **45** 2c. lake 27·00 1·00

1910. Dated "1610 1910".

109 **46** 1c. green 2·00 30
107 **47** 2c. red 5·50 40
97 – 3c. olive 6·00 17·00
98 **49** 4c. violet 16·00 16·00
108 – 5c. blue 8·00 2·75
111 – 6c. purple 18·00 48·00
112 – 8c. bistre 50·00 75·00
102 – 9c. green 48·00 80·00
103 – 10c. grey 55·00 £100

115	–	12c. brown	65·00	65·00
105	–	15c. black	65·00	£100

DESIGNS—HORIZ: 5c. Cupids; 8c. Mosquito; 9c. Logging camp, Red Indian Lake; 10c. Paper mills, Grand Falls. VERT: 3c. John Guy; 6c. Sir Francis Bacon; 12c. King Edward VII; 15c. King George V. (Cupids and Mosquito are places).

57 Queen Mary

58 King George V

67 Seal of Newfoundland

1911. Coronation.

117	**57**	1c. green	10·00	30
118	**58**	2c. red	6·00	20
119	–	3c. brown	21·00	35·00
120	–	4c. purple	19·00	27·00
121	–	5c. blue	7·00	1·50
122	–	6c. grey	13·00	25·00
123	–	8c. blue	55·00	75·00
124	–	9c. blue	22·00	28·00
125	–	10c. green	30·00	42·00
126	–	12c. plum	25·00	48·00
127	**67**	15c. lake	22·00	48·00

PORTRAITS—VERT (As Type **57/8**): 3c. Duke of Windsor when Prince of Wales; 4c. King George VI when Prince Albert; 5c. Princess Mary, the Princess Royal; 6c. Duke of Gloucester when Prince Henry; 8c. Duke of Kent when Prince George; 9c. Prince John; 10c. Queen Alexandra; 12c. Duke of Connaught.

68 Caribou

1919. Newfoundland Contingent, 1914–18.

130	**68**	1c. green	3·75	20
131		2c. red	3·75	85
132		3c. brown	8·00	20
133		4c. mauve	9·50	80
134		5c. blue	9·50	1·25
135		6c. grey	7·50	42·00
136		8c. purple	12·00	48·00
137		10c. green	7·00	4·50
138		12c. orange	19·00	65·00
139		15c. blue	18·00	65·00
140		24c. brown	22·00	28·00
141		36c. olive	16·00	32·00

DESIGNS—Each inscr with the name of a different action: 1c. Suvla Bay; 3c. Gueudecourt; 4c. Beaumont Hamel; 6c. Monchy; 10c. Steenbeck; 15c. Langemarck; 24c. Cambrai; 36c. Combles. The 2, 5, 8 and 12c. are inscribed "Royal Naval Reserve-Ubique".

1919. Air. Hawker Flight. No. 132a optd **FIRST TRANS- ATLANTIC AIR POST April, 1919.**

142	**68**	3c. brown	£16000	£8500

1919. Air. Alcock and Brown Flight. Surch **Trans-Atlantic AIR POST, 1919. ONE DOLLAR.**

143		$1 on 15c. red (No. 75)	£110	£110

1920. Surch in words between bars.

144		2c. on 30c. blue (No. 77)	4·75	21·00
146		3c. on 15c. red (No. 75)	24·00	20·00
147		3c. on 35c. red (No. 78)	10·00	16·00

1921. Air. Optd **AIR MAIL to Halifax, N.S. 1921.**

148a		35c. red (No. 78)	95·00	80·00

73 Twin Hills, Tor's Cove

75 Statue of Fighting Newfoundlander, St. John's

1923.

149	**73**	1c. green	2·00	20
150	–	2c. red	1·00	10
151	**75**	3c. brown	1·50	10
152	–	4c. purple	1·00	30
153	–	5c. blue	2·75	1·75
154	–	6c. grey	6·00	9·00
155	–	8c. purple	7·50	3·50
156	–	9c. green	18·00	29·00
157	–	10c. violet	8·50	4·00
158	–	11c. olive	3·75	19·00
159	–	12c. lake	3·50	11·00
160	–	15c. blue	3·50	22·00
161	–	20c. brown	12·00	13·00
162	–	24c. brown	48·00	75·00

DESIGNS—HORIZ: 2c. South-west Arm, Trinity; 6c. Upper Steadies, Humber River; 8c. Quidi Vidi, near St. John's; 9c. Caribou crossing lake; 11c. Shell Bird Island; 12c. Mount Moriah, Bay of Islands; 20c. Placentia. VERT: 4c. Humber River; 5c. Coast at Trinity; 10c. Humber River Canon; 15c. Humber River, near Little Rapids; 24c. Topsail Falls.

1927. Air. Optd **Air Mail DE PINEDO 1927**.

163		60c. black (No. 79)	£30000	£8500

88 Newfoundland and Labrador

89 S.S. "Caribou"

90 King George V and Queen Mary

91 Duke of Windsor when Prince of Wales

1928. Publicity issue.

164	**88**	1c. green	2·25	1·25
180	**89**	2c. red	1·75	40
181	**90**	3c. brown	1·00	20
201	**91**	4c. mauve	2·00	1·25
183	–	5c. grey	7·00	3·75
184a	–	6c. blue	2·25	16·00
170	–	8c. brown	3·75	32·00
171	–	9c. green	2·00	17·00
185	–	10c. violet	4·25	3·75
173	–	12c. lake	2·00	22·00
174a	–	14c. purple	8·00	8·50
175	–	15c. blue	4·50	30·00
176a	–	20c. black	3·00	7·00
177	–	28c. green	28·00	50·00
178	–	30c. brown	6·00	17·00

DESIGNS—HORIZ: 5c. Express train; 6c. Newfoundland Hotel, St. John's; 8c. Heart's Content; 10c. War Memorial, St. John's; 15c. Vickers Vimy aircraft; 20c. Parliament House, St. John's. VERT: 9, 14c. Cabot Tower, St. John's; 12, 28c. G.P.O., St. John's; 30c. Grand Falls, Labrador.

1929. Surch **THREE CENTS**.

188		3c. on 6c. (No. 154)	1·00	6·50

1930. Air. No. 141 surch **Trans-Atlantic AIR MAIL By B. M. "Columbia" September 1930 Fifty Cents**.

191	**68**	50c. on 36c. olive	£5500	£4750

103 Westland Limousine III and Dog-team

104 Vickers Vimy Biplane and early Sailing Packet

105 Routes of historic Trans-Atlantic Flights

1931. Air.

192	**103**	15c. brown	9·00	16·00
193	**104**	50c. green	32·00	55·00
194	**105**	$1 blue	50·00	95·00

107 Codfish

108 King George V

110 Duke of Windsor when Prince of Wales

111 Reindeer

112 Queen Elizabeth II when Princess

121 Corner Brook Paper Mills

1932.

209	**107**	1c. green	3·25	30
276		1c. grey	20	1·75
210	**108**	2c. red	1·50	20
223		2c. green	2·25	10
211	–	3c. brown	1·50	20
212	**110**	4c. lilac	7·50	2·00
224		4c. red	4·50	40
213	**111**	5c. purple	6·50	2·75
225c		5c. violet	1·00	30
214	**112**	6c. blue	4·00	14·00
226	–	7c. lake	3·00	3·75
282	**121**	8c. red	2·25	3·50
215	–	10c. brown	70	65
216	–	14c. black	4·25	5·50
217	–	15c. purple	1·25	2·00
218	–	20c. green	1·00	1·00
228	–	24c. blue	1·00	3·25
219	–	25c. grey	2·00	2·25
220	–	30c. blue	40·00	35·00
289	–	48c. brown	4·00	7·50

DESIGNS—VERT: 3c. Queen Mary; 7c. Queen Mother when Duchess of York. HORIZ: 10c. Salmon; 14c. Newfoundland dog; 15c. Harp seal; 20c. Cape Race; 24c. Loading iron ore, Bell Island; 25c. Sealing fleet; 30, 48c. Fishing fleet.

1932. Air. Surch **TRANS-ATLANTIC WEST TO EAST Per Dornier DO-X May, 1932. One Dollar and Fifty Cents**.

221	**105**	$1.50 on $1 blue	£225	£225

1933. Optd **L. & S. Post.** ("Land and Sea") between bars.

229	**103**	15c. brown	4·25	14·00

124 Put to Flight

1933. Air.

230	**124**	5c. brown	19·00	20·00
231	–	10c. yellow	14·00	35·00
232	–	30c. blue	32·00	48·00
233	–	60c. green	50·00	£110
234	–	75c. brown	50·00	£110

DESIGNS: 10c. Land of Heart's Delight; 30c. Spotting the herd; 60c. News from home; 75c. Labrador.

1933. Air. Balbo Trans-Atlantic Mass Formation Flight. No. 234 surch **1933 GEN. BALBO FLIGHT. $4.50.**

235		$4.50 on 75c. brown	£275	£325

130 Sir Humphrey Gilbert

131 Compton Castle, Devon

1933. 350th Anniv of Annexation. Dated "1583 1933".

236	**130**	1c. black	1·00	1·50
237	**131**	2c. green	1·75	70
238	–	3c. brown	2·50	1·25
239	–	4c. red	80	50
240	–	5c. violet	2·00	80
241	–	7c. blue	15·00	17·00
242	–	8c. orange	8·00	15·00
243	–	9c. blue	7·00	16·00
244	–	10c. brown	4·00	11·00
245	–	14c. black	16·00	30·00
246w	–	15c. red	7·50	24·00
247	–	20c. green	14·00	19·00
248	–	24c. purple	17·00	24·00
249	–	32c. black	8·00	50·00

DESIGNS—VERT: 3c. Gilbert coat of arms; 5c. Anchor token; 14c. Royal Arms; 15c. Gilbert in the "Squirrel"; 24c. Queen Elizabeth I; 32c. Gilbert's statue at Truro. HORIZ: 4c. Eton College; 7c. Gilbert commissioned by Elizabeth; 8c. Fleet leaving Plymouth, 1583; 9c. Arrival at St. John's; 10c. Annexation, 5 August, 1583; 20c. Map of Newfoundland.

1935. Silver Jubilee.

250	**143a**	4c. red	1·00	1·75
251		5c. violet	1·25	3·00
252		7c. blue	2·25	7·00
253		24c. olive	5·00	14·00

1937. Coronation.

254	**143b**	2c. green	1·00	3·00
255		4c. red	1·60	4·00
256		5c. purple	3·00	4·00

144 Atlantic Cod

155 King George VI

1937. Coronation.

257	**144**	1c. grey	3·00	30
258e	–	3c. brown	6·50	3·75
259	–	7c. blue	2·50	1·25
260	–	8c. red	2·00	4·00
261	–	10c. black	5·00	9·00
262	–	14c. black	1·40	3·00
263	–	15c. red	13·00	4·50
264f	–	20c. green	2·50	9·50
265	–	24c. blue	2·50	3·00
266	–	25c. black	2·75	2·75
267	–	48c. purple	8·50	6·50

DESIGNS: 3c. Map of Newfoundland; 7c. Rein-deer; 8c. Corner Brook Paper Mills; 10c. Atlantic salmon; 14c. Newfoundland dog; 15c. Harp seal; 20c. Cape Race; 24c. Bell Island; 25c. Sealing fleet; 48c. The Banks fishing fleet.

1938.

277	**155**	2c. green	30	75
278	–	3c. red	30	30
279	–	4c. blue	2·25	40
271	–	7c. blue	1·00	6·50

DESIGNS: 3c. Queen Mother; 4c. Queen Elizabeth II, aged 12; 7c. Queen Mary.

159 King George VI and Queen Elizabeth

1938. Royal Visit.

272	**159**	5c. blue	3·25	1·00

1939. Surch in figures and triangles.

273	**159**	2c. on 5c. blue	2·50	50
274		4c. on 5c. blue	2·00	1·00

161 Grenfell on the "Strathcona" (after painting by Gribble)

1941. 50th Anniv of Sir Wilfred Grenfell's Labrador Mission.

275	**161**	5c. blue	30	1·00

162 Memorial University College

1942.

290	**162**	30c. red	1·00	3·25

163 St. John's

165 Queen Elizabeth II when Princess

1943. Air.
291 163 7c. blue . . . 50 1·00

1946. Surch **TWO CENTS**.
292 162 2c. on 30c. red . . . 30 1·00

1947. 21st Birthday of Princess Elizabeth.
293 165 4c. blue . . . 30 1·00

166 Cabot off Cape Bonavista

1947. 450th Anniv of Cabot's Discovery of Newfoundland.
294 166 5c. violet . . . 20 1·00

POSTAGE DUE STAMPS

D 1

1939.
D1 D 1 1c. green . . . 2·25 12·00
D2 2c. red . . . 13·00 7·50
D3 3c. blue . . . 5·00 25·00
D4 4c. orange . . . 9·00 20·00
D5 5c. brown . . . 5·50 28·00
D6 10c. purple . . . 7·00 20·00

NEW GUINEA Pt. 1

Formerly a German Colony, part of the island of New Guinea. Occupied by Australian forces during the 1914–18 war and subsequently joined with Papua and administered by the Australian Commonwealth under trusteeship. After the Japanese defeat in 1945 Australian stamps were used until 1952 when the combined issue appeared for Papua and New Guinea (q.v.). The stamps overprinted "N.W. PACIFIC ISLANDS" were also used in Nauru and other ex-German islands.

12 pence = 1 shilling;
20 shillings = 1 pound.

1914. "Yacht" key-types of German New Guinea surch **G.R.I.** and value in English currency.
16 N 1d. on 3pf. brown . . . 45·00 55·00
17 1d. on 5pf. green . . . 18·00 32·00
18 2d. on 10pf. red . . . 24·00 40·00
19 2d. on 20pf. blue . . . 28·00 45·00
5 2½d. on 10pf. red . . . 65·00 £140
6 2½d. on 20pf. blue . . . 75·00 £150
22 3d. on 25pf. blk & red on yell . . . £110 £160
23 3d. on 30pf. blk & orge on buff . . . 90·00 £140
24 4d. on 40pf. black and red . . . £100 £170
25 5d. on 50pf. black & pur on buff . . . £160 £200
26 8d. on 80pf. blk & red on rose . . . £325 £400
12 O 1s on 1m. red . . . £1600 £2500
13 2s. on 2m. blue . . . £1700 £2500
14 3s. on 3m. black . . . £3250 £4250
15 5s. on 5m. red and black . . . £7500 £9000

Nos. 3/4 surch **1**.
31 N "1" on 2d. on 10pf. red . . . £15000 £15000
32 "1" on 2d. on 20pf. blue . . . £15000 £9500

4

1914. Registration labels with names of various towns surch **G.R.I. 3d.**
33 4 3d. black and red . . . £180 £200

1914. "Yacht" key-types of German Marshall Islands surch **G.R.I.** and value in English currency.
50 N 1d. on 3pf. brown . . . 50·00 85·00
51 1d. on 5pf. green . . . 50·00 55·00
52 2d. on 10pf. red . . . 17·00 26·00
53 2d. on 20pf. blue . . . 18·00 30·00
64g 2½d. on 10pf. red . . . £10000
64h 2½d. on 20pf. blue . . . £11500
54 3d. on 25pf. black and red on yellow . . . £275 £375
55 3d. on 30pf. black and orange on buff . . . £300 £400
56 4d. on 40pf. black and red . . . £100 £140
57 5d. on 50pf. black and purple on buff . . . £140 £190
58 8d. on 80pf. black and red on rose . . . £400 £500
59 O 1s. on 1m. red . . . £2000 £3250
60 2s. on 2m. blue . . . £1200 £2500
61 3s. on 3m. black . . . £3750 £5500
62 5s. on 5m. red and black . . . £7500 £9500

1915. Nos. 52 and 53 surch **1**.
63 N "1" on 2d. on 10pf. red . . . £140 £170
64 "1" on 2d. on 20pf. blue . . . £3000 £2250

1915. Stamps of Australia optd **N. W. PACIFIC ISLANDS**.
119 3 ½d. green . . . 1·25 3·50
103 1d. red . . . 3·75 1·60
120 1d. violet . . . 1·75 6·50
94 1 2d. grey . . . 6·00 17·00
121 3 2d. orange . . . 7·00 2·75
122 2d. red . . . 9·50 3·75
74 1 2½d. blue . . . 2·75 16·00
96 3d. olive . . . 5·50 11·00
70 3 4d. orange . . . 4·00 15·00
123 4d. violet . . . 20·00 40·00
124 4d. blue . . . 11·00 60·00
105 5d. brown . . . 3·00 12·00
110 1 6d. blue . . . 4·50 14·00
89 9d. violet . . . 16·00 21·00
90 1s. green . . . 11·00 24·00
115 2s. brown . . . 21·00 38·00
116 5s. grey and yellow . . . 60·00 65·00
84 10s. grey and pink . . . £110 £160
99 £1 brown and blue . . . £250 £400

1918. Nos. 105 and 90 surch **One Penny**.
100 3 1d. on 5d. brown . . . 90·00 80·00
101 1 1d. on 1s. green . . . 90·00 75·00

12 Native Village

14 Raggiana Bird of Paradise (Dates either side of value)

1925.
125 12 ½d. orange . . . 2·50 7·00
126 1d. green . . . 2·50 5·50
126a 1½d. red . . . 3·25 2·75
127 2d. red . . . 2·50 4·50
128 3d. blue . . . 4·50 4·00
129 4d. olive . . . 13·00 21·00
130b 6d. brown . . . 5·00 48·00
131 9d. purple . . . 13·00 45·00
132 1s. green . . . 15·00 27·00
133 2s. lake . . . 30·00 48·00
134 5s. brown . . . 48·00 65·00
135 10s. pink . . . £100 £180
136 £1 grey . . . £190 £300

1931. Air. Optd with biplane and **AIR MAIL**.
137 12 ½d. orange . . . 1·50 7·00
138 1d. green . . . 1·60 5·00
139 1½d. red . . . 1·25 5·00
140 2d. red . . . 1·25 7·00
141 3d. blue . . . 1·75 13·00
142 4d. olive . . . 1·25 9·00
143 6d. brown . . . 1·75 14·00
144 9d. purple . . . 3·00 17·00
145 1s. green . . . 3·00 17·00
146 2s. lake . . . 7·00 42·00
147 5s. brown . . . 20·00 65·00
148 10s. pink . . . 75·00 £100
149 £1 grey . . . £140 £250

1931. 10th Anniv of Australian Administration. Dated "1921–1931".
150 14 1d. green . . . 4·00 2·00
151 1½d. red . . . 5·00 10·00
152 2d. red . . . 5·00 2·25
153 3d. blue . . . 5·00 4·75
154 4d. olive . . . 6·50 21·00
155 5d. green . . . 5·00 21·00
156 6d. brown . . . 5·00 19·00
157 9d. violet . . . 8·50 19·00
158 1s. grey . . . 6·00 15·00
159 2s. lake . . . 10·00 32·00
160 5s. brown . . . 42·00 55·00
161 10s. pink . . . 85·00 £130
162 £1 grey . . . £190 £250

1931. Air. Optd with biplane and **AIR MAIL**.
163 14 ½d. orange . . . 3·25 3·25
164 1d. green . . . 4·00 4·75
165 1½d. red . . . 3·75 10·00
166 2d. red . . . 3·75 3·00
167 3d. blue . . . 6·00 6·50
168 4d. olive . . . 6·00 6·00
169 5d. green . . . 6·00 11·00
170 6d. brown . . . 7·00 26·00
171 9d. violet . . . 8·00 15·00
172 1s. grey . . . 7·50 15·00
173 2s. lake . . . 16·00 48·00
174 5s. brown . . . 42·00 70·00
175 10s. pink . . . 60·00 £120
176 £1 grey . . . £110 £250

1932. As T **14**, but without dates.
177 1d. green . . . 2·50 20
178 1½d. red . . . 2·50 11·00
179 2d. red . . . 2·50 20
179a 2½d. green . . . 6·50 21·00
180 3d. blue . . . 3·25 1·00
180a 3½d. red . . . 13·00 11·00
181 4d. olive . . . 3·25 6·00
182 5d. green . . . 3·50 70
183 6d. brown . . . 4·50 3·25
184 9d. violet . . . 9·50 22·00
185 1s. grey . . . 4·50 10·00
186 2s. lake . . . 4·00 17·00
187 5s. brown . . . 27·00 45·00
188 10s. pink . . . 48·00 70·00
189 £1 grey . . . 95·00 £100

1932. Air. T **14**, but without dates, optd with biplane and **AIR MAIL**.
190 ½d. orange . . . 60 1·50
191 1d. green . . . 1·25 1·50
192 1½d. mauve . . . 1·75 7·50
193 2d. red . . . 1·75 30
193a 2½d. green . . . 6·00 2·50
194 3d. blue . . . 3·25 3·00
194a 3½d. red . . . 4·50 3·25
195 4d. olive . . . 4·50 10·00
196 5d. green . . . 7·00 7·50
197 6d. brown . . . 4·50 15·00
198 9d. violet . . . 6·00 9·00
199 1s. grey . . . 6·00 9·00
200 2s. lake . . . 10·00 48·00
201 5s. brown . . . 48·00 60·00
202 10s. pink . . . 80·00 80·00
203 £1 grey . . . 75·00 55·00

16 Bulolo Goldfields

18 King George VI

1935. Air.
204 16 £2 violet . . . £225 £130
205 £5 green . . . £550 £400

1935. Silver Jubilee. Nos. 177 and 179 optd **HIS MAJESTY'S JUBILEE. 1910–1935.**
206 1d. green . . . 75 50
207 2d. red . . . 1·75 50

1937. Coronation.
208 18 2d. red . . . 50 1·00
209 3d. blue . . . 50 1·75
210 5d. green . . . 50 1·75
211 1s. purple . . . 50 1·50

1939. Air. As T **16** but inscr "AIR MAIL POSTAGE".
212 ½d. orange . . . 3·75 7·00
213 1d. green . . . 3·25 4·50
214 1½d. purple . . . 4·00 9·50
215 2d. red . . . 8·00 3·50
216 3d. blue . . . 13·00 18·00
217 4d. olive . . . 14·00 8·50
218 5d. green . . . 13·00 4·00
219 6d. brown . . . 26·00 20·00
220 9d. violet . . . 26·00 26·00
221 1s. green . . . 26·00 21·00
222 2s. red . . . 65·00 48·00
223 5s. brown . . . £130 95·00
224 10s. pink . . . £400 £250
225 £1 olive . . . £100 £110

OFFICIAL STAMPS

1915. Nos. 16 and 17 optd **O. S.**
O1 N 1d on 3pf. brown . . . 26·00 75·00
O2 1d. on 3pf. green . . . 80·00 £140

1925. Optd **O S**.
O22 12 1d. green . . . 1·00 4·50
O23 1½d. red . . . 5·50 17·00
O24 2d. red . . . 1·75 3·75
O25 3d. blue . . . 3·50 8·00
O26 4d. olive . . . 4·50 8·50
O27a 6d. brown . . . 7·00 35·00
O28 9d. purple . . . 4·00 35·00
O29 1s. green . . . 5·50 35·00
O30 2s. lake . . . 28·00 60·00

1931. Optd **O S**.
O31 14 1d. green . . . 7·00 13·00
O32 1½d. red . . . 8·00 12·00
O33 2d. red . . . 10·00 7·00
O34 3d. blue . . . 6·50 6·00
O35 4d. olive . . . 6·50 8·50
O36 5d. green . . . 10·00 12·00
O37 6d. brown . . . 14·00 17·00
O38 9d. violet . . . 16·00 28·00
O39 1s. grey . . . 16·00 28·00
O40 2s. lake . . . 40·00 70·00
O41 5s. brown . . . £100 £170

1932. T **14**, but without dates, optd **O S**.
O42 1d. green . . . 9·00 10·00
O43 1½d. red . . . 10·00 12·00
O44 2d. red . . . 10·00 3·25
O45 2½d. green . . . 3·75 6·00
O46 3d. blue . . . 9·00 27·00
O47 3½d. red . . . 3·75 9·00
O48 4d. olive . . . 10·00 21·00
O49 5d. green . . . 8·50 21·00
O50 6d. brown . . . 15·00 42·00
O51 9d. violet . . . 14·00 42·00
O52 1s. grey . . . 15·00 29·00
O53 2s. lake . . . 30·00 75·00
O54 5s. brown . . . £110 £170

For later issues see **PAPUA NEW GUINEA**.

NEW HEBRIDES Pt. 1

A group of islands in the Pacific Ocean, E. of Australia, under joint administration of Gt. Britain and France. The Condominium ended in 1980, when the New Hebrides became independent as the Republic of Vanuatu.

1908. 12 pence = 1 shilling;
20 shillings = 1 pound.
1938. 100 gold centimes = 1 gold franc.
1977. 100 centimes = 1 New Hebrides franc.

BRITISH ADMINISTRATION

1908. Stamps of Fiji optd. (a) **NEW HEBRIDES. CONDOMINIUM.** (with full points).
1a 23 ½d. green . . . 40 7·00
2 1d. red . . . 50 40
5 2d. purple and orange . . . 60 70
6 2½d. purple and blue on blue . . . 60 70
7 5d. purple and green . . . 80 2·00
8 6d. purple and red . . . 70 1·25
3 1s. green and red . . . 19·00 3·75

(b) **NEW HEBRIDES CONDOMINIUM** (without full points).
10 23 ½d. green . . . 3·50 24·00
11 1d. red . . . 10·00 8·50
12 2d. grey . . . 60 3·00
13 2½d. blue . . . 65 4·25
14 5d. purple and green . . . 1·50 5·50
15 6d. purple and deep purple . . . 1·25 5·00
16 1s. black and green . . . 1·25 7·50

3 Weapons and Idols

1911.
18 3 ½d. green . . . 85 1·75
19 1d. red . . . 3·75 2·00
20 2d. grey . . . 8·00 4·00
21 2½d. blue . . . 3·00 5·50
24 5d. green . . . 4·50 7·00
25 6d. purple . . . 3·00 5·00
26 1s. black on green . . . 2·75 13·00
27 2s. purple on blue . . . 24·00 22·00
28 5s. green on yellow . . . 35·00 48·00

1920. Surch. (a) On T **3**.
40 3 1d. on ½d. green . . . 4·00 22·00
30 1d. on 5d. green . . . 7·00 60·00
31 1d. on 1s. black on green . . . 1·25 13·00
32 1d. on 2s. purple on blue . . . 1·00 10·00
33 1d. on 5s. green on yellow . . . 1·00 10·00
41 3d. on 1d. red . . . 4·00 11·00
42 5d. on 2½d. blue . . . 7·50 21·00

(b) On No. F16 of French New Hebrides.
34 3 2d. on 40c. red on yellow . . . 1·00 19·00

5

1925.
43 5 ½d. (5c.) black . . . 1·25 14·00
44 1d. (10c.) green . . . 1·00 12·00
45 2d. (20c.) grey . . . 1·75 2·50
46 2½d. (25c.) brown . . . 1·00 13·00
47 5d. (50c.) blue . . . 3·00 2·75
48 6d. (60c.) purple . . . 3·50 14·00
49 1s. (1f.25) black on green . . . 3·25 19·00
50 2s. (2f.50) purple on blue . . . 6·00 22·00
51 5s. (6f.25) green on yellow . . . 6·00 25·00

6 Lopevi Islands and Outrigger Canoe

1938.
52 6 5c. green . . . 2·50 4·50
53 10c. orange . . . 1·25 4·25
54 15c. violet . . . 3·50 4·50
55 20c. red . . . 1·60 2·75
56 25c. brown . . . 1·60 3·00
57 30c. blue . . . 2·50 2·75
58 40c. olive . . . 4·50 6·50
59 50c. purple . . . 1·60 2·75
60 1f. red on green . . . 4·00 9·00
61 2f. blue on green . . . 30·00 19·00
62 5f. red on yellow . . . 70·00 48·00
63 10f. violet on blue . . . £200 75·00

1949. U.P.U. As T **4d/g** of Pitcairn Islands.
64 10c. orange . . . 30 1·00
65 15c. violet . . . 30 1·00
66 30c. blue . . . 30 1·00
67 50c. purple . . . 40 1·00

7 Outrigger Sailing Canoes

1953.
68 7 5c. green . . . 60 20
69 10c. red . . . 60 10
70 15c. yellow . . . 60 10
71 20c. blue . . . 60 10

72 – 25c. olive 60 10
73 – 30c. brown 60 10
74 – 40c. sepia 60 10
75 – 50c. violet . . . . 1·00 10
76 – 1f. orange . . . . 5·00 1·00
77 – 2f. purple . . . . 5·00 8·00
78 – 5f. red . . . . 7·00 22·00
DESIGNS: 25c. to 50c. Native carving; 1f. to 5f. Two natives outside hut.

1953. Coronation. As T **4h** of Pitcairn Islands.
79 10c. black and red 60 50

10 "San Pedro y San Paulo" (Quiros) and Map

1956. 50th Anniv of Condominium. Inscr "1906 1956".
80 **10** 5c. green 15 10
81 10c. red 15 10
82 – 20c. blue 10 10
83 – 50c. lilac 15 15
DESIGN: 20, 50c. "Marianne", "Talking Drum" and "Britannia".

12 Port Villa; Iririki Islet

1957.
84 **12** 5c. green . . . . 40 1·25
85 10c. red 30 10
86 15c. yellow . . . . 50 1·25
87 20c. blue 40 10
88 – 25c. olive 45 10
89 – 30c. brown 45 10
90 – 40c. sepia 45 10
91 – 50c. violet 45 10
92 – 1f. orange . . . . 1·00 1·00
93 – 2f. mauve . . . . 4·00 3·00
94 – 5f. black . . . . 9·00 4·75
DESIGNS: 25c. to 50c. River scene and spear fisherman; 1f. to 5f. Woman drinking from coconut.

1963. Freedom from Hunger. As T **20a** of Pitcairn Islands.
95 60c. green 50 15

1963. Centenary of Red Cross. As T **20b** of Pitcairn Islands, but with British and French cyphers in place of the Queen's portrait.
96 15c. red and black 20 10
97 45c. red and blue 35 20

17 Cocoa Beans

1963.
98 – 5c. red, brown and blue . . 1·00 50
99 **17** 10c. brown, buff and green 15 10
100 – 15c. bistre, brown and violet 15 10
101 – 20c. black, green and blue 55 10
102 – 25c. violet, brown and red 50 70
103 – 30c. brown, bistre and violet 75 10
104 – 40c. red and blue . . . . 80 1·40
105 – 50c. green, yellow and blue 60 10
129 – 60c. red and blue 40 15
106 – 1f. red, black and green . . 2·00 3·25
107 – 2f. black, purple and green 2·00 1·75
108 – 3f. multicoloured . . . . . 10·00 6·00
109 – 5f. blue, deep blue and black . . . . 10·00 21·00
DESIGNS: 5 c Exporting manganese, Forari; 15c. Copra; 20c. Fishing from Palikulo Point; 25c. Picasso triggerfish; 30c. New Caledonian nautilus shell; 40, 60c. Lionfish; 50c. Clown surgeonfish; 1f. Cardinal honeyeater (bird); 2f. Buff-bellied flycatcher; 3f. Thicket warbler; 5f. White-collared kingfisher.

1965. Centenary of I.T.U. As T **24a** of Pitcairn Islands, but with British and French cyphers in place of the Queen's portrait.
110 15c. red and drab 20 10
111 60c. blue and red 35 20

1965. I.C.Y. As T **24b** of Pitcairn Islands, but with British and French cyphers in place of the Queen's portrait.
112 5c. purple and turquoise . . 15 10
113 55c. green and lavender . . . 20 20

1966. Churchill Commemoration. As T **24c** of Pitcairn Islands, but with British and French cyphers in place of the Queen's portrait.
114 5c. blue 20 10
115 15c. green 40 10
116 25c. brown 50 10
117 30c. violet 50 10

1966. World Cup Football Championship. As T **25** of Pitcairn Islands, but with British and French cyphers in place of the Queen's portrait.
118 20c. multicoloured 30 15
119 40c. multicoloured 70 15

1966. Inauguration of W.H.O. Headquarters, Geneva. As T **25a** of Pitcairn Islands, but with British and French cyphers in place of the Queen's portrait.
120 25c. black, green and blue . . 15 10
121 60c. black, purple and ochre 40 20

1966. 20th Anniv of UNESCO. As T **25b/d** of Pitcairn Islands, but with British and French cyphers in place of the Queen's portrait.
122 15c. multicoloured 25 10
123 30c. yellow, violet and olive 65 10
124 45c. black, purple and orange 75 15

36 The Coast Watchers

1967. 25th Anniv of Pacific War. Multicoloured.
125 15c. Type **36** 20 10
126 25c. Map of war zone, U.S. marine and Australian soldier 45 20
127 60c. H.M.A.S. "Canberra" (cruiser) 50 30
128 1f. Boeing B-17 "Flying Fortress" 50 80

40 Globe and Hemispheres

1968. Bicent of Bougainville's World Voyage.
130 **40** 15c. green, violet and red 15 10
131 – 25c. olive, purple and blue 30 10
132 – 60c. brown, purple & green 35 10
DESIGNS: 25c. Ships "La Boudeuse" and "L'Etoile", and map; 60c. Bougainville, ship's figure-head and bougainvillea flowers.

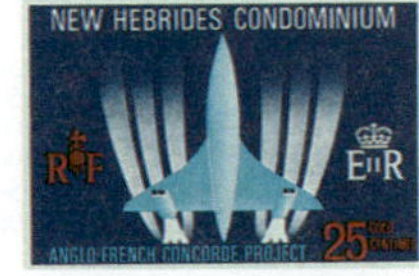

43 Concorde and Vapour Trails

1968. Anglo-French Concorde Project.
133 **43** 25c. blue, red and blue . . 35 20
134 – 60c. red, black and blue . . 40 25
DESIGN: 60c. Concorde in flight.

45 Kauri Pine

1969. Timber Industry.
135 **45** 20c. multicoloured 10 10

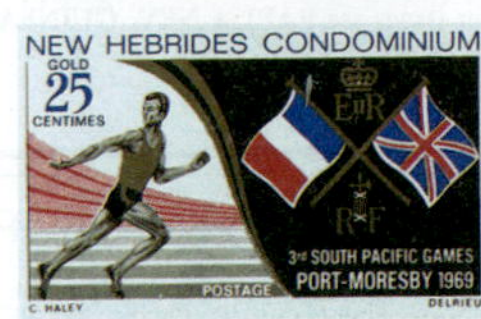

46 Cyphers, Flags and Relay Runner receiving Baton

1969. 3rd South Pacific Games, Port Moresby. Multicoloured.
136 25c. Type **46** 10 10
137 1f. Runner passing baton . . 20 20

48 Diver on Platform

52 General Charles de Gaulle

51 U.P.U. Emblem and Headquarters Building

1969. Pentecost Island Land Divers. Mult.
138 15c. Type **48** 10 10
139 25c. Diver jumping 10 10
140 1f. Diver at end of fall . . . 20 20

1970. New U.P.U. Headquarters Building.
141 **51** 1f.05 slate, orange & purple 20 20

1970. 30th Anniv of New Hebrides' Declaration for the Free French Government.
142 **52** 65c. multicoloured 35 70
143 1f.10 multicoloured 45 70

1970. No. 101 surch **35**.
144 35c. on 20c. black, green and blue 30 30

54 "The Virgin and Child" (Bellini)

57 Kauri Pine, Cone and Arms of Royal Society

56 Football

1970. Christmas. Multicoloured.
145 15c. Type **54** 10 10
146 50c. "The Virgin and Child" (Cima) 20 20

1971. Death of General Charles de Gaulle. Nos. 142/3 optd **1890-1970 IN MEMORIAM 9-11-70**.
147 **52** 65c. multicoloured 15 10
148 1f.10 multicoloured 15 20

1971. 4th South Pacific Games, Papeete, French Polynesia.
149 20c. Type **56** 10 10
150 65c. Basketball (vert) 30 20

1971. Royal Society's Expedition to New Hebrides.
151 **57** 65c. multicoloured 20 15

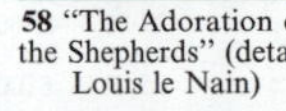

58 "The Adoration of the Shepherds" (detail, Louis le Nain)

60 Ceremonial Headdress, South Malekula

59 De Havilland Drover 3

1971. Christmas. Multicoloured.
152 25c. Type **58** 10 10
153 50c. "The Adoration of the Shepherds" (detail, Tintoretto) 30 90

1972. Aircraft. Multicoloured.
154 20c. Type **59** 30 15
155 25c. Short S25 Sandringham 4 flying boat 30 15
156 30c. De Havilland Dragon Rapide 30 15
157 65c. Sud Aviation SE 210 Caravelle . . . . 75 1·25

1972. Multicoloured.
158 5c. Type **60** 10 20
159 10c. Baker's pigeon 25 20
160 15c. Gong and carving, North Ambrym 15 20
161 20c. Red-headed parrot finch 40 25
162 25c. Graskoin's cowrie (shell) 40 25
163 30c. Red-lip olive (shell) . . . 50 30
164 35c. Chestnut-bellied kingfisher 65 40
165 65c. Pretty conch (shell) . . . 75 60
166 1f. Gong (North Malekula) and carving (North Ambrym) . . . . 50 1·00
167 2f. Palm lorikeet . . . . . . 3·50 4·50
168 3f. Ceremonial headdress, South Malekula (different) 1·50 6·00
169 5f. Great green turban (shell) 4·00 13·00

61 "Adoration of the Kings" (Spranger)

63 "Dendrobium teretifolium"

1972. Christmas. Multicoloured.
170 25c. Type **61** 10 10
171 70c. "The Virgin and Child in a Landscape" (Provoost) 20 20

1972. Royal Silver Wedding. As T **98** of Gibraltar, but with Royal and French cyphers in background.
172 35c. violet 15 10
173 65c. green 20 10

1973. Orchids. Multicoloured.
174 25c. Type **63** 25 10
175 30c. "Ephemerantha comata" 25 10
176 35c. "Spathoglottis petri" . . 30 10
177 65c. "Dendrobium mohlianum" 60 55

64 New Wharf at Vila

65 Wild Horses

1973. Opening of New Wharf at Villa. Mult.
178 25c. Type **64** 20 10
179 70c. As Type **64** but horiz . . 40 30

1973. Tanna Island. Multicoloured.
180 35c. Type **65** 45 15
181 70c. Yasur Volcano 55 20

66 Mother and Child

1973. Christmas. Multicoloured.
182 35c. Type **66** 10 10
183 70c. Lagoon scene 20 20

67 Pacific Pigeon

1974. Wild Life. Multicoloured.
184 25c. Type **67** 60 25
185 35c. "Lyssa curvata" (moth) 60 60
186 70c. Green sea turtle 60 70
187 1f.15 Grey-headed flying fox 80 1·50

1974. Royal Visit. Nos. 164 and 167 optd **ROYAL VISIT 1974**.
188 35c. multicoloured 40 10
189 2f. multicoloured 60 40

69 Old Post Office

1974. Inaug of New Post Office, Vila. Mult.
190 35c. Type **69** 15 50
191 70c. New Post Office 15 60

70 Capt. Cook and Map

1974. Bicent of Discovery. Multicoloured.
192 35c. Type **70** 1·25 2·00
193 35c. William Wales and beach landing 1·25 2·00
194 35c. William Hodges and island scene 1·25 2·00
195 1f.15 Capt. Cook, map and H.M.S. "Resolution" (59 × 34 mm) 2·50 3·50

71 U.P.U. Emblem and Letters

1974. Centenary of U.P.U.
196 **71** 70c. multicoloured 30 70

72 "Adoration of the Magi" (Velazquez)

74 Canoeing

73 Charolais Bull

1974. Christmas. Multicoloured.
197 35c. Type **72** 10 10
198 70c. "The Nativity" (Gerard van Honthorst) 20 20

1975.
199 **73** 10f. brown, green and blue 7·00 18·00

1975. World Scout Jamboree, Norway. Mult.
200 25c. Type **74** 15 10
201 35c. Preparing meal 15 10
202 1f. Map-reading 35 15
203 5f. Fishing 1·25 2·50

75 "Pitti Madonna" (Michelangelo)

77 Telephones of 1876 and 1976

76 Concorde in British Airways Livery

1975. Christmas. Michelangelo's Sculptures. Mult.
204 35c. Type **75** 10 10
205 70c. "Bruges Madonna" 15 10
206 2f.50 "Taddei Madonna" 70 50

1976. 1st Commercial Flight of Concorde.
207 **76** 5f. multicoloured 4·00 5·00

1976. Centenary of Telephone. Multicoloured.
208 25c. Type **77** 15 10
209 70c. Alexander Graham Bell 30 10
210 1f.15 Satellite and Noumea Earth Station 50 50

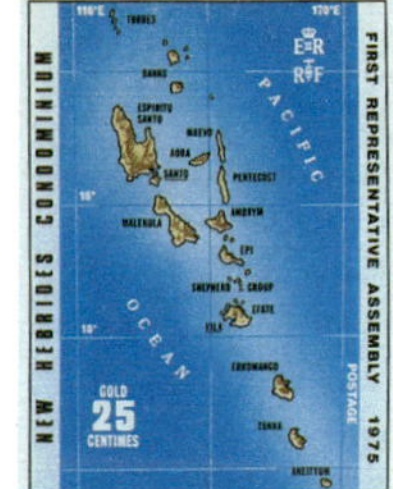

78 Map of the Islands

1976. Constitutional Changes. Multicoloured.
211 25c. Type **78** 40 15
212 1f. View of Santo (horiz) 75 60
213 2f. View of Vila (horiz) 1·10 2·25
Nos. 212/13 are smaller, 36 × 26 mm.

79 "The Flight into Egypt" (Lusitano)

80 Royal Visit, 1974

1976. Christmas. Multicoloured.
214 35c. Type **79** 10 10
215 70c. "Adoration of the Shepherds" 15 10
216 2f.50 "Adoration of the Magi" 45 50
Nos. 215/16 show retables by the Master of Santos-o-Novo.

1977. Silver Jubilee. Multicoloured.
217 35c. Type **80** 10 10
218 70c. Imperial State Crown 15 10
219 2f. The Blessing 30 65

1977. Currency change. Nos. 158/69 and 199 surch.
233 5f. on 5c. Type **60** 50 15
234 10f. on 10c. Baker's pigeon 50 15
222 15f. on 15c. Gong and carving 60 1·50
223 20f. on 20c. Red-headed parrot finch 1·25 55

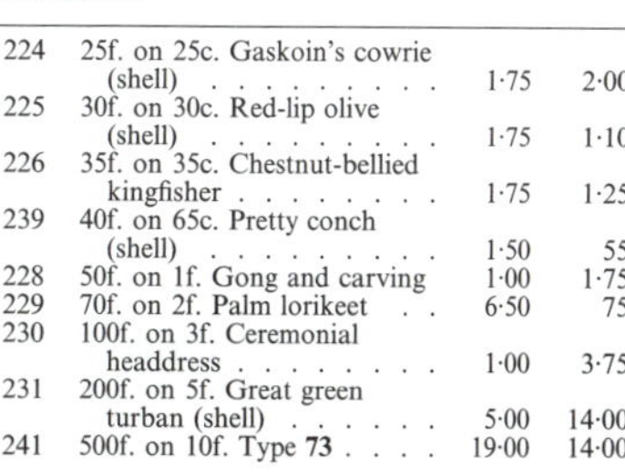

224 25f. on 25c. Gaskoin's cowrie (shell) 1·75 2·00
225 30f. on 30c. Red-lip olive (shell) 1·75 1·10
226 35f. on 35c. Chestnut-bellied kingfisher 1·75 1·25
239 40f. on 65c. Pretty conch (shell) 1·50 55
228 50f. on 1f. Gong and carving 1·00 1·75
229 70f. on 2f. Palm lorikeet 6·50 75
230 100f. on 3f. Ceremonial headdress 1·00 3·75
231 200f. on 5f. Great green turban (shell) 5·00 14·00
241 500f. on 10f. Type **73** 19·00 14·00

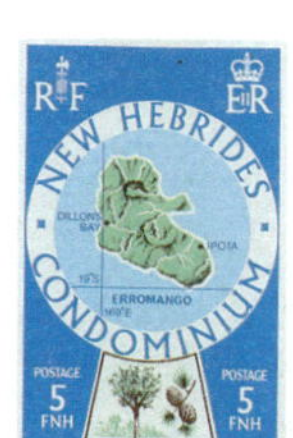

89 Island of Erromango and Kauri Pine

90 "Tempi Madonna" (Raphael)

1977. Islands. Multicoloured.
242 5f. Type **89** 30 10
243 10f. Territory map and copra-making 40 30
244 15f. Espiritu Santo and cattle 30 30
245 20f. Efate and Vila P.O. 30 25
246 25f. Malekula and headdresses 40 40
247 30f. Aobe, Maewo and pigs' tusks 45 50
248 35f. Pentecost and land diver 50 65
249 40f. Tanna and John Frum Cross 70 60
250 50f. Shepherd Is. and canoe 1·50 40
251 70f. Banks Is. and dancers 1·75 3·50
252 100f. Ambrym and idols 1·75 90
253 200f. Aneityum and baskets 1·75 2·50
254 500f. Torres Is. and archer fisherman 3·50 7·50

1977. Christmas. Multicoloured.
255 10f. Type **90** 20 45
256 15f. "The Flight into Egypt" (Gerard David) 30 60
257 30f. "Virgin and Child" (Batoni) 40 90

91 Concorde over New York

1978. Concorde Commemoration.
258 10f. Type **91** 1·00 75
259 20f. Concorde over London 1·00 1·00
260 30f. Concorde over Washington 1·25 1·40
261 40f. Concorde over Paris 1·50 1·60

92 White Horse of Hanover

93 "Madonna and Child"

1978. 25th Anniv of Coronation.
262 **92** 40f. brown, blue and silver 15 30
263 – 40f. multicoloured 15 30
264 – 40f. brown, blue and silver 15 30
DESIGNS: No. 263, Queen Elizabeth II; 264, Gallic Cock.

1978. Christmas. Paintings by Durer. Mult.
265 10f. Type **93** 10 10
266 15f. "The Virgin and Child with St. Anne" 10 10
267 30f. "Madonna of the Siskin" 15 10
268 40f. "Madonna of the Pear" 20 15

1979. 1st Anniv of Internal Self-Government. Surch **166°E 11.1.79 FIRST ANNIVERSARY INTERNAL SELF-GOVERNMENT** and new value.
269 **78** 10f. on 25f. multicoloured (blue background) 10 10
270 40f. on 25f. multicoloured (green background) 20 20

95 1938 5c. Stamp and Sir Rowland Hill

96 Chubwan Mask

1979. Death Centenary of Sir Rowland Hill. Mult.
271 10f. Type **95** 10 10
272 20f. 1969 25c. Pentecost Island Land Divers commemorative 20 10
273 40f. 1925 2d. (20c.) 25 20
MS274 143 × 94 mm. Nos. 272 and F286 75 90

1979. Arts Festival. Multicoloured.
275 5f. Type **96** 10 10
276 10f. Nal-Nal clubs and spears 10 10
277 20f. Ritual puppet 15 10
278 40f. Neqatmalow headdress 25 15

97 "Native Church" (Metas Masongo)

1979. Christmas and International Year of the Child. Children's Drawings. Multicoloured.
279 5f. Type **97** 10 10
280 10f. "Priest and Candles" (Herve Rutu) 10 10
281 20f. "Cross and Bible" (Mark Deards) (vert) 10 10
282 40f. "Green Candle and Santa Claus" (Dev Raj) (vert) 15 15

98 White-bellied Honeyeater

1980. Birds. Multicoloured.
283 10f. Type **98** 50 10
284 20f. Scarlet robin 70 10
285 30f. Yellow-fronted white-eye 90 45
286 40f. Fan-tailed cuckoo 1·00 70

POSTAGE DUE STAMPS

1925. Optd **POSTAGE DUE.**
D1 **5** 1d. (10c.) green 30·00 1·00
D2 2d. (20c.) grey 32·00 1·00
D3 3d. (30c.) red 32·00 2·50
D4 5d. (50c.) blue 35·00 4·50
D5 10d. (1c.) red on blue 40·00 5·50

1938. Optd **POSTAGE DUE.**
D 6 **6** 5c. green 25·00 40·00
D 7 10c. orange 25·00 40·00
D 8 20c. red 28·00 55·00
D 9 40c. olive 35·00 65·00
D10 1f. red on green 45·00 75·00

1953. Nos. 68/9, 71, 74 and 76 optd **POSTAGE DUE.**
D11 **7** 5c. green 4·00 13·00
D12 10c. red 1·75 10·00
D13 20c. blue 5·00 19·00
D14 – 40c. sepia (No. 74) 7·00 29·00
D15 – 1f. orange (No. 76) 4·50 29·00

1957. Optd **POSTAGE DUE.**
D16 **12** 5c. green 30 1·50
D17 10c. red 30 1·50
D18 20c. blue 75 1·75
D19 – 40c. sepia (No. 90) 1·00 2·50
D20 – 1f. orange (No. 92) 1·25 3·25

FRENCH ADMINISTRATION

1908. Stamps of New Caledonia optd **NOUVELLES HEBRIDES.**
F1 **15** 5c. green 5·00 4·75
F2 10c. red 6·50 3·50
F3 **16** 25c. blue on green 6·50 2·25
F4 50c. red on green 7·00 4·75
F5 **17** 1f. blue on green 17·00 20·00

1910. Nos. F1/5 further optd **CONDOMINIUM.**
F 6 **15** 5c. green 3·00 3·00
F 7 10c. red 3·00 1·25
F 8 **16** 25c. blue on green 2·25 3·75
F 9 50c. red on orange 6·50 9·75
F10 **17** 1f. blue on green 15·00 22·00

The following issues are as stamps of British Administration but are inscr "NOUVELLES HEBRIDES" except where otherwise stated.

1911.

F11 3 5c. green 1·00 2·75
F12 10c. red 50 75
F13 20c. grey 1·00 2·25
F25 25c. blue 1·25 5·50
F15 30c. brown on yellow 6·50 5·25
F16 40c. red on yellow 1·40 3·75
F17 50c. olive 2·00 4·00
F18 75c. orange 7·00 23·00
F19 1f. red on blue 2·50 3·00
F20 2f. violet 8·50 22·00
F21 5f. red on green 12·00 35·00

1920. Surch in figures.

F34 5c. on 40c. red on yellow (No. F16) 27·00 95·00
F32a 5c. on 50c. red on orange (No. F4) £450 £475
F33 5c. on 50c. red on orange (No. F9) 2·40 13·00
F38 10c. on 5c. green (No. F11) 1·00 6·00
F33a 10c. on 25c. blue on green (No. F8) 50 1·50
F35 20c. on 30c. brown on yellow (No. F26) 11·00 65·00
F39 30c. on 10c. red (No. F12) 1·00 2·50
F41 50c. on 25c. blue (No. F25) 2·50 24·00

1921. Stamp of New Hebrides (British) surch **10c.**

F37 10c. on 5d. green (No. 24) 11·00 50·00

1925.

F42 5 5c. (½d.) black 75 10·00
F43 10c. (1d.) green 1·00 9·00
F44 20c. (2d.) grey 1·75 2·75
F45 25c. (2½d.) brown 1·50 9·00
F46 30c. (3d.) red 1·50 9·00
F47 40c. (4d.) red on yellow 1·50 9·00
F48 50c. (5d.) blue 1·50 1·75
F49 75c. (7½d.) brown 1·50 14·00
F50 1f. (10d.) red on blue 1·50 2·50
F51 2f. (1s.8d.) violet 2·50 25·00
F52 5f. (4d.) red on green 3·50 25·00

1938.

F53 6 5c. green 2·50 6·50
F54 10c. orange 2·25 1·75
F55 15c. violet 2·25 4·00
F56 20c. red 2·50 3·50
F57 25c. brown 5·50 4·50
F58 30c. blue 5·50 5·00
F59 40c. olive 2·25 9·00
F60 50c. purple 2·25 3·25
F61 1f. red on green 2·75 5·50
F62 2f. blue on green 30·00 30·00
F63 5f. red on yellow 50·00 50·00
F64 10f. violet and blue £200 £100

1941. Free French Issue. As last, optd **France Libre**.

F65 6 5c. green 2·00 25·00
F66 10c. orange 3·75 24·00
F67 15c. violet 6·50 40·00
F68 20c. red 18·00 32·00
F69 25c. brown 21·00 42·00
F70 30c. blue 21·00 38·00
F71 40c. olive 21·00 40·00
F72 50c. purple 19·00 38·00
F73 1f. red on green 20·00 38·00
F74 2f. blue on green 18·00 38·00
F75 5f. red on yellow 17·00 38·00
F76 10f. violet on blue 17·00 38·00

1949. 75th Anniv of U.P.U.

F77 10c. orange 2·50 5·50
F78 15c. violet 3·75 9·00
F79 30c. blue 5·50 12·00
F80 50c. purple 6·50 15·00

1953.

F81 7 5c. green 2·00 2·75
F82 10c. red 3·00 2·75
F83 15c. yellow 3·00 3·00
F84 20c. blue 3·00 2·75
F85 – 25c. olive 1·25 2·75
F86 – 30c. brown 1·25 3·00
F87 – 40c. sepia 1·75 3·00
F88 – 50c. violet 1·25 2·75
F89 – 1f. orange 9·50 7·50
F90 – 2f. purple 16·00 45·00
F91 – 5f. red 18·00 85·00

1956. 50th Anniv of Condominium.

F92 10 5c. green 1·00 2·00
F93 10c. red 1·00 2·25
F94 – 20c. blue 65 2·50
F95 – 50c. violet 1·00 2·50

1957.

F 96 12 5c. green 40 2·25
F 97 10c. red 1·25 2·25
F 98 15c. yellow 1·50 2·75
F 99 20c. blue 1·40 2·00
F100 – 25c. olive 1·25 1·75
F101 – 30c. brown 1·40 1·75
F102 – 40c. sepia 2·00 1·25
F103 – 50c. violet 2·00 1·60
F104 – 1f. orange 5·50 4·00
F105 – 2f. mauve 11·00 21·00
F106 – 5f. black 28·00 48·00

1963. Freedom from Hunger. As T **51** of New Caledonia.

F107 60c. green and brown 10·00 16·00

1963. Centenary of Red Cross. As T **53** of New Caledonia.

F108 15c. red, grey and orange 7·25 9·00
F109 45c. red, grey and bistre 9·75 25·00

1963.

F110 – 5c. lake, brown and blue 55 65
F111 – 10c. brown, buff and green* 2·00 2·50
F112 – 10c. brown, buff and green 75 1·60
F113 18 15c. bistre, brown and violet 6·00 1·25
F114 – 20c. black, green and blue* 2·25 4·00
F115 – 20c. black, green and blue 1·50 1·60
F116 – 25c. violet, brown and red 70 1·10
F117 – 30c. brown, bistre and violet 7·50 1·25
F118 – 40c. red and blue 3·25 7·50
F119 – 50c. green, yellow and turquoise 8·50 1·60
F120 – 60c. red and blue 1·75 1·90
F121 – 1f. red, black and green 2·00 4·50
F122 – 2f. black, brown and olive 17·00 9·00
F123 – 3f. multicoloured* 10·50 26·00
F124 – 3f. multicoloured 8·50 12·00
F125 – 5f. blue, indigo and black 24·00 29·00

The stamps indicated by an asterisk have "RF" wrongly placed on the left.

1965. Centenary of I.T.U. As T **56** of New Caledonia.

F126 15c. blue, green and brown 7·00 9·00
F127 60c. red, grey and green 18·00 30·00

1965. I.C.Y. As Nos. 112/13.

F128 5c. purple and turquoise 2·50 6·00
F129 55c. green and lavender 9·50 12·00

1966. Churchill Commem. As Nos. 114/17.

F130 5c. multicoloured 2·10 5·50
F131 15c. multicoloured 3·00 2·25
F132 25c. multicoloured 3·50 7·00
F133 30c. multicoloured 4·25 7·50

1966. World Cup Football Championship. As Nos. 118/19.

F134 20c. multicoloured 1·90 4·25
F135 40c. multicoloured 3·50 4·25

1966. Inauguration of W.H.O. Headquarters, Geneva. As Nos. 120/1.

F136 25c. black, green and blue 2·50 3·50
F137 60c. black, mauve and ochre 3·50 7·50

1966. 20th Anniv of UNESCO. As Nos. 122/4.

F138 15c. multicoloured 1·50 2·50
F139 30c. yellow, violet and olive 2·25 4·00
F140 45c. black, purple and orange 2·25 4·50

1967. 25th Anniv of Pacific War. As Nos. 125/8.

F141 15c. multicoloured 1·25 1·50
F142 25c. multicoloured 1·60 3·00
F143 60c. multicoloured 1·75 2·50
F144 1f. multicoloured 2·00 2·75

1968. Bicentenary of Bougainville's World Voyage. As Nos. 130/2.

F145 15c. green, violet and red 55 1·10
F146 25c. olive, purple and blue 65 1·25
F147 60c. brown, purple and green 1·10 1·50

1968. Anglo-French Concorde Project. As Nos. 133/4.

F148 25c. blue, red and violet 1·90 2·40
F149 60c. red, black and blue 2·25 4·25

1969. Timber Industry. As No. 135.

F150 20c. multicoloured 45 1·00

1969. 3rd South Pacific Games, Port Moresby, Papua New Guinea. As Nos. 136/7.

F151 25c. multicoloured 50 1·40
F152 1f. multicoloured 1·50 2·00

1969. Land Divers of Pentecost Island. As Nos. 138/40.

F153 15c. multicoloured 55 1·25
F154 25c. multicoloured 45 1·25
F155 1f. multicoloured 1·10 2·00

1970. Inauguration of New U.P.U. Headquarters Building, Berne. As No. 141.

F156 1f.05 slate, orange & purple 1·00 2·75

1970. New Hebrides' Declaration for the Free French Government. As Nos. 142/3.

F157 65c. multicoloured 2·00 2·00
F158 1f.10 multicoloured 2·25 2·25

1970. No. F115 surch **35**.

F159 35c. on 20c. black, green and blue 65 1·75

1970. Christmas. As Nos. 145/6.

F160 15c. multicoloured 25 1·00
F161 50c. multicoloured 45 1·25

1971. Death of General Charles de Gaulle. Nos. F157/8 optd **1890-1970 IN MEMORIAM 9-11-70**.

F162 65c. multicoloured 1·00 1·50
F163 1f.10 multicoloured 1·50 2·00

1971. 4th South Pacific Games, Papeete, French Polynesia. As Nos. 149/50.

F164 20c. multicoloured 75 1·00
F165 65c. multicoloured 1·00 1·50

1971. Royal Society Expedition to New Hebrides. As No. 151.

F166 65c. multicoloured 1·00 1·50

1971. Christmas. As Nos. 152/3.

F167 25c. multicoloured 50 75
F168 50c. multicoloured 60 1·25

1972. Aircraft. As Nos. 154/7.

F169 20c. multicoloured 1·00 1·60
F170 25c. multicoloured 1·00 1·60
F171 30c. multicoloured 1·10 1·60
F172 65c. multicoloured 2·75 5·00

1972. As Nos. 158/69.

F173 5c. multicoloured 85 1·40
F174 10c. multicoloured 1·90 1·75
F175 15c. multicoloured 90 1·25
F176 20c. multicoloured 2·50 1·50
F177 25c. multicoloured 1·90 1·60
F178 30c. multicoloured 1·90 1·50
F179 35c. multicoloured 3·00 1·50
F180 65c. multicoloured 2·40 2·00
F181 1f. multicoloured 2·40 2·75
F182 2f. multicoloured 15·00 13·50
F183 3f. multicoloured 7·50 17·00
F184 5f. multicoloured 10·00 30·00

1972. Christmas. As Nos. 170/1.

F185 25c. multicoloured 45 1·00
F186 70c. multicoloured 65 1·50

1972. Royal Silver Wedding. As Nos. 172/3.

F187 35c. multicoloured 50 50
F188 65c. multicoloured 60 1·25

1973. Orchids. As Nos. 174/7.

F189 25c. multicoloured 2·75 1·40
F190 30c. multicoloured 2·75 1·60
F191 35c. multicoloured 2·75 1·60
F192 65c. multicoloured 4·75 5·00

1973. Opening of New Wharf at Vila. As Nos. 178/9.

F193 25c. multicoloured 80 1·10
F194 70c. multicoloured 1·10 2·25

1973. Tanna Island. As Nos. 180/1.

F195 35c. multicoloured 2·25 2·25
F196 70c. multicoloured 3·25 3·25

1973. Christmas. As Nos. 182/3.

F197 35c. multicoloured 50 1·00
F198 70c. multicoloured 75 2·75

1974. Wild Life. As Nos. 184/7.

F199 25c. multicoloured 4·50 3·25
F200 35c. multicoloured 5·75 2·40
F201 70c. multicoloured 6·00 4·75
F202 1f.15 multicoloured 7·50 11·00

1974. Royal Visit of Queen Elizabeth II. Nos. F179 and F182 optd **VISITE ROYALE 1974**.

F203 35c. Chestnut-bellied kingfisher 3·00 90
F204 2f. Green palm lorikeet 6·50 8·25

1974. Inauguration of New Post Office, Vila. As Nos. 190/1.

F205 35c. multicoloured 1·00 2·00
F206 70c. multicoloured 1·00 2·00

1974. Bicent of Discovery. As Nos. 192/5.

F207 35c. multicoloured 4·00 5·75
F208 35c. multicoloured 4·00 5·75
F209 35c. multicoloured 4·00 5·75
F210 1f.15 multicoloured 8·50 12·00

1974. Centenary of U.P.U. As No. 196.

F210a 70c. blue, red and black 1·75 3·00

1974. Christmas. As Nos. 197/8.

F211 35c. multicoloured 40 75
F212 70f. multicoloured 60 1·25

1975. Charolais Bull. As No. 199.

F213 10f. brown, green and blue 30·00 45·00

1975. World Scout Jamboree, Norway. As Nos. 200/3.

F214 25c. multicoloured 70 50
F215 35c. multicoloured 75 60
F216 1f. multicoloured 1·25 1·25
F217 5f. multicoloured 6·50 10·00

1975. Christmas. As Nos. 204/6.

F218 35c. multicoloured 35 50
F219 70c. multicoloured 55 90
F220 2f.50 multicoloured 1·90 3·00

1976. 1st Commercial Flight of Concorde. As No. 207, but Concorde in Air France livery.

F221 5f. multicoloured 13·00 12·00

1976. Centenary of Telephone. As Nos. 208/10.

F222 25c. multicoloured 60 50
F223 70c. multicoloured 1·50 1·50
F224 1f.15 multicoloured 1·75 2·75

1976. Constitutional Changes. As Nos. 211/13.

F225 25c. multicoloured 60 50
F226 1f. multicoloured 1·50 1·25
F227 2f. multicoloured 2·50 2·75

1976. Christmas. Paintings. As Nos. 214/16.

F228 35c. multicoloured 30 30
F229 70c. multicoloured 50 50
F230 2f.50 multicoloured 1·75 3·00

1977. Silver Jubilee. As Nos. F217/9.

F231 35c. multicoloured 30 20
F232 70c. multicoloured 55 35
F233 2f. multicoloured 55 65

1977. Currency change. Nos. F173/84 and F213, surch.

F234 5f. on 5c. multicoloured 1·00 1·25
F235 10f. on 10c. multicoloured 2·50 1·25
F236 15f. on 15c. multicoloured 1·25 1·25
F237 20f. on 20c. multicoloured 3·00 1·50
F238 25f. on 25c. multicoloured 2·50 1·75
F239 30f. on 30c. multicoloured 2·50 2·25
F240 35f. on 35c. multicoloured 4·25 2·25
F241 40f. on 65c. multicoloured 3·25 3·00
F242 50f. on 1f. multicoloured 2·50 3·00
F243 70f. on 2f. multicoloured 7·50 4·00
F244 100f. on 3f. multicoloured 3·50 6·00
F245 200f. on 5f. multicoloured 13·00 25·00
F246 500f. on 10f. multicoloured 23·00 45·00

1977. Islands. As Nos. 242/54.

F256 5f. multicoloured 1·25 1·75
F257 10f. multicoloured 1·00 1·75
F258 15f. multicoloured 2·00 1·75
F259 20f. multicoloured 2·00 1·75
F260 25f. multicoloured 2·00 1·75
F261 30f. multicoloured 2·00 1·75
F262 35f. multicoloured 2·75 1·75
F263 40f. multicoloured 1·50 2·25
F264 50f. multicoloured 2·75 2·25
F265 70f. multicoloured 5·50 4·50
F266 100f. multicoloured 4·50 4·00
F267 200f. multicoloured 6·00 12·00
F268 500f. multicoloured 10·00 18·00

1977. Christmas. As Nos. 255/7.

F269 10f. multicoloured 30 30
F270 15f. multicoloured 50 50
F271 30f. multicoloured 80 1·40

1978. Concorde. As Nos. 258/61.

F272 10f. multicoloured 2·50 1·50
F273 20f. multicoloured 2·75 1·75
F274 30f. multicoloured 3·25 2·25
F275 40f. multicoloured 3·75 3·50

1978. Coronation. As Nos. 262/4.

F276 40f. brown, blue and silver 25 70
F277 40f. multicoloured 25 70
F278 40f. brown, blue and silver 25 70

1978. Christmas. As Nos. 265/8.

F279 10f. multicoloured 15 30
F280 15f. multicoloured 20 35

F281 30f. multicoloured 30 70
F282 40f. multicoloured 35 85

1979. Internal Self-Government. As T **37** surch **166°E PREMIER GOUVERNEMENT AUTONOME 11.1.78. 11.1.79** and new value.
F283 10f. on 25f. multicoloured (blue background) . . . 90 1·00
F284 40f. on 25f. multicoloured (green background) . . . 1·60 1·75

1979. Death Centenary of Sir Rowland Hill. As Nos. 271/3.
F285 10f. multicoloured 35 50
F286 20f. multicoloured 35 60
F287 40f. multicoloured . . . . 40 1·00

1979. Arts Festival. As Nos. 275/8.
F288 5f. multicoloured 30 60
F289 10f. multicoloured 30 60
F290 20f. multicoloured 40 80
F291 40f. multicoloured . . . . 60 1·25

1979. Christmas and International Year of the Child. As Nos. 279/82.
F292 5f. multicoloured 85 60
F293 10f. multicoloured . . . . 1·00 60
F294 20f. multicoloured . . . . 1·10 80
F295 40f. multicoloured . . . . 1·90 2·00

1980. Birds. As Nos. 283/6.
F296 10f. multicoloured . . . . 1·10 1·75
F297 20f. multicoloured . . . . 1·40 2·00
F298 30f. multicoloured . . . . 1·75 2·75
F299 40f. multicoloured . . . . 1·90 3·25

POSTAGE DUE STAMPS

1925. Nos. F32 etc, optd **CHIFFRE TAXE.**
FD53 **5** 10c. (1d.) green . . . . . 50·00 3·00
FD54 20c. (2d.) grey . . . . . 55·00 3·00
FD55 30c. (3d.) red . . . . . 55·00 3·00
FD56 50c. (5d.) blue . . . . . 50·00 3·00
FD57 1f. (10d.) red on blue . . 50·00 3·00

1938. Optd **CHIFFRE TAXE.**
FD65 **6** 5c. green . . . . 14·00 60·00
FD66 10c. orange . . . . 17·00 60·00
FD67 20c. red . . . . 23·00 65·00
FD68 40c. olive . . . . 48·00 £130
FD69 1f. red on green . . . . . 48·00 £140

1941. Free French Issue. As last optd **France Libre.**
FD77 **6** 5c. green . . . . 15·00 38·00
FD78 10c. orange . . . . 15·00 38·00
FD79 20c. red . . . . 15·00 38·00
FD80 40c. olive . . . . 19·00 38·00
FD81 1f. red on green . . . . . 18·00 38·00

1953. Optd **TIMBRE-TAXE.**
FD92 **7** 5c. green . . . . 8·00 21·00
FD93 10c. red . . . . 6·50 20·00
FD94 20c. blue . . . . 20·00 30·00
FD95 – 40c. sepia (No. F87) . . . 13·00 28·00
FD96 – 1f. orange (No. F89) . . . 17·00 50·00

1957. Optd **TIMBRE-TAXE.**
FD107 **12** 5c. green . . . . 90 9·00
FD108 10c. red . . . . 1·40 9·00
FD109 20c. blue . . . . 2·75 13·00
FD110 – 40c. sepia (No. F102) . . 6·50 26·00
FD111 – 1f. orange (No. F104) . . 5·50 32·00

For later issues see **VANUATU.**

NEW REPUBLIC Pt. 1

A Boer republic originally part of Zululand. It was incorporated with the South African Republic in 1888 and annexed to Natal in 1903.

12 pence = 1 shilling;
20 shillings = 1 pound.

1

1886. On yellow or blue paper.
1 **1** 1d. black . . . . — £3000
2 1d. violet . . . . 11·00 13·00
73 2d. violet . . . . 10·00 10·00
79 3d. violet . . . . 16·00 17·00
75 4d. violet . . . . 14·00 14·00
81 6d. violet . . . . 9·00 10·00
82 9d. violet . . . . 12·00 13·00
83 1s. violet . . . . 12·00 12·00
84 1s.6d. violet . . . . 22·00 20·00
85 2s. violet . . . . 19·00 18·00
86 2s.6d. violet . . . . 25·00 25·00
87 3s. violet . . . . 48·00 48·00
88b 4s. violet . . . . 45·00 45·00
16 5s. violet . . . . 30·00 40·00
90 5s.6d. violet . . . . 16·00 17·00
91 7s.6d. violet . . . . 20·00 22·00
92 10s. violet . . . . 16·00 17·00
93 10s.6d. violet . . . . . . 17·00 17·00
44 12s. violet £300
23 13s. violet £450
94 £1 violet . . . . 55·00 55·00
25 30s. violet £100

Some stamps are found with Arms embossed in the paper, and others with the Arms and without a date above "ZUID-AFRIKA".

NEW SOUTH WALES Pt. 1

A S.E. state of the Australian Commonwealth, whose stamps it now uses.

12 pence = 1 shilling;
20 shillings = 1 pound.

1 Seal of the Colony

8

1850. Imperf.
11 **1** 1d. red £3250 £275
25 2d. blue £2750 £130
42 3d. green £3500 £225

1851. Imperf.
47 **8** 1d. red £1000 £120
83 1d. orange . . . . £225 20·00
86 2d. blue . . . . £150 9·50
87 3d. green . . . . £275 32·00
76 6d. brown £1800 £250
79 8d. yellow £4750 £600

16

11

1854. Imperf.
109 **16** 1d. red . . . . £170 23·00
112 2d. blue . . . . £150 10·00
115 3d. green . . . . £800 80·00
88 **11** 5d. green £1000 £650
90 6d. grey . . . . £600 35·00
96 6d. brown . . . . £650 35·00
98 8d. orange £5000 £1100
100 1s. red . . . . £1200 70·00

For these stamps perforated, see No. 134 etc.

24

1860. Perf.
195 **16** 1d. red . . . . 55·00 21·00
134 2d. blue . . . . £120 10·00
226e 3d. green . . . . 6·00 1·00
233d **11** 5d. green . . . . 9·00 1·00
143 6d. brown . . . . £400 48·00
165 6d. violet . . . . 75·00 4·75
236 8d. yellow . . . . £120 16·00
170 1s. red . . . . £110 8·00
297c **24** 5s. purple . . . . 48·00 13·00

26

28

1862. Queen Victoria. Various frames.
223f **26** 1d. red . . . . 6·00 50
225g **28** 2d. blue . . . . 13·00 50
230c – 4d. brown . . . . 42·00 1·75
234 – 6d. lilac . . . . 55·00 1·25
346a – 10d. lilac . . . . 13·00 46·00
237 – 1s. black . . . . 75·00 4·00

1871. As No. 346a, surch **NINEPENCE.**
322 9d. on 10d. brown . . . . . 9·50 4·00

42

1885.
238b **42** 5s. green and lilac . . . . £425 90·00
275 10s. red and violet . . . £180 50·00
242 £1 red and lilac £3500 £2250

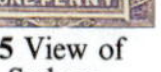
45 View of Sydney

46 Emu

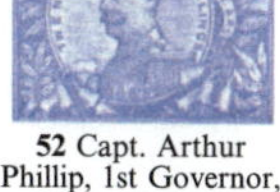
52 Capt. Arthur Phillip, 1st Governor, and Lord Carrington, Governor in 1888

55 Allegorical Figure of Australia

1888. Cent of New South Wales.
253 **45** 1d. mauve . . . . 5·50 80
254e **46** 2d. blue . . . . 8·50 30
338 – 4d. brown . . . . 10·00 3·50
256 – 6d. red . . . . 24·00 3·50
297fb – 6d. green . . . . 23·00 9·50
306 – 6d. yellow . . . . 12·00 2·75
257 – 8d. purple . . . . 20·00 4·25
347 – 1s. brown . . . . 27·00 1·75
263 – 5s. violet . . . . £150 29·00
350b **52** 20s. blue . . . . £190 60·00

DESIGNS—As Type **45**: 4d. Capt. Cook; 6d. Queen Victoria and Arms; 8d. Superb lyrebird; 1s. Kangaroo. As Type **52**: 5s. Map of Australia.

1890.
265 **55** 2½d. blue . . . . 5·00 50

1891. Types as 1862, but new value and colours, surch in words.
266 **26** ½d. on 1d. grey . . . . . 3·00 4·00
267a – 7½d. on 6d. brown . . . . 5·00 4·00
268d – 12½d. on 1s. red . . . . 12·00 11·00

58

62

63

64

66 Superb Lyrebird

67

1892.
272 **58** ½d. grey . . . . 2·50 20
298 ½d. green . . . . 1·50 60
300 **62** 1d. red . . . . 1·75 10
335 **63** 2d. blue . . . . 2·00 20
296b **64** 2½d. violet . . . . 10·00 1·25
303 2½d. blue . . . . 4·00 70
352 **67** 9d. brown and blue . . . 13·00 1·75
349a **66** 2s.6d. green . . . . . . 35·00 18·00

60

1897. Diamond Jubilee and Hospital Charity.
280 **60** 1d. (1s.) green and brown 40·00 40·00
281 – 2½d. (2s.6d.) gold & blue £170 £170

DESIGN—VERT: 2½d. Two female figures.

OFFICIAL STAMPS

1879–92. Various issues optd **O S.**

A. Issues of 1854 to 1871.
O20b **26** 1d. red . . . . 9·00 1·40
O21c **28** 2d. blue . . . . 8·50 1·00
O25c **16** 3d. green . . . . 5·00 3·75
O26a – 4d. brown (No. 230c) . . 12·00 3·50
O28 **11** 5d. green . . . . 14·00 15·00
O31b – 6d. lilac (No. 234) . . . 20·00 5·50
O32b **11** 8d. orange . . . . 22·00 10·00
O11 – 9d. on 10d. (No. 322) . . £500
O18a – 10d. lilac (No. 346a) . . £180 £100
O33 – 1s. black (No. 237) . . . 25·00 8·50
O18 **24** 5s. purple . . . . £225 85·00

B. Fiscal stamps of 1885.
O37 **24** 10s. red and violet £2500 £1000
O38 £1 red and violet £11000 £6500

C. Issue of 1888 (Nos. 253/350b).
O39 1d. mauve . . . . 3·50 75
O40 2d. blue . . . . 4·50 40
O41 4d. brown . . . . 11·00 3·75
O42 6d. red . . . . 8·50 5·50
O43 8d. purple . . . . 21·00 12·00
O44 1s. brown . . . . 22·00 4·00
O49a 5s. violet . . . . 19·00 70·00
O50 20s. blue £2000 £600

D. Issues of 1890 and 1892.
O58a **58** ½d. grey . . . . 5·00 11·00
O55 **26** ½d. on 1d. grey . . . . 55·00 55·00
O54 **55** 2½d. blue . . . . 11·00 9·50
O56 – 7½d. on 6d. (No. 283) . . 35·00 45·00
O57 – 12½d. on 1s. (No. 284c) 60·00 75·00

POSTAGE DUE STAMPS

D 1

1891.
D 1 **D 1** ½d. green . . . . 5·00 4·00
D 2b 1d. green . . . . 9·50 1·75
D 3e 2d. green . . . . 14·00 2·25
D 4 3d. green . . . . 27·00 5·50
D 5 4d. green . . . . 18·00 2·25
D 6 6d. green . . . . 27·00 7·00
D 7 8d. green . . . . 85·00 20·00
D 8 5s. green . . . . £140 48·00
D 9 10s. green . . . . £300 65·00
D10b 20s. green £300 £200

REGISTRATION STAMPS

15

1856.
102 **15** (6d.) red and blue (Imp) £900 £170
106 (6d.) orange and blue (Imp) £1000 £180
127 (6d.) red and blue (Perf) £100 20·00
120 (6d.) orange and blue (Perf) . . . . £425 65·00

NEW ZEALAND Pt. 1

A group of islands in the south Pacific Ocean. A Commonwealth Dominion.

1855. 12 pence = 1 shilling;
20 shillings = 1 pound.
1967. 100 cents = 1 dollar.

1

3

1855. Imperf.
35 **1** 1d. red £400 £250
34 1d. orange £600 £225
39 2d. blue . . . . £500 80·00
40 3d. lilac £450 £150
43 6d. brown £1000 £100
45 1s. green £1300 £325

1862. Perf.
110 **1** 1d. orange . . . . £180 35·00
132 1d. brown . . . . £180 32·00
114 2d. blue . . . . £180 22·00
133 2d. orange . . . . £160 29·00
117 3d. lilac . . . . £120 35·00
119 4d. red £2500 £250
120 4d. yellow £190 £110
122 6d. brown . . . . £250 28·00
136 6d. blue . . . . £180 60·00
125 1s. green £225 £100

1873.
151 **3** ½d. pink . . . . 12·00 1·75

5 6 7 8 9 10 11

1874. Inscr "POSTAGE".

180	5	1d. lilac	50·00	6·00
181	6	2d. red	50·00	6·00
154	7	3d. brown	£110	60·00
182	8	4d. purple	£140	45·00
183	9	6d. blue	85·00	11·00
184	10	1s. green	£130	42·00
185	11	2s. red	£350	£300
186		5s. grey	£375	£300

13 16

19 F 4

1882. Inscr "POSTAGE & REVENUE".

236	13	½d. black	4·50	15
237	10	1d. red	4·00	10
238	9	2d. mauve	13·00	75
239	16	2½d. blue	50·00	3·75
198	10	3d. yellow	48·00	8·00
222	6	4d. green	55·00	45·00
200	19	5d. black	60·00	15·00
224b	8	6d. brown	60·00	8·50
202	9	8d. blue	70·00	45·00
226	7	1s. brown	90·00	7·50

1882.

F 90	F 4	2s. blue	35·00	5·00
F 99		2s.6d. brown	35·00	5·50
F100		3s. mauve	80·00	7·00
F102		5s. green	80·00	9·50
F 87		10s. brown	£140	22·00
F 77		£1 red	£200	60·00

The above are revenue stamps authorised for use as postage stamps as there were no other postage stamps available in these denominations. Other values in this and similar types were mainly used for revenue purposes.

23 Mount Cook or Aorangi

24 Lake Taupo and Mount Ruapehu

26 Lake Wakatipu and Mount Earnslaw

25 Pembroke Peak, Milford Sound

28 Sacred Huia Birds

29 White Terrace, Rotomahana

30 Otira Gorge and Mount Ruapehu

31 Brown Kiwi

32 Maori War Canoe

33 Pink Terrace, Rotomahana

34 Kea and Kaka

35 Milford Sound

1898.

246	23	½d. purple	7·00	1·25
302		½d. green	6·50	80
247	24	1d. blue and brown	5·50	40
248	25	2d. red	30·00	25
249	26	2½d. blue (A)*	9·50	32·00
320		2½d. blue (B)*	18·00	3·50
309	28	3d. brown	27·00	1·50
252	29	4d. red	14·00	19·00
311a	30	5d. brown	29·00	6·00
254	31	6d. green	60·00	35·00
265		6d. red	38·00	4·25
325	32	8d. blue	27·00	11·00
326	33	9d. purple	27·00	8·00
268a	34	1s. orange	60·00	4·00
328	35	2s. green	85·00	24·00
329	–	5s. red	£190	£225

DESIGN—As Type **30**: 5s. Mount Cook.
*Type A of 2½d. is inscr "WAKITIPU", Type B "WAKATIPU".

40 Commemorative of the New Zealand Contingent in the South African War

1900.

274	29	1d. red	13·00	20
275b	40	1½d. brown	9·50	4·00
319	25	2d. purple	5·50	1·75
322d	24	4d. blue and brown	4·00	2·50

The 1d., 2d. and 4d. are smaller than the illustrations of their respective types.

42

44 Maori Canoe "Te Arawa"

1901.

303	42	1d. red	3·00	10

1906. New Zealand Exhibition, Christchurch. Inscr "COMMEMORATIVE SERIES OF 1906".

370	44	½d. green	24·00	32·00
371	–	1d. red	16·00	16·00
372	–	3d. brown and blue	50·00	80·00
373	–	6d. red and green	£180	£275

DESIGNS: 1d. Maori art; 3d. Landing of Cook; 6d. Annexation of New Zealand.

50 51 King Edward VII

53 Dominion

1907.

386	50	1d. red	23·00	2·00
383	28	3d. brown	35·00	15·00
376	31	6d. red	40·00	8·00
385	34	1s. orange	£110	24·00

These are smaller in size than the 1898 and 1901 issues. Type **50** also differs from Type **42** in the corner ornaments.

1909.

387	51	½d. green	4·25	50
405	53	1d. red	1·75	10
388	51	2d. mauve	9·50	6·50
389		3d. brown	23·00	1·25
390a		4d. yellow	6·00	6·50
396		4d. orange	20·00	14·00
391		5d. brown	17·00	3·50
392		6d. red	40·00	1·25
393		8d. blue	11·00	1·75
394		1s. red	48·00	2·75

1913. Auckland Industrial Exhibition. Optd AUCKLAND EXHIBITION, 1913.

412	51	½d. green	15·00	55·00
413	53	1d. red	21·00	45·00
414	51	3d. brown	£130	£250
415		6d. red	£160	£300

62 King George V

1915.

446	62	½d. green	1·00	30
416		1½d. grey	3·50	1·75
438		1½d. brown	2·25	20
417a		2d. violet	7·00	35·00
439		2d. yellow	2·25	20
419		2½d. blue	3·25	5·00
449		3d. brown	7·50	1·00
421		4d. yellow	4·25	50·00
422e		4d. violet	7·00	50
423		4½d. green	12·00	24·00
424		5d. blue	6·50	1·00
425		6d. red	8·50	50
426		7½d. brown	10·00	23·00
427		8d. blue	11·00	50·00
428		8d. brown	20·00	1·50
429		9d. green	17·00	2·75
430c		1s. orange	14·00	50

1915. No. 446 optd WAR STAMP and stars.

452	62	½d. green	2·25	50

64 "Peace" and Lion

65 "Peace" and Lion

1920. Victory. Inscr "VICTORY" or dated "1914 1919" (6d.).

453	64	½d. green	3·00	2·50
454	65	1d. red	4·50	60
455	–	1½d. orange	3·00	50
456	–	3d. brown	12·00	14·00
457	–	6d. violet	13·00	17·00
458	–	1s. orange	20·00	48·00

DESIGNS—HORIZ (As Type **65**): 1½d. Maori chief. (As Type **64**): 3d. Lion; 1s. King George V. VERT (As Type **64**): 6d. "Peace" and "Progress".

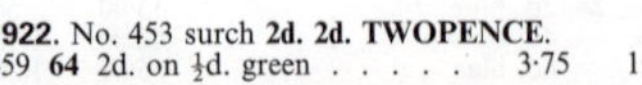

1922. No. 453 surch 2d. 2d. TWOPENCE.

459	64	2d. on ½d. green	3·75	1·40

69 New Zealand

70 Exhibition Buildings

1923. Restoration of Penny Postage.

460	69	1d. red	3·00	60

1925. Dunedin Exhibition.

463	70	½d. green on green	3·00	11·00
464		1d. red on rose	3·75	5·50
465		4d. mauve on mauve	30·00	70·00

71 73 Nurse

1926.

468	71	1d. red	75	20
469	–	2s. blue	55·00	25·00
470	–	3s. mauve	90·00	£150

The 2s. and 3s. are larger, 21 × 25 mm.

1929. Anti-T.B. Fund.

544	73	1d.+1d. red	11·00	18·00

1930. Inscr "HELP PROMOTE HEALTH".

545	73	1d.+1d. red	20·00	38·00

74 Smiling Boy F 6 "Arms" Type

75 New Zealand Lake Scenery

1931. Health Stamps.

546	74	1d.+1d. red	75·00	75·00
547		2d.+1d. blue	75·00	60·00

1931. Air.

548	75	3d. brown	25·00	15·00
549		4d. purple	25·00	20·00
550		7d. orange	27·00	9·00

1931. Air. Surch FIVE PENCE.

551	75	5d. on 3d. green	10·00	8·00

1931. Various frames.

F191	F 6	1s.3d. yellow	13·00	2·25
F192		1s.3d. yellow and black	4·00	1·25
F193		2s.6d. brown	8·50	80
F194		4s. red	19·00	1·50
F195		5s. green	20·00	1·00
F196		6s. red	35·00	3·25
F197		7s. blue	35·00	5·50
F198		7s.6d. grey	65·00	55·00
F153		8s. violet	28·00	32·00
F154		9s. orange	30·00	29·00
F201		10s. red	35·00	2·25
F156		12s.6d. purple	£130	£130
F202		15s. green	45·00	19·00
F203		£1 pink	28·00	3·75
F159		25s. blue	£375	£475
F205w		30s. brown	£250	£110
F161		35s. yellow	£3000	£3500
F206		£2 violet	£110	22·00
F207		£2 10s. red	£300	£325
F208w		£3 green	£150	48·00
F165		£3 10s. red	£1400	£1400
F210		£4 blue	£160	£120
F167		£4 10s. grey	£1200	£1300
F211w		£5 blue	£200	45·00

77 Hygeia Goddess of Health

78 The Path to Health

1932. Health Stamp.

552	77	1d.+1d. red	20·00	27·00

1933. Health Stamp.

553	78	1d.+1d. red	13·00	17·00

1934. Air. Optd TRANS-TASMAN AIR MAIL "FAITH IN AUSTRALIA.".

554	75	7d. blue	35·00	40·00

80 Crusader

1934. Health Stamp.

555	**80**	1d.+1d. red	11·00	17·00

81 Collared Grey Fantail — **83** Maori Woman — **86** Maori Girl

85 Mt. Cook — **87** Mitre Peak

89 Harvesting — **91** Maori Panel

93 Capt. Cook at Poverty Bay

1935.

556	**81**	½d. green	1·50	1·25
557	–	1d. red	1·75	1·00
558a	**83**	1½d. brown	8·50	8·50
580	–	2d. orange	30	10
581c	**85**	2½d. brown and grey	50	4·00
561	**86**	3d. brown	12·00	3·25
583d	**87**	4d. black and brown	1·00	20
584c	–	5d. blue	2·00	1·75
585c	**89**	6d. red	1·25	20
586d	–	8d. brown	3·75	1·25
631	**91**	9d. red and black	3·75	3·50
588	–	1s. green	2·50	60
589e	**93**	2s. olive	5·50	1·50
590c	–	3s. chocolate and brown	3·50	2·25

DESIGNS—As Type **81**: 1d. Brown kiwi; 2d. Maori carved house; 1s. Parson bird. As Type **87**: 8d. Tuatara lizard. As Type **85**: 5d. Swordfish; 3s. Mt. Egmont.

95 Bell Block Aerodrome

1935. Air.

570	**95**	1d. red	1·00	70
571		3d. violet	5·00	3·00
572		6d. blue	9·50	3·00

96 King George V and Queen Mary

1935. Silver Jubilee.

573	**96**	½d. green	75	1·00
574		1d. red	1·00	80
575		6d. orange	18·00	28·00

97 "The Key to Health" — **99** N.Z. Soldier at Anzac Cove

1935. Health Stamp.

576	**97**	1d.+1d. red	2·50	2·75

1936. Charity. 21st Anniv of "Anzac" Landing at Gallipoli.

591	**99**	½d.+½d. green	60	1·75
592		1d.+1d. red	60	1·40

100 Wool

1936. Congress of British Empire Chambers of Commerce, Wellington. Inscr as in T **100**.

593	**100**	½d. green	30	30
594	–	1d. red (Butter)	30	20
595	–	2½d. blue (Sheep)	1·25	8·00
596	–	4d. violet (Apples)	1·00	5·50
597	–	6d. brown (Exports)	2·50	4·50

105 Health Camp

1936. Health Stamp.

598	**105**	1d.+1d. red	1·75	3·75

106 King George VI and Queen Elizabeth

1937. Coronation.

599	**106**	1d. red	30	10
600		2½d. blue	80	2·50
601		6d. orange	1·10	2·25

107 Rock climbing — **108** King George VI

1937. Health Stamp.

602	**107**	1d.+1d. red	3·00	3·75

1938.

603	**108**	½d. green	6·50	10
604		½d. brown	20	40
605		1d. red	5·00	10
606		1d. green	20	10
607		1½d. brown	26·00	2·75
608		1½d. red	20	60
680		2d. orange	15	10
609		3d. blue	20	10
681		4d. purple	70	60
682		5d. grey	50	90
683		6d. red	50	10
684		8d. violet	75	65
685		9d. brown	1·75	50
686b	–	1s. brown and red	50	80
687	–	1s.3d. brown and blue	1·25	1·25
688	–	2s. orange and green	3·75	2·50
689	–	3s. brown and grey	4·50	3·50

The shilling values are larger, 22×25½ mm, and "NEW ZEALAND" appears at the top.

109 Children playing — **110** Beach Ball

1938. Health Stamp.

610	**109**	1d.+1d. red	6·50	3·00

1939. Health Stamps. Surch.

611	**110**	1d. on ½d.+½d. green	4·75	4·50
612		2d. on 1d.+1d. red	5·50	4·50

1939. Surch in bold figures.

F212	**F 6**	3/6 on 3s.6d. green	20·00	7·00
F214		5/6 on 5s.6d. lilac	48·00	18·00
F215		11/- on 11s. yellow	80·00	48·00
F216		22/- on 22s. red	£300	£140
F186		35/- on 35s. orange	£475	£250

112 "Endeavour", Chart of N.Z. and Captain Cook

1940. Centenary of Proclamation of British Sovereignty. Inscr "CENTENNIAL OF NEW ZEALAND 1840 1940".

613	–	½d. green	30	10
614	**112**	1d. brown and red	2·75	10
615	–	1½d. blue and mauve	30	60
616	–	2d. green and brown	1·50	10
617	–	2½d. green and blue	2·00	1·00
618	–	3d. purple and red	3·75	1·00
619	–	4d. brown and red	13·00	1·50
620	–	5d. blue and brown	7·00	3·75
621	–	6d. green and violet	11·00	1·25
622	–	7d. black and red	1·75	4·00
623	–	8d. black and red	11·00	3·00
624	–	9d. green and orange	7·50	2·00
625	–	1s. green and deep green	13·00	3·75

DESIGNS—HORIZ (as T **112**): ½d. Arrival of the Maoris, 1350; 1½d. British Monarchs; 2d. Abel Tasman with "Heemskerk" and chart; 3d. Landing of immigrants, 1840; 4d. Road, rail, ocean and air transport; 6d. "Dunedin" and "frozen mutton" sea route to London; 7, 8d. Maori council; 9d. Gold mining methods, 1861 and 1940. (25×21 mm): 5d. H.M.S. "Britomart" at Akaroa, 1840. VERT (21×25 mm): 2½d. Treaty of Waitangi. (As T **112**): 1s. Giant kauri tree.

1940. Health Stamps.

626	**110**	1d.+½d. green	14·00	16·00
627		2d.+1d. orange	14·00	16·00

1941. Surch.

628	**108**	1d. on ½d. green	1·75	10
629		2d. on 1½d. brown	1·75	10

1941. Health Stamps. Optd **1941**.

632	**110**	1d.+½d. green	50	2·25
633		2d.+1d. orange	50	2·25

125 Boy and Girl on Swing

1942. Health Stamps.

634	**125**	1d.+½d. green	30	1·25
635		2d.+1d. orange	30	1·25

126 Princess Margaret

1943. Health Stamps.

636	**126**	1d.+½d. green	20	1·50
637	–	2d.+1d. brown	20	25

DESIGN: 2d. Queen Elizabeth II as Princess.

1944. Surch **TENPENCE** between crosses.

662		10d. on 1½d. blue and mauve (No. 615)	15	10

129 Queen Elizabeth II as Princess and Princess Margaret — **130** Peter Pan Statue, Kensington Gardens

1944. Health Stamps.

663	**129**	1d.+½d. green	30	40
664		2d.+1d. blue	30	30

1945. Health Stamps.

665	**130**	1d.+½d. green and buff	15	20
666		2d.+1d. red and buff	15	20

131 Lake Matheson — **132** King George VI and Parliament House, Wellington

133 St. Paul's Cathedral — **139** "St. George" (Wellington College War Memorial window)

1946. Peace Issue.

667	**131**	½d. green and brown	20	65
668	**132**	1d. green	10	10
669	**133**	1½d. red	10	50
670	–	2d. purple	15	10
671	–	3d. blue and grey	30	15
672	–	4d. green and orange	20	20
673	–	5d. green and blue	50	1·00
674	–	6d. brown and red	15	30
675	**139**	8d. black and red	15	30
676	–	9d. blue and black	15	30
677	–	1s. grey	40	40

DESIGNS—As Type **132**: 2d. The Royal Family. As Type **131**: 3d. R.N.Z.A.F. badge and airplanes; 4d. Army badge, tank and plough; 5d. Navy badge, H.M.N.Z.S. "Achilles" (cruiser) and "Dominion Monarch" (liner); 6d. N.Z. coat of arms, foundry and farm; 9d. Southern Alps and Franz Josef Glacier. As T **139**: 1s. National Memorial campanile.

142 Soldier helping Child over Stile — **145** Statue of Eros

1946. Health Stamps.

678	**142**	1d.+½d. green and orange	15	15
679		2d.+1d. brown & orange	15	15

1947. Health Stamps.

690	**145**	1d.+½d. green	15	15
691		2d.+1d. red	15	15

146 Port Chalmers, 1848

1948. Centenary of Otago. Various designs inscr "CENTENNIAL OF OTAGO".

692	**146**	1d. blue and green	25	35
693	–	2d. green and brown	25	35
694	–	3d. purple	30	60
695	–	6d. black and red	30	60

DESIGNS—HORIZ: 2d. Cromwell, Otago; 6d. Otago University. VERT: 3d. First Church, Dunedin.

150 Boy sunbathing and Children playing — **151** Nurse and Child

1948. Health Stamps.

696	**150**	1d.+½d. blue and green	15	20
697		2d.+1d. purple and red	15	20

1949. Health Stamps.

698	**151**	1d.+½d. green	25	20
699		2d.+1d. blue	25	20

1950. As Type **F 6**, but without value, surch **1½d. POSTAGE.**

700		1½d. red	40	30

Type **F 6** is illustrated next to Type **74**.

153 Queen Elizabeth II and Prince Charles

155 Cairn on Lyttleton Hills

1950. Health Stamps.
701 **153** 1d.+½d. green 25 20
702 2d.+1d. purple 25 20

1950. Centenary of Canterbury, N.Z.
703 – 1d. green and blue 40 55
704 **155** 2d. red and orange 40 55
705 – 3d. deep blue and blue 40 75
706 – 6d. brown and blue 50 75
707 – 1s. purple and blue 50 1·00
DESIGNS—VERT: 1d. Christchurch Cathedral; 3d. John Robert Godley. HORIZ: 6d. Canterbury University College; 1s. Aerial view of Timaru.

159 "Takapuna" class Yachts

1951. Health Stamps.
708 **159** 1½d.+½d. red and yellow 20 1·00
709 2d.+1d. green and yellow 25 25

160 Princess Anne

161 Prince Charles

1952. Health Stamps.
710 **160** 1½d.+½d. red 15 30
711 **161** 2d.+1d. brown 15 20

1952. Surch in figures.
712 **108** 1d. on ½d. orange 30 90
713 3d. on 1d. green 10 10

164 Queen Elizabeth II

166 Westminster Abbey

165 Coronation State Coach

1953. Coronation.
714 – 2d. blue 30 30
715 **164** 3d. brown 30 10
716 **165** 4d. red 1·25 2·50
717 **166** 8d. grey 80 1·60
718 – 1s.6d. purple and blue 2·00 2·75
DESIGNS—As Type **165**: 2d. Queen Elizabeth II and Buckingham Palace; 1s.6d. St. Edward's Crown and Royal Sceptre.

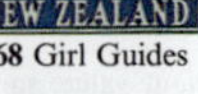
168 Girl Guides

169 Boy Scouts

1953. Health Stamps.
719 **168** 1½d.+½d. blue 15 10
720 **169** 2d.+1d. green 15 40

170 Queen Elizabeth II

171 Queen Elizabeth II and Duke of Edinburgh

1953. Royal Visit.
721 **170** 3d. purple 10 10
722 **171** 4d. blue 10 60

172

173

174 Queen Elizabeth II

1953. Small figures of value.
723 **172** ½d. black 15 30
724 1d. orange 15 10
725 1½d. brown 20 10
726 2d. green 20 10
727 3d. red 20 10
728 4d. blue 40 50
729 6d. purple 70 1·60
730 8d. red 60 60
731 **173** 9d. brown and green 60 60
732 1s. black and red 65 10
733 1s.6d. black and blue 1·25 60
733c 1s.9d. black and orange 7·00 1·50
733d **174** 2s.6d. brown 18·00 8·00
734 3s. green 12·00 30
735 5s. red 18·00 4·50
736 10s. blue 40·00 19·00

175 Young Climber and Mts. Aspiring and Everest

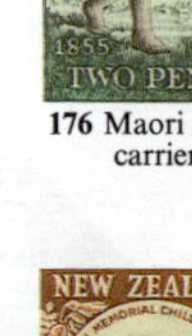

176 Maori Mail-carrier

177 Queen Elizabeth II

179 Children's Health Camps Federation Emblem

1954. Health Stamps.
737 **175** 1½d.+½d. brown and violet 15 30
738 2d.+1d. brown and blue 15 30

1955. Centenary of First New Zealand Stamps. Inscr "1855–1955".
739 **176** 2d. brown and green 10 10
740 **177** 3d. red 10 10
741 – 4d. black and blue 60 1·00
DESIGN—HORIZ (As Type **176**): 4d. Douglas DC-3 airliner.

1955. Health Stamps.
742 **179** 1½d.+½d. brown and chestnut 10 60
743 2d.+1d. red and green 10 35
744 3d.+1d. brown and red 15 15

180

183 Takahe

181 "The Whalers of Foveaux Strait"

1955. As 1953 but larger figures of value and stars omitted from lower right corner.
745 **180** 1d. orange 50 10
746 1½d. brown 60 60
747 2d. green 40 10
748b 3d. red 50 10
749 4d. blue 1·00 80
750 6d. purple 10·00 20
751 8d. brown 6·50 8·00

1956. Southland Centennial.
752 **181** 2d. green 30 15
753 – 3d. brown 10 10
754 **183** 8d. violet and red 1·25 1·75
DESIGN—As Type **181**: 3d. Allegory of farming.

184 Children picking Apples

185 New Zealand Lamb and Map

1956. Health Stamps.
755 **184** 1½d.+½d. brown 15 70
756 2d.+1d. green 15 55
757 3d.+1d. red 15 15

1957. 75th Anniv of First Export of N.Z. Lamb.
758 **185** 4d. blue 50 1·00
759 – 8d. red 75 1·25
DESIGN—HORIZ: 8d. Lamb, sailing ship "Dunedin" and "Port Brisbane" (refrigerated freighter).

187 Sir Truby King

188 Life-savers in Action

1957. 50th Anniv of Plunket Society.
760 **187** 3d. red 10 10

1957. Health Stamps.
761 **188** 2d.+1d. black and green 15 70
762 – 3d.+1d. blue and red 15 10
MS762b Two sheets, each 112×96 mm, with Nos. 761 and 762 in blocks of 6 (2×3) Per pair 9·00 25·00
DESIGN: 3d. Children on seashore.

1958. Surch.
763a **180** 2d. on 1½d. brown 15 10
808 2½d. on 3d. red 25 15

192 Boys' Brigade Bugler

193 Sir Charles Kingsford-Smith and Fokker F.IIa/3m Southern Cross

1958. Health Stamps.
764 – 2d.+1d. green 20 40
765 **192** 3d.+1d. blue 20 40
MS765a Two sheets, each 104×124 mm, with Nos. 764/5 in blocks of 6 (3×2) Per pair 7·00 18·00
DESIGN: 2d. Girls' Life Brigade cadet.

1958. 30th Anniv of 1st Air Crossing of Tasman Sea.
766 **193** 6d. blue 50 75

194 Seal of Nelson

1958. Centenary of City of Nelson.
767 **194** 3d. red 10 10

195 "Pania" Statue, Napier

196 Australian Gannets on Cape Kidnappers

1958. Centenary of Hawke's Bay Province.
768 **195** 2d. green 10 10
769 **196** 3d. blue 20 10
770 – 8d. brown 55 1·50
DESIGN—As Type **195**: 8d. Maori sheep-shearer.

197 "Kiwi", Jamboree Badge

198 Careening H.M.S. "Endeavour" at Ship Cove

1959. Pan-Pacific Scout Jamboree, Auckland.
771 **197** 3d. brown and red 30 10

1959. Centenary of Marlborough Province. Inscr as in T **198**.
772 **198** 2d. green 30 10
773 – 3d. blue 30 10
774 – 8d. brown 1·00 2·25
DESIGNS: 3d. Shipping wool, Wairau Bar, 1857; 8d. Salt industry, Grassmere.

201 Red Cross Flag

1959. Red Cross Commemoration.
775 **201** 3d.+1d. red and blue 20 10

202 Grey Teal

204 "The Explorer"

1959. Health Stamps.
776 **202** 2d.+1d. yellow, olive and red 50 65
777 – 3d.+1d. black, pink and blue 50 65
MS777c Two sheets, each 95×109 mm, with Nos. 776/7 in blocks of 6 (3×2) Per pair 8·50 24·00
DESIGN: 3d. New Zealand stilt.

1960. Centenary of Westland Province.
778 **204** 2d. green 20 10
779 – 3d. salmon 20 10
780 – 8d. black 70 3·00
DESIGNS: 3d. "The Gold Digger"; 8d. "The Pioneer Woman".

207 Manuka (Tea Tree)

215 Timber Industry

219 Taniwha (Maori Rock Drawing)

225 Sacred Kingfisher

1960.
781 **207** ½d. green and red 10 10
782 – 1d. multicoloured 10 10
783 – 2d. multicoloured 10 10
784 – 2½d. multicoloured 1·00 10
785 – 3d. multicoloured 30 10

786 – 4d. multicoloured 40 10
787 – 5d. multicoloured 1·25 10
788 – 6d. lilac, green and turquoise 50 10
788d – 7d. red, green and yellow 65 1·40
789 – 8d. multicoloured 40 10
790 – 9d. red and blue 40 10
791 **215** 1s. brown and green 30 10
792b – 1s.3d. red, sepia and blue 2·00 25
793 – 1s.6d. olive and brown 75 10
794 – 1s.9d. brown 10·00 15
795 – 1s.9d. multicoloured 5·50 1·00
796 **219** 2s. black and buff 2·50 10
797 – 2s.6d. yellow and brown 1·75 1·00
798 – 3s. sepia 23·00 1·00
799 – 3s. bistre, blue and green 3·25 1·75
800 – 5s. myrtle 2·25 80
801 – 10s. blue 4·50 3·25
802 – £1 mauve 9·50 7·50

DESIGNS—VERT (as Type **207**): 1d. Karaka; 2d. Kowhai Ngutu-kaka (Kaka Beak); 2½d. Titoki (plant); 3d. Kowhai; 4d. Puarangi (Hibiscus); 5d. Matua tikumu (Mountain daisy); 6d. Pikiarero (Clematis); 7d. Koromiko; 8d. Rata. (As T **215**): 1s.3d. Rainbow trout; 1s.6d. Tiki. (As T **219**): 5s. Sutherland Falls; £1 Potutu Geyser. HORIZ (as T **215**): 9d. National flag; 1s.9d. Aerial top-dressing. (As Type **219**): 2s.6d. Butter-making; 3s. Tongariro National Park and Chateau; 10s. Tasman Glacier.

1960. Health Stamps.
803 **225** 2d.+1d. sepia and blue 50 75
804 – 3d.+1d. purple & orange 50 75
MS804b Two sheets, each 95 × 107 mm, with Nos. 803/4 in blocks of 6 Per pair 26·00 38·00
DESIGN: 3d. New Zealand pigeon.

227 "The Adoration of the Shepherds" (Rembrandt)

228 Great Egret

1960. Christmas.
805 **227** 2d. red & brown on cream 15 10

1961. Health Stamps.
806 **228** 2d.+1d. black and purple 50 70
807 – 3d.+1d. sepia and green 50 70
MS807a Two sheets, each 97 × 121 mm, with Nos. 806/7 in blocks of 6 (3 × 2) Per pair 26·00 30·00
DESIGN: 3d. New Zealand falcon.

232 "Adoration of the Magi" (Durer)

236 Tieke Saddleback

233 Morse Key and Port Hills, Lyttleton

1961. Christmas.
809 **232** 2½d. multicoloured 10 10

1962. Telegraph Centenary.
810 **233** 3d. sepia and green 10 10
811 – 8d. black and red 90 90
DESIGN: 8d. Modern teleprinter.

1962. Health Stamps.
812 – 2½d.+1d. multicoloured 50 70
813 **236** 3d.+1d. multicoloured 50 70
MS813b Two sheets, each 96 × 101 mm, with Nos. 812/13 in blocks of 6 (3 × 2) Per pair 45·00 50·00
DESIGN: 2½d. Red-fronted parakeet.

237 "Madonna in Prayer" (Sassoferrato)

238 Prince Andrew

1962. Christmas.
814 **237** 2½d. multicoloured 10 10

1963. Health Stamps.
815 **238** 2½d.+1d. blue 30 70
816 – 3d.+1d. red 30 10
MS816a Two sheets, each 93 × 100 mm, with Nos. 815/16 in blocks of 6 (3 × 2) Per pair 24·00 38·00
DESIGN: 3d. Prince Andrew (different).

240 "The Holy Family" (Titian)

1963. Christmas.
817 **240** 2½d. multicoloured 10 10

241 Steam Locomotive "Pilgrim" (1863) and Class DG Diesel Locomotive

1963. Centenary of New Zealand Railway. Inscr as in T **241**. Multicoloured.
818 3d. Type **241** 40 10
819 1s.9d. Diesel express and Mt. Ruapehu 1·50 1·50

243 "Commonwealth Cable"

1963. Opening of COMPAC (Trans-Pacific Telephone Cable).
820 **243** 8d. multicoloured 50 1·25

244 Road Map and Car Steering-wheel

1964. Road Safety Campaign.
821 **244** 3d. black, yellow and blue 30 10

245 Silver Gulls

1964. Health Stamps. Multicoloured.
822 2½d.+1d. Type **245** 40 50
823 3d.+1d. Little penguin 40 50
MS823b Two sheets, each 171 × 84 mm, with Nos. 822/3 in blocks of 8 (4 × 2) Per pair 48·00 60·00

246 Rev. S. Marsden taking first Christian Service at Rangihoua Bay, 1814

1964. Christmas.
824 **246** 2½d. multicoloured 10 10

1964. Surch **7D POSTAGE**.
825 F **6** 7d. on (–) red 50 1·50

248 Anzac Cove

1965. 50th Anniv of Gallipoli Landing.
826 **248** 4d. brown 10 10
827 – 5d. green and red 10 60
DESIGN: 5d. Anzac Cove and poppy.

249 I.T.U. Emblem and Symbols

250 Sir Winston Churchill

1965. Centenary of I.T.U.
828 **249** 9d. blue and brown 55 35

1965. Churchill Commemoration.
829 **250** 7d. black, grey and blue 30 50

251 Wellington Provincial Council Building

252 Kaka

1965. Centenary of Government in Wellington.
830 **251** 4d. multicoloured 20 10

1965. Health Stamps. Multicoloured.
831 3d.+1d. Type **252** 40 65
832 4d.+1d. Collared grey fantail 40 65
MS832b Two sheets, each 100 × 109 mm, with Nos. 831/2 in blocks of 6 (3 × 2) Per pair 38·00 48·00

254 I.C.Y. Emblem

255 "The Two Trinities" (Murillo)

1965. International Co-operation Year.
833 **254** 4d. red and olive 20 10

1965. Christmas.
834 **255** 3d. multicoloured 10 10

256 Arms of New Zealand

1965. 11th Commonwealth Parliamentary Conf. Multicoloured.
835 4d. Type **256** 25 20
836 9d. Parliament House, Wellington, and Badge 65 1·25
837 2s. Wellington from Mt. Victoria 4·50 6·50

259 "Progress" Arrowhead

260 New Zealand Bell Bird

1966. 4th National Scout Jamboree, Trentham.
838 **259** 4d. gold and green 15 10

1966. Health Stamps. Multicoloured.
839 3d.+1d. Type **260** 50 75
840 4d.+1d. Weka rail 50 75
MS841 Two sheets, each 107 × 91 mm. Nos. 839/40 in blocks of 6 (3 × 2) Per pair 22·00 48·00

262 "The Virgin with Child" (Maratta)

263 Queen Victoria and Queen Elizabeth II

1966. Christmas.
842 **262** 3d. multicoloured 10 10

1967. Centenary of New Zealand Post Office Savings Bank.
843 **263** 4d. black, gold and purple 10 10
844 – 9d. multicoloured 10 20
DESIGN: 9d. Half-sovereign of 1867 and commemorative dollar coin.

265 Manuka (Tea Tree)

268 Running with Ball

1967. Decimal Currency. Designs as earlier issues, but with values inscr in decimal currency as T **265**.
845 **265** ½c. blue, green and red 10 10
846 – 1c. mult (No. 782) 10 10
847 – 2c. mult (No. 783) 10 10
848 – 2½c. mult (No. 785) 10 10
849 – 3c. mult (No. 786) 10 10
850 – 4c. mult (No. 787) 30 10
851 – 5c. lilac, olive and green (No. 788) 50 30
852 – 6c. mult (No. 788d) 50 70
853 – 7c. mult (No. 789) 60 70
854 – 8c. red and blue (No. 790) 60 40
855 **215** 10c. brown and green 60 40
856 – 15c. green and brown (No. 793) 1·75 1·25
857 **219** 20c. black and buff 1·00 10
858 – 25c. yellow and brown (No. 797) 1·25 2·00
859 – 30c. yellow, green and blue (No. 799) 1·25 25
860 – 50c. green (No. 800) 1·75 50
861 – $1 blue (No. 801) 9·00 1·00
862 – $2 mauve (No. 802) 4·00 6·00
F219a F **6** $4 violet 2·50 1·50
F220a $6 green 3·00 3·00
F221a $8 blue 4·00 4·50
F222a $10 blue 5·00 3·75
For 15c. in different colours, see No. 874.

1967. Health Stamps. Rugby Football.
867 **268** 2½c.+1c. multicoloured 15 15
868 – 3c.+1c. multicoloured 15 15
MS869 Two sheets. (a) 76 × 130 mm (867). (b) 130 × 76 mm (868). Containing blocks of six Per pair 23·00 38·00
DESIGN—HORIZ: 3c. Positioning for place-kick.

271 Brown Trout

273 Forest and Timber

1967.
870 – 7c. multicoloured 1·50 90
871 **271** 7½c. multicoloured 50 70
872 – 8c. multicoloured 75 70
873 **273** 10c. multicoloured 50 10

874 – 15c. green, deep green and red (as No. 793) . . . 1·00 1·00
875 – 18c. multicoloured . . . . 1·00 55
876 – 20c. multicoloured . . . . 1·00 20
877 – 25c. multicoloured . . . . 1·75 2·00
878 – 28c. multicoloured 60 10
879 – $2 black, ochre and blue (as No. 802) . . . . . 13·00 13·00

DESIGNS: 7c. "Kaitia" (trawler) and catch; 8c. Apples and orchard; 18c. Sheep and the "Woolmark"; 20c. Consignments of beef and herd of cattle; 25c. Dairy farm, Mt. Egmont and butter consignment. VERT: 28c. Fox Glacier, Westland National Park.

No. 871 was originally issued to commemorate the introduction of the brown trout into New Zealand.

No. 874 is slightly larger than No. 793, measuring 21 × 25 mm, and the inscr and numerals differ in size.

278 "The Adoration of the Shepherds" (Poussin)

279 Mount Aspiring, Aurora Australis and Southern Cross

1967. Christmas.
880 **278** 2½c. multicoloured 10 10

1967. Cent of Royal Society of New Zealand.
881 **279** 4c. multicoloured 25 20
882 – 8c. multicoloured 25 80
DESIGN: 8c. Sir James Hector (founder).

281 Open Bible

282 Soldiers and Tank

1968. Centenary of Maori Bible.
883 **281** 3c. multicoloured 10 10

1968. New Zealand Armed Forces. Multicoloured.
884 4c. Type **282** 25 15
885 10c. Airmen, Fairey Firefly and English Electric Canberra aircraft 35 70
886 28c. Sailors and H.M.N.Z.S. "Achilles", 1939, and H.M.N.Z.S. "Waikato", 1968 . . . . 50 2·50

285 Boy breasting Tape and Olympic Rings

1968. Health Stamps. Multicoloured.
887 2½c.+1c. Type **285** 20 15
888 3c.+1c. Girl swimming and Olympic rings 20 15
MS889 Two sheets, each 145 × 95 mm. Nos. 887/8 in blocks of 6 Per pair . . . . 16·00 42·00

287 Placing Votes in Ballot Box

288 Human Rights Emblem

1968. 75th Anniv of Universal Suffrage in New Zealand.
890 **287** 3c. ochre, green and blue 10 10

1968. Human Rights Year.
891 **288** 10c. red, yellow and green 10 30

289 "Adoration of the Holy Child" (G. van Honthorst)

1968. Christmas.
892 **289** 2½c. multicoloured 10 10

290 I.L.O. Emblem

1969. 50th Anniv of Int Labour Organization.
893 **290** 7c. black and red 15 30

291 Supreme Court Building, Auckland

1969. Centenary of New Zealand Law Society.
894 **291** 3c. multicoloured 10 10
895 – 10c. multicoloured 20 60
896 – 18c. multicoloured . . . . 30 1·50
DESIGNS—VERT: 10c. Law Society's coat of arms; 18c. "Justice" (from Memorial Window in University of Canterbury, Christchurch).

295 Student being conferred with Degree

1969. Centenary of Otago University. Mult.
897 3c. Otago University (vert) 10 10
898 10c. Type **295** 20 25

296 Boys playing Cricket

1969. Health Stamps.
899 **296** 2½c.+1c. multicoloured . . 40 65
900 – 3c.+1c. multicoloured . . 40 65
901 – 4c.+1c. brown and ultramarine . . . . . . 40 2·00
MS902 Two sheets, each 144 × 84 mm. Nos. 899/900 in blocks of 6 Per pair . . . . . 16·00 48·00
DESIGNS—HORIZ: 3c. Girls playing cricket. VERT: 4c. Dr. Elizabeth Gunn (founder of first Children's Health Camp).

299 Oldest existing House in New Zealand, and Old Stone Mission Store, Kerikeri

1969. Early European Settlement in New Zealand, and 150th Anniv of Kerikeri. Multicoloured.
903 4c. Type **299** 20 25
904 6c. View of Bay of Islands 30 1·75

301 "The Nativity" (Federico Fiori Barocci)

306 Girl, Wheat Field and C.O.R.S.O. Emblem

302 Captain Cook, Transit of Venus and "Octant"

1969. Christmas.
905 **301** 2½c. multicoloured 10 10

1969. Bicentenary of Captain Cook's Landing in New Zealand.
906 **302** 4c. black, red and blue . . 75 35
907 – 6c. green, brown and black . . . . 1·00 2·50
908 – 18c. brown, green and black . . . . 1·75 2·50
909 – 28c. red, black and blue 2·75 4·00
MS910 109 × 90 mm. Nos. 906/9 18·00 35·00
DESIGNS: 6c. Sir Joseph Banks (naturalist) and outline of H.M.S. "Endeavour"; 18c. Dr. Daniel Solander (botanist) and his plant; 28c. Queen Elizabeth II and Cook's chart, 1769.

1969. 25th Anniv of C.O.R.S.O. (Council of Organizations for Relief Services Overseas). Multicoloured.
911 7c. Type **306** . . . . 35 1·10
912 8c. Mother feeding her child, dairy herd and C.O.R.S.O. emblem (horiz) . . . . . . 35 1·25

308 "Cardigan Bay" (champion trotter)

1970. Return of "Cardigan Bay" to New Zealand.
913 **308** 10c. multicoloured 30 30

309 "Vanessa gonerilla" (butterfly)

310 Queen Elizabeth II and New Zealand Coat of Arms

1970.
914 – ½c. multicoloured . . . 10 20
915 **309** 1c. multicoloured . . . 10 10
916 – 2c. multicoloured . . . 10 10
917 – 2½c. multicoloured . . . 30 20
918 – 3c. multicoloured . . . 15 10
919 – 4c. multicoloured . . . 15 10
920 – 5c. multicoloured . . . 30 10
921 – 6c. black, green and red 30 1·00
922 – 7c. multicoloured . . . 50 1·00
923 – 7½c. multicoloured . . . 75 1·50
924 – 8c. multicoloured . . . 50 1·00
925 **310** 10c. multicoloured . . . 50 15
926 – 15c. black, flesh and brown 75 50
927 – 18c. green, brown & black 75 50
928 – 20c. black and brown . . 75 15
929 – 23c. multicoloured . . . 60 30
930b – 25c. multicoloured . . . 50 40
931 – 30c. multicoloured . . . 50 15
932 – 50c. multicoloured . . . 50 20
933 – $1 multicoloured . . . . 1·00 1·25
934 – $2 multicoloured . . . . 2·50 1·75
DESIGNS—VERT (as T **309**): ½c. "Lycaena salustius" (butterfly); 2c. "Argyrophenga antipodum" (butterfly); 2½c. "Nyctemera annulata (moth); 3c. "Detunda egregia" (moth); 4c. Charagia virescens" (moth); 5c. Scarlet wrasse ("Scarlet parrot fish"); 6c. Big-bellied sea horses; 7c. Leather-jacket (fish); 7½c. Intermediate halfbeak ("Garfish"); 8c. John Dory (fish). (As T **310**): 18c. Maori club; 25c. Hauraki Gulf Maritime Park; 30c. Mt. Cook National Park. HORIZ (as T **310**): 15c. Maori fish hook; 20c. Maori tattoo pattern; 23c. Egmont National Park; 50c. Abel Tasman National Park; $1 Geothermal power; $2 Agricultural technology.

311 Geyser Restaurant

312 U.N. H.Q. Building

1970. World Fair, Osaka. Multicoloured.
935 7c. Type **311** 20 75
936 8c. New Zealand Pavilion . . 20 75
937 18c. Bush Walk 40 75

1970. 25th Anniv of United Nations.
938 **312** 3c. multicoloured 10 10
939 – 10c. red and yellow . . . 20 20
DESIGN: 10c. Tractor on horizon.

313 Soccer

314 "The Virgin adoring the Child" (Correggio)

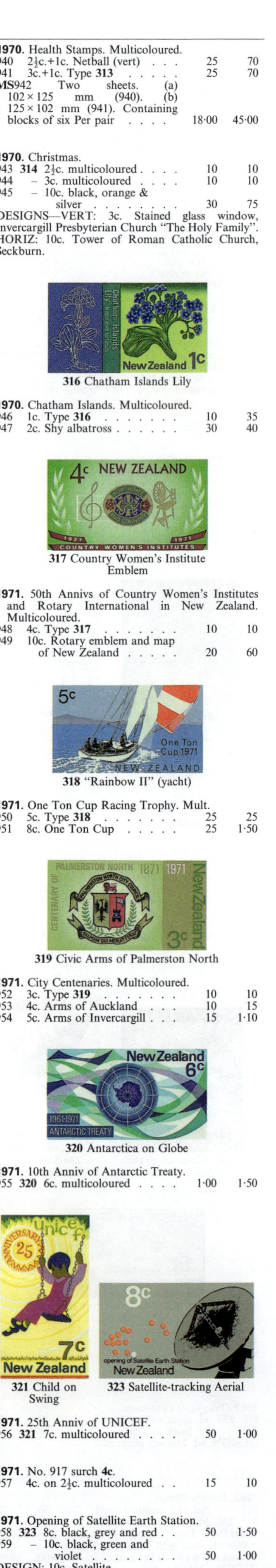

1970. Health Stamps. Multicoloured.
940 2½c.+1c. Netball (vert) . . . 25 70
941 3c.+1c. Type **313** 25 70
MS942 Two sheets. (a) 102 × 125 mm (940). (b) 125 × 102 mm (941). Containing blocks of six Per pair . . . . 18·00 45·00

1970. Christmas.
943 **314** 2½c. multicoloured 10 10
944 – 3c. multicoloured 10 10
945 – 10c. black, orange & silver 30 75
DESIGNS—VERT: 3c. Stained glass window, Invercargill Presbyterian Church "The Holy Family". HORIZ: 10c. Tower of Roman Catholic Church, Seckburn.

316 Chatham Islands Lily

1970. Chatham Islands. Multicoloured.
946 1c. Type **316** 10 35
947 2c. Shy albatross 30 40

317 Country Women's Institute Emblem

1971. 50th Annivs of Country Women's Institutes and Rotary International in New Zealand. Multicoloured.
948 4c. Type **317** 10 10
949 10c. Rotary emblem and map of New Zealand 20 60

318 "Rainbow II" (yacht)

1971. One Ton Cup Racing Trophy. Mult.
950 5c. Type **318** 25 25
951 8c. One Ton Cup . . . . . 25 1·50

319 Civic Arms of Palmerston North

1971. City Centenaries. Multicoloured.
952 3c. Type **319** 10 10
953 4c. Arms of Auckland . . . 10 15
954 5c. Arms of Invercargill . . . 15 1·10

320 Antarctica on Globe

1971. 10th Anniv of Antarctic Treaty.
955 **320** 6c. multicoloured . . . . 1·00 1·50

321 Child on Swing

323 Satellite-tracking Aerial

1971. 25th Anniv of UNICEF.
956 **321** 7c. multicoloured . . . . 50 1·00

1971. No. 917 surch **4c**.
957 4c. on 2½c. multicoloured . . 15 10

1971. Opening of Satellite Earth Station.
958 **323** 8c. black, grey and red . . 50 1·50
959 – 10c. black, green and violet . . . . 50 1·00
DESIGN: 10c. Satellite.

324 Girls playing Hockey

1971. Health Stamps. Multicoloured.

960	3c.+1c. Type **324**	45	65
961	4c.+1c. Boys playing hockey	45	65
962	5c.+1c. Dental health	1·10	2·00
MS963	Two sheets, each 122 × 96 mm. Nos. 960/1 in blocks of six Per pair	19·00	45·00

325 "Madonna bending over the Crib" (Maratta)

1971. Christmas. Multicoloured.

964	3c. Type **325**	10	10
965	4c. "The Annunciation" (stained-glass window)	10	10
966	10c. "The Three Kings"	70	1·25

Nos. 965/6 are smaller, size 21½ × 38 mm.

326 "Tiffany" Rose **327** Lord Rutherford and Alpha Particles

1971. 1st World Rose Convention, Hamilton. Mult.

967	2c. Type **326**	15	30
968	5c. "Peace"	35	35
969	8c. "Chrysler Imperial"	60	1·10

1971. Birth Centenary of Lord Rutherford (scientist). Multicoloured.

970	1c. Type **327**	20	50
971	7c. Lord Rutherford and formula	55	1·75

328 Benz (1895) **329** Coat of Arms of Wanganui

1972. International Vintage Car Rally. Mult.

972	3c. Type **328**	20	10
973	4c. Oldsmobile (1904)	20	10
974	5c. Ford "Model T" (1914)	20	10
975	6c. Cadillac Service car (1915)	25	45
976	8c. Chrysler (1924)	40	2·00
977	10c. Austin "7" (1923)	40	1·50

1972. Anniversaries.

978	**329** 3c. multicoloured	15	10
979	– 4c. orange, brown & black	15	10
980	– 5c. multicoloured	25	10
981	– 8c. multicoloured	40	1·10
982	– 10c. multicoloured	40	1·10

DESIGNS AND EVENTS—VERT: 3c. Type **329** (centenary of Wanganui Council); 5c. De Havilland D.H.89 Dragon Rapide and Boeing 737 (25th anniv of National Airways Corp); 8c. French frigate and Maori palisade (bicentenary of landing by Marion du Fresne). HORIZ: 4c. Postal Union symbol (10th anniv of Asian–Oceanic Postal Union); 10c. Stone cairn (150th anniv of New Zealand Methodist Church).

330 Black Scree Cotula **331** Boy playing Tennis

1972. Alpine Plants. Multicoloured.

983	4c. Type **330**	30	10
984	6c. North Island edelweiss	40	40
985	8c. Haast's buttercup	60	85
986	10c. Brown Mountain daisy	70	1·25

1972. Health Stamps.

987	**331** 3c.+1c. grey and brown	30	50
988	– 4c.+1c. brown, grey and yellow	30	50
MS989	Two sheets, each 107 × 123 mm. Nos. 987/8 in blocks of six Per pair	18·00	40·00

DESIGN: No. 988, Girl playing tennis.

332 "Madonna with Child" (Murillo) **333** Lake Waikaremoana

1972. Christmas. Multicoloured.

990	3c. Type **332**	10	10
991	5c. "The Last Supper" (stained-glass window, St. John's Church, Levin)	15	10
992	10c. Pohutukawa flower	35	70

1972. Lake Scenes. Multicoloured.

993	6c. Type **333**	75	1·00
994	8c. Lake Hayes	85	1·00
995	18c. Lake Wakatipu	1·25	2·00
996	23c. Lake Rotomahana	1·40	2·25

334 Old Pollen Street

1973. Commemorations.

997	**334** 3c. multicoloured	10	10
998	– 4c. multicoloured	15	10
999	– 5c. multicoloured	15	15
1000	– 6c. multicoloured	50	50
1001	– 8c. grey, blue and gold	35	50
1002	– 10c. multicoloured	50	80

DESIGNS AND EVENTS: 3c. (centenary of Thames Borough); 4c. Coalmining and pasture (centenary of Westport Borough); 5c. Cloister (centenary of Canterbury University); 6c. Forest, birds and lake (50th anniv of Royal Forest and Bird Protection Society); 8c. Rowers (Success of N.Z. rowers in 1972 Olympics); 10c. Graph and people (25th anniv of E.C.A.F.E.).

335 Class W Locomotive

1973. New Zealand Steam Locomotives. Mult.

1003	3c. Type **335**	25	10
1004	4c. Class X	25	10
1005	5c. Class Ab	25	10
1006	10c. Class Ja No. 1274	1·50	1·40

336 "Maori Woman and Child" **337** Prince Edward

1973. Paintings by Frances Hodgkins. Mult.

1027	5c. Type **336**	25	15
1028	8c. "Hilltop"	40	80
1029	10c. "Barn in Picardy"	40	65
1030	18c. "Self-portrait Still Life"	75	2·00

1973. Health Stamps.

1031	**337** 3c.+1c. green & brown	30	50
1032	4c.+1c. red and brown	30	50
MS1033	Two sheets, each 96 × 121 mm, with Nos. 1031/2 in blocks of 6 (3 × 2) Per pair	16·00	38·00

338 "Tempi Madonna" (Raphael) **339** Mitre Peak

1973. Christmas. Multicoloured.

1034	3c. Type **338**	10	10
1035	5c. "Three Kings" (stained-glass window, St. Theresa's Church, Auckland)	10	10
1036	10c. Family entering church	25	50

1973. Mountain Scenery. Multicoloured.

1037	6c. Type **339**	45	80
1038	8c. Mt. Ngauruhoe	55	1·25
1039	18c. Mt. Sefton (horiz)	70	2·00
1040	23c. Burnett Range (horiz)	80	2·50

340 Hurdling **341** Queen Elizabeth II

1974. 10th British Commonwealth Games, Christchurch.

1041	**340** 4c. multicoloured	10	10
1042	– 5c. black and violet	10	10
1043	– 10c. multicoloured	20	15
1044	– 18c. multicoloured	15	50
1045	– 23c. multicoloured	20	80

DESIGNS: 5c. Ball-player (4th Paraplegic Games, Dunedin); 10c. Cycling; 18c. Rifle-shooting; 23c. Bowls.

1974. New Zealand Day. Sheet 131 × 74 mm, containing T **341** and similar horiz designs, size 37 × 20 mm. Multicoloured.

MS1046	4c. × 5 Treaty House, Waitangi; Signing Waitangi Treaty; Type **341**; Parliament Buildings extensions; Children in class	70	2·50

342 "Spirit of Napier" Fountain **344** Children, Cat and Dog

343 Boeing Seaplane, 1919

1974. Centenaries of Napier and U.P.U. Mult.

1047	4c. Type **342**	10	10
1048	5c. Clock Tower, Berne	20	30
1049	8c. U.P.U. Monument, Berne	55	1·60

1974. History of New Zealand Airmail Transport. Multicoloured.

1050	3c. Type **343**	25	10
1051	4c. Lockheed 10 Electra "Kauha", 1937	30	10
1052	5c. Bristol Type 170 Freighter Mk 31, 1958	30	30
1053	23c. Short S.30 modified "G" Class flying boat "Aotearoa", 1940	1·40	2·00

1974. Health Stamps.

1054	**344** 3c.+1c. multicoloured	20	50
1055	– 4c.+1c. multicoloured	25	50
1056	– 5c.+1c. multicoloured	1·00	1·50
MS1057	145 × 123 mm. No. 1055 in block of ten	21·00	40·00

Nos. 1055/6 are similar to Type **344**, showing children with pets.

345 "The Adoration of the Magi" (Konrad Witz) **346** Great Barrier Island

1974. Christmas. Multicoloured.

1058	3c. Type **345**	10	10
1059	5c. "The Angel Window" (stained glass window, Old St. Pauls Church, Wellington)	10	10
1060	10c. Madonna lily	30	90

1974. Offshore Islands. Multicoloured.

1061	6c. Type **346**	25	40
1062	8c. Stewart Island	40	1·25
1063	18c. White Island	50	1·50
1064	23c. The Brothers	55	1·75

347 Crippled Child

1975. Anniversaries and Events. Multicoloured.

1065	3c. Type **347**	10	10
1066	5c. Farming family	10	10
1067	10c. I.W.Y. symbols	15	65
1068	18c. Medical School Building, Otago University	40	1·75

COMMEMORATIONS: 3c. 40th anniv of New Zealand Crippled Children Society; 5c. 50th anniv of Women's Division, Federated Farmers of New Zealand; 10c. International Women's Year; 18c. Centenary of Otago Medical School.

348 Scow "Lake Erie"

1975. Historic Sailing Ships.

1069	**348** 4c. black and red	30	10
1070	– 5c. black and blue	30	10
1071	– 8c. black and yellow	40	70
1072	– 10c. black and yellow	45	70
1073	– 18c. black and brown	75	2·25
1074	– 23c. black and lilac	85	2·25

SHIPS: 5c. Schooner "Herald"; 8c. Brigantine "New Zealander"; 10c. Topsail schooner "Jessie Kelly"; 18c. Barque "Tory"; 23c. Full-rigged clipper "Rangitiki".

349 Lake Sumner Forest Park

1975. Forest Park Scenes. Multicoloured.

1075	6c. Type **349**	30	60
1076	8c. North-west Nelson	40	1·00
1077	18c. Kaweka	65	1·75
1078	23c. Coromandel	90	1·75

350 Girl feeding Lamb **351** "Virgin and Child" (Zanobi Machiavelli)

1975. Health Stamps. Multicoloured.

1079	3c.+1c. Type **350**	15	30
1080	4c.+1c. Boy with hen and chicks	15	30
1081	5c.+1c. Boy with duck and duckling	40	1·50
MS1082	123 × 146 mm. No. 1080 × 10	15·00	40·00

1975. Christmas. Multicoloured.
1083 3c. Type **351** 10 10
1084 5c. "Cross in Landscape" (stained-glass window, Greendale Church) (horiz) 10 10
1085 10c. "I saw three ships" (carol) (horiz) 35 65

352 "Sterling Silver"

353 Queen Elizabeth II (photograph by W. Harrison)

353a Maripi (knife)

353b Rainbow Abalone or Paua

1975. (a) Garden Roses. Multicoloured.
1086 1c. Type **352** 10 10
1087 2c. "Lilli Marlene" 10 20
1088 3c. "Queen Elizabeth" . . 60 10
1089 4c. "Super Star" 10 60
1090 5c. "Diamond Jubilee" . . 10 10
1091a 6c. "Cresset" . . . . . . 40 1·00
1092a 7c. "Michele Meilland" . . 40 10
1093a 8c. "Josephine Bruce" . . 30 10
1094 9c. "Iceberg" 30 60

(b) Type **353**.
1094ab 10c. multicoloured . . . 30 10

(c) Maori Artefacts.
1095 **353a** 11c. brown, yellow & black 30 80
1096 – 12c. brown, yellow & black 30 50
1097 – 13c. brown, mauve & black . . . . 40 1·00
1098 – 14c. brown, yellow & black 30 20
DESIGNS: 12c. Putorino (flute); 13c. Wahaika (club); 14c. Kotiate (club).

(d) Sea Shells. Multicoloured.
1099 20c. Type **353b** 15 20
1100 30c. Toheroa clam 25 50
1101 40c. Old woman or coarse dosinia 30 45
1102 50c. New Zealand or spiny murex 40 45
1103 $1 New Zealand scallop . . 70 1·00
1104 $2 Circular saw . . . . . 1·00 1·75

(e) Building. Multicoloured.
1105 $5 "Beehive" (section of Parliamentary Buildings, Wellington) (22 × 26 mm) 1·75 1·50

354 Family and League of Mothers Badge

1976. Anniversaries and Metrication. Mult.
1110 6c. Type **354** 10 10
1111 7c. Weight, temperature, linear measure and capacity 10 10
1112 8c. "William Bryon" (immigrant ship), mountain and New Plymouth 15 10
1113 10c. Two women shaking hands and Y.W.C.A. badge 15 60
1114 25c. Map of the world showing cable links . . . 30 1·25
ANNIVERSARIES: 6c. 50th anniv of League of Mothers; 7c. Metrication; 8c. Centenary of New Plymouth; 10c. 50th anniv of New Zealand Y.W.C.A.; 25c. Link with International Telecommunications Network.

355 Gig

1976. Vintage Farm Transport. Multicoloured.
1115 6c. Type **355** 15 40
1116 7c. Thornycroft lorry . . . 15 10
1117 8c. Scandi wagon 30 15
1118 9c. Traction engine 20 40
1119 10c. Wool wagon 20 40
1120 25c. Cart . . . . 65 2·25

356 Purakaunui Falls

357 Boy and Pony

1976. Waterfalls. Multicoloured.
1121 10c. Type **356** 25 10
1122 14c. Marakopa Falls 40 95
1123 15c. Bridal Veil Falls . . . 45 1·10
1124 16c. Papakorito Falls . . . 55 1·25

1976. Health Stamps. Multicoloured.
1125 7c.+1c. Type **357** 20 30
1126 8c.+1c. Girl and calf 20 30
1127 10c.+1c. Girls and bird . . 40 90
MS1128 96 × 121 mm. Nos. 1125/7 × 2 . . . . 2·50 6·00

358 "Nativity" (Spanish carving)

359 Arms of Hamilton

1976. Christmas. Multicoloured.
1129 7c. Type **358** 15 10
1130 11c. "Resurrection" (stained-glass window, St. Joseph's Catholic Church, Grey Lynn) (horiz) 25 30
1131 18c. Angels (horiz) . . . . 40 1·00

1977. Anniversaries. Multicoloured.
1132 8c. Type **359** 15 10
1133 8c. Arms of Gisborne . . . 15 10
1134 8c. Arms of Masterton . . . 15 10
1135 10c. A.A. emblem 15 40
1136 10c. Arms of the Royal Australasian College of Surgeons 15 40
ANNIVERSARIES: No. 1132, Cent of Hamilton; 1133, Cent of Gisborne; 1134, Cent of Masterton; 1135, 75th anniv of Automobile Association in New Zealand; 1136, 50th anniv of R.A.C.S.

360 Queen Elizabeth II

361 Physical Education and Maori Culture

1977. Silver Jubilee. Sheet 178 × 82 mm, containing T **360** and similar vert designs showing different portraits.
MS1137 8c. × 5 multicoloured . . 65 1·60

1977. Education. Multicoloured.
1138 8c. Type **361** 40 70
1139 8c. Geography, science and woodwork 40 70
1140 8c. Teaching the deaf, kindergarten and woodwork 40 70
1141 8c. Tertiary and language classes 40 70
1142 8c. Home science, correspondence school and teacher training . . . 40 70

1977. Nos. 918/19 surch.
1143 7c. on 3c. "Detunda egregia" (moth) 40 70
1144 8c. on 4c. "Charagia virescens" (moth) 40 70

363 Karitane Beach

1977. Seascapes. Multicoloured.
1145 10c. Type **363** 15 10
1146 16c. Ocean Beach, Mount Maunganui 30 30
1147 18c. Piha Beach 30 30
1148 30c. Kaikoura Coast 35 40

364 Girl with Pigeon

365 "The Holy Family" (Correggio)

1977. Health Stamps. Multicoloured.
1149 7c.+2c. Type **364** 20 50
1150 8c.+2c. Boy with frog . . . 20 55
1151 10c.+2c. Girl with butterfly 40 1·00
MS1152 97 × 120 mm. Nos. 1149/51 × 2 . . . . 1·40 6·50
Stamps from No. **MS**1152 are without white border and together form a composite design.

1977. Christmas. Multicoloured.
1153 7c. Type **365** 15 10
1154 16c. "Madonna and Child" (stained-glass window, St. Michael's and All Angels, Dunedin) (vert) 25 25
1155 23c. "Partridge in a Pear Tree" (vert) . . . . . . 40 1·25

366 Merryweather Manual Pump, 1860

1977. Fire Fighting Appliances. Multicoloured.
1156 10c. Type **366** 15 10
1157 11c. 2-wheel hose, reel and ladder, 1880 . . . . . . 15 25
1158 12c. Shand Mason steam fire engine, 1873 . . . . 20 30
1159 23c. Chemical fire engine, 1888 . . . . 30 90

367 Town Clock and Coat of Arms, Ashburton

368 Students and Ivey Hall, Lincoln College

1978. Centenaries.
1160 **367** 10c. multicoloured . . . 15 10
1161 – 10c. multicoloured . . . 15 10
1162 – 12c. red, yellow and black 15 15
1163 – 20c. multicoloured . . . 20 30
DESIGNS—VERT: No. 1161, Mount Egmont (cent of Stratford); 1162, Early telephone (cent of telephone in New Zealand). HORIZ: No. 1163, Aerial view of Bay of Islands (cent of Bay of Islands County).

1978. Land Resources and Centenary of Lincoln College of Agriculture. Multicoloured.
1164 10c. Type **368** 15 10
1165 12c. Sheep grazing 15 30
1166 15c. Fertiliser ground spreading 15 30
1167 16c. Agricultural Field Days 15 40
1168 20c. Harvesting grain . . . 20 40
1169 30c. Dairy farming 30 90

369

370 Maui Gas Drilling Platform

1978. Coil Stamps.
1170 **369** 1c. purple 10 65
1171 2c. orange 10 65
1172 5c. brown 10 65
1173 10c. blue 30 80

1978. Resources of the Sea. Multicoloured.
1174 12c. Type **370** 15 15
1175 15c. Trawler 15 20
1176 20c. Map of 200 mile fishing limit 20 30
1177 23c. Humpback whale and bottle-nosed dolphins . . 25 35
1178 35c. Kingfish, snapper, grouper and squid 40 60

371 First Health Charity Stamp

372 "The Holy Family" (El Greco)

1978. Health Stamps.
1179 **371** 10c.+2c. black, red and gold 20 35
1180 – 12c.+2c. multicoloured 20 40
MS1181 97 × 124 mm. Nos. 1179/80 × 3 . . . . 1·00 4·00
DESIGNS: 10c. Type **371** (50th anniv of Health Stamps); 12c. Heart Operation (National Heart Foundation).

1978. Christmas. Multicoloured.
1182 7c. Type **372** 10 10
1183 16c. All Saint's Church, Howick (horiz) 25 35
1184 23c. Beach scene (horiz) . . 30 50

373 Sir Julius Vogel

374 Riverlands Cottage, Blenheim

1979. Statesmen. Designs each brown and drab.
1185 10c. Type **373** 25 50
1186 10c. Sir George Grey . . . 25 50
1187 10c. Richard John Seddon 25 50

1979. Architecture (1st series).
1188 **374** 10c. black, light blue and blue 10 10
1189 – 12c. black, light green and green 15 25
1190 – 15c. black and grey . . . 20 40
1191 – 20c. black, brown and sepia 25 40
DESIGNS: 12c. The Mission House, Waimate North; 15c. "The Elms", Tauranga; 20c. Provincial Council Buildings, Christchurch.
See also Nos. 1217/20 and 1262/5.

375 Whangaroa Harbour

1979. Small Harbours. Multicoloured.
1192 15c. Type **375** 15 10
1193 20c. Kawau Island 20 40
1194 23c. Akaroa Harbour (vert) 20 50
1195 35c. Picton Harbour (vert) 30 70

376 Children with Building Bricks

1979. International Year of the Child.
1196 **376** 10c. multicoloured . . . 15 10

377 Two-spotted Chromis

1979. Health Stamps. Marine Life. Multicoloured.
1197 10c.+2c. Type **377** 30 60
1198 10c.+2c. Sea urchin 30 60

1199	12c.+2c. Red goatfish and underwater cameraman (vert)	30	60
MS1200	144×72 mm. Nos. 1197/9, each×2	1·00	2·75

1979. Nos. 1091a/3a and 1094ab surch.

1201	4c. on 8c. "Josephine Bruce"	10	50
1202	14c. on 10c. Type **353**	30	10
1203	17c. on 6c. "Cresset"	30	1·00
1203a	20c. on 7c. "Michele Meilland"	30	10

379 "Madonna and Child" (sculpture, Ghiberti)

380 Chamber, House of Representatives

1979. Christmas. Multicoloured.

1204	10c. Type **379**	15	10
1205	25c. Christ Church, Russell	30	50
1206	35c. Pohutukawa (tree)	40	70

1979. 25th Commonwealth Parliamentary Conf, Wellington. Multicoloured.

1207	14c. Type **380**	15	10
1208	20c. Mace and Black Rod	20	30
1209	30c. "Beehive" wall hanging	30	75

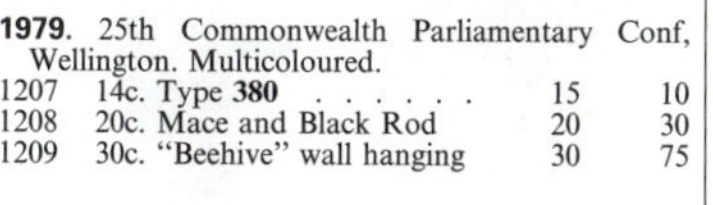

381 1855 1d. Stamp

1980. Anniversaries and Events.

1210	**381** 14c. black, red and yellow	20	30
1211	– 14c. black, blue & yellow	20	30
1212	– 14c. black, green & yellow	20	30
1213	– 17c. multicoloured	20	30
1214	– 25c. multicoloured	25	35
1215	– 30c. multicoloured	25	40
MS1216	146×96 mm. Nos. 1210/12 (as horiz strip) (sold at 52c.)	1·00	4·00

DESIGNS: No. 1211, 1855 2d. stamp; 1212, 1855 1s. stamp (125th anniv of New Zealand stamps); 1213, Geyser, wood-carving and building (Centenary of Rotorua (town)); 1214, "Earina autumnalis" and "Thelymitra venosa" (International Orchid Conference, Auckland); 1215, Ploughing and Golden Plough Trophy (World Ploughing Championships, Christchurch).

382 Ewelme Cottage, Parnell

1980. Architecture (2nd series). Multicoloured.

1217	14c. Type **382**	15	10
1218	17c. Broadgreen, Nelson	15	25
1219	25c. Courthouse, Oamaru	20	35
1220	30c. Government Buildings, Wellington	25	40

383 Auckland Harbour

1980. Large Harbours. Multicoloured.

1221	25c. Type **383**	20	20
1222	30c. Wellington Harbour	25	30
1223	35c. Lyttelton Harbour	25	35
1224	50c. Port Chalmers	30	1·10

384 Surf-fishing

385 "Madonna and Child with Cherubim" (sculpture, Andrea della Robbia)

1980. Health Stamps. Fishing. Multicoloured.

1225	14c.+2c. Type **384**	25	85
1226	14c.+2c. Wharf-fishing	25	85
1227	17c.+2c. Spear-fishing	25	55
MS1228	148×75 mm. Nos. 1225/7, each×2	1·25	3·25

1980. Christmas. Multicoloured.

1229	10c. Type **385**	15	10
1230	25c. St. Mary's Church, New Plymouth	25	25
1231	35c. Picnic scene	40	1·00

386 Te Heu Heu (chief)

387 Lt. Col. the Hon. W. H. A. Feilding and Borough of Feilding Crest (cent)

1980. Maori Personalities. Multicoloured.

1232	15c. Type **386**	15	10
1233	25c. Te Hau (chief)	15	20
1234	35c. Te Puea (princess)	20	10
1235	45c. Ngata (politician)	30	30
1236	60c. Te Ata-O-Tu (warrior)	30	50

1981. Commemorations.

1237	**387** 20c. multicoloured	20	20
1238	– 25c. orange and black	25	25

DESIGN AND COMMEMORATION: 25c. I.Y.D. emblem and cupped hands (International Year of the Disabled).

388 The Family at Play

389 Kaiauai River

1981. "Family Life". Multicoloured.

1239	20c. Type **388**	15	10
1240	25c. The family young and old	20	20
1241	30c. The family at home	20	35
1242	35c. The family at church	25	45

1981. River Scenes. Multicoloured.

1243	30c. Type **389**	20	25
1244	35c. Mangahao	20	30
1245	40c. Shotover (horiz)	25	40
1246	60c. Cleddau (horiz)	35	65

390 St. Paul's Cathedral

1981. Royal Wedding. Multicoloured.

1247	20c. Type **390**	30	30
1248	20c. Prince Charles and Lady Diana Spencer	30	30

391 Girl with Starfish

392 "Madonna suckling the Child" (painting, d'Oggiono)

1981. Health Stamps. Children playing by the Sea. Multicoloured.

1249	20c.+2c. Type **391**	20	65
1250	20c.+2c. Boy fishing	20	65
1251	25c.+2c. Children exploring rock pool	20	35
MS1252	100×125 mm. Nos. 1249/51, each×2	1·00	3·00

Nos. 1249/50 were printed together, se-tenant, forming a composite design.

The stamps from No. **MS**1252 were printed together, se-tenant, in horizontal strips, each forming a composite design.

1981. Christmas. Multicoloured.

1253	14c. Type **392**	15	10
1254	30c. St. John's Church, Wakefield	20	25
1255	40c. Golden tainui (flower)	35	35

393 Tauranga Mission House

394 Map of New Zealand

1981. Commemorations. Multicoloured.

1256	20c. Type **393**	20	10
1257	20c. Water tower, Hawera	20	10
1258	25c. Cat	25	35
1259	30c. "Dunedin" (refrigerated sailing ship)	25	40
1260	35c. Scientific research equipment	25	45

COMMEMORATIONS: No. 1256, Centenary of Tauranga (town); 1257, Centenary of Hawera (town); 1258, Centenary of S.P.C.A. (Society for the Prevention of Cruelty to Animals in New Zealand); 1259, Centenary of frozen meat exports; 1260, International Year of Science.

1982.

1261	**394** 24c. green and blue	30	10

395 Alberton, Auckland

1982. Architecture (3rd series). Multicoloured.

1262	20c. Type **395**	15	15
1263	25c. Caccia Birch, Palmerston North	15	25
1264	30c. Railway station, Dunedin	40	30
1265	35c. Post Office, Ophir	25	40

396 Kaiteriteri Beach, Nelson (Summer)

1982. New Zealand Scenes. Multicoloured.

1266	35c. Type **396**	20	30
1267	40c. St. Omer Park, Queenstown (Autumn)	25	35
1268	45c. Mt. Ngauruhoe, Tongariro National Park (Winter)	25	40
1269	70c. Wairarapa farm (Spring)	40	60

397 Labrador

398 "Madonna with Child and Two Angels" (painting by Piero di Cosimo)

1982. Health Stamps. Dogs. Multicoloured.

1270	24c.+2c. Type **397**	65	1·00
1271	24c.+2c. Border collie	65	1·00
1272	30c.+2c. Cocker spaniel	65	1·00
MS1273	98×125 mm. Nos. 1270/2, each×2	3·25	6·50

1982. Christmas. Multicoloured.

1274	18c. Type **398**	15	10
1275	35c. Rangiatea Maori Church, Otaki	25	30
1276	45c. Surf life-saving	40	40

399 Nephrite

399a Grapes

399b Kokako

400 Old Arts Building, Auckland University

1982. (a) Minerals. Multicoloured.

1277	1c. Type **399**	10	10
1278	2c. Agate	10	10
1279	3c. Iron pyrites	10	10
1280	4c. Amethyst	10	10
1281	5c. Carnelian	10	10
1282	9c. Native sulphur	20	10
	(b) Fruits. Multicoloured.		
1283	10c. Type **399a**	50	10
1284	20c. Citrus fruit	35	10
1285	30c. Nectarines	30	10
1286	40c. Apples	35	10
1287	50c. Kiwifruit	40	10
	(c) Native Birds. Multicoloured.		
1288	30c. Kakapo	60	25
1289	40c. Mountain ("Blue") duck	60	35
1290	45c. New Zealand falcon	1·25	35
1291	60c. New Zealand teal	2·25	1·25
1292	$1 Type **399b**	1·00	30
1293	$2 Chatham Island robin	1·00	50
1294	$3 Stitchbird	1·25	1·40
1295	$4 Saddleback	1·50	2·00
1296	$5 Takahe	3·75	3·25
1297	$10 Little spotted kiwi	5·00	6·00

1983. Commemorations. Multicoloured.

1303	24c. Salvation Army Centenary logo	20	10
1304	30c. Type **400**	20	40
1305	35c. Stylized kangaroo and kiwi	20	40
1306	40c. Rainbow trout	25	55
1307	45c. Satellite over Earth	25	55

COMMEMORATIONS: 24c. Salvation Army centenary; 30c. Auckland University centenary; 35c. Closer Economic Relationship agreement with Australia; 40c. Centenary of introduction of rainbow trout into New Zealand; 45c. World Communications Year.

401 Queen Elizabeth II

1983. Commonwealth Day. Multicoloured.

1308	24c. Type **401**	20	10
1309	35c. Maori rock drawing	30	50
1310	40c. Woolmark and woolscouring symbols	30	80
1311	45c. Coat of arms	30	80

402 "Boats, Island Bay" (Rita Angus)

403 Mt. Egmont

1983. Paintings by Rita Angus. Multicoloured.

1312	24c. Type **402**	20	10
1313	30c. "Central Otago Landscape"	25	45
1314	35c. "Wanaka Landscape"	30	50
1315	45c. "Tree"	35	70

1983. Beautiful New Zealand. Multicoloured.

1316	35c. Type **403**	20	35
1317	40c. Cooks Bay	25	40

1318 45c. Lake Matheson (horiz) 25 45
1319 70c. Lake Alexandrina (horiz) 40 70

404 Tabby

405 "The Family of the Holy Oak Tree" (Raphael)

1983. Health Stamps. Cats. Multicoloured.
1320 24c.+2c. Type **404** 35 75
1321 24c.+2c. Siamese 35 75
1322 30c.+2c. Persian 50 1·00
MS1323 100 × 126 mm. Nos. 1320/2, each × 2 1·75 3·00

1983. Christmas. Multicoloured.
1324 18c. Type **405** 15 10
1325 35c. St. Patrick's Church, Greymouth 30 45
1326 45c. "The Glory of Christmas" 35 80

406 Geology

1984. Antarctic Research. Multicoloured.
1327 24c. Type **406** 30 10
1328 40c. Biology 35 40
1329 58c. Glaciology 50 1·50
1330 70c. Meteorology 60 85
MS1331 126 × 110 mm. Nos. 1327/30 1·50 3·50

407 "Mountaineer", Lake Wakatipu

1984. New Zealand Ferry Boats. Multicoloured.
1332 24c. Type **407** 20 10
1333 40c. "Waikana", Otago 25 45
1334 58c. "Britannia", Waitemata 30 1·40
1335 70c. "Wakatere", Firth of Thames 45 85

408 Mount Hutt

1984. Ski-slope Scenery. Multicoloured.
1336 35c. Type **408** 20 25
1337 40c. Coronet Park 25 30
1338 45c. Turoa 25 30
1339 70c. Whakapapa 40 75

409 Hamilton's Frog

1984. Amphibians and Reptiles. Multicoloured.
1340 24c. Type **409** 30 30
1341 24c. Great Barrier skink 30 30
1342 30c. Harlequin gecko 30 35
1343 58c. Otago skink 45 70
1344 70c. Gold-striped gecko 60 75

410 Clydesdales ploughing

1984. Health Stamps. Horses. Multicoloured.
1345 24c.+2c. Type **410** 40 75
1346 24c.+2c. Shetland ponies 40 75
1347 30c.+2c. Thoroughbreds 40 75
MS1348 148 × 75 mm. Nos. 1345/7, each × 2 1·75 3·25

411 "Adoration of the Shepherds" (Lorenzo di Credi)

1984. Christmas. Multicoloured.
1349 18c. Type **411** 15 10
1350 35c. Old St. Paul's, Wellington (vert) 30 30
1351 45c. "The Joy of Christmas" (vert) 40 70

412 Mounted Riflemen, South Africa, 1901

1984. New Zealand Military History. Mult.
1352 24c. Type **412** 20 10
1353 40c. Engineers, France, 1917 30 45
1354 58c. Tanks of 2nd N.Z. Divisional Cavalry, North Africa, 1942 40 1·50
1355 70c. Infantryman in jungle kit, and 25-pounder gun, Korea and South-East Asia, 1950–72 45 90
MS1356 122 × 106 mm. Nos. 1352/5 1·00 2·25

413 St. John Ambulance Badge

1985. Centenary of St. John Ambulance in New Zealand.
1357 **413** 24c. black, gold and red 20 15
1358 30c. black, silver and blue 25 45
1359 40c. black and grey 30 1·10

The colours of the badge depicted are those for Bailiffs and Dames Grand Cross (24c.), Knights and Dames of Grace (30c.) and Commanders, Officer Brothers and Sisters (40c.).

414 Nelson Horse Tram, 1862

1985. Vintage Trams. Multicoloured.
1360 24c. Type **414** 30 10
1361 30c. Graham's Town steam tram, 1871 40 60
1362 35c. Dunedin cable car, 1881 40 70
1363 40c. Auckland electric tram, 1902 40 70
1364 45c. Wellington electric tram, 1904 50 90
1365 58c. Christchurch electric tram, 1905 55 1·75

415 Shotover Bridge

416 Queen Elizabeth II (from photo by Camera Press)

1985. Bridges of New Zealand. Multicoloured.
1366 35c. Type **415** 40 60
1367 40c. Alexandra Bridge 45 60
1368 45c. South Rangitikei Railway Bridge (vert) 50 1·25
1369 70c. Twin Bridges (vert) 60 1·25

1985. Multicoloured, background colours given.
1370 **416** 25c. red 50 10
1371 35c. blue 90 10

417 Princess of Wales and Prince William

418 The Holy Family in the Stable

1985. Health Stamps. Designs showing photographs by Lord Snowdon. Multicoloured.
1372 25c.+2c. Type **417** 90 1·25
1373 25c.+2c. Princess of Wales and Prince Henry 90 1·25
1374 35c.+2c. Prince and Princess of Wales with Princes William and Henry 90 1·25
MS1375 118 × 84 mm. Nos. 1372/4, each × 2 4·25 6·00

1985. Christmas. Multicoloured.
1376 18c. Type **418** 20 10
1377 40c. The shepherds 45 85
1378 50c. The angels 45 1·00

419 H.M.N.Z.S. "Philomel" (1914–47)

1985. New Zealand Naval History. Multicoloured.
1379 25c. Type **419** 60 15
1380 45c. H.M.N.Z.S. "Achilles" (1936–46) 80 1·40
1381 60c. H.M.N.Z.S. "Rotoiti" (1949–65) 1·10 2·00
1382 75c. H.M.N.Z.S. "Canterbury" (from 1971) 1·40 2·25
MS1383 124 × 108 mm. Nos. 1379/82 4·50 5·25

420 Police Computer Operator

1986. Centenary of New Zealand Police. Designs showing historical aspects above modern police activities. Multicoloured.
1384 25c. Type **420** 35 55
1385 25c. Detective and mobile control room 35 55
1386 25c. Policewoman and badge 35 55
1387 25c. Forensic scientist, patrol car and policeman with child 35 55
1388 25c. Police College, Porirua, "Lady Elizabeth II" (patrol boat) and dog handler 35 55

421 Indian "Power Plus" 1000cc Motor Cycle (1920)

1986. Vintage Motor Cycles. Multicoloured.
1389 35c. Type **421** 40 45
1390 45c. Norton "CS1" 500cc (1927) 45 65
1391 60c. B.S.A. "Sloper". 500cc (1930) 55 1·50
1392 75c. Triumph "Model H" 550cc (1915) 60 1·75

422 Tree of Life

1986. International Peace Year. Multicoloured.
1393 25c. Type **422** 30 30
1394 25c. Peace dove 30 30

423 Knights Point

424 "Football" (Kylie Epapara)

1986. Coastal Scenery. Multicoloured.
1395 55c. Type **423** 55 65
1396 60c. Becks Bay 55 80
1397 65c. Doubtless Bay 60 1·25
1398 80c. Wainui Bay 75 1·25
MS1399 124 × 99 mm. No. 1398 (sold at $1.20) 1·00 1·25

1986. Health Stamps. Children's Paintings (1st series). Multicoloured.
1400 30c.+3c. Type **424** 40 65
1401 30c.+3c. "Children at Play" (Philip Kata) 40 65
1402 45c.+3c. "Children Skipping" (Mia Flannery) (horiz) 50 65
MS1403 144 × 81 mm. Nos. 1400/2, each × 2 2·25 2·75
See also Nos. 1433/5.

425 "A Partridge in a Pear Tree"

426 Conductor and Orchestra

1986. Christmas. "The Twelve Days of Christmas" (carol). Multicoloured.
1404 25c. Type **425** 20 10
1405 55c. "Two turtle doves" 45 55
1406 65c. "Three French hens" 50 1·00

1986. Music in New Zealand.
1407 **426** 30c. multicoloured 25 10
1408 – 60c. black, blue & orange 45 70
1409 – 80c. multicoloured 70 1·75
1410 – $1 multicoloured 80 1·25

DESIGNS: 60c. Cornet and brass band; 80c. Piper and Highland pipe band; $1 Guitar and country music group.

427 Jetboating

428 Southern Cross Cup

1987. Tourism. Multicoloured.
1411 60c. Type **427** 50 50
1412 70c. Sightseeing flights 60 60
1413 80c. Camping 70 75
1414 85c. Windsurfing 70 85
1415 $1.05 Mountaineering 90 1·10
1416 $1.30 River rafting 1·10 1·40

1987. Yachting Events. Designs showing yachts. Multicoloured.
1417 40c. Type **428** 30 15
1418 80c. Admiral's Cup 60 80
1419 $1.05 Kenwood Cup 70 1·25
1420 $1.30 America's Cup 75 1·40

429 Hand writing Letter and Postal Transport

1987. New Zealand Post Ltd Vesting Day. Mult.
1421 40c. Type **429** 1·00 1·50
1422 40c. Posting letter, train and mailbox 1·00 1·50

430 Avro Type 626 and Wigram Airfield, 1937

1987. 50th Anniv of Royal New Zealand Air Force. Multicoloured.
1423 40c. Type **430** 65 15
1424 70c. Curtiss Kittyhawk I over World War II Pacific airstrip 90 1·75
1425 80c. Short S25 Sunderland flying boat and Pacific lagoon 1·00 1·75
1426 85c. Douglas A-4F Skyhawk and Mt. Ruapehu 1·10 1·60
MS1427 115 × 105 mm. Nos. 1423/6 5·00 6·00

431 Urewera National Park and Fern Leaf
432 "Kite Flying" (Lauren Baldwin)

1987. Centenary of National Parks Movement. Multicoloured.
1428 70c. Type **431** 70 55
1429 80c. Mt. Cook and buttercup 75 60
1430 85c. Fiordland and pineapple shrub 80 65
1431 $1.30 Tongariro and tussock 1·40 95
MS1432 123 × 99 mm. No. 1431 (sold at $1.70) 1·25 1·75

1987. Health Stamps. Children's Paintings (2nd series). Multicoloured.
1433 40c.+3c. Type **432** 80 1·50
1434 40c.+3c. "Swimming" (Ineke Schoneveld) 80 1·50
1435 60c.+3c. "Horse Riding" (Aaron Tylee) (vert) 1·25 1·50
MS1436 100 × 117 mm. Nos. 1433/5, each × 2 5·00 7·00

433 "Hark the Herald Angels Sing"
434 Knot ("Pona")

1987. Christmas. Multicoloured.
1437 35c. Type **433** 45 10
1438 70c. "Away in a Manger" 90 70
1439 85c. "We Three Kings of Orient Are" 1·10 85

1987. Maori Fibre-work. Multicoloured.
1440 40c. Type **434** 25 10
1441 60c. Binding ("Herehere") 35 55
1442 80c. Plait ("Whiri") 45 1·25
1443 85c. Cloak weaving ("Korowai") with flax fibre ("Whitau") 50 1·40

435 "Geothermal"

1988. Centenary of Electricity. Each shows radiating concentric circles representing energy generation.
1444 **435** 40c. multicoloured 25 20
1445 – 60c. black, red and brown 35 45
1446 – 70c. multicoloured 40 70
1447 – 80c. multicoloured 45 60
DESIGNS: 60c. "Thermal"; 70c. "Gas"; 80c. "Hydro".

436 Queen Elizabeth II and 1882 Queen Victoria 1d. Stamp

1988. Centenary of Royal Philatelic Society of New Zealand. Multicoloured.
1448 40c. Type **436** 35 75
1449 40c. As Type **436**, but 1882 Queen Victoria 2d. 35 75
MS1450 107 × 160 mm. $1 "Queen Victoria" (Chalon) (vert) 3·00 3·50

437 "Mangopare"
438 "Good Luck"

1988. Maori Rafter Paintings. Multicoloured.
1451 40c. Type **437** 30 45
1452 40c. "Koru" 30 45
1453 40c. "Raupunga" 30 45
1454 60c. "Koiri" 45 75

1988. Greetings Stamps. Multicoloured.
1455 40c. Type **438** 70 85
1456 40c. "Keeping in touch" 70 85
1457 40c. "Happy birthday" 70 85
1458 40c. "Congratulations" (41 × 27 mm) 70 85
1459 40c. "Get well soon" (41 × 27 mm) 70 85

439 Paradise Shelduck
440 Milford Track

1988. Native Birds. Multicoloured.
1459a 5c. Sooty crake 15 40
1460 10c. Double-banded plover 15 30
1461 20c. Yellowhead 20 30
1462 30c. Grey-backed white-eye ("Silvereye") 30 30
1463 40c. Brown kiwi 35 40
1463b 45c. Rock wren 50 50
1464 50c. Sacred kingfisher 50 60
1465 60c. Spotted cormorant ("Spotted shag") 50 70
1466 70c. Type **439** 70 1·00
1467 80c. Victoria penguin ("Fiordland Crested Penguin") 1·00 1·00
1467a 80c. New Zealand falcon 2·00 1·40
1468 90c. New Zealand robin 1·25 1·50
The 40 and 45c. also exist self-adhesive.

1988. Scenic Walking Trails. Multicoloured.
1469 70c. Type **440** 50 60
1470 80c. Heaphy Track 55 75
1471 85c. Copland Track 60 80
1472 $1.30 Routeburn Track 90 1·25
MS1473 124 × 99 mm. No. 1472 (sold at $1.70) 1·50 1·50

441 Kiwi and Koala at Campfire

1988. Bicentenary of Australian Settlement.
1474 **441** 40c. multicoloured 40 35
A stamp in a similar design was also issued by Australia.

442 Swimming
443 "O Come All Ye Faithful"

1988. Health Stamps. Olympic Games, Seoul. Mult.
1475 40c.+3c. Type **442** 40 70
1476 60c.+3c. Athletics 60 1·10
1477 70c.+3c. Canoeing 70 1·10
1478 80c.+3c. Show-jumping 90 1·40
MS1479 120 × 90 mm. Nos. 1475/8 3·25 4·50

1988. Christmas. Carols. Designs showing illuminated verses. Multicoloured.
1480 35c. Type **443** 30 30
1481 70c. "Hark the Herald Angels Sing" 50 65
1482 80c. "Ding Dong Merrily on High" 50 85
1483 85c. "The First Nowell" 55 95

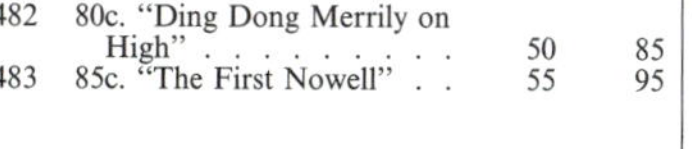

444 "Lake Pukaki" (John Gully)

1988. New Zealand Heritage (1st issue). "The Land". Designs showing 19th-century paintings. Multicoloured.
1484 40c. Type **444** 35 20
1485 60c. "On the Grass Plain below Lake Arthur" (William Fox) 45 45
1486 70c. "View of Auckland" (John Hoyte) 55 70
1487 80c. "Mt. Egmont from the Southward" (Charles Heaphy) 60 70
1488 $1.05 "Anakiwa, Queen Charlotte Sound" (John Kinder) 80 1·40
1489 $1.30 "White Terraces, Lake Rotomahana", (Charles Barraud) 95 1·60
See also Nos. 1505/10, 1524/9, 1541/6, 1548/53 and 1562/7.

445 Brown Kiwi

1988.
1490 **445** $1 green 2·00 3·25
1490b $1 red 2·00 2·75
1490c $1 blue 1·00 1·50
2090 $1 violet 1·00 1·00
2090a $1.10 gold 80 85
2090b £1.50 brown 1·10 1·20
See also Nos. **MS**1745, **MS**1786 and **MS**2342.

446 Humpback Whale and Calf

1988. Whales. Multicoloured.
1491 60c. Type **446** 80 85
1492 70c. Killer whales 90 1·10
1493 80c. Southern right whale 90 1·25
1494 85c. Blue whale 95 1·50
1495 $1.05 Southern bottlenose whale and calf 1·25 2·00
1496 $1.30 Sperm whale 1·40 2·25
Although inscribed "ROSS DEPENDENCY" Nos. 1491/6 were available from post offices throughout New Zealand.

447 Clover
448 Katherine Mansfield

1989. Wild Flowers. Multicoloured.
1497 40c. Type **447** 40 20
1498 60c. Lotus 50 65
1499 70c. Montbretia 60 1·25
1500 80c. Wild ginger 70 1·25

1989. New Zealand Authors. Multicoloured.
1501 40c. Type **448** 30 25
1502 60c. James K. Baxter 40 50
1503 70c. Bruce Mason 50 70
1504 80c. Ngaio Marsh 55 70

449 Moriori Man and Map of Chatham Islands

1989. New Zealand Heritage (2nd issue). The People.
1505 **449** 40c. multicoloured 45 25
1506 – 60c. brown, grey and deep brown 60 75
1507 – 70c. green, grey and deep green 65 90
1508 – 80c. blue, grey and deep blue 75 90
1509 – $1.05 grey, light grey and black 1·00 1·60
1510 – $1.30 red, grey and brown 1·25 2·00
DESIGNS: 60c. Gold prospector; 70c. Settler ploughing; 80c. Whaling; $1.05, Missionary preaching to Maoris; $1.30, Maori village.

450 White Pine (Kahikatea)
451 Duke and Duchess of York with Princess Beatrice

1989. Native Trees. Multicoloured.
1511 80c. Type **450** 65 80
1512 85c. Red pine (Rimu) 70 85
1513 $1.05 Totara 80 1·10
1514 $1.30 Kauri 1·00 1·40
MS1515 102 × 125 mm. No. 1514 (sold at $1.80) 1·75 1·75

1989. Health Stamps. Multicoloured.
1516 40c.+3c. Type **451** 80 1·50
1517 40c.+3c. Duchess of York with Princess Beatrice 80 1·50
1518 80c.+3c. Princess Beatrice 1·40 1·75
MS1519 120 × 89 mm. Nos. 1516/18, each × 2 5·50 7·50

452 One Tree Hill, Auckland through Bedroom Window

1989. Christmas. Designs showing Star of Bethlehem. Multicoloured.
1520 35c. Type **452** 30 15
1521 65c. Shepherd and dog in mountain valley 65 70
1522 80c. Star over harbour 75 1·10
1523 $1 Star over globe 1·00 1·40

453 Windsurfing

1989. New Zealand Heritage (3rd issue). The Sea. Multicoloured.
1524 40c. Type **453** 50 25
1525 60c. Fishes of many species 85 70
1526 65c. Striped marlin and game fishing launch 90 85
1527 80c. Rowing boat and yachts in harbour 1·00 90
1528 $1 Coastal scene 1·25 1·10
1529 $1.50 "Rotoiti" (container ship) and tug 1·90 2·25

454 Games Logo

1989. 14th Commonwealth Games, Auckland. Mult.
1530 40c. Type **454** 40 35
1531 40c. Goldie (games kiwi mascot) 40 35
1532 40c. Gymnastics 40 35
1533 50c. Weightlifting 45 40
1534 65c. Swimming 50 55
1535 80c. Cycling 80 70
1536 $1 Lawn bowling 90 90
1537 $1.80 Hurdling 1·25 1·90
MS1538 Two sheets, each 105 × 92 mm, with different margin designs. (a) Nos. 1530/1 (horiz pair). (b) Nos. 1530/1 (vert pair) Set of 2 sheets 5·00 5·50

455 Short S.30 modified "G" Class Flying Boat "Aotearoa" and Boeing 747-200

1990. 50th Anniv of Air New Zealand.
1539 **455** 80c. multicoloured . . . 1·40 1·10

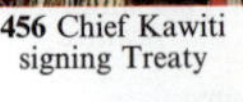

456 Chief Kawiti signing Treaty **458** *Thelymitra pulchella*

457 Maori Voyaging Canoe

1990. 150th Anniv of Treaty of Waitangi. Sheet 80 × 118 mm, containing T **456** and similar multicoloured design.
MS1540 40c. Type **456**; 40c. Chief Hone Heke (first signatory) and Lieut-Governor Hobson (horiz) 2·50 3·75

1990. New Zealand Heritage (4th issue). The Ships. Multicoloured.
1541 40c. Type **457** 60 25
1542 50c. H.M.S. "Endeavour" (Cook), 1769 . . . . . . 85 80
1543 60c. "Tory" (barque), 1839 95 1·00
1544 80c. "Crusader" (full-rigged immigrant ship), 1871 . . 1·40 1·50
1545 $1 "Edwin Fox" (full-rigged immigrant ship), 1873 . . 1·60 1·50
1546 $1.50 "Arawa" (steamer), 1884 . . . . 2·00 3·00

1990. "New Zealand 1990" International Stamp Exhibition, Auckland. Native Orchids. Sheet 179 × 80 mm, containing T **458** and similar vert designs. Multicoloured.
MS1547 40c. Type **458**; 40c. "Corybas macranthus"; 40c. "Dendrobium cunninghamii"; 40c. "Pterostylis banksii"; 80c. "Aporostylis bifolia" (sold at $4.90) . . . . 4·50 4·50
The stamps in No. **MS**1547 form a composite design.

459 Grace Neill (social reformer) and Maternity Hospital, Wellington

1990. New Zealand Heritage (5th issue). Famous New Zealanders. Multicoloured.
1548 40c. Type **459** 55 30
1549 50c. Jean Batten (pilot) and Percival P.3 Gull Six aircraft 65 85
1550 60c. Katherine Sheppard (suffragette) and 19th-century women . . . 85 1·50
1551 80c. Richard Pearse (inventor) and early flying machine . . . . 1·10 1·50
1552 $1 Lt.-Gen. Sir Bernard Freyberg and tank . . . 1·25 1·50
1553 $1.50 Peter Buck (politician) and Maori pattern . . . 1·50 2·50

460 Akaroa **461** Jack Lovelock (athlete) and Race

1990. 150th Anniv of European Settlements. Mult.
1554 80c. Type **460** 75 75
1555 $1 Wanganui 95 95
1556 $1.50 Wellington . . . . . 1·40 2·25
1557 $1.80 Takapuna Beach, Auckland . . . . 1·60 2·25
MS1558 125 × 100 mm. No. 1557 (sold at $2.30) . . . . 3·50 3·50

1990. Health Stamps. Sportsmen (1st series). Mult.
1559 40c.+5c. Type **461** 50 85
1560 80c.+5c. George Nepia (rugby player) and match 75 1·40
MS1561 115 × 96 mm. Nos. 1559/60, each × 2 . . . . 3·25 4·00
See also Nos. 1687/8.

462 Creation Legend of Rangi and Papa

1990. New Zealand Heritage (6th issue). The Maori. Multicoloured.
1562 40c. Type **462** 40 30
1563 50c. Pattern from Maori feather cloak 55 80
1564 60c. Maori women's choir 60 90
1565 80c. Maori facial tattoos . . 75 1·00
1566 $1 War canoe prow (detail) 90 1·25
1567 $1.50 Maori haka . . . . . 1·40 2·75

463 Queen Victoria **464** Angel

1990. 150th Anniv of the Penny Black. Sheet 169 × 70 mm, containing T **463** and similar vert designs.
MS1568 40c. × 6 blue (Type **463**, King Edward VII, King George V, King Edward VIII, King George VI, Queen Elizabeth II) 4·00 5·00

1990. Christmas.
1569 **464** 40c. purple, blue & brn 40 10
1570 – $1 purple, green & brown 80 50
1571 – $1.50 purple, red & brown . . . . 1·40 2·50
1572 – $1.80 purple, red & brown . . . . 1·60 2·50
DESIGNS: $1 to $1.80, Different angels.

465 Antarctic Petrel **466** Coopworth Ewe and Lambs

1990. Antarctic Birds. Multicoloured.
1573 40c. Type **465** 80 30
1574 50c. Wilson's storm petrel 90 75
1575 60c. Snow petrel . . . . . 1·10 1·25
1576 80c. Southern fulmar . . . 1·25 1·25
1577 $1 Bearded penguin ("Chinstrap Penguin") . . 1·40 1·25
1578 $1.50 Emperor penguin . . 1·60 3·00
Although inscribed "Ross Dependency" Nos. 1573/8 were available from post offices throughout New Zealand.

1991. New Zealand Farming and Agriculture. Sheep Breeds. Multicoloured.
1579 40c. Type **466** 40 20
1580 60c. Perendale 55 75
1581 80c. Corriedale 70 85
1582 $1 Drysdale 85 90
1583 $1.50 South Suffolk . . . . 1·25 2·50
1584 $1.80 Romney . . . . . . 1·50 2·50

467 Moriori, Royal Albatross, Nikau Palm and Artefacts **469** Tuatara on Rocks

468 Goal and Footballers

1991. Bicentenary of Discovery of Chatham Islands. Multicoloured.
1585 40c. Type **467** 75 50
1586 80c. Carvings, H.M.S. "Chatham", Moriori house of 1870, and Tommy Solomon . . . . 1·50 2·00

1991. Centenary of New Zealand Football Association. Multicoloured.
1587 80c. Type **468** . . . . . . 1·40 1·75
1588 80c. Five footballers and referee . . . . 1·40 1·75
Nos. 1587/8 were printed together, se-tenant, forming a composite design.

1991. Endangered Species. The Tuatara. Mult.
1590 40c. Type **469** 40 60
1591 40c. Tuatara in crevice . . . 40 60
1592 40c. Tuatara with foliage . . 40 60
1593 40c. Tuatara in dead leaves 40 60

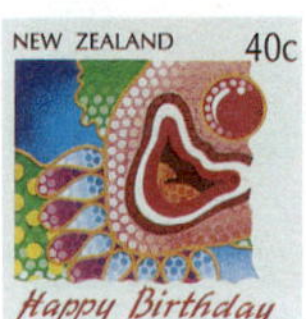

470 Clown **471** Cat at Window

1991. "Happy Birthday". Multicoloured.
1594 40c. Type **470** 75 85
1595 40c. Balloons 75 85
1596 40c. Party hat 75 85
1597 40c. Birthday present (41 × 27 mm) 75 85
1598 40c. Birthday cake (41 × 27 mm) 75 85
1599 45c. Type **470** 75 85
1600 45c. As No. 1595 . . . . . 75 85
1601 45c. As No. 1596 . . . . . 75 85
1602 45c. As No. 1597 . . . . . 75 85
1603 45c. As No. 1598 . . . . . 75 85

1991. "Thinking of You". Multicoloured.
1604 40c. Type **471** 75 85
1605 40c. Cat playing with slippers 75 85
1606 40c. Cat with alarm clock 75 85
1607 40c. Cat in window (41 × 27 mm) 75 85
1608 40c. Cat at door (41 × 27 mm) 75 85
1609 45c. Type **471** 75 85
1610 45c. As No. 1605 . . . . . 75 85
1611 45c. As No. 1606 . . . . . 75 85
1612 45c. As No. 1607 . . . . . 75 85
1613 45c. As No. 1608 . . . . . 75 85

472 Punakaiki Rocks

1991. Scenic Landmarks. Multicoloured.
1614 40c. Type **472** 40 30
1615 50c. Moeraki Boulders . . . 55 55
1616 80c. Organ Pipes 85 85
1617 $1 Castle Hill 95 95
1618 $1.50 Te Kaukau Point . . 1·50 1·60
1619 $1.80 Ahuriri River Clay Cliffs . . . . 1·75 1·90

473 Dolphins Underwater

1991. Health Stamps. Hector's Dolphin. Mult.
1620 45c.+5c. Type **473** . . . . 90 1·25
1621 80c.+5c. Dolphins leaping 1·25 2·00
MS1622 115 × 100 mm. Nos. 1620/1, each × 2 . . . . 5·00 6·50

474 Children's Rugby **475** "Three Shepherds"

1991. World Cup Rugby Championship. Mult.
1623 80c. Type **474** . . . . . . 1·00 1·25
1624 $1 Women's rugby . . . . 1·10 1·00
1625 $1.50 Senior rugby . . . . 1·75 2·75
1626 $1.80 "All Blacks" (national team) . . . . 2·00 2·75
MS1627 113 × 90 mm. No. 1626 (sold at $2.40) . . . . 4·00 5·00

1991. Christmas. Multicoloured.
1628 45c. Type **475** 55 80
1629 45c. Two Kings on camels 55 80
1630 45c. Mary and Baby Jesus 55 80
1631 45c. King with gift 55 80
1632 65c. Star of Bethlehem . . . 70 80
1633 $1 Crown 85 95
1634 $1.50 Angel . . . . 1·40 2·25

476 "Dodonidia helmsii"

1991. Butterflies. Multicoloured.
1635 $1 Type **476** . . . . 1·00 60
1641 $2 "Zizina otis oxleyi" . . . 2·50 1·75
1642 $3 "Vanessa itea" . . . . . 3·25 3·00
1643 $4 "Lycaena salustius" . . . 2·25 2·40
1644 $5 "Bassaris gonerilla" . . . 3·25 3·25

479 Yacht "Kiwi Magic", 1987

1992. New Zealand Challenge for America's Cup. Multicoloured.
1655 45c. Type **479** 45 20
1656 80c. Yacht "New Zealand", 1988 . . . . 80 70
1657 $1 Yacht "America", 1851 95 85
1658 $1.50 "America's Cup" Class yacht, 1992 . . . . 1·60 1·60

480 "Heemskerk"

1992. Great Voyages of Discovery. Mult.
1659 45c. Type **480** 55 25
1660 80c. "Zeehan" . . . . . . 90 1·10
1661 $1 "Santa Maria" . . . . . 1·25 1·10
1662 $1.50 "Pinta" and "Nina" 1·50 2·50
Nos. 1659/60 commemorate the 350th anniv of Tasman's discovery of New Zealand and Nos. 1661/2 the 500th anniv of discovery of America by Columbus.

481 Sprinters

1992. Olympic Games, Barcelona (1st issue).
1663 **481** 45c. multicoloured . . . 50 50
See also Nos. 1670/3.

482 Weddell Seal and Pup

1992. Antarctic Seals. Multicoloured.
1664 45c. Type **482** 70 30
1665 50c. Crabeater seals swimming 80 60
1666 65c. Leopard seal and Adelie penguins 1·00 1·25
1667 80c. Ross seal 1·25 1·25
1668 $1 Southern elephant seal and harem 1·40 1·25
1669 $1.80 Hooker's sea lion and pup 2·25 3·25

Although inscribed "ROSS DEPENDENCY" Nos. 1664/9 were available from post offices throughout New Zealand.

483 Cycling

1992. Olympic Games, Barcelona (2nd issue). Multicoloured.
1670 45c. Type **483** 65 35
1671 80c. Archery 90 70
1672 $1 Equestrian three-day eventing 1·00 85
1673 $1.50 Sailboarding 1·50 1·40
MS1674 125 × 100 mm. Nos. 1670/3 4·00 5·00

484 Ice Pinnacles, Franz Josef Glacier

1992. Glaciers. Multicoloured.
1675 45c. Type **484** 40 25
1676 50c. Tasman Glacier 50 45
1677 80c. Snowball Glacier, Marion Plateau 70 70
1678 $1 Brewster Glacier 85 85
1679 $1.50 Fox Glacier 1·40 1·60
1680 $1.80 Franz Josef Glacier 1·50 1·60

485 "Grand Finale" Camellia

486 Tree and Hills

1992. Camellias. Multicoloured.
1681 45c. Type **485** 60 25
1682 50c. "Showa-No-Sakae" 70 60
1683 80c. "Sugar Dream" 90 80
1684 $1 "Night Rider" 1·10 85
1685 $1.50 "E.G. Waterhouse" 1·50 2·75
1686 $1.80 "Dr. Clifford Parks" 1·75 3·00

1992. Health Stamps. Sportsmen (2nd series). As T **461**. Multicoloured.
1687 45c.+5c. Anthony Wilding (tennis player) and match 1·00 1·25
1688 80c.+5c. Stewie Dempster (cricketer) and batsman 1·00 1·50
MS1689 115 × 96 mm. Nos. 1687/8, each × 2 4·50 5·50

1992. Landscapes. Multicoloured.
1690 45c. Type **486** 60 65
1691 45c. River and hills 60 65
1692 45c. Hills and mountain 60 65
1693 45c. Glacier 60 65
1694 45c. Hills and waterfall 60 65
1695 45c. Tree and beach 60 65
1696 45c. Estuary and cliffs 60 65
1697 45c. Fjord 60 65
1698 45c. River delta 60 65
1699 45c. Ferns and beach 60 65

487 Reindeer over Houses

488 1920s Fashions

1992. Christmas. Multicoloured.
1700 45c. Type **487** 90 1·00
1701 45c. Santa Claus on sleigh over houses 90 1·00
1702 45c. Christmas tree in window 90 1·00
1703 45c. Christmas wreath and children at window 90 1·00
1704 65c. Candles and fireplace 1·10 90
1705 $1 Family going to church 1·40 1·00
1706 $1.50 Picnic under Pohutukawa tree 2·00 2·75

1992. New Zealand in the 1920s. Multicoloured.
1707 45c. Type **488** 50 20
1708 50c. Dr. Robert Jack and early radio announcer 55 65
1709 80c. "All Blacks" rugby player, 1924 85 1·00
1710 $1 Swaggie and dog 95 1·00
1711 $1.50 Ford "Model A" car and young couple 1·75 2·25
1712 $1.80 Amateur aviators and biplane 2·00 2·75

489 "Old Charley" Toby Jug

490 Women's Fashions of the 1930s

1993. Royal Doulton Ceramics Exhibition, New Zealand. Multicoloured.
1713 45c. Type **489** 50 20
1714 50c. "Bunnykins" nursery plate 55 60
1715 80c. "Maori Art" tea set 85 85
1716 $1 "Ophelia" handpainted plate 1·00 90
1717 $1.50 "St. George" figurine 1·60 2·50
1718 $1.80 "Lambeth" salt-glazed stoneware vase 1·90 2·50
MS1719 125 × 100 mm. No. 1718 1·60 2·50

1993. New Zealand in the 1930s. Multicoloured.
1720 45c. Type **490** 50 25
1721 50c. Unemployed protest march 55 75
1722 80c. "Phar Lap" (racehorse) 85 95
1723 $1 State housing project 1·00 1·00
1724 $1.50 Boys drinking free school milk 1·75 3·00
1725 $1.80 Cinema queue 1·90 2·75

491 Women signing Petition

492 Champagne Pool

1993. Centenary of Women's Suffrage. Mult.
1726 45c. Type **491** 50 20
1727 80c. Aircraft propeller and woman on tractor 1·00 85
1728 $1 Housewife with children 1·00 95
1729 $1.50 Modern women 1·60 2·00

1993. Thermal Wonders, Rotorua. Multicoloured.
1730 45c. Type **492** 60 25
1731 50c. Boiling mud 60 40
1732 80c. Emerald pool 85 70
1733 $1 Hakereteke Falls 95 80
1734 $1.50 Warbrick Terrace 1·50 1·75
1735 $1.80 Pohutu Geyser 1·60 1·75
See also No. **MS**1770.

493 Yellow-eyed Penguin, Hector's Dolphin and New Zealand Fur Seal

1993. Endangered Species Conservation. Mult.
1736 45c. Type **493** 85 1·00
1737 45c. Taiko (bird), Mount Cook lily and mountain duck ("Blue Duck") 85 1·00
1738 45c. Giant snail, rock wren and Hamilton's frog 85 1·00
1739 45c. Kaka (bird), New Zealand pigeon and giant weta 85 1·00
1740 45c. Tusked weta (23 × 28 mm) 85 1·00

494 Boy with Puppy

495 Christmas Decorations (value at left)

1993. Health Stamps. Children's Pets. Mult.
1741 45c.+5c. Type **494** 60 90
1742 80c.+5c. Girl with kitten 90 1·50
MS1743 115 × 96 mm. Nos. 1741/2, each × 2 2·75 4·25

1993. "Taipei '93" Asian International Stamp Exhibition, Taiwan. (a) No. **MS**1743 optd **TAIPEI '93** and emblem on sheet margin. Mult.
MS1744 Nos. 1741/2, each × 2 12·00 13·00

(b) Sheet 125 × 100 mm, containing Nos. 1490/c.
MS1745 **445** $1 green, $1 blue, $1 red 5·00 5·00

1993. Christmas. Multicoloured.
1746 45c. Type **495** 60 85
1747 45c. Christmas decorations (value at right) 60 85
1748 45c. Sailboards, gifts and Christmas pudding (value at left) 60 85
1749 45c. Sailboards, gifts and Christmas pudding (value at right) 60 85
1750 $1 Sailboards, baubles and Christmas cracker 1·50 1·25
1751 $1.50 Sailboards, present and wreath 2·00 3·25

496 Rainbow Abalone or Paua

497 Sauropod

1993. Marine Life. Multicoloured.
1752 45c. Type **496** 1·00 1·00
1753 45c. Green mussels 1·00 1·00
1754 45c. Tarakihi 1·00 1·00
1755 45c. Salmon 1·00 1·00
1756 45c. Southern blue-finned tuna, yellow-finned tuna and kahawai 1·00 1·00
1757 45c. Rock lobster 1·00 1·00
1758 45c. Snapper 1·00 1·00
1759 45c. Grouper 1·00 1·00
1760 45c. Orange roughy 1·00 1·00
1761 45c. Squid, hoki and black oreo 1·10 1·00

1993. Prehistoric Animals. Multicoloured.
1762 45c. Type **497** 60 45
1763 45c. Carnosaur and sauropod (30 × 25 mm) 75 60
1764 80c. Pterosaur 1·10 85
1765 $1 Ankylosaur 1·25 95
1766 $1.20 Mauisaurus 1·50 2·50
1767 $1.50 Carnosaur 1·60 2·50
MS1768 125 × 100 mm. $1.50 No. 1767 1·75 1·75

1993. "Bangkok '93" International Stamp Exhibition, Thailand. (a) No. **MS**1768 optd **BANGKOK '93** and emblem on sheet margin. Multicoloured.
MS1769 $1.50 No. 1767 1·60 2·00

(b) Sheet 115 × 100 mm, containing No. 1735.
MS1770 $1.80 multicoloured 2·75 3·75

498 Soldiers, National Flag and Pyramids

499 Bungy Jumping

1993. New Zealand in the 1940s. Multicoloured.
1771 45c. Type **498** 80 25
1772 50c. Aerial crop spraying 85 60
1773 80c. Hydro-electric scheme 1·10 80
1774 $1 Marching majorettes 1·40 90
1775 $1.50 American troops 1·90 2·00
1776 $1.80 Crowd celebrating victory 2·00 2·25

1994. Tourism. Multicoloured.
1777 45c. Type **499** 50 25
1778 45c. White water rafting (25 × 25 mm) 50 55
1779 80c. Trout fishing 70 70
1780 $1 Jet boating (horiz) 80 80
1781 $1.50 Tramping 1·40 2·00
1782 $1.80 Heli-skiing 1·90 2·00
See also No. **MS**1785.

500 "New Zealand Endeavour" (yacht)

503 Rock and Roll Dancers

501 Mt. Cook and New Zealand Symbols

1994. Round the World Yacht Race.
1783 **500** $1 multicoloured 1·40 1·60

1994.
1784 **501** $20 blue and gold 11·50 12·00

1994. "Hong Kong '94" International Stamp Exhibition. Multicoloured.
MS1785 95 × 115 mm. $1.80 No. 1782 3·50 3·50
MS1786 100 × 125 mm. $1 × 3 As Nos. 1490/c 4·50 5·00

1994. New Zealand in the 1950s. Multicoloured.
1787 45c. Type **503** 45 25
1788 80c. Sir Edmund Hillary on Mt. Everest 75 75
1789 $1 Aunt Daisy (radio personality) 85 85
1790 $1.20 Queen Elizabeth II during 1953 royal visit 1·25 1·25
1791 $1.50 Children playing with Opo the dolphin 1·60 2·00
1792 $1.80 Auckland Harbour Bridge 1·90 2·00

504 Mt. Cook and Mt. Cook Lily ("Winter")

1994. The Four Seasons. Multicoloured.
1793 45c. Type **504** 45 25
1794 70c. Lake Hawea and Kowhai ("Spring") 65 65
1795 $1.50 Opononi Beach and Pohutukawa ("Summer") 1·40 1·40
1796 $1.80 Lake Pukaki and Puriri ("Autumn") 1·75 1·75

505 Rainbow Abalone or Paua Shell

506 Maui pulls up Te Ika

1994. New Zealand Life. Multicoloured.
1797 45c. Type **505** (25 × 20 mm) 40 45
1798 45c. Pavlova dessert (35 × 20 mm) 40 45
1799 45c. Hokey pokey ice cream (25 × 20 mm) 40 45
1800 45c. Fish and chips (35 × 20 mm) 40 45
1801 45c. Jandals (30 × 20 mm) 40 45
1802 45c. Bush shirt (25 × 30½ mm) 40 45
1803 45c. Buzzy Bee (toy) (35 × 30½ mm) 40 45

1804 45c. Gumboots and black singlet (25 × 30½ mm) . . 40 45
1805 45c. Rugby boots and ball (35 × 30½ mm) 40 45
1806 45c. Kiwifruit (30 × 30½ mm) 40 45
See also Nos. 2318/27.

1994. Maori Myths. Multicoloured.
1807 45c. Type **506** 50 25
1808 80c. Rona snatched up by Marama 85 85
1809 $1 Maui attacking Tuna . . 1·00 1·00
1810 $1.20 Tane separating Rangi and Papa . . . . 1·40 2·00
1811 $1.50 Matakauri slaying the Giant of Wakatipu . . . 1·50 2·00
1812 $1.80 Panenehu showing crayfish to Tangaroa . . 1·75 2·00

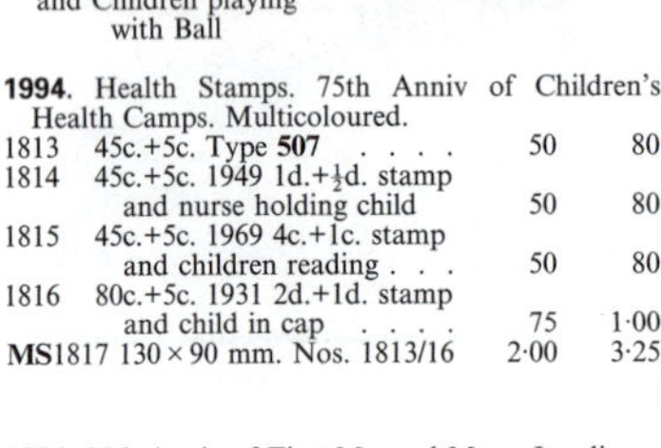

507 1939 2d. on 1d.+1d. Health Stamp and Children playing with Ball
508 Astronaut on Moon (hologram)

1994. Health Stamps. 75th Anniv of Children's Health Camps. Multicoloured.
1813 45c.+5c. Type **507** 50 80
1814 45c.+5c. 1949 1d.+½d. stamp and nurse holding child 50 80
1815 45c.+5c. 1969 4c.+1c. stamp and children reading . . . 50 80
1816 80c.+5c. 1931 2d.+1d. stamp and child in cap . . . . 75 1·00
MS1817 130 × 90 mm. Nos. 1813/16 2·00 3·25

1994. 25th Anniv of First Manned Moon Landing.
1818 **508** $1.50 multicoloured . . 2·25 2·50

509 "people reaching people"

1994. Self-adhesive.
1818ab **509** 40c. multicoloured . . 75 55
1819 45c. multicoloured . . 1·00 65

510 African Elephants

1994. Stamp Month. Wild Animals. Multicoloured.
1820 45c. Type **510** 90 80
1821 45c. White rhinoceros . . . 90 80
1822 45c. Lions 90 80
1823 45c. Common zebras . . . 90 80
1824 45c. Giraffe and calf 90 80
1825 45c. Siberian tiger 90 80
1826 45c. Hippopotamuses . . . 90 80
1827 45c. Spider monkey 90 80
1828 45c. Giant panda 90 80
1829 45c. Polar bear and cub . . 90 80

1994. "Philakorea '94" International Stamp Exhibition, Seoul. Multicoloured.
MS1830 125 × 100 mm. Nos. 1459a/65 . . . . 6·50 6·00
MS1831 125 × 100 mm. Nos. 1820, 1822, 1824/5 and 1828/9 . . . 3·75 4·50

511 Children with Crib
512 Batsman

1994. Christmas. Multicoloured.
1832 45c. Father Christmas and children (30 × 25 mm) . . 45 40
1833 45c. Type **511** 45 20
1834 70c. Man and toddler with crib 65 80
1835 80c. Three carol singers . . 70 85
1836 $1 Five carol singers 90 90
1837 $1.50 Children and candles 1·25 2·00
1838 $1.80 Parents with child . . 1·60 2·00
MS1839 125 × 100 mm. Nos. 1833/6 2·75 2·75

1994. Centenary of New Zealand Cricket Council. (a) Horiz designs, each 30 × 25 mm. Multicoloured.
1840 45c. Bathers catching balls 65 80
1841 45c. Child on surf board at top 65 80
1842 45c. Young child with rubber ring at top 65 80
1843 45c. Man with beach ball at top 65 80
1844 45c. Woman with cricket bat at right 65 80
1845 45c. Boy in green cap with bat 65 80
1846 45c. Man in spotted shirt running 65 80
1847 45c. Woman in striped shorts with bat 65 80
1848 45c. Boy in wet suit with surf board at right . . . 65 80
1849 45c. Sunbather with newspaper at right . . . 65 80
(b) T **512** and similar vert designs. Multicoloured.
1850 45c. Type **512** 75 40
1851 80c. Bowler . . . . 1·25 80
1852 $1 Wicket keeper . . . . . 1·50 1·00
1853 $1.80 Fielder . . . . 2·50 2·25

1995. "POST X '95" Postal History Exhibition, Auckland. Sheet 130 × 90 mm, containing No. 1297 and a reproduction of No. 557 optd "SPECIMEN".
MS1854 $10 multicoloured . . . 17·00 17·00

513 Auckland

1995. New Zealand by Night. Multicoloured.
1855 45c. Type **513** 60 25
1856 80c. Wellington 90 65
1857 $1 Christchurch . . . . . . 1·25 85
1858 $1.20 Dunedin . . . . . . 1·40 1·40
1859 $1.50 Rotorua . . . . . . 1·50 1·60
1860 $1.80 Queenstown . . . . . 1·75 1·60
See also No. **MS**1915.

514 The 15th Hole, Waitangi
515 New Zealand Pigeon and Nest

1995. New Zealand Golf Courses. Multicoloured.
1861 45c. Type **514** 65 30
1862 80c. The 6th hole, New Plymouth . . . . 1·00 90
1863 $1.20 The 9th hole, Rotorua 1·50 2·50
1864 $1.80 The 5th hole, Queenstown . . . . . . 2·40 3·00

1995. Environment. Multicoloured.
1865 45c. Type **515** 65 65
1866 45c. Planting sapling 65 65
1867 45c. Dolphins and whales . 65 65
1868 45c. Thunderstorm 65 65
1869 45c. Backpackers 65 65
1870 45c. Animal pests 65 65
1871 45c. Noxious plants 65 65
1872 45c. Undersized fish and shellfish 65 65
1873 45c. Pollution from factories 65 65
1874 45c. Family at picnic site . . 65 65

516 Teacher with Guitar and Children
517 Map of Australasia and Asia

1995. Maori Language Year. Multicoloured.
1875 45c. Type **516** 50 20
1876 70c. Singing group 75 75
1877 80c. Mother and baby . . . 85 85
1878 $1 Women performing traditional welcome . . . 1·10 1·10
1879 $1.50 Grandfather reciting family genealogy . . . . 1·75 2·25
1880 $1.80 Tribal orator . . . . 2·00 2·25

1995. Meetings of Asian Development Bank Board of Governors and International Pacific Basin Economic Council, Auckland. Multicoloured.
1881 $1 Type **517** . . . . 1·25 1·00
1882 $1.50 Map of Australasia and Pacific . . . . 1·75 2·75

518 "Black Magic" (yacht)

1995. New Zealand's Victory in 1995 America's Cup.
1883 **518** 45c. multicoloured . . . 55 55

519 Boy on Skateboard

1995. Health Stamps. Children's Sports. Mult.
1884 45c.+5c. Type **519** . . . . 75 1·25
1885 80c.+5c. Girl on bicyle . . . 1·75 1·75
MS1886 130 × 90 mm. Nos. 1884/5, each × 2 . . . . 4·00 5·00

1995. "Stampex '95" National Stamp Exhibition, Wellington. No. **MS**1886 additionally inscr with "Stampex '95" and emblem on sheet margin. Mult.
MS1887 130 × 90 mm. Nos. 1884/5, each × 2 . . . . 5·50 6·50

520 Lion Red Cup and Players

1995. Centenary of Rugby League. Multicoloured.
1888 45c. Trans Tasman test match (30 × 25 mm) . . . 60 60
1889 45c. Type **520** 50 20
1890 $1 Children's rugby and mascot . . . . 1·25 1·10
1891 $1.50 George Smith, Albert Baskerville and early match . . . . 2·00 2·50
1892 $1.80 Courtney Goodwill Trophy and match against Great Britain . . . . . . 2·25 2·50
MS1893 125 × 100 mm. No. 1892 3·00 3·00

521 Sheep and Lamb
522 Archangel Gabriel

1995. Farmyard Animals. Multicoloured.
1894 40c. Type **521** 75 75
1895 40c. Deer 75 75
1896 40c. Mare and foal 75 75
1897 40c. Cow with calf 75 75
1898 40c. Goats and kid 75 75
1899 40c. Common turkey . . . 75 75
1900 40c. Ducks 75 75
1901 40c. Red junglefowl 75 75
1902 40c. Sow with piglets . . . 75 75
1903 40c. Border collie 75 75
1904 45c. As Type **521** 75 75
1905 45c. As No. 1895 . . . . . 75 75
1906 45c. As No. 1896 . . . . . 75 75
1907 45c. As No. 1897 . . . . . 75 75
1908 45c. As No. 1898 . . . . . 75 75
1909 45c. As No. 1899 . . . . . 75 75
1910 45c. As No. 1900 . . . . . 75 75
1911 45c. As No. 1901 . . . . . 75 75
1912 45c. As No. 1902 . . . . . 75 75
1913 45c. As No. 1903 . . . . . 75 75

1995. "Singapore '95" International Stamp Exhibition. Multicoloured.
MS1914 170 × 70 mm. Nos. 1909/13 3·25 4·00
MS1915 148 × 210 mm. Nos. 1855/60 11·00 14·00

No. **MS**1915 also includes the "JAKARTA '95" logo.

1995. Christmas. Stained Glass Windows from St. Mary's Anglican Church, Merivale (Nos. 1916/18), The Lady Chapel of St. Luke's Anglican Church, Christchurch (Nos. 1919/22) or St. John the Evangelist Church, Cheviot (No. 1923). Multicoloured. (a) As T **522**.
1916 40c. Type **522** 70 25
1917 45c. Type **522** 70 25
1918 70c. Virgin Mary . . . . . 1·00 90
1919 80c. Shepherds . . . . . . 1·10 1·00
1920 $1 Virgin and Child . . . . 1·40 1·10
1921 $1.50 Two Wise Men . . . 2·25 2·75
1922 $1.80 Wise Man kneeling . . 2·50 2·75
(b) Smaller design, 25 × 30 mm.
1923 40c. Angel with trumpet . . 60 50

523 Face and Nuclear Disarmament Symbol
524 Mt. Cook

1995. Nuclear Disarmament.
1924 **523** $1 multicoloured . . . . 1·00 1·00

1995. New Zealand Scenery. Multicoloured.
1925 5c. Type **524** 10 10
1926 10c. Champagne Pool . . 10 10
1927 20c. Cape Reinga 15 20
1928 30c. Mackenzie Country 20 25
1929 40c. Mitre Peak (vert) . . 30 35
1930 50c. Mt. Ngauruhoe . . . 35 40
1931 60c. Lake Wanaka (vert) 45 50
1932 70c. Giant kauri tree (vert) 50 55
1933 80c. Doubtful Sound (vert) 60 65
1934 90c. Waitomo Limestone Cave (vert) 65 70
1934a 90c. Rangitoto Island . . . 65 70
1934b $1 Taiaroa Head (27 × 22 mm) 75 80
1934c $1.10 Kaikoura Coast (27 × 22 mm) 80 85
1934d $1.30 Lake Camp, South Canterbury (27 × 22 mm) 95 1·00
1934e $2 Great Barrier Island (27 × 22 mm) . . . . . 1·50 1·60
1934f $3 Cape Kidnappers (27 × 22 mm) . . . . . 2·20 2·30
1935 $10 Mt. Ruapehu (38 × 32 mm) . . . . . 7·25 7·50
For similar self-adhesive designs see Nos. 1984b/91b.
For miniature sheets containing some of these designs see Nos. **MS**1978, **MS**1998, **MS**2005, **MS**2328 and **MS**2401.

525 Dame Kiri te Kanawa (opera singer)
526 National Flags, Peace Dove and "50"

1995. Famous New Zealanders. Multicoloured.
1936 40c. Type **525** 75 40
1937 80c. Charles Upham, V.C. (war hero) . . . . 1·00 85
1938 $1 Barry Crump (author) . . 1·25 1·00
1939 $1.20 Sir Brian Barratt-Boyes (surgeon) . . . . . 1·75 1·25
1940 $1.50 Dame Whina Cooper (Maori leader) . . . . . 1·75 1·75
1941 $1.80 Sir Richard Hadlee (cricketer) . . . . 2·75 2·25

1995. 50th Anniv of United Nations.
1942 **526** $1.80 multicoloured . . 2·75 2·50

527 Fern and Globe

1995. Commonwealth Heads of Government Meeting, Auckland. Multicoloured.
1943 40c. Type **527** 75 40
1944 $1.80 Fern and New Zealand flag . . . . . 3·50 2·75

528 "Kiwi"

1996. Famous Racehorses. Multicoloured.

1945 40c. Type **528** 55 25
1946 80c. "Rough Habit" 95 95
1947 $1 "Blossom Lady" . . . . 1·25 1·25
1948 $1.20 "Il Vicolo" . . . . . 1·60 1·60
1949 $1.50 "Horlicks" . . . . . 1·75 2·00
1950 $1.80 "Bonecrusher" . . . . 2·50 2·50
MS1951 Seven sheets, each 162 × 110 mm. (a) No. 1945. (b) No. 1946. (c) No. 1947. (d) No. 1948. (e) No. 1949. (f) No. 1950. (g) Nos. 1945/50 Set of 7 sheets . . . . 16·00 19·00

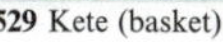

529 Kete (basket) **530** Southern Black-backed Gulls

1996. Maori Crafts. Multicoloured.

1952 40c. Type **529** 50 25
1953 80c. Head of Taiaha (spear) 90 90
1954 $1 Taniko (embroidery) . . 1·25 1·25
1955 $1.20 Pounamu (greenstone) 1·50 1·75
1956 $1.50 Hue (gourd) . . . . . 1·75 2·50
1957 $1.80 Korowai (feather cloak) . . . . 2·00 2·50
See also No. **MS**2049.

1996. Marine Life. Multicoloured. Self-adhesive or ordinary gum.

1968 40c. Type **530** 55 60
1969 40c. Children, sea cucumber and spiny starfish 55 60
1970 40c. Yacht, gull and common shrimps 55 60
1971 40c. Gaudy nudibranch . . 55 60
1972 40c. Large rock crab and clingfish 55 60
1973 40c. Snake skin chiton and red rock crab 55 60
1974 40c. Estuarine triplefin and cat's-eye shell 55 60
1975 40c. Cushion star and sea horses 55 60
1976 40c. Blue-eyed triplefin and Yaldwyn's triplefin . . . 55 60
1977 40c. Common octopus . . . 55 60

1996. "SOUTHPEX '96" Stamp Show, Invercargill. Sheet 100 × 215 mm, containing No. 1929 × 10.

MS1978 40c. × 10 multicoloured 5·50 5·50

531 Fire and Ambulance Services **532** Mt. Egmont, Taranaki

1996. Rescue Services. Multicoloured.

1979 40c. Type **531** 50 40
1980 80c. Civil Defence 90 90
1981 $1 Air-sea rescue . . . . 1·10 1·10
1982 $1.50 Air ambulance and rescue helicopter . . . . 1·60 2·50
1983 $1.80 Mountain rescue and Red Cross . . . . 2·25 2·50

1996. New Zealand Scenery. Self-adhesive. Mult.

1983a 10c. Champagne Pool . . 10 10
1984b 40c. Type **532** 25 30
1985 40c. Piercy Island, Bay of Islands 40 45
1986 40c. Tory Channel, Marlborough Sounds . . 40 45
1987 40c. "Earnslaw" (ferry), Lake Wakatipu 40 45
1988 40c. Lake Matheson . . . 40 45
1989 40c. Fox Glacier 40 45
1990 80c. Doubtful Sound (as No. 1933) 60 65
1990b 90c. Rangitoto Island (as No. 1934a) 60 65
1991 $1 Pohutukawa tree (33 × 22 mm) 85 85
1991b $1.10 Kaikoura Coast . . 80 85

533 Yellow-eyed Penguin **534** Baby in Car Seat

1996. Marine Wildlife. Multicoloured.

1992 40c. Type **533** 50 50
1993 80c. Royal albatross (horiz) 90 90
1994 $1 Great egret (horiz) . . . 95 1·10
1995 $1.20 Flukes of sperm whale (horiz) . . . . 1·10 1·60
1996 $1.50 Fur seals . . . . . . 1·25 2·00
1997 $1.80 Bottlenose dolphin . . 1·50 2·00
See also Nos. **MS**1999 and **MS**2037.

1996. "CHINA '96" 9th International Stamp Exhibition, Peking. Multicoloured.

MS1998 180 × 80 mm. Nos. 1926/8 and 1930 . . . . 1·75 2·00
MS1999 140 × 90 mm. Nos. 1994 and 1996 . . . . 2·75 3·00
No. **MS**1999 also shows designs as Nos. 1992/3, 1995 and 1997, but without face values.

1996. Health Stamps. Child Safety. Multicoloured. Self-adhesive (2003) or ordinary (others) gum.

2000 40c.+5c. Type **534** 50 75
2003 40c.+5c. Type **534** (21½ × 38 mm) 50 75
2001 80c.+5c. Child and adult on zebra crossing . . . . . 90 1·25
MS2002 130 × 90 mm. Nos. 2000/1, each × 2 . . . . 2·75 2·75
Stamps from No. **MS**2002 are slightly larger with "NEW ZEALAND" and the face values redrawn.

1996. "CAPEX '96" International Stamp Exhibition, Toronto. (a) No. **MS**2002 optd **CAPEX '96** and emblem on sheet margin. Mult.

MS2004 Nos. 2000/1, each × 2 . . 3·25 2·75

(b) Sheet 180 × 80 mm, containing Nos. 1931/4.

MS2005 $3 multicoloured . . . . 3·25 3·25

535 Violin

1996. 50th Anniv of New Zealand Symphony Orchestra. Multicoloured.

2006 40c. Type **535** 40 40
2007 80c. French horn . . . . . 1·00 1·50

536 Swimming **537** "Hinemoa"

1996. Centennial Olympic Games, Atlanta. Mult.

2008 40c. Type **536** 50 25
2009 80c. Cycling . . . . 1·25 1·00
2010 $1 Running . . . . 1·25 1·00
2011 $1.50 Rowing . . . . 1·75 3·00
2012 $1.80 Dinghy racing . . . . 2·00 3·00
MS2013 120 × 80 mm. Nos. 2008/12 6·00 6·50

1996. Centenary of New Zealand Cinema. Mult.

2014 40c. Type **537** 50 40
2015 80c. "Broken Barrier" . . . 1·00 1·00
2016 $1.50 "Goodbye Pork Pie" 1·75 2·50
2017 $1.80 "Once Were Warriors" . . . . 1·75 2·50

538 Danyon Loader (swimmer) and Blyth Tait (horseman) **539** Beehive Ballot Box

1996. New Zealand Olympic Gold Medal Winners, Atlanta.

2018 **538** 40c. multicoloured . . . 50 50

1996. New Zealand's First Mixed Member Proportional Representation Election.

2019 **539** 40c. black, red and yellow 50 50

540 King following Star

1996. Christmas. Multicoloured. (a) Size 35 × 35 mm.

2020 40c. Type **540** 50 20
2021 70c. Shepherd and Baby Jesus 80 80
2022 80c. Angel and shepherd . . 90 90
2023 $1 Mary, Joseph and Baby Jesus . . . . 1·25 1·00
2024 $1.50 Mary and Joseph with donkey . . . . 2·00 2·50
2025 $1.80 The Annunciation . . 2·00 2·25

(b) Size 30 × 24 mm. Self-adhesive.

2026 40c. Angels with trumpets 50 80
2027 40c. King with gift 70 50

541 Adzebill

1996. Extinct Birds. Multicoloured. (a) Size 40 × 28 mm.

2028 40c. Type **541** 60 40
2029 80c. South Island whekau ("Laughing Owl") . . . . 1·25 1·25
2030 $1 Piopio . . . . 1·25 1·10
2031 $1.20 Huia . . . . 1·50 1·75
2032 $1.50 Giant eagle . . . . . 1·75 2·50
2033 $1.80 Giant moa . . . . . 2·00 2·50
MS2034 105 × 92 mm. No. 2033 2·00 2·00

(b) Size 30 × 24 mm. Self-adhesive.

2035 40c. Stout-legged wren . . . 70 50

1996. "TAIPEI '96" 10th Asian International Stamp Exhibition, Taiwan. (a) No. **MS**2034 overprinted with "TAIPEI '96" logo on sheet margin. Multicoloured.

MS2036 105 × 92 mm. No. 2033 2·75 2·75

(b) Sheet 140 × 90 mm, containing Nos. 1993 and 1997. Multicoloured.

MS2037 Nos. 1993 and 1997 . . 2·75 2·75
No. **MS**2037 also shows designs as Nos. 1992 and 1994/6, but without face values.

542 Seymour Square, Blenheim **543** Holstein Friesian Cattle

1996. Scenic Gardens. Multicoloured.

2038 40c. Type **542** 50 25
2039 80c. Pukekura Park, New Plymouth . . . . 1·00 1·00
2040 $1 Wintergarden, Auckland 1·25 1·10
2041 $1.50 Botanic Garden, Christchurch . . . . . . 1·75 2·25
2042 $1.80 Marine Parade Gardens, Napier . . . . 1·90 2·25

1997. Cattle Breeds. Multicoloured.

2043 40c. Type **543** 70 40
2044 80c. Jersey . . . . 1·40 1·00
2045 $1 Simmental . . . . 1·60 1·00
2046 $1.20 Ayrshire . . . . 1·90 1·60
2047 $1.50 Angus . . . . 1·90 2·00
2048 $1.80 Hereford . . . . . . 2·25 2·00

1997. "HONG KONG '97" International Stamp Exhibition. Multicoloured.

MS2049 130 × 110 mm. Nos. 1952/3 and 1956 . . . . 3·00 3·00
MS2050 101 × 134 mm. Nos. 2044/5 and 2047 . . . . 3·50 3·50
No. **MS**2050 is also inscribed for the Chinese New Year ("Year of the Ox").

544 James Cook and Sextant

1997. Millennium Series (1st issue). Discoverers of New Zealand. Multicoloured.

2051 40c. Type **544** 80 45
2052 80c. Kupe and ocean-going canoe . . . . 1·00 90
2053 $1 Carved panel depicting Maui (vert) . . . . 1·25 1·00
2054 $1.20 Anchor and "St. Jean Baptiste" (Jean de Surville) (vert) . . . . . 1·75 1·60
2055 $1.50 Dumont d'Urville, crab and "Lastrolabe" . . 2·00 2·00
2056 $1.80 Abel Tasman and illustration from journal 2·00 2·00
See also Nos. 2140/5, 2216/21, 2239/44, 2304/9 and 2310.

545 Rippon Vineyard, Central Otago

1997. New Zealand Vineyards. Multicoloured.

2057 40c. Type **545** 60 25
2058 80c. Te Mata Estate, Hawke's Bay . . . . 1·00 90
2059 $1 Cloudy Bay Vineyard, Marlborough . . . . . . 1·25 1·00
2060 $1.20 Pegasus Bay Vineyard, Waipara . . . . 1·50 1·75
2061 $1.50 Milton Vineyard, Gisborne . . . . 1·75 2·50
2062 $1.80 Goldwater Estate, Waiheke Island . . . . . 1·90 2·50
MS2063 Seven sheets, each 150 × 110 mm. (a) No. 2057. (b) No. 2058. (c) No. 2059. (d) No. 2060. (e) No. 2061. (f) No. 2062. (g) Nos. 2057/62 Set of 7 sheets . . . . 13·00 14·00
See also No. **MS**2081.

546 Cottage Letterbox

1997. Curious Letterboxes. Multicoloured. Self-adhesive.

2064 40c. Type **546** 50 50
2065 40c. Owl letterbox 50 50
2066 40c. Blue whale letterbox . . 50 50
2067 40c. "Kilroy is Back" letterbox 50 50
2068 40c. Nesting box letterbox 50 50
2069 40c. Piper letterbox 50 50
2070 40c. Diver's helmet letterbox 50 50
2071 40c. Aircraft letterbox . . . 50 50
2072 40c. Water tap letterbox . . 50 50
2073 40c. Indian palace letterbox 50 50

547 "The Promised Land", 1948 (Colin McCahon)

1997. Contemporary Paintings by Colin McCahon. Multicoloured.

2074 40c. Type **547** 50 35
2075 $1 "Six Days in Nelson and Canterbury", 1950 . . . 1·10 90
2076 $1.50 "Northland Panels" (detail), 1958 . . . . . 1·75 2·25
2077 $1.80 "Moby Dick is sighted off Muriwai Beach", 1972 2·25 2·25

548 Carrier Pigeon (based on 1899 "Pigeon-gram" local stamp)

1997. Centenary of Great Barrier Island Pigeon Post.
2078 **548** 40c. red 50 70
2079 80c. blue . . . . 90 1·40
See also Nos. **MS**2080 and **MS**2122.

1997. "Pacific '97" International Stamp Exhibition, San Francisco. Multicoloured.
MS2080 137 × 120 mm. Nos. 2078/9, each × 2 . . . . 2·50 2·50
MS2081 140 × 100 mm. Nos. 2057, 2059 and 2061 . . . . 3·00 3·00
No. **MS**2080 is in a triangular format.

549 Rainbow Trout and Red Setter Fly

1997. Fly Fishing. Multicoloured.
2082 40c. Type **549** 40 35
2083 $1 Sea-run brown trout and grey ghost fly 90 90
2084 $1.50 Brook charr and twilight beauty fly . . . . 1·40 2·50
2085 $1.80 Brown trout and Hare and Cooper fly . . . . . 1·60 2·50
See also No. **MS**2172.

550 "Beach Scene" (Fern Petrie)

1997. Children's Health. Children's paintings. Mult.
(a) Ordinary gum.
2086 40c.+5c. Type **550** 45 75
2087 80c.+5c. "Horse-riding on the Waterfront" (Georgia Dumergue) . . . . 80 1·25
MS2088 130 × 90 mm. Nos. 2086/7 and 40c.+5c. As No. 2089 (25 × 36 mm) . . . . 1·75 1·75

(b) Self-adhesive.
2089 40c.+5c. "Picking Fruit" (Anita Pitcher) 70 60

551 The "Overlander" at Paremata, Wellington

1997. Scenic Railway Services. Multicoloured.
2091 40c. Type **551** 50 35
2092 80c. The "Tranz Alpine" in the Southern Alps 90 80
2093 $1 The "Southener" at Canterbury . . . . 1·00 90
2094 $1.20 The "Coastal Pacific" on the Kaikoura Coast . . 1·40 2·00
2095 $1.50 The "Bay Express" at Central Hawke's Bay . . 1·60 2·25
2096 $1.80 The "Kaimai Express" at Tauranga Harbour . . 1·75 2·25
See also No. **MS**2173.

552 Samuel Marsden's "Active", Bay of Islands
553 Huhu Beetle

1997. Christmas. Multicoloured. (a) Ordinary gum.
2097 40c. Type **552** 45 20
2098 70c. Revd. Marsden preaching 75 65
2099 80c. Marsden and Maori chiefs 85 75
2100 $1 Maori family . . . . 1·00 90
2101 $1.50 Handshake and cross 1·60 2·00
2102 $1.80 Pohutukawa (flower) and Rangihoua Bay . . . 1·75 2·00

(b) Smaller design, 29 × 24 mm. Self-adhesive.
2103 40c. Memorial cross, Pohutukawa and Bay of Islands 40 40

1997. Insects. Multicoloured. Self-adhesive.
2104 40c. Type **553** 50 50
2105 40c. Giant land snail . . . 50 50
2106 40c. Giant weta 50 50
2107 40c. Giant dragonfly 50 50
2108 40c. Peripatus 50 50
2109 40c. Cicada 50 50
2110 40c. Puriri moth 50 50
2111 40c. Veined slug 50 50
2112 40c. Katipo 50 50
2113 40c. Flax weevil 50 50

554 "Rosa rugosa"
555 Queen Elizabeth II and Prince Philip

1997. New Zealand–China Joint Issue. Roses. Mult.
2114 40c. Type **554** 50 50
2115 40c. "Aotearoa" 50 50
MS2116 115 × 95 mm. 80c. Nos. 2114/15 . . . . 1·00 1·00

1997. Golden Wedding of Queen Elizabeth and Prince Philip.
2117 **555** 40c. multicoloured . . . 50 50

556 Cartoon Kiwi on Busy-bee

1997. New Zealand Cartoons. "Kiwis Taking on the World". Multicoloured.
2118 40c. Type **556** 60 25
2119 $1 "Let's have 'em for Breakfast" . . . . 1·10 80
2120 $1.50 Kiwi dinghy winning race . . . . 1·40 1·75
2121 $1.80 "CND" emblem cut in forest . . . . 1·75 1·75

1997. "Aupex '97" National Stamp Exhibtion, Auckland. Sheet 140 × 120 mm. Multicoloured.
MS2122 Nos. 2078/9, each × 2 . . 2·10 2·10
No. **MS**2122 is in a triangular format.

1997. International Stamp and Coin Exhibition 1997, Shanghai. Sheet as No. **MS**2116, but redrawn to include "Issued by New Zealand Post to commemorate the International Stamp and Coin Expo. Shanghai, China. 19–23 November 1997" inscr in English and Chinese with additional die-stamped gold frame and logo.
MS2123 115 × 95 mm. Nos. 2114/15 1·00 1·00

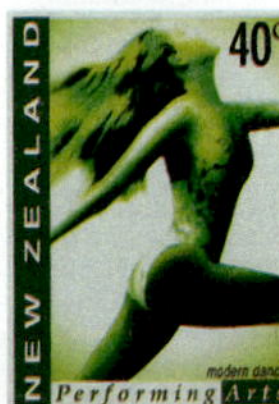

557 Modern Dancer

1998. Performing Arts. Multicoloured.
2124 40c. Type **557** 50 25
2125 80c. Trombone player . . . 85 75
2126 $1 Opera singer . . . . . . 1·50 85
2127 $1.20 Actor . . . . 1·50 1·50
2128 $1.50 Singer . . . . 1·75 2·50
2129 $1.80 Ballet dancer . . . . 2·25 2·50
MS2130 Seven sheets, each 150 × 110 mm. (a) No. 2124. (b) No. 2125. (c) No. 2126. (d) No. 2127. (e) No. 2128. (f) No. 2129. (g) Nos. 2124/9 Set of 7 sheets . . . . 15·00 18·00

558 Museum of New Zealand

1998. Opening of Museum of New Zealand, Wellington. Multicoloured.
2131 40c. Type **558** 30 35
2132 $1.80 Museum, spotted cormorant and silver gull 1·40 1·40

559 Domestic Cat
560 Maoris and Canoe

1998. Cats. Multicoloured.
2133 40c. Type **559** 40 35
2134 80c. Burmese 75 80
2135 $1 Birman 85 80
2136 $1.20 British blue . . . . . 1·00 1·40
2137 $1.50 Persian . . . . 1·25 2·00
2138 $1.80 Siamese . . . . 1·75 2·00

1998. Chinese New Year ("Year of the Tiger"). Multicoloured.
MS2139 100 × 135 mm. Nos. 2133, 2135 and 2138 . . . . 3·00 3·00

1998. Millennium Series (2nd issue). Immigrants. Multicoloured.
2140 40c. Type **560** 35 25
2141 80c. 19th-century European settlers and immigrant ship 75 65
2142 $1 Gold miners and mine 1·00 80
2143 $1.20 Post 1945 European migrants and liner . . . . 1·25 1·10
2144 $1.50 Pacific islanders and church . . . . 1·40 1·60
2145 $1.80 Asian migrant and jumbo jet . . . . 1·60 1·60

561 "With Great Respect to the Mehmetcik" Statue, Gallipoli
562 Mother and Son Hugging

1998. Joint Issue New Zealand–Turkey. Memorial Statues. Multicoloured.
2146 40c. Type **561** 40 35
2147 $1.80 "Mother with Children", National War Memorial, Wellington . . 1·25 1·40

1998. "Stay in Touch" Greetings Stamps. Mult. Self-adhesive.
2148 40c. Type **562** 35 35
2149 40c. Couple on beach . . . 35 35
2150 40c. Boys striking hands . . 35 35
2151 40c. Grandmother and grandson 35 35
2152 40c. Young boys in pool (horiz) 35 35
2153 40c. "I'LL MISS YOU ... PLEASE WRITE" (horiz) 35 35
2154 40c. Symbolic couple and clouds (horiz) 35 35
2155 40c. Young couple kissing (horiz) 35 35
2156 40c. Couple sat on sofa (horiz) 35 35
2157 40c. Maoris rubbing noses (horiz) 35 35

563 Mount Cook or Aorangi
565 Girl wearing Lifejacket

564 "Wounded at Cassino"

1998. Centenary of 1898 Pictorial Stamps. Designs as T **23/26** and **28/35** with modern face values as T **563**.
2158 **563** 40c. brown 50 50
2159 **24** 40c. blue and brown . . 50 50
2160 **25** 40c. brown 50 50
2161 **28** 40c. brown 50 50
2162 **29** 40c. red 50 50
2163 **31** 40c. green 50 50
2164 **32** 40c. blue 50 50
2165 **34** 40c. orange 50 50
2166 **26** 80c. blue (inscr "LAKE WAKITIPU") (35 × 23 mm) 85 75
2167 80c. blue (inscr "LAKE WAKATIPU") (35 × 23 mm) 85 75
2168 **30** $1 brown (23 × 35 mm) 95 85
2169 **33** $1.20 brown (35 × 23 mm) . . . . 1·00 1·60
2170 **35** $1.50 green (35 × 23 mm) 1·25 1·75
2171 – $1.80 red (as No. 329) (23 × 35 mm) . . . . 1·40 1·75
See also Nos. **MS**2188 and **MS**2214.

1998. "Israel '98" World Stamp Exhibition, Tel Aviv. Multicoloured.
MS2172 112 × 90 mm. Nos. 2082 and 2085 . . . . 2·50 2·75
MS2173 125 × 100 mm. Nos. 2092/3 and 2095 . . . . 4·00 4·00

1998. Paintings by Peter McIntyre. Multicoloured.
2174 40c. Type **564** 35 30
2175 $1 "The Cliffs of Rangitikei" 85 75
2176 $1.50 "Maori Children, King Country" . . . . 1·25 1·40
2177 $1.80 "The Anglican Church, Kakahi" . . . . 1·40 1·50
See also No. **MS**2215.

1998. Children's Health. Water Safety. Mult.
(a) Ordinary gum.
2178 40c.+5c. Type **565** 40 50
2179 80c.+5c. Boy learning to swim 60 75
MS2180 125 × 90 mm. Nos. 2178/9, each × 2 . . . . 2·00 2·00

(b) Smaller design, 25 × 37 mm. Self-adhesive.
2181 40c.+5c. Type **565** 30 50

566 Sunrise near Cambridge

1998. Scenic Skies. Multicoloured.
2182 40c. Type **566** 40 20
2183 80c. Clouds over Lake Wanaka 75 65
2184 $1 Sunset over Mount Maunganui 85 75
2185 $1.20 Rain clouds over South Bay, Kaikoura . . 1·00 1·10
2186 $1.50 Sunset near Statue of Wairaka, Whakatane Harbour . . . . 1·40 1·25
2187 $1.80 Cloud formation above Lindis Pass . . . . 1·60 1·75
See also No. **MS**2245.

1998. "TARAPEX '98" National Stamp Exhibition, New Plymouth.
MS2188 90 × 80 mm. Nos. 2166/7 1·60 1·75

567 Virgin Mary and Christ Child
568 Lemon and Mineral Water Bottle, Paeroa

1998. Christmas. Multicoloured. (a) Ordinary gum.
2189 40c. Type **567** 35 15
2190 70c. Shepherds approaching the stable 55 55
2191 80c. Virgin Mary, Joseph and Christ Child 65 65
2192 $1 Magi with gift of gold 80 80
2193 $1.50 Three magi . . . . . 1·25 1·40
2194 $1.80 Angel and shepherds 1·40 1·50

(b) Smaller design, 24 × 29 mm. Self-adhesive.
2195 40c. Type **567** 35 30

1998. Town Icons. Multicoloured. Self-adhesive.
2196 40c. Type **568** 35 35
2197 40c. Carrot, Ohakune . . . 35 35
2198 40c. Brown Trout, Gore (25 × 36 mm) 35 35
2199 40c. Crayfish, Kaikoura (25 × 36 mm) 35 35
2200 40c. Sheep-shearer, Te Kuiti (25 × 36 mm) 35 35
2201 40c. "Pania of the Reef" (Maori legend), Napier (25 × 36 mm) 35 35
2202 40c. Paua Shell, Riverton (24 × 29 mm) 35 35
2203 40c. Kiwifruit, Te Puke (24 × 29 mm) 35 35

2204 40c. Border Collie, Lake Tekapo (24 × 29 mm) 35 35
2205 40c. "Big Cow", Hawera (24 × 29 mm) 35 35

569 Moonfish

571 "Fuchsia excorticata"

570 Wellington in 1841 and 1998

1998. International Year of the Ocean. Mult.
2206 40c. Type **569** 35 50
2207 40c. Mako shark 35 50
2208 40c. Yellowfin tuna 35 50
2209 40c. Giant squid 35 50
2210 80c. Striped marlin 60 70
2211 80c. Porcupine fish 60 70
2212 80c. Eagle ray 60 70
2213 80c. Sandager's wrasse 60 70
Nos. 2206/9 and 2210/13 respectively were printed together, se-tenant, forming composite designs.
See also Nos. **MS**2246 and **MS**2277.

1998. "Italia '98" International Philatelic Exhibition, Milan. Multicoloured.
MS2214 90 × 80 mm. Nos. 2167 and 2170 3·00 3·25
MS2215 112 × 90 mm. Nos. 2176/7 2·00 2·25

1998. Millennium Series (3rd issue). Urban Transformations. Multicoloured.
2216 40c. Type **570** 70 30
2217 80c. Auckland in 1852 and 1998 95 55
2218 $1 Christchurch in 1851 and 1998 1·10 70
2219 $1.20 Westport in 1919 and 1998 1·40 1·25
2220 $1.50 Tauranga in 1880 and 1998 1·60 1·50
2221 $1.80 Dunedin in 1862 and 1998 1·75 1·75

1999. Flowering Trees of New Zealand. Mult.
2222 40c. Type **571** 40 20
2223 80c. "Solanum laciniatum" 65 55
2224 $1 "Sophora tetraptera" 75 70
2225 $1.20 "Carmichaelia stevensonii" 85 1·00
2226 $1.50 "Olearia angustfolia" 1·25 1·60
2227 $1.80 "Metrosideros umbellata" 1·40 1·60
See also No. **MS**2286.

572 Civic Theatre, Auckland

573 Labrador Puppy and Netherland Dwarf Rabbit

1999. Art Deco Architecture. Multicoloured.
2228 40c. Type **572** 50 20
2229 $1 Masonic Hotel, Napier 2·00 80
2230 $1.50 Medical and Dental Chambers, Hastings 1·40 1·60
2231 $1.80 Buller County Chambers, Westport 1·40 1·60

1999. Popular Pets. Multicoloured.
2232 40c. Type **573** 40 30
2233 80c. Netherland dwarf rabbit 80 55
2234 $1 Tabby kitten and Netherland dwarf rabbit 90 70
2235 $1.20 Lamb 1·25 1·25
2236 $1.50 Welsh pony 1·40 1·50
2237 $1.80 Two budgerigars 1·50 1·60
MS2238 100 × 135 mm. Nos. 2232/4 1·75 1·75
No. **MS**2238 also commemorates the Chinese New Year ("Year of the Rabbit").
See also No. **MS**2287.

574 Toy Fire Engine and Marbles

1999. Millennium Series (4th issue). Nostalgia. Multicoloured.
2239 40c. Type **574** 40 30
2240 80c. Commemorative tin of biscuits and cereal packet 70 55
2241 $1 Tram, tickets and railway crockery 85 70
2242 $1.20 Radio and "Woman's Weekly" magazine 1·00 1·25
2243 $1.50 Coins, postcards and stamps 1·25 1·40
2244 $1.80 Lawn mower and seed packets 1·40 1·60

1999. "Australia '99" World Stamp Exhibition, Melbourne. Multicoloured.
MS2245 130 × 70 mm. Nos. 2182 and 2187 1·90 1·90
MS2246 130 × 90 mm. Nos. 2206/7 and 2210/11 2·00 2·00

575 Hunter Building, Victoria University

576 Auckland Blues Player kicking Ball

1999. Centenary of Victoria University, Wellington.
2247 **575** 40c. multicoloured 30 30

1999. New Zealand U-Bix Rugby Super 12 Championship. Multicoloured. Ordinary or self-adhesive gum.
2248 40c. Type **576** 40 40
2249 40c. Auckland Blues player being tackled 40 40
2250 40c. Chiefs player being tackled 40 40
2251 40c. Chiefs lineout jump 40 40
2252 40c. Wellington Hurricanes player being tackled 40 40
2253 40c. Wellington Hurricanes player passing ball 40 40
2254 40c. Canterbury Crusaders lineout jump 40 40
2255 40c. Canterbury Crusaders player kicking ball 40 40
2256 40c. Otago Highlanders player diving for try 40 40
2257 40c. Otago Highlanders player running with ball 40 40

577 "The Lake, Tuai"

1999. Paintings by Doris Lusk. Multicoloured.
2268 40c. Type **577** 35 30
2269 $1 "The Pumping Station" 80 70
2270 $1.50 "Arcade Awning, St. Mark's Square, Venice (2)" 1·10 1·25
2271 $1.80 "Tuam St. II" 1·25 1·40
See also No. **MS**2276.

578 "A Lion in the Meadow" (Margaret Mahy)

1999. Children's Health. Children's Books. Mult. (a) Ordinary gum.
2272 40c.+5c. Type **578** 55 55
2273 80c.+5c. "Greedy Cat" (Joy Cowley) 70 70
MS2274 130 × 90 mm. 40c. + 5c. Type **578**; 40c. + 5c. As No. 2275 (37 × 25 mm); 80c. + 5c. No. 2273 1·40 1·40

(b) Smaller design, 37 × 25 mm. Self-adhesive.
2275 40c.+5c. "Hairy Maclary's Bone" (Lynley Dodd) (37 × 25 mm) 50 50

1999. "PhilexFrance '99" International Stamp Exhibiton, Paris. Multicoloured.
MS2276 112 × 90 mm. Nos. 2268 and 2271 1·75 1·75
MS2277 130 × 90 mm. Nos. 2208/9 and 2212/13 2·00 2·00

579 "APEC"

1999. 10th Asia-Pacific Economic Co-operation Meeting, New Zealand.
2278 **579** 40c. multicoloured 30 30

580 West Ruggedy Beach, Stewart Island

1999. Scenic Walks. Multicoloured.
2279 40c. Type **580** 35 30
2280 80c. Ice lake, Butler Valley, Westland 60 55
2281 $1 Tonga Bay, Abel Tasman National Park 75 70
2282 $1.20 East Matakitaki Valley, Nelson Lakes National Park 85 90
2283 $1.50 Great Barrier Island 1·10 1·25
2284 $1.80 Mt. Egmont, Taranki 1·40 1·40
MS2285 Seven sheets, each 150 × 110 mm. (a) No. 2279. (b) No. 2280. (c) No. 2281. (d) No. 2282. (e) No. 2283. (f) No. 2284. (g) Nos. 2279/84 Set of 7 sheets 11·00 12·00
See also No. **MS**2295.

1999. "China '99" International Stamp Exhibition, Peking. Multicoloured.
MS2286 112 × 90 mm. Nos. 2222/3 1·00 1·00
MS2287 100 × 135 mm. Nos. 2232 and 2234 1·00 1·00

581 Baby Jesus with Animals

1999. Christmas. Multicoloured. (a) Ordinary gum.
2288 40c. Type **581** 30 15
2289 80c. Virgin Mary praying 65 55
2290 $1.10 Mary and Joseph on way to Bethlehem 80 75
2291 $1.20 Angel playing harp 85 80
2292 $1.50 Three shepherds 1·10 1·25
2293 $1.80 Three wise men with gifts 1·40 1·40

(b) Smaller design, 23 × 28 mm. Self-adhesive.
2294 40c. Type **581** 30 30

1999. "Palmpex '99" National Stamp Exhibition, Palmerston North. Sheet 130 × 90 mm, containing No. 2284. Multicoloured.
MS2295 $1.80, Mt. Egmont, Taranaki 1·40 1·40

582 "P" Class Dinghy

1999. Yachting. Multicoloured. (a) Size 28 × 39 mm. Ordinary gum.
2296 40c. Type **582** 35 15
2297 80c. Laser dinghy 60 55
2298 $1.10 18ft skiff 80 75
2299 $1.20 Hobie catamaran 85 80
2300 $1.50 Racing yacht 1·10 1·25
2301 $1.80 Cruising yacht 1·25 1·40
MS2302 125 × 100 mm. Nos. 2296/301 4·50 5·00

(b) Size 23 × 28 mm. Self-adhesive.
2303 40c. Optimist dinghy 30 30

583 Group of Victorian Women (female suffrage, 1893)

1999. Millenium Series (5th issue). New Zealand Achievements. Multicoloured.
2304 40c. Type **583** 40 15
2305 80c. Richard Pearse's aircraft (powered flight, 1903) 75 55
2306 $1.10 Lord Rutherford (splitting the atom, 1919) 85 85
2307 $1.20 Boat on lake (invention of jet boat, 1953) 90 90
2308 $1.50 Sir Edmund Hillary (conquest of Everest, 1953) 1·40 1·50
2309 $1.80 Protesters and warship (nuclear free zone, 1987) 1·40 1·60

584 Sunrise and World Map

2000. Millennium Series (6th issue).
2310 **584** 40c. multicoloured 65 30

585 Araiteuru (North Island sea guardian)

586 Chilly Bin (cool box)

2000. Chinese New Year ("Year of the Dragon"). Maori Spirits and Guardians. Multicoloured.
2311 40c. Type **585** 35 15
2312 80c. Kurangaituku (giant bird woman) 60 55
2313 $1.10 Te Hoata and Te Pupu (volcanic taniwha sisters) 80 75
2314 $1.20 Patupaiarehe (mountain fairy tribe) 85 80
2315 $1.50 Te Ngarara-huarau (giant first lizard) 1·10 1·25
2316 $1.80 Tuhirangi (South Island sea guardian) 1·25 1·40
MS2317 125 × 90 mm. Nos. 2315/16 2·50 2·50

2000. New Zealand Life (2nd series). Each including a cartoon kiwi. Multicoloured. Self-adhesive.
2318 40c. Type **586** 35 35
2319 40c. Pipis (seafood delicacy) 35 35
2320 40c. "Lilo" 35 35
2321 40c. Chocolate fish 35 35
2322 40c. Bach or Crib (holiday home) 35 35
2323 40c. Barbeque 35 35
2324 40c. Ug (fur-lined) boots 35 35
2325 40c. Anzac biscuits 35 35
2326 40c. Hot dog 35 35
2327 40c. Meat pie 35 35

2000. "The Stamp Show 2000" International Stamp Exhibition, London. Sheet 110 × 80 mm, containing Nos. 1934b and 1934e/f. Multicoloured.
MS2328 $1 Taiaroa Head; $2 Great Barrier Island; $3 Cape kidnappers 4·00 4·50

587 Volkswagen Beetle

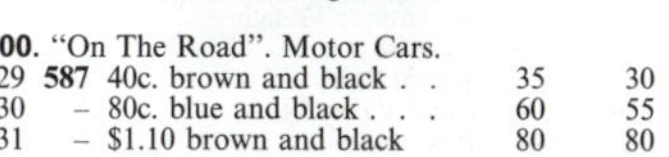

2000. "On The Road". Motor Cars.
2329 **587** 40c. brown and black 35 30
2330 – 80c. blue and black 60 55
2331 – $1.10 brown and black 80 80

2332 – $1.20 green and black . . 85 85
2333 – $1.50 brown and black 1·10 1·25
2334 – $1.80 lilac and black . . 1·25 1·40
DESIGNS: 80c. Ford Zephyr Mk I; $1.10, Morris Mini Mk II; $1.20, Holden HQ Kingswood; $1.50, Honda Civic; $1.80, Toyota Corolla.

588 Lake Lyndon, Canterbury

2000. Scenic Reflections. Multicoloured.
2336 40c. Type **588** 50 30
2337 80c. Lion (cruising launch) on Lake Wakatipu . . . 85 55
2338 $1.10 Eruption of Mount Ruapehu . . . . 1·00 80
2339 $1.20 Rainbow Mountain Scenic Reserve, Rotorua 1·10 85
2340 $1.50 Tairua Harbour, Coromandel Peninsula . . 1·40 1·50
2341 $1.80 Lake Alexandrina . . 1·50 1·50
See also No. **MS**2368.

2000. "EXPO 2000" World Stamp Exhibition, Anaheim, U.S.A. Sheet 132 × 78 mm, containing Nos. 1490, 1490b/c and 2090/a.
MS2342 $1 red; $1 blue; $1 violet; $1 green; $1.10 gold . . . . . . 3·00 3·25

589 Lady Elizabeth Bowes-Lyon and Glamis Castle, 1907

2000. Queen Elizabeth the Queen Mother's 100th Birthday. Multicoloured.
2343 40c. Type **589** 60 30
2344 $1.10 Fishing in New Zealand, 1966 . . . . . 1·10 70
2345 $1.80 Holding bunch of daisies, 1997 . . . . . . 1·75 1·60
MS2346 115 × 60 mm. Nos. 2343/5 2·40 2·40

590 Rowing

2000. Olympic Games, Sydney, and other Sporting Events. Multicoloured.
2347 40c. Type **590** 35 30
2348 80c. Show jumping 65 55
2349 $1.10 Cycling 80 80
2350 $1.20 Triathlon 85 85
2351 $1.50 Bowling . . . . . . 1·10 1·25
2352 $1.80 Netball . . . . 1·25 1·40
Nos. 2351/2 omit the Olympic logo.

591 Virgin Mary and Baby Jesus

2000. Christmas. Multicoloured. (a) Ordinary gum.
2353 40c. Type **591** 35 30
2354 80c. Mary and Joseph on way to Bethlehem 60 55
2355 $1.10 Baby Jesus in manger 85 80
2356 $1.20 Archangel Gabriel . . 95 90
2357 $1.50 Shepherd with lamb 1·25 1·40
2358 $1.80 Three Wise Men . . . 1·40 1·60

(b) Self-adhesive. Size 30 × 25 mm.
2359 40c. Type **591** 30 30

592 Geronimo (teddy bear)

2000. Children's Health. Teddy Bears and Dolls. Multicoloured. (a) Ordinary gum.
2360 40c.+5c. Type **592** 45 50
2361 80c.+5c. Antique French doll and wooden Schoenhut doll 70 80
2362 $1.10 Chad Valley bear . . 75 70
2363 $1.20 Poppy (doll) 80 80
2364 $1.50 Swanni (large bear) and Dear John (small bear) . . . . 90 1·25
2365 $1.80 Lia (doll) and bear . . 1·10 1·25
MS2366 100 × 60 mm. 40c. + 5c. Type **592**; 80c. + 5c. As No. 2361 1·00 1·00

(b) Self-adhesive. Size 29 × 24 mm.
2367 40c.+5c. Type **592** 35 40

2000. "CANPEX 2000" National Stamp Exhibition, Christchurch. Sheet 95 × 80 mm, containing Nos. 2336 and 2341. Multicoloured.
MS2368 40c. Type **588**; $1.80 Lake Alexandrina . . . . 1·40 1·50

593 Lesser Kestrel

2000. Threatened Birds. Multicoloured.
2369 40c. Type **593** 50 30
2370 40c. Yellow-fronted parakeet 50 30
2371 80c. New Zealand stilt ("Black Stilt") 70 55
2372 $1.10 Fernbird ("Stewart Island Fernbird") 75 70
2373 $1.20 Kakapo . . . . . . 90 1·00
2374 $1.50 Weka rail ("North Island Weka") . . . . . 1·10 1·25
2375 $1.80 Brown kiwi ("Okarito Brown Kiwi") . . . . . 1·25 1·25
Nos. 2369 and 2375 form a joint issue with France.
See also No. **MS**2393.

594 *Sonoma* (mail ship) at Quay

2001. Moving the Mail in the 20th Century.
2376 **594** 40c. purple and red . . . 30 35
2377 – 40c. green 30 35
2378 – 40c. agate 30 35
2379 – 40c. blue 30 35
2380 – 40c. brown 30 35
2381 – 40c. purple 30 35
2382 – 40c. black and cinnamon 30 35
2383 – 40c. multicoloured 30 35
2384 – 40c. mauve 30 35
2385 – 40c. multicoloured . . . 30 35
DESIGNS: No. 2377, Stagecoach crossing river; 2378, Early postal lorry; 2379, Paddle steamer on River Wanganui; 2380, Railway T.P.O.; 2381, Loading mail through nose door of aircraft; 2382, Postwoman with bicycle; 2383, Loading lorry by fork-lift truck; 2384, Aircraft at night; 2385, Computer mouse.
See also No. **MS**2424.

595 Green Turtle

2001. Chinese New Year ("Year of the Snake"). Marine Reptiles. Multicoloured.
2386 40c. Type **595** 55 30
2387 80c. Leathery turtle 80 55
2388 90c. Loggerhead turtle . . . 80 60
2389 $1.30 Hawksbill turtle . . . 1·25 1·10
2390 $1.50 Banded sea-snake . . 1·50 1·25
2391 $2 Yellow-bellied sea-snake . . 1·60 1·40
MS2392 125 × 90 mm. Nos. 2390/1 2·75 2·75

2001. "Hong Kong 2001" Stamp Exhibition. Sheet 100 × 80 mm, containing Nos. 2374/5. Multicoloured.
MS2393 $1.50, North Island weka; $1.80, Okarito brown kiwi . . 2·50 2·50

596 Camellia

2001. Garden Flowers. Multicoloured.
2394 40c. Type **596** 30 25
2395 80c. Siberian iris 60 55
2396 90c. Daffodil 65 60
2397 $1.30 Chrysanthemum . . . 85 1·10
2398 $1.50 Sweet pea . . . . . . 90 1·25
2399 $2 Petunia . . . . 1·10 1·25
MS2400 95 × 125 mm. Nos. 2394/9 4·00 4·25

2001. Invercargill "Stamp Odyssey 2001" National Stamp Exhibition. Sheet 133 × 81 mm, containing Nos. 1934a/d. Multicoloured.
MS2401 90c. Rangitoto Island; $1 Taiaroa Head; $1.10, Kaikoura Coast; $1.30, Lake Camp, South Canterbury . . . . 2·50 2·75

597 Greenstone Amulet

2001. Art from Nature. Multicoloured.
2402 40c. Type **597** 35 30
2403 80c. Oamaru stone sculpture 65 55
2404 90c. Paua ornament 70 60
2405 $1.30 Kauri ornament . . . 95 1·10
2406 $1.50 Flax basket . . . . . 1·10 1·25
2407 $2 Silver-dipped fern frond 1·25 1·25
Nos. 2402/7 were each printed in sheets of 25 (5 × 5) in which the stamps were included in four different orientations so that four blocks of 4 in each sheet showed the complete work of art.

598 Douglas DC-3

2001. Aircraft. Multicoloured.
2408 40c. Type **598** 35 30
2409 80c. Fletcher FU24 Topdresser 65 55
2410 90c. De Havilland DH82A Tiger Moth 70 60
2411 $1.30 Fokker FVIIb/3m Southern Cross . . . . . 90 1·10
2412 $1.50 De Havilland DH100 Vampire . . . . 1·00 1·25
2413 $2 Boeing & Westervelt seaplane . . . . 1·25 1·25

599 Parcel

2001. Greetings Stamps. Multicoloured.
2414 40c. Type **599** 25 30
2415 40c. Trumpet 25 30
2416 40c. Heart and ribbon . . . 25 30
2417 40c. Balloons 25 30
2418 40c. Flower 25 30
2419 90c. Photo frame 60 65
2420 90c. Fountain pen and letter 60 65
2421 90c. Candles on cake . . . 60 65
2422 90c. Star biscuits 60 65
2423 90c. Candle and flowers . . 60 65

2001. "Belgica 2001" International Stamp Exhibition, Brussels. Sheet 180 × 90 mm, containing Nos. 2376/85. Multicoloured.
MS2424 40c. × 10, Nos. 2376/85 3·50 4·00

600 Bungy Jumping, Queenstown

2001. Tourism Centenary. Multicoloured. (a) Size 38 × 32 mm. Ordinary gum.
2425 40c. Type **600** 25 30
2426 80c. Maori Canoe on Lake Rotoiti 45 50
2427 90c. Sightseeing from Mount Alfred 55 60
2428 $1.30 Fishing on Glenorchy river 75 80
2429 $1.50 Sea-kayaking in Abel Tasman National Park . . 85 90
2430 $2 Fiordland National Park 1·10 1·25

(b). Size 30 × 25 mm. Self-adhesive.
2431 40c. Type **600** 35 35
2432 90c. Sightseeing from Mount Alfred 65 70
2433 $1.50 Sea-kayaking in Abel Tasman National Park . . 1·25 1·40

2001. "Philanippon '01" International Stamp Exhibition, Tokyo. Sheet 90 × 82 mm, containing Nos. 2429/30. Multicoloured.
MS2434 $1.50 Sea-kayaking in Abel Tasman National Park; $2 Fiordland National Park . . . 2·50 2·75

601 Family cycling

2001. Children's Health. Cycling. Multicoloured. (a) Size 39 × 29 mm. Ordinary gum.
2435 40c. + 5c. Type **601** 40 35
2436 90c. + 5c. Mountain bike stunt 85 75
MS2437 Circular, 100 mm diameter. Nos. 2435/6 . . . . 1·00 1·10

(b) Size 29 × 231/2. Self-adhesive.
2438 40c. + 5c. Boy on bike . . . 40 30

602 "When Christ was born of Mary free"

2001. Christmas. Carols. Multicoloured. (a) Size 29 × 34 mm. Ordinary gum.
2439 40c. Type **602** 40 20
2440 80c. "Away in a manger" 70 40
2441 90c. "Joy to the world" . . 80 55
2442 $1.30 "Angels we have heard on high" . . . . 1·10 80
2443 $1.50 "O holy night" . . . 1·25 90
2444 $2 "While shepherds watched" . . . . 1·50 1·50

(b) Size 21 × 26 mm. Self-adhesive.
2445 40c. Type **602** 35 30

603 Queen Elizabeth II at State Opening of Parliament, 1954

605 Gandalf (Sir Ian McKellen) and Saruman (Christopher Lee)

604 Rockhopper Penguins

2001. Queen Elizabeth II's 75th Birthday. Multicoloured (except 40c.).
2446 40c. Type **603** (black and silver) 50 30
2447 80c. Queen Elizabeth II on walkabout, 1970 . . . 80 50
2448 90c. Queen Elizabeth II wearing Maori cloak, 1977 . . . . 90 55
2449 $1.30 Queen Elizabeth II with bouquet, 1986 . . . 1·25 80
2450 $1.50 Queen Elizabeth II at Commonwealth Games, 1990 . . . . 1·40 90
2451 $2 Queen Elizabeth II, 1997 1·60 1·25

2001. New Zealand Penguins. Multicoloured.
2452 40c. Type **604** 50 30
2453 80c. Little penguin ("Little Blue Penguin") 75 50

2454 90c. Snares Island penguins ("Snares Crested Penguins") 85 60
2455 $1.30 Big-crested penguins ("Erect-crested Penguins") 1·10 85
2456 $1.50 Victoria penguins ("Fiordland Crested Penguins") . . . . 1·25 1·10
2457 $2 Yellow-eyed penguins . . 1·60 1·40

2001. Making of *The Lord of the Rings* Film Trilogy (1st issue): *The Fellowship of the Ring.* Multicoloured. (a) Designs 24 × 50 mm or 50 × 24 mm.

2458 40c. Type **605** 75 30
2459 80c. The Lady Galadriel (Cate Blanchett) . . . . 1·40 60
2460 90c. Sam Gamgee (Sean Austin) and Frodo Baggins (Elijah Wood) (horiz) . . . . 1·50 75
2461 $1.30 Guardian of Rivendell 2·25 2·00
2462 $1.50 Strider (Viggo Mortensen) . . . . 2·50 2·50
2463 $2 Boromir (Sean Bean) (horiz) . . . . 3·25 3·50

(b) Designs 26 × 37 mm or 37 × 26 mm. Self-adhesive.

2464 40c. Type **605** 40 30
2465 80c. The Lady Galadriel (Cate Blanchett) 60 50
2466 90c. Sam Gamgee (Sean Austin) and Frodo Baggins (Elijah Wood) (horiz) 75 75
2467 $1.30 Guardian of Rivendell 1·25 1·50
2468 $1.50 Strider (Viggo Mortensen) . . . . 1·50 2·00
2469 $2 Boromir (Sean Bean) (horiz) . . . . 1·60 2·50

See also No. **MS**2490, 2652/63 and 2713/25.

606 "Christian Cullen" (harness racing)

2002. Chinese New Year ("Year of the Horse"). New Zealand Racehorses. Multicoloured.

2470 40c. Type **606** 30 30
2471 80c. "Lyell Creek" (harness racing) 50 50
2472 90c. "Yulestar" (harness racing) 55 55
2473 $1.30 "Sunline" 80 80
2474 $1.50 "Ethereal" 90 90
2475 $2 "Zabeel" . . . . 1·25 1·25
MS2476 127 × 90 mm. Nos. 2473/4 3·75 4·25

607 *Hygrocybe rubrocarnosa*

608 War Memorial Museum, Auckland

2002. Fungi. Multicoloured.

2477 40c. Type **607** 45 30
2478 80c. *Entoloma hochstetteri* 75 50
2479 90c. *Aseroe rubra* 85 60
2480 $1.30 *Hericium coralloides* 1·10 1·10
2481 $1.50 *Thaxterogaster porphyreus* . . . . 1·25 1·40
2482 $2 *Ramaria aureorhiza* . . . 1·60 1·60
MS2483 114 × 104 mm. Nos. 2477/82 5·50 5·50

2002. Architectural Heritage. Multicoloured.

2484 40c. Type **608** 35 30
2485 80c. Stone Store, Kerikeri (25 × 30 mm) 60 50
2486 90c. Arts Centre, Christchurch (50 × 30 mm) 65 55
2487 $1.30 Government Buildings, Wellington (50 × 30 mm) 95 80
2488 $1.50 Dunedin Railway Station (25 × 30 mm) . . 1·10 90
2489 $2 Sky Tower, Auckland . . 1·25 1·25

2002. "Northpex 2002" Stamp Exhibition. Sheet 130 × 95 mm, containing Nos. 2458, 2461 and 2463. Multicoloured.

MS2490 40c. Gandalf (Sir Ian Mckellen) and Saruman (Christopher Lee); $1.30 Guardian of Rivendell; $2 Boromir (Sean Bean) (horiz) . . . . 4·25 4·25

No. **MS**2490 was sold at face value.

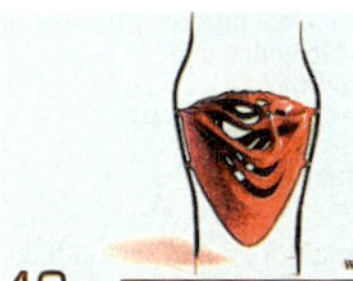

609 "Starfish Vessel" (wood sculpture) (Graeme Priddle)

2002. Artistic Crafts. Joint Issue with Sweden. Multicoloured.

2491 40c. Type **609** 35 30
2492 40c. Flax basket (Willa Rogers) (37 × 29 mm) . . 35 30
2493 80c. "Catch II" (clay bowl) (Raewyn Atkinson) . . . 55 50
2494 90c. "Vessel Form" (silver brooch) (Gavin Hitchings) 60 55
2495 $1.30 Glass towers from "Immigration" series (Emma Camden) 85 85
2496 $1.50 "Pacific Rim" (clay vessel) (Merilyn Wiseman) 95 1·10
2497 $2 Glass vase (Ola and Maria Höglund) (37 × 29 mm) . . . . . . 1·25 1·40

Nos. 2492 and 2497 are additionally inscribed "JOINT ISSUE WITH SWEDEN".

610 *Brodie* (Anna Poland, Cardinal McKeefry School) (National Winner)

2002. Children's Book Festival. Stamp Design Competition. Designs illustrating books. Multicoloured.

2498 40c. Type **610** 30 35
2499 40c. *The Last Whale* (Hee Su Kim, Glendowie Primary School) 30 35
2500 40c. *Scarface Claw* (Jayne Bruce, Rangiora Borough School) 30 35
2501 40c. *Which New Zealand Bird?* (Teigan Stafford-Bush, Ararimu School) . . 30 35
2502 40c. *Which New Zealand Bird?* (Hazel Gilbert, Gonville School) 30 35
2503 40c. *The Plight of the Penguin* (Gerard Mackle, Temuka High School) . . 30 35
2504 40c. *Scarface Claw* (Maria Rodgers, Salford School) 30 35
2505 40c. *Knocked for Six* (Paul Read, Ararimu School) 30 35
2506 40c. *Grandpa's Shorts* (Jessica Hitchings, Ashleigh Bree, Malyna Sengdara and Aniva Kini, Glendene Primary School) 30 35
2507 40c. *Which New Zealand Bird?* (Olivia Duncan, Takapuna Intermediate School) 30 35
MS2508 230 × 90 mm. Nos. 2498/507 2·75 3·25

611 Queen Elizabeth the Queen Mother, 1992

2002. Queen Elizabeth the Queen Mother Commemoration.

2509 **611** $2 multicoloured . . . . 1·75 1·60

612 Tongaporutu Cliffs, Taranaki

2002. Coastlines. Multicoloured. (a) Size 38 × 29 mm. Ordinary gum.

2510 40c. Type **612** 25 30
2511 80c. Lottin Point, East Cape 50 55
2512 90c. Curio Bay, Catlins . . 60 65
2513 $1.30 Kaikoura Coast . . . 85 90
2514 $1.50 Meybille Bay, West Coast . . . . 95 1·00
2515 $2 Papanui Point, Raglan 1·25 1·40

(b) Size 28 × 21 mm. Self-adhesive.

2516 40c. Type **612** 30 30
2517 90c. Curio Bay, Catlins . . 65 75
2518 $1.50 Meybille Bay, West Coast . . . . 1·10 1·40

613 Basket of Fruit

2002. Children's Health. Healthy Eating. Multicoloured. (a) Ordinary gum.

2519 40c.+5c. Type **613** 50 55
2520 90c.+5c. Selection of vegetables 75 80
MS2521 90 × 75 mm. Nos. 2519/20 and as No. 2522 (22 × 26 mm) 1·75 2·00

(b) Self-adhesive.

2522 40c.+5c. Fruit and vegetables (22 × 26 mm) 30 35

2002. "Amphilex 2002" International Stamp Exhibition, Amsterdam. Sheet 130 × 95 mm, containing Nos. 2462/3. Multicoloured.

MS2523 $1.50 Strider (Viggo Mortensen); $2 Boromir (Sean Bean) (horiz) . . . . 2·00 2·00

No. **MS**2523 was sold at face value.

614 St. Werenfried, Tokaanu

2002. Christmas. Church Interiors. Multicoloured. (a) Size 35 × 35 mm. Ordinary gum.

2524 40c. Type **614** 25 30
2525 80c. St. David's, Christchurch 50 55
2526 90c. Orthodox Church of Transfiguration of Our Lord, Masterton 60 65
2527 $1.30 Cathedral of the Holy Spirit, Palmerston North 85 90
2528 $1.50 St. Paul's Cathedral, Wellington . . . . . . 95 1·00
2529 $2 Cathedral of the Blessed Sacrament, Christchurch 1·25 1·40

(b) Size 25 × 30 mm. Self-adhesive.

2530 40c. St. Werenfried, Tokaanu 30 30

615 *KZ 1* (racing yacht)

2002. Racing and Leisure Craft. Multicoloured.

2531 40c. Type **615** 30 35
2532 80c. *High 5* (ocean racing yacht) 65 55
2533 90c. *Gentle Spirit* (sports fishing and diving boat) 75 70
2534 $1.30 *North Star* (luxury motor cruiser) . . . . . 1·00 1·00
2535 $1.50 *Ocean Runner* (powerboat) . . . . . . 1·25 1·40
2536 $2 *Salperton* (ocean-going yacht) . . . . 1·40 1·50
MS2537 140 × 80 mm. Nos. 2531/6 4·75 5·00

616 *Black Magic* (New Zealand) and *Luna Rossa* (Italy)

2002. America's Cup, 2003 (1st issue). Scenes from 2000 final, between New Zealand and Italy. Multicoloured.

2538 $1.30 Type **616** 95 90
2539 $1.50 Aerial view of race . . 1·00 1·00
2540 $2 Yachts turning . . . . . 1·40 1·60
MS2541 140 × 80 mm. Nos. 2538/40 4·50 4·75

See also Nos. 2562/5.

2002. "Stampshow 02" International Stamp Exhibition, Melbourne. No. **MS**2541 with "Stampshow 02" emblem and inscription on the margin. Multicoloured.

MS2542 140 × 80 mm. Nos. 2538/40 3·75 4·00

617 Green-roofed Holiday Cottage and Paua Shell

2002. Holiday Homes. Multicoloured.

2543 40c. Type **617** 30 35
2544 40c. Red-roofed cottage and sunflower 30 35
2545 40c. White-roofed cottage and life-belt 30 35
2546 40c. Cottage with orange door, boat and fishing fly 30 35
2547 40c. Blue-roofed cottage and fish 30 35
2548 40c. Cottage and caravan 30 35

618 "The Nativity" (15th-cent painting in style of Di Baldese)

2002. New Zealand–Vatican City Joint Issue.

2549 **618** $1.50 multicoloured . . 1·25 1·40

2002. Making of *The Lord of the Rings* Film Trilogy (2nd issue): The Two Towers. As T **605**. Multicoloured. (a) Designs 50 × 24 mm or 24 × 50 mm. Ordinary gum.

2550 40c. Aragorn (Viggo Mortenson) and Eowyn (Miranda Otto) (horiz) . . 50 30
2551 80c. Orc raider (horiz) . . . 90 55
2552 90c. Gandalf the White (Sir Ian McKellen) . . . . . 1·00 70
2553 $1.30 Easterling warriors (horiz) . . . . 1·25 1·25
2554 $1.50 Frodo (Elijah Wood) 1·40 1·40
2555 $2 Eowyn, Shield Maiden of Rohan (Miranda Otto) (horiz) . . . . 1·75 2·00

(b) Designs 37 × 26 mm or 26 × 37 mm. Self-adhesive.

2556 40c. Strider (Viggo Mortenson) and Eowyn (Miranda Otto) (horiz) . . 25 30
2557 80c. Orc raider (horiz) . . . 50 55
2558 90c. Gandalf the White (Sir Ian McKellen) 60 65
2559 $1.30 Easterling warriors (horiz) . . . . 85 1·10
2560 $1.50 Frodo (Elijah Wood) 95 1·25
2561 $2 Eowyn, Shield Maiden of Rohan (Miranda Otto) (horiz) . . . . 1·25 1·75

2003. America's Cup (2nd issue). The Defence. As T **616**. Multicoloured.

2562 40c. Aerial view of Team New Zealand yacht . . . 25 30
2563 80c. Two Team New Zealand yachts 50 55
2564 90c. Team New Zealand yacht tacking 60 65
MS2565 140 × 80 mm. Nos. 2562/4 1·75 1·75

619 Shepherd with Flock in High Country

2003. Chinese New Year ("Year of the Sheep"). Sheep Farming. Multicoloured.

2566 40c. Type **619** 35 30
2567 90c. Mustering the sheep . . 65 55
2568 $1.30 Sheep in pen with sheep dog . . . . 1·10 1·10
2569 $1.50 Sheep shearing . . . 1·25 1·40
2570 $2 Sheep shearing (different) 1·50 1·60
MS2571 125 × 85 mm. Nos. 2568 and 2570 . . . . 2·75 2·75

620 Jon Trimmer in *Carmina Burana*

621 Officer, Forest Rangers, 1860s

2003. 50th Anniv of Royal New Zealand Ballet. Scenes from past productions. Multicoloured.
2572 40c. Type **620** 35 30
2573 90c. *Papillon* (horiz) 75 65
2574 $1.30 *Cinderella* 1·10 1·10
2575 $1.50 *FrENZy* 1·25 1·40
2576 $2 *Swan Lake* (horiz) 1·50 1·60

2003. New Zealand Military Uniforms. Multicoloured.
2577 40c. Type **621** 40 40
2578 40c. Lieutenant, Napier Naval Artillery Volunteers, 1890s 40 40
2579 40c. Officer, 2nd Regt, North Canterbury Mounted Rifles, 1900–10 40 40
2580 40c. Mounted Trooper, New Zealand Mounted Rifles, South Africa 1899–1902 40 40
2581 40c. Staff Officer, New Zealand Division, France, 1918 40 40
2582 40c. Petty Officer, Royal New Zealand Navy, 1914–18 40 40
2583 40c. Rifleman, New Zealand Rifle Brigade, France, 1916–18 40 40
2584 40c. Sergeant, New Zealand Engineers, 1939–45 40 40
2585 40c. Matron, Royal New Zealand Navy Hospital, 1940s 40 40
2586 40c. Private, New Zealand Women's Auxiliary Army Corps, Egypt, 1942 40 40
2587 40c. Pilot serving with R.A.F. Bomber Command, Europe, 1943 40 40
2588 40c. Fighter Pilot, No. 1 (Islands) Group, Royal New Zealand Air Force, Pacific, 1943 40 40
2589 40c. Driver, Women's Auxiliary Air Force, 1943 40 40
2590 40c. Gunner, 16th Field Regt, Royal New Zealand Artillery, Korea, 1950–53 40 40
2591 40c. Acting Petty Officer, H.M.N.Z.S. *Tamaki*, 1957 40 40
2592 40c. Scouts, New Zealand Special Air Service, Malaya, 1955–57 40 40
2593 40c. Canberra Pilot serving with R.A.F. Far East Command, Malaya, 1960 40 40
2594 40c. Infantrymen, 1st Bn, Royal New Zealand Infantry Regt, South Vietnam, 1960s 40 40
2595 40c. Infantryman, New Zealand Bn, UNTAET, East Timor, 2000 40 40
2596 40c. Monitor, Peace Monitoring Group, Bougainville, 2001 40 40

Nos. 2577/96 were printed together, se-tenant, with detailed descriptions of the designs printed on the reverse.

622 Ailsa Mountains

2003. New Zealand Landscapes (1st series). Each including the fern symbol after the country inscr. Multicoloured.
2597 45c. Kaikoura 45 35
2598 50c. Type **622** 30 35
2599 $1 Coromandel 60 65
2600 $1.35 Church of the Good Shepherd, Lake Tekapo 1·30 1·30
2601 $1.50 Arrowtown 95 1·00
2602 $2 Tongariro National Park 1·25 1·40
2603 $5 Castlepoint Lighthouse 3·25 3·50

Nos. 2597 and 2601 also come self-adhesive.
See also Nos. 2868/2873.

623 Sir Edmund Hillary and Mount Everest

2003. 50th Anniv of Conquest of Everest. Multicoloured.
2616 40c. Type **623** 50 60
2617 40c. Climbers reaching summit and Tenzing Norgay 50 60

624 Buckingham Palace

2003. 50th Anniv of Coronation. As Nos. 714/18 (Coronation issue of 1953) but face values in decimal currency as T **624**.
2618 **624** 40c. ultramarine 45 35
2619 – 90c. brown 80 70
2620 – $1.30 red 1·25 1·25
2621 – $1.50 blue 1·40 1·40
2622 – $2 violet and ultramarine 1·60 1·60

DESIGNS—VERT: (as T **164**)—90c. Queen Elizabeth II; $1.50, Westminster Abbey. HORIZ: (as T **624**)—$1.30, Coronation State Coach; $2 St. Edward's Crown and Royal Sceptre.

625 New Zealand vs. South Africa Match, 1937

2003. Centenary of New Zealand Test Rugby. Multicoloured.
2623 40c. Type **625** 50 35
2624 90c. New Zealand vs. Wales match, 1963 75 70
2625 $1.30 New Zealand vs. Australia, 1985 1·10 1·10
2626 $1.50 New Zealand vs. France, 1986 1·25 1·40
2627 $1.50 All Blacks jersey 1·25 1·75
2628 $2 New Zealand vs. England, 1997 1·60 1·75
MS2629 100 × 180 mm. Nos. 2623/8 5·75 6·00

626 Papaaroha, Coromandel Peninsula

2003. New Zealand Waterways. Multicoloured.
2630 40c. Type **626** 45 35
2631 90c. Waimahana Creek, Chatham Islands 75 70
2632 $1.30 Blue Lake, Central Otago 1·25 1·25
2633 $1.50 Waikato River 1·40 1·40
2634 $2 Hooker River, Canterbury 1·60 1·75

627 Boy on Swing

2003. Children's Health. Playgrounds. Multicoloured. (a) Size 39 × 29 mm. Ordinary gum.
2635 40c.+5c. Type **627** 50 60
2636 90c.+5c. Girls playing hopscotch 90 1·00
MS2637 88 × 90 mm. Nos. 2635/6 and 40c.+5c. Girl on climbing frame 2·00 2·00

(b) Size 24 × 29 mm. Self-adhesive.
2638 40c.+5c. Girl on climbing frame 60 40

628 Benz Velo (1895)

2003. Veteran Vehicles. Multicoloured.
2639 40c. Type **628** 45 35
2640 90c. Oldsmobile (1903) 75 70
2641 $1.30 Wolseley (1911) 1·25 1·25
2642 $1.50 Talbot (1915) 1·40 1·40
2643 $2 Model T Ford (1915) 1·60 1·75

629 Christ Child in Crib

630 Hamadryas Baboon

2003. Christmas Decorations. Multicoloured. (a) Size 30 × 30 mm. Ordinary gum.
2644 40c. Type **629** 45 25
2645 90c. Silver and gold bird 75 70
2646 $1.30 Silver candle 1·25 1·25
2647 $1.50 Bells 1·40 1·40
2648 $2 Angel 1·60 1·75

(b) Size 21 × 26 mm. Self-adhesive.
2649 40c. Type **629** 45 35
2650 $1 Filigree metalwork decoration with baubles 1·00 1·00

2003. "Bangkok 2003" World Philatelic Exhibition. Sheet, 110 × 80 mm, containing Nos. 2572/3 and 2576.
MS2651 40c. Type **620**; 90c. *Papillon* (horiz); $2 *Swan Lake* (horiz) 3·00 3·00

2003. Making of The Lord of the Rings Film Trilogy (3rd issue): *The Return of the King*. As T **605**. Multicoloured. (a) Designs 24 × 49 mm or 49 × 50 mm. Ordinary gum.
2652 40c. Legolas 50 35
2653 80c. Frodo Baggins 85 70
2654 90c. Merry and Pippin (horiz) 95 75
2655 $1.30 Aragorn 1·25 1·25
2656 $1.50 Gandalf the White 1·50 1·50
2657 $2 Gollum (horiz) 2·00 2·75

(b) Designs 24 × 35 mm or 35 × 24 mm. Self-adhesive.
2658 40c. Legolas 50 35
2659 80c. Frodo Baggins 85 70
2660 90c. Merry and Pippin (horiz) 95 75
2661 $1.30 Aragorn 1·25 1·25
2662 $1.50 Gandalf the White 1·50 1·50
2663 $2 Gollum (horiz) 2·00 2·75

2003. "Welpex 2003" National Stamp Exhibition, Wellington. Sheet 120 × 100 mm, containing Nos. 2626/8.
MS2664 $1.50 New Zealand vs. France, 1986; $1.50 All Blacks jersey; $2 New Zealand vs. England, 1997 5·50 5·50

2004. New Zealand Zoo Animals. Multicoloured. (a) Ordinary gum. Size 29 × 39 mm.
2665 40c. Type **630** 45 35
2666 90c. Malayan sun bear 85 70
2667 $1.30 Red panda 1·25 1·25
2668 $1.50 Ring-tailed lemur 1·40 1·40
2669 $2 Spider monkey 1·60 1·75
MS2670 125 × 90 mm. Nos. 2668/9 3·00 3·00

No. **MS**2670 commemorates Chinese New Year, "Year of the Monkey".

(b) Self-adhesive. Size 24 × 29 mm.
2671 40c. Type **631** 45 35

2004. Hong Kong 2004 International Stamp Exhibition. Sheet, 110 × 80 mm, containing Nos. 2627/8.
MS2672 $1.50 All Blacks jersey; $2 New Zealand vs. England, 1997 3·50 3·50

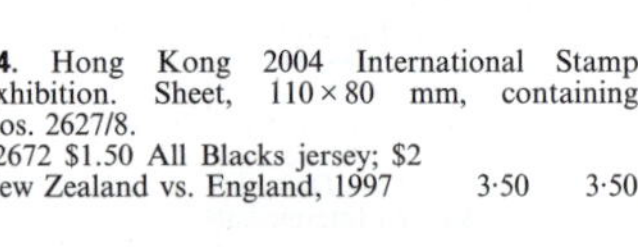

631 New Zealand Team

2004. Rugby Sevens. Multicoloured.
2673 40c. Type **631** 45 35
2674 90c. Hong Kong team 85 70
2675 $1.50 Hong Kong Stadium 1·40 1·40
2676 $2 Westpac Stadium, Wellington 1·75 2·00
MS2677 125 × 85 mm. Nos. 2673/6 4·00 4·00

Stamps of the same design were issued by Hong Kong.

632 Parliament Building, Auckland, 1854

2004. 150th Anniv of First Official Parliament in New Zealand.
2678 **632** 40c. purple and black 45 35
2679 – 45c. purple and black 55 60
2680 – 90c. lilac and black 85 70
2681 – $1.30 grey and black 1·25 1·25
2682 – $1.50 blue and black 1·40 1·40
2683 – $2 green and black 1·60 1·75
MS2684 186 × 65 mm. Nos. 2678/82 5·00 5·00

DESIGNS:45c. As No. 2678; 90c. Parliament Buildings, Wellington, 1865; $1.30 Parliament Buildings, Wellington, 1899; $1.50 Parliament House, Wellington, 1918; $2 The Beehive, Wellington, 1977.

633

2004. "Draw it Yourself" Postcard Labels. Multicoloured. Self-adhesive.
2685 $1.50 Type **633** 1·40 1·60
2686 $1.50 Rosine with "New Zealand Post" at bottom left 1·40 1·60
2687 $1.50 As Type **633** but emerald 1·40 1·60
2688 $1.50 Reddish violet with "New Zealand Post" at bottom left 1·40 1·60

634 Mountain Oysters

2004. Wild Food Postcard Labels. Multicoloured. Self-adhesive.
2689 $1.50 Type **634** 1·40 1·60
2690 $1.50 Huhu grubs 1·40 1·60
2691 $1.50 Possum pate 1·40 1·60

635 Local Man outside Post Office on Tractor

2004. Kiwi Characters Postcard Labels. Multicoloured. Self-adhesive.
2692 $1.50 Type **635** 1·40 1·60
2693 $1.50 Children on horseback 1·40 1·60
2694 $1.50 Elderly couple outside their home 1·40 1·60

636 Kinnard Haines Tractor

2004. Historic Farm Equipment. Multicoloured.
2695 45c. Type **636** 45 40
2696 90c. Fordson F tractor with plough 80 70
2697 $1.35 Burrell traction engine 1·25 1·40
2698 $1.50 Threshing mill 1·25 1·40
2699 $2 Duncan's Seed Drill 1·60 1·75

637 "Dragon Fish"

638 Magnolia

2004. World of Wearable Arts. Multicoloured.
2701 45c. Type **637** 45 40
2702 90c. "Persephone's Descent" (man in armour costume) 80 70
2703 $1.35 "Meridian" (woman in silk costume) 1·25 1·40
2704 $1.50 "Taunga Ika" (woman in net costume) 1·25 1·40
2705 $2 "Cailleach Na Mara" (woman in sea witch costume) 1·60 1·75

2004. Garden Flowers. Multicoloured.
2706 45c. Type **638** 45 40
2707 90c. Helleborus 80 70
2708 $1.35 Nerine 1·25 1·40
2709 $1.50 Rhododendron 1·25 1·40
2710 $2 Delphinium 1·60 1·75
MS2711 160 × 65 mm. Nos. 2706/2710 4·75 5·00

The 45c. stamp in No. **MS**2711 was impregnated with the fragrance of Magnolia.

2004. Salon du Timbre International Stamp Exhibition, Paris. Sheet 125 × 95 mm, containing designs from **MS**2664 and No. 2676.
MS2712 $1.50 New Zealand vs. France 1986, $1.50 All Blacks jersey; $2 Westpac Stradium . . . 3·50 3·75

639

2004. Emergency 5c. Provisional Stamp.
2713 **639** 5c. blue and vermilion . . . 10 10

640 Skippers Canyon (The Ford of Bruinen)

2004. Making of The Lord of the Rings Film Trilogy (4th issue): *Home of Middle Earth*. Multicoloured. Designs 40 × 30 mm. (a) Ordinary gum.
2714 45c. Type **640** 35 40
2715 45c. Arwen facing Black Riders 35 40
2716 90c. Mount Olympus (South of Rivendell) 65 70
2717 90c. Gimley and Legolas . . 65 70
2718 $1.50 Erewhon (Edoras) . . 1·10 1·20
2719 $1.50 Gandalf the White, Legolas, Gimley and Aragorn riding to Rohan . . . 1·10 1·20
2720 $2 Tongariro (Emyn Muil, Mordor) . . . . 1·50 1·60
2721 $2 Frodo and Sam . . . . 1·50 1·60
MS2722 100 × 180 mm. Nos. 2714/21 7·25 7·50

(b) Designs 29 × 24 mm. Self-adhesive.
2723 45c. Skippers Canyon (The Ford of Bruinen) 35 40
2724 45c. Arwen facing Black Riders 35 40
2725 90c. Mount Olympus (South of Rivendell) 65 70
2726 90c. Gimley and Legolas . . 65 70

641 John Walker winning 1500 Metre Race

2004. Olympic Games, Athens. Gold Medal Winners. Multicoloured. Self-adhesive.
2727 45c. Type **641** 50 40
2728 90c. Yvette Williams (long jump) 85 70
2729 $1.50 Ian Ferguson and Paul MacDonald (kayaking) . . . . 1·40 1·60
2730 $2 Peter Snell (800 metre race) . . . . 1·60 1·75

2004. World Stamp Exhibition, Singapore. Sheet 125 × 95 mm containing Nos. 2717/19. Multicoloured.
MS2731 90c. Gimley and Legolas; 90c. Mount Olympus (South of Rivendell); $1.50 Gandalf the White, Legolas, Gimley and Aragorn riding to Rohan; $1.50 Erewhon (Edoras) . . . . . . 3·25 3·75

2004. Tourism (1st series). As T **622**. Multicoloured.
2732 $1.50 The Bath House, Rotorua . . . . 1·25 1·40
2733 $1.50 Pohutu Geyser, Rotorua . . . . 1·25 1·40
2734 $1.50 Hawke's Bay . . . . 1·25 1·40
2735 $1.50 Lake Wakatipu, Queenstown . . . . . . 1·25 1·40
2736 $1.50 Mitre Peak, Milford Sound . . . . 1·25 1·40
2737 $1.50 Kaikoura . . . . . . 1·25 1·40
See also Nos. 2868/73.

642 Children playing in the Sea

2004. Children's Health. A Day at the Beach. Multicoloured. (a) Size 30 × 40 mm. Ordinary gum.
2738 45c.+5c. Type **642** 35 40
2739 90c.+5c. People in dinghy and swimmer 65 70
MS2740 102 × 90 mm. Nos. 2738/9 and 45c.+5c. Children fishing (25 × 30 mm) . . . . 1·40 1·50

(b) Size 24 × 29 mm. Self-adhesive.
2741 45c.+5c. Children fishing . . 35 40

643 Christmas Dinner

2004. Christmas. Multicoloured. Designs 49 × 49 mm. (a) Ordinary gum.
2742 45c. Type **643** 50 40
2743 90c. Traditional Maori meal 80 70
2744 $1.35 Barbecued prawns and salmon . . . . 1·25 1·25
2745 $1.50 Pie and salad . . . . 1·25 1·40
2746 $2 Plum pudding and pavlova . . . . 1·60 1·75

644 Christmas Dinner

(b) Vert designs as T **644**. Self-adhesive.
2747 45c. Type **644** 35 40
2748 90c. Traditional Maori meal 65 70
2749 $1 Christmas cake and cards 70 75

2004. "Baypex 2004 Hawke's Bay Stamp Show". Sheet 130 × 70 mm, containing Nos. 1934f and 2733. Multicoloured.
MS2750 $1.50 Hawke's Bay, $3 Cape Kidnappers . . . . . . 3·00 3·25

645 Whitewater Rafting

2004. Extreme Sports. Multicoloured.
2751 45c. Type **645** 50 40
2752 90c. Snowsports 80 70
2753 $1.35 Skydiving . . . . . . 1·25 1·25
2754 $1.50 Jet boating . . . . . 1·25 1·40
2755 $2 Bungy jumping . . . . . 1·60 1·75

646 Sheep

2005. Farmyard Animals and Chinese New Year ("Year of the Rooster"). Multicoloured. (a) Ordinary gum.
2757 45c. Type **646** 45 40
2758 90c. Dogs 80 70
2759 $1.35 Pigs . . . . 1·25 1·25
2760 $1.50 Rooster . . . . . . 1·25 1·40
2761 $2 Rooster perched on farm equipment . . . . 1·60 1·75
MS2762 126 × 90 mm. Nos. 2757/2761 . . . . 5·50 5·50

(b) Size 24 × 30 mm. Self-adhesive.
2763 45c. Sheep 35 40

647 Beneficiaries (Centenary of Rotary International)

2005. Anniversaries of Organisations. Multicoloured.
2764 45c. Type **647** 45 40
2765 45c. Rural development (50th Anniv of the Lions) 45 40
2766 45c. Canoeists (150th Anniv of YMCA) 45 40
2767 $1.50 Building development (Centenary of Rotary International) . . . . . 1·25 1·25
2768 $1.50 Miniature train (50th Anniv of the Lions) . . . 1·25 1·25
2769 $1.50 Beneficiaries jumping (150th Anniv of YMCA) 1·20 1·25
MS2770 130 × 100 mm. Nos. 2764/9 and central gutter . . . . . . 4·25 4·50

648 1855 Full Face Queen, London Print (No. 1)

2005. 150th Anniv of New Zealand Stamps (1st issue). Stamps of 1855–1905. Multicoloured.
2771 45c. Type **648** 35 40
2772 90c. 1873 Newspaper (Nos. 143/5) 65 70
2773 $1.35 1891 Government Life (No. L 5) . . . . 1·00 1·10
2774 $1.50 1989 Pictorial, Mt. Cook (No. 259) . . . . . 1·10 1·20
2775 $2 1901 Universal Postage (No. 277) . . . . 1·50 1·60
MS2776 160 × 80 mm. Nos. 2771/75 4·50 4·75
See also Nos. 2777/2781 and 2791/**MS**2796.

2005. 150th Anniv of New Zealand Stamps (2nd issue). Stamps of 1905–1955. As T **648**. Multicoloured. Ordinary gum.
2777 45c. 1906 New Zealand Exhibition (No. 371) . . . 35 40
2778 90c. 1931 Health (No. 546) 65 70
2779 $1.35 1935 Airmail (No. 571) . . . . 1·00 1·10
2780 $1.50 1946 Peace (No. 676) 1·10 1·20
2781 $2 1954 Queen Elizabeth II (No. 736) . . . . 1·50 1·60
MS2782 160 × 80 mm. Nos. 2766/70 4·50 4·75

(b) Designs 25 × 30 mm. Self-adhesive.
2783 45c. As No. 2777 . . . . . 35 40
2784 90c. As No. 2778 . . . . . 65 70

2005. Pacific Explorer World Stamp Exhibition, Sydney.
MS2785 109 × 90 mm. Nos. 2775 and 2780 . . . . 3·00 3·25

649 Cafe, 1910s

2005. Cafe Culture. Multicoloured. Self-adhesive.
2786 45c. Type **649** 45 30
2787 90c. Cafe, 1940s 80 70
2788 $1.35 Cafe, 1970s . . . . . 1·25 1·25
2789 $1.50 Tables outside cafe on pavement, 1990s . . . . 1·25 1·40
2790 $2 Internet cafe, 2005 . . . 1·60 1·75

2005. 150th Anniv of New Zealand Stamps (3rd issue). Stamps of 1955—2005. As T **648**. Multicoloured.
2791 45c. 1965 50th Anniversary of the Gallipoli Landing (No. 827) 40 30
2792 90c. 1988 Round Kiwi (No. 1490) 80 70
2793 $1.35 1990 The Achievers Katherine Sheppard (No. 1550) . . . . 1·25 1·25
2794 $1.50 1994 Maori Myths Maui (No. 1807) . . . . 1·25 1·40
2795 $2 2003 Centenary of New Zealand Test Rugby (No. 2627) . . . . 1·60 1·75
MS2796 160 × 80 mm. Nos. 2791/5 4·75 5·00

650 All Blacks Jersey

2005. DHL New Zealand Lions Rugby Series. Self-adhesive.
2797 **650** 45c. black and grey . . . 45 50
2798 – 45c. multicoloured . . . 45 50
2799 – $1.50 black and grey . . 1·10 1·25
2800 – $1.50 multicoloured . . 1·10 1·25
DESIGNS: No. 2797, Type **650**; 2798, Red Lions jersey; 2799, As No. 2797; No. 2800, As No. 2798.

651 Kiwi

653 Child and Horse

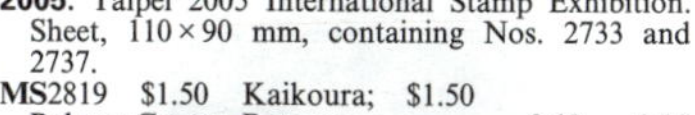

652 Kakapo ("Relies heavily on camouflage for defence")

2005. Personalised Stamps. Multicoloured.
2801 45c. Type **651** 45 45
2802 45c. Pohutukawa (native Christmas tree) 45 45
2803 45c. Champagne glasses . . 45 45
2804 45c. Balloons 45 45
2805 45c. Wedding bands 45 45
2806 45c. Gift box 45 45
2807 45c. Baby's hand 45 45
2808 $1.50 Globe . . . . 1·25 1·40
2809 $2 As Type **651** . . . . . 1·60 1·75
2810 $2 Fern . . . . 1·60 1·75

2005. Endangered Species. Kakapo. Designs showing the Kakpo with different facts inscribed. Multicoloured.
2811 45c. Type **652** 60 60
2812 45c. "Night Parrot unique to New Zealand" 60 60
2813 45c. "Nocturnal bird living on the forest floor" . . . 60 60
2814 45c. "Endangered – only 86 known surviving" 60 60

2005. Children's Health. Pets. Multicoloured. (a) Size 30 × 40 mm. Ordinary gum.
2815 45c.+5c. Type **653** 55 55
2816 90c.+5c. Child holding rabbit 90 95
MS2817 100 × 90 mm. Nos. 2815/16 and 45c.+5c. Children and dog (25 × 30 mm) . . . . 1·75 2·00

(b) Size 25 × 30 mm. Self-adhesive.
2818 45c.+5c. Children and dog 50 55

2005. Taipei 2005 International Stamp Exhibition. Sheet, 110 × 90 mm, containing Nos. 2733 and 2737.
MS2819 $1.50 Kaikoura; $1.50 Pohutu Geyser, Rotorua . . . 2·10 2·20

654 Baby Jesus

2005. Christmas. Multicoloured. (a) 35 × 35 mm. Ordinary gum.
2820 45c. Type **654** 30 35
2821 90c. Mary and Joseph . . . 65 70
2822 $1.35 Shepherd . . . . . . 95 1·00
2823 $1.50 Wise Men . . . . . . 1·00 1·10
2824 $2 Star . . . . 1·40 1·50

(b) Size 24 × 29 mm. Self-adhesive.
2825 45c. Type **654** 30 35
2826 $1 Gifts on straw 70 75

655 King Kong

2005. *King Kong* (film). Multicoloured.
2827 45c. Type **655** 30 35
2828 90c. Carl Denham 65 70
2829 $1.35 Ann Darrow . . . . 95 1·00
2830 $1.50 Jack Driscoll . . . . 1·00 1·10
2831 $2 Ann Darrow and Jack Driscoll . . . . 1·40 1·50
MS2832 180 × 65 mm. Nos. 2827/31 4·25 4·50

2005. National Stamp Show, Auckland. Sheet, 120 × 90 mm, containing Nos. 2774, 2780 and 2794.
MS2833 $1.50 1989 Pictorial, Mt Cook (No. 259); $1.50 1946 Peace (No. 676); $1.50 1994 Maori Myths – Maui (No. 1807) . . . 4·00 4·25

656 Lucy opening the Wardrobe **657** Labrador Retriever Guide Dog

2005. Making of *The Chronicles of Narnia*: *The Lion the Witch and the Wardrobe* (film). Multicoloured. (a) Ordinary gum.
2834 45c. Type **656** 30 35
2835 90c. Lucy, Edmund, Peter and Susan in snowy forest (horiz) 65 70
2836 $1.35 The White Witch tempting Edmund with Turkish delight (horiz) . . 95 1·00
2837 $1.50 Dissenters turned to stone statues in courtyard of White Witch's castle 1·00 1·10
2838 $2 Lucy and body of Aslan (horiz) . . . . 1·40 1·50

(b) As Nos. 2834/8 but smaller. Self-adhesive.
MS2839 200 × 70 mm. 45c. Type **656** (25 × 35 mm); 90c. As No. 2835 (35 × 25 mm); $1.35 As No. 2836 (35 × 25 mm); $1.50 As No. 2837 (25 × 35 mm); $2 As No. 2838 (35 × 25 mm) . . . . 4·25 4·50

2006. Chinese New Year ("Year of the Dog"). Multicoloured. (a) Ordinary gum.
2840 45c. Type **657** 35 45
2841 90c. German Shepherd Dog 70 80
2842 $1.35 Jack Russell Terrier 1·25 1·25
2843 $1.50 Golden Retriever . . 1·25 1·40
2844 $2 Huntaway (New Zealand Sheepdog) . . . . 1·60 1·75
MS2845 124 × 89 mm. Nos. 2844/5 4·75 5·00

(b) Size 25 × 30 mm. Self-adhesive.
2846 45c. Type **657** 30 35

658 Street Scene, c. 1930

2006. 75th Anniv of Hawke's Bay Earthquake. Multicoloured.
2848 45c. Type **658** 45 50
2849 45c. Aerial view of devastated city of Napier 45 50
2850 45c. Aerial view with roofless church and intact Public Trust Building, Napier 45 50
2851 45c. Fire engine and crew 45 50
2852 45c. HMS *Veronica* 45 50
2853 45c. Sailors from HMS *Veronica* clearing debris 45 50
2854 45c. Red Cross nurses with hospital patient 45 50
2855 45c. Rescue services 45 50
2856 45c. Abandoned vehicles on broken road ("Devastation") 45 50
2857 45c. Outdoor hospital ward, Botanical Gardens, Napier ("Medical services") 45 50
2858 45c. Emergency mail plane 45 50
2859 45c. Refugees on road . . . 45 50
2860 45c. Refugee tents, Nelson Park 45 50
2861 45c. Makeshift cooking facilities, Hastings 45 50
2862 45c. Maori women ("Community spirit") . . 45 50
2863 45c. Refugees boarding train 45 50
2864 45c. Reconstruction work ("Building industry") . . 45 50
2865 45c. Hastings Street rebuilt in Art Deco style, 1933 45 50
2866 45c. Carnival procession ("Celebrations") 45 50
2867 45c. Entrance to National Tobacco Company building, Ahuriri, 2005 . . 45 50

Nos. 2849/50 form a composite design showing an aerial view of Napier after the earthquake.

2006. Tourism (2nd series). As T **622**. Multicoloured.
2868 $1.50 Lake Wanaka . . . . 1·40 1·60
2869 $1.50 Mount Taranaki . . . 1·40 1·60
2870 $1.50 Halfmoon Bay, Stewart Island . . . . . 1·40 1·60
2871 $1.50 Franz Josef Glacier, West Coast . . . . 1·40 1·60
2872 $1.50 Huka Falls, Taupo . . 1·40 1·60
2873 $1.50 Cathedral Cove, Coromandel . . . . . . 1·40 1·60

659 Queen Elizabeth II

2006. 80th Birthday of Queen Elizabeth II.
2874 **659** $5 multicoloured . . . . 3·50 3·75
MS2875 105 × 100 mm. No. 1272 of Jersey; $5 Type **659** (sold at $17.50) . . . . 12·00 12·50
No. **MS**2875 is identical to **MS**1273 of Jersey.

660 Champagne Glasses

2006. Personalised Stamps. Multicoloured.
2876 45c. Type **660** 30 35
2877 45c. Buzzy Bee (toy) 30 35
2878 45c. Silver fern 30 35
2879 45c. Pohutukawa flower . . 30 35
2880 45c. Christmas star decorations 30 35
2881 45c. Engagement and wedding rings 30 35
2882 45c. Red rose 30 35
2883 $1.50 As No. 2878 . . . . 1·00 1·10
2884 $2 As No. 2879 . . . . . . 1·40 1·50
2885 $2 As No. 2880 . . . . . . 1·40 1·50

2006. Washington 2006 World Philatelic Exhibition. Sheet, 120 × 80 mm containing designs as Nos. 2809/10 but without imprint date.
MS2886 $2 Fern; $2 Type **651** 2·75 3·00

EXPRESS DELIVERY STAMPS

E 1

1903.
E1 E **1** 6d. red and violet . . . . 38·00 23·00

E **2** Express Mail Delivery Van

1939.
E6 E **2** 6d. violet . . . . 1·50 1·75

LIFE INSURANCE DEPARTMENT

L 1 L **3** Castlepoint Lighthouse

1891.
L13 L **1** ½d. purple . . . . 60·00 4·00
L14 1d. blue . . . . 60·00 75
L15 2d. brown . . . . 90·00 3·50
L 4 3d. brown . . . . £180 22·00
L 5 6d. green . . . . £300 60·00
L 6 1s. pink £500 £120

1905. Similar type but "V.R." omitted.
L24 ½d. green . . . . 16·00 2·25
L22 1d. blue . . . . £170 30·00
L38 1d. red . . . . 3·25 2·00
L26 1½d. black . . . . 40·00 8·00
L27 1½d. brown . . . . 1·50 3·00
L21 2d. brown . . . . £1100 95·00
L28 2d. purple . . . . 50·00 29·00
L29 2d. yellow . . . . 7·00 2·00
L30 3d. brown . . . . 45·00 26·00
L35 3d. red . . . . 18·00 28·00
L41 6d. pink . . . . 14·00 35·00

1947. Lighthouses.
L42 L **3** ½d. green and orange . . 1·75 70
L43 – 1d. olive and blue . . . 1·75 1·25
L44 – 2d. blue and black . . . 1·50 1·00
L45 – 2½d. black and blue . . . 9·50 13·00
L46 – 3d. mauve and blue . . . 3·50 1·00
L47 – 4d. brown and orange . . 4·25 1·75
L48 – 6d. brown and blue . . . 4·00 2·75
L49 – 1s. brown and blue . . . 4·00 3·50
LIGHTHOUSES—HORIZ: 1d. Taiaroa; 2d. Cape Palliser; 6d. The Brothers. VERT: 2½d. Cape Campbell; 3d. Eddystone; 4d. Stephens Island; 1s. Cape Brett.

1967. Decimal currency. Stamps of 1947–65 surch.
L50a 1c. on 1d. (No. L43) . . . 1·00 4·25
L51 2c. on 2½d. (No. L45) . . . 8·50 14·00
L52 2½c. on 3d. (No. L46) . . . 1·25 4·00
L53 3c. on 4d. (No. L47) . . . 3·25 5·00
L54 5c. on 6d. (No. L48) . . . 75 6·00
L55a 10c. on 1s. (No. L49) . . . 75 4·00

L **13** Moeraki Point Lighthouse

1969.
L56 L **13** ½c. yellow, red and violet . . . . 65 1·75
L57 – 2½c. blue, green and buff 50 1·25
L58 – 3c. stone, yellow & brn 50 75
L59 – 4c. green, ochre and blue . . . . 50 1·00
L60 – 8c. multicoloured . . . 40 2·75
L61 – 10c. multicoloured . . . 40 2·75
L62 – 15c. multicoloured . . . 40 2·00
DESIGNS—HORIZ: 2½c. Puysegur Point Lighthouse; 4c. Cape Egmont Lighthouse. VERT: 3c. Baring Head Lighthouse; 8c. East Cape; 10c. Farewell Spit; 15c. Dog Island Lighthouse.

1978. No. L57 surch **25c**.
L63 25c. on 2½c. blue, green and buff . . . . 75 1·75

L 17

1981.
L64 L **17** 5c. multicoloured . . . 10 10
L65 10c. multicoloured . . . 10 10
L66 20c. multicoloured . . . 15 15
L67 30c. multicoloured . . . 25 25
L68 40c. multicoloured . . . 30 30
L69 50c. multicoloured . . . 30 35

OFFICIAL STAMPS

1891. Optd **O.P.S.O.**
O 1 **3** ½d. pink . . . . — £550
O 2 **13** ⅛d. black . . . . — £325
O13 **23** ½d. green . . . . — £325
O 4 **10** 1d. pink . . . . — £325
O19 **42** 1d. red . . . . — £350
O 6 **9** 2d. mauve . . . . — £425
O 8 **16** 2½d. blue . . . . — £375
O14 **26** 2½d. blue (A) . . . . . — £600
O21 2½d. blue (B) . . . . . — £400
O22 **28** 3d. brown . . . . — £550
O16 **24** 4d. blue and brown . . . — £500
O11 **19** 5d. black . . . . — £500
O17a **30** 5d. brown . . . . — £500
O12 **8** 6d. brown (No. 224b) . . — £700
O18 **32** 8d. blue . . . . — £650
O23 **34** 1s. red . . . . — £1100
O24 **35** 2s. green . . . . — £1800

Optd **OFFICIAL**.

1907. Pictorials.
O59 **23** ½d. green . . . . 9·00 75
O61a **25** 2d. purple . . . . 8·50 1·60
O63 **28** 3d. brown . . . . 48·00 1·75
O64 **31** 6d. red . . . . £170 21·00
O65 **34** 1s. orange . . . . 95·00 15·00
O66 **35** 2s. green . . . . 80·00 £100
O67 – 5s. red (No. 329) £150 £180

1907. "Universal" type.
O60b **42** 1d. red . . . . 12·00 50

1908.
O70 **50** 1d. red . . . . 65·00 3·25
O72 **31** 6d. red (No. 254) . . . . £160 35·00

1910. King Edward VII etc.
O73 **51** ½d. green . . . . 6·50 30
O78 **53** 1d. red . . . . 3·25 10
O74 **51** 3d. brown . . . . 14·00 80
O75 6d. red . . . . 19·00 5·50
O76 8d. blue . . . . 12·00 20·00
O77 1s. orange . . . . 48·00 15·00

1913. Queen Victoria.
O82 F **4** 2s. blue . . . . 50·00 48·00
O83 5s. green . . . . 75·00 £100
O84 £1 red £600 £550

1915. King George V.
O 96 **62** ½d. green . . . . 2·00 10
O 90 1½d. grey . . . . 5·50 90
O 91 1½d. brown . . . . . . 5·00 30
O 98 2d. yellow . . . . 2·50 50
O 99 3d. brown . . . . 5·00 50
O101 4d. violet . . . . 14·00 4·00
O102 6d. red . . . . 5·00 75
O103 8d. brown . . . . 65·00 £180
O104 9d. green . . . . 40·00 38·00
O105b 1s. orange . . . . 7·00 2·00

1927. King George V.
O111 **71** 1d. red . . . . 2·00 20
O112 2s. blue . . . . 75·00 £110

1933. "Arms".
O113 F **6** 5s. green £250 £300

Optd **Official.**

1936. "Arms".
O133aw F **6** 5s. green . . . . . . 40·00 6·00

1936. As 1935.
O120 **81** ½d. green . . . . 7·50 4·50
O115 – 1d. red (No. 557) . . . 4·25 1·25
O122 **83** 1½d. brown . . . . . . 24·00 4·75
O123 – 2d. orange (No. 580) . . 4·75 10
O124a **85** 2½d. brown and grey . . 14·00 21·00
O125 **86** 3d. brown . . . . 48·00 3·50
O126c **87** 4d. black and brown . . 4·50 1·00
O127c **89** 6d. red . . . . 12·00 30
O128a – 8d. brown (No. 586b) 8·50 16·00
O130 **91** 9d. red and black . . . 20·00 22·00
O131b – 1s. green (No. 588) . . 28·00 2·25
O132d **93** 2s. olive . . . . 42·00 8·50

1938. King George VI.
O134 **108** ½d. green . . . . 20·00 2·25
O135 ½d. orange . . . . 1·60 3·50
O136 1d. red . . . . 21·00 15
O137 1d. green . . . . 3·50 10
O138 1½d. brown . . . . . . 75·00 18·00
O139 1½d. red . . . . 10·00 6·50
O152 2d. orange . . . . 2·75 10
O140 3d. blue . . . . 3·50 10
O153 4d. purple . . . . 4·25 2·50
O154 6d. red . . . . 14·00 50
O155 8d. violet . . . . 8·00 6·50
O156 9d. brown . . . . 9·00 6·50
O157a – 1s. brown and red (No. 686b) . . . . . . 8·50 9·00
O158 – 2s. orange and green (No. 688) . . . . . 30·00 16·00

1940. Centenary stamps.
O141 ½d. green . . . . 2·75 35
O142 1d. brown and red . . . . 6·00 10
O143 1½d. blue and mauve . . . 3·75 2·00
O144 2d. green and brown . . . 5·50 10
O145 2½d. green and blue . . . . 5·00 2·75
O146 3d. purple and red . . . . 8·00 1·00
O147 4d. brown and red . . . . 40·00 1·50
O148 6d. green and violet . . . 26·00 1·50
O149 8d. black and red . . . . 30·00 17·00
O150 9d. olive and red . . . . 11·00 5·00
O151 1s. green . . . . 48·00 3·00

O **6** Queen Elizabeth II

1954.
O159 O **6** 1d. orange 75 40
O160 1½d. brown . . . . . 3·75 5·00
O161a 2d. green 40 30
O162 2½d. olive . . . . . . 3·00 1·50
O163a 3d. red 40 10
O164 4d. blue . . . . 1·50 75
O165 9d. red . . . . 7·00 2·50
O166 1s. purple . . . . . . 1·25 30
O167 3s. slate . . . . 22·00 40·00

1959. Surch.
O169 O **6** 2½d. on 2d. green . . . 1·25 1·50
O168 6d. on 1½d. brown . . . 50 1·10

POSTAGE DUE STAMPS

D 1 D 2

1899.
D 9 D **1** ½d. red and green . . . 3·00 16·00
D10 1d. red and green . . . 13·00 2·25
D15 2d. red and green . . . 45·00 6·00
D12 3d. red and green . . . 13·00 3·75
D16 4d. red and green . . . 32·00 9·00
D 6 5d. red and green . . . 22·00 25·00
D 7 6d. red and green . . . 29·00 28·00
D 2 8d. red and green . . . 60·00 75·00

D 8 10d. red and green 70·00 85·00
D 3 1s. red and green 65·00 85·00
D 4 2s. red and green £120 £140

1902.

D18 D 2 ½d. red and green 1·75 2·50
D30 1d. red and green 3·75 80
D22a 2d. red and green 5·50 2·50
D36 3d. red and green 15·00 42·00

D 3

1939.

D41 D 3 ½d. green 5·00 5·00
D42 1d. red 2·75 1·25
D46 2d. blue 8·00 2·00
D47aw 3d. brown 9·00 10·00

NICARAGUA Pt. 15

A republic of Central America, independent since 1821.

1862. 100 centavos = 1 peso (paper currency).
1912. 100 centavos de cordoba = 1 peso de cordoba (gold currency).
1925. 100 centavos = 1 cordoba.

2 Volcanoes 5

1862. Perf or roul.

13 2 1c. brown 1·50 75
4 2c. blue 2·25 75
14 5c. black 6·00 1·25
18 10c. red 2·25 1·40
19 25c. green 2·25 2·40

1882.

20 5 1c. green 15 20
21 2c. red 15 20
22 5c. blue 15 15
23 10c. violet 15 60
24 15c. yellow 30 1·50
25 20c. grey 50 3·00
26 50c. violet 70 6·00

6 Steam Locomotive and Telegraph Key 7

1890.

27 6 1c. brown 25 30
28 2c. red 25 30
29 5c. blue 25 20
30 10c. grey 25 25
31 20c. red 25 1·75
32 50c. violet 25 5·50
33 1p. brown 40 7·75
34 2p. green 40 10·00
35 5p. red 50 19·00
36 10p. orange 50 27·00

1891.

37 7 1c. brown 15 30
38 2c. red 15 30
39 5c. blue 15 25
40 10c. grey 15 35
41 20c. lake 15 1·75
42 50c. violet 15 3·00
43 1p. sepia 15 4·50
44 2p. green 15 5·00
45 5p. red 15 12·00
46 10p. orange 15 15·00

8 First Sight of the New World

1892. Discovery of America.

47 8 1c. brown 15 25
48 2c. red 15 25
49 5c. blue 15 20
50 10c. grey 15 25
51 20c. red 15 1·75
52 50c. violet 15 4·25
53 1p. brown 15 4·25
54 2p. green 15 5·00
55 5p. red 15 14·00
56 10p. orange 15 18·00

9 Volcanoes 10

1893.

57 9 1c. brown 15 25
58 2c. red 15 25
59 5c. blue 15 20
60 10c. grey 15 25
61 20c. brown 15 1·40
62 50c. violet 15 3·50
63 1p. brown 15 4·25
64 2p. green 15 5·00
65 5p. red 15 11·00
66 10p. orange 15 14·00

1894.

67 10 1c. brown 15 25
68 2c. red 15 25
69 5c. blue 15 20
70 10c. grey 15 25
71 20c. red 15 1·50
72 50c. violet 15 3·50
73 1p. brown 15 4·25
74 2p. green 15 7·50
75 5p. brown 15 9·00
76 10p. orange 15 12·00

11 12 Map of Nicaragua 13 Arms of Republic of Central America

1895.

77 11 1c. brown 15 20
78 2c. red 15 20
79 5c. blue 15 15
80 10c. grey 15 20
81 20c. red 15 70
82 50c. violet 15 3·00
83 1p. brown 15 4·50
84 2p. green 15 4·75
85 5p. red 15 9·25
86 10p. orange 15 14·50

1896. Date "1896".

90 12 1c. violet 15 75
91 2c. green 15 50
92 5c. red 15 35
93 10c. blue 30 65
94 20c. brown 1·75 3·50
95 50c. grey 35 4·75
96 1p. black 35 6·50
97 2p. red 35 9·00
98 5p. blue 35 9·00

1897. As T 12, dated "1897".

99 12 1c. violet 25 35
100 2c. green 25 35
101 5c. red 25 20
102 10c. blue 3·75 65
103 20c. brown 1·50 2·25
104 50c. grey 5·25 5·75
105 1p. black 5·25 8·75
106 2p. red 11·50 11·00
107 5p. blue 11·50 25·00

1898.

108 13 1c. brown 20 20
109 2c. grey 20 20
110 4c. lake 20 30
122 5c. olive 15·00 15
112 10c. purple 8·75 40
113 15c. blue 25 1·00
114 20c. blue 6·00 1·00
115 50c. yellow 6·00 5·75
116 1p. blue 30 9·50
117 2p. brown 11·00 13·00
118 5p. orange 15·00 19·00

14 15 Mt. Momotombo

1899.

126 14 1c. green 10 25
127 2c. brown 10 25
128 4c. red 20 25
129 5c. blue 15 25
130 10c. orange 15 25
131 15c. brown 15 40
132 20c. green 20 70
133 50c. red 15 1·75
134 1p. orange 15 5·00
135 2p. violet 15 12·00
136 5p. blue 15 14·50

1900.

137 15 1c. red 35 10
138 2c. orange 65 15
139 3c. green 75 20
140 4c. olive 95 25
184 5c. red 1·50 45
185 5c. blue 1·50 45
142 6c. red 19·00 5·50
186 10c. mauve 1·50 45
144 15c. blue 10·00 35
145 20c. brown 9·00 30
146 50c. lake 9·00 1·60
147 1p. yellow 20·00 6·75
148 2p. red 8·00 75
149 5p. black 14·00 2·50

1901. Surch **1901** and value.

151 15 2c. on 1p. yellow 11·00 8·50
169 3c. on 6c. red 8·00 5·00
163 4c. on 6c. red 7·00 4·00
173 5c. on 1p. yellow 11·50 5·75
168 10c. on 2p. red 8·00 1·75
152 10c. on 5p. black 14·00 11·00
153 20c. on 2p. red 22·00 20·00
176 20c. on 5p. black 6·00 3·75

1901. Postage Due stamps of 1900 optd **1901 Correos.**

177 D 16 1c. red 60 30
178 2c. orange 45 30
179 5c. blue 55 45
180 10c. violet 55 45
181 20c. brown 75 1·00
182 30c. green 70 1·00
183 50c. lake 70 1·00

1902. Surch **1902** and value.

187 15 15c. on 2c. orange 4·00 1·50
188 30c. on 1c. red 1·50 4·25

27 Pres. Santos Zelaya 37 Arms

1903. 10th Anniv of Revolution against Sacaza and 1st election of Pres. Zelaya.

189 27 1c. black and green 25 45
190 2c. black and red 50 45
191 5c. black and blue 25 45
192 10c. black and orange 25 70
193 15c. black and lake 45 1·40
194 20c. black and violet 45 1·40
195 50c. black and olive 45 3·00
196 1p. black and brown 45 3·50

1904. Surch **15 Centavos.**

200 15 15c. on 10c. mauve 5·75 3·00

1904. Surch **Vale**, value and wavy lines.

203 15 5c. on 10c. mauve 1·90 50
204 15c. on 10c. mauve 60 40

1905. No. 186 surch **5 CENTS.**

205 15 5c. on 10c. mauve 75 50

1905.

206 37 1c. green 20 15
207 2c. red 20 15
208 3c. violet 25 20
280 3c. orange 25 15
209 4c. orange 25 20
281 4c. violet 25 15
282 5c. blue 25 15
211 6c. grey 45 30
283 6c. brown 1·75 1·10
212 10c. brown 55 20
284 10c. lake 60 10
213 15c. olive 55 25
285 15c. black 60 10
214 20c. lake 45 25
286 20c. olive 60 10
215 50c. orange 1·75 1·40
287 50c. green 70 35
216 1p. black 90 90
288 1p. yellow 70 35
217 2p. green 90 1·25
289 2p. red 70 35
218 5p. violet 1·00 1·50

1906. Surch **Vale** (or **VALE**) and value in one line.

292 37 2c. on 3c. orange 90 75
293 5c. on 20c. olive 30 25
247 10c. on 2c. red 1·10 45
223 10c. on 3c. violet 30 15
248 10c. on 4c. orange 1·25 55
291 10c. on 15c. black 30 25
250 10c. on 20c. lake 1·90 85
252 10c. on 50c. orange 1·40 45
234 10c. on 2p. green 12·00 7·00
235 10c. on 5p. violet 60·00 42·00
226 15c. on 1c. green 30 20
229 20c. on 2c. red 40 25
230 20c. on 5c. blue 45 35
236 35c. on 6c. grey 1·60 1·60
232 50c. on 6c. grey 45 35
238 1p. on 5p. violet 25·00 14·50

51 50 64

1908. Fiscal stamps as T **51** optd **CORREO–1908** or surch **VALE** and value also.

260 51 1c. on 5c. yellow 35 20
261 2c. on 5c. yellow 35 25
262 4c. on 5c. yellow 65 30
256 5c. yellow 45 35
257 10c. blue 35 20
263 15c. on 50c. green 45 30
264 35c. on 50c. green 2·50 65
258 1p. brown 20 1·40
259 2p. grey 20 1·50

1908. Fiscal stamps as T **50** optd **CORREOS–1908** or surch **VALE** and value also.

268 50 2c. orange 2·10 1·00
269 4c. on 2c. orange 1·00 65
270 5c. on 2c. orange 1·10 45
271 10c. on 2c. orange 1·10 25

1909. Surch **CORREOS–1909 VALE** and value.

273 51 1c. on 50c. green 2·25 95
274 2c. on 50c. green 4·00 1·75
275 4c. on 50c. green 4·00 1·75
276 5c. on 50c. green 2·25 1·10
277 10c. on 50c. green 65 40

1910. Surch **Vale** and value in two lines.

296 37 2c. on 3c. orange 65 35
300 2c. on 4c. violet 25 15
301 5c. on 20c. olive 25 15
302 10c. on 15c. black 30 15
303 10c. on 50c. green 20 15
299 10c. on 1p. yellow 65 35
305 10c. on 2p. red 45 35

1911. Surch **Correos 1911** (or **CORREOS 1911**) and value.

307 51 2c. on 5p. blue 25 30
312 5c. on 2p. grey 90 70
308 5c. on 10p. pink 55 30
309 10c. on 25c. lilac 30 20
310 10c. on 2p. grey 30 20
311 35c. on 1p. brown 30 25

1911. Surch **VALE POSTAL de 1911** and value.

313 51 5c. on 25c. lilac 90 70
314 5c. on 50c. green 3·00 3·00
315 5c. on 5p. blue 4·00 4·00
317 5c. on 50p. red 3·00 3·00
318 10c. on 50c. green 70 45

1911. Railway tickets as T **64**, with fiscal surch on the front, further surch for postal use. (a) Surch **vale CORREO DE 1911** and value on back.

319 64 2c. on 5c. on 2nd class blue 55 65
320 05c. on 5c. on 2nd class blue 30 40
321 10c. on 5c. on 2nd class blue 30 40
322 15c. on 10c. on 1st class red 40 50

(b) Surch **vale CORREO DE 1911** and value on front.

322c 64 2c. on 5c. on 2nd class blue 8·00 8·00
322d 05c. on 5c. on 2nd class blue £170 £170
322e 10c. on 5c. on 2nd class blue 80·00 80·00
322f 15c. on 10c. on 1st class red 22·00 22·00

(c) Surch **CORREO** and value on front.

323 64 2c. on 10c. on 1st class red 80 80
324 20c. on 10c. on 1st class red 4·00 4·00
325 50c. on 10c. on 1st class red 7·50 7·50

(d) Surch **Correo Vale 1911** and value on front.

326 64 2c. on 10c. on 1st class red 15 15
328 5c. on 5c. on 2nd class blue 90 80
327 5c. on 10c. on 1st class red 20 1·25
330 10c. on 10c. on 1st class red 70 50

(e) Surch **Vale CORREO DE 1911** and value on back.

331 64 5c. on 10c. on 1st class red 18·00
332 10c. on 10c. on 1st class red 7·00

(f) Surch **CORREO Vale 10 cts. 1911** and bar obliterating **oficial** on front.

333 64 10c. on 10c. on 1st class red 1·25 1·00

70 71

1912.

337 70 1c. green 25 15
338 2c. red 25 15

339 3c. brown 25 15
340 4c. purple 25 15
341 5c. black and blue 25 15
342 6c. brown 25 70
343 10c. brown 25 15
344 15c. violet 25 15
345 20c. brown 25 15
346 25c. black and green 25 15
347 **71** 35c. brown and green 1·10 1·10
348 **70** 50c. blue 65 30
349 1p. orange 90 1·40
350 2p. green 90 1·75
351 5p. black 1·60 2·10

1913. Surch **Vale 15 cts Correos 1913**.
352 **71** 15c. on 35c. brown & green 30 20

1913. Surch **VALE 1913** and value in "centavos de cordoba". A. On stamps of 1912 issue.
353 **70** ½c. on 3c. brown 35 25
354 ½c. on 15c. violet 20 15
355 ½c. on 1p. orange 20 15
356 1c. on 3c. brown 55 45
357 1c. on 4c. purple 20 15
358 1c. on 50c. blue 20 15
359 1c. on 5p. black 20 15
360 2c. on 4c. purple 25 20
361 2c. on 20c. brown 2·25 2·75
362 2c. on 25c. black & green 25 15
363 **71** 2c. on 35c. brown & green 20 35
364 **70** 2c. on 50c. blue 20 90
365 2c. on 2p. green 15 15
366 3c. on 6c. brown 15 10

B. On Silver Currency stamps of 1912 (Locomotive type).
367 **Z 1** ½c. on 2c. red 3·25 2·50
368 1c. on 3c. brown 2·10 1·60
369 1c. on 4c. red 2·10 1·60
370 1c. on 6c. red 2·10 1·60
371 1c. on 20c. blue 2·10 1·60
372 1c. on 25c. black & green 2·10 1·60
384 2c. on 1c. green 25·00 19·00
373 2c. on 25c. black & green 11·25 8·50
374 5c. on 35c. black & green 2·10 1·60
375 5c. on 50c. olive 2·10 1·60
376 6c. on 1p. orange 2·10 1·60
377 10c. on 2p. brown 2·10 1·60
378 1p. on 5p. green 2·10 1·60

1914. No. 352 surch with new value and **Cordoba** and thick bar over old surch.
385 **71** ½c. on 15c. on 35c. 15 10
386 1c. on 15c. on 35c. 20 15

1914. Official stamps of 1913 surch with new value and thick bar through "OFICIAL".
387 **70** 1c. on 25c. blue 30 20
388 **71** 1c. on 35c. blue 30 20
389 **70** 1c. on 1p. blue 20 15
391 2c. on 50c. blue 30 15
392 2c. on 2p. blue 20 15
393 5c. on 5p. blue 20 15

79 National Palace, Managua

80 Leon Cathedral

1914. Various frames.
394 **79** ½c. blue 50 15
395 1c. green 50 15
396 **80** 2c. orange 50 15
397 **79** 3c. brown 80 25
398 **80** 4c. red 80 25
399 **79** 5c. grey 30 10
400 **80** 6c. sepia 5·25 3·25
401 10c. yellow 55 15
402 **79** 15c. violet 3·50 1·40
403 **80** 20c. grey 6·50 3·25
404 **79** 25c. orange 85 20
405 **80** 50c. blue 85 25
See also Nos. 465/72, 617/27 and 912/24.

1915. Surch **VALE 5 cts. de Cordoba 1915**.
406 **80** 5c. on 6c. sepia 1·10 35

1918. Stamps of 1914 surch **Vale centavos de cordoba**.
407 **80** ½c. on 6c. sepia 2·00 75
408 ½c. on 10c. yellow 1·40 25
409 **79** ½c. on 15c. violet 1·40 45
410 ½c. on 25c. orange 3·00 85
411 **80** ½c. on 50c. blue 1·40 25
440 1c. on 2c. orange 90 20
413 **79** 1c. on 3c. brown 1·50 25
414 **80** 1c. on 6c. sepia 7·00 2·10
415 1c. on 10c. yellow 13·00 4·75
416 **79** 1c. on 15c. violet 2·40 55
418 **80** 1c. on 20c. grey 1·40 25
420 **79** 1c. on 25c. orange 2·40 70
421 **80** 1c. on 50c. blue 7·75 2·25
422 2c. on 4c. red 1·75 25
423 2c. on 6c. sepia 13·00 4·75
424 2c. on 10c. yellow 13·00 2·50
425 2c. on 20c. grey 7·00 2·10
426 **79** 2c. on 25c. orange 3·00 30
427 **80** 5c. on 6c. sepia 5·00 2·50
428 **79** 5c. on 15c. violet 1·75 45

1919. Official stamps of 1915 surch **Vale centavo de cordoba** and with bar through "OFICIAL".
444 **80** ½c. on 2c. blue 30 15
445 ½c. on 4c. blue 70 15
446 **79** 1c. on 3c. blue 70 25
432 1c. on 25c. blue 1·10 20
433 **80** 2c. on 50c. blue 1·10 20
443a 10c. on 20c. blue 1·00 40

1921. Official stamps of 1913 optd **Particular** and wavy lines through "OFICIAL".
441 **70** 1c. blue 90 45
442 5c. blue 90 35

1921. No. 399 surch **Vale medio centavo**.
447 **79** ½c. on 5c. black 35 15

1921. Official stamp of 1915 optd **Particular R de C** and bars.
448 **79** 1c. blue 3·50 1·00

1921. Official stamps of 1915 surch **Vale un centavo R de C** and bars.
449 **79** 1c. on 5c. blue 95 35
450 **80** 1c. on 6c. blue 50 20
451 1c. on 10c. blue 65 20
452 **79** 1c. on 15c. blue 1·10 20

90

91 Jose C. del Valle

1921. Fiscal stamps as T **23** surch **R de C Vale** and new value.
453 **90** 1c. on 1c. red and black 10 10
454 1c. on 2c. green and black 10 10
455 1c. on 4c. orange and black 10 10
456 1c. on 15c. blue and black 10 10
No. 456 is inscr "TIMBRE TELEGRAFICO".

1921. Independence Centenary.
457 – ½c. black and blue 30 25
458 **91** 1c. black and green 30 25
459 – 2c. black and red 30 25
460 – 5c. black and violet 30 25
461 – 10c. black and orange 20 25
462 – 25c. black and yellow 30 25
463 – 50c. black and violet 30 25
DESIGNS: ½c. Arce; 2c. Larreinaga; 5c. F. Chamorro; 10c. Jerez; 25c. J. P. Chamorro; 50c. Dario.

1922. Surch **Vale un centavo R. de C.**
464 **80** 1c. on 10c. yellow 10 10

1922. As Nos. 394, etc, but colours changed.
465 **79** ½c. green 15 10
466 1c. violet 15 10
467 **80** 2c. red 15 10
468 **79** 3c. olive 25 15
469 **80** 6c. brown 15 15
470 **79** 15c. brown 25 15
471 **80** 20c. brown 35 15
472 1cor. brown 65 35
Nos. 465/72 are size 27 × 22¾ mm.
For later issues of these types, see Nos. 617/27 and 912/24.

1922. Optd **R. de C.**
473 **79** 1c. violet 10 10

1922. Independence issue of 1921 surch **R. de C. Vale un centavo**.
474 **91** 1c. on 1c. black and green 55 45
475 – 1c. on 5c. black and violet 55 55
476 – 1c. on 10c. black and orange 55 30
477 – 1c. on 25c. black and yellow 55 25
478 – 1c. on 50c. black and violet 25 20

94

99 F. Hernandez de Cordoba

1922. Surch **Nicaragua R. de C. Vale un cent.**
479 **94** 1c. yellow 10 10
480 1c. mauve 10 10
481 1c. blue 10 10

1922. Surch **Vale 0.01 de Cordoba** in two lines.
482 **80** 1c. on 10c. yellow 70 25
483 2c. on 10c. yellow 70 20

1923. Surch **Vale 2 centavos de cordoba** in three lines.
484 **79** 1c. on 5c. black 70 15
485 **80** 2c. on 10c. yellow 70 15

1923. Optd **Sello Postal**.
486 – ½c. black and blue (No. 457) 5·50 4·25
487 **91** 1c. black and green 1·40 70

1923. Independence issue of 1921 surch **R. de C. Vale un centavo de cordoba**.
488 1c. on 2c. black and red 30 30
489 1c. on 5c. black and violet 35 15
490 1c. on 10c. black and orange 15 15
491 1c. on 25c. black and yellow 25 25
492 1c. on 50c. black and violet 15 10

1923. Fiscal stamp optd **R. de C.**
493 **90** 1c. red and black 15 10

1924. Optd **R. de C. 1924** in two lines.
494 **79** 1c. violet 15 15

1924. 400th Anniv of Foundation of Leon and Granada.
495 **99** 1c. green 90 25
496 2c. red 90 25
497 5c. blue 65 25
498 10c. brown 65 45

1925. Optd **R. de C. 1925** in two lines.
499 **79** 1c. violet 15 10

1927. Optd **Resello 1927**.
525 **79** ½c. green 10 10
528 1c. violet (No. 466) 10 10
555 1c. violet (No. 473) 15 10
532 **80** 2c. red 15 10
533 **79** 3c. green 20 10
537 **80** 4c. red 9·50 8·00
539 **79** 5c. grey 55 20
542 **80** 6c. brown 7·75 6·50
543 10c. yellow 25 15
545 **79** 15c. brown 55 25
547 **80** 20c. brown 25 15
549 **79** 25c. orange 30 15
551 **80** 50c. blue 30 15
553 1cor. brown 35 15

1928. Optd **Resello 1928**.
559 **79** ½c. green 20 15
560 1c. violet 10 10
561 **80** 2c. red 15 10
562 **79** 3c. green 15 10
563 **80** 4c. red 15 10
564 **79** 5c. grey 15 10
565 **80** 6c. brown 15 10
566 10c. yellow 20 10
567 **79** 15c. brown 25 20
568 **80** 20c. brown 35 20
569 **79** 25c. orange 55 20
570 **80** 50c. blue 90 10
571 1cor. brown 75 25

1928. Optd **Correos 1928**.
574 **79** ½c. green 15 10
575 1c. violet 10 10
576 3c. olive 55 20
577 **80** 4c. red 25 10
578 **79** 5c. grey 20 10
579 **80** 6c. brown 30 15
580 10c. yellow 35 15
581 **79** 15c. brown 1·00 15
582 **80** 20c. brown 1·00 15
583 **79** 25c. orange 1·00 20
584 **80** 50c. blue 1·00 20
585 1cor. brown 3·00 1·50

1928. No. 577 surch **Vale 2 cts.**
586 **80** 2c. on 4c. red 90 25

1928. Fiscal stamp as T **90**, but inscr "TIMBRE TELEGRAFICO" and surch **Correos 1928 Vale** and new value.
587 **90** 1c. on 5c. blue and black 25 15
588 2c. on 5c. blue and black 25 15
589 3c. on 5c. blue and black 25 15

1928. Obligatory Tax. No. 587 additionally optd **R. de T.**
590 **90** 1c. on 5c. blue and black 45 10

1928. As Nos. 465/72 but colours changed.
591 **79** ½c. red 30 15
592 1c. orange 30 15
593 **80** 2c. green 30 15
594 **79** 3c. purple 30 20
595 **80** 4c. brown 30 20
596 **79** 5c. yellow 30 15
597 **80** 6c. blue 30 20
598 10c. blue 65 20
599 **79** 15c. red 85 35
600 **80** 20c. green 85 35
601 **79** 25c. purple 16·00 3·75
602 **80** 50c. brown 1·90 70
603 1cor. violet 3·75 1·75
See also Nos. 617/27 and 912/24.

106

1928.
604 **106** 1c. purple 20 10
647 1c. red 25 10
For 1c. green see No. 925.

1929. Optd **R. de C.**
605 **79** 1c. orange 10 10
628 1c. olive 15 10

1929. Optd **Correos 1929**.
606 **79** ½c. green 20 15

1929. Optd **Correos 1928**.
607 **99** 10c. brown 55 45

1929. Fiscal stamps as T **90**, but inscr "TIMBRE TELEGRAFICO". A. Surch **Correos 1929 R. de C. C$ 0.01** vert.
613 **90** 1c. on 5c. blue and black 10 15

B. Surch **Correos 1929** and value.
611 **90** 1c. on 10c. green and black 20 15
612 2c. on 5c. blue and black 20 10

C. Surch **Correos 1929** and value vert and **R. de C.** or **R. de T.** horiz.
608 **90** 1c. on 5c. blue and black (R. de T.) 20 15
609 2c. on 5c. blue and black (R. de T.) 15 15
610 2c. on 5c. blue and black (R. de C.) 13·00 70

1929. Air. Optd **Correo Aereo 1929. P.A.A.**
614 **79** 25c. sepia 1·40 1·40
615 25c. orange 1·00 1·00
616 25c. violet 90 70

1929. As Nos. 591/603 but colours changed.
617 **79** 1c. green 10 10
618 3c. blue 25 15
619 **80** 4c. blue 25 15
620 **79** 5c. brown 30 15
621 **80** 6c. drab 30 15
622 10c. brown 45 15
623 **79** 15c. red 65 20
624 **80** 20c. orange 80 25
625 **79** 25c. violet 20 10
626 **80** 50c. green 35 15
627 1cor. yellow 2·75 90
See also Nos. 912/24.

112 Mt. Momotombo

1929. Air.
629 **112** 15c. purple 25 10
630 20c. green 70 45
631 25c. olive 50 30
632 50c. sepia 80 45
633 1cor. red 1·10 55
See also Nos. 926/30.

1930. Air. Surch **Vale** and value.
634 **112** 15c. on 25c. olive 40 30
635 20c. on 25c. olive 60 45

114 G.P.O. Managua

1930. Opening of the G.P.O., Managua.
636 **114** ½c. sepia 80 60
637 1c. red 80 60
638 2c. orange 65 45
639 3c. orange 1·00 90
640 4c. yellow 1·00 90
641 5c. olive 1·60 1·10
642 6c. green 1·60 1·10
643 10c. black 1·60 1·00
644 25c. blue 3·25 2·40
645 50c. blue 5·25 3·50
646 1cor. violet 15·00 7·25

1931. Optd **1931** and thick bar obliterating old overprint "1928".
648 **99** 10c. brown (No. 607) 45 90

1931. No. 607 surch **C$ 0.02**.
649 **99** 2c. on 10c. brown 55 45

1931. Optd **1931** and thick bar.
650 **99** 2c. on 10c. brown (No. 498) 55 1·75

1931. Air. Nos. 614/16 surch **1931 Vale** and value.
651 **79** 15c. on 25c. sepia 90·00 90·00
652 15c. on 25c. orange 45·00 45·00
653 15c. on 25c. violet 9·00 9·00
654 20c. on 25c. violet 9·00 9·00

1931. Optd **1931**.
656 **79** ½c. green 35 10
657 1c. olive 35 10
665 1c. orange (No. 605) 10 10
658 **80** 2c. red 35 10
659 **79** 3c. blue 35 15

660 5c. yellow 2·10 1·40
661 5c. sepia 65 20
662 15c. orange 70 45
663 25c. sepia 9·00 3·75
664 25c. violet 3·50 1·50

1931. Air. Surch **1931** and value.
667 **80** 15c. on 25c. olive 4·75 4·75
668 15c. on 50c. sepia 36·00 36·00
669 15c. on 1cor. red 90·00 90·00
666 15c. on 20c. on 25c. olive (No. 635) 7·50 7·50

120 G.P.O. before and after the Earthquake

1932. G.P.O. Reconstruction Fund.
670 **120** ½c. green (postage) 90 90
671 1c. brown 1·25 1·25
672 2c. red 90 90
673 3c. blue 90 90
674 4c. blue 90 90
675 5c. brown 1·40 1·40
676 6c. brown 1·40 1·40
677 10c. brown 2·25 1·50
678 15c. red 3·50 2·25
679 20c. orange 2·10 2·10
680 25c. violet 2·25 2·25
681 50c. green 2·25 2·25
682 1cor. yellow 4·50 4·50
683 15c. mauve (air) 90 75
684 20c. green 1·10 1·10
685 25c. brown 5·50 5·50
686 50c. brown 7·00 7·00
687 1cor. red 10·50 10·50

1932. Air. Surch **Vale** and value.
688 **112** 30c. on 50c. sepia 1·40 1·40
689 35c. on 50c. sepia 1·40 1·40
690 40c. on 1cor. red 1·60 1·60
691 55c. on 1cor. red 1·60 1·60
For similar surcharges on these stamps in different colours see Nos. 791/4 and 931/4.

1932. Air. International Air Mail Week. Optd **Semana Correo Aereo Internacional 11–17 Septiembre 1932**.
692 **112** 15c. violet 40·00 40·00

1932. Air. Inauguration of Inland Airmail Service. Surch **Inauguracion Interior 12 Octubre 1932 Vale C$0.08.**
693 **112** 8c. on 1cor. red 13·00 13·00

1932. Air. Optd **Interior–1932** or surch **Vale** and value also.
705 **120** 25c. brown 4·75 4·75
706 32c. on 50c. brown 5·50 5·50
707 40c. on 1cor. red 4·25 4·25

1932. Air. Nos. 671, etc, optd **Correo Aereo Interior** in one line and **1932**, or surch **Vale** and value also.
694 **120** 1c. brown 12·00 12·00
695 2c. red 12·00 12·00
696 3c. blue 5·50 5·50
697 4c. blue 5·50 5·50
698 5c. brown 5·50 5·50
699 6c. brown 5·50 5·50
700 8c. on 10c. brown 5·25 5·25
701 16c. on 20c. orange 5·25 5·25
702 24c. on 25c. violet 5·25 5·25
703 50c. green 5·25 5·25
704 1cor. yellow 5·50 5·50

1932. Air. Surch **Correo Aereo Interior–1932** in two lines and **Vale** and value below.
710 **80** 1c. on 2c. red 40 40
711 **79** 2c. on 3c. blue 40 40
712 **80** 3c. on 4c. blue 40 40
713 **79** 4c. on 5c. sepia 40 40
714 **80** 5c. on 6c. brown 40 40
715 6c. on 10c. brown 40 40
716 **79** 8c. on 15c. orange 40 40
717 **80** 16c. on 20c. orange 40 40
718 **79** 24c. on 25c. violet 85 60
719 25c. on 25c. violet 85 60
720 **80** 32c. on 50c. green 85 75
721 40c. on 50c. green 95 85
722 50c. on 1cor. yellow 1·25 1·25
723 100c. on 1cor. yellow 2·50 2·50

127 Wharf, Port San Jorge

128 La Chocolata Cutting

1932. Opening of Rivas Railway.
726 **127** 1c. yellow (postage) 19·00
727 – 2c. red 19·00
728 – 5c. sepia 19·00
729 – 10c. brown 19·00
730 – 15c. yellow 19·00
731 **128** 15c. violet (air) 25·00
732 – 20c. green 25·00
733 – 25c. brown 25·00
734 – 50c. sepia 25·00
735 – 1cor. red 25·00
DESIGNS—HORIZ: 2c. El Nacascolo Halt; 5c. Rivas Station; 10c. San Juan del Sur; 15c. (No. 730), Arrival platform at Rivas; 20c. El Nacascolo; 25c. La Cuesta cutting; 50c. San Juan del Sur quay; 1cor. El Estero.

1932. Surch **Vale** and value in words.
736 **79** 1c. on 3c. blue 35 15
737 **80** 2c. on 4c. blue 30 15

130 Railway Construction

1932. Opening of Leon–Sauce Railway.
739 – 1c. yellow (postage) 19·00
740 – 2c. red 19·00
741 – 5c. sepia 19·00
742 **130** 10c. brown 19·00
743 – 15c. yellow 19·00
744 – 15c. violet (air) 25·00
745 – 20c. green 25·00
746 – 25c. brown 25·00
747 – 50c. sepia 25·00
748 – 1cor. red 25·00
DESIGNS—HORIZ: 1c. El Sauce; 2c., 15c. (No. 744), Bridge at Santa Lucia; 5c. Santa Lucia; 15c. (No. 743), Santa Lucia cutting; 20c. Santa Lucia River Halt; 25c. Malpaicillo Station; 50c. Railway panorama; 1cor. San Andres.

1933. Surch **Resello 1933 Vale** and value in words.
749 **79** 1c. on 3c. blue 20 15
750 1c. on 5c. sepia 20 15
751 **80** 2c. on 10c. brown 20 15

133 Flag of the Race

1933. 441st Anniv of Columbus' Departure from Palos. Roul.
753 **133** ½c. green (postage) 95 95
754 1c. green 80 80
755 2c. red 80 80
756 3c. red 80 80
757 4c. orange 80 80
758 5c. yellow 95 95
759 10c. brown 95 95
760 15c. brown 95 95
761 20c. blue 95 95
762 25c. blue 95 95
763 30c. violet 2·40 2·40
764 50c. purple 2·40 2·40
765 1cor. brown 2·40 2·40
766 1c. brown (air) 90 90
767 2c. purple 90 90
768 4c. violet 1·50 1·40
769 5c. blue 1·40 1·40
770 6c. blue 1·40 1·40
771 8c. brown 45 45
772 15c. brown 45 45
773 20c. yellow 1·40 1·40
774 25c. orange 1·40 1·40
775 50c. red 1·40 1·40
776 1cor. green 9·00 9·00

(**134**) (Facsimile signatures of R. E. Deshon, Minister of Transport and J. R. Sevilla, P.M.G.)

1933. Optd with T **134**.
777 **79** ½c. green 30 15
778 1c. green 15 10
779 **80** 2c. red 40 15
780 **79** 3c. blue 15 10
781 **80** 4c. blue 20 15
782 **79** 5c. brown 20 10
783 **80** 6c. drab 25 20
784 10c. brown 25 15
785 **79** 15c. red 30 20
786 **80** 20c. orange 40 30
787 **79** 25c. violet 45 25
788 **80** 50c. green 75 50
789 1cor. yellow 4·00 1·60

1933. No. 605 optd with T **134**.
790 **79** 1c. orange 25 15

1933. Air. Surch **Vale** and value.
791 **112** 30c. on 50c. orange 35 15
792 35c. on 50c. blue 45 20
793 40c. on 1cor. yellow 70 15
794 55c. on 1cor. green 70 30

135 Lake Xolotlan

1933. Air. International Airmail Week.
795 **135** 10c. brown 90 90
796 15c. violet 75 75
797 25c. red 85 85
798 50c. blue 90 90

(**136**)

1933. Air. Inland service. Colours changed. Surch as T **136** and optd with T **134**.
799 **80** 1c. on 2c. green 15 15
800 **79** 2c. on 3c. olive 15 15
801 **80** 3c. on 4c. red 15 15
802 **79** 4c. on 5c. blue 15 15
803 **80** 5c. on 6c. blue 15 15
804 6c. on 10c. sepia 15 10
805 **79** 8c. on 15c. brown 20 15
806 **80** 16c. on 20c. brown 20 15
807 **79** 24c. on 25c. red 15 15
808 25c. on 25c. orange 30 30
809 **80** 32c. on 50c. violet 30 25
810 40c. on 50c. green 40 25
811 50c. on 1cor. yellow 40 30
812 1cor. on 1cor. red 95 80

1933. Obligatory Tax. As No. 647 optd with T **134**. Colour changed.
813 **106** 1c. orange 25 15

1934. Air. Surch **Servicio Centroamericano Vale 10 centavos.**
814 **112** 10c. on 20c. green 35 35
815 10c. on 25c. olive 35 35
See also No. 872.

1935. Optd **Resello 1935**. (a) Nos. 778/9.
816 **79** 1c. green 10 10
817 **80** 2c. red 15 10
(b) No. 813 but without T **134** opt.
818 **106** 1c. orange 15 10

1935. No. 783 surch **Vale Medio Centavo.**
819 **80** ½c. on 6c. brown 35 15

1935. Optd with T **134** and **RESELLO – 1935** in a box.
820 **79** ½c. green 20 15
821 **80** ½c. on 6c. brown (No. 819) 15 10
822 **79** 1c. green 25 10
823 **80** 2c. red 55 10
824 2c. red (No. 817) 30 10
825 **79** 3c. blue 30 15
826 **80** 4c. blue 30 15
827 **79** 5c. brown 25 10
828 **80** 6c. drab 30 10
829 10c. brown 55 20
830 **79** 15c. red 15 10
831 **80** 20c. orange 90 25
832 **79** 25c. violet 30 15
833 **80** 50c. green 35 25
834 1cor. yellow 45 35

1935. Obligatory Tax. No. 605 optd with **RESELLO – 1935** in a box.
835 **79** 1c. orange 25·00

1935. Obligatory Tax. Optd **RESELLO – 1935** in a box. (a) No. 813 without T **134** opt.
836 **106** 1c. orange 25 15
(b) No. 818.
868 **106** 1c. orange 20 15

1935. Air. Nos. 799/812 optd with **RESELLO – 1935** in a box.
839 **80** 1c. on 2c. green 10 10
840 **79** 2c. on 3c. olive 20 20
879 **80** 3c. on 4c. red 15 15
880 **79** 4c. on 5c. blue 15 15
881 **80** 5c. on 6c. blue 15 15
882 6c. on 10c. sepia 15 15
883 **79** 8c. on 15c. brown 15 15
884 **80** 16c. on 20c. brown 15 15
847 **79** 24c. on 25c. red 35 30
848 25c. on 25c. orange 25 25
849 **80** 32c. on 50c. violet 20 20
850 40c. on 50c. green 30 25
851 50c. on 1cor. yellow 45 35
852 1cor. on 1cor. red 85 40

1935. Air. Optd with **RESELLO – 1935** in a box. (a) Nos. 629/33.
853 **112** 15c. purple 30 10
873 20c. green 40 30
855 25c. green 40 35
856 50c. sepia 40 35
857 1cor. red 65 35
(b) Nos. 791/4.
858 **112** 30c. on 50c. orange 40 35
859 35c. on 50c. blue 40 25
860 40c. on 1cor. yellow 40 35
861 55c. on 1cor. green 40 30
(c) Nos. 814/5.
862 **112** 10c. on 20c. green £300 £300
863 10c. on 25c. olive 60 50

1935. Optd with **RESELLO – 1935** in a box.
864 **79** ½c. green (No. 465) 15 10
865 1c. green (No. 617) 20 10
866 **80** 2c. red (No. 467) 55 10
867 **79** 3c. blue (No. 618) 20 15

1936. Surch **Resello 1936 Vale** and value.
869 **79** 1c. on 3c. blue (No. 618) 15 10
870 2c. on 5c. brown (No. 620) 15 10

1936. Air. Surch **Servicio Centroamericano Vale diez centavos** and **RESELLO – 1935** in a box.
871 **112** 10c. on 25c. olive 30 30

1936. Obligatory Tax. No. 818 optd **1936**.
874 **106** 1c. orange 50 20

1936. Obligatory Tax. No. 605 optd with T **134** and **1936**.
875 **79** 1c. orange 50 20

1936. Air. No. 622 optd **Correo Aereo Centro-Americano Resello 1936**.
876 **80** 10c. brown 20 20

1936. Air. Nos. 799/800 and 805 optd **Resello 1936**.
885 **80** 1c. on 2c. green 25 20
886 **79** 2c. on 3c. olive 10 10
887 8c. on 15c. brown 25 25

1936. Optd with or without T **37**, surch **1936 Vale** and value.
888 **79** ½c. on 15c. red 20 15
889 **80** 1c. on 4c. blue 25 15
890 **79** 1c. on 5c. brown 25 20
891 **80** 1c. on 6c. drab 45 20
892 **79** 1c. on 15c. red 25 20
893 **80** 1c. on 20c. orange 20 15
895 2c. on 10c. brown 30 20
896 **79** 2c. on 15c. red 60 50
897 **80** 2c. on 20c. orange 55 45
898 **79** 2c. on 25c. violet 35 20
900 **80** 2c. on 50c. green 35 25
901 2c. on 1cor. yellow 35 30
902 3c. on 4c. blue 40 30

1936. Optd **Resello 1936**.
903 **79** 3c. blue (No. 618) 35 25
904 5c. brown (No. 620) 30 15
905 **80** 10c. brown (No. 784) 30 20

1936. Air. Surch **1936 Vale and value.**
906 **112** 15c. on 50c. brown 30 25
907 15c. on 1cor. red 30 25

1936. Fiscal stamps surch **RECONSTRUCCION COMUNICACIONES 5 CENTAVOS DE CORDOBA** and further surch **Vale dos centavos Resello 1936**.
908 **90** 1c. on 5c. green 25 10
909 2c. on 5c. green 25 10

1936. Obligatory Tax. Fiscal stamps surch **RECONSTRUCCION COMUNICACIONES 5 CENTAVOS DE CORDOBA** and further surch. (a) **1936 R. de C. Vale Un Centavo.**
910 **90** 1c. on 5c. green 15 10
(b) **Vale un centavo R. de C. 1936.**
911 **90** 1c. on 5c. green 20 10

1937. Colours changed. Size 27×22¾ mm.
912 **79** ½c. black 15 10
913 1c. red 15 10

No.	Type	Description	Unused	Used
914	80	2c. blue	15	10
915	79	3c. brown	15	10
916	80	4c. yellow	20	10
917	79	5c. red	15	10
918	80	6c. violet	20	10
919		10c. green	20	10
920	79	15c. green	15	10
921	80	20c. brown	30	10
922	79	25c. orange	30	10
923	80	50c. brown	35	15
924		1cor. blue	40	25

1937. Obligatory Tax. Colour changed.

No.	Type	Description	Unused	Used
925	106	1c. green	15	10

1937. Air. Colours changed.

No.	Type	Description	Unused	Used
926	112	15c. orange	20	10
927		20c. red	20	15
928		25c. black	25	15
929		50c. violet	45	15
930		1cor. orange	65	15

1937. Air. Surch **Vale** and value. Colours changed.

No.	Type	Description	Unused	Used
931	112	30c. on 50c. red	30	10
932		35c. on 50c. olive	35	10
933		40c. on 1cor. green	35	15
934		55c. on 1cor. blue	35	30

1937. Air. Surch **Servicio Centroamericano Vale Diez Centavos**.

No.	Type	Description	Unused	Used
949	112	10c. on 1cor. red	30	15

1937. Air. No. 805 (without T **134**) optd **1937**.

No.	Type	Description	Unused	Used
950	79	8c. on 15c. brown	50	15

142 Baseball Player

1937. Obligatory Tax. For 1937 Central American Olympic Games. Optd with ball in red under "OLIMPICO".

No.	Type	Description	Unused	Used
951	142	1c. red	35	15
952		1c. yellow	35	15
953		1c. blue	35	15
953a		1c. green	35	15
MS953b		134×90 mm. Nos. 951/3a	3·25	3·25

1937. Nos. 799/809 optd **Habilitado 1937**.

No.	Type	Description	Unused	Used
954	80	1c. on 2c. green	10	10
955	79	2c. on 3c. olive	10	10
956	80	3c. on 4c. red	10	10
957	79	4c. on 5c. blue	10	10
958	80	5c. on 6c. blue	10	10
959		6c. on 10c. brown	10	10
960	79	8c. on 15c. brown	10	10
961	80	16c. on 20c. brown	20	20
962	79	24c. on 25c. red	20	20
963		25c. on 25c. orange	20	25
964	80	32c. on 50c. violet	20	25

144 Presidential Palace, Managua

1937. Air. Inland.

No.	Type	Description	Unused	Used
965	144	1c. red	15	10
966		2c. blue	15	10
967		3c. olive	15	10
968		4c. black	15	10
969		5c. purple	20	10
970		6c. brown	20	10
971		8c. violet	20	10
972		16c. orange	35	25
973		24c. yellow	20	15
974		25c. green	50	25

145 Nicaragua

1937. Air. Abroad.

No.	Type	Description	Unused	Used
975	145	10c. green	25	10
976		15c. blue	25	10
977		20c. yellow	30	25
978		25c. violet	30	25
979		30c. red	40	25
980		50c. orange	60	25
981		1cor. olive	65	45

146 Presidential Palace

1937. Air. Abroad. 150th Anniv of U.S. Constitution.

No.	Type	Description	Unused	Used
982	–	10c. blue and green	1·10	70
983	146	15c. blue and orange	1·10	70
984	–	20c. blue and red	80	65
985	–	25c. blue and brown	80	65
986	–	30c. blue and green	80	65
987	–	35c. blue and yellow	35	25
988	–	40c. blue and green	55	40
989	–	45c. blue and purple	55	40
990	–	50c. blue and mauve	55	40
991	–	55c. blue and green	2·25	1·25
992	–	75c. blue and green	55	30
993	–	1cor. red and blue	75	30

DESIGNS: 10c. Children's Park, Managua; 20c. S. America; 25c. C. America; 30c. N. America; 35c. Lake Tiscapa; 40c. Pan-American motor-road; 45c. Priniomi Park; 50c. Piedrecitas Park; 55c. San Juan del Sur; 75c Rio Tipitapa; 1cor. Granade landscape.

146b Diriangen

1937. Air. Day of the Race.

No.	Type	Description	Unused	Used
993a	146b	1c. green (inland)	15	10
993b		4c. lake	15	10
993c		5c. violet	25	15
993d		8c. blue	15	10
993e		10c. brown (abroad)	20	10
993f		15c. blue	20	10
993g		20c. pink	30	15

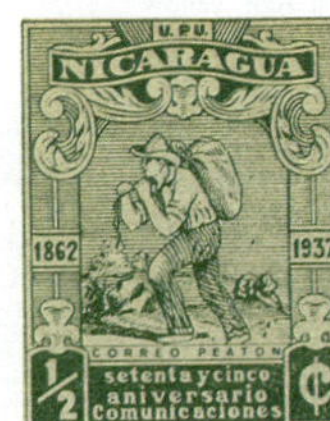

147 Letter Carrier

1937. 75th Anniv of Postal Administration.

No.	Type	Description	Unused	Used
994	147	½c. green	15	10
995	–	1c. mauve	15	10
996	–	2c. brown	15	10
997	–	3c. violet	65	20
998	–	5c. blue	65	20
999	–	7½c. red	2·50	75

DESIGNS: 1c. Mule transport; 2c. Diligence; 3c. Yacht; 5c. Packet steamer; 7½c. Steam mail train.

147a Gen. Tomas Martinez

1938. Air. 75th Anniv of Postal Administration.

No.	Type	Description	Unused	Used
999a	147a	1c. blk & orge (inland)	25	20
999b		5c. black and violet	25	20
999c		8c. black and blue	30	30
999d		16c. black and brown	40	35
999e	–	10c. blk & grn (abroad)	30	25
999f	–	15c. black and blue	40	35
999g	–	25c. black and violet	25	25
999h	–	50c. black and red	40	30

DESIGNS: 10c. to 50c. Gen. Anastasio Somoza.

1938. Surch **1938** and **Vale**, new value in words and **Centavos**.

No.	Type	Description	Unused	Used
1000	79	3c. on 25c. orange	10	10
1001	80	5c. on 50c. brown	10	10
1002		6c. on 1 cor. blue	15	15

149 Dario Park

150 Lake Managua

151 President Somoza

1939.

No.	Type	Description	Unused	Used
1003	149	1½c. green (postage)	10	10
1004		2c. red	10	10
1005		3c. blue	10	10
1006		6c. brown	10	10
1007		7½c. green	10	10
1008		10c. brown	15	10
1009		15c. orange	15	10
1010		25c. violet	15	15
1011		50c. green	30	20
1012		1cor. yellow	60	45
1013	150	2c. blue (air: inland)	15	15
1014		3c. olive	15	15
1015		8c. mauve	15	15
1016		16c. orange	25	15
1017		24c. yellow	25	15
1018		32c. green	35	15
1019		50c. red	40	15
1020	151	10c. brown (air: abroad)	15	10
1021		15c. blue	15	10
1022		20c. yellow	15	20
1023		25c. violet	15	15
1024		30c. red	20	20
1025		50c. orange	30	20
1026		1cor. olive	45	35

1939. Nos. 920/1. Surch **Vale un Centavo 1939**.

No.	Type	Description	Unused	Used
1027	79	1c. on 15c. green	10	10
1028	80	1c. on 20c. brown	10	10

153 Will Rogers and Managua Airport

1939. Air. Will Rogers Commemorative. Inscr "WILL ROGERS/1931/1939".

No.	Type	Description	Unused	Used
1029	153	1c. green	10	10
1030	–	2c. red	10	10
1031	–	3c. blue	10	10
1032	–	4c. blue	15	10
1033	–	5c. red	10	10

DESIGNS: 2c. Rogers at Managua; 3c. Rogers in P.A.A. hut; 4c. Rogers and U.S. Marines; 5c. Rogers and street in Managua.

156 Senate House and Pres. Somoza

1940. Air. President's Visit to U.S.A. (a) Inscr "AEREO INTERIOR".

No.	Type	Description	Unused	Used
1034	–	4c. brown	15	10
1035	156	8c. brown	10	10
1036	–	16c. green	15	10
1037	156	20c. mauve	30	15
1038	–	32c. red	20	20

(b) Inscr "CORREO AEREO INTERNACIONAL".

No.	Type	Description	Unused	Used
1039	–	25c. blue	20	15
1040	–	30c. black	20	10
1041	156	50c. red	25	40
1042	–	60c. green	30	35
1043	–	65c. brown	30	20
1044	–	90c. olive	40	35
1045	–	1cor. violet	60	30

DESIGNS: 4c., 16c., 25c., 30c., 65c., 90c. Pres. Somoza addressing Senate; 32c., 60c., 1cor. Portrait of Pres. Somoza between symbols of Nicaragua and New York World's Fair.

158 L. S. Rowe, Statue of Liberty and Union Flags

1940. Air. 50th Anniv of Pan-American Union.

No.	Type	Description	Unused	Used
1046	158	1cor.25 multicoloured	40	35

159 First Issue of Nicaragua and Sir Rowland Hill

1941. Air. Centenary of First Adhesive Postage stamps.

No.	Type	Description	Unused	Used
1047	159	2cor. brown	2·25	75
1048		3cor. blue	7·00	80
1049		5cor. red	20·00	2·10

1941. Surch **Servicio ordinario Vale Diez Centavos de Cordoba**.

No.	Type	Description	Unused	Used
1050	153	10c. on 1c. green	15	10

161 Rube Dario

1941. 25th Death Anniv of Ruben Dario (poet).

No.	Type	Description	Unused	Used
1051	161	10c. red (postage)	20	15
1052		20c. mauve (air)	25	15
1053		35c. green	30	20
1054		40c. orange	35	25
1055		60c. blue	40	35

1943. Surch **Servicio Ordinario Vale Diez Centavos**.

No.	Type	Description	Unused	Used
1056	153	10c. on 1c. green	10	10

162 "V" for Victory **163** Red Cross

164 Red Cross Workers and Wounded

1943. Victory.

No.	Type	Description	Unused	Used
1057	162	10c. red and violet (postage)	10	10
1058		30c. red and brown	15	10
1059		40c. red and green (air)	15	10
1060		60c. red and blue	20	10

1944. Air. 80th Anniv of Int Red Cross Society.

No.	Type	Description	Unused	Used
1061	163	25c. red	40	15
1062	–	50c. bistre	65	35
1063	164	1cor. green	1·25	1·00

DESIGN—VERT: 50c. Two Hemispheres.

165 Columbus and Lighthouse **166** Columbus's Fleet and Lighthouse

1945. Honouring Columbus's Discovery of America and Erection of Columbus Lighthouse near Trujillo City, Dominican Republic.

No.	Type	Description	Unused	Used
1064	165	4c. black & green (postage)	15	10
1065		6c. black and orange	20	10
1066		8c. black and red	20	15
1067		10c. black and blue	30	15
1068	166	20c. grey and green (air)	60	20
1069		35c. black and red	95	25
1070		75c. pink and green	1·75	55
1071		90c. blue and red	2·00	85
1072		1cor. blue and black	2·25	50
1073		2cor.50 red and blue	6·00	2·50

168 Roosevelt as a Stamp Collector

1946. President Roosevelt Commemorative Inscr "HOMENAJE A ROOSEVELT".

No.	Type	Description	Unused	Used
1074	168	4c. green & black (postage)	15	15
1075	–	8c. violet and black	20	20
1076	–	10c. blue and black	30	25
1077	–	16c. red and black	40	30
1078	–	32c. brown and black	50	25
1079	–	50c. grey and black	50	25

1080 – 25c. orange & black (air) 20 10
1081 – 75c. red and black 25 20
1082 – 1cor. green and black 30 30
1083 – 3cor. violet and black 2·25 2·25
1084 – 5cor. blue and black 3·00 3·00

DESIGNS—portraying Roosevelt. HORIZ: 8c., 25c. with Churchill at the Atlantic Conference; 16c., 1cor. with Churchill, De Gaulle and Giraud at the Casablanca Conference; 32c., 3cor. with Churchill and Stalin at the Teheran Conference. VERT: 10c., 75c. Signing Declaration of War against Japan; 50c., 5cor. Head of Roosevelt.

171 Managua Cathedral

172 G.P.O., Managua

1947. Managua Centenary. Frames in black.
1085 **171** 4c. red (postage) 10 10
1086 – 5c. blue 15 10
1087 – 6c. green 20 15
1088 – 10c. olive 20 15
1089 – 75c. brown 30 25

1090 – 5c. violet (air) 10 10
1091 **172** 20c. green 15 15
1092 – 35c. orange 15 15
1093 – 90c. purple 30 20
1094 – 1cor. brown 45 35
1095 – 2cor.50 purple 1·00 1·10

DESIGNS—POSTAGE (as Type **171**): 5c. Health Ministry; 6c. Municipal Building; 10c. College; 75c. G.P.O., Managua. AIR (as Type **172**): 5c. College; 35c. Health Ministry; 90c. National Bank; 1cor. Municipal Building; 2cor.50, National Palace.

173 San Cristobal Volcano

174 Ruben Dario Monument, Managua

1947. (a) Postage.
1096 **173** 2c. orange and black 10 10
1097 – 3c. violet and black 10 10
1098 – 4c. grey and black 10 10
1099 – 5c. red and black 20 10
1100 – 6c. green and black 15 10
1101 – 8c. brown and black 15 10
1102 – 10c. red and black 25 15
1103 – 20c. blue and black 1·10 25
1104 – 30c. purple and black 70 25
1105 – 50c. red and black 1·90 70
1106 – 1cor. brown and black 60 35

DESIGNS—as Type **173**: 3c. Lion on Ruben Dario's tomb, Leon Cathedral; 4c. Race stand; 5c. Soldiers' Monument; 6c. Sugar cane; 8c. Tropical fruits; 10c. Cotton; 20c. Horses; 30c. Coffee plant; 50c. Prize bullock; 1cor. Agricultural landscape.

(b) Air.
1107 **174** 5c. red and green 10 10
1108 – 6c. orange and black 10 10
1109 – 8c. brown and red 10 10
1110 – 10c. blue and brown 15 10
1111 – 20c. orange and blue 15 10
1112 – 25c. green and red 20 15
1113 – 35c. brown and black 30 15
1114 – 50c. black and violet 20 10
1115 – 1cor. red and black 45 25
1116 – 1cor.50 green and red 50 45
1117 – 5cor. red and brown 3·75 3·75
1118 – 10cor. brown and violet 3·00 3·00
1119 – 25cor. yellow and green 6·00 6·00

DESIGNS—As Type **174**: 6c. Baird's tapir; 8c. Highway and Lake Managua; 10c. Genizaro Dam; 20c. Ruben Dario Monument, Managua; 25c. Sulphur Lagoon, Nejapa; 35c. Managua Airport; 50c. Mouth of Rio Prinzapolka; 1cor. Thermal Baths, Tipitapa; 1cor.50, Rio Tipitapa; 5cor. Embassy building; 10cor. Girl carrying basket of fruit; 2cor. Franklin D. Roosevelt Monument, Managua.

175 Softball

176 Pole-vaulting

177 Tennis

178 National Stadium, Managua

1949. 10th World Amateur Baseball Championships. (a) Postage as T **175/6**.
1120 **175** 1c. brown 10 10
1121 – 2c. blue 50 15
1122 **176** 3c. green 25 10
1123 – 4c. purple 15 15
1124 – 5c. orange 40 15
1125 – 10c. green 40 15
1126 – 15c. red 50 15
1127 – 25c. blue 50 20
1128 – 35c. green 80 20
1129 – 40c. violet 1·75 30
1130 – 60c. black 1·40 35
1131 – 1cor. red 1·50 90
1132 – 2cor. purple 2·75 1·50
MS1132a Thirteen sheets 140×105 or 105×140 mm (vert designs). Nos. 1120/32 in blocks of four 60·00 60·00

DESIGNS—VERT: 2c. Scout; 5c. Cycling; 25c. Boxing; 35c. Basketball. HORIZ: 4c. Diving; 10c. Stadium; 15c. Baseball; 40c. Yachting; 60c. Table tennis; 1cor. Football; 2cor. Tennis.

(b) Air as T **177**.
1133 **177** 1c. red 10 10
1134 – 2c. black 10 10
1135 – 3c. red 10 10
1136 – 4c. black 10 10
1137 – 5c. blue 35 15
1138 – 15c. green 65 10
1139 – 25c. purple 1·25 25
1140 – 30c. brown 1·00 25
1141 – 40c. violet 50 25
1142 – 75c. mauve 2·50 1·60
1143 – 1cor. blue 3·00 80
1144 – 2cor. olive 1·25 1·00
1145 – 5cor. green 2·10 2·10
MS1145a Thirteen sheets each 125×115 mm. Nos. 1133/45 in blocks of four £120 £120

DESIGNS—SQUARE: 2c. Football; 3c. Table tennis; 4c. Stadium; 5c. Yachting; 15c. Basketball; 25c. Boxing; 30c. Baseball; 40c. Cycling; 75c. Diving; 1cor. Pole-vaulting; 2cor. Scout; 5cor. Softball.

1949. Obligatory Tax stamps. Stadium Construction Fund.
1146 **178** 5c. blue 20 10
1146a 5c. red 20 10
MS1146b 87×97 mm. No. 1146 in block of four 3·00 3·00

179 Rowland Hill

180 Heinrich von Stephan

1950. 75th Anniv of U.P.U. Frames in black.
1147 **179** 20c. red (postage) 15 10
1148 – 25c. green 15 10
1149 – 75c. blue 50 50
1150 – 80c. green 30 25
1151 – 4cor. blue 85 80
MS1151a Five sheets each 114×126 mm. Nos. 1147/51 in blocks of four 24·00 24·00

DESIGNS—VERT: 25c. Portrait as Type **180**; 75c. Monument, Berne; 80c., 4cor. Obverse and reverse of Congress Medal.

1152 – 16c. red (air) 15 10
1153 **180** 20c. orange 15 10
1154 – 25c. black 15 15
1155 – 30c. red 25 10
1156 – 85c. green 55 50
1157 – 1cor.10 brown 50 35
1158 – 2cor.14 green 1·25 1·25
MS1158a Seven sheets each 126×114 mm. Nos. 1152/8 in blocks of four 28·00 28·00

DESIGNS—HORIZ: 16c. Rowland Hill; 25, 30c. U.P.U. Offices, Berne; 85c. Monument, Berne; 1cor.10 and 2cor.14,Obverse and reverse of Congress Medal.

181 Queen Isabella and Columbus's Fleet

182 Isabella the Catholic

1952. 500th Birth Anniv of Isabella the Catholic.
1159 – 10c. mauve (postage) 10 10
1160 **181** 96c. blue 1·50 65
1161 – 98c. red 1·50 65
1162 – 1cor.20 brown 50 40
1163 **182** 1cor.76 purple 60 60
MS1163a 160×128 mm. Nos. 1159/63 2·40 2·40

1164 2cor.30 red (air) 1·40 1·10
1165 – 2cor.80 orange 1·00 95
1166 – 3cor. green 4·25 1·75
1167 **181** 3cor.30 blue 4·25 2·00
1168 – 3cor.60 green 1·50 1·25
MS1168a 160×128 mm. Nos. 1164/8 5·50 5·50

DESIGNS—VERT: 10c., 3cor.60, Queen facing right; 98c., 3cor. Queen and "Santa Maria"; 1cor.20, 2cor.80, Queen and Map of Americas.

183 O.D.E.C.A. Flag

1953. Foundation of Organization of Central American States.
1169 **183** 4c. blue (postage) 10 10
1170 – 5c. green 10 10
1171 – 6c. brown 10 10
1172 – 15c. olive 20 15
1173 – 50c. sepia 25 15

1174 – 20c. red (air) 10 10
1175 **183** 25c. blue 15 10
1176 – 30c. brown 15 15
1177 – 60c. green 25 20
1178 – 1cor. purple 35 45

DESIGNS: 5c., 1cor. Map of C. America; 6c., 20c. Hands holding O.D.E.C.A. arms; 15c., 30c. Five presidents of C. America; 50c., 60c. Charter and flags.

184 Pres. Solorzano

185 Pres. Arguello

1953. Presidential Series. Portraits in black. (a) Postage. As T **184**.
1179 **184** 4c. red 10 10
1180 – 6c. blue (D. M. Chamorro) 10 10
1181 – 8c. brown (Diaz) 10 10
1182 – 15c. red (Somoza) 15 10
1183 – 50c. green (E. Chamorro) 20 15

(b) Air. As T **185**.
1184 **185** 4c. red 10 10
1185 – 5c. orange (Moncada) 10 10
1186 – 20c. blue (J. B. Sacasa) 10 10
1187 – 25c. blue (Zelaya) 10 10
1188 – 30c. lake (Somoza) 10 10
1189 – 35c. green (Martinez) 20 20
1190 – 40c. plum (Guzman) 20 20
1191 – 45c. olive (Cuadra) 20 20
1192 – 50c. red (P. J. Chamorro) 35 25
1193 – 60c. blue (Zavala) 40 40
1194 – 85c. brown (Cardenas) 40 40
1195 – 1cor.10 purple (Carazo) 60 55
1196 – 1cor.20 bistre (R. Sacasa) 65 55

186 Sculptor and U.N. Emblem

1954. U.N.O. Inscr "HOMENAJE A LA ONU".
1197 **186** 3c. drab (postage) 10 10
1198 A 4c. green 15 10
1199 B 5c. green 20 10
1200 C 15c. green 55 20
1201 D 1cor. turquoise 45 40

1202 E 3c. red (air) 10 10
1203 F 4c. orange 10 10
1204 C 5c. red 15 10
1205 D 30c. pink 75 15
1206 B 2cor. red 80 70
1207 A 3cor. brown 1·50 1·00
1208 **186** 5cor. purple 1·75 1·40

DESIGNS: A, Detail from Nicaragua's coat of arms; B, Globe; C, Candle and Nicaragua's Charter; D, Flags of Nicaragua and U.N.; E, Torch; F, Trusting hands.

187 Capt. D. L. Ray

188 North American Sabre

1954. National Air Force. Frames in black. (a) Postage. Frames as T **187**.
1209 **187** 1c. black 10 10
1210 – 2c. black 10 10
1211 – 3c. myrtle 10 10
1212 – 4c. orange 15 10
1213 – 5c. green 20 10
1214 – 15c. turquoise 15 10
1215 – 1cor. violet 35 25

(b) Air. Frames as T **188**.
1216 – 10c. black 10 10
1217 **188** 15c. black 15 10
1218 – 20c. mauve 15 10
1219 – 25c. red 20 10
1220 – 30c. blue 10 10
1221 – 50c. blue 75 50
1222 – 1cor. green 65 35

DESIGNS—POSTAGE: 2c. North American Sabre; 3c. Douglas Boston; 4c. Consolidated Liberator; 5c. North American Texan trainer; 15c. Pres. Somoza; 1cor. Emblem. AIR: 10c. D. L. Ray; 20c. Emblem; 25c. Hangars; 30c. Pres. Somoza; 50c. North American Texan trainers; 1cor. Lockheed Lightning airplanes.

189 Rotary Slogans

190a

1955. 50th Anniv of Rotary International.
1223 **189** 15c. orange (postage) 10 10
1224 A 20c. olive 15 15
1225 B 35c. violet 15 15
1226 C 40c. red 15 15
1227 D 90c. black 30 25
MS1227a 127×102 mm. Nos. 1223/7 2·50 2·50

1228 D 1c. red (air) 10 10
1229 A 2c. blue 10 10
1230 C 3c. green 10 10
1231 **189** 4c. violet 10 10
1232 B 5c. brown 10 10
1233 25c. turquoise 15 15
1234 **189** 30c. black 15 10
1235 C 45c. mauve 30 25
1236 A 50c. green 25 20
1237 D 1cor. blue 45 30
MS1237a 127×102 mm. Nos. 1233/7 5·00 5·00

DESIGNS—VERT: A, Clasped hands; B, Rotarian and Nicaraguan flags; D, Paul P. Harris. HORIZ: C, World map and winged emblem.

1956. National Exhibition. Surch **Conmemoracion Exposicion Nacional Febrero 4-16, 1956** and value.
1238 5c. on 6c. brown (No. 1171) (postage) 10 10
1239 5c. on 6c. black & bl (No. 1180) 10 10
1240 5c. on 8c. brn & blk (No. 1101) 10 10
1241 15c. on 35c. violet (No. 1225) 15 10
1242 15c. on 80c. grn & blk (No. 1150) 15 10
1243 15c. on 90c. black (No. 1227) 15 10
1244 30c. on 35c. black and green (No. 1189) (air) 10 15
1245 30c. on 45c. blk & ol (No. 1191) 25 15
1246 30c. on 45c. mauve (No. 1235) 25 15
1247 2cor. on 5cor. purple (No. 1208) 50 35

1956. Obligatory Tax. Social Welfare Fund.
1247a **190a** 5c. blue 10 10

191 Gen. J. Dolores Estrada

192 President Somoza

1956. Cent of War of 1856. Inscr as in T **191**.
1248 – 5c. brown (postage) 10 10
1249 – 10c. lake 10 10
1250 – 15c. grey 10 10
1251 – 25c. red 15 15
1252 – 50c. purple 30 20

1253 **191** 30c. red (air) 10 10
1254 – 60c. brown 20 15

No.	Type	Description	Unused	Used
1255	–	1cor.50 green	20	35
1256	–	2cor.50 blue	30	30
1257	–	10cor. orange	1·90	1·75

DESIGNS—VERT: 5c. Gen. M. Jerez; 10c. Gen. F. Chamorro; 50c. Gen. J. D. Estrada; 1cor.50, E. Mangalo; 10cor. Commodore H. Paulding. HORIZ: 15c. Battle of San Jacinto; 25c. Granada in flames; 60c. Bas-relief; 2cor.50, Battle of Rivas.

1957. Air. National Mourning for Pres. G. A. Somoza. Various frames. Inscr as in T **192**. Centres in black.

No.	Type	Description	Unused	Used
1258	–	15c. black	10	10
1259	–	30c. blue	15	15
1260	**192**	2cor. violet	80	70
1261	–	3cor. olive	1·25	1·10
1262	–	5cor. sepia	1·90	1·90

193 Scout and Badge

194 Clasped Hands, Badge and Globe

1957. Birth Centenary of Lord Baden-Powell.

No.	Type	Description	Unused	Used
1263	**193**	10c. olive & vio (postage)	10	10
1264	–	15c. sepia and purple	15	15
1265	–	20c. brown and blue	15	15
1266	–	25c. brown and turquoise	15	15
1267	–	50c. olive and red	35	35
MS1267a		127 × 102 mm. Nos. 1263/7. Imperf	1·50	1·50
1268	**194**	3c. olive and red (air)	15	15
1269	–	4c. blue and brown	15	15
1270	–	5c. brown and green	15	15
1271	–	6c. drab and violet	15	15
1272	–	8c. red and black	15	15
1273	–	30c. black and green	15	15
1274	–	40c. black and blue	15	15
1275	–	75c. sepia and purple	35	35
1276	–	85c. grey and red	40	40
1277	–	1cor. brown and green	40	40
MS1277a		127 × 102 mm. Nos. 1273/7. Imperf	2·50	2·50

DESIGNS—VERT: 4c. Scout badge; 5c., 15c. Wolf cub; 6c. Badge and flags; 8c. Badge and emblems of scouting 20c. Scout; 25., 1cor. Lord Baden-Powell; 30., 50c. Joseph A. Harrison; 75c. Rover Scout; 85c. Scout. HORIZ: 40c. Presentation to Pres. Somoza.

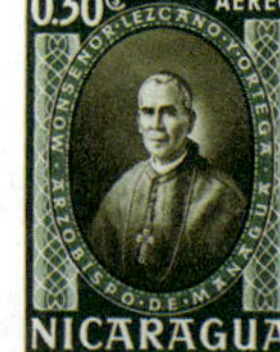

195 Pres. Luis Somoza

197 Archbishop of Managua

196 Managua Cathedral

1957. Election of Pres. Somoza. Portrait in brown.

(a) Postage. Oval frame.

No.	Type	Description	Unused	Used
1278	**195**	10c. red	10	10
1279		15c. blue	10	10
1280		35c. purple	10	10
1281		50c. brown	15	15
1282		75c. green	40	40

(b) Air. Rectangular frame.

No.	Type	Description	Unused	Used
1283	–	20c. blue	10	10
1284	–	25c. mauve	15	10
1285	–	30c. sepia	15	15
1286	–	40c. turquoise	15	15
1287	–	2cor. violet	95	95

1957. Churches and Priests. Centres in olive.

No.	Type	Description	Unused	Used
1288	**196**	5c. green (postage)	10	10
1289	–	10c. purple	10	10
1290	**197**	15c. blue	10	10
1291	–	20c. sepia	10	10
1292	–	50c. green	20	15
1293	–	1cor. violet	30	30
1294	**197**	30c. green (air)	10	10
1295	**196**	60c. brown	15	15
1296	–	75c. blue	25	25
1297	–	90c. red	30	30
1298	–	1cor.50 turquoise	35	35
1299	–	2cor. purple	40	40

DESIGNS—HORIZ: As Type **196**: 20, 90c. Leon Cathedral; 50c., 1cor.50, La Merced, Granada Church. VERT: As Type **197**: 10, 75c. Bishop of Nicaragua; 1, 2cor. Father Mariano Dubon.

198 "Honduras" (freighter)

1957. Nicaraguan Merchant Marine Commemoration. Inscr as in T **198**.

No.	Type	Description	Unused	Used
1300	**198**	4c. black, blue and myrtle (postage)	30	10
1301	–	5c. violet, blue and brown	30	10
1302	–	6c. black, blue and red	30	10
1303	–	10c. black, green and sepia	30	10
1304	–	15c. brown, blue and red	50	10
1305	–	50c. brown, blue and violet	60	20
1306	–	25c. purple, blue and ultramarine (air)	60	20
1307	–	30c. grey, buff and brown	15	10
1308	–	50c. bistre, blue and violet	20	20
1309	–	60c. black, turquoise and purple	85	30
1310	–	1cor. black, blue and red	1·10	30
1311	–	2cor.50 brown, blue and black	2·25	1·25

DESIGNS: 5c. Gen. A. Somoza, founder of Mamenic (National) Shipping Line, and "Guatemala" (freighter); 6c. "Guatemala"; 10c. "Salvador" (freighter); 15c. Freighter between hemispheres; 25c. "Managua" (freighter); 30c. Ship's wheel and world map; 50c. (No. 1305), Hemispheres and ship; 50c. (No. 1308), Mamenic Shipping Line flag; 60c. "Costa Rica" (freighter); 1cor. "Nicarao" (freighter); 2cor.50, Map, freighter and flag.

199 Exhibition Emblem

1958. Air. Brussels International Exn. Inscr "EXPOSICION MUNDIAL DE BELGICA 1958".

No.	Type	Description	Unused	Used
1312	**199**	25c. black, yellow & green	10	10
1313	–	30c. multicoloured	15	15
1314	–	45c. black, ochre and blue	15	15
1315	**199**	1cor. black, blue and dull purple	25	25
1316	–	2cor. multicoloured	25	25
1317	–	10cor. sepia, purple and blue	1·40	1·00
MS1317a		130 × 119 mm. Nos. 1312/17	12·00	12·00

DESIGNS: As Type **199**: 30c., 20cor. Arms of Nicaragua; 45c., 10cor. Nicaraguan pavilion.

200 Emblems of C. American Republics

1958. 17th Central American Lions Convention. Inscr as in T **200**. Emblems (5c., 60c.) multicoloured; Lions badge (others) in blue, red, yellow (or orange and buff).

No.	Type	Description	Unused	Used
1318	**200**	5c. blue (postage)	10	10
1319	–	10c. blue and orange	10	10
1320	–	20c. blue and green	10	10
1321	–	50c. blue and purple	15	15
1322	–	75c. blue and mauve	30	25
1323	–	1cor.50 blue, salmon and drab	45	45
MS1323a		157 × 90 mm. Nos. 1318/23	1·75	1·75
1324	–	30c. blue and orange (air)	10	10
1325	**200**	60c. blue and pink	20	15
1326	–	90c. blue	25	20
1327	–	1cor.25 blue and olive	35	30
1328	–	2cor. blue and green	60	50
1329	–	3cor. blue, red and violet	95	90
MS1329a		157 × 90 mm. Nos. 1324/9	3·00	3·00

DESIGNS—HORIZ: 10c., 1cor.25, Melvin Jones; 20, 30c. Dr. T. A. Arias; 50, 90c. Edward G. Barry; 75c., 2cor. Lions emblem; 1cor.50, 3cor. Map of C. American Isthmus.

201 Arms of La Salle

202 U.N. Emblem

1958. Brothers of the Nicaraguan Christian Schools Commemoration. Inscr as in T **201**.

No.	Type	Description	Unused	Used
1330	**201**	5c. red, blue and yellow (postage)	10	10
1331	–	10c. sepia, blue and green	10	10
1332	–	15c. sepia, brown & bistre	10	10
1333	–	20c. black, red and bistre	10	10
1334	–	50c. sepia, orange & bis	15	15
1335	–	75c. sepia, turquoise & green	25	20
1336	–	1cor. black, violet & bis	40	30
1337	**201**	30c. blue, red & yellow (air)	10	10
1338	–	60c. sepia, purple & grey	25	20
1339	–	85c. black, red and blue	30	25
1340	–	90c. black, green & ochre	35	35
1341	–	1cor.25 black, red and ochre	50	45
1342	–	1cor.50 sepia, green and grey	60	55
1343	–	1cor.75 black, brn & bl	65	55
1344	–	2cor. sepia, green & grey	65	65

DESIGNS—HORIZ: 10, 60c. Managua Teachers Institute. VERT: 15, 85c. De La Salle (founder); 20, 90c. Brother Carlos; 50c., 1cor.50, Brother Antonio; 75c., 1cor.25, Brother Julio; 1cor., 1cor.75, Brother Argeo; 2cor. Brother Eugenio.

1958. Inauguration of UNESCO Headquarters Building, Paris. Inscr as in T **202**.

No.	Type	Description	Unused	Used
1345	**202**	10c. blue & mauve (postage)	10	10
1346	–	15c. mauve and blue	10	10
1347	–	25c. brown and green	10	10
1348	–	40c. black and red	15	15
1349	–	45c. mauve and blue	20	20
1350	**202**	50c. green and brown	25	25
MS1350a		85 × 103 mm. Nos. 1345/50	1·25	1·25
1351	–	60c. blue and mauve (air)	25	15
1352	–	75c. brown and green	25	20
1353	–	90c. green and brown	30	25
1354	–	1cor. mauve and blue	40	30
1355	–	3cor. red and black	60	60
1356	–	5cor. blue and mauve	1·00	85
MS1356a		85 × 103 mm. Nos. 1351/6	3·75	3·75

DESIGNS—VERT: 15c. Aerial view of H.Q. 25, 45c. Facade composed of letters "UNESCO"; 40c. H.Q. and Eiffel Tower. In oval vignettes—60c. As 15c.; 75c., 5cor. As 25c.; 90c., 3cor. As 40c.; 1cor. As Type **202**.

203

204

1959. Obligatory Tax. Consular Fiscal stamps surch. Serial Nos. in red.

No.	Type	Description	Unused	Used
1357	**203**	5c. on 50c. blue	10	10
1358	**204**	5c. on 50c. blue	10	10

205

206 Cardinal Spellman with Pope John XXIII

207 Abraham Lincoln

1959. Obligatory Tax.

No.	Type	Description	Unused	Used
1359	**205**	5c. blue	15	10

1959. Cardinal Spellman Commemoration.

No.	Type	Description	Unused	Used
1360	**206**	5c. flesh & green (postage)	10	10
1361	A	10c. multicoloured	10	10
1362	B	15c. red, black and green	10	10
1363	C	20c. yellow and blue	10	10
1364	D	25c. red and blue	10	10
MS1364a		116 × 128 mm. Nos. 1360/4	35	35
1365	E	30c. blue, red & yell (air)	10	10
1366	**206**	35c. bronze and orange	10	10
1367	A	1cor. multicoloured	30	30
1368	B	1cor.5 red and black	35	30
1369	C	1cor.50 yellow and blue	45	35
1370	D	2cor. blue, violet and red	55	45
1371	E	5cor. multicoloured	75	55
MS1371a		116 × 128 mm. Nos. 1365/71. Perf or imperf	3·25	3·25

DESIGNS—VERT: A, Cardinal's Arms; B, Cardinal; D, Cardinal wearing sash. HORIZ: C, Cardinal and Cross; E, Flags of Nicaragua, Vatican City and U.S.A.

1960. 150th Birth Anniv of Abraham Lincoln. Portrait in black.

No.	Type	Description	Unused	Used
1372	**207**	5c. red (postage)	10	10
1373		10c. green	10	10
1374		15c. orange	10	10
1375		1cor. purple	25	25
1376		2cor. blue	30	45
MS1376a		152 × 116 mm. Nos. 1372/6. Imperf	1·10	1·10
1377		30c. blue (air)	10	10
1378		35c. red	15	10
1379		70c. purple	20	20
1380		1cor.5 green	35	35
1381		1cor.50 violet	50	45
1382	–	5cor. ochre and black	55	55
MS1382a		152 × 116 mm. Nos. 1377/82. Imperf	3·00	3·00

DESIGN—HORIZ: 5cor. Scroll inscr "Dar al que necesite—A. Lincoln".

1960. Air. 10th Anniv of San Jose (Costa Rica) Philatelic Society. Optd **X Aniversario Club Filatelico S. J.—C. R.**

No.	Type	Description	Unused	Used
1383		2cor. red (No. 1206)	70	60
1384		2cor.50 blue (No. 1256)	75	75
1385		3cor. green (No. 1166)	1·40	90

1960. Red Cross Fund for Chilean Earthquake Relief. Nos. 1372/82 optd **Resello** and Maltese Cross. Portrait in black.

No.	Type	Description	Unused	Used
1386	**207**	5c. red (postage)	10	10
1387		10c. green	10	10
1388		15c. orange	10	10
1389		1cor. purple	25	25
1390		2cor. blue	30	25
1391		30c. blue (air)	25	20
1392		35c. red	20	20
1393		70c. purple	25	25
1394		1cor.5 green	30	30
1395		1cor.50 violet	40	35
1396	–	5cor. ochre and black	1·00	1·00

210

1961. Air. World Refugee Year. Inscr "ANO MUNDIAL DEL REFUGIADO".

No.	Type	Description	Unused	Used
1397	–	2cor. multicoloured	20	20
1398	**210**	5cor. ochre, blue & green	60	60
MS1398a		100 × 70 mm. Nos. 1397/8	4·00	4·00

DESIGN: 2cor. Procession of refugees.

211 Pres. Roosevelt, Pres. Somoza and Officer

1961. Air. 20th Anniv of Nicaraguan Military Academy.

No.	Type	Description	Unused	Used
1399	**211**	20c. multicoloured	10	10
1400	–	25c. red, blue and black	10	10
1401	–	30c. multicoloured	10	10
1402	–	35c. multicoloured	10	10
1403	–	40c. multicoloured	10	10
1404	–	45c. black, flesh and red	15	15
1405	**211**	60c. multicoloured	15	15
1406	–	70c. multicoloured	20	20
1407	–	1cor.5 multicoloured	25	25
1408	–	1cor.50 multicoloured	35	35
1409	–	2cor. multicoloured	50	50
1410	–	5cor. black, flesh & grey	70	60
MS1410a		Two sheets each 160 × 100 mm. Nos. 1399/1404 and 1405/10. Imperf	4·50	4·50

DESIGNS—VERT: 25, 70c. Flags; 35c., 1cor.50, Standard bearers; 40c., 2cor. Pennant and emblem. HORIZ: 30c., 1cor.5 Group of officers; 45c., 5cor. Pres. Somoza and Director of Academy.

1961. Air. Consular Fiscal stamps as T **203/4** with serial Nos. in red, surch **Correo Aereo** and value.

No.	Type	Description	Unused	Used
1411		20c. on 50c. blue	15	10
1412		20c. on 1cor. olive	15	10
1413		20c. on 2cor. green	15	10
1414		20c. on 3cor. red	15	10
1415		20c. on 5cor. red	15	10
1416		20c. on 10cor. violet	15	10
1417		20c. on 20cor. brown	15	10
1418		20c. on 50cor. brown	15	10
1419		20c. on 100cor. lake	15	10

213 I.J.C. Emblem and Global Map of the Americas

1961. Air. Junior Chamber of Commerce Congress.

No.	Type	Description	Unused	Used
1420		2c. multicoloured	10	10
1421		3c. black and yellow	10	10
1422		4c. multicoloured	10	10
1423		5c. black and red	10	10
1424		6c. multicoloured	15	10
1425		10c. multicoloured	10	10
1426		15c. black, green and blue	10	10
1427		30c. black and blue	15	10
1428		35c. multicoloured	15	10
1429		70c. black, red and yellow	20	20
1430		1cor.5 multicoloured	35	30
1431		5cor. multicoloured	70	70

DESIGNS—HORIZ: 2c., 15c. Type **213**; 4c., 35c. "J.C.I." upon Globe. VERT: 3c., 30c. I.J.C. emblem; 5c., 70c. Scroll; 6c., 1cor.5, Handclasp; 10c., 5cor. Regional map of Nicaragua.

1961. Air. 1st Central American Philatelic Convention, San Salvador. Optd **Convencion Filatelica–Centro–America–Panama–San Salvador–27 Julio 1961.**
1432 **158** 1cor.25 multicoloured . . 25 25

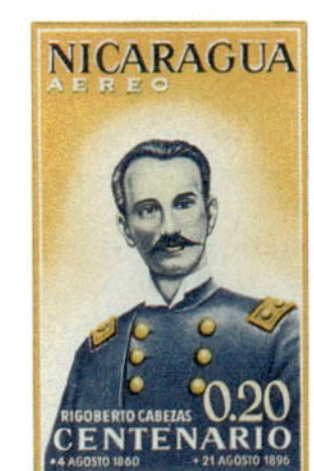

215 R. Cabezas

1961. Air. Birth Centenary of Cabezas.
1433 **215** 20c. blue and orange . . 10 10
1434 – 40c. purple and blue . . 15 15
1435 – 45c. sepia and green . . 15 15
1436 – 70c. green and brown . . 25 20
1437 – 2cor. blue and pink . . . 60 40
1438 – 10cor. purple and turquoise . . . . . . 1·50 1·50
DESIGNS—HORIZ: 40c. Map and view of Cartago; 45c. 1884 newspaper; 70c. Assembly outside building; 2cor. Scroll; 10cor. Map and view of Masaya.

216 Official Gazettes

219 "Cattleya skinneri"

1961. Centenary of Regulation of Postal Rates.
1439 **216** 5c. brown and turquoise 10 10
1440 – 10c. brown and green . . 10 10
1441 – 15c. brown and red . . . 10 10
DESIGNS: 10c. Envelopes and postmarks; 15c. Martinez and Somoza.

1961. Air. Dag Hammarskjold Commemoration. Nos. 1351/6 optd **Homenaje a Hammarskjold Sept. 18-1961.**
1442 60c. blue and mauve 30 30
1443 75c. brown and green . . . 35 35
1444 90c. green and brown . . . 45 45
1445 1cor. mauve and blue . . . 50 50
1446 3cor. red and black 80 80
1447 5cor. blue and mauve . . . 1·50 1·50

1962. Air. Surch **RESELLO C$ 1.00.**
1448 – 1cor. on 1cor.10 brown (No. 1157) 30 25
1449 **207** 1cor. on 1cor.5 black and green 30 25
See also Nos. 1498/1500a, 1569/70, 1608/14, 1669/76 and 1748/62.

1962. Obligatory Tax. Nicaraguan Orchids. Mult.
1450 5c. Type **219** 10 10
1451 5c. "Bletia roezlii" 10 10
1452 5c. "Sobralia pleiantha" . . 10 10
1453 5c. "Lycaste macrophylla" 10 10
1454 5c. "Schomburgkia tibicinus" 10 10
1455 5c. "Maxillaria tenuifolia" 10 10
1456 5c. "Stanhopea ecornuta" 10 10
1457 5c. "Oncidium ascendens" and "O. cebolleta" . . . 10 10
1458 5c. "Cycnoches egertonianum" 10 10
1459 5c. "Hexisia bidentata" . . 10 10

220 UNESCO "Audience"

222 Arms of Nueva Segovia

221a Reproduction of Nos. 1/2 and Early Postmarks (½-size illustration)

1962. Air. 15th Anniv of UNESCO.
1460 **220** 2cor. multicoloured . . . 15 15
1461 – 5cor. multicoloured . . . 80 80
MS1461a 90 × 65 mm. Nos. 1460/1. Imperf . . . . 1·90 1·90
DESIGN: 5cor. U.N. and UNESCO emblems.

1962. Air. Malaria Eradication. Nos. 1425, 1428/31 optd with mosquito surrounded by **LUCHA CONTRA LA MALARIA.**
1462 – 10c. 35 30
1463 – 35c. 45 30
1464 – 70c. 60 45
1465 – 1cor.5 . . . . 80 65
1466 – 5cor. . . . . 1·00 1·25

1962. Air. Centenary of First Nicaraguan Postage Stamps. Sheet 85 × 95 mm. Imperf.
MS1466a **221a** 7cor. multicoloured 3·50 3·50

1962. Urban and Provincial Arms. Arms mult; inscr black; background colours below.
1467 **222** 2c. mauve (postage) . . 10 10
1468 – 3c. blue 10 10
1469 – 4c. lilac 10 10
1470 – 5c. yellow 10 10
1471 – 6c. brown 10 10
1472 **222** 30c. red (air) 10 10
1473 – 50c. orange 15 10
1474 – 1cor. green 25 20
1475 – 2cor. grey 45 40
1476 – 5cor. blue 75 60
ARMS: 3c., 50c. Leon; 4c., 1cor. Managua; 5c., 2cor. Granada; 6c., 5cor. Rivas.

223 Liberty Bell

1963. Air. 150th Anniv of Independence.
1477 **223** 30c. drab, blue & black 15 10

224 Blessing

1963. Air. Death Tercentenary of St. Vincent de Paul and St. Louise de Marillac.
1478 – 60c. black and orange 15 10
1479 **224** 1cor. olive and orange 25 20
1480 – 2cor. black and red . . . 50 45
DESIGNS—VERT: 60c. "Comfort" (St. Louise and woman). HORIZ: 2cor. St. Vincent and St. Louise.

225 "Map Stamp"

226 Cross on Globe

1963. Air. Central American Philatelic Societies Federation Commemoration.
1481 **225** 1cor. blue and yellow . . 30 20

1963. Air. Ecumenical Council, Vatican City.
1482 **226** 20c. red and yellow . . . 15 10

227 Ears of Wheat

228 Boxing

1963. Air. Freedom from Hunger.
1483 **227** 10c. green and light green 10 10
1484 – 25c. sepia and yellow . . 15 10
DESIGN: 25c. Barren tree and campaign emblem.

1963. Air. Sports. Multicoloured.
1485 2c. Type **228** 10 10
1486 3c. Running 10 10
1487 4c. Underwater harpooning 10 10
1488 5c. Football 10 10
1489 6c. Baseball 15 10
1490 10c. Tennis 20 10
1491 15c. Cycling 20 10
1492 20c. Motor-cycling 20 10
1493 35c. Chess 30 15
1494 60c. Angling 45 20
1495 1cor. Table-tennis 55 35
1496 2cor. Basketball 75 55
1497 5cor. Golf . . . . 1·90 1·10

1964. Air. Surch **Resello** or **RESELLO** (1500a) and value.
1498 – 5c. on 6c. (No. 1424) 35 10
1499 – 10c. on 30c. (No. 1365) 45 15
1500 **207** 15c. on 30c. 70 20
1500a **201** 20c. on 30c. 15 10
See also Nos. 1448/9, 1569/70, 1608/14 and 1669/76.

1964. Optd **CORREOS.**
1501 5c. multicoloured (No. 1451) 10 10

231 Flags

232 "Alliance Emblem"

1964. Air. "Centro America".
1502 **231** 40c. multicoloured . . . 15 15

1964. Air. "Alliance for Progress". Multicoloured.
1503 5c. Type **232** 10 10
1504 10c. Red Cross post (horiz) 10 10
1505 15c. Highway (horiz) . . . 10 10
1506 20c. Ploughing (horiz) . . . 10 10
1507 25c. Housing (horiz) 15 10
1508 30c. Presidents Somoza and Kennedy and Eugene Black (World Bank) (horiz) 15 10
1509 35c. School and adults (horiz) 20 15
1510 40c. Chimneys (horiz) . . . 25 15

233 Map of Member Countries

1964. Air. Central American "Common Market". Multicoloured.
1511 15c. Type **233** 10 10
1512 25c. Ears of wheat 10 10
1513 40c. Cogwheels 10 10
1514 50c. Heads of cattle 15 10

1964. Air. Olympic Games, Tokyo. Nos. 1485/7, 1489 and 1495/6 optd **OLIMPIADAS TOKYO - 1964.**
1515 2c. Type **108** 10 10
1516 3c. Running 10 10
1517 4c. Underwater harpooning 10 10
1518 6c. Baseball 10 10
1519 1cor. Table-tennis . . . . . 1·10 1·10
1520 2cor. Basketball . . . . . 2·25 2·25

235 Rescue of Wounded Soldier

1965. Air. Red Cross Centenary. Multicoloured.
1521 20c. Type **235** 10 10
1522 25c. Blood transfusion . . . 15 10
1523 40c. Red Cross and snowbound town 15 15
1524 10cor. Red Cross and map of Nicaragua . . . . . . 1·50 1·50

236 Statuettes

1965. Air. Nicaraguan Antiquities. Multicoloured.
1525 5c. Type **236** 10 10
1526 10c. Totem 10 10
1527 15c. Carved dog (horiz) . . 10 10
1528 20c. Composition of "objets d'art" 10 10
1529 25c. Dish and vase (horiz) 10 10
1530 30c. Pestle and mortar . . . 10 10
1531 35c. Statuettes (different) (horiz) 10 10
1532 40c. Deity 15 10
1533 50c. Wine vessel and dish 15 10
1534 60c. Bowl and dish (horiz) 20 10
1535 1cor. Urn 45 15

237 Pres. Kennedy

238 A. Bello

1965. Air. Pres. Kennedy Commemorative.
1536 **237** 35c. black and green . . 15 10
1537 75c. black and mauve . . 25 15
1538 1cor.10 black and blue 35 25
1539 2cor. black and brown 90 55
MS1539a Four sheets each 90 × 116 mm. Nos. 1536/9 in blocks of four. Imperf . . . . 7·50 7·50

1965. Air. Death Centenary of Andres Bello (poet and writer).
1540 **238** 10c. black and brown . . 10 10
1541 15c. black and blue . . . 10 10
1542 45c. black and purple . . 15 10
1543 80c. black and green . . 20 15
1544 1cor. black and yellow 25 20
1545 2cor. black and grey . . 45 45

1965. 9th Central American Scout Camporee. Nos. 1450/9 optd with scout badge and **CAMPOREE SCOUT 1965.**
1546 5c. multicoloured 20 20
1547 5c. multicoloured 20 20
1548 5c. multicoloured 20 20
1549 5c. multicoloured 20 20
1550 5c. multicoloured 20 20
1551 5c. multicoloured 20 20
1552 5c. multicoloured 20 20
1553 5c. multicoloured 20 20
1554 5c. multicoloured 20 20
1555 5c. multicoloured 20 20
MS1555a 127 × 102 mm. Sheet No. **MS**1277a optd **CAMPOREE SCOUT 1965** on each stamp 10·00 10·00

240 Sir Winston Churchill

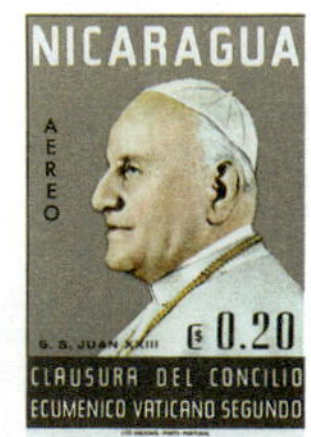

241 Pope John XXIII

1966. Air. Churchill Commemorative.
1556 **240** 20c. mauve and black . . 10 10
1557 – 35c. green and black . . 15 10
1558 – 60c. ochre and black . . 15 15
1559 – 75c. red 20 20
1560 – 1cor. purple 30 25

1561	**240** 2cor. violet, lilac & black	60	55
1562	– 3cor. blue and black	65	60
MS1563	99×95 mm. Nos. 1558/61. Imperf	1·75	1·75

DESIGNS—HORIZ: 35c., 1cor. Churchill broadcasting. VERT: 60c., 3cor. Churchill crossing the Rhine; 75c. Churchill in Hussars' uniform.

1966. Air. Closure of Vatican Ecumenical Council. Multicoloured.

1564	20c. Type **241**	10	10
1565	35c. Pope Paul VI	15	15
1566	1cor. Archbishop Gonzalez y Robleto	30	25
1567	2cor. St. Peter's, Rome	30	25
1568	3cor. Papal arms	60	40

1967. Air. Nos. 1533/4 surch **RESELLO** and value.

1569	10c. on 50c. multicoloured	10	10
1570	15c. on 60c. multicoloured	10	10

See also Nos. 1448/9, 1498/1500a, 1608/14 and 1669/76.

243 Dario and Birthplace

1967. Air. Birth Centenary of Ruben Dario (poet). Designs showing Dario and view. Multicoloured.

1571	5c. Type **243**	10	10
1572	10c. Monument, Managua	10	10
1573	20c. Leon Cathedral (site of Dario's tomb)	10	10
1574	40c. Allegory of the centaurs	15	10
1575	75c. Allegory of the mute swans	30	20
1576	1cor. Roman triumphal march	25	20
1577	2cor. St. Francis and the wolf	45	40
1578	5cor. "Faith" opposing "Death"	65	60
MS1579	Two sheets each 130×107 mm. Nos. 1571/4 and 1575/8	4·75	4·75

244 "Megalura peleus"

1967. Air. Butterflies. Multicoloured.

1580	5c. "Heliconius petiveranua" (vert)	10	10
1581	10c. "Colaenis julia" (vert)	10	10
1582	15c. Type **244**	10	10
1583	20c. "Aneyluris jurgensii"	10	10
1584	25c. "Thecla regalis"	10	10
1585	30c. "Doriana thia" (vert)	10	10
1586	35c. "Lymnias pixae" (vert)	15	10
1587	40c. "Metamorpho dido"	25	10
1588	50c. "Papilio arcas" (vert)	25	15
1589	60c. "Ananea cleomestra"	35	15
1590	1cor. "Victorina epaphaus" (vert)	60	30
1591	2cor. "Prepona demophon"	1·10	50

245 McDivitt and White

1967. Air. Space Flight of McDivitt and White. Multicoloured.

1592	5c. Type **245**	10	10
1593	10c. Astronauts and "Gemini 5" on launching pad	10	10
1594	15c. "Gemini 5" and White in Space	10	10
1595	20c. Recovery operation at sea	15	10
1596	35c. Type **245**	10	10
1597	40c. As 10c.	15	10
1598	75c. As 15c.	20	20
1599	1cor. As 20c.	35	25

246 National Flower of Costa Rica

1967. Air. 5th Year of Central American Economic Integration. Designs showing national flowers of Central American countries. Multicoloured.

1600	40c. Type **246**	15	10
1601	40c. Guatemala	15	10
1602	40c. Honduras	15	10
1603	40c. Nicaragua	15	10
1604	40c. El Salvador	15	10

247 Presidents Diaz and Somoza

1968. Air. Visit of Pres. Diaz of Mexico.

1605	– 20c. black	10	10
1606	**247** 40c. olive	20	10
1607	– 1cor. brown	35	20

DESIGNS—VERT: 20c. Pres. Somoza greeting Pres. Diaz; 1cor. Pres. Diaz of Mexico.

1968. Surch **RESELLO** and value.

1608	– 5c. on 6c. (No. 1180) (postage)	10	10
1609	– 5c. on 6c. (No. 1471)	10	10
1610	– 5c. on 6c. (No. 1424) (air)	10	10
1611	– 5c. on 6c. (No. 1489)	10	10
1612	**156** 5c. on 8c. (No. 1035)	10	10
1614	– 1cor. on 1cor.50 (No. 1369)	25	20

See also Nos. 1448/9, 1498/1500a, 1569/70 and 1669/76.

249 Mangoes

1968. Air. Nicaraguan Fruits. Multicoloured.

1615	5c. Type **249**	10	10
1616	10c. Pineapples	10	10
1617	15c. Oranges	10	10
1618	20c. Pawpaws	10	10
1619	30c. Bananas	10	10
1620	35c. Avocado pears	15	10
1621	50c. Water-melons	15	10
1622	75c. Cashews	25	15
1623	1cor. Sapodilla plums	35	20
1624	2cor. Cocoa beans	45	20

250 "The Crucifixion" (Fra Angelico)

1968. Air. Religious Paintings. Multicoloured.

1625	10c. Type **250**	10	10
1626	15c. "The Last Judgement" (Michelangelo) (vert)	10	10
1627	35c. "The Beautiful Gardener" (Raphael) (vert)	15	15
1628	2cor. "The Spoliation of Christ" (El Greco) (vert)	45	30
1629	3cor. "The Conception" (Murillo) (vert)	60	45
MS1630	100×80 mm. 5cor. "The Crucifixion" (Dali)	3·50	3·50

1968. Air. Pope Paul's Visit to Bogota. Nos. 1625/8 optd **Visita de S. S. Paulo VI C. E. de Bogota 1968**.

1631	**250** 10c. multicoloured	10	10
1632	– 15c. multicoloured	10	10
1633	– 35c. multicoloured	10	10
1634	– 2cor. multicoloured	30	20

252 Basketball

1969. Air. Olympic Games, Mexico. Mult.

1635	10c. Type **252**	10	10
1636	15c. Fencing (horiz)	10	10
1637	20c. High-diving	10	10
1638	35c. Running	10	10
1639	50c. Hurdling (horiz)	15	10
1640	75c. Weightlifting	20	15
1641	1cor. Boxing (horiz)	35	20
1642	2cor. Football	55	55
MS1643	100×120 mm. Nos. 1639/42	2·00	2·00

253 Midas Cichlid

1969. Air. Fishes. Multicoloured.

1644	10c. Type **253**	10	10
1645	15c. Moga cichlid	10	10
1646	20c. Common carp	20	10
1647	30c. Tropical gar	25	10
1648	35c. Swordfish	30	10
1649	50c. Big-mouthed sleeper	35	15
1650	75c. Atlantic tarpon	40	20
1651	1cor. Lake Nicaragua shark	60	25
1652	2cor. Sailfish	75	45
1653	3cor. Small-toothed sawfish	1·40	70
MS1654	83×137 mm. Nos. 1650/3	2·00	2·00

1969. Air. Various stamps surch **RESELLO** and value.

1655	10c. on 25c. (No. 1507)	10	10
1656	10c. on 25c. (No. 1512)	10	10
1657	15c. on 25c. (No. 1529)	10	10
1658	50c. on 70c. (No. 1379)	15	10

255 Scenery, Tower and Emblem

258 "Minerals"

1969. Air. "Hemisfair" (1968) Exhibition.

1659	**255** 30c. blue and red	10	10
1660	35c. purple and red	10	10
1661	75c. red and blue	15	10
1662	1cor. purple and black	30	20
1663	2cor. purple and green	55	40
MS1664	75×111 mm. Nos. 1659/60, 1662/3. Perf or imperf	1·75	1·75

1969. Various stamps surch. (a) Optd **CORREO**.

1665	5c. (No. 1450)	10	10
1666	5c. (No. 1453)	10	10
1667	5c. (No. 1454)	10	10
1668	5c. (No. 1459)	10	10

(b) Optd **RESELLO** and surch.

1669	10c. on 25c. (No. 1529)	10	10
1670	10c. on 30c. (No. 1324)	10	10
1671	10c. on 30c. (No. 1427)	10	10
1672	10c. on 30c. (No. 1530)	10	10
1673	15c. on 35c. (No. 1531)	10	10
1674	20c. on 30c. (No. 1307)	10	10
1675	20c. on 30c. (No. 1401)	10	10
1676	20c. on 35c. (No. 1509)	10	10

1969. Air. Nicaraguan Products. Multicoloured.

1677	5c. Type **258**	10	10
1678	10c. "Fish"	10	10
1679	15c. "Bananas"	10	10
1680	20c. "Timber"	10	10
1681	35c. "Coffee"	10	10
1682	40c. "Sugar-cane"	15	10
1683	60c. "Cotton"	20	10
1684	75c. "Rice and Maize"	20	15
1685	1cor. "Tobacco"	30	20
1686	2cor. "Meat"	35	25

1969. 50th Anniv of I.L.O. Obligatory tax stamps. Nos. 1450/9 optd **O.I.T. 1919-1969**.

1687	5c. multicoloured	10	10
1688	5c. multicoloured	10	10
1689	5c. multicoloured	10	10
1690	5c. multicoloured	10	10
1691	5c. multicoloured	10	10
1692	5c. multicoloured	10	10
1693	5c. multicoloured	10	10
1694	5c. multicoloured	10	10
1695	5c. multicoloured	10	10
1696	5c. multicoloured	10	10

260 Girl carrying Tinaja

261 Pele (Brazil)

1970. Air. 8th Inter-American Savings and Loans Conference, Managua.

1697	**260** 10c. multicoloured	10	10
1698	15c. multicoloured	10	10
1699	20c. multicoloured	10	10
1700	35c. multicoloured	10	10
1701	50c. multicoloured	15	10
1702	75c. multicoloured	20	15
1703	1cor. multicoloured	30	20
1704	2cor. multicoloured	60	40

1970. World Football "Hall of Fame" Poll-winners. Multicoloured.

1705	5c. Type **261** (postage)	10	10
1706	10c. Puskas (Hungary)	10	10
1707	15c. Matthews (England)	10	10
1708	40c. Di Stefano (Argentina)	10	10
1709	2cor. Facchetti (Italy)	55	45
1710	3cor. Yashin (Russia)	70	65
1711	5cor. Beckenbauer (West Germany)	70	90
1712	20c. Santos (Brazil) (air)	10	10
1713	80c. Wright (England)	20	15
1714	1cor. Flags of 16 World Cup finalists	25	20
1715	4cor. Bozsik (Hungary)	90	75
1716	5cor. Charlton (England)	1·10	90

262 Torii (Gate)

263 Module and Astronauts on Moon

1970. Air. EXPO 70, World Fair, Osaka, Japan.

1717	**262** 25c. multicoloured	10	10
1718	30c. multicoloured	10	10
1719	35c. multicoloured	10	10
1720	75c. multicoloured	25	15
1721	1cor.50 multicoloured	35	30
1722	3cor. multicoloured	45	35
MS1723	108×78 mm. Nos. 1720/2. Imperf	1·50	1·50

1970. Air. "Apollo 11" Moon Landing (1969). Mult.

1724	35c. Type **263**	10	10
1725	40c. Module landing on Moon	10	10
1726	60c. Astronauts with U.S. flag	20	15
1727	75c. As 40c.	25	15
1728	1cor. As 60c.	35	20
1729	2cor. Type **263**	40	35

264 F. D. Roosevelt

265 "The Annunciation" (Grunewald)

1970. Air. 25th Death Anniv of Franklin D. Roosevelt.

1730	**264** 10c. black	10	10
1731	– 15c. brown and black	10	10
1732	– 20c. green and black	10	10
1733	**264** 35c. purple and black	10	10
1734	– 50c. brown	15	10
1735	**264** 75c. blue	20	15
1736	– 1cor. red	25	20
1737	– 2cor. black	30	35

PORTRAITS: 15c., 1cor. Roosevelt with stamp collection; 20c., 50c., 2cor. Roosevelt (full-face).

1970. Air. Christmas. Paintings. Multicoloured.

1738	10c. Type **265**	10	10
1739	10c. "The Nativity" (detail, El Greco)	10	10
1740	10c. "The Adoration of the Magi" (detail, Durer)	10	10
1741	10c. "Virgin and Child" (J. van Hemessen)	10	10
1742	10c. "The Holy Shepherd" (Portuguese School, 16th cent)	10	10
1743	15c. Type **265**	10	10
1744	20c. As No. 1739	10	10
1745	35c. As No. 1740	15	10
1746	75c. As No. 1741	20	15
1747	1cor. As No. 1742	30	20

1971. Surch **RESELLO** and new value.

1748	30c. on 90c. black (No. 1227) (postage)	10·00	10·00
1749	10c. on 1cor.5 red, black & red (No. 1368) (air)	10	10
1750	10c. on 1cor.5 mult (No. 1407)	10	10
1751	10c. on 1cor.5 mult (No. 1430)	10	10
1752	15c. on 1cor.50 green and red (No. 1116)	10	10
1753	15c. on 1cor.50 green (No. 1255)	10	10

1754 15c. on 1cor.50 yellow and blue (No. 1369) 10 10
1755 15c. on 1cor.50 black and violet (No. 1381) 10 10
1756 20c. on 85c. black and red (No. 1276) 15 10
1757 20c. on 85c. black, red and blue (No. 1339) 15 10
1758 25c. on 90c. black, green and ochre (No. 1440) . . 15 15
1759 30c. on 1cor.10 black and purple (No. 1195) 15 15
1760 40c. on 1cor.10 brown and black (No. 1157) 65 65
1761 40c. on 1cor.50 mult (No. 1408) 65 65
1762 1cor. on 1cor.10 black and blue (No. 1538) . . . . . 1·60 1·60

266 Basic Mathematical Equation

1971. Scientific Formulae. "The Ten Mathematical Equations that changed the Face of the Earth". Multicoloured.
1763 10c. Type **266** (postage) . . 10 10
1764 15c. Newton's Law 10 10
1765 20c. Einstein's Law 10 10
1766 1cor. Tsiolkovsky's Law . . 25 25
1767 2cor. Maxwell's Law . . . 90 75
1768 25c. Napier's Law (air) . . 10 10
1769 30c. Pythagoras' Law . . . 10 10
1770 40c. Boltzmann's Law . . . 15 10
1771 1cor. Broglie's Law 30 20
1772 2cor. Archimedes' Law . . . 55 40

267 Peace Emblem

1971. "Is There a Formula for Peace?".
1773 **267** 10c. blue and black . . . 10 10
1774 15c. blue, black and violet 10 10
1775 20c. blue, black & brown 10 10
1776 40c. blue, black and green 10 10
1777 50c. blue, black & purple 15 10
1778 80c. blue, black and red 15 15
1779 1cor. blue, black & green 30 20
1780 2cor. blue, black & violet 55 35

268 Montezuma Oropendola
269 "Moses with the Tablets of the Law" (Rembrandt)

1971. Air. Nicaraguan Birds. Multicoloured.
1781 10c. Type **268** 45 20
1782 15c. Turquoise-browed motmot 45 20
1783 20c. White-throated magpie-jay 55 20
1784 25c. Scissor-tailed flycatcher 55 20
1785 30c. Spotted-breasted oriole (horiz) 70 20
1786 35c. Rufous-naped wren . . 85 20
1787 40c. Great kiskadee 85 20
1788 75c. Red-legged honeycreeper (horiz) . . . 1·50 40
1789 1cor. Great-tailed grackle (horiz) . . . . 1·75 50
1790 2cor. Belted kingfisher . . . 5·50 1·00

1971. "The Ten Commandments". Paintings. Multicoloured.
1791 10c. Type **269** (postage) . . 10 10
1792 15c. "Moses and the Burning Bush" (Botticelli) (1st Commandment) . . . 10 10
1793 20c. "Jepthah's Daughter" (Degas) (2nd Commandment) (horiz) 10 10
1794 30c. "St. Vincent Ferrer preaching in Verona" (Morone) (3rd Commandment) (horiz) 10 10
1795 35c. "Noah's Drunkenness" (Michelangelo) (4th Commandment) (horiz) 10 10
1796 40c. "Cain and Abel" (Trevisani) (5th Commandment) (horiz) 10 10
1797 50c. "Joseph accused by Potiphar's Wife" (Rembrandt) (6th Commandment) 10 10
1798 60c. "Isaac blessing Jacob" (Eeckhout) (7th Commandment) (horiz) 15 10
1799 75c. "Susannah and the Elders" (Rubens) (8th Commandment) (horiz) 25 20
1800 1cor. "Bathsheba after her Bath" (Rembrandt) (9th Commandment) (air) . . 25 20
1801 2cor. "Naboth's Vineyard" (Smetham) (10th Commandment) 40 35

270 U Thant and Pres. Somoza

1971. Air. 25th Anniv of U.N.O.
1802 **270** 10c. brown and red . . . 10 10
1803 15c. green and emerald 10 10
1804 20c. blue and light blue 10 10
1805 25c. red and purple . . . 10 10
1806 30c. brown and orange 10 10
1807 40c. green and grey . . . 15 10
1808 1cor. green and sage . . 25 20
1809 2cor. brown & light brown 30 35

1972. Olympic Games, Munich. Nos. 1709, 1711, 1713 and 1716 surch **OLIMPIADAS MUNICH 1972**, emblem and value or optd only (5cor.).
1810 40c. on 2cor. multicoloured (postage) 10 10
1811 50c. on 3cor. multicoloured 15 10
1812 20c. on 80c. mult (air) . . . 10 10
1813 60c. on 4cor. multicoloured 15 10
1814 5cor. multicoloured 65 65

272 Figurine and Apoyo Site on Map

1972. Air. Pre-Columbian Art. A. H. Heller's Pottery Discoveries. Multicoloured.
1815 10c. Type **272** 10 10
1816 15c. Cana Castilla 10 10
1817 20c. Catarina 10 10
1818 25c. Santa Helena 10 10
1819 30c. Mombacho 10 10
1820 35c. Tisma 10 10
1821 40c. El Menco 10 10
1822 50c. Los Placeres 15 10
1823 60c. Masaya 15 15
1824 80c. Granada 20 15
1825 1cor. Las Mercedes 30 20
1826 2cor. Nindiri 55 35

273 "Lord Peter Wimsey" (Dorothy Sayers)

1972. Air. 50th Anniv of International Criminal Police Organization (INTERPOL). Famous Fictional Detectives. Multicoloured.
1827 5c. Type **273** 10 10
1828 10c. "Philip Marlowe" (Raymond Chandler) . . 10 10
1829 15c. "Sam Spade" (D. Hammett) . . . . . 6·00 20
1830 20c. "Perry Mason" (Erle Stanley Gardner) 10 10
1831 25c. "Nero Wolfe" (Rex Stout) 10 10
1832 35c. "C. Auguste Dupin" (Edgar Allan Poe) 10 10
1833 40c. "Ellery Queen" (F. Dannay and M. Lee) 10 10
1834 50c. "Father Brown" (G. K. Chesterton) 10 10
1835 60c. "Charlie Chan" (Earl D. Biggers) 15 10
1836 80c. "Inspector Maigret" (Georges Simenon) . . . 25 15
1837 1cor. "Hercule Poirot" (Agatha Christie) 25 20
1838 2cor. "Sherlock Holmes" (A. Conan Doyle) 70 70

274 "The Shepherdess and her Brothers"

1972. Air. Christmas. Scenes from Legend of the Christmas Rose. Multicoloured.
1839 10c. Type **274** 10 10
1840 15c. Adoration of the Wise Men 10 10
1841 20c. Shepherdess crying . . 10 10
1842 35c. Angel appears to Shepherdess 10 10
1843 40c. Christmas Rose 10 10
1844 60c. Shepherdess thanks angel for roses 15 10
1845 80c. Shepherdess takes roses to Holy Child 15 15
1846 1cor. Holy Child receiving roses 20 15
1847 2cor. Nativity scene 45 35
MS1848 132 × 132 mm. Nos. 1839/47 1·40 1·40

275 Sir Walter Raleigh and Elizabethan Galleon

1973. Air. Causes of the American Revolution. Multicoloured.
1849 10c. Type **275** 40 10
1850 15c. Signing "Mayflower Compact" 10 10
1851 20c. Acquittal of Peter Zenger (vert) 10 10
1852 25c. Acclaiming American resistance (vert) 10 10
1853 30c. Revenue stamp (vert) 10 10
1854 35c. "Serpent" slogan—"Join or die" 10 10
1855 40c. Boston Massacre (vert) 10 10
1856 50c. Boston Tea-party . . . 10 10
1857 60c. Patrick Henry on trial (vert) 15 10
1858 75c. Battle of Bunker Hill 20 10
1859 80c. Declaration of Independence 20 15
1860 1cor. Liberty Bell 30 20
1861 2cor. US seal (vert) 90 60

1973. Nos. 1450/54, 1456 and 1458/9 optd **CORREO**.
1862 **219** 5c. multicoloured 25 10
1863 – 5c. multicoloured 25 10
1864 – 5c. multicoloured 25 10
1865 – 5c. multicoloured 25 10
1866 – 5c. multicoloured 25 10
1867 – 5c. multicoloured 25 10
1868 – 5c. multicoloured 25 10
1869 – 5c. multicoloured 25 10

277 Baseball, Player and Map
278 Givenchy, Paris

1973. Air. 20th International Baseball Championships, Managua (1972).
1870 **277** 15c. multicoloured . . . 10 10
1871 20c. multicoloured . . . 10 10
1872 40c. multicoloured . . . 10 10
1873 10cor. multicoloured . . . 1·50 90
MS1874 105 × 134 mm. Nos. 1870/3 2·50 2·50

1973. World-famous Couturiers. Mannequins. Mult.
1875 1cor. Type **278** (postage) . . 25 20
1876 2cor. Hartnell, London . . . 40 40
1877 5cor. Balmain, Paris . . . . 1·00 90
1878 10c. Lourdes, Nicaragua (air) 10 10
1879 15c. Halston, New York . . 10 10
1880 20c. Pino Lancetti, Rome . . 10 10
1881 35c. Madame Gres, Paris . . 10 10
1882 40c. Irene Galitzine, Rome 10 10
1883 80c. Pedro Rodriguez, Barcelona 15 15
MS1884 170 × 170 mm. Nos. 1875/82 2·50 2·50

279 Diet Chart

1973. Air. Child Welfare. Multicoloured.
1885 5c.+5c. Type **279** 10 10
1886 10c.+5c. Senora Samoza with baby, and Children's Hospital 10 10
1887 15c.+5c. "Childbirth" . . . 10 10
1888 20c.+5c. "Immunization" . . 10 10
1889 30c.+5c. Water purification 10 10
1890 35c.+5c. As No. 1886 . . . 10 10
1891 50c.+10c. Alexander Fleming and "Antibiotics" 30 10
1892 60c.+15c. Malaria control 15 10
1893 70c.+10c. Laboratory analysis 15 15
1894 80c.+20c. Gastroenteritis . . 20 15
1895 1cor.+50c. As No. 1886 . . 30 25
1896 2cor. Pediatric surgery . . . 45 35

280 Virginia and Father

1973. Christmas. "Does Santa Claus exist?" (Virginia O'Hanlon's letter to American "Sun" newspaper). Multicoloured.
1897 2c. Type **280** (postage) . . . 10 10
1898 3c. Text of letter 10 10
1899 4c. Reading the reply . . . 10 10
1900 5c. Type **280** 10 10
1901 15c. As 3c. 10 10
1902 20c. As 4c. 10 10
1903 1cor. Type **280** (air) 20 15
1904 2cor. As 3c. 35 30
1905 4cor. As 4c. 75 65
MS1906 197 × 143 mm. Nos. 1903/5 2·00 2·00
No MS1906 has an inscription in English on the reverse.

281 Churchill making Speech, 1936

1974. Birth Cent of Sir Winston Churchill.
1907 **281** 2c. multicoloured (postage) 10 10
1908 – 3c. black, blue and brown 10 10
1909 – 4c. multicoloured 10 10
1910 – 5c. multicoloured 10 10
1911 – 10c. brown, green & blue 30 10
1912 – 5cor. multicoloured (air) 90 80
1913 – 6cor. black, brown & bl 1·00 90
MS1914 Two sheets each 85 × 64 mm. (a) 4cor. black, yellow and green; (b) 4cor. multicoloured 2·25 2·25
DESIGNS: 3c. "The Four Churchills" (wartime cartoon); 4c. Candle, cigar and "Action" stickers; 5c. Churchill, Roosevelt and Stalin at Yalta; 10c. Churchill landing in Normandy, 1944; 5cor. Churchill giving "V" sign; 6cor. "Bulldog Churchill" (cartoon); MS1914 (a) Churchill and 10 Downing Street; (b) Churchill House of Parliament.

282 Presentation of World Cup to Uruguay, 1930

1974. World Cup Football Championship. Mult.
1915 1c. Type **282** (postage) . . 10 10
1916 2c. Victorious Italian team, 1934 . . . . 10 10
1917 3c. Presentation of World Cup to Italy, 1938 . . . . 10 10
1918 4c. Uruguay's winning goal, 1950 . . . . 10 10
1919 5c. Victorious West Germany, 1954 . . . . . 10 10
1920 10c. Rejoicing Brazilian players, 1958 . . . . . . 10 10
1921 15c. Brazilian player holding World Cup, 1962 . . . . 10 10
1922 20c. Queen Elizabeth II presenting Cup to Bobby Moore, 1966 . . . . . . 10 10

1923 25c. Victorious Brazilian players, 1970 10 10
1924 10cor. Football and flags of participating countries, 1974 (air) 1·75 1·75
MS1925 Two sheets each 115 × 112 mm. (a) 4cor. As 10c.; (b) 5cor. As 20c. 2·50 2·50

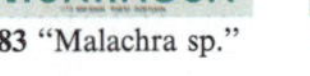

283 "Malachra sp."

284 Nicaraguan 7½c. Stamp of 1937

1974. Wild Flowers and Cacti. Multicoloured.
1926 2c. Type **283** (postage) 10 10
1927 3c. "Paguira insignis" 10 10
1928 4c. "Convolvulus sp." 10 10
1929 5c. "Pereschia autumnalis" 10 10
1930 10c. "Ipomea tuberosa" 10 10
1931 15c. "Hibiscus elatus" 10 10
1932 20c. "Plumeria acutifolia" 10 10
1933 1cor. "Centrosema sp." (air) 20 20
1934 3cor. "Hylocereus undatus" 60 55

1974. Centenary of U.P.U.
1935 **284** 2c. red, green & blk (postage) 10 20
1936 – 3c. blue, green and black 10 10
1937 – 4c. multicoloured 10 10
1938 – 5c. brown, mauve & blk 10 10
1939 – 10c. red, brown and black 10 10
1940 – 20c. green, blue and black 10 10
1941 – 40c. multicoloured (air) 10 10
1942 – 3cor. green, black & pink 50 40
1943 – 5cor. blue, black and lilac 1·00 80
MS1944 108 × 128 mm. 1cor. As 20c.; 2cor. As 4c.; 4cor. Jet Airliner over Globe (horiz). Imperf 2·00 2·00
DESIGNS—VERT: 3c. 5c. stamp of 1937; 5c. 2c. stamp of 1937; 10c. 1c. stamp of 1937; 20c. ½c. stamp of 1937; 40c. 10c. stamp of 1961; 5cor. 4cor. U.P.U. stamp of 1950. HORIZ: 4c. 10c. air stamp of 1934; 3cor. 85c. U.P.U. air stamp of 1950.

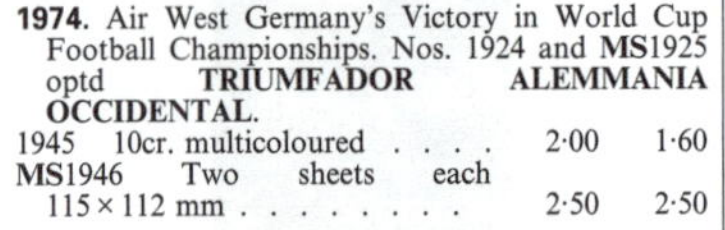

1974. Air West Germany's Victory in World Cup Football Championships. Nos. 1924 and **MS**1925 optd **TRIUMFADOR ALEMMANIA OCCIDENTAL.**
1945 10cr. multicoloured 2·00 1·60
MS1946 Two sheets each 115 × 112 mm 2·50 2·50

286 Tamandua

1974. Nicaraguan Fauna. Multicoloured.
1947 1c. Type **286** (postage) 10 10
1948 2c. Puma 10 10
1949 3c. Common raccoon 10 10
1950 4c. Ocelot 10 10
1951 5c. Kinkajou 10 10
1952 10c. Coypu 10 10
1953 15c. Collared peccary 15 10
1954 20c. Baird's tapir 15 10
1955 3cor. Red brocket (air) 1·50 1·40
1956 5cor. Jaguar 2·40 2·00

287 "Prophet Zacharias"

1975. Christmas. 500th Birth Anniv of Michelangelo. Multicoloured.
1957 1c. Type **287** (postage) 10 10
1958 2c. "Christ amongst the Jews" 10 10
1959 3c. "The Creation of Man" (horiz) 10 10
1960 4c. Interior of Sistine Chapel, Rome 10 10
1961 5c. "Moses" 10 10
1962 10c. "Mouscron Madonna" 10 10
1963 15c. "David" 10 10
1964 20c. "Doni Madonna" 10 10
1965 40c. "Madonna of the Steps" (air) 10 10
1966 80c. "Pitti Madonna" 15 15
1967 2cor. "Christ and Virgin Mary" 35 30
1968 5cor. "Michelangelo" (self-portrait) 75 75
MS1969 101 × 87 mm. Nos. 1967/8. Imperf 2·00 2·00

288 Giovanni Martinelli ("Othello")

1975. Great Opera Singers. Multicoloured.
1970 1c. Type **288** (postage) 10 10
1971 2c. Tito Gobbi ("Simone Boccanegra") 10 10
1972 3c. Lotte Lehmann ("Der Rosenkavalier") 10 10
1973 4c. Lauritz Melchior ("Parsifal") 10 10
1974 5c. Nellie Melba ("La Traviata") 10 10
1975 15c. Jussi Bjoerling ("La Boheme") 10 10
1976 20c. Birgit Nilsson ("Turandot") 10 10
1977 25c. Rosa Ponselle ("Norma") (air) 10 10
1978 35c. Guiseppe de Luca ("Rigoletto") 10 10
1979 40c. Joan Sutherland ("La Figlia del Reggimiento") 10 10
1980 50c. Enzio Pinza ("Don Giovanni") 10 10
1981 60c. Kirsten Flagstad ("Tristan and Isolde") 15 10
1982 80c. Maria Callas ("Tosca") 15 15
1983 2cor. Fyodor Chaliapin ("Boris Godunov") 60 35
1984 5cor. Enrico Caruso ("La Juive") 1·10 60
MS1985 137 × 119 mm. 1cor. As 80c.; Nos. 1983/4. Perf or imperf 2·50 2·50

289 The First Station

290 "The Spirit of 76"

1975. Easter. The 14 Stations of the Cross.
1986 **289** 1c. multicoloured (postage) 10 10
1987 – 2c. multicoloured 10 10
1988 – 3c. multicoloured 10 10
1989 – 4c. multicoloured 10 10
1990 – 5c. multicoloured 10 10
1991 – 15c. multicoloured 10 10
1992 – 20c. multicoloured 10 10
1993 – 25c. multicoloured 10 10
1994 – 35c. multicoloured 10 10
1995 – 40c. multicoloured (air) 10 10
1996 – 50c. multicoloured 10 10
1997 – 80c. multicoloured 15 15
1998 – 1cor. multicoloured 20 15
1999 – 5cor. multicoloured 80 65
DESIGNS: 2c. to 5cor. Different Stations of the Cross.

1975. Bicentenary of American Independence (1st series). Multicoloured.
2000 1c. Type **290** (postage) 10 10
2001 2c. Pitt addressing Parliament 10 10
2002 3c. Paul Revere's Ride (horiz) 10 10
2003 4c. Demolishing statue of George III (horiz) 10 10
2004 5c. Boston Massacre 10 10
2005 10c. Tax stamp and George III 3d. coin (horiz) 10 10
2006 15c. Boston Tea Party (horiz) 10 10
2007 20c. Thomas Jefferson 10 10
2008 25c. Benjamin Franklin 10 10
2009 30c. Signing of Declaration of Independence (horiz) 10 10
2010 35c. Surrender of Cornwallis at Yorktown (horiz) 10 10
2011 40c. Washington's Farewell (horiz) (air) 10 10
2012 50c. Washington addressing Congress (horiz) 10 10
2013 2cor. Washington arriving for Presidential Inauguration (horiz) 70 30
2014 5cor. Statue of Liberty and flags 75 45
MS2015 133 × 128 mm. 7cor. As 1c. Perf or imperf 1·75 1·75
See also Nos. 2506/**MS**2072.

291 Saluting the Flag

1975. "Nordjamb 75" World Scout Jamboree, Norway. Multicoloured.
2016 1c. Type **291** (postage) 10 10
2017 2c. Scout canoe 10 10
2018 3c. Scouts shaking hands 10 10
2019 4c. Scout preparing meal 10 10
2020 5c. Entrance to Nicaraguan camp 10 10
2021 20c. Scouts meeting 10 10
2022 35c. Aerial view of camp (air) 10 10
2023 40c. Scouts making music 10 10
2024 1cor. Camp-fire 20 15
2025 10cor. Lord Baden-Powell 1·25 1·10
MS2026 Two sheets each 126 × 112 mm. (a) 2cor. as 4c. and 3cor. as 2c. (Perf); (b) 2cor. as 5c. and 3cor. as 1cor. (Imperf) 2·00 2·00

292 President Somoza

1975. President Somoza's New Term of Office, 1974–81.
2027 **292** 20c. multicoloured (postage) 10 10
2028 40c. multicoloured 10 10
2029 1cor. multicoloured (air) 20 20
2030 10cor. multicoloured 1·25 1·10
2031 20cor. multicoloured 3·25 2·75

293 "Chess Players" (L. Carracci)

1975. Chess. Multicoloured.
2032 1c. Type **293** (postage) 10 10
2033 2c. "Arabs playing Chess" (Delacroix) 10 10
2034 3c. "Cardinals playing Chess" (V. Marais-Milton) 10 10
2035 4c. "Duke Albrecht V of Bavaria and Anna of Austria at Chess" (H. Muelich) (vert) 10 10
2036 5c. "Chess game" (14th-century Persian manuscript) 10 10
2037 10c. "Origins of Chess" (India, 1602) 10 10
2038 15c. "Napoleon playing Chess in Schonbrunn Palace in 1809" (A. Uniechowski) (vert) 10 10
2039 20c. "The Chess Game in the House of Count Ingenheim" (J.E. Hummel) 10 10
2040 40c. "The Chess-players" (T. Eakins) (air) 10 10
2041 2cor. Fischer v Spassky match, Reykjavik, 1972 55 35
2042 5cor. "William Shakespeare and Ben Jonson playing Chess" (K. van Mander) 60 50
MS2043 142 × 67 mm. Nos. 2041/2 Perf or imperf 1·75 1·75

294 Choir of King's College, Cambridge

1975. Christmas. Famous Choirs. Multicoloured.
2044 1c. Type **294** (postage) 10 10
2045 2c. Abbey Choir, Einsiedeln 10 10
2046 3c. Regensburg Cathedral choir 10 10
2047 4c. Vienna Boys' choir 10 10
2048 5c. Sistine Chapel choir 10 10
2049 15c. Westminster Cathedral choir 10 10
2050 20c. Mormon Tabernacle choir 10 10
2051 50c. School choir, Montserrat (air) 10 10
2052 1cor. St. Florian children's choir 20 15
2053 2cor. "Little Singers of the Wooden Cross" (vert) 45 35
2054 5cor. Pope with choristers of Pueri Cantores 60 50
MS2055 163 × 127 mm. 10cor. First performance of "Stille Nacht", Obendorf Church, Austria, 1818 (40 × 47 mm). Imperf 2·50 2·50

295 "The Smoke Signal" (F. Remington)

1976. Bicent of American Revolution (2nd series). "200 Years of Progress". Multicoloured.
2056 1c. Type **295** (postage) 10 10
2057 1c. Houston Space Centre 10 10
2058 2c. Lighting candelabra, 1976 10 10
2059 2c. Edison's lamp and houses 10 10
2060 3c. "Agriculture 1776" 10 10
2061 3c. "Agriculture 1976" 10 10
2062 4c. Harvard College, 1776 10 10
2063 4c. Harvard University, 1976 10 10
2064 5c. Horse and carriage 15 10
2065 5c. Boeing 747-100 airliner 15 10
2066 80c. Philadelphia, 1776 (air) 25 15
2067 80c. Washington, 1976 25 15
2068 2cor.75 "Bonhomme Richard" (American frigate) (John Paul Jones's flagship) and H.M.S. "Seraphis" (frigate), Battle of Flamborough Head 1·50 70
2069 2cor.75 U.S.S. "Glenard Phipscomp" (nuclear submarine) 1·50 70
2070 4cor. Wagon train 90 70
2071 4cor. Amtrak gas turbine train, 1973 3·25 1·75
MS2072 140 × 111 mm. 10cor. George Washington and Family; 10cor. President Ford and Family 7·00 7·00

296 Italy, 1968

1976. Olympic Games, Victors in Rowing and Sculling. Multicoloured.
2073 1c. Denmark 1964 (postage) 10 10
2074 2c. East Germany 1972 10 10
2075 3c. Type **296** 10 10
2076 4c. Great Britain 1936 10 10
2077 5c. France 1952 (vert) 10 10
2078 35c. U.S.A. 1920 (vert) 10 10
2079 55c. Russia 1956 (vert) (air) 20 10
2080 70c. New Zealand 1972 (vert) 20 15
2081 90c. New Zealand 1968 25 20
2082 20cor. U.S.A. 1956 2·75 2·50
MS2083 157 × 109 mm. 10cor. First Women's Rowing "Eights" Event; part of U.S.A. crew, 1976 (39 × 52 mm) 2·75 2·75

1976. Air. East Germany Victory in Rowing Event at Montreal Olympics. Nos. 2082 and **MS**2083 optd **REPUBLICA DEMOCRATIC ALEMANA VENCEDOR EN. 1976.**
2084 20cor. multicoloured 4·25 3·50
MS2085 157 × 109 mm. 10cor. multicoloured 2·25 2·25

298 Buce Jenner

1976. Air. Decathlon Winner at Montreal Olympics.
MS2086 **298** 165 × 165 mm. 25cor. multicoloured 4·25 4·25

299 Mauritius 1847 2d. "Post Office"

1976. Rare and Famous Stamps. Multicoloured.
2087 1c. Type **299** (postage) . . . 10 10
2088 2c. Western Australia 1854 "Inverted Mute Swan" . . 85 15
2089 3c. Mauritius 1847 1d. "Post Office" 10 10
2090 4c. Jamaica 1920 1s. inverted frame 10 10
2091 5c. U.S 1918 24c. inverted aircraft 10 10
2092 10c. Swiss 1845 Basel "Dove" 10 10
2093 25c. Canada 1959 Seaway inverted centre 10 10
2094 40c. Hawaiian 1851 2c. "Missionary" (air) 10 10
2095 1cor. G.B. 1840 "Penny Black" 20 20
2096 2cor. British Guiana 1850 1c. black on magenta . . 40 35
2097 5cor. Honduras 1925 airmail 25c. on 10c. . . . . . . 3·50 1·10
2098 10cor. Newfoundland 1919 "Hawker" airmail stamp 1·25 1·10
MS2099 140 × 101 mm. 4cor. Nicaragua 1881 "Grey-town" cover with G.B./Nicaragua stamps 75 70

300 Olga Nunez de Saballos (Member of Parliament)

1977. Air. International Women's Year. Multicoloured.
2100 35c. Type **300** 10 10
2101 1cor. Josefa Toledo de Aguerri (educator) 20 20
2102 10cor. Hope Portocarreo de Samoza (President's wife) 1·25 1·00

1977. 50th Anniv of National Guard. Designs as **MS**1410a with revised inscription "1927–1977 Aniversario Guardia Nacional de Nicaragua".
MS2103 Two sheets each 160 × 100 mm. Nos. 1399/1404 and 1405/10. Imperf . . . . 2·50 2·50

301 "Graf Zeppelin" in Hangar

1977. 75th Anniv of First Zeppelin Flight. Mult.
2104 1c. Type **301** (postage) . . . 10 10
2105 2c. "Graf Zeppelin" in flight 10 10
2106 3c. Giffard's steam-powered dirigible airship, 1852 . . 15 10
2107 4c. "Graf Zeppelin" in mooring hangar 15 10
2108 5c. "Graf Zeppelin" on ground 15 10
2109 35c. Astra airship "Ville de Paris" (air) 35 15
2110 70c. "Schwaben" 40 20
2111 3cor. "Graf Zeppelin" over Lake Constance . . . . . 1·00 65
2112 10cor. LZ-2 on Lake Constance . . . . 3·75 2·25
MS2113 101 × 65 mm. 20cor. Mooring crew handling "Graf Zeppelin". Perf or imperf . . . 6·50 6·50

302 Lindbergh and Map

1977. 50th Anniv of Lindbergh's Transatlantic Flight. Multicoloured.
2114 1c. Type **302** (postage) . . . 10 10
2115 2c. Map and "Spirit of St. Louis" 10 10
2116 3c. Charles Lindbergh (vert) 10 10
2117 4c. "Spirit of St. Louis" crossing Atlantic 10 10
2118 5c. Charles Lindbergh standing by "Spirit of St. Louis" 10 10
2119 20c. Lindbergh, route and "Spirit of St. Louis" . . . 20 15
2120 55c. Lindbergh landing in Nicaragua (1928) (air) . . 20 15
2121 80c. "Spirit of St. Louis" and route map 35 15
2122 2cor. "Spirit of St. Louis" flying along Nicaraguan coast 65 35
2123 10cor. Passing Momotombo (Nicaragua) . . . . . . 1·90 1·25
MS2124 124 × 80 mm. 20cor. "Spirit of St. Louis" in flight . . . . 4·25 4·25

303 Christmas Festival

1977. Christmas. Scenes from Tchaikovsky's "Nutcracker" Suite. Multicoloured.
2125 1c. Type **303** 10 10
2126 2c. Doll's dance 10 10
2127 3c. Clara and snowflakes . . 10 10
2128 4c. Snow fairy and prince 10 10
2129 5c. Snow fairies 10 10
2130 15c. Sugar fairy and prince 10 10
2131 40c. Waltz of the Flowers 10 10
2132 90c. Chinese dance 20 15
2133 1cor. Senora Bonbonierre 20 20
2134 10cor. Arabian dance . . . 1·40 1·25
MS2135 130 × 109 mm. 20cor. Finale (air) . . . . 4·25 4·25

304 "Mr. and Mrs. Andrews". (Gainsborough)

1978. Paintings. Multicoloured.
2136 1c. Type **304** (postage) . . . 10 10
2137 2c. "Giovanna Bacelli" (Gainsborough) 10 10
2138 3c. "Blue Boy" (Gainsborough) 10 10
2139 4c. "Francis I" (Titian) . . 10 10
2140 5c. "Charles V at Battle of Muhlberg" (Titian) . . . 10 10
2141 25c. "Sacred Love" (Titian) 10 10
2142 5cor. "Hippopotamus and Crocodile Hunt" (Rubens) (air) 60 50
2143 10cor. "Duke of Lerma on Horseback" (Rubens) . . 1·75 1·40
MS2144 130 × 105 mm. 20cor. Rubens (from painting of Rubens and Isabella Brandt) . . . . . 4·25 4·25

305 Gothic Portal with Rose Window, Small Basilica of St. Francis

1978. 750th Anniv of Canonisation of St. Francis of Assisi. Multicoloured.
2145 1c. Type **305** (postage) . . . 10 10
2146 2c. St. Francis preaching to birds 10 10
2147 3c. Painting of St. Francis 10 10
2148 4c. Franciscan genealogical tree 10 10
2149 5c. Portiuncola 10 10
2150 15c. Autographed blessing 10 10
2151 25c. Windows of Large Basilica 10 10
2152 80c. St. Francis and wolf (air) 15 10
2153 10cor. St. Francis . . . . . 1·60 1·50
MS2154 121 × 105 mm. 20cor. Our Lady of Conception (patron saint of Nicaragua) . . . . 4·00 4·00

306 Locomotive No. 6, 1921

1978. Centenary of Railway. Multicoloured.
2155 1c. Type **306** (postage) . . . 10 10
2156 2c. Lightweight cargo locomotive 10 10
2157 3c. Steam locomotive No. 10, 1909 . . . . . . 10 10
2158 4c. Baldwin steam locomotive No. 31, 1906 10 10
2159 5c. Baldwin steam locomotive No. 21, 1911 10 10
2160 15c. Presidential Pullman coach 15 10
2161 35c. Steam locomotive No. 33, 1907 (air) 20 15
2162 4cor. Baldwin steam locomotive No. 36, 1907 2·50 90
2163 10cor. Juniata steam locomotive, 1914, U.S.A. 6·25 2·25
MS2164 140 × 107 mm. 20cor. Map of Nicaraguan railway system 4·00 4·00

307 Mongol Warriors ("Michael Strogoff")

1978. 150th Birth Anniv of Jules Verne. Mult.
2165 1c. Type **307** (postage) . . . 10 10
2166 2c. Sea scene ("The Mysterious Island") . . . 10 10
2167 3c. Sea monsters ("Journey to the Centre of the Earth") 10 10
2168 4c. Balloon and African elephant ("Five Weeks in a Balloon") 20 10
2169 90c. Submarine ("Twenty Thousand Leagues Under the Sea") (air) 75 20
2170 10cor. Balloon, Indian, steam locomotive and elephant ("Around the World in Eighty Days") 6·50 4·00
MS2171 113 × 87 mm. 20cor. Space ship ("From Earth to Moon") 6·50 6·50

308 Icarus

1978. 75th Anniv of History of Aviation. First Powered Flight. Multicoloured.
2172 1c. Type **308** (postage) . . . 10 10
2173 2c. Montgolfier balloon (vert) 10 10
2174 3c. Wright Flyer I 10 10
2175 4c. Orville Wright in Wright Type A (vert) 10 10
2176 55c. Vought-Sikorsky VS-300 helicopter prototype (air) 30 10
2177 10cor. Space Shuttle . . . . 2·10 1·00
MS2178 143 × 114 mm. 20cor. "Flyer" III . . . . 6·50 6·50

309 Ernst Ocwirk and Alfredo di Stefano

310 "St. Peter" (Goya)

1978. World Cup Football Championship, Argentina. Multicoloured.
2179 20c. Type **309** (postage) . . 10 10
2180 25c. Ralk Edstrom and Oswaldo Piazza 10 10
2181 50c. Franz Beckenbauer and Dennis Law (air) 10 10
2182 5cor. Dino Zoff and Pele . . 65 50
MS2183 102 × 77 mm. 20cor. Dominique Rocheteau and Johan Neeskens . . . . 4·00 4·00

1978. Christmas. Multicoloured.
2184 10c. Type **310** (postage) . . 10 10
2185 15c. "St. Gregory" (Goya) 10 10
2186 3cor. "The Apostles John and Peter" (Durer) (air) 40 30
2187 10cor. "The Apostles Paul and Mark" (Durer) . . . 1·40 1·00
MS2188 143 × 104 mm. 20cor. "The Child with Garland" (Durer) 6·50 6·50

311 San Cristobal

1978. Volcanoes and Lakes. Multicoloured.
2189 5c. Type **311** (postage) . . . 10 10
2190 5c. Lake de Cosiguina . . . 10 10
2191 20c. Telica 10 10
2192 20c. Lake Jiloa 10 10
2193 35c. Cerro Negro (air) . . . 10 10
2194 35c. Lake Masaya 10 10
2195 90c. Momotombo 20 15
2196 90c. Lake Asososca 20 15
2197 1cor. Mombacho 20 15
2198 1cor. Lake Apoyo 20 15
2199 10cor. Concepcion . . . . 1·60 80
2200 10cor. Lake Tiscapa . . . . 1·60 80

312 General O'Higgins

1979. Air. Birth Bicentenary of Bernardo O'Higgins (liberation hero).
2201 **312** 20cor. multicoloured . . 3·75 1·90

313 Ginger Plant and Broad-tailed Hummingbird

1979. Air. Flowers. Multicoloured.
2202 50c. Type **313** 60 20
2203 55c. Orchids 10 10
2204 70c. Poinsettia 15 10
2205 80c. "Poro poro" 15 10
2206 2cor. "Morpho cypris" (butterfly) and Guayacan flowers 50 30
2207 4cor. Iris 45 30

314 Children with football

315 Indian Postal Runner

316 Einstein and Albert Schweitzer

317 Loggerhead Turtle

1980. Year of Liberation (1979) and Nicaragua's Participation in Olympic Games. Unissued stamps overprinted. (a) International Year of the Child. Mult.
2208 20c. Children on roundabout (postage) . . 15 15
2209 90c. Type **314** (air) 65 65
2210 2cor. Children with stamp albums . . . . 1·50 1·50

2211 2cor.20 Children playing with toy steam train and aircraft 14·00 14·00
2212 10cor. Baseball 7·50 7·50
MS2213 130×105 mm. 5cor. As No. 2211 (30×47 mm); 15cor. Dr. Hermann Gmeiner (30×47 mm) 20·00 20·00

(b) Death Centenary of Sir Rowland Hill. Mult.
2214 20c. Type **315** (postage) 20 20
2215 35c. Pony express 40 40
2216 1cor. Pre-stamp letter (horiz) 1·10 1·10
2217 1cor.80 Sir Rowland Hill examining sheet of Penny Black stamps (air) 1·90 1·90
2218 2cor.20 Penny Blacks (horiz) 2·40 2·40
2219 5cor. Nicaraguan Zeppelin flight cover (horiz) 5·50 5·50
MS2220 130×105 mm. 20cor. Sir Rowland Hill and Indian postal runner (36×47 mm) 20·00 20·00

(c) Birth Centenary of Albert Einstein (physicist). Multicoloured.
2221 5c. Type **316** (postage) 15 15
2222 10c. Einstein and equation 25 25
2223 15c. Einstein and 1939 World Fair pavilion 40 40
2224 20c. Einstein and Robert Oppenheimer 50 50
2225 25c. Einstein in Jerusalem 65 65
2226 1cor. Einstein and Nobel Prize medal (air) 2·50 2·50
2227 2cor.75 Einstein and space exploration 7·00 7·00
2228 10cor. Einstein and Mahatma Gandhi 15·00 15·00
MS2229 130×105 mm. 5cor. Einstein at work (53×36 mm); 15cor. As No. 2228 (53×36 mm) 20·00 20·00

(d) Endangered Turtles. Multicoloured.
2230 90c. Type **317** 1·00 80
2231 2cor. Leatherback turtle 2·25 1·75
2232 2cor.30 Ridley turtle 1·75 1·75
2233 10cor. Hawksbill turtle 7·50 7·50
MS2234 150×105 mm. 5cor. As No. 2231 (51×32 mm); 15cor. Green turtles (51×32 mm) 20·00 20·00

318 Rigoberto Lopez Perez and Crowds pulling down Statue

1980. 1st Anniv of the Revolution. Multicoloured.
2235 40c. Type **318** 10 10
2236 75c. Street barricade 10 10
2237 1cor. "Learn to Read" emblem (vert) 15 10
2238 1cor.25 German Pomares Ordonez and jungle fighters 20 15
2239 1cor.85 Victory celebrations (vert) 25 15
2240 2cor.50 Carlos Fonesca and camp-fire 35 35
2241 5cor. Gen. Augusto Sandino and flag (vert) 70 55
MS2242 118×90 mm. 10cor. Nicaraguan landscape 1·75 1·75

1980. Literacy Year. Unissued stamps optd **1980 ANO DE LA ALFABETIZACION**.
(a) International Year of the Child. As Nos. 2208/12.
2243 – 20c. Children on roundabout (postage) 1·00 1·00
2244 **314** 90c. Children with football (air) 1·00 1·00
2245 – 2cor. Children with stamp albums 1·00 1·00
2246 – 2cor.20 Children playing with toy steam train and airplane 2·00 2·00
2247 – 10cor. Baseball 4·50 4·50
MS2248 105×90 mm. 10cor. Dr. Hermann Gmeiner 6·50 6·50

(b) Death Centenary of Sir Rowland Hill. Nos. 2214/16.
2249 **315** 20c. Indian postal runner 70 70
2250 – 35c. Pony express 70 70
2251 – 1cor. Pre-stamp letter (horiz) 70 70
MS2252 83×100 mm. 10cor. Penny Black and Nicaraguan 2c. stamp 3·75 3·75

(c) Birth Centenary of Albert Einstein (physicist). As Nos. 2221/8.
2253 5c. Optd **"YURI GAGARIN/12/IV/1961/ LER HOMBRE EN EL ESPACIO"** (postage) 1·10 1·10
2254 10c. Optd **"LURABA 1981"** and space shuttle 1·10 1·10
2255 15c. Optd **"SPACE SHUTTLE"** and craft 1·10 1·10
2256 20c. Optd **ANO DE LA ALFABETIZACION** 1·10 1·10
2257 25c. Optd **"16/VII/1969/LER HOMBRE A LA LUNA"** and **"APOLLO XI"** 1·10 1·10
2258 1cor. Optd As No. 2256 (air) 1·10 1·10
2259 2cor.75 Optd As No. 2256 1·10 1·10
2260 10cor.75 Optd **"LUNOJOD 1"** and vehicle 1·10 1·10
MS2261 111×85 mm. 10cor. Einstein at work 18·00 18·00

(d) Air. Endangered Species. Turtles. As Nos. 2230/3. Multicoloured.
2262 **317** 90c. Loggerhead turtle 1·00 1·00
2263 – 2cor. Leatherback turtle 1·00 1·00
2264 – 2cor.20 Ridley turtle 1·00 1·00
2265 – 10cor. Hawksbill turtle 1·00 1·00
MS2266 140×105 mm. 5cor. Green turtles 18·00 18·00

320 Resplendent Quetzal

1981. "WIPA" 1981 International Stamp Exhibition, Vienna. Sheet 93×55 mm.
MS2267 **320** 10cor. multicoloured 1·75 1·50

321 Footballer and El Molinon Stadium

1981. World Cup Football Championship, Spain. (1st issue). Venues. Multicoloured.
2268 5c. Type **321** 10 10
2269 20c. Sanchez Pizjuan, Seville 10 10
2270 25c. San Mames, Bilbao 10 10
2271 30c. Vincent Calderon, Madrid 10 10
2272 50c. R.C.D. Espanol, Barcelona 10 10
2273 4cor. New Stadium, Valladolid 55 35
2274 5cor. Balaidos, Vigo 55 35
2275 10cor. Santiago Bernabeu, Madrid 1·10 65
MS2276 65×79 mm. 10cor. Nou Camp, Barcelona (36×28 mm) 1·40 1·10
See also Nos. 2325/**MS**2332.

322 Adult Education

1981. 2nd Anniv of Revolution. Multicoloured.
2277 50c. Type **322** (postage) 10 10
2278 2cor.10 Workers marching (air) 30 15
2279 3cor. Roadbuilding and container ship 65 30
2280 6cor. Medical services 50 25

323 Allegory of Revolution

1981. 20th Anniv of Sandinista National Liberation Front. Multicoloured.
2281 50c. Type **323** (postage) 10 10
2282 4cor. Sandinista guerrilla (air) 25 10

324 Postman

1981. 12th Postal Union of the Americas and Spain Congress, Managua. Multicoloured.
2283 50c. Type **324** (postage) 10 10
2284 2cor.10 Pony Express (air) 30 15
2285 3cor. Postal Headquarters, Managua 45 25
2286 6cor. Government building, globe and flags of member countries 50 25

325 Reliefs depicting Bulgarian History (½-size illustration)

1981. Air. 1300th Anniv of Bulgarian State. Sheet 96×70 mm. Imperf.
MS2287 **325** 10cor. multicoloured 1·40 1·10

326 "Nymphaea capensis"

1981. Water Lilies. Multicoloured.
2288 50c. Type **326** (postage) 10 10
2289 1cor. "Nymphaea daubenyana" 15 10
2290 1cor.20 "Nymphaea Marliacea Chromat" 20 10
2291 1cor.80 "Nymphaea Dir. Geo. T. Moore" 25 15
2292 2cor. "Nymphaea lotus" 30 15
2293 2cor.50 "Nymphaea B.G. Berry" 35 20
2294 10cor. "Nymphaea Gladstoniana" (air) 60 40

327 Giant Panda

1981. Air. "Philatokyo 81 International Stamp Exhibition". Sheet 100×61 mm.
MS2295 **327** 10cor. multicoloured 1·40 1·10

328 Cardinal Tetra

1981. Tropical Fishes. Multicoloured.
2296 50c. Type **328** (postage) 15 10
2297 1cor. Guppy 30 20
2298 1cor.85 Striped headstander 50 30
2299 2cor.10 Skunk corydoras 65 35
2300 2cor.50 Black-finned pearlfish 75 40
2301 3cor.50 Long-finned killie (air) 1·10 65
2302 4cor. Red swordtail 1·25 80

329 Frigate

1981. Air. "Espamer 81 Stamp Exhibition, Buenos Aires". Sheet 98×59 mm.
MS2303 **329** 10cor. multicoloured 1·40 1·10

330 Lineated Woodpecker

331 Satellite in Orbit

1981. Birds. Multicoloured.
2304 50c. Type **330** (postage) 35 15
2305 1cor.20 Keel-billed toucan (horiz) 70 25
2306 1cor.80 Finsch's conure (horiz) 80 35
2307 2cor. Scarlet macaw 1·10 40
2308 3cor. Slaty-tailed trogon (air) 1·25 50
2309 4cor. Violet sabrewing (horiz) 1·75 60
2310 6cor. Blue-crowned motmot 3·50 1·00

1981. Satellite Communications. Multicoloured.
2311 50c. Type **331** (postage) 10 10
2312 1cor. "Intelsat IVA" 15 10
2313 1cor.50 "Intelsat V" moving into orbit 20 15
2314 2cor. Rocket releasing "Intelsat V" 30 20
2315 3cor. Satellite and Space Shuttle (air) 45 25
2316 4cor. "Intelsat V" and world maps 55 30
2317 5cor. Tracking stations 70 45

332 Steam Locomotive at Lake Granada

1981. Locomotives. Multicoloured.
2318 50c. Type **332** (postage) 20 10
2319 1cor. Vulcan Iron Works steam locomotive No. 35, 1946 40 10
2320 1cor.20 Baldwin steam locomotive No. 21, 1911 (inscribed "Philadelphia Iron Works") 45 10
2321 1cor.80 Steam crane, 1909 70 10
2322 2cor. General Electric Model "U10B" diesel locomotive, 1960s 75 10
2323 2cor.50 German diesel railbus, 1954 (dated "1956") 90 15
2324 6cor. Japanese-built diesel railbus, 1967 (air) 2·40 35

333 Heading Ball

1982. World Cup Football Championship, Spain (2nd issue). Multicoloured.
2325 5c. Type **333** (postage) 10 10
2326 20c. Running with ball 10 10
2327 25c. Running with ball (different) 10 10
2328 2cor.50 Saving goal 35 20
2329 3cor.50 Goalkeeper diving for ball (horiz) 50 30
2330 4cor. Kicking ball (air) 55 35
2331 10cor. Tackle (horiz) 60 40
MS2332 98×61 mm. 10cor. Goalkeeper attempting save (39×31 mm) 1·40 1·10

334 Cocker Spaniel

1982. Pedigree Dogs. Multicoloured.
2333 5c. Type **334** (postage) 10 10
2334 20c. Alsatian 10 10

2335 25c. English setter 10 10
2336 2cor.50 Brittany spaniel . . 35 20
2337 3cor. Boxer (air) 45 25
2338 3cor.50 Pointer 50 30
2339 6cor. Collie 60 30

335 Satellite Communications

1982. Air. I.T.U. Congress.
2340 **335** 25cor. multicoloured . . 2·10 1·50

336 "Dynamine myrrhina"

1982. Butterflies. Multicoloured.
2341 50c. Type **336** (postage) . . 20 10
2342 1cor.20 "Eunica alcmena" 40 10
2343 1cor.50 "Callizona acesta" 40 10
2344 2cor. "Adelpha leuceria" . . 60 20
2345 3cor. "Parides iphidamas" (air) . . . . 1·00 30
2346 3cor.50 "Consul hippona" 1·10 35
2347 4cor. "Morpho peleides" . . 1·25 40

337 Dog and Russian Rocket

1982. Space Exploration. Multicoloured.
2348 5c. Type **337** (postage) . . . 10 10
2349 15c. Satellite (vert) 10 10
2350 50c. "Apollo–Soyuz" link 10 10
2351 1cor.50 Satellite 20 15
2352 2cor.50 Docking in space . . 35 20
2353 5cor. Russian space station (air) 45 20
2354 6cor. Space shuttle "Columbia" (vert) 60 30

338 Mailcoach

1982. Centenary of U.P.U. Membership. Mult.
2355 50c. Type **338** (postage) . . 10 10
2356 1cor.20 "Victoria" (packet steamer) . . . . 1·10 35
2357 3cor.50 Steam locomotive, 1953 (air) . . . . 2·75 25
2358 10cor. Boeing 727-100 airliner . . . . 1·50 1·10

339 Cyclists

1982. 14th Central American and Caribbean Games. Multicoloured.
2359 10c. Type **339** (postage) . . 10 10
2360 15c. Swimming (horiz) . . . 10 10
2361 25c. Basketball 10 10
2362 50c. Weightlifting 10 10
2363 2cor.50 Handball (air) . . . 35 20
2364 3cor. Boxing (horiz) 45 25
2365 9cor. Football (horiz) . . . 75 45
MS2366 65 × 90 mm. 10cor. Baseball (30 × 39 mm) . . . . 1·40 90

340 Balloon

1982. Air. "Philexfrance 82 International Stamp Exhibition, Paris". Sheet 79 × 91 mm.
MS2367 **340** 15cor. multicoloured 2·10 1·25

341 Washington passing through Trenton

1982. 250th Birth Anniv of George Washington. Multicoloured.
2368 50c. Mount Vernon, Washington's house (39 × 49 mm) (postage) . . 10 10
2369 1cor. Washington signing the Constitution (horiz) 15 10
2370 2cor. Type **341** 30 20
2371 2cor.50 Washington crossing the Delaware (horiz) (air) 35 20
2372 3cor.50 Washington at Valley Forge (horiz) . . . 50 30
2373 4cor. Washington at the Battle of Trenton 55 35
2374 6cor. Washington at Princeton 60 55

342 Carlos Fonseca, Dove and Flags

1982. 3rd Anniv of Revolution. Multicoloured.
2375 50c. Type **342** (postage) . . 10 10
2376 2cor.50 Ribbons forming dove (vert) (air) 35 20
2377 1cor. Augusto Sandino and dove (vert) 55 30
2378 6cor. Dove 60 55

343 "Vase of Flowers" (R. Penalba)

1982. Paintings. Multicoloured.
2379 25c. Type **343** (postage) . . 10 10
2380 50c. "El Gueguense" (M. Garcia) (horiz) . . . 10 10
2381 1cor. "The Couple" (R. Perez) 15 10
2382 1cor.20 "Canales Valley" (A. Mejias) (horiz) . . . 20 10
2383 1cor.85 "Portrait of Senora Castellon" (T. Jerez) . . . 25 15
2384 2cor. "The Vendors" (L. Cerrato) 30 20
2385 9cor. "Sitting Woman" (A. Morales) (horiz) (air) 55 35
MS2386 86 × 64 mm. 10cor. "Roosters" (P. Ortiz) (horiz) 1·40 90

344 Lenin and Dimitrov, Moscow, 1921

1982. Birth Centenary of Georgi Dimitrov (Bulgarian statesman). Multicoloured.
2387 50c. Type **344** (postage) . . 10 10
2388 2cor.50 Dimitrov & Todor Yikov, Sofia, 1946 (air) 35 20
2389 4cor. Dimitrov and flag . . 55 35

345 Ausberto Narvaez

1982. 26th Anniv of State of Resistance Movement. Multicoloured.
2390 50c. Type **345** (postage) . . 10 10
2391 2cor.50 Cornelio Silva . . . 35 20
2392 4cor. Rigoberto Lopez Perez (air) 55 35
2393 6cor. Edwin Castro 60 55

346 Old Ruins at Leon

1982. Tourism. Multicoloured.
2394 50c. Type **346** (postage) . . 10 10
2395 1cor. Ruben Dario Theatre and Park, Managua . . . 15 10
2396 1cor.20 Independence Square, Granada 20 10
2397 1cor.80 Corn Island 25 15
2398 2cor. Carter Santiago Volcano, Masaya 30 20
2399 2cor.50 El Coyotepe Fortress, Masaya (air) . . 35 20
2400 3cor.50 Luis A. Velazquez Park, Managua 50 30

347 Karl Marx and View of Trier

1982. Death Centenary of Karl Marx. Mult.
2401 1cor. Type **347** (postage) . . 15 10
2402 4cor. Marx and grave in Highgate Cemetery (air) 55 35

348 Stacking Cane and Fruit

1982. World Food Day. Multicoloured.
2403 50c. Picking Fruit (horiz) . . 10 10
2404 1cor. Type **348** 15 10
2405 2cor. Cutting sugar cane (horiz) 30 20
2406 10cor. F.A.O. and P.A.N. emblems (horiz) 85 65

349 "Santa Maria"

1982. 490th Anniv of Discovery of America. Multicoloured.
2407 50c. Type **349** (postage) . . 65 20
2408 1cor. "Nina" . . . . 1·25 30
2409 1cor.50 "Pinta" . . . . . . 1·75 45
2410 2cor. Columbus and fleet . . 2·00 70
2411 2cor.50 Fleet and map of route (air) . . . . 2·00 70
2412 4cor. Arrival in America . . 55 35
2413 7cor. Death of Columbus 65 60
MS2414 71 × 56 mm. 10cor. "Santa Maria" (vert) . . . . 1·40 90

350 "Lobelia laxiflora"

351 "Micrurus lemniscatus"

1982. Woodland Flowers. Multicoloured.
2415 50c. Type **350** (postage) . . 10 10
2416 1cor.20 "Bombacopsis quinata" 20 10
2417 1cor.80 "Mimosa albida" 25 15
2418 2cor. "Epidendrum alatum" 30 20
2419 2cor.50 Passion flower "Passiflora foetida" wrongly inscr "Pasiflora" (air) 35 20
2420 3cor.50 "Clitoria sp." . . . 50 30
2421 5cor. "Russelia sarmentosa" 70 45

1982. Reptiles. Multicoloured.
2422 10c. Type **351** (postage) . . 10 10
2423 50c. Common iguana "Iguana iguana" (horiz) 10 10
2424 2cor. "Lachesis muta" (snake) (horiz) 30 20
2425 2cor.50 Hawksbill turtle "Eretmochelys imbricata" (horiz) (air) 35 20
2426 3cor. Boa constrictor "Constrictor constrictor" 45 25
2427 3cor.50 American crocodile "Crocodilus acutus" (horiz) 50 30
2428 5cor. Diamond-back rattlesnake "Sistrurus catenatus" (horiz) 70 45

352 Tele-cor Building, Managua

1982. Telecommunications Day. Multicoloured.
2429 1cor. Type **352** (postage) . . 15 10
2430 50c. Interior of radio transmission room (air) 10 10

353 Girl with Dove

1983. Air. Non-Aligned States Conference.
2431 **353** 4cor. multicoloured . . . 55 35

354 Jose Marti and Birthplace

1983. 130th Birth Anniv of Jose Marti (Cuban revolutionary).
2432 **354** 1cor. multicoloured . . . 15 10

355 Boxing

356 "Neomarica coerulea"

1983. Olympic Games, Los Angeles (1st issue). Multicoloured.
2433 50c. Type **355** (postage) . . 10 10
2434 1cor. Gymnastics 15 10
2435 1cor.50 Running 20 15
2436 2cor. Weightlifting 30 20
2437 4cor. Discus (air) 55 35
2438 5cor. Basketball 70 45
2439 6cor. Cycling 90 55
MS2440 60 × 88 mm. 15cor. Sailing (31 × 39 mm) . . . . 2·10 1·25
See also Nos 2609/**MS**2616.

1983. Flowers.
2441 **356** 1cor. blue 15 10
2442 – 1cor. violet 15 10
2443 – 1cor. mauve 15 10
2444 – 1cor. brown 15 10
2445 – 1cor. green 15 10
2446 – 1cor. blue 15 10
2447 – 1cor. green 15 10
2448 – 1cor. green 15 10
2449 – 1cor. mauve 15 10
2450 – 1cor. red 15 10
2451 – 1cor. grey 15 10
2452 – 1cor. yellow 15 10
2453 – 1cor. brown 15 10
2454 – 1cor. purple 15 10
2455 – 1cor. green 15 10
2456 – 1cor. black 15 10
DESIGNS: No. 2442, "Tabebula ochraceae"; 2443, "Laella sp"; 2444, "Plumeria rubra"; 2445, "Brassavola nodosa"; 2446, "Stachytarpheta indica"; 2447, "Cochiospermum sp"; 2448, "Malvaviscus arboreus"; 2449, "Telecoma stans"; 2450, "Hibiscus rosa-sinensis"; 2451, "Cattleya lueddemanniana"; 2452, "Tagetes erecta"; 2453, "Senecio sp"; 2454, "Sobralia macrantha"; 2455, "Thumbergia alata"; 2456, "Bixa orellana".
See also Nos. 2739/54, 2838/53 and 3087/3102.

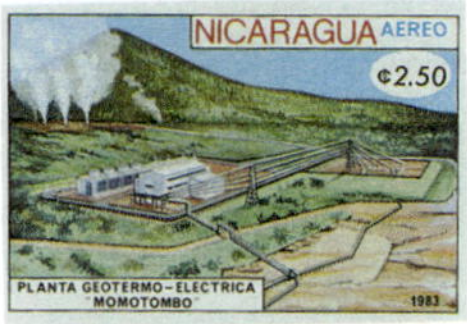

357 Momotombo Geothermal Electrical Plant

1983. Air. Energy.
2457 **357** 2cor.50 multicoloured . . 35 20

358 Map of Nicaragua and Girl picking Coffee

1983. Papal Visit.
2458 – 50c. red, black and blue (postage) 10 10
2459 **358** 1cor. multicoloured . . . 15 10
2460 – 4cor. multicoloured (air) 55 35
2461 – 7cor. multicoloured . . . 1·40 1·40
MS2462 80 × 66 mm. 15cor. multicoloured (31 × 39 mm) . . 2·10 1·25
DESIGNS: 50c. Demonstrating crowd; 4cor. Pres. Cordova Rivas and Pope John Paul II; 7cor. Pope outside Managua Cathedral; Pope John Paul II.

359 "Xilophanes chiron"

1983. Moths. Multicoloured.
2463 15c. Type **359** (postage) . . 10 10
2464 50c. "Protoparce ochus" . . 15 10
2465 65c. "Pholus lasbruscae" . . 25 10
2466 1cor. "Amphypterus gannascus" 30 10
2467 1cor.50 "Pholus licaon" . . 40 15
2468 2cor. "Agrius cingulata" . . 60 25
2469 10cor. "Rothschildia jurulla" (vert) (air) . . . 3·25 95

360 La Recoleccion Church, Leon

1983. Monuments. Multicoloured.
2470 50c. Subtiava Church, Leon (horiz) (postage) 10 10
2471 1cor. La Inmaculada Castle, Rio San Juan (horiz) . . 15 10
2472 2cor. Type **360** 30 20
2473 4cor. Ruben Dario Monument, Managua (air) 55 35

361 Passenger Carriage

1983. Railway Wagons. Multicoloured.
2474 15c. Type **361** (postage) . . 10 10
2475 65c. Goods wagon No. 1034 25 10
2476 1cor. Tanker wagon No. 931 30 10
2477 1cor.50 Xolotlan hopper wagon 45 10
2478 4cor. Railcar (air) . . . . . 1·25 35
2479 5cor. Tipper truck . . . . . 1·50 40
2480 7cor. Railbus . . . . 2·25 60

362 Helping Earthquake Victim

1983. Red Cross. Multicoloured.
2481 50c. Aiding flood victims (horiz) (postage) 10 10
2482 1cor. Placing stretcher patient into ambulance (horiz) 15 10
2483 4cor. Type **362** (air) 55 35
2484 5cor. Doctor examining wounded soldier (horiz) 70 45

363 Raising Telephone Pole

1983. World Communications Year.
2485 **363** 1cor. multicoloured . . . 15 10

364 Ibex

1983. Air. "Tembal 83 International Stamp Exhibition, Basel". Sheet 79 × 64 mm.
MS2486 **364** 15cor. multicoloured 2·10 1·25

365 Basketball

1983. 9th Pan-American Games. Multicoloured.
2487 15c. Basketball (horiz) (postage) 10 10
2488 50c. Water polo (horiz) . . 10 10
2489 65c. Running (horiz) 15 10
2490 1cor. Type **365** 15 10
2491 2cor. Weightlifting 30 20
2492 7cor. Fencing (horiz) (air) 65 30
2493 8cor. Gymnastics (horiz) . . 70 40
MS2494 75 × 85 mm. 15cor. Boxing (39 × 31 mm) . . . . 2·10 1·25

366 Boeing 727-100

1983. Air. "Expo Filnic National Stamp Exhibition". Sheet 79 × 60 mm.
MS2495 **366** 10cor. multicoloured 1·40 90

367 Container Ship being Unloaded

1983. 4th Anniv of Revolution. Multicoloured.
2496 1cor. Type **367** 55 15
2497 2cor. Telcor building, Leon 30 20

368 Carlos Fonseca

369 Simon Bolivar on Horseback

1983. Founders of Sandinista National Liberation Front. Multicoloured.
2498 50c. Escobar, Navarro, Ubeda, Pomares and Ruiz (postage) 10 10
2499 1cor. Santos Lopez, Borge, Buitrago and Mayorga . . 15 10
2500 4cor. Type **368** (air) 55 35

1983. Birth Bicentenary of Simon Bolivar. Mult.
2501 50c. Bolivar and Sandinista guerrilla 10 10
2502 1cor. Type **369** 15 10

370 Jaguar

1983. Air. "Brasiliana 83 International Stamp Exhibition, Rio de Janeiro. Sheet 95 × 65 mm.
MS2503 **370** 15cor. multicoloured 2·10 1·25

371 Movements of a Pawn

1983. Chess. Multicoloured.
2504 15c. Type **371** (postage) . . 10 10
2505 65c. Knight's movements . . 10 10
2506 1cor. Bishop's movements 15 10
2507 2cor. Rook's movements . . 30 20
2508 4cor. Queen's movements (air) 55 35
2509 5cor. King's movements . . 70 45
2510 7cor. Game in progress . . 75 60

372 Speed Skating

1983. Winter Olympic Games, Sarajevo (1984) (1st issue). Multicoloured.
2511 50c. Type **372** (postage) . . 10 10
2512 1cor. Slalom 15 10
2513 1cor.50 Luge 20 15
2514 2cor. Ski jumping 30 20
2515 4cor. Figure skating (air) . . 55 35
2516 5cor. Downhill skiing . . . 70 45
2517 6cor. Biathlon 90 55
MS2518 51 × 80 mm. 15cor. Ice hockey (31 × 39 mm) . . . . . 2·10 1·25

373 Soldiers with German Shepherd Dog

374 "Madonna of the Chair"

1983. Armed Forces.
2519 **373** 4cor. multicoloured . . . 55 35

1983. 500th Birth Anniv of Raphael. Multicoloured.
2520 50c. Type **374** (postage) . . 10 10
2521 1cor. "Esterhazy Madonna" 15 10
2522 1cor.50 "Sistine Madonna" 20 15
2523 2cor. "Madonna of the Linnet" 30 20
2524 4cor. "Madonna of the Meadow" (air) 55 35
2525 5cor. "Madonna of the Garden" 70 45
2526 6cor. "Adoration of the Kings" 90 55
MS2527 86 × 123 mm. 15cor. "Foligno Madonna" . . . . . 2·10 1·25

375 Pottery Idol

1983. Archaeological Finds. Multicoloured.
2528 50c. Type **375** (postage) . . 10 10
2529 1cor. Pottery dish with ornamental lid 15 10
2530 2cor. Vase with snake design 30 20
2531 4cor. Pottery dish (air) . . . 55 35

376 Metal being poured into Moulds

1983. Nationalization of Mines. Multicoloured.
2532 1cor. Type **376** (postage) . . 15 10
2533 4cor. Workers and mine (air) 55 35

377 Radio Operator and Sinking Liner

1983. "Fracap '83" Congress of Radio Amateurs of Central America and Panama. Multicoloured.
2534 1cor. Type **377** 70 15
2535 4cor. Congress emblem and town destroyed by earthquake 55 35

378 Tobacco

1983. Agrarian Reform.
2536 **378** 1cor. green 15 10
2537 – 2cor. orange 30 20
2538 – 4cor. brown 35 35
2539 – 5cor. blue 45 45
2540 – 6cor. lavender 55 55
2541 – 7cor. purple 60 60

2542 – 8cor. purple 70 65
2543 – 10cor. brown 90 90
DESIGNS: 2cor. Cotton; 4cor. Maize; 5cor. Sugar; 6cor. Cattle; 7cor. Rice; 8cor. Coffee; 10cor. Bananas.
See also Nos. 2755/62 and 2854/61.

379 Fire Engine with Ladder

1983. Fire Engines. Multicoloured.
2544 50c. Type **379** (postage) 10 10
2545 1cor. Water tanker 15 10
2546 6cor. Crew vehicle, 1930 90 55
2547 1cor.50 Pump with extension fire hoses (air) 20 15
2548 2cor. Pump with high-pressure tank 30 20
2548a 4cor. Water tanker 60 40
2549 5cor. Fire engine, 1910 70 45

380 Jose Marti and General Sandino

1983. Nicaragua–Cuba Solidarity. Multicoloured.
2550 1cor. Type **380** (postage) 15 10
2551 4cor. Teacher, doctor and welder (air) 55 35

381 "Adoration of the Shepherds" (Hugo van der Gaes)
382 Anniversary Emblem

1983. Christmas. Multicoloured.
2552 50c. Type **381** (postage) 10 10
2553 1cor. "Adoration of the Kings" (Domenico Ghirlandaio) 15 10
2554 2cor. "Adoration of the Shepherds" (El Greco) 30 20
2555 7cor. "Adoration of the Kings" (Konrad von Soest) (air) 65 30

1984. Air. 25th Anniv of Cuban Revolution.
2557 **382** 4cor. red, blue and black 45 20
2558 – 6cor. multicoloured 55 30
DESIGN: 6cor. Fidel Castro and Che Guevara.

383 Bobsleigh

1984. Winter Olympic Games, Sarajevo. Mult.
2559 50c. Type **383** (postage) 10 10
2560 50c. Biathlon 10 10
2561 1cor. Slalom 20 15
2562 1cor. Speed skating 20 15
2563 4cor. Skiing (air) 45 45
2564 5cor. Ice-dancing 55 55
2565 10cor. Ski-jumping 90 60
MS2566 64 × 73 mm. 15cor. Ice hockey (31 × 35 mm) 2·10 1·25

384 Chinchilla

1984. Cats. Multicoloured.
2567 50c. Type **384** (postage) 10 10
2568 50c. Longhaired white 10 10
2569 1cor. Red tabby 20 15
2570 2cor. Tortoiseshell 35 20
2571 4cor. Burmese 70 45
2572 3cor. Siamese (air) 50 35
2573 7cor. Longhaired silver 70 35

385 National Arms
386 Blanca Arauz

1984. 50th Death Anniv of Augusto Sandino. Mult.
2574 1cor. Type **385** (postage) 20 15
2575 4cor. Augusto Sandino (air) 35 20

1984. International Women's Day.
2576 **386** 1cor. multicoloured 20 15

387 Sunflower
388 "Soyuz"

1984. Agricultural Flowers. Multicoloured.
2577 50c. Type **387** (postage) 10 10
2578 50c. "Poinsettia pulcherrima" 10 10
2579 1cor. "Cassia alata" 20 15
2580 1cor. "Antigonon leptopus" 20 15
2581 3cor. "Bidens pilosa" (air) 50 35
2582 4cor. "Althaea rosea" 70 45
2583 5cor. "Rivea corymbosa" 85 55

1984. Space Anniversaries. Multicoloured.
2584 50c. Type **388** (15th anniv of "Soyuz 6", "7" and "8" flights) (postage) 10 10
2585 50c. "Soyuz" (different) (15th anniv of "Soyuz 6", "7" and "8" flights) 10 10
2586 1cor. "Apollo 11" approaching Moon (15th anniv of 1st manned landing) 20 15
2587 2cor. "Luna I" (25th anniv of 1st Moon satellite) 35 20
2588 3cor. "Luna II" (25th anniv of 1st Moon landing) (air) 50 35
2589 4cor. "Luna III" (25th anniv of 1st photographs of far side of Moon) 70 45
2590 9cor. Rocket (50th anniv of Korolev's book on space flight) 1·25 75

389 "Noli me Tangere" (detail)
390 Daimler, 1886

1984. 450th Death Anniv of Correggio (artist). Multicoloured.
2591 50c. Type **389** (postage) 10 10
2592 50c. "Madonna of St. Jerome" (detail) 10 10
2593 1cor. "Allegory of Virtue" 20 15
2594 2cor. "Allegory of Pleasure" 35 20
2595 3cor. "Ganymedes" (detail) (air) 50 35
2596 5cor. "The Danae" (detail) 55 55
2597 8cor. "Leda and the Swan" (detail) 1·00 60
MS2598 116 × 81 mm. 15cor. "St. John the Evangelist" 2·10 1·25

1984. 150th Birth Anniv of Gottlieb Daimler (automobile designer). Multicoloured.
2599 1cor. Type **390** (postage) 10 10
2600 1cor. Abadal, 1914 (horiz) 10 10
2601 2cor. Ford, 1903 1·50 45
2602 2cor. Renault, 1899 35 20
2603 3cor. Rolls Royce, 1910 (horiz) (air) 50 35
2604 4cor. Metallurgique, 1907 (horiz) 70 45
2605 7cor. Bugatti "Mod 40" (horiz) 75 50

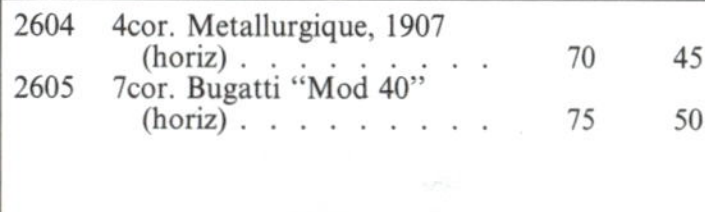

391 "Cardinal Infante Dom Fernando"

1984. Air. "Espana 84 International Stamp Exhibition, Madrid". Sheet 76 × 98 mm.
MS2606 **391** 15cor. multicoloured 2·10 1·25

1984. 19th Universal Postal Union Congress Philatelic Salon, Hamburg. Multicoloured.
2607 15cor. Type **392** 5·75 2·10
MS2608 101 × 60 mm. 5cor. Zeppelin "Bodensee" 4·00 2·50

392 Mail Transport

1984. Air. 19th Universal Postal Union Congress Philatelic Salon, Hamburg.
2607 **392** 15cor. multicoloured 5·75 2·10

393 Basketball

1984. Olympic Games, Los Angeles (2nd issue). Multicoloured.
2609 50c. Type **393** (postage) 10 10
2610 50c. Volleyball 10 10
2611 1cor. Hockey 20 15
2612 2cor. Tennis (air) 35 20
2613 3cor. Football (horiz) 50 35
2614 4cor. Water polo (horiz) 70 45
2615 9cor. Soccer (horiz) 1·10 75
MS2616 105 × 67 mm. 15cor. Baseball (horiz) 2·10 1·25

394 Horses and Carriage

1984. Air. "Expofilnic 84 National Stamp Exhibition". Sheet 86 × 66 mm.
MS2617 **394** 15cor. multicoloured 2·10 1·25

395 Rural Construction Site

1984. 5th Anniv of Revolution. Multicoloured.
2618 5c. Type **395** (postage) 10 10
2619 1cor. Diesel locomotive, Pacific–Atlantic line 1·50 30
2620 4cor. Ploughing with oxen and tractor (Agrarian reform) (air) 40 20
2621 7cor. State Council building 75 35

396 "Children defending Nature" (Pablo Herrera Berrios)

1984. UNESCO Environmental Protection Campaign. Multicoloured.
2622 50c. Type **396** (postage) 10 10
2623 1cor. Living and dead forests 20 15
2624 2cor. Fisherman and dried river bed 35 20
2625 10cor. Hands holding plants (vert) (air) 85 75

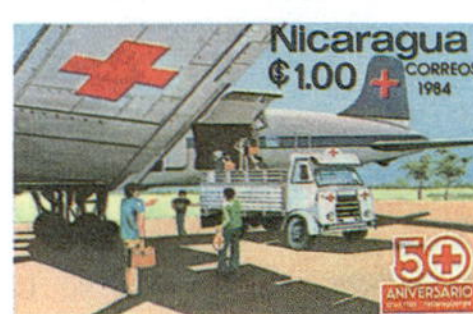

397 Red Cross Airplane and Ambulance

1984. 50th Anniv of Nicaraguan Red Cross. Mult.
2626 1cor. Type **397** (postage) 30 15
2627 7cor. Battle of Solferino (125th anniv) (air) 90 45

398 "Discovery"

1984. Air. "Ausipex 84 International Stamp Exhibition, Melbourne". Sheet 74 × 94 mm.
MS2628 **398** 15cor. multicoloured 2·10 1·25

399 Ventura Escalante and Dominican Republic Flag

1984. Baseball. Multicoloured.
2629 50c. Type **399** (postage) 10 10
2630 50c. Danial Herrera and Mexican flag 10 10
2631 1cor. Adalberto Herrera and Venezuelan flag 20 15
2632 1cor. Roberto Clemente and Nicaraguan flag 20 15
2633 3cor. Carlos Colas and Cuban flag (air) 30 35
2634 4cor. Stanley Cayasso and Argentinian flag 45 45
2635 5cor. Babe Ruth and U.S.A. flag 55 55

400 Central American Tapir

1984. Wildlife Protection. Multicoloured.
2636 25c. Type **400** (postage) 10 10
2637 25c. Young tapir 10 10
2638 3cor. Close-up of tapir (air) 15 10
2639 4cor. Mother and young 20 15

401 Football in 1314

1985. World Cup Football Championship, Mexico (1986) (1st issue). Multicoloured.
2640 50c. Type **401** (postage) 10 10
2641 50c. Football in 1500 10 10
2642 1cor. Football in 1872 10 10
2643 1cor. Football in 1846 10 10

2644 2cor. Football in 1883 (air) 10 10
2645 4cor. Football in 1890 . . . 20 15
2646 6cor. Football in 1953 . . . 30 20
MS2647 92×81 mm. 10cor. Footballers 50 35

See also Nos. 2731/MS2738 and 2812/MS2819.

402 "Strobilomyces retisporus"

1985. Fungi. Multicoloured.

2648 50c. Type **402** (postage) . . 10 10
2649 50c. "Boletus calopus" . . . 10 10
2650 1cor. "Boletus luridus" . . 15 10
2651 1cor. "Xerocomus illudens" (air) 15 10
2652 4cor. "Gyrodon merulioides" 55 25
2653 5cor. "Tylopilus plumbeoviolaceus" . . . 65 30
2654 8cor. "Gyroporus castaneus" . . . . 1·10 40

403 Postal Runner and Map

1985. 13th Postal Union of the Americas and Spain Congress. Multicoloured.

2655 1cor. Type **403** (postage) . . 10 10
2656 7cor. Casa Aviocar mail plane over map (air) . . . 45 20

404 Cyclist

1985. Air. "Olymphilex 85 International Stamp Exhibition, Lausanne". Sheet 53×82 mm.

MS2657 **404** 15cor. multicoloured 1·10 55

405 Cuban Crocodile

1985. Air. "Espamer 85 International Stamp Exhibition, Havana". Sheet 94×60 mm.

MS2658 **405** 10cor. multicoloured 1·00 50

406 Steam Locomotive, Oldenburg

1985. 150th Anniv of German Railway. Mult.

2659 1cor. Type **406** (postage) . . 20 10
2660 1cor. Electric locomotive, Prussia 20 10
2661 9cor. Steam locomotive No. 88, Prussia (air) . . . 75 15
2662 9cor. Double-deck tram . . 75 15
2663 15cor. Steam locomotive, Wurttemberg . . . . . . 1·10 25
2664 21cor. Steam locomotive, Germany . . . . 1·75 40
MS2665 80×60 mm. 42cor. Steam engine with tender (35×26 mm) 3·50 1·75

The Miniature sheets also commemorates centenary of Nicaraguan railways.

407 Douglas, 1928

1985. Centenary of Motor Cycle. Multicoloured.

2666 50c. Type **407** (postage) . . 10 10
2667 50c. FN, 1928 . . . . . . 10 10
2668 1cor. Puch, 1938 . . . . . 10 10
2669 2cor. Wanderer, 1939 (air) 10 10
2670 4cor. Honda, 1949 . . . . 10 10
2671 5cor. BMW, 1984 . . . . . 10 10
2672 7cor. Honda, 1984 . . . . 40 10

408 "Matelea quirosii"

409 "Capitulation of German Troops" (P. Krivonogov)

1985. Flowers. Multicoloured.

2673 50c. Type **408** (postage) . . 10 10
2674 50c. "Ipomea nil" 10 10
2675 1cor. "Lysichitum americanum" 10 10
2676 2cor. "Clusia sp." (air) . . . 10 10
2677 4cor. "Vanilla planifolia" . . 10 10
2678 7cor. "Stemmadenia obovata" 75 40

1985. 40th Anniv of End of World War II. Mult.

2679 9cor.50 Type **409** (postage) 1·00 50
2680 28cor. Woman behind barbed wire and Nuremberg trial (air) . . 3·00 1·50

410 Lenin and Red Flag

1985. 115th Birth Anniv of Lenin. Multicoloured.

2681 4cor. Type **410** 10 10
2682 21cor. Lenin addressing crowd 45 30

411 Bassett Hound

1985. "Argentina 85 International Stamp Exhibition, Buenos Aires. Sheet 76×96 mm.

MS2683 **411** 75cor. multicoloured (4.47) . . . . 4·50 2·50

412 Victoria de Julio Sugar Factory

1985. Air. 6th Anniv of Revolution. Multicoloured.

2684 9cor. Type **412** 20 15
2685 9cor. Soldier and flag . . . 20 15

413 Common Pheasant

1985. Domestic Birds. Multicoloured.

2686 50c. Type **413** 25 20
2687 50c. Hen 50 10
2688 1cor. Helmeted guineafowl 35 20
2689 2cor. Swan goose 65 20
2690 6cor. Ocellated turkey . . . 2·10 35
2691 8cor. Duck . . . . 1·75 10

414 Luis A. Delgadillo

415 Zeledon

1985. International Music Year. Multicoloured.

2692 1cor. Type **414** (postage) . . 10 10
2693 1cor. Masked dancer with floral headdress 10 10
2694 9cor. Masked procession (air) 65 40
2695 9cor. Crowd outside church 65 40
2696 15cor. Masked dancer in brimmed hat . . . . . . 1·10 55
2697 21cor. Procession resting . . 1·50 75

1985. Air. Birth Centenary of Benjamin Zeledon.

2698 **415** 15cor. multicoloured . . 1·00 55

416 Dunant and Lifeboat

1985. 75th Death Anniv of Henri Dunant (founder of Red Cross). Multicoloured.

2699 3cor. Type **416** 40 10
2700 15cor. Dunant and Ilyushin Il-86 and Tupolev Tu-154 aircraft . . . . 1·25 55

417 Fire Engine

1985. 6th Anniv of SINACOI Fire Service. Mult.

2701 1cor. Type **417** (postage) . . 10 10
2702 1cor. Fire station 10 10
2703 1cor. Engine with water jet 10 10
2704 3cor. Foam tender (air) . . 10 10
2705 9cor. Airport fire engine . . 50 15
2706 15cor. Engine at fire 85 45
2707 21cor. Fireman in protective clothing . . . . 1·10 75

418 Halley, Masaya Volcano and Comet

1985. Appearance of Halley's Comet. Mult.

2708 1cor. Type **418** (postage) . . 10 10
2709 3cor. Armillary sphere and 1910 trajectory 10 10
2710 3cor. "Venus" space probe and Tycho Brahe underground observatory 10 10
2711 9cor. Habermel's astrolabe and comet's path through solar system (air) 50 15
2712 15cor. Hale Telescope, Mt. Palomar, and Herschel's telescope 85 45
2713 21cor. Galileo's telescope and sections through telescopes of Newton, Cassegrain and Ritchey 1·25 60

419 Tapir eating

1985. Protected Animals. Baird's Tapir. Mult.

2714 1cor. Type **419** (postage) . . 10 10
2715 3cor. Tapir in water (air) . . 10 10
2716 5cor. Tapir in undergrowth 10 10
2717 9cor. Mother and calf . . . 20 15

420 "Rosa spinosissima"

1986. Wild Roses. Multicoloured.

2718 1cor. Type **420** 10 10
2719 1cor. Dog rose ("R. canina") 10 10
2720 3cor. "R. eglanteria" . . . 10 10
2721 5cor. "R. rubrifolia" 10 10
2722 9cor. "R. foetida" 20 15
2723 100cor. "R. rugosa" . . . . 2·00 1·10

421 Crimson Topaz

422 Footballer and Statue

1986. Birds. Multicoloured.

2724 1cor. Type **421** 10 10
2725 3cor. Orange-billed nightingale thrush 10 10
2726 3cor. Troupial 10 10
2727 5cor. Painted bunting . . . 20 15
2728 10cor. Frantzius's nightingale thrush 60 40
2729 21cor. Great horned owl . . 1·25 1·00
2730 75cor. Great kiskadee . . . 5·50 3·00

1986. World Cup Football Championship, Mexico (2nd issue). Multicoloured.

2731 1cor. Type **422** (postage) . . 10 10
2732 1cor. Footballer and sculptured head 10 10
2733 3cor. Footballer and water holder with man as stem (air) 10 10
2734 3cor. Footballer and sculpture 10 10
2735 5cor. Footballer and sculptured head (different) 10 10
2736 9cor. Footballer and sculpture (different) . . . 20 15
2737 100cor. Footballer and sculptured snake's head 3·00 1·50
MS2738 83×93 mm. 100cor. Footballer's leg and ball . . . 3·00 1·50

1986. (a) Flowers. As Nos. 2441/56 but values changed.

2739 5cor. blue 10 10
2740 5cor. violet 10 10
2741 5cor. purple 10 10
2742 5cor. orange 10 10
2743 5cor. green 10 10
2744 5cor. blue 10 10
2745 5cor. green 10 10
2746 5cor. green 10 10
2747 5cor. mauve 10 10
2748 5cor. red 10 10
2749 5cor. grey 10 10
2750 5cor. orange 10 10
2751 5cor. brown 10 10
2752 5cor. brown 10 10
2753 5cor. green 10 10
2754 5cor. black 10 10

DESIGNS: No. 2739, Type **356**; 2740, "Tabebula ochraceae"; 2741, "Laella sp"; 2742, Frangipani ("Plumeria rubra"); 2743, "Brassavola nodosa"; 2744, "Strachytarpheta indica"; 2745, "Cochlospermum sp"; 2746, "Malvaviscus arboreus"; 2747, "Tecoma stans"; 2748, Chinese hibiscus ("Hibiscus rosa-sinensis"); 2749, "Cattleya lueddemanniana"; 2750, African marigold ("Tagetes erecta"); 2751, "Senecio sp"; 2752, "Sobralia macrantha"; 2753, "Thumbergia alata"; 2754, "Bixa orellana".

(b) Agrarian Reform. As T **378**.
2755 1cor. brown 10 10
2756 9cor. violet 20 15
2757 15cor. purple 30 20
2758 21cor. red 45 30
2759 33cor. orange 65 45
2760 42cor. green 90 55
2761 50cor. brown . . . . . . 1·00 65
2762 100cor. blue . . . . . . 2·00 1·50
DESIGNS: 1cor. Type **378**; 9cor. Cotton; 15cor. Maize; 21cor. Sugar; 33cor. Cattle; 42cor. Rice; 50cor. Coffee; 100cor. Bananas.

423 Alfonso Cortes

1986. National Libraries. Latin American Writers. Multicoloured.
2763 1cor. Type **423** (postage) . . 10 10
2764 3cor. Azarias H. Pallais . . 10 10
2765 3cor. Salomon de la Selva 10 10
2766 5cor. Ruben Dario 10 10
2767 9cor. Pablo Neruda 10 10
2768 15cor. Alfonso Reyes (air) 45 25
2769 100cor. Pedro Henriquez Urena . . . . 3·00 1·50

424 Great Britain Penny Black and Nicaragua 1929 25c. Stamp

1986. Air. 125th Anniv of Nicaraguan Stamps. Designs showing G.B. Penny Black and Nicaragua stamps.
2770 **424** 30cor. multicoloured . . 90 45
2771 – 40cor. brown, black and grey . . . . 1·25 60
2772 – 50cor. red, black and grey . . . . 1·50 75
2773 – 100cor. blue, black and grey . . . . 3·00 1·50
DESIGNS: 40c. 1903 1p. stamp; 50c. 1892 5p. stamp; 1p. 1862 2c. stamp.

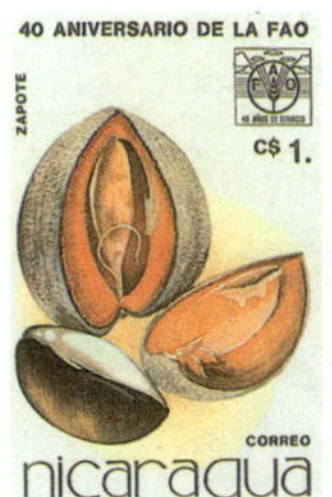

425 Sapodilla

426 Rainbow and Globe

1986. 40th Anniv of F.A.O. Multicoloured.
2774 1cor. Type **425** (postage) . . 10 10
2775 1cor. Maranon 10 10
2776 3cor. Tree-cactus 10 10
2777 3cor. Granadilla 10 10
2778 5cor. Custard-apple (air) . . 10 10
2779 21cor. Melocoton 65 35
2780 100cor. Mamey . . . . . . 3·00 1·50

1986. Air. International Peace Year. Multicoloured.
2781 5cor. Type **426** 10 10
2782 10cor. Dove and globe . . . 30 10

427 Lockheed L-1011 TriStar 500

1986. "Stockholmia 86" International Stamp Exhibition. Multicoloured.
2783 1cor. Type **427** (postage) . . 10 10
2784 1cor. Yakovlev Yak-40 . . 10 10
2785 3cor. B.A.C. One Eleven . . 10 10
2786 3cor. Boeing 747-100 . . . 10 10
2787 9cor. Airbus Industrie A300 (air) 30 10
2788 15cor. Tupolev Tu-154 . . . 45 10
2789 100cor. Concorde (vert) . . 3·00 1·50
MS2790 60 × 73 mm. 100cor. SAAb "FAirchild 340" (39 × 31 mm) 3·00 1·50

428 "Pinta" and 16th-century Map

1986. 500th Anniv (1992) of Discovery of America by Columbus (1st issue). Multicoloured.
2791 1cor. Type **428** (postage) . . 80 30
2792 1cor. "Santa Maria" and "Nina" 80 30
2793 9cor. Juan de la Cosa (air) 30 10
2794 9cor. Christopher Columbus 30 10
2795 21cor. King and Queen of Spain 65 35
2796 100cor. Courtiers behind Columbus and Indians . . 3·00 1·50
MS2797 Two sheets each 155 × 80 mm. (a) Nos. 2971/2; (b) Nos. 2793/6 . . . . 6·00 3·00
The designs of the same value and Nos. 2795/6 were printed together in se-tenant pairs within their sheets, Nos. 2791/2 and 2795/6 forming composite designs.
See also Nos. 2911/16.

429 Fonseca and Flags

1986. Air. 25th Anniv of Sandinista Front and 10th Death Anniv of Carlos Fonseca (co-founder).
2798 **429** 15cor. multicoloured . . 10 10

430 Rhinoceros

431 "Theritas coronata"

1986. Air. Endangered Animals. Multicoloured.
2799 15cor. Type **430** 45 10
2800 15cor. Zebra 45 10
2801 25cor. Elephant 75 40
2802 25cor. Giraffe 75 40
2803 50cor. Tiger . . . . 1·50 75
2804 50cor. Mandrill . . . . . . 1·50 75

1986. Butterflies. Multicoloured.
2805 10cor. Type **431** (postage) 20 10
2806 15cor. "Salamis cacta" (air) 20 10
2807 15cor. "Charayes nitebis" 20 10
2808 15cor. "Papilio maacki" . . 20 10
2809 25cor. "Palaeochrysophonus hippothoe" 20 10
2810 25cor. "Euphaedro cyparissa" 20 10
2811 30cor. "Ritra aurea" . . . 20 10

432 Player and French Flag

433 Ernesto Mejia Sanchez

1986. Air. World Cup Football Championship, Mexico (3rd issue). Finalists. Multicoloured. Designs showing footballers and national flags.
2812 10cor. Type **432** 10 10
2813 10cor. Argentina 10 10
2814 10cor. West Germany . . . 10 10
2815 15cor. England 10 10
2816 15cor. Brazil 10 10
2817 25cor. Spain 10 10
2818 50cor. Belgium (horiz) . . . 10 10
MS2819 95 × 65 mm. 100cor. Players 3·00 1·50

1987. Ruben Dario Cultural Order of Independence. Multicoloured.
2820 10cor. Type **433** (postage) 10 10
2821 10cor. Fernando Gordillo 10 10
2822 10cor. Francisco Perez Estrada 10 10
2823 15cor. Order medal (air) . . 10 10
2824 30cor. Julio Cortazar . . . 20 20
2825 60cor. Enrique Fernandez Morales 35 25

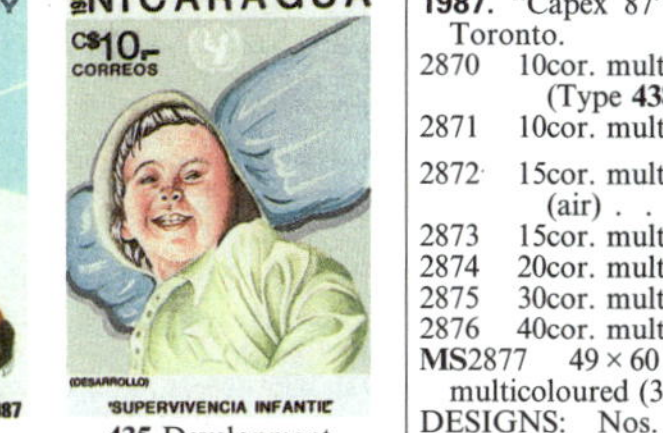

434 Ice Hockey **435** Development

1987. Winter Olympic Games, Calgary (1988). Multicoloured.
2826 10cor. Type **434** (postage) 10 10
2827 10cor. Speed skating 10 10
2828 15cor. Downhill skiing (air) 10 10
2829 15cor. Figure skating . . . 10 10
2830 20cor. Shooting 15 10
2831 30cor. Slalom 20 10
2832 40cor. Ski jumping 25 10
MS2833 75 × 66 mm. 110cor. Ice hockey (different) (39 × 31 mm) 70 35

1987. UNICEF Child Survival Campaign. Multicoloured.
2834 10cor. Type **435** (postage) 10 10
2835 25cor. Vaccination (air) . . 75 40
2836 30cor. Oral rehydration therapy 90 45
2837 50cor. Breast-feeding . . . 1·50 75

1987. (a) Flowers. As Nos. 2441/56 and 2739/54 but values changed.
2838 10cor. blue 10 10
2839 10cor. violet 10 10
2840 10cor. purple 10 10
2841 10cor. red 10 10
2842 10cor. green 10 10
2843 10cor. blue 10 10
2844 10cor. green 10 10
2845 10cor. green 10 10
2846 10cor. mauve 10 10
2847 10cor. red 10 10
2848 10cor. green 10 10
2849 10cor. orange 10 10
2850 10cor. brown 10 10
2851 10cor. purple 10 10
2852 10cor. turquoise 10 10
2853 10cor. black 10 10
DESIGNS: No. 2838, Type **356**; 2839, "Tabebula ochraceae"; 2840, "Laella sp"; 2841, Frangipani; 2842, "Brassavola nodosa"; 2843, "Stachytarpheta indica"; 2844, "Cochlospermum sp"; 2845, "Malvaviscus arboreus"; 2846, "Tecoma stans"; 2847, Chinese hibiscus; 2848, "Cattleya lueddemanniana"; 2849, African marigold; 2850, "Senecio sp"; 2851, "Sobralla macrantha"; 2852, "Thumbergia alata"; 2853, "Bixa orellana".

(b) Agrarian Reform. As T **378**. Dated "1987".
2854 10cor. brown 10 10
2855 10cor. violet 10 10
2856 15cor. purple 10 10
2857 25cor. red 15 10
2858 30cor. orange 20 10
2859 50cor. brown 30 20
2860 60cor. green 35 25
2861 100cor. blue 65 45
DESIGNS: No. 2854, Type **378**; 2855, Cotton; 2856, Maize; 2857, Sugar; 2858, Cattle; 2859, Coffee; 2860, Rice; 2861, Bananas.

436 Flags and Buildings

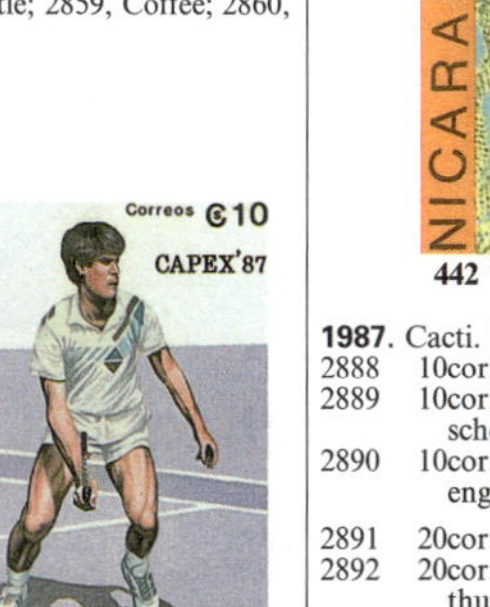

438 Tennis Player

437 "Mammuthus columbi"

1987. 77th Interparliamentary Conf, Managua.
2862 **436** 10cor. multicoloured . . 10 10

1987. Prehistoric Animals. Multicoloured.
2863 10cor. Type **437** (postage) 10 10
2864 10cor. Triceratops 10 10
2865 10cor. Dimetrodon 10 10
2866 15cor. Uintaterium (air) . . 10 10
2867 15cor. Dinichthys 10 10
2868 30cor. Pteranodon 60 35
2869 40cor. Tilosaurus 85 45

1987. "Capex 87" International Stamp Exhibition, Toronto.
2870 10cor. multicoloured (Type **438**) (postage) . . . 10 10
2871 10cor. mult 10 10
2872 15cor. mult (male player) (air) 45 10
2873 15cor. mult (female player) 45 10
2874 20cor. multicoloured 60 30
2875 30cor. multicoloured 60 45
2876 40cor. multicoloured 85 60
MS2877 49 × 60 mm. 110cor. multicoloured (31 × 39 mm) . . 70 35
DESIGNS: Nos. 2871/**MS**2877, Various tennis players.

439 Dobermann Pinscher **441** Levski

440 Modern Wooden Houses

1987. Dogs. Multicoloured.
2878 10cor. Type **439** (postage) 10 10
2879 10cor. Bull mastiff 10 10
2880 15cor. Japanese spaniel (air) 45 10
2881 15cor. Keeshond 45 10
2882 20cor. Chihuahua 60 30
2883 30cor. St. Bernard 90 45
2884 40cor. West Gotha spitz . . 85 60

1987. Air. International Year of Shelter for the Homeless. Multicoloured.
2885 20cor. Type **440** 15 10
2886 30cor. Modern brick-built houses 20 10

1987. Air. 150th Birth Anniv of Vasil Levski (revolutionary).
2887 **441** 30cor. multicoloured . . 20 10

442 "Opuntia acanthocarpa major"

1987. Cacti. Multicoloured.
2888 10cor. Type **442** (postage) 10 10
2889 10cor. "Lophocereus schottii" 10 10
2890 10cor. "Echinocereus engelmanii" 10 10
2891 20cor. Saguaros (air) . . . 60 30
2892 20cor. "Lemaireocereus thurberi" 60 30
2893 30cor. "Opuntia fulgida" . . 90 45
2894 50cor. "Opuntia ficus indica" . . . . 1·50 75

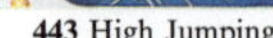

443 High Jumping

1987. 10th Pan-American Games, Indiana. Mult.
2895 10cor. Type **443** (postage) 10 10
2896 10cor. Handball 10 10
2897 15cor. Running (air) 45 10
2898 15cor. Gymnastics 45 10
2899 20cor. Baseball 60 30
2900 30cor. Synchronized swimming (vert) 90 45
2901 40cor. Weightlifting (vert) 1·25 60
MS2902 57 × 67 mm 110cor. Gymnastics (different) (31 × 39 mm) 2·75 1·50

444 Television Tower, East Berlin

1987. Air. 750th Anniv of Berlin. Sheet 69 × 96 mm.
MS2903 **443** 130cor. multicoloured 3·00 1·50

445 "Cosmos"

1987. Cosmonautics Day. Multicoloured.
2904 10cor. Type **445** (postage) 10 10
2905 10cor. "Sputnik" 10 10
2906 15cor. "Proton" (air) 45 10
2907 25cor. "Luna" 75 40
2908 25cor. "Meteor" 75 40
2909 30cor. "Electron" 90 45
2910 50cor. "Mars-1" 1·50 75

446 Native Huts and Terraced Hillside

1987. Air. 500th Anniv (1992) of Discovery of America by Columbus (2nd issue). Mult.
2911 15cor. Type **446** 45 20
2912 15cor. Columbus's fleet 90 30
2913 20cor. Spanish soldiers in native village 60 30
2914 30cor. Mounted soldiers killing natives 90 45
2915 40cor. Spanish people and houses 1·25 60
2916 50cor. Church and houses 1·50 75

447 Tropical Gar

1987. World Food Day. Fishes. Multicoloured.
2917 10cor. Type **447** (postage) 20 10
2918 10cor. Atlantic tarpon ("Tarpon atlanticus") 20 10
2919 10cor. Jaguar guapote ("Cichlasoma managuense") 20 10
2920 15cor. Banded astyanax ("Astyana fasciatus") (air) 90 45
2921 15cor. Midas cichlid ("Cichlasoma citrimellum") 90 45
2922 20cor. Wolf cichlid 1·25 65
2923 50cor. Lake Nicaragua shark 3·00 1·50

448 Lenin

449 "Nativity"

1987. 70th Anniv of Russian Revolution. Mult.
2924 10cor. Type **448** (postage) 10 10
2925 30cor. "Aurora" (cruiser) (horiz) (air) 50 15
2926 50cor. Russian arms 30 20

1987. Christmas. Details of Painting by L. Saenz. Multicoloured.
2927 10cor. Type **449** 10 10
2928 20cor. "Adoration of the Magi" 60 30
2929 25cor. "Adoration of the Magi" (close-up detail) 75 40
2930 50cor. "Nativity" (close-up detail) 1·50 75

1987. Surch.
2931 **435** 400cor. on 10cor. mult (postage) 30 15
2935 **440** 200cor. on 20cor. multicoloured (air) 15 10
2932 – 600cor. on 50cor. mult (No. 2837) 40 20
2933 – 1000cor. on 25cor. mult (No. 2835) 70 35
2936 – 3000cor. on 30cor. mult (No. 2886) 2·10 1·00
2934 – 5000cor. on 30cor. mult (No. 2836) 3·50 1·75

451 Cross-country Skiing

452 Flag around Globe

1988. Winter Olympic Games, Calgary. Mult.
2937 10cor. Type **451** 10 10
2938 10cor. Rifle-shooting (horiz) 10 10
2939 15cor. Ice hockey 45 10
2940 20cor. Ice skating 60 30
2941 25cor. Downhill skiing 75 40
2942 30cor. Ski jumping (horiz) 90 45
2943 40cor. Slalom 1·25 60
MS2944 66 × 74 mm. 100cor. Ice skating (pairs) (39 × 27 mm) 1·50 75

1988. 10th Anniv of Nicaragua Journalists' Association. Multicoloured.
2945 1cor. Type **452** (postage) 10 10
2946 5cor. Churches of St. Francis Xavier, Sandino and Fatima, Managua, and speaker addressing journalists (42 × 27 mm) (air) 1·25 60

453 Basketball

1988. Olympic Games, Seoul. Multicoloured.
2947 10cor. Type **453** 10 10
2948 10cor. Gymnastics 10 10
2949 15cor. Volleyball 45 10
2950 20cor. Long jumping 60 30
2951 25cor. Football 75 40
2952 30cor. Water polo 90 45
2953 40cor. Boxing 1·25 60
MS2954 70 × 60 mm. 100cor. Baseball (39 × 31 mm) 1·50 75

454 Brown Bear

1988. Mammals and their Young. Multicoloured.
2955 10c. Type **454** (postage) 10 10
2956 15c. Lion 10 10
2957 25c. Cocker spaniel 10 10
2958 50c. Wild boar 15 10
2959 4cor. Cheetah (air) 55 20
2960 7cor. Spotted hyena 1·00 40
2961 8cor. Red fox 1·25 50
MS2962 61 × 71 mm. 15cor. Kittens (31 × 39 mm) 2·10 1·10

455 Slide Tackle

1988. "Essen '88" International Stamp Fair and European Football Championship, Germany. Mult.
2963 50c. Type **455** (postage) 10 10
2964 1cor. Footballers 15 10
2965 2cor. Lining up shot (vert) (air) 30 10
2966 3cor. Challenging for ball (vert) 50 20
2967 4cor. Heading ball (vert) 65 25
2968 5cor. Tackling (vert) 80 30
2969 6cor. Opponent winning possession 1·00 40
MS2970 58 × 71 mm. 15cor. Players challenging goalkeeper (31 × 39 mm) 2·20 1·10

456 Bell JetRanger III (½-size illustration)

1988. "Finlandia 88" International Stamp Exhibition, Helsinki. Helicopters. Multicoloured.
2971 4cor. Type **456** (postage) 15 10
2972 12cor. MBB-Kawasaki BK-117A-3 (air) 20 10
2973 16cor. Boeing-Vertol B-360 30 10
2974 20cor. Agusta A.109 MR11 40 10
2975 24cor. Sikorsky S-61N 55 20
2976 28cor. Aerospatiale SA.365 Dauphin 2 60 25
2977 56cor. Sikorsky S-76 Spirit 1·25 50
MS2978 97 × 52 mm. 120cor. "NH-90" (39 × 31 mm) 2·40 1·25

457 Flags and Map

458 Casimiro Sotelo Montenegro

1988. 9th Anniv of Revolution. Multicoloured.
2979 1cor. Type **457** (postage) 20 10
2980 5cor. Landscape and hands releasing dove (air) 80 30

1988. Revolutionaries.
2981 **458** 4cor. blue (postage) 15 10
2982 – 12cor. mauve (air) 20 10
2983 – 16cor. green 30 10
2984 – 20cor. red 45 15
2985 – 24cor. brown 55 20
2986 – 28cor. violet 65 25
2987 – 50cor. red 1·25 45
2988 – 100cor. purple 2·40 1·00
DESIGNS: 12cor. Ricardo Morales Aviles; 16cor. Silvio Mayorga Delgado; 20cor. Pedro Arauz Palacios; 24cor. Oscar A. Turcios Chavarrias; 28cor. Julio C. Buitrago Urroz; 50cor. Jose B. Escobar Perez; 100cor. Eduardo E. Contreras Escobar.

459 "Acacia baileyana"

460 West Indian Fighting Conch

1988. Flowers. Multicoloured.
2989 4cor. Type **459** (postage) 15 10
2990 12cor. "Anigozanthos manglesii" (air) 20 10
2991 16cor. "Telopia speciosissima" 30 10
2992 20cor. "Eucalyptus ficifolia" 45 15
2993 24cor. "Boronia heterophylla" 60 30
2994 28cor. "Callistemon speciosus" 70 35
2995 30cor. "Nymphaea caerulea" (horiz) 80 40
2996 50cor. "Clianthus formosus" 1·25 60

1988. Molluscs. Multicoloured.
2997 4cor. Type **460** (postage) 20 10
2998 12cor. Painted polymita (air) 30 10
2999 16cor. Giant sundial 40 10
3000 20cor. Japanese baking oyster 55 10
3001 24cor. Yoka star shell 75 20
3002 28cor. Gawdy frog shell 80 25
3003 50cor. Mantled top 1·75 50

461 Zapotecan Funeral Urn

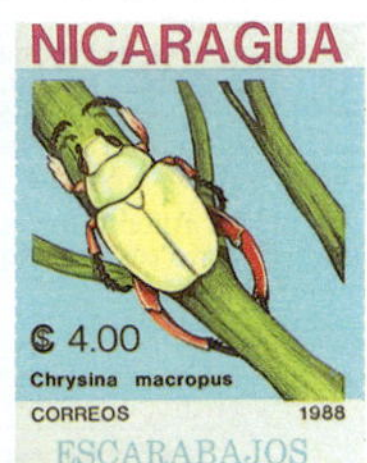

462 "Chrysina macropus"

1988. 500th Anniv (1992) of Discovery of America by Columbus (3rd issue). Multicoloured.
3004 4cor. Type **461** (postage) 15 10
3005 12cor. Mochican ceramic seated figure (air) 20 10
3006 16cor. Mochican ceramic head 30 10
3007 20cor. Tainan ceramic vessel 45 10
3008 28cor. Nazcan vessel (horiz) 65 20
3009 100cor. Incan ritual pipe (horiz) 2·40 1·00
MS3010 100 × 65 mm. 120cor. Aztec ceramic head (39 × 31 mm) 2·50 1·25

1988. Beetles. Multicoloured.
3011 4cor. Type **462** (postage) 15 10
3012 12cor. "Plusiotis victoriana" (air) 20 10
3013 16cor. "Ceratotrupes bolivari" 30 10
3014 20cor. "Gymnetosoma stellata" 50 15
3015 24cor. "Euphoria lineoligera" 60 20
3016 28cor. "Euphoria candezei" 70 30
3017 50cor. "Sulcophanaeus chryseicollis" 1·25 50

463 Dario

1988. Air. Centenary of Publication of "Blue" by Ruben Dario.
3018 **463** 25cor. multicoloured 60 20

464 Simon Bolivar, Jose Marti, Gen. Sandino and Fidel Castro

1989. Air. 30th Anniv of Cuban Revolution.
3019 **464** 20cor. multicoloured . . 50 20

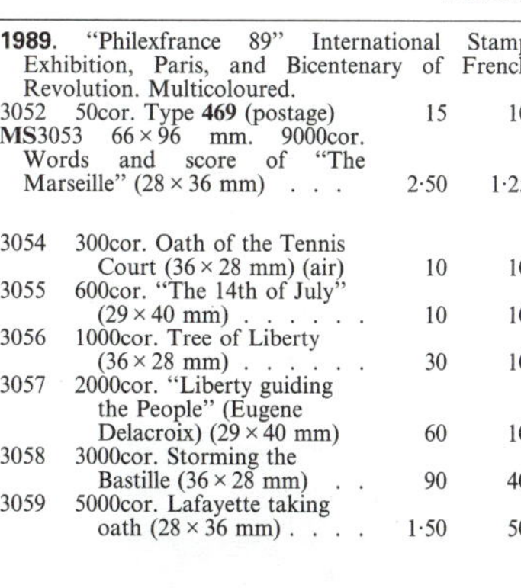

465 Pochomil Tourist Centre

1989. Tourism. Multicoloured.
3020 4cor. Type **465** (postage) . . 15 10
3021 12cor. Granada Tourist Centre (air) 45 15
3022 20cor. Olof Palme Convention Centre . . . 65 30
3023 24cor. Masaya Volcano National Park 55 20
3024 28cor. La Boquita Tourist Centre 70 25
3025 30cor. Xiloa Tourist Centre 75 30
3026 50cor. Managua Hotel . . . 1·25 60
MS3027 101 × 50 mm. 160cor. Beach, Montelimar International Tourist Centre (39 × 31 mm) 3·50 1·75

466 Footballers

467 Downhill Skiing

1989. Air. World Cup Football Championship, Italy (1990).
3028 **466** 100cor. multicoloured . . 10 10
3029 – 200cor. multicoloured . . 10 10
3030 – 600cor. multicoloured . . 10 10
3031 – 1000cor. multicoloured 30 10
3032 – 2000cor. multicoloured 60 10
3033 – 3000cor. multicoloured 90 40
3034 – 5000cor. multicoloured 1·50 50
MS3035 90 × 70 mm. 9000cor. multicoloured (31 × 39 mm) . . 2·50 1·25
DESIGNS: 200cor. to 9000cor. Different footballers.

1989. Air. Winter Olympic Games, Albertville (1992) (1st issue). Multicoloured.
3036 50cor. Type **467** 10 10
3037 300cor. Ice hockey 10 10
3038 600cor. Ski jumping 10 10
3039 1000cor. Ice skating 30 10
3040 2000cor. Biathlon 60 10
3041 3000cor. Slalom 90 40
3042 5000cor. Skiing . . . . . . 1·50 50
MS3043 86 × 65 mm. 9000cor. Two-man bobsleighing (31 × 39 mm) 2·50 1·25
See also Nos. 3184/**MS**3191.

468 Water Polo

1989. Air. Olympic Games, Barcelona (1992). Mult.
3044 100cor. Type **468** 10 10
3045 200cor. Running 10 10
3046 600cor. Diving 10 10
3047 1000cor. Gymnastics 30 10
3048 2000cor. Weightlifting . . . 60 10
3049 3000cor. Volleyball 90 40
3050 5000cor. Wrestling . . . . 1·50 50
MS3051 80 × 60 mm. 9000cor. Hockey (31 × 39 mm) . . . . 2·50 1·25
See also Nos. 3192/**MS**3199.

469 Procession of States General at Versailles

470 American Darter

1989. "Philexfrance 89" International Stamp Exhibition, Paris, and Bicentenary of French Revolution. Multicoloured.
3052 50cor. Type **469** (postage) 15 10
MS3053 66 × 96 mm. 9000cor. Words and score of "The Marseille" (28 × 36 mm) . . . 2·50 1·25
3054 300cor. Oath of the Tennis Court (36 × 28 mm) (air) 10 10
3055 600cor. "The 14th of July" (29 × 40 mm) 10 10
3056 1000cor. Tree of Liberty (36 × 28 mm) 30 10
3057 2000cor. "Liberty guiding the People" (Eugene Delacroix) (29 × 40 mm) 60 10
3058 3000cor. Storming the Bastille (36 × 28 mm) . . 90 40
3059 5000cor. Lafayette taking oath (28 × 36 mm) . . . . 1·50 50

1989. Air. "Brasiliana 89" International Stamp Exhibition, Rio de Janeiro. Birds. Multicoloured.
3060 100cor. Type **470** 20 20
3061 200cor. Swallow-tailed kite 20 20
3062 600cor. Turquoise-browed motmot 25 20
3063 1000cor. Painted redstart . . 40 20
3064 2000cor. Great antshrike (horiz) 80 20
3065 3000cor. Northern royal flycatcher . . . . 1·10 90
3066 5000cor. White-flanked antwren (horiz) . . . . . 2·00 1·10
MS3067 61 × 91 mm. 9000cor. Yellow-crowned amazon (31 × 39 mm) . . . . 2·50 1·25

471 Anniversary Emblem

472 Animal-shaped Vessel

1989. Air. 10th Anniv of Revolution. Multicoloured.
3068 300r. Type **471** 10 10
MS3069 97 × 77 mm. 9000cor. Concepcion volcano (36 × 28 mm) 2·50 1·25

1989. Air. America. Pre-Columbian Artefacts.
3070 **472** 2000cor. multicoloured 60 10

Currency Reform. 150000 (old) cordoba = 1 (new) cordoba
The following issues, denominated in the old currency, were distributed by agents but were not issued (each set consists of seven values and is dated "1990"):
"London 90" International Stamp Exn. Ships
World Cup Football Championship, Italy
Olympic Games, Barcelona (1992)
Fungi
Winter Olympic Games, Albertville (1992)

473 Little Spotted Kiwi

1991. "New Zealand 1990" International Stamp Exhibition, Auckland. Birds. Multicoloured.
3071 5c. Type **473** 15 10
3072 5c. Takahe 15 10
3073 10c. Red-fronted parakeet 20 15
3074 20c. Weka rail 45 25
3075 30c. Kagu (vert) 25 40
3076 60c. Kea . . . . 1·25 90
3077 70c. Kakapo . . . . 1·50 1·00
MS3078 90 × 68 mm. 1cor.51 Black swan (40 × 31 mm) . . . . . . 2·75 1·40

474 Jaguar

1991. 45th Anniv of Food and Agriculture Organization. Animals. Multicoloured.
3079 5c. Type **474** 10 10
3080 5c. Ocelot (vert) 10 10
3081 10c. Black-handed spider monkey (vert) 15 10
3082 20c. Baird's tapir 30 15
3083 30c. Nine-banded armadillo 45 20
3084 60c. Coyote 85 45
3085 70c. Two-toed sloth . . . . 1·00 50

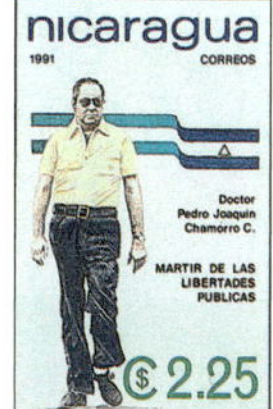

475 Dr. Chamorro

476 Steam Locomotive, 1920s, Peru

1991. Dr. Pedro Joaquin Chamorro (campaigner for an independent Press).
3086 **475** 2cor.25 multicoloured . . 50 20

1991. Flowers. As T **356** but with currency inscribed in "oro".
3087 – 1cor. blue 25 10
3088 – 2cor. green 45 20
3089 – 3cor. brown 70 30
3090 – 4cor. purple 95 40
3091 – 5cor. red . . . . 1·10 45
3092 – 6cor. green . . . . . . 1·40 55
3093 **356** 7cor. blue . . . . . . 1·60 65
3094 – 8cor. green . . . . . . 1·90 75
3095 – 9cor. green . . . . . . 2·10 85
3096 – 10cor. violet . . . . . . 2·25 90
3097 – 11cor. mauve . . . . . 2·50 1·00
3098 – 12cor. yellow . . . . . 2·75 1·10
3099 – 13cor. red . . . . . . 3·00 1·25
3100 – 14cor. green . . . . . 3·25 1·25
3101 – 15cor. mauve . . . . . 3·50 1·40
3102 – 16cor. black . . . . . 3·75 1·50
DESIGNS: 1cor. "Stachytarpheta indica"; 2cor. "Cochlospermum sp."; 3cor. "Senecio sp."; 4cor. "Sobralia macrantha"; 5cor. Frangipani; 6cor. "Brassavola nodosa"; 8cor. "Malvaviscus arboreus"; 9cor. "Cattleya lueddemanniana"; 10cor. "Tabebula ochraceae"; 11cor. "Laelia sp."; 12cor. African marigold; 13cor. Chinese hibiscus; 14cor. "Thumbergia alata"; 15cor. "Tecoma stans"; 16cor. "Bixa orellana".

1991. Steam Locomotives of South and Central America. Multicoloured.
3103 25c. Type **476** 30 10
3104 25c. Locomotive No. 508, 1917, Bolivia 30 10
3105 50c. Class N/O locomotive, 1910s, Argentina 50 10
3106 1cor.50 Locomotive, 1952, Chile 90 20
3107 2cor. Locomotive No. 61, 1944, Colombia . . . . 1·25 25
3108 3cor. Locomotive No. 311, 1947, Brazil . . . . . . 2·00 35
3109 3cor.50 Locomotive No. 60, 1910, Paraguay . . . . 2·25 45
MS3110 Two sheets each 100 × 70 mm. (a) 7cor.50 Guatemala; (b) 7cor.50 Nicaragua 11·00 5·50

477 Match Scene (West Germany versus Netherlands)

1991. West Germany, Winners of World Cup Football Championship (1990). Multicoloured.
3111 25c. Type **477** 10 10
3112 25c. Match scene (West Germany versus Colombia) (vert) 10 10
3113 50c. West German players and referee 10 10
3114 1cor. West German players forming wall (vert) . . . 25 10
3115 1cor.50 Diego Maradona (Argentina) (vert) 35 15
3116 3cor. Argentinian players and Italian goalkeeper (vert) 70 30
3117 3cor.50 Italian players . . . 80 30
MS3118 100 × 70 mm. 7cor.50 West German team celebrating with World Cup trophy . . . . . . 1·70 80

478 "Prepona praeneste"

1991. Butterflies. Multicoloured.
3119 25c. Type **478** 10 10
3120 25c. "Anartia fatima" . . . 10 10
3121 50c. "Eryphanis aesacus" . . 10 10
3122 1cor. "Heliconius melpomene" 25 10
3123 1cor.50 "Chlosyne janais" 35 15
3124 3cor. "Marpesia iole" . . . 70 30
3125 3cor.50 Rusty-tipped page 80 30
MS3126 100 × 70 mm. 7cor.50 Emperor . . . . 1·75 85

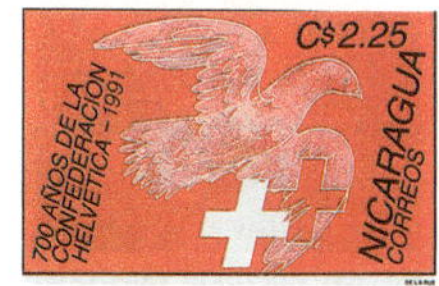

479 Dove and Cross

1991. 700th Anniv of Swiss Confederation.
3127 **479** 2cor.25 red, black and yellow 50 20

480 Yellow-headed Amazon

1991. "Rainforest is Life". Fauna. Multicoloured.
3128 2cor.25 Type **480** 50 20
3129 2cor.25 Keel-billed toucan 50 20
3130 2cor.25 Scarlet macaw . . . 50 20
3131 2cor.25 Resplendent quetzal 50 20
3132 2cor.25 Black-handed spider monkey 50 20
3133 2cor.25 White-throated capuchin 50 20
3134 2cor.25 Three-toed sloth . . 50 20
3135 2cor.25 Chestnut-headed oropendola 50 20
3136 2cor.25 Violet sabrewing . . 50 20
3137 2cor.25 Tamandua 50 20
3138 2cor.25 Jaguarundi 50 20
3139 2cor.25 Boa constrictor . . 50 20
3140 2cor.25 Common iguana . . 50 20
3141 2cor.25 Jaguar 50 20
3142 2cor.25 White-necked jacobin 50 20
3143 2cor.25 "Doxocopa clothilda" (butterfly) . . . 50 20
3144 2cor.25 "Dismorphia deione" (butterfly) 50 20
3145 2cor.25 Golden arrow-poison frog 50 20
3146 2cor.25 "Callithomia hezia" (butterfly) 50 20
3147 2cor.25 Chameleon 50 20
Nos. 3128/47 were issued together, se-tenant, forming a composite design.

481 "Isochilus major"

1991. Orchids. Multicoloured.
3148 25c. Type **481** 10 10
3149 25c. "Cycnoches ventricosum" 10 10
3150 50c. "Vanilla odorata" . . . 10 10
3151 1cor. "Helleriella nicaraguensis" 25 10
3152 1cor.50 "Barkeria spectabilis" 35 15
3153 3cor. "Maxillaria hedwigae" 70 30
3154 3cor.50 "Cattleya aurantiaca" 80 30
MS3155 100 × 70 mm. 7cor.50 *Psygmorchis pusilla* (27 × 41 mm) 1·75 85

482 Concepcion Volcano

1991. America (1990).
3156 **482** 2cor.25 multicoloured . . 50 20

483 Warehouse and Flags

1991. 30th Anniv of Central American Bank of Economic Integration.
3157 **483** 1cor.50 multicoloured . . 35 15

484 "The One-eyed Man"

1991. Death Centenary (1990) of Vincent van Gogh (painter). Multicoloured.
3158 25c. Type **484** 10 10
3159 25c. "Head of Countrywoman with Bonnet" 10 10
3160 50c. "Self-portrait" 10 10
3161 1cor. "Vase with Carnations and other Flowers" . . . 25 10
3162 1cor.50 "Vase with Zinnias and Geraniums" 35 15
3163 3cor. "Portrait of Tanguy Father" 70 30
3164 3cor.50 "Portrait of a Man" (horiz) 80 30
MS3165 127 × 102 mm. 7cor.50 "Footpath with Poplars". Imperf 1·75 85

485 Painting by Rafaela Herrera (1st-prize winner)

1991. National Children's Painting Competition.
3166 **485** 2cor.25 multicoloured . . 50 20

486 Golden Pavilion

1991. "Phila Nippon '91" International Stamp Exhibition, Tokyo. Multicoloured.
3167 25c. Type **486** 10 10
3168 50c. Himaji Castle 10 10
3169 1cor. Head of Bunraku doll 25 10
3170 1cor.50 Japanese cranes . . 35 15
3171 2cor.50 Phoenix pavilion . . 60 25
3172 3cor. "The Guardian" (statue) 70 30
3173 3cor.50 Kabuki actor . . . 80 30
MS3174 100 × 71 mm. 7cor.50 Mizusahi vase . . . . 1·75 85

487 Turquoise-browed Motmot
488 Columbus's Fleet

1992. Birds. Multicoloured.
3175 50c. Type **487** 15 10
3176 75c. Collared trogon 20 10
3177 1cor. Broad-billed motmot 25 10
3178 1cor.50 Wire-tailed manakin 40 15
3179 1cor.75 Paradise tanager (horiz) 45 20
3180 2cor.25 Resplendent quetzal 60 25
3181 2cor.25 Black-spotted bare-eye 60 25
MS3182 Two sheets each 100 × 70 mm. (a) 7cor.50 Crimson-rumped toucanet; (b) 7cor.50 Spotted antbird . . . . 11·00 5·50

1992. America (1991). Voyages of Discovery.
3183 **488** 2cor.25 multicoloured . . 35 15

489 Ice Hockey

1992. Winter Olympic Games, Albertville (2nd issue). Multicoloured.
3184 25c. Type **489** 10 10
3185 25c. Four-man bobsleighing 10 10
3186 50c. Skiing (vert) 15 10
3187 1cor. Speed skating 25 10
3188 1cor.50 Cross-country skiing 40 15
3189 3cor. Double luge 75 30
3190 3cor.50 Ski jumping (vert) 90 35
MS3191 100 × 70 mm. 7cor.50 Skiing. Imperf . . . . 1·75 85

490 Fencing
491 Ceramic Vase with Face (Lorenza Pineda Co-operative)

1992. Olympic Games, Barcelona (2nd issue) Mult.
3192 25c. Type **490** 10 10
3193 25c. Throwing the javelin (horiz) 10 10
3194 50c. Basketball 15 10
3195 1cor.50 Running 40 15
3196 2cor. Long jumping 50 20
3197 3cor. Running 75 30
3198 3cor.50 Show jumping . . . 90 35
MS3199 100 × 70 mm. 7cor.50 Canoeing. Imperf . . . . . . 1·75 85

1992. Contemporary Arts and Crafts. Mult.
3200 25c. Type **491** 10 10
3201 25c. Ceramic spouted vessel (Jose Oritz) (horiz) 10 10
3202 50c. Blue-patterned ceramic vase (Elio Gutierrez) . . . 15 10
3203 1cor. "Christ" (Jose de los Santos) 25 10
3204 1cor.50 "Family" (sculpture, Erasmo Moya) 40 15
3205 3cor. "Bird-fish" (Silvio Chavarria Co-operative) (horiz) 85 30
3206 3cor.50 Filigree ceramic vessel (Maria de los Angeles Bermudez) . . . 90 35
MS3207 100 × 70 mm., 7cor.50 Masks (Jose Flores). Imperf . . 1·75 85

492 "Picnic Table with Three Objects" (Alejandro Arostegui)
493 Rivoli's Hummingbird

1992. Contemporary Paintings. Multicoloured.
3208 25c. Type **492** 10 10
3209 25c. "Prophetess of the New World" (Alberto Ycaza) 10 10
3210 50c. "Flames of Unknown Origin" (Bernard Dreyfus) (horiz) 15 10
3211 1cor.50 "Owl" (Orlando Sobalvarro) (horiz) . . . 40 15
3212 2cor. "Pegasus at Liberty" (Hugo Palma) (horiz) . . 50 20
3213 3cor. "Avocados" (Omar d'Leon) (horiz) 75 30
3214 3cor.50 "Gueguense" (Carlos Montenegro) . . 90 35
MS3215 100 × 71 mm. 7cor.50 "Shipment" (Federico Nordalm). Imperf . . . . 1·75 85

1992. 2nd U.N. Conference on Environment and Development, Rio de Janeiro. Tropical Forest Wildlife. Multicoloured.
3216 1cor.50 Type **493** 40 15
3217 1cor.50 Harpy eagle ("Aguila arpia") 40 15
3218 1cor.50 Orchid 40 15
3219 1cor.50 Keel-billed toucan and morpho butterfly . . 40 15
3220 1cor.50 Resplendent quetzal 40 15
3221 1cor.50 Guardabarranco . . 40 15
3222 1cor.50 Howler monkey ("Mono aullador") . . . 40 15
3223 1cor.50 Sloth ("Perezoso") 40 15
3224 1cor.50 Squirrel monkey ("Mono ardilla") 40 15
3225 1cor.50 Blue and yellow macaw ("Guacamaya") 40 15
3226 1cor.50 Emerald boa and scarlet tanager 40 15
3227 1cor.50 Poison-arrow frog 40 15
3228 1cor.50 Jaguar 40 15
3229 1cor.50 Anteater 40 15
3230 1cor.50 Ocelot 40 15
3231 1cor.50 Coati 40 15
Nos. 3216/31 were issued together, se-tenant, forming a composite design of a forest.

494 Fabretto with Children

1992. Father Fabretto, "Benefactor of Nicaraguan Children".
3232 **494** 2cor.25 multicoloured . . 60 25

495 "Nicaraguan Identity" (Claudia Gordillo)

1992. Winning Entry in Photography Competition.
3233 **495** 2cor.25 multicoloured . . 60 25

496 "The Indians of Nicaragua" (Milton Jose Cruz)

1992. Winning Entry in Children's Painting Competition.
3234 **496** 2cor.25 multicoloured . . 60 25

497 Eucharistical Banner
498 Rivas Cross, 1523

1993. 460th Anniv of Catholic Church in Nicaragua. Multicoloured.
3235 25c. Type **497** 10 10
3236 50c. "Shrine of the Immaculate Conception" 10 10
3237 1cor. 18th-century document 20 10
3238 1cor.50 16th-century baptismal font 30 10
3239 2cor. "The Immaculate Conception" 40 15
3240 2cor.25 Monsignor Diego Alvarez Osorio (1st Bishop of Leon) 50 20
3241 3cor. "Christ on the Cross" 65 25

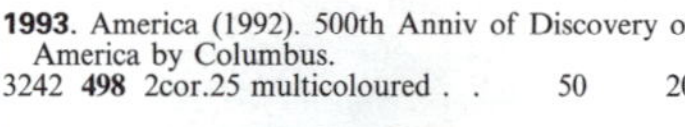

1993. America (1992). 500th Anniv of Discovery of America by Columbus.
3242 **498** 2cor.25 multicoloured . . 50 20

499 Cathedral

1993. Inauguration of Cathedral of the Immaculate Conception of Mary, Managua. Multicoloured.
3243 3cor. Type **499** 65 25
3244 4cor. Cross, Virgin Mary and map of Nicaragua (2nd Provincial Council) 85 35
Nos. 3243/4 were issued together, se-tenant, forming a composite design.

500 Emblem and Voters queueing outside Poll Station

1993. 23rd General Assembly of Organization of American States.
3245 **500** 3cor. multicoloured . . . 85 45

501 Anniversary Emblem

1993. 90th Anniv of Pan-American Health Organization.
3246 **501** 3cor. multicoloured . . . 85 45

502 "Sonatina" (Alma Iris Perez)

1993. Winning Entry in Children's Painting Competition.
3247 **502** 3cor. multicoloured . . . 85 45

503 Racoon Buttterflyfish

1993. Butterflyfishes. Multicoloured.
3248 1cor.50 Type **503** 50 25
3249 1cor.50 Rainford's butterflyfish ("Chaetodon rainfordi") 50 25
3250 1cor.50 Mailed butterflyfish ("Chaetodon reticulatus") 50 25
3251 1cor.50 Thread-finned butterflyfish ("Chaetodon auriga") 50 25
3252 1cor.50 Pennant coralfish ("Heniochus acuminatus") 50 25
3253 1cor.50 Dark-banded butterflyfish ("Coradion fulvocinctus") 50 25
3254 1cor.50 Mirror butterflyfish ("Chaetodon speculum") 50 25
3255 1cor.50 Lined butterflyfish ("Chaetodon lineolatus") 50 25
3256 1cor.50 Bennett's butterflyfish ("Chaetodon bennetti") 50 25
3257 1cor.50 Black-backed butterflyfish ("Chaetodon melanotus") 50 25
3258 1cor.50 Golden butterflyfish ("Chaetodon aureus") . . 50 25
3259 1cor.50 Saddle butterflyfish ("Chaetodon ephippium") 50 25
3260 1cor.50 Pyramid butterflyfish ("Hemitaurichthys polylepis") 50 25
3261 1cor.50 Dotted butterflyfish ("Chaetodon semeion") 50 25
3262 1cor.50 Klein's butterflyfish ("Chaetodon kleinii") . . 50 25
3263 1cor.50 Copper-banded butterflyfish ("Chelmon rostratus") 50 25

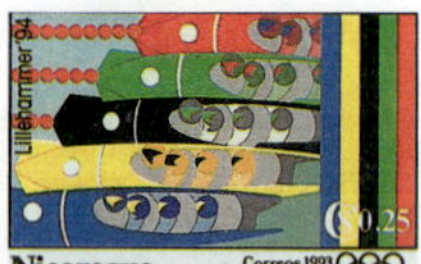

504 Four-man Bobsleigh

1993. Multicoloured. (a) Winter Olympic Games, Lillehammer, Norway (1994).
3264 25c. Type **504** 10 10
3265 25c. Skiing 10 10
3266 50c. Speed skating 15 10
3267 1cor.50 Ski jumping 45 20
3268 2cor. Women's figure skating 55 25
3269 3cor. Pairs' figure skating 85 45
3270 3cor.50 Shooting (biathlon) 1·00 45

(b) Olympic Games, Atlanta (1996).
3271 25c. Swimming 10 10
3272 25c. Diving 10 10
3273 50c. Long distance running 15 10
3274 1cor. Hurdling 30 15
3275 1cor.50 Gymnastics 45 20
3276 3cor. Throwing the javelin 85 45
3277 3cor.50 Sprinting . . . . . 1·00 50
MS3278 Two sheets each 100 × 70 mm. (a) 7cor.50 Flags; (b) 7cor.50 Olympic torch and hands 2·10 1·10

505 "Bromeliaceae sp." **506** Tomas Brolin (Sweden)

1994. Tropical Forest Flora and Fauna. Mult.
3279 2cor. Type **505** 50 25
3280 2cor. Sparkling-tailed hummingbird ("Tilmatura dupontii") 50 25
3281 2cor. "Anolis biporcatus" (lizard) 50 25
3282 2cor. Lantern fly ("Fulgara laternaria") 50 25
3283 2cor. Sloth ("Bradypus sp.") 50 25
3284 2cor. Ornate hawk eagle ("Spizaetus ornatus") . . 50 25
3285 2cor. Lovely cotinga ("Cotinga amabilis") . . 50 25
3286 2cor. Schegel's lance-head snake ("Bothrops schlegelii") 50 25
3287 2cor. "Odontoglossum sp." (orchid) and bee 50 25
3288 2cor. Red-eyed tree frog ("Agalychnis callidryas") 50 25
3289 2cor. "Heliconius sapho" (butterfly) 50 25
3290 2cor. Passion flower ("Passiflora vitifolia") . . 50 25
MS3291 Two sheets each 105 × 77 mm. (a) 10cor. Agouti; (b) 10cor. "Melinaea lilies" (butterfly) . . . . 2·25 1·10
Nos. 3279/90 were issued together, se-tenant, forming a composite design.

1994. World Cup Football Championship, U.S.A. Players.
3292 50c. Type **506** 15 10
3293 1cor. Jan Karas (Poland) and Antonio Luiz Costa (Brazil) 30 15
3294 1cor. Maxime Bossis and Michel Platini (France) 30 15
3295 1cor.50 Harold Schumacher (Germany) 45 20
3296 2cor. Andoni Zubizarreta (Spain) 55 30
3297 2cor.50 Lothar Matthaeus (Germany) and Diego Maradona (Argentine Republic) 75 35
3298 3cor.50 Bryan Robson (England) and Carlos Santos (Portugal) . . . . . 1·00 50
MS3299 71 × 100 mm. 10cor. Carlos Valderrama (Colombia) . . . 2·25 1·10

507 "Four in One" (Julio Lopez)

1994. Contemporary Arts. Multicoloured.
3300 50c. Rush mat (Rosalia Sevilla) (horiz) 15 10
3301 50c. Type **507** 15 10
3302 1cor. Ceramic church (Auxiliadora Bush) . . . 30 15
3303 1cor. Statuette of old woman (Indiana Robleto) 30 15
3304 2cor.50 "Santiago" (Jose de los Santos) 55 30
3305 3cor. "Gueguense" (Ines Gutierrez de Chong) . . . 85 45
3306 4cor. Ceramic hornet's nest (Elio Gutierrez) 95 45
MS3307 100 × 70 mm. 10cor. "Metate" (grinding stone) (Saul Carballo). Imperf . . . . . . 2·25 1·10

508 "Callicore patelina"

1994. "Hong Kong '94" International Stamp Exhibition. Butterflies. Multicoloured.
3308 1cor.50 Type **508** 35 15
3309 1cor.50 "Chlosyne narva" 35 15
3310 1cor.50 Giant brimstone ("Anteos maerula") . . . 35 15
3311 1cor.50 Diadem ("Marpesia petreus") 35 15
3312 1cor.50 "Pierella helvetia" 35 15
3313 1cor.50 "Eurytides epidaus" 35 15
3314 1cor.50 Doris ("Heliconius doris") 35 15
3315 1cor.50 "Smyrna blomfildia" 35 15
3316 1cor.50 "Eueides lybia olympia" 35 15
3317 1cor.50 "Adelpha heraclea" 35 15
3318 1cor.50 "Heliconius hecale zuleika" 35 15
3319 1cor.50 "Parides montezuma" 35 15
3320 1cor.50 "Morpho polyphemus" 35 15
3321 1cor.50 "Eresia alsina" . . . 35 15
3322 1cor.50 "Prepona omphale octavia" 35 15
3323 1cor.50 "Morpho grenadensis" 35 15

509 "The Holy Family" (anonymous)

1994. Christmas (1993). Paintings. Multicoloured.
3324 1cor. Type **509** 25 15
3325 4cor. "Nativity" (Lezamon) 95 45

510 Sculpture

1994. Chontal Culture Statuary. Multicoloured, colour of frame given.
3326 **510** 50c. yellow 15 10
3327 – 50c. yellow 15 10
3328 – 1cor. emerald 30 15
3329 – 1cor. green 30 15
3330 – 2cor.50 blue 55 35
3331 – 3cor. blue 85 45
3332 – 4cor. green 95 45
MS3333 100 × 70 mm. 10cor. Twin totems. Imperf . . . . 2·25 1·10
DESIGNS: 50c. (3327) to 10cor. Different sculptures.

511 "Virgin of Nicaragua" (Celia Lacayo)

1994. Contemporary Paintings. Multicoloured.
3334 50c. Type **511** 15 10
3335 50c. "Woman embroidering" (Guillermo Rivas Navas) 15 10
3336 1cor. "Couple dancing" (June Beer) 30 15
3337 1cor. "Song of Peace" (Alejandro Canales) . . . 30 15
3338 2cor.50 "Sapodilla Plums" (Genaro Lugo) (horiz) . . 55 30
3339 3cor. "Figure and Fragments" (Leonel Vanegas) 85 45
3340 4cor. "Eruption of Agua Volcano" (Asilia Guillen) (horiz) 95 45
MS3341 100 × 70 mm. 10cor. "Still-life" (Alejandro Alonso Rochi). Imperf . . . . 2·25 1·10

512 Nicolas Copernicus and Satellite

1994. Astronomers. Multicoloured.
3342 1cor.50 Type **512** 35 15
3343 1cor.50 Tycho Brahe and astronomers 35 15
3344 1cor.50 Galileo Galilei and "Galileo" space probe . . 35 15
3345 1cor.50 Sir Isaac Newton and telescope 35 15
3346 1cor.50 Edmond Halley, space probe and Halley's Comet 35 15
3347 1cor.50 James Bradley and Greenwich Observatory 35 15
3348 1cor.50 William Herschel and telescope 35 15
3349 1cor.50 John Goodricke and Algol (star) 35 15
3350 1cor.50 Karl Friedrich Gauss and Gottingen Observatory 35 15
3351 1cor.50 Friedrich Bessel and 1838 star telescope . . . 35 15
3352 1cor.50 William Cranch Bond (wrongly inscr "Granch") and Harvard College Observatory . . . 35 15
3353 1cor.50 Sir George Airy and stellar disk 35 15
3354 1cor.50 Percival Lowell and Flagstaff Observatory, Arizona, U.S.A. 35 15
3355 1cor.50 George Hale (wrongly inscr "Halle") and solar spectroscope . . 35 15
3356 1cor.50 Edwin Hubble and Hubble telescope 35 15
3357 1cor.50 Gerard Kuiper and Miranda (Uranus moon) 35 15
MS3358 144 × 84 mm. 10cor. Nicolas Copernicus and interstellar probe . . . . . . 2·25 1·10
Nos. 3342/57 were issued together, se-tenant, forming a composite design.

513 1886 Benz Tricycle

1994. Automobiles. Multicoloured.
3359 1cor.50 Type **513** 35 15
3360 1cor.50 1909 Benz Blitzen 35 15
3361 1cor.50 1923 Mercedes Benz 24/100/140 . . . . 35 15
3362 1cor.50 1928 Mercedes Benz SSK 35 15
3363 1cor.50 1934 Mercedes Benz 500K Cabriolet 35 15
3364 1cor.50 1949 Mercedes Benz 170S 35 15
3365 1cor.50 1954 Mercedes Benz W196 . . . . 35 15
3366 1cor.50 1954 Mercedes Benz 300SL 35 15
3367 1cor.50 1896 Ford Quadricycle 35 15
3368 1cor.50 1920 Ford taxi cab 35 15
3369 1cor.50 1928 Ford Roadster 35 15
3370 1cor.50 1932 Ford V-8 . . . 35 15
3371 1cor.50 1937 Ford V-8 78 35 15
3372 1cor.50 1939 Ford 91 Deluxe Tudor Sedan . . . 35 15
3373 1cor.50 1946 Ford V-8 Sedan Coupe 35 15
3374 1cor.50 1958 Ford Custom 300 . . . . 35 15
MS3375 120 × 84 mm. 10cor. Henry Ford, 1903 Ford Model A, Karl Benz and 1897 5CH . . . . . 2·25 1·10

514 Hugo Eckener and Count Ferdinand von Zeppelin

1994. Zeppelin Airships. Multicoloured.
3376 1cor.50 Type **514** 35 15
3377 1cor.50 "Graf Zeppelin" over New York, 1928 . . 35 15
3378 1cor.50 "Graf Zeppelin" over Tokyo, 1929 . . . . 35 15
3379 1cor.50 "Graf Zeppelin" over Randolph Hearst's villa, 1929 . . . . 35 15
3380 1cor.50 Charles Lindbergh, Hugo Eckener and "Graf Zeppelin" at Lakehurst, 1929 . . . . 35 15
3381 1cor.50 "Graf Zeppelin" over St. Basil's Cathedral, Moscow (wrongly inscr "Santra Sofia") 35 15
3382 1cor.50 "Graf Zeppelin" over Paris, 1930 . . . . . 35 15
3383 1cor.50 "Graf Zeppelin" over Cairo, Egypt, 1931 35 15
3384 1cor.50 "Graf Zeppelin" over Arctic Sea 35 15
3385 1cor.50 "Graf Zeppelin" over Rio de Janeiro, 1932 35 15
3386 1cor.50 "Graf Zeppelin" over St. Paul's Cathedral, London, 1935 . . . . . 35 15
3387 1cor.50 "Graf Zeppelin" over St. Peter's Cathedral, Rome 35 15
3388 1cor.50 "Graf Zeppelin" over Swiss Alps 35 15
3389 1cor.50 "Graf Zeppelin over Brandenburg Gate, Berlin 35 15
3390 1cor.50 Hugo Eckener piloting "Graf Zeppelin" 35 15
3391 1cor.50 Captain Ernest Lehman, "Graf Zeppelin" and Dornier Do-X flying boat 35 15
MS3392 Two sheets each 96 × 69 mm. (a) 10cor. Hugo Eckener and *Graf Zeppelin*; (b) 10cor. Count Ferdinand von Zeppelin and Airship . . . . . 4·50 2·25

515 Gabriel Horvilleur

1994. Nicaraguan Philatelists. Multicoloured.
3393 1cor. Type **515** 15 10
3394 3cor. Jose Cauadra 85 45
3395 4cor. Alfredo Pertz 95 45

516 August 21 1955 Sighting at Kentucky

1994. Alien Sightings. Eight sheets each 105 × 75 mm containing horiz designs as T **516**.
MS3396 Eight sheets. (a) 60cor. Type **516**; (b) 60cor. September 19 1961 sighting, New Hampshire, USA; (c) 60cor. 28 July 1965 sighting, Argentina; (d) 60cor. May 8 1973 sighting, Texas, USA; (e) 60cor. September 22 1976 sighting, Canary Islands; (f) 60cor. October 26 1978 sighting, Pennsylvania, USA; (g) 60cor. November 7 1989 sighting, Kansas, USA; (h) 61cor. July 21 1991 sighting, Missouri, USA 12·00 12·00

517 "Poponjoche" (Thelma Gomez) **518** Conference Emblem

1994. 1st Nicaraguan Tree Conference.
3397 **517** 4cor. multicoloured . . . 95 45

1994. 2nd International Conference on New and Restored Democracies, Managua.
3398 **518** 3cor. multicoloured . . . 55 55

518a Chocolate Point Himalayan

1994. Cats. Two sheets containing T **518a** and similar vert designs. Multicoloured.
MS3399 (a) 146×203 mm. 1cor.50×12, Type **518a**; Somali; American shorthair; Russian blue; Scottish fold; Persian; Egyptian mau; Blue cream Manx; Blue Birman; Seal point Balinese; Blue oriental shorthair; Persian; Angora; Siamese; Two seal point Birman kittens; Devon rex. (b) 136×100 mm. 15cor. Golden Persian (38×50 mm). Set of 2 sheets . . . . 4·25 4·25
The stamps of **MS**3399a form a composite design.

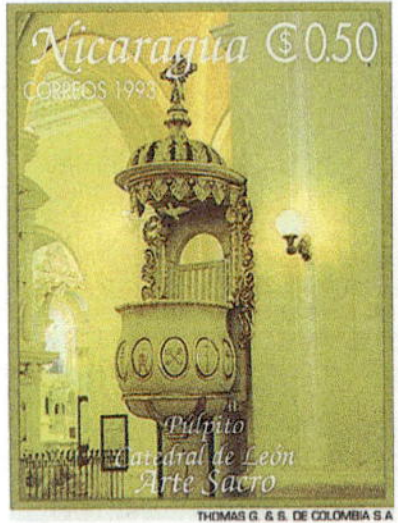

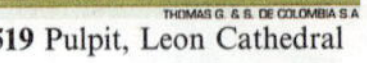

519 Pulpit, Leon Cathedral **520** Mascot and Emblem

1994. Religious Art. Multicoloured.
3400 50c. Type **519** 15 10
3401 50c. "St. Anna" (porcelain figure), Chinandega Church 15 10
3402 1cor. "St. Joseph and Child" (porcelain figure), St. Peter's Church, Rivas 30 15
3403 1cor. "St. James", Jinotepe Church 30 15
3404 2cor.50 Gold chalice, Subtiava Temple, Leon 55 30
3405 3cor. Processional cross, Niquinohomo Church, Masaya 85 45
3406 4cor. "Lord of Miracles" (crucifix), Lord of Miracles Temple, Managua 95 45
MS3407 100×70 mm. 10cor. Silver altar hanging, St. Peter's Church, Rivas. Imperf . . . . 2·25 1·10

1994. 32nd World Amateur Baseball Championship.
3408 **520** 4cor. multicoloured . . . 1·00 1·00

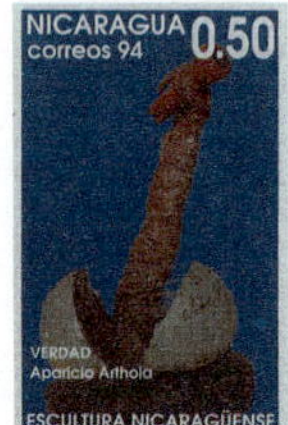

520a "Verdad" (Aparicio Arthola)

1994. Sculpture. Multicoloured.
3409 50c. Type **520a** 10 10
3410 1cor. "Buho" (Oelando Sobalvarro) 15 10
3411 1cor.50 "Pequeno Lustrador" (Noel Flores Castro) 20 10
3412 2cor. "Exodo II" (Miguel Angel Abarca) 25 10
3413 2cor.50 "Raza" (Fernando Saravia) 35 15
3414 3cor. "Dolor Incognito" (Edith Gron) 40 15
3415 4cor. "Garza" (Ernesto Cardenal) 55 20
MS3416 Two sheets, each 70×100 mm. (a) 15cor. "Atlante" (Jorge Navas Cordonero). Imperf. (b) 15cor. "Maternidad" (Rodrigo Penalba). Imperf. Set of 2 sheets 4·00 4·00

521 Mt. Sorak

1994. "Philakorea 1994" International Stamp Exhibition, Seoul. Views of South Korea. Mult.
3417 1cor.50 Type **521** 25 10
3418 1cor.50 Bronze Statue of Kim Yu-Shin 25 10
3419 1cor.50 Woedolgae (solitary rock) 25 10
3420 1cor.50 Stream, Mt. Hallasan, Cheju Island . . 25 10
3421 1cor.50 Mirukpong and Pisondae 25 10
3422 1cor.50 Ch'onbuldong Valley 25 10
3423 1cor.50 Bridge of the Seven Nymphs 25 10
3425 1cor.50 Piryong Waterfall 25 10
MS3425 106×76 mm. 10cor. Child surrounded by food on first birthday . . . . 2·25 2·25

522 Piano on Stage

1994. 25th Anniv of Ruben Dario National Theatre, Managua.
3426 **522** 3cor. multicoloured . . . 55 20

523 Tyrannosaurus Rex

1994. Prehistoric Animals. Multicoloured.
3427 1cor.50 Type **523** 25 10
3428 1cor.50 Plateosaurus 25 10
3429 1cor.50 Pteranodon 25 10
3430 1cor.50 Camarasaurus . . . 25 10
3431 1cor.50 Euplocephalus . . . 25 10
3432 1cor.50 Sacuanjoche 25 10
3433 1cor.50 Deinonychus . . . 25 10
3434 1cor.50 Chasmosaurus . . . 25 10
3435 1cor.50 Dimorphodon . . . 25 10
3436 1cor.50 Ametriorhynchids 25 10
3437 1cor.50 Ichthyosaurus . . . 25 10
3438 1cor.50 Pterapsis and compsognathus 25 10
3439 1cor.50 Cephalopod 25 10
3440 1cor.50 Archelon 25 10
3441 1cor.50 Griphognatus and gyroptychius 25 10
3442 1cor.50 Plesiosaur and nautiloid 25 10
Nos. 3427/42 were issued together, se-tenant, forming a composite design.

523a Chapel, Granada **523b** Rai (Brazil)

1994. Cultural Heritage. Multicoloured.
3443 50c. Type **523a** 10 10
3444 1cor. San Francisco Convent, Granada (horiz) 15 10
3445 1cor.50 Santiago tower, Leon 20 10
3446 2cor. Santa Ana parish church, Nindiri (horiz) . . 25 10
3447 2cor.50 Santa Ana parish church, Nandaime 35 10
3448 3cor. Arched doorway, Los Leones, Granada (horiz) 40 15
3449 4cor. La Inmaculada Concepcion castle, Rio San Juan (horiz) 55 20
MS3450 100×70 mm. 15cor. San Jacinto hacienda, Managua. Imperf . . . . 2·00 2·00

1994. World Cup Football Championships, USA. Three sheets containing T **523** and similar multicoloured designs showing players.
MS3451 (a) 149×120 mm. 3cor.×8, Type **523b**; Freddy Rincon (Colombia); Luis Garcia (Mexico); Thomas Dooley (USA); Franco Barest (Italy); Tony Meola (USA); Enzo Francescoli (Uruguay); Roy Wegerle (USA). (b) 70×100 mm. 10cor. Faustino Asprilla (Colombia). (c) 106×76 mm. 10cor. Aldolfo Valencia (Colombia) (horiz). Set of 3 sheets 4·50 4·50

524 Hawker Typhoon 1B

1994. 50th Anniv of D-Day. Multicoloured.
3452 3cor. Type **524** 55 20
3453 3cor. Douglas C-47 Skytrain transport dropping paratroops 55 20
3454 3cor. H.M.S. "Mauritius" (cruiser) bombarding Houlgate, Normandy . . 55 20
3455 3cor. Formation of Mulberry Harbours to transport supplies to beach 55 20
3456 3cor. British AVRE Churchill tank 55 20
3457 3cor. Tank landing craft . . 55 20

525 Renate Stecher (women's 200 m, 1972) **526** Detachment of Command module "Eagle"

1994. Centenary of International Olympic Committee. Gold Medal Winners. Multicoloured.
3458 3cor.50 Type **525** 60 25
3459 3cor.50 Cassius Clay (Muhammad Ali) (boxing, 1960) 60 25
MS3460 106×76 mm. 10cor. Claudia Pechstein (5000 metres speed skating, 1994) . . . . . 1·75 1·75

1994. 25th Anniv of First Manned Moon Landing. Multicoloured.
3461 3cor. Type **526** 55 20
3462 3cor. Launch of "Saturn V", Cape Canaveral, Florida 55 20
3463 3cor. Command module orbiting Moon 55 20
3464 3cor. Footprint on Moon 55 20
3465 3cor. Primary space capsule separating 55 20
3466 3cor. Command module . . 55 20
3467 3cor. Lunar module landing on Moon 55 20
3468 3cor. Astronaut on Moon 55 20
MS3469 Two sheets each 81×116 mm. (a) 10cor. Buzz Aldrin, Neil Armstrong and Michael Collins (crew) (46×28 mm); (b) 10cor. Astronaut on Moon saluting American flag (28×46 mm) . . . . 3·50 3·50

527 "The Death Cart" (Erick Joanello Montoya)

1994. 1st Prize in Children's Painting Competition.
3470 **527** 4cor. multicoloured . . . 70 30

528 Black-crowned Night Heron

1994. Woodland Animals. Multicoloured.
3471 2cor. Type **528** 35 15
3472 2cor. Scarlet macaw ("Ara macao") 35 15
3473 2cor. Cattle egrets ("Bubulcus ibis") (wrongly inscr "Bulbulcus") 35 15
3474 2cor. American black vultures ("Coragyps atratus") 35 15
3475 2cor. Brazilian rainbow boa ("Epicrates cenchria") . . 35 15
3476 2cor. Red-legged honeycreepers ("Cyanerpes cyaneus") . . 35 15
3477 2cor. Plain chachalaca ("Ortalis vetula") 35 15
3478 2cor. Sloth ("Bradypus griseus") 35 15
3479 2cor. Jaguar ("Felis onca") 35 15
3480 2cor. American darter ("Anhinga anhinga") . . 35 15
3481 2cor. Baird's tapir ("Tapirus bairdi") 35 15
3482 2cor. Anteater ("Myrmecophaga jubata") 35 15
3483 2cor. Iguana ("Iguana iguaana") 35 15
3484 2cor. Snapping turtle ("Chelydra serpentina") 35 15
3485 2cor. Red-billed whistling ducks ("Dendrocygna autumnalis") 35 15
3486 2cor. Ocelot ("Felis pardalis") 35 15
MS3487 100×70 mm. 15cor. American anhingas (as central motif of No. 3462) . . . . . . 2·25 2·25
Nos. 3471/86 were issued together, se-tenant, forming a composite design.

529 "The Kid" (dir. Charlie Chaplin) **530** "Discovery of America"

1994. Centenary of Motion Pictures. Multicoloured.
3488 2cor. Type **529** 35 15
3489 2cor. "Citizen Kane" (dir. Orson Welles) 35 15
3490 2cor. "Lawrence of Arabia" (dir. David Lean) 35 15
3491 2cor. "Ivan the Terrible" (dir. Sergio Eisenstein) . . 35 15
3492 2cor. "Metropolis" (dir. Fritz Lang) 35 15
3493 2cor. "The Ten Commandments" (dir. Cecil B. De Mille) 35 15
3494 2cor. "Gandhi" (dir. Richard Attenborough) 35 15
3495 2cor. "Casablanca" (dir. Michael Curtiz) 35 15
3496 2cor. "Platoon" (dir. Oliver Stone) 35 15
3497 2cor. "The Godfather" (dir. Francis Ford Coppola) 35 15
3498 2cor. "2001: A Space Odyssey" (dir. Stanley Kubrick) 35 15
3499 2cor. "The Ocean Depths" (dir. Jean Renoir) 35 15
MS3500 80×109 mm. 15cor. "Gone with the Wind" (dir. Victor Fleming) . . . . 2·25 2·25

1994. 15th Death Anniv of Rodrigo Penalba (artist). Multicoloured.
3501 50c. Type **530** 10 10
3502 1cor. "Portrait of Mauricio" 20 10
3503 1cor.50 "Portrait of Franco" 25 10
3504 2cor. "Portrait of Mimi Hammer" 35 15
3505 2cor.50 "Seated Woman" 45 20
3506 3cor. "Still-life" (horiz) . . 55 20
3507 4cor. "Portrait of Maria Augusta" 70 30
MS3508 70×100 mm. 15cor. "Entrance to Anticoli" (66×96 mm). Imperf . . . . . 2·25 2·25

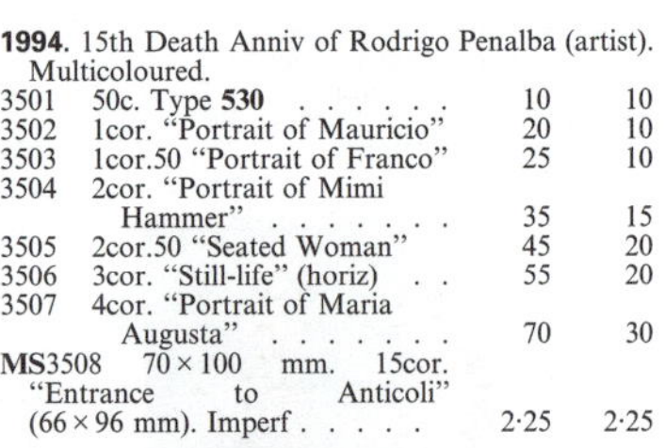

531 Hen and Cock

1994. Endangered Species. The Highland Guan. Multicoloured.
3509 50c. Type **531** 10 10
3510 1cor. Cock 20 10
3511 2cor.50 Hen 45 20
3512 3cor. Cock and hen (different) 55 25
MS3513 100×70 mm. 15cor. Heads of cock and hen . . . . 2·25 2·25

532 M.W. Jung

1995. Korea Baseball Championship. Eight sheets, each 147 × 200 mm containing T **532** and similar vert designs showing players and team emblems. Multicoloured.

MS3514 (a) 3cor.50 × 9, Type **532**; K.K. Kim; H.J. Kim; M.T. Chung; Pacific Dolphins emblem; B.W. An; D.G. Yoon; S.D. Choi; D.K. Kim. (b) 3cor.50 × 9, J.H. Jang; Y.D. Han; K.D. Lee; J.S. Park; Hanwha Eagles emblem; M.C. Jeong; J.W. Song; J.G. Kang; D.S. Koo. (c) 3cor.50 × 9, R.J. Park; K.J. Cho; K.T. Kim; W.H. Kim; Raiders emblem; I.H. Baik; S.K. Park; K.L. Kim; J.S. Park. (d) 3cor.50 × 9, J.I. Ryu; S.Y. Kim; S.R. Kim; B.C. Dong; Samsung Lions emblem; K.W. Kang; C.S. Park; J.H. Yang; T.H. Kim.(e) 3cor.50 × 9, D.H. Han; Y.S. Kim; J.H. Yoo; Y.B. Seo; LG Twins emblem; J.H. Park; S.H. Lee; D.S. Kim; J.H. Kim. (f) 3cor.50 × 9, H.K. Yoon; D.H. Park; H.K. Joo; E.G. Kim; Lotte Giants emblem; J.T. Park; P.S. Kong; J.S. Yeom; M.H. Kim. (g) 3.50 × 9, D.Y Sun; J.B. Lee; J.S. Kim; S.H. Kim; Haitai Tigers emblem; G.C. Lee; G.H. Cho; S.H. Kim (different); S.C. Lee. (h) 3cor.50 × 9, M.S. Lee; C.S. Park; H.S. Lim; K.W. Kim; OB Bears emblem; J.S. Kim; T.H. Kim; H.S. Kim; S.J. Kim. Set of 8 sheets . . . 25·00 25·00

533 "Avanzamos Hacia El Siglo 21" (Maria Jose Zamora)

534 Greater Bird of Paradise (*Paradisaea apoda*)

1995. FUNCOD (environmental organization) Art Prize. Multicoloured.

3515 1cor. Type**533** 15 10
3516 2cor. "Naturaleza Muerta" (Rafael Castellon) 20 10
3517 4cor. "Aguas Cautivas" (Alvaro Gutierrez) 55 20

1995. Birds. Two sheets containing T **534** and similar vert designs. Multicoloured.

MS3518 (a) 120 × 164 mm. 2cor. × 12, Type **534**; *Dryocopus galeatus*; Montezuma oropendola (*Psarocolius Montezuma*); Black-capped kingfisher (*Halcyon pileata*); White-throated magpie jay (*Calocitta Formosa*); Green-winged macaw (*Ara chloroptera*); Eastern rosella (*Platycercus eximius*); Palawan peacock pheasant (*Polyplectron emphanum*); Red-legged seriema (*Cariama cristata*); Hoatzin (*Opisthocomus hoatzin*); Blue-bellied roller (*Coracias cyanogaster*). (b) 75 × 102 mm. 10cor. *Dryocopus galeatus* (different). Set of 2 sheets . . . 4·25 4·25

The stamps of **MS**3518a form a composite design.

535 Hovercraft

1995. British–Nicaraguan San Juan River Expedition.

3519 **535** 4cor. multicoloured . . . 55 20

536 "Fiesta de Boaco" (Ernesto Brown)

1995. Centenary of Boaco City.

3520 **536** 4cor. multicoloured . . . 55 20

537 Villa Rivas and Cannon

1995. 275th Anniv of Villa Rivas. 160th Anniv of Rivas City.

3521 **537** 3cor. multicoloured . . . 40 15

538 Louis Pasteur

1995. Death Centenary of Louis Pasteur (research scientist).

3522 **538** 4cor. multicoloured . . . 55 20

539 Crocodile

1995. Fauna. Three sheets containing T **541** and similar multicoloured designs.

MS3523 (a) 140 × 100 mm. 2cor.50 × 9, Type **539**; Opossum; Peccary; Paca; Tree frog; Iguana; Scarlet macaw; Capybara; Vampire bat. (b) 110 × 80 mm. 15cor. Jaguar (vert). (c) 110 × 80 mm. 15cor. Ornate hawk eagle (vert). Set of 3 sheets . . 7·00 7·00

540 "Children love Nature" (Brenda Gutierrez)

1995. Winning Design in Children's Drawing Competition.

3524 **540** 3cor. multicoloured . . . 40 15

541 Carlos Drummond De Andrade

542 Child and Maize

1995. Twentieth Century Writers. Sheet 112 × 210 mm containing T **541** and similar vert designs showing writers and their country flags. Multicoloured.

MS3525 3cor. × 12, Type **541**; Cesar Vallejo; Jorge Luis Borges; James Joyce; Marcel Proust; William Faulkner; Vladimir Maiakovski; Ezra Pound; Franz Kafka; T.S. Eliot; Rainer Maria Rilke; Federico Garcia Lorca . . . . 4·75 4·75

1995. 50th Anniv of United Nations Food and Agriculture Organization (FAO).

3526 **542** 4cor. multicoloured . . . 55 20

543 "Ferry Boat"

1995. Paintings by Armando Morales. Multicoloured.

3527 50c. Type **543** 10 10
3528 1cor. "Oliverio Castaneda" (vert) 15 10
3529 1cor. 50 "Desnudo Sentado" (vert) 20 10
3530 2cor. "Las Senoritas de Puerto Cabezas" 25 10
3531 2cor. 50 "El Automovil de la Compania" (vert) . . . 35 10
3532 3cor. "Paisaje Taurino" (vert) 40 15
3533 4cor. "Anonas" 55 20
MS3534 100 × 70 mm. 15cor. "Mujer Dormida". Imperf . . . . . . 2·00 2·00

544 Doves and UN Flag

546 Paul Harris (founder) and Emblem

545 African Map Butterfly (*Cyrestis Camillus*)

1995. 50th Anniv of United Nations. Multicoloured.

3535 3cor. Type **544** 40 15
3536 4cor. Lion and lamb 55 20
3537 5cor. Dove sitting on UN helmet 70 30
MS3538 70 × 100 mm. 10cor. Dove and children . . . . 1·30 1·30

Nos. 3535/7 were issued together, se-tenant, forming a composite design.

1995. Butterflies. Two sheets containing T **545** and similar multicoloured designs.

MS3539 (a) 138 × 125 mm. 2cor.50 × 12, Type **545**; Lilac beauty (*Salamis cacta*); Giant charaxes (*Charaxes castor*); Beautiful monarch (*Danaus Formosa*); Red swallowtail (*Graphium ridleyanus*); Hewitson's forest blue (*Hewitsonia boisduvali*); Club-tailed charaxes (*Charaxes zoolina*); *Kalima cymodoce*; Blue spot commodore (*Precis westermanni*); African giant swallowtail (*Papilio antimachus*); Red glider (*Cymothoe sangaris*); Giant blue swallowtail (*Papilio zalmoxis*). (b) 106 × 76 mm. *Danaus Formosa* (vert). Set of 2 sheets . . . . 4·25 4·25

The stamps of **MS**3539a form a composite design.

1995. 90th Anniv of Rotary International (charitable organization). Multicoloured.

3540 15cor. Type **546** . . . . . 2·00 80
MS3541 106 × 76 mm. 25cor. Emblems from 1905 and 1995 . . . 2·35 3·35

547 Michael Jordan (basketball)

548 John Lennon

1995. Olympic Games, Atlanta. Three sheets containing T **547** and similar vert designs. Multicoloured.

MS3542 (a) 110 × 100 mm. 5cor. × 6, Type **547**; Heike Henkel (high jump); Linford Christie (running); Vitaly Chterchbo (gymnastic); Heike Drechsler (long jump); Mark Tewksbury (swimming). (b) 112 × 78 mm. 20cor. Pierre de Coubertin (founder) and Runner. (c) 112 × 78 mm. 20cor. Javelin throw and Pierre de Coubertin (horiz). Set of 3 sheets . . . . 7·25 7·25

1995. 15th Death Anniv of John Lennon (musician).

3543 **548** 2cor. multicoloured . . . 25 10

549 Stylized Nativity

1995. Christmas.

3544 **549** 4cor. multicoloured . . . 55 20

550 Otto Meyerhof (medicine, 1922)

1995. Centenary of the Nobel Prize. Five sheets containing T **550** and similar vert designs showing prize winners. Multicoloured.

MS3545 (a) 102 × 180 mm. 2cor.50 × 9, Type **550**; Leon Bourgeois (peace, 1920); James Frank (physics, 1925); Leo Esaki (physics, 1973); Miguel Angel Asturias (literature, 1967); Henri Bergson (literature, 1927); Friedrich Bergius (chemistry, 1931); Klaus von Klitzing (physics, 1985); Eisaku Sato (peace, 1974). (b) 130 × 179 mm. 2cor.50 × 2, Wilhelm Rontgen (physics, 1901); Theodor Mommsen (literature, 1902); Philipp von Lenard (physics, 1905); Walther Nernst (chemistry, 1920); Hans Spemann (medicine,1935); Jean-Paul Sartre (literature, 1964); T.S. Eliot (literature, 1948); Albert Camus (literature, 1957); Ludwig Quidde (peace, 1927); Werner Heisenberg (physics, 1932); Joseph Brodsky (literature, 1987); Carl von Ossietzky (peace, 1935). (c) 107 × 76 mm.15cor. Johannes Stark (physics, 1919). (d) 107 × 76 mm. 15cor. Sin-itiro Tomonaga (physics, 1965). (e) 107 × 76 mm. 15cor. Oscar Arias Sanchez (peace, 1987) . . . . 9·75 9·75

The stamps of **MS**3545a/b, respectively, each form a composite design.

551 *Cattleya downiana*

1995. Orchids. Three sheets containing T **551** and similar horiz designs. Multicoloured.

MS3546 (a) 139 × 95 mm. 2cor.50 × 9, Type **551**; *Odontoglossum maculatum*; *Barkeria Lindleyana*; *Rossioglossum grande*; *Brassavola digbyana* (inscr "Brassavp"); *Miltonia Schroederiana*; *Oncidium ornithorhynchum*; *Odontoglossum cervantesii*; *Chysis Tricostata*. (b) 139 × 95 mm. 3cor. × 9, *Lycaste Auburn*; *Lemboglossum cordatum*; *Cyrtochilum macranthum*; *Miltassia Aztec*; *Masdevallia ignea*; *Oncidium Sniffen*; *Brassolaeliocattleya*; *Ascocenda*; *Phalaenopsis*. (c) 106 × 76 mm. 15cor. *Odontoglossum uro-skinneri*. Set of 3 sheets . . . . 8·25 8·25

The stamps of **MS**3546b form a composite design.

SILVER CURRENCY

The following were for use in all places on the Atlantic coast of Nicaragua where the silver currency was in use. This currency was worth about 50c. to the peso.

Earlier issues (overprints on Nicaraguan stamps) were also issued for Zelaya. These are listed in the Stanley Gibbons Part 15 (Central America) Catalogue.

G 1 Steam Locomotive

1912.

G 1	**Z 1**	1c. green	1·75	90
G 2		2c. red	1·25	55
G 3		3c. brown	1·75	85
G 4		4c. lake	1·75	70
G 5		5c. blue	1·75	70
G 6		6c. red	9·75	5·00
G 7		10c. grey	1·75	70
G 8		15c. lilac	1·75	1·10
G 9		20c. blue	1·75	1·10
G10		25c. black and green . .	2·25	1·60
G11		35c. black and brown . .	3·25	1·90
G12		50c. green	3·25	1·90
G13		1p. orange	5·00	3·25
G14		2p. brown	9·75	6·00
G15		5p. green	20·00	12·50

OFFICIAL STAMPS

Overprinted **FRANQUEO OFICIAL**.

1890. Stamps of 1890.
O37 **6** 1c. blue 30 60
O38 2c. blue 30 60
O39 5c. blue 30 70
O40 10c. blue 30 75
O41 20c. blue 35 90
O42 50c. blue 35 1·10
O43 1p. blue 40 1·75
O44 2p. blue 40 2·75
O45 5p. blue 45 6·00
O46 10p. blue 45 11·50

1891. Stamps of 1891.
O47 **7** 1c. green 15 40
O48 2c. green 15 40
O49 5c. green 15 40
O50 10c. green 15 40
O51 20c. green 15 70
O52 50c. green 15 75
O53 1p. green 15 90
O54 2p. green 15 90
O55 5p. green 15 2·25
O56 10p. green 15 3·50

1892. Stamps of 1892.
O57 **8** 1c. brown 15 30
O58 2c. brown 15 30
O59 5c. brown 15 30
O60 10c. brown 15 30
O61 20c. brown 15 50
O62 50c. brown 15 70
O63 1p. brown 15 1·10
O64 2p. brown 15 1·75
O65 5p. brown 15 2·75
O66 10p. brown 15 3·50

1893. Stamps of 1893.
O67 **9** 1c. black 15 30
O68 2c. black 15 30
O69 5c. black 15 30
O70 10c. black 15 30
O71 20c. black 15 50
O72 25c. black 15 65
O73 50c. black 15 70
O74 1p. black 15 1·00
O75 2p. black 15 1·25
O76 5p. black 15 2·75
O77 10p. black 15 3·50

1894. Stamps of 1894.
O78 **10** 1c. orange 15 30
O79 2c. orange 15 30
O80 5c. orange 15 30
O81 10c. orange 15 30
O82 20c. orange 15 30
O83 50c. orange 15 45
O84 1p. orange 15 1·00
O85 2p. orange 15 1·75
O86 5p. orange 15 3·50
O87 10p. orange 15 4·50

1895. Stamps of 1895.
O88 **11** 1c. green 15 30
O89 2c. green 15 30
O90 5c. green 15 30
O91 10c. green 15 30
O92 20c. green 15 50
O93 50c. green 15 80
O94 1p. green 15 80
O95 2p. green 15 1·25
O96 5p. green 15 1·90
O97 10p. green 15 2·40

1896. Stamps of 1896, dated "1896", optd **FRANQUEO OFICIAL** in oval frame.
O 99 **12** 1c. red 1·50 1·90
O100 2c. red 1·50 1·90
O101 5c. red 1·50 1·90
O102 10c. red 1·50 1·90
O103 20c. red 1·90 1·90
O104 50c. red 3·00 3·00
O105 1p. red 7·25 7·25
O106 2p. red 7·25 7·25
O107 5p. red 9·50 9·50

1896. Nos. D99/103 handstamped **Franqueo Oficial**.
O108 **D 13** 1c. orange — 4·25
O109 2c. orange — 4·25
O110 5c. orange — 3·00
O111 10c. orange — 3·00
O112 20c. orange — 3·00

1897. Stamps of 1897, dated "1897", optd **FRANQUEO OFICIAL** in oval frame.
O113 **12** 1c. red 2·00 2·00
O114 2c. red 2·00 2·00
O115 5c. red 2·00 2·00
O116 10c. red 1·90 2·10
O117 20c. red 1·90 2·40
O118 50c. red 3·00 3·00
O119 1p. red 8·25 8·25
O120 2p. red 9·75 9·75
O121 5p. red 15·00 15·00

1898. Stamps of 1898 optd **FRANQUEO OFICIAL** in oval frame.
O124 **13** 1c. red 2·00 2·00
O125 2c. red 2·00 2·00
O126 4c. red 2·00 2·00
O127 5c. red 1·50 1·50
O128 10c. red 2·40 2·40
O129 15c. red 3·75 3·75
O130 20c. red 3·75 3·75
O131 50c. red 5·00 5·00
O132 1p. red 6·50 6·50
O133 2p. red 6·50 6·50
O134 5p. red 6·50 6·50

1899. Stamps of 1899 optd **FRANQUEO OFICIAL** in scroll.
O137 **14** 1c. green 15 60
O138 2c. brown 15 60
O139 4c. red 15 60
O140 5c. blue 15 40
O141 10c. orange 15 60
O142 15c. brown 15 1·25
O143 20c. green 15 2·00
O144 50c. red 15 2·00
O145 1p. orange 15 6·00
O146 2p. violet 15 6·00
O147 5p. blue 15 9·00

O 16   O 38

1900.
O148 **O 16** 1c. purple 45 45
O149 2c. orange 35 35
O150 4c. olive 45 45
O151 5c. blue 90 30
O152 10c. violet 90 25
O153 20c. brown 65 25
O154 50c. lake 90 35
O155 1p. blue 2·10 1·50
O156 2p. orange 2·40 2·40
O157 5p. black 3·00 3·00

1903. Stamps of 1900 surch **OFICIAL** and value, with or without ornaments.
O197 **15** 1c. on 10c. mauve 1·25 1·50
O198 2c. on 3c. green 1·50 1·90
O199 4c. on 3c. green 5·75 5·75
O200 4c. on 10c. mauve 5·75 5·75
O201 5c. on 3c. green 70 70

1903. Surch.
O202 **O 16** 10c. on 20c. brown 15 15
O203 30c. on 20c. brown 15 15
O204 50c. on 20c. brown 35 25

1905.
O219 **O 38** 1c. green 20 20
O220 2c. red 20 20
O221 5c. blue 20 20
O222 10c. brown 20 25
O223 20c. orange 20 25
O224 50c. olive 20 25
O225 1p. lake 20 20
O226 2p. violet 20 20
O227 5p. black 20 20

1907. Surch **Vale 10 c**.
O239 **O 38** 10c. on 1c. green 55 55
O241 10c. on 2c. red 15·00 11·50
O243 20c. on 2c. red 13·50 9·00
O245 50c. on 1c. green 1·10 1·10
O247 50c. on 2c. red 13·50 6·50

1907. Surch **Vale 20 cts** or **Vale $1.00**.
O249 **O 38** 20c. on 1c. green 70 70
O250 $1 on 2c. red 1·10 1·10
O251 $2 on 2c. red 1·10 1·10
O252 $3 on 2c. red 1·10 1·10
O253 $4 on 5c. blue 1·40 1·40

1907. No. 206 surch **OFICIAL** and value.
O256 **49** 10c. on 1c. green 9·00 7·75
O257 15c. on 1c. green 9·00 7·75
O258 20c. on 1c. green 9·00 7·75
O259 50c. on 1c. green 9·00 7·75
O260 1p. on 1c. green 8·25 7·75
O261 2p. on 1c. green 8·25 7·75

1907. Fiscal stamps as T **50** surch **10 cts. CORREOS 1907 OFICIAL 10 CTS.**
O262 **50** 10c. on 2c. orange 10 10
O263 35c. on 1c. blue 10 10
O264 70c. on 1c. blue 10 10
O266 1p. on 2c. orange 10 15
O267 2p. on 2c. orange 10 15
O268 3p. on 5c. brown 10 15
O269 4p. on 5c. brown 15 15
O270 5p. on 5c. brown 15 15

1908. Stamp of 1905 surch **OFICIAL VALE** and value.
O271 **37** 10c. on 3c. violet 9·00 7·75
O272 15c. on 3c. violet 9·00 7·75
O273 20c. on 3c. violet 9·00 7·75
O274 35c. on 3c. violet 9·00 7·75
O275 50c. on 3c. violet 9·00 7·75

1908. Fiscal stamps as T **50** surch as last but dated 1908.
O276 **50** 10c. on 1c. blue 55 35
O277 10c. on 2c. orange 75 30
O278 35c. on 1c. blue 55 35
O279 35c. on 2c. orange 80 45
O280 50c. on 1c. blue 55 35
O281 50c. on 2c. orange 80 45
O282 70c. on 2c. orange 80 45
O283 1p. on 1c. blue 23·00 23·00
O284 1p. on 2c. orange 80 45
O285 2p. on 1c. blue 65 55
O286 2p. on 2c. orange 80 45

1909. Stamps of 1905 optd **OFICIAL**.
O290 **37** 10c. lake 15 15
O291 15c. black 45 35
O292 20c. olive 70 55
O293 50c. green 1·10 70
O294 1p. yellow 1·25 90
O295 2p. red 1·75 1·40

1911. Stamps of 1905 optd **OFICIAL** and surch **Vale** and value.
O296 **37** 5c. on 3c. orange 3·75 3·75
O297 10c. on 4c. violet 3·00 3·00

1911. Railway tickets, surch **Timbre Fiscal Vale 10 ctvs.** further surch for official postal use. Printed in red. (a) Surch **Correo oficial Vale** and value on front.
O334 **64** 10c. on 10c. on 1st class 5·25 4·50
O335 15c. on 10c. on 1st class 5·25 4·50
O336 20c. on 10c. on 1st class 5·25 4·50
O337 50c. on 10c. on 1st class 7·00 6·25
O338 $1 on 10c. on 1st class 8·00 11·00
O339 $2 on 10c. on 1st class 11·50 16·00

(b) Surch **CORREO OFICIAL** and new value on front.
O340 **64** 10c. on 10c. on 1st class 30·00 27·00
O341 15c. on 10c. on 1st class 30·00 27·00
O342 20c. on 10c. on 1st class 30·00 28·00
O343 50c. on 10c. on 1st class 27·00 24·00

(c) No. 322 surch on front **Correo Oficial Vale 1911** and new value and with **15 cts.** on back obliterated by heavy bar.
O344 **64** 5c. on 10c. on 1st class 10·00 9·50
O345 10c. on 10c. on 1st class 11·50 11·00
O346 15c. on 10c. on 1st class 13·00 12·00
O347 20c. on 10c. on 1st class 15·00 18·00
O348 50c. on 10c. on 1st class 17·00 16·00

(d) No. 322 surch on front **Correo Oficial 1912** and new value and with the whole surch on back obliterated.
O349 **64** 5c. on 10c. on 1st class 12·00 9·50
O350 10c. on 10c. on 1st class 12·00 9·50
O351 15c. on 10c. on 1st class 12·00 9·50
O352 20c. on 10c. on 1st class 12·00 9·50
O353 25c. on 10c. on 1st class 12·00 9·50
O354 50c. on 10c. on 1st class 12·00 9·50
O355 $1 on 10c. on 1st class 12·00 9·50

1913. Stamps of 1912 optd **OFICIAL**.
O356 **70** 1c. blue 10 10
O357 2c. blue 10 10
O358 3c. blue 10 10
O359 4c. blue 10 10
O360 5c. blue 10 10
O361 6c. blue 10 15
O362 10c. blue 10 15
O363 15c. blue 10 15
O364 20c. blue 15 20
O365 25c. blue 15 15
O366 **71** 35c. blue 20 20
O367 **70** 50c. blue 1·10 1·10
O368 1p. blue 25 25
O369 2p. blue 25 25
O370 5p. blue 35 35

1915. Optd **OFICIAL**.
O406 **79** 1c. blue 15 15
O407 **80** 2c. blue 15 15
O408 **79** 3c. blue 15 15
O409 **80** 4c. blue 15 15
O410 **79** 5c. blue 15 15
O411 **80** 6c. blue 15 15
O412 10c. blue 15 15
O413 **79** 15c. blue 15 15
O414 **80** 20c. blue 15 15
O415 **79** 25c. blue 25 25
O416 **80** 50c. blue 45 45

1925. Optd **Oficial** or **OFICIAL**.
O513 **79** ½c. green 10 10
O514 1c. violet 10 10
O515 **80** 2c. red 10 10
O516 **79** 3c. olive 10 10
O517 **80** 4c. red 10 10
O518 **79** 5c. black 10 10
O519 **80** 6c. brown 10 10
O520 10c. yellow 10 10
O521 **79** 15c. brown 10 10
O522 **80** 20c. brown 10 10
O523 **79** 25c. orange 40 40
O524 **80** 50c. blue 45 45

1929. Air. Official stamps of 1925 additionally optd **Correo Aereo**.
O618 **79** 25c. orange 35 35
O619 **80** 50c. blue 55 55

1931. Stamp of 1924 surch **OFICIAL C$ 0.05 Correos 1928**.
O651 **99** 5c. on 10c. brown 25 25

1931. No. 648 additionally surch **OFICIAL** and value.
O652 **99** 5c. on 10c. brown 25 25

1931. Stamps of 1914 optd **1931** (except 6c., 10c.), and also optd **OFICIAL**.
O670 **79** 1c. olive (No. 762) 20 20
O707 **80** 2c. red 6·50 6·50
O671 **79** 3c. blue 20 20
O672 5c. sepia 20 20
O673 **80** 6c. brown 25 25
O675 10c. brown 25 25
O674 10c. blue (No. 697) 1·10 1·10
O710 **79** 15c. orange 70 70
O711 25c. sepia 70 70
O712 25c. violet 1·75 1·75

1932. Air. Optd **Correo Aereo OFICIAL** only.
O688 **79** 15c. orange 45 45
O689 **80** 20c. orange 50 50
O690 **79** 25c. violet 50 50
O691 **80** 50c. green 60 60
O692 1cor. yellow 60 60

1932. Air. Optd **1931 Correo Aereo OFICIAL**.
O693 **79** 25c. sepia 25·00 25·00

1932. Optd **OFICIAL**.
O694 **79** 1c. olive 10 10
O695 **80** 2c. red 10 10
O696 **79** 3c. blue 15 10
O697 **80** 4c. blue 15 10
O698 **79** 5c. sepia 15 15
O699 **80** 6c. brown 20 10
O700 10c. brown 30 25
O701 **79** 15c. orange 40 25
O702 **80** 20c. orange 40 30
O703 **79** 25c. violet 1·25 50
O704 **80** 50c. green 15 15
O705 1cor. yellow 20 20

1933. 441st Anniv of Columbus's Departure from Palos. As T **133**, but inscr "CORREO OFICIAL". Roul.
O777 1c. yellow 60 60
O778 2c. yellow 60 60
O779 3c. brown 60 60
O780 4c. brown 60 60
O781 5c. brown 60 60
O782 6c. blue 75 75
O783 10c. violet 75 75
O784 15c. purple 75 75
O785 20c. green 75 75
O786 25c. green 1·75 1·75
O787 50c. red 2·25 2·25
O788 1cor. red 3·50 3·50

1933. Optd with T **134** and **OFICIAL**.
O814 **79** 1c. green 10 10
O815 **80** 2c. red 10 10
O816 **79** 3c. blue 10 10
O817 **80** 4c. blue 10 10
O818 **79** 5c. brown 10 10
O819 **80** 6c. grey 10 10
O820 10c. brown 10 10
O821 **79** 15c. red 15 15
O822 **80** 20c. orange 15 15
O823 **79** 25c. violet 15 15
O824 **80** 50c. green 25 25
O825 1cor. yellow 50 45

1933. Air. Optd with T **134** and **CORREO Aereo OFICIAL**.
O826 **79** 15c. violet 20 20
O827 **80** 20c. green 20 20
O828 **79** 25c. olive 20 20
O829 **80** 50c. green 35 35
O830 1cor. red 60 50

1935. Nos. O814/25 optd **RESELLO – 1935** in a box.
O864 **79** 1c. green 10 10
O865 **80** 2c. red 10 10
O866 **79** 3c. blue 10 10
O867 **80** 4c. blue 10 10
O868 **79** 5c. brown 10 10
O869 **80** 6c. grey 10 10
O870 10c. brown 10 10
O871 **79** 15c. red 15 15
O872 **80** 20c. orange 15 15
O873 **79** 25c. violet 15 15
O874 **80** 50c. green 20 20
O875 1cor. yellow 35 35

1935. Air. Nos. O826/30 optd **RESELLO – 1935** in a box.
O877 **79** 15c. violet 30 25
O878 **80** 20c. green 30 25
O879 **79** 25c. olive 30 30
O880 **80** 50c. green 90 90
O881 1cor. red 90 90

(O 141)   O 151 Islets in the Great Lake

1937. Nos. 913, etc, optd with Type O **141**.
O935 **79** 1c. red 25 15
O936 **80** 2c. blue 25 15
O937 **79** 3c. brown 30 25
O938 5c. red 35 30
O939 **80** 10c. green 40 35
O940 **79** 15c. green 50 40
O941 25c. orange 60 45
O942 **80** 50c. brown 85 50
O943 1cor. blue 2·25 1·00

1937. Air. Nos. 926/30 optd with Type O **141**.
O944 **112** 15c. orange 50 35
O945 20c. red 50 35
O946 25c. black 50 45
O947 50c. violet 50 45
O948 1cor. orange 50 45

1939.
O1020 **O 151** 2c. red 15 15
O1021 3c. blue 15 15
O1022 6c. brown 15 15
O1023 7½c. green 15 15
O1024 10c. brown 15 15
O1025 15c. orange 15 15
O1026 25c. violet 30 30
O1027 50c. green 45 45

O **152** Pres. Somoza

1939. Air.
O1028 O **152** 10c. brown 30 30
O1029 15c. blue 30 30
O1030 20c. yellow 30 30
O1031 25c. violet 30 30
O1032 30c. red 30 30
O1033 50c. orange 40 40
O1034 1cor. olive 75 75

O **175** Managua Airport

1947. Air.
O1120 O **175** 5c. brown and black 15 10
O1121 – 10c. blue and black 15 15
O1122 – 15c. violet and black 15 10
O1123 – 20c. orange & black 20 10
O1124 – 25c. blue and black 15 15
O1125 – 50c. red and black 15 15
O1126 – 1cor. grey and black 40 35
O1127 – 2cor.50 brown and black 75 90
DESIGNS: 10c. Sulphur lagoon, Nejapa; 15c. Ruben Dario Monument, Managua; 20c. Baird's tapir; 25c. Genizaro Dam; 50c. Thermal baths, Tipitapa; 1cor. Highway and Lake Managua; 2cor.50, Franklin D. Roosevelt Monument, Managua.

O **181** U.P.U. Offices, Berne

1950. Air. 75th Anniv of U.P.U. Inscr as in Type O **181**. Frames in black.
O1159 – 5c. purple 10 10
O1160 – 10c. green 10 10
O1161 – 25c. purple 10 10
O1162 O **181** 50c. orange 15 10
O1163 – 1cor. blue 35 30
O1164 – 2cor.60 black . . . 2·10 1·75
MSO1165 Six sheets each 121 × 96 mm. Nos. O1159/64 in blocks of four . . . . 25·00 25·00
DESIGNS—HORIZ: 5c. Rowland Hill; 10c. Heinrich von Stephan; 25c. Standehaus, Berne; 1cor. Monument, Berne; 2cor.60, Congress Medal.

1961. Air. Consular Fiscal stamps as T **203/4** with serial Nos. in red, surch **Oficial Aereo** and value.
O1448 10c. on 1cor. olive 10 10
O1449 15c. on 20cor. brown . . . 10 10
O1450 20c. on 100cor. lake . . . 10 10
O1451 25c. on 50c. blue 15 10
O1452 35c. on 50cor. brown . . . 15 15
O1453 50c. on 3cor. red 15 15
O1454 1cor. on 2cor. green . . . 25 20
O1455 2cor. on 5cor. red 25 45
O1456 5cor. on 10cor. violet . . 60 60

POSTAGE DUE STAMPS

D **13** D **16**

1896.
D 99 D **13** 1c. orange . . . . . . 45 1·10
D100 2c. orange . . . . . . 45 1·10
D101 5c. orange . . . . . . 45 1·10
D102 10c. orange . . . . . 45 1·10
D103 20c. orange . . . . . 45 1·10
D104 30c. orange . . . . . 45 1·10
D105 50c. orange . . . . . 45 1·40

1897.
D108 D **13** 1c. violet . . . . . . 45 1·10
D109 2c. violet . . . . . . 45 1·10
D110 5c. violet . . . . . . 45 1·10
D111 10c. violet . . . . . 45 1·10
D112 20c. violet . . . . . 75 1·25
D113 30c. violet 45 90
D114 50c. violet 45 90

1898.
D124 D **13** 1c. green . . . . . . 15 1·25
D125 2c. green . . . . . . 15 1·25
D126 5c. green . . . . . . 15 1·25
D127 10c. green . . . . . 15 1·25
D128 20c. green . . . . . 15 1·25
D129 30c. green . . . . . . 15 1·25
D130 50c. green . . . . . . 15 1·25

1899.
D137 D **13** 1c. red . . . . 15 1·25
D138 2c. red . . . . 15 1·25
D139 5c. red . . . . 15 1·25
D140 10c. red . . . . . . 15 1·25
D141 20c. red . . . . . . 15 1·25
D142 50c. red . . . . . . 15 1·25

1900.
D146 D **16** 1c. red 70
D147 2c. orange 70
D148 5c. blue 70
D149 10c. violet 70
D150 20c. brown 70
D151 30c. green . . . . . 1·40
D152 50c. lake . . . . . . 1·40

NIGER Pt. 6, Pt. 14

Area south of the Sahara. In 1920 was separated from Upper Senegal and Niger to form a separate colony. From 1944 to 1959 used the stamps of French West Africa.

In 1958 Niger became an autonomous republic within the French Community and on 3 August 1960 an independent republic.

100 centimes = 1 franc.

1921. Stamps of Upper Senegal and Niger optd **TERRITOIRE DU NIGER**.
1 **7** 1c. violet and purple . . . . 30 2·75
2 2c. purple and grey . . . . . 15 3·25
3 4c. blue and black . . . . . 45 4·00
4 5c. chocolate and brown . . . 70 2·30
5 10c. green and light green . . 1·60 3·50
25 10c. pink on blue . . . . . 55 4·00
6 15c. yellow and brown . . . 60 2·75
7 20c. black and purple . . . . 75 3·00
8 25c. green and black . . . . 70 2·50
9 30c. carmine and red . . . . 2·50 4·50
26 30c. red and green . . . . . 30 3·75
10 35c. violet and red . . . . . 1·20 3·25
11 40c. red and grey . . . . . 80 4·00
12 45c. brown and blue . . . . 50 4·75
13 50c. blue and ultramarine . . 1·80 4·00
27 50c. blue and grey . . . . . 35 4·00
28 60c. red . . . . 75 3·75
14 75c. brown and yellow . . . 75 5·50
15 1f. purple and brown . . . . 1·00 4·00
16 2f. blue and green . . . . . 85 5·75
17 5f. black and violet . . . . . 1·30 5·50

1922. Stamps of 1921 surch.
18 **7** 25c. on 15c. yellow & brown 40 4·75
19 25c. on 2f. blue and green . . 1·60 4·25
20 25c. on 5f. black and violet 1·10 4·75
21 60 on 75c. violet on pink . . 10 3·00
22 65 on 45c. brown and blue 1·70 5·75
23 85c. on 75c. brown & yellow 1·40 6·25
24 1f.25 on 1f. light blue & blue 70 5·50

3 Wells **5** Zinder Fort

4 Canoe on River Niger

1926.
29 **3** 1c. green and purple . . . . 10 2·00
30 2c. red and grey . . . . . . 10 2·75
31 3c. brown and mauve . . . . 10 3·50
32 4c. black and brown . . . . 15 3·75
33 5c. green and red . . . . . 55 2·50
34 10c. green and blue 10 80
35 15c. light green and green . . 50 2·50
36 15c. red and lilac . . . . . . 10 2·75
37 **4** 20c. brown and blue . . . . 30 3·75
38 25c. pink and black . . . . . 90 2·30
39 30c. light green and green . . 2·00 3·75
40 30c. mauve and yellow . . . 1·00 3·50
41 35c. blue and red on blue . . 65 2·75
42 35c. green and deep green . . 1·70 4·75
43 40c. grey and purple . . . . 10 2·30
44 45c. mauve and yellow . . . 1·00 4·00
45 45c. green and turquoise . . 1·30 5·25
46 50c. green and red on green 20 30
47 55c. brown and red . . . . . 1·80 5·50
48 60c. brown and red . . . . . 55 5·00
49 65c. red and green . . . . . 1·10 4·00
50 70c. red and green . . . . . 1·80 5·50
51 75c. mauve and green on pink . . . . 1·40 3·50
52 80c. green and purple . . . . 2·00 5·25
53 90c. red and carmine . . . . 1·20 5·50
54 90c. green and red . . . . . 1·70 4·25
55 **5** 1f. green and red . . . . . . 5·50 10·00
56 1f. orange and red . . . . . 1·60 2·30
57 1f. red and green . . . . . . 1·40 4·75
58 1f.10 green and brown . . . . 5·00 8·25
59 1f.25 red and green . . . . . 2·30 2·50
60 1f.25 orange and red . . . . 2·75 5·75
61 1f.40 brown and mauve . . . 2·30 5·75
62 1f.50 light blue and blue . . 1·40 2·00
63 1f.60 green and brown . . . 2·00 5·75
64 1f.75 brown and mauve . . . 2·00 4·25
65 1f.75 ultramarine and blue . . 1·40 2·00
66 2f. brown and orange . . . . 1·60 2·00
67 2f.25 ultramarine and blue . . 1·80 4·50
68 2f.50 brown . . . . 2·75 4·50
69 3f. grey and mauve . . . . . 2·00 1·60
70 5f. black and purple on pink 1·10 2·50
71 10f. mauve and lilac . . . . 1·40 4·00
72 20f. orange and green . . . . 2·00 5·00

1931. "Colonial Exhibition" key types inscr "NIGER".
73 E 40c. green . . . . 5·00 9·50
74 F 50c. mauve . . . . 4·75 7·50
75 G 90c. red . . . . 1·50 11·00
76 H 1f.50 blue . . . . 6·75 11·00

4a

1937. International Exhibition, Paris.
77 **4a** 20c. violet . . . . 85 4·25
78 30c. green . . . . 90 5·00
79 40c. red . . . . 60 3·50
80 50c. brown and agate . . . 65 3·25
81 90c. red . . . . 80 3·25
82 1f.50 blue . . . . 50 3·50
MS82a 120 × 100 mm. 3f. mauve Imperf . . . . 9·25 17·00

1938. Int Anti-cancer Fund. As T **17a** of Oceanic Settlements.
83 1f.75+50c. blue . . . . 9·25 34·00

4b

1939. Caille.
84 **4b** 90c. orange . . . . 35 3·75
85 2f. violet . . . . 30 2·75
86 2f.25 blue . . . . 25 3·75

1939. New York World's Fair. As T **17b** of Oceanic Settlements.
87 1f.25 red . . . . 1·40 4·25
88 2f.25 blue . . . . 35 5·25

1939. 150th Anniv of French Revolution. As T **17c** of Oceanic Settlements.
89 45c.+25c. green and black . . 8·00 21·00
90 70c.+30c. brown and black . . 6·75 20·00
91 90c.+35c. orange and black . . 8·25 21·00
92 1f.25+1f. red and black . . . 7·75 21·00
93 2f.25+2f. blue and black . . . 8·75 21·00

4c

1940. Air.
94 **4c** 1f.90 blue . . . . 1·30 3·50
95 2f.90 red . . . . 75 3·50
96 4f.50 green . . . . 1·20 3·75
97 4f.90 olive . . . . 65 4·75
98 6f.90 orange . . . . 80 3·00

1941. National Defence Fund. Surch **SECOURS NATIONAL** and additional value.
98a **4** +1f. on 50c. green and red on green . . . . 5·00 6·25
98b +2f. on 80c. green & pur . . 7·75 12·50
98c **5** +2f. on 1f.50 lt blue & bl 14·50 18·00
98d +3f. on 2f. brown & orge 10·50 18·00

5a Zinder Fort **5c** "Vocation"

5b Weighing Baby

1942. Marshal Petain issue.
98e **5a** 1f. green . . . . 55 3·75
98f 2f.50 blue . . . . 55 3·75

1942. Air. Colonial Child Welfare Fund.
98g – 1f.50+3f.50 green . . . . 75 4·00
98h – 2f.+6f. brown . . . . . . 90 4·00
98i **5b** 3f.+9f. red . . . . 1·00 3·75
DESIGNS: 49 × 28 mm: 1f.50, Maternity Hospital, Dakar; 2f. Dispensary, Mopti.

1942. Air. Imperial Fortnight.
98j **5c** 1f.20+1f.80 blue and red . . 1·00 4·75

5e

1942. Air. As T **5e** but inscr "NIGER" at foot.
98k **5e** 50f. red and yellow . . . . 2·30 5·00

7 Giraffes

8 Carmine Bee Eater

1959. Wild Animals and Birds. Inscr "PROTECTION DE LA FAUNE".
99 – 50c. turquoise, green and black (postage) . . . . . 1·50 3·50
100 – 1f. multicoloured . . . . . 1·60 3·50
101 – 2f. multicoloured . . . . . 1·60 3·50
102 – 5f. mauve, black and brown 2·50 2·30
103 – 7f. red, black and green . . 3·50 3·50
104 – 10f. multicoloured . . . . . 2·75 2·75
105 – 15f. sepia and turquoise . . 3·00 2·75
106 – 20f. black and violet . . . . 2·75 2·30
107 **7** 25f. multicoloured . . . . . 3·50 2·00
108 30f. brown, bistre and green 3·00 2·50
109 – 50f. blue and brown . . . . 10·00 2·75
110 – 60f. sepia and green . . . . 14·00 5·00
111 – 85f. brown and bistre . . . 6·75 3·50
112 – 100f. bistre and green . . . 9·00 4·25
113 **8** 200f. multicoloured (air) . . 44·00 17·00
114 – 500f. green, brown and blue 21·00 16·00
DESIGNS—As Type **7**: HORIZ: 50c., 10f. African manatee. VERT: 1, 2f. Crowned cranes; 5, 7f. Saddle-bill stork; 15, 20f. Barbary sheep; 50, 60f. Ostriches; 85, 100f. Lion. As Type **8**: VERT: 500f. Game animals.

8a

1960. 10th Anniv of African Technical Co-operation Commission.
115 **8a** 25f. brown and ochre . . . 2·50 3·75

9 Conseil de l'Entente Emblem

11 Pres. Diori Hamani

1960. 1st Anniv of Conseil de l'Entente.
116 **9** 25f. multicoloured . . . . . 1·20 3·75

1960. Independence. No. 112 surch **200 F Independance 3-8-60**.
117 200f. on 100f. bistre and green . . . . 9·00 9·00

1960.
118 **11** 25f. black and bistre . . . 35 25

12 U.N. Emblem and Niger Flag

1961. Air. 1st Anniv of Admission into U.N.
119 **12** 25f. red, green and orange 40 25
120 100f. green, red and emerald . . . . 1·40 90

12a

1962. Air. "Air Afrique" Airline.
121 **12a** 100f. violet, black and brown . . . . 1·50 75

12b

1962. Malaria Eradication.
122 **12b** 25f.+5f. brown 45 45

13 Athletics

1962. Abidjan Games, 1961. Multicoloured.
123 15f. Boxing and cycling (vert) 25 15
124 25f. Basketball and football (vert) 35 20
125 85f. Type **13** . . . . 1·10 55

13a

1962. 1st Anniv of Union of African and Malagasy States.
126 **13a** 30f. mauve 40 30

14 Pres. Hamani and Map

1962. 4th Anniv of Republic.
127 **14** 25f. multicoloured 35 25

14a

1963. Freedom from Hunger.
128 **14a** 25f.+5f. purple, brn & olive 55 55

15 Running

17 Wood-carving

16 Agadez Mosque

1963. Dakar Games.
129 – 15f. brown and blue . . . 25 15
130 **15** 25f. red and brown 35 20
131 – 45f. black and green . . . 70 40
DESIGNS—HORIZ: 15f. Swimming. VERT: 45f. Volleyball.

1963. Air. 2nd Anniv of Admission to U.P.U. Multicoloured.
132 50f. Type **16** 75 40
133 85f. Gaya Bridge . . . . . . 1·25 60
134 100f. Presidential Palace, Niamey . . . . 1·25 70

1963. Traditional Crafts. Multicoloured.
135 5f. Type **17** (postage) 15 15
136 10f. Skin-tanning (horiz) . . 20 15
137 25f. Goldsmith 40 20
138 30f. Mat-making (horiz) . . . 60 30
139 85f. Potter . . . . 1·40 80
140 100f. Canoe building (horiz) (47 × 27 mm) (air) . . . . 2·00 1·10

17a

1963. Air. African and Malagasy Posts and Telecommunications Union.
141 **17a** 85f. multicoloured 95 55

1963. Air. Red Cross Centenary. Optd with cross and **Centenaire de la Croix-Rouge** in red.
142 **12** 25f. red, green and orange 60 40
143 100f. green, red and emerald . . . . 1·40 85

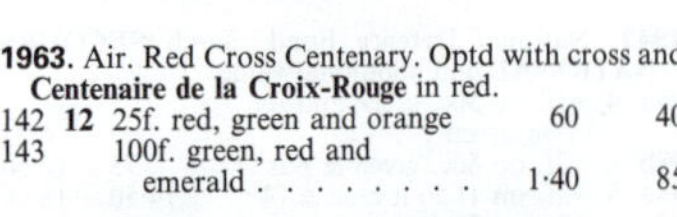

19 Costume Museum

1963. Opening of Costume Museum, Niamey. Vert costume designs. Multicoloured.
144 15f. Berber woman 20 15
145 20f. Haussa woman 35 15
146 25f. Tuareg woman 45 20
147 30f. Tuareg man 55 20
148 60f. Djerma woman . . . . 1·25 50
149 85f. Type **19** . . . . 1·50 60

20 "Europafrique"

1963. Air. European–African Economic Convention.
150 **20** 50f. multicoloured . . . . 2·50 2·00

21 Groundnut Cultivation

1963. Air. Groundnut Cultivation Campaign.
151 **21** 20f. blue, brown and green 35 20
152 – 45f. brown, blue and green 75 25
153 – 85f. multicoloured . . . . 1·40 65
154 – 100f. olive, brown and blue 1·50 90
DESIGNS: 45f. Camel transport; 85f. Fastening sacks; 100f. Dispatch of groundnuts by lorry.

21a

1963. Air. 1st Anniv of "Air Afrique" and DC-8 Service Inauguration.
155 **21a** 50f. multicoloured 70 45

22 Man and Globe

1963. 15th Anniv of Declaration of Human Rights.
156 **22** 25f. blue, brown and green 45 25

23 "Telstar"

1964. Air. Space Telecommunications.
157 **23** 25f. olive and violet . . . 40 20
158 – 100f. green and purple . . 1·10 80
DESIGN: 100f. "Relay".

24 "Parkinsonia aculeata"

25 Statue, Abu Simbel

1964. Flowers. Multicoloured.
159 5f. Type **24** 60 30
160 10f. "Russelia equisetiformis" 50 30
161 15f. "Lantana camara" . . . 1·00 45
162 20f. "Agryeia nervosa" . . . 1·00 45
163 25f. "Luffa cylindrica" . . . 1·00 45
164 30f. "Hibiscus rosa-sinensis" 1·40 60
165 45f. "Plumierai rubra" . . . 2·00 1·25
166 50f. "Catharanthus roseus" 2·00 1·25
167 60f. "Caesalpinia pulcherrima" . . . . . . 3·50 1·50

Nos. 164/7 have "REPUBLIQUE DU NIGER" at the top and the value at bottom right.

1964. Air. Nubian Monuments Preservation.
168 **25** 25f. green and brown . . . 65 45
169 30f. brown and blue . . . 1·00 70
170 50f. blue and purple . . . 2·00 1·25

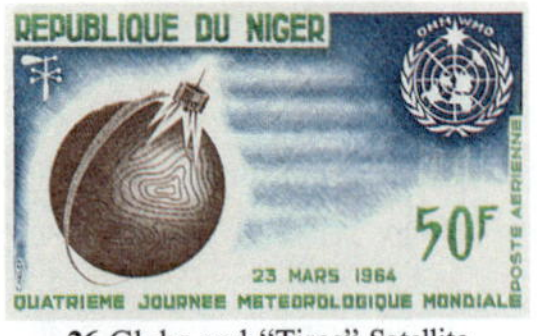
26 Globe and "Tiros" Satellite

1964. Air. World Meteorological Day.
171 **26** 50f. brown, blue and green 1·10 65

27 Sun Emblem and Solar Flares

28 Convoy of Lorries

1964. International Quiet Sun Years.
172 **27** 30f. red, violet and sepia 50 35

1964. O.M.N.E.S. (Nigerian Mobile Medical and Sanitary Organization) Commemoration.
173 **28** 25f. orange, olive and blue 40 20
174 – 30f. multicoloured 50 20
175 – 50f. multicoloured 80 30
176 – 60f. purple, orange & turq 90 35
DESIGNS: 30f. Tending children; 50f. Tending women; 60f. Open-air laboratory.

29 Rocket, Stars and Stamp Outline

1964. Air. "PHILATEC 1964" Int Stamp Exn, Paris.
177 **29** 50f. mauve and blue . . . 85 60

30 European, African and Symbols of Agriculture and Industry

31 Pres. Kennedy

1964. Air. 1st Anniv of European–African Economic Convention.
178 **30** 50f. multicoloured 65 40

1964. Air. Pres. Kennedy Commemoration.
179 **31** 100f. multicoloured . . . . 1·25 1·10

32 Water-polo

1964. Air. Olympic Games, Tokyo.
180 **32** 60f. brown, deep green and purple 60 50
181 – 85f. brown, blue and red 1·00 60
182 – 100f. blue, red and green 1·25 70
183 – 250f. blue, brown and green . . . . 2·50 1·75
DESIGNS—HORIZ: 85f. Relay-racing. VERT: 100f. Throwing the discus; 250f. Athlete holding Olympic Torch.

32a

1964. French, African and Malagasy Co-operation.
184 **32a** 50f. brown, orange and violet 65 40

33 Azawak Tuareg Encampment

1964. Native Villages. Multicoloured.
185 15f. Type **33** 20 20
186 20f. Songhai hut 25 20
187 25f. Wogo and Kourtey tents 30 20
188 30f. Djerma hut 40 25
189 60f. Sorkawa fishermen's encampment . . . . 1·00 30
190 85f. Hausa urban house . . . 1·25 50

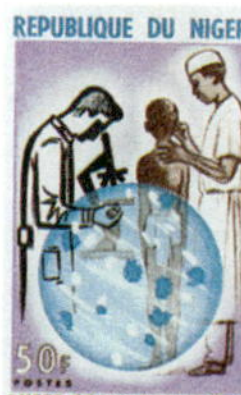

34 Doctors and Patient and Microscope Slide

35 Abraham Lincoln

1964. Anti-leprosy Campaign.
191 **34** 50f. multicoloured 50 45

1965. Death Centenary of Abraham Lincoln.
192 **35** 50f. multicoloured 60 50

36 Instruction by "Radio-Vision"

1965. "Human Progress". Inscr as in T **36**.
193 **36** 20f. brown, yellow and blue 30 20
194 – 25f. sepia, brown and green 35 20
195 – 30f. purple, red and green 45 25
196 – 50f. purple, blue and brown 70 35
DESIGNS: 25f. Student; 30f. Adult class; 50f. Five tribesmen ("Alphabetization").

37 Ader's Telephone

38 Pope John XXIII

1965. I.T.U. Centenary.
197 **37** 25f. black, lake and green 50 25
198 – 30f. green, purple and red 60 30
199 – 50f. green, purple and red 1·00 50
DESIGNS: 30f. Wheatstone's telegraph; 50f. "Telautographe".

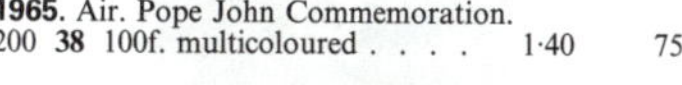

1965. Air. Pope John Commemoration.
200 **38** 100f. multicoloured . . . . 1·40 75

39 Hurdling

1965. 1st African Games, Brazzaville.
201 **39** 10f. purple, green & brown 20 15
202 – 15f. red, brown and grey 30 15
203 – 20f. purple, blue and green 40 20
204 – 30f. purple, green and lake 50 25
DESIGNS—VERT: 15f. Running; 30f. Long-jumping. HORIZ: 20f. Pole-vaulting.

40 "Capture of Cancer" (the Crab)

41 Sir Winston Churchill

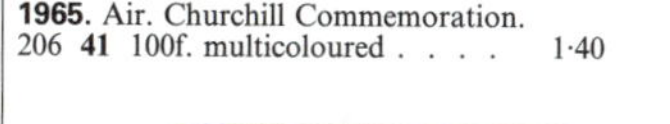

1965. Air. Campaign against Cancer.
205 **40** 100f. brown, black & green 1·40 80

1965. Air. Churchill Commemoration.
206 **41** 100f. multicoloured . . . . 1·40 80

42 Interviewing

1965. Radio Club Promotion.
207 **42** 30f. brown, violet and green 30 15
208 – 45f. red, black and buff . . 45 25
209 – 50f. multicoloured 55 30
210 – 60f. purple, blue and ochre 60 40
DESIGNS—VERT: 45f. Recording; 50f. Listening to broadcast. HORIZ: 60f. Listeners' debate.

43 "Agricultural and Industrial Workers"

44 Fair Scene and Flags

1965. Air. International Co-operation Year.
211 **43** 50f. brown, black and bistre 70 35

1965. Air. International Fair, Niamey.
212 **44** 100f. multicoloured . . . . 1·10 70

45 Dr. Schweitzer and Diseased Hands

1966. Air. Schweitzer Commemoration.
213 **45** 50f. multicoloured 80 45

46 "Water Distribution and Control"

1966. Int Hydrological Decade Inauguration.
214 **46** 50f. blue, orange and violet 70 35

47 Weather Ship "France I"

1966. Air. 6th World Meteorological Day.
215 **47** 50f. green, purple and blue 1·50 70

48 White and "Gemini" Capsule

1966. Air. Cosmonauts.
216 **48** 50f. black, brown and green 75 40
217 – 50f. blue, violet and orange 75 40
DESIGN: No. 217, Leonov and "Voskhod" capsule.

49 Head-dress and Carvings

1966. World Festival of Negro Arts, Dakar.
218 **49** 30f. black, brown and green 45 25
219 – 50f. violet, brown and blue 60 35
220 – 60f. lake, violet and brown 70 40
221 – 100f. black, red and blue 1·25 70
DESIGNS: 50f. Carved figures and mosaics; 60f. Statuettes, drums and arch; 100f. Handicrafts and church.

50 "Diamant" Rocket and Gantry

52 Cogwheel Emblem and Hemispheres

51 Goalkeeper saving Ball

1966. Air. French Space Vehicles. Multicoloured designs each showing different satellites.
222 45f. Type **50** 70 40
223 60f. "A 1" (horiz) 80 45
224 90f. "FR 1" (horiz) . . . . 1·00 50
225 100f. "D 1" (horiz) . . . . 1·50 75

1966. World Cup Football Championship.
226 – 30f. red, brown and blue 55 25
227 **51** 50f. brown, blue and green 75 35
228 – 60f. blue, purple and bistre 85 50
DESIGNS—VERT: 30f. Player dribbling ball; 60f. Player kicking ball.

1966. Air. Europafrique.
229 **52** 50f. multicoloured 70 45

53 Parachutist

1966. 5th Anniv of National Armed Forces. Mult.
230 20f. Type **53** 35 15
231 30f. Soldiers with standard (vert) 45 20
232 45f. Armoured patrol vehicle (horiz) 70 30

53a

1966. Air. Inauguration of DC-8F Air Services.
233 **53a** 30f. olive, black and grey 60 25

54 Inoculating cattle

1966. Campaign for Prevention of Cattle Plague.
234 **54** 45f. black, brown and blue 1·00 50

55 "Voskhod 1"

56 UNESCO "Tree"

1966. Air. Astronautics.
235 **55** 50f. blue, indigo and lake 65 35
236 – 100f. violet, blue and lake 1·25 75
DESIGN—HORIZ: 100f. "Gemini 6" and "7".

1966. 20th Anniv of UNESCO.
237 **56** 50f. multicoloured 70 25

57 Japanese Gate, Atomic Symbol and Cancer ("The Crab")

58 Furnace

1966. Air. International Cancer Congress, Tokyo.
238 **57** 100f. multicoloured . . . . 1·40 75

1966. Malbaza Cement Works.
239 **58** 10f. blue, orange and brown 15 10
240 – 20f. blue and green 30 15
241 – 30f. brown, grey and blue 45 20
242 – 50f. indigo, brown and blue 65 30
DESIGNS—HORIZ: 20f. Electrical power-house; 30f. Works and cement silos; 50f. Installation for handling raw materials.

59 Niamey Mosque

1967. Air.
243 **59** 100f. blue, green and grey 1·10 70

60 Durer (self-portrait)

1967. Air. Paintings. Multicoloured.
244 50f. Type **60** 80 60
245 100f. David (self-portrait) . . 1·50 90
246 250f. Delacroix (self-portrait) 3·00 2·00
See also Nos. 271/2 and 277/9.

61 Red-billed Hornbill

62 Bobsleigh Course, Villard-de-Lans

1967. Birds.
247 **61** 1f. bistre, red and green (postage) 25 20
248 – 2f. black, brown and green 25 20
249 – 30f. multicoloured . . . . 1·25 35
249a – 40f. purple, orange and green . . . . 1·40 60
250 – 45f. brown, green and blue . . . . 1·75 35
250a – 65f. yellow, brown & pur 2·00 80
251 – 70f. multicoloured . . . . 2·40 1·00
251a – 250f. blue, purple and green (48 × 27 mm) (air) 7·25 2·25
BIRDS: 2f. Lesser pied kingfishers; 30f. Common gonolek; 40f. Red bishop; 45f., 65f. Little masked weaver; 70f. Chestnut-bellied sandgrouse; 250f. Splendid glossy starlings.

1967. Grenoble—Winter Olympics Town (1968).
252 **62** 30f. brown, blue and green 40 25
253 – 45f. brown, blue and green 60 30
254 – 60f. brown, blue and green 80 50
255 – 90f. brown, blue and green 1·10 65
DESIGNS: 45f. Ski-jump, Autrans; 60f. Ski-jump, St. Nizier du Moucherotte; 90f. Slalom course, Chamrousse.

63 Family and Lions Emblem

64 Weather Ship

1967. 50th Anniv of Lions International.
256 **63** 50f. blue, red and green . . 60 35

1967. Air. World Meteorological Day.
257 **64** 50f. red, black and blue . . 1·50 70

65 View of World Fair

1967. Air. World Fair, Montreal.
258 **65** 100f. black, blue and purple . . . . 2·75 75

66 I.T.Y. Emblem and Jet Airliner

67 Scouts around Campfire

1967. International Tourist Year.
259 **66** 45f. violet, green and purple 45 35

1967. World Scout Jamboree, Idaho, U.S.A.
260 **67** 30f. brown, lake and blue 40 20
261 – 45f. blue, brown and orange 60 30
262 – 80f. lake, slate and bistre 1·25 50
DESIGNS—HORIZ: 45f. Jamboree emblem and scouts. VERT: 80f. Scout cooking meal.

68 Audio-Visual Centre

1967. Air. National Audio-Visual Centre, Niamey.
263 **68** 100f. violet, blue and green 90 50

69 Carrying Patient

70 "Europafrique"

1967. Nigerian Red Cross.
264 **69** 45f. black, red and green 60 20
265 – 50f. black, red and green 75 25
266 – 60f. black, red and green 1·00 35
DESIGNS: 50f. Nurse with mother and child; 60f. Doctor giving injection.

1967. Europafrique.
267 **70** 50f. multicoloured 60 30

71 Dr. Konrad Adenauer

72 African Women

71a

1967. Air. Adenauer Commemoration.
268 **71** 100f. brown and blue . . . 1·40 70

1967. Air. 5th Anniv of African and Malagasy Post and Telecommunications Union (U.A.M.P.T.).
270 **71a** 100f. violet, green and red 1·10 60

1967. Air. Death Centenary of Jean Ingres (painter). Paintings by Ingres. As T **60**. Multicoloured.
271 100f. "Jesus among the Doctors" (horiz) . . . . . 1·60 1·00
272 150f. "Jesus restoring the Keys to St. Peter" (vert) 2·25 1·50

1967. U.N. Women's Rights Commission.
273 **72** 50f. brown, yellow and blue 60 35

72a

73 Nigerian Children

1967. 5th Anniv of West African Monetary Union.
274 **72a** 30f. green and purple . . 35 20

1967. Air. 21st Anniv of UNICEF.
275 **73** 100f. brown, blue and green . . . . 1·25 95

74 O.C.A.M. Emblem

1968. Air. O.C.A.M. Conference, Niamey.
276 **74** 100f. orange, green and blue . . . . 1·10 60

1968. Air. Paintings (self-portraits). As T **60**. Multicoloured.
277 50f. J.-B. Corot 70 40
278 150f. Goya . . . . 1·90 1·00
279 200f. Van Gogh . . . . . . 2·50 1·50

75 Allegory of Human Rights

1968. Human Rights Year.
280 **75** 50f. indigo, brown and blue 60 30

76 Breguet 27 Biplane over Lake

1968. Air. 35th Anniv of 1st France–Niger Airmail Service.
281 **76** 45f. blue, green and mauve 95 35
282 – 80f. slate, brown and blue 1·60 55
283 – 100f. black, green and blue 2·50 75
DESIGNS—Potez 25TOE biplane: 80f. On ground; 100f. In flight.

77 "Joyous Health"

1968. 20th Anniv of W.H.O.
284 **77** 50f. indigo, blue and brown 60 35

78 Cyclists of 1818 and 1968

1968. Air. 150th Anniv of Bicycle.
285 **78** 100f. green and red . . . . 1·50 70

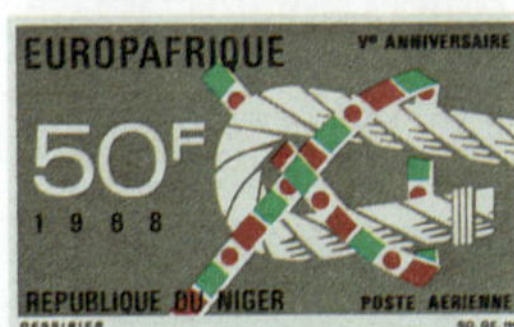

79 Beribboned Rope

1968. Air. 5th Anniv of Europafrique.
286 **79** 50f. multicoloured 65 40

80 Fencing

1968. Air. Olympic Games, Mexico.
287 **80** 50f. purple, violet and green 50 35
288 – 100f. black, purple and blue 85 50
289 – 150f. purple and orange . . 1·25 70
290 – 200f. blue, brown and green . . . . 1·75 1·25
DESIGNS—VERT: 100f. High-diving; 150f. Weight-lifting. HORIZ: 200f. Horse-jumping.

81 Woodland Kingfisher

1969. Birds. Dated "1968". Multicoloured.
292 5f. African grey hornbill (postage) 20 10
293 10f. Type **81** 30 15
294 15f. Senegal coucal 70 25
295 20f. Rose-ringed parakeets . . 85 45
296 25f. Abyssinian roller . . . . 1·10 60
297 50f. Cattle egret . . . . . . 1·60 85
298 100f. Violet starling (27 × 49 mm) (air) . . . . 3·50 1·75
See also Nos. 372/7, 567/8 and 714/15.

82 Mahatma Gandhi

1968. Air. "Apostles of Non-Violence".
299 **82** 100f. black and yellow . . 1·75 60
300 – 100f. black and turquoise 1·00 50
301 – 100f. black and grey . . . 1·00 50
302 – 100f. black and orange . . 1·00 50
PORTRAITS: No. 300, President Kennedy; No. 301, Martin Luther King; No. 302, Robert F. Kennedy.

82a "Pare, Minister of the Interior" (J. L. La Neuville)

1968. Air. "Philexafrique" Stamp Exhibition, Abidjan (Ivory Coast, 1969) (1st issue).
304 **82a** 100f. multicoloured . . . 1·60 1·60

83 Arms of the Republic

1968. Air. 10th Anniv of Republic.
305 **83** 100f. multicoloured . . . . 1·00 50

83a "Napoleon as First Consul" (Ingres)

1969. Air. Napoleon Bonaparte. Birth Bicentenary. Multicoloured.
306 50f. Type **83a** . . . . 1·50 90
307 100f. "Napoleon visiting the plague victims of Jaffa" (Gros) . . . . 2·50 1·25

308 150f. "Napoleon Enthroned" (Ingres) . . . . 3·50 1·75
309 200f. "The French Campaign" (Meissonier) 5·00 2·50

83b Giraffes and stamp of 1926

1969. Air. "Philexafrique" Stamp Exhibition, Abidjan, Ivory Coast (2nd issue).
310 **83b** 50f. brown, blue and orange . . . . 1·25 1·00

84 Boeing 707 over Rain-cloud and Anemometer

1969. Air. World Meteorological Day.
311 **84** 50f. black, blue and green 90 35

85 Workers supporting Globe

1969. 50th Anniv of I.L.O.
312 **85** 30f. red and green 40 20
313 50f. green and red 50 35

86 Panhard and Levassor (1909)

1969. Air. Veteran Motor Cars.
314 **86** 25f. green 45 20
315 – 45f. violet, blue and grey 55 25
316 – 50f. brown, ochre and grey 1·10 35
317 – 70f. purple, red and grey 1·50 45
318 – 100f. green, brown and grey . . . . 1·75 65
DESIGNS: 45f. De Dion Bouton 8 (1904); 50f. Opel "Doktor-wagen" (1909); 70f. Daimler (1910); 100f. Vermorel 12/16 (1912).

87 Mother and Child

88 Mouth and Ear

1969. 50th Anniv of League of Red Cross Societies.
319 **87** 45f. red, brown and blue 60 25
320 – 50f. red, grey and green . . 70 25
321 – 70f. red, brown and ochre 1·00 40
DESIGNS—VERT: 70f. Man with Red Cross parcel. HORIZ: 50f. Symbolic Figures, Globe and Red Crosses.

1969. 1st French Language Cultural Conf, Niamey.
322 **88** 100f. multicoloured . . . . 1·25 60

89 School Building

1969. National School of Administration.
323 **89** 30f. black, green and orange 30 20

1969. Air. 1st Man on the Moon. No. 114 optd **L'HOMME SUR LA LUNE JUILLET 1969 APOLLO 11** and moon module.
324 500f. green, brown and blue 6·50 6·50

91 "Apollo 8" and Rocket

1969. Air. Moon Flight of "Apollo 8". Embossed on gold foil.
325 **91** 1000f. gold . . . . 15·00 15·00

91a

1969. 5th Anniv of African Development Bank.
326 **91a** 30f. brown, green and violet 35 15

92 Child and Toys

1969. Air. International Toy Fair, Nuremburg.
327 **92** 100f. blue, brown and green . . . . 2·75 75

93 Linked Squares

1969. Air. "Europafrique".
328 **93** 50f. yellow, black and violet 55 30

94 Trucks crossing Sahara

1969. Air. 45th Anniv of "Croisiere Noire" Trans-Africa Expedition.
329 **94** 50f. brown, violet & mauve 75 35
330 – 100f. violet, red and blue 1·50 65
331 – 150f. multicoloured . . . . 2·00 1·25
332 – 200f. green, indigo and blue . . . . 3·00 1·50
DESIGNS: 100f. Crossing the mountains; 150f. African children and expedition at Lake Victoria; 200f. Route Map, European greeting African and Citroen truck.

94a Aircraft, Map and Airport

1969. 10th Anniv of Aerial Navigation Security Agency for Africa and Madagascar (A.S.E.C.N.A.).
333 **94a** 100f. red . . . . 1·50 70

95 Classical Pavilion

1970. National Museum.
334 **95** 30f. blue, green and brown 30 15
335 – 45f. blue, green and brown 45 25
336 – 50f. blue, brown and green 50 25
337 – 70f. brown, blue and green 70 40
338 – 100f. brown, blue and green . . . . 1·10 60
DESIGNS: 45f. Temporary exhibition pavilion; 50f. Audio-visual pavilion; 70f. Local musical instruments gallery; 100f. Handicrafts pavilion.

96 Niger Village and Japanese Pagodas

97 Hypodermic "Gun" and Map

1970. Air. "EXPO 70" World Fair, Osaka, Japan (1st issue).
339 **96** 100f. multicoloured 90 45

1970. One Hundred Million Smallpox Vaccinations in West Africa.
340 **97** 50f. blue, purple and green 70 30

98 Education Symbols

1970. Air. International Education Year.
341 **98** 100f. slate, red and purple 1·00 45

99 Footballer

1970. World Cup Football Championship, Mexico.
342 **99** 40f. green, brown and purple 60 25
343 – 70f. purple, brown and blue . . . . 1·00 40
344 – 90f. red and black . . . . 1·25 60
DESIGNS: 70f. Football and Globe; 90f. Two footballers.

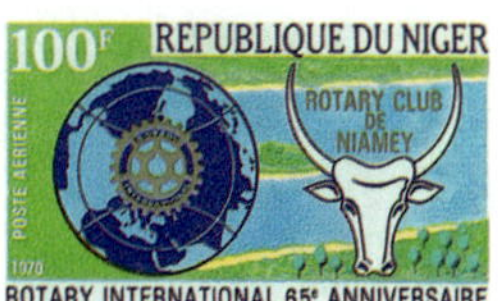

100 Rotary Emblems

1970. Air. 65th Anniv of Rotary International.
345 **100** 100f. multicoloured . . . 1·25 55

101 Bay of Naples and Niger Stamp

1970. Air. 10th "Europafrique" Stamp Exn, Naples.
346 **101** 100f. multicoloured . . . 1·00 60

102 Clement Ader's "Avion III" and Modern Airplane

1970. Air. Aviation Pioneers.
347 **102** 50f. grey, blue and red . . 70 25
348 – 100f. red, grey and blue 1·50 60
349 – 150f. lt brown, brn & grn 1·50 75
350 – 200f. red, bistre and violet 2·25 1·00
351 – 250f. violet, grey and red 3·50 1·40
DESIGNS: 100f. Joseph and Etienne Montgolfier balloon and rocket; 150f. Isaac Newton and gravity diagram; 200f. Galileo and rocket in planetary system; 250f. Leonardo da Vinci's drawing of a "flying machine" and Chanute's glider.

103 Cathode Ray Tube illuminating Books, Microscope and Globe

1970. Air. World Telecommunications Day.
352 **103** 100f. brown, green and red . . . . 1·25 50

1970. Inauguration of New U.P.U. Headquarters Building, Berne. As T **81** of New Caledonia.
353 30f. red, slate and brown . . 35 20
354 60f. violet, red and blue . . . 60 30

1970. Air. Safe Return of "Apollo 13". Nos. 348 and 350 optd **Solidarite Spatiale Apollo XIII 11-17 Avril 1970**.
355 100f. red, slate and blue . . . 1·00 50
356 200f. red, bistre and violet . . 1·75 75

105 U.N. Emblem, Man, Woman and Doves

1970. Air. 25th Anniv of U.N.O.
357 **105** 100f. multicoloured . . . 1·00 50
358 150f. multicoloured . . . 1·50 75

106 Globe and Heads

1970. Air. International French Language Conference, Niamey. Die-stamped on gold foil.
359 **106** 250f. gold and blue . . . 2·50 2·50

107 European and African Women

1970. Air. "Europafrique".
360 **107** 50f. red and green 55 30

108 Japanese Girls and "EXPO 70" Skyline

1970. Air. "EXPO 70" World Fair, Osaka, Japan. (2nd issue).
361 **108** 100f. purple, orange & grn 90 40
362 – 150f. blue, brown & green 1·25 60
DESIGN: 150f. "No" actor and "EXPO 70" by night.

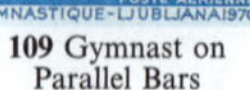

109 Gymnast on Parallel Bars   **111** Beethoven, Keyboard and Manuscripts

1970. Air. World Gymnastic Championships, Ljubljiana.
363 **109** 50f. blue 50 30
364 – 100f. green . . . . 1·10 55
365 – 150f. purple . . . . . . 1·75 75
366 – 200f. red . . . . 2·00 95
GYMNASTS—HORIZ: 100f. Gymnast on vaulting-horse; 150f. Gymnast in mid-air. VERT: 200f. Gymnast on rings.

1970. Air. Moon Landing of "Luna 16". Nos. 349 and 351 surch **LUNA 16 – Sept. 1970 PREMIERS PRELEVEMENTS AUTOMATIQUES SUR LA LUNE** and value.
367 100f. on 150f. light brown, brown and green . . . . . 1·10 50
368 200f. on 250f. violet, grey and red . . . . 2·40 1·00

1970. Air. Birth Bicentenary of Beethoven. Mult.
369 100f. Type **111** . . . . . . 1·40 55
370 150f. Beethoven and allegory, "Hymn of Joy" . . . . . 2·25 85

112 John F. Kennedy Bridge, Niamey

1970. Air. 12th Anniv of Republic.
371 **112** 100f. multicoloured . . . 1·10 45

1971. Birds. Designs similar to T **81**. Variously dated between 1970 and 1972. Multicoloured.
372 5f. African grey hornbill . . 65 30
373 10f. Woodland kingfisher . . 85 30
374 15f. Senegal coucal . . . . . 1·75 1·00
375 20f. Rose-ringed parakeet . . 2·10 1·00
376 35f. Broad-tailed paradise whydah . . . . 3·00 1·50
377 50f. Cattle egret . . . . . . 3·75 2·75
The Latin inscription on No. 377 is incorrect, reading "Bulbucus ibis" instead of "Bubulcus ibis".
See also Nos. 714/15.

114 Pres. Nasser

1971. Air. Death of Pres. Gamal Nasser (Egyptian statesman). Multicoloured.
378 100f. Type **114** 75 40
379 200f. Nasser waving . . . . 1·50 75

115 Pres. De Gaulle

1971. Air. De Gaulle Commemoration. Embossed on gold foil.
380 **115** 1000f. gold . . . . 38·00 38·00

116 "MUNICH" and Olympic Rings

1971. Air. Publicity for 1972 Olympic Games, Munich.
381 **116** 150f. purple, blue & green 1·25 70

117 "Apollo 14" leaving Moon   **118** Symbolic Masks

1971. Air. Moon Mission of "Apollo 14".
382 **117** 250f. green, orange & blue 2·25 1·25

1971. Air. Racial Equality Year.
383 **118** 100f. red, green and blue 90 40
384 – 200f. brown, green & blue 1·75 80
DESIGN: 200f. "Peoples" and clover-leaf emblem.

119 Niamey on World Map

1971. 1st Anniv of French-speaking Countries Co-operative Agency.
385 **119** 40f. multicoloured 50 25

120 African Telecommunications Map

1971. Air. Pan-African Telecommunications Network.
386 **120** 100f. multicoloured . . . 75 40

121 African Mask and Japanese Stamp

1971. Air. "PHILATOKYO 71" International Stamp Exhibition, Japan.
387 **121** 50f. olive, purple and green 65 30
388 – 100f. violet, red and green 1·10 45
DESIGN: 100f. Japanese scroll painting and Niger stamp.

122 "Longwood House, St. Helena" (C. Vernet)

1971. Air. 150th Anniv of Napoleon's Death. Paintings. Multicoloured.
389 150f. Type **122** . . . . . . 1·75 70
390 200f. "Napoleon's Body on his Camp-bed" (Marryat) 2·50 90

123 Satellite, Radio Waves, and Globe

1971. Air. World Telecommunications Day.
391 **123** 100f. multicoloured . . . 1·10 50

124 Pierre de Coubertin and Discus-throwers

1971. Air. 75th Anniv of Modern Olympic Games.
392 **124** 50f. red and blue 50 25
393 – 100f. multicoloured . . . 90 40
394 – 150f. blue and purple . . 1·40 65
DESIGNS—VERT: 100f. Male and female athletes holding torch. HORIZ: 150f. Start of race.

125 Scout Badges and Mount Fuji

1971. 13th World Scout Jamboree, Asagiri, Japan.
395 **125** 35f. red, purple and orange 40 20
396 – 40f. brown, plum and green 45 20
397 – 45f. green, red and blue 60 25
398 – 50f. green, violet and red 70 30
DESIGNS—VERT: 40f. Scouts and badge; 45f. Scouts converging on Japan. HORIZ: 50f. "Jamboree" in rope, and marquee.

126 "Apollo 15" on Moon

1971. Air. Moon Mission of "Apollo 15".
399 **126** 150f. blue, violet & brown 1·50 70

127 Linked Maps

1971. 2nd Anniv of Renewed "Europafrique" Convention, Niamey.
400 **127** 50f. multicoloured 60 30

128 Gouroumi (Hausa)   **129** De Gaulle in Uniform

1971. Musical Instruments.
401 **128** 25f. brown, green and red 30 10
402 – 30f. brown, violet & green 35 15
403 – 35f. blue, green and purple 35 25
404 – 40f. brown, orange & grn 45 25
405 – 45f. ochre, brown and blue 55 35
406 – 50f. brown, red and black 95 45
DESIGNS: 30f. Molo (Djerma); 35f. Garaya (Hausa); 40f. Godjie (Djerma-Sonrai); 45f. Inzad (Tuareg); 50f. Kountigui (Sonrai).

1971. Air. 1st Death Anniv of Gen. Charles De Gaulle (French statesman).
407 **129** 250f. multicoloured . . . 5·00 4·00

129a U.A.M.P.T. H.Q. and Rural Scene

1971. Air. 10th Anniv of African and Malagasy Posts and Telecommunications Union.
408 **129a** 100f. multicoloured . . . 90 45

130 "Audience with Al Hariri" (Baghdad, 1237)

1971. Air. Moslem Miniatures. Multicoloured.
409 100f. Type **130** . . . . . . 1·00 45
410 150f. "Archangel Israfil" (Iraq, 14th-cent) (vert) . . 1·50 70
411 200f. "Horsemen" (Iraq, 1210) . . . . 2·25 1·25

131 Louis Armstrong   **132** "Children of All Races"

1971. Air. Death of Louis Armstrong (American jazz musician). Multicoloured.
412 100f. Type **131** . . . . . . 1·50 55
413 150f. Armstrong playing trumpet . . . . 2·00 85

1971. 25th Anniv of UNICEF.
414 **132** 50f. multicoloured 60 45

133 "Adoration of the Magi" (Di Bartolo)

1971. Air. Christmas. Paintings. Multicoloured.
415 100f. Type **133** . . . . . . 1·00 45
416 150f. "The Nativity" (D. Ghirlandaio) (vert) . . 1·50 70
417 200f. "Adoration of the Shepherds" (Perugino) . . 2·00 1·00

134 Presidents Pompidou and Hamani

1972. Air. Visit of Pres. Pompidou of France.
418 **134** 250f. multicoloured . . . 4·75 3·50

135 Ski "Gate" and Cherry Blossom

1972. Air. Winter Olympic Games, Sapporo, Japan.
419 **135** 100f. violet, red and green . . . 90 40
420 – 150f. red, purple and violet . . . . 1·25 70
DESIGN—HORIZ: 150f. Snow crystals and Olympic flame.

135a "The Masked Ball"

1972. Air. UNESCO "Save Venice" Campaign.
422 **135a** 50f. multicoloured (vert) 50 25
423 – 100f. multicoloured (vert) 1·00 45
424 – 150f. multicoloured (vert) 1·50 70
425 – 200f. multicoloured . . . 2·00 1·00
DESIGNS: Nos. 422/5 depict various details of Guardi's painting, "The Masked Ball".

136 Johannes Brahms and Music
137 Saluting Hand

1972. Air. 75th Death Anniv of Johannes Brahms (composer).
426 **136** 100f. green, myrtle and red . . . . 1·50 55

1972. Air. Int Scout Seminar, Cotonou, Dahomey.
427 **137** 150f. violet, blue & orange . . . . 1·50 60

138 Star Symbol and Open Book

1972. International Book Year.
428 **138** 35f. purple and green . . 35 20
429 – 40f. blue and lake . . . . 1·40 35
DESIGN: 40f. Boy reading, 16th-century galleon and early aircraft.

139 Heart Operation

1972. Air. World Heart Month.
430 **139** 100f. brown and red . . . 1·50 55

140 Bleriot XI crossing the Channel, 1909

1972. Air. Milestones in Aviation History.
431 **140** 50f. brown, blue and lake 1·10 50
432 – 75f. grey, brown and blue 1·75 60
433 – 100f. ultramarine, blue and purple . . . . . . 3·25 1·40
DESIGNS: 75f. Lindbergh crossing the Atlantic in "Spirit of St. Louis"; 100f. First flight of Concorde, 1969.

141 Satellite and Universe

1972. Air. World Telecommunications Day.
434 **141** 100f. brown, purple & red 1·10 45

142 Boxing

1972. Air. Olympic Games, Munich. Sports and Munich Buildings.
435 **142** 50f. brown and blue . . . 50 20
436 – 100f. brown and green . . 75 40
437 – 150f. brown and red . . . 1·25 60
438 – 200f. brown and mauve 1·75 85
DESIGNS—VERT: 100f. Long-jumping; 150f. Football. HORIZ: 200f. Running.

143 A. G. Bell and Telephone

1972. Air. 50th Death Anniv of Alexander Graham Bell (inventor of telephone).
440 **143** 100f. blue, purple and red 1·10 55

144 "Europe on Africa" Map

1972. Air. "Europafrique" Co-operation.
441 **144** 50f. red, green and blue 50 25

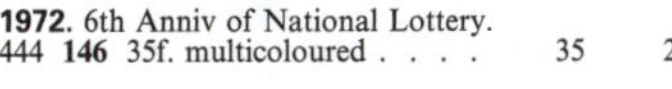

145 Herdsman and Cattle
146 Lottery Wheel

1972. Medicinal Salt-ponds at In-Gall. Multicoloured.
442 35f. Type **145** 50 25
443 40f. Cattle in salt-pond . . . 60 25

1972. 6th Anniv of National Lottery.
444 **146** 35f. multicoloured 35 25

147 Postal Runner

1972. Air. U.P.U. Day. Postal Transport.
445 **147** 50f. brown, green and lake 60 25
446 – 100f. green, blue and lake 90 45
447 – 150f. green, violet and lake . . . . 1·75 70
DESIGNS: 100f. Rural mail van; 150f. Loading Fokker Friendship mail plane.

147a

1972. 10th Anniv of West African Monetary Union.
448 **147a** 40f. grey, violet and brown 40 25

1972. Air. Gold Medal Winners. Munich Olympic Games. Nos. 435/8 optd with events and names, etc.
449 **142** 50f. brown and blue . . . 50 20
450 – 100f. brown and green . . 85 40
451 – 150f. brown and red . . . 1·40 60
452 – 200f. brown and mauve 1·75 80
OVERPRINTS: 50f. **WELTER CORREA MEDAILLE D'OR**; 100f. **TRIPLE SAUT SANEIEV MEDAILLE D'OR**; 150f. **FOOTBALL POLOGNE MEDAILLE D'OR**; 200f. **MARATHON SHORTER MEDAILLE D'OR**.

148 "The Raven and the Fox"

1972. Air. Fables of Jean de la Fontaine.
453 **148** 25f. black, brown & green 1·10 40
454 – 50f. brown, green & purple 60 25
455 – 75f. brown, green & brown . . . . 1·00 45
DESIGNS: 50f. "The Lion and the Rat"; 75f. "The Monkey and the Leopard".

149 Astronauts on Moon

1972. Air. Moon Flight of "Apollo 17".
456 **149** 250f. multicoloured . . . 2·75 1·25

150 Dromedary Race

1972. Niger Sports.
457 **150** 35f. purple, red and blue 75 40
458 – 40f. lake, brown and green . . . . 1·00 60
DESIGN: 40f. Horse race.

151 Pole Vaulting
153 Knight and Pawn

152 "Young Athlete"

1973. 2nd African Games, Lagos, Nigeria. Mult.
459 35f. Type **151** 30 25
460 40f. Basketball 35 25
461 45f. Boxing 45 25
462 75f. Football 70 45

1973. Air. Antique Art Treasures.
463 **152** 50f. red 50 25
464 – 100f. violet . . . . 1·00 40
DESIGN: 100f. "Head of Hermes".

1973. World Chess Championships, Reykjavik, Iceland.
465 **153** 100f. green, blue and red 2·50 1·00

154 "Abutilon pannosum"
155 Interpol Badge

1973. Rare African Flowers. Multicoloured.
466 30f. Type **154** 70 30
467 45f. "Crotalaria barkae" . . 80 30
468 60f. "Dichrostachys cinerea" 1·40 45
469 80f. "Caralluma decaisneana" 1·60 55

1973. 50th Anniv of International Criminal Police Organization (Interpol).
470 **155** 50f. multicoloured 85 30

156 Scout with Radio

1973. Air. Scouting in Niger.
471 **156** 25f. brown, green and red 25 20
472 – 50f. brown, green and red 55 25
473 – 100f. brown, green and red . . . . 1·25 50
474 – 150f. brown, green and red . . . . 2·25 90
DESIGNS: 50f. First aid; 100f. Care of animals; 150f. Care of the environment.

157 Hansen and Microscope
158 Nurse tending Child

1973. Centenary of Dr. Hansen's Discovery of Leprosy Bacillus.
475 **157** 50f. brown, green and blue 85 35

1973. 25th Anniv of W.H.O.
476 **158** 50f. brown, red and blue 65 25

159 "The Crucifixion" (Hugo van der Goes)

1973. Air. Easter. Paintings. Multicoloured.
477 50f. Type **159** 55 25
478 100f. "The Deposition" (Cima de Conegliano) (horiz) . . . . 1·10 50
479 150f. "Pieta" (Bellini) (horiz) 1·60 65

160 Douglas DC-8 and Mail Van

1973. Air. Stamp Day.
480 **160** 100f. brown, red and green . . . . 1·50 55

161 W.M.O. Emblem and "Weather Conditions"

1973. Air. Centenary of W.M.O.
481 **161** 100f. brown, red and green . . . . 1·10 45

162 "Crouching Lioness" (Delacroix)

1973. Air. Paintings by Delacroix. Multicoloured.
482 150f. Type **162** . . . . . . 2·00 1·00
483 200f. "Tigress and Cub" . . 3·25 1·50

163 Crocodile

1973. Wild Animals from "Park W".
484 **163** 25f. multicoloured 45 20
485 – 35f. grey, gold and black 75 30
486 – 40f. multicoloured 75 30
487 – 80f. multicoloured . . . . 1·25 50
DESIGNS: 35f. African elephant; 40f. Hippopotamus; 80f. Warthog.

164 Eclipse over Mountain

1973. Total Eclipse of the Sun.
488 **164** 40f. violet 60 30

1973. Air. 24th International Scouting Congress, Nairobi, Kenya. Nos. 473/4 optd **24 Conference Mondiale du Scoutisme NAIROBI 1973**.
489 100f. brown, green and red 1·00 40
490 150f. brown, green and red 2·00 90

166 Palomino

1973. Horse-breeding. Multicoloured.
491 50f. Type **166** 90 30
492 75f. French trotter . . . . . 1·40 40
493 80f. English thoroughbred . . 1·50 55
494 100f. Arab thoroughbred . . 2·00 65

1973. Pan-African Drought Relief. African Solidarity. No. 436 surch **SECHERESSE SOLIDARITE AFRICAINE** and value.
495 **145** 100f. on 35f. multicoloured . . . . . 1·40 1·00

168 Rudolf Diesel and Oil Engine

1973. 60th Death Anniv of Rudolf Diesel (engineer).
496 **168** 25f. blue, purple and grey 80 45
497 – 50f. grey, green and blue 1·40 65
498 – 75f. blue, black and mauve . . . . 2·10 1·00
499 – 125f. blue, red and green 3·50 1·25
DESIGNS: 50f. Series "BB 100" diesel locomotive; 75f. Type "060-DB1" diesel locomotive, France; 125f. Diesel locomotive No. 72004, France.

168a

1973. African and Malagasy Posts and Telecommunications Union.
500 **168a** 100f. red, green and brown 75 50

168b African Mask and Old Town Hall, Brussels

171 "Apollo"

1973. Air. African Fortnight, Brussels.
501 **168b** 100f. purple, blue and red . . . . 1·00 50

169 T.V. Set and Class

1973. Schools Television Service.
502 **169** 50f. black, red and blue 60 30

1973. 3rd International French Language and Culture Conf, Liege. No. 385 optd **3e CONFERENCE DE LA FRANCOPHONIE LIEGE OCTOBRE 1973**.
503 **110** 40f. multicoloured 50 25

1973. Classical Sculptures.
504 **171** 50f. green and brown . . 60 30
505 – 50f. black and brown . . 60 30
506 – 50f. brown and red . . . 60 30
507 – 50f. purple and red . . . 60 30
DESIGNS: No. 505, "Atlas"; No. 506, "Hercules"; No. 507, "Venus".

172 Bees and Honeycomb

1973. World Savings Day.
508 **172** 40f. brown, red and blue 45 25

173 "Food for the World"

1973. Air. 10th Anniv of World Food Programme.
509 **173** 50f. violet, red and blue 60 30

174 Copernicus and "Sputnik 1"

175 Pres. John Kennedy

1973. Air. 500th Birth Anniv of Copernicus (astonomer).
510 **174** 150f. brown, blue and red 1·40 70

1973. Air. 10th Death Anniv of U.S. President Kennedy.
511 **175** 100f. multicoloured . . . 1·00 50

176 Kounta Songhai Blanket

178 Lenin

177 Barges on River Niger

1973. Niger Textiles. Multicoloured.
513 35f. Type **176** 50 30
514 40f. Tcherka Snghai blanket (horiz) 70 40

1974. Air. 1st Anniv of Ascent of Niger by "Fleet of Hope".
515 **177** 50f. blue, green and red 75 35
516 – 75f. purple, blue and green . . . . 1·00 45
DESIGN: 75f. "Barban Maza" (tug) and barge.

1974. Air. 50th Death Anniv of Lenin.
517 **178** 50c. brown 50 30

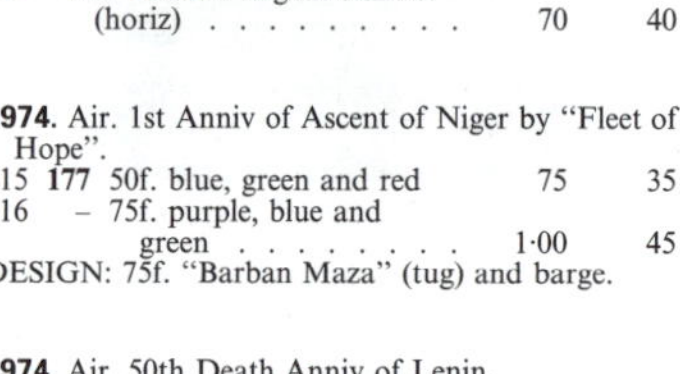

179 Slalom Skiing

1974. Air. 50th Anniv of Winter Olympic Games.
518 **179** 200f. red, brown and blue 2·50 1·00

180 Newly-born Baby

1974. World Population Year.
519 **180** 50f. multicoloured 50 25

181 Footballers and "Global" Ball

1974. Air. World Cup Football Championship, West Germany.
520 **181** 75f. violet, black & brown 65 35
521 – 150f. brown, green & turq 1·40 55
522 – 200f. blue, orange & green 1·75 1·00
DESIGNS: 150, 200f. Football scenes similar to Type **181**.

182 "The Crucifixion" (Grunewald)

1974. Air. Easter. Paintings. Multicoloured.
524 50f. Type **182** 50 25
525 75f. "Avignon Pieta" (attributed to E. Quarton) 75 35
526 125f. "The Entombment" (G. Isenmann) . . . . . . 1·25 65

183 Class 230K Locomotive, 1948, France and Locomotive No. 5511, 1938, U.S.A.

1974. Famous Railway Locomotives of the Steam Era.
527 **183** 50f. green, black and violet . . . . 1·25 40
528 – 75f. green, black & brown 1·90 55
529 – 100f. multicoloured . . . 2·50 85
530 – 150f. brown, black and red . . . . 3·75 1·25
DESIGNS: 75f. Class 21 locomotive, 1893, France; 100f. Locomotive, 1866, U.S.A. and "Mallard", Great Britain; 150f. Marc Seguin locomotive, 1829, France and Stephenson's "Rocket", 1829.

184 Map of Member Countries

1974. 15th Anniv of Conseil de l'Entente.
531 **184** 40f. multicoloured 40 20

185 Knights

1974. Air. 21st Chess Olympiad, Nice.
532 **185** 50f. brown, blue & indigo 1·25 65
533 – 75f. purple, brown & green . . . . 1·75 75
DESIGN: 75f. Kings.

186 Marconi and "Elettra" (steam yacht)

1974. Birth Centenary of Guglielmo Marconi (radio pioneer).
534 **186** 50f. blue, brown & mauve 50 30

187 Astronaut on Palm of Hand

1974. Air. 5th Anniv of 1st Landing on Moon.
535 **187** 150f. brown, blue & indigo . . . . 1·25 60

188 Tree on Palm of Hand

190 Camel Saddle

189 "The Rhinoceros" (Longhi)

1974. National Tree Week.
536 **188** 35f. turquoise, grn & brn 40 30

1974. Air. Europafrique.
537 **189** 250f. multicoloured . . . 5·00 3·00

1974. Handicrafts.
538 **190** 40f. red, blue and brown 45 20
539 – 50f. blue, red and brown 55 30
DESIGN: 50f. Statuettes of horses.

192 Frederic Chopin

1974. 125th Death Anniv of Frederic Chopin.
541 **192** 100f. black, red and blue 1·50 55

1974. Beethoven's Ninth Symphony Commemoration. As T **192**.
542 100f. lilac, blue and indigo 1·50 55
DESIGN: 100f. Beethoven.

193 European Woman and Douglas DC-8 Airliners

194 "Skylab" over Africa

1974. Air. Centenary of U.P.U.
543 **193** 50f. turquoise, grn & pur 50 25
544 – 100f. blue, mauve & ultram . . . . 2·25 75
545 – 150f. brown, blue & indigo . . . . 1·50 80
546 – 200f. brown, orange & red 1·60 1·25
DESIGNS: 100f. Japanese woman and electric locomotives; 150f. American Indian woman and liner; 200f. African woman and road vehicles.

1974. Air. "Skylab" Space Laboratory.
547 **194** 100f. violet, brown & blue 1·00 45

195 Don-don Drum

197 "Virgin and Child" (Correggio)

196 Tree and Compass Rose

1974.
548 **195** 60f. purple, green and red 90 45

1974. 1st Death Anniv of Tenere Tree (desert landmark).
549 **196** 50f. brown, blue and ochre . . . . 2·00 1·00

1974. Air. Christmas. Multicoloured.
550 100f. Type **197** . . . . . . 1·00 35
551 150f. "Virgin and Child, and St. Hilary" (F. Lippi) . . . 1·50 55
552 200f. "Virgin and Child" (Murillo) . . . . 2·00 95

198 "Apollo" Spacecraft

1975. Air. "Apollo–Soyuz" Space Test Project.
553 **198** 50f. green, red and blue 50 25
554 – 100f. grey, red and blue 80 40
555 – 150f. purple, plum & blue 1·25 60
DESIGNS: 100f. "Apollo" and "Soyuz" docked; 150f. "Soyuz" spacecraft.

199 European and African Women

1975. Air. Europafrique.
556 **199** 250f. brown, purple & red 2·25 1·75

200 Communications Satellite and Weather Map

1975. World Meteorological Day.
557 **200** 40f. red, black and blue 40 20

201 "Christ in the Garden of Olives" (Delacroix)

1975. Air. Easter. Multicoloured.
558 75f. Type **201** 65 35
559 125f. "The Crucifixion" (El Greco) (vert) . . . . . 1·10 50
560 150f. "The Resurrection" (Limousin) (vert) . . . . . 1·25 75

202 Lt-Col. S. Kountche, Head of State

1975. Air. 1st Anniv of Military Coup.
561 **202** 100f. multicoloured . . . 1·00 50

203 "City of Truro", 1903, Great Britain

1975. Famous Locomotives. Multicoloured.
562 50f. Type **203** . . . . 1·25 35
563 75f. Class 05 steam locomotive No. 003, 1937, Germany . . . . 1·60 50
564 100f. "General", 1855, U.S.A. (dated "1863") . . . . . 2·50 75
565 125f. Series BB 15000 electric locomotive, 1971, France 3·00 90

1975. Birds. As Nos. 296 and 298, but dated "1975". Multicoloured.
567 25f. Abyssinian roller (postage) . . . . 1·25 35
568 100f. Violet starlings (air) . . 3·25 90

205 "Zabira" Leather Bag

1975. Niger Handicrafts. Multicoloured.
569 35f. Type **205** 30 20
570 40f. Chequered rug 45 25
571 45f. Flower pot 50 30
572 60f. Gourd 75 35

206 African Woman and Child

1975. International Women's Year.
573 **206** 50f. blue, brown and red 75 50

207 Dr. Schweitzer and Lambarene Hospital

1975. Birth Centenary of Dr. Albert Schweitzer.
574 **207** 100f. brown, green & black . . . . 1·00 55

208 Peugeot, 1892

1975. Early Motor-cars.
575 **208** 50f. blue and mauve . . . 60 30
576 – 75f. purple and blue . . . 1·00 40
577 – 100f. mauve and green . . 1·40 60
578 – 125f. green and red . . . 1·50 70
DESIGNS: 75f. Daimler, 1895; 100f. Fiat, 1899; 125f. Cadillac, 1903.

209 Tree and Sun

1975. National Tree Week.
579 **209** 40f. green, orange and red 40 25

210 Boxing

1975. Traditional Sports.
580 **210** 35f. brown, orange & black 35 20
581 – 40f. brown, green & black 40 20
582 – 45f. brown, blue and black 50 25
583 – 50f. brown, red and black 55 30
DESIGNS—VERT: 40f. Boxing; 50f. Wrestling. HORIZ: 45f. Wrestling.

211 Leontini Tetradrachme

1975. Ancient Coins.
584 **211** 50f. grey, blue and red . . 60 20
585 – 75f. grey, blue and mauve 85 30
586 – 100f. grey, orange and blue . . . . 1·25 40
587 – 125f. grey, purple & green 1·50 60
COINS: 75f. Athens tetradrachme; 100f. Himer diadrachme; 125f. Gela tetradrachme.

212 Putting the Shot

1975. Air. "Pre-Olympic Year". Olympic Games, Montreal (1976).
588 **212** 150f. brown and red . . . 1·10 55
589 – 200f. red, chestnut and brown . . . . 1·50 85
DESIGN: 200f. Gymnastics.

213 Starving Family

1975. Pan-African Drought Relief.
590 **213** 40f. blue, brown & orange 55 30
591 – 45f. brown and blue . . . 1·10 50
592 – 60f. blue, green and orange . . . . 1·00 40
DESIGNS: 45f. Animal skeletons; 60f. Truck bringing supplies.

214 Trading Canoe crossing R. Niger

1975. Tourism. Multicoloured.
593 40f. Type **214** 50 25
594 45f. Boubon Camp entrance 55 25
595 50f. Boubon Camp view . . 60 35

215 U.N. Emblem and Peace Dove

1975. Air. 30th Anniv of U.N.O.
596 **215** 100f. light blue and blue 85 40

216 "Virgin of Seville" (Murillo)

1975. Air. Christmas. Multicoloured.
597 50f. Type **216** 50 35
598 75f. "Adoration of the Shepherds" (Tintoretto) (horiz) 75 45
599 125f. "Virgin with Angels" (Master of Burgo d'Osma) 1·25 75

1975. Air. "Apollo–Soyuz" Space Link. Nos. 533/5 optd **JONCTION 17 Juillet 1975**.
600 **198** 50f. green, red and blue 50 25
601 – 100f. grey, red and blue 75 45
602 – 150f. purple, plum & blue 1·25 75

218 "Ashak"

1976. Literacy Campaign. Multicoloured.
603 25f. Type **218** 15 10
604 30f. "Kaska" 20 15
605 40f. "Iccee" 25 15
606 50f. "Tuuri-nya" 30 20
607 60f. "Lekki" 35 25

219 Ice Hockey

1976. Winter Olympic Games, Innsbruck, Austria. Multicoloured.
608 40f. Type **219** (postage) . . . 35 20
609 50f. Tobogganing 40 20
610 150f. Ski-jumping . . . . . 1·25 50
611 200f. Figure-skating (air) . . 1·50 75
612 300f. Cross-country skiing . . 2·00 1·00

220 Early Telephone and Satellite

1976. Telephone Centenary.
614 **220** 100f. orange, blue & green 85 50

221 Baby and Ambulance

1976. World Health Day.
615 **221** 50f. red, brown and purple 50 25

222 Washington crossing the Delaware (after Leutze)

1976. Bicentenary of American Revolution. Mult.
616 40f. Type **222** (postage) . . . 30 15
617 50f. First soldiers of the Revolution 40 20
618 150f. Joseph Warren – martyr of Bunker Hill (air) . . . . 1·10 35
619 200f. John Paul Jones aboard the "Bonhomme Richard" 1·50 60
620 300f. Molly Pitcher – heroine of Monmouth . . . . . . 2·00 90

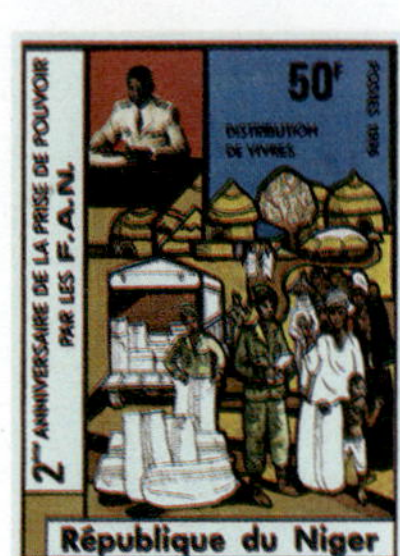

223 Distribution of Provisions

1976. 2nd Anniv of Military Coup. Multicoloured.
622 50f. Type **223** 35 25
623 100f. Soldiers with bulldozer (horiz) . . . . 1·10 45

224 "Hindenburg" crossing Lake Constance

1976. Air. 75th Anniv of Zeppelin Airships. Multicoloured.
624 40f. Type **224** 40 15
625 50f. LZ-3 over Wurzberg . . 50 25
626 150f. L-9 over Friedrichshafen . . . . . 1·40 55
627 200f. LZ-2 over Rothenburg (vert) . . . . 1·75 70
628 300f. "Graf Zeppelin II" over Essen . . . . 4·25 90

225 "Europafrique" Symbols

1976. "Europafrique".
630 **225** 100f. multicoloured . . . 1·40 50

226 Plant Cultivation

1976. Communal Works. Multicoloured.
631 25f. Type **226** 15 10
632 30f. Harvesting rice 20 15

227 Boxing

1976. Olympic Games, Montreal. Multicoloured.
633 40f. Type **227** 25 15
634 50f. Basketball 40 20
635 60f. Football 45 25
636 80f. Cycling (horiz) 60 20
637 100f. Judo (horiz) 70 30

228 Motobecane "125"

1976. Motorcycles.
639 **228** 50f. violet, brown & turq 60 25
640 – 75f. green, red & turquoise 85 35
641 – 100f. brown, orange & pur . . . . 1·25 50
642 – 125f. slate, olive and black . . . . 1·50 75
DESIGNS: 75f. Norton "Challenge"; 100f. B.M.W. "903"; 125f. Kawasaki "1000".

229 Cultivation Map

1976. Operation "Sahel Vert". Multicoloured.
643 40f. Type **229** 30 15
644 45f. Tending plants (vert) . . 35 20
645 60f. Planting sapling (vert) . . 55 30

1976. International Literacy Day. Nos. 603/7 optd **JOURNEE INTERNATIONALE DE L'ALPHABETISATION.**
646 **218** 25f. multicoloured 15 15
647 – 30f. multicoloured 15 15
648 – 40f. multicoloured 20 15
649 – 50f. multicoloured 25 20
650 – 60f. multicoloured 30 20

231 Basket Making

1976. Niger Women's Association. Multicoloured.
651 40f. Type **231** 35 20
652 45f. Hairdressing (horiz) . . 40 25
653 50f. Making pottery 50 35

232 Wall Paintings

1976. "Archaeology". Multicoloured.
654 40f. Type **232** 45 25
655 50f. Neolithic statuettes . . . 50 25
656 60f. Dinosaur skeleton . . . 90 35

233 "The Nativity" (Rubens)

1976. Air. Christmas. Multicoloured.
657 50f. Type **233** 50 25
658 100f. "Holy Night" (Correggio) . . . . 1·10 45
659 150f. "Adoration of the Magi" (David) (horiz) . . 1·50 90

234 Benin Ivory Mask

1977. 2nd World Festival of Negro-African Arts, Lagos.
660 **234** 40f. brown 40 20
661 – 50f. blue 60 30
DESIGNS—HORIZ: 50f. Nigerian stick dance.

235 Students in Class

236 Examining Patient

1977. Alphabetization Campaign.
662 **235** 40f. multicoloured 30 15
663 50f. multicoloured 40 20
664 60f. multicoloured 60 20

1977. Village Health. Multicoloured.
665 40f. Type **236** 50 20
666 50f. Examining baby 60 30

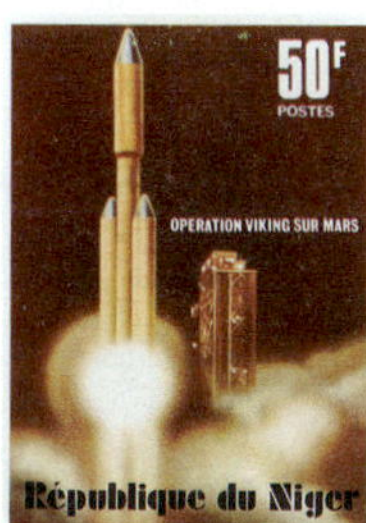

237 Rocket Launch

1977. "Viking" Space Mission. Multicoloured.
667 50f. Type **237** (postage) . . . 45 15
668 80f. "Viking" approaching Mars (horiz) 65 20
669 100f. "Viking" on Mars (horiz) (air) 65 25
670 150f. Parachute descent . . . 1·00 30
671 200f. Rocket in flight . . . . 1·40 45

238 Marabou Stork

1977. Fauna Protection.
673 **238** 80f. sepia, bistre and red 2·00 80
674 – 90f. brown and turquoise 1·25 60
DESIGN: 90f. Bushbuck.

239 Satellite and Weather Symbols

1977. World Meteorological Day.
675 **239** 100f. blue, black & turq 1·00 50

240 Gymnastic Exercise

1977. 2nd Youth Festival, Tahoua. Multicoloured.
676 40f. Type **240** 35 20
677 50f. High jumping 40 25
678 80f. Choral ensemble 70 35

241 Red Cross and Children playing

1977. World Health Day. Child Immunization Campaign.
679 **241** 80f. red, mauve and orange 75 35

242 Fly, Dagger, and W.H.O. Emblem in Eye

1977. Fight against Onchocerciais (blindness caused by worm infestation).
680 **242** 100f. blue, grey and red 1·40 55

243 Guirka Tahoua Dance

1977. "Popular Arts and Traditions". Multicoloured.
681 40f. Type **243** 45 25
682 50f. Maifilafili Gaya 50 20
683 80f. Naguihinayan Loga . . 80 45

244 Four Cavalrymen

1977. Chiefs' Traditional Cavalry. Multicoloured.
684 40f. Type **244** 55 25
685 50f. Chieftain at head of cavalry 65 30
686 60f. Chieftain and cavalry . . 90 45

245 Planting Crops

1977. "Operation Green Sahel" (recovery of desert).
687 **245** 40f. multicoloured 50 25

246 Albert John Luthuli (Peace, 1960)

1977. Nobel Prize Winners. Multicoloured.
688 50f. Type **246** 30 15
689 80f. Maurice Maeterlinck (Literature, 1911) 55 20
690 100f. Allan L. Hodgkin (Medicine, 1963) 70 25
691 150f. Albert Camus (Literature, 1957) . . . . 1·00 35
692 200f. Paul Ehrlich (Medicine, 1908) . . . . 1·50 40

247 Mao Tse-tung

1977. 1st Death Anniv of Mao Tse-tung (Chinese leader).
694 **247** 100f. black and red . . . 80 50

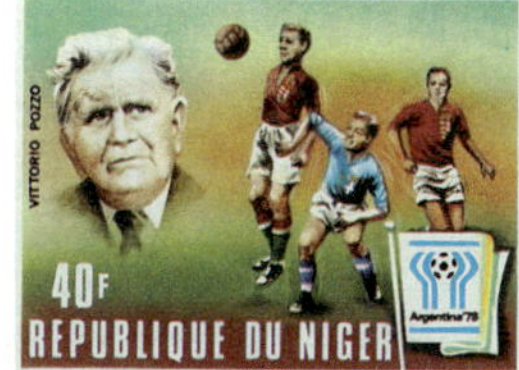

248 Vittorio Pozzo (Italy)

1977. World Football Cup Elimination Rounds. Multicoloured.
695 40f. Type **248** 30 10
696 50f. Vincente Feola, Spain . . 35 15
697 80f. Aymore Moreira, Portugal 50 20
698 100f. Sir Alf Ramsey, England 75 25
699 200f. Helmut Schon, West Germany . . . . 1·40 45

249 Horse's Head and Parthenon

1977. UNESCO Commemoration.
701 **249** 100f. blue, red and pale blue . . . . 1·25 60

250 Carrying Water **252** Paul Follereau and Leper

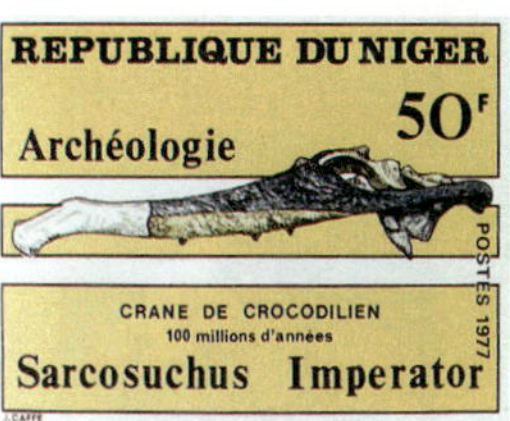

251 Crocodile Skull

1977. Women's Work. Multicoloured.
702 40f. Type **250** 35 30
703 50f. Pounding maize 40 25

1977. Archaeology. Multicoloured.
704 50f. Type **251** 60 40
705 80f. Neolithic tools 90 60

1978. 25th Anniv of World Leprosy Day.
706 **252** 40f. red, blue and orange 30 15
707 – 50f. black, red and orange 40 20
DESIGN—HORIZ: 50f. Follereau and two lepers.

253 "The Assumption"

1978. 400th Birth Anniv of Peter Paul Rubens. Paintings. Multicoloured.
708 50f. Type **253** 30 15
709 70f. "The Artist and his Friends" (horiz) 40 20
710 100f. "History of Maria de Medici" 70 25
711 150f. "Alathea Talbot" . . . 1·10 35
712 200f. "Portrait of the Marquise de Spinola" . . . 1·50 40

1978. As Nos. 376/7 but redrawn and background colour of 35f. changed to blue, 35f. undated, 50f. dated "1978".
714 35f. Broad-tailed paradise whydah . . . . 1·50 75
715 50f. Cattle egret . . . . . . 2·50 95
The 50f. is still wrongly inscribed "Balbucus".

254 Putting the Shot

1978. National Schools and University Sports Championships. Multicoloured.
716 40f. Type **254** 20 15
717 50f. Volleyball 30 20
718 60f. Long-jumping 35 20
719 100f. Throwing the javelin . . 55 35

255 Nurse assisting Patient

1978. Niger Red Cross.
720 **255** 40f. multicoloured 30 20

256 Station and Dish Aerial

1978. Goudel Earth Receiving Station.
721 **256** 100f. multicoloured . . . 65 40

257 Football and Flags of Competing Nations

1978. World Cup Football Championship, Argentina. Multicoloured.
722 40f. Type **257** 25 10
723 50f. Football in net 35 15
724 100f. Globe and goal 75 25
725 200f. Tackling (horiz) . . . . 1·40 55

258 "Fireworks"

1978. Air. 3rd African Games, Algiers. Multicoloured.
727 40f. Type **258** 25 20
728 150f. Olympic rings emblem 1·00 60

259 Niamey Post Office

1978. Niamey Post Office. Multicoloured.
729 40f. Type **259** 25 15
730 60f. Niamey Post Office (different) 35 25

260 Aerial View of Water-works

1978. Goudel Water-works.
731 **260** 100f. multicoloured . . . 55 40

261 R.T.N. Emblem

1978. Air. 20th Anniv of Niger Broadcasting.
732 **261** 150f. multicoloured . . . 90 60

262 Golden Eagle and Oldenburg 2g. Stamp of 1859

1978. Air. "Philexafrique" Stamp Exhibition, Libreville, Gabon (1st issue) and Int Stamp Fair, Essen, West Germany. Multicoloured.
733 100f. Type **262** . . . . . . 2·50 1·25
734 100f. Giraffes and Niger 1959 2f. stamp . . . . 2·50 1·25
See also Nos. 769/70.

263 Giraffe

265 Dome of the Rock, Jerusalem

1978. Endangered Animals. Multicoloured.
735 40f. Type **263** 45 25
736 50f. Ostrich 85 25
737 70f. Cheetah 75 35
738 150f. Scimitar oryx (horiz) . . 1·50 75
739 200f. Addax (horiz) . . . . . 2·00 95
740 300f. Hartebeest (horiz) . . . 2·50 1·25

1978. World Cup Football Championship Finalists. Nos. 695/9 optd.
741 **248** 40f. multicoloured 30 20
742 – 50f. multicoloured 40 20
743 – 80f. multicoloured 55 25
744 – 100f. multicoloured . . . 65 40
745 – 200f. multicoloured . . . 1·40 75
OVERPRINTS: 40f. **EQUIPE QUATRIEME: ITALIE**; 50f. **EQUIPE TROISIEME: BRESIL**; 80f. **EQUIPE SECONDE: PAYS BAS**; 100f. **EQUIPE VAINQUEUR: ARGENTINE**. 200 f; **ARGENTINE - PAYS BAS 3 - 1**.

1978. Palestinian Welfare.
747 **265** 40f.+5f. multicoloured . . 40 30

266 Laying Foundation Stone, and View of University

1978. Air. Islamic University of Niger.
748 **266** 100f. multicoloured . . . 60 40

267 Tinguizi

268 "The Homecoming" (Daumier)

1978. Musicians. Multicoloured.
749 100f. Type **267** 75 40
750 100f. Chetima Ganga (horiz) 75 40
751 100f. Dan Gourmou 75 40

1979. Paintings. Multicoloured.
752 50f. Type **268** 50 20
753 100f. "Virgin in Prayer" (Durer) 60 20
754 150f. "Virgin and Child" (Durer) 90 30
755 200f. "Virgin and Child" (Durer) (different) . . . . 1·25 40

269 Feeder Tanks

1979. Solar Energy. Multicoloured.
757 40f. Type **269** 30 20
758 50f. Solar panels on house roofs (horiz) 40 25

270 Langha Contestants

1979. Traditional Sports. Multicoloured.
759 40f. Type **270** 25 15
760 50f. Langha contestants clasping hands 35 20

271 Children with Building Bricks

1979. International Year of the Child. Multicoloured.
761 40f. Type **271** 25 15
762 100f. Children with book . . 60 25
763 150f. Children with model airplane . . . . 1·25 45

272 Rowland Hill, Peugeot Mail Van and French "Ceres" Stamp of 1849

1979. Death Centenary of Sir Rowland Hill. Mult.
764 40f. Type **272** 25 15
765 100f. Canoes and Austrian newspaper stamp, 1851 . . 60 25
766 150f. "DC-3" aircraft & U.S. "Lincoln" stamp, 1869 . . 1·10 35
767 200f. Advanced Passenger Train (APT), Great Britain and Canada 7½d. stamp, 1857 . . . . 2·25 40

273 Zabira Decorated Bag and Niger 45f. Stamp, 1965

1979. "Philexafrique 2" Exhibition, Gabon (2nd issue).
769 **273** 50f. multicoloured 65 40
770 – 150f. blue, red and carmine . . . . 1·60 1·10
DESIGN: 150f. Talking Heads, world map, satellite and U.P.U. emblem.

274 Alcock and Brown Statue and Vickers Vimy Aircraft

1979. 60th Anniv of First Transatlantic Flight.
771 **274** 100f. multicoloured . . . 1·00 35

275 Djermakoye Palace

1979. Historic Monuments.
772 **275** 100f. multicoloured . . . 55 40

276 Bororos in Festive Headdress

1979. Annual Bororo Festival. Multicoloured.
773 45f. Type **276** 30 20
774 60f. Bororo women in traditional costume (vert) 35 25

277 Boxing

1979. Pre-Olympic Year.
775 **277** 45f. multicoloured 30 15
776 – 100f. multicoloured . . . 55 25
777 – 150f. multicoloured . . . 85 35
778 – 250f. multicoloured . . . 1·25 45
DESIGNS: 100f. to 250f. Various boxing scenes.

278 Class of Learner-drivers

1979. Driving School.
780 **278** 45f. multicoloured 30 20

279 Douglas DC-10 over Map of Niger

1979. Air. 20th Anniv of ASECNA (African Air Safety Organization).
781 **279** 150f. multicoloured . . . 1·10 60

1979. "Apollo 11" Moon Landing. Nos. 667/8, 670/1 optd **alunissage apollo XI juillet 1969** and lunar module.
782 50f. Type **237** (postage) . . . 30 20
783 80f. "Viking" approaching Mars (horiz) 50 35
784 150f. Parachute descent (air) 90 60
785 200f. Rocket in flight . . . . 1·25 80

281 Four-man Bobsleigh

1979. Winter Olympic Games, Lake Placid (1980). Multicoloured.
787 40f. Type **281** 25 15
788 60f. Downhill skiing 35 15
789 100f. Speed skating 60 25
790 150f. Two-man bobsleigh . . 90 35
791 200f. Figure skating . . . . 1·10 45

282 Le Gaweye Hotel

1980. Air.
793 **282** 100f. multicoloured . . . 60 40

283 Sultan and Court

1980. Sultan of Zinder's Court. Multicoloured.
794 45f. Type **283** 30 20
795 60f. Sultan and court (different) 40 20

284 Chain Smoker and Athlete

285 Walking

1980. World Health Day. Anti-smoking Campaign.
796 **284** 100f. multicoloured . . . 65 40

1980. Olympic Games, Moscow. Multicoloured.
797 60f. Throwing the javelin . . 35 15
798 90f. Type **285** 50 20
799 100f. High jump (horiz) . . . 55 25
800 300f. Running (horiz) . . . . 1·50 55

1980. Winter Olympic Games Medal Winners. Nos. 787/91 optd.
802 **281** 40f. **VAINQUEUR R.D.A.** 25 15
803 – 60f. **VAINQUEUR STENMARK SUEDE** 30 20
804 – 100f. **VAINQUEUR HEIDEN Etats-Unis** 60 30
805 – 150f. **VAINQUEURS SCHERER-BENZ Suisse** 90 45
806 – 200f. **VAINQUEUR COUSINS Grande Bretagne** . . . . . . 1·25 65

287 Village Scene

1980. Health Year.
808 **287** 150f. multicoloured . . . 75 50

288 Class 150 (first locomotive in Japan, 1871)

1980. Steam Locomotives. Multicoloured.
809 45f. Type **288** 80 10
810 60f. "Fred Merril", 1848, U.S.A. . . . . 1·10 10
811 90f. Series 61, 1934, Germany 1·75 20
812 100f. Type P2, 1900, Prussia 2·25 20
813 130f. "Aigle", 1846, France 3·25 30

289 Steve Biko and Map of Africa **292** U.A.P.T. Emblem

291 Footballer

1980. 4th Death Anniv of Steve Biko (South African Anti-apartheid Worker).
815 **289** 150f. multicoloured . . . 80 60

1980. Olympic Medal Winners. Nos. 787/800 optd.
816 **285** 60f. **KULA (URSS)** . . . 35 15
817 – 90f. **DAMILANO (IT)** 55 25
818 – 100f. **WZSOLA (POL)** 60 30
819 – 300f. **YIFTER (ETH)** . . 1·60 90

1980. World Cup Football Championship, Spain (1982). Various designs showing Football.
821 **291** 45f. multicoloured 25 15
822 – 60f. multicoloured 30 15
823 – 90f. multicoloured 55 20
824 – 100f. multicoloured . . . 60 25
825 – 130f. multicoloured . . . 80 30

1980. 5th Anniv of African Posts and Telecommunications Union.
827 **292** 100f. multicoloured . . . 55 40

293 Earthenware Statuettes

1981. Kareygorou Culture Terracotta Statuettes. Multicoloured.
828 45f. Type **293** 25 20
829 60f. Head (vert) 35 20
830 90f. Head (different) (vert) . . 50 30
831 150f. Three heads 90 50

294 "Self-portrait"

1981. Paintings by Rembrandt. Multicoloured.
832 60f. Type **294** 40 15
833 90f. "Portrait of Hendrickje at the Window" 60 20
834 100f. "Portrait of an Old Man" 65 25
835 130f. "Maria Trip" 90 35
836 200f. "Self-portrait" (different) . . . . 1·25 45
837 400f. "Portrait of Saskia" . . 2·25 1·00

295 Ostrich

1981. Animals. Multicoloured.
839 10f. Type **295** 55 25
840 20f. Scimitar oryx 25 15
841 25f. Addra gazelle 20 15
842 30f. Arabian bustard 95 45
843 60f. Giraffe 50 20
844 150f. Addax . . . . 1·00 45

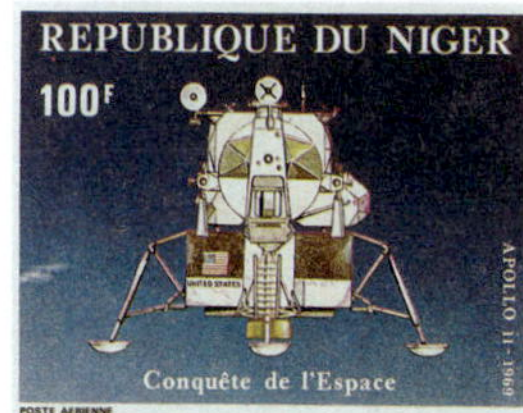

296 "Apollo 11"

1981. Air. Conquest of Space. Multicoloured.
845 100f. Type **296** 60 25
846 150f. Boeing 747 SCA carrying space shuttle . . . 1·00 40
847 200f. Rocket carrying space shuttle . . . . 1·25 40
848 300f. Space shuttle flying over planet . . . . 3·00 1·00

297 Tanks

1981. 7th Anniv of Military Coup.
849 **297** 100f. multicoloured . . . 1·00 40

298 Disabled Archer

1981. International Year of Disabled People.
850 **298** 50f. dp brown, red & brown 50 20
851 – 100f. brown, red and green 75 40
DESIGN: 100f. Disabled draughtsman.

299 Ballet Mahalba

1981. Ballet Mahalba. Multicoloured.
852 100f. Type **299** 70 35
853 100f. Ballet Mahalba (different) 70 35

300 "Portrait of Olga in an Armchair"

1981. Air. Birth Centenary of Pablo Picasso (artist). Multicoloured.
854 60f. Type **300** 40 20
855 90f. "The Family of Acrobats" 55 25
856 120f. "The Three Musicians" 70 35
857 200f. "Paul on a Donkey" . . 1·10 55
858 400f. "Young Girl drawing in an Interior" (horiz) . . . . 2·40 1·25

301 Mosque and Ka'aba

1981. 15th Centenary of Hejira.
859 **301** 100f. multicoloured . . . 60 35

302 Carriage

1981. British Royal Wedding.
860 **302** 150f. multicoloured . . . 60 35
861 – 200f. multicoloured . . . 1·00 55
862 – 300f. multicoloured . . . 1·25 1·00
DESIGNS: 200f., 300f. Similar designs showing carriages.

303 Sir Alexander Fleming

1981. Birth Centenary of Sir Alexander Fleming (discoverer of Penicillin).
864 **303** 150f. blue, brown and green . . . . 1·50 60

304 Pen-nibs, Envelope, Flower and U.P.U. Emblem

1981. International Letter Writing Week.
865 **304** 65f. on 45f. blue and red 40 20
866 – 85f. on 60f. blue, orange and black 50 30
DESIGN: 85f. Quill, hand holding pen and U.P.U. emblem.

305 Crops, Cattle and Fish

1981. World Food Day.
867 **305** 100f. multicoloured . . . 1·00 35

306 Tackling

1981. World Cup Football Championship, Spain (1982). Multicoloured.
868 40f. Type **306** 25 20
869 65f. Goalkeeper fighting for ball 40 30
870 85f. Passing ball 55 35
871 150f. Running with ball . . . 1·00 60
872 300f. Jumping for ball . . . 2·25 1·10

307 Peugeot, 1912

1981. 75th Anniv of French Grand Prix Motor Race. Multicoloured.
874 20f. Type **307** 25 15
875 40f. Bugatti, 1924 . . . . . 35 20
876 65f. Lotus-Climax, 1962 . . . 55 30
877 85f. Georges Boillot 75 35
878 150f. Phil Hill . . . . 1·10 60

308 "Madonna and Child" (Botticelli) **309** Children watering Plants

1981. Christmas. Various Madonna and Child Paintings by named artists. Multicoloured.
880 100f. Type **308** 60 40
881 200f. Botticini . . . . 1·25 75
882 300f. Botticini (different) . . 2·00 1·10

1982. School Gardens. Multicoloured.
883 65f. Type **309** 50 30
884 85f. Tending plants and examining produce 60 35

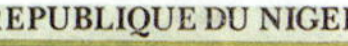

310 Arturo Toscanini (conductor, 25th death anniv)

1982. Celebrities' Anniversaries. Multicoloured.
885 120f. Type **310** . . . . . . 1·00 45
886 140f. "Fruits on a Table" (Manet, 150th birth anniv) (horiz) 80 55
887 200f. "L'Estaque" (Braque, birth centenary) (horiz) . . 1·25 60
888 300f. George Washington (250th birth anniv) . . . . 2·00 90
889 400f. Goethe (poet, 150th death anniv) . . . . . . 2·50 1·25
890 500f. Princess of Wales (21st birthday) . . . . 2·75 1·50

311 Palace of Congresses

1982. Palace of Congresses.
892 **311** 150f. multicoloured . . . 90 60

312 Martial Arts

1982. 7th Youth Festival, Agadez. Multicoloured.
893 65f. Type **312** 40 30
894 100f. Traditional wrestling . . 60 40

313 Planting a Tree

315 Map of Africa showing Member States

314 Scouts in Pirogue

1982. National Re-afforestation Campaign. Multicoloured.
895 150f. Type **313** . . . . . . 1·00 60
896 200f. Forest and desert . . . 1·25 75

1982. 75th Anniv of Boy Scout Movement. Mult.
897 65f. Type **314** 55 30
898 85f. Scouts in inflatable dinghy 65 30
899 130f. Scouts in canoe . . . . 1·25 45
900 200f. Scouts on raft . . . . 1·75 60

1982. Economic Community of West African States.
902 **315** 200f. yellow, black and blue . . . . 1·25 75

316 Casting Net

1982. Niger Fishermen. Multicoloured.
903 65f. Type **316** 85 30
904 85f. Net fishing 70 40

1982. Birth of Prince William of Wales. Nos. 860/2 optd **NAISSANCE ROYALE 1982.**
905 **302** 150f. multicoloured . . . 75 60
906 – 200f. multicoloured . . . 1·00 75
907 – 300f. multicoloured . . . 1·40 1·10

318 Hands reaching towards Mosque

1982. 13th Islamic Foreign Ministers Meeting, Niamey.
909 **318** 100f. multicoloured . . . 60 40

319 "Flautist"

1982. Norman Rockwell Paintings. Multicoloured.
910 65f. Type **319** 40 25
911 85f. "Clerk" 50 25
912 110f. "Teacher and Pupil" . . 70 35
913 150f. "Girl Shopper" 90 50

320 World Map and Satellite

1982. I.T.U. Delegates' Conference, Nairobi.
914 **320** 130f. blue, light blue and black . . . . 1·00 50

1982. World Cup Football Championship Winners. Nos. 868/72 optd.
915 40f. Type **306** 25 20
916 65f. Goalkeeper fighting for ball 40 30
917 85f. Passing ball 45 25
918 150f. Running with ball . . . 90 50
919 300f. Jumping for ball . . 1·75 1·10
OVERPRINTS: 40f. **1966 VAINQUEUR GRANDE - BRETAGNE**; 65f. **"1970 VAINQUEUR BRESIL"**; 85f. **"1974 VAINQUEUR ALLEMAGNE (RFA)"**; 150f. **"1978 VAINQUEUR ARGENTINE"**; 300f. **"1982 VAINQUEUR ITALIE"**.

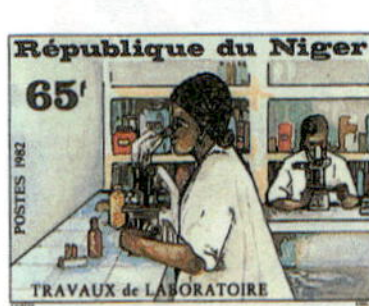
322 Laboratory Workers with Microscopes

1982. Laboratory Work. Multicoloured.
921 65f. Type **322** 60 40
922 115f. Laboratory workers . . 80 50

323 "Adoration of the Kings"

1982. Air. Christmas. Paintings by Rubens. Multicoloured.
923 200f. Type **323** . . . . . . 1·25 50
924 300f. "Mystic Marriage of St. Catherine" . . . . . . 2·00 75
925 400f. "Virgin and Child" . . 2·50 1·00

324 Montgolfier Balloon

1983. Air. Bicent of Manned Flight. Mult.
926 65f. Type **324** 45 15
927 85f. Charles's hydrogen balloon 60 20
928 200f. Goodyear Aerospace airship (horiz) . . . . . . 1·25 60
929 250f. Farman H.F.III biplane (horiz) . . . . 1·50 70
930 300f. Concorde . . . . . . 3·00 1·40
931 500f. "Apollo 11" spacecraft 3·00 1·40
No. 928 is wrongly inscribed "Zeppelin".

325 Harvesting Rice

326 E.C.A. Anniversary Emblem

1983. Self-sufficiency in Food. Multicoloured.
932 65f. Type **325** 60 30
933 85f. Planting rice 80 40

1983. 25th Anniv of Economic Commission for Africa.
934 **326** 120f. multicoloured . . . 75 40
935 200f. multicoloured . . . 1·25 70

327 "The Miraculous Draught of Fishes"

1983. 500th Birth Anniv of Raphael. Multicoloured.
936 65f. Type **327** 50 20
937 85f. "Grand Ducal Madonna" (vert) 50 20
938 100f. "The Deliverance of St. Peter" 60 25
939 150f. "Sistine Madonna" (vert) . . . . 1·00 45
940 200f. "The Fall on the Way to Calvary" (vert) . . . . 1·10 60
941 300f. "The Entombment" . . 1·75 80
942 400f. "The Transfiguration" (vert) . . . . 2·25 1·10
943 500f. "St. Michael fighting the Dragon" (vert) . . . . 3·00 1·40

328 Surveying

1983. The Army in the Service of Development. Multicoloured.
944 85f. Type **328** 60 25
945 150f. Road building . . . . 1·00 50

329 Palace of Justice

1983. Palace of Justice, Agadez.
946 **329** 65f. multicoloured 40 20

330 Javelin

1983. Air. Olympic Games, Los Angeles. Mult.
947 85f. Type **330** 50 20
948 200f. Shotput . . . . 1·10 60
949 250f. Throwing the hammer (vert) . . . . 1·50 70
950 300f. Discus . . . . 1·75 80

331 Rural Post Vehicle

332 Dome of the Rock

1983. Rural Post Service. Multicoloured.
952 65f. Type **331** 50 20
953 100f. Post vehicle and map 75 30

1983. Palestine.
954 **332** 65f. multicoloured 65 20

333 Class watching Television

1983. International Literacy Day. Multicoloured.
955 40f. Type **333** 25 15
956 65f. Teacher at blackboard (vert) 40 25
957 85f. Learning weights (vert) 55 30
958 100f. Outdoor class 60 35
959 150f. Woman reading magazine (vert) . . . . . 1·00 50

334 Three Dancers

1983. 7th Dosso Dance Festival. Multicoloured.
960 65f. Type **334** 50 25
961 85f. Four dancers 60 35
962 120f. Two dancers 90 50

335 Post Van

1983. World Communications Year. Multicoloured.
963 80f. Type **335** 60 40
964 120f. Sorting letters 80 40
965 150f. W.C.Y. emblem (vert) 1·00 50

336 Television Antenna and Solar Panel

1983. Solar Energy in the Service of Television. Multicoloured.
966 85f. Type **336** 60 30
967 130f. Land-rover and solar panel 90 45

337 "Hypolimnas misippus"

1983. Butterflies. Multicoloured.
968 75f. Type **337** 70 35
969 120f. "Papilio demodocus" 1·10 50
970 250f. "Vanessa antiopa" . . 2·00 90
971 350f. "Charexes jasius" . . 2·75 1·40
972 500f. "Danaus chrisippus" . . 4·50 1·75

338 "Virgin and Child with Angels"

339 Samariya Emblem

1983. Air. Christmas. Paintings by Botticelli. Multicoloured.
973 120f. Type **338** 75 40
974 350f. "Adoration of the Magi" (horiz) . . . . . . 2·25 1·00
975 500f. "Virgin of the Pomegranate" . . . . . . 3·00 1·25

1984. Samariya.
976 **339** 80f. black, orange & green 50 30

340 Running

1984. Air. Olympic Games, Los Angeles. Mult.
977 80f. Type **340** 40 20
978 120f. Pole vault 60 30
979 140f. High jump 80 30
980 200f. Triple jump (vert) . . . 1·25 45
981 350f. Long jump (vert) . . . 2·00 1·00

341 Boubon's Tetra

1984. Fish.
983 **341** 120f. multicoloured . . . 2·75 80

342 Obstacle Course

1984. Military Pentathlon. Multicoloured.
984 120f. Type **342** 80 40
985 140f. Shooting 95 50

343 Radio Station

1984. New Radio Station.
986 **343** 120f. multicoloured . . . 85 40

344 Flags, Agriculture and Symbols of Unity and Growth

1984. 25th Anniv of Council of Unity.
987 **344** 65f. multicoloured 40 25
988 85f. multicoloured 50 40

345 "Paris" (early steamer)

1984. Ships. Multicoloured.
989 80f. Type **345** 75 30
990 120f. "Jacques Coeur" (full-rigged ship) 85 40
991 150f. "Bosphorus" (full-rigged ship) . . . . 1·40 50
992 300f. "Comet" (full-rigged ship) . . . . 2·50 1·10

346 Daimler

1984. Motor Cars. Multicoloured.
993 100f. Type **346** 75 30
994 140f. Renault . . . . 1·10 45
995 250f. Delage "D 8" . . . . . 1·75 70
996 400f. Maybach "Zeppelin" 2·75 90

347 "Rickmer Rickmers" (full-rigged ship)

1984. Universal Postal Union Congress, Hamburg.
997 **347** 300f. blue, brown and green . . . . 2·75 1·75

348 Cattle

1984. Ayerou Market. Multicoloured.
998 80f. Type **348** 60 40
999 120f. View of market . . . . 1·00 60

349 Viper

1984.
1000 **349** 80f. multicoloured . . . 75 40

350 Carl Lewis (100 and 200 m)

1984. Air. Olympic Games Medal Winners. Multicoloured.
1001 80f. Type **350** 50 20
1002 120f. J. Cruz (800 m) . . . 70 40
1003 140f. A. Cova (10,000 m) . . 80 45
1004 300f. Al Joyner (Triple jump) . . . . 1·75 90

351 Emblem

1984. 10th Anniv of Economic Community of West Africa.
1006 **351** 80f. multicoloured . . . 50 30

352 Emblem and Extract from General Kountche's Speech

1984. United Nations Disarmament Decennials.
1007 **352** 400f. black and green . . 2·50 1·75
1008 500f. black and blue . . 3·00 1·75

353 Football

1984. Air. Preliminary Rounds of World Cup Football Championship, Mexico.
1009 **353** 150f. multicoloured . . . 1·00 45
1010 – 250f. multicoloured . . . 1·75 80
1011 – 450f. multicoloured . . . 2·50 1·25
1012 – 500f. multicoloured . . . 3·00 1·75
DESIGNS: 250 to 500f. Footballing scenes.

354 "The Visitation" (Ghirlandaio)

1984. Air. Christmas. Multicoloured.
1013 100f. Type **354** 60 30
1014 200f. "Virgin and Child" (Master of Saint Verdiana) . . . . 1·25 65
1015 400f. "Virgin and Child" (J. Koning) . . . . 2·50 1·25

1984. Drought Relief. Nos. 895/6 optd **Aide au Sahel 84**.
1016 150f. multicoloured . . . . 1·00 80
1017 200f. multicoloured . . . . 1·25 1·10

356 Organization Emblem

1985. 10th Anniv of World Tourism Organization.
1018 **356** 100f. black, orange and green 70 40

357 Breast-feeding Baby

360 Profile and Emblem

1985. Infant Survival Campaign. Multicoloured.
1019 85f. Type **357** 70 30
1020 110f. Feeding baby and changing nappy 90 40

358 Black-necked Stilt

1985. Air. Birth Centenary of John J. Audubon (ornithologist). Multicoloured.
1021 110f. Type **358** . . . . . . 1·10 45
1022 140f. Greater flamingo (vert) 1·50 65
1023 200f. Atlantic puffin . . . . 2·25 95
1024 350f. Arctic tern (vert) . . . 4·25 1·25

1985. 15th Anniv of Technical and Cultural Co-operation Agency.
1026 **360** 110f. brown, red & violet 65 40

361 Dancers

1985. 8th Niamey Festival. Multicoloured.
1027 85f. Type **361** 60 40
1028 110f. Four dancers (vert) . . 70 50
1029 150f. Dancers (different) . . 1·00 65

362 Wolf ("White Fang") and Jack London

1985. International Youth Year. Multicoloured.
1030 85f. Type **362** 60 25
1031 105f. Woman with lion and Joseph Kessel 75 30
1032 250f. Capt. Ahab harpooning white whale ("Moby Dick") . . . . . 1·75 90
1033 450f. Mowgli on elephant ("Jungle Book") . . . . 2·75 1·50

363 Two Children on Leaf

1985. "Philexafrique" Stamp Exhibition, Lome, Togo (1st issue). Multicoloured.
1034 200f. Type **363** . . . . . . 1·25 1·00
1035 200f. Mining . . . . 1·25 1·00
See also Nos. 1064/5.

364 "Hugo with his Son Francois" (A. de Chatillon)

1985. Death Centenary of Victor Hugo (writer).
1036 **364** 500f. multicoloured . . . 3·00 1·75

365 French Turbotrain TGV 001, Satellite and Boeing 737 on Map

1985. Europafrique.
1037 **365** 110f. multicoloured . . . 2·75 55

366 Addax

1985. Endangered Animals. Multicoloured.
1038 50f. Type **366** 40 15
1039 60f. Addax (different) (horiz) 45 25
1040 85f. Two scimitar oryxes (horiz) 55 25
1041 110f. Oryx 75 35

367 "Oedaleus sp" on Millet **368** Cross of Agadez

1985. Vegetation Protection. Multicoloured.
1042 85f. Type **367** 55 20
1043 110f. "Dysdercus volkeri" (beetle) 75 35
1044 150f. Fungi attacking sorghum and millet (horiz) . . . . 2·50 60
1045 210f. Sudan golden sparrows in tree . . . . 2·10 85
1046 390f. Red-billed queleas in tree . . . . 4·25 2·10

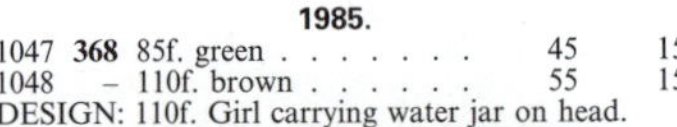

1985.
1047 **368** 85f. green 45 15
1048 – 110f. brown 55 15
DESIGN: 110f. Girl carrying water jar on head.

369 Arms, Flags and Agriculture

1985. 25th Anniv of Independence.
1049 **369** 110f. multicoloured . . . 70 40

370 Baobab **373** "Boletus"

371 Man watching Race

1985. Protected Trees. Multicoloured.
1050 110f. Type **370** 80 50
1051 210f. "Acacia albida" . . . 1·40 1·00
1052 390f. Baobab (different) . . 3·00 1·60

1985. Niamey–Bamako Powerboat Race. Mult.
1053 110f. Type **371** 70 45
1054 150f. Helicopter and powerboat . . . . 1·60 85
1055 250f. Powerboat and map 1·75 1·25

1985. "Trees for Niger". As Nos. 1050/2 but new values and optd **DES ARBRES POUR LE NIGER**.
1056 **370** 30f. multicoloured . . . 25 20
1057 – 85f. multicoloured . . . 55 40
1058 – 110f. multicoloured . . . 70 55

1985. Fungi. Multicoloured.
1059 85f. Type **373** . . . . . . 1·40 30
1060 110f. "Hypholoma fasciculare" . . . . . 2·10 45
1061 200f. "Coprinus comatus" 3·00 1·10
1062 300f. "Agaricus arvensis" (horiz) . . . . 4·50 1·50
1063 400f. "Geastrum fimbriatum" (horiz) . . . 5·75 2·10

374 First Village Water Pump

1985. "Philexafrique" Stamp Exhibition, Lome, Togo (2nd issue). Multicoloured.
1064 250f. Type **374** . . . . . . 1·75 1·25
1065 250f. Handicapped youths playing dili (traditional game) . . . . 1·75 1·25

375 "Saving Ant" and Savings Bank Emblem **376** Gouroumi

1985. World Savings Day.
1066 **375** 210f. multicoloured . . . 1·40 85

1985. Musical Instruments. Multicoloured.
1067 150f. Type **376** . . . . . . 1·10 60
1068 210f. Gassou (drums) (horiz) 1·60 1·00
1069 390f. Algaita (flute) . . . . 2·75 1·50

377 "The Immaculate Conception" **379** National Identity Card

378 Comet over Paris, 1910

1985. Air. Christmas. Paintings by Murillo. Mult.
1071 110f. "Madonna of the Rosary" 65 35
1072 250f. Type **377** . . . . . 1·75 90
1073 390f. "Virgin of Seville" . . 2·50 1·25

1985. Air. Appearance of Halley's Comet. Multicoloured.
1074 110f. Type **378** 70 35
1075 130f. Comet over New York 85 40
1076 200f. "Giotto" satellite . . . 1·50 70
1077 300f. "Vega" satellite . . . 2·25 1·00
1078 390f. "Planet A" space probe . . . . 2·50 1·25

1986. Civil Statutes Reform. Each black, green and orange.
1079 85f. Type **379** 65 30
1080 110f. Civil registration emblem 75 40

380 Road Signs **381** Oumarou Ganda (film producer)

1986. Road Safety Campaign.
1081 **380** 85f. black, yellow and red 75 30
1082 – 110f. black, red and green . . . . 1·00 40
DESIGN: 110f. Speed limit sign, road and speedometer ("Watch your speed").

1986. Honoured Artists. Multicoloured.
1083 60f. Type **381** 35 20
1084 85f. Idi na Dadaou 50 30
1085 100f. Dan Gourmou 60 40
1086 130f. Koungoui (comedian) 80 45

382 Martin Luther King **384** Statue and F. A. Bartholdi

383 Footballer and 1970 40f. Stamp

1986. Air. 18th Death Anniv of Martin Luther King (human rights activist).
1087 **382** 500f. multicoloured . . . 3·25 1·90

1986. Air. World Cup Football Championship, Mexico. Multicoloured.
1088 130f. Type **383** . . . . . . 1·00 30
1089 210f. Footballer and 1970 70f. stamp . . . . 1·25 45
1090 390f. Footballer and 1970 90f. stamp . . . . 2·75 1·00
1091 400f. Footballer and Mexican figure on "stamp" . . . . 2·75 1·00

1986. Air. Centenary of Statue of Liberty.
1093 **384** 300f. multicoloured . . . 2·25 1·10

385 Truck

1986. "Trucks of Hope". Multicoloured.
1094 85f. Type **385** 75 30
1095 110f. Mother and baby (vert) . . . . 1·00 40

386 Nelson Mandela and Walter Sisulu **387** Food Co-operatives

1986. International Solidarity with S. African and Namibian Political Prisoners Day. Multicoloured.
1096 200f. Type **386** . . . . . . 1·50 80
1097 300f. Nelson Mandela . . . 2·25 1·00

1986. 40th Anniv of F.A.O. Multicoloured.
1098 50f. Type **387** 30 20
1099 60f. Anti-desertification campaign 35 25
1100 85f. Irrigation 50 35
1101 100f. Rebuilding herds of livestock 60 40
1102 110f. Reafforestation . . . 75 45

388 Trees and Woman with Cooking Pots **389** "Sphodromantis sp."

1987. "For a Green Niger". Multicoloured.
1103 85f. Type **388** 55 30
1104 110f. Trees, woman and cooking pots (different) 70 40

1987. Protection of Vegetation. Useful Insects. Multicoloured.
1105 85f. Type **389** 60 40
1106 110f. "Delta sp." 85 50
1107 120f. "Cicindela sp." . . . 95 65

390 Transmitter, Map and Woman using Telephone

1987. Liptako–Gourma Telecommunications Network.
1108 **390** 110f. multicoloured . . . 80 50

391 Morse Key and Operator, 19th-century

1987. 150th Anniv of Morse Telegraph. Mult.
1109 120f. Type **391** 75 40
1110 200f. Samuel Morse (inventor) (vert) . . . . . 1·25 70
1111 350f. Morse transmitter and receiver . . . . 2·25 1·25

392 Tennis Player

1987. Olympic Games, Seoul (1988). Multicoloured.
1112 85f. Type **392** 50 40
1113 110f. Pole vaulter 70 40
1114 250f. Footballer . . . . . . 1·50 90

393 Ice Hockey

1987. Winter Olympic Games, Calgary (1988) (1st issue). Multicoloured.
1116 85f. Type **393** 60 35
1117 110f. Speed skating 70 35
1118 250f. Figure skating (pairs) 1·75 90
See also Nos. 1146/9.

394 Long-distance Running

1987. African Games, Nairobi. Multicoloured.
1120 85f. Type **394** 50 35
1121 110f. High jumping 60 35
1122 200f. Hurdling . . . . . . 1·25 70
1123 400f. Javelin throwing . . . 2·50 1·40

395 Chief's Stool, Sceptre and Crown

1987. 10th Anniv of National Tourism Office. Multicoloured.
1124 85f. Type **395** 50 35
1125 110f. Nomad, caravan and sceptre handle 60 35
1126 120f. Houses 70 40
1127 200f. Bridge over River Niger . . . . 1·25 70

396 Yaama Mosque at Dawn

1987. Aga Khan Prize.
1128 **396** 85f. multicoloured . . . 50 35
1129 – 110f. multicoloured . . . 60 35
1130 – 250f. multicoloured . . . 1·50 90
DESIGNS: 110, 250f. Yaama mosque at various times of the day.

397 Court Building

398 "Holy Family of the Sheep" (Raphael)

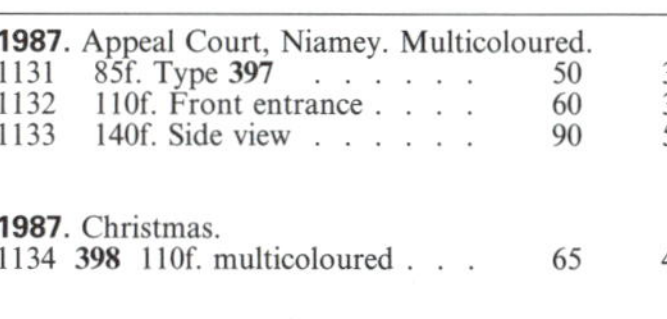

1987. Appeal Court, Niamey. Multicoloured.
1131 85f. Type **397** 50 30
1132 110f. Front entrance 60 35
1133 140f. Side view 90 55

1987. Christmas.
1134 **398** 110f. multicoloured . . . 65 40

399 Water Drainage

1988. Health Care. Multicoloured.
1136 85f. Type **399** 70 40
1137 110f. Modern sanitation . . 80 40
1138 165f. Refuse collection . . . 1·25 65

400 Singer and Band

402 New Great Market, Niamey

1988. Award of Dan-Gourmou Music Prize.
1139 **400** 85f. multicoloured . . . 80 50

1988. Winter Olympic Games Winners. Nos. 1116/18 optd.
1140 85f. **Medaille d'or URSS** . . 50 35
1141 110f. **Medaille d'or 5.000-10.000 m-GUSTAFSON (Suede)** . . 60 40
1142 250f. **Medaille d'or E. GORDEEVA - S. GRINKOV URSS** . . . 1·50 90

1988.
1143 **402** 85f. multicoloured . . . 60 40

403 Mother and Child

1988. UNICEF Child Vaccination Campaign and 40th Anniv of W.H.O. Multicoloured.
1144 85f. Type **403** 70 40
1145 110f. Doctor and villagers 90 50

404 Kayak

405 Emblem

1988. Air. Olympic Games, Seoul (2nd issue) and 125th Birth Anniv of Pierre de Coubertin (founder of modern Olympic Games). Multicoloured.
1146 85f. Type **404** 50 20
1147 165f. Rowing (horiz) 90 50
1148 200f. Two-man kayak (horiz) . . . . 1·25 70
1149 600f. One-man kayak . . . 3·50 2·00

1988. 25th Anniv of Organization of African Unity.
1151 **405** 85f. multicoloured . . . 50 30

406 Team working

407 Anniversary Emblem

1988. Dune Stabilization.
1152 **406** 85f. multicoloured . . . 60 40

1988. 125th Anniv of International Red Cross.
1153 **407** 85f. multicoloured . . . 60 30
1154 110f. multicoloured . . . 80 40

409 Emblem

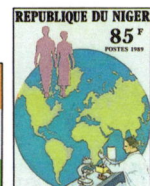

410 Couple, Globe and Laboratory Worker

1989. Niger Press Agency.
1159 **409** 85f. black, orange & grn 45 30

1989. Campaign against AIDS.
1160 **410** 85f. multicoloured . . . 55 30
1161 110f. multicoloured . . . 85 40

411 Radar, Tanker and Signals

412 General Ali Seybou (Pres.)

1989. 30th Anniv of International Maritime Organization.
1162 **411** 100f. multicoloured . . . 1·75 75
1163 120f. multicoloured . . . 2·10 1·00

1989. 15th Anniv of Military Coup. Mult.
1164 85f. Type **412** 45 25
1165 110f. Soldiers erecting flag 65 35

413 Eiffel Tower

1989. "Philexfrance 89" International Stamp Exhibition, Paris. Multicoloured.
1166 100f. Type **413** 60 40
1167 200f. Flags on stamps . . . 1·25 65

414 "Planting a Tree of Liberty"

1989. Bicentenary of French Revolution.
1168 **414** 250f. multicoloured . . . 1·50 1·00

415 Telephone Dial, Radio Mast, Map and Stamp

417 Emblem

416 "Apollo 11" Launch

1989. 30th Anniv of West African Posts and Telecommunications Association.
1169 **415** 85f. multicoloured . . . 45 30

1989. Air. 20th Anniv of First Manned Landing on Moon. Multicoloured.
1170 200f. Type **416** . . . . . . 1·25 65
1171 300f. Crew . . . . 2·00 1·00
1172 350f. Astronaut and module on lunar surface . . . . 2·25 1·25
1173 400f. Astronaut and U.S. flag on lunar surface . . . 2·50 1·25

1989. 25th Anniv of African Development Bank.
1174 **417** 100f. multicoloured . . . 60 30

418 Before and After Attack, and "Schistocerca gregaria"

1989. Locusts.
1175 **418** 85f. multicoloured . . . 50 30

419 Auguste Lumiere and 1st Cine Performance, 1895

1989. 35th Death Anniv of Auguste Lumiere and 125th Birth Anniv of Louis Lumiere (photo-graphy pioneers). Multicoloured.
1176 150f. Type **419** 90 55
1177 250f. Louis Lumiere and first cine-camera, 1894 . . 1·50 85
1178 400f. Lumiere brothers and first colour cine-camera, 1920 . . . . 2·50 1·25

420 Tractor, Map and Pump

1989. 30th Anniv of Agriculture Development Council.
1179 **420** 75f. multicoloured . . . 45 30

421 Zinder Regional Museum

422 "Russelia equisetiformis"

1989. Multicoloured.
1180 85f. Type **421** 45 30
1181 145f. Carawan 60 40
1182 165f. Temet dunes 90 60

1989. Flowers. Multicoloured.
1183 10f. Type **422** 15 10
1184 20f. "Argyreia nervosa" . . 15 10
1185 30f. "Hibiscus rosa-sinensis" 20 10
1186 50f. "Catharanthus roseus" 35 20
1187 100f. "Cymothoe sangaris" (horiz) 75 35

423 Emblem

424 Adults learning Alphabet

1990. 10th Anniv of Pan-African Postal Union.
1188 **423** 120f. multicoloured . . . 70 40

1990. International Literacy Year. Multicoloured.
1189 85f. Type **424** 45 25
1190 110f. Adults learning arithmetic 65 35

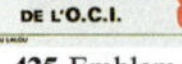
425 Emblem

427 Leland and Child

426 Footballers and Florence

1990. 20th Anniv of Islamic Conference Organization.
1191 **425** 85f. multicoloured . . . 50 30

1990. Air. World Cup Football Championship, Italy. Multicoloured.
1192 130f. Type **426** . . . . . . 1·00 40
1193 210f. Footballers and Verona . . . . 1·40 75
1194 500f. Footballers and Bari 3·25 1·75
1195 600f. Footballers and Rome 3·75 2·00

1990. Mickey Leland (American Congressman) Commemoration.
1196 **427** 300f. multicoloured . . . 1·75 1·00
1197 500f. multicoloured . . . 3·00 1·75

428 Emblem

429 Flags and Envelopes on Map

1990. 1st Anniv of National Movement for the Development Society.
1198 **428** 85f. multicoloured . . . 50 30

1990. 20th Anniv of Multinational Postal Training School, Abidjan.
1199 **429** 85f. multicoloured . . . 65 30

430 Gymnastics

1990. Olympic Games, Barcelona (1992). Mult.
1200 85f. Type **430** 40 25
1201 110f. Hurdling 60 35
1202 250f. Running . . . . . . 1·50 90
1203 400f. Show jumping . . . . 2·75 1·40
1204 500f. Long jumping . . . . 3·00 1·75

431 Arms, Map and Flag

432 Emblem

1990. 30th Anniv of Independence.
1206 **431** 85f. multicoloured . . . 45 30
1207 110f. multicoloured . . . 65 40

1990. 40th Anniv of United Nations Development Programme.
1208 **432** 100f. multicoloured . . . 50 30

433 The Blusher

434 Christopher Columbus and "Santa Maria"

1991. Butterflies and Fungi. Multicoloured.
1209 85f. Type **433** (postage) . . 1·00 30
1210 110f. "Graphium pylades" (female) 75 25
1211 200f. "Pseudacraea hostilia" 1·25 55
1212 250f. Cracked green russula 2·50 1·10
1213 400f. "Boletus impolitus" (air) . . . . 3·75 1·60
1214 500f. "Precis octavia" . . . 2·75 1·25

1991. 540th Birth of Christopher Columbus. Mult.
1216 85f. Type **434** (postage) . . 70 25
1217 110f. 15th-century Portuguese caravel . . . 1·00 30
1218 200f. 16th-century four-masted caravel . . . . . 1·60 65
1219 250f. "Estremadura" (Spanish caravel), 1511 . . 2·00 85
1220 400f. "Vija" (Portuguese caravel), 1600 (air) . . . 3·25 1·10
1221 500f. "Pinta" . . . . 3·50 1·50

435 Speed Skating

1991. Winter Olympic Games, Albertville (1992). Multicoloured.
1223 110f. Type **435** 60 25
1224 300f. Ice-hockey . . . . . 1·25 80
1225 500f. Women's downhill skiing . . . . 2·50 1·25
1226 600f. Two-man luge . . . . 2·75 1·25

436 Flag and Boy holding Stone

437 Hairstyle

1991. Palestinian "Intifada" Movement.
1227 **436** 110f. multicoloured . . . 75 30

1991. Traditional Hairstyles. Multicoloured.
1228 85f. Type **437** 20 10
1229 110f. Netted hairstyle . . . 25 15
1230 165f. Braided hairstyle . . . 40 20
1231 200f. Plaited hairstyle . . . 45 25

438 Boubon Market

1991. African Tourism Year. Multicoloured.
1232 85f. Type **438** 20 10
1233 110f. Timia waterfalls (vert) 25 15
1234 130f. Ruins at Assode . . . 30 15
1235 200f. Tourism Year emblem (vert) 45 25

439 Anatoly Karpov and Gary Kasparov

1991. Anniversaries and Events. Multicoloured.
1236 85f. Type **439** (World Chess Championship) (postage) 20 10
1237 110f. Ayrton Senna and Alain Prost (World Formula 1 motor racing championship) 25 15
1238 200f. Reading of Declaration of Human Rights and Comte de Mirabeau (bicentenary of French Revolution) . . . 45 25
1239 250f. Dwight D. Eisenhower, Winston Churchill and Field-Marshal Montgomery (50th anniv of America's entry into Second World War) . . . . 3·50 85
1240 400f. Charles de Gaulle and Konrad Adenauer (28th anniv of Franco-German Co-operation Agreement) (air) 95 55
1241 500f. Helmut Kohl and Brandenburg Gate (2nd anniv of German reunification) . . . . . . 1·10 60

440 Japanese "ERS-1" Satellite

1991. Satellites and Transport. Multicoloured.
1243 85f. Type **440** (postage) . . 20 10
1244 110f. Japanese satellite observing Aurora Borealis 25 15
1245 200f. Louis Favre and "BB 415" diesel locomotive . . 2·50 45
1246 250f. "BB-BB 301" diesel locomotive . . . . 3·00 55
1247 400f. "BB 302" diesel locomotive (air) . . . . . 4·50 70
1248 500f. Lockheed Stealth fighter-bomber and Concorde . . . . 1·10 60

441 Crowd and Emblem on Map

443 Couple adding Final Piece to Globe Jigsaw

442 Timberless House

1991. National Conference (to determine new constitution).
1250 **441** 85f. multicoloured . . . 20 10

1992.
1251 **442** 85f. multicoloured . . . 20 10

1992. World Population Day. Multicoloured.
1252 85f. Type **443** 20 10
1253 110f. Children flying globe kite (after Robert Parker) 25 15

444 Columbus and Fleet

1992. 500th Anniv of Discovery of America by Columbus.
1254 **444** 250f. multicoloured . . . 60 35

445 Zaleye

1992. 2nd Death Anniv of Hadjia Haqua Issa (Zaleye) (singer).
1255 **445** 150f. multicoloured . . . 35 20

446 Conference Emblem

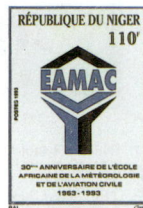

447 College Emblem

1992. International Nutrition Conference, Rome.
1256 **446** 145f. multicoloured . . . 35 20
1257 350f. multicoloured . . . 80 45

1993. 30th Anniv of African Meteorology and Civil Aviation College.
1258 **447** 110f. blue, black & green 25 15

448 Girl planting Sapling

1993. Anti-desertification Campaign.
1259 **448** 85f. multicoloured . . . 20 10
1260 165f. multicoloured . . . 40 20

449 Aerosol spraying Globe (Patricia Charets)

1993. World Population Day. Children's Drawings. Multicoloured.
1261 85f. Type **449** 20 10
1262 110f. Tree and person with globe as head looking at high-rise tower blocks (Mathieu Chevrault) . . . 25 15

450 Jerusalem

1993. "Jerusalem, Holy City".
1268 **450** 110f. multicoloured . . . 30 15

451 People of Different Races

1994. Award of Nobel Peace Prize to Nelson Mandela and F. W. de Klerk (South African statesmen).
1269 **451** 270f. multicoloured . . . 70 40

OFFICIAL STAMPS

O **13** Djerma Women

1962. Figures of value in black.
O121 O **13** 1f. violet 10 10
O122 2f. green 10 10
O123 5f. blue 15 10
O124 10f. red 15 10
O125 20f. blue 20 15
O126 25f. orange 25 20
O127 30f. blue 30 25
O128 35f. green 35 30
O129 40f. brown 35 35
O130 50f. slate 40 40
O131 60f. turquoise 50 45
O132 85f. turquoise 70 40
O133 100f. purple 85 40
O134 200f. blue . . . . . . 1·50 80

1988. As Type O **13**, but figures of value in same colour as remainder of design.
O1155 O **13** 5f. blue 10 10
O1156 10f. red 10 10
O1157 15f. yellow 10 10
O1158 20f. blue 20 10
O1159 45f. orange 25 20
O1160 50f. green 30 20

POSTAGE DUE STAMPS

1921. Postage Due stamps of Upper Senegal and Niger "Figure" key-type optd **TERRITOIRE DU NIGER**.
D18 M 5c. green . . . . 10 4·25
D19 10c. red . . . . 10 4·25
D20 15c. grey . . . . 10 4·25
D21 20c. brown . . . . 10 2·75
D22 30c. blue . . . . 20 4·25
D23 50c. black . . . . 50 4·00
D24 60c. orange . . . . 15 6·00
D25 1f. violet . . . . 30 4·00

D **6** Zinder Fort

1927.
D73 D **6** 2c. red and blue . . . . 15 3·75
D74 4c. black and orange . . 15 3·25
D75 5c. violet and yellow . . 15 3·25
D76 10c. violet and red . . . 10 3·00
D77 15c. orange and green 10 4·25
D78 20c. sepia and red . . . 20 3·00
D79 25c. sepia and black . . 20 3·00
D80 30c. grey and violet . . 65 4·75
D81 50c. red on green . . . . 45 5·25
D82 60c. orange & lilac on bl 45 5·25
D83 1f. violet & blue on blue 60 3·75
D84 2f. mauve and red . . . 1·40 5·50
D85 3f. blue and brown . . . 1·70 6·25

D **13** Cross of Agadez

1962.
D123 D **13** 50c. green 10 10
D124 1f. violet 10 10
D125 2f. myrtle 10 10
D126 A 3f. mauve 10 10
D127 5f. green 15 15
D128 10f. orange 15 15
D129 B 15f. blue 15 15
D130 20f. red 20 20
D131 50f. brown 40 40
DESIGNS: A, Cross of Iferouane; B, Cross of Tahoua.

D **450** Cross of Iferouane

1993.
D1263 D **450** 5f. multicoloured . . 10 10
D1264 10f. orange and black 10 10
D1265 – 15f. multicoloured 10 10
D1266 – 20f. mve, yell & blk 10 10
D1267 – 50f. multicoloured 10 10
DESIGN: 15 to 50f. Cross of Tahoua.

NIGER COAST PROTECTORATE

Pt. 1

A district on the west coast of Africa. In 1900 became part of Southern Nigeria.

12 pence = 1 shilling;
20 pence = 1 pound.

1892. Stamps of Gt. Britain (Queen Victoria) optd **BRITISH PROTECTORATE OIL RIVERS**.
1 **71** ½d. red . . . . 12·00 8·00
2 **57** 1d. lilac . . . . 7·00 8·00
3 **73** 2d. green and red . . . . . 25·00 8·00
4 **74** 2½d. purple and blue . . . . 6·50 2·25
5 **78** 5d. purple and blue . . . . . 10·00 6·50
6 **82** 1s. green . . . . 55·00 80·00

1893. Half of No. 2 surch **½d.**
7 **57** ½d. on half of 1d. lilac . . . £150 £140

1893. Nos. 1 to 6 surch in words (½d., 1s.) or figures (others).
20 **73** ½d. on 2d. green and red . . £400 £250
21 **74** ½d. on 2½d. purple on blue £325 £180
37 **73** 1s. on 2d. green and red . . £450 £350
40 5s. on 2d. green and red . . £9000 £10000
41 **78** 10s. on 5d. purple and blue £6500 £8500
42 **82** 20s. on 1s. green £110000

13

14

1893. Various frames with "OIL RIVERS" barred out and "NIGER COAST" above.
45 **13** ½d. red . . . . 4·25 4·75
46b 1d. blue . . . . 3·75 3·25
47d 2d. green . . . . 19·00 13·00
48 2½d. red . . . . 8·50 3·50
49b 5d. lilac . . . . 14·00 13·00
50 1s. black . . . . 14·00 12·00

1894. Various frames.
66 **14** ½d. green . . . . 3·50 1·50
67d 1d. red . . . . 2·50 2·75
68 2d. red . . . . 1·75 2·00
69 2½d. blue . . . . 7·50 2·00
55a 5d. purple . . . . 6·00 5·50
71 6d. brown . . . . 7·00 6·50
72 1s. black . . . . 15·00 29·00
73b 2s.6d. brown . . . . . . 22·00 80·00
74b 10s. violet . . . . 90·00 £170

1894. Surch with large figures.
58 ½ on half 1d. (No. 46) £800 £325
59 1 on half 2d. (No. 2) £1700 £350

1894. No. 67 bisected and surch.
64 **14** ½d. on half of 1d. red £2500 £425

1894. Surch **ONE HALF PENNY** and bars.
65 **14** ½d. on 2½d. blue £375 £225

NIGERIA

Pt. 1

A former British colony on the west coast of Africa, comprising the territories of Northern and Southern Nigeria and Lagos. Attained full independence within the British Commonwealth in 1960 and became a Federal Republic in 1963.

The Eastern Region (known as Biafra (q.v)) seceded in 1967, remaining independent until overrun by Federal Nigerian troops during January 1970.

1914. 12 pence = 1 shilling;
20 shillings = 1 pound.
1973. 100 kobo = 1 naira.

1

1914.
15 **1** ½d. green . . . . 1·25 40
16b 1d. red . . . . 1·75 35
17 1½d. orange . . . . 4·50 15
18 2d. grey . . . . 1·50 6·00
20 2d. brown . . . . 1·50 15
21 2½d. blue . . . . 1·00 6·50
5a 3d. purple on yellow . . . . 1·50 2·75
22 3d. violet . . . . 5·00 3·25
23 3d. blue . . . . 6·50 1·00
24 4d. black and red on yellow 65 55
25a 6d. purple . . . . 7·00 8·00
26 1s. black on green . . . . . 1·25 2·00
9 2s.6d. black and red on blue 16·00 6·50
10 5s. green and red on yellow 13·00 55·00
11d 10s. green and red on green 35·00 £100
12a £1 purple and black on red £170 £200

1935. Silver Jubilee. As T **143a** of Newfoundland.
30 1½d. blue and grey . . . . . 80 1·00
31 2d. green and blue . . . . . 1·50 1·00
32 3d. brown and blue . . . . . 3·00 15·00
33 1s. grey and purple . . . . . 3·00 30·00

3 Apapa Wharf

11 Victoria–Buea Road

1936.
34 **3** ½d. green . . . . 1·50 1·40
35 – 1d. red 50 40
36 – 1½d. brown . . . . 2·00 40
37 – 2d. black 50 80
38 – 3d. blue . . . . 2·00 1·50
39 – 4d. brown . . . . 2·00 2·00
40 – 6d. violet 50 60
41 – 1s. green . . . . 1·75 4·75
42 **11** 2s.6d. black and blue . . . 3·75 25·00
43 – 5s. black and green . . . . 9·00 32·00
44 – 10s. black and grey . . . . 55·00 80·00
45 – £1 black and orange . . . . 80·00 £160
DESIGNS—VERT: 1d. Cocoa; 1½d. Tin dredger; 2d. Timber industry; 3d. Fishing village; 4d. Cotton ginnery; 6d. Habe minaret; 1s. Fulani cattle. HORIZ: 5s. Oil palms; 10s. River Niger at Jebba; £1 Canoe pulling.

1937. Coronation. As T **143b** of Newfoundland.
46 1d. red . . . . 60 2·50
47 1½d. brown . . . . 1·60 3·00
48 3d. blue . . . . 1·60 3·00

15 King George VI

1938.
49 **15** ½d. green 10 10
50a 1d. red 75 40
50b 1d. lilac 10 20
51a 1½d. brown 10 10
52 2d. black . . . . 10 1·60
52ab 2d. red 10 50
52b 2½d. orange . . . . 10 1·50
53 3d. blue 10 10
53b 3d. black . . . . 15 1·00
54 4d. orange . . . . 48·00 3·00
54a 4d. blue . . . . 15 2·50
55 6d. purple 40 10
56a 1s. olive 30 10
57 1s.3d. blue 90 30
58b – 2s.6d. black and blue . . 2·25 3·50
59c – 5s. black and orange . . 5·50 4·00
DESIGNS: 2s.6d., 5s. As Nos. 42 and 44 but with portrait of King George VI.

1946. Victory. As T **4a** of Pitcairn Islands.
60 1½d. brown 35 10
61 4d. blue . . . . 35 2·25

1948. Royal Silver Wedding. As T **4b/c** of Pitcairn Islands.
62 1d. mauve 35 30
63 5s. orange . . . . 6·00 12·00

1949. U.P.U. As T **4d/g** of Pitcairn Islands.
64 1d. purple 15 25
65 3d. blue . . . . 1·25 3·00
66 6d. purple . . . . 30 3·00
67 1s. olive . . . . 50 2·00

1953. Coronation. As T **4h** of Pitcairn Islands.
68 1½d. black and green 40 10

18 Old Manilla Currency

26 Victoria Harbour

29 New and Old Lagos

1953.
69 **18** ½d. black and orange . . 15 30
70 – 1d. black and bronze . . 20 10
71 – 1½d. turquoise 50 40
72 – 2d. black and ochre . . . 4·00 30
72cb – 2d. slate . . . . 3·50 40
73 – 3d. black and purple . . . 55 10
74 – 4d. black and blue . . . 2·50 20
75 – 6d. brown and black . . . 30 10
76 – 1s. black and purple . . . 40 10
77 **26** 2s.6d. black and green . . 6·00 50
78 – 5s. black and orange . . . 3·50 1·40
79 – 10s. black and brown . . 13·00 2·50
80 **29** £1 black and violet . . . 23·00 8·00
DESIGNS—HORIZ (As Type **18**): 1d. Bornu horsemen; 1½d. "Groundnuts"; 2d. "Tin"; 3d. Jebba Bridge and R. Niger; 4d. "Cocoa"; 1s. "Timber". (As Type **26**): 5s. "Palm oil"; 10s. "Hides and skins". VERT (As Type **18**): 6d. Ife bronze.

1956. Royal Visit. No. 72 optd **ROYAL VISIT 1956**.
81 2d. black and ochre 40 30

31 Victoria Harbour

1958. Centenary of Victoria, S. Cameroons.
82 **31** 3d. black and purple 20 30

32 Lugard Hall

1959. Attainment of Self-government. Northern Region of Nigeria.
83 **32** 3d. black and purple 15 10
84 – 1s. black and green 55 60
DESIGN: 1s. Kano Mosque.

35 Legislative Building

1960. Independence Commemoration.
85 **35** 1d. black and red 10 10
86 – 3d. black and blue 15 10
87 – 6d. green and brown 20 20
88 – 1s.3d. blue and yellow . . . 40 20
DESIGNS—As Type **35**: 3d. African paddling canoe; 6d. Federal Supreme Court. LARGER (40 × 24 mm): 1s.3d. Dove, torch and map.

39 Groundnuts

48 Central Bank

1961.
89 **39** ½d. green 10 60
90 – 1d. violet 80 10
91 – 1½d. red . . . . 80 2·25
92 – 2d. blue 30 10

93 – 3d. green 40 10
94 – 4d. blue 40 2·00
95 – 6d. yellow and black 80 10
96 – 1s. green 4·50 10
97 – 1s.3d. orange 1·50 10
98 **48** 2s.6d. black and yellow 2·75 15
99 – 5s. black and green 65 1·25
100 – 10s. black and blue 3·50 4·25
101 – £1 black and red 12·00 15·00

DESIGNS—VERT (as Type **39**): 1d. Coal mining; 1½d. Adult education; 2d, Pottery; 3d. Oyo carver; 4d. Weaving; 6d. Benin mask; 1s. Yellow casqued hornbill; 1s.3d. Camel train. HORIZ (as Type **48**: 5s. Nigeria Museum; 10s. Kano airport; £1 Lagos railway station.

52 Globe and Diesel-electric Locomotive

1961. Admission into U.P.U. Inscr as in T **52**.
102 **52** 1d. orange and blue 30 10
103 – 3d. olive and black 30 10
104 – 1s.3d. blue and red 80 20
105 – 2s.6d. green and blue 85 2·00

DESIGNS: 3d. Globe and mail van; 1s.3d. Globe and Bristol 175 Britannia aircraft; 2s.6d. Globe and liner.

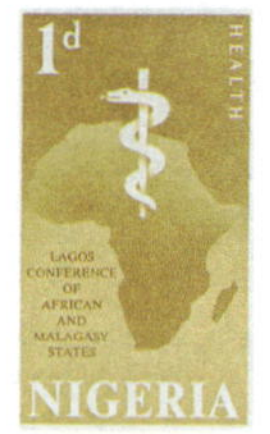

56 Coat of Arms **61** "Health"

1961. 1st Anniv of Independence.
106 **56** 3d. multicoloured 10 10
107 – 4d. green and orange 20 10
108 – 6d. green 30 10
109 – 1s.3d. grey and blue 35 10
110 – 2s.6d. green and blue 40 2·00

DESIGNS—HORIZ: 4d. Natural resources map; 6d. Nigerian eagle; 1s 3d. Eagles in flight; 2s.6d. Nigerians and flag.

1962. Lagos Conf of African and Malagasy States.
111 **61** 1d. bistre 10 10
112 – 3d. purple 10 10
113 – 6d. green 15 10
114 – 1s. brown 20 10
115 – 1s.3d. blue 25 20

DESIGNS: Map and emblems symbolising Culture (3d.); Commerce (6d.); Communications (1s.); Co-operation (1s.3d.).

66 Malaria Eradication Emblem and Parasites

1962. Malaria Eradication.
116 **66** 3d. green and red 15 10
117 – 6d. blue and purple 20 10
118 – 1s.3d. mauve and blue 20 10
119 – 2s.6d. blue and brown 30 90

DESIGNS (embodying emblem): 6d. Insecticide-spraying; 1s.3d. Aerial spraying; 2s.6d. Mother, child and microscope.

70 National Monument

1962. 2nd Anniv of Independence.
120 **70** 3d. green and blue 10 10
121 – 5s. red, green and violet 1·00 1·00

DESIGN—VERT: 5s. Benin bronze.

72 Fair Emblem **76** "Arrival of Delegates"

1962. International Trade Fair, Lagos.
122 **72** 1d. red and olive 10 10
123 – 6d. black and red 15 10
124 – 1s. black and brown 15 10
125 – 2s.6d. yellow and blue 60 20

DESIGNS—HORIZ: 6d. "Cogwheels of Industry"; 1s. "Cornucopia of Industry"; 2s.6d. Oilwells and tanker.

1962. 8th Commonwealth Parliamentary Conference, Lagos.
126 **76** 2½d. blue 15 1·10
127 – 4d. blue and rose 15 30
128 – 1s.3d. sepia and yellow 20 20

DESIGNS—HORIZ: 4d. National Hall. VERT: 1s.3d. Mace as Palm Tree.

80 Tractor and Maize **81** Mercury Capsule and Kano Tracking Station

1963. Freedom from Hunger.
129 – 3d. olive 1·00 20
130 **80** 6d. mauve 1·50 20

DESIGN—VERT: 3d. Herdsman.

1963. "Peaceful Use of Outer Space".
131 **81** 6d. blue and green 25 10
132 – 1s.3d. black and turquoise 35 20

DESIGN: 1s.3d. Satellite and Lagos Harbour.

83 Scouts shaking Hands

1963. 11th World Scout Jamboree. Marathon.
133 **83** 3d. red and bronze 30 20
134 – 1s. black and red 95 80
MS134a 93×95 mm. Nos. 133/4 1·75 1·75

DESIGN: 1s. Campfire.

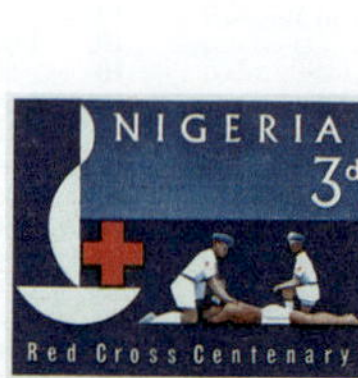

85 Emblem and First Aid Team **88** President Azikiwe and State House

1963. Centenary of Red Cross.
135 **85** 3d. red and blue 40 10
136 – 6d. red and green 60 10
137 – 1s.3d. red and sepia 80 70
MS137a 102×102 mm. No. 137 (block of four) 8·50 11·00

DESIGNS: 6d. Emblem and "Hospital Services"; 1s.3d. Patient and emblem.

1963. Republic Day.
138 **88** 3d. olive and green 10 10
139 – 1s.3d. brown and sepia 10 10
140 – 2s.6d. turquoise and blue 15 15

The buildings on the 1s.3d. and the 2s.6d. are the Federal Supreme Court and the Parliament Building respectively.

90 "Freedom of worship" **93** Queen Nefertari

1963. 15th Anniv of Declaration of Human Rights.
141 – 3d. red 10 10
142 **90** 6d. green 15 10
143 – 1s.3d. blue 30 10
144 – 2s.6d. purple 45 30

DESIGNS—HORIZ: 3d. (Inscr "1948–1963"), Charter and broken whip. VERT: 1s.3d. "Freedom from Want"; 2s.6d. "Freedom of Speech".

1964. Nubian Monuments Preservation.
145 **93** 6d. olive and green 50 10
146 – 2s.6d. brown, olive & green 1·75 2·25

DESIGN: 2s.6d. Rameses II.

95 President Kennedy **98** President Azikiwe

1964. Pres. Kennedy Memorial Issue.
147 **95** 1s.3d. lilac and black 30 15
148 – 2s.6d. multicoloured 40 65
149 – 5s. multicoloured 70 1·75
MS149a 154×135 mm. No. 149 (block of four). Imperf 7·00 12·00

DESIGNS: 2s.6d. Kennedy and flags; 5s. Kennedy (U.S. coin head) and flags.

1964. 1st Anniv of Republic.
150 **98** 3d. brown 10 10
151 – 1s.3d. green 35 10
152 – 2s.6d. green 70 90

DESIGNS—25×42 mm: 1s.3d. Herbert Macaulay; 2s.6d. King Jaja of Opobo.

101 Boxing Gloves

1964. Olympic Games, Tokyo.
153 **101** 3d. sepia and green 45 10
154 – 6d. green and blue 60 10
155 – 1s.3d. sepia and olive 1·00 15
156 – 2s.6d. sepia and brown 1·75 3·75
MS156a 102×102 mm. No. 156 (block of four). Imperf 3·00 4·25

DESIGNS—HORIZ: 6d. High-jumping. VERT: 1s.3d. Running. TRIANGULAR (60×30 mm): 2s.6d. Hurdling.

105 Scouts on Hill-top **109** "Telstar"

1965. 50th Anniv of Nigerian Scout Movement.
157 **105** 1d. brown 10 10
158 – 3d. red, black and green 15 10
159 – 6d. red, sepia and green 25 20
160 – 1s.3d. brown, yellow and deep green 40 85
MS160a 76×104 mm. No. 160 (block of four). Imperf 5·00 8·50

DESIGNS: 3d. Scout badge on shield; 6d. Scout badges; 1s.3d. Chief Scout and Nigerian scout.

1965. International Quiet Sun Years.
161 **109** 6d. violet and turquoise 15 15
162 – 1s.3d. green and lilac 15 15

DESIGN: 1s.3d. Solar satellite.

111 Native Tom-tom and Modern Telephone

1965. Centenary of I.T.U.
163 **111** 3d. black, red and brown 20 10
164 – 1s.3d. black, green & blue 2·00 1·00
165 – 5s. multicoloured 5·00 7·00

DESIGNS—VERT: 1s.3d. Microwave aerial. HORIZ: 5s. Telecommunications satellite and part of globe.

114 I.C.Y. Emblem and Diesel-hydraulic Locomotive

1965. International Co-operation Year.
166 **114** 3d. green, red and orange 3·00 20
167 – 1s. black, blue and lemon 3·00 40
168 – 2s.6d. green, blue & yellow 9·00 7·00

DESIGNS: 1s. Students and Lagos Teaching Hospital; 2s.6d. Kainji (Niger) Dam.

117 Carved Frieze

1965. 2nd Anniv of Republic.
169 **117** 3d. black, red and yellow 10 10
170 – 1s.3d. brown, green & blue 25 10
171 – 5s. brown, sepia and green 60 1·25

DESIGNS—VERT: 1s.3d. Stone Images at Ikom; 5s. Tada bronze.

121 African Elephants

1965.
172 – ½d. multicoloured 1·00 2·75
173 **121** 1d. multicoloured 50 15
174 – 1½d. multicoloured 8·00 8·50
222 – 2d. multicoloured 2·25 90
176 – 3d. multicoloured 1·25 30
177a – 4d. multicoloured 30 10
225 – 6d. multicoloured 2·25 20
179 – 9d. blue and red 3·00 60
227 – 1s. multicoloured 2·50 20
181 – 1s.3d. multicoloured 8·50 1·50
182 **227** 2s.6d. light brown, buff and brown 75 1·75
183 – 5s. chestnut, yellow and brown 1·75 3·00
184 – 10s. multicoloured 6·50 3·25
185 – £1 multicoloured 17·00 9·00

DESIGNS—VERT (as T **121**): ½d. Lion and cubs; 6d. Saddle-bill stork. (26½×46mm): 10s. Hippopotamus. HORIZ (as T **121**): 1½d. Splendid sunbird; 2d. Village weaver and red-headed malimbe; 3d. Cheetah; 4d. Leopards; 9d. Grey parrots. (46×26½ mm): 1s. Blue-breasted kingfishers; 1s.3d. Crowned cranes; 2s.6d. Kobs; 5s. Giraffes; £1 African buffalo.

The 1d., 3d., 4d., 1s., 1s.3d., 2s.6d., 5s. and £1 exist optd **F.G.N.** (Federal Government of Nigeria) twice in black. They were prepared in November 1968 as official stamps, but the scheme was abandoned. Some stamps held at a Head Post Office were sold in error and passed through the post. The Director of Posts then decided to put limited supplies on sale, but they had no postal validity.

1966. Commonwealth Prime Ministers' Meeting, Lagos. Optd **COMMONWEALTH P. M. MEETING 11. JAN. 1966.**
186 **48** 2s.6d. black and yellow 30 30

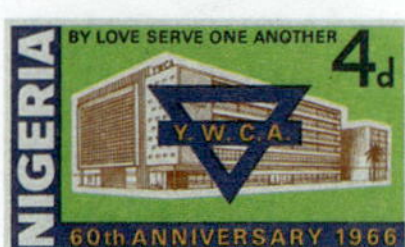

135 Y.W.C.A. Emblem and H.Q., Lagos

1966. Diamond Jubilee of Nigerian Y.W.C.A.
187 **135** 4d. multicoloured 15 10
188 9d. multicoloured 15 60

137 Telephone Handset and Linesman

1966. 3rd Anniv of Republic.

189 – 4d. green 10 10
190 137 1s.6d. black, brown & violet 30 50
191 – 2s.6d. multicoloured . . . 1·00 2·25

DESIGNS—VERT: 4d. Dove and flag. HORIZ: 2s.6d. North Channel Bridge over River Niger, Jebba.

139 "Education, Science and Culture"

1966. 20th Anniv of UNESCO.

192 139 4d. black, lake and orange 40 10
193 1s.6d. black, lake & turq 1·75 2·50
194 2s.6d. black, lake and pink . . . . 2·75 5·00

140 Children drinking

1966. Nigerian Red Cross.

195 140 4d.+1d. black, vio & red 30 30
196 – 1s.6d.+3d. multicoloured 55 3·75
197 – 2s.6d.+3d. multicoloured 65 4·25

DESIGNS—VERT: 1s.6d. Tending patient. HORIZ: 2s.6d. Tending casualties and badge.

143 Surveying

1967. Int Hydrological Decade. Mult.

198 4d. Type **143** 10 10
199 2s.6d. Water gauge on dam (vert) . . . . 25 1·50

145 Globe and Weather Satellite

1967. World Meteorological Day.

200 145 4d. mauve and blue . . . 15 10
201 – 1s.6d. black, yellow & blue 65 90

DESIGN: 1s.6d. Passing storm and sun.

147 Eyo Masqueraders

1967. 4th Anniv of Republic. Multicoloured.

202 4d. Type **147** 15 10
203 1s.6d. Crowds watching acrobat . . . . 50 1·50
204 2s.6d. Stilt dancer (vert) . . . 75 3·25

150 Tending Sick Animal

1967. Rinderpest Eradication Campaign.

205 150 4d. multicoloured 15 10
206 1s.6d. multicoloured . . . 55 1·50

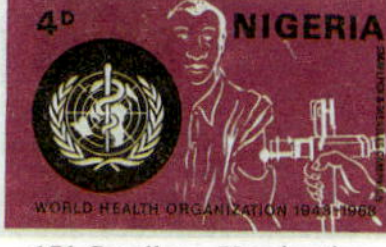

151 Smallpox Vaccination

1968. 20th Anniv of W.H.O.

207 151 4d. mauve and black . . 15 10
208 – 1s.6d. orange, lemon & blk . . . . 55 1·00

DESIGN: 1s.6d. African and mosquito.

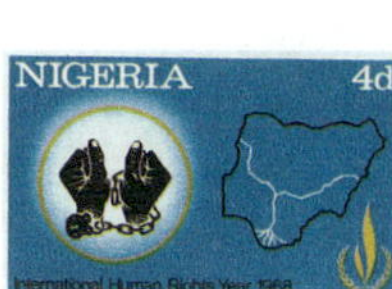

153 Chained Hands and Outline of Nigeria

155 Hand grasping at Doves of Freedom

1968. Human Rights Year.

209 153 4d. blue, black and yellow 10 10
210 – 1s.6d. green, red and black . . . . 20 1·00

DESIGN—VERT: 1s.6d. Nigerian flag and Human Rights emblem.

1968. 5th Anniv of Federal Republic.

211 155 4d. multicoloured 10 10
212 1s.6d. multicoloured . . . 20 1·00

156 Map of Nigeria and Olympic Rings

1968. Olympic Games, Mexico.

213 156 4d. black, green and red 20 10
214 – 1s.6d. multicoloured . . . 80 30

DESIGN: 1s.6d. Nigerian athletes, flag and Olympic rings.

158 G.P.O., Lagos

1969. Inauguration of Philatelic Service.

215 158 4d. black and green . . . 10 10
216 1s.6d. black and blue . . 20 50

159 Yakubu Gowon and Victoria Zakari

160 Bank Emblem and "5th Anniversary"

1969. Wedding of General Gowon.

217 159 4d. brown and green . . . 15 10
218 1s.6d. black and green . . 90 30

1969. 5th Anniv of African Development Bank.

233 160 4d. orange, black and blue 10 10
234 – 1s.6d. yellow, black and purple . . . . 20 1·25

DESIGN: 1s.6d. Bank emblem and rays.

162 I.L.O. Emblem

1969. 50th Anniv of I.L.O.

235 162 4d. black and violet . . . 10 10
236 – 1s.6d. green and black . . 75 1·50

DESIGN: 1s.6d. World map and I.L.O. emblem.

164 Olumo Rock

1969. International Year of African Tourism.

237 164 4d. multicoloured 15 10
238 – 1s. black and green . . . 20 10
239 – 1s.6d. multicoloured . . . 1·25 95

DESIGNS—VERT: 1s. Traditional musicians; 1s.6d. Assob Falls.

167 Symbolic Tree

169 Scroll

168 U.P.U. Headquarters Building

1970. "Stamp of Destiny". End of Civil War.

240 167 4d. gold, blue and black 10 10
241 – 1s. multicoloured 10 10
242 – 1s.6d. green and black . . 15 10
243 – 2s. multicoloured 20 20

DESIGNS—VERT: 1s. Symbolic wheel; 1s.6d. United Nigerians supporting map. HORIZ: 2s. Symbolic torch.

1970. New U.P.U. Headquarters Building.

244 168 4d. violet and yellow . . 10 10
245 1s.6d. blue and indigo . . 40 20

1970. 25th Anniv of United Nations.

246 169 4d. brown, buff and black 10 10
247 – 1s.6d. blue, brown & gold 30 20

DESIGN: 1s.6d. U.N. Building.

170 Oil Rig

172 Ibibio Face Mask

171 Children and Globe

1970. 10th Anniv of Independence.

248 2d. Type **170** 25 10
249 4d. University graduate . . . 15 10
250 6d. Durbar horsemen 30 10
251 9d. Servicemen raising flag 40 10
252 1s. Footballer 40 10
253 1s.6d. Parliament building . . 40 40
254 2s. Kainji Dam 70 90
255 2s.6d. Agricultural produce 70 1·00

1971. Racial Equality Year. Multicoloured.

256 4d. Type **171** 10 10
257 1s. Black and white men uprooting "Racism" (vert) 10 10
258 1s.6d. "The World in Black and White" (vert) 15 75
259 2s. Black and white men united . . . . 15 1·50

1971. Antiquities of Nigeria.

260 172 4d. black and blue . . . 10 10
261 – 1s.3d. brown and ochre 15 30
262 – 1s.9d. green, brown & yell 20 1·25

DESIGNS: 1s.3d. Benin bronze; 1s.9d. Ife bronze.

173 Children and Symbol

174 Mast and Dish Aerial

1971. 25th Anniv of UNICEF.

263 173 4d. multicoloured 10 10
264 – 1s.3d. orange, red & brn 15 40
265 – 1s.9d. turquoise and deep turquoise . . . . 15 1·00

DESIGNS: Each with UNICEF symbol: 1s.3d. Mother and child; 1s.9d. Mother carrying child.

1971. Opening of Nigerian Earth Satellite Station.

266 174 4d. multicoloured 15 10
267 – 1s.3d. green, blue & black 25 50
268 – 1s.9d. brown, orange & blk . . . . 25 1·00
269 – 3s. mauve, black and purple . . . . 45 2·00

DESIGNS: Nos. 267/9 as Type **174**, but showing different views of the Satellite Station.

175 Trade Fair Emblem

177 Nok Style Terracotta Head

176 Traffic

1972. All-Africa Trade Fair.

270 175 4d. multicoloured 10 10
271 – 1s.3d. lilac, yellow & gold 15 35
272 – 1s.9d. yellow, orange & blk . . . . 15 1·60

DESIGNS—HORIZ: 1s.3d. Map of Africa with pointers to Nairobi. VERT: 1s.9d. Africa on globe.

1972. Change to Driving on the Right.

273 176 4d. orange, brown & black 50 10
274 – 1s.3d. multicoloured . . . 1·25 70
275 – 1s.9d. multicoloured . . . 1·25 1·25
276 – 3s. multicoloured . . . . 1·75 3·00

DESIGNS: 1s.3d. Roundabout; 1s.9d. Highway; 3s. Road junction.

1972. All-Nigeria Arts Festival. Multicoloured.

277 4d. Type **177** 10 10
278 1s.3d. Bronze pot from Igbo-Ukwu 25 60
279 1s.9d. Bone harpoon (horiz) 30 1·75

178 Hides and Skins

1973.

290 178 1k. multicoloured . . . 10 20
281 – 2k. multicoloured . . . 35 10
292 – 3k. multicoloured . . . 15 10
282a – 5k. multicoloured . . . 50 10
294 – 7k. multicoloured . . . 30 1·25
295 – 8k. multicoloured . . . 40 10
344 – 10k. multicoloured . . . 1·00 20
297 – 12k. black, green and blue . . . . 30 3·25
298 – 15k. multicoloured . . . 30 60
299 – 18k. multicoloured . . . 50 30
300 – 20k. multicoloured . . . 65 30
301 – 25k. multicoloured . . . 85 45
302 – 30k. black, yellow & blue . . . . 40 1·50
303 – 35k. multicoloured . . . 6·00 4·75
288a – 50k. multicoloured . . . 50 90
305 – 1n. multicoloured . . . 50 75
306 – 2n. multicoloured . . . 75 2·00

DESIGNS—HORIZ: 2k. Natural gas tanks; 3k. Cement works; 5k. Cattle-ranching; 7k. Timber mill; 8k. Oil refinery; 10k. Cheetahs, Yankari Game Reserve; 12k. New Civic Building; 15k. Sugar-cane harvesting; 20k. Vaccine production; 25k. Modern wharf; 35k. Textile machinery; 1n. Eko Bridge; 2n. Teaching Hospital, Lagos. VERT: 18k. Palm oil production; 30k. Argungu Fishing Festival; 50k. Pottery.

179 Athlete

1973. 2nd All-African Games, Lagos.

307 179 5k. lilac, blue and black 15 10
308 – 12k. multicoloured . . . 20 50
309 – 18k. multicoloured . . . 45 1·00
310 – 25k. multicoloured . . . 50 1·50

DESIGNS—HORIZ: 12k. Football; 18k. Table tennis. VERT: 25k. National stadium.

180 All-Africa House, Addis Ababa

1973. 10th Anniv of O.A.U. Multicoloured.
311 5k. Type **180** 10 10
312 18k. O.A.U. flag (vert) 30 40
313 30k. O.A.U. emblem and symbolic flight of ten stairs (vert) 50 80

181 Dr. Hansen **182** W.M.O. Emblem and Weather-vane

1973. Cent of Discovery of Leprosy Bacillus.
314 **181** 5k.+2k. brown, pink and black 30 85

1973. Centenary of I.M.O./W.M.O.
315 **182** 5k. multicoloured 30 10
316 30k. multicoloured 1·50 2·25

183 University Complex

1973. 25th Anniv of Ibadan University. Multicoloured.
317 5k. Type **183** 10 10
318 12k. Students' population growth (vert) 15 20
319 18k. Tower and students 25 35
320 30k. Teaching Hospital 35 65

184 Lagos 1d. Stamp of 1874

1974. Stamp Centenary.
321 – 5k. green, orange & black 15 10
322 – 12k. multicoloured 30 40
323 **184** 18k. green, mauve & black 50 70
324 – 30k. multicoloured 1·50 2·00
DESIGNS: 5k. Graph of mail traffic growth; 12k. Northern Nigeria £25 stamp of 1904; 30k. Forms of mail transport.

185 U.P.U. Emblem on Globe

1974. Centenary of U.P.U.
325 **185** 5k. blue, orange and black 15 10
326 – 18k. multicoloured 2·00 60
327 – 30k. brown, green & black 1·75 1·75
DESIGNS: 18k. World transport map; 30k. U.P.U. emblem and letters.

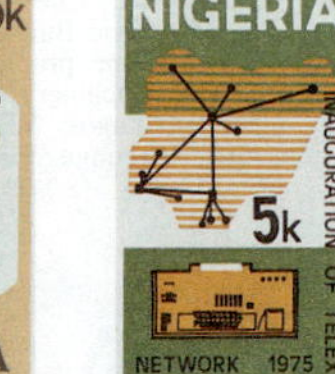

186 Starving and Well-fed Children **187** Telex Network and Teleprinter

1974. Freedom from Hunger Campaign.
328 **186** 5k. green, buff and black 10 10
329 – 12k. multicoloured 30 50
330 – 30k. multicoloured 80 1·75
DESIGNS—HORIZ: 12k. Poultry battery. VERT: 30k. Water-hoist.

1975. Inauguration of Telex Network.
331 **187** 5k. black, orange & green 10 10
332 – 12k. black, yellow & brn 20 20
333 – 18k. multicoloured 30 30
334 – 30k. multicoloured 50 50
DESIGNS: 12, 18, 30k. are as Type **187** but with the motifs arranged differently.

188 Queen Amina of Zaria **190** Alexander Graham Bell

1975. International Women's Year.
335 **188** 5k. green, yellow and blue 35 10
336 18k. purple, blue & mauve 1·00 80
337 30k. multicoloured 1·25 1·60

1976. Centenary of Telephone.
355 **190** 5k. multicoloured 10 10
356 – 18k. multicoloured 40 55
357 – 25k. blue, light blue and brown 70 1·00
DESIGNS—HORIZ: 18k. Gong and modern telephone system. VERT: 25k. Telephones, 1876 and 1976.

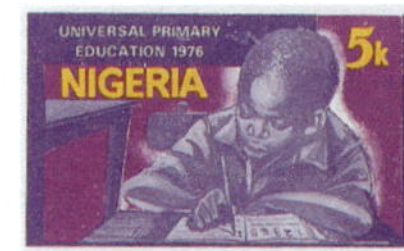

191 Child writing

1976. Launching of Universal Primary Education.
358 **191** 5k. yellow, violet & mauve 10 10
359 – 18k. multicoloured 45 60
360 – 25k. multicoloured 70 1·00
DESIGNS—VERT: 18k. Children entering school; 25k. Children in class.

192 Festival Emblem

1976. 2nd World Black and African Festival of Arts and Culture, Nigeria.
361 **192** 5k. gold and brown 35 10
362 – 10k. brown, yellow & blk 35 55
363 – 12k. multicoloured 80 90
364 – 18k. yellow, brown & blk 90 90
365 – 30k. red and black 1·00 1·50
DESIGNS: 10k. National Arts Theatre; 12k. African hair-styles; 18k. Musical instruments; 30k. "Nigerian arts and crafts".

193 General Murtala Muhammed and Map of Nigeria **194** Scouts saluting

1977. 1st Death Anniv of General Muhammed (Head of State). Multicoloured.
366 5k. Type **193** 10 10
367 18k. General in dress uniform (vert) 20 35
368 30k. General in battle dress (vert) 30 70

1977. 1st All-African Scout Jamboree, Jos, Nigeria. Multicoloured.
369 5k. Type **194** 15 10
370 18k. Scouts cleaning street (horiz) 60 70
371 25k. Scouts working on farm (horiz) 70 1·25
372 30k. Jamboree emblem and map of Africa (horiz) 80 2·00

195 Trade Fair Complex

1977. 1st Lagos Int Trade Fair.
373 **195** 5k. black, blue and green 10 10
374 – 18k. black, blue and purple 20 25
375 – 30k. multicoloured 30 45
DESIGNS: 18k. Globe and Trade Fair emblem; 30k. Weaving and basketry.

196 Map showing Nigerian Universities

1978. Global Conference on Technical Co-operation between Developing Countries, Buenos Aires.
376 **196** 5k. multicoloured 10 10
377 – 12k. multicoloured 15 15
378 – 18k. multicoloured 25 25
379 – 30k. yellow, violet & black 45 60
DESIGNS: 12k. Map of West African highways and telecommunications; 18k. Technologists undergoing training; 30k. World map.

197 Microwave Antenna

1978. 10th World Telecommunications Day.
380 **197** 30k. multicoloured 50 60

198 Students on "Operation Feed the Nation"

1978. "Operation Feed the Nation" Campaign. Multicoloured.
381 5k. Type **198** 10 10
382 18k. Family backyard farm 20 20
383 30k. Plantain farm (vert) 35 60

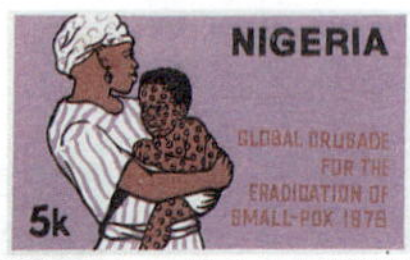

199 Mother with Infected Child

1978. Global Eradication of Smallpox.
384 **199** 5k. black, brown and lilac 15 10
385 – 12k. multicoloured 25 40
386 – 18k. black, brown & yell 40 55
387 – 30k. black, silver and pink 55 1·40
DESIGNS—HORIZ: 12k. Doctor and infected child; 18k. Group of children being vaccinated. VERT: 30k. Syringe.

200 Nok Terracotta Human Figure, Bwari (900 B.C.–100 A.D.) **201** Anti-Apartheid Emblem

1978. Antiquities.
388 **200** 5k. black, blue and red 10 10
389 – 12k. multicoloured 15 10
390 – 18k. black, blue and red 20 15
391 – 30k. multicoloured 25 20
DESIGNS—HORIZ: 12k. Igbo-Ukwu bronze snail shell, Igbo Isaiah (9th-century A.D.). VERT: 18k. Ife bronze statue of a king (12th–15th century A.D.); 30k. Benin bronze equestrian figure (about 1700 A.D.).

1978. International Anti-Apartheid Year.
392 **201** 18k. black, yellow and red 15 15

202 Wright Brothers and Wright Type A

1978. 75th Anniv of Powered Flight.
393 **202** 5k. multicoloured 20 10
394 – 18k. black, blue and light blue 60 20
DESIGN: 18k. Nigerian Air Force formation.

203 Murtala Muhammed Airport

1979. Opening of Murtala Muhammed Airport.
395 **203** 5k. black, grey and blue 40 30

204 Child with Stamp Album

1979. 10th Anniv of National Philatelic Service.
396 **204** 5k. multicoloured 10 20

205 Mother and Child

1979. International Year of the Child. Multicoloured.
397 5k. Type **205** 10 10
398 18k. Children studying 35 30
399 25k. Children playing (vert) 40 50

206 Trainee Teacher making Audio Visual Aid Materials **207** Necom House

1979. 50th Anniv of International Bureau of Education. Multicoloured.
400 10k. Type **206** 10 10
401 30k. Adult education class 25 30

1979. 50th Anniv of Consultative Committee of International Radio.
402 **207** 10k. multicoloured 15 20

208 Trainees of the Regional Air Survey School, Ile-Ife

1979. 21st Anniv of Economic Commission for Africa.
403 **208** 10k. multicoloured 20 20

209 Football Cup and Map of Nigeria

1980. African Cup of Nations Football Competition, Nigeria. Multicoloured.
404 10k. Type **209** 20 10
405 30k. Footballer (vert) 60 50

210 Wrestling

1980. Olympic Games, Moscow.
406 **210** 10k. multicoloured 10 10
407 – 20k. black and green 10 10

408 – 30k. black, orange & blue 15 15
409 – 45k. multicoloured . . . 20 20
DESIGNS—VERT: 20k. Long jump; 45k. Netball. HORIZ: 30k. Swimming.

211 Figures supporting O.P.E.C. Emblem

1980. 20th Anniv of O.P.E.C. (Organization of Petroleum Exporting Countries).
410 **211** 10k. black, blue and yellow 15 10
411 – 45k. black, blue and mauve 70 60
DESIGN—VERT: 45k. O.P.E.C. emblem and globe.

212 Tank Locomotive No. 2, Wushishi Tramway

1980. 25th Anniv of Nigerian Railway Corporation. Multicoloured.
412 10k. Type **212** 75 10
413 20k. Loading goods train . . 1·00 85
414 30k. Freight train . . . . . 1·40 1·25

213 Metric Scales

215 Disabled Woman sweeping

1980. World Standards Day.
415 **213** 10k. red and black . . . 10 10
416 – 30k. multicoloured . . . 35 40
DESIGN—HORIZ: 30k. Quality control.

214 "Communication" Symbols and Map of West Africa

1980. 5th Anniv of Economic Community of West African States.
417 **214** 10k. black, orange & olive 10 10
418 – 25k. black, green and red 30 10
419 – 30k. black, yellow & brn 20 15
420 – 45k. black, turquoise & bl 25 25
DESIGNS: 25k. "Transport"; 30k. "Agriculture"; 45k. "Industry".

1981. International Year for Disabled Persons.
421 **215** 10k. multicoloured . . . 20 10
422 – 30k. black, brown and blue 65 65
DESIGN: 30k. Disabled man filming.

216 President launching "Green Revolution" (food production campaign)

1981. World Food Day.
423 **216** 10k. multicoloured . . . 10 10
424 – 25k. black, yellow & green 20 50
425 – 30k. multicoloured . . . 25 55
426 – 45k. black, brown & yell 45 85
DESIGNS—VERT: 25k. Food crops; 30k. Harvesting tomatoes. HORIZ: 45k. Pig farming.

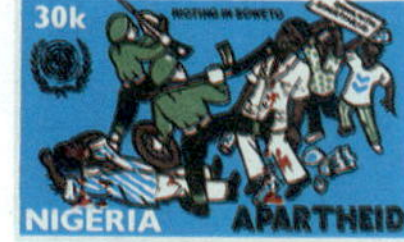

217 Rioting in Soweto

1981. Anti-Apartheid Movement.
427 **217** 30k. multicoloured . . . 35 55
428 – 45k. black, red and green 50 1·25
DESIGN—VERT: 45k. "Police brutality".

218 "Preservation of Wildlife"

1982. 75th Anniv of Boy Scout Movement. Multicoloured.
429 30k. Type **218** 50 55
430 45k. Lord Baden-Powell taking salute 75 95

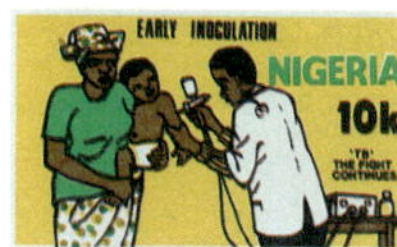

219 Early Inoculation

1982. Centenary of Robert Koch's Discovery of Tubercle Bacillus.
431 **219** 10k. multicoloured . . . 20 15
432 – 30k. black, brown and green 50 65
433 – 45k. black, brown and green . . . . 80 1·40
DESIGNS—HORIZ: 30k. Technician and microscope. VERT: 45k. Patient being X-rayed.

220 "Keep Your Environment Clean"

1982. 10th Anniv of U.N. Conference on Human Environment.
434 **220** 10k. multicoloured . . . 10 10
435 – 20k. orange, grey and black 20 40
436 – 30k. multicoloured . . . 35 60
437 – 45k. multicoloured . . . 55 85
DESIGNS: 20k. "Check air pollution"; 30k. "Preserve natural environment"; 45k. "Reafforestation concerns all".

221 "Salamis parhassus"

222 Carving of "Male and Female Twins"

1982. Nigerian Butterflies. Multicoloured.
438 10k. Type **221** 15 10
439 20k. "Iterus zalmoxis" . . . 30 30
440 30k. "Cymothoe beckeri" . . 40 40
441 45k. "Papilio hesperus" . . . 70 70

1982. 25th Anniv of National Museum. Multicoloured.
442 10k. Type **222** 10 10
443 20k. Royal bronze leopard (horiz) 20 35
444 30k. Soapstone seated figure 35 90
445 45k. Wooden helmet mask 50 1·75

223 Three Generations

1983. Family Day. Multicoloured.
446 10k. Type **223** 15 10
447 30k. Parents with three children (vert) 50 65

224 Satellite View of Globe

1983. Commonwealth Day.
448 **224** 10k. brown and black . . 10 10
449 – 25k. multicoloured . . . 20 30
450 – 30k. black, purple and grey 55 35
451 – 45k. multicoloured . . . 35 45
DESIGNS—HORIZ: 25k. National Assembly Buildings. VERT: 30k. Drilling for oil; 45k. Athletics.

225 Corps Members on Building Project

226 Postman on Bicycle

1983. 10th Anniv of National Youth Service Corps. Multicoloured.
452 10k. Type **225** 15 10
453 25k. On the assault-course (vert) 30 30
454 30k. Corps members on parade 40 40

1983. World Communications Year. Multicoloured.
455 10k. Type **226** 15 10
456 25k. Newspaper kiosk (horiz) 30 45
457 30k. Town crier blowing elephant tusk (horiz) . . . 35 80
458 45k. T.V. newsreader (horiz) 45 1·10

227 Pink Shrimp

1983. World Fishery Resources.
459 **227** 10k. red, blue and black 15 10
460 – 25k. multicoloured . . . 30 40
461 – 30k. multicoloured . . . 30 45
462 – 45k. multicoloured . . . 40 70
DESIGNS: 25k. Long-necked croaker; 30k. Barracuda; 45k. Fishing techniques.

228 On Parade

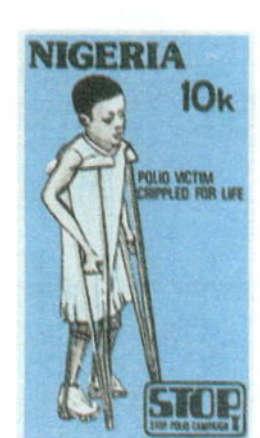

229 Crippled Child

1983. Centenary of Boys' Brigade and 75th Anniv of Founding in Nigeria. Multicoloured.
463 10k. Type **228** 40 10
464 30k. Members working on cassava plantation (horiz) 1·50 1·50
465 45k. Skill training (horiz) . . 2·25 2·75

1984. Stop Polio Campaign.
466 **229** 10k. blue, black and brown 20 15
467 – 25k. orange, black & yell 40 75
468 – 30k. red, black and brown 60 1·10
DESIGNS—HORIZ: 25k. Child receiving vaccine. VERT: 30k. Healthy child.

230 Waterbuck

232 Boxing

231 Obverse and Reverse of 1969 £1 Note

1984. Nigerian Wildlife.
469 **230** 10k. green, brown & black 15 10
470 – 25k. multicoloured . . . 30 50
471 – 30k. brown, black & green 40 90
472 – 45k. blue, orange & black 45 1·50
DESIGNS—HORIZ: 25k. Hartebeest; 30k. African buffalo. VERT: 45k. Diademed monkey.

1984. 25th Anniv of Nigerian Central Bank.
473 **231** 10k. multicoloured . . . 20 10
474 – 25k. brown, black & green 45 60
475 – 30k. red, black and green 55 75
DESIGNS: 25k. Central Bank; 30k. Obverse and reverse of 1959 £5 note.

1984. Olympic Games, Los Angeles. Mult.
476 10k. Type **232** 15 10
477 25k. Discus-throwing 35 50
478 30k. Weightlifting 40 60
479 45k. Cycling 60 90

233 Irrigation Project, Lesotho

234 Pin-tailed Whydah

1984. 20th Anniv of African Development Bank.
480 **233** 10k. multicoloured . . . 15 10
481 – 25k. multicoloured . . . 30 50
482 – 30k. black, yellow and blue 35 60
483 – 45k. black, brown and blue . . . . 1·75 90
DESIGNS—HORIZ: 25k. Bomi Hills Road, Liberia; 30k. School building project, Seychelles; 45k. Coal mining, Niger.

1984. Rare Birds. Multicoloured.
484 10k. Type **234** 75 20
485 25k. Spur-winged plover . . 1·50 70
486 30k. Red bishop . . . . . . 1·50 1·75
487 45k. Double-spurred francolin 1·75 2·50

235 Boeing 747 Airliner taking-off

1984. 40th Anniv of International Civil Aviation Organization. Multicoloured.
488 10k. Type **235** 40 10
489 45k. Boeing 707 airliner circling globe . . . . . . 1·50 2·25

236 Office Workers and Clocks ("Punctuality")

1985. "War against Indiscipline". Mult.
490 20k. Type **236** 30 35
491 50k. Cross over hands passing banknotes ("Discourage Bribery") . . 55 75

237 Footballers receiving Flag from Major-General Buhari

239 Globe and O.P.E.C. Emblem

238 Rolling Mill

1985. International Youth Year. Mult.
492 20k. Type **237** 30 20
493 50k. Girls of different tribes with flag (vert) 55 70
494 55k. Members of youth organizations with flags (vert) 55 80

1985. 25th Anniv of Independence. Mult.
495 20k. Type **238** 25 10
496 50k. Map of Nigeria 40 45
497 55k. Remembrance Arcade 40 50
498 60k. Eleme, first Nigerian oil refinery . . . . 1·00 1·25
MS499 101 × 101 mm. Nos. 495/8 5·00 6·50

1985. 25th Anniv of Organization of Petroleum Exporting Countries.
500 **239** 20k. blue and red 75 35
501 – 50k. black and blue . . . 1·50 75
DESIGN—HORIZ: 50k. World map and O.P.E.C. emblem.

240 Waterfall

241 Map of Nigeria and National Flag

1985. World Tourism Day. Multicoloured.
502 20k. Type **240** 35 10
503 50k. Pottery, carved heads and map of Nigeria (horiz) 45 50
504 55k. Calabash carvings and Nigerian flag 45 50
505 60k. Leather work 45 55

1985. 40th Anniv of United Nations Organization and 25th Anniv of Nigerian Membership.
506 **241** 20k. black, green and blue 20 10
507 – 50k. black, blue and red 35 75
508 – 55k. black, blue and red 35 85
DESIGNS—HORIZ: 50k. United Nations Building, New York; 55k. United Nations logo.

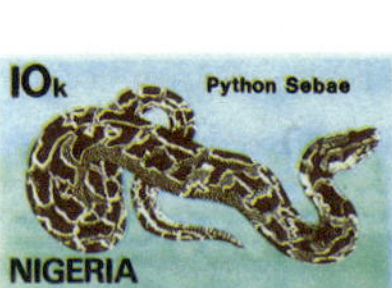

242 Rock Python

243 Social Worker with Children

1986. African Reptiles.
509 **242** 10k. multicoloured . . . 30 10
510 – 20k. black, brown and blue 50 90
511 – 25k. multicoloured . . . 50 1·00
512 – 30k. multicoloured . . . 50 1·00
DESIGNS: 20k. Long snouted crocodile; 25k. Gopher tortoise; 30k. Chameleon.

1986. Nigerian Life. Multicoloured.
513 1k. Type **243** 10 10
514 2k. Volkswagen motor assembly line (horiz) . . 10 10
515 5k. Modern housing estate (horiz) 10 10
516 10k. Harvesting oil palm fruit 10 10
517 15k. Unloading freighter (horiz) 15 10
518 20k. "Tecoma stans" (flower) 15 10
519 25k. Hospital ward (horiz) 15 10
519a 30k. Birom dancers (horiz) 15 10
520 35k. Telephonists operating switchboard (horiz) . . . 15 10
521 40k. Nkpokiti dancers . . 15 10
522 45k. Hibiscus (horiz) . . . 15 10
523a 50k. Post Office counter (horiz) 15 10
524 1n. Stone quarry (horiz) 15 15
525a 2n. Students in laboratory (horiz) 15 15
525ba 10n. Lekki Beach (horiz) 20 15
525c 20n. Ancient wall, Kano (horiz) . . . . 4·50 1·75
525d 50n. Rock bridge (horiz) 4·00 3·50
525e 100n. Ekpe masquerader 2·50 3·25
525f 500n. National Theatre (horiz) . . . . 8·00 8·50

244 Emblem and Globe

1986. International Peace Year. Mult.
526 10k. Type **244** 20 10
527 20k. Hands of five races holding globe . . . . . . 60 1·50

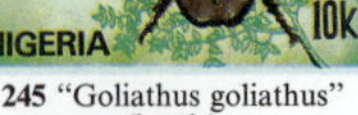
245 "Goliathus goliathus" (beetle)

246 Oral Rehydration Therapy

1986. Nigerian Insects. Multicoloured.
528 10k. Type **245** 30 10
529 20k. "Vespa vulgaris" (wasp) 40 40
530 25k. "Acheta domestica" (cricket) 45 90
531 30k. "Anthrenus verbasci" (beetle) . . . . 55 1·50
MS532 119 × 101 mm. Nos. 528/31 4·50 6·50

1986. 40th Anniv of UNICEF.
533 **246** 10k. multicoloured . . . 30 10
534 – 20k. black, brown & yell 40 40
535 – 25k. multicoloured . . . 45 70
536 – 30k. multicoloured . . . 55 1·00
DESIGNS: 20k. Immunization; 25k. Breast-feeding; 30k. Mother and child.

247 Stylized Figures on Wall ("International Understanding")

1986. 25th Anniv of Nigerian Institute of International Affairs.
537 **247** 20k. black, blue and green 50 50
538 – 30k. multicoloured . . . 75 1·25
DESIGN—VERT: 30k. "Knowledge" (bronze sculpture).

248 Freshwater Clam

1987. Shells.
539 **248** 10k. multicoloured . . . 65 10
540 – 20k. black, brown and pink . . . . 1·00 1·75
541 – 25k. multicoloured . . . 1·00 2·00
542 – 30k. multicoloured . . . 1·25 2·50
DESIGNS: 20k. Periwinkle; 25k. Bloody cockle (inscr "BLODDY COCKLE"); 30k. Mangrove oyster.

249 "Clitoria ternatea"

250 Doka Hairstyle

1987. Nigerian Flowers.
543 **249** 10k. multicoloured . . . 10 10
544 – 20k. brown, yellow and green 15 25
545 – 25k. multicoloured . . . 15 45
546 – 30k. multicoloured . . . 20 1·00
DESIGNS: 20k. "Hibiscus tiliaceus"; 25k. "Acanthus montanus"; 30k. "Combretum racemosum".

1987. Women's Hairstyles.
547 **250** 10k. black, brown and grey 10 10
548 – 20k. multicoloured . . . 15 25
549 – 25k. black, brown and red 20 55
550 – 30k. multicoloured . . . 20 1·00
DESIGNS: 20k. Eting; 25k. Agogo; 30k. Goto.

251 Family sheltering under Tree

252 Red Cross Worker distributing Food

1987. International Year of Shelter for the Homeless. Multicoloured.
551 20k. Type **251** 15 15
552 30k. Family and modern house 15 90

1988. 125th Anniv of International Red Cross. Multicoloured.
553 20k. Type **252** 65 30
554 30k. Carrying patient to ambulance . . . . 65 1·75

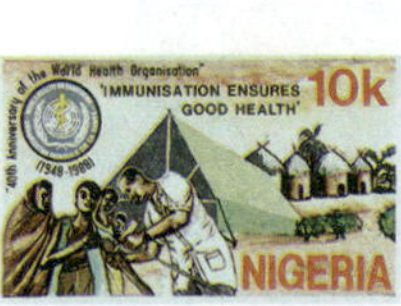

253 Doctor vaccinating Baby

254 O.A.U. Logo

1988. 40th Anniv of W.H.O. Multicoloured.
555 10k. Type **253** 25 10
556 20k. W.H.O. logo and outline map of Nigeria 60 60
557 30k. Doctor and patients at mobile clinic 60 60

1988. 25th Anniv of Organization of African Unity.
558 **254** 10k. brown, green & orge 15 15
559 – 20k. multicoloured . . . 15 15
DESIGN: 20k. Four Africans supporting map of Africa.

255 Pink Shrimp

1988. Shrimps.
560 **255** 10k. multicoloured . . . 20 10
561 – 20k. black and green . . 25 15
562 – 25k. black, red and brown 25 25
563 – 30k. orange, brown & blk 30 60
MS564 120 × 101 mm. Nos. 560/3 1·50 2·00
DESIGNS: 20k. Tiger shrimp; 25k. Deepwater roseshrimp; 30k. Estuarine prawn.

256 Weightlifting

1988. Olympic Games, Seoul. Multicoloured.
565 10k. Type **256** 25 10
566 20k. Boxing 35 35
567 30k. Athletics (vert) 50 65

257 Banknote Production Line (½-size illustration)

1988. 25th Anniv of Nigerian Security Printing and Minting Co. Ltd.
568 **257** 10k. multicoloured . . . 10 10
569 – 20k. black, silver and green 20 20
570 – 25k. multicoloured . . . 30 30
571 – 30k. multicoloured . . . 50 50
DESIGNS—HORIZ (As T **257**): 20k. Coin production line. VERT (37 × 44 mm): 25k. Montage of products; 30k. Anniversary logos.

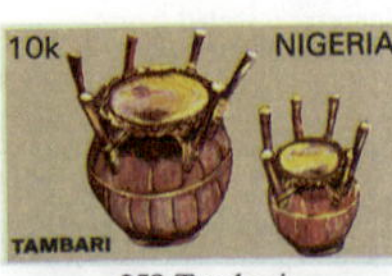

258 Tambari

1989. Nigerian Musical Instruments.
572 **258** 10k. multicoloured . . . 10 10
573 – 20k. multicoloured . . . 20 20
574 – 25k. brown, green & black 30 30
575 – 30k. brown and black . . 50 50
DESIGNS: 20k. Kundung; 25k. Ibid; 30k. Dundun.

259 Construction of Water Towers, Mali

1989. 25th Anniv of African Development Bank. Multicoloured.
576 10k. Type **259** 10 10
577 20k. Paddy field, Gambia . . 15 15
578 25k. Bank Headquarters, Abidjan, Ivory Coast . . . 25 25
579 30k. Anniversary logo (vert) 35 35

260 Lighting Campfire

1989. 70th Anniv of Nigerian Girl Guides Association. Multicoloured.
580 10k. Type **260** 30 10
581 20k. Guide on rope bridge (vert) 70 60

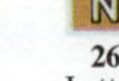
261 Etubom Costume

262 Dove with Letter and Map of Africa

1989. Traditional Costumes. Multicoloured.
582 10k. Type **261** 40 10
583 20k. Fulfulde 45 25
584 25k. Aso-Ofi 50 85
585 30k. Fuska Kura . . . . . . 60 1·75

1990. 10th Anniv of Pan African Postal Union. Multicoloured.
586 10k. Type **262** 25 10
587 20k. Parcel and map of Africa 50 50

263 Oil Lamps

1990. Nigerian Pottery.
588 **263** 10k. black, brown & violet 10 10
589 – 20k. black, brown & violet 20 20
590 – 25k. brown and violet . . 25 25
591 – 30k. multicoloured . . . 35 35
MS592 120 × 100 mm. Nos. 588/91 80 90
DESIGNS: 20k. Water pots; 25k. Musical pots; 50k. Water jugs.

264 Teacher and Class

1990. International Literacy Year.
593 **264** 20k. multicoloured . . . 20 10
594 – 30k. brown, blue & yellow 30 30
DESIGN: 30k. Globe and book.

265 Globe and OPEC Logo

1990. 30th Anniv of the Organization of Petroleum Exporting Countries. Multicoloured.
595 10k. Type **265** 10 10
596 20k. Logo and flags of member countries (vert) . . 20 20
597 25k. World map and logo . . 25 25
598 30k. Logo within inscription "Co-operation for Global Energy Security" (vert) . . 35 35

266 Grey Parrot

267 Eradication Treatment

1990. Wildlife. Multicoloured.
599 20k. Type **266** 20 10
600 30k. Roan antelope 20 10

601 1n.50 Grey-necked bald crow ("Rockfowl") 60 80
602 2n.50 Mountain gorilla . . . 85 1·25
MS603 118 × 119 mm. Nos. 599/602 1·75 2·25

1991. National Guineaworm Eradication Day. Multicoloured.
604 10k. Type **267** 15 10
605 20k. Women collecting water from river (horiz) 25 25
606 30k. Boiling pot of water . . 25 25

268 Hand holding Torch (Progress) **269** National Flags

1991. Organization of African Unity Heads of State and Governments Meeting, Abuja. Each showing outline map of Africa. Multicoloured.
607 20k. Type **268** 15 10
608 30k. Cogwheel (Unity) . . . 20 25
609 50k. O.A.U. flag (Freedom) 20 45

1991. Economic Community of West African States Summit Meeting, Abuja. Multicoloured.
610 20k. Type **269** 15 10
611 50k. Map showing member states 30 45

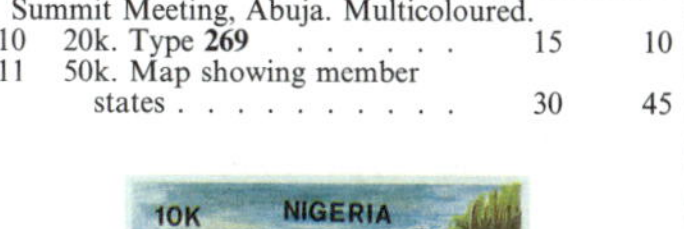

270 Electric Catfish

1991. Nigerian Fishes. Multicoloured.
612 10k. Type **270** 15 10
613 20k. Nile perch 25 25
614 30k. Nile mouthbrooder ("Talapia") 35 35
615 50k. Sharp-toothed catfish . . 50 55
MS616 121 × 104 mm. Nos. 612/15 2·00 2·50

271 Telecom '91 Emblem

1991. "Telecom '91" 6th World Telecommunication Exhibition, Geneva.
617 **271** 20k. black, green and violet 30 10
618 – 50k. multicoloured . . . 40 30
DESIGN—VERT: 50k. Emblem and patchwork.

272 Boxing

1992. Olympic Games, Barcelona (1st issue). Multicoloured.
619 50k. Type **272** 15 15
620 1n. Nigerian athlete winning race 25 25
621 1n.50 Table tennis 35 35
622 2n. Taekwondo 45 45
MS623 120 × 117 mm. Nos. 619/22 1·75 2·00
See also No. 624.

273 Football **274** Blood Pressure Gauge

1992. Olympic Games, Barcelona (2nd issue).
624 **273** 1n.50 multicoloured . . . 50 50

1992. World Health Day. Multicoloured.
625 50k. Type **274** 15 15
626 1n. World Health Day '92 emblem 20 20
627 1n.50 Heart and lungs . . . 30 30
628 2n. Interior of heart 45 45
MS629 123 × 111 mm. Nos. 625/8 1·10 1·25

275 Map of World and Stamp on Globe

1992. "Olymphilex '92" Olympic Stamp Exhibition, Barcelona. Multicoloured.
630 50k. Type **275** 20 10
631 1n.50 Examining stamps . . 40 40
MS632 120 × 109 mm. Nos. 630/1 1·60 1·75

276 Gathering Plantain Fruit **277** Centre Emblem

1992. 25th Anniv of International Institute of Tropical Agriculture.
633 **276** 50k. multicoloured . . . 10 10
634 – 1n. multicoloured 15 15
635 – 1n.50 black, brown & grn 20 20
636 – 2n. multicoloured 25 25
MS637 121 × 118 mm. Nos. 633/6 1·25 1·50
DESIGNS—VERT: 1n.50, Harvesting cassava tubers; 2n. Stacking yams. HORIZ: 1n. Tropical foods.

1992. Commissioning of Maryam Babangida National Centre for Women's Development.
638 **277** 50k. gold, emerald and green 10 10
639 – 1n. multicoloured 15 15
640 – 1n.50 multicoloured . . . 20 20
641 – 2n. multicoloured 30 30
DESIGNS—VERT: 1n. Women working in fields; 2n. Woman at loom. HORIZ: 1n.50, Maryam Babangida National Centre.
All examples of No. 641 are without a "NIGERIA" inscription.

278 Healthy Food and Emblem **279** Sabada Dance

1992. International Conference on Nutrition, Rome. Multicoloured.
642 50k. Type **278** 10 10
643 1n. Child eating 15 15
644 1n.50 Fruit (vert) 20 20
645 2n. Vegetables 25 25
MS646 120 × 100 mm. Nos. 642/5 1·50 1·75

1992. Traditional Dances. Multicoloured.
647 50k. Type **279** 10 10
648 1n. Sato 15 15
649 1n.50 Asian Ubo Ikpa . . . 20 20
650 2n. Dundun 25 25
MS651 126 × 107 mm. Nos. 647/50 1·50 1·75

280 African Elephant

1993. Wildlife. Multicoloured.
652 1n.50 Type **280** . . . . . . 1·50 40
653 5n. Stanley crane (vert) . . . 2·00 50
654 20n. Roan antelope . . . . . 2·75 2·00
655 30n. Lion . . . . 3·00 3·00

281 Suburban Garden

1993. World Environment Day. Multicoloured.
656 1n. Type **281** 10 10
657 1n.50 Water pollution 15 10
658 5n. Forest road 50 60
659 10n. Rural house . . . . . . 90 1·25

282 Oni Figure **283** "Bulbophyllum distans"

1993. 50th Anniv of National Museums and Monuments Commission. Multicoloured.
660 1n. Type **282** 10 10
661 1n.50 Bronze head of Queen Mother 10 10
662 5n. Bronze pendant (horiz) 30 50
663 10n. Nok head . . . . 70 1·00

1993. Orchids. Multicoloured.
664 1n. Type **283** 10 10
665 1n.50 "Eulophia cristata" . . 15 10
666 5n. "Eulophia horsfalli" . . . 45 55
667 10n. "Eulophia quartiniana" 1·00 1·25
MS668 103 × 121 mm. Nos. 664/7 1·75 2·00

284 Children in Classroom and Adults carrying Food

1994. International Year of the Family. Mult.
669 1n.50 Type **284** 10 10
670 10n. Market . . . . 1·00 1·50

285 Hand with Tweezers holding 1969 4d. Philatelic Service Stamp

1994. 25th Anniv of Nat Philatelic Service. Mult.
671 1n. Type **285** 10 10
672 1n.50 Philatelic Bureau . . . 15 10
673 5n. Stamps forming map of Nigeria 45 60
674 10n. Philatelic counter . . . 1·00 1·40

286 "I Love Stamps"

1994. 120th Anniv of First Postage Stamps in Nigeria. Multicoloured.
675 1n. Type **286** 10 10
676 1n.50 "I Collect Stamps" . . 15 15
677 5n. 19th-century means of communication 45 60
678 10n. Lagos stamp of 1874 . . 1·00 1·40

287 Magnifying Glass over Globe

1994. "Philakorea '94" International Stamp Exhibition, Seoul.
679 **287** 30n. multicoloured . . . 1·75 2·40
MS680 127 × 115 mm. **287** 30n. multicoloured . . . . 2·25 4·00

288 Geryon Crab

1994. Crabs. Multicoloured.
681 1n. Type **288** 10 10
682 1n.50 Spider crab 10 10
683 5n. Red spider crab 45 55
684 10n. Geryon maritae crab . . 90 1·25

289 Sewage Works **290** Letterbox

1994. 30th Anniv of African Development Bank. Multicoloured.
685 1n.50 Type **289** 15 10
686 30n. Development Bank emblem and flowers . . . 1·75 2·40

1995. 10th Anniv of Nigerian Post and Telecommunication Corporations. Multicoloured.
687 1n. Type **290** 10 10
688 1n.50 Letter showing "1 JAN 1985" postmark (horiz) . . 10 10
689 5n. Nipost and Nitel emblems (horiz) 30 45
690 10n. Mobile telephones . . . 60 1·00

291 Woman preparing Food **292** "Candlestick" Telephone

1995. Family Support Programme. Multicoloured.
691 1n. Type **291** 10 10
692 1n.50 Mother teaching children 10 10
693 5n. Family meal 30 45
694 10n. Agricultural workers and tractor 60 90

1995. Cent of First Telephone in Nigeria. Mult.
695 1n.50 Type **292** 10 10
696 10n. Early equipment . . . . 60 1·00

293 F.A.O. Emblem **294** "Justice" and 50th Anniversary Emblem

1995. 50th Anniv of F.A.O. Multicoloured.
697 1n.50 Type **293** 10 10
698 30n. Fishing canoes . . . . 1·90 2·50

1995. 50th Anniv of United Nations. Multicoloured.
699 1n. Type **294** 10 10
700 1n.50 Toxic waste (horiz) . . 10 10
701 5n. Tourist hut (horiz) . . . 30 40
702 10n. Nigerian armoured car on U.N. duty (horiz) . . . 1·50 1·60

295 Container Ship in Dock

1996. 10th Anniv of Niger Dock. Multicoloured.
703 5n. Type **295** 35 30
704 10n. "Badagri" (tourist launch) on crane 65 60
705 20n. Shipping at dock . . . 1·00 1·50
706 30n. "Odoragushin" (ferry) 1·50 2·50

296 Scientist and Crops

1996. 21st Anniv of E.C.O.W.A.S. (Economic Community of West African States). Multicoloured.
707 5n. Type **296** 30 30
708 30n. Queue at border crossing . . . . 1·50 2·25

297 Judo

298 Nigerian Flag and Exhibition Emblem

1996. Olympic Games, Atlanta. Multicoloured.
709 5n. Type **297** 35 30
710 10n. Tennis 80 60
711 20n. Relay race . . . . . . 1·00 1·50
712 30n. Football . . . . 1·50 2·25

1996. "ISTANBUL '96" International Stamp Exhibition.
713 **298** 30n. mauve, green and black . . . . 1·50 2·25

299 "Volvariella esculenta"

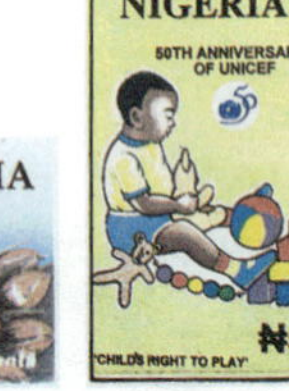

300 Boy with Toys

1996. Fungi. Multicoloured.
714 5n. Type **299** 45 30
715 10n. "Lentinus subnudus" . . 90 60
716 20n. "Tricholoma lobayensis" 1·25 1·50
717 30n. "Pleurotus tuber-regium" . . . . 1·50 2·25

1996. 50th Anniv of UNICEF. Multicoloured.
718 5n. Type **300** 30 30
719 30n. Girl reading book (horiz) . . . . 1·50 2·25

301 Literacy Logo

1996. 5th Anniv of Mass Literacy Commission.
720 **301** 5n. emerald, green and black 30 30
721 – 30n. emerald, green and black . . . . 1·50 2·25
DESIGN: 30n. Hands holding book and literacy logo.

302 Three Footballers

1998. World Cup Football Championship, France. Multicoloured.
722 5n. Type **302** 25 30
723 10n. Player with ball (vert) 55 60
724 20n. Player receiving ball (vert) . . . . 1·10 1·25
725 30n. Two opposing players 1·60 2·25

303 University Tower and Complex

1998. 50th Anniv of Ibadan University. Mult.
726 5n. Type **303** 25 30
727 30n. Anniversary logo and University crest . . . . . 1·60 2·25

304 Ship and Logo

1998. 8th Anniv of Economic Community of West African States Military Arm (ECOMOG). Multicoloured.
728 5n. Type **304** 25 30
729 30n. Logo and original member states . . . . . . 1·25 1·75
730 50n. Current member states 2·25 3·50

305 Caged Steam Locomotive

1999. Centenary of Nigerian Railway Corporation. Multicoloured.
731 5n. Type **305** 25 30
732 10n. Iddo Terminus 55 60
733 20n. Diesel locomotive No. 2131 . . . . 1·10 1·25
734 30n. Passenger train pulling into station . . . . 1·60 2·25

306 Football and Globe

1999. 11th World Youth Football Championship, Nigeria. Multicoloured.
735 5n.+5n. Type **306** 15 30
736 10n.+5n. Player throwing ball 20 35
737 20n.+5n. Player scoring goal 35 50
738 30n.+5n. Map of Nigeria showing venues 50 70
739 40n.+5n. World Youth Football Championship logo 60 80
740 50n.+5n. Player being tackled 75 95
MS741 120 × 115 mm. Nos. 735/40 2·50 2·75

307 Sea Life and F.E.P.A. Emblem

308 Nicon Emblem

1999. 10th Anniv of Federal Environmental Protection Agency. Multicoloured.
742 5n. Type **307** 30 30
743 10n. Forest 65 60
744 20n. Monkeys . . . . 1·40 1·10
745 30n. Villagers and wildlife . . 2·75 2·75

1999. 30th Anniv of Nicon Insurance Corporation. Multicoloured.
746 5n. Type **308** 25 30
747 30n. Emblem and Nicon Building (horiz) . . . . . 1·00 1·50

309 Map of Nigeria in 1900

310 Sunshine Hour Recorder

2000. New Millennium (1st Issue). Multicoloured.
748 10n. Type **309** 45 15
749 20n. Map of Nigeria in 1914 65 40
750 30n. Coat of arms 70 80
751 40n. Map of Nigeria in 1996 1·00 1·40
See also Nos. 786/9.

2000. 50th Anniv of World Meteorological Organization.
752 **310** 10n. multicoloured . . . 15 15
753 – 30n. brown and blue . . . 55 75
DESIGN—HORIZ: 30n. Meteorological station.

311 "Freedom of the Press"

312 Boxing

2000. Return to Democracy. Multicoloured.
754 10n. Type **311** 10 15
755 20n. "Justice for All" (horiz) 25 30
756 30n. Parliamentary Mace . . 35 50
757 40n. President Olusegun Obasanjo 50 70
MS758 99 × 109 mm. Nos. 754/7 1·10 1·40

2000. Olympic Games, Sydney. Multicoloured.
759 10n. Type **312** 10 15
760 20n. Weightlifting 25 30
761 30n. Women's football . . . 35 50
762 40n. Men's football 50 65
MS763 136 × 118 mm. Nos. 759/62 1·10 1·40

313 Obafemi Awolowo

314 Hug Plum

2000. 40th Anniv of Nigeria's Independence.
764 **313** 10n. black, emerald and green 10 15
765 – 20n. black, emerald and green 25 30
766 – 30n. black, emerald and green 35 40
767 – 40n. multicoloured . . . 80 70
768 – 50n. multicoloured . . . 95 1·00
DESIGNS—VERT: 20n. Abubakar Tafawa Balewa; 30n. Nnamdi Azikiwe. HORIZ: 40n. Liquified gas station; 50n. Container ships.

2001. Fruits. Multicoloured.
769 20n. Type **314** 45 30
770 30n. White star apple 55 40
771 40n. African breadfruit . . . 75 80
772 50n. Akee apple . . . . . . 85 1·00

315 *Daily Times* Headquarters, Lagos

316 Broad-tailed Paradise Whydah

2001. 75th Anniv of *The Daily Times of Nigeria*. Multicoloured.
773 20n. Type **315** 25 30
774 30n. First issue of *Nigerian Daily Times*, 1926 . . . . 35 40
775 40n. *Daily Times* printing works, Lagos 50 55
776 50n. *Daily Times* masthead, 1947 . . . . 60 65

2001. Wildlife. Multicoloured.
777 10n. Type **316** 10 15
778 15n. Fire-bellied woodpecker 15 20
779 20n. Grant's zebra (horiz) . . 15 20
780 25n. Aardvark (horiz) 20 25
781 30n. Preuss's guenon (monkey) 25 30
782 40n. Great ground pangolin (horiz) 35 40
783 50n. Pygmy chimpanzee (*Pan paniscus*) (horiz) 45 50
784 100n. Red-eared guenon (monkey) 90 95

317 "Children encircling Globe" (Urska Golob)

318 Map of Nigeria and Dove

2001. U.N. Year of Dialogue among Civilisations.
785 **317** 20n. multicoloured . . . 25 30

2002. New Millennium (2nd issue). Multicoloured.
786 20n. Type **318** 40 30
787 30n. Globe and satellite dish 55 40
788 40n. Handshake across flag in shape of Nigeria 85 80
789 50n. Two overlapping hearts 85 1·00

319 Kola Nuts

2002. Cash Crops. Multicoloured.
790 20n. Type **319** 30 25
791 30n. Oil palm 40 35
792 40n. Cassava 50 50
793 50n. Maize (vert) 60 70

320 Nigerian Player dribbling Ball

2002. World Cup Football Championship, Japan and Korea. Multicoloured.
794 20n. Type **320** 30 25
795 30n. Footballs around Globe 40 35
796 40n. Footballer's legs and World Cup Trophy (horiz) 50 55
797 50n. World Cup Trophy . . 60 70

321 Nurse caring for Patient

2003. World AIDS Day. Multicoloured.
798 20n. Type **321** 30 20
799 50n. Counselling on AIDS 70 80

322 Girl and Boy in Class

323 Athlete running

2003. Universal Basic Education. Multicoloured.
800 20n. Type **322** 30 20
801 50n. Boy writing in book (horiz) 70 80

2003. 8th All Africa Games, Abuja. Multicoloured.
802 20n. Type **323** 30 20
803 30n. High jump (horiz) . . . 40 30
804 40n. Taekwondo (horiz) . . . 55 60
805 50n. Long jump 70 85
MS806 172 × 98 mm. Nos. 802/5 2·00 2·25

324 Logo and Map of Nigeria

2003. Commonwealth Heads of Government Meeting, Abuja. Multicoloured.
807 20n. Type **324** 30 20
808 50n. Logo (vert) 70 80

325 Female with Cubs

2003. Endangered Species. Side-Striped Jackal. Multicoloured.
809 20n. Type **325** 35 20
810 40n. Adult jackal 65 40
811 80n. Two jackals . . . . . . 1·25 1·25
812 100n. Adult jackal (with head lowered, looking through grass) . . . . 1·50 1·75

326 Athletes

327 Children carrying Water and Food (Zainab Jalloh)

2004. Olympic Games, Athens. Multicoloured.
813 50n. Type **326** 70 50
814 120n. Basketball . . . . . . 1·60 1·75

2004. Children's Day. Multicoloured.
815 50n. Type **327** 70 45
816 90n. Book with lightening bolt and hand-cuffed hands (Jessica Umaru) (horiz) . . 1·25 90
817 120n. Skulls, outline of Nigeria and forbidden weapons (Chinonso Chukwougor)(horiz) . . . 1·50 1·75
818 150n. Skull smoking, drugs and alcohol (Sanusi Omolola) . . . . 1·75 2·00
MS819 170 × 104 mm. Nos. 815/18 4·75 5·00

328 Emblems in "100"

2005. Centenary of Rotary International. Mult.
820 50n. Type **328** 70 50
821 120n. Map of world and Rotary and centenary emblems . . . . 1·50 1·75

329 Outline of Stamp

2005. 131st Year of Commemorative Postage Stamps. Multicoloured.
823 50n. Type **329** 70 50
824 90n. Outlines of Nigeria and postage stamp . . . . . . 1·25 90
825 120n. "1874 2005" and Nigerian flag in outline map . . . . 1·50 1·75
826 150n. 1961 3d. 1st anniv of independence and 2002 50n. maize stamps . . . . 1·75 2·00

POSTAGE DUE STAMPS

D 1

1959.
D1 **D 1** 1d. orange . . . . 15 1·00
D2 2d. orange . . . . 20 1·00
D3 3d. orange . . . . 25 1·50
D4 6d. orange . . . . 25 5·00
D5 1s. black . . . . 50 6·50

1961.
D 6 **D 1** 1d. red 15 40
D 7 2d. blue 20 45
D 8 3d. green 25 60
D 9 6d. yellow . . . . 30 1·40
D10 1s. blue . . . . 50 2·25

1973. As Type **D 1**.
D11 2k. red 10 10
D12 3k. blue 10 10
D13 5k. yellow 10 10
D14 10k. green 10 10

NIUAFO'OU Pt. 1

A remote island, part of the Kingdom of Tonga, with local autonomy.

100 seniti = 1 pa'anga.

1 Map of Niuafo'ou

2a SPIA De Havilland D.H.C. 6 Turin Otter 300

1983.
1 **1** 1s. stone, black and red . . . 30 90
2 2s. stone, black and green . . 30 90
3 3s. stone, black and blue . . 30 90
4 3s. stone, black and brown 30 90
5 5s. stone, black and purple 40 90
6 6s. stone, black and blue . . 40 90
7 9s. stone, black and green . . 40 90
8 10s. stone, black and blue . . 40 90
9 13s. stone, black and green 65 90
10 15s. stone, black and brown 70 1·25
11 20s. stone, black and blue . . 75 1·25
12 29s. stone, black and purple 1·00 80
13 32s. stone, black and green 1·00 90
14 47s. stone, black and red . . 1·40 1·40

1983. No. 820 of Tonga optd **NIUAFO'OU KINGDOM OF TONGA** or surch also.
15 1p. on 2p. green and black . . 2·50 3·50
16 2p. green . . . . 3·50 5·00

1983. Inauguration of Niuafo'ou Airport.
17 **2a** 29s. multicoloured . . . . . 1·50 1·00
18 1p. multicoloured . . . . . 3·00 3·25

1983. As T **1**, but without value, surch.
19 3s. stone, black and blue . . . 30 50
20 5s. stone, black and blue . . . 30 50
21 32s. stone, black and blue . . 1·75 1·25
22 2p. stone, black and blue . . . 8·50 10·00

4 Eruption of Niuafo'ou

1983. 25th Anniv of Re-settlement. Mult.
23 5s. Type **4** 40 30
24 29s. Lava flow . . . . 1·00 1·00
25 32s. Islanders fleeing to safety 1·10 1·00
26 1p.50 Evacuation by canoe . . 3·50 5·00

5 Purple Swamphen

6 Green Turtle

1983. Birds of Niuafo'ou.
27 **5** 1s. black and mauve . . . . 1·25 1·25
28 – 2s. black and blue . . . . 1·25 1·25
29 – 3s. black and green . . . . 1·25 1·25
30 – 5s. black and yellow . . . . 1·50 1·25
31 – 6s. black and orange . . . . 1·75 1·60
32 – 9s. multicoloured . . . . . 2·00 1·25
33 – 10s. multicoloured . . . . 2·00 2·00
34 – 13s. multicoloured . . . . 2·50 1·60
35 – 15s. multicoloured . . . . 2·50 2·50
36 – 20s. multicoloured . . . . 2·75 2·75
37 – 29s. multicoloured . . . . 2·75 1·50
38 – 32s. multicoloured . . . . 2·75 1·60
39 – 47s. multicoloured . . . . 3·25 2·25
40 – 1p. multicoloured . . . . 6·00 8·50
41 – 2p. multicoloured . . . . 8·00 12·00

DESIGNS—VERT (22 × 29 mm): 2s. White collared kingfisher; 3s. Red-headed parrot finch; 5s. Buff-banded rail ("Banded Rail"); 6s. Polynesian scrub hen ("Niuafo'ou megapode"); 9s. Green honeyeater; 10s. Purple swamphen (different). (22 × 36 mm): 29s. Red-headed parrot finch (different); 32s. White-collared kingfisher (different). (29 × 42 mm): 1p. As 10s. HORIZ (29 × 22 mm): 13s. Buff-banded rail ("Banded Rail") (different): 15s. Polynesian scrub hen (different). (36 × 22 mm): 20s. As 13s.; 47s. As 15s. (42 × 29 mm): 2p. As 15s.

1984. Wildlife and Nature Reserve. Mult.
42 29s. Type **6** 70 70
43 32s. Insular flying fox (vert) 70 70
44 47s. Humpback whale . . . . 3·50 1·75
45 1p.50 Polynesian scrub hen ("Niuafo'ou megapode") (vert) . . . . 5·50 7·50

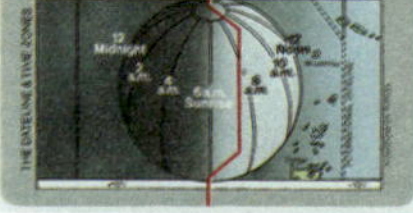

7 Diagram of Time Zones

1984. Cent of International Dateline. Mult.
46 47s. Type **7** 75 50
47 2p. Location map showing Niuafo'ou . . . . 2·25 3·50

8 Australia 1913 £2 Kangaroo Definitive

9 Dutch Brass Band entertaining Tongans

1984. "Ausipex" International Stamp Exhibition, Melbourne. Multicoloured.
48 32s. Type **8** 75 60
49 1p.50 Niuafo'ou 1983 10s. map definitive . . . . . . 2·25 3·00
MS50 90 × 100 mm. As Nos. 48/9, but without exhibition logo and with face value at foot . . . . 1·75 2·50

1985. 400th Birth Anniv of Jacob Le Maire (discoverer of Niuafo'ou).
51 **9** 13s. brown, yellow & orange 25 40
52 – 32s. brown, yellow and blue 55 60
53 – 47s. brown, yellow and green 75 80
54 – 1p.50 brown, cinnamon and yellow . . . . 2·25 3·00
MS55 90 × 90 mm. 1p.50 brown, light brown and blue. Imperf 1·50 2·00

DESIGNS: 32s. Tongans preparing kava; 47s. Tongan canoes and outriggers; 1p.50, "Eendracht" at anchor off Tafahi Island.

10 "Ysabel", 1902

1985. Mail Ships. Multicoloured.
56B 9s. Type **10** 35 55
57A 13s. "Tofua I", 1908 . . . . 70 55
58B 47s. "Mariposa", 1934 . . . 1·10 1·60
59B 1p.50 "Matua", 1936 . . . . 2·50 4·00

11 Preparing to fire Rocket

1985. Niuafo'ou Rocket Mails. Multicoloured.
60B 32s. Type **11** . . . . 1·00 80
61A 42s. Rocket in flight . . . . 1·25 1·00
62B 57s. Ship's crew watching rocket's descent . . . . . 1·60 1·40
63A 1p.50 Islanders reading mail 3·50 4·50

12 Halley's Comet, 684 A.D.

1986. Appearance of Halley's Comet. Multicoloured.
64 42s. Type **12** . . . . 5·00 3·00
65 42s. Halley's Comet, 1066, from Bayeux Tapestry . . . 5·00 3·00
66 42s. Edmond Halley . . . . . 5·00 3·00
67 42s. Halley's Comet, 1910 . . 5·00 3·00
68 42s. Halley's Comet, 1986 . . 5·00 3·00
69 57s. Type **12** . . . . 5·00 3·50
70 57s. As No. 65 . . . . 5·00 3·50
71 57s. As No. 66 . . . . 5·00 3·50
72 57s. As No. 67 . . . . 5·00 3·50
73 57s. As No. 68 . . . . 5·00 3·50

Nos. 64/8 and 69/73 were printed together, se-tenant, forming composite designs.

1986. Nos. 32/9 surch.
74 4s. on 9s. Green honeyeater 85 2·00
75 4s. on 10s. Purple swamphen 85 2·00
76 42s. on 13s. Buff-banded rail ("Banded Rail") . . . . 2·75 2·00
77 42s. on 15s. Polynesian scrub hen . . . . 2·75 2·00
78 57s. on 29s. Red-headed parrot finch . . . . . . 3·25 2·25
79 57s. on 32s. White-collared kingfisher . . . . 3·25 2·25
80 2p.50 on 20s. Buff-banded rail ("Banded Rail") . . . . 9·00 11·00
81 2p.50 on 47s. Polynesian scrub hen . . . . 9·00 11·00

13a Peace Corps Surveyor and Pipeline

1986. "Ameripex '86" International Stamp Exhibition, Chicago. 25th Anniv of United States Peace Corps. Multicoloured.
82 57s. Type **13a** . . . . 1·25 1·25
83 1p.50 Inspecting crops . . . . 2·25 3·00
MS84 90 × 90 mm. Nos. 82/3, magnifying glass and tweezers. Imperf . . . . 3·75 5·00

14 Swimmers with Mail

1986. Centenary of First Tonga Stamps. Designs showing Niuafo'ou mail transport. Multicoloured.
85 42s. Type **14** 90 90
86 57s. Collecting tin can mail . . 1·10 1·10
87 1p. Ship firing mail rocket . . 2·00 2·50
88 2p.50 "Collecting the Mails" (detail) (C. Mayger) . . . . 3·50 4·75
MS89 135 × 80 mm. No. 88 . . . 5·00 7·00

15 Woman with Nourishing Foods ("Eat a balanced diet")

1987. Red Cross. Preventive Medicine. Mult.
90 15s. Type **15** 60 60
91 42s. Nurse with baby ("Give them post-natal care") . . . 1·60 1·60
92 1p. Man with insecticide ("Insects spread disease") 2·50 3·25
93 2p.50 Boxer ("Say no to alcohol, drugs, tobacco") . . 4·00 5·50

16 Hammerhead

1987. Sharks. Multicoloured.
94 29s. Type **16** . . . . 2·00 1·75
95 32s. Tiger shark . . . . 2·00 1·75
96 47s. Grey nurse shark . . . . 2·50 2·25
97 1p. Great white shark . . . . 4·00 6·00
MS98 90 × 90 mm. 2p. Shark and fishes . . . . 11·00 12·00

17 Capt. E. C. Musick and Sikorsky S.42A Flying Boat "Samoan Clipper"

1987. Air Pioneers of the South Pacific. Multicoloured.
99 42s. Type **17** . . . . 2·00 1·40
100 57s. Capt. J. W. Burgess and Short S. 30 modified "G" Class flying boat "Aotearoa" . . . . 2·25 1·75
101 1p.50 Sir Charles Kingsford Smith and Fokker F.VIIa/3m "Southern Cross" . . . 3·50 4·00
102 2p. Amelia Earhart and Lockheed 10E Electra . . 3·75 5·00

18 Polynesian Scrub Hen and 1983 1s. Map Definitive

1988. 5th Annivs of First Niuafo'ou Postage Stamp (42, 57s.) and Niuafo'ou Airport Inauguration (1, 2p.). Multicoloured.
103 42s. Type **18** . . . . 1·00 75
104 57s. As Type **18**, but with stamp at left . . . . . . 1·00 95
105 1p. Concorde and 1983 Airport Inauguration 29s. stamp . . . . 4·50 3·25
106 2p. As 1p. but with stamp at left . . . . 5·00 4·00

19 Sailing Ship and Ship's Boat

20 Audubon's Shearwaters and Blowholes, Houma, Tonga

1988. Bicentenary of Australian Settlement. Sheet 115 × 110 mm containing T **19** and similar vert designs. Multicoloured.

MS107 42s. Type **19**; 42s. Aborigines; 42s. Early settlement; 42s. Marine and convicts; 42s. Sheep station; 42s. Mounted stockman; 42s. Kangaroos and early Trans Continental locomotive; 42s. Kangaroos and train carriages; 42s. Flying Doctor aircraft; 42s. Cricket match; 42s. Wicket and Sydney skyline; 42s. Fielders and Sydney Harbour Bridge . . . . 35·00 35·00

Each horizontal strip of 4 within No. **MS**107 shows a composite design.

1988. Islands of Polynesia. Multicoloured.

108	42s. Type **20**	1·50	95
109	57s. Brown kiwi at Akaroa Harbour, New Zealand . .	2·25	1·40
110	90s. Red-tailed tropic birds at Rainmaker Mountain, Samoa	2·50	2·50
111	2p.50 Laysan albatross at Kapoho Volcano, Hawaii	4·75	6·00

21 Sextant

23 Formation of Earth's Surface

22 Spiny Hatchetfish

1989. Bicentenary of Mutiny on the Bounty. Sheet 115 × 110 mm containing T **21** and similar vert designs. Multicoloured.

MS112 42s. Type **21**; 42s. Capt. Bligh; 42s. Lieutenant, 1787; 42s. Midshipman, 1787; 42s. Tahitian woman and contemporary newspaper; 42s. Breadfruit plant; 42s. Pistol and extract from "Mutiny on the Bounty"; 42s. Book illustration of Bligh cast adrift; 42s. Profile of Tahitian woman and extract from contemporary newspaper; 42s. Signatures of "Bounty officers"; 42s. Fletcher Christian; 42s. Tombstone of John Adams, Pitcairn Island . . . . 14·00 16·00

1989. Fishes of the Deep. Multicoloured.

113	32s. Type **22**	85	1·00
114	42s. Snipe eel	1·00	1·00
115	57s. Viperfish	1·25	1·50
116	1p.50 Football anglerfish . .	3·00	4·00

1989. The Evolution of the Earth. Multicoloured.

(a) Size 27 × 35½ mm.

117	1s. Type **23**	40	70
118	2s. Cross-section of Earth's crust	40	70
119	5s. Volcano	50	70
120	10s. Cross-section of Earth during cooling	50	70
120a	13s. Gem stones	75	50
121	15s. Sea	50	50
122	20s. Mountains	50	50
123	32s. River gorge	60	40
124	42s. Early plant life, Silurian era	80	45
124a	45s. Early marine life . . .	80	70
125	50s. Fossils and Cambrian lifeforms	90	55
126	57s. Carboniferous forest and coal seams	1·00	55
126a	60s. Dinosaurs feeding . . .	1·25	85
126b	80s. Tyrannosaurus and triceratops fighting . . .	1·50	1·40
	(b) Size 25½ × 40 mm.		
127	1p. Dragonfly and amphibians, Carboniferous era	1·50	1·50
128	1p.50 Dinosaurs, Jurassic era	2·50	2·75
129	2p. Archaeopteryx and mammals, Jurassic era . .	3·00	3·00
130	5p. Human family and domesticated dog, Pleistocene era	4·50	5·50
130a	10p. Mammoth and sabre-tooth tiger	7·50	9·00

24 Astronaut on Moon and Newspaper Headline

1989. "World Stamp Expo '89" International Stamp Exhibition, Washington.

131	**24**	57s. multicoloured	2·00	1·50

1989. 20th Universal Postal Union Congress, Washington. Miniature sheet, 185 × 150 mm, containing designs as Nos. 117/20, 121/4, 125/6 and 127/30, but wuth U.P.U. emblem at top right and some new values.

MS132 32s. × 5 (as Nos. 117/20, 121); 42s. × 5 (as Nos. 122/4, 125/6); 57s. × 5 (as Nos. 127/30, 131) . . . . 22·00 24·00

25 Lake Vai Lahi

1990. Niuafo'ou Crater Lake. Multicoloured.

133	42s. Type **25**	70	1·00
134	42s. Islands in centre of lake	70	1·00
135	42s. South-west end of lake and islet	70	1·00
136	1p. Type **25**	1·40	1·60
137	1p. As No. 134	1·40	1·60
138	1p. As No. 135	1·40	1·60

Nos. 133/8 were printed together in se-tenant strips of each value, forming a composite design.

26 Penny Black and Tin Can Mail Service

1990. 150th Anniv of the Penny Black. Mult.

139	42s. Type **26**	1·25	1·00
140	57s. U.S.A. 1847 10c. stamp	1·40	1·25
141	75s. Western Australia 1854 1d. stamp	1·60	2·00
142	2p.50 Mafeking Siege 1900 1d. stamp	5·00	6·00

27 Humpback Whale surfacing

1990. Polynesian Whaling. Multicoloured.

143	15s. Type **27**	2·25	1·75
144	42s. Whale diving under canoe	2·75	1·90
145	57s. Tail of Blue whale . . .	3·00	1·90
146	2p. Old man and pair of whales	8·00	9·00

MS147 120 × 93 mm. 1p. Pair of whales (38 × 30 mm) . . . . . 10·00 11·00

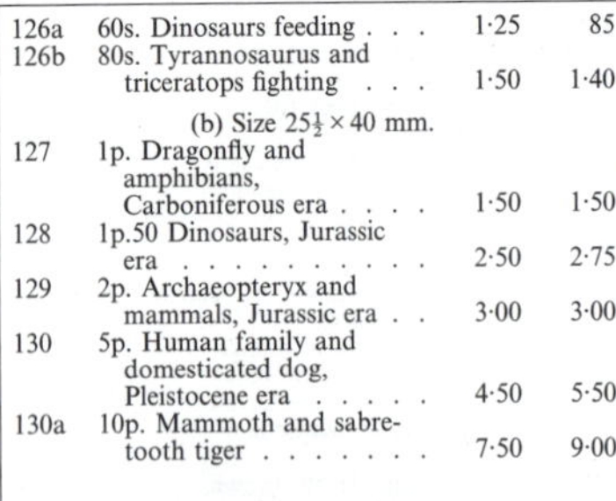

27a Agriculture and Fisheries

1990. 40th Anniv of U.N. Development Programme. Multicoloured.

148	57s. Type **27a**	90	1·40
149	57s. Education	90	1·40
150	2p.50 Healthcare	3·25	4·00
151	2p.50 Communications . . .	3·25	4·00

28 H.M.S. "Bounty"

30 Longhorned Beetle Grub

1991. Bicentenary of Charting of Niuafo'ou. Multicoloured.

152	32s. Type **28**	1·25	1·75
153	42s. Chart of "Pandora's" course	1·40	1·75
154	57s. H.M.S. "Pandora" (frigate)	1·75	1·75

MS155 120 × 93 mm. 2p. Capt. Edwards of the "Pandora"; 3p. Capt. Bligh of the "Bounty" . . . 11·00 12·00

1991. Ornithological and Scientific Expedition to Niuafo'ou. No. MS147 surch **1991 ORNITHOLOGICAL AND SCIENTIFIC EXPEDITION T $1**.

MS156 120 × 93 mm. 1p. on 1p. multicoloured . . . . 3·25 4·00

1991. Longhorned Beetle. Multicoloured.

157	42s. Type **30**	80	1·00
158	57s. Adult beetle	90	1·00
159	1p.50 Grub burrowing . . .	2·75	3·25
160	2p.50 Adult on tree trunk . .	4·00	4·50

31 Heina meeting the Eel

1991. Christmas. The Legend of the Coconut Tree. Multicoloured.

161	15s. Type **31**	35	60
162	42s. Heina crying over the eel's grave	90	1·00

MS163 96 × 113 mm. 15s. Type **31**; 42s. No. 162; 1p.50, Heina's son collecting coconuts; 3p. Milk flowing from coconut . . . . 9·00 10·00

31a Columbus

1992. 500th Anniv of Discovery of America by Columbus. Sheet 119 × 109 mm. containing vert designs as T **31a**. Multicoloured.

MS164 57s. Columbus; 57s. Queen Isabella and King Ferdinand; 57s. Columbus being blessed by Abbot of Palos; 57s. 15th-century compass; 57s. Wooden traverse, windrose and the "Nina"; 57s. Bow of "Santa Maria"; 57s. Stern of "Santa Maria"; 57s. The "Pinta"; 57s. Crew erecting cross; 57s. Sailors and Indians; 57s. Columbus reporting to King and Queen; 57s. Coat of Arms . . 17·00 18·00

31b American Battleship Ablaze, Pearl Harbor

1992. 50th Anniv of War in the Pacific. Multicoloured.

165	42s. Type **31b**	1·40	1·40
166	42s. Destroyed American Douglas B-18 Bolo aircraft, Hawaii	1·40	1·40
167	42s. Newspaper and Japanese Mitsubishi A6M Zero-Sen fighter	1·40	1·40
168	42s. Pres. Roosevelt signing Declaration of War	1·40	1·40
169	42s. Japanese T95 light tank and Gen. MacArthur . . .	1·40	1·40
170	42s. Douglas SBD Dauntless dive bomber and Admiral Nimitz	1·40	1·40
171	42s. Bren gun and Gen. Sir Thomas Blamey	1·40	1·40
172	42s. Australian mortar crew, Kokoda	1·40	1·40
173	42s. U.S.S. "Mississippi" in action and Maj. Gen. Julian C. Smith	1·40	1·40
174	42s. U.S.S. "Enterprise" (aircraft carrier)	1·40	1·40
175	42s. American marine and Maj. Gen. Curtis Lemay	1·40	1·40
176	42s. Boeing B-29 Superfortress bomber and Japanese surrender, Tokyo Bay	1·40	1·40

Nos. 165/76 were printed together, se-tenant, forming a composite design.

31c King Taufa'ahau Tupou IV and Queen Halaevalu During Coronation

1992. 25th Anniv of the Coronation of King Tupou IV.

177	**31c**	45s. multicoloured	75	75
178	–	80s. multicoloured	1·50	1·75
179	–	80s. black and brown . .	1·50	1·75
180	–	80s. multicoloured	1·50	1·75
181	–	2p. multicoloured	2·50	3·00

DESIGNS—(34 × 23 mm): No. 177, Type **31c**. (48 × 35 mm): No. 178, King Tupou IV and Tongan national anthem; 179, Extract from Investiture ceremony; 180, Tongan choir; 181, As 45s.

Nos. 177/81 show the King's first name incorrectly spelt as "Tauf'ahau".

32 Male and Female Scrub Hens searching for Food

1992. Endangered Species. Polynesian Scrub Hen. Multicoloured.

182	45s. Type **32**	1·00	1·25
183	60s. Female guarding egg . .	1·25	1·40
184	80s. Chick	1·60	1·75
185	1p.50 Head of male	2·75	3·50

33 1983 2s. Map Definitive and 1993 60s. Dinosaur Definitive

1993. 10th Anniv of First Niuafo'ou Stamp. Multicoloured.

186	60s. Type **33**	1·00	1·10
187	80s. 1983 5s. definitive and 1993 80s. dinosaurs definitive	1·25	1·40

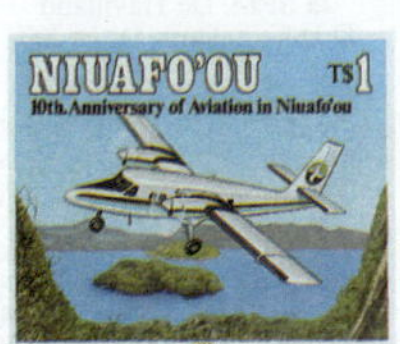

34 De Havilland Twin Otter 200/300 of South Pacific Island Airways

34a King Tupou IV and "Pangai" (patrol boat)

1993. 10th Anniv of First Flight to Niuafo'ou. Multicoloured.
188 1p. Type **34** . . . . 1·50 2·00
189 2p.50 De Havilland Twin Otter 200/300 of Friendly Islands Airways . . . . . 3·50 4·50

1993. 75th Birthday of King Taufa'ahau Tupou IV. Multicoloured.
190 45s. Type **34a** 55 65
191 80s. King Tupou IV and musical instruments (38½ × 51 mm) . . . . . . 1·25 1·75
192 80s. King Tupou IV and sporting events (38½ × 51 mm) . . . . 1·25 1·75
193 80s. King Tupou IV with De Havilland Twin Otter 200/300 airplane and telecommunications . . . . 1·25 1·75
194 2p. As 45s. but larger (38½ × 51 mm) . . . . . . 2·75 3·25

35 Blue-crowned Lorikeets

35a "Crater Lake Megapode and Volcano" (Paea Puletau)

1993. Natural History of Lake Vai Lahi. Multicoloured.
195 60s. Type **35** . . . . 1·00 1·25
196 60s. White-tailed tropic bird and reef heron . . . . . . 1·00 1·25
197 60s. Black admiral (butterfly) and Niuafo'ou coconut beetle . . . . 1·00 1·25
198 60s. Niuafo'ou dragonfly, pacific black ducks and Niuafo'ou moths . . . . 1·00 1·25
199 60s. Niuafo'ou megapode . . 1·00 1·25
Nos. 195/9 were printed together, se-tenant, forming a composite design.

1993. Children's Painting Competition Winners.
200 **35a** 10s. multicoloured . . . . 50 1·00
201 – 10s. black and grey . . . 50 1·00
202 – 1p. multicoloured . . . . 3·50 3·75
203 – 1p. multicoloured . . . . 3·50 3·75
DESIGNS: Nos. 200 and 202, Type **35a**; Nos. 201 and 203, "Ofato Beetle Grubs of Niuafo'ou" (Peni Finau).

36 "Scarabaeidea"

1994. Beetles. Multicoloured.
204 60s. Type **36** . . . . 85 1·00
205 80s. "Coccinellidea" . . . . 1·10 1·40
206 1p.50 "Cerambycidea" . . . 2·00 2·50
207 2p.50 "Pentatomidae" . . . 3·75 4·25

37 Stern of H.M.S. "Bounty"

38 Blue-crowned Lory and Lava Flows

1994. Sailing Ships. Multicoloured.
208 80s. Type **37** . . . . 1·75 2·25
209 80s. Bow of H.M.S. "Bounty" . . . . 1·75 2·25
210 80s. H.M.S. "Pandora" (frigate) . . . . 1·75 2·25
211 80s. Whaling ship . . . . . 1·75 2·25
212 80s. Trading schooner . . . 1·75 2·25

1994. Volcanic Eruptions on Niuafo'ou. Multicoloured.
213 80s. Type **38** . . . . 1·25 1·75
214 80s. Pacific ducks over lava flows . . . . 1·25 1·75
215 80s. Megapodes and palm trees . . . . 1·25 1·75
216 80s. White-tailed tropic birds and inhabitants . . . . . 1·25 1·75
217 80s. Reef heron and evacuation, 1946 . . . . . 1·25 1·75

Nos. 213/17 were printed together, se-tenant, forming a composite design.

1995. Visit South Pacific Year '95. Save the Whales. Nos. 143/6 surch **SAVE THE WHALES VISIT SOUTH PACIFIC YEAR '95**, emblem and value.
218 60s. on 42s. Whale diving under canoe . . . . 2·00 1·75
219 80s. on 15s. Type **27** . . . . 2·25 2·25
220 80s. on 57s. Tail of blue whale . . . . 2·25 2·25
221 2p. on 2p. Old man and pair of whales . . . . 4·25 4·50
MS222 120 × 93 mm. 1p.50 on 1p. Pair of whales (38 × 30 mm) . . 3·50 4·25

39a American Marine

1995. 50th Anniv of End of World War II in the Pacific.
223 **39a** 60s. yellow, black and blue . . . . 1·25 1·50
224 – 60s. yellow, black and blue . . . . 1·25 1·50
225 – 60s. yellow, black and blue . . . . 1·25 1·50
226 – 60s. yellow, black and blue . . . . 1·25 1·50
227 – 60s. yellow, black and blue . . . . 1·25 1·50
228 **39a** 80s. yellow, black and red 1·25 1·50
229 – 80s. yellow, black and red 1·25 1·50
230 – 80s. yellow, black and red 1·25 1·50
231 – 80s. yellow, black and red 1·25 1·50
232 – 80s. yellow, black and red 1·25 1·50
DESIGNS: Nos. 224 and 229, Marine firing and side of tank; 225 and 230, Tank; 226 and 231, Marines leaving landing craft; 227 and 232, Beach assault and palm trees.
Nos. 223/32 were printed together, se-tenant, forming two composite designs.

39b Dinosaurs Feeding

1995. "Singapore '95" International Stamp Exhibitions. Designs showing exhibition emblem. Multicoloured.
233 45s. Type **39b** (as No. 126a) 1·00 1·50
234 60s. Tyrannosaurus fighting Triceratops (as No. 126b) 1·00 1·50
MS235 110 × 70 mm. 2p. Plesiosaurus . . . . 2·50 3·50

39c Great Wall of China (½-size illustration)

1995. Beijing International Coin and Stamp Show '95. Sheet 143 × 87 mm.
MS236 **39c** 1p.40 multicoloured 2·25 3·00

39d St. Paul's Cathedral and Searchlights

1995. 50th Anniv of United Nations and End of Second World War.
237 **39d** 60s. multicoloured . . . . 1·25 1·75
238 – 60s. black and blue . . . 1·25 1·75
239 – 60s. multicoloured . . . 1·25 1·75
240 – 80s. multicoloured . . . 1·50 1·75
241 – 80s. blue and black . . . 1·50 1·75
242 – 80s. multicoloured . . . 1·50 1·75

DESIGNS—HORIZ: No. 239, Concorde; 240, Allied prisoners of war and Burma Railway; 242, Mt. Fuji and express train. VERT—25 × 35 mm: Nos. 238 and 241, U.N. anniversary emblem.

40 Charles Ramsay and Swimmers with Poles

1996. Tin Can Mail Pioneers. Multicoloured.
243 45s. Type **40** 90 90
244 60s. Charles Ramsay and encounter with shark . . . 1·25 1·25
245 1p. Walter Quensell and transferring mail from canoes to ship . . . . . . 2·00 2·00
246 3p. Walter Quensell and Tin Can Mail cancellations . . 6·00 6·50

40a Cave Painting, Lake Village and Hunter

1996. 13th Congress of International Union of Prehistoric and Protohistoric Sciences, Forli, Italy. Multicoloured.
247 1p. Type **40a** . . . . 2·25 2·25
248 1p. Egyptians with Pyramid, Greek temple, and Romans with Colosseum . . . . . 2·25 2·25

40b Dolls, Model Truck and Counting Balls

41 Island and Two Canoes

1996. 50th Anniv of UNICEF. Children's Toys. Multicoloured.
249 80s. Type **40b** . . . . 1·75 2·00
250 80s. Teddy bear, tricycle and model car . . . . 1·75 2·00
251 80s. Book, model helicopter, pedal car and roller skates 1·75 2·00
Nos. 249/51 were printed together, se-tenant, forming a composite design.

1996. 50th Anniv of Evacuation of Niuafo'ou. Multicoloured.
252 45s. Type **41** . . . . 85 1·10
253 45s. Erupting volcano and canoes . . . . 85 1·10
254 45s. End of island, volcanic cloud and canoe . . . . . 85 1·10
255 45s. Family and livestock in outrigger canoe . . . . . 85 1·10
256 45s. Islanders reaching "Matua" (inter-island freighter) . . . . 85 1·10
257 60s. Type **41** . . . . 95 1·10
258 60s. As No. 253 . . . . . . 95 1·10
259 60s. As No. 254 . . . . . . 95 1·10
260 60s. As No. 255 . . . . . . 95 1·10
261 60s. As No. 256 . . . . . . 95 1·10
Nos. 252/6 and 257/61 respectively were printed together, se-tenant, forming the same composite design.

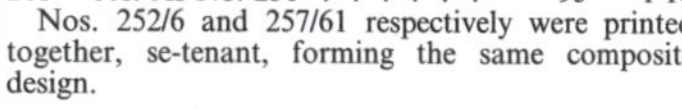

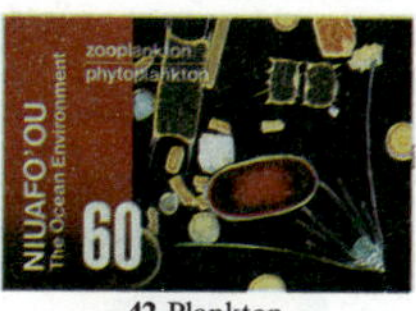
42 Plankton

1997. The Ocean Environment.
262 **42** 60s. multicoloured . . . . 1·00 1·00
263 – 80s. multicoloured . . . . 1·25 1·25
264 – 1p.50 multicoloured . . . 2·25 2·50
265 – 2p.50 multicoloured . . . 3·00 3·50
DESIGNS: 80s. to 2p.50, Different plankton.

42a Black-naped Tern

1997. "Pacific '97" International Stamp Exhibition, San Francisco. Sheet 85 × 110 mm.
MS266 **42a** 2p. multicoloured . . 3·00 3·75

42b King and Queen on Wedding Day

1997. King and Queen of Tonga's Golden Wedding and 30th Anniv of Coronation. Multicoloured.
267 80s. Type **42b** . . . . 1·75 1·75
268 80s. King Tupou in Coronation robes . . . . 1·75 1·75
MS269 82 × 70 mm. 5p. King Tupou with pages (horiz) . . . . . . 7·00 7·50

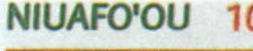

43 Blue-crowned Lory Nestlings

43a King Taufa'ahau Tupou IV

1998. Endangered Species. Blue-crowned Lory. Multicoloured.
270 10s. Type **43** . . . . 1·50 1·50
271 55s. Feeding on flowers . . . 3·00 1·25
272 80s. Perched on branch . . . 4·00 2·00
273 3p. Pair on branch . . . . . 8·00 9·00
MS274 160 × 112 mm. Nos. 270/3 × 2 30·00 30·00

1998. Diana, Princess of Wales Commemoration. Sheet, 145 × 70 mm, containing vert designs as T **91** of Kiribati. Multicoloured.
MS275 10s. Princess Diana in tartan jacket, 1987; 80s. Wearing white dress, 1992; 1p. Wearing check jacket, 1993; 2p.50, Wearing black jacket (sold at 4p.40+50s. charity premium) . . . . 5·50 6·00

1998. 80th Birthday of King Taufa'ahau Tupou IV.
276 **43a** 2p.70 multicoloured . . . 2·50 3·25

43b Tiger and Top Left Quarter of Clock Face

1998. Chinese New Year ("Year of the Tiger"). Sheet, 126 × 85 mm, containing horiz designs as T **43b**, each showing tiger and quarter segment of clock face. Multicoloured.
MS277 55s. Type **43b**; 80s. Top right quarter; 1p. Bottom left quarter; 1p. Bottom right quarter . . . 4·00 4·75
No. **MS**277 also includes "SINGPEX '98" Stamp Exhibition, Singapore emblem on the sheet margin.

43c "Amphiprion melanopus"

1998. International Year of the Ocean. Multicoloured.
278 10s. Type **43c** 40 50
279 55s. "Amphiprion perideraion" 80 90
280 80s. "Amphiprion chrysopterus" . . . . . . 1·00 1·10

43d Angel playing lute (inscr in Tongan)

1998. Christmas. Multicoloured.
281 20s. Type **43d** 70 55
282 55s. Angel playing violin (inscr in English) . . . . . 1·10 60
283 1p. Children and bells (inscr in Tongan) . . . . 1·60 1·75
284 1p.60 Children and candles (inscr in English) . . . . . 2·25 3·00

43e Rabbit on Hind Legs

1999. Chinese New Year ("Year of the Rabbit"). Sheet 126 × 85 mm, containing horiz designs as T **43e**, showing rabbits and segments of flower (each red, yellow and grey). Multicoloured.
MS285 10s. Type **43e**; 55s. Rabbit facing left; 80s. Rabbit facing right; 1p. Two rabbits . . . . 2·50 3·25

44 "Eendracht" (Le Maire)

1999. Early Explorers. Multicoloured.
286 80s. Type **44** . . . . 2·25 1·00
287 2p.70 Tongiaki (outrigger canoe) . . . . 3·50 4·00
MS288 120 × 72 mm. Nos. 286/7 5·50 6·50
No. **MS**288 also includes the "Australia '99" emblem on the sheet margin.

44a "Cananga odorata"

1999. Fragrant Flowers. Multicoloured.
289 55s. Type **44a** 75 60
290 80s. "Gardenia tannaensis" (vert) . . . . 1·00 80
291 1p. "Coleus amboinicus" (vert) . . . . 1·40 1·50
292 2p.50 "Hernandia moerenhoutiana" . . . . . 2·75 3·75

45 Dove over Tafahi Island

2000. New Millennium. Sheet, 120 × 80 mm, containing T **45** and similar vert design. Multicoloured.
MS293 1p. Type **45**; 2p.50, Kalia (traditional canoe) passing island 3·50 4·00

45a Dragon in the Sky

2000. Chinese New Year ("Year of the Dragon"). Sheet, 126 × 85 mm, containing horiz designs as T **46a**. Multicoloured.
MS294 10s. Type **45a**; 55s. Dragon in the sky (facing left); 80s. Sea dragon (facing right); 1p. Sea dragon (facing left) . . . . . 2·25 2·75

45b Queen Elizabeth the Queen Mother

46 Tongan Couple

2000. "The Stamp Show 2000" International Stamp Exhibition, London. Queen Elizabeth the Queen Mother's 100th Birthday. Sheet, 105 × 71 mm, containing designs as T **45b**.
MS295 1p.50, Type **45b**; 2p.50, Queen Salote Tupou III of Tonga 3·50 4·00

2000. "EXPO 2000" World Stamp Exhibition, Anaheim, U.S.A. Space Communications. Sheet, 120 × 90 mm, containing T **46** and similar vert designs. Multicoloured.
MS296 10s. Type **46**; 2p.50, Telecom dish aerial; 2p.70, "Intelsat" satelite . . . . 4·50 5·50

47 *Jamides bochus* (butterfly)

2000. Butterflies. Multicoloured.
297 55s. Type **47** 85 70
298 80s. *Hypolimnas bolina* . . . 1·10 90
299 1p. *Eurema hecabe aprica* . . 1·40 1·40
300 2p.70 *Danaus plexippus* . . . 2·50 3·00

48 Snake

2001. Chinese New Year ("Year of the Snake") and "Hong Kong 2001" Stamp Exhibition. Sheet, 125 × 87 mm, containing horiz designs as T **48** showing decorative snakes.
MS301 10s. multicoloured; 55s. multicoloured; 80s. multicoloured; 1p. multicoloured . . . . . . 3·00 3·25

49 Seale's Flying Fish

2001. Fishes. Multicoloured.
302 80s. Type **49** . . . . 1·40 90
303 1p. Swordfish . . . . 1·60 1·60
304 2p.50 Skipjack tuna . . . . 3·00 3·50
MS305 121 × 92 mm. Nos. 302/4 5·50 6·00

50 Pawpaw

2001. Tropical Fruit. Sheet, 120 × 67 mm, containing T **50** and similar vert designs. Multicoloured.
MS306 55s. Type **50**; 80s. Limes; 1p. Mango; 2p.50, Bananas . . . 4·00 5·00

51 Barn Owl in Flight

2001. Barn Owls. Multicoloured.
307 10s. Type **51** 40 60
308 55s. Adult feeding young in nest . . . . 1·00 55
309 2p.50 Adult and fledglings in nest . . . . 2·50 2·75
310 2p.70 Barn owl in palm tree 2·50 2·75
MS311 170 × 75 mm. Nos. 307/10 6·00 6·50

51a Queen Elizabeth with Princess Elizabeth, Coronation, 1937

2002. Golden Jubilee. Sheet 162 × 95 mm, containing designs as T **51a**.
MS312 15s. brown, violet and gold; 90s. multicoloured; 1p.20, multicoloured; 1p.40, multicoloured; 2p.25, multicoloured . . . . 8·00 8·50
DESIGNS—HORIZ (as Type **51a**): 15s. Type **51a**; 90s. Queen Elizabeth in lilac outfit; 1p.20, Princess Elizabeth in garden; 1p.40, Queen Elizabeth in red hat and coat. VERT (38 × 51 mm): 2p.25, Queen Elizabeth after Annigoni.

51b Two Horses with Foal

2002. Chinese New Year ("Year of the Horse"). Sheet, 126 × 89 mm, containing vert designs as T **51b**. Multicoloured.
MS313 65s. Two horses with foal; 80s. Horse drinking from river; 1p. Horse standing in river; 2p.50 Horse and foal on river bank 6·00 6·50

52 Polynesian Scrub Fowl with Eggs

2002. Polynesian Scrub Fowl. Multicoloured.
314 15s. Type **52** 30 50
315 70s. Two birds on rocks . . 90 90
316 90s. Polynesian scrub fowl by tree (vert) . . . . 1·10 1·10
317 2p.50 Two birds in undergrowth (vert) . . . . 2·25 2·75
MS318 72 × 95 mm. Nos. 316/17 4·50 5·00

53 Octopus (*Octopus vulgaris*)

2002. Cephalopods. Multicoloured.
319 80s. Type **53** 90 75
320 1p. Squid (*Sepioteuthis lessoniana*) . . . . 1·10 1·10
321 2p.50 Nautilus (*Nautilus belauensis*) . . . . 2·50 3·00
MS322 120 × 83 mm. Nos. 319/21 4·50 5·00

54 CASA C-212 Aviocar

2002. Mail Planes. Sheet, 140 × 80 mm, containing T **54** and similar horiz designs. Multicoloured.
MS323 80s. Type **54**; 1p.40 Britten-Norman Islander; 2p.50 DHC 6-300 Twin Otter . . . . . . 4·75 5·50

54a Ram

2003. Chinese New Year ("Year of the Sheep"). Sheet 128 × 88 mm, containing horiz designs as T **54a**. Multicoloured.
MS324 65s. Type **54a**, 80s. Three ewes; 1p. Three black-faced ewes; 2p.50 Two ewes . . . . 4·25 4·75

54b Queen Elizabeth II

2004. 50th Anniv of Coronation.
325 **54b** 90s. purple, blue and bistre 70 60
326 – 1p.20 green, blue and bistre . . . . 1·00 90
327 – 1p.40 blue, purple and bistre . . . . 1·25 1·25
328 – 2p.50 multicoloured . . . 2·75 3·00
DESIGNS: 1p.20 Queen Elizabeth II on throne; 1p.40 Queen Salote in open-top car; 2p.50 Queen Salote.

54c Spider Monkey

2004. Chinese New Year ("Year of the Monkey"). Sheet 95 × 85 mm containing horiz designs as T **54c**. Each azure, black and scarlet.
MS329 60s. Spider monkey; 80s; Ring-tailed Lemur; 1p. Cotton-top tamarin; 2p.50 White-cheeked gibbon . . . . 4·50 4·75

56 Pawpaw Tree

2004. Fruit Trees. Multicoloured.
335 45s. Type **56** 50 45
336 60s. Banana tree 65 65
337 80s. Coconut tree 80 80
338 1p.80 Lime tree . . . . . . 1·75 2·00

57 Mary and Baby Jesus

2004. Christmas. Multicoloured.
339 15s. Type **57** 25 20
340 90s. Mary and Joseph on the way to Bethlehem 90 70
341 1p.20 The Shepherds . . . . 1·10 1·25
342 2p.60 The Three Wise Men 2·40 2·75

58 Rooster and Hen

2005. Chinese New Year ("Year of the Rooster"). Sheet 95×85 mm, containing T **58** and similar horiz designs. Multicoloured.
MS343 65s. Type **58**; 80s. Rooster, hen and three chicks; 1p. Rooster, hen and chick; 2p.50 Rooster and hen on nest . . . . 4·75 5·00

NIUE — Pt. 1

One of the Cook Is. group in the S. Pacific. A dependency of New Zealand, the island achieved local self-government in 1974.

1902. 12 pence = 1 shilling;
20 shillings = 1 pound.
1967. 100 cents = 1 dollar.

1902. T **42** of New Zealand optd **NIUE** only.
1 **42** 1d. red £300 £300

Stamps of New Zealand surch **NIUE.** and value in native language.

1902. Pictorials of 1898 etc.
8 **23** ½d. green . . . . 1·00 1·00
9 **42** 1d. red . . . . 60 1·00
2 **26** 2½d. blue (B) . . . . . . 1·50 4·00
13 **28** 3d. brown . . . . 9·50 5·00
14 **31** 6d. red . . . . 12·00 11·00
16 **34** 1s. orange . . . . 35·00 35·00

1911. King Edward VII stamps.
17 **51** ½d. green 50 50
18 6d. red . . . . 2·00 7·00
19 1s. orange . . . . 6·50 48·00

1917. Dominion and King George V stamps.
21 **53** 1d. red . . . . 14·00 5·50
22 **62** 3d. brown . . . . 45·00 85·00

1917. Stamps of New Zealand (King George V, etc) optd **NIUE.** only.
23 **62** ½d. green . . . . 70 2·50
24 **53** 1d. red . . . . 10·00 8·50
25 **62** 1½d. grey . . . . 1·00 2·25
26 1½d. brown . . . . 70 4·50
28a 2½d. blue . . . . 1·25 7·00
29a 3d. brown . . . . 1·25 1·50
30a 6d. red . . . . 4·75 24·00
31a 1s. orange . . . . 5·50 27·00

1918. Stamps of New Zealand optd **NIUE.**
33 F **4** 2s. blue . . . . 16·00 32·00
34 2s.6d. brown . . . . . . 21·00 48·00
35 5s. green . . . . 25·00 50·00
37b 10s. red . . . . 90·00 £140
37 £1 red £150 £225

1920. Pictorial types as Cook Islands (1920), but inscr "NIUE".
38 **9** ½d. black and green . . . . 3·75 3·75
45 – 1d. black and red . . . . 1·75 1·00
40 – 1½d. black and red . . . . 2·50 9·50
46 – 2½d. black and blue . . . . 4·25 11·00
41 – 3d. black and blue . . . . 75 14·00
47 **7** 4d. black and violet . . . . 7·00 20·00
42 – 6d. brown and green . . . . 1·75 18·00
43 – 1s. black and brown . . . . 1·75 18·00

1927. Admiral type of New Zealand optd **NIUE.**
49 **71** 2s. blue . . . . 18·00 32·00

1931. No. 40 surch **TWO PENCE.**
50 2d. on 1½d. black and red . . 3·00 1·00

1931. Stamps of New Zealand (Arms types) optd **NIUE.**
83 F **6** 2s.6d. brown . . . . . . 3·50 10·00
84 5s. green . . . . 7·50 11·00
53 10s. red . . . . 35·00 £100
86 £1 pink . . . . 48·00 60·00

1932. Pictorial stamps as Cook Islands (1932) but inscr additionally "NIUE".
89 **20** ½d. black and green . . . . 50 2·50
90 – 1d. black and red . . . . 50 1·75
64 **22** 2d. black and brown . . . . 50 1·75
92 – 2½d. black and blue . . . . 60 1·25
93 – 4d. black and blue . . . . 4·25 1·00
67 – 6d. black and orange . . . 70 75
61 – 1s. black and violet . . . . 2·25 5·00

1935. Silver Jubilee. As Nos. 63, 92 and 67, with colours changed, optd **SILVER JUBILEE OF KING GEORGE V. 1910-1935.**
69 1d. red . . . . 60 3·50
70 2½d. blue . . . . 3·50 8·00
71 6d. green and orange . . . . 3·25 6·50

1937. Coronation. New Zealand stamps optd **NIUE.**
72 **106** 1d. red 30 10
73 2½d. blue . . . . 40 1·50
74 6d. orange 40 20

1938. As 1938 issue of Cook Islands, but inscr "NIUE COOK ISLANDS".
95 **29** 1s. black and violet . . . . 1·50 85
96 **30** 2s. black and brown . . . . 8·50 3·00
97 – 3s. blue and green . . . . . 15·00 7·00

1940. As No. 132 of Cook Islands but inscr "NIUE COOK ISLANDS".
78 **32** 3d. on 1½d. black and purple 75 20

1946. Peace. New Zealand stamps optd **NIUE** (twice on 2d.).
98 **132** 1d. green 40 10
99 – 2d. purple (No. 670) . . . 40 10
100 – 6d. brown & red (No. 674) 40 80
101 **139** 8d. black and red 50 80

18 Map of Niue

19 H.M.S. "Resolution"

1950.
113 **18** ½d. orange and blue . . . 10 1·00
114 **19** 1d. brown and green . . . 2·25 2·25
115 – 2d. black and red . . . . 1·25 1·75
116 – 3d. blue and violet 10 20
117 – 4d. olive and purple . . . 10 20
118 – 6d. green and orange . . . 80 1·25
119 – 9d. orange and brown . . 10 1·40
120 – 1s. purple and black . . . 10 20
121 – 2s. brown and green . . . 2·50 4·75
122 – 3s. blue and black . . . . 4·50 4·50
DESIGNS—HORIZ: 2d. Alofi landing; 3d. Native hut; 4d. Arch at Hikutavake; 6d. Alofi bay; 1s. Cave, Makefu. VERT: 9d. Spearing fish; 2s. Bananas; 3s. Matapa Chasm.

1953. Coronation. As Types of New Zealand but inscr "NIUE".
123 **164** 3d. brown 65 40
124 **168** 6d. grey 95 40

26

27 "Pua"

1967. Decimal Currency. (a) Nos. 113/22 surch.
125 **17** ½c. on ½d. 10 10
126 **18** 1c. on 1d. . . . . 1·10 15
127 – 2c. on 2d. 10 10
128 – 2½c. on 3d. 10 10
129 – 3c. on 4d. 10 10
130 – 5c. on 6d. 10 10
131 – 8c. on 9d. 10 10
132 – 10c. on 1s. 10 10
133 – 20c. on 2s. . . . . . . 35 1·00
134 – 30c. on 3s. . . . . . . 65 1·50
(b) Arms type of New Zealand without value, surch as in T **26**.
135 **26** 25c. brown 30 55
136 50c. green 70 80
137 $1 mauve . . . . 45 1·25
138 $2 pink . . . . 50 2·00

1967. Christmas. As T **278** of New Zealand but inscr "NIUE".
139 2½c. multicoloured 10 10

1969. Christmas. As No. 905 of New Zealand but inscr "NIUE".
140 2½c. multicoloured 10 10

1969. Flowers. Multicoloured; frame colours given.
141 **27** ½c. green 10 10
142 – 1c. red 10 10
143 – 2c. olive 10 10
144 – 2½c. brown 10 10
145 – 3c. blue 10 10
146 – 5c. red 10 10
147 – 8c. violet 10 10
148 – 10c. yellow 10 10
149 – 20c. blue . . . . 35 1·25
150 – 30c. green . . . . 1·10 1·75
DESIGNS: 1c. "Golden Shower"; 2c. Flamboyant; 2½c. Frangipani; 3c. Niue crocus; 5c. Hibiscus; 8c. "Passion Fruit"; 10c. "Kampui"; 20c. Queen Elizabeth II (after Anthony Buckley); 30c. Tapeu orchid.
For 20c. design as 5c. see No. 801.

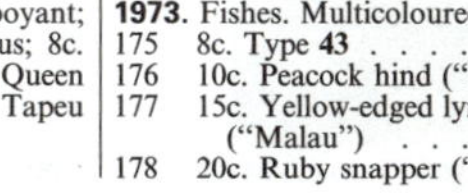

37 Kalahimu

1970. Indigenous Edible Crabs. Mult.
151 3c. Type **37** 10 10
152 5c. Kalavi 10 10
153 30c. Unga 30 25

1970. Christmas. As T **314** of New Zealand, but inscr "NIUE".
154 2½c. multicoloured 10 10

38 Outrigger Canoe, and Fokker F.27 Friendship over Jungle

1970. Opening of Niue Airport. Multicoloured.
155 3c. Type **38** 10 20
156 5c. "Tofua II" (cargo liner) and Fokker F.27 Friendship over harbour 15 20
157 8c. Fokker F.27 Friendship over airport 15 30

39 Spotted Triller

1971. Birds. Multicoloured.
158 5c. Type **39** 15 35
159 10c. Purple-capped fruit dove . 40 20
160 20c. Blue-crowned lory . . . 60 20

1971. Christmas. As T **325** of New Zealand, but inscr "Niue".
161 3c. multicoloured 10 10

40 Niuean Boy

41 Octopus Lure

1971. Niuean Portraits. Multicoloured.
162 4c. Type **40** 10 10
163 6c. Girl with garland 10 20
164 9c. Man 10 40
165 14c. Woman with garland . . 15 80

1972. South Pacific Arts Festival, Fiji. Multicoloured.
166 3c. Type **41** 10 10
167 5c. War weapons 15 15
168 10c. Sika throwing (horiz) . . 20 15
169 25c. Vivi dance (horiz) . . . 30 25

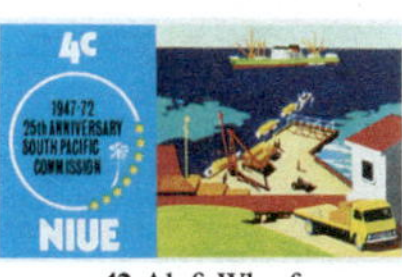
42 Alofi Wharf

1972. 25th Anniv of South Pacific Commission. Multicoloured.
170 4c. Type **42** 10 10
171 5c. Medical services 15 10
172 6c. Schoolchildren 15 10
173 18c. Dairy cattle 25 20

1972. Christmas. As T **332** of New Zealand, but inscr "NIUE".
174 3c. multicoloured 10 10

43 Silver Sweeper

1973. Fishes. Multicoloured.
175 8c. Type **43** 25 25
176 10c. Peacock hind ("Loi") . . 25 30
177 15c. Yellow-edged lyretail ("Malau") 30 40
178 20c. Ruby snapper ("Palu") . . 30 45

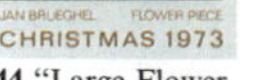
44 "Large Flower Piece" (Jan Brueghel)

46 King Fataaiki

45 Capt. Cook and Bowsprit

1973. Christmas. Flower studies by the artists listed. Multicoloured.
179 4c. Type **44** 10 10
180 5c. Bollongier 10 10
181 10c. Ruysch 20 20

1974. Bicent of Capt. Cook's Visit. Mult.
182 2c. Type **45** 20 20
183 3c. Niue landing place . . . 20 20
184 8c. Map of Niue 20 30
185 20c. Ensign of 1774 and Administration Building . . 30 65

1974. Self-government. Multicoloured.
186 4c. Type **46** 10 15
187 8c. Annexation Ceremony, 1900 . . . . 10 15
188 10c. Legislative Assembly Chambers (horiz) 10 15
189 20c. Village meeting (horiz) . 15 25

47 Decorated Bicycles

48 Children going to Church

1974. Christmas. Multicoloured.
190 3c. Type **47** 10 10
191 10c. Decorated motorcycle . . 10 10
192 20c. Motor transport to church 20 30

1975. Christmas. Multicoloured.
193 4c. Type **48** 10 10
194 5c. Child with balloons on bicycle 10 10
195 10c. Balloons and gifts on tree 20 20

49 Hotel Buildings

1975. Opening of Tourist Hotel. Mult.
196 8c. Type **49** 10 10
197 20c. Ground-plan and buildings 20 20

50 Preparing Ground for Taro

1976. Food Gathering. Multicoloured.
198 1c. Type **50** 10 10
199 2c. Planting taro 10 10
200 3c. Banana gathering 10 10
201 4c. Harvesting taro 10 10
202 5c. Gathering shellfish . . . 30 10
203 10c. Reef fishing 10 10
204 20c. Luku gathering 15 15
205 50c. Canoe fishing 20 60
206 $1 Coconut husking 25 80
207 $2 Uga gathering . . . . . . 45 1·40
See also Nos. 249/58 and 264/73.

51 Water

1976. Utilities. Multicoloured.
208 10c. Type **51** 10 10
209 15c. Telecommunications . . 15 15
210 20c. Power 15 15

52 Christmas Tree, Alofi

1976. Christmas. Multicoloured.
211 9c. Type **52** 15 15
212 15c. Church service, Avatele 15 15

53 Queen Elizabeth II and Westminster Abbey

1977. Silver Jubilee. Multicoloured.
213 $1 Type **53** 60 50
214 $2 Coronation regalia 80 75
MS215 72 × 104 mm. Nos. 213/14 1·10 1·60
Stamps from the miniature sheet have a blue border.

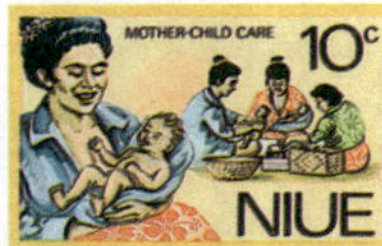

54 Child Care

1977. Personal Services. Multicoloured.
216 10c. Type **54** 15 10
217 15c. School dental clinic . . . 20 20
218 20c. Care of the aged 20 20

55 "The Annunciation" **58** "The Deposition of Christ" (Caravaggio)

57 "An Island View in Atooi"

1977. Christmas. Paintings by Rubens. Multicoloured.
219 10c. Type **55** 20 10
220 12c. "Adoration of the Magi" 20 15
221 20c. "Virgin in a Garland" 35 40
222 35c. "The Holy Family" . . 55 90
MS223 82 × 129 mm. Nos. 219/22 1·10 1·25

1977. Nos. 198/207, 214, 216 and 218 surch.
224 12c. on 1c. Type **50** 25 25
225 16c. on 2c. Planting taro . . 30 30
226 20c. on 3c. Banana gathering 30 40
227 35c. on 4c. Harvesting taro 30 45
228 40c. on 5c. Gathering shellfish 30 50
229 60c. on 20c. Luku gathering 30 55
230 70c. on $1 Coconut husking 30 55
231 85c. on $2 Uga gathering . . 30 60
232 $1.10 on 10c. Type **22** . . . 30 60
233 $2.60 on 20c. Care of the aged 50 70
234 $3.20 on $2 Coronation regalia 60 80

1978. Bicent of Discovery of Hawaii. Paintings by John Webber. Multicoloured.
235 12c. Type **57** 85 40
236 16c. "A View of Karakaooa, in Owhyhee" 95 50
237 20c. "An Offering before Capt. Cook in the Sandwich Islands" . . . . 1·00 60
238 30c. "Tereoboo, King of Owhyhee bringing presents to Capt. Cook" . . . . . 1·10 70
239 35c. "A Canoe in the Sandwich Islands, the rowers masked" . . . . . 1·25 80
MS240 121 × 121 mm. Nos. 235/9 4·75 2·75

1978. Easter. Paintings from the Vatican Galleries. Multicoloured.
241 10c. Type **58** 20 10
242 20c. "The Burial of Christ" (Bellini) 40 25
MS243 102 × 68 mm. Nos. 241/2 1·00 1·00

1978. Easter. Children's Charity. Designs as Nos. 241/2 in separate miniature sheets 64 × 78 mm, each with a face value of 70c.+5c.
MS244 As Nos. 241/2 Set of 2 sheets 1·00 2·00

59 Flags of Niue and U.K.

1978. 25th Anniv of Coronation. Mult.
245 $1.10 Type **59** 60 90
246 $1.10 Coronation portrait by Cecil Beaton 60 90
247 $1.10 Queen's personal flag for New Zealand 60 90
MS248 87 × 98 mm. Nos. 245/7 with white borders . . . . 2·50 1·50

1978. Designs as Nos. 198/207 but margin colours changed and silver frame.
249 12c. Type **50** 20 20
250 16c. Planting taro 20 20
251 30c. Banana gathering . . . 30 25
252 35c. Harvesting taro 30 30
253 40c. Gathering shellfish . . . 40 40
254 60c. Reef fishing 40 35
255 75c. Luku gathering 40 40
256 $1.10 Canoe fishing 50 80
257 $3.20 Coconut husking . . . 60 90
258 $4.20 Uga gathering 65 95

60 "Festival of the Rosary"

1978. Christmas. 450th Death Anniv of Durer. Multicoloured.
259 20c. Type **60** 40 20
260 30c. "The Nativity" 50 30
261 35c. "Adoration of the Magi" 60 35
MS262 143 × 82 mm. Nos. 259/61 1·50 2·00

1978. Christmas. Children's Charity. Designs as Nos. 259/61 in separate miniature sheets 74 × 66 mm., each with a face value of 60c.+5c.
MS263 As Nos. 259/61 Set of 3 sheets . . . . 1·00 2·00

1979. Air. Designs as Nos. 249/58 but gold frames and additionally inscr "AIRMAIL".
264 15c. Planting taro 20 15
265 20c. Banana gathering . . . 20 15
266 23c. Harvesting taro 25 15
267 50c. Canoe fishing 65 20
268 90c. Reef fishing 65 35
269 $1.35 Type **50** . . . . 65 1·50
270 $2.10 Gathering shellfish . . 65 1·75
271 $2.60 Luku gathering . . . 65 1·75
272 $5.10 Coconut husking . . . 80 1·75
273 $6.35 Uga gathering . . . . 80 1·75

61 "Pieta" (Gregorio Fernandez)

1979. Easter. Paintings. Multicoloured.
274 30c. Type **61** 30 25
275 35c. "Burial of Christ" (Pedro Roldan) 35 25
MS276 82 × 82 mm. Nos. 274/5 1·00 1·00

1979. Easter. Children's Charity. Designs as Nos. 274/5 in separate miniature sheets 86 × 69 mm., each with a face value of 70c.+5c.
MS277 As Nos. 274/5 Set of 2 sheets 1·10 1·75

62 "The Nurse and Child" (Franz Hals) **63** Penny Black Stamp

1979. International Year of the Child. Details of Paintings. Multicoloured.
278 16c. Type **62** 20 15
279 20c. "Child of the Duke of Osuna" (Goya) 20 20
280 30c. "Daughter of Robert Strozzi" (Titian) 35 35
281 35c. "Children eating Fruit" (Murillo) 45 40
MS282 80 × 115 mm. Nos. 278/81 1·25 2·25

1979. International Year of the Child. Children's Charity. Designs as Nos. 278/81 in separate miniature sheets 99 × 119 mm, each with a face value of 70c.+5c.
MS283 As Nos. 278/81 Set of 4 sheets . . . . 1·00 1·50

1979. Death Cent of Sir Rowland Hill. Mult.
284 20c. Type **63** 15 15
285 20c. Sir Rowland Hill and original Bath mail coach 15 15
286 30c. Basel 1845 2½r. stamp 15 20
287 30c. Sir Rowland Hill and Alpine village coach . . . 15 20
288 35c. U.S.A. 1847 5c. stamp 20 20
289 35c. Sir Rowland Hill and "Washington" (first transatlantic U.S.A. mail vessel) 20 20
290 50c. France 1849 20c. stamp 25 20
291 50c. Sir Rowland Hill and French Post Office railway van, 1849 . . . . 25 20
292 60c. Bavaria 1849 1k. stamp 25 20
293 60c. Sir Rowland Hill and Bavarian coach with mail 25 20
MS294 143 × 149 mm. Nos. 284/93 2·50 3·00
The two versions of each value were issued se-tenant within the sheet, forming composite designs.

64 Cook's Landing at Botany Bay

1979. Death Bicentenary of Captain Cook. Multicoloured.
295 20c. Type **64** 55 30
296 30c. Cook's men during a landing on Erromanga . . 75 40
297 35c. H.M.S. "Resolution" and H.M.S. "Discovery" in Queen Charlotte's Sound 85 45
298 75c. Death of Captain Cook, Hawaii . . . . 1·50 70
MS299 104 × 80 mm. Nos. 295/8 3·75 2·50

65 Launch of "Apollo 11" **66** "Virgin of Tortosa" (P. Serra)

1979. 10th Anniv of First Manned Moon Landing. Multicoloured.
300 30c. Type **65** 35 20
301 35c. Lunar module on Moon 45 25
302 60c. Sikorsky Sea King helicopter, recovery ship and command module after splashdown 90 40
MS303 120 × 82 mm. Nos. 300/2 1·25 1·60
Stamps from No. **MS**303 have the inscription in gold on a blue panel.

1979. Christmas. Paintings. Multicoloured.
304 20c. Type **66** 10 10
305 25c. "Virgin with Milk" (R. di Mur) 15 15
306 30c. "Virgin and Child" (S. di G. Sassetta) 20 20
307 50c. "Virgin and Child" (J. Huguet) 25 25
MS308 95 × 113 mm. Nos. 304/7 75 1·25

1979. Christmas Children's Charity. Designs as Nos. 304/7 in separate miniature sheets, 49 × 84 mm, each with a face value of 85c.+5c.
MS309 As Nos. 304/7 Set of 4 sheets 1·00 2·00

1980. Hurricane Relief. Surch **HURRICANE RELIEF Plus 2c.** (a) On Nos. 284/93 **HURRICANE RELIEF** spread over each se-tenant pair.
310 **63** 20c.+2c. multicoloured . . 20 40
311 – 20c.+2c. multicoloured (No. 285) 20 40
312 – 30c.+2c. multicoloured (No. 286) 25 45
313 – 30c.+2c. multicoloured (No. 287) 25 45
314 – 35c.+2c. multicoloured (No. 288) 30 50
315 – 35c.+2c. multicoloured (No. 289) 30 50
316 – 50c.+2c. multicoloured (No. 290) 35 65
317 – 50c.+2c. multicoloured (No. 291) 35 65
318 – 60c.+2c. multicoloured (No. 292) 35 70
319 – 60c.+2c. multicoloured (No. 293) 35 70

(b) On Nos. 295/8.
320 **64** 20c.+2c. multicoloured . . 40 50
321 – 30c.+2c. multicoloured . . 40 60
322 – 35c.+2c. multicoloured . . 40 65
323 – 75c.+2c. multicoloured . . 70 1·10

(c) On Nos. 300/2.
324 **65** 30c.+2c. multicoloured . . 25 40
325 – 35c.+2c. multicoloured . . 25 45
326 – 60c.+2c. multicoloured . . 50 75

(d) On Nos. 304/7.
327 **66** 20c.+2c. multicoloured . . 20 35
328 – 25c.+2c. multicoloured . . 20 40
329 – 30c.+2c. multicoloured . . 20 45
330 – 50c.+2c. multicoloured . . 30 70

68 "Pieta" (Bellini)

1980. Easter. "Pieta". Paintings. Mult.
331 25c. Type **68** 20 15
332 30c. Botticelli 25 20
333 35c. A. van Dyck 25 20
MS334 75 × 104 mm. As Nos. 331/3, but each with additional premium of **+ 2c.** 55 90
The premiums on No. **MS**334 were used to support Hurricane Relief.

1980. Easter. Hurricane Relief. Designs as Nos. 331/3 in separate miniature sheets, 75 × 52 mm, each with a face value of 85c.+5c.
MS335 As Nos. 331/3 Set of 3 sheets 1·00 1·50

69 Ceremonial Stool, New Guinea **72** Queen Elizabeth the Queen Mother

1980. South Pacific Festival of Arts, New Guinea. Multicoloured.
336 20c. Type **69** 10 10
337 20c. Ku-Tagwa plaque, New Guinea 10 10
338 20c. Suspension hook, New Guinea 10 10
339 20c. Ancestral board, New Guinea 10 10
340 25c. Platform post, New Hebrides 10 10
341 25c. Canoe ornament, New Ireland 10 10
342 25c. Carved figure, Admiralty Islands 10 10
343 25c. Female with child, Admiralty Islands 10 10
344 30c. The God A'a, Rurutu (Austral Islands) 15 15
345 30c. Statue of Tangaroa, Cook Islands 15 15
346 30c. Ivory pendant, Tonga 15 15

347 30c. Tapa (Hiapo) cloth, Niue 15 15
348 35c. Feather box (Waka), New Zealand 15 15
349 35c. Hei-Tiki amulet, New Zealand 15 15
350 35c. House post, New Zealand 15 15
351 35c. Feather image of god Ku, Hawaii 15 15
MS352 Four sheets, each 86 × 124 mm. (a) Nos. 336, 340, 344, 348; (b) Nos. 337, 341, 345, 349; (c) Nos. 338, 342, 346, 350; (d) Nos. 339, 343, 347, 351. Each stamp with an additional premium of 2c. Set of 4 sheets 1·50 2·00

1980. "Zeapex '80" International Stamp Exhibition, Auckland. Nos. 284/93 optd (A) **ZEAPEX'80 AUCKLAND** or (B) **NEW ZEALAND STAMP EXHIBITION** and emblem.
353 **63** 20c. multicoloured (A) 25 15
354 – 20c. multicoloured (B) 25 15
355 – 30c. multicoloured (A) 25 15
356 – 30c. multicoloured (B) 25 15
357 – 35c. multicoloured (A) 25 15
358 – 35c. multicoloured (B) 25 15
359 – 50c. multicoloured (A) 30 20
360 – 50c. multicoloured (B) 30 20
361 – 60c. multicoloured (A) 30 20
362 – 60c. multicoloured (B) 30 20
MS363 143 × 149 mm. Nos. 353/62, each additionally surcharged **+ 2c.** 3·50 2·75

1980. 80th Birthday of The Queen Mother.
364 **72** $1.10 multicoloured 80 1·50
MS365 55 × 80 mm. **72** $3 multicoloured 1·00 1·75

73 100 m Dash

74 "The Virgin and Child"

1980. Olympic Games, Moscow.
366 **73** 20c. multicoloured 20 15
367 – 20c. multicoloured 20 15
368 – 25c. multicoloured 20 20
369 – 25c. multicoloured 20 20
370 – 30c. multicoloured 25 20
371 – 30c. multicoloured 25 20
372 – 35c. multicoloured 25 25
373 – 35c. multicoloured 25 25
MS374 119 × 128 mm. Nos. 366/73, each stamp including premium of 2c. 1·00 1·00

DESIGNS: No. 367, Allen Wells, Great Britain (winner 100 m dash); 368, 400 m freestyle 369, Ines Diers (winner, D.D.R.); 370, Soling Class; 371, Winner, Denmark; 372, Football; 373, Winner, Czechoslovakia.

Nos. 366/7, 368/9, 370/1 and 372/3 were printed se-tenant in pairs each pair forming a composite design. On the 25c. and 35c. stamps the face value is at right on the first design and at left on the second in each pair. For the 30c. No. 370 has a yacht with a green sail at left and No. 371 a yacht with a red sail.

1980. Christmas.
375 **74** 20c. multicoloured 15 15
376 – 25c. multicoloured 15 15
377 – 30c. multicoloured 20 20
378 – 35c. multicoloured 20 20
MS379 87 × 112 mm. Nos. 375/8 85 1·25

DESIGNS: 25c. to 35c. Various Virgin and Child paintings by Andrea del Sarto.

1980. Christmas. Children's Charity. Designs as Nos. 375/8 in separate miniature sheets 62 × 84 mm, each with a face value of 80c.+5c.
MS380 As Nos. 375/8 Set of 4 sheets 1·25 1·75

75 "Phalaenopsis sp."

77 Prince Charles

76 "Jesus Defiled" (El Greco)

1981. Flowers (1st series). Multicoloured.
381 2c. Type **75** 10 10
382 2c. Moth orchid 10 10
383 5c. "Euphorbia pulcherrima" 10 10
384 5c. Poinsettia 10 10
385 10c. "Thunbergia alata" 10 10
386 10c. Black-eyed Susan 10 10
387 15c. "Cochlospermum hibiscoides" 15 15
388 15c. Buttercup tree 15 15
389 20c. "Begonia sp." 20 20
390 20c. Begonia 20 20
391 25c. "Plumeria sp." 25 25
392 25c. Frangipani 25 25
393 30c. "Strelitzia reginae" 30 30
394 30c. Bird of Paradise 30 30
395 35c. "Hibiscus syriacus" 30 30
396 35c. Rose of Sharon 30 30
397 40c. "Nymphaea sp." 35 35
398 40c. Water lily 35 35
399 50c. "Tibouchina sp." 45 45
400 50c. Princess flower 45 45
401 60c. "Nelumbo sp." 55 55
402 60c. Lotus 55 55
403 80c. "Hybrid hibiscus" 75 75
404 80c. Yellow hibiscus 75 75
405 $1 Golden shower tree ("cassia fistula") 1·00 1·00
406 $2 "Orchid var" 3·50 2·50
407 $3 "Orchid sp." 3·75 3·50
408 $4 "Euphorbia pulcherrima poinsettia" 2·25 4·00
409 $6 "Hybrid hibiscus" 2·75 6·00
410 $10 Scarlet hibiscus ("hibiscus rosa-sinensis") 4·25 9·00

Nos. 405/10 are larger, 47 × 35 mm.
See also Nos. 527/36.

1981. Easter. Details of Paintings. Mult.
425 35c. Type **76** 40 30
426 50c. "Pieta" (Fernando Gallego) 60 50
427 60c. "The Supper of Emmaus" (Jacopo de Pontormo) 65 55
MS428 69 × 111 mm. As Nos. 425/7, but each with charity premium of 2c. 1·00 1·75

1981. Easter. Children's Charity. Designs as Nos. 425/7 in separate miniature sheets 78 × 86 mm, each with a face value of 80c.+5c.
MS429 As Nos. 425/7 Set of 3 sheets 1·00 2·00

1981. Royal Wedding. Multicoloured.
430 75c. Type **77** 25 60
431 95c. Lady Diana Spencer 30 70
432 $1.20 Prince Charles and Lady Diana Spencer 30 80
MS433 78 × 85 mm. Nos. 430/2 2·00 2·50

78 Footballer Silhouettes

1981. World Cup Football Championship, Spain (1982).
434 **78** 30c. green, gold and blue 20 20
435 – 30c. green, gold and blue 20 20
436 – 30c. green, gold and blue 20 20
437 – 35c. blue, gold and orange 20 20
438 – 35c. blue, gold and orange 20 20
439 – 35c. blue, gold and orange 20 20
440 – 40c. orange, gold and green 20 20
441 – 40c. orange, gold and green 20 20
442 – 40c. orange, gold and green 20 20
MS443 162 × 122 mm. 30c.+3c., 35c.+3c., 40c.+3c. (each × 3). As Nos. 434/42 1·60 2·00

DESIGNS—Various footballer silhouettes: 435, gold figure 3rd from left; 436, gold figure 4th from left; 437, gold figure 3rd from left; 438, gold figure 4th from left; 439, gold figure 2nd from left; 440, gold figure 3rd from left displaying close control; 441, gold figure 2nd from left; 442, gold figure 3rd from left, heading.

1982. International Year for Disabled Persons. Nos. 430/2 surch **+5c.**
444 75c.+5c. Type **77** 50 85
445 95c.+5c. Lady Diana Spencer 60 1·00
446 $1.20+5c. Prince Charles and Lady Diana 60 1·25
MS447 78 × 85 mm. As Nos. 444/6, with each surcharged **+ 10c.** 1·75 4·50

80 "The Holy Family with Angels" (detail)

81 Prince of Wales

1981. Christmas. 375th Birth Anniv of Rembrandt. Multicoloured.
448 20c. Type **80** 65 45
449 35c. "Presentation in the Temple" 85 55
450 50c. "Virgin and Child in Temple" 95 1·10
451 60c. "The Holy Family" 1·25 1·50
MS452 79 × 112 mm. Nos. 448/51 3·25 3·75

1982. Christmas. Children's Charity. Designs as Nos. 448/51 in separate miniature sheets 66 × 80 mm, each with a face value of 80c.+5c.
MS453 As Nos. 448/51 Set of 4 sheets 2·00 2·50

1982. 21st Birthday of Princess of Wales. Multicoloured.
454 50c. Type **81** 40 55
455 $1.25 Prince and Princess of Wales 60 90
456 $2.50 Princess of Wales 1·50 1·40
MS457 81 × 101 mm. Nos. 454/6 4·75 3·50

The stamps from No. **MS**457 are without white borders.

1982. Birth of Prince William of Wales (1st issue). Nos. 430/3 optd.
458 75c. Type **77** 1·50 2·00
459 75c. Type **77** 1·50 2·00
460 95c. Lady Diana Spencer 2·50 2·50
461 95c. Lady Diana Spencer 2·50 2·50
462 $1.20 Prince Charles and Lady Diana Spencer 2·50 2·75
463 $1.20 Prince Charles and Lady Diana Spencer 2·50 2·75
MS464 78 × 85 mm. Nos. 430/2 6·00 6·00

OVERPRINTS: Nos. 458, 460 and 462 **COMMEMORATING THE ROYAL BIRTH 21 JUNE 1982**; 459, 461 and 463 **BIRTH OF PRINCE WILLIAM OF WALES 21 JUNE 1982**; **MS**464 **PRINCE WILLIAM OF WALES 21 JUNE 1982**.

1982. Birth of Prince William of Wales (2nd issue). As Nos. 454/6, but with changed inscriptions. Multicoloured.
465 50c. Type **81** 50 65
466 $1.25 Prince and Princess of Wales 1·00 1·25
467 $2.50 Princess of Wales 4·00 3·25
MS468 81 × 101 mm. As Nos. 465/7 7·00 5·50

83 Infant

1982. Christmas. Paintings of Infants by Bronzion, Murillo and Boucher.
469 **83** 40c. multicoloured 1·50 80
470 – 52c. multicoloured 1·60 95
471 – 83c. multicoloured 2·50 2·50
472 – $1.05 multicoloured 2·75 2·75
MS473 110 × 76 mm. Designs as Nos. 469/72 (each 31 × 27 mm), but without portrait of Princess and Prince William 5·00 2·75

84 Prince and Princess of Wales with Prince William

86 Scouts signalling

85 Prime Minister Robert Rex

1982. Christmas. Children's Charity. Sheet 72 × 58 mm.
MS474 **84** 80c.+5c. multicoloured 1·50 1·50

1983. Commonwealth Day. Multicoloured.
475 70c. Type **85** 50 55
476 70c. H.M.S. "Resolution" and H.M.S. "Adventure" off Niue, 1774 50 55
477 70c. Passion flower 50 55
478 70c. Limes 50 55

1983. 75th Anniv of Boy Scout Movement and 125th Birth Anniv of Lord Baden-Powell. Multicoloured.
479 40c. Type **86** 35 40
480 50c. Planting sapling 45 50
481 83c. Map-reading 85 90
MS482 137 × 90 mm. As Nos. 479/81, but each with premium of 3c. 1·25 1·75

1983. 15th World Scout Jamboree, Alberta, Canada. Nos. 479/81 optd **XV WORLD JAMBOREE CANADA.**
483 40c. Type **86** 35 40
484 50c. Planting sapling 45 50
485 83c. Map-reading 85 90
MS486 137 × 90 mm. As Nos. 483/5, but each with premium of 3c. 1·60 1·75

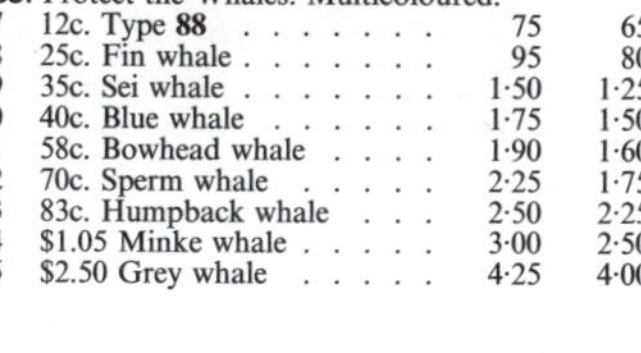

88 Black Right Whale

1983. Protect the Whales. Multicoloured.
487 12c. Type **88** 75 65
488 25c. Fin whale 95 80
489 35c. Sei whale 1·50 1·25
490 40c. Blue whale 1·75 1·50
491 58c. Bowhead whale 1·90 1·60
492 70c. Sperm whale 2·25 1·75
493 83c. Humpback whale 2·50 2·25
494 $1.05 Minke whale 3·00 2·50
495 $2.50 Grey whale 4·25 4·00

89 Montgolfier Balloon, 1783

1983. Bicentenary of Manned Flight. Mult.
496 25c. Type **89** (postage) 55 25
497 40c. Wright Brothers Flyer I, 1903 1·40 45
498 58c. Airship "Graf Zeppelin", 1928 1·50 60
499 70c. Boeing 247, 1933 1·75 85
500 83c. "Apollo 8", 1968 1·75 1·00
501 $1.05 Space shuttle "Columbia", 1982 2·00 1·40
MS502 118 × 130 mm. Nos. 496/501 (air) 3·00 3·25

90 "The Garvagh Madonna"

91 Morse Key Transmitter

1983. Christmas. 500th Birth Anniv of Raphael. Multicoloured.
503 30c. Type **90** 85 40
504 40c. "Madonna of the Granduca" 90 45
505 58c. "Madonna of the Goldfish" 1·25 60
506 70c. "The Holy Family of Francis I" 1·40 70
507 83c. "The Holy Family with Saints" 1·50 80
MS508 120 × 114 mm. As Nos. 503/7 but each with a premium of 3c. 3·25 2·75

1983. Various stamps surch. (a) Nos. 393/4, 399/404 and 407.
509 52c. on 30c. "Strelitzia reginae" 70 45
510 52c. on 30c. Bird of paradise 70 45
511 58c. on 50c. "Tibouchina sp." 70 55
512 58c. on 50c. Princess flower 70 55
513 70c. on 60c. "Nelumbo sp." 85 60
514 70c. on 60c. Lotus 85 60
515 83c. on 80c. "Hybrid hibiscus" 1·00 75
516 83c. on 80c. Yellow hibiscus 1·00 75
517 $3.70 on $3 "Orchid sp." 6·00 3·25

(b) Nos. 431/2 and 455/6.
518 $1.10 on 95c. Lady Diana Spencer 2·50 2·25
519 $1.10 on $1.25 Prince and Princess of Wales 1·50 2·00

520 $2.60 on $1.20 Prince Charles and Lady Diana . . . . . 3·00 3·50
521 $2.60 on $2.50 Princess of Wales . . . . 2·75 3·25

1983. Christmas. 500th Birth Anniv of Raphael. Children's Charity. Designs as Nos. 503/7 in separate miniature sheets, 65 × 80 mm, each with face value of 85c.+5c.
MS522 As Nos. 503/7 Set of 5 sheets 3·50 3·25

1984. World Communications Year. Multicoloured.
523 40c. Type **91** 30 35
524 52c. Wall-mounted phone . . 40 45
525 83c. Communications satellite 60 65
MS526 114 × 90 mm. Nos. 523/5 1·10 1·50

92 "Phalaenopsis sp."

93 Discus throwing

1984. Flowers (2nd series). Multicoloured.
527 12c. Type **92** 25 15
528 25c. "Euphorbia pulcherrima" 35 20
529 30c. "Cochlospermum hibiscoides" 40 25
530 35c. "Begonia sp." 40 25
531 40c. "Plumeria sp." 50 30
532 52c. "Strelitzia reginae" . . . 65 40
533 58c. "Hibiscus syriacus" . . . 70 45
534 70c. "Tibouchina sp." . . . 1·00 60
535 83c. "Nelumbo sp." . . . . 1·10 70
536 $1.05 "Hybrid hibiscus" . . . 1·25 85
537 $1.75 "Cassia fistula" . . . . 2·00 1·50
538 $2.30 "Orchid var" . . . . . 4·50 2·00
539 $3.90 "Orchid sp." . . . . . 6·00 4·00
540 $5 "Euphorbia pulcherrima poinsettia" . . . . . . 5·00 4·50
541 $6.60 "Hybrid hibiscus" . . . 6·00 6·00
542 $8.30 "Hibiscus rosa-sinensis" 8·00 7·00
Nos. 537/42 are larger, 39 × 31 mm.

1984. Olympic Games, Los Angeles. Multicoloured.
547 30c. Type **93** 25 30
548 35c. Sprinting (horiz) 30 35
549 40c. Horse racing (horiz) . . 35 40
550 58c. Boxing (horiz) 50 55
551 70c. Javelin-throwing 60 65

94 Koala

98 "The Nativity" (A. Vaccaro)

96 Niue National Flag and Premier Sir Robert Rex

1984. "Ausipex" International Stamp Exhibition, Melbourne. (a) Designs showing Koala Bears.
552 **94** 25c. multicoloured (postage) 70 50
553 – 35c. multicoloured 80 55
554 – 40c. multicoloured 90 60
555 – 58c. multicoloured . . . . 1·00 85
556 – 70c. multicoloured . . . . 1·25 1·00
(b) Vert designs showing Kangaroos.
557 – 83c. multicoloured (air) . . 1·50 1·25
558 – $1.05 multicoloured . . . . 1·75 1·60
559 – $2.50 multicoloured . . . . 3·00 4·00
MS560 110 × 64 mm. $1.75 Wallaby; $1.75 Koala bear . . . . . . 4·00 4·00
See also Nos. **MS**566/7.

1984. Olympic Gold Medal Winners, Los Angeles. Nos. 547/51 optd.
561 30c. Type **93** 65 30
562 35c. Sprinting 70 35
563 40c. Horse racing 75 35
564 58c. Boxing 80 50
565 70c. Javelin-throwing 85 60

OPTS: 30c. **Discus Throw Rolf Danneberg Germany**; 35c. **1,500 Metres Sebastian Coe Great Britain**; 40c. **Equestrian Mark Todd New Zealand**; 58c. **Boxing Tyrell Biggs United States**; 70c. **Javelin Throw Arto Haerkoenen Finland**.

1984. "Ausipex" International Stamp Exhibition, Melbourne (2nd issue). Designs as Nos. 552/60 in miniature sheets of six or four. Multicoloured.
MS566 109 × 105 mm. Nos. 552/6 and $1.75 Koala bear (as No. **MS**560) . . . . 6·00 4·75
MS567 80 × 105 mm. Nos. 557/9 and $1.75 Wallaby (as No. **MS**560) 6·00 4·75

1984. 10th Anniv of Self-government. Mult.
568 40c. Type **96** . . . . 1·10 50
569 58c. Map of Niue and Premier Rex . . . . 1·10 60
570 70c. Premier Rex receiving proclamation of self-government . . . . 1·10 70
MS571 110 × 83 mm. Nos. 568/70 2·00 2·00
MS572 100 × 74 mm. $2.50 As 70c. (50 × 30 mm) . . . . 2·00 2·00

1984. Birth of Prince Henry. Nos. 430 and 454 surch **$2 Prince Henry 15. 9. 84.**
573 $2 on 50c. Type **81** . . . . 2·50 2·75
574 $2 on 75c. Type **77** . . . . . 2·50 2·75

1984. Christmas. Multicoloured.
575 40c. Type **98** 70 35
576 58c. "Virgin with Fly" (anon, 16th-century) 85 50
577 70c. "The Adoration of the Shepherds" (B. Murillo) . . 95 60
578 80c. "Flight into Egypt" (B. Murillo) . . . . 1·10 70
MS579 115 × 111 mm. As Nos. 575/8 but each stamp with a 5c. premium 2·50 2·25
MS580 Four sheets, each 66 × 98 mm. As Nos. 575/8, but each stamp 30 × 42 mm. with a face value of 95c.+10c. Set of 4 sheets . . . . 3·75 3·00

99 House Wren

1985. Birth Bicentenary of John J. Audubon (ornithologist). Multicoloured.
581 40c. Type **99** . . . . 2·75 1·00
582 70c. Veery . . . . 3·00 1·60
583 83c. Grasshopper sparrow . . 3·25 2·00
584 $1.50 Henslow's sparrow . . . 3·50 2·25
585 $2.50 Vesper sparrow . . . . 5·00 4·25
MS586 Five sheets, each 54 × 60 mm. As Nos. 581/5 but each stamp 34 × 26 mm with a face value of $1.75 and without the commemorative inscription Set of 5 sheets . . . . 13·00 8·50

100 The Queen Mother in Garter Robes

1985. Life and Times of Queen Elizabeth the Queen Mother. Multicoloured.
587 70c. Type **100** . . . . 1·50 1·50
588 $1.15 In open carriage with the Queen . . . . 1·60 1·60
589 $1.50 With Prince Charles during 80th birthday celebrations . . . . . . 1·75 1·75
MS590 70 × 70 mm. $3 At her desk in Clarence House (38 × 35 mm) 6·50 2·75
See also No. **MS**627.

1985. South Pacific Mini Games, Rarotonga. Nos. 547/8 and 550/1 surch **MINI SOUTH PACIFIC GAMES, RAROTONGA** and emblem.
591 52c. on 70c. Javelin throwing 40 55
592 83c. on 58c. Boxing 65 80
593 95c. on 35c. Sprinting 75 90
594 $2 on 30c. Type **93** . . . . 1·50 2·00

1985. Pacific Islands Conference, Rarotonga. Nos. 475/8 optd **PACIFIC ISLANDS CONFERENCE, RAROTONGA** and emblem.
595 70c. Type **85** 55 75
596 70c. "Resolution" and "Adventure" off Niue, 1774 . . . . 55 75
597 70c. Passion flower 55 75
598 70c. Limes 55 75
Nos. 595 also shows an overprinted amendment to the caption which now reads **Premier Sir Robert Rex K.B.E.**.

103 "R. Strozzi's Daughter" (Titian)

104 "Virgin and Child"

1985. International Youth Year. Mult.
599 58c. Type **103** . . . . 2·00 90
600 70c. "The Fifer" (E. Manet) 2·25 1·00
601 $1.15 "Portrait of a Young Girl" (Renoir) . . . . . 3·00 1·90
602 $1.50 "Portrait of M. Berard" (Renoir) . . . 3·25 2·50
MS603 Four sheets, each 63 × 79 mm. As Nos. 599/602 but each with a face value of $1.75+10c. Set of 4 sheets . . . 14·00 11·00

1985. Christmas. Details of Paintings by Correggio. Multicoloured.
604 58c. Type **104** . . . . 1·50 85
605 85c. "Adoration of the Magi" 1·75 1·40
606 $1.05 "Virgin with Child and St. John" . . . . 2·25 2·50
607 $1.45 "Virgin and Child with St. Catherine" . . . . . . 2·75 3·50
MS608 83 × 123 mm. As Nos. 604/7 but each stamp with a face value of 60c.+10c. . . . . 3·00 2·75
MS609 Four sheets, each 80 × 90 mm. 65c. Type **104**; 95c. As No. 605; $1.20, As No. 606; $1.75, As No. 607 (each stamp 49 × 59 mm). Imperf Set of 4 sheets . . . . 4·00 4·00

105 "The Constellations" (detail)

1986. Appearance of Halley's Comet. Designs showing details from ceiling painting "The Constellations" by Giovanni de Vecchi. Nos. 611/13 show different spacecraft at top left. Multicoloured.
610 60c. Type **105** 50 50
611 75c. "Vega" spacecraft . . . 65 65
612 $1.10 "Planet A" spacecraft . 90 90
613 $1.50 "Giotto" spacecraft . . 1·25 1·25
MS614 125 × 91 mm. As Nos. 610/13 but each stamp with a face value of 95c. . . . . 4·75 4·25
Stamps from No. **MS**614 are without borders.

106 Queen Elizabeth II and Prince Philip

107 U.S.A. 1847 Franklin 5c. Stamp and Washington Sculpture, Mt. Rushmore, U.S.A.

1986. 60th Birthday of Queen Elizabeth II. Multicoloured.
615 $1.10 Type **106** . . . . . . 80 1·00
616 $1.50 Queen and Prince Philip at Balmoral . . . . 1·00 1·25
617 $2 Queen at Buckingham Palace . . . . 1·50 1·75
MS618 110 × 70 mm. As Nos. 615/17, but each stamp with a face value of 75c. . . . . . 2·75 3·25
MS619 58 × 89 mm. $3 Queen and Prince Philip at Windsor Castle 3·50 4·25

1986. "Ameripex '86" International Stamp Exhibition, Chicago. Multicoloured.
620 $1 Type **107** . . . . 3·25 3·25
621 $1 Flags of Niue and U.S.A. and Mt. Rushmore sculptures . . . . 3·25 3·25
Nos. 620/1 were printed together, se-tenant, forming a composite design.

108 "Statue under Construction, Paris, 1883" (Victor Dargaud)

1986. Centenary of Statue of Liberty. Multicoloured.
622 $1 Type **108** . . . . 2·00 2·00
623 $2.50 "Unveiling of Statue of Liberty" (Edmund Morand) . . . . 2·75 3·50
MS624 107 × 73 mm. As Nos. 622/3, but each stamp with a face value of $1.25 . . . . 2·50 3·00
See also No. **MS**648.

109 Prince Andrew, Miss Sarah Ferguson and Westminster Abbey

1986. Royal Wedding.
625 **109** $2.50 multicoloured . . . 3·25 3·50
MS626 106 × 68 mm. $5 Prince Andrew and Miss sarah Ferguson (43 × 30 mm) . . . . 7·50 8·00

1986. 86th Birthday of Queen Elizabeth the Queen Mother. Nos. 587/9 in miniature sheet, 109 × 83 mm.
MS627 Nos. 587/9 . . . . 12·00 12·00

110 Great Egret

111 "Virgin and Child" (Perugino)

1986. "Stampex '86" Stamp Exhibition, Adelaide. Australian Birds. Multicoloured.
628 40c. Type **110** . . . . 3·00 1·75
629 60c. Painted finch (horiz) . . 3·25 2·00
630 75c. Australian king parrot 3·50 2·25
631 80c. Variegated wren (horiz) 3·75 2·50
632 $1 Peregrine falcon . . . . . 4·25 2·75
633 $1.65 Azure kingfisher (horiz) 6·00 4·00
634 $2.20 Budgerigars . . . . . 6·50 6·00
635 $4.25 Emu (horiz) . . . . . 8·00 7·50

1986. Christmas. Paintings from Vatican Museum. Multicoloured.
636 80c. Type **111** . . . . 2·00 1·75
637 $1.15 "Virgin of St. N. dei Frari" (Titian) . . . . . 2·25 2·00
638 $1.80 "Virgin with Milk" (Lorenzo di Credi) . . . . 3·25 3·50
639 $2.60 "Madonna of Foligno" (Raphael) . . . . 4·00 5·00
MS640 87 × 110 mm. As Nos. 636/9, but each stamp with a face value of $1.50 . . . . 8·50 6·00
MS641 70 × 100 mm. $7.50 As No. 639, but 27 × 43 mm . . . 8·00 9·00

1986. Visit of Pope John Paul II to South Pacific. Nos. 636/9 surch **CHRISTMAS VISIT TO SOUTH PACIFIC OF POPE JOHN PAUL II NOVEMBER 21 24 1986.**
642 80c.+10c. Type **111** . . . . 3·00 2·50
643 $1.15+10c. "Virgin of St. N. dei Frari" (Titian) . . . . 3·50 3·00
644 $1.80+10c. "Virgin with Milk" (Lorenzo di Credi) 4·75 4·00
645 $2.60+10c. "Madonna of Foligno" (Raphael) . . . . 6·00 5·00
MS646 87 × 110 mm. As Nos. 642/5, but each stamp with a face value of $1.50+10c. . . . . 15·00 12·00
MS647 70 × 100 mm. $7.50+50c. As No. 645, but 27 × 43 mm . . . 15·00 12·00

112a Sailing Ship under Brooklyn Bridge

1987. Centenary of Statue of Liberty (1986) (2nd issue). Two sheets, each 122 × 122 mm, containing T **112a** and similar multicoloured designs.

MS648 Two sheets. (a) 75c. Type **112a**; 75c. Restoring Statue's flame; 75c. Steam-cleaning Statue's torch; 75c. "Esmerelda" (children cadet barquentine) off Manhattan; 75c. Cadet barque at dusk. (b) 75c. Statue of Liberty at night (vert); 75c. Statue at night (side view) (vert); 75c. Cleaning Statue's crown (vert); 75c. Statue at night (rear view) (vert); 75c. Cleaning a finial (vert) Set of 2 sheets . . 8·00 9·00

113 Boris Becker, Olympic Rings and Commemorative Coin

1987. Olympic Games, Seoul (1988). Tennis (1st issue). Designs showing Boris Becker in play.

649 **113** 80c. multicoloured . . . 2·75 2·00
650 – $1.15 multicoloured . . . 3·00 2·25
651 – $1.40 multicoloured . . . 3·25 2·50
652 – $1.80 multicoloured . . . 4·00 3·25

1987. Olympic Games, Seoul (1988). Tennis (2nd issue). As T **113** but showing Steffi Graf.

653 85c. multicoloured . . . . . 2·75 1·75
654 $1.05 multicoloured . . . . 3·00 2·00
655 $1.30 multicoloured . . . . 3·25 2·25
656 $1.75 multicoloured . . . . 3·50 2·75

1987. Royal Ruby Wedding. Nos. 616/17 surch **40TH WEDDING ANNIV. 4.85.**

657 $4.85 on $1.50 Queen and Prince Philip at Balmoral 4·75 4·50
658 $4.85 on $2 Queen at Buckingham Palace . . . . 4·75 4·50

115 "The Nativity"

1987. Christmas. Religious Paintings by Durer. Multicoloured.

659 80c. Type **115** . . . . 1·50 1·25
660 $1.05 "Adoration of the Magi" . . . . 1·75 1·75
661 $2.80 "Celebration of the Rosary" . . . . 3·25 3·75
MS662 100 × 140 mm. As Nos. 659/61, but each size 48 × 37 mm with a face value of $1.30 . . . . 7·50 4·50
MS663 90 × 80 mm. $7.50 As No. 661, but size 51 × 33 mm 7·50 7·00

Nos. 659/61 each include detail of an angel with lute as in T **115**.

Stamps from the miniature sheets are without this feature.

116 Franz Beckenbauer in Action

1988. West German Football Victories. Mult.

664 20c. Type **116** 70 70
665 40c. German "All Star" team in action 90 90
666 60c. Bayern Munich team with European Cup, 1974 1·10 1·10
667 80c. World Cup match, England, 1966 . . . . . . 1·40 1·40
668 $1.05 World Cup match, Mexico, 1970 . . . . . . 1·60 1·60
669 $1.30 Beckenbauer with pennant, 1974 . . . . . . 2·00 2·00
670 $1.80 Beckenbauer and European Cup, 1974 . . . 2·25 2·25

1988. Steffi Graf's Tennis Victories. Nos. 653/6 optd.

671 85c. mult (optd **Australia 24 Jan 88 French Open 4 June 88**) . . . . 2·25 1·50
672 $1.05 multicoloured (optd **Wimbledon 2 July 88 U S Open 10 Sept. 88**) . . . . 2·75 1·75
673 $1.30 multicoloured (optd **Women's Tennis Grand Slam: 10 September 88**) . . 2·75 1·90
674 $1.75 mult (optd **Seoul Olympic Games Gold Medal Winner**) . . . . . . 2·75 2·10

118 Angels

1988. Christmas. Details from "The Adoration of the Shepherds" by Rubens. Multicoloured.

675 60c. Type **118** . . . . 1·75 1·50
676 80c. Shepherds . . . . 2·00 1·75
677 $1.05 Virgin Mary . . . . . 2·75 2·50
678 $1.30 Holy Child . . . . . . 3·50 3·00
MS679 83 × 103 mm. $7.20 The Nativity (38 × 49 mm) . . . . 6·00 7·50

119 Astronaut and "Apollo 11" Emblem

1989. 20th Anniv of First Manned Landing on Moon. Multicoloured.

680 $1.50 Type **119** . . . . . . 4·50 4·50
681 $1.50 Earth and Moon . . . 4·50 4·50
682 $1.50 Astronaut and "Apollo 11" emblem . . . 4·50 4·50
MS683 160 × 64 mm. As Nos. 680/2, but each stamp with a face value of $1.15 . . . . 5·00 5·00

120 Priests

1989. Christmas. Details from "Presentation in the Temple" by Rembrandt. Multicoloured.

684 70c. Type **120** . . . . 3·00 2·75
685 80c. Virgin and Christ Child in Simeon's arms . . . . . 3·00 2·75
686 $1.05 Joseph . . . . 3·50 3·25
687 $1.30 Simeon and Christ Child . . . . 4·00 3·75
MS688 84 × 110 mm. $7.20 "Presentation in the Temple" (39 × 49 mm) . . . . 12·00 13·00

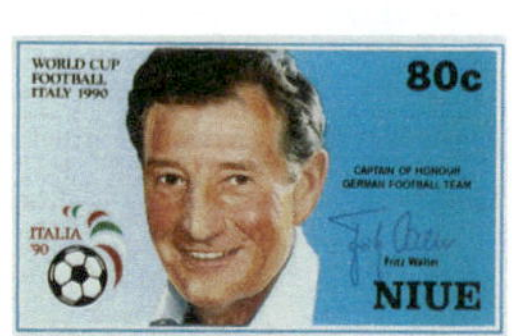

121 Fritz Walter

1990. World Cup Football Championship, Italy. German Footballers. Multicoloured.

689 80c. Type **121** . . . . 2·50 2·50
690 $1.15 Franz Beckenbauer . . 2·75 2·75
691 $1.40 Uwe Seeler . . . . . . 3·00 3·00
692 $1.80 German team emblem and signatures of former captains . . . . 4·00 4·00

122 "Merchant Maarten Looten" (Rembrandt)

123 Queen Elizabeth the Queen Mother

1990. 150th Anniv of the Penny Black. Rembrandt Paintings. Multicoloured.

693 80c. Type **122** . . . . 3·25 2·50
694 $1.05 "Rembrandt's Son Titus with Pen in Hand" 3·50 3·00
695 $1.30 "The Shipbuilder and his Wife" . . . . 3·75 3·25
696 $1.80 "Bathsheba with King David's Letter" . . . . 4·00 3·50
MS697 82 × 143 mm. As Nos. 693/6, but each with a face value of $1.50 7·50 7·50

1990. 90th Birthday of Queen Elizabeth the Queen Mother.

698 **123** $1.25 multicoloured . . . 4·75 4·00
MS699 84 × 64 mm. **123** $7 multicoloured . . . . 13·00 11·00

124 "Adoration of the Magi" (Dirk Bouts)

129 "The Virgin and Child with Sts. Jerome and Dominic" (Lippi)

1990. Christmas. Religious Paintings. Mult.

700 70c. Type **124** . . . . 3·00 2·75
701 80c. "Holy Family" (Fra Bartolommeo) . . . . . . 3·25 3·00
702 $1.05 "Nativity" (Memling) 3·50 3·50
703 $1.30 "Adoration of the Kings" (Bruegel the Elder) 4·50 4·50
MS704 100 × 135 mm. $7.20 "Virgin and Child Enthroned" (detail, Cosimo Tura) . . . . 11·00 12·00

1990. "Birdpex '90" Stamp Exhibition, Christchurch, New Zealand. No. 410 optd **Birdpex '90** and logo.

705 $10 Scarlet hibiscus . . . . . 12·00 13·00

1991. 65th Birthday of Queen Elizabeth II. No. 409 optd **SIXTY FIFTH BIRTHDAY QUEEN ELIZABETH II.**

706 $6 "Hybrid hibiscus" . . . . 12·00 12·00

1991. 10th Wedding Anniv of Prince and Princess of Wales. Nos. 430/2 optd **TENTH ANNIVERSARY.**

707A 75c. Type **77** . . . . . . 2·25 1·75
708A 95c. Lady Diana Spencer 3·25 2·75
709A $1.20 Prince Charles and Lady Diana . . . . . . 3·25 2·75

1991. Christmas. Religious Paintings. Mult.

710 20c. Type **129** . . . . 1·25 85
711 50c. "The Isenheim Altarpiece" (M. Grunewald) . . . . . 2·25 1·75
712 $1 "The Nativity" (G. Pittoni) . . . . 3·50 3·50
713 $2 "Adoration of the Kings" (J. Brueghel the Elder) . . 4·50 5·50
MS714 79 × 104 mm. $7 "Adoration of the Sheperds" (G. Reni) . . 10·00 12·00

130 Buff-banded Rail

1992. Birds. Multicoloured.

718 20c. Type **130** . . . . 1·50 80
719 50c. Red-tailed tropic bird . . 1·75 1·10
720 70c. Purple swamphen . . . 2·25 1·25
721 $1 Pacific pigeon . . . . . . 2·75 1·75
722 $1.50 White-collared kingfisher . . . . 2·50 2·25
723 $2 Blue-crowned lory . . . . 2·50 2·50
724 $3 Purple-capped fruit dove 2·50 3·00
726 $5 Barn owl . . . . 5·50 5·50
727 $7 Longtailed koel ("Cockoo") (48½ × 35 mm) 5·50 7·50
728 $10 Reef heron (48½ × 35 mm) . . . . . . 7·50 9·50
729 $15 Spotted triller ("Polynesian Triller") (48½ × 35 mm) . . . . . . 11·00 14·00

131 Columbus before King Ferdinand and Queen Isabella

1992. 500th Anniv of Discovery of America by Columbus. Multicoloured.

731 $2 Type **131** . . . . 3·50 3·00
732 $3 Fleet of Columbus . . . . 6·00 5·50
733 $5 Claiming the New World for Spain . . . . 7·00 6·50

132 Tennis and $10 Commemorative Coin

1992. Olympic Games, Barcelona. Mult.

734 $2.50 Type **132** . . . . . . 6·00 5·00
735 $2.50 Olympic flame and national flags . . . . . . 6·00 5·00
736 $2.50 Gymnastics and different $10 coin . . . . 6·00 5·00
MS737 152 × 87 mm. $5 Water polo 11·00 12·00

1992. 6th Festival of Pacific Arts, Rarotonga. Nos. 336/51 surch **$1.**

738 $1 on 20c. Type **69** . . . . . 1·00 1·00
739 $1 on 20c. Ku-Tagwa plaque, New Guinea . . . . 1·00 1·00
740 $1 on 20c. Suspension hook, New Guinea . . . . 1·00 1·00
741 $1 on 20c. Ancestral board, New Guinea . . . . 1·00 1·00
742 $1 on 25c. Platform post, New Hebrides . . . . . . 1·00 1·00
743 $1 on 25c. Canoe ornament, New Ireland . . . . 1·00 1·00
744 $1 on 25c. Carved figure, Admiralty Islands . . . . 1·00 1·00
745 $1 on 25c. Female with child, Admiralty Islands . . . . 1·00 1·00
746 $1 on 30c. The God A'a, Rurutu, Austral Islands . . 1·00 1·00
747 $1 on 30c. Statue of Tangaroa, Cook Islands . . 1·00 1·00
748 $1 on 30c. Ivory pendant, Tonga . . . . 1·00 1·00
749 $1 on 30c. Tapa (Hiapo) cloth, Niue . . . . 1·00 1·00
750 $1 on 35c. Feather box (Waka), New Zealand . . 1·00 1·00
751 $1 on 35c. Hei-Tiki amulet, New Zealand . . . . . . 1·00 1·00
752 $1 on 35c. House post, New Zealand . . . . 1·00 1·00
753 $1 on 35c. Feather image of god Ku, Hawaii . . . . . 1·00 1·00

134 "St. Catherine's Mystic Marriage" (detail) (Memling)

135 Queen on Official Visit

1992. Christmas.

754 **134** 20c. multicoloured . . . . 1·25 75
755 – 50c. multicoloured . . . . 2·00 1·50
756 – $1 multicoloured . . . . 3·00 3·00
757 – $2 multicoloured . . . . 4·50 5·50
MS758 87 × 101 mm. $7 multicoloured (as 50c., but larger (36 × 47 mm) . . . . 11·00 12·00

DESIGNS: 50c., $1, $2 Different details from "St. Catherine's Mystic Marriage" by Hans Memling.

1992. 40th Anniv of Queen Elizabeth II's Accession. Multicoloured.

759 70c. Type **135** . . . . 2·25 1·75
760 $1 Queen in green evening dress . . . . 2·75 2·25
761 $1.50 Queen in white embroidered evening dress 3·25 2·75
762 $2 Queen with bouquet . . . 3·75 3·25

136 Rough-toothed Dolphin

1993. Endangered Species. South Pacific Dolphins. Multicoloured.
763 20c. Type **136** . . . . 1·25 90
764 50c. Fraser's dolphin . . . . 2·00 1·60
765 75c. Pantropical spotted dolphin . . . . 2·50 2·75
766 $1 Risso's dolphin . . . . . 3·00 3·50

1993. Premier Sir Robert Rex Commemoration. Nos. 568/70 optd **1909 IN MEMORIAM 1992 SIR ROBERT R REX K.B.E.** or surch also.
767 40c. Type **96** . . . . 2·50 2·50
768 58c. Map of Niue and Premier Rex . . . . 2·50 2·50
769 70c. Premier Rex receiving proclamation of self-government . . . . . . 2·50 2·50
770 $1 on 40c. Type **96** . . . . 2·75 2·75
771 $1 on 58c. Map of Niue and Premier Rex . . . . . . 2·75 2·75
772 $1 on 70c. Premier Rex receiving proclamation of self-government . . . . . 2·75 2·75

138 Queen Elizabeth II in Coronation Robes and St. Edward's Crown

1993. 40th Anniv of Coronation.
773 **138** $5 multicoloured . . . . 12·00 12·00

139 "Virgin of the Rosary" (detail) (Guido Reni)

1993. Christmas.
774 **139** 20c. multicoloured 85 75
775 – 70c. multicoloured . . . . 2·00 1·25
776 – $1 multicoloured . . . . 2·25 1·50
777 – $1. 50 multicoloured . . . 3·00 3·50
778 – $3 multicoloured (32 × 47 mm) . . . . . . 4·75 6·50
DESIGNS: 70c. to $3 Different details of "Virgin of the Rosary" (Reni).

140 World Cup and Globe with Flags of U.S.A. and Previous Winners

1994. World Cup Football Championship, U.S.A.
779 **140** $4 multicoloured . . . . 6·50 7·50

141 "Apollo 11" and Astronaut on Moon

1994. 25th Anniv of First Manned Moon Landing. Multicoloured.
780 $2.50 Type **141** . . . . . 6·00 6·00
781 $2.50 Astronaut and flag . . 6·00 6·00
782 $2.50 Astronaut and equipment . . . . 6·00 6·00

142 "The Adoration of the Kings" (Jan Gossaert)

1994. Christmas. Religious Paintings. Multicoloured.
783 70c. Type **142** . . . . 1·00 1·25
784 70c. "Madonna and Child with Sts. John and Catherine" (Titian) . . . . 1·00 1·25
785 70c. "The Holy Family and Shepherd" (Titian) . . . . 1·00 1·25
786 70c. "The Virgin and Child with Saints" (Gerard David) . . . . 1·00 1·25
787 $1 "The Adoration of the Shepherds" (cherubs detail) (Poussin) . . . . 1·25 1·50
788 $1 "The Adoration of the Shepherds" (Holy Family detail) (Poussin) . . . . . 1·25 1·50
789 $1 "Madonna and Child with Sts. Joseph and John" (Sebastiano) . . . . 1·25 1·50
790 $1 "The Adoration of the Kings" (Veronese) . . . . 1·25 1·50

143 Long John Silver and Jim Hawkins ("Treasure Island")

145 Tapeu Orchid

1994. Death Centenary of Robert Louis Stevenson (author). Multicoloured.
791 $1.75 Type **143** . . . . . . 3·50 3·00
792 $1.75 Transformation of Dr. Jekyll ("Dr. Jekyll and Mr. Hyde") . . . . 3·50 3·00
793 $1.75 Attack on David Balfour ("Kidnapped") . . 3·50 3·00
794 $1.75 Robert Louis Stevenson, tomb and inscription . . . . 3·50 3·00

1996. Nos. 720 and 722 surch.
795 50c. on 70c. Purple swamphen . . . . 7·00 4·00
796 $1 on $1.50 White-collared kingfisher . . . . 8·00 6·50

1996. Flowers. Multicoloured.
797 70c. Type **145** 80 80
798 $1 Frangipani . . . . 1·00 1·00
799 $1.20 "Golden Shower" . . . 1·40 1·75
800 $1.50 "Pua" . . . . 1·90 2·50

1996. Redrawn design as No. 146.
801 20c. red and green . . . . . 1·75 1·25

146 "Jackfish" (yacht)

1996. Sailing Ships. Multicoloured.
802 70c. Type **146** . . . . 1·10 1·10
803 $1 "Jennifer" (yacht) . . . . 1·60 1·60
804 $1.20 "Mikeva" (yacht) . . . 1·90 2·00
805 $2 "Eye of the Wind" (cadet brig) . . . . 2·50 3·00

147 "Desert Star" (ketch)

149 Ox

148 "Acropora gemmifera"

1996. "Taipei '96" International Philatelic Exhibition, Taiwan. Sheet 90 × 80 mm.
MS806 **147** $1.50 multicoloured 2·00 2·50

1996. Corals. Multicoloured.
807 20c. Type **148** 70 70
808 50c. "Acropora nobilis" . . 1·00 75
809 70c. "Goniopora lobata" . . 1·25 85
810 $1 "Sylaster sp." . . . . . . 1·50 1·25
811 $1.20 "Alveopora catalai" . . 1·75 1·75
812 $1.50 "Fungia scutaria" . . . 2·00 2·00
813 $2 "Porites solida" . . . . . 2·50 2·75
814 $3 "Millepora sp." . . . . . 3·25 3·75
815 $4 "Pocillopora eydouxi" . . 3·75 4·50
816 $5 "Platygyra pini" . . . . . 4·00 4·75

1997. "HONG KONG '97" International Stamp Exhibition. Chinese New Year ("Year of the Ox"). Sheet 120 × 90 mm.
MS817 **149** $1.50 multicoloured 1·50 2·25

150 Steps to Lagoon

1997. Island Scenes. Multicoloured.
818 $1 Type **150** . . . . 1·25 1·50
819 $1 Islands in lagoon . . . . 1·25 1·50
820 $1 Beach with rocks in foreground . . . . 1·25 1·50
821 $1 Over-hanging rock on beach . . . . 1·25 1·50
Nos. 818/21 were printed together, se-tenant, forming a composite design.

151 Humpback Whale

1997. Whales (1st series). Multicoloured.
822 20c. Type **151** 50 45
823 $1 Humpback whale and calf (vert) . . . . 1·25 1·25
824 $1.50 Humpback whale surfacing (vert) . . . . . 1·75 2·00
MS825 120 × 90 mm. Nos. 822/4 3·00 3·50
No. **MS**825 shows the "Pacific '97" International Stamp Exhibition, San Francisco, emblem on the margin.
See also Nos. 827/9.

152 Niue 1902 Ovpt on New Zealand 1d.

153 Niue 1918–29 Overprint on New Zealand £1

1997. "Aupex '97" Stamp Exhibition, Auckland (1st issue). Sheet 136 × 90 mm.
MS826 **152** $2+20c. multicoloured 2·10 2·50

1997. Whales (2nd series). As T **151**. Multicoloured.
827 50c. Killer whale (vert) . . . 85 85
828 70c. Minke whale (vert) . . . 1·00 1·00
829 $1.20 Sperm whale (vert) . . 1·25 1·25

1997. "Aupex '97" Stamp Exhibition, Auckland (2nd issue). Sheet 90 × 135 mm.
MS830 **153** $2+20c. multicoloured 1·90 2·50

154 Floral Display in Woven Basket

1997. Christmas. Floral Displays. Multicoloured.
831 20c. Type **154** 45 40
832 50c. Display in white pot . . 70 60
833 70c. Display in white basket 90 90
834 $1 Display in purple vase . . 1·25 1·50

1998. Diana, Princess of Wales Commemoration. Sheet 145 × 70 mm, containing vert designs as T **91** of Kiribati. Multicoloured.
MS835 20c. Wearing white jacket, 1992; 50c. Wearing pearl-drop earrings, 1988; $1 In raincoat, 1990; $2 With Mother Theresa, 1992 (sold at $3.70+50c. charity premium) . . . . 3·00 3·50

155 Divers and Turtle

1998. Diving. Multicoloured.
836 20c. Type **155** 45 45
837 70c. Diver exploring coral reef 75 75
838 $1 Exploring underwater chasm (vert) 90 90
839 $1.20 Divers and coral fronds 1·10 1·25
840 $1.50 Divers in cave . . . . 1·40 1·75

157 Pacific Black Duck

1998. Coastal Birds (1st series). Multicoloured.
841 20c. Type **157** 70 60
842 70c. White tern ("Fairy Tern") . . . . 1·25 80
843 $1 Great frigate bird (vert) 1·25 1·10
844 $1.20 Pacific golden plover ("Lesser Golden Plover") 1·40 1·50
845 $2 Common noddy ("Brown Noddy") . . . . 2·00 2·50
See also Nos. 875/8.

158 Golden Cowrie

1998. Shells. Multicoloured.
846 20c. Type **158** 40 30
847 70c. Cowrie shell 75 65
848 $1 Spider conch . . . . . . 1·00 1·00
849 $5 Helmet shell . . . . . . 5·00 7·00

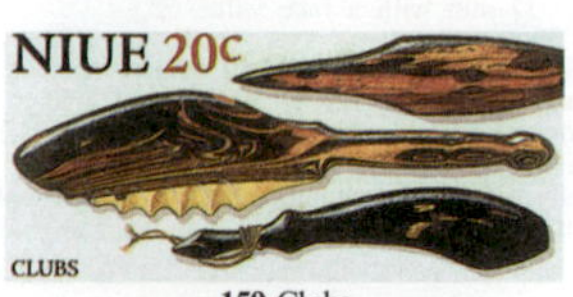

159 Clubs

1998. Ancient Weapons. Multicoloured.
850 20c. Type **159** 40 30
851 $1.20 Three spears (59 × 24 mm) . . . . . . 1·00 1·00
852 $1.50 Five spears (59 × 24 mm) . . . . . . 1·25 1·75
853 $2 Throwing stones . . . . . 1·50 2·25

160 Outrigger Canoe (first migration of Niue Fekai)

1999. "Australia '99" World Stamp Exhibition, Melbourne. Maritime History. Each blue.

854 70c. Type **160** 70 60
855 $1 H.M.S. "Resolution" (Cook) . . . . 1·25 1·00
856 $1.20 "John Williams" (missionary sailing ship) . . 1·40 1·60
857 $1.50 Captain James Cook 1·60 2·00

161 "Risbecia tryoni"

1999. Endangered Species. Nudibranchs. Mult.

858 20c. Type **161** 45 40
859 $1 "Chromodoris lochi" . . 1·10 1·00
860 $1.20 "Chromodoris elizabethina" . . . . . . 1·25 1·40
861 $1.50 "Chromodoris bullocki" . . . . 1·50 2·00
MS862 190 × 105 mm. Nos. 858/61 × 2 . . . . 6·50 8·00

162 Togo Chasm

1999. Scenic Views. Multicoloured.

863 $1 Type **162** . . . . . . 1·10 1·00
864 $1.20 Matapa Chasm . . . . 1·25 1·25
865 $1.50 Tufukia (horiz) . . . . 1·50 2·00
866 $2 Talava Arches (horiz) . . 1·75 2·50

163 Shallow Baskets

1999. Woven Baskets. Multicoloured.

867 20c. Type **163** 70 90
868 70c. Tray and bowl . . . . . 80 1·10
869 $1 Tall basket and deep bowls (44 × 34 mm) . . . . 1·00 1·40
870 $3 Tall basket and shallow bowls (44 × 34 mm) . . . . 2·10 2·50

164 Children, Yachts and Forest

1999. 25th Anniv of Self-Government. Sheet, 120 × 74 mm, containing T **164** and similar horiz design. Multicoloured.

MS871 20c. Type **164**; $5 Scuba diver, young child and sunset 4·00 5·00

165 Family and Man in Canoe

1999. New Millennium. Multicoloured.

872 20c. Type **165** . . . . 1·00 1·25
873 70c. People pointing up . . . 1·60 1·90
874 $4 Diver and man in traditional dress . . . . . 2·75 3·25

Nos. 872/4 were printed together, se-tenant, with the backgrounds forming a composite design.

166 Purple-capped Fruit Dove **167** Queen Elizabeth the Queen Mother

2000. Coastal Birds (2nd series). Multicoloured.

875 20c. Type **166** 45 40
876 $1 Purple swamphen . . . . 1·00 90
877 $1.20 Barn owl . . . . . . 1·40 1·40
878 $2 Blue-crowned lory . . . . 1·75 2·25

2000. 100th Birthday of Queen Elizabeth the Queen Mother and 18th Birthday of Prince William. Multicoloured.

879 $1.50 Type **167** . . . . . . 1·75 1·75
880 $3 Queen Elizabeth the Queen Mother and Prince William (horiz) . . . . . 2·50 3·25

168 Pole Vault

2000. Olympic Games, Sydney. Multicoloured.

881 50c. Type **168** 60 45
882 70c. Diving 75 65
883 $1 Hurdling . . . . 1·10 1·10
884 $3 Gymnastics . . . . 2·25 3·25

169 Couple in Traditional Costumes

2000. Island Dances. Multicoloured.

885 20c. Type **169** 45 70
886 70c. Woman in red costume 80 1·10
887 $1.50 Woman in white costume . . . . 1·25 1·40
888 $3 Child in costume made of leaves . . . . 1·75 1·90

Nos. 885/8 were printed together, se-tenant, with the backgrounds forming a composite design of flowers.

170 New Zealand Overprinted 1d. of 1902

2001. Centenary of First Niue Stamps. Multicoloured.

889 70c. Type **170** 75 75
890 $3 New Zealand overprinted £1 stamp of 1918–29 . . . 2·00 2·75

171 Large Green-banded Blue

2001. Butterflies. Multicoloured.

891 20c. Type **171** 40 35
892 70c. Leafwing 80 70
893 $1.50 Cairns birdwing . . . 1·25 1·40
894 $2 Meadow argus . . . . . 1·50 2·00

172 Green Turtle

2001. Turtles. Multicoloured.

895 50c. Type **172** 60 60
896 $1 Hawksbill turtle . . . . . 1·00 1·00
897 $3 Green turtle on beach . . 2·50 3·00

173 Coconut Crab emerging from Sea

2001. Coconut Crabs. Multicoloured.

898 20c. Type **173** 40 30
899 70c. Crab on beach with coconut palms 80 70
900 $1.50 Crab climbing coconut palm . . . . 1·25 1·50
901 $3 Crab with coconut . . . . 2·50 3·00

174 Government Offices

2001. Centenary of Annexation to New Zealand. Multicoloured.

902 $1.50 Type **174** . . . . . . 1·25 1·40
903 $2 New Zealand Commissioner and Niue Chief . . . . 1·50 2·00

175 Three Wise Men

2001. Christmas. Multicoloured.

904 20c. Type **175** 35 25
905 70c. Dove 80 60
906 $1 Angel . . . . 1·10 90
907 $2 Star . . . . 2·00 2·50

2002. World Wildlife Fund. No. 858 surch **$10.00**.

908 $10 on 20c. *Risbecia tryoni* 10 10

177 Great Clam

2002. Great Clam. Multicoloured.

909 50c. Type **177** 35 40
910 70c. Clam with black spots around opening 50 55
911 $1 Clam with barnacles attached 75 80
912 $1.50 Clam with white coral attached . . . . 1·10 1·30
MS913 163 × 101 mm. Nos. 909/12, each × 2 . . . . 5·50 6·00

178 Cadillac Eldorado (1953)

2003. Centenary of the Cadillac. Multicoloured.

MS916 115 × 155 mm. $1.50 Type **178**; $1.50 Cadillac Eldorado (2002); $1.50 Cadillac Eldorado (1967); $1.50 Cadillac Sedan DeVille (1961) . . . . 6·00 6·25
MS917 108 × 82 mm. $4 Cadillac Seville (1978) . . . . 3·00 3·25

179 Corvette Convertible (1954)

2003. 50th Anniv of the Corvette. Multicoloured.

MS918 117 × 156 mm. $1.50 Type **179**; $1.50 Corvette (1979); $1.50 Corvette Convertible (1956); $1.50 Corvette Stingray (1964) 6·00 6·25
MS919 109 × 82 mm. $4 Corvette (1979) . . . . 3·00 3·25

180 Queen Elizabeth II **181** Nicholas Frantz (1927)

2003. Golden Jubilee. Multicoloured.

MS920 147 × 78 mm. $1.50 Type **180**; $1.50 Wearing tiara; $1.50 Wearing Imperial State Crown . . . . 3·25 3·40
MS921 97 × 68 mm. $4 Holding bouquet . . . . 3·00 3·25

2003. Centenary of Tour de France Cycle Race. Multicoloured.

MS922 156 × 96 mm. $1.50 Type **181**; $1.50 Nicholas Frantz (1928); $1.50 Maurice De Waele (1929); $1.50 Andre Leducq wearing round neck t-shirt (1930) 4·25 5·50
MS923 106 × 76 mm. $4 Andre Leducq wearing collared shirt (1930) . . . . 3·35 3·00

182 Wrinkled Hornbill

2004. Birds. Two sheets containing T **182** and similar multicoloured designs.

MS924 79 × 104 mm. $1.50 Type **182**; $1.50 Toco toucan; $1.50 Roseate spoonbill; $1.50 Blue and yellow ("Gold") macaw 4·25 4·50
MS925 52 × 76 mm. $3 Green-winged Macaw (horiz) . . . . 2·20 2·30

183 Garibaldi Fish

2004. Fish. Two sheets containing T **183** and similar horiz designs. Multicoloured.

MS926 104 × 79 mm. $1.50 Type **183**; $1.50 Golden dddamselfish; $1.50 Squarespot anthias; $1.50 Orange-fin anemonefish . . . . 4·25 4·50
MS927 76 × 52 mm. $3 Maculosus angel . . . . 2·20 2·30

184 *Agrias beata*

2004. Butterflies. Two sheets containing T **184** and similar horiz designs. Multicoloured.
MS928 104 × 79 mm. $1.50 Type **184**; $1.50 *Papilio blume*; $1.50 *Cethosia bibbis*; $1.50 *Cressida Cressida* . . . . . . 4·25 4·50
MS929 52 × 76 mm. $3 *Morpho rhetenor rhetenor* . . . . . . 2·20 2·30

185 Prince William

2004. 21st Birthday of Prince William. Two sheets containing T **185** and similar vert designs. Multicoloured.
MS930 147 × 78 mm. $1.50 Wearing suit and white spotted tie; $1.50 Type **185**; $1.50 Wearing suit and square patterned tie . . . . . 3·25 3·50
MS931 68 × 98 mm. $4 Wearing blue patterned shirt . . . . 3·00 3·35

186 Boeing 737-200

2004. Centenary of Powered Flight. Two sheets containing T **186** and similar horiz designs. Multicoloured.
MS932 107 × 176 mm. 80c. Type **186**; 80c. Boeing Stratocruiser; 80c. Boeing Model SA-307B; 80c. Douglas DC-2; 80c. Wright Flyer 1; 80c. DeHavilland D.H.4A . . . . 4·75 5·00
MS933 106 × 76 mm. $4 Boeing 767 3·00 3·25

187 Allied Air Forces

2004. 60th Anniv of D-Day Landings. Two sheets containing T **187** and similar horiz designs. Multicoloured.
MS934 140 × 100 mm. $1.50 Type **187**; $1.50 Allied naval guns; $1.50 Paratroopers; $1.50 Advance of Allies . . . . . . 4·25 4·50
MS935 98 × 68 mm. $3 Landing on Normandy . . . . 2·20 2·30

188 520 Class 4-8-4, Australia

2004. Bicentenary of Steam Locomotives. Two sheets containing T **188** and similar horiz designs. Multicoloured.
MS936 200 × 103 mm. $1.50 Type **188**; $1.50 FEF-2 Class 4-8-4, U.S.A; $1.50 Royal Scot Class 4-6-0, Great Britain; $1.50A4 Class 4-6-2, Great Britain . . . 4·25 4·50
MS937 100 × 70 mm. $3 Class GS-4 4-8-4, U.S.A . . . . 2·20 2·30

189 Pope John Paul II

2004. 25th Anniv of the Pontificate of Pope John Paul II. Sheet 126 × 198 mm containing T **189** and similar vert designs.
MS938 $1.50 Type **189**; $1.50 Waving; $1.50 At the Wailing Wall; $1.50 Holding Crucifix 4·25 4·50

190 Lily

2004. United Nations International Year of Peace. Flowers. Sheet 139 × 177 mm containing T **190** and similar vert designs. Multicoloured.
MS939 75c. Type **190**; 75c. Thistle; 75c. Lily of the Valley; 75c. Rose; 75c. Garland flower; 75c. Crocus; 75c. Lotus; 75c. Iris . . . . . 3·75 4·00

OFFICIAL STAMPS

1985. Nos. 409/10 and 527/42 optd **O.H.M.S.**
O 1 12c. Type **92** 35 30
O 2 25c. "Euphorbia pulcherrima" 40 35
O 3 30c. "Cochlospermum hibiscoides" 45 35
O 4 35c. "Begonia sp." 50 40
O 5 40c. "Plumeria sp." 50 45
O 6 52c. "Strelitzia reginae" . . 60 50
O 7 58c. "Hibiscus syriacus" . . 60 55
O 8 70c. "Tibouchina sp." . . . 75 70
O 9 83c. "Nelumbo sp." 90 80
O10 $1.05 "Hybrid hibiscus" . . 1·25 1·00
O11 $1.75 "Cassia fistula" . . . 1·75 1·75
O12 $2.30 Orchid var. . . . . . 5·50 2·75
O13 $3.90 Orchid sp. . . . . . . 6·00 4·25
O14 $4 "Euphorbia pulcherrima poinsettia" . . . . 5·50 6·00
O15 $5 "Euphorbia pulcherrima poinsettia" . . . . 5·50 6·00
O16 $6 "Hybrid hibiscus" . . . . 8·00 9·00
O17 $6.60 "Hybrid hibiscus" . . 8·00 9·00
O18 $8.30 "Hibiscus rosa-sinensis" . . . . 9·00 10·00
O19 $10 Scarlet hibiscus . . . . 10·00 11·00

1993. Nos. 718/29 optd **O.H.M.S.**
O20 20c. Type **130** . . . . . . 1·75 1·50
O21 50c. Red-tailed tropic bird 2·25 1·75
O22 70c. Purple swamphen . . . 3·00 2·00
O23 $1 Pacific pigeon . . . . . 3·25 2·00
O24 $1.50 White-collared kingfisher . . . . 4·00 3·00
O25 $2 Blue-crowned lory . . . 4·00 3·25
O26 $3 Crimson-crowned fruit dove . . . . 2·75 3·50
O27 $5 Barn owl . . . . 9·50 6·50
O28 $7 Longtailed cuckoo (48½ × 35 mm) . . . . . . 6·50 8·50
O29 $10 Eastern reef heron (48½ × 35 mm) . . . . . . 7·50 10·00
O30 $15 Spotted triller ("Polynesian Triller") (48½ × 35 mm) . . . . . . 16·00 18·00

NORFOLK ISLAND Pt. 1

A small island East of New South Wales, administered by Australia until 1960 when local government was established.

1947. 12 pence = 1 shilling;
20 shillings = 1 pound.
1966. 100 cents = $1 Australian.

1 Ball Bay

1947.
1 **1** ½d. orange 85 60
2 1d. violet 50 60
3 1½d. green 50 70
4 2d. mauve 55 40
5 2½d. red 80 30
6 3d. brown 70 70
6a 3d. green . . . . 13·00 7·50
7 4d. red . . . . 1·75 40
8 5½d. blue 70 30
9 6d. brown 70 30
10 9d. pink . . . . 1·25 40
11 1s. green 70 40
12 2s. brown . . . . 1·00 1·00
12a 2s. blue . . . . 17·00 8·00

12 "Hibiscus insularis"

2 Warder's Tower

4 Old Stores (Crankmill)

17 Queen Elizabeth II (after Annigoni) and Cereus

22 Red-tailed Tropic Bird

1953.
24 **12** 1d. green 15 10
25 – 2d. red and green 20 10
26 – 3d. green 70 15
13 **2** 3½d. red . . . . 1·00 90
27 – 5d. purple 55 20
14 – 6½d. green . . . . 2·25 3·25
15 **4** 7½d. blue . . . . 1·50 3·00
28 – 8d. red 80 50
16 – 8½d. brown . . . . 1·75 4·75
29 **17** 9d. blue 80 45
17 – 10d. violet . . . . 1·00 75
30 – 10d. brown and violet . . . 1·25 1·00
31 – 1s.1d. red 80 35
32 – 2s. brown . . . . 5·00 1·00
33 – 2s.5d. violet . . . . 1·00 40
34 – 2s.8d. brown and green . . 2·25 55
18 – 5s. brown . . . . 32·00 8·00
35 – 5s. brown and green . . . . 3·50 75
36 **22** 10s. green . . . . 30·00 32·00
DESIGNS—VERT: 2d. "Lagunaria patersonii"; 5d. Lantana; 8d. Red hibiscus; 8½d. Barracks entrance; 10d. Salt house; 1s.1d. Fringed hibiscus; 2s. Solander's petrel; 2s.5d. Passion-flower; 2s.8d. Rose apple. HORIZ: 3d. White tern; 6½d. Airfield; 5s. Bloody Bridge.

For Nos. 25 and 28 with face values in decimal currency see Nos. 600/1.

8 Norfolk Is. Seal and Pitcairners Landing

1956. Cent of Landing of Pitcairners on Norfolk Is.
19 **8** 3d. green 75 40
20 2s. violet . . . . 1·00 1·00

1958. Surch.
21 **4** 7d. on 7½d. blue . . . . . . 75 1·00
22 – 8d. on 8½d. brown (No. 16) 75 1·00

1959. 150th Anniv of Australian P.O. No. 331 of Australia surch **NORFOLK ISLAND 5D.**
23 **143** 5d. on 4d. slate 35 30

1960. As Nos. 13 and 14/15 but colours changed and surch.
37 **2** 1s.1d. on 3½d. blue . . . . . 2·00 1·00
38 2s.5d. on 6½d. turquoise . . . 3·00 1·00
39 **4** 2s.8d. on 7½d. sepia . . . . 6·00 5·50

26 Queen Elizabeth II and Map

1960. Introduction of Local Government.
40 **26** 2s.8d. purple . . . . 5·50 6·50

27 Open Bible and Candle

29 Stripey

28 Open Prayer Book and Text

1960. Christmas.
41 **27** 5d. mauve 60 50

1961. Christmas.
42 **28** 5d. blue 30 70

1962. Fishes.
43 **29** 6d. sepia, yellow and green 60 25
44 – 11d. orange, brown and blue 1·00 80
45 – 1s. blue, pink and olive . . 60 25
46 – 1s.3d. blue, brown and green . . . . 1·00 1·75
47 – 1s.6d. sepia, violet and blue 1·25 80
48 – 2s.3d. multicoloured . . . . 2·50 80
DESIGNS: 11d. Gold-mouthed emperor; 1s. Surge wrasse ("Po'ov"); 1s.3d. Seachub ("Dreamfish"); 1s.6d. Giant grouper; 2s.3d. White trevally.

30 "Madonna and Child"

31 "Peace on Earth ..."

1962. Christmas.
49 **30** 5d. blue 45 80

1963. Christmas.
50 **31** 5d. red 40 70

32 Overlooking Kingston

33 Norfolk Pine

1964. Multicoloured.
51 5d. Type **32** 60 60
52 8d. Kingston . . . . 1·00 1·50
53 9d. The Arches (Bumboras) 1·25 30
54 10d. Slaughter Bay . . . . . 1·25 30

1964. 50th Anniv of Norfolk Island as Australian Territory.
55 **33** 5d. black, red and orange 40 15
56 8d. black, red and green . . 40 1·10

34 Child looking at Nativity Scene

35 Nativity Scene

1964. Christmas.
57 **34** 5d. multicoloured 30 40

1965. 50th Anniv of Gallipoli Landing. As T **22** of Nauru, but slightly larger (22 × 34½ mm).
58 5d. brown, black and green . . 15 10

1965. Christmas.
59 **35** 5d. multicoloured 15 10

38 "Hibiscus insularis"

39 Headstone Bridge

1966. Decimal Currency. As earlier issue but with values in cents and dollars. Surch in black on silver tablets obliterating old value as in T **38**.
60 **38** 1c. on 1d. 20 10
61 – 2c. on 2d. (No. 25) 20 10
62 – 3c. on 3d. (No. 26) 75 90
63 – 4c. on 5d. (No. 27) 25 10
64 – 5c. on 8d. (No. 28) 30 10
65 – 10c. on 10d. (No. 30) . . . 1·00 15
66 – 15c. on 1s.1d. (No. 31) . . 50 50
67 – 20c. on 2s. (No. 32) . . . 2·75 2·75
68 – 25c. on 2s.5d. (No. 33) . . 1·00 40
69 – 30c. on 2s.8d. (No. 34) . . 1·00 50

70 – 50c. on 5s. (No. 35) . . . 2·50 75
71a **22** $1 on 10s. . . . . 2·25 2·50

1966. Multicoloured.
72 7c. Type **39** 40 15
73 9c. Cemetery Road 40 15

41 St. Barnabas' Chapel (interior)

43 Star over Philip Island

1966. Centenary of Melanesian Mission. Mult.
74 4c. Type **41** 10 10
75 25c. St. Barnabas' Chapel (exterior) 20 20

1966. Christmas.
76 **43** 4c. multicoloured 10 10

44 H.M.S. "Resolution", 1774

1967. Multicoloured.
77 1c. Type **44** 10 10
78 2c. "La Boussole" and "L'Astrolabe", 1788 . . . . 15 10
79 3c. H.M.S. "Supply" (brig), 1788 . . . . 15 10
80 4c. H.M.S. "Sirius" (frigate), 1790 . . . . 75 10
81 5c. "Norfolk" (sloop), 1798 . . . 20 10
82 7c. H.M.S. "Mermaid" (survey cutter), 1825 . . . . 20 10
83 9c. "Lady Franklin" (full-rigged ship), 1853 . . . . . 20 10
84 10c. "Morayshire" (full-rigged transport), 1856 . . . . . 20 50
85 15c. "Southern Cross" (missionary ship), 1866 . . . 50 30
86 20c. "Pitcairn" (missionary schooner), 1891 . . . . . . 60 40
87 25c. "Black Billy" (Norfolk Island whaleboat), 1895 . . 1·50 75
88 30c. "Iris" (cable ship), 1907 1·50 2·00
89 50c. "Resolution" (schooner), 1926 . . . . 2·50 2·75
90 $1 "Morinda" (freighter), 1931 3·00 2·75

45 Lions Badge and 50 Stars

47 Queen Elizabeth II

46 Prayer of John Adams and Candle

1967. 50th Anniv of Lions International.
91 **45** 4c. black, green and yellow 10 10

1967. Christmas.
92 **46** 5c. black, olive and red . . 10 10

1968.
93 **47** 3c. black, brown and red 10 10
94 4c. black, brown and green 10 10
95 5c. black, brown and violet 10 10
95a 6c. black, brown and lake 30 60

59 Avro Type 691 Lancastrian and Douglas DC-4 Aircraft

1968. 21st Anniv of QANTAS Air Service, Sydney–Norfolk Island.
96 **59** 5c. black, red and blue . . . 15 10
97 7c. brown, red and turquoise 15 10

60 Bethlehem Star and Flowers

61 Captain Cook, Quadrant and Chart of Pacific Ocean

1968. Christmas.
98 **60** 5c. multicoloured 10 10

1969. Captain Cook Bicentenary (1st issue). Observation of the transit of Venus across the Sun from Tahiti.
99 **61** 10c. multicoloured 10 10
See also Nos. 118/19, 129, 152/5, 200/2 and 213/14.

62 Van Diemen's Land, Norfolk Island and Sailing Cutter

63 "The Nativity" (carved mother-of-pearl plaque)

1969. 125th Anniv of Annexation of Norfolk Island to Van Diemen's Land.
100 **62** 5c. multicoloured 10 10
101 30c. multicoloured . . . . 50 1·00

1969. Christmas.
102 **63** 5c. multicoloured 10 10

64 New Zealand Grey Flyeater

1970. Birds. Multicoloured.
103 1c. Scarlet robin (vert) . . . 30 10
104 2c. Golden whistler (vert) . . 30 20
105 3c. Type **64** 30 10
106 4c. Long-tailed koels 60 10
107 5c. Red-fronted parakeet (vert) . . . . 1·50 60
108 7c. Long-tailed triller (vert) 45 10
109 9c. Island thrush 70 10
110 10c. Boobook owl (vert) . . 1·75 3·00
111 15c. Norfolk Island pigeon (vert) . . . . 1·25 65
112 20c. White-chested white-eye 8·00 3·25
113 25c. Norfolk Island parrots (vert) . . . . 1·75 40
114 30c. Collared grey fantail . . 8·00 1·75
115 45c. Norfolk Island starlings 1·50 80
116 50c. Crimson rosella (vert) . . 2·00 1·75
117 $1 Sacred kingfisher . . . . 10·00 10·00

65 Cook and Map of Australia

1970. Captain Cook Bicentenary (2nd issue). Discovery of Australia's East Coast. Mult.
118 5c. Type **65** 15 10
119 20c. H.M.S. "Endeavour" and aborigine 40 10

66 First Christmas Service, 1788

68 Rose Window, St. Barnabas Chapel, Kingston

67 Bishop Patteson, and Martyrdom of St. Stephen

1970. Christmas.
120 **66** 5c. multicoloured 10 10

1971. Death Cent of Bishop Patteson. Multicoloured.
121 6c. Type **67** 10 35
122 6c. Bible, Martyrdom of St. Stephen and knotted palm-frond 10 35
123 10c. Bishop Patteson and stained glass 10 35
124 10c. Cross and Bishop's Arms 10 35

1971. Christmas.
125 **68** 6c. multicoloured 10 10

69 Map and Flag

1972. 25th Anniv of South Pacific Commission.
126 **69** 7c. multicoloured 15 20

70 "St. Mark" (stained glass window) (All Saints, Norfolk Is.)

71 Cross and Pines (stained-glass window, All Saints Church)

1972. Christmas.
127 **70** 7c. multicoloured 10 10

1972. Cent of First Pitcairner-built Church.
128 **71** 12c. multicoloured 10 10

72 H.M.S. "Resolution" in the Antarctic

1973. Capt. Cook Bicentenary (3rd issue). Crossing of the Antarctic Circle.
129 **72** 35c. multicoloured . . . . 2·25 2·25

73 Child and Christmas Tree

1973. Christmas. Multicoloured.
130 7c. Type **73** 20 10
131 12c. Type **73** 25 10
132 35c. Fir trees and star . . . 70 90

74 Protestant Clergyman's Quarters

1973. Historic Buildings. Multicoloured.
133 1c. Type **74** 10 10
134 2c. Royal Engineers' Office 10 10
135 3c. Double Quarters for Free Overseers . . . . 25 1·00
136 4c. Guard House 20 20
137 5c. Entrance to Pentagonal Gaol 25 15
138 7c. Pentagonal Gaol 35 35
139 8c. Prisoners' Barracks . . . 1·25 2·25
140 10c. Officers' Quarters, New Military Barracks 50 55
141 12c. New Military Barracks 50 30
142 14c. Beach Stores 50 70
143 15c. The Magazine . . . . . 1·25 50
144 20c. Entrance, Old Military Barracks . . . . 50 1·00
145 25c. Old Military Barracks 1·25 1·50
146 30c. Old Stores (Crankmill) 50 60
147 50c. Commissariat Stores . . 50 2·00
148 $1 Government House . . . 1·00 4·00

75 Royal Couple and Map

1974. Royal Visit.
149 **75** 7c. multicoloured 40 20
150 25c. multicoloured 70 80

76 Chichester's De Havilland Gipsy Moth Seaplane "Madame Elijah"

1974. 1st Aircraft Landing on Norfolk Island.
151 **76** 14c. multicoloured 75 70

77 "Captain Cook" (engraving by J. Basire)

78 Nativity Scene (pearl-shell pew carving)

1974. Capt. Cook Bicentenary (4th issue). Discovery of Norfolk Is. Multicoloured.
152 7c. Type **77** 55 65
153 10c. H.M.S. "Resolution" (H. Roberts) . . . . 1·00 1·25
154 14c. Norfolk Island pine . . 75 1·25
155 25c. "Norfolk Island flax" (G. Raper) . . . . 75 1·50

1974. Christmas.
156 **78** 7c. multicoloured 15 10
157 30c. multicoloured 60 75

79 Norfolk Pine

1974. Centenary of Universal Postal Union. Multicoloured. Imperf. Self-adhesive.
158 10c. Type **79** 35 50
159 15c. Offshore islands 45 55
160 35c. Crimson rosella and sacred kingfisher 85 85
161 40c. Pacific map 85 95
MS162 106×101 mm. Map of Norfolk Is. cut-to-shape with reduced size replicas of Nos. 158/61 . . . . 20·00 24·00

80 H.M.S. "Mermaid" (survey cutter)

1975. 150th Anniv of Second Settlement. Multicoloured.
163 10c. Type **80** . . . . 40 1·10
164 35c. Kingston, 1835 (from painting by T. Seller) . . . 60 1·25

81 Star on Norfolk Island Pine

82 Memorial Cross

1975. Christmas.
165 **81** 10c. multicoloured 15 10
166 15c. multicoloured 20 10
167 35c. multicoloured 30 35

1975. Cent of St. Barnabas Chapel. Mult.
168 30c. Type **82** 20 15
169 60c. Laying foundation stone, and Chapel in 1975 . . . . 40 40

83 Launching of "Resolution"

1975. 50th Anniv of Launching of "Resolution" (schooner). Multicoloured.
170 25c. Type **83** 25 40
171 45c. "Resolution" at sea . . 40 70

84 Whaleship "Charles W. Morgan"

1976. Bicent of American Revolution. Mult.
172 18c. Type **84** 20 35
173 25c. Thanksgiving Service . . 20 35
174 40c. Boeing B-17 Flying Fortress over Norfolk Island 30 85
175 45c. California quail 45 85

85 Antarctic Tern and Sun

86 "Vanessa ita"

1976. Christmas.
176 **85** 18c. multicoloured 25 15
177 25c. multicoloured 35 20
178 45c. multicoloured 50 50

1977. Butterflies and Moths. Multicoloured.
179 1c. Type **86** 10 40
180 2c. "Utetheisa pulchelloides" 10 40
181 3c. "Agathia asterias" . . . 10 20
182 4c. "Cynthia kershawi" . . . 10 25
183 5c. "Leucania loreyimima" . 15 1·10
184 10c. "Hypolimnas bolina" . . 30 1·10
185 15c. "Pyrrhorachis pyrrhogona" 30 30
186 16c. "Austrocarea iocephala" 30 30
187 17c. "Pseudocoremia christiani" 35 30
188 18c. "Cleora idiocrossa" . . 35 30
189 19c. "Simplicia caeneusalis" 35 30
190 20c. "Austrocidaria ralstonae" 40 30
191 30c. "Hippotion scrofa" . . . 50 60
192 40c. "Papilio amynthor (ilioneus)" 50 40
193 50c. "Tiracola plagiata" . . . 50 75
194 $1 "Precis villida" 60 75
195 $2 "Cepora perimale" . . . 75 1·40

87 Queen's View, Kingston

1977. Silver Jubilee.
196 **87** 25c. multicoloured 35 30

88 Hibiscus Flowers and Oil Lamp

89 Captain Cook (from a portrait by Nathaniel Dance)

1977. Christmas.
197 **88** 18c. multicoloured 15 10
198 25c. multicoloured 15 10
199 45c. multicoloured 30 35

1978. Capt. Cook Bicentenary (5th issue). Discovery of Hawaii. Multicoloured.
200 18c. Type **89** 30 20
201 25c. Discovery of northern Hawaiian islands 30 30
202 80c. British flag against island background 60 70

90 Guide Flag and Globe

1978. 50th Anniv of Girl Guides. Multicoloured. Imperf. Self-adhesive.
203 18c. Type **90** 25 45
204 25c. Trefoil and scarf badge 30 55
205 35c. Trefoil and Queen Elizabeth 45 75
206 45c. Trefoil and Lady Baden-Powell 55 75

91 St. Edward's Crown

1978. 25th Anniv of Coronation. Mult.
207 25c. Type **91** 15 15
208 70c. Coronation regalia . . . 40 45

92 View of Duncombe Bay with Scout at Camp Fire

1978. 50th Anniv of Boy Scout Movement. Multicoloured. Imperf. Self-adhesive.
209 20c. Type **92** 30 45
210 25c. View from Kingston and emblem 35 55
211 35c. View of Anson Bay and Link Badge 50 90
212 45c. Sunset scene and Lord Baden-Powell 55 95

93 Chart showing Route of Arctic Voyage

1978. Captain Cook Bicentenary (6th issue). Northern-most Voyages. Multicoloured.
213 25c. Type **93** 30 30
214 90c. "H.M.S. "Resolution" and H.M.S. "Discovery" in Pack Ice" (Webber) . . . 80 80

94 Poinsettia and Bible

95 Cook and Village of Staithes near Marton

1978. Christmas. Multicoloured.
215 20c. Type **94** 15 10
216 30c. Native oak and bible . . 20 15
217 55c. Hibiscus and bible . . . 30 30

1978. 250th Birth Anniv of Captain Cook. Multicoloured.
218 20c. Type **95** 30 25
219 80c. Cook and Whitby Harbour . . . . 70 1·25

96 H.M.S. "Resolution"

1979. Death Bicent of Captain Cook. Mult.
220 20c. Type **96** 25 30
221 20c. Cook (statue) 25 30
222 40c. Cook's death 30 50
223 40c. Cook's death (different) 30 50
Nos. 220/1 were issued se-tenant, in horizontal pairs throughout the sheet, forming a composite design. A chart of Cook's last voyage is shown in the background. Nos. 222/3 were also issued se-tenant, the horizontal pair forming a composite design taken from an aquatint by John Clevely.

97 Assembly Building

1979. First Norfolk Island Legislative Assembly.
224 **97** $1 multicoloured 50 50

98 Tasmania 1853 1d. Stamp and Sir Rowland Hill

1979. Death Centenary of Sir Rowland Hill.
225 **98** 20c. blue and brown . . . 20 10
226 – 30c. red and grey 25 15
227 – 55c. violet and indigo . . . 40 30
MS228 142 × 91 mm. No. 227 . . 55 1·25
DESIGNS: 30c. Great Britain 1841 1d. red; 55c. 1947 "Ball Bay" 1d. stamp.

99 I.Y.C. Emblem and Map of Pacific showing Norfolk Island as Pine Tree

1979. International Year of the Child.
229 **99** 80c. multicoloured 40 45

100 Emily Bay

1979. Christmas.
230 **100** 15c. multicoloured 15 15
231 – 20c. multicoloured 15 15
232 – 30c. multicoloured 15 15
MS233 152 × 83 mm. Nos. 230/2 1·00 1·75
DESIGNS: 20, 30c. Different scenes.

Nos. 230/2 were printed together, se-tenant, forming a composite design.

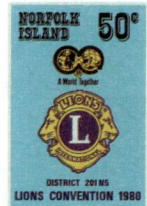

101 Lions International Emblem

1980. Lions Convention.
234 **101** 50c. multicoloured 35 30

102 Rotary International Emblem

1980. 75th Anniv of Rotary International.
235 **102** 50c. multicoloured 35 30

103 De Havilland Gipsy Moth Seaplane "Madame Elijah"

1980. Airplanes. Multicoloured.
236 1c. Hawker Siddeley H.S.748 15 20
237 2c. Type **103** 15 20
238 3c. Curtis P-40E Kittyhawk I 15 20
239 4c. Chance Vought F4U-1 Corsair 15 30
240 5c. Grumman TBF Avenger 15 30
241 15c. Douglas SBD-5 Dauntless 30 30
242 20c. Cessna 172D Skyhawk 30 30
243 25c. Lockheed 414 Hudson 30 35
244 30c. Lockheed PV-1 Ventura 40 2·00
245 40c. Avro Type 685 York . . 50 55
246 50c. Douglas DC-3 . . . . . 65 65
247 60c. Avro Type 691 Lancastrian 75 75
248 80c. Douglas DC-4 . . . . . 1·00 1·00
249 $1 Beech 200 Super King Air 1·00 1·00
250 $2 Fokker F.27 Friendship 2·00 3·00
251 $5 Lockheed C-130 Hercules 3·00 2·00

104 Queen Elizabeth the Queen Mother

1980. 80th Birthday of The Queen Mother.
252 **104** 22c. multicoloured 20 20
253 60c. multicoloured 35 40

105 Red-tailed Tropic Birds

1980. Christmas. Birds. Multicoloured.
254 15c. Type **105** 30 25
255 22c. White terns 30 25
256 35c. White-capped noddys . . 30 25
257 60c. White terns (different) 40 45

106 "Morayshire" and View of Norfolk Island

1981. 125th Anniv of Pitcairn Islanders' Migration to Norfolk Island. Multicoloured.
258 5c. Type **106** 15 15
259 35c. Islanders arriving ashore 40 30
260 60c. View of new settlement 60 45
MS261 183 × 127 mm. Nos. 258/60 1·25 1·75

107 Wedding Bouquet from Norfolk Island

1981. Royal Wedding. Multicoloured.
262 35c. Type **107** 15 15
263 55c. Prince Charles at horse trials 25 25
264 60c. Prince Charles and Lady Diana Spencer 25 35

108 Uniting Church in Australia

1981. Christmas. Churches. Multicoloured.
265 18c. Type **108** 10 10
266 24c. Seventh Day Adventist Church 15 15
267 30c. Church of the Sacred Heart 15 20
268 $1 St. Barnabas Chapel . . . 35 70

109 Pair of White-chested White-Eyes

1981. White-chested White-Eye ("Silvereye"). Mult.
269 35c. Type **109** 25 35
270 35c. Bird on nest 25 35
271 35c. Bird with egg 25 35
272 35c. Parents with chicks . . . 25 35
273 35c. Fledgelings 25 35

110 Aerial view of Philip Island

1982. Philip and Nepean Islands. Mult.
274 24c. Type **110** 20 20
275 24c. Close-up view of Philip Island landscape 20 20
276 24c. Gecko ("Phyllodactylus guentheri"), Philip Island 20 20
277 24c. Sooty tern, Philip Island 20 20
278 24c. Philip Island hibiscus ("hibiscus insularis") . . . 20 20
279 35c. Aerial view of Nepean Island 25 25
280 35c. Close-up view of Nepean Island landscape 25 25
281 35c. Gecko ("phyllodactylus guentheri"), Nepean Island 25 25
282 35c. Blue-faced boobies, Nepean Island 25 25
283 35c. "Carpobrotus glaucescens" (flower), Nepean Island 25 25

111 Sperm Whale

1982. Whales.
284 **111** 24c. multicoloured 50 35
285 – 55c. multicoloured 75 95
286 – 80c. black, mauve & stone 1·00 2·00
DESIGNS: 55c. Black right whale; 80c. Humpback whale.

112 "Diocet", Wrecked 20 April 1873

1982. Shipwrecks. Multicoloured.
287 24c. H.M.S. "Sirius", wrecked 19 March 1790 . . 50 50
288 27c. Type **112** 50 50
289 35c. "Friendship", wrecked 17 May 1835 . . . . . . 90 80
290 40c. "Mary Hamilton", wrecked 6 May 1873 . . . 90 1·25
291 55c. "Fairlie", wrecked 14 February 1840 . . . . 1·25 1·25
292 65c. "Warrigal", wrecked 18 March 1918 . . . . . 1·25 1·75

113 R.N.Z.A.F. Lockheed 414 Hudson dropping Christmas Supplies, 1942

1982. Christmas. 40th Anniv of First Supply-plane Landings on Norfolk Island (Christmas Day 1942). Multicoloured.
293 27c. Type **113** 75 35
294 40c. R.N.Z.A.F. Lockheed 414 Hudson landing Christmas supplies 1942 . . 95 65
295 75c. Christmas, 1942 . . . . 1·10 1·40

114 50th (Queen's Own) Regiment

115 "Panaeolus papilionaceus"

1982. Military Uniforms. Multicoloured.
296 27c. Type **114** 25 35
297 40c. 58th (Rutlandshire) Regiment 30 75
298 55c. 80th (Staffordshire Volunteers) Battalion Company 35 95
299 65c. 11th (North Devonshire) Regiment . . . . 40 1·25

1983. Fungi. Multicoloured.
300 27c. Type **115** 30 35
301 40c. "Coprinus domesticus" 40 50
302 55c. "Marasmius niveus" . . 45 70
303 65c. "Cymatoderma elegans var lamellatum" 50 85

116 Beechcraft 18

1983. Bicentenary of Manned Flight. Mult.
304 10c. Type **116** 15 15
305 27c. Fokker F.28 Fellowship 25 35
306 45c. French military Douglas C-54 . . . . 40 60
307 75c. Sikorsky S-61N helicopter 60 95
MS308 105 × 100 mm. Nos. 304/7 1·75 2·75

117 St. Matthew

119 Popwood

118 Cable Ship "Chantik"

1983. Christmas. 150th Birth Anniv of Sir Edward Burne-Jones.
309 5c. Type **117** 10 10
310 24c. St. Mark 20 30
311 30c. Jesus Christ 25 40
312 45c. St. Luke 35 55
313 85c. St. John . . . . 55 1·10
DESIGNS: showing stained glass windows from St. Barnabas Chapel, Norfolk Island.

1983. World Communications Year. ANZCAN Cable. Multicoloured.
314 30c. Type **118** 25 40
315 45c. "Chantik" during in-shore operations 30 55
316 75c. Cable ship "Mercury" 40 95
317 85c. Diagram of cable route 40 1·10

1984. Flowers. Multicoloured.
318 1c. Type **119** 30 70
319 2c. Strand morning glory . . 40 70
320 3c. Native phreatia 45 70
321 4c. Philip Island wisteria . . 45 70
322 5c. Norfolk Island palm . . . 70 70
323 10c. Evergreen 50 70
324 15c. Bastard oak 60 70
325 20c. Devil's guts 60 70
326 25c. White oak 60 80
327 30c. Ti . . . . 60 1·00
328 35c. Philip Island hibiscus . . 60 1·00
329 40c. Native wisteria . . . . . 60 1·25
330 50c. Native jasmine . . . . . 70 1·25
331 $1 Norfolk Island hibiscus . . 70 1·75
332 $3 Native oberonia . . . . . 1·10 4·00
333 $5 Norfolk Island pine . . . 1·50 4·50

120 Morwong

1984. Reef Fishes. Multicoloured.
334 30c. Type **120** 30 45
335 45c. Black-spotted goatfish 30 65
336 75c. Surgeonfish . . . . . . 40 1·10
337 85c. Three-striped butterflyfish . . . . 45 1·40

121 Owl with Eggs

123 Font, Kingston Methodist Church

122 1953 7½d. and 1974 Cook Bicent 10c. Stamps

1984. Boobook Owl. Multicoloured.
338 30c. Type **121** 75 90
339 30c. Fledgeling 75 90
340 30c. Young owl on stump . . 75 90
341 30c. Adult on branch 75 90
342 30c. Owl in flight 75 90

1984. "Ausipex" International Stamp Exhibition, Melbourne. Multicoloured.
343 30c. Type **122** 30 35
344 45c. John Buffett commemorative postal stationery envelope 50 75
345 75c. Design from Presentation Pack for 1982 Military Uniforms issue . . 90 1·75
MS346 151 × 93 mm. Nos. 343/5 4·00 4·50

1984. Christmas. Centenary of Methodist Church on Norfolk Island. Multicoloured.
347 5c. Type **123** 10 25
348 24c. Church service in Old Barracks, Kingston, late 1800s 25 40
349 30c. The Revd. & Mrs. A. H. Phelps and sailing ship . . 35 45
350 45c. The Revd. A. H. Phelps and First Congregational Church, Chester, U.S.A. 40 65
351 85c. Interior of Kingston Methodist Church . . . . 80 1·40

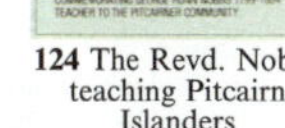
124 The Revd. Nobbs teaching Pitcairn Islanders

126 The Queen Mother (from photo by Norman Parkinson)

125 "Fanny Fisher"

1984. Death Centenary of Revd. George Hunn Nobbs (leader of Pitcairn community). Multicoloured.
352 30c. Type **124** 25 45
353 45c. The Revd. Nobbs with sick islander 30 65
354 75c. Baptising baby . . . . . 45 1·10
355 85c. Presented to Queen Victoria, 1852 . . . . . . 55 1·40

1985. 19th-Century Whaling Ships (1st series). Multicoloured.
356 5c. Type **125** 30 50
357 33c. "Costa Rica Packet" . . 60 55
358 50c. "Splendid" . . . . . . 1·00 1·50
359 90c. "Onward" . . . . . . 1·25 2·25
See also Nos. 360/3.

1985. 19th-Century Whaling Ships (2nd series). As T **125**. Multicoloured.
360 15c. "Waterwitch" 50 70
361 20c. "Canton" 55 80
362 60c. "Aladdin" . . . . 1·10 1·75
363 80c. "California" . . . . . . 1·10 2·25

1985. Life and Times of Queen Elizabeth the Queen Mother. Multicoloured.
364 5c. The Queen Mother (from photo by Dorothy Wilding) 10 10
365 33c. With Princess Anne at Trooping the Colour . . . 25 25
366 50c. Type **126** 40 55
367 90c. With Prince Henry at his christening (from photo by Lord Snowdon) . . . . . 60 1·00
MS368 91 × 73 mm. $1 With Princess Anne at Ascot Races . . . . . 1·75 1·75

127 "Swimming"

1985. International Youth Year. Children's Paintings. Multicoloured.
369 33c. Type **127** 40 40
370 50c. "A Walk in the Country" 70 85

128 Prize-winning Cow and Owner

1985. 125th Anniv of Royal Norfolk Island Agricultural and Horticultural Show. Mult.
371 80c. Type **128** 75 80
372 90c. Show exhibits 85 90
MS373 132 × 85 mm. Nos. 371/2 1·75 2·50

129 Shepherds with Flock

131 "Giotto" Spacecraft

130 Long-spined Sea Urchin

1985. Christmas. Multicoloured.
374 27c. Type **129** 40 30
375 33c. Mary and Joseph with donkey 50 40
376 50c. The Three Wise Men . . 80 65
377 90c. The Nativity . . . . . 1·25 1·25

1986. Marine Life. Multicoloured.
378 5c. Type **130** 10 10
379 33c. Blue starfish 30 35

380 55c. Southern eagle ray . . . 50 85
381 75c. Snowflake moray . . . 70 1·25
MS382 100 × 95 mm. Nos. 378/81 3·00 4·00

1986. Appearance of Halley's Comet. Mult.
383 $1 Type **131** . . . . 75 1·50
384 $1 Halley's Comet . . . . . 75 1·50
Nos. 383/4 were printed together, se-tenant, forming a composite design.

132 Isaac Robinson (U.S. Consul 1887–1908)
133 Princess Elizabeth and Dog

1986. "Ameripex '86" International Stamp Exhibition, Chicago. Multicoloured.
385 33c. Type **132** 30 35
386 50c. Ford "Model T" (first vehicle on island) (horiz) 50 50
387 80c. Statue of Liberty 55 80
MS388 125 × 100 mm. Nos. 385/7 1·25 2·25
No. 387 also commemorates the Centenary of the Statue of Liberty.

1986. 60th Birthday of Queen Elizabeth II. Multicoloured.
389 5c. Type **133** 10 10
390 33c. Queen Elizabeth II . . . 40 35
391 80c. Opening Norfolk Island Golf Club . . . . 1·60 1·40
392 90c. With Duke of Edinburgh in carriage . . . . 1·25 1·60

134 Stylized Dove and Norfolk Island
135 British Convicts, 1787

1986. Christmas.
393 **134** 30c. multicoloured 25 30
394 40c. multicoloured 30 45
395 $1 multicoloured . . . . 70 1·50

1986. Bicentenary (1988) of Norfolk Island Settlement (1st issue). Governor Phillip's Commission. Multicoloured.
396 36c. Type **135** 80 35
397 55c. Judge passing sentence of transportation . . . . . 1·50 85
398 90c. Governor Phillip meeting Home Secretary (inscr "Home Society") . . . . . 2·50 3·50
399 90c. As No. 398, but correctly inscr "Home Secretary" . . . . 2·25 3·25
400 $1 Captain Arthur Phillip . . 2·50 2·50
See also Nos. 401/4, 421/4, 433/5, 436/7 and 438/43.

136 Stone Tools

1986. Bicentenary (1988) of Norfolk Island Settlement (2nd issue). Pre-European Occupation. Multicoloured.
401 36c. Type **136** 50 85
402 36c. Bananas and taro . . . 50 85
403 36c. Polynesian outrigger canoe 50 85
404 36c. Maori chief 50 85

137 Philip Island from Point Ross
138 Male Red-fronted Parakeet

1987. Norfolk Island Scenes. Multicoloured.
405 1c. Cockpit Creek Bridge . . 50 1·50
406 2c. Cemetery Bay Beach . . 50 1·50
407 3c. Island guesthouse . . . . 50 1·50
408 5c. Type **137** . . . . 30 1·00
409 15c. Cattle in pasture . . . . 80 2·00
410 30c. Rock fishing . . . . . . 30 1·25
411 37c. Old Pitcairner-style house . . . . 1·40 2·00
412 40c. Shopping centre . . . . 35 1·25
413 50c. Emily Bay . . . . . . 45 1·25
414 60c. Bloody Bridge . . . . . 2·00 3·00
415 80c. Pitcairner-style shop . . 1·75 2·75
416 90c. Government House . . . 1·25 2·25
417 $1 Melanesian Memorial Chapel . . . . 1·00 1·75
418 $2 Convict Settlement, Kingston . . . . 1·25 3·50
419 $3 Ball Bay . . . . 2·00 5·00
420 $5 Northern cliffs . . . . . 2·50 7·00

1987. Bicentenary of Norfolk Island Settlement (1988) (3rd issue). The First Fleet. As T **135**. Multicoloured.
421 5c. Loading supplies, Deptford 50 75
422 55c. Fleet leaving Spithead 1·75 2·25
423 55c. H.M.S. "Sirius" leaving Spithead . . . . 1·75 2·25
424 $1 Female convicts below decks . . . . 2·25 3·00
Nos. 422/3 were printed together, se-tenant, forming a composite design.

1987. Red-fronted Parakeet ("Green Parrot"). Multicoloured.
425 5c. Type **138** . . . . 2·00 1·75
426 15c. Adult with fledgeling and egg . . . . 2·50 2·25
427 36c. Young parakeets . . . . 3·50 3·25
428 55c. Female parakeet . . . . 4·50 3·75

139 Christmas Tree and Restored Garrison Barracks
140 Airliner, Container Ship and Sydney Harbour Bridge

1987. Christmas. Multicoloured.
429 30c. Type **139** 30 30
430 42c. Children opening presents 45 55
431 58c. Father Christmas with children . . . . 60 1·00
432 63c. Children's party . . . . 70 1·25

1987. Bicentenary of Norfolk Island Settlement (1988) (4th issue). Visit of La Perouse (navigator). As T **135**. Multicoloured.
433 37c. La Perouse with King Louis XVI 95 55
434 90c. "L'Astrolabe" and "La Boussole" off Norfolk Island . . . . 2·75 3·00
435 $1 "L'Astrolabe" wrecked in Solomon Islands . . . . . 2·75 3·00

1988. Bicentenary of Norfolk Island Settlement (5th issue). Arrival of First Fleet at Sydney. As T **135**. Multicoloured.
436 37c. Ship's cutter approaching Port Jackson 1·50 75
437 $1 Landing at Sydney Cove 3·00 3·50

1988. Bicentenary of Norfolk Island Settlement (6th issue). Foundation of First Settlement. As T **135**. Multicoloured.
438 5c. Lt. Philip Gidley King . . 20 50
439 37c. Raising the flag, March 1788 . . . . 85 75
440 55c. King exploring . . . . 1·75 1·50
441 70c. Landing at Sydney Bay, Norfolk Island . . . . . 2·00 2·50
442 90c. H.M.S. "Supply" (brig) 2·25 2·75
443 $1 Sydney Bay settlement, 1788 . . . . 2·25 2·75

1988. "Sydpex '88" National Stamp Exhibition, Sydney. Multicoloured.
444 37c. Type **140** . . . . 95 1·25
445 37c. Exhibition label under magnifying glass (horiz) . . 95 1·25
446 37c. Telephone and dish aerial . . . . 95 1·25
MS447 118 × 84 mm. Nos. 444/6 4·50 5·00

141 Flowers and Decorations
142 Pier Store and Boat Shed

1988. Christmas. Multicoloured.
448 30c. Type **141** 50 40
449 42c. Flowers 70 70
450 58c. Fishes and beach 85 95
451 63c. Norfolk Island . . . . . 95 1·25

1988. Restored Buildings from the Convict Era. Multicoloured.
452 39c. Type **142** 45 40
453 55c. Royal Engineers Building 60 60
454 90c. Old Military Barracks 1·00 1·60
455 $1 Commissariat Store and New Military Barracks . . 1·10 1·60

143 "Lamprima aenea"

1989. Endemic Insects. Multicoloured.
456 39c. Type **143** 65 40
457 55c. "Insulascirtus nythos" 90 75
458 90c. "Caedicia araucariae" 1·40 2·25
459 $1 "Thrincophora aridela" 1·60 2·25

144 H.M.S. "Bounty" off Tasmania

1989. Bicentenary of the Mutiny on the "Bounty". Multicoloured.
460 5c. Type **144** 60 60
461 39c. Mutineers and Polynesian women, Pitcairn Island . . . . 1·75 1·25
462 55c. Lake Windermere, Cumbria (Christian's home county) . . . . 2·25 2·25
463 $1.10 "Mutineers casting Bligh adrift" (Robert Dodd) . . . . 3·50 4·50
MS464 110 × 85 mm. 39c. No. 461; 90c. Isle of Man 1989 Mutiny 35p., No. 414; $1 Pitcairn Islands 1989 Settlement Bicent 90c., No. 345 . . . . 6·00 7·00

145 Norfolk Island Flag
146 Red Cross

1989. 10th Anniv of Internal Self-government. Multicoloured.
465 41c. Type **145** 90 55
466 55c. Old ballot box 95 65
467 $1 Norfolk Island Act, 1979 1·75 2·00
468 $1.10 Island crest . . . . . 1·75 2·75

1989. 75th Anniv of Red Cross on Norfolk Island.
469 **146** $1 red and blue . . . . . 3·00 3·25

147 "Gethsemane"

1989. Christmas. Designs showing opening lines of hymns and local scenes. Multicoloured.
470 36c. Type **147** 90 40
471 60c. "In the Sweet Bye and Bye" . . . . 1·75 2·00
472 75c. "Let the Lower Lights be Burning" . . . . 2·25 3·00
473 80c. "The Beautiful Stream" 2·25 3·00

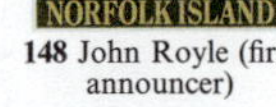

148 John Royle (first announcer)
149 H.M.S. "Bounty" on fire, Pitcairn Island, 1790

1989. 50th Anniv of Radio Australia. Designs each showing Kingston buildings. Mult.
474 41c. Type **148** 95 65
475 65c. Radio waves linking Australia and Norfolk Island . . . . 1·75 2·50
476 $1.10 Anniversary kookaburra logo . . . . . 2·75 4·25

1990. History of the Norfolk Islanders (1st series). Settlement on Pitcairn Island. Mult.
477 70c. Type **149** . . . . 2·50 3·00
478 $1.10 Arms of Norfolk Island 2·75 3·50
See also Nos. 503/4 and 516/17.

150 H.M.S. "Sirius" striking Reef

1990. Bicentenary of Wreck of H.M.S. "Sirius". Multicoloured.
479 41c. Type **150** . . . . 1·75 2·00
480 41c. H.M.S. "Sirius" failing to clear bay . . . . 1·75 2·00
481 65c. Divers at work on wreck 2·50 3·00
482 $1 Recovered artifacts and chart of site . . . . 2·75 3·25
Nos. 479/80 were printed together, se-tenant, forming a composite design.

151 Unloading Lighter, Kingston
152 "Ile de Lumiere" (freighter)

1990. Ships.
483 **151** 5c. brown 20 50
484 10c. brown 20 50
485 – 45c. multicoloured . . . . 1·00 60
486 – 50c. multicoloured . . . . 1·00 1·00
487 – 65c. multicoloured . . . . 1·00 1·25
488 **152** 70c. multicoloured . . . . 1·00 1·25
489 – 75c. multicoloured . . . . 2·00 2·00
490 – 80c. multicoloured . . . . 2·00 2·25
491 – 90c. multicoloured . . . . 2·00 2·25
492 – $1 multicoloured . . . . 2·00 2·00
493 – $2 multicoloured . . . . 2·25 3·50
494 – $5 multicoloured . . . . 5·00 7·00
DESIGNS—As T **152**: 45c. "La Dunkerquoise" (French patrol vessel); 50c. "Dmitri Mendeleev" (Russian research vessel); 65c. "Pacific Rover" (tanker); 75c. "Norfolk Trader" (freighter); 80c. "Roseville" (transport); 90c. "Kalia" (container ship); $1 "Bounty" (replica); $2 H.M.A.S. "Success" (supply ship); $5 H.M.A.S. "Whyalla" (patrol vessel).

153 Santa on House Roof
154 William Charles Wentworth

1990. Christmas. Multicoloured.
499 38c. Type **153** 75 45
500 43c. Santa at Kingston Post Office 80 50
501 65c. Santa over Sydney Bay, Kingston (horiz) . . . . . 1·75 2·25
502 85c. Santa on Officers' Quarters (horiz) . . . . . 2·00 2·75

1990. History of the Norfolk Islanders (2nd series). The First Generation.
503 **154** 70c. brown and cinnamon 1·25 1·50
504 – $1.20 brown and cinnamon . . . . 2·00 2·50
DESIGN: $1.20, Thursday October Christian.

155 Adult Robin and Chicks in Nest
156 Map of Norfolk Island

1990. "Birdpex '90" Stamp Exhibition, Christchurch, New Zealand. Scarlet Robin. Multicoloured.
505 65c. Type **155** . . . . 1·25 1·50
506 $1 Hen on branch . . . . . 1·75 2·00
507 $1.20 Cock on branch . . . 1·75 2·25
MS508 70 × 90 mm. $1 Hen; $1 Cock and hen . . . . 4·50 4·75
Each inscribed "Norfolk Island Robin".

1991. Ham Radio Network. Multicoloured.
509 43c. Type **156** . . . . 1·25 70
510 $1 Globe showing Norfolk Island . . . . 2·75 3·00
511 $1.20 Map of south-west Pacific . . . . 2·75 4·00

157 Display in "Sirius" Museum
158 H.M.S. "Pandora" wrecked on Great Barrier Reef (1791)

1991. Norfolk Island Museums. Mult.
512 43c. Type **157** 90 65
513 70c. 19th-century sitting room, House Museum (horiz) . . . . 1·75 2·50
514 $1 Carronade, "Sirius" Museum (horiz) . . . . . 2·50 3·25
515 $1.20 Reconstructed jug and beaker, Archaeological Museum . . . . 2·50 3·75

1991. History of the Norfolk Islanders (3rd series). Search for the "Bounty". Multicoloured.
516 $1 Type **158** . . . . 2·75 2·50
517 $1.20 H.M.S. "Pandora" leaving bay . . . . 2·75 3·00

159 Hibiscus and Island Scene

1991. Christmas.
518 **159** 38c. multicoloured 90 45
519 43c. multicoloured . . . . 1·00 55
520 65c. multicoloured . . . . 1·50 2·00
521 85c. multicoloured . . . . 1·75 2·50

160 Tank and Soldier in Jungle
161 Coat of Arms

1991. 50th Anniv of Outbreak of Pacific War. Multicoloured.
522 43c. Type **160** . . . . 1·25 65
523 70c. Boeing B-17 Flying Fortress on jungle airstrip 2·25 2·75
524 $1 Warships . . . . 2·75 3·50

1992. 500th Anniv of Discovery of America by Columbus. Multicoloured.
525 45c. Type **161** 85 55
526 $1.05 "Santa Maria" . . . . 2·00 2·75
527 $1.20 Columbus and globe 2·50 3·25

162 Deployment Map
163 Norfolk Pines above Ball Bay

1992. 50th Anniv of Battle of the Coral Sea. Multicoloured.
528 45c. Type **162** . . . . 1·25 60
529 70c. H.M.A.S. "Australia" (cruiser) . . . . 2·00 2·50
530 $1.05 U.S.S. "Yorktown" (aircraft carrier) . . . . . 2·75 3·50

1992. 50th Anniv of Battle of Midway. As T **162**. Multicoloured.
531 45c. Battle area . . . . . . 1·25 60
532 70c. Consolidated PBY-5 Catalina flying boat over task force . . . . 2·00 2·50
533 $1.05 Douglas SBD Dauntless dive bomber and "Akagi" (Japanese aircraft carrier) burning . . . . . 2·75 3·50

1992. 50th Anniv of Battle of Guadalcanal. As T **162**. Multicoloured.
534 45c. American troops landing (horiz) . . . . 1·25 60
535 70c. Machine-gun crew (horiz) . . . . 2·00 2·50
536 $1.05 Map of Pacific with Japanese and American flags (horiz) . . . . 2·75 3·50

1992. Christmas. Multicoloured.
537 40c. Type **163** 70 40
538 45c. Headstone Creek 75 45
539 75c. South side of Ball Bay 1·50 2·25
540 $1.20 Rocky Point Reserve 2·00 3·00

164 Boat Shed and Flaghouses, Kingston

1993. Tourism. Historic Kingston. Mult.
541 45c. Type **164** . . . . 80 1·00
542 45c. Old Military Barracks 80 1·00
543 45c. All Saints Church . . . 80 1·00
544 45c. Officers' Quarters . . . 80 1·00
545 45c. Quality Row . . . . . 80 1·00
Nos. 541/5 were printed together, se-tenant, forming a composite design.

165 Fire Engine

1993. Emergency Services. Multicoloured.
546 45c. Type **165** . . . . 1·00 60
547 70c. Cliff rescue squad . . . 1·10 1·75
548 75c. Ambulance . . . . 1·40 1·90
549 $1.20 Police car . . . . . . 2·50 3·00

166 Blue Sea Lizard ("Glaucus atlanticus")

1993. Nudibranchs. Multicoloured.
550 45c. Type **166** 80 55
551 45c. Ocellate nudibranch ("Phyllidia ocellata") . . . 80 55
552 75c. "Bornella sp." . . . . . 1·50 1·75
553 85c. "Glossodoris rubroannolata" . . . . . 1·75 2·25
554 95c. "Halgerda willeyi" . . . 2·00 2·50
555 $1.05 "Ceratosoma amoena" 2·00 3·00

167 Christmas Wreath
168 Maori Stone Clubs

1993. Christmas.
556 **167** 40c. multicoloured 60 50
557 45c. multicoloured 60 50
558 75c. multicoloured . . . . 1·00 1·50
559 $1.20 multicoloured . . . 1·90 2·75

1993. Bicentenary of Contact with New Zealand. Multicoloured.
560 70c. Type **168** . . . . 1·25 1·50
561 $1.20 First Maori map of New Zealand, 1793 . . . . 2·00 2·75

169 Alvaro de Saavedra, Route Map and "Florida"

1994. Pacific Explorers. Multicoloured.
562 5c. Vasco Nunez de Balboa, map and "Barbara" . . . 55 65
563 10c. Ferdinand Magellan, map and "Vitoria" 70 65
564 20c. Juan Sebastian del Cano, map and "Vitoria" . . . . 1·00 85
565 50c. Type **169** . . . . 1·00 1·00
566 70c. Ruy Lopez de Villalobos, map and "San Juan" . . . . 1·25 1·25
567 75c. Miguel Lopez de Legaspi, map and "San Lesmes" . . . . 1·25 1·25
568 80c. Sir Francis Drake, map and "Golden Hind" . . . 1·25 1·25
569 85c. Alvaro de Mendana, map and "Santiago" . . . 1·25 1·25
570 90c. Pedro Fernandes de Quiros, map and "San Pedro y Pablo" . . . . . 1·25 1·25
571 $1 Luis Baez de Torres, map and "San Pedrico" . . . . 1·40 1·40
572 $2 Abel Tasman, map and "Heemskerk" . . . . . . 2·00 2·50
573 $5 William Dampier, map and "Cygnet" . . . . . . 4·25 5·50
MS574 100 × 80 mm. $1.20 "Golden Hind" (Drake) (32 × 52 mm) 3·00 3·00

170 Sooty Tern
171 House and Star

1994. Sea Birds. Multicoloured.
575 45c. Type **170** . . . . 95 1·10
576 45c. Red-tailed tropic bird . . 95 1·10
577 45c. Australian gannet . . . 95 1·10
578 45c. Wedge-tailed shearwater 95 1·10
579 45c. Masked booby . . . . . 95 1·10
Nos. 575/9 were printed together, se-tenant, forming a composite design.

1994. Christmas. Multicoloured. Self-adhesive.
580 45c. Type **171** 80 55
581 75c. Figures from stained-glass windows . . . . . . 1·50 2·00
582 $1.20 Rainbow and "The Church of God" (missionary sailing ship) . . 2·50 3·00

172 Chevrolet, 1926

1995. Vintage Motor Vehicles. Multicoloured.
583 45c. Type **172** 75 55
584 75c. Ford Model "A", 1928 1·25 1·75
585 $1.05 Ford Model "A A/C", 1929 . . . . 1·60 2·00
586 $1.20 Ford Model "A", 1930 1·75 2·25

173 Tail Flukes of Humpback Whale

1995. Humpback Whale Conservation. Multicoloured.
587 45c. Type **173** . . . . 1·00 55
588 75c. Mother and calf . . . . 1·50 2·00
589 $1.05 Whale breaching (vert) 1·75 2·50
MS590 107 × 84 mm. $1.20 Humpback whale (29 × 49 mm) 2·50 3·00

174 Dot-and-Dash Butterflyfish

1995. Butterflyfishes. Multicoloured.
591 5c. Type **174** 30 75
592 45c. Blue-spotted butterflyfish 85 50
593 $1.20 Three-belted butterflyfish . . . . 2·25 2·75
594 $1.50 Three-finned butterflyfish . . . . 2·50 3·25

1995. "JAKARTA '95" Stamp Exhibition, Indonesia. No. **MS**590 optd "Selamat Hari Merdeka" and emblem on sheet margin in gold.
MS595 107 × 84 mm. $1.20 Humpback whale . . . . . . 1·75 2·50

175 International 4 × 4 Refueller, 1942

1995. Second World War Vehicles. Multicoloured.
596 5c. Type **175** 30 75
597 45c. Ford Sedan, 1942 . . . 75 45
598 $1.20 Ford 3 ton tipper, 1942 2·00 2·50
599 $2 D8 caterpillar with scraper 3·00 4·00

1995. Flower designs as 1960 issues, but with face values in decimal currency.
600 5c. pink and green (as No. 25) 20 30
601 5c. red (as No. 28) 20 30

176 Servicing Fighter
177 Peace Dove and Anniversary Emblem

1995. 50th Anniv of End of Second World War in the Pacific. Multicoloured.
602 5c. Type **176** 40 50
603 45c. Sgt. Tom Derrick, VC (vert) 70 45
604 75c. Gen. Douglas MacArthur (vert) . . . . 1·25 1·50
605 $1.05 Girls celebrating victory 1·75 2·00
606 $10 Pacific War medals (50 × 30 mm) . . . . . . 16·00 19·00
The $10 also includes the "Singapore '95" International stamp exhibition logo.

1995. Christmas. 50th Anniv of United Nations. Each including U.N. anniversary emblem.
607 **177** 45c. gold and blue 75 45
608 – 75c. gold and violet . . . 1·10 1·25
609 – $1.05 gold and red . . . 1·60 2·00
610 – $1.20 gold and green . . 1·75 2·25
DESIGNS: 75c. Star of Bethlehem; $1.05, Symbolic candles on cake; $1.20, Olive branch.

178 Skink on Bank

1996. Endangered Species. Skinks and Geckos. Multicoloured.
611 5c. Type **178** 60 85
612 5c. Gecko on branch 60 85
613 45c. Skink facing right . . . 80 85
614 45c. Gecko on flower 80 85

179 Sopwith Pup Biplane and Emblem
181 "Naticarlus oncus"

1996. 75th Anniv of Royal Australian Air Force. Aircraft. Multicoloured.
615 45c. Type **179** 70 70
616 45c. Wirraway fighter 70 70
617 75c. F-111C jet fighter . . . 1·25 1·50
618 85c. F/A-18 Hornet jet fighter 1·40 1·60

180 Rat

1996. Chinese New Year ("Year of the Rat"). Sheet 100 × 75 mm.
MS619 **180** $1 black, red and brown 1·50 2·25

1996. Shells. Multicoloured.
620 45c. Type **181** 70 85
621 45c. "Janthina janthina" . . 70 85
622 45c. "Cypraea capitserpentis" 70 85
623 45c. "Argonauta nodosa" . . 70 85

182 Shopping

183 The Nativity

1996. Tourism. Multicoloured.
624 45c. Type **182** 50 50
625 75c. Celebrating Bounty Day 1·00 1·00
626 $2.50 Horse riding . . . . . 3·75 4·50
627 $3.70 Unloading lighter . . . 4·50 5·75

1996. Christmas. Multicoloured.
628 45c. Type **183** 50 50
629 45c. Star and boat sheds . . 50 50
630 75c. Star, bungalow and ox 90 1·50
631 85c. Star, fruit, flowers and ox . . . . 1·10 1·75

184 Coat of Arms

185 Calf

1997.
632 **184** 5c. blue and yellow . . . 20 30
633 – 5c. brown 20 30
DESIGN: No. 633, Great Seal of Norfolk Island.

1997. Beef Cattle. Sheet 67 × 67 mm.
MS634 **185** $1.20 multicoloured 2·00 2·50

1997. "HONG KONG '97" International Stamp Exhibition. As No. **MS**634, but with exhibition emblem on sheet margin.
MS635 67 × 67 mm. **185** $1.20 multicoloured . . . . 2·50 3·25

186 "Cepora perimale"

1997. Butterflies. Multicoloured.
636 75c. Type **186** . . . . 1·00 1·00
637 90c. "Danaus chrysippus" . . 1·25 1·60
638 $1 "Danaus hamata" . . . . 1·40 1·60
639 $1.20 "Danaus plexippus" . . 1·50 2·25

187 Dusky Dolphins

1997. Dolphins. Multicoloured.
640 45c. Type **187** 75 60
641 75c. Common dolphin and calf . . . . 1·25 1·40
MS642 106 × 80 mm. $1.05 Dolphin 2·00 2·50

1997. "Pacific '97" International Stamp Exhibition, San Francisco. As No. **MS**642, but with exhibition emblem on sheet margin.
MS643 106 × 80 mm. $1.05 Dolphin 3·00 3·50

188 Ball Bay, Norfolk Island

1997. 50th Anniv of Norfolk Island Stamps. Multicoloured.
644 $1 Type **188** . . . . 1·25 1·75
645 $1.50 1947 2d. stamp . . . . 1·25 1·75
646 $8 Ball Bay and 1947 2s. bistre stamp (90 × 45 mm) 7·50 11·00

188a Queen Elizabeth II

1997. Golden Wedding of Queen Elizabeth and Prince Philip. Multicoloured.
647 20c. Type **188a** 50 60
648 25c. Prince Philip in carriage-driving trials 50 60
649 25c. Prince Philip 55 65
650 50c. Queen in phaeton at Trooping the Colour . . . 70 80
MS651 110 × 70 mm. $1.50 Queen Elizabeth and Prince Philip in landau (horiz) . . . . 2·25 2·75
Nos. 647/8 and 649/50 were each printed together, se-tenant, with the backgrounds forming composite designs.

189 Royal Yacht "Britannia" leaving Hong Kong

1997. Return of Hong Kong to China. Sheet 126 × 91 mm.
MS652 **189** 45c. multicoloured 1·00 1·50
No. **MS**652 is inscribed "Brittania" in error.

190 Christmas Tree

191 Oriental Pearl T.V. Tower, Shanghai

1997. Annual Festivals. Multicoloured.
653 45c. Type **190** 60 45
654 75c. Fireworks (New Year's Eve) . . . . 90 1·25
655 $1.20 Rose (Valentine's Day) 1·40 1·75

1997. "Shanghai '97" International Stamp and Coin Exhibition, shanghai. Sheet 103 × 138 mm.
MS656 **191** 45c. multicoloured 1·00 1·50

192 Tiger Mask

1998. Chinese New Year ("Year of the Tiger"). Sheet 75 × 95 mm.
MS657 **192** 45c. multicoloured 1·00 1·50

193 "Pepper"

194 Entrance to Pentagonal Gaol

1998. Cats. Multicoloured.
658 45c. Type **193** 65 65
659 45c. "Tabitha" at window . . 65 65
660 75c. "Midnight" . . . . . . 85 1·00
661 $1.20 "Rainbow" with flower pot . . . . 1·25 1·50

1998.
662 **194** 5c. black and blue 20 30
663 – 5c. black and green . . . 20 30
DESIGN: No. 663, Ruined First Settlement cottage.

194a Princess Diana with Bouquet, 1991

1998. Diana, Princess of Wales Commemoration. Multicolured.
664 45c. Type **194a** 50 50
MS665 145 × 70 mm. 45c. Wearing blue and white dress, 1989; 45c. Wearing pearl earrings, 1990; 45c. No. 664; 45c. Wearing striped dress (sold at $1.80+45c. charity premium) . . . . 1·60 2·00

195 Tweed Trousers

196 Hammer Throwing

1998. Reef Fishes. Multicoloured.
666 10c. Type **195** 30 40
667 20c. Conspicuous angelfish 55 50
668 30c. Moon wrasse 65 50
669 45c. Wide-striped clownfish 75 50
670 50c. Racoon butterflyfish . . 80 80
671 70c. Artooti (juvenile) . . . . 1·00 1·00
672 75c. Splendid hawkfish . . . 1·00 1·00
673 85c. Scorpion fish . . . . . 1·25 1·25
674 90c. Orange fairy basslet . . 1·25 1·25
675 $1 Sweetlips . . . . 1·25 1·25
676 $3 Moorish idol . . . . . . 2·75 3·50
677 $4 Gold-ribbon soapfish . . 3·25 4·25
MS678 110 × 85 mm. $1.20 Shark (29 × 39 mm) . . . . 1·50 1·75
Nos. 672 and 675 are incorrectly inscribed "Splendid Hawkefish" and "Sweetlip".

1998. 16th Commonwealth Games, Kuala Lumpur.
679 **196** 75c. red and black . . . . 85 1·00
680 – 95c. violet and black . . . 1·00 1·25
681 – $1.05 mauve and black . . 1·10 1·40
MS682 80 × 100 mm. 85c. green and black . . . . 1·00 1·50
DESIGNS—HORIZ: 95c. Trap shooting. VERT: 85c. Flag bearer; $1.05, Lawn bowls.

197 "Norfolk" (sloop)

1998. Bicentenary of the Circumnavigation of Tasmania by George Bass and Matthew Flinders.
683 **197** 45c. multicoloured . . . . 1·50 1·00
MS684 101 × 69 mm. **197** $1.20 multicoloured . . . . 2·50 2·75

198 Blue whale

1998. Whales of the Southern Oceans (joint issue with Namibia and South Africa). Sheet 103 × 70 mm.
MS685 **198** $1.50 multicoloured 1·90 2·25

199 "Peace on Earth"

1998. Christmas. Multicoloured.
686 45c. Type **199** 55 50
687 75c. "Joy to the World" . . 85 80
688 $1.05 "A Season of Love" . . 1·25 1·75
689 $1.20 "Light of the World" 1·25 1·75

200 Short S.23 Sandringham (flying boat)

201 Soft Toy Rabbit

1999. Aircraft. Each red and green.
690 5c. Type **200** 25 40
691 5c. DC-4 "Norfolk Trader" 25 40

1999. Chinese New Year ("Year of the Rabbit"). Sheet 80 × 100 mm.
MS692 **201** 95c. multicoloured 1·00 1·50

202 Hull of "Resolution" under Construction

1999. "Australia '99" International Stamp Exhibition, Melbourne. Schooner "Resolution". Multicoloured.
693 45c. Type **202** . . . . 1·50 1·50
694 45c. After being launched . . 1·50 1·50
695 45c. In Emily Bay . . . . . 1·50 1·50
696 45c. Off Cascade . . . . . . 1·50 1·50
697 45c. Alongside at Auckland 1·50 1·50

203 Pacific Black Duck

204 Solander's Petrel in Flight

1999. "iBRA '99" International Stamp Exhibition, Nuremburg. Sheet 80 × 100 mm.
MS698 **203** $2.50 multicoloured 3·50 4·25

1999. Endangered Species. Solander's Petrel ("Providence Petrel"). Multicoloured.
699 75c. Type **204** . . . . 1·50 1·00
700 $1.05 Head of Solander's petrel (horiz) . . . . . . 1·60 1·40

701 $1.20 Adult and fledgling (horiz) . . . . 1·60 1·60
MS702 130 × 90 mm. $4.50 Solander's petrel in flight (35 × 51 mm) . . . . 6·50 6·50
See also No. MS738.

205 "Cecile Brunner" Rose

206 Pottery

1999. Roses. Multicoloured.
703 45c. Type **205** 60 40
704 75c. Green rose 85 90
705 $1.05 "David Buffett" rose 1·25 1·75
MS706 60 × 81 mm. $1.20 "A Country Woman" Rose . . . 1·40 1·75
No. **MS**706 also commemorates the 50th anniversary of the Country Women's Association on Norfolk Island.

1999. "China '99" International Stamp Exhibition, Beijing. No. **MS**692 with "China '99" logo optd on the margin in red.
MS707 80 × 100 mm. 95c. Type **201** 1·00 1·25

1999. Handicrafts of Norfolk Island. Multicoloured.
708 45c. Type **206** 50 50
709 45c. Woodcarving 50 50
710 75c. Quilting 75 90
711 $1.05 Basket-weaving . . . . 1·00 1·50

206a Inspecting Bomb Damage, Buckingham Palace, 1940

1999. "Queen Elizabeth the Queen Mother's Century". Multicoloured (except $1.20).
712 45c. Type **206a** 70 70
713 45c. At Abergeldy Castle sale of work, 1955 . . . . . . 70 70
714 75c. Queen Mother, Queen Elizabeth and Prince William, 1994 . . . . . . 95 95
715 $1.20 Inspecting the King's Regiment (black) . . . . . 1·50 1·75
MS716 145 × 70 mm. $3 Queen Elizabeth, 1937, and Amy Johnson's flight to Australia, 1930 3·25 3·50

207 Bishop George Augustus Selwyn

1999. Christmas. 150th Anniv of Melanesian Mission. Multicoloured (except 75c.).
717 45c. Type **207** 80 90
718 45c. Bishop John Coleridge Patteson 80 90
719 75c. "150 YEARS MELANESIAN MISSION" (black) . . . . 90 1·00
720 $1.05 Stained-glass windows 1·00 1·40
721 $1.20 "Southern Cross" (missionary ship) and religious symbols . . . . . 1·00 1·40
Nos. 717/21 were printed together, se-tenant, with the backgrounds forming a composite design.

208 Basket of Food (Thanksgiving)

2000. Festivals.
722 **208** 5c. black and blue 20 30
723 – 5c. black and blue 20 30
DESIGN: No. 723, Musician playing guitar (Country Music Festival).

209 Dragon

2000. Chinese New Year ("Year of the Dragon"). Sheet 106 × 86 mm.
MS724 **209** $2 multicoloured . . 1·75 2·00

210 Domestic Goose

2000. Ducks and Geese. Multicoloured.
725 45c. Type **210** 55 50
726 75c. Pacific black duck . . . 1·00 1·00
727 $1.05 Mallard drake . . . . 1·25 1·50
728 $1.20 Aylesbury duck . . . . 1·25 1·50

211 Honour Roll for First World War

2000. Anzac Day. Multicoloured.
729 45c. Type **211** 60 50
730 75c. Honour rolls for Second World War and Korea . . 80 1·10

212 Young Boy, Shipwright and Whaleboat

2000. "Whaler Project 2000". Two sheets, each 96 × 76 mm, containing T **212**. Multicoloured.
MS731 **212** $4 multicoloured . . 4·50 5·00
MS732 $4 mult ("THE STAMP SHOW 2000" and Crown Agents logos added in gold) Imperf . . 4·50 5·00

213 Captain William Bligh and Bounty

2000. "Bounty" Day. Multicoloured.
733 45c. Type **213** 70 55
734 75c. Fletcher Christian and Tahiti . . . . 90 1·10

214 Turtle

215 Malcolm Champion (Olympic Gold Medal Winner, Stockholm, 1912)

2000. 8th Festival of Pacific Arts, New Caledonia. Multicoloured. (a) Size 24 × 29 mm. Self-adhesive.
735 45c. Urn and swat 50 50

(b) Sheet 130 × 70 mm.
MS736 75c. Type **214**; $1.05 Traditional mosaic; $1.20 Mask and spearhead; $2 Decorated utensils . . . . 5·00 5·50

2000. "Olymphilex 2000" International Stamp Exhibition, Sydney. Sheet 120 × 70 mm.
MS737 **215** $3 multicoloured . . 3·00 3·50

2000. "Canpex 2000" National Stamp Exhibition, Christchurch, New Zealand. Sheet 120 × 90 mm.
MS738 $2.40 No. 701 × 2 . . . . 2·50 3·00

216 Sun over Pines

2000. Christmas. Multicoloured.
739 45c. Type **216** 80 45
740 75c. Candle over pines . . . 1·25 80
741 $1.05 Moon over pines . . . 1·40 1·40
742 $1.20 Star over pines . . . . 1·60 1·75

217 "Norfolk Island in 1825 and 2001" (Jessica Wong and Mardi Pye)

2000. New Millennium. Children's drawings. Mult.
743 45c. Type **217** . . . . 1·00 1·00
744 45c. "Seabirds over Norfolk Island" (Roxanne Spreag) 1·00 1·00
745 75c. "Trees and Clothes" (Tara Grube) . . . . . . 1·40 1·40
746 75c. "Underwater Scene" (Thomas Greenwood) . . . 1·40 1·40

218 Red-fronted Parakeet ("Green Parrot")

219 Purple Swamphen

2001. Green Parrot.
747 **218** 5c. red and green 25 35

2001. Chinese New Year "Year of the Snake" and International Stamp Exhibition, Hong Kong.
748 **219** 45c. multicoloured . . . . 1·50 1·00
MS749 110 × 70 mm. $2.30 Norfolk Island eel and purple swamphen (as Type **219**, but without country inscr and face value). Imperf 2·00 2·50

220 "Old Clothes"

222 Woman and Child in Victorian Dress

221 Satellite over China

2001. Centenary of Australian Federation. Cartoons from *The Bulletin Magazine*. Multicoloured.
750 45c. Type **220** 65 70
751 45c. "Tower of Babel" . . . 65 70
752 45c. "The Political Garotters" 65 70
753 45c. "Promises, Promises!" 65 70
754 45c. "The Gout of Federation" 65 70
755 45c. "The Federal Spirit" . . 65 70
756 75c. "Australia Faces the Dawn" 80 90
757 $1.05 "The Federal Capital Question" . . . . 1·00 1·40
758 $1.20 "The Imperial Fowl-Yard" . . . . 1·10 1·50

2001. Invercargill "Stamp Odyssey 2001" National Stamp Exhibition, New Zealand. Sheet, 136 × 105 mm, containing T **221** and similar vert designs. Multicoloured.
MS759 75c. Type **221**; 75c. Satellite over Pacific; 75c. Satellite over Australia . . . . 2·50 3·00

2001. Bounty Day.
760 **222** 5c. black and green . . . 20 30

223 *Jasminium simplicifolium*

2001. Perfume from Norfolk Island. Multicoloured.
761 45c. Type **223** 40 30
762 75c. Girl's face in perfume bottle 65 60
763 $1.05 Girl and roses . . . . 85 1·00
764 $1.20 Taylor's Road, Norfolk Island . . . . 1·00 1·25
765 $1.50 Couple shopping for perfume . . . . 1·25 1·75
MS766 145 × 98 mm. $3 Girl and perfume bottle ("NORFOLK ISLAND" in two lines) (60 × 72 mm) . . . . 2·75 3·25
Nos. 761/5 were printed on paper impregnated with the Jasmine fragrance.

224 Whaleboat

226 Miamiti (cartoon owl) holding Island Flag

225 Australian Soldiers playing Cards

2001. Local Boats. Multicoloured.
768 45c. Type **224** 60 40
769 $1 Motor launch . . . . . . 1·25 1·40
770 $1 Family rowing boat (horiz) . . . . 1·25 1·40
771 $1.50 Sailing cutter (horiz) . . 1·50 1·75
No. 768 also comes self-adhesive.

2001. Centenary of Australian Army. B.C.O.F. Japan.
773 **225** 45c. brown and blue . . . 60 65
774 – 45c. brown and blue . . . 60 65
775 – $1 brown and green . . . 1·40 1·50
776 – $1 brown and green . . . 1·40 1·50
DESIGNS: No. 774, Christmas float; 775, Birthday cake; 776, Australian military policeman directing traffic.

2001. 6th South Pacific Mini Games (1st issue).
777 **226** 10c. brown and green . . 25 35
See also Nos. 794/5.

227 Strawberry Guava

228 Sacred Kingfisher

2001. Christmas. Island Plants. Each incorporating carol music. Multicoloured.
778 45c. Type **227** 60 50
779 45c. Poinsettia 60 50
780 $1 Christmas croton . . . . 1·25 1·40

781 $1 Hibiscus . . . . 1·25 1·40
782 $1.50 Indian shot . . . . . 1·50 1·75
No. 779 is inscribed "Pointsettia" in error.

2002. "Nuffka" (Sacred Kingfisher).
783 **228** 10c. deep blue and blue 35 45

229 Red-tailed Tropic Bird

2002. Cliff Ecology. Multicoloured.
784 45c. Type **229** 75 45
785 $1 White oak blossom . . . 1·25 1·40
786 $1 White oak tree . . . . . 1·25 1·40
787 $1.50 Eagle ray . . . . . . 1·75 1·90

229a Elizabeth Duchess of York with Princesses Elizabeth and Margaret, 1930

2002. Golden Jubilee.
788 **229a** 45c. black, red and gold 60 40
789 – 75c. multicoloured . . . 90 80
790 – $1 black, red and gold 1·10 1·00
791 – $1.50 multicoloured . . 1·50 1·75
MS792 162 × 95 mm. Nos. 788/91 and $3 multicoloured . . . . . 6·50 7·00
DESIGNS:—HORIZ: 75c. Queen Elizabeth in multicoloured hat, 1977; $1 Queen Elizabeth wearing Imperial State Crown, Coronation 1953; $1.50, Queen Elizabeth at Windsor Horse Show, 2000. VERT (38 × 51 mm)— $3 Queen Elizabeth after Annigoni.
Designs as Nos. 788/91 in No. **MS**792 omit the gold frame around each stamp and the "Golden Jubilee 1952-2002" inscription.

230 Derelict Steam Engine

2002. Restoration of Yeaman's Mill Steam Engine.
793 **230** $4.50 multicoloured . . . 5·00 5·50

231 Miamiti (cartoon owl) running

232 Lawn Bowls Player

2002. 6th South Pacific Mini Games (2nd issue). Multicoloured.
794 50c. Type **231** 75 60
795 $1.50 Miamiti playing tennis 1·75 1·90

2002. Bounty Bowls Tournament.
796 **232** 10c. black and green . . . 20 30

233 *Streblorrhiza speciosa*

234 Running

2002. Phillip Island Flowers. Multicoloured.
797 10c. Type **233** 25 40
798 20c. *Plumbago zeylanica* . . . 30 20
799 30c. *Canavalia rosea* 40 30
800 40c. *Ipomea pes-caprae* . . . 45 45
801 45c. *Hibiscus insularis* 50 45
802 50c. *Solanum laciniatum* . . . 75 45
803 95c. *Phormium tenax* . . . . 1·00 1·00
804 $1 *Lobelia anceps* . . . . . 1·00 1·00
805 $1.50 *Carpobrotus glaucescens* 2·00 2·25
806 $2 *Abutilon julianae* . . . . 2·50 2·75
807 $3 *Wollastonia biflora* . . . . 3·00 3·25
808 $5 *Oxalis corniculata* . . . . 6·00 6·50
No. 797 is inscribed "specioca" in error.

2002. 17th Commonwealth Games, Manchester. Multicoloured.
809 10c. Type **234** 20 30
810 45c. Cycling (horiz) . . . . . 1·00 55
811 $1 Lawn bowls . . . . 1·25 1·10
812 $1.50 Shooting (horiz) . . . 1·60 1·75

235 Adult Sperm Whale and Calf

2002. Norfolk Island—New Caledonia Joint Issue. Operation Cetaces (marine mammal study). Multicoloured.
813 $1 Type **235** . . . . 1·25 1·40
814 $1 Sperm whale attacked by giant squid . . . . 1·25 1·40
A similar set was issued by New Caledonia.

236 White Tern incubating Egg

2002. Christmas. White Tern. Multicoloured.
815 45c. Type **236** 60 45
816 45c. White tern chick 60 45
817 $1 Two White terns in flight 1·25 1·00
818 $1.50 White tern landing . . 1·50 1·75

237 Horses in Riding School

2003. Horses on Norfolk Island. Multicoloured.
819 45c. Type **237** 60 60
820 45c. Mares and foals in paddock 60 60
821 45c. Showjumpers 60 60
822 75c. Racehorses . . . . . . 1·10 1·25
823 75c. Draught horses . . . . 1·10 1·25

238 Old Warehouse Buildings at Seashore

2003. Photographic Scenes of Norfolk Island (1st series). Multicoloured.
824 50c. Type **238** 70 50
825 95c. Beached boat (with rainbow markings) and sandy shore . . . . . . 1·25 1·25
826 $1.10 Grazing cattle and pine trees . . . . 1·40 1·40
827 $1.65 Sandy shore and headland with single pine tree . . . . 2·00 2·50
See also Nos. 859/62.

239 "Southern Prize"

2003. Day Lilies. Multicoloured.
828 50c. Type **239** 65 70
829 50c. "Becky Stone" 65 70
830 50c. "Cameroons" 65 70
831 50c. "Chinese Autumn" . . . 65 70
832 50c. "Scarlet Orbit" 65 70
833 50c. "Ocean Rain" 65 70
834 50c. "Gingerbread Man" . . 65 70
835 50c. "Pink Corduroy" . . . 65 70
836 50c. "Elizabeth Hinrichsen" 65 70
837 50c. "Simply Pretty" 65 70

240 Maeve and Gil Hitch

241 Seashore with Trees and Stream

2003. 1st Norfolk Island Writer's Festival. Black, violet and lilac (Nos. 838/9 and 844/5) or multicoloured (Nos. 840/3).
838 10c. Type **240** 25 35
839 10c. Alice Buffett 25 35
840 10c. Nan Smith 25 35
841 10c. Archie Bigg 25 35
842 50c. Colleen McCullough . . 70 75
843 50c. Peter Clarke 70 75
844 50c. Bob Tofts 70 75
845 50c. Merval Hoare 70 75

2004. Island Landscapes. Multicoloured.
846 50c. Type **241** 85 90
847 50c. Sandy shore with wooden post and small boat 85 90
848 50c. Rocky bay with pine trees on headland 85 90
849 50c. Grazing cattle, pine trees and ruined building . . . 85 90

242 Queen Elizabeth II wearing Imperial State Crown

243 Globe ("Peace on Earth")

2003. 50th Anniv of Coronation.
MS850 115 × 85 mm. 10c. Type **242** (black, deep violet and violet); $3 Queen wearing flowered hat and dress (multicoloured) . . . . . 3·50 3·75

2003. Christmas. Multicoloured.
851 50c. Type **243** 70 55
852 50c. Bird and rainbow ("Joy to the World") 70 55
853 $1.10 Heart-shaped Christmas present ("Give the gift of Love") . . . . 1·40 1·25
854 $1.65 Candle ("Trust in Faith") . . . . 2·25 2·75

244 De Havilland D.H.60G Gipsy Moth Floatplane (first aircraft at Norfolk Island, 1931)

2003. Centenary of Powered Flight. Multicoloured (except Type **244**).
855 50c. Type **244** (black, brown and violet) 75 50
856 $1.10 Boeing 737 (Norfolk Island–Australia service) 1·40 1·40
857 $1.65 Douglas DC-4 (passenger service 1949–977) . . . . 2·25 2·75
MS858 110 × 83 mm. $1.65 Wright *Flyer I*, 1903 (47 × 29 mm) . . 2·50 3·00

245 Timbers from Prow of Boat and Houses

2004. Photographic Scenes of Norfolk Island (2nd series). Multicoloured.
859 50c. Type **245** 75 50
860 95c. Waterfall . . . . 1·40 1·25
861 $1.10 Cattle and pine trees 1·50 1·50
862 $1.65 Beach and headland at sunset . . . . 2·00 2·50

246 Whale Shark

2004. Sharks. Multicoloured.
863 10c. Type **246** 25 30
864 50c. Hammerhead shark . . 65 45
865 $1.10 Tiger shark . . . . . 1·25 1·25
866 $1.65 Bronze whaler shark 1·75 2·00

247 Golden Orb Spider

2004. Spiders. Multicoloured.
867 50c. Type **247** 70 55
868 50c. Community spider . . . 70 55
869 $1 St. Andrews Cross . . . . 1·25 1·25
870 $1.65 Red-horned spider . . 1·75 2·00
MS871 120 × 80 mm. $1.50 Red-horned spider (48 × 40 mm) . . 2·00 2·25

248 Loading Cargo into Light Craft

2004. Werken Dar Shep. Multicoloured.
872 50c. Type **248** 70 50
873 $1.10 Transporting cargo . . 1·40 1·40
874 $1.65 Two light craft . . . . 1·75 2·00
MS875 130 × 85 mm. $1.65 Craft moored alongside dock . . . . 2·25 2·50

249 Apple Blossom

2004. Hippeastrums. Multicoloured.
876 50c. Type **249** 70 75
877 50c. Carnival 70 75
878 50c. Cherry blossom 70 75
879 50c. Lilac wonder 70 75
880 50c. Millennium star 70 75
881 50c. Cocktail 70 75
882 50c. Milady 70 75
883 50c. Pacific sunset 70 75
884 50c. Geisha girl 70 75
885 50c. Lady Jane 70 75

250 Three Children

2004. 25th Anniv of Quota International (humanitarian organisation). Sheet 135 × 73 mm containing T **250** and similar horiz designs. Multicoloured.
MS886 50c. Type **250**; $1.10 Feet painted with "WE CARE"; $1.65 Boy drawing "Quota" in sand 3·50 3·75

2004. Perfume from Norfolk Island. Special Edition. No. **MS**766 optd with **SPECIAL EDITION**.
MS887 145 × 98 mm. $3 Girl and perfume bottle . . . . 3·00 3·50

251 Tree Fern

252 Tree and "Twas the Night Before Christmas"

2004. Norfolk Island Palm and Fern.
888 **251** 10c. green and black . . . 20 30
889 – 10c. yellow and black . . 20 30
DESIGNS: No. 888, Type **251**; 889, Palm.

2004. Christmas. Designs showing Christmas tree and excerpt of carol.
890 **252** 50c. green and silver . . . 70 55
891 – 50c. lilac and silver . . . 70 55
892 – $1.10 carmine and silver 1·40 1·10
893 – $1.65 orange and silver 1·90 2·25
DESIGNS: No. 890, Type **252**; 891, "Silent Night"; 892, "Twelve Days of Christmas"; 893, "Oh Holy Night".

253 Sacred Kingfisher

2004. Sacred Kingfisher. Multicoloured.
894 50c. Type **253** 85 60
895 50c. Two sacred kingfishers 85 60
896 $1 Sacred kingfisher perched 1·60 1·60
897 $2 Sacred kingfisher from back 3·00 3·25
MS898 130 × 158 mm. Nos. 894/7, each × 2 11·00 12·00

254 Coat of Arms and Flag

2004. 25th Anniv of Self-Government.
899 **254** $5 multicoloured 6·00 6·50

255 Boat Race

2005. Centenary of Rotary International (humanitarian organisation). Multicoloured.
900 50c. Type **255** 70 55
901 50c. Tree planting (vert) 70 55
902 $1.20 Paul Harris (founder) 1·40 1·40
903 $1.80 Rotary Youth Leadership Awards (vert) 1·90 2·25
MS904 110 × 80 mm. $2 District 9910 (Rotary community) 2·50 2·75

256 Tea Cup, 1856

2005. Norfolk Island Museum, Kingston. Multicoloured.
905 50c. Type **256** 80 55
906 50c. Salt cellar from HMS *Bounty*, 1856 80 55
907 $1.10 Medicine cups, 1825–55 1·40 1·40
908 $1.65 Stoneware jar, 1825–55 1·90 2·25

257 Polynesian Explorer and Voyaging Canoe

2005. Pacific Explorers. Multicoloured.
909 50c. Type **257** 70 50
910 $1.20 *Vitoria* (Magellan) 1·60 1·60
911 $1.80 Captain Cook ashore at Norfolk Island and HMS *Resolution* 2·40 2·75
MS912 140 × 85 mm. $2 Early map of Pacific (45 × 31 mm) 2·75 3·00
No. **MS**912 also commemorates Pacific Explorer 2005 World Stamp Expo, Sydney.

258 Branka House

2005. Old Island Houses. Multicoloured.
913 50c. Type **258** 60 50
914 50c. Greenacres 60 50
915 $1.20 Ma Annas 1·40 1·40
916 $1.80 Naumai 2·00 2·25

259 Red-tailed Tropic Bird

260 "Marjory Brown"

2005. Seabirds of Norfolk Island. Multicoloured.
917 10c. Type **259** 15 20
919 50c. Australasian gannet 60 40
922 $1.50 Grey ternlet 1·50 1·25
924 $2 Masked booby 2·00 2·25
926 $5 White-necked petrel 4·75 5·00
MS927 100 × 70 mm. $4 Red-tailed tropic bird (horiz) 4·50 4·75

2005. Hibiscus Varieties. Multicoloured.
928 50c. Type **260** 60 65
929 50c. "Aloha" 60 65
930 50c. "Pulau Tree" 60 65
931 50c. "Ann Miller" 60 65
932 50c. "Surfrider" 60 65
933 50c. "Philip Island" 60 65
934 50c. "Rose of Sharon" 60 65
935 50c. "D. J. O'Brien" 60 65
936 50c. "Elaine's Pride" 60 65
937 50c. "Castle White" 60 65
938 50c. Skeleton Hibiscus 60 65
939 50c. "Pink Sunset" 60 65

261 Anson Bay

2005. Christmas. Multicoloured.
940 50c. Type **261** 60 40
941 $1.20 Cascade Bay 1·40 1·40
942 $1.80 Ball Bay 2·00 2·25

262 Drummer

2005. Norfolk Island Jazz Festival. Multicoloured.
943 50c. Type **262** 60 45
944 $1.20 Saxophone player 1·40 1·40
945 $1.80 Guitarist and pine tree 2·00 2·25

NORTH BORNEO Pt. 1

A territory in the north of the Island of Borneo in the China Sea, formerly under the administration of the British North Borneo Company. A Crown Colony since 1946. Joined Malaysia in 1963 and renamed Sabah in 1964.

100 cents = 1 dollar (Malayan).

1

1883. "POSTAGE NORTH BORNEO" at top.
8 **1** ½c. mauve 95·00 £180
9 1c. orange £180 £325
10 2c. brown 30·00 27·00
11 4c. pink 17·00 50·00
12 8c. green 19·00 50·00
13 10c. blue 32·00 50·00

1883. Surch **8 Cents.** vert.
2 **1** 8c. on 2c. brown £1000 £650

1883. Surch **EIGHT CENTS**.
3 **1** 8c. on 2c. brown £475 £190

Where there are three price columns, prices in the second column are for postally used stamps and those in the third column are for stamps cancelled with black bars.

4

5

1883. Inscr "NORTH BORNEO".
4 **4** 50c. violet £150 — 27·00
5 **5** $1 red £130 — 14·00
For these designs with "BRITISH" in place of value in words at top, see Nos. 46/7.

1886. Optd **and Revenue**.
14 **1** ½c. mauve £140 £225
15 10c. blue £190 £225

1886. Surch in words and figures.
18 **1** 3c. on 4c. pink £120 £130
19 5c. on 8c. green £120 £130

9

10

13

19

1886. Inscr "BRITISH NORTH BORNEO".
22 **9** ½c. red 3·50 13·00
24 1c. orange 2·00 9·00
25 2c. brown 2·00 8·50
26 4c. pink 3·00 12·00
27 8c. green 14·00 21·00
28 10c. blue 7·50 28·00
45 **10** 25c. blue 65·00 80·00 75
46 – 50c. violet 90·00 £130 75
47 – $1 red 30·00 £110 75
48 **13** $2 green £140 £180 1·50
49 **19** $5 purple £200 £250 8·50
50 – $10 brown £275 £350 12·00
DESIGNS: 50c. As Type **4**; $1, As Type **5**. $10 As Type **19** but with different frame.

14

1888. Inscr "POSTAGE & REVENUE".
36b **14** ½c. red 1·50 4·75 60
37 1c. orange 2·75 4·25 50
38b 2c. brown 4·25 16·00 50
39 3c. violet 2·50 12·00 50
40 4c. pink 6·00 32·00 50
41 5c. grey 2·75 22·00 50
42 6c. red 9·00 23·00 50
43a 8c. green 21·00 27·00 50
44b 10c. blue 6·50 21·00 50

1890. Surch in words.
51 **10** 2c. on 25c. blue 70·00 90·00
52 8c. on 25c. blue 95·00 £110

1891. Surch in figures and words.
63 **14** 1c. on 4c. pink 23·00 14·00
64 1c. on 5c. grey 7·00 6·00
54 **9** 6c. on 8c. green £8000 £4250
55 **14** 6c. on 8c. green 24·00 10·00
56 **9** 6c. on 10c. blue 60·00 22·00
57 **14** 6c. on 10c. blue £170 26·00
65 **10** 8c. on 25c. blue £150 £160

24 Dyak Chief

25 Sambar Stag ("Cervus unicolor")

26 Sago Palm

27 Great Argus Pheasant

28 Arms of the Company

29 Malay Prau

30 Estuarine Crocodile

31 Mt. Kinabalu

32 Arms of the Company with Supporters

1894.
66 **24** 1c. black and bistre 1·25 9·50 50
69 **25** 2c. black and red 5·50 4·75 50
70 **26** 3c. green and mauve 2·75 8·50 50
72 **27** 5c. black and red 14·00 11·00 60
73a **28** 6c. black and brown 4·50 18·00 60
74 **29** 8c. black and lilac 6·50 11·00 60
75a **30** 12c. black and blue 28·00 80·00 2·50
78 **31** 18c. black and green 27·00 50·00 2·00
79c **32** 24c. blue and red 23·00 70·00 2·00

1894. As Nos. 47, etc, but inscr "THE STATE OF NORTH BORNEO".
81 25c. blue 9·00 30·00 1·00
82 50c. violet 26·00 60·00 2·00
83 $1 red 12·00 24·00 1·25
84 $2 green 20·00 75·00 2·50
85b $5 purple £225 £300 9·00
86 $10 brown £250 £350 15·00

1895. No. 83 surch in figures and words.
87 4 cents on $1 red 6·50 1·50 50
88 10 cents on $1 red 23·00 1·75 50
89 20 cents on $1 red 42·00 17·00 50
90 30 cents on $1 red 30·00 27·00 65
91 40 cents on $1 red 32·00 48·00 65

37 Orang-utan

41 Sun Bear

43 Borneo Steam Train

1897. As 1894 issue with insertion of native inscriptions.
92a **24** 1c. black and bistre 11·00 2·75 40
94a **25** 2c. black and red 22·00 2·50 40
95 2c. black and green 48·00 2·00 60
97 **26** 3c. green and mauve 18·00 3·00 50
98 **37** 4c. black and green 9·00 — 1·50
99 4c. black and red 35·00 9·00 50
100a **27** 5c. black & orange 95·00 3·00 60
101a **28** 6c. black and brown 32·00 4·00 50
103 **29** 8c. black and brown 12·00 28·00 75
104 **41** 10c. brown and grey £100 42·00 2·75
106b **30** 12c. black and blue 90·00 35·00 1·50
107 **43** 16c. green & brown £130 90·00 3·25
108 **31** 18c. black and green 22·00 75·00 2·00

110b 18c. black & green* . . . . 80·00 12·00 1·50
109 32 24c. blue and red* . . . . 20·00 90·00 2·00
111b 24c. blue and red* . . . . 45·00 55·00 2·50

*No. 110b is inscribed "POSTAGE & REVENUE" at the sides instead of "POSTAL REVENUE" as in No. 108. No. 111b has the words "POSTAGE & REVENUE" at the sides below the Arms; these words were omitted in No. 109.

1899. Stamps of 1897 and Nos. 81/6 surch **4 CENTS.**
112a 4c. on 5c. black and orange 28·00 10·00
113 4c. on 6c. black and brown 19·00 24·00
114 4c. on 8c. black and lilac . . 15·00 10·00
115 4c. on 12c. black and blue 24·00 13·00
116 4c. on 18c. black and green (110) . . . . 12·00 14·00
117 4c. on 24c. blue and red (111) . . . . 24·00 18·00
118 4c. on 25c. blue . . . . . 5·50 8·50
119 4c. on 50c. violet . . . . 11·00 16·00
121 4c. on $1 red . . . . . 5·50 12·00
122 4c. on $2 green . . . . . 5·50 13·00
125 4c. on $5 purple . . . . 6·50 14·00
126 4c. on $10 brown . . . . 6·50 14·00

1901. Stamps of 1897 and Nos. 81/6 optd **BRITISH PROTECTORATE.**
127a 1c. black and bistre 2·50 1·75 30
128 2c. black and green 3·75 1·25 30
129 3c. green and mauve . . . . . 1·75 5·50 30
130 4c. black and red 9·00 1·50 30
131a 5c. black and orange . . . . . 14·00 2·50 30
132b 6c. black and brown 4·00 15·00 70
133 8c. black and lilac 3·75 3·75 50
134 10c. brown and grey 60·00 5·00 1·00
135 12c. black and blue 50·00 12·00 1·50
136 16c. green and brown . . . . . £140 26·00 2·25
137 18c. black & green (110b) . . . . . 12·00 25·00 1·25
138 24c. blue and red (111b) . . . . . 16·00 40·00 1·50
139 25c. blue . . . . . 2·00 10·00 50
140 50c. violet . . . . 2·75 11·00 55
141 $1 red . . . . . 6·50 38·00 2·50
143 $2 green . . . . . 30·00 95·00 3·50
144 $5 purple (with full point) . . . . . £225 £475 8·00
184 $5 purple (without full point) . . . . £1200 £1400 8·50
145 $10 brown (with full point) . . . . . £425 £750 11·00
185 $10 brown (without full point) . . . . £1600 — 8·50

1904. Stamps of 1897 and Nos. 81/6 surch **4 cents.**
146 4c. on 5c. blk & orge . . . . . . 38·00 48·00 12·00
147 4c. on 6c. black & brn . . . . . . 7·00 21·00 12·00
148 4c. on 8c. blk & lilac . . . . . . 13·00 26·00 12·00
149 4c. on 12c. black & bl . . . . . . 28·00 40·00 12·00
150 4c. on 18c. black and green (110b) 14·00 38·00 12·00
151a 4c. on 24c. bl & red (111b) . . . . . 17·00 50·00 12·00
152 4c. on 25c. blue . . 4·50 25·00 12·00
153 4c. on 50c. violet . . 5·00 38·00 12·00
154 4c. on $1 red . . . 6·00 48·00 12·00
155 4c. on $2 green . . 6·00 48·00 12·00
156 4c. on $5 purple . . 12·00 48·00 12·00
157 4c. on $10 brown 12·00 48·00 12·00

51 Malayan Tapir

52 Traveller's Tree

64

(68)

1909. No. 177 is surch **20 CENTS.**
277 51 1c. black and brown . . . . . 1·00 70 —
160 52 2c. black and green 1·00 70 30
278 2c. black and red 85 60 —
162 – 3c. black and red 2·75 2·75 40
279 – 3c. black and green 3·00 75 —
280 – 4c. black and red 50 10 —
281 – 5c. black and brown . . . . . 5·50 2·75 —
282 – 6c. black and green 6·50 90 —
283 – 8c. black and red 3·50 50 —
284 – 10c. black and blue 3·75 90 —
285 – 12c. black and blue 21·00 80 —
174 – 16c. black and brown . . . . 26·00 7·00 1·00
175 – 18c. black and green . . . . . 95·00 32·00 1·00
177 – 20c. on 18c. blk & grn . . . . . 7·00 1·00 30
176 – 24c. black and mauve . . . . . 28·00 3·50 1·75

289 64 25c. black and green . . . . . 9·50 4·25 —
179 – 50c. black and blue 12·00 4·50 2·25
180 – $1 black and brown . . . . . 17·00 4·00 3·00
181 – $2 black and lilac 65·00 17·00 4·75
182 – $5 black and red £120 £130 32·00
183 – $10 black and orange . . . . £400 £450 75·00

DESIGNS—As T **51**: 3c. Jesselton railway station; 4c. Sultan of Sulu, his staff and W. C. Cowie, first Chairman of the Company; 5c. Asiatic elephant; 8c. Ploughing with buffalo; 24c. Dwarf cassowary. As T **52**: 6c. Sumatran rhinoceros; 10c. Wild boar; 12c. Palm cockatoo; 16 c Rhinoceros hornbill; 18 c Banteng. As T **64** but Arms with supporters: $5, $10.

1916. Stamps of 1909 surch.
186 2c. on 3c. black and red . . 25·00 15·00
187 4c. on 6c. black and olive . . 22·00 17·00
188 10c. on 12c. black and blue 55·00 65·00

1916. Nos. 277 etc, optd with T **68**.
189 1c. black and brown . . . . 7·50 35·00
203 2c. black and green . . . . . 27·00 50·00
191 3c. black and red . . . . . 27·00 48·00
192 4c. black and red . . . . . 5·50 32·00
193 5c. black and brown . . . . 40·00 55·00
206 6c. black and green . . . . . 50·00 65·00
207 8c. black and red . . . . . 27·00 55·00
196 10c. black and blue . . . . 45·00 70·00
197 12c. black and blue . . . . 90·00 90·00
198 16c. black and brown . . . . 90·00 90·00
199 20c. on 18c. black and green 42·00 90·00
200 24c. black and mauve £110 £110
201 25c. black and green £350 £425

1918. Nos. 159, etc, surch **RED CROSS TWO CENTS.**
214 1c.+2c. black and brown . . 3·50 12·00
215 2c.+2c. black and green . . . 1·00 8·50
216 3c.+2c. black and red . . . . 14·00 19·00
218 4c.+2c. black and red . . . . 70 5·00
219 5c.+2c. black and brown . . 8·00 23·00
221 6c.+2c. black and olive . . . 5·00 24·00
222 8c.+2c. black and red . . . . 5·50 11·00
223 10c.+2c. black and blue . . . 8·00 24·00
224 12c.+2c. black and blue . . . 21·00 45·00
225 16c.+2c. black and brown . . 22·00 45·00
226 24c.+2c. black and mauve . . 22·00 45·00
229 25c.+2c. black and green . . 10·00 42·00
230 50c.+2c. black and blue . . . 12·00 42·00
231 $1+2c. black and brown . . 45·00 50·00
232 $2+2c. black and lilac . . . 75·00 95·00
233 $5+2c. black and red £350 £550
234 $10+2c. black and orange . . £375 £550

The premium of 2c. on each value was for Red Cross Funds.

1918. Nos. 159, etc. surch **FOUR CENTS** and a red cross.
235 1c.+4c. black and brown . . 60 5·00
236 2c.+4c. black and green . . . 65 8·00
237 3c.+4c. black and red . . . . 1·00 3·75
238 4c.+4c. black and red . . . . 40 4·75
239 5c.+4c. black and brown . . 2·00 22·00
240 6c.+4c. black and olive . . . 1·90 12·00
241 8c.+4c. black and red . . . . 1·25 9·50
242 10c.+4c. black and blue . . . 3·75 12·00
243 12c.+4c. black and blue . . . 14·00 14·00
244 16c.+4c. black and brown . . 8·00 16·00
245 24c.+4c. black and mauve . . 11·00 20·00
246 25c.+4c. black and green . . 6·00 50·00
248 50c.+4c. black and blue . . . 15·00 45·00
249 $1+4c. black and brown . . 18·00 60·00
250 $2+4 c black and lilac . . . 50·00 80·00
251 $5+4c. black and red £275 £400
252 $10+4c. black and orange . . £300 £400

The premium of 4c. on each value was for Red Cross Funds.

1922. Nos. 159, etc, optd **MALAYA-BORNEO EXHIBITION 1922.**
253 1c. black and brown . . . . 14·00 65·00
255 2c. black and green . . . . . 2·00 23·00
256 3c. black and red . . . . . 15·00 60·00
257 4c. black and red . . . . . 3·00 38·00
258 5c. black and brown . . . . 9·00 60·00
260 6c. black and green . . . . . 9·00 65·00
261 8c. black and red . . . . . 6·00 42·00
263 10c. black and blue . . . . 14·00 60·00
265 12c. black and blue . . . . 9·00 21·00
267 16c. black and brown . . . . 20·00 65·00
268 20c. on 18c. black and green 21·00 8·00
270 24c. black and mauve . . . . 38·00 70·00
274 25c. black and green . . . . 8·00 60·00
275 50c. black and blue . . . . 12·00 60·00

1923. No. 280 surch **THREE CENTS** and bars.
276 – 3c. on 4c. black and red . . 1·50 6·00

73 Head of a Murut

76 Mount Kinabalu

1931. 50th Anniv of North Borneo Company.
295 73 3c. black and green . . . . 1·25 80
296 – 6c. black and orange . . . 16·00 3·25
297 – 10c. black and red . . . . 4·25 13·00
298 76 12c. black and blue . . . . 4·75 8·00
299 – 25c. black and violet . . . 38·00 35·00
300 – $1 black and green . . . . 27·00 £100
301 – $2 black and brown . . . . 48·00 £110
302 – $5 black and purple £150 £450

DESIGNS—VERT: 6c. Orang-utan; 10c. Dyak warrior; $1, $2, $5 Arms. HORIZ: 25c. Clouded leopard.

81 Buffalo Transport

82 Palm Cockatoo

1939.
303 81 1c. green and brown . . . 3·50 1·75
304 82 2c. purple and blue . . . . 5·00 1·75
305 – 3c. blue and green . . . . 4·00 2·00
306 – 4c. green and violet . . . . 9·00 50
307 – 6c. blue and red . . . . . 8·50 9·50
308 – 8c. red . . . . 12·00 1·50
309 – 10c. violet and green . . . 38·00 6·00
310 – 12c. green and blue . . . . 30·00 6·50
311 – 15c. green and brown . . . 25·00 9·00
312 – 20c. violet and blue . . . . 18·00 4·50
313 – 25c. green and brown . . . 23·00 12·00
314 – 50c. brown and violet . . . 26·00 9·50
315 – $1 brown and red . . . . 85·00 19·00
316 – $2 violet and olive £130 £110
317 – $5 indigo and blue £350 £225

DESIGNS—VERT: 3c. Native; 4c. Proboscis monkey; 6c. Mounted Bajaus; 10c. Orang-utan; 15c. Dyak; $1, $2 Arms. HORIZ: 8c. Map of Eastern Archipelago; 12c. Murut with blow-pipe; 20c. River scene; 25c. Native boat; 50c. Mt. Kinabalu; $5 Arms with supporters.

1941. Optd **WAR TAX.**
318 81 1c. green and brown . . . 1·75 3·50
319 82 2c. purple and blue . . . . 7·00 4·00

1945. British Military Administration. Stamps of 1939 optd **BMA.**
320 81 1c. green and brown . . . 9·00 2·00
321 82 2c. purple and blue . . . . 14·00 2·00
322 – 3c. blue and green . . . . 1·25 1·25
323 – 4c. green and violet . . . . 16·00 16·00
324 – 6c. blue and red . . . . . 1·25 1·25
325 – 8c. red . . . . 3·00 75
326 – 10c. violet and green . . . 3·00 40
327 – 12c. green and blue . . . . 6·00 2·75
328 – 15c. green and brown . . . 1·50 1·00
329 – 20c. violet and blue . . . . 4·50 1·50
330 – 25c. green and brown . . . 6·50 1·50
331 – 50c. brown and violet . . . 3·00 1·75
332 – $1 brown and red . . . . 48·00 40·00
333 – $2 violet and olive . . . . 50·00 32·00
334 – $5 indigo and blue . . . . 23·00 14·00

1947. Stamps of 1939 optd with Crown over GR monogram and bars obliterating "THE STATE OF" and "BRITISH PROTECTORATE".
335 81 1c. green and brown . . . 15 1·00
336 82 2c. purple and blue . . . . 1·75 90
337 – 3c. blue and green 15 90
338 – 4c. green and violet 70 90
339 – 6c. blue and red 25 20
340 – 8c. red 30 20
341 – 10c. violet and green . . . 1·50 40
342 – 12c. green and blue . . . . 2·00 2·75
343 – 15c. green and brown . . . 2·25 30
344 – 20c. violet and blue . . . . 2·75 85
345 – 25c. green and brown . . . 2·75 50
346 – 50c. brown and violet . . . 2·75 85
347 – $1 brown and red . . . . 6·50 1·75
348 – $2 violet and olive . . . . 15·00 17·00
349 – $5 indigo and blue . . . . 23·00 17·00

1948. Silver Wedding. As T **4b/c** of Pitcairn Islands.
350 8c. red 30 80
351 $10 mauve . . . . 23·00 35·00

1949. U.P.U. As T **4d/g** of Pitcairn Islands.
352 8c. red 60 30
353 10c. brown . . . . 3·25 1·50
354 30c. brown . . . . 1·25 1·75
355 55c. blue . . . . 1·25 2·50

100 Mt. Kinabalu

102 Coconut Grove

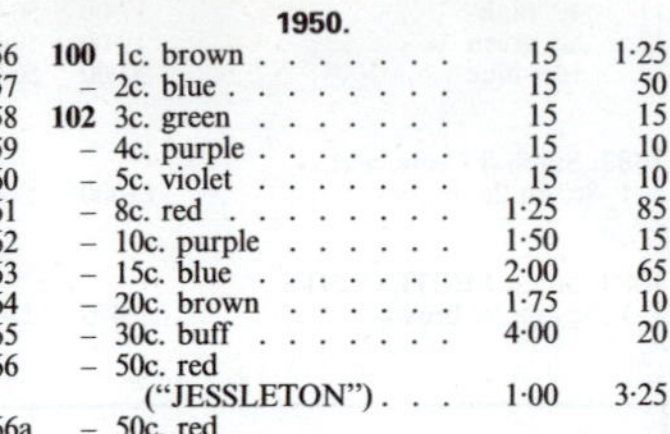

1950.
356 100 1c. brown . . . . 15 1·25
357 – 2c. blue 15 50
358 102 3c. green 15 15
359 – 4c. purple 15 10
360 – 5c. violet 15 10
361 – 8c. red . . . . 1·25 85
362 – 10c. purple . . . . 1·50 15
363 – 15c. blue . . . . 2·00 65
364 – 20c. brown . . . . 1·75 10
365 – 30c. buff . . . . 4·00 20
366 – 50c. red ("JESSLETON") . . 1·00 3·25
366a – 50c. red ("JESSELTON") . . . 10·00 2·75
367 – $1 orange . . . . 4·00 1·00
368 – $2 green . . . . 7·00 14·00
369 – $5 green . . . . 16·00 22·00
370 – $10 blue . . . . 40·00 65·00

DESIGNS—VERT: 4c. Hemp drying; 5c. Cattle at Kota Belud; 30c. Suluk river canoe; 50c. Clock tower, Jesselton; $1 Bajau horsemen. HORIZ: 2c. Musician; 8c. Map; 10c. Log pond; 15c. Malay prau, Sandakan; 20c. Bajau chief; $2 Murut with blowpipe; $5 Net fishing; $10, King George VI and arms.

1953. Coronation. As T **4h** of Pitcairn Islands.
371 10c. black and red . . . . . 1·25 60

1954. As 1950 but with portrait of Queen Elizabeth II.
372 1c. brown 10 30
373 2c. blue 60 15
374 3c. green . . . . 1·00 2·00
375 4c. purple 75 20
376 5c. violet 75 10
377 8c. red 60 30
378 10c. purple 30 10
379 15c. blue . . . . 1·00 10
380 20c. brown 30 15
381 30c. buff . . . . 2·00 20
382 50c. red (No. 366a) . . . . 5·00 20
383 $1 orange . . . . 6·50 20
384 $2 green . . . . 12·00 1·25
385 $5 green . . . . 10·00 26·00
386 $10 blue . . . . 24·00 35·00

117 Malay Prau

1956. 75th Anniv of Foundation of British North Borneo Co. Inscr "CHARTER 1ST NOVEMBER 1881".
387 – 10c. black and red . . . . 1·00 40
388 117 15c. black and brown . . 30 30
389 – 35c. black and green . . . 30 1·50
390 – $1 black and slate . . . . 65 2·50

DESIGNS—HORIZ: 10c. Borneo Railway, 1902; 35c. Mt. Kinabalu. VERT: $1 Arms of Chartered Company.

120 Sambar Stag

1961.
391 120 1c. green and red 20 10
392 – 4c. olive and orange . . . 20 90
393 – 5c. sepia and violet . . . 30 10
394 – 6c. black and turquoise 50 40
395 – 10c. green and red 50 10
396 – 12c. brown and myrtle . . 30 10
397 – 20c. turquoise and blue 3·50 10
398 – 25c. black and red . . . . 80 1·00
399 – 30c. sepia and olive . . . 70 20
400 – 35c. slate and brown . . . 1·75 1·25
401 – 50c. green and bistre . . . 1·75 20
402 – 75c. blue and purple . . . 10·00 90
403 – $1 brown and green . . . 13·00 80
404 – $2 brown and slate . . . 30·00 3·00
405 – $5 green and purple . . . 38·00 18·00
406 – $10 red and blue . . . . 32·00 35·00

DESIGNS—HORIZ: 4c. Sun bear; 5c. Clouded leopard; 6c. Dusun woman with gong; 10c. Map of Borneo; 12c. Banteng; 20c. Butterfly orchid; 25c. Sumatran rhinoceros; 30c. Murut with blow-pipe; 35c. Mt. Kinabalu; 50c. Dusun and buffalo transport; 75c. Bajau horseman. VERT: $1 Orang-utan; $2 Rhinoceros hornbill; $5 Crested wood partridge; $10 Arms of N. Borneo.

1963. Freedom from Hunger. As T **20a** of Pitcairn Islands.
407 12c. blue . . . . 1·50 75

POSTAGE DUE STAMPS

Overprinted **POSTAGE DUE**.

1895. Issue of 1894.
D 2 25 2c. black and red 18·00 24·00 2·25
D 3 26 3c. green & mve 6·00 16·00 1·00
D 5 27 5c. black and red 55·00 25·00 3·00
D 6a 28 6c. black & brn 16·00 48·00 2·50
D 7 29 8c. black and lilac . . . . 50·00 50·00 2·75
D 8b 30 12c. black & blue . . . . . 70·00 50·00 2·50
D10 31 18c. black & grn 70·00 60·00 4·00
D11b 32 24c. blue and red 29·00 55·00 4·00

1897. Issue of 1897.
D12 25 2c. black and red 8·50 9·00 1·50
D13 2c. black & green 50·00 † 70
D14 26 3c. green & mve 20·00 † 50
D16a 4c. black and red 45·00 † 50
D17a 27 5c. black & orge 20·00 48·00 1·75
D18 28 6c. black & brn 5·50 30·00 70
D20 29 8c. black & lilac 7·00 † 50
D21a 30 12c. black & blue £100 † 4·00
D22 31 18c. black and green (No. 108) . . † † £750
D23 18c. black and green (No. 110b) . . 55·00 † 4·00

No.	Type	Description			
D24	32	24c. blue and red (No. 109)	—	†	£350
D25		24c. blue and red (No. 111b)	27·00	†	2·25

1902. Issue of 1901.

No.	Type	Description			
D37		1c. black and bistre	—	†	28·00
D38		2c. black and green	16·00	3·75	30
D39		3c. green and mauve	5·50	3·25	30
D40		4c. black and red	14·00	6·50	30
D41		5c. black and orange	26·00	4·50	30
D42		6c. black and brown	18·00	11·00	40
D43		8c. black and lilac	20·00	4·25	40
D45		10c. brown and grey	90·00	20·00	1·40
D46		12c. black and blue	28·00	17·00	2·50
D47		16c. green & brown	48·00	22·00	2·50
D48		18c. black and green	11·00	19·00	1·50
D49		24c. blue and red	11·00	26·00	2·50

1919. Issue of 1909.

No.	Type	Description		
D52		2c. black and green	11·00	75·00
D66		2c. black and red	75	1·75
D67		3c. black and green	9·00	27·00
D55		4c. black and red	1·00	1·25
D57		5c. black and brown	9·50	24·00
D80		6c. black and olive	6·50	2·50
D62		8c. black and red	1·50	1·50
D63		10c. black and blue	13·00	19·00
D64		12c. black and blue	60·00	50·00
D65a		16c. black and brown	19·00	50·00

POSTAGE DUE

D 2 Crest of the Company

1939.

No.	Type	Description		
D85	D 2	2c. brown	6·50	75·00
D86		4c. red	6·50	£100
D87		6c. violet	23·00	£130
D88		8c. green	24·00	£225
D89		10c. blue	50·00	£350

For later issues see **SABAH**.

JAPANESE OCCUPATION

1942. Stamps of North Borneo optd as T **1** of Japanese Occupation of Brunei. (a) Issue of 1939.

No.	Type	Description		
J 1	81	1c. green and brown	£160	£225
J 2	82	2c. purple and blue	£160	£225
J 3	–	3c. blue and green	£130	£225
J 4a	–	4c. green and violet	50·00	£130
J 5	–	6c. blue and red	£140	£275
J 6	–	8c. red	£180	£190
J 7	–	10c. violet and green	£160	£275
J 8	–	12c. green and blue	£180	£425
J 9	–	15c. green and brown	£170	£425
J10	–	20c. violet and blue	£200	£500
J11	–	25c. green and brown	£200	£500
J12	–	50c. brown and violet	£275	£600
J13	–	$1 brown and red	£275	£750
J14	–	$2 violet and olive	£475	£1000
J15	–	$5 blue	£550	£950

(b) War Tax Issue of 1941.

No.	Type	Description		
J16	81	1c. green and brown	£550	£300
J17	82	2c. purple and blue	£1400	£500

2 Mt. Kinabalu

3 Borneo Scene

1943.

No.	Type	Description		
J18	2	4c. red	19·00	42·00
J19	3	8c. blue	16·00	42·00

(4) ("Imperial Japanese Postal Service, North Borneo")

(5) ("Imperial Japanese Postal Service, North Borneo")

1944. Optd with T **4**. (a) On stamps of North Borneo.

No.	Type	Description		
J20	81	1c. green and brown	5·00	12·00
J21	82	2c. purple and blue	7·50	9·00
J22	–	3c. blue and green	4·75	9·50
J23	–	4c. green and violet	9·00	17·00
J24	–	6c. blue and red	6·00	6·50
J25	–	8c. red	8·50	17·00
J26	–	10c. violet and green	8·50	13·00
J27	–	12c. green and blue	12·00	13·00
J28	–	15c. green and brown	11·00	16·00
J29	–	20c. violet and blue	24·00	45·00
J30	–	25c. green and brown	24·00	45·00
J31	–	50c. brown and violet	70·00	£120
J32	–	$1 brown and red	90·00	£150

(b) On stamps of Japanese Occupation of North Borneo.

No.	Type	Description		
J21a		2c. purple and blue (J2)	£425	
J22a		3c. blue and green (J3)	£425	
J25a		8c. red (J6)	£425	
J26b		10c. violet and green (J7)	£200	£375
J27a		12c. green and blue (J8)	£425	
J28a		15c. green and brown (J9)	£425	

1944. No. J1 surch with T **5**.

No.	Type	Description		
J33	81	$2 on 1c. green and brown	£4500	£3750

(6)

1944. No. 315 of North Borneo surch with T **6**.

No.	Type	Description		
J34		$5 on $1 brown and red	£4000	£2750

1944. Stamps of Japan optd as bottom line in T **4**.

No.	Type	Description		
J35	126	1s. brown	8·00	24·00
J36	84	2s. red	7·00	19·00
J37	–	3s. green (No. 319)	7·00	24·00
J38	129	4s. green	12·00	20·00
J39	–	5s. red (No. 396)	9·00	23·00
J40	–	6s. orange (No. 322)	11·00	24·00
J41	–	8s. violet (No. 324)	6·50	24·00
J42	–	10s. red (No. 399)	7·50	24·00
J43	–	15s. blue (No. 401)	9·50	24·00
J44	–	20s. blue (No. 328)	80·00	90·00
J45	–	25s. brown (No. 329)	55·00	75·00
J46	–	30s. blue (No. 330)	£170	95·00
J47	–	50s. olive and brown (No. 331)	65·00	70·00
J48	–	1y. brown (No. 332)	65·00	£100

NORTH GERMAN CONFEDERATION Pt. 7

The North German Confederation was set up on 1 January 1868, and comprised the postal services of Bremen, Brunswick, Hamburg Lubeck, Mecklenburg (both), Oldenburg, Prussia (including Hanover, Schleswig-Holstein with Bergedorf and Thurn and Taxis) and Saxony.

The North German Confederation joined the German Reichspost on 4 May 1871, and the stamps of Germany were brought into use on 1 January 1872.

Northern District: 30 groschen = 1 thaler.
Southern District: 60 kreuzer = 1 gulden.

1

3

1868. Roul or perf. (a) Northern District.

No.	Type	Description		
19	1	¼g. mauve	18·00	13·50
22		⅓g. green	5·00	1·80
23		½g. orange	5·00	1·80
25		1g. red	4·50	90
27		2g. blue	7·50	1·30
29		5g. bistre	8·75	8·75

(b) Southern District.

No.	Type	Description		
30	–	1k. green	13·50	8·50
13	–	2k. orange	60·00	44·00
33	–	3k. red	7·50	1·80
36	–	7k. blue	11·00	8·75
18	–	18k. bistre	38·00	65·00

The 1k. to 18k. have the figures in an oval.

1869. Perf.

No.	Type	Description		
38	3	10g. grey	£350	70·00
39	–	30g. blue	£275	£140

The frame of the 30g. is rectangular.

OFFICIAL STAMPS

O 5

1870. (a) Northern District.

No.	Type	Description		
O40	O 5	¼g. black and brown	29·00	49·00
O41		⅓g. black and brown	11·00	22·00
O42		½g. black and brown	3·00	3·50
O43		1g. black and brown	3·00	90
O44		2g. black and brown	7·50	5·00

(b) Southern District.

No.	Type	Description		
O45		1k. black and grey	33·00	£300
O46		2k. black and grey	90·00	£950
O47		3k. black and grey	27·00	49·00
O48		7k. black and grey	49·00	£300

NORTH INGERMANLAND Pt. 10

Stamps issued during temporary independence of this Russian territory, which adjoins Finland.

100 pennia = 1 mark.

1 18th-century Arms of Ingermanland

4 Gathering Crops

1920.

No.	Type	Description		
1	1	5p. green	2·25	4·25
2		10p. red	2·25	4·25
3		25p. brown	2·25	4·25
4		50p. blue	2·25	4·25
5		1m. black and red	26·00	45·00
6		5m. black and purple	£100	£160
7		10m. black and brown	£180	£250

1920. Inscr as in T **2**.

No.	Type	Description		
8	–	10p. blue and green	3·00	7·50
9	–	30p. green and brown	3·00	7·50
10	–	50p. brown and blue	3·00	7·50
11	–	80p. grey and red	3·00	7·50
12	4	1m. grey and red	14·00	40·00
13	–	5m. red and violet	8·00	19·00
14	–	10m. violet and brown	7·75	19·00

DESIGNS—VERT: 10p. Arms; 30p. Reaper; 50p. Ploughing; 80p. Milking. HORIZ: 5m. Burning church; 10m. Zither players.

NORTH WEST RUSSIA Pt. 10

Issues made for use by the various Anti-bolshevist Armies during the Russian Civil War, 1918–20.

100 kopeks = 1 rouble.

NORTHERN ARMY

1 "OKCA" = Osobiy Korpus Severnoy Armiy—(trans "Special Corps, Northern Army")

1919. As T **1** inscr "OKCA".

No.	Type	Description		
1	1	5k. purple	10	40
2		10k. blue	10	40
3		15k. yellow	10	40
4		20k. red	10	40
5		50k. green	10	40

NORTH-WESTERN ARMY

(2)

1919. Arms types of Russia optd as T **2**. Imperf or perf.

No.	Type	Description		
6	22	2k. green	3·00	7·50
16		3k. red	3·00	7·50
7		5k. lilac	3·00	7·50
8	23	10k. blue	4·50	10·00
9	10	15k. blue and brown	4·00	7·50
10	14	20k. red and blue	5·00	8·50
11	10	20k. on 14k. red and blue	£250	
12		25k. violet and green	8·00	12·00
13	14	50k. green and purple	8·00	12·00
14	15	1r. orange & brown on brn	16·00	24·00
17	11	3r.50 green and red	32·00	45·00
18	22	5r. blue on green	24·00	32·00
19	11	7r. pink and green	90·00	£160
15	20	10r. grey and red on yellow	60·00	85·00

1919. No. 7 surch.

No.	Type	Description		
20	22	10k. on 5k. lilac	4·00	7·50

WESTERN ARMY

1919. Stamps of Latvia optd with Cross of Lorraine in circle with plain background. Imperf. (a) Postage stamps.

No.	Type	Description		
21	1	3k. lilac	30·00	40·00
22		5k. red	30·00	40·00
23		10k. blue	£110	£190
24		20k. orange	30·00	40·00
25		25k. grey	30·00	40·00
26		35k. brown	30·00	40·00
27		50k. violet	30·00	40·00
28		75k. green	30·00	55·00

(b) Liberation of Riga issue.

No.	Type	Description		
29	4	5k. red	25·00	45·00
30		15k. green	15·00	35·00
31		35k. brown	15·00	35·00

1919. Stamps of Latvia optd with Cross of Lorraine in circle with burele background and characters **3. A** (= "Z. A."). Imperf. (a) Postage stamps.

No.	Type	Description		
32	1	3k. lilac	4·00	8·00
33		5k. red	4·00	8·00
34		10k. blue	90·00	£170
35		20k. orange	8·00	16·00
36		25k. grey	22·00	45·00
37		35k. brown	14·00	24·00
38		50k. violet	14·00	24·00
39		75k. green	14·00	24·00

(b) Liberation of Riga issue.

No.	Type	Description		
40	4	5k. red	2·75	6·50
41		15k. green	2·75	6·50
42		35k. brown	2·75	6·50

1919. Arms type of Russia surch with Cross of Lorraine in ornamental frame and **LP** with value in curved frame. Imperf or perf.

No.	Type	Description		
43	22	10k. on 2k. green	4·50	6·00
54		20k. on 3k. red	4·00	7·50
44	23	30k. on 4k. red	4·50	7·00
45	22	40k. on 5k. lilac	4·50	7·00
46	23	50k. on 10k. blue	4·50	6·00
47	10	70k. on 15k. blue and brown	4·50	6·00
48	14	90k. on 20k. red and blue	6·00	8·00
49	10	1r. on 25k. violet and green	4·50	6·00
50		1r.50 on 35k. green & brown	35·00	55·00
51	14	2r. on 50k. green and purple	6·00	10·00
52	10	4r. on 70k. red and brown	16·00	24·00
53	15	6r. on 1r. orange, brown on brown	16·00	25·00
56	11	10r. on 3r.50 green & pur	40·00	48·00

NORTHERN NIGERIA Pt. 1

A British protectorate on the west coast of Africa. In 1914 incorporated into Nigeria.

12 pence = 1 shilling;
20 shillings = 1 pound.

1

5

1900.

No.	Type	Description		
1	1	½d. mauve and green	3·25	14·00
2		1d. mauve and red	3·50	3·75
3		2d. mauve and yellow	12·00	48·00
4		2½d. mauve and blue	10·00	38·00
5		5d. mauve and brown	24·00	50·00
6		6d. mauve and violet	21·00	32·00
7		1s. green and black	24·00	70·00
8		2s.6d. green and blue	£110	£425
9		10s. green and brown	£250	£650

1902. As T **1**, but portrait of King Edward VII.

No.	Type	Description		
10		½d. purple and green	2·00	1·00
11		1d. purple and red	2·25	75
12		2d. purple and yellow	2·00	3·00
13		2½d. purple and blue	1·50	9·50
14		5d. purple and brown	3·00	5·00
15		6d. purple and violet	9·00	4·50
16		1s. green and black	3·50	6·00
17		2s.6d. green and blue	8·00	50·00
18		10s. green and brown	48·00	55·00

1910. As last. New colours etc.

No.	Type	Description		
28		½d. green	2·00	1·25
29		1d. red	2·00	1·25
30		2d. grey	4·50	2·25
31		2½d. blue	2·25	7·00
32		3d. purple on yellow	3·50	75
34		5d. purple and green	4·00	13·00
35a		6d. purple	5·00	6·00
36		1s. black and green	2·25	75
37		2s.6d. black and red on blue	10·00	30·00
38		5s. green and red on yellow	23·00	75·00
39		10s. green and red on green	42·00	48·00

1912.

No.	Type	Description		
40	5	½d. green	1·75	60
41		1d. red	1·75	60
42		2d. grey	3·00	8·50
43		3d. purple on yellow	2·25	1·25
44		4d. black and red on yellow	1·25	2·25
45		5d. purple and olive	4·00	12·00
46		6d. purple and violet	4·00	4·25
47		9d. purple and red	2·00	12·00
48		1s. black on green	4·50	2·25
49		2s.6d. black and red on blue	7·00	45·00
50		5s. green and red on yellow	20·00	80·00
51		10s. green and red on green	38·00	48·00
52		£1 purple and black on red	£170	£110

NORTHERN RHODESIA Pt. 1

A British territory in central Africa, north of the Zambesi. From 1954 to 1963 part of the central African Federation and using the stamps of Rhodesia and Nyasaland (q.v.). A new constitution was introduced on 3 January 1964, with internal self-government and independence came on 24 October 1964 when the country was renamed Zambia (q.v.).

12 pence = 1 shilling;
20 shillings = 1 pound.

1

1925. The shilling values are larger and the view is in first colour.

No.	Type	Description	Unused	Used
1	1	½d. green	1·75	80
2		1d. brown	1·75	10
3		1½d. red	2·00	30
4		2d. orange	2·00	10
5		3d. blue	2·00	1·25
6		4d. violet	4·25	50
7		6d. grey	4·50	40
8		8d. purple	4·00	48·00
9		10d. olive	4·50	42·00
10		1s. orange and black	3·75	1·75
11		2s. brown and blue	16·00	25·00
12		2s.6d. black and green	17·00	10·00
13		3s. violet and blue	24·00	19·00
14		5s. grey and violet	35·00	17·00
15		7s.6d. purple and black	£120	£170
16		10s. green and black	75·00	80·00
17		20s. red and purple	£170	£190

1935. Silver Jubilee. As T **143a** of Newfoundland.

No.	Type	Description	Unused	Used
18		1d. blue and olive	80	1·50
19		2d. green and blue	1·25	1·50
20		3d. brown and blue	2·50	5·50
21		6d. grey and purple	4·75	1·50

1937. Coronation. As T **143b** of Newfoundland.

No.	Type	Description	Unused	Used
22		1½d. red	30	35
23		2d. brown	40	35
24		3d. blue	60	1·25

1938. As 1925, but with portrait of King George VI facing right and "POSTAGE & REVENUE" omitted.

No.	Type	Description	Unused	Used
25		½d. green	10	10
26		½d. brown	75	1·50
27		1d. brown	20	20
28		1d. green	75	1·50
29		1½d. red	45·00	75
30		1½d. orange	30	10
31		2d. orange	45·00	1·75
32		2d. red	30	50
33		2d. purple	45	1·50
34		3d. blue	40	30
35		3d. red	50	2·75
36		4d. violet	30	40
37		4½d. blue	1·00	7·00
38		6d. grey	30	10
39		9d. violet	1·00	5·50
40		1s. orange and black	3·50	60
41		2s.6d. black and green	7·00	4·25
42		3s. violet and blue	15·00	10·00
43		5s. grey and violet	15·00	10·00
44		10s. green and black	18·00	15·00
45		20s. red and purple	45·00	48·00

1946. Victory. As T **4a** of Pitcairn Islands.

No.	Type	Description	Unused	Used
46		1½d. orange	50	50
47		2d. red	10	50

1948. Silver Wedding. As T **4b/c** of Pitcairn Islands.

No.	Type	Description	Unused	Used
48		1½d. orange	30	10
49		20s. red	45·00	50·00

1949. U.P.U. As T **4d/g** of Pitcairn Islands.

No.	Type	Description	Unused	Used
50		2d. red	20	30
51		3d. blue	1·50	1·75
52		6d. grey	55	1·75
53		1s. orange	55	1·00

5 Cecil Rhodes and Victoria Falls

1953. Birth Centenary of Cecil Rhodes.

No.	Type	Description	Unused	Used
54	5	½d. brown	50	1·00
55		1d. green	40	1·00
56		2d. mauve	40	30
57		4½d. blue	40	3·25
58		1s. orange and black	75	4·50

6 Arms of the Rhodesias and Nyasaland  9 Arms

1953. Rhodes Centenary Exhibition.

No.	Type	Description	Unused	Used
59	6	6d. violet	70	1·25

1953. Coronation. As T **4h** of Pitcairn Islands.

No.	Type	Description	Unused	Used
60		1½d. black and orange	70	20

1953. As 1938 but with portrait of Queen Elizabeth II facing left.

No.	Type	Description	Unused	Used
61		½d. brown	65	10
62		1d. green	65	10
63		1½d. orange	1·25	10
64		2d. purple	1·25	10
65		3d. red	80	10
66		4d. violet	1·25	2·00
67		4½d. blue	1·50	4·25
68		6d. grey	1·25	10
69		9d. violet	1·25	4·25
70		1s. orange and black	70	10
71		2s.6d. black and green	9·00	4·50
72		5s. grey and purple	9·50	12·00
73		10s. green and black	7·50	26·00
74		20s. red and purple	24·00	29·00

1963. Arms black, gold and blue; portrait and inscriptions black; background colours given.

No.	Type	Description	Unused	Used
75	9	½d. violet	70	1·25
76		1d. blue	1·00	10
77		2d. brown	70	10
78		3d. yellow	30	10
79		4d. green	70	30
80		6d. green	1·00	10
81		9d. bistre	60	1·60
82		1s. purple	50	10
83		1s.3d. purple	2·25	10
84		2s. orange	2·25	3·50
85		2s.6d. lake	2·25	2·00
86		5s. mauve	8·00	8·00
87		10s. mauve	9·00	17·00
88		20s. blue	11·00	21·00

Nos. 84/88 are larger (27 × 23 mm).

POSTAGE DUE STAMPS

D 1 D 2

1929.

No.	Type	Description	Unused	Used
D1	D 1	1d. black	2·50	2·50
D2		2d. black	3·00	3·00
D3		3d. black	3·00	26·00
D4		4d. black	9·50	30·00

1963.

No.	Type	Description	Unused	Used
D 5	D 2	1d. orange	1·40	4·75
D 6		2d. blue	1·40	4·00
D 7		3d. lake	1·40	6·00
D 8		4d. blue	1·40	10·00
D 9		6d. purple	6·50	9·00
D10		1s. green	7·50	25·00

For later issues see **ZAMBIA**.

NORWAY Pt. 11

In 1814 Denmark ceded Norway to Sweden, from 1814 to 1905 the King of Sweden was also King of Norway after which Norway was an independent Kingdom.

1855. 120 skilling = 1 speciedaler.
1877. 100 ore = 1 krone.

1 3 King Oscar I

1855. Imperf.

No.	Type	Description	Unused	Used
1	1	4s. blue	£4000	75·00

1856. Perf.

No.	Type	Description	Unused	Used
4	3	2s. yellow	£500	75·00
6		3s. lilac	£250	42·00
7		4s. blue	£225	6·50
11		8s. red	£950	18·00

4 5

1863.

No.	Type	Description	Unused	Used
12	4	2s. yellow	£550	£100
13		3s. lilac	£425	£250
16		4s. blue	£150	5·25
17		8s. pink	£600	28·00
18		24s. brown	55·00	70·00

1867.

No.	Type	Description	Unused	Used
21	5	1s. black	60·00	29·00
23		2s. buff	26·00	26·00
26		3s. lilac	£250	55·00
27		4s. blue	60·00	4·75
29		8s. red	£300	21·00

6 10 With background shading

A

1872. Value in "Skilling".

No.	Type	Description	Unused	Used
33	6	1s. green	11·00	18·00
36		2s. blue	12·00	34·00
39		3s. red	55·00	5·75
42		4s. mauve	21·00	31·00
44		6s. brown	£300	29·00
45		7s. brown	32·00	33·00

1877. Letters without serifs as Type A. Value in "ore".

No.	Type	Description	Unused	Used
47	10	1ore brown	4·75	3·75
83		2ore brown	4·75	4·25
84c		3ore orange	36·00	2·10
52		5ore blue	19·00	7·25
85d		5ore green	21·00	80
86a		10ore red	43·00	75
55		12ore green	75·00	10·50
75b		12ore brown	13·00	8·00
76		20ore brown	85·00	12·00
87		20ore blue	45·00	1·40
88		25ore mauve	43·00	6·75
61		35ore green	19·00	6·25
62		50ore purple	35·00	5·75
63		60ore blue	30·00	9·25

9 King Oscar II

1878.

No.	Type	Description	Unused	Used
68	9	1k. green and light green	32·00	5·50
69		1k.50 blue and ultramarine	65·00	24·00
70		2k. brown and pink	46·00	15·00

1888. Surch **2 ore**.

No.	Type	Description	Unused	Used
89a	6	2ore on 12ore brown	2·00	2·20

D

1893. Letters with serifs as Type D.

No.	Type	Description	Unused	Used
133	10	1ore drab	70	40
134		2ore brown	45	30
135		3ore orange	60	30
136		5ore green	6·75	20
529		5ore purple	20	15
138		7ore green	85	25
139		10ore red	6·50	15
140		10ore green	10·50	40
529a		10ore grey	20	15
141		12ore violet	80	90
530		15ore brown	35	20
143		15ore blue	60	30
144		20ore blue	9·50	20
530a		20ore green	20	15
146		25ore mauve	60·00	25
147		25ore red	9·50	50
531		25ore blue	15	15
148		30ore grey	16·00	35
149		30ore blue	7·50	3·00
119		35ore green	15·00	4·50
150		35ore brown	22·00	30
151		40ore green	11·00	35
152		40ore blue	32·00	30
531b		50ore purple	10	10
154		60ore blue	38·00	55
531c		60ore orange	10	10
531d		70ore orange	20	20
531e		80ore brown	20	15
531f		90ore brown	25	25

See also Nos. 279 etc and 1100/3.

1905. Surch.

No.	Type	Description	Unused	Used
122	5	1k. on 2s. buff	55·00	27·00
123		1k.50 on 2s. buff	80·00	55·00
124		2k. on 2s. buff	95·00	47·00

1906. Surch.

No.	Type	Description	Unused	Used
162	10	5ore on 25ore mauve	70	50
125	6	15ore on 4s. mauve	5·50	3·25
126		30ore on 7s. brown	12·00	6·00

15 King Haakon VII  16 King Haakon VII

1907.

No.	Type	Description	Unused	Used
127	15	1k. green	48·00	25·00
128		1½k. blue	70·00	65·00
129		2k. red	95·00	90·00

1910.

No.	Type	Description	Unused	Used
155a	16	1k. green	70	15
156		1½k. blue	2·30	40
157		2k. red	3·00	55
158		5k. violet	4·75	3·50

17 Constitutional Assembly (after O. Wergeland) 19

1914. Centenary of Independence.

No.	Type	Description	Unused	Used
159	17	5ore green	1·90	40
160		10ore red	4·25	55
161		20ore blue	11·00	5·00

1922.

No.	Type	Description	Unused	Used
163	19	10ore green	15·00	45
164		20ore purple	24·00	20
165		25ore red	30·00	60
166		45ore blue	2·75	70

20 21 22

1925. Air. Amundsen's Polar Flight.

No.	Type	Description	Unused	Used
167	20	2ore brown	2·00	1·80
168		3ore orange	3·75	3·00
169		5ore mauve	7·00	5·75
170		10ore green	9·50	10·50
171		15ore blue	9·50	11·50
172		20ore mauve	12·50	16·00
173		25ore red	3·50	3·50

1925. Annexation of Spitzbergen.

No.	Type	Description	Unused	Used
183	21	10ore green	6·25	6·75
184		15ore blue	6·25	3·75
185		20ore purple	6·25	1·10
186		45ore blue	7·25	4·75

1926. Size 16 × 19½ mm.

No.	Type	Description	Unused	Used
187	22	10ore green	85	15
187a		14ore orange	1·00	1·70
188		15ore brown	1·00	20
189		20ore purple	38·00	14·50
189a		20ore red	1·30	15
190		25ore red	14·00	1·60
190a		25ore brown	1·70	20
190b		30ore blue	1·90	25
191		35ore brown	85·00	20
191a		35ore violet	3·25	15
192		40ore blue	7·25	95
193		40ore grey	2·50	15
194		50ore pink	2·75	20
195		60ore blue	3·00	20

For stamps as Type **22** but size 17 × 21 mm, see Nos. 284, etc.

1927. Surcharged with new value and bar.

No.	Type	Description	Unused	Used
196	22	20ore on 25ore red	4·75	1·00
197	19	30ore on 45ore blue	13·50	1·10
198	21	30ore on 45ore blue	5·50	3·25

24 Akershus Castle 25 Ibsen  28 Abel

1927. Air.

No.	Type	Description	Unused	Used
199a	24	45ore blue (with frame-lines)	7·25	1·80
323		45ore blue (without frame-lines)	1·20	30

1928. Ibsen Centenary.

No.	Type	Description	Unused	Used
200	25	10ore green	7·75	1·40
201		15ore brown	3·25	1·80
202		20ore red	3·75	40
203		30ore blue	4·25	2·10

1929. Postage Due stamps optd **Post Frimerke** (204/6 and 211) or **POST** and thick bar (others).

No.	Type	Description	Unused	Used
204	D 12	1ore brown	40	60
205		4ore mauve (No. D96a)	40	35
206		10ore green	1·80	1·90
207		15ore brown	3·25	2·75
208		20ore purple	1·40	45
209		40ore blue	3·75	60
210		50ore purple	7·75	6·50
211		100ore yellow	3·00	1·90
212		200ore violet	4·50	2·50

1929. Death Cent of N. H. Abel (mathematician).

No.	Type	Description	Unused	Used
213	28	10ore green	4·25	60
214		15ore brown	3·25	1·20
215		20ore red	1·10	25
216		30ore blue	2·25	1·30

1929. Surch **14 ORE 14**.

No.	Type	Description	Unused	Used
217	5	14ore on 2s. buff	1·70	3·00

30 St. Olaf (sculpture, Brunlanes Church)

31 Nidaros Trondhjem Cathedral

32 Death of St. Olaf (after P. N. Arbo)

1930. 9th Death Centenary of St. Olaf.

219	30	10ore green	8·50	30
220	31	15ore sepia and brown	1·10	45
221	30	20ore red	1·40	35
222	32	30ore blue	6·75	1·80

33 North Cape and "Bergensfjord" (liner)

1930. Norwegian Tourist Association Fund. Size $35\frac{1}{2} \times 21\frac{1}{2}$ mm.

223	33	15ore+25ore brown	1·70	2·30
224		20ore+25ore red	21·00	22·00
225		30ore+25ore blue	55·00	50·00

For smaller stamps in this design see Nos. 349/51, 442/66 and 464/6.

34 Radium Hospital

1931. Radium Hospital Fund.

226	34	20ore+10ore red	9·50	3·75

35 Bjornson

36 L. Holberg

1932. Birth Cent of Bjornstjerne Bjornson (writer).

227	35	10ore green	9·75	45
228		15ore brown	95	90
229		20ore red	1·80	30
230		30ore blue	2·75	1·60

1934. 250th Birth Anniv of Holberg (writer).

231	36	10ore green	3·25	25
232		15ore brown	60	50
233		20ore red	14·50	20
234		30ore blue	2·75	1·50

37 Dr. Nansen

38 No background shading

38b King Haakon VII

1935. Nansen Refugee Fund.

235	37	10ore+10ore green	2·10	2·00
236		15ore+10ore brown	7·25	7·25
237		20ore+10ore red	1·20	1·00
238		30ore+10ore blue	7·50	7·00

See also Nos. 275/8.

1937.

279	38	1ore green	80	45
280		2ore brown	45	55
281		3ore orange	70	65
282		5ore mauve	40	15
283		7ore green	60	20
413		10ore grey	45	15
285		12ore violet	75	1·20
414		15ore green	1·20	40
415		15ore brown	30	15
416		20ore brown	2·75	1·50
417		20ore green	30	15

1937. As T **22**, but size 17×21 mm.

284	22	10ore green	45	15
286		14ore orange	1·80	2·40
287		15ore green	1·70	20
288a		20ore red	35	15
289		25ore brown	1·90	20
289a		25ore red	95	15
290		30ore blue	2·20	20
290a		30ore grey	6·25	25
291		35ore violet	2·20	20
292		40ore grey	3·50	20
292a		40ore blue	3·25	20
293		50ore purple	2·10	30
293a		55ore orange	17·00	20
294		60ore blue	2·75	20
294a		80ore brown	17·00	15

1937.

255	38b	1k. green	10	20
256		1k.50 blue	70	1·50
257		2k. red	60	3·75
258		5k. purple	6·00	22·00

39 Reindeer

41 Joelster in Sunnfjord

1938. Tourist Propaganda.

262	39	15ore brown	1·00	55
263	–	20ore red	90	25
264	41	30ore blue	1·00	75

DESIGN—As T **39** but VERT: 20ore, Stave Church, Borgund.

42 Queen Maud

43 Lion Rampant

44 Dr. Nansen

1939. Queen Maud Children's Fund.

267	42	10ore+5ore green	45	3·75
268		15ore+5ore brown	45	3·75
269		20ore+5ore red	45	3·00
270		30ore+5ore blue	45	3·75

1940.

271	43	1k. green	80	15
272		$1\frac{1}{2}$k. blue	1·70	30
273		2k. red	2·50	85
274		5k. purple	3·75	3·50

See also Nos. 318/21.

1940. National Relief Fund.

275	44	10ore+10ore green	1·50	2·40
276		15ore+10ore brown	1·50	3·00
277		20ore+10ore red	45	80
278		30ore+10ore blue	95	1·60

46 Femboring (fishing boat) and Iceberg

47 Colin Archer (founder) and Lifeboat "Colin Archer"

1941. Haalogaland Exhibition and Fishermen's Families Relief Fund.

295	46	15ore+10ore blue	1·10	2·50

1941. 50th Anniv of National Lifeboat Institution.

296	47	10ore+10ore green	80	1·10
297		15ore+10ore brown	1·10	1·80
298	–	20ore+10ore red	1·00	55
299	–	30ore+10ore blue	2·30	4·25

DESIGN—VERT: 20ore, 30ore, "Osloskoyta" (lifeboat).

48 Soldier and Flags

51 Oslo University

1941. Norwegian Legion Support Fund.

300	48	20ore+80ore red	29·00	42·00

1941. Stamps of 1937 optd **V** (= Victory).

301B	38	1ore green	35	2·50
302B		2ore brown	35	3·75
303B		3ore orange	35	3·00
304B		5ore mauve	35	30
305A		7ore green	75	2·75
306B	22	10ore green	35	25
307B	38	12ore violet	70	12·00
308A	22	14ore orange	1·30	8·75
309A		15ore green	60	1·10
310B		20ore red	25	25
311B		25ore brown	50	45
312B		30ore blue	1·20	1·80
313A		35ore violet	1·50	85
314B		40ore grey	85	50
315B		50ore purple	1·20	1·90
316A		60ore blue	1·90	1·40
317B	43	1k. green	1·50	45
318B		$1\frac{1}{2}$k. blue	3·25	10·50
319B		2k. red	10·50	34·00
320B		5k. purple	18·00	75·00

1941. As No. 413, but with "V" incorporated in the design.

321		10ore green	80	8·25

1941. Centenary of Foundation of Oslo University Building.

322	51	1k. green	24·00	32·00

52 Queen Ragnhild's Dream

53 Stiklestad Battlefield

1941. 700th Death Anniv of Snorre Sturlason (historian).

324	52	10ore green	25	15
325	–	15ore brown	30	50
326	–	20ore red	25	15
327	–	30ore blue	1·40	1·80
328	–	50ore violet	1·00	1·30
329	53	60ore blue	1·00	1·40

DESIGNS (illustrations from "Sagas of Kings")—As T **53**: 15ore Einar Tambarskjelve at Battle of Svolder; 30ore King Olav II sails to his wedding; 50ore Svipdag's men enter Hall of the Seven Kings. As T **52**: 20ore Snorre Sturlason.

55 Vidkun Quisling

1942. (a) Without opt.

330	55	20ore+30ore red	4·00	13·50

(b) Optd **1-2-1942.**

331	55	20ore+30ore red	4·00	13·50

See also No. 336.

56 Rikard Nordraak

57 Embarkation of the Viking Fleet

1942. Birth Centenary of Rikard Nordraak (composer).

332	56	10ore green	1·10	1·40
333	57	15ore brown	1·10	1·70
334	56	20ore red	1·10	1·40
335	–	30ore blue	1·10	1·40

DESIGN—As Type **57**: 30ore Mountains across sea and two lines of the National Anthem.

1942. War Orphans' Relief Fund. As T **55** but inscr "RIKSTINGET 1942".

336		20ore+30ore red	45	3·25

58 J. H. Wessel

59 Reproduction of Types **55** and **1**

1942. Birth Bicentenary of Wessel (poet).

337	58	15ore brown	10	20
338		20ore red	10	20

1942. Inaug of European Postal Union, Vienna.

339	59	20ore red	15	45
340		30ore blue	15	1·00

60 "Sleipner" (Destroyer)

61 Edvard Grieg

1943.

341	60	5ore purple	20	15
342	–	7ore green	30	30
343	60	10ore green	20	10
344	–	15ore green	60	65
345	–	20ore red	20	20
346	–	30ore blue	80	90
347	–	40ore green	65	80
348	–	60ore blue	70	85

DESIGNS: 7ore, 30ore Merchant ships in convoy; 15ore Airman; 20ore "Vi Vil Vinne" (We will win) written on the highway; 40ore Soldiers on skis; 60ore King Haakon VII.

For use on correspondence posted at sea on Norwegian merchant ships and (in certain circumstances) from Norwegian camps in Gt. Britain during the German Occupation of Norway. After liberation all values were put on sale in Norway.

1943. Norwegian Tourist Association Fund. As T **33**, but reduced to 27×21 mm.

349	33	15ore+25ore brown	65	80
350		20ore+25ore red	80	1·50
351		30ore+25ore blue	1·20	1·50

1943. Birth Centenary of Grieg (composer).

352	61	10ore green	20	25
353		20ore red	20	25
354		40ore green	20	25
355		60ore blue	20	25

62 Soldier's Emblem

63 Fishing Station

1943. Soldiers' Relief Fund.

356	62	20ore+30ore red	40	3·00

1943. Winter Relief Fund.

357	63	10ore+10ore green	75	2·20
358	–	20ore+10ore red	70	2·50
359	–	40ore+10ore grey	70	2·50

DESIGNS: 20ore Mountain scenery; 40ore Winter landscape.

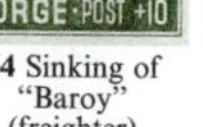

64 Sinking of "Baroy" (freighter)

65 Gran's Bleriot XI "Nordsjoen"

1944. Shipwrecked Mariners' Relief Fund.

360	64	10ore+10ore green	65	3·25
361	–	15ore+10ore brown	65	3·25
362	–	20ore+10ore red	65	3·25

DESIGNS—HORIZ: 15ore "Sanct Svithun" (cargo liner) attacked by Bristol Type 142 Blenheim Mk IV airplane. VERT: 20ore Sinking of "Irma" (freighter).

1944. 30th Anniv of First North Sea Flight, by Tryggve Gran.

363	65	40ore blue	55	1·20

66 Girl Spinning

67 Arms

68 Henrik Wergeland

1944. Winter Relief Fund. Inscr as in T **66**.

364	66	5ore+10ore mauve	55	1·80
365	–	10ore+10ore green	55	1·80
366	–	15ore+10ore purple	55	1·80
367	–	20ore+10ore red	55	1·80

DESIGNS: 10ore Ploughing; 15ore Tree felling; 20ore Mother and children.

1945.

368	67	$1\frac{1}{2}$k. blue	1·70	45

1945. Death Centenary of Wergeland (poet).

369	68	10ore green	15	25
370		15ore brown	40	70
371		20ore red	10	20

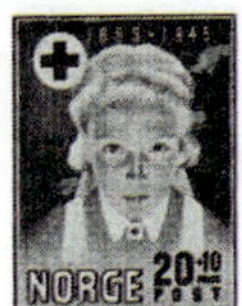
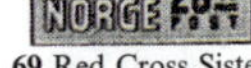
69 Red Cross Sister

70 Folklore Museum Emblem

1945. Red Cross Relief Fund and Norwegian Red Cross Jubilee.

372	**69**	20ore+10ore red	35	40

1945. 50th Anniv of National Folklore Museum.

373	**70**	10ore green	35	25
374		20ore red	35	25

71 Crown Prince Olav

72 "R.N.A.F."

1946. National Relief Fund.

375	**71**	10ore+10ore green	35	35
376		15ore+10ore brown	35	35
377		20ore+10ore red	35	35
378		30ore+10ore blue	90	1·20

1946. Honouring Norwegian Air Force trained in Canada.

379	**72**	15ore red	45	75

73 King Haakon VII

74 Fridtjof Nansen, Roald Amundsen and "Fram"

1946.

380	**73**	1k. green	1·10	15
381		1½k. blue	3·00	15
382		2k. brown	20·00	15
383		5k. violet	13·50	50

1947. Tercentenary of Norwegian Post Office.

384	–	5ore mauve	30	15
385	–	10ore green	30	15
386	–	15ore brown	60	15
387	–	25ore red	50	15
388	–	30ore grey	75	15
389	–	40ore blue	1·80	25
390	–	45ore violet	1·50	55
391	–	50ore brown	2·20	35
392	**74**	55ore orange	3·25	25
393	–	60ore grey	2·75	1·10
394	–	80ore brown	3·00	40

DESIGNS: 5ore Hannibal Sehested (founder of postal service) and Akershus Castle; 10ore "Postal-peasant"; 15ore Admiral Tordenskiold and 18th-century warship; 25ore Christian M. Falsen; 30ore Cleng Peerson and "Restaurationen" (emigrant sloop), 1825; 40ore "Constitutionen" (paddle-steamer), 1827; 45ore First Norwegian locomotive "Caroline"; 50ore Svend Foyn and "Spes et Fides" (whale catcher); 60ore Coronation of King Haakon and Queen Maud in Nidaros Cathedral; 80ore King Haakon and Oslo Town Hall.

75 Petter Dass

76 King Haakon VII

1947. Birth Tercentenary of Petter Dass (poet).

395	**75**	25ore red	60	60

1947. 75th Birthday of King Haakon VII.

396	**76**	25ore orange	45	55

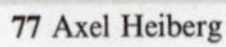
77 Axel Heiberg

80 A. L. Kielland

1948. 50th Anniv of Norwegian Forestry Society and Birth Centenary of Axel Heiberg (founder).

397	**77**	25ore red	55	35
398		80ore brown	1·30	30

1948. Red Cross. Surch **25+5** and bars.

399	**69**	25+5 ore on 20+10 ore red	50	65

1949. Nos. 288a and 292a surch.

400	**22**	25ore on 20ore red	30	15
401		45ore on 40ore blue	1·80	50

1949. Birth Centenary of Alexander L. Kielland (author).

402	**80**	25ore red	85	20
403		40ore blue	85	45
404		80ore brown	1·40	65

81 Symbolising Universe

82 Pigeons and Globe

1949. 75th Anniv of U.P.U.

405	**81**	10ore green and purple	45	45
406	**82**	25ore red	25	20
407	–	40ore blue	25	45

DESIGN—37 × 21 mm: 40ore Dove, globe and signpost.

84 King Harald Haardraade and Oslo Town Hall

85 Child with Flowers

1950. 900th Anniv of Founding of Oslo.

408	**84**	15ore green	45	55
409		25ore red	35	20
410		45ore blue	45	55

1950. Infantile Paralysis Fund.

411	**85**	25ore+5ore red	35	65
412		45ore+5ore blue	3·50	3·75

87 King Haakon VII

88 Arne Garborg (after O. Rusti)

1950.

418	**87**	25ore red	50	15
419		25ore grey	11·00	20
419a		25ore green	65	15
420		30ore grey	5·25	60
421		30ore red	50	15
422a		35ore red	3·00	15
422b		40ore purple	1·10	25
423		45ore blue	95	1·50
424		50ore brown	1·50	15
425		55ore orange	1·60	95
426		55ore blue	1·00	45
427		60ore blue	7·75	15
427a		65ore blue	70	25
427b		70ore brown	8·50	25
428		75ore purple	1·50	25
429		80ore brown	1·60	25
430		90ore orange	95	25

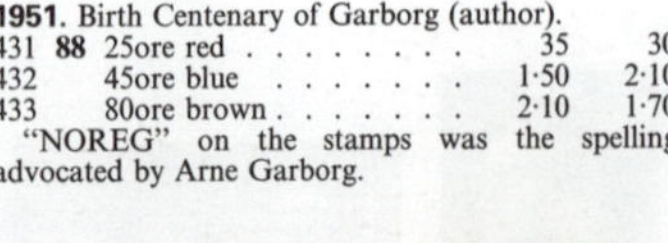

1951. Birth Centenary of Garborg (author).

431	**88**	25ore red	35	30
432		45ore blue	1·50	2·10
433		80ore brown	2·10	1·70

"NOREG" on the stamps was the spelling advocated by Arne Garborg.

89 Ice Skater

92 King Haakon VII

1951. 6th Winter Olympic Games. Inscr "OSLO 1952".

434	**89**	15ore+5ore green	1·80	2·50
435	–	30ore+10ore red	1·80	2·50
436	–	55ore+20ore blue	6·00	9·00

DESIGNS—As T **89**: 30ore Ski jumping. 38 × 21 mm: 55ore Winter landscape.

1951. Surch in figures.

440	**38**	20ore on 15ore green	45	20
437	**87**	30ore on 25ore red	50	15

1952. 80th Birthday of King Haakon.

438	**92**	30ore scarlet and red	25	20
439		55ore blue and grey	70	75

94 "Supplication"

95 Medieval Sculpture

1953. Anti-cancer Fund.

441	**94**	30ore+10ore red and cream	1·00	1·30

1953. Norwegian Tourist Association Fund. As T **33** but smaller 27½ × 21 mm.

442	**33**	20ore+10ore green	5·50	7·25
464		25ore+10ore green	2·50	3·50
443		30ore+15ore red	5·50	7·25
465		35ore+15ore red	3·50	4·75
444		55ore+25ore blue	10·00	11·00
466		65ore+25ore blue	2·50	3·00

1953. 8th Cent of Archbishopric of Nidaros.

445	**95**	30ore red	50	45

96 Stephenson Locomotive on Hoved Railway, 1854, and Horse-drawn Sledge

97 C. T. Nielsen (first Director)

1954. Centenary of Norwegian Railways.

446	**96**	20ore green	45	25
447	–	30ore red	45	20
448	–	55ore blue	1·10	1·00

DESIGNS: 30ore Diesel-hydraulic express train; 55ore Alfred Andersen (engine driver) in locomotive cab.

1954. Centenary of Telegraph Service.

449	**97**	20ore black and green	15	25
450	–	30ore red	15	20
451	–	55ore blue	80	75

DESIGNS: 30ore Radio masts at Tryvannshogda; 55ore Telegraph lineman on skis.

98 "Posthorn" Type Stamp

100 King Haakon and Queen Maud

1955. Norwegian Stamp Centenary.

452	–	20ore blue and green	15	25
453	**98**	30ore deep red and red	15	10
454	–	55ore blue and grey	35	50

DESIGNS: 20ore Norway's first stamp; 55ore "Lion" type stamp.

1955. Stamp Cent and Int Stamp Exn, Oslo. Nos. 452/4 with circular opt **OSLO NORWEX**.

455	–	20ore blue and green	6·75	8·25
456	**98**	30ore deep red and red	6·75	8·25
457	–	55ore blue and grey	6·75	8·25

Nos. 455/7 were only on sale at the Exhibition P.O. at face plus 1k. entrance fee.

1955. Golden Jubilee of King Haakon.

458	**100**	30ore red	25	20
459		55ore blue	35	45

101 Crown Princess Martha

101a Whooper Swans

1956. Crown Princess Martha Memorial Fund.

460	**101**	35ore+10ore red	50	65
461		65ore+10ore blue	2·10	2·20

1956. Northern Countries' Day.

462	**101a**	35ore red	35	40
463		65ore blue	35	55

102 Jan Mayen Island (after aquarell, H. Mohn)

103 Map of Spitzbergen

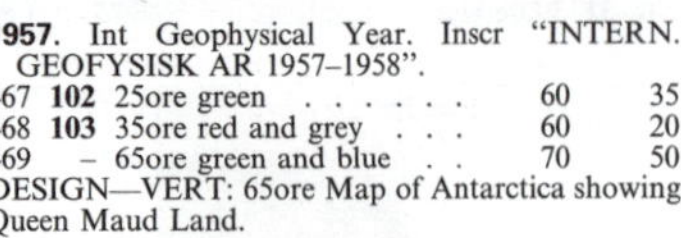

1957. Int Geophysical Year. Inscr "INTERN. GEOFYSISK AR 1957–1958".

467	**102**	25ore green	60	35
468	**103**	35ore red and grey	60	20
469	–	65ore green and blue	70	50

DESIGN—VERT: 65ore Map of Antarctica showing Queen Maud Land.

104 King Haakon VII

1957. 85th Birthday of King Haakon.

470	**104**	35ore red	15	20
471		65ore blue	50	60

105 King Olav V

106 King Olav V

1958.

472	**105**	25ore green	60	15
473		30ore violet	95	20
474		35ore red	45	25
474a		35ore green	2·00	15
475		40ore red	45	20
475a		40ore grey	2·20	1·10
476		45ore red	50	15
477		50ore brown	3·75	15
478		50ore red	4·00	15
479		55ore grey	1·10	80
480		60ore violet	2·75	80
481		65ore blue	95	40
482		80ore brown	4·50	55
483		85ore brown	1·00	25
484		90ore orange	50	15
485	**106**	1k. green	45	30
486		1k.50 blue	1·80	15
487		2k. red	1·30	40
488		5k. purple	23·00	15
489		10k. orange	3·25	15

107 Asbjorn Kloster (founder)

108 Society's Centenary Medal

1959. Cent of Norwegian Temperance Movement.

490	**107**	45ore brown	30	25

1959. 150th Anniv of Royal Norwegian Agricultural Society.

491	**108**	45ore brown and red	30	40
492		90ore grey and blue	1·20	1·50

109 Sower

110 White Anemone

1959. Centenary of Norwegian Royal College of Agriculture.
493 **109** 45ore black and brown . . . 45 40
494 – 90ore black and blue . . 85 90
DESIGN—VERT: 90ore Ears of corn.

1960. Tuberculosis Relief Funds.
495 **110** 45ore+10ore yellow, green and red . . . . 1·60 1·70
496 – 90ore+10ore mult . . . . 3·00 5·00
DESIGN: 90ore Blue anemone.

111 Society's Original Seal

112 Refugee Mother and Child

1960. Bicentenary of Royal Norwegian Society of Scientists.
497 **111** 45ore red on grey 35 35
498 90ore blue on grey . . . 1·00 1·20

1960. World Refugee Year.
499 **112** 45ore+25ore black and pink . . . . 2·40 3·50
500 90ore+25ore blk & bl . . 5·50 7·00

113 Viking Longship

1960. Norwegian Ships.
501 **113** 20ore black and grey . . 90 65
502 – 25ore black and green . . 80 65
503 – 45ore black and red . . . 80 50
504 – 55ore black and brown 1·90 2·00
505 – 90ore black and blue . . 1·60 1·40
SHIPS: 25ore Hanse kogge; 45ore "Skomvaer" (barque); 55ore "Dalfon" (tanker); 90ore "Bergensfjord" (liner).

113a Conference Emblem

113b Douglas DC-8

1960. Europa.
506 **113a** 90ore blue 45 45

1961. 10th Anniv of Scandinavian Airlines System (SAS).
507 **113b** 90ore blue 35 55

114 Throwing the Javelin

1961. Centenary of Norwegian Sport.
508 **114** 20ore brown 40 45
509 – 25ore green 40 55
510 – 45ore red 40 20
511 – 90ore mauve . . . . . 2·30 85
DESIGNS: 25ore Ice skating; 45ore Ski jumping; 90ore Yachting.

115 Haakonshallen Barracks and Rosencrantz Tower

1961. 700th Anniv of Haakonshallen, Bergen.
512 **115** 45ore black and red . . . 35 20
513 1k. black and green . . . 35 35

116 Oslo University

1961. 150th Anniv of Oslo University.
514 **116** 45ore red 20 20
515 1k.50 blue 30 35

117 Nansen

119 Frederic Passy and Henri Dunant (winners in 1901)

118 Amundsen, "Fram" and Dog-team

1961. Birth Centenary of Fridtjof Nansen (polar explorer).
516 **117** 45ore black and red . . . 25 20
517 90ore black and blue . . 50 50

1961. 50th Anniv of Amundsen's Arrival at South Pole.
518 **118** 45ore red and grey . . . 35 30
519 – 90ore deep blue and blue 65 85
DESIGN: 90ore Amundsen's party and tent at South Pole.

1961. Nobel Peace Prize.
520 **119** 45ore red 35 20
521 1k. green 45 35

120 Prof. V. Bjerknes

1962. Birth Centenary of Prof. Vilhelm Bjerknes (physicist).
522 **120** 45ore black and red . . . 30 20
523 1k.50 black and blue . . 55 35

121 Etrich/Rumpler Taube Monoplane "Start"

1962. 50th Anniv of Norwegian Aviation.
524 **121** 1k.50 brown and blue . . 95 45

122 Branch of Fir, and Cone

125 Reef Knot

123 Europa "Tree"

1962. Cent of State Forestry Administration.
525 **122** 45ore grey, black and red 60 45
526 1k. grey, black and green 3·00 25

1962. Europa.
527 **123** 50ore red 35 20
528 90ore blue 55 95

1962.
531g – 25ore green 70 15
532 – 30ore drab . . . . . . 2·50 2·40
532a – 30ore green 25 25
533 **125** 35ore green 20 15
533a – 40ore red 95 30
534 – 40ore green 20 15
534a – 45ore green 30 50
535 **125** 50ore red . . . . . . 2·10 15
535a 50ore grey 20 15
536 – 55ore brown 35 55
536a **125** 60ore green . . . . . . 4·50 15
537 60ore red 60 30
537b – 65ore violet 75 30
538 **125** 65ore red 35 15
538a 70ore brown 20 15
539 – 75ore green 20 15
539a – 80ore purple . . . . . 1·50 1·40
539b – 80ore brown 30 15
540 – 85ore brown 30 25
540a – 85ore buff 30 25
540b – 90ore blue 30 20
541 – 100ore violet 30 15
541a – 100ore red 30 15
542 – 110ore red 30 15
542a – 115ore brown 45 35
543 – 120ore blue 40 25
543a – 125ore red 30 15
544 – 140ore blue 40 25
544a – 750ore brown . . . . . 1·20 15
DESIGNS: 25, 40, 90, 100 (2), 110, 120, 125ore, Runic drawings; 30, 45, 55, 75, 85ore, Ear of wheat and Atlantic cod; 65 (537b), 80, 140ore, "Stave" (wooden) church and "Aurora Borealis"; 115ore Fragment of Urnes stave-church; 750ore Sigurd Farnesbane (the Dragon killer) and Regin (the blacksmith), portal from Hylestad stave-church.

126 Camilla Collett

127 Boatload of Wheat

1963. 150th Birth Anniv of Camilla Collett (author).
545 **126** 50ore red 20 30
546 90ore blue . . . . 55 1·70

1963. Freedom from Hunger.
547 **127** 25ore bistre 35 40
548 35ore green 45 60
549 – 50ore red 35 30
550 – 90ore blue . . . . . . 1·00 1·10
DESIGN—$37\frac{1}{2} \times 21$ mm: 50, 90ore Birds carrying food on cloth.

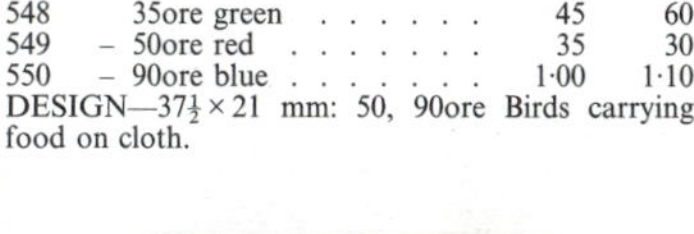

128 River Mail Boat

1963. Tercentenary of Southern-Northern Norwegian Postal Services.
551 **128** 50ore red . . . . 1·10 50
552 – 90ore blue . . . . 2·10 2·00
DESIGN: 90ore Femboring (Northern sailing vessel).

129 Ivar Aasen

130 "Co-operation"

1963. 150th Birth Anniv of Ivar Aasen (philologist).
553 **129** 50ore red and grey . . . 35 20
554 90ore blue and grey . . . 80 75
The note after No. 433 re "NOREG" also applies here.

1963. Europa.
555 **130** 50ore orange and purple 50 20
556 90ore green and blue . . 1·50 1·50

131 "Herringbone" Pattern

1963. 150th Anniv of Norwegian Textile Industry.
557 **131** 25ore green and bistre . . 55 55
558 35ore ultramarine and blue 65 75
559 50ore purple and red . . 55 45

132 Edvard Munch (self-portrait)

133 Eilert Sundt (founder)

1963. Birth Centenary of Edvard Munch (painter and engraver).
560 **132** 25ore black 30 25
561 – 35ore green 30 25
562 – 50ore brown 30 15
563 – 90ore blue and indigo . . 65 65
DESIGNS (woodcuts)—HORIZ: 35ore "Fecundity"; 50ore "The Solitaries". VERT: 90ore "The Girls on the Bridge".

1964. Centenary of Oslo Workers' Society.
564 **133** 25ore green 40 40
565 – 50ore purple 40 25
DESIGN: 50ore Beehive emblem of O.W.S.

134 C. M. Guldberg and P. Waage (chemists)

1964. Centenary of Law of Mass Action.
566 **134** 35ore green 55 45
567 55ore stone . . . . 1·30 1·20

135 Eidsvoll Manor

1964. 150th Anniv of Norwegian Constitution.
568 **135** 50ore grey and red . . . 35 30
569 – 90ore black and blue . . 80 95
DESIGN: 90ore Storting (Parliament House), Oslo.

On 1 June 1964 a stamp depicting the U.N. refugee emblem and inscr "PORTO BETALT ... LYKKEBREVET 1964" was put on sale. It had a franking value of 50ore but was sold for 2k.50, the balance being for the Refugee Fund. In addition, each stamp bore a serial number representing participation in a lottery which took place in September. The stamp was on sale until 15 July and had validity until 10 August.

136 Harbour Scene

137 Europa "Flower"

1964. Cent of Norwegian Seamen's Mission.
570 **136** 25ore green and yellow 50 50
571 90ore blue and cream . . 1·20 1·40

1964. Europa.
572 **137** 90ore deep blue and blue 1·70 1·70

138 H. Anker and O. Arvesen (founders)

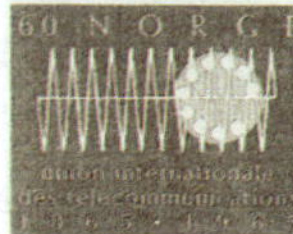

139 "Radio-telephone"

1964. Cent of Norwegian Folk High Schools.
573 **138** 50ore pink 55 30
574 90ore blue . . . . 1·90 1·90
The note after No. 433 re "NOREG" also applies here.

1965. Centenary of I.T.U.
575 **139** 60ore purple 55 25
576 – 90ore grey . . . . . . 1·00 1·00
DESIGN: 90ore "T.V. transmission".

140 Dove of Peace and Broken Chain

1965. 20th Anniv of Liberation.
577 **140** 30ore+10ore brown, green and sepia 25 30
578 – 60ore+10ore blue and red 25 30
DESIGN: 60ore Norwegian flags.

141 Mountain Landscapes

1965. Centenary of Norwegian Red Cross.
579 **141** 60ore brown and red . . 35 25
580 – 90ore blue and red . . . 2·50 2·10
DESIGN: 90ore Coastal view.

142 Europa "Sprig"

144 Rondane Mountains (after H. Sohlberg)

143 St. Sunniva and Bergen Buildings

1965. Europa.
581 **142** 60ore red 50 30
582 90ore blue . . . . 1·10 1·10

1965. Bicentenary of Harmonien Philharmonic Society.
583 – 30ore black and green . . 45 25
584 **143** 90ore black and blue . . 90 95
DESIGN—VERT: 30ore St. Sunniva.

1965. Rondane National Park.
585 **144** 1k.50 blue . . . . 1·00 25

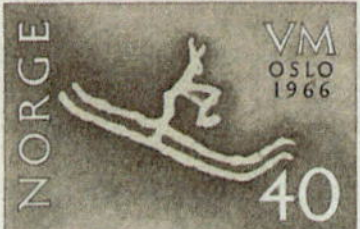

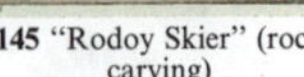
145 "Rodoy Skier" (rock carving)

146 "The Bible"

1966. World Skiing Championships, Oslo. Inscr "VM OSLO 1966".
586 **145** 40ore brown 45 85
587 – 55ore green . . . . . . 1·20 1·20
588 – 60ore brown 45 25
589 – 90ore blue . . . . . . 85 1·10
DESIGNS—HORIZ: 55ore Ski jumper; 60ore Cross-country skier. VERT: 90ore Holmenkollen ski jumping tower, Oslo.

1966. 150th Anniv of Norwegian Bible Society.
590 **146** 60ore red 45 25
591 90ore blue . . . . 70 1·10

147 Guilloche Pattern

148 J. Sverdrup (after C. Krohg)

1966. 150th Anniv of Bank of Norway.
592 **147** 30ore green 45 40
593 – 60ore red (Bank building) 30 15
No. 593 is size $27\frac{1}{2} \times 21$ mm.

1966. 150th Birth Anniv of Johan Sverdrup (statesman).
594 **148** 30ore green 35 25
595 60ore purple 30 25

149 Europa "Ship"

150 Molecules in Test-tube

1966. Europa.
596 **149** 60ore red 50 25
597 90ore blue . . . . 1·10 95

1966. Birth Centenaries of S. Eyde (industrialist) (1966) and K. Birkeland (scientist) (1967), founders of Norwegian Nitrogen Industry.
598 **150** 40ore blue and light blue 1·20 1·10
599 – 55ore mauve and red . . 1·60 1·40
DESIGN: 55ore Ear of wheat and conical flask.

151 E.F.T.A. Emblem

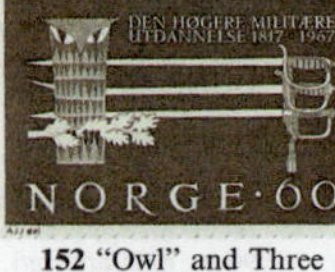

152 "Owl" and Three Swords

1967. European Free Trade Association.
600 **151** 60ore red 40 20
601 90ore blue . . . . 1·30 1·40

1967. 150th Anniv of Higher Military Training.
602 **152** 60ore brown 50 40
603 90ore green . . . . . . 1·60 1·60

153 Cogwheels

154 Johanne Dybwad

1967. Europa.
604 **153** 60ore deep plum, plum and purple 35 20
605 90ore deep violet, violet and blue . . . . 1·00 1·10

1967. Birth Centenary of J. Dybwad (actress).
606 **154** 40ore blue 40 30
607 60ore red 40 10

155 I. Skrefsrud (missionary and founder)

156 Climbers on Mountain-top

1967. Centenary of Norwegian Santal Mission.
608 **155** 60ore brown 40 20
609 – 90ore blue 90 75
DESIGN—HORIZ: 90ore Ebenezer Church, Benagaria, Santal, India.

1968. Centenary of Norwegian Mountain Touring Association.
610 **156** 40ore brown 75 75
611 – 60ore red 75 25
612 – 90ore blue . . . . 1·40 1·10
DESIGNS: 60ore Mountain cairn and scenery; 90ore Glitretind peak.

157 "The Blacksmiths"

158 Vinje

1968. Norwegian Handicrafts.
613 **157** 65ore brown, black & red 45 25
614 90ore brown, black & blue . . . . 95 1·10

1968. 150th Birth Anniv of Aasmund Vinje (poet).
615 **158** 50ore brown 35 40
616 65ore red 35 15
See note below No. 433.

159 Cross and Heart

160 Cathinka Guldberg (first deaconess)

1968. Centenary of Norwegian Lutheran Home Mission Society.
617 **159** 40ore red and green . . . 2·40 2·40
618 65ore red and violet . . . 50 15

1968. Centenary of Deaconess House, Oslo.
619 **160** 50ore blue 40 30
620 65ore red 40 20

161 K. P. Arnoldson and F. Bajer

1968. Nobel Peace Prize Winners of 1908.
621 **161** 65ore brown 40 25
622 90ore blue 75 75

161a Viking Ships (from old Swedish coin)

1969. 50th Anniv of Northern Countries' Union.
623 **161a** 65ore red 45 20
624 90ore blue 75 80

162 Transport

1969. Centenary of "Rutebok for Norge" ("Communications of Norway") and Road Safety Campaign.
625 **162** 50ore green 30 50
626 – 65ore red and green . . . 20 25
DESIGN: 65ore Pedestrian-crossing.

163 Colonnade

1969. Europa.
627 **163** 65ore black and red . . . 75 20
628 90ore black and blue . . 45 95

164 J. Hjort and Atlantic Cod Eggs

1969. Birth Centenary of Professor Johan Hjort (fisheries pioneer).
629 **164** 40ore brown and blue . . 75 60
630 – 90ore blue and green . . 2·40 1·20
DESIGN: 90ore Hjort and polyp.

165 Traena Islands

1969.
631 **165** 3k.50 black 70 20

166 King Olav V

167 "Mother and Child"

1969.
632 **166** 1k. green 30 15
633 1k.50 blue 45 15
634 2k. red 45 15
635 5k. blue 95 15
636 10k. brown . . . . . . 2·75 15
637 20k. brown . . . . . . 2·50 15
637a 50k. green . . . . 9·75 40

1969. Birth Centenary of Gustav Vigeland (sculptor).
638 **167** 65ore black and red . . . 25 20
639 – 90ore black and blue . . 75 85
DESIGN: 90ore "Family" (sculpture).

168 Punched Cards

169 Queen Maud

1969. Bicentenary of 1st National Census. Mult.
640 65ore Type **168** 25 20
641 90ore "People" (diagram) . . 75 85

1969. Birth Centenary of Queen Maud.
642 **169** 65ore purple 25 10
643 90ore blue 75 75

170 Wolf ("Canis lupus")

171 "V" Symbol

1970. Nature Conservation Year.
644 **170** 40ore brown and blue . . 75 80
645 – 60ore grey and brown . . 75 1·50
646 – 70ore brown and blue . . 1·00 45
647 – 100ore brown and blue 2·30 1·00
DESIGNS—VERT: 60ore Pale pasque flower ("Pulsatilla vernalis"); 70ore Voringsfossen Falls. HORIZ: 100ore White-tailed sea eagle ("Haliaeetus albicilla").

1970. 25th Anniv of Liberation.
648 **171** 70ore red and violet . . . 1·20 40
649 – 100ore blue and green . . 1·20 1·10
DESIGN—HORIZ: 100ore Merchant ships in convoy.

172 "Citizens"

173 Hands reaching for Globe

1970. 900th Anniv of Bergen.
650 **172** 40ore green 95 80
651 – 70ore purple . . . . . . 1·70 40
652 – 1k. blue . . . . 1·30 1·50
DESIGNS: 70ore "City between the Mountains"; 1k. "Ships".

1970. 25th Anniv of United Nations.
653 **173** 70ore red . . . . 1·80 45
654 100ore green . . . . . . 1·20 1·20

174 G. O. Sars

175 Ball-game

1970. Norwegian Zoologists.
655 **174** 40ore brown 75 95
656 – 50ore lilac 85 70
657 – 70ore brown . . . . . . 1·00 25
658 – 100ore blue . . . . . . 1·00 1·00
ZOOLOGISTS: 50ore Hans Strom; 70ore J. E. Gunnerus; 100ore Michael Sars.

1970. Centenary of Central School of Gymnastics, Oslo.
659 **175** 50ore brown and blue . . 50 40
660 – 70ore brown and red . . 75 10
DESIGN—HORIZ: 70ore "Leapfrog" exercise.

176 Tonsberg's Seal c. 1340

1971. 1100th Anniv of Tonsberg.
661 **176** 70ore red 50 20
662 100ore blue 75 70

177 Parliament House, Oslo

1971. Centenary of Introduction of Annual Parliamentary Sessions.
663 **177** 70ore lilac and red . . . 40 30
664 100ore green and blue . . 75 65

178 "Helping Hand"

1971. "Help for Refugees".

665 **178** 50ore green and black 45 60

666 70ore red and black 30 25

179 "Hauge addressing Followers" (A. Tidemand)

1971. Birth Centenary of Hans Nielson Hauge (church reformer).

667 **179** 60ore black 45 35

668 70ore brown 30 25

180 Bishop welcoming Worshippers

1971. 900th Anniv of Oslo Bishopric.

669 – 70ore black and red 35 20

670 **180** 1k. black and blue 1·00 95

DESIGN—VERT: 70ore Masons building first church.

181 Roald Amundsen and Treaty Emblem

1971. 10th Anniv of Antarctic Treaty.

671 **181** 100ore red and blue 1·30 1·30

182 "The Preacher and the King"

184 3s. "Posthorn" Stamp

183 Anniversary Symbol

1971. Norwegian Folk Tales. Drawings by Erik Werenskiold.

672 – 40ore black and green 30 20

673 **182** 50ore black and blue 35 15

674 – 70ore black and purple 45 20

DESIGNS—VERT: 40ore "The Farmer and the Woman"; 70ore "The Troll and the Girl".

1972. 150th Anniv of Norwegian Savings Banks.

675 **183** 80ore gold and red 45 20

676 1k.20 gold and blue 45 65

1972. Centenary of Norwegian "Posthorn" Stamps.

677 **184** 80ore red and brown 35 9·00

678 1k. blue and violet 55 45

MS679 120×71 mm. Nos. 677/8 (sold at 2k.50) 3·25 4·25

185 Alstad "Picture" Stone (detail)

186 King Haakon VII

1972. 1100th Anniv of Norway's Unification. Relics.

680 **185** 50ore green 55 60

681 – 60ore brown 80 85

682 – 80ore red 1·10 35

683 – 1k.20 blue 35 95

DESIGNS: 60ore Portal, Hemsedal Church (detail); 80ore Figurehead of Oseberg Viking ship; 1k.20, Sword-hilt (Lodingen).

1972. Birth Centenary of King Haakon VII.

684 **186** 80ore red 1·00 25

685 1k.20 blue 75 1·00

187 "Joy" (Ingrid Ekrem)

189 "Maud"

1972. "Youth and Leisure".

686 **187** 80ore mauve 45 20

687 – 1k.20 blue 75 1·20

DESIGN: 1k.20, "Solidarity" (Ole Instefjord).

1972. "Interjunex 1972" Stamp Exhibition, Oslo. Nos. 686/7 optd **INTERJUNEX 72**.

688 **187** 80ore mauve 1·90 2·40

689 – 1k.20 blue 1·90 2·40

1972. Norwegian Polar Ships.

690 **189** 60ore olive and green 1·10 75

691 – 80ore red and black 1·20 30

692 – 1k.20 blue and red 1·20 1·10

DESIGNS: 80ore "Fram" (Amundsen and Nansen's ship); 1k.20, "Gjoa".

190 "Little Man"

191 Dr. Hansen and Bacillus Diagram

1972. Norwegian Folk Tales. Drawings of Trolls by Th. Kittelsen.

693 **190** 50ore black and green 30 20

694 – 60ore black and blue 45 35

695 – 80ore black and pink 30 15

TROLLS: 60ore "The troll who wonders how old he is"; 80ore "Princess riding on a bear".

1973. Centenary of Hansen's Identification of Leprosy Bacillus.

696 **191** 1k. red and blue 45 20

697 – 1k.40 blue and red 65 95

DESIGN: 1k.40, As Type **191** but bacillus as seen in modern microscope.

192 Europa "Posthorn"

193 King Olav V

192a "The Nordic House", Reykjavik

1973. Europa.

698 **192** 1k. red, scarlet and carmine 1·10 25

699 1k.40 emerald, green and blue 1·10 1·10

1973. Nordic Countries' Postal Co-operation.

700 **192a** 1k. multicoloured 35 15

701 1k.40 multicoloured 35 85

1973. King Olav's 70th Birthday.

702 **193** 1k. brown and purple 45 20

703 1k.40 brown and blue 45 75

194 J. Aall

195 Bone Carving

1973. Birth Centenary of Jacob Aall (industrialist).

704 **194** 1k. purple 30 20

705 1k.40 blue 30 65

1973. Lapp Handicrafts.

706 **195** 75ore brown and cream 25 30

707 – 1k. red and cream 35 15

708 – 1k.40 black and blue 40 65

DESIGNS: 1k. Detail of weaving; 1k.40, Detail of tin-ware.

196 Yellow Wood Violet

197 Land Surveying

1973. Mountain Flowers. Multicoloured.

709 65ore Type **196** 15 20

710 70ore Rock speedwell 20 60

711 1k. Mountain heath 20 15

1973. Bicent of Norwegian Geographical Society.

712 **197** 1k. red 25 15

713 – 1k.40 blue 45 70

DESIGN: 1k.40, Old map of Hestbraepiggene (mountain range).

198 Lindesnes

199 "Bridal Procession on Hardanger Fjord" (A. Tidemand and H. Gude)

1974. Norwegian Capes.

714 **198** 1k. green 45 25

715 – 1k.40 blue 1·00 1·00

DESIGN: 1k.40, North Cape.

1974. Norwegian Paintings. Multicoloured.

716 1k. Type **199** 30 15

717 1k.40 "Stugunoset from Filefjell" (J. Dahl) 35 65

200 Gulating Law Manuscript, 1325

201 Trees and Saw Blade

1974. 700th Anniv of King Magnus Lagaboter National Legislation.

718 **200** 1k. red and brown 30 15

719 – 1k.40 blue and brown 50 70

DESIGN: 1k.40, King Magnus Lagaboter (sculpture in Stavanger Cathedral).

1974. Industrial Accident Prevention.

720 **201** 85ore green, deep green and emerald 1·00 1·50

721 – 1k. carmine, red and orange 75 30

DESIGN: 1k. Flower and cogwheel.

202 J. H. L. Vogt

203 Buildings of the World

1974. Norwegian Geologists.

722 **202** 65ore brown and green 25 25

723 – 85ore brown and purple 70 1·00

724 – 1k. brown and orange 50 20

725 – 1k.40 brown and blue 75 80

DESIGNS: 85ore V. M. Goldschmidt; 1k. Th. Kjerulf; 1k.40, W. C. Brogger.

1974. Centenary of Universal Postal Union.

726 **203** 1k. brown and green 45 20

727 – 1k.40 blue and brown 50 65

DESIGN: 1k.40, People of the World.

204 Detail of Chest of Drawers

205 Woman Skier, 1900

1974. Norwegian Folk Art. Rose Painting. Mult.

728 85ore Type **204** 45 50

729 1k. Detail of cupboard 25 15

1975. Norwegian Skiing.

730 **205** 1k. red and green 50 25

731 – 1k.40 blue and brown 50 65

DESIGN: 1k.40, Skier making telemark turn.

206 "Three Women with Ivies" Gate, Vigeland Park, Oslo

207 Nusfjord Fishing Harbour, Lofoten Islands

1975. International Women's Year.

732 **206** 1k.25 violet and purple 30 15

733 1k.40 ultramarine and blue 30 70

1975. European Architectural Heritage Year.

734 **207** 1k. green 30 45

735 – 1k.25 red 25 15

736 – 1k.40 blue 30 60

DESIGNS: 1k.25, Old Stavanger; 1k.40, Roros.

208 Norwegian 1k. Coin, 1875 (Monetary Convention)

1975. Cent of Monetary and Metre Conventions.

737 **208** 1k.25 red 20 20

738 – 1k.40 blue 40 55

DESIGN: 1k.40, O. J. Broch (original Director of the International Bureau of Weights and Measures) (Metre Convention).

209 Camping and Emblem

1975. World Scout Jamboree, Lillehammer. Mult.

739 1k.25 Type **209** 25 20

740 1k.40 Skiing and emblem 45 75

210 Colonist's Peat House

1975. 150th Anniv of First Emigrations to America.

741 **210** 1k.25 brown 45 20

742 – 1k.40 blue 45 55

DESIGNS: 1k.40, C. Peerson and extract from letter to America, 1874.

211 "Templet" (Temple Mountain), Tempelfjord, Spitzbergen

212 "Television Screen" (T. E. Johnsen)

1975. 50th Anniv of Norwegian Administration of Spitzbergen.

743 **211** 1k. grey 30 45

744 – 1k.25 purple 30 10

745 – 1k.40 blue 80 1·20

DESIGNS: 1k.25, Miners leaving pit; 1k.40, Polar bear.

1975. 50th Anniv of Norwegian Broadcasting System. Multicoloured.

746 1k.25 Type **212** 15 20

747 1k.40 Telecommunications antenna (N. Davidsen) (vert) 25 50

213 "The Annunciation"

1975. Paintings from "Altaket" (wooden vault) of "Al" Stave Church, Hallingdal.

748 80ore Type **213** 20 20

749 1k. "The Visitation" 20 25

750 1k.25 "The Nativity" (30×38 mm) 20 10

751 1k.40 "The Adoration" (30×38 mm) 45 55

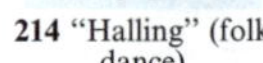

214 "Halling" (folk dance)

215 Silver Sugar Caster, Stavanger, 1770

1976. Norwegian Folk Dances. Multicoloured.

752		80ore Type **214**	30	50
753		1k. "Springar"	30	25
754		1k.25 "Gangar"	30	10

1976. Centenary of Oslo Museum of Applied Art.

755	**215**	1k.25 brown, red and pink	20	20
756	–	1k.40 lilac, blue and azure	35	65

DESIGN: 1k.40, Goblet, Nøstetangen Glass-works, 1770.

216 Bishop's "Mitre" Bowl, 1760

217 "The Pulpit", Lyse Fjord

1976. Europa. Early Products of Herrebo Potteries, Halden.

757	**216**	1k.25 red and mauve	30	20
758	–	1k.40 ultramarine & blue	50	65

DESIGN: 1k.40, Decorative plate, 1760.

1976. Norwegian Scenery. Multicoloured.

759		1k. Type **217**	30	45
760		1k.25 Peak of Gulleplet ("The Golden Apple"), Balestrand, Sognefjord	45	25

218 Social Development Graph

219 Olav Duun and Cairn, Dun Mountain, Joa Island, Namsen Fjord

1976. Cent of Norwegian Central Bureau of Statistics.

761	**218**	1k.25 red	40	15
762	–	2k. blue	45	35

DESIGN: 2k. National productivity graph.

1976. Birth Centenary of Olav Duun (novelist).

763	**219**	1k.25 multicoloured	40	25
764		1k.40 multicoloured	45	80

220 "Slindebirkin" (T. Fearnley)

221 Details of "April"

1976. Norwegian Paintings. Multicoloured.

765		1k.25 Type **220**	45	20
766		1k.40 "Gamle Furutraer" (L. Hertervig)	55	65

1976. Tapestry from Baldishol Stave Church. Mult.

767		80ore Type **221**	25	20
768		1k. Detail of "May"	25	25
769		1k.25 "April" and "May" section of tapestry (48 × 30 mm)	25	15

222 Five Water-lilies

223 Akershus Castle, Oslo

1977. Nordic Countries Co-operation in Nature Conservation and Environment Protection.

770	**222**	1k.25 multicoloured	30	15
771		1k.40 multicoloured	30	65

1977.

772	–	1k. green	25	20
773	–	1k.10 purple	25	20
774	**223**	1k.25 red	20	15
775	–	1k.30 brown	30	15
776	–	1k.40 lilac	25	20
777	–	1k.50 red	30	15
778	–	1k.70 green	40	40
779	–	1k.75 green	35	15
780	–	1k.80 blue	45	35
781	–	2k. red	45	15
782	–	2k.20 blue	45	40
783	–	2k.25 violet	45	35
784	–	2k.50 red	45	15
785	–	2k.75 red	50	60
786	–	3k. blue	50	25
787	–	3k.50 violet	60	25

DESIGNS—HORIZ: 1k. Austraat Manor; 1k.10, Trondenes Church, Harstad; 1k.30, Steinviksholm Fortress, Asen Fjord; 1k.40, Ruins of Hamar Cathedral; 2k.20, Tromsdalen Church; 2k.50, Loghouse, Breiland; 2k.75, Damsgard Palace, Laksevag, near Bergen; 3k. Ruins of Selje Monastery; 3k.50, Lindesnes lighthouse. VERT: 1k.50, Stavanger Cathedral; 1k.70, Rosenkrantz Tower, Bergen; 1k.75, Seamen's commemoration hall, Stavern; 1k.80, Torungen lighthouses, Arendal; 2k. Tofte royal estate, Dovre; 2k.25, Oscarshall (royal residence), Oslofjord.

224 Hamnoy, Lofoten Islands

225 Spruce

1977. Europa. Multicoloured.

795		1k.25 Type **224**	50	25
796		1k.80 Huldrefossen, Nordfjord (vert)	50	55

1977. Norwegian Trees.

797	**225**	1k. green	25	25
798	–	1k.25 brown	25	20
799	–	1k.80 black	35	45

DESIGNS: 1k.25, Fir; 1k.80, Birch.

See note below No. 433.

226 "Constitutionen" (paddle-steamer) at Arendal

1977. Norwegian Coastal Routes.

800	**226**	1k. brown	20	20
801	–	1k.25 red	30	25
802	–	1k.30 green	90	85
803	–	1k.80 blue	45	40

DESIGNS: 1k.25, "Vesteraalen" (coaster) off Bodo; 1k.30, "Kong Haakon" and "Dronningen" at Stavanger, 1893 (ferries); 1k.80, "Nordstjernen" and "Harald Jarl" (ferries).

227 "From the Herring Fishery" (after photo by S. A. Borretzen)

1977. Fishing Industry.

804	**227**	1k.25 brown on orange	20	20
805	–	1k.80 blue on blue	30	60

DESIGN: 1k.80, Saithe and fish hooks.

See note below No. 433.

228 "Saturday Evening" (H. Egedius)

1977. Norwegian Paintings. Multicoloured.

806		1k.25 Type **228**	30	20
807		1k.80 "Forest Lake in Lower Telemark" (A. Cappelen)	40	65

229 "David with the Bells"

230 "Peer and the Buck Reindeer" (after drawing by P. Krohg for "Peer Gynt")

1977. Miniatures from the Bible of Aslak Bolt. Mult.

808		80ore Type **229**	20	15
809		1k. "Singing Friars"	20	30
810		1k.25 "The Holy Virgin with the Child" (34 × 27 mm)	20	25

1978. 150th Birth Anniv of Henrik Ibsen (dramatist).

811	**230**	1k.25 black and stone	25	25
812	–	1k.80 multicoloured	35	50

DESIGN: 1k.80, Ibsen (after E. Werenskiold).

231 Heddal Stave Church, Telemark

232 Lenangstindene and Jaegervasstindene, Troms

1978. Europa.

813	**231**	1k.25 brown and orange	40	20
814	–	1k.80 green and blue	75	65

DESIGN: 1k.80, Borgund stave church, Sogn.

1978. Norwegian Scenery. Multicoloured.

815		1k. Type **232**	30	25
816		1k.25 Gaustatoppen, Telemark	30	25

233 King Olav in Sailing-boat

1978. 75th Birthday of King Olav V.

817	**233**	1k.25 brown	30	30
818	–	1k.80 violet	30	40

DESIGN—VERT: 1k.80, King Olav delivering royal speech at opening of Parliament.

234 Amundsen's Polar Flight Stamp of 1925

1978. "Norwex 80" International Stamp Exhibition (1st issue).

819	**234**	1k.25 green and grey	40	60
820		1k.25 blue and grey	40	60
821	–	1k.25 green and grey	40	60
822	–	1k.25 blue and grey	40	60
823	**234**	1k.25 purple and grey	40	60
824		1k.25 red and grey	40	60
825	–	1k.25 purple and grey	40	60
826	–	1k.25 blue and grey	40	60

DESIGNS: Nos. 821/2, 825/6, Annexation of Spitzbergen stamp of 1925.

On Nos. 819/26 each design incorporates a different value of the 1925 issues.

See also Nos. **MS**847 and **MS**862.

235 Willow Pipe Player

236 Wooden Doll, c. 1830

1978. Musical Instruments.

827	**235**	1k. green	20	20
828	–	1k.25 red	30	20
829	–	1k.80 blue	45	45
830	–	7k.50 grey	1·20	25
831	–	15k. brown	2·50	25

DESIGNS: 1k.25, Norwegian violin; 1k.80, Norwegian zither; 7k.50, Ram's horn; 15k. Jew's harp.

See note below No. 433.

1978. Christmas. Antique Toys from Norwegian Folk Museum. Multicoloured.

835		80ore Type **236**	20	20
836		1k. Toy town, 1896/7	20	30
837		1k.25 Wooden horse from Torpo, Hallingdal	20	15

237 Ski Jumping at Huseby, 1879

238 "Portrait of Girl" (M. Stoltenberg)

1979. Centenary of Skiing Competitions at Huseby and Holmenkollen.

838	**237**	1k. green	30	25
839	–	1k.25 red	30	25
840	–	1k.80 blue	25	55

DESIGNS: 1k.25, Crown Prince Olav ski jumping at Holmenkollen, 1922; 1k.80, Cross-country skiing at Holmenkollen, 1976.

1979. International Year of the Child. Mult.

841		1k.25 Type **238**	25	20
842		1k.80 "Portrait of Boy" (H. C. F. Hosenfelder)	35	60

239 Road to Briksdal Glacier

240 Falkberget (after Harald Dal)

1979. Norwegian Scenery. Multicoloured.

843		1k. Type **239**	30	25
844		1k.25 Skjernoysund, near Mandal	30	15

1979. Birth Centenary of Johan Falkberget (novelist).

845	**240**	1k.25 brown	30	20
846	–	1k.80 blue	40	60

DESIGN: 1k.80, "Ann-Magritt and the Hovi Bullock" (statue by Kristofer Leirdal).

241 Dornier Do-J Wal Flying Boat N-25

1979. "Norwex 80" International Stamp Exhibition, Oslo (2nd issue). Arctic Aviation. Sheet 113 × 91 mm containing T **241** and similar horiz designs, each black, yellow and ultramarine.

MS847	1k.25 Type **241** (Amundsen and Ellsworth, 1925); 2k. Airship N.1 *Norge* (Amundsen, Ellsworth and Nobile, 1926); 2k.80, Loening OA-2 amphibian *Live Eriksson* (Thor Solberg, 1935); 4k. Douglas DC-7C *Reider Viking* (first scheduled flight over North Pole, 1957) (sold at 15k.)	3·75	4·50

242 Steam Train on Kylling Bridge, Verma, Romsdal

243 Glacier Buttercup ("Ranunculus glacialis")

1979. Norwegian Engineering.

848	**242**	1k.25 black and brown	30	15
849	–	2k. black and blue	30	15
850	–	10k. brown and bistre	1·60	40

DESIGNS: 2k. Vessingsjo Dam, Nea, Sor-Trondelag; 10k. Statfjord A offshore oil drilling and production platform.

1979. Flowers. Multicoloured.

851		80ore Type **243**	25	15
852		1k. Alpine cinquefoil ("Potentilla crantzii")	20	25
853		1k.25 Purple saxifrage ("Saxifraga oppositifolia")	20	15

See also Nos. 867/8.

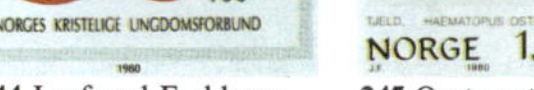

244 Leaf and Emblems

245 Oystercatcher Chick ("Haematopus ostralegus")

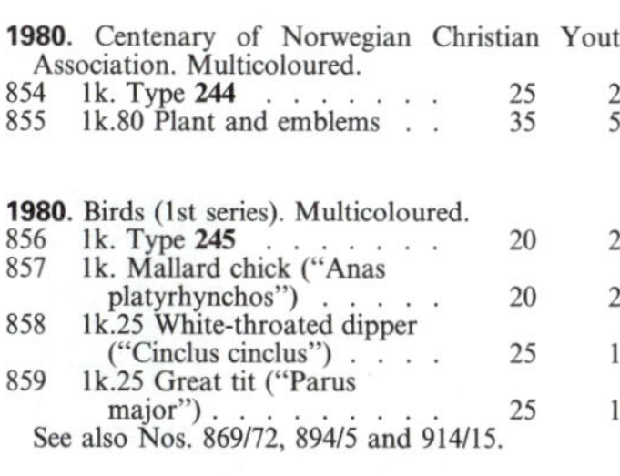

1980. Centenary of Norwegian Christian Youth Association. Multicoloured.
854 1k. Type **244** 25 25
855 1k.80 Plant and emblems . . 35 50

1980. Birds (1st series). Multicoloured.
856 1k. Type **245** 20 25
857 1k. Mallard chick ("Anas platyrhynchos") 20 25
858 1k.25 White-throated dipper ("Cinclus cinclus") 25 15
859 1k.25 Great tit ("Parus major") 25 15
See also Nos. 869/72, 894/5 and 914/15.

246 Telephone and Dish Aerial

1980. Centenary of Norwegian Telephone Service.
860 **246** 1k.25 brown, purple & bl 25 25
861 – 1k.80 multicoloured . . . 35 45
DESIGN: 1k.80, Erecting a telephone pole.

247 *Bergen* (paddle-steamer)

1980. "Norwex 80" International Stamp Exhibition, Oslo (3rd issue). Sheet 113×90 mm containing T **247** and similar horiz designs.
MS862 1k.25, red and black; 2k. yellow and black; 2k.80, yellow, green and black; 4k. dull blue and black (sold at 15k.) . . . . . 3·50 3·50
DESIGNS: 2k. Steam locomotive and carriages, 1900; 2k.80, Motor coach, 1940; 4k. Boeing 737 and Douglas DC-9 aircraft.

248 "Vulcan as an Armourer" (Hassel Jerverk after Bech)

1980. Nordic Countries' Postal Co-operation. Cast-iron Stove Ornaments.
863 **248** 1k.25 brown 25 10
864 – 1k.80 violet 35 55
DESIGN: 1k.80, "Hercules at a burning Altar" (Moss Jerverk after Henrich Bech).

249 "Jonsokbal" (Nikolai Astrup)

1980. Norwegian Paintings. Multicoloured.
865 1k.25 Type **249** 25 20
866 1k.80 "Seljefloyten" (Christian Skredsvig) . . . 40 50

1980. Flowers. As T **243**. Multicoloured.
867 80ore Rowan berries ("Sorbus aucparia") . . . 20 20
868 1k. Dog rose hips ("Rosa canina") 20 20

1981. Birds (2nd series). As T **245**. Multicoloured.
869 1k.30 Lesser white-fronted goose ("Anser erythropus") 25 25
870 1k.30 Peregrine falcon ("Falco peregrinus") . . . 25 25
871 1k.50 Atlantic puffin ("Fratercula arctica") . . . 30 25
872 1k.50 Black guillemot ("Cepphus grylle") 30 25

250 Cow

251 "The Mermaid" (painting by Kristen Aanstad on wooden dish from Hol)

1981. Centenary of Norwegian Milk Producers' National Association. Multicoloured.
873 1k.10 Type **250** 30 25
874 1k.50 Goat 30 15
See note below No. 433.

1981. Europa. Multicoloured.
875 1k.50 Type **251** 40 20
876 2k.20 "The Proposal" (painting by Ola Hansson on box from Nes) 60 55
See note below No. 433.

252 Weighing Anchor

1981. Sailing Ship Era.
877 **252** 1k.30 green 55 25
878 – 1k.50 red 45 25
879 – 2k.20 blue . . . . 1·00 60
DESIGNS—VERT: 1k.50, Climbing the rigging. HORIZ: 2k.20, "Christian Radich" (cadet ship).

253 "Skibladner" (paddle-steamer)

1981. Norwegian Lake Shipping.
880 **253** 1k.10 brown 45 20
881 – 1k.30 green 45 35
882 – 1k.50 red 45 20
883 – 2k.30 blue 90 45
DESIGNS: 1k.30, "Victoria" (ferry); 1k.50, "Faemund II" (ferry); 2k.30, "Storegut" (train ferry).

254 Handicapped People as Part of Community

1981. International Year of Disabled Persons.
884 **254** 1k.50 pink, red and blue 30 25
885 – 2k.20 blue, deep blue and red 45 50
DESIGN: 2k.20, Handicapped and non-handicapped people walking together.

255 "Interior in Blue" (Harriet Backer)

1981. Norwegian Paintings. Multicoloured.
886 1k.50 Type **255** 30 25
887 1k.70 "Peat Moor on Jaeren" (Kitty Lange Kielland) . . 45 50

256 Hajalmar Branting and Christian Lange

1981. Nobel Peace Prize Winners of 1921.
888 **256** 5k. black 90 25

257 "One of the Magi" (detail from Skjak tapestry, 1625)

258 Ski Sticks

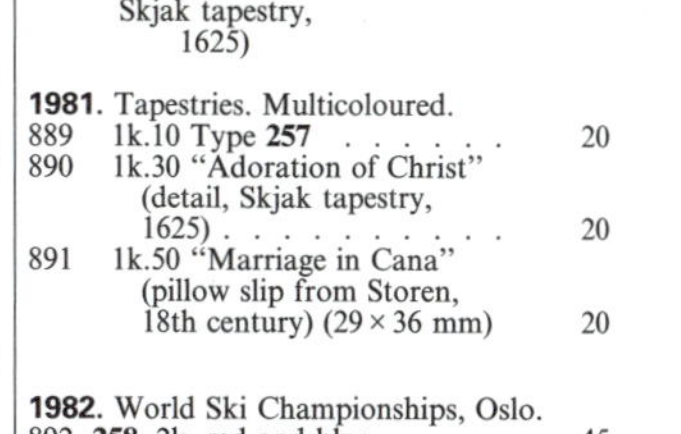

1981. Tapestries. Multicoloured.
889 1k.10 Type **257** 20 15
890 1k.30 "Adoration of Christ" (detail, Skjak tapestry, 1625) 20 35
891 1k.50 "Marriage in Cana" (pillow slip from Storen, 18th century) (29×36 mm) 20 15

1982. World Ski Championships, Oslo.
892 **258** 2k. red and blue 45 25
893 – 3k. blue and red 50 40
DESIGN: 3k. Skis.

1982. Birds (3rd series). As T **245**. Multicoloured.
894 2k. Bluethroat ("Luscinia svecica") 35 15
895 2k. European robin ("Erithacus rubecula") . . 35 15

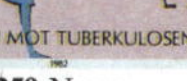

259 Nurse

260 King Haakon VII disembarking from "Heimdal" after Election, 1905

1982. Anti-tuberculosis Campaign. Mult.
896 2k. Type **259** 45 15
897 3k. Microscope 50 45
See note below No. 433.

1982. Europa.
898 **260** 2k. brown 95 25
899 – 3k. blue . . . . 1·10 50
DESIGN: 3k. Crown Prince Olav greeting King Haakon VII after liberation, 1945.

261 "Girls from Telemark" (Erik Werenskiold)

1982. Norwegian Paintings. Multicoloured.
900 1k.75 Type **261** 40 40
901 2k. "Tone Veli by Fence" (Henrik Sorenson) (vert) 40 25
See note below No. 433.

262 Consecration Ceremony, Nidaros Cathedral, Trondheim

1982. 25th Anniv of King Olav V's Reign.
902 **262** 3k. violet 50 55

263 "Bjornstjerne Bjornson on Balcony at Aulestad" (Erik Werenskiold)

1982. Writers' Birth Anniversaries. Multicoloured.
903 1k.75 Type **263** (150th anniv) 45 25
904 2k. "Sigrid Undset" (after A. C. Svarstad) (birth centenary) 45 25

264 Construction of Letter "A"

265 Fridtjof Nansen

1982. Centenary of Graphical Union of Norway.
905 **264** 2k. yellow, green and black 45 25
906 – 3k. multicoloured 50 45
DESIGN: 3k. Offset litho printing rollers.

1982. 1922 Nobel Peace Prize Winner.
907 **265** 3k. blue 50 40
See note below No. 433.

266 "Christmas Tradition" (Adolf Tidemand)

267 Buhund (farm dog)

1982. Christmas.
908 **266** 1k.75 multicoloured . . . 35 15

1983. Norwegian Dogs. Multicoloured.
909 2k. Type **267** 45 35
910 2k.50 Elkhound 45 15
911 3k.50 Lundehund (puffin hunter) 45 60
See note below No. 433.

268 Mountain Scenery

269 Edvard Grieg with Concerto in A minor

1983. Nordic Countries' Postal Co-operation. "Visit the North". Multicoloured.
912 2k.50 Type **268** 45 15
913 3k.50 Fjord scenery 60 55

1983. Birds (4th series). As T **245**. Mult.
914 2k.50 Barnacle goose ("Branta leucopsis") . . . 45 15
915 2k.50 Little auk ("Alle alle") 45 15

1983. Europa.
916 **269** 2k.50 red . . . . 1·00 25
917 – 3k.50 blue and green . . 1·00 75
DESIGN—VERT: 3k.50, Statue of Niels Henrik Abel (mathematician) by Gustav Vigeland.

270 Arrows forming Posthorn

1983. World Communications Year. Multicoloured.
918 2k.50 Type **270** 45 20
919 3k.50 Arrows circling globe 60 60

271 King Olav V and Royal Birch, Molde

1983. 80th Birthday of King Olav V.
920 **271** 5k. green . . . . 1·00 25

272 Lie

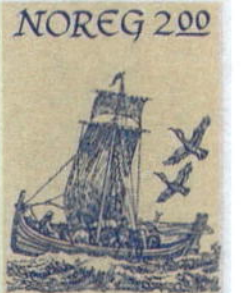

273 Northern Femboring

1983. 150th Birth Anniv of Jonas Lie (author).
921 **272** 2k.50 red 45 25

1983. North Norwegian Ships.
922 **273** 2k. blue and brown . . . 45 35
923 – 3k. brown and blue . . . 50 50
DESIGNS: 3k. Northern jekt.
See note below No. 433.

274 "The Sleigh Ride" (Axel Ender) **275** Post Office Counter

1983. Christmas. Multicoloured.
924 2k. Type **274** 45 25
925 2k.50 "The Guests are arriving" (Gustav Wendel) 45 15

1984. Postal Work. Multicoloured.
926 2k. Type **275** 35 25
927 2k.50 Postal sorting 45 25
928 3k.50 Postal delivery 60 50

276 Freshwater Fishing **277** Magnetic Meridians and Parallels

1984. Sport Fishing.
929 **276** 2k.50 red 30 10
930 – 3k. green 35 40
931 – 3k.50 blue 90 45
DESIGNS: 3k. Atlantic salmon fishing; 3k.50, Sea fishing.

1984. Birth Bicentenary of Christopher Hansteen (astronomer and geophysicist).
932 **277** 3k.50 blue 60 45
933 – 5k. red . . . . 1·00 40
DESIGN—VERT: 5k. Portrait of Hansteen by Johan Gorbitz.

278 Bridge **279** Vegetables, Fruit and Herbs

1984. Europa. 25th Anniv of European Post and Telecommunications Conference.
934 **278** 2k.50 multicoloured . . . 75 15
935 3k.50 multicoloured . . . 95 55

1984. Centenary of Norwegian Horticultural Society. Multicoloured.
936 2k. Type **279** 25 30
937 2k.50 Rose and garland of flowers 50 15

280 Honey Bees **281** Holberg (after J. M. Bernigeroth)

1984. Centenaries of Norwegian Beekeeping Society and Norwegian Poultry-breeding Society. Mult.
938 2k.50 Type **280** 45 15
939 2k.50 Leghorn cock 45 15
See note below No. 433.

1984. 300th Birth Anniv of Ludvig Holberg (writer).
940 **281** 2k.50 red 45 25

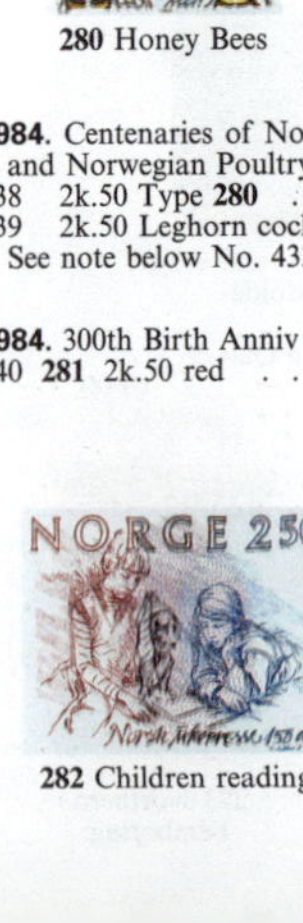

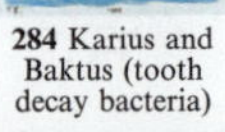

282 Children reading **284** Karius and Baktus (tooth decay bacteria)

283 Entering Parliamentary Chamber, 2 July 1884

1984. 150th Anniv of "Norsk Penning-Magazin" (1st weekly magazine in Norway).
941 **282** 2k.50 purple, blue and red 45 15
942 – 3k.50 orange and violet 60 45
DESIGN: 3k.50, 1st edition of "Norsk Penning-Magazin".

1984. Cent of Norwegian Parliament.
943 **283** 7k.50 brown . . . . . . 1·50 70

1984. Characters from Stories by Thorbjorn Egner. Multicoloured.
944 2k. Type **284** 60 20
945 2k. The tree shrew playing guitar 60 20
946 2k.50 Kasper, Jesper and Jonatan (Rovers) in Kardemomme Town . . . 65 15
947 2k.50 Chief Constable Bastian 65 15

285 Mount Sagbladet (Saw Blade)

1985. Antarctic Mountains. Multicoloured.
948 2k.50 Type **285** 50 10
949 3k.50 Mount Hoggestabben (Chopping Block) 65 70

286 Return of Crown Prince Olav, 1945

1985. 40th Anniv of Liberation.
950 **286** 3k.50 red and blue . . . 60 50

287 Kongsten Fort

1985. 300th Anniv of Kongsten Fort.
951 **287** 2k.50 multicoloured . . . 45 15

288 Bronze Cannon, 1596 **289** "Boy and Girl" (detail)

1985. Artillery Anniversaries. Multicoloured.
952 3k. Type **288** (300th anniv of Artillery) 50 50
953 4k. Cannon on sledge carriage, 1758 (bicentenary of Artillery Officers Training School) 70 40

1985. International Youth Year. Sculptures in Vigeland Park, Oslo. Multicoloured.
954 2k. Type **289** 35 25
955 3k.50 Bronze fountain (detail) 70 55
See note below No. 433.

290 Torgeir Augundsson (fiddler) **291** Workers at Glomfjord

1985. Europa. Music Year.
956 **290** 2k.50 red 75 20
957 – 3k.50 blue 90 50
DESIGN: 3k.50, Ole Bull (composer and violinist).

1985. Centenary of Electricity in Norway.
958 **291** 2k.50 red and scarlet . . 45 15
959 – 4k. blue and green . . . 70 35
DESIGN: 4k. Men working on overhead cable.

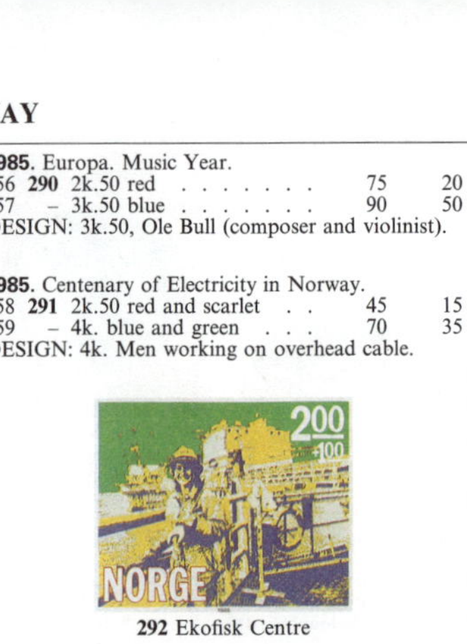

292 Ekofisk Centre

1985. Stamp Day. Norwegian Working Life (1st series). Offshore Oil Industry. Sheet 112×91 mm containing T **292** and similar horiz designs. Multicoloured.
MS960 2k.+1k. Type **292**; 2k.+1k. Drilling rig *Treasure Scout* and supply ship *Odin Viking*; 2k.+1k. Towing *Stratfjord C* platform to oil field, 1984; 2k.+1k. Drilling team on rig *Neptuno Nordraug* 3·25 5·00
See also Nos. **MS**989 and **MS**1012.

293 Carl Deichman on Book Cover **294** Wreath

1985. Bicentenary of Public Libraries.
961 **293** 2k.50 sepia and brown . . 50 15
962 – 10k. green . . . . 1·90 50
DESIGN—HORIZ: 10k. Library interior.

1985. Christmas. Multicoloured.
963 2k. Type **294** 60 25
964 2k.50 Northern bullfinches 60 15

295 "Berghavn" (dredger) **296** Sun

1985. 250th Anniv of Port Authorities and Bicentenary of Hydrography in Norway.
965 **295** 2k.50 purple, orange & bl 55 5·00
966 – 5k. blue, green and brown 75 45
DESIGN: 5k. Sextant and detail of chart No. 1 of Lt. F.C. Grove showing Trondheim sealane, 1791.

1986.
967 **296** 2k.10 orange and brown 45 15
968 – 2k.30 green and blue . . 45 15
970 – 2k.70 pink and red . . . 60 20
971 – 4k. blue and green . . . 85 15
DESIGNS: 2k.30, Atlantic cod and herring; 2k.70, Flowers; 4k. Star ornaments.

297 Marksman in Prone Position

1986. World Biathlon Championships. Mult.
977 2k.50 Type **297** 70 10
978 3k.50 Marksman standing to take aim 55 55

298 Industry and Countryside **299** Stone Cutter

1986. Europa. Multicoloured.
979 2k.50 Type **298** 60 20
980 3k.50 Dead and living forest, mountains and butterflies 1·00 70

1986. Centenary of Norwegian Craftsmen's Federation.
981 **299** 2k.50 lake and red . . . 45 15
982 – 7k. blue and red . . . . 1·10 60
DESIGN: 7k. Carpenter.

300 Moss

1986. Nordic Countries' Postal Co-operation. Twinned Towns. Multicoloured.
983 2k.50 Type **300** 50 15
984 4k. Alesund 60 40
See note below No. 433.

301 Hans Polson Egede (missionary) and Map **303** "Olav Kyrre founds Diocese in Nidaros"

302 Timber being debarked and cut

1986. Birth Anniversaries.
985 **301** 2k.10 brown and red . . 45 50
986 – 2k.50 red, green and blue 50 15
987 – 3k. brown and red . . . 50 40
988 – 4k. purple and lilac . . . 70 40
DESIGNS: 2k.10, Type **301** (300th anniv); 2k.50, Herman Wildenvey (poet) and poem carved in wall at Stavern (centenary); 3k. Tore Ojasaeter (poet) and old cupboard from Skjak (centenary); 4k. Engebret Soot (engineer) and lock gates, Orje (centenary).
See note below No. 433.

1986. Stamp Day. Norwegian Working Life (2nd series). Paper Industry. Sheet 113×91 mm containing T **302** and similar horiz designs. Multicoloured.
MS989 2k.50+1k. Type **302**; 2k.50+1k. Boiling plant; 2k.50+1k. Paper factory; 2k.50+1k. Paper being dried and rolled into bales . . . . 4·50 5·25

1986. Christmas. Stained Glass Windows by Gabriel Kielland in Nidaros Cathedral, Trondheim. Multicoloured.
990 2k.10 Type **303** 50 20
991 2k.50 "The King and the Peasant at Sul" 50 15

304 Doves **305** Numeral

1986. International Peace Year.
992 **304** 15k. red, blue and green 3·25 60

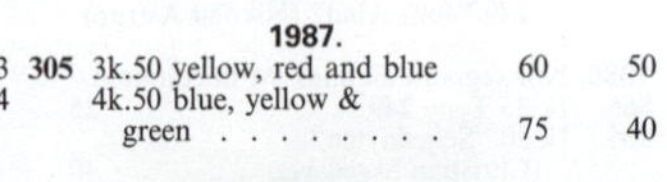

1987.
993 **305** 3k.50 yellow, red and blue 60 50
994 4k.50 blue, yellow & green 75 40

306 Wooden Building

1987. Europa. Multicoloured.
1000 2k.70 Type **306** 75 15
1001 4k.50 Building of glass and stone . . . . 1·30 40

307 The Final Vote

309 Funnel-shaped Chanterelle ("Cantharellus tubaeformis")

308 Rehabilitation Centre, Mogadishu

1987. 150th Anniv of Laws on Local Councils (granting local autonomy).
1002 **307** 12k. green . . . . 2·40 50

1987. Norwegian Red Cross in Somalia. Sheet 113×92 mm.
MS1003 **308** 4k.50 multicoloured 90 1·00

1987. Fungi (1st series). Multicoloured.
1004 2k.70 Type **309** 45 15
1005 2k.70 The gypsy ("Rozites caperata") 45 15
See also Nos. 1040/1 and 1052/3.

310 Bjornstad Farm from Vaga

1987. Centenary of Sandvig Collections, Maihaugen.
1006 **310** 2k.70 sepia and brown 50 15
1007 – 3k.50 purple and blue . . 60 50
DESIGN: 3k.50, "Horse and Rider" (wooden carving, Christen Erlandsen Listad).

311 Valevag Churchyard

1987. Birth Centenary of Fartein Valen (composer).
1008 **311** 2k.30 blue and green . . 45 40
1009 – 4k.50 brown 90 25
DESIGN—VERT: 4k.50, Fartein Valen.
See note below No. 433.

312 "Storm at Sea" (Christian Krohg)

1987. Paintings. Multicoloured.
1010 2k.70 Type **312** 50 15
1011 5k. "The Farm" (Gerhard Munthe) . . . . 1·00 40

313 Eggs and Alevin

1987. Stamp Day. Norwegian Working Life (3rd series). Atlantic Salmon Farming. Sheet 113×91 mm containing T **313** and similar horiz designs. Multicoloured.
MS1012 2k.30+50ore Type **313**; 2k.70+50ore Hatching tanks and parr; 3k.50+50ore Marine stage; 4k.50+50ore Harvested salmon 4·25 4·75

314 Cat with Children making Decorations

1987. Christmas. Multicoloured.
1013 2k.30 Type **314** 50 40
1014 2k.70 Dog with children making gingersnaps . . . 50 15

315 Dales Pony **316** Western Capercaillie

1987. Native Ponies.
1015 **315** 2k.30 deep brown, green and brown 45 50
1016 – 2k.70 buff, brown & blue 50 20
1017 – 4k.50 brown, red and blue 70 40
DESIGNS: 2k.70, Fjord pony; 4k.50, Nordland pony.
See note below No. 433.

1988. Wildlife.
1018 – 2k.60 deep brown, brown and green . . . 50 20
1019 **316** 2k.90 black, brn & grn 50 15
1020 – 3k. brown, grey and green 50 15
1021 – 3k.20 ultramarine, green and blue 50 15
1022 – 3k.80 brown, blue & blk 60 15
1023 – 4k. brown, red and green 70 15
1024 – 4k.50 brown, green & bl 75 25
1025 – 5k.50 brown, grey & grn 95 25
1026 – 6k.40 brown, blk & grn 1·10 35
DESIGNS: 2k.60, Fox; 3k. Stoat; 3k.20, Mute swan; 3k.80, Reindeer; 4k. Eurasian red squirrel; 4k.50, Beaver; 5k.50, Lynx; 6k.40, Tengmalm's owl.

317 Band

1988. Centenary of Salvation Army in Norway. Multicoloured.
1035 2k.90 Type **317** 50 15
1036 4k.80 Othilie Tonning (early social worker) and Army nurse 85 55

318 Building Fortress

1988. Military Anniversaries.
1037 **318** 2k.50 green 45 25
1038 – 2k.90 brown 50 15
1039 – 4k.60 blue 75 45
DESIGNS: 2k.50, Type **318** (300th anniv of Defence Construction Service); 2k.90, Corps members in action (centenary of Army Signals corps); 4k.60, Making pontoon bridge (centenary of Engineer Corps).

1988. Fungi (2nd series). As T **309**. Mult.
1040 2k.90 Wood blewits ("Lepista nuda") 50 15
1041 2k.90 "Lactarius deterrimus" 50 15

319 Globe

320 King Olav V

1988. European Campaign for Interdependence and Solidarity of North and South.
1042 **319** 25k. multicoloured . . . 5·25 75

1988. 85th Birthday of King Olav V. Multicoloured.
1043 2k.90 Type **320** 50 15
MS1044 121×91 mm. 2k.90 King Olav arriving as baby; 2k.90 Type **320**; 2k.90 King Olav at Holmenkollen . . . . 2·10 2·40

321 "Prinds Gustav" (paddle-steamer)

322 King Christian IV

1988. Europa. Transport and Communications.
1045 **321** 2k.90 black, red and blue 85 15
1046 – 3k.80 blue, red & yellow 1·30 75
DESIGN: 3k.80, Heroybrua Bridge.

1988. 400th Anniv of Christian IV's Accession to Danish and Norwegian Thrones.
1047 **322** 2k.50 black, stone & vio 60 20
1048 – 10k. multicoloured . . . 1·75 40
DESIGN: 10k. 1628 silver coin and extract from decree on mining in Norway.

323 Handball

1988. Stamp Day. Sport. Sheet 113×91 mm containing T **323** and similar horiz designs. Multicoloured.
MS1049 2k.90 Type **323**; 2k.90 Football; 2k.90 Basketball; 2k.90 Volleyball (sold at 15k.) . . . 3·75 4·00

324 Ludvig with Ski Stick

325 Start and Finish of Race

1988. Christmas. Multicoloured.
1050 2k.90 Type **324** 55 15
1051 2k.90 Ludvig reading letter 55 15

1989. Fungi (3rd series). As T **309**. Multicoloured.
1052 3k. Chanterelle ("Cantharellus cibarius") 50 15
1053 3k. Butter mushroom ("Suillus luteus") 50 15

1989. World Cross-country Championship, Stavanger.
1054 **325** 5k. multicoloured . . . 90 35

326 Vardo **327** Setesdal Woman

1989. Town Bicentenaries.
1055 **326** 3k. blue, red & light blue 50 15
1056 – 4k. purple, blue & orange 60 50
DESIGN: 4k. Hammerfest.

1989. Nordic Countries' Postal Co-operation. Traditional Costumes. Multicoloured.
1057 3k. Type **327** 50 25
1058 4k. Kautokeino man 85 55

328 Children making Snowman

329 Rooster and Cover of 1804 First Reader

1989. Europa. Children's Games. Multicoloured.
1059 3k.70 Type **328** . . . . . 1·00 60
1060 5k. Cat's cradle . . . . . . 1·50 70
See note below No. 433.

1989. 250th Anniv of Primary Schools.
1061 **329** 2k.60 multicoloured . . 50 45
1062 – 3k. brown 50 15
DESIGN: 3k. Pocket calculator and child writing.

330 "Impressions of the Countryside" (detail)

1989. Stamp Day. Sheet 107×85 mm. containing T **330** and similar horiz designs, forming a composite design of the painting by Jakob Weidemann.
MS1063 3k.×4 multicoloured (sold at 15k.) . . . . 3·75 5·25

331 Bjorg Eva Jensen (300m. speed skating 1980)

1989. Winter Olympic Games, Lillehammer (1994) (1st issue). Norwegian Gold Medallists. Sheet 113×91 mm containing T **331** and similar horiz designs. Multicoloured.
MS1064 4k. Type **331**; 4k. Eirik Kvalfoss (biathlon, 1984); 4k. Tom Sandberg (combined cross-country and ski-jumping, 1984); 4k. Women's team (10km cross-country relay, 1984) (sold at 20k.) 4·50 6·00
See also Nos. **MS**1083, **MS**1097, **MS**1143, 1150/1, **MS**1157, 1169/70 and 1175/80.

332 Arnulf Overland (poet, centenary) **333** Star Decoration

1989. Writers' Birth Anniversaries.
1065 **332** 3k. red and blue 50 15
1066 – 25k. blue, orange & green . . . . 4·50 75
DESIGN: 25k. Hanna Winsnes (pseudonym Hugo Schwartz) (bicentenary).

1989. Christmas. Tree Decorations. Mult.
1067 3k. Type **333** 50 15
1068 3k. Bauble 50 15

334 Larvik Manor

335 Emblem

1989. Manor Houses.
1069 **334** 3k. brown 50 15
1070 – 3k. green 50 15
DESIGN: No. 1070, Rosendal Barony.

1990. Winter Cities Events, Tromso.
1071 **335** 5k. multicoloured . . . 90 35

336 Common Spotted Orchid ("Dactylorhiza fuchsii")

337 Merchant Navy, Airforce, Home Guard, "Moses" (coastal gun) and Haakon VII's Monogram

1990. Orchids (1st series). Multicoloured.
1072 3k.20 Type **336** 50 15
1073 3k.20 Dark red helleborine ("Epipactis atrorubens") 50 15
See also Nos. 1141/2.

1990. 50th Anniv of Norway's Entry into Second World War. Multicoloured.
1074 3k.20 Type **337** 50 15
1075 4k. Second Battle of Narvik, 1940 . . . . 70 50

338 Penny Black

1990. 150th Anniv of the Penny Black. Sheet 113×91 mm containing T **338** and similar vert design.
MS1076 5k. Type **338**; 5k. First Norwegian stamp (sold at 15k.) 3·50 3·75

339 Trondheim Post Office

340 "Tordenskiold" (from print by J. W. Tegner after Balthazar Denner)

1990. Europa. Post Office Buildings. Mult.
1077 3k.20 Type **339** 85 25
1078 4k. Longyearbyen Post Office . . . . 1·30 50

1990. 300th Birth Anniv of Admiral Tordenskiold (Peter Wessel). Multicoloured.
1079 3k.20 Type **340** 50 15
1080 5k. Tordenskiold's coat-of-arms 75 40

341 Svendsen

343 "Children and Snowman" (Ragni Engstrom Nilsen)

342 Thoreleif Haug (cross-country skiing, 1924)

1990. 150th Birth Anniv of Johan Svendsen (composer and conductor).
1081 **341** 2k.70 black and red . . 50 40
1082 – 15k. brown and yellow 2·50 45
DESIGN: 15k. Svendsen Monument (Stinius Fredriksen), Oslo.

1990. Winter Olympic Games, Lillehammer (1994) (2nd issue). Norwegian Gold Medallists. Sheet 113×91 mm containing T **342** and similar horiz designs. Multicoloured.
MS1083 4k. Type **342**; 4k. Sonja Henie (figure skating, 1928, 1932, 1936); 4k. Ivar Ballangrud (speed skating, 1928, 1936); 4k. Hjalmar Andersen (speed skating, 1952) (sold at 20k.) . . . . 5·00 6·00

1990. Christmas. Children's Prize-winning Drawings. Multicoloured.
1084 3k.20 Type **343** 55 15
1085 3k.20 "Christmas Church" (Jorgen Ingier) 55 15

344 Nobel Medal and Soderblom

1990. 60th Anniv of Award of Nobel Peace Prize to Nathan Soderblom, Archbishop of Uppsala.
1086 **344** 30k. brown, blue and red 5·75 70

345 Plan and Elevation of Container Ship and Propeller

1991. Centenaries of Federation of Engineering Industries (1989) and Union of Iron and Metal Workers.
1087 **345** 5k. multicoloured . . . 85 60

346 Satellite transmitting to Tromso

1991. Europa. Europe in Space. Mult.
1088 3k.20 Type **346** 85 25
1089 4k. Rocket leaving Andoya rocket range . . . . . . 1·20 40
See note below No. 433.

347 Christiansholm Fortress (late 17th- century)

348 Fountain, Vigeland Park, Oslo

1991. 350th Anniv of Kristiansand. Each black, blue and red.
1090 3k.20 Type **347** 60 25
1091 5k.50 Present day view of Christiansholm Fortress 95 30

1991. Nordic Countries' Postal Co-operation. Tourism. Multicoloured.
1092 3k.20 Type **348** 60 15
1093 4k. Globe, North Cape Plateau 95 65

349 "Skomvaer III" (lifeboat)

1991. Centenary of Norwegian Society for Sea Rescue.
1094 **349** 3k.20 brown, black & grn 50 25
1095 – 27k. brown, grey & purple . . . . 5·50 85
DESIGN—VERT: 27k. "Colin Archer" (first lifeboat).

350 Engraving on Steel

1991. Stamp Day. Stamp Engraving. Sheet 113×91 mm containing T **350** and similar horiz designs.
MS1096 2k.70 Type **350**; 3k.20 Engraver using magnifying glass; 4k. Engraver's hands seen through magnifying glass; 5k. Positive impression of engraving and burin (sold at 20k.) . . . . 4·00 4·75

351 Birger Ruud (ski jumping, 1932, 1936; downhill, 1936)

1991. Winter Olympic Games, Lillehammer (1994) (3rd issue). Norwegian Gold Medallists. Sheet 113×91 mm containing T **351** and similar horiz designs. Multicoloured.
MS1097 4k. Type **351**; 4k. Johann Grottumsbraten (cross-country skiing, 1928, 1932); 4k. Knut Johannesen (speed skaing, 1960, 1964); 4k. Magnar Solberg (biathlon, 1960, 1968, 1972) (sold at 20k.) . . . . 4·75 5·75

352 Posthorn

1991.
1098 **352** 1k. black and orange . . 30 15
1099 2k. red and green . . . 45 25
1100 3k. green and blue . . . 50 15
1101 4k. red and orange . . . 70 15
1102 5k. blue and green . . . 90 25
1103 6k. red and green . . . 1·00 25
1104 7k. blue and brown . . . 1·30 25
1105 8k. green and purple . . 1·40 40
1106 9k. brown and blue . . . . 1·60 35

353 Guisers with Goat Head

1991. Christmas. Guising. Multicoloured.
1120 3k.20 Type **353** 55 25
1121 3k.20 Guisers with lantern 55 25

354 Queen Sonja

355 King Harald

356 King Harald

1992.
1122 **354** 2k.80 lake, purple & red 50 25
1123 3k. green, deep green and turquoise 50 15
1124 **355** 3k.30 blue, ultramarine and light blue 60 15
1125 3k.50 black and grey . . 60 15
1127 4k.50 deep red and red 75 50
1128 5k.50 brown, sepia & blk 95 25
1129 5k.60 orange, red and vermilion . . . . . . 1·00 25
1131 6k.50 emerald, green and turquoise . . . . . . 1·10 55
1132 6k.60 maroon, purple and brown . . . . . 1·10 25
1133 7k.50 violet, lilac and purple 50 65
1134 8k.50 chestnut, deep brown and brown . . 60 60
1135 **356** 10k. green . . . . 1·75 25
1438 20k. violet . . . . 3·25 1·30
1138 30k. blue . . . . 4·75 50
1139 50k. green . . . . 9·50 1·30

1992. Orchids (2nd series). As T **336**. Mult.
1141 3k.30 Lady's slipper orchid ("Cypripedium calceolus") 60 25
1142 3k.30 Fly orchid ("Ophrys insectifera") 60 25

357 Hallgeir Brenden (cross-country skiing, 1952, 1956)

1992. Winter Olympic Games, Lillehammer (4th issue). Norwegian Gold Medallists. Sheet 113×91 mm containing T **357** and similar horiz designs. Multicoloured.
MS1143 4k. Type **357**; 4k. Arnfinn Bergmann (ski jumping, 1952); 4k. Stein Eriksen (super slalom, 1952); 4k. Simon Slattvik (combined, 1952) (sold at 20k.) . . . . . 4·25 5·50

358 "Restaurationen" (emigrant sloop)

1992. Europa. 500th Anniv of Discovery of America by Columbus. Transatlantic Ships. Multicoloured.
1144 3k.30 Type **358** 95 25
1145 4k.20 "Stavangerfjord" (liner) and American skyline . . . . 1·40 45
See note below No. 433.

359 Norwegian Pavilion, Rainbow and Ship

360 Molde

1992. "Expo '92" World's Fair, Seville. Mult.
1146 3k.30 Type **359** 60 25
1147 5k.20 Mountains, rainbow, fish and oil rig 95 45

1992. 250th Anniversaries of Molde and Kristiansund.
1148 **360** 3k.30 blue, green & brn 50 25
1149 – 3k.30 blue, brown & lt bl 60 25
DESIGN: No. 1149, Kristiansund.

361 Banners and Lillehammer Buildings

363 Gnomes below Pillar Box

362 Flask with Etched Figures (Serre Petersen)

1992. Winter Olympic Games, Lillehammer (1994) (5th issue). Multicoloured.
1150 3k.30 Type **361** 60 25
1151 4k.20 Flags 70 50

1992. Stamp Day. Sheet 113×91 mm containing T **362** and similar horiz designs. Multicoloured.
MS1152 2k.80 Type **362**; 3k.30 Monogrammed carafe; 4k.20 Cut-glass salad bowl; 5k.20 Engraved goblet (Heinrich Gottlieb Kohler) (sold at 20k.) . . . . 5·00 4·00

1992. Christmas. Christmas card designs by Otto Moe. Multicoloured.
1153 3k.30 Type **363** 55 25
1154 3k.30 Gnome posting letter 55 25

364 Orange-tip ("Anthocaris cardamines")

366 Grieg

365 Finn Chr. Jagge (slalom)

1993. Butterflies (1st series). Multicoloured.
1155 3k.50 Type **364** 60 25
1156 3k.50 Small tortoiseshell ("Aglais urticae") 60 25
See also Nos. 1173/4.

1993. Winter Olympic Games, Lillehammer (1994) (6th issue). Norwegian Gold Medallists at 1992 Games. Sheet 113×91 mm containing T **365** and similar horiz designs. Multicoloured.
MS1157 4k.50 Type **365**; 4k.50 Bjorn Daehlie (cross-country skiing); 4k.50 Geir Karlstad (speed skating); 4k.50 Vegard Ulvang (cross-country skiing) . . . . 4·25 6·00

1993. 150th Birth Anniv of Edvard Grieg (composer). Multicoloured.
1158 3k.50 Type **366** 60 25
1159 5k.50 "Spring" 95 40

367 Two-man Kayak on Lake

368 Richard With (founder) and "Vesteraalen"

1993. Nordic Countries' Postal Co-operation. Tourist Activities. Multicoloured.
1160 4k. Type **367** 70 25
1161 4k.50 White-water rafting 90 40

1993. Centenary of Express Coaster Service.
1162 **368** 3k.50 blue, violet and red 60 25
1163 – 4k.50 multicoloured . . 90 45
DESIGN: 4k.50, "Kong Harald".

369 Handball

370 Johann Castberg (politician)

1993. Sports Events. Multicoloured.
1164 3k.50 Type **369** (Women's World Championship, Norway) 60 25
1165 5k.50 Cycling (World Championships, Oslo and Hamar) 95 40

1993. Centenary of Workforce Protection Legislation.
1166 **370** 3k.50 brown and blue . . 60 25
1167 – 12k. blue and brown . . 2·25 55
DESIGN: 12k. Betzy Kjelsberg (first woman factory inspector).

371 Deail of Altarpiece (Jakob Klukstad), Lesja Church

1993. Stamp Day. Wood Carvings of Acanthus Leaves. Sheet 113×91 mm containing T **371** and similar horiz designs. Multicoloured.
MS1168 3k. Type **371**; 3k.50 Detail of dresser (Ola Teigeroen); 4k.50 Detail of Fliksaker chest (Jens Strammerud); 5k.50 Detail of pulpit, Our Saviour's Church, Oslo (sold at 21k.) . . . . . . 4·75 4·75

372 Torch Bearer on Skis

373 Store Mangen Chapel

1993. Winter Olympic Games, Lillehammer (1994) (7th issue). Morgedal–Lillehammer Torch Relay. Multicoloured.
1169 3k.50 Type **372** 60 25
1170 3k.50 Lillehammer 60 25

Nos. 1169/70 were issued together, se-tenant, forming a composite design.

1993. Christmas. Multicoloured.
1171 3k.50 Type **373** 60 25
1172 3k.50 Stamnes church, Sandnessjoen 60 25

1994. Butterflies (2nd series). As T **364**. Mult.
1173 3k.50 Northern clouded yellow ("Colias hecla") 60 25
1174 3k.50 Freya's fritillary ("Clossiana freija") . . . 60 25

374 Flags

375 Cross-country Skiing

1994. Winter Olympic Games, Lillehammer (8th issue). Multicoloured.
1175 3k.50 Type **374** 80 30
1176 3k.50 Flags (different) . . . 80 30
1177 3k.50 Lillehammer (church and rings 80 30
1178 3k.50 Lillehammer (ski jump) and rings 80 30
1179 4k.50 Flags of European countries 75 50
1180 5k.50 Flags of non-European countries . . . 95 40
Nos. 1175/8 were issued together, se-tenant, forming a composite design.

1994. Paralympic Games, Lillehammer. Mult.
1181 4k.50 Type **375** . . . . . 1·10 50
1182 5k.50 Downhill skiing . . . 1·00 45

376 King Christian VII's Signature and Seal

1994. Bicentenary of Tromso.
1183 **376** 3k.50 red, bistre & brn 60 25
1184 – 4k.50 blue, yellow and light blue 75 55
DESIGN: 4k.50, Tromsdalen church.

377 Mount Floy Incline Railway Cars, Bergen

1994. Tourism. Multicoloured.
1185 4k. Type **377** 70 40
1186 4k.50 "Svolvaer Goat" (rock formation), Lofoten . . . 85 55
1187 5k.50 Beacon, World's End, Tjome 95 35

378 Osterdal Farm Buildings

1994. Cent of Norwegian Folk Museum, Bygdoy.
1188 **378** 3k. multicoloured . . . 50 40
1189 – 3k.50 blue, yellow and purple 60 25
DESIGN: 3k.50, Horse-drawn sleigh, 1750 (Torsten Hoff).

379 Technological Symbols and Formula ("Glass Flasks")

1994. EUREKA (European technology co-operation organization) Conference of Ministers, Lillehammer. Multicoloured.
1190 4k. Type **379** 60 45
1191 4k.50 Technological symbols ("Electronic Chips") . . . 85 45

380 Electric Tram and Street Plan of Oslo, 1894

382 Sledge

381 Engraved Brooch

1994. Centenary of Electric Trams. Multicoloured.
1192 3k.50 Type **380** 60 25
1193 12k. Articulated tram and Oslo route map . . . . . 3·50 85

1994. Stamp Day. Jewellery. Sheet 113×91 mm containing T **381** and similar horiz designs. Multicoloured.
MS1194 3k. Type **381**; 3k.50 Silver and gem studded brooch; 4k.50 "Rings" brooch; 5k.50 Brooch with medallions and central stone (sold at 21k.) . . . . 4·75 3·35

1994. Christmas.
1195 **382** 3k.50 red and black . . 60 25
1196 – 3k.50 ultramarine, blue and black 60 25
DESIGN: No. 1196, Kick-sledge.

383 Cowberry ("Vaccinium vitis-idaea")

384 Swan Pharmacy, Bergen

1995. Wild Berries (1st Series). Multicoloured.
1197 3k.50 Type **383** 60 25
1198 3k.50 Bilberry ("Vaccinium myrtillus") 60 25
See also Nos. 1224/5.

1995. 400th Anniv of Norwegian Pharmacies. Multicoloured.
1199 3k.50 Type **384** 60 25
1200 25k. Scales, pestle and mortar and ingredients . . 5·25 1·90

385 German Commander saluting Terje Rollem (Home Guard commander)

1995. 50th Anniv of Liberation of Norway.
1201 **385** 3k.50 silver, green and black 60 25
1202 – 4k.50 silver, blue and black 90 70
1203 – 5k.50 silver, red and black 95 40
DESIGNS: 4k.50, King Haakon VII and family returning to Norway; 5k.50, Children waving Norwegian flags.

386 Old Moster Church

387 Skudeneshavn

1995. Millenary of Christianity in Norway. Multicoloured.
1204 3k.50 Type **386** 60 25
1205 15k. Slettebakken Church, Bergen . . . . 3·00 1·20

1995. Nordic Countries' Postal Co-operation. Tourism. Multicoloured.
1206 4k. Type **387** 70 55
1207 4k.50 Hole in the Hat (coastal rock formation) 85 55

388 Flagstad as Isolde

389 Disputants in Conflict

1995. Birth Centenary of Kirsten Flagstad (opera singer). Multicoloured.
1208 3k.50 Type **388** 60 25
1209 5k.50 Flagstad in scene from "Lohengrin" (Wagner) . . 95 40

1995. Bicentenary of Conciliation Boards. Multicoloured.
1210 7k. Type **389** . . . . . . 1·25 70
1211 12k. Disputants in conciliation with mediator 60 85

390 Letter and Vice-regent Hannibal Sehested (founder)

1995. 350th Anniv (1997) of Norwegian Postal Service (1st issue). Multicoloured.
1212 3k.50 Type **390** (letter post, 1647) 80 55
1213 3k.50 Wax seal (registered post, 1745) 80 55
1214 3k.50 Postmarks (1845) . . 80 55
1215 3k.50 Banknotes, coins and money orders (transfer of funds, 1883) 80 55
1216 3k.50 Editions of "Norska Intelligenz-Sedler" and "Arkiv" (newspapers and magazines, 1660) 80 55
1217 3k.50 Address label, cancellations and "Constitutionen" (paddle-steamer) (parcel post, 1827) 80 55
1218 3k.50 Stamps (1855) 80 55
1219 3k.50 Savings book (Post Office Savings Bank, 1950) 80 55
The dates are those of the introduction of the various services.
See also Nos. 1237/44 and 1283/90.

391 Trygve Lie (first Secretary-General) and Emblem

392 Woolly Hat

1995. 50th Anniv of U.N.O. Multicoloured.
1220 3k.50 Type **391** 60 25
1221 5k.50 Relief worker, water pump and emblem . . . 95 40

1995. Christmas. Multicoloured.
1222 3k.50 Type **392** 60 25
1223 3k.50 Mitten 65 25

1996. Wild Berries (2nd series). As T **383**. Multicoloured.
1224 3k.50 Wild strawberries ("Fragaria vesca") 60 25
1225 3k.50 Cloudberries ("Rubus chamaemorus") 60 25

393 Advent Bay

394 Cross-country Skier (Hakon Paulsen)

1996. Svalbard Islands. Multicoloured.
1226 10k. Type **393** . . . . . . 1·90 70
1227 20k. Polar bear . . . . . . 4·25 1·40

1996. Centenary of Modern Olympic Games. Children's Drawings. Multicoloured.
1228 3k.50 Type **394** 60 25
1229 5k.50 Athlete (Emil Tanem) 95 40

395 Besseggen **396** Steam Train, Urskog-Holand Line

1996. Tourism. UNESCO World Heritage Sites. Multicoloured.
1230 4k. Type **395** 70 50
1231 4k.50 Stave church, Urnes 75 50
1232 5k.50 Rock carvings, Alta 95 40
See also Nos. 1291/3.

1996. Railway Centenaries. Multicoloured.
1233 3k. Type **396** 50 35
1234 4k.50 Steam train, Setesdal line 90 60

397 Location Map and Height Indicator

1996. Natural Gas Production at Troll, near Bergen. Multicoloured.
1235 3k.50 Type **397** 60 30
1236 25k. Planned route map of pipelines to Europe for next 200 years . . . . . 4·75 1·90

398 Postal Courier crossing Mountains

1996. 350th Anniv (1997) of Postal Service (2nd issue). Multicoloured.
1237 3k.50 Type **398** 75 65
1238 3k.50 "Framnaes" (fjord steamer) 75 65
1239 3k.50 Postal truck in Oslo 75 65
1240 3k.50 Taking mail on board "Ternen" (seaplane) on Jonsvatn Lake, Trondheim 75 65
1241 3k.50 Loading mail train at East Station, Oslo 75 65
1242 3k.50 Rural postman at Mago farm, Nittedal . . . 75 65
1243 3k.50 Serving customer, Elverum post office . . . 75 65
1244 3k.50 Computer, letters and globe 75 65

399 Leif Juster, Sean Connery, Liv Ullmann and Olsen Gang

1996. Centenary of Motion Pictures. Multicoloured.
1245 3k.50 Type **399** 60 25
1246 5k.50 Wenche Foss, Jack Fjeldstad, Marilyn Monroe, blood and gun 95 40
1247 7k. Charlie Chaplin in "Modern Times", Ottar Gladvedt, Laurel and Hardy and Marlene Dietrich . . . . 1·25 65

400 Left Detail of Embroidery **401** Skram

1996. Christmas. Embroidery Details from Telemark Folk Costume. Multicoloured.
1248 3k.50 Type **400** 60 25
1249 3k.50 Right detail 60 25
Nos. 1248/9 were issued together, se-tenant, forming a composite design.

1996. 150th Birth Anniv of Amalie Skram (writer).
1250 **401** 3k.50 red 60 40
1251 – 15k. violet and red . . . 3·50 1·20

DESIGN: 15k. Scene from dramatisation of "People of Hellemyr".

402 Posthorn **403** Coltsfoot

1997. Multicoloured, colour of oval given.
1252 **402** 10ore red 10 15
1253 20ore blue 10 15
1254 30ore orange 10 15
1255 40ore black 10 20
1256 50ore green 10 20

1997. Flowers. Multicoloured.
1259 3k.20 Red clover 50 25
1260 3k.40 Marsh marigold . . 50 20
1261 3k.60 Red campion 65 25
1262 3k.70 Type **403** 65 20
1263 3k.80 Wild pansy 70 30
1264 4k. Wood anemone . . . 70 25
1265 4k.30 Lily of the valley . . 70 35
1266 4k.50 White clover 75 25
1267 5k. Harebell 75 25
1268a 5k.40 Oeder's lousewort . . 70 25
1269 5k.50 Hepatica 95 45
1270 6k. Ox-eye daisy 70 40
1271 7k. Yellow wood violet . . 75 60
1272 7k.50 Pale pasque flower 95 35
1273a 8k. White water-lily . . . 1·50 40
1274 13k. Purple saxifrage . . . 2·20 60
1275a 14k. Globe flower . . . . 2·50 80
1276b 25k. Melancholy thistle . . 2·20 1·40

404 Bumble Bee **405** Ski Jumping

1997. Insects (1st series). Multicoloured.
1277 3k.70 Type **404** 60 25
1278 3k.70 Ladybird 60 25
See also Nos. 1306/7.

1997. World Nordic Skiing Championships, Trondheim. Multicoloured.
1279 3k.70 Type **405** 60 25
1280 5k. Speed skiing 75 35

406 King Harald (photo by Erik Johansen)

1997. 60th Birthdays of King Harald and Queen Sonja. Multicoloured.
1281 3k.70 Type **406** 60 25
1282 3k.70 Queen Sonja and King Harald (photo by Knut Falch) (horiz) . . . 60 25

407 Hammer, Plumb Line and Hook (post-war reconstruction)

1997. 350th Anniv of Postal Service (3rd issue). Post-war History. Multicoloured.
1283 3k.70 Type **407** 70 75
1284 3k.70 "Kon Tiki" (replica of balsa raft) (Thor Heyerdahl's expedition from Peru to Polynesia, 1947) 70 75
1285 3k.70 Grouse feather (official bird of Rondane National Park (first National Park, 1962)) . . 70 75
1286 3k.70 Hands of man and woman (Welfare State (introduction of National Insurance, 1967)) 70 75
1287 3k.70 Drilling platform, Ekofisk oil field (discovery of oil in Norwegian sector of North Sea, 1969) . . . 70 75
1288 3k.70 Grete Waitz (first women's world Marathon champion, 1983) 70 75
1289 3k.70 Askoy Bridge, 1992 (communications) 70 75
1290 3k.70 Crown Prince Haakon Magnus lighting Olympic flame (Winter Olympic Games, Lillehammer, 1994) 70 75

1997. Tourism. As T **395**. Multicoloured.
1291 4k.30 Roros 70 90
1292 5k. Faerder Lighthouse . . 75 60
1293 6k. Nusfjord . . . . 1·20 45

408 University, Cathedral, Statue of King Olav, City Gate and Broadcasting Tower **409** Gerhardsen and Storting (Parliament House)

1997. Millenary of Trondheim. Multicoloured.
1294 3k.70 Type **408** 60 25
1295 12k. Trees, mine, King Olav, pilgrims, burning buildings and harbour . . 2·00 1·20

1997. Birth Centenary of Einar Gerhardsen (Prime Minister 1945–51, 1955–63 and 1963–65).
1296 **409** 3k.70 black, stone and red 60 25
1297 – 25k. black, flesh and green . . . . 4·00 1·90
DESIGN: 25k. Gerhardsen, mountain, factory and electricity pylon.

410 Thematic Subjects **411** Harald Saeverud (composer)

1997. Inauguration of National Junior Stamp Club. Multicoloured.
1298 3k.70 Type **410** 60 25
1299 3k.70 Thematic subjects including fish and tiger . . 60 25

1997. Birth Centenaries.
1300 **411** 10k. blue . . . . 1·60 95
1301 – 15k. green . . . . 2·75 1·40
DESIGN: 15k. Tarjei Vesaas (writer).

412 Dass in Rowing Boat

1997. 350th Birth Anniv of Petter Dass (priest and poet). Multicoloured.
1302 **412** 3k.20 blue and brown . . 60 45
1303 – 3k.70 green, blue and brown 60 25
DESIGN: 3k.70, Dass and Alstahaug Church.

413 Golden Calendar Stick Symbols against Candle Flames **414** Roses

1997. Christmas. Multicoloured. Self-adhesive.
1304 3k.70 Type **413** 60 40
1305 3k.70 Silver calendar stick symbols against night sky 60 40

1998. Insects (2nd series). As T **404**. Multicoloured.
1306 3k.80 Dragonfly 60 25
1307 3k.80 Grasshopper 60 25

1998. St. Valentine's Day. Self-adhesive.
1308 **414** 3k.80 multicoloured . . 75 35

415 "Hornelen" (passenger and mail steamer) **416** Holmenkollen Ski Jump, Oslo

1998. Nordic Countries' Postal Co-operation. Ships.
1309 **415** 3k.80 blue and green . . 60 25
1310 – 4k.50 green and blue . . 75 65
DESIGN: No. 1310, "Kommandoren" (passenger catamaran).

1998. Tourist Sights. Multicoloured.
1311 3k.80 Type **416** 60 40
1312 4k.50 Fisherman, Alesund Harbour 75 90
1313 5k.50 Mt Hamaroyskaftet 95 95

417 Egersund Harbour

1998. Bicentenary of Egersund.
1314 **417** 3k.80 blue and pink . . 30 35
1315 – 6k. blue and mauve . . 1·00 45
DESIGN: No. 1315, Egersund ceramics.

418 Silver

1998. Minerals. Multicoloured.
1316 3k.40 Type **418** 60 40
1317 5k.20 Cobalt 95 55

419 "Water Rider" (Frans Widerberg)

1998. Contemporary Art. Multicoloured.
1318 6k. Type **419** . . . . . . 1·00 65
1319 7k.50 "Red Moon" (carpet, Synnove Anker Aurdal) 1·20 80
1320 13k. "King Haakon VII" (sculpture, Nils Aas) . . . 2·20 1·50

420 Hopscotch

1998. Children's Games (1st series). Multicoloured.
1321 3k.80 Type **420** 60 25
1322 5k.50 Throwing coins at a stick 95 80
See also Nos 1355/6.

421 Boeing 747, Douglas DC-3 and Junkers Ju 52 Airliners

1998. Inauguration of Oslo Airport, Gardermoen. Multicoloured.
1323 3k.80 Type **421** 45 25
1324 6k. Boeing 737 airliner and map of former approaches to Gardermoen Airport 1·00 60
1325 24k. Terminal building, control tower and wings drawn by Leonardo da Vinci . . . . 3·75 2·10

422 Main Entrance and Guard

1998. 150th Anniv of Royal Palace, Oslo.
1326 **422** 3k.40 purple 60 50
1327 – 3k.80 blue, pink and yellow 70 25
DESIGN: 3k.80, Main front of palace.

423 Music Score

424 Cheese Slicer (Thor Bjorklund)

1998. Christmas. Multicoloured. Self-adhesive.
1328 3k.80 Type **423** (red background) 65 25
1329 3k.80 Music score (blue background) 65 25

1999. Norwegian Inventions. Self-adhesive.
1330 **424** 3k.60 black and blue . . 60 30
1331 – 4k. black and red . . . 70 30
1332 – 4k.20 black and green 70 25
DESIGNS: 4k. Paper clip (Johan Vaaler); 4k.20 Aerosol can (Erik Rotheim).

425 Salmon and Fly

1999. Fishes and Fishing Flies. Multicoloured. Self-adhesive.
1333 4k. Type **425** 70 25
1334 4k. Cod and fly 70 30

426 Heart blowing Flowers out of Posthorn

427 "The Pioneer" (statue, Per Palle Storm)

1999. St. Valentine's Day.
1335 **426** 4k. multicoloured . . . 70 40

1999. Centenary of Norwegian Confederation of Trade Unions.
1336 **427** 4k. multicoloured . . . 70 25

428 Poland v Norway, Class B Championship, 1998

1999. World Ice Hockey Championships, Norway. Multicoloured.
1337 4k. Type **428** 70 65
1338 7k. Switzerland v Sweden, Class A Championship, 1998 . . . . 1·20 65

429 Mute Swans

1999. Tourism. Multicoloured.
1339 4k. Type **429** 70 65
1340 5k. Hamar Cathedral . . . 75 45
1341 6k. Sami man from Troms 1·00 35

430 Emigration

1999. "Norway 2000" (1st issue). Norwegian History. Multicoloured.
1342 4k. Type **430** 70 55
1343 6k. King Olav and Bible (conversion to Christianity, 11th century) 1·00 95
1344 14k. Medal of King Christian IV and quarry workers (union of Norway and Denmark) 2·30 1·90
1345 26k. Oslo at Beier Bridge, 1850s (industrialization) 4·25 90

431 Horse Ferry, Amli, East Agder, 1900

1999. "Norway 2000" (2nd issue). Photographs of Everyday Life. Multicoloured.
1346 4k. Type **431** . . . . . . 65 16·00
1347 4k. Men hewing rock during construction of Valdres railway line, 1900 . . . . 65 16·00
1348 4k. Taxi driver Aarseth Odd filling up car with petrol, Kleive, 1930 . . . . . . 65 16·00
1349 4k. Dairymaid Mathea Isaksen milking cow, Karmoy, 1930 . . . . . 65 16·00
1350 4k. Haymakers, Hemsedal, 1943 . . . . 65 16·00
1351 4k. Cross-country skier Dagfinn Knutsen, 1932 65 16·00
1352 4k. "Bolgen" (coastal fishing boat), Varanger Fjord, 1977 . . . . 65 16·00
1353 4k. Boy Jon Andre Koch holding football, 1981 . . 65 16·00
MS1354 136 × 148 mm. Nos. 1346/53 5·00 6·00

432 Skateboarding

434 Family bringing in Logs

433 Wenche Foss and Per Haugen in "An Ideal Husband" (Oscar Wilde)

1999. Children's Games (2nd series). Multicoloured.
1355 4k. Type **432** 70 75
1356 6k. Inline skating . . . . . 1·00 60

1999. Centenary of National Theatre.
1357 **433** 3k.60 purple and orange 60 60
1358 – 4k. ultramarine and blue 70 50
DESIGN: 4k. Toralv Maurstad and Tore Segelcke in "Per Gynt" (Henrik Ibsen).

1999. Christmas. Multicoloured. Self-adhesive.
1359 4k. Type **434** 70 50
1360 4k. Family sitting by window 70 30

435 "Sunset" (Sverre Simonsen)

1999. Year 2000. Winning entries in photographic competition. Multicoloured. Self-adhesive.
1361 4k. Type **435** 75 45
1362 4k. "Winter Nights" (Poul Christensen) 75 40

436 Eye within Heart

2000. St. Valentine's Day.
1363 **436** 4k. multicoloured . . . 70 30

437 "Angry Child" (statue, Gustav Vigeland)

2000. Millenary of Oslo City. Multicoloured.
1364 4k. Type **437** 70 70
1365 6k. Christian IV statue . . . 1·00 95
1366 8k. City Hall and clock face 1·50 2·20
1367 27k. Oslo Stock Exchange and Mercury (statue) . . 4·75 1·30

438 Golden Eagle

2000. Endangered Species. Multicoloured.
1368 5k. Type **438** 95 80
1369 6k. European moose . . . . 1·00 60
1370 7k. Sperm whale . . . . . 1·30 40

439 "Power and Energy"

2000. "EXPO 2000" World's Fair, Hanover, Germany. Paintings by Marianne Heske. Mult.
1371 4k.20 "The Quiet Room" 70 45
1372 6k.30 Type **439** . . . . . 1·10 60

440 Cadets, 1750

441 Mackerel

2000. 250th Anniv of Royal Norwegian Military Academy.
1373 **440** 3k.60 multicoloured . . 60 80
1374 – 8k. blue, yellow and red 1·50 45
DESIGN: 8k. Cadets, 2000.

2000. Fishes. Multicoloured. Self-adhesive.
1375 4k.20 Type **441** . . . . . 1·10 25
1376 4k.20 Herring . . . . 1·10 25

442 Spaceman (May-Therese Vorland)

443 "Monument to Log Drivers" (sculpture, Trygve M. Barstad)

2000. "Stampin the Future". Winning Entries in Children's International Painting Competition. Multicoloured.
1377 4k.20 Type **442** 70 30
1378 6k.30 Rocket and Earth (Jann Fredrik Ronning) 1·10 50

2000. Millennium of Skien City. Multicoloured.
1379 4k.20 Type **443** 70 40
1380 15k. Skien Church . . . . 2·50 1·60

444 Laestadius, Lifelong Saxifrage and Laestadius Poppy

445 Nils og Blamann with Goat and Cart

2000. Birth Bicentenary of Lars Levi Laestadius (clergyman and botanist).
1381 **444** 5k. multicoloured . . . 75 65

2000. Cartoon Characters. Multicoloured. Self-adhesive.
1382 4k.20 Type **445** 75 25
1383 4k.20 Soldier No. 91 Stomperud and birds . . 75 30

446 Woven Altar Piece, Hamaroy Church

2000. Altar Pieces. Multicoloured.
1384 3k.60 Type **446** 60 55
1385 4k.20 Ski Church 75 40

2000.
1388 **352** 1k. multicoloured . . . 30 35
1389 2k. multicoloured . . . 45 25
1389a 3k. multicoloured . . . 70 50
1389b 5k. multicoloured . . . 85 40
1390 6k. multicoloured . . . 1·00 55
1391 7k. multicoloured . . . 1·20 60
1392 9k. multicoloured . . . 1·50 60

447 Sekel Rose

448 Place Mat

2001. Roses (1st series). Multicoloured. Self-adhesive.
1395 4k.50 Type **447** 75 70
1396 4k.50 Namdal rose 75 55
See also Nos 1418/19 and 1491/2.

2001. Crafts (1st series). Multicoloured. Self-adhesive.
1397 4k. Type **448** 70 25
1398 4k.50 Pot with lid 85 35
1399 7k. Bunad (woven cloth) . . 1·20 55
See also Nos. 1415/17.

449 Aase Bye

2001. Thespians (1st series).
1400 **449** 4k. black and brown . . 70 30
1401 – 4k.50 black and blue . . 85 25
1402 – 5k.50 black and brown 95 60
1403 – 7k. black and purple . . 1·20 60
1404 – 8k. black and grey . . . 1·50 70
DESIGNS: 4k.50, Per Aabel; 5k.50, Alfred Maurstad; 7k. Lillebil Ibsen; 8k. Tore Segelcke.
See also Nos 1410/14 and 1450/4.

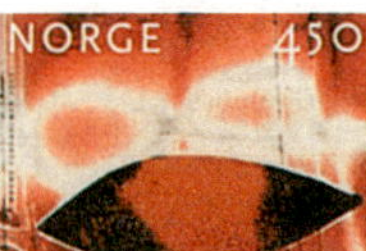
450 "Ties that Bind" (Magne Furuholmen)

2001. St. Valentine's Day.
1405 **450** 4k.50 multicoloured . . 75 25

451 Whitewater Kayaking

453 Lalla Carlsen

452 Tuba Player

2001. Sports. Multicoloured. Self-adhesive.
1406 4k.50 Type **451** 85 40
1407 7k. Rock climbing . . . . . 1·20 1·00

2001. Centenary of School Bands. Multicoloured.
1408 4k.50 Type **452** 85 40
1409 9k. Majorette . . . . 1·50 1·10

2001. Thespians (2nd series). Multicoloured.
1410 5k. Type **453** 75 50
1411 5k.50 Leif Juster 95 40
1412 7k. Kari Diesen . . . . . . 1·20 90

1413 9k. Arvid Nilssen . . . . . 1·50 80
1414 10k. Einar Rose . . . . . 1·70 85

2001. Crafts (2nd series). As T **449**. Multicoloured.
1415 5k. Wooden drinking vessel 95 40
1416 6k.50 Crocheted doll's clothing . . . . 1·20 80
1417 8k.50 Knitted woollen hat 1·50 1·10

454 Rose "Heidekonigin" **456** Kittens

455 Old Bank of Norway

2001. Roses (2nd series). Multicoloured. Self-adhesive.
1418 5k.50 Type **454** . . . . . . 1·00 35
1419 5k.50 Rose "Old Master" 1·00 35
Nos. 1418/19 are impregnated with the scent of roses.

2001. Norwegian Architecture. Multicoloured.
1420 5k.50 Type **455** 95 35
1421 8k.50 Ivar Aasen Centre . . 1·50 75

2001. Pets. Multicoloured.
1422 5k.50 Type **456** . . . . . . 1·00 45
1423 7k.50 Goat . . . . 1·40 70

457 Aung San Suu Kyi (Burmese opposition leader), 1991

2001. Centenary of Nobel Prizes. Peace Prize Winners (Nos. 1424/5 and 1427). Multicoloured.
1424 5k.50 Type **457** . . . . . . 1·10 40
1425 5k.50 Nelson Mandela (South African President), 1993 . . . . 1·10 40
1426 7k. Alfred Nobel (Prize Fund founder) . . . . . 1·40 65
1427 7k. Henry Dunant (founder of Red Cross), 1901 . . . 1·40 65
1428 9k. Fridtjof Nansen (Norwegian organizer for League of Nations refugee relief), 1922 . . . . . . 1·90 80
1429 9k. Mikhail Gorbachev (Soviet President), 1990 1·40 80
1430 10k. Martin Luther King (Civil Rights leader), 1964 1·40 95
1431 10k. Rigoberta Menchu Tum (Guatemalan Civil Rights leader), 1992 . . . 1·30 1·00
MS1432 170 × 64 mm. No. 1426 1·10 45
Dates are those on which the Prize was awarded.

458 Snow-covered Trees and Lights

2001. Northern Lights. Multicoloured.
1433 5k. Type **458** 95 45
1434 5k.50 Lights and reindeer 1·00 50

459 Gingerbread Man **460** Tordis Maurstad

2001. Christmas. Multicoloured. Self-adhesive.
1435 5k.50 Type **459** . . . . . . 1·10 40
1436 5k.50 Gingerbread house . . 1·10 40

2002. Thespians (3rd series). Showing caricatures by Arne Roar Lund.
1450 **460** 5k. black and lilac . . . 85 40
1451 – 5k.50 black and grey . . 95 40
1452 – 7k. black and green . . 1·20 50
1453 – 9k. black and green . . 1·50 60
1454 – 10k. black and brown . . 1·70 70
DESIGNS: 5k.50 Rolf Just Nilsen; 7k. Lars Tvinde; 9k. Henry Gleditsch; 10k. Norma Balean.

461 Boys tackling **462** Scene from "Askeladden and the Good Helpers" (animated film by Ivo Caprino)

2002. Centenary of Norwegian Football Association (1st issue). Multicoloured. Self-adhesive.
1455 5k.50 Type **461** 90 40
1456 5k.50 German referee Peter Hertel and player 90 40
1457 5k.50 Girls tackling 90 40
1458 5k.50 Boy kicking ball . . . 90 40
See also Nos. 1469/**MS**1475.

2002. Fairytale Characters. Multicoloured. Self-adhesive.
1459 5k.50 Type **462** 90 40
1460 9k. Giant troll (drawing by Theodor Kittelsen) . . . 1·50 60

463 "Monument to Whaling" (Sivert Donali)

2002. Nordic Countries' Postal Co-operation. Modern Art. Sculptures. Multicoloured.
1461 7k.50 Type **463** . . . . . . 1·30 50
1462 8k.50 "Throw" (Kåre Groven) . . . . 1·40 55

464 Holmestrand

2002. City Charter Anniversaries. Multicoloured.
1463 5k.50 Type **464** (300th anniv) 90 40
1464 5k.50 Kongsberg (200th anniv) 90 40

465 Abel

2002. Birth Bicentenary of Niels Henrik Abel (mathematician). Multicoloured.
1465 5k.50 Type **465** 90 40
1466 22k. Mathematical rosette 3·75 2·25

466 Johan Borgen **468** Clown on Tightrope

467 Norwegian Team (Olympic Games, Berlin, 1936)

2002. Writers' Birth Centenaries. Portraits by Nils Aas.
1467 **466** 11k. yellow and green . . 1·80 75
1468 – 20k. green and blue . . 3·50 2·00
DESIGN: 20k. Nordahl Grieg.

2002. Centenary of Norwegian Football Association (2nd issue). Multicoloured.
1469 5k. Type **467** 85 35
1470 5k.50 No. 9 player and Brazil No. 4 player (World Cup, France, 1998) 90 35
1471 5k.50 Norway and U.S.A. women players (Olympic Games, Sydney, 2000) . . 90 35
1472 7k. Player capturing ball from Sweden No. 11 player (Norway–Sweden, 1960) . . . . 1·20 45
1473 9k. Player with chevron sleeves (Norway–England, 1981) . . . . 1·50 60
1474 10k. Winning team members (Rosenborg–Milan (Champions League, 1996)) . . . . 1·70 65
MS1475 140 × 127 mm. Nos. 1469/74 7·00 7·00

2002. Europa. Circus. Multicoloured.
1476 5k.50 Type **468** 90 35
1477 8k.50 Elephant, horse and chimpanzee . . . . 1·40 55

2002. "Nordia 2002" Nordic Stamp Exhibition, Kristiansand. Nos. 1465/6 surch **NORDIC 2002**.
1478 5k.50 multicoloured 90 35
1479 22k. multicoloured . . . . 3·75 2·20

470 Landstad on Horseback and Frontispiece of "Norske Folkeviser"

2002. Birth Bicentenary of Magnus Brostrup Landstad (folk-song collector and hymn writer). Multicoloured.
1480 5k. Type **470** 85 35
1481 5k.50 Landstad and frontispiece of Kirkefalmebog 90 35

471 Straw Heart-shaped Decoration

2002. Christmas. Multicoloured. Self-adhesive.
1482 5k.50 Type **471** 90 35
1483 5k.50 Paper star-shaped decoration 90 35

472 "Nordmandens Krone" (Kare Espolin Johnson)

2003. Graphic Art (1st series). Multicoloured.
1484 5k. Type **472** 85 35
1485 8k.50 "Bla Hester" (Else Hagen) . . . . 1·40 55
1486 9k. "Dirigent og Solist" (Niclas Gulbrandsen) . . 1·50 60
1487 11k. "Olympia" (Svein Strand) . . . . 1·80 75
1488 22k. "Still Life XVII" (Rigmor Hansen) . . . . 3·75 2·20
See also Nos. 1515/16.

473 Heart

2003. St. Valentine.
1489 **473** 5k.50 multicoloured . . 90 35

474 Doudji Knife Handle (Havard Larsen) **475** Rose "Grand Prix"

2003. Crafts. Coil stamp. Self-adhesive.
1490 **474** 5k.50 multicoloured . . 90 35

2003. Roses (3rd series). Multicoloured. Self-adhesive.
1491 5k.50 Type **475** 90 35
1492 5k.50 Rose "Champagne" 90 35

476 Operating Theatre **477** Forest Troll

2003. 400th Anniv of Public Health Service. Multicoloured.
1493 5k.50 Type **476** 85 35
1494 7k. Doctor examining baby 1·10 45

2003. Fairytale Characters (2nd series). Showing drawings by Theodor Kittelsen. Self-adhesive. Multicoloured.
1495 5k.50 Type **477** 85 35
1496 9k. Water sprite (horiz) . . 1·40 45

478 Hand and Violin

2003. Bergen International Festival. Multicoloured.
1497 5k.50 Type **478** 85 35
1498 10k. Children's faces . . . . 1·60 65

479 Child holding Bread

2003. World Refugee Day. Multicoloured.
1499 5k.50 Type **479** 85 35
1500 10k. Refugees . . . . 1·60 65

480 Crown Prince Olav as a Child **482** Dagbladet (Per Krohg)

481 Baby

2003. Birth Centenary of King Olav V (1903–1991). Multicoloured.
1501 5k.50 Type **480** 85 35
1502 8k.50 Crown Prince Olav and Crown Princess Martha . . . . 1·40 60
1503 11k. King Olav V . . . . . 1·80 75
MS1504 170 × 101 mm. Nos. 1501/3 4·00 4·00

2003. Greetings Stamps. Multicoloured. Self-adhesive.
1505 5k.50 Type **481** 85 35
1506 5k.50 Hand wearing ring . . 85 35
1507 5k.50 Lily 85 35
1508 5k.50 Couple 85 35
1509 5k.50 Children and cake . . 85 35

2003. Europa. Poster Art. Multicoloured.
1510 8k.50 Type **482** . . . . . 1·40 60
1511 9k. Winter Olympics, Oslo (Knut Yran) . . . . . . 1·50 60
1512 10k. Music festival (Willibald Storn) . . . . 1·60 65

483 Bjornstjerne Bjornson (literature, 1903)

2003. Norwegian Nobel Prize Winners (1st series). Multicoloured.
1513 11k. Type **483** . . . . . . 1·80 70
1514 22k. Lars Onsager (chemistry, 1968) . . . . 3·50 1·40
See also Nos. 1549/50.

484 "Winter Landscape 1980" (Terje Grostad)

2003. Graphic Art (2nd series). Multicoloured.
1515 5k. Type **484** 80 30
1516 5k.50 "Goatherd and Goats" (Rolf Nesch) . . . 85 35

485 Santa Claus

2003. Christmas. Self-adhesive gum. Multicoloured.
1517 5k.50 Type **485** 85 35
1518 5k.50 Present 85 35

486 Coronet Medusa (*Periphylla periphylla*)

2004. Marine Life (1st series). Multicoloured. Self-adhesive.
1519 5k.50 Type **486** 95 50
1520 6k. Catfish (*Anarhichas lupus*) 95 50
1521 9k. Little cuttlefish (*Sepiola atlantica*) . . . . 1·40 70
See also Nos. 1576/7 and 1608.

487 Couple

2004. Greetings Stamps. Self-adhesive gum. Each green and grey.
1522 6k. Type **487** 95 50
1523 6k. Globe 95 50

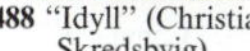

488 "Idyll" (Christian Skredsbvig) **489** Heart

2004. Painters' Birth Anniversaries. Multicoloured.
1524 6k. Type **488** (150th anniv) 95 50
1525 9k.50 "Stetind in Fog" (Peder Balke) (bicentenary) . . . . . . 1·50 75
1526 10k.50 "Workers' Protest" (Reidar Aulie) (centenary) 1·60 80

2004. St. Valentine's Day.
1527 **489** 6k. multicoloured . . . 95 50

490 Cyclist

2004. Europa. Holidays. Multicoloured.
1528 6k. Type **490** 95 50
1529 7k.50 Canoeist . . . . 1·20 60
1530 9k.50 Skiers . . . . 1·50 75

491 Otto Sverdrup **492** Sea God Njord

2004. 150th Birth Anniv of Otto Sverdrup (polar explorer). Each purple and buff.
1531 6k. Type **491** 95 50
1532 9k.50 *Fram* (polar research ship) . . . . 1·50 75
MS1533 166 × 60 mm. Nos. 1541/2 plus 1 label . . . . 2·50 2·50
No. **MS**1533 was issued with a stamp-sized label showing design of Greenland stamp.
Stamps of similar designs were issued by Greenland and Canada.

2004. Nordic Mythology. Multicoloured.
1534 7k.50 Type **492** . . . . . . 1·20 60
1535 10k.50 Balder's funeral . . . 1·60 80
MS1536 106 × 70 mm. Nos. 1544/5 2·40 2·40
Stamps of a similar theme were issued by Aland Islands, Denmark, Faeroe Islands, Finland, Greenland, Iceland and Sweden.

493 Princess Ingrid Alexandra

2004. Birth of Princess Ingrid Alexandra of Norway. Sheet 94 × 61 mm.
MS1537 **493** 6k. multicoloured 2·75 2·75

494 Steam Locomotive, Koppang Station

2004. 150th Anniv of Norwegian Railways. Multicoloured.
1538 6k. Type **494** 95 50
1539 7k.50 Passengers and staff, Dovre station . . . . 1·20 60
1540 9k.50 Early diesel locomotive, Flatmark halt 1·40 70
1541 10k.50 Airport Express locomotive . . . . 1·60 80

495 Hakon Hakonsson **496** Smiley (emblem)

2004. 800th Birth Anniv of Hakon Hakonsson (Viking leader). Multicoloured.
1542 12k. Type **495** . . . . 1·90 90
1543 22k. Outline of Hakon's hall and sword . . . . 3·25 2·75

2004. Youth Stamps. Multicoloured.
1544 6k. Type **496** 95 50
1545 9k. Badges . . . . 1·40 70

497 Ship's Prow and Barrels

2004. Centenary of Archaeological Discovery, Oseberg. Multicoloured.
1546 7k.50 Type **497** . . . . . . 1·20 60
1547 9k.50 Sled . . . . 1·40 70
1548 12k. Bed . . . . 1·90 90

2004. Norwegian Nobel Prize Winners (2nd series). As T **483**. Multicoloured.
1549 5k.50 Odd Hassel (chemistry, 1969) 90 45
1550 6k. Christian Lous Lange (peace, 1921) 95 50

498 "Friends" (Hanne Soteland) **499** Princesses and Guard

2004. Christmas. Winning Designs in UNICEF Painting Competition. Multicoloured. Self-adhesive.
1551 6k. Type **498** 90 45
1552 6k. "Caring" (Synne Amalie Lund Kallak) 90 45

2005. 150th Birth Anniv of Erik Werenskiold (artist). Illustrations from "The Three Princesses in the Blue Hill" fairytale by Peter Christen Asbjornsen and Jorgen Moe. Multicoloured.
1553 7k.50 Type **499** . . . . . . 1·20 60
1554 9k.50 Royal cradle . . . . 1·40 70

500 Soup Kitchen, Møllergata (1953)

2005. 150th Anniv of Church City Missions (humanitarian organization). Multicoloured.
1555 5k.50 Type **500** 90 45
1556 6k. Ministers giving communion at street service, Oslo 95 50

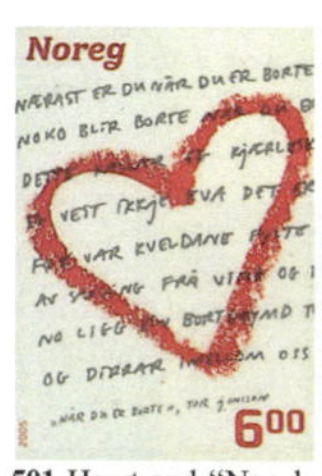

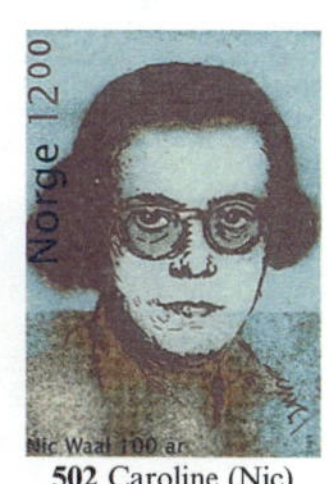

501 Heart and "Nar du er Borte" (poem by Tor Jonsson) **502** Caroline (Nic) Waal

2005. St. Valentine's Day.
1557 **501** 6k. carmine and silver 95 50

2005. Birth Centenaries. Multicoloured.
1558 12k. Type **502** (first child psychiatrist) . . . . . 1·90 90
1559 22k. Aase Gruda Skard (first child psychologist) 3·25 2·75

503 "City of the Future" (Maja Anna Marszalek) **504** Fjord, Geiranger

2005. Winning Entries in Children's Drawing Competition. Multicoloured.
1560 6k. Type **503** 95 50
1561 7k.50 "The Modern Classroom" (Tobias Abrahamsen) . . . . . . 1·20 60

2005. Tourism. Self-adhesive. Multicoloured.
1562 6k. Type **504** 95 50
1563 9k.50 Kjosfossen, Flam . . 1·40 70
1564 10k.50 Polar bear, Svalbard 1·60 80

505 Prime Minister Christian Michelsen (Norway)

2005. Centenary of Dissolution of Union with Sweden. Multicoloured.
1565 6k. Type **505** . . . . . . 1·00 50
1566 7k.50 King Haakon VII (Sweden) . . . . 1·30 65
MS1567 162 × 94 mm. Nos. 1565/56 2·30 2·30

506 King Haakon VII taking Oath (1905)

2005. 20th-century Events. Multicoloured.
1568 6k. Type **506** . . . . 1·00 50
1569 6k. Crown Prince Olav riding through Oslo (1945) . . . . 1·00 50
1570 6k. King Olav V appearing on first Norwegian television broadcast (1960) 1·00 50
1571 6k. Prime Minster Trygve Bratteli opening Ekofisk oilfield (1971) . . . . . . 1·00 50
1572 9k. Kjetil Rekdal scoring winning goal in World Cup match against Brazil (1998) . . . . 1·40 70

507 *Christian Radich*

2005. Ships. Multicoloured.
1573 6k. Type **507** . . . . 1·00 50
1574 9k.50 *Sorlandet* . . . . . . 1·60 80
1575 10k.50 *Statsraad Lehmkuhl* 1·80 90

508 Killer Whale (*Orcinus orca*)

2005. Marine Life (2nd series). Multicoloured. Self-adhesive.
1576 (5k.50) Type **508** 95 50
1577 (6k.) Sea anemone (*Urticina eques*) . . . . 1·00 50

509 Jomfruland Lighthouse

2005. Lighthouses. Self-adhesive. Multicoloured.
1578 (6k.) Type **509** . . . . . . 1·00 50
1579 (6k.) Tranoy . . . . 1·00 50

510 Thortveitite (rare mineral)

2005. Centenary of Geological Society. Mult.
1580 5k.50 Type **510** 95 50
1581 6k. Drilling rig, ship, continental shelf, stylized rock section and *Lamprocyclas maritalis* . . 1·00 50

511 Transmitting Apparatus

2005. 150th Anniv of Telegraph in Norway. Multicoloured.
1582 6k. Type **511** . . . . 1·00 50
1583 10k.50 Girl using mobile phone . . . . 1·80 90

512 Fish

2005. Europa. Gastronomy. Multicoloured.
1584 9k.50 Type **512** . . . . . . 1·60 80
1585 10k.50 Decorated table . . . 1·80 90

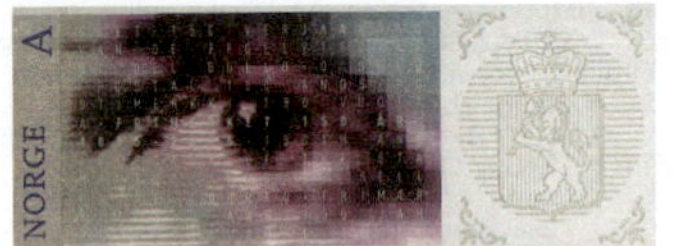

513 Eye and "150th Anniversary" (⅔-size illustration)

2005. 150th Anniv of Norwegian Stamps. Mult.
1586 (6k.) Type **513** . . . . . . 1·00 50
MS1587 170×60 mm. (6k.) Type **513**; 12k. First stamp and woman writing letter . . . . . 3·00 3·00

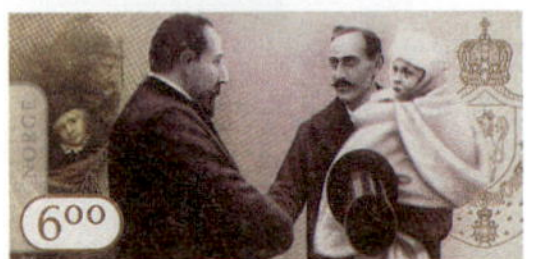

514 King Haakon holding Crown Prince Olav and Prime Minister Christian Michelsen

2005. Centenary of Norwegian Royal House. Multicoloured.
1588 6k. Type **514** . . . . 1·00 50
1589 6k. King Harald VII and Crown Prince Haakon holding Princess Ingrid Alexandra . . . . 1·00 50

515 Gingerbread Christmas Tree

2005. Christmas. Multicoloured. Self-adhesive.
1590 (6k.) Type **515** . . . . . . 1·00 50
1591 (6k.) Spiced oranges . . . . 1·00 50

516 Comet and "Tanke og draum er himmelske køyrety" (Olav Hauge)

2006. Centenary of Language Society.
1592 **516** 6k. multicoloured . . . 1·00 50

517 Kari Traa performing Iron Cross

519 Flower

518 Heart and Blossom

2006. Winter Olympic Games, Turin. Multicoloured.
1593 6k. Type **517** . . . . 1·00 50
1594 22k. Elinar Bjørndalen (biathlete) . . . . 2·00 1·00

2006. St. Valentine's Day.
1595 **5187** A (6k.) multicoloured 1·00 50

2006. Greetings Stamps. Multicoloured. Self-adhesive.
1596 A (6k.) Type **519** . . . . . 1·00 50
1597 A (6k.) Baby . . . . 1·00 50
1598 A (6k.) Heart and rings . . 1·00 50
1599 A (6k.) Cake . . . . 1·00 50

520 Lifeguard carrying Victim

2006. Centenary of Lifesaving Society. Mult.
1600 10k. Type **520** . . . . 1·70 85
1601 10k.50 Baby swimming . . 1·80 90

521 Shaman's Drum (detail)

2006. Nordic Mythology. Sheet 105×70 mm containing T **521** and similar horiz design. Multicoloured.
MS1602 A (6k.) Type **521**; 10k.50 Fafnir (dragon) (carved door panel) . . . . 3·00 3·00
Stamps of a similar theme were issued by Aland Islands, Denmark, Faroe Islands, Finland, Greenland, Iceland and Sweden.

522 Lynx

2006. Wildlife. Multicoloured.
1603 6k.50 Type **522** . . . . . . 1·10 55
1604 8k.50 Capercaillie . . . . . 1·50 75
1605 10k. Golden eagle . . . . . 1·70 85
1606 10k.50 Artic fox . . . . . 1·80 90
1607 13k. Mountain hare . . . . 2·20 1·10

523 *Polycera quadrilineata*

2006. Marine Life. (3rd series). Self-adhesive.
1608 **523** 10k. multicoloured . . . 1·70 85

OFFICIAL STAMPS

O **22**

O **36**

1925.
O187 O **22** 5ore mauve 70 65
O188 10ore green 35 20
O189 15ore blue . . . . . 1·50 1·70
O190 20ore purple 40 20
O191 30ore grey . . . . . 2·00 3·25
O192 40ore blue . . . . . 1·00 1·00
O193 60ore blue . . . . . 3·50 3·75

1929. Surch **2 2**.
O219 O **22** 2ore on 5ore mauve 40 60

1933.
O231 O **36** 2ore brown . . . . . 55 1·10
O243 5ore purple . . . . . 75 1·10
O233 7ore orange . . . . . 4·25 4·50
O245 10ore green 60 30
O235 15ore green 65 45
O247 20ore red 75 30
O237 25ore brown 50 50
O238 30ore blue 65 50
O248 35ore violet 60 40
O249 40ore grey 90 50
O250 60ore blue 90 80
O241 70ore brown . . . . . 1·10 1·70
O242 100ore blue . . . . . 1·25 1·50

O **39**

O **58** Quisling Emblem

1937.
O267 O **39** 5ore mauve 25 25
O268 7ore orange 40 60
O269 10ore green 25 20
O270 15ore brown 25 20
O271 20ore red 25 20
O260 25ore brown 95 65
O273 25ore red 25 20
O261 30ore blue 70 60
O275 30ore grey 80 40
O276 35ore purple 40 25
O277 40ore grey 40 25
O278 40ore blue . . . . . . 2·75 25
O279 50ore lilac 60 20
O280 60ore blue 45 20
O281 100ore blue . . . . . 1·10 35
O282 200ore orange . . . . 1·40 30

1942.
O336 O **58** 5ore mauve . . . . . 70 1·30
O337 7ore orange . . . . . 70 1·30
O338 10ore green 20 25
O339 15ore brown . . . . . 1·40 9·25
O340 20ore red 20 25
O341 25ore brown . . . . . 2·50 13·50
O342 30ore blue . . . . . . 2·10 12·00
O343 35ore purple . . . . . 2·10 7·25
O344 40ore grey 35 30
O345 60ore blue . . . . . . 1·90 6·75
O346 1k. blue . . . . 2·10 9·50

1949. Surch **25** and bar.
O402 O **39** 25ore on 20ore red . . 30 30

O **89**

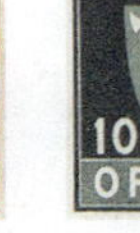

O **99**

1951.
O434 O **89** 5ore mauve 60 20
O435 10ore grey 60 10
O436 15ore brown 75 35
O437 30ore red 60 10
O438 35ore brown 90 45
O439 60ore blue 90 25
O440 100ore violet . . . . . 2·10 35

1955.
O458 O **99** 5ore purple 20 15
O459 10ore grey 20 15
O460 15ore brown . . . . . 45 1·30
O461 20ore green 50 15
O736 25ore green 20 20
O463 30ore red . . . . . . 1·40 55
O464 30ore green . . . . . 1·25 20
O465 35ore red 45 15
O466 40ore lilac 60 15
O467 40ore green 30 75
O468 45ore red . . . . . . 1·00 15
O469 50ore brown . . . . . 1·60 25
O470 50ore red 95 25
O471 50ore blue 45 25
O738 50ore grey 20 25
O739 60ore blue . . . . . . 85 3·50
O473 60ore red 50 15
O475 65ore red 75 30
O476 70ore brown . . . . . 3·00 65
O477 70ore red 20 20
O478 75ore purple . . . . . 9·00 9·00
O479 75ore green 60 55
O481 80ore brown 55 20
O741 80ore red 30 15
O482 85ore brown . . . . . 60 1·60
O483 90ore orange 70 15
O484 1k. violet 70 15
O485 1k. red 20 15
O486 1k.10 red 60 55
O744 1k.25 red 60 15
O745 1k.30 purple . . . . . 95 1·20
O746 1k.50 red 45 15
O747 1k.75 green . . . . . 1·00 1·00
O748 2k. green 50 15
O749 2k. red 60 15
O750 3k. violet 85 45
O488 5k. violet . . . . . . 9·75 6·00
O752 5k. blue 70 25

POSTAGE DUE STAMPS

D **12**

1889. Inscr "at betale" and "PORTOMAERKE".
D95 D **12** 1ore green 70 75
D96a 4ore mauve 95 45
D97 10ore red . . . . . . 5·25 40
D98 15ore brown . . . . . 5·00 60
D99 20ore blue . . . . . . 5·50 35
D94 50ore purple . . . . . 3·00 1·30

1922. Inscr "a betale" and "PORTOMERKE".
D162 D **12** 4ore purple . . . . . 4·75 6·50
D163 10ore green . . . . . 3·50 1·10
D164 20ore purple . . . . . 5·25 3·00
D165 40ore blue . . . . . . 10·50 60
D166 100ore yellow . . . . 38·00 6·75
D167 200ore violet . . . . 46·00 16·00

NOSSI-BE Pt. 6

An island north-west of Madagascar, declared a French protectorate in 1840. In 1901 it became part of Madagascar and Dependencies.

100 centimes = 1 franc.

1889. Stamp of French Colonies, "Peace and Commerce" type, surch.
8 H 25c. on 40c. red on yellow . . £1900 £550

1889. Stamps of French Colonies, "Commerce" type, surch.
4 J 5c. on 10c. black on lilac . . . £2500 £550
2 5c. on 20c. red on green . . . £2500 £750
6 15 on 20c. red on green . . . £2500 £550
7 25 on 30c. brown on drab . . £2250 £450
9 25 on 40c. red on yellow . . . £1900 £450

1890. Stamps of French Colonies, "Commerce" type, surch. (a) **N S B 0 25**.
10 J 0 25 on 20c. red on green . . £275 £190
11 0 25 on 75c. red on pink . . £180 £200
12 0 25 on 1f. green £275 £200

(b) **N S B 25 c**.
13 J 25c. on 20c. red on green . . £275 £190
14 25c. on 75c. red on pink . . £250 £190
15 25c. on 1f. green £250 £200

(c) **N S B 25** in frame.
16 J 25 on 20c. red on green . . . £650 £450
17 25 on 75c. red on pink . . . £650 £450
18 25 on 1f. green £650 £450

1893. Stamps of French Colonies, "Commerce" type, surch **NOSSI-BE** and bar over value in figures.
36 J 25 on 20c. red on green . . . 50·00 44·00
37 50 on 10c. black on lilac . . 55·00 44·00
38 75 on 15c. blue £170 £140
39 1f. on 5c. green . . . . . . £100 80·00

1893. Stamps of French Colonies, "Commerce" type, optd **Nossi Be**.
40a J 10c. black on lilac . . . . . 27·00 6·50
41 15c. blue . . . . 27·00 11·50
42 20c. red on green . . . . . £350 15·00

1894. "Tablet" key-type inscr "NOSSI-BE" in red (1, 5, 15, 25, 75c., 1f.) or blue (others).
44 D 1c. black on blue . . . . . 1·60 90
45 2c. brown on buff . . . . . 1·80 2·30
46 4c. brown on grey . . . . . 2·50 3·50
47 5c. green on green . . . . . 2·30 2·75
48 10c. black on lilac . . . . . 2·30 4·50
49 15c. blue . . . . 9·75 3·00
50 20c. red on green . . . . . 9·25 7·50
51 25c. black on pink . . . . . 10·00 9·25
52 30c. brown on drab . . . . 7·25 13·00
53 40c. red on yellow . . . . . 11·00 16·00
54 50c. red on pink . . . . . . 5·50 7·00
55 75c. brown on orange . . . 26·00 18·00
56 1f. green . . . . 9·50 32·00

POSTAGE DUE STAMPS

1891. Stamps of French Colonies, "Commerce" type, surch **NOSSI-BE chiffre-taxe A PERCEVOIR** and value.
D19 J 0.20 on 1c. black on blue . . £225 £160
D20 0.30 on 2c. brown on buff . £225 £160
D21 0.35 on 4c. brown on grey . £250 £180
D22 0.35 on 20c. red on green . £275 £180
D23 0.50 on 30c. brn on drab . 80·00 70·00
D24 1f. on 35c. black on orge . £150 £120

1891. Stamps of French Colonies, "Commerce" type, surch **Nossi-Be A PERCEVOIR** and value.
D25 J 5c. on 20c. red on green . . £120 £120
D26 10c. on 15c. blue on blue . £130 £130
D33 0.10 on 5c. green . . . . . 23·00 13·50
D27 15c. on 10c. black on lilac . £120 £120
D34 0.15 on 20c. red on green . 28·00 30·00
D28 25c. on 5c. green on green . £120 £120
D35 0.25 on 75c. red on pink . . £375 £350

NOVA SCOTIA Pt. 1

An eastern province of the Dominion of Canada, whose stamps it now uses.

Currency: As Canada.

1

2 Emblem of the United Kingdom

1853. Imperf.
1 **1** 1d. brown £2000 £400
4 **2** 3d. blue £750 £140
5 6d. green £4000 £450
8 1s. purple £14000 £2750

3 4

1860. Perf.
10 **3** 1c. black . . . . 3·75 14·00
23 2c. purple . . . . 4·50 12·00
13 5c. blue . . . . £375 19·00
14 **4** 8½c. green . . . . 3·50 42·00
28 10c. red . . . . 4·50 26·00
17 12½c. black . . . . 30·00 28·00

NYASALAND PROTECTORATE Pt. 1

A British Protectorate in central Africa. Formerly known as British Central Africa. From 1954 to 1963 part of the Central African Federation using the stamps of Rhodesia and Nyasaland (q.v.). From July 1964 independent within the Commonwealth under its new name of Malawi.

12 pence = 1 shilling;
20 shillings = 1 pound.

1891. Stamps of Rhodesia optd **B.C.A.**
1 **1** 1d. black . . . . 7·00 5·50
2 2d. green and red . . . . 7·00 4·00
3 4d. brown and black . . . . 7·50 5·00
5 6d. blue . . . . 10·00 8·00
6 8d. red and blue . . . . . 15·00 28·00
7 1s. brown . . . . 17·00 11·00
8 2s. red . . . . 28·00 50·00
9 2s.6d. purple . . . . 65·00 85·00
10 3s. brown and green . . . . 65·00 65·00
11 4s. black and red . . . . . 60·00 85·00
12 5s. yellow . . . . 70·00 75·00
13 10s. green £140 £190
14 – £1 blue £700 £550
15 – £2 red £950
16 – £5 olive £1600
17 – £10 brown £3500 £4500

1892. Stamps of Rhodesia surch **B.C.A.** and value in words.
18 **1** 3s. on 4s. black and red . . . £325 £325
19 4s. on 5s. yellow . . . . . . 75·00 85·00

1895. No. 2 surch **ONE PENNY.** and bar.
20 **1** 1d. on 2d. green and red . . 11·00 35·00

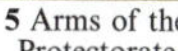

5 Arms of the Protectorate **7** Arms of the Protectorate

1895. The 2s.6d. and higher values are larger.
32 **5** 1d. black . . . . 3·25 5·50
33 2d. black and green . . . . 15·00 5·00
34 4d. black and orange . . . . 24·00 17·00
35 6d. black and blue . . . . . 28·00 13·00
36 1s. black and red . . . . . 28·00 17·00
37 2s.6d. black and mauve . . . £140 £130
38 3s. black and yellow . . . . £110 55·00
39 5s. black and olive £160 £200
29 £1 black and orange £950 £375
40 £1 black and blue £900 £500
30 £10 black and orange £5500 £4000
31 £25 black and green £10000

1897. The 2s.6d. and higher values are larger.
43 **7** 1d. black and blue . . . . 3·25 1·25
57d 1d. purple and red . . . . 2·50 50
44 2d. black and yellow . . . 2·00 2·00
45 4d. black and red . . . . . 6·50 1·50
57e 4d. purple and olive . . . . 8·50 11·00
46 6d. black and green . . . . 45·00 4·25
58 6d. purple and brown . . . 3·75 3·00
47 1s. black and purple . . . . 11·00 7·00
48 2s.6d. black and blue . . . 55·00 42·00
49 3s. black and green £200 £250
50 4s. black and red . . . . . 70·00 80·00
50a 10s. black and olive £160 £160
51 £1 black and purple £275 £160
52 £10 black and yellow . . . £4750 £1800

1897. No. 49 surch **ONE PENNY.**
53 **7** 1d. on 3s. black and green 6·50 9·50

10 11

1898.
56a **10** 1d. red and blue (imperf) £3000 £170
57 1d. red and blue (perf) . . £3000 23·00

1903. The 2s.6d. and higher values are larger.
68 **11** 1d. grey and red . . . . . 6·50 2·75
60 2d. purple . . . . 3·50 1·00
61 4d. green and black . . . 2·50 9·00
62 6d. grey and brown . . . 3·25 2·00
62b 1s. grey and blue . . . . . 3·75 12·00
63 2s.6d. green . . . . 50·00 80·00
64 4s. purple . . . . 70·00 80·00
65 10s. green and black . . . £140 £225
66 £1 grey and red £275 £180
67 £10 grey and blue £5000 £3500

13 14

1908.
73 **13** ½d. green . . . . 1·75 2·25
74 1d. red . . . . 4·00 1·00
75 3d. purple on yellow . . . . 1·50 4·25
76 4d. black and red on yellow 1·50 1·50
77 6d. purple . . . . 3·75 11·00
72 1s. black on green . . . . . 2·75 12·00
78 **14** 2s.6d. black and red on blue 55·00 85·00
79 4s. red and black . . . . . 85·00 £130
80 10s. green and red on green £130 £250
81 £1 purple and black on red £475 £600
82 £10 purple and blue £8500 £6000

1913. As 1908, but portrait of King George V.
100 ½d. green . . . . 1·50 50
101 1d. red . . . . 2·25 50
102 1½d. orange . . . . 3·25 17·00
103 2d. grey . . . . 1·00 50
89 2½d. blue . . . . 2·25 7·00
90 3d. purple on yellow . . . . 4·50 4·50
91 4d. black and red on yellow 2·00 2·50
107 6d. purple . . . . 3·00 3·25
93a 1s. black on green . . . . . 5·50 1·50
109 2s. purple and blue on blue 15·00 12·00
94 2s.6d. black and red on blue 11·00 15·00
111 4s. red and black . . . . . 19·00 28·00
112 5s. green and red on yellow 40·00 75·00
113 10s. green and red on green 90·00 95·00
98 £1 purple and black on red £180 £140
99e £10 purple and blue £3250 £1700

17 King George V and Symbol of the Protectorate

1934.
114 **17** ½d. green . . . . 75 1·25
115 1d. brown 75 75
116 1½d. red . . . . 75 3·00
117 2d. grey . . . . 80 1·25
118 3d. blue . . . . 2·50 1·75
119 4d. mauve . . . . 2·50 3·50
120 6d. violet . . . . 2·50 50
121 9d. olive . . . . 6·50 9·00
122 1s. black and orange . . . 9·50 14·00

1935. Silver Jubilee. As T **143a** of Newfoundland.
123 1d. blue and grey . . . . . 1·00 2·00
124 2d. green and blue . . . . . 1·00 1·50
125 3d. brown and blue . . . . 7·00 17·00
126 1s. grey and purple . . . . . 20·00 50·00

1937. Coronation. As T **143b** of Newfoundland.
127 ½d. green . . . . 30 1·50
128 1d. brown . . . . 50 1·00
129 2d. grey . . . . 50 2·50

1938. As T **17** but with head of King George VI and "POSTAGE REVENUE" omitted.
130 ½d. green . . . . 30 1·50
130a ½d. brown . . . . 10 2·25
131 1d. brown . . . . 2·75 30
131a 1d. green . . . . 30 1·00
132 1½d. red . . . . 4·75 4·50
132a 1½d. grey . . . . 30 6·00
133 2d. grey . . . . 8·00 1·25
133a 2d. red . . . . 30 1·75
134 3d. blue 60 70
135 4d. mauve . . . . 2·75 1·50
136 6d. violet . . . . 2·75 1·50
137 9d. olive . . . . 2·75 3·25
138 1s. black and orange . . . . 3·50 2·00

1938. As T **14** but with head of King George VI facing right.
139 2s. purple and blue on blue 10·00 12·00
140 2s.6d. black and red on blue 12·00 14·00
141 5s. green and red on yellow 45·00 23·00
142 10s. green and red on green 50·00 50·00
143 £1 purple and black on red 40·00 32·00

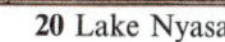

20 Lake Nyasa **21** King's African Rifles

1945.
144 **20** ½d. black and brown . . . 50 10
145 **21** 1d. black and green . . . 20 70
160 – 1d. brown and green . . . 50 20
146 – 1½d. black and grey . . . 30 50
147 – 2d. black and red . . . . 1·50 85
148 – 3d. black and blue 20 30
149 – 4d. black and red . . . . 2·00 80
150 – 6d. black and violet . . . 2·50 90
151 **20** 9d. black and olive . . . . 1·75 3·00
152 – 1s. blue and green . . . . 1·50 20
153 – 2s. green and purple . . . 6·00 4·75
154 – 2s.6d. green and blue . . . 7·50 5·00
155 – 5s. purple and blue . . . . 4·50 6·50
156 – 10s. red and green . . . . 15·00 14·00
157 – 20s. red and black . . . . 21·00 28·00

DESIGNS—HORIZ: 1½d., 6d. Tea estate; 2d., 1s., 10s. Map of Nyasaland; 4d., 2s.6d. Tobacco; 5s., 20s. Badge of Nyasaland. VERT: 1d. (No. 160), Leopard and sunrise; 3d., 2s. Fishing village.

1946. Victory. As T **4a** of Pitcairn Islands.
158 1d. green 10 30
159 2d. red 30 10

1948. Silver Wedding. As T **4b/c** of Pitcairn Islands.
161 1d. green 15 10
162 10s. mauve . . . . 15·00 26·00

1949. U.P.U. As T **4d/g** of Pitcairn Islands.
163 1d. green 30 20
164 3d. blue . . . . 2·00 3·25
165 6d. purple 50 50
166 1s. blue 30 50

27 Arms in 1891 and 1951

1951. Diamond Jubilee of Protectorate.
167 **27** 2d. black and red . . . . 1·25 1·50
168 3d. black and blue . . . . 1·25 1·50
169 6d. black and violet . . . 1·25 2·00
170 5s. black and blue . . . . 3·75 7·00

1953. Rhodes Centenary Exhibition. As T **6** of Northern Rhodesia.
171 6d. violet 50 30

1953. Coronation. As T **4h** of Pitcairn Islands.
172 2d. black and orange 70 80

29 Grading Cotton

1953. As 1945 but with portrait of Queen Elizabeth II as in T **29**. Designs as for corresponding values except where stated.
173 **20** ½d. black and brown . . . 10 1·50
174 – 1d. brn & grn (as No. 160) 65 40
175 – 1½d. black and grey . . . 20 1·90
176a – 2d. black and orange . . 30 30
177 **29** 2½d. green and black . . . 20 50
178 – 3d. black and red (as 4d.) 30 20
179 – 4½d. black and blue (as 3d.) 30 40
180 – 6d. black and violet . . . 90 1·50
181 **20** 9d. black and olive . . . 1·00 2·50
182 – 1s. blue and green . . . 2·25 50
183 – 2s. green and red . . . . 2·00 3·75
184 – 2s.6d. green and blue . . 3·25 6·00
185 – 5s. purple and blue . . . 7·00 6·00
186 – 10s. red and green . . . 4·50 19·00
187 – 20s. red and black . . . 17·00 29·00

30 **32** Mother and Child

34 Tea Industry

1963. Revenue stamps optd **POSTAGE** as in T **30** or surch also.
188 **30** ½d. on 1d. blue 30 30
189 1d. green 30 10
190 2d. red 30 30
191 3d. blue 30 10
192 6d. purple 30 10
193 9d. on 1s. red 40 25
194 1s. purple 45 10
195 2s.6d. black . . . . 1·25 2·50
196 5s. brown . . . . 3·25 1·50
197 10s. olive . . . . 4·50 7·00
198 £1 violet . . . . 5·00 7·00

1964.
199 **32** ½d. violet 10 30
200 – 1d. black and green . . . 10 10
201 – 2d. brown 10 10
202 – 3d. brown, green and bistre 10 10
203 – 4d. blue and yellow 20 30
204 **34** 6d. purple, green and blue 70 70
205 – 1s. brown, blue and yellow 15 10
206 – 1s.3d. bronze and brown 3·25 10
207 – 2s.6d. brown and blue . . 3·25 50
208 – 5s. blue, green, yellow & blk . . . . 1·50 1·75
209 – 10s. green, salmon and black . . . . 2·50 3·25
210 – £1 brown and yellow . . . 7·00 11·00

DESIGNS—HORIZ (as Type **32**): 1d. Chambo (fish); 2d. Zebu bull; 3d. Groundnuts; 4d. Fishing. (As Type **34**): 1s. Timber; 1s.3d. Turkish tobacco industry; 2s.6d. Cotton industry; 5s. Monkey Bay, Lake Nyasa; 10s. Forestry, Afzelia. VERT (as Type **34**): £1 Nyala.

POSTAGE DUE STAMPS

1950. As Type D **1** of Gold Coast, but inscr "NYASALAND".
D1 1d. red . . . . 3·75 25·00
D2 2d. blue . . . . 13·00 25·00
D3 3d. green . . . . 13·00 6·00
D4 4d. purple . . . . 23·00 48·00
D5 6d. orange . . . . 30·00 £130

For later issues see **MALAWI**.

NYASSA COMPANY Pt. 9

In 1894 Portugal granted a charter to the Nyassa Company to administer an area in the Northern part of Mozambique, including the right to issue its own stamps. The lease was terminated in 1929 and the administration was transferred to Mozambique whose stamps were used there.

1898. 1000 reis = 1 milreis.
1913. 100 centavos = 1 escudo.

1898. "Figures" and "Newspaper" key-types inscr "MOCAMBIQUE" optd **NYASSA**.
1 **V** 2½r. brown . . . . 2·10 1·90
2 **R** 5r. orange . . . . 2·10 1·90
3 10r. mauve . . . . 2·10 1·90
4 15r. brown . . . . 2·10 1·90
5 20r. lilac . . . . 2·10 1·90
6 25r. green . . . . 2·10 1·90
7 50r. blue . . . . 2·10 1·90
8 75r. pink . . . . 2·50 2·30
9 80r. green . . . . 2·50 2·30
10 100r. brown on buff . . . . 2·50 2·30
11 150r. red on pink . . . . . 7·50 7·00
12 200r. blue on blue . . . . . 4·50 4·25
13 300r. blue on brown . . . . 6·75 4·25

1898. "King Carlos" key-type inscr "MOCAMBIQUE" optd **NYASSA**.
14 **S** 2½r. grey . . . . 1·40 1·30
15 5r. red . . . . 1·40 1·30
16 10r. green . . . . 1·40 1·30
17 15r. brown . . . . 1·90 1·60
18 20r. lilac . . . . 1·90 1·60
19 25r. green . . . . 1·90 1·60
20 50r. blue . . . . 1·90 1·60
21 75r. pink . . . . 2·10 1·90
22 80r. mauve . . . . 2·50 1·40
23 100r. blue on blue . . . . . 2·50 1·40
24 150r. brown on yellow . . . 2·50 1·40
25 200r. purple on pink . . . . 2·50 1·50
26 300r. blue on pink . . . . . 3·50 1·50

2 Giraffe **3** Dromedaries

1901.
27 **2** 2½r. brown and black . . . . 1·30 65
28 5r. violet and black . . . . . 1·30 65
29 10r. green and black . . . . 1·30 65
30 15r. brown and black . . . . 1·30 65
31 20r. red and black . . . . . 1·30 80
32 25r. orange and black . . . . 1·30 80

33 50r. blue and black . . . . . 1·30 80
34 3 75r. red and black . . . . . 1·50 1·10
35 80r. bistre and black . . . . 1·50 1·10
36 100r. brown and black . . . 1·50 1·10
37 150r. brown and black . . . 1·70 1·20
38 200r. green and black . . . . 1·70 1·20
39 300r. green and black . . . . 1·70 1·20

1903. (a) Surch in figures and words.
40 3 65r. on 80r. mauve and black 1·20 90
41 115r. on 150r. brown & black 1·20 90
42 130r. on 300r. green & black 1·20 90

(b) Optd **PROVISORIO**.
43 2 15r. brown and black . . . . 1·20 90
44 25r. orange and black . . . . 1·20 90

1910. Optd **PROVISORIO** and surch in figures and words.
50 2 5r. on 2½r. brown and black 1·20 95
51 3 50r. on 100r. bistre and black 1·20 95

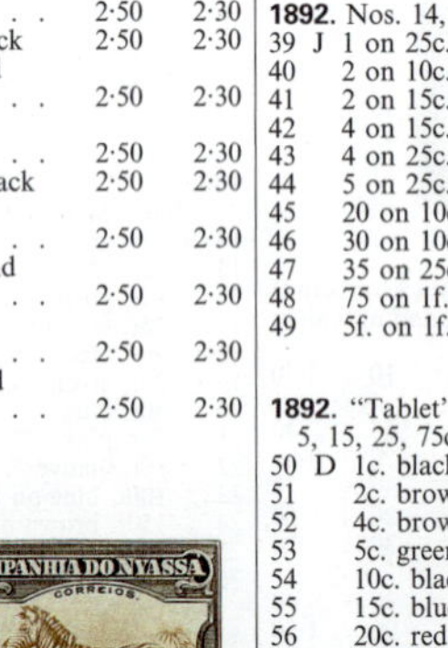

9 Dromedaries

12 Vasco de Gama's Flagship "Sao Gabriel"

1911. Optd **REPUBLICA**.
53 9 2½r. violet and black . . . . 1·10 70
54 5r. black . . . . 1·10 70
55 10r. green and black . . . . 1·10 70
56 – 20r. red and black . . . . 1·10 70
57 – 25r. brown and black . . . 1·10 70
58 – 50r. blue and black . . . . 1·10 70
59 – 75r. brown and black . . . 1·10 70
60 – 100r. brown & black on green . . . . 1·10 70
61 – 200r. green & black on orge 1·30 1·20
62 12 300r. black on blue . . . . 2·75 1·90
63 400r. brown and black . . . 3·25 2·10
64 500r. violet and green . . . 4·25 3·25
DESIGNS—HORIZ: 20, 25, 50r. Common zebra. VERT: 75, 100, 200r. Giraffe.

1918. Surch **REPUBLICA** and value in figures.
(a) Stamps of 1901.
65 2 ¼c. on 2½c. brown and black £150 £110
66 ½c. on 5r. violet and black . . £150 £110
67 1c. on 10r. green and black £150 £110
68 1½c. on 15r. brown and black 2·40 1·30
69 2c. on 20r. red and black . . 4·75 3·50
70 3½c. on 25r. orange and black 1·50 1·10
71 5c. on 50r. blue and black . . 1·50 1·10
72 3 7½c. on 75r. red and black . . 1·70 1·10
73 8c. on 80r. mauve and black 1·50 1·10
74 10c. on 100r. bistre and black 1·50 1·10
75 15c. on 150r. brown & black 1·50 1·10
76 20c. on 200r. green and black 1·50 1·10
77 30c. on 300r. green and black 2·50 2·30

(b) Nos. 43/4 and 40/2.
78 2 1½c. on 15r. brown and black 2·30 2·30
79 3½c. on 25r. orange and black 3·50 2·75
80 3 40c. on 65r. on 80r. . . . . 21·00 19·00
81 50c. on 115r. on 150r. . . . 3·00 2·30
82 1c. on 130r. on 300r. . . . 3·00 2·30

1921. Stamps of 1911 surch in figures and words.
83A 9 ¼c. on 2½r. violet and black . . . . 2·50 2·30
85A ½c. on 5r. black . . . . . . 2·50 2·30
86A 1c. on 10r. green and black . . . . 2·50 2·30
87A 12 1½c. on 300r. black on blue . . . . 2·50 2·30
88A – 2c. on 20r. red and black 2·50 2·30
89A – 2½c. on 25r. brown and black . . . . 2·50 2·30
90A 12 3c. on 400r. brown & black . . . . 2·50 2·30
91A – 5c. on 50r. blue and black 2·50 2·30
92A – 7½c. on 75r. brown & black . . . . 2·50 2·30
93A – 10c. on 100r. brown and black on green . . . . 2·50 2·30
94A 12 12c. on 500r. violet & green . . . . 2·50 2·30
95A – 20c. on 200r. green and black on orange . . . . 2·50 2·30

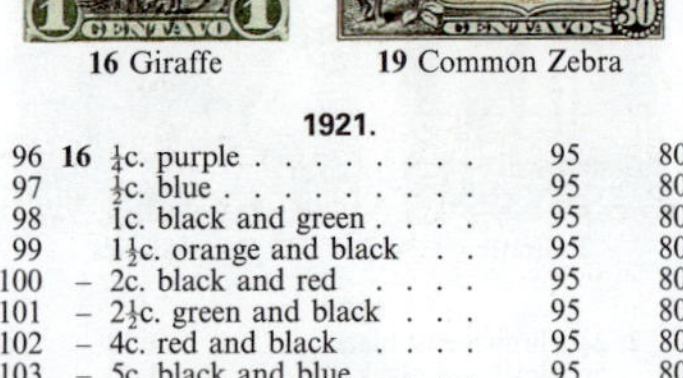

16 Giraffe

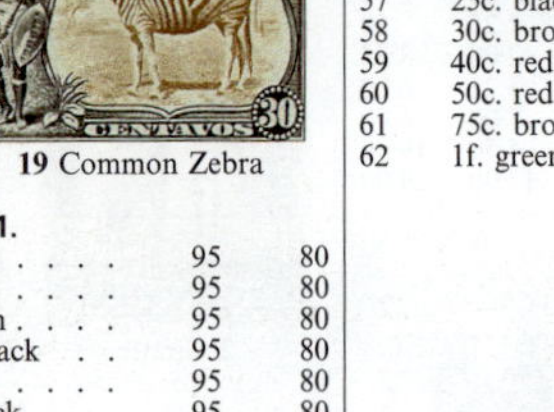

19 Common Zebra

1921.
96 16 ¼c. purple 95 80
97 ½c. blue 95 80
98 1c. black and green 95 80
99 1½c. orange and black . . 95 80
100 – 2c. black and red 95 80
101 – 2½c. green and black . . . 95 80
102 – 4c. red and black 95 80
103 – 5c. black and blue 95 80
104 – 6c. violet and black 95 80
123 – 7½c. brown and black . . . 90 65
124 – 8c. green and black . . . 90 65
125 – 10c. brown and black . . . 90 65
126 – 15c. red and black 90 65
127 – 20c. blue and black 90 65
110 19 30c. brown and black . . . 95 80
111 40c. blue and black 95 80
112 50c. green and black . . . 95 80
113 1e. brown and black . . . 95 80
114 – 2e. black and brown . . . 3·75 3·00
115 – 5e. brown and blue . . . . 3·50 2·50
DESIGNS—As Type **16**: 2c. to 6c. Vasco da Gama; 7½c. to 20c. Vasco da Gama's flagship "Sao Gabriel". As Type **19**: 2, 5e. Native dhow.

CHARITY TAX STAMPS

The notes under this heading in Portugal also apply here.

1925. Marquis de Pombal Commem. Nos. C327/9 of Mozambique optd **NYASSA**.
C141 C 22 15c. brown . . . . . 7·25 6·00
C142 – 15c. brown . . . . . 7·25 6·00
C143 C 25 15c. brown . . . . . 7·25 6·00

POSTAGE DUE STAMPS

D 21 "Sao Gabriel"

1924.
D132 – ½c. green . . . . . . 2·50 2·10
D133 – 1c. blue . . . . 2·50 2·10
D134 – 2c. red . . . . 2·50 2·10
D135 – 3c. red . . . . 2·50 2·10
D136 D 21 5c. brown . . . . . . 2·50 2·10
D137 6c. brown . . . . . . 2·50 2·10
D138 10c. purple . . . . . 2·50 2·10
D139 – 20c. red . . . . . . 2·50 2·10
D140 – 50c. purple . . . . . 2·50 2·10
DESIGNS: ½c., 1c. Giraffe; 2c., 3c. Common zebra; 20c., 50c. Vasco da Gama.

1925. De Pombal stamps of Mozambique, Nos. D327/9, optd **NYASSA**.
D144 C 22 30c. brown . . . . . 8·75 8·75
D145 – 30c. brown . . . . . 8·75 8·75
D146 C 25 30c. brown . . . . . 8·75 8·75

OBOCK Pt. 6

A port and district on the Somali Coast. During 1894 the administration was moved to Djibouti, the capital of French Somali Coast, and the Obock post office was closed.

1892. Stamps of French Colonies, "Commerce" type, optd **OBOCK**.
1 J 1c. black on blue . . . . . . 48·00 44·00
2 2c. brown on buff . . . . . 48·00 48·00
12 4c. brown on grey . . . . . 11·50 18·00
13 5c. green on green . . . . . 16·00 16·00
14 10c. black on lilac . . . . . 20·00 30·00
15 15c. blue . . . . 11·00 21·00
16 20c. red on green . . . . . . 55·00 48·00
17 25c. black on pink . . . . . 17·00 23·00
8 35c. black on orange £275 £250
18 40c. red on buff . . . . . . 55·00 55·00
19 75c. red on pink £200 £170
20 1f. green . . . . 65·00 65·00

1892. Nos. 14, 15, 17 and 20 surch.
39 J 1 on 25c. black on red . . . 6·50 10·00
40 2 on 10c. black on lilac . . . 65·00 55·00
41 2 on 15c. blue . . . . 6·00 20·00
42 4 on 15c. blue . . . . 10·00 28·00
43 4 on 25c. black on red . . . 11·50 9·75
44 5 on 25c. black on red . . . 22·00 27·00
45 20 on 10c. black on lilac . . 80·00 80·00
46 30 on 10c. black on lilac . . 95·00 85·00
47 35 on 25c. black on red . . . 90·00 65·00
48 75 on 1f. olive . . . . 85·00 95·00
49 5f. on 1f. olive £550 £450

1892. "Tablet" key-type inscr "OBOCK" in red (1, 5, 15, 25, 75c., 1f.) or blue (others).
50 D 1c. black on blue . . . . . 4·50 4·75
51 2c. brown on buff . . . . . 1·80 2·50
52 4c. brown on grey . . . . . 2·00 1·80
53 5c. green on green . . . . . 4·75 6·25
54 10c. black on lilac . . . . . 6·75 8·75
55 15c. blue . . . . 17·00 12·00
56 20c. red on green . . . . . . 28·00 32·00
57 25c. black on pink . . . . . 25·00 29·00
58 30c. brown on drab . . . . . 20·00 17·00
59 40c. red on yellow . . . . . 18·00 17·00
60 50c. red on pink . . . . . . 13·00 16·00
61 75c. brown on orange . . . 36·00 20·00
62 1f. green . . . . 30·00 50·00

5

1893.
63 5 2f. grey . . . . 60·00 60·00
64 5f. red £120 £120
The 5f. stamp is larger than the 2f.

6

7

1894.
65 6 1c. black and red 20 35
66 2c. red and green . . . . . 2·00 1·30
67 4c. red and orange . . . . . 1·20 1·00
68 5c. green and brown . . . . 1·70 90
69 10c. black and green . . . . 4·75 2·50
70 15c. blue and red . . . . . 2·00 80
71 20c. orange and purple . . . 6·25 95
72 25c. black and blue . . . . . 8·50 1·70
73 30c. yellow and green . . . . 21·00 7·25
74 40c. orange and green . . . 9·25 6·00
75 50c. red and blue . . . . . 8·00 4·50
76 75c. lilac and orange . . . . 10·00 4·50
77 1f. olive and purple . . . . . 8·50 6·75
78 7 2f. orange and lilac £120 £100
79 5f. red and blue £120 £100
80 10f. lake and red £120 £120
81 25f. blue and brown £600 £600
82 50f. green and lake £650 £600
Length of sides of Type 7: 2f. 37 mm; 5f. 42 mm; 10f. 46 mm; 25, 50f. 49 mm.

POSTAGE DUE STAMPS

1892. Postage Due stamps of French Colonies optd **OBOCK**.
D25 U 1c. black . . . . 55·00 60·00
D26 2c. black . . . . 46·00 55·00
D27 3c. black . . . . 50·00 55·00
D28 4c. black . . . . 34·00 44·00
D29 5c. black . . . . 12·50 11·00
D30 10c. black . . . . 46·00 48·00
D31 15c. black . . . . 22·00 29·00
D32 20c. black . . . . 26·00 40·00
D33 30c. black . . . . 44·00 46·00
D34 40c. black . . . . 65·00 65·00
D35 60c. black . . . . 75·00 75·00
D36 1f. brown £150 £150
D37 2f. brown £160 £160
D38 5f. brown £325 £325

For later issues see **DJIBOUTI**.

OCEANIC SETTLEMENTS Pt. 6

Scattered French islands in the E. Pacific Ocean, including Tahiti and the Marquesas.

In 1957 the Oceanic Settlements were renamed French Polynesia.

1892. "Tablet" key-type.
1 D 1c. black and red on blue . . 40 45
2 2c. brown and blue on buff 1·50 1·00
3 4c. brown and blue on grey 1·30 1·20
14 5c. green and red . . . . . 1·60 45
5 10c. black and blue on lilac 21·00 8·50
15 10c. red and blue . . . . . 1·00 30
6 15c. blue and red . . . . . 19·00 7·75
16 15c. grey and red . . . . . 1·30 3·25
7 20c. red and blue on green 5·75 12·50
8 25c. black and red on pink 38·00 12·00
17 25c. blue and red . . . . . 7·25 2·00
9 30c. brown and blue on drab 15·00 14·00
18 35c. black and red on yellow 2·30 4·75
10 40c. red and blue on yellow 90·00 £100
19 45c. black and red on green 1·30 6·50
11 50c. red and blue on pink 4·25 6·75
20 50c. brown and red on blue £140 £150
12 75c. brown and red on orange . . . . 8·75 14·50
13 1f. green and red . . . . . 18·00 23·00

2 Tahitian Woman

3 Kanakas

4 Valley of Fautaua

1913.
21 2 1c. brown and violet 30 30
22 2c. grey and brown 70 95
23 4c. blue and orange . . . . 90 1·50
24 5c. light green and green . . 1·50 1·60
46 5c. black and blue . . . . . 1·30 1·80
25 10c. orange and red . . . . 3·00 1·90
47 10c. light green and green 2·75 3·75
48 10c. purple and red on blue 2·50 3·25
25a 15c. black and orange . . . 2·50 2·50
26 20c. violet and black . . . . 85 3·50
49 20c. green . . . . 1·90 4·50
50 20c. brown and red . . . . 3·00 3·00
27 3 25c. blue and ultramarine 3·75 2·30
51 25c. red and violet . . . . 1·30 2·30
28 30c. brown and grey . . . . 5·50 6·00
52 30c. red and carmine . . . 2·50 6·00
53 30c. red and black . . . . 2·30 2·50
54 30c. green and blue . . . . 2·75 5·50
29 35c. red and green . . . . 2·00 3·50
30 40c. green and black . . . . 2·50 2·75
31 45c. red and orange . . . . 2·50 4·00
32 50c. black and brown . . . 12·50 14·50
55 50c. blue and ultramarine 2·30 2·75
56 50c. blue and grey . . . . . 1·90 1·80
57 60c. black and green . . . . 1·70 4·75
58 65c. mauve and brown . . . 4·00 4·00
33 75c. violet and purple . . . 3·00 3·00
59 90c. mauve and red . . . . 10·50 26·00
34 4 1f. black and red . . . . . 3·25 2·50
60 1f.10 brown and mauve . . 3·25 5·25
61 1f.40 violet and brown . . . 5·50 7·00
62 1f.50 light blue and blue . . 15·00 8·75
35 2f. green and brown . . . . 6·75 6·00
36 5f. blue and violet . . . . . 9·00 18·00

1915. "Tablet" key-type optd **E F O 1915** and bar.
37 D 10c. red . . . . 95 3·25

1915. Red Cross. No. 37 surch **5c** and red cross.
38 D 10c.+5c. red . . . . 10·50 23·00

1915. Red Cross. Surch **5c** and red cross.
41 2 10c.+5c. orange and red . . . 2·50 4·50

1916. Surch.
42 2 10c. on 15c. black and orange 85 3·00
67 4 25c. on 2f. green and brown 95 5·25
68 25c. on 5f. blue and violet . . 95 5·25
63 3 60 on 75c. brown and blue 45 2·50
64 4 65 on 1f. brown and blue . . 1·40 4·50
65 85 on 1f. brown and blue . . 1·30 3·00
66 3 90 on 75c. mauve and red . . 2·50 4·50
69 4 1f.25 on 1f. ultramarine & bl 80 3·50
70 1f.50 on 1f. light blue & blue 2·30 3·00
71 20f. on 5f. mauve and red . . 10·00 32·00

1921. Surch **1921** and new value.
43 2 05 on 2c. grey and brown . . 30·00 30·00
44 3 10 on 45c. red and orange . . 36·00 40·00
45 2 25 on 15c. black and orange 4·25 10·50

1924. Surch **45c. 1924**.
72 2 45c. on 10c. orange and red 4·00 6·00

1926. Surch in words.
73 4 3f. on 5f. blue and grey . . . 50 5·00
74 10f. on 5f. black and green 4·25 8·00

13 Papetoia Bay

1929.
75 13 3f. sepia and green . . . . 5·75 7·00
76 5f. sepia and blue . . . . . 7·50 16·00
77 10f. sepia and red . . . . . 10·00 50·00
78 20f. sepia and mauve . . . 32·00 70·00

1931. "International Colonial Exhibition", Paris, key-types.
79 E 40c. black and green . . . . 5·75 11·00
80 F 50c. black and mauve . . . 6·50 12·00
81 G 90c. black and red . . . . . 6·75 13·00
82 H 1f.50 black and blue . . . . 7·00 10·00

14 Spearing Fish

15 Tahitian Girl

16 Native Gods

1934.

83 **14** 1c. black . . . . 10 2·00
84 2c. red . . . . 10 2·75
85 3c. blue . . . . 25 4·75
86 4c. orange . . . . 10 4·50
87 5c. mauve . . . . 40 3·00
88 10c. brown . . . . 25 3·75
89 15c. green . . . . 15 4·00
90 20c. red . . . . 35 3·25
91 **15** 25c. blue . . . . 2·00 2·75
92 30c. green . . . . 2·00 5·00
93 30c. orange . . . . 90 4·00
94 **16** 35c. green . . . . 3·50 7·75
95 **15** 40c. mauve . . . . 50 3·75
96 45c. red . . . . 11·50 14·00
97 45c. green . . . . 1·90 5·00
98 50c. violet . . . . 95 1·10
99 55c. blue . . . . 6·25 11·50
100 60c. black . . . . 1·20 3·75
101 65c. brown . . . . 5·50 5·25
102 70c. pink . . . . 2·50 5·00
103 75c. olive . . . . 8·50 11·00
104 80c. purple . . . . 2·30 5·25
105 90c. red . . . . 1·20 3·25
106 **16** 1f. brown . . . . 1·70 2·50
107 1f.25 purple . . . . 12·00 10·00
108 1f.25 red . . . . 1·90 5·25
109 1f.40 orange . . . . 1·50 6·00
110 1f.50 blue . . . . 1·50 1·80
111 1f.60 violet . . . . 1·40 5·25
112 1f.75 green . . . . 8·25 7·75
113 2f. red . . . . 1·30 3·00
114 2f.25 blue . . . . 1·80 5·25
115 2f.50 black . . . . 2·30 5·25
116 3f. orange . . . . 1·20 5·50
117 5f. mauve . . . . 1·80 5·75
118 10f. green . . . . 1·90 7·75
119 20f. brown . . . . 1·60 8·25

17 Flying Boat

1934. Air.
120 **17** 5f. green . . . . 1·50 4·00

1937. International Exhibition, Paris. As Nos. 168/73 of St.-Pierre et Miquelon.
121 20c. violet . . . . 2·30 6·00
122 30c. green . . . . 1·00 5·25
123 40c. red . . . . 45 4·25
124 50c. brown . . . . 95 3·00
125 90c. red . . . . 50 4·25
126 1f.50 blue . . . . 1·30 7·75

17a Pierre and Marie Curie

1938. International Anti-cancer Fund.
127 **17a** 1f.75+50c. blue . . . . . 9·00 30·00

17b

1939. New York World's Fair.
128 **17b** 1f.25 red . . . . 1·10 6·25
129 2f.25 blue . . . . 95 5·00

17c Storming the Bastille

1939. 150th Anniv of French Revolution.
130 **17c** 45c.+25c. green and black (postage) . . . . . . 6·50 38·00
131 70c.+30c. brown & black 10·00 38·00
132 90c.+35c. orange & black 10·00 38·00
133 1f.25+1f. red and black 12·00 38·00
134 2f.25+2f. blue and black 12·00 38·00

135 5f.+4f. black & orge (air) 21·00 30·00

1941. Adherence to General de Gaulle. Optd **FRANCE LIBRE**. (a) Nos. 75/8.
136 **13** 3f. brown and green . . . 1·30 6·50
137 5f. brown and blue . . . . 90 10·50
138 10f. brown and red . . . . 5·25 19·00
139 20f. brown and mauve . . 42·00 £110

(b) Nos. 106 and 115/19.
140 **16** 1f. brown . . . . 85 10·50
141 2f.50 black . . . . 1·00 14·50
142 3f. red . . . . 1·80 14·50
143 5f. mauve . . . . 3·25 13·50
144 10f. green . . . . 13·50 75·00
145 20f. brown . . . . 14·00 75·00

(c) Air stamp of 1934.
146 **17** 5f. green . . . . 1·80 4·50

19 Polynesian Travelling Canoe

19a Airplane

1942. Free French Issue. (a) Postage.
147 **19** 5c. brown . . . . 10 4·50
148 10c. blue . . . . 10 3·25
149 25c. green . . . . 50 4·50
150 30c. red . . . . 10 4·00
151 40c. green . . . . 10 4·50
152 80c. purple . . . . 75 4·75
153 1f. mauve 85 85
154 1f.50 red . . . . 1·30 3·50
155 2f. black . . . . 1·30 2·00
156 2f.50 blue . . . . 1·50 5·25
157 4f. violet . . . . 1·20 4·00
158 5f. yellow . . . . 1·00 4·00
159 10f. brown . . . . 2·30 4·50
160 20f. green . . . . 1·90 5·00

(b) Air. As T **19a**.
161 1f. orange . . . . 1·70 4·00
162 1f.50 red . . . . 1·80 4·50
163 5f. purple . . . . 1·80 5·25
164 10f. black . . . . 2·50 6·00
165 25f. blue . . . . 3·00 7·00
166 50f. green . . . . 4·00 7·00
167 100f. red . . . . 3·75 7·00

19b

1944. Mutual Aid and Red Cross Funds.
168 **19b** 5f.+20f. blue . . . . . . 65 6·00

1945. Surch in figures.
169 **19** 50c. on 5c. brown . . . . 20 4·75
170 60c. on 5c. brown . . . . 20 4·75
171 70c. on 5c. brown . . . . 40 5·00
172 1f.20 on 5c. brown . . . . 45 4·75
173 2f.40 on 25c. green . . . . 65 4·75
174 3f. on 25c. green . . . . . 80 3·25
175 4f.50 on 25c. green . . . . 1·30 5·75
176 15f. on 2f.50 blue . . . . 85 4·75

20a Felix Eboue

1945. Eboue.
177 **20a** 2f. black . . . . 10 5·00
178 25f. green . . . . 95 6·50

20b "Victory"

1946. Air. Victory.
179 **20b** 8f. green . . . . 25 6·25

20c Legionaries by Lake Chad

1946. Air. From Chad to the Rhine.
180 **20c** 5f. red . . . . 1·40 6·75
181 – 10f. brown . . . . 80 6·75
182 – 15f. green . . . . 1·30 6·50
183 – 20f. red . . . . 1·70 6·50
184 – 25f. purple . . . . 1·00 7·50
185 – 50f. black . . . . 1·30 9·25
DESIGNS: 10f. Battle of Koufa; 15f. Tank Battle, Mareth; 20f. Normandy Landings; 25f. Liberation of Paris; 50f. Liberation of Strasbourg.

21 Mooréa Coastline

22 Tahitian Girl

23 Wandering Albatross over Mooréa

1948. (a) Postage as T **21/22**.
186 **21** 10c. brown 10 35
187 30c. green 45 35
188 40c. blue . . . . 60 3·25
189 – 50c. lake . . . . 60 3·00
190 – 60c. olive . . . . 45 4·50
191 – 80c. blue . . . . 50 5·00
192 – 1f. lake . . . . 2·50 90
193 – 1f.20 blue . . . . 2·50 5·00
194 – 1f.50 blue . . . . 70 2·50
195 **22** 2f. brown . . . . 2·75 75
196 2f.40 lake . . . . 2·75 5·50
197 3f. violet . . . . 7·75 60
198 4f. blue . . . . 2·30 60
199 – 5f. brown . . . . 3·25 80
200 – 6f. blue . . . . 3·50 70
201 – 9f. brown, black and red 2·50 5·00
202 – 10f. olive . . . . 4·25 45
203 – 15f. red . . . . 5·25 1·10
204 – 20f. blue . . . . 6·00 65
205 – 25f. brown . . . . 5·50 1·20

(b) Air. As T **23**.
206 – 13f. light blue and deep blue . . . . 3·00 1·30
207 **23** 50f. lake . . . . 28·00 23·00
208 – 100f. violet . . . . 25·00 18·00
209 – 200f. blue . . . . 48·00 18·00
DESIGNS: As T **22**: 50c. to 80c. Kanaka fisherman; 9f. Bora-Bora girl; 1f. to 1f.50, Faa village; 5, 6, 10f. Bora-Bora and Pandanus pine; 15f. to 25f. Polynesian girls. As T **23**: 13f. Pahia Peak and palms; 100f. Airplane over Mooréa; 200f. Wandering albatross over Maupiti Island.

24a People of Five Races, Aircraft and Globe

1949. Air. 75th Anniv of U.P.U.
210 **24a** 10f. blue . . . . 3·25 34·00

24b Doctor and Patient

1950. Colonial Welfare.
211 **24b** 10f.+2f. green and blue 7·00 11·50

24c **25** "Nafea" (after Gauguin)

1952. Centenary of Military Medals.
212 **24c** 3f. violet, yellow and green . . . . 10·00 10·50

1953. Air. 50th Death Anniv of Gauguin (painter).
213 **25** 14f. sepia, red and turquoise . . . . 30·00 65·00

25a Normandy Landings, 1944

1954. Air. 10th Anniv of Liberation.
214 **25a** 3f. green and turquoise 9·25 6·75

26 Schooner in Dry Dock, Papeete

1956. Economic and Social Development Fund.
215 **26** 3f. turquoise . . . . 1·00 1·10

POSTAGE DUE STAMPS

1926. Postage Due stamps of France surch **Etabts Francais de l'Oceanie 2 francs a percevoir** (No. D80) or optd **Etablissements Francais de l'Oceanie** (others).
D73 **D 11** 5c. blue . . . . 10 3·50
D74 10c. brown . . . . . . 10 3·25
D75 20c. olive . . . . 35 4·25
D76 30c. red . . . . 35 5·00
D77 40c. red . . . . 1·00 7·00
D78 60c. green . . . . . . 65 6·75
D79 1f. red on yellow . . . 55 7·00
D80 2f. on 1f. red . . . . . 75 7·75
D81 3f. mauve . . . . 3·25 19·00

D 14 Fautaua Falls **D 24**

1929.
D82 **D 14** 5c. brown and blue . . 20 2·75
D83 10c. green and orange 10 4·00
D84 30c. red and brown . . 50 4·25
D85 50c. brown and green 1·20 4·00
D86 60c. green and violet . . 2·00 8·25
D87 – 1f. mauve and blue . . 2·00 5·50
D88 – 2f. brown and red . . . 1·70 5·75
D89 – 3f. green and blue . . . 1·30 6·00
DESIGN: 1 to 3f. Polynesian man.

1948.
D210 **D 24** 10c. green . . . . . . 10 1·90
D211 30c. brown . . . . . . 10 4·75
D212 50c. red . . . . 20 4·75
D213 1f. blue . . . . 75 4·75
D214 2f. green . . . . 75 5·50
D215 3f. red . . . . 1·60 5·75
D216 4f. violet . . . . 1·40 6·00
D217 5f. mauve . . . . 1·80 7·00
D218 10f. blue . . . . 3·00 9·50
D219 20f. lake . . . . 2·30 11·50

For later issues see **FRENCH POLYNESIA**.

OLDENBURG — Pt. 7

A former Grand Duchy in North Germany. In 1867 it joined the North German Federation.

72 grote = 1 thaler.

1

2

3

1852. Imperf.

1	1	⅓sgr. black on green	£1300	£1300
2		1/30th. black on blue	£375	26·00
5		1/15th. black on red	£800	85·00
8		1/10th. black on yellow	£800	85·00

1859. Imperf.

17	2	¼g. yellow	£325	£4000
10		⅓g. black on green	£2500	£3000
19		⅓g. green	£475	£850
21		½g. brown	£425	£550
11		1g. black on blue	£700	43·00
23		1g. blue	£225	£170
15		2g. black on red	£950	£650
26		2g. red	£450	£450
16		3g. black on yellow	£950	£650
28		3g. yellow	£450	£450

1862. Roul.

30	3	⅓g. green	£225	£225
32		½g. orange	£225	£110
42		1g. red	10·50	50·00
36		2g. blue	£225	50·00
39		3g. bistre	£225	50·00

OMAN (SULTANATE) — Pt. 19

In January 1971, the independent Sultanate of Muscat and Oman was renamed Sultanate of Oman.

NOTE. Labels inscribed "State of Oman" or "Oman Imamate State" are said to have been issued by a rebel administration under the Imam of Oman. There is no convincing evidence that these labels had any postal use within Oman and they are therefore omitted. They can be found, however, used on covers which appear to emanate from Amman and Baghdad.

1971. 1000 baizas = 1 rial saidi.
1972. 1000 baizas = 1 rial omani.

1971. Nos. 110/21 of Muscat and Oman optd SULTANATE of OMAN in English and Arabic.

122	12	5b. purple	30	10
142		10b. brown	45	15
124		20b. brown	1·20	30
125	A	25b. black and violet	1·20	30
126		30b. black and blue	1·80	55
127		40b. black and orange	2·30	60
128	14	50b. mauve and blue	30	85
129	B	75b. green and brown	4·50	1·20
130	C	100b. blue and orange	6·25	1·90
131		¼r. brown and green	15·00	5·00
132	E	½r. violet and red	31·00	8·50
133	F	1r. red and violet	60·00	17·00

19 Sultan Qabus and Buildings ("Land Development")

1971. National Day. Multicoloured.

134	10b. Type 19	1·50	25
135	40b. Sultan in military uniform and Omanis ("Freedom")	6·25	55
136	50b. Doctors and patients ("Health Services")	7·75	90
137	100b. Children at school ("Education")	15·00	3·00

1971. No. 94 of Muscat and Oman surch SULTANATE of OMAN 5 in English and Arabic.

138	5b. on 3b. purple	£120	14·00

21 Child in Class

1971. 25th Anniv of UNICEF.

139	21	50b.+25b. multicoloured	14·00	3·75

22 Book Year Emblem

1972. International Book Year.

140	22	25b. multicoloured	14·00	1·90

(24)

1972. Nos. 102 of Muscat and Oman and 127 of Oman optd with T 24.

144	25b. on 1r. blue and orange	£100	£100
145	25b. on 40b. black and orange	£100	£100

26 Matrah, 1809

1972.

158	26	5b. multicoloured	25	10
147		10b. multicoloured	55	15
148		20b. multicoloured	90	15
149		25b. multicoloured	1·20	15
150	–	30b. multicoloured	1·50	15
151	–	40b. multicoloured	1·50	15
152	–	50b. multicoloured	1·90	25
153	–	75b. multicoloured	4·50	45
154	–	100b. multicoloured	6·25	75
155	–	¼r. multicoloured	14·00	1·50
156	–	½r. multicoloured	27·00	4·50
157	–	1r. multicoloured	42·00	9·25

DESIGNS—26×21 mm: 30b. to 75b. Shinas, 1809. 42×25 mm: 100b. to 1r. Muscat, 1809.

29 Government Buildings

1973. Opening of Ministerial Complex.

170	29	25b. multicoloured	1·90	75
171		100b. multicoloured	7·00	1·90

30 Oman Crafts (dhow building)

1973. National Day. Multicoloured.

172	15b. Type 30	1·20	40
173	50b. Seeb International Airport	5·75	1·50
174	65b. Dhow and tanker	6·25	1·50
175	100b. "Ship of the Desert" (camel)	8·50	2·50

31 Aerial View of Port

1974. Inauguration of Port Qabus.

176	31	100b. multicoloured	7·75	2·75

32 Map on Open Book

1974. Illiteracy Eradication Campaign. Mult.

177	25b. Type 32	2·30	40
178	100b. Hands reaching for open book (vert)	7·00	2·30

33 Sultan Qabus bin Said and Emblems

1974. Centenary of U.P.U.

179	33	100b. multicoloured	2·30	1·50

34 Arab Scribe

1975. "Eradicate Illiteracy".

180	34	25b. multicoloured	5·75	1·90

35 New Harbour, Mina Raysoot

1975. National Day. Multicoloured.

181	30b. Type 35	75	40
182	50b. Stadium and map	1·50	45
183	75b. Water desalination plant	1·90	85
184	100b. Television station	2·75	1·30
185	150b. Satellite Earth station and map	3·75	2·00
186	250b. Telecommunications symbols and map	7·75	3·75

36 Arab Woman and Child with Nurse

1975. International Women's Year. Mult.

187	75b. Type 36	1·90	75
188	150b. Mother and children (vert)	3·00	1·50

37 Presenting Colours and Opening of Seeb–Nizwa Highway

1976. National Day. Multicoloured.

201	25b. Type 37	75	25
202	40b. Parachutists and harvesting	2·30	55
203	75b. Agusta-Bell AB-212 helicopters and Victory Day procession	4·50	1·20
204	150b. Road construction and Salalah T.V. Station	5·50	2·00

38 Great Bath, Moenjodaro

1977. "Save Moenjodaro" Campaign.

205	38	125b. multicoloured	5·00	2·30

39 A.P.U. Emblem

40 Coffee Pots

1977. 25th Anniv of Arab Postal Union.

206	39	30b. multicoloured	1·90	55
207		75b. multicoloured	3·75	1·50

1977. National Day. Multicoloured.

208	40b. Type 40	1·10	40
209	75b. Earthenware pots	2·30	75
210	100b. Khor Rori inscriptions	3·75	1·20
211	150b. Silver jewellery	6·25	1·50

1978. Surch in English and Arabic.

212	40b. on 150b. mult (No. 185)	£225	£225
213	50b. on 150b. mult (No. 188)	£225	£225
214	75b. on 250b. mult (No. 186)	£400	£400

42 Mount Arafat, Pilgrims and Kaaba

1978. Pilgrimage to Mecca.

215	42	40b. multicoloured	3·75	1·70

43 Jalali Fort

1978. National Day. Forts. Multicoloured.

216	20b. Type 43	75	25
217	25b. Nizwa Fort	75	30
218	40b. Rostaq Fort	1·80	55
219	50b. Sohar Fort	2·00	60
220	75b. Bahla Fort	2·50	1·00
221	100b. Jibrin Fort	3·75	1·30

44 World Map, Koran and Symbols of Arab Achievements

1979. The Arabs.

222	44	40b. multicoloured	1·50	40
223		100b. multicoloured	3·00	90

45 Child on Swing

1979. International Year of the Child.

224	45	40b. multicoloured	2·75	1·90

46 Gas Plant

1979. National Day. Multicoloured.

225	25b. Type 46	1·90	70
226	75b. Dhow and modern trawler	5·75	1·90

47 Sultan Qabus on Horseback

1979. Armed Forces Day. Multicoloured.
227 40b. Type **47** . . . . 3·75 1·20
228 100b. Soldier . . . . 7·75 2·75

48 Mosque, Mecca

1980. 1400th Anniv of Hegira. Multicoloured.
229 50b. Type **48** . . . . 3·00 75
230 150b. Mosque and Kaaba . . 5·50 2·50

49 Bab Alkabir

1980. National Day. Multicoloured.
231 75b. Type **49** . . . . 1·50 75
232 100b. Corniche . . . . . . 1·90 1·20
233 250b. Polo match . . . . . 4·25 3·50
234 500b. Omani women . . . . 7·75 6·25

50 Sultan and Naval Patrol Boat

1980. Armed Forces Day. Multicoloured.
235 150b. Type **50** . . . . . . 4·50 2·30
236 750b. Sultan and mounted soldiers . . . . 23·00 11·00

51 Policewoman helping Children across Road

1981. National Police Day. Multicoloured.
237 50b. Type **51** . . . . 2·75 75
238 100b. Police bandsmen . . . 3·00 1·50
239 150b. Mounted police . . . . 3·50 2·30
240 ½r. Police headquarters . . . 10·00 7·25

1981. Nos. 231, 234 and 235/6 surch **POSTAGE** and new value in English and Arabic.
241 **50** 20b. on 150b. multicoloured . . . . . 3·00 60
242 – 30b. on 750b. multicoloured . . . . . 3·75 90
243 **49** 50b. on 75b. multicoloured 4·50 1·50
244 – 100b. on 500b. multicoloured . . . . . 7·75 2·75

53 Sultan's Crest

1981. Welfare of Blind.
245 **53** 10b. black, blue and red 15·00 1·90

54 Palm Tree, Fishes and Wheat

1981. World Food Day.
246 **54** 50b. multicoloured . . . . 4·50 1·90

55 Pilgrims at Prayer

1981. Pilgrimage to Mecca.
247 **55** 50b. multicoloured . . . . 5·50 2·30

56 Al Razha

1981. National Day. Multicoloured.
248 160b. Type **56** . . . . . . 3·75 2·30
249 300b. Sultan Qabus bin Said 7·00 3·50

57 Muscat Port, 1981

1981. Retracing the Voyage of Sinbad. Mult.
250 50b. Type **57** . . . . 1·50 75
251 100b. The "Sohar" (replica of medieval dhow) . . . . . 3·00 1·90
252 130b. Map showing route of voyage . . . . 3·75 2·50
253 200b. Muscat Harbour, 1650 5·50 3·50
MS254 172 × 130 mm. Nos. 250/3 46·00 23·00

58 Parachute-drop

1981. Armed Forces Day. Multicoloured.
255 100b. Type **58** . . . . 3·75 1·90
256 400b. Missile-armed corvettes 10·00 4·50

59 Police Launch

1982. National Police Day. Multicoloured.
257 50b. Type **59** . . . . 2·30 1·20
258 100b. Royal Oman Police Band at Cardiff . . . . . 4·50 2·30

60 "Nerium mascatense"

1982. Flora and Fauna. Multicoloured.
259 5b. Type **60** 25 15
260 10b. "Dionysia mira" 25 15
261 20b. "Teucrium mascatense" 40 15
262 25b. "Geranium mascatense" 40 15
263 30b. "Cymatium boschi" (horiz) 60 30
264 40b. Eloise's acteon (horiz) 60 30
265 50b. Teulere's cowrie (horiz) 70 40
266 75b. Lovely cowrie (horiz) . . 90 60
267 100b. Arabian chukar (25 × 33 mm) . . . . . . 3·00 1·10
268 ¼r. Hoopoe (25 × 33 mm) . . 7·75 4·25
269 ½r. Arabian tahr (25 × 39 mm) . . . . . . 9·25 5·75
270 1r. Arabian oryx (25 × 39 mm) . . . . . . 15·00 11·50

Nos. 259/62 show flowers, Nos. 263/6 shells, Nos. 267/8 birds and Nos. 269/70 animals.

61 Palm Tree

1982. Arab Palm Tree Day. Multicoloured.
271 40b. Type **61** 70 40
272 100b. Palm tree and nuts . . 1·60 95

62 I.T.U. Emblem

1982. I.T.U. Delegates Conference, Nairobi.
273 **62** 100b. multicoloured . . . 7·00 2·75

63 Emblem and Cups

1982. Municipalities Week.
274 **63** 40b. multicoloured . . . . 4·50 1·90

64 State Consultative Council Inaugural Session

1982. National Day. Multicoloured.
275 40b. Type **64** . . . . 3·00 1·50
276 100b. Petroleum refinery . . 6·25 2·75

65 Sultan meeting Troops

1982. Armed Forces Day. Multicoloured.
277 50b. Type **65** . . . . 2·30 1·20
278 100b. Mounted army band 4·50 2·30

66 Police Motorcyclist and Headquarters

1983. National Police Day.
279 **66** 50b. multicoloured . . . . 5·50 1·90

67 Satellite, W.C.Y. Emblem and Dish Aerial

1983. World Communications Year.
280 **67** 50b. multicoloured . . . . 4·50 2·30

68 Bee Hives

1983. Bee-keeping. Multicoloured.
281 50b. Type **68** . . . . 3·00 2·30
282 50b. Bee collecting nectar . . 3·00 2·30

Nos. 281/2 were issued together, se-tenant, each pair forming a composite design.

69 Pilgrims at Mudhalfa

1983. Pilgrimage to Mecca.
283 **69** 40b. multicoloured . . . . 5·50 1·90

70 Emblem, Map and Sultan

1983. Omani Youth Year.
284 **70** 50b. multicoloured . . . . 4·50 1·90

71 Sohar Copper Mine

1983. National Day. Multicoloured.
285 50b. Type **71** . . . . 2·30 1·20
286 100b. Sultan Qabus University and foundation stone . . . . 4·50 2·30

72 Machine Gun Post

1983. Armed Forces Day.
287 **72** 100b. multicoloured . . . 6·25 2·30

73 Police Cadets Parade

1984. National Police Day.
288 **73** 100b. multicoloured . . . 6·25 2·30

74 Footballers and Cup

1984. 7th Arabian Gulf Cup Football Tournament. Multicoloured.
289 40b. Type **74** . . . . 2·30 1·20
290 50b. Emblem and pictograms of footballers . . . . . . 3·75 1·50

75 Stoning the Devil

1984. Pilgrimage to Mecca.
291 **75** 50b. multicoloured . . . . 1·20 70

76 New Central Post Office and Automatic Sorting Machine

1984. National Day. Multicoloured.
292 130b. Type **76** 95 85
293 160b. Map of Oman with telecommunications symbols . . . . 1·50 1·30

77 Scouts reading Map

1984. 16th Arab Scouts Conference, Muscat. Multicoloured.
294 50b. Scouts pegging tent . . 1·20 45
295 50b. Type **77** . . . . 1·20 45
296 130b. Scouts assembled round flag . . . . 3·75 1·30
297 130b. Scout, cub, guide, brownie and scout leaders 3·75 1·30

78 Sultan, Jet Fighters and "Al Munassir" (landing craft)

1984. Armed Forces Day.
298 **78** 100b. multicoloured . . . 6·25 2·75

79 Bell 214ST Helicopter lifting Man from "Al-Ward" (tanker)

1985. National Police Day.
299 **79** 100b. multicoloured . . . 6·25 2·75

80 Al-Khaif Mosque and Tent, Mina

1985. Pilgrimage to Mecca.
300 **80** 50b. multicoloured . . . . 3·00 1·20

81 I.Y.Y. Emblem and Youth holding Olive Branches

1985. International Youth Year. Mult.
301 50b. Type **81** . . . . 1·90 75
302 100b. Emblem and young people at various activities 3·50 1·50

82 Palace before and after Restoration

1985. Restoration of Jabrin Palace. Mult.
303 100b. Type **82** . . . . . . 2·30 1·20
304 250b. Restored ceiling . . . 5·50 3·50

83 Drummers

1985. International Omani Traditional Music Symposium.
305 **83** 50b. multicoloured . . . . 3·00 1·20

84 Scenes of Child Care and Emblem

1985. UNICEF Child Health Campaign.
306 **84** 50b. multicoloured . . . . 3·00 1·20

85 Flags around Map of Gulf

1985. 6th Supreme Council Session of Gulf Co-operation Council, Muscat. Multicoloured.
307 40b. Type **85** . . . . 1·70 75
308 50b. Portraits of rulers of Council member countries 2·20 90

86 Sultan Qabus University and Students

1985. National Day. Multicoloured.
309 20b. Type **86** 60 30
310 50b. Tractor and oxen ploughing field . . . . . . 1·20 75
311 100b. Port Qabus cement factory and Oman Chamber of Commerce . . 2·00 1·20
312 200b. Road bridge, Douglas DC-10 airliner and communications centre . . 3·50 2·30
313 250b. Portrait of Sultan Qabus (vert) . . . . 4·25 2·75

87 Military Exercise at Sea

1985. Armed Forces Day.
314 **87** 100b. multicoloured . . . 6·25 1·50

88 Red-tailed Butterflyfish

1985. Marine Life. Multicoloured.
315 20b. Type **88** 45 15
316 50b. Black-finned melon butterflyfish 90 40
317 100b. Gardiner's butterflyfish 1·40 90
318 150b. Narrow-barred Spanish mackerel . . . . 2·00 1·50
319 200b. Lobster (horiz) . . . . 3·00 2·00

89 Frankincense Tree

1985. Frankincense Production.
320 **89** 100b. multicoloured . . . 90 90
321 3r. multicoloured . . . . . 26·00 23·00

90 Camel Corps Member

1986. National Police Day.
322 **90** 50b. multicoloured . . . . 3·50 1·20

91 Cadet Barquentine "Shabab Oman", 1986

1986. Participation of "Shabab Oman" in Statue of Liberty Centenary Celebrations. Multicoloured.
323 50b. "Sultana" (full-rigged sailing ship), 1840 . . . . 3·00 1·20
324 100b. Type **91** . . . . . . 4·50 1·90
MS325 162 × 128 mm. Nos. 323/4 (sold at 250b.) . . . . 17·00 9·25

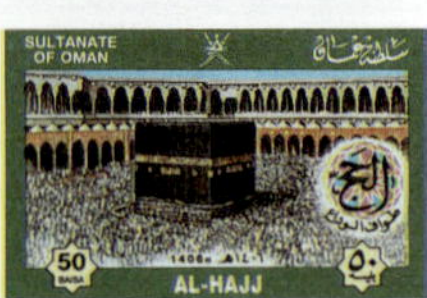

92 Crowd around Holy Kaaba

1986. Pilgrimage to Mecca.
326 **92** 50b. multicoloured . . . . 2·30 90

93 Scouts erecting Tent

1986. 17th Arab Scout Camp, Salalah. Multicoloured.
327 50b. Type **93** . . . . 1·90 75
328 100b. Scouts making survey 3·00 1·50

94 Sports Complex

1986. Inauguration of Sultan Qabus Sports Complex.
329 **94** 100b. multicoloured . . . 2·75 1·40

95 Mother and Baby, Emblem and Tank on Globe

1986. International Peace Year.
330 **95** 130b. multicoloured . . . 2·30 1·20

96 Al-Sahwa Tower

1986. National Day. Multicoloured.
331 50b. Type **96** . . . . 1·20 60
332 100b. Sultan Qabus University (inauguration) 2·75 1·30
333 130b. 1966 stamps and F.D.C. cancellation (20th anniv of first Oman stamp issue) (57 × 27 mm) . . . . 3·00 1·50

97 Camel Corps

1987. National Police Day.
334 **97** 50b. multicoloured . . . . 2·50 1·20

98 Family

1987. Arabian Gulf Social Work Week.
335 **98** 50b. multicoloured . . . . 2·30 90

99 Aqueduct

101 Examples of Work and Hand holding Cup

100 Crowd around Holy Kaaba

1987. International Environment Day. Mult.
336 50b. Greater flamingoes . . . 2·30 75
337 130b. Type **99** . . . . . . 3·75 1·20

1987. Pilgrimage to Mecca. Multicoloured.
338 50b. Type **100** . . . . . . 1·20 75
339 50b. Al-Khaif Mosque and tents, Mina . . . . 1·20 75
340 50b. Stoning the Devil . . . 1·20 75

341 50b. Pilgrims at Mudhalfa . . 1·20 75
342 50b. Pilgrims at prayer . . . 1·20 75
343 50b. Mount Arafat, pilgrims and Kaaba . . . . 1·20 75

1987. 3rd Municipalities Month.
344 **101** 50b. multicoloured . . . 1·70 75

102 Marine Science and Fisheries Centre

1987. National Day. Multicoloured.
345 50b. Type **102** 60 40
346 130b. Royal Hospital . . . . 1·70 1·00

103 Radio Operators

1987. 15th Anniv of Royal Omani Amateur Radio Society.
347 **103** 130b. multicoloured . . . 2·30 1·20

104 Weaver

1988. Traditional Crafts. Multicoloured.
348 50b. Type **104** 90 55
349 100b. Potter . . . . 1·40 75
350 150b. Halwa maker . . . . . 1·90 1·20
351 200b. Silversmith . . . . . . 2·30 1·40
MS352 165 × 135 mm. Nos. 348/51 (sold at 600b.) . . . . 11·50 7·75

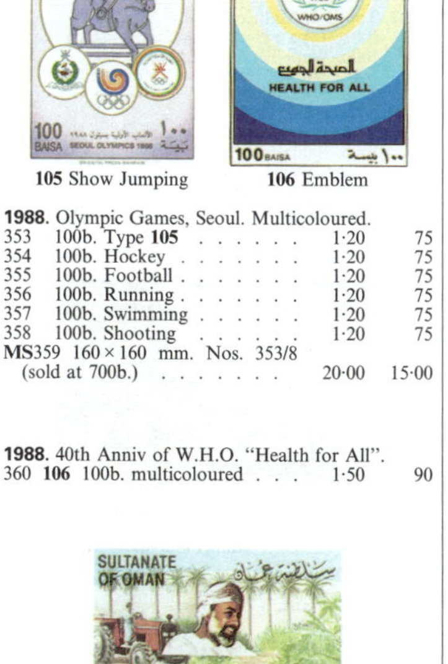

105 Show Jumping 106 Emblem

1988. Olympic Games, Seoul. Multicoloured.
353 100b. Type **105** . . . . . . 1·20 75
354 100b. Hockey . . . . 1·20 75
355 100b. Football . . . . 1·20 75
356 100b. Running . . . . 1·20 75
357 100b. Swimming . . . . . . 1·20 75
358 100b. Shooting . . . . . . 1·20 75
MS359 160 × 160 mm. Nos. 353/8 (sold at 700b.) . . . . 20·00 15·00

1988. 40th Anniv of W.H.O. "Health for All".
360 **106** 100b. multicoloured . . . 1·50 90

107 Tending Land and Crops

1988. National Day. Agriculture Year. Mult.
361 100b. Type **107** . . . . . . 1·00 75
362 100b. Livestock . . . . . . 1·00 75

108 Dhahira Region (woman's)

1989. Costumes. Multicoloured.
363 30b. Type **108** 60 30
364 40b. Eastern region (woman's) 75 45
365 50b. Batinah region (woman's) 90 60
366 100b. Interior region (woman's) . . . . 1·80 1·20
367 130b. Southern region (woman's) . . . . 2·30 1·70
368 150b. Muscat region (woman's) . . . . 2·75 1·90
369 200b. Dhahira region (man's) 1·50 1·20
370 ¼r. Eastern region (man's) . . 1·80 1·70
371 ½r. Southern region (man's) 3·50 3·25
372 1r. Muscat region (man's) . . 7·00 6·25
MS373 210 × 145 mm. Nos. 363/8 (sold at 700b.) . . . . 14·00 9·25
MS374 210 × 145 mm. Nos. 369/72 (sold at 2r.) . . . . 20·00 15·00

109 Fishing

1989. National Day. Agriculture Year. Mult.
375 100b. Type **109** 90 60
376 100b. Agriculture 90 60

110 Flags and Omani State Arms

1989. 10th Supreme Council Session of Arab Co-operation Council, Muscat. Multicoloured.
377 50b. Type **110** 60 45
378 50b. Council emblem and Sultan Qabus 60 45

111 Emblem and Map

1990. 5th Anniv (1989) of Gulf Investment Corporation.
379 **111** 50b. multicoloured . . . 1·50 75
380 130b. multicoloured . . . 2·30 1·20

112 Emblem and Douglas DC-10 Airliner 113 Map

1990. 40th Anniv of Gulf Air.
381 **112** 80b. multicoloured . . . 3·00 1·20

1990. Omani Ophiolite Symposium, Muscat.
382 **113** 80b. multicoloured . . . 90 60
383 150b. multicoloured . . . 1·80 1·30

114 Ahmed bin Na'aman al-Ka'aby (envoy), "Sultana" and Said bin Sultan al-Busaidi

1990. 150th Anniv of First Omani Envoy's Journey to U.S.A.
384 **114** 200b. multicoloured . . . 1·90 1·20

115 Sultan Qabus Rose

1990. 20th Anniv of Sultan Qabus's Accession.
385 **115** 200b. multicoloured . . . 1·90 1·20

116 National Day Emblem

1990. National Day.
386 **116** 100b. red and green on gold foil . . . . 1·20 60
387 – 200b. green and red on gold foil . . . . 2·30 1·30
MS388 160 × 114 mm. Nos. 386/7 (sold at 500b.) . . . . 4·50 4·50
DESIGN: 200b. Sultan Qabus.

117 Donor and Recipient

1991. Blood Donation.
389 **117** 50b. multicoloured . . . 45 40
390 200b. multicoloured . . . 1·90 1·20

118 Industrial Emblems

1991. National Day and Industry Year. Mult.
391 100b. Type **118** . . . . . . 2·30 75
392 200b. Sultan Qabus . . . . . 3·75 1·50
MS393 172 × 123 mm. Nos. 391/2 (sold at 400b.) . . . . 6·25 3·75

119 Weapons, Military Transport and Sultan Qabus

1991. Armed Forces Day.
394 **119** 100b. multicoloured . . . 1·50 75

120 Interior of Museum and National Flags 121 Satellite Picture of Asia

1992. Inaug of Omani-French Museum, Muscat.
395 **120** 100b. multicoloured . . . 1·20 75
MS396 141 × 100 mm. No. 395 (sold at 300b.) . . . . 7·75 3·75

1992. World Meteorological Day.
397 **121** 220b. multicoloured . . . 2·30 1·50

122 Emblem and Hands 123 Emblem and Hands protecting Handicapped Child

1992. World Environment Day.
398 **122** 100b. multicoloured . . . 1·50 90

1992. Welfare of Handicapped Children.
399 **123** 70b. multicoloured . . . 1·20 60

124 Sultan Qabus and Books

1992. Publication of Sultan Qabus "Encyclopedia of Arab Names".
400 **124** 100b. multicoloured . . . 1·40 75

125 Sultan Qabus, Factories and Industry Year Emblem

1992. National Day. Multicoloured.
401 100b. Type **125** . . . . . . 1·20 75
402 200b. Sultan Qabus and Majlis As'shura (Consultative Council) emblem . . . . 1·90 1·20

126 Mounted Policemen and Sultan Qabus

1993. National Police Day.
403 **126** 80b. multicoloured . . . 1·40 75

127 Census Emblem

1993. Population, Housing and Establishments Census.
404 **127** 100b. multicoloured . . . 1·20 75

128 Frigate and Sultan Qabus presenting Colours

1993. Navy Day.
405 **128** 100b. multicoloured . . . 1·50 75

129 Youth Year Emblem

1993. National Day and Youth Year. Multi.
406 100b. Type **129** . . . . . . 1·20 75
407 200b. Sultan Qabus . . . . . 1·90 1·20

130 Scout Headquarters and Emblem

1993. 61st Anniv of Scouting in Oman (408) and 10th Anniv of Sultan Qabus as Chief Scout (409). Multicoloured.
408 100b. Type **130** 90 75
409 100b. Scout camp and Sultan Qabus 90 75
Nos. 408/9 were issued together, se-tenant, forming a composite design.

131 Sei Whale and School of Dolphins

1993. Whales and Dolphins in Omani Waters. Multicoloured.
410 100b. Type **131** . . . . . . 1·90 1·20
411 100b. Sperm whale and dolphins . . . . 1·90 1·20
MS412 160 × 120 mm. Nos. 410/11 (sold at 400b.) . . . . . . 27·00 19·00
Nos. 410/11 were issued together, se-tenant, forming a composite design.

132 Water Drops and Falaj (ancient water system)

133 Municipality Building

1994. World Water Day.
413 **132** 50b. multicoloured . . . 90 45

1994. 70th Anniv of Muscat Municipality.
414 **133** 50b. multicoloured . . . 90 45

134 Centenary Emblem and Sports Pictograms

1994. Centenary of International Olympic Committee.
415 **134** 100b. multicoloured . . . 7·75 3·75

135 Emblem

1994. National Day. Multicoloured.
416 50b. Type **135** 60 40
417 50b. Sultan Qabus 60 40

136 Airplane and Emblem

1994. 50th Anniv of I.C.A.O.
418 **136** 100b. multicoloured . . . 3·00 1·50

137 Arms

139 Emblem and National Colours

138 Meeting

1994. 250th Anniv of Al-Busaid Dynasty. Multicoloured.
419 50b. Type **137** dated "1744–1775" . . . . 1·10 40
420 50b. Type **137** dated "1775–1779" . . . . 1·10 40
421 50b. Type **137** dated "1779–1792" . . . . 1·10 40
422 50b. Type **137** dated "1792–1804" . . . . 1·10 40
423 50b. Type **137** dated "1804–1807" . . . . 1·10 40
424 50b. Said bin Sultan (1807–1856) . . . . 1·10 40
425 50b. Type **137** dated "1856–1866" . . . . 1·10 40
426 50b. Type **137** dated "1866–1868" . . . . 1·10 40
427 50b. Type **137** dated "1868–1871" . . . . 1·10 40
428 50b. Turki bin Said (1871–1888) . . . . 1·10 40
429 50b. Feisal bin Turki (1888–1913) . . . . 1·10 40
430 50b. Taimur bin Feisal (1913–1932) . . . . . . 1·10 40
431 50b. Arms, Sultan Qabus and family tree . . . . . . 1·10 40
432 50b. Said bin Taimur (1932–1970) . . . . 1·10 40
433 50b. Sultan Qabus (1970–) 1·10 40
MS434 140 × 110 mm. 200d. As No. 431. Imperf . . . . 3·50 2·30

1995. Open Parliament.
435 **138** 50b. multicoloured . . . 90 55

1995. 50th Anniv of Arab League.
436 **139** 100b. multicoloured . . . 1·20 60

140 Anniversary Emblem

1995. 50th Anniv of U.N.O.
437 **140** 100b. multicoloured . . . 1·90 90

141 Sultan Qabus in Robes

1995. National Day. Multicoloured.
438 50b. Type **141** 75 45
439 100b. Sultan Qabus in military uniform . . . . . 1·20 60
MS440 150 × 110 mm. Nos. 438/9 (sold at 300b.) . . . . 3·00 2·30

142 Council Emblem

1995. 16th Supreme Council Session of Gulf Co-operation Council, Oman. Multicoloured.
441 100b. Type **142** . . . . . . 1·50 75
442 200b. Sultan Qabus, members' flags and map 2·30 1·20

143 Ash'shashah

1996. Omani Sailing Vessels. Multicoloured.
443 50b. Type **143** 25 15
444 100b. Al-Battil 45 40
445 200b. Al-Boum 90 75
446 250b. Al-Badan . . . . . . 1·20 90
447 350b. As'sanbuq . . . . . . 1·70 1·30
448 450b. Al-Galbout . . . . . 2·00 1·70
449 650b. Al-Baghlah . . . . . 2·75 2·50
450 1r. Al-Ghanjah . . . . . . 4·50 3·75

144 Emblem, Poppy Head, Skull-like Face smoking Cigarette and Syringe

1996. United Nations Decade against Drug Abuse.
451 **144** 100b. multicoloured . . . 9·25 7·00

145 Shooting

1996. Olympic Games, Atlanta. Multicoloured.
452 100b. Type **145** . . . . . . 3·75 1·90
453 100b. Swimming . . . . . . 3·75 1·90
454 100b. Cycling . . . . 3·75 1·90
455 100b. Running . . . . 3·75 1·90
Nos. 452/5 were issued together, se-tenant, forming a composite design.

146 Tournament Emblem and Flags of Participating Countries

1996. 13th Arabian Gulf Cup Football Championship.
456 **146** 100b. multicoloured . . . 1·30 75

147 Sultan Qabus and Sur (left detail)

1996. National Day. Multicoloured.
457 50b. Type **147** 60 45
458 50b. Sultan Qabus and Sur (right detail) 60 45
Nos. 457/8 were issued together, se-tenant, forming a composite design.

148 Mother with Children

1996. 50th Anniv of UNICEF.
459 **148** 100b. multicoloured . . . 90 60

149 Nakl Fort

1997. Tourism. Multicoloured.
460 100b. Type **149** . . . . . . 1·10 75
461 100b. Wadi Tanuf (waterfall in centre of stamp) . . . . 1·10 75
462 100b. Fort on Muthrah Corniche . . . . 1·10 75
463 100b. Wadi Dayqah Dam . . 1·10 75
464 100b. Bahla fort (overlooking tree-covered plain) . . . . 1·10 75
465 100b. Wadi Darbut waterfall (near top of stamp) . . . . 1·10 75

150 Sultan Qabus and Dhofar Waterfalls

1997. National Day. Multicoloured.
466 100b. Type **150** . . . . . . 1·20 75
467 100b. Sultan Qabus seated by waterfalls . . . . 1·20 75

151 Guide Activities

1997. 25th Anniv of Oman Girl Guides.
468 **151** 100b. multicoloured . . . 1·40 90

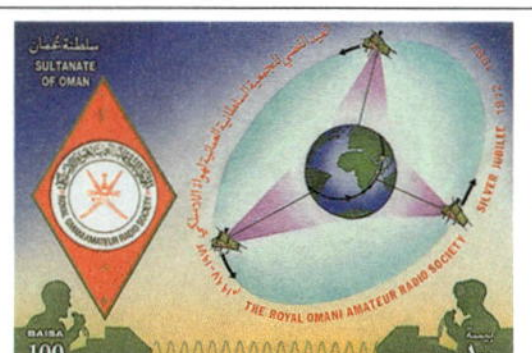

152 Society and Anniversary Emblems

1997. 25th Anniv of Royal Omani Amateur Radio Society.

469	**152**	100b. multicoloured	1·50	90

153 Dagger and Sheath

1998. Al-Khanjar Assaidi. Multicoloured, background colours given.

470	**153**	50b. green	45	40
471		50b. red	45	40
471a		80b. yellow	75	70
472		100b. violet	90	75
473		200b. brown	1·80	1·50

154 Car, Traffic Lights, Hand and Police Motor Cycle

1998. Gulf Co-operation Council Traffic Week.

474	**154**	100b. multicoloured	3·00	1·50

155 Sohar Fort

1998. Tourism. Multicoloured.

475	100b. Type **155**	1·20	75
476	100b. Wadi Shab	1·20	75
477	100b. Nizwa town	1·20	75
478	100b. Eid celebration (religious holiday)	1·20	75
479	100b. View of river	1·20	75
480	100b. Three young girls by an aqueduct	1·20	75

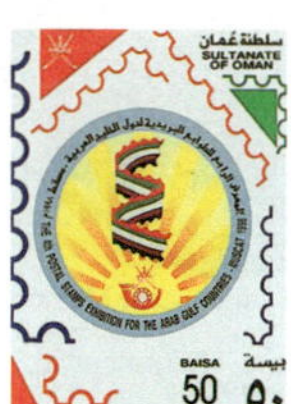

156 Exhibition Emblem

1998. 4th Arab Gulf Countries Stamp Exhibition, Muscat.

481	**156**	50b. multicoloured	75	55

157 U.P.U. Emblem and Doves

1998. World Stamp Day.

482	**157**	100b. multicoloured	90	75

158 Year Emblem

1998. National Day. Year of the Private Sector. Multicoloured.

483	100b. Sultan Qabus	1·20	75
484	100b. Type **158**	1·20	75
MS485	160 × 80 mm. Nos. 483/4	15·00	15·00

159 Map and Container Ship at Quayside

1998. Inauguration of Salalah Port Container Terminal.

486	**159**	50b. multicoloured	2·30	1·20

160 Sultan Qabus, Dove and Olive Branch

1998. International Peace Award.

487	**160**	500b. multicoloured	7·75	5·75

161 Military Aircraft and Sultan Qabus

1999. 40th Anniv of Royal Air Force of Oman.

488	**161**	100b. multicoloured	1·50	90

162 African Monarch

1999. Butterflies. Multicoloured.

489	100b. Type **162**	1·30	90
490	100b. Chequered swallowtail (*Papilio demoleus*)	1·30	90
491	100b. Blue pansy (*Precis orithya*)	1·30	90
492	100b. Yellow pansy (*Precis hierta*)	1·30	90
MS493	110 × 110 mm. Nos. 489/92	19·00	11·50

163 Longbarbel Goatfish

1999. Marine Life. Multicoloured.

494	100b. Type **163**	75	75
495	100b. Red-eyed round herring (*Etrumeus teres*)	75	75
496	100b. Brown-spotted grouper (*Epinephelus chlorostigma*)	75	75
497	100b. Blue-spotted emperor (*Lethrinus lentjan*)	75	75
498	100b. Blood snapper (*Lutjanus erythropterus*)	75	75
499	100b. Wahoo (*Acanthocybium solandri*)	75	75
500	100b. Long-tailed tuna (*Thunnus tonggol*)	75	75
501	100b. Crimson jobfish (*Pristipomoides filamentosus*)	75	75
502	100b. Yellow-finned tuna (*Thunnus albacares*)	75	75
503	100b. Cultured shrimp (*Penaeus indicus*)	75	75
504	100b. Pharaoh cuttlefish (*Sepia pharaonis*)	75	75
505	100b. Tropical rock lobster (*Panulirus homarus*)	75	75

164 Sand Cat

1999. Wildlife. Multicoloured.

506	100b. Type **164**	75	75
507	100b. Genet	75	75
508	100b. Leopard	75	75
509	100b. Sand fox	75	75
510	100b. Caracal lynx	75	75
511	100b. Hyena	75	75
MS512	175 × 96 mm. Nos. 506/11	15·00	11·50

165 Globe and Emblem

1999. 125th Anniv of Universal Postal Union.

513	**165**	200b. multicoloured	1·50	1·50

166 Sultan Qabus and Musicians

1999. National Day. Multicoloured.

514	100b. Type **166**	1·20	75
515	100b. Sultan Qabus and horsemen	1·20	75

Nos. 514/15 were issued together, se-tenant, forming a composite design.

167 Sultan Qabus, Globe and "2000"

2000. New Year. Sheet 80 × 95 mm.

MS516	**167**	500b. multicoloured	10·00	10·00

168 Water Droplet and Dried Earth

2000. World Water Week.

517	**168**	100b. multicoloured	85	75

169 Emblem, Airplane and Silhouette of Bird

2000. 50th Anniv of Gulf Air.

518	**169**	100b. multicoloured	1·00	75

170 Crimson-tip Butterfly (*Colotis danae*)

2000. Butterflies. Multicoloured.

519	100b. Type **170**	1·20	75
520	100b. *Anaphaeis aurota*	1·20	75
521	100b. *Tarucus rosaceus*	1·20	75
522	100b. Long-tailed blue (*Lampides boeticus*)	1·20	75
MS523	110 × 110 mm. Nos. 519/22	14·00	9·25

171 Yellow Seahorse (*Hippocampus kuda*)

2000. Marine Life. Multicoloured.

524	100b. Type **171**	1·30	85
525	100b. Yellow boxfish (*Ostracion cubicus*)	1·30	85
526	100b. Japanese pineconefish (*Monocentris japonica*)	1·30	85
527	100b. Broad-barred lionfish (*Pterois antennata*)	1·30	85
528	100b. *Rhinecanthus assasi*	1·30	85
529	100b. Blue-spotted stingray (*Taeniura lymma*)	1·30	85
MS530	130 × 125 mm. Nos. 524/9	11·00	7·75

172 Arabian Tahr

2000. Mammals. Multicoloured.

531	100b. Type **172**	1·20	85
532	100b. Nubian ibex	1·20	85
533	100b. Arabian oryx	1·20	85
534	100b. Arabian gazelle	1·20	85
MS535	130 × 96 mm. Nos. 531/4	11·00	7·75

173 Emblem

2000. Olympic Games, Sydney. Multicoloured.

536	100b. Type **173**	1·30	1·20
537	100b. Running	1·30	1·20
538	100b. Swimming	1·30	1·20
539	100b. Rifle-shooting	1·30	1·20
MS540	121 × 100 mm. Nos. 536/9	15·00	11·50

174 Sultan Qabus

2000. National Day. Multicoloured.

541	100b. Type **174**	1·10	75
542	100b. Sitting	1·10	75
543	100b. Wearing uniform including red beret	1·10	75
544	100b. Wearing (white) naval uniform	1·10	75
545	100b. Anniversary emblem	1·10	75
546	100b. Wearing (beige) police uniform	1·10	75
MS547	175 × 120 mm. Nos. 541/6	6·25	4·50

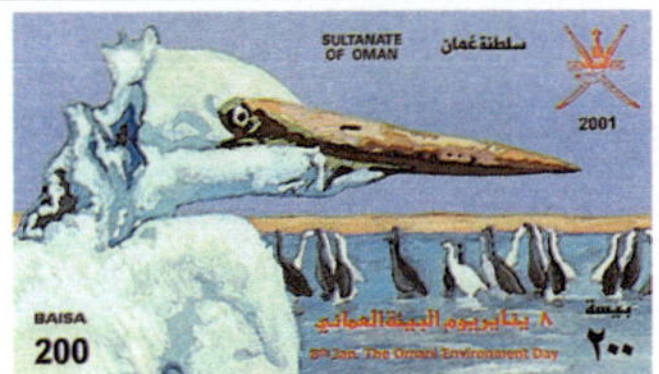

175 Egret and Sea Birds

2001. Environment Day. Sheet 83 × 46 mm.
MS548 **175** 200b. multicoloured 6·25 6·25

176 Dagger and Sheath
177 Child and Tank

2001. Al-Khanjar A'suri. Multicoloured, background colours given. (a) Size 24 × 27 mm.
549 **176** 50b. red 45 40
550 80b. yellow 75 70

(b) Size 26 × 34 mm.
551 **176** 100b. blue 90 85
552 200b. white . . . . 1·70 1·50
MS553 80 × 100 mm. Nos. 549/552 3·75 3·50

2001. Al Aqsa Uprising. Sheet 105 × 100 mm.
MS554 **177** 100b. multicoloured 3·00 1·50

178 Children encircling Globe
180 *Cerithium caeruleum*

179 Globe, Tree, Map and Sunrise

2001. United Nations Year of Dialogue among Civilizations.
555 **178** 200b. multicoloured . . . 1·50 1·50

2001. National Day. Year of the Environment. Multicoloured.
556 100b. Type **179** 75 75
557 100b. Sunrise and Sultan Qabas 75 75
Nos. 556/7 were issued together, se-tenant, forming a composite design.

2001. Shells. Multicoloured.
558 100b. Type **180** 75 75
559 100b. *Nassarius coronatus* . . 75 75
560 100b. *Cerithdea cingulata* . . 75 75
561 100b. *Epitoneum pallash* . . . 75 75

181 Necklace

2001. Traditional Jewellery. Four sheets, each 71 × 71 mm containing T **181** and similar multicoloured designs.
MS562 (a) 100b. Type **181**; (b) 100b. Necklace with barred pendant (horiz) (63 × 28 mm); (c) 100b. "Mazrad" necklace (circular) (38 × 38 mm); (d) 100b. Hair decoration (triangular) (64 × 32 mm) . . . . 4·50 3·75

182 Map enclosed in Circle

2001. 22nd Supreme Session of Gulf Co-operation Council, Oman. Multicoloured.
563 50b. Type **182** 40 40
564 100b. Sultan Qabas 75 75

183 Interior of Dome

2002. Inauguration of Sultan Qabus Grand Mosque, Baushar. Multicoloured.
565 50b. Type **183** 55 40
566 50b. Dome 55 40
567 50b. Entrance 55 40
568 50b. Decorated roof 55 40
MS569 120 × 90 mm. 100b. Aerial view of mosque. Imperf . . . 2·30 1·20

184 Olive Ridley Turtle

2002. Turtles. Multicoloured.
570 100b. Type **184** 75 75
571 100b. Atlantic green turtle . . 75 75
572 100b. Hawksbill 75 75
573 100b. Loggerhead 75 75
MS574 130 × 98 mm. Nos. 570/3. Imperf . . . . 4·50 3·75

185 Adult and Child's Hands
187 Collared Dove (*Streptopelia decaocto*)

186 Sultan Qabus and Cheetah

2002. Early Intervention for Children with Special Needs. Ordinary or self-adhesive gum.
575 **185** 100b. multicoloured . . . 90 75

2002. National Day. Year of the Environment. Sheet 100 × 80 mm.
MS577 **186** 100b. multicoloured 30 25

2002. Birds. Multicoloured.
578 50b. Type **187** 45 40
579 50b. Black-headed tchagra (*Tchagra senegala*) 45 40
580 50b. Ruppell's weaver (*Ploceus galbula*) 45 40
581 50b. Bonelli's eagle (*Hieraetus fasciatus*) 45 40
582 50b. White-eyed bulbul (*Pycnontus xanthopygos*) 45 40
583 50b. Northern eagle owl (*Bubo bubo*) 45 40
584 50b. Dunn's lark (*Eremalauda dunni*) 45 40
585 50b. Cape dikkop (*Burhinus capensis*) 45 40
586 50b. Graceful prinia (*Prinia gracilis*) 45 40
587 50b. Indian grey francolin (*Francolinus pondicerianus*) 45 40
588 50b. Tristram's grackle (*Onychognathus tristramii*) 45 40
589 50b. Red-wattled plover (*Vanellus indicus* (inscr "Hoplopterus indicus")) . . 45 40
590 50b. House crow (*Corvus splendens*) 45 40
591 50b. Houbara bustard (*Chlamydotis undulate*) . . 45 40
592 50b. White-collared kingfisher (*Halcyon chloris*) 45 40
593 50b. Crowned sand grouse (*Pterocles coronatus*) . . . 45 40

188 Muscat Gate and Festival Emblem

2003. Muskat Festival.
594 **188** 100b. multicoloured . . . 45 40

189 Horse's Head

2003. Arabian Horses. Four sheets, each 95 × 80 mm containing T **189** and similar vert designs. Multicoloured.
MS595 (a) 100b. Type **189**; (b) 100b. Chestnut; (c) 100b. Grey; (d) 100b. Wearing tasselled breast harness 4·50 3·00

190 Chinese and Omani Buildings (½-size illustration)

2003. 25th Anniv of Oman—China Diplomatic Relations.
596 **190** 70b. multicoloured . . . 60 55

191 Census Emblem

2003. National Census. Multicoloured.
597 50b. Type **191** 45 40
598 50b. Emblem and numbers 45 40

192 Dove, Globe and Hands

2003. International Day of Peace.
599 **192** 200b. multicoloured . . . 1·50 1·20

193 Emblem

2003. Organization of Islamic Conference.
600 **193** 100b. multicoloured . . . 75 60

194 Emblem

2003. SANAD (Self-employment and national autonomous development) Project. (a) Self-adhesive gum.
601 **194** 100b. multicoloured . . . 75 60

(b) Miniature sheet. Ordinary gum.
MS602 120 × 95 mm. **194** 100b. multicoloured 85 85

195 Illuminated Manuscript

2003. Manuscripts. Multicoloured.
603 100b. Type **195** 75 75
604 100b. Mathematical drawing 75 75
605 100b. Compass 75 75
606 100b. Diagram 75 75
MS607 151 × 122 mm. 50b. × 4, Showing ships; As No. 606; As No. 603; Script enclosed in circle 1·90 1·90
Nos. 603/6 were issued together, se-tenant forming a composite design.

196 Sultan Qabus

2003. National Day. Multicoloured.
608 50b. Type **196** 45 40
609 50b. Wearing dark robe facing left 45 40

610 50b. Wearing white robe and multicoloured turban . . . 45 40
611 50b. Wearing white turban facing right 45 40

197 *Anogeissus* (inscr "dhoafrica")

2004. Flowers. Multicoloured.
612 50b. Type **197** 45 40
613 50b. *Tecomella undulate* . . . 45 40
614 50b. *Euyrops pinifolius* . . . 45 40
615 50b. *Aloe dhofarensis* 45 40
616 50b. *Cleome glaucescens* . . . 45 40
617 50b. *Cassia italica* 45 40
618 50b. *Cibirhiza dhofarensis* . . 45 40
619 50b. *Ipomoea nil* 45 40
620 50b. *Viola cinera* 45 40
621 50b. *Dyschoriste dalyi* 45 40
622 50b. *Calotropis procera* . . . 45 40
623 50b. *Lavandula dhofarensis* 45 40
624 50b. *Teucrium mascatense* . . 45 40
625 50b. *Capparis mucronifolia* . . 45 40
626 50b. *Geranium mascatense* . . 45 40
627 50b. *Convolvulus arvensis* . . 45 40

198 Emblem

2004. Centenary of FIFA (Federation Internationale de Football Association).
628 **198** 250b. multicoloured . . . 1·20 90

199 Leopard

2004. Arabian Leopard. Multicoloured.
629 50b. Type **199** 45 40
630 50b. Two leopards 45 40
631 50b. Leopard facing left . . . 45 40
632 50b. Leopard with raised paw 45 40
Nos. 629/32 were issued together, se-tenent, forming a composite design.

200 *Montipora*

2004. Corals. Multicoloured.
633 100b. Type **200** 75 75
634 100b. *Porites* 75 75
635 100b. *Acropora* 75 75
636 100b. *Cycloeris* 75 75

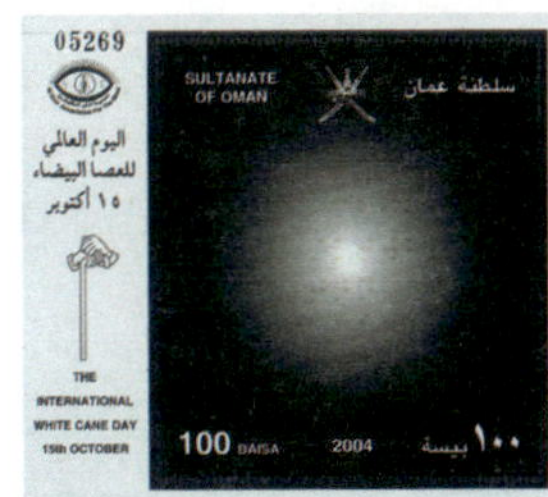

201 Dove holding Olive Branch

2004. International Day of Peace. Multicoloured.
637 50b. Type **201** 45 40
638 100b. Doves becoming olive branch and globe 75 60

202 Sun in Black Sky (¼-size illustration)

2004. International White Cane Day. Sheet 118 × 105 mm.
MS639 **202** 100b. black 75 60
No. **MS**639 was embossed with Braille letters.

203 Emblem

2004. 10th Gulf Cooperation Council Stamp Exhibition, Muscat. Ordinary or self-adhesive gum.
640 **203** 50c. multicoloured 45 40

204 Sultan Qabus

2004. National Day. Multicoloured.
642 100b. Type **204** 75 60
643 100b. Facing left 75 60
644 100b. Wearing blue turban facing right 75 60
645 100b. Wearing pink turban facing right 75 60

205 Oasis (Al Masarrat Water Supply Scheme)

2004. Al Masarrat and Ash'Sharqiyah Water Supply Schemes. Multicoloured.
646 50b. Type **205** 45 40
647 50b. Oasis (Ash'Sharqiyah Water Supply Scheme) . . 45 40
Nos. 646/7 were issued together, se-tenant, forming a composite design.

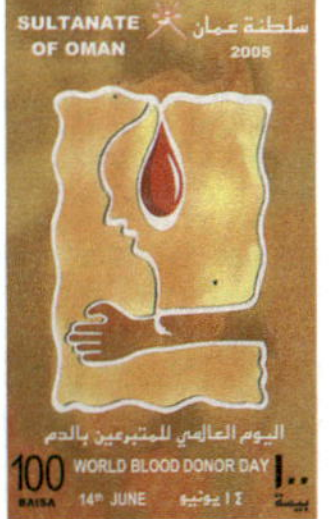

206 Children and Rescue Workers

2005. Civil Defence. Multicoloured.
648 50b. Type **206** 45 40
649 100b. Fire fighters and rescue team 75 60

207 Blood Droplet and Arm

2005. International Blood Donor Day.
650 **207** 100b. multicoloured . . . 75 60

208 Animals and Census Recorders

2005. Agricultural Census. Multicoloured.
651 100b. Type **208** 75 60
652 100b. Recorder, farmer, palm and shrub 75 60
Nos. 651/2 were issued together, se-tenant, forming a composite design.

ORANGE FREE STATE (ORANGE RIVER COLONY) Pt. 1

British possession 1848–54. Independent 1854–99. Annexed by Great Britain, 1900. Later a province of the Union of South Africa.

12 pence = 1 shilling;
20 shillings = 1 pound.

1

38 King Edward VII, Springbok and Gnu

1869.
48 **1** ½d. brown . . . . 2·50 50
84 ½d. yellow . . . . 2·00 35
2 1d. brown . . . . 12·00 45
68 1d. purple . . . . 3·00 30
50 2d. mauve . . . . 14·00 30
51 3d. blue . . . . 3·00 2·00
19 4d. blue . . . . 4·00 2·50
7 6d. red . . . . 12·00 2·00
9 1s. orange . . . . 38·00 1·50
87 1s. brown . . . . 21·00 1·50
20 5s. green . . . . 9·00 11·00

1877. Surch in figures.
75 **1** ½d. on 3d. blue . . . . . . 6·50 3·50
36 ½d. on 5s. green . . . . . . 17·00 3·75
54 1d. on 3d. blue . . . . . . 5·00 60
57 1d. on 4d. blue . . . . . . 27·00 5·50
22 1d. on 5s. green . . . . . . 55·00 21·00
53 2d. on 3d. blue . . . . . . 35·00 2·00
67 2½d. on 3d. blue . . . . . . 14·00 70
83 2½d. on 3d. blue . . . . . . 6·00 80
40 3d. on 4d. blue . . . . . . 32·00 16·00
12 4d. on 6d. red . . . . £180 27·00

1896. Surch **Halve Penny.**
77 **1** ½d. on 3d. blue . . . . 1·00 50

1900. Surch **V.R.I.** and value in figures.
112 **1** ½d. on ½d. orange 30 20
113 1d. on 1d. purple 30 20
114 2d. on 2d. mauve . . . . . 1·25 30
104 2½d. on 3d. blue (No. 83) 15·00 12·00
117 3d. on 3d. blue 60 30
118 4d. on 4d. blue . . . . . . 2·75 2·75
108 6d. on 6d. red . . . . . . 38·00 35·00
120 6d. on 6d. blue 70 40
121 1s. on 1s. brown . . . . . 4·50 45
122 5s. on 5s. green . . . . . . 8·00 8·50

1900. Stamps of Cape of Good Hope optd **ORANGE RIVER COLONY.**
133 **17** ½d. green 50 10
134 1d. red . . . . 1·50 10
135 **6** 2½d. blue . . . . 1·50 35

1902. No. 120 surch **4d** and bar.
136 **1** 4d. on 6d. blue . . . . . . 1·50 75

1902. Surch **E. R. I. 6d.**
137 **1** 6d. on 6d. blue . . . . . . 3·75 11·00

1902. No. 20 surch **One Shilling** and star.
138 **1** 1s. on 5s. green . . . . . . 7·50 14·00

1903.
148 **38** ½d. green . . . . 9·00 50
140 1d. red . . . . 5·00 10
141 2d. brown . . . . 6·50 80
142 2½d. blue . . . . 1·60 50
143 3d. mauve . . . . 8·00 90
150 4d. red and green . . . . 4·50 2·75
145 6d. red and mauve . . . . 8·50 1·00
146 1s. red and brown . . . . 28·00 1·75
147 5s. blue and brown . . . . 80·00 22·00

MILITARY FRANK STAMP

M 1

1899.
M1 **M 1** (–) black on yellow . . . 17·00 55·00

POLICE FRANK STAMPS

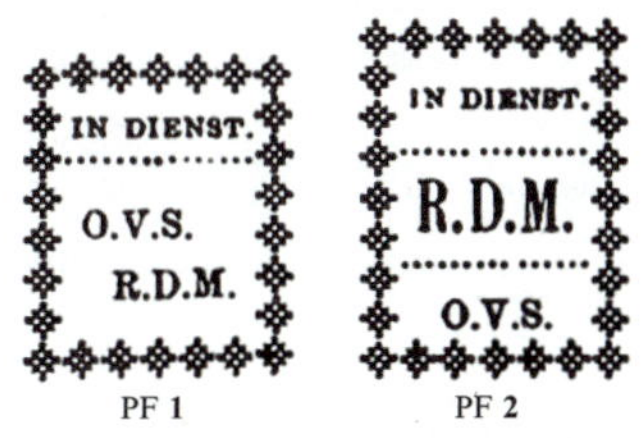

PF 1 **PF 2**

1896.
PF2 **PF 1** (–) black £140 £200

1899.
PF3 **PF 2** (–) black on yellow . . £130 £150

ORCHHA Pt. 1

A state of Central India. Now uses Indian stamps.

12 pies = 1 anna; 16 annas = 1 rupee.

1

2

1913. Imperf.
1 **1** ½a. green . . . . 35·00 £100
2 1a. red . . . . 20·00 £180

1914. Imperf.
3a **2** ¼a. blue . . . . 40 4·25
4 ½a. green . . . . 55 5·50
5c 1a. red . . . . 2·50 6·50
6 2a. brown . . . . 4·50 25·00
7b 4a. yellow . . . . 10·00 35·00

3 Maharaja Vir Singh II

5 Maharaja Vir Singh II

1935.
8b **3** ¼a. purple and grey . . . . 50 3·00
9 ½a. grey and green . . . . 50 2·25
10 ¾a. mauve and green . . . 50 2·25
11 – 1a. green and brown . . . 50 2·25
12 **3** 1¼a. grey and mauve . . . 50 2·25
13 1½a. brown and red . . . . 50 2·25

14 2a. blue and orange 50 2·25
15 2½a. brown and orange 65 2·50
16 3a. blue and mauve 65 2·50
17 4a. purple and green 65 4·50
18 6a. black and buff 70 4·50
19 8a. brown and purple 2·25 5·50
20 12a. green and purple 1·00 5·50
21 12a. blue and purple 28·00 80·00
22 1r. brown and green 80 6·50
24 2r. brown and yellow 3·00 17·00
25 3r. black and blue 1·50 17·00
26 4r. black and brown 3·00 19·00
27 5r. blue and purple 3·00 20·00
28 – 10r. green and red 7·00 27·00
29 – 15r. black and green 12·00 65·00
30 – 25r. orange and blue 16·00 75·00

DESIGN: 1a., 10r. to 25r. As Type **3**, but inscr "POSTAGE & REVENUE". There are two different versions of the portrait for the 1r. value.

1939.
31 **5** ¼a. brown 3·75 75·00
32 ½a. green 3·75 60·00
33 ¾a. blue 4·75 95·00
34 1a. red 3·75 19·00
35 1¼a. blue 4·00 95·00
36 1½a. mauve 4·25 £120
37 2a. red 3·75 75·00
38 2½a. green 5·00 £200
39 3a. violet 6·50 £110
40 4a. slate 7·50 27·00
41 8a. mauve 12·00 £200
42 – 1r. green 20·00
43 – 2r. violet 42·00 £550
44 – 5r. orange £140
45 – 10r. green £500
46 – 15r. lilac £11000
47 – 25r. purple £7500

The rupee values are larger (25 × 30 mm) and have different frame.

PAHANG Pt. 1

A state of the Federation of Malaya, incorporated in Malaysia in 1963.

100 cents = 1 dollar (Straits or Malayan).

1889. Nos. 52/3 and 63 of Straits Settlements optd **PAHANG**.
4a 2c. red 6·00 8·00
2 8c. orange £1700 £1700
3 10c. grey £225 £250

1891. No. 68 of Straits Settlements surch **PAHANG Two CENTS**.
7 2c. on 24c. green £180 £200

9 Tiger

10 Tiger

1891.
11 **9** 1c. green 4·25 3·25
12 2c. red 4·50 3·25
13 5c. blue 11·00 40·00

1895.
14 **10** 3c. purple and red 7·50 2·75
15 4c. purple and red 17·00 12·00
16 5c. purple and yellow 27·00 21·00

1897. No. 13 divided, and each half surch.
18 **9** 2c. on half of 5c. blue £1500 £375
18d 3c. on half of 5c. blue £1500 £375

1898. Stamps of Perak optd **Pahang**.
19 **44** 10c. purple and orange 20·00 25·00
20 25c. green and red 85·00 £160
21 50c. purple and black £400 £450
22 50c. green and black £250 £325
23 **45** $1 green £350 £475
24 $5 green and blue £1300 £2000

1898. Stamp of Perak surch **Pahang Four cents**.
25 **44** 4c. on 8c. purple and blue 4·75 5·50

1899. No. 16 surch **Four cents**.
28 **10** 4c. on 5c. purple and yellow 17·00 60·00

15 Sultan Sir Abu Bakar

16 Sultan Sir Abu Bakar

1935.
29 **15** 1c. black 20 40
30 2c. green 1·25 50
31 3c. green 15·00 15·00
32 4c. orange 70 50
33 5c. brown 70 10
34 6c. red 16·00 1·75
35 8c. grey 60 10
36 8c. red 2·75 55·00
37 10c. purple 80 10
38 12c. blue 2·25 1·25
39 15c. blue 15·00 50·00
40 25c. purple and red 1·25 1·50
41 30c. purple and orange 1·00 1·10
42 40c. red and purple 85 2·00
43 50c. black on green 3·00 1·50
44 $1 black and red on blue 2·50 8·00
45 $2 green and red 22·00 30·00
46 $5 green and red on green 8·00 65·00

1948. Silver Wedding. As T **4b/c** of Pitcairn Islands.
47 10c. violet 15 60
48 $5 green 25·00 40·00

1949. U.P.U. As T **4d/g** of Pitcairn Islands.
49 10c. purple 30 20
50 15c. blue 1·10 1·25
51 25c. orange 35 1·50
52 50c. black 70 2·00

1950.
53 **16** 1c. black 10 10
54 2c. orange 20 10
55 3c. green 30 80
56 4c. brown 1·00 10
57a 5c. purple 50 15
58 6c. grey 40 30
59 8c. red 50 1·50
60 8c. green 85 75
61 10c. mauve 25 10
62 12c. red 85 1·25
63 15c. blue 75 10
64 20c. black and green 50 2·75
65 20c. blue 1·00 10
66 25c. purple and orange 50 10
67 30c. red and purple 1·25 35
68 35c. red and purple 60 25
69 40c. red and purple 1·50 7·50
70 50c. black and blue 1·50 10
71 $1 blue and purple 2·75 3·25
72 $2 green and red 13·00 21·00
73 $5 green and brown 55·00 70·00

1953. Coronation. As T **4h** of Pitcairn Islands.
74 10c. black and purple 1·25 10

1957. As Nos. 92/102 of Kedah but inset portrait of Sultan Sir Abu Bakar.
75 1c. black 10 10
76 2c. red 10 10
77 4c. sepia 10 10
78 5c. lake 10 10
79 8c. green 1·00 2·25
80 10c. sepia 1·25 10
81 10c. purple 3·50 30
82 20c. blue 2·25 20
83 50c. black and blue 45 75
84 $1 blue and purple 6·00 2·00
85 $2 green and red 4·00 9·00
86 $5 brown and green 11·00 15·00

17 "Vanda hookeriana"

1965. As Nos. 115/21 of Kedah but with inset portrait of Sultan Sir Abu Bakar as in T **17**.
87 **17** 1c. multicoloured 10 1·25
88 – 2c. multicoloured 10 1·25
89 – 5c. multicoloured 15 10
90 – 6c. multicoloured 30 1·25
91 – 10c. multicoloured 20 10
92 – 15c. multicoloured 1·00 10
93 – 20c. multicoloured 1·60 40

The higher values used in Pahang were Nos. 20/7 of Malaysia (National Issue).

18 "Precis orithya"

19 Sultan Haji Ahmad Shah

1971. Butterflies. As Nos. 124/30 of Kedah, but with portrait of Sultan Sir Abu Bakar as in T **18**.
96 – 1c. multicoloured 20 2·00
97 – 2c. multicoloured 50 2·25
98 – 5c. multicoloured 1·00 50
99 – 6c. multicoloured 1·50 2·25
100 – 10c. multicoloured 1·00 30
101 **18** 15c. multicoloured 1·75 10
102 – 20c. multicoloured 2·00 50

The higher values in use with this issue were Nos. 64/71 of Malaysia (National Issues).

1975. Installation of the Sultan.
103 **19** 10c. green, lilac and gold 50 1·25
104 15c. black, yellow and green 60 10
105 50c. black, blue and green 1·75 4·50

1977. As Nos. 97/8, 100/102 but with portrait of Sultan Haji Ahmad Shah.
106 – 2c. multicoloured 60·00 55·00
107 – 5c. multicoloured 70 1·25
108 – 10c. multicoloured 1·00 75
109 **18** 15c. multicoloured 1·00 30
110 – 20c. multicoloured 4·00 1·75

20 "Rhododendron scortechinii"

21 Rice

1979. Flowers. As Nos. 135/41 of Kedah but with portrait of Sultan Haji Ahmad Shah as in T **20**.
111 1c. "Rafflesia hasseltii" 10 1·00
112 2c. "Pterocarpus indicus" 10 1·00
113 5c. "Lagerstroemia speciosa" 10 30
114 10c. "Durio zibethinus" 15 10
115 15c. "Hibiscus rosa-sinensis" 15 10
116 20c. Type **20** 20 10
117 25c. "Etlingera elatior" (inscr "Phaeomeria speciosa") 40 40

1986. As Nos. 152/8 of Kedah but with portrait of Sultan Ahmad Shah as in T **21**.
125 1c. Coffee 10 20
126 2c. Coconuts 15 20
127 5c. Cocoa 20 20
128 10c. Black pepper 20 10
129 15c. Rubber 30 10
130 20c. Oil palm 35 10
131 30c. Type **21** 35 15

PAKHOI Pt. 17

An Indo-Chinese Post Office in China, closed in 1922.

1903. Stamps of Indo-China, "Tablet" key-type, surch **PACKHOI** and value in Chinese.
1 D 1c. black and red on blue 9·25 10·00
2 2c. brown and blue on buff 4·75 5·25
3 4c. brown and blue on grey 5·25 5·00
4 5c. green and red 2·75 4·00
5 10c. red and blue 1·75 4·50
6 15c. grey and red 3·50 5·50
7 20c. red and blue on green 8·50 11·00
8 25c. blue and red 5·50 8·50
9 25c. black and red on pink 6·50 9·50
10 30c. brown and blue on drab 15·00 13·00
11 40c. red and blue on yellow 55·00 55·00
12 50c. red and blue on pink £275 £275
13 50c. brown and red on blue 80·00 65·00
14 75c. brown and red on orange 70·00 65·00
15 1f. green and red 75·00 65·00
16 5f. mauve and blue on lilac £110 £110

1906. Stamps of Indo-China surch **PAK-HOI** and value in Chinese.
17 **8** 1c. green 2·50 2·75
18 2c. red on yellow 2·25 2·25
19 4c. mauve on blue 2·50 2·50
20 5c. green 3·00 1·90
21 10c. red 2·75 2·50
22 15c. brown on blue 6·25 6·50
23 20c. red on green 3·75 3·75
24 25c. blue 3·50 3·75
25 30c. brown on cream 4·50 4·00
26 35c. black on yellow 4·00 4·00
27 40c. black on grey 3·75 4·25
28 50c. olive on green 8·00 6·50
29 D 75c. brown on orange 60·00 60·00
30 **8** 1f. green 26·00 26·00
31 2f. brown on yellow 45·00 42·00
32 D 5f. mauve on lilac £100 £110
33 **8** 10f. red on green £110 £110

1908. Stamps of Indo-China (Native types) surch **PAKHOI** and value in Chinese.
34 **10** 1c. black and brown 1·50 1·00
35 2c. black and brown 1·00 1·25
36 4c. black and blue 1·00 1·50
37 5c. black and green 1·40 1·75
38 10c. black and red 1·75 3·25
39 15c. black and violet 2·50 3·25
40 **11** 20c. black and violet 2·50 2·75
41 25c. black and blue 2·75 3·50
42 30c. black and brown 3·25 4·25
43 35c. black and green 3·25 4·25
44 40c. black and brown 3·00 4·25
45 50c. black and red 3·75 4·25
46 **12** 75c. black and orange 6·25 6·25
47 – 1f. black and red 8·00 8·00
48 – 2f. black and green 17·00 18·00
49 – 5f. black and blue 80·00 £100
50 – 10f. black and violet £110 £110

1919. As last, surch in addition in figures and words.
51 **10** ⅖c. on 1c. black and green 50 2·75
52 ⅘c. on 2c. black and brown 1·25 3·00
53 1⅗c. on 4c. black and blue 1·50 2·75
54 2c. on 5c. black and green 2·00 3·25
55 4c. on 10c. black and red 3·75 4·00
56 6c. on 15c. black and violet 3·00 3·00
57 **11** 8c. on 20c. black and violet 4·25 4·25
58 10c. on 25c. black and blue 4·50 4·25
59 12c. on 30c. black & brown 3·00 3·25
60 14c. on 35c. black and green 2·50 3·00
61 16c. on 40c. black & brown 3·50 3·75
62 20c. on 50c. black and red 2·75 3·25
63 **12** 30c. on 75c. black & orange 3·50 4·00
64 – 40c. on 1f. black and red 12·50 12·50
65 – 80c. on 2f. black and green 5·25 5·25
66 – 2pi. on 5f. black and blue 12·00 14·00
67 – 4pi. on 10f. black and violet 24·00 29·00

PAKISTAN Pt. 1

A Dominion created in 1947 from territory with predominantly Moslem population in Eastern and Western India. Became an independent Islamic Republic within the British Commonwealth in 1956. The eastern provinces declared their independence in 1971 and are now known as Bangladesh.

On 30 January 1972 Pakistan left the Commonwealth but rejoined on 1 October 1989.

1947. 12 pies = 1 anna;
16 annas = 1 rupee.
1961. 100 paisa = 1 rupee.

1947. King George VI stamps of India optd **PAKISTAN**.
1 **100a** 3p. grey 10 10
2 ½a. purple 10 10
3 9p. green 10 10
4 1a. red 10 10
5 **101** 1½a. violet 30 10
6 2a. red 10 20
7 3a. violet 10 20
8 3½a. blue 65 2·25
9 **102** 4a. brown 20 20
10 6a. green 1·00 1·25
11 8a. violet 30 60
12 12a. red 1·00 20
13 – 14a. purple (No. 277) 3·00 3·50
14 **93** 1r. grey and brown 2·00 1·25
15 2r. purple and brown 3·25 2·25
16 5r. green and blue 4·00 4·00
17 10r. purple and claret 4·00 3·50
18 15r. brown and green 48·00 80·00
19 25r. violet and purple 55·00 45·00

3 Constituent Assembly Building, Karachi

1948. Independence.
20 **3** 1½a. blue 1·25 1·25
21 – 2½a. green 1·25 20
22 – 3a. brown 1·25 35
23 – 1r. red 1·25 70

DESIGNS—HORIZ: 2½a. Entrance to Karachi Airport; 3a. Gateway to Lahore Fort. VERT: 1r. Crescent and Stars in foliated frame.

7 Scales of Justice

9 Lloyds Barrage

12 Salimullah Hostel, Dacca University

13 Khyber Pass

1948. Designs with crescent moon pointing to right.
24 **7** 3p. red 10 10
25 6p. violet 80 10
26 9p. green 50 10
27 – 1a. blue 10 50
28 – 1½a. green 10 10
29 – 2a. red 1·50 70
30 **9** 2½a. green 3·25 6·50
31 – 3a. green 7·50 1·00
32 **9** 3½a. blue 3·75 5·50
33 4a. brown 65 10
34 – 6a. blue 1·00 50
35 – 8a. black 65 1·25
36 – 10a. red 5·50 8·00
37 – 12a. red 7·50 1·00
38 **12** 1r. blue 6·50 10
39 2r. brown 20·00 60
40a 5r. red 12·00 25
41b **13** 10r. mauve 18·00 1·50
42 15r. green 18·00 17·00
210b 25r. violet 3·00 4·00

DESIGNS—VERT (as Type **7**): 1a., 1½a., 2a. Star and Crescent; 6a., 8a., 12a. Karachi Port Trust. HORIZ (as Type **12**): 3a., 10a. Karachi Airport.

1949. As 1948 but with crescent moon pointing to left.
44a – 1a. blue 4·50 10
45a – 1½a. green 3·00 10
46a – 2a. red 4·00 10
47 – 3a. green 13·00 1·00
48 – 6a. blue 10·00 1·50
49 – 8a. black 10·00 2·00
50 – 10a. red 19·00 2·50
51 – 12a. red 23·00 50

16

1949. 1st Death Anniv of Mohammed Ali Jinnah.
52 **16** 1½a. brown 2·00 1·50
53 3a. green 2·00 1·50
54 – 10a. black 6·00 8·00
DESIGN: 10a. inscription reads "QUAID-I-AZAM MOHAMMAD ALI JINNAH" etc.

17 Pottery

1951. 4th Anniv of Independence.
55 **17** 2½a. red 1·75 1·25
56 – 3a. purple 1·00 10
57 **17** 3½a. blue (A) 1·25 4·50
57a – 3½a. blue (B) 3·50 5·00
58 – 4a. green 75 10
59 – 6a. orange 1·00 10
60 – 8a. sepia 4·50 25
61 – 10a. violet 2·00 1·75
62 – 12a. slate 2·00 10
DESIGNS—VERT: 3, 12a. Airplane and hour-glass; 4, 6a. Saracenic leaf pattern. HORIZ: 8, 10a. Archway and lamp.
(A) has Arabic fraction on left as in Type **17**, (B) has it on right.
For similar 3½a. see No. 88.

21 "Scinde Dawk" Stamp and Ancient and Modern Transport

1952. Cent of "Scinde Dawk" Issue of India.
63 **21** 3a. green on olive 75 85
64 12a. brown on salmon 1·00 15

22 Kaghan Valley

24 Tea Plantation, East Pakistan

1954. 7th Anniv of Independence.
65 **22** 6p. violet 10 10
66 – 9p. blue 3·25 2·00
67 – 1a. red 10 10
68 – 1½a. red 10 10
69 **24** 14a. myrtle 1·50 10
70 – 1r. green 11·00 10
71 – 2r. orange 2·75 10
DESIGNS—HORIZ (as Type **22**): 9p. Mountains, Gilgit; 1a. Badshahi Mosque, Lahore. (As Type **24**): 1r. Cotton plants, West Pakistan; 2r. Jute fields and river, East Pakistan. VERT (as Type **22**): 1½a. Mausoleum of Emperor Jehangir, Lahore.

29 View of K2

1954. Conquest of K2 (Mount Godwin-Austen).
72 **29** 2a. violet 40 30

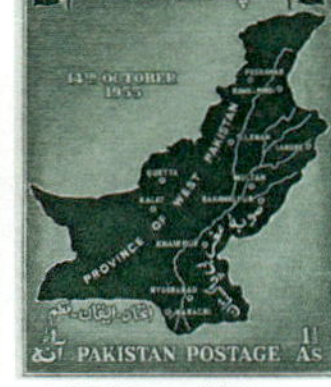

30 Karnaphuli Paper Mill, East Bengal
35 Map of West Pakistan

1955. 8th Anniv of Independence.
73 **30** 2½a. red (A) 50 1·40
73a – 2½a. red (B) 30 1·40
74 – 6a. blue 1·00 10
75 – 8a. violet 3·75 10
76 – 12a. red and orange 4·00 10
DESIGNS: 6a. Textile mill, W. Pakistan; 8a. Jute mill, E. Pakistan; 12a. Main Sui gas plant.
(A) has Arabic fraction on left as in Type **30**, (B) has it on right.
For similar 2½a. see No. 87.

1955. 10th Anniv of U.N. Nos. 68 and 76 optd **TENTH ANNIVERSARY UNITED NATIONS 24.10.55.**
77 1½a. red 1·50 5·00
78 12a. red and orange 50 3·50

1955. West Pakistan Unity.
79 **35** 1½a. green 40 1·25
80 2a. brown 50 10
81 12a. red 1·25 50

36 Constituent Assembly Building, Karachi

1956. Republic Day.
82 **36** 2a. green 80 10

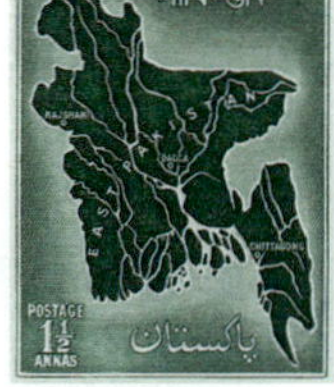
37
38 Map of East Pakistan

1956. 9th Anniv of Independence.
83 **37** 2a. red 65 10

1956. 1st Session of National Assembly of Pakistan at Dacca.
84 **38** 1½a. green 40 1·50
85 2a. brown 40 10
86 12a. red 40 1·25

41 Orange Tree
42 Pakistani Flag

1957. 1st Anniv of Republic.
87 – 2½a. red 20 10
88 – 3½a. blue 30 10
89 **41** 10r. green and orange 80 20
DESIGNS: 2½a. as Type **30** without value in Arabic at right; 3½a. as Type **17** without value in Arabic at right.

1957. Centenary of Struggle for Independence (Indian Mutiny).
90 **42** 1½a. green 50 10
91 12a. blue 1·25 10

43 Pakistani Industries

1957. 10th Anniv of Independence.
92 **43** 1½a. blue 20 30
93 4a. salmon 45 1·50
94 12a. mauve 45 50

1958. 2nd Anniv of Republic. As T **41**.
209 15r. red and purple 2·00 3·00
DESIGN: 15r. Coconut tree.

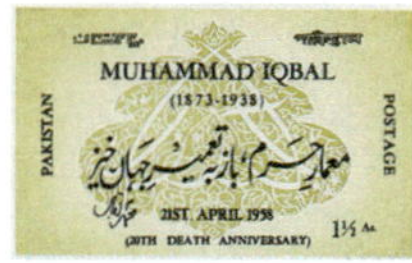

45

1958. 20th Death Anniv of Mohammed Iqbal (poet).
96 **45** 1½a. olive and black 55 40
97 2a. brown and black 55 10
98 14a. turquoise and black 90 10

46 U.N. Charter and Globe

1958. 10th Anniv of Declaration of Human Rights.
99 **46** 1½a. turquoise 10 10
100 14a. sepia 45 10

1958. Scout Jamboree. Optd **PAKISTAN BOY SCOUT 2nd NATIONAL JAMBOREE CHITTAGONG Dec. 58-Jan. 59.**
101 **22** 6p. violet 20 10
102 – 8a. violet (No. 75) 40 10

1959. Revolution Day. No. 74 optd **REVOLUTION DAY Oct. 27, 1959.**
103 6a. blue 80 10

49 "Centenary of An Idea"
50 Armed Forces Badge

1959. Red Cross Commemoration.
104 **49** 2a. red and green 30 10
105 10a. red and blue 55 10

1960. Armed Forces Day.
106 **50** 2a. red, blue and green 50 10
107 14a. red and blue 1·00 10

51 Map of Pakistan

1960.
108 **51** 6p. purple 40 10
109 2a. red 60 10
110 8a. green 1·25 10
111 1r. blue 2·00 10

52 "Uprooted Tree"
55 "Land Reforms, Rehabilitation and Reconstruction"

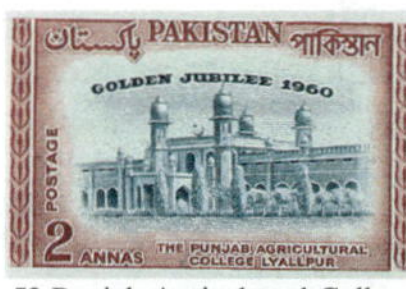

53 Punjab Agricultural College

1960. World Refugee Year.
112 **52** 2a. red 20 10
113 10a. green 30 10

1960. Golden Jubilee of Punjab Agricultural College, Lyallpur.
114 **53** 2a. blue and red 10 10
115 – 8a. green and violet 20 10
DESIGN: 8a. College arms.

1960. Revolution Day.
116 **55** 2a. green, pink and brown 10 10
117 14a. green, yellow and blue 50 75

56 Caduceus
57 "Economic Co-operation"

1960. Centenary of King Edward Medical College, Lahore.
118 **56** 2a. yellow, black and blue 50 10
119 14a. green, black and red 1·75 1·00

1960. Int Chamber of Commerce C.A.F.E.A. Meeting, Karachi.
120 **57** 14a. brown 50 10

58 Zam-Zama Gun, Lahore ("Kim's Gun" after Rudyard Kipling)

1960. 3rd Pakistan Boy Scouts' National Jamboree, Lahore.
121 **58** 2a. red, yellow and green 80 10

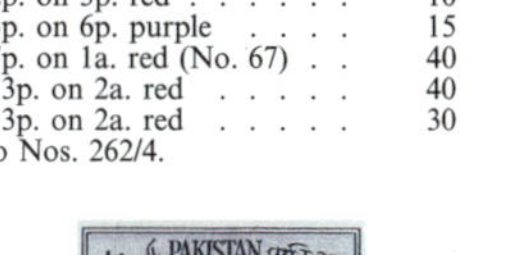
1961. Surch in "PAISA".
122 – 1p. on 1½a. red (No. 68) 40 10
123 **7** 2p. on 3p. red 10 10
124 **51** 3p. on 6p. purple 15 10
125 – 7p. on 1a. red (No. 67) 40 10
126 **51** 13p. on 2a. red 40 10
127 **37** 13p. on 2a. red 30 10
See also Nos. 262/4.

60 Khyber Pass

61 Shalimar Gardens, Lahore
62 Chota Sona Masjid (gateway)

1961.
170 **60** 1p. violet 10 10
132 2p. red 1·00 10
133 3p. purple 75 10
173 5p. blue 10 10
135 7p. green 2·00 10
175 **61** 10p. brown 10 10
176 13p. violet 10 10
176a 15p. purple 20 10
176b 20p. green 30 10
138 25p. blue 5·50 10
178 40p. purple 15 30
179 50p. green 15 10
141 75p. red 40 70
142 90p. green 70 70
204 **62** 1r. red 30 10
144 1r.25 violet 75 80
206 2r. orange 55 15
207 5r. green 5·50 65

1961. Lahore Stamp Exn. No. 110 optd **LAHORE STAMP EXHIBITION 1961** and emblem.
145 **51** 8a. green 1·00 1·75

64 Warsak Dam and Power Station

1961. Completion of Warsak Hydro-electric Project.
146 **64** 40p. black and blue 60 10

65 Narcissus

1961. Child Welfare Week.
147 **65** 13p. turquoise 50 10
148 90p. mauve . . . . 1·25 20

66 Ten Roses **67** Police Crest and "Traffic Control"

1961. Co-operative Day.
149 **66** 13p. red and green 40 10
150 90p. red and blue 85 90

1961. Police Centenary.
151 **67** 13p. silver, black and blue 50 10
152 40p. silver, black and red 1·00 20

68 Locomotive "Eagle", 1861

1961. Railway Centenary.
153 **68** 13p. green, black and yellow 75 80
154 – 50p. yellow, black and green . . . . 1·00 1·50
DESIGN: 50p. Diesel locomotive No. 20 and tracks forming "1961".

1962. 1st Karachi–Dacca Jet Flight. No. 87 surch with Boeing 720B airliner and **FIRST JET FLIGHT KARACHI–DACCA 13 Paisa**.
155 13p. on $2\frac{1}{2}$a. red . . . . . . 1·75 1·25

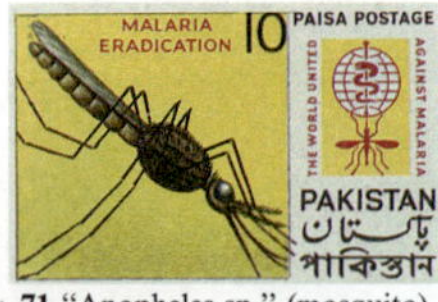

71 "Anopheles sp." (mosquito)

1962. Malaria Eradication.
156 **71** 10p. black, yellow and red 35 10
157 – 13p. black, lemon and red 35 10
DESIGN: 13p. Mosquito pierced by blade.

73 Pakistan Map and Jasmine

1962. New Constitution.
158 **73** 40p. green, turquoise & grey 70 10

74 Football

1962. Sports.
159 **74** 7p. black and blue 10 10
160 – 13p. black and green . . . 60 1·50
161 – 25p. black and purple . . . 20 10
162 – 40p. black and brown . . . 2·00 2·50
DESIGNS: 13p. Hockey; 25p. Squash; 40p. Cricket.

78 Marble Fruit Dish and Bahawalpuri Clay Flask

1962. Small Industries.
163 **78** 7p. lake 10 10
164 – 13p. green . . . . 2·50 2·50
165 – 25p. violet 10 10
166 – 40p. green 10 10
167 – 50p. red 10 10
DESIGNS: 13p. Sports equipment; 25p. Camelskin lamp and brassware; 40p. Wooden powder-bowl and basket-work; 50p. Inlaid cigarette-box and brassware.

83 "Child Welfare"

1962. 16th Anniv of UNICEF.
168 **83** 13p. black, blue and purple 35 10
169 40p. black, yellow and blue 35 10

1963. Pakistan U.N. Force in West Irian. Optd **U.N. FORCE W. IRIAN**.
182 **61** 13p. violet 10 75

85 "Dancing" Horse, Camel and Bull

1963. National Horse and Cattle Show.
183 **85** 13p. blue, sepia and pink 10 10

86 Wheat and Tractor

1963. Freedom from Hunger.
184 **86** 13p. brown . . . . 2·00 10
185 – 50p. bistre . . . . 3·50 55
DESIGN: 50p. Lifting rice.

1963. 2nd International Stamp Exhibition, Dacca. Surch **13 PAISA INTERNATIONAL DACCA STAMP EXHIBITION 1963**.
186 **51** 13p. on 2a. red 50 50

89 Centenary Emblem

1963. Centenary of Red Cross.
187 **89** 40p. red and olive . . . . 2·00 15

90 Paharpur

1963. Archaeological Series.
188 **90** 7p. blue 55 10
189 – 13p. sepia 55 10
190 – 40p. red 90 10
191 – 50p. violet 95 10
DESIGNS—VERT: 13p. Moenjodaro. HORIZ: 40p. Taxila; 50p. Mainamati.

1963. Centenary of Pakistan Public Works Department. Surch **100 YEARS OF P.W.D. OCTOBER, 1963 13**.
192 **60** 13p. on 3p. purple 10 10

95 Ataturk's Mausoleum

1963. 25th Death Anniv of Kemal Ataturk.
193 **95** 50p. red 50 10

96 Globe and UNESCO Emblem

1963. 15th Anniv of Declaration of Human Rights.
194 **96** 50p. brown, red and blue 40 10

97 Thermal Power Installations

1963. Completion of Multan Thermal Power Station.
195 **97** 13p. blue 10 10

99 Temple of Thot, Queen Nefertari and Maids

1964. Nubian Monuments Preservation.
211 **99** 13p. blue and red 30 10
212 – 50p. purple and black . . . 70 10
DESIGN: 50p. Temple of Abu Simbel.

101 "Unisphere" and Pakistan Pavilion

1964. New York World's Fair.
213 **101** 13p. blue 10 10
214 – 1r.25 blue and orange . . 40 20
DESIGN—VERT: 1r.25, Pakistan Pavilion on "Unisphere".

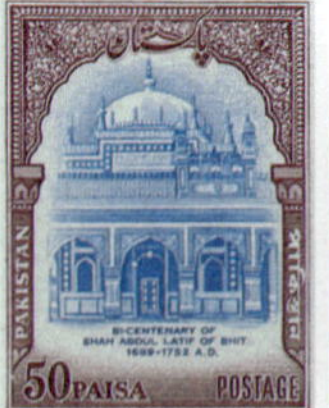

103 Shah Abdul Latif's Mausoleum **106** Bengali and Urdu Alphabets

104 Mausoleum of Quaid-i-Azam

1964. Death Bicentenary of Shah Abdul Latif of Bhit.
215 **103** 50p. blue and red . . . . 1·00 10

1964. 16th Death Anniv of Mohammed Ali Jinnah (Quaid-i-Azam).
216 **104** 15p. green . . . . 1·00 10
217 – 50p. green . . . . 2·25 10
DESIGN: 50p. As Type **104**, but $26\frac{1}{2}\times31\frac{1}{2}$ mm.

1964. Universal Children's Day.
218 **106** 15p. brown 10 10

107 University Building

1964. 1st Convocation of the West Pakistan University of Engineering and Technology, Lahore.
219 **107** 15p. brown 10 10

108 "Help the Blind"

1965. Blind Welfare.
220 **108** 15p. blue and yellow . . . 20 10

109 I.T.U. Emblem and Symbols

1965. Centenary of I.T.U.
221 **109** 15p. purple . . . . 1·50 30

110 I.C.Y. Emblem

1965. International Co-operation Year.
222 **110** 15p. black and blue . . . 50 15
223 50p. green and yellow . . 1·50 40

111 "Co-operation"

1965. 1st Anniv of Regional Development Co-operation Pact. Multicoloured.
224 15p. Type **111** 20 10
225 50p. Globe and flags of Turkey, Iran and Pakistan ($54\frac{1}{2}\times30\frac{1}{4}$ mm) . . . . . 1·10 10

113 Soldier and Tanks

1965. Pakistan Armed Forces. Multicoloured.
226 7p. Type **113** 75 30
227 15p. Naval Officer and "Tughril" (destroyer) . . . 1·50 10
228 50p. Pilot and Lockheed F-104C Starfighters . . . . 2·50 30

116 Army, Navy and Air Force Crests

1966. Armed Forces Day.
229 **116** 15p. blue, green and buff 1·00 10

117 Atomic Reactor, Islamabad

119 Children

118 Bank Crest

1966. Inauguration of Pakistan's 1st Atomic Reactor.
230 **117** 15p. black 10 10

1966. Silver Jubilee of Habib Bank.
231 **118** 15p. green, orange & sepia 10 10

1966. Universal Children's Day.
232 **119** 15p. black, red and yellow 10 10

120 UNESCO Emblem

1966. 20th Anniversary of UNESCO.
233 **120** 15p. multicoloured . . . 2·75 30

121 Flag, Secretariat Building and President Ayub

1966. Islamabad (new capital).
234 **121** 15p. multicoloured . . . 35 10
235 50p. multicoloured . . . 65 10

122 Avicenna

123 Mohammed Ali Jinnah

1966. Foundation of Health and Tibbi Research Institute.
236 **122** 15p. green and salmon . . 40 10

1966. 90th Birth Anniv of Mohammed Ali Jinnah.
237 **123** 15p. black, orange & blue 15 10
238 – 50p. black, purple and blue 35 10
DESIGN: 50p. Same portrait as 15p. but different frame.

124 Tourist Year Emblem

1967. International Tourist Year.
239 **124** 15p. black, blue and brown 10 10

125 Emblem of Pakistan T.B. Association

126 Scout Salute and Badge

1967. Tuberculosis Eradication Campaign.
240 **125** 15p. red, sepia and brown 10 10

1967. 4th National Scout Jamboree.
241 **126** 15p. brown and purple . . 15 10

127 "Justice"

1967. Cent of West Pakistan High Court.
242 **127** 15p. multicoloured . . . 10 10

128 Dr. Mohammed Iqbal (philosopher)

1967. Iqbal Commemoration.
243 **128** 15p. sepia and red 15 10
244 1r. sepia and green . . . 35 10

129 Hilal-i-Isteqlal Flag

1967. Award of Hilal-i-Isteqlal (for Valour) to Lahore, Sialkot and Sargodha.
245 **129** 15p. multicoloured . . . 10 10

130 "20th Anniversary"

1967. 20th Anniv of Independence.
246 **130** 15p. red and green . . . 10 10

131 "Rice Exports"

1967. Pakistan Exports. Multicoloured.
247 10p. Type **131** 10 15
248 15p. Cotton plant, yarn and textiles (vert) (27 × 45 mm) 10 10
249 50p. Raw jute, bale and bags (vert) (27 × 45 mm) 20 15

134 Clay Toys

1967. Universal Children's Day.
250 **134** 15p. multicoloured . . . 10 10

135 Shah and Empress of Iran and Gulistan Palace, Teheran

1967. Coronation of Shah Mohammed Riza Pahlavi and Empress Farah of Iran.
251 **135** 50p. purple, blue and ochre . . . . 1·00 10

136 "Each For All–All for Each"

1967. Co-operative Day.
252 **136** 15p. multicoloured . . . 10 10

137 Mangla Dam

1967. Indus Basin Project.
253 **137** 15p. multicoloured . . . 10 10

138 Crab pierced by Sword

139 Human Rights Emblem

1967. The Fight Against Cancer.
254 **138** 15p. red and black . . . 70 10

1968. Human Rights Year.
255 **139** 15p. red and blue 10 15
256 50p. red, yellow and grey 10 15

140 Agricultural University, Mymensingh

1968. First Convocation of East Pakistan Agricultural University.
257 **140** 15p. multicoloured . . . 10 10

141 W.H.O. Emblem

1968. 20th Anniv of W.H.O.
258 **141** 15p. orange and red . . . 10 15
259 50p. orange and blue . . 10 15

142 Kazi Nazrul Islam (poet, composer and patriot)

1968. Nazrul Islam Commemoration.
260 **142** 15p. sepia and yellow . . 35 15
261 50p. sepia and red 65 15

1968. Nos. 56, 74 and 61 surch.
262 4p. on 3a. purple . . . . . . 1·00 1·75
263 4p. on 6a. blue . . . . . . 1·25 1·75
264 60p. on 10a. violet . . . . . 1·00 35

144 Children running with Hoops

1968. Universal Children's Day.
265 **144** 15p. multicoloured . . . 10 10

145 National Assembly

1968. "A Decade of Development".
266 **145** 10p. multicoloured . . . 10 10
267 – 15p. multicoloured . . . 10 10
268 – 50p. multicoloured . . . 2·00 20
269 – 60p. blue, purple and red 50 35
DESIGNS: 15p. Industry and Agriculture; 50p. Army, Navy and Air Force; 60p. Minaret and atomic reactor plant.

149 Chittagong Steel Mill

1969. Pakistan's First Steel Mill, Chittagong.
270 **149** 15p. grey, blue and olive 10 10

150 "Family"

1969. Family Planning.
271 **150** 15p. purple and blue . . . 10 10

151 Olympic Gold Medal and Hockey Player

1969. Olympic Hockey Champions.
272 **151** 15p. multicoloured . . . 75 50
273 1r. multicoloured . . . . 2·25 1·00

152 Mirza Ghalib and Lines of Verse

1969. Death Centenary of Mirza Ghalib (poet).
274 **152** 15p. multicoloured . . . 20 15
275 50p. multicoloured . . . 50 15
The lines of verse on No. 275 are different from those in Type **152**.

153 Dacca Railway Station

1969. 1st Anniv of New Dacca Railway Station.
276 **153** 15p. multicoloured . . . 30 10

154 I.L.O. Emblem and "1919–1969"

1969. 50th Anniv of I.L.O.
277 **154** 15p. buff and green . . . 10 10
278 50p. brown and red . . . 40 10

155 "Ladyon Balcony" (18th-cent Mogul)

1969. 5th Anniv of Regional Co-operation for Development. Miniatures. Multicoloured.
279 20p. Type **155** 15 10
280 50p. "Kneeling Servant" (17th-cent Persian) 15 10
281 1r. "Suleiman the Magnificent holding Audience" (16th-cent Turkish) 20 10

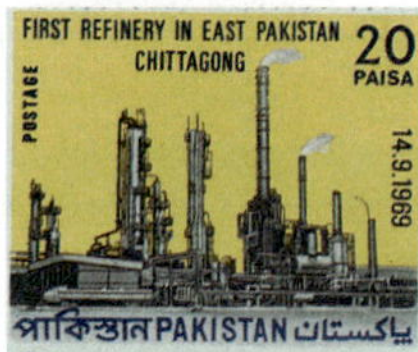

158 Eastern Refinery, Chittagong

1969. 1st East Pakistan Oil Refinery.
282 **158** 20p. multicoloured . . . 10 10

159 Children playing outside "School"

1969. Universal Children's Day.
283 **159** 20p. multicoloured . . . 10 10

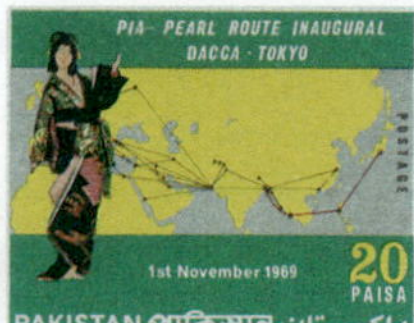

160 Japanese Doll and P.I.A. Air Routes

1969. Inauguration of P.I.A. Pearl Route, Dacca–Tokyo.
284 **160** 20p. multicoloured . . . 40 10
285 50p. multicoloured . . . 60 40

161 "Reflection of Light" Diagram

1969. Millenary Commemorative of Ibn-al-Haitham (physicist).
286 **161** 20p. black, yellow and blue 10 10

162 Vickers Vimy and Karachi Airport

1969. 50th Anniv of 1st England–Australia Flight.
287 **162** 50p. multicoloured . . . 70 35

163 Flags, Sun Tower and Expo Site Plan

1970. "Expo-70" World Fair, Osaka.
288 **163** 50p. multicoloured . . . 20 30

164 New U.P.U. H.Q. Building

1970. New U.P.U. Headquarters Building.
289 **164** 20p. multicoloured . . . 15 10
290 50p. multicoloured . . . 25 25

165 U.N. H.Q. Building

1970. 25th Anniv of United Nations. Mult.
291 20p. Type **165** 10 10
292 50p. U.N. emblem 15 20

167 I.E.Y. Emblem, Book and Pen

1970. International Education Year.
293 **167** 20p. multicoloured . . . 10 10
294 50p. multicoloured . . . 20 20

168 Saiful Malook Lake (Pakistan)

1970. 6th Anniv of Regional Co-operation for Development. Multicoloured.
295 20p. Type **168** 15 10
296 50p. Seeyo-Se-Pol Bridge, Esfahan (Iran) 20 10
297 1r. View from Fethiye (Turkey) 20 15

171 Asian Productivity Symbol

1970. Asian Productivity Year.
298 **171** 50p. multicoloured . . . 20 20

172 Dr. Maria Montessori

1970. Birth Centenary of Dr. Maria Montessori (educationist).
299 **172** 20p. multicoloured . . . 15 10
300 50p. multicoloured . . . 15 30

173 Tractor and Fertilizer Factory

1970. 10th Near East F.A.O. Regional Conference, Islamabad.
301 **173** 20p. green and brown . . 15 30

174 Children and Open Book **175** Pakistan Flag and Text

1970. Universal Children's Day.
302 **174** 20p. multicoloured . . . 15 10

1970. Elections for National Assembly.
303 **175** 20p. green and violet . . 15 10

1970. Elections for Provincial Assemblies. As No. 303 but inscr "PROVINCIAL ASSEMBLIES".
304 **175** 20p. green and red . . . 15 10

176 Conference Crest and burning Al-Aqsa Mosque

1970. Conference of Islamic Foreign Ministers, Karachi.
305 **176** 20p. multicoloured . . . 15 15

177 Coastal Embankments

1971. East Pakistan Coastal Embankments Project.
306 **177** 20p. multicoloured . . . 15 15

178 Emblem and United Peoples of the World **180** Chaharbagh School (Iran)

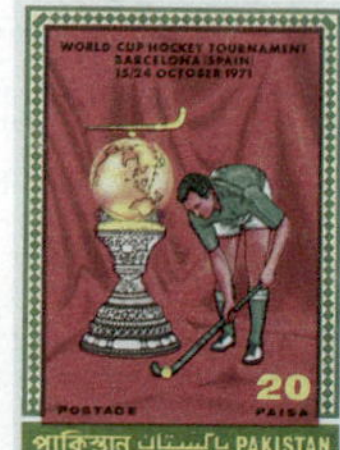

179 Maple Leaf Cement Factory, Daudkhel

1971. Racial Equality Year.
307 **178** 20p. multicoloured . . . 10 15
308 50p. multicoloured . . . 20 45

1971. 20th Anniv of Colombo Plan.
309 **179** 20p. brown, black & violet 10 10

1971. 7th Anniv of Regional Co-operation for Development. Multicoloured.
310 10p. Selimiye Mosque (Turkey) (horiz) 10 15
311 20p. Badshahi Mosque, Lahore (horiz) 20 25
312 50p. Type **180** 30 35

181 Electric Train and Boy with Toy Train

1971. Universal Children's Day.
313 **181** 20p. multicoloured . . . 1·75 50

182 Horseman and Symbols

1971. 2500th Anniv of Persian Monarchy.
314 **182** 10p. multicoloured . . . 20 30
315 20p. multicoloured . . . 30 40
316 50p. multicoloured . . . 40 75

183 Hockey-player and Trophy

1971. World Cup Hockey Tournament, Barcelona.
317 **183** 20p. multicoloured . . . 1·75 1·00

184 Great Bath, Moenjodaro

1971. 25th Anniv of UNESCO and Campaign to save the Moenjodaro Excavations.
318 **184** 20p. multicoloured . . . 20 30

185 UNICEF Symbol

1971. 25th Anniv of UNICEF.
319 **185** 50p. multicoloured . . . 30 60

186 King Hussein and Jordanian Flag

1971. 50th Anniv of Hashemite Kingdom of Jordan.
320 **186** 20p. multicoloured . . . 15 20

187 Badge of Hockey Federation and Trophy

1971. Hockey Championships Victory.
321 **187** 20p. multicoloured . . . 2·50 1·00

188 Reading Class

1972. International Book Year.
322 **188** 20p. multicoloured . . . 20 40

189 View of Venice

1972. UNESCO Campaign to Save Venice.
323 **189** 20p. multicoloured . . . 30 40

190 E.C.A.F.E. Emblem and Discs

1972. 25th Anniv of E.C.A.F.E.
324 **190** 20p. multicoloured . . . 15 30

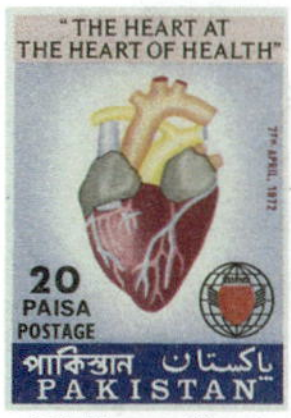

191 Human Heart **192** "Only One Earth"

1972. World Health Day.
325 **191** 20p. multicoloured . . . 20 30

1972. U.N. Conference on the Human Environment, Stockholm.
326 **192** 20p. multicoloured . . . 20 30

193 "Fisherman" (Cevat Dereli) **194** Mohammed Ali Jinnah and Tower

1972. 8th Anniv of Regional Co-operation for Development. Multicoloured.
327 10p. Type **193** 20 20
328 20p. "Iranian Woman" (Behzad) 35 25
329 50p. "Will and Power" (A. R. Chughtai) 55 70

1972. 25th Anniv of Independence. Mult.
330 10p. Type **194** 10 10
331 20p. "Land Reform" (74 × 23½) 15 30
332 20p. "Labour Reform" (74 × 23½) 15 30
333 20p. "Education Policy" (74 × 23½) 15 30
334 20p. "Health Policy" (74 × 23½) 15 30
335 60p. National Assembly Building (46 × 28 mm) . . 25 40

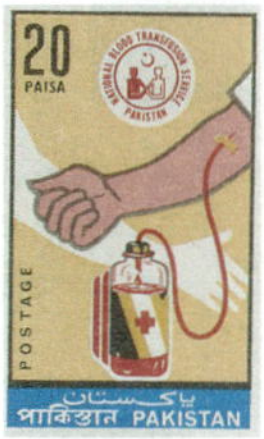

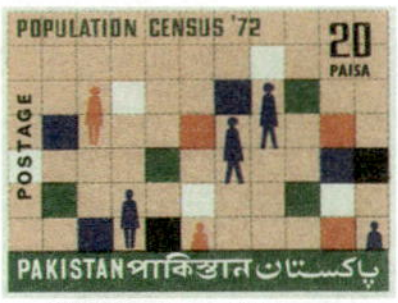

195 Donating Blood **196** People and Squares

1972. National Blood Transfusion Service.
336 **195** 20p. multicoloured . . . 20 30

1972. Centenary of Population Census.
337 **196** 20p. multicoloured . . . 20 20

197 Children from Slums

1972. Universal Children's Day.
338 **197** 20p. multicoloured . . . 20 30

198 People and Open Book

1972. Education Week.
339 **198** 20p. multicoloured . . . 20 30

199 Nuclear Power Plant

1972. Inauguration of Karachi Nuclear Power Plant.
340 **199** 20p. multicoloured . . . 20 40

200 Copernicus in Observatory

1973. 500th Birth Anniv of Nicholas Copernicus (astronomer).
341 **200** 20p. multicoloured . . . 20 30

201 Moenjodaro Excavations

1973. 50th Anniv of Moenjodaro Excavations.
342 **201** 20p. multicoloured . . . 20 30

202 Elements of Meteorology

1973. Centenary of I.M.O./W.M.O.
343 **202** 20p. multicoloured . . . 30 40

203 Prisoners-of-war

1973. Prisoners-of-war in India.
344 **203** 1r.25 multicoloured . . . 1·75 2·50

204 National Assembly Building and Constitution Book

1973. Constitution Week.
345 **204** 20p. multicoloured . . . 70 65

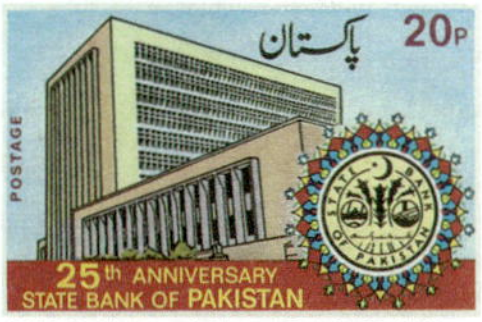

205 Badge and State Bank Building

1973. 25th Anniv of Pakistan State Bank.
346 **205** 20p. multicoloured . . . 15 30
347 1r. multicoloured 30 50

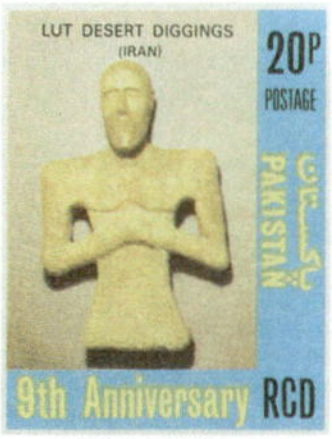

206 Lut Desert Excavations (Iran) **207** Constitution Book and Flag

1973. 9th Anniv of Regional Co-operation for Development. Multicoloured.
348 20p. Type **206** 30 20
349 60p. Main Street, Moenjodaro (Pakistan) . . 55 50
350 1r.25 Mausoleum of Antiochus I (Turkey) . . . 75 1·25

1973. Independence Day and Enforcement of the Constitution.
351 **207** 20p. multicoloured . . . 15 30

208 Mohammed Ali Jinnah (Quaid-i-Azam)

1973. 25th Death Anniv of Mohammed Ali Jinnah.
352 **208** 20p. green, yellow & black 15 30

209 Wallago

1973. Fishes. Multicoloured.
353 10p. Type **209** . . . . . . 1·10 1·10
354 20p. Rohu . . . . 1·25 1·25
355 60p. Mozambique mouthbrooder . . . . . . 1·40 1·40
356 1r. Catla . . . . 1·40 1·40

210 Children's Education

1973. Universal Children's Day.
357 **210** 20p. multicoloured . . . 15 40

211 Harvesting

1973. 10th Anniv of World Food Programme.
358 **211** 20p. multicoloured . . . 60 40

212 Ankara and Kemal Ataturk

1973. 50th Anniv of Turkish Republic.
359 **212** 50p. multicoloured . . . 45 35

213 Boy Scout **214** "Basic Necessities"

1973. National Silver Jubilee Jamboree.
360 **213** 20p. multicoloured . . . 1·75 50

1973. 25th Anniv of Declaration of Human Rights.
361 **214** 20p. multicoloured . . . 30 40

215 Al-Biruni and Nandana Hill

1973. Al-Biruni Millennium Congress.
362 **215** 20p. multicoloured . . . 50 20
363 1r.25 multicoloured . . . 1·25 90

216 Dr. Hansen, Microscope and Bacillus
218 Conference Emblem

217 Family and Emblem

1973. Centenary of Hansen's Discovery of Leprosy Bacillus.
364 **216** 20p. multicoloured . . . 1·00 80

1974. World Population Year.
365 **217** 20p. multicoloured . . . 10 10
366 1r.25 multicoloured . . . 30 40

1974. Islamic Summit Conference, Lahore. Multicoloured.
367 20p. Type **218** 10 10
368 65p. Emblem on "Sun" (42 × 30 mm) 25 60
MS369 102 × 102 mm. Nos. 367/8. Imperf . . . . 1·50 4·75

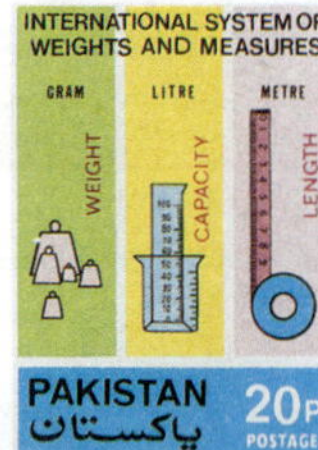

219 Units of Weight and Measurement

1974. Adoption of Int Weights and Measures System.
370 **219** 20p. multicoloured . . . 15 25

220 "Chand Chauthai" Carpet, Pakistan

1974. 10th Anniversary of Regional Co-operation for Development. Multicoloured.
371 20p. Type **220** 20 15
372 60p. Persian carpet, 16th-century 40 55
373 1r.25 Anatolian carpet, 15th-century . . . . . . 65 1·25

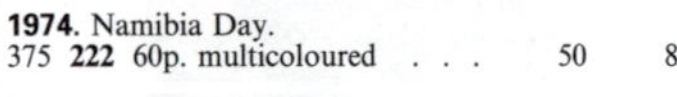

221 Hands protecting Sapling
222 Torch and Map

1974. Tree Planting Day.
374 **221** 20p. multicoloured . . . 50 60

1974. Namibia Day.
375 **222** 60p. multicoloured . . . 50 80

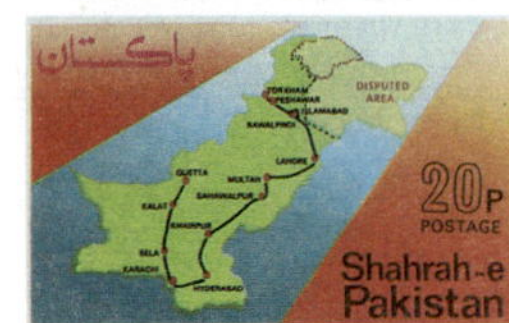

223 Highway Map

1974. Shahrah-e-Pakistan (Pakistan Highway).
376 **223** 20p. multicoloured . . . 1·25 1·00

224 Boy at Desk
225 U.P.U. Emblem

1974. Universal Children's Day.
377 **224** 20p. multicoloured . . . 30 40

1974. Centenary of U.P.U. Multicoloured.
378 20p. Type **225** 20 20
379 2r.25 U.P.U. emblem, Boeing 707 and mail-wagon (30 × 41 mm) . . . . . . 55 1·40
MS380 100 × 101 mm. Nos. 378/9. Imperf . . . . 1·25 5·00

226 Liaquat Ali Khan
227 Dr. Mohammed Iqbal (poet and philosopher)

1974. Liaquat Ali Khan (First Prime Minister of Pakistan).
381 **226** 20p. black and red . . . 30 40

1974. Birth Centenary of Dr. Iqbal (1977) (1st issue).
382 **227** 20p. multicoloured . . . 30 40
See also Nos. 399, 433 and 445/9.

228 Dr. Schweitzer and River Scene

1975. Birth Centenary of Dr. Albert Schweitzer.
383 **228** 2r.25 multicoloured . . . 4·25 3·25

229 Tourism Year Symbol

1975. South East Asia Tourism Year.
384 **229** 2r.25 multicoloured . . . 60 1·00

230 Assembly Hall, Flags and Prime Minister Bhutto

1975. 1st Anniv of Islamic Summit Conference, Lahore.
385 **230** 20p. multicoloured . . . 35 35
386 1r. multicoloured . . . . 75 1·40

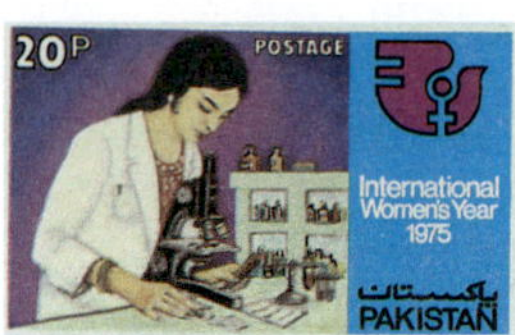

231 "Scientific Research"

1975. International Women's Year. Mult.
387 20p. Type **231** 20 25
388 2r.25 Girl teaching woman ("Adult Education") . . . 1·10 2·00

232 "Globe" and Algebraic Symbol
233 Pakistani Camel-skin Vase

1975. International Congress of Mathematical Sciences, Karachi.
389 **232** 20p. multicoloured . . . 50 60

1975. 11th Anniv of Regional Co-operation for Development. Multicoloured.
390 20p. Type **233** 25 30
391 60p. Iranian tile (horiz) . . . 50 1·00
392 1r.25 Turkish porcelain vase 75 1·50

234 Sapling and Dead Trees
235 Black Partridge

1975. Tree Planting Year.
393 **234** 20p. multicoloured . . . 35 60

1975. Wildlife Protection (1st series).
394 **235** 20p. multicoloured . . . 1·25 35
395 2r.25 multicoloured . . . 4·00 4·75
See also Nos. 400/1, 411/12, 417/18, 493/6, 560, 572/3, 581/2, 599, 600, 605, 621/2, 691, 702, 752, 780/3, 853 and 1027.

236 "Today's Girls"
238 Dr. Mohammed Iqbal

237 Hazrat Amir Khusrau, Sitar and Tabla (½-size illustration)

1975. Universal Children's Day.
396 **236** 20p. multicoloured . . . 30 50

1975. 700th Birth Anniv of Hazrat Amir Khusrau (poet and musician).
397 **237** 20p. multicoloured . . . 20 50
398 2r.25 multicoloured . . . 80 2·00

1975. Birth Cent (1977) of Dr. Iqbal (2nd issue).
399 **238** 20p. multicoloured . . . 30 50

239 Urial (wild sheep)
241 Dome and Minaret of the Rauza-e-Mubarak

240 Moenjodaro Remains

1975. Wildlife Protection (2nd series).
400 **239** 20p. multicoloured . . . 30 30
401 3r. multicoloured . . . . 1·75 3·25

1976. "Save Moenjodaro" (1st issue). Multicoloured.
402 10p. Type **240** 65 80
403 20p. Remains of houses . . . 75 90
404 65p. The Citadel 75 90
405 3r. Well inside a house . . . 75 90
406 4r. The "Great Bath" . . . . 85 1·00
See also Nos. 414 and 430.

1976. International Congress on Seerat.
407 **241** 20p. multicoloured . . . 15 20
408 3r. multicoloured 55 90

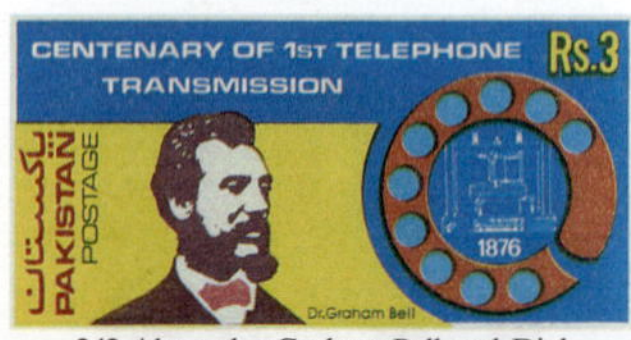

242 Alexander Graham Bell and Dial

1976. Telephone Centenary.
409 **242** 3r. multicoloured . . . . 1·25 2·00

243 College Arms within "Sun"

1976. Cent of National College of Arts, Lahore.
410 **243** 20p. multicoloured . . . 30 50

244 Common Peafowl

1976. Wildlife Protection (3rd series).
411 **244** 20p. multicoloured . . . 1·00 35
412 3r. multicoloured . . . . 3·50 4·50

245 Human Eye

1976. Prevention of Blindness.
413 **245** 20p. multicoloured . . . 1·00 70

246 Unicorn and Ruins

1976. "Save Moenjodaro" (2nd series).
414 **246** 20p. multicoloured . . . 30 40

247 Jefferson Memorial

1976. Bicent of American Revolution. Mult.
415 90p. Type **247** 75 60
416 4r. "Declaration of Independence" (47 × 36 mm) . . . . . . 3·00 5·00

248 Ibex

1976. Wildlife Protection (4th series).
417 **248** 20p. multicoloured . . . 30 35
418 3r. multicoloured . . . . 1·25 2·50

249 Mohammed Ali Jinnah

1976. 12th Anniv of Regional Co-operation for Development. Multicoloured.
419 20p. Type **249** 65 90
420 65p. Reza Shah the Great (Iran) 65 90
421 90p. Kemal Ataturk (Turkey) 65 90

250 Urdu Text

251 Mohammed Ali Jinnah and Wazir Mansion

1976. Birth Cent of Mohammed Ali Jinnah (1st issue). (a) Type **250**.
422 **250** 5p. black, blue and yellow 20 25
423 10p. black, yellow & pur 20 25
424 15p. black and blue . . . 20 25
425 1r. black, yellow and blue 30 30

(b) Type **251**. Background Buildings given. Mult.
426 20p. Type **251** 20 25
427 40p. Sind Madressah 20 25
428 50p. Minar Qarardad-e-Pakistan 20 25
429 3r. Mausoleum 45 50
See also No. 436.

252 Dancing-girl, Ruins and King Priest

1976. "Save Moenjodaro" (3rd series).
430 **252** 65p. multicoloured . . . 35 80

253 U.N. Racial Discrimination Emblem

1976. U.N. Decade to Combat Racial Discrimination.
431 **253** 65p. multicoloured . . . 30 60

254 Child in Maze and Basic Services

1976. Universal Children's Day.
432 **254** 20p. multicoloured . . . 60 60

255 Verse from "Allama Iqbal"

1976. Birth Centenary (1977) of Dr. Iqbal (3rd issue).
433 **255** 20p. multicoloured . . . 15 30

256 Mohammed Ali Jinnah giving Scout Salute

257 Children Reading

1976. Quaid-i-Azam Centenary Jamboree.
434 **256** 20p. multicoloured . . . 1·00 60

1976. Children's Literature.
435 **257** 20p. multicoloured . . . 65 65

258 Mohammed Ali Jinnah

1976. Birth Centenary of Mohammed Ali Jinnah (2nd issue).
436 **258** 10r. green and gold . . . 2·75 3·50

259 Rural Family

261 Forest

260 Turkish Vase, 1800 B.C.

1977. Social Welfare and Rural Development Year.
437 **259** 20p. multicoloured . . . 40 10

1977. 13th Anniv of Regional Co-operation for Development.
438 **260** 20p. orange, blue & black 45 10
439 – 65p. multicoloured . . . 65 40
440 – 90p. multicoloured . . . 90 1·50
DESIGNS: 60p. Pakistani toy bullock cart from Moenjodaro; 90p. Pitcher with spout from Sialk Hill, Iran.

1977. National Tree Plantation Campaign.
441 **261** 20p. multicoloured . . . 20 30

262 Desert Scene

1977. U.N. Conference on Desertification, Nairobi.
442 **262** 65p. multicoloured . . . 1·00 45

263 "Water for Children of the World"

265 Iqbal and Spirit of the Poet Roomi (from painting by Behzad)

264 Aga Khan III

1977. Universal Children's Day.
443 **263** 50p. multicoloured . . . 40 30

1977. Birth Centenary of Aga Khan III.
444 **264** 2r. multicoloured . . . . 55 1·00

1977. Birth Centenary of Dr. Mohammed Iqbal (4th issue). Multicoloured.
445 20p. Type **265** 60 70
446 65p. Iqbal looking at Jamaluddin Afghani and Saeed Haleem Pasha at prayer (Behzad) 60 70
447 1r.25 Urdu verse 65 75
448 2r.25 Persian verse 70 85
449 3r. Iqbal 75 95

266 The Holy "Khana-Kaaba" (House of God, Mecca)

1977. Haj (pilgrimage to Mecca).
450 **266** 65p. multicoloured . . . 30 30

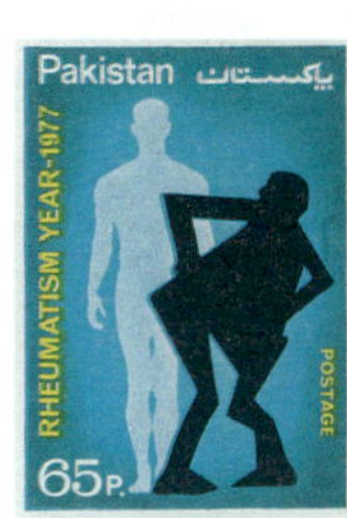

267 Rheumatic Patient and Healthy Man

268 Woman in Costume of Rawalpindi-Islamabad

1977. World Rheumatism Year.
451 **267** 65p. blue, black and yellow 30 20

1978. Indonesia–Pakistan Economic and Cultural Co-operation Organization.
452 **268** 75p. multicoloured . . . 30 20

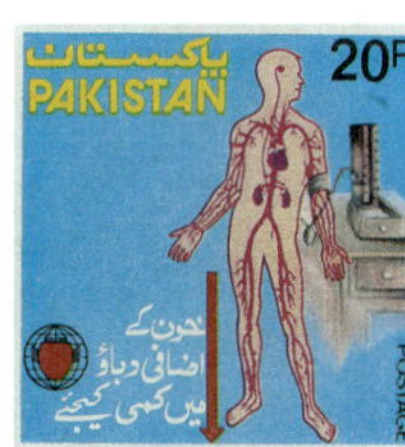

269 Human Body and Sphygmomanometer

1978. World Hypertension Month.
453 **269** 20p. multicoloured . . . 15 10
454 – 2r. multicoloured 60 90
The 2r. value is as Type **269** but has the words "Down with high blood pressure" instead of the Urdu inscription at bottom left.

270 Henri Dunant

1978. 150th Birth Anniv of Henri Dunant (founder of the Red Cross).
455 **270** 1r. multicoloured . . . . 1·00 20

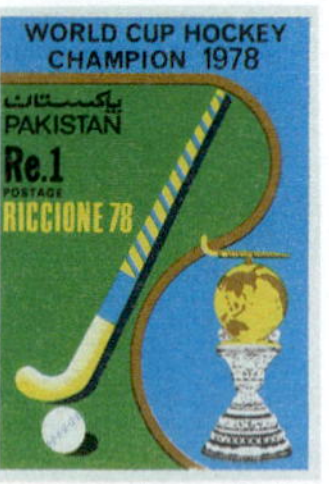

271 Red Roses (Pakistan) 272 "Pakistan, World Cup Hockey Champions"

1978. 14th Anniv of Regional Co-operation for Development. Roses. Multicoloured.
456 20p. Type **271** 35 20
457 90p. Pink roses (Iran) 50 20
458 2r. Yellow rose (Turkey) . . 75 25

1978. "Riccione '78" International Stamp Fair. Multicoloured.
459 1r. Type **272** . . . . 1·25 25
460 2r. Fountain at Piazza Turismo 50 35

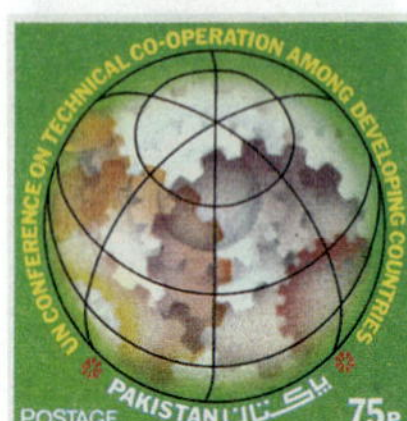

273 Cogwheels within Globe Symbol

1978. U.N. Technical Co-operation amongst Developing Countries Conference.
461 **273** 75p. multicoloured . . . 15 10

274 St. Patrick's Cathedral, Karachi 275 Minar-i-Qarardad-e-Pakistan

1978. Centenary of St. Patrick's Cathedral, Karachi. Multicoloured.
462 1r. Type **274** 10 10
463 2r. Stained glass window . . 25 25

1978.
464 **275** 2p. green 10 10
465 3p. black 10 10
466 5p. blue 10 10
467 – 10p. blue and turquoise . . 10 10
468 – 20p. green 60 10
469 – 25p. green and mauve . . 1·25 10
470 – 40p. blue and mauve . . 10 10
471 – 50p. lilac and green . . 30 10
472 – 60p. black 10 10
473b – 75p. red . . . . . . 1·50 10
474 – 90p. mauve and blue . . 30 10
475 – 1r. green 60 10
476 – 1r.50 orange 20 10
477 – 2r. red 20 10
478 – 3r. blue 20 10
479 – 4r. black 20 10
480 – 5r. brown 20 10
DESIGNS—HORIZ (25 × 20 mm): 10p. to 90p. Tractor. VERT (21 × 25 mm): 1r. to 5r. Mausoleum of Ibrahim Khan Makli, Thatta.

277 Emblem and "United Races" Symbol 278 Maulana Mohammad Ali Jauhar

1978. International Anti-Apartheid Year.
481 **277** 1r. multicoloured 15 15

1978. Birth Centenary of Maulana Mohammad Ali Jauhar (patriot).
482 **278** 50p. multicoloured . . . 50 20

279 Panavia MRCA Tornado, De Havilland Dragon Rapide and Wright Flyer I

1978. 75th Anniv of Powered Flight. Mult.
483 65p. Type **279** . . . . . . 1·00 1·75
484 1r. McDonnell Douglas Phantom II, Lockheed Tristar 500 and Wright Flyer I . . . . 1·10 1·75
485 2r. North American X-15, Tupolev Tu-104 and Wright Flyer I . . . . . . 1·25 2·00
486 2r.25 Mikoyan Gurevich MiG-15, Concorde and Wright Flyer I . . . . . . 1·25 2·25

280 "Holy Koran illuminating Globe" and Raudha-e-Mubarak (mausoleum)

1979. "12th Rabi-ul-Awwal" (Prophet Mohammed's birthday).
487 **280** 20p. multicoloured . . . 40 15

281 "Aspects of A.P.W.A."

1979. 30th Anniv of A.P.W.A. (All Pakistan Women's Association).
488 **281** 50p. multicoloured . . . 75 15

282 Tippu Sultan Shaheed of Mysore

1979. Pioneers of Freedom (1st series). Multicoloured.
490 10r. Type **282** . . . . 75 1·60
491 15r. Sir Syed Ahmad Khan 1·00 2·25
492 25r. Altaf Hussain Hali . . . 1·50 2·25
See also Nos. 757, 801/27, 838/46, 870/2, 904/6, 921/8, 961/2, 1007, 1019/20 and 1075/7.

283 Himalayan Monal Pheasant

1979. Wildlife Protection (5th series). Pheasants. Multicoloured.
493 20p. Type **283** . . . . . . 1·25 60
494 25p. Kalij pheasant . . . . . 1·25 80
495 40p. Koklass pheasant . . . 1·60 1·75
496 1r. Cheer pheasant . . . . . 3·00 2·00

284 "Pakistan Village Scene" (Ustad Bakhsh)

1979. 15th Anniv of Regional Co-operation for Development. Multicoloured.
497 40p. Type **284** 20 25
498 75p. "Iranian Goldsmith" (Kamal al Molk) 20 25
499 1r.60 "Turkish Harvest" (Namik Ismail) 25 30

285 Guj Embroidered Shirt (detail)

1979. Handicrafts (1st series). Multicoloured.
500 40p. Type **285** 20 20
501 1r. Enamel inlaid brass plate 25 25
502 1r.50 Baskets 30 30
503 2r. Chain-stitch embroidered rug (detail) 40 40
See also Nos. 578/9, 595/6 and 625/8.

286 Children playing on Climbing-frame

1979. S.O.S. Children's Village, Lahore.
504 **286** 50p. multicoloured . . . 40 40

287 "Island" (Z. Maloof)

1979. International Year of the Child. Children's Paintings. Multicoloured.
505 40p. Type **287** 15 15
506 75p. "Playground" (R. Akbar) 25 25
507 1r. "Fairground" (M. Azam) 25 25
508 1r.50 "Hockey Match" (M. Tayyab) 30 30
MS509 79 × 64 mm. 2r. "Child looking at Faces in the Sky" (M. Mumtaz) (vert). Imperf . . 1·00 2·00

288 Warrior attacking Crab 289 Pakistan Customs Emblem

1979. "Fight Against Cancer".
510 **288** 40p. black, yellow and purple 70 70

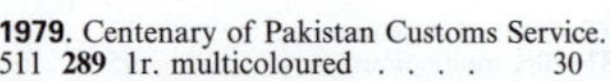

1979. Centenary of Pakistan Customs Service.
511 **289** 1r. multicoloured 30 30

290 Boeing 747-200 and Douglas DC-3 Airliners

1980. 25th Anniv of Pakistan International Air Lines.
512 **290** 1r. multicoloured . . . . 1·75 90

291 Islamic Pattern 292 Young Child

1980.
513 **291** 10p. green and yellow . . 10 10
514 15p. deep green and green 10 10
515 25p. violet and red . . . 10 50
516 35p. red and green . . . 10 50
517 – 40p. red and brown . . . 15 10
518 – 50p. violet and green . . 10 50
519 – 80p. green and black . . 15 50
The 40 to 80p. values also show different Islamic patterns, the 40p. being horizontal and the remainder vertical.

1980. 5th Asian Congress of Paediatric Surgery, Karachi.
530 **292** 50p. multicoloured . . . 75 1·50

293 Conference Emblem

1980. 11th Islamic Conference of Foreign Ministers, Islamabad.
531 **293** 1r. multicoloured . . . . 1·00 75

294 Karachi Port (½-size illustration)

1980. Centenary of Karachi Port Authority.
532 **294** 1r. multicoloured . . . . 1·75 1·40

1980. "Riccione 80" International Stamp Exhibition. Nos. 505/8 optd **RICCIONE 80**.
533 **287** 40p. multicoloured . . . 30 80
534 – 75p. multicoloured . . . 40 90
535 – 1r. multicoloured 45 90
536 – 1r.50 multicoloured . . . 60 1·10

296 College Emblem with Old and New Buildings

1980. 75th Anniv of Command and Staff College, Quetta.
537 **296** 1r. multicoloured 20 15

1980. World Tourism Conference, Manila. No. 496 optd **WORLD TOURISM CONFERENCE MANILA 80**.
538 1r. Cheer pheasant . . . . . 1·25 40

298 Birth Centenary Emblem

1980. Birth Cent of Hafiz Mahmood Shairani.
539 **298** 40p. multicoloured . . . 30 1·00

299 Shalimar Gardens, Lahore

1980. Aga Khan Award for Architecture.
540 **299** 2r. multicoloured . . . . 40 1·75

300 Rising Sun

1980. 1400th Anniv of Hegira (1st issue). Multicoloured.
541 40p. Type **300** 10 10
542 2r. Ka'aba and symbols of Moslem achievement (33 × 33 mm) 25 45
543 3r. Holy Koran illuminating the World (30 × 54 mm) . . 30 80
MS544 106 × 84 mm. 4r. Candles. Imperf . . . . 45 1·00
See also No. 549.

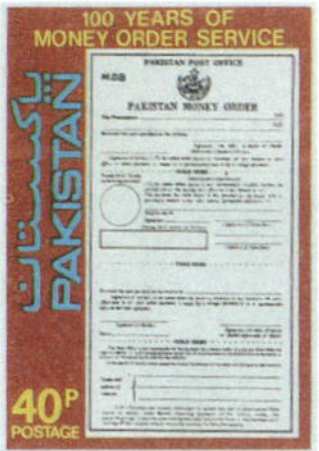

301 Money Order Form **302** Postcards encircling Globe

1980. Centenary of Money Order Service.
545 **301** 40p. multicoloured . . . 20 60

1980. Centenary of Postcard Service.
546 **302** 40p. multicoloured . . . 20 60

303 Heinrich von Stephan and U.P.U. Emblem

1981. 150th Birth Anniv of Heinrich von Stephan (U.P.U. founder).
547 **303** 1r. multicoloured 30 20

304 Aircraft and Airmail Letters

1981. 50th Anniv of Airmail Service.
548 **304** 1r. multicoloured 60 20

305 Mecca

1981. 1400th Anniv of Hegira (2nd issue).
549 **305** 40p. multicoloured . . . 20 60

306 Conference Emblem and Afghan Refugees

1981. Islamic Summit Conference (1st issue). Multicoloured.
550 40p. Type **306** 30 10
551 40p. Conference emblem encircled by flags and Afghan refugees (28 × 58 mm) 30 10
552 1r. Type **306** 50 10
553 1r. As No. 551 . . . . . . 50 10
554 2r. Conference emblem and map showing Afghanistan (48 × 32 mm) 65 50

307 Conference Emblem

1981. Islamic Summit Conference (2nd issue). Multicoloured.
555 40p. Type **307** 10 15
556 40p. Conference emblem and flags (28 × 46 mm) 10 15
557 85p. Type **307** 20 40
558 85p. As No. 556 . . . . . . 20 40

308 Kemal Ataturk

1981. Birth Centenary of Kemal Ataturk (Turkish statesman).
559 **308** 1r. multicoloured 50 15

309 Green Turtle

1981. Wildlife Protection (6th series).
560 **309** 40p. multicoloured . . . 1·25 40

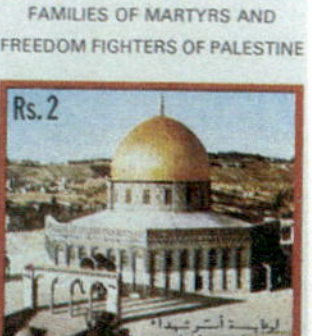

310 Dome of the Rock

1981. Palestinian Welfare.
561 **310** 2r. multicoloured 35 35

311 Malubiting West

1981. Mountain Peaks (1st series). Karakoram Range. Multicoloured.
562 40p. Type **311** 40 40
563 40p. Malubiting West (24 × 31 mm) 40 40
564 1r. Haramosh 55 75
565 1r. Haramosh (24 × 31 mm) 55 75
566 1r.50 K6 . . . . 70 1·00
567 1r.50 K6 (24 × 31 mm) . . . 70 1·00
568 2r. K2, Broad Peak, Gasherbrum 4 and Gasherbrum 2 . . . . . 70 1·40
569 2r. K2 (24 × 31 mm) . . . . 70 1·40
See also Nos. 674/5.

312 Pakistan Steel "Furnace No. 1"

1981. 1st Firing of Pakistan Steel "Furnace No. 1", Karachi.
570 **312** 40p. multicoloured . . . 20 10
571 2r. multicoloured . . . . 60 1·75

313 Western Tragopan

1981. Wildlife Protection (7th series).
572 **313** 40p. multicoloured . . . 2·25 75
573 – 2r. multicoloured . . . . 4·25 4·25
DESIGN: 2r. As Type **313** but with background showing a winter view.

314 Disabled People and I.Y.D.P. Emblem

1981. International Year for Disabled Persons.
574 **314** 40p. multicoloured . . . 30 50
575 2r. multicoloured . . . . 1·10 1·75

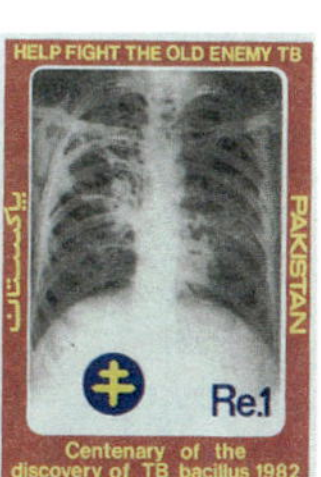

315 World Hockey Cup below Flags of participating Countries **317** Chest X-Ray of Infected Person

316 Camel Skin Lamp

1982. Pakistan—World Cup Hockey Champions. Multicoloured.
576 1r. Type **315** . . . . 2·00 1·50
577 1r. World Hockey Cup above flags of participating countries . . . . 2·00 1·50

1982. Handicrafts (2nd series). Multicoloured.
578 1r. Type **316** 70 80
579 1r. Hala pottery 70 80
See also Nos. 595/6.

1982. Centenary of Robert Koch's Discovery of Tubercle Bacillus.
580 **317** 1r. multicoloured . . . . 1·25 1·50

318 Indus Dolphin

1982. Wildlife Protection (8th series).
581 **318** 40p. multicoloured . . . 1·50 1·25
582 – 1r. multicoloured . . . . 3·00 2·50
DESIGN: 1r. As Type **318** but with design reversed.

319 "Apollo–Soyuz" Link-up, 1975

1982. Peaceful Use of Outer Space.
583 **319** 1r. multicoloured . . . . 2·00 1·25

320 Sukkur Barrage

1982. 50th Anniv of Sukkur Barrage.
584 **320** 1r. multicoloured 30 30

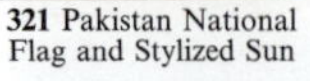

321 Pakistan National Flag and Stylized Sun

324 Scout Emblem and Tents

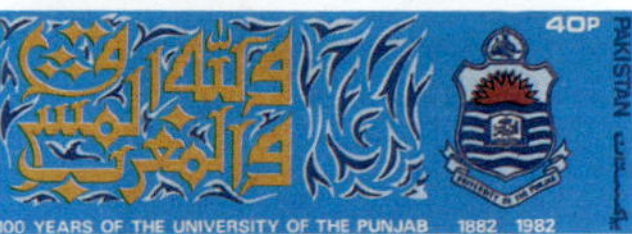

323 Arabic Inscription and University Emblem (⅔-size illustration)

1982. Independence Day. Multicoloured.
585 40p. Type **321** 20 30
586 85p. Map of Pakistan and stylized torch . . . . . . 45 1·25

1982. "Riccione '82" Stamp Exhibition. No. 584 optd **RICCIONE-82.**
587 **320** 1r. multicoloured 20 20

1982. Centenary of the Punjab University.
588 **323** 40p. multicoloured . . . 1·25 1·00

1983. 75th Anniv of Boy Scout Movement.
589 **324** 2r. multicoloured 50 50

325 Laying Pipeline

1983. Inaug of Quetta Natural Gas Pipeline Project.
590 **325** 1r. multicoloured 30 30

326 "Papilio polyctor"

1983. Butterflies. Multicoloured.
591 40p. Type **326** . . . . . . 1·25 20
592 50p. "Atrophaneura aristolochiae" . . . . . . 1·50 20
593 60p. "Danaus chrysippus" . . 1·75 60
594 1r.50 "Papilio demoleus" . . 2·50 2·25

1983. Handicrafts (3rd series). As T **316**. Multicoloured.
595 1r. Five flower motif needlework, Sind 15 15
596 1r. Straw mats 15 15

327 School of Nursing and University Emblem

1983. Presentation of Charter to Aga Khan University, Karachi.
597 **327** 2r. multicoloured . . . . 1·50 2·00

328 Yak Caravan crossing Zindiharam-Darkot Pass, Hindu Kush

1983. Trekking in Pakistan.
598 **328** 1r. multicoloured . . . . 1·50 1·50

329 Marsh Crocodile

331 Floral Design

330 Goitred Gazelle

1983. Wildlife Protection (9th series).
599 **329** 3r. multicoloured . . . . 3·50 2·00

1983. Wildlife Protection (10th series).
600 **330** 1r. multicoloured . . . . 2·50 2·00

1983. 36th Anniv of Independence. Mult.
601 60p. Type **331** 10 10
602 4r. Hand holding flaming torch 40 45

332 Traditional Weaving, Pakistan

1983. Indonesian–Pakistan Economic and Cultural Co-operation Organization, 1969–1983. Mult.
603 2r. Type **332** 20 25
604 2r. Traditional weaving, Indonesia 20 25

333 "Siberian Cranes" (Great White Cranes) (Sir Peter Scott)

1983. Wildlife Protection (11th series).
605 **333** 3r. multicoloured . . . . 3·00 3·25

334 W.C.Y. Emblem

1983. World Communications Year. Multicoloured.
606 2r. Type **334** 20 25
607 3r. W.C.Y. emblem (different) (33 × 33 mm) 30 35

335 Farm Animals

1983. World Food Day. Multicoloured.
608 3r. Type **335** . . . . 1·50 1·75
609 3r. Fruit . . . . 1·50 1·75
610 3r. Crops . . . . 1·50 1·75
611 3r. Sea food . . . . 1·50 1·75

336 Agriculture Produce and Fertilizer Factory

337 Lahore, 1852

1983. National Fertilizer Corporation.
612 **336** 60p. multicoloured . . . 15 30

1983. National Stamp Exn, Lahore. Mult.
613 60p. Musti Durwaza Dharmsala 60 75
614 60p. Khabgha 60 75
615 60p. Type **337** 60 75
616 60p. Summan Burj Hazuri . . 60 75
617 60p. Flower Garden, Samadhi Northern Gate . . 60 75
618 60p. Budda Darya, Badshahi Masjid 60 75

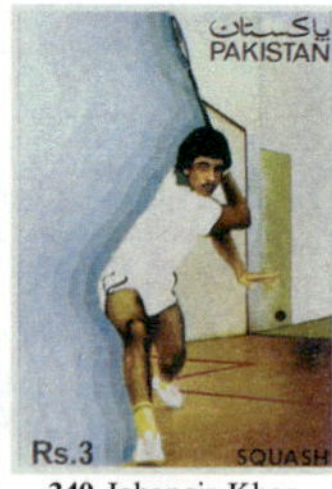

338 Winner of "Enterprise" Event

340 Jahangir Khan (World Squash Champion)

339 Snow Leopard

1983. Yachting Champions, Asian Games, Delhi. Multicoloured.
619 60p. Type **338** . . . . . . 1·75 1·75
620 60p. Winner of "OK" Dinghy event . . . . . . 1·75 1·75

1984. Wildlife Protection (12th series).
621 **339** 40p. multicoloured . . . 1·75 90
622 1r.60 multicoloured . . . 4·75 6·00

1984. Squash.
623 **340** 3r. multicoloured . . . . 2·25 1·75

341 P.I.A. Boeing 707 Airliner

1984. 20th Anniv of Pakistan International Airways Service to China.
624 **341** 3r. multicoloured . . . . 5·00 5·50

342 Glass-work

343 Attock Fort

1984. Handicrafts (4th series). Multicoloured, frame colours given.
625 **342** 1r. blue 25 15
626 – 1r. red 25 15
627 – 1r. green 25 15
628 – 1r. violet 25 15

DESIGNS: showing glass-work in Sheesh Mahal, Lahore Fort. Nos. 627/8 are horizontal designs.

1984. Forts.
629 – 5p. black and purple . . . 20 40
630 – 10p. black and red . . . 20 10
631 – 15p. violet and brown . . 75 10
632 **343** 20p. black and violet . . 60 10
633 – 50p. brown and red . . . 1·50 10
634 – 60p. light brown & brown 1·00 10
635 – 70p. blue . . . . 1·50 10
636 – 80p. brown and red . . . 1·50 10

DESIGNS: 5p. Kot Diji Fort; 10p. Rohtas Fort; 15p. Bala Hissar Fort; 50p. Hyderabad Fort; 60p. Lahore Fort; 70p. Sibi Fort; 80p. Ranikot Fort.

344 Shah Rukn i Alam's Tomb, Multan

1984. Aga Khan Award for Architecture.
647 **344** 60p. multicoloured . . . 2·00 2·25

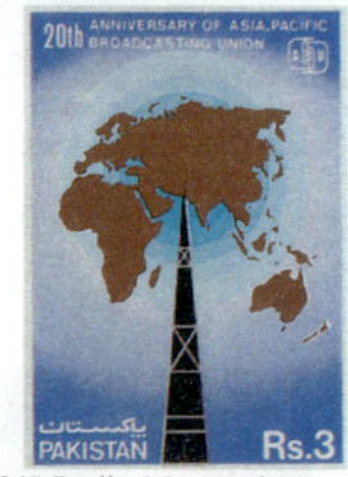

345 Radio Mast and Map of World

1984. 20th Anniv of Asia–Pacific Broadcasting Union.
648 **345** 3r. multicoloured . . . . 1·00 60

346 Wrestling

1984. Olympic Games, Los Angeles. Mult.
649 3r. Type **346** . . . . 1·25 1·50
650 3r. Boxing . . . . 1·25 1·50
651 3r. Athletics . . . . 1·25 1·50
652 3r. Hockey . . . . 1·25 1·50
653 3r. Yachting . . . . 1·25 1·50

347 Jasmine (National flower) and Inscription

1984. Independence Day. Multicoloured.
654 60p. Type **347** 10 10
655 4r. Symbolic torch 45 50

348 Gearwheel Emblem and Flags of Participating Nations

1984. Pakistan International Trade Fair.
656 **348** 60p. multicoloured . . . 1·00 30

349 Interior of Main Dome

1984. Tourism Convention, Shahjahan Mosque, Thatta. Multicoloured.
657 1r. Type **349** 50 60
658 1r. Brick and glazed tile work 50 60
659 1r. Gateway 50 60
660 1r. Symmetrical archways . . 50 60
661 1r. Interior of a dome . . . 50 60

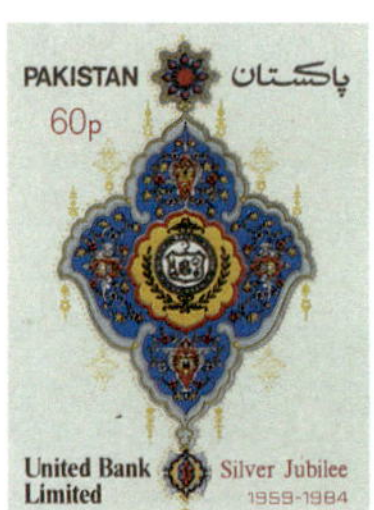

350 Bank Emblem in Floral Pattern

1984. 25th Anniv of United Bank Ltd.
662 **350** 60p. multicoloured . . . 80 80

351 Conference Emblem

1984. 20th United Nations Conference of Trade and Development.
663 **351** 60p. multicoloured . . . 80 40

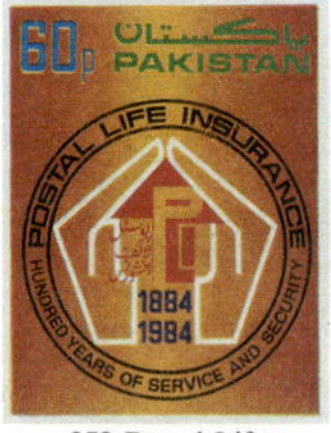

352 Postal Life Insurance Emblem within Hands

353 Bull (wall painting)

1984. Centenary of Postal Life Insurance. Multicoloured.
664 60p. Type **352** 70 15
665 1r. "100" and Postal Life Insurance emblem 90 15

1984. UNESCO Save Moenjadoro Campaign. Multicoloured.
666 2r. Type **353** . . . . 1·40 1·00
667 2r. Bull (seal) . . . . 1·40 1·00

354 International Youth Year Emblem and "75"

1985. 75th Anniv of Girl Guide Movement.
668 **354** 60p. multicoloured . . . 3·25 1·50

355 Smelting Ore

1985. Inauguration of Pakistan Steel Corporation. Multicoloured.
669 60p. Type **355** 65 25
670 1r. Pouring molten steel from ladle (28 × 46 mm) . . . . 1·10 25

356 Map of Pakistan and Rays of Sun

1985. Presidential Referendum of 19 December 1984.
671 **356** 60p. multicoloured . . . 1·75 55

357 Ballot Box and Voting Paper

1985. March Elections. Multicoloured.
672 1r. Type **357** 65 15
673 1r. Minar-e-Qarardad-e-Pakistan Tower, and word "Democracy" (31 × 43 mm) 65 15

1985. Mountain Peaks (2nd series). As T **311**. Multicoloured.
674 40p. Rakaposhi (Karakoram Range) . . . . 1·75 75
675 2r. Nangaparbat (Western Himalayas) . . . . 3·75 5·00

358 Trophy and Medals from Olympic Games 1984, Asia Cup 1985 and World Cup 1982

1985. Pakistan Hockey Team "Grand Slam" Success.
676 **358** 1r. multicoloured . . . . 2·50 2·00

359 King Edward Medical College

1985. 125th Anniv of King Edward Medical College, Lahore.
677 **359** 3r. multicoloured . . . . 1·75 1·00

360 Illuminated Inscription in Urdu

1985. Independence Day. Multicoloured.
678 60p. Type **360** 40 65
679 60p. Illuminated "XXXVIII" (inscr in English) 40 65

361 Sind Madressah-tul-Islam, Karachi

1985. Centenary of Sind Madressah-tul-Islam (theological college), Karachi.
680 **361** 2r. multicoloured . . . . 1·75 85

362 Jamia Masjid Mosque by Day

1985. Inauguration of New Jamia Masjid Mosque, Karachi. Multicoloured.
681 1r. Type **362** 90 50
682 1r. Jamia Masjid illuminated at night 90 50

363 Lawrence College, Murree

1985. 125th Anniv of Lawrence College, Murree.
683 **363** 3r. multicoloured . . . . 2·00 85

364 United Nations Building, New York

1985. 40th Anniv of United Nations Organization. Multicoloured.
684 1r. Type **364** 30 15
685 2r. U.N. Building and emblem 40 50

365 Tents and Jamboree Emblem

1985. 10th National Scout Jamboree.
686 **365** 60p. multicoloured . . . 2·25 2·50

366 Islamabad

1985. 25th Anniv of Islamabad.
687 **366** 3r. multicoloured . . . . 2·50 1·00

367 Map of S.A.A.R.C. Countries and National Flags

1985. 1st Summit Meeting of South Asian Association for Regional Co-operation, Dhaka, Bangladesh. Multicoloured.
688 1r. Type **367** . . . . 1·50 4·00
689 2r. National flags (39 × 39 mm) . . . . . . 75 2·00

368 Globe and Peace Dove

1985. 25th Anniv of U.N. General Assembly's Declaration on Independence for Colonial Territories.
690 **368** 60p. multicoloured . . . 1·00 60

369 Peregrine Falcon

1986. Wildlife Protection (13th series). Peregrine Falcon.
691 **369** 1r.50 multicoloured . . . 4·25 4·25

370 A.D.B.P. Building, Islamabad

1986. 25th Anniv of Agricultural Development Bank of Pakistan.
692 **370** 60p. multicoloured . . . 1·75 50

371 Government S.E. College

1986. Centenary of Government Sadiq Egerton College, Bahawalpur.
693 **371** 1r. multicoloured . . . . 2·75 50

372 Emblem and Bar Graph

373 "1947 1986"

1986. 25th Anniv of Asian Productivity Organization.
694 **372** 1r. multicoloured . . . . 2·75 30

1986. 39th Anniv of Independence. Multicoloured.
695 80p. Type **373** . . . . . . 1·50 25
696 1r. Illuminated inscription in Urdu . . . . 1·50 25

374 Open Air Class

375 Mother and Child

1986. International Literacy Day.
697 **374** 1r. multicoloured . . . . 1·75 30

1986. UNICEF Child Survival Campaign.
698 **375** 80p. multicoloured . . . 2·00 65

376 Aitchison College

1986. Centenary of Aitchison College, Lahore.
699 **376** 2r.50 multicoloured . . . 1·75 1·00

377 Two Doves carrying Olive Branches

378 Table Tennis Players

1986. International Peace Year.

700 **377** 4r. multicoloured 60 75

1986. 4th Asian Cup Table Tennis Tournament, Karachi.

701 **378** 2r. multicoloured . . . . 2·00 1·00

379 Argali

1986. Wildlife Protection (14th series). Argali.

702 **379** 2r. multicoloured . . . . 3·00 3·00

380 Selimiye Mosque, Edirne, Turkey

382 Mistletoe Flowerpecker and Defence Symbols

381 St. Patrick's School

1986. "Ecophilex '86" International Stamp Exhibition, Islamabad. Multicoloured.

703 3r. Type **380** . . . . 1·40 1·60

704 3r. Gawhar Shad Mosque, Mashhad, Iran . . . . . 1·40 1·60

705 3r. Grand Mosque, Bhong, Pakistan . . . . 1·40 1·60

1987. 125th Anniv of St. Patrick's School, Karachi.

706 **381** 5r. multicoloured . . . . 2·75 1·50

1987. Post Office Savings Bank Week. Multicoloured.

707 5r. Type **382** . . . . 1·10 1·25

708 5r. Spotted pardalote and laboratory apparatus . . . 1·10 1·25

709 5r. Black-throated blue warbler and agriculture symbols . . . . 1·10 1·25

710 5r. Red-capped manakin and industrial skyline . . . . . 1·10 1·25

383 New Parliament House, Islamabad

1987. Inauguration of New Parliament House, Islamabad.

711 **383** 3r. multicoloured 50 60

384 Opium Poppies and Flames

1987. Campaign Against Drug Abuse.

712 **384** 1r. multicoloured 65 30

385 Flag and National Anthem Score

1987. 40th Anniv of Independence. Mult.

713 80p. Type **385** . . . . . . 1·25 20

714 3r. Text of speech by Mohammed Ali Jinnah, Minar-e-Qardad-e-Pakistan Tower and arms . . . . . 1·50 50

386 Hawker Tempest Mk II

1987. Air Force Day. Military Aircraft. Mult.

715 3r. Type **386** . . . . 1·25 1·25

716 3r. Hawker Fury . . . . . 1·25 1·25

717 3r. Supermarine Attacker . . 1·25 1·25

718 3r. North American F-86 Sabre . . . . 1·25 1·25

719 3r. Lockheed F-104C Starfighter . . . . 1·25 1·25

720 3r. Lockheed C-130 Hercules 1·25 1·25

721 3r. Shenyang/Tianjin F-6 . . . 1·25 1·25

722 3r. Dassault Mirage III . . . 1·25 1·25

723 3r. North American A-5A Vigilante . . . . 1·25 1·25

724 3r. General Dynamics F-16 Fighting Falcon . . . . . 1·25 1·25

387 Pasu Glacier

1987. Pakistan Tourism Convention. Views along Karakoram Highway. Multicoloured.

725 1r.50 Type **387** 60 55

726 1r.50 Apricot trees 60 55

727 1r.50 Karakoram Highway 60 55

728 1r.50 View from Khunjerab Pass 60 55

388 Shah Abdul Latif Bhitai Mausoleum

1987. Shah Abdul Latif Bhitai (poet) Commem.

729 **388** 80p. multicoloured . . . 30 30

389 D. J. Sind Science College, Karachi

1987. Centenary of D. J. Sind Science College, Karachi.

730 **389** 80p. multicoloured . . . 20 20

390 College Building

1987. 25th Anniv of College of Physicians and Surgeons.

731 **390** 1r. multicoloured . . . . 1·75 30

391 Homeless People, Houses and Rising Sun

1987. International Year of Shelter for the Homeless.

732 **391** 3r. multicoloured 50 50

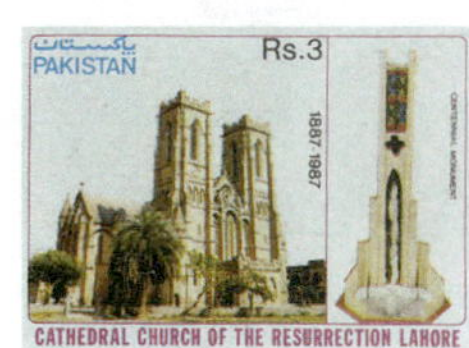

392 Cathedral Church of the Resurrection, Lahore

1987. Centenary of Cathedral Church of the Resurrection, Lahore.

733 **392** 3r. multicoloured 50 50

393 Honeycomb and Arms

1987. 40th Anniv of Pakistan Post Office.

734 **393** 3r. multicoloured 50 50

394 Corporation Emblem

1987. Radio Pakistan's New Programme Schedules.

735 **394** 80p. multicoloured . . . 15 15

395 Jamshed Nusserwanjee Mehta and Karachi Municipal Corporation Building

1988. Birth Centenary (1986) of Jamshed Nusserwanjee Mehta (former President of Karachi Municipal Corporation).

736 **395** 3r. multicoloured 50 50

396 Leprosy Symbols within Flower

398 Globe

397 W.H.O. Building, Geneva

1988. World Leprosy Day.

737 **396** 3r. multicoloured 75 50

1988. 40th Anniv of W.H.O.

738 **397** 4r. multicoloured 60 50

1988. 125th Anniv of Int Red Cross and Crescent.

739 **398** 3r. multicoloured 50 50

399 Crescent, Leaf Pattern and Archway

1988. Independence Day.

740 **399** 80p. multicoloured . . . 10 10

741 4r. multicoloured 45 50

400 Field Events

1988. Olympic Games, Seoul. Multicoloured.

742 10r. Type **400** . . . . 1·10 1·10

743 10r. Track events . . . . . . 1·10 1·10

744 10r. Jumping and pole vaulting . . . . 1·10 1·10

745 10r. Gymnastics . . . . . . 1·10 1·10

746 10r. Table tennis, tennis, hockey and baseball . . . 1·10 1·10

747 10r. Volleyball, football, basketball and handball . . 1·10 1·10

748 10r. Wrestling, judo, boxing and weightlifting . . . . . 1·10 1·10

749 10r. Shooting, fencing and archery . . . . 1·10 1·10

750 10r. Water sports . . . . . 1·10 1·10

751 10r. Equestrian events and cycling . . . . 1·10 1·10

401 Markhor

1988. Wildlife Protection (15th series).

752 **401** 2r. multicoloured 65 50

402 Islamia College, Peshawar

1988. 75th Anniv of Islamia College, Peshawar.

753 **402** 3r. multicoloured 50 50

403 Symbols of Agriculture, Industry and Education with National Flags

1988. South Asian Association for Regional Co-operation 4th Summit Meeting, Islamabad. Multicoloured.
754 25r. Type **403** . . . . 1·50 1·50
755 50r. National flags on globe and symbols of communications (33 × 33 mm) . . . . . . 3·75 3·25
756 75r. Stamps from member countries (52 × 29 mm) . . 4·00 4·50

1989. Pioneers of Freedom (2nd series). As T **282**. Multicoloured.
757 3r. Maulana Hasrat Mohani 30 30

404 Logo

1989. "Adasia 89" 16th Asian Advertising Congress, Lahore.
758 **404** 1r. multicoloured ("Pakistan" in yellow) 1·10 1·40
759 1r. multicoloured ("Pakistan" in blue) . . 1·10 1·40
760 1r. multicoloured ("Pakistan" in white) 1·10 1·40

405 Zulfikar Ali Bhutto

1989. 10th Death Anniv of Zulfikar Ali Bhutto (statesman). Multicoloured.
761 1r. Type **405** 20 10
762 2r. Zulfikar Ali Bhutto (different) 30 30

406 "Daphne" Class Submarine

1989. 25 Years of Pakistan Navy Submarine Operations. Multicoloured.
763 1r. Type **406** . . . . 1·40 1·50
764 1r. "Fleet Snorkel" class submarine . . . . 1·40 1·50
765 1r. "Agosta" class submarine 1·40 1·50

407 "The Oath of the Tennis Court" (David)

1989. Bicentenary of French Revolution.
766 **407** 7r. multicoloured . . . . 1·75 1·00

408 Pitcher, c. 2200 B.C.

1989. Archaeological Artefacts. Terracotta pottery from Baluchistan Province. Mult.
767 1r. Type **408** 30 30
768 1r. Jar, c. 2300 B.C. 30 30
769 1r. Vase, c. 3600 B.C. 30 30
770 1r. Jar, c. 2600 B.C. 30 30

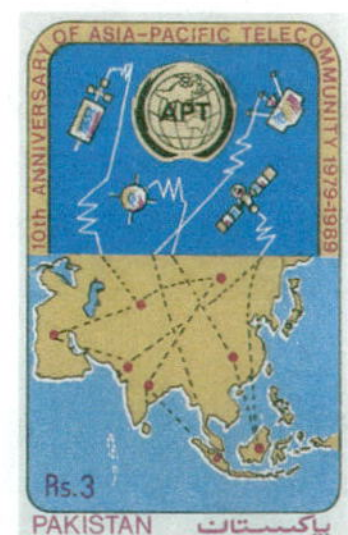

409 Satellites and Map of Asian Telecommunications Network

1989. 10th Anniv of Asia–Pacific Telecommunity.
771 **409** 3r. multicoloured 50 50

410 Container Ship at Wharf

1989. Construction of Integrated Container Terminal, Port Qasim.
772 **410** 6r. multicoloured . . . . 3·00 3·75

411 Mohammed Ali Jinnah

412 Mausoleum of Shah Abdul Latif Bhitai

1989.
773 **411** 1r. multicoloured 80 10
774 1r.50 multicoloured . . . 90 50
775 2r. multicoloured . . . . 1·00 30
776 3r. multicoloured . . . . 1·25 50
777 4r. multicoloured . . . . 1·50 70
778 5r. multicoloured . . . . 1·50 70

1989. 300th Birth Anniv of Shah Abdul Latif Bhitai (poet).
779 **412** 2r. multicoloured 50 50

413 Asiatic Black Bear

414 Ear of Wheat encircling Globe

1989. Wildlife Protection (16th series). Asiatic Black Bear. Multicoloured.
780 4r. Type **413** . . . . 90 1·10
781 4r. Bear among boulders . . 90 1·10
782 4r. Standing on rock . . . . 90 1·10
783 4r. Sitting by trees . . . . . 90 1·10

1989. World Food Day.
784 **414** 1r. multicoloured 35 35

415 Games Emblem and Flags of Member Countries

1989. 4th South Asian Sports Federation Games, Islamabad.
785 **415** 1r. multicoloured 35 35

416 Patchwork Kamblee (cloth) entering Gate of Heaven

1989. 800th Birth Anniv of Baba Farid (Muslim spiritual leader).
786 **416** 3r. multicoloured 40 40

417 Pakistan Television Logo

1989. 25th Anniv of Television Broadcasting in Pakistan.
787 **417** 3r. multicoloured 40 40

418 Family of Drug Addicts in Poppy Bud

1989. South Asian Association for Regional Co-operation Anti-Drugs Campaign.
788 **418** 7r. multicoloured . . . . 2·25 1·40

419 Murray College, Sialkot

1989. Centenary of Murray College, Sialkot.
789 **419** 6r. multicoloured . . . . 1·25 1·00

420 Government College, Lahore

1989. 125th Anniv of Government College, Lahore.
790 **420** 6r. multicoloured . . . . 75 1·25

421 Fields, Electricity Pylons and Rural Buildings

1989. 10th Anniv of Centre for Asia and Pacific Integrated Rural Development.
791 **421** 3r. multicoloured 65 75

422 Emblem and Islamic Patterns

1990. 20th Anniv of Organization of the Islamic Conference.
792 **422** 1r. multicoloured . . . . 1·50 20

423 Hockey Match

1990. 7th World Hockey Cup, Lahore.
793 **423** 2r. multicoloured . . . . 4·50 4·25

424 Mohammed Iqbal addressing Crowd and Liaquat Ali Khan taking Oath

1990. 50th Anniv of Passing of Pakistan Resolution. Multicoloured.
794 1r. Type **424** . . . . 1·00 1·25
795 1r. Maulana Mohammad Ali Jauhar and Mohammed Ali Jinnah with banner . . . . 1·00 1·25
796 1r. Women with Pakistan flag, and Mohammed Ali Jinnah taking Governor-General's oath, 1947 . . . 1·00 1·25
797 7r. Minar-i-Qarardad-e-Pakistan Monument and Resolution in Urdu and English (86 × 42 mm) . . . 2·50 3·00
Nos. 794/6 were printed together, se-tenant, forming a composite design.

425 Pregnant Woman resting

1990. "Safe Motherhood" South Asia Conference, Lahore.
798 **425** 5r. multicoloured . . . . 75 1·00

426 "Decorated Verse by Ghalib" (Shakir Ali)

1990. Painters of Pakistan (1st series). Shakir Ali.
799 **426** 1r. multicoloured . . . . 2·25 1·25
See also Nos. 856/7.

427 Satellite in Night Sky

1990. Launch of "Badr I" Satellite.
800 **427** 3r. multicoloured . . . . 3·50 3·50

428 Allama Mohammed Iqbal

1990. Pioneers of Freedom (3rd series). Each brown and green.

801 1r. Type **428** 40 45
802 1r. Mohammed Ali Jinnah 40 45
803 1r. Sir Syed Ahmad Khan . . 40 45
804 1r. Nawab Salimullah 40 45
805 1r. Mohtarma Fatima Jinnah 40 45
806 1r. Aga Khan III 40 45
807 1r. Nawab Mohammad Ismail Khan 40 45
808 1r. Hussain Shaheed Suhrawardy 40 45
809 1r. Syed Ameer Ali 40 45
810 1r. Nawab Bahadur Yar Jung 40 45
811 1r. Khawaja Nazimuddin . . 40 45
812 1r. Maulana Obaidullah Sindhi 40 45
813 1r. Sahibzada Abdul Qaiyum Khan 40 45
814 1r. Begum Jahanara Shah Nawaz 40 45
815 1r. Sir Ghulam Hussain Hidayatullah 40 45
816 1r. Qazi Mohammad Isa . . 40 45
817 1r. Sir M. Shahnawaz Khan Mamdot 40 45
818 1r. Pir Sahib of Manki Sharif 40 45
819 1r. Liaquat Ali Khan 40 45
820 1r. Maulvi A. K. Fazl-ul-Haq 40 45
821 1r. Allama Shabbir Ahmad Usmani 40 45
822 1r. Sadar Abdur Rab Nishtar 40 45
823 1r. Bi Amma 40 45
824 1r. Sir Abdullah Haroon . . 40 45
825 1r. Chaudhry Rahmat Ali . . 40 45
826 1r. Raja Sahib of Mahmudabad 40 45
827 1r. Hassanally Effendi . . . 40 45

See also Nos. 838/46, 870/2, 904/6, 921/8, 961/2, 1007, 1019/20 and 1075/7.

429 Cultural Aspects of Indonesia and Pakistan

1990. Indonesia–Pakistan Economic and Cultural Co-operation Organization.

828 **429** 7r. multicoloured . . . . 2·25 2·25

430 Globe, Open Book and Pen

1990. International Literacy Year.

829 **430** 3r. multicoloured . . . . 1·00 1·50

431 College Crests 432 Children and Globe

1990. Joint Meeting between Royal College of Physicians, Edinburgh, and College of Physicians and Surgeons, Pakistan.

830 **431** 2r. multicoloured 60 75

1990. U.N. World Summit for Children, New York.

831 **432** 7r. multicoloured . . . . 75 1·50

433 Girl within Members' Flags

1990. South Asian Association for Regional Co-operation Year of Girl Child.

832 **433** 2r. multicoloured 70 75

434 Paper passing over Rollers 435 Civil Defence Worker protecting Islamabad

1990. 25th Anniv of Security Papers Limited.

833 **434** 3r. multicoloured . . . . 3·00 1·50

1991. International Civil Defence Day.

834 **435** 7r. multicoloured . . . . 1·25 1·50

436 Logo and Flags of Member Countries

1991. South and West Asia Postal Union Commemoration.

835 **436** 5r. multicoloured . . . . 1·60 1·90

437 Globe and Figures

1991. World Population Day.

836 **437** 10r. multicoloured . . . . 1·90 2·50

438 Mentally Handicapped Athlete 439 Habib Bank Headquarters and Emblem

1991. Pakistan Participation in Special Olympic Games.

837 **438** 7r. multicoloured . . . . 1·75 2·50

1991. Pioneers of Freedom (4th series). As T **428**. Each brown and green.

838 1r. Maulana Zafar Ali Khan 65 75
839 1r. Maulana Mohamed Ali Jauhar 65 75
840 1r. Chaudhry Khaliquzzaman 65 75
841 1r. Hameed Nizami 65 75
842 1r. Begum Ra'ana Liaquat Ali Khan 65 75
843 1r. Mirza Abol Hassan Ispahani 65 75
844 1r. Raja Ghazanfar Ali Khan 65 75
845 1r. Malik Barkat Ali 65 75
846 1r. Mir Jaffer Khan Jamali 65 75

1991. 50th Anniv of Habib Bank.

847 **439** 1r. multicoloured . . . . 1·25 10
848 5r. multicoloured . . . . 4·00 4·25

440 St. Joesph's Convent School

1991. 130th Anniv (1992) of St. Joesph's Convent School, Karachi.

849 **440** 5r. multicoloured . . . . 3·75 3·75

441 Emperor Sher Shah Suri 443 Houbara Bustard

442 Jinnah Antarctic Research Station

1991. Emperor Sher Shah Suri (founder of road network) Commemoration.

850 **441** 5r. multicoloured . . . . 1·50 2·00
MS851 92 × 80 mm. 7r. Emperor on horseback and portrait as Type **441**. Imperf . . . . . . 1·40 2·25

1991. Pakistan Scientific Expedition to Antarctica.

852 **442** 7r. multicoloured . . . . 2·50 2·50

1991. Wildlife Protection (17th series).

853 **443** 7r. multicoloured . . . . 2·00 2·50

444 Mosque

1991. 300th Death Anniv of Hazrat Sultan Bahoo.

854 **444** 7r. multicoloured . . . . 2·00 2·50

445 Development Symbols and Map of Asia

1991. 25th Anniv of Asian Development Bank.

855 **445** 7r. multicoloured . . . . 2·75 3·00

1991. Painters of Pakistan (2nd series). As T **426**. Multicoloured.

856 1r. "Procession" (Haji Muhammad Sharif) . . . . 2·00 1·50
857 1r. "Women harvesting" (Ustad Allah Bux) . . . . 2·00 1·50

446 American Express Travellers Cheques of 1891 and 1991 (¾-size illustration)

1991. Centenary of American Express Travellers Cheques.

858 **446** 7r. multicoloured . . . . 1·75 2·50

447 Flag, Banknote and Banking Equipment

1992. 1st Anniv of Muslim Commercial Bank Privatization. Multicoloured.

859 1r. Type **447** 20 10
860 7r. Flag with industrial and commercial scenes . . . . 1·25 1·40

448 Imran Khan (team captain) and Trophy

1992. Pakistan's Victory in World Cricket Championship. Multicoloured.

861 2r. Type **448** 70 70
862 5r. Trophy and national flags (horiz) . . . . 1·50 1·50
863 7r. Pakistani flag, trophy and symbolic cricket ball . . . 1·75 2·00

449 "Rehber-1" Rocket and Satellite View of Earth

1992. International Space Year. Mult.

864 1r. Type **449** 25 10
865 2r. Satellite orbiting Earth and logo 35 50

450 Surgical Instruments

1992. Industries. Multicoloured.

866 10r. Type **450** . . . . 1·00 1·40
867 15r. Leather goods . . . . . 1·40 2·00
868 25r. Sports equipment . . . 2·50 3·00

451 Globe and Symbolic Family

1992. Population Day.

869 **451** 6r. multicoloured . . . . 1·00 1·25

1992. Pioneers of Freedom (5th series). As T **428**. Each brown and green.

870 1r. Syed Suleman Nadvi . . 1·25 1·40
871 1r. Nawab Iftikhar Hussain Khan Mamdot . . . . . . 1·25 1·40
872 1r. Maulana Muhammad Shibli Naumani . . . . . 1·25 1·40

452 Scout Badge and Salute

1992. 6th Islamic Scout Jamboree and 4th Islamic Scouts Conference. Multicoloured.

873 6r. Type **452** 50 75
874 6r. Conference centre and scout salute 50 75

453 College Building

1992. Centenary of Islamia College, Lahore.
875 **453** 3r. multicoloured 50 70

454 "Viola odorata" (flower) and Symbolic Drug Manufacture

1992. Medicinal Plants (1st series).
876 **454** 6r. multicoloured . . . . 2·75 2·00
See also Nos. 903, 946, 1010, 1026, 1037, 1099, 1123, 1142 and 1159.

455 Emblem

1992. Extraordinary Ministerial Council Session of Economic Co-operation Organization, Islamabad.
877 **455** 7r. multicoloured . . . . 1·00 1·75

456 Emblems and Field **457** Alhambra Palace, Granada, Spain

1992. International Conference on Nutrition, Rome.
878 **456** 7r. multicoloured . . . . 70 1·25

1992. Cultural Heritage of Muslim Granada.
879 **457** 7r. multicoloured . . . . 70 1·25

458 Mallard **459** Baluchistan Costume

Four different versions of designs as T **458**:
Type A. "Rs.5" at right with rainbow 8 mm beneath "P" of "PAKISTAN"
Type B. "Rs.5" at right with rainbow 2 mm beneath "P"
Type C. "Rs.5" at left with rainbow 2 mm beneath "N" of "PAKISTAN"
Type D. "Rs.5" at left with rainbow 8 mm beneath "N"

1992. Water Birds. Multicoloured.
880 5r. Type **458** (A) 60 70
881 5r. Type **458** (B) 60 70
882 5r. Type **458** (C) 60 70
883 5r. Type **458** (D) 60 70
884 5r. Greylag goose (A) 60 70
885 5r. As No. 884 (B) 60 70
886 5r. As No. 884 (C) 60 70
887 5r. As No. 884 (D) 60 70
888 5r. Gadwall (A) 60 70
889 5r. As No. 888 (B) 60 70
890 5r. As No. 888 (C) 60 70
891 5r. As No. 888 (D) 60 70
892 5r. Common shelduck (A) . . 60 70
893 5r. As No. 892 (B) 60 70
894 5r. As No. 892 (C) 60 70
895 5r. As No. 892 (D) 60 70
Nos. 880/95 were printed together, se-tenant, each horizontal row having a composite design of a rainbow.

1993. Women's Traditional Costumes. Multicoloured.
896 6r. Type **459** . . . . 1·25 1·50
897 6r. Punjab . . . . 1·25 1·50
898 6r. Sindh . . . . 1·25 1·50
899 6r. North-west Frontier Province . . . . 1·25 1·50

460 Clasped Hands and Islamic Symbols **461** I.T.U. Emblem

1993. 21st Conference of Islamic Foreign Ministers, Karachi.
900 **460** 1r. multicoloured 65 10
901 6r. multicoloured . . . . 2·00 2·50

1993. 25th Anniv of World Telecommunication Day.
902 **461** 1r. multicoloured . . . . 1·50 30

1993. Medicinal Plants (2nd issue). As T **454**. Multicoloured.
903 6r. Fennel and symbolic drug manufacture . . . . 3·00 2·25

1993. Pioneers of Freedom (6th series). As T **428**. Each brown and red.
904 1r. Ghulam Mohammad Bhurgri . . . . 1·25 1·25
905 1r. Ahmed Yar Khan . . . . 1·25 1·25
906 1r. Mohammad Pir Sahib Zakori Sharif . . . . . . 1·25 1·25

462 College Building and Arms

1993. Centenary of Gordon College, Rawalpindi.
907 **462** 2r. multicoloured . . . . 1·75 1·75

463 Juniper Forest

1993. Campaign to Save the Juniper Forest, Ziarat.
907a **463** 1r. multicoloured . . . . 1·50 30
908 7r. multicoloured . . . . 3·50 3·00

464 Globe, Produce and Emblem

1993. World Food Day.
909 **464** 6r. multicoloured . . . . 1·25 1·40

465 Burn Hall Institution, Abbottabad **466** Peace Dove carrying Letter and National Flags

1993. 50th Anniv of Burn Hall Institutions.
910 **465** 7r. multicoloured . . . . 2·50 2·75

1993. South and West Asia Postal Union Commemoration.
911 **466** 7r. multicoloured . . . . 2·50 2·75

467 Congress Emblem **468** Wazir Mansion (birthplace)

1993. Pakistan College of Physicians and Surgeons International Medical Congress.
912 **467** 1r. multicoloured . . . . 2·00 30

1993. 45th Death Anniv of Mohammed Ali Jinnah.
913 **468** 1r. multicoloured . . . . 1·50 30

469 Emblem and National Flag

1994. 75th Anniv of I.L.O.
914 **469** 7r. multicoloured . . . . 1·75 2·00

470 Ratan Jot (flower)

1994. Ratification of International Biological Diversity Convention. Multicoloured.
915 6r. Type **470** 50 65
916 6r. Wetlands habitat 50 65
917 6r. Golden mahseer ("Tor puttitora") (fish) 50 65
918 6r. Brown bear 50 65

471 Silhouette of Family and Emblem

1994. International Year of the Family.
919 **471** 7r. multicoloured 70 80

472 Symbolic Globe and Logo

1994. World Population Day.
920 **472** 7r. multicoloured 70 80

1994. Pioneers of Freedom (7th series). As T **428**. Each brown and green.
921 1r. Nawab Mohsin-Ul-Mulk 30 40
922 1r. Sir Shahnawaz Bhutto . . 30 40
923 1r. Nawab Viqar-Ul-Mulk . . 30 40
924 1r. Pir Ilahi Bux 30 40
925 1r. Sheikh Abdul Qadir . . . 30 40
926 1r. Dr. Sir Ziauddin Ahmed 30 40
927 1r. Jam Mir Ghulam Qadir Khan 30 40
928 1r. Sardar Aurangzeb Khan 30 40

473 Hala Pottery, Pakistan **474** Boy writing and Globe

1994. Indonesia–Pakistan Economic and Cultural Co-operation Organization. Multicoloured.
929 10r. Type **473** . . . . 1·75 2·00
930 10r. Lombok pottery, Indonesia . . . . 1·75 2·00

1994. International Literacy Day.
931 **474** 7r. multicoloured 75 85

475 Mohammed Ali Jinnah and Floral Pattern

1994.
932 **475** 1r. multicoloured 20 10
933 2r. multicoloured 25 10
934 3r. multicoloured 30 10
935 4r. multicoloured 30 10
936 5r. multicoloured 30 15
937 7r. multicoloured 30 20
938 10r. multicoloured 20 25
939 12r. multicoloured 25 30
940 15r. multicoloured 30 35
941 20r. multicoloured 40 45
942 25r. multicoloured 45 50
943 30r. multicoloured 55 60

476 Gateway and Emblem **477** Engraver

1994. 2nd South Asian Association for Regional Co-operation and 12th National Scout Jamborees, Quetta.
944 **476** 7r. multicoloured . . . . 1·00 1·10

1994. 1st Int Festival of Islamic Artisans at Work.
945 **477** 2r. multicoloured . . . . 1·25 60

478 Henbane **479** Abu-I Kasim Firdausi (poet)

1994. Medicinal Plants (3rd issue).
946 **478** 6r. multicoloured 75 80

1994. Millenary of "Shah Namah" (poem).
947 **479** 1r. multicoloured 25 15

480 Museum Building

1994. Centenary of Lahore Museum.
948 **480** 4r. multicoloured 60 70

481 World Cup Trophies for 1971, 1978, 1982 and 1994

1994. Victory of Pakistan in World Cup Hockey Championship.
949 **481** 5r. multicoloured 75 80

482 Tourist Attractions

1995. 20th Anniv of World Tourism Organization.
950 **482** 4r. multicoloured . . . . 1·00 1·10

483 Khan Khushal of Khattak and Army

1995. Khan Khushal of Khattak (poet) Commemoration.
951 **483** 7r. multicoloured . . . . 1·75 1·75

484 E.C.O. Emblem

1995. 3rd Economic Co-operation Organization Summit, Islamabad.
952 **484** 6r. multicoloured . . . . 1·25 1·40

485 Common Indian Krait

1995. Snakes. Multicoloured.
953 6r. Type **485** 70 85
954 6r. Indian cobra 70 85
955 6r. Indian python 70 85
956 6r. Russell's viper 70 85

486 Globe and Environments

1995. Earth Day.
957 **486** 6r. multicoloured 70 75

487 Victoria Carriage, Karachi

1995. Traditional Transport.
958 **487** 5r. multicoloured 65 70

488 Prime Minister Tansu Ciller of Turkey and Rose

1995. 1st Muslim Women Parliamentarians' Conference, Islamabad. Multicoloured.
959 5r. Type **488** . . . . 80 1·00
960 5r. Prime Minister Benazir Bhutto and jasmine . . . . 80 1·00

1995. Pioneers of Freedom (8th series). As T **428**. Each brown and green.
961 1r. Maulana Shaukat Ali . . 80 70
962 1r. Chaudhry Ghulam Abbas 80 70

489 Oil Sardine

1995. Fishes. Multicoloured.
963 6r. Type **489** 70 75
964 6r. Mozambique mouthbrooder ("Tilapia") 70 75
965 6r. Brown trout 70 75
966 6r. Rohu 70 75

490 "Erasmia pulchella"

1995. Butterflies. Multicoloured.
967 6r. Type **490** 70 80
968 6r. "Callicore astarte" (inscr "Catogramme") 70 80
969 6r. "Ixias pyrene" 70 80
970 6r. "Heliconius" 70 80

491 Major Raja Aziz Bhatti Shaheed and Medal

1995. Defence Day.
971 **491** 1r.25 multicoloured . . . 1·50 1·00

492 Presentation Convent School, Rawalpindi

1995. Centenary of Presentation Convent School, Rawalpindi.
972 **492** 1r.25 multicoloured . . . 1·25 1·00

493 Women Soldiers, Golfer and Scientist

494 "Louis Pasteur in Laboratory" (Edelfelt)

1995. 4th World Conference on Women, Peking. Multicoloured.
973 1r.25 Type **493** 30 45
974 1r.25 Women graduates, journalist, computer operator and technicians 30 45
975 1r.25 Sewing machinist and women at traditional crafts 30 45
976 1r.25 Army officer and women at traditional tasks 30 45

1995. Death Centenary of Louis Pasteur (chemist).
977 **494** 5r. multicoloured . . . . 1·00 1·00

495

496 Liaquat Ali Khan

1995.
978 **495** 5p. blue, orange and brown 10 10
979 15p. orange, violet and brown 20 10
980 25p. blue, mauve and purple 30 10
981 75p. green, brown and deep brown 90 10

1995. Birth Centenary (1995) of Liaquat Ali Khan (statesman).
987 **496** 1r.25 multicoloured . . . 70 30

497 Village and Irrigated Fields

1995. 50th Anniv of F.A.O.
988 **497** 1r.25 multicoloured . . . 70 30

498 Pakistani Soldier treating Somali Refugees

1995. 50th Anniv of United Nations.
989 **498** 7r. multicoloured . . . . 1·00 1·40

499 Education Emblem

500 Hand holding Book, Eye and Pen Nib

1995. 80th Anniv (1993) of Kinnaird College for Women, Lahore.
990 **499** 1r.25 multicoloured . . . 70 30

1995. International Conference of Writers and Intellectuals, Islamabad.
991 **500** 1r.25 multicoloured . . . 70 30

501 Children holding Hands and S.A.A.R.C. Logo

502 Jet Skier

1995. 10th Anniv of South Asian Association for Regional Co-operation.
992 **501** 1r.25 multicoloured . . . 50 30

1995. National Water Sports Gala, Karachi. Multicoloured.
993 1r.25 Type **502** 30 45
994 1r.25 Local punts 30 45
995 1r.25 Sailboard 30 45
996 1r.25 Water skier 30 45

503 Mortar Board and Books

1995. 20th Anniv of Allama Iqbal Open University.
997 **503** 1r.25 multicoloured . . . 50 30

504 Balochistan Quetta University Building

1995. 25th Anniv of Balochistan Quetta University.
998 **504** 1r.25 multicoloured . . . 50 30

505 Zulfikar Ali Bhutto, Flag and Crowd

1996. 17th Death Anniv of Zulfikar Ali Bhutto (former Prime Minister). Multicoloured.
999 1r.25 Type **505** . . . . . . 1·25 20
1000 4r. Zulfikar Ali Bhutto and flag (53 × 31 mm) . . . . 2·50 1·75
MS1001 118 × 74 mm. 8r. Zulfikar Ali Bhutto and crowd. Imperf 2·00 2·00

506 Wrestling

1996. Olympic Games, Atlanta. Multicoloured.
1002 5r. Type **506** 60 70
1003 5r. Boxing 60 70
1004 5r. Pierre de Coubertin . . . 60 70
1005 5r. Hockey 60 70
MS1006 112 × 100 mm. 25r. Designs as Nos. 1002/5, but without face values. Imperf . . . . 2·25 2·75

1996. Pioneers of Freedom (9th series). Allama Abdullah Yousuf Ali. As T **428**.
1007 1r. brown and green 30 10

507 G.P.O. Building, Lahore

1996. Restoration of G.P.O. Building, Lahore.
1008 **507** 5r. multicoloured 45 60

508 Symbolic Open Book and Text

1996. International Literacy Day.
1009 **508** 2r. multicoloured 40 25

509 Yarrow **510** Faiz Ahmed Faiz

1996. Medicinal Plants (4th series).
1010 **509** 3r. multicoloured . . . . 1·25 1·00

1997. 86th Birth Anniv of Faiz Ahmed Faiz (poet).
1011 **510** 3r. multicoloured 50 50

511 Golden Jubilee and O.I.C. Emblems **512** Amir Timur

1997. Special Summit Conference of Organization of Islamic Countries commemorating 50th anniv of Pakistan.
1012 **511** 2r. multicoloured 35 35

1997. 660th Birth Anniv of Timur (founder of Timurid Empire).
1013 **512** 3r. multicoloured 50 50

513 Jalal-al-din Moulana Rumi **514** Apple

1997. Pakistan–Iran Joint Issue.
1014 3r. Type **513** 40 50
1015 3r. Allama Mohammad Iqbal (poet) 40 50

1997. Fruit.
1016 **514** 2r. multicoloured 35 35

515 People on Globe

1997. World Population Day.
1017 **515** 2r. multicoloured 35 35

516 Stylized Dove of Peace

1997. 40th Anniv of Co-operation between International Atomic Energy Agency and Pakistan Atomic Energy Corporation.
1018 **516** 2r. multicoloured 50 35

1997. Pioneers of Freedom (10th series). As T **428**. Each brown and green.
1019 1r. Mohammad Ayub Khuhro 75 75
1020 1r. Begum Salma Tassaduq Hussain 75 75

517 Mohammed Ali Jinnah

1997. 50th Anniv of Independence. Multicoloured.
1021 3r. Type **517** 50 60
1022 3r. Allama Mohammad Iqbal 50 60
1023 3r. Mohtarma Fatima Jinnah 50 60
1024 3r. Liaquat Ali Khan . . . 50 60

518 College Building

1997. 75th Anniv of Lahore College for Women.
1025 **518** 3r. multicoloured . . . . 1·25 1·00

519 Garlic

1997. Medicinal Plants (5th series).
1026 **519** 2r. multicoloured . . . . 1·00 65

520 Himalayan Monal Pheasant **521** Globe and Cracked Ozone Layer

1997. Wildlife Protection (18th series).
1027 **520** 2r. multicoloured . . . . 1·75 1·00

1997. Save Ozone Layer Campaign.
1028 **521** 3r. multicoloured . . . . 1·40 1·10

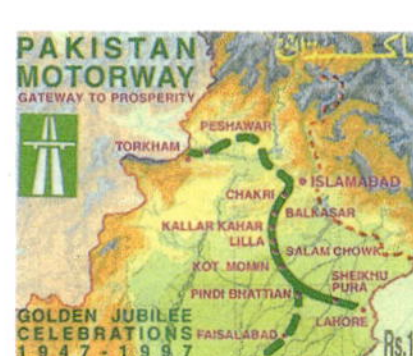

522 Map of Pakistan Motorway Project

1997. Pakistan Motorway Project.
1029 **522** 10r. multicoloured . . . 1·50 1·60
MS1030 117 × 97 mm. No. 1029 (sold at 15r.) . . . . 2·50 2·75

523 Emblem and Disabled People

1997. International Day for the Disabled.
1031 **523** 4r. multicoloured 60 60

524 Karachi Grammar School

1997. 150th Anniv of Karachi Grammar School.
1032 **524** 2r. multicoloured . . . . 1·25 70

525 Mirza Ghalib

1998. Birth Bicentenary (1997) of Mirza Ghalib (poet).
1033 **525** 2r. multicoloured 30 25
No. 1033 is inscr "DEATH ANNIVERSARY".

526 Servicemen, Pakistan Flag and "50"

1998. 50th Anniv (1997) of Armed Forces.
1034 **526** 7r. multicoloured 70 70

527 Sir Syed Ahmed Khan

1998. Death Centenary of Sir Syed Ahmed Khan (social reformer).
1035 **527** 7r. brown, green & stone 60 70

528 Olympic Torch and Sports

1998. 27th National Games, Peshawar.
1036 **528** 7r. multicoloured 70 70

529 Thornapple

1998. Medicinal Plants (6th series).
1037 **529** 2r. multicoloured 60 30

530 Silver Jubilee Emblem **531** Mohammed Ali Jinnah

1998. 25th Anniv of Senate.
1038 **530** 2r. multicoloured 25 15
1039 5r. multicoloured 55 65

1998.
1039a **531** 1r. red and black . . . 10 10
1040 2r. blue and red 10 10
1041 3r. green and brown . . 10 10
1042 4r. purple and orange 10 10
1043 5r. brown and green . . 10 10
1044 6r. green and blue . . . 10 15
1045 7r. red and violet . . . 15 20

532 College Building

1998. Cent of Government College, Faisalabad.
1046 **532** 5r. multicoloured 40 40

533 "Mohammed Ali Jinnah" (S. Akhtar)

1998. 50th Death Anniv of Mohammed Ali Jinnah.
1047 **533** 15r. multicoloured . . . 1·50 1·75
MS1048 72 × 100 mm. **533** 15r. multicoloured (sold at 20r.) . . 2·00 2·25

534 Cross-section of Eye

1998. 21st International Ophthalmology Congress, Islamabad.
1049 **534** 7r. multicoloured . . . . 1·00 1·00

535 United Nations Emblems and Bukhari

1998. Birth Centenary of Syed Ahmed Shah Patrus Bukhari.
1050 **535** 5r. multicoloured 40 40

536 Map, "50 years" and Stamps **538** Dr. Abdus Salam

537 Mother and Child

1998. 50th Anniv of Philately in Pakistan.
1051 **536** 6r. multicoloured 50 50

1998. World Food Day.
1052 **537** 6r. multicoloured 50 50

1998. Scientists of Pakistan (1st series). Dr. Abdus Salam.
1053 **538** 2r. multicoloured 30 25
See also No. 1068.

539 Satellite Dish Aerial

1998. "Better Pakistan" Development Plan. Mult.
1054 2r. Type **539** 35 40
1055 2r. Combine harvester . . . 35 40
1056 2r. Airliner 35 40
1057 2r. Children and doctor . . 35 40

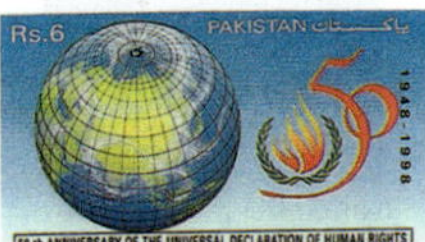

540 Globe and Human Rights Emblem

1998. 50th Anniv of Universal Declaration of Human Rights.
1058 **540** 6r. multicoloured 70 60

541 Pakistani Woman carrying Water Pot

1998. 50th Anniv of UNICEF in Pakistan. Multicoloured.
1059 2r. Type **541** 30 40
1060 2r. Woman reading 30 40
1061 2r. Woman with goitre 30 40
1062 2r. Young boy receiving oral vaccine 30 40

542 Earth seen from Space

1998. International Year of the Ocean.
1063 **542** 5r. multicoloured 70 50

543 Marchers and Route Map

1998. Qaumi Parcham March, Khyber to Chaghi.
1064 **543** 2r. multicoloured 30 25

544 Centenary Logo

545 Dr. Salimuz Zaman Siddiqui

1999. Centenary of Saudi Dynasty of Saudi Arabia. Multicoloured.
1065 2r. Type **544** 25 10
1066 15r. As Type **544**, but with mosaic pattern in corners 1·25 1·50
MS1067 73 × 100 mm. 15r. No. 1066 (sold at 20r.) . . . . 2·00 2·25

1999. Scientists of Pakistan (2nd series). Dr. Salimuz Zaman Siddiqui.
1068 **545** 5r. multicoloured 40 40

546 Mountains and Pakistan Flag

1999. "Atoms for Peace".
1069 **546** 5r. multicoloured 40 40

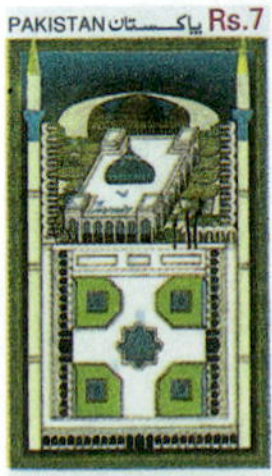

547 Plan and View of Mosque

548 Fasting Buddha Statue (drapery on left knee)

1999. Completion of Data Darbar Mosque Complex, Lahore.
1070 **547** 7r. multicoloured 50 50

1999. Archaeological Heritage. Multicoloured.
1071 7r. Type **548** 55 65
1072 7r. Fasting Buddha (drapery on right knee) 55 65
MS1073 107 × 90 mm. Nos. 1071/2 (sold at 25r.) . . . . 2·00 2·50
No. **MS**1073 includes the "China '99" International Stamp Exhibition, Beijing, logo on the margin.

549 Red Cross International Committee Emblem and "50"

1999. 50th Anniv of Geneva Conventions.
1074 **549** 5r. red and black 40 40

1999. Pioneers of Freedom (11th series). As T **428**. Each brown and green.
1075 2r. Maulana Abdul Hamid Badayuni 35 40
1076 2r. Chaudhry Muhammad Ali 35 40
1077 2r. Sir Adamjee Haji Dawood 35 40

550 Ustad Nusrat Fateh Ali Khan

1999. Ustad Nusrat Fateh Ali Khan (musician) Commemoration.
1078 **550** 2r. multicoloured 75 40

551 Islamic Development Bank Building

552 Crowd celebrating

1999. 25th Anniv of Islamic Development Bank.
1079 **551** 5r. multicoloured 40 40

1999. 50th Anniv of People's Republic of China. Multicoloured.
1080 2r. Type **552** 20 10
1081 15r. Bust of Mao Tse-tung (Chinese leader) and emblem (horiz) . . . . . 1·25 1·50

553 "Enterprise" Sailing Dinghy

554 "Optimist" Sailing Dinghies

1999. 9th Asian Sailing Championship. Sailing Craft. Multicoloured.
1082 2r. Type **553** 40 40
1083 2r. "470" dinghy 40 40
1084 2r. "Optimist" dinghy . . . 40 40
1085 2r. "Laser" dinghy 40 40
1086 2r. "Mistral" sailboard . . . 40 40

1999. 10th Asian "Optimist" Sailing Championship.
1087 **554** 2r. multicoloured 30 20

555 U.P.U. Emblem

1999. 125th Anniv of Universal Postal Union.
1088 **555** 10r. multicoloured . . . 75 80

556 Hakim Mohammed Said

557 National Bank of Pakistan Building

1999. 1st Death Anniv of Hakim Mohammed Said.
1089 **556** 5r. multicoloured 40 40

1999. 50th Anniv of National Bank of Pakistan.
1090 **557** 5r. multicoloured 40 40

558 Evolution of the "Shell" Emblem

559 Profiles of Children in "10"

1999. Centenary of Shell in Pakistan.
1091 **558** 4r. multicoloured 70 60

1999. 10th Anniv of United Nations Rights of the Child Convention.
1092 **559** 2r. emerald, green and red 30 20

560 Science Equipment, Books and Computer

1999. 25th Anniv of Allama Iqbal Open University. Multicoloured.
1093 2r. Type **560** 20 15
1094 3r. Scholastic symbols as Type **560** 30 25
1095 5r. Map of Pakistan . . . . 1·00 65

561 Josh Malihabadi

1999. Birth Centenary of Josh Malihabadi (poet).
1096 **561** 5r. multicoloured 40 40

562 Dr. Afzal Qadri and Locusts

1999. 25th Death Anniv of Dr. Afzal Qadri (scientist).
1097 **562** 3r. multicoloured 30 25

563 Ghulam Bari Aleeg

564 Plantain

1999. 50th Death Anniv of Ghulam Bari Aleeg (writer).
1098 **563** 5r. multicoloured 50 50

1999. Medicinal Plants (7th series).
1099 **564** 5r. multicoloured . . . . 1·00 60

565 Mosque (½-size illustration)

1999. Eid-ul-Fitr Greetings.
1100 **565** 2r. multicoloured 25 10
1101 15r. multicoloured . . . 1·75 2·00

566 Woman and Young Boy

2000. 25th Anniv of S.O.S. Children's Villages in Pakistan.
1102 **566** 2r. multicoloured 40 25

567 Racing Cyclists

2000. Centenary of International Cycling Union.
1103 **567** 2r. multicoloured . . . . 1·00 65

568 Doves

2000. Pakistan Convention on Human Rights and Human Dignity.
1104 **568** 2r. multicoloured 40 25

569 College Building

2000. Centenary of Edwardes College, Peshawar.
1105 **569** 2r. multicoloured 30 20

570 Mahomed Ali Habib

2000. Mahomed Ali Habib (founder of Habib Bank Ltd) Commemoration.
1106 **570** 2r. multicoloured 30 20

571 Emblems and Symbols

2000. 50th Anniv of Institute of Cost and Management Accountants. Multicoloured.
1107 2r. Type **571** 25 10
1108 15r. Emblems, graph, keyboard and globe . . . 1·50 1·75

572 Ahmed Jaffer

2000. 10th Death Anniv of Ahmed Jaffer (prominent businessman).
1109 **572** 10r. multicoloured . . . 75 80

573 "Sarfaroshaane Tehreeke Pakistan" (detail)

2000. "Sarfaroshaane Tehreeke Pakistan" (painting). Showing different details. Multicoloured.
1110 5r. Type **573** 40 45
1111 5r. Bullock carts with tree in foreground 40 45
1112 5r. Bullock carts and crowd carrying Pakistan flag . . 40 45
1113 5r. Unloading bullock cart 40 45

574 Captain Muhammad Sarwar

2000. Defence Day. Showing winners of Nishan-e-Haider medal. Multicoloured.
1114 5r. Type **574** 50 50
1115 5r. Major Tufail Muhammad 50 50
See also No. 1173/4.

575 Athletics

2000. Olympic Games, Sydney. Multicoloured.
1116 4r. Type **575** 40 45
1117 4r. Hockey 40 45
1118 4r. Weightlifting 40 45
1119 4r. Cycling 40 45

576 Emblem and Building

577 Conference Emblem

2000. 125th Anniv of National College of Arts, Lahore.
1120 **576** 5r. multicoloured 30 40

2000. "Creating the Future" Business Conference.
1121 **577** 5r. multicoloured 40 40

578 Exhibition Emblem

2000. "Ideas 2000" International Defence Exhibition and Seminar.
1122 **578** 7r. multicoloured 70 70

579 Liquorice

2000. Medicinal Plants (8th series).
1123 **579** 2r. multicoloured 50 25

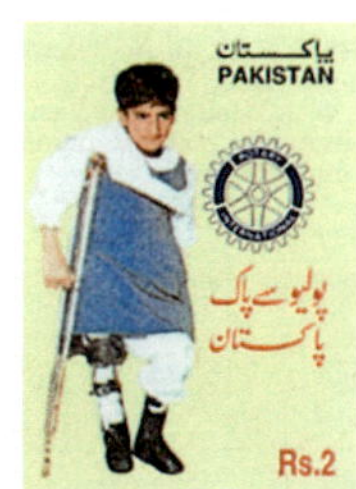

580 Crippled Child and Rotary Emblem

2000. "A World Without Polio" Campaign.
1124 **580** 2r. multicoloured 30 20

581 Refugee Family and Emblems

2000. 50th Anniv of United Nations High Commissioner for Refugees.
1125 **581** 2r. multicoloured 25 20

582 Hafeez Jalandhri

2001. Birth Centenary of Hafeez Jalandhri (poet).
1126 **582** 2r. multicoloured 40 25

583 Habib Bank AG Zurich Head Office

2001. Habib Bank AG Zurich Commemoration.
1127 **583** 5r. multicoloured 50 50

584 Chashma Nuclear Power Station

2001. Opening of Chashma Nuclear Power Station.
1128 **584** 4r. multicoloured 50 50

585 S.A.F. Games Emblem

2001. 9th S.A.F. Games, Islamabad.
1129 **585** 4r. multicoloured (blue background) 50 60
1130 4r. multicoloured (pink background) 50 60

586 "Ma Gu's Birthday Offering"

2001. 50th Anniv of Pakistan–China Friendship. Multicoloured.
1131 4r. Type **586** 50 55
1132 4r. "Two Pakistani Women drawing Water" 50 55
1133 4r. Girls in traditional Yugur and Hunza costumes 50 55
No. 1131 is inscribed "BIRTTHDAY" in error.

587 Mohammad Ali Jinnah

589 Khawaja Ghulam Farid

588 Goat Emblem and Traditional Architecture

2001. 125th Birth Anniv of Mohammad Ali Jinnah ("Quaid-e-Azam") (1st issue).
1134 **587** 4r. multicoloured 40 40
See also Nos. 1152/6.

2001. Defence Day. As T **574** showing winners of Nishan-e-Haider medal. Multicoloured.
1135 4r. Major Shabbir Sharif Shaheed 50 55
1136 4r. Major Mohammad Akram Shaheed 50 55

2001. Sindh Festival, Karachi.
1137 **588** 4r. yellow, black and green 40 40

2001. Death Centenary of Khawaja Ghulam Farid (poet).
1138 **589** 5r. multicoloured 45 45

590 "Children encircling Globe"(Urska Golob)

591 Syed Imitaz Ali Taj

2001. U.N. Year of Dialogue among Civilizations.
1139 **590** 4r. multicoloured 40 40

2001. Syed Imitaz Ali Taj (writer) Commemoration.
1140 **591** 5r. multicoloured 45 45

592 Pres. Saparmurat Niyazov of Turkmenistan

593 Peppermint

2001. 10th Anniv of Turkmenistan Independence.
1141 **592** 5r. multicoloured 45 45

2001. Medicinal Plants (9th series).
1142 **593** 4r. multicoloured . . . . 1·00 50

594 Convent of Jesus and Mary, Lahore

2001. 125th Anniv of Convent of Jesus and Mary, Lahore.
1143 **594** 4r. multicoloured 40 40

595 Dr. Ishtiaq Husain Qureshi

596 Blue Throat

2001. 20th Death Anniv of Dr. Ishtiaq Husain Qureshi (historian).
1144 **595** 4r. multicoloured 40 40

2001. Birds. Multicoloured.
1145 4r. Type **596** 70 70
1146 4r. Hoopoe 70 70
1147 4r. Pin-tailed sandgrouse . . 70 70
1148 4r. Magpie robin 70 70

597 Handshake beneath Flags of U.A.E. and Pakistan

598 Nishtar Medical College, Multan

2001. 30th Anniv of Diplomatic Relations between Pakistan and United Arab Emirates. Multicoloured.

1149 5r. Type **597** 40 20
1150 30r. Pres. Sheikh Zayed bin Sultan Al Nahyan of U.A.E. and Mohammed Ali Jinnah (horiz) . . . . 2·25 2·75

2001. 50th Anniv of Nishtar Medical College, Multan.

1151 **598** 5r. multicoloured 50 45

599 Mohammad Ali Jinnah taking Oath as Governor General, 1947

600 Troops and Ordnance

2001. 125th Birth Anniv of Mohammad Ali Jinnah ("Quaid-e-Azam") (2nd issue). Multicoloured.

1152 4r. Type **599** 30 35
1153 4r. Opening State Bank, Karachi, 1948 . . . . . 30 35
1154 4r. Taking salute, Peshawar, 1948 . . . . 30 35
1155 4r. Inspecting guard of honour, 1948 (55 × 27 mm) 30 35
1156 4r. With anti-aircraft gun crew, 1948 (55 × 27 mm) 30 35

2001. 50th Anniv of Pakistan Ordnance Factories.

1157 **600** 4r. multicoloured 40 40

601 Samandar Khan Samandar

2002. Samandar Khan Samandar (poet) Commemoration.

1158 **601** 5r. multicoloured 45 45

602 Hyssop

2002. Medicinal Plants (10th series).

1159 **602** 5r. multicoloured 75 50

603 Statues of Buddha

2002. 50th Anniv of Diplomatic Relations between Pakistan and Japan.

1160 **603** 5r. multicoloured 40 40

604 Pakistan and Kyrgyzstan Flags

605 Anwar Ratol Mangoes

2002. 10th Anniv of Diplomatic Relations between Pakistan and Kyrgyzstan.

1161 **604** 5r. multicoloured 40 40

2002. Fruits of Pakistan. Mangoes. Multicoloured.

1162 4r. Type **605** 40 45
1163 4r. Dusehri mangoes 40 45
1164 4r. Chaunsa mangoes . . . 40 45
1165 4r. Sindhri mango 40 45

606 Begum Noor us Sabah

607 Children with Animals and Pakistan Flag

2002. 55th Independence Day Celebrations. Political Figures. Multicoloured.

1166 4r. Type **606** 40 45
1167 4r. I. Chundrigar 40 45
1168 4r. Habib Ibrahim Rahimtoola 40 45
1169 4r. Qazi Mureed Ahmed . . 40 45

2002. World Summit on Sustainable Development, Johannesburg. Multicoloured.

1170 4r. Type **607** 50 50
1171 4r. Mountain and cartoon character (37 × 37 mm) . . 50 50

608 Mohammad Aly Rangoonwala (politician/ philanthropist)

2002. Mohammad Aly Rangoonwala Commem.

1172 **608** 4r. multicoloured 40 40

2002. Defence Day. As T **574** showing winners of Nishan-e-Haider medal. Multicoloured.

1173 4r. Lance Naik Muhammad Mahfuz Shaheed 50 50
1173b 4r. Sawar Muhammad Hussain Shaheed 50 50

609 Muhammad Iqbal in Academic Gown

610 "Eid Mubarak"

2002. 125th Birth Anniv of Muhammad Iqbal (writer). Multicoloured.

1174 4r. Type **609** 50 50
1175 4r. Muhammad Iqbal in library 50 50

2002. Eid-ul-Fitr Festival.

1176 **610** 4r. multicoloured 40 40

611 Hakim Muhammad Hassan Qarshi and Plants

2002. Hakim Muhammad Hassan Qarshi (pioneer of Tibb homeopathic medicine) Commemoration.

1177 **611** 4r. multicoloured 75 50

612 Red-legged Partridge, Markhor and White Flowers

2003. National Philatelic Exhibition, Karachi.

1178 **612** 4r. multicoloured 75 50

613 Anniversary Emblem

614 Minaret Emblem

2003. 50th Anniv of Pakistan Academy of Sciences.

1179 **613** 4r. multicoloured 50 50

2003. Centenary Celebrations of North West Frontier Province.

1180 **614** 4r. multicoloured 40 40

615 Golden Jubilee Emblem

2003. 50th Anniv of Pakistan Council of Scientific and Industrial Research, Islamabad.

1181 **615** 4r. brown, green and yellow 40 40

616 Prof. A. B. A. Haleem

2003. Prof. A. B. A. Haleem (1st Vice Chancellor of Karachi University) Commemoration.

1182 **616** 2r. multicoloured 25 20

617 Flowers and Anti Narcotics Force Badge

2003. "Say No to Drugs".

1183 **617** 2r. multicoloured 50 25

618 Sir Syed Memorial, Islamabad

2003. Sir Syed Memorial, Islamabad.

1184 **618** 2r. multicoloured 25 20

619 *Rosa damascene*

620 Fatima Jinnah

2003. Medicinal Plants (11th series).

1185 **619** 2r. multicoloured 70 30

2003. 110th Birth Anniv of Fatima Jinnah (politician and campaigner for women's rights).

1186 **620** 4r. multicoloured 35 30

621 Abdul Rahman (PO employee killed in raid, 2002)

622 Moulana Abdul Sattar Khan Niazi (politician, 88th)

2003. Commemorations. Multicoloured.

1187 2r. Type **621** 25 25
1188 2r. M. A. Rahim (trade union leader and philanthropist) 25 25

2003. Birth Anniversaries. Multicoloured.

1189 2r. Type **622** 35 35
1190 2r. Muhammad Yousaf Khattak (politician, 86th) 35 35
1191 2r. Moulana Muhammad Ismail Zabeeh (politician, centenary) 35 35

623 Emblem

2003. United Nations Literacy Decade.

1192 **623** 1r. multicoloured 15 10

624 Pilot Officer Rashid Minhas and Nishan-e-Haider Medal

2003. 32nd Death Anniv of Pilot Officer Rashid Minhas.

1193 **624** 2r. multicoloured 50 25

625 Pakistan Academy of Letters, Islamabad

2003. 25th Anniv of Pakistan Academy of Letters (2001).

1194 **625** 2r. multicoloured 30 25

626 Karakoram Highway

2003. 25th Anniv of Karakoram Highway.

1195 **626** 2r. multicoloured 30 25

627 Nanga Parbat

2003. 50th Anniv of First Ascent of Nanga Parbat Mountain.
1196 **627** 2r. multicoloured 30 25

628 PAF Public School, Sargodha

2003. 50th Anniv of PAF Public School, Sargodha.
1197 **628** 4r. multicoloured 40 40

629 Leather Coats

2003. Achievement of 10 Billion US Dollar Exports Target, 2002–3. Multicoloured.
1198 1r. Type **629** 15 20
1199 1r. Towels 15 20
1200 1r. Readymade garments . . 15 20
1201 1r. Cargo ship being loaded by crane, Port Qasim . . 15 20
1202 1r. Fisheries 15 20
1203 1r. Yarn 15 20
1204 1r. Sports equipment . . . 15 20
1205 1r. Fabrics 15 20
1206 1r. Furniture 15 20
1207 1r. Surgical instruments . . 15 20
1208 1r. Gems and jewellery . . . 15 20
1209 1r. Leather goods 15 20
1210 1r. Information technology 15 20
1211 1r. Rice 15 20
1212 1r. Auto parts 15 20
1213 1r. Carpets 15 20
1214 1r. Marble and granite . . . 15 20
1215 1r. Fruits 15 20
1216 1r. Cutlery 15 20
1217 1r. Engineering goods . . . 15 20

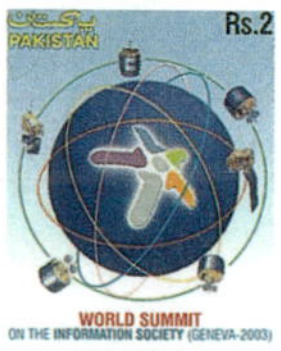

630 Boy in Wheelchair with Boy and Girl

631 Globe

2003. International Day for Disabled.
1218 **630** 2r. multicoloured 30 25

2003. World Summit on the Information Society, Geneva (Switzerland) and Tunis (Tunisia).
1219 **631** 2r. multicoloured 30 25

632 Khalid Class Submarine (Agosta 90B)

633 Pakistan Air Force Plane, Siachen, 1988–90

2003. Submarine Construction in Pakistan. Multicoloured.
1220 1r. Type **632** 20 10
1221 2r. Khalid Class submarine (Agosta 90B) and Pakistan flag (horiz) . . . 35 40

2003. Centenary of Powered Flight. Pakistan Air Force. Multicoloured.
1222 2r. Type **633** 35 40
1223 2r. Old and modern Pakistan Air Force planes 35 40

634 Emblem

2004. 12th Summit Meeting of South Asian Association for Regional Co-operation, Islamabad.
1224 **634** 4r. multicoloured 40 40

635 Sadiq Public School, Bahawalpur

2004. 50th Anniv of Sadiq Public School, Bahawalpur.
1225 **635** 4r. multicoloured 40 40

636 South Asian Federation Games Medal

637 Justice Pir Muhammad Karam Shah Al-Azhari

2004. 9th South Asian Federation (S.A.F.) Games, Islamabad. Multicoloured.
1226 2r. Type **636** 25 30
1227 2r. Sprinting 25 30
1228 2r. Squash 25 30
1229 2r. Boxing 25 30
1230 2r. Wrestling 25 30
1231 2r. Judo 25 30
1232 2r. Javelin throwing 25 30
1233 2r. Football 25 30
1234 2r. Rowing 25 30
1235 2r. Shooting 25 30
1236 2r. Shot-putting 25 30
1237 2r. Badminton 25 30
1238 2r. Weight lifting 25 30
1239 2r. Volleyball 25 30
1240 2r. Table tennis 25 30
1241 2r. Swimming 25 30

2004. Justice Pir Muhammad Karam Shah Al-Azhari Commemoration.
1242 **637** 2r. multicoloured 25 20

638 Cadet College, Hasanabdal

639 Central Library, Bahawalpur

2004. 50th Anniv of Cadet College, Hasanabdal.
1243 **638** 4r. multicoloured 35 35

2004. 80th Anniv of Central Library, Bahawalpur.
1244 **639** 2r. multicoloured 25 20

640 Bhong Mosque, Rahim Yar Khan

2004. Bhong Mosque.
1245 **640** 4r. multicoloured 35 35

641 Footballer and FIFA Emblem

2004. Centenary of FIFA (Federation Internationale de Football Association). Multicoloured.
1246 5r. Type **641** 55 60
1247 5r. FIFA emblem 55 60
1248 5r. As No. 1246 with stadium background extended behind FIFA emblem 55 60

642 Silk Road alongside Indus River

2004. Silk Road. Multicoloured.
1249 4r. Type **642** 50 50
1250 4r. Silk Road and Haramosh Peak (vert) . . 50 50

643 Juniper Forest and Emblems

2004. 50th Anniv of Sui Southern Gas Company. Protecting National Heritage.
1251 **643** 4r. multicoloured 40 40

644 K2

645 Running

2004. 50th Anniv of First Ascent of K2. Multicoloured.
1252 5r. Type **644** 60 50
MS1253 **1253** 96 × 64 mm. 30r. Views of K2. Imperf . . . . . 1·75 2·25

2004. Olympic Games, Athens. Multicoloured.
1254 5r. Type **645** 50 50
1255 5r. Boxing 50 50
1256 5r. Hockey 50 50
1257 5r. Wrestling 50 50

646 Muhammad Ali Jinnah

647

648 Muhammad Ali Jinnah

649

2004. 57th Anniv of Independence.
1258 **646** 5r. multicoloured 40 45
1259 **647** 5r. multicoloured 40 45
1260 **648** 5r. multicoloured 40 45
1261 **649** 5r. multicoloured 40 45
Nos. 1258/61 each show Muhammad Ali Jinnah beside Urdu text, which differs on each stamp.

650 Maulvi Abdul Haq

2004. Maulvi Abdul Haq (scholar) Commemoration.
1262 **650** 4r. multicoloured 30 30

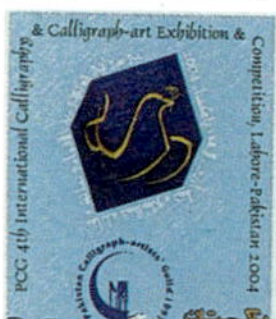

651 Calligraphic Dove with Olive Branch and Emblem

652 Striped Gourami

2004. 4th International Calligraphy and Calligraph-Art Exhibition and Competition.
1263 **651** 5r. multicoloured 35 35

2004. Fish. Multicoloured.
1264 2r. Type **652** 30 35
1265 2r. Black widow 30 35
1266 2r. Yellow dwarf cichlid . . 30 35
1267 2r. Tiger barb 30 35
1268 2r. Neon tetra 30 35

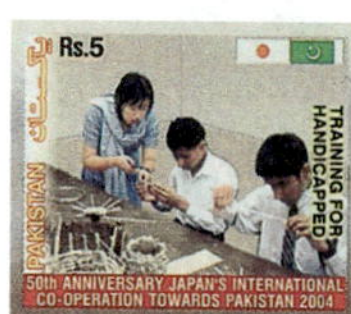

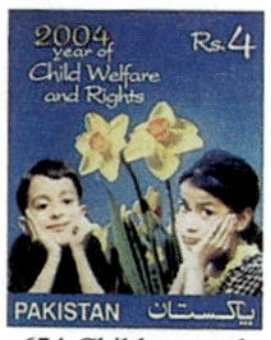

653 Training for Handicapped

654 Children and Daffodils

2004. 50th Anniv of Japan's International Co-Operation and Assistance. Multicoloured.
1269 5r. Type **653** 40 45
1270 5r. Polio eradication 40 45
1271 5r. Ghazi Barotha hydropower 40 45
1272 5r. Friendship tunnel (Kohat) 40 45
MS1273 128 × 68 mm. 30r. Looking down Friendship Tunnel and designs as Nos. 269/72 . . . . 1·75 2·25

2004. Year of Child Welfare and Rights.
1274 **654** 4r. multicoloured 35 35

655 Open University Emblems

2004. 30th Anniv of Allama Iqbal Open University, Islamabad.
1275 **655** 20r. multicoloured . . . 1·25 1·40

656 Khyber Medical College

657 Prof. Ahmed Ali

2004. Centenary of Khyber Medical College.
1276 **656** 5r. multicoloured 50 45

2005. 95th Birth Anniv of Prof. Ahmed Ali.
1277 **657** 5r. multicoloured 40 40

658 Allama Iqbal (Pakistani), Mihai Emineseu (Romanian) and Monument

659 Saadat Hasan Manto

2005. Pakistani and Romanian Poets. Multicoloured.
1278 5r. Type **658** 10 15
1279 5r. Allama Iqbal, Mihai Emineseu and book title 10 15

2005. 50th Death Anniv of Saadat Hasan Manto (short story writer).
1280 **659** 5r. multicoloured 10 15

660 Muhammad Ali Jinnah and Tempest II Airplane

2005. Air Force. Multicoloured.
1281 5r. Type **660** 40 45
1282 5r. Visit of Muhammad Ali Jinnah to the Air Force academy (vert) 40 45
1283 5r. Fighter plane and air force base facilities . . . 40 45
1284 5r. Roundel and fighter plane 40 45

661 Command and Staff College

2005. Centenary of Command and Staff College, Quetta.
1285 **661** 5r. multicoloured 40 40

662 Muhammad Ali Jinnah and Mustafa Kemal Atatürk

2005. 85th Anniversary of Turkish Grand National Assembly. Multicoloured.
1286 10r. Type **662** 65 70
1287 10r. Mustafa Kemal Atatürk 65 70

663 Institute of Business Administration, Karachi
664 Entrance

2005. 50th Anniv of Institute of Business Administration, Karachi. Multicoloured.
1288 3r. Type **663** 25 25
1289 3r. Entrance to Institute . . 25 25

2005. 95th Anniv of Islamia High School, Quetta. Paper with fluorescent fibres.
1290 **664** 5r. multicoloured 40 40

665 Akhtar Shairani
666 Emblem

2005. Birth Centenary of Akhtar Shairani (poet).
1291 **665** 5r. multicoloured 40 40

2005. World Summit on the Information Society, Tunis.
1292 **666** 5r. multicoloured 40 40

667 Abdul Rehman Baba
668 Marathon Runners

2005. Abdul Rehman Baba (poet) Commemoration.
1293 **667** 5r. multicoloured 40 40

2005. Lahore Marathon.
1294 **668** 5r. multicoloured 40 40

669 *Lepiota procera*
671 Emblem and Clasped Hands

670 Silhouettes and Sports Equipment

2005. Mushrooms. Multicoloured.
1295 5r. Type **669** 35 40
1296 5r. *Tricholoma gambosum* 35 40
1297 5r. *Amanita caesarea* 35 40
1298 5r. *Cantharellus cibarius* . . 35 40
1299 5r. *Boletus luridus* 35 40
1300 5r. *Morchella vulgaris* . . . 35 40
1301 5r. *Amanita vaginata* 35 40
1302 5r. *Agaricus arvensis* 35 40
1303 5r. *Coprinus comatus* 35 40
1304 5r. *Clitocybe geotropa* . . . 35 40

2005. International Year of Sports and Physical Education.
1305 **670** 5r. multicoloured 40 40

2005. 20th Anniv of South Asian Association for Regional Co-operation.
1306 **671** 5r. multicoloured 40 40

672 Khwaja Sarwar Hasan
673 Emblem and Silhouettes of Children

2005. Khwaja Sarwar Hasan (founder of Pakistan Institute of International Affairs) Commemoration.
1307 **672** 5r. multicoloured 45 40

2005. 30th Anniv of SOS Children's Villages of Pakistan.
1308 **673** 5r. multicoloured 40 40

OFFICIAL STAMPS

1947. King George VI Official stamps of India optd **PAKISTAN**.
O 1 O **20** 3p. slate . . . . 2·00 1·50
O 2 ½a. purple 30 10
O 3 9p. green . . . . . . 5·00 3·25
O 4 1a. red 30 10
O 5 1½a. violet 30 10
O 6 2a. orange 30 30
O 7 2½a. violet . . . . . 7·00 9·00
O 8 4a. brown . . . . . 1·25 1·00
O 9 8a. violet . . . . . 1·75 2·50
O10 **93** 1r. slate and brown (No. O138) . . . . . . 80 2·00
O11 2r. purple and brown (No. O139) . . . . . 5·50 4·50
O12 5r. green and blue (No. O140) . . . . . . 21·00 38·00
O13 10r. purple and red (No. O141) . . . . . 55·00 £110

1948. Optd **SERVICE**. Crescent moon pointing to right.
O14 **7** 3p. red 10 10
O15 6p. violet 10 10
O37 9p. green 10 10
O17 – 1a. blue . . . . 3·75 10
O18 – 1½a. green . . . . . . 3·50 10
O19 – 2a. red . . . . 1·50 10
O20 – 3a. green . . . . . . 26·00 10·00
O21 **9** 4a. brown . . . . . . 1·25 10
O22 – 8a. black . . . . . . 2·25 9·50
O23 **12** 1r. blue . . . . 1·25 10
O42 2r. brown . . . . 4·25 20
O61 5r. red . . . . 7·50 15
O26 **13** 10r. mauve . . . . . . 17·00 48·00

1949. Optd **SERVICE**. Crescent moon pointing to left.
O38 – 1a. blue 10 10
O39 – 1½a. green 10 10
O40 – 2a. red 15 10
O30 – 3a. green . . . . 29·00 6·00
O31 – 8a. black . . . . 48·00 19·00

1951. 4th Anniv of Independence. As Nos. 56, 58 and 60 but inscr "SERVICE" instead of "PAKISTAN POSTAGE".
O32 3a. purple . . . . 7·50 10·00
O33 4a. green . . . . 2·00 10
O34 8a. sepia . . . . 8·00 4·00

1954. 7th Anniv of Independence. Nos. 65/71 optd **SERVICE**.
O53 6p. violet 10 10
O54 9p. blue 10 10
O55 1a. red 10 10
O56 1½a. red 10 10
O57 14a. myrtle . . . . . . 50 4·00
O58 1r. green 50 10
O51 2r. orange . . . . . . 2·25 15

1955. 8th Anniv of Independence. Nos. 74/5 optd **SERVICE**.
O63 6a. blue 15 10
O64 8a. violet 15 10

1959. 9th Anniv of Independence. Optd **SERVICE**.
O65 **37** 2a. red 10 10

1961. 1st Anniv of Republic. Optd **SERVICE**.
O62 **41** 10r. green and orange . . 7·00 8·50

1961. Optd **SERVICE**.
O66 **51** 8a. green 20 10
O67 1r. blue 20 10

1961. New currency. Provisional stamps. Nos. 122 etc. optd **SERVICE**.
O68 – 1p. on 1½a. red 10 10
O69 **7** 2p. on 3p. red 10 10
O70 **51** 3p. on 6p. purple 10 10
O71 – 7p. on 1a. red 10 10
O72 **51** 13p. on 2a. red 10 10
O73 **37** 13p. on 2a. red 10 10

1961. Definitive issue optd **SERVICE**.
O 74 **60** 1p. violet 10 10
O 75 2p. red 10 10
O 79 3p. purple 10 10
O 94 5p. blue 10 10
O 81 7p. green 10 10
O 82 **61** 10p. brown 10 10
O 83 13p. violet 10 10
O 98 15p. purple . . . . . . 10 2·00
O 99 20p. green 10 40
O100 25p. blue . . . . 10·00 3·25
O 85 40p. purple 10 10
O102 50p. turquoise 10 15
O 87 75p. red 20 10
O104 90p. green . . . . . . 6·00 4·50
O 88 **62** 1r. red 35 10
O 89 2r. orange . . . . . . 1·50 20
O 90 5r. green . . . . 4·25 7·00

1979. Optd **SERVICE**.
O109 **275** 2p. green 10 30
O110 – 3p. black 10 30
O111 – 5p. blue 10 30
O112 **275** 10p. blue and turquoise 10 30
O113 – 20p. green (No. 468) . . 10 10
O114 – 25p. green and mauve (No. 489) 10 10
O115 – 40p. blue and mauve (No. 470) 30 10
O116 – 50p. lilac and green (No. 471) 10 10
O117 – 60p. black (No. 472) . . 1·00 10
O118 – 75p. red (No. 473) . . 1·00 10
O119 – 1r. green (No. 475) . . 2·25 10
O120 – 1r.50 orange (No. 476) 20 30
O121 – 2r. red (No. 477) . . . 20 10
O122 – 3r. blue (No. 478) . . . 30 30
O123 – 4r. black (No. 479) . . 3·00 50
O124 – 5r. brown (No. 480) . . 3·00 50

1980. As Nos. 513/19 but inscr "SERVICE".
O125 **291** 10p. green and yellow 1·00 10
O126 15p. deep green & green 1·00 10
O127 25p. violet and red . . . 15 70
O128 35p. red and green . . . 20 80
O129 – 40p. red and brown . . 1·00 10
O130 – 50p. red and green . . 20 40
O131 – 80p. green and black . . 30 1·50

1984. Nos. 629/30 and 632/6 optd **SERVICE**.
O132 – 5p. black and purple . . 10 60
O133 – 10p. black and red . . . 15 40
O135 **343** 20p. black and violet . . 30 40
O136 – 50p. brown and red . . 40 40
O137 – 60p. lt brown & brown 45 50
O138 – 70p. blue 50 70
O139 – 80p. brown and red . . 55 70

1989. No. 773 optd **SERVICE**.
O140 **411** 1r. multicoloured . . . 4·00 85

O 7 State Bank of Pakistan Building, Islamabad

1990.
O141 O **7** 1r. red and green . . . 10 10
O142 2r. red and pink 10 10
O143 3r. red and blue 10 10
O144 4r. red and brown . . . 10 10
O145 5r. red and purple . . . 10 10
O146 10r. red and brown . . 20 25

PALAU Pt. 22

Formerly part of the United States Trust Territory of the Pacific Islands, Palau became an autonomous republic on 1 January 1981. Until 1983 it continued to use United States stamps.

Palau became an independent republic on 1 October 1994.

100 cents = 1 dollar.

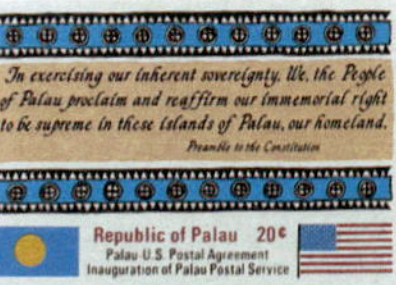

1 Preamble to Constitution

1983. Inaug of Postal Independence. Mult.
1 20c. Type **1** 50 40
2 20c. Natives hunting (design from Koror meeting house) 50 40
3 20c. Preamble to Constitution (different) 50 40
4 20c. Three fishes (design from Koror meeting house) 50 40

2 Palau Fruit Dove
3 Map Cowrie

1983. Birds. Multicoloured.
5 20c. Type **2** 45 35
6 20c. Morning bird 45 35
7 20c. Palau white-eye (inscr "Giant White-eye") 45 35
8 20c. Palau fantail 45 35

1983. Marine Life. Multicoloured.
9 1c. Sea fan 15 15
10 3c. Type **3** 15 15
11 5c. Jellyfish . . . . 1·70 15
12 10c. Hawksbill turtle 15 15
13 13c. Giant clam 15 15
14 14c. Trumpet triton 25 25
15 20c. Parrotfish 30 25
16 22c. Indo-Pacific hump-headed ("Bumphead") parrotfish 50 40
17 25c. Soft coral and damselfishes 50 45
17a 28c. Chambered nautilus . . 50 40
18 30c. Dappled sea cucumber 50 40
18a 33c. Sea anemone and anemonefishes ("Clownfish") 70 55
19 37c. Sea urchin 55 45
19a 39c. Green sea turtle 85 70
19b 44c. Sailfish 95 75
20 50c. Starfish 85 65
21 $1 Common squid . . . . . 1·60 1·10
22 $2 Dugong . . . . 3·75 3·00
23 $5 Pink sponge . . . . . . 8·25 6·50
24 $10 Spinner dolphin . . . . 15·00 12·00

4 Humpback Whale

1983. World Wildlife Fund. Whales. Mult.
25 20c. Type **4** 55 40
26 20c. Blue whale 55 40
27 20c. Fin whale 55 40
28 20c. Sperm whale 55 40

5 "Spear fishing at New Moon"
6 King Abba Thulle

1983. Christmas. Paintings by Charlie Gibbons. Mult.
29 20c. Type **5** 55 40
30 20c. "Taro Gardening" . . . 55 40
31 20c. "First Child Ceremony" 55 40

32 20c. "Traditional Feast at the Bai" 55 40
33 20c. "Spear Fishing from Red Canoe" 55 40

1983. Bicentenary of Captain Henry Wilson's Voyage to Palau.

34 **6** 20c. brown, blue & deep blue 55 40
35 – 20c. brown, blue & deep blue 55 40
36 – 20c. brown, blue & deep blue 55 40
37 – 20c. brown, blue & deep blue 55 40
38 – 20c. brown, blue & deep blue 55 40
39 – 20c. brown, blue & deep blue 55 40
40 – 20c. brown, blue & deep blue 55 40
41 – 20c. brown, blue & deep blue 55 40

DESIGNS—VERT: No. 37, Ludec (King Abba Thulle's wife); 38, Capt. Henry Wilson; 41, Prince Lee Boo. HORIZ: (47 × 20 mm): 35, Mooring in Koror; 36, Village scene in Pelew Islands; 39, Approaching Pelew; 40, Englishman's camp on Ulong.

7 Trumpet Triton

1984. Sea Shells (1st series). Multicoloured.

42 20c. Type **7** 50 35
43 20c. Horned helmet 50 35
44 20c. Giant clam 50 35
45 20c. Laciniate conch 50 35
46 20c. Royal oak ("cloak") scallop 50 35
47 20c. Trumpet triton (different) 50 35
48 20c. Horned helmet (different) 50 35
49 20c. Giant clam (different) 50 35
50 20c. Laciniate conch (different) 50 35
51 20c. Royal oak ("cloak") scallop (different) 50 35

Nos. 43/6 have mauve backgrounds, Nos. 48/51 blue backgrounds.

See also Nos. 145/9, 194/8, 231/5, 256/60 and 515/19.

8 White-tailed Tropic Bird

1984. Air. Birds. Multicoloured.

52 40c. Type **8** 1·10 75
53 40c. White tern (inscr "Fairy Tern") 1·10 75
54 40c. White-capped noddy (inscr "Black Noddy") 1·10 75
55 40c. Black-naped tern 1·10 75

9 "Oroolong" (Wilson's schooner)

1984. 19th Universal Postal Union Congress Philatelic Salon, Hamburg. Multicoloured.

56 40c. Type **9** 75 65
57 40c. Missionary ship "Duff" 75 65
58 40c. German expeditionary steamer "Peiho" 75 65
59 40c. German gunboat "Albatros" 75 65

10 Spear Fishing

1984. "Ausipex 84" International Stamp Exhibition, Melbourne. Fishing. Multicoloured.

60 20c. Type **10** 35 30
61 20c. Kite fishing 35 30
62 20c. Underwater spear fishing 35 30
63 20c. Net fishing 35 30

11 Mountain Apple

1984. Christmas. Multicoloured.

64 20c. Type **11** 35 30
65 20c. Beach morning glory 35 30
66 20c. Turmeric 35 30
67 20c. Plumeria 35 30

12 Chick

1985. Birth Bicentenary of John J. Audubon (ornithologist). Designs showing Audubon's Shearwater. Multicoloured.

68 22c. Type **12** (postage) 75 65
69 22c. Head of shearwater 75 65
70 22c. Shearwater flying 75 65
71 22c. Shearwater on lake 75 65
72 44c. "Audubon's Shearwater" (Audubon) (air) 1·10 75

13 Borotong (cargo canoe)

1985. Traditional Canoes and Rafts. Multicoloured.

73 22c. Type **13** 55 50
74 22c. Kabeki (war canoe) 55 50
75 22c. Olechutel (bamboo raft) 55 50
76 22c. Kaeb (racing/sailing canoe) 55 50

14 Boy with Guitar

16 Mother cuddling Child

15 Raising German Flag at Palau, 1885, and German 1880 20pf. Stamp

1985. International Youth Year. Multicoloured.

77 44c. Type **14** 75 60
78 44c. Boy with fishing rod 75 60
79 44c. Boy with baseball bat 75 60
80 44c. Boy with spade 75 60

Nos. 77/80 were issued together se-tenant, each block forming a composite design showing a ring of children of different races.

1985. Air. Centenary of Vatican Treaty (granting German trading privileges in Caroline Islands). Multicoloured.

81 44c. Type **15** 80 80
82 44c. Early German trading post, Angaur, and Marshall Islands 1899 5pf. overprinted stamp 80 80
83 44c. Abai (village meeting house) and Caroline Islands 1901 5m. yacht stamp 80 80
84 44c. "Cormoran" (German cruiser), 1914, and Caroline Islands 1901 40pf. yacht stamp 80 80

1985. Christmas. Multicoloured.

85 14c. Mother with child on lap 30 25
86 22c. Type **16** 45 35
87 33c. Mother supporting child in arms 70 55
88 44c. Mother lifting child in air 95 75

17 Consolidated Catalina Amphibian over Natural Bridge

1985. Air. 50th Anniv of First Trans-Pacific Airmail Flight. Multicoloured.

89 44c. Type **17** 75 65
90 44c. Douglas DC-6B approaching Airai–Koror Passage 75 65
91 44c. Grumman Albatross flying boat over Airai Village 75 65
92 44c. Douglas DC-4 landing at Airai 75 65
MS93 85 × 69 mm. $1 Martin M-130 flying boat "China Clipper" on first flight (postage) 2·20 1·90

18 Comet and Kaeb, 1758

1985. Appearance of Halley's Comet. Multicoloured.

94 44c. Type **18** 85 60
95 44c. Comet and U.S.S. "Vincennes", 1835 85 60
96 44c. Comet and "Scharnhorst" (German cruiser), 1910 85 60
97 44c. Comet and tourist cabin cruiser, 1986 85 60

19 Micronesian Flycatchers

1986. Songbirds. Multicoloured.

98 44c. Type **19** ("Mangrove Flycatchers") 75 65
99 44c. Cardinal honeyeaters 75 65
100 44c. Blue-faced parrot finches 75 65
101 44c. Grey-brown white-eye ("Dusky White-eye") and bridled white eye 75 65

20 Spear Fisherman

1986. "Ameripex '86" International Stamp Exhibition, Chicago. Sea and Reef World. Multicoloured.

102 14c. Type **20** 50 30
103 14c. Olechutel (native raft) 50 30
104 14c. Kaebs (sailing canoes) 50 30
105 14c. Rock islands and sailfish 50 30
106 14c. Inter-island ferry and two-winged flyingfishes 50 30
107 14c. Bonefishes 50 30
108 14c. Jacks 50 30
109 14c. Japanese mackerel 50 30
110 14c. Sailfishes 50 30
111 14c. Barracuda 50 30
112 14c. Undulate triggerfishes 50 30
113 14c. Dolphin (fish) 50 30
114 14c. Spear fisherman with grouper 50 30
115 14c. Manta ray 50 30
116 14c. Striped marlin 50 30
117 14c. Black-striped parrotfishes 50 30
118 14c. Red-breasted wrasse 50 30
119 14c. Malabar blood snappers 50 30
120 14c. Malabar blood snapper and clupeid ("Herring") school 50 30
121 14c. Dugongs 50 30
122 14c. Powder-blue surgeonfishes 50 30
123 14c. Spotted eagle ray 50 30
124 14c. Hawksbill turtle 50 30
125 14c. Needlefishes 50 30
126 14c. Tuna 50 30
127 14c. Octopus 50 30
128 14c. Anemonefishes ("Clownfish") 50 30
129 14c. Squid 50 30
130 14c. Groupers 50 30
131 14c. Moorish idols 50 30
132 14c. Queen conch and starfish 50 30
133 14c. Diadem soldierfishes 50 30
134 14c. Starfish and stingrays 50 30
135 14c. Lionfish 50 30
136 14c. Emperor angelfishes 50 30
137 14c. Saddle butterflyfishes 50 30
138 14c. Spiny lobster 50 30
139 14c. Mangrove crab 50 30
140 14c. Giant clam ("Tridacna gigas") 50 30
141 14c. Moray 50 30

Nos. 102/41 are each inscribed on the back (over the gum) with the name of the subject featured on the stamp.

Nos. 102/41 were printed together, se-tenant, forming a composite design.

21 Presidential Seal

1986. Air. Haruo I. Remeliik (first President) Commemoration. Multicoloured.

142 44c. Type **21** 95 85
143 44c. Kabeki (war canoe) passing under Koror–Babeldaob Bridge 95 85
144 44c. Presidents Reagan and Remeliik 95 85

1986. Sea Shells (2nd series). As T **7**. Multicoloured.

145 22c. Commercial trochus 50 40
146 22c. Marble cone 50 40
147 22c. Fluted giant clam 50 40
148 22c. Bullmouth helmet 50 40
149 22c. Golden cowrie 50 40

23 Crab inhabiting Soldier's rusting Helmet

1986. International Peace Year. Multicoloured.

150 22c. Type **23** (postage) 55 50
151 22c. Marine life inhabiting airplane 55 50
152 22c. Rusting tank behind girl 55 50
153 22c. Abandoned assault landing craft, Airai 55 50
154 22c. Statue of Liberty, New York (centenary) (air) 85 75

24 Gecko

1986. Reptiles. Multicoloured.

155 22c. Type **24** 50 45
156 22c. Emerald tree skink 50 45
157 22c. Estuarine crocodile 50 45
158 22c. Leatherback turtle 50 45

25 Girl with Guitar and Boy leading Child on Goat

26 Tailed Jay on Soursop

1986. Christmas. Multicoloured.

159 22c. Type **25** 35 30
160 22c. Boys singing and girl carrying flowers 35 30
161 22c. Mother holding baby 35 30
162 22c. Children carrying baskets of fruit 35 30
163 22c. Girl with white terns 35 30

Nos. 159/63 were issued together, se-tenant, forming a composite design.

1987. Butterflies (1st series). Multicoloured.

164 44c. Type **26** 80 70
165 44c. Common mormon on sweet orange 80 70
166 44c. Common eggfly on swamp cabbage 80 70
167 44c. Oleander butterfly on fig 80 70

See also Nos. 223/6.

27 Bat flying

1987. Air. Palau Fruit Bat. Multicoloured.

168	44c. Type **27**	85	65
169	44c. Bat hanging from branch	85	65
170	44c. Bat feeding	85	65
171	44c. Head of bat	85	65

28 *Ixora casei*

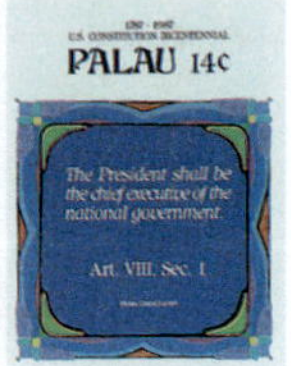

31 "The President shall be the chief executive ..."

29 Babeldaob

1987. Flowers. Multicoloured.

172	1c. Type **28**	15	15
173	3c. *Lumnitzera littorea*	15	15
174	5c. *Sonneratia alba*	15	15
175	10c. Woody vine	15	15
176	14c. *Bikkia palauensis*	15	15
177	15c. *Limophila aromatica*	20	10
178	22c. *Bruguiera gymnorhiza*	35	30
179	25c. *Fragraea ksid*	45	40
180	36c. *Ophiorrhiza palauensis*	55	50
181	39c. *Cerbera manghas*	60	55
182	44c. *Samadera indica*	75	65
183	45c. *Maesa canfieldiae*	75	65
184	50c. *Dolichandrone spathacea*	85	75
185	$1 *Barringtonia racemosa*	1·70	1·40
186	$2 *Nepenthes mirabilis*	3·50	3·00
187	$5 Orchid	8·25	7·25
188	$10 Bouquet of mixed flowers	14·00	12·00

1987. "Capex '87" International Stamp Exhibition, Toronto. Multicoloured.

190	22c. Type **29**	45	40
191	22c. Floating Garden Islands	45	40
192	22c. Rock Island	45	40
193	22c. Koror	45	40

1987. Sea Shells (3rd series). As T **7**. Multicoloured.

194	22c. Black-striped triton	50	40
195	22c. Tapestry turban	50	40
196	22c. Adusta murex	50	40
197	22c. Little fox mitre	50	40
198	22c. Cardinal mitre	50	40

1987. Bicentenary of United States of America Constitution. Multicoloured.

199	14c. Type **31**	15	15
200	14c. Palau and U.S. Presidents' seals (24 × 37 mm)	15	15
201	14c. "The executive power shall be vested ..."	15	15
202	22c. "The legislative power of Palau ..."	35	30
203	22c. Palau Olbiil Era Kelulau and U.S. Senate seals (24 × 37 mm)	35	30
204	22c. "All legislative powers herein granted ..."	35	30
205	44c. "The judicial power of Palau ..."	65	55
206	44c. Palau and U.S. Supreme Court seals (24 × 37 mm)	65	55
207	44c. "The judicial power of the United States ..."	65	55

The three designs of the same value were printed together in se-tenant strips, the top stamp of each strip bearing extracts from the Palau Constitution and the bottom stamp extracts from the U.S. Constitution.

32 Japanese Mobile Post Office and 1937 Japan ½s. Stamp

1987. Links with Japan. Multicoloured.

208	14c. Type **32**	25	25
209	22c. Phosphate mine and Japan 1942 5s. stamp	40	35
210	33c. Douglas DC-2 flying over Badrulchau monuments and Japan 1937 2s.+2s. stamp	55	50
211	44c. Japanese Post Office, Koror, and Japan 1927 10s. stamp	75	65
MS212	80 × 94 mm. $1 Japanese visitors at the Aviator's Grave, Japanese Cemetery, Peleliu	2·00	1·80

33 Huts, White Tern and Outrigger Canoes

34 Snapping Shrimp and Watchman Goby

1987. Christmas. Multicoloured.

213	22c. Type **33**	40	35
214	22c. Flying white tern carrying twig	40	35
215	22c. Holy Family in kaeb	40	35
216	22c. Angel and kaeb	40	35
217	22c. Outrigger canoes and hut	40	35

Nos. 213/17 were issued together, se-tenant, forming a composite design; each stamp bears a verse of the carol "I Saw Three Ships".

1987. 25th Anniv of World Ecology Movement. Multicoloured.

218	22c. Type **34**	45	40
219	22c. Mauve vase sponge and sponge crab	45	40
220	22c. Lemon ("Pope's") damselfish and blue-streaked cleaner wrasse	45	40
221	22c. Clown anemonefishes and sea anemone	45	40
222	22c. Four-coloured nudibranch and banded coral shrimp	45	40

1988. Butterflies (2nd series). As T **26**.

223	44c. Orange tiger on "Tournefotia argentia"	65	55
224	44c. Swallowtail on "Citrus reticulata"	65	55
225	44c. Lemon migrant on "Crataeva speciosa"	65	55
226	44c. "Appias ada" (wrongly inscr "Colias philodice") on "Crataeva speciosa"	65	55

35 Whimbrel

1988. Ground-dwelling Birds. Multicoloured.

227	44c. Type **35**	65	55
228	44c. Chinese little bittern ("Yellow Bittern")	65	55
229	44c. Nankeen ("Rufous Night Heron")	65	55
230	44c. Buff-banded rail ("Banded Rail")	65	55

1988. Sea Shells (4th series). As T **7**. Mult.

231	25c. Striped engina	45	40
232	25c. Ivory cone	45	40
233	25c. Plaited mitre	45	40
234	25c. Episcopal mitre	45	40
235	25c. Isabelle cowrie	45	40

36 Palauan Kaeb

37 Baseball

1988. 5th Anniv of Palau Postal Independence and "Finlandia 88" International Stamp Exhibition, Helsinki. Sheet 149 × 97 mm containing T **36** and similar horiz designs. Multicoloured.

MS236	25c. Type **36**; 25c. Spanish "Vizcaya" class cruiser; 25c. German cruiser "Cormoran"; 25c. Japanese street mailbox, Koror Museum; 25c. U.S Trust Territory freighter at Malakal; 25c. Koror Post Office	2·20	1·90

1988. Olympic Games, Seoul. Multicoloured.

237	25c.+5c. Type **37**	45	40
238	25c.+5c. Running	45	40
239	45c.+5c. Diving	75	60
240	45c.+5c. Swimming	75	60

38 Man's Head and Artwork for Finlandia'88 Stamp

39 Angel Violinist and Singing Cherubs

1988. 10th Anniv of U.S. Possessions Philatelic Society. "Praga 88" International Stamp Exhibition, Czechoslovakia. Sheet 149 × 97 mm containing T **38** and similar horiz designs. Multicoloured.

MS241	45c. Type **38**; 45c. Society emblem; 45c. Artwork for first set of Palau stamps; 45c. Artwork for "China Clipper" miniature sheet; 45c. Man examining cover and boy holding envelope; 45c. Woman cancelling cover	3·75	3·25

1988. Christmas. Multicoloured.

242	25c. Type **39**	45	40
243	25c. Angels and children singing	45	40
244	25c. Children adoring child	45	40
245	25c. Angels and birds flying	45	40
246	25c. Running children and angels playing trumpets	45	40

Nos. 242/6 were issued together, se-tenant, forming a composite design.

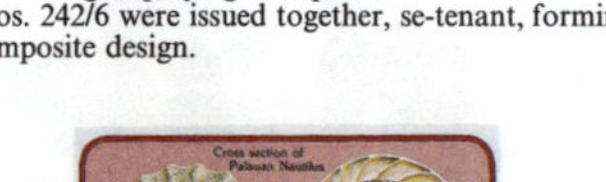

40 Ammonite and Cross Section of Palauan Nautilus

1988. Chambered Nautilus. Sheet 133 × 121 mm containing T **40** and similar designs.

MS247	25c. multicoloured (Type **40**); 25c. brown, black and black (Palauan bai symbols for nautilus) (25 × 53 mm); 25c. multicoloured (Palauan nautilus in cage); 25c. multicoloured (Different species); 25c. multicoloured (Releasing tagged nautilus)	2·50	2·30

41 Nicobar Pigeon

43 Robin-redbreast Triton

42 False Chanterelle

1989. Endangered Birds. Multicoloured.

248	45c. Type **41**	65	55
249	45c. Palau ground dove	65	55
250	45c. Marianas scrub hen	65	55
251	45c. Palau scops owl	65	55

1989. Fungi. Multicoloured.

252	45c. Type **42** (inscr "Gilled Auricularia)	70	60
253	45c. Black fellows' bread ("Rock mushroom")	70	60
254	45c. Chicken mushroom ("Polyporous")	70	60
255	45c. Veiled stinkhorn	70	60

1989. Sea Shells (5th series). Multicoloured.

256	25c. Type **43**	45	40
257	25c. Hebrew cone	45	40
258	25c. Tadpole triton	45	40
259	25c. Lettered cone	45	40
260	25c. Rugose mitre	45	40

44 Cessna 207 Stationair 7

1989. Air. Aircraft. Multicoloured.

261	36c. Type **44**	55	50
262	39c. Embraer Bandeirante airliner	55	50
264	45c. Boeing 727 jetliner	55	50

No. 261 is wrongly inscribed "Skywagon".

45 "Little Bird amidst Chrysanthemum" (Ando Hiroshige)

1989. Emperor Hirohito of Japan Commemoration. Sheet 67 × 101 mm.

MS266	**45** $1 multicoloured	1·80	1·60

46 Jettison of Third Stage

1989. 20th Anniv of First Manned Landing on Moon. Multicoloured.

267	25c. Type **46**	40	30
268	25c. Command Module adjusting position	40	30
269	25c. Lunar Excursion Module "Eagle" docking	40	30
270	25c. Space module docking	40	30
271	25c. Propulsion for entry into lunar orbit	40	30
272	25c. Third stage burn	40	30
273	25c. Command Module orbiting Moon	40	30
274	25c. Command Module and part of "Eagle"	40	30
275	25c. Upper part of "Eagle" on Moon	40	30
276	25c. Descent of "Eagle"	40	30
277	25c. Nose of rocket	40	30
278	25c. Reflection in Edwin "Buzz" Aldrin's visor	40	30
279	25c. Neil Armstrong and flag on Moon	40	30
280	25c. Footprints and astronaut's oxygen tank	40	30
281	25c. Upper part of astronaut descending ladder	40	30
282	25c. Launch tower and body of rocket	40	30
283	25c. Survival equipment on Aldrin's space suit	40	30
284	25c. Blast off from lunar surface	40	30

285 25c. View of Earth and astronaut's legs 40 30
286 25c. Leg on ladder 40 30
287 25c. Lift off 40 30
288 25c. Spectators at launch . . 40 30
289 25c. Capsule parachuting into Pacific 40 30
290 25c. Re-entry 40 30
291 25c. Space Module jettison 40 30
292 $2.40 "Buzz" Aldrin on Moon (photo by Neil Armstrong) (34 × 47 mm) 40 30

Nos. 267/91 were issued together, se-tenant, forming a composite design.

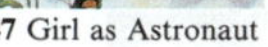

47 Girl as Astronaut 48 Bridled Tern

1989. Year of the Young Reader. Multicoloured.
293 25c. Type **47** 35 30
294 25c. Boy riding dolphin . . . 35 30
295 25c. Cheshire Cat in tree . . 35 30
296 25c. Mother Goose 35 30
297 25c. Baseball player 35 30
298 25c. Girl reading 35 30
299 25c. Boy reading 35 30
300 25c. Mother reading to child 35 30
301 25c. Girl holding flowers listening to story 35 30
302 25c. Boy in baseball strip . . 35 30

1989. "World Stamp Expo '89" International Stamp Exhibition, Washington D.C. Stilt Mangrove. Multicoloured.
303 25c. Type **48** 40 30
304 25c. Lemon migrant (inscr "Sulphur Butterfly") . . . 40 30
305 25c. Micronesian flycatcher ("Mangrove Flycatcher") 40 30
306 25c. White-collared kingfisher 40 30
307 25c. Fruit bat 40 30
308 25c. Estuarine crocodile . . . 40 30
309 25c. Nankeen ("Rufous Night Heron") 40 30
310 25c. Stilt mangrove 40 30
311 25c. Bird's nest fern 40 30
312 25c. Beach hibiscus tree . . . 40 30
313 25c. Common eggfly (butterfly) 40 30
314 25c. Dog-faced watersnake 40 30
315 25c. Mangrove jingle shell . . 40 30
316 25c. Palau bark cricket . . . 40 30
317 25c. Periwinkle and mangrove oyster 40 30
318 25c. Jellyfish 40 30
319 25c. Flat-headed grey ("Striped") mullet 40 30
320 25c. Mussels, sea anemones and algae 40 30
321 25c. Pajama cardinalfish . . 40 30
322 25c. Black-tailed snappers . . 40 30

Nos. 303/22 are each inscribed on the back (over the gum) with the name of the subject featured on the stamp.

Nos. 303/22 were issued together, se-tenant, forming a composite design.

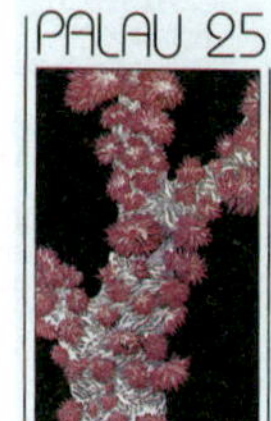

49 Angels, Sooty Tern and Audubon's Shearwater 50 Pink Coral

1989. Christmas. Carol of the Birds. Mult.
323 25c. Type **49** 45 40
324 25c. Palau fruit dove and angel 45 40
325 25c. Madonna and child, cherub and birds 45 40
326 25c. Angel, blue-faced parrot finch, Micronesian flycatcher and cardinal honeyeater 45 40
327 25c. Angel, Micronesian flycatcher and black-headed gulls 45 40

Nos. 323/7 were printed together, se-tenant, forming a composite design.

1990. Soft Corals. Multicoloured.
328 25c. Type **50** 45 40
329 25c. Mauve coral 45 40
330 25c. Yellow coral 45 40
331 25c. Orange coral 45 40

See also Nos. 392/5.

51 Siberian Rubythroat

1990. Forest Birds. Multicoloured.
332 45c. Type **51** 65 55
333 45c. Palau bush warbler . . . 65 55
334 45c. Micronesian starling . . 65 55
335 45c. Common cicdabird ("Cicadabird") 65 55

52 Prince Lee Boo, Capt. Henry Wilson and H.M.S. "Victory"

1990. "Stamp World London 90" International Stamp Exhibition. Prince Lee Boo's Visit to England, 1784, and 150th Anniv of the Penny Black. Multicoloured.
336 25c. Type **52** 40 35
337 25c. St. James's Palace . . . 40 35
338 25c. Rotherhithe Docks . . . 40 35
339 25c. Ooroolong House, Devon (Capt. Wilson's home) . . 40 35
340 25c. Vincenzo Lunardi's balloon 40 35
341 25c. St. Paul's Cathedral . . 40 35
342 25c. Prince Lee Boo's grave 40 35
343 25c. St. Mary's Church, Rotherhithe 40 35
344 25c. Memorial tablet to Prince Lee Boo 40 35
MS345 115 × 85 mm. $1 Penny Black (vert) . . . . 1·50 1·30

53 "Corymborkis veratrifolia" 55 White Tern, Pacific Golden Plover and Sanderling

54 Plane Butterfly on Beach Sunflower

1990. "Expo 90" International Garden and Greenery Exposition, Osaka. Orchids. Multicoloured.
346 45c. Type **53** 65 55
347 45c. "Malaxis setipes" . . . 65 55
348 45c. "Dipodium freycinetianum" 65 55
349 45c. "Bulbophyllum micronesiacum" 65 55
350 45c. "Vanda teres" 65 55

1990. Butterflies. Multicoloured.
351 45c. Type **54** 60 55
352 45c. Painted lady on coral tree 60 55
353 45c. "Euploea nemertes" on sorcerer's flower 60 55
354 45c. Meadow argus (inscr "Buckeye") on beach pea 60 55

1990. Lagoon Life. Multicoloured.
355 25c. Type **55** 35 25
356 25c. Bidekill fisherman . . . 35 25
357 25c. Yacht and insular halfbeaks 35 25
358 25c. Palauan kaebs 35 25
359 25c. White-tailed tropic bird 35 25
360 25c. Spotted eagle ray . . . 35 25
361 25c. Great barracudas . . . 35 25
362 25c. Reef needlefish 35 25
363 25c. Reef needlefish and black-finned reef ("Reef Blacktip") shark 35 25
364 25c. Hawksbill turtle 35 25
365 25c. Six-feelered threadfins and octopus 35 25
366 25c. Narrow-banded batfish and six-feelered threadfins 35 25
367 25c. Lionfish and six-feelered threadfins 35 25
368 25c. Snowflake moray and six-feelered threadfins . . . 35 25
369 25c. Inflated and uninflated porcupinefishes and six-feelered threadfins 35 25
370 25c. Regal angelfish, blue-streaked cleaner wrasse, blue sea star and corals . . 35 25
371 25c. Clown triggerfish and spotted garden eels 35 25
372 25c. Anthias and spotted garden eels 35 25
373 25c. Sail-finned snapper ("Bluelined sea bream"), blue-green chromis, blue ("Sapphire") damselfish and spotted garden eel . . 35 25
374 25c. Masked ("Orange-spine") unicornfish and ribbon-striped ("White-tipped") soldierfish 35 25
375 25c. Slatepencil sea urchin and leopard sea cucumber 35 25
376 25c. Pacific partridge tun (shell) 35 25
377 25c. Mandarin fish and spotted garden eel 35 25
378 25c. Tiger cowrie 35 25
379 25c. Feather starfish and orange-finned anemonefish 35 25

Nos. 355/79 were printed together, se-tenant, forming a composite design.

56 *Delphin*, 1890, and Card

1990. Pacifica. Mail Transport. Multicoloured.
380 45c. Type **56** 85 75
381 45c. Right-hand half of card flown on 1951 inaugural U.S. civilian airmail flight and forklift unloading mail from Boeing 727 . . . . . 85 75

Nos. 380/1 were issued together, se-tenant, forming a composite design.

57 Girls singing and Boy with Butterfly

1990. Christmas. Multicoloured.
382 25c. Type **57** 35 30
383 25c. White terns perching on girl's songbook 35 30
384 25c. Girl singing and boys playing flute and guitar . . 35 30
385 25c. Couple with baby 35 30
386 25c. Three girls singing . . . 35 30

58 Consolidated B-24S Liberator Bombers over Peleliu

1990. 46th Anniv of U.S. Action in Palau Islands during Second World War.
387 45c. Type **58** 75 65
388 45c. Landing craft firing rocket barrage 75 65
389 45c. 1st Marine division attacking Peleliu 75 65
390 45c. U.S. Infantryman and Palauan children 75 65
MS391 105 × 53 mm. $1 U.S.S. "Peleliu" (helicopter carrier) (50 × 38 mm) . . . . 2·00 1·70

1991. Hard Corals. As T **50**.
392 30c. Staghorn coral 50 40
393 30c. Velvet leather coral . . . 50 40
394 30c. Van Gogh's cypress coral 50 40
395 30c. Violet lace coral 50 40

59 Statue of Virgin Mary, Nkulangelul Point

1991. Angaur, The Phosphate Island. Mult.
396 30c. Type **59** 45 30
397 30c. Angaur Post Office opening day cancellation and kaeb (sailing canoe) (41 × 27 mm) 45 30
398 30c. Billfish and Caroline Islands 40pf. "Yacht" stamp (41 × 27 mm) . . . 45 30
399 30c. Steam locomotive at phosphate mine 45 30
400 30c. Lighthouse Hill and German copra freighter . . 45 30
401 30c. Dolphins and map showing phosphate mines (41 × 27 mm) 45 30
402 30c. Estuarine crocodile (41 × 27 mm) 45 30
403 30c. Workers cycling to phosphate plant 45 30
404 30c. Freighter loading phosphate 45 30
405 30c. Hammerhead shark and German overseer (41 × 27 mm) 45 30
406 30c. Angaur cancellation and Marshall Islands 10pf. "Yacht" stamp (41 × 27 mm) 45 30
407 30c. Rear Admiral Graf von Spee and "Scharnhorst" (German cruiser) 45 30
408 30c. "Emden" (German cruiser) and Capt. Karl von Muller 45 30
409 30c. Crab-eating macaque (41 × 27 mm) 45 30
410 30c. Sperm whale (41 × 27 mm) 45 30
411 30c. H.M.A.S. "Sydney" (cruiser) shelling radio tower 45 30

Nos. 396/411 were issued together, se-tenant, with the centre block of eight stamps forming a composite design of a map of the island.

60 Moorhen 61 Pope Leo XIII and 19th-century Spanish and German Flags

1991. Birds. Multicoloured.
412 1c. Palau bush warbler . . . 15 15
413 4c. Type **60** 15 15
414 6c. Buff-banded rail ("Banded Rail") 15 15
415 19c. Palau fantail 25 15
416 20c. Micronesian flycatcher ("Mangrove Flycatcher") 25 25
417 23c. Purple swamphen . . . 30 25
418 29c. Palau fruit dove 40 35
419 35c. Crested tern 50 40
420 40c. Reef herons (inscr "Pacific Reef-Heron") . . 50 45
421 45c. Micronesian pigeon . . 60 55
422 50c. Great frigate bird . . . 65 55
423 52c. Little pied cormorant . . 70 60
424 75c. Jungle nightjar 95 85
425 95c. Cattle egret . . . . . . 1·20 1·10
426 $1.34 Sulphur-crested cockatoo . . . . 1·70 1·50
427 $2 Blue-faced parrot finch . . 2·50 2·30
428 $5 Eclectus parrots . . . . . 6·75 6·00
429 $10 Palau bush warblers feeding chicks (51 × 28 mm) 13·00 11·50

1991. Centenary of Christianity in Palau Islands. Multicoloured.
432 29c. Type **61** 40 35
433 29c. Ibedul Ilengelekei and Church of the Sacred Heart, Koror, 1920 . . . . 40 35
434 29c. Marino de la Hoz, Emilio Villar and Elias Fernandez (Jesuit priests executed in Second World War) 40 35
435 29c. Centenary emblem and Fr. Edwin G. McManus (compiler of Palauan–English dictionary) 40 35
436 29c. Present Church of the Sacred Heart, Koror . . . 40 35
437 29c. Pope John Paul II and Palau and Vatican flags . . 40 35

62 Pacific White-sided Dolphin

1991. Pacific Marine Life. Multicoloured.
438 29c. Type **62** 45 30
439 29c. Common dolphin . . . 45 30
440 29c. Rough-toothed dolphin 45 30
441 29c. Bottle-nosed dolphin . . 45 30
442 29c. Common (inscr "Harbor") porpoise . . . 45 30
443 29c. Head and body of killer whale 45 30

444 29c. Tail of killer whale, spinner dolphin and yellow-finned tuna 45 30
445 29c. Dall's porpoise 45 30
446 29c. Finless porpoise 45 30
447 29c. Map of Palau Islands and bottle-nosed dolphin 45 30
448 29c. Dusky dolphin 45 30
449 29c. Southern right whale dolphin 45 30
450 29c. Striped dolphin 45 30
451 29c. Fraser's dolphin 45 30
452 29c. Peale's dolphin 45 30
453 29c. Spectacled porpoise . . 45 30
454 29c. Spotted dolphin 45 30
455 29c. Hourglass dolphin . . . 45 30
456 29c. Risso's dolphin 45 30
457 29c. Hector's dolphin 45 30

63 McDonnell Douglas Wild Weasel Fighters

1991. Operation Desert Storm (liberation of Kuwait). Multicoloured.
458 20c. Type **63** 30 30
459 20c. Lockheed Stealth fighter-bomber 30 30
460 20c. Hughes Apache helicopter 30 30
461 20c. "M-109 TOW" missile on "M998 HMMWV" vehicle 30 30
462 20c. President Bush of U.S.A. 30 30
463 20c. M2 "Bradley" tank . . 30 30
464 20c. U.S.S. "Ranger" (aircraft carrier) 30 30
465 20c. "Pegasus" (patrol boat) 30 30
466 20c. U.S.S. "Wisconsin" (battleship) 30 30
467 $2.90 Sun, dove and yellow ribbon 30 30
MS468 101 × 127 mm. No. 467 4·00 3·50

64 Bai Gable

66 "Silent Night, Holy Night!"

65 Bear's-paw Clam, China Clam, Fluted Giant Clam and "Tridacna derasa"

1991. 10th Anniv of Republic of Palau and Palau–Pacific Women's Conference, Koror. Bai (community building) Decorations. Mult. Imperf (self-adhesive) (50c.), perf (others).
469 29c. Type **64** (postage) . . . 45 40
470 29c. Interior of bai (left side) (32 × 48 mm) 45 40
471 29c. Interior of bai (right side) (32 × 48 mm) 45 40
472 29c. God of construction . . 45 40
473 29c. Bubuu (spider) (value at left) (30 × 23 mm) 45 40
474 29c. Delerrok, the money bird (facing right) (31 × 23 mm) 45 40
475 29c. Delerrok (facing left) (31 × 23 mm) 45 40
476 29c. Bubuu (value at right) (30 × 23 mm) 45 40
477 50c. Bai gable (as in Type **64**) (24 × 51 mm) (air) 45 40
Nos. 469/76 were issued together, se-tenant, Nos. 470/1 forming a composite design.

1991. Conservation and Cultivation of Giant Clams. Multicoloured.
478 50c. Type **65** 70 60
479 50c. Symbiotic relationship between giant clam and "Symbiodinium microadriaticum" 70 60
480 50c. Hatchery 70 60
481 50c. Diver measuring clams in sea-bed nursery 70 60
482 50c. Micronesian Mariculture Demonstration Center, Koror (108 × 16 mm) . . . 70 60

1991. Christmas. Multicoloured.
483 29c. Type **66** 40 35
484 29c. "All is calm, all is bright;" 40 35
485 29c. "Round yon virgin mother and child!" 40 35
486 29c. "Holy Infant, so tender and mild," 40 35
487 29c. "Sleep in heavenly peace." 40 35
Nos. 483/7 were issued together, se-tenant, forming a composite design.

67 Flag, Islands and Children

1991. 25th Anniv of Presence of United States Peace Corps in Palau. Children's paintings.
488 29c. Type **67** 45 40
489 29c. Volunteers arriving by airplane 45 40
490 29c. Health care 45 40
491 29c. Fishing 45 40
492 29c. Agriculture 45 40
493 29c. Education 45 40

68 *Zuiho Maru* (commercial trochus shell breeding and marine research)

1991. "Phila Nippon '91" International Stamp Exhibition, Tokyo. Japanese Heritage in Palau. Multicoloured.
494 29c. Type **68** 40 35
495 29c. Man carving story board (traditional arts) 40 35
496 29c. Tending pineapple crop (agricultural training) . . . 40 35
497 29c. Klidm (stone carving), Koror (archaeological research) 40 35
498 29c. Teaching carpentry and building design 40 35
499 29c. Kawasaki "Mavis" flying boat (air transport) 40 35
MS500 71 × 102 mm. $1 Map, yellow-finned tuna and 1941 cancellation . . . . 1·30 1·10

69 Mitsubishi Zero-Sen attacking Shipping at Pearl Harbor

70 *Troides criton*

1991. Pacific Theatre in Second World War (1st issue). Multicoloured.
501 29c. Type **69** 45 40
502 29c. U.S.S. "Nevada" underway from Pearl Harbor 45 40
503 29c. U.S.S. "Shaw" exploding at Pearl Harbor 45 40
504 29c. Douglas Dauntless dive bombers attacking Japanese carrier "Akagi" 45 40
505 29c. U.S.S. "Wasp" sinking off Guadalcanal 45 40
506 29c. Battle of Philippine Sea 45 40
507 29c. Landing craft storming Saipan Beach 45 40
508 29c. U.S. 1st Cavalry on Leyte 45 40
509 29c. Battle of Bloody Nose Ridge, Peleliu 45 40
510 29c. U.S. troops landing at Iwo Jima 45 40
See also Nos. 574/83, 601/10 and 681/90.

1992. Butterflies. Multicoloured.
511 50c. Type **70** 65 55
512 50c. *Alcides zodiaca* 65 55
513 50c. *Papilio poboroi* 65 55
514 50c. *Vindula arsinoe* 65 55

71 Common Hairy Triton

73 "And darkness was upon the face of the deep ..."

72 Christopher Columbus

1992. Sea Shells (6th series). Multicoloured.
515 29c. Type **71** 45 40
516 29c. Eglantine cowrie 45 40
517 29c. Sulcate swamp cerith . . 45 40
518 29c. Black-spined murex . . 45 40
519 29c. Black-mouth moon . . . 45 40

1992. Age of Discovery from Columbus to Drake. Multicoloured.
520 29c. Type **72** 45 40
521 29c. Ferdinand Magellan . . 45 40
522 29c. Sir Francis Drake . . . 45 40
523 29c. Cloud blowing northerly wind 45 40
524 29c. Compass rose 45 40
525 29c. Dolphin and "Golden Hind" (Drake's ship) . . . 45 40
526 29c. Corn cobs and "Santa Maria" (Columbus's ship) 45 40
527 29c. Mythical fishes 45 40
528 29c. Betel palm, cloves and black pepper 45 40
529 29c. "Vitoria" (Magellan's ship), Palau Islands, Audubon's shearwater and crested tern 45 40
530 29c. White-tailed tropic bird, bicoloured parrotfish, pineapple and potatoes . . 45 40
531 29c. Compass 45 40
532 29c. Mythical sea monster . . 45 40
533 29c. Paddles and astrolabe 45 40
534 29c. Parallel ruler, divider and Inca gold treasure . . 45 40
535 29c. Backstaff 45 40
536 29c. Cloud blowing southerly wind 45 40
537 29c. Amerigo Vespucci . . . 45 40
538 29c. Francisco Pizarro . . . 45 40
539 29c. Vasco Nunez de Balboa 45 40
With the exception of Nos. 523 and 536 each stamp is inscribed on the back (over the gum) with the name of the subject featured on the stamp.
Nos. 520/39 were issued together, se-tenant, the backgrounds forming a composite design of the hemispheres.

1992. 2nd U.N. Conference on Environment and Development, Rio de Janeiro. The Creation of the World from the Book of Genesis, Chapter 1. Multicoloured.
540 29c. Type **73** 45 40
541 29c. Sunlight 45 40
542 29c. "Let there be a firmament in the midst of the waters, ..." 45 40
543 29c. Sky and clouds 45 40
544 29c. "Let the waters under the heaven ..." 45 40
545 29c. Tree 45 40
546 29c. Waves and sunlight (no inscr) 45 40
547 29c. Waves and sunlight ("... and it was good.") 45 40
548 29c. Waves and clouds (no inscr) 45 40
549 29c. Waves and clouds ("... and it was so.") 45 40
550 29c. Plants on river bank (no inscr) 45 40
551 29c. Plants on river bank ("... and it was good.") 45 40
552 29c. "Let there be lights in the firmament ..." 45 40
553 29c. Comet, planet and clouds 45 40
554 29c. "Let the waters bring forth abundantly the moving creature ..." . . . 45 40
555 29c. Great frigate bird and red-tailed tropic bird flying and collared lory on branch 45 40
556 29c. "Let the earth bring forth the living creature after his kind ..." 45 40
557 29c. Woman, man and rainbow 45 40
558 29c. Mountains ("... and it was good.") 45 40
559 29c. Sun and hills 45 40
560 29c. Killer whale and fishes 45 40
561 29c. Fishes ("... and it was good.") 45 40
562 29c. Elephants and squirrel 45 40
563 29c. Orchard and cat ("... and it was very good.") . . 45 40

Nos. 540/63 were issued together, se-tenant, forming six composite designs each covering four stamps.

74 Greg Louganis (diving)

1992. Olympic Games, Barcelona. Six sheets, each 80 × 110 mm containing horiz design as T **74** showing outstanding competitors.
MS564 Six sheets. (a) 50c. Type **74**; (b) 50c. Dawn Fraser (swimming); (c) 50c. Carl Lewis (track and field); (d) 50c. Bob Beamon (long jumping); (e) 50c. Olga Korbutt (gymnast); (f) 50c. Dick Fosbury (high jumping) . . . . 4·75 4·00

75 Presley and Dove

1992. 15th Death Anniv of Elvis Presley (entertainer). Multicoloured.
565 29c. Type **75** 55 50
566 29c. Presley and dove's wing 55 50
567 29c. Presley in yellow cape 55 50
568 29c. Presley in white and red shirt ($\frac{3}{4}$ face) 55 50
569 29c. Presley singing into microphone 55 50
570 29c. Presley crying 55 50
571 29c. Presley in red shirt ($\frac{3}{4}$ face) 55 50
572 29c. Presley in purple shirt (full face) 55 50
573 29c. Presley (left profile) . . . 55 50

76 Grumman Avenger

1992. Air. Pacific Theatre in Second World War (2nd issue). Aircraft. Multicoloured.
574 50c. Type **76** 85 75
575 50c. Curtiss P-40C of the Flying Tigers fighters . . . 85 75
576 50c. Mitsubishi Zero-Sen fighter 85 75
577 50c. Hawker Hurricane Mk I fighter 85 75
578 50c. Consolidated Catalina flying boat 85 75
579 50c. Curtiss Hawk 75 fighter 85 75
580 50c. Boeing Flying Fortress bomber 85 75
581 50c. Brewster Buffalo fighter 85 75
582 50c. Vickers Supermarine Walrus flying boat 85 75
583 50c. Curtiss Kittyhawk I fighter 85 75

77 "Thus Every Beast"

1992. Christmas. "The Friendly Beasts" (carol). Multicoloured.
584 29c. Type **77** 45 40
585 29c. "By Some Good Spell" 45 40
586 29c. "In the Stable Dark was Glad to Tell" 45 40
587 29c. "Of the Gift He Gave Emanuel" (angel on donkey) 45 40
588 29c. "The Gift He Gave Emanuel" (Palau fruit doves) 45 40

78 Dugong

1993. Animals. Multicoloured.
589 50c. Type **78** 70 60
590 50c. Blue-faced booby ("Masked Booby") 70 60
591 50c. Crab-eating macaque . . 70 60
592 50c. New Guinea crocodile 70 60

79 Giant Deepwater Crab

1993. Seafood. Multicoloured.
593 29c. Type **79** 45 40
594 29c. Scarlet shrimp 45 40
595 29c. Smooth nylon shrimp . . 45 40
596 29c. Armed nylon shrimp . . 45 40

80 Oceanic White-tipped Shark

1993. Sharks. Multicoloured.
597 50c. Type **80** 70 60
598 50c. Great hammerhead . . . 70 60
599 50c. Zebra ("Leopard") shark 70 60
600 50c. Black-finned reef shark 70 60

81 U.S.S. "Tranquility" (hospital ship) **82** Girl with Goat

1993. Pacific Theatre in Second World War (3rd issue). Multicoloured.
601 29c. Capture of Guadalcanal 50 45
602 29c. Type **81** 50 45
603 29c. New Guineans drilling 50 45
604 29c. Americans land in New Georgia 50 45
605 29c. U.S.S. "California" (battleship) 50 45
606 29c. Douglas Dauntless dive bombers over Wake Island 50 45
607 29c. Flame-throwers on Tarawa 50 45
608 29c. American advance on Makin 50 45
609 29c. North American B-25 Mitchells bomb Simpson Harbour, Rabaul 50 45
610 29c. Aerial bombardment of Kwajalein 50 45

1992. Christmas. Multicoloured.
611 29c. Type **82** 45 40
612 29c. Children with garlands and goats 45 40
613 29c. Father Christmas . . . 45 40
614 29c. Musicians and singer . . 45 40
615 29c. Family carrying food . . 45 40

83 Pterosaur **85** Flukes of Whale's Tail

84 "After Child-birth Ceremony" (Charlie Gibbons)

1993. Monsters of the Pacific. Multicoloured.
616 29c. Type **83** 45 40
617 29c. Outrigger canoe 45 40
618 29c. Head of plesiosaur . . . 45 40
619 29c. Pterosaur and neck of plesiosaur 45 40
620 29c. Pterosaur (flying towards left) 45 40
621 29c. Giant crab 45 40
622 29c. Tentacles of squid and two requiem sharks 45 40
623 29c. Hammerhead shark, tentacle of squid and neck of plesiosaur 45 40
624 29c. Head of lake serpent . . 45 40
625 29c. Hammerhead shark and neck of serpent 45 40
626 29c. Squid ("Kraken") . . . 45 40
627 29c. Manta ray, tentacles of squid and body of plesiosaur 45 40
628 29c. Three barracudas and body of plesiosaur 45 40
629 29c. Angelfishes and serpent's claw 45 40
630 29c. Octopus and body of serpent 45 40
631 29c. Nautilus and body of plesiosaur 45 40
632 29c. Moorish idols (two striped fishes) 45 40
633 29c. Lionfish 45 40
634 29c. Squid 45 40
635 29c. Requiem shark and body of kronosaur 45 40
636 29c. Zebra shark and sea-bed 45 40
637 29c. Squid and sea-bed . . . 45 40
638 29c. Giant nautilus and tail of serpent 45 40
639 29c. Head of kronosaur . . . 45 40
640 29c. Lionfish, body of kronosaur and sea-bed . . 45 40

Nos. 616/40 were issued together, se-tenant, forming a composite design.

1993. International Year of Indigenous Peoples. Multicoloured.
641 29c. Type **84** 85 75
642 29c. "Village in Early Palau" (Charlie Gibbons) 85 75
MS643 112 × 96 mm. $290 "Quarrying of Stone Money" (storyboard carving, Ngiraibuuch Skebong) (37 × 50 mm) . . . . 4·25 3·75

1993. Jonah and The Whale. Multicoloured.
644 29c. Type **85** 45 40
645 29c. Bird and part of fluke 45 40
646 29c. Two birds 45 40
647 29c. Kaeb (canoe) 45 40
648 29c. Sun, birds and dolphin 45 40
649 29c. Shark and whale's tail 45 40
650 29c. Shoal of brown fishes and part of whale 45 40
651 29c. Hammerhead shark, shark's tail and fishes . . . 45 40
652 29c. Dolphin (fish) and shark's head 45 40
653 29c. Dolphin and fishes . . . 45 40
654 29c. Scombroid and other fishes and part of whale . . 45 40
655 29c. Two turtles swimming across whale's body 45 40
656 29c. Shoal of pink fishes and whale's back 45 40
657 29c. Spotted eagle ray, manta ray and top of whale's head 45 40
658 29c. Two groupers and shoal of small brown fishes . . . 45 40
659 29c. Jellyfish and wrasse (blue fish) 45 40
660 29c. Wrasse, other fishes and whale's dorsal fin 45 40
661 29c. Whale's eye and corner of mouth 45 40
662 29c. Opened mouth 45 40
663 29c. Jonah 45 40
664 29c. Convict tang (yellow and black striped fish) and brain corals on sea bed . . 45 40
665 29c. Hump-headed bannerfishes and sea anenome 45 40
666 29c. Undulate triggerfish (blue-striped) and corals on sea bed 45 40
667 29c. Brown and red striped fish, corals and part of whale's jaw 45 40
668 29c. Two groupers (spotted) on sea bed 45 40

Nos. 644/68 were issued together, se-tenant, forming a composite design.

86 Alfred's Manta

1994. "Hong Kong '94" International Stamp Exhibition. Rays. Multicoloured.
669 40c. Type **86** 60 55
670 40c. Spotted eagle ray . . . 60 55
671 40c. Coachwhip stingray . . 60 55
672 40c. Black-spotted stingray 60 55

87 Crocodile's Head

1994. The Estuarine Crocodile. Multicoloured.
673 20c. Type **87** 45 40
674 20c. Hatchling and eggs . . . 45 40
675 20c. Crocodile swimming underwater 45 40
676 20c. Crocodile half-submerged 45 40

88 Red-footed Booby

1994. Sea Birds. Multicoloured.
677 50c. Type **88** 65 55
678 50c. Great frigate bird . . . 65 55
679 50c. Brown booby 65 55
680 50c. Little pied cormorant . . 65 55

89 U.S. Marines capture Kwajalein

1994. Pacific Theatre in Second World War (4th issue). Multicoloured.
681 29c. Type **89** 45 40
682 29c. Aerial bombardment of Japanese airbase, Truk . . 45 40
683 29c. U.S.S. 284 "Tullibee" (submarine) (Operation Desecrate) 45 40
684 29c. Landing craft storming Saipan beach 45 40
685 29c. Shooting down Japanese Mitsubishi Zero-Sen bombers, Mariana Islands (Turkey Shoot) 45 40
686 29c. Liberated civilians, Guam 45 40
687 29c. U.S. troops taking Peleliu 45 40
688 29c. Securing Angaur 45 40
689 29c. General Douglas MacArthur 45 40
690 29c. U.S. Army memorial . . 45 40

90 Allied Warships

1994. 50th Anniv of D-day (Allied Landings in Normandy). Multicoloured.
691 50c. C-47 transport aircraft dropping paratroopers . . 75 65
692 50c. Type **90** 75 65
693 50c. Troops disembarking from landing craft 75 65
694 50c. Tanks coming ashore . . 75 65
695 50c. Sherman tank crossing minefield 75 65
696 50c. Aircraft attacking German positions 75 65
697 50c. Gliders dropping paratroops behind lines . . 75 65
698 50c. Pegasus Bridge 75 65
699 50c. Allied forces pushing inland 75 65
700 50c. Beach at end of 6 June 1944 . . . . 75 65

91 Baron Pierre de Coubertin (founder of modern games)

1994. Centenary of International Olympic Committee. Multicoloured.
701 29c. Type **91** 50 45
MS702 Six sheets each 110 × 80 mm. (a) 50c. Anne-Marie Moser (skater) (vert); (b) 50c. James Craig (ice hockey) (vert); (c) $1 Eric Heiden (speed skater) (vert); (d) $1 Nancy Kerrigan (ice skater); (f) $2 Dan Jansen (speed skater) holding child and flowers . . . 8·50 7·50

92 Top of "Saturn V" Rocket and Command and Lunar Modules joined **93** Sail-finned Goby

1994. 25th Anniv of First Manned Moon Landing. Multicoloured.
703 29c. Type **92** 50 40
704 29c. Lunar module preparing to land (side view) 50 40
705 29c. Lunar module leaving surface (top view) 50 40
706 29c. Command module (view of circular end) 50 40
707 29c. Earth viewed from Moon 50 40
708 29c. "Saturn V" third stage 50 40
709 29c. Neil Armstrong descending ladder to lunar surface 50 40
710 29c. Footprint in lunar surface 50 40
711 29c. Alan Shepard and lunar module on Moon 50 40
712 29c. Command module separating from service module 50 40
713 29c. "Saturn V" second stage (rocket inscr "USA USA") 50 40
714 29c. Rear view of "Apollo 17" astronaut at Splitrock Valley of Taurus-Littrow 50 40
715 29c. Lunar module reflected in visor of Edwin Aldrin 50 40
716 29c. James Irwin and David Scott raising flag on "Apollo 15" mission . . . 50 40
717 29c. Command module descending with parachutes deployed 50 40
718 29c. "Saturn V" lifting off from Kennedy Space Center 50 40
719 29c. "Apollo 17" astronaut Harrison Schmitt collecting lunar surface samples with shovel 50 40
720 29c. "Apollo 16" astronaut John Young and lunar rover vehicle 50 40
721 29c. "Apollo 12" astronaut Charles Conrad collecting samples with machine . . . 50 40
722 29c. Command module after splashdown 50 40

Nos. 703/22 were issued together, se-tenant, forming a composite design.

1994. "Philakorea 1994" International Stamp Exhibition, Seoul. Philatelic Fantasies. Designs showing named animal with various postal items. Multicoloured.
723 29c. Type **93** (postage) . . . 50 45
724 29c. Black-saddled ("Sharpnose") puffers . . . 50 45
725 29c. Lightning butterflyfish 50 45
726 29c. Clown anemonefish . . 50 45
727 29c. Parrotfish 50 45
728 29c. Narrow-banded batfish 50 45
729 29c. Clown triggerfish 50 45
730 29c. Twin-spotted wrasse . . 50 45
731 40c. Palau fruit bat 70 60
732 40c. Crocodile 70 60
733 40c. Dugong 70 60
734 40c. Banded sea snake . . . 70 60
735 40c. Bottle-nosed dolphin . . 70 60
736 40c. Hawksbill turtle 70 60
737 40c. Common octopus . . . 70 60
738 40c. Manta ray 70 60
739 50c. Palau fantail and chicks (air) 85 75
740 50c. Banded crake 85 75
741 50c. Grey-rumped ("Island") swiftlets 85 75
742 50c. Micronesian kingfisher 85 75
743 50c. Red-footed booby . . . 85 75
744 50c. Great frigate bird . . . 85 75

745 50c. Palau scops owl 85 75
746 50c. Palau fruit dove 85 75

1994. 50th Anniv of American Invasion of Peleliu. No. **MS**391 optd **50th ANNIVERSARY INVASION OF PELEUU SEPTEMBER 1994**.
MS747 105 × 53 mm. $1 multicoloured 1·70 1·50

95 Micronesian Monument (Henrik Starcke), U.N. Headquarters

97 Tebruchel in Mother's Arms

96 Mickey and Minnie Mouse at Airport

1994. Attainment of Independence. Multicoloured.
748 29c. Type **95** 45 40
749 29c. Presidential seal 45 40
750 29c. Pres. Kuniwo Nakamura of Palau and Pres. William Clinton of United States shaking hands (56 × 41 mm) 45 40
751 29c. Palau and United States flags 45 40
752 29c. Score of "Belau Er Kid" (national anthem) 45 40
Nos. 748/52 were issued together, se-tenant, forming a composite design.

1994. Tourism. Walt Disney cartoon characters. Multicoloured.
753 29c. Type **96** 50 40
754 29c. Goofy on way to hotel 50 40
755 29c. Donald Duck on beach 50 40
756 29c. Minnie Mouse and Daisy Duck learning Ngloik (dance) 50 40
757 29c. Mickey and Minnie rafting to natural bridge 50 40
758 29c. Uncle Scrooge finding stone money in Babeldaob Jungle 50 40
759 29c. Goofy and napoleon wrasse after collision 50 40
760 29c. Minnie visiting clam garden 50 40
761 29c. Grandma Duck weaving basket 50 40
MS762 Three sheets each 127 × 101 mm. (a) $1 Mickey diving on shipwreck; (b) $1 Donald visiting Airai Bai on Babeldaob; (c) $2.90 Pluto and Mickey visiting Second World War aircraft wreck 6·25 5·50

1994. International Year of the Family. Illustrating story of Tebruchel. Multicoloured.
763 20c. Type **97** 30 25
764 20c. Tebruchel's father (kneeling on beach) 30 25
765 20c. Tebruchel as youth 30 25
766 20c. Tebruchel's wife (standing on beach) 30 25
767 20c. Tebruchel with catch of fish 30 25
768 20c. Tebruchel's pregnant wife sitting in house 30 25
769 20c. Tebruchel's aged mother in dilapidated house 30 25
770 20c. Tebruchel's aged father (standing) 30 25
771 20c. Tebruchel holding first child 30 25
772 20c. Tebruchel's wife (sitting on beach mat) 30 25
773 20c. Tebruchel with aged mother 30 25
774 20c. Tebruchel's father (sitting cross-legged) and wife holding child 30 25
Nos. 763/74 were issued together, se-tenant, forming a composite design.

98 Wise Men and Cherubs

99 Bora Milutinovic (coach)

1994. Christmas. "O Little Town of Bethlehem" (carol). Multicoloured.
775 29c. Type **98** 45 40
776 29c. Angel, shepherds with sheep and cherub 45 40
777 29c. Angels and Madonna and Child 45 40
778 29c. Angels, Bethlehem and shepherd with sheep 45 40
779 29c. Cherubs and Palau fruit doves 45 40
Nos. 775/9 were issued together, se-tenant, forming a composite design.

1994. World Cup Football Championship, U.S.A. Multicoloured.
780 29c. Type **99** 45 40
781 29c. Cle Kooiman 45 40
782 29c. Ernie Stewart 45 40
783 29c. Claudio Reyna 45 40
784 29c. Thomas Dooley 45 40
785 29c. Alexi Lalas 45 40
786 29c. Dominic Kinnear 45 40
787 29c. Frank Klopas 45 40
788 29c. Paul Caligiuri 45 40
789 29c. Marcelo Balboa 45 40
790 29c. Cobi Jones 45 40
791 29c. U.S.A. flag and World Cup trophy 45 40
792 29c. Tony Meola 45 40
793 29c. John Doyle 45 40
794 29c. Eric Wynalda 45 40
795 29c. Roy Wegerle 45 40
796 29c. Fernando Clavijo 45 40
797 29c. Hugo Perez 45 40
798 29c. John Harkes 45 40
799 29c. Mike Lapper 45 40
800 29c. Mike Sorber 45 40
801 29c. Brad Friedel 45 40
802 29c. Tab Ramos 45 40
803 29c. Joe-Max Moore 45 40
804 50c. Babeto (Brazil) 75 65
805 50c. Romario (Brazil) 75 65
806 50c. Franco Baresi (Italy) 75 65
807 50c. Roberto Baggio (Italy) 75 65
808 50c. Andoni Zubizarreta (Spain) 75 65
809 50c. Oleg Salenko (Russia) 75 65
810 50c. Gheorghe Hagi (Rumania) 75 65
811 50c. Dennis Bergkamp (Netherlands) 75 65
812 50c. Hristo Stoichkov (Bulgaria) 75 65
813 50c. Tomas Brolin (Sweden) 75 65
814 50c. Lothar Matthaus (Germany) 75 65
815 50c. Arrigo Sacchi (Italy coach), Carlos Alberto Parreira (Brazil coach), flags and World Cup trophy 75 65

100 Yellow Boxfish ("Cube Trunkfish")

101 Presley

1995. Fishes. Multicoloured.
816 1c. Type **100** 15 15
817 2c. Lionfish 15 15
818 3c. Scarlet-finned ("Long-jawed") squirrelfish 15 15
819 4c. Harlequin ("Longnose") filefish 15 15
820 5c. Ornate butterflyfish 15 15
821 10c. Yellow seahorse 15 15
822 20c. Magenta dottyback (22 × 30 mm) 25 25
836 20c. Magenta dottyback ($17\frac{1}{2}$ × 21 mm) 25 15
823 32c. Reef lizardfish (22 × 30 mm) 40 35
837 32c. Reef lizardfish ($17\frac{1}{2}$ × 21 mm) 40 30
824 50c. Multibarred goatfish 60 55
825 55c. Barred blenny 65 55
826 $1 Fingerprint pufferfish 1·30 1·10
827 $2 Long-nosed hawkfish 2·50 2·30
828 $3 Mandarin fish 4·00 3·50
829 $5 Palette ("Blue") surgeonfish 6·75 6·00
830 $10 Coral hind (47 × 30 mm) 14·00 12·00

1995. 60th Birth Anniv of Elvis Presley (entertainer). Multicoloured.
838 32c. Type **101** 50 45
839 32c. Presley wearing white shirt and blue jacket 50 45
840 32c. Presley with microphone and flower 50 45
841 32c. Presley wearing blue shirt and jumper 50 45
842 32c. Presley with rose 50 45
843 32c. Presley with brown hair wearing white shirt 50 45
844 32c. Presley wearing blue open-necked shirt 50 45
845 32c. Presley (in green shirt) singing 50 45
846 32c. Presley as boy (with fair hair) 50 45

102 Grey-rumped ("Palau") Swiftlets

1995. Air. Birds. Multicoloured.
847 50c. Type **102** 75 65
848 50c. Barn swallows 75 65
849 50c. Jungle nightjar 75 65
850 50c. White-breasted wood swallow 75 65

103 "Unyu Maru 2" (tanker)

1995. Japanese Fleet Sunk off Rock Islands (1944). Multicoloured.
851 32c. Type **103** 50 40
852 32c. "Wakatake" (destroyer) 50 40
853 32c. "Teshio Maru" (freighter) 50 40
854 32c. "Raizan Maru" (freighter) 50 40
855 32c. "Chuyo Maru" (freighter) 50 40
856 32c. "Shinsei Maru" (No. 18 freighter) 50 40
857 32c. "Urakami Maru" (freighter) 50 40
858 32c. "Ose Maru" (tanker) 50 40
859 32c. "Iro" (tanker) 50 40
860 32c. "Shosei Maru" (freighter) 50 40
861 32c. Patrol Boat 31 50 40
862 32c. "Kibi Maru" (freighter) 50 40
863 32c. "Amatsu Maru" (tanker) 50 40
864 32c. "Gozan Maru" (freighter) 50 40
865 32c. "Matuei Maru" (freighter) 50 40
866 32c. "Nagisan Maru" (freighter) 50 40
867 32c. "Akashi" (repair ship) 50 40
868 32c. "Kamikazi Maru" (freighter) 50 40
Nos. 851/68 were issued together, se-tenant, forming a composite design.

104 "Pteranodon sternbergi"

1995. 25th Anniv of Earth Day. Prehistoric Winged Animals. Multicoloured.
869 32c. Type **104** 50 40
870 32c. "Pteranodon ingens" 50 40
871 32c. Pterodactyls 50 40
872 32c. Dorygnathus 50 40
873 32c. Dimorphodon 50 40
874 32c. Nyctosaurus 50 40
875 32c. "Pterodactylus kochi" 50 40
876 32c. Ornithodesmus 50 40
877 32c. "Diatryma" sp. 50 40
878 32c. Archaeopteryx 50 40
879 32c. Campylognathoides 50 40
880 32c. Gallodactylus 50 40
881 32c. Batrachognathus 50 40
882 32c. Scaphognathus 50 40
883 32c. Peteinosaurus 50 40
884 32c. "Ichthyornis" sp. 50 40
885 32c. Ctenochasma 50 40
886 32c. Rhamphorhynchus 50 40
Nos. 869/86 were issued together, se-tenant, forming a composite design.

105 Fairey Delta 2

1995. Research and Experimental Jet-propelled Aircraft. Multicoloured.
887 50c. Type **105** 75 65
888 50c. B-70 Valkyrie 75 65
889 50c. Douglas X-3 Stiletto 75 65
890 50c. Northrop/Nasa HL-10 75 65
891 50c. Bell XS-1 75 65
892 50c. Tupolev Tu-144 75 65
893 50c. Bell X-1 75 65
894 50c. Boulton Paul P.111 75 65
895 50c. EWR VJ 101C 75 65
896 50c. Handley Page HP-115 75 65
897 50c. Rolls Royce TMR "Flying Bedstead" 75 65
898 50c. North American X-15 75 65
MS899 $2 Concorde (84 × 28 mm) (postage) 3·00 2·75

106 Scuba Gear

1995. Submersibles. Multicoloured.
900 32c. Type **106** 50 40
901 32c. Cousteau midget submarine "Denise" 50 40
902 32c. Jim suit 50 40
903 32c. Beaver IV 50 40
904 32c. "Ben Franklin" 50 40
905 32c. U.S.S. "Nautilus" (submarine) 50 40
906 32c. Deep Rover 50 40
907 32c. Beebe bathysphere 50 40
908 32c. "Deep Star IV" 50 40
909 32c. U.S. Navy Deep Submergence Rescue Vehicle 50 40
910 32c. "Aluminaut" (aluminium submarine) 50 40
911 32c. "Nautile" 50 40
912 32c. "Cyana" 50 40
913 32c. French Navy (F.N.R.S.) bathyscaphe 50 40
914 32c. Woods Hole Oceanographic Institute's "Alvin" 50 40
915 32c. "Mir I" (research submarine) 50 40
916 32c. "Archimede" (bathyscaphe) 50 40
917 32c. "Trieste" (bathyscaphe) 50 40
Nos. 900/917 were issued together, se-tenant, forming a composite design.

107 Dolphins, Diver and Pufferfish

1995. "Singapore'95" International Stamp Exhibition. Marine Life. Multicoloured.
918 32c. Type **107** 50 40
919 32c. Turtle and diver 50 40
920 32c. Grouper, anemonefish and crab on sea-bed (emblem on right) 50 40
921 32c. Parrotfish, lionfish and angelfish (emblem on left) 50 40

108 Dove in Helmet (Peace)

1995. 50th Annivs of U.N.O. and F.A.O. Mult.
922 60c. Type **108** 85 75
923 60c. Ibedul Gibbons (Palau chief) in flame (human rights) 85 75
924 60c. Palau atlas in open book (education) 85 75
925 60c. Bananas in tractor (agriculture) 85 75
MS926 Two sheets each 116 × 83 mm. (a) $2 National flag and Palau fruit dove; (b) $2 Irrigation of crops and anniversary emblem (FAO) (vert) 5·75 5·00
Nos. 922/5 were issued together, se-tenant, the centre of each block forming a composite design of the U.N. emblem.

109 Palau Fruit Doves

1995. 1st Anniv of Independence. Each showing Palau national flag. Multicoloured.
927 20c. Type **109** 35 30
928 20c. Rock Islands 35 30
929 20c. Map of Palau islands . . 35 30
930 20c. Orchid and hibiscus . . 35 30
931 32c. Raccoon butterflyfish, soldierfish and conch shell 35 30

110 "Preparing Tin-Fish" (William Draper)

1995. 50th Anniv of the End of Second World War. Multicoloured.
932 32c. Type **110** 50 45
933 32c. "Hellcat's Take-off into Palau's Rising Sun" (Draper) 50 45
934 32c. "Dauntless Dive Bombers over Malakal Harbor" (Draper) 50 45
935 32c. "Planes Return from Palau" (Draper) 50 45
936 32c. "Communion Before Battle" (Draper) 50 45
937 32c. "The Landing" (Draper) 50 45
938 32c. "First Task Ashore" (Draper) 50 45
939 32c. "Fire Fighters save Flak-torn Pilot" (Draper) . . . 50 45
940 32c. "Young Marine Headed for Peleliu" (Tom Lea) . . 50 45
941 32c. "Peleliu" (Lea) 50 45
942 32c. "Last Rites" (Lea) . . . 50 45
943 32c. "The Thousand Yard Stare" (Lea) 50 45
944 60c. "Admiral Chester W. Nimitz" (Albert Murray) (vert) . . . . . . 1·00 90
945 60c. "Admiral William F. Halsey" (Murray) (vert) 1·00 90
946 60c. "Admiral Raymond A. Spruance" (Murray) (vert) . . . . 1·00 90
947 60c. "Vice-Admiral Marc A. Mitscher" (Murray) (vert) . . . . 1·00 90
948 60c. "General Holland M. Smith" (Murray) (vert) 1·00 90
MS949 129 × 90 mm. $3 Nose art on B-29 bomber Bock's Car (38 × 24½ mm) . . . . 4·25 3·75

111 Angel with Animals

1995. Christmas. "We Three Kings of Orient Are" (carol). Multicoloured.
950 32c. Type **111** 50 40
951 32c. Two wise men 50 40
952 32c. Shepherd at crib 50 40
953 32c. Wise man and shepherd 50 40
954 32c. Children with goat . . . 50 40
Nos. 950/4 were issued together, se-tenant, forming a composite design.

112 Mother and Young in Feeding Area

1995. Year of the Sea Turtle. Multicoloured.
955 32c. Type **112** 60 55
956 32c. Young adult females meeting males 60 55
957 32c. Sun, cockerel in tree and mating area 60 55
958 32c. Woman and hatchlings 60 55
959 32c. Couple and nesting area 60 55
960 32c. House and female swimming to lay eggs . . . 60 55

Nos. 955/60 were issued together, se-tenant, forming a composite design of the turtle's life cycle.

113 Lennon

114 Rats leading Procession

1995. 15th Death Anniv of John Lennon (entertainer).
961 **113** 32c. multicoloured 85 75

1996. Chinese New Year. Year of the Rat. Multicoloured.
962 10c. Type **114** 25 25
963 10c. Three rats playing instruments 25 25
964 10c. Rats playing tuba and banging drum 25 25
965 10c. Family of rats outside house 25 25
MS966 131 × 63 mm. 60c. Family of rats outside house and rats playing tuba and banging drum (56 × 42 mm); (b) 60c. Rats playing instruments and leading procession (56 × 42 mm) (air) 2·20 1·90
Nos. 962/5 were issued together, se-tenant, forming a composite design of a procession.

115 Girls

1996. 50th Anniv of UNICEF. Each showing three children. Multicoloured.
967 32c. Type **115** 50 45
968 32c. Girl in centre wearing lei around neck 50 45
969 32c. Girl in centre wearing headscarf 50 45
970 32c. Boy in centre and girls holding bunches of grass 50 45
Nos. 967/70 were issued together, se-tenant, forming a composite design of the children around a globe and the UNICEF emblem.

116 Basslet and Vermiculate Parrotfish ("P")

1996. Underwater Wonders. Illuminated letters spelling out PALAU. Multicoloured.
971 32c. Type **116** 50 45
972 32c. Yellow-striped cardinalfish ("A") 50 45
973 32c. Pair of atoll butterflyfish ("L") 50 45
974 32c. Starry moray and slate-pencil sea urchin ("A") . . 50 45
975 32c. Blue-streaked cleaner wrasse and coral hind ("Grouper") ("U") 50 45

117 Ferdinand Magellan and "Vitoria"

1996. "CAPEX'96" International Stamp Exhibition, Toronto, Canada. Circumnavigators. Multicoloured.
976 32c. Type **117** (postage) . . . 50 45
977 32c. Charles Wilkes and U.S.S. "Vincennes" (sail frigate) 50 45
978 32c. Joshua Slocum and "Spray" (yacht) 50 45
979 32c. Ben Carlin and "Half-Safe" (amphibian) 50 45
980 32c. Edward Beach and U.S.S. "Triton" (submarine) 50 45
981 32c. Naomi James and "Express Crusader" (yacht) 50 45
982 32c. Sir Ranulf Fiennes and snow vehicle 50 45
983 32c. Rick Hansen and wheelchair 50 45
984 32c. Robin Knox-Johnson and "Enza New Zealand" (catamaran) 50 45
MS985 Two sheets each 110 × 80 mm. (a) $3 Sir Francis Chichester and "Gypsy Moth IV" (yacht); (b) $3 Bob Martin, Mark Sullivan and Troy Bradley and "Odyssey" (helium balloon) . . 9·50 8·25

986 60c. Lowell Smith and Douglas world cruiser seaplanes (air) 95 85
987 60c. Ernst Lehmann and "Graf Zeppelin" (dirigible airship) 95 85
988 60c. Wiley Post and Lockheed Vega "Winnie Mae" 95 85
989 60c. Yuri Gagarin and "Vostok I" (spaceship) . . 95 85
990 60c. Jerrie Mock and Cessna 180 "Spirit of Columbus" 95 85
991 60c. H. Ross Perot jnr. and Bell LongRanger III helicopter "Spirit of Texas" 95 85
992 60c. Brooke Knapp and Gulfstream III "The American Dream" 95 85
993 60c. Jeana Yeager and Dick Rutan and "Voyager" . . 95 85
994 60c. Fred Lasby and Piper Commanche 95 85

118 Simba, Nala and Timon ("The Lion King")

1996. Disney Sweethearts. Multicoloured.
995 1c. Type **118** 15 10
996 2c. Georgette, Tito and Oliver ("Oliver & Company") 15 10
997 3c. Duchess, O'Malley and Marie ("The Aristocats") 15 10
998 4c. Bianca, Jake and Polly ("The Rescuers Down Under") 15 10
999 5c. Tod, Vixey and Copper ("The Fox and the Hound") 15 10
1000 6c. Thumper, Flower and their Sweethearts ("Bambi") 15 10
1001 60c. As No. 995 . . . . . 1·00 90
1002 60c. Bernard, Bianca and Mr. Chairman ("The Rescuers") 85 60
1003 60c. As No. 996 . . . . . 1·00 90
1004 60c. As No. 997 . . . . . 1·00 90
1005 60c. As No. 998 . . . . . 1·00 90
1006 60c. As No. 999 . . . . . 1·00 90
1007 60c. Robin Hood, Maid Marian and Alan-a-Dale ("Robin Hood") . . . . 1·00 90
1008 60c. As No. 1000 . . . . . 1·00 90
1009 60c. Pongo, Perdita and the Puppies ("101 Dalmatians") . . . . . . 1·00 90
MS1010 Two sheets each 110 × 131 mm. (a) $2 Bambi and Faline; (b) $2 Lady ("Lady and the Tramp") (vert) . . . . . . 7·50 6·50

119 Hakeem Olajuwan (basketball)

1996. Centenary of Modern Olympic Games and Olympic Games, Atlanta. Multicoloured.
1011 32c. Type **119** 50 40
1012 32c. Pat McCormick (gymnastics) 50 40
1013 32c. Jim Thorpe (pentathlon and decathlon) 50 40
1014 32c. Jesse Owens (athletics) 50 40
1015 32c. Tatyana Gutsu (gymnastics) 50 40
1016 32c. Michael Jordan (basketball) 50 40
1017 32c. Fu Mingxia (diving) . . 50 40
1018 32c. Robert Zmelik (decathlon) 50 40
1019 32c. Ivan Pedroso (long jumping) 50 40
1020 32c. Nadia Comaneci (gymnastics) 50 40
1021 32c. Jackie Joyner-Kersee (long jumping) 50 40
1022 32c. Michael Johnson (running) 50 40
1023 32c. Kristin Otto (swimming) 50 40
1024 32c. Vitai Scherbo (gymnastics) 50 40
1025 32c. Johnny Weissmuller (swimming) 50 40
1026 32c. Babe Didrikson (track and field athlete) 50 40
1027 32c. Eddie Tolan (track athlete) 50 40
1028 32c. Krisztina Egerszegi (swimming) 50 40
1029 32c. Sawao Kato (gymnastics) . . . . . . 50 1·90
1030 32c. Aleksandr Popov (swimming) 50 45
1031 40c. Fanny Blankers-Koen (track and field athlete) (vert) 60 55
1032 40c. Bob Mathias (decathlon) (vert) 60 55
1033 60c. Torchbearer entering Wembley Stadium, 1948 60 55
1034 60c. Entrance to Olympia Stadium, Athens, and flags 60 55
Nos. 1011/30 were issued together, se-tenant, forming a composite design of the athletes and Olympic rings.

120 The Creation

1996. 3000th Anniv of Jerusalem. Illustrations by Guy Rowe from "In Our Image: Character Studies from the Old Testament". Mult.
1035 20c. Type **120** 35 30
1036 20c. Adam and Eve 35 30
1037 20c. Noah and his Wife . . 35 30
1038 20c. Abraham 35 30
1039 20c. Jacob's Blessing 35 30
1040 20c. Jacob becomes Israel 35 30
1041 20c. Joseph and his Brethren 35 30
1042 20c. Moses and Burning Bush 35 30
1043 20c. Moses and the Tablets 35 30
1044 20c. Balaam 35 30
1045 20c. Joshua 35 30
1046 20c. Gideon 35 30
1047 20c. Jephthah 35 30
1048 20c. Samson 35 30
1049 20c. Ruth and Naomi . . . 35 30
1050 20c. Saul anointed 35 30
1051 20c. Saul denounced 35 30
1052 20c. David and Jonathan . . 35 30
1053 20c. David and Nathan . . 35 30
1054 20c. David mourns 35 30
1055 20c. Solomon praying . . . 35 30
1056 20c. Solomon judging . . . 35 30
1057 20c. Elijah 35 30
1058 20c. Elisha 35 30
1059 20c. Job 35 30
1060 20c. Isaiah 35 30
1061 20c. Jeremiah 35 30
1062 20c. Ezekiel 35 30
1063 20c. Nebuchadnezzar's Dream 35 30
1064 20c. Amos 35 30

121 Nankeen Night Heron

1996. Birds over Palau Lagoon. Multicoloured.
1065 50c. Eclectus parrot (female) ("Iakkotsiang") 85 70
1066 50c. Type **121** 85 70
1067 50c. Micronesian pigeon ("Belochel") 85 70
1068 50c. Eclectus parrot (male) ("Iakkotsiang") 85 70
1069 50c. White tern ("Sechosech") 85 70
1070 50c. Common noddy ("Mechadelbedaoch") . . 85 70
1071 50c. Nicobar pigeon ("Laib") 85 70
1072 50c. Chinese little bittern ("Cheloteachel") 85 70
1073 50c. Little pied cormorant ("Deroech") 85 70
1074 50c. Black-naped tern ("Kerkirs") 85 70
1075 50c. White-tailed tropic bird ("Dudek") 85 70
1076 50c. Sulphur-crested cockatoo ("Iakkotsiang") (white bird) 85 70
1077 50c. White-capped noddy ("Bedaoch") 85 70
1078 50c. Bridled tern ("Bedebedchakl") 85 70

1079 50c. Reef heron (grey) ("Sechou") 85 70
1080 50c. Grey-tailed tattler ("Kekereielderariik") . . 85 70
1081 50c. Reef heron (white) ("Sechou") 85 70
1082 50c. Audubon's shearwater ("Ochaieu") 85 70
1083 50c. Black-headed gull ("Oltirakladial") 85 70
1084 50c. Ruddy turnstone ("Omechederiibabad") . . 85 70

Nos. 1065/84 were issued together, se-tenant, forming a composite design.

122 Lockheed U-2

1996. Spy Planes. Multicoloured.
1085 40c. Type **122** 70 60
1086 40c. General Dynamics EF-111A 70 60
1087 40c. Lockheed YF-12A . . 70 60
1088 40c. Lockheed SR-71 . . . 70 60
1089 40c. Teledyne Ryan Tier II Plus 70 60
1090 40c. Lockheed XST 70 60
1091 40c. Lockheed ER-2 . . . . 70 60
1092 40c. Lockheed F-117A Nighthawk 70 60
1093 40c. Lockheed EC-130E . . 70 60
1094 40c. Ryan Firebee 70 60
1095 40c. Lockheed Martin/ Boeing Darkstar 70 60
1096 40c. Boeing E-3A Sentry . . 70 60
MS1097 120 × 90 mm. $3 Northrop B-2A Stealth Bomber (41 × 56 mm) . . . . 5·25 4·50

123 "The Birth of a New Nation"

1996. 2nd Anniv of Independence. Illustrations from "Kirie" by Koh Sekiguchi. Multicoloured.
1098 20c. Type **123** 35 30
1099 20c. "In the Blue Shade of Trees" 35 30

124 Pandanus

1996. Christmas. "O Tannenbaum" (carol). Decorated Trees. Multicoloured.
1100 32c. Type **124** 55 50
1101 32c. Mangrove 55 50
1102 32c. Norfolk Island pine . . 55 50
1103 32c. Papaya 55 50
1104 32c. Casuarina 55 50

Nos. 1100/4 were issued together, se-tenant, forming a composite design.

125 "Viking I" in Orbit (½-size illustration)

1996. Space Missions to Mars. Multicoloured.
1105 32c. Type **125** 55 50
1106 32c. "Viking I" emblem (top half) 55 50
1107 32c. "Mars Lander" firing de-orbit engines 55 50
1108 32c. "Viking I" emblem (bottom half) 55 50
1109 32c. Phobos (Martian moon) 55 50
1110 32c. "Mars Lander" entering Martian atmosphere 55 50
1111 32c. "Mariner 9" (first mission, 1971) 55 50
1112 32c. Parachute opens for landing and heat shield jettisons 55 50
1113 32c. Projected U.S./Russian manned spacecraft, 21st century (top half) 55 50
1114 32c. "Lander" descent engines firing 55 50
1115 32c. Projected U.S./Russian spacecraft (bottom half) 55 50
1116 32c. "Viking I Lander" on Martian surface, 1976 . . 55 50
MS1117 Two sheets each 98 × 78 mm. (a) $3 Mars Rover (projected 1997 mission) (37 × 30 mm); (b) $3 Water probe (projected 1999 mission) . . . 10·50 9·25

Nos. 1105/16 were issued together, se-tenant, forming several composite designs.

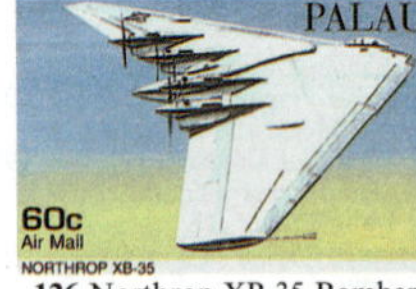

126 Northrop XB-35 Bomber

1996. Oddities of the Air. Aircraft Designs. Multicoloured.
1118 60c. Type **126** . . . . . . 1·00 90
1119 60c. Leduc O.21 . . . . . 1·00 90
1120 60c. Convair Model 118 flying car . . . . 1·00 90
1121 60c. Blohm und Voss BV 141 . . . . 1·00 90
1122 60c. Vought V-173 . . . . 1·00 90
1123 60c. McDonnell XF-85 Goblin . . . . 1·00 90
1124 60c. North American F-82B Twin Mustang fighter . . 1·00 90
1125 60c. Lockheed XFV-1 vertical take-off fighter . . 1·00 90
1126 60c. Northrop XP-79B . . . 1·00 90
1127 60c. Saunders Roe SR/A1 flying boat fighter . . . . 1·00 90
1128 60c. "Caspian Sea Monster" hovercraft . . . . 1·00 90
1129 60c. Grumman X-29 demonstrator . . . . . . 1·00 90
MS1130 $3 Martin Marieeta X-24B (84 × 28 mm) . . . . 5·25 4·50

127 Ox Cart

1997. Chinese New Year. Year of the Ox. Sheet 76 × 106 mm.
MS1131 **127** $2 multicoloured . . 3·50 3·00

128 Emblem

1997. 50th Anniv of South Pacific Commission. Sheet 103 × 70 mm.
MS1132 **128** $1 multicoloured . . 1·70 1·50

129 Pemphis

130 "Apollo 15" Command Module splashing-down

1997. "Hong Kong '97" Stamp Exhibition. Flowers. Multicoloured.
1133 1c. Type **129** 15 15
1134 2c. Sea lettuce 15 15
1135 3c. Tropical almond 15 15
1136 4c. Guettarda 15 15
1137 5c. Pacific coral bean . . . 15 15
1138 32c. Black mangrove . . . 50 45
1139 32c. Cordia 50 45
1140 32c. Lantern tree 50 45
1141 32c. Palau rock-island flower 50 45
1142 50c. Fish-poison tree 70 60
1143 50c. Indian mulberry . . . 70 60
1144 50c. Pacific poison-apple . . 70 60
1145 50c. "Ailanthus" sp. 70 60
1146 $3 Sea hibiscus (73 × 48 mm) 3·75 2·75

1997. Bicentenary of the Parachute. Multicoloured.
1147 32c. Type **130** (postage) . . 55 50
1148 32c. Skydiving team in formation (40 × 23 mm) 55 50
1149 32c. Cargo drop from airplane 55 50
1150 32c. Parasailing (40 × 23 mm) 55 50
1151 32c. Parachutist falling to earth 55 50
1152 32c. Parachute demonstration team (40 × 23 mm) 55 50
1153 32c. Parachutist falling into sea 55 50
1154 32c. Drag-racing car (40 × 23mm) 55 50
MS1155 Two sheets. (a) 72 × 102 mm. $2 Training tower, Fort Benning, Georgia (27 × 84 mm); (b) 102 × 72 mm. $2 "Funny Car" safety parachute (56 × 42 mm) . . . . 7·00 6·00
1156 60c. Parachuting demonstration (air) . . . 1·00 90
1157 60c. "The Blue Flame" (world land-speed record attempt) (40 × 23 mm) . . 1·00 90
1158 60c. Atmospheric Re-entry Demonstrator (capsule with three canopies) . . . 1·00 90
1159 60c. Spies parachuting behind enemy lines during Second World War (40 × 23 mm) . . . . . . 1·00 90
1160 60c. Andre Jacques Garnerin's first successful parachute descent (from balloon), 1797 . . . . . 1·00 90
1161 60c. C-130E airplane demonstrating Low Altitude Parachute Extraction System (airplane and capsule with four canopies) (40 × 23 mm) . . . . . . 1·00 90
1162 60c. U.S. Army parachutist flying parafoil . . . . . 1·00 90
1163 60c. Parachute (one canopy) slowing high performance airplane (40 × 23mm) . . 1·00 90

131 Pacific Black Duck beneath Banana Tree

1997. Palau's Avian Environment. Multicoloured.
1164 20c. Type **131** 35 30
1165 20c. Pair of red junglefowl beneath calamondin (clustered orange fruits) 35 30
1166 20c. Nicobar pigeon in parinari tree (single orange fruits) 35 30
1167 20c. Cardinal honeyeater in wax apple tree (clustered brown fruits) 35 30
1168 20c. Purple swamphen and Chinese little bittern amid taro plants 35 30
1169 20c. Eclectus parrot in pangi football fruit tree (single brown fruits) 35 30
1170 20c. Micronesian pigeon in rambutan (clustered red fruits) 35 30
1171 20c. Micronesian starlings in mango tree (clustered green fruits) 35 30
1172 20c. Fruit bat in breadfruit tree 35 30
1173 20c. White-collared kingfisher in coconut palm (with sailing dinghy) . . . 35 30
1174 20c. Palau fruit dove in sweet orange tree (single green fruits) 35 30
1175 20c. Chestnut mannikins flying around sour-sop tree and nest 35 30

132 Himeji Temple, Japan

1997. 50th Anniv of UNESCO. Multicoloured.
1176 32c. Type **132** 55 50
1177 32c. Kyoto, Japan 55 50
1178 32c. Pagoda roofs, Himeji Temple (white inscr at left) 55 50
1179 32c. Garden, Himeji Temple 55 50
1180 32c. Path and doorway, Himeji Temple 55 50
1181 32c. Pagoda roofs, Himeji Temple (white inscr at right) 55 50
1182 32c. Roof ridge and decoration, Himeji Temple 55 50
1183 32c. Inscribed post and veranda, Himeji Temple 55 50
1184 60c. Ceiling, Augustusburg Castle, Germany (horiz) 1·00 90
1185 60c. Augustusburg Castle (horiz) . . . . 1·00 90
1186 60c. Falkenlust Castle, Germany (horiz) . . . . 1·00 90
1187 60c. Roman ruins, Trier, Germany (horiz) . . . . 1·00 90
1188 60c. House, Trier (horiz) . . 1·00 90
MS1189 Two sheets each 127 × 102 mm. (a) $2 Tree trunk, Yakushims, Japan (horiz); (b) $2 Forest, Shirakami-Sanchi, Japan (horiz) . . . . 7·00 6·00

133 Darago, Philippines
134 "Swallows and Peach Blossoms under a Full Moon"

1997. "Pacific 97" International Stamp Exhibition, San Francisco. Volcano Goddesses of the Pacific. Multicoloured.
1190 32c. Type **133** 50 45
1191 32c. Fuji, Japan 50 45
1192 32c. Pele, Hawaii 50 45
1193 32c. Pare and Hutu, Polynesia 50 45
1194 32c. Dzalarhons, Haida tribe, North America . . 50 45
1195 32c. Chuginadak, Aleutian Islands, Alaska 50 45

1997. Birth Bicentenary of Ando Hiroshige (Japanese painter). Multicoloured.
1196 32c. Type **134** 65 55
1197 32c. "Parrot on a Flowering Branch" 65 55
1198 32c. "Crane and Rising Sun" 65 55
1199 32c. "Cock, Unbrella and Morning Glories" 65 55
1200 32c. "Titmouse hanging Head Downward on a Camellia Branch" 65 55
MS1201 Two sheets each 102 × 127 mm. (a) $2 Kingfisher and Iris; (b) $2 "Falcon on a Pine Tree with Rising Sun" . . . . 7·00 6·00

135 Bai (community building)

1997. 3rd Anniv of Independence.
1202 **135** 32c. multicoloured . . . 55 50

136 "Albatross" (U.S.A.)

1997. Oceanic Research. Research Vessels (1203/11) or Personalities (**MS**1212). Multicoloured.

1203 32c. Type **136** 55 50
1204 32c. "Mabahiss" (Egypt) . . 55 50
1205 32c. "Atlantis II" (U.S.A.) 55 50
1206 32c. Hans Hass's "Xarifa" (schooner) 55 50
1207 32c. "Meteor" (Germany) 55 50
1208 32c. "Egabras III" (U.S.A.) 55 50
1209 32c. "Discoverer" (U.S.A.) 55 50
1210 32c. "Kaiyo" (Japan) . . . 55 50
1211 32c. "Ocean Defender" (Great Britain) 55 50
MS1212 Three sheets each 110 × 80 mm. (a) $2 Jacques-Yves Cousteau (undersea researcher) (looking to right); (b) $2 Cousteau wearing diving suit (vert); (c) $2 Pete Seeger (folk singer and ecologist) (vert) . . . . 10·50 9·25

137 "I Can Read by Myself"

1997. Literacy Campaign. Walt Disney cartoon characters. Multicoloured.

1213 1c. Type **137** 15 10
1214 2c. "Start Them Young" . . 15 10
1215 3c. "Share your Knowledge" 15 10
1216 4c. "The insatiable Reader" 15 10
1217 5c. "Reading is the ultimate Luxury" 15 10
1218 10c. "Real Men read" . . . 15 10
1219 32c. "Exercise your Right to Read" 50 45
1220 32c. As No. 1217 . . . . . 50 45
1221 32c. As No. 1215 . . . . . 50 45
1222 32c. As No. 1214 . . . . . 50 45
1223 32c. "Reading is fundamental" 50 45
1224 32c. As No. 1216 . . . . . 50 45
1225 32c. "Reading Time is Anytime" 50 45
1226 32c. As No. 1218 . . . . . 50 45
1227 32c. Type **137** 50 45
MS1228 Two sheets. (a) 139 × 114 mm. $2 Daisy Duck carrying books ("The Library is for Everyone"); (b) $3 Mickey Mouse holding book ("Books are Magical") . . . . 8·75 7·50

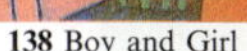

138 Boy and Girl **139** Diana, Princess of Wales

1997. Christmas. "Some Children See Him" (carol). Multicoloured.

1229 32c. Type **138** 55 50
1230 32c. Asian boy and white girl 55 50
1231 32c. Madonna and Child behind boy and girl . . . 55 50
1232 32c. White girl and Oriental children 55 50
1233 32c. Asian boy and Palauan girl 55 50

Nos. 1229/33 were issued together, se-tenant, forming a composite design.

1997. Diana, Princess of Wales Commemoration.
1234 **139** 60c. multicoloured . . . 1·10 95

140 Tiger (paper cutting)

1998. Chinese New Year. Year of the Tiger. Two sheets each 92 × 117 mm.
MS1235 Two sheets. (a) 50c. Type **140**; (b) 50c. Tiger (toy) 1·70 1·50

141 Nucleus of Galaxy M100

1998. Hubble Space Telescope. Multicoloured.

1236 32c. Type **141** 50 45
1237 32c. Top of Hubble telescope 50 45
1238 32c. Astronaut on robot arm 50 45
1239 32c. Astronaut fixing new camera to telescope . . . 50 45
1240 32c. Astronaut in cargo space of shuttle "Endeavour" 50 45
1241 32c. Hubble released after repair 50 45
MS1242 Three sheets each 71 × 110 mm. (a) $2 Edwin Hubble (astronomer); (b) $2 Hubble telescope; (c) $2 Astronauts servicing Hubble telescope . . 10·50 9·25

142 Mother Teresa

1998. Mother Teresa (founder of Missionaries of Charity) Commemoration. Portraits of Mother Teresa. Multicoloured.

1243 60c. Type **142** . . . . . . 1·00 90
1244 60c. Facing right . . . . . 1·00 90
1245 60c. Wearing cross . . . . 1·00 90
1246 60c. Wearing cardigan . . . 1·00 90

143 Ladybird Remotely Operated Vehicle, Japan

1998. International Year of the Ocean. Deep-sea Robots. Multicoloured.

1247 32c. Type **143** 55 50
1248 32c. Slocum Glider 55 50
1249 32c. "Hornet" 55 50
1250 32c. "Scorpio" 55 50
1251 32c. "Odyssey" Autonomous Underwater Vehicle 55 50
1252 32c. Jamstec Survey System launcher, Japan 55 50
1253 32c. "Scarab II" (servicer of undersea telephone cables) 55 50
1254 32c. U.S. Navy torpedo finder 55 50
1255 32c. Jamstec Survey System vehicle, Japan 55 50
1256 32c. Cetus tether for undersea cables 55 50
1257 32c. Deep-sea remotely operated vehicle 55 50
1258 32c. Abe (autonomous benthic explorer) 55 50
1259 32c. OBSS 55 50
1260 32c. Remote controlled vehicle 225G "Swimming Eyeball" (for inspection of undersea oil rigs) 55 50
1261 32c. Japanese Underwater Remotely Operated Vehicle 55 50
1262 32c. Benthos remotely piloted vehicle 55 50
1263 32c. Curv III (cable-controlled underwater research vehicle) 55 50
1264 32c. "Smartie", Great Britain 55 50
MS1265 Two sheets each 88 × 118 mm. (a) $2 "Dolphin 3K", Japan; (b) $2 "Jason jr." 7·00 6·00

1998. "Israel 98" International Stamp Exhibition, Tel Aviv. Nos. 1035/64 optd with emblem.

1266 20c. multicoloured 35 30
1267 20c. multicoloured 35 30
1268 20c. multicoloured 35 30
1269 20c. multicoloured 35 30
1270 20c. multicoloured 35 30
1271 20c. multicoloured 35 30
1272 20c. multicoloured 35 30
1273 20c. multicoloured 35 30
1274 20c. multicoloured 35 30
1275 20c. multicoloured 35 30
1276 20c. multicoloured 35 30
1277 20c. multicoloured 35 30
1278 20c. multicoloured 35 30
1279 20c. multicoloured 35 30
1280 20c. multicoloured 35 30
1281 20c. multicoloured 35 30
1282 20c. multicoloured 35 30
1283 20c. multicoloured 35 30
1284 20c. multicoloured 35 30
1285 20c. multicoloured 35 30
1286 20c. multicoloured 35 30
1287 20c. multicoloured 35 30
1288 20c. multicoloured 35 30
1289 20c. multicoloured 35 30
1290 20c. multicoloured 35 30
1291 20c. multicoloured 35 30
1292 20c. multicoloured 35 30
1293 20c. multicoloured 35 30
1294 20c. multicoloured 35 30
1295 20c. multicoloured 35 30

145 Hut **146** Footballer

1998. The Legend of Orachel. Multicoloured.

1296 40c. Type **145** 70 60
1297 40c. Outrigger canoes moored by hut 55 45
1298 40c. Hut and man in canoe 70 60
1299 40c. Bird in tree 70 60
1300 40c. Front half of three-man canoe 70 60
1301 40c. Rear half of canoe and head of snake 70 60
1302 40c. Crocodile, fishes and coral 70 60
1303 40c. Shark and fishes . . . 70 60
1304 40c. Turtle, jellyfish and body of snake 70 60
1305 40c. Underwater bai (community building) . . 70 60
1306 40c. Orachel swimming underwater and fishes . . 70 60
1307 40c. Coral, fishes and seaweed 70 60

1998. World Cup Football Championship, France. Multicoloured.

1308 50c. Type **146** 85 75
1309 50c. Player in blue and white striped shirt 85 75
1310 50c. Player in green shirt and white shorts 85 75
1311 50c. Player in white shirt and blue shorts 85 75
1312 50c. Player in green shirt and black shorts 85 75
1313 50c. Player in red short-sleeved shirt 85 75
1314 50c. Player in yellow shirt and blue shorts 85 75
1315 50c. Player in red long-sleeved shirt 85 75
MS1316 70 × 64 mm. $3 Pele being tackled . . . . 5·25 4·50

147 Scuba Fishing

1998. 4th Micronesian Islands Games, Palau. Multicoloured.

1317 32c. Type **147** 50 45
1318 32c. Spear throwing 50 45
1319 32c. Swimming 50 45
1320 32c. Coconut throwing . . . 50 45
1321 32c. Games emblem 50 45
1322 32c. Coconut tree climbimg 50 45
1323 32c. Canoe racing 50 45
1324 32c. Coconut husking . . . 50 45
1325 32c. Diving 50 45

148 Rudolph and other Reindeer

1998. Christmas. "Rudolph the Red Nosed Reindeer" (carol). Multicoloured.

1326 32c. Type **148** 55 50
1327 32c. Two reindeer and girl in yellow dress 55 50
1328 32c. Two reindeer, boy and girl 55 50
1329 32c. Two reindeer, girl in long pink dress and star 55 50
1330 32c. Father Christmas and sleigh 55 50

Nos. 1326/30 were issued together, se-tenant, forming a composite design.

149 Princess Dot (ant)

1998. "A Bug's Life" (computer animated film). Multicoloured.

1331 20c. Type **149** 35 30
1332 20c. Heimlich (caterpillar), Francis (ladybird) and Slim (stick insect) 35 30
1333 20c. Hopper (grasshopper) 35 30
1334 20c. Princess Atta (ant) . . 35 30
1335 32c. Princess Atta and Flick (ant) in boat 50 45
1336 32c. Princess Atta and Flick sitting on heart 50 45
1337 32c. Flick with Princess Atta sitting on leaf 50 45
1338 32c. Flick handing Princess Atta a flower 50 45
1339 50c. Butterfly, Heimlich, Francis and other bugs (horiz) 85 75
1340 50c. Slim, Francis and Heimlich (horiz) 85 75
1341 50c. Manny (praying mantis) (horiz) 85 75
1342 50c. Francis (horiz) 85 75
1343 60c. Slim and Flick juggling 1·00 90
1344 60c. Francis on cycle, Heimlich and Slim . . . 1·00 90
1345 60c. Manny hynotizing Flick 1·00 90
1346 60c. Manny, Rosie (spider) and other bugs . . . . 1·00 90
MS1347 Four sheets. (a) 127 × 102 mm. $2 Slim, Francis and Heimlich (75 × 50 mm); (b)127 × 102 mm. $2 Princess Atta and Flick (horiz); (c) 127 × 102 mm. $2 Butterfly; (d) 102 × 127 mm. $2 Francis, Flick and Heimlich (75 × 50 mm) . . 14·00 12·00

150 Group Photograph of Astronauts, 1962

1999. John Glenn's Return to Space. Multicoloured.

1348 60c. Type **150** . . . . . . 1·00 90
1349 60c. Glenn in space helmet (looking straight ahead) 1·00 90
1350 60c. Group photograph of five astronauts . . . . . 1·00 90
1351 60c. Glenn in space helmet (head turned to left) . . . 1·00 90
1352 60c. Glenn in civilian suit 1·00 90
1353 60c. Glenn in space helmet (eyes looking right) . . . 1·00 90

1354 60c. Glenn with Pres. John Kennedy . . . . 1·00 90
1355 60c. Glenn in space suit (bare-headed) ("John Glenn, 1962") . . . . . 1·00 90
1356 60c. Glenn (head raised) . . 1·00 90
1357 60c. "Discovery" (space shuttle) on launch pad . . 1·00 90
1358 60c. Glenn and two fellow astronauts with three NASA employees . . . . 1·00 90
1359 60c. Glenn (wearing glasses and looking straight ahead) . . . . 1·00 90
1360 60c. "Discovery" in hangar 1·00 90
1361 60c. Glenn in space suit (bare-headed) ("John Glenn") . . . . 1·00 90
1362 60c. Glenn (wearing glasses and looking down) . . . 1·00 90
1363 60c. Glenn in space suit and inner helmet . . . . . . 1·00 90
MS1364 Two sheets. (a) 80 × 120 mm. $2 Glenn in 1962 (28 × 41 mm); (b) 110 × 90 mm $2 Glenn in 1998 (28 × 41 mm) . . 7·00 6·00

151 Rachel Carson (naturalist)

1999. Environmental Heroes of the 20th Century. Multicoloured.
1365 33c. Type **151** 55 50
1366 33c. Ding Darling (President of U.S. National Wildlife Federation, 1936) 55 50
1367 33c. David Brower 55 50
1368 33c. Jacques Cousteau (oceanologist) 55 50
1369 33c. Roger Tory Peterson (ornithologist) 55 50
1370 33c. Prince Philip, Duke of Edinburgh (President of World Wide Fund for Nature) 55 50
1371 33c. Joseph Wood Krutch 55 50
1372 33c. Aldo Leopold 55 50
1373 33c. Dian Fossey (zoologist) (wrongly inscr "Diane") 55 50
1374 33c. Al Gore 55 50
1375 33c. Sir David Attenborough (naturalist and broadcaster) 55 50
1376 33c. Paul MacCready (aeronautical engineer) (wrongly inscr "McCready") 55 50
1377 33c. Sting 55 50
1378 33c. Paul Winter 55 50
1379 33c. Ian MacHarg 55 50
1380 33c. Denis Hayes 55 50

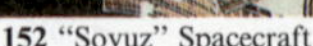

152 "Soyuz" Spacecraft

153 Haruo Remeliik

1999. "Mir" Space Station. Multicoloured.
1381 33c. Type **152** 50 45
1382 33c. "Specktr" science module 50 45
1383 33c. Rear of space shuttle 50 45
1384 33c. "Kuant 2" scientific and air lock module . . . 50 45
1385 33c. "Kristall" technological module 50 45
1386 33c. Front of "Atlantis" (space shuttle) and docking module 50 45
MS1387 Four sheets each 76 × 108 mm. (a) $2 Cosmonaut Valery Polyakov watching from "Mir", 1995; (b) $2 Shannon Lucid and Yury Usachov, 1996; (c) $2 Anatoly Solovyov inspecting damage to "Mir", 1997; (d) $2 Charles Precourt and Talgat Musabayev, 1998 . . . . . . 14·00 12·00

1999.
1388 **153** 1c. multicoloured . . . 15 15
1389 – 2c. multicoloured . . . 15 15
1390 – 20c. multicoloured . . . 35 30
1391 – 22c. multicoloured . . . 40 35
1392 – 33c. multicoloured . . . 55 50
1393 – 50c. multicoloured . . . 85 75
1394 – 55c. multicoloured . . . 95 85
1395 – 60c. multicoloured . . . 1·10 95
1395a – 70c. violet and deep violet . . . . 1·20 1·10
1396 – 77c. multicoloured . . . 1·30 1·10
1396a – 80c. green and emerald 1·40 1·20
1400 – $3.20 multicoloured . . 5·75 5·00
1400a – $12.25 rose and red . . 16·00 13·50
DESIGNS: 2c. Lazarus Salii; 20c. Charlie Gibbons; 22c. Admiral Raymond Spuance; 33c. Pres. Kuniwo Nakamura; 50c. Admiral William Halsey; 55c. Colonel Lewis Puller; 60c. Franklin Roosevelt (US President 1933–45); 70c. General Douglas MacArthur; 77c. Harry Truman (US President 1945–53); 80c. Admiral Chester W. Nimitz; $3.20 Jimmy Carter (US President 1977–81); $12.25 President John F. Kennedy.

154 Leatherback Turtle

1999. Endangered Reptiles and Amphibians. Multicoloured.
1405 33c. Type **154** 60 55
1406 33c. Kemp's Ridley turtle 60 55
1407 33c. Green turtles 60 55
1408 33c. Marine iguana 60 55
1409 33c. Table Mountain ghost frog 60 55
1410 33c. Spiny turtle 60 55
1411 33c. Hewitt's ghost frog . . 60 55
1412 33c. Geometric tortoise . . 60 55
1413 33c. Limestone salamander 60 55
1414 33c. Desert rain frog 60 55
1415 33c. Cape plantanna 60 55
1416 33c. Long-toed tree frog . . 60 55
MS1417 Two sheets each 110 × 80 mm. (a) $2 Hawksbill Turtle; (b) $2 Marine crocodile 7·00 6·00

155 Caroline Islands 1901 5 and 20pf. Stamps and Golsdorf Steam Railway Locomotive

1999. "iBRA '99" International Stamp Exhibition, Nuremberg, Germany. Multicoloured.
1418 55c. Type **155** . . . . . . 1·00 90
1419 55c. Caroline Islands 1901 5m. yacht stamp and carriage of Leipzig–Dresden Railway . . . . 1·00 90
MS1420 160 × 106 mm. $2 Caroline Islands 1900 3pf. Stamp on cover 3·50 3·00

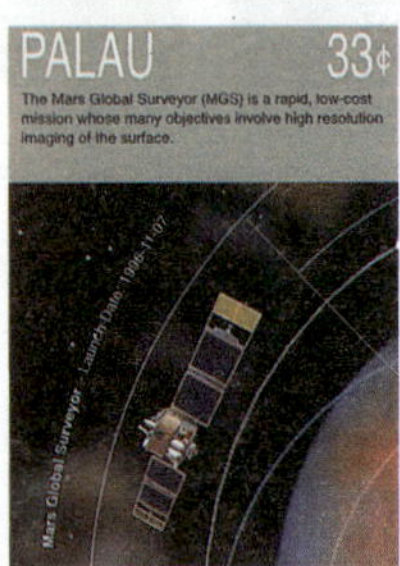

156 "Mars Global Surveyor" in Orbit

1999. Space Missions to Mars. Multicoloured.
1421 33c. Type **156** 60 55
1422 33c. "Mars Climate" Orbiter 60 55
1423 33c. "Mars Polar" Lander 60 55
1424 33c. "Deep Space 2" 60 55
1425 33c. "Mars Surveyor 2001" Orbiter 60 55
1426 33c. "Mars Surveyor 2001" Lander 60 55
MS1427 Four sheets, each 76 × 111 mm. (a) $2 "Mars Global Surveyor"; (b) $2 "Mars Climate" Orbiter; (c) "Mars Polar" Lander; (d) $2 "Mars Surveyor 2001" Lander . . . . 14·00 12·00
Nos. 1421/6 were issued together, se-tenant, forming a composite design.

157 "Banza natida"

1999. Earth Day. Pacific Insects. Multicoloured.
1428 33c. Type **157** 60 55
1429 33c. "Drosophila heteroneura" (fruit-fly) . . 60 55
1430 33c. "Nesomicromus lagus" 60 55
1431 33c. "Megalagrian leptodemus" 60 55
1432 33c. "Pseudopsectra cookeorum" 60 55
1433 33c. "Ampheida neocaledonia" 60 55
1434 33c. "Pseudopsectra swezeyi" 60 55
1435 33c. "Deinacrida heteracantha" 60 55
1436 33c. Beech forest butterfly 60 55
1437 33c. Hercules moth 60 55
1438 33c. Striped sphinx moth . . 60 55
1439 33c. Tussock butterfly . . . 60 55
1440 33c. Weevil 60 55
1441 33c. Bush cricket 60 55
1442 33c. Longhorn beetle . . . 60 55
1443 33c. "Abathrus bicolor" . . 60 55
1444 33c. "Stylogymnusa subantartica" 60 55
1445 33c. Moth butterfly 60 55
1446 33c. "Paraconosoma naviculare" 60 55
1447 33c. Cairn's birdwing ("Ornithoptera priamus") 60 55

158 Launch 1R (living quarters)

1999. International Space Station, 1998–2004. Multicoloured.
1448 33c. Type **158** 55 50
1449 33c. Launch 14A (final solar arrays) 55 50
1450 33c. Launch 8A (mechanical arm) 55 50
1451 33c. Launch 1J (Japanese experiment module) . . . 55 50
1452 33c. Launch 1E (Colombus Orbital Facility laboratory) 55 50
1453 33c. Launch 16A (habitation module) 55 50
MS1454 Four sheets each 76 × 111 mm. (a) $2 Complete International Space Station; (b) $2 Commander Bob Cabana and Sergei Krikalev; (c) $2 Crew of Flight 2R (horiz); (d) $2 X-38 Crew Return Vehicle (horiz) . . 14·00 12·00

159 William Gibson

161 Queen Mother and Attendants

160 "Women Divers"

1999. The Information Age: Visionaries in the Twentieth Century. Multicoloured.
1455 33c. Type **159** 60 55
1456 33c. Danny Hillis 60 55
1457 33c. Steve Wozntak 60 55
1458 33c. Steve Jobs 60 55
1459 33c. Nolan Bushnell 60 55
1460 33c. John Warnock 60 55
1461 33c. Ken Thompson 60 55
1462 33c. Al Shugart 60 55
1463 33c. Rand and Robyn Miller 60 55
1464 33c. Nicolas Negroponte . . 60 55
1465 33c. Bill Gates 60 55
1466 33c. Arthur C. Clarke . . . 60 55
1467 33c. Marshall McLuhan . . 60 55
1468 33c. Thomas Watson Jr . . 60 55
1469 33c. Gordon Moore 60 55
1470 33c. James Gosling 60 55
1471 33c. Sabeer Bhatia and Jack Smith 60 55
1472 33c. Esther Dyson 60 55
1473 33c. Jerry Young and David Filo 60 55
1474 33c. Jeff Bezos 60 55
1475 33c. Bob Kahn 60 55
1476 33c. Jaron Lanier 60 55
1477 33c. Andy Grove 60 55
1478 33c. Jim Clark 60 55
1479 33c. Bob Metcalfe 60 55

1999. 150th Death Anniv of Katsushika Hokusai (Japanese artist). Multicoloured.
1480 33c. Type **160** 55 50
1481 33c. "Bull and Parasol" . . 55 50
1482 33c. Drawing of bare-breasted woman 55 50
1483 33c. Drawing of fully-clothed woman (sitting) 55 50
1484 33c. "Japanese Spaniel" . . 55 50
1485 33c. "Porter in Landscape" 55 50
1486 33c. "Bacchanalian Revelry" (musician in bottom right corner) 55 50
1487 33c. "Bacchanalian Revelry" (different) 55 50
1488 33c. Drawing of woman (crouching) 55 50
1489 33c. Drawing of woman (reclining on floor) . . . 55 50
1490 33c. "Ox-herd" (ox) 55 50
1491 33c. "Ox-herd" (man on bridge) 55 50
MS1492 Two sheets each 102 × 73 mm. (a) $2 "At Swan Lake in Shainani"; (b) $2 "Mount Fuji in a Thunderstorm" (vert) 7·00 6·00

1999. "Queen Elizabeth the Queen Mother's Century".
1493 **161** 60c. black and gold . . . 95 85
1494 – 60c. black and gold . . . 95 85
1495 – 60c. multicoloured . . . 95 85
1496 – 60c. multicoloured . . . 95 85
MS1497 152 × 154 mm. $2 black 7·00 6·00
DESIGNS: No. 1494, Queen Mother with corgi dog; 1495, Queen Mother in pink coat and hat; 1496, Queen Mother in yellow evening dress and tiara. 37 × 49 mm—Queen Mother holding open book.

162 Launch of Rocket

1999. 30th Anniv of First Manned Moon Landing. Multicoloured.
1498 33c. Type **162** 55 50
1499 33c. Spacecraft above Earth and Moon's surface . . . 55 50
1500 33c. Astronaut descending ladder 55 50
1501 33c. Distant view of rocket launch 55 50
1502 33c. Astronaut planting flag on Moon 55 50
1503 33c. "Apollo 11" crew members 55 50
MS1504 Four sheets each 78 × 101 mm. (a) $2 Rocket on launch-pad; (b) $2 Astronaut descending ladder (different); (c) $2 Lunar module; (d) $2 Splash down . . . . 14·00 12·00

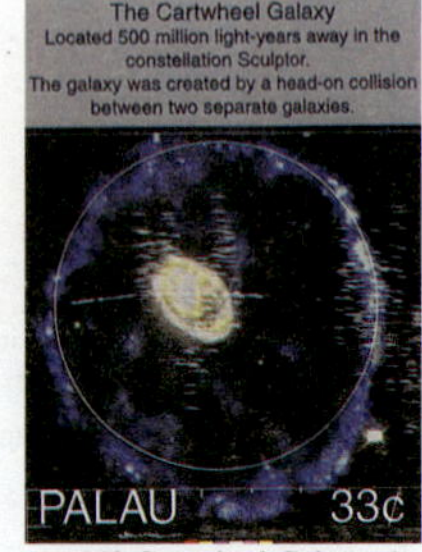

163 Cartwheel Galaxy

1999. Images from Space: Hubble Telescope. Multicoloured.
1505 33c. Type **163** 55 50
1506 33c. Stingray Nebula 55 50
1507 33c. Planetary Nebula NGC 3918 . . . . 55 50
1508 33c. Cat's Eye Nebula . . . 55 50
1509 33c. Galaxy NGC 7742 . . . 55 50
1510 33c. Eight-burst Nebula . . 55 50
MS1511 Four sheets each 77 × 100 mm. (a) $2 Supernova 1987-A; (b) Saturn (infrared aurora); (c) $2 Planetary Nebula M2-9; (d) $2 Eta Carinae . . . 14·00 12·00

164 Calves and Chickens

165 "Keep Safe"

1999. Christmas. "Puer Nobis" (carol). Mult.
1512 20c. Type **164** 35 30
1513 20c. Donkey, geese and rabbit 35 30
1514 20c. Child Jesus, cats and lambs 35 30
1515 20c. Geese, goat and sheep 35 30
1516 20c. Donkey and cockerel 35 30

Nos. 1512/16 were issued together, se-tenant, forming a composite design.

1999. "How to Love Your Dog". Multicoloured.
1517 33c. Type **165** 60 55
1518 33c. Girl with puppies (Show affection) 60 55
1519 33c. Dog asleep (A place of one's own) 60 55
1520 33c. Girl with Scottish terrier (Communicate) . . 60 55
1521 33c. Dog eating (Good food) 60 55
1522 33c. Vet examining dog (Annual check-up) 60 55
1523 33c. Girl with prone dog (Teach rules) 60 55
1524 33c. Dog with disc (Exercise and play) 60 55
1525 33c. Dog with basket (Let him help) 60 55
1526 33c. Dog with heart on collar (Unconditional love) 60 55
MS1527 Two sheets each 100 × 69 mm. (a) $2 Puppies (Love is a gentle thing); (b) $2 Puppy (Pleasure of your company) . . 7·00 6·00

166 Deep Space Probe

2000. Projected Space Probes. Multicoloured.
1528 55c. Type **166** 50 45
1529 55c. Piggy back probe . . . 50 45
1530 55c. Deep space telescope probe 50 45
1531 55c. Space probe on course to rendezvous with comet 50 45
1532 55c. Yellow space probe orbiting planet 50 45
1533 55c. Deep space probe with advanced onboard artificial intelligence . . . 50 45
MS1534 Four sheets each 98 × 138 mm. (a) $2 Space probe in storm (horiz); (b) $2 Insect-shaped lander (horiz); (c) $2 Space probe with dish aerial; (d) Secondary probe disengaging from parent probe . . . . 14·00 12·00

167 Native Brazilian Indians, 1800

168 Lech Walesa and Shipyard Workers

2000. New Millennium (1st series). The Nineteenth Century 1800–1850. Multicoloured.
1535 20c. Type **167** 35 30
1536 20c. Broken manacles (Haiti slave revolt, 1800) 35 30
1537 20c. Napoleon I (assumption of title of Emperor of France, 1804) 35 30
1538 20c. Shaka (Zulu leader) . . 35 30
1539 20c. Monster (publication of *Frankenstein* (novel) by Mary Shelley, 1818) . . . 35 30
1540 20c. Simon Bolivar (revolutionary) 35 30
1541 20c. Camera (development of photography) 35 30
1542 20c. Dripping tap (introduction of water purification system, 1829) 35 30
1543 20c. Steam locomotive (inauguration in Great Britain of first passenger-carrying railway, 1830) . . 35 30
1544 20c. Discovery of electromagnetic induction by Michael Faraday, 1831 35 30
1545 20c. First use of anaesthesia in surgery by Crawford Williamson Long, 1842 35 30
1546 20c. Morse key (transmission of first message by Samuel Morse, 1844) 35 30
1547 20c. Poster (first convention on Women's Rights, Seneca Falls, U.S.A., 1848) 35 30
1548 20c. Karl Marx (publication of the *Communist Manifesto*), 1848 . . . . 35 30
1549 20c. Charles Darwin's (naturalist) voyage on *Beagle* (56 × 36 mm) . . . 35 30
1550 20c. Revolution in Germany, 1848 . . . . . 35 30
1551 20c. Commencement of Taiping Rebellion, China, 1850 . . . . 35 30

There are a number of errors in the stamp inscriptions and descriptions.

See also Nos. 1552/68, 1691/1702 and 1741/57.

2000. New Millennium (2nd series). The Twentieth Century 1980–1989. Multicoloured.
1552 20c. Type **168** (foundation of Solidarity (trade union), 1980) 35 30
1553 20c. First photographic image taken by *Voyager I* of Saturn, 1980 . . . . . 35 30
1554 20c. Election of Ronald Reagan as President of the United States of America, 1980 . . . . . 35 30
1555 20c. A.I.D.S. virus (identification of A.I.D.S.) 35 30
1556 20c. Marriage of Prince Charles and Lady Diana Spencer, 1981 . . . . . . 35 30
1557 20c. Production of the compact disc, 1983 . . . 35 30
1558 20c. Leak of poisonous gas from insecticide plant, Bhopal, India, 1984 . . . 35 30
1559 20c. Inauguration of Pai's Pyramid, 1984 . . . . . 35 30
1560 20c. Mikhail Gorbachev elected Secretary General of the Soviet Communist Party, 1985 . . . . 35 30
1561 20c. Explosion at the Chernobyl nuclear power plant, 1986 . . . . 35 30
1562 20c. Explosion of space shuttle *Challenger*, 1986 35 30
1563 20c. Klaus Barbie, ((former chief of German Gestapo in France) sentenced to life imprisonment), 1987 35 30
1564 20c. Salman Rushdie (author) (publication of *The Satanic Verses*, 1988) 35 30
1565 20c. Election of Benazir Bhutto as Prime Minister of Pakistan, 1988 . . . . 35 30
1566 20c. Tiananmen Square (student demonstrations, 1989) 35 30
1567 20c. Demonstrators breaching Berlin Wall, 1989 (59 × 39 mm) 35 30
1568 20c. Development of the World Wide Web 35 30

169 Dragon

2000. Chinese New Year. Year of the Dragon. Sheet 80 × 60 mm.
MS1569 **169** $2 multicoloured . . 3·50 3·00

170 Bill Clinton (1992–2000)

171 Australopithecine (Southern Ape species, Africa)

2000. Former United States Presidents.
1570 **170** $1 black and brown . . 1·70 1·50
1571 – $2 black and blue . . . 3·50 3·00
1572 – $3 black and mauve . . 5·25 4·50
1574 – $5 black and brown . . 8·75 7·50
1575 – $11.75 black and brown (40 × 23 mm) . . . . 20·00 17·00

DESIGNS: $2 Ronald Reagan (1980–88); $3 Gerald Ford (1974–76); $5 George Bush (1988–92); $11.75 John F. Kennedy (1960–63).

2000. Pre-historic Discoveries of the 20th-Century. Multicoloured.
1580 20c. Type **171** 35 30
1581 20c. Australopithecine skull 35 30
1582 20c. Homo habilis using hand axe 35 30
1583 20c. Hand-axe 35 30
1584 20c. Homo habilis skull . . 35 30
1585 20c. Australo pithecine skeleton "Lucy" 35 30
1586 20c. Archaic Homo sapien skull 35 30
1587 20c. Diapithicine skull . . . 35 30
1588 20c. Homo erectus family 35 30
1589 20c. Wood hut 35 30
1590 20c. Australopithecine ethopis skull 35 30
1591 20c. Homo sapien 35 30
1592 20c. Homo sapien skull . . 35 30
1593 20c. Discovery of Taung Baby, 1924 . . . . 35 30
1594 20c. Homo erectus skull . . 35 30
1595 20c. Louis Leaky (archaeologist) 35 30
1596 20c. Neanderthal skull . . . 35 30
1597 20c. Neanderthal man . . . 35 30
1598 20c. Development of the fully bipedal foot 35 30
1599 20c. Raymond Dart (discoverer of Taung Baby) 35 30

172 Tennis Player

2000. Olympic Games, Sydney. Multicoloured.
1600 33c. Type **172** 55 50
1601 33c. Shot put 55 50
1602 33c. Greek flag and stadium 55 50
1603 33c. Ancient Olympic athletes 55 50

173 Re-usable Launch Vehicle

2000. Projected Unmanned Craft and Space Exploration. Multicoloured.
1604 33c. Type **173** 55 50
1605 33c. Single stage vertical take-off craft 55 50
1606 33c. Robotic rocket plane 55 50
1607 33c. Single-stage craft . . . 55 50
1608 33c. Fully-automated deep-space exploration craft . . 55 50
1609 33c. Magnetohydrodynamics-powered launch craft . . 55 50
MS1610 Four sheets, each 100 × 135 mm. (a) $2 Spacecraft taking-off (privately funded launch craft); (b) $2 Emergency crew return craft using parachutes (horiz); (c) $2 Interplanetary space craft (horiz); (d) $2 Space shuttle leaving space station . . . . . 13·00 11·50

174 Banded Crake (*Rallina eurizonoides*)

2000. Birds. Multicoloured.
1611 20c. Type **174** 35 30
1612 20c. Micronesian kingfisher (*Halcyon cinnamomina*) . . 35 30
1613 20c. Little pied cormorant (*Phalacrocorax melanoleucos*) 35 30
1614 20c. Eastern reef heron (*Egretta sacra*) 35 30
1615 20c. Nicobar pigeon (*Caloenas nicobarica*) . . 35 30
1616 20c. Rufous night heron (*Nycticorax caledonicus*) 35 30
1617 33c. Palau ground dove (*Gallicolumba canifrons*) 55 50
1618 33c. Palau scops owl (*Pyrroglaux podargina*) . . 55 50
1619 33c. Mangrove flycatcher (*Cyornis rufigastra*) (wrongly inscr "Pyrrboglaux podargina") 55 50
1620 33c. Palau bushwarbler (*Cettia annae*) 55 50
1621 33c. Palau fantail (*Rhipidura lepida*) 55 50
1622 33c. Morning bird (*Celluricincla tenebrosa*) 55 50
MS1623 Two sheets, each 76 × 126 mm. (a) $2 Palau whiteeye (*Megazosterops palauensis*) (horiz); (b) $2 Palau fruitdove (*Ptilinopus pelewensis*) (horiz) . . . . 6·50 5·75

No. 1611 is inscribed "Slatey-legged Crake" and No. 1614 "Pacific reef egret" both in error. There are also several errors in the Latin names.

175 Booker T. Washington (educationist)

2000. 20th-Century Personalities. Multicoloured.
1624 33c. Type **175** 55 50
1625 33c. Buckmeister Fuller (inventor and designer) . . 55 50
1626 33c. Marie Curie (physicist) 55 50
1627 33c. Walt Disney (animator and producer) 55 50
1628 33c. Franklin D. Roosevelt (32nd United States President) 55 50
1629 33c. Henry Ford (car manufacturer) 55 50
1630 33c. Betty Friedan (author and feminist leader) . . . 55 50
1631 33c. Sigmund Freud (founder of psychoanalysis) 55 50
1632 33c. Mahatma Ghandi (Indian leader) 55 50
1633 33c. Mikhail Gorbachev (Soviet President) 55 50
1634 33c. Stephan Hawkings (theoretical physicist) . . 55 50
1635 33c. Martin Luther King Jr. (civil rights leader) . . . 55 50
1636 33c. Toni Morrison (writer) 55 50
1637 33c. Georgia O'Keeffe (artist) 55 50
1638 33c. Rosa Parks (civil rights activist) 55 50
1639 33c. Carl Sagan (astronomer) 55 50
1640 33c. Jonas Salk (immunologist) 55 50
1641 33c. Sally Ride (astronaut and astrophysicist) . . . 55 50
1642 33c. Nikola Tesla (electrical engineer and physicist) . . 55 50
1643 33c. Wilbur and Orville Wright (aviation pioneer) 55 50

176 Reef Bass (*Pseudogramma gregoryi*)

2000. Marine Life of the Atlantic and Pacific Oceans. Multicoloured.
1644 20c. Type **176** 55 50
1645 20c. Great white shark (*Carcharodon carcharias*) 55 50
1646 20c. Sharptail eel (*Myrichthys breviceps*) . . 55 50
1647 20c. Sailfish (*Istiophorus platypterus*) 55 50
1648 20c. Southern stingray (*Dasyatis americana*) . . . 55 50
1649 20c. Ocean triggerfish (*Canthidermis sufflamen*) 55 50
1650 55c. Scalloped hammerhead (*Sphyrna lewini*) (vert) . . 75 70
1651 55c. White-tipped reef shark (*Triaenodon obesus*) (vert) 75 70
1652 55c. Moon jellyfish (*Aurelia aurita*) (vert) 75 70
1653 55c. Lionfish (*Pterois volitans*) (vert) 75 70
1654 55c. Seahorse (*Hippocampus abdominalis*) (vert) 75 70
1655 55c. Spotted eagle ray (*Aetobatus narinari*) (vert) 75 70
MS1656 Two sheets, each 110 × 85 mm. (a) $2 Short bigeye (*Pristigenys alta*) (vert); (b) $2 Gaff-topsail catfish (*Bagre marinus*) (vert) . . . . 6·50 5·75

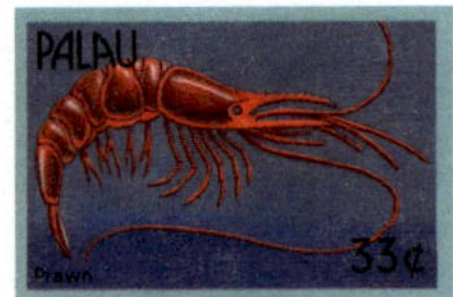

177 Prawn

2000. Marine Life. Multicoloured.

1657 33c. Type **177** 55 50
1658 33c. Deep sea angler 55 50
1659 33c. Rooster fish 55 50
1660 33c. Grenadier 55 50
1661 33c. *Platyberix opalescens* 55 50
1662 33c. Lantern fish 55 50
1663 33c. Emperor angelfish . . . 55 50
1664 33c. Nautilus 55 50
1665 33c. Moorish idol 55 50
1666 33c. Seahorse 55 50
1667 33c. Clown triggerfish . . . 55 50
1668 33c. Clown fish 55 50
MS1669 Two sheets, each 106 × 75 mm. (a) $2 Giant squid; (b) $2 Manta ray . . . . . . 6·50 5·75

178 James Watson (co-discoverer of structure of D.N.A.)

2000. Advances in Science and Medicine. Multicoloured.

1670 33c. Type **178** 55 50
1671 33c. Har Gobing Khorana and Robert Holley (work on genetic code) 55 50
1672 33c. Hamilton Smith and Werner Arber (discovered restriction enzymes) . . . 55 50
1673 33c. Centrifugation machine and D.N.A. double helix 55 50
1674 33c. Richard Roberts (discovered R.N.A. splicing and split genes) 55 50
1675 33c. Maurice Wilkins (co-discoverer of structure of D.N.A.) 55 50
1676 33c. D.N.A. double helix . . 55 50
1677 33c. Frederick Sanger and Walter Gilbert (developed methods for determining nucleotide sequences for D.N.A. molecules) . . . 55 50
1678 33c. Kary Mullis (discovered polymerase chain reaction) 55 50
1679 33c. D.N.A. double helix and frogs (mapping location of genes) 55 50
1680 33c. Francis Crick (co-discoverer of structure of D.N.A.) 55 50
1681 33c. Marshall Nirenberg (work on genetic code) . . 55 50
1682 33c. Daniel Nathans (discovered restriction enzymes) 55 50
1683 33c. Harold Varmus and Michael Bishop (identified several genes involved in cancer) 55 50
1684 33c. Phillip Sharp (discovered polymerase chain reaction) 55 50
1685 33c. Sheep (cloning sheep to produce Dolly, 1997) . . 55 50
1686 33c. D.N.A. being separated by electrophoresis . . . 55 50
1687 33c. Paul Berg (first developed methods for cloning genes, 1980) . . . 55 50
1688 33c. Michael Smith and D.N.A. (discovered polymerase chain reaction) 55 50
1689 33c. D.N.A. and deer (human genome project) 55 50
MS1690 Two sheets, each 97 × 117 mm. (a) $2 Dolly (cloned sheep) (37 × 50 mm). (b) $2 D.N.A. and deer (37 × 50 mm) 6·50 5·75

179 Hourglass and Map of South East Asia

2000. New Millennium (3rd series). Multicoloured.

1691 20c. Type **179** 35 30
1692 20c. Hourglass and map of North America 35 30
1693 20c. Hourglass and map of Europe 35 30
1694 20c. Hourglass and map of Australia 35 30
1695 20c. Hourglass and map of South America 35 30
1696 20c. Hourglass and map of Africa 35 30
1697 55c. Clock face and clouds (vert) 90 80
1698 55c. Clock face and building faade (vert) 90 80
1699 55c. Clock face and coastline (vert) 90 80
1700 55c. Clock face and farm buildings (vert) 90 80
1701 55c. Clock face and forest (vert) 90 80
1702 55c. Clock face and desert (vert) 90 80

180 American Bald Eagle

181 Rhamphorhynchus

2000. Endangered Species. Multicoloured.

1703 33c. Type **180** 55 50
1704 33c. Small whorled pogonia 55 50
1705 33c. Arctic peregrine falcon 55 50
1706 33c. Golden lion tamarin . . 55 50
1707 33c. American alligator . . 55 50
1708 33c. Brown pelican 55 50
1709 33c. Aleutian Canada goose 55 50
1710 33c. Western grey kangaroo 55 50
1711 33c. Palau scops owl 55 50
1712 33c. Jocotoco antpitta . . . 55 50
1713 33c. Orchid 55 50
1714 33c. Red lechwe 55 50
MS1715 Two sheets, each 120 × 92 mm. (a) $2 Lahontan cutthroat trout (horiz); (b) $2 Leopard . . . . 6·50 5·75

2000. Dinosaurs. Multicoloured.

1716 33c. Type **181** 35 30
1717 33c. Ceratosaurus 35 30
1718 33c. Apatosaurus 35 30
1719 33c. Stegosaurus 35 30
1720 33c. Archaeopteryx 35 30
1721 33c. Allosaurus 35 30
1722 33c. Parasaurolophus . . . 35 50
1723 33c. Pteranodonrus 35 30
1724 33c. Tyrannosaurus 35 30
1725 33c. Triceratops 35 30
1726 33c. Ankylosaurus 35 30
1727 33c. Velociraptor 35 30
MS1728 Two sheets, each 94 × 71 mm. (a) $2 Jurassic landscape; (b) $2 Cretaceous landscape . . . . 6·50 5·75

Nos. 1716/21 and 1722/7 were each issued together, se-tenant, forming a composite design.

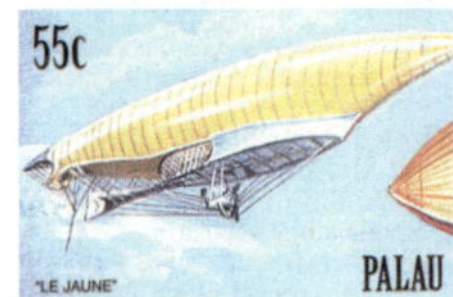

182 Lebaudy–Juillot Airship Le Jaune

2000. Centenary of First Zeppelin Flight and Airship Development. Multicoloured.

1729 55c. Type **182** 90 80
1730 55c. Forlanini airship *Leonardo DaVinci* 90 80
1731 55c. Thomas Baldwin's airship U.S. Military No. 1, 1908 . . . . . . 90 80
1732 55c. Astra-Torres 1 . . . . . 90 80
1733 55c. Rear of Astra-Torres 1 and Parseval PL VII . . . 90 80
1734 55c. Rear of Parseval PL VII and Lebaudy airship *Liberte* 90 80
MS1735 Two sheets, each 110 × 85 mm. (a) $2 Santos-Dumont airship Ballon No. 9 La Badaleuse; (b) $2 Santos-Dumont Ballon No. 6 circling Eiffel Tower 13·00 11·50

Nos. 1729/34 were issued together, se-tenant, forming a composite design.

183 Duke and Duchess of York

184 Viking Diver attacking Danish Ship

2000. 100th Birthday of Queen Elizabeth the Queen Mother. Multicoloured.

1736 55c. Type **183** . . . . . . 1·80 1·70
1737 55c. As Duchess of York wearing cloche hat . . . 1·80 1·70
1738 55c. Wearing green floral hat . . . . 1·80 1·70
1739 55c. Wearing blue hat . . . 1·80 1·70
MS1740 99 × 84 mm. $2 Wearing yellow coat and hat . . . . . 3·25 3·00

2000. New Millennium (4th series). Development of Diving Equipment. Multicoloured.

1741 33c. Type **184** 55 50
1742 33c. Issa (12th-century Arab diver) 55 50
1743 33c.15 th-century salvage diver using breathing tube 55 50
1744 33c. 17 th-century diver wearing leather suit and carrying halberd 55 50
1745 33c. Edmund Halley's wooden diving bell, 1690 55 50
1746 33c. David Bushnell's diving bell Turtle, 1776 . . . . 55 50
1747 33c. Diver wearing suit and Siebe helmet,1819 . . . . 55 50
1748 33c. *Hunley* (Confederate submarine) 55 50
1749 33c. Argonaut (first underwater salvage vehicle), 1899 . . . . . . 55 50
1750 33c. John Williamson's underwater filming vehicle photosphere, 1914 . . . . 55 50
1751 33c. Diver wearing brass helmet, weighted boots, with air supply and safety lines (circa 1930) 55 50
1752 33c. William Beebe and Otis Barton's bathysphere, 1934 . . . . 55 50
1753 33c. Coelacanth (prehistoric fish previously thought extinct) 55 50
1754 33c. Italian divers on chariot planting explosive charges on ship hull during World War II 55 50
1755 33c. *Trieste* (bathyscaphe) (record dive by Jaques Picard and Lt. Don Walsh, 1960) 55 50
1756 33c. *Alvin* (submersible) surveying thermal vents in Galapagos Rift (1977) (60 × 40 mm) 55 50
1757 33c. Sylvia Earle wearing Jim Suit, 1979 . . . . . 55 50

185 "Dancers" (S. Adelbai)

2000. 8th Pacific Arts Festival, Noumea, New Caledonia. Sheet 192 × 153 mm containing T **185** and similar horiz designs. Multicoloured.

MS1758 33c. Type **185**; 33c. "Storyboard Art" (D. Inabo); 33c. "Traditional Money" (M. Takeshi); 33c. "Clay Lamp and Bowl" (W. Watanabe); 33c. "Meeting House" (P. Tiakl); "Outrigger Canoe" (S. Adelbai); 33c. "Weaver" (M. Vitarelli); 33c. "Rock Island Scene" (W. Marcil); 33c. "Contemporary Music" (J. Imetuker) . . . . 5·00 4·50

186 Turtle Shell Bracelet

187 Top of Head

2000. 45th Anniv of Belau National Museum. Multicoloured.

1759 33c. Type **186** 55 50
1760 33c. Bust (sculpture) (H. Hijikata) 55 50
1761 33c. "Turtle Shell Women's Money" 55 50
1762 33c. "Cherecheroi" (T. Suzuki) 55 50
1763 33c. Money jar (B. Sylvester) 55 50
1764 33c. "Prince Lebu" (Ichikawa) 55 50
1765 33c. "Beach at Lild" (H. Hijikata) 55 50
1766 33c. Traditional mask . . . 55 50
1767 33c. Taro platter (T. Rebluud) 55 50
1768 33c. "Meresebang" (Ichikawa) 55 50
1769 33c. Woman and child (sculpture) (B. Sylvester) 55 50
1770 33c. "Birth Ceremony" (I. Kishigawa) 55 50

2000. 80th Birthday of Pope John Paul II. Sheet 158 × 243 mm containing T **187** and similar vert designs showing collage of miniature religious photographs. Multicoloured, country inscription and face value at left (a) or right (b).

MS1771 50c. Type **187**; 50c. Ear (a); 50c. Neck and collar (a); 50c. Shoulder (a); 50c. Forehead (b); 50c. Forehead and eye (b); 50c. Nose and cheek (b); 50c. Hands (b) . . . . 6·50 5·75

No. **MS**1771 was issued with the stamps arranged in two vertical columns separated by a gutter also containing miniature photographs. When viewed as a whole, the miniature sheet forms a portrait of Pope John Paul II.

188 Face enclosed by Snake

2000. Chinese New Year. Year of the Snake. Two sheets, each 69 × 99 mm containing T **188** and similar horiz design.

MS1772 (a) 60c. Type **188**; (b) 60c. Face with snake head-dress . . 2·00 1·80

189 Indian Red Admiral (*Vanessa indica*)

2000. Butterflies. Multicoloured.

1773 33c. Type **189** 55 50
1774 33c. Chequered swallowtail (*Papilio demoleus*) 55 50
1775 33c. Yamfly (*Loxura atymnus*) 55 50
1776 33c. Fiery jewel (*Hypochrysops ignite*) . . 55 50
MS1777 Four sheets. (a) 119 × 134 mm. 33c. Cairn's birdwing (*Ornithoptera priamus*); 33c. Meadow argus (*Junonia villida*); 33c. Orange albatross (*Appias nero*); 33c. Glasswing (*Acraea andromacha*); 33c. Beak butterfly (*Libythea geoffroyi*); 33c. Great eggfly (*Hypolimnas bolina*); (b) 119 × 134 mm. 33c. Large green-banded blue (*Danis danis*); 33c. Union jack (*Delias mysis*); 33c. Broad-bordered grass yellow (*Eurema brigitta*); 33c. Striped blue crow (*Euploea mulciber*); 33c. Red lacewing (*Cethosia bibles*); 33c. Palmfly (*Elyminias hypermnestra*) (inscr "Elyminas agondas"); (c) 107 × 77 mm. $2 Clipper (*Parthenos Sylvia*); (d) 107 × 77 mm. $2 Blue triangle (*Graphium sarpedon*) . . . . . 6·50 5·75

190 Little Kingfisher

2000. Flora and Fauna. Four sheets containing T **190** and similar multicoloured designs.

MS1778 (a) 132 × 80 mm. 33c. Type **190**; 33c. Mangrove snake; 33c. Bats and breadfruit; 33c. Giant tree frog; 33c. Giant centipede; 33c. Crab-eating macaque; (b) 90 × 112 mm. 33c. Giant spiral ginger; 33c. Good luck plant; 33c. Leaves and green coconuts; 33c. Orchid and butterfly; 33c. Crocodile; 33c. Orchid; (c) 120 × 93 mm. $2 Claw and mouth of land crab (vert); (d) 119 × 93 mm. $2 Head and fin of fish . . . . 6·50 5·75

2001. As T **153** with additional imprint date at foot. Multicoloured.
1779 1c. Type **153** 20 20
1780 11c. As No. 1389 . . . . . 20 20
1781 60c. As No. 1395 . . . . . 75 65

191 "Washing the Copybook" (Torii Kiyomitsu)

192 *Teracotona euprepia*

2001. Japanese Art. Six sheets containing T **191** and similar vert designs. Multicoloured.
MS1795 (a) 161 × 120 mm. 60c. × 5 Type **191**; "Woman playing Shamisen and woman reading letter" (Iwasa Matabei); "Ichikawa Danjuro (actor) as Samurai" (Katasukawa Shunsho); "Gentleman entertained by courtesans" (Torrii Kiyonaga); "Geisha at teahouse" (Torrii Kiyonaga); (b) 161 × 120 mm. 60c. × 5 "Preparing Sashimi" (Kitagawa Utamaro); "Sanogawa Ichimatsu and Onoe Kikugoro (actors) in Plum Blossoms and Young Herbs" (Ishikawa Toyonobu); "Courtesan adjusting her comb" (Kaigetsudo Dohan); "Nakamura Tomijuro (actor) as woman dancing" (Katsukawa Shunsho); "Woman with poem card and writing brush" (Yashima Gakutei); (c) 187 × 113 mm. 60c. × 6 "Kitano Shrine, Kyoto" (Anon.); (d) 91 × 104 mm. $2 "Raiko attacks demon kite" (detail, Totoya Hokkei); (e) 123 × 105 mm. $2 "Beauty writing letter" (detail, Kaigetsudo Doshin) (28 × 42 mm); (e) 150 × 102 mm. $2 "Fireworks at Ikenohata" (detail, Kobayashi Kiyochika) (28 × 42 mm) . . . . 20·00 18·00
No. **MS**1795c was made up of six stamps, each stamp forming part of the composite design of the painting.

2001. Moths. Multicoloured.
1796 20c. Type **192** 35 30
1797 21c. Basker (*Euchromia lethe*) 35 30
1798 80c. White-lined sphinx (*Hyles lineate*) 80 70
1799 $1 Isabella Tiger Moth (*Pyrrharctia Isabella*) (Inscr "Pyrrrharctia") . . 2·40 2·00
MS1800 (a) 133 × 115 mm. 34c. × 6 Cinnabar moth (*Tyria jacobeae*); Beautiful tiger moth (*Amphicallia bellatrix*); Garden tiger moth (*Arctia caja*); *Zygaena occitanica*; Jersey tiger moth (*Euplagia quadripunctaria*); *Utetheisa ornatrix*; (b) 133 × 115 mm. 70c. × 6 Milionia isodoxa (inscr "Milonia"); *Cephonodes kingi*; *Anaphe panda*; Io moth (*Automeris io*); Tau emperor (*Aglia tau*); Lime hawk moth (*Mimas tiliae*); (c) 98 × 71 mm. $2 Owl moth (*Brahmaea wallichii*); (d) 98 × 71 mm. $2 Isabel moth (*Graellsia isabellae*) (inscr "Graaellsia") . . . . 10·00 9·25

193 Ivo Andric (1961)

194 Communal Meeting House (Bai)

2001. Centenary of the First Nobel Prize for Literature. Six sheets containing T **193** and similar vert designs. Multicoloured.
MS1801 (a) 148 × 209 mm. 34c. × 6 Type **193**; Eyvind Johnson (1974); Salvatore Quasimodo (1959); Mikhael Sholokhov (1965); Pablo Neruda (1971); Saul Bellow (1976); (b) 148 × 209 mm. 70c. × 6 Boris Pasternak (1958); Francois Mauriac (1952); Frans Eemil Sillanpaa (1939); Roger Martin du Gard (1937); Pearl Buck (1938); Andre Gide (1947); (c) 148 × 209 mm. 80c. × 6 Karl Gjellerup (1917); Anatole France (1921); Sinclair Lewis (1930); Jacinto Benavente (1922); John Galsworthy (1932); Erik A. Karlfeldt (1931); (d) 108 × 128 mm. $2 Bertrand Russell (1950); (e) 108 × 128 mm. $2 Luigi Pirandello (1934); (f) 108 × 128 mm. $2 Harry Martinson (1974) . . . . . . 18·00 17·00

2001. Christmas. Multicoloured.
1802 20c. Type **194** 35 25
1803 34c. No. 1786 . . . . . . 55 35

195 Foot and Football (1950)

197 Yellow-faced Mynah (*Mino dumontii*)

196 "Groom taking Horses to Pasture" (Han Kan)

2001. History of Football World Cup Championships. Poster Designs. Four sheets containing T **195** and similar vert designs. Multicoloured.
MS1804 (a) 154 × 109 mm. 34c. × 6 Type **195**; Goalkeeper and ball (1954); Ball enclosed in scarf of flags (1958); Globe and ball (1962); Championship mascot (1966); Silhouette of ball (1970); (b) 154 × 109 mm. Player with raised arms (1978); Stylized player (1982); Silhouette of player against statues (1986); Amphitheatre (1990); "94", ball and player (1994); Championship emblem (1998); (c) 88 × 75 mm. $2 Trophy (detail); (d) 88 × 75 mm. $2 "Uruguay" (1930) . . . . . . 11·50 10·50

2001. Sheet 200 × 136 mm containing T **196**. Multicoloured.
MS1805 60c. × 4 Type **196** . . . 2·00 1·80

2001. Birds. Four sheets containing T **197** and similar vert designs. Multicoloured.
MS1806 (a) 120 × 120 mm. 55c. × 6 Type **197**; Red-breasted pitta (*Pitta erythogaster*); Red-bearded Bee-eater (*Nyctyornis amictus*); Superb fruit dove (*Ptilinopus superbus*); Coppersmith barbet (*Megalaima haemacephala*); Diard's trogon (*Harpactes diardii*); (b) 120 × 120 mm. 60c. × 6 Spectacled monarch (*Monarcha trivirgatus*); Blue-tailed pitta (*Pitta guajana*) (inscr "Banded pitta"); Rufous-backed kingfisher (*Ceyx rufidorsa*); Scarlet robin (*Petroica multicolour*); Golden whistler (*Pachycephala pectoralis*); Mid-mountain rail babbler (*Ptilorrhoa castanonota*) (inscr "Jewel babbler"); (c) 105 × 75 mm. $2 River kingfisher (*Alcedo atthis*); (d) 105 × 75 mm. $2 Asiatic paradise flycatcher (*Tersiphone paradise*) . . . 11·50 10·50

198 Seagull on Rock

2002. Inauguration of Japanese sponsored Koror—Babeldaob Bridge. Multicoloured.
1807 20c. Type **198** 45 40
1808 20c. Palm tree on island . . 45 40
1809 20c. Three palm trees on island 45 40
1810 20c. Rocks and prow of boat 45 40
1811 20c. Boat, bird and island . . 45 40
1812 20c. Shoreline 45 40
1813 20c. Two people in row boat 45 40
1814 20c. Buoy and birds 45 40
1815 20c. Birds and dolphin's tail 45 40
1816 20c. Dolphins 45 40
1817 20c. Boy on raft 45 40
1818 20c. Two men wading . . . 45 40
1819 20c. Man fishing 45 40
1820 20c. Bridge supports 45 40
1821 20c. Cyclist and part of car 45 40
1822 20c. Car 45 40
1823 20c. Two people and bridge supports 45 40
1824 20c. Motor boat and truck 45 40
1825 20c. Coach 45 40
1826 20c. Base of bridge support 45 40
1827 20c. Canoe paddle and two birds 45 40
1828 20c. One bird 45 40
1829 20c. Top of sail and base of bridge 45 40
1830 20c. Treetops, motorcyclist and palm trees 45 40
1831 20c. Two pelicans on rock 45 40
1832 20c. Bird's wing, rock and canoes 45 40
1833 20c. Prow of canoe and motor boat 45 40
1834 20c. Rear of boat and rear of outrigger canoe 45 40
1835 20c. Outrigger canoe 45 40
1836 20c. Jet ski, boat slip and base of trees 45 40
1837 34c. No. 1807 . . . . . . 45 40
1838 34c. No. 1808 . . . . . . 45 40
1839 34c. No. 1809 . . . . . . 45 40
1840 34c. No. 1810 . . . . . . 45 40
1841 34c. No. 1811 . . . . . . 45 40
1842 34c. No. 1812 . . . . . . 45 40
1843 34c. No. 1813 . . . . . . 45 40
1844 34c. No. 1814 . . . . . . 45 40
1845 34c. No. 1815 . . . . . . 45 40
1846 34c. No. 1816 . . . . . . 45 40
1847 34c. No. 1817 . . . . . . 45 40
1848 34c. No. 1808 . . . . . . 45 40
1849 34c. No. 1819 . . . . . . 45 40
1850 34c. No. 1820 . . . . . . 45 40
1851 34c. No. 1821 . . . . . . 45 40
1852 34c. No. 1822 . . . . . . 45 40
1853 34c. No. 1823 . . . . . . 45 40
1854 34c. No. 1824 . . . . . . 45 40
1855 34c. No. 1825 . . . . . . 45 40
1856 34c. No. 1826 . . . . . . 45 40
1857 34c. No. 1827 . . . . . . 45 40
1858 34c. No. 1828 . . . . . . 45 40
1859 34c. No. 1829 . . . . . . 45 40
1860 34c. No. 1830 . . . . . . 45 40
1861 34c. No. 1831 . . . . . . 45 40
1862 34c. No. 1832 . . . . . . 45 40
1863 34c. No. 1833 . . . . . . 45 40
1864 34c. No. 1834 . . . . . . 45 40
1865 34c. No. 1835 . . . . . . 45 40
1866 34c. No. 1836 . . . . . . 45 40
Nos. 1807/36 and 1837/66, respectively, each form a composite design of Koror and Babeldaob islands, the bridge and bay.

199 Statue of Liberty wrapped in Flag

2002. "United We Stand" Support for Victims of Terrorist Attacks on World Trade Centre, New York.
1867 **199** $1 multicoloured . . . . 1·60 1·50

200 Queen Elizabeth II

2002. Golden Jubilee. 50th Anniv of Queen Elizabeth II's Accession to the Throne. Two sheets containing T **200** and similar square designs. Multicoloured.
MS1868 (a) 132 × 100 mm. 80c. × 4, Type **200**; Queen Elizabeth wearing flowered hat; Prince Phillip; Wearing tiara and diamond jewellery. (b) 76 × 109 mm. $2 Queen Elizabeth with hand extended. Set of 2 sheets 3·25 3·00

201 Grey-backed White Eye

202 *Euanthe sanderiana*

2002. Birds. Multicoloured.
1869 1c. Type **201** 15 15
1870 2c. Great frigate bird . . . 15 15
1871 3c. Eclectus parrot 15 15
1872 4c. Red-footed booby . . . 15 15
1873 5c. Cattle egret 15 15
1874 10c. Cardinal honey eater 15 15
1875 11c. Blue-faced parrot-finch 15 15
1876 15c. Rufous fantail 25 20
1877 20c. White-faced storm petrel 35 30
1878 21c. Willie wagtail 35 30
1879 23c. Black-headed gull . . 35 35
1879a 26c. Great tit 40 35
1879b 50c. Pale white-eye 80 75
1880 50c. Sanderling 80 75
1881 57c. White-tailed tropicbird 90 80
1882 70c. Rainbow lorikeet . . 1·10 1·00
1883 80c. Moorhen . . . . . . 1·30 1·20
1884 $1 Buff-banded rail . . . . 1·60 1·50
1885 $2 *Esacus magnirostris* . . 3·25 3·00
1886 $3 Common tern . . . . . 5·00 4·50
1887 $3.50 Ruddy turnstone . . 5·75 5·25
1888 $3.95 White-collared kingfisher . . . . 6·50 5·75
1889 $5 Sulphur-crested cockatoo . . . . 8·25 7·25
1890 $10 Swallow . . . . 16·00 14·50

2002. Flowers. Multicoloured.
1891 20c. Type **202** 35 30
1892 34c. *Ophiorrhiza palauensis* 55 50
1893 60c. *Cerbera manghas* . . . 1·10 95
1894 80c. Inscr "Mendinilla pterocaula" . . . . . . 1·30 1·20
MS1895 Four sheets. (a) 87 × 158 mm. 60c. × 6, *Bruguiera gymnorhiza*; *Samadera indica* (inscr "indical"); Inscr "Maesa canfieldiae"; *Lumnitzera litorea*; *Dolichandrone palawense*; Orchid (inscr "Limnophila aromatica"). (b) 96 × 171 mm. 60c. × 6 *Sonneratia alba*; *Barringtonia racemosa*; *Ixora casei*; *Tristellateia australasiae*; *Nepenthes mirabilisi*; *Limnophila aromaticai*. (c) 100 × 90 mm. $2 *Fagraea ksid*. (d) 100 × 90 mm. $2 *Cerbera manghas* (horiz). Set of 4 sheets . . . . 18·00 17·00
The stamps and margins of **MS**1895a/b, respectively, each form a composite design.

203 Great Dane

2002. Dogs and Cats. Four sheets containing T **203** and similar multicoloured designs.
MS1896 Two sheets (a/b), each 199 × 105 mm. (a) Dogs. 50c. × 6, Type **203**; Whippet; Bedlington terrier; Golden retriever; Papillon; Doberman. (b) Cats. 50c. × 6, Persian Himalayan; Norwegian Forest Cat; Havana; Exotic shorthair; Persian; Maine coon. Two sheets (c/d), each 105 × 75 mm. (c) $2 British shorthair cat. (d) $2 Shetland sheepdog . . . . 16·00 14·50

204 Male Super-G Skier

2002. Winter Olympic Games, Salt Lake City (1st issue). Multicoloured.
1897 $1 Type **204** . . . . 1·60 1·50
1898 $1 Female Super-G skier . . 1·60 1·50
MS1899 88 × 119 mm. Nos. 1897/8 3·25 3·00
See also Nos. 1918/**MS**1920.

205 Mount Fuji, Japan

2002. International Year of Mountains. Two sheets containing T **205** and similar horiz designs. Multicoloured.
MS1900 (a) 152 × 112 mm. 80c. × 4 Type **205**; Mount Everest, Nepal/China; Mount Owen, USA; Mount Huascaran, Peru (inscr "Huascarran", Nepal). (b) 90 × 68 mm. $2 Mount Eiger, Switzerland. Set of 2 sheets . . 3·25 3·00

206 Kayangel

2002. 21st Anniv of Constitutional Day. Showing flags of Palau states.

1901	**206**	37c. multicoloured . . .	60	55
1902	–	37c. red, ultramarine and black	60	55
1903	–	37c. multicoloured . . .	60	55
1904	–	37c. multicoloured . . .	60	55
1905	–	37c. blue, yellow and black	60	55
1906	–	37c. multicoloured . . .	60	55
1907	–	37c. yellow, blue and black	60	55
1908	–	37c. multicoloured . . .	60	55
1909	–	37c. scarlet, ultramarine and black	60	55
1910	–	37c. green and black . .	60	55
1911	–	37c. black, green and ultramarine	60	55
1912	–	37c. multicoloured . . .	60	55
1913	–	37c. multicoloured . . .	60	55
1914	–	37c. multicoloured . . .	60	55
1915	–	37c. multicoloured . . .	60	55
1916	–	37c. ultramarine, scarlet and black	60	55
1917	–	37c. blue and black . . .	60	55

DESIGNS: Type **206**; Ngarchelong; Ngaraard; Ngardmau; Ngaremlengui; Ngiwal; Republic of Palau; Ngatpang; Melekeor; Ngchesar; Aimeliik; Airai; Koror; Peleliu; Angaur; Sonsorol; Hatohobei.

207 Male Super-G Skier

2002. Winter Olympic Games, Salt Lake City (2nd issue). Multicoloured.

1918	$1 Type **207**	1·60	1·50
1919	$1 Female Super-G skier . .	1·60	1·50
MS1920	88 × 119 mm. Nos. 1918/19	3·25	3·00

Nos. 1918/**MS**1920 differ from 1897/**MS**1899, in the design of the Olympic rings.

2002. International Year of Eco Tourism. Two sheets containing T **208** and similar vert designs. Multicoloured.
MS1921 (a) 108 × 144 mm. 60c. × 6, Type **208**; Ray; Sea slug; Angelfish (different); Turtle; Nautilus. (b) 76 × 104 mm. $2 Canoeist. Set of 2 sheets . . . . 9·25 8·25
The stamps and margins of **MS**1921a/b, respectively, each form a composite design.

209 "Bando Shuka as the Courtesan Shirato" (Utagawa Kunisada)

2002. Japanese Art. Five sheets containing T **209** and similar multicoloured designs.
MS1922 (a) 190 × 143 mm. 60c. × 6, Type **209**; "Ichikawa Danjuro VII as Sugawara No Michizane" (Utagawa Kunisada); "Sawamura Sojuro III as Oboshi Yuranosuke" (Utagawa Toyokuni); "Kataoka Nizaemon Vii as Fujiwara Shihei" (Utagawa Toyokuni); "Portrait of Nakamura Noshio II" (Utagawa Kunimasa); "Kawarazaki Gon-Nosuke as Daroku" (Toyohara Kunichika). (b) 177 × 110 mm. 80c. × 4, "Gaslight Hall" (Kobayashi Kiyochika) (horiz); "Cherry Blossom at Night at Shin Yoshiwara" (Inoue Yasuji) (horiz); "Night Rain at Oyama" (Utagawa Toyokuni II) (horiz); "Kintai Bridge" (Keisai Eisen) (horiz). (c) 150 × 127 mm. 80c. × 4, "Bush-clover Branch and Sweetfish" (Utagawa Kuniyoshi) (28 × 89 mm); "Catfish" (Utagawa Kuniyoshi) (28 × 89 mm); "Scene at Takanawa" (Keisai Eisen) (28 × 89 mm); "Ochanomizu" (Keisai Eisen) (28 × 89 mm). (d) 105 × 85 mm. $2 "Okane, Strong Woman of Omi" (Utagawa Kuniyoshi). Imperf. (e) 105 × 85 mm. $2 "Scenes on the Banks of the Oumaya River" (Utagawa Kuniyoshi). Imperf 17·00 15·00

210 Wimpy 211 Elvis Presley

2002. Popeye (cartoon character created by Elzie Segar). Two sheets containing T **210** and similar multicoloured designs showing characters.
MS1923 (a) 198 × 128 mm. 60c. × 6, Type **210**; Swee'pea; Popeye; Marlin; Jeep; Brutus (Bluto). (b) 125 × 92 mm. $2 Popeye playing golf (horiz) . . . . 9·25 8·25
The stamps and margin of **MS**1923a form a composite design.

2002. 25th Death Anniv of Elvis Presley (entertainer). Sheet 156 × 152 mm containing T **211** similar vert designs. Multicoloured.
MS1924 37c. × 6, Type **211**; Seated holding guitar; Wearing white jacket and black hat; Standing holding two-necked electric guitar; Holding acoustic guitar; Wearing open-necked shirt . . . . . . 3·75 3·25

212 "Presentation of Jesus in the Temple" (detail) (Perugino) 213 Teddy Bear dressed as Accountant

2002. Christmas. Paintings.Multicoloured.

1925	23c. Type **212**	45	35
1926	37c. "Madonna and Child enthroned between Angels and Saints" (Domenico Chirlandio)	60	45
1927	60c. "Maesta, Madonna and Child" (Simone Martini)	80	75
1928	80c. "Sacred Conversation" (Giovanni Bellini (inscr "Giovanna")) (horiz) . .	1·20	1·10
1929	$1 "Nativity" (Domenico Ghirlandaio) (horiz) . . .	1·80	1·60
MS1930	104 × 78 mm. $2 "Sacred Conversation" (detail) (horiz)	3·25	3·00

2002. Centenary of the Teddy Bear. Sheet 149 × 194 mm containing T **213** and imilar vert designs showing dressed bears.
MS1931 60c. × 4, Type **213**; Computer programmer; Business woman; Lawyer . . . . 4·00 3·75
No.**MS**1931 was cut around in the shape of a teddy bear.

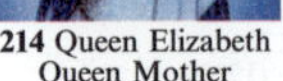

214 Queen Elizabeth Queen Mother 216 *Lethocerus grandis*

215 Rock Climbing

2002. Queen Elizabeth the Queen Mother Commemoration. Two sheets containing T **214** and similar multicoloured designs. Multicoloured.
MS1932 (a) 140 × 156 mm. 80c. × 4, Type **214**; Wearing pearls; Wearing purple outfit; Wearing tiara and sash (b) 108 × 82 mm. $2 Wearing flowered hat. Set of 2 sheets . . . . 5·25 4·75

2003. 20th World Scout Jamboree, Thailand. Multicoloured.

1933/8	60c. × 6; Type **215**; Emblem and penknife; Rope knots; Cub Scout; Square Knot; Boy Scout	6·00	5·25
MS1939	100 × 72 mm. $2 Robert Baden-Powell (founder) (vert)	3·25	3·00

2003. Flora and Fauna. Multicoloured.

1940/5	60c. × 6 Type **216**; *Cyrtotrachelus;Lytta vesicatoria*; *Aulacocylus*; *Phalacrognathus mulleri*; *Mormolyce phyllodes*	6·00	5·25
1946/51	60c. × 6 *Murex brevifrons*; *Charonia variegate*; *Tonna galea*; *Strombus gigas*; *Tonna maculova*; *Cassis madagasariensis* . . .	6·00	5·25
1952/7	60c. × 6 *Phalaenopsis grex*; *Cattlya loddigesii*; *Phalaenopsis*; *Dendrobium*; *Laelia anceps*; *Cymbidium* . .	6·00	5·25
MS1958	Three sheets. (a) 70 × 96 mm. $2 *Catacanthus incarnates*. (b) 66 × 96 mm. $2 *Cymatium femorale*. (c) 66 × 96 mm. $2 *Vanda rothchidiana* (horiz). Set of 3 sheets	9·75	8·75

217 White Goat

2003. New Year. "Year of the Ram" (stamps show goats and sheep). Multicoloured.

1959/61	37c. × 3 Type **217**; Sheep with curved horns; Angora goat	1·80	1·70

218 Charles Lindbergh, Donald Hall and *Spirit of St. Louis*

2003. 75th Anniv of First Transatlantic Flight. Sheet 135 × 118 mm containing T **218** and similar horiz designs. Multicoloured.

1962/7	60c. × 6, Type **218**; *Spirit of St. Louis*; *Spirit of St. Louis* on Curtis Field; *Spirit of St. Louis* airborne; Arriving in Paris; Ticker tape parade, New York . . .	6·00	5·25

219 Diana, Princess of Wales

2003. Anniversaries. Three sheets, each 136 × 96 mm containing T **219** and similar multicoloured designs.
MS1968 (a) Diana, Princess of Wales (5th death anniv). 80c. × 4, Type **219** (India); Wearing orange outfit (Canada); Wearing blue-patterned outfit (Egypt); Facing left (Italy). (b) John F. Kennedy (40th death anniv). 80c. × 4, Wearing naval uniform; Facing left; Facing right; Holding ship's wheel. (c) Ronald Reagan (92nd birth anniv). 80c. × 4, As young man, horses at right (horiz); In middle age, horses at left (horiz); As older man, one horse (horiz); Facing left, two horses (horiz) 5·25 4·75
Nos. **MS**1968a/c, respectively, each form a composite design.

220 David Brown 221 Queen Elizabeth II

2003. Columbia Space Shuttle Commemoration. Sheet 184 × 146 mm containing T **220** and similar vert designs. Multicoloured.
MS1969 37c. × 7, Type **220**; Rick Husband; Laurel Blair Salton Clark; Kalpana Chawla; Michael Anderson; William McCool; Ilan Ramon . . . . 4·25 3·75
The stamps and margin of No. **MS**1969 form a composite design.

2003. 50th Anniv of Coronation (2002) of Queen Elizabeth II. Two sheets containing T **221** and similar vert designs. Multicoloured.
MS1970 (a) 161 × 104 mm. $1 × 3, Type **221**; Wearing pink dress; Wearing Order of the Garter robes. (b) 71 × 106 mm. Wearing tiara and robe . . . . 8·25 7·25
The stamps and margins of Nos. **MS**1970a/b, respectively, each form a composite design.

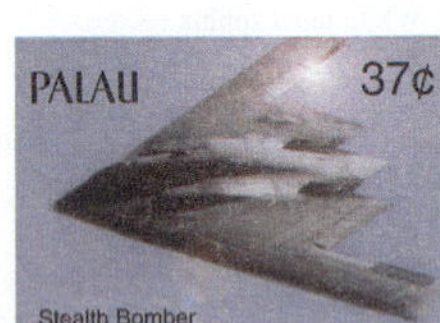

222 Stealth Bomber

2003. Military Action in Iraq. Sheet 136 × 136 mm containing T **222** and similar horiz designs. Multicoloured.

1971/6	37c. × 6, Type **222**; F-18 fighter; M1 Abrams tank; 203 mm M 110s artillery; *Donald Cook* (destroyer); Tomahawk missile	3·75	3·25

223 Prince William 224 Henri Pelissier

2003. 21st Birthday of Prince William. Multicoloured.
1977/9 $1 × 3, Type **223**; As baby; Wearing dark sweater . . . 5·00 4·50
MS1980 68 × 98 mm. $2 As baby in Princess Diana's arms . . . . 3·25 3·00

2003. Centenary of Tour de France Cycle Race. Multicoloured.
1981/4 60c. × 4, Type **224** (1923); Ottavio Bottecchia (1924); Ottavio Bottecchia (1925); Lucien Buysse (1926) . . 4·00 3·75
MS1985 161 × 100 mm. $2 Philippe Thys (1920) . . . . 3·25 3·00

225 Fokker 70

2003. Centenary of Powered Flight. Two sheets containing T **225** and similar horiz designs. Multicoloured.
MS1986 (a) 108 × 175 mm. 55c. × 6, Type **225**; Boeing 747 217B; Curtiss T-32 *Condor*; Vickers Viscount; *Wright Flyer III*; Avro Ten Achilles. (b) 106 × 76 mm. $2 *Wright Flyer III* (different) . . 3·25 3·00

226 "Blue and Silver: Trouville"

2003. Death Centenary of James McNeil Whistler (artist). Multicoloured.
1987 37c. Type **226** 75 70
1988 55c. "The Last of Old Westminster" 80 75
1989 60c. "Wapping" . . . . . 1·10 95
1990 $1 "Cremorne Gardens" . . 1·60 1·50
MS1991 Two sheets. (a) 186 × 97 mm. Size 36 × 72 mm. 80c. × 4, "Arrangement in Flesh Colour and Black: Portrait of Theodore Duret"; "Arrangement in White and Black"; "Harmony in Pink and Grey: Portrait of Lady Meux"; "Arrangement in Black and Gold; Comte Robert de Montesquiou-Fezensac". (b) 114 × 88 mm. $2 "Portrait of the Artist's Mother" (vert) . . . . 8·50 7·75

227 Apes (clown)

2003. Circus. Two sheets containing T **227** and similar vert designs. Multicoloured.
MS1992 (a) 120 × 195 mm. Clowns. 80c. × 4, Type **227**; Mo Lite; Gigi; Buttons. (b) 147 × 218 mm. Performers. 80c. × 4, Performing dogs; Trapeze artiste; Performing goat; Balancing act . . . . . 10·50 9·50

228 "Madonna Della Melagrana" (Sandro Botticelli)

2003. Christmas. Multicoloured.
1993 37c. Type **228** 75 70
1994 60c. "Madonna del Magnificat" (Sandro Botticelli) 90 80
1995 80c. "Madonna and Child with the Saints and the Angels" (Andrea del Sarto) . . . . 1·30 1·20
1996 $1 "La Madonna del Roseto" (Sandro Botticelli) . . . . 1·70 1·50
MS1997 106 × 84 mm. $2 "Madonna and Child with Angels and Saints" (Domenico Ghirlandaio) . . . 3·25 3·00

229 Mating Turtles

2004. Turtles. Two sheets containing T **229** and similar horiz designs. Multicoloured.
MS1998 (a) 146 × 107 mm. 80c. × 6, Type **229**; Laying eggs; Hatching; Hatchlings going to sea; Growing up; Returning. (b) 100 × 87 mm. $2 Turtle . . . . 3·25 3·00
The stamps and margins of Nos. **MS**1998a/b, respectively, each form a composite design.

230 "The Connoisseur" (1962)

2004. 25th Death Anniv of Norman Rockwell (artist). Two sheets containing T **230** and similar multicoloured designs.
MS1999 (a) 146 × 177 mm. 80c. × 4, Type **230**; "Artist facing Blank Canvas" (Deadline) (1938); "Art Critic" (1955); Stained glass (1960). (b) 95 × 102 mm. $2 "Painting Tavern Sign" (1926) (horiz) . . . . 3·25 3·00

231 "Antonia Zarate" (Francisco Jose de Goya y Lucientes)

2004. Treasures of Hermitage Museum, St. Petersburg. Multicoloured.
2000 37c. Type **231** 65 60
2001 55c. "Portrait of a Lady" (Antonio Correggio) . . . 80 75
2002 80c. "Portrait of Count Olivarez" (Diego Velasquez) . . . . 1·30 1·20
2003 $1 "Portrait of a Young Man with a Lace Collar" (Rembrandt Harmensz van Rijn) . . . . 1·70 1·50
MS2004 62 × 81 mm. $2 "Family Portrait" (Anthony van Dyck). Imperf . . . . 3·25 3·00

232 Coral Hind

2004. Marine Life (1st issue). Two sheets containing T **232** and similar horiz designs. Multicoloured.
MS2005 (a) 146 × 107 mm. 55c. × 6, Type **232**; Octopus; Manta ray; Dugong; Crab; Grouper. (b) 100 × 87 mm. $2 Grey reef shark 7·25 6·50
Nos. **MS**2005a/b, respectively each form a composite design. See also Nos. 2031/6.

233 Phosphate

2004. Minerals. Two sheets containing T **233** and similar horiz designs. Multicoloured.
MS2006 (a) 146 × 107 mm. 55c. × 6, Type **233**; Antimony; Limonite; Chalcopyrite (inscr "Calcopyrite"); Bauxite; Manganite. (b) 100 × 87 mm. $2 Gold 3 . . . . 7·25 6·50

234 "Dora Maar" (1938)

2004. 30th Death Anniv of Pablo Picasso (artist). Two sheets containing T **234** and similar vert designs.
MS2007 (a) 180 × 130 mm. 80c. × 4, Type **234**; "The Yellow Sweater" (1939); "Woman in Green" (1944); "Woman in Armchair" (1941). (b) 52 × 82 mm. $2 "Woman dressing her Hair" (1940). Imperf . . . 8·50 7·75

235 *Cethosia hypsea*

2004. Fauna. Six sheet containing T **235** and similar multicoloured.
MS2008 (a) 154 × 119 mm. Butterflies. 80c. × 4 Type **235**; *Cethosia myrina*; *Charaxes durnfordi*; Charaxes nitebis. (b) 154 × 119 mm. Snakes. 80c. × 4, Bull snake; Garter snake; Yellow-lipped sea snake; Yellow-bellied sea snake. (c) 154 × 119 mm. Birds. 80c. × 4, Blue-faced parrot finch (vert); Mangrove flycatcher (vert); Palau swiftlet (vert); Bridled white-eye (vert). (d) 105 × 76 mm. $2 Inscr "Charaxes nitesbis". (e) 105 × 76 mm. $2 Glass frog (f) 105 × 76 mm. $2 Dusky white-eye 13·00 11·50

236 "Green Bamboo and White Ape" (Ren Yu) (detail)

2004. New Year. Year of the Monkey. Muliticoloured.
2009 50c. Type **236** 80 75
MS2010 71 × 100 mm. $2 "Green Bamboo and White Ape" (Ren Yu) (24 × 80 mm) . . . . . . 1·60 1·50

237 Orsachel (M. Takeshi)

2004. 9th Pacific Arts Festival. Multicoloured.
2011/20 26c. × 10, Type **237**; Flute (Sim Adelbai); Rur (W. Watanabe); Bamboo Raft (P. Tiaki); Story Telling (A. Murret); Yek (A. Imetuker); Canoe House (W. Marsil); Carving Axe (W. Watanabe); Weaving (W. Marsil); Dancing Props (Sam Adelbai) . . . . 5·25 4·75
2021/30 37c. × 10, Ongall (P. Tiaki); Bai (S. Weers); Taro Plant (S. Smaserui); Toluk (W. Watanabe); Medicinal Plants (S. Smaserui); War Canoe (M. Takeshi); Painting (Sim Adelbai); Ponding Taro (A. Imetuker); Llengel (M. Takeshi); Speer Technique (A. Imeuker) . . . . . 5·25 4·75

238 Cuttle Fish

2004. Marine Life (2nd issue). Multicoloured.
2031/6 26c. × 6, Type **238**; Pennant coralfish (inscr "Longfin bannerfish") (*Heniochus acuminatus*); Red sponge and medusa worm; Sea slug (*Risbecia tryoni*); Emperor angel fish; Sea slug (*Chromodoris coi*) . . . . 6·25 5·75
2037/42 37c. × 6, Spotted eagle ray (*Aetobatis narinari*); Jelly fish (*Mastigias*); Nautilus (*Nautilus belauensis*); Grey reef shark (*Carcharchinus amblyrhynchos*); Tunicales; Manta ray (*Manta birostris*) . . . 6·25 5·75
MS2043 Two sheets (a) 107 × 66 mm. $2 Pink anemonefish (*Amphiprion perideraion*). (b) 77 × 107 mm. $2 Fire (inscr "Dusky") anemonefish (*Amphiprion melanopus*) . . . 6·50 5·75

239 Dove holding Olive Branch

2004. International Year of Peace. Two sheets containing T **239** and similar multicoloured designs.
MS2044 (a) 68 × 99 mm. $2 Type **239**; (b) 148 × 87 mm. $3 × 3, Mahatma Gandhi; Nelson Mandela; Martin Luther King 3·25 3·00

240 Early Greek Athletes

2004. Olympic Games, Athens. Multicoloured.
2045 37c. Type **240** 65 60
2046 55c. Gold medals (Atlanta, 1996) 90 80
2047 80c. Sigfrid Edstrom (IOC president 1942–1952) (vert) . . . . 1·30 1·20
2048 $1 Women footballers . . . 1·60 1·50

241 Landing Craft LCA 1377

2004. 60th Anniv of D-Day (the Normandy invasion). Two sheets containing T **241** and similar horiz designs. Multicoloured.
MS2049 (a) 136 × 136 mm. 50c. × 6, Type **241**; Landing craft, infantry; LCVP (landing craft, vehicle and personnel); Conning tower, Submarine U 309; HMS *Begonia*; HMS *Roberts*. (b) 97 × 77 mm. $2 LST (tank landing ship) . . . 8·25 7·25

242 Pope John Paul II and Mehmet Ali Agca (Turkish man who shot and wounded Pope John Paul II)

2004. 25th Anniv of Pontificate of Pope John Paul II (2003). Sheet 95 × 117 mm containing T **242** and similar horiz designs. Multicoloured.
MS2050 80c. × 4, Type **242**; Facing left (visit to Poland); Wearing shawl (concert, Ischia); With Patriach Zakka . . . . 5·25 4·75

243 Rinus Michels

245 "Babe" Ruth

244 Deng Xiaoping

2004. European Football Championship. Two sheets containing T **243** and similar multicoloured designs.
MS2051 (a) 147 × 86 mm. 80c. × 4, Type **243**; Rinat Dasaev; Marco van Basten; Olympiastadion, Berlin. (b) 98 × 85 mm. Netherlands team, 1988 Cup Winners (51 × 38 mm) . . . . 8·50 7·75
The stamps and margin of Nos. **MS**1267a/b, respectively, form composite designs.

2004. Birth Centenary of Deng Xiaoping (leader of China, 1978–89). Sheet 97 × 67 mm.
MS2052 **244** $2 multicoloured . . 3·25 3·00

2004. Centenary of World Series Baseball Championships. George Herman (Babe) Ruth Commemoration. Multicoloured.
2053 37c. Type **245** 60 55
2054 37c. Facing right 60 55

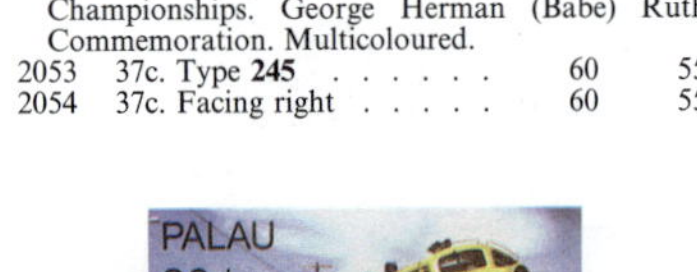

246 Locomotive ATSF 315

2004. Bicentenary of Steam Locomotives. Multicoloured.
2055/8 26c. × 4, Type **246**; Amtrak 464; Electric rail car N52; Diesel electric locomotive SD70MAC . . . . . 1·70 1·50
2059/62 50c. × 4, Locomotive CS SO2002; Locomotive P 36 NO032; Locomotive SW600; Steam locomotive (inscr "Gambler LNV 9703 440 NG") . . . . 3·25 3·00
2063/6 80c. × 4, Birney n62 Interurban; Steam locomotive (inscr "c 62-2-103103"); Locomotive (inscr "WRMO 2007"); ATSF 314 Santa Fe . . 5·25 4·75
MS2067 Three sheets. (a) 100 × 70 mm. $2 *Eurostar*. (b) 98 × 68 mm. $2 Locomotive CN 5700. (c) 101 × 70 mm. $2 *Royal Hudson* 2860 (vert) . . . . . . 9·75 8·75

247 Hadrosaurus

2004. Dinosaurs. Two sheets containing T **247** and similar horiz designs. Multicoloured.
MS2068 (a) 154 × 119 mm. 80c. × 4, Type **247**; Pterodaustro; Agilisaurus; Amargasaurus. (b) 106 × 76 mm. $2 Archaeopteryx 22·00 20·00
The stamps and margins of **MS**2068a/b, respectively, form composite designs.

248 Diego Maradona (Argentina) (3/5-size illustration)

2004. Centenary of FIFA (Federation Internationale de Football Association). Two sheets containing T **248** and similar horiz designs showing players. Multicoloured.
MS2069 (a) 193 × 97 mm. 80c. × 4, Type **248**; David Seaman (England); Andreas Brehme (Germany); Paul Ince (England). (b) 108 × 87 mm. $2 Fernando Redondo (Argentina) . . . . . 8·50 7·75

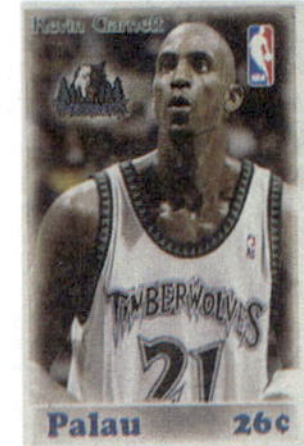

249 Kevin Garnett

2004. Basketball Players. Multicoloured.
2070 26c. Type **249** 45 40
2071 26c. Tim Duncan 45 40
2072 26c. Chris Bosh 45 40

250 "Virgin and Child" (Quentin Metsys (Massys))

2004. Christmas. Multicoloured.
2073 37c. Type **250** 75 70
2074 60c. "Virgin and Child" (Adolphe William Bouguereau) 90 80
2075 80c. "Madonna and Child" (William Dyce) . . . . . 1·30 1·20
2076 $1 Madonna and child (Carlo Crivelli) . . . . . 1·70 1·50
MS2077 76 × 107 mm. $2 Madonna and child (Peter Paul Rubens) (vert) . . . . 3·25 3·00

251 Fruit and Vegetables

2004. 5th Anniv of Diplomatic Relations with Republic of China (Taiwan). Multicoloured.
2078/81 80c. × 4, Type **251**; Destroyer; Ngarachamayong Cultural Centre; Belau National Museum . . 5·25 4·75

252 Rooster

2005. New Year. Year of the Rooster. Multicoloured.
2082 50c. Type **252** 85 60
2083 50c. As No. 2082 but design reversed 85 60

253 "Battle of Trafalgar" (Thomas Luny)

2005. Bicentenary of Battle of Trafalgar. Multicoloured.
2084 37c. Type **253** 75 70
2085 55c. *Redoubtable* surrendering (painting) . . 1·10 90
2086 80c. *Victory* firing on *Redoubtable* (painting) . . 1·30 1·20
2087 $1 "*Victory* returning Home" (J. M. W. Turner) 1·70 1·50
MS2088 86 × 122 mm. $2 Nelson wounded (painting) . . . . . 3·25 3·25

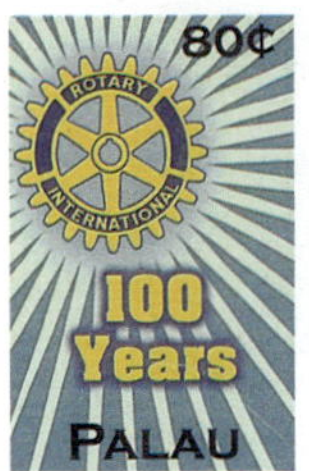

254 Emblem

255 Book Cover for "Andersen Fairy Tales"

2005. Centenary of Rotary International. Sheet 120 × 110 mm containing T **254** and similar vert designs. Multicoloured.
MS2089 80c. × 4, Type **254**; Rotary centennial bell; Flags; James Wheeler Davidson (rotary pioneer) . . . . 5·25 4·25

2005. Birth Bicentenary of Hans Christian Andersen (writer). Book covers. Multicoloured.
2090/2092 $1 × 3, Type **255**; *The Ugly Duckling*; *Tales of Hans Christian Andersen* . . . . 5·00 4·00
MS2093 67 × 97 mm. $2 *The Little Match Girl* . . . . 3·25 3·25

256 Friedrich Von Schiller

2005. Death Bicentenary of Friedrich Von Schiller (writer). Multicoloured.
MS2094 116 × 142 mm. $1 × 3, Type **256**; Facing right; Standing 5·00 4·00
MS2095 53 × 72 mm. $2 Facing left 3·25 3·25

257 Pilots reviewing Route

2005. 60th Anniv of End of World War II. Multicoloured.
2096/2099 80c. × 4, Type **257**; "Dambuster" crew; Ground crew; Lancaster bomber over Mohne Dam ("Dambuster" raid—May 16/17 1945) . . 5·25 4·25
2100/2103 80c. × 4, Russian tanks; Tank commanders; Russian and German tanks; Destroyed German tank (Kursk Battle—July 1943) 5·25 4·25
MS2104 Two sheets, each 107 × 97 mm. (a) $2 Squadron 617 Leader Guy Gibson and "Bouncing bomb" ("Dambuster" raid). (b) $2 Russian troops and destroyed German tank (Kursk Battle) . . . . 6·50 6·50

258 Audie Murphy

2005. 60th Anniv of Victory in Japan Day (VJ day—15 August 1945). Multicoloured.
2105/2108 80c. × 4, Type **258**; John F. Kennedy; Admiral Chester William Nimitz; US Marines recapture Guam . . . . 5·25 4·25
MS2109 100 × 70 mm. $2 Sailors returning home (horiz) . . . . 3·25 3·25

259 *Nautilus* ("20000 Leagues under the Sea")

2005. Death Centenary of Jules Verne (writer). Two sheets containing T **259** and similar multicoloured designs.
MS2110 145 × 56 mm. $1 × 3, Type **259**; Cliff face ("Mysterious Island"); Dinosaurs ("Journey to the Centre of the Earth") . . . 5·00 5·00
MS2111 56 × 145 mm. $2 Air balloon ("Around the World in Eighty Days") (vert) . . . . . 3·25 3·25

260 Seagulls

2005. EXPO 2005, Aichi, Japan. Multicoloured.
2112/2115 80c. × 4, Type **260**; Cosmos; Koala bear; Baby in incubator . . . 5·25 4·25

261 Tepukei

2005. Boats. Two sheets containing T **261** and similar horiz designs. Multicoloured.
MS2116 203 × 173 mm. 80c. × 4, Type **261**; Tainui; Palaun canoe; Yap outrigger . . . . 5·25 4·25
MS2117 89 × 101 mm. $2 *Kon-tiki* 3·25 3·25

262 Pope John Paul II

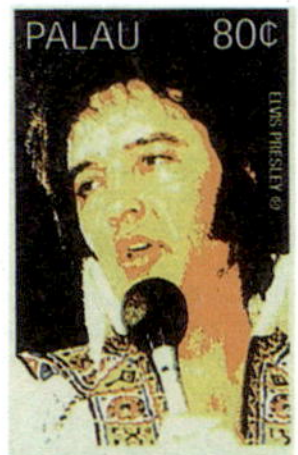

263 Elvis Presley

2005. Pope John Paul II Commemoration.
2118 **262** $1 multicoloured . . . . 1·70 1·50

2005. 70th Birth Anniv of Elvis Presley (entertainer). Multicoloured.
2119 80c. Type **263** . . . . 1·30 1·20
2120/2123 80c. × 4, Facing right (blue); As No. 2119 (green); As No. 2119 (yellow); As No. 2119 (red) . . . 5·25 4·25

264 2002 World Cup Final (Brazil–Germany)

2005. 75th Anniv of World Cup Football Championships. Multicoloured.
2124/2126 $1 × 3, Type **264**; Lothar Matthaus (Germany) holding trophy; Gerd Muller (top scorer) . . . . 5·00 4·00
MS2127 100 × 70 mm. $2 Franz Beckenbauer (German player and manager) (43 × 29 mm) . . . . 3·25 3·25

265 1939 5c. Vatican City Stamp

2005. Vacant See.
2128 **265** 37c. multicoloured . . . 75 70

266 "Wildeve Rose"

2005. Taipei 2005 International Stamp Exhibition. Roses. Multicoloured.
2129/2133 80c. × 4, Type **266**; "Graham Thomas"; "Crocus"; "Tess of the d'Urbervilles" . . 5·25 4·25

PALESTINE Pt. 1

A territory at the extreme east of the Mediterranean Sea, captured from the Turks by Great Britain in 1917 and under Military Occupation until 1920. It was a British Mandate of the League of Nations from 1923 to May 1948 when the State of Israel was proclaimed.

1918. 10 milliemes = 1 piastre.
1927. 1,000 mills = £P1.

1

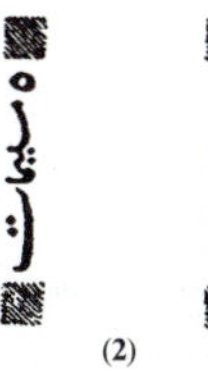

(2)

1918.
3 **1** 1p. blue . . . . 2·00 2·00

1918. Surch with T **2**.
4 **1** 5m. on 1p. blue . . . . 4·75 2·75

3 "E.E.F." = Egyptian Expeditionary Force

فلسطين
PALESTINE
פלשתינה א״י
(4)

1918.
5 **3** 1m. brown 30 40
6 2m. green 30 45
7 3m. brown 35 35
8 4m. red 35 40
9a 5m. orange 65 30
10 1p. blue 35 25
11 2p. olive . . . . 1·25 60
12 5p. purple . . . . 1·75 2·25
13 9p. ochre . . . . 4·75 5·00
14 10p. blue . . . . 4·25 3·25
15 20p. grey . . . . 11·00 16·00
Nos. 1/15 were also valid in Transjordan, Cilicia, Lebanon and Syria.

1920. Optd with T **4**.
71 **3** 1m. brown . . . . 1·00 30
61 2m. green . . . . 1·75 30
72 2m. yellow . . . . 1·00 30
62 3m. brown . . . . 1·75 30
73 3m. blue . . . . 1·75 15
74 4m. red . . . . 1·75 20
64 5m. orange . . . . 2·00 30
76 6m. green . . . . 1·75 30
77 7m. brown . . . . 1·50 30
78 8m. red . . . . 1·50 30
79 1p. grey . . . . 2·00 30
65 1p. blue . . . . 1·75 35
80 13m. blue . . . . 2·25 15
66 2p. olive . . . . 2·50 40
82 5p. purple . . . . 4·75 1·25
87 9p. ochre . . . . 9·00 9·00
88 10p. blue . . . . 7·50 2·50
26 20p. grey . . . . 27·00 42·00
89 20p. violet . . . . 9·00 5·50

9 Rachel's Tomb

10 Dome of the Rock

11 Citadel, Jerusalem

12 Sea of Galilee

1927.
90 **9** 2m. blue . . . . 1·50 10
91 3m. green . . . . 1·00 10
92 **10** 4m. red . . . . 5·50 1·25
104 4m. purple . . . . 1·25 10
93 **11** 5m. orange . . . . 2·50 10
94a **10** 6m. green 75 20
95 **11** 7m. red . . . . 7·00 60
105 7m. violet 75 10
96 **10** 8m. brown . . . . 13·00 6·00
106 8m. red . . . . 1·25 20
97 **9** 10m. grey . . . . 1·50 10
98 **10** 13m. blue . . . . 8·00 30
107 13m. brown . . . . 1·25 10
108a 15m. blue . . . . 3·25 40
99a **11** 20m. olive . . . . 1·50 15
100 **12** 50m. purple . . . . 1·50 30
101 90m. bistre . . . . 60·00 60·00
102 100m. blue . . . . 2·25 70
103b 200m. violet . . . . 9·00 3·50
109 250m. brown . . . . 4·00 2·25
110 500m. red . . . . 4·50 3·00
111 £P1 black . . . . 6·00 3·50

POSTAGE DUE STAMPS

D 1

D 2

1920.
D1 **D 1** 1m. brown . . . . 16·00 25·00
D2 2m. green . . . . 12·00 10·00
D3 4m. red . . . . 10·00 10·00
D4 8m. mauve . . . . 7·00 7·00
D5 13m. blue . . . . 6·00 6·00

1924.
D 6 **D 2** 1m. brown . . . . . . 90 2·00
D 7 2m. yellow . . . . . . 2·25 1·75
D 8 4m. green . . . . 2·00 1·25
D 9 8m. red . . . . 3·00 90
D10 13m. blue . . . . 2·75 2·50
D11 5p. violet . . . . 8·50 1·75

1928. As Type **D 2**, but inscr "MIL" instead of "MILLIEME".
D12 **D 2** 1m. brown . . . . . . 1·00 85
D13 2m. yellow . . . . . . 1·50 60
D14 4m. green . . . . . . 2·00 1·60
D15 6m. brown . . . . . . 16·00 5·00
D16 8m. red . . . . . . 2·00 1·00
D17 10m. grey . . . . . . 1·50 60
D18 13m. blue . . . . . . 2·50 1·75
D19 20m. olive . . . . . . 2·50 1·25
D20 50m. violet . . . . . . 2·75 1·25

PALESTINIAN AUTHORITY Pt. 19

Following negotiations in Oslo, during which the Israeli government recognized the Palestine Liberation Organization as representing the Arab inhabitants of those areas occupied by Israel since 1967 and the P.L.O. accepted Israel's right to exist within secure borders, an agreement was signed in Washington on 13 September 1993 under which there was to be limited Palestinian self-rule in the Gaza Strip and in an enclave around Jericho on the West Bank. Further talks followed, leading to the Cairo Agreement of 4 May 1994, which inaugurated Palestinian Authority rule in Gaza and Jericho.

Under the Taba Accord of 28 September 1995 the Israeli army progressively withdrew from much of the remainder of the West Bank, which was then placed under Palestinian Authority administration.

CURRENCY Israeli currency continued to be used in the Palestinian Authority areas. The first stamp issues had face values in mils, the currency of the Palestine Mandate period, but the Israeli authorities objected to this notional currency with the result that the face values were subsequently shown in the Jordanian currency of 1000 fils = 1 dinar.

PA 1 Monument from Hisham Palace, Jericho

1994. Multicoloured.
PA 1 5m. Type **PA 1** 10 10
PA 2 10m. Type **PA 1** 10 10
PA 3 20m. Type **PA 1** 10 10
PA 4 30m. Church of the Holy Sepulchre, Jerusalem . . 10 10
PA 5 40m. As No. PA4 . . . . 10 10
PA 6 50m. As No. PA4 . . . . 15 15
PA 7 75m. As No. PA4 . . . . 25 25
PA 8 125m. Flags of Palestinian Authority 30 30
PA 9 150m. As No. PA8 . . . . 40 40
PA10 250m. As No. PA8 . . . . 75 75
PA11 300m. As No. PA8 . . . . 1·00 1·00
PA12 500m. Flags of Palestinian Authority (51 × 29 mm) 1·40 1·40
PA13 1000m. Dome of the Rock, Jerusalem (51 × 29 mm) 3·00 3·00

PA 2 Arms of Palestinian Authority

PA 3 Prime Minister Rabin of Israel and Chairman Arafat of P.L.O. with Pres. Clinton

1994.
PA14 **PA 2** 50m. yellow 15 15
PA15 100m. green 25 25
PA16 125m. blue 30 30
PA17 200m. orange 60 60
PA18 250m. yellow 75 75
PA19 400m. purple . . . . 1·20 1·20

1994. Gaza and Jericho Peace Agreement. Sheet 105 × 70 mm.
MSPA20 **PA 3** 750m.+250m. multicoloured . . . . 3·00 3·00

PA 4 "Land of My Dreams" (Ibrahim Hazimeh)

1995. 50th Anniv of Arab League. Sheet 105 × 70 mm.
MSPA21 **PA 4** 750f.+250f. multicoloured . . . . 3·00 3·00

1995. Award of Nobel Peace Prize to Yasser Arafat, Yitzhak Rabin and Shimon Peres. No. **MS**PA20 surch **FILS** English and Arabic.
MSPA22 **PA 3** 740f.+250f. multicoloured . . . . 3·00 3·00

NEW CURRENCY. From No. PA23 the face values are expressed as 1000 fils = 1 Jordanian dinar.

PA 6 Palestine Mandate 1927 2m. Stamp

PA 7 Woman in Embroidered Costume

1995. Palestine Postal History.
PA23 **PA 6** 150f. green and black 3·75 45
PA24 – 350f. orange and black 1·10 1·10
PA25 – 500f. red and black . . 1·40 1·40
DESIGNS: 350f. Palestine Mandate 1927; 5m. stamp; 500f. Palestine Mandate 1932; 8m. stamp.

1995. Traditional Palestinian Women's Costumes. Multicoloured.
PA26 250f. Type **PA 7** 75 75
PA27 300f. Woman carrying basket 95 95
PA28 550f. Woman in cloak . . 1·80 1·80
PA29 900f. Woman in veiled headdress . . . . 2·75 2·75

1995. Nos. PA1/13 surch **FILS** in English and Arabic.
PA30 **PA 1** 5f. on 5m. mult . . . 10 10
PA31 10f. on 10m. mult . . 10 10
PA32 20f. on 20m. mult . . 10 10
PA33 – 30f. on 30m. mult . . 10 10
PA34 – 40f. on 40m. mult . . 10 10
PA35 – 50f. on 50m. mult . . 15 15
PA36 – 75f. on 75m. mult . . 25 25
PA37 – 125f. on 125m. mult 30 30
PA38 – 150f. on 150m. mult 40 40
PA39 – 250f. on 250m. mult 75 75
PA40 – 300f. on 300m. mult 1·00 1·00
PA41 – 500f. on 500m. mult 1·40 1·40
PA42 – 1000f. on 1000m. mult 3·00 3·00

1995. Handstamped **Fils** within circle in English and Arabic, twice on each stamp. (a) On Nos. PA1/13.
PA43 **PA 1** 5f. on 5m. mult . . . 10 10
PA44 10f. on 10m. mult . . 10 10
PA45 20f. on 20m. mult . . 10 10
PA46 – 30f. on 30m. mult . . 10 10
PA47 – 40f. on 40m. mult . . 10 10
PA48 – 50f. on 50m. mult . . 20 20
PA49 – 75f. on 75m. mult . . 30 30
PA50 – 125f. on 125m. mult 35 35
PA51 – 150f. on 150m. mult 45 45
PA52 – 250f. on 250m. mult 80 80
PA53 – 300f. on 300m. mult 1·10 1·10
PA54 – 500f. on 500m. mult 1·50 1·50
PA55 – 1000f. on 1000m. mult 3·00 3·00

(b) On Nos. PA14/19.
PA56 **PA 2** 50f. on 50m. yellow 20 20
PA57 100f. on 100m. green 25 25
PA58 125f. on 125m. blue 35 35
PA59 200f. on 200m. orange 80 80
PA60 250f. on 250m. yellow 85 85
PA61 400f. on 400m. purple 1·50 1·50
MSPA62 **PA 3** 750f.+250f. on 750m.+250m. multicoloured . . 3·00 3·00

PA **10** Bethlehem (old print)

1995. Christmas. Multicoloured.
PA63 10f. Type **PA10** 10 10
PA64 20f. Manger Square, Bethlehem 15 15
PA65 50f. Entrance to Church of the Nativity (vert) . . . 15 15
PA66 100f. Pope John Paul II with Yasser Arafat . . . 40 40
PA67 1000f. Site of the Nativity 3·50 3·50

PA **11** Yasser Arafat

1996.
PA68 **PA 11** 10f. black and lilac 10 10
PA69 20f. black and yellow 15 15
PA70 50f. black and blue 15 15

PA71 100f. black and green 40 40
PA72 1000f. black & brown 3·50 3·50

PA 12 Summer Palace, Peking

1996. Int Stamp Exhibitions and Fairs. Mult.
PA73 20f. Type PA **12** ("China '96") 15 15
PA74 50f. Hagia Sofia Mosque, Istanbul ("Istanbul '96") 25 25
PA75 100f. Villa Hugel, Essen (Essen stamp fair) . . . 40 40
PA76 1000f. Modern skyline, Toronto ("Capex '96") 3·75 3·75

PA 13 Crowd of Palestinians

1996. 1st Presidential Legislative and Presidential Elections. Sheet 105 × 70 mm.
MSPA77 PA **13** 1250f. multicoloured . . . . 4·75 4·75

PA 14 Boxing

1996. Olympic Games, Atlanta. Multicoloured.
PA78 30f. Type PA **14** . . . 10 10
PA79 40f. Olympic medal of 1896 . . . . 15 15
PA80 50f. Running 25 25
PA81 150f. Olympic flame and flag 55 55
PA82 1000f. Palestinian Olympic Committee emblem . . . . . . 4·00 4·00
PAPA83 140 × 105 mm. Nos. PA78 and PA80/1 . . 3·00 3·00

PA 15 Poppy

PA 17 Great Tits

PA 16 Three Wise Men

1996. Flowers and Fruits. Multicoloured.
PA84 10f. Type PA**15** 10 10
PA85 25f. Hibiscus 10 10
PA86 100f. Thyme 40 40
PA87 150f. Lemon 60 60
PA88 750f. Orange . . . . 3·00 3·00
MSPA89 105 × 70 mm. 1000f. Olive 3·75 3·75

1996. Christmas. Sheet 165 × 105 mm containing Type PA **16** and similar square designs. Multicoloured.
MSPA90 150f. Type PA **16**; 350f. Bethlehem; 500f. Shepherds; 750f. The Nativity . . . . 6·25 6·25
No. **MSPA90** form a composite design.

1997. Birds. Multicoloured.
PA91 25f. Type PA **17** 15 15
PA92 75f. Blue rock thrushes . . 25 25
PA93 150f. Golden orioles . . . 45 45
PA94 350f. Hoopoes . . . . . 1·00 1·00
PA95 600f. Peregrine falcons . . 1·40 1·40

PA 18 Gaza

1997. Palestinian Towns in 1839. Each brown and black.
PA96 350f. Type PA **18** . . . . 1·00 1·00
PA97 600f. Hebron . . . . . . 1·70 1·70

PA **19** Chinese Junk

PA **21** "The Young Jesus in the Temple" (Anton Wollenek)

PA **20** Yasser Arafat and Wischnewski

1997. Return of Hong Kong to China. Sheet 140X90 mm.
MSPA98 PA **19** 225f. multicoloured 60 60

1997. Friends of Palestine (1st series). Hans-Jurgen Wischnewski (German politician). Multicoloured.
PA 99 600f. Type PA **20** . . . . 1·40 1·40
PA100 600f. Wischnewski congratulating Yasser Arafat . . . . 1·40 1·40
See also Nos. PA103/4.

1997. Christmas.
PA101 PA **21** 350f. multicoloured 85 85
PA102 700f. multicoloured 1·70 1·70

PA **22** Mother Teresa and Street Scene

1997. Friends of Palestine (2nd series). Mother Teresa (founder of Missionaries of Charity). Multicoloured.
PA103 600f. Type PA **22** . . . . 1·40 1·40
PA104 600f. Mother Teresa with Yasser Arafat . . . . . 1·40 1·40

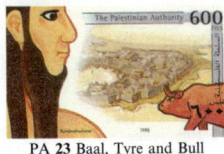

PA **23** Baal, Tyre and Bull

1998. Baal (Canaanite god). Sheet 72 × 109 mm.
MSPA105 PA **23** 600f. multicoloured . . . . 1·70 1·70

PA **24** Hare and Palm Tree

1998. Mosaics from Jabalia. Multicoloured.
PA106 50f. Type PA **24** 15 15
PA107 125f. Goat, hare and hound 40 40
PA108 200f. Lemon tree and baskets 60 60
PA109 400f. Lion . . . . 1·20 1·20

PA **25** Sea Onion

PA **26** Emblem

1998. Medicinal Plants. Multicoloured.
PA110 40f. Type PA **25** 10 10
PA111 80f. "Silybum marianum" 25 25
PA112 500f. "Foeniculum vulgare" . . . . 1·40 1·40
PA113 800f. "Inula viscosa" . . . 2·30 2·30

1998. Admission of Palestinian Authority as Non-voting Member to United Nations Organization. Sheet 82 × 65 mm.
MSPA114 PA **26** 700f. multicoloured . . . . 2·00

PA **27** Bonelli's Eagle

PA **28** Southern Swallowtail (Papilio alexanor)

1998. Birds of Prey. Multicoloured.
PA115 20f. Type PA **27** 10 10
PA116 60f. Northern hobby ("Hobby") 15 15
PA117 340f. Verreaux's eagle . . 95 95
PA118 600f. Bateleur . . . . . . 1·70 1·70
PA119 900f. Common buzzard ("Buzzard") . . . . . 2·50 2·50

1998. Butterflies. Sheet 106 × 84 mm containing Type PA**28** and similar horiz designs. Multicoloured.
MSPA120 100f. Type PA **28**; 200f. African monarch; 300f. *Gonepteryx cleopatra*; 400f. *Melanargia titea* . . . . 2·75 2·75

PA **29** Ornamental Star

1998. Christmas. Sheet 90 × 140 mm.
MSPA21 PA **29** 1000f. multicoloured . . . . 2·75 2·75

PA **30** Yasser Arafat and U.S. Pres Clinton signing Agreement

PA **31** Control Tower

1999. Wye River Middle East Peace Agreement. Sheet 83 × 65 mm.
MSPA122 PA **30** 900f. multicoloured . . . . 2·30 2·30

1999. Inauguration of Gaza International Airport. Multicoloured.
PA123 80f. Type PA **31** 15 15
PA124 300f. Fokkar F.27 Friendship airliner (horiz) 70 70
PA125 700f. Terminal building (horiz) . . . . 1·90 1·90

PA **32** Peking ("China'99")

1999. International Stamp Exhibitions and Anniversary. Multicoloured.
PA126 20f. Type PA **32** 15 15
PA127 80f. Melbourne ("Australia 99") 25 25
PA128 260f. Nuremberg ("iBRA'99") 85 85
PA129 340f. Paris ("Philexfrance 99") . . . . 1·10 1·10
PA130 400f. Emblem and landscape (face value at right) (125th anniv of U.P.U.) . . . . 1·20 1·20
PA131 400f. As No. PA130 but face value at left . . . 1·20 1·20

PA **33** Relief by Anton Wollenek

PA **34** Horse and Foal

1999. Hebron.
PA132 PA **33** 400f. multicoloured 1·20 1·20
PA133 500f. multicoloured 1·70 1·70

1999. Arabian Horses. Multicoloured.
PA134 25f. Type PA **34** 10 10
PA135 75f. Black horse 15 15
PA136 150f. Horse rearing . . . 30 30
PA137 350f. Horse trotting . . . 75 75
PA138 800f. Brown horse . . . . 1·90 1·90

PA **35** Madonna and Child

PA **37** Palestine Sunbird

PA **36** Nativity

1999. Christmas (1st series).
PA139 PA **35** 60f. blue, black and ochre 15 15
PA140 80f. multicoloured 15 15
PA141 100f. multicoloured 25 25
PA142 280f. multicoloured 60 60
PA143 300f. multicoloured 70 70
PA144 400f. multicoloured 95 95
PA145 500f. multicoloured 1·20 1·20
PA146 560f. multicoloured 1·40 1·40
See also Nos. PA147/57.

1999. Christmas (2nd series). Designs with frames and face values in colours indicated.
PA147 PA **36** 200f. multicoloured (black) 25 25
PA148 200f. multicoloured (silver) 70 70
PA149 280f. multicoloured (white) 30 30
PA150 280f. multicoloured (silver) 95 95
PA151 – 380f. multicoloured (black) 40 40
PA152 – 380f. multicoloured (silver) . . . . . 1·20 1·20
PA153 – 460f. multicoloured (white) 45 55
PA154 – 460f. multicoloured (silver) . . . . . 1·40 1·50
PA155 – 560f. multicoloured (lemon) 60 60
PA156 – 560f. multicoloured (silver) . . . . . 2·30 2·30
PA157 PA **36** 2000f. multicoloured 5·50 5·50
DESIGNS: 380, 460f. Adoration of the Magi; 560f. Flight into Egypt.

1999. Sheet 105 × 70 mm.
MSPA158 PA **37** 750f. multicoloured . . . . 1·70 1·70

PANAMA Pt. 15

Country situated on the C. American isthmus. Formerly a State or Department of Colombia, Panama was proclaimed an independent republic in 1903.

1878. 100 centavos = 1 peso.
1906. 100 centesimos = 1 balboa.

1 Coat of Arms

3 Map

1878. Imperf. The 50c. is larger.
1 **1** 5c. green 15·00 13·50
2 10c. blue 38·00 35·00
3 20c. red 24·00 21·00
4 50c. yellow 9·75

1887. Perf.
5 **3** 1c. black on green 50 65
6 2c. black on pink 1·25 1·00
7 5c. black on blue 90 35
7a 5c. black on grey 1·50 45
8 10c. black on yellow 90 45
9 20c. black on lilac 90 45
10 50c. brown 1·50 75

5 Map of Panama

38 Map of Panama

1892.
12a **5** 1c. green 15 15
12b 2c. red 20 20
12c 5c. blue 90 45
12d 10c. orange 20 20
12e 20c. violet 25 25
12f 50c. brown 30 25
12g 1p. lake 3·75 2·40

1894. Surch **HABILITADO 1894** and value.
13 **5** 1c. on 2c. red 35 35
15 **3** 5c. on 20c. black on lilac 1·50 1·00
18 10c. on 50c. brown 1·90 1·90

1903. Optd **REPUBLICA DE PANAMA**.
70 **5** 1c. green 1·25 75
36 2c. red 55 55
37 5c. blue 1·25 55
38 10c. orange 1·25 1·25
39 20c. violet 2·40 2·40
75 **3** 50c. brown 14·00 14·00
40 **5** 50c. brown 6·00 4·25
41 1p. lake 29·00 24·00

1903. Optd **PANAMA** twice.
53 **5** 1c. green 25 25
54 2c. red 25 25
55 5c. blue 30 30
56 10c. orange 30 30
64 20c. violet 90 90
65 50c. brown 1·50 1·50
66 1p. lake 3·50 2·75

1904. Optd **Republica de Panama**.
94 **5** 1c. green 35 35
97 2c. red 45 45
98 5c. blue 45 45
99 10c. orange 45 45
100 20c. violet 45 45
103 **3** 50c. brown 1·75 1·75
104 **5** 1p. lake 9·50 8·25

1905.
151 **38** ½c. orange 55 45
136 1c. green 55 40
137 2c. red 70 55

1906. Surch **PANAMA** twice and new value and thick bar.
138 **5** 1c. on 20c. violet 25 25
139 2c. on 50c. brown 25 25
140 5c. on 1p. lake 55 45

41 Panamanian Flag

42 Vasco Nunez de Balboa

43 F. de Cordoba
44 Arms of Panama

45 J. Arosemena

46 M. J. Hurtado

47 J. de Obaldia

1906.
142 **41** ½c. multicoloured 40 35
143 **42** 1c. black and green 40 35
144 **43** 2c. black and red 55 35
145 **44** 2½c. red 55 35
146 **45** 5c. black and blue 1·00 35
147 **46** 8c. black and purple 55 40
148 **47** 10c. black and violet 55 35
149 – 25c. black and brown 1·50 60
150 – 50c. black 3·75 2·10
DESIGNS: 25c. Tomas Herrera; 50c. Jose de Fabrega.

48 Balboa

49 De Cordoba

50 Arms

51 Arosemena

52 Hurtado

53 Obaldia

1909.
152 **48** 1c. black and green 65 50
153 **49** 2c. black and red 65 30
154 **50** 2½c. red 90 30
155 **51** 5c. black and blue 1·10 30
156 **52** 8c. black and purple 4·25 2·50
157 **53** 10c. black and purple 2·10 1·10

56 Balboa viewing Pacific Ocean

57 Balboa reaches the Pacific

1913. 400th Anniv of Discovery of Pacific Ocean.
160 **56** 2½c. yellow and green 45 40

1915. Panama Exhibition and Opening of Canal.
161 – ½c. black and olive 45 35
162 – 1c. black and green 55 35
163 **57** 2c. black and red 65 35
164 – 2½c. black and red 65 35
165 – 3c. black and violet 1·00 35
166 – 5c. black and blue 2·50 50
167 – 10c. black and orange 1·50 50
168 – 20c. black and brown 7·25 2·40
DESIGNS: ½c. Chorrera Falls; 1c. Relief Map of Panama Canal; 2½c. Cathedral ruins, Old Panama; 3c. Palace of Arts, National Exhibition; 5c. Gatun Locks; 10c. Culebra Cut; 20c. Archway, S. Domingo Monastery.

62 Balboa Docks

1918. Views of Panama Canal.
178 – 12c. black and violet 20·00 5·50
179 – 15c. black and blue 12·00 2·75
180 – 24c. black and brown 35·00 9·00
181 **62** 50c. black and orange 42·00 20·00
182 – 1b. black and violet 45·00 22·00
DESIGNS: 12c. "Panama" (cargo liner) in Gaillard Cut, north; 15c. "Panama" in Gaillard Cut, south; 24c. "Cristobal" (cargo liner) in Gatun Locks; 1b. "Nereus" (U.S. Navy collier) in Pedro Miguel Locks.

1919. 400th Anniv of Founding of City of Panama. No. 164 surch **1519 1919 2 CENTESIMOS 2**.
183 2c. on 2½c. black and red 45 45

64 Arms of Panama

65 Vallarino

68 Bolivar's Speech

70 Hurtado

1921. Independence Centenary. Dated "1821 1921".
184 **64** ½c. orange 55 30
185 **65** 1c. green 55 25
186 – 2c. red ("Land Gate", Panama City) 70 30
187 **65** 2½c. red (Bolivar) 95 75
188 – 3c. violet (Cervantes statue) 95 75
189 **68** 5c. blue 90 45
190 **65** 8c. olive (Carlos Ycaza) 3·50 2·10
191 – 10c. violet (Government House 1821–1921) 2·40 85
192 – 15c. blue (Balboa statue) 3·00 1·25
193 – 20c. brown (Los Santos Church) 5·00 2·40
194 **65** 24c. sepia (Herrera) 5·00 3·00
195 – 50c. black (Fabrega) 8·75 4·50

1921. Birth Centenary of Manuel Jose Hurtado (writer).
196 **70** 2c. green 55 35

1923. No. 164 surch **1923 2 CENTESIMOS 2**.
197 2c. on 2½c. black and red 35 35

72

73 Simon Bolivar

74 Statue of Bolivar

75 Congress Hall, Panama

1924.
198 **72** ½c. orange 20 10
199 1c. green 20 10
200 2c. red 25 10
201 5c. blue 35 15
202 10c. violet 40 20
203 12c. olive 45 45
204 15c. blue 55 45
205 24c. brown 2·25 65
206 50c. orange 3·75 90
207 1b. black 5·50 2·25

1926. Bolivar Congress.
208 **73** ½c. orange 35 15
209 1c. green 35 15
210 2c. red 40 25
211 4c. grey 40 25
212 5c. blue 65 40
213 **74** 8c. purple 75 65
214 10c. violet 60 60
215 12c. olive 90 90
216 15c. blue 1·25 1·10
217 20c. brown 2·40 1·25
218 **75** 24c. slate 3·00 1·50
219 50c. black 7·00 3·50

78 "Spirit of St. Louis" over Map

1928. Lindbergh's Flying Tour.
222 – 2c. red on rose 55 35
223 **78** 5c. blue on green 75 55
DESIGN—VERT: 2c. "Spirit of St. Louis" over Old Panama with opt **HOMENAJE A LINDBERGH**.

1928. 25th Anniv of Independence. Optd **1903 NOV 3 BRE 1928**.
224 **70** 2c. green 30 20

1929. Air. No. E226 surch with Fokker Universal airplane and **CORREO AEREO 25 25 VEINTICINCO CENTESIMOS**.
225 E **81** 25c. on 10c. orange 1·10 90

1929. Air. Nos. E226/7 optd **CORREO AEREO** or additionally surch with new value in **CENTESIMOS**.
238 E **81** 5c. on 10c. orange 55 55
228 10c. orange 55 55
268 10c. on 20c. brown 90 55
229 15c. on 10c. orange 55 55
269 20c. brown 90 55
230 25c. on 20c. brown 1·25 1·10

83

87

1930. Air.
231 **83** 5c. blue 20 10
232 5c. orange 35 10
233 7c. red 35 10
234 8c. black 35 10
235 15c. green 45 10
236 20c. red 50 10
237 25c. blue 55 55

1930. No. 182 optd with airplane and **CORREO AEREO**.
239 1b. black and violet 20·00 16·00

1930. Air.
244 **87** 5c. blue 20 10
245 10c. orange 35 25
246 30c. violet 6·75 4·00
247 50c. red 1·25 35
248 1b. black 6·75 4·25

1930. Bolivar's Death Centenary. Surch **1830 - 1930 17 DE DICIEMBRE UN CENTESIMO**.
249 **73** 1c. on 4c. grey 25 20

89 Seaplane over Old Panama

92 Manuel Amador Guerrero

1931. Air. Opening of service between Panama City and western provinces.
250 **89** 5c. blue 1·00 90

1932. Optd **HABILITADA** or surch also.
251 **64** ½c. orange (postage) 35 20
252 **73** ½c. orange 20 20
253 1c. green 25 20
270 **68** 1c. on 5c. blue 45 35
254 **73** 2c. red 20 20
255 5c. blue 45 30
256 – 10c. violet (No. 191) 70 35
258 **74** 10c. on 12c. olive 75 40
259 10c. on 15c. blue 70 35
257 20c. brown 1·00 1·10
260 **83** 20c. on 25c. blue (air) 4·00 55

1932. Birth Centenary of Dr. Guerrero (first president of republic).
261 **92** 2c. red 45 20

95 National Institute

1934. 25th Anniv of National Institute.
262 – 1c. green 55 55
263 – 2c. red 55 55
264 – 5c. blue 75 60
265 **95** 10c. brown 2·10 1·00
266 – 12c. green 3·50 1·50
267 – 15c. blue 4·75 1·75
DESIGNS—VERT: 1c. J. D. de Obaldia; 2c. E. A. Morales; 5c. Sphinx and Quotation from Emerson. HORIZ: 12c. J. A. Facio; 15c. P. Arosemena.

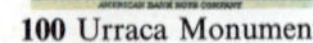

(98) **100** Urraca Monument

99 Custom House Ruins, Portobelo

1936. Birth Centenary of Pablo Arosemena. (a) Postage. Surch as T **98**, but without **CORREO AEREO**.
271 **72** 2c. on 24c. brown 55 45

(b) Air. Surch with T **98**.
272 **72** 5c. on 50c. orange 60 50

1936. 4th Spanish–American Postal Congress (1st issue). Inscr "IV CONGRESO POSTAL AMERICO-ESPANOL".
273 **99** ½c. orange (postage) . . . 40 25
274 – 1c. green 40 25
275 – 2c. red 40 25
276 – 5c. blue 45 30
277 – 10c. violet 75 45
278 – 15c. blue 75 60
279 – 20c. red . . . . 95 1·00
280 – 25c. brown . . . . 1·50 1·40
281 – 50c. orange . . . . 8·50 2·75
282 – 1b. black . . . . 9·00 7·00
DESIGNS: 1c. "Panama" (Old tree); 2c. "La Pollera" (woman in costume); 5c. Bolivar; 10c. Ruins of Old Panama Cathedral; 15c. Garcia y Santos; 20c. Madden Dam; 25c. Columbus; 50c. "Resolute" (liner) in Gaillard Cut; 1b. Panama Cathedral.

283 **100** 5c. blue (air) 70 40
284 – 10c. orange 90 65
285 – 20c. red . . . . 1·25 1·00
286 – 30c. violet . . . . 2·10 1·90
287 – 50c. red . . . . 30·00 18·00
288 – 1b. black . . . . 9·00 6·50
DESIGNS—HORIZ: 10c. "Man's Genius Uniting the Oceans"; 20c. Panama; 50c. San Pedro Miguel Locks; 1b. Courts of Justice. VERT: 30c. Balboa Monument.

1937. 4th Spanish–American Postal Congress (2nd issue). Nos. 273/88 optd **UPU**.
289 **99** ½c. orange (postage) . . . 35 20
290 – 1c. green 45 20
291 – 2c. red 45 20
292 – 5c. blue 45 30
293 – 10c. violet 75 45
294 – 15c. blue . . . . 4·75 2·40
295 – 20c. red . . . . 1·10 1·10
296 – 25c. brown . . . . 1·75 90
297 – 50c. orange . . . . 7·00 4·25
298 – 1b. black . . . . 8·75 7·50

299 **99** 5c. blue (air) 45 45
300 – 10c. orange 70 55
301 – 20c. red 95 75
302 – 30c. violet . . . . 3·50 2·40
303 – 50c. red . . . . 25·00 20·00
304 – 1b. black . . . . 11·50 9·50

1937. Optd **1937-38**.
305 **73** ½c. orange 50 45
306 **65** 1c. green 30 25
307 **73** 1c. green 30 25
308 **70** 2c. green 35 25
309 **73** 2c. red 35 30

1937. Surch **1937-38** and value.
310 **73** 2c. on 4c. grey 45 30
311 **78** 2c. on 8c. olive 45 30
312 **74** 2c. on 8c. purple 45 30
313 2c. on 10c. violet 45 30
314 2c. on 12c. olive 45 30
315 – 2c. on 15c. blue (No. 192) 45 30
316 **65** 2c. on 24c. sepia 45 30
317 2c. on 50c. black 45 30

1937. Air. Optd **CORREO AEREO** or surch also.
318 **73** 5c. blue 45 45
319 **74** 5c. on 15c. blue 45 45
320 5c. on 20c. brown 45 45
321 **75** 5c. on 24c. slate 45 45
322 **62** 5c. on 1b. black and violet 6·75 3·75
323 – 10c. on 10c. violet (No. 191) . . . . . . 1·40 90
324 **75** 10c. on 50c. black . . . . 1·40 90

105 Fire-Engine

106 Firemen's Monument

107 Fire-Brigade Badge

1937. 50th Anniv of Fire Brigade.
325 – ½c. orange (postage) . . . 45 25
326 – 1c. green 45 25
327 – 2c. red 45 30
328 **105** 5c. blue 65 30
329 **106** 10c. violet . . . . . . 1·10 65
330 – 12c. green . . . . . . 1·50 1·10

331 **107** 5c. blue (air) 55 35
332 – 10c. orange 70 45
333 – 20c. red 90 55
DESIGNS—VERT: ½c. R. Arango; 1c. J. A. Guizado; 10c. (No. 332), F. Arosemena; 12c. D. H. Brandon; 20c. J. G. Duque. HORIZ: 2c. House on fire.

108 Basketball Player

111 Old Panama Cathedral and Statue of Liberty

1938. Air. Central American and Caribbean Olympic Games.
334 **108** 1c. red 80 30
335 – 2c. green (Baseball player) (horiz) 80 15
336 – 7c. grey (Swimmer) (horiz) 1·10 35
337 – 8c. brown (Boxers) (horiz) 1·10 35
338 – 15c. blue (Footballer) . . 2·60 1·10
MS339 140×140 mm. Nos. 334/8 (sold at 35c.) . . . . 15·00 15·00

1938. Opening of Aguadulce Normal School, Santiago. Optd **NORMAL DE SANTIAGO JUNIO 5 1938** or surch also.
340 **72** 2c. red (postage) 30 25
341 **87** 7c. on 30c. violet (air) . . 45 45
342 **83** 8c. on 15c. green 45 45

1938. 150th Anniv of U.S. Constitution. Flags in red, white and blue.
343 **111** 1c. black and green (postage) 45 20
344 2c. black and red 55 25
345 5c. black and blue 60 45
346 12c. black and olive . . . 1·10 65
347 15c. black and blue . . . 1·40 75
348 7c. black and grey (air) 50 30
349 8c. black and blue 70 30
350 15c. black and brown . . 90 70
351 50c. black and orange . . 12·00 9·00
352 1b. black . . . . 12·00 9·00
Nos. 343/7 are without the Douglas DC-3 airliner.

112 Pierre and Marie Curie

1939. Obligatory Tax. Cancer Research Fund. Dated "1939".
353 **112** 1c. red 55 15
354 1c. green 55 15
355 1c. orange 55 15
356 1c. blue 55 15

113 Gatun Locks

1939. 25th Anniv of Opening of Panama Canal.
357 **113** ½c. yellow (postage) . . . 2·10 2·10
358 – 1c. green . . . . 2·25 1·75
359 – 2c. red 55 15
360 – 5c. blue . . . . 1·75 20
361 – 10c. violet . . . . 5·50 90
362 – 12c. olive 75 55
363 – 15c. blue 75 70
364 – 50c. orange . . . . . . 1·75 1·25
365 – 1b. brown . . . . 3·50 2·25
DESIGNS: 1c. "Santa Elena" (liner) in Pedro Miguel Locks; 2c. Allegory of canal construction; 5c. "Rangitata" (liner) in Culebra Cut; 10c. Panama canal ferry; 12c. Aerial view; 15c. Gen. Gorgas; 50c. M. A. Guerrero; 1b. Woodrow Wilson.

366 – 1c. red (air) 35 10
367 – 2c. green 35 15
368 – 5c. blue 55 20
369 – 10c. violet 70 25
370 – 15c. blue 95 35
371 – 20c. red . . . . 2·50 95
372 – 50c. brown . . . . 3·00 90
373 – 1b. black . . . . 6·00 4·00
PORTRAITS: 1c. B. Porras; 2c. Wm. H. Taft; 5c. P. J. Sosa; 10c. L. B. Wise; 15c. A. Reclus; 20c. Gen. Goethals; 50c. F. de Lesseps; 1b. Theodore Roosevelt.

115 Flags of American Republics

120a "Liberty"

1940. Air. 50th Anniv of Pan-American Union.
374 **115** 15c. blue 45 30

1940. Air. No. 370 surch **55**.
375 5c. on 15c. blue 25 25

No. 363 surch **AEREO SIETE**.
376 7c. on 15c. blue 40 30

No. 371 surch **SIETE**.
377 7c. on 20c. red 40 30

No. 374 surch **8–8**.
378 **115** 8c. on 15c. blue 40 30

1941. Obligatory Tax. Cancer Research Fund. Optd **LUCHA CONTRA EL CANCER**.
379 **72** 1c. green . . . . 1·40 1·10

1941. Enactment of New Constitution. (a) Postage. Optd **CONSTITUCION 1941**.
380 **72** ½c. orange 35 20
381 1c. green 35 20
382 2c. red 35 25
383 5c. blue 45 20
384 10c. violet 65 45
385 15c. blue . . . . 1·00 65
386 50c. orange . . . . 5·50 2·50
387 1b. black . . . . 13·00 4·50

(b) Air. Surch **CONSTITUCION 1941 AEREO** and value in figures.
388 E **81** 7c. on 10c. orange . . . 65 65
389 **72** 15c. on 24c. brown . . . 2·25 1·50

(c) Air. Optd **CONSTITUCION 1941**.
390 **83** 20c. red . . . . 3·25 2·25
391 **87** 50c. red . . . . 7·50 4·25
392 1b. black . . . . 17·00 9·00

1941. Obligatory Tax. Cancer Research Fund. Dated "1940".
393 **112** 1c. red 45 10
394 1c. green 45 10
395 1c. orange 45 10
396 1c. blue 45 10

1942. Telegraph stamps as T **120a** optd or surch. (a) Optd **CORREOS 1942** and (No. 397) surch **2c.**
397 2c. on 5c. blue 70 55
398 10c. violet 90 70

(b) Air. Optd **CORREO AEREO 1942**.
399 20c. brown . . . . 1·75 1·50

123 Flags of Panama and Costa Rica

1942. 1st Anniv of Revised Frontier Agreement between Panama and Costa Rica.
400 **123** 2c. red (postage) 30 25
401 15c. green (air) 60 15

1942. Obligatory Tax. Cancer Research Fund. Dated "1942".
402 **112** 1c. violet 45 15

127 Balboa reaches Pacific

129 J. D. Arosemena Normal School

131 A. G. Melendez

1942. (a) Postage stamps.
403 – ½c. red, blue and violet . . 10 10
404 – ½c. blue, orange and red 15 10
405 – 1c. green 10 10
406 – 1c. red 10 10
407 – 2c. red ("ACARRERO") 20 10
408 – 2c. red ("ACARREO") 45 10
409 – 2c. black and red 15 10
410 **127** 5c. black and blue 20 10
411 – 5c. blue 30 10
412 – 10c. orange and red . . . 45 20
413 – 10c. orange and purple . . 35 20
414 – 15c. black and blue . . . 35 55
415 – 15c. black 35 20
416 – 50c. black and red 85 60
417 – 1b. black . . . . 1·75 70
DESIGNS—VERT: ½c. National flag; 1c. Farm girl; 10c. Golden Altar, Church of St. Jose; 50c. San Blas Indian woman and child. HORIZ: 2c. Oxen drawing sugar cart; 15c. St. Thomas's Hospital; 1b. National highway.

(b) Air.
418 – 2c. red 45 10
419 – 7c. red 55 20
420 – 8c. black and brown . . . 20 10
421 – 10c. black and blue . . . 20 15
422 – 15c. violet 30 10
423 – 15c. grey 35 15
424 **129** 20c. brown 35 10
425 20c. green 35 20
426 – 50c. green . . . . 1·25 45
427 – 50c. red . . . . 3·50 2·60
428 – 50c. blue 60 40
429 – 1b. orange, yellow and black . . . . 1·40 65
DESIGNS—HORIZ: 2c., 7c. Black marlin; 8c., 10c. Gate of Glory, Portobelo; 15c. Taboga Is; 50c. Fire Brigade H.Q., Panama City; 1b. Idol (Golden Beast).

1943. Obligatory Tax. Cancer Research Fund. Dated "1943".
433 **112** 1c. green 45 15
434 1c. red 45 15
435 1c. orange 45 15
436 1c. blue 45 15

1943. Air.
437 **131** 3b. grey . . . . 5·50 5·50
438 – 5b. blue (T. Lefevre) . . . 8·50 7·00

1945. Obligatory Tax. Cancer Research Fund. Dated "1945".
439 **112** 1c. red 45 20
440 1c. green 45 20
441 1c. orange 45 20
442 1c. blue 45 20

1946. Obligatory Tax. Cancer Research Fund. Surch **CANCER B/. 0.01 1947**.
443 **72** 1c. on ½c. orange 55 15
444 1c. on 1c. green 55 15
445 – 1c. on ½c. red, blue and violet (No. 403) 45 10
446 **72** 1c. on 12c. olive 45 15
447 1c. on 24c. brown 45 15

1947. Air. Surch **AEREO 1947** and value.
448 – 5c. on 7c. red (No. 419) . . 20 20
449 **83** 5c. on 8c. black 20 20
450 – 5c. on 8c. black and brown (No. 420) 20 20
451 **83** 10c. on 15c. green 55 35
452 – 10c. on 15c. violet (422) . . 30 25

134 Flag of Panama

135 National Theatre

1947. 2nd Anniv of National Constitutional Assembly.
453 **134** 2c. red, deep red and blue (postage) 15 10
454 – 5c. blue 20 20
455 **135** 8c. violet (air) 45 30
DESIGN—As Type **134**: 5c. Arms of Panama.

1947. Cancer Research Fund. Dated "1947".
456 **112** 1c. red 45 10
457 1c. green 45 10

458 1c. orange 45 10
459 1c. blue 45 10

1947. Surch **HABILITADA CORREOS** and value.
460 **83** ½c. on 8c. black 10 10
461 – ½c. on 8c. black and brown (No. 420) . . . 10 10
462 – 1c. on 7c. red (No. 419) 15 15
463 **135** 2c. on 8c. violet 20 15

1947. Surch **Habilitada CORREOS B/. 0.50.**
464 **72** 50c. on 24c. brown 65 65

138 J. A. Arango

1948. Air. Honouring members of the Revolutionary Junta of 1903.
465 – 3c. black and blue 35 25
466 **138** 5c. black and brown . . . 35 25
467 – 10c. black and orange . . 35 25
468 – 15c. black and red 35 55
469 – 20c. black and red 40 40
470 – 50c. black . . . . 3·75 1·60
471 – 1b. black and green . . . 3·00 2·75
472 – 2b. black and yellow . . . 7·00 6·00
PORTRAITS—HORIZ: 3c. M. A. Guerrero; 10c. F. Boyd; 15c. R. Arias. VERT: 20c. M. Espinosa; 50c. Carlos Arosemena (engineer); 1b. N. de Obarrio; 2b. T. Arias.

140 Firemen's Monument

1948. 50th Anniv of Colon Fire Brigade.
473 **140** 5c. black and red 20 15
474 – 10c. black and orange . . 35 20
475 – 20c. black and blue . . . 70 40
476 – 25c. black and brown . . 70 55
477 – 50c. black and violet . . . 90 55
478 – 1b. black and green . . . 1·50 90
DESIGNS—HORIZ: 10c. Fire engine; 20c. Fire hose; 25c. Fire Brigade Headquarters. VERT: 50c. Commander Walker; 1b. First Fire Brigade Commander.

142 F. D. Roosevelt and J. D. Arosemena

144 Roosevelt Monument, Panama

1948. Air. Homage to F. D. Roosevelt.
479 **142** 5c. black and red 20 15
480 – 10c. orange 30 30
481 **144** 20c. green 35 35
482 – 50c. black and blue . . . 40 35
483 – 1b. black 90 75
DESIGNS—HORIZ: 10c. Woman with palm symbolizing "Four Freedoms"; 50c. Map of Panama Canal. VERT: 1b. Portrait of Roosevelt.

147 Cervantes

148 Monument to Cervantes

1948. 400th Birth Anniv of Cervantes.
484 **147** 2c. black and red (postage) 30 15
485 **148** 5c. black and blue (air) 20 10
486 – 10c. black and mauve . . 35 30
DESIGN—HORIZ: 10c. Don Quixote and Sancho Panza (inscr as Type **148**).

1949. Air. Jose Gabriel Duque (philanthropist). Birth Centenary. No. 486 optd **"CENTENARIO DE JOSE GABRIEL DUQUE" "18 de Enero de 1949"**.
487 10c. black and mauve 40 40

1949. Obligatory Tax. Cancer Research Fund. Surch **LUCHA CONTRA EL CANCER** and value.
488 **142** 1c. on 5c. black and red 35 10
489 – 1c. on 10c. orange (No. 480) 35 10

1949. Incorporation of Chiriqui Province Cent. Stamps of 1930 and 1942 optd **1849 1949 CHIRIQUI CENTENARIO**. (a) On postage stamps as No. 407. (i) Without surcharge.
491 – 2c. red 20 10

(ii) Surch **1 UN CENTESIMO 1** also.
490 – 1c. on 2c. red 20 10

(b) Air.
492 – 2c. red (No. 418) 20 20
493 **83** 5c. blue 30 30
494 – 15c. grey (No. 423) 40 40
495 – 50c. red (No. 427) . . . . 1·75 1·75

1949. 75th Anniv of U.P.U. Stamps of 1930 and 1942/3 optd **1874 1949 U.P.U.** No. 625 is also surch **B/0.25**.
496 – 1c. green (No. 405) (postage) 20 10
497 – 2c. red (No. 407) 30 15
498 **127** 5c. blue 45 25
499 – 2c. red (No. 418) (air) . . 20 20
500 **83** 5c. orange 55 35
501 – 10c. black and blue (No. 421) 20 20
502 **131** 25c. on 3b. grey 30 30
503 – 50c. red (No. 427) . . . . 1·60 1·60

1949. Cancer Research Fund. Dated "1949".
504 **112** 1c. brown 45 10

153 Father Xavier

154 St. Xavier University

1949. Bicentenary of Founding of St. Xavier University.
505 **153** 2c. black and red (postage) 25 15
506 **154** 5c. black and blue (air) 35 15

155 Dr. Carlos J. Finlay

156 "Aedes aegypti"

1950. Dr. Finlay (medical research worker).
507 **155** 2c. black and red (postage) 35 15
508 **156** 5c. black and blue (air) 85 40

1950. Death Centenary of San Martin. Optd **CENTENARIO del General** (or **Gral.**) **Jose de San Martin 17 de Agosto de 1950** or surch also. The 50c. is optd **AEREO** as well.
509 – 1c. green (No. 405) (postage) 15 10
510 – 2c. on ½c. blue, orange and red (No. 404) . . . 20 10
511 **127** 5c. black and blue 25 20
512 – 2c. red (No. 418) (air) . . 35 30
513 **83** 5c. orange 35 35
514 – 10c. black & blue (No. 421) 55 45
515 **83** 25c. blue 90 70
516 – 50c. black & violet (No. 477) . . . . . . 1·40 1·00

158 Badge

159 Stadium

1950. Obligatory Tax. Physical Culture Fund. Dated "1950".
517 – 1c. black and red 70 20
518 **158** 1c. black and blue 70 20
519 **159** 1c. black and green . . . 70 20
520 – 1c. black and orange . . 70 20
521 – 1c. black and violet . . . 70 20
DESIGNS—VERT: No. 520, as Type **159** but medallion changed and incorporating four "F"'s; 521, Discus thrower. HORIZ: No. 517, as Type **159** but front of stadium.

1951. Birth Tercentenary of Jean-Baptiste de La Salle (educational reformer). Optd **Tercer Centenario del Natalicio de San Juan Baptista de La Salle. 1651-1951.**
522 2c. black and red (No. 409) 15 15
523 5c. blue (No. 411) 25 15

1952. Air. Surch **AEREO 1952** and value.
524 2c. on 10c. black and blue (No. 421) 20 15
525 5c. on 10c. black and blue (No. 421) 25 10
526 1b. on 5b. blue (No. 438) . . 23·00 23·00

1952. Surch **1952** and figure of value.
527 1c. on ½c. (No. 404) 15 10

Air. Optd **AEREO** also.
528 5c. on 2c. (No. 408) 15 10
529 25c. on 10c. (No. 413) . . . 70 65

164 Isabella the Catholic

167 Masthead of "La Estrella"

1952. 500th Birth Anniv of Isabella the Catholic.
530 **164** 1c. black & grn (postage) 10 10
531 2c. black and red 15 10
532 5c. black and blue 20 15
533 10c. black and violet . . . 25 20
534 4c. black and orange (air) 10 10
535 5c. black and olive . . . 15 10
536 10c. black and buff . . . 35 30
537 25c. black and slate . . . 55 35
538 50c. black and brown . . 75 45
539 1b. black . . . . 3·00 3·00

1953. Surch **B/.0.01 1953.**
540 1c. on 10c. (No. 413) 10 10
541 1c. on 15c. black (No. 415) 15 10

1953. Air. No. 421 surch **5 1953.**
542 5c. on 10c. black and blue . . 35 10

1953. Air. Centenary of "La Estrella de Panama", Newspaper.
543 **167** 5c. red 20 15
544 10c. blue 25 25

168 Pres. and Senora Amador Guerrero

1953. 50th Anniv of Panama Republic.
545 – 2c. violet (postage) . . . 15 10
546 **168** 5c. orange 20 10
547 – 12c. purple 35 15
548 – 20c. indigo . . . . 2·25 45
549 – 50c. yellow 90 65
550 – 1b. blue . . . . 2·25 1·00
DESIGNS—VERT: 2c. Blessing the flat; 50c. Old Town Hall. HORIZ: 12c. J. A. Santos and J. De La Ossa; 20c. Revolutionary council; 1b. Obverse and reverse of coin.

551 – 2c. blue (air) 10 10
552 – 5c. green 15 10
553 – 7c. grey 20 15
554 – 25c. black . . . . 1·40 70
555 – 50c. brown 65 70
556 – 1b. orange . . . . 2·25 1·00
DESIGNS—VERT: 2c. Act of Independence. HORIZ: 5c. Pres. and Senora Remon Cantera; 7c. Girl in national costume; 25c. National flower; 50c. Salazar, Huertas and Domingo; 1b. National dance.

1954. Surch in figures.
557 – 3c. on 1c. red (No. 406) (postage) 10 10
558 **167** 1c. on 5c. red (air) . . . 10 10
559 1c. on 10c. blue 10 10

170 Gen. Herrera at Conference Table

1954. Death Centenary of Gen. Herrera.
560 – 3c. violet (postage) . . . 20 10
561 **170** 6c. green (air) 15 10
562 – 1b. black and red . . . . 2·25 2·10
DESIGNS—VERT: 3c. Equestrian statue. HORIZ: 1b. Cavalry charge.

171 Rotary Emblem and Map

1955. Air. 50th Anniv of Rotary International.
563 **171** 6c. violet 15 10
564 21c. red 55 35
565 1b. black . . . . 3·50 1·90

172 Tocumen Airport

173 President Remon Cantera

1955.
566 **172** ½c. brown 10 10

1955. National Mourning for Pres. Remon Cantera.
567 **173** 3c. black & pur (postage) 15 10
568 6c. black and violet (air) 20 15

174 V. de la Guardia y Azala and M. Chiaria

175 F. de Lesseps

1955. Centenary of Cocle Province.
569 **174** 5c. violet 20 10

1955. 150th Birth Anniv of De Lesseps (engineer).
570 **175** 3c. lake on pink (postage) 30 10
571 – 25c. blue on blue . . . . 4·25 2·50
572 – 50c. violet on lilac 90 60
573 – 5c. myrtle on green (air) 20 10
574 – 1b. black and mauve . . 3·00 1·75
DESIGNS—VERT: 5c. P. J. Sosa; 50c. T. Roosevelt. HORIZ: 25c. First excavations for Panama Canal; 1b. "Ancon I" (first ship to pass through canal) and De Lesseps.

1955. Air. No. 564 surch.
575 **171** 15c. on 21c. red 45 35

177 Pres. Eisenhower (United States)

178 Bolivar Statue

1956. Air. Pan-American Congress, Panama and 30th Anniv of First Congress.
576 – 6c. black and blue 30 20
577 – 6c. black and bistre . . . 30 20
578 – 6c. black and green . . . 30 20
579 – 6c. sepia and green . . . 30 20
580 – 6c. green and yellow . . . 30 20
581 – 6c. green and violet . . . 30 20
582 – 6c. blue and lilac 30 20
583 – 6c. green and purple . . . 30 20
584 – 6c. blue and olive 30 20
585 – 6c. sepia and yellow . . . 30 20
586 – 6c. blue and sepia 30 20
587 – 6c. green and mauve . . . 30 20
588 – 6c. sepia and red 30 20
589 – 6c. green and blue 30 20
590 – 6c. sepia and blue 30 20
591 – 6c. black and orange . . . 30 20
592 – 6c. sepia and grey 30 20
593 – 6c. black and pink 30 20
594 **177** 6c. blue and red 70 35
595 – 6c. blue and grey 30 20
596 – 6c. green and brown . . . 30 20
597 **178** 20c. grey 40 55

598 – 50c. green 75 75
599 – 1b. sepia 1·50 95
PRESIDENTIAL PORTRAITS as Type **177**: No. 576, Argentina; 577, Bolivia; 578, Brazil; 579, Chile; 580, Colombia; 581, Costa Rica; 582, Cuba; 583, Dominican Republic; 584, Ecuador; 585, Guatemala; 586, Haiti; 587, Honduras; 588, Mexico; 589, Nicaragua; 590, Panama; 591, Paraguay; 592, Peru; 593, Salvador; 595, Uruguay; 596, Venezuela. As Type **178**—HORIZ: No. 598, Bolivar Hall. VERT: No. 599, Bolivar Medallion.

179 Arms of Panama City

180 Pres. Carlos A. Mendoza

1956. 6th Inter-American Congress of Municipalities, Panama City.
600 **179** 3c. green (postage) 15 10
601 – 25c. red (air) 55 35
602 – 50c. black 65 55
MS603 125×76 mm. Nos. 600/2. Imperf (sold at 85c.) 2·50 2·50
DESIGNS: 25c. Stone bridge, Old Panama; 50c. Town Hall, Panama.

1956. Birth Centenary of Pres. Carlos A. Mendoza.
604 **180** 10c. green and red 20 15

182 Dr. Belisario Porras

1956. Birth Centenary of Dr. Porras.
605 – 15c. grey (postage) 45 20
606 **182** 25c. blue and red 65 45
607 – 5c. green (air) 10 10
608 – 15c. red 30 25
DESIGNS—HORIZ: 15c. (No. 605), National Archives; 15c. (No. 608), St. Thomas's Hospital. VERT: 5c. Porras Monument.

183 Isthmus Highway

185 Manuel E. Batista

1957. 7th Pan-American Highway Congress.
609 **183** 3c. green (postage) 15 10
610 – 10c. black (air) 20 15
611 – 20c. black and blue 35 35
612 – 1b. green 1·75 1·75
MS613 85c. No. **MS**603 optd **VII CONGRESO INTERAMERICANO DE CARRETERAS 1957** 7·00 7·00
DESIGNS—VERT: 10c. Highway under construction; 20c. Darien Forest; 1b. Map of Pan-American Highway.

1957. Air. Surch **1957 x 10c x**.
614 **173** 10c. on 6c. black & violet 20 20

1957. Birth Centenary of Manuel Espinosa Batista (independence leader).
615 **185** 5c. blue and green 15 10

186 Portobelo Castle

189 U.N. Emblem

1957. Air. Buildings. Centres in black.
616 **186** 10c. grey 25 15
617 – 10c. purple 25 15
618 – 10c. violet 25 15
619 – 10c. grey and green 25 15
620 – 10c. blue 25 15
621 – 10c. brown 25 15
622 – 10c. orange 25 15
623 – 10c. light blue 25 15
624 – 1b. red 2·10 95
DESIGNS—HORIZ: No. 617, San Jeronimo Castle; 618, Portobelo Customs-house; 619, Panama Hotel; 620, Pres. Remon Cantera Stadium; 621, Palace of Justice; 622, Treasury; 623, San Lorenzo Castle. VERT: No. 624, Jose Remon Clinics.

1957. Surch **1957** and value.
625 **172** 1c. on ½c. brown 10 10
626 3c. on ½c. brown 10 10

1958. Air. Surch **1958** and value.
627 **170** 5c. on 6c. green 20 10

1958. Air. 10th Anniv of U.N.O.
628 **189** 10c. green 20 10
629 21c. blue 45 35
630 50c. orange 45 45
631 – 1b. red, blue and grey 1·75 1·40
MS632 127×102 mm. Nos. 628/31. Imperf (sold at 2b.) 6·50 6·50
DESIGN: 1b. Flags of Panama and United Nations.

1958. No. 547 surch **3c 1958**.
633 3c. on 12c. purple 10 10

191 Flags Emblem

192 Brazilian Pavilion

1958. 10th Anniv of Organization of American States. Emblem (T **191**) multicoloured within yellow and black circular band; background colours given below.
634 **191** 1c. grey (postage) 10 10
635 2c. green 10 10
636 3c. red 15 10
637 7c. blue 25 10
638 5c. blue (air) 15 10
639 10c. red 20 15
640 – 50c. black, yellow and grey 35 35
641 **191** 1b. black 1·75 1·40
DESIGN—VERT: 50c. Headquarters building.

1958. Brussels International Exhbition.
642 **192** 1c. green & yellow (postage) 10 10
643 – 3c. green and blue 15 10
644 – 5c. slate and brown 15 10
645 – 10c. brown and blue 20 20
646 – 15c. violet and grey (air) 35 35
647 – 50c. brown and slate 60 60
648 – 1b. turquoise and lilac 1·25 1·25
MS649 130×105 mm. Nos. 642/8 (sold at 2b.) 4·25 4·25
DESIGNS—PAVILIONS: As Type **192**: 3c. Argentina; 5c. Venezuela; 10c. Great Britain; 15c. Vatican City; 50c. United States; 1b. Belgium.

193 Pope Pius XII

194 Children on Farm

1959. Pope Pius XII Commemoration.
650 **193** 3c. brown (postage) 15 10
651 – 5c. violet (air) 15 15
652 – 30c. mauve 30 25
653 – 50c. grey 75 60
MS654 127×86 mm. Nos. 650/3. Imperf (sold at 1b.) 2·10 2·10
PORTRAITS (Pope Pius XII): 5c. when Cardinal; 30c. wearing Papal tiara; 50c. enthroned.

1959. Obligatory Tax. Youth Rehabilitation Institute. Size 35×24 mm.
655 **194** 1c. grey and red 15 10

195 U.N. Headquarters, New York

197 J. A. Facio

1959. 10th Anniv of Declaration of Human Rights.
656 **195** 3c. olive & brown (postage) 10 10
657 – 15c. green and orange 35 25
658 – 5c. blue and green (air) 15 10
659 – 10c. brown and grey 20 15
660 – 20c. slate and brown 35 35
661 – 50c. blue and green 60 60
662 **195** 1b. blue and red 1·40 1·25
DESIGNS: 5c., 15c. Family looking towards light; 10c., 20c. U.N. emblem and torch; 50c. U.N. flag.

1959. 8th Latin-American Economic Commission Congress. Nos. 656/61 optd **8A REUNION C.E.P.A.L. MAYO 1959** or surch also.
663 **195** 3c. olive and brown (postage) 10 10
664 – 15c. green and orange 35 20
665 – 5c. blue and green (air) 10 10
666 – 10c. brown and grey 25 15
667 – 20c. slate and brown 45 35
668 – 1b. on 50c. blue and green 1·60 1·60
MS669 No. **MS**654, but larger in two lines (sold at 1b.) 5·00 5·00

1959. 50th Anniv of National Institute.
670 – 3c. red (postage) 10 10
671 – 13c. green 30 15
672 – 21c. blue 40 30
673 **197** 5c. black (air) 10 10
674 – 10c. black 20 20
DESIGNS—VERT: 3c. E. A. Morales (founder); 10c. Ernesto de la Guardia, Nr; 13c. A. Bravo. HORIZ: 21c. National Institute building.

1959. Obligatory Tax. Youth Rehabilitation Institute. As No. 655, but colours changed and inscr "1959".
675 **194** 1c. green and black 10 10
676 1c. blue and black 10 10
See also No. 690.

198 Football

200 Administration Building

1959. 3rd Pan-American Games, Chicago. Inscr "III JUEGOS DEPORTIVOS PANAMERICANOS".
677 **198** 1c. green & grey (postage) 10 10
678 – 3c. brown and blue 15 10
679 – 20c. brown and green 50 45
680 – 5c. brown and black (air) 15 10
681 – 10c. brown and grey 25 20
682 – 50c. brown and blue 45 40
DESIGNS: 3c. Swimming; 5c. Boxing; 10c. Baseball; 20c. Hurdling; 50c. Basketball.

1960. Air. World Refugee Year. Nos. 554/6 optd **NACIONES UNIDAS ANO MUNDIAL REFUGIADOS. 1959–1960.**
683 25c. black 35 35
684 50c. brown 70 55
685 1b. orange 1·50 1·10

1960. Air. 25th Anniv of National University.
686 **200** 10c. green 15 15
687 – 21c. blue 30 20
688 – 25c. blue 50 35
689 – 30c. black 55 40
DESIGNS: 21c. Faculty of Science; 25c. Faculty of Medicine; 30c. Statue of Dr. Octavio Mendez Pereira (first rector) and Faculty of Law.

1960. Obligatory Tax. Youth Rehabilitation Institute. As No. 655 but smaller (32×22 mm) and inscr "1960".
690 **194** 1c. grey and red 10 10

202 Fencing

204 "Population"

1960. Olympic Games.
691 **202** 3c. purple & violet (postage) 10 10
692 – 5c. green and turquoise 20 10
693 – 5c. red and orange (air) 10 10
694 – 10c. black and bistre 20 15
695 – 25c. deep blue and blue 45 40
696 – 50c. black and brown 60 45
MS697 127×76 mm. Nos. 695/6. Imperf (sold at 80c.) 2·50 2·50
DESIGNS—VERT: 5c. (No. 692), Football; (No. 693), Basketball; 25c. Javelin-throwing; 50c. Runner with Olympic Flame. HORIZ: 10c. Cycling.

1960. Air. 6th National Census (5c.) and Central American Census.
698 **204** 5c. black 10 10
699 – 10c. brown 20 15
DESIGN: 10c. Two heads and map.

205 Boeing 707 Airliner

1960. Air.
700 **205** 5c. blue 15 10
701 10c. green 40 20
702 20c. brown 85 40

206 Pastoral Scene

1961. Agricultural Census (16th April).
703 **206** 3c. turquoise 10 10

206a U.N. Emblem

1961. Air. 15th Anniv of United Nations (1960). Sheet 65×77 mm. Imperf.
MS704 80c. cerise and black 1·60 1·60

207 Helen Keller School

1961. 25th Anniv of Lions Club.
705 – 3c. blue (postage) 10 10
706 **207** 5c. black (air) 10 10
707 – 10c. green 20 10
708 – 21c. blue, red and yellow 40 30
DESIGNS: 3c. Nino Hospital; 10c. Children's Colony, Verano; 21c. Lions emblem, arms and slogan.

1961. Air. Obligatory Tax. Youth Rehabilitation Fund. Surch **1 c "Rehabilitacion de Menores"**.
709 – 1c. on 10c. black and bistre (No. 694) 10 10
710 **205** 1c. on 10c. green 10 10

1961. Air. World Refugee Year (1959–60). Sheet No. **MS**704 optd with uprooted oak emblem and **ANO DE LOS REFUGIADOS**.
MS711 80c. cerise and black 3·50 3·50

1961. Air. Surch **HABILITAD. en** and value.
712 **200** 1c. on 10c. green 10 10
713 – 1b. on 25c. blue and blue (No. 695) 1·25 1·25

210 Flags of Costa Rica and Panama

1961. Meeting of Presidents of Costa Rica and Panama.
715 **210** 3c. red and blue (postage) 15 10
716 – 1b. black and gold (air) 1·25 75
DESIGN: 1b. Pres. Chiari of Panama and Pres. Echandi of Costa Rica.

211 Girl using Sewing-machine

212 Campaign Emblem

1961. Obligatory Tax. Youth Rehabilitation Fund.
717 **211** 1c. violet 10 10
718 1c. yellow 10 10
719 1c. green 10 10
720 1c. blue 10 10
721 1c. purple 10 10
722 – 1c. mauve 10 10
723 – 1c. grey 10 10
724 – 1c. blue 10 10
725 – 1c. orange 10 10
726 – 1c. red 10 10
DESIGN: Nos. 722/6, Boy sawing wood.

1961. Air. Malaria Eradication.
727 **212** 5c.+5c. red 60 30
728 10c.+10c. blue 60 30
729 15c.+15c. green 60 30

213 Dag Hammarskjold

214 Arms of Panama

1961. Air. Death of Dag Hammarskjold.
730 **213** 10c. black and grey . . . 20 15

1962. Air. (a) Surch **Vale B/.0.15**.
731 **200** 15c. on 10c. green 30 20
(b) No. 810 surch **XX** over old value and **VALE B/ .1.00**.
732 – 1b. on 25c. deep blue and blue . . . . 1·25 75

1962. 3rd Central American Inter-Municipal Co-operation Assembly.
733 **214** 3c. red, yellow and blue (postage) 10 10
734 – 5c. black and blue (air) 20 10
DESIGN—HORIZ: 5c. City Hall, Colon.

215 Mercury on Cogwheel

217 Social Security Hospital

1962. 1st Industrial Census.
735 **215** 3c. red 10 10

1962. Surch **VALE** and value with old value obliterated.
736 **212** 10c. on 5c.+5c. red . . . 90 45
737 20c. on 10c.+10c. blue . . 1·50 90

1962. Opening of Social Security Hospital, Panama City.
738 **217** 3c. black and red 10 10

218 Colon Cathedral

221 Col. Glenn and Capsule "Friendship 7"

220 Thatcher Ferry Bridge nearing Completion

1962. "Freedom of Worship". Inscr "LIBERTAD DE CULTOS". Centres in black.
739 – 1c. red and blue (postage) 10 10
740 – 2c. red and cream 10 10
741 – 3c. blue and cream 10 10
742 – 5c. red and green 10 10
743 – 10c. green and cream . . 20 15
744 – 10c. mauve and blue . . 20 15
745 – 15c. blue and green . . . 30 20
746 **218** 20c. red and pink 35 25
747 – 25c. green and pink . . . 45 35
748 – 50c. blue and pink . . . 60 55
749 – 1b. violet and cream . . . 1·75 1·40
DESIGNS—HORIZ: 1c. San Francisco de Veraguas Church; 3c. David Cathedral; 25c. Orthodox Greek Temple; 1b. Colon Protestant Church. VERT: 2c. Panama Old Cathedral; 5c. Nata Church; 10c. Don Bosco Temple; 15c. Virgin of Carmen Church; 50c. Panama Cathedral.

750 – 5c. violet and flesh (air) . . 10 10
751 – 7c. light mauve and mauve 15 10
752 – 8c. violet and blue 15 10
753 – 10c. violet and salmon . . . 20 10
754 – 10c. green and purple . . . 20 20
755 – 15c. red and orange 25 20
756 – 21c. sepia and blue 35 30
757 – 25c. blue and pink 45 35
758 – 30c. mauve and blue 50 45
759 – 50c. purple and green . . . 70 70
760 – 1b. blue and salmon . . . . 1·25 1·10
MS761 132 × 107 mm. Nos. 747/8, 757 and 759. Imperf . . . . . 2·10 2·10
DESIGNS—HORIZ: 5c. Cristo Rey Church; 7c. San Miguel Church; 21c. Canal Zone Synagogue; 25c. Panama Synagogue; 50c. Canal Zone Protestant Church. VERT: 8c. Santuario Church; 10c. Los Santos Church; 15c. Santa Ana Church; 30c. San Francisco Church; 1b. Canal Zone Catholic Church.

1962. Air. 9th Central American and Caribbean Games, Jamaica. Nos. 693 and 695 optd **"IX JUEGOS C.A. Y DEL CARIBE KINGSTON - 1962"** or surch also.
762 5c. red and orange 15 15
764 10c. on 25c. deep blue & blue 55 50
765 15c. on 25c. deep blue & blue 40 35
766 20c. on 25c. deep blue & blue 45 45
763 25c. deep blue and blue . . . 55 50

1962. Opening of Thatcher Ferry Bridge, Canal Zone.
767 **220** 3c. black and red (postage) 10 10
768 – 10c. black and blue (air) 20 15
DESIGN: 10c. Completed bridge.

1962. Air. Col. Glenn's Space Flight.
769 **221** 5c. red 10 10
770 – 10c. yellow 20 20
771 – 31c. blue 45 40
772 – 50c. green 65 65
MS773 77 × 110 mm. Nos. 769/72. Imperf (sold at 1b.) . . . . . . 2·50 2·50
DESIGNS—HORIZ: "Friendship": 10c. Over Earth; 31c. In space. VERT: 50c. Col. Glenn.

222 U.P.A.E. Emblem

225 F.A.O. Emblem

223 Water Exercise

1963. Air. 50th Anniv of Postal Union of Americas and Spain.
774 **222** 10c. multicoloured 20 15

1963. 75th Anniv of Panama Fire Brigade.
775 **223** 1c. black & green (postage) 10 10
776 – 3c. black and blue 10 10
777 – 5c. black and red 10 10
778 – 10c. black and orange (air) 15 15
779 – 15c. black and purple . . 20 20
780 – 21c. blue, gold and red . . 50 45
DESIGNS: 3c. Brigade officers; 5c. Brigade president and advisory council; 10c. "China" pump in action, 1887; 15c. "Cable 14" station and fire-engine; 21c. Fire Brigade badge.

1963. Air. Red Cross Cent (1st issue). Nos. 769/71 surch with red cross **1863 1963** and premium.
781 **215** 5c.+5c. red . . . . . . 1·40 1·40
782 – 10c.+10c. yellow . . . . 2·75 2·75
783 – 31c.+15c. blue . . . . . 2·75 2·75
See also No. 797.

1963. Air. Freedom from Hunger.
784 **225** 10c. red and green 20 20
785 15c. red and blue 30 25

1963. Air. 22nd Central American Lions Convention. Optd **"XXII Convencion Leonistica Centroamericana Panama, 18-21 Abril 1963"**.
786 **207** 5c. black 10 10

1963. Air. Surch **HABILITADO Vale B./0.04.**
789 **200** 4c. in 10c. green 10 10

1963. Air. Nos. 743 and 769 optd **AEREO** vert.
790 10c. green and cream 20 15
791 20c. brown and green 30 25

1963. Air. Freedom of the Press. No. 693 optd **LIBERTAD DE PRENSA 20-VIII-63.**
792 5c. red and orange 10 10

1963. Air. Visit of U.S. Astronauts to Panama. Optd **"Visita Astronautas Glenn-Schirra Sheppard Cooper a Panama"** or surch also.
793 **221** 5c. red . . . . 2·50 2·50
794 10c. on 5c. red . . . . . 3·25 3·25
MS795 77 × 100 mm. No. **MS**773 (sold at 1b.) . . . . 30·00 30·00

1963. Air. Surch **HABILITADO 10c.**
796 **221** 10c. on 5c. red . . . . . 5·50 5·50

1963. Air. Red Cross Centenary (2nd issue). No. 781 surch **"Centenario Cruz Roja Internacional 10c"** with premium obliterated.
797 **221** 10c. on 5c.+5c. red . . . 6·00 6·00

1963. Surch **VALE** and value.
798 **217** 4c. on 3c. black and red (postage) 15 10
799 – 4c. on 3c. black, blue and cream (No. 741) . . . 15 10
800 **220** 4c. on 3c. black and red 15 10
801 – 4c. on 3c. black and blue (No. 776) 15 10
802 **182** 10c. on 25c. blue and red 35 15
803 – 10c. on 25c. blue (No. 688) (air) 20 15

234 Pres. Orlich (Costa Rica) and Flags

236 Vasco Nunez de Balboa

235 Innsbruck

1963. Presidential Reunion, San Jose (Costa Rica). Multicoloured. Presidents and flags of their countries.
804 1c. Type **234** (postage) . . . 10 10
805 2c. Somoza (Nicaragua) . . . 15 15
806 3c. Villeda (Honduras) . . . 20 15
807 4c. Chiari (Panama) 25 20
808 5c. Rivera (El Salvador) (air) 30 30
809 10c. Ydigoras (Guatemala) 55 45
810 21c. Kennedy (U.S.A.) . . . 1·60 1·40

1963. Winter Olympic Games, Innsbruck.
811 ½c. red and blue (postage) . . 10 10
812 1c. red, brown and turquoise 10 10
813 3c. red and blue 25 15
814 4c. red, brown and green . . 35 20
815 5c. red, brown and mauve (air) 45 25
816 15c. red, brown and blue . . 1·10 90
817 21c. red, brown and myrtle 2·25 1·90
818 31c. red, brown and blue . . 3·00 2·25
MS819 100 × 65 mm. Nos. 817/18 but colours changed. Imperf 14·00 12·00

DESIGNS: ½c. (expressed "B/0.005"), 3c. Type **235**; 1, 4c. Speed-skating; 5c. to 31c. Skiing (slalom).

1964. 450th Anniv of Discovery of Pacific Ocean.
820 **236** 4c. green on flesh (postage) 10 10
821 10c. violet on pink (air) 20 20

237 Boy Scout

238 St. Paul's Cathedral, London

1964. Obligatory Tax for Youth Rehabilitation Institute.
822 **237** 1c. red 10 10
823 1c. grey 10 10
824 1c. light blue 10 10
825 1c. olive 10 10
826 1c. violet 10 10
827 – 1c. brown 10 10
828 – 1c. orange 10 10
829 – 1c. turquoise 10 10
830 – 1c. violet 10 10
831 – 1c. yellow 10 10
DESIGN: Nos. 827/31, Girl guide.

1964. Air. Ecumenical Council, Vatican City (1st issue). Cathedrals. Centres in black.
832 21c. red (Type **238**) 55 35
833 21c. blue (Kassa, Hungary) 55 35
834 21c. green (Milan) 55 35
835 21c. black (St. John's, Poland) 55 35
836 21c. brown (St. Stephen's, Vienna) 55 35
837 21c. brown (Notre Dame, Paris) 55 35
838 21c. violet (Moscow) 55 35
839 21c. violet (Lima) 55 35
840 21c. red (Stockholm) 55 35
841 21c. mauve (Cologne) 55 35
842 21c. bistre (New Delhi) . . . 55 35
843 21c. deep turquoise (Basel) 55 35
844 21c. green (Toledo) 55 35
845 21c. red (Metropolitan, Athens) 55 35
846 21c. olive (St. Patrick's, New York) 55 35
847 21c. green (Lisbon) 55 35
848 21c. turquoise (Sofia) 55 35
849 21c. deep brown (New Church, Delft, Netherlands) 55 35
850 21c. deep sepia (St. George's Patriarchal Church, Istanbul) 55 35
851 21c. blue (Basilica, Guadalupe, Mexico) . . . 55 35
852 1b. blue (Panama) . . . . . 1·75 1·75
853 2b. green (St. Peter's, Rome) 3·00 3·00
MS854 198 × 138 mm. Nos. 832, 837/8, 846 and 852/3. Imperf (sold at 3b.85) . . . . 9·00 9·00
See also Nos. 822/**MS**888.

1964. As Nos. 749 and 760 but colours changed and optd **HABILITADA**.
855 1b. black, red & blue (postage) . . . . 1·75 1·60
856 1b. black, green & yellow (air) . . . . 1·75 1·25

1964. Air. No. 756 surch **VALE B/. 0.50.**
857 50c. on 21c. black, sepia and blue 65 40

241 Discus-thrower

1964. Olympic Games, Tokyo.
858 ½c. ("B/0.005") purple, red, brown and green (postage) 10 10
859 1c. multicoloured 10 10
860 5c. black, red and olive (air) 35 25
861 10c. black, red and yellow . . 70 45
862 21c. multicoloured . . . . . 1·40 90
863 50c. multicoloured . . . . . 2·75 1·75
MS864 66 × 95 mm. No. 863 . . 14·00 14·00

DESIGNS: ½c. Type **241**; 1c. Runner with Olympic Flame; 5c. to 50c. Olympic Stadium, Tokyo, and Mt. Fuji.

1964. Air. Nos. 692 and 742 surch **Aereo B/.0.10**.
865 10c. on 5c. green and turquoise 20 15
866 10c. on 5c. black, red and green 20 15

243 Space Vehicles (Project "Apollo")

1964. Space Exploration. Multicoloured.
867 ½c. ("B/0.005") Type **243** (postage) 10 10
868 1c. Rocket and capsule (Project "Gemini") 10 10
869 5c. W. M. Schirra (air) . . . 20 20
870 10c. L. G. Cooper 30 30
871 21c. Schirra's capsule 75 75
872 50c. Cooper's capsule . . . . 3·25 3·00
MS873 60 × 95 mm. No. 872 . . 14·00 14·00

1964. No. 687 surch **Correos B/. 0.10**.
874 10c. on 21c. blue 15 15

245 Water-skiing

1964. Aquatic Sports. Multicoloured.
875 ½c. ("B/0.005") Type **245** (postage) 10 10
876 1c. Underwater swimming . . 10 10
877 5c. Fishing (air) 20 10
878 10c. Sailing (vert) . . . . . 1·50 60
879 21c. Speedboat racing . . . . 2·75 1·50
880 31c. Water polo at Olympic Games, 1964 . . . . . . 3·50 1·75
MS881 95 × 65 mm. No. 880 . . 10·00 10·00

1964. Air. Ecumenical Council, Vatican City (2nd issue). Stamps of 1st issue optd **1964**. Centres in black.
882 21c. red (No. 832) 70 50
883 21c. green (No. 834) 70 50
884 21c. olive (No. 836) 70 50
885 21c. deep sepia (No. 850) . . 70 50
886 1b. blue (No. 852) . . . . . 2·75 2·00
887 2b. green (No. 853) . . . . . 5·50 4·50
MS888 No. **MS**854 optd **1964** and coat-of-arms (sold at 3b.65) . . 18·00 18·00

247 General View

248 Eleanor Roosevelt

1964. Air. New York's World Fair.
889 **247** 5c. black and yellow . . . 30 25
890 – 10c. black and red . . . 75 60
891 – 15c. black and green . . . 1·25 80
892 – 21c. black and blue . . . 1·90 1·50
MS893 127 × 76 mm. No. 892 . . 3·75 3·50
DESIGNS: 10c., 15c. Fair pavilions (different); 21c. Unisphere.

1964. Mrs. Eleanor Roosevelt Commemoration.
894 **248** 4c. black and red on yellow (postage) 15 10
895 20c. black and green on buff (air) 50 45
MS896 87 × 76 mm. Nos. 894/5Imperf (sold at 25c.) 7·00 7·00

249 Dag Hammarskjold

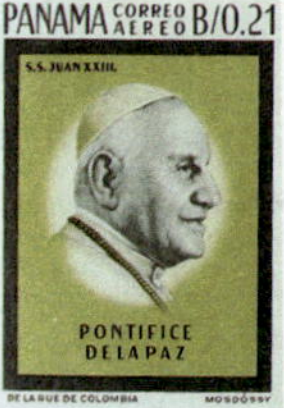

250 Pope John XXIII

1964. Air. U.N. Day.
897 **249** 21c. black and blue . . . 70 50
898 – 21c. blue and black . . . 70 50
MS899 98 × 80 mm. No. 897/8. Imperf . . . . 4·25 4·25
DESIGN: No. 898, U.N. Emblem.

1964. Air. Pope John Commemoration.
900 **250** 21c. black and bistre . . . 70 50
901 – 21c. mult (Papal Arms) 70 50
MS902 97 × 80 mm. Nos. 900/1 7·00 7·00

251 Slalom Skiing Medals

1964. Winter Olympic Winners' Medals. Medals in gold, silver and bronze.
903 **251** ½c. ("B/0.005") turquoise (postage) 10 10
904 – 1c. deep blue 10 10
905 – 2c. brown 20 15
906 – 3c. mauve 25 15
907 – 4c. lake 35 20
908 – 5c. violet (air) 45 25
909 – 6c. blue 55 30
910 – 7c. violet 65 35
911 – 10c. green 90 50
912 – 21c. red . . . . 1·40 95
913 – 31c. blue . . . . 2·50 1·40
MS914 142 × 103 mm. Nos. 911/13 8·00 8·00
DESIGNS—Medals for: 1c., 7c. Speed-skating; 2c., 21c. Bobsleighing; 3c., 10c. Figure-skating; 4c. Ski-jumping; 5c., 6c., 31c. Cross-country skiing. Values in the same design show different medal-winners and country names.

252 Red-billed Toucan

1965. Birds. Multicoloured.
915 1c. Type **252** (postage) . . . 65 10
916 2c. Scarlet macaw 65 10
917 3c. Woodpecker sp. . . . . 1·00 15
918 4c. Blue-grey tanager (horiz) 1·00 25
919 5c. Troupial (horiz) (air) . . 1·25 40
920 10c. Crimson-backed tanager (horiz) . . . . 2·60 55

253 Red Snapper

1965. Marine Life. Multicoloured.
921 1c. Type **253** (postage) . . . 10 10
922 2c. Dolphin (fish) 10 10
923 8c. Shrimp (air) 20 15
924 12c. Smooth hammerhead . . 60 25
925 13c. Sailfish 65 30
926 25c. Lined seahorse (vert) . . 80 35

254 Double Daisy and Emblem

1966. Air. 50th Anniv of Junior Chamber of Commerce. Flowers. Multicoloured: background colour given.
927 **254** 30c. mauve 55 45
928 – 30c. flesh (Hibiscus) . . . 55 45
929 – 30c. olive (Mauve orchid) 55 45
930 – 40c. green (Water lily) . . 60 55
931 – 40c. blue (Gladiolus) . . . 60 55
932 – 40c. pink (White orchid) 60 55

Each design incorporates the Junior Chamber of Commerce Emblem.

1966. Surch. (a) Postage.
933 13c. on 25c. (No. 747) . . . 30 20

(b) Air.
934 3c. on 5c. (No. 680) 10 10
935 13c. on 25c. (No. 695) . . . 30 25

256 Chicken

1967. Domestic Animals. Multicoloured.
936 1c. Type **256** (postage) . . . 10 10
937 3c. Cockerel 10 10
938 5c. Pig (horiz) 10 10
939 8c. Cow (horiz) 15 10
940 10c. Pekingese dog (air) . . . 25 20
941 13c. Zebu (horiz) 30 20
942 30c. Cat 60 50
943 40c. Horse (horiz) 75 60

257 American Darter

1967. Wild Birds. Multicoloured.
944 ½c. Type **257** 70 15
945 1c. Resplendent quetzal . . . 70 15
946 3c. Turquoise-browed motmot 90 20
947 4c. Red-necked aracari (horiz) . . . . 1·00 30
948 5c. Chestnut-fronted macaw 1·40 30
949 13c. Belted kingfisher . . . . 5·00 1·40

258 "Deer" (F. Marc)

1967. Wild Animals. Paintings. Multicoloured.
950 1c. Type **258** (postage) . . . 10 10
951 3c. "Cougar" (F. Marc) (vert) 10 10
952 5c. "Monkeys" (F. Marc) . . 10 10
953 8c. "Fox" (F. Marc) 20 10
954 10c. "St. Jerome and the Lion" (Durer) (vert) (air) 20 15
955 13c. "The Hare" (Durer) (vert) 30 20
956 20c. "Lady with the Ermine" (Da Vinci) (vert) 45 25
957 30c. "The Hunt" (Delacroix) 65 45

259 Map of Panama and People

1969. National Population Census.
958 **259** 5c. blue 10 10
959 – 10c. purple 20 15
DESIGN—VERT: 10c. People and map of the Americas.

260 Cogwheel

1969. 50th Anniv of Rotary Int in Panama.
960 **260** 13c. black, yellow and blue 20 20

261 Cornucopia and Map

1969. 1st Anniv of 11 October Revolution.
961 **261** 10c. multicoloured 20 10

262 Tower and Map

1969.
962 **262** 3c. black and orange . . 10 10
963 – 5c. green 10 10
964 – 8c. brown 20 15
965 – 13c. black and green . . . 25 15
966 – 20c. brown 35 25
967 – 21c. yellow 35 25
968 – 25c. green 45 30
969 – 30c. black 50 45
970 – 34c. brown 55 45
971 – 38c. blue 60 45
972 – 40c. yellow 65 45
973 – 50c. black and purple . . 85 65
974 – 59c. purple . . . . . . 1·00 60
DESIGNS—HORIZ: 5c. Peasants; 13c. Hotel Continental; 25c. Del Rey Bridge; 34c. Panama Cathedral; 38c. Municipal Palace; 40c. French Plaza; 50c. Thatcher Ferry Bridge; 59c. National Theatre. VERT: 8c. Nata Church; 20c. Virgin of Carmen Church; 21c. Altar, San Jose Church; 30c. Dr. Arosemena statue.

263 Discus-thrower and Stadium

1970. 11th Central American and Caribbean Games, Panama (1st series).
975 **263** 1c. multicoloured (postage) 10 10
976 2c. multicoloured 10 10
977 3c. multicoloured 10 10
978 5c. multicoloured 10 10
979 10c. multicoloured 20 15
980 13c. multicoloured 25 15
981 – 13c. multicoloured 25 15
982 **263** 25c. multicoloured 45 35
983 30c. multicoloured 55 45
984 – 13c. multicoloured (air) 1·00 25
985 – 30c. multicoloured 60 45
DESIGNS—VERT: No. 981, "Flor del Espirited Santo" (flowers); 985, Indian girl. HORIZ: No. 984, Thatcher Ferry Bridge and palm.
See also Nos. 986/94.

264 J. D. Arosemena and Stadium

1970. Air. 11th Central American and Caribbean Games, Panama (2nd series). Multicoloured.
986 1c. Type **264** 10 10
987 2c. Type **264** 10 10
988 3c. Type **264** 10 10
989 5c. Type **264** 10 10
990 13c. Basketball 20 15
991 13c. New Gymnasium . . . 20 15
992 13c. Revolution Stadium . . 20 15
993 13c. Panamanian couple in festive costume 20 15
994 30c. Eternal Flame and stadium 45 35
MS995 85 × 75 mm. No. 994. Imperf 55 55

265 A. Tapia and M. Sosa (first comptrollers)

1971. 40th Anniv of Panamanian Comptroller-General's Office. Multicoloured.
996 3c. Comptroller-General's Building (1970) (vert) . . . 10 10
997 5c. Type **265** 10 10
998 8c. Comptroller-General's emblem (vert) 15 10
999 13c. Comptroller-General's Building (1955–70) 30 15

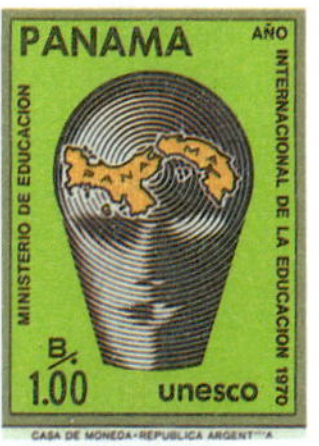

266 "Man and Alligator" 267 Map of Panama on I.E.Y. Emblem

1971. Indian Handicrafts.
1000 **266** 8c. multicoloured 20 15

1971. International Education Year.
1001 **267** 1b. multicoloured . . . 1·50 1·50

268 Astronaut on Moon 269 Panama Pavilion

1971. Air. "Apollo 11" and "Apollo 12" Moon Missions. Multicoloured.
1002 13c. Type **268** 35 25
1003 13c. "Apollo 12" astronauts 35 25

1971. Air. "EXPO 70" World Fair, Osaka, Japan.
1004 **269** 10c. multicoloured . . . 15 15

270 Conference Text and Emblem

1971. 9th Inter-American Loan and Savings Association Conference, Panama City.
1005 **270** 25c. multicoloured . . . 60 35

271 Panama Flag

1971. Air. American Tourist Year. Multicoloured.
1006 5c. Type **271** 10 10
1007 13c. Map of Panama and Western Hemisphere . . . 30 20

272 New U.P.U. H.Q. Building

1971. Inauguration of New U.P.U. Headquarters Building, Berne. Multicoloured.
1008 8c. Type **272** 20 10
1009 30c. U.P.U. Monument, Berne (vert) 60 35

273 Cow and Pig

1971. 3rd Agricultural Census.
1010 **273** 3c. multicoloured 10 10

274 Map and "4S" Emblem

1971. "4S" Programme for Rural Youth.
1011 **274** 2c. multicoloured 10 10

275 Gandhi 276 Central American Flags

1971. Air. Birth Centenary (1969) of Mahatma Gandhi.
1012 **275** 10c. multicoloured . . . 20 15

1971. Air. 150th Anniv of Central American States' Independence from Spain.
1013 **276** 13c. multicoloured . . . 30 20

277 Early Panama Stamp 278 Altar, Nata Church

1971. Air. 2nd National, Philatelic and Numismatic Exhibition, Panama.
1014 **277** 8c. blue, black and red 20 15

1972. Air. 450th Anniv of Nata Church.
1015 **278** 40c. multicoloured . . . 50 45

279 Telecommunications Emblem

1972. Air. World Telecommunications Day.
1016 **279** 13c. black, blue & lt blue 20 15

280 "Apollo 14" Badge

1972. Air. Moon Flight of "Apollo 14".
1017 **280** 13c. multicoloured . . . 60 25

281 Children on See-saw

1972. 25th Anniv (1971) of UNICEF. Mult.
1018 1c. Type **281** (postage) . . . 10 10
1019 5c. Boy sitting by kerb (vert) (air) 10 10
1020 8c. Indian mother and child (vert) 15 10
1021 50c. UNICEF emblem (vert) 70 45
MS1022 86 × 75 mm. No. 1021. Imperf . . . . 1·25 1·25

282 Tropical Fruits

1972. Tourist Publicity. Multicoloured.
1023 1c. Type **282** (postage) . . . 10 10
1024 2c. "Isle of Night" 10 10
1025 3c. Carnival float (vert) . . 10 10
1026 5c. San Blas textile (air) . . 10 10
1027 8c. Chaquira (beaded collar) 20 10
1028 25c. Ruined fort, Portobelo 35 30
MS1029 96 × 120 mm. Nos. 1026 and 1028. Imperf 90

283 Map and Flags 284 Baseball Players

1973. Obligatory Tax. Panama City Post Office Building Fund. 7th Bolivar Games.
1030 **283** 1c. black 10 10

1973. Air. 7th Bolivar Games.
1031 **284** 8c. red and yellow . . . 15 10
1032 – 10c. black and blue . . . 20 15
1033 – 13c. multicoloured . . . 30 20
1034 – 25c. black, red and green 55 30
1035 – 50c. multicoloured . . . 1·25 55
1036 – 1b. multicoloured . . . 2·50 1·10
DESIGNS—VERT: 10c. Basketball; 13c. Flaming torch. HORIZ: 25c. Boxing; 50c. Panama map and flag, Games emblem and Bolivar; 1b. Games' medals.

1973. U.N. Security Council Meeting, Panama City. Various stamps surch **O.N.U.** in laurel leaf, **CONSEJO DE SEGURIDAD 15 - 21 Marzo 1973** and value.
1037 8c. on 59c. (No. 974) (postage) 10 10
1038 10c. on 1b. (No. 1001) . . . 15 15
1039 13c. on 30c. (No. 969) . . . 20 15
1040 13c. on 40c. (No. 1015) (air) 25 15

286 Farming Co-operative

1973. Obligatory Tax. Post Office Building Fund.
1041 **286** 1c. green and red . . . 10 10
1042 – 1c. grey and red 10 10
1043 – 1c. yellow and red . . . 10 10
1044 – 1c. orange and red . . . 10 10
1045 – 1c. blue and red 10 10
DESIGNS: No. 1042, Silver coins; 1043, V. Lorenzo; 1044, Cacique Urraca; 1045, Post Office building.
See also Nos. 1061/2.

287 J. D. Crespo (educator) 290 Women's upraised Hands

1973. Famous Panamanians. Multicoloured.
1046 3c. Type **287** (postage) . . . 10 10
1047 5c. Isabel Obaldia (educator) (air) 10 10
1048 8c. N. V. Jaen (educator) . . 20 15
1049 10c. "Forest Scene" (Roberto Lewis, painter) 20 15
1050 13c. R. Miro (poet) 35 20
1051 13c. "Portrait of a Lady" (M. E. Amador, painter) 35 20
1052 20c. "Self-Portrait" (Isaac Benitez, painter) 55 20
1053 21c. M. A. Guerrero (statesman) 55 25
1054 25c. Dr. B. Porras (statesman) 55 30
1055 30c. J. D. Arosemena (statesman) 70 35
1056 34c. Dr. O. M. Pereira (writer) 90 45
1057 38c. Dr. R. J. Alfaro (writer) . . . . 1·10 50

1973. Air. 50th Anniv of Isabel Obaldia Professional School. Nos. 1047, 1054 and 1056 optd **1923 1973 Godas de Oro Escuela Profesional Isabel Herrera Obaldia** and EP emblem.
1058 5c. multicoloured 15 10
1059 25c. multicoloured 55 30
1060 34c. multicoloured 60 55

1974. Obligatory Tax. Post Office Building Fund. As Nos. 1044/5.
1061 1c. orange 10 10
1062 2c. blue 10 10

1974. Surch **VALE** and value.
1063 5c. on 30c. black (No. 969) (postage) 10 10
1064 10c. on 34c. brown (No. 970) 15 10
1065 13c. on 21c. yellow (No. 967) 20 15
1066 1c. on 25c. multicoloured (No. 1028) (air) 10 10
1067 3c. on 20c. mult (No. 1052) 10 10
1068 8c. on 38c. mult (No. 1057) 15 10
1069 10c. on 34c. mult (No. 1056) 15 15
1070 13c. on 21c. mult (No. 1053) 20 15

1975. Air. International Women's Year.
1071 **290** 17c. multicoloured . . . 45 20

291 Bayano Dam

1975. Air. 7th Anniv of October 1968 Revolution.
1073 **291** 17c. black, brown & blue 20 15
1074 – 27c. blue and green . . . 30 25
1075 – 33c. multicoloured . . . 1·10 30
DESIGNS—VERT: 27c. Victoria sugar plant, Veraguas, and sugar cane. HORIZ: 33c. Tocumen International Airport.

1975. Obligatory Tax. Various stamps surch **VALE PRO EDIFICIO** and value.
1076 – 1c. on 30c. black (No. 969) (postage) . . 10 10
1077 – 1c. on 40c. yellow (No. 972) 10 10
1078 – 1c. on 50c. black and purple (No. 973) . . . 10 10
1079 – 1c. on 30c. mult (No. 1009) 10 10
1080 **282** 1c. on 1c. multicoloured 10 10
1081 – 1c. on 2c. multicoloured (No. 1024) 10 10
1082 **278** 1c. on 40c. mult (air) . . 10 10
1083 – 1c. on 25c. mult (No. 1028) 10 10
1084 – 1c. on 25c. mult (No. 1052) 10 10
1085 – 1c. on 20c. mult (No. 1054) 10 10
1086 – 1c. on 30c. mult (No. 1055) 10 10

1975. Obligatory Tax. Post Office Building Fund. As No. 1045.
1087 1c. red 10 10

294 Bolivar and Thatcher Ferry Bridge

1976. 150th Anniv of Panama Congress (1st issue). Multicoloured.
1088 6c. Type **294** (postage) . . . 10 10
1089 23c. Bolivar Statue (air) . . 30 25
1090 35c. Bolivar Hall, Panama City (horiz) 50 30
1091 41c. Bolivar and flag . . . 60 40

295 "Evibacus princeps"

1976. Marine Fauna. Multicoloured.
1092 2c. Type **295** (postage) . . . 10 10
1093 3c. "Ptitosarcus sinuosus" (vert) 10 10

1094 4c. "Acanthaster planci" 10 10
1095 7c. "Oreaster reticulatus" 10 10
1096 17c. Porcupinefish (vert) (air) 60 20
1097 27c. "Pocillopora damicornis" 40 25
MS1098 100 × 100 mm. 1b. *Mithrax spinossimus*. Imperf 3·25 3·25

296 "Simon Bolivar"

1976. 150th Anniv of Panama Congress (2nd issue). Designs showing details of Bolivar Monument or flags of Latin-American countries. Multicoloured.
1099 20c. Type **296** 30 20
1100 20c. Argentina 30 20
1101 20c. Bolivia 30 20
1102 20c. Brazil 30 20
1103 20c. Chile 30 20
1104 20c. "Battle scene" 30 20
1105 20c. Colombia 30 20
1106 20c. Costa Rica 30 20
1107 20c. Cuba 30 20
1108 20c. Ecuador 30 20
1109 20c. El Salvador 30 20
1110 20c. Guatemala 30 20
1111 20c. Guyana 30 20
1112 20c. Haiti 30 20
1113 20c. "Congress assembly" 30 20
1114 20c. "Liberated people" 30 20
1115 20c. Honduras 30 20
1116 20c. Jamaica 30 20
1117 20c. Mexico 30 20
1118 20c. Nicaragua 30 20
1119 20c. Panama 30 20
1120 20c. Paraguay 30 20
1121 20c. Peru 30 20
1122 20c. Dominican Republic 30 20
1123 20c. "Bolivar and standard-bearer" 30 20
1124 20c. Surinam 30 20
1125 20c. Trinidad and Tobago 30 20
1126 20c. Uruguay 30 20
1127 20c. Venezuela 30 20
1128 20c. "Indian Delegation" 30 20
MS1129 81 × 122 mm. 30c. Bolivar and flag-bearer; 30c. Top of Monument; 40c. Inscribed tablet. Perf or Imperf 2·50 2·50

297 Nicanor Villalaz (designer of Panama Arms) **298** National Lottery Building, Panama City

1976. Villalaz Commemoration.
1130 **297** 5c. blue 10 10

1976. "Progressive Panama".
1131 **298** 6c. multicoloured 10 10

299 Cerro Colorado, Copper Mine

1976. Air.
1132 **299** 23c. multicoloured 30 20

300 Contadora Island

1977. Tourism.
1133 **300** 3c. multicoloured 10 10

301 Secretary-General of Pan-American Union, A. Orfila

1978. Signing of Panama–U.S.A. Treaty. Mult.
1134 3c. Type **301** 10 10
1135 23c. Treaty signing scene (horiz) 30 25
1136 40c. President Carter 55 30
1137 50c. Gen. O. Torrijos of Panama 70 50
Nos. 1134 and 1136/7 were issued together se-tenant in horizontal stamps of three showing Treaty signing as No. 1135.

302 Signing Ratification of Panama Canal Treaty

1978. Ratification of Panama Canal Treaty.
1138 **302** 3c. multicoloured 10 10
1139 – 5c. multicoloured 10 10
1140 – 35c. multicoloured 50 25
1141 – 41c. multicoloured 60 30
DESIGNS: 5, 35, 41c. As Type **302**, but with the design of the Ratification Ceremony spread over the three stamps, issued as a se-tenant strip in the order 5c. (29 × 39 mm), 41c. (44 × 39 mm), 35c. (29 × 39 mm).

303 Colon Harbour and Warehouses

1978. 30th Anniv of Colon Free Zone.
1142 **303** 6c. multicoloured 10 10

304 Children's Home and Melvin Jones

1978. Birth Centenary of Melvin Jones (founder of Lions International).
1143 **304** 50c. multicoloured 70 55

305 Pres. Torrijos, "Flavia" (liner) and Children

1979. Return of Canal Zone. Multicoloured.
1144 3c. Type **305** 1·25 55
1145 23c. Presidents Torrijos and Carter, liner and flags of Panama and U.S.A. 50 25

306 "75" and Bank Emblem

1979. 75th Anniv of National Bank.
1146 **306** 6c. black, red and blue 10 10

307 Rotary Emblem **308** Children inside Heart

1979. 75th Anniv of Rotary International.
1147 **307** 17c. blue and yellow 25 20

1979. International Year of the Child.
1148 **308** 50c. multicoloured 70 45

309 U.P.U. Emblem and Globe **310** Colon Station

1979. 18th Universal Postal Union Congress, Rio de Janeiro.
1149 **309** 35c. multicoloured 50 30

1980. Centenary of Trans-Panamanian Railway.
1150 **310** 1c. purple and lilac 20 35

311 Postal Headquarters, Balboa (inauguration) **318** Boys in Children's Village

1980. Anniversaries and Events.
1151 **311** 3c. multicoloured 10 10
1152 – 6c. multicoloured 10 10
1153 – 17c. multicoloured 25 20
1154 – 23c. multicoloured 30 20
1155 – 35c. blue, black and red 50 30
1156 – 41c. pink and black 60 40
1157 – 50c. multicoloured 70 45
DESIGNS—HORIZ: 17c. Map of Central America and flags (census of the Americas); 23c. Tourism and Convention Centre (opening); 35c. Bank emblem (Inter-American Development Bank, 25th anniv); 41c. F. de Lesseps (Panama Canal cent); 50c. Olympic Stadium, Moscow (Olympic Games). VERT: 6c. National flag (return of Canal Zone).

1980. Olympic Games, Lake Placid and Moscow.
(a) Optd **1980 LAKE PLACID MOSCU** and venue emblems.
1158 20c. (No. 1099) 80 80
1159 20c. (1101) 80 80
1162 20c. (1103) 80 80
1164 20c. (1105) 80 80
1166 20c. (1107) 80 80
1168 20c. (1109) 80 80
1170 20c. (1111) 80 80
1172 20c. (1113) 80 80
1174 20c. (1115) 80 80
1176 20c. (1117) 80 80
1178 20c. (1119) 80 80
1180 20c. (1121) 80 80
1182 20c. (1123) 80 80
1184 20c. (1125) 80 80
1186 20c. (1127) 80 80

(b) Optd with Lake Placid Olympic emblems and medals total of country indicated.
1159 20c. "**ALEMANIA D.**" (1101) 80 80
1161 20c. "**AUSTRIA**" (1102) 80 80
1163 20c. "**SUECIA**" (1104) 80 80
1165 20c. "**U.R.S.S.**" (1106) 80 80
1167 20c. "**ALEMANIA F.**" (1108) 80 80
1169 20c. "**ITALIA**" (1110) 80 80
1171 20c. "**U.S.A.**" (1112) 80 80
1173 20c. "**SUIZA**" (1114) 80 80
1175 20c. "**CANADA/GRAN BRETANA**" (1116) 80 80
1177 20c. "**NORUEGA**" (1118) 80 80
1179 20c. "**LICHTENSTEIN**" (1120) 80 80
1181 20c. "**HUNGRIA/BULGARIA**" (1122) 80 80
1183 20c. "**FINLANDIA**" (1124) 80 80
1185 20c. "**HOLANDIA**" (1126) 80 80
1187 20c. "**CHECOS-LOVAQUIA/FRANCIA**" (1128) 80 80
Nos. 1158, etc, occur on 1st, 3rd and 5th rows and Nos. 1159, etc, occur on the others.

(c) Lake Placid and Moscow and venue with Olympic rings.
1188 20c. (No. 1099) 80 80
1190 20c. (1101) 80 80
1192 20c. (1103) 80 80
1194 20c. (1105) 80 80
1196 20c. (1107) 80 80
1198 20c. (1109) 80 80
1200 20c. (1111) 80 80
1202 20c. (1113) 80 80
1204 20c. (1115) 80 80
1206 20c. (1117) 80 80
1208 20c. (1119) 80 80
1210 20c. (1121) 80 80
1212 20c. (1123) 80 80
1214 20c. (1125) 80 80
1216 20c. (1127) 80 80

(d) Optd with country names as indicated.
1189 20c. "**RUSIA/ALEMANIA D.**" (1101) 80 80
1191 20c. "**SUECIA/FINLANDIA**" (1102) 80 80
1193 20c. "**GRECIA/BELGICA/INDIA**" (1104) 80 80
1195 20c. "**BULGARIA/CUBA**" (1106) 80 80
1197 20c. "**CHECOS-LOVAQUIA/YUGOSLAVIA**" (1108) 80 80
1199 20c. "**ZIMBAWE/COREA DEL NORTE/MONGOLIA**" (1110) 80 80
1201 20c. "**ITALIA/HUNGRIA**" (1112) 80 80
1203 20c. "**AUSTRALIA/DINAMARCA**" (1114) 80 80
1205 20c. "**TANZANIA/MEXICO/HOLANDA**" (1116) 80 80
1207 20c. "**RUMANIA/FRANCIA**" (1118) 80 80
1209 20c. "**BRASIL/ETIOPIA**" (1120) 80 80
1211 20c. "**IRLANDA/UGANDA/VENEZUELA**" (1122) 80 80
1213 20c. "**GRAN BRETANA/POLONIA**" (1124) 80 80
1215 20c. "**SUIZA/ESPANA/AUSTRIA**" (1126) 80 80
1217 20c. "**JAMAICA/LIBANO/GUYANA**" (1128) 80 80
MS1218 No. **MS**1129 optd in gold 30c. with Olympic emblems; 30c. with Concorde and Lindbergh's aircraft; 40c. with Apollo I and space shuttle 23·00 23·00
Nos. 1188, etc, occur on 1st, 3rd and 5th rows and Nos. 1189, etc, on the others.

1980. Medal Winners at Winter Olympic Games, Lake Placid. (a) Optd with 1980, medals and venue emblems.
1219 20c. 1980 medals and venue and emblems (No. 1099) 80 80
1221 20c. As No. 1219 (1101) 80 80
1223 20c. As No. 1219 (1103) 80 80
1225 20c. As No. 1219 (1105) 80 80
1227 20c. As No. 1219 (1107) 80 80
1229 20c. As No. 1219 (1109) 80 80
1231 20c. As No. 1219 (1111) 80 80
1233 20c. As No. 1219 (1113) 80 80
1235 20c. As No. 1219 (1115) 80 80
1237 20c. As No. 1219 (1117) 80 80
1239 20c. As No. 1219 (1119) 80 80
1241 20c. As No. 1219 (1121) 80 80
1243 20c. As No. 1219 (1123) 80 80
1245 20c. As No. 1219 (1125) 80 80
1247 20c. As No. 1219 (1127) 80 80

(b) Optd with 1980 medals and venue emblems and Olympic torch and country indicated.
1220 20c. "**ALEMANIA D.**" (1100) 80 80
1222 20c. "**AUSTRIA**" (1102) 80 80
1224 20c. "**SUECIA**" (1104) 80 80
1226 20c. "**U.R.S.S.**" (1106) 80 80
1228 20c. "**ALEMANIA F.**" (1108) 80 80
1230 20c. "**ITALIA**" (1110) 80 80
1232 20c. "**U.S.A.**" (1112) 80 80
1234 20c. "**SUIZA**" (1114) 80 80
1236 20c. "**CANADA/GRAN BRETANA**" (1116) 80 80
1238 20c. "**NORUEGA**" (1118) 80 80
1240 20c. "**LICHTENSTEIN**" (1120) 80 80
1242 20c. "**HUNGRIA/BULGARIA**" (1122) 80 80
1244 20c. "**FINLANDIA**" (1124) 80 80
1246 20c. "**HOLANDIA**" (1126) 80 80
1248 20c. "**CHECOS-LOVAQUIA/FRANCIA**" (1128) 80 80
Nos. 1219, etc, occur on 1st, 3rd and 5th rows and Nos. 1220, etc, on the others.

1980. World Cup Football Championship, Argentina (1978) and Spain (1980). Optd with: A. Football cup emblems. B. "**ESPAMER 80**" and "Argentina '78" emblems and inscriptions "**ESPANA '82/CAMPEONATO/MUNDIAL DE FUTBOL**". C. World Cup Trophy and "**ESPANA '82.**". D. "**ESPANA 82/Football/Argentina '78/BESPAMER '80 MADRID**". E. FIFA globes emblem and "**ESPANA '82/ARGENTINA '78/ESPANA '82**". F. With ball and inscription as for B.
1249 20c. No. 1099 (A, C, E) 80 80
1250 20c. No. 1100 (B, D, F) 80 80
1251 20c. No. 1101 (A, C, E) 80 80
1252 20c. No. 1102 (B, D, F) 80 80
1253 20c. No. 1103 (A, C, E) 80 80
1254 20c. No. 1104 (B, D, F) 80 80
1255 20c. No. 1105 (A, C, E) 80 80
1256 20c. No. 1106 (B, D, F) 80 80
1257 20c. No. 1107 (A, C, E) 80 80
1258 20c. No. 1108 (B, D, F) 80 80
1259 20c. No. 1109 (A, C, E) 80 80
1260 20c. No. 1110 (B, D, F) 80 80
1261 20c. No. 1111 (A, C, E) 80 80
1262 20c. No. 1112 (B, D, F) 80 80
1263 20c. No. 1113 (A, C, E) 80 80
1264 20c. No. 1114 (B, D, F) 80 80
1265 20c. No. 1115 (A, C, E) 80 80
1266 20c. No. 1116 (B, D, F) 80 80
1267 20c. No. 1117 (A, C, E) 80 80

1268 20c. No. 1118 (B, D, F) . . 80 80
1269 20c. No. 1119 (A, C, E) . . 80 80
1270 20c. No. 1120 (B, D, F) . . 80 80
1271 20c. No. 1121 (A, C, E) . . 80 80
1272 20c. No. 1122 (B, D, F) . . 80 80
1273 20c. No. 1123 (A, C, E) . . 80 80
1274 20c. No. 1124 (B, D, F) . . 80 80
1275 20c. No. 1125 (A, C, E) . . 80 80
1276 20c. No. 1126 (B, D, F) . . 80 80
1277 20c. No. 1127 (A, C, E) . . 80 80
1278 20c. No. 1128 (B, D, F) . . 80 80
MS1279 No. **MS**1129 optd in silver. 30c. with World Cup embelms; 30c. with "Viking-Mars" emblem and space shuttle; 40c. with Zeppelin . . . . 23·00 23·00

1980. Obligatory Tax. Children's Village. Mult.
1280 2c. Type **318** 10 10
1281 2c. Boy with chicks 10 10
1282 2c. Working in the fields . . 10 10
1283 2c. Boys with pig 10 10
MS1284 154 × 170 mm. 2c. Type **318**; 2c. Boys cleaning cages; 2c. As No. 1160; 2c. Woodwork (sold at 1b.) . . . . 1·40 1·40

319 Jean Baptiste de la Salle and Map showing La Salle Schools

320 Louis Braille

1981. Education in Panama by the Christian Schools.
1285 **319** 17c. blue, black and red 25 20

1981. International Year of Disabled People.
1286 **320** 23c. multicoloured . . . 30 20

321 Statue of the Virgin

1981. 150th Anniv of Apparition of Miraculous Virgin to St. Catharine Laboure.
1287 **321** 35c. multicoloured . . . 50 35

322 Crimson-backed Tanager

1981. Birds. Multicoloured.
1288 3c. Type **322** 55 10
1289 6c. Chestnut-fronted macaw (vert) 70 15
1290 41c. Violet sabrewing (vert) 2·75 1·00
1291 50c. Keel-billed toucan . . . 3·75 1·25

323 "Boy feeding Donkey" (Ricardo Morales)

324 Banner

1981. Obligatory Tax. Christmas. Children's Village. Multicoloured.
1292 2c. Type **323** 10 10
1293 2c. "Nativity" (Enrique Daniel Austin) 10 10
1294 2c. "Bird in Tree" (Jorge Gonzalez) 10 10
1295 2c. "Church" (Eric Belgrane) 10 10
MS1296 131 × 140 mm. 2c. The Wise Men (Eliecer Antonio Osorio); 2c. Nativity (Ricardo Correoso); 2c. House (Samuel Carter Ruiz); 2c. Family in House (John A. Calvo) (sold for 5b.) . . . . 7·00 7·00

1981. National Reaffirmation.
1297 **324** 3c. multicoloured 10 10

325 General Herrera

326 Ricardo J. Alfaro

1982. 1st Death Anniv of General Omar Torrijos Herrera. Multicoloured.
1298 5c. Aerial view of Panama (postage) 10 10
1299 6c. Colecito army camp . . 10 10
1300 17c. Bayano river barrage 25 20
1301 50c. Felipillo engineering works 70 45
1302 23c. Type **325** (air) 35 25
1303 35c. Security Council reunion 50 30
1304 41c. Gen. Omar Torrijos airport . . . . 1·25 45
MS1305 84 × 75 mm. No. 1302 (sold at 1b.) . . . . 1·40 1·10

1982. Birth Cent of Ricardo J. Alfaro (statesman).
1306 **326** 3c. black, mauve and blue (postage) 10 10
1307 – 17c. black and mauve (air) 25 15
1308 – 23c. multicoloured . . . 30 20
DESIGNS: 17c. Profile of Alfaro wearing spectacles (as humanist); 23c. Portrait of Alfaro (as lawyer).

328 Pig Farming

329 Pele (Brazilian footballer)

1982. Obligatory Tax. Christmas. Children's Village. Multicoloured.
1309 2c. Type **328** 10 10
1310 2c. Gardening 10 10
1311 2c. Metalwork (horiz) . . . 10 10
1312 2c. Bee-keeping (horiz) . . . 10 10
MS1313 Two sheets each 70 × 95 mm.(a) 2b. Football and classroom; (b) 2b. Scouts and musicians. Imperf . . . . . . 9·50 9·50

1982. World Cup Football Championship, Spain. Multicoloured.
1314 50c. Italian team (horiz) (postage) 70 45
1315 23c. Football emblem and map of Panama (air) . . 30 20
1316 35c. Type **329** 50 30
1317 41c. World Cup Trophy . . 60 35
MS1318 85 × 75 mm. No. 1316. Imperf (sold at 1b.) . . . . . 1·40 1·10

330 Chamber of Trade Emblem

1983. "Expo Comer" Chamber of Trade Exhibition.
1319 **330** 17c. lt blue, blue, & gold 25 15

331 Dr. Nicolas Solano

332 Pope John Paul II giving Blessing

1983. Air. Birth Centenary (1982) of Dr. Nicolas Solano (anti-tuberculosis pioneer).
1320 **331** 23c. brown 35 20

1983. Papal Visit. Multicoloured.
1321 6c. Type **332** (postage) . . . 10 10
1322 17c. Pope John Paul II . . . 25 15
1323 35c. Pope and map of Panama (air) 50 30

333 Map of Americas and Sunburst

334 Simon Bolivar

1983. 24th Assembly of Inter-American Development Bank Governors.
1324 **333** 50c. light blue, blue and gold 70 45

1983. Birth Bicentenary of Simon Bolivar.
1325 **334** 50c. multicoloured . . . 70 45
MS1326 85 × 75 mm. **334** 1b. multicoloured. Impref . . . . 1·40 1·10

335 Postal Union of the Americas and Spain Emblem

336 Moslem Mosque

1983. World Communications Day. Mult.
1327 30c. Type **335** 45 25
1328 40c. W.C.Y. emblem 60 40
1329 50c. Universal Postal Union emblem 70 45
1330 60c. "Flying Dove" (Alfredo Sinclair) 85 55
MS1331 150 × 150 mm. 1b. As Nos. 1327/30. Imperf . . . . . 1·40 1·10

1983. Freedom of Worship. Multicoloured.
1332 3c. Type **336** 10 10
1333 5c. Bahai temple 10 10
1334 6c. Church of St. Francis of the Mountains, Veraguas 10 10
1335 17c. Shevet Ahim synagogue 25 15

337 "The Annunciation" (Dagoberto Moran)

338 Ricardo Miro (writer)

1983. Obligatory Tax. Christmas. Children's Village. Multicoloured.
1336 2c. Type **337** 10 10
1337 2c. Church and houses (Leonidas Molinar) (vert) 10 10
1338 2c. Bethlehem and star (Colon Olmedo Zambrano) (vert) 10 10
1339 2c. Flight into Egypt (Hector Ulises Velasquez) (vert) 10 10
MS1340 Two sheets each 70 × 95 mm. (a) 2b. As Nos. 1336/7; (b) 2b. As Nos. 1338/9 . . . . 9·50 5·50

1983. Famous Panamanians. Multicoloured.
1341 1c. Type **338** 10 10
1342 3c. Richard Newman (educationalist) 10 10
1343 5c. Cristobal Rodriguez (politician) 10 10
1344 6c. Alcibiades Arosemena (politician) 10 10
1345 35c. Cirilo Martinez (educationalist) 50 30

339 "Rural Architecture" (Juan Manuel Cedero)

1983. Paintings. Multicoloured.
1346 1c. Type **339** 10 10
1347 1c. "Large Nude" (Manuel Chong Neto) 10 10
1348 3c. "On another Occasion" (Spiros Vamvas) 10 10
1349 6c. "Punta Chame" (Guillermo Trujillo) . . . 10 10
1350 28c. "Neon Light" (Alfredo Sinclair) 30 20
1351 35c. "The Prophet" (Alfredo Sinclair) (vert) 50 30
1352 41c. "Highland Girls" (Al Sprague) (vert) 60 40
1353 1b. "One Morning" (Ignacio Mallol Pibernat) . . . . 1·40 75

340 Tonosi Double Jug

1984. Archaeological Finds. Multicoloured.
1354 30c. Type **340** 35 10
1355 40c. Dish on stand 60 20
1356 50c. Jug decorated with human face (vert) 70 25
1357 60c. Waisted bowl (vert) . . 85 35
MS1358 85 × 75 mm. 1b. As No. 1355. Imperf . . . . . . 1·40 1·10

341 Boxing

1984. Olympic Games, Los Angeles. Mult.
1359 19c. Type **341** 35 25
1360 19c. Baseball 35 25
1361 19c. Basketball (vert) . . . 35 25
1362 19c. Swimming (vert) . . . 35 25

342 Roberto Duran

1984. Roberto Duran (boxer) Commem.
1363 **342** 26c. multicoloured . . . 45 30

343 Shooting

1984. Olympic Games, Los Angeles (2nd series). Multicoloured.
1364 6c. Type **343** (postage) . . . 15 10
1366 30c. Weightlifting (air) . . . 50 30
1367 37c. Wrestling 65 45
1368 1b. Long jump . . . . . . 1·25 90
MS1365 75 × 85 mm. 1b. Running (53 × 26 mm) . . . . 1·40 1·10

344 "Pensive Woman" (Manuel Chong Neto)

1984. Paintings. Multicoloured.
1369 1c. Type **344** 10 10
1370 3c. "The Child" (Alfredo Sinclair) (horiz) 10 10
1371 6c. "A Day in the Life of Rumalda" (Brooke Alfaro) (horiz) 15 10
1372 30c. "Highlanders" (Al Sprague) 50 10
1373 37c. "Ballet Interval" (Roberto Sprague) (horiz) 65 15
1374 44c. "Wood on Chame Head" (Guillermo Trujillo) (horiz) 75 25
1375 50c. "La Plaza Azul" (Juan Manuel Cedeno) (horiz) 60 25
1376 1b. "Ira" (Spiros Vamvas) (horiz) . . . . 1·25 90

345 Map, Pres. Torrijos Herrera and Liner in Canal Lock

1984. 5th Anniv of Canal Zone Postal Sovereignty.
1377 **345** 19c. multicoloured . . . 1·10 1·10

346 Emblem as Seedling

347 Boy

1984. Air. World Food Day.
1378 **346** 30c. red, green and blue 50 45

1984. Obligatory Tax. Christmas. Children's Village. Multicoloured.
1379 2c. Type **347** 10 10
1380 2c. Boy in tee-shirt . . . 10 10
1381 2c. Boy in checked shirt . . 10 10
1382 2c. Cub scout 10 10
MS1383 75×84 mm. 4×2c. Designs showing children (sold at 2b.) 2·75 1·40

348 American Manatee

1984. Animals. Each in black.
1384 3c. Type **348** (postage) . . . 10 10
1385 30c. "Tayra" (air) 60 25
1386 44c. Jaguarundi 85 40
1387 50c. White-lipped peccary 90 40
MS1388 75×85 mm. 1b. Three-toed sloth (*Bradypus griseus*) (vert) 1·40 1·10

349 Copper One Centesimo Coins, 1935

1985. Coins. Multicoloured.
1389 3c. Type **349** (postage) . . . 10 10
1390 3c. Silver ten centesimo coins, 1904 . . . . 10 10
1391 3c. Silver five centesimo coins, 1916 . . . . 10 10
1392 30c. Silver 50 centesimo coins, 1904 (air) 50 30
1393 37c. Silver half balboa coins, 1962 . . . . 65 45
1394 44c. Silver balboa coins, 1953 . . . . 75 50

350 Figures on Map reaching for Dove

352 Scouts with Statue of Christ

351 Tanker in Dock

1985. Contadora Peace Movement.
1395 **350** 10c. multicoloured . . . 15 10
1396 20c. multicoloured . . . 30 20
1397 30c. multicoloured . . . 40 25
MS1398 85×75 mm. 1b. multicoloured (Dove over flags on map) (air) . . . . 1·40 1·10

1985. 70th Anniv of Panama Canal.
1399 **351** 19c. multicoloured . . . 2·75 90

1985. Obligatory Tax. Christmas. Children's Village. Multicoloured.
1400 2c. Type **352** 10 10
1401 2c. Children holding cards spelling "Feliz Navidad" 10 10
1402 2c. Children holding balloons 10 10
1403 2c. Group of cub scouts . . 10 10
MS1404 95×70 mm. Nos. 1400/3. Perf or imperf (sold at 2b.) . . 2·75 1·40

353 "40" on Emblem

1986. 40th Anniv (1985) of U.N.O.
1405 **353** 23c. multicoloured . . . 30 20

354 Boys in Cab of Crane

1986. International Youth Year (1985).
1406 **354** 30c. multicoloured . . . 40 25

355 "Awaiting Her Turn" (Al Sprague)

1986. Paintings. Multicoloured.
1407 3c. Type **355** 10 10
1408 5c. "Aerobics" (Guillermo Trujillo) (horiz) 10 10
1409 19c. "House of Cardboard" (Eduardo Augustine) . . 30 20
1410 30c. "Tierra Gate" (Juan Manuel Cedeno) (horiz) 40 25
1411 36c. "Supper for Three" (Brood Alfaro) 50 30
1412 42c. "Tenderness" (Alfredo Sinclair) 60 40
1413 50c. "Lady of Character" (Manuel Chong Neto) . . 70 45
1414 60c. "Calla Lilies No. 1" (Maigualida de Diaz) (horiz) 80 55

356 Atlapa Convention Centre

1986. Miss Universe Contest. Multicoloured.
1415 23c. Type **356** 30 20
1416 60c. Emblem 80 55

357 Comet and Globe

358 Angels

1986. Appearance of Halley's Comet.
1417 **357** 23c. multicoloured . . . 25 15
1418 – 30c. blue, brown and yellow 35 25
MS1419 75×85 mm. 1b. multicoloured. Imperf . . . . 1·40 1·10
DESIGNS: 30c., 1b. Panama la Vieja Cathedral tower.

1986. Obligatory Tax. 20th Anniv of Children's Village. Children's drawings. Multicoloured.
1420 2c. Type **358** 10 10
1421 2c. Cupids 10 10
1422 2c. Indians 10 10
1423 2c. Angels (different) . . . 10 10
MS1424 75×85 mm. 2b. Dancers (54×62 mm). Perf or imperf 2·75 1·40

359 Basketball

360 Argentina Player

1986. 15th Central American and Caribbean Games, Santiago. Multicoloured.
1425 20c. Type **359** 20 10
1426 23c. Sports 25 15

1986. World Cup Football Championship, Mexico. Multicoloured.
1427 23c. Type **360** 25 15
1428 30c. West Germany player 35 25
1429 37c. West Germany and Argentina players 45 30
MS1430 75×85 mm. 1b. Ball and players legs . . . . 1·40 1·10

361 Crib

362 Dove and Globe

1986. Christmas. Multicoloured.
1431 23c. Type **361** 25 15
1432 36c. Tree and presents . . . 40 25
1433 42c. As No. 1432 . . . . . 45 30

1986. International Peace Year. Multicoloured.
1434 8c. Type **362** 10 10
1435 19c. Profiles and emblem . . 20 10

363 Mask

365 Mountain Rose

364 Headquarters Building

1987. Tropical Carnival. Multicoloured.
1436 20c. Type **363** 20 10
1437 35c. Sun with eye mask . . 40 25
MS1438 75×85 mm. 1b. As No. 363. Imperf . . . . 1·40 1·10

1987. 50th Anniv (1985) of Panama Lions Club.
1439 **364** 37c. multicoloured . . . 45 30

1987. Flowers and Birds. Multicoloured.
1440 3c. Type **365** 10 10
1441 5c. Blue-grey tanager (horiz) 40 10
1442 8c. Golden cup 10 10
1443 15c. Tropical kingbird (horiz) 80 25
1444 19c. "Barleria micans" (flower) 20 10
1445 23c. Brown pelican (horiz) 1·10 40
1446 30c. "Cordia dentata" (flower) 35 25
1447 36c. Rufous pigeon (horiz) 1·50 65

366 Octavio Menendez Pereira (founder) and Anniversary Monument

1987. 50th Anniv (1986) of Panama University.
1448 **366** 19c. multicoloured . . . 20 10

367 Emblem in "40"

1987. 40th Anniv (1985) of F.A.O.
1449 **367** 10c. brown, yellow and black 10 10
1450 45c. brown, green and black 50 30

368 Heinrich Schutz

369 Development Projects

1987. Composers and 7th Anniv (1986) of National Theatre.
1451 **368** 19c. multicoloured . . . 20 10
1452 – 30c. green, mauve & brown 35 25
1453 – 37c. brown, blue and deep blue 45 30
1454 – 60c. green, yellow & black 70 45
DESIGNS—HORIZ: 30c. National Theatre. VERT: 37c. Johann Sebastian Bach; 60c. Georg Friedrich Handel.

1987. 25th Anniv (1986) of Inter-American Development Bank.
1455 **369** 23c. multicoloured . . . 25 15

370 Horse-drawn Fire Pump, 1887, and Modern Appliance

372 "Adoration of the Magi" (Albrecht Nentz)

371 Wrestling

1987. Centenary of Fire Service. Multicoloured.
1456 25c. Type **370** 30 20
1457 35c. Fireman carrying boy 40 25

1987. 10th Pan-American Games, Indianapolis. Mult.
1458 15c. Type **371** 20 10
1459 25c. Tennis (vert) 25 15
1460 30c. Swimming 35 25
1461 41c. Basketball (vert) . . . 45 30
1462 60c. Cycling (vert) 70 45
MS1463 74×84 mm. 1b. Weightlifting . . . . 1·40 1·10

1987. Christmas. Multicoloured.
1464 22c. Type **372** 25 15
1465 35c. "The Virgin adored by Angels" (Matthias Grunewald) 40 25
1466 37c. "Virgin and Child" (Konrad Witz) 45 30

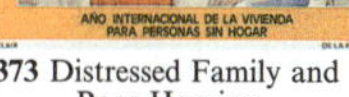

373 Distressed Family and Poor Housing

374 Heart falling into Crack

1987. International Year of Shelter for the Homeless. Multicoloured.
1467 45c. Type **373** 50 30
1468 50c. Happy family and stylized modern housing 50 30

1988. Anti-drugs Campaign.
1469 **374** 10c. red and orange . . 10 10
1470 17c. red and green . . . 20 10
1471 25c. red and blue 30 20

375 Hands and Sapling

376 Breastfeeding

1988. Reafforestation Campaign.
1472 **375** 35c. deep green and green 40 25
1473 40c. red and purple . . . 45 30
1474 45c. brown and bistre . . 50 30

1988. UNICEF Infant Survival Campaign. Mult.
1475 20c. Type **376** 25 15
1476 31c. Vaccination 35 25
1477 45c. Children playing by lake (vert) 50 30

377 Rock Beauty and Cuban Hogfish

1988. Fishes. Multicoloured.
1478 7c. Type **377** 15 10
1479 35c. French angelfish . . . 65 30
1480 60c. Black-barred soldierfish 1·10 55
1481 1b. Spotted drum . . . . . 2·00 1·25

378 Emblem and Clasped Hands

379 "Virgin with Donors"

1988. 75th Anniv of Girl Guide Movement.
1482 **378** 35c. multicoloured . . . 35 25

1988. Christmas. Anonymous Paintings from Museum of Colonial Religious Art. Mult.
1483 17c. Type **379** (postage) . . 20 10
1484 45c. "Virgin of the Rosary with St. Dominic" 50 30
1485 35c. "St. Joseph with the Child" (air) 35 25

380 Athletes and Silver Medal (Brazil)

1989. Seoul Olympic Games Medals. Mult.
1486 17c. Type **380** (postage) . . 20 10
1487 25c. Wrestlers and gold medal (Hungary) 30 20
1488 60c. Weightlifter and gold medal (Turkey) 70 45
1490 35c. Boxers and bronze medal (Colombia) (air) . . 35 25
MS1489 120 × 80 mm. 1b. Swimmer 1·40 1·10

381 St. John Bosco

382 Anniversary Emblem

1989. Death Centenary of St. John Bosco (founder of Salesian Brothers). Multicoloured.
1491 10c. Type **381** 15 10
1492 20c. Menor Basilica and St. John with people . . . 25 15

1989. 125th Anniv of Red Cross Movement.
1493 **382** 40c. black and red . . . 50 30
1494 – 1b. multicoloured . . . 1·50 90
DESIGN: 1b. Red Cross workers putting patient in ambulance.

383 "Ancon I" (first ship through Canal)

1989. Air. 75th Anniv of Panama Canal.
1495 **383** 35c. red, black and yellow . . . . 2·25 80
1496 – 60c. multicoloured . . . 3·25 1·25
DESIGN: 60c. Modern tanker.

384 Barriles Ceremonial Statue

1989. America. Pre-Columbian Artefacts. Mult.
1497 20c. Type **384** 25 15
1498 35c. Ceramic vase 45 30

385 "March of the Women on Versailles" (engraving)

1989. Bicent of French Revolution. Mult.
1499 25c. Type **385** (postage) . . 30 20
1500 35c. "Storming the Bastille" (air) 45 30
1501 45c. Birds 55 35

386 "Holy Family"

1989. Christmas. Multicoloured.
1502 17c. Type **386** 20 10
1503 35c. 1988 crib in Cathedral 45 30
1504 45c. "Nativity" 55 35
The 17 and 45c. show children's paintings.

387 "Byrsonima crassifolia"

1990. Fruit. Multicoloured.
1505 20c. Type **387** 20 10
1506 35c. "Bactris gasipaes" . . . 40 25
1507 40c. "Anacardium occidentale" 40 25

388 Sinan

1990. 88th Birthday of Rogelio Sinan (writer).
1508 **388** 23c. brown and blue . . 25 15

389 Pond Turtle

1990. Reptiles. Multicoloured.
1509 35c. Type **389** 40 25
1510 45c. Olive loggerhead turtle 50 35
1511 60c. Red-footed tortoise . . 65 40

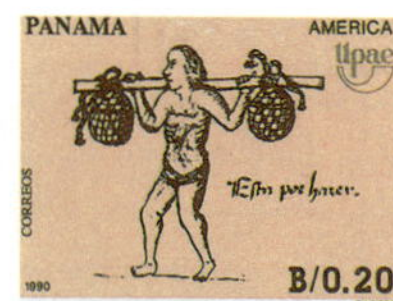

390 Carrying Goods on Yoke (after Oviedo)

1990. America.
1512 **390** 20c. brown, light brown and gold 20 10
1513 – 35c. multicoloured . . . 70 50
DESIGN—VERT: 35c. Warrior wearing gold chest ornament and armbands.

391 Dr. Guillermo Patterson, jun., "Father of Chemistry"

393 St. Ignatius

392 In Sight of Land

1990. Chemistry in Panama.
1514 **391** 25c. black and turquoise 25 15
1515 – 35c. multicoloured . . . 40 25
1516 – 45c. multicoloured . . . 50 35
DESIGNS: 35c. Evaporation experiment; 45c. Books and laboratory equipment.

1991. America. 490th Anniv of Discovery of Panama Isthmus by Rodrigo Bastidas.
1517 **392** 35c. multicoloured . . . 50 35

1991. 450th Anniv of Society of Jesus and 500th Birth Anniv of St. Ignatius de Loyola (founder).
1518 **393** 20c. multicoloured . . . 30 20

394 Declaration of Women's Right to Vote

1991. 50th Anniv of First Presidency of Dr. Arnulfo Arias Madrid.
1519 **394** 10c. brown, stone & gold 15 10
1520 – 10c. brown, stone & gold 15 10
DESIGN: No. 1520, Department of Social Security headquarters.

395 "Glory to God ..." (Luke 2: 14) and Score of "Gloria in Excelsis"

1991. Christmas. Multicoloured.
1521 35c. Type **395** 50 35
1522 35c. Nativity 50 35

396 Adoration of the Kings

1992. Epiphany.
1523 **396** 10c. multicoloured . . . 15 10

397 Family and Housing Estate

1992. "New Lives" Housing Project.
1524 **397** 5c. multicoloured 10 10

398 Costa Rican and Panamanian shaking Hands

1992. 50th Anniv (1991) of Border Agreement with Costa Rica. Multicoloured.
1525 20c. Type **398** 30 20
1526 40c. Map showing Costa Rica and Panama 55 35
1527 50c. Presidents Calderon and Arias and national flags 70 45

399 Pollutants and Hole over Antarctic

1992. "Save the Ozone Layer".
1528 **399** 40c. multicoloured . . . 55 35

400 Exhibition Emblem

1992. "Expocomer 92" 10th International Trade Exhibition, Panama City.
1529 **400** 10c. multicoloured . . . 15 10

401 Portrait

402 Maria Olimpia de Obaldia

1992. 1st Death Anniv of Dame Margot Fonteyn (ballet dancer). Portraits by Pietro Annigoni. Multicoloured.
1530 35c. Type **401** 50 35
1531 45c. On stage 60 40

1992. Birth Centenary of Maria Olimpia de Obaldia (poet).
1532 **402** 10c. multicoloured . . . 15 10

403 Athletics Events and Map of Spain

1992. Olympic Games, Barcelona.
1533 **403** 10c. multicoloured . . . 15 10

404 Paca

1992. Endangered Animals.
1534 **404** 5c. brown, stone & black 10 10
1535 – 10c. black, brn & stone 25 25
1536 – 15c. brown, blk & stone 20 15
1537 – 20c. multicoloured . . . 30 20
DESIGNS: 10c. Harpy eagle; 15c. Jaguar; 20c. Iguana.

405 Zion Baptist Church, Bocas del Toro

1992. Centenary of Baptist Church in Panama.
1538 **405** 20c. multicoloured . . . 30 20

406 Columbus's Fleet

1992. America. 500th Anniv of Discovery of America by Columbus. Multicoloured.
1539 20c. Type **406** 45 30
1540 35c. Columbus planting flag 75 50

407 Flag and Map of Europe

408 Mascot

1992. European Single Market.
1541 **407** 10c. multicoloured . . . 15 10

1992. "Expo '92" World's Fair, Seville.
1542 **408** 10c. multicoloured . . . 15 10

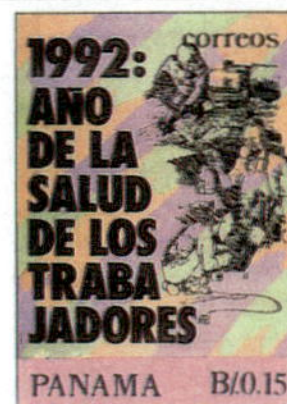

409 Occupations

1992. American Workers' Health Year.
1543 **409** 15c. multicoloured . . . 20 15

410 Angel and Shepherds

1992. Christmas. Multicoloured.
1544 20c. Type **410** 30 20
1545 35c. Mary and Joseph arriving at Bethlehem . . 50 35

411 Jesus lighting up the Americas

1993. 500th Anniv (1992) of Evangelization of the American Continent.
1546 **411** 10c. multicoloured . . . 15 10

412 Woman on Crutches and Wheelchair-bound Man

1993. National Day of Disabled Persons.
1547 **412** 5c. multicoloured 10 10

413 Herrera (bust)

1993. 32nd Death Anniv of Dr. Jose de la Cruz Herrera (essayist).
1548 **413** 5c. multicoloured 10 10

414 Nutritious Foods and Emblems

1993. International Nutrition Conference, Rome.
1549 **414** 10c. multicoloured . . . 15 10

415 Caravel and Columbus in Portobelo Harbour

1994. 490th Anniv (1992) of Columbus's Fourth Voyage and Exploration of the Panama Isthmus.
1550 **415** 50c. multicoloured . . . 65 45

416 Panama Flag and Greek Motifs

418 Chinese Family and House

1995. 50th Anniv of Greek Community in Panama. Multicoloured.
1551 20c. Type **416** 25 15
MS1552 100 × 50 mm. 75c. Acropolis, Athens; 75c. Greek Orthodox Church, Panama (horiz) 1·75 1·40

1995. Various stamps surch.
1553 – 20c. on 23c. multicoloured (1459) 25 15
1554 **373** 25c. on 45c. multicoloured 30 20
1555 – 30c. on 45c. multicoloured (1510) 40 25
1556 **375** 35c. on 45c. brown and bistre 45 30
1557 – 35c. on 45c. multicoloured (1477) 45 30
1558 – 40c. on 41c. multicoloured (1461) 50 35
1559 – 50c. on 60c. multicoloured (1511) 65 45
1560 – 1b. on 50c. multicoloured (1480) 1·25 85

1996. Chinese Presence in Panama. 142nd Anniv of Arrival of First Chinese Immigrants. Multicoloured.
1561 60c. Type **418** 75 50
MS1562 90 × 78 mm. 1b.50 Motifs for winter, spring, summer and autumn. Imperf . . . . 1·75 1·40

419 The King's Bridge from the North (16th century)

1996. 475th Anniv (1994) of Founding by the Spanish of Panama City. Multicoloured.
1563 15c. Type **419** 20 15
1564 20c. City arms, 1521 (vert) 25 15
1565 25c. Plan of first cathedral 30 20
1566 35c. Present-day ruins of Cathedral of the Assumption of Our Lady 45 30

420 "60", Campus and Emblem

1996. 60th Anniv of Panama University.
1567 **420** 40c. multicoloured . . . 50 35

421 Anniversary Emblem

1996. 75th Anniv of Panama Chapter of Rotary International.
1568 **421** 5b. multicoloured . . . 6·25 4·25

422 Great Tinamou

1996. America (1993). Endangered Species.
1569 **422** 20c. multicoloured . . . 25 15

423 Northern Coati

1996. Mammals. Multicoloured.
1570 25c. Type **423** 30 20
1571 25c. Collared anteater ("Tamandua mexicana") 30 20
1572 25c. Two-toed anteater ("Cyclopes didactylus") 30 20
1573 25c. Puma 30 20

424 De Lesseps

425 "50" and Emblem

1996. Death Centenary of Ferdinand, Vicomte de Lesseps (builder of Suez Canal).
1574 **424** 35c. multicoloured . . . 45 30

1996. 50th Anniv of U.N.O.
1575 **425** 45c. multicoloured . . . 55 35

426 Emblem and Motto

427 Bello

1996. 25th Anniv (1993) of Panama Chapter of Kiwanis International.
1576 **426** 40c. multicoloured . . . 50 35

1996. 25th Anniv (1995) of Andres Bello Covenant for Education, Science, Technology and Culture.
1577 **427** 35c. multicoloured . . . 45 30

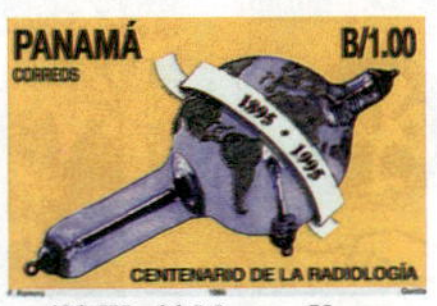

428 World Map on X-ray Equipment

1996. Centenary of Discovery of X-rays by Wilhelm Rontgen.
1578 **428** 1b. multicoloured . . . 1·25 85

429 Madonna and Child

1996. Christmas.
1579 **429** 35c. multicoloured . . . 45 30

430 Diesel Train and Panama Canal

1996. America (1994). Postal Transport.
1580 **430** 30c. multicoloured . . . 35 25

431 "Panama, More than a Canal" (C. Gonzalez)

1997. 20th Anniv of Torrijos–Carter Treaty (transferring Control of Canal Zone to Panama in Year 2000). Multicoloured.

1581	20c. Type **431**	25	15
1582	30c. "A Curtain of Our Flag" (A. Siever) (vert)	35	25
1583	45c. "Perpetual Steps" (R. Martinez)	55	35
1584	50c. Kurt Waldheim (U.N. Secretary-General), President Carter of U.S.A. and President Torrijos of Panama at signing ceremony	60	40
MS1585	127×102 mm. 3, 40, 50c. Composite design as No. 1584 (sold at 1b.50)	1·75	1·40

432 Pedro Miguel Locks

1997. World Congress on Panama Canal. Mult.

1586	45c. Type **432**	55	35
1587	45c. Miraflores Locks	55	35
MS1588	100×75 mm. 1b.50 Gatun Locks (75×30 mm)	1·75	1·40

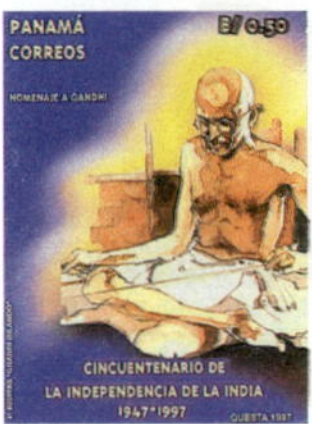
433 "Gandhi Spinning" (P. Biswas)

435 Mary and Joseph searching for Lodgings

434 Crocodile on Rock

1997. 50th Anniv of Independence of India.

1589	**433** 50c. multicoloured	60	40

1997. The American Crocodile. Multicoloured.

1590	25c. Type **434**	30	20
1591	25c. Looking across water	30	20
1592	25c. Two crocodiles	30	20
1593	25c. Head with mouth open	30	20

1997. Christmas.

1594	**435** 35c. multicoloured	45	30

436 Fire Engines from 1941 and 1948

1997. Centenary of Colon City Fire Brigade.

1595	**436** 20c. multicoloured	25	15

437 "Eleutherodactylus biporcatus" (robber frog)

1997. Frogs. Multicoloured.

1596	25c. Type **437**	30	20
1597	25c. "Hyla colymba" (tree frog)	30	20
1598	25c. "Hyla rufitela" (tree frog)	30	20
1599	25c. "Nelsonephryne aterrima"	30	20

438 Women wearing Polleras

1997. America (1996). Traditional Costumes.

1600	**438** 20c. multicoloured	25	15

439 Arosemena

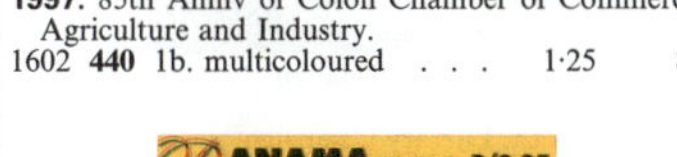
440 Emblem

1997. Death Centenary of Justo Arosemena (President, 1855–56).

1601	**439** 40c. multicoloured	50	35

1997. 85th Anniv of Colon Chamber of Commerce, Agriculture and Industry.

1602	**440** 1b. multicoloured	1·25	85

441 Douglas DC-3

1997. 50th Anniv of Panamanian Aviation Company. Multicoloured.

1603	35c. Type **441**	45	30
1604	35c. Martin 4-0-4	45	30
1605	35c. Avro HS-748	45	30
1606	35c. Lockheed L-168 Electra	45	30
1607	35c. Boeing 727-100	45	30
1608	35c. Boeing 737-200 Advanced	45	30

442 Wailing Wall

444 Central Avenue, San Felipe

443 Building Facade and Emblem

1997. 3000th Anniv of Jerusalem. Multicoloured.

1609	20c. Type **442**	25	15
1610	25c. Service in the Basilica of the Holy Sepulchre	30	20
1611	60c. Dome of the Rock	75	50
MS1612	100×75 mm. 2b.50 Motifs of Nos. 1609/11	2·25	1·75

1998. 50th Anniv of Organization of American States.

1613	**443** 40c. multicoloured	10	10

1998. Tourism. Multicoloured.

1614	10c. Type **444**	10	10
1615	20c. Tourists in rainforest	25	15
1616	25c. Gatun Locks, Panama Canal (horiz)	30	20
1617	35c. Panama City (horiz)	45	30
1618	40c. San Jeronimo Fort, San Felipe de Portobelo (horiz)	50	30
1619	45c. Rubber raft, River Chagres (horiz)	55	35
1620	60c. Beach, Dog's Island, Kuna Yala (horiz)	75	50

445 Nativity

2000. Christmas.

1621	**445** 40c. multicoloured	45	25

446 Pavilion

2000. "World Expo'98" World's Fair, Lisbon, Portugal.

1622	**446** 45c. multicoloured	50	30

447 Harpy Eagle (L. Melillo)

2000. The Harpy Eagle. Entries in painting competition by named artist.

1623	**447** 20c. black and green	25	15
1624	– 20c. multicoloured	25	15
1625	– 20c. multicoloured	25	15
1626	– 20c. multicoloured	25	15

DESIGNS: No. 1624, J. JimEnez; 1625, S. Castro; 1626, J. Ramos.

448 Emblem

2000. 40th Anniv of Business Executives' Association.

1627	**448** 50c. multicoloured	60	35

449 Emblem

2000. 50th Anniv of Colon Free Trade Zone.

1628	**449** 15c. multicoloured	20	15

450 Emblem

2000. 50th Anniv of Universal Declaration of Human Rights.

1629	**450** 15c. multicoloured	20	15

451 *Platyphora haroldi*

2000. Beetles. Multicoloured.

1630	30c. Type **451**	35	20
1631	30c. *Stilodes leoparda*	35	20
1632	30c. *Stilodes fuscolineata*	35	20
1633	30c. *Platyphora boucardi*	35	20

452 Cruise Ship

2000. Return of Control of Panama Canal to Panama (1999). Multicoloured.

1634	20c. Type **452**	25	15
1635	35c. Cruise ship at lock gate	40	25
1636	40c. View down canal	45	25
1637	45c. Cruise ship passing through lock	50	30

453 Constructing Canal

2000. 85th Anniv of Panama Canal. Multicoloured.

1638	40c. Type **453**	45	25
1639	40c. Construction of canal (different)	45	25
MS1640	106×56 mm. 1b.50 View of canal at early stage of construction	1·75	1·75

454 Crowd and Madrid wearing surgical mask

2001. Birth Centenary of Dr. Arnulfo Arias Madrid.

1641	**454** 20c. black and brown	25	15
1642	– 20c. black and sepia	25	15
1643	– 30c. multicoloured	35	20
1644	– 30c. multicoloured	35	20

DESIGNS: No. 1642, Crowd and Madrid holding glasses; 1643, Flag, building faade and Madrid; 1644, Crowd and Madrid.

Nos. 1641/25 and 1643/4 respectively were each issued together, se-tenant, forming a composite design.

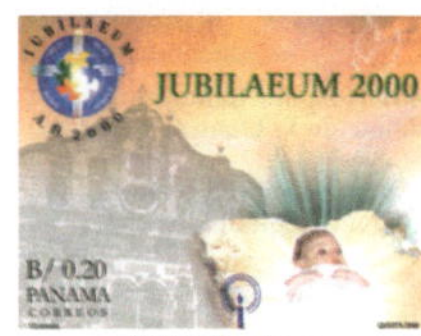
455 Baby Jesus

2001. Year 2000.

1645	**455** 20c. multicoloured	25	15

456 Crowned Globe, Rainbow and Birds (D. Ortega)

2001. "Dreaming of the Future". Winning Entries in Stamp Design Competition. Multicoloured.

1646	20c. Type **456**	25	15
1647	20c. Globe in flower (L. Guerra)	25	15
MS1648	105×54 mm. 75c. Tree, birds, globe and children (J. Aguilar) (horiz); 75c. Blue birds holding ribbons, globe and children holding hands (S. Sitton) (horiz)	90	90

457 Angel and Baby Jesus

458 Banco General Tower (Carlos Medina)

2001. Christmas.
1649 **457** 35c. multicoloured . . . 40 25

2001. Architecture of 1990s. Multicoloured.
1650 35c. Type **458** 40 25
1651 35c. Los Delfines condominium (Edwin Brown) 40 25
MS1652 104 × 54 mm. 75c. Circular building (Ricardo Moreno and Jesus Santamaria) (horiz); 75c. Building with three gables (Ricardo Moreno and Jesus Santamaria) (horiz) . . . . . 1·75 1·75

459 *Psychopsis krameriana*

2001. Orchids. Multicoloured.
1653 35c. Type **459** 40 25
1654 35c. *Cattleya dowiana* . . . 40 25
MS1655 104 × 54 mm. 75c. *Peristeria elata*; 75c. *Miltoniopsis roezlii* 1·75 1·75

460 1878 50c. Sovereign State and 1904 1c. Republic of Panama Stamps

2001. 18th U. P. A. E. P. Congress, Panama.
1656 **460** 5b. multicoloured . . . 6·00 6·00

461 Hospital Buildings and Dr Jaime de la Guardia (founder)

2001. 50th Anniv of San Fernando Clinical Hospital.
1657 **461** 20c. multicoloured . . . 25 15

462 Pres. Moscoso and Cornucopia

2002. Mireya Moscoso, First Woman President of Panama.
1658 **462** 35c. multicoloured . . . 40 25

463 Couple and Drums

2002. Christmas, 2001. Multicoloured.
1659 60c. Type **463** 65 40
1660 1b. Hat, instruments and candles . . . . 1·10 65
1661 2b. Vase, gourds and holly 2·10 1·30

464 Helmeted Warrior (allegorical painting)

2002. 180th Anniv of Independence. Multicoloured.
1662 15c. Type **464** 15 10
1663 15c. Woman charioteer (allegorical painting) . . . 15 10

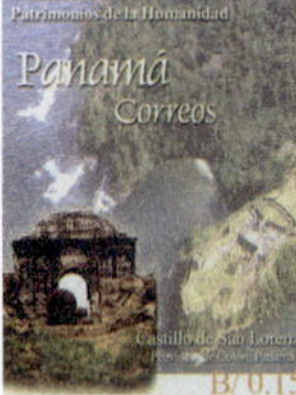

465 San Lorenzo Castle

466 Natives and Ship

2002. America.Cultural Heritage. Multicoloured.
1664 15c. Type **465** 15 10
1665 15c. Panama city 15 10
1666 1b. 50 Metropolitan Cathedral church (horiz) 1·60 95
1667 1b. 50 Portobelo fortifications (horiz) . . . 1·60 95

2002. 500th Anniv of Discovery of Panama Isthmus. Multicoloured.
1668 50c. Type **466** 55 30
1669 5b. Native woman and Spanish conquistador . . 5·50 3·25

467 Spaniard and Natives (allegorical painting)

2002. Artistic Treasures of Las Garzas Palace. Painting by Robert Lewis. Multicoloured.
1670 5c. Type **467** 10 10
1671 5c. Battle scene 10 10
1672 5c. Mythical figures 10 10
1673 5c. Spanish women 10 10

468 *Montastraea annualaris*

2002. Corals. Multicoloured.
1674 10c. Type **468** 10 10
1675 10c. *Pavona chiriquiensis* . . 10 10
1676 1b. *Siderastrea glynni* . . . 1·10 65
1677 2b. *Pocillopora* . . . . . . 2·20 1·30

469 *Ophioderes maternal*

2002. Butterflies and Moths. Multicoloured.
1678 10c. Type **469** 10 10
1679 10c. *Rhuda focula* 10 10
1680 1b. *Morpho peleides* . . . 1·10 65
1681 2b. *Tarchon felderi* . . . . 2·20 1·30

470 "100" enclosing Jean Baptiste de La Salle (founder) and Children

2003. Air. Centenary of La Salle Christian Schools.
1682 **470** 5b. multicoloured . . . 5·50 3·25

471 Nata Church

2003. Air. 480th Anniv of Nata.
1683 **471** 1b. multicoloured . . . 1·10 65

472 Girl and Nativity Figures

2003. Christmas (2002).
1684 **472** 15c. multicoloured . . . 15 10

473 Children

2003. America. Literacy Campaign.
1685 **473** 45c. multicoloured . . . 50 30

474 Clara Gonzalez de Behringer

2003. Famous Women. Clara Gonzalez de Behringer (first woman lawyer).
1686 **474** 30c. multicoloured . . . 30 20

475 "Colon" (steam locomotive)

2003. Air. First Transcontinental Railway. Multicoloured.
1687 40c. Type **475** 40 25
1688 50c. Locomotive in station (vert) 55 35

476 Columbus Monument

2003. 150th Anniv of Colon City (2002).
1689 **476** 15c. multicoloured . . . 15 10

477 Spanish Soldiers and Native Americans

2003. Air. 500th Anniv of Santa Maria de Belen.
1690 **477** 1b.50 multicoloured . . 1·60 95

478 Christopher Columbus and his Ships

2003. Air. 500th Anniv of Fourth Voyage of Christopher Columbus (2002).
1691 **478** 2b. multicoloured . . . 2·20 1·30

479 Luis Russell

2003. Birth Centenary of Luis Russell (musician).
1692 **479** 10c. multicoloured . . . 10 10

480 Muse of Music (statue)

482 Josemaria Escriva de Balaguer

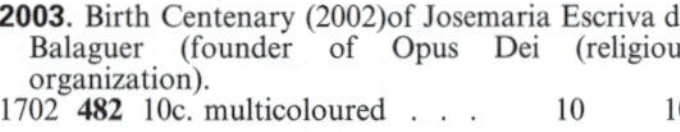

481 Village and Woman's Face

2003. Artistic Treasures of National Theatre. Multicoloured.
1693 5c. Type **480** (postage) . . . 10 10
1694 5c. Muse of theatre (statue) 10 10

(b) Size 40 × 30 mm.
1695 50c. Decorated balcony (air) 55 35
1696 60c. Portico and decorated ceiling 65 40

2003. Kuna Indians of San Blas Archipelago. Multicoloured.
1697 50c. Type **481** 55 35
1698 50c. Couple wearing traditional costume (vert) 55 35
1699 60c. Traditional dance . . . 65 40
1700 60c. Woman's hands sewing mola (traditional cloth) 65 40
MS1701 100 × 50 mm. 1b.50 Fish (mola design) (50 × 46mm) . . 1·60 1·60

2003. Birth Centenary (2002)of Josemaria Escriva de Balaguer (founder of Opus Dei (religious organization).
1702 **482** 10c. multicoloured . . . 10 10

483 Hospital Building and St. Tomas de Villanueva (founder)

2003. Air. Panamanian Medicine Multicoloured.
1703 50c. Type **483** (300th anniv of St. Tomas Hospital) . . 55 35
1704 50c. Building facade and William Crawford Gorgas (founder) (75th anniv of Gorgas Medical Institute) 55 35

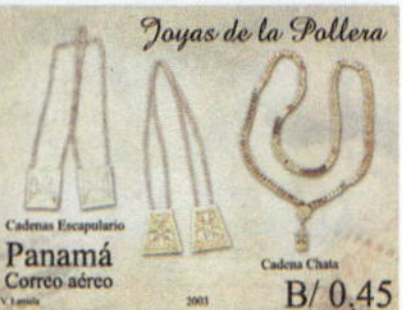

484 Necklaces

2003. Air. Pollera (Latin American folk costume) Jewellery. Multicoloured.
1705 45c. Type **484** 50 30
1706 60c. Broaches 65 40

485 National Arms (¾-size illustration)

2003. Centenary of Panama Republic (1st issue). Multicoloured.
1707 5c. Type **485** 10 10
1708 10c. National flag 10 10
1709 15c. Manuel Amador Guerrero (president, 1903) 15 10
1710 15c. Mireya Mascoso (president, 2003) 15 10
1711 25c. Act of Independence . . 25 15
1712 30c. Sterculia apetala . . . 30 20
1713 30c. Peristeria elata 30 20
1714 35c. Revolutionary junta . . 40 25
1715 45c. Constitutional conference members . . . 50 30
See also No. 1717.

486 Harpy Eagle (*Harpia harpia*) and Harlequin Frog (*Atelopus varius*)

2003. America. Endangered Species.
1716 **486** 2b. multicoloured . . . 2·20 1·30

487 Panama City and Nativity

2003. Centenary of Panama Republic (2nd issue). Christmas.
1717 **487** 10c. multicoloured . . . 10 10

488 Building Facade

2003. 150th Anniv of "La Estrella" Newspaper.
1718 **488** 40c. multicoloured . . . 40 25

489 Panama City and Emblems

2003. Panama City, Ibero-American Cultural Capital, 2003.
1719 **489** 5c. multicoloured 10 10

ACKNOWLEDGEMENT OF RECEIPT STAMPS

1898. Handstamped **A. R. COLON COLOMBIA**.
AR24 **5** 5c. blue . . . . 4·50 3·75
AR25 10c. orange . . . . 8·00 8·00

1902. Handstamped **AR** in circle.
AR32 **5** 5c. blue . . . . 3·00 3·00
AR33 10c. orange . . . . 6·00 6·00

1903. No. AR169 of Colombia handstamped **AR** in circle.
AR34 **AR 60** 5c. red . . . . . . 11·00 11·00

AR 37

1904.
AR135 **AR 37** 5c. blue 90 90

1916. Optd **A.R.**
AR177 **50** 2½c. red 90 90

EXPRESS LETTER STAMPS

1926. Optd **EXPRESO**.
E220 **57** 10c. black and orange . . 4·25 2·10
E221 20c. black and brown . . 5·50 2·10

E 81 Cyclist Messenger

1929.
E226 **E 81** 10c. orange 90 70
E227 20c. brown . . . . . . 1·75 1·10

INSURANCE STAMPS

1942. Surch **SEGURO POSTAL HABILITADO** and value.
IN430 5c. on 1b. black (No. 373) 45 35
IN431 10c. on 1b. brown (No. 365) 70 55
IN432 25c. on 50c. brown (No. 372) . . . . 1·25 1·25

POSTAGE DUE STAMPS

D 58 San Geronimo Castle Gate, Portobelo

1915.
D169 **D 58** 1c. brown . . . . . . 1·90 30
D170 – 2c. brown . . . . . . 2·75 25
D171 – 4c. brown . . . . . . 3·75 55
D172 – 10c. brown . . . . . 2·75 1·10
DESIGNS—VERT: 2c. Statue of Columbus. HORIZ: 4c. House of Deputies. VERT: 10c. Pedro J. Sosa.
No. D169 is wrongly inscr "CASTILLO DE SAN LORENZO CHAGRES".

D 86

1930.
D240 **D 86** 1c. green 70 25
D241 2c. red 70 20
D242 4c. blue 75 30
D243 10c. violet 75 40

REGISTRATION STAMPS

R 4

1888.
R12 **R 4** 10c. black on grey . . . 6·00 4·00

1897. Handstamped **R COLON** in circle.
R22 **5** 10c. orange . . . . 4·25 4·00

R 15

1900.
R29 **R 15** 10c. black on blue . . . 2·50 2·10
R30 10c. red . . . . 18·00 15·00

1902. No. R30 surch by hand.
R31 **R 15** 20c. on 10c. red . . . . 15·00 12·00

1903. Type R **85** of Colombia optd **REPUBLICA DE PANAMA**.
R42 20c. red on blue . . . . . . 27·00
R43 20c. blue on blue . . . . . 27·00

1903. Nos. R42/3 surch.
R46 10c. on 20c. red on blue . . 50·00 50·00
R47 10c. on 20c. blue on blue . . 50·00 50·00

1904. Optd **PANAMA**.
R60 **5** 10c. orange . . . . 2·10 2·10

1904. Type R **6** of Colombia surch **Panama 10** and bar.
R67 10c. on 20c. red on blue . . 38·00 35·00
R68 10c. on 20c. blue on blue . . 38·00 35·00

1904. Type R **85** of Colombia optd **Republica de Panama**.
R106 20c. red on blue . . . . . 5·00 5·00

R 35

1904.
R133 **R 35** 10c. green 70 30

1916. Stamps of Panama surch **R 5 cts**.
R175 **46** 5c. on 8c. black & purple 2·10 1·40
R176 **52** 5c. on 8c. black & purple 2·10 50

TOO LATE STAMPS

1903. Too Late stamp of Colombia optd **REPUBLICA DE PANAMA**.
L44 **L 86** 5c. violet on red . . . . 7·50 5·50

L 36

1904.
L134 **L 36** 2½c. red 70 40

1910. Typewritten optd **Retardo**.
L158 **50** 2½c. red . . . . 75·00 75·00

1910. Optd **RETARDO**.
L159 **50** 2½c. red . . . . 38·00 30·00

1916. Surch **RETARDO UN CENTESIMO**.
L174 **38** 1c. on ½c. orange . . . . 15·00 12·00

APPENDIX

The following stamps have either been issued in excess of postal needs or have not been available to the public in reasonable quantities at face value. Such stamps may later be given full listing if there is evidence of regular postal use.

1964.
Satellites. Postage ½, 1c.; Air 5, 10, 21, 50c.

1965.
Tokyo Olympic Games Medal Winners. Postage ½, 1, 2, 3, 4c.; Air 5, 6, 7, 10, 21, 31c.

Space Research. Postage ½, 1, 2, 3c.; Air 5, 10, 11, 31c.

400th Birth Anniv of Galileo. Air 10, 21c.

Peaceful Uses of Atomic Energy. Postage ½, 1, 4c.; Air 6, 10, 21c.

Nobel Prize Medals. Air 10, 21c.

Pres. John Kennedy. Postage ½, 1c.; Air 10+5c., 21+10c., 31+15c.

1966.
Pope Paul's Visit to U.N. in New York. Postage ½, 1c.; Air 5, 10, 21, 31c.

Famous Men. Postage ½c.; Air 10, 31c.

Famous Paintings. Postage ½c.; Air 10, 31c.

World Cup Football Championship. Postage ½, ½c.; Air 10, 10, 21, 21c.

Italian Space Research. Postage ½, 1c.; Air 5, 10, 21c.

Centenary of I.T.U. Air 31c.

World Cup Winners. Optd on 1966 World Cup Issue. Postage ½, ½c.; Air 10, 10, 21, 21c.

Religious Paintings. Postage ½, 1, 2, 3c.; Air 21, 21c.

Churchill and Space Research. Postage ½c.; Air 10, 31c.

3rd Death Anniv of Pres. John Kennedy. Postage ½, 1c.; Air 10, 31c.

Jules Verne and Space Research. Postage ½, 1c.; Air 5, 10, 21, 31c.

1967.
Religious Paintings. Postage ½, 1c.; Air 5, 10, 21, 31c.

Mexico Olympics. Postage ½, 1c.; Air 5, 10, 21, 31c.

Famous Paintings. Postage 5c. × 3; Air 21c. × 3.

Goya's Paintings. Postage 2, 3, 4c.; Air 5, 8, 10, 13, 21c.

1968.
Religious Paintings. Postage 1, 1, 3c.; Air 4, 21, 21c.

Mexican President's Visit. Air 50c., 1b.

Winter Olympic Games, Grenoble. Postage ½, 1c.; Air 5, 10, 21, 31c.

Butterflies. Postage ½, 1, 3, 4c.; Air 5, 13c.

Ship Paintings. Postage ½, 1, 3, 4c.; Air 5, 13c.

Fishes. Postage ½, 1, 3, 4c.; Air 5, 13c.

Winter Olympic Medal Winners. Postage 1, 2, 3, 4, 5, 6, 8c.; Air 13, 30c.

Paintings of Musicians. Postage 5, 10, 15, 20, 25, 30c.

Satellite Transmissions from Panama T.V. (a) Olympic Games, Mexico. Optd on 1964 Satellites issue. Postage ½c.; Air 50c. (b) Pope Paul's Visit to Latin America. Postage ½c.; Air 21c. (c) Panama Satellite Transmissions. Inauguration. (i) optd on Space Research issue of 1965. Postage 5c.; Air 31c. (ii) optd on Churchill and Space Research issue of 1966. Postage ½c.; Air 10c.

Hunting Paintings. Postage 1, 3, 5, 10c.; Air 13, 30c.

Horses and Jockeys. Postage 5, 10, 15, 20, 25, 30c.

Mexico Olympics. Postage 1, 2, 3, 4, 5, 6, 8c.; Air 13, 30c.

1969.
1st International Philatelic and Numismatic Exhibition. Optd on 1968 Issue of Mexican President's Visit. Air 50c., 1b.

Telecommunications Satellites. Air 5, 10, 15, 20, 25, 30c.

Provisionals. Surch "Decreto No. 112 (de 6 de marzo de 1969)" and new values on No. 781 and 10c.+5c. and 21c.+10c. of 1965 Issue of 3rd Death Anniv of Pres. John Kennedy. Air 5c. on 5c.+5c., 5c. on 10c.+5c., 10c. on 21c.+10c.

Pope Paul VI Visit to Latin America. Religious Paintings. Postage 1, 2, 3, 4, 5c.; Air 6, 7, 8, 10c.

PAPAL STATES Pt. 8

Parts of Italy under Papal rule till 1870 when they became part of the Kingdom of Italy.

1852. 100 bajocchi = 1 scudo.
1866. 100 centesimi = 1 lira.

1

2

1852. Papal insignia as in T **1** and **2** in various shapes and frames. Imperf.
2 ½b. black on grey . . . . . . £425 42·00
5 ½b. black on lilac . . . . . . 35·00 £120
10 1b. black on green . . . . . 46·00 55·00
11 2b. black on green . . . . . £130 11·00
14 2b. black on white . . . . . 8·50 50·00
15 3b. black on brown . . . . . 60·00 26·00
16 3b. black on yellow . . . . . 23·00 £160
17 4b. black on brown . . . . . £4500 65·00
19 4b. black on yellow . . . . . £120 34·00
20 5b. black on pink . . . . . . £150 7·50
22 6b. black on lilac £850 £190
23 6b. black on grey . . . . . . £550 48·00
25 7b. black on blue . . . . . . £850 60·00
26 8b. black on white . . . . . £400 32·00
27 50b. blue £12000 £1500
29 1s. pink £3000 £3000

1867. Same types. Imperf.
30 2c. black on green £110 £200
32 3c. black on grey £1800 £2250
33 5c. black on blue £130 £170
34 10c. black on red . . . . . . £850 55·00
35 20c. black on red . . . . . . £120 75·00
36 40c. black on yellow £140 £170
37 80c. black on pink £140 £450

1868. Same types. Perf.
42 2c. black on green . . . . . . 8·00 60·00
43 3c. black on grey . . . . . . 35·00 £3000
45 5c. black on blue . . . . . . 9·75 38·00
46 10c. black on orange . . . . 2·75 11·00
49 20c. black on mauve . . . . . 3·75 30·00
50 20c. black on red . . . . . . 2·20 13·00
52 40c. black on yellow . . . . . 5·50 85·00
55 80c. black on pink . . . . . 25·00 £325

PAPUA Pt. 1

(Formerly **BRITISH NEW GUINEA**)

The eastern portion of the island of New Guinea, to the North of Australia, a territory of the Commonwealth of Australia, now combined with New Guinea. Australian stamps were used after the Japanese defeat in 1945 until the combined issue appeared in 1952.

12 pence = 1 shilling;
20 shilling = 1 pound.

1 Lakatoi (native canoe) with Hanuabada Village in Background

6

1901.

9	1	½d. black and green	10·00	3·75
10		1d. black and red	4·25	2·00
11		2d. black and violet	10·00	4·00
12		2½d. black and blue	15·00	12·00
13		4d. black and brown	35·00	50·00
6		6d. black and green	45·00	35·00
7		1s. black and orange	60·00	65·00
8		2s.6d. black and brown	£550	£500

1906. Optd **Papua**.

38	1	½d. black and green	11·00	12·00
39		1d. black and red	4·00	5·00
40		2d. black and violet	4·50	2·25
24		2½d. black and blue	3·75	15·00
42		4d. black and brown	30·00	50·00
43		6d. black and green	32·00	42·00
19		1s. black and orange	20·00	38·00
37		2s.6d. black and brown	32·00	50·00

1907.

66	6	½d. black and green	1·75	3·75
94		1d. black and red	1·40	1·25
68		2d. black and purple	3·75	5·50
51a		2½d. black and blue	6·50	6·50
63		4d. black and brown	4·75	9·00
80		6d. black and green	8·50	7·50
81		1s. black and orange	7·00	19·00
82		2s.6d. black and brown	38·00	45·00

1911.

84a	6	½d. green	50	2·25
85		1d. red	70	75
86		2d. mauve	70	75
87		2½d. blue	4·75	8·50
88		4d. olive	2·25	11·00
89		6d. brown	3·75	5·00
90		1s. yellow	9·00	15·00
91		2s.6d. red	32·00	38·00

1916.

93	6	½d. green and olive	80	1·00
95		1½d. blue and brown	1·50	80
96		2d. purple and red	1·75	75
97		2½d. green and blue	4·75	12·00
98		3d. black and turquoise	2·25	1·75
99		4d. brown and orange	2·50	5·00
100		5d. grey and brown	4·25	16·00
101		6d. purple	3·25	9·50
127		9d. lilac and violet	4·50	32·00
102		1s. brown and olive	3·50	7·00
128		1s.3d. lilac and blue	7·50	32·00
103		2s.6d. red and pink	21·00	40·00
104		5s. black and green	48·00	48·00
105		10s. green and blue	£140	£160

1917. Surch **ONE PENNY**.

106a	6	1d. on ½d. green	1·00	1·25
107		1d. on 2d. mauve	12·00	15·00
108		1d. on 2½d. blue	1·25	3·75
109		1d. on 4d. green	1·75	4·50
110		1d. on 6d. brown	8·50	17·00
111		1d. on 2s.6d. red	1·50	6·00

1929. Air. Optd **AIR MAIL**.

114	6	3d. black and turquoise	1·00	7·00

(11)

1930. Air. Optd with T **11**.

118	6	3d. black and turquoise	1·00	6·00
119		6d. purple	7·00	10·00
120		1s. brown and olive	4·25	15·00

1931. Surch in words or figures and words.

122	6	2d. on 1½d. blue and brown	1·00	2·00
125		5d. on 1s. brown and olive	1·00	1·75
126		9d. on 2s.6d. red and pink	5·50	8·50
123		1s.3d. on 5d. black and green	4·25	9·00

15 Motuan Girl

18 Raggiana Bird of Paradise

20 Native Mother and Child

1932.

130	15	½d. black and orange	1·50	3·25
131	–	1d. black and green	1·75	60
132	–	1½d. black and red	1·50	8·00
133	18	2d. red	11·00	30
134	–	3d. black and blue	3·25	6·50
135	20	4d. olive	6·00	9·50
136	–	5d. black and green	3·00	3·00
137	–	6d. brown	7·50	5·50
138	–	9d. black and violet	10·00	21·00
139	–	1s. green	4·00	8·50
140	–	1s.3d. black and purple	15·00	27·00
141	–	2s. black and green	15·00	24·00
142	–	2s.6d. black and mauve	25·00	38·00
143	–	5s. black and brown	55·00	55·00
144	–	10s. violet	85·00	85·00
145	–	£1 black and grey	£190	£150

DESIGNS—VERT (as T **15**): 1d. Chieftain's son; 1½d. Tree houses; 3d. Papuan dandy; 5d. Masked dancer; 9d. Shooting fish; 1s. Ceremonial platform; 1s.3d. Lakatoi; 2s. Papuan art; 2s.6d. Pottery-making; 5d. Native policeman; £1 Delta house. VERT (as T **18**): 6d. Papuan mother. HORIZ: (as T **20**): 10s. Lighting fire.

31 Hoisting the Union Jack

35 King George VI

1934. 50th Anniv of Declaration of British Protectorate. Inscr "1884 1934".

146	31	1d. green	1·00	3·50
147	–	2d. red	1·75	3·00
148	31	3d. blue	1·75	3·00
149	–	5d. purple	11·00	16·00

DESIGN: 2d., 5d. Scene on H.M.S. "Nelson".

1935. Silver Jubilee. Optd **HIS MAJESTY'S JUBILEE 1910 1935 (1910 – 1935** on 2d.).

150	–	1d. black & green (No. 131)	75	3·00
151	18	2d. red	2·50	3·00
152	–	3d. black and blue (No. 134)	1·75	3·00
153	–	5d. black & green (No. 136)	2·50	3·00

1937. Coronation.

154	35	1d. green	45	20
155		2d. red	45	1·25
156		3d. blue	45	1·25
157		5d. purple	45	1·75

36 Port Moresby

1938. Air. 50th Anniv of Declaration of British Possession.

158	36	2d. red	3·00	2·50
159		3d. blue	3·00	2·25
160		5d. green	3·50	3·25
161		8d. red	6·00	15·00
162		1s. mauve	19·00	16·00

37 Natives poling Rafts

1939. Air.

163	37	2d. red	3·00	4·50
164		3d. blue	3·00	8·50
165		5d. green	3·00	2·25
166		8d. red	8·00	3·25
167		1s. mauve	10·00	8·50
168		1s.6d. olive	30·00	35·00

OFFICIAL STAMPS

1931. Optd **O S**.

O55	6	½d. green and olive	2·25	4·75
O56a		1d. black and red	4·00	9·00
O57		1½d. blue and brown	1·60	12·00
O58		2d. brown and purple	3·75	11·00
O59		3d. black and turquoise	2·50	22·00
O60		4d. brown and orange	2·50	18·00
O61		5d. grey and brown	6·00	38·00
O62		6d. purple and red	4·00	8·50
O63		9d. lilac and violet	30·00	48·00
O64		1s. brown and olive	9·00	30·00
O65		1s.3d. lilac and blue	30·00	48·00
O66		2s.6d. red and pink	40·00	85·00

PAPUA NEW GUINEA Pt. 1

Combined territory on the island of New Guinea administered by Australia under trusteeship. Self-government was established during 1973.

1952. 12 pence = 1 shilling;
20 shillings = 1 pound.
1966. 100 cents = $1 Australian.
1975. 100 toea = 1 kina.

1 Matschie's Tree Kangaroo

7 Kiriwina Chief House

1952.

1	1	½d. green	30	10
2	–	1d. brown	20	10
3	–	2d. blue	35	10
4	–	2½d. orange	3·75	50
5	–	3d. myrtle	50	10
6	–	3½d. red	50	10
6a	–	3½d. black	6·00	90
18	–	4d. red	75	10
19	–	5d. green	75	10
7	7	6½d. purple	1·25	10
20	–	7d. green	3·75	10
8	–	7½d. blue	2·50	1·00
21	–	8d. blue	75	1·50
9	–	9d. brown	2·75	40
10	–	1s. green	1·75	10
11	–	1s.6d. myrtle	5·00	60
22	–	1s.7d. brown	8·50	4·50
12	–	2s. blue	3·00	10
23	–	2s.5d. red	2·00	1·50
13	–	2s.6d. purple	3·00	40
24	–	5s. red and olive	7·00	1·00
14	–	10s. slate	32·00	13·00
15	–	£1 brown	32·00	13·00

DESIGNS—VERT (as T **1**): 1d. Buka head-dresses; 2d. Native youth; 2½d. Greater bird of paradise; 3d. Native policeman; 3½d. Papuan head-dress; 4d., 5d. Cacao plant. (As T **7**): 7½d. Kiriwina Yam house; 1s.6d. Rubber tapping; 2s. Sepik dancing masks; 5s. Coffee beans; £1 Papuan shooting fish. HORIZ (as T **7**): 7, 8d. Klinki plymill; 9d. Copra making; 1s. Lakatoi; 1s.7d., 2s.5d. Cattle; 2s.6d. Native shepherd and flock; 10s. Map of Papua and New Guinea.

1957. Nos. 4, 1 and 10 surch.

16	–	4d. on 2½d. orange	1·50	10
25	1	5d. on ½d. green	75	10
17	–	7d. on 1s. green	40	10

23 Council Chamber, Port Moresby

1961. Reconstitution of Legislative Council.

26	23	5d. green and yellow	1·00	25
27		2s.3d. green and salmon	2·50	1·50

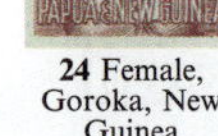

24 Female, Goroka, New Guinea

26 Female Dancer

39 Waterfront, Port Moresby

28 Traffic Policeman

1961.

28	24	1d. lake	70	10
29	–	3d. blue	30	10
47	39	8d. green	30	15
30	26	1s. green	1·00	15
31	–	2s. purple	45	15
48	–	2s.3d. blue	30	30
32	28	3s. green	1·00	1·75

DESIGNS—As Type **24**: 3d. Tribal elder, Tari, Papua. As Type **39**: 2s.3d. Piaggio P-166B Portofino aircraft landing at Tapini. As Type **26**: 2s. Male dancer.

29 Campaign Emblem

30 Map of South Pacific

1962. Malaria Eradication.

33	29	5d. lake and blue	30	15
34		1s. red and brown	50	25
35		2s. black and green	60	70

1962. 5th South Pacific Conference, Pago Pago.

36	30	5d. red and green	50	15
37		1s.6d. violet and yellow	75	70
38		2s.6d. green and blue	75	1·40

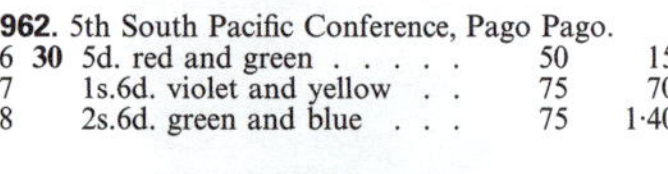

31 Throwing the Javelin

1962. 7th British Empire and Commonwealth Games, Perth.

39	31	5d. brown and blue	20	10
40	–	5d. brown and orange	20	10
41	–	2s.3d. brown and green	70	75

SPORTS—As T **31**: No. 40, High jump. 32 × 23 mm: No. 41, Runners.

34 Raggiana Bird of Paradise

37 Queen Elizabeth II

36 Rabaul

1963.

42	34	5d. yellow, brown and sepia	1·00	10
43	–	6d. red, brown and grey	60	1·25
44	36	10s. multicoloured	12·00	6·00
45	37	£1 brown, gold and green	2·00	1·75

DESIGN—As Type **34**: 6d. Common phalanger.

38 Centenary Emblem

40 Games Emblem

1963. Centenary of Red Cross.
46 **38** 5d. red, grey and green . . 60 10

1963. 1st South Pacific Games, Suva.
49 **40** 5d. brown 10 10
50 1s. green 30 60

41 Watam Head **45** Casting Vote

1964. Native Artefacts. Multicoloured.
51 11d. Type **41** 25 10
52 2s.5d. Watam head (different) 30 1·75
53 2s.6d. Bosmun head 30 10
54 5s. Medina head 35 20

1964. Common Roll Elections.
55 **45** 5d. brown and drab 10 10
56 2s.3d. brown and blue . . . 20 25

46 "Health Centres" **50** Striped Gardener Bowerbird

1964. Health Services.
57 **46** 5d. violet 10 10
58 – 8d. green 10 10
59 – 1s. blue 15 10
60 – 1s.2d. red 20 35
DESIGNS: 8d. "School health"; 1s. "Infant child and maternal health"; 1s.2d. "Medical training".

1964. Multicoloured.
61 1d. Type **50** 40 10
62 3d. Adelbert bowerbird . . . 50 10
63 5d. Blue bird of paradise . . . 55 10
64 6d. Lawes's parotia 75 10
65 8d. Black-billed sicklebill . . . 1·00 20
66 1s. Emperor of Germany bird of paradise . . . . 1·00 10
67 2s. Brown sicklebill 75 30
68 2s.3d. Lesser bird of paradise 75 85
69 3s. Magnificent bird of paradise . . . . 75 1·25
70 5s. Twelve-wired bird of paradise . . . . 7·00 1·50
71 10s. Magnificent riflebird . . . 2·75 9·00
Nos. 66/71 are larger, 25½ × 36½ mm.

61 Canoe Prow

1965. Sepik Canoe Prows in Port Moresby Museum.
72 **61** 4d. multicoloured 50 10
73 – 1s.2d. multicoloured . . . . 1·00 1·75
74 – 1s.6d. multicoloured 50 10
75 – 4s. multicoloured 50 50
Each show different carved prows as Type **61**.

61a "Simpson and his Donkey"

1965. 50th Anniv of Gallipoli Landing.
76 **61a** 2s.3d. brown, black & green 20 10

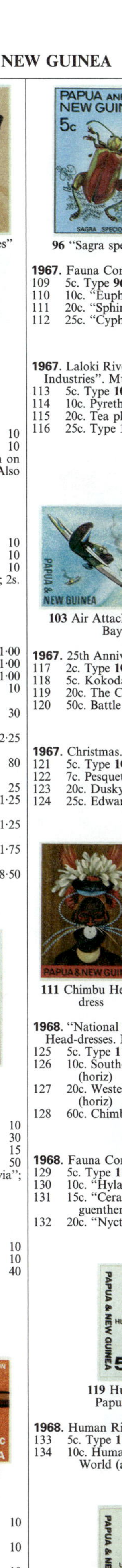

65 Urban Plan and Native House **69** "Papilio ulysses"

66 Mother and Child

1965. 6th South Pacific Conference, Lae.
77 **65** 6d. multicoloured 10 10
78 – 1s. multicoloured 10 10
No. 78 is similar to Type **65** but with the plan on the right and the house on the left. Also "URBANISATION" reads downwards.

1965. 20th Anniv of U.N.O.
79 **66** 6d. sepia, blue and turquoise 10 10
80 – 1s. brown, blue and violet 10 10
81 – 2s. blue, green and olive . . 10 10
DESIGNS—VERT: 1s. Globe and U.N. emblem; 2s. U.N. emblem and globes.

1966. Decimal Currency. Butterflies. Mult.
82 1c. Type **69** . . . . 40 1·00
83 3c. "Cyrestis acilia" . . . . 40 1·00
84 4c. "Graphium weiskei" . . . 40 1·00
85 5c. "Terinos alurgis" 40 10
86 10c. "Ornithoptera priamus" (horiz) 50 30
86a 12c. "Euploea callithoe" (horiz) . . . . 2·50 2·25
87 15c. "Papilio euchenor" (horiz) . . . . 1·00 80
88 20c. "Parthenos sylvia" (horiz) 50 25
89 25c. "Delias aruna" (horiz) 70 1·25
90 50c. "Apaturina erminea" (horiz) . . . . 10·00 1·25
91 $1 "Doleschallia dascylus" (horiz) . . . . 3·00 1·75
92 $2 "Ornithoptera paradisea" (horiz) . . . . 6·00 8·50

80 "Molala Harai" **84** Throwing the Discus

1966. Folklore. Elema Art (1st series).
93 **80** 2c. black and red 10 10
94 – 7c. black, yellow and blue 10 30
95 – 30c. black, red and green . . 15 15
96 – 60c. black, red and yellow 40 50
DESIGNS: 7c. "Marai"; 30c. "Meavea Kivovia"; 60c. "Toivita Tapaivita".

1966. South Pacific Games, Noumea. Mult.
97 5c. Type **84** 10 10
98 10c. Football 15 10
99 20c. Tennis 20 40

87 "Mucuna novoguineensis" **91** "Fine Arts"

1966. Flowers. Multicoloured.
100 5c. Type **87** 15 10
101 10c. "Tecomanthe dendrophila" 15 10
102 20c. "Rhododendron macgregoriae" 20 10
103 60c. "Rhododendron konori" 50 1·40

1967. Higher Education. Multicoloured.
104 1c. Type **91** 10 10
105 3c. "Surveying" 10 10
106 4c. "Civil Engineering" . . . 10 10
107 5c. "Science" 10 10
108 20c. "Law" 10 10

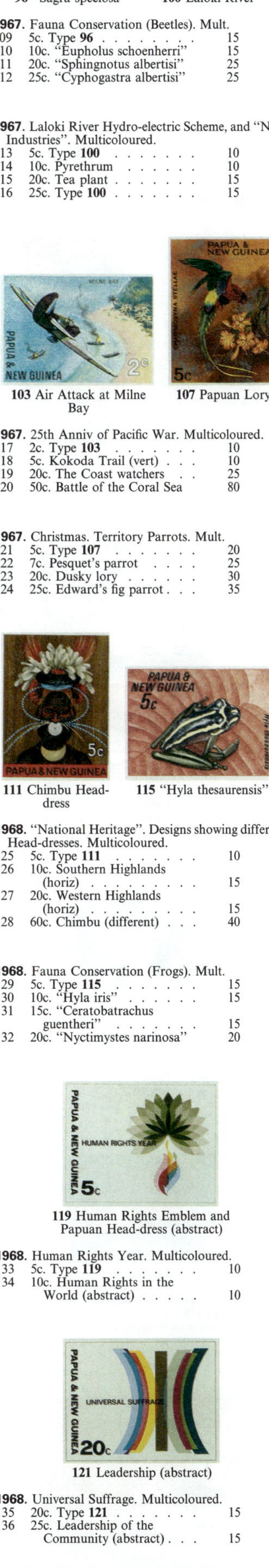

96 "Sagra speciosa" **100** Laloki River

1967. Fauna Conservation (Beetles). Mult.
109 5c. Type **96** 15 10
110 10c. "Eupholus schoenherri" 15 10
111 20c. "Sphingnotus albertisi" 25 10
112 25c. "Cyphogastra albertisi" 25 10

1967. Laloki River Hydro-electric Scheme, and "New Industries". Multicoloured.
113 5c. Type **100** 10 10
114 10c. Pyrethrum 10 10
115 20c. Tea plant 15 10
116 25c. Type **100** 15 10

103 Air Attack at Milne Bay **107** Papuan Lory

1967. 25th Anniv of Pacific War. Multicoloured.
117 2c. Type **103** 10 50
118 5c. Kokoda Trail (vert) . . . 10 10
119 20c. The Coast watchers . . 25 10
120 50c. Battle of the Coral Sea 80 70

1967. Christmas. Territory Parrots. Mult.
121 5c. Type **107** 20 10
122 7c. Pesquet's parrot 25 90
123 20c. Dusky lory 30 10
124 25c. Edward's fig parrot . . . 35 10

111 Chimbu Head-dress **115** "Hyla thesaurensis"

1968. "National Heritage". Designs showing different Head-dresses. Multicoloured.
125 5c. Type **111** 10 10
126 10c. Southern Highlands (horiz) 15 10
127 20c. Western Highlands (horiz) 15 10
128 60c. Chimbu (different) . . . 40 45

1968. Fauna Conservation (Frogs). Mult.
129 5c. Type **115** 15 50
130 10c. "Hyla iris" 15 10
131 15c. "Ceratobatrachus guentheri" 15 10
132 20c. "Nyctimystes narinosa" 20 50

119 Human Rights Emblem and Papuan Head-dress (abstract)

1968. Human Rights Year. Multicoloured.
133 5c. Type **119** 10 20
134 10c. Human Rights in the World (abstract) 10 10

121 Leadership (abstract)

1968. Universal Suffrage. Multicoloured.
135 20c. Type **121** 15 20
136 25c. Leadership of the Community (abstract) . . . 15 30

123 Common Egg Cowrie

1968. Sea Shells. Multicoloured.
137 1c. Type **123** 10 10
138 3c. Laciniate conch . . . . . 30 1·25
139 4c. Lithograph cone . . . . 20 1·25
140 5c. Marbled cone 25 10
141 7c. Episcopal mitre 35 10
142 10c. "Cymbiola rutila ruckeri" 45 10
143 12c. Checkerboard bonnet . . 1·25 2·00
144 15c. Scorpion conch . . . . 60 1·00
145 20c. Fluted giant clam or scale tridacna 70 10
146 25c. Camp pitar venus . . . 70 70
147 30c. Ramose murex . . . . 70 1·00
148 40c. Chambered or pearly nautilus . . . . 75 1·00
149 60c. Trumpet triton 70 60
150 $1 Manus green papuina . . 1·00 75
151 $2 Glory of the sea cone . . 10·00 3·25

138 Tito Myth **142** "Fireball" Class Dinghy

1969. Folklore. Elema Art (2nd series).
152 **138** 5c. black, yellow and red 10 50
153 – 5c. black, yellow and red 10 50
154 – 10c. black, grey and red 15 50
155 – 10c. black, grey and red 15 50
DESIGNS: No. 153, Iko Myth; 154, Luvuapo Myth; 155, Miro Myth.

1969. 3rd South Pacific Games, Port Moresby.
156 **142** 5c. black 10 25
157 – 10c. violet 10 10
158 – 20c. green 15 20
DESIGNS—HORIZ: 10c. Swimming pool, Boroko; 20c. Games arena, Konedobu.

145 "Dendrobium ostrinoglossum" **149** Bird of Paradise

1969. Flora Conservation (Orchids). Multicoloured.
159 5c. Type **145** 25 10
160 10c. "Dendrobium lawesii" 25 70
161 20c. "Dendrobium pseudofrigidum" 30 90
162 30c. "Dendrobium conanthum" 30 70

1969.
162a **149** 2c. blue, black and red 10 65
163 5c. green, brown & orge 10 10

150 Native Potter **151** Tareko

1969. 50th Anniv of I.L.O.
164 **150** 5c. multicoloured 10 10

1969. Musical Instruments.
165 **151** 5c. multicoloured 10 10
166 – 10c. black, green & yellow 10 10
167 – 25c. black, yellow & brown 15 15
168 – 30c. multicoloured 25 15
DESIGNS: 10c. Garamut; 25c. Iviliko; 30c. Kundu.

155 Prehistoric Ambun Stone **159** King of Saxony Bird of Paradise

1970. "National Heritage". Multicoloured.

169	5c. Type **155**	10	10
170	10c. Masawa canoe of Kula Circuit	10	10
171	25c. Torres' map, 1606	40	15
172	30c. H.M.S. "Basilisk" (paddle-sloop), 1873	65	25

1970. Fauna Conservation. Birds of Paradise. Mult.

173	5c. Type **159**	60	15
174	10c. King bird of paradise	60	60
175	15c. Raggiana bird of paradise	80	1·00
176	25c. Sickle-crested bird of paradise	1·00	70

163 Douglas DC-6B and Mt. Wilhelm

1970. Australian and New Guinea Air Services. Multicoloured.

177	5c. Type **163**	25	30
178	5c. Lockheed Electra and Mt. Yule	25	30
179	5c. Boeing 727-100 and Mt. Giluwe	25	30
180	5c. Fokker Friendship and Manam Island	25	30
181	25c. Douglas DC-3 and Matupi Volcano	35	40
182	30c. Boeing 707 and Hombrom's Bluff	35	60

169 N. Miklouho-Maclay (scientist) and Effigy

1970. 42nd A.N.Z.A.A.S. Congress, Port Moresby. Multicoloured.

183	5c. Type **169**	10	10
184	10c. B. Malinowski (anthropologist) and native hut	20	10
185	15c. T. Salvadori (ornithologist) and double-wattled cassowary	90	25
186	20c. F. R. R. Schlechter (botanist) and flower	60	25

A.N.Z.A.A.S. = Australian–New Zealand Association for the Advancement of Science.

170 Wogeo Island Food Bowl **171** Eastern Highlands Dwelling

1970. Native Artefacts. Multicoloured.

187	5c. Type **170**	10	10
188	10c. Lime pot	20	10
189	15c. Albom sago storage pot	20	10
190	30c. Manus island bowl (horiz)	25	30

1971. Native Dwellings. Multicoloured.

191	5c. Type **171**	10	10
192	7c. Milne Bay stilt dwelling	15	90
193	10c. Purari Delta dwelling	15	10
194	40c. Sepik dwelling	25	90

172 Spotted Phalanger **173** "Basketball"

1971. Fauna Conservation. Multicoloured.

195	5c. Type **172**	30	10
196	10c. Long-fingered possum	35	10
197	15c. Feather-tailed possum	50	80
198	25c. Long-tailed echidna	70	80
199	30c. Ornate tree kangaroo (horiz)	70	50

1971. 4th South Pacific Games, Papeete. Mult.

200	7c. Type **173**	10	10
201	14c. "Sailing"	15	20
202	21c. "Boxing"	15	30
203	28c. "Athletics"	15	40

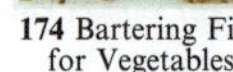

174 Bartering Fish for Vegetables **175** Sia Dancer

1971. Primary Industries. Multicoloured.

204	7c. Type **174**	10	10
205	9c. Man stacking yams	15	30
206	14c. Vegetable market	25	10
207	30c. Highlanders cultivating garden	45	65

1971. Native Dancers. Multicoloured.

208	7c. Type **175**	20	10
209	9c. Urasena dancer	20	20
210	20c. Siassi Tubuan dancers (horiz)	50	75
211	28c. Sia dancers (horiz)	65	90

176 Papuan Flag over Australian Flag

1971. Constitutional Development.

212	**176**	7c. multicoloured	30	10
213	–	7c. multicoloured	30	10

DESIGN: No. 213, Crest of Papua New Guinea and Australian coat of arms.

177 Map of Papua New Guinea and Flag of South Pacific Commission

1972. 25th Anniv of South Pacific Commission.

214	**177**	15c. multicoloured	45	55
215	–	15c. multicoloured	45	55

DESIGN: No. 215, Man's face and flag of the Commission.

178 Turtle

1972. Fauna Conservation (Reptiles). Mult.

216	7c. Type **178**	35	10
217	14c. Rainforest dragon	50	1·25
218	21c. Green python	55	1·50
219	30c. Salvador's monitor	60	1·25

179 Curtiss MF-6 Seagull and "Eureka" (schooner)

1972. 50th Anniv of Aviation. Multicoloured.

220	7c. Type **179**	40	10
221	14c. De Havilland D.H.37 and native porters	60	1·25
222	20c. Junkers G.31 and gold dredger	70	1·25
223	25c. Junkers F-13 and mission church	70	1·25

180 New National Flag **181** Rev. Copland King

1972. National Day. Multicoloured.

224	7c. Type **180**	20	10
225	10c. Native drum	25	25
226	30c. Trumpet triton	45	50

1972. Christmas. Missionaries. Multicoloured.

227	7c. Type **181**	25	40
228	7c. Rev. Dr. Flierl	25	40
229	7c. Bishop Verjus	25	40
230	7c. Pastor Ruatoka	25	40

182 Mt. Tomavatur Station **183** Queen Carola's Parotia

1973. Completion of Telecommunications Project, 1968–72. Multicoloured.

231	7c. Type **182**	15	20
232	7c. Mt. Kerigomma Station	15	20
233	7c. Sattelburg Station	15	20
234	7c. Wideru Station	15	20
235	9c. Teleprinter	15	20
236	30c. Network map	35	50

Nos. 235/6 are larger, 36 × 26 mm.

1973. Birds of Paradise. Multicoloured.

237	7c. Type **183**	1·00	35
238	14c. Goldie's bird of paradise	2·25	1·00
239	21c. Ribbon-tailed bird of paradise	2·50	1·50
240	28c. Princess Stephanie's bird of paradise	3·00	2·00

Nos. 239/40 are size 18 × 49 mm.

184 Wood Carver

1973. Multicoloured.

241	1c. Type **184**	10	10
242	3c. Wig-makers	30	10
243	5c. Mt. Bagana	55	10
244	6c. Pig exchange	80	1·50
245	7c. Coastal village	20	10
246	8c. Arawe mother	25	30
247	9c. Fire dancers	20	20
248	10c. Tifalmin hunter	40	10
249	14c. Crocodile hunters	35	70
250	15c. Mt. Elimbari	50	30
251	20c. Canoe-racing, Manus	60	40
252	21c. Making sago	30	1·00
253	25c. Council House	30	45
254	28c. Menyamya bowmen	30	1·00
255	30c. Shark-snaring	30	50
256	40c. Fishing canoes, Madang	30	40
257	60c. Tapa cloth-making	40	50
258	$1 Asaro Mudmen	45	1·10
259	$2 Enga "Sing Sing"	1·75	6·00

185 Stamps of German New Guinea, 1897

1973. 75th Anniv of Papua New Guinea Stamps.

260	**185**	1c. multicoloured	10	15
261	–	6c. indigo, blue and silver	15	30
262	–	7c. multicoloured	15	30
263	–	9c. multicoloured	15	30
264	–	25c. orange and gold	30	80
265	–	30c. plum and silver	30	90

DESIGNS—As Type **185**: 6c. 2 mark stamp of German New Guinea, 1900; 7c. Surcharged registration label of New Guinea, 1914. 46 × 35 mm: 9c. Papuan 1s. stamp, 1901. 45 × 38 mm: 25c. ½d. stamp of New Guinea, 1925; 30c. Papuan 10s. stamp, 1932.

186 Native Carved Heads **187** Queen Elizabeth II (from photo by Karsh)

1973. Self-government.

266	**186**	7c. multicoloured	30	15
267		10c. multicoloured	50	65

1974. Royal Visit.

268	**187**	7c. multicoloured	25	15
269		30c. multicoloured	75	1·50

188 Blyth's Hornbill

1974. Birds' Heads. Multicoloured.

270	7c. Type **188**	1·25	70
271	10c. Double-wattled cassowary (33 × 49 mm)	2·00	3·25
272	30c. New Guinea harpy eagle	4·00	8·50

189 "Dendrobium bracteosum" **191** 1-toea Coin

190 Motu Lakatoi

1974. Flora Conservation. Multicoloured.

273	7c. Type **189**	30	10
274	10c. "D. anosmum"	40	60
275	20c. "D. smillieae"	50	1·40
276	30c. "D. insigne"	60	1·75

1974. National Heritage. Canoes. Multicoloured.

277	7c. Type **190**	30	10
278	10c. Tami two-master morobe	30	55
279	25c. Aramia racing canoe	60	3·00
280	30c. Buka Island canoe	60	1·00

1975. New Coinage. Multicoloured.

281	1t. Type **191**	10	30
282	7t. New 2t. and 5t. coins	25	10
283	10t. New 10t. coin	25	30
284	20t. New 20t. coin	40	80
285	1k. New 1k. coin	1·25	4·50

SIZES: 10, 20t. As Type **191**; 7t., 1k. 45 × 26 mm.

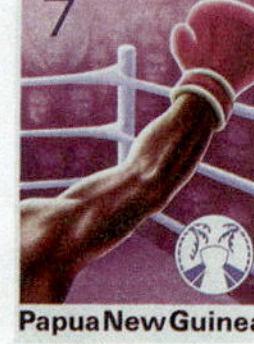

192 "Ornithoptera alexandrae" **193** Boxing

1975. Fauna Conservation (Birdwing Butterflies). Multicoloured.

286	7t. Type **192**	30	10
287	10t. "O. victoriae"	40	65

288 30t. "O. allottei" . . . . . . 70 2·00
289 40t. "O. chimaera" . . . . . 90 3·50

1975. 5th South Pacific Games, Guam. Mult.
290 7t. Type **193** 10 10
291 20t. Running 15 30
292 25t. Basketball 30 45
293 30t. Swimming 30 50

194 Map and National Flag

1975. Independence. Multicoloured.
294 7t. Type **194** 20 10
295 30t. Map and National emblem 40 65
MS296 116 × 58 mm. Nos. 294/5 1·10 1·75

195 M.V. "Bulolo"

1976. Ships of the 1930s. Multicoloured.
297 7t. Type **195** 20 10
298 15t. M.V. "Macdhui" 30 30
299 25t. M.V. "Malaita" 35 65
300 60t. S.S. "Montoro" . . . . 50 2·50

196 Rorovana Carvings

1976. Bougainville Art. Multicoloured.
301 7t. Type **196** 10 10
302 20t. Upe hats 20 35
303 25t. Kapkaps . . . . 25 1·00
304 30t. Canoe paddles 30 80

197 Rabaul House

1976. Native Dwellings. Multicoloured.
305 7t. Type **197** 10 10
306 15t. Aramia house 15 20
307 30t. Telefomin house 25 60
308 40t. Tapini house . . . . . 25 1·50

198 Landscouts

1976. 50th Annivs of Survey Flight and Scouting in Papua New Guinea. Multicoloured.
309 7t. Type **198** 15 10
310 10t. De Havilland D.H.50A seaplane 15 20
311 15t. Seascouts 20 40
312 60t. De Havilland D.H.50A seaplane on water . . . . 60 3·00

199 Father Ross and New Guinea Highlands

1976. William Ross Commemoration.
313 **199** 7t. multicoloured 40 15

200 Picture Wrasse

1976. Fauna Conservation (Tropical Fish). Mult.
314 5t. Type **200** 15 10
315 15t. Emperor angelfish . . . 25 45
316 30t. Six-blotched hind 40 80
317 40t. Thread-finned butterflyfish . . . . 45 1·10

201 Man from Kundiawa

202 Headdress, Wasara Tribe

1977. Headdresses. Multicoloured.
318 1t. Type **201** 10 10
319 5t. Masked dancer, Abelam area of Maprik 10 10
320 10t. Headdress from Koiari 20 15
321 15t. Woman with face paint, Hanuabada 25 20
322 20t. Orokaiva dancer 40 30
323 25t. Haus Tambaran dancer, Abelam area of Maprik . . 30 30
324 30t. Asaro Valley headdress 30 35
325 35t. Singsing costume, Garaina 30 45
326 40t. Waghi Valley headdress 30 35
327 50t. Trobriand Island dancer 40 60
328 1k. Type **202** . . . . 50 1·50
329 2k. Headdress, Meko tribe 75 3·00
SIZES: 1, 5, 20t. 25 × 31 mm; 35, 40t. 23 × 38 mm; 1k. 28 × 35 mm; 2k. 33 × 23 mm; others 26 × 26 mm.

203 National Flag and Queen Elizabeth II

1977. Silver Jubilee. Multicoloured.
330 7t. Type **203** 20 10
331 15t. The Queen and national emblem 25 35
332 35t. The Queen and map of P.N.G. 40 70

204 White-breasted Ground Pigeon

1977. Fauna Conservation (Birds). Mult.
333 5t. Type **204** 35 10
334 7t. Victoria crowned pigeon 35 10
335 15t. Pheasant pigeon 65 65
336 30t. Orange-fronted fruit dove . . . . 80 1·10
337 50t. Banded imperial pigeon 1·25 3·50

205 Guides and Gold Badge

206 Kari Marupi Myth

1977. 50th Anniv of Guiding in Papua New Guinea. Multicoloured.
338 7t. Type **205** 20 10
339 15t. Guides mapping 25 20
340 30t. Guides washing 40 50
341 35t. Guides cooking 40 60

1977. Folklore. Elema Art (3rd series).
342 **206** 7t. multicoloured 15 10
343 – 20t. multicoloured 35 35
344 – 30t. red, blue and black 40 75
345 – 35t. red, yellow and black 40 75
DESIGNS: 20t. Savoripi clan myth; 30t. Oa-Laea myth; 35t. Oa-Iriarapo myth.

207 Blue-tailed Skink

1978. Fauna Conservation (Skinks). Mult.
346 10t. Type **207** 20 10
347 15t. Green tree skink 25 25
348 35t. Crocodile skink 30 70
349 40t. New Guinea blue-tongued skink 45 85

208 "Roboastra arika"

1978. Sea Slugs. Multicoloured.
350 10t. Type **208** 20 10
351 15t. "Chromodoris fidelis" . . 25 30
352 35t. "Flabellina macassarana" 45 85
353 40t. "Chromodoris marginata" . . . . 50 1·00

209 Present Day Royal Papua New Guinea Constabulary

1978. History of Royal Papua New Guinea Constabulary. Uniformed Police and Constabulary Badges. Multicoloured.
354 10t. Type **209** 20 10
355 15t. Mandated New Guinea Constabulary, 1921–41 . . 25 15
356 20t. British New Guinea Armed Constabulary, 1890–1906 . . . . 25 40
357 25t. German New Guinea Police, 1899–1914 . . . . 30 45
358 30t. Royal Papua and New Guinea Constabulary, 1906–64 . . . . 30 60

210 Ocarina

211 East New Britain Canoe Prow

1979. Musical Instruments. Mult.
359 7t. Type **210** 10 10
360 20t. Musical bow (horiz) . . 20 20
361 28t. Launut 25 30
362 35t. Nose flute (horiz) . . . 30 45

1979. Traditional Canoe Prows and Paddles. Mult.
363 14t. Type **211** 20 15
364 21t. Sepik war canoe 30 25
365 25t. Trobriand Island canoe 30 30
366 40t. Milne Bay canoe 40 60

212 Katudababila (waist belt)

213 "Aenetus cyanochlora"

1979. Traditional Currency. Multicoloured.
367 7t. Type **212** 10 10
368 15t. Doga (chest ornament) 20 30
369 25t. Mwali (armshell) 35 55
370 35t. Soulava (necklace) . . . 45 75

1979. Fauna Conservation. Moths. Multicoloured.
371 7t. Type **213** 20 10
372 15t. "Celerina vulgaris" . . . 30 35
373 20t. "Alcidis aurora" (vert) 30 75
374 25t. "Phyllodes conspicillator" . . . . . . 35 1·00
375 30t. "Lyssa patroclus" (vert) 40 1·00

214 "The Right to Affection and Love"

216 Detail from Betrothal Ceremony Mural, Minj District, Western Highlands Province

215 "Post Office Service"

1979. International Year of the Child. Mult.
376 7t. Type **214** 10 10
377 15t. "The right to adequate nutrition and medical care" 15 15
378 30t. "The right to play" . . . 20 20
379 60t. "The right to a free education" 45 60

1980. Admission to U.P.U. (1979). Multicoloured.
380 7t. Type **215** 10 10
381 25t. "Wartime mail" 25 25
382 35t. "U.P.U. emblem 35 40
383 40t. "Early postal services" 40 50

1980. South Pacific Festival of Arts.
384 **216** 20t. yellow, orange & blk 15 35
385 – 20t. mult (two figures, left-hand in black and yellow; right-hand in black, yellow and red) 15 35
386 – 20t. mult (two figures, left-hand in black and orange; right-hand in black) 15 35
387 – 20t. mult (two figures, one behind the other) . . . 15 35
388 – 20t. mult (one figure) . . 15 35
DESIGNS: Nos. 385/8, further details of Betrothal Ceremony.
Nos. 384/8 were issued together in horizontal se-tenant strips of five within the sheet, forming a composite design.

217 Family being Interviewed

1980. National Census. Multicoloured.
389 7t. Type **217** 10 10
390 15t. Population symbol . . . 15 15
391 40t. Papua New Guinea map 30 40
392 50t. Heads symbolizing population growth 35 50

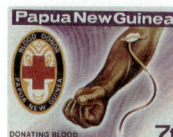

218 Donating Blood

1980. Red Cross Blood Bank. Multicoloured.
393 7t. Type **218** 15 10
394 15t. Receiving transfusion . . 20 20
395 30t. Map of Papua New Guinea showing blood transfusion centres 25 25
396 60t. Blood and its components 40 60

219 Dugong

1980. Mammals. Multicoloured.
397 7t. Type **219** 10 10
398 30t. New Guinea marsupial cat (vert) 30 45
399 35t. Tube-nosed bat (vert) . . 30 45
400 45t. Rufescent bandicoot . . 40 55

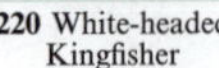

220 White-headed Kingfisher

221 Native Mask

1981. Kingfishers. Multicoloured.

401 3t. Type **220** 25 60
402 7t. Forest kingfisher 25 10
403 20t. Sacred kingfisher 30 50
404 25t. White-tailed kingfisher (26 × 46 mm) 30 85
405 60t. Blue-winged kookaburra 60 3·00

1981.

406 **221** 2t. violet and orange 10 20
407 – 5t. red and green 10 20
DESIGN: 5t. Hibiscus flower.

222 Mortar Team

1981. Defence Force. Multicoloured.

408 7t. Type **222** 15 10
409 15t. Douglas DC-3 and aircrew 25 25
410 40t. "Aitape" (patrol boat) and seamen 35 65
411 50t. Medical team examining children 35 75

223 M.A.F. (Missionary Aviation Fellowship) Cessna Super Skywagon

1981. "Mission Aviation". Multicoloured.

412 10t. Type **223** 20 10
413 15t. Catholic mission British Aircraft Swallow "St. Paulus" 25 15
414 20t. S.I.L. (Summer Institute of Linguistics) Hiller 12E helicopter 25 25
415 30t. Lutheran mission Junkers F-13 35 40
416 35t. S.D.A. (Seventh Day Adventist Church) Piper PA-23 Aztec 35 55

224 Scoop Net Fishing

1981. Fishing. Multicoloured.

417 10t. Type **224** 15 10
418 15t. Kite fishing 20 30
419 30t. Rod fishing 30 50
420 60t. Scissor net fishing 55 85

225 Buhler's Papuina

1981. Land Snail Shells. Multicoloured.

421 5t. Type **225** 10 10
422 15t. Yellow naninia 20 25
423 20t. Adonis papuina and Hermoine papuina 20 35
424 30t. Hinde's papuina and New Pommeranian papuina 30 50
425 40t. "Papuina strabo" 40 80

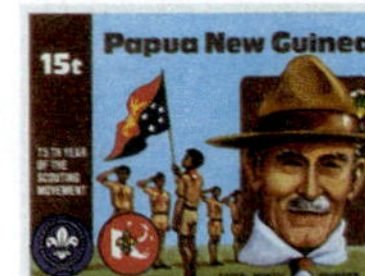

226 Lord Baden-Powell and Flag-raising Ceremony

1981. 75th Anniv of Boy Scout Movement. Mult.

426 15t. Type **226** 20 15
427 25t. Scout leader and camp 20 30
428 35t. Scout and hut building 20 45
429 50t. Percy Chaterton and Scouts administering first aid 30 75

227 Yangoru and Boiken Bowls, East Sepik

1981. Native Pottery. Multicoloured.

430 10t. Type **227** 10 10
431 20t. Utu cooking pot and small Gumalu pot, Madang 20 30
432 40t. Wanigela pots, Northern (37 × 23 mm) 40 55
433 50t. Ramu Valley pots, Madang (37 × 23 mm) 45 80

228 "Eat Healthy Foods"

1982. Food and Nutrition. Multicoloured.

434 10t. Type **228** 10 10
435 15t. Protein foods 20 30
436 30t. Protective foods 40 55
437 40t. Energy foods 45 70

229 "Stylophora sp."

1982. Multicoloured.

438 1t. Type **229** 10 20
439 3t. "Dendrophyllia sp." (vert) 60 1·50
440 5t. "Acropora humilis" 15 10
441 10t. "Dendronephthya sp." (vert) 80 80
442 12t. As 10t. 3·50 6·00
443 15t. "Distichopora sp." 20 20
444 20t. "Isis sp" (vert) 90 25
445 25t. "Acropora sp." (vert) 50 50
446 30t. "Dendronephthya sp." (different) (vert) 1·25 90
447 35t. "Stylaster elegans" (vert) 1·25 50
448 40t. "Antipathes sp." (vert) 1·25 1·50
449 45t. "Turbinarea sp." (vert) 2·00 1·00
450 1k. "Xenia sp." 1·00 85
451 3k. "Distichopora sp." (vert) 2·25 3·50
452 5k. Raggiana bird of paradise (33 × 33 mm) 7·00 9·00

230 Missionaries landing on Beach

231 Athletics

1982. Centenary of Catholic Church in Papua New Guinea. Mural on Wall of Nordup Catholic Church, East New Britain. Multicoloured.

457 10t. Type **230** 20 65
458 10t. Missionaries talking to natives 20 65
459 10t. Natives with slings and spears ready to attack 20 65

Nos. 457/9 were issued together, se-tenant, forming a composite design.

1982. Commonwealth Games and "Anpex 82" Stamp Exhibition, Brisbane. Multicoloured.

460 10t. Type **231** 15 10
461 15t. Boxing 20 25
462 45t. Rifle-shooting 40 70
463 50t. Bowls 45 75

232 National Flag

1983. Commonwealth Day. Multicoloured.

464 10t. Type **232** 15 10
465 15t. Basket-weaving and cabbage-picking 20 30
466 20t. Crane hoisting roll of material 25 35
467 50t. Lorries and ships 60 75

233 Transport Communications

1983. World Communications Year. Multicoloured.

468 10t. Type **233** 30 10
469 25t. "Postal service" 50 25
470 30t. "Telephone service" 55 30
471 60t. "Transport service" 1·10 90

234 "Chelonia depressa"

1984. Turtles. Multicoloured.

472 5t. Type **234** 20 10
473 10t. "Chelonia mydas" 25 10
474 15t. "Eretmochelys imbricata" 30 30
475 20t. "Lepidochelys olivacea" 40 35
476 25t. "Caretta caretta" 45 50
477 40t. "Dermochelys coriacea" 60 75

235 Avro Type 618 Ten "Faith in Australia"

237 Ceremonial Shield and Club, Central Province

236 Parliament House

1984. 50th Anniv of First Airmail Australia–Papua New Guinea. Multicoloured.

478 20t. Type **235** 40 30
479 25t. De Havilland Dragon Express "Carmania" 40 45
480 40t. Westland Widgeon 50 80
481 60t. Consolidated PBY-5 Catalina flying boat 70 1·25

1984. Opening of New Parliament House.

482 **236** 10t. multicoloured 30 30

1984. Ceremonial Shields. Multicoloured.

483 10t. Type **237** 20 10
484 20t. Ceremonial shield, West New Britain 30 35
485 30t. Ceremonial shield, Madang Province 45 75
486 50t. Ceremonial shield, East Sepik 75 3·00

See also Nos. 558/61.

238 H.M.S. "Nelson" at Port Moresby, 1884

239 Fergusson Island

1984. Centenary of Protectorate Proclamations for British New Guinea and German New Guinea. Multicoloured.

487 10t. Type **238** 35 55
488 10t. Papua New Guinea flag and Port Moresby, 1984 35 55
489 45t. Papua New Guinea flag and Rabaul, 1984 50 1·90
490 45t. German warship "Elizabeth" at Rabaul, 1884 50 1·90

Nos. 487/8 and 489/90 were issued in se-tenant pairs, each pair forming a composite picture.

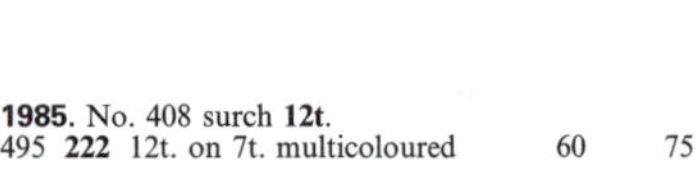

1985. Tourist Scenes. Multicoloured.

491 10t. Type **239** 25 10
492 25t. Sepik River 50 60
493 40t. Chimbu Gorge (horiz) 75 1·40
494 60t. Dali Beach, Vanimo (horiz) 1·25 1·90

1985. No. 408 surch **12t.**

495 **222** 12t. on 7t. multicoloured 60 75

241 Dubu Platform, Central Province

242 Head of New Britain Collared Sparrow Hawk

1985. Ceremonial Structures. Multicoloured.

496 15t. Type **241** 35 15
497 20t. Tamuniai house, West New Britain 50 50
498 30t. Traditional yam tower, Trobriand Island 65 80
499 60t. Huli grave, Tari 1·00 1·75

1985. Birds of Prey. Multicoloured.

500 12t. Type **242** 70 1·50
501 12t. New Britain collared sparrow hawk in flight 70 1·50
502 30t. Doria's goshawk 1·00 1·75
503 30t. Doria's goshawk in flight 1·00 1·75
504 60t. Long-tailed honey buzzard 1·50 2·25
505 60t. Long-tailed honey buzzard in flight 1·50 2·25

243 National Flag and Parliament House

244 Early Postcard, Aerogramme, Inkwell and Spectacles

1985. 10th Anniv of Independence.

506 **243** 12t. multicoloured 60 1·00

1985. Centenary of Papua New Guinea Post Office. Multicoloured.

507 12t. Type **244** 45 10
508 30t. Queensland 1897 1d. die with proof and modern press printing stamps 1·10 1·00
509 40t. Newspaper of 1885 announcing shipping service and loading mail into aircraft 1·75 2·25
510 60t. Friedrich-Wilhelmshafen postmark of 1892 and Port Moresby F.D.C. postmark of 9 October 1985 2·00 3·75
MS511 As Nos. 507/10, but designs continue on sheet margins 6·00 7·00

245 Figure with Eagle

246 Valentine or Prince Cowrie

1985. Nombowai Wood Carvings. Mult.
512 12t. Type **245** 50 10
513 30t. Figure with clam shell 1·25 75
514 60t. Figure with dolphin . . 2·00 3·00
515 80t. Figure of woman with cockerel . . . . 2·50 5·00

1986. Sea Shells. Multicoloured.
516 15t. Type **246** 75 15
517 35t. Bulow's olive . . . . . 1·60 1·40
518 45t. Parkinson's olive . . . . 2·00 2·25
519 70t. Golden cowrie . . . . . 2·50 5·75

246a Princess Elizabeth in A.T.S. Uniform, 1945

1986. 60th Birthday of Queen Elizabeth II. Mult.
520 15t. Type **246a** 15 15
521 35t. Silver Wedding Anniversary photograph (by Patrick Lichfield), Balmoral, 1972 . . . . . 20 40
522 50t. Queen inspecting guard of honour, Port Moresby, 1982 . . . . 40 85
523 60t. On board Royal Yacht "Britannia", Papua New Guinea, 1982 . . . . . . 65 1·00
524 70t. At Crown Agents' Head Office, London, 1983 . . . 40 1·25

247 Rufous Fantail

248 Martin Luther nailing Theses to Cathedral Door, Wittenberg and Modern Lutheran Pastor

1986. "Ameripex '86" International Stamp Exhibition, Chicago. Small Birds (1st series). Multicoloured.
525 15t. Type **247** 90 30
526 35t. Streaked berry pecker . . 1·75 1·25
527 45t. Red-breasted pitta . . . 1·90 1·25
528 70t. Olive-yellow robin (vert) 2·50 6·50
See also Nos. 597/601.

1986. Centenary of Lutheran Church in Papua New Guinea. Multicoloured.
529 15t. Type **248** 75 15
530 70t. Early church, Finschhafen, and modern Martin Luther Chapel, Lae Seminary . . . . 2·25 3·75

249 "Dendrobium vexillarius"

250 Maprik Dancer

1986. Orchids. Multicoloured.
531 15t. Type **249** 95 20
532 35t. "Dendrobium lineale" 2·00 75
533 45t. "Dendrobium johnsoniae" . . . . 2·00 1·10
534 70t. "Dendrobium cuthbertsonii" . . . . . . 2·75 6·00

1986. Papua New Guinea Dancers. Multicoloured.
535 15t. Type **250** 80 15
536 35t. Kiriwina . . . . 1·60 80
537 45t. Kundiawa . . . . 1·75 95
538 70t. Fasu . . . . 3·00 4·25

251 White-bonnet Anemonefish

1987. Anemonefish. Multicoloured.
539 17t. Type **251** 70 25
540 30t. Orange-finned anemonefish . . . . 1·40 1·10
541 35t. Fire anemonefish ("Tomato clownfish") . . . 1·50 1·40
542 70t. Spine-cheeked anemonefish . . . . 2·50 6·00

252 "Roebuck" (Dampier), 1700

1987. Ships. Multicoloured.
543 1t. "La Boudeuse" (De Bougainville, 1768) . . . . 50 1·25
544 5t. Type **252** . . . . 1·00 1·75
545 10t. H.M.S. "Swallow" (Philip Carteret), 1767 . . 1·25 1·75
546 15t. H.M.S. "Fly" (Blackwood), 1845 . . . . 1·75 1·00
547 17t. As 15t. . . . . 1·75 75
548 20t. H.M.S. "Rattlesnake" (Owen Stanley), 1849 . . . 1·75 1·00
549 30t. "Vitiaz" (Maclay), 1871 1·75 2·50
550 35t. "San Pedrico" (Torres) and zabra, 1606 . . . . . 70 1·00
551 40t. "L'Astrolabe" (D'Urville), 1827 . . . . . 2·00 2·75
552 45t. "Neva" (D. Albertis), 1876 . . . . 75 1·25
553 60t. Spanish galleon (Jorge de Meneses), 1526 . . . . . 2·50 3·50
554 70t. "Eendracht" (Schouten and Le Maire), 1616 . . . 1·75 2·75
555 1k. H.M.S. "Blanche" (Simpson), 1872 . . . . . 2·50 3·00
556 2k. "Merrie England" (steamer), 1889 . . . . . 3·25 3·00
557 3k. "Samoa" (German colonial steamer), 1884 . . 4·00 6·00
For some of these designs redrawn for "Australia '99" World Stamp Exhibition see Nos. 857/60.

1987. War Shields. As T **237**. Multicoloured.
558 15t. Gulf Province 20 25
559 35t. East Sepik 45 50
560 45t. Madang Province . . . 55 60
561 70t. Telefomin 85 90

1987. No. 442 surch **15t**.
562 15t. on 12t. "Dendronephthya sp." (vert) 65 65

254 "Protoreaster nodosus"

1987. Starfish. Multicoloured.
563 17t. Type **254** 55 25
564 35t. "Gomophia egeriae" . . 1·10 70
565 45t. "Choriaster granulatus" 1·25 80
566 70t. "Neoferdina ocellata" . . 1·75 3·50

255 Cessna Stationair 6 taking off, Rabaraba

1987. Aircraft in Papua New Guinea. Mult.
567 15t. Type **255** . . . . 1·00 25
568 35t. Britten Norman Islander over Hombrum Bluff . . . 1·75 90
569 45t. De Havilland Twin Otter 100 over Highlands . . . 1·75 1·00
570 70t. Fokker F.28 Fellowship over Madang . . . . . 2·75 6·50

256 Pre-Independence Policeman on Traffic Duty and Present-day Motorcycle Patrol

1988. Centenary of Royal Papua New Guinea Constabulary. Multicoloured.
571 17t. Type **256** 45 25
572 35t. British New Guinea Armed Constabulary, 1890, and Governor W. MacGregor 80 50
573 45t. Police badges 90 65
574 70t. German New Guinea Police, 1888, and Dr. A Hahl (founder) . . . . . . 1·50 1·75

257 Lakatoi (canoe) and Sydney Opera House

1988. "Sydpex '88" Nat Stamp Exn, Sydney.
575 **257** 35t. multicoloured . . . . 80 1·25

258 Papua New Guinea Flag on Globe and Fireworks

1988. Bicent of Australian Settlement. Mult.
576 35t. Type **258** . . . . 1·00 1·50
577 35t. Australian flag on globe and fireworks . . . . . 1·00 1·50
MS578 90 × 50 mm. Nos. 576/7 1·50 2·25
Nos. 576/7 were printed together, se-tenant, forming a composite design.

259 Male and Female Butterflies in Courtship

1988. Endangered Species. "Ornithoptera alexandrae" (butterfly). Multicoloured.
579 5t. Type **259** . . . . 1·00 1·75
580 17t. Female laying eggs and mature larva (vert) . . . . 2·00 40
581 25t. Male emerging from pupa (vert) . . . . . . 2·75 3·50
582 35t. Male feeding . . . . . 3·25 3·50

260 Athletics

1988. Olympic Games, Seoul. Multicoloured.
583 17t. Type **260** 30 30
584 45t. Weightlifting 70 70

261 "Rhododendron zoelleri"

263 Writing Letter

1989. Rhododendrons. Multicoloured.
585 3t. Type **261** 10 10
586 20t. "Rhododendron cruttwellii" 50 30
587 60t. "Rhododendron superbum" . . . . 1·25 1·50
588 70t. "Rhododendron christianae" . . . . 1·50 1·75

1989. Int Letter Writing Week. Multicoloured.
589 20t. Type **263** 30 30
590 35t. Stamping letter 55 50
591 60t. Posting letter . . . . . 90 1·10
592 70t. Reading letter . . . . . 1·10 1·40

264 Village House, Buka Island, North Solomons

1989. Traditional Dwellings. Multicoloured.
593 20t. Type **264** 40 35
594 35t. Tree house, Koiari, Central Province 70 60
595 60t. Longhouse, Lauan, New Ireland . . . . 1·25 1·40
596 70t. Decorated house, Basilaki, Milne Bay . . . 1·50 1·60

265 Tit Berrypecker (female)

266 Motu Motu Dancer, Gulf Province

1989. Small Birds (2nd issue). Multicoloured.
597 20t. Type **265** . . . . 1·00 1·00
598 20t. Tit berrypecker (male) 1·00 1·00
599 35t. Blue-capped babbler . . 1·50 80
600 45t. Black-throated robin . . 1·50 1·00
601 70t. Large mountain sericornis . . . . 2·25 2·50

1989. No. 539 surch **20t.**
602 20t. on 17t. Type **251** . . . 60 70

1989. Traditional Dancers. Multicoloured.
603 20t. Type **266** 65 35
604 35t. Baining, East New Britain . . . . 1·10 90
605 60t. Vailala River, Gulf Province . . . . 2·00 2·25
606 70t. Timbunke, East Sepik Province . . . . 2·00 2·50

267 Hibiscus, People going to Church and Gope Board

1989. Christmas. Designs showing flowers and carved panels. Multicoloured.
607 20t. Type **267** 40 35
608 35t. Rhododendron, Virgin and Child and mask . . . 60 60
609 60t. D'Albertis creeper, Christmas candle and war shield . . . . 1·25 1·60
610 70t. Pacific frangipani, peace dove and flute mask . . . 1·40 1·90

268 Guni Falls

270 Gwa Pupi Dance Mask

269 Boys and Census Form

1990. Waterfalls. Multicoloured.
611 20t. Type **268** 60 35
612 35t. Rouna Falls 85 75
613 60t. Ambua Falls . . . . . 1·40 1·50
614 70t. Wawoi Falls . . . . . . 1·60 1·75

1990. National Census. Multicoloured.
615 20t. Type **269** 40 30
616 70t. Family and census form 1·50 2·25

1990. Gogodala Dance Masks. Multicoloured.
617 20t. Type **270** 80 30
618 35t. Tauga paiyale . . . . . 1·25 70
619 60t. A: ga . . . . 2·00 3·25
620 70t. Owala . . . . 2·00 3·75

271 Sepik and Maori Kororu Masks

1990. "New Zealand 1990" International Stamp Exhibition, Auckland.
621 **271** 35t. multicoloured . . . . 75 1·00

272 Dwarf Cassowary and Great Spotted Kiwi

1990. 150th Anniv of Treaty of Waitangi. Mult.
622 20t. Type **272** . . . . 1·25 50
623 35t. Double-wattled cassowary and brown kiwi 1·50 1·50

273 Whimbrel

1990. Migratory Birds. Multicoloured.
624 20t. Type **273** 85 40
625 35t. Sharp-tailed sandpiper 1·25 80
626 60t. Ruddy turnstone . . . . 2·25 3·25
627 70t. Terek sandpiper . . . . 2·50 3·25

274 Jew's Harp **276** Magnificent Riflebird

275 Weigman's Papuina

1990. Musical Instruments. Multicoloured.
628 20t. Type **274** 60 30
629 35t. Musical bow 90 50
630 60t. Wantoat drum . . . . . 1·75 2·25
631 70t. Gogodala rattle . . . . 1·75 2·50

1991. Land Shells. Multicoloured.
632 21t. Type **275** 65 30
633 40t. "Papuina globula" and "Papuina azonata" . . . . 1·00 85
634 50t. "Planispira deaniana" . . 1·40 1·60
635 80t. Chance's papuina and golden-mouth papuina . . 2·00 2·75

1991. Birds of Paradise. Multicoloured. (a) Face values shown as "t" or "K".
636 1t. Type **276** 15 40
637 5t. Loria's bird of paradise 20 40
638 10t. Sickle-crested bird of paradise 20 40
639 20t. Wahnes' parotia 50 30
640 21t. Crinkle-collared manucode . . . . 1·50 30
641 30t. Goldie's bird of paradise 30 40
642 40t. Wattle-billed bird of paradise 50 50
643 45t. King bird of paradise . . 5·00 80
644 50t. Short-tailed paradigalla bird of paradise 50 55
645 60t. Queen Carola's parotia 7·50 2·75
646 90t. Emperor of Germany bird of paradise . . . . . 8·00 4·00
647 1k. Magnificent bird of paradise . . . . 1·75 1·75
648 2k. Superb bird of paradise 1·90 2·00
649 5k. Trumpet bird . . . . . . 2·25 6·50
650 10k. Lesser bird of paradise (32 × 32 mm) . . . . . . 5·00 10·00

(b) Face values shown as "T".
650a 21t. Crinkle-collared manucode 90 40
650b 45t. King bird of paradise 2·00 1·00
650c 60t. Queen Carola's parotia 2·25 2·25
650d 90t. Emperor of Germany bird of paradise . . . . . 2·75 3·50

For designs as Nos. 642, 644 and 647/8 but without "1992 BIRD OF PARADISE" at foot, see Nos. 704/7.

277 Cricket

1991. 9th South Pacific Games. Multicoloured.
651 21t. Type **277** . . . . 1·75 40
652 40t. Athletics . . . . 1·50 1·00
653 50t. Baseball . . . . 1·75 2·25
654 80t. Rugby Union . . . . . 2·75 4·00

278 Cathedral of St. Peter and St. Paul, Dogura

1991. Cent of Anglican Church in Papua New Guinea. Multicoloured.
655 21t. Type **278** 70 30
656 40t. Missionaries landing, 1891, and Kaieta shrine . . 1·40 1·40
657 80t. First church and Modawa tree . . . . . . 2·25 3·50

279 Rambusto Headdress, Manus Province **281** Canoe Prow Shield, Bamu

280 "Nina"

1991. Tribal Headdresses. Multicoloured.
658 21t. Type **279** 60 30
659 40t. Marawaka, Eastern Highlands . . . . . . 1·10 1·40
660 50t. Tufi, Oro Province . . . 1·25 2·00
661 80t. Sina Sina, Simbu Province . . . . 2·00 4·00

1992. 500th Anniv of Discovery of America by Columbus and "EXPO '92" World's Fair, Seville. Multicoloured.
662 21t. Type **280** 60 30
663 45t. "Pinta" . . . . 1·25 1·00
664 60t. "Santa Maria" . . . . . 1·75 2·00
665 90t. Christopher Columbus and ships . . . . 2·25 3·50

1992. "World Columbian Stamp Expo '92", Chicago. Sheet, 110 × 80 mm, containing Nos. 664/5.
MS666 60t. "Santa Maria"; 90t. Christopher Columbus and ships (sold at 1k. 70) . . . . 4·25 5·50

1992. Papuan Gulf Artifacts. Multicoloured.
667 21t. Type **281** 40 30
668 45t. Skull rack, Kerewa . . . 85 75
669 60t. Ancestral figure, Era River . . . . 1·25 1·50
670 90t. Gope (spirit) board, Urama . . . . 1·60 2·75

282 Papuan Infantryman **283** "Hibiscus tiliaceus"

1992. 50th Anniv of Second World War Campaigns in Papua New Guinea. Multicoloured.
671 21t. Type **282** 60 30
672 45t. Australian militiaman . . 1·25 90
673 60t. Japanese infantryman . . 1·75 2·25
674 90t. American infantryman 2·50 3·75

1992. Flowering Trees. Multicoloured.
675 21t. Type **283** 65 30
676 45t. "Castanospermum australe" . . . . 1·50 1·00
677 60t. "Cordia subcordata" . . 2·50 2·75
678 90t. "Acacia auriculiformis" 2·75 4·00

284 Three-striped Dasyure

1993. Mammals. Multicoloured.
679 21t. Type **284** 40 30
680 45t. Striped bandicoot 90 80
681 60t. Dusky black-eared giant rat . . . . 1·25 1·50
682 90t. Painted ringtail possum 1·75 2·75

285 Rufous Wren Warbler

1993. Small Birds. Multicoloured.
683 21t. Type **285** 45 30
684 45t. Superb pitta 90 80
685 60t. Mottled whistler . . . . 1·25 1·50
686 90t. Slaty-chinned longbill . . 1·60 2·75

1993. "Taipei '93" Asian Int Stamp Exn, Taiwan. Nos. 683/6 optd **TAIPEI'93** and emblem.
687 21t. Type **285** 75 30
688 45t. Superb pitta . . . . . . 1·40 80
689 60t. Mottled whistler . . . . 1·60 2·75
690 90t. Slaty-chinned longbill . . 2·00 4·00

287 Thread-finned Rainbowfish

1993. Freshwater Fishes. Multicoloured.
691 21t. Type **287** 60 30
692 45t. Peacock gudgeon . . . . 1·25 80
693 60t. Northern rainbowfish . . 1·60 2·25
694 90t. Popondetta blue-eye . . 2·25 4·00

288 Blue Bird of Paradise

1993. "Bangkok '93" Asian International Stamp Exhibition, Thailand. Sheet 100 × 65 mm.
MS695 **288** 2k. multicoloured . . 6·00 7·50

289 Douglas DC-3

1993. 20th Anniv of Air Niugini. Multicoloured.
696 21t. Type **289** 75 25
697 45t. Fokker F.27 Friendship 1·75 70
698 60t. De Havilland D.H.C.7 Dash Seven . . . . 2·00 2·25
699 90t. Airbus Industrie A310 2·75 4·25

290 Girl holding Matschie's Tree Kangaroo **292** Hagen Axe, Western Highlands

1994. Matschie's (Huon Gulf) Tree Kangaroo. Mult.
700 21t. Type **290** 35 25
701 45t. Adult male 90 60
702 60t. Female with young in pouch . . . . 1·25 1·75
703 90t. Adolescent on ground 1·90 3·25

1994. "Hong Kong '94 International Stamp Exhibition. Designs as Nos. 642, 644 and 647/8, but without "1992 BIRD OF PARADISE" at foot. Multicoloured.
704 40t. Yellow-breasted bird of paradise . . . . 85 1·25
705 50t. Short-tailed paradigalla bird of paradise . . . . . 1·25 1·50
706 1k. Magnificent bird of paradise . . . . 2·00 2·75
707 2k. Superb bird of paradise 3·00 4·00

1994. Nos. 541 and 551 surch.
708 21t. on 35t. Fire anemonefish 7·00 50
709 1k.20 on 40t. "L'Astrolabe" (D'Urville) . . . . 1·50 1·50

1994. Artifacts. Multicoloured.
710 1t. Type **292** 10 50
711 2t. Telefomin shield, West Sepik 10 50
712 20t. Head mask, Gulf Province 80 30
713 21t. Kanganaman stool, East Sepik 30 10
714 45t. Trobriand lime gourd, Milne Bay 50 25
715 60t. Yuat River flute stopper, East Sepik . . . . 1·00 30
716 90t. Tami Island dish, Morobe 60 40
717 1k. Kundu (drum), Ramu River estuary . . . . . . 3·50 2·50
723 5k. Gogodala dance mask, Western Province . . . . 1·70 1·80
724 10k. Malanggan mask, New Ireland . . . . 3·50 3·75

293 Ford Model "T", 1920

1994. Historical Cars. Multicoloured.
725 21t. Type **293** 35 25
726 45t. Chevrolet "490", 1915 90 60
727 60t. Austin "7", 1931 . . . . 1·25 1·75
728 90t. Willys jeep, 1942 . . . . 1·90 3·00

294 Grizzled Tree Kangaroo **298** Peter To Rot

297 "Daphnis hypothous pallescens"

1994. "Phila Korea '94" International Stamp Exhibition, Seoul. Tree Kangaroos. Sheet 106 × 70 mm, containing T **294** and similar vert design. Multicoloured.
MS729 90t. Type **294**; 1k.20, Doria's tree kangaroo 70 75

1994. Surch.
730 – 5t. on 35t. mult (No. 604) 1·00 75
731 – 5t. on 35t. mult (No. 629) 14·00 10·00
732 **271** 10t. on 35t. mult . . . . 22·00 5·50
733 – 10t. on 35t. mult (No. 623) . . . . . . 10·00 3·50
734 – 21t. on 80t. mult (No. 635) . . . . . . 40·00 75
735 – 50t. on 35t. mult (No. 612) . . . . . . 27·00 13·00
736 – 50t. on 35t. mult (No. 618) . . . . . . 90·00 18·00
737 – 65t. on 70t. mult (No. 542) . . . . . . 2·00 1·40
738 – 65t. on 70t. mult (No. 616) . . . . . . 2·00 1·40
739 – 1k. on 70t. mult (No. 614) 17·00 5·00
740 – 1k. on 70t. mult (No. 620) 2·00 3·00

1994. Moths. Multicoloured.
741 21t. Type **297** 35 25
742 45t. "Tanaorhinus unipuncta" 80 65
743 60t. "Neodiphthera sciron" 1·10 1·50
744 90t. "Parotis marginata" . . 1·60 2·50

1995. Beatification of Peter To Rot (catechist) and Visit of Pope John Paul II. Multicoloured.
745 21t. Type **298** 10 10
746 1k. on 90t. Pope John Paul II 35 40
No. 746 was not issued without surcharge.

299 Airliner over Holiday Village

1995. Tourism. Multicoloured.
747 21t. "Melanesian Discoverer" (cruise ship) and launch . . 10 10
748 21t. Tourist taking photo of traditional mask 10 10
749 50t. on 45t. Type **299** . . . 15 20
750 50t. on 45t. Holiday homes 15 20
751 65t. on 60t. Tourists and guide crossing river 20 25
752 65t. on 60t. White water rafting 20 25
753 1k. on 90t. Scuba diver and "Chertan" (launch) 35 40
754 1k. on 90t. Divers and wreck of aircraft 35 40
Nos. 749/54 were not issued without surcharge.

1995. Nos. 643, 646, 650b, 650d and 692/4 surch **21t.**
755 21t. on 45t. King bird of paradise (643) . . . . . . 1·50 1·00
757 21t. on 45t. King bird of paradise (650b) . . . . . 4·75 3·00
759 21t. on 45t. Peacock gudgeon 55 40
760 21t. on 60t. Northern rainbowfish . . . . 1·50 2·00
756 21t. on 90t. Emperor of Germany bird of paradise (646) . . . . 1·50 1·00
758 21t. on 90t. Emperor of Germany bird of paradise (650d) . . . . 6·00 1·00
761 21t. on 90t. Popondetta blue-eye 55 60

302 "Lentinus umbrinus"

302a "Lentinus umbrinus"

1995. Fungi. Multicoloured.
762 25t. Type **302** 45 30
765a 25t. Type **302a** 35 35
763 50t. "Amanita hemibapha" 80 80
764 65t. "Boletellus emodensis" 95 1·25
765 1k. "Ramaria zippellii" . . 1·60 2·25
On Type **302a** the fungi illustration is larger, 26 × 32 mm instead of 27 × 30½ mm, face value and inscriptions are in a different type and there is no imprint date at foot.

303 Anniversary Emblem and Map of Papua New Guinea

1995. 20th Anniv of Independence. Multicoloured.
766 21t. Type **303** 30 25
767 50t. Emblem and lines on graph 70 80
768 1k. As 50t. . . . . 1·40 2·25

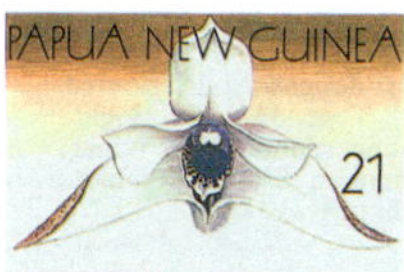

304 "Dendrobium rigidifolium"

1995. "Singapore '95" International Stamp Exhibition. Orchids. Sheet 150 × 95 mm, containing T **304** and similar horiz designs. Multicoloured.
MS769 21t. Type **304**; 45t. "Dendrobium convolutum"; 60t. "Dendrobium spectabile"; 90t. "Dendrobium tapiniense" (sold at 3k.) 75 80

305 Pig

1995. Chinese New Year ("Year of the Pig"). Sheet 150 × 95 mm.
MS770 **305** 3k. multicoloured . . 1·00 1·10
No. **MS**770 is inscribed "BEIJING '95" on the sheet margin.

306 Volcanic Eruption, Tavarvur

1995. 1st Anniv of Volcanic Eruption, Rabaul.
771 **306** 2k. multicoloured 70 75

307 "Zosimus aeneus"

1995. Crabs. Multicoloured.
772 21t. Type **307** 40 25
773 50t. "Cardisoma carnifex" . . 75 60
774 65t. "Uca tetragonon" . . . 90 1·25
775 1k. "Eriphia sebana" . . . . 1·25 2·00

308 Pesquet's Parrot

309 "Lagriomorpha indigacea"

1996. Parrots. Multicoloured.
776 25t. Type **308** . . . . 1·25 30
777 50t. Rainbow lory . . . . . 1·75 65
778 65t. Green-winged king parrot . . . . 2·00 1·75
779 1k. Red-winged parrot . . . 2·50 3·25

1996. Beetles. Multicoloured.
780 25t. Type **309** 10 15
781 50t. "Eupholus geoffroyi" . . 15 20
782 65t. "Promechus pulcher" . . 20 25
783 1k. "Callistola pulchra" . . . 35 40

310 Guang Zhou Zhong Shang Memorial Hall

1996. "China '96" 9th Asian International Stamp Exhibition, Peking. Sheet 105 × 70 mm.
MS784 **310** 70t. multicoloured . . 25 30

311 Rifle-shooting

1996. Olympic Games, Atlanta. Multicoloured.
785 25t. Type **311** 10 15
786 50t. Athletics 15 20
787 65t. Weightlifting 20 25
788 1k. Boxing 35 40

312 Air Traffic Controller

1996. Centenary of Radio. Multicoloured.
789 25t. Type **312** 10 15
790 50t. Radio disc-jockey . . . 15 20
791 65t. Dish aerials 20 25
792 1k. Early radio transmitter 35 40

313 Dr. Sun Yat-sen

1996. "TAIPEI '96" 10th Asian International Stamp Exhibition, Taiwan. Sheet 105 × 70 mm, containing T **313** and similar vert design. Multicoloured.
MS793 65t. Type **313**; 65t. Dr. John Guise (former speaker of Papua New Guinea House of Assembly) 45 50

314 "Hibiscus rosa-sinensis"

1996. Flowers. Multicoloured.
794 1t. Type **314** 10 10
795 5t. "Bougainvillea spectabilis" 10 10
796 10t. "Thunbergia fragrans" (vert) 10 10
797 20t. "Caesalpinia pulcherrima" (vert) 10 10
798 25t. "Hoya sp." (vert) . . . 10 15
799 30t. "Heliconia spp." (vert) 10 15
800 50t. "Amomum goliathensis" (vert) 15 20
801 65t. "Plumeria rubra" . . . 20 25
802 1k. "Mucuna novoguineensis" 35 40

315 Ox and National Flag

1997. "HONG KONG '97" International Stamp Exhibition. Sheet 130 × 90 mm.
MS808 **315** 1k.50 multicoloured 50 55

316 Gogodala Canoe Prow

1997. Canoe Prows. Multicoloured.
809 25t. Type **316** 10 15
810 50t. East New Britain 15 20
811 65t. Trobriand Island 20 25
812 1k. Walomo 35 40

1997. Golden Wedding of Queen Elizabeth and Prince Philip. As T **87** of Kiribati. Multicoloured.
813 25t. Prince Philip on polo pony, 1972 . . . . 10 15
814 25t. Queen Elizabeth at Windsor Polo Club 10 15
815 50t. Prince Philip carriage-driving, 1995 . . . . . . 15 20
816 50t. Queen Elizabeth and Prince Edward on horseback 15 20
817 1k. Prince Philip waving and Peter and Zara Phillips on horseback 35 40
818 1k. Queen Elizabeth waving and Prince Harry on horseback 35 40
MS819 105 × 71 mm. 2k. Queen Elizabeth and Prince Philip in landau (horiz) 70 75
Nos. 813/14, 815/16 and 818/19 respectively were printed together, se-tenant, with the backgrounds forming composite designs.

317 Air Niugini Airliner over Osaka

1997. Inaugural Air Niugini Port moresby to Osaka Flight. Sheet 110 × 80 mm.
MS820 **317** 3k. multicoloured . . 1·00 1·10

318 "Pocillopora woodjonesi"

1997. Pacific Year of the Coral Reef. Corals. Mult.
821 25t. Type **318** 10 15
822 50t. "Subergorgia mollis" . . 15 20
823 65t. "Oxypora glabra" . . . 20 25
824 1k. "Turbinaria reinformis" 35 40

319 Greater Sooty Owl

1998. Birds. Multicoloured.
825 25t. Type **319** 50 20
826 50t. Wattled brush turkey . . 70 45
827 65t. New Guinea grey-headed goshawk . . . . 80 1·00
828 1k. Forest bittern . . . . . 1·25 2·00

1998. Diana, Princess of Wales Commemoration. Sheet, 145 × 70 mm, containing vert designs as T **91** of Kiribati. Multicoloured.
MS829 1k., Wearing pink jacket, 1992; 1k. Wearing purple dress; 1988; 1k. wearing tartan jacket, 1990; 1k. Carrying bouquets, 1990 (sold at 4k.+50t. charity premium) 1·50 1·60

320 Mother Teresa and Child

1998. Mother Teresa Commemoration. Mult.
830 65t. Type **320** 20 25
831 1k. Mother Teresa 35 40

1998. No. 774 surch **25t**.
832 25t. on 65t. "Uca tetragonon" 10 15

322 "Daphnis hypothous pallescens"

1998. Moths. Multicoloured.
833 25t. Type **322** 10 15
834 50t. "Theretra polistratus" 15 20
835 65t. "Psilogramma casurina" 20 25
836 1k. "Meganoton hyloicoides" 35 40

323 "Coelogyne fragrans" 324 Weightlifting

1998. Orchids. Multicoloured.
837 25t. Type **323** 10 15
838 50t. "Den cuthbertsonii" . . 15 20
839 65t. "Den vexillarius "var" retroflexum" 20 25
840 1k. "Den finisterrae" 35 40

1998. 16th Commonwealth Games, Kuala Lumpur, Malaysia. Multicoloured.
841 25t. Type **324** 10 15
842 50t. Lawn bowls 15 20
843 65t. Rugby Union 20 25
844 1k. Squash 35 40

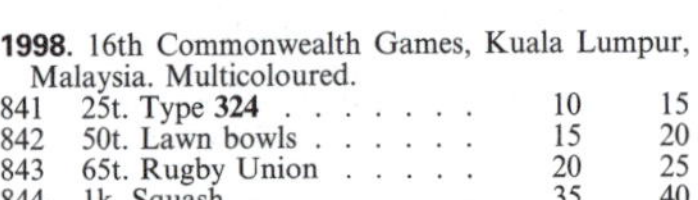

325 Double Kayak

1998. Sea Kayaking World Cup, Manus Island. Multicoloured.
845 25t. Type **325** 10 15
846 50t. Running 15 20
847 65t. Traditional canoe and modern kayak 20 25
848 1k. Single kayak and stylized bird of paradise 35 40

326 The Holy Child

1998. Christmas. Multicoloured.
849 25t. Type **326** 10 15
850 50t. Mother breast-feeding baby 15 20
851 65t. Holy Child and tribal elders 20 25
852 1k. Map of Papua New Guinea and festive bell . . 35 40

1999. "Australia '99" World Stamp Exhibition, Melbourne. Designs as Nos. 543, 552 and 556/7, showing ships, redrawn to include exhibition emblem at top right and with some face values changed. Multicoloured.
853 25t. "La Boudeuse" (De Bougainville) (as No. 543) 10 15
854 50t. "Neva" (D'Albertis) (as No. 552) 15 20
855 65t. "Merrie England" (steamer) (as No. 556) . . 20 25
856 1k. "Samoa" (German colonial steamer) (as No. 557) 35 40
MS857 165 × 110 mm. 5t. H.M.S. "Rattlesnake" (Owen Stanley) (as No. 548); 10t. H.M.S. "Swallow" (Philip Carteret) (as No. 545); 15t. "Roebuck" (Dampier) (as No. 544); 20t. H.M.S. "Blanche" (SImpson) (as No. 55); 30t. "Vitaz" (Maclay) (as No. 549); 40t. "San Pedrico" (Torres) and zabra (as No. 550); 60t. Spanish galleon (Jorge de Meneses) (as No. 553); 1k.20, "L' Astrolabe" (D' Urville) (as No. 551) . . . 1·00 1·10

No. 855 is inscribed "Merrir England" in error. Of the designs in No. **MS**857 the 5t. is inscribed "Simpson Blanche 1872", 10t. "Carterel", 15t. "Dampien", 40t. "eabra" and 60t. "Menesis", all in error.

327 German New Guinea 1900 Yacht Type 2m. Stamp

1999. "iBRA '99" International Stamp Exhibition, Nuremberg. Multicoloured.
858 1k. Type **327** 35 40
859 1k. German New Guinea 1897 3pf. and 5pf. optd on Germany 35 40

328 Father Jules Chevalier

1999. "PhilexFrance '99" International Stamp Exhibition, Paris. Famous Frenchmen. Mult.
860 25t. Type **328** 10 15
861 50t. Bishop Alain-Marie . . . 15 20
862 65t. Joseph-Antoine d'Entrecasteaux (explorer) 20 25
863 1k. Louis de Bougainville (explorer) 35 40

329 Hiri Claypot and Traditional Dancer

1999. Hiri Moale Festival. Multicoloured (except No. **MS**686).
864 25t. Type **329** 10 15
865 50t. Three dancers 15 20
866 65t. Hiri Lagatoi (trading canoe) and dancer 20 25
867 1k. Hiri Sorcerer and dancer 35 40
MS868 140 × 64mm. 1k. Hiri Sorcerer (deep blue and blue); 1k. Hiri Claypot (deep purple and blue); 1k. Hiri Lagatoi (green and blue) . . . . 1·00 1·10

330 Lap-top Computer, Globe and Watch

1999. New Millennium. Modern Technology. Each showing Globe. Multicoloured.
869 25t. Type **330** 10 15
870 50t. Globe within concentric circles 15 20
871 65t. Compact disc, web site and man using computer 20 25
872 1k. Keyboard, dish aerial and solar eclipse 35 40

331 *Turbo petholatus*

2000. Sea Shells. Multicoloured.
873 25t. Type **331** 10 15
874 50t. *Charonia tritonis* 15 20
875 65t. *Cassis cornuta* 20 25
876 1k. *Ovula ovum* 35 40

332 Rabbit 333 Shell

2000. Chinese New Year ("Year of the Rabbit") (1999). Sheet, 145 × 70mm, containing T **332** and similar vert designs. Multicoloured.
MS877 65t. Type **332**; 65t. Light brown rabbit running; 65t. White rabbit grinning; 65t. Pink rabbit hiding behind grass knoll . . . 90 95

2000. 25th Anniv of Independence. Multicoloured.
878 25t. Type **333** 10 15
879 50t. Raggiana bird of Paradise 15 20
880 65t. Ornament 20 25
881 1k. Red bird of Paradise perched on spear and drums 35 40
MS882 145 × 75 mm. Nos. 878/81 80 1·00

334 Athletics

2000. Olympic Games, Sydney. Multicoloured.
883 25t. Type **334** 10 15
884 50t. Swimming 15 20
885 65t. Boxing 20 25
886 1k. Weightlifting 35 40
MS887 80 × 90 mm. 3k. Runner with Olympic Torch (34 × 45 mm) (sold at 3k.50) . . . . 1·10 1·25

No. **MS**887 includes the "Olymphilex 2000" stamp exhibition logo on the sheet margin.

335 Queen Mother in Yellow Coat and Hat

2000. Queen Elizabeth the Queen Mother's 100th Birthday. Multicoloured.
888 25t. Type **335** 10 15
889 50t. Queen Mother with bouquet of roses 15 20
890 65t. Queen Mother in green coat 20 25
891 1k. Lady Elizabeth Bowes-Lyon 35 40

336 Comb-crested Jacana

2001. Water Birds. Multicoloured.
892 35t. Type **336** 10 15
893 70t. Masked lapwing 25 30
894 90t. Australian white ibis . . 30 35
895 1k.40 Black-tailed godwit . . 50 55

337 Cessna 170 Aircraft

2001. 50th Anniv of Mission Aviation Fellowship. Multicoloured.
896 35t. Type **337** 10 15
897 70t. Auster Autocar 25 30
898 90t. Cessna 260 . . . . . . 30 35
899 1k.40 Twin Otter 50 55

338 Flags of China and Papua New Guinea

2001. 25th Anniv of Diplomatic Relations between Papua New Guinea and China. Multicoloured.
900 10t. Type **338** 10 10
901 50t. Dragon and bird of paradise 15 20
902 2k. Tian An Men (Gate of Heavenly Peace), Beijing, and Parliament House, Port Moresby 70 75

2001. Nos. 745, 862, 866, 871 and 883 surch.
903 50t. on 21t. Type **248** 75 50
904 50t. on 25t. Type **334** 15 20
905 50t. on 65t. Compact disc, web site and man using computer 15 20
906 2k.65 on 65t. Joseph-Antoine d'Entrecasteaux 90 95
907 2k.65 on 65t. Hiri Lagatoi (trading canoe) and dancer 90 95

341 Flag of Enga Province

2001. Provincial Flags. Multicoloured.
908 10t. Type **341** 20 10
909 15t. Simbu Province 20 10
910 20t. Manus Province 20 10
911 50t. Central Province 50 20
912 2k. New Ireland Province . . 1·75 1·50
913 5k. Sandaun Province . . . . 3·00 3·50

2002. Golden Jubilee. As T **211** of St. Helena.
914 1k.25 multicoloured 40 45
915 1k.45 multicoloured 50 55
916 2k. black, brown and gold . . 70 75
917 2k.65 multicoloured 90 95
MS918 162 × 95 mm. Nos. 914/17 and 5k. multicoloured . . . . . 4·00 4·25

DESIGNS—HORIZ:1k.25, Queen Elizabeth with Princesses Elizabeth and Margaret, 1941; 1k.45, Queen Elizabeth in evening dress, 1975; 2k. Princess Elizabeth, Duke of Edinburgh and children, 1951; 2k.65, Queen Elizabeth at Henley-on-Thames. VERT (38 × 51 mm)—5k. Queen Elizabeth after Annigoni.

Designs as Nos. 914/17 in No. **MS**918 omit the gold frame around each stamp and the "Golden Jubilee 1952–2002" inscription.

342 Lakotoi (trading canoe) and Hanuabada Village

2002. Centenary of First Papuan Stamps (2001).
919 **342** 5t. black and mauve . . . 10 10
920 15t. black and brown . . . 10 10
921 20t. black and blue 10 10
922 1k.25 black and brown . . 40 45
923 1k.45 black and green . . 50 55
924 10k. black and orange . . 3·50 3·75
MS925 127 × 99 mm. Nos. 919/24 4·50 5·00

The design of Type **342** is adapted from that of the first Papua issue of 1901.

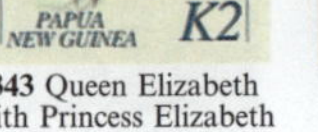

343 Queen Elizabeth with Princess Elizabeth in South Africa

344 *Cadetia taylori*

2002. Queen Elizabeth the Queen Mother Commemoration. Multicoloured (No. 929) or black and blue (others).
926 2k. Type **343** 70 75
927 2k. Queen Elizabeth with Princess Elizabeth at Balmoral, 1951 . . . . . 70 75
928 2k. Queen Mother at Sandown races, 2001 (26 × 30 mm) 70 75
929 2k. Queen Mother with Irish Guards, 1988 (41 × 30 mm) 70 75

930 2k. Queen Mother at the Derby, 1988 (26 × 30 mm) 70 75
931 2k. Queen Mother at Ascot races, 1966 . . . . 70 75
932 2k. King George VI with Queen Elizabeth at Balmoral, 1951 . . . . . 70 75
MS933 Two sheets, each 65 × 101 mm. (a) 3k. Queen Mother at Lord Linley's wedding, 1993; 3k. At Aintree racecourse, 1991 (wearing brooch). (b) 3k. Lady Elizabeth Bowes-Lyon as a young girl; 3k. Queen Mother on Remembrance Day, 1988 (each 26 × 40 mm) . . . . 4·00 4·25

2002. Orchids. Multicoloured.
934 5t. Type **344** 10 10
935 30t. *Dendrobium anosmum* . . 10 10
936 45t. *Dendrobium bigibbum* . . 15 20
937 1k.25 *Dendrobium cuthbertsonii* 40 45
938 1k.45 *Spiranthes sinensis* . . 50 55
939 2k.65 *Thelymitra carnea* . . . 75 80
MS940 135 × 135 mm. 2k. *Dendrobium bracteosum*; 2k. *Calochilus campestris*; 2k. *Anastomus oscitans*; 2k. *Thelymitra carnea*; 2k. *Dendrobium macrophyllum*; 2k. *Dendrobium johnsoniae* (all horiz) 4·00 4·25

345 *Ornithoptera chimaera*

2002. Birdwing Butterflies. Multicoloured.
941 50t. Type **345** 15 20
942 50t. *Ornithoptera goliath* . . 15 20
943 1k.25 *Ornithoptera meridionalis* 40 45
944 1k.45 *Ornithoptera paradisea* 50 55
945 2k.65 *Ornithoptera victoriae* 75 80
946 5k. *Ornithoptera alexandrae* 1·70 1·80

346 Globe covered in National Flags and New York Skyline

2002. "United We Stand". Support for Victims of 11 September 2001 Terrorist Attacks. Sheet 174 × 123 mm.
MS947 **346** 50t. × 4 multicoloured 60 65

347 Mt. Wilhelm, Papua New Guinea

2003. International Year of Mountains. Multicoloured.
948 50t. Type **347** 15 20
949 1k.25 Matterhorn, Switzerland 40 45
950 1k.45 Mount Fuji, Japan . . 50 55
951 2k.65 Massif des Aravis, France 75 80

348 Sago Storage Pot

349 Papuan Scout Troop

2003. Clay Pots. Multicoloured.
952 65t. Type **348** 20 25
953 1k. Smoking pot 35 40
954 1k.50 Water jar 50 55
955 2k.50 Water jar on stand . . 75 80
956 4k. Ridge pot . . . . 1·40 1·50

2003. 20th World Scout Jamboree, Thailand. Multicoloured.
957 50t. Type **349** 15 20
958 1k.25 Scouts in workshop . . 40 45
959 1k.45 Scouts on wooden platform with banner . . . 50 55
960 2k.65 Scouts 75 80

350 Princess Elizabeth

351 Prince William

2003. 50th Anniv of Coronation.
961 **350** 65t. brown, bistre and black 20 25
962 – 65t. deep lilac, lilac and black 20 25
963 – 1k.50 deep blue, blue and black 50 55
964 – 2k. deep purple, purple and black 70 75
965 – 2k.50 black and grey . . . 75 80
966 – 4k. brown, cinnamon and black . . . . 1·40 1·50
MS967 146 × 116 mm. 2k. multicoloured; 2k. multicoloured; 2k. multicoloured; 2k. multicoloured; 2k. multicoloured; 2k. multicoloured . . . . . . 4·25 4·50
MS968 97 × 67 mm. 8k. multicoloured . . . . 4·00 4·00

DESIGNS: No. 962, Queen Elizabeth II in Coronation robes and crown; 963, Queen wearing white evening dress, sash and tiara; 964, Queen seated, wearing tiara; 965, Queen in Coronation robes, with Imperial State Crown and sceptre; 966, Princess Elizabeth as teenager; **MS**967, Princess Elizabeth aged 21; Queen wearing diadem, 1952; Wearing hat with blue flowers, c. 1958; Wearing tiara, c. 1970; Wearing red hat with black bow, c. 1985; Wearing black robes and hat with white cockade, c. 1992; **MS**968, Wearing garter robes (from painting by Annigoni).

2003. 21st Birthday of Prince William of Wales. Multicoloured.
969 65t. Type **351** 20 25
970 65t. Wearing red and blue t-shirt 20 25
971 1k.50 As toddler 50 55
972 2k. Wearing grey jacket and blue tie 70 75
973 2k.50 Prince William 75 80
974 4k. Playing polo . . . . . . 1·40 1·50
MS975 146 × 116 mm. 2k. As toddler; 2k. Wearing sunglasses; 2k. Wearing blue jacket and tie (facing forwards); 2k. Wearing blue jacket and tie (facing right); 2k. Wearing blue shirt; 2k. Wearing black and yellow t-shirt 4·00 4·25
MS976 95 × 66 mm. 8k. Prince William . . . . 2·75 3·00

352 Gabagaba Village

2003. Coastal Villages. Multicoloured.
977 65t. Type **352** 20 25
978 65t. Wanigela (Koki) 20 25
979 1k.50 Tubuserea 50 55
980 2k. Hanuabada 70 75
981 2k.50 Barakau 75 80
982 4k. Porebada . . . . 1·40 1·50

353 Orville Wright circling Fort Myer, Virginia, 1908

2003. Centenary of Powered Flight. Multicoloured (except No. **MS**987).
983 65t. Type **353** 20 25
984 1k.50 Orville Wright piloting "Baby Grand" biplane, Belmont New York, 1910 50 55
985 2k.50 Wilbur Wright holding anemometer, Pau, France, 1909 . . . . 75 80
986 4k. Wilbur Wright piloting Wright Model A, Pau, France, 1909 . . . . . . 1·40 1·50
MS987 176 × 96 mm. 2k.50 Wright *Flyer I* outside hangar, Kitty Hawk, North Carolina, 1903 (multicoloured); 2k.50 Wright *Flyer I* rolled out from hangar (black, grey and brown); 2k.50 Wright *Flyer I* being prepared for takeoff (black, green and brown); 2k.50 Wright *Flyer I* taking off, 1903 (multicoloured) . . . . . . 3·50 3·75
MS988 105 × 76 mm. 10k. Wright *Flyer I*, 1903 . . . . 3·50 3·75

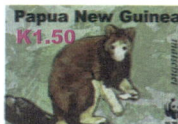

354 Matschie's Tree Kangaroo

2003. Endangered Species. Tree Kangaroos. Multicoloured.
989 65t. Grizzled tree kangaroo 20 25
990 1k.50 Type **354** 50 55
991 2k.50 Doria's tree kangaroo 75 80
992 4k. Goodfellow's tree kangaroo . . . . 1·40 1·50
MS993 168 × 127 mm. As Nos. 989/92, each × 2, but without white margins . . . . 5·75 6·25

355 Indo-Pacific Hump-backed Dolphin

2003. Protected Species. Dolphins. Multicoloured.
994 65t. Type **355** 20 25
995 65t. Two Indo-Pacific bottlenose dolphins 20 25
996 1k.50 Indo-Pacific bottlenose dolphin leaping 50 55
997 2k. Irrawaddy dolphin . . . 70 75
998 2k.50 Indo-Pacific hump-backed dolphin leaping . . 75 80
999 4k. Irrawaddy dolphin with diver . . . . 1·40 1·50
MS1000 147 × 112 mm. 1k.50 Indo-Pacific hump-backed dolphin; 1k.50 Indo-Pacific bottlenose dolphin; 1k.50 Two Indo-Pacific bottlenose dolphins; 1k.50 Irrawaddy dolphin with diver; 1k.50 Irrawaddy dolphin; 1k.50 Indo-Pacific hump-backed dolphin 3·00 3·25

2004. Nos. 977/8 surch.
1001 70t. on 65t. Type **352** . . . 25 30
1002 70t. on 65t.Wanigela (Koki) 25 30

357 Lake Wanam Rainbowfish

2004. Freshwater Fish. Multicoloured.
1003 70t. Type **357** 25 30
1004 70t. Kokoda mogurnda . . 25 30
1005 1k. Sepik grunter 35 40
1006 2k.70 Papuan black bass . . 95 1·00
1007 4k.60 Lake Tebera rainbowfish . . . . 1·50 1·60
1008 20k. Wichmann's mouth almighty . . . . 7·00 7·25

358 Ankylosaurus

2004. Prehistoric Animals. Multicoloured.
1009 70t. Type **358** 25 30
1010 1k. Oviraptor 35 40
1011 2k. Tyranosaurus 70 75
1012 2k.65 Gigantosaurus 90 95
1013 2k.70 Centrosaurus . . . . 95 1·00
1014 4k.60 Carcharodontsaurus 1·50 1·60
MS1015 146 × 106 mm. 1k.50 Edmontonia; 1k.50 Struthiomimus; 1k.50 Psittacosaurus; 1k.50 Gastonia; 1k.50 Shunosaurus; 1k.50 Iguanadon . . . . 3·00 3·25
MS1016 116 × 86 mm. 7k. Afrovenator . . . . 2·20 2·30

359 *Phalaenopsis amabilis*

2004. Orchids. Multicoloured.
1017 70k. Type **359** 25 30
1018 1k. *Phaius tankervilleae* . . 35 40
1019 2k. *Bulbophyllum macranthum* 70 75
1020 2k.65 *Dendrobium rhodostictum* 90 95
1021 2k.70 *Diplocaulobium ridleyanum* . . . . 95 1·00
1022 4k.60 *Spathoglottis papuana* 1·50 1·60
MS1023 146 × 106 mm. 2k. *Dendrobium cruttwellii*; 2k. *Dendrobium coeloglossum*; 2k. *Dendrobium alaticaulinum*; 2k. *Dendrobium Obtusisepalum*; 2k. *Dendrobium johnsoniae*; 2k. *Dendrobium insigne* . . . . . 5·00 5·25
MS1024 116 × 86 mm. 7k. *Dendrobium biggibum* . . . . 2·20 2·30

360 Headdress from East Sepik Province

2004. Local Headdresses. Multicoloured.
1025 70t. Type **360** 25 30
1026 70t. Simbu Province 25 30
1027 2k.65 Southern Highlands Province 90 95
1028 2k.70 Western Highlands Province . . . . 95 1·00
1029 4k.60 Eastern Highlands Province . . . . 1·50 1·60
1030 5k. Central Province . . . . 1·70 1·80

2004. No. 910 and Nos. 994/5 surch.
1031 5t. on 20t. Manus Province (910) 10 10
1032 70t. on 65t. Type **355** (994) 25 30
1033 70t. on 65t. Two Indo-Pacific bottlenose dolphins (995) 25 30

363 Swimming

2004. Olympic Games, Athens. Multicoloured.
1034 70t. Type **363** 25 30
1035 2k.65 Weight lifting (vert) 90 95
1036 2k.70 "The Torch Race" (Greek art) (vert) . . . . 95 1·00
1037 4k.60 Olympic poster, Helsinki 1952 (vert) . . . 1·50 1·60

364 Papua New Guinea Football Player

2004. Centenary of FIFA (Federation Internationale de Football Association). Multicoloured.
1038 70t. Type **364** 25 30
1039 2k.65 Shooting at goal . . . 90 95
1040 2k.70 Two players . . . . . 95 1·00
1041 4k.60 Players and referee . . 1·50 1·60
MS1042 165 × 85 mm. 2k.50 Bruno Conti, Italy; 2k.50 Oliver Kahn, Germany; 2k.50 Mario Kempes, Argentina; 2k.50 Bobby Moore, England (51 × 20 mm) . . . . 3·50 3·75
MS1043 93 × 76 mm. 10k. Bobby Robson, England (51 × 20 mm) 3·50 3·75

365 Flag of East New Britain Province

2004. Provincial Flags. Multicoloured.
1044 70t. Type **365** 25 30
1045 70t. Madang Province . . . 25 30
1046 2k.65 Eastern Highlands Province 90 95
1047 2k.70 Morobe Province . . 95 1·00
1048 4k.60 Milne Bay Province . 1·50 1·60
1049 10k. East Sepik Province . . 3·50 3·75

366 *Phalium areola*

2004. Sea Shells. Multicoloured.
1050 70t. Type **366** 40 50
1051 70t. *Conus auratus* 40 50
1052 2k.65 *Oliva miniacea* 1·40 1·40
1053 2k.70 *Lambis chiragra* 1·40 1·40
1054 4k.60 *Conus suratensis* 2·40 2·40
1055 10k. *Architectonica perspective* 5·00 5·50

2005. Nos. 1003/4 and 1025/6 surch **75t**.
1056 75t. on 70t. Type **357** 60 60
1057 75t. on 70t. Kokoda mogurnda 60 60
1058 75t. on 70t. Type **360** 60 60
1059 75t. on 70t. Simbu Province 60 60

369 Little Egret

2005. Coastal Birds. Multicoloured.
1060 5t. Type **369** 30 50
1061 75t. White-faced heron 75 60
1062 75t. Nankeen night heron 75 60
1063 3k. Crested tern 1·75 1·75
1064 3k.10 Bar-tailed godwit 1·75 1·75
1065 5k.20 Little pied heron 2·75 3·25

370 Children, Handwriting and Rotary Emblem

2005. Centenary of Rotary International (Humanitarian organisation). Multicoloured.
1066 75t. Type **370** 75 35
1067 3k. Child and PolioPlus emblem 1·75 1·75
1068 3k.10 Co-Founders of the first Rotary club 1·75 1·75
1069 4k. Silvester Schiele (1st Rotary Pres.) (vert) 2·00 2·25
1070 4k. Paul Harris (Founder of Rotary International) (vert) 2·00 2·25
1071 4k. Three children (vert) 2·00 2·25
1072 5k.20 Chicago skyline 2·50 3·00
MS1073 107×74 mm. 10k. Globe and "Mankind is our Business" (vert) 5·00 5·50

371 Lady in Pink

2005. Frangipani Flowers. Multicoloured.
1074 75t. Type **371** 75 45
1075 75t. Evergreen 75 45
1076 1k. Carmine flush 95 50
1077 3k. *Cultivar acutifolia* 2·00 2·25
1078 3k.10 American beauty 2·00 2·25
1079 5k.20 Golden kiss 3·00 3·25

373 *Promechus pulcher*

2005. Beetles. Multicoloured.
1091 75t. Type **373** 75 45
1092 75t. *Callistola pulchra* 75 45
1093 1k. *Lagriomorpha indigacea* 75 45
1094 3k. *Hellerhinus papuanus* 2·00 2·25
1095 3k.10 *Aphorina australis* 2·20 2·25
1096 5k.20 *Bothricara pulchella* 3·00 3·25

374 Pope John Paul II on Visit to Papua New Guinea

2005. Pope John Paul II Commemoration. Multicoloured. Country name and value colour given.
1097 **374** 2k. blue 1·75 1·75
1098 2k. green 1·75 1·75
1099 2k. orange 1·75 1·75
1100 2k. mauve 1·75 1·75

375 Flag of Southern Highlands Province

2005. Provincial Flags. Multicoloured.
1101 75t. Type **375** 90 45
1102 75t. Gulf Province 90 45
1103 1k. North Solomons Province 1·25 50
1104 3k. Oro Province 2·50 2·50
1105 3k.10 Western Highlands Province 2·50 2·50
1106 5k.20 Western Province 2·00 2·10

376 Ruddy Somali (inscr "Rudy")

2005. Cats and Dogs. Multicoloured.
1107 75t. Type **376** 75 45
1108 75t. Balinese seal lynx point 75 45
1109 3k. Sphynx brown mackerel tabby and white 2·00 2·25
1110 3k.10 Korat blue 2·00 2·25
1111 5k.20 Bengal brown spotted tabby 3·00 3·25
MS1112 232×100 mm. 2k.50 Yorkshire terrier; 2k.50 Basenji; 2k.50 Neapolitan mastiff (wrongly inscr "Msastiff"); 2k.50 Poodle 6·00 6·50
MS1113 100×70 mm. 10k. Boston terrier (horiz) 6·00 6·50

The stamps and margins of No. **MS**1112 form a composite background design spelling "DOGS".

POSTAGE DUE STAMPS

1960. Stamps of 1952 surch **POSTAL CHARGES** and value.
D2 1d. on 6½d. purple 3·25 4·50
D3 3d. on ½d. green 3·50 1·75
D1 6d. on 7½d. blue (A) £800 £425
D4 6d. on 7½d. blue (B) 27·00 6·50
D5 1s.3d. on 3½d. black 4·00 2·00
D6 3s. on 2½d. orange 14·00 3·50

In (A) value and "POSTAGE" is obliterated by a solid circle and a series of "IX's" but these are omitted in (B).

D 3

1960.
D 7 **D 3** 1d. orange 65 75
D 8 3d. brown 70 75
D 9 6d. blue 75 40
D10 9d. red 75 1·75
D11 1s. green 75 50
D12 1s.3d. violet 1·00 2·00
D13 1s.6d. blue 4·00 6·00
D14 3s. yellow 2·50 75

PARAGUAY Pt. 20

A republic in the centre of S. America, independent since 1811.

1870. 8 reales = 1 peso.
1878. 100 centavos = 1 peso.
1944. 100 centimos = 1 guarani.

1

7

1870. Various frames. Values in "reales". Imperf.
1 **1** 1r. red 4·00 2·25
3 2r. blue 55·00 32·00
4 3r. black 90·00 55·00

1878. Handstamped with large **5**. Imperf.
5 **1** 5c. on 1r. red 40·00 26·00
9 5c. on 2r. blue £140 75·00
13 5c. on 3r. black £110 70·00

1879. Prepared for use but not issued (wrong currency). Values in "reales". Perf.
14 **7** 5r. orange 40
15 10r. brown 50

1879. Values in "centavos". Perf.
16 **7** 5c. brown 1·10 70
17 10c. green 1·60 95

1881. Handstamped with large figures.
18 **7** 1 on 10c. green 8·00 4·75
19 2 on 10c. green 8·00 4·75

1881. As T **1** (various frames), but value in "centavos". Perf.
20 **1** 1c. blue 40 40
21a 2c. red 30 40
22 4c. brown 40 50

1884. No. 1 handstamped with large **1**. Imperf.
23 **1** 1c. on 1r. red 2·40 1·40

13

24

1884. Perf.
24 **13** 1c. green 30 15
25 2c. red 40 15
26 5c. blue 40 15

1887.
32 **24** 1c. green 15 15
33a 2c. red 15 15
34 5c. blue 30 20
35 7c. brown 30 25
36 10c. mauve 45 30
37 15c. orange 45 30
38 20c. pink 45 30
50 40c. blue 2·00 70
51 60c. orange 95 30
52 80c. blue 80 30
53 1p. green 85 30

25

27 C. Rivarola

1889. Imperf or perf.
40 **25** 15c. purple 1·60 95

1892.
42 **27** 1 CENTAVOS grey 15 10
54 1 CENTAVO grey 15 10
43 – 2c. green 15 10
44 – 4c. red 10 10
57 – 5c. purple 15 10
46 – 10c. violet 30 25
47 – 14c. brown 55 30
48 – 20c. red 95 30
49 – 30c. green 1·25 30
84 – 1p. blue 40 25

PORTRAITS: 2c. S. Jovellano; 4c. J. Bautista Gil; 5c. H. Uriarte; 10c. C. Barreiro; 14c. Gen. B. Caballero; 20c. Gen. P. Escobar; 30c. J. Gonzales; 1p. J. B. Egusquisa.

1892. 400th Anniv of Discovery of America. No. 46 optd **1492 12 DE OCTUBRE 1892** in oval.
41 10c. violet 5·75 1·50

1895. Surch **PROVISORIO 5**.
59 **24** 5c. on 7c. brown 30 30

30

39

1896. Telegraph stamps as T **30** surch **CORREOS 5 CENTAVOS** in oval.
60 **30** 5c. on 2c. brown, blk & grey 45 20
61 5c. on 4c. orange, blk & grey 45 20

1898. Surch **Provisorio 10 Centavos**.
63 **24** 10c. on 15c. orange 35 35
62 10c. on 40c. blue 25 25

1900. Telegraph stamps as T **30** surch with figures of value twice and bar.
64 **30** 5c. on 30c. green, blk & grey 1·60 70
65 10c. on 50c. lilac, blk & grey 3·50 1·50

1900.
76 **39** 1c. green 10 10
67 2c. grey 10 10
73 2c. pink 20 15
68 3c. brown 10 10
78 4c. blue 15 10
69 5c. green 10 10
74 5c. brown 20 10
79 5c. lilac 25 10
80 8c. brown 20 15
71 10c. red 20 15
72 24c. blue 45 20
82 28c. orange 25 35
83 40c. blue 25 10

1902. Surch **Habilitado en** and new values.
88 – 1c. on 14c. brown (No. 47) 30 20
91 – 1c. on 1p. blue (No. 84) 20 15
86 **39** 5c. on 8c. brown (No. 80) 35 20
87 5c. on 28c. orange (No. 82) 20 30
89 **24** 5c. on 60c. orange (No. 51) 20 25
90 5c. on 80c. blue (No. 52) 30 25
85 **39** 20c. on 24c. blue (No. 72) 35 20

46

47

1903.
92 **46** 1c. grey 20 15
93 2c. green 25 20
94a 5c. blue 25 10
95 10c. brown 45 20
96 20c. red 45 25
97 30c. blue 50 25
98 60c. violet 1·25 55

1903.
99 **47** 1c. green 15 10
100 2c. orange 15 10
101 5c. blue 20 15
102 10c. violet 30 20
103 20c. green 50 25
104 30c. blue 90 30
105 60c. brown 95 35

48

50

51 National Palace, Asuncion

1904.
106 **48** 10c. blue 35 20

1904. End of successful Revolt against Govt. (begun in August). Surch **PAZ 12 Dic. 1904. 30 centavos.**
107 **48** 30c. on 10c. blue 50 35

1905.
108 **50** 1c. orange 15 10
109 1c. red 15 10
110 1c. blue 15 10
112 2c. green 40·00
113 2c. red 15 10
114 5c. blue 15 10
116 5c. yellow 15 10
117 10c. brown 15 10
118 10c. green 15 10
119 10c. blue 15 10
120 20c. lilac 45 35
121 20c. brown 45 35
122 20c. green 35 20
123 30c. blue 45 20
124 30c. grey 45 20
125 30c. lilac 50 35
126 60c. brown 35 25
128 60c. pink 4·00 1·40
129 **51** 1p. black and red 1·75 80
130 1p. black and brown 65 35
131 1p. black and green 35 35
132 2p. black and blue 35 25
133 2p. black and red 35 25
134 2p. black and brown 40 30
135 5p. black and red 90 35

136 5p. black and blue 90 35
137 5p. black and green . . . 90 35
138 10p. black and brown . . . 80 35
139 10p. black and blue . . . 80 35
141 20p. black and green . . . 2·25 1·25
142 20p. black and yellow . . . 2·25 1·25
143 20p. black and purple . . . 2·25 1·25

1907. Surch **Habilitado en** and value and bars.
159 **50** 5c. on 1c. blue 10 10
160 5c. on 2c. red 15 10
145 5c. on 2c. green 40 25
172 **39** 5c. on 28c. orange . . . . 1·60 60
173 5c. on 40c. blue 30 25
163 **50** 5c. on 60c. brown 15 10
162 5c. on 60c. pink 20 15
175 20c. on 1c. blue 20 15
180 **24** 20c. on 2c. red . . . . . . 4·00 2·10
177 **50** 20c. on 2c. red . . . . . . 6·75 3·50
178 20c. on 30c. blue . . . . . 2·00 1·10
179 20c. on 30c. lilac 30 30

1907. Official stamps surch **Habilitado en**, value and bars. Where not otherwise stated, the design is as T **50** but with "OFICIAL" below the lion.
164 – 5c. on 10c. green 30 20
149 – 5c. on 10c. brown 30 20
150 – 5c. on 10c. lilac 30 20
181 **24** 5c. on 15c. orange (No. O63) . . . . 3·00 2·40
182 5c. on 20c. pink (No. O64) 45·00 32·00
166 – 5c. on 20c. brown 30 25
151 – 5c. on 20c. green 30 20
167 – 5c. on 20c. pink 30 25
152 – 5c. on 20c. lilac 30 20
157 **46** 5c. on 30c. blue (No. O104) 95 85
154 – 5c. on 30c. blue 50 50
169 – 5c. on 30c. yellow 10 10
168 – 5c. on 30c. grey 20 15
183 **24** 5c. on 50c. grey (No. O65) 21·00 15·00
158 **46** 5c. on 60c. violet (No. O105) 35 25
155 – 5c. on 60c. brown 20 15
171 – 5c. on 60c. blue 20 10
184 **24** 20c. on 5c. blue (No. O60) 1·90 1·50
174 **46** 20c. on 5c. blue (No. O101) . . . . 1·90 1·50

1907. Official stamps, as T **50** and **51** with "OFICIAL" added, optd **Habilitado** and one bar.
146 5c. grey 30 20
148 5c. blue 25 15
185 1p. black and orange 35 35
186 1p. black and red 30 25

1907. Official stamps, as T **51** with "OFICIAL" added, surch **Habilitado 1908 UN CENTAVO** and bar.
188 1c. on 1p. black and red . . 20 20
189 1c. on 1p. black and brown 1·00 50

1908. Optd **1908**.
190 **50** 1c. green 10 10
191 5c. yellow 10 10
192 10c. brown 10 10
193 20c. orange 10 10
194 30c. red 40 30
195 60c. mauve 30 30
196 **51** 1p. blue 15 15

1909. Optd **1909**.
197 **50** 1c. blue 10 10
198 1c. red 10 10
199 5c. green 10 10
200 5c. orange 10 10
201 10c. red 20 15
202 10c. brown 20 15
203 20c. lilac 20 20
204 20c. yellow 10 10
205 30c. brown 45 30
206 30c. blue 45 30

62 **63** **65**

1910.
207 **62** 1c. brown 10 10
208 5c. lilac 10 10
209 5c. green 10 10
210 5c. blue 10 10
211 10c. green 10 10
212 10c. violet 10 10
213 10c. red 10 10
214 20c. red 10 10
215 50c. red 45 20
216 75c. blue 15 10

1911. No. 216 perf diagonally and each half used as 20c.
217 **62** 20c. (½ of 75c.) blue . . . 15 10

1911. Independence Centenary.
218 **63** 1c. black and olive 10 10
219 2c. black and blue 10 10
220 5c. black and red 20 10
221 10c. brown and blue . . . 30 15
222 20c. blue and olive 30 15
223 50c. blue and lilac 45 30
224 75c. purple and olive . . . 45 30

1912. Surch **Habilitada en VEINTE** and thin bar.
225 **62** 20c. on 50c. red 10 10

1913.
226 **65** 1c. black 10 10
227 2c. orange 10 10
228 5c. mauve 10 10
229 10c. green 10 10
230 20c. red 10 10
231 40c. red 10 10
232 75c. blue 10 10
233 80c. yellow 10 10
234 1p. blue 10 10
235 1p.25 blue 30 10
236 3p. green 30 10

1918. No. D242 surch **HABILITADO EN 0.05 1918** and bar.
237 5c. on 40c. brown 10 10

1918. Nos. D239/42 optd **HABILITADO 1918**.
238 5c. brown 10 10
239 10c. brown 10 10
240 20c. brown 10 10
241 40c. brown 15 10

1918. Surch **HABILITADO EN 0.30 1918** and bar.
242 **65** 30c. on 40c. red 10 10

1920. Surch **HABILITADO en**, value and **1920**.
243 **65** 50c. on 80c. yellow 15 10
244 1p.75 on 3p. green 60 50

1920. Nos. D243/4 optd **HABILITADO 1920** or surch also.
245 1p. brown 20 10
246 1p. on 1p.50 brown 35 10

72 Parliament House, Asuncion

1920. Jubilee of Constitution.
247 **72** 50c. black and red 30 20
248 1p. black and blue 50 40
249 1p.75 black and blue . . . 20 15
250 3p. black and yellow . . . 75 25

1920. Surch **50**.
251 **65** 50 on 75c. blue 45 10

1921. Surch **50** and two bars.
252 **62** 50 on 75c. blue 10 10
253 **65** 50 on 75c. blue 25 10

75

1922.
254 **75** 50c. blue and red 10 10
255 1p. brown and blue 10 10

Between 1922 and 1936 many regular postage stamps were overprinted **C** (= Campana—country), these being used at post offices outside Asuncion but not for mail sent abroad. The prices quoted are for whichever is the cheapest.

77 Starting-point of Conspirators

80 Map

1922. Independence.
256 **77** 1p. blue 20 10
258 1p. blue and red 30 10
259 1p. grey and purple 30 10
260 1p. grey and orange . . . 30 10
257 5p. purple 30 25
261 5p. brown and blue 30 25
262 5p. black and green . . . 30 25
263 5p. blue and red 30 25

1924. Surch **Habilitado en**, value and **1924**.
265 **65** 50c. on 75c. blue 10 10
266 $1 on 1p.25 blue 10 10
267 – $1 on 1p.50 brown (No. D244) 10 10

1924.
268 **80** 1p. blue 10 10
269 2p. red 15 10
270 4p. blue 30 10

81 Gen. Jose E. Diaz

82 Columbus

1925.
271 **81** 50c. red 10 10
272 1p. blue 10 10
273 1p. green 10 10

1925.
274 **82** 1p. blue 15 10

1926. Surch **Habilitado en** and new value.
275 **62** 1c. on 5c. blue 10 10
276 $0.02 on 5c. blue 10 10
277 **65** 7c. on 40c. red 10 10
278 15c. on 75c. blue 10 10
279 **50** $0.50 on 60c. purple (No. 195) 10 10
280 – $0.50 on 75c. blue (No. O243) 10 10
281 – $1.50 on 1p.50 brown (No. D244) 15 10
282 **80** $1.50 on 4p. blue 10 10

86

87 P. J. Caballero

88 Paraguay

89 Cassel Tower, Asuncion

90 Columbus

92 Arms of De Salazarde Espinosa, founder of Asuncion

1927.
283 **86** 1c. red 10 10
284 2c. orange 10 10
285 7c. lilac 10 10
286 7c. green 10 10
287 10c. green 10 10
288 10c. red 10 10
290 10c. blue 10 10
291 20c. blue 10 10
292 20c. purple 10 10
293 20c. violet 10 10
294 20c. pink 10 10
295 50c. blue 10 10
296 50c. red 10 10
323 50c. orange 10 10
326 50c. green 10 10
299 50c. mauve 10 10
300 50c. pink 10 10
301 70c. blue 10 10
328 **87** 1p. green 10 10
329 1p. red 10 10
330 1p. purple 10 10
331 1p. blue 10 10
304 1p. orange 10 10
332 1p. violet 10 10
333 **88** 1p.50 brown 10 10
334 1p.50 lilac 10 10
307 1p.50 pink 10 10
335 1p.50 blue 10 10
308 – 2p.50 bistre 10 10
337 – 2p.50 violet 10 10
338 – 3p. grey 10 10
310 – 3p. red 10 10
311 – 3p. violet 10 10
312 **89** 5p. brown 25 20
340 5p. violet 10 10
314 5p. orange 10 10
315 **90** 10p. red 35 35
317 10p. blue 35 35
318 **88** 20p. red . . . . 1·60 85
319 20p. green . . . . 1·60 85
320 20p. purple . . . . 1·60 85
DESIGNS—As Type **87**: 2p.50, Fulgencio Yegros; 3p. V. Ignacio Yturbe.

1928. Foundation of Asuncion, 1537.
342 **92** 10p. purple 95 70

93 Pres. Hayes of U.S.A. and Villa Hayes

1928. 50th Anniv of Hayes's Decision to award Northern Chaco to Paraguay.
343 **93** 10p. brown . . . . 3·75 1·40
344 10p. grey . . . . 3·75 1·40

1929. Air. Surch **Correo Aereo Habilitado en** and value.
357 **86** $0.95 on 7c. lilac 20 20
358 $1.90 on 20c. blue 20 20
345 – $2.85 on 5c. purple (No. O239) 95 70
348 – $3.40 on 3p. grey (No. 338) 1·90 85
359 **80** $3.40 on 4p. blue 30 30
360 $4.75 on 4p. blue 55 30
346 – $5.65 on 10c. green (No. O240) 35 45
361 – $6.80 on 3p. grey (No. 338) 35 35
349 **80** $6.80 on 4p. blue . . . . 1·90 85
347 – $11.30 on 50c. red (No. O242) 60 50
350 **89** $17 on 5p. brown (A) . . . 1·90 85
362 $17 on 5p. brown (B) . . . 1·50 1·10
On No. 350 (A) the surcharge is in four lines, and on No. 362 (B) it is in three lines.

95

1929. Air.
352 **95** 2.85p. green 35 30
353 – 5.65p. brown 60 30
354 – 5.65p. red 40 35
355 – 11.30p. purple 70 55
356 – 11.30p. blue 35 35
DESIGNS: 5.65p. Carrier pigeon; 11.30p. Stylized airplane.

1930. Air. Optd **CORREO AEREO** or surch also in words.
363 **86** 5c. on 10c. green 10 10
364 5c. on 70c. blue 10 10
365 10c. green 10 10
366 20c. blue 20 20
367 **87** 20c. on 1p. red 30 30
368 **86** 40c. on 50c. orange 15 10
369 **87** 1p. green 35 35
370 – 3p. grey (No. 338) 35 35
371 **90** 6p. on 10p. red 60 50
372 **88** 10p. on 20p. red . . . . . 5·50 3·25
373 10p. on 20p. purple . . . . 6·50 4·75

101 **103**

1930. Air.
374 **101** 95c. blue on blue 40 35
375 95c. red on pink 40 35
376 – 1p.90 purple on blue . . . 40 35
377 – 1p.90 red on pink 40 35
378 **103** 6p.80 black on blue . . . 40 35
379 6p.80 green on pink . . . 45 40
DESIGN: 1p.90, Asuncion Cathedral.

104 Declaration of Independence

105

1930. Air. Independence Day.

380	**104**	2p.85 blue	40	35
381		3p.40 green	35	25
382		4p.75 purple	35	25

1930. Red Cross Fund.

383	**105**	1p.50+50c. blue	1·10	70
384		1p.50+50c. red	1·10	70
385		1p.50+50c. lilac	1·10	70

106 Portraits of Archbishop Bogarin

1930. Consecration of Archbishop Bogarin.

386	**106**	1p.50 blue	1·10	60
387		1p.50 red	1·10	60
388		1p.50 violet	1·10	60

1930. Surch **Habilitado en CINCO**.

389	**86**	5c. on 7c. green	10	10

108 Planned Agricultural College at Ypacarai

1931. Agricultural College Fund.

390	**108**	1p.50+50c. blue on red	30	30

109 Arms of Paraguay

1931. 60th Anniv of First Paraguay Postage Stamps.

391	**109**	10p. brown	30	25
392		10p. red on blue	35	25
393		10p. blue on red	35	25
395		10p. grey	50	20
396		10p. blue	20	20

110 Gunboat "Paraguay"

1931. Air. 60th Anniv of Constitution and Arrival of new Gunboats.

397	**110**	1p. red	25	20
398		1p. blue	25	20
399		2p. orange	30	25
400		2p. brown	30	25
401		3p. green	65	40
402		3p. blue	65	45
403		3p. red	60	40
404		6p. green	75	60
405		6p. mauve	95	65
406		6p. blue	70	50
407		10p. red	2·00	1·40
408		10p. green	2·50	1·90
409		10p. blue	1·40	1·00
410		10p. brown	2·25	1·60
411		10p. pink	2·00	1·40

1931. As T **110**.

412	–	1p.50 violet	95	35
413	–	1p.50 blue	15	10

DESIGN: Gunboat "Humaita".
No. 413 is optd with large **C**.

112 War Memorial

113 Orange Tree and Yerba Mate

114 Yerba Mate

115 Palms

116 Yellow-headed Caracara

1931. Air.

414	**112**	5c. blue	15	10
415		5c. green	15	10
416		5c. red	20	10
417		5c. purple	15	10
418	**113**	10c. violet	10	10
419		10c. red	10	10
420		10c. brown	10	10
421		10c. blue	10	10
422	**114**	20c. red	15	10
423		20c. blue	20	10
424		20c. green	20	15
425		20c. brown	15	10
426	**115**	40c. green	20	10
426a		40c. blue	15	10
426b		40c. red	20	10
427	**116**	80c. blue	35	30
428		80c. green	35	20
428a		80c. red	25	20

1931. Air. Optd with airship "Graf Zeppelin" and **Correo Aereo "Graf Zeppelin"** or surch also.

429	**80**	3p. on 4p. blue	7·75	6·25
430		4p. blue	7·75	6·25

118 Farm Colony

1931. 50th Anniv of Foundation of San Bernardino.

431	**118**	1p. green	35	20
432		1p. red	10	10

1931. New Year. Optd **FELIZ ANO NUEVO 1932**.

433	**106**	1p.50 blue	60	60
434		1p.50 red	60	60

120 "Graf Zeppelin"

1932. Air.

435	**120**	4p. blue	1·40	1·75
436		8p. red	2·40	2·00
437		12p. green	1·90	1·75
438		16p. purple	3·75	3·00
439		20p. brown	4·00	3·75

121 Red Cross H.Q.

122 (Trans: "Has been, is and will be")

1932. Red Cross Fund.

440	**121**	50c.+50c. pink	25	25

1932. Chaco Boundary Dispute.

441	**122**	1p. purple	20	10
442		1p.50 pink	10	10
443		1p.50 brown	10	10
444		1p.50 green	10	10
445		1p.50 blue	10	10

Nos. 443/5 are optd with a large **C**.

1932. New Year. Surch **CORREOS FELIZ ANO NUEVO 1933** and value.

446	**120**	50c. on 4p. blue	35	30
447		1p. on 8p. red	35	30
448		1p.50 on 12p. green	35	30
449		2p. on 16p. purple	35	30
450		5p. on 20p. brown	1·25	75

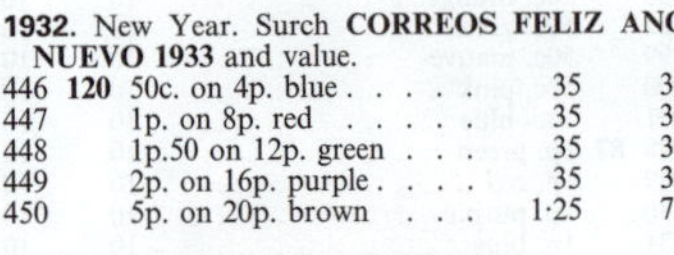

124 "Graf Zeppelin" over Paraguay

125 "Graf Zeppelin" over Atlantic

1933. Air. "Graf Zeppelin" issue.

451	**124**	4p.50 blue	1·25	75
452		9p. red	2·50	1·90
453		13p.50 green	2·50	1·90
454	**125**	22p.50 brown	6·00	4·50
455		45p. violet	8·25	6·75

126 Columbus's Fleet

1933. 441st Anniv of Departure of Columbus from Palos. Maltese Crosses in violet.

456	**126**	10c. olive and red	45	15
457		20c. blue and lake	45	15
458		50c. red and green	75	35
459		1p. brown and blue	60	40
460		1p.50 green and blue	60	40
461		2p. green and sepia	1·75	70
462		5p. lake and olive	3·75	1·40
463		10p. sepia and blue	3·75	1·40

127 G.P.O., Asuncion

1934. Air.

464	**127**	33p.75 blue	1·60	95
468		33p.75 red	1·60	95
466		33p.75 green	1·40	85
467		33p.75 brown	1·40	85

1934. Air. Optd **1934**.

469	**124**	4p.50 blue	1·75	1·75
470		9p. red	2·25	2·25
471		13p.50 green	6·50	6·50
472	**125**	22p.50 brown	5·25	5·25
473		45p. violet	11·00	11·00

1935. Air. Optd **1935**.

474	**124**	4p.50 red	2·25	2·25
475		9p. green	3·25	3·25
476		13p.50 brown	9·25	9·25
477	**125**	22p.50 purple	8·75	8·75
478		45p. blue	23·00	23·00

131 Tobacco Plant

1935. Air.

479	**131**	17p. brown	3·75	3·00
480		17p. red	6·75	5·00
481		17p. blue	4·25	3·50
482		17p. green	2·10	1·75

132 Church of the Incarnation

1935. Air.

483	**132**	102p. red	5·00	3·75
485		102p. blue	2·50	1·90
486		102p. brown	2·50	1·90
487		102p. violet	1·10	80
487a		102p. orange	1·10	85

1937. Air. Surch **Habilitado en** and value in figures.

488	**127**	$24 on 33p.75 blue	40	50
489	**132**	$65 on 102p. grey	1·25	95
490		$84 on 102p. green	1·25	95

134 Arms of Asuncion

135 Monstrance

1937. 4th Centenary of Asuncion (1st issue).

491	**134**	50c. purple and violet	10	10
492		1p. green and bistre	10	10
493		3p. blue and red	10	10
494		10p. yellow and red	15	10
495		20p. grey and blue	20	20

1937. 1st National Eucharistic Congress.

496	**135**	1p. red, yellow and blue	10	10
497		3p. red, yellow and blue	10	10
498		10p. red, yellow and blue	15	10

136 Oratory of the Virgin of Asuncion

137 Asuncion

1938. 4th Centenary of Asuncion (2nd issue).

499	**136**	5p. olive	25	10
500		5p. red	35	10
501		11p. brown	25	10

1939. Air.

502	**137**	3p.40 blue	75	45
503		3p.40 green	75	45
504		3p.40 brown	75	45

138 J. E. Diaz

1939. Reburial in National Pantheon of Ashes of C. A. Lopez and J. E. Diaz.

505	**138**	2p. brown and blue	25	15
506	–	2p. brown and blue	25	15

DESIGN—VERT: No. 506, C. A. Lopez.

139 Pres. Caballero and Senator Decoud

1939. 50th Anniv of Asuncion University.

507	–	50c. blk & orge (postage)	10	10
508	–	1p. black and blue	15	10
509	–	2p. black and red	25	10
510	**139**	5p. black and blue	35	20
511		28p. black and red (air)	4·75	3·75
512		90p. black and green	8·00	6·50

DESIGN: Nos. 507/9, Pres. Escobar and Dr. Zubizarreta.

140 Coats of Arms

141 Pres. Baldomir and Flags of Paraguay and Uruguay

1939. Chaco Boundary Peace Conference, Buenos Aires (1st issue).

513	**140**	50c. blue (postage)	15	10
514	**141**	1p. olive	15	10
515	A	2p. green	20	10
516	B	3p. brown	35	25
517	C	5p. orange	25	20
518	D	6p. violet	40	30
519	E	10p. brown	50	35
520	F	1p. brown (air)	10	10
521	**140**	3p. blue	10	10
522	E	5p. olive	10	15

523 D 10p. violet 15 15
524 C 30p. orange 25 15
525 B 50p. brown 15 25
526 A 100p. green 60 25
527 **141** 200p. green . . . . 2·75 1·75
528 – 500p. black . . . . 13·00 10·50
DESIGNS (flag on right is that of country named): A, Benavides (Peru); B, Eagle (USA); C, Alessandri (Chile); D, Vargas (Brazil); E, Ortiz (Argentina); F, Figure of "Peace" (Bolivia); 500p. (30 × 40 mm), Map of Chaco frontiers.
See also Nos. 536/43.

143 Arms of New York

144 Asuncion–New York Air Route

1939. New York World's Fair.
529 **143** 5p. red (postage) 20 15
530 10p. blue 40 30
531 11p. green 25 45
532 22p. grey 35 30
533 **144** 30p. brown (air) . . . . 3·25 2·40
534 80p. orange . . . . . . 4·25 3·00
535 90p. violet . . . . 7·00 5·50

145 Soldier

147 Waterfall

1940. Chaco Boundary Peace Conference, Buenos Aires (2nd issue). Inscr "PAZ DEL CHACO".
536 **145** 50c. orange 15 10
537 – 1p. purple 15 15
538 – 3p. green 25 20
539 – 5p. brown 10 25
540 – 10p. mauve 35 20
541 – 20p. blue 30 25
542 – 50p. green . . . . 1·10 35
543 **147** 100p. black . . . . 2·50 1·60
DESIGNS: As Type **145**: VERT: 1p. Water-carrier; 5p. Ploughing with oxen. HORIZ: 3p. Cattle Farming. As Type **147**: VERT: 10p. Fishing in the Paraguay River. HORIZ: 20p. Bullock-cart; 50p. Cattle-grazing.

148 Western Hemisphere

149 Reproduction of Paraguay No. 1

1940. 50th Anniv of Pan-American Union.
544 **148** 50c. orange (postage) . . 10 10
545 1p. green 10 10
546 5p. blue 25 10
547 10p. brown 30 30
548 20p. red (air) 35 25
549 70p. blue 35 30
550 100p. green 80 65
551 500p. violet . . . . 2·75 1·40

1940. Cent of First Adhesive Postage Stamps. Inscr "CENTENARIO DEL SELLO POSTAL 1940".
552 **149** 1p. purple and green . . . 65 35
553 – 5p. brown and green . . . 85 45
554 – 6p. blue and brown . . . 1·75 50
555 – 10p. black and red . . . 1·90 60
DESIGNS: 5p. Sir Rowland Hill; 6p., 10p. Early Paraguayan stamps.

1940. National Mourning for Pres. Estigarribia. Surch **7-IX-40/DUELO NACIONAL/5 PESOS** in black border.
556 **145** 5p. on 50c. orange . . . 25 25

152 Dr. Francia

154 Our Lady of Asuncion

1940. Death Centenary of Dr. Francia (dictator).
557 **152** 50c. red 15 10
558 – 50c. purple 15 10
559 **152** 1p. green 15 10
560 – 5p. blue 15 10
PORTRAIT: Nos. 558 and 560, Dr. Francia seated in library.

1941. Visit of President Vargas of Brazil. Optd **Visita al Paraguay Agosto de 1941**.
560a 6p. violet (No. 518) 25 25

1941. Mothers' Fund.
561 **154** 7p.+3p. brown 35 25
562 7p.+3p. violet 35 25
563 7p.+3p. red 35 25
564 7p.+3p. blue 35 25

1942. Nos. 520/2 optd **Habilitado** and bar(s).
565 – 1p. brown 15 10
566 **140** 3p. blue 20 10
567 – 5p. olive 25 10

156 Arms of Paraguay

158 Irala's Vision

1942.
568 **156** 1p. green 10 10
569 1p. orange 10 10
570 7p. blue 10 10
571 7p. brown 10 10
For other values as Type **156** see Nos. 631, etc.

1942. 4th Centenary of Asuncion.
572 – 2p. green (postage) . . . 75 40
573 **158** 5p. red 75 40
574 – 7p. blue 75 35
575 – 20p. purple (air) 95 30
576 **158** 70p. brown . . . . 2·40 1·25
577 – 500p. olive . . . . 7·25 5·25
DESIGNS—VERT: 2p., 20p. Indian hailing ships; 7p., 500p. Irala's Arms.

160 Columbus sighting America

161 Pres. Morinigo and Symbols of Progress

1943. 450th Anniv of Discovery of America by Columbus.
578 **160** 50c. violet 25 20
579 1p. brown 20 10
580 5p. green 65 20
581 7p. blue 35 10

1943. Three Year Plan.
582 **161** 7p. blue 10 10

NOTE: From No. 583 onwards, the currency having been changed, the letter "c" in the value description indicates "centimos" instead of "centavos".

1944. St. Juan Earthquake Fund. Surch **U.P.A.E. Adhesion victimas San Juan y Pueblo Argentino centimos** and bar.
583 E 10c. on 10p. brown (No. 519) 40 25

1944. No. 311 surch **Habilitado en un centimo**.
584 1c. on 3p. violet 10 10

1944. Surch **1944/5 Centimos 5**.
585 **160** 5c. on 7p. blue 15 10
586 **161** 5c. on 7p. blue 15 10

164 Primitive Indian Postmen

181 Jesuit Relics of Colonial Paraguay

1944.
587 **164** 1c. black (postage) . . . 10 10
588 – 2c. brown 15 10
589 – 5c. olive . . . . 3·25 80
590 – 7c. blue 15 20
591 – 10c. green . . . . 1·50 45
592 – 15c. blue 40 25
593 – 50c. black 35 35
594 – 1g. red 70 40
DESIGNS—HORIZ: 2c. Ruins of Humaita Church; 7c. Marshal Francisco S. Lopez; 1g. Ytororo Heroes' Monument. VERT: 5c. First Paraguayan railway locomotive; 10c. "Tacuary" (paddle-steamer); 15c. Port of Asuncion; 50c. Meeting place of Independence conspirators.

595 – 1c. blue (air) 20 15
596 – 2c. green 10 10
597 – 3c. purple 80 20
598 – 5c. green 20 10
599 – 10c. violet 20 15
600 – 20c. brown . . . . 4·00 1·60
601 – 30c. blue 25 25
602 – 40c. olive 15 15
603 – 70c. red 25 20
604 **181** 1g. orange 90 40
605 – 2g. brown . . . . 2·25 55
606 – 5g. brown . . . . 5·50 2·75
607 – 10g. blue . . . . 13·00 9·75
DESIGNS—HORIZ: 1c. Port of Asuncion; 2c. First telegraphic apparatus in S. America; 3c. Paddle-steamer "Tacuary"; 5c. Meeting place of Independence Conspirators; 10c. Antequera Monument; 20c. First Paraguayan railway locomotive; 40c. Government House. VERT: 30c. Ytororo Heroes' Monument; 70c. As Type **164** but vert: 2g. Ruins of Humaita Church; 5g. Oratory of the Virgin; 10g. Marshal Francisco S. Lopez.
See also Nos. 640/51.

1945. No. 590 surch with figure **5** over ornaments deleting old value.
608 5c. on 7c. blue 10 10

186 Clasped Hands and Flags

1945. President Morinigo's Goodwill Visits. Designs of different sizes inscr "CONFRATERNIDAD" between crossed flags of Paraguay and another American country, mentioned in brackets.
(a) Postage.
609 **186** 1c. green (Panama) . . . 10 10
610 3c. red (Venezuela) . . . 10 10
611 5c. grey (Ecuador) 10 10
612 2g. brown (Peru) . . . . 1·50 90

(b) Air.
613 20c. orange (Colombia) . . . 10 30
614 40c. olive (Bolivia) 10 25
615 70c. red (Mexico) 40 40
616 1g. blue (Chile) 50 50
617 2g. violet (Brazil) 75 75
618 5g. green (Argentina) . . . . 2·25 2·25
619 10g. brown (U.S.A.) . . . . 6·50 6·50
The 5 and 10g. are larger, 32 × 28 and 33½ × 30 mm respectively.

1945. Surch **1945 5 Centimos 5**.
620 **160** 5c. on 7p. blue 50 20
621 **161** 5c. on 7p. blue 50 20
622 – 5c. on 7p. blue (No. 590) 50 20

1945. Surch **1945** and value.
623 **154** 2c. on 7p.+3p. brown . . 10 10
624 2c. on 7p.+3p. violet . . . 10 10
625 2c. on 7p.+3p. red 10 10
626 2c. on 7p.+3p. blue . . . 10 10
627 5c. on 7p.+3p. brown . . 20 10
628 5c. on 7p.+3p. violet . . . 20 10
629 5c. on 7p.+3p. red 20 10
630 5c. on 7p.+3p. blue . . . 20 10

1946. As T **156** but inscr "U.P.U." at foot.
631 **156** 5c. grey 10 10
631a 5c. pink 10 10
631b 5c. brown 10 10
686 10c. blue 10 10
687 10c. pink 10 10
631c 30c. green 10 10
631d 30c. brown 10 10
775 45c. green 10 10
631e 50c. mauve 10 10
776 50c. purple 10 10
858 70c. brown 10 10
777 90c. blue 10 10
778 1g. violet 10 10
860 1g.50 mauve 10 10
814 2g. ochre 10 10
780 2g.20 mauve 10 10
781 3g. brown 10 10
782 4g.20 green 10 10
862 4g.50 blue 15 10
816 5g. red 10 10
689 10g. orange 20 30
784 10g. green 20 15
818 12g.45 green 20 10
819 15g. orange 25 15
786 20g. blue 40 30
820 30g. bistre 20 30
812 50g. brown 30 25
821 100g. blue 90 50
See also Nos. 1037/49.

1946. Surch **1946 5 Centimos 5**.
632 **154** 5c. on 7p.+3p. brown . . 25 35
633 5c. on 7p.+3p. violet . . . 25 35
634 5c. on 7p.+3p. red 25 35
635 5c. on 7p.+3p. blue . . . 25 35

1946. Air. Surch **1946 5 Centimos 5**.
636 5c. on 20c. brown (No. 600) 5·50 5·75
637 5c. on 30c. blue (No. 601) . . 30 30
638 5c. on 40c. olive (No. 602) 30 30
639 5c. on 70c. red (No. 603) . . 30 30

1946. As Nos. 587/607 but colours changed and some designs smaller.
640 – 1c. red (postage) 20 15
641 – 2c. violet 10 10
642 **164** 5c. blue 10 10
643 – 10c. orange 10 10
644 – 15c. olive 15 15
645 **181** 50c. green 50 30
646 – 1g. blue 95 30
DESIGNS—VERT: 1c. Paddle-steamer "Tacuary"; 1g. Meeting place of Independence Conspirators. HORIZ: 2c. First telegraphic apparatus in S. America; 10c. Antequera Monument; 15c. Ytororo Heroes' Monument.

647 – 10c. red (air) 10 10
648 – 20c. green 80 20
649 – 1g. brown 25 25
650 – 5g. purple . . . . 2·25 1·40
651 – 10g. red . . . . 7·25 4·00
DESIGNS—VERT: 10c. Ruins of Humaita Church. HORIZ: 20c. Port of Asuncion; 1g. Govt. House; 5g. Marshal Francisco S. Lopez; 10g. Oratory of the Virgin.

189 Marshal Francisco Lopez

190 Archbishop of Paraguay

1947. Various frames.
652 **189** 1c. violet (postage) . . . 10 10
653 2c. red 10 10
654 5c. green 10 10
655 15c. blue 10 10
656 50c. green 40 40
657 32c. red (air) 10 10
658 64c. brown 25 25
659 1g. blue 40 40
660 5g. purple and blue . . . 1·60 60
661 10g. green and red . . . 2·75 95

1947. 50th Anniv of Archbishopric of Paraguay.
662 **190** 2c. grey (postage) 10 10
663 – 5c. red 10 10
664 – 10c. black 10 10
665 – 15c. green 25 15
666 – 20c. black (air) 10 10
667 – 30c. grey 10 10
668 – 40c. mauve 15 10
669 **190** 70c. red 25 25
670 – 1g. lake 30 30
671 – 2g. red 95 40
672 **190** 5g. slate and red . . . . 1·60 70
673 – 10g. brown and green . . 3·75 1·75
DESIGNS: 5, 20c., 10g. Episcopal Arms; 10, 30c., 1g. Sacred Heart Monument; 15, 40c., 2g. Vision of projected monument.

194 Torchbearer

195 C. A. Lopez, J. N. Gonzalez and "Paraguari" (freighter)

1948. Honouring the "Barefeet" (political party). Badge in red and blue.
674 **194** 5c. red (postage) 10 10
675 15c. orange 15 10
676 69c. green (air) 40 40
677 5g. blue . . . . 3·25 1·50

1948. Centenary of Paraguay's Merchant Fleet. Centres in black, red and blue.
678 **195** 2c. orange 15 10
679 5c. blue 20 10
680 10c. black 25 10
681 15c. violet 40 10
682 50c. green 60 20
683 1g. red 90 25

1949. Air. National Mourning for Archbishop of Paraguay. Surch **DUELO NACIONAL 5 CENTIMOS 5**.
684 **190** 5c. on 70c. red 15 15

1949. Air. Aid to Victims of Ecuadorean Earthquake. No. 667 surch **AYUDA AL ECUADOR 5 + 5** and two crosses.
685 5c.+5c. on 30c. slate 10 10

198 "Postal C-ommunications"

199 President Roosevelt

1950. Air. 75th Anniv of U.P.U.

691 **198** 20c. violet and green . . . 1·50 1·60
692 30c. brown and purple . . 45 50
693 50c. green and grey . . . 50 50
694 1g. brown and blue . . . 50 50
695 5g. black and red . . . . 1·50 1·60

1950. Air. Honouring F. D. Roosevelt. Flags in red and blue.

696 **199** 20c. orange 10 10
697 30c. black 10 10
698 50c. purple 15 10
699 1g. green 25 25
700 5g. blue 30 30

1951. 1st Economic Congress of Paraguay. Surch **PRIMER CONGRESO DE ENTIDADES ECONOMICAS DEL PARAGUAY 18-IV-1951** and shield over a block of four stamps.

700a **156** 5c. pink 20 10
700b 10c. blue 35 25
700c 30c. green 50 40

Prices are for single stamps. Prices for blocks of four, four times single prices.

200 Columbus Lighthouse

201 Urn

1952. Columbus Memorial Lighthouse.

701 **200** 2c. brown (postage) . . . 10 10
702 5c. blue 10 10
703 10c. pink 10 10
704 15c. blue 10 10
705 20c. purple 10 10
706 50c. orange 15 10
707 1g. green 25 25
708 **201** 10c. blue (air) 10 10
709 20c. green 10 10
710 30c. purple 10 10
711 40c. pink 10 10
712 50c. bistre 10 10
713 1g. blue 15 10
714 2g. orange 25 20
715 5g. lake 25 40

202 Isabella the Catholic

1952. Air. 500th Birth Anniv of Isabella the Catholic.

716 **202** 1g. blue 10 10
717 2g. brown 20 20
718 5g. green 40 40
719 10g. purple 40 40

203 S. Pettirossi (aviator)

204 San Roque Church, Asuncion

1954. Pettirossi Commemoration.

720 **203** 5c. blue (postage) 10 10
721 20c. red 10 10
722 50c. purple 10 10
723 60c. violet 15 10
724 40c. brown (air) 10 10
725 55c. green 10 10
726 80c. blue 10 10
727 1g.30 grey 35 35

1954. Air. San Roque Church Centenary.

728 **204** 20c. red 10 10
729 30c. purple 10 10
730 50c. blue 10 10
731 1g. purple and brown . . 10 10
732 1g. black and brown . . . 10 10
733 1g. green and brown . . . 10 10
734 1g. orange and brown . . 10 10
735 5g. yellow and brown . . 20 20
736 5g. olive and brown . . . 20 20
737 5g. violet and brown . . . 20 20
738 5g. buff and brown . . . 20 20
MS738a Two sheets each 124 × 108 mm. Nos. 731/4 and 735/8. No gum . . . . 1·40 1·40

205 Marshal Lopez, C. A. Lopez and Gen. Caballero

1954. National Heroes.

739 **205** 5c. violet (postage) . . . 10 10
740 20c. blue 10 10
741 50c. mauve 10 10
742 1g. brown 10 10
743 2g. green 15 10
744 5g. violet (air) 20 15
745 10g. olive 35 35
746 20g. grey 35 30
747 50g. pink . . . . 1·60 1·25
748 100g. blue . . . . 5·50 4·50

206 Presidents Stroessner and Peron

1955. Visit of President Peron. Flags in red and blue.

749 **206** 5c. brown & buff (postage) 10 10
750 10c. lake and buff 10 10
751 50c. grey 10 10
752 1g.30 lilac and buff . . . 10 10
753 2g.20 blue and buff . . . 20 10
754 60c. olive and buff (air) . . 10 10
755 2g. green 10 10
756 3g. red 20 10
757 4g.10 mauve and buff . . 30 20

207 Trinidad Campanile

1955. Sacerdotal Silver Jubilee of Mgr. Rodriguez.

758 **207** 5c. brown (postage) . . . 10 10
759 – 20c. brown 10 10
760 – 50c. brown 10 10
761 – 2g.50 green 10 10
762 – 5g. brown 15 10
763 – 15g. green 30 20
764 – 25g. green 35 35
765 **207** 2g. blue (air) 10 10
766 – 3g. green 10 10
767 – 4g. green 10 10
768 – 6g. brown 10 10
769 – 10g. red 20 10
770 – 20g. brown 30 10
771 – 30g. green 95 70
772 – 50g. blue . . . . 2·40 1·60

DESIGNS—HORIZ: 20c., 3g. Cloisters in Trinidad; 5, 10g. San Cosme Portico; 15, 20g. Church of Jesus. VERT: 50c., 4g. Cornice in Santa Maria; 2g.50, 6g. Santa Rosa Tower; 25, 30g. Niche in Trinidad; 50g. Trinidad Sacristy.

208 Angel and Marching Soldiers

209 Soldier and Flags

1957. Chaco Heroes. Inscr "HOMENAJE A LOS HEROES DEL CHACO". Flags in red, white and blue.

787 **208** 5c. green (postage) . . . 10 10
788 10c. red 10 10
789 15c. blue 10 10
790 20c. purple 10 10
791 25c. black 10 10
792 – 30c. blue 10 10
793 – 40c. black 10 10
794 – 50c. lake 10 10
795 – 1g. turquoise 10 10
796 – 1g.30 blue 10 10
797 – 1g.50 purple 10 10
798 – 2g. green 10 10
799 **209** 10c. blue (air) 10 10
800 15c. purple 10 10
801 20c. red 10 10
802 25c. blue 10 10
803 50c. turquoise 10 10
804 1g. red 10 10
805 – 1g.30 purple 10 10
806 – 1g.50 blue 10 10
807 – 2g. green 10 10
808 – 4g.10 vermilion and red . . 10 10
809 – 5g. black 10 10
810 – 10g. turquoise 15 15
811 – 25g. blue 40 15

DESIGNS—HORIZ: Nos. 792/8, Man, woman and flags; 805/11, "Paraguay" and kneeling soldier.

212 R. Gonzalez and St. Ignatius

213 President Stroessner

1958. 4th Centenary of St. Ignatius of Loyola.

822 **212** 50c. green 10 10
823 – 50c. brown 10 10
824 – 1g.50 violet 10 10
825 – 3g. blue 10 10
826 **212** 6g.25 red 15 10

DESIGNS—VERT: 50c. brown; 3g. Statue of St. Ignatius. HORIZ: 1g.50, Jesuit Fathers' house, Antigua.

See also Nos. 1074/81.

1958. Re-election of Pres. Stroessner. Portrait in black.

827 **213** 10c. red (postage) 10 10
828 15c. violet 10 10
829 25c. green 10 10
830 30c. lake 10 10
831 50c. mauve 10 10
832 75c. blue 10 10
833 5g. turquoise 10 10
834 10g. brown 10 15
835 12g. mauve (air) 40 35
836 18g. orange 25 40
837 23g. brown 65 40
838 36g. green 65 40
839 50g. olive 80 50
840 65g. grey . . . . 1·25 75

1959. Nos. 758/72 surch with star enclosed by palm leaves and value.

841 1g.50 on 5c. ochre (postage) 10 10
842 1g.50 on 20c. brown 10 10
843 1g.50 on 50c. purple . . . 10 10
844 3g. on 2g.50 olive 10 10
845 6g.25 on 5g. brown 10 10
846 20g. on 15g. turquoise . . . 35 35
847 30g. on 25g. green 50 50
848 4g. on 2g. blue (air) . . . 10 10
849 12g.45 on 3g. olive 25 20
850 18g.15 on 6g. brown 35 30
851 23g.40 on 10g. red 25 35
852 34g.80 on 20g. bistre . . . 40 50
853 36g. on 4g. green 40 30
854 43g.95 on 30g. green . . . 75 60
855 100g. on 50g. blue . . . . 1·90 1·10

215 U.N. Emblem

216 U.N. Emblem and Map of Paraguay

1959. Air. Visit of U.N. Secretary-General.

856 **215** 5g. blue and orange . . . 75 30

1959. Air. U.N. Day.

857 **216** 12g.45 orange and blue 25 20

217 Football

218 "Uprooted Tree"

1960. Olympic Games, Rome. Inscr "1960".

863 **217** 30c. red & green (postage) 10 10
864 50c. purple and blue . . . 10 10
865 75c. green and orange . . 10 10
866 1g.50 violet and green . . 10 10
867 – 12g.45 blue and red (air) 25 25
868 – 18g.15 green and purple 35 35
869 – 36g. red and green . . . 80 30

DESIGN—AIR: Basketball.

1960. World Refugee Year (1st issue).

870 **218** 25c. pink and green (postage) 10 10
871 50c. green and red 10 10
872 70c. brown and mauve . . 30 25
873 1g.50 blue and deep blue 30 30
874 3g. grey and brown . . . 65 35
875 – 4g. pink and green (air) 95 70
876 – 12g.45 green and blue . . 1·90 1·25
877 – 18g.15 orange and red . . 2·75 2·00
878 – 23g.40 blue and red . . . 3·50 2·75

DESIGN—AIR. As Type **218** but with "ANO MUNDIAL" inscr below tree.

See also Nos. 971/7.

219 U.N. Emblem

220 U.N. Emblem and Flags

1960. "Human Rights". Inscr "DERECHOS HUMANOS".

879 **219** 1g. red and blue (postage) 10 10
880 – 3g. orange and blue . . . 10 10
881 – 6g. orange and green . . 10 10
882 – 20g. yellow and red . . . 15 15
MS882a 140 × 95 mm. Nos. 879/82 2·00 2·00
883 **219** 40g. blue and red (air) . . 30 30
884 – 60g. red and green . . . 75 65
885 – 100g. red and blue . . . 1·40 95
MS885a 140 × 95 mm. Nos. 883/5 8·00 8·00

DESIGNS: 3g., 60g. Hand holding scales; 6g. Hands breaking chain; 20g., 100g. "Freedom flame".

1960. U.N. Day. Flags and inscr in blue and red.

886 **220** 30c. blue (postage) . . . 10 10
887 75c. yellow 10 10
888 90c. mauve 10 10
889 3g. orange (air) 10 10
890 4g. green 10 10

221 Bridge with Arms of Brazil and Paraguay

222 Timber Truck

1961. Inauguration of International Bridge between Brazil and Paraguay.

891 **221** 15c. green (postage) . . . 10 10
892 30c. blue 10 10
893 50c. orange 10 10
894 75c. blue 15 10
895 1g. violet 10 10
896 – 3g. red (air) 15 10
897 – 12g.45 lake 30 25
898 – 18g.15 green 35 30
899 – 36g. blue 75 25
MS899a 125 × 181 mm. Nos. 896/9. Imperf . . . . 1·50 1·50

DESIGN—HORIZ: Nos. 896/9, Aerial view of bridge.

1961. Paraguayan Progress. Inscr "PARAGUAY EN MARCHA".

900 **222** 25c. red & green (postage) 10 10
901 – 90c. yellow and blue . . . 10 10
902 – 1g. red and orange . . . 10 10
903 – 2g. green and pink . . . 10 10
904 – 5g. violet and green . . . 15 10
905 **222** 12g.45 blue and buff (air) 40 25
906 – 18g.15 violet and buff . . 55 35
907 – 22g. blue and orange . . 30 40
908 – 36g. yellow, green and blue 60 50

DESIGNS: 90c., 2g., 18g.15, Motorized timber barge; 1, 5, 22g. Radio mast; 36g. Boeing 707 jetliner.

223 P. J. Caballero, J. G. R. de Francia and F. Yegros

224 "Chaco Peace"

1961. 150th Anniv of Independence. (a) 1st issue.
909 **223** 30c. green (postage) . . . 10 10
910 50c. mauve 10 10
911 90c. violet 10 10
912 1g.50 blue 10 10
913 3g. bistre 10 10
914 4g. blue 10 10
915 5g. brown 10 10
916 – 12g.45 red (air) 20 15
917 – 18g.15 blue 30 25
918 – 23g.40 green 40 30
919 – 30g. violet 45 35
920 – 36g. red 65 50
921 – 44g. brown 70 35
DESIGN: Nos. 916/21, Declaration of Independence.

(b) 2nd issue. Inscr "PAZ DEL CHACO".
922 **224** 25c. red (postage) 10 10
923 30c. green 10 10
924 50c. brown 10 10
925 1g. violet 10 10
926 2g. blue 10 10
927 – 3g. blue (air) 20 15
928 – 4g. purple 20 20
929 – 100g. green . . . . . . 1·40 1·00
DESIGN: Nos. 927/9, Clasped hands.

225 Puma

226 Arms of Paraguay

(c) 3rd issue.
930 **225** 75c. violet (postage) . . . 10 10
931 1g.50 brown 10 10
932 4g.50 green 15 10
933 10g. blue 25 20
934 – 12g.45 purple (air) 90 40
935 – 18g.15 blue . . . . . . 1·25 75
936 – 34g.80 brown . . . . . . 2·25 1·25
DESIGN: Nos. 934/6, Brazilian tapir.

(d) 4th issue.
937 **226** 15c. blue (postage) . . . 10 10
938 25c. red 10 10
939 75c. green 10 10
940 1g. red 10 10
941 3g. brown (air) 10 10
942 12g.45 mauve 25 25
943 36g. turquoise 65 30
The air stamps have a background pattern of horiz lines.

227 Grand Hotel, Guarani

(e) 5th issue.
944 **227** 50c. grey (postage) . . . 10 10
945 1g. green 10 10
946 4g.50 violet 10 10
947 – 3g. brown (air) 10 10
948 – 4g. blue 10 10
949 – 18g.15 orange 40 35
950 – 36g. red 30 50
The air stamps are similar to Type **227** but inscr "HOTEL GUARANI" in upper left corner. See also Nos. 978/85 and 997/1011.

228 Racquet, Net and Balls

1961. 28th South American Tennis Championships, Asuncion (1st issue). Centres multicoloured; border colours given.
951 **228** 35c. pink (postage) . . . 10 10
952 75c. yellow 10 10
953 1g.50 blue 10 10
954 2g.25 turquoise 10 10
955 4g. grey 15 10
MS955a 105 × 160 mm. Nos. 951/5 in block of 4 with colours changed. Imperf . . . . 8·00
956 12g.45 orange (air) 90 40
957 20g. orange . . . . 1·40 40
958 50g. orange . . . . 2·25 75
See also Nos. 978/85.

229

1961. "Europa".
959 **229** 50c. red, blue and mauve 10 10
960 75c. red, blue and green 10 10
961 1g. red, blue and brown 10 10
962 1g.50 red, blue & lt blue 10 10
963 4g.50 red, blue and yellow 20 20
MS963a 180 × 139 mm. Nos. 959/63. Imperf . . . . 4·75 4·75

230 Comm. Alan Shepard and Solar System

231

1961. Commander Shepard's Space Flight.
964 – 10c. brown and blue (postage) 10 10
965 – 25c. mauve and blue . . . 10 10
966 – 50c. orange and blue . . . 10 10
967 – 75c. green and blue . . . 10 10
968 **230** 18g.15 blue and green (air) . . . . 4·00 3·00
969 36g. blue and orange . . 4·00 3·00
970 50g. blue and mauve . . . 5·50 3·50
MS970a 124 × 94 mm. No. 970 23·00
DESIGN—HORIZ: Nos. 964/7, Comm. Shepard.

1961. World Refugee Year (2nd issue).
971 **231** 10c. deep blue and blue (postage) 10 10
972 25c. purple and orange . . 10 10
973 50c. mauve and pink . . 10 10
974 75c. blue and green . . . 10 10
975 – 18g.15 red and brown (air) 55 25
976 – 36g. green and red . . . 1·25 55
977 – 50g. orange and green . . 1·50 1·10
MS977a 119 × 80 mm. No. 977 4·25
Nos. 975/7 have a different background and frame.

232 Tennis-player

233 Scout Bugler

1962. 150th Anniv of Independence (6th issue) and 28th South American Tennis Championships, Asuncion (2nd issue).
978 **232** 35c. blue (postage) . . . 10 10
979 75c. violet 10 10
980 1g.50 brown 10 10
981 2g.25 green 10 10
982 – 4g. red (air) 10 10
983 – 12g.45 purple 60 30
984 – 20g. turquoise 80 25
985 – 50g. brown . . . . 1·60 40
Nos. 982/5 show tennis-player using backhand stroke.

1962. Boy Scouts Commemoration.
986 **233** 10c. green & pur (postage) 10 10
987 20c. green and red 10 10
988 25c. green and brown . . 10 10
989 30c. green and emerald 10 10
990 50c. green and blue . . . 10 10
991 – 12g.45 mauve & blue (air) 50 40
992 – 36g. mauve and green . . 1·50 90
993 – 50g. mauve and yellow . . 1·90 90
MS993a 128 × 101 mm. No. 993 9·50
DESIGN: Nos. 991/3, Lord Baden-Powell.

234 Pres. Stroessner and the Duke of Edinburgh

235 Map of the Americas

1962. Air. Visit of Duke of Edinburgh.
994 **234** 12g.45 blue, buff & green 20 15
995 18g.15 blue, pink and red 30 25
996 36g. blue, yellow & brown 25 20
MS996a 130 × 80 mm. No. 995 4·50

1962. 150th Anniv of Independence (7th issue) and Day of the Americas.
997 **235** 50c. orange (postage) . . 10 10
998 75c. blue 10 10
999 1g. violet 10 10
1000 1g.50 green 10 10
1001 4g.50 red 10 10
1002 – 20g. mauve (air) 30 20
1003 – 50g. orange 70 50
DESIGN: 20g., 50g. Hands supporting Globe.

236 U.N. Emblem

238 Football Stadium

237 Mosquito and W.H.O. Emblem

1962. 150th Anniv of Independence (8th issue).
1004 **236** 50c. brown (postage) . . 10 10
1005 75c. purple 10 10
1006 1g. blue 10 10
1007 2g. brown 10 10
1008 – 12g.45 violet (air) . . . 35 35
1009 – 18g.15 green 25 25
1010 – 23g.40 red 35 35
1011 – 30g. red 80 65
DESIGN: Nos. 1008/11, U.N. Headquarters, New York.

1962. Malaria Eradication.
1012 **237** 30c. black, blue and pink (postage) 10 10
1013 50c. black, green & bistre 10 10
1014 – 75c. black, bistre and red 10 10
1015 – 1g. black, bistre and green 10 10
1016 – 1g.50 black, bistre & brown 10 10
1017 **237** 3g. black, red & blue (air) 10 10
1018 4g. black, red and green 10 10
1019 – 12g.45 black, grn & brn 25 10
1020 – 18g.15 black, red and purple 90 55
1021 – 36g. black, blue and red 1·25 85
MS1021a 105 × 70 mm. No. 1021 7·50
DESIGN: Nos. 1014/16, 1019/21, Mosquito on U.N. emblem, and microscope.

1962. World Cup Football Championship, Chile.
1022 **238** 15c. brown & yell (postage) 10 10
1023 25c. brown and green . . 10 10
1024 30c. brown and violet . . 10 10
1025 40c. brown and orange 10 10
1026 50c. brown and green . . 10 10
1027 – 12g.45 black, red and violet (air) . . . . . 1·10 25
1028 – 18g.15 black, brn & vio 90 45
1029 – 36g. black, grey & brown 2·00 80
MS1029a 105 × 70 mm. No. 1029 7·50 6·50
DESIGN—HORIZ: Nos. 1027/9, Footballers and Globe.

239 "Lago Ypoa" (freighter)

1962. Paraguayan Merchant Marine Commem.
1030 **239** 30c. brown (postage) . . 15 10
1031 – 90c. blue 20 10
1032 – 1g.50 purple 25 10
1033 – 2g. green 35 15
1034 – 4g.20 blue 50 20
1035 – 12g.45 red (air) 30 15
1036 – 44g. blue 30 45
DESIGNS—HORIZ: 90c. Freighter; 1g.50, "Olympo" (freighter); 2g. Freighter (diff); 4g.20, "Rio Apa" (freighter). VERT: 12g.45, 44g. Ship's wheel.

1962. As Nos. 631, etc, but with taller figures of value.
1037 **156** 50c. blue 10 10
1038 70c. lilac 10 10
1039 1g.50 violet 10 10
1040 3g. blue 10 10
1041 4g.50 brown 10 10
1042 5g. mauve 10 10
1043 10g. mauve 20 10
1044 12g.45 blue 20 10
1045 15g.45 red 25 10
1046 18g.15 purple 10 15
1047 20g. brown 10 15
1048 50g. brown 25 30
1049 100g. grey 90 30

241 Gen. A. Stroessner

242 Popes Paul VI, John XXIII and St. Peter's

1963. Re-election of Pres. Stroessner to Third Term of Office.
1050 **241** 50c. brown and drab (postage) 10 10
1051 75c. brown and pink . . 10 10
1052 1g.50 brown and mauve 10 10
1053 3g. brown and green . . 10 10
1054 12g.45 red and pink (air) 25 20
1055 18g.15 green and pink 65 30
1056 36g. violet and pink . . 85 40

1964. Popes Paul VI and John XXIII.
1057 **242** 1g.50 yellow and red (postage) 10 10
1058 3g. green and red . . . 10 10
1059 4g. brown and red . . . 10 10
1060 – 12g.45 olive & grn (air) 35 20
1061 – 18g.15 green and violet 45 30
1062 – 36g. green and blue . . . 1·25 60
DESIGNS: Nos. 1060/2, Cathedral, Asuncion.

243 Arms of Paraguay and France

245 Map of the Americas

1964. Visit of French President.
1063 **243** 1g.50 brown (postage) 10 10
1064 – 3g. blue 40 10
1065 **243** 4g. grey 10 10
1066 – 12g.45 violet (air) . . . 25 20
1067 **243** 18g.15 green 70 30
1068 – 36g. red . . . . 1·25 60
DESIGNS: 3, 12g.45, 36g. Presidents Stroessner and De Gaulle.

1965. 6th Reunion of the Board of Governors of the Inter-American Development Bank. Optd **Centenario de la Epopeya Nacional 1,864–1,870** as in T **245**.
1069 **245** 1g.50 green (postage) . . 10 10
1070 3g. pink 10 10
1071 4g. blue 10 10
1072 12g.45 brown (air) . . . 20 10
1073 36g. violet 65 45
The overprint refers to the National Epic of 1864–70, the war with Argentina, Brazil and Uruguay and this inscription occurs on many other issues from 1965 onwards.
Nos. 1069/73 without the overprint were not authorized.

246 R. Gonzalez and St. Ignatius

247 Ruben Dario

1966. 350th Anniv of Founding of San Ignacio Guazu Monastery.
1074 **246** 15c. blue (postage) . . . 10 10
1075 25c. blue 10 10
1076 75c. blue 10 10
1077 90c. blue 10 10
1078 – 3g. brown (air) 10 10
1079 – 12g.45 brown 10 10
1080 – 18g.15 brown 20 10
1081 – 23g.40 brown 35 25
DESIGNS: Nos. 1078/81, Jesuit Fathers' house, Antigua.
For similar stamps with different inscriptions, see Nos. 822, 824 and 826.

1966. 50th Death Anniv of Ruben Dario (poet).
1082 **247** 50c. blue 10 10
1083 70c. brown 10 10
1084 1g.50 lake 10 10
1085 3g. violet 10 10
1086 4g. turquoise 10 10
1087 5g. black 10 10
1088 – 12g.45 blue (air) 10 10

1089 – 18g.15 violet 10 10
1090 – 23g.40 brown 35 10
1091 – 36g. green 65 25
1092 – 50g. red 75 25
DESIGNS: Nos. 1088/92, Open book inscr "Paraguay de Fuego ..." by Dario.

248 Lions' Emblem on Globe 249 W.H.O. Emblem

1967. 50th Anniv of Lions International.
1093 **248** 50c. violet (postage) . . 10 10
1094 70c. blue 10 10
1095 – 1g.50 blue 10 10
1096 – 3g. brown 10 10
1097 – 4g. blue 10 10
1098 – 5g. brown 10 10
1099 – 12g.45 brown (air) . . . 10 10
1100 – 18g.15 violet 15 10
1101 – 23g.40 purple 20 10
1102 – 36g. blue 25 25
1103 – 50g. red 25 25
DESIGNS—VERT: 1g.50, 3g. M. Jones; 4, 5g. Lions headquarters, Chicago. HORIZ: 12g.45, 18g.15, Library–"Education"; 23g.40, 36g., 50g. Medical laboratory–"Health".

1968. 20th Anniv of W.H.O.
1104 **249** 3g. turquoise (postage) 10 10
1105 4g. purple 10 10
1106 5g. brown 10 10
1107 10g. violet 10 10
1108 – 36g. brown (air) 40 25
1109 – 50g. red 45 30
1110 – 100g. blue 60 35
DESIGN—VERT: Nos. 1108/10, W.H.O. emblem on scroll.

250 251

1969. World Friendship Week.
1111 **250** 50c. red 10 10
1112 70c. blue 10 10
1113 1g.50 brown 10 10
1114 3g. mauve 10 10
1115 4g. green 10 10
1116 5g. violet 10 10
1117 10g. purple 20 10

1969. Air. Campaign for Houses for Teachers.
1118 **251** 36g. blue 40 20
1119 50g. brown 75 30
1120 100g. red . . . . 1·40 50

252 Pres. Lopez 253 Paraguay 2r. Stamp of 1870

1970. Death Centenary of Pres. F. Solano Lopez.
1121 **252** 1g. brown (postage) . . 10 10
1122 2g. violet 10 10
1123 3g. pink 10 10
1124 4g. red 10 10
1125 5g. blue 10 10
1126 10g. green 10 10
1127 15g. blue (air) 10 10
1128 20g. brown 20 10
1129 30g. green 55 20
1130 40g. purple 60 25

1970. Centenary of First Paraguayan Stamps.
1131 **253** 1g. red (postage) 10 10
1132 A 2g. blue 10 10
1133 B 3g. brown 10 10
1134 **253** 5g. violet 10 10
1135 A 10g. lilac 20 10
1136 B 15g. purple (air) 65 25
1137 **253** 30g. green 80 50
1138 A 36g. red 90 30
DESIGNS: First Paraguay stamps. A, 1r.; B, 3r.

254 Teacher and Pupil 255 UNICEF Emblem

1971. International Education Year–UNESCO.
1139 **254** 3g. blue (postage) . . . 10 10
1140 5g. lilac 10 10
1141 10g. green 10 10
1142 20g. red (air) 20 10
1143 25g. mauve 25 15
1144 30g. brown 25 20
1145 50g. green 40 35

1972. 25th Anniv of UNICEF.
1146 **255** 1g. brown (postage) . . 10 10
1147 2g. blue 10 10
1148 3g. red 10 10
1149 4g. purple 10 10
1150 5g. green 10 10
1151 10g. purple 10 10
1152 20g. blue (air) 20 10
1153 25g. green 25 15
1154 30g. brown 25 20

256 Acaray Dam

1972. Tourist Year of the Americas.
1155 **256** 1g. brown (postage) . . 10 10
1156 – 2g. brown 10 10
1157 – 3g. blue 10 10
1158 – 5g. red 10 10
1159 – 10g. green 10 10
1160 – 20g. red (air) 25 10
1161 – 25g. grey 30 15
1162 – 50g. lilac . . . . 1·40 45
1163 – 100g. mauve 80 40
DESIGNS: 2g. Statue of Lopez; 3g. Friendship Bridge; 5g. Rio Tebicuary Bridge; 10g. Grand Hotel, Guarani; 20g. Motor coach; 25g. Social Service Institute Hospital; 50g. Liner "Presidente Stroessner"; 100g. Lockheed Electra airliner.

257 O.E.A. Emblem

1973. 25th Anniv of Organization of American States (O.E.A.).
1164 **257** 1g. mult (postage) . . . 10 10
1165 2g. multicoloured . . . 10 10
1166 3g. multicoloured . . . 10 10
1167 4g. multicoloured . . . 10 10
1168 5g. multicoloured . . . 10 10
1169 10g. multicoloured . . . 10 10
1170 20g. multicoloured (air) 20 10
1171 25g. multicoloured . . . 30 15
1172 50g. multicoloured . . . 25 35
1173 100g. multicoloured . . 1·00 40

258 Exhibition Emblem

1973. International Industrial Exhibition, Paraguay.
1174 **258** 1g. brown (postage) . . 10 10
1175 2g. red 10 10
1176 3g. blue 10 10
1177 4g. green 10 10
1178 5g. lilac 10 10
1179 20g. mauve (air) 20 10
1180 25g. red 25 10

259 Carrier Pigeon with Letter

1975. Centenary of U.P.U.
1181 **259** 1g. violet & blk (postage) 10 10
1182 2g. red and black . . . 10 10
1183 3g. blue and black . . . 10 10
1184 5g. blue and black . . . 10 10
1185 10g. purple and black . . 10 10
1186 20g. brown & black (air) 25 15
1187 25g. green and black . . 30 20

260 Institute Buildings

1976. Inauguration (1974) of Institute of Higher Education.
1188 **260** 5g. violet, red and black (postage) 10 10
1189 10g. blue, red and black 10 10
1190 30g. brn, red & blk (air) 25 15

261 Rotary Emblem

1976. 70th Anniv of Rotary International.
1191 **261** 3g. blue, bistre and black (postage) 10 10
1192 4g. blue, bistre and mauve 10 10
1193 25g. blue, bistre and green (air) 30 15

262 Woman and I.W.Y. Emblem

1976. International Women's Year.
1194 **262** 1g. brown & blue (postage) 10 10
1195 2g. brown and red . . . 10 10
1196 20g. brown & green (air) 25 10

263 Black Palms

1977. Flowering Plants and Trees. Multicoloured.
1197 2g. Type **263** (postage) . . . 10 10
1198 3g. Mburucuya flowers . . . 10 10
1199 20g. Marsh rose (tree) (air) 35 25

264 Nanduti Lace

1977. Multicoloured.
1200 1g. Type **264** (postage) . . . 10 10
1201 5g. Nanduti weaver 10 10
1202 25g. Lady holding jar (air) 40 25

265 F. S. Lopez

1977. 150th Birth Anniv of Marshal Francisco Solano Lopez.
1203 **265** 10g. brown (postage) . . 10 10
1204 50g. blue (air) 40 50
1205 100g. green 75 60

266 General Bernardino Caballero National College

1978. Cent of National College of Asuncion.
1206 **266** 3g. red (postage) 10 10
1207 4g. blue 10 10
1208 5g. violet 10 10
1209 20g. brown (air) 20 15
1210 25g. purple 25 20
1211 30g. green 35 25

267 Marshal Jose F. Estigarribia, Trumpeter and Flag 268 Congress Emblem

1978. "Salon de Bronce" Commemoration.
1212 **267** 3g. purple, blue and red (postage) 10 10
1213 5g. violet, blue and red 10 10
1214 10g. grey, blue and red 10 10
1215 20g. green, bl & red (air) 25 15
1216 25g. violet, blue and red 30 20
1217 30g. purple, blue and red 35 25

1979. 22nd Latin American Tourism Congress, Asuncion.
1218 **268** 10g. black, blue and red (postage) 10 10
1219 50g. black, blue and red (air) 30 40

269 Spanish Colonial House, Pilar

1980. Bicentenary of Pilar City.
1220 **269** 5g. mult (postage) . . . 10 10
1221 25g. multicoloured (air) 30 20

270 Boeing 707

1980. Inauguration of Paraguayan Airlines Boeing 707 Service.
1222 **270** 20g. mult (postage) . . . 30 10
1223 100g. multicoloured (air) 1·40 70

271 Seminary, Communion Cup and Bible

1981. Air. Centenary of Metropolitan Seminary, Asuncion.
1224 **271** 5g. blue 10 10
1225 10g. brown 10 10
1226 25g. green 30 20
1227 50g. black 60 40

272 U.P.U. Monument, Berne

1981. Centenary of Admission to U.P.U.
1228 **272** 5g. red and black (postage) 10 10
1229 10g. mauve and black . . 10 10
1230 20g. green and black (air) 50 15
1231 25g. red and black . . . 60 20
1232 50g. blue and black . . . 60 40

273 St. Maria Mazzarello **275** Sun and Map of Americas

274 Stroessner and Bridge over River Itaipua

1981. Air. Death Centenary of Mother Maria Mazzarello (founder of Daughters of Mary).
1233 **273** 20g. green and black . . 50 15
1234 25g. red and black . . . 60 20
1235 50g. violet and black . . 60 40

1983. 25th Anniv of President Stroessner City.
1236 **274** 3g. green, blue & blk (postage) 10 10
1237 5g. red, blue and black 10 10
1238 10g. violet, blue and black 10 10
1239 20g. grey, blue & blk (air) 25 15
1240 25g. purple, blue & black 30 20
1241 50g. blue, grey and black 30 40

1985. Air. 25th Anniv of Inter-American Development Bank.
1242 **275** 3g. orange, yellow & pink 10 10
1243 5g. orange, yellow & mauve 10 10
1244 10g. orange, yellow & mauve 10 10
1245 50g. orange, yellow & brown 10 10
1246 65g. orange, yellow & bl 15 10
1247 95g. orange, yellow & green 20 15

276 U.N. Emblem **277** 1886 1c. Stamp

1986. Air. 40th Anniv of U.N.O.
1248 **276** 5g. blue and brown . . . 10 10
1249 10g. blue and grey . . . 10 10
1250 50g. blue and black . . . 10 10

1986. Centenary of First Official Stamp.
1251 **277** 5g. deep blue, brown and blue (postage) 10 10
1252 15g. deep blue, brown and blue 10 10
1253 40g. deep blue, brown and blue 10 10
1254 – 65g. blue, green and red (air) 15 15
1255 – 100g. blue, green and red 50 25
1256 – 150g. blue, green and red 70 40
DESIGNS: 65, 100, 150g. 1886 7c. stamp.

278 Integration of the Nations Monument, Colmena

1986. Air. 50th Anniv of Japanese Immigration. Multicoloured.
1257 5g. La Colmena vineyards (horiz) 10 10
1258 10g. Flowers of cherry tree and lapacho (horiz) . . . 10 10
1259 20g. Type **278** 10 10

279 Caballero, Stroessner and Road

1987. Centenary of National Republican Association (Colorado Party).
1260 **279** 5g. multicoloured (postage) 10 10
1261 10g. multicoloured . . . 10 10
1262 25g. multicoloured . . . 10 10
1263 – 150g. multicoloured (air) 25 40
1264 – 170g. multicoloured . . 55 20
1265 – 200g. multicoloured . . 60 25
DESIGN: 150 to 200g. Gen. Bernardino Caballero (President 1881–86 and founder of party), Pres. Alfredo Stroessner and electrification of countryside.

280 Emblem of Visit **281** Silver Mate

1988. Visit of Pope John Paul II.
1266 **280** 10g. blue and black (postage) 10 10
1267 20g. blue and black . . . 10 10
1268 50g. blue and black . . . 15 10
1269 – 100g. multicoloured (air) 55 20
1270 – 120g. multicoloured . . 65 25
1271 – 150g. multicoloured . . 80 35
DESIGN—HORIZ: 100 to 150g. Pope and Caacupe Basilica.

1988. Air. Centenary of New Germany Colony. Multicoloured.
1272 90g. Type **281** 25 10
1273 105g. Mate ("Ilex paraguayensis") plantation 30 20
1274 120g. As No. 1273 . . . . 35 25

1988. Air. 75th Anniv of Paraguay Philatelic Centre. No. 1249 optd *** 75o ANIVERSARIO DE FUNDACION CENTRO FILATELICO DEL PARAGUAY 15 JUNIO-1913 - 1988.**
1275 **276** 10g. blue and grey . . . 10 10

283 Pres. Stroessner and Government Palace

1988. Air. Re-election of President Stroessner.
1276 **283** 200g. multicoloured . . 55 25
1277 500g. multicoloured . . 1·40 90
1278 1000g. multicoloured . . 2·75 1·50

1989. "Parafil 89" Stamp Exhibition. Nos. 1268 and 1270 optd **PARAFIL 89**.
1279 **280** 50g. blue and black (postage) 15 10
1280 – 120g. multicoloured (air) 35 25

285 Green-winged Macaw

1989. Birds. Multicoloured.
1281 50g. Type **285** (postage) . . 20 20
1282 100g. Brazilian merganser (horiz) (air) 20 20
1283 300g. Greater rhea (horiz) 60 60
1284 500g. Toco toucan (horiz) 95 95
1285 1000g. Bare-faced curassow (horiz) . . . . 2·10 2·10
1286 2000g. Wagler's macaw and blue and yellow macaw 4·00 4·00

286 Anniversary Emblem

1990. Centenary of Organization of American States. Multicoloured.
1287 50g. Type **286** 10 10
1288 100g. Organization and anniversary emblems (vert) 10 10
1289 200g. Map of Paraguay . . 45 15

287 Basket **288** Flags on Map

1990. America. Pre-Columbian Life. Mult.
1290 150g. Type **287** (postage) . . 15 10
1291 500g. Guarani post (air) . . 1·10 95

1990. Postal Union of the Americas and Spain Colloquium. Multicoloured.
1292 200g. Type **288** 20 15
1293 250g. First Paraguay stamp 25 15
1294 350g. Paraguay 1990 America first day cover (horiz) 35 25

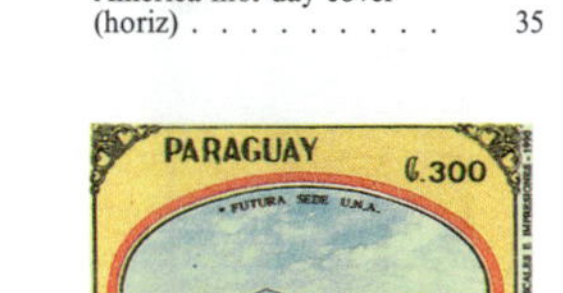

289 Planned Building

1990. Centenary of National University. Mult.
1295 300g. Type **289** 70 55
1296 400g. Present building . . . 95 75
1297 600g. Old building . . . . 1·40 1·10

290 Guarambare Church

1990. Franciscan Churches. Multicoloured.
1298 50g. Type **290** 10 10
1299 100g. Yaguaron Church . . 25 20
1300 200g. Ita Church 45 35

1991. Visit of King and Queen of Spain. Nos. 1290/1 optd **Vista de sus Majestades Los Reyes de Espana 22-24 Octubre 1990.**
1301 **287** 150g. mult (postage) . . 15 10
1302 – 500g. multicoloured (air) 1·10 95

292 "Human Rights" (Hugo Pistilli)

1991. 40th Anniv of United Nations Development Programme. Multicoloured.
1303 50g. Type **292** 10 10
1304 100g. "United Nations" (sculpture, Hermann Guggiari) 10 20
1305 150f. First Miguel de Cervantes prize, awarded to Augusto Roa Bastos, 1989 . . . . 15 10

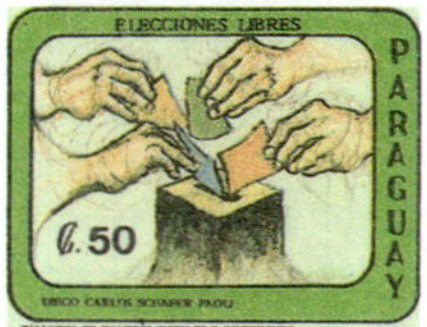

294 Hands and Ballot Box (free elections)

1991. Democracy. Multicoloured.
1308 50g. Type **294** (postage) . . 10 10
1309 100g. Sun (State and Catholic Church) (vert) 10 10
1310 200g. Arrows and male and female symbols (human rights) (vert) 55 10
1311 300g. Dove and flag (freedom of the press) (vert) (air) 50 20
1312 500g. Woman and child welcoming man (return of exiles) 70 25
1313 3000g. Crowd with banners (democracy) . . . . . . 4·75 2·75

295 Julio Manuel Morales (gynaecologist)

1991. Medical Professors.
1314 **295** 50g. mult (postage) . . . 10 10
1315 – 100g. multicoloured . . 10 10
1316 – 200g. multicoloured . . 50 10
1317 – 300g. brown, black & green 70 20
1318 – 350g. brown, black and green (air) 75 20
1319 – 500g. multicoloured . . 1·10 50
DESIGNS: 100g. Carlos Gatti (surgeon); 200g. Gustavo Gonzalez (symptomatologist); 300g. Juan Max Boettner (physician and musician); 350g. Juan Boggino (pathologist); 500g. Andres Barbero (founder of Paraguayan Red Cross).

1991. "Espamer '91" Spain–Latin America Stamp Exhibition, Buenos Aires. Nos. 1298/1300 optd **ESPAMER 91 BUENOS AIRES 5 14 Jul** and Conquistador in oval.
1323 50g. multicoloured 10 10
1324 100g. multicoloured 10 10
1325 200g. multicoloured 60 10

298 Ruy Diaz de Guzman (historian)

1991. Writers and Musicians. Multicoloured.
1326 50g. Type **298** (postage) . . 10 10
1327 100g. Maria Talavera (war chronicler) (vert) 10 10
1328 150g. Augusto Roa Bastos (writer and 1989 winner of Miguel de Cervantes Prize) (vert) 40 10
1329 200g. Jose Asuncion Flores (composer of "La Guarania") (vert) (air) . . 45 10
1330 250g. Felix Perez Cardozo (harpist and composer) . . 65 40
1331 300g. Juan Carlos Moreno Gonzalez (composer) . . 85 45

299 Battle of Tavare

1991. America. Voyages of Discovery. Mult.
1332 100g. Type **299** (postage) . . 10 10
1333 300g. Arrival of Domingo Martinez de Irala in Paraguay (air) 75 50

300 "Compass of Life" (Alfredo Moraes)

1991. Paintings. Multicoloured.
1334 50g. Type **300** (postage) . . 10 10
1335 100g. "Callejon Illuminated" (Michael Burt) 35 10
1336 150g. "Arete" (Lucy Yegros) 45 10
1337 200g. "Itinerants" (Hugo Bogado Barrios) (air) . . 50 10
1338 250g. "Travellers without a Ship" (Bernardo Ismachoviez) 65 15
1339 300g. "Guarani" (Lotte Schulz) 75 50

301 Chaco Peccary

1992. Endangered Mammals. Multicoloured.
1340 50g. Type **301** 10 10
1341 100g. Ocelot (horiz) 10 10
1342 150g. Brazilian tapir 35 10
1343 200g. Maned wolf 40 10

302 Geometric Design, Franciscan Church, Caazapa

1992. 500th Anniv of Discovery of America by Columbus (1st series). Church Roof Tiles. Mult.
1344 50g. Type **302** 10 10
1345 100g. Church, Jesuit church, Trinidad 10 10
1346 150g. Missionary ship, Jesuit church, Trinidad 50 10
1347 200g. Plant, Franciscan church, Caazapa 50 10
See also Nos. 1367/71.

1992. "Granada '92" International Thematic Stamp Exhibition. Nos. 1344/7 optd **GRANADA '92** and emblem.
1348 50g. multicoloured 10 10
1349 100g. multicoloured 10 10
1350 150g. multicoloured 40 10
1351 200g. multicoloured 50 10

304 Malcolm L. Norment (founder) and Emblem

1992. 68th Anniv of Paraguay Leprosy Foundation. Multicoloured.
1352 50g. Type **304** 10 10
1353 250g. Gerhard Hansen (discoverer of leprosy bacillus) 50 15

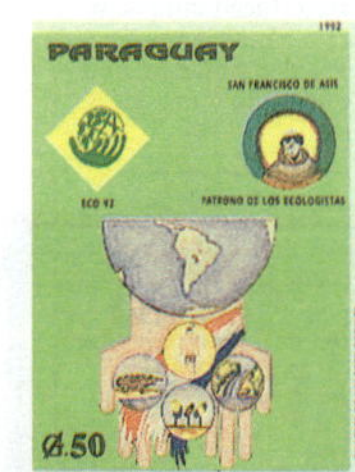

305 Southern Hemisphere and Ecology Symbols on Hands

1992. 2nd United Nations Conference on Environment and Development, Rio de Janeiro. Multicoloured.
1354 50g. Type **305** 10 10
1355 100g. Butterfly and chimneys emitting smoke 10 10
1356 250g. Tree and map of South America on globe 45 15

306 Factories and Cotton (economy)

1992. National Population and Housing Census. Multicoloured.
1357 50g. Type **306** 10 10
1358 200g. Houses (vert) 15 10
1359 250g. Numbers and stylized people (population) (vert) 20 15
1360 300g. Abacus (education) . . 50 20

307 Football

1992. Olympic Games, Barcelona. Multicoloured.
1361 50g. Type **307** 10 10
1362 100g. Tennis 10 10
1363 150g. Running 10 10
1364 200g. Swimming (horiz) . . 15 10
1365 250g. Judo 20 15
1366 350g. Fencing (horiz) . . . 50 20

308 Brother Luis Bolanos

1992. 500th Anniv of Discovery of America by Columbus (2nd series). Evangelists. Mult.
1367 50g. Type **308** (translator of Catechism into Guarani and founder of Guarani Christian settlements) . . 10 10
1368 100g. Brother Juan de San Bernardo (Franciscan and first Paraguayan martyr) 10 10
1369 150g. St. Roque Gonzalez de Santa Cruz (Jesuit missionary and first Paraguayan saint) 10 10
1370 200g. Fr. Amancio Gonzalez (founder of Melodia settlement) 15 10
1371 250g. Mgr. Juan Sinforiano Bogarin (first Archbishop of Asuncion) (vert) . . . 45 15

309 Fleet approaching Shore

1992. America. 500th Anniv of Discovery of America by Columbus. Multicoloured.
1372 150g. Type **309** (postage) . . 30 10
1373 350g. Christopher Columbus (vert) (air) 50 20

1992. 30th Anniv of United Nations Information Centre in Paraguay. Nos. 1354/6 optd **NACIONES UNIDAS 1992 - 30 AÑOS CENTRO INFORMACION ONU EN PARAGUAY**.
1374 50g. multicoloured 10 10
1375 100g. multicoloured 10 10
1376 250g. multicoloured 45 15

1992. Christmas. Nos. 1367/9 optd **Navidad 92**.
1377 50g. multicoloured 10 10
1378 100g. multicoloured 10 10
1379 150g. multicoloured 35 10

1992. "Parafil 92" Paraguay–Argentina Stamp Exhibition, Buenos Aires. Nos. 1372/3 optd **PARAFIL 92**.
1380 150g. multicoloured (postage) 35 10
1381 350g. multicoloured (air) . . 50 20

313 Planting and Hoeing

1992. 50th Anniv of Pan-American Agricultural Institute. Multicoloured.
1382 50g. Type **313** 10 10
1383 100g. Test tubes 10 10
1384 200g. Cotton plant in cupped hands 15 10
1385 250g. Cattle and maize plant 45 15

314 Yolanda Bado de Artecona

1992. Centenary of Paraguayan Writers' College. Multicoloured.
1386 50g. Type **314** 10 10
1387 100g. Jose Ramon Silva . . 10 10
1388 150g. Abelardo Brugada Valpy 10 10
1389 200g. Tomas Varela 15 10
1390 250g. Jose Livio Lezcano . . 45 15
1391 300g. Francisco I. Fernandez 50 20

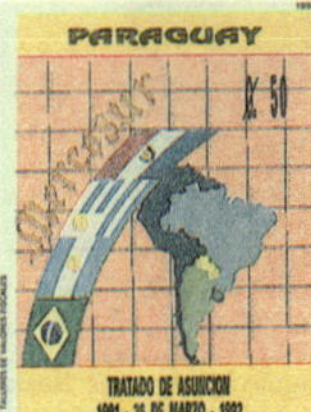

315 Members' Flags and Map of South America

316 Orange Flowers (Gilda Hellmers)

1993. 1st Anniv (1992) of Treaty of Asuncion forming Mercosur (common market of Argentina, Brazil, Paraguay and Uruguay). Multicoloured.
1392 50g. Type **315** 10 10
1393 350g. Flags encircling globe showing map of South America 65 20

1993. 50th Anniv of St. Isabel Leprosy Association. Flower paintings by artists named. Multicoloured.
1394 50g. Type **316** 10 10
1395 200g. Luis Alberto Balmelli 15 10
1396 250g. Lili del Monico . . . 20 15
1397 350g. Brunilde Guggiari . . 50 20

317 Goethe (after J. Lips) and Manuscript of Poem

1993. Centenary of Goethe College.
1398 **317** 50g. brown, black & blue 10 10
1399 – 200g. multicoloured . . 40 10
DESIGN: 200g. Goethe (after J. Tischbein).

1993. "Brasiliana 93" International Stamp Exhibition, Rio de Janeiro. Nos. 1398/9 optd **BRASILIANA 93**.
1400 50g. brown, black and blue 10 10
1401 200g. multicoloured 15 10

319 Palace (Michael Burt)

1993. Centenary (1992) of Los Lopez (Government) Palace, Asuncion. Paintings of palace by artists named. Multicolured.
1402 50g. Type **319** 10 10
1403 100g. Esperanza Gill 10 10
1404 200g. Emili Aparici 15 10
1405 250g. Hugo Bogado Barrios (vert) 15 10

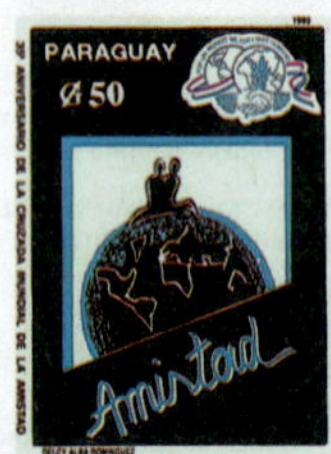

320 Couple sitting on Globe and Emblem

1993. 35th Anniv of World Friendship Crusade.
1406 **320** 50g. black, blue and mauve 10 10
1407 – 100g. multicoloured . . 10 10
1408 – 200g. multicoloured . . 15 10
1409 – 250g. multicoloured . . 15 10
DESIGNS: 100g. Dr. Ramon Artemio Bracho (founder), map of Americas and emblem; 200g. Children and sun emerging from cloud; 250g. Couple hugging and emblem.

1993. Inauguration of President Juan Carlos Wasmosy. Nos. 1402/5 optd **TRANSMISION DEL MANDO PRESIDENCIAL GRAL. ANDRES RODRIGUEZ ING. JUAN C. WASMOSY 15 DE AGOSTO 1993.**
1410 50g. multicoloured 10 10
1411 100g. multicoloured 10 10
1412 200g. multicoloured 15 10
1413 250g. multicoloured 15 10

322 "Church of the Incarnation" (Juan Guerra Gaja)

1993. Centenary of Church of the Incarnation. Paintings. Multicoloured.
1414 50g. Type **322** 10 10
1415 350g. "Church of the Incarnation" (Hector Blas Ruiz) (horiz) 25 20

323 Bush Dog

1993. America. Endangered Animals. Mult.
1416 250g. Type **323** (postage) . . 40 10
1417 50g. Great anteater (air) . . 10 10

1993. 80th Anniv of World Food Programme. Nos. 1383/4 optd **'30 ANOS DEL PROGRAMA MUNDIAL DE ALIMENTOS'** and emblem.
1418 100g. multicoloured 10 10
1419 200g. multicoloured 15 10

325 Children Carol-singing

1993. Christmas. Multicoloured.
1420 50g. Type **325** 10 10
1421 250g. Wise men following star 15 10

326 Boy and Girl Scouts

1993. 80th Anniv of Paraguay Scouts Association. Multicoloured.
1422 50g. Type **326** 10 10
1423 100g. Boy scouts in camp 10 10
1424 200g. Lord Robert Baden-Powell (founder of Scouting movement) . . . 15 10
1425 250g. Girl scout with flag 15 10

327 Cecilio Baez

1994. Centenary of First Graduation of Lawyers from National University, Asuncion.
1426 **327** 50g. red and crimson . . 10 10
1427 – 100g. yellow and orange 10 10
1428 – 250g. yellow and green 15 10
1429 – 500g. blue and deep blue 30 20
DESIGNS—VERT: 100g. Benigno Riquelme. HORIZ: 250g. Emeterio Gonzalez; 500g. J. Gaspar Villamayor.

328 Basketball 329 Penalty Kick

1994. 50th Anniv of Phoenix Sports Association. Multicoloured.
1430 50g. Type **328** 10 10
1431 200g. Football 15 10
1432 250g. Pedro Andres Garcia Arias (founder) and tennis (horiz) 15 10

1994. World Cup Football Championship, U.S.A. Multicoloured.
1433 250g. Type **329** 15 10
1434 500g. Tackle 55 20
1435 1000g. Dribbling ball past opponent . . . . 1·10 75

330 Runner

1994. Centenary of International Olympic Committee. Multicoloured.
1436 350g. Type **330** 25 20
1437 400g. Athlete lighting Olympic Flame 55 20

331 World Map and Emblem

1994. World Congress of International Federation for Physical Education, Asuncion. Multicoloured.
1438 200g. Type **331** 15 10
1439 1000g. Family exercising and flag (vert) . . . . . 1·25 80

1994. Brazil, Winners of World Cup Football Championship. Nos. 1433/5 optd **BRASIL Campeon Mundial de Futbol Estados Unidos '94**.
1440 250g. multicoloured 40 10
1441 500g. multicoloured 80 50
1442 1000g. multicoloured . . . 1·60 95

1994. 25th Anniv of First Manned Moon Landing. No. 1407 optd **25 Anos, Conquista de la Luna por el hombre 1969 - 1994**.
1443 100g. multicoloured 10 10

334 Barrios

1994. 50th Death Anniv of Agustin Pio Barrios Mangore (guitarist). Multicoloured.
1444 250g. Type **334** 15 10
1445 500g. Barrios wearing casual clothes and a hat 65 20

335 Police Commandant, 1913

1994. 151st Anniv of Police Force. Multicoloured.
1446 50g. Type **335** 10 10
1447 250g. Carlos Bernardino Cacabelos (first Commissioner) and Pedro Nolasco Fernandez (first Chief of Asuncion Police Dept) 15 10

336 Maguari Stork

1994. "Parafil 94" Stamp Exhibition. Birds. Mult.
1448 100g. Type **336** 35 35
1449 150g. Yellow-billed cardinal 35 35
1450 400g. Green kingfisher (vert) 2·00 75
1451 500g. Jabiru (vert) . . . . . 2·25 75

337 Nicolas Copernicus and Eclipse

1994. Total Eclipse of the Sun, November 1994. Astronomers. Multicoloured.
1452 50g. Type **337** 10 10
1453 200g. Johannes Kepler and sun dial, St. Cosmas and Damian Jesuit settlement 15 10

338 Steam Locomotive

1994. America. Postal Transport. Multicoloured.
1454 100g. Type **338** . . . . . . 1·00 60
1455 1000g. Express mail motor cycle . . . . 1·25 80

339 Mother and Child

1994. International Year of the Family. Details of paintings by Olga Blinder. Multicoloured.
1456 50g. Type **339** 10 10
1457 250g. Mother and children 15 10

340 Holy Family and Angels

1994. Christmas. Ceramic Figures. Multicoloured.
1458 150g. Type **340** 10 10
1459 700g. Holy Family (vert) . . 80 55

341 Red Cross Workers and Dr. Andres Barbero (founder)

1994. 75th Anniv of Paraguay Red Cross. Mult.
1460 150g. Scouts, anniversary emblem and Henri Dunant (founder of International Red Cross) 10 10
1461 700g. Type **341** 80 55

342 Sculpture by Herman Guggiari and Pope John Paul II

1994. 90th Anniv of San Jose College. Mult.
1462 200g. Type **342** 15 10
1463 250g. College entrance and Pope John Paul II 15 10

343 Pasteur and Hospital Facade

1995. Paraguayan Red Cross. Death Centenary of Louis Pasteur (chemist) and Centenary of Clinical Hospital.
1464 **343** 1000g. multicoloured . . 1·10 75

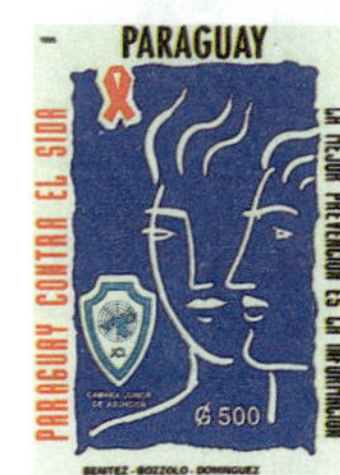

344 Couple

1995. Anti-AIDS Campaign. Multicoloured.
1465 500g. Type **344** 60 20
1466 1000g. Sad and happy blood droplets . . . . 1·00 50

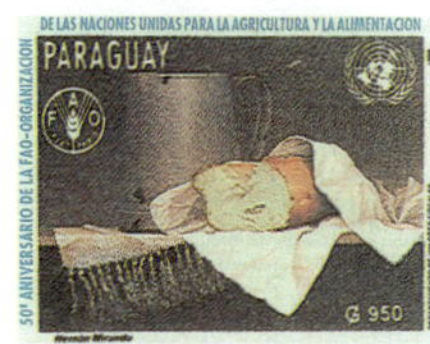

345 Jug and Loaf

1995. 50th Anniv of F.A.O. Paintings by Hernan Miranda. Multicoloured.
1467 950g. Type **345** . . . . . . 1·00 75
1468 2000g. Melon and leaf . . . 2·10 1·40

346 Olive-backed Warbler

1995. 5th Neo-tropical Ornithological Congress, Asuncion. Multicoloured.
1469 100g. Type **346** 10 10
1470 200g. Swallow-tailed manakin 15 10
1471 600g. Troupial 65 30
1472 1000g. Hooded siskin . . . 1·00 75

347 River Monday Rapids

348 "100"

1995. 5th International Town, Ecology and Tourism Symposium. Multicoloured.
1473 1150g. Type **347** 1·25 85
1474 1300g. Aregua railway station 4·50 2·75

1995. Centenary of Volleyball.
1475 **348** 300g. multicoloured 20 15
1476 – 600g. blue and black 40 30
1477 – 1000g. multicoloured 1·00 75
DESIGNS: 600g. Ball hitting net; 1000g. Hands, ball and net.

349 Macizo, Acahay

1995. America. Environmental Protection. Mult.
1478 950g. Type **349** 85 45
1479 2000g. Tinfunque Reserve, Chaco (vert) 1·60 1·00

350 Anniversary Emblem

1995. 50th Anniv of U.N.O. Multicoloured.
1480 200g. Type **350** 15 10
1481 3000g. Stylized figures supporting emblem 3·25 2·00

351 Couple holding Star

1995. Christmas. Multicoloured.
1482 200g. Type **351** 15 10
1483 1000g. Crib 95 50

352 Marti and "Hedychium coronarium"

1995. Birth Cent of Jose Marti (revolutionary). Multicoloured.
1484 200g. Type **352** 10 10
1485 1000g. Marti, Cuban national flag and "Hedychium coronarium" (horiz) 1·10 50

353 "Railway Station" (Asuncion)

1996. 25th Latin American and Caribbean Forum of Lions International. Paintings by Esperanza Gill. Multicoloured.
1486 200g. Type **353** 10 10
1487 1000g. "Viola House" 1·10 70

354 "Cattleya nobilior"

1996. Orchids. Multicoloured.
1488 100g. Type **354** 10 10
1489 200g. "Oncidium varicosum" 10 10
1490 1000g. "Oncidium jonesianum" (vert) 1·00 45
1491 1150g. "Sophronitis cernua" 1·10 55

355 Emblems and Gymnast on "Stamp"

1996. Centenary of Modern Olympic Games and Olympic Games, Atlanta. Multicoloured.
1492 500g. Type **355** 30 20
1493 1000g. Emblems and runner on "stamp" 60 45

356 Bosco, Monks and Boys

1996. Centenary of Salesian Brothers in Paraguay. Multicoloured.
1494 200g. Type **356** 10 10
1495 300g. Madonna and Child, Pope John Paul II and St. John Bosco (vert) 15 10
1496 1000g. St. John Bosco (founder) and map 40 20

357 Family Outing (Silvia Cacares Baez)

1996. 50th Anniv of UNICEF. Multicoloured.
1497 1000g. Type **357** 50 30
1498 1300g. Families (Cinthia Perez Alderete) 65 40

358 Pope John Paul II, Caacupe Cathedral and Virgin

359 Woman

1996. Our Lady of Caacupe. Multicoloured.
1499 200g. Type **358** 10 10
1500 1300g. Pope John Paul II, floodlit cathedral and Virgin (horiz) 65 40

1996. America. Traditional Costumes. Mult.
1501 500g. Type **359** 25 20
1502 1000g. Couple 50 30

360 Boxes and Food

1996. International Year for Eradication of Poverty. Multicoloured.
1503 1000g. Type **360** 50 30
1504 1150g. Boy with boxes and food (vert) 55 30

361 Mother and Baby

362 "Eryphanis automedon"

1996. Christmas. Multicoloured.
1505 200g. Type **361** 10 10
1506 1000g. Mother with smiling child 50 30

1997. Butterflies. Multicoloured.
1507 200g. Type **362** 10 10
1508 500g. "Dryadula phaetusa" 25 15
1509 1000g. "Vanessa myrinna" 50 30
1510 1150g. Rare tiger 55 30

363 First Government Palace (legislative building)

1997. Buildings. Multicoloured.
1511 200g. Type **363** 10 10
1512 1000g. Patri Palace (postal headquarters) 50 30

364 Crucifix, Piribebuy

1997. Year of Jesus Christ.
1513 **364** 1000g. multicoloured 50 30

365 Summit Emblem

1997. 11th Group of Rio Summit Meeting, Asuncion.
1514 **365** 1000g. multicoloured 40 20

366 Cactus

1997. "The Changing Climate—Everyone's Concern". Plants. Multicoloured.
1515 300g. Type **366** 15 10
1516 500g. "Bromelia balansae" (vert) 20 10
1517 1000g. "Monvillea kroenlaini" 40 20

367 Tiger Cat

1997. 1st Mercosur (South American Common Market), Chile and Bolivia Stamp Exhibition, Asuncion. Mammals. Multicoloured.
1518 200g. Type **367** 10 10
1519 1000g. Black howler monkey (vert) 40 20
1520 1150g. Paca 50 30

368 Members' Flags and Southern Cross

1997. 6th Anniv of Mercosur (South American Common Market).
1521 **368** 1000g. multicoloured 40 20

369 Postman and Letters circling Globe

370 Neri Kennedy (javelin)

1997. America. The Postman. Multicoloured.
1522 1000g. Type **369** 40 20
1523 1150g. Weather and terrain aspects of postal delivery and postman (horiz) 50 30

1997. 50th Anniv of National Sports Council. Multicoloured.
1524 200g. Type **370** 10 10
1525 1000g. Ramon Milciades Gimenez Gaona (discus) 40 20

1997. "Mevifil '97" First International Exhibition of Philatelic Audio-visual and Computer Systems, Buenos Aires, Argentina. Nos. 1446/7 optd **MEVIFIL '97**.
1526 50g. multicoloured 10 10
1527 250g. multicoloured 10 10

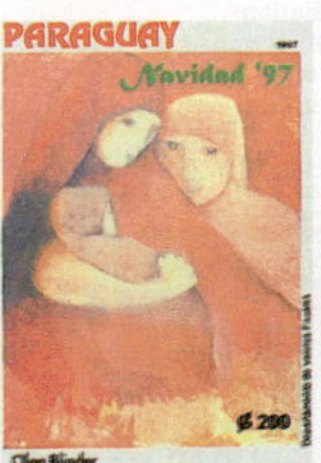

372 Mother and Child (Olga Blinder)

373 Boy

1997. Christmas. Multicoloured.
1528 200g. Type **372** 10 10
1529 1000g. Mother and child (Hernan Miranda) 40 20

1997. "Children of the World with AIDS". Children's Paintings. Multicoloured.
1530 500g. Type **373** 20 10
1531 1000g. Girl 40 20

374 Drinking Vessel and Emblem forming "70"

375 Julio Cesar Romero (1986 World Cup team member)

1997. 70th Anniv of Asuncion Rotary Club.
1532 **374** 1150g. multicoloured . . 50 30

1998. World Cup Football Championship, France. Multicoloured.
1533 200g. Type **375** 10 10
1534 500g. Carlos Gamarra (World Cup team member) tackling opponent 20 10
1535 1000g. World Cup team (horiz) 40 20

376 Silver Tetra

1998. Fishes. Multicoloured.
1536 200g. Type **376** 10 10
1537 300g. Spotted sorubim . . . 15 10
1538 500g. Dorado 20 10
1539 1000g. Pira jagua 40 20

377 Painting by Carlos Colombino

378 Cep

1998. Paintings by artists named. Multicoloured.
1540 200g. Type **377** 10 10
1541 300g. Felix Toranzos . . . 15 10
1542 400g. Edith Gimenez . . . 15 10
1543 1000g. Ricardo Migliorisi (horiz) 40 20

1998. Fungi. Multicoloured.
1544 400g. Type **378** 15 10
1545 600g. Parasol mushroom . . 25 15
1546 1000g. Collared earthstar . . 40 20

379 Carlos Lopez's House, Botanical and Zoological Gardens, Asuncion

1998. 50th Anniv of Organization of American States. Multicoloured.
1547 500g. Type **379** 20 10
1548 1000g. Villa Palmerola, Aregua 40 20

380 Door of Sanctuary, Caazapa Church

1998. 400th Anniv of Ordination of First Paraguayan Priests by Brother Hernando de Trejo y Sanabria. Multicoloured.
1549 400g. Type **380** 15 10
1550 1700g. Statue of St. Francis of Assisi, Atyra Church (horiz) 70 40

381 "Acacia caven"

1998. Flowers. Multicoloured.
1551 100g. Type **381** 10 10
1552 600g. "Cordia trichotoma" 25 15
1553 1900g. "Glandularia" sp. . . 80 45

382 Ruins of the Mission of Jesus, Itapua

1998. Mercosur (South American Common Market) Heritage Sites.
1554 **382** 5000g. multicoloured . . 2·10 1·25

383 Serafina Davalos (first female lawyer in Paraguay) and National College

1998. America. Famous Women. Multicoloured.
1555 1600g. Type **383** 60 35
1556 1700g. Adela Speratti (first director) and Teachers' Training College 65 35

384 Abstract (Carlos Colombino)

1998. 50th Anniv of Universal Declaration of Human Rights. Multicoloured.
1557 500g. Type **384** 20 10
1558 1000g. Man on crutches (after Joel Filartiga) . . . 40 20

385 Crib

1998. Christmas. Multicoloured.
1559 300g. Type **385** 10 10
1560 1600g. Crib (different) (vert) 60 35

386 Coral Cobra

1999. Reptiles. Multicoloured.
1561 100g. Type **386** 10 10
1562 300g. Ground lizard 10 10
1563 1600g. Red-footed tortoise 65 35
1564 1700g. Paraguay caiman . . 70 40

1999. "Chaco Peace 99" Stamp Exhibition, Paraguay and Bolivia. No. 1542 optd **1era. Exposicion Filatelica Paraguayo-Boliviana PAZ DEL CHACO 99**.
1565 400g. multicoloured 15 10

388 Painting by Ignacio Nunes Soler

1999. Paintings. Showing paintings by named artists.
1566 500g. Type **388** 20 10
1567 1600g. Modesto Delgado Rodas 65 35
1568 1700g. Jaime Bestard . . . 70 40

389 Carlos Humberto Parades being tackled

1999. American Cup Football Championship, Paraguay. Multicoloured.
1569 300g. Type **389** 10 10
1570 500g. South American Football Federation Building, Luque, Paraguay (horiz) 20 10
1571 1900g. Feliciano Caceres Stadium, Luque (horiz) 75 45

390 Toucan

1999. 50th Anniv of S.O.S. Children's Villages. Multicoloured.
1572 1700g. Type **390** 70 40
1573 1900g. Toucan (different) (vert) 75 45

391 Government Palace

1999. Assassination of Dr. Luis Marua Argana (Vice-president, 1998–99). Multicoloured.
1574 100g. Type **391** 10 10
1575 500g. Dr. Argana (vert) . . 20 10
1576 1500g. Crowd before National Congress building 60 35

392 *Cochlospermum regium*

1999. Medicinal Plants. Multicoloured.
1577 600g. Type **392** 25 10
1578 700g. *Borago officinalis* . . 30 15
1579 1700g. *Passiflora cincinnata* 70 40

393 "The Man who carries the Storm"

1999. America. A New Millennium without Arms. Showing paintings by Ricardo Migliorisi. Mult.
1580 1500g. Type **393** 60 35
1581 3000g. "The Man who dominates the Storm" (vert) . . . . 1·25 75

394 "Couple" (Olga Blinder)

1999. International Year of the Elderly. Mult.
1582 1000g. Type **394** 40 20
1583 1900g. "Old Woman" (Marma de los Reyes Omella Herrero) (vert) . . 75 45

395 "Mother and Child" (Manuel Viedma)

1999. Christmas. Multicoloured.
1584 300g. Type **395** 10 10
1585 1600g. "Nativity" (Federico Ordinana) 65 35

396 *Tabebuia impetiginosa*

1999. Centenary of Pedro Juan Caballero City. Multicoloured.
1586 1000g. Type **396** 40 20
1587 1600g. *Tabebuia pulcherrima* (vert) 65 35

397 Oratory of the Virgin Our Lady of the Assumption and National Mausoleum

1999. 40th Anniv of Inter-American Development Bank. Multicoloured.
1588 600g. Type **397** 25 15
1589 700g. Government Palace 30 15

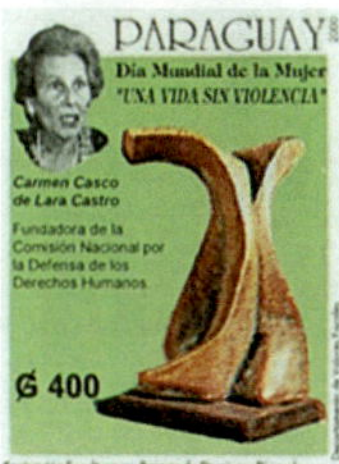

398 Carmen Casco de Lara Castro and "Conjunction" (bronze sculpture, Domingo Rivarola)

2000. International Women's Day. Carmen Casco de Lara Castro (founder of National Commission for Human Rights). Multicoloured.

1590 400g. Type **398** 15 10
1591 2000g. Carmen Casco de Lara Castro and "Violation" (bronze sculpture, Gustavo Beckelman) 80 45

399 Hydroelectric Dam, Yacyreta, and Marsh Deer

2000. "EXPO 2000" World's Fair, Hanover, Germany. Showing bi-lateral development projects. Multicoloured.

1592 500g. Type **399** (Paraguay–Argentine Republic) . . . 20 10
1593 2500g. Hydroelectric dam, Itaipu and Brazilian tapir (Paraguay–Brazil) . . . . 1·00 60

400 Students and Pope John Paul II

2000. Centenary of the Daughters of Maria Auxiliadora College. Multicoloured.

1594 600g. Type **400** 25 15
1595 2000g. College building . . 80 45

401 Footballers chasing Ball

2000. Olympic Games, Sydney. Multicoloured.

1596 2500g. Type **401** 70 40
1597 3000g. Francisco Rojas Soto (athlete), Munich Olympics, 1972 (horiz) . . 85 50

402 Adult Hands protecting Child (Nahuel Moreno Lezcano)

2000. 10th Anniv of United Nations Convention on the Rights of the Child. Multicoloured.

1598 1500g. Type **402** 45 25
1599 1700g. Hand prints (Claudia Alessandro Irala Chavez) (horiz) 50 30

403 Firemen attending to Fire

2000. 95th Anniv of Fire Service. Multicoloured.

1600 100g. Type **403** 10 10
1601 200g. Badge and fireman wearing 1905 dress uniform 10 10
1602 1500g. Firemen attending fire (horiz) 45 25
1603 1600g. Firemen using hose (horiz) 45 25

404 Stretch of Road from San Bernardino to Altos

2000. Road Development Scheme. Multicoloured.

1604 500g. Type **404** 15 10
1605 3000g. Gaspar Rodriguez de Francia motorway 85 50

405 Signpost and Emblem

2000. America. AIDS Awareness Campaign. Mult.

1606 1500g. Type **405** 45 25
1607 2500g. Ribbon emblem on noughts and crosses grid 70 40

406 "Love and Peace" (metal sculpture, Hugo Pistilli)

2000. International Year of Culture and Peace. Multicoloured.

1608 500g. Type **406** 15 10
1609 2000g. "For Peace" (metal sculpture, Herman Guggiari) 60 35

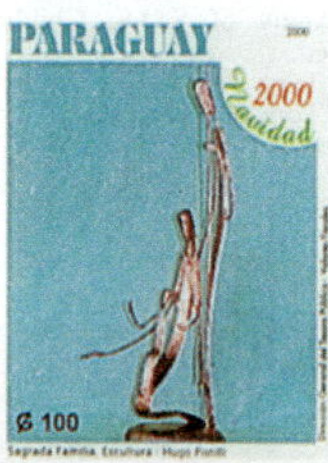

407 "Holy Family" (metal sculpture, Hugo Pistilli)

2000. Christmas. Multicoloured.

1610 100g. Type **407** 10 10
1611 500g. Poem, pen and Jose Luis Appleyard (poet and writer) 15 10
1612 2000g. Nativity (crib firgures) (horiz) 65 35

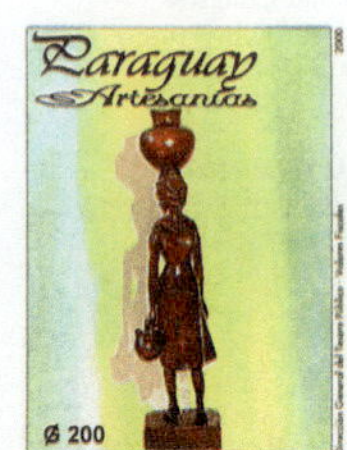

408 Country Woman (sculpture, Behage)

2000. Art. Multicoloured.

1613 200g. Type **408** 10 10
1614 1500g. Drinking vessels (Quintin Velazquez) (horiz) 45 25
1615 2000g. Silver orchid brooch (Quirino Torres) 65 35

409 Flores

2000. 30th Birth Anniv (2002) of Jose Asuncion Flores (musician). Multicoloured.

1616 100g. Type **409** 10 10
1617 1500g. Violin 45 25
1618 2500g. Trombone 70 40

410 Presidents of Argentina, Brazil, Paraguay and Uruguay signing Treaty

2001. 10th Anniv of Asuncion Treaty (cooperation treaty). Multicoloured.

1619 500g. Type **410** 15 10
1620 2500g. Map of South America (vert) 70 40

411 *Opuntia*

2001. Cacti. Multicoloured.

1621 2000g. Type **411** 65 35
1622 2500g. *Cerus stenogonus* . . 70 40

412 Three Players

2001. Under 20's Football Championship, Argentina. Multicoloured.

1623 2000g. Type **412** 65 35
1624 2500g. Two players (vert) 70 40

413 Holando Cow (Friesian)

2001. Cattle. Multicoloured.

1625 200g. Type **413** 10 10
1626 500g. Nelore bull (Brahmin) 15 10
1627 1500g. Pampa Chaqueno bull 45 25

414 Donkey Riders (Josefina Pla)

2001. Xylographs (wood engravings).

1628 **414** 500g. multicoloured . . 15 10
1629 – 500g. multicoloured (vert) 15 10
1630 – 1500g. black, green and lemon 45 25
1631 – 2000g. multicoloured . . 65 35

DESIGNS: 500g. Type **414**; 500g. Women (Leonor Cecotto); 1500g. Frog (Jacinta Rivero); 2000g. (Livio Abramo).

415 Eichu (Pleiades)

2001. Guarani (Native Americans) Mythology. Multicoloured.

1632 100g. Type **415** 10 10
1633 600g. Mborevi Rape (Milky Way) 25 15
1634 1600g. Jagua Ho'u Jasy (Eclipse of the moon) . . 50 30

416 Inocencio Lezcano

2001. Teachers' Day. Multicoloured.

1635 200g. Type **416** 10 10
1636 1600g. Ramon Cardozo . . 50 30

417 Jesuit Mission Ruins, Trinidad and St. Ignacio de Loyola (statue)

2001. America. Cultural Heritage. Multicoloured.

1637 500g. Type **417** 15 10
1638 2000g. Ruins (different) . . 65 35

Nos. 1637/8 were issued together, se-tenant, in strips of two stamps and two labels, the whole forming a composite design.

418 Children encircling Globe

2001. United Nations Year of Dialogue among Civilization.

1639 **418** 3000g. multicoloured . . 1·00 55

419 Dough Nativity (Gladys Feliciangeli)

2001. Christmas. Multicoloured.

1640 700g. Type **419** 35 20
1641 4000g. Clay and banana leaf Nativity (Mercedes Servin) 1·30 70

420 World Trade Buildings, New York

2001. "No to Terrorism". Multicoloured.
1642 500g. Type **420** 15 10
1643 5000g. Chain links changing to doves and flags (horiz) 1·40 80

421 *Passiflora carulea*

2001. 10th Anniv of Mercosur (South American Common Market).
1644 **421** 4000g. multicoloured . . 1·30 70

422 Tree Frog (*Phyllomedusa sauvagei*)

2002. Scout Jamboree, Loma Plata.
1645 **422** 6000g. multicoloured . . 2·00 95

423 Rowers, Club Building and Cormorant

2002. Centenary of "El Mbigua" (cormorant) Social Club.
1646 **423** 700g. multicoloured . . 35 20

424 "The Pieta" (statue)

2002. 25th Anniv of Juan de Salzar Cultural Centre, Asuncion. Multicoloured.
1647 2500g. Type **424** 70 40
1648 5000g. St. Michael (statue) 1·40 80

425 Team Members

2002. Football World Cup Championships, Japan and South Korea.
1649 **425** 3000g. multicoloured . . 90 50

426 Mennonite Church, Filadelfia

2002. 75th Anniv of Arrival of Mennonite Christians. Multicoloured.
1650 2000g. Type **426** 65 35
1651 4000g. Church, Loma Plata 1·30 70

427 Criollo Mare and Foal

2002. Horses. Multicoloured.
1652 700g. Type **427** 35 20
1653 1000g. Quarto de Milla . . 40 25
1654 6000g. Arabian . . . . . . 2·00 95

428 Players holding Cup

2002. Centenary of Olimpia Football Club.
1655 **428** 700g. multicoloured . . 35 20

429 *Stevia rebaudiana*

2002. Centenary of Pan American Health Organization. Multicoloured.
1656 4000g. Type **429** 90 50
1657 5000g. *Ilex paraguayensis* . . 1·30 70

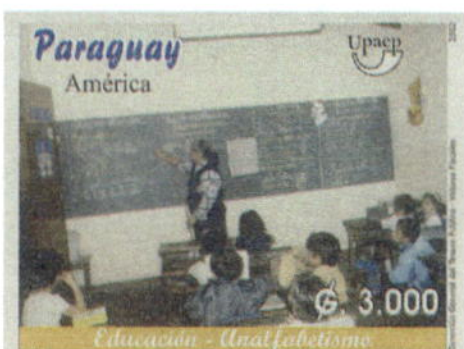

432 Teacher and Class

2002. America. Literacy Campaign. Multicoloured.
1661 3000g. Type **432** 90 50
1662 6000g. Children playing . . 2·00 95

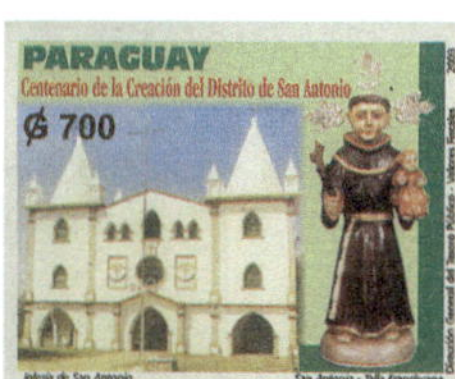

435 San Antonio Church and Saint Anthony (statue)

2003. Centenary of San Antonio District.
1667 **435** 700g. multicoloured . . 35 20

436 Decorated Plate and Josefina Pla

2003. Birth Centenary of Josefina Pla (ceramist and writer). Multicoloured.
1668 700g. Type **436** 35 20
1669 6000g. Josefina Pla and engraving . . . . 2·00 95

437 Blue-fronted Amazon (*Amazona aestiva*)

2003. Parrots. Multicoloured.
1670 1000g. Type **437** 40 25
1671 2000g. Monk parrot (*Myiopsitta monachus*) . . 65 35
1673 4000g. White-eyed conure (*Aratinga leucophtalmus*) 90 50

438 Legislative Palace

2003. Inauguration of New Legislative Palace.
1674 **438** 4000g. multicoloured . . 90 50

439 Pope John Paul II and Our Lady of Ascuncion Church

2003. 25th Anniv of Pontificate of Pope John Paul II.
1675 **439** 6000g. multicoloured . . 2·00 95

440 Pig

2003. Domestic Animals. Multicoloured.
1676 1000g. Type **440** 40 25
1677 3000g. Sheep 90 50
1678 8000g. Goat . . . . 2·50 1·40

441 Sweets

2003. Gastronomy. Multicoloured.
1679 700g. Type **441** 35 20
1680 2000g. Sopa Paraguaya (cake) 65 35
1681 3000g. Chipa (bread) . . . 90 50

442 Julio Correa

2003. Folklorists. Multicoloured.
1682 700g. Type **442** 35 20
1683 1000g. Emilano Rivarola Fernadez 40 25
1684 2000g. Manuel Ortiz Guerrero 65 35

443 La Golondriana

2003. National Dances. Multicoloured.
1685 700g. Type **443** 35 20
1686 3000g. Polca 90 50
1687 4000g. Galopera 90 50

444 Footballers

2003. Centenary of Guarani Football Club.
1688 **444** 700g. multicoloured . . 35 20

445 Poncho Para i (60 stripe poncho)

2003. Mercosur. Crafts. Multicoloured.
1689 4000g. Type **445** 90 50
1690 5000g. Shirt made from Ao Poi fabric . . . . 1·30 1·70

446 Flight into Egypt

2003. Christmas. Patchwork designs made by Santa Maria de Fe Mission. Multicoloured.
1691 700g. Type **446** 35 20
1692 1000g. Shepherd and star . . 40 25
1693 4000g. Holy Family 90 50

447 Footballers

2003. Futsal (Indoor Football) Championship, Sol de America Stadium, Asuncion, Paraguay. Multicoloured.
1694 4000g. Type **447** 90 50
1695 5000g. Two players . . . . 1·30 70

2003. Paraguay's Qualification for Futsal World Cup Championship, Taiwan . Nos. 1694/5 optd **PARAGUAY CAMPEON MUNDIAL**. Multicoloured.
1696 4000g. As Type **447** 90 50
1697 5000g. As No. 1695 . . . . 1·30 70

449 *Cordia bordasii*

2003. America. Endangered Species. Multicoloured.
1698 1000g. Type **449** 40 25
1699 5000g. *Chorisia insignis* 1·30 75
1700 5000g. *Bulnesia sarmientoi* 1·30 70

450 Anahi (C. Gomez)

2004. Comics written by Robin Wood. Mult.
1701 1000g. Type **450** 40 25
1702 3000g. Nippur de Lagash (L. Olivera) 90 50
1703 5000g. Dago (A. Salinas) 1·30 70

451 Footballer

2004. Centenary of National Football Team.
1704 **451** 700g. multicoloured 35 20

452 Statues, Alter Piece, San Jose Church

2004. Centenary of San Jose College, Asuncion.
1705 **452** 700g. multicoloured 35 20

453 Pablo Neruda (statue) (Hugo Pistilli)

2004. Birth Centenary of Ricardo Eliecer Neftali Reyes Basoalto. (Pablo Neruda) (writer).
1706 **453** 5000g. multicoloured 1·30 70

454 Monday Waterfall

2004. Tourism. Multicoloured.
1707 700g. Type **454** 35 20
1708 6000g. Tobati 2·00 95

455 Asuncion (fresco) (Jose Laterza Parodi)

2004. Museum of Independence. Multicoloured.
1709 700g. Type **455** 35 20
1710 5000g. Museum building 1·30 70

456 Abstract (Enrique Careaga)

2004. Centenary of Museo del Barro (art museum). Multicoloured.
1711 2000g. Type **456** 65 35
1712 3000g. Female figure (Mercedes Noguera) (vert) 90 50
1713 4000g. Crucified Christ (Jesuit Mission) (vert) 90 50

457 Jose Flores and Musical Score

2004. Birth Centenary of Jose Asuncion Flores (composer).
1714 **457** 5000g. multicoloured 1·30 70

458 Camello Locomotive (1911)

2004. 150th Anniv of Railways. Multicoloured.
1715 2000g. Type **458** 65 35
1716 3000g. El Coqueto locomotive (1911) (horiz) 90 50
MS1717 117×82 mm. 6000g. Sapucai locomotive (1886) (50×40 mm) 2·00 2·00

459 *Procias nudicollis*

2004. America. Environmental Protection. Mult.
1718 6000g. Type **459** 2·00 95
MS1719 117×82 mm. 6000g. *Ceratophys cranwelli* (50×40 mm) 2·00 2·00

460 Ocelot (*Felis pardalis*)

2004. Mercosur. Aquifer Conservation. Mult.
1720 2000g. Type **460** 65 35
1721 4000g. Giant anteater (*Myrmecophaga tridactyla*), Hippopotamus (*Hydrochoerus hydrochaeris*) and crested screamer (*Chauna torquata*) 90 50

461 Maize (Zea mays)

2004. Agricultural Crops. Multicoloured.
1722 2000g. Type **461** 65 35
1723 4000g. Cotton (*Gossypium hirsutum*) 90 50
1724 6000g. Soya bean (*Glicine max*) 2·00 95

462 Mary and Jesus

2004. Christmas. Paintings by Ricardo Migliorisi. Multicoloured.
1725 3000g. Type **462** 90 50
1726 5000g. Angel (vert) 1·30 70

463 1870 3r. Stamp and Emblem

2004. 40th Anniv of Latin American Parliament.
1727 **463** 4000g. multicoloured 90 50

464 Turbines

2004. 30th Anniv of Paraguay—Brazil Hydro-Electric Generation (ITAIPU). Multicoloured.
1728 4000g. Type **464** 90 50
1729 5000g. Dam (vert) 1·30 70

OFFICIAL STAMPS

O 14 O 19

O 20 O 37

1886. Various types as O **14**, O **19** and O **20** optd **OFICIAL**. (a) Imperf.
O32 1c. orange 3·50 2·25
O33 2c. violet 3·50 2·25
O34 5c. orange 3·50 2·25
O35 7c. green 3·50 2·25
O36 10c. brown 3·50 2·25
O37 15c. blue 8·50 11·00
O38 20c. lake 3·50 2·25

(b) New colours. Perf.
O39 1c. green 80 65
O40 2c. red 80 65
O41 5c. blue 80 65
O42 7c. orange 80 65
O43 10c. lake 80 65
O44 15c. brown 15·00 9·00
O45 20c. blue 80 65

1889. Stamp of 1889 surch **OFICIAL** and value. Perf.
O47 **25** 1 on 15c. purple 1·60 75
O48 2 on 10c. purple 1·60 75

1889. Stamp of 1889 surch **OFICIAL** and value. Imperf.
O49 **25** 3 on 15c. purple 1·60 75
O50 5 on 15c. brown 1·60 75

1890. Stamps of 1887 optd **OFICIAL** or **Oficial**.
O58 **24** 1c. green 10 10
O59 2c. red 15 10
O60 5c. blue 15 10
O61 7c. brown 1·40 75
O55 10c. mauve 20 15
O63 15c. orange 20 15
O64 20c. pink 25 15
O65 50c. grey 15 15
O86 1p. green 10 10

1901.
O73 O **37** 1c. blue 30 30
O74 2c. red 10 10
O75 4c. brown 10 10
O76 5c. green 10 10
O77 8c. brown 10 10
O78 10c. red 10 10
O79 20c. blue 20 15

1903. Stamps of 1903, optd **OFICIAL**.
O 99 **46** 1c. grey 10 10
O100 2c. green 10 10
O101 5c. blue 15 10
O102 10c. brown 10 10
O103 20c. red 10 10
O104 30c. blue 10 10
O105 60c. violet 20 20

1904. As T **50**, but inscr "OFICIAL".
O106 1c. green 20 10
O107 1c. olive 30 10
O108 1c. orange 35 15
O109 1c. red 30 20
O110 2c. orange 20 10
O111 2c. green 20 10
O112 2c. red 60 40
O113 2c. grey 50 30
O114 5c. blue 25 20
O116 5c. grey 1·10 75
O117 10c. lilac 15 10
O118 20c. lilac 50 30

1913. As T **65**, but inscr "OFICIAL".
O237 1c. grey 10 10
O238 2c. orange 10 10
O239 5c. purple 10 10
O240 10c. green 10 10
O241 20c. red 10 10
O242 50c. red 10 10
O243 75c. blue 10 10
O244 1p. blue 10 10
O245 2p. yellow 20 20

1935. Optd **OFICIAL**.
O474 **86** 10c. blue 10 10
O475 50c. mauve 10 10
O476 **87** 1p. orange 10 10
O477 **122** 1p.50 green 10 10
O478 – 2p.50 violet (No. 337) 10 10

1940. 50th Anniv of Asuncion University. As T **139**, inscr "SERVICIO OFICIAL", but portraits of Pres. Escobar and Dr. Zubizarreta.
O513 50c. black and red 10 10
O514 1p. black and red 10 10
O515 2p. black and blue 10 10
O516 5p. black and blue 10 10
O517 10p. black and blue 10 10
O518 50p. black and orange 40 10

POSTAGE DUE STAMPS

D 48

1904.
D106 D **48** 2c. green 30 30
D107 4c. green 30 30
D108 10c. green 30 30
D109 20c. green 30 30

1913. As T **65**, but inscr "DEFICIENTE".
D237 1c. brown 10 10
D238 2c. brown 10 10
D239 5c. brown 10 10
D240 10c. brown 10 10
D241 20c. brown 10 10
D242 40c. brown 10 10
D243 1p. brown 10 10
D244 1p.50 brown 10 10

APPENDIX

The following stamps have either been issued in excess of postal needs or have not been available to the public in reasonable quantities at face value. Such stamps may later be given full listing if there is evidence of regular postal use.

1962.

Manned Spacecraft. Postage 15, 25, 30, 40, 50c.; Air 12g.45, 18g.15, 36g.

Previous Olympic Games (1st series). Vert designs. Postage 15, 25, 30, 40, 50c.; Air 12g.45, 18g.15, 36g.

Vatican Council. Postage 50, 70c., 1g.50, 2, 3g.; Air 5, 10g., 12g.45, 18g.15, 23g.40, 36g.

Europa. Postage 4g.; Air 36g.

Solar System. Postage 10, 20, 25, 30, 50c.; Air 12g.45, 36g., 50g.

1963.

Previous Olympic Games (2nd series). Horiz designs. Postage 15, 25, 30, 40, 50c.; Air 12g.45, 18g.15, 36g.

Satellites and Space Flights. Vert designs. Postage 10, 20, 25, 30, 50c.; Air 12g.45, 36, 50g.

Previous Winter Olympic Games. Postage 10, 20, 25, 30, 50c.; Air 12g.45, 36, 50g.

Freedom from Hunger. Postage 10, 25, 50, 75c.; Air 18g.15, 36, 50g.

"Mercury" Space Flights. Postage 15, 25, 30, 40, 50c.; Air 12g.45, 18g.15, 50g.

Winter Olympic Games. Postage 15, 25, 30, 40, 50c.; Air 12g.45, 18g.15, 50g.

1964.

Tokyo Olympic Games. Postage 15, 25, 30, 40, 50c.; Air 12g.45, 18g.15, 50g.

Red Cross Centenary. Postage 10, 25, 30, 50c.; Air 18g.15, 36, 50g.

"Gemini", "Telstar" and "Apollo" Projects. Postage 15, 25, 30, 40, 50c.; Air 12g.45, 18g.15, 50g.

Spacecraft Developments. Postage 15, 25, 30, 40, 50c.; Air 12g.45, 18g.15, 50g.

United Nations. Postage 15, 25, 30, 40, 50c.; Air 12g.45, 18g.15, 50g.

American Space Research. Postage 10, 15, 20, 30, 40c.; Air 12g.45+6g., 18g.15+9g., 20g.+20g.

Eucharistic Conference. Postage 20g.+10g., 30g.+15g., 50g.+25g., 100g.+50g.

Pope John Memorial Issue. Postage 20g.+10g., 30g.+15g., 50g.+25g., 100g.+50g.

1965.

Scouts. Postage 10, 15, 20, 30, 50c.; Air 12g.45, 18g.15, 36g.

Tokyo Olympic Games Medals. Postage 15, 25, 30, 40, 50c.; Air 12g.45, 18g.15, 50g.

Famous Scientists. Postage 10, 15, 20, 30, 40c.; Air 12g.45+6g., 18g.15+9g., 20g.+20g.

Orchids and Trees. Postage 20, 30, 90c., 1g.50, 4g.50.; Air 3, 4, 66g.

Kennedy and Churchill. Postage 15, 25, 30, 40, 50c.; Air 12g.45, 18g.15, 50g.

I.T.U. Centenary. Postage 10, 15, 20, 30, 40c.; Air 12g.45+6g., 18g.15+9g., 20g.+10g.

Pope Paul VI. Visit to United Nations. Postage 10, 15, 20, 30, 50c.; Air 12g.45, 18g.15, 36g.

1966.

"Gemini" Space Project. Postage 15, 25, 30, 40, 50c.; Air 12g.45, 18g.15, 50g.

Events of 1965. Postage 10, 15, 20, 30, 50c.; Air 12g.45, 18g.15, 36g.

Mexico Olympic Games. Postage 10, 15, 20, 30, 50c.; Air 12g.45, 18g.15, 36g.

German Space Research. Postage 10, 15, 20, 30, 50c.; Air 12g.45, 18g.15, 36g.

Famous Writers. Postage 10, 15, 20, 30, 50c.; Air 12g.45, 18g.15, 36g.

Italian Space Research. Postage 10, 15, 20, 30, 50c.; Air 12g.45, 18g.15, 36g.

Moon Missions. Postage 10, 15, 20, 30, 50c.; Air 12g.45, 18g.15, 36g.

Sports Commemorative Issue. Postage 10, 15, 20, 30, 50c.; Air 12g.45, 18g.15, 36g.

3rd Death Anniv of Pres. John Kennedy. Postage 10, 15, 20, 30, 50c.; Air 12g.45, 18g.15, 36g.

Famous Paintings. Postage 10, 15, 20, 30, 50c.; Air 12g.45, 18g.15, 36g.

1967.

Religious Paintings. Postage 10, 15, 20, 30, 50c.; Air 12g.45, 18g.15, 36g.

16th-century. Religious Paintings. Postage 10, 15, 20, 30, 50c.; Air 12g.45, 18g.15, 36g.

Impressionist Paintings. Postage 10, 15, 20, 30, 50c.; Air 12g.45, 18g.15, 36g.

European Paintings of 17th and 18th Cent. Postage 10, 15, 20, 25, 30, 50c.; Air 12g.45, 18g.15, 36g.

Birth Anniv of Pres. John Kennedy. Postage 10, 15, 20, 25, 30, 50c.; Air 12g.45, 18g.15, 36g.

Sculpture. Postage 10, 15, 20, 25, 30, 50c.; Air 12g.45, 18g.15, 50g.

Mexico Olympic Games. Archaeological Relics. Postage 10, 15, 20, 25, 30, 50c.; Air 12g.45, 18g.15, 36g.

1968.

Religious Paintings. Postage 10, 15, 20, 25, 30, 50c.; Air 12g.45, 18g.15, 36g.

Winter Olympic Games, Grenoble. Paintings. Postage 10, 15, 20, 25, 30, 50c.; Air 12g.45, 18g.15, 36g.

Paraguayan Stamps from 1870–1970. Postage 10, 15, 20, 25, 30, 50c.; Air 12g.45, 18g.15, 36g.

Mexico Olympic Games, Paintings of Children. Postage 10, 15, 20, 25, 30, 50c.; Air 12g.45, 18g.15, 36g. (Sailing ship and Olympic Rings).

Visit of Pope Paul VI to Eucharistic Congress. Religious Paintings. Postage 10, 15, 20, 25, 30, 50c.; Air 12g.45, 18g.15, 36g.

Important Events of 1968. Postage 10, 15, 20, 25, 30, 50c.; Air 12g.45, 18g.15, 50g.

1969.

Gold Medal Winners of 1968 Mexico Olympic Games. Postage 10, 15, 20, 25, 30, 50c.; Air 12g.45, 18g.15, 50g.

Int. Projects in Outer Space. Postage 10, 15, 20, 25, 30, 50c.; Air 12g.45, 18g.15, 50g.

Latin American Wildlife. Postage 10, 10, 15, 15, 20, 20, 25, 25, 30, 30, 50, 50, 75, 75 c; Air 12g.45 × 2, 18g.15 × 2.

Gold Medal Winners in Olympic Football, 1900–1968. Postage 10, 15, 20, 25, 30, 50, 75c.; Air 12g.45, 18g.15.

Paraguayan Football Champions, 1930–1966. Postage 10, 15, 20, 25, 30, 50, 75c.; Air 12g.45, 18g.15.

Paintings by Goya. Postage 10, 15, 20, 25, 30, 50, 75c.; Air 12g.45, 18g.15.

Christmas. Religious Paintings. Postage 10, 15, 20, 25, 30, 50, 75c.; Air 12g.45, 18g.15.

1970.

Moon Walk. Postage 10, 15, 20, 25, 30, 50, 75c.; Air 12g.45, 18g.15.

Easter. Paintings. Postage 10, 15, 20, 25, 30, 50, 75c.; Air 12g.45, 18g.15.

Munich Olympic Games. Postage 10, 15, 20, 25, 30, 50, 75c.; Air 12g.45, 18g.15.

Paintings from the Pinakothek Museum in Munich. Postage 10, 15, 20, 25, 30, 50, 75c.; Air 12g.45, 18g.15.

"Apollo" Space Programme. Postage 10, 15, 20, 25, 30, 50, 75c.; Air 12g.45, 18g.15.

Space Projects in the Future. Postage 10, 15, 20, 25, 30, 50, 75c.; Air 12g.45, 18g.15.

"Expo 70" World Fair, Osaka, Japan. Japanese Paintings. Postage 10, 15, 20, 25, 30, 50, 75c.; Air 12g.45, 18g.15, 50g.

Flower Paintings. Postage 10, 15, 20, 25, 30, 50, 75c.; Air 12g.45, 18g.15, 50g.

Paintings from Prado Museum, Madrid. Postage 10, 15, 20, 25, 30, 50, 75c.; Air 12g.45, 18g.15, 50g.

Paintings by Durer. Postage 10, 15, 20, 25, 30, 50, 75c.; Air 12g.45, 18g.15, 50g.

1971.

Christmas 1970/71. Religious Paintings. Postage 10, 15, 20, 25, 30, 50, 75c.; Air 12g.45, 18g.15, 50g.

Munich Olympic Games, 1972. Postage 10, 15, 20, 25, 30, 50, 75c.; Air 12g.45, 18g.15, 50g.

Paintings of Horses and Horsemen. Postage 10, 15, 20, 25, 30, 50, 75c.; Air 12g.45, 18g.15, 50g.

Famous Paintings from the Louvre, Paris. Postage 10, 15, 20, 25, 30, 50, 75c.; Air 12g.45, 18g.15, 50g.

Paintings in the National Museum, Asuncion. Postage 10, 15, 20, 25, 30, 50, 75c.; Air 12g.45, 18g.15, 50g.

Hunting Paintings. Postage 10, 15, 20, 25, 30, 50, 75c.; Air 12g.45, 18g.15, 50g.

Philatokyo '71, Stamp Exhibition, Tokyo. Japanese Paintings. Postage 10, 15, 20, 25, 30, 50, 75c.; Air 12g.45, 18g.15, 50g.

Winter Olympic Games, Sapporo, 1972. Japanese Paintings. Postage 10, 15, 20, 25, 30, 50, 75c.; Air 12g.45, 18g.15, 50g.

150th Death Anniv of Napoleon. Paintings. Postage 10, 15, 20, 25, 30, 50, 75c.; Air 12g.45, 18g.15, 50g.

Famous Paintings from the Dahlem Museum, Berlin. Postage 10, 15, 20, 25, 30, 50, 75c.; Air 12g.45, 18g.15, 50g.

1972.

Locomotives (1st series). Postage 10, 15, 20, 25, 30, 50, 75c.; Air 12g.45, 18g.15, 50g.

Winter Olympic Games, Sapporo. Postage 10, 15, 20, 25, 30, 50, 75c.; Air 12g.45, 18g.15, 50g.

Racing Cars. Postage 10, 15, 20, 25, 30, 50, 75c.; Air 12g.45, 18g.15, 50g.

Famous Sailing Ships. Postage 10, 15, 20, 25, 30, 50, 75c.; Air 12g.45, 18g.15, 50g.

Famous Paintings from the Vienna Museum. Postage 10, 15, 20, 25, 30, 50, 75c.; Air 12g.45, 18g.15, 50g.

Famous Paintings from the Asuncion Museum. Postage 10, 15, 20, 25, 30, 50, 75c.; Air 12g.45, 18g.15, 50g.

Visit of the Argentine President to Paraguay. Postage 10, 15, 20, 25, 30, 50, 75c.; Air 12g.45, 18g.15.

Visit of President of Paraguay to Japan. Postage 10, 15, 20, 25, 30, 50, 75c.; Air 12g.45, 18g.15.

Paintings of Animals and Birds. Postage 10, 15, 20, 25, 30, 50, 75c.; Air 12g.45, 18g.15.

Locomotives (2nd series). Postage 10, 15, 20, 25, 30, 50, 75c.; Air 12g.45, 18g.15.

South American Fauna. Postage 10, 15, 20, 25, 30, 50, 75c.; Air 12g.45, 18g.15.

1973.

Famous Paintings from the Florence Museum. Postage 10, 15, 20, 25, 30, 50, 75c.; Air 5, 10, 20g.

South American Butterflies. Postage 10, 15, 20, 25, 30, 50, 75c.; Air 5, 10, 20g.

Cats. Postage 10, 15, 20, 25, 30, 50, 75c.; Air 5, 10, 20g.

Portraits of Women. Postage 10, 15, 20, 25, 30, 50, 75c.; Air 5, 10, 20g.

World Cup Football Championship, West Germany (1974) (1st issue). Postage 10, 15, 20, 25, 30, 50, 75c.; Air 5, 10, 20g.

Paintings of Women. Postage 10, 15, 20, 25, 30, 50, 75c.; Air 5, 10, 20g.

Birds. Postage 10, 15, 20, 25, 30, 50, 75c.; Air 5, 10, 20g.

"Apollo" Moon Missions and Future Space Projects. Postage 10, 15, 20, 25, 30, 50, 75c.; Air 5, 10, 20g.

Visit of Pres. Stroessner to Europe and Morocco. Air 5, 10, 25, 50, 150g.

Folk Costume. Postage 25, 50, 75c., 1g., 1g.50, 1g.75, 2g.25.

Flowers. Postage 10, 20, 25, 30, 40, 50, 75c.

1974.

World Cup Football Championship, West Germany (2nd issue). Air 5, 10, 20g.

Roses. Postage 10, 15, 20, 25, 30, 50, 75c.

Famous Paintings from the Gulbenkian Museum, New York. Postage 10, 15, 20, 25, 30, 50, 75 c; Air 5, 10, 20g.

U.P.U. Centenary. Postage 10, 15, 20, 25, 30, 50, 75c.; Air 5, 10, 20g.

Famous Masterpieces. Postage 10, 15, 20, 25, 30, 50, 75c.; Air 5, 10, 20g.

Visit of Pres. Stroessner to France. Air 100g.

World Cup Football Championship, West Germany (3rd issue). Air 4, 5, 10g.

Ships. Postage 5, 10, 15, 20, 25, 35, 40, 50c.

Events of 1974. Air 4g. (U.P.U.), 5g. (President of Chile's visit), 10g. (President Stroessner's visit to South Africa).

Centenary of U.P.U. Air 4, 5, 10, 20g.

1975.

Paintings. Postage 5, 10, 15, 20, 25, 35, 40, 50c.

Christmas (1974). Postage 5, 10, 15, 20, 25, 35, 40, 50c.

"Expo '75" Okinawa, Japan. Air 4, 5, 10g.

Paintings from National Gallery, London. Postage 5, 10, 15, 20, 25, 35, 40, 50c.

Dogs. Postage 5, 10, 15, 20, 25, 35, 40, 50c.

South American Fauna. Postage 5, 10, 15, 20, 25, 35, 40, 50c.

"Espana '75". Air 4, 5, 10g.

500th Birth Anniv of Michelangelo. Postage 5, 10, 15, 20, 25, 35, 40, 50c.; Air 4, 5, 10g.

Winter Olympic Games, Innsbruck (1976). Postage 1, 2, 3, 4, 5g.; Air 10, 15, 20g.

Olympic Games, Montreal (1976). Gold borders. Postage 1, 2, 3, 4, 5g.; Air 10, 15, 20g.

Various Commemorations. Air 4g. (Zeppelin), 5g. (1978 World Cup), 10g. (Nordposta Exhibition).

Bicent (1976) of American Revolution (1st issue). Paintings of Sailing Ships. Postage 5, 10, 15, 20, 25, 35, 40, 50c.

Bicent (1976) of American Revolution (2nd issue). Paintings. Postage 5, 10, 15, 20, 25, 35, 40, 50c.

Bicent (1976) of American Revolution (3rd issue). Lunar Rover and American Cars. Air 4, 5, 10g.

Various Commemorations. Air 4g. (Concorde), 5g. (Lufthansa), 10g. ("Exfilmo" and "Espamer" Stamp Exhibitions).

Paintings by Spanish Artists. Postage 1, 2, 3, 4, 5g.; Air 10, 15, 20g.

1976.

Holy Year. Air 4, 5, 10g.

Cats. Postage 5, 10, 15, 20, 25, 35, 40, 50c.

Railway Locomotives (3rd series). Postage 1, 2, 3, 4, 5g.; Air 10, 15, 20g.

Butterflies. Postage 5, 10, 15, 20, 25, 35, 40, 50c.

Domestic Animals. Postage 1, 2, 3, 4, 5g.; Air 10, 15, 20g.

Bicent of American Revolution (4th issue) and U.S. Postal Service. Postage 1, 2, 3, 4, 5g.; Air 10, 15, 20g.

"Paintings and Planets". Postage 1, 2, 3, 4, 5g.; Air 10, 15, 20g.

Ship Paintings. Postage 1, 2, 3, 4, 5g.; Air 10, 15, 20g.

German Ship Paintings (1st issue). Postage 1, 2, 3, 4, 5g.; Air 10, 15, 20g.

Bicentenary of American Revolution (5th issue). Paintings of Cowboys and Indians. Postage 1, 2, 3, 4, 5g.; Air 10, 15, 20g.

Gold Medal Winners. Olympic Games, Montreal. Postage 1, 2, 3, 4, 5g.; Air 10, 15, 20g.

Paintings by Titian. Postage 1, 2, 3, 4, 5g.; Air 10, 15, 20g.

History of the Olympics. Postage 1, 2, 3, 4, 5g.; Air 10, 15, 20g.

1977.

Paintings by Rubens (1st issue). Postage 1, 2, 3, 4, 5g.; Air 10, 15, 20g.

Bicent of American Revolution (6th issue). Astronautics. Postage 1, 2, 3, 4, 5g.; Air 10, 15, 20g.

"Luposta 77" Stamp Exn. Zeppelin and National Costumes. Postage 1, 2, 3, 4, 5g.; Air 10, 15, 20g.

History of Aviation. Postage 1, 2, 3, 4, 5g.; Air 10, 15, 20g.

Paintings. Postage 1, 2, 3, 4, 5g.; Air 10, 15, 20g.

German Ship Paintings (2nd issue). Postage 1, 2, 3, 4, 5g.; Air 10, 15, 20g.

Nobel Prize-winners for Literature. Postage 1, 2, 3, 4, 5g.; Air 10, 15, 20g.

History of World Cup (1st issue). Postage 1, 2, 3, 4, 5g.; Air 10, 15, 20g.

History of World Cup (2nd issue). Postage 1, 2, 3, 4, 5g.; Air 10, 15, 20g.

1978.

Paintings by Rubens (2nd issue). Postage 1, 2, 3, 4, 5g.; Air 10, 15, 20g.

Chess Olympiad, Buenos Aires. Paintings of Chess Games. Postage 1, 2, 3, 4, 5g.; Air 10, 15, 20g.

Paintings by Jordaens. Postage 3, 4, 5, 6, 7, 8, 20g.; Air 10, 25g.

450th Death Anniv of Durer (1st issue). Postage 3, 4, 5, 6, 7, 8, 20g.; Air 10, 25g.

Paintings by Goya. Postage 3, 4, 5, 6, 7, 8, 20g.; Air 10, 25g.

Astronautics of the Future. Postage 3, 4, 5, 6, 7, 8, 20g.; Air 10, 25g.

Racing Cars. Postage 3, 4, 5, 6, 7, 8, 20g.; Air 10, 25g.

Paintings by Rubens (3rd issue). Postage 3, 4, 5, 6, 7, 8, 20g.; Air 10, 25g.

25th Anniv of Queen Elizabeth's Coronation (reproduction of stamps). Postage 3, 4, 5, 6, 7, 8, 20g.; Air 10, 25g.

Paintings and Stamp Exhibition Emblems. Postage 3, 4, 5, 6, 7, 8, 20g.; Air 10, 25g.

Various Commemorations. Air 75g. (Satellite Earth Station), 500g. (Coat of Arms), 1000g. (Pres. Stroessner).

International Year of the Child (1st issue). Snow White and the Seven Dwarfs. Postage 3, 4, 5, 6, 7, 8, 20g.; Air 10, 25g.

Military Uniforms. Postage 3, 4, 5, 6, 7, 8, 20g.; Air 10, 25g.

1979.

World Cup Football Championship, Argentina. Postage 3, 4, 5, 6, 7, 8, 20g.; Air 10, 25g.

Christmas (1978). Paintings of Madonnas. Postage 3, 4, 5, 6, 7, 8, 20g.; Air 10, 25g.

History of Aviation. Postage 3, 4, 5, 6, 7, 8, 20g.; Air 10, 25g.

450th Death Anniv of Durer (2nd issue). Postage 3, 4, 5, 6, 7, 8, 20g.; Air 10, 25g.

Death Centenary of Sir Rowland Hill (1st issue). Reproduction of Stamps. Postage 3, 4, 5, 6, 7, 8, 20g.; Air 10, 25g.

International Year of the Child (2nd issue). Cinderella. Postage 3, 4, 5, 6, 7, 8, 20g.; Air 10, 25g.

Winter Olympic Games, Lake Placid (1980). Postage 3, 4, 5, 6, 7, 8, 20g.; Air 10, 25g.

Sailing Ships. Postage 3, 4, 5, 6, 7, 8, 20g.; Air 10, 25g.

International Year of the Child (3rd issue). Cats. Postage 3, 4, 5, 6, 7, 8, 20g.; Air 10, 25g.

International Year of the Child (4th issue). Little Red Riding Hood. Postage 3, 4, 5, 6, 7, 8, 20g.; Air 10, 25g.

Olympic Games, Moscow (1980). Greek Athletes. Postage 3, 4, 5, 6, 7, 8, 20g.; Air 10, 25g.

Centenary of Electric Locomotives. Postage 3, 4, 5, 6, 7, 8, 20g.; Air 10, 25g.

1980.

Death Centenary of Sir Rowland Hill (2nd issue). Military Aircraft. Postage 3, 4, 5, 6, 7, 8, 20 g; Air 10, 25g.

Death Centenary of Sir Rowland Hill (3rd issue). Stamps. Postage 3, 4, 5, 6, 7, 8, 20g.; Air 10, 25g.

Winter Olympic Games Medal Winners (1st issue). Postage 3, 4, 5, 6, 7, 8, 20g.; Air 10, 25g.

Composers. Scenes from Ballets. Postage 3, 4, 5, 6, 7, 8, 20g.; Air 20, 25g.

International Year of the Child (1979) (5th issue). Christmas. Postage 3, 4, 5, 6, 7, 8, 20g.; Air 10, 25g.

Exhibitions. Paintings of Ships. Postage 3, 4, 5, 6, 7, 8, 20g.; Air 10, 25g.

World Cup Football Championship, Spain (1982) (1st issue). Postage 3, 4, 5, 6, 7, 8, 20g.; Air 10, 25g.

World Chess Championship, Merano. Postage 3, 4, 5, 6, 7, 8, 20g.; Air 10, 25g.

1981.

Winter Olympic Games Medal Winners (2nd issue). Postage 25, 50c., 1, 2, 3, 4, 5g.; Air 5, 10, 30g.

International Year of the Child (1979) (6th issue). Children and Flowers. Postage 10, 25, 50, 100, 200, 300, 400g.; Air 75, 500, 1000g.

"WIPA 1981" International Stamp Exhibition, Vienna. 1980 Composers stamp optd. Postage 4g.; Air 10g.

Wedding of Prince of Wales (1st issue). Postage 25, 50c., 1, 2, 3, 4, 5g.; Air 5, 10, 30g.

Costumes and Treaty of Itaipu. Postage 10, 25, 50, 100, 200, 300, 400g.

Paintings by Rubens. Postage 25, 50c., 1, 2, 3, 4, 5g.

Anniversaries and Events. Air 5g. (250th birth anniv

of George Washington), 10g. (80th birthday of Queen Mother), 30g. ("Philatokyo '81").

Flight of Space Shuttle. Air 5, 10, 30g.

Birth Bicentenary of Ingres. Postage 25, 50c., 1, 2, 3, 4, 5g.

World Cup Football Championship, Spain (1982) (2nd issue). Air 5, 10, 30g.

Birth Centenary of Picasso. Postage 25, 50c., 1, 2, 3, 4, 5g.

"Philatelia '81" International Stamp Exhibition, Frankfurt. Picasso stamps optd. Postage 25, 50c., 1, 2, 3, 4g.

"Espamer '81" International Stamp Exhibition. Picasso stamps optd. Postage 25, 50c., 1, 2, 3, 4g.

Wedding of Prince of Wales (2nd issue). Postage 25, 50c., 1, 2, 3, 4, 5g.; Air 5, 10, 30g.

International Year of the Child (1979) (7th issue). Christmas. Postage 25, 50c., 1, 2, 3, 4, 5g.

Christmas. Paintings. Air 5, 10, 30g.

1982.

International Year of the Child (1979) (8th issue). Puss in Boots. Postage 25, 50c., 1, 2, 3, 4, 5g.

World Cup Football Championship, Spain (3rd issue). Air 5, 10, 30g.

75th Anniv of Boy Scout Movement and 125th Birth Anniv of Lord-Baden Powell (founder). Postage 25, 50c., 1, 2, 3, 4, 5g.; Air 5, 10, 30g.

"Essen 82" International Stamp Exhibition, 1981 International Year of the Child (7th issue) Christmas stamps optd. Postage 25, 50c., 1, 2, 3, 4g.

Cats. Postage 25, 50c., 1, 2, 3, 4, 5g.

Chess paintings. Air 5, 10, 30g.

"Philexfrance 82" International Stamp Exhibition. 1981 Ingres stamps optd. Postage 25, 50c., 1, 2, 3g.

World Cup Football Championship, Spain (4th issue). Postage 25, 50c., 1, 2, 3, 4, 5g.; Air 5, 10, 30g.

"Philatelia 82" International Stamp Exhibition, Hanover. 1982 Cats issue optd. Postage 25, 50c., 1, 2, 3, 4, 5g.

500th Birth Anniv of Raphael (1st issue). Postage 25, 50c., 1, 2, 3, 4, 5g.

500th Birth Anniv of Raphael (2nd issue) and Christmas (1st issue). Postage 25, 50c., 1, 2, 3, 4, 5g.

World Cup Football Championship Results. Air 5, 10, 30g.

Christmas (2nd issue). Paintings by Rubens. Air 5, 10, 30g.

Paintings by Durer. Life of Christ. Postage 25, 50c., 1, 2, 3, 4, 5g.

500th Birth Anniv of Raphael (3rd issue) and Christmas (3rd issue). Air 5, 10, 30g.

1983.

Third International Railways Congress, Malaga (1982). Postage 25, 50c., 1, 2, 3, 4, 5g.

Racing Cars. Postage 25, 50c., 1, 2, 3, 4, 5g.

Paintings by Rembrandt. Air 5, 10, 30g.

German Astronautics. Air 5, 10, 30g.

Winter Olympic Games, Sarajevo (1984). Postage 25, 50c., 1, 2, 3, 4, 5g.

Bicentenary of Manned Flight. Air 5, 10, 30g.

Pope John Paul II. Postage 25, 50c., 1, 2, 3, 4, 5g.

Olympic Games, Los Angeles (1984). Air 5, 10, 30g.

Veteran Cars. Postage 25, 50c., 1, 2, 3, 4, 5g.; Air 5, 10, 30g.

"Brasiliana '83" International Stamp Exhibition and 52nd F.I.P. Congress (1st issue). 1982 World Cup (4th issue) stamps optd. Postage 25, 50c., 1, 2, 3, 4g.

"Brasiliana '83" International Stamp Exhibition and 52nd F.I.P. Congress (2nd issue). 1982 Raphael/Christmas stamps optd. Postage 25, 50c., 1, 2, 3, 4g.

Aircraft Carriers. Postage 25, 50c., 1, 2, 3, 4, 5g.

South American Flowers. Air 5, 10, 30g.

South American Birds. Postage 25, 50c., 1, 2, 3, 4, 5g.

25th Anniv of International Maritime Organization. Air 5, 10, 30g.

"Philatelia '83" International Stamp Exhibition, Dusseldorf. 1983 International Railway Congress stamps optd. Postage 25, 50c., 1, 2, 3, 4g.

"Exfivia - 83" International Stamp Exn, Bolivia. 1982 Durer paintings optd. Postage 25, 50c., 1, 2, 3, 4g.

Flowers, Postage 10, 25g.; Chaco soldier, Postage 50g.; Dams, Postage 75g; Air 100g.; President, Air 200g.

1984.

Bicent of Manned Flight. Postage 25, 50c., 1, 2, 3, 4, 5g.

World Communications Year. Air 5, 10, 30g.

Dogs. Postage 25, 50c., 1, 2, 3, 4, 5g.

Olympic Games, Los Angeles. Air 5, 10, 30g.

Animals. Postage 10, 25, 50, 75g.

1983 Anniversaries. Air 100g. (birth bicentenary of Bolivar), 200g. (76th anniv of boy scout movement).

Christmas (1983) and New Year. Postage 25, 50c., 1, 2, 3, 4, 5g.

Winter Olympic Games, Sarajevo. Air 5, 10, 30g.

Troubador Knights. Postage 25, 50c., 1, 2, 3, 4, 5g.

World Cup Football Championship, Spain (1982) and Mexico (1986). Air 5, 10, 30g.

International Stamp Fair, Essen. 1983 Racing Cars stamps optd. Postage 25, 50c., 1, 2, 3, 4g.

Extinct Animals. Postage 25, 50c., 1, 2, 3, 4, 5g.

60th Anniv of International Chess Federation. Air 5, 10, 30g.

19th Universal Postal Union Congress Stamp Exhibition, Hamburg (1st issue). Sailing Ships. Postage 25, 50c., 1, 2, 3, 4, 5g.

19th Universal Postal Union Congress Stamp Exhibition, Hamburg (2nd issue). Troubadour Knights stamp optd. Postage 5g.

Leaders of the World. British Railway Locomotives. Postage 25, 50c., 1, 2, 3, 4, 5g.

50th Anniv of First Lufthansa Europe–South America Direct Mail Flight. Air 5, 10, 30g.

30th Anniv of Presidency of Alfredo Stroessner. Dam stamp optd. Air 100g.

"Ausipex 84" International Stamp Exhibition, Melbourne. 1974 U.P.U. Centenary stamps optd. Postage 10, 15, 20, 25, 30, 50, 75c.

"Phila Korea 1984" International Stamp Exhibition, Seoul. Olympic Games, Los Angeles, and Extinct Animals stamps optd. Postage 5g.; Air 30g.

German National Football Championship and Sindelfingen Stamp Bourse. 1974 World Cup stamps (1st issue) optd. Postage 10, 15, 20, 25, 30, 50, 75c.

Cats. Postage 25, 50c., 1, 2, 3, 4, 5g.

Winter Olympic Games Medal Winners. Air 5, 10, 30g.

Centenary of Motor Cycle. Air 5, 10, 30g.

1985.

Olympic Games Medal Winners. Postage 25, 50c., 1, 2, 3, 4, 5g.

Christmas (1984). Costumes. Air 5, 10, 30g.

Fungi. Postage 25, 50c., 1, 2, 3, 4, 5g.

Participation of Paraguay in Preliminary Rounds of World Cup Football Championship. Air 5, 10, 30g.

"Interpex 1985" and "Stampex 1985" Stamp Exhibitions. 1981 Queen Mother's Birthday stamp optd. Postage 10g. × 2.

International Federation of Aero-Philatelic Societies Congress, Stuttgart. 1984 Lufthansa Europe–South America Mail Flight stamp optd. Air 10g.

Paraguayan Animals and Extinct Animals. Postage 25, 50c., 1, 2, 3, 4, 5g.

"Olymphilex 85" Olympic Stamps Exhibition, Lausanne. 1984 Winter Olympics Games Medal Winners stamp optd. Postage 10g.

"Israphil 85" International Stamp Exhibition, Tel Aviv. 1982 Boy Scout Movement stamp optd. Postage 5g.

Music Year. Air 5, 10, 30g.

Birth Bicentenary of John J. Audubon (ornithologist). Birds. Postage 25, 50c., 1, 2, 3, 4, 5g.

Railway Locomotives. Air 5, 10, 30g.

"Italia '85" International Stamp Exhibition, Rome (1st issue). 1983 Pope John Paul II stamp optd. Postage 5g.

50th Anniv of Chaco Peace (1st issue). 1972 Visit of Argentine President stamp optd. Postage 30c.

"Mophila 85" Stamp Exhibition, Hamburg. 1984 U.P.U. Congress Stamp Exhibition (1st issue) stamp optd. Postage 5g.

"Lupo 85" Stamp Exhibition, Lucerne. 1984 Bicentenary of Manned Flight stamp optd. Postage 5g.

"Expo 85" World's Fair, Tsukuba. 1981 "Philatokyo '81" stamp optd. Air 30g.

International Youth Year. Mark Twain. Postage 25, 50c., 1, 2, 3, 4, 5g.

75th Death Anniv of Henri Dunant (founder of Red Cross). Air 5, 10, 30g.

150th Anniv of German Railways (1st issue). Postage 25, 50c., 1, 2, 3, 4, 5g.

International Chess Federation Congress, Graz. Air 5, 10, 30g.

50th Anniv of Chaco Peace (2nd issue) and Government Achievements. Postage 10, 25, 50, 75g.; Air 100, 200g.

Paintings by Rubens. Postage 25, 50c., 1, 2, 3, 4, 5g.

Explorers and their Ships. Air 5, 10, 30g.

"Italia '85" International Stamp Exhibition, Rome (2nd issue). Paintings. Air 5, 10, 30g.

1986.

Paintings by Titian. Postage 25, 50c., 1, 2, 3, 4, 5g.

International Stamp Fair, Essen. 1985 German Railways stamps optd. Postage 25, 50c., 1, 2, 3, 4g.

Fungi. Postage 25, 50c., 1, 2, 3, 4, 5g.

"Ameripex '86" International Stamp Exhibition, Chicago. Air 5, 10, 30g.

Lawn Tennis (1st issue). Inscriptions in black or red. Air 5, 10, 30g.

Centenary of Motor Car. Postage 25, 50c., 1, 2, 3, 4, 5g.

Appearance of Halley's Comet. Air 5, 10, 30g.

Qualification of Paraguay for World Cup Football Championship Final Rounds, Mexico (1st issue). Postage 25, 50c., 1, 2, 3, 4, 5g.

Tenth Pan-American Games, Indianapolis (1987). 1985 Olympic Games Medal Winners stamp optd. Postage 5g.

Maybach Cars. Postage 25, 50c., 1, 2, 3, 4, 5g.

Freight Trains. Air 5, 10, 30g.

Qualification of Paraguay for World Cup Football Championship Final Rounds (2nd issue). Air 5, 10, 30g.

Winter Olympic Games, Calgary (1988) (1st issue). 1983 Winter Olympic Games stamp optd. Postage 5g.

Centenary of Statue of Liberty. Postage 25, 50c., 1, 2, 3, 4, 5g.

Dogs. Postage 25, 50c., 1, 2, 3, 4, 5g.

150th Anniv of German Railways (2nd issue). Air 5, 10, 30g.

Lawn Tennis (2nd issue). Postage 25, 50c., 1, 2, 3, 4, 5g.

Visit of Prince Hitachi of Japan. 1972 Visit of President of Paraguay to Japan stamps optd. Postage 10, 15, 20, 25, 30, 50, 75c.

International Peace Year. Paintings by Rubens. Air 5, 10, 30g.

Olympic Games, Seoul (1988) (1st issue). Postage 25, 50c., 1, 2, 3, 4, 5g.

27th Chess Olympiad, Dubai. 1982 Chess Paintings stamp optd. Air 10g.

1987.

World Cup Football Championship, Mexico (1986) and Italy (1990). Air 5, 10, 20, 25, 30g.

12th Spanish American Stamp and Coin Exhibition, Madrid, and 500th Anniv of Discovery of America by Columbus. 1975 South American Fauna and 1983 25th Anniv of I.M.O. stamps optd. Postage 15, 20, 25, 35, 40g.; Air 10g.

Tennis as Olympic Sport. 1986 Lawn Tennis (1st issue) stamps optd. Air 10, 30g.

Olympic Games, Barcelona (1992). 1985 Olympic Games Medal Winners stamps optd. Postage 25, 50c., 1, 2, 3, 4g.

"Olymphilex '87" Olympic Stamps Exhibition, Rome. 1985 Olympic Games Medal Winners stamp optd. Postage 5g.

Cats. Postage 1, 2, 3, 5, 60g.

Paintings by Rubens (1st issue). Postage 1, 2, 3, 5, 60g.

Saloon Cars. Air 5, 10, 20, 25, 30g.

National Topics. Postage 10g. (steel plant), 25g. (Franciscan monk), 50g. (400th anniv of Ita and Yaguaron), 75g. (450th Anniv of Asuncion); Air 100g. (airliner), 200g. (Pres. Stroessner).

"Capex 87" International Stamp Exhibition, Toronto. Cats stamps optd. Postage 1, 2, 3, 5g.

500th Anniv of Discovery of America by Columbus. Postage 1, 2, 3, 5, 60g.

Winter Olympic Games, Calgary (1988) (2nd issue). Air 5, 10, 20, 25, 30g.

Centenary of Colorado Party. National Topics and 1978 Pres. Stroessner stamps optd. Air 200, 1000g.

750th Anniv of Berlin (1st issue) and "Luposta '87" Air Stamps Exhibition, Berlin. Postage 1, 2, 3, 5, 60g.

Olympic Games, Seoul (1988) (2nd issue). Air 5, 10, 20, 25, 30g.

Rally Cars. Postage 1, 2, 3, 5, 60g.

"Exfivia 87" Stamp Exhibition, Bolivia. National Topics stamps optd. Postage 75g.; Air 100g.

"Olymphilex '88" Olympic Stamps Exhibition, Seoul. 1986 Olympic Games, Seoul (1st issue) stamps optd. Postage 2, 3, 4, 5g.

"Philatelia '87" International Stamp Exhibition, Cologne. 1986 Lawn Tennis (2nd issue) stamps optd. Postage 25, 50c., 1, 2, 3, 4g.

Italy–Argentina Match at Zurich to Launch 1990 World Cup Football Championship, Italy. 1986 Paraguay Qualification (2nd issue) stamps optd. Air 10, 30g.

"Exfilna '87" Stamp Exhibition, Gerona. 1986 Olympic Games, Seoul (1st issue) stamps optd. Postage 25, 50c.

Spanish Ships. Postage 1, 2, 3, 5, 60g.

Paintings by Rubens (2nd issue). Air 5, 10, 20, 25, 30g.

Christmas. Air 5, 10, 20, 25, 30g.

Winter Olympic Games, Calgary (1988) (3rd issue). Postage 1, 2, 3, 5, 60g.

1988.

150th Anniv of Austrian Railways. Air 5, 10, 20, 25, 30g.

"Aeropex 88" Air Stamps Exhibition, Adelaide, 1987. 750th Anniv of Berlin and "Luposta '87" stamps optd. Postage 1, 2, 3, 5g.

"Olympex" Stamp Exhibition, Calgary. 1987 Winter Olympic Games (3rd issue) stamps optd. Postage 1, 2, 3g.

Olympic Games, Seoul (3rd issue). Equestrian Events. Postage 1, 2, 3, 5, 60g.

Space Projects. Air 5, 10, 20, 25, 30g.

750th Anniv of Berlin (2nd issue). Paintings. Postage 1, 2, 3, 5, 60g.

Visit of Pope John Paul II. Postage 1, 2, 3, 5, 60g.

"Lupo Wien 88" Stamp Exhibition, Vienna. 1987 National Topics stamp optd. Air 100g.

World Wildlife Fund. Extinct Animals. Postage 1, 2, 3, 5g.

Paintings in West Berlin State Museum. Air 5, 10, 20, 25, 30g.

Bicentenary of Australian Settlement. 1981 Wedding of Prince of Wales (1st issue) optd. Postage 25, 50c., 1, 2g.

History of World Cup Football Championship (1st issue). Air 5, 10, 20, 25, 30g.

New Presidential Period, 1988–1993. 1985 Chaco Peace and Government Achievements issue optd. Postage 10, 25, 50, 75g.; Air 100, 200g.

Olympic Games, Seoul (4th issue). Lawn Tennis and Medal. Postage 1, 2, 3, 5, 60g.

Calgary Winter Olympics Gold Medal Winners. Air 5, 10, 20, 25, 30g.

History of World Cup Football Championship (2nd issue). Air 5, 10, 20, 25, 30g.

"Prenfil '88" International Philatelic Press Exhibition, Buenos Aires. "Ameripex '86" stamp optd. Air 30g.

"Philexfrance 89" International Stamp Exhibition, Paris. 1985 Explorers stamp optd. Air 30g.

PARMA Pt. 8

A former Grand Duchy of N. Italy, united with Sardinia in 1860 and now part of Italy.

100 centesimi = 1 lira.

1 Bourbon "fleur-de-lis"

2

3

1852. Imperf.

2	**1**	5c. black on yellow	42·00	85·00
11		5c. yellow	£5000	£600
4		10c. black	70·00	95·00
5		15c. black on pink	£1900	42·00
13		15c. red	£6000	£130
7		25c. black on purple	£9500	£140
14		25c. brown		£275
9		40c. black on blue	£1700	£225

1857. Imperf.

17	**2**	15c. red	£200	£325
19		25c. purple	£375	£150
20		40c. blue	46·00	£400

1859. Imperf.

28	**3**	5c. green	£1900	£3250
29		10c. brown	£700	£350
32		20c. blue	£1000	£160
33		40c. red	£475	£7000
35		80c. yellow	£6000	

NEWSPAPER STAMPS

1853. As T **3**. Imperf.

N1	**3**	6c. black on pink	£1100	£250
N3		9c. black on blue	70·00	95·00

PATIALA Pt. 1

A "convention" state in the Punjab, India.

12 pies = 1 anna;
16 annas = 1 rupee.

1884. Stamps of India (Queen Victoria) with curved opt **PUTTIALLA STATE** vert.

1	**23**	½a. turquoise	3·75	4·25
2	–	1a. purple	48·00	65·00
3	–	2a. blue	13·00	14·00
4	–	4a. green (No. 96)	80·00	90·00
5	–	8a. mauve	£400	£950
6	–	1r. grey (No. 101)	£130	£550

1885. Stamps of India (Queen Victoria) optd **PUTTIALLA STATE** horiz.

7	**23**	½a. turquoise	2·25	30
11	–	1a. purple	60	30
8	–	2a. blue	5·00	1·75
9	–	4a. green (No. 96)	3·25	3·50
12	–	8a. mauve	20·00	45·00
10	–	1r. grey (No. 101)	13·00	75·00

Stamps of India optd **PATIALA STATE**.

1891. Queen Victoria.

32	**40**	3p. red	30	15
13	**23**	½a. turquoise (No. 84)	40	10
33	–	½a. green (No. 114)	1·00	40
14	–	9p. red	1·00	2·25
15	–	1a. purple	1·40	30
34	–	1a. red	2·50	1·25
17	–	1a.6p. brown	1·25	1·50
18	–	2a. blue	1·25	30
20	–	3a. orange	2·25	60
21	–	4a. green (No. 95)	2·25	60
23	–	6a. brown (No. 80)	2·50	13·00
26	–	8a. mauve	2·75	13·00
27	–	12a. purple on red	2·50	14·00
28	**37**	1r. green and red	4·25	48·00
29	**38**	2r. red and orange	£120	£750

30 3r. brown and green £170 £800
31 5r. blue and violet £200 £850

1903. King Edward VII.
35 3p. grey 40 10
37 ½a. green (No. 122) 1·10 15
38 1a. red (No. 123) 90 10
39 2a. lilac 1·40 65
40 3a. orange 1·60 35
41 4a. olive 2·75 1·25
42 6a. bistre 3·25 8·50
43 8a. mauve 3·75 2·25
44 12a. purple on red 7·00 23·00
45 1r. green and red 4·00 5·00

1912. King Edward VII. Inscr "INDIA POSTAGE & REVENUE".
46 ½a. green (No. 149) 40 25
47 1a. red (No. 150) 1·75 1·00

1912. King George V. Optd in two lines.
48 **55** 3p. grey 25 10
49 **56** ½a. green 1·00 20
50 **57** 1a. red 1·75 20
61 1a. brown 2·75 40
51 **58** 1½d. brown (A) 30 55
52 **59** 2a. purple 1·25 1·00
53 **62** 3a. orange 2·50 1·25
62 3a. blue 3·25 8·00
54 **63** 4a. olive 3·50 3·00
55 **64** 6a. ochre 1·75 3·75
56 **65** 8a. mauve 3·00 2·25
57 **66** 12a. red 3·75 8·50
58 **67** 1r. brown and green 7·50 13·00
59 2r. red and brown 14·00 £140
60 5r. blue and violet 30·00 £170

1928. King George V. Optd in one line.
63 **55** 3p. grey 2·00 10
64 **56** ½a. green 25 10
75 **79** ½a. green 85 30
65a **80** 9p. green 2·25 75
66 **57** 1a. brown 75 25
76 **81** 1a. brown 1·10 20
67 **82** 1a.3p. mauve 3·00 15
77 **59** 2a. red 40 1·50
68 **70** 2a. lilac 1·75 40
69 **61** 2a.6p. orange 4·50 2·25
70 **62** 3a. blue 3·00 2·25
78w 3a. red 5·50 8·00
71 **71** 4a. green 4·50 1·50
79 **63** 4a. olive 1·75 2·50
72 **65** 8a. mauve 6·00 3·25
73 **66** 1r. brown and green 7·00 9·50
74w 2r. red and orange 11·00 50·00

1937. King George VI. Optd in one line.
80 **91** 3p. grey 25·00 35
81 ½a. brown 10·00 50
82 9p. green 5·00 1·00
83 1a. red 2·75 20
84 **92** 2a. red 1·50 8·50
85 – 2a.6p. violet 4·50 18·00
86 – 3a. green 4·50 8·00
87 – 3a.6p. blue 6·00 22·00
88 – 4a. brown 23·00 15·00
89 – 6a. green 22·00 50·00
90 – 8a. violet 24·00 38·00
91 – 12a. red 23·00 60·00
92 **93** 1r. grey and brown 22·00 40·00
93 2r. purple and brown 26·00 95·00
94 5r. green and blue 32·00 £200
95 10r. purple and red 45·00 £350
96 15r. brown and green £100 £550
97 25r. grey and purple £130 £550

1943. King George VI. Optd **PATIALA** only.
(a) Issue of 1938.
98 **94** 3p. grey 10·00 2·25
99 ½a. brown 6·50 1·75
100 9p. green £250 6·50
101 1a. red 23·00 2·00
102 **93** 1r. grey and brown 13·00 80·00

(b) Issue of 1940.
103 **92** 3p. grey 4·00 15
104 ½a. mauve 4·00 15
105 9p. green 1·50 15
106 1a. red 1·00 10
107 **101** 1a.3p. bistre 1·60 3·25
108 1½a. violet 12·00 3·25
109 2a. red 9·00 50
110 3a. violet 8·00 2·50
111 3½a. blue 19·00 35·00
112 **102** 4a. brown 8·00 3·50
113 6a. green 3·25 26·00
114 8a. violet 3·00 13·00
115 12a. purple 18·00 75·00

OFFICIAL STAMPS
Overprinted **SERVICE**.

1884. Nos. 1 to 3 (Queen Victoria).
O1 **23** ½a. turquoise 15·00 30
O2 – 1a. purple 1·00 10
O3 – 2a. blue £4500 £120

1885. Nos. 7, 11 and 8 (Queen Victoria).
O4 **23** ½a. turquoise 1·00 25
O5 – 1a. purple 1·00 10
O7 – 2a. blue 75 30

1891. Nos. 13 to 28 and No. 10 (Queen Victoria).
O 8 **23** ½a. turquoise (No. 13) 40 10
O 9 – 1a. purple 5·00 10
O20 – 1a. red 75 10
O10a – 2a. blue 3·25 2·00
O12 – 3a. orange 1·50 2·75
O13a – 4a. green 1·40 30
O15 – 6a. brown 1·60 35
O16 – 8a. mauve 2·75 1·25
O18 – 12a. purple on red 1·50 60
O19 – 1r. grey 2·00 65
O21 **37** 1r. green and red 6·00 9·50

1903. Nos. 36 to 45 (King Edward VII).
O22 3p. grey 40 10
O24 ½a. green 75 10
O25 1a. red 60 10
O26a 2a. lilac 80 10
O28 3a. brown 3·50 3·00
O29 4a. olive 2·00 20
O30 8a. mauve 1·75 75
O32 1r. green and red 1·75 80

1907. Nos. 46/7 (King Edward VII). Inscr "INDIA POSTAGE & REVENUE".
O33 ½a. green 50 20
O34 1a. red 50 10

1913. Official stamps of India (King George V). Optd **PATIALA STATE** in two lines.
O35 **55** 3p. grey 10 20
O36 **56** ½a. green 10 10
O37 **57** 1a. red 10 10
O38 1a. brown 7·50 1·00
O39 **59** 2a. mauve 90 60
O40 **63** 4a. olive 50 35
O41 **64** 6a. bistre 1·75 2·50
O42 **65** 8a. mauve 55 70
O43 **67** 1r. brown and green 1·40 1·40
O44 2r. red and brown 18·00 50·00
O45 5r. blue and violet 10·00 20·00

1927. Postage stamps of India (King George V) optd **PATIALA STATE SERVICE** in two lines.
O47 **55** 3p. grey 10 10
O48 **56** ½a. green 1·00 55
O58 **79** ½a. green 10 10
O49 **57** 1a. brown 15 10
O59 **81** 1a. brown 35 30
O50 **82** 1a.3p. mauve 40 10
O51 **70** 2a. purple 20 30
O52 2a. red 30 35
O60 **59** 2a. red 15 30
O53w **61** 2½a. orange 80 80
O54 **71** 4a. green 50 30
O62 **63** 4a. olive 2·25 1·25
O55 **65** 8a. purple 1·00 65
O56w **66** 1r. brown and green 2·75 3·00
O57 2r. red and orange 12·00 28·00

1938. Postage stamps of India (King George VI) optd **PATIALA STATE SERVICE**.
O63 **91** ½a. brown 75 20
O64 9p. green 13·00 55·00
O65 1a. red 75 40
O66 **93** 1r. grey and brown 1·00 6·50
O67 2r. purple and green 4·50 5·00
O68 5r. green and blue 15·00 55·00

1939. Surch **1A SERVICE 1A**.
O70 **82** 1a. on 1¼a. mauve 9·00 2·75

1940. Official stamps of India optd **PATIALA**.
O71 **O 20** 3p. grey 1·75 10
O72 ½a. brown 5·00 10
O73 ½a. purple 75 10
O74 9p. green 75 40
O75 1a. red 3·25 10
O76 1a.3p. bistre 1·00 25
O77 1½a. violet 6·50 1·00
O78 2a. orange 10·00 35
O79 2½a. violet 3·50 75
O80 4a. brown 1·75 2·50
O81 8a. violet 4·00 6·00

1940. Postage stamps of India (King George VI) optd **PATIALA SERVICE**.
O82 **93** 1r. slate and brown 5·00 10·00
O83 2r. purple and brown 12·00 60·00
O84 5r. green and blue 20·00 80·00

PENANG Pt. 1

A British Settlement which became a state of the Federation of Malaya, incorporated in Malaysia in 1963.

100 cents = 1 dollar (Straits or Malayan).

1948. Silver Wedding. As T **4b/c** of Pitcairn Islands.
1 10c. violet 30 20
2 $5 brown 30·00 30·00

1949. As Nos. 278/92 of Straits Settlement.
3 1c. black 20 30
4 2c. orange 85 20
5 3c. green 30 1·00
6 4c. brown 30 10
7 5c. purple 2·25 2·75
8 6c. grey 30 20
9 8c. red 60 4·00
10 8c. green 1·50 1·75
11 10c. mauve 30 10
12 12c. red 2·25 6·00
13 15c. blue 60 30
14 20c. black and green 60 1·25
15 20c. blue 70 1·25
16 25c. purple and orange 1·75 30
17 35c. red and purple 1·25 1·25
18 40c. red and purple 1·75 12·00
19 50c. black and blue 2·75 20
20 $1 blue and purple 17·00 2·00
21 $2 green and red 22·00 2·00
22 $3 green and brown 48·00 3·00

1949. U.P.U. As T **4d/g** of of Pitcairn Islands.
23 10c. purple 20 10
24 15c. blue 2·00 3·00
25 25c. orange 45 3·00
26 30c. black 1·50 3·50

1953. Coronation. As T **4h** of Pitcairn Islands.
27 10c. black and purple 1·50 10

1954. As T **1** of Malacca, but inscr "PENANG".
28 1c. black 10 70
29 2c. orange 50 30
30 4c. brown 70 10
31 5c. mauve 2·00 3·25
32 6c. grey 15 80
33 8c. green 20 3·50
34 10c. purple 20 10
35 12c. red 30 3·50
36 20c. blue 50 10
37 25c. purple and orange 30 10
38 30c. red and purple 30 10
39 35c. red and purple 70 60
40 50c. black and blue 50 10
41 $1 blue and purple 2·50 30
42 $2 green and red 10·00 3·75
43 $5 green and brown 45·00 3·75

1957. As Nos. 92/102 of Kedah, but inset portrait of Queen Elizabeth II.
44 1c. black 10 1·25
45 2c. red 10 1·00
46 4c. sepia 10 10
47 5c. lake 10 30
48 8c. green 1·25 2·25
49 10c. brown 30 10
50 20c. blue 60 40
51 50c. black and blue 60 70
52 $1 blue and purple 5·50 1·00
53 $2 green and red 18·00 13·00
54 $5 brown and green 21·00 12·00

1 Copra

1960. As Nos. 44/54, but with inset Arms of Penang as in T **1**.
55 1c. black 10 1·60
56 2c. red 10 1·60
57 4c. brown 10 10
58 5c. lake 10 10
59 8c. green 2·75 4·50
60 10c. purple 30 10
61 20c. blue 40 10
62 50c. black and blue 30 30
63 $1 blue and purple 4·25 1·75
64 $2 green and red 4·25 6·00
65 $5 brown and green 10·00 8·50

2 "Vanda hookeriana"

1965. As Nos. 115/21 of Kedah, but with Arms of Penang inset and inscr "PULAU PINANG" as in T **2**.
66 **2** 1c. multicoloured 10 1·25
67 – 2c. multicoloured 10 1·25
68 – 5c. multicoloured 20 10
69 – 6c. multicoloured 30 1·25
70 – 10c. multicoloured 20 10
71 – 15c. multicoloured 1·00 10
72 – 20c. multicoloured 1·60 30

The higher values used in Penang were Nos. 20/7 of Malaysia (National Issues).

3 "Valeria valeria"

1971. Butterflies. As Nos. 124/30 of Kedah but with Arms of Penang inset and inscr "pulau pinang" as in T **3**.
75 – 1c. multicoloured 40 2·25
76 – 2c. multicoloured 70 2·25
77 – 5c. multicoloured 1·50 40
78 – 6c. multicoloured 1·50 2·00
79 – 10c. multicoloured 1·50 15
80 – 15c. multicoloured 1·50 10
81 **3** 20c. multicoloured 1·75 60

The higher values in use with this issue were Nos. 64/71 of Malaysia (National Issues).

4 "Etlingera elatior" (inscr "Phaeomeria speciosa")

5 Cocoa

1979. Flowers. As Nos. 135/41 of Kedah, but with Arms of Penang and inscr "pulau pinang" as in T **4**.
86 1c. "Rafflesia hasseltii" 10 1·00
87 2c. "Pterocarpus indicus" 10 1·00
88 5c. "Lagerstroemia speciosa" 10 35
89 10c. "Durio zibethinus" 15 10
90 15c. "Hibiscus rosa-sinensis" 15 10
91 20c. "Rhododendron scortechinii" 20 10
92 25c. Type **4** 40 30

1986. As Nos. 152/8 of Kedah but with Arms of Penang and inscr "PULAU PINANG" as in T **5**.
100 1c. Coffee 10 20
101 2c. Coconuts 15 20
102 5c. Type **5** 20 20
103 10c. Black pepper 20 10
104 15c. Rubber 40 10
105 20c. Oil palm 30 10
106 30c. Rice 30 15

PENRHYN ISLAND Pt. 1

One of the Cook Islands in the South Pacific. A dependency of New Zealand. Used Cook Islands stamps until 1973 when further issues for use in the Northern group of the Cook Islands issues appeared.

A. NEW ZEALAND DEPENDENCY

1902. Stamps of New Zealand (Pictorials) surch **PENRHYN ISLAND.** and value in native language.
4 **23** ½d. green 80 7·00
10 **42** 1d. red 1·25 4·50
1 **26** 2½d. blue (No. 249) 4·00 8·00
14 **28** 3d. brown 10·00 24·00
15 **31** 6d. red 15·00 35·00
16a **34** 1s. orange 42·00 42·00

1914. Stamps of New Zealand (King Edward VII) surch **PENRHYN ISLAND.** and value in native language.
19 **51** ½d. green 80 8·00
22 6d. red 23·00 70·00
23 1s. orange 42·00 95·00

1917. Stamps of New Zealand (King George V) optd **PENRHYN ISLAND.**
28 **62** ½d. green 1·00 2·00
29 1½d. grey 6·50 20·00
30 1½d. brown 60 20·00
24a 2½d. blue 2·00 7·00
31 3d. brown 3·50 24·00
26a 6d. red 5·00 20·00
27a 1s. orange 12·00 32·00

1920. Pictorial types as Cook Islands (1920), but inscr "PENRHYN".
32 **9** ½d. black and green 1·00 17·00
33 – 1d. black and red 1·50 15·00
34 – 1½d. black and violet 6·50 19·00
40 – 2½d. brown and black 5·00 28·00
35 – 3d. black and red 2·50 8·50
36 – 6d. brown and red 3·25 20·00
37 – 1s. black and blue 10·00 26·00

B. PART OF COOK ISLANDS

1973. Nos. 228/9, 231, 233/6, 239/40 and 243/5 of Cook Is. optd **PENRHYN NORTHERN** or **PENRHYN** ($1, 2).
41B 1c. multicoloured 10 10
42B 2c. multicoloured 10 10
43B 3c. multicoloured 20 10
44B 4c. multicoloured 10 10
45B 5c. multicoloured 10 10
46B 6c. multicoloured 15 30
47B 8c. multicoloured 20 40
48B 15c. multicoloured 30 50
49B 20c. multicoloured 1·50 80
50B 50c. multicoloured 50 1·75
51B $1 multicoloured 50 2·00
52B $2 multicoloured 50 2·25

1973. Nos. 450/2 of Cook Is. optd **PENRHYN NORTHERN.**
53 **138** 25c. multicoloured 30 20
54 – 30c. multicoloured 30 20
55 – 50c. multicoloured 30 20

10 "Ostracion sp."

1974. Fishes. Multicoloured.
56 ½c. Type **10** 50 75
57 1c. "Monodactylus argenteus" 70 75
58 2c. "Pomacanthus imperator" 80 75
59 3c. "Chelmon rostratus" 80 50
60 4c. "Chaetodon ornatissimus" 80 50
61 5c. "Chaetodon melanotus" 80 50
62 8c. "Chaetodon raffessi" 80 50
63 10c. "Chaetodon ephippium" 85 50
64 20c. "Pygoplites diacanthus" 1·75 50
65 25c. "Heniochus acuminatus" 1·75 50
66 60c. "Plectorhynchus chaetodonoides" 2·50 90
67 $1 "Balistipus undulatus" 3·25 1·25
68 $2 Bird's-eye view of Penrhyn 3·00 12·00
69 $5 Satellite view of Australasia 3·00 5·00

Nos. 68/9 are size 63 × 25 mm.

11 Penrhyn Stamps of 1902

13 Churchill giving "V" sign

12 "Adoration of the Kings" (Memling)

1974. Cent of Universal Postal Union. Mult.
70 25c. Type **11** 20 45
71 50c. Stamps of 1920 . . . . . 35 55

1974. Christmas. Multicoloured.
72 5c. Type **12** 20 30
73 10c. "Adoration of the Shepherds" (Hugo van der Goes) 25 30
74 25c. "Adoration of the Magi" (Rubens) 40 45
75 30c. "The Holy Family" (Borgianni) 45 65

1974. Birth Cent of Sir Winston Churchill.
76 **13** 30c. brown and gold 35 85
77 – 50c. green and gold 45 90
DESIGN: 50c. Full-face portrait.

1975. "Apollo–Soyuz" Space Project. Optd **KIA ORANA ASTRONAUTS** and emblem.
78 $5 Satellite view of Australasia 1·75 2·50

15 "Virgin and Child" (Bouts)

16 "Pieta"

1975. Christmas. Paintings of the "Virgin and Child" by artists given below. Multicoloured.
79 7c. Type **15** 40 10
80 15c. Leonardo da Vinci . . . 70 20
81 35c. Raphael . . . . 1·10 35

1976. Easter. 500th Birth Anniv of Michelangelo.
82 **16** 15c. brown and gold 25 15
83 – 20c. lilac and gold 30 15
84 – 35c. green and gold 40 20
MS85 112 × 72 mm. Nos. 82/4 . . . 85 1·25
DESIGNS: Nos. 83/4 show different views of the "Pieta".

17 "Washington crossing the Delaware" (E. Leutze)

18 Running

1976. Bicentenary of American Revolution.
86 **17** 30c. multicoloured 25 15
87 – 30c. multicoloured 25 15
88 – 30c. multicoloured 25 15
89 – 50c. multicoloured 30 20
90 – 50c. multicoloured 30 20
91 – 50c. multicoloured 30 20
MS92 103 × 103 mm. Nos. 86/91 1·25 1·25
DESIGNS: Nos. 86/88, "Washington crossing the Delaware" (E. Leutze); Nos. 89/91, "The Spirit of "76" (A. M. Willard).
Nos. 86/88 and 89/91 were each printed together, se-tenant, forming a composite design of the complete painting. Type **17** shows the left-hand stamp of the 30c. design.

1976. Olympic Games, Montreal. Multicoloured.
93 25c. Type **18** 25 15
94 30c. Long jumping 30 15
95 75c. Throwing the javelin . . 55 25
MS96 86 × 128 mm. Nos. 93/5 . . 1·10 2·00

19 "The Flight into Egypt"

1976. Christmas. Durer Engravings.
97 **19** 7c. black and silver 15 10
98 – 15c. blue and silver 25 15
99 – 35c. violet and silver 35 25
DESIGNS: 15c. "Adoration of the Magi"; 35c. "The Nativity".

20 The Queen in Coronation Robes

1977. Silver Jubilee. Multicoloured.
100 50c. Type **20** 25 60
101 $1 The Queen and Prince Philip 35 65
102 $2 Queen Elizabeth II . . . 50 80
MS103 128 × 87 mm. Nos. 100/2 1·00 1·50
Stamps from the miniature sheet have silver borders.

21 "The Annunciation"

1977. Christmas. Illustrations by J. S. von Carolsfeld.
104 **21** 7c. brown, purple and gold 40 15
105 – 15c. red, purple and gold 60 15
106 – 35c. deep green, green and gold . . . . 1·00 30
DESIGNS: 15c. "The Announcement to the Shepherds"; 35c. "The Nativity".

22 Iiwi

23 "The Road to Calvary"

1978. Bicentenary of Discovery of Hawaii. Birds and Artefacts. Multicoloured.
107 20c. Type **22** 80 30
108 20c. Elgin cloak 80 30
109 30c. Apapane 90 40
110 30c. Feather image of a god 90 40
111 35c. Moorhen 90 45
112 35c. Feather cape, helmet and staff 90 45
113 75c. Hawaii O-o . . . . . . 1·50 80
114 75c. Feather image and cloak 1·50 80
MS115 Two sheets, each 78 × 119 mm. containing. (a) Nos. 107, 109, 111, 113. (b) Nos. 108, 110, 112, 114 . . . . 5·00 7·00

1978. Easter. 400th Birth Anniv of Rubens. Multicoloured.
116 10c. Type **23** 20 10
117 15c. "Christ on the Cross" 25 15
118 35c. "Christ with Straw" . . 45 25
MS119 87 × 138 mm. Nos. 116/18 1·00 1·60
Stamps from No. **MS**119 are slightly larger (28 × 36 mm).

1978. Easter. Children's Charity. Designs as Nos. 116/18 in separate miniature sheets, 49 × 68 mm, each with a face value of 60c.+5c.
MS120 As Nos. 116/18. Set of 3 sheets . . . . 90 1·50

24 Royal Coat of Arms

25 "Madonna of the Pear"

1978. 25th Anniv of Coronation.
121 **24** 90c. black, gold and mauve 30 60
122 – 90c. multicoloured 30 60
123 – 90c. black, gold and green 30 60
MS124 75 × 122 mm. Nos. 121/3 1·10 2·00
DESIGNS: No. 122, Queen Elizabeth II; No. 123, New Zealand coat of arms.

1978. Christmas. 450th Death Anniv of Albrecht Durer. Multicoloured.
125 30c. Type **25** 65 30
126 35c. "The Virgin and Child with St. Anne" (Durer) . . 65 30
MS127 101 × 60 mm. Nos. 125/6 1·00 1·25

26 Sir Rowland Hill and G.B. Penny Black Stamp

27 Max and Moritz

1979. Death Centenary of Sir Rowland Hill. Mult.
128 75c. Type **26** 40 55
129 75c. 1974 U.P.U. Centenary 25c. and 50c. commemoratives 40 55
130 90c. Sir Rowland Hill 45 70
131 90c. 1978 Coronation Anniversary 90c. commemorative 45 70
MS132 116 × 58 mm. Nos. 128/31 1·25 1·50
Stamps from No. **MS**132 have cream backgrounds.

1979. International Year of the Child. Illustrations from "Max and Moritz" stories by Wilhelm Busch. Multicoloured.
133 12c. Type **27** 15 15
134 12c. Max and Moritz looking down chimney 15 15
135 12c. Max and Moritz making off with food 15 15
136 12c. Cook about to beat dog 15 15
137 15c. Max sawing through bridge 20 15
138 15c. Pursuer approaching bridge 20 15
139 15c. Collapse of bridge . . . 20 15
140 15c. Pursuer in river 20 15
141 20c. Baker locking shop . . . 20 20
142 20c. Max and Moritz emerge from hiding 20 20
143 20c. Max and Moritz falling in dough 20 20
144 20c. Max and Moritz made into buns 20 20

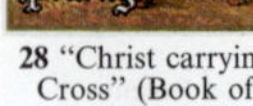

28 "Christ carrying Cross" (Book of Ferdinand II)

29 "Queen Elizabeth, 1937" (Sir Gerald Kelly)

1980. Easter. Scenes from 15th-cent Prayer Books. Multicoloured.
145 12c. Type **28** 15 20
146 20c. "The Crucifixion" (William Vrelant, Book of Duke of Burgundy) 20 25
147 35c. "Descent from the Cross" (Book of Ferdinand II) 30 45
MS148 111 × 65 mm. Nos. 145/7 55 1·00
Stamps from No. **MS**148 have cream borders.

1980. Easter. Children's Charity. Designs as Nos. 145/7 in separate miniature sheets 54 × 85 mm, each with a face value of 70c.+5c.
MS149 As Nos. 145/7. Set of 3 sheets 75 1·00

1980. 80th Birthday of The Queen Mother.
150 **29** $1 multicoloured . . . . . 1·25 1·25
MS151 55 × 84 mm. **29** $2.50 multicoloured . . . . 1·60 1·60

30 Falk Hoffman, East Germany (platform diving) (gold)

31 "The Virgin of Counsellors" (Luis Dalmau)

1980. Olympic Medal Winners. Multicoloured.
152 10c. Type **30** 30 10
153 10c. Martina Jaschke, East Germany (platform diving) 30 10
154 20c. Tomi Polkolainen, Finland (archery) 35 15
155 20c. Kete Losaberidse, U.S.S.R. (archery) 35 15
156 30c. Czechoslovakia (football) 40 20
157 30c. East Germany (football) 40 20
158 50c. Barbel Wockel, East Germany (200 m) 50 30
159 50c. Pietro Mennea, Italy (200 m) 50 30
MS160 150 × 106 mm. Nos. 152/9 1·40 1·75
Stamps from No. **MS**160 have gold borders.

1980. Christmas. Mult.
161 20c. Type **31** 15 15
162 35c. "Virgin and Child" (Serra brothers) 20 20
163 50c. "The Virgin of Albocacer" (Master of the Porciuncula) 30 30
MS164 135 × 75 mm. Nos. 161/3 1·50 1·50

1980. Christmas. Children's Charity. Design as Nos. 161/3 in separate miniature sheets, 54 × 77 mm, each with a face value of 70c.+5c.
MS165 As Nos. 161/3. Set of 3 sheets 1·50 1·50

32 Amatasi

33 "Jesus at the Grove" (Veronese)

1981. Sailing Craft and Ships (1st series). Mult.
166 1c. Type **32** 20 15
167 1c. Ndrua (canoe) 20 15
168 1c. Waka (canoe) 20 15
169 1c. Tongiaki (canoe) 20 15
170 3c. Va'a Teu'ua (canoe) . . . 40 15
171 3c. "Vitoria" (Del Cano's ship) 40 15
172 3c. "Golden Hind" (Drake's ship) 40 15
173 3c. "La Boudeuse" (Bougainville's ship) . . . 40 15
174 4c. H.M.S. "Bounty" 50 15
175 4c. "L'Astrolabe" (Dumont d'Urville's ship) 50 15
176 4c. "Star of India" (full-rigged ship) 50 15
177 4c. "Great Republic" (clipper) 50 15
178 6c. "Balcutha" (clipper) . . . 50 20
179 6c. "Coonatto" (clipper) . . 50 20
180 6c. "Antiope" (clipper) . . . 50 20
181 6c. "Taeping" (clipper) . . . 50 20
182 10c. "Preussen" (full-rigged ship) 50 75
183 10c. "Pamir" (barque) . . . 50 75
184 10c. "Cap Hornier" (full-rigged ship) 50 75
185 10c. "Patriarch" (clipper) . . 50 75
186 15c. Type **32** 50 85
187 15c. As No. 167 . . . . . . 50 85
188 15c. As No. 168 . . . . . . 50 85
189 15c. As No. 169 . . . . . . 50 85
190 20c. As No. 170 . . . . . . 50 85
191 20c. As No. 171 . . . . . . 50 85
192 20c. As No. 172 . . . . . . 50 85
193 20c. As No. 173 . . . . . . 50 85
194 30c. As No. 174 . . . . . . 50 95
195 30c. As No. 175 . . . . . . 50 95
196 30c. As No. 176 . . . . . . 50 95
197 30c. As No. 177 . . . . . . 50 95
198 50c. As No. 178 . . . . . . 1·00 1·75
199 50c. As No. 179 . . . . . . 1·00 1·75
200 50c. As No. 180 . . . . . . 1·00 1·75
201 50c. As No. 181 . . . . . . 1·00 1·75
202 $1 As No. 182 . . . . 2·50 1·50
203 $1 As No. 183 . . . . 2·50 1·50
204 $1 As No. 184 . . . . 2·50 1·50
205 $1 As No. 185 . . . . 2·50 1·50
206 $2 "Cutty Sark" (clipper) . . 4·50 3·25
207 $4 "Mermerus" (clipper) . . 9·00 5·00
208 $6 H.M.S. "Resolution" and H.M.S. "Discovery" (Cook's ships) . . . . . . 15·00 12·00
Nos. 186/201 are 41 × 35 mm, Nos. 202/5 41 × 25 mm and Nos. 206/8 47 × 33 mm in size.
Nos. 181 and 201 are wrongly inscribed "TEAPING".
See also Nos. 337/55.

1981. Easter. Paintings. Multicoloured.
218 30c. Type **33** 40 20
219 40c. "Christ with Crown of Thorns" (Titian) 55 25
220 50c. "Pieta" (Van Dyck) 60 30
MS221 110 × 68 mm. Nos. 218/20 2·75 2·00

1981. Easter. Children's Charity. Designs as Nos. 218/20 in separate miniature sheets 70 × 86 mm, each with a face value of 70c.+5c.
MS222 As Nos. 218/20. Set of 3 sheets 1·25 1·50

34 Prince Charles as Young Child

35 Footballers

1981. Royal Wedding. Multicoloured.
223 40c. Type **34** 15 35
224 50c. Prince Charles as schoolboy 15 40
225 60c. Prince Charles as young man 20 40
226 70c. Prince Charles in ceremonial Naval uniform 20 45
227 80c. Prince Charles as Colonel-in-Chief, Royal Regiment of Wales 20 45
MS228 99 × 89 mm. Nos. 223/7 90 2·00

1981. International Year for Disabled Persons. Nos. 223/7 surch **+5c.**
229 **34** 40c.+5c. multicoloured 15 50
230 – 50c.+5c. multicoloured 15 55
231 – 60c.+5c. multicoloured 20 55
232 – 70c.+5c. multicoloured 20 60
233 – 80c.+5c. multicoloured 20 65
MS234 99 × 89 mm. As Nos. 229/33, but 10c. premium on each stamp 80 2·50

1981. World Cup Football Championship, Spain (1982). Multicoloured.
235 15c. Type **35** 20 15
236 15c. Footballer wearing orange jersey with black and mauve stripes 20 15
237 15c. Player in blue jersey 20 15
238 35c. Player in blue jersey 30 25
239 35c. Player in red jersey 30 25
240 35c. Player in yellow jersey with green stripes 30 25
241 50c. Player in orange jersey 40 35
242 50c. Player in mauve jersey 40 35
243 50c. Player in black jersey 40 35
MS244 113 × 151 mm. As Nos. 235/43, but each stamp with a premium of 3c. 4·75 2·75

36 "The Virgin on a Crescent"

37 Lady Diana Spencer as Baby

1981. Christmas. Engravings by Durer.
245 **36** 30c. violet, purple and stone 90 1·00
246 – 40c. violet, purple and stone 1·25 1·40
247 – 50c. violet, purple and stone 1·50 1·75
MS248 134 × 75 mm. As Nos. 245/7, but each stamp with a premium of 2c. 2·00 2·25
MS249 Designs as Nos. 245/7 in separate miniature sheets, 58 × 85 mm, each with a face value of 70c.+5c. Set of 3 sheets 1·50 1·75
DESIGNS: 40c. "The Virgin at the Fence"; 50c. "The Holy Virgin and Child".

1982. 21st Birthday of Princess of Wales. Multicoloured.
250 30c. Type **37** 30 30
251 50c. As young child 40 45
252 70c. As schoolgirl 60 60
253 80c. As teenager 70 80
254 $1.40 As a young lady 1·10 1·25
MS255 87 × 110 mm. Nos. 250/4 6·50 3·50

1982. Birth of Prince William of Wales (1st issue). Nos. 223/7 optd **BIRTH OF PRINCE WILLIAM OF WALES 21 JUNE 1982.**
256 40c. Type **34** 30 35
257 50c. Prince Charles as schoolboy 40 45
258 60c. Prince Charles as young man 45 55
259 70c. Prince Charles in ceremonial Naval uniform 50 60
260 80c. Prince Charles as Colonel-in-Chief, Royal Regiment of Wales 50 65
MS261 99 × 89 mm. Nos. 256/60 6·00 7·00

1982. Birth of Prince William of Wales (2nd issue). As Nos. 250/5 but with changed inscriptions. Multicoloured.
262 30c. As Type **37** (A) 60 55
263 30c. As Type **37** (B) 60 55
264 50c. As No. 251 (A) 70 65
265 50c. As No. 251 (B) 70 65
266 70c. As No. 252 (A) 90 80
267 70c. As No. 252 (B) 90 80
268 80c. As No. 253 (A) 95 85
269 80c. As No. 253 (B) 95 85
270 $1.40 As No. 254 (A) 1·40 1·25
271 $1.40 As No. 254 (B) 1·40 1·25
MS272 88 × 109 mm. As No. **MS**255 (c) 4·75 3·25
INSCR: A. "21 JUNE 1982. BIRTH OF PRINCE WILLIAM OF WALES"; B. "COMMEMORATING THE BIRTH OF PRINCE WILLIAM OF WALES"; C. "21 JUNE 1982. ROYAL BIRTH PRINCE WILLIAM OF WALES".

39 "Virgin and Child" (detail, Joos Van Cleve)

40 Red Coral

1982. Christmas. Details from Renaissance Paintings of "Virgin and Child". Multicoloured.
273 25c. Type **39** 30 40
274 48c. "Virgin and Child" (Filippino Lippi) 45 55
275 60c. "Virgin and Child" (Cima da Conegliano) 60 70
MS276 134 × 73 mm. As Nos. 273/5 but each with 2c. charity premium 1·00 2·00

1982. Christmas. Children's Charity. Designs as Nos. 273/5, but without frames, in separate miniature sheets, 60 × 85 mm, each with a face value of 70c.+5c.
MS277 As Nos. 273/5. Set of 3 sheets 1·25 1·60

1983. Commonwealth Day. Multicoloured.
278 60c. Type **40** 40 45
279 60c. Aerial view of Penrhyn atoll 40 45
280 60c. Eleanor Roosevelt on Penrhyn during Second World War 40 45
281 60c. Map of South Pacific 40 45

41 Scout Emblem and Blue Tropical Flower

1983. 75th Anniv of Boy Scout Movement. Multicoloured.
282 36c. Type **41** 1·50 65
283 48c. Emblem and pink flower 1·75 75
284 60c. Emblem and orange flower 1·75 1·00
MS285 86 × 46 mm. $2 As 48c., but with elements of design reversed 1·50 3·00

1983. 15th World Scout Jamboree, Alberta, Canada. Nos. 282/4 optd **XV WORLD JAMBOREE CANADA 1983.**
286 36c. Type **41** 1·25 40
287 48c. Emblem and pink flower 1·50 55
288 60c. Emblem and orange flower 1·60 75
MS289 86 × 46 mm. $2 As 48c., but with elements of design reversed 1·50 3·50

43 School of Sperm Whales

1983. Whale Conservation. Multicoloured.
290 8c. Type **43** 1·00 70
291 15c. Harpooner preparing to strike 1·40 95
292 35c. Whale attacking boat 2·00 1·40
293 60c. Dead whales marked with flags 3·00 2·00
294 $1 Dead whales on slipway 3·75 3·00

44 "Mercury" (cable ship)

1983. World Communications Year. Multicoloured.
295 36c. Type **44** 80 35
296 48c. Men watching cable being laid 85 45
297 60c. "Mercury" (different) 1·10 60
MS298 115 × 90 mm. As Nos. 295/7 but each with charity premium of 3c. 1·25 1·60
On No. **MS**298 the values are printed in black and have been transposed with the World Communications Year logo.

1983. Various stamps surch. (a) Nos. 182/5, 190/7 and 206.
299 18c. on 10c. "Preussen" 1·00 30
300 18c. on 10c. "Pamir" 1·00 30
301 18c. on 10c. "Cap Hornier" 1·00 30
302 18c. on 10c. "Patriarch" 1·00 30
303 36c. on 20c. Va'a Teu'ua 1·25 45
304 36c. on 20c. "Vitoria" 1·25 45
305 36c. on 20c. "Golden Hind" 1·25 45
306 36c. on 20c. "La Boudeuse" 1·25 45
307 36c. on 30c. H.M.S. "Bounty" 1·25 45
308 36c. on 30c. "L'Astrolabe" 1·25 45
309 36c. on 30c. "Star of India" 1·25 45
310 36c. on 30c. "Great Republic" 1·25 45
311 $1.20 on $2 "Cutty Sark" 4·50 1·60
(b) Nos. 252/3.
312 72c. on 70c. Princess Diana as schoolgirl 4·00 1·50
313 96c. on 80c. Princess Diana as teenager 4·00 1·75

1983. Nos. 225/6, 268/9, 253 and 208 surch.
314 48c. on 60c. Prince Charles as young man 3·75 1·75
315 72c. on 70c. Prince Charles in ceremonial Naval uniform 4·25 1·90
316 96c. on 80c. As No. 253 (inscr "21 JUNE 1982 ...") 3·00 1·10
317 96c. on 80c. As No. 253 (inscr "COMMEMORATING ...") 2·00 1·10
318 $1.20 on $4.40 As young lady 3·50 1·60
319 $5.60 on $6 H.M.S. "Resolution" and "Discovery" 18·00 10·00

45 George Cayley's Airship Design, 1837

1983. Bicentenary of Manned Flight. Mult. A. Inscr "NORTHERN COOK ISLANDS".
320A 36c. Type **45** 1·00 80
321A 48c. Dupuy de Lome's man-powered airship, 1872 1·25 90
322A 60c. Santos Dumont's airship "Ballon No. 6", 1901 1·50 1·25
323A 96c. Lebaudy-Juillot's airship, No. 1 "La Jaune", 1902 2·25 1·75
324A $1.32 Airship LZ-127 "Graf Zeppelin", 1929 3·00 2·50
MS325A 113 × 138 mm. Nos. 320A/4A 6·50 11·00
B. Corrected spelling optd in black on silver over original inscription.
320B 36c. Type **45** 35 30
321B 48c. Dupuy de Lome's man-powered airship, 1872 40 45
322B 60c. Santos Dumont's airship "Ballon No. 6", 1901 45 50
323B 96c. Lebaudy-Juillot's airship No. 1 "La Jaune", 1902 75 80
324B $1.32 Airship LZ-127 "Graf Zeppelin", 1929 1·00 1·10
MS325B 113 × 138 mm. Nos. 320B/4B 2·25 4·25

46 "Madonna in the Meadow"

47 Waka

1983. Christmas. 500th Birth Anniv of Raphael. Multicoloured.
326 36c. Type **46** 60 40
327 42c. "Tempi Madonna" 60 40
328 48c. "The Smaller Cowper Madonna" 80 50
329 60c. "Madonna della Tenda" 95 60
MS330 87 × 115 mm. As Nos. 326/9 but each with a charity premium of 3c. 3·00 2·50

1983. Nos. 266/7, 227 and 270 surch.
331 72c. on 70c. As No. 252 (inscr "21 JUNE 1982 ...") 1·75 80
332 72c. on 70c. As No. 252 (inscr "COMMEMORATING ...") 1·00 60
333 96c. on 80c. Prince Charles as Colonel-in-Chief, Royal Regiment of Wales 1·75 65
334 $1.20 on $1.40 As No. 254 (inscr "21 JUNE 1982 ...") 2·00 70
335 $1.20 on $1.40 As No. 254 (inscr "COMMEMORATING ...") 1·50 65

1983. Christmas. 500th Birth Anniv of Raphael. Children's Charity. Designs as Nos. 326/9 in separate miniature sheets, 65 × 84 mm, each with a face value of 75c.+5c.
MS336 As Nos. 326/9. Set of 4 sheets 1·75 3·00

1984. Sailing Craft and Ships (2nd series). Multicoloured.
337 2c. Type **47** 70 70
338 4c. Amatasi 70 70
339 5c. Ndrua 70 70
340 8c. Tongiaki 70 70
341 10c. "Vitoria" 70 60
342 18c. "Golden Hind" 1·00 70
343 20c. "La Boudeuse" 70 70
344 30c. H.M.S. "Bounty" 1·00 70
345 36c. "L'Astrolabe" 70 70
346 48c. "Great Republic" 70 70
347 50c. "Star of India" 70 70
348 60c. "Coonatto" 70 70
349 72c. "Antiope" 70 70
350 80c. "Balcutha" 70 70
351 96c. "Cap Hornier" 85 85
352 $1.20 "Pamir" 2·50 1·40
353 $3 "Mermerus" (41 × 31 mm) 5·00 3·00
354 $5 "Cutty Sark" (41 × 31 mm) 5·50 5·00
355 $9.60 H.M.S. "Resolution" and H.M.S. "Discovery" (41 × 31 mm) 21·00 18·00

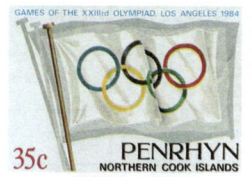

48 Olympic Flag

1984. Olympic Games, Los Angeles. Mult.
356 35c. Type **48** 30 35
357 60c. Olympic torch and flags 50 55
358 $1.80 Ancient athletes and Coliseum 1·50 1·60
MS359 103 × 86 mm. As Nos. 356/8 but each with a charity premium of 5c. 2·40 2·50

49 Penrhyn Stamps of 1978, 1979 and 1981

1984. "Ausipex" International Stamp Exhibition, Melbourne. Multicoloured.
360 60c. Type **49** 50 75
361 $1.20 Location map of Penrhyn 1·00 1·25
MS362 90 × 90 mm. As Nos. 360/1, but each with a face value of 96c. 1·75 2·00

1984. Birth of Prince Harry. Nos. 223/4 and 250/1 surch **$2 Birth of Prince Harry 15 Sept. 1984.**
363 $2 on 30c. Type **37** 1·60 1·50
364 $2 on 40c. Type **34** 1·75 1·75

365 $2 on 50c. Prince Charles as schoolboy . . . . 1·75 1·75
366 $2 on 50c. Lady Diana as young child . . . . 1·60 1·50

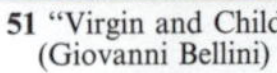

51 "Virgin and Child" (Giovanni Bellini)

53 Lady Elizabeth Bowes-Lyon, 1921

52 Harlequin Duck

1984. Christmas. Paintings of the Virgin and Child by different artists. Multicoloured.
367 36c. Type **51** 60 35
368 48c. Lorenzo di Credi 75 45
369 60c. Palma the Older 80 50
370 96c. Raphael . . . . 1·00 80
MS371 93 × 118 mm. As Nos. 367/70, but each with a charity premium of 5c. . . . . 2·50 3·00

1984. Christmas. Children's Charity. Designs as Nos. 367/70, but without frames, in separate miniature sheets 67 × 81 mm, each with a face value of 96c.+10c.
MS372 As Nos. 367/70. Set of 4 sheets . . . . 3·00 3·50

1985. Birth Bicentenary of John J. Audubon (ornithologist). Multicoloured.
373 20c. Type **52** . . . . 2·00 1·75
374 55c. Sage grouse . . . . . . 2·75 2·75
375 65c. Solitary sandpiper . . . 3·00 3·00
376 75c. Dunlin . . . . 3·25 3·50
MS377 Four sheets, each 70 × 53 mm. As Nos. 373/6, but each with a face value of 95c. 9·00 6·50
Nos. 373/6 show original paintings.

1985. Life and Times of Queen Elizabeth the Queen Mother. Each violet, silver and yellow.
378 75c. Type **53** 40 65
379 95c. With baby Princess Elizabeth, 1926 . . . . . 50 80
380 $1.20 Coronation Day, 1937 65 1·00
381 $2.80 On her 70th birthday 1·25 2·00
MS382 66 × 90 mm. $5 The Queen Mother . . . . 2·40 3·25
See also No. **MS**403.

54 "The House in the Wood"

1985. International Youth Year. Birth Centenary of Jacob Grimm (folklorist). Multicoloured.
383 75c. Type **54** . . . . 2·50 2·25
384 95c. "Snow-White and Rose-Red" . . . . 2·75 2·50
385 $1.15 "The Goose Girl" . . . 3·00 2·75

55 "The Annunciation"

1985. Christmas. Paintings by Murillo. Mult.
386 75c. Type **55** . . . . 1·25 1·25
387 $1.15 "Adoration of the Shepherds" . . . . 1·75 1·75
388 $1.80 "The Holy Family" . . 2·50 2·50
MS389 66 × 131 mm. As Nos. 386/8, but each with a face value of 95c. 2·75 3·00
MS390 Three sheets, each 66 × 72 mm. As Nos. 386/8, but with face values of $1.20, $1.45 and $2.75. Set of 3 sheets . . . 4·50 4·75

56 Halley's Comet

1986. Appearance of Halley's Comet. Design showing details of the painting "Fire and Ice" by Camille Rendal. Multicoloured.
391 $1.50 Type **56** . . . . 2·75 1·50
392 $1.50 Stylized "Giotto" spacecraft . . . . 2·75 1·50
MS393 108 × 43 mm. $3 As Nos. 391/2 (104 × 39 mm). Imperf 2·25 2·50
Nos. 391/2 were printed together, forming a composite design of the complete painting.

57 Princess Elizabeth aged Three, 1929, and Bouquet

1986. 60th Birthday of Queen Elizabeth II. Multicoloured.
394 95c. Type **57** . . . . 1·50 80
395 $1.45 Profile of Queen Elizabeth and St. Edward's Crown . . . . 2·00 1·25
396 $2.50 Queen Elizabeth aged three and in profile with Imperial State Crown (56 × 30 mm) . . . . 2·50 2·00

58 Statue of Liberty under Construction, Paris

59 Prince Andrew and Miss Sarah Ferguson

1986. Centenary of Statue of Liberty. Each black, gold and green.
397 95c. Type **58** 65 70
398 $1.75 Erection of Statue, New York . . . . 1·10 1·25
399 $3 Artist's impression of Statue, 1876 . . . . 2·10 2·25
See also No. **MS**412.

1986. Royal Wedding. Multicoloured.
400 $2.50 Type **59** . . . . 3·50 3·50
401 $3.50 Profile of Prince Andrew and Miss Sarah Ferguson . . . . 4·00 4·00

1986. "Stampex '86" Stamp Exhibition, Adelaide. No. **MS**362 surch **$2** in black on gold.
MS402 $2 on 96c. × 2 . . . . . 6·00 7·00
The "Stampex '86" exhibition emblem is overprinted on the sheet margin.

1986. 86th Birthday of Queen Elizabeth the Queen Mother. Nos. 378/81 in miniature sheet, 90 × 120 mm.
MS403 Nos. 378/81 . . . . . . 13·00 9·50

61 "Adoration of the Shepherds"

65 "The Garvagh Madonna"

1986. Christmas. Engravings by Rembrandt. Each brown, ochre and gold.
404 65c. Type **61** . . . . 1·75 1·75
405 $1.75 "Virgin and Child" . . 3·00 3·00
406 $2.50 "The Holy Family" . . 4·25 4·25
MS407 120 × 87 mm. As Nos. 404/6, but each size 31 × 39 mm with a face value of $1.50 . . . . . . 12·00 9·00

1986. Visit of Pope John Paul II to **South Pacific**. Nos. 404/6 surch **SOUTH PACIFIC VISIT 21 TO 24 NOVEMBER 1986 +10c**.
408 65c.+10c. Type **61** . . . . 3·50 2·50
409 $1.75+10c. "Virgin and Child" . . . . 5·00 3·75
410 $2.50+10c. "The Holy Family" . . . . 6·00 4·25
MS411 120 × 87 mm. As Nos. 408/10, but each size 31 × 39 mm with a face value of $1.50+10c. . . . . 15·00 9·00

1987. Centenary of Statue of Liberty (1986) (2nd issue). Two sheets, each 122 × 122 mm, containing multicoloured designs as T **112a** of Niue.
MS412 Two sheets. (a) 65c. Head and torch of Statue; 65c. Torch at sunset; 65c. Restoration workers with flag; 65c. Statue and Manhattan skyline; 65c. Workers and scaffolding. (b) 65c. Workers on Statue crown (horiz); 65c. Aerial view of Ellis Island (horiz); 65c. Ellis Island Immigration Centre (horiz); 65c. View from Statue to Ellis Island and Manhattan (horiz); 65c. Restoration workers (horiz). Set of 2 sheets . . . . 7·50 11·00

1987. Royal Ruby Wedding. Nos. 68/9 optd **Fortieth Royal Wedding Anniversary 1947–87**.
413 $2 Birds-eye view of Penrhyn 2·00 2·25
414 $5 Satellite view of Australasia . . . . 3·50 4·25

1987. Christmas. Religious Paintings by Raphael. Multicoloured.
415 95c. Type **65** . . . . 1·50 1·50
416 $1.60 "The Alba Madonna" 2·00 2·00
417 $2.25 "The Madonna of the Fish" . . . . 3·00 3·00
MS418 91 × 126 mm. As Nos. 415/17, but each with a face value of $1.15 . . . . 13·00 13·00
MS419 70 × 86 mm. $4.80 As No. 417, but size 36 × 39 mm. 13·00 13·00

66 Athletics

1988. Olympic Games, Seoul. Multicoloured.
420 55c. Type **66** 75 65
421 95c. Pole vaulting (vert) . . . 1·25 1·00
422 $1.25 Shot putting . . . . . 1·50 1·40
423 $1.50 Lawn tennis (vert) . . 2·50 1·75
MS424 110 × 70 mm. As Nos. 421 and 423, but each with a face value of $2.50 . . . . 4·00 5·00

1988. Olympic Gold Medal Winners, Seoul. Nos. 420/3 optd.
425 55c. Type **66** (optd **CARL LEWIS UNITED STATES 100 METERS**) 80 60
426 95c. Pole vaulting (optd **LOUISE RITTER UNITED STATES HIGH JUMP**) . . . . 1·25 90
427 $1.25 Shot putting (optd **ULF TIMMERMANN EAST GERMANY SHOT-PUT**) 1·50 1·25
428 $1.50 Lawn tennis (optd **STEFFI GRAF WEST GERMANY WOMEN'S TENNIS**) . . . . 4·50 1·75
MS429 110 × 70 mm. $2.50 As No. 421 (optd **JACKIE JOYNER-KERSEE United States Heptathlon**); $2.50 As No. 423 (optd **STEFFI GRAF West Germany Women's Tennis MILOSLAV MECIR Czechoslovakia Men's Tennis**) 5·50 5·50

67 "Virgin and Child"

69 Virgin Mary

68 Neil Armstrong stepping onto Moon

1988. Christmas. Designs showing different "Virgin and Child" paintings by Titian.
430 **67** 70c. multicoloured 90 90
431 – 85c. multicoloured . . . . 1·00 1·00
432 – 95c. multicoloured . . . . 1·25 1·25
433 – $1.25 multicoloured . . . 1·50 1·50
MS434 100 × 80 mm. $6.40 As type **67**, but diamond-shaped (57 × 57 mm) . . . . 6·00 7·00

1989. 20th Anniv of First Manned Moon Landing. Multicoloured.
435 55c. Type **68** . . . . 1·60 70
436 75c. Astronaut on Moon carrying equipment . . . . 1·75 85
437 95c. Conducting experiment on Moon . . . . 2·25 1·10
438 $1.25 Crew of "Apollo 11" 2·50 1·40
439 $1.75 Crew inside "Apollo 11" . . . . 2·75 1·90

1989. Christmas. Details from "The Nativity" by Durer. Multicoloured.
440 55c. Type **69** 80 80
441 70c. Christ Child and cherubs 90 90
442 85c. Joseph . . . . 1·25 1·25
443 $1.25 Three women . . . . . 1·60 1·60
MS444 88 × 95 mm. $6.40 "The Nativity" (31 × 50 mm) . . . . 6·50 7·50

70 Queen Elizabeth the Queen Mother

1990. 90th Birthday of Queen Elizabeth the Queen Mother.
445 **70** $2.25 multicoloured . . . 2·50 2·50
MS446 85 × 73 mm. **70** $7.50 multicoloured . . . . 13·00 13·00

71 "Adoration of the Magi" (Veronese)

1990. Christmas. Religious Paintings. Multicoloured.
447 55c. Type **71** . . . . 1·00 1·00
448 70c. "Virgin and Child" (Quentin Metsys) . . . . . 1·40 1·40
449 85c. "Virgin and Child Jesus" (Hugo van der Goes) . . . 1·60 1·60
450 $1.50 "Adoration of the Kings" (Jan Gossaert) . . 2·50 2·50
MS451 108 × 132 mm. $6.40 "Virgin and Child with Saints, Francis, John the Baptist, Zenobius and Lucy" (Domenico Veneziano) 8·00 9·00

1990. "Birdpex '90" Stamp Exhibition, Christchurch, New Zealand. Nos. 373/6 surch **Birdpex '90** and emblem.
452 $1.50 on 20c. Type **52** . . . 1·90 2·25
453 $1.50 on 55c. Sage grouse . . 1·90 2·25
454 $1.50 on 65c. Solitary sandpiper . . . . 1·90 2·25
455 $1.50 on 75c. Dunlin . . . . 1·90 2·25

1991. 65th Birthday of Queen Elizabeth II. No. 208 optd **COMMEMORATING 65th BIRTHDAY OF H.M. QUEEN ELIZABETH II**.
456 $6 H.M.S. "Resolution" and "Discovery", 1776–80 . . . 12·00 13·00

74 "The Virgin and Child with Saints" (G. David)

1991. Christmas. Religious Paintings. Multicoloured.
457 55c. Type **74** . . . . 1·00 1·00
458 85c. "Nativity" (Tintoretto) 1·50 1·50
459 $1.15 "Mystic Nativity" (Botticelli) . . . . 1·75 1·75
460 $1.85 "Adoration of the Shepherds" (B. Murillo) . . 2·75 3·25
MS461 79 × 103 mm. $6.40 "The Madonna of the Chair" (Raphael) (vert) . . . . 11·00 11·00

74a Running

1992. Olympic Games, Barcelona. Multicoloured.
462 75c. Type **74a** . . . . 1·60 1·60
463 95c. Boxing . . . . 1·75 1·75
464 $1.15 Swimming . . . . . . 2·00 2·00
465 $1.50 Wrestling . . . . . . 2·25 2·25

75 Marquesan Canoe

1992. 6th Festival of Pacific Arts, Rarotonga. Multicoloured.
466 $1.15 Type **75** . . . . 1·60 1·60
467 $1.75 Tangaroa statue from Rarotonga . . . . 2·00 2·00
468 $1.95 Manihiki canoe . . . . 2·25 2·25

1992. Royal Visit by Prince Edward. Nos. 466/8 optd **ROYAL VISIT.**
469 $1.15 Type **75** . . . . 2·25 2·00
470 $1.75 Tangaroa statue from Rarotonga . . . . 3·00 2·75
471 $1.95 Manihiki canoe . . . . 3·75 3·50

76 "Virgin with Child and Saints" (Borgognone)

1992. Christmas. Religious Paintings by Ambrogio Borgognone. Multicoloured.
472 55c. Type **76** 75 75
473 85c. "Virgin on Throne" . . 1·10 1·10
474 $1.05 "Virgin on Carpet" . . 1·40 1·40
475 $1.85 "Virgin of the Milk" . . 2·25 2·25
MS476 101 × 86 mm. $6.40 As 55c., but larger (36 × 46 mm) . . . . 7·00 8·00

77 Vincente Pinzon and "Nina"

1992. 500th Anniv of Discovery of America by Columbus. Multicoloured.
477 $1.15 Type **77** . . . . 2·00 2·00
478 $1.35 Martin Pinzon and "Pinta" . . . . 2·25 2·25
479 $1.75 Christopher Columbus and "Santa Maria" . . . . 3·00 3·00

78 Queen Elizabeth II in 1953

80 "Virgin on Throne with Child" (detail) (Tura)

79 Bull-mouth Helmet

1993. 40th Anniv of Coronation.
480 **78** $6 multicoloured . . . . . 6·50 8·50

1993. Marine Life. Multicoloured.
481 5c. Type **79** 10 10
482 10c. Daisy coral 10 10
483 15c. Hydroid coral 10 15
484 20c. Feather-star 15 20
485 25c. Sea star 20 25
486 30c. Varicose nudibranch . . 20 25
487 50c. Smooth sea star 35 40
488 70c. Black-lip pearl oyster . . 50 55
489 80c. Four-coloured nudibranch 60 65
490 85c. Prickly sea cucumber . . 60 65
491 90c. Organ pipe coral 65 70
492 $1 Blue sea lizard 75 80
493 $2 Textile cone shell . . . . 1·50 1·60
494 $3 Starfish . . . . 2·20 2·30
495 $5 As $3 . . . . 3·75 4·00
496 $8 As $3 . . . . 5·00 5·25
497 $10 As $3 . . . . 7·25 7·50
Nos. 494/7 are larger, 47 × 34 mm, and include a portrait of Queen Elizabeth II at top right.

1993. Christmas.
499 **80** 55c. multicoloured . . . . 1·00 1·00
500 – 85c. multicoloured . . . . 1·50 1·50
501 – $1.05 multicoloured . . . 1·75 1·75
502 – $1.95 multicoloured . . . 2·75 3·00
503 – $4.50 mult (32 × 47 mm) 6·00 7·00
DESIGNS: 80c. to $4.50, Different details from "Virgin on Throne with Child" (Cosme Tura).

81 Neil Armstrong stepping onto Moon

1994. 25th Anniv of First Manned Moon Landing.
504 **81** $3.25 multicoloured . . . 7·50 8·00

82 "The Virgin and Child with Sts. Paul and Jerome" (Vivarini)

84 Queen Elizabeth the Queen Mother at Remembrance Day Ceremony

83 Battleship Row burning, Pearl Harbor

1994. Christmas. Religious Paintings. Multicoloured.
505 90c. Type **82** . . . . 1·10 1·25
506 90c. "The Virgin and Child with St. John" (Luini) . . 1·10 1·25
507 90c. "The Virgin and Child with Sts. Jerome and Dominic" (Lippi) . . . . 1·10 1·25
508 90c. "Adoration of the Shepherds" (Murillo) . . . 1·10 1·25
509 $1 "Adoration of the Kings" (detail of angels) (Reni) . . 1·10 1·25
510 $1 "Madonna and Child with the Infant Baptist" (Raphael) . . . . 1·10 1·25
511 $1 "Adoration of the Kings" (detail of manger) (Reni) 1·10 1·25
512 $1 "Virgin and Child" (Borgognone) . . . . . . 1·10 1·25

1995. 50th Anniv of End of Second World War. Multicoloured.
513 $3.75 Type **83** . . . . 8·00 8·00
514 $3.75 Boeing B-25 Superfortress "Enola Gay" over Hiroshima . . . . . 8·00 8·00

1995. 95th Birthday of Queen Elizabeth the Queen Mother.
515 **84** $4.50 multicoloured . . . 9·50 9·50

85 Anniversary Emblem, United Nations Flag and Headquarters

1995. 50th Anniv of United Nations.
516 **85** $4 multicoloured . . . . . 4·00 5·50

86 Loggerhead Turtle

1995. Year of the Sea Turtle. Multicoloured.
517 $1.15 Type **86** . . . . 1·75 2·00
518 $1.15 Hawksbill turtle . . . 1·75 2·00
519 $1.65 Olive ridley turtle . . . 2·25 2·50
520 $1.65 Green turtle . . . . . 2·25 2·50

87 Queen Elizabeth II and Rose

1996. 70th Birthday of Queen Elizabeth.
521 **87** $4.25 multicoloured . . . 5·00 6·50

88 Olympic Flame, National Flags and Sports

1996. Centenary of Modern Olympic Games.
522 **88** $5 multicoloured . . . . . 6·50 8·00

89 Royal Wedding, 1947

1997. Golden Wedding of Queen Elizabeth and Prince Philip.
523 **89** $3 multicoloured . . . . . 4·00 3·75
MS524 42 × 28 mm. **89** $4 multicoloured . . . . 4·25 5·00

90 Diana, Princess of Wales with Sons

90a King George VI and Queen Elizabeth on Wedding Day

1998. Diana, Princess of Wales Commemoration.
525 **90** $1.50 multicoloured . . . 1·50 1·75
MS526 70 × 100 mm. **90** $3.75 multicoloured . . . . 3·50 4·00

1998. Children's Charities. No. **MS**526 surch **+$1 CHILDREN'S CHARITIES.**
MS527 70 × 100 mm. **90** $3.75+$1 multicoloured . . . . 3·50 4·25

1999. New Millennium. Nos. 466/8 optd **KIA ORANA THIRD MILLENNIUM.**
528 $1.15 Type **75** . . . . 1·25 1·25
529 $1.75 Tangaroa statue from Rarotonga . . . . 1·60 1·60
530 $1.95 Manihiki canoe . . . . 1·75 1·75

2000. Queen Elizabeth the Queen Mother's 100th Birthday.
531 **90a** $2.50 purple and brown 2·75 2·75
532 – $2.50 brown . . . . . . 2·75 2·75
533 – $2.50 green and brown . . 2·75 2·75
534 – $2.50 blue and brown . . 2·75 2·75
MS535 72 × 100 mm. $10 multicoloured . . . . 8·50 9·50
DESIGNS: No. 532, Queen Elizabeth with young Princess Elizabeth; 533, Royal Family in 1930; 534, Queen Elizabeth with Princesses Elizabeth and Margaret; **MS**535, Queen Elizabeth wearing blue gown.

90b Ancient Greek Javelin-throwers

2000. Olympic Games, Sydney. Multicoloured.
536 $2.75 Type **90b** . . . . . . 2·40 2·50
537 $2.75 Modern javelin-thrower 2·40 2·50
538 $2.75 Ancient Greek discus-thrower . . . . 2·40 2·50
539 $2.75 Modern discus-thrower 2·40 2·50
MS540 90 × 99 mm. $3.50 Cook Islands Olympic Torch Relay runner in traditional costume (vert) . . . . 3·00 3·50

91 Ocean Sunfish

2003. Endangered Species. Ocean Sunfish.
541 **91** 80c. multicoloured . . . . 1·00 1·10
542 – 90c. multicoloured . . . . 1·10 1·25
543 – $1.15 multicoloured . . . 1·25 1·40
544 – $1.95 multicoloured . . . 1·75 1·90
DESIGNS: 90c. to $1.95, Ocean sunfish.

91a Statue of Liberty

2003. "United We Stand". Support for Victims of 11 September 2001 Terrorist Attacks. Multicoloured.
MS545 75 × 109 mm. **91a** $1.50 × 4 Statue of Liberty, Twin Towers and flags of USA and Cook Islands . . . . 5·50 6·00

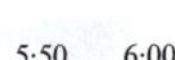

92 Pope John Paul II

2005. Pope John Paul II Commemoration.
546 **92** $1.45 multicoloured . . . 1·75 1·75

OFFICIAL STAMPS

1978. Optd or surch **O.H.M.S.**
O 1 1c. multicoloured (No. 57) 15 10
O 2 2c. multicoloured (No. 58) 15 10
O 3 3c. multicoloured (No. 59) 25 10
O 4 4c. multicoloured (No. 60) 25 10
O 5 5c. multicoloured (No. 61) 30 10
O 6 8c. multicoloured (No. 62) 35 15
O 7 10c. multicoloured (No. 63) 40 15
O 8 15c. on 60c. mult (No. 66) 45 25
O 9 18c. on 60c. mult (No. 66) 50 25
O10 20c. multicoloured (No. 64) 50 25
O11 25c. multicoloured (No. 65) 55 30
O12 30c. on 60c. mult (No. 66) 55 35
O13 50c. multicoloured (No. 89) 1·10 55
O14 50c. multicoloured (No. 90) 1·10 55
O15 50c. multicoloured (No. 91) 1·10 55
O16 $1 multicoloured (No. 101) 1·75 45
O17 $2 multicoloured (No. 102) 3·00 50

1985. Nos. 206/8, 278/81, 337/47 and 349/55 optd **O.H.M.S.** or surch also.
O18 2c. Type **47** 70 80
O19 4c. Amatasi 70 80
O20 5c. Ndrua 70 80
O21 8c. Tongiaki 70 80
O22 10c. "Vitoria" 70 80
O23 18c. "Golden Hind" . . . . 2·00 90
O24 20c. "La Boudeuse" . . . . 1·75 90
O25 30c. H.M.S. "Bounty" . . . 2·75 1·00
O26 40c. on 36c. "L'Astrolabe" 1·75 90
O27 50c. "Star of India" . . . . 1·75 90
O28 55c. on 48c. "Great Republic" . . . . 1·75 90
O39 65c. on 60c. Type **40** . . . 80 1·00
O40 65c. on 60c. Aerial view of Penrhyn atoll . . . . . . 80 1·00
O41 65c. on 60c. Eleanor Roosevelt on Penrhyn during Second World War 80 1·00
O42 65c. on 60c. Map of South Pacific . . . . 80 1·00
O29 75c. on 72c. "Antiope" . . . 2·50 1·60
O30 75c. on 96c. "Cap Hornier" 2·50 1·60
O31 80c. "Balcutha" . . . . . . 2·50 1·60
O32 $1.20 "Pamir" . . . . . . 2·75 1·60
O33 $2 "Cutty Sark" . . . . . . 5·50 3·25
O34 $3 "Mermerus" . . . . . . 4·25 3·50
O35 $4 "Mermerus" . . . . . . 5·50 5·00
O36 $5 "Cutty Sark" . . . . . . 8·00 6·50
O37 $6 H.M.S. "Resolution" and H.M.S. "Discovery" . . . 11·00 9·50
O38 $9.60 H.M.S. "Resolution" and H.M.S. "Discovery" 14·00 13·00

1998. Nos. 481/93 optd **O.H.M.S.**
O43 5c. Type **79** 10 10
O44 10c. Daisy coral 10 10
O45 15c. Hydroid coral 10 15
O46 20c. Feather-star 15 20
O47 25c. Sea star 20 25
O48 30c. Varicose nudibranch . . 20 25
O49 50c. Smooth sea star 35 40
O50 70c. Black-lip pearl oyster 50 55
O51 80c. Four-coloured nudibranch 60 65
O52 85c. Prickly sea cucumber . . 60 65
O53 90c. Organ pipe coral . . . 65 70
O54 $1 Blue sea lizard 75 80
O55 $2 Textile cone shell . . . . 1·50 1·60

PERAK Pt. 1

A state of the Federation of Malaya, incorporated in Malaysia in 1963.

100 cents = 1 dollar (Straits or Malayan).
Stamps of Straits Settlement optd or surch.

1878. No. 11 optd with crescent and star and **P** in oval.
1 2c. brown £1800 £1400

1880. Optd **PERAK**.
10 **9** 2c. brown . . . . 19·00 55·00
17 2c. red . . . . 4·00 3·00

1883. Surch **2 CENTS PERAK**.
16 2c. on 4c. red £550 £250

1886. No. 63a surch **ONE CENT PERAK**.
(a) Without full point.
29 1c. on 2c. red . . . . 3·50 10·00

(b) With final full point.
26 1c. on 2c. red . . . . 65·00 85·00

1886. No. 63a surch **1 CENT PERAK**.
28 1c. on 2c. red £130 £130

1886. No. 63a surch **One CENT PERAK**.
33b 1c. on 2c. red . . . . 2·75 2·75

1889. No. 17 surch **ONE CENT** (with full point).
41 1c. on 2c. red £250 £130

1891. Surch **PERAK One CENT**.
57 1c. on 2c. red . . . . 2·25 8·00
43 1c. on 6c. lilac . . . . 48·00 27·00

1891. Surch **PERAK Two CENTS**.
48 2c. on 24c. green . . . . . . 18·00 11·00

42 Tiger

44 Tiger

45 Elephants

1892.
61 **42** 1c. green . . . . 2·25 15
62 2c. red . . . . 1·75 30
63 2c. orange . . . . 50 3·25
64 5c. blue . . . . 3·25 7·50

1895. Surch **3 CENTS**.
65 **42** 3c. red . . . . 3·75 3·00

1895.
66 **44** 1c. purple and green . . . . 2·50 50
67 2c. purple and brown . . . 2·75 50
68 3c. purple and red . . . . . 2·75 50
69 4c. purple and red . . . . . 12·00 4·75
70 5c. purple and yellow . . . 4·00 55
71 8c. purple and blue . . . . 45·00 65
72 10c. purple and orange . . . 15·00 50
73 25c. green and red . . . . . £150 12·00
74 50c. purple and black . . . 48·00 32·00
75 50c. green and black £200 £160
76 **45** $1 green £180 £180
77 $2 green and red £325 £300
78 $3 green and yellow £375 £400
79 $5 green and blue £500 £500
80 $25 green and orange . . . £8500 £3000

1900. Surch in words.
81 **44** 1c. on 2c. purple and brown 60 2·25
82 1c. on 4c. purple and red . . 1·00 11·00
83 1c. on 5c. purple and yellow 2·25 12·00
84 3c. on 8c. purple and blue 4·50 9·50
85 3c. on 50c. green and black 2·75 6·50
86 **45** 3c. on $1 green . . . . . . 55·00 £140
87 3c. on $2 green and red . . 30·00 85·00

50 Sultan Iskandar

51 Sultan Iskandar

1935.
88 **50** 1c. black . . . . 1·25 10
89 2c. green . . . . 1·25 10
90 4c. orange . . . . 1·50 10
91 5c. brown 60 10
92 6c. red . . . . 11·00 4·25
93 8c. grey . . . . 1·00 10
94 10c. purple 70 15
95 12c. blue . . . . 2·75 1·00
96 25c. purple and red . . . . 2·25 1·00
97 30c. purple and orange . . 3·00 1·50
98 40c. red and purple . . . . 4·50 4·50
99 50c. black on green . . . . 5·00 1·25
100 $1 black and red on blue 2·50 1·25
101 $2 green and red . . . . . 23·00 8·50
102 $5 green and red on green £100 40·00

1938.
103 **51** 1c. black . . . . 10·00 10
104 2c. green . . . . 5·50 10
105 2c. orange . . . . 3·50 6·00
106a 3c. green . . . . 2·75 4·75
107 4c. orange . . . . 38·00 10
108 5c. brown . . . . 6·00 10
109 6c. red . . . . 27·00 10
110 8c. grey . . . . 26·00 10
111 8c. red . . . . 1·00 65·00
112 10c. purple . . . . 28·00 10
113 12c. blue . . . . 21·00 1·00
114 15c. blue . . . . 4·25 13·00
115 25c. purple and red . . . 50·00 3·25
116 30c. purple and orange . . 9·50 2·25
117 40c. red and purple . . . 50·00 2·00
118 50c. black on green . . . 32·00 75
119 $1 black and red on blue £130 16·00
120 $2 green and red . . . . £150 60·00
121 $5 green and red on green £225 £300

1948. Silver Wedding. As T **4b/c** of Pitcairn Islands.
122 10c. violet 15 10
123 $5 green . . . . 23·00 29·00

1949. U.P.U. As T **4d/g** of Pitcairn Islands.
124 10c. purple 15 10
125 15c. blue . . . . 1·50 2·00
126 25c. orange . . . . 30 2·75
127 50c. black . . . . 1·25 3·50

52 Sultan Yussuf 'Izzuddin Shah

53 Sultan Idris Shah

1950.
128 **52** 1c. black 10 10
129 2c. orange 20 10
130 3c. green . . . . 2·50 10
131 4c. brown 50 10
132 5c. purple . . . . 50 2·00
133 6c. grey 30 10
134 8c. red . . . . 65 2·25
135 8c. green . . . . 1·00 1·00
136 10c. purple 20 10
137 12c. red . . . . 1·00 4·00
138 15c. blue . . . . 1·00 10
139 20c. black and green . . . 1·00 65
140 20c. blue 75 10
141 25c. purple and orange . . 60 10
142 30c. red and purple . . . . 1·50 20
143 35c. red and purple . . . . 1·00 25
144 40c. red and purple . . . . 3·25 6·00
145 50c. black and blue . . . . 3·25 10
146 $1 blue and purple . . . . 7·00 1·00
147 $2 green and red . . . . . 13·00 7·00
148 $5 green and brown . . . 38·00 15·00

1953. Coronation. As T **4h** of Pitcairn Islands.
149 10c. black and purple . . . . 1·50 10

1957. As Nos. 92/102 of Kedah, but portrait of Sultan Yussuf Izzuddin Shah.
150 1c. black 10 20
151 2c. orange . . . . 30 1·00
152 4c. brown 20 10
153 5c. lake 20 10
154 8c. green . . . . 2·00 3·50
155 10c. sepia . . . . 1·50 10
156 10c. purple . . . . 3·50 10
157 20c. blue . . . . 2·25 10
158a 50c. black and blue 40 10
159 $1 blue and purple . . . . 6·50 40
160a $2 green and red . . . . . 3·25 2·25
161a $5 brown and green . . . . 8·00 8·00

1963. Installation of Sultan of Perak.
162 **53** 10c. multicoloured 10 10

54 "Vanda hookeriana"

1965. As Nos. 115/21 of Kedah, but with inset portrait of Sultan Idris as in T **54**.
163 **54** 1c. multicoloured 10 50
164 – 2c. multicoloured 10 70
165 – 5c. multicoloured 10 10
166 – 6c. multicoloured 15 40
167 – 10c. multicoloured 15 10
168 – 15c. multicoloured 80 10
169 – 20c. multicoloured . . . . 1·25 10
The higher values used in Perak were Nos. 20/7 of Malaysia (National Issues).

55 "Delias ninus"

1971. Butterflies. As Nos. 124/30 of Kedah, but with portrait of Sultan Idris as In T **55**.
172 **55** 1c. multicoloured . . . . . 40 2·25
173 – 2c. multicoloured . . . . . 1·00 2·25
174 – 5c. multicoloured . . . . . 1·25 10
175 – 6c. multicoloured . . . . . 1·25 2·00
176 – 10c. multicoloured . . . . 1·25 10
177 – 15c. multicoloured . . . . 1·00 10
178 – 20c. multicoloured . . . . 1·75 30
The higher values in use with this issue were Nos. 64/71 of Malaysia (National Issues).

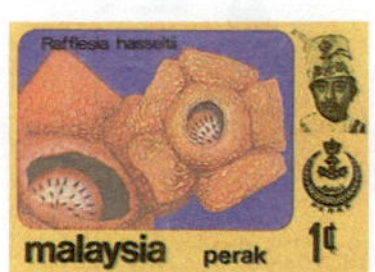

56 "Rafflesia hasseltii"

57 Coffee

1979. Flowers. As Nos. 135/41 of Kedah but with portrait of Sultan Idris as in T **56**.
184 1c. Type **56** 10 85
185 2c. "Pterocarpus indicus" . . 10 85
186 5c. "Lagerstroemia speciosa" 10 20
187 10c. "Durio zibethinus" . . . 15 10
188 15c. "Hibiscus rosa-sinensis" 15 10
189 20c. "Rhododendron scortechinii" 20 10
190 25c. "Etlingera elatior" (inscr "Phaeomeria speciosa") 40 20

1986. As Nos. 152/8 of Kedah but with portrait of Sultan Azlan Shah as in T **57**.
198 1c. Type **57** 10 20
199 2c. Coconuts 15 20
200 5c. Cocoa 20 10
201 10c. Black pepper 25 10
202 15c. Rubber 40 10
203 20c. Oil palm 30 10
204 30c. Rice 40 15

OFFICIAL STAMPS

1889. Stamps of Straits Settlements optd **P.G.S.**
O1 **30** 2c. red . . . . 4·25 5·50
O2 4c. brown . . . . 13·00 22·00
O3 6c. lilac . . . . 25·00 50·00
O4 8c. orange . . . . 32·00 65·00
O5 **38** 10c. grey . . . . 75·00 75·00
O6 **30** 12c. blue £200 £250
O7 12c. purple £250 £325
O9 24c. green £190 £225

1894. No. 64 optd **Service**.
O10 **30** 5c. blue . . . . 70·00 1·00

1895. No. 70 optd **Service**.
O11 **31** 5c. purple and yellow . . 2·50 50

PERLIS Pt. 1

A state of the Federation of Malaya, incorporated in Malaysia in 1963.

100 cents = 1 dollar (Straits or Malayan).

1948. Silver Wedding. As T **4b/c** of Pitcairn Islands.
1 10c. violet . . . . 30 2·75
2 $5 brown . . . . 29·00 48·00

1949. U.P.U. As T **4d/g** of Pitcairn Islands.
3 10c. purple . . . . 30 1·50
4 15c. blue . . . . 1·25 3·75
5 25c. orange . . . . 45 2·00
6 50c. black . . . . 1·00 3·75

1 Raja Syed Putra

2 "Vanda hookeriana"

1951.
7 **1** 1c. black . . . . 20 1·00
8 2c. orange 75 50
9 3c. green . . . . 1·50 2·75
10 4c. brown . . . . 1·25 30
11 5c. purple . . . . 50 3·00
12 6c. grey . . . . 1·50 1·25
13 8c. red . . . . 2·25 4·75
14 8c. green . . . . 75 3·50
15 10c. purple 50 30
16 12c. red . . . . 75 3·00
17 15c. blue . . . . 4·00 4·75
18 20c. black and green . . . . 2·25 7·50
19 20c. blue . . . . 1·00 70
20 25c. purple and orange . . . 1·75 1·75
21 30c. red and purple . . . . . 1·75 10·00
22 35c. red and purple . . . . . 75 4·00
23 40c. red and purple . . . . . 3·25 20·00
24 50c. black and blue . . . . . 4·00 4·25
25 $1 blue and purple . . . . . 7·50 22·00

26 $2 green and red 14·00 38·00
27 $5 green and brown 50·00 95·00

1953. Coronation. As T **4h** of Pitcairn Islands.
28 10c. black and purple 1·25 3·00

1957. As Nos. 92/102 of Kedah, but inset portrait of Raja Syed Putra.
29 1c. black 10 30
30 2c. red 10 30
31 4c. brown 10 30
32 5c. lake 10 10
33 8c. green 2·00 1·75
34 10c. brown 1·50 2·25
35 10c. purple 5·00 3·25
36 20c. blue 2·50 3·25
37 50c. black and blue 60 3·50
38 $1 blue and purple 7·00 11·00
39 $2 green and red 7·00 8·00
40 $5 brown and green 10·00 11·00

1965. As Nos. 115/21 of Kedah, but with inset portrait of Tunku Bendahara Abu Bakar as in T **2**.
41 **2** 1c. multicoloured 10 1·00
42 – 2c. multicoloured 10 1·50
43 – 5c. multicoloured 15 40
44 – 6c. multicoloured 65 1·50
45 – 10c. multicoloured 65 40
46 – 15c. multicoloured 1·00 40
47 – 20c. multicoloured 1·00 1·75
The higher values used in Perlis were Nos. 20/7 of Malaysia (National Issues).

3 "Danaus melanippus"

4 Raja Syed Putra

1971. Butterflies. As Nos. 124/30 of Kedah, but with portrait of Raja Syed Putra as in T **3**.
48 – 1c. multicoloured 20 1·25
49 **3** 2c. multicoloured 40 2·25
50 – 5c. multicoloured 1·25 1·25
51 – 6c. multicoloured 1·50 3·00
52 – 10c. multicolored 1·50 1·25
53 – 15c. multicoloured 1·50 50
54 – 20c. multicoloured 1·50 2·25
The higher values in use with this issue were Nos. 64/71 of Malaysia (National Issues).

1971. 25th Anniv of Installation of Raja Syed Putra.
56 **4** 10c. multicoloured 30 2·25
57 15c. multicoloured 30 75
58 50c. multicoloured 80 4·00

5 "Pterocarpus indicus"

6 Coconuts

1979. Flowers. As Nos. 135/41 of Kedah, but with portrait of Raja Syed Putra as in T **5**.
59 1c. "Rafflesia hasseltii" 10 1·00
60 2c. Type **5** 10 1·00
61 5c. "Lagerstroemia speciosa" 10 1·00
62 10c. "Durio zibethinus" 15 30
63 15c. "Hibiscus rosa-sinensis" 15 10
64 20c. "Rhododendron scortechinii" 20 10
65 25c. "Etlingera elatior" (inscr "Phaeomeria speciosa") 40 85

1986. As Nos. 152/8 of Kedah, but with portrait of Raja Syed Putra as in T **6**.
73 1c. Coffee 10 25
74 2c. Type **6** 15 25
75 5c. Cocoa 20 20
76 10c. Black pepper 25 25
77 15c. Rubber 40 10
78 20c. Oil palm 35 10
79 30c. Rice 35 15

7 Raja Syed Putra and Aspects of Perlis

1995. 50th Anniv of Raja Syed Putra's Accession. Multicoloured.
80 30c. Type **7** 60 50
81 $1 Raja Syed Putra and Palace 1·75 3·00

PERU Pt. 20

A republic on the N.W. coast of S. America independent since 1821.

1857. 8 reales = 1 peso.
1858. 100 centavos = 10 dineros = 5 pesetas = 1 peso.
1874. 100 centavos = 1 sol.
1985. 100 centimos = 1 inti.
1991. 100 centimos = 1 sol.

7

8

1858. T **7** and similar designs with flags below arms. Imperf.
8 **7** 1d. blue 75·00 5·00
13 1 peseta red 90·00 11·00
5 ½ peso yellow £1300 £225

1862. Various frames. Imperf.
14 **8** 1d. red 10·00 1·75
20 1d. green 10·00 2·10
16 1 peseta, brown 55·00 17·00
22 1 peseta, yellow 70·00 21·00

10 Vicuna

13

14

1866. Various frames. Perf.
17 **10** 5c. green 5·00 60
18 – 10c. red 5·00 1·10
19 – 20c. brown 17·00 3·50
See also No. 316.

1871. 20th Anniv of First Railway in Peru (Callao–Lima–Chorillos). Imperf.
21a **13** 5c. red £110 28·00

1873. Roul by imperf.
23 **14** 2c. blue 25·00 £200

15 Sun-god

16

20

21

1874. Various frames. Perf.
24 **15** 1c. orange 40 40
25a **16** 2c. violet 40 40
26 5c. blue 70 25
27 10c. green 15 15
28 20c. red 1·60 40
29 **20** 50c. green 7·50 2·10
30 **21** 1s. pink 1·25 1·25
For further stamps in these types, see Nos. 278, 279/84 and 314/5.

(24)

(27) Arms of Chile

1880. Optd with T **24**.
36 **15** 1c. green 40 40
37 **16** 2c. red 1·10 45
39 5c. blue 1·60 70
40 **20** 50c. green 23·00 14·50
41 **21** 1s. red 80·00 38·00

1881. Optd as T **24**, but inscr "LIMA" at foot instead of "PERU".
42 **15** 1c. green 95 30
43 **16** 2c. red 15·00 7·50
44 5c. blue 1·75 45
286 10c. green 40 50
45 **20** 50c. green £375 £200
46 **21** 1s. red 85·00 45·00

1881. Optd with T **27**.
57 **15** 1c. orange 60 85
58 **16** 2c. violet 60 3·50
59 2c. red 1·90 16·00
60 5c. blue 55·00 60·00
61 10c. green 1·50 2·00
62 20c. red £100 £100

(28)

(28a)

1882. Optd with T **27** and **28**.
63 **15** 1c. green 80 65
64 **16** 5c. blue 1·10 65
66 **20** 50c. red 2·25 1·60
67 **21** 1s. blue 4·75 3·75

1883. Optd with T **28** only.
200 **15** 1c. green 1·60 1·00
201 **16** 2c. red 1·40 3·25
202 5c. blue 2·25 1·60
203 **20** 50c. pink 65·00
204 **21** 1s. blue 30·00

1883. Handstamped with T **28a** only.
206 **15** 1c. orange 1·00 65
210 **16** 5c. blue 8·50 4·25
211 10c. green 95 65
216 **20** 50c. green 7·50 3·00
220 **21** 1s. red 11·50 5·00

1883. Optd with T **24** and **28a**, the inscription in oval reading "PERU".
223 **20** 50c. green £100 50·00
225 **21** 1s. red £120 75·00

1883. Optd with T **24** and **28a**, the inscription in oval reading "LIMA".
227 **15** 1c. green 4·50 3·25
228 **16** 2c. red 4·50 3·25
232 5c. blue 7·75 5·00
234 **20** 50c. green £120 75·00
236 **21** 1s. red £160 £100

1883. Optd with T **28** and **28a**.
238 **15** 1c. green 1·25 65
241 **16** 2c. red 1·25 60
246 5c. blue 1·40 65

1884. Optd **CORREOS LIMA** and sun.
277 **16** 5c. blue 75 25

1886. Re-issue of 1866 and 1874 types.
278 **15** 1c. violet 60 20
314 1c. red 30 20
279 **16** 2c. green 85 10
315 2c. blue 25 20
280 5c. orange 70 10
316 **10** 5c. lake 1·60 35
281 **16** 10c. black 50 10
317 – 10c. orange (Llamas) 1·10 25
282 **16** 20c. blue 5·25 35
318 – 20c. blue (Llamas) 7·50 1·10
283 **20** 50c. red 1·90 35
284 **21** 1s. brown 1·50 35

(71 Pres. R. M. Bermudez)

73

1894. Optd with T **71**.
294 **15** 1c. orange 75 25
295 1c. green 45 20
296c **16** 2c. violet 45 15
297 2c. red 50 20
298 5c. blue 2·75 1·50
299 10c. green 50 20
300 **20** 50c. green 1·60 1·00

1894. Optd with T **28** and **71**.
301 **16** 2c. red 45 20
302 5c. blue 1·10 30
303 **20** 50c. red 38·00 25·00
304 **21** 1s. blue 95·00 75·00

1895. Installation of Pres. Nicolas de Pierola.
328 **73** 1c. violet 1·75 75
329 2c. green 1·75 75
330 5c. yellow 1·75 75
331 10c. blue 1·75 75
332 – 20c. orange 1·90 80
333 – 50c. blue 10·50 3·75
334 – 1s. lake 42·00 21·00
Nos. 332/4 are larger (30 × 36 mm) and the central device is in a frame of laurel.
See also Nos. 352/4.

75 Atahualpa

76 Pizarro

77 General de la Mar

1896.
335 **75** 1c. blue 55 15
336 1c. green 55 10
337 2c. blue 60 15
338 2c. red 60 10
341 **76** 5c. blue 85 10
340 5c. green 85 10
342 10c. yellow 1·40 20
343 10c. black 1·40 10
344 20c. orange 2·75 25
345 **77** 50c. red 5·25 50
346 1s. red 7·00 85
347 2s. lake 3·00 65

1897. No. D31 optd **FRANQUEO**.
348 D **22** 1c. brown 50 25

82 Suspension Bridge at Paucartambo

83 Pres. D. Nicolas de Pierola

1897. Opening of New Postal Building. Dated "1897".
349 **82** 1c. blue 80 30
350 – 2c. brown 80 25
351 **83** 5c. red 1·25 30
DESIGN: 2c. G.P.O. Lima.

1899. As Nos. 328/34, but vert inscr replaced by pearl ornaments.
352 **73** 22c. green 30 15
353 – 5s. red 1·90 1·40
354 – 10s. green £425 £275

84 President Eduardo Lopez de Romana

85 Admiral Grau

1900.
357 **84** 22c. black and green 10·00 70

1901. Advent of the Twentieth Century.
358 **85** 1c. black and green 1·10 25
359 – 2c. black and red 1·10 25
360 – 5c. black and lilac 1·25 25
PORTRAITS: 2c. Col. Bolognesi; 5c. Pres. Romana.

90 Municipal Board of Health Building

1905.
361 **90** 12c. black and blue 1·25 25

1907. Surch.
362 **90** 1c. on 12c. black and blue 25 20
363 2c. on 12c. black and blue 50 35

97 Bolognesi Monument

98 Admiral Grau

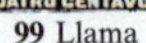
99 Llama

101 Exhibition Buildings

103 G.P.O., Lima

107 Columbus

1907.

364 **97** 1c. black and green . . . 25 15
365 **98** 2c. purple and red 25 15
366 **99** 4c. olive . . . . 5·00 60
367 – 5c. black and blue 40 10
368 **101** 10c. black and brown . . 1·00 25
369 – 20c. black and green . . . 19·00 90
370 **103** 50c. black . . . . 21·00 95
371 – 1s. green and violet . . . £100 2·10
372 – 2s. black and blue . . . . £100 85·00

DESIGNS—VERT: As Type **98**: 5c. Statue of Bolivar. (24 × 33 mm): 2c. Columbus Monument. HORIZ: As Type **101**: 20c. Medical School, Lima. (33 × 24 mm): 1s. Grandstand, Santa Beatrice Racecourse, Lima.

1909. Portraits.

373 – 1c. grey (Manco Capac) 15 15
374 **107** 2c. green 15 15
375 – 4c. red (Pizarro) 40 15
376 – 5c. purple (San Martin) 15 10
377 – 10c. blue (Bolivar) 55 15
378 – 12c. blue (de la Mar) . . 85 25
379 – 20c. brown (Castilla) . . 90 40
380 – 50c. orange (Grau) . . . 5·50 30
381 – 1s. black and lake (Bolognesi) . . . . . . 9·50 30

See also Nos. 406/13, 431/5, 439/40 and 484/9.

1913. Surch **UNION POSTAL 8 Cts. Sud Americana** in oval.

382 **90** 8c. on 12c. black and blue 55 20

1915. As 1896, 1905 and 1907, surch **1915** and value.

383 **75** 1c. on 1c. green . . . . . 13·50 10·00
384 **97** 1c. on 1c. black and green 70 50
385 **98** 1c. on 2c. purple and red 1·00 85
386 **76** 1c. on 10c. black 85 60
387 **99** 1c. on 4c. green . . . . . 2·00 1·75
388 **101** 1c. on 10c. black & brown 35 20
389 2c. on 10c. black & brown 80·00 65·00
390 **90** 2c. on 12c. black and blue 65 50
391 – 2c. on 20c. black and green (No. 369) . . . . . 11·50 10·00
392 **103** 2c. on 50c. black . . . . 3·00 3·00

1916. Surch **VALE**, value and **1916**.

393 1c. on 12c. blue (378) 15 15
394 1c. on 20c. brown (379) . . . 15 15
395 1c. on 50c. orange (380) . . . 15 15
396 2c. on 4c. red (375) 15 15
397 10c. on 1s. black & lake (381) 40 25

1916. Official stamps of 1909 optd **FRANQUEO 1916** or surch **VALE 2 Cts** also.

398 **O 108** 1c. red 15 15
399 2c. on 50c. olive . . . 15 15
400 10c. brown 20 15

1916. Postage Due stamps of 1909 surch **FRANQUEO VALE 2 Cts. 1916.**

401 **D 109** 2c. on 1c. brown . . . 40 40
402 2c. on 5c. brown . . . 15 15
403 2c. on 10c. brown . . . 15 15
404 2c. on 50c. brown . . . 15 15

1917. Surch **Un Centavo.**

405 1c. on 4c. (No. 375) 20 15

1918. Portraits as T **107**.

406 1c. black & orge (San Martin) 10 10
407 2c. black and green (Bolivar) 15 10
408 4c. black and red (Galvez) . . 25 10
409 5c. black and blue (Pardo) 15 10
410 8c. black and brown (Grau) 90 25
411 10c. black and blue (Bolognesi) 35 10
412 12c. black and lilac (Castilla) 1·10 15
413 20c. black and green (Caceres) . . . . 1·50 15

126 Columbus at Salamanca University

129 A. B. Leguia

1918.

414 **126** 50c. black and brown . . 4·25 35
415a – 1s. black and green . . . 13·00 50
416 – 2s. black and blue . . . 22·00 55

DESIGNS: 1s. Funeral of Atahualpa; 2s. Battle of Arica.

1920. New Constitution.

417 **129** 5c. black and blue 15 15
418 5c. black and brown . . . 15 15

130 San Martin

131 Oath of Independence

132 Admiral Cochrane

137 J. Olaya

1921. Centenary of Independence.

419 **130** 1c. brown (San Martin) 25 15
420 2c. green (Arenales) . . . 25 15
421 4c. red (Las Heras) . . . 85 50
422 **131** 5c. brown 35 15
423 **132** 7c. violet 70 35
424 **130** 10c. blue (Guisse) 70 35
425 12c. black (Vidal) . . . . 2·75 40
426 20c. black and red (Leguia) . . . . 2·75 70
427 50c. violet and purple (S. Martin Monument) 7·75 2·00
428 **131** 1s. green and red (San Martin and Leguia) . . 11·00 3·00

1923. Surch **CINCO Centavos 1923.**

429 5c. on 8c. black & brn (No. 410) 40 20

1924. Surch **CUATRO Centavos 1924.**

430 4c. on 5c. (No. 409) 25 15

1924. Portraits as T **107**. Size 18½ × 23 mm.

431 2c. olive (Rivadeneyra) . . . 10 10
432 4c. green (Melgar) 10 10
433 8c. black (Iturregui) . . . . 1·60 90
434 10c. red (A. B. Leguia) . . . 15 10
435 15c. blue (De la Mar) 50 15
439 1s. brown (De Saco) . . . . 7·50 85
440 2s. blue (J. Leguia) . . . . . 19·00 4·25

1924. Monuments.

436 **137** 20c. blue 95 10
437 20c. yellow . . . . 1·25 15
438 – 50c. purple (Bellido) . . . 4·25 35

See also Nos. 484/9.

139 Simon Bolivar

140

1924. Cent of Battle of Ayacucho. Portraits of Bolivar.

441 – 2c. olive 35 10
442 **139** 4c. green 65 10
443 5c. black . . . . 1·25 10
444 **140** 10c. red 70 10
445 – 20c. blue . . . . 1·40 15
446 – 50c. lilac . . . . 4·00 50
447 – 1s. brown . . . . 10·00 2·00
448 – 2s. blue . . . . 21·00 8·25

1925. Surch **DOS Centavos 1925.**

449 **137** 2c. on 20c. blue . . . . . 1·25 50

1925. Optd**Plebiscito.**

450 10c. red (No. 434) 70 70

143 The Rock of Arica

1925. Obligatory Tax. Tacna–Arica Plebiscite.

451 **143** 2c. orange . . . . 1·50 40
452 5c. blue . . . . 2·50 50
453 5c. red . . . . 1·90 40
454 5c. green . . . . 2·25 60
455 – 10c. brown . . . . 3·00 60
456 – 50c. green . . . . 16·00 7·50

DESIGNS—HORIZ: 39 × 30 mm: 10c. Soldiers with colours. VERT: 27 × 33 mm: 50c. Bolognesi Statue.

146 The Rock of Arica

1927. Obligatory Tax. Figures of value not encircled.

457 **146** 2c. orange . . . . 2·25 50
458 2c. brown . . . . 2·75 50
459 2c. blue . . . . 2·50 50
460 2c. violet . . . . 1·75 50
461 **146** 2c. green . . . . 1·25 50
462 20c. red . . . . 6·00 1·50

1927. Air. Optd **Servicio Aereo.**

463 **9** 50c. purple (No. 438) . . . 32·00 20·00

148 Pres. A. B. Leguia

149 The Rock of Arica

1927. Air.

464 **148** 50c. green 70 35

1928. Obligatory Tax. Plebiscite Fund.

465 **149** 2c. mauve 60 20

1929. Surch **Habilitada 2 Cts. 1929.**

466 – 2c. on 8c. (No. 410) . . . 50 50
468 **137** 15c. on 20c. (No. 437) . . 70 70

1929. Surch **Habilitada 2 centavos 1929.**

467 2c. on 8c. (No. 410) 70 70

1930. Optd **Habilitada Franqueo.**

469 **149** 2c. mauve 85 85

1930. Surch **Habilitada 2 Cts. 1930.**

470 **137** 2c. on 20c. yellow 25 25

1930. Surch **Habilitada Franqueo 2 Cts. 1930.**

471 **148** 2c. on 50c. green 25 25

156 Arms of Peru

157 Lima Cathedral

1930. 6th (inscribed "seventh") Pan-American Child Congress.

472 **156** 2c. green 60 55
473 **157** 5c. red . . . . 2·00 1·00
474 – 10c. blue . . . . 1·25 85
475 – 50c. brown . . . . 17·00 10·00

DESIGNS—HORIZ: 10c. G.P.O., Lima. VERT: 50c. Madonna and Child.

1930. Fall of Leguia Govt. No. 434 optd with Arms of Peru or surch with new value in four corners also.

477 2c. on 10c. red 10 10
478 4c. on 10c. red 20 20
479 10c. red 15 10
476 15c. on 10c. red 20 15

159 Simon Bolivar

161 Pizarro

162 The Old Stone Bridge, Lima

1930. Death Centenary of Bolivar.

480 **159** 2c. brown 35 20
481 4c. red 70 30
482 10c. green 35 25
483 15c. grey 70 50

1930. As T **107** and **137** but smaller, 18 × 22 mm.

484 – 2c. olive (Rivadeneyra) . . 15 10
485 – 4c. green (Melgar) 15 10
486 – 15c. blue (De la Mar) . . 50 10
487 **137** 20c. yellow (Olaya) . . . 1·00 20
488 – 50c. purple (Bellido) . . . 1·25 25
489 – 1s. brown (De Saco) . . . 1·60 35

1931. Obligatory Tax. Unemployment Fund. Surch **Habilitada Pro Desocupados 2 Cts.**

490 **159** 2c. on 4c. red 70 35
491 2c. on 10c. green 50 35
492 2c. on 15c. grey 50 35

1931. 1st Peruvian Philatelic Exhibition.

493 **161** 2c. slate . . . . 1·90 1·10
494 4c. brown . . . . 1·90 1·10
495 **162** 10c. red . . . . 1·90 1·10
496 10c. green and mauve . . 1·90 1·10
497 **161** 15c. green . . . . 1·90 1·10
498 **162** 15c. red and grey . . . . 1·90 1·10
499 15c. blue and orange . . 1·90 1·10

163 Manco Capac

164 Oil Well

170

1931.

500 **163** 2c. olive 20 10
501 **164** 4c. green 40 30
502 – 10c. orange 85 10
503 – 15c. blue . . . . 1·50 25
504 – 20c. yellow . . . . 6·00 40
505 – 50c. lilac . . . . 5·00 40
506 – 1s. brown . . . . 11·00 85

DESIGNS—VERT: 10c. Sugar Plantation; 15c. Cotton Plantation; 50c. Copper Mines. 1s. Llamas. HORIZ: 20c. Guano Islands.

1931. Obligatory Tax. Unemployment Fund.

507 **170** 2c. green 10 10
508 2c. red 10 10

171 Arms of Piura

172 Parakas

1932. 4th Centenary of Piura.

509 **171** 10c. blue (postage) . . . 5·50 5·00
510 15c. violet . . . . 5·50 5·00
511 50c. red (air) . . . . . . 18·00 16·00

1932. 400th Anniv of Spanish Conquest of Peru. Native designs.

512 **172** 10c. purple (22 × 19½ mm) 15 10
513 – 15c. lake (25 × 19½ mm) 35 10
514 – 50c. brown (19½ × 22 mm) 75 15

DESIGNS: 15c. Chimu; 50c. Inca.

175 Arequipa and El Misti

176 Pres. Sanchez Cerro

1932. 1st Anniv of Constitutional Government.

515 **175** 2c. blue 15 10
527 2c. black 15 10
528 2c. green 15 10
516 4c. brown 15 10
529 4c. orange 15 10
517 **176** 10c. red . . . . 15·00 8·25
530 – 10c. red 50 10
518 – 15c. blue 35 10
531 – 15c. mauve 35 10
519 – 20c. lake 50 10
532 – 20c. violet 50 15
520 – 50c. green 70 15
521 – 1s. orange . . . . 5·50 35
533 – 1s. brown . . . . 6·25 40

DESIGNS—VERT: 10c. (No. 530), Statue of Liberty; 15c. to 1s. Bolivar Monument, Lima.

178 Blacksmith

179 Monument of 2nd May to Battle of Callao

1932. Obligatory Tax. Unemployment Fund.
522 **178** 2c. grey 10 10
523 2c. violet 10 10

1933. Obligatory Tax. Unemployment Fund.
524 **179** 2c. violet 15 10
525 2c. orange 15 10
526 2c. purple 15 10

181 Hawker Hart Bomber

184 F. Pizarro

185 Coronation of Huascar

186 The Inca

1934. Air.
534 **181** 2s. blue 4·50 35
535 5s. brown 9·50 70

1934. Obligatory Tax. Unemployment Fund. Optd **Pro-Desocupados.** (a) In one line.
536 **176** 2c. green 10 10
585 – 2c. purple (No. 537) 10 10
(b) In two lines.
566 – 2c. purple (No. 537) 10 10

1934.
537 – 2c. purple 10 10
538 – 4c. green 15 10
539 **184** 10c. red 15 10
540 15c. blue 50 10
541 **185** 20c. blue 1·00 15
542 50c. brown 1·00 15
543 **186** 1s. violet 2·75 35
DESIGNS: 2, 4c. show the scene depicted in Type **189**.

187 Lake of the Marvellous Cure

188 Grapes

1935. Tercentenary of Founding of Ica.
544 – 4c. black 65 65
545 **187** 5c. red 65 65
546 **188** 10c. mauve 3·75 1·40
547 **187** 20c. green 1·60 1·00
548 – 35c. red 7·50 3·50
549 – 50c. brown and orange 5·00 3·50
550 – 1s. red and violet 14·50 8·25
DESIGNS—HORIZ: 4c. City of Ica; 50c. Don Diego Lopez and King Philip IV of Spain. VERT: 35c. Cotton blossom; 1s. Supreme God of the Nazcas.

189 Pizarro and "The Thirteen"

192 Funeral of Atahualpa

1935. 4th Centenary of Founding of Lima.
551 **189** 2c. brown (postage) 35 20
552 – 4c. violet 50 35
553 – 10c. red 50 20
554 – 15c. blue 85 40
555 **189** 20c. grey 1·40 50
556 – 50c. green 1·90 1·25
557 – 1s. blue 4·00 2·40
558 – 2s. brown 11·00 6·75
DESIGNS—HORIZ: 4c. Lima Cathedral. VERT: 10c., 50c. Miss L. S. de Canevaro; 15c., 2s. Pizarro; 1s. The "Tapada" (a veiled woman).

559 **192** 5c. green (air) 35 20
560 – 35c. brown 75 35
561 – 50c. yellow 1·25 70
562 – 1s. purple 1·75 75
563 – 2s. orange 1·75 1·50
564 **192** 5s. purple 7·75 4·25
565 **189** 10s. blue 30·00 20·00
DESIGNS—HORIZ: 35c. Airplane near San Cristobal Hill; 50c., 1s. Airplane over Avenue of Barefoot Friars. VERT: 2s. Palace of Torre Tagle.

207 "San Cristobal" (caravel)

1936. Callao Centenary.
567 **207** 2c. black (postage) 1·25 20
568 – 4c. green 45 15
569 – 5c. brown 45 15
570 – 10c. blue 45 20
571 – 15c. green 2·00 25
572 – 20c. brown 45 25
573 – 50c. lilac 1·25 45
574 – 1s. olive 23·00 1·60
575 – 2s. purple 15·00 5·00
576 – 5s. red 21·00 12·00
577 – 10s. brown and red 45·00 30·00

578 – 35c. slate (air) 8·00 4·00
DESIGNS—HORIZ: 4c. La Punta Naval College; 5c. Independence Square, Callao; 10c. Aerial view of Callao; 15c. "Reina del Pacifico" (liner) in Callao Docks and Custom House; 20c. Plan of Callao, 1746; 35c. "La Callao" (locomotive); 1s. Gunboat "Sacramento"; 10s. Real Felipe Fortifications. VERT: 50c. D. Jose de la Mar; 2s. Don Jose de Velasco; 5s. Fort Maipo and miniature portraits of Galvez and Nunez.

1936. Obligatory Tax. St. Rosa de Lima Cathedral Construction Fund. Optd **"Ley 8310".**
579 **179** 2c. purple 10 10

1936. Surch **Habilitado** and value in figures and words.
580 – 2c. on 4c. green (No. 538) (postage) 10 10
581 **185** 10c. on 20c. blue 15 15
582 **186** 10c. on 1s. violet 20 20
583 **181** 5c. on 2s. blue (air) 35 15
584 25c. on 5s. brown 70 25

211 Guanay Cormorants

217 Mail Steamer "Inca" on Lake Titicaca

1936.
586 **211** 2c. brown (postage) 1·40 25
616 2c. green 1·75 25
587 – 4c. brown 50 25
617 – 4c. black 25 15
618 – 10c. red 10 10
619 – 15c. blue 50 25
590 – 20c. black 70 15
620 – 20c. brown 25 15
591 – 50c. yellow 2·10 50
621 – 50c. grey 70 15
592 – 1s. purple 4·25 70
622 – 1s. blue 1·40 35
593 – 2s. blue 9·00 2·00
623 – 2s. violet 3·00 35
594 – 5s. blue 9·00 3·00
595 – 10s. brown and violet 50·00 19·00
DESIGNS—VERT: 4c. Oil well; 10c. Inca postal runner; 1s. G.P.O., Lima; 2s. M. de Amat y Junyent; 5s. J. A. de Pando y Riva; 10s. J. D. Condemarin. HORIZ: 15c. Paseo de la Republica, Lima; 20c. Municipal Palace and Natural History Museum; 50c. University of San Marcos, Lima.

596 – 5c. green (air) 25 10
625 **217** 15c. blue 90 15
598 – 20c. grey 90 15
626 – 20c. green 85 15
627 – 25c. red 40 10
628 – 30c. brown 80 15
600 – 35c. brown 1·60 1·40
601 – 50c. yellow 75 45
629 – 50c. red 1·10 30
630 – 70c. green 1·25 50
603 – 80c. black 14·00 7·00
631 – 80c. green 4·50 1·00
604 – 1s. blue 9·00 1·50
632 – 1s. brown 6·00 60
605 – 1s.50 brown 9·00 5·50
633 – 1s.50 orange 5·50 40
606 – 2s. blue 15·00 6·50
634 – 2s. green 11·00 70
607 – 5s. green 20·00 3·25
608 – 10s. brown and red £100 65·00
DESIGNS—HORIZ: 5c. La Mar Park; 20c. Native recorder player and llama; 30c. Chuquibambilla ram; 25, 35c. J. Chavez; 50c. Mining Area; 70c. Ford "Tin Goose" airplane over La Punta; 1s. Steam train at La Cima; 1s.50, Aerodrome at Las Palmas, Lima. 2s. Douglas DC-2 mail plane; 5s. Valley of R. Inambari. VERT: 80c. Infiernillo Canyon, Andes; 10s. St. Rosa de Lima.

223 St. Rosa de Lima

1937. Obligatory Tax. St. Rosa de Lima Construction Fund.
609 **223** 2c. red 15 10

1937. Surch **Habilit.** and value in figures and words. (a) Postage.
610 1s. on 2s. blue (593) 3·25 3·25
(b) Air.
611 15c. on 30c. brown (599) 45 40
612 15c. on 35c. brown (600) 45 25
613 15c. on 70c. green (630) 3·50 2·25
614 25c. on 80c. black (603) 7·50 6·00
615 1s. on 2s. blue (606) 5·50 3·00

225 Bielovucic over Lima

226 Jorge Chavez

1937. Air. Pan-American Aviation Conference.
635 **225** 10c. violet 40 10
636 **226** 15c. green 50 10
637 – 25c. brown 40 10
638 – 1s. black 1·90 1·00
DESIGNS—As T **225**: 25c. Limatambo Airport; 1s. Peruvian air routes.

229 "Protection" (by John Q. A. Ward)

230 Children's Holiday Camp

1938. Obligatory Tax. Unemployment Fund.
757c **229** 2c. brown 10 10

1938. Designs as T **230**.
693 **230** 2c. green 10 10
694 – 4c. brown 10 10
642 – 10c. red 20 10
696 – 15c. blue 10 10
727 – 15c. turquoise 10 10
644 – 20c. purple 15 10
740 – 20c. violet 10 10
698 – 50c. blue 15 10
741 – 50c. brown 15 10
699 – 1s. purple 85 10
742 – 1s. brown 25 10
700 – 2s. green 2·50 10
731 – 2s. blue 55 10
701 – 5s. brown and violet 5·75 35
732 – 5s. purple and blue 75 35
702 – 10s. blue and black 10·00 50
733 – 10s. black and green 2·50 70
DESIGNS—VERT: 4c. Chavin pottery; 10c. Automobile roads in Andes; 20c. (2) Industrial Bank of Peru; 1s. (2) Portrait of Toribio de Luzuriaga; 5s. (2) Chavin Idol. HORIZ: 15c. (2) Archaeological Museum, Lima; 50c. (2) Labourers' homes at Lima; 2s. (2) Fig Tree; 10s. (2) Mt. Huascaran.

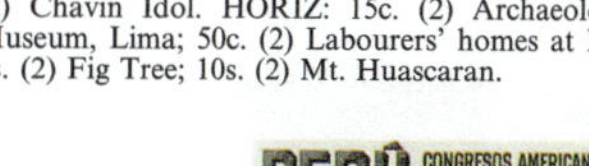

240 Monument on Junin Plains

248 Seal of City of Lima

1938. Air. As T **240**.
650 – 5c. brown 15 10
743 – 5c. green 10 10
651 **240** 15c. brown 15 10
652 – 20c. red 40 10
653 – 25c. green 20 10
654 – 30c. orange 20 10
735 – 30c. red 15 10
655 – 50c. green 35 30
656 – 70c. grey 50 25
736 – 70c. blue 30 10
657 – 80c. green 60 10
737 – 80c. red 55 15
658 – 1s. green 5·00 2·75
705 – 1s.50 violet 45 35
738 – 1s.50 purple 45 30
660 – 2s. red and blue 1·60 50
661 – 5s. purple 10·50 1·10
662 – 10s. blue and green 55·00 27·00
DESIGNS—VERT: 20c. Rear-Admiral M. Villar; 70c. (No. 656, 736), Infiernillo Canyon; 2s. Stele from Chavin Temple. HORIZ: 5c. People's restaurant, Callao; 25c. View of Tarma; 30c. Ica River irrigation system; 50c. Port of Iquitos; 80c. Mountain roadway; 1s. Plaza San Martin, Lima; 1s.50, Nat. Radio Station, San Miguel; 5s. Ministry of Public Works; 10s. Heroe's Crypt, Lima.

1938. 8th Pan-American Congress, Lima.
663 – 10c. grey (postage) 50 20
664 **248** 15c. gold, blue, red & blk 85 25
665 – 1s. brown 1·90 85
DESIGNS (39 × 32½ mm): 10c. Palace and Square, 1864; 1s. Palace, 1938.

666 – 25c. blue (air) 55 50
667 – 1s.50 lake 1·90 1·25
668 – 2s. black 90 45
DESIGNS—VERT: 26 × 37 mm: 25c. Torre Tagle Palace. HORIZ: 39 × 32½ mm: 1s.50, National Congress Building, Lima; 2s. Congress Presidents, Ferreyros, Paz Soldan and Arenas.

1940. No. 642 surch **Habilitada 5 cts.**
669 5c. on 10c. red 15 10

251 National Broadcasting Station

1941. Optd **FRANQUEO POSTAL.**
670 **251** 50c. yellow 1·60 15
671 1s. violet 1·60 20
672 2s. green 3·25 50
673 5s. brown 19·00 5·50
674 10s. mauve 29·00 4·75

1942. Air. No. 653 surch **Habilit 0.15.**
675 15c. on 25c. green 85 10

253 Map of S. America showing R. Amazon

254 Francisco de Orellana

255 Francisco Pizarro

257 Samuel Morse

1943. 400th Anniv of Discovery of R. Amazon.
676 – 2c. red 10 10
677 **254** 4c. grey 15 10
678 **255** 10c. brown 20 10
679 **253** 15c. blue 50 20
680 – 20c. olive 20 15
681 – 25c. orange 2·00 35
682 **254** 30c. red 35 20
683 **253** 50c. green 35 40
685 – 70c. violet 2·50 70
686 – 80c. blue 2·50 70
687 – 1s. brown 4·75 70
688 **255** 5s. black 9·50 4·00
DESIGNS—As Type **254**: 2, 70c. Portraits of G. Pizarro and Orellana in medallion; 20, 80c. G. Pizarro. As Type **253**: 25c., 1s. Orellana's Discovery of the R. Amazon.

1943. Surch with Arms of Peru (as Nos. 483, etc) above **10 CTVS.**
689 10c. on 10c. red (No. 642) 15 10

1944. Centenary of Invention of Telegraphy.
691 **257** 15c. blue 15 15
692 30c. brown 50 20

1946. Surch **Habilitada S/o 0.20.**
706 20c. on 1s. purple (No. 699) 25 10

259

261

1947. 1st National Tourist Congress, Lima. Unissued designs inscr "V Congreso Pan Americano de Carreteras 1944" optd **Habilitada I Congreso Nac. de Turismo Lima–1947**.
707 **259** 15c. black and red 25 15
708 – 1s. brown 35 20
709 – 1s.35 green 35 25
710 **261** 3s. blue 85 50
711 – 5s. green . . . . 2·10 1·25
DESIGNS—VERT: 1s. Mountain road; 1s.35, Forest road. HORIZ: 5s. Road and house.

1947. Air. 1st Peruvian Int Airways Lima–New York Flight. Optd with PIA badge and **PRIMER VUELO LIMA - NUEVA YORK**.
712 5c. brown (No. 650) 10 10
713 50c. green (No. 655) 15 10

263 Basketball Players

1948. Air. Olympic Games.
714 – 1s. blue . . . . 3·75 2·25
715 **263** 2s. brown . . . . 5·75 3·00
716 – 5s. green . . . . 11·50 5·00
717 – 10s. yellow . . . . 15·00 6·50
MS717a 116 × 151 mm. Nos. 714/17 28·00 28·00
DESIGNS: 1s. Map showing air route from Peru to Great Britain; 5s. Discus thrower; 10s. Rifleman.
No. 714 is inscr "AEREO" and Nos. 715/17 are optd **AEREO**.
The above stamps exist overprinted **MELBOURNE 1956** but were only valid for postage on one day.

1948. Air. Nos. 653, 736 and 657 surch **Habilitada S/o.** and value.
722 5c. on 25c. green 10 10
723 10c. on 25c. green 30 10
718 10c. on 70c. blue 65 20
719 15c. on 70c. blue 30 10
720 20c. on 70c. blue 30 10
724 30c. on 80c. green 90 15
721 55c. on 70c. blue 30 10

263a

263b

1949. Anti-tuberculosis Fund. Surch **Decreto Ley No. 18** and value.
724a **263a** 3c. on 4c. blue 55 10
724b **263b** 3c. in 10c. blue 55 10

264 Statue of Admiral Grau

264a "Education"

1949.
726 **264** 10c. blue and green . . . 10 10

1950. Obligatory Tax. National Education Fund.
851 **264a** 3c. lake (16½ × 21 mm) 10 10
897 3c. lake (18 × 21½ mm) 15 10

265 Park, Lima

1951. Air. 75th Anniv of U.P.U. Unissued stamps inscr "VI CONGRESO DE LA UNION POSTAL DE LAS AMREICAS Y ESPANA-1949" optd **U.P.U. 1874–1949**.
745 **265** 5c. green 10 10
746 – 30c. red and black 15 10
747 – 55c. green 15 10
748 – 95c. turquoise 20 15
749 – 1s.50 red 30 25
750 – 2s. blue 35 30
751 – 5s. red . . . . 3·00 2·10
752 – 10s. violet . . . . 4·75 3·00
753 – 20s. blue and brown . . . 8·50 5·00
DESIGNS: 30c. Peruvian flag; 55c. Huancayo Hotel; 95c. Ancash Mtns; 1s.50, Arequipa Hotel; 2s. Coaling Jetty; 5s. Town Hall, Miraflores; 10s. Congressional Palace; 20s. Pan-American flags.

1951. Air Surch **HABILITADA S/o. 0.25**.
754 25c. on 30c. red (No. 735) . . 15 10

1951. Surch **HABILITADA S/.** and figures.
755 1c. on 2c. (No. 693) 10 10
756 5c. on 15c. (No. 727) 10 10
757 10c. on 15c. (No. 727) . . . 10 10

268 Obrero Hospital, Lima

1951. 5th Pan-American Highways Congress. Unissued "VI CONGRESO DE LA UNION POSTAL" stamps, optd **V Congreso Panamericano de Carreteras 1951**.
758 – 2c. green 10 10
759 **268** 4c. red 10 10
760 – 15c. grey 15 10
761 – 20c. brown 10 10
762 – 50c. purple 15 10
763 – 1s. blue 20 10
764 – 2s. blue 30 10
765 – 5s. red . . . . 1·50 1·00
766 – 10s. brown . . . . 3·25 85
DESIGNS—HORIZ: 2c. Aguas Promenade; 50c. Archiepiscopal Palace, Lima; 1s. National Judicial Palace; 2s. Municipal Palace; 5s. Lake Llanganuco, Ancash. VERT: 15c. Inca postal runner; 20c. Old P.O., Lima; 10s. Machu-Picchu ruins.

269 Father Tomas de San Martin and Capt. J. de Aliaga

1951. Air. 4th Cent of S. Marcos University.
767 **269** 30c. black 10 10
768 – 40c. blue 15 10
769 – 50c. mauve 20 10
770 – 1s.20 green 30 15
771 – 2s. grey 35 15
772 – 5s. multicoloured . . . . 1·50 20
DESIGNS: 40c. San Marcos University; 50c. Santo Domingo Convent; 1s.20, P. de Peralto Barnuevo, Father Tomas de San Martin and Jose Baquijano; 2s. Toribio Rodriguez, Jose Hipolito Unanue and Jose Cayetano Heredia; 5s. University Arms in 1571 and 1735.

270 Engineer's School

1952. (a) Postage.
774 – 2c. purple 10 10
775 – 5c. green 30 10
776 – 10c. green 30 10
777 – 15c. grey 25 15
777a – 15c. brown . . . . 1·25 50
829 – 20c. brown 20 10
779 **270** 25c. red 15 10
779a 25c. green 30 10
780 – 30c. blue 10 10
780a – 30c. red 15 10
830 – 30c. mauve 15 10
924 – 50c. green 10 10
831 – 50c. purple 15 10
782 – 1s. brown 30 10
782a – 1s. blue 30 10
783 – 2s. turquoise 40 10
783a – 2s. grey 55 15
DESIGNS—As Type **270**: HORIZ: 2c. Hotel, Tacna; 5c. Tuna fishing boat and indigenous fish; 10c. View of Matarani; 15c. Steam train; 30c. Public Health and Social Assistance. VERT: 20c. Vicuna. Larger (35 × 25 mm): HORIZ: 50c. Inca maize terraces; 1s. Inca ruins, Paramonga Fort; 2s. Agriculture Monument, Lima.

(b) Air.
784 – 40c. green 65 10
785 – 75c. brown . . . . 1·10 25
834 – 80c. red 50 10
786 – 1s.25 blue 25 10
787 – 1s.50 red 20 10
788 – 2s.20 blue 65 15
789 – 3s. brown 75 25
835 – 3s. green 50 30
836 – 3s.80 orange 85 35
790 – 5s. brown 50 15
791 – 10s. brown . . . . 1·50 35
838 – 10s. red . . . . 1·00 45
DESIGNS—As Type **270**. HORIZ: 40c. Gunboat "Maranon"; 1s.50, Housing Complex. VERT: 75c., 80c. Colony of Guanay cormorants. Larger (25 × 25 mm.): HORIZ: 1s.25, Corpac-Limatambo Airport; 2s.20, 3s.80, Inca Observatory, Cuzco; 5s. Garcilaso (portrait). VERT: 3s. Tobacco plant, leaves and cigarettes; 10s. Manco Capac Monument (25 × 37 mm).
See also Nos. 867, etc.

271 Isabella the Catholic

272 "Santa Maria", "Pinta" and "Nina"

273

1953. Air. 500th Birth Anniv of Isabella the Catholic.
792 **271** 40c. red 20 10
793 **272** 1s.25 green . . . . . . 2·25 50
794 **271** 2s.15 purple 35 25
795 **272** 2s.20 black . . . . . . 4·25 75

1954. Obligatory Tax. National Marian Eucharistic Congress Fund. Roul.
796 **273** 5c. blue and red 25 10

274 Gen. M. Perez Jimenez

275 Arms of Lima and Bordeaux

1956. Visit of President of Venezuela.
797 **274** 25c. brown 10 10

1957. Air. Exhibition of French Products, Lima.
798 **275** 40c. lake, blue and green 10 10
799 – 50c. black, brown & green 15 10
800 – 1s.25 deep blue, green and blue . . . . 1·75 35
801 – 2s.20 brown and blue . . 40 30
DESIGNS—HORIZ: 50c. Eiffel Tower and Lima Cathedral; 1s.25, Admiral Dupetit-Thouars and frigate "La Victorieuse"; 2s.20, Exhibition building, Pres. Prado and Pres. Coty.

276 1857 Stamp

277 Carlos Paz Soldan (founder)

1957. Air. Centenary of First Peruvian Postage Stamp.
802 – 5c. black and grey 10 10
803 **276** 10c. turquoise and mauve 10 10
804 – 15c. brown and green . . 10 10
805 – 25c. blue and yellow . . . 10 10
806 – 30c. brown and chocolate 10 10
807 – 40c. ochre and black . . . 15 10
808 – 1s.25 brown and blue . . 35 25
809 – 2s.20 red and blue 50 30
810 – 5s. red and mauve . . . . 1·25 1·00
811 – 10s. violet and green . . . 3·25 2·00
DESIGNS: 5c. Pre-stamp Postmarks; 15c. 1857 2r. stamp; 25c. 1d. 1858; 30c. 1p. 1858 stamp; 40c. ½ peso 1858 stamp; 1s.25, J. Davila Condemarin, Director of Posts, 1857; 2s.20, Pres. Ramon Castilla; 5s. Pres. D. M. Prado; 10s. Various Peruvian stamps in shield.

1958. Air. Centenary of Lima–Callao Telegraph Service.
812 **277** 40c. brown and red . . . 10 10
813 – 1s. green 15 10
814 – 1s.25 blue and purple . . 25 15
DESIGNS—VERT: 1s. Marshal Ramon Castilla. HORIZ: 1s.25, Pres. D. M. Prado and view of Callao.
No. 814 also commemorates the political centenary of the Province of Callao.

278 Flags of France and Peru

279 Father Martin de Porras Velasquez

1958. Air. "Treasures of Peru" Exhibition, Paris.
815 **278** 50c. red, blue & deep blue 10 10
816 – 65c. multicoloured 10 10
817 – 1s.50 brown, purple & bl 25 10
818 – 2s.50 purple, turq & grn 45 20
DESIGNS—HORIZ: 65c. Lima Cathedral and girl in national costume; 1s.50, Caballero and ancient palace. VERT: 2s.50, Natural resources map of Peru.

1958. Air. Birth Centenary of D. A. Carrion Garcia (patriot).
819 **279** 60c. multicoloured 10 10
820 – 1s.20 multicoloured . . . 15 10
821 – 1s.50 multicoloured . . . 25 10
822 – 2s.20 black 30 20
DESIGNS—VERT: 1s.20, D. A. Carrion Garcia. 1s.50, J. H. Unanue Pavon. HORIZ: 2s.20, First Royal School of Medicine (now Ministry of Government Police, Posts and Telecommunications).

280 Gen. Alvarez Thomas

281 Association Emblems

1958. Air. Death Centenary of Gen. Thomas.
823 **280** 1s.10 purple, red & bistre 20 15
824 1s.20 black, red and bistre 25 15

1958. Air. 150th Anniv of Advocates' College, Lima. Emblems in bistre and blue.
825 **281** 80c. green 10 10
826 1s.10 red 15 10
827 1s.20 blue 15 10
828 1s.50 purple 20 10

282 Piura Arms and Congress Emblem

283

1960. Obligatory Tax. 6th National Eucharistic Congress Fund.
839 **282** 10c. multicoloured . . . 20 10
839a 10c. blue and red 20 10

1960. Air. World Refugee Year.
840 **283** 80c. multicoloured 30 30
841 4s.30 multicoloured . . . 50 50

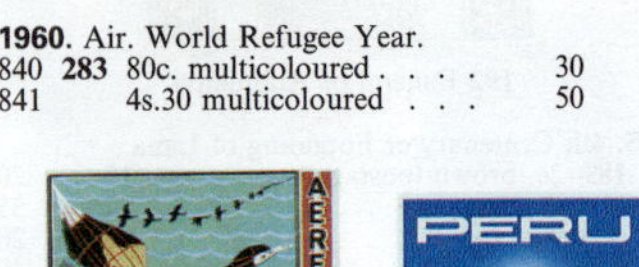

284 Sea Bird bearing Map

285 Congress Emblem

1960. Air. International Pacific Fair, Lima.
842 **284** 1s. multicoloured 40 15

1960. 6th National Eucharistic Congress, Piura.
843 **285** 50c. red, black and blue 15 10
844 – 1s. multicoloured (Eucharistic symbols) 25 10

286 1659 Coin

1961. Air. 1st National Numismatic Exhibition, Lima.
845 – 1s. grey and brown . . . 20 10
846 **286** 2s. grey and blue 25 15
DESIGNS: 1s. 1659 coin.

287 "Amazonas"

1961. Air. Centenary of World Tour of Cadet Sailing Ship "Amazonas".
847 **287** 50c. green and brown . . 35 10
848 80c. red and purple . . . 50 10
849 1s. black and green . . . 70 15

288 Globe, Moon and Stars **289** Olympic Torch

1961. Air. I.G.Y.
850 **288** 1s. multicoloured 15 15

1961. Air. Olympic Games, 1960.
852 **289** 5c. blue and black 40 35
853 10s. red and black 95 60
MS853a 100 × 80 mm. Nos. 852/3. Imperf . . . . 2·50 2·75

290 "Balloon"

291 Fair Emblem

1961. Christmas and New Year.
854 **290** 20c. blue 30 10

1961. Air. 2nd International Pacific Fair, Lima.
855 **291** 1s. multicoloured 20 15

292 Symbol of Eucharist

293 Sculptures "Cahuide" and "Cuauhtemoc"

1962. Obligatory Tax. 7th National Eucharistic Congress Fund. Roul.
857 **292** 10c. blue and yellow . . . 10 10

1962. Air. Peruvian Art Treasures Exhibition, Mexico 1960. Flags red and green.
859 **293** 1s. red 15 10
860 – 2s. turquoise 25 15
861 – 3s. brown 30 15
DESIGNS: 2s. Tupac-Amaru and Hidalgo; 3s. Presidents Prado and Lopez.

294 Frontier Maps

1962. Air. 20th Anniv of Ecuador–Peru Border Agreement.
862 **294** 1s.30 black & red on grey 25 15
863 1s.50 multicoloured . . . 25 15
864 2s.50 multicoloured . . . 30 30

295 The Cedar, Pomabamba

296 "Man"

1962. Centenary of Pomabamba and Pallasca Ancash.
865 **295** 1s. green and red (postage) 35 15
866 – 1s. black and grey (air) 10 10
DESIGN: No. 866, Agriculture, mining, etc, Pallasca Ancash (31½ × 22 mm.).

1962. As Nos. 774/91 but colours and some designs changed and new values. (a) Postage.
867 20c. purple 20 10
921 20c. red 10 10
922 30c. blue (as No. 776) . . . 10 10
923 40c. orange (as No. 784) . . 60 10
871 60c. black (as No. 774) . . . 25 10
925 1s. red 10 10

(b) Air.
873 1s.30 ochre (as No. 785) . . 60 20
874 1s.50 purple 35 10
875 1s.80 blue (as No. 777) . . . 1·25 40
876 2s. green 40 15
926 2s.60 green (as No. 783) . . 30 15
877 3s. purple 40 15
927 3s.60 purple (as No. 789) . . 45 20
878 4s.30 orange 80 30
928 4s.60 orange (as No. 788) . . 35 25
879 5s. green 80 35
880 10s. blue . . . . 1·60 40

1963. Air. Chavin Excavations Fund. Pottery.
881 – 1s.+50c. grey and pink . . 15 15
882 – 1s.50+1s. grey and blue 15 15
883 – 3s.+2s.50 grey & green . . 50 50
884 **296** 4s.30+3s. grey and green 85 65
885 – 6s.+4s. grey and olive . . 1·25 85
FIGURES—HORIZ: 1s. "Griffin"; 1s.50, "Eagle"; 3s. "Cat". VERT: 6s. "Deity".

297 Campaign and Industrial Emblems

1963. Freedom from Hunger.
886 **297** 1s. bistre and red (postage) 15 10
887 4s.30 bistre and green (air) 40 40

298 Henri Dunant and Centenary Emblem

1964. Air. Red Cross Centenary.
888 **298** 1s.30+70c. multicoloured 25 25
889 4s.30+1s.70 multicoloured 55 55

299 Chavez and Wing

300 Alliance Emblem

1964. Air. 50th Anniv of Jorge Chavez's Trans-Alpine Flight.
890 **299** 5s. blue, purple and brn 75 35

1964. "Alliance for Progress". Emblem black, green and blue.
891 **300** 40c. black & yell (postage) 10 10
892 – 1s.30 black & mauve (air) 15 10
893 **300** 3s. black and blue 30 25
DESIGN—HORIZ: 1s.30, As Type **300**, but with inscription at right.

301 Fair Poster

302 Net, Flag and Globe

1965. Air. 3rd International Pacific Fair, Lima.
894 **301** 1s. multicoloured 10 10

1965. Air. Women's World Basketball Championships, Lima.
895 **302** 1s.30 violet and red . . . 30 15
896 4s.30 bistre and red . . . 45 30

303 St. Martin de Porras (anonymous)

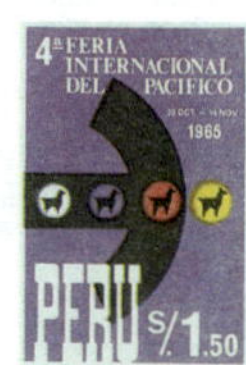

304 Fair Emblem

1965. Air. Canonization of St. Martin de Porras (1962). Paintings. Multicoloured.
898 1s.30 Type **303** 15 10
899 1s.80 "St. Martin and the Miracle of the Animals" (after painting by Camino Brent) 25 10
900 4s.30 "St. Martin and the Angels" (after painting by Fausto Conti) 50 25
Porras is wrongly spelt "Porres" on the stamps.

1965. 4th International Pacific Fair, Lima.
901 **304** 1s.50 multicoloured . . . 15 10
902 2s.50 multicoloured . . . 20 10
903 3s.50 multicoloured . . . 30 20

305 Father Christmas and Postmarked Envelope

312 2nd May Monument and Battle Scene

1965. Christmas.
904 **305** 20c. black and red 15 10
905 50c. black and green . . . 20 10
906 1s. black and blue 30 10
The above stamps were valid for postage only on November 2nd. They were subsequently used as postal employees' charity labels.

1966. Obligatory Tax. Journalists' Fund. (a) Surch **HABILITADO "Fondo del Periodista Peruano" Ley 16078 S/o. 0.10.**
907 **264a** 10c. on 3c. (No. 897) . . 65 10

(b) Surch **Habilitado "Fondo del Periodista Peruano" Ley 16078 S/. 0.10.**
909 **264a** 10c. on 3c. (No. 897) . . 25 10

1966. Obligatory Tax. Journalists' Fund. No. 857 optd **Periodista Peruano LEY 16078**.
910 **292** 10c. blue and yellow . . . 10 10

1966. Nos. 757c, 851 and 897 surch **XX Habilitado S/. 0.10.**
911 **229** 10c. on 2c. brown . . . 10 10
912 **264a** 10c. on 3c. lake (No. 897) 10 10
912b 10c. on 3c. lake (No. 851) . . . . . 2·00 70

1966. Air. Centenary of Battle of Callao. Mult.
913 1s.90 Type **312** 30 20
914 3s.60 Monument and sculpture 45 30
915 4s.60 Monument and Jose Galvez 50 40

313 Funerary Mask

1966. Gold Objects of Chimu Culture. Multicoloured.
916 1s.90+90c. Type **313** 35 35
917 2s.60+1s.30 Ceremonial knife (vert) 40 40
918 3s.60+1s.80 Ceremonial urn 90 90
919 4s.60+2s.30 Goblet (vert) . . 1·25 1·25
920 20s.+10s. Ear-ring . . . . . 4·75 4·75

314 Civil Guard Emblem

1966. Air. Civil Guard Centenary Multicoloured.
929 90c. Type **314** 10 10
930 1s.90 Emblem and activities of Civil Guard 20 10

315 Map and Mountains

1966. Opening of Huinco Hydro-electric Scheme.
931 **315** 70c. black, deep blue and blue (postage) 10 10
932 1s.90 black, blue and violet (air) 20 15

316 Globe

1967. Air. Peruvian Photographic Exhibition, Lima.
933 – 2s.60 red and black . . . 25 15
934 – 3s.60 black and blue . . . 35 25
935 **316** 4s.60 multicoloured . . . 40 30
DESIGNS: 2s.60, "Sun" carving; 3s.60, Map of Peru within spiral.

317 Symbol of Construction

1967. Six-year Construction Plan.
936 **317** 90c. black, gold and mauve (postage) . . . 10 10
937 1s.90 black, gold and ochre (air) 15 15

318 "St. Rosa" (from painting by A. Medoro)

319 Vicuna within Figure "5"

1967. Air. 350th Death Anniv of St. Rosa of Lima. Designs showing portraits of St. Rosa by artists given below. Multicoloured.

938 1s.90 Type **318** 30 15
939 2s.60 C. Maratta 40 15
940 3s.60 Anon., Cusquena School 55 25

1967. 5th International Pacific Fair, Lima.

941 **319** 1s. black, green and gold (postage) 10 10
942 1s. purple, black and gold (air) 10 10

320 Pen-nib made of Newspaper

321 Wall Reliefs (fishes)

1967. Obligatory Tax. Journalists' Fund.

943 **320** 10c. black and red 10 10

1967. Obligatory Tax. Chan-Chan Excavation Fund.

944 **321** 20c. black and blue . . . 10 10
945 – 20c. black and mauve . . 10 10
946 – 20c. black and brown . . 10 10
947 – 20c. multicoloured 10 10
948 – 20c. multicoloured 10 10
949 – 20c. black and green . . . 10 10

DESIGNS: No. 945, Ornamental pattern; No. 946, Carved "bird"; No. 947, Temple on hillside; No. 948, Corner of Temple; No. 949, Ornamental pattern (birds).

322 Lions' Emblem

323 Nazca Jug

1967. Air. 50th Anniv of Lions International.

950 **322** 1s.60 violet, blue and grey 15 10

1968. Air. Ceramic Treasures of Nazca Culture. Designs showing painted pottery jugs. Mult.

951 1s.90 Type **323** 15 15
952 2s.60 Falcon 20 15
953 3s.60 Round jug decorated with bird 25 20
954 4s.60 Two-headed snake . . 30 25
955 5s.60 Sea Bird 40 35

324 Alligator

325 "Antarqui" (Airline Symbol)

1968. Gold Sculptures of Mochica Culture. Mult.

956 1s.90 Type **324** 15 10
957 2s.60 Bird (vert) 15 10
958 3s.60 Lizard 25 15
959 4s.60 Bird (vert) 30 15
960 5s.60 Jaguar 35 20

1968. Air. 12th Anniv of APSA (Peruvian Airlines).

961 **325** 3s.60 multicoloured . . . 30 15
962 – 5s.60 brown, black & red 45 20

DESIGN: 5s.60, Alpaca and stylized Boeing 747.

326 Human Rights Emblem

327 "The Discus-thrower"

1968. Air. Human Rights Year.

963 **326** 6s.50 red, green & brown 25 20

1968. Air. Olympic Games, Mexico.

964 **327** 2s.30 brown, blue & yell 15 10
965 3s.50 blue, red and green 20 15
966 5s. black, blue and pink 25 15
967 6s.50 purple, brown & bl 35 20
968 8s. blue, mauve and lilac 40 25
969 9s. violet, green and orange 45 30

328

331 Indian's Head and Wheat

1968. Obligatory Tax. Unissued stamps surch as in T **328**.

970 **328** 20c. on 50c. violet, orange and black 40 40
971 20c. on 1s. blue, orange and black 40 40

1968. Obligatory Tax. Journalists' Fund. No. 897 surch **Habilitado Fondo Periodista Peruano Ley 17050 S/.** and value.

972 **264a** 20c. on 3c. lake 10 10

1968. Christmas. No. 900 surch **PRO NAVIDAD Veinte Centavos R.S. 5-11-68.**

973 20c. on 4s.30 multicoloured 25 20

1969. Unissued Agrarian Reform stamps, surch as in T **331**. Multicoloured.

974 2s.50 on 90c. Type **331** (postage) 15 10
975 3s. on 90c. Man digging . . 15 15
976 4s. on 90c. As No. 975 . . . 25 15
977 5s.50 on 1s.90 Corn-cob and hand scattering cobs (air) 30 15
978 6s.50 on 1s.90 As No. 977 . . 40 20

333 First Peruvian Coin (obverse and reverse)

1969. Air. 400th Anniv of 1st Peruvian Coinage.

979 **333** 5s. black, grey and yellow 25 15
980 5s. black, grey and green 25 15

334 Worker holding Flag and Oil Derrick

1969. Nationalization of International Petroleum Company's Oilfields and Refinery (9 October 1968).

981 **334** 2s.50 multicoloured . . . 15 10
982 3s. multicoloured 20 10
983 4s. multicoloured 25 15
984 5s.50 multicoloured . . . 30 20

335 Castilla Monument

336 Boeing 707, Globe and "Kon Tiki" (replica of balsa raft)

1969. Air. Death Centenary of President Ramon Castilla.

985 **335** 5s. blue and green 30 15
986 – 10s. brown and purple . . 70 30

DESIGN—(21×37 mm): 10s. President Castilla.

1969. 1st A.P.S.A. (Peruvian Airlines) Flight to Europe.

987 **336** 2s.50 mult (postage) . . . 20 10
988 3s. multicoloured (air) . . 30 10
989 4s. multicoloured 40 10
990 5s.50 multicoloured . . . 50 15
991 6s.50 multicoloured . . . 60 25

337 Dish Aerial, Satellite and Globe

1969. Air. Inauguration of Lurin Satellite Telecommunications Station, Lima.

992 **337** 20s. multicoloured . . . . 1·50 60
MS993 110×81 mm. No. 992. Imperf . . . . 1·40 1·40

338 Captain Jose A. Quinones Gonzales (military aviator)

1969. Quinones Gonzales Commemoration.

994 **338** 20s. mult (postage) . . . 1·50 70
995 20s. multicoloured (air) 1·50 45

339 W.H.O. Emblem

1969. Air. 20th Anniv (1968) of W.H.O.

996 **339** 5s. multicoloured 15 15
997 6s.50 multicoloured . . . 20 15

340 Peasant breaking Chains

341 Arms of the Inca Garcilaso de la Vega (historian)

1969. Agrarian Reform Decree.

998 **340** 2s.50 deep blue, blue and red (postage) 10 10
999 3s. purple, lilac and black (air) 10 10
1000 4s. brown and light brown 15 10

1969. Air. Garcilaso de la Vega Commemoration.

1001 **341** 2s.40 black, silver & grn 10 10
1002 – 3s.50 black, buff and blue 15 10
1003 – 5s. multicoloured 20 15
MS1004 127×88 mm. Nos. 1001/1003. Imperf 90 90

DESIGNS: 3s.50, Title page, "Commentarios Reales", Lisbon, 1609; 5s. Inca Garcilaso de la Vega.

342 Admiral Grau and Ironclad Warship "Huascar"

1969. Navy Day.

1005 **342** 50s. multicoloured . . . 4·50 2·50

343 "6" and Fair Flags

1969. 6th International Pacific Fair, Lima.

1006 **343** 2s.50 mult (postage) . . 10 10
1007 3s. multicoloured (air) 15 10
1008 4s. multicoloured 15 10

344 Father Christmas and Greetings Card

345 Col. F. Bolognesi and Soldier

1969. Christmas.

1009 **344** 20c. black and red . . . 10 10
1010 20c. black and orange 10 10
1011 20c. black and brown . . 10 10

1969. Army Day.

1012 **345** 1s.20 black, gold and blue (postage) 10 10
1013 50s. black, gold and brown (air) . . . . . 3·00 1·10

346 Arms of Amazonas

1970. Air. 150th Anniv (1971) of Republic (1st issue).

1014 **346** 10s. multicoloured . . . 35 30

See also Nos. 1066/70, 1076/80 and 1081/90.

347 I.L.O. Emblem on Map

1970. Air. 50th Anniv of I.L.O.

1015 **347** 3s. deep blue and blue 15 10

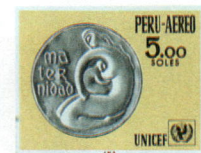

348 "Motherhood"

1970. Air. 24th Anniv of UNICEF.

1016 **348** 5s. black and yellow . . 25 15
1017 6s.50 black and pink . . 35 20

349 "Puma" Jug

350 Ministry Building

1970. Vicus Culture. Ceramic Art. Multicoloured.

1018 2s.50 Type **349** (postage) . . 15 10
1019 3s. Squatting warrior (statuette) (air) 20 15
1020 4s. Animal jug 25 15
1021 5s.50 Twin jugs 30 20
1022 6s.50 Woman with jug (statuette) 40 25

1970. Ministry of Transport and Communications.

1023 **350** 40c. black and purple . . 10 10
1024 40c. black and yellow . . 10 10
1025 40c. black and grey . . . 10 10
1026 40c. black and red . . . 10 10
1027 40c. black and brown . . 10 10

351 Peruvian Anchovy

352 Telephone and Skyline

1970. Fishes. Multicoloured.
1028 2s.50 Type **351** (postage) . . 35 10
1029 2s.50 Chilean hake 35 10
1030 3s. Swordfish (air) 40 15
1031 3s. Yellow-finned tuna . . . 40 15
1032 5s.50 Atlantic wolffish . . . 1·00 25

1970. Air. Nationalization of Lima Telephone Service.
1033 **352** 5s. multicoloured 30 15
1034 10s. multicoloured . . . 55 25

353 "Soldier and Farmer"

354 U.N. Headquarters and Dove

1970. Unity of Armed Forces and People.
1035 **353** 2s.50 mult (postage) . . 15 10
1036 3s. multicoloured (air) 25 10
1037 5s.50 multicoloured . . . 35 15

1970. Air. 25th Anniv of U.N.O.
1038 **354** 3s. blue and light blue 15 10

355 Rotary Emblem

1970. Air. 50th Anniv of Lima Rotary Club.
1039 **355** 10s. gold, red and black 75 25

356 Military Parade (Army Staff College, Chorrillos)

1970. Military, Naval and Air Force Academies. Multicoloured.
1040 2s.50 Type **356** 35 20
1041 2s.50 Parade, Naval Academy, La Punta . . . 35 20
1042 2s.50 Parade, Air Force Officer Training School, Las Palmas 35 20

357 Puruchuco, Lima

1970. Tourism. Multicoloured.
1043 2s.50 Type **357** (postage) . . 15 10
1044 3s. Chan-Chan-Trujillo, La Libertad (air) 15 10
1045 4s. Sacsayhuaman, Cuzco (vert) 25 10
1046 5s.50 Lake Titicaca, Pomata, Puno (vert) 30 15
1047 10s. Machu-Picchu, Cuzco (vert) 60 30
MS1048 127 × 95 mm. Nos. 1043/7. Imperf . . . . 1·75 1·75

358 Festival Procession

1970. Air. October Festival, Lima. Multicoloured.
1049 3s. Type **358** 15 10
1050 4s. "The Cock-fight" (T. Nunez Ureta) 25 10
1051 5s.50 Altar, Nazarenas Shrine (vert) 30 20
1052 6s.50 "The Procession" (J. Vinatea Reinoso) . . . 35 25
1053 8s. "The Procession" (Jose Sabogal) (vert) 50 20

359 "The Nativity" (Cuzco School)

1970. Christmas. Paintings by Unknown Artists. Multicoloured.
1054 1s.20 Type **359** 30 25
1055 1s.50 "The Adoration of the Magi" (Cuzquena School) 10 10
1056 1s.80 "The Adoration of the Shepherds" (Peruvian School) 10 10

360 "Close Embrace" (petroglyph)

1971. Air. "Gratitude for World Help in Earthquake of May 1970".
1057 **360** 4s. olive, black and red 25 15
1058 5s.50 blue, flesh and red 35 15
1059 6s.50 grey, blue and red 40 20

361 "St. Rosa de Lima" (F. Laso)

1971. 300th Anniv of Canonization of St. Rosa de Lima.
1060 **361** 2s.50 multicoloured . . . 15 10

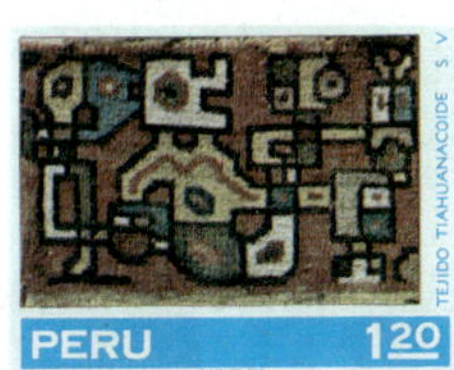

362 Tiahuanaco Fabric

1971. Ancient Peruvian Textiles.
1061 **362** 1s.20 mult (postage) . . 15 10
1062 – 2s.50 multicoloured . . . 25 10
1063 – 3s. multicoloured (air) 30 10
1064 – 4s. pink, green & dp grn 40 10
1065 – 5s.50 multicoloured . . . 55 15
DESIGNS—HORIZ: 2s.50, Chancay fabric; 4s. Chancay lace. VERT: 3s. Chancay tapestry; 5s.50, Paracas fabric.

363 M. Garcia Pumacahua

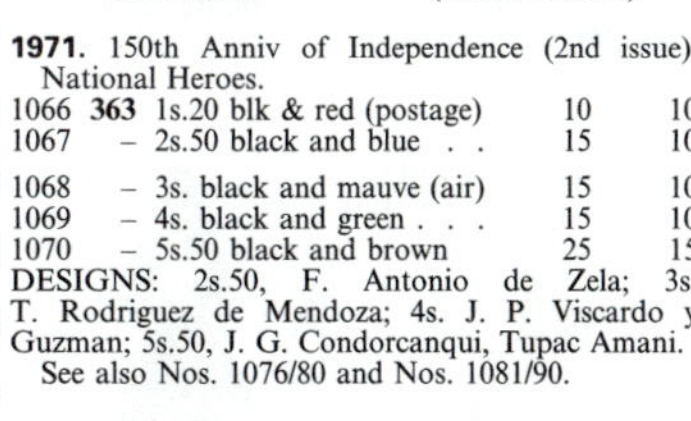

364 Violet Amberjack (Nazca Culture)

1971. 150th Anniv of Independence (2nd issue). National Heroes.
1066 **363** 1s.20 blk & red (postage) 10 10
1067 – 2s.50 black and blue . . 15 10
1068 – 3s. black and mauve (air) 15 10
1069 – 4s. black and green . . . 15 10
1070 – 5s.50 black and brown 25 15
DESIGNS: 2s.50, F. Antonio de Zela; 3s. T. Rodriguez de Mendoza; 4s. J. P. Viscardo y Guzman; 5s.50, J. G. Condorcanqui, Tupac Amani.
See also Nos. 1076/80 and Nos. 1081/90.

1971. "Traditional Fisheries of Peru". Piscatorial Ceramics. Multicoloured.
1071 1s.50 Type **364** (postage) . . 25 10
1072 3s.50 Pacific bonito (Chimu Inca) (air) 55 15
1073 4s. Peruvian anchovy (Mochica) 75 20
1074 5s.50 Chilian hake (Chimu) 1·10 35
1075 8s.50 Peruvian menhaden (Nazca) . . . . 1·75 60

1971. 150th Anniv of Independence. National Heroes (3rd issue). As T **363**. Multicoloured.
1076 1s.20 M. Melgar (postage) 10 10
1077 2s.50 J. Baquijano y Carrillo 15 10
1078 3s. J. de la Riva Aguero (air) 15 10
1079 4s. H. Unanue 15 10
1080 5s.50 F. J. de Luna Pizarro 25 15

366 Liberation Expedition Monument

367 R. Palma (author and poet)

1971. 150th Anniv of Independence (4th issue). As T **366**. Multicoloured.
1081 1s.50 M. Bastidas (postage) 10 10
1082 2s. J. F. Sanchez Carrion . . 10 10
1083 2s.50 M. J. Guise 15 10
1084 3s. F. Vidal (air) 15 10
1085 3s.50 J. de San Martin . . . 15 15
1086 4s.50 Type **366** 20 15
1087 6s. "Surrender of the 'Numancia Battalion'" (horiz) (42 × 35 mm) . . . 30 15
1088 7s.50 Alvarez de Arenales Monument (horiz) (42 × 39 mm) 35 20
1089 9s. Monument to Founders of the Republic, Lima (horiz) (42 × 39 mm) . . . 40 20
1090 10s. "Proclamation of Independence" (horiz) (46 × 35 mm) 50 20

1971. Air. 150th Anniv of National Library.
1091 **367** 7s.50 black and brown 60 25

368 Weightlifting

369 "Gongora portentosa"

1971. Air. 25th World Weightlifting Championships, Huampani, Lima.
1092 **368** 7s.50 black and blue . . 60 25

1971. Peruvian Flora (1st series). Orchids. Mult.
1093 1s.50 Type **369** 25 10
1094 2s. "Odontoglossum cristatum" 30 10
1095 2s.50 "Mormolyca peruviana" 35 10
1096 3s. "Trichocentrum pulchrum" 45 15
1097 3s.50 "Oncidium sanderae" 35 20
See also Nos. 1170/4 and 1206/10.

370 Family and Flag

371 Schooner "Sacramento" of 1821

1971. Air. 3rd Anniv of October 3rd Revolution.
1098 **370** 7s.50 black, red and blue 50 30
MS1099 110 × 82 mm. No. 1089. Imperf . . . . 1·00 1·00

1971. Air. 150th Anniv of Peruvian Navy and "Order of the Peruvian Sun".
1100 **371** 7s.50 blue and light blue 1·50 30
1101 – 7s.50 multicoloured . . . 50 25
DESIGN: No. 1101, Order of the Peruvian Sun.

372 "Development and Liberation" (detail)

1971. 2nd Ministerial Meeting of "The 77" Group.
1102 **372** 1s.20 multicoloured (postage) 10 10
1103 – 3s.50 multicoloured . . . 25 10
1104 – 50s. multicoloured (air) 3·00 1·50
DESIGNS—As Type **372**: 3s.50, 50s. Detail from the painting "Development and Liberation".

373 "Plaza de Armas, 1843" (J. Rugendas)

1971. "Exfilima" Stamp Exhibition, Lima.
1105 **373** 3s. black and green . . . 30 10
1106 – 3s.50 black and pink . . 40 15
DESIGN: 3s.50, "Plaza de Armas, 1971" (C. Zeiter).

374 Fair Emblem

375 Army Crest

1971. Air. 7th International Pacific Fair, Lima.
1107 **374** 4s.50 multicoloured . . . 20 15

1971. 150th Anniv of Peruvian Army.
1108 **375** 8s.50 multicoloured . . . 60 20

376 "The Flight into Egypt"

1971. Christmas. Multicoloured.
1109 1s.80 Type **376** 20 10
1110 2s.50 "The Magi" 25 10
1111 3s. "The Nativity" 35 10

377 "Fishermen" (J. Ugarte Elespuru) 378 Chimu Idol

1971. Social Reforms. Paintings. Multicoloured.
1112 3s.50 Type **377** 45 10
1113 4s. "Threshing Grain in Cajamarca" (Camilo Blas) 45 10
1114 6s. "Hand-spinning Huanca Native Women" (J. Sabogal) 60 15

1972. Peruvian Antiquities. Multicoloured.
1115 3s.90 Type **378** 35 15
1116 4s. Chimu statuette 35 15
1117 4s.50 Lambayeque idol . . . 45 15
1118 5s.40 Mochica collar 55 15
1119 6s. Lambayeque "spider" pendant 60 15

379 Peruvian Bigeye

1972. Peruvian Fishes. Multicoloured.
1120 1s.20 Type **379** (postage) . . 30 10
1121 1s.50 Common guadana . . 30 15
1122 2s.50 Jack mackerel 55 20
1123 3s. Diabolico (air) 65 20
1124 5s.50 Galapagos hogfish . . 1·25 35

380 "Peruvian Family" (T. Nunez Ureta)

1972. Air. Education Reforms.
1125 **380** 6s.50 multicoloured . . . 35 20

381 Mochica Warrior 382 White-tailed Trogon

1972. Peruvian Art (1st series). Mochica Ceramics. Multicoloured.
1126 1s.20 Type **381** 15 10
1127 1s.50 Warrior's head 15 10
1128 2s. Kneeling deer 25 10
1129 2s.50 Warrior's head (different) 35 10
1130 3s. Kneeling warrior 40 15
See also Nos. 1180/4.

1972. Air. Peruvian Birds. Multicoloured.
1131 2s. Type **382** . . . . 1·50 20
1132 2s.50 Amazonian umbrellabird . . . . . . 1·75 20
1133 3s. Andean cock of the rock 2·00 25
1134 6s.50 Red-billed toucan . . 3·75 45
1135 8s.50 Blue-crowned motmot 4·75 55

383 "The Harvest" (July) 384 "Quipu" on Map

1972. 400th Anniv of G. Poma de Ayala's "Inca Chronicles". Woodcuts.
1136 **383** 2s.50 black and red . . . 35 10
1137 – 3s. black and green . . . 60 10
1138 – 2s.50 black and pink . . . 30 10
1139 – 3s. black and blue . . . 50 10
1140 – 2s.50 black and orange 50 10
1141 – 3s. black and lilac . . . 50 10
1142 – 2s.50 black and brown 35 10
1143 – 3s. black and green . . . 50 10
1144 – 2s.50 black and blue . . 35 10
1145 – 3s. black and orange . . 50 10
1146 – 2s.50 black and mauve 35 10
1147 – 3s. black and yellow . . 50 10

DESIGNS: No. 1137, "Land Purification" (August); No. 1138, "Sowing" (September); No. 1139, "Invocation of the Rains" (October); No. 1140, "Irrigation" (November); No. 1141, "Rite of the Nobility" (December); No. 1142, "Maize Cultivation Rights" (January); No. 1143, "Ripening of the Maize" (February); No. 1144, "Birds in the Maize" (March); No. 1145, "Children as camp-guards" (April); No. 1146, "Gathering the harvest" (May); No. 1147, "Removing the harvest" (June).

1972. Air. "Exfibra 72" Stamp Exn, Rio de Janeiro.
1148 **384** 5s. multicoloured 25 15

385 "The Messenger" 386 Catacaos Woman

1972. Air. Olympic Games, Munich.
1149 **385** 8s. multicoloured 55 20

1972. Air. Provincial Costumes (1st series). Mult.
1150 2s. Tupe girl 15 10
1151 3s.50 Type **386** 30 10
1152 4s. Conibo Indian 40 10
1153 4s.50 Agricultural worker playing "quena" and drum 40 15
1154 5s. "Moche" (Trujillo) girl 40 15
1155 6s.50 Ocongate (Cuzco) man and woman 55 40
1156 8s. "Chucupana" (Ayacucho) girl 60 50
1157 8s.50 "Cotuncha" (Junin) girl 70 55
1158 10s. "Pandilla" dancer . . . 60 60
See also Nos. 1248/9.

387 Ruins of Chavin (Ancash)

1972. Air. 25th Death Anniv Julio C. Tello (archaeologist). Multicoloured.
1159 1s.50 "Stone of the 12 Angles", Cuzco (vert) . . 15 10
1160 3s.50 Type **387** 30 10
1161 4s. Burial-tower, Sillustani (Puno) (vert) 30 10
1162 5s. Gateway, Chavin (Ancash) 45 15
1163 8s. "Wall of the 3 Windows", Machu Picchu (Cuzco) 55 25

388 "Territorial Waters"

1972. 4th Anniv of Armed Forces Revolution. Mult.
1164 2s. Agricultural Workers ("Agrarian Reform") (vert) 10 10
1165 2s.50 Type **388** 50 10
1166 3s. Oil rigs ("Nationalization of Petroleum Industry") (vert) 20 10

389 "The Holy Family" (wood-carving) 390 "Ipomoea purpurea"

1972. Christmas. Multicoloured.
1167 1s.50 Type **389** 15 10
1168 2s. "The Holy Family" (carved Huamanga stone) (horiz) 15 10
1169 2s.50 "The Holy Family" (carved Huamanga stone) 20 10

1972. Peruvian Flora (2nd series). Multicoloured.
1170 1s.50 Type **390** 15 10
1171 2s.50 "Amaryllis ferreyrae" 20 10
1172 3s. "Liabum excelsum" . . 30 10
1173 3s.50 "Bletia catenulata" . . 55 10
1174 5s. "Cantua buxifolia cantuta" 35 20

391 Inca Poncho 392 Mochica Cameo and Cups

1973. Air. Ancient Inca Textiles.
1175 **391** 2s. multicoloured 15 10
1176 – 3s.50 multicoloured . . . 25 10
1177 – 4s. multicoloured 25 10
1178 – 5s. multicoloured 30 10
1179 – 8s. multicoloured 55 25
DESIGNS: Nos. 1176/9, similar to T **391**.

1973. Air. Peruvian Art (2nd series). Jewelled Antiquities. Multicoloured.
1180 1s.50 Type **392** 10 10
1181 2s.50 Gold-plated arms and hands (Lambayeque) . . 15 10
1182 4s. Bronze effigy (Mochica) 25 10
1183 5s. Gold pendants (Nazca) 30 15
1184 8s. Gold cat (Mochica) . . . 60 25

393 Andean Condor 394 "The Macebearer" (J. Sabogal)

1973. Air. Fauna Protection (1st series). Mult.
1185 2s.50 Lesser rhea . . . . . 1·00 30
1186 3s.50 Giant otter 45 10
1187 4s. Type **393** 40 20
1188 5s. Vicuna 60 15
1189 6s. Chilian flamingo . . . . 2·25 40
1190 8s. Spectacled bear 70 25
1191 8s.50 Bush dog (horiz) . . . 60 25
1192 10s. Short-tailed chinchilla (horiz) 75 30
See also Nos. 1245/6.

1973. Air. Peruvian Paintings. Multicoloured.
1193 1s.50 Type **394** 10 10
1194 8s. "Yananacu Bridge" (E. C. Brent) (horiz) . . 30 15
1195 8s.50 "Portrait of a Lady" (D. Hernandez) 35 15
1196 10s. "Peruvian Birds" (T. N. Ureta) . . . . 1·25 40
1197 20s. "The Potter" (F. Laso) 1·10 40
1198 50s. "Reed Boats" (J. V. Reinoso) (horiz) . . . . . 3·50 1·50

395 Basketball Net and Map

1973. Air. 1st World Basketball Festival.
1199 **395** 5s. green 35 10
1200 20s. purple . . . . . . 1·40 40

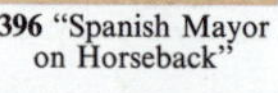

396 "Spanish Mayor on Horseback" 398 Fair Emblem (poster)

1973. 170th Birth Anniv of Pancho Fierro (painter). Multicoloured.
1201 1s.50 Type **396** 10 10
1202 2s. "Peasants" 15 10
1203 2s.50 "Father Abregu" . . . 20 10
1204 3s.50 "Dancers" 30 10
1205 4s.50 "Esteban Arredondo on horseback" 45 20

1973. Air. Peruvian Flora (3rd series). Orchids. As T **390**. Multicoloured.
1206 1s.50 "Lycaste reichenbachii" 20 10
1207 2s.50 "Masdevallia amabilis" 30 10
1208 3s. "Sigmatostalix peruviana" 40 10
1209 3s.50 "Porrogossum peruvianum" 40 10
1210 8s. "Oncidium incarum" . . 60 25

1973. Air. 8th International Pacific Fair, Lima.
1211 **398** 8s. red, black and grey 60 20

399 Symbol of Flight

1973. Air. 50th Anniv of Air Force Officers' School.
1212 **399** 8s.50 multicoloured . . . 60 15

400 "The Presentation of the Child"

1973. Christmas. Paintings of the Cuzco School. Multicoloured.
1213 1s.50 Type **400** 10 10
1214 2s. "The Holy Family" (vert) 15 10
1215 2s.50 "The Adoration of the Kings" 15 10

401 Freighter "Ilo"

1973. Air. National Development. Multicoloured.
1216 1s.50 Type **401** 75 20
1217 2s.50 Trawlers 85 20
1218 8s. B.A.C. One Eleven 200 airliner and seagull . . . 1·00 25

402 House of the Mulberry Tree, Arequipa

1974. Air. "Landscapes and Cities". Mult.
1219 1s.50 Type **402** 10 10
1220 2s.50 El Misti (peak), Arequipa 15 10
1221 5s. Giant puya, Cordillera Blanca, Ancash (vert) . . 30 15
1222 6s. Huascaran (peak), Cordillera Blanca, Ancash 35 15
1223 8s. Lake Querococha, Cordillera Blanca, Ancash 55 20

403 Peruvian 2c. Stamp of 1873 405 Church of San Jeronimo, Cuzco

404 Room of the Three Windows, Machu Picchu

1974. Stamp Day and 25th Anniv of Peruvian Philatelic Association.
1224 **403** 6s. blue and grey 40 15

1974. Air. Archaeological Discoveries. Mult.
(a) Cuzco Relics.
1225 3s. Type **404** 15 10
1226 5s. Baths of Tampumacchay 25 15
1227 10s. "Kencco" 45 25
(b) Dr. Tello's Discoveries at Chavin de Huantar. Stone carvings.
1228 3s. Mythological jaguar (vert) 15 10
1229 5s. Rodent ("Vizcacha") (vert) 25 15
1230 10s. Chavin warrior (vert) 45 25

1974. Air. Architectural Treasures. Multicoloured.
1231 1s.50 Type **405** 10 10
1232 3s.50 Cathedral of Santa Catalina, Cajamarca . . . 20 10
1233 5s. Church of San Pedro, Zepita, Puno (horiz) . . . 25 10
1234 6s. Cuzco Cathedral 30 15
1235 8s.50 Wall of the Coricancha, Cuzco . . . 80 20

406 "Colombia" Bridge, Tarapoto–Juanjui Highway

1974. "Structural Changes". Multicoloured.
1236 2s. Type **406** 15 10
1237 8s. Tayacaja hydro-electric scheme 40 20
1238 10s. Tablachaca dam . . . 50 25

407 "Battle of Junin" (F. Yanez)

1974. 150th Anniv of Battle of Junin.
1239 **407** 1s.50 mult (postage) . . 10 10
1240 2s.50 multicoloured . . . 10 10
1241 6s. multicoloured (air) 30 10

408 "Battle of Ayacucho" (F. Yanez)

1974. 150th Anniv of Battle of Ayacucho.
1242 **408** 2s. mult (postage) . . . 10 10
1243 3s. multicoloured 15 10
1244 7s.50 multicoloured (air) 45 15

1974. Air. Fauna Protection (2nd series). As T **393**. Multicoloured.
1245 8s. Red uakari 50 15
1246 20s. As 8s. 85 50

409 Chimu Gold Mask

1974. Air. 8th World Mining Congress, Lima.
1247 **409** 8s. multicoloured 45 15

1974. Air. Provincial Costumes (2nd series). As T **386**. Multicoloured.
1248 5s. Horseman in "chalan" (Cajamarca) 35 15
1249 8s.50 As 5s. 60 15

410 Pedro Paulet and Spacecraft

1974. Air. Centenary of U.P.U. and Birth Centenary of Pedro E. Paulet (aviation scientist).
1250 **410** 8s. violet and blue . . . 40 15

411 Copper Smelter, La Oroya

1974. Expropriation of Cerro de Pasco Mining Complex.
1251 **411** 1s.50 blue and deep blue 10 10
1252 3s. red and brown . . . 15 10
1253 4s.50 green and grey . . 25 15

412 "Capitulation of Ayacucho" (D. Hernandez)

1974. Air. 150th Anniv of Spanish Forces' Capitulation at Ayacucho.
1254 **412** 3s.50 multicoloured . . . 20 10
1255 8s.50 multicoloured . . . 60 20
1256 10s. multicoloured . . . 80 25

413 "Madonna and Child" **415** Map and Civic Centre, Lima

414 "Andean Landscape" (T. Nunez Ureta)

1974. Christmas. Paintings of the Cuzco Shool. Multicoloured.
1257 1s.50 Type **413** (postage) . . 10 10
1258 6s.50 "Holy Family" (air) 30 15

1974. Air. Andean Pact Communications Ministers' Meeting, Cali, Colombia.
1259 **414** 6s.50 multicoloured . . . 35 15

1975. Air. 2nd General Conference of U.N. Organization for Industrial Development.
1260 **415** 6s. black, red and grey 25 15

1975. Air. Various stamps surch.
1261 – 1s.50 on 3s.60 purple (No. 927) 10 10
1262 – 2s. on 2s.60 green (No. 926) 15 10
1263 – 2s. on 3s.60 purple (No. 927) 15 10
1263a – 2s. on 3s.60 black and blue (No. 934) . . . 10 10
1264 – 2s. on 4s.30 orange (No. 878) 10 10
1265 – 2s. on 4s.30 multicoloured (No. 900) 15 10
1266 – 2s. on 4s.60 orange (No. 928) 10 10
1267 – 2s.50 on 4s.60 orange (No. 928) 25 10
1268 – 3s. on 2s.60 green (No. 926) 15 10
1294 – 3s.50 on 4s.60 orange (No. 928) 20 10
1269 – 4s. on 2s.60 green (No. 926) 20 10
1270 – 4s. on 3s.60 purple (No. 927) 20 10
1271 – 4s. on 4s.60 orange (No. 928) 15 10
1295 – 4s.50 on 3s.80 orange (No. 836) 20 10
1272 – 5s. on 3s.60 purple (No. 927) 20 10
1273 – 5s. on 3s.80 orange (No. 836) 35 10
1296 – 5s. on 4s.30 orange (No. 878) 30 10
1297 – 6c. on 4s.60 orange (No. 928) 40 15
1277 **316** 6s. on 4s.60 multicoloured (No. 935) 45 10
1278 – 7s. on 4s.30 orange (No. 878) 40 15
1279 – 7s.50 on 3s.60 purple (No. 927) 50 15
1280 – 8s. on 3s.60 purple (No. 927) 50 15
1281 **271** 10s. on 2s.15 purple (No. 794) 40 25
1298 – 10s. on 2s.60 green (No. 926) 60 20
1282 – 10s. on 3s.60 purple (No. 927) 60 25
1283 – 10s. on 3s.60 multicoloured (No. 940) 50 25
1284 – 10s. on 4s.30 orange (No. 878) 25 25
1285 – 10s. on 4s.60 orange (No. 928) 60 25
1286 – 20s. on 3s.60 purple (No. 927) 40 15
1287 – 24s. on 3s.60 multicoloured (No. 953) . . . . . 1·40 45
1288 – 28s. on 4s.60 multicoloured (No. 954) . . . . . 1·50 55
1289 – 32s. on 5s.60 multicoloured (No. 955) . . . . . 1·50 65
1290 – 50s. on 2s.60 green (No. 926) . . . . . 2·75 1·00
1299 – 50s. on 3s.60 purple (No. 927) . . . . . 2·25 1·50
1292 – 100s. on 3s.80 orange (No. 836) . . . . . 3·50 1·50

417 Lima on World Map

1975. Air. Conference of Non-aligned Countries' Foreign Ministers, Lima.
1311 **417** 6s.50 multicoloured . . . 40 15

418 Maria Parado de Bellido

1975. "Year of Peruvian Women" and International Women's Year. Multicoloured.
1312 1s.50 Type **418** 15 10
1313 2s. Micaela Bastidas (vert) 15 10
1314 2s.50 Juana Alarco de Dammert 20 10
1315 3s. I.W.Y. emblem (vert) . . 35 10

419 Route Map of Flight

1975. Air. 1st "Aero Peru" Flight, Rio de Janeiro–Lima–Los Angeles.
1316 **419** 8s. multicoloured 60 15

420 San Juan Macias **421** Fair Poster

1975. Canonization of St. Juan Macias.
1317 **420** 5s. multicoloured 30 10

1975. Air. 9th International Pacific Fair, Lima.
1318 **421** 6s. red, brown and black 50 15

422 Col. F. Bolognesi **423** "Nativity"

1975. Air. 159th Birth Anniv of Colonel Francisco Bolognesi.
1319 **422** 20s. multicoloured . . . 1·25 35

1976. Air. Christmas (1975).
1320 **423** 6s. multicoloured 35 15

424 Louis Braille

1976. 150th Anniv of Braille System for Blind.
1321 **424** 4s.50 red, black and grey 30 10

426 Inca Postal Runner **427** Map on Riband

1976. Air. 11th UPAE Congress, Lima.
1322 **426** 5s. black, brown and red 50 10

1976. Air. Reincorporation of Tacna.
1323 **427** 10s. multicoloured . . . 30 15

428 Peruvian Flag

1976. 1st Anniv of Second Phase of Revolution.
1324 **428** 5s. red, black and grey 15 10

429 Police Badge

1976. Air. 54th Anniv of Peruvian Special Police.
1325 **429** 20s. multicoloured . . . 1·00 40

430 "Tree of Badges" **431** Chairman Pal Losonczi

1976. Air. 10th Anniv of Bogota Declaration.
1326 **430** 10s. multicoloured . . . 30 20

1976. Air. Visit of Hungarian Head of State.
1327 **431** 7s. black and blue . . . 40 15

432 "St. Francis of Assisi" (El Greco) **434** "Nativity"

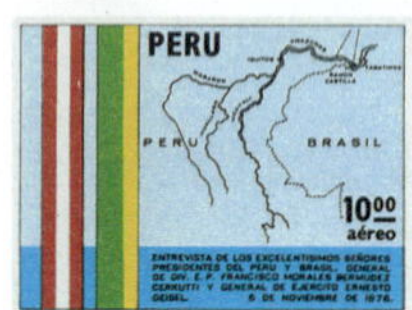

433 Map and National Colours

1976. 750th Death Anniv of St. Francis of Assisi.
1328 **432** 5s. brown and gold . . . 35 10

1976. Air. Meeting of Presidents of Peru and Brazil.
1329 **433** 10s. multicoloured . . . 30 20

1976. Christmas.
1330 **434** 4s. multicoloured 30 10

435 Military Monument and Symbols

1977. Air. Army Day.
1331 **435** 20s. black, buff and red 40 40

436 Map and Scroll

1977. Air. Visit of Peruvian President to Venezuela.
1332 **436** 12s. multicoloured . . . 60 25

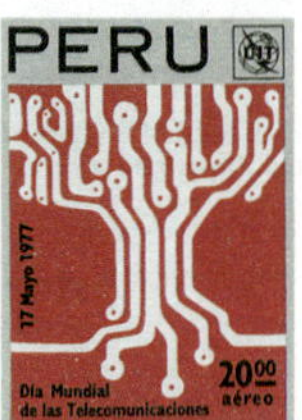

437 Printed Circuit

1977. Air. World Telecommunications Day.
1333 **437** 20s. red, black and silver 1·10 40

438 Inca Postal Runner **439** Petrochemical Plant, Map and Tanker

1977.
1334 **438** 6s. black and turquoise (postage) 40 15
1335 8s. black and red . . . 40 15
1336 10s. black and blue . . . 55 25
1337 12s. black and green . . 55 35
1338 24s. black and red (air) 1·00 50
1339 28s. black and blue . . . 1·10 50
1340 32s. black and brown . . 1·50 70

1977. Air. Bayovar Petrochemical Complex.
1341 **439** 14s. multicoloured . . . 1·50 30

440 Arms of Arequipa **441** President Videla

1977. Air. "Gold of Peru" Exhibition, Arequipa.
1342 **440** 10s. multicoloured . . . 20 10

1977. Air. Visit of President Videla of Argentina.
1343 **441** 36s. multicoloured . . . 75 25

1977. Various stamps surch **FRANQUEO** and new value.
1344 **325** 6s. on 3s.60 multicoloured 40 15
1345 8s. on 3s.60 multicoloured 45 15
1346 – 10s. on 5s.60 brown, black and red (No. 962) 50 25
1347 **305** 10s. on 50c. black & grn 30 10
1348 20s. on 20c. black and red 50 20
1349 30s. on 1s. black and blue 70 35

444 Fair Emblem and Flags **445** Republican Guard Badge

1977. 10th International Pacific Fair.
1350 **444** 10s. multicoloured . . . 20 10

1977. 58th Anniv of Republican Guard.
1351 **445** 12s. multicoloured . . . 25 15

446 Admiral Miguel Grau **447** "The Holy Family"

1977. Air. Navy Day.
1352 **446** 28s. multicoloured . . . 35 25

1977. Christmas. Multicoloured.
1353 8s. Type **447** (postage) . . . 10 10
1354 20s. "The Adoration of the Shepherds" (air) 50 20

448 Open Book of Flags **449** Inca Head

1978. Air. 8th Meeting of Education Ministers.
1355 **448** 30s. multicoloured . . . 40 25

1978.
1356 **449** 6s. green (postage) . . . 10 10
1357 10s. red 15 10
1358 16s. brown 20 20
1359 24s. mauve (air) 30 25
1360 30s. pink 40 30
1361 65s. blue 90 70
1362 95s. blue . . . . 1·50 1·00

450 Emblem and Flags of West Germany, Argentina, Austria and Brazil

1978. World Cup Football Championship, Argentina (1st issue). Multicoloured.
1367 10s. Type **450** 20 10
1368 10s. Emblem and flags of Hungary, Iran, Italy and Mexico 20 10
1369 10s. Emblem and flags of Scotland, Spain, France and Netherlands 20 10
1370 10s. Emblem and flags of Peru, Poland, Sweden and Tunisia 20 10
See also Nos. 1412/15.

451 Microwave Antenna

1978. Air. 10th World Telecommunications Day.
1371 **451** 50s. grey, deep blue and blue 75 50

1978. Various stamps surch **Habilitado Dif.-Porte** and value (Nos. 1372/4), **Habilitado R.D. No. 0118** and value (Nos. 1377/8, 1381, 1384, 1390) or with value only (others).
1372 **229** 2s. on 2c. brown (postage) 10 10
1373 **229** 4s. on 2c. brown 10 10
1374 5s. on 2c. brown 10 10
1375 **313** 20s. on 1s.90+90c. multicoloured 75 60
1376 – 30s. on 2s.60+1s.30 multicoloured (No. 917) 60 60
1377 **229** 35s. on 2c. brown . . . 1·25 20
1378 50s. on 2c. brown . . . 4·00 60
1379 – 55s. on 3s.60+1s.80 multicoloured (No. 918) . . . . . . 1·10 55
1380 – 65s. on 4s.60+2s.30 multicoloured (No. 919) . . . . . . 1·75 1·10
1381 – 80s. on 5s.60 mult (No. 960) . . . . . . 1·40 40
1382 – 85s. on 20s.+10s. multicoloured (No. 920) . . . . . . 2·00 1·25
1383 – 25s. on 4s.60 mult (No. 954) (air) 20 15
1384 **316** 34s. on 4s.60 mult . . . 50 15
1385 **302** 40s. on 4s.30 bistre and red 50 20
1386 **449** 45s. on 28s. green . . . 45 25
1387 – 70s. on 2s.60 green (No. 926) . . . . . . 2·75 40
1388 **449** 75s. on 28s. green . . . 75 40
1389 – 105s. on 5s.60 mult (No. 955) . . . . . . 1·00 85
1390 – 110s. on 3s.60 purple (No. 927) . . . . . . 1·90 60
1391 – 265s. on 4s.30 mult (No. 900) . . . . . . 4·00 1·50
The 28s. value as Type **449** was not issued without a surcharge.

1978. Surch **SOBRE TASA OFICIAL** and value.
1400 **229** 3s. on 2s. brown 10 10
1401 6s. on 2c. brown 15 10

456 San Martin **457** Elmer Faucett and Stinson-Faucett F-19 and Boeing 727-200 Aircraft

1978. Air. Birth Bicentenary of General Jose de San Martin.
1410 **456** 30s. multicoloured . . . 40 30

1978. 50th Anniv of Faucett Aviation.
1411 **457** 40s. multicoloured . . . 50 30

1978. World Cup Football Championship, Argentina (2nd issue). Multicoloured.
1412 16s. As Type **450** 15 10
1413 16s. As No. 1368 . . . . . 15 10
1414 16s. As No. 1369 . . . . . 15 10
1415 16s. As No. 1370 . . . . . 15 10

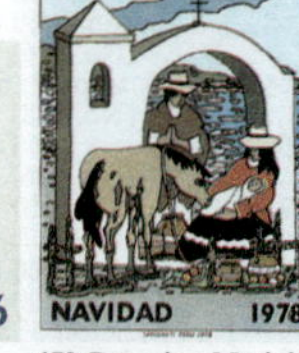

458 Nazca Bowl **459** Peruvian Nativity

1978.
1416 **458** 16s. blue 15 10
1417 20s. green 15 10
1418 25s. green 20 15
1419 35s. red 35 15
1420 45s. brown 40 25
1421 50s. black 50 25
1422 55s. mauve 50 25
1423 70s. mauve 60 35
1424 75s. blue 55 40
1425 80s. brown 55 40
1426 200s. violet . . . . . . 1·90 1·50

1978. Christmas.
1436 **459** 16s. multicoloured . . . 15 10

460 Ministry of Education, Lima **461** Queen Sophia and King Juan Carlos

1979. National Education.
1437 **460** 16s. multicoloured . . . 15 10

1979. Air. Visit of King and Queen of Spain.
1438 **461** 75s. multicoloured . . . 60 25

462 Red Cross Emblem

1979. Centenary of Peruvian Red Cross Society.
1439 **462** 16s. multicoloured . . . 10 10

463 "Naval Battle of Iquique" (E. Velarde)

1979. Pacific War Centenary. Multicoloured.
1440 14s. Type **463** 40 10
1441 25s. "Col. Jose Joaquin Inclan" (vert) 30 15
1442 25s. "Arica Blockade-runner, the Corvette "Union" 60 15
1443 25s. "Heroes of Angamos" 60 15
1444 25s. "Lt. Col. Pedro Ruiz Gallo" (vert) 30 15
1445 85s. "Marshal Andres H. Caceres" (vert) 45 40
1446 100s. "Battle of Angamos" (T. Castillo) . . . . . . 1·75 60
1447 100s. "Battle of Tarapaca" 55 45
1448 115s. "Admiral Miguel Grau" (vert) . . . . . . 1·40 50
1449 200s. "Bolognesi's Reply" (Leppiani) . . . . 1·25 90
1450 200s. "Col. Francisco Bolognesi" (vert) . . . . 1·60 1·10
1451 200s. "Col. Alfonso Ugarte" (Morizani) . . . . 1·60 1·10
A similar 200s. value, showing the Crypt of the Fallen was on sale for a very limited period only.

464 Billiard Balls and Cue **465** Arms of Cuzco

1979. 34th World Billiards Championship, Lima.
1456 **464** 34s. multicoloured . . . 30 15

1979. Inca Sun Festival, Cuzco.
1457 **465** 50s. multicoloured . . . 35 20

466 Flag and Arch

468 Exposition Emblem

1979. 50th Anniv of Reincorporation of Tacna into Peru.
1458 **466** 16s. multicoloured . . . 15 10

1979. Surch in figures only.
1459 **229** 7s. on 2c. brown 10 10
1460 9s. on 2c. brown 10 10
1461 15s. on 2c. brown . . . 15 10

1979. 3rd World Telecommunications Exhibition, Geneva.
1467 **468** 15s. orange, blue and grey 10 10

469 Caduceus

1979. Int Stomatology Congress, Lima, and 50th Anniv of Peruvian Academy of Stomatology.
1468 **469** 25s. gold, black & turq 20 15

470 Fair Emblem on World Map

1979. 11th International Pacific Fair.
1469 **470** 55s. multicoloured . . . 40 30

471 Regalia of Chimu Chief (Imperial period)

472 Angel with Lute

1979. Rafael Larco Herrera Museum of Archaeology.
1470 **471** 85s. multicoloured . . . 60 40

1980. Christmas.
1471 **472** 25s. multicoloured . . . 20 10

1980. Various stamps surch.
1472 **466** 20s. on 16s. multicoloured (postage) 15 10
1473 **463** 25s. on 14s. multicoloured 30 15
1474 **464** 65s. on 34s. multicoloured 45 35
1475 **458** 80s. on 70s. mauve 55 40
1476 **449** 35s. on 24s. mauve (air) 25 15
1477 **438** 45s. on 32s. black and brown 30 20

474 "Respect and Comply with the Constitution"

475 Ceramic Vase (Chimu Culture)

1980. Citizens' Duties.
1478 **474** 15s. turquoise 10 10
1479 – 20s. red 15 10
1480 – 25s. blue 20 15
1481 – 30s. mauve 20 15
1482 – 35s. black 25 20
1483 – 45s. green 30 25
1484 – 50s. brown 35 25
INSCRIPTIONS: 20s. "Honour your country and protect your interests"; 25s. "Comply with the elective process"; 30s. "Comply with your military service"; 35s. "Pay your taxes"; 45s. "Work and contribute to national progress"; 50s. "Respect the rights of others".

1980. Rafael Larco Herrera Archaeological Museum.
1485 **475** 35s. multicoloured . . . 25 20

476 "Liberty" and Map of Peru

478 Rebellion Memorial, Cuzco (Joaquin Ugarte)

477 Machu Picchu

1980. Return to Democracy.
1486 **476** 25s. black, buff and red 20 15
1487 – 35s. black and red . . . 25 20
DESIGN: 35s. Handshake.

1980. World Tourism Conference, Manila.
1488 **477** 25s. multicoloured . . . 20 15

1980. Bicentenary of Tupac Amaru Rebellion.
1489 **478** 25s. multicoloured . . . 20 15
See also No. 1503.

479 Nativity

1980. Christmas.
1490 **479** 15s. multicoloured . . . 10 10

480 Bolivar and Flags

482 Presidential Badge of Office, Laurel Leaves and Open Book

1981. 150th Death Anniv of Simon Bolivar.
1491 **480** 40s. multicoloured . . . 30 20

1981. Various stamps surch.
1492 – 25s. on 35s. black and red (No. 1487) 20 15
1493 **482** 40s. on 25s. multicoloured 30 20
1494 **458** 85s. on 200s. violet . . . 60 45
1495 – 100s. on 115s. mult (No. 1448) 95 50
1496 **482** 130s. on 25s. mult . . . 95 40
1497 140s. on 25s. mult . . . 1·10 50

1981. Re-establishment of Constitutional Government.
1498 **482** 25s. multicoloured . . . 20 15

483 Stone Head, Pallasca

1981.
1499 **483** 30s. violet 20 15
1500 – 40s. blue 30 20
1501 – 100s. mauve 70 45
1502 – 140s. green 95 60
DESIGNS—VERT: 40s. Stone head, Huamachuco; 100s. Stone head (Chavin culture). HORIZ: 140s. Stone puma head (Chavin culture).

484 Tupac Amaru and Micaela Bastidas (sculptures by Miguel Boca Rossi)

1981. Bicentenary of Revolution of Tupac Amaru and Micaela Bastidas.
1503 **484** 60s. multicoloured . . . 40 30

485 Post Box, 1859

486 Map of Peru and I.Y.D.P. Emblem

1981. 50th Anniv of Postal and Philatelic Museum, Lima.
1504 **485** 130s. multicoloured . . . 95 60

1981. International Year of Disabled Persons.
1505 **486** 100s. violet, mauve and gold 70 45

487 Victor Raul Haya de la Torre (President of Constitutional Assembly)

490 Inca Messenger (drawing by Guaman Ponce de Ayala)

1981. Constitution.
1506 **487** 30s. violet and grey . . . 20 15

1981. No. 801 surch.
1507 30s. on 2s.20 brown & blue 20 15
1508 40s. on 2s.20 brown & blue 30 20

1981. 12th International Pacific Fair. No. 801 surch with **12 Feria Internacional del Pacifico 1981 140**.
1509 140s. on 2s.20 brown & blue 95 70

1981. Christmas.
1510 **490** 30s. black and mauve . . 20 10
1511 40s. black and red . . . 35 10
1512 130s. black and green . . 75 35
1513 140s. black and blue . . 90 40
1514 200s. black and brown 1·25 60

1982. Various stamps surch **Habilitado Franq. Postal** and value (Nos. 1520/1) or with value only (others).
1515 **229** 10s. on 2c. brown (postage) 15 10
1516 – 10s. on 10c. red (No. 642) 10 10
1517 **292** 40s. on 10c. blue and yellow 15 10
1518 **273** 70s. on 5c. blue and red 35 20
1519 **264a** 80s. on 3c. lake . . . 30 15
1520 D **109** 80s. on 10c. green . . 30 15
1521 O **108** 80s. on 10c. brown 30 15
1522 **292** 100s. on 10c. blue and yellow 40 20
1523 – 140s. on 50c. brown, yellow and red . . 50 25
1524 – 140s. on 1s. mult . . 50 25
1525 **264a** 150s. on 3c. lake . . 40 20
1526 180s. on 3c. lake . . 55 30
1527 200s. on 3c. lake . . 70 40
1528 **273** 280s. on 5c. blue and red 85 55
1529 – 40s. on 1s.25 blue and purple (No. 814) (air) . . 30 15
1530 – 100s. on 2s.20 (No. 801) brown and blue 40 20
1531 – 240s. on 1s.25 blue and purple (No. 814) . . . . 1·25 85
Nos. 1523/4 are surcharged on labels for the Seventh Eucharistic Congress which previously had no postal validity.

493 Inca Pot

494 Jorge Basadre (after Oscar Lopez Aliaga)

1982. Indian Ceramics.
1532 **493** 40s. orange 30 15
1533 80s. lilac 50 25
1534 – 80s. red 60 25
1535 **493** 180s. green . . . . . . 1·25 70
1536 – 240s. blue . . . . . . 1·25 60
1537 – 280s. violet . . . . . 1·40 70
DESIGNS: 80s., (No. 1534), 240, 280s. Nazca fish ceramic.

1982. Jorge Basadre (historian) Commemoration.
1538 **494** 100s. black and green . . 25 20

495 Julio C. Tello (bust, Victoria Macho)

1982. Birth Centenary of Julio C. Tello (archaeologist).
1539 **495** 200s. green and blue . . 45 30

496 Championship Emblem

497 Disabled Person in Wheelchair

1982. 9th World Women's Volleyball Championship, Peru.
1540 **496** 80s. red and black . . . 20 15

1982. Rights for the Disabled Year.
1541 **497** 200s. blue and red . . . 50 30

498 Andres A. Caceres Medallion

1982. Centenary of Brena Campaign.
1542 **498** 70s. brown and grey . . 20 15

499 Footballers

500 Congress Emblem

1982. World Cup Football Championship, Spain.
1543 **499** 80s. multicoloured . . . 20 15

1982. 16th Int Latin Notaries Congress, Lima.
1544 **500** 500s. black, gold and red 1·10 50

501 Bull (clay jar)

502 Pedro Vilcapaza

1982. Handicrafts Year.
1545 **501** 200s. red, brown and black 50 30

1982. Death Bicentenary of Pedro Vilcapaza (Indian leader).
1546 **502** 240s. brown and black 35 35

503 Jose Davila Condemarin (after J. Y. Pastor)

504 "Nativity" (Hilario Mendivil)

1982. Death Centenary of Jose Davila Condemarin (Director General of Posts).
1547 **503** 150s. black and blue . . 40 25

1982. Christmas.
1548 **504** 280s. multicoloured . . . 40 30

505 Centre Emblem and Hand holding Potatoes

1982. 10th Anniv of International Potato Centre.
1549 **505** 240s. brown and grey . . 35 35

506 Arms of Piura

1982. 450th Anniv of San Miguel de Piura.
1550 **506** 280s. multicoloured . . . 40 40

507 Microscope

1982. Centenary of Discovery of Tubercule Bacillus.
1551 **507** 240s. green 35 35

508 "St. Theresa of Avila" (Jose Espinoza de los Monteros)

1983. 400th Death Anniv of St. Theresa of Avila.
1552 **508** 100s. multicoloured . . . 25 15

509 Civil Defence Badge and Interlocked Hands

1983. 10th Anniv of Civil Defence System.
1553 **509** 100s. blue, orange & blk 25 15

510 Silver Shoe

1983. "Peru, Land of Silver".
1554 **510** 250s. silver, black & blue 55 35

511 Map of Signatories and 200 Mile Zone

513 "75"

512 Boeing 747-200

1983. 30th Anniv of Santiago Declaration.
1555 **511** 280s. brown, blue & black 40 40

1983. 25th Anniv of Lima–Bogota Airmail Service.
1556 **512** 150s. multicoloured . . . 60 25

1983. 75th Anniv of Lima and Callao State Lotteries.
1557 **513** 100s. blue and purple . . 20 15

514 Cruiser "Almirante Grau"

1983. Peruvian Navy. Multicoloured.
1558 150s. Type **514** 95 25
1559 350s. Submarine "Ferre" . . 1·50 55

1983. Various stamps surch.
1560 **493** 100s. on 40s. orange . . 20 15
1561 **498** 100s. on 70s. brown and grey 20 15
1562 **496** 100s. on 80s. red and black 20 15
1563 **502** 100s. on 240s. brown and black 20 15
1564 **505** 100s. on 240s. ochre, deep brown and brown 20 15
1565 **507** 100s. on 240s. green . . 20 15
1566 **506** 150s. on 280s. mult . . 30 15
1567 **511** 150s. on 280s. brown, blue and black 30 15
1568 **504** 200s. on 280s. mult . . 40 25
1569 **493** 300s. on 180s. green . . 55 35
1570 400s. on 180s. green . . 75 50
1571 **499** 500s. on 80s. mult . . . 95 65

516 Simon Bolivar

517 "Virgin and Child" (Cuzquena School)

1983. Birth Bicentenary of Simon Bolivar.
1572 **516** 100s. blue and black . . 20 15

1983. Christmas.
1573 **517** 100s. multicoloured . . . 20 10

518 Fair Emblem

520 Leoncio Prado

519 W.C.Y. Emblem

1983. 14th International Pacific Fair.
1574 **518** 350s. multicoloured . . . 40 15

1984. World Communications Year.
1575 **519** 700s. multicoloured . . . 75 30

1984. Death Centenary (1983) of Colonel Leoncio Prado.
1576 **520** 150s. bistre and brown 15 10

521 Container Ship "Presidente Jose Pardo" at Wharf

1984. Peruvian Industry.
1577 **521** 250s. purple 65 20
1578 – 300s. blue 90 25
DESIGN: 300s. "Presidente Jose Pardo" (container ship).

522 Ricardo Palma

523 Pistol Shooting

1984. 150th Birth Anniv (1983) of Ricardo Palma (writer).
1579 **522** 200s. violet 15 10

1984. Olympic Games, Los Angeles.
1580 **523** 500s. mauve and black 45 25
1581 – 750s. red and black . . . 60 30
DESIGN: 750s. Hurdling.

524 Arms of Callao

525 Water Jar

1984. Town Arms.
1582 **524** 350s. grey 25 15
1583 – 400s. brown 55 25
1584 – 500s. brown 65 30
DESIGNS: 400s. Cajamarca; 500s. Ayacucho.

1984. Wari Ceramics (1st series).
1585 **525** 100s. brown 10 10
1586 – 150s. brown 15 10
1587 – 200s. brown 20 10
DESIGNS: 150s. Llama; 200s. Vase.
See also Nos. 1616/18.

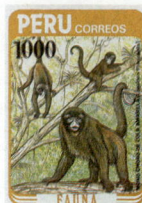

526 Hendee's Woolly Monkeys

1984. Fauna.
1588 **526** 1000s. multicoloured . . 75 40

527 Signing Declaration of Independence

1984. Declaration of Independence.
1589 **527** 350s. black, brown & red 25 15

528 General Post Office, Lima

529 "Canna edulis"

1984. Postal Services.
1590 **528** 50s. olive 10 10

1984. Flora.
1591 **529** 700s. multicoloured . . . 45 25

530 Grau (after Pablo Muniz)

531 Hipolito Unanue

1984. 150th Anniv of Admiral Miguel Grau. Mult.
1592 600s. Type 35 20
1593 600s. Battle of Angamos (45 × 35 mm) 85 30
1594 600s. Grau's seat, National Congress 35 20
1595 600s. "Battle of Iquique" (Guillermo Spier) (45 × 35 mm) 85 30

1984. 150th Death Anniv (1983) of Hipolito Unanue (founder of School of Medicine).
1596 **531** 50s. green 10 10

532 Destroyer "Almirante Guise"

1984. Peruvian Navy.
1597 **532** 250s. blue 35 20
1598 – 400s. turquoise and blue 75 25
DESIGN: 400s. River gunboat "America".

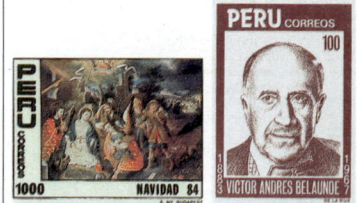

533 "The Adoration of the Shepherds"

534 Belaunde

1984. Christmas.
1599 **533** 1000s. multicoloured . . 40 15

1984. Birth Centenary (1983) of Victor Andres Belaunde (diplomat).
1600 **534** 100s. purple 15 10

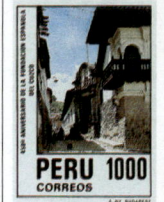

535 Street in Cuzco

536 Fair Emblem

1984. 450th Anniv of Founding of Cuzco by the Spanish.
1601 **535** 1000s. multicoloured . . 40 25

1984. 15th International Pacific Fair, Lima.
1602 **536** 1000s. blue and red . . . 40 25

537 "Foundation of Lima" (Francisco Gonzalez Gamarra)

538 Pope John Paul II

1985. 450th Anniv of Lima.
1603 **537** 1500s. multicoloured . . 55 30

1985. Papal Visit.
1604 **538** 2000s. multicoloured . . 45 35

539 Dish Aerial, Huancayo

540 Jose Carlos Mariategui

1985. 15th Anniv (1984) of Entel Peru (National Telecommunications Enterprise).
1605 **539** 1100s. multicoloured . . 25 15

1985. 60th Death Anniv (1984) of Jose Carlos Mariategui (writer).
1606 **540** 800s. red 20 15

541 Emblem

1985. 25th Meeting of American Airforces Co-operation System.
1607 **541** 400s. multicoloured . . . 15 10

542 Captain Quinones

1985. 44th Death Anniv of Jose Abelardo Quinones Gonzales (airforce captain).
1608 **542** 1000s. multicoloured . . 25 15

543 Arms of Huancavelica

544 Globe and Emblem

1985.
1609 **543** 700s. orange 15 15
See also Nos. 1628/9.

1985. 14th Latin-American Air and Space Regulations Days, Lima.
1610 **544** 900s. blue 25 15

545 Francisco Garcia Calderon (head of 1881 Provisional Government)

546 Cross, Flag and Map

1985. Personalities.
1611 **545** 500s. green 20 10
1612 – 800s. green 35 15
DESIGN: 800s. Oscar Miro Quesada (philosopher and jurist).

1985. 1st Anniv of Constitucion City.
1613 **546** 300s. multicoloured . . . 15 10

547 General Post Office, Lima

548 Society Emblem, Satellite and Radio Equipment

1985. Postal Services.
1614 **547** 200s. grey 10 10

1985. 55th Anniv of Peruvian Radio Club.
1615 **548** 1300s. blue and orange 35 20

549 Robles Moqo Style Cat Vase

550 St. Francis's Monastery, Lima

1985. Wari Ceramics (2nd series).
1616 **549** 500s. brown 15 10
1617 – 500s. brown 15 10
1618 – 500s. brown 15 10
DESIGNS: No. 1617, Cat, Huaura style; No. 1618, Llama's head, Robles Moqo Style.

1985. Tourism Day.
1619 **550** 1300s. multicoloured . . 30 15

551 Title Page of "Doctrina Christiana"

552 Emblem and Curtiss "Jenny" Airplane

1985. 400th Anniv of First Book printed in South America.
1620 **551** 300s. black and stone . . 15 10

1985. 40th Anniv of I.C.A.O.
1621 **552** 1100s. black, blue and red 40 15

553 Humboldt Penguin

554 "Virgin and Child" (Cuzquena School)

1985. Fauna.
1622 **553** 1500s. multicoloured . . 2·10 20

1985. Christmas.
1623 **554** 2i.50 multicoloured . . . 20 10

555 Postman lifting Child

556 Cesar Vallejo

1985. Postal Workers' Christmas and Children's Restaurant Funds.
1624 **555** 2i.50 multicoloured . . . 30 20

1986. Poets.
1625 **556** 800s. blue 20 10
1626 – 800s. brown 20 10
DESIGN: No. 1626, Jose Santos Chocano.

557 Arms

1986. 450th Anniv of Trujillo.
1627 **557** 3i. multicoloured 30 15

1986. Town Arms. As T **543**.
1628 700s. blue 15 10
1629 900s. brown 25 15
DESIGNS: 700s. Huanuco; 900s. Puno.

558 Stone Carving of Fish

559 "Hymenocallis amancaes"

1986. Restoration of Chan-Chan.
1630 **558** 50c. multicoloured . . . 15 10

1986. Flora.
1631 **559** 1100s. multicoloured . . 25 15

560 Alpaca and Textiles

561 St. Rosa de Lima (Daniel Hernandez)

1986. Peruvian Industry.
1632 **560** 1100s. multicoloured . . 25 15

1986. 400th Birth Anniv of St. Rosa de Lima.
1633 **561** 7i. multicoloured 95 40

562 Daniel Alcides Carrion

563 Emblems and "16"

1986. Death Centenary (1985) of Daniel Alcides Carrion.
1634 **562** 50c. brown 10 10

1986. 16th International Pacific Fair, Lima.
1635 **563** 1i. multicoloured 10 10

564 Woman Handspinning and Boy in Reed Canoe

1986. International Youth Year.
1636 **564** 3i.50 multicoloured . . . 65 20

565 Pedro Vilcapaza

567 Fernando and Justo Albujar Fayaque and Manuel Guarniz

566 U.N. Building, New York

1986. 205th Anniv of Vilcapaza Rebellion.
1637 **565** 50c. brown 10 10

1986. 40th Anniv (1985) of U.N.O.
1638 **566** 3i.50 multicoloured . . . 30 20

1986. National Heroes.
1639 **567** 50c. brown 10 10

568 Nasturtium

570 Tinta Costumes, Canchis Province

569 Submarine "Casma (R-1)", 1926

1986. Flora.
1640 **568** 80c. multicoloured . . . 10 10

1986. Peruvian Navy. Each blue.
1641 1i.50 Type **569** 80 20
1642 2i.50 Submarine "Abtao", 1954 . . . . 1·40 35

1986. Costumes.
1643 **570** 3i. multicoloured 30 20

571 Sacsayhuaman Fort, Cuzco

1986. Tourism Day (1st issue).
1644 **571** 4i. multicoloured 40 30
See also No. 1654.

572 La Tomilla Water Treatment Plant

1986. 25th Anniv of Inter-American Development Bank.
1645 **572** 1i. multicoloured 10 10

573 "Datura candida"

575 Chavez, Bleriot XI and Simplon Range

574 Pope John Paul and Sister Ana

1986. Flora.
1646 **573** 80c. multicoloured . . . 10 10

1986. Beatification of Sister Ana of the Angels Monteagudo.
1647 **574** 6i. multicoloured 90 45

1986. 75th Anniv of Trans-Alpine Flight by Jorge Chavez Dartnell.
1648 **575** 5i. multicoloured . . . . 1·00 35

576 Emblem

577 "Martyrs of Uchuraccay"

1986. National Vaccination Days.
1649 **576** 50c. blue 10 10

1986. Peruvian Journalists' Fund.
1650 **577** 1i.50 black and blue . . 15 10

578 "Canis nudus"

579 Brigantine "Gamarra"

1986. Fauna.
1651 **578** 2i. multicoloured 20 15

1986. Navy Day.
1652 **579** 1i. blue and light blue 75 25
1653 – 1i. blue and red 75 25
DESIGN: No. 1653, Battleship "Manco Capac".

580 Intihuatana Cuzco

1986. Tourism Day (2nd issue).
1654 **580** 4i. multicoloured 40 30

581 Institute Building

1986. 35th Anniv (1985) of Institute of Higher Military Studies.
1655 **581** 1i. multicoloured 15 10

582 Children

583 White-winged Guan

1986. Postal Workers' Christmas and Children's Restaurant Funds.
1656 **582** 2i.50 black and brown 30 20

1986. Fauna.
1657 **583** 2i. multicoloured . . . . 2·00 40

584 Galvez

585 "St. Joseph and Child" (Cuzquena School)

1986. Birth Centenary (1985) of Jose Galvez Barrenechea (poet).
1658 **584** 50c. brown 10 10

1986. Christmas.
1659 **585** 5i. multicoloured 75 30

586 Flags, and Hands holding Cogwheel

587 Shipibo Costumes

1986. 25th Anniv of "Senati" (National Industrial Training Organization).
1660 **586** 4i. multicoloured 40 30

1987. Christmas.
1661 **587** 3i. multicoloured 30 25

588 Harvesting Mashua

590 Santos

589 Dr. Reiche and Diagram of Nazca Lines

1987. World Food Day.
1662 **588** 50c. multicoloured . . . 10 10

1987. Dr. Maria Reiche (Nazca Lines researcher).
1663 **589** 8i. multicoloured 80 60

1987. Mariano Santos (Hero of War of the Pacific).
1664 **590** 50c. violet 10 10

591 Show Jumping

1987. 50th Anniv of Peruvian Horse Club.
1665 **591** 3i. multicoloured 30 25

592 Salaverry

593 Colca Canyon

1987. 150th Death Anniv (1986) of General Felipe Santiago Salaverry (President, 1835–36).
1666 **592** 2i. multicoloured 20 15

1987. "Arequipa 87" National Stamp Exhibition.
1667 **593** 6i. multicoloured 50 30

594 1857 1 & 2r. Stamps

595 Arguedas

1987. "Amifil 87" National Stamp Exhibition, Lima.
1668 **594** 1i. brown, blue and grey 10 10

1987. 75th Birth Anniv (1986) of Jose Maria Arguedas (writer).
1669 **595** 50c. brown 10 10

596 Carving, Emblem and Nasturtium

1987. Centenary of Arequipa Chamber of Commerce and Industry.
1670 **596** 2i. multicoloured 20 15

597 Vaccinating Child

598 De la Riva Aguero

1987. Child Vaccination Campaign.
1671 **597** 50c. red 10 10

1987. Birth Centenary (1985) of Jose de la Riva Aguero (historian).
1672 **598** 80c. brown 10 10

599 Porras Barrenechea

600 Footballers

1987. 90th Birth Anniv of Raul Porras Barrenechea (historian).
1673 **599** 80c. brown 10 10

1987. World Cup Football Championship, Mexico (1986).
1674 **600** 4i. multicoloured 20 15

601 Stone Carving of Man

1987. Restoration of Chan-Chan.
1675 **601** 50c. multicoloured . . . 10 10

602 Comet and "Giotto" Space Probe

1987. Appearance of Halley's Comet (1986).
1676 **602** 4i. multicoloured 45 15

603 Chavez

604 Osambela Palace

1987. Birth Centenary of Jorge Chavez Dartnell (aviator).
1677 **603** 2i. brown, ochre and gold 10 10

1987. 450th Birth Anniv of Lima.
1678 **604** 2i.50 multicoloured . . . 15 10

605 Machu Picchu

1987. 75th Anniv (1986) of Discovery of Machu Picchu.
1679 **605** 9i. multicoloured 40 30

606 St. Francis's Church

1987. Cajamarca, American Historical and Cultural Site.
1680 **606** 2i. multicoloured 10 10

607 National Team, Emblem and Olympic Rings

1988. 50th Anniv (1986) of First Peruvian Participation in Olympic Games (at Berlin).
1681 **607** 1i.50 multicoloured . . . 10 10

608 Children

1988. 150th Anniv of Ministry of Education.
1682 **608** 1i. multicoloured 10 10

609 Statue and Pope

1988. Coronation of Virgin of Evangelization, Lima.
1683 **609** 10i. multicoloured . . . 40 30

610 Emblems

611 Postman and Lima Cathedral

1988. Rotary International Anti-Polio Campaign.
1684 **610** 2i. blue, gold and red . . 10 10

1988. Postal Workers' Christmas and Children's Restaurant Funds.
1685 **611** 9i. blue 30 20

612 Flags

613 St. John Bosco

1988. 1st Meeting of Eight Latin American Presidents of Contadora and Lima Groups, Acapulco, Mexico.
1686 **612** 9i. multicoloured 30 20

1988. Death Centenary of St. John Bosco (founder of Salesian Brothers).
1687 **613** 5i. multicoloured 20 15

614 Supply Ship "Humboldt" and Globe

1988. 1st Peruvian Scientific Expedition to Antarctica.
1688 **614** 7i. multicoloured 90 20

615 Clay Wall

1988. Restoration of Chan-Chan.
1689 **615** 4i. brown and black . . 15 10

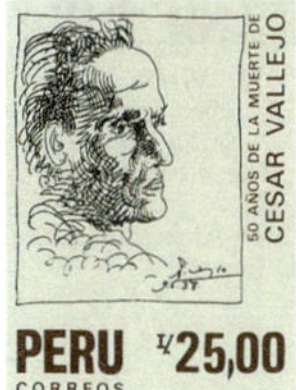

616 Vallejo (after Picasso)

617 Journalists at Work

1988. 50th Death Anniv of Cesar Vallejo (poet).
1690 **616** 25i. black, yellow & brn 50 40

1988. Peruvian Journalists' Fund.
1691 **617** 4i. blue and brown . . . 10 10

618 1908 2s. Columbus Monument Stamp

619 "17" and Guanaco

1988. "Exfilima 88" Stamp Exhibition, Lima, and 500th Anniv of Discovery of America by Christopher Columbus.
1692 **618** 20i. blue, pink and black 20 10

1988. 17th International Pacific Fair, Lima.
1693 **619** 4i. multicoloured 10 10

620 "Village Band"

621 Dogs

1988. Birth Centenary of Jose Sabogal (painter).
1694 **620** 12i. multicoloured . . . 15 10

1988. "Canino '88" International Dog Show, Lima.
1695 **621** 20i. multicoloured . . . 20 10

622 Silva and Score of "Splendour of Flowers"

623 Pope

1988. 50th Death Anniv (1987) of Alfonso de Silva (composer).
1696 **622** 20i. grey, deep brown and brown 20 10

1988. 2nd Visit of Pope John Paul II.
1697 **623** 50i. multicoloured . . . 35 25

624 Volleyball

625 Volleyball

1988. Olympic Games, Seoul.
1698 **624** 25i. multicoloured . . . 20 10

1988. Postal Workers' Christmas and Children's Restaurant Funds. Unissued stamp surch as in T **625**.
1699 **625** 95i. on 300s. black and red 60 50

626 Ceramic Vase

627 Map

1988. Chavin Culture. Unissued stamps surch as in T **626**.
1700 **626** 40i. on 100s. red 30 20
1701 80i. on 10s. black . . . 25 15

1989. Forest Boundary Road. Unissued stamp surch as in T **627**.
1702 **627** 70i. on 80s. green, black and blue 40 30

628 Arm

629 Huari Weaving

1989. Laws of the Indies. Unissued stamp surch as in T **628**.
1703 **628** 230i. on 300s. brown . . 60 15

1989. Centenary of Credit Bank of Peru.
1704 **629** 500i. multicoloured . . . 85 20

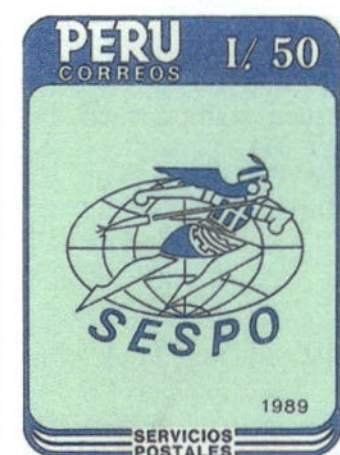

630 Special Postal Services Emblem

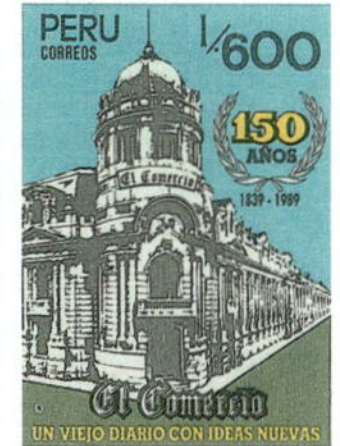

631 Newspaper Offices

1989. Postal Services.
1705 **630** 50i. blue and green . . . 10 10
1706 – 100i. red and pink . . . 10 10
DESIGN: 100i. National Express Post emblem.

1989. 150th Anniv of "El Comercio" (newspaper).
1707 **631** 600i. multicoloured . . . 50 10

632 Garcilaso de la Vega

1989. 450th Birth Anniv of Garcilaso de la Vega (writer).
1708 **632** 300i. multicoloured . . . 10 10

633 Emblem

1989. Express Mail Service.
1709 **633** 100i. red, blue and orange 10 10

634 Dr. Luis Loli Roca (founder of Journalists' Federation)

1989. Peruvian Journalists' Fund.
1710 **634** 100i. blue, deep blue and black 10 10

635 Relief of Birds

1989. Restoration of Chan-Chan.
1711 **635** 400i. multicoloured . . . 35 10

636 Old Map of South America

1989. Centenary of Lima Geographical Society.
1712 **636** 600i. multicoloured . . . 1·40 20

637 Painting

1989. 132nd Anniv of Society of Founders of Independence.
1713 **637** 300i. multicoloured . . . 10 10

638 Lake Huacachina

1989. 3rd Meeting of Latin American Presidents of Contadora and Lima Groups, Ica.
1714 **638** 1300i. multicoloured . . 1·10 60

639 Children buying Stamps for Commemorative Envelopes

641 Vessel with Figure of Doctor examining Patient

640 "Corryocactus huincoensis"

1989. Postal Workers' Christmas and Children's Restaurant Funds.
1715 **639** 1200i. multicoloured . . 30 20

1989. Cacti. Multicoloured.
1716 500i. Type **640** 15 10
1717 500i. "Haagocereus clavispinus" (vert) 15 10
1718 500i. "Loxanthocereus acanthurus" 15 10
1719 500i. "Matucana cereoides" (vert) 15 10
1720 500i. "Trichocereus peruvianus" (vert) 15 10

1989. America. Pre-Columbian Ceramics. Mult.
1721 5000i. Type **641** . . . . . 1·60 1·00
1722 5000i. Vessel with figure of surgeon performing cranial operation . . . . 1·60 1·00

642 Bethlehem Church

1990. Cajamarca, American Historical and Cultural Site.
1723 **642** 600i. multicoloured . . . 15 10

643 Climber in Andes

644 Pope and Virgin of Evangelization

1990. Huascaran National Park. Multicoloured.
1724 900i. Type **643** 20 15
1725 900i. Llanganuco Lake (horiz) 20 15
1726 1000i. "Puya raimondi" (plant) 25 20

1727 1000i. Snow-covered mountain peak (horiz) . . 25 20
1728 1100i. Huascaran Mountain (horiz) 30 25
1729 1100i. Andean condor over mountain slopes (horiz) 50 30

1990. 2nd Visit of Pope John Paul II.
1730 **644** 1250i. multicoloured . . 30 25

645 "Agrias beata" (female)

1990. Butterflies. Multicoloured.
1731 1000i. Type **645** 35 25
1732 1000i. "Agrias beata" (male) 35 25
1733 1000i. "Agrias amydon" (female) 35 25
1734 1000i. "Agrias sardanapalus" (female) . . 35 25
1735 1000i. "Agrias sardanapalus" (male) . . 35 25

646 Victor Raul Haya de la Torre (President of Constituent Assembly)

647 Emblem

1990. 10th Anniv of Political Constitution.
1736 **646** 2100i. multicoloured . . 45 10

1990. 40th Anniv of Peruvian Philatelic Association.
1737 **647** 300i. brown, blk & cream 60 20

648 Globe and Exhibition Emblem

1990. "Prenfil '88" International Philatelic Literature Exhibition, Buenos Aires.
1738 **648** 300i. multicoloured . . . 10 10

649 "Republic" (Antoine-Jean Gros)

1990. Bicentenary of French Revolution. Paintings. Multicoloured.
1739 2000i. Type **649** 40 10
1740 2000i. "Storming the Bastille" (Hubert Robert) 40 10
1741 2000i. "Lafayette at the Festival of the Republic" (anon) 40 10
1742 2000i. "Jean Jacques Rousseau and Symbols of the Revolution" (E. Jeaurat) 40 10

650 "Founding Arequipa" (Teodoro Nunez Ureta)

1990. 450th Anniv of Arequipa.
1743 **650** 50000i. multicoloured . . 10 10

651 Pelado Island Lighthouse

1990. Peruvian Navy. Unissued stamps, each light blue and blue, surch as in T **651**.
1744 110000i. on 200i. Type **651** 1·25 25
1745 230000i. on 400i. "Morona" (hospital ship) . . . . . 3·00 50

652 Games Mascot

653 1857 1r. Stamp and Container Ship

1990. 4th South American Games (1st issue). Multicoloured.
1746 110000i. Type **652** 25 20
1747 280000i. Shooting . . . . . 1·10 60
1748 290000i. Athletics (horiz) . . 1·25 65
1749 300000i. Football . . . . . 1·25 65
See also Nos. 1753/6.

1990. 150th Anniv of Pacific Steam Navigation Company. Multicoloured. Self-adhesive.
1750 250000i. Type **653** . . . . 1·90 75
1751 350000i. 1857 2r. stamp and container ship . . . . . 2·75 1·00

654 Postal Van

1990. Postal Workers' Christmas and Children's Restaurant Funds.
1752 **654** 310000i. multicoloured 1·25 70

1991. 4th South American Games (2nd issue). As T **652**. Multicoloured.
1753 560000i. Swimming . . . . 1·90 1·10
1754 580000i. Show jumping (vert) . . . . 2·00 1·25
1755 600000i. Yachting (vert) . . 3·00 1·40
1756 620000i. Tennis (vert) . . . 2·10 1·40

655 Maria Jesus Castaneda de Pardo

1991. Red Cross. Unissued stamp surch.
1757 **655** 0.15i/m. on 2500i. red . . 50 25

Note. "i/m" on No. 1757 onwards indicates face value in million intis.

656 Adelie Penguins, Scientist and Station

1991. 2nd Peruvian Scientific Expedition to Antarctica. Unissued stamps surch. Multicoloured.
1758 0.40i/m. on 50000i. Type **656** . . . . 3·00 80
1759 0.45i/m. on 80000i. Station and Pomarine skua . . . 3·50 1·00
1760 0.50i/m. on 100000i. Whale, map and station . . . . 1·60 10

657 "Siphoonandra elliptica" (plant No. 1 in University herbarium)

658 "Virgin of the Milk"

1991. 300th Anniv of National University of St. Anthony Abad del Cusco. Multicoloured.
1761 10c. Type **657** 15 10
1762 20c. Bishop Manuel de Mollinedo y Angulo (first Chancellor) 50 20
1763 1s. University arms . . . . 2·50 1·00

1991. Postal Workers' Christmas and Children's Restaurant Funds. Paintings by unknown artists. Multicoloured.
1764 70c. Type **658** . . . . . . 1·25 50
1765 70c. "Divine Shepherdess" 1·25 50

659 Lake

1991. America (1990). The Natural World. Mult.
1766 0.50i/m. Type **659** 90 40
1767 0.50i/m. Waterfall (vert) . . 90 40

660 Sir Rowland Hill and Penny Black

1992. 150th Anniv (1990) of the Penny Black.
1768 **660** 0.40i/m. black, grey & bl 70 35

661 Arms and College

662 Arms

1992. 150th Anniv (1990) of Our Lady of Guadalupe College.
1769 **661** 0.30i/m. multicoloured 55 10

1992. 80th Anniv (1991) of Entre Nous Society, Lima (literature society for women).
1770 **662** 10c. multicoloured . . . 10 10

663 Map

1992. Bolivia–Peru Presidential Meeting, Ilo.
1771 **663** 20c. multicoloured . . . 15 10

664 Tacaynamo Idol

665 Raimondi

1992. Restoration of Chan-Chan.
1772 **664** 0.15i/m. multicoloured 10 10
See note below No. 1757.

1992. Death Centenary of Jose Antonio Raimondi (naturalist).
1773 **665** 0.30i/m. multicoloured 25 20
See note below No. 1757.

666 First Issue

668 1568 Eight Silver Reales Coin

667 Melgar

1992. Bicentenary (1990) of "Diario de Lima" (newspaper).
1774 **666** 35c. black and yellow . . 35 15

1992. Birth Bicentenary (1990) of Mariano Melgar (poet).
1775 **667** 60c. multicoloured . . . 50 25

1992. 1st Peruvian Coinage.
1776 **668** 70c. multicoloured . . . 1·00 35

669 Emblem

1992. 75th Anniv of Catholic University of Peru.
1777 **669** 90c. black and stone . . 1·25 35

670 Emblem

672 "Virgin of the Spindle" (painting, Santa Clara Monastery, Cuzco)

1992. 90th Anniv of Pan-American Health Organization. Self-adhesive. Imperf.
1778 **670** 3s. multicoloured . . . . 3·25 1·10

1992. Various stamps surch.
1779 – 40c. on 500i. multicoloured (1717) 30 15
1780 – 40c. on 500i. multicoloured (1718) 30 15
1781 – 40c. on 500i. multicoloured (1719) 30 15
1782 – 40c. on 500i. multicoloured (1720) 30 15
1783 **493** 50c. on 180s. green . . . 40 20
1784 **648** 50c. on 300i. mult . . . 40 20
1785 **645** 50c. on 1000i. mult . . . 40 20
1786 – 50c. on 1000i. mult (1732) 40 20
1787 – 50c. on 1000i. mult (1733) 40 20
1788 – 50c. on 1000i. mult (1734) 40 20
1789 – 50c. on 1000i. mult (1735) 40 20
1790 **647** 1s. on 300i. brown, black and cream . . . . . 3·00 90
1791 **644** 1s. on 1250i. mult . . . 1·60 80
1792 **638** 1s. on 1300i. mult . . . 2·10 1·00

1993. Self-adhesive. Imperf.
1793 **672** 80c. multicoloured . . . 65 30

673 Gold Figures

1993. Sican Culture (1st series). Multicoloured. Self-adhesive. Imperf.
1794 2s. Type **673** . . . . 2·75 80
1795 5s. Gold foil figure (vert) . . 5·00 2·00
See also Nos. 1814/15.

674 Incan Gold Decoration and Crucifix on Chancay Robe

1993. 500th Anniv of Evangelization of Peru.
1796 **674** 1s. multicoloured . . . . 1·25 65

675 "The Marinera" (Monica Rojas)
676 "Madonna and Child" (statue)

1993. Paintings of Traditional Scenes. Multicoloured. Self-adhesive. Imperf.
1797 1s.50 Type **675** . . . . . . 1·50 60
1798 1s.50 "Fruit Sellers" (Angel Chavez) . . . . 1·50 60

1993. Centenary (1991) of Salesian Brothers in Peru. Self-adhesive. Imperf.
1799 **676** 70c. multicoloured . . . 95 25

677 Francisco Pizarro and Spanish Galleon

1993. America (1991). Voyages of Discovery. Multicoloured.
1800 90c. Type **677** . . . . . . 1·25 30
1801 1s. Spanish galleon and route map of Pizarros' second voyage . . . . . 1·50 40
Nos. 1800/1 were issued together, se-tenant, forming a composite design.

678 Gold Mask

1993. Jewels from Funerary Chamber of "Senor of Sipan" (1st series).
1802 **678** 50c. multicoloured . . . 55 15
See also Nos. 1830/1.

679 Escriva

1993. 1st Anniv of Beatification of Josemaria Escriva (founder of Opus Dei). Self-adhesive. Imperf.
1803 **679** 30c. multicoloured . . . 45 10

1993. 120th Anniv of Diplomatic Relations and Peace, Friendship, Commerce and Navigation Treaty with Japan. Multicoloured.
1804 1s.50 Type **680** . . . . . . 1·75 45
1805 1s.70 Peruvian and Japanese children and Mts. Huascaran (Peru) and Fuji (Japan) . . . . . . 1·90 55

681 Sea Lions
682 Delgado

1993. Stamp Exhibitions. Multicoloured.
1806 90c. Type **681** ("Amifil '93" National Stamp Exhibition, Lima) . . . . 1·10 25
1807 1s. Blue and yellow macaw ("Brasiliana '93" International Stamp Exhibition, Rio de Janeiro) (vert) . . . . . 2·00 80

1993. Birth Centenary of Dr. Honorio Delgado (psychiatrist and neurologist). Self-adhesive. Imperf.
1808 **682** 50c. brown 30 15

683 Morales Macedo
684 "The Sling" (Quechua Indians)

1993. Birth Centenary of Rosalia de Lavalle de Morales Macedo (founder of Society for Protection of Children and of Christian Co-operation Bank). Self-adhesive. Imperf.
1809 **683** 80c. orange 80 25

1993. Ethnic Groups (1st series). Statuettes by Felipe Lettersten. Multicoloured. Self-adhesive. Imperf.
1810 2s. Type **684** . . . . . . 1·60 60
1811 3s.50 "Fire" (Orejon Indians) . . . . 3·25 1·50
See also Nos. 1850/1.

685 "20" on Stamp
686 "Virgin of Loreta"

1993. 20th International Pacific Fair.
1812 **685** 1s.50 multicoloured . . . 1·40 70

1993. Christmas.
1813 **686** 1s. multicoloured . . . . 1·00 55

687 Artefacts from Tomb, Poma
688 Ceramic Figure

1993. Sican Culture (2nd series). Multicoloured. Self-adhesive. Imperf.
1814 2s.50 Type **687** . . . . . . 2·25 1·10
1815 4s. Gold mask . . . . . . 4·00 2·00

1993. Chancay Culture. Multicoloured. Self-adhesive. Imperf.
1816 10s. Type **688** . . . . . . 9·25 4·50
1817 20s. Textile pattern (horiz) 19·00 9·50

689 "With AIDS There is No Tomorrow"
690 Computer Graphics

1993. International AIDS Day.
1818 **689** 1s.50 multicoloured . . . 1·40 70

1994. 25th Anniv of National Council for Science and Technology. Self-adhesive. Imperf.
1819 **690** 1s. multicoloured . . . . 1·40 25

691 "The Bridge" (woodcut from "New Chronicle and Good Government" by Poma de Ayala)
692 Engraved Mate Dish

1994. Self-adhesive. Imperf.
1820 **691** 20c. blue 35 10
1821 40c. orange 55 10
1822 50c. violet 70 15
For similar design see Nos. 1827/9.

1994. Multicoloured. Self-adhesive. Imperf.
1823 1s.50 Type **692** . . . . . . 2·00 40
1824 1s.50 Engraved silver and mate vessel (vert) . . . . 2·00 40
1825 3s. Figure of bull from Pucara . . . . 3·75 85
1826 3s. Glazed plate decorated with fishes . . . . 3·75 85

693 "The Bridge" (Poma de Ayala)
694 Gold Trinkets

1994.
1827 **693** 30c. brown 45 10
1828 40c. black 60 10
1829 50c. red 70 15

1994. Jewels from Funerary Chamber of Senor de Sipan (2nd series). Multicoloured.
1830 3s. Type **694** . . . . 3·75 85
1831 5s. Gold mask (vert) . . . . 6·50 1·25

695 El Brujo

1994. Archaeology. El Brujo Complex, Trujillo.
1832 **695** 70c. multicoloured . . . 75 20

696 "Baby Emmanuel" (Cuzco sculpture)
697 Brazilian Player

1995. Christmas (1994). Multicoloured.
1833 1s.80 Type **696** . . . . . . 1·40 50
1834 2s. "Nativity" (Huamanga ceramic) . . . . 1·50 55

1995. World Cup Football Championship, U.S.A. (1994). Multicoloured.
1835 60c. Type **697** 35 15
1836 4s.80 Mascot, pitch and flags . . . . 3·50 1·50

698 Jauja–Huancayo Road

1995. 25th Anniv (1994) of Ministry of Transport, Communications, Housing and Construction.
1837 **698** 20c. multicoloured . . . 10 10

699 Mochican Pot (Rafael Larco Herrera Museum of Archaeology)
700 Juan Parra del Reigo (poet) (after David Alfaro)

1995. Museum Exhibits. Multicoloured.
1838 40c. Type **699** 20 10
1839 80c. Mochican gold and gemstone ornament of man with slingshot (Rafael Larco Herrera Museum of Archaeology, Lima) 70 20
1840 90c. Vessel in shape of beheaded man (National Museum) 80 25

1995. Writers' Birth Centenaries (1994). Mult.
1841 90c. Type **700** 75 50
1842 90c. Jose Carlos Mariategui 75 50

701 Church
702 Violoncello and Music Stand

1995. 350th Anniv (1993) of Carmelite Monastery, Lima.
1843 **701** 70c. multicoloured . . . 70 20

1995. Musical Instruments. Multicoloured.
1844 20c. Type **702** 10 10
1845 40c. Andean drum 45 10

703 Steam-powered Fire Engine

1995. Volunteer Firemen. Multicoloured.
1846 50c. Type **703** 55 10
1847 90c. Modern fire engine . . 95 25

704 Union Club and Plaza de Armas

1995. World Heritage Site. Lima. Multicoloured.
1848 90c. Type **704** 95 25
1849 1s. Cloisters of Dominican Monastery . . . . 1·10 25

705 "Bora Child"

1995. Ethnic Groups (2nd series). Statuettes by Felipe Lettersten. Multicoloured.
1850 1s. Type **705** . . . . 1·10 25
1851 1s.80 "Aguaruna Man" . . 1·90 50

706 Woman fishing

1995. 30th Anniv (1993) of World Food Programme.
1852 **706** 1s.80 multicoloured . . . 1·90 50

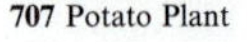

707 Potato Plant **708** Reed Sailing Canoe

1995. The Potato. Multicoloured.
1853 1s.80 Type **707** . . . . . . 1·90 50
1854 2s. Mochican ceramic of potato tubers . . . . . . 2·10 55

1995. Tourism and Ecology. Lake Titicaca.
1855 **708** 2s. multicoloured . . . . 2·25 75

709 Great Horned Owl **710** Anniversary Emblem

1995. Endangered Animals. Multicoloured.
1856 1s. Type **709** . . . . 1·25 25
1857 1s.80 Jaguar on branch (horiz) . . . . 1·90 50

1995. 25th Anniv of Andean Development Corporation.
1858 **710** 5s. multicoloured . . . . 5·00 1·25

711 Ollantaytambo

1995. World Tourism Day.
1859 **711** 5s.40 multicoloured . . . 5·25 1·50

712 Ancient Letterbox, Head Post Office

1995. World Post Day.
1860 **712** 1s.80 multicoloured . . . 1·75 50

713 Columbus landing on Beach

1995. America (1992 and 1993). Multicoloured.
1861 1s.50 Type **713** (500th anniv of discovery of America) 1·50 40
1862 1s.70 Guanaco (vert) . . . 1·75 60

714 Cart

1995. America (1994). Postal Transport. Mult.
1863 1s.80 Type **714** . . . . . . 1·75 60
1864 2s. Post vans . . . . 2·00 55

715 Lima Cathedral (rear entrance)

1995. Doorways. Multicoloured.
1865 30c. Type **715** 40 10
1866 70c. St. Francis's Church (side entrance) 75 20

716 Peruvian Delegation, San Francisco Conference, 1945

1995. 50th Anniv of U.N.O.
1867 **716** 90c. multicoloured . . . 95 25

717 Ceramic Church (National Culture Museum) **718** Lady Olave Baden-Powell (Girl Guides)

1995. Museum Exhibits. Multicoloured.
1868 20c. Type **717** 10 10
1869 20c. "St. John the Apostle" (figurine) (Riva Aguero Institute Museum of Popular Art) 10 10
1870 40c. "Allegory of Asia" (alabaster figurine) (National Culture Museum) 45 10
1871 50c. "Archangel Moro" (figurine) (Riva Aguero Institute Museum of Popular Art) 50 10

1995. Scouting. Multicoloured.
1872 80c. Type **718** 85 20
1873 1s. Lord Robert Baden Powell (founder of Boy Scouts) 90 25

Nos. 1872/3 were issued together, se-tenant, forming a composite design.

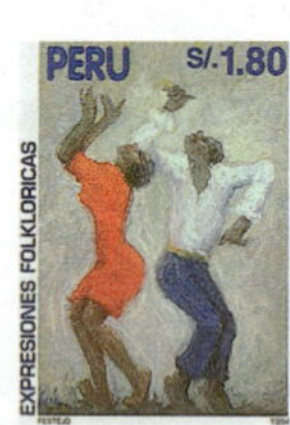

719 "Festejo" **720** Stream in Sub-tropical Forest

1995. Folk Dances. Multicoloured.
1874 1s.80 Type **719** . . . . . . 1·75 50
1875 2s. "Marinera Limena" (horiz) . . . . 1·90 55

1995. Manu National Park, Madre de Dios. Multicoloured.
1876 50c. Type **720** 55 10
1877 90c. American chamaeleon (horiz) 95 25

721 Toma de Huinco **722** St. Toribio de Mogrovejo (Archbishop of Lima)

1995. Electricity and Development. Multicoloured.
1878 20c. Type **721** 10 10
1879 40c. Antacoto Lake 45 10

1995. Saints. Multicoloured.
1880 90c. Type **722** 90 25
1881 1s. St. Francisco Solano (missionary) 95 25

723 Cultivating Crops

1996. 50th Anniv (1995) of F.A.O.
1882 **723** 60c. multicoloured . . . 55 15

724 Crib

1996. Christmas (1995). Porcelain Figures. Multicoloured.
1883 30c. Type **724** 15 10
1884 70c. Three Wise Men (horiz) 70 15

725 Lachay National Park

1996. America (1995). Environmental Protection. Multicoloured.
1885 30c. Type **725** 15 10
1886 70c. Black caiman 70 15

726 "21" **727** Rifle Shooting

1996. 21st International Pacific Fair, Lima.
1887 **726** 60c. multicoloured . . . 60 15

1996. Olympic Games, Barcelona (1992). Multicoloured.
1888 40c. Type **727** 45 10
1889 40c. Tennis 45 10
1890 60c. Swimming 55 15
1891 60c. Weightlifting 55 15

Nos. 1888/91 were issued together, se-tenant, forming a composite design of the sports around the games emblem.

728 Archaeological Find from Sipan

1996. "Expo'92" World's Fair, Seville.
1892 **728** 1s.50 multicoloured . . . 1·40 35

729 Vallejo (after Gaston Garreu)

1996. Birth Centenary of Cesar Vallejo (writer).
1893 **729** 50c. black 50 10

730 Avenue of the Descalzos

1996. UNESCO World Heritage Site. Lima.
1894 **730** 30c. brown and stone . . 15 10

731 "Kon Tiki" (replica of balsa raft)

1997. 50th Anniv of Thor Heyerdahl's "Kon Tiki" Expedition (voyage from Peru to Tuamoto Island, South Pacific).
1895 **731** 3s.30 multicoloured . . . 1·90 70

732 Child **733** Owl

1997. 50th Anniv (1996) of UNICEF.
1896 **732** 1s.80 multicoloured . . . 1·50 40

1997. Mochica Culture.
1897 **733** 20c. green 10 10
1898 – 30c. violet 15 10
1899 – 50c. black 45 10
1900 – 1s. orange 75 20
1901 – 1s.30 red . . . . 1·10 25
1902 – 1s.50 brown . . . . . . 1·25 30

DESIGNS—Vessels in shape of: 30c. Crayfish; 50c. Cormorant; 1s. Monkeys; 1s.30, Duck; 1s.50, Jaguar.

See also Nos. 1942/6.

734 Shooting

1997. Olympic Games, Atlanta, U.S.A. (1996). Multicoloured.
1903 2s.70 Type **734** . . . . . . 1·25 60
1904 2s.70 Volleyball . . . . . . 1·25 60
1905 2s.70 Boxing . . . . 1·25 60
1906 2s.70 Football . . . . . . 1·25 60

735 White-bellied Caique **736** Scout Badge and Tents

1997. 25th Anniv of Peru Biology College.
1907 **735** 5s. multicoloured . . . . 2·50 1·10

1997. 90th Anniv of Boy Scout Movement.
1908 **736** 6s.80 multicoloured . . . 3·25 1·50

737 Man on Reed Raft

1997. 8th International Anti-corruption Conference, Lima.
1909 **737** 2s.70 multicoloured . . . 1·50 60

738 Emblem

1997. 10th Anniv of Montreal Protocol (on reduction of use of chlorofluorocarbons).
1910 **738** 6s.80 multicoloured . . . 3·25 1·50

739 Pectoral

1997. Funerary Chamber of "Senor of Sipan". Multicoloured.
1911 2s.70 Type **739** . . . . . . 2·10 50
1912 3s.30 Ear-cap (vert) . . . . 2·75 60
MS1913 80 × 59 mm. 10s. Open tomb . . . . 8·00 1·75

740 Von Stephan
741 Shipibo Woman

1997. Death Centenary of Heinrich von Stephan (founder of U.P.U.).
1914 **740** 10s. multicoloured . . . 8·00 1·75

1997. America (1996). Traditional Costumes. Multicoloured.
1915 2s.70 Type **741** . . . . . . 2·25 50
1916 2s.70 Shipibo man . . . . 2·25 50

742 Inca Messenger
743 Castilla

1997. America. The Postman. Multicoloured.
1917 2s.70 Type **742** . . . . . . 2·25 50
1918 2s.70 Modern postman . . . 2·25 50

1997. Birth Bicentenary of Ramon Castilla (President, 1845–51 and 1855–62).
1919 **743** 1s.80 multicoloured . . . 1·50 30

744 Tennis
745 River Kingfisher

1997. 13th Bolivarian Games, Arequipa. Mult.
1920 2s.70 Type **744** . . . . . . 2·25 50
1921 2s.70 Football . . . . . . 2·25 50
1922 2s.70 Basketball . . . . . . 2·25 50
1923 2s.70 Volleyball . . . . . . 2·25 50
Nos. 1920/3 were issued together, se-tenant, containing a composite design of a ball in the centre.

1997. Manu National Park. Birds. Multicoloured.
1924 3s.30 Type **745** . . . . . . 2·75 60
1925 3s.30 Green woodpecker . . 2·75 60
1926 3s.30 Red crossbill . . . . 2·75 60
1927 3s.30 Eagle . . . . 2·75 60
1928 3s.30 Jabiru . . . . 2·75 60
1929 3s.30 Cuban screech owl . . 2·75 60

746 Concentric Circles over Map
747 Map and Krill

1997. 30th Anniv of Treaty of Tlatelolco (banning nuclear weapons in Latin America and the Caribbean).
1930 **746** 20s. multicoloured . . . 16·00 3·50

1997. 8th Peruvian Scientific Expedition to Antarctica.
1931 **747** 6s. multicoloured . . . . 5·00 1·00

748 Holy Family
749 Map, Emblem and Unanue

1997. Christmas.
1932 **748** 2s.70 multicoloured . . . 2·10 50

1997. 25th Anniv (1996) of Hipolito Unanue Agreement (health co-operation in Andes region).
1933 **749** 1s. multicoloured 80 15

750 Obverse and Reverse of 1897 1 Libra Coin

1997. Centenary of Gold Libra in Peru. Sheet 80 × 59 mm.
MS1934 **750** 10s. multicoloured 8·00 1·75

751 Facade
753 Map and Emblem

752 School and Cadets

1997. Cent of Posts and Telegraph Headquarters.
1935 **751** 1s. multicoloured 80 15

1998. Centenary of Chorrillos Military School.
1936 **752** 2s.70 multicoloured . . . 2·10 50

1998. 50th Anniv of Organization of American States.
1937 **753** 2s.70 multicoloured . . . 2·10 50

754 Cuzco Cathedral

1998. 25th Anniv of Aeroperu. Multicoloured.
1938 1s.50 Type **754** . . . . . . 1·25 25
1939 2s.70 Airbus Industrie A320 jetliner . . . . 2·25 50

755 "Paso Horse" (Enrique Arambur Ferreyros)
756 Lima Cathedral

1998. 50th Anniv of National Association of Breeders and Owners of Paso Horses.
1940 **755** 2s.70 violet . . . . . . 2·00 50

1998. Centenary of Restoration of Lima Cathedral.
1941 **756** 2s.70 red, yellow and black . . . . 2·00 50

1998. Mochica Culture. As Nos. 1897 and 1899/1902 but values and/or colours changed.
1942 1s. blue 80 15
1943 1s.30 purple . . . . 1·00 20
1944 1s.50 blue . . . . 1·25 25
1945 2s.70 bistre . . . . 2·10 50
1946 3s.30 black . . . . 2·50 60
DESIGNS: 1s.30, Type **733**; 1s.50, Jaguar; 2s.70, Cormorant; 3s.30, Duck.

757 Ceremony, Sacsayhuaman, Cuzco
758 Goalkeeper

1998. "Inti-Raymi" Inca Festival.
1947 **757** 5s. multicoloured . . . . 3·50 85

1998. World Cup Football Championship, France. Multicoloured.
1948 2s.70 Type **758** . . . . . . 2·00 50
1949 3s.30 Two players . . . . . 2·50 60
MS1950 100 × 79 mm. 10s. Player kicking ball (horiz) . . . . . . 8·00 1·75
Nos. 1948/9 were issued together, se-tenant, forming a composite design.

759 Lloque Yupanqui

1998. Inca Chiefs (1st issue). Multicoloured.
1951 2s.70 Type **759** 95 45
1952 2s.70 Sinchi Roca 95 45
1953 9s.70 Mancoc Capau . . . 3·50 1·75
See also Nos. 2008/11.

760 Soldiers

1998. Heroes of (River) Cenepa (Peru-Ecuador border dispute). Sheet 110 × 80 mm.
MS1954 **760** 10s. multicoloured 4·00 1·75

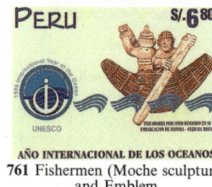

761 Fishermen (Moche sculpture) and Emblem

1998. International Year of the Ocean.
1955 **761** 6s.80 multicoloured . . . 4·50 1·25

762 Bars of Music and Conductor's Hands
763 Mother Teresa and Baby

1998. 60th Anniv of National Symphony Orchestra.
1956 **762** 2s.70 multicoloured . . . 95 45

1998. 1st Death Anniv of Mother Teresa (founder of Missionaries of Charity).
1957 **763** 2s.70 multicoloured . . . 95 45

764 Children with Toys
766 Tropical Forest

765 Princess of Ampato (Inca mummy)

1998. Peruvian Children's Foundation.
1958 **764** 8s.80 multicoloured . . . 3·25 1·60

1998. 3rd Anniv of Discovery by Johann Reinhard of Best Preserved Pre-Hispanic Corpse. Sheet 100 × 80 mm.
MS1959 **765** 10s. multicoloured 4·00 1·75

1998. Manu National Park.
1960 **766** 1s.50 multicoloured . . . 55 25

767 1858 1 Dinero Stamp
768 Chabuca Granda (singer)

1998. World Stamp Day.
1961 **767** 6s.80 multicoloured . . . 2·40 1·20

1998. America. Famous Women.
1962 **768** 2s.70 multicoloured . . . 95 45

769 "Agalychnis craspedopus"

1998. Frogs. Multicoloured.
1963 3s.30 Type **769** . . . . . . 1·25 60
1964 3s.30 Amazonian horned frog ("Ceratophrys cornuta") . . . . 1·25 60
1965 3s.30 "Epipedobates macero" . . . . 1·25 60
1966 3s.30 "Phyllomedusa vaillanti" (leaf frog) . . . 1·25 60
1967 3s.30 "Dendrobates biolat" (poison arrow frog) . . . 1·25 60
1968 3s.30 "Hemiphractus proboscideus" (horned frog) . . . . 1·25 60
Nos. 1963/8 were issued together, se-tenant, forming a composite design.

770 "Chulucanas Nativity" (Lizzy Lopez)

1998. Christmas.
1969 **770** 3s.30 multicoloured . . . 1·25 60

771 Dove and Flags of Peru, Ecuador and Guarantor Countries

1998. Signing of Peru–Ecuador Peace Agreement, Brasilia.
1970 **771** 2s.70 multicoloured . . . 95 45

772 Children on Hillside

1998. 50th Anniv of Universal Declaration of Human Rights.
1971 **772** 5s. multicoloured . . . . 1·75 85

773 Scout Badge and Tents

1999. 19th World Scout Jamboree, Chile. Multicoloured.
1972 5s. Type **773** . . . . 1·75 85
1973 5s. Emblem and tents . . . 1·75 85

774 Emblem

1999. 50th Anniv of Peruvian Philatelic Association.
1974 **774** 2s.70 multicoloured . . . 95 45

775 "Evening Walk"

1999. 120th Death Anniv of Pancho Fierro (artist). Multicoloured.
1975 2s.70 Type **775** 95 45
1976 3s.30 "The Sound of the Devil" . . . . 1·25 60

776 Dancer and Detail from Costume

1999. "Puno" (traditional dance).
1977 **776** 3s.30 multicoloured . . . 1·25 60

1999. Mochica Culture. As Nos. 1943/46 but values and or colours changed.
1978 1s. red 35 15
1979 1s.50 blue 55 25
1980 1s.80 brown 65 30
1981 2s. orange 70 35
DESIGNS: Vessels in shape of—1s. Jaguar; 1s.50, Duck; 1s.80, Type **733**; 2s. Cormorant.

777 Inca blowing Conch Shell

1999. 25th Anniv of Peruvian Folklore Centre (CENDAF).
1982 **777** 1s.80 multicoloured . . . 65 30

778 Malinowski and Train crossing Bridge

1999. Death Centenary of Ernest Malinowski (designer of iron bridge between Lima and La Oroya).
1983 **778** 5s. multicoloured . . . . 1·75 85

779 Sick and Healthy Hearts with Smiling Face

1999. Child Heart Care.
1984 **779** 2s.70 multicoloured . . . 95 45

780 Origami Birds

1999. Centenary of Japanese Immigration.
1985 **780** 6s.80 multicoloured . . . 2·40 1·25

781 Miner and Crowbars

1999. 50th Anniv of Milpo S.A. Mining Company.
1986 **781** 1s.50 multicoloured . . . 55 25

782 Wildlife

1999. Flora and Fauna.
1987 **782** 5s. multicoloured . . . . 1·75 1·00
MS1988 79 × 98 mm. 10s. Jaguar, Manu National Park (horiz) 3·50 3·30

1999. Nos. 1888/91 surch.
1989 1s. on 40c. Rifle shooting 35 20
1990 1s. on 40c. Tennis 35 20
1991 1s. on 60c. Swimming . . . 35 20
1992 1s. on 60c. Weightlifting . . 35 20
1993 1s.50 on 40c. Rifle shooting 35 20
1994 1s.50 on 40c. Tennis 35 20
1995 1s.50 on 60c. Swimming . . 35 20
1996 1s.50 on 60c. Weightlifting 35 20
1997 2s.70 on 40c. Rifle shooting 35 20
1998 2s.70 on 40c. Tennis 35 20
1999 2s.70 on 60c. Swimming . . 35 20
2000 2s.70 on 60c. Weightlifting 35 20
2001 3s.30 on 40c. Rifle shooting 35 20
2002 3s.30 on 40c. Tennis 35 20
2003 3s.30 on 60c. Swimming . . 35 20
2004 3s.30 on 60c. Weightlifting 35 20

1999. No. 1894 surch.
2005 2s.40 on 30c. brown and ochre 80 45

785 Penguin and Antarctic Vessel

1999. 40th Anniv of Antarctic Treaty.
2006 **785** 6s.80 multicoloured . . . 2·40 1·40

786 Bird

1999. Nazca Lines. Sheet 98 × 79 mm.
MS2007 **786** 10s. multicoloured 3·50 3·50

1999. Inca Chiefs (2nd issue). As T **759**. Multicoloured.
2008 3s.30 Maita Capac 80 45
2009 3s.30 Inca Roca 80 45
2010 3s.30 Capac Yupanqui . . . 80 45
2011 3s.30 Yahuar Huaca 80 45

787 Galena

1999. Minerals. Multicoloured.
2012 2s.70 Type **787** 95 55
2013 3s.30 Scheelita . . . . . . 1·10 65
2014 5s. Virgotrigonia peterseni 1·75 1·00

788 Virgin of Carmen

1999.
2015 **788** 3s.30 multicoloured . . . 1·10 65

789 Building

1999. St. Catalina Monastery, Arequipa.
2016 **789** 2s.70 multicoloured . . . 95 35

790 Emblem and Dragon

1999. 150th Anniv of Chinese Immigration to Peru.
2017 **790** 1s.50 red and black . . . 55 35

791 Taking Pulse

1999. 25th Anniv of Peruvian Medical Society.
2018 **791** 1s.50 multicoloured . . . 55 35

792 Emblem

1999. 125th Anniv of Universal Postal Union.
2019 **792** 3s.30 multicoloured . . . 1·10 65

793 Sunflower growing out of Gun

1999. America. A New Millennium without Arms. Multicoloured.
2020 2s.70 Type **793** 95 55
2021 3s.30 Man emerging from Globe (horiz) . . . . . . 1·10 65

794 Woman with Fumigator

1999. Seor de los Milagros Festival, Lima. Multicoloured.
2022 1s. Type **794** 35 20
2023 1s.50 Procession 55 30

795 Young Child and Emblem

1999. 40th Anniv of Inter-American Development Bank.
2024 **795** 1s.50 multicoloured . . . 55 30

796 *Pterourus zagreus chrysomelus*

1999. Butterflies. Multicoloured.
2025 3s.30 Type **796** . . . . . . 1·10 65
2026 3s.30 *Asterope buckleyi* . . . 1·10 65
2027 3s.30 *Parides chabrias* . . . 1·10 65
2028 3s.30 *Mimoides pausanias* . . 1·10 65
2029 3s.30 *Nessaea obrina* . . . . 1·10 65
2030 3s.30 *Pterourus zagreus zagreus* . . . . 1·10 65

797 Map of Cunhuime Sur Sub-sector

1999. 1st Anniv of Peru–Ecuador Border Peace Agreement. Multicoloured.
2031 1s. Type **797** 35 20
2032 1s. Map of Lagartococha-Gueppi sector 35 20
2033 1s. Map of Cusumasa Bumbuiza-Yaupi Santiago sub-sector (horiz) 35 20

798 Globe

1999. 5th Anniv of Serpost S.A. (Peruvian postal services).
2034 **798** 2s.70 multicoloured . . . 95 55

799 Virgin of Belen

1999. Christmas.
2035 **799** 2s.70 multicoloured . . . 95 55

800 Mujica and Factory

1999. Birth Centenary of Ricardo Bentin Mujica (industrialist).
2036 **800** 2s.70 multicoloured . . . 95 55

801 Flags encircling Globe

2000. New Millennium. Sheet 79 × 99 mm.
MS2037 **801** 10s. multicoloured 3·50 3·50

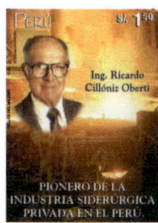

802 Oberti and Foundry

2000. Ricardo Cilloniz Oberti (founder of Peruvian steel industry).
2038 **802** 1s.50 multicoloured . . . 55 30

803 Llamas

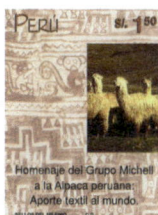

2000. Michell Group (Peruvian alpaca exporters). Multicoloured.
2039 1s.50 Type **803** 55 30
2040 1s.50 Llamas (different) . . 55 30
Nos. 2039/40 were issued together, se-tenant, forming a composite design.

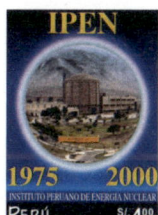

804 Power Station

2000. 25th Anniv of Peruvian Institute of Nuclear Energy (I.P.E.N.).
2041 **804** 4s. multicoloured . . . . 1·40 80

805 Miner

2000. Mining Industry. Multicoloured.
2042 1s. Type **805** 35 20
2043 1s. View of mine 35 20
Nos. 2042/3 were issued together, se-tenant, forming a composite design.

806 Stylized Outline of Peru

2000. 70th Anniv of Comptroller General of Republic.
2044 **806** 3s.30 multicoloured . . . 1·10 65

807 Field and Emilio Guimoye Hernandez

2000. Poblete Agriculture Group.
2045 **807** 1s.50 multicoloured . . . 55 30

808 Pupils carrying Flags

2000. National School Sports Games.
2046 **808** 1s.80 multicoloured . . . 60 35

809 Machu Picchu

2000. World Heritage Sites.
2047 **809** 1s.30 multicoloured . . . 45 25

810 Emblem

2000. Campaign Against Domestic Violence.
2048 **810** 3s.80 multicoloured . . . 1·25 75

811 Emblem

2000. Year.
2049 **811** 3s.20 multicoloured . . . 1·10 65

812 "Cataratas de Ahuashiyacu" (Susan Hidalgo Bacalla)

2000. Winning Entries in Students' Painting Competition. Multicoloured.
2050 3s.20 Type **812** . . . . . . 1·10 65
2051 3s.20 "Laguna Yarinacocha" (Mari Trini Ramos Vargas) (horiz) . . 1·10 65
2052 3s.80 "La Campina Arequipena" (Anibal Lajo Yanez) (horiz) . . . . . 1·25 75

813 Member Flags and Emblem

2000. United Nations Millennium Summit, New York, U.S.A.
2053 **813** 3s.20 multicoloured . . . 1·10 65

814 San Martín

2000. 150th Death Anniv of General Jose de San Martin.
2054 **814** 3s.80 multicoloured . . . 1·25 75

815 Bus, Map of South America and Road

2000. 30th Anniv of Peru—North America Bus Route. Multicoloured.
2055 1s. Type **815** 35 20
2056 2s.70 Bus, map of North America and road 95 55
Nos. 2055/6 were issued together, se-tenant, forming a composite design.

816 Cyclist

2000. Centenary of International Cycling Union.
2057 **816** 3s.20 multicoloured . . . 1·10 65

817 Sun Dial

2000. 50th Anniv of World Meteorological Organization.
2058 **817** 1s.50 multicoloured . . . 55 30

818 Western Leaf Lizard (*Tropidurus plica*)

2000. Lizards. Multicoloured.
2059 3s.80 Type **818** . . . . . . 1·25 75
2060 3s.80 Haitian ameiva (*Ameiva ameiva*) . . . . 1·25 75
2061 3s.80 Two-lined skink (*Mabouya bistriata*) . . . 1·25 75
2062 3s.80 *Neusticurus ecpleopus* 1·25 75
2063 3s.80 Blue-lipped forest anole (*Anolis fuscoauratus*) 1·25 75
2064 3s.80 Horned wood lizard (*Enyalioides palpebralis*) 1·25 75
Nos. 2059/64 were issued together, se-tenant, forming a composite design.

819 *Matucana madisoniorum*

2000. Cacti.
2065 **819** 3s.80 multicoloured . . . 1·25 75

820 Noriega and Space Shuttle

2000. Carlos Noriega (first Peruvian astronaut).
2066 **820** 3s.80 multicoloured . . . 1·25 75

821 De Mendoza and Library

2000. 250th Birth Anniv Toribio Rodríguez de Mendoza.
2067 **821** 3s.20 multicoloured . . . 1·10 65

822 Symbols of Ucayali

2000. Centenary of Ucayali Province.
2068 **822** 3s.20 multicoloured . . . 1·10 65

823 Grape Vine and Flag

2000. Wines of Peru.
2069 **823** 3s.80 multicoloured . . . 1·25 75

824 Flags on Watch Parts

2000. 20th Anniv of ALADI (Latin-American integration association).
2070 **824** 10s.20 multicoloured . . 3·30 3·50

825 Emblem

2000. 50th Anniv of Federation of Journalists.
2071 **825** 1s.50 multicoloured . . . 55 30

826 Petrified Forest, Santa Cruz

2000.
2072 **826** 1s.50 multicoloured . . . 45 25

827 Male and Female Symbols

2000. America. Anti-AIDS Campaign.
2073 **827** 3s.80 multicoloured . . . 1·20 70

828 Justice Palace, Trujillo

2000. New Judicial Powers.
2074 **828** 1s.50 multicoloured . . . 45 25

829 Child at Table

2000. 90th Anniv of Peruvian Salvation Army.
2075 **829** 1s.50 multicoloured . . . 45 25

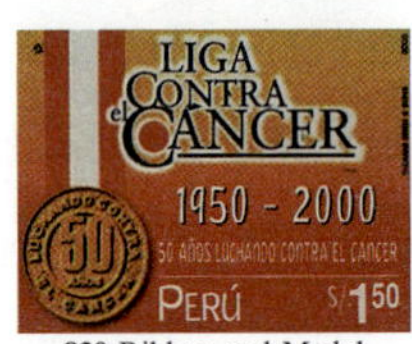

830 Ribbon and Medal

2000. 50th Anniv of League against Cancer.
2076 **830** 1s.50 multicoloured . . . 45 25

831 Steam Locomotive

2000. 150th Anniv of Peruvian Railways.
2077 **831** 1s.50 multicoloured . . . 45 25

832 Monument, Parliament Building

2000. National Congress.
2078 **832** 3s.80 multicoloured . . . 1·20 75

833 Doris Gibson (first editor)

2000. 50th Anniv of "Caretas" Magazine.
2079 **833** 3s.20 multicoloured . . . 1·10 65

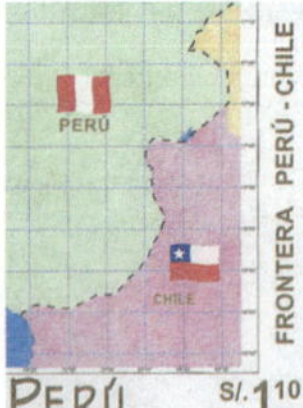

834 Map showing Peru—Chile Border

2000. National Borders. Multicoloured. Designs showing maps of borders.
2080 1s.10 Type **834** 40 25
2081 1s.50 Peru—Brazil 45 25
2082 2s.10 Peru—Colombia (horiz) 80 50
2083 3s.20 Peru—Ecuador (horiz) 1·10 65
2084 3s.80 Peru—Bolivia . . . . 1·20 75

835 Luis Alberto Sanchez

2000. Birth Centenary of Luis Alberto Sanchez (writer).
2085 **835** 3s.20 multicoloured . . . 1·10 65

836 *Haageocereus acranthus*

2000. Cacti. Multicoloured.
2086 1s.10 Type **836** 40 25
2087 1s.50 *Cleistocactus xylorhizus* 45 25
2088 2s.10 *Mila caespitose* . . . 80 50
2089 2s.10 *Haageocereus setosus* (horiz) 80 50
2090 3s.20 *Opuntia pachypus* (horiz) . . . . 1·10 65
2091 3s.80 *Haageocereus tenuis* 1·20 75

837 University Arms

2001. 450th Anniv of San Marco University.
2092 **837** 1s.50 multicoloured . . . 45 25

838 Footballers

2001. Centenary of Club Alianza Lima (Lima football club). Multicoloured.
2093 3s.20 Type **838** . . . . . . 1·10 65
2094 3s.20 Two players and ball 1·10 65
Nos. 2093/4 were issued together, se-tenant, forming a composite design.

839 Symbols of Abuse and Family

2001. International Day against Drug Abuse.
2095 **839** 1s.10 multicoloured . . . 40 25

840 Roque Saenz Pena

2001. 150th Birth Anniv of Roque Saenz Pena (Argentinean general).
2096 **840** 3s.80 multicoloured . . . 1·20 75

841 Walls, Sun, Tree and Horseman

2001. Rio Lurin Valley.
2097 **841** 1s.10 multicoloured . . . 40 25

842 *Hyalella* (amphipod crustacean)

2001.
2098 **842** 1s.80 multicoloured . . . 70 40

843 Early Post Cart

2001. 70th Anniv of Post and Philately Museum.
2099 **843** 3s.20 multicoloured . . . 1·10 65

844 Names of Participating Countries

2002. Ibero-American Conference, Lima.
2100 **844** 1s.10 black and scarlet 40 25
2101 – 2s.70 scarlet and orange 1·00 60
DESIGN: 2s.70, Triangle.

845 Ruins and Hand

2002. 150th Anniv of Peru—Costa Rica Diplomatic Relations. Multicoloured.
2102 1s.10 Type **845** 40 25
2103 2s.70 Hand and grassland 90 55
Nos. 2102/3 were issued, together, se-tenant, forming a composite design.

846 People from Many Races

2005. International Conference to Combat Racism.
2104 **846** 3s.80 multicoloured . . . 1·30 80

847 Multicultural Symbols

848 Airplane and Passengers

2002. International Day of Indigenous Peoples.
2105 **847** 5s.80 multicoloured . . . 2·25 1·40

2002. 50th Anniv of International Organization for Migration.
2106 **848** 3s.80 multicoloured . . . 1·20 75

849 "100" enclosing Map of Americas

2002. Centenary of Pan American Health Organization.
2107 **849** 3s.20 multicoloured . . . 1·10 65

850 Early University Building

852 *Stanhopea*

851 Distillation Equipment

2002. Centenary of La Molina Agricultural University. Multicoloured.
2108 1s.10 Type **850** 40 25
2109 2s.70 Modern building . . . 1·00 60

2002. Pisco (brandy) Distilling. Multicoloured.
2110 3s.20 Type **851** . . . . . . 1·10 65
2111 3s.80 Amphora . . . . . . 1·20 75
MS2112 100 × 80 mm. 10s. "Pisco Festival" (Jose Sabogal) . . . 4·00 4·00

2002. Orchids. Multicoloured.
2113 1s.50 Type **852** 45 25
2114 3s.20 *Chloraea pavoni* . . . 1·10 65
2115 3s.80 *Psychopsis* . . . . . 1·20 75

853 *Solanum stenotomum*

2002. Native Tuberous Plants. Multicoloured.
2116 1s.10 Type **853** 40 25
2117 1s.50 *Ipomea batatas* 45 25
2118 2s.10 *Ipomea purpurea* . . . 80 50

854 Balcony, Osambela Palace

2002. America. Cultural Heritage. Multicoloured.
2119 2s.70 Type **854** 90 55
2120 5s.80 Balcony, Torre Tagle Palace . . . . 1·90 1·10

855 Flower enclosing Globe

856 Blue-faced Booby (*Sula dactiilatra*)

2002. United Nations Year (2001) of Dialogue among Civilizations. Multicoloured.
2121 1s.50 Type **855** 45 25
2122 1s.80 Children encircling globe 70 40

2002. Paracus National Reserve. Multicoloured.
2123 1s.10 Type **856** 40 25
2124 1s.50 Peruvian booby (*Sula variegate*) (horiz) 45 25
2125 3s.20 American oystercatcher (*Haematopus palliates*) (horiz) . . . . . 1·10 65
2126 3s.80 *Grapus grapus* (crab) (horiz) . . . . 1·20 75

857 Giant Otter (*Pteronura brasiliensis*)

2002. Endangered Species. Sheet 80 × 100 mm.
MS2127 **857** 8s. multicoloured . . 2·75 2·75

858 Figure with Crab's Claws, Sipan

859 La Zamacueca

2002. Tourism. Archaeological Sites. Multicoloured.
2128 1s.50 Type **858** 50 30
2129 3s.20 Warrior (metal decoration), Sican . . . . 1·10 65
2130 3s.80 Gold pectoral decoration, Kuntur Wasi (horiz) . . . . 1·30 80
MS2131 80 × 100 mm. 10s.20 Los Pinchudos, Gran Pajaten (horiz) 3·50 3·50

2002. Peruvian Dances. Multicoloured.
2132 2s.10 Type **859** 70 40
2133 2s.70 El Alcatraz 90 55

860 Robert Baden Powell (founder of Scout movement)

2002. 90th Anniv of Peruvian Scouts. Multicoloured.
2134 3s.20 Type **860** . . . . . . 1·10 65
2135 3s.20 Juan Luis Rospigliosi (co-founder of Peruvian Scouts) . . . . 1·10 65
MS2136 100 × 80 mm. 10s.20 First Peruvian Scout group . . . . 3·50 3·50

Nos. 2134/5 were issued together, se-tenant, forming a composite design.

861 Globe and Postal Emblems

2002. Postal Services.
2137 **861** 20s. multicoloured . . . 6·75 4·00

862 Viracocha

863 Peruvian Red-necked Owl Monkey (*Aotus nancymai* (inscr "nancymaea"))

2002. Ancient Rulers (1st series). Multicoloured.
2138 1s.50 Type **862** 50 30
2139 2s.70 Pachacutec 90 55
2140 3s.20 Inca Yupanqui . . . . 1·10 65
2141 3s.80 Tupac Inca Yupanqui 1·30 80
See also Nos. 2191/3.

2002. Primates. Multicoloured.
2142 3s.80 Type **863** . . . . . . 1·30 80
2143 3s.80 Grey monk saki (*Pithecia irrorata*) . . . . 1·30 80
2144 3s.80 Equatorial saki (*Pithecia aequatorialis*) . . 1·30 80
2145 3s.80 White-fronted capuchin (*Cebus albifrons*) 1·30 80
2146 3s.80 Bolivian squirrel monkey (*Saimiri boliviensis*) . . . . 1·30 80
2147 3s.80 Owl monkey (*Aotus vociferans*) . . . . 1·30 80

864 Chalcopyrite (CuFeS2)

2002. Minerals (1st series). Multicoloured.
2148 1s.80 Type **864** 60 35
2149 3s.20 Zinc sulphide (Zns) . . 1·10 65
2150 3s.20 Pyrargyrite (inscr "AgSbS3") . . . . 1·10 65
See also Nos. 2187/8.

865 Miguel Grau

2002. Miguel Grau (naval hero) Commemoration.
2151 **865** 3s.80 multicoloured . . . 1·30 80

866 Spanish and Peruvian Flags and Coins

2002. Peru—Spain Business Conference.
2152 **866** 3s.80 multicoloured . . . 1·30 80

867 Flags, Bridge and Map

2002. Peru—Bolivia Integrated Development Plan.
2153 **867** 3s.20 multicoloured . . . 1·10 65

868 Andean and Amazonian People

2002. National Commission for Andean and Amazonian Peoples.
2154 **868** 1s.50 multicoloured . . . 50 30

869 Fishermen

2002. 50th Anniv of National Fishing Society.
2155 **869** 3s.20 multicoloured . . . 1·10 65

870 Alexander von Humboldt

871 Surveyor

2002. Bicentenary of Visit by Alexander von Humboldt (geologist).
2156 **870** 3s.20 multicoloured . . . 1·10 65

2003. Centenary of Hydro-graphic Mapping.
2157 **871** 1s.10 multicoloured . . . 40 25

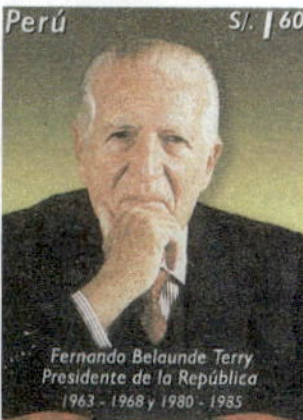

872 Emblem

874 Fernando Terry

873 Transmitter

2003. 25th Anniv of Movimiento Manuela Ramos (organization for sexual equality).
2158 **872** 3s.80 scarlet and black 1·30 80

2003. 40th Anniv of RPP Radio.
2159 **873** 4s. multicoloured . . . . 1·40 85

2003. 1st Death Anniv of Fernando Belaunde Terry (president 1963—68 and 1980—1985).
2160 **874** 1s.60 multicoloured . . . 55 35

875 Jose Maria Escriva de Balaguer

2003. Canonization of Jose Maria Escriva de Balaguer (founder of Opus Dei (religious organization)).
2161 **875** 1s.20 multicoloured . . . 40 25

876 Teresa de la Cruz

2003. 50th Death Anniv of Teresa de la Cruz Candamo.
2162 **876** 4s. brown and yellow . . 1·40 85

877 Map of the Americas

2003. 150th Anniv of Peru—Italy Treaty of Friendship and Trade. Multicoloured.
2163 2s. Type **877** 70 40
2164 2s. Map of Europe, Africa and Asia 70 40
Nos. 2163/4 were issued together, se-tenant, forming a composite design.

878 Emblems

2003. Serpente de Agua Exhibition (cultural project). Multicoloured.
2165 2s. Type **878** 70 40
2166 2s. Early and modern children 70 40

879 Emblem and Children

2003. 50th Anniv of UNESCO Associated Schools.
2167 **879** 1s.20 multicoloured . . . 40 25

880 Four Birds

2003. Endangered Species. Andean Cock of the Rock (*Rupicola peruviana*). Multicoloured.
2168 2s. Type **880** 70 40
2169 2s. Single bird 70 40
Nos. 2168/9 were issued together, se-tenant, forming a composite design.

881 1570 Map (Diego Mendez)

2003. 150th Anniv of Peru—Panama Diplomatic Relations.
2170 **881** 4s. multicoloured . . . . 1·40 85

882 *Wright Flyer*, Orville and Wilbur Wright

2003. Centenary of Powered Flight. Multicoloured.
2171 4s.80 Type **882** . . . . . . 1·60 95
2172 4s.80 "Arriba siempre arriba hasta alcanzar la gloria" 1·60 95
Nos. 2171/2 were issued together, se-tenant, forming a composite design.

883 Musician and Notes

2003. Cajon (wooden box played as musical instrument).
2173 **883** 4s.80 multicoloured . . . 1·60 95

884 Chess Board and Globe

2004. Chess.
2174 **884** 1s.20 multicoloured . . . 40 25

885 Free-style Crawl

887 Antonio de Mendoza

886 Wheelchair User, Amputee and Boy using Crutches

2004. Swimming.
2175 **885** 1s.20 multicoloured . . . 40 25

2004. National Institute of Rehabilitation. Year of the Rights for the Disabled.
2176 **886** 1s.20 multicoloured . . . 40 25

2004. Viceroys. Multicoloured.
2177 1s.20 Type **887** 40 25
2178 1s.20 Andreas Hurtado de Mendoza 40 25
2179 1s.20 Deigo Lopez de Zuniga y Velasco 40 25
2180 4s.80 Blasco Nunez de Vela 1·60 95

888 The Nativity

2004. Christmas (2003).
2181 **888** 4s.80 multicoloured . . . 1·60 95

889 Emblem

2004. 30th Anniv of Civil Defence Organization.
2182 **889** 4s.80 multicoloured . . . 1·60 95

890 Cebiche (fish)

2004. Traditional Dishes.
2183 **890** 4s.80 multicoloured . . . 1·60 95

891 *Chaubardia heteroclite*

2004. Orchids. Multicoloured.
2184 1s.20 Type **891** 40 25
2185 2s.20 *Cochleanthes amazonica* (incr "Cochleanther") 75 45
2186 4s.80 *Sobralia* (horiz) . . . 1·60 95

892 Orpiment

2004. Minerals (2nd series). Multicoloured.
2187 1s.20 Type **892** 40 25
2188 4s.80 Rodocrosita . . . . . 1·40 85

893 St. Martin de Porres

2004. Peruvian Saints. Multicoloured.
2189 4s.80 Type **893** . . . . . . 1·60 95
2190 4s.80 St. Rosa de Lima (horiz) . . . . 1·60 95

2004. Ancient Rulers (2nd series). As T **862**. Multicoloured.
2191 1s.20 Huascar 40 25
2192 1s.20 Atahualpa 40 25
2193 3s.20 Huayna Capac . . . . 1·10 65

894 Locomotive

2004. Railways. Multicoloured.
2194 1s.20 Type **894** 40 25
2195 4s.80 "Puente Galeros" viaduct . . . . 1·60 95

895 Marine Otter (*Lontra feline*) (inscr "Londra")

2004. Endangered Species. Multicoloured.
2196 1s.80 Type **895** 60 35
2197 1s.80 Ara couloni (vert) . . 60 35

896 Fire Fighters

2004. Fire Service. Multicoloured.
2198 2s.20 Type **896** 75 45
2199 2s.20 Fire appliance 75 45

897 Jorge Basadre

898 *Matucana haynei*

2004. Birth Centenary of Jorge Basadre Grohmann (writer) (2003).
2200 **897** 4s.80 indigo . . . . . . 1·60 95

2004. Cacti (2nd series). Multicoloured.
2201 1s.20 Type **898** 40 25
2202 1s.20 *Eriosyce islayensis* . . 40 25
2203 4s.80 *Pymaeocereus bylesianus* (inscr "Pigmaeocereus") . . . . 1·60 95

899 Gentoo Penguin (*Pygoscelis papua*) (inscr "Pygosceles")

2004. Antarctic Fauna. Multicoloured.
2204 1s.80 Type **899** 60 35
2205 1s.80 *Asteroidea* 60 35
2206 1s.80 *Leucocarbo atriceps* (horiz) 60 35

900 Tree and Children

2004. Environmental Awareness. Multicoloured.
2207 4s.80 Type **900** (Population Control Day) . . . . . 1·60 95
2208 4s.80 Plants and animals (National Biological Diversity Day) . . . . . 1·60 95

901 Stadium

2004. Football. Multicoloured.
2209 4s.80 Type **901** (50th anniv of National Stadium, Lima) . . . . 1·60 95
2210 4s.80 Players, emblem and trophy (World Cup Football Championships, Japan and South Korea (2002)) . . . . 1·60 90

902 Ruben Vargas Ugarte (historian)

2004. Personalities. Multicoloured.
2211 4s.80 Type **902** . . . . . . 1·60 95
2212 4s.80 Jose Jimenez Borja (writer) (vert) . . . . . . 1·60 95

903 Glass

2004. Pisco Sour National Drink.
2213 **903** 4s.80 multicoloured . . . 1·60 95

904 Daniel Carrion

2004. Daniel Alcides Carrion (medical student who died after inoculation experiment) Commemoration.
2214 **904** 4s.80 multicoloured . . . 1·60 95

905 "Founding of Juaja" (Wenceslao Hinostroza)

2004. 470th Anniv of Founding of Juaja. Sheet 100 × 80 mm.
MS2215 **905** 7s. multicoloured . . 2·50 2·50

906 Alpaca

907 *Bothros roedingeri*

2004. Llamas. Multicoloured.
2216 20c. Type **906** 10 10
2217 30c. Vicuna 10 10
2218 40c. Guanaco 10 10
2219 50c. Llama 10 10

2004. Snakes. Multicoloured.
2220 1s.80 Type **907** 60 35
2221 1s.80 *Micrurus lemniscalus* 60 35
2222 1s.80 *Bothrops atrox* 60 35
2223 1s.80 *Bothrops microphtalmus* 60 35
2224 1s.80 *Micrurus surinamensis* 60 35
2225 1s.80 *Bothrops barnetti* . . . 60 35
Nos. 2220/5 were issued together, se-tenant, forming a composite design.

908 Mount Huascaran

2004. International Year of Mountains (2002). Sheet 100 × 80 mm.
MS2226 **908** 7s. multicoloured . . 2·50 1·50

909 Artefacts and Building

2004. Royal Tombs of Sipan Museum, Lambayeque.
2227 **909** 4s.80 multicoloured . . . 1·60 95

910 Punta Capones Lighthouse

2004. Lighthouses (1st issue). Multicoloured.
2228 2s. Type **910** 70 40
2229 2s. Islas Chincha 70 40
See also Nos. 2286/7.

911 Fire Fighter

2004. 130th Anniv of Volunteer Fire Brigades.
2230 **911** 4s.80 multicoloured . . . 1·60 95

912 *Trachurus murphyi*

2004. Fish. Sheet 140 × 112 mm containing T **912** and similar horiz designs. Multicoloured.
MS2231 1s.60 × 5, Type **912**; *Mugil cephalus*; *Engraulis ringens*; *Odontesthes regia*; *Merluccius peruanus* . . . . 2·75 2·75
The stamps and margin of **MS**2231 form a composite design.

913 Cathedral Tower, Arequipa

2004. Tourism. Sheet 100 × 80 mm containing T **913** and similar multicoloured design.
MS2232 4s. × 2, Type **913**; El Misti volcano . . . . 2·75 2·75
The stamps and margin of **MS**2232 form a composite design.

914 Solar Clock, Intihuatana

2004. World Heritage Site. Machu Picchu. Multicoloured.
2233 1s.20 Type **914** 40 25
2234 1s.20 Temple 40 25
2235 1s.20 Waterfall, Huayna Picchu 40 25
2236 4s.80 Ciudadela . . . . . . 1·60 95

915 *Myrciaria dubia*

2004. Medicinal Plants. Multicoloured.
2237 4s.80 Type **915** . . . . . . 1·60 95
2238 4s.80 *Lepidium meyenii* . . . 1·60 95
2239 4s.80 *Uncaria tomentosa* . . 1·60 95

916 Map and Emblem

2004. Inter-American Development Bank Governors' Assembly Annual Reunion.
2240 **916** 4s.80 multicoloured . . . 1·60 95

917 Italian Volpino Spitz

2004. Dogs. Multicoloured.
2241 4s.80 Type **917** . . . . . . 1·60 95
2242 4s.80 Peruvian Inca Orchid 1·60 95
2243 4s.80 Beauceron (Pastor de Beauce) . . . . 1·60 95
2244 4s.80 Italian Spinone . . . 1·60 95

918 Huaylash

2004. Traditional Dances. Multicoloured.
2245 1s.20 Type **918** 40 25
2246 1s.20 Huayno 40 25

919 Scientists and Weather Map

2004. Preparation for "El Nino".
2247 **919** 4s.80 multicoloured . . . 1·60 95

920 Paca Lake, Jauja

2004. Tourism. Multicoloured.
2248 4s.80 Type **920** . . . . . . 1·60 95
2249 4s.80 Banos del Inca (thermal springs), Cajamarca (vert) . . . . 1·60 95
2250 4s.80 Ballestas island, Paracas, Ica (vert) . . . . 1·60 95
2251 4s.80 Caballitos (handmade totora reed boats) (vert) 1·60 95

921 Santiago Apostol Church, Pomata

2004. Cultural Heritage.
2252 **921** 1s.80 multicoloured . . .

922 Flower containing Children

2004. America. Literacy Campaign. Multicoloured.
2253 1s.20 Type **922** 40 25
2254 1s.20 Child and computer (horiz) 40 25

923 Aboriginal Footballer

2004. Americas' Cup Football Championship, Peru. Sheet 74 × 74 mm.
MS2255 **923** 5s. multicoloured . . 1·60 1·60
No. **MS**2255 was cut round in the shape of a football.

924 SR Orfeo

2004. Peruvian Gaited Horses. Multicoloured.
2256 1s.20 Type **924** 40 25
2257 1s.20 JyEP Pretencioso . . . 40 25
2258 1s.20 MSP Morenita 40 25
2259 4s.80 Horse's head . . . . 1·60 90

925 Otter

2004. Endangered Species. Giant Otter (*Pteronura brasiliensis*). Sheet 90 × 115 mm containing T **925** and similar vert designs. Multicoloured.
MS2260 30c. Type **925**; 50c. Snarling; 1s.50 Eating fish; 1s.50 Mother and cubs . . . . . . 1·40 1·40

926 Living and Dead Trees

2004. America. Environmental Protection.
2261 **926** 4s.50 multicoloured . . . 1·50 90

927 Central Railway (1870)

2004. National Railways. Multicoloured.
2262 5s. Type **927** . . . . 1·60 95
MS2263 80 × 60 mm. 10s. Train on Puente Infiernillo bridge (horiz) 3·25 3·25

928 Musical Instruments

2004. 60th Anniv of Cancion Criolla Day.
2264 **928** 5s. multicoloured . . . . 1·60 95

929 Pope John Paul II and Mother Teresa

2004. Canonization of Mother Teresa.
2265 **929** 5s. multicoloured . . . . 1·60 95

930 Anniversary Emblem

2004. Centenary of FIFA (Federation Internationale de Football Association).
2266 **930** 5s. multicoloured . . . . 1·60 95

931 Pope John Paul II

2004. 25th Anniv of Pope John Paul II's Pontificate.
2267 **931** 5s. multicoloured . . . . 1·60 95

932 Flora Tristan (women's rights activist)

2004. 25th Anniv of Women's Centre.
2268 **932** 5s. multicoloured . . . . 1·60 95

933 World Map and Exports

2004. Exporters Day.
2269 **933** 5s. multicoloured . . . . 1·60 95

934 Piranha (*Serrasalmus*)

2004. Fish. Multicoloured.
2270 2s. Type **934** 70 40
2271 4s.50 La Plata river dolphin (*Pontoporia blainvillei*) . . 1·50 90
2272 5s. Pirarucu (*Arapaima gigas*) (vert) . . . . . . 1·60 95

935 "40"

2004. 40th Anniv of Latin American Parliament. Multicoloured.
2273 2s.50 Type **935** 80 45
2274 2s.50 Andres Townsend Escurra (first president) and flags 80 45

936 Couple

937 Gavel and Regalia

2004. Mochica Ceramics. Designs showing jugs. Multicoloured.
2275 4s.50 Type **936** . . . . . . 1·50 90
2276 4s.50 Couple (different) . . 1·50 90
2277 5s. Two animals (horiz) . . 1·60 95

2004. Bicentenary of Law College.
2278 **937** 5s. multicoloured . . . . 1·60 95

938 Envelope

2004. 10th Anniv of Serpost.
2279 **938** 5s. multicoloured . . . . 1·60 95

939 Juan Diego Florez

940 Machu Picchu Base

2004. Musicians. Sheet 121 × 95 mm containing T **939** and similar multicoloured designs.
MS2280 2s. × 5, Type **939**; Susana Baca; Gian Marco; Eva Ayllon (horiz); Libido (horiz) . . . . 3·25 3·25

2004. Antarctic. Multicoloured.
2281 1s.50 Type **940** 55 30
2282 2s. *Megaptera novaeagliae* (horiz) 70 40
2283 4s.50 *Orcinus orca* (horiz) 1·50 90

941 Smilodon neogaeus

942 The Nativity

2004. Pre-historic Animals. Multicoloured.
2284 1s.80 Type **941** 60 35
2285 3s.20 Toxodon platensis . . 1·10 65
Nos. 2284/5 were issued together, se-tenant, forming a composite design.

2004. Lighthouses (2nd issue). As T **910**. Multicoloured.
2286 4s.50 Pijuayal . . . . 1·50 90
2287 4s.50 Suana . . . . 1·50 90

2004. Christmas.
2288 **942** 5s. multicoloured . . . . 1·60 95

943 Flags

944 Map and Battle of Ayacucho

2004. Latin-American Presidential Summit.
2289 **943** 5s. multicoloured . . . . 1·60 95

2004. 180th Anniv of Battles. Multicoloured.
2290 1s.80 Type **944** 60 35
2291 3s.20 Battle of Junin . . . . 1·10 65

945 Emblem

947 *Cantua buxifolia*

946 Ruins

2004. 50th Anniv of Art Museum, Lima.
2292 **945** 5s. multicoloured . . . . 1·60 95

2004. Caral Archaeological Site. Sheet 80 × 60 mm.
MS2293 **946** 10s. multicoloured 3·25 3·25

2005. 40th Anniv of Las Leyendas Park. Multicoloured.
2294 5s. Type **947** . . . . 1·60 95
2295 5s. Puma (*Puma concolor*) 1·60 95
Nos. 2294/5 were issued together, se-tenant, forming a composite design.

948 Trophies and Emblem

949 Dental Examination

2005. Cienciano Football Club—South American Cup Champions, 2003 and South American Recopa Champions, (2004).
2296 **948** 5s. multicoloured . . . . 1·60 95

2005. 75th Anniv (2004) of Stomatology Academy.
2297 **949** 5s. multicoloured . . . . 1·60 95

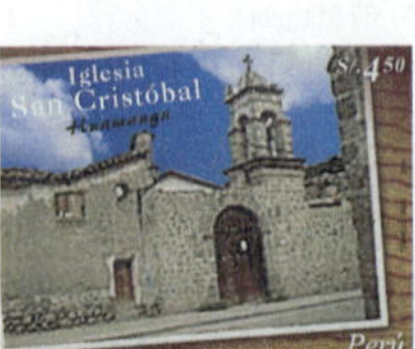

950 Children and Teacher

2005. Campaign for Rights and Responsibilities for Health.
2298 **950** 2s. multicoloured 70 40

951 San Cristobal Church, Huamanga

2005. Churches. Multicoloured.
2299 4s.50 Type **951** . . . . . 1·50 90
2300 5s. Huancayo Cathedral . . 1·60 95

952 Don Ramon Castilla (president 1845—51 and 1855—62) and Slaves

2005. 150th Anniv of Abolition of Slavery.
2301 **952** 5s. crimson . . . . . . 1·60 95

953 Tank

2005. Armed Forces. Multicoloured.
2302 1s.80 Type **953** 30 35
2305 1s.80 Submarine 30 35
2306 1s.80 Mirage fighters and ship 30 35
2303 3s.20 Sukoi aircraft . . . . 1·10 65
2304 3s.20 Soldiers . . . . 1·10 65
2307 3s.20 Missile frigate . . . . 1·10 65
Nos. 2302/4 and 2305/7, respectively were issued together, se-tenant, forming a composite design.

954 *Eugenia stipitata*

2005. Fruit. Multicoloured.
2308 4s.50 Type **954** . . . . . . 1·50 90
2309 4s.50 *Maurita flexuosa* . . . 1·50 90
2310 5s. *Solanum sessiliflorum* (vert) . . . . 1·60 95

955 Luis Alva Talledo

2005. Luis Alva Talledo (singer and founder of Prolirica (music association)).
2311 **955** 1s.50 multicoloured . . . 55 30

956 Northern Chestnut-tailed Ant Bird

957 Soldier and Woman (Pancho Fierro)

2005. Allpahuayo-Mishana Reserve. Multicoloured.
2312 4s.50 Type **956** . . . . . . 1·50 90
2313 4s.50 *Mishana tyrannulet* . . 1·50 90
2314 4s.50 Tree frog . . . . . . 1·50 90
2315 4s.50 Iguana . . . . 1·50 90
Nos. 2312/15 were issued together, se-tenant, forming a composite design.

2005. Art. Multicoloured.
2316 2s. Type **957** 70 40
2317 2s. Old woman, child, old man and woman wearing fur trimmed robe (Ignacio Merino) 70 40
2318 2s. Portrait of man (Daniel Hernandes) 70 40
2319 2s. Mountains and church (Camilo Blas) 70 40
2320 2s. Portrait of woman (Ricardo Grau) 70 40
2321 2s. Abstract (Fernando de Szyszlo) 70 40

958 Stone Carvings, Chavin de Huantar

959 White-winged Guan (*Penelope albipennis*)

2005. 180th Birth Anniv (2004) of Antonio Raimondi (scientist). Multicoloured.
2322 1s.80 Type **958** 60 35
2323 3s.20 Inca tern and bat . . 1·10 65

2324		4s.50 *Stanhophea*	1·50	90
2325		5s. Huallanca periwinkle fossil (*Roemoceras subplanum*)	1·60	95

2005. Rediscovery of White-winged Guan (presumed extinct) in Laquipampa Reserve. Sheet 81 × 60 mm.

MS2326	**959**	10s. multicoloured	3·25	3·25

EXPRESS LETTER STAMPS

1908. Optd **EXPRESO**.

E373	**76**	10c. black	17·00	12·50
E382	–	10c. blue (No. 377)	21·00	11·50
E383	**101**	10c. black and brown	11·50	10·00

OFFICIAL STAMPS

1890. Stamps of 1866 optd **GOBIERNO** in frame.

O287	**15**	1c. violet	1·10	1·10
O324		1c. red	7·00	7·00
O288	**16**	2c. green	1·10	1·10
O325		2c. blue	7·00	7·00
O289		5c. orange	1·60	1·60
O326	**10**	5c. lake	5·50	5·50
O290	**16**	10c. black	85	45
O291		20c. blue	2·50	1·60
O327		20c. blue (as T **10**)	5·50	5·50
O292	**20**	50c. red	3·50	1·75
O293	**21**	1s. brown	4·25	3·75

1894. Stamps of 1894 (with "Head" optd) optd **GOBIERNO** in frame.

O305	**15**	1c. orange (No. 294)	19·00	19·00
O306		1c. green (No. 295)	1·10	1·10
O307	**16**	2c. violet (No. 296)	1·10	1·10
O308		2c. red (No. 297)	90	90
O309		5c. blue (No. 298)	8·50	7·50
O310		10c. green (No. 299)	3·00	3·00
O311	**20**	50c. green (No. 300)	4·25	4·25

1894. Stamps of 1894 (with "Head" and "Horseshoe" optd) optd **GOBIERNO** in frame.

O312	**16**	2c. red (No. 301)	1·60	1·60
O313		5c. blue (No. 302)	1·60	1·60

1896. Stamps of 1896 optd **GOBIERNO**.

O348	**75**	1c. blue	10	10
O349	**76**	10c. yellow	1·00	25
O350		10c. black	10	10
O351	**77**	50c. red	25	20

O 108

1909.

O382	**108**	1c. red	10	10
O572		10c. brown	40	30
O385		10c. purple	15	10
O573		50c. green	35	20

1935. Optd **Servicio Oficial**.

O567	**184**	10c. red	10	10

PARCEL POST STAMPS

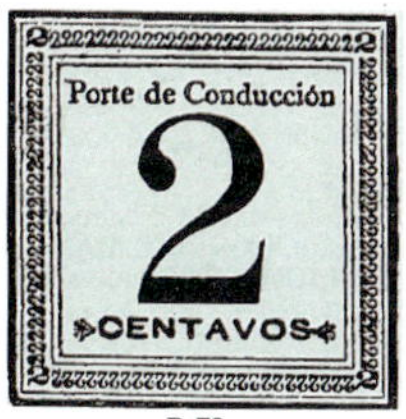

P 79

1895. Different frames.

P348	**79**	1c. purple	1·90	1·60
P349		2c. brown	2·10	1·90
P350		5c. blue	8·50	5·50
P351		10c. brown	11·50	8·25
P352		20c. pink	14·50	12·00
P353		50c. green	38·00	32·00

1903. Surch in words.

P361	**79**	1c. on 20c. pink	12·50	10·00
P362		1c. on 50c. green	12·50	10·00
P363		5c. on 10c. brown	75·00	60·00

POSTAGE DUE STAMPS

D 22  D 23  D 109

1874.

D31	**D 22**	1c. brown	10	10
D32	**D 23**	5c. red	30	15
D33		10c. orange	30	15
D34		20c. blue	50	30
D35		50c. brown	10·00	3·00

1881. Optd with T **24** ("LIMA" at foot instead of "PERU").

D47	**D 22**	1c. brown	3·00	2·00
D48	**D 23**	5c. red	5·50	5·00
D49		10c. orange	5·50	5·50
D50		20c. blue	21·00	17·00
D51		50c. brown	45·00	42·00

1881. Optd **LIMA CORREOS** in double-lined circle.

D52	**D 22**	1c. brown	4·25	4·25
D53	**D 23**	5c. red	5·50	5·00
D54		10c. orange	6·75	5·50
D55		20c. blue	21·00	17·00
D56		50c. brown	65·00	55·00

1883. Optd with T **24** (inscr "LIMA" instead of "PERU") and also with T **28a**.

D247	**D 22**	1c. brown	4·25	3·00
D250	**D 23**	5c. red	6·25	5·75
D253		10c. orange	6·25	5·75
D256		20c. blue	£400	£375
D258		50c. brown	55·00	45·00

1884. Optd with T **28a** only.

D259	**D 22**	1c. brown	40	40
D262	**D 23**	5c. red	30	20
D267		10c. orange	35	25
D269		20c. blue	1·00	35
D271		50c. brown	3·00	75

1894. Optd **LIMA CORREOS** in double-lined circle and with T **28a**.

D275	**D 22**	1c. brown	10·50	9·25

1896. Optd **DEFICIT**.

D348	**D 22**	1c. brown (D31)	15	15
D349	**D 23**	5c. red (D32)	20	15
D350		10c. orange (D33)	55	15
D351		20c. blue (D34)	70	20
D352	**20**	50c. red (283)	60	20
D353	**21**	1s. brown (284)	85	35

1899. As T **73**, but inscr "DEFICIT" instead of "FRANQUEO".

D355		5s. green	1·40	4·25
D356		10s. brown	£800	£800

1902. Surch **DEFICIT** and value in words.

D361		1c. on 10s. (D356)	85	50
D362		5c. on 10s. (354)	50	40

1902. Surch **DEFICIT** and value in words.

D363	**23**	1c. on 20c. (D34)	60	40
D364		5c. on 20c. (D34)	1·50	1·00

1909.

D382	**109**	1c. brown	35	15
D419		1c. purple	15	15
D420		2c. purple	15	15
D570		2c. brown	15	15
D383		5c. brown	35	15
D421		5c. purple	25	20
D384		10c. brown	40	15
D422		10c. purple	40	15
D571		10c. green	40	15
D385		50c. brown	60	20
D423		50c. purple	1·40	50
D424		1s. purple	10·00	3·00
D425		2s. purple	19·00	6·75

1935. Optd **Deficit**.

D568	–	2c. purple (No. 537)	40	40
D569	**184**	10c. red	50	40

PHILIPPINES

Pt. 9, Pt. 22, Pt. 21

A group of islands in the China Sea, E. of Asia, ceded by Spain to the United States after the war of 1898. Under Japanese Occupation from 1941 until 1945. An independent Republic since 1946.

1854. 20 cuartos = 1 real; 8 reales = 1 peso plata fuerte.
1864. 100 centimos = 1 peso plata fuerte.
1871. 100 centimos = 1 escudo (= ½ peso).
1872. 100 centimos = 1 peseta (=1/5peso).
1876. 1000 milesimas = 100 centavos or centimos = 1 peso.
1899. 100 cents = 1 dollar.
1906. 100 centavos = 1 peso.
1962. 100 sentimos = 1 piso.

SPANISH ADMINISTRATION

1 Queen Isabella II  4 Queen Isabella II  5 Queen Isabella II

1854. Imperf.

1	**1**	5c. red	£1300	£225
3		10c. red	£425	£160
5		1r. blue	£500	£170
7		2r. green	£700	£130

On the 1r. the inscriptions are reversed.

1859. Imperf.

13	**4**	5c. red	13·50	6·25
14		10c. pink	12·50	13·50

1861. Larger lettering. Imperf.

17	**5**	5c. red	25·00	8·00

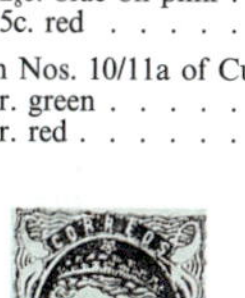

7 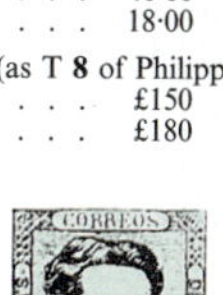 8

1863. Imperf.

19	**7**	5c. red	10·00	4·25
20		10c. red	30·00	30·00
21		1r. mauve	£550	£325
22		2r. blue	£425	£300

1863. Imperf.

25	**8**	1r. green	£110	38·00

1864. As T **14** of Spain, but value in "centimos de peso". Imperf.

26		$3\frac{1}{8}$c. black on buff	2·75	1·50
27		$6\frac{2}{8}$c. green on pink	2·75	75
28		$12\frac{4}{8}$c. blue on pink	5·50	60
29		25c. red on pink	10·50	4·25
30		25c. red on white	7·50	2·50

1868. Optd **HABILITADO POR LA NACION**.

(a) On 1854 to 1863 issues of Philippines.

41	**7**	5c. red	50·00	35·00
53	**4**	10c. pink	90·00	50·00
36	**8**	1r. green	50·00	14·50
42	**7**	1r. mauve	£550	£325
52	**1**	1r. blue	£2000	£1000
43	**7**	2r. blue	£450	£180

(b) On 1864 issues of Philippines.

31		$3\frac{1}{8}$c. black on buff	17·00	3·25
32		$6\frac{2}{8}$c. green on pink	17·00	3·25
33		$12\frac{4}{8}$c. blue on pink	46·00	21·00
34		25c. red	18·00	12·50

(c) On Nos. 10/11a of Cuba (as T **8** of Philippines).

44		1r. green	£150	80·00
45		2r. red	£180	70·00

12  13 King Amadeo

1871.

37	**12**	5c. blue	46·00	5·00
38		10c. green	6·75	4·25
39		20c. brown	50·00	29·00
40		40c. red	70·00	15·00

1872.

46	**13**	12c. pink	10·00	4·25
47		16c. blue	£100	27·00
48a		25c. grey	8·25	4·00
49		62c. mauve	25·00	7·25
50		1p.25 brown	46·00	22·00

14

1874.

54	**14**	12c. grey	11·50	3·50
55		25c. blue	4·25	1·50
56		62c. pink	35·00	3·50
57		1p.25 brown	£170	50·00

15  16

1875. With rosettes each side of "FILIPINAS".

58	**15**	2c. pink	1·70	60
59		2c. blue	£150	70·00
60		6c. orange	8·00	1·80
61		10c. blue	21·00	50
62		12c. mauve	2·20	50
63		20c. brown	11·00	2·50
64		25c. green	8·00	50

1878. Without rosettes.

65	**16**	25m. black	2·10	35
66		25m. green	50·00	22·00
67		50m. purple	22·00	9·25
68a		(62½m.) 0.0625 lilac	42·00	14·50
69		100m. red	85·00	35·00
70		100m. green	7·50	2·10
71		125m. blue	3·75	35
72		200m. pink	25·00	5·00
74		250m. brown	9·25	2·10

1877. Surch **HABILITADO 12 CS. PTA.** in frame.

75	**15**	12c. on 2c. pink	70·00	22·00
76	**16**	12c. on 25m. black	70·00	21·00

1879. Surch **CONVENIO UNIVERSAL DE CORREOS HABILITADO** and value in figures and words.

78	**16**	2c. on 25m. green	38·00	8·50
79		8c. on 100m. red	23·00	4·25

1880. "Alfonso XII" key-type inscr "FILIPINAS".

97	X	1c. green	35	15
82a		2c. red	75	1·30
83		2½c. brown	6·25	1·30
95		$2\frac{4}{8}$c. blue	35	10
99		50m. bistre	35	15
85		5c. grey	65	1·30
100		6c. brown	8·50	1·30
87		$6\frac{2}{8}$c. green	5·00	8·00
88		8c. brown	28·00	16·00
89		10c. brown	2·75	1·30
90		10c. purple	5·25	10·50
91		10c. green	£325	£180
92		$12\frac{4}{8}$c. pink	1·50	1·20
93		20c. brown	2·10	1·00
94		25c. brown	2·75	1·00

1881. "Alfonso XII" key-type inscr "FILIPINAS" with various circular surcharges. (a) **HABILITADO U. POSTAL** and value.

111	X	1c. on $2\frac{4}{8}$c. blue	65	40
102		10c. on $2\frac{4}{8}$c. blue	6·25	1·30

(b) **HABILITADO CORREOS 2 CENTS. DE PESO.**

101	X	2c. on 2½c. brown	3·25	1·30

(c) **HABILITADO PA. U. POSTAL 8 CMOS.**

106	X	8c. on 2c. red	6·25	1·50

(d) **HABILITADO PA. CORREOS DE** and value.

107	X	10c. cuartos on 2c. red	3·75	1·30
112		16 cuartos on $2\frac{4}{8}$c. blue	10·00	2·50
103		20c. on 8c. brown	8·50	2·75
113		1r. on 2c. red	6·75	2·50
109		1r. on 5c. lilac	5·25	2·30
110		1r. on 8c. brown	10·00	3·75
105		2r. on $2\frac{4}{8}$c. blue	5·25	1·40

25  29  30

31  34

1881. Fiscal and telegraph stamps. (a) with circular surch **HABILITADO CORREOS**, **HABILITADO PARA CORREOS**, **HABILITADO PA. U. POSTAL** or **HABILITADO PA. CORREOS** and value in figures and words.

115	**25**	2c. on 10 cuartos bistre	22·00	14·00
129	**29**	2c. on 200m. green	5·00	2·50
116	**25**	$2\frac{4}{8}$c. on 10 cuartos bistre	3·25	70
117		$2\frac{4}{8}$c. on 2r. blue	£160	70·00
124		$6\frac{2}{8}$c. on $12\frac{4}{8}$c. lilac	5·00	3·00
118		8c. on 2r. blue	8·75	2·40
119		8c. on 10c. brown	£180	£140
123		16 cmos. on 2r. blue	6·00	2·50
137	**31**	20c. on 150m. blue	27·00	22·00
134		20c. on 250m. blue	£110	90·00
127	**25**	1r. on 10 cuartos bistre	12·00	4·25
121		1r. on $12\frac{4}{8}$c. lilac	8·00	3·75
130	**29**	1r. on 200m. green	60·00	37·00
131		1r. on 1 peso green	13·00	14·50
132	**30**	1r. on 10 pesetas bistre	44·00	23·00
133	**31**	2r. on 250m. blue	10·00	3·25

(b) With two circular surcharges as above, showing two different values.

128	**25**	8c. on 2r. on 2r. blue	20·00	12·00
136	**31**	1r. on 20c. on 250m. blue	9·00	4·50

(c) Optd **HABILITADO PARA CORREOS** in straight lines.

122	**25**	10 cuartos bistre	£160	70·00
126		1r. green	90·00	65·00

1887. Various stamps with oval surch **UNION GRAL. POSTAL HABILITADO** (No. 142) or **HABILITADO PARA COMMUNICACIONES** and new value. (a) "Alfonso XII" key-type inscr "FILIPINAS".

138	X	$2\frac{4}{8}$c. on 1c. green	2·10	1·20
139		$2\frac{4}{8}$c. on 5c. lilac	1·40	65
140		$2\frac{4}{8}$c. on 50m. bistre	1·90	1·30

141 2⅜c. on 10c. green . . . . . 1·40 70
142 8c. on 2⅜c. blue 80 50

(b) "Alfonso XII" key-type inscr "FILIPAS-IMPRESOS".

143 X 2⅜c. on⅛c. green 50 20

(c) Fiscal and telegraph stamps.

144 **29** 2⅜c. on 200m. green . . . 4·00 1·80
145 2⅜c. on 20c. brown . . . 11·00 5·00
146 **34** 2⅜c. on 1c. bistre 80 60

1889. Various stamps with oval surch **RECARGO DE CONSUMOS HABILITADO** and new value.

(a) "Alfonso XII" key-type inscr "FILIPINAS".

147 X 2⅜c. on 1c. green 20 20
148 2⅜c. on 2c. red 15 15
149 2⅜c. on 2⅜c. blue 10 10
150 2⅜c. on 5c. lilac 15 15
151 2⅜c. on 50m. bistre 15 15
152 2⅜c. on 12⅛c. pink 75 75

(b) "Alfonso XII" key-type inscr "FILIPAS-IMPRESOS".

160 X 2⅜c. on⅛c. green 15 15

(c) Fiscal and telegraph stamps.

153 **34** 2⅜c. on 1c. bistre 40 40
154 2⅜c. on 2c. red 40 40
155 2⅜c. on 2⅜c. brown 15 15
156 2⅜c. on 5c. blue 15 15
157 2⅜c. on 10c. green 15 15
158 2⅜c. on 10c. mauve 80 70
159 2⅜c.on 20c. mauve 30 30
161 – 17⅜c. on 5p. green . . . . 75·00

No. 161 is a fiscal stamp inscribed "DERECHO JUDICIAL" with a central motif as T **43** of Spain.

1890. "Baby" key-type inscr "FILIPINAS".

176 Y 1c. violet 85 25
188 1c. red . . . . 13·50 7·25
197 1c. green . . . . 1·80 50
162 2c. red 15 15
177 2c. violet 40 15
190 2c. brown 15 15
198 2c. blue 25 15
163 2⅜c. blue 40 15
178 2⅜c. grey 25 15
165 5c. blue 40 15
163 5c. green 40 15
199 5c. brown . . . . 8·50 2·50
181 6c. purple 25 15
192 6c. red . . . . 1·60 75
166 8c. green 25 15
182 8c. blue 65 25
193 8c. red 80 25
167 10c. green . . . . 1·40 25
172 10c. pink 65 15
202 10c. brown 60 25
173 12⅜c. green 20 15
184 12⅜c. orange 65 15
185 15c. brown 85 25
195 15c. red . . . . 1·70 80
203 15c. green . . . . 2·10 1·40
169 20c. red . . . . 60·00 30·00
186 20c. brown . . . . 2·10 35
196 20c. purple . . . . 14·00 7·25
204 20c. orange . . . . . . 4·25 1·40
170 25c. brown . . . . 4·50 85
175 25c. blue . . . . 1·70 20
205 40c. purple . . . . 14·50 4·25
206 80c. red . . . . 25·00 10·00

1897. Surch **HABILITADO CORREOS PARA** 1897 and value in frame. (a) "Baby" key-type inscr "FILIPINAS".

212 Y 5c. on 5c. green . . . . . 4·50 2·50
208 15c. on 15c. red . . . . 2·50 1·40
213 15c. on 15c. brown . . . . 3·75 2·30
209 20c. on 20c. purple . . . . 18·00 10·00
214 20c. on 20c. brown . . . . 6·25 4·00
210 20c. on 25c. brown . . . . 12·50 8·50

(b) "Alfonso XII" key-type inscr "FILIPINAS".

215 X 5c. on 5c. lilac . . . . . 5·00 2·40

1898. "Curly Head" key-type inscr "FILIPNAS 1898 y 99".

217 Z 1m. brown 15 15
218 2m. brown 15 15
219 3m. brown 15 15
220 4m. brown . . . . 6·75 1·50
221 5m. brown 15 15
222 1c. purple 15 15
223 2c. green 15 15
224 3c. brown 15 15
225 4c. orange . . . . 11·00 8·00
226 5c. red 25 15
227 6c. blue 65 35
228 8c. brown 25 15
229 10c. red . . . . 1·70 60
230 15c. grey . . . . 1·30 40
231 20c. purple . . . . 1·30 60
232 40c. lilac 65 40
233 60c. black . . . . 3·00 1·40
234 80c. brown . . . . 3·00 1·40
235 1p. green . . . . 16·00 10·00
236 2p. blue . . . . 22·00 12·50

STAMPS FOR PRINTED MATTER

1886. "Alfonso XII" key-type inscr "FILIPAS-IMPRESOS".

P138 X 1m. red 25 15
P139 ⅛c. green 25 15
P140 2m. blue 25 15
P141 5m. brown 25 15

1890. "Baby" key-type inscr "FILIPAS-IMPRESOS".

P171 Y 1m. purple 15 15
P172 ⅛c. purple 15 15
P173 2m. purple 15 15
P174 5m. purple 15 15

1892. "Baby" key-type inscr "FILIPAS-IMPRESOS".

P192 Y 1m. green . . . . 2·30 40
P193 ⅛c. green 90 20
P194 2m. green . . . . 2·40 45
P191 5m. green . . . . £225 50·00

1894. "Baby" key-type inscr "FILIPAS-IMPRESOS".

P197 Y 1m. grey 20 20
P198 ⅛c. brown 20 20
P199 2m. grey 20 20
P200 5m. grey 20 20

1896. "Baby" key-type inscr "FILIPAS-IMPRESOS".

P205 Y 1m. blue 25 15
P206 ⅛c. blue 95 50
P207 2m. brown 35 15
P208 5m. blue . . . . 2·50 1·30

UNITED STATES ADMINISTRATION

1899. United States stamps of 1894 (No. 267 etc) optd **PHILIPPINES**.

252 – 1c. green . . . . 2·50 50
253 – 2c. red . . . . 1·70 75
255 – 3c. violet . . . . 5·00 1·00
256 – 4c. brown . . . . 20·00 4·25
257 – 5c. blue . . . . 5·00 75
258 – 6c. purple . . . . 25·00 5·75
259 – 8c. brown . . . . 25·00 6·25
260 – 10c. brown . . . . 15·00 3·25
262 – 15c. green . . . . 26·00 6·50
263 **83** 50c. orange . . . . £110 33·00
264 – $1 black £350 £225
266 – $2 blue £425 £300
267 – $5 green £800 £700

1903. United States stamps of 1902 optd **PHILIPPINES**.

268 **103** 1c. green . . . . 3·25 35
269 **104** 2c. red . . . . 6·25 1·00
270 **105** 3c. violet . . . . 60·00 10·00
271a **106** 4c. brown . . . . 60·00 17·00
272 **107** 5c. blue . . . . 10·00 85
273 **108** 6c. lake . . . . 65·00 18·00
274 **109** 8c. violet . . . . 37·00 12·50
275 **110** 10c. brown . . . . 17·00 2·10
276 **111** 13c. purple . . . . 29·00 15·00
277 **112** 15c. olive . . . . 50·00 12·50
278 **113** 50c. orange . . . . £110 29·00
279 **114** $1 black £300 £170
280 **115** $2 blue £700 £700
281 **116** $5 green £900 £850

1904. United States stamp of 1903 optd **PHILIPPINES**.

282a **117** 2c. red . . . . 4·50 1·80

45 Rizal

46 Arms of Manila

1906. Various portraits as T **45** and T **46**.

337 **45** 2c. green 15 15
338 – 4c. red (McKinley) . . . 15 15
339 – 6c. violet (Magellan) . . . 25 15
340 – 8c. brown (Legaspi) . . . 15 15
341 – 10c. blue (Lawton) . . . 25 15
288 – 12c. red (Lincoln) . . . 4·25 1·70
342 – 12c. orange (Lincoln) . . 25 25
289 – 16c. black (Sampson) . . 3·25 25
298 – 16c. green (Sampson) . . 3·00 1·00
344 – 16c. olive (Dewey) . . . 85 15
290 – 20c. brown (Washington) . 3·25 25
345 – 20c. yellow (Washington) . 25 15
291 – 26c. brown (Carriedo) . . 5·00 2·10
346 – 26c. green (Carriedo) . . 40 40
292 – 30c. green (Franklin) . . 4·25 1·20
313 – 30c. blue (Franklin) . . . 3·00 40
347 – 30c. grey (Franklin) . . . 50 25
293 **46** 1p. orange . . . . 25·00 5·75
363a 1p. violet . . . . 3·25 3·25
294 2p. black . . . . 35·00 1·20
364 2p. brown . . . . £170 60·00
350 4p. blue . . . . 20·00 40
351 10p. green . . . . 46·00 4·50

Nos. 288, 289, 298, 290, 291, 292, 313, 293 and 294 exist perf only, the other values perf or imperf.

1926. Air. Madrid–Manila Flight. Stamps as last, optd **AIR MAIL 1926 MADRID-MANILA** and aeroplane propeller.

368 **45** 2c. green . . . . 6·50 6·50
369 4c. red . . . . 10·00 10·00
370 – 6c. violet . . . . 41·00 25·00
371 – 8c. brown . . . . 41·00 25·00
372 – 10c. blue . . . . 41·00 25·00
373 – 12c. orange . . . . 41·00 41·00
374 – 16c. green (Sampson) . . . £2500 £1300
375 – 16c. olive (Dewey) . . . 60·00 60·00
376 – 20c. yellow . . . . 60·00 60·00
377 – 26c. green . . . . 60·00 60·00
378 – 30c. grey . . . . 60·00 60·00
383 **46** 1p. violet £170 £150
379 2p. brown £425 £250
380 4p. blue £600 £400
381 10p. green £1000 £550

49 Legislative Palace

1926. Inauguration of Legislative Palace.

384 **49** 2c. black and green 40 25
385 4c. black and red 40 25
386 16c. black and olive . . . 85 65
387 18c. black and brown . . . 85 65
388 20c. black and orange . . 1·20 1·00
389 24c. black and grey . . . 2·50 65
390 1p. black and mauve . . . 37·00 26·00

1928. Air. London–Orient Flight by British Squadron of Seaplanes. Stamps of 1906 optd **L.O.F.** (= London Orient Flight), **1928** and Fairey IIID seaplane.

402 **45** 2c. green 40 25
403 – 4c. red 50 40
404 – 6c. violet . . . . 1·70 1·50
405 – 8c. brown . . . . 2·00 1·70
406 – 10c. blue . . . . 2·00 1·70
407 – 12c. orange . . . . 2·75 2·50
408 – 16c. olive (Dewey) . . . 2·00 1·70
409 – 20c. yellow . . . . 2·75 2·50
410 – 26c. green . . . . 8·25 5·50
411 – 30c. grey . . . . 8·25 5·50
412 **46** 1p. violet . . . . 41·00 31·00

54 Mayon Volcano

57 Vernal Falls, Yosemite National Park, California, wrongly inscr "PAGSANJAN FALLS"

1932.

424 **54** 2c. green 40 60
425 – 4c. red 35 35
426 – 12c. orange 50 50
427 **57** 18c. red . . . . 21·00 8·25
428 – 20c. yellow 65 65
429 – 24c. violet . . . . 1·20 75
430 – 32c. brown . . . . 1·20 85

DESIGNS—HORIZ: 4c. Post Office, Manila; 12c. Freighters at Pier No. 7, Manila Bay; 20c. Rice plantation; 24c. Rice terraces; 32c. Baguio Zigzag.

1932. No. 350 surch in words in double circle.

431 **46** 1p. on 4p. blue . . . . . 1·70 40
432 2p. on 4p. blue . . . . . 3·00 65

1932. Air. Nos. 424/30 optd with Dornier Do-J flying boat "Gronland Wal" and **ROUND-THE-WORLD FLIGHT VON GRONAU 1932**.

433 2c. green 35 35
434 4c. red 35 35
435 12c. orange 50 50
436 18c. red . . . . 3·00 3·00
437 20c. yellow . . . . 1·50 1·50
438 24c. violet . . . . 1·50 1·50
439 32c. brown . . . . 1·50 1·50

1933. Air. Stamps of 1906 optd **F. REIN MADRID-MANILA FLIGHT-1933** under propeller.

440 **45** 2c. green 35 35
441 – 4c. red 40 35
442 – 6c. violet 65 65
443 – 8c. brown . . . . 2·10 1·30
444 – 10c. blue . . . . 1·80 85
445 – 12c. orange . . . . 1·70 85
446 – 16c. olive (Dewey) . . . 1·70 85
447 – 20c. orange . . . . 1·70 1·00
448 – 26c. green . . . . 1·80 1·30
449 – 30c. grey . . . . 2·50 1·70

1933. Air. Nos. 337 and 425/30 optd with **AIR MAIL** on wings of airplane.

450 2c. green 40 40
451 4c. red 15 15
452 12c. orange 25 15
453 20c. yellow 25 15
454 24c. violet 35 25
455 32c. brown 40 35

66 Baseball

1934. 10th Far Eastern Championship Games.

456 **66** 2c. brown . . . . 1·20 65
457 – 6c. blue 25 15
458 – 16c. purple 40 40

DESIGNS—VERT: 6c. Tennis; 16c. Basketball.

69 Dr. J. Rizal

72 Pearl Fishing

1935. Designs as T **69/70** in various sizes (sizes in millimetres).

459 2c. red (19 × 22) 15 15
460 4c. green (34 × 22) 15 15
461 6c. brown (22½ × 28) 15 15
462 8c. violet (34 × 22) 15 15
463 10c. red (34 × 22) 25 15
464 12c. black (34 × 22) 25 15
465 16c. blue (34 × 22) 25 15
466 20c. bistre (19 × 22) 25 15
467 26c. blue (34 × 22) 35 25
468 30c. red (34 × 22) 35 25
469 1p. black and orange (37 × 27) . . . . . . 2·10 1·50
470 2p. black and brown (37 × 27) 4·25 1·50
471 4p. black and blue (37 × 27) 4·25 3·00
472 5p. black and green (27 × 37) 8·25 2·10

DESIGNS: 4c. Woman, Carabao and Rice-stalks; 6c. Filipino girl; 10c. Fort Santiago; 12c. Salt springs; 16c. Magellan's landing; 20c. "Juan de la Cruz"; 26c. Rice terraces; 30c. Blood Compact; 1p. Barasoain Church; 2p. Battle of Manila Bay; 4p. Montalban Gorge; 5p. George Washington (after painting by John Faed).

COMMONWEALTH OF THE PHILIPPINES

83 "Temples of Human Progress"

1935. Inauguration of Commonwealth of the Philippines.

483 **83** 2c. red 15 15
484 6c. violet 15 15
485 16c. blue 25 25
486 36c. green 35 35
487 50c. brown 50 50

1935. Air. "China Clipper" Trans-Pacific Air Mail Flight. Optd **P.I. U.S. INITIAL FLIGHT December-1935** and Martin M-130 flying boat.

488 10c. red (No. 463) 25 15
489 30c. red (No. 468) 40 40

85 J. Rizal y Mercado

89 Manuel L. Quezon

1936. 75th Birth Anniv of Rizal.

490 **85** 2c. yellow 15 15
491 6c. blue 15 15
492 36c. brown 50 50

1936. Air. Manila–Madrid Flight by Arnaiz and Calvo. Stamps of 1906 surch **MANILA-MADRID ARNACAL FLIGHT–1936** and value.

493 **45** 2c. on 4c. red 15 15
494 6c. on 12c. orange 15 15
495 16c. on 26c. green 25 25

1936. Stamps of 1935 (Nos. 459/72) optd **COMMON-WEALTH** (2c., 6c., 20c.) or **COMMONWEALTH** (others).

496 2c. red 15 15
497 4c. green 40 40
526 6c. brown 15 15
527 8c. violet 15 15
528 10c. red 15 15
529 12c. black 15 15
530 16c. blue 15 15
531 20c. bistre 15 15
532 26c. blue 25 25
505 30c. red 35 15
534 1p. black and orange 40 15
535 2p. black and brown . . . . 2·50 65
508 4p. black and blue . . . . 17·00 4·25
509 5p. black and green . . . . 2·50 1·20

1936. 1st Anniv of Autonomous Government.

510 **89** 2c. brown 15 15
511 6c. green 15 15
512 12c. blue 25 25

90 Philippine Is

92 Arms of Manila

1937. 33rd International Eucharistic Congress.
513 **90** 2c. green 15 15
514 6c. brown 15 15
515 12c. blue 15 15
516 20c. orange 25 15
517 36c. violet 40 40
518 50c. red 60 35

1937.
522 **92** 10p. grey . . . . 3·25 1·70
523 20p. brown . . . . 1·70 1·20

1939. Air. 1st Manila Air Mail Exhibition. Surch **FIRST AIR MAIL EXHIBITION Feb 17 to 19, 1939** and value.
548a – 8c. on 26c. green (346) . . 65 40
549 **92** 1p. on 10p. grey . . . . 2·50 2·10

1939. 1st National Foreign Trade Week. Surch **FIRST FOREIGN TRADE WEEK MAY 21-27, 1939** and value.
551 – 2c. on 4c. green (460) . . 15 15
552a **45** 6c. on 26c. green (346) . . 25 20
553 **92** 50c. on 20p. brown . . . 85 85

101 Triumphal Arch

102 Malacanan Palace

103 Pres. Quezon taking Oath of Office

1939. 4th Anniv of National Independence.
554 **101** 2c. green 15 15
555 6c. red 15 15
556 12c. blue 25 15
557 **102** 2c. green 15 15
558 6c. orange 15 15
559 12c. red 25 15
560 **103** 2c. orange 15 15
561 6c. green 15 15
562 12c. violet 25 15

104 Jose Rizal

105 Filipino Vinta and Boeing 314 Flying Boat

1941.
563 **104** 2c. green 15 15
623 – 2c. brown 25 15
In No. 623 the head faces to the right.

1941. Air.
566 **105** 8c. red 85 50
567 20c. blue . . . . 1·00 40
568 60c. green . . . . 1·20 85
569 1p. sepia 65 40

For Japanese Occupation issues of 1941–45 see **JAPANESE OCCUPATION OF PHILIPPINE ISLANDS.**

1945. Victory issue. Nos. 496, 525/31, 505, 534 and 522/3 optd **VICTORY**.
610 2c. red 15 15
611 4c. green 15 15
612 6c. brown 25 15
613 8c. violet 25 15
614 10c. red 25 15
615 12c. black 15 15
616 16c. blue 35 15
617 20c. bistre 40 15
618 30c. red 50 40
619 1p. black and orange . . . . 1·50 35
620 10p. grey . . . . 50·00 11·50
621 20p. brown . . . . 46·00 12·50

INDEPENDENT REPUBLIC

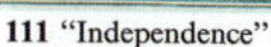
111 "Independence"

113 Bonifacio Monument

1946. Proclamation of Independence.
625 **111** 2c. red 30 30
626 6c. green 60 30
627 12c. blue 90 45

1946. Optd **PHILIPPINES 50TH ANNIVERSARY MARTYRDOM OF RIZAL 1896–1946.**
628 **104** 2c. brown (No. 623) . . . 30 20

1947.
629 – 4c. brown 15 15
630 **113** 10c. red 15 15
631 – 12c. blue 20 15
632 – 16c. grey . . . . 1·60 95
633 – 20c. brown 45 15
634 – 50c. green . . . . . . 1·20 10
635 – 1p. violet . . . . 2·40 60
DESIGNS—VERT: 4c. Rizal Monument; 50c., 1p. Avenue of Palm Trees. HORIZ: 12c. Jones Bridge; 16c. Santa Lucia Gate; 20c. Mayon Volcano.

115 Manuel L. Quezon

117 Presidents Quezon and Roosevelt

116 Pres. Roxas taking Oath of Office

1947.
636 **115** 1c. green 15 10
MS637 64 × 85 mm. No. 636 in block of four. Imperf . . . . 1·50 1·50

1947. 1st Anniv of Independence.
638 **116** 4c. red 20 15
639 6c. green 50 50
640 16c. purple . . . . 1·20 80

1947. Air.
641 **117** 6c. green 60 60
642 40c. orange . . . . 1·30 1·30
643 80c. blue . . . . 3·25 3·25

119 United Nations Emblem

121 General MacArthur

1947. Conference of Economic Commission for Asia and Far East, Baguio. Imperf or perf.
648 **119** 4c. red and pink . . . . 1·60 1·60
649 6c. violet and light violet 2·40 2·40
650 12c. blue and light blue 2·75 2·75

1948. 3rd Anniv of Liberation.
652 **121** 4c. violet 60 20
653 6c. red . . . . 1·10 75
654 16c. blue . . . . 1·60 75

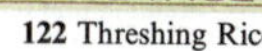
122 Threshing Rice

125 Dr. Jose Rizal

1948. United Nations Food and Agriculture Organization Conference, Baguio.
655 **122** 2c. green & yell (postage) 90 60
656 6c. brown and stone . . . 1·10 80
657 18c. blue and light blue 3·00 2·40
658 40c. red and pink (air) . . 15·00 8·00

1948.
662 **125** 2c. green 20 15

126 Pres. Manuel Roxas

127 Scout and Badge

1948. President Roxas Mourning Issue.
663 **126** 2c. black 20 15
664 4c. black 35 20

1948. 25th Anniv of Philippine Boy Scouts. Perf or imperf.
665 **127** 2c. green and brown . . . 1·10 60
666 4c. pink and brown . . . 1·50 90

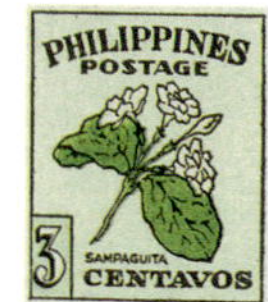
128 Sampaguita, National Flower

1948. Flower Day.
667 **128** 3c. green and black . . . 35 30

130 Santos, Tavera and Kalaw

131 "Doctrina Christiana" (first book published in Philippines)

1949. Library Rebuilding Fund.
671 **130** 4c.+2c. brown . . . . . 1·10 80
672 **131** 6c.+4c. violet . . . . . 3·25 2·20
673 – 18c.+7c. blue . . . . . 4·50 3·75
DESIGN—VERT: 18c. Title page of Rizal's "Noli Me Tangere".

132 U.P.U. Monument, Berne

1949. 75th Anniv of U.P.U.
674 **132** 4c. green 20 10
675 6c. violet 20 15
676 18c. blue 80 30
MS677 106 × 92 mm. Nos. 674/6. Imperf . . . . 1·50 1·50

133 General del Pilar at Tirad Pass

134 Globe

1949. 50th Death Anniv of Gen. Gregorio del Pilar.
678 **133** 2c. brown 15 15
679 4c. green 35 30

1950. 5th International Congress of Junior Chamber of Commerce.
680 **134** 2c. violet (postage) . . . 20 10
681 6c. green 30 15
682 18c. blue 65 20
683 30c. orange (air) 50 20
684 50c. red 90 20

135 Red Lauan Trees

136 Franklin D. Roosevelt

1950. 15th Anniv of Forestry Service.
685 **135** 2c. green 35 20
686 4c. violet 75 30

1950. 25th Anniv of Philatelic Association.
687 **136** 4c. brown 30 20
688 6c. pink 60 35
689 18c. blue . . . . 1·30 95
MS690 61 × 51 mm. **136** 80c. green. Imperf . . . . 2·50 2·50

137 Lions Emblem

138 President Quirino taking Oath of Office

1950. "Lions" International Convention, Manila.
691 **137** 2c. orange (postage) . . . 65 65
692 4c. lilac . . . . 1·00 1·00
693 30c. green (air) . . . . . 1·00 75
694 50c. blue . . . . 1·10 1·00
MS695 91 × 88 mm. Nos. 693/4 2·20 2·20

1950. Pres. Quirino's Inauguration.
696 **138** 2c. red 15 10
697 4c. purple 15 15
698 6c. green 20 15

1950. Surch **ONE CENTAVO**.
699 **125** 1c. on 2c. green 15 10

140 Dove and Map

141 War Widow and Children

1950. Baguio Conference.
701 **140** 5c. green 30 20
702 6c. red 30 20
703 18c. blue 75 50

1950. Aid to War Victims.
704 **141** 2c.+2c. red 10 10
705 – 4c.+4c. violet 45 45
DESIGN: 4c. Disabled veteran.

142 Arms of Manila

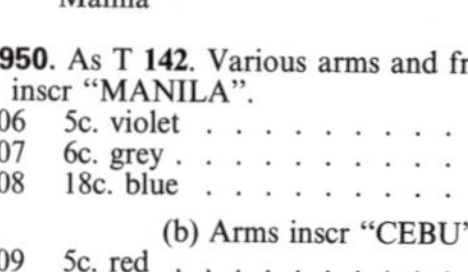
143 Soldier and Peasants

1950. As T **142**. Various arms and frames. (a) Arms inscr "MANILA".
706 5c. violet 60 50
707 6c. grey 50 35
708 18c. blue 60 50

(b) Arms inscr "CEBU".
709 5c. red 60 50
710 6c. brown 50 35
711 18c. violet 60 50

(c) Arms inscr "ZAMBOANGA".
712 5c. green 60 50
713 6c. brown 50 35
714 18c. blue 60 50

(d) Arms inscr "ILOILO".
715 5c. green 60 50
716 6c. violet 50 35
717 18c. blue 60 50

1951. Guarding Peaceful Labour. Perf or imperf.
718 **143** 5c. green 20 20
719 6c. purple 35 35
720 18c. blue . . . . 1·00 1·00

144 Philippines Flag and U.N. Emblem

145 Statue of Liberty

1951. U.N. Day.
721 **144** 5c. red 90 35
722 6c. green 60 35
723 18c. blue . . . . 1·60 1·10

1951. Human Rights Day.
724 **145** 5c. green 50 30
725 6c. orange 75 50
726 18c. blue . . . . 1·30 80

146 Schoolchildren

147 M. L. Quezon

1952. 50th Anniv of Philippine Educational System.
727 **146** 5c. orange 60 50

1952. Portraits.
728 **147** 1c. brown 15 15
729 – 2c. black (J. Abad Santos) 15 15
730 – 3c. red (A. Mabini) . . . 15 15
731 – 5c. red (M. H. del Pilar) 15 15
732 – 10c. blue (Father J. Burgos) 15 15
733 – 20c. red (Lapu-Lapu) . . 30 15
734 – 25c. green (Gen. A. Luna) 45 20
735 – 50c. red (C. Arellano) . . 90 30
736 – 60c. red (A. Bonifacio) . . 1·00 45
737 – 2p. violet (G. L. Jaena) 3·25 1·10

149 Aurora A. Quezon

1952. Fruit Tree Memorial Fund.
742 **149** 5c.+1c. blue 15 15
743 6c.+2c. pink 45 45
See also No. 925.

150 Milkfish and Map of Oceania

1952. Indo-Pacific Fisheries Council.
744 **150** 5c. brown . . . . 1·20 75
745 6c. blue 75 60

151 "A Letter from Rizal"

1952. Pan-Asiatic Philatelic Exhibition, Manila.
746 **151** 5c. blue (postage) 65 15
747 6c. brown 65 20
748 30c. red (air) . . . . . . 1·30 1·10

152 Wright Park, Baguio City

153 F. Baltazar (poet)

1952. 3rd Lions District Convention.
749 **152** 5c. red 95 95
750 6c. green . . . . 1·30 1·10

1953. National Language Week.
751 **153** 5c. bistre 50 35

154 "Gateway to the East"

155 Pres. Quirino and Pres. Sukarno

1953. International Fair, Manila.
752 **154** 5c. turquoise 35 15
753 6c. red 35 15

1953. Visit of President to Indonesia. Flags in yellow, blue and red.
754 **155** 5c. blue, yellow and black 20 10
755 6c. green, yellow and black 30 30

156 Doctor examining patient

1953. 50th Anniv of Philippines Medical Association.
756 **156** 5c. mauve 30 30
757 6c. blue 45 35

1954. Optd **FIRST NATIONAL BOY SCOUTS JAMBOREE APRIL 23-30, 1954** or surch also.
758 5c. red (No. 731) . . . . . . 1·30 1·10
759 18c. on 50c. green (No. 634) 2·20 1·60

158 Stamp of 1854, Magellan and Manila P.O.

1954. Stamp Centenary. Central stamp in orange.
760 **158** 5c. violet (postage) . . . 80 60
761 18c. blue . . . . 1·60 1·30
762 30c. green . . . . 3·75 2·40
763 10c. brown (air) . . . . . 1·60 1·30
764 20c. green . . . . 2·75 2·20
765 50c. red . . . . 5·50 4·75

159 Diving

1954. 2nd Asian Games, Manila.
766 – 5c. blue on blue (Discus) 90 65
767 **159** 18c. green on green . . . 1·50 1·10
768 – 30c. red on pink (Boxing) 2·20 1·90

1954. Surch **MANILA CONFERENCE OF 1954** and value.
769 **113** 5c. on 10c. red 20 15
770 – 18c. on 20c. brown (No. 633) 80 75

161 "Independence"

162 "The Immaculate Conception" (Murillo)

1954. Independence Commemoration.
771 **161** 5c. red 30 20
772 18c. blue 95 60

1954. Marian Year.
773 **162** 5c. blue 60 35

163 Mayon Volcano and Filipino Vinta

1955. 50th Anniv of Rotary International.
774 **163** 5c. blue (postage) 35 15
775 18c. red . . . . 1·30 65
776 50c. green (air) . . . . . 2·50 1·10

164 "Labour"

165 Pres. Magsaysay

1955. Labour-Management Congress, Manila.
777 **164** 5c. brown . . . . 1·50 60

1955. 9th Anniv of Republic.
778 **165** 5c. blue 20 20
779 20c. red 75 75
780 30c. green . . . . 1·30 1·30

166 Lt. J. Gozar

1955. Air. Air Force Heroes.
781 **166** 20c. violet 80 15
782 – 30c. red (Lt. C. F. Basa) 1·30 30
783 **166** 50c. green . . . . 1·10 20
784 – 70c. blue (Lt. C. F. Basa) 1·90 1·30

167 Liberty Well

1956. Artesian Wells for Rural Areas.
785 **167** 5c. violet 35 35
786 20c. green 80 75

1956. 5th Conference of World Confederation of Organizations of the Teaching Profession. No. 731 optd **WCOTP CONFERENCE MANILA.**
787 5c. red 35 35

169 Nurse and War Victims

170 Monument (landing marker) in Leyte

1956. 50th Anniv of Philippines Red Cross.
788 **169** 5c. violet and red 50 50
789 20c. brown and red . . . 75 60

1956. Liberation Commem. Perf or imperf.
790 **170** 5c. red 15 15

171 St. Thomas's University

172 Statue of the Sacred Heart

1956. University of St. Thomas.
791 **171** 5c. brown and red 25 20
792 60c. brown and mauve . . 1·10 1·00

1956. 2nd National Eucharistic Congress and Centenary of the Feast of the Sacred Heart.
793 **172** 5c. green 35 30
794 20c. pink 80 80

1956. Surch **5 5.**
795 5c. on 6c. brown (No. 710) 15 15
796 5c. on 6c. brown (No. 713) 15 15
797 5c. on 6c. violet (No. 716) . . 15 15

174 Girl Guide, Badge and Camp

175 Pres. Ramon Magsaysay

1957. Girl Guides' Pacific World Camp, Quezon City, and Birth Centenary of Lord Baden-Powell. Perf or imperf.
798 **174** 5c. blue 50 50

1957. Death of Pres. Magsaysay.
799 **175** 5c. black 15 10

176 Sergio Osmena (Speaker) and First Philippine Assembly

1957. 50th Anniv of First Philippine Assembly.
800 **176** 5c. green 15 15

177 "The Spoliarium" after Juan Luna

1957. Birth Centenary of Juan Luna (painter).
801 **177** 5c. red 15 10

1957. Inauguration of President C. P. Garcia and Vice-President D. Macapagal. Nos. 732/3 surch **GARCIA-MACAPAGAL INAUGURATION DEC. 30, 1957** and value.
802 5c. on 10c. blue 20 20
803 10c. on 20c. red 30 30

179 University of the Philippines

1958. Golden Jubilee of University of the Philippines.
804 **179** 5c. red 35 15

180 Pres. Garcia

1958. 12th Anniv of Republic.
805 **180** 5c. multicoloured 15 15
806 20c. multicoloured 60 45

181 Main Hospital Building, Quezon Institute

1958. Obligatory Tax. T.B. Relief Fund.
807 **181** 5c.+5c. green and red . . 20 20
808 10c.+5c. violet and red . . 45 45

182 The Immaculate Conception and Manila Cathedral

1958. Inauguration of Manila Cathedral.
809 **182** 5c. multicoloured 20 15

1959. Surch **One Centavo**.
810 1c. on 5c. red (No. 731) . . . 15 10

1959. 14th Anniv of Liberation. Nos. 704/5 surch.
812 **141** 1c. on 2c.+2c. red 10 10
813 – 6c. on 4c.+4c. violet . . . 15 15

186 Philippines Flag 187 Bulacan Seal

1959. Adoption of Philippine Constitution.
814 **186** 6c. red, blue and yellow 15 10
815 20c. red, blue and yellow 20 20

1959. Provincial Seals. (a) Bulacan Seal and 60th Anniv of Malolos Constitution.
816 **187** 6c. green 15 10
817 20c. red 30 20

(b) Capiz Seal and 11th Death Anniv of Pres. Roxas.
818 6c. brown 10 10
819 25c. violet 30 30
The shield within the Capiz seal bears the inset portrait of Pres. Roxas.

(c) Bacolod Seal.
820 6c. green 15 10
821 10c. purple 20 15

188 Scout at Campfire

1959. 10th World Scout Jamboree, Manila.
822 **188** 6c.+4c. red on yellow (postage) 15 15
823 6c.+4c. red 35 35
824 – 25c.+5c. blue on yellow 60 60
825 – 25c.+5c. blue 75 75
826 – 30c.+10c. green (air) . . . 60 60
827 – 70c.+20c. brown . . . . 1·30 1·30
828 – 80c.+20c. violet . . . . . 1·90 1·90
MS829 171 × 90 mm. Nos. 823, 825/8 (sold at 4p.) . . . . 12·50 12·50
DESIGNS: 25c. Scout with bow and arrow; 30c. Scout cycling; 70c. Scout with model airplane; 80c. Pres. Garcia with scout.

190 Bohol Sanatorium

1959. Obligatory Tax. T.B. Relief Fund. Nos. 807/8 surch **HELP FIGHT T B** with Cross of Lorraine and value and new design (T **190**).
830 **181** 3c.+5c. on 5c.+5c. . . . 20 20
831 6c.+5c. on 10c.+5c. . . . 20 20
832 **190** 6c.+5c. green and red . . 20 20
833 25c.+5c. blue and red . . 45 35

191 Pagoda and Gardens at Camp John Hay

1959. 50th Anniv of Baguio.
834 **191** 6c. green 15 10
835 25c. red 35 20

1959. U.N. Day. Surch **6c UNITED NATIONS DAY**.
836 **132** 6c. on 18c. blue 15 10

193 Maria Cristina Falls 196 Dr. Jose Rizal

195

1959. World Tourist Conference, Manila.
837 **193** 6c. green and violet . . . 15 15
838 30c. green and brown . . 60 45

1959. No. 629 surch **One** and bars.
839 1c. on 4c. brown 15 10

1959. Centenary of Manila Athenaeum (school).
840 **195** 6c. blue 10 10
841 30c. red 50 35

1959.
842 **196** 6c. blue 15 10

197 Book of the Constitution

1960. 25th Anniv of Philippines Constitution.
844 **197** 6c. brn & gold (postage) 15 15
845 30c. blue and silver (air) 45 30

198 Congress Building

1960. 5th Anniv of Manila Pact.
846 **198** 6c. green 10 10
847 25c. orange 45 35

199 Sunset, Manila Bay

1960. World Refugee Year.
848 **199** 6c. multicoloured 15 15
849 25c. multicoloured 45 30

200 North American F-86 Sabre and Boeing P-12 Fighters

1960. Air. 25th Anniv of Philippine Air Force.
850 **200** 10c. red 15 15
851 20c. blue 45 30

1960. Surch.
852 **134** 1c. on 18c. blue 20 15
853 **161** 5c. on 18c. blue 20 20
854 **163** 5c. on 18c. red 30 15
855 **158** 10c. on 18c. orange & blue 20 15
856 **140** 10c. on 18c. blue 30 20

202 Lorraine Cross 204 Pres. Quezon

1960. 50th Anniv of Philippine Tuberculosis Society. Lorraine Cross and wreath in red and gold.
857 **202** 5c. green 15 10
858 6c. blue 15 10

1960. Obligatory Tax. T.B. Relief Fund. Surch **6+5 HELP PREVENT TB**.
859 **181** 6c.+5c. on 5c.+5c. green and red 35 15

1960.
860 **204** 1c. green 15 10

205 Basketball

1960. Olympic Games.
861 **205** 6c. brown & grn (postage) 15 10
862 – 10c. brown and purple . . 20 15
863 – 30c. brown and orange (air) 60 50
864 – 70c. purple and blue . . . 1·30 1·10
DESIGNS: 10c. Running; 30c. Rifle-shooting; 70c. Swimming.

206 Presidents Eisenhower and Garcia

1960. Visit of President Eisenhower.
865 **206** 6c. multicoloured 20 15
866 20c. multicoloured 50 30

207 "Mercury" and Globe

1961. Manila Postal Conference.
867 **207** 6c. multicoloured (postage) 15 10
868 30c. multicoloured (air) 35 30

1961. Surch **20 20**.
869 20c. on 25c. green (No. 734) 30 15

1961. 2nd National Scout Jamboree, Zamboanga. Nos. 822/5 surch **2nd National Boy Scout Jamboree Pasonanca Park** and value.
870 10c. on 6c.+4c. red on yellow 15 15
871 10c. on 6c.+4c. red 50 50
872 30c. on 25c.+5c. blue on yellow 35 35
873 30c. on 25c.+5c. blue 60 60

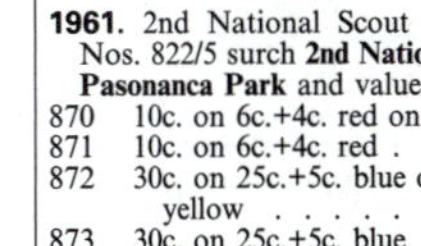

210 La Salle College

1961. 50th Anniv of La Salle College.
874 **210** 6c. multicoloured 15 10
875 10c. multicoloured 20 15

211 Rizal when Student, School and University Buildings

1961. Birth Centenary of Dr. Jose Rizal.
876 **211** 5c. multicoloured 10 10
877 – 6c. multicoloured 10 10
878 – 10c. brown and green . . 20 20
879 – 20c. turquoise and brown 30 30
880 – 30c. multicoloured 50 35
DESIGNS: 6c. Rizal and birthplace at Calamba, Laguna; 10c. Rizal, mother and father; 20c. Rizal extolling Luna and Hidalgo at Madrid; 30c. Rizal's execution.

1961. 15th Anniv of Republic. Optd **IKA 15 KAARAWAN Republika ng Pilipinas Hulyo 4, 1961**.
881 **198** 6c. green 20 20
882 25c. orange 45 45

213 Roxas Memorial T.B. Pavilion

1961. Obligatory Tax. T.B. Relief Fund.
883 **213** 6c.+5c. brown and red . . 35 15

214 Globe, Plan Emblem and Supporting Hand

1961. 7th Anniv of Admission of Philippines to Colombo Plan.
884 **214** 5c. multicoloured 10 10
885 6c. multicoloured 15 15

1961. Philippine Amateur Athletic Federation's Golden Jubilee. Surch with P.A.A.F. monogram and **6c PAAF GOLDEN JUBILEE 1911 1961**.
886 **200** 6c. on 10c. red 20 20

216 Typist

1961. Government Employees' Association.
887 **216** 6c. violet and brown . . . 20 10
888 10c. blue and brown . . . 35 20

1961. Inauguration of Pres. Macapagal and Vice-Pres. Pelaez. Surch **MACAPAGAL-PELAEZ DEC. 30, 1961 INAUGURATION 6c**.
889 6c. on 25c. violet (No. 819) 15 10

1962. Cross obliterated by Arms and surch **6s**.
890 **181** 6c. on 5c.+5c. green and red 15 15

220 Waling-Waling 221 A. Mabini (statesman)

1962. Orchids. Multicoloured.
892 5c. Type **220** 15 15
893 6c. White Mariposa 15 15
894 10c. "Dendrobium sanderii" 20 20
895 20c. Sanggumay 35 35

1962. New Currency.
896 – 1s. brown 10 10
897 **221** 3s. red 10 10
898 – 5s. red 10 10
899 – 6s. brown 15 10
900 – 6s. blue 15 10
901 – 10s. purple 15 10
902 – 20s. blue 20 10
903 – 30s. red 50 15
904 – 50s. violet 90 15
905 – 70s. blue 1·10 50
906 – 1p. green 2·20 45
907 – 1p. orange 75 35
PORTRAITS: 1s. M. L. Quezon; 5s. M. H. del Pilar; 6s. (2) J. Rizal (different); 10s. Father J. Burgos; 20s. Lapu-Lapu; 30s. Rajah Soliman; 50s. C. Arellano; 70s. S. Osmena; 1p. (No. 906) E. Jacinto; 1p. (No. 907) J. M. Panganiban.

225 Pres. Macapagal taking Oath

1962. Independence Day.
915 **225** 6s. multicoloured 15 10
916 10s. multicoloured 20 15
917 30s. multicoloured 35 20

226 Valdes Memorial T.B. Pavilion

1962. Obligatory Tax Stamps. T.B. Relief Fund. Cross in red.
918 **226** 6s.+5s. purple 15 15
919 30s.+5s. blue 45 30
920 70s.+5s. blue 1·00 90

227 Lake Taal

1962. Malaria Eradication.
921 **227** 6s. multicoloured 15 15
922 10s. multicoloured 20 15
923 70s. multicoloured 1·50 1·10

1962. Bicentenary of Diego Silang Revolt. No. 734 surch **1762 1962 BICENTENNIAL Diego Silang Revolt 20.**
924 20s. on 25c. green 30 20

1962. No. 742 with premium obliterated.
925 **149** 5c. blue 20 15

230 Dr. Rizal playing Chess

1962. Rizal Foundation Fund.
926 **230** 6s.+4s. green and mauve 20 20
927 – 30s.+5s. blue and purple 50 50
DESIGN: 30s. Dr. Rizal fencing.

1963. Surch.
928 **221** 1s. on 3s. red 15 10
929 – 5s. on 6s. brown (No. 899) 15 15

1963. Diego Silang Bicentenary Art and Philatelic Exhibition, G.P.O., Manila. No. 737 surch **1763 1963 DIEGO SILANG BICENTENNIAL ARPHEX** and value.
930 6c. on 2p. violet 15 15
931 20c. on 2p. violet 30 30
932 70c. on 2p. violet 90 75

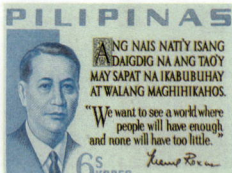

233 "We want to see ..." (Pres. Roxas)

1963. Presidential Sayings (1st issue).
933 **233** 6s. blue and black 15 10
934 30s. brown and black 45 15
See also Nos. 959/60, 981/2, 1015/16, 1034/5, 1055/6, 1148/9 and 1292/3.

234 Lorraine Cross on Map

1963. Obligatory Tax. T.B. Relief Fund. Cross in red.
935 **234** 6s.+5s. pink and violet 15 10
936 10s.+5s. pink and green 15 15
937 50s.+5s. pink & brown 75 50

235 Globe and Flags
236 Centenary Emblem

1963. 1st Anniv of Asian-Oceanic Postal Union.
938 **235** 6s. multicoloured 15 15
939 20s. multicoloured 20 15

1963. Red Cross Centenary. Cross in red.
940 **236** 5s. grey and violet 15 10
941 6s. grey and blue 15 15
942 20s. grey and green 45 20

237 Tinikling (dance)

1963. Folk Dances. Multicoloured.
943 5s. Type **237** 15 15
944 6s. Pandanggo sa Ilaw 15 15
945 10s. Itik-Itik 15 15
946 20s. Singkil 30 30

238 Pres. Macapagal and Philippine Family

1963. President's Social-Economic Programme.
947 **238** 5s. multicoloured 15 15
948 6s. multicoloured 15 15
949 20s. multicoloured 35 20

239 Presidents' Meeting

1963. Visit of President Mateos of Mexico.
950 **239** 6s. multicoloured 15 15
951 30s. multicoloured 45 15

240 Bonifacio and Flag

1963. Birth Cent of Andres Bonifacio (patriot).
952 **240** 5s. multicoloured 15 10
953 6s. multicoloured 15 15
954 25s. multicoloured 35 30

1963. 15th Anniv of Declaration of Human Rights. Sheet No. **MS**677 optd with **UN ADOPTION OF HUMAN RIGHTS 15TH ANNIVERSARY DEC. 10, 1963**, by Philippine Bureau of Printing.
MS955 106 × 92 mm 1·30 1·30

241 Harvester
242 Bamboo Organ, Catholic Church, Las Pinas

1963. Freedom from Hunger.
956 **241** 6s. multicoloured (postage) 15 10
957 30s. multicoloured (air) 60 45
958 50s. multicoloured 95 75

1963. Presidential Sayings (2nd issue). As T **233** but with portrait and saying changed.
959 6s. black and violet 15 10
960 30s. black and green 35 15
PORTRAIT AND SAYING: Pres. Magsaysay, "I believe ...".

1964. Las Pinas Organ Commemoration.
961 **242** 5s. multicoloured 15 10
962 6s. multicoloured 15 15
963 20s. multicoloured 45 20

243 A. Mabini (patriot)
245 S.E.A.T.O. Emblems and Flags

244 Negros Oriental T.B. Pavilion

1964. Birth Centenary of A. Mabini.
964 **243** 6s. gold and violet 15 10
965 10s. gold and brown 15 15
966 30s. gold and green 35 15

1964. Obligatory Tax. T.B. Relief Fund. Cross in red.
967 **244** 5s.+5s. purple 15 10
968 6s.+5s. blue 15 10
969 30s.+5s. brown 45 30
970 70s.+5s. green 90 80

1964. 10th Anniv of S.E.A.T.O.
971 **245** 6s. multicoloured 15 10
972 10s. multicoloured 20 15
973 25s. multicoloured 30 15

246 President signing the Land Reform Code
247 Basketball

1964. Agricultural Land Reform Code. President and inscr at foot in brown, red and sepia.
974 **246** 3s. green (postage) 15 10
975 6s. blue 15 15
976 30s. brown (air) 35 20

1964. Olympic Games, Tokyo. Sport in brown. Perf or imperf.
977 **247** 6s. blue and gold 15 15
978 – 10s. pink and gold 20 15
979 – 20s. yellow and gold 50 20
980 – 30s. green and gold 65 50
SPORTS: 10s. Relay-racing; 20s. Hurdling; 30s. Football.

1965. Presidential Sayings (3rd issue). As T **233** but with portrait and saying changed.
981 6s. black and green 15 15
982 30s. black and purple 35 15
PORTRAIT AND SAYING: Pres. Quirino, "So live ...".

248 Presidents Luebke and Macapagal

1965. Visit of President of German Federal Republic.
983 **248** 6s. multicoloured 15 10
984 10s. multicoloured 20 15
985 25s. multicoloured 35 30

249 Meteorological Emblems
250 Pres. Kennedy

1965. Cent of Philippines Meteorological Services.
986 **249** 6s. multicoloured 15 15
987 20s. multicoloured 15 15
988 50s. multicoloured 60 30

1965. John F. Kennedy (U.S. President) Commemoration.
989 **250** 6s. multicoloured 15 15
990 10s. multicoloured 20 15
991 30s. multicoloured 50 20

251 King Bhumibol and Queen Sirikit, Pres. Macapagal and Wife

1965. Visit of King and Queen of Thailand.
992 **251** 2s. multicoloured 10 10
993 6s. multicoloured 15 15
994 30s. multicoloured 50 20

252 Princess Beatrix and Mrs. Macapagal

1965. Visit of Princess Beatrix of the Netherlands.
995 **252** 2s. multicoloured 10 10
996 6s. multicoloured 15 15
997 10s. multicoloured 20 15

1965. Obligatory Tax. T.B. Relief Fund. Surch.
998 **244** 1s.+5s. on 6s.+5s. 15 10
999 3s.+5s. on 6s.+5s. 20 15

254 Hand holding Cross and Rosary
256 Signing Agreement

1965. 400th Anniv of Philippines Christianisation. Multicoloured.
1000 3s. Type **254** (postage) 15 10
1001 6s. Legaspi-Urdaneta, monument 20 10

1002 30s. Baptism of Filipinos by Father Urdaneta, Cebu (horiz) (48 × 27 mm) (air) 50 30
1003 70s. "Way of the Cross"– ocean map of Christian voyagers' route, Spain to the Philippines (horiz) (48 × 27 mm) 1·30 1·20
MS1004 170 × 105 mm. Nos. 1000/3. Imperf 3·00 3·00

1965. "MAPILINDO" Conference, Manila.
1005 **256** 6s. blue, red and yellow 15 15
1006 10s. multicoloured 15 15
1007 25s. multicoloured 45 20
The above stamps depict Pres. Sukarno of Indonesia, former Pres. Macapagal of the Philippines and Prime Minister Tunku Abdul Rahman of Malaysia.

257 Cyclists and Globe

259 Dr. A. Regidor

1965. 2nd Asian Cycling Championships, Philippines.
1008 **257** 6s. multicoloured 10 10
1009 10s. multicoloured 20 15
1010 25s. multicoloured 45 30

1965. Inauguration of Pres. Marcos and Vice-Pres. Lopez. Nos. 926/7 surch **MARCOS-LOPEZ INAUGURATION DEC. 30, 1965** and value.
1011 **230** 10s. on 6s.+4s. 20 20
1012 – 30s. on 30s.+5s. 50 50

1966. Regidor (patriot) Commemoration.
1013 **259** 6s. blue 15 15
1014 30s. brown 30 20

1966. Presidential Sayings (4th issue). As T **233** but with portrait and saying changed.
1015 6s. black and red 15 10
1016 30s. black and blue 35 20
PORTRAIT AND SAYING: Pres. Aguinaldo, "Have faith ...".

1966. Campaign Against Smuggling. No. 900 optd **HELP ME STOP SMUGGLING Pres. MARCOS.**
1017 6s. blue 20 15

261 Girl Scout

1966. Silver Jubilee of Philippines Girl Scouts.
1018 **261** 3s. multicoloured 15 10
1019 6s. multicoloured 15 15
1020 20s. multicoloured 45 20

262 Pres. Marcos taking Oath

1966. Inauguration (1965) of Pres. Marcos.
1021 **262** 6s. multicoloured 15 15
1022 20s. multicoloured 15 15
1023 30s. multicoloured 30 20

263 Manila Seal and Historical Scenes

1966. Introduction of New Seal for Manila.
1024 **263** 6s. multicoloured 15 15
1025 30s. multicoloured 30 15

264 Bank Facade and 1 peso Coin

265 "Progress"

1966. 50th Anniv of Philippines National Bank. Mult.
1026 6s. Type **264** 15 10
1027 10s. Old and new bank buildings 20 15
MS1028 157 × 70 mm. **265** 70s. multicoloured 1·90 1·90

266 Bank Building

1966. 60th Anniv of Postal Savings Bank.
1029 **266** 6s. violet, yellow & green 15 10
1030 10s. red, yellow and green 20 15
1031 20s. blue, yellow & green 45 20

1966. Manila Summit Conference. Nos. 1021 and 1023 optd **MANILA SUMMIT CONFERENCE 1966 7 NATIONS** and emblem.
1032 **262** 6s. multicoloured 20 15
1033 30s. multicoloured 30 30

1966. Presidential Sayings (5th issue). As T **233** but with portrait and saying changed.
1034 6s. black and brown 15 10
1035 30s. black and blue 35 15
PORTRAIT AND SAYING: Pres. Laurel; "No one can love the Filipinos better ...".

1967. 50th Anniv of Lions International. Nos. 977/80 optd with Lions emblem and **50th ANNIVERSARY LIONS INTERNATIONAL 1967**. Imperf.
1036 **247** 6c. blue and gold 15 15
1037 – 10c. pink and gold 20 15
1038 – 20c. yellow and gold 45 20
1039 – 30c. green and gold 65 65

269 "Succour" (after painting by F. Amorsolo)

1967. 25th Anniv of Battle of Bataan.
1040 **269** 5s. multicoloured 15 10
1041 20s. multicoloured 20 15
1042 2p. multicoloured 2·40 1·30

1967. Nos. 900 and 975 surch.
1043 – 4s. on 6s. blue 15 10
1044 **246** 5s. on 6s. blue 15 10

271 Stork-billed Kingfisher

1967. Obligatory Tax. T.B. Relief Fund. Birds. Multicoloured.
1045 1s.+5s. Type **271** 15 15
1046 5s.+5s. Rufous hornbill 20 20
1047 10s.+5s. Philippine eagle 35 20
1048 30s.+5s. Great-billed parrot 75 50
See also Nos. 1113/16.

272 Gen. MacArthur and Paratroopers landing on Corregidor

1967. 25th Anniv of Battle of Corregidor.
1049 **272** 6s. multicoloured 10 10
1050 5p. multicoloured 4·50 3·75

273 Bureau of Posts Building, Manila

1967. 65th Anniv of Philippines Bureau of Posts.
1051 **273** 4s. multicoloured 20 20
1052 20s. multicoloured 20 15
1053 50s. multicoloured 60 45

274 Escaping from Eruption

1967. Obligatory Tax. Taal Volcano Eruption (1965) (1st issue).
1054 **274** 70s. multicoloured 95 80
For compulsory use on foreign air mail where the rate exceeds 70s. in aid of Taal Volcano Rehabilitation Committee.
See also No. 1071.

1967. Presidential Sayings (6th issue). As T **233** but with portrait and saying changed.
1055 10s. black and blue 15 10
1056 30s. black and violet 35 15
PORTRAIT AND SAYING: Pres. Quezon. "Social justice is far more beneficial ...".

275 "The Holy Family" (Filipino version)

1967. Christmas.
1057 **275** 10s. multicoloured 20 15
1058 40s. multicoloured 50 45

276 Pagoda, Pres. Marcos and Chiang Kai-shek

1967. China–Philippines Friendship.
1059 **276** 5s. multicoloured 10 10
1060 – 10s. multicoloured 15 15
1061 – 20s. multicoloured 20 15
DESIGNS (with portraits of Pres. Marcos and Chiang Kai-shek): 10s. Gateway, Chinese Garden, Rizal Park, Luneta; 20s. Chinese Garden, Rizal Park, Luneta.

277 Ayala Avenue, Manila, Inaugural Ceremony and Rotary Badge

1968. 1st Anniv of Makati Centre Post Office, Manila.
1062 **277** 10s. multicoloured 15 15
1063 20s. multicoloured 20 20
1064 40s. multicoloured 60 60

1968. Surch.
1065 – 5s. on 6s. (No. 981) 15 10
1066 – 5s. on 6s. (No. 1034) 15 10
1067 **244** 10s. on 6s.+5s. 15 10

280 Calderon, Barasoain Church and Constitution

1968. Birth Centenary of Felipe G. Calderon (lawyer and author of Malolos Constitution).
1068 **280** 10s. multicoloured 15 10
1069 40s. multicoloured 60 45
1070 75s. multicoloured 1·20 1·10

281 Eruption

282 "Philcomsat", Earth Station and Globe

1968. Taal Volcano Eruption (1965) (2nd issue).
1071 **281** 70s. multicoloured 95 95

Two issues were prepared by an American Agency under a contract signed with the Philippine postal authority but at the last moment this contract was cancelled by the Philippine Government. In the meanwhile the stamps had been on sale in the U.S.A. but they were never issued in the Philippines and they had no postal validity.
They comprise a set for the Mexican Olympic Games in the values 1, 2, 3 and 15s. postage and 50, 75s., 1, 2p. airmail and a set in memory of J. F. Kennedy and Robert Kennedy in the values 1, 2, 3s. postage and 5, 10p. airmail.

1968. Inauguration of "Philcomsat"–POTC Earth Station, Tanay, Rizal, Luzon.
1072 **282** 10s. multicoloured 20 15
1073 40s. multicoloured 60 45
1074 75s. multicoloured 1·00 90

283 "Tobacco Production" (mural)

1968. Philippines Tobacco Industry.
1075 **283** 10s. multicoloured 15 15
1076 40s. multicoloured 60 50
1077 70s. multicoloured 1·10 90

284 "Kudyapi"

1968. St. Cecilia's Day. Musical Instruments. Mult.
1078 10s. Type **284** 10 10
1079 20s. "Ludag" 10 10
1080 30s. "Kulintangan" 25 20
1081 50s. "Subing" 35 35

285 Concordia College

286 Children singing Carols

1968. Centenary of Concordia Women's College.
1082 **285** 10s. multicoloured 10 10
1083 20s. multicoloured 15 10
1084 70s. multicoloured 50 35

1968. Christmas.
1085 **286** 10s. multicoloured 15 15
1086 40s. multicoloured 50 45
1087 75s. multicoloured 95 80

287 Philippine Tarsier

1969. Philippines Fauna. Multicoloured.
1088 2s. Type **287** 15 15
1089 10s. Tamarau 15 15
1090 20s. Water buffalo 20 20
1091 75s. Greater Malay chevrotain 1·30 1·00

288 President Aguinaldo and Cavite Building

1969. Birth Centenary of President Amilio Aguinaldo.
1092 **288** 10s. multicoloured . . . 20 15
1093 40s. multicoloured . . . 60 35
1094 70s. multicoloured . . . 1·00 80

289 Rotary Emblem and "Bastion of San Andres"

1969. 50th Anniv of Manila Rotary Club.
1095 **289** 10s. mult (postage) . . . 15 15
1096 40s. multicoloured (air) 45 30
1097 75s. multicoloured . . . 95 75

290 Senator C. M. Recto **292** Jose Rizal College

1969. Recto Commemoration.
1098 **290** 10s. purple 15 10

1969. Philatelic Week. No. 1051 optd **PHILATELIC WEEK NOV. 24-30, 1968.**
1099 **273** 4s. multicoloured 20 10

1969. 50th Anniv of Jose Rizal College, Mandaluyong, Rizal.
1100 **292** 10s. multicoloured . . . 15 15
1101 40s. multicoloured . . . 60 45
1102 50s. multicoloured . . . 90 65

1969. 4th National Boy Scout Jamboree, Palayan City. No. 1019 surch **4th NATIONAL BOY SCOUT JAMBOREE PALAYAN CITY–MAY, 1969 5s.**
1103 5s. on 6s. multicoloured . . 20 15

294 Red Cross Emblems and Map **295** Pres. and Mrs. Marcos harvesting Rice

1969. 50th Anniv of League of Red Cross Societies.
1104 **294** 10s. red, blue and grey 15 15
1105 40s. red, blue and cobalt 50 30
1106 75s. red, brown and buff 80 75

1969. "Rice for Progress".
1107 **295** 10s. multicoloured . . . 15 15
1108 40s. multicoloured . . . 50 35
1109 75s. multicoloured . . . 80 75

296 "The Holy Child of Leyte" (statue)

1969. 80th Anniv of Return of the "Holy Child of Leyte" to Tacloban.
1110 **296** 5s. mult (postage) . . . 15 10
1111 10s. multicoloured . . . 15 15
1112 40s. multicoloured (air) 50 35

1969. Obligatory Tax. T.B. Relief Fund. Birds as T **271.**
1113 1s.+5s. Common gold-backed woodpecker . . . 20 15
1114 5s.+5s. Philippine trogon . . 20 15
1115 10s.+5s. Johnstone's (inscr "Mt. Apo") lorikeet . . . 35 20
1116 40s.+5s. Scarlet (inscr "Johnstone's") minivet . . 50 35

297 Bank Building

1969. Inauguration of Philippines Development Bank, Makati, Rizal.
1117 **297** 10s. black, blue and green 15 10
1118 40s. black, purple and green 90 45
1119 75s. black, brown & grn 1·30 95

298 "Philippine Birdwing"

1969. Philippine Butterflies. Multicoloured.
1120 10s. Type **298** 20 15
1121 20s. Tailed jay 30 20
1122 30s. Red Helen 50 30
1123 40s. Birdwing 80 45

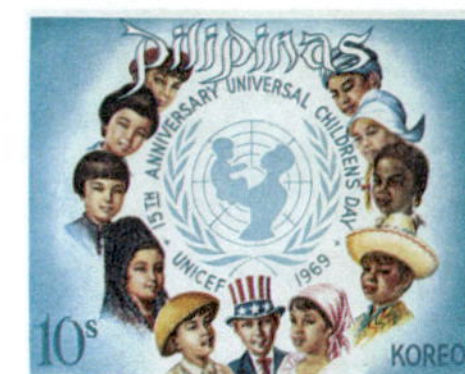

299 Children of the World

1969. 15th Anniv of Universal Children's Day.
1124 **299** 10s. multicoloured . . . 15 10
1125 20s. multicoloured . . . 20 15
1126 30s. multicoloured . . . 20 20

300 Memorial and Outline of Landing **303** Melchora Aquino

301 Cultural Centre

1969. 25th Anniv of U.S. Forces' Landing on Leyte.
1127 **300** 5s. multicoloured 15 10
1128 10s. multicoloured . . . 20 15
1129 40s. multicoloured . . . 50 30

1969. Cultural Centre, Manila.
1130 **301** 10s. blue 15 15
1131 30s. purple 35 20

1969. Philatelic Week. Nos. 943/6 (Folk Dances) optd **1969 PHILATELIC WEEK** or surch also.
1132 5s. multicoloured 15 15
1133 5s. on 6s. multicoloured . . 15 15
1134 10s. multicoloured 20 20
1135 10s. on 20s. multicoloured 20 20

1969. 50th Death Anniv of Melchora Aquino, "Tandang Sora" (Grand Old Woman of the Revolution).
1136 **303** 10s. multicoloured . . . 15 15
1137 20s. multicoloured . . . 20 15
1138 30s. multicoloured . . . 50 20

1969. 2nd-term Inaug of President Marcos. Surch **PASINAYA, IKA-2 PANUNUNGKULAN PANGULONG FERDINAND E. MARCOS DISYEMBRE 30, 1969.**
1139 **262** 5s. on 6s. multicoloured 20 10

305 Ladle and Steel Mills

1970. Iligan Integrated Steel Mills.
1140 **305** 10s. multicoloured . . . 15 15
1141 20s. multicoloured . . . 35 20
1142 30s. multicoloured . . . 65 30

1970. Nos. 900, 962 and 964 surch.
1143 – 4s. on 6s. blue 15 10
1144 **242** 5s. on 6s. multicoloured 15 10
1145 **243** 5s. on 6s. multicoloured 15 10

307 New U.P.U. Headquarters Building

1970. New U.P.U. Headquarters Building, Berne.
1146 **307** 10s. ultramarine, yellow and blue 15 15
1147 30s. blue, yellow and green 60 30

1970. Presidential Sayings (7th issue). As T **233** but with portrait and saying changed.
1148 10s. black and purple . . . 15 10
1149 40s. black and green 35 15
PORTRAIT AND SAYING: Pres. Osmena, "Ante todo el bien de nuestro pueblo" ("The well-being of our nation comes above all").

308 Dona Julia V. de Ortigas and T.B. Society Headquarters

1970. Obligatory Tax. T.B. Relief Fund.
1150 **308** 1s.+5s. multicoloured . . 15 10
1151 5s.+5s. multicoloured . . 20 20
1152 30s.+5s. multicoloured 75 50
1153 70s.+5s. multicoloured 95 65

309 I.C.S.W. Emblem

1970. 15th Int Conference on Social Welfare.
1154 **309** 10s. multicoloured . . . 15 15
1155 20s. multicoloured . . . 30 20
1156 30s. multicoloured . . . 60 20

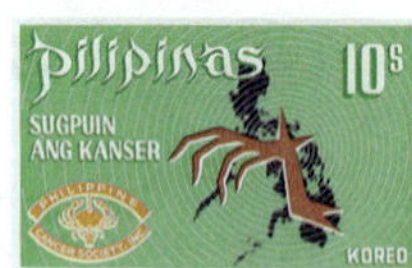

310 "Crab" (after sculpture by A. Calder)

1970. "Fight Cancer" Campaign.
1157 **310** 10s. multicoloured . . . 20 15
1158 40s. multicoloured . . . 45 20
1159 50s. multicoloured . . . 65 35

311 Scaled Tridacna

1970. Sea Shells. Multicoloured.
1160 5s. Type **311** 15 10
1161 10s. Royal spiny oyster . . 15 10
1162 20s. Venus comb murex . . 20 15
1163 40s. Glory-of-the-sea cone 60 35

1970. Nos. 986, 1024 and 1026 surch with new values in figures and words.
1164 **249** 4s. on 6s. 15 10
1165 **263** 4s. on 6s. 15 10
1166 **264** 4s. on 6s. 15 10

313 The "Hundred Islands" and Ox-cart

1970. Tourism (1st series). Multicoloured.
1167 10s. Type **313** 15 15
1168 20s. Tree-house, Pasonanca Park, Zamboanga City . . 20 15
1169 30s. "Filipino" (statue) and sugar plantation, Negros Island 30 30
1170 2p. Calesa (horse-carriage) and Miagao Church, Iloilo . . . . 1·90 1·20
See also Nos. 1186/9, 1192/5 and 1196/9.

314 Map of the Philippines **318** Mariano Ponce

317 Pope Paul VI and Map

1970. Golden Jubilee of Philippine Pharmaceutical Association.
1171 **314** 10s. multicoloured . . . 15 10
1172 50s. multicoloured . . . 75 35

1970. U.P.U./A.O.P.U. Regional Seminar, Manila. No. 938 surch **UPU-AOPU REGIONAL SEMINAR NOV. 23 - DEC. 5, 1970 TEN 10s.**
1173 **235** 10s. on 6s. multicoloured 15 15

1970. Philatelic Week. No. 977 surch **1970 PHILATELIC WEEK 10s TEN.**
1174 **247** 10s. on 6s. brown, blue and gold 15 10

1970. Pope Paul's Visit to the Philippines.
1175 **317** 10s. mult (postage) . . . 15 15
1176 30s. multicoloured . . . 30 20
1177 40s. multicoloured (air) 45 20

1970.
1178 **318** 10s. red 15 10
1179 – 15s. brown 15 10
1180 – 40s. red 35 10
1181 – 1p. blue 95 35
DESIGNS: 15s. Josefa Llanes Escoda; 40s. Gen. Miguel Malvar; 1p. Julian Felipe.

320 "PATA" Horse and Carriage

1971. 20th PATA Conference and Workshop, Manila.
1183 **320** 5s. multicoloured 15 10
1184 10s. multicoloured . . . 15 15
1185 70s. multicoloured . . . 50 35

1971. Tourism (2nd series). Views as T **313.** Multicoloured.
1186 10s. Nayong Pilipino resort 10 10
1187 20s. Fish farm, Iloilo . . . 15 10
1188 30s. Pagsanjan Falls 20 15
1189 5p. Watch-tower, Punta Cruz . . . . 1·80 1·60

321 Emblem and Family

1971. Regional Conference of International Planned Parenthood Federation for South-East Asia and Oceania.
1190 **321** 20s. multicoloured 15 10
1191 40s. multicoloured 20 15

1971. Tourism (3rd series). As T **313**. Mult.
1192 10s. Aguinaldo pearl farm 15 15
1193 20s. Coral-diving, Davao 15 15
1194 40s. Taluksengay Mosque 20 20
1195 1p. Ifugao woman and Banaue rice-terraces 1·60 65

1971. Tourism (4th series). As T **313**. Mult.
1196 10s. Cannon and Filipino vintas, Fort del Pilar 15 15
1197 30s. Magellan's Cross, Cebu City 15 15
1198 50s. "Big Jar", Calamba, Laguna (Rizal's birthplace) 30 20
1199 70s. Mayon Volcano and diesel train 1·60 45

1971. Surch **FIVE 5s.**
1200 **264** 5s. on 6s. multicoloured 15 10

323 G. A. Malcolm (founder) and Law Symbols

1971. 60th Anniv of Philippines College of Law.
1201 **323** 15s. mult (postage) 15 15
1202 1p. multicoloured (air) 80 75

324 Commemorative Seal

1971. 400th Anniv of Manila.
1203 **324** 10s. multicoloured (postage) 15 15
1204 1p. multicoloured (air) 1·20 80

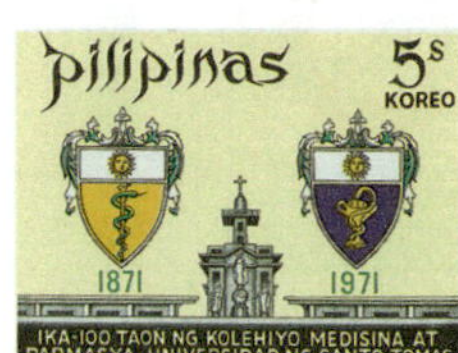

325 Arms of Faculties

1971. Centenaries of Faculties of Medicine and Surgery, and of Pharmacy, Santo Tomas University.
1205 **325** 5s. mult (postage) 15 10
1206 2p. multicoloured (air) 1·60 1·50

1971. University Presidents' World Congress, Manila. Surch **MANILA MCMLXXI CONGRESS OF UNIVERSITY PRESIDENTS 5s FIVE** and emblem.
1207 **266** 5s. on 6s. violet, yellow and green 15 10

327 "Our Lady of Guia"

1971. 400th Anniv of "Our Lady of Guia", Ermita, Manila.
1208 **327** 10s. multicoloured 15 15
1209 75s. multicoloured 60 50

328 Bank and "Customers"

1971. 70th Anniv of First National City Bank.
1210 **328** 10s. multicoloured 15 15
1211 30s. multicoloured 30 20
1212 1p. multicoloured 75 60

1971. Surch in figure and word.
1213 **259** 4s. on 6s. blue 15 10
1214 5s. on 6s. blue 15 10

1971. Philatelic Week. Surch **1971 - PHILATELIC WEEK 5s FIVE**.
1215 **266** 5s. on 6s. violet, yellow and green 15 10

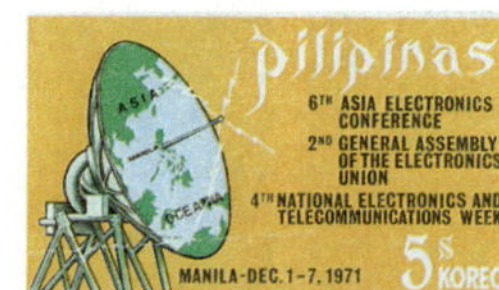

331 Dish Aerial and Events

1972. 6th Asian Electronics Conference, Manila (1971) and Related Events.
1216 **331** 5s. multicoloured 15 10
1217 40s. multicoloured 60 35

332 Fathers Burgos, Gomez and Zamora

1972. Centenary of Martyrdom of Fathers Burgos, Gomez and Zamora.
1218 **332** 5s. multicoloured 10 10
1219 60s. multicoloured 45 45

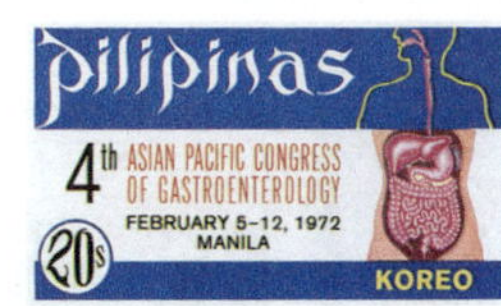

333 Human Organs

1972. 4th Asian–Pacific Gastro-enterological Congress, Manila.
1220 **333** 20s. mult (postage) 20 15
1221 40s. multicoloured (air) 45 35

1972. Surch **5s FIVE**.
1222 **263** 5s. on 6s. multicoloured 15 10

1972. No. O914 with optd **G.O.** obliterated by bars.
1223 50s. violet 45 20

1972. Surch.
1224 **245** 10s. on 6s. multicoloured 15 10
1225 **251** 10s. on 6s. multicoloured 15 10
1226 – 10s. on 6s. black and red (No. 1015) 15 10

336 Memorial Gardens, Manila

1972. Tourism. "Visit Asean Lands" Campaign.
1227 **336** 5s. multicoloured 15 10
1228 50s. multicoloured 90 20
1229 60s. multicoloured 1·20 35

337 "KKK" Flag

1972. Evolution of Philippines' Flag.
1230 **337** 30s. red and blue 30 20
1231 – 30s. red and blue 30 20
1232 – 30s. red and blue 30 20
1233 – 30s. black and blue 30 20
1234 – 30s. red and blue 30 20
1235 – 30s. red and blue 30 20
1236 – 30s. red and blue 30 20
1237 – 30s. red and blue 30 20
1238 – 30s. black, red and blue 30 20
1239 – 30s. yellow, red and blue 30 20
FLAGS: No. 1231, Three "K"'s in pyramid; No. 1232, Single "K"; No. 1233, "K", skull and crossbones; No. 1234, Three "K"'s and sun in triangle; No. 1235, Sun and three "K"'s; No. 1236, Ancient Tagalog "K" within sun; No. 1237, Face in sun; No. 1238, Tricolor; No. 1239, Present national flag—sun and stars within triangle, two stripes.

338 Mabol, Santol and Papaya

1972. Obligatory Tax. T.B. Relief Fund. Fruits. Mult.
1240 1s.+5s. Type **338** 10 10
1241 10s.+5s. Bananas, balimbang and mangosteen 15 15
1242 40s.+5s. Guava, mango, duhat and susongkalabac 30 30
1243 1p.+5s. Orange, pineapple, lanzones and sirhuelas 65 65

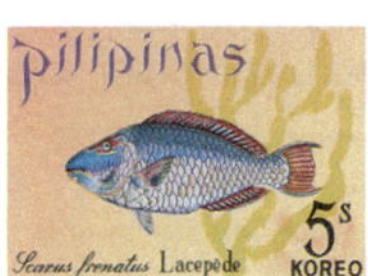

339 Bridled Parrotfish

1972. Fishes. Multicoloured.
1244 5s. Type **339** (postage) 15 10
1245 10s. Klein's butterflyfish 15 10
1246 20s. Moorish idol 20 15
1247 50s. Two-spined angelfish (air) 75 35

340 Bank Headquarters

1972. 25th Anniv of Philippines Development Bank.
1248 **340** 10s. multicoloured 15 10
1249 20s. multicoloured 15 15
1250 60s. multicoloured 60 35

341 Pope Paul VI

1972. 1st Anniv of Pope Paul's Visit to Philippines.
1251 **341** 10s. mult (postage) 10 10
1252 50s. multicoloured 45 35
1253 60s. multicoloured (air) 60 60

1972. Various stamps surch.
1254 **240** 10s. on 6s. (No. 953) 15 10
1255 – 10s. on 6s. (No. 959) 15 10
1256 **250** 10s. on 6s. (No. 989) 15 10

343 "La Barca de Aqueronte" (Hidalgo)

1972. 25th Anniv of Stamps and Philatelic Division, Philippines Bureau of Posts. Filipino Paintings. Multicoloured.
1257 5s. Type **343** 10 10
1258 10s. "Afternoon Meal of the Rice Workers" (Amorsolo) 15 15
1259 30s. "Espana y Filipinas" (Luna) (27 × 60 mm) 20 20
1260 70s. "The Song of Maria Clara" (Amorsolo) 60 60

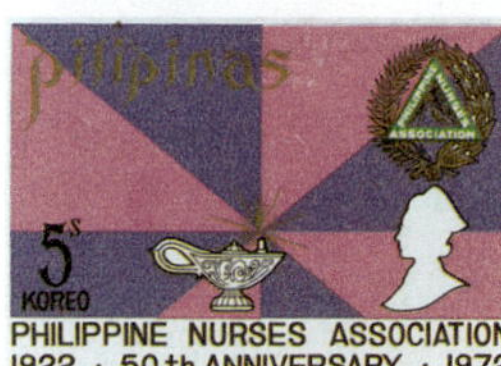

344 Lamp, Emblem and Nurse

1972. 50th Anniv of Philippine Nurses Assn.
1261 **344** 5s. multicoloured 10 10
1262 10s. multicoloured 15 15
1263 70s. multicoloured 45 35

345 Heart on Map

1972. World Heart Month.
1264 **345** 5s. red, green and violet 10 10
1265 10s. red, green and blue 15 10
1266 30s. red, blue and green 20 20

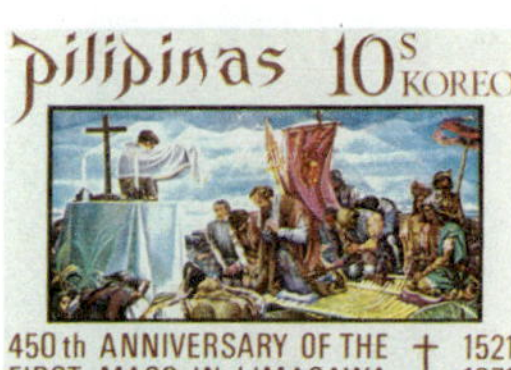

346 "The First Mass" (C. V. Francisco)

1972. 450th Anniv of 1st Mass in Limasawa (1971).
1267 **346** 10s. mult (postage) 15 15
1268 60s. multicoloured (air) 50 45

1972. Asia-Pacific Scout Conference, Manila. Various stamps surch **ASIA PACIFIC SCOUT CONFERENCE NOV, 1972** and value.
1269 **233** 10s. on 6s. (No. 933) 15 10
1270 **240** 10s. on 6s. (No. 953) 15 10
1271 – 10s. on 6s. (No. 981) 15 10

348 Olympic Emblems and Torch

1972. Olympic Games, Munich.
1272 **348** 5s. multicoloured 10 10
1273 10s. multicoloured 15 15
1274 70s. multicoloured 60 45

1972. Philatelic Week. Nos. 950 and 983 surch **1972 PHILATELIC WEEK TEN 10s.**
1275 **239** 10s. on 6s. multicoloured 15 10
1276 **248** 10s. on 6s. multicoloured 15 10

350 Manunggul Burial Jar

1972. Philippine Archaeological Discoveries. Multicoloured.
1277 10s. Type **350** 15 10
1278 10s. Ritual earthenware vessel 15 10
1279 10s. Metal pot 15 10
1280 10s. Earthenware vessel . . 15 10

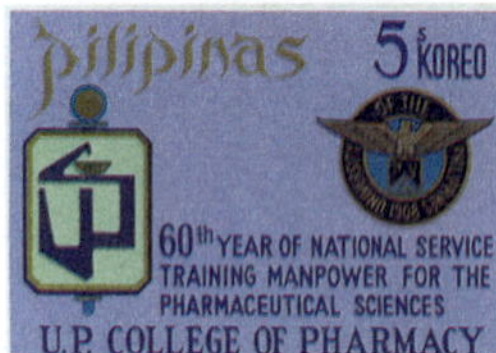

351 Emblems of Pharmacy and University of the Philippines

1972. 60th Anniv of National Training for Pharmaceutical Sciences, University of the Philippines.
1281 **351** 5s. multicoloured 10 10
1282 10s. multicoloured . . . 15 15
1283 30s. multicoloured . . . 20 15

352 "The Lantern-makers" (J. Pineda)

1972. Christmas.
1284 **352** 10s. multicoloured . . . 15 15
1285 30s. multicoloured . . . 20 15
1286 50s. multicoloured . . . 45 35

353 President Roxas and Wife

1972. 25th Anniv of Philippines Red Cross.
1287 **353** 5s. multicoloured 15 10
1288 20s. multicoloured . . . 15 15
1289 30s. multicoloured . . . 20 20

1973. Nos. 948 and 1005 surch **10s**.
1290 **238** 10s. on 6s. multicoloured 15 10
1291 **256** 10s. on 6s. blue. red and yellow 15 10

1973. Presidential Sayings (8th issue). As **T 233** but with portrait and saying changed.
1292 10s. black and bistre 15 10
1293 30s. black and mauve . . . 35 15
PORTRAIT AND SAYING: 10s., 30s. Pres. Garcia, "I would rather be right than successful".

355 University Building

1973. 60th Anniv of St. Louis University, Baguio City.
1294 **355** 5s. multicoloured 10 10
1295 10s. multicoloured . . . 10 10
1296 75s. multicoloured . . . 60 50

356 Col. J. Villamor and Air Battle

1973. Villamor Commemoration.
1297 **356** 10s. multicoloured . . . 15 10
1298 2p. multicoloured . . . 1·30 1·30

1973. Various stamps surch.
1299 **252** 5s. on 6s. multicoloured 15 10
1300 **266** 5s. on 6s. violet, yellow and green 15 10
1301 **318** 15s. on 10s. red (No. O1182) 15 10

359 Actor and Stage Performance

1973. 1st "Third-World" Theatre Festival, Manila.
1302 **359** 5s. multicoloured 10 10
1303 10s. multicoloured . . . 10 10
1304 50s. multicoloured . . . 35 20
1305 70s. multicoloured . . . 60 35

1973. President Marcos's Anti-smuggling Campaign. No. 1017 surch **5s**.
1306 5s. on 6s. blue 15 10

1973. 10th Death Anniv of John F. Kennedy. No. 989 surch **5s**.
1307 5s. on 6s. multicoloured . . 15 10

1973. Compulsory Tax Stamps. T.B. Relief Fund. Nos. 1241/2 surch.
1308 15s.+5s. on 10s.+5s. mult 15 15
1309 60s.+5s. on 40s.+5s. mult 45 45

364 M. Agoncillo (maker of first national flag)

365 Imelda Marcos

1973. 75th Anniv of Philippine Independence.
1310 **363** 15s. multicoloured . . . 15 15
1311 45s. multicoloured . . . 20 20
1312 90s. multicoloured . . . 65 65

1973. Perf or imperf.
1313 – 15s. violet 15 10
1314 **364** 60s. brown 35 35
1315 – 90s. blue 60 30
1316 – 1p.10 blue 75 35
1317 – 1p.50 red 95 80
1318 – 1p.50 brown 95 35
1319 – 1p.80 green . . . . . 1·10 1·00
1320 – 5p. blue . . . . 3·00 3·00
DESIGNS: 15s. Gabriela Silang (revolutionary); 90s. Teodoro Yangco (businessman); 1p.10, Pio Valenzuela (physician); 1p.50 (No. 1317), Pedro Paterno (revolutionary); 1p.50 (No. 1318), Teodora Alonso (mother of Jose Rizal); 1p.80, E. Evangelista (revolutionary); 5p. F. M. Guerrero (writer).
For similar designs see Nos. 1455/8.

363 Proclamation Scenes

1973. Projects Inaugurated by Sra Imelda Marcos.
1321 **365** 15s. multicoloured . . . 15 15
1322 50s. multicoloured . . . 30 30
1323 60s. multicoloured . . . 35 35

366 Malakanyang Palace

1973. Presidential Palace, Manila.
1324 **366** 15s. mult (postage) . . . 15 15
1325 50s. multicoloured . . . 20 20
1326 60s. multicoloured (air) 35 35

367 Interpol Emblem **368** Scouting Activities

1973. 50th Anniv of International Criminal Police Organization (Interpol).
1327 **367** 15s. multicoloured . . . 15 10
1328 65s. multicoloured . . . 45 20

1973. Golden Jubilee of Philippine Boy Scouts. Perf or imperf.
1329 **368** 15s. bistre and green . . 15 15
1330 – 65s. blue and yellow . . 45 30
DESIGN: 65s. Scouts reading brochure.

369 Bank Emblem, Urban and Agricultural Landscapes

1974. 25th Anniv of Central Bank of the Philippines. Multicoloured.
1331 15s. Type **369** 15 10
1332 60s. Bank building, 1949 . . 35 20
1333 1p.50 Bank complex, 1974 95 60

370 "Maria Clara" Costume **373** Map of South-East Asia

1974. Centenary of U.P.U. Philippine Costumes. Multicoloured.
1334 15s. Type **370** 15 15
1335 60s. "Balintawak" 35 20
1336 80s. "Malong" 60 30

1974. Philatelic Week (1973). No. 1303 surch **1973 PHILATELIC WEEK 15s**.
1337 **359** 15s. on 10s. multicoloured 15 10

1974. 25th Anniv of Philippine "Lionism". Nos. 1297 and 1180 surch **PHILIPPINE LIONISM 1949-1974 15s** and Lions emblem.
1338 **356** 15s. on 10s. multicoloured 15 10
1339 – 45s. on 40s. red 20 20

1974. Asian Paediatrics Congress, Manila. Perf or imperf.
1340 **373** 30s. red and blue 20 15
1341 1p. red and green . . . 60 35

374 Gen. Valdes and Hospital

1974. Obligatory Tax. T.B. Relief Fund. Perf or imperf.
1342 **374** 15s.+5s. green and red 15 15
1343 1p.10+5s. blue and red 35 30

1974. Nos. 974, 1024 and 1026 surch.
1344 **246** 5s. on 3s. green 15 10
1345 **263** 5s. on 6s. multicoloured 15 10
1346 **264** 5s. on 6s. multicoloured 15 10

378 W.P.Y. Emblem

1974. World Population Year. Perf or imperf.
1347 **378** 5s. black and orange . . 15 15
1348 2p. blue and green . . . 1·10 60

379 Red Feather Emblem

1974. 25th Anniv of Community Chest Movement in the Philippines. Perf or imperf.
1349 **379** 15s. red and blue 15 15
1350 40s. red and green . . . 20 15
1351 45s. red and brown . . . 35 15

381 Sultan Mohammad Kudarat, Map, Malayan Prau and Order

1975. Sultan Kudarat of Mindanao Commem.
1352 **381** 15s. multicoloured . . . 15 10

382 Association Emblem **383** Rafael Palma

1975. 25th Anniv of Philippine Mental Health Association. Perf or imperf.
1353 **382** 45s. green and orange . . 20 15
1354 1p. green and purple . . 45 30

1975. Birth Centenary of Rafael Palma (educationalist and statesman). Perf or imperf (15s.), perf (30s.).
1355 **383** 15s. green 20 15
1436 30s. brown 15 10

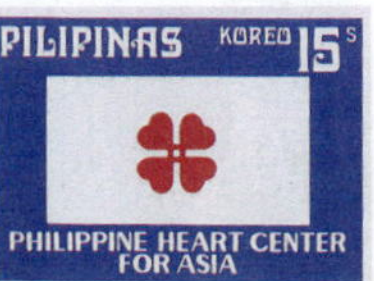

384 Heart Centre Emblem

1975. Inauguration of Philippine Heart Centre for Asia, Quezon City. Perf or imperf.
1356 **384** 15s. red and blue 15 15
1357 50s. red and green . . . 20 20

385 Cadet in Full Dress, and Academy Building

1975. 70th Anniv of Philippine Military Academy.
1358 **385** 15s. multicoloured . . . 15 15
1359 45s. multicoloured . . . 45 20

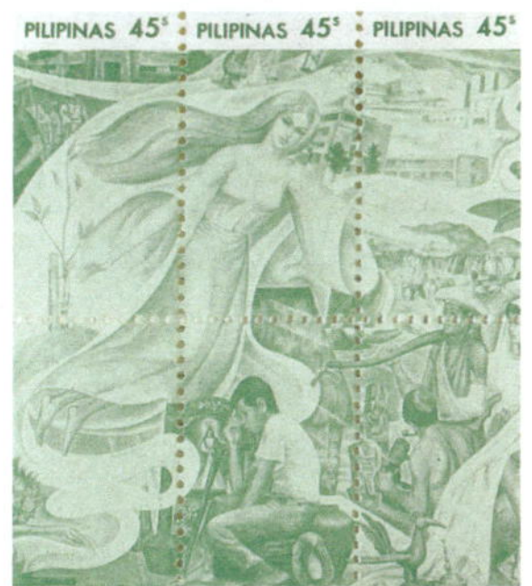

387/9, 392/4 "Helping the Disabled"

1975. 25th Anniv (1974) of Philippines Orthopaedic Association. Perf or imperf.
1360 – 45s. green (inscr at left and top) 20 15
1361 **387** 45s. green 20 15
1362 **388** 45s. green 20 15
1363 **389** 45s. green 20 15
1364 – 45s. green (inscr at top and right) 20 15
1365 – 45s. green (inscr at left and bottom) 20 15
1366 **392** 45s. green 20 15
1367 **393** 45s. green 20 15
1368 **394** 45s. green 20 15
1369 – 45s. green (inscr at bottom and right) . . 20 15
DESIGNS—23 × 30 mm: Nos. 1360, 1364/5, 1369, Details of corners of the mural.
Nos. 1360/9 were issued together, se-tenant, forming a composite design.

1975. Nos. 1153 and 1342/3 surch.
1370 **374** 5s. on 15s.+5s. green and red 10 10
1371 **308** 60s. on 70s.+5s. multicoloured 35 20
1372 **374** 1p. on 1p.10+5s. blue and red 45 30

397 Planting Sapling

398 Jade Vine

1975. Forest Conservation. Multicoloured.
1373 45s. Type **397** 20 15
1374 45s. Sapling and tree-trunks 20 15

1975.
1375 **398** 15s. multicoloured . . . 15 10

399 Imelda Marcos and I.W.Y. Emblem

400 Commission Badge

1975. International Women's Year. Perf or imperf.
1376 **399** 15s. black, blue & dp blue 15 15
1377 80s. black, blue and pink 45 35

1975. 75th Anniv of Civil Service Commission. Perf or imperf.
1378 **400** 15s. multicoloured . . . 15 15
1379 50s. multicoloured . . . 30 20

401 Angat River Barrage

1975. 25th Anniv of International Irrigation and Drainage Commission. Perf or imperf.
1380 **401** 40s. blue and orange . . 20 15
1381 1p.50 blue and mauve 60 45

402 "Welcome to Manila"

403 N. Romualdez (legislator and writer)

1975. Centenary of Hong Kong and Shanghai Banking Corporation's Service in the Philippines.
1382 **402** 1p.50 multicoloured . . 1·30 35

1975. Birth Centenaries. Perf or imperf.
1383 **403** 60s. lilac 20 15
1384 – 90s. mauve 35 15
DESIGN: 90s. General G. del Pilar.

405 Boeing 747-100 Airliner and Martin M-130 Flying Boat

1975. 40th Anniv of First Trans-Pacific China Clipper Airmail Flight. San Francisco–Manila.
1385 **405** 60s. multicoloured . . . 45 20
1386 1p.50 multicoloured . . 1·20 60

1975. Airmail Exn. Nos. 1314 and 1318 optd **AIRMAIL EXHIBITION NOV 22-DEC 9.**
1387 **364** 60s. brown 20 20
1388 – 1p.50 brown 65 65

407 APO Emblem

408 E. Jacinto

1975. 25th Anniv of APO Philatelic Society. Perf or imperf.
1389 **407** 5s. multicoloured 15 15
1390 1p. multicoloured . . . 50 35

1975. Birth Centenary of Emilio Jacinto (military leader). Perf or imperf.
1391 **408** 65s. mauve 20 15

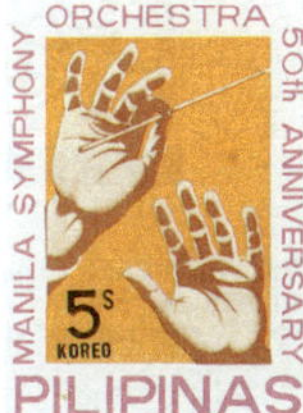

409 San Agustin Church

410 "Conducting" Hands

1975. Holy Year. Churches. Perf or imperf.
1392 **409** 20s. blue 15 15
1393 – 30s. black and yellow . . 15 15
1394 – 45s. red, pink and black 20 15
1395 – 60s. bistre, yellow & black 30 20
DESIGNS—HORIZ: 30s. Morong Church; 45s. Taal Basilica. VERT: 60s. San Sebastian Church.

1976. 50th Anniv of Manila Symphony Orchestra.
1396 **410** 5s. multicoloured 10 10
1397 50s. multicoloured . . . 35 30

411 Douglas DC-3 and DC-10

1976. 30th Anniv of Philippines Airlines (PAL).
1398 **411** 60s. multicoloured . . . 30 15
1399 1p.50 multicoloured . . 1·20 65

412 Felipe Agoncillo (statesman)

413 University Building

1976. Felipe Agoncillo Commemoration.
1400 **412** 1p.60 black 95 20

1976. 75th Anniv of National University.
1401 **413** 45s. multicoloured . . . 20 15
1402 60s. multicoloured . . . 35 20

414 "Foresight Prevents Blindness"

415 Emblem on Book

1976. World Health Day.
1403 **414** 15s. multicoloured . . . 15 10

1976. 75th Anniv of National Archives.
1404 **415** 1p.50 multicoloured . . 80 75

416 College Emblem and University Tower

1976. 50th Anniv of Colleges of Education and Science, Saint Thomas's University.
1405 **416** 15s. multicoloured . . . 15 10
1406 50s. multicoloured . . . 20 20

417 College Building

1976. 50th Anniv of Maryknoll College.
1407 **417** 15s. multicoloured . . . 15 10
1408 1p.50 multicoloured . . 80 60

1976. Olympic Games, Montreal. Surch **15s Montreal 1976 21st OLYMPICS, CANADA** and emblem.
1409 **348** 15s. on 10s. mult 15 10

419 Constabulary Headquarters, Manila

1976. 75th Anniv of Philippine Constabulary. Perf or imperf.
1410 **419** 15s. multicoloured . . . 15 15
1411 60s. multicoloured . . . 35 20

420 Land and Aerial Surveying

1976. 75th Anniv of Lands Bureau.
1412 **420** 80s. multicoloured . . . 25 25

1976. Air. Bicentenary of American Revolution. No. **MS**1004 optd **U.S.A. BICENTENNIAL 1776—1976** and individual stamps surch.
MS1413 170 × 105 mm. 5s. on 3s., 5s. on 6s., 15s. on 30s., 50s. on 70s. Imperf . . . . 3·75 3·75

422 Badges of Banking Organizations

1976. International Monetary Fund and World Bank Joint Board of Governors Annual Meeting, Manila.
1414 **422** 60s. multicoloured . . . 20 20
1415 1p.50 multicoloured . . 80 60

423 Virgin of Antipolo

426 Facets of Education

425 "Going to Church"

1976. 350th Anniv of "Virgin of Antipolo".
1416 **423** 30s. multicoloured . . . 15 15
1417 90s. multicoloured . . . 35 35

1976. Philatelic Week. Surch **1976 PHILATELIC WEEK 30s.**
1418 **355** 30s. on 10s. mult 15 15

1976. Christmas.
1419 **425** 15s. multicoloured . . . 10 10
1420 30s. multicoloured . . . 20 15

1976. 75th Anniv of Philippine Educational System.
1421 **426** 30s. multicoloured . . . 15 15
1422 75s. multicoloured . . . 45 20

1977. Surch.
1423 1p.20 on 1p.10 blue (No. 1316) 60 35
1424 3p. on 5p. blue (No. 1320) 1·30 1·10

428 Jose Rizal

429 Flags, Map and Emblem

1977. Famous Filipinos. Multicoloured.
1425 30s. Type **428** 15 10
1426 2p.30 Dr. Galicano Apacible 95 65

1977. 15th Anniv of Asian–Oceanic Postal Union.
1427 **429** 50s. multicoloured . . . 15 10
1428 1p.50 multicoloured . . 60 45

430 Worker and Cogwheels **431** Commission Emblem

1977. 10th Anniv of Asian Development Bank.
1429 **430** 90s. multicoloured . . . 45 35
1430 2p.30 multicoloured . . 95 80

1977. National Rural Credit Commission.
1431 **431** 30s. multicoloured . . . 15 10

432 Dutch Windmill and First Stamps of The Netherlands and the Philippines

1977. Air. "Amphilex77" International Stamp Exhibition, Amsterdam. Sheet 73 × 90 mm.
MS1432 **432** 7p.50 × 3, multicoloured . . . . 11·00 11·00

433 Solicitor-General's Emblem

1977. 75th Anniv of Office of Solicitor-General.
1433 **433** 1p.65 multicoloured . . 45 20

434 Conference Emblem

1977. World Law Conference, Manila.
1434 **434** 2p.20 multicoloured . . 75 30

435 A.S.E.A.N. Emblem

1977. 10th Anniv of Association of South East Asian Nationals (A.S.E.A.N.).
1435 **435** 1p.50 multicoloured . . 65 35

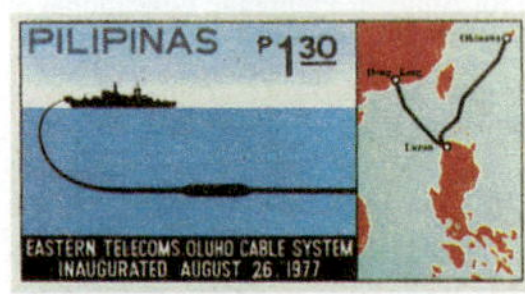

436 Cable Ship "Mercury" and Map

1977. Inauguration of OLUHO Cable (Okinawa–Luzon–Hong Kong).
1437 **436** 1p.30 multicoloured . . 60 35

437 President Marcos

1977. 60th Birthday of President Marcos.
1438 **437** 30s. multicoloured . . . 15 10
1439 2p.30 multicoloured . . 1·00 65

438 People raising Flag **439** Bishop Gregorio Aglipay (founder)

1977. 5th Anniv of "New Society".
1440 **438** 30s. multicoloured . . . 15 10
1441 2p.30 multicoloured . . 1·00 65

1977. 75th Anniv of Aglipayan Church.
1442 **439** 30s. multicoloured . . . 15 10
1443 90s. multicoloured . . . 35 20

440 Bull and early Spanish Stamps

1977. Air. "Espamer 77" International Stamp Exhibition, Barcelona. Sheet 75 × 90 mm.
MS1444 **440** 7p.50 × 3, multicoloured . . . . 15·00 15·00

441 Fokker F.7 Trimotor "General New" and World Map

1977. 50th Anniv of 1st Pan-Am International Air Service.
1445 **441** 2p.30 multicoloured . . 95 60

442 Eight-pointed Star and Children **445** University Badge

444 Scouts and Map of Philippines

1977. Christmas.
1446 **442** 30s. multicoloured . . . 15 10
1447 45s. multicoloured . . . 20 15

1977. Philatelic Week. Surch **90s 1977 PHILATELIC WEEK.**
1448 **407** 90s. on 1p. multicoloured 35 20

1977. National Scout Jamboree.
1449 **444** 30s. multicoloured . . . 50 15

1978. 50th Anniv of Far Eastern University.
1450 **445** 30s. multicoloured . . . 15 10

446 Sipa Player

1978. "Sipa" (Filipino ball game).
1451 **446** 5s. multicoloured 10 10
1452 – 10s. multicoloured . . . 10 10
1453 – 40s. multicoloured . . . 30 15
1454 – 75s. multicoloured . . . 45 20
DESIGNS: Nos. 1452/4, Different players.

Nos. 1451/4 were issued together, se-tenant, forming a composite design.

447 Jose Rizal **448** Arms of Meycauayan

1978.
1455 **447** 30s. blue 15 10
1456 – 30s. mauve 15 10
1457 – 90s. green 20 10
1458 – 1p.20 red 35 15
DESIGNS: No. 1456, Rajah Kalantiaw (Panay chief); 1457, Lope K. Santos ("Father of Filipino grammar"); 1458, Gregoria de Jesus (patriot).

1978. 400th Anniv of Meycauayan.
1459 **448** 1p.05 multicoloured . . 35 20

449 Horse-drawn Mail Cart

1978. "CAPEX 78" International Stamp Exhibition, Toronto. Multicoloured.
1460 2p.50 Type **449** . . . . . 1·10 75
1461 5p. Filipino vinta (sailing canoe) . . . . 3·00 1·90
MS1462 Two sheets, each 90 × 73 mm, each containing 4 × 7p.50. (a) With blue backgrounds; (b) With green backgrounds . . . . 18·00 18·00
DESIGNS—36 × 22 mm : 7p.50 (i) As No. 1461; (ii) As No. 1460; (iii) Early staem locomotive; (iv) Schooner.

450 Andres Bonifacio Monument (Guillermo Tolentino)

1978. Andres Bonifacio Monument.
1463 **450** 30s. multicoloured . . . 15 10

451 Knight, Rook and Globe

1978. World Chess Championship, Baguio City.
1464 **451** 30s. red and violet . . . 15 10
1465 2p. red and violet . . . 60 35

452 Miner

1978. 75th Anniv of Benguet Consolidated Mining Company.
1466 **452** 2p.30 multicoloured . . 1·20 45

453 Pres. Quezon **455** Pres. Osmena

454 Law Association and Conference Emblems

1978. Birth Centenary of Manuel L. Quezon (former President).
1467 **453** 30s. multicoloured . . . 15 10
1468 1p. multicoloured . . . 35 15

1978. 58th Int Law Association Conf, Manila.
1469 **454** 2p.30 multicoloured . . 80 60

1978. Birth Centenary of Sergio Osmena (former President).
1470 **455** 30s. multicoloured . . . 15 10
1471 1p. multicoloured . . . 35 20

456 Map of Cable Route and Cable Ship "Mercury"

1978. Inauguration of Philippines–Singapore Submarine Cable.
1472 **456** 1p.40 multicoloured . . 60 20

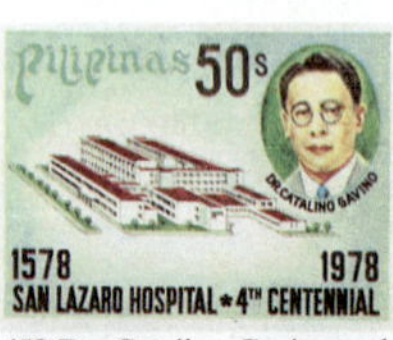

457 Basketball

1978. 8th Men's World Basketball Championship, Manila.
1473 **457** 30s. multicoloured . . . 15 10
1474 2p.30 multicoloured . . 80 60

458 Dr. Catalino Gavino and Hospital

1978. 400th Anniv of San Lazaro Hospital.
1475 **458** 50s. multicoloured . . . 20 10
1476 90s. multicoloured . . . 35 20

459 Nurse vaccinating Child **461** Man on Telephone, Map and Satellite

1978. Global Eradication of Smallpox.
1477 **459** 30s. multicoloured . . . 10 10
1478 1p.50 multicoloured . . 65 35

1978. Philatelic Week. No. 1391 surch **1978 PHILATELIC WEEK 60s.**
1479 **408** 60s. on 65s. mauve . . . 20 10

1978. 50th Anniv of Philippine Long Distance Telephone Company. Multicoloured.
1480 30s. Type **461** 10 10
1481 2p. Woman on telephone and globe 75 50
Nos. 1480/1 were issued together, se-tenant, forming a composite design.

462 Family travelling in Ox-drawn Cart

1978. Decade of the Filipino Child.
1482 **462** 30s. multicoloured . . . 10 10
1483 1p.35 multicoloured . . 60 20

463 Spanish Colonial Church and Arms

1978. 400th Anniv of Agoo Town.
1484 **463** 30s. multicoloured . . . 10 15
1485 45s. multicoloured . . . 15 20

464 Church and Arms

1978. 400th Anniv of Balayan Town.
1486 **464** 30s. multicoloured . . . 15 10
1487 90s. multicoloured . . . 35 15

465 Dr. Sison **466** Family and Houses

1978. Dr. Honoria Acosta Sison (first Filipino woman physician) Commemoration.
1488 **465** 30s. multicoloured . . . 15 10

1978. 30th Anniv of Declaration of Human Rights.
1489 **466** 30s. multicoloured . . . 10 10
1490 3p. multicoloured . . . 1·30 75

467 Melon butterflyfish

1978. Fishes. Multicoloured.
1491 30s. Type **467** 15 10
1492 1p.20 Black triggerfish . . . 45 15
1493 2p.20 Picasso triggerfish . . 80 35
1494 2p.30 Copper-banded butterflyfish 80 45
1495 5p. Atoll butterflyfish ("Chaetodon mertensi") 1·80 1·00
1496 5p. Yellow-faced butterflyfish ("Euxiphipops xanthometapon") . . . . 1·80 1·00

468 Carlos P. Romulo

1979. 80th Anniv of Carlos P. Romulo (1st Asian President of U.N. General Assembly).
1497 **468** 30s. multicoloured . . . 10 10
1498 2p. multicoloured . . . 95 45

469 Cogwheel (Rotary Emblem) **470** Rosa Sevilla de Alvero

1979. 60th Anniv of Manila Rotary Club.
1499 **469** 30s. multicoloured . . . 10 10
1500 2p.30 multicoloured . . 70 25

1979. Birth Centenary of Rosa Sevilla de Alvero (writer and educator).
1501 **470** 30s. mauve 10 10

471 Burning-off Gas and Map

1979. 1st Oil Production. Nido Complex, Palawan.
1502 **471** 30s. multicoloured . . . 15 10
1503 45s. multicoloured . . . 20 10

472 Merrill's Fruit Dove

1979. Birds. Multicoloured.
1504 30s. Type **472** 30 15
1505 1p.20 Brown tit-babbler . . 50 45
1506 2p.20 Mindoro zone-tailed (inscr "Imperial") pigeon 95 45
1507 2p.30 Steere's pitta . . . . 1·00 50
1508 5p. Koch's pitta and red-breasted pitta . . . . . . 2·20 1·20
1509 5p. Great eared nightjar . . 2·20 1·20

473 Association Emblem

1979. 25th Anniv of Association of Special Libraries of the Philippines.
1510 **473** 30s. green, black & yell 15 10
1511 75s. green, black & yell 30 10
1512 1p. green, black & orange 35 20

474 Conference Emblem

1979. 5th U.N. Conference on Trade and Development, Manila.
1513 **474** 1p.20 multicoloured . . 35 15
1514 2p.30 multicoloured . . 95 35

475 Malay Civet

1979. Animals. Multicoloured.
1515 30s. Type **475** 15 10
1516 1p.20 Crab-eating macaque 45 15
1517 2p.20 Javan pig 80 35
1518 2p.30 Leopard cat 80 45
1519 5p. Oriental small-clawed otter . . . . 1·80 1·00
1520 5p. Malayan pangolin . . . 1·80 1·00

476 Dish Aerial

1979. World Telecommunications Day. Mult.
1521 90s. Type **476** 30 10
1522 1p.30 Hemispheres 45 20

477 Mussaenda "Dona Evangelina"

1979. Cultivated Mussaendas. Multicoloured.
1523 30s. Type **477** 15 10
1524 1p.20 "Dona Esperanza" . . 45 15
1525 2p.20 "Dona Hilaria" . . . 80 35
1526 2p.30 "Dona Aurora" . . . 80 45
1527 5p. "Gining Imelda" . . . . 1·80 1·00
1528 5p. "Dona Trining" . . . . 1·80 1·00

478 Manila Cathedral

1979. 400th Anniv of Archdiocese of Manila.
1529 **478** 30s. multicoloured . . . 15 10
1530 75s. multicoloured . . . 20 10
1531 90s. multicoloured . . . 35 20

479 "Bagong Lakas" (patrol boat)

1979. Philippine Navy Foundation Day.
1532 **479** 30s. multicoloured . . . 20 10
1533 45s. multicoloured . . . 30 15

1979. Air. 1st Scout Philatelic Exhibition and 25th Anniv of 1st National Jamboree. Surch **1ST SCOUT PHILATELIC EXHIBITION JULY 4.14, 1979 QUEZON CITY AIRMAIL 90s.**
1534 **188** 90s. on 6c.+4c. red on yellow 30 30
MS1535 171 × 90 mm. Nos. 823, 825/8 each surch **50s.** . . . . . 2·75 2·75

481 Drug Addict breaking Manacles

1979. "Fight Drug Abuse" Campaign.
1536 **481** 30s. multicoloured . . . 15 10
1537 90s. multicoloured . . . 35 15
1538 1p.05 multicoloured . . 45 20

482 Afghan Hound

1979. Cats and Dogs. Multicoloured.
1539 30s. Type **482** 10 10
1540 90s. Tabby cats 35 15
1541 1p.20 Dobermann pinscher 45 20
1542 2p.20 Siamese cats 80 20
1543 2p.30 German shepherd dog 95 80
1544 5p. Chinchilla cats . . . . 1·80 95

483 Children flying Kites

1979. International Year of the Child. Paintings by Rod Dayao. Multicoloured.
1545 15s. Type **483** 10 10
1546 20s. Boys fighting with catapults 15 10
1547 25s. Girls dressing-up . . . 15 15
1548 1p.20 Boy playing policeman 35 20

484 Hands holding Emblems

1979. 80th Anniv of Methodism in the Philippines.
1549 **484** 30s. multicoloured . . . 15 10
1550 1p.35 multicoloured . . 45 15

485 Anniversary Medal and 1868 Coin

1979. 50th Anniv of Philippine Numismatic and Antiquarian Society.
1551 **485** 30s. multicoloured . . . 15 10

486 Concorde over Manila and Paris

1979. 25th Anniv of Air France Service to the Philippines. Multicoloured.
1552 1p.05 Type **486** 50 20
1553 2p.20 Concorde over monument . . . . 1·30 60

1979. Philatelic Week. Surch **1979 PHILATELIC WEEK 90s.**
1554 **412** 90s. on 1p.60 black . . . 35 15

488 "35" and I.A.T.A. Emblem

1979. 35th Annual General Meeting of International Air Transport Association, Manila.
1555 **488** 75s. multicoloured . . . 30 15
1556 2p.30 multicoloured . . 95 65

489 Bureau of Local Government Emblem **490** Christmas Greetings

1979. Local Government Year.
1557 **489** 30s. multicoloured . . . 15 15
1558 45s. multicoloured . . . 20 65

1979. Christmas. Multicoloured.
1559 30s. Type **490** 15 10
1560 90s. Stars 45 30

491 Rheumatism Victim

1980. 4th Congress of Southeast Asia and Pacific Area League Against Rheumatism, Manila.
1561 **491** 30s. multicoloured . . . 15 10
1562 90s. multicoloured . . . 50 20

492 Birthplace and MacArthur Memorial Foundation

1980. Birth Centenary of General Douglas MacArthur (U.S. Army Chief of Staff). Mult.
1563 30s. Type **492** 15 10
1564 75s. General MacArthur . . 35 15
1565 2p.30 Hat, pipe and glasses 1·30 75
MS1566 76 × 76 mm. 5p. Landing in the Philippines (horiz). Imperf 3·00 2·50

493 Columbus and Emblem

495 Tirona, Benitez and University

494 Soldiers and Academy Emblem

1980. 75th Anniv of Knights of Columbus Organization in Philippines.
1567 **493** 30s. multicoloured . . . 15 10
1568 1p.35 multicoloured . . 80 45

1980. 75th Anniv of Philippine Military Academy.
1569 **494** 30s. multicoloured . . . 15 10
1570 1p.20 multicoloured . . 75 30

1980. 60th Anniv of Philippine Women's University.
1571 **495** 30s. multicoloured . . . 15 10
1572 1p.05 multicoloured . . 65 30

496 Boats and Burning City

1980. 75th Anniv of Rotary International. Details of painting by Carlos Francisco. Multicoloured.
1573 30s. Type **496** 15 10
1574 30s. Priest with cross, swordsmen and soldier . . 15 10
1575 30s. "K K K" flag and group around table . . . 15 10
1576 30s. Man in midst of spearmen and civilian scenes 15 10
1577 30s. Reading the Constitution, soliders and U.S. and Philippine flags 15 10
1578 2p.30 Type **496** . . . . . 1·30 60
1579 2p.30 As No. 1574 . . . . 1·30 60
1580 2p.30 As No. 1575 . . . . 1·30 60
1581 2p.30 As No. 1576 . . . . 1·30 60
1582 2p.30 As No. 1577 . . . . 1·30 60
Nos. 1573/7 and 1578/82 were issued together in se-tenant strips of five, each strip forming a composite design.

497 Mosque and Koran

498 Hand stubbing out Cigarette

1980. 600th Anniv of Islam in the Philippines.
1583 **497** 30s. multicoloured . . . 15 10
1584 1p.30 multicoloured . . 75 30

1980. World Health Day. Anti-smoking Campaign.
1585 **498** 30s. multicoloured . . . 15 10
1586 75s. multicoloured . . . 45 20

499 Scouting Activities and Badge

1980. 40th Anniv of Girl Scouting in the Philippines.
1587 **499** 30s. multicoloured . . . 15 10
1588 2p. multicoloured . . . 65 30

500 Jeepney

502 Association Emblem

1980. Philippine Jeepneys (decorated jeeps). Multicoloured.
1589 30s. Type **500** 15 10
1590 1p.20 Side view of Jeepney 65 30

1980. 82nd Anniv of Independence. Surch **PHILIPPINE INDEPENDENCE 82ND ANNIVERSARY 1898 1980.**
1591 **412** 1p.35 on 1p.60 black . . 80 45
1592 1p.50 on 1p.80 green (No. 1319) . . . . . 1·00 50

1980. 7th General Conference of International Association of Universities, Manila.
1593 **502** 30s. multicoloured . . . 15 10
1594 2p.30 multicoloured . . 1·30 1·30

503 Map and Emblems

504 Filipinos and Emblem

1980. 46th Congress of International Federation of Library Associations and Institutions, Manila.
1595 **503** 30s. green and black . . 20 10
1596 75s. blue and black . . 45 20
1597 2p.30 red and black . . 1·50 80

1980. 5th Anniv of Kabataang Barangay (national council charged with building the "New Society").
1598 **504** 30s. multicoloured . . . 20 10
1599 40s. multicoloured . . . 20 15
1600 1p. multicoloured . . . 65 30

1980. Nos. 1433, 1501, 1536, 1557 and 1559 surch.
1601 **470** 40s. on 30s. mauve . . . 20 10
1602 **481** 40s. on 30s. multicoloured 20 10
1603 **489** 40s. on 30s. multicoloured 20 10
1604 **490** 40s. on 30s. multicoloured 20 10
1605 **433** 2p. on 1p.65 mult . . . 1·30 65

506 Sunset, Filipino Vinta and Conference Emblem

1980. World Tourism Conference, Manila.
1606 **506** 30s. multicoloured . . . 20 15
1607 2p.30 multicoloured . . 1·40 80

507 Magnifying Glass and Stamps

508 U.N. Headquarters and Philippines Flag

1980. Postage Stamp Day.
1608 **507** 40s. multicoloured . . . 20 15
1609 1p. multicoloured . . . 65 30
1610 2p. multicoloured . . . 1·30 65

1980. 35th Anniv of U.N.O.
1611 40s. Type **508** 30 15
1612 3p.20 U.N. Headquarters and U.N. and Philippines flags . . . . 1·90 1·30

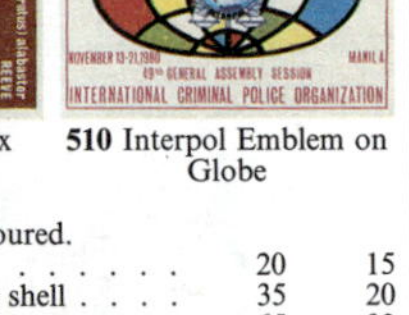

509 Alabaster Murex

510 Interpol Emblem on Globe

1980. Shells. Multicoloured.
1613 40s. Type **509** 20 15
1614 60s. Giant frog shell 35 20
1615 1p.20 Zambo's murex . . . 65 30
1616 2p. Pallid carrier shell . . . 1·30 60

1980. 49th General Assembly of Interpol, Manila.
1617 **510** 40s. multicoloured . . . 20 10
1618 1p. multicoloured . . . 65 30
1619 3p.20 multicoloured . . 2·10 1·30

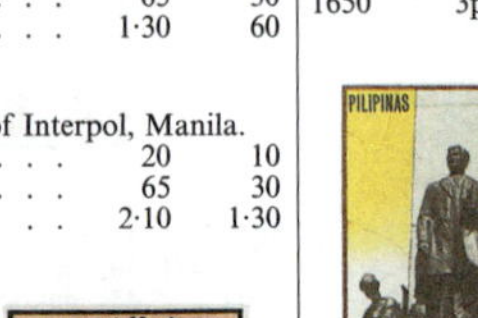

511 University and Faculty Emblems

513 Christmas Tree and Presents

1980. 75th Anniv of Central Philippine University. Multicoloured, background colour given.
1620 **511** 40s. blue 30 10
1621 3p.20 green . . . . . . 1·20 1·30

1980. Philatelic Week. No. 1377 surch **1980 PHILATELIC WEEK P1.20.**
1622 **399** 1p.20 on 80s. black, blue and pink 60 30

1980. Christmas.
1623 **513** 40s. multicoloured . . . 20 10

1981. Various stamps surch.
1624 **244** 10s. on 6s.+5s. blue . . 15 10
1625 **462** 10s. on 30s. mult 10 10
1626 **408** 40s. on 65s. mauve . . . 20 10
1627 **458** 40s. on 90s. mult 20 10
1628 **481** 40s. on 90s. mult 20 10
1629 – 40s. on 90s. mult (No. 1560) 20 10
1630 **448** 40s. on 1p.05 mult . . . 20 10
1631 **462** 40s. on 1p.35 mult . . . 20 15
1632 **399** 85s. on 80s. black, blue and pink 50 30
1633 **408** 1p. on 65s. mauve . . . 75 30
1634 **401** 1p. on 1p.50 blue and mauve 75 30
1635 **422** 1p. on 1p.50 mult . . . 60 20
1636 – 1p.20 on 1p.50 brown (No. 1318) 75 35
1637 **433** 1p.20 on 1p.65 mult . . 75 35
1638 – 1p.20 on 1p.80 green (No. 1319) 75 35
1639 **401** 2p. on 1p.50 blue and mauve . . . . 1·30 60
1640 **434** 3p.20 on 2p.20 mult . . 1·90 1·00

1981. 30th Anniv of APO Philatelic Society. Surch **NOV. 30, 1980 APO PHILATELIC SOCIETY PEARL JUBILEE 40s.**
1641 **455** 40s. on 30s. mult 20 10

516 Von Stephan and U.P.U. Emblem

1981. 150th Birth Anniv of Heinrich von Stephan (founder of U.P.U.).
1642 **516** 3p.20 multicoloured . . 1·90 95

1981. Girl Scouts Camp. No. 1589 surch **GSP RJASIA-PACIFIC REGIONAL CAMP PHILIPPINES DECEMBER 23, 1980 40s.**
1643 **500** 40s. on 30s. mult 20 10

518 Pope John Paul II

519 Parliamentary Debate

1981. Papal Visit. Multicoloured.
1644 90s. Type **518** 50 20
1645 1p.20 Pope and cardinals . . 65 30
1646 2p.30 Pope blessing crowd (horiz) . . . . 1·30 65
1647 3p. Pope and Manila Cathedral (horiz) . . . . 1·60 80
MS1648 75 × 91 mm. 7p.50 Pope and map of Philippines . . . . . . 6·00 3·00

1981. Interparliamentary Union Meeting, Manila.
1649 **519** 2p. multicoloured . . . 1·40 60
1650 3p.20 multicoloured . . 1·90 1·00

520 Monument

521 President Aguinaldo's Car

1981. Jose Rizal Monument, Luneta Park.
1651 **520** 40s. black, yellow & brn 20 10

1981. 50th Anniv of Philippine Motor Association. Multicoloured.
1652 40s. Type **521** 20 10
1653 40s. 1930 model car 20 10
1654 40s. 1937 model car 20 10
1655 40s. 1937 model car (different) 20 10

522 Bubble Coral

1981. Corals. Multicoloured.
1656 40s. Type **522** 20 10
1657 40s. Branching corals . . . 20 10
1658 40s. Brain coral 20 10
1659 40s. Table coral 20 10

523 President Marcos and Flag

1981. Inauguration of President Marcos. Perf or imperf.
1660 **523** 40s. multicoloured . . . 20 10
MS1661 78 × 78 mm. 5p. As No. 1660 but design smaller with inscriptions below. Imperf 3·00 1·30

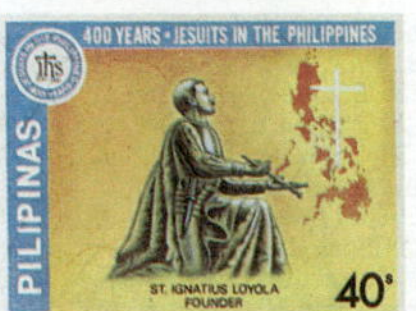

524 St. Ignatius de Loyola (founder)

1981. 400th Anniv of Jesuits in the Philippines. Mult.
1662 40s. Type **524** 20 10
1663 40s. Dr. Jose P. Rizal and Intramuros Ateneo 20 10
1664 40s. Father Frederico Faura (director) and Manila Observatory 20 10
1665 40s. Father Saturnino Urios (missionary) and map of Mindanao 20 10
MS1666 89 × 89 mm. As Nos. 1662/5 but smaller. Imperf (sold at 2p.) 2·20 75

525 F. R. Castro

526 Pres. Ramon Magsaysay

1981. Chief Justice Fred Ruiz Castro.
1667 **525** 40s. multicoloured 20 10

1981.
1668 – 1p. brown and black 65 30
1669 **526** 1p.20 brown and black 75 35
1670 – 2p. purple and black 1·40 60
DESIGNS: 1p. General Gregorio del Pilar; 2p. Ambrosio R. Bautista.
See also Nos. 1699/1704, 1807 etc and 2031/3.

527 Man in Wheelchair

528 Early Filipino Writing

1981. International Year of Disabled Persons.
1671 **527** 40s. multicoloured 30 15
1672 3p.20 multicoloured 1·90 1·00

1981. 24th International Red Cross Conference.
1673 **528** 40s. black, red and bistre 15 10
1674 2p. black and red 1·30 50
1675 3p.20 black, red and mauve 1·90 90

529 Isabel II Gate, Manila

1981.
1676 **529** 40s. black 20 10

530 Concert in Park

1981. Opening of Concert at Park 200.
1677 **530** 40s. multicoloured 20 10

1981. Philatelic Week. No. 1435 surch **P120 1981 PHILATELIC WEEK**.
1678 **435** 1p.20 on 1p.50 mult 75 35

532 Running

1981. 11th South-east Asian Games, Manila.
1679 **532** 40s. yellow, green & brn 20 10
1680 – 1p. multicoloured 75 30
1681 – 2p. multicoloured 1·50 60
1682 – 2p.30 multicoloured 1·50 65
1683 – 2p.80 multicoloured 1·80 80
1684 – 3p.20 violet and blue 1·90 1·00
DESIGNS: 1p. Cycling; 2p. President Marcos and Juan Antonio Samaranch (president of International Olympic Committee); 2p.30, Football; 2p.80, Shooting; 3p.20, Bowling.

533 Manila Film Centre

1982. Manila International Film Festival. Mult.
1685 40s. Type **533** 30 10
1686 2p. Front view of trophy 1·50 60
1687 3p.20 Side view of trophy 1·90 1·00

534 Carriedo Fountain

1982. Centenary of Manila Metropolitan Waterworks and Sewerage System.
1688 **534** 40s. blue 20 10
1689 1p.20 brown 75 35

535 Lord Baden-Powell (founder)

537 President Marcos presenting Sword of Honour

536 Embroidered Banner

1982. 75th Anniv of Boy Scout Movement. Mult.
1690 40s. Type **535** 20 10
1691 2p. Scout 1·50 60

1982. 25th Anniv of Children's Museum and Library Inc. Multicoloured.
1692 40s. Type **536** 20 10
1693 1p.20 Children playing 75 35

1982. Military Academy.
1694 **537** 40s. multicoloured 20 15
1695 1p. multicoloured 75 30

538 Soldier and Memorial

1982. Bataan Day.
1696 **538** 40s. multicoloured 20 10
1697 – 2p. multicoloured 1·50 60
MS1698 76 × 76 mm. 3p.20 purple and black. Imperf 2·20 1·60
DESIGNS: 2p. Doves and rifles; 3p.20, Field gun and flag.

1982. Portraits. As T **526**.
1699 40s. blue 20 10
1700 1p. red 75 30
1701 1p.20 brown 75 35
1702 2p. mauve 1·30 60
1703 2p.30 purple 1·50 60
1704 3p.20 blue 1·90 1·00
DESIGNS: 40s. Isabelo de los Reyes (founder of first workers' union); 1p. Aurora Aragon Quezon (social worker and former First Lady); 1p.20, Francisco Dagohoy; 2p. Juan Sumulong (politician); 2p.30, Professor Nicanor Abelardo (composer); 3p.20, General Vicente Lim.
For these designs in other values, see Nos. 1811/15.

539 Worker with Tower Award

1982. Tower Awards (for best "Blue Collar" Workers). Multicoloured.
1705 40s. Type **539** (inscr "MANGGAGAWA") 20 10
1705d 40s. Type **539** (inscr "MANGAGAWA") 60 10
1706 1p.20 Cogwheel and tower award (inscr "MANGGAGAWA") 75 35
1706b 1p.20 As No. 1706 but inscr "Mangagawa" 1·25 20

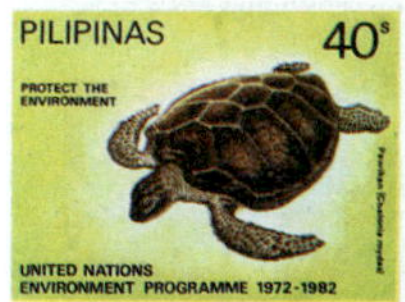

541 Green Turtle

1982. 10th Anniv of United Nations Environment Programme. Multicoloured.
1707 40s. Type **541** 30 15
1708 3p.20 Philippine eagle 2·75 1·00

542 K.K.K. Emblem

1982. Inauguration of Kilusang Kabuhayan at Kaunlaran (national livelihood movement).
1709 **542** 40s. green, light green and black 20 10
1816 60s. green, light green and black 15 15
1817 60s. green, red and black 15 15

543 Chemistry Apparatus and Emblem

1982. 50th Anniv of Adamson University.
1710 **543** 40s. multicoloured 20 10
1711 1p.20 multicoloured 75 35

544 Dr. Fernando G. Calderon and Emblems

1982. 75th Anniv of College of Medicine, University of the Philippines.
1712 **544** 40s. multicoloured 30 15
1713 3p.20 multicoloured 1·90 1·00

545 President Marcos

546 Hands supporting Family

1982. 65th Birthday of President Ferdinand Marcos.
1714 **545** 40s. multicoloured 20 10
1715 3p.20 multicoloured 1·90 1·00
MS1716 76 × 76 mm. Nos. 1714/15. Imperf 2·50 1·60

1982. 25th Anniv of Social Security System.
1717 **546** 40s. black, orange & blue 20 10
1718 1p.20 black, orange and green 75 35

547 Emblem and Flags forming Ear of Wheat

1982. 15th Anniv of Association of South East Asian Nations.
1719 **547** 40s. multicoloured 20 10

548 St. Theresa of Avila

1982. 400th Death Anniv of St. Theresa of Avila. Multicoloured.
1720 40s. Type **548** 20 10
1721 1p.20 St. Theresa and map of Europe, Africa and Asia 75 35
1722 2p. As 1p.20 1·50 60

549 St. Isabel College

1982. 350th Anniv of St. Isabel College.
1723 **549** 40s. multicoloured 20 15
1724 1p. multicoloured 75 30

550 President Marcos signing Decree and Tenant Family

1982. 10th Anniv of Tenant Emancipation Decree.
1725a **550** 40s. green, brown and black (37 × 27 mm) 20 10
1726 40s. green, brown and black (32 × 22½ mm) 20 10

551 "Reading Tree"

1982. Literacy Campaign.
1727 **551** 40s. multicoloured 20 10
1728 2p.30 multicoloured 1·50 60

552 Helmeted Heads

1982. 43rd World Congress of Skal Clubs, Manila.
1729 40s. Type **552** 20 10
1730 2p. Head in feathered head-dress 1·50 60

553 Dancers with Parasols

1982. 25th Anniv of Bayanihan Folk Arts Centre. Multicoloured.
1731 40s. Type **553** 20 10
1732 2p.80 Dancers (different) . . 1·80 80

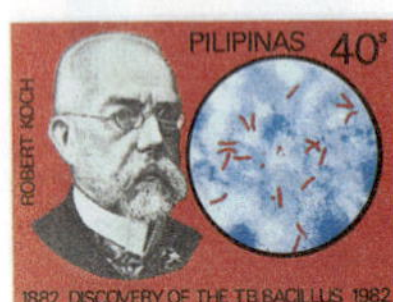

554 Dr. Robert Koch and Bacillus

1982. Cent of Discovery of Tubercule Bacillus.
1733 **554** 40s. red, blue and black 20 10
1734 2p.80 multicoloured . . 1·80 80

555 Father Christmas in Sleigh

1982. Christmas.
1735 **555** 40s. multicoloured . . . 20 15
1736 1p. multicoloured . . . 75 30

556 Presidential Couples and Flags

1982. State Visit of Pres. Marcos to United States.
1737 **556** 40s. multicoloured . . . 15 15
1738 3p.20 multicoloured . . 1·30 90
MS1739 76×75 mm. Nos. 1737/8. Imperf . . . . 2·75 1·30

557 Woman with Sewing Machine
559 Eulogio Rodriguez

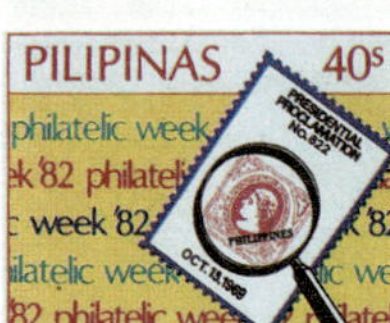

558 Stamp and Magnifying Glass

1982. U.N. World Assembly on Ageing.
1740a **557** 1p.20 green and orange 75 35
1741a – 2p. pink and blue . . . 1·50 60
DESIGN: 2p. Man with carpentry tools.

1983. Philatelic Week.
1742 **558** 40s. multicoloured . . . 20 10
1743 1p. multicoloured . . . 45 30

1983. Birth Centenary of Eulogio Rodriguez (former President of Senate).
1744a **559** 40s. multicoloured . . 20 10
1745 1p.20 multicoloured . . 75 35

560 Symbolic Figure and Film Frame

1983. Manila International Film Festival.
1746a **560** 40s. multicoloured . . . 20 10
1747a 3p.20 multicoloured . . 1·50 95

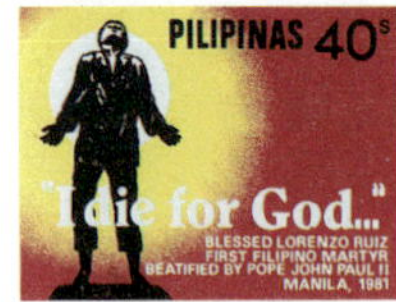

561 Monument

1983. 2nd Anniv of Beatification of Lorenzo Ruiz.
1748 **561** 40s. yellow, red and black 20 10
1749 1p.20 multicoloured . . 75 35

562 Early Printing Press

1983. 390th Anniv of First Local Printing Press.
1750 **562** 40s. green and black . . 20 10

563 Emblem and Ship

1983. 25th Anniv of International Maritime Organization.
1751 **563** 40s. red, black and blue 20 10

1983. 7th National Scout Jamboree. No. 1709 optd **7TH BSP NATIONAL JAMBOREE 1983**.
1752 **542** 40s. green, light green and black 20 10

1983. Nos. 1360/9 surch **40s**.
1753 – 40s. on 45c. green . . . 20 10
1754 **387** 40s. on 45c. green . . . 20 10
1755 **388** 40s. on 45c. green . . . 20 10
1756 **389** 40s. on 45c. green . . . 20 10
1757 – 40s. on 45c. green . . . 20 10
1758 – 40s. on 45c. green . . . 20 10
1759 **392** 40s. on 45c. green . . . 20 10
1760 **393** 40s. on 45c. green . . . 20 10
1761 **394** 40s. on 45c. green . . . 20 10
1762 – 40s. on 45c. green . . . 20 10

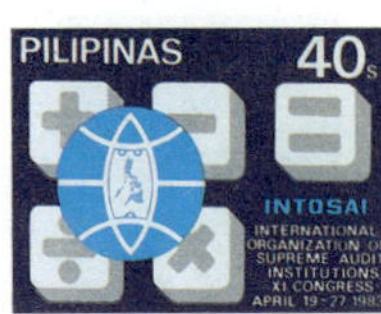

566 Calculator Keys

1983. 11th International Organization of Supreme Audit Institutions Congress.
1763 **566** 40s. blue, light blue and silver 20 10
1764 – 2p.80 multicoloured . . 1·80 80
MS1765 77×76 mm. Nos. 1763/4. Imperf . . . . 2·20 1·50
DESIGN: 2p.80, Congress emblem.

567 Smiling Children
568 Detail of Statue

1983. 75th Anniv of Philippine Dental Association.
1766 **567** 40s. green, mauve & brn 20 15

1983. 75th Anniv of University of the Philippines.
1767 **568** 40s. brown and green . . 20 15
1768 – 1p.20 multicoloured . . 65 30
DESIGN: 1p.20, Statue and diamond.

569 Yasuhiro Nakasone and Pres. Marcos

1983. Visit of Japanese Prime Minister.
1769 **569** 40s. multicoloured . . . 20 15

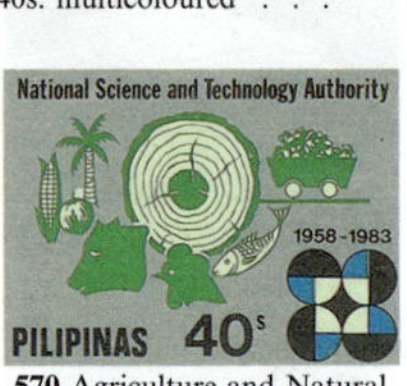

570 Agriculture and Natural Resources

1983. 25th Anniv of National Science and Technology Authority. Multicoloured.
1770 40s. Type **570** 30 15
1771 40s. Heart, medical products and food (Health and nutrition) 30 15
1772 40s. Industrial complex and air (Industry and energy) 30 15
1773 40s. House, scientific equipment and book (Sciences and social science) 30 15

571 Globes and W.C.Y. Emblem

1983. World Communication Year.
1774 **571** 3p.20 multicoloured . . 1·90 90

572 Postman

1983. Bicent of Philippine Postal System.
1775 **572** 40s. multicoloured . . . 20 15

573 Woman with Tambourine
575 Woman casting Vote

574 University Activities

1983. Christmas. Multicoloured.
1776 40s. Type **573** 20 15
1777 40s. Man turning spit (left side) 20 15
1778 40s. Pig on spit 20 15
1779 40s. Man turning spit (right side) 20 15
1780 40s. Man with guitar . . . 20 15
MS1781 153×77 mm. Nos. 1776/80. Imperf . . . . 1·80 1·80
Nos. 1776/80 were issued together, se-tenant, forming a composite design.

1983. 50th Anniv of Xavier University.
1782 **574** 40s. multicoloured . . . 20 15
1783 60s. multicoloured . . . 35 15

1983. 50th Anniv of Female Suffrage.
1784 **575** 40s. multicoloured . . . 20 15
1785 60s. multicoloured . . . 35 15

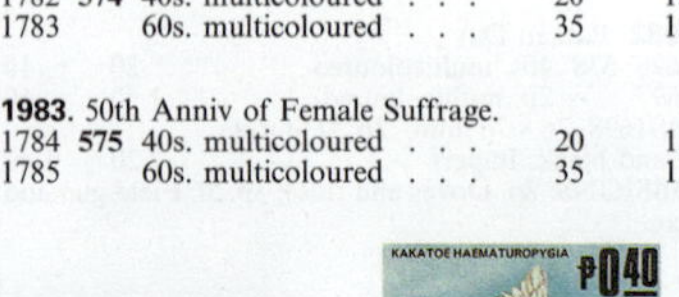

576 Workers
578 Red-vented Cockatoo

577 Cutting Stamp from Envelope

1983. 50th Anniv of Ministry of Labour and Employment.
1786 **576** 40s. multicoloured . . . 20 15
1787 60s. multicoloured . . . 35 15

1983. Philatelic Week. Multicoloured.
1788 50s. Type **577** 45 15
1789 50s. Sorting stamps 45 15
1790 50s. Soaking stamps 45 15
1791 50s. Hinging stamp 45 15
1792 50s. Mounting stamp in album 15 15

1984. Parrots. Multicoloured.
1793 40s. Type **578** 60 30
1794 2p.30 Guaiabero 80 30
1795 2p.80 Mountain racket-tailed parrot 95 35
1796 3p.20 Great-billed parrot . . 1·20 35
1797 3p.60 Muller's parrot . . . 1·50 75
1798 5p. Philippine hanging parrot . . . . 1·30 65

579 Princess Tarhata Kiram
580 Nun and Congregation

1984. 5th Death Anniv of Princess Tarhata Kiram.
1799 **579** 3p. deep green, green and red 75 30

1984. 300th Anniv of Religious Congregation of the Virgin Mary.
1800 **580** 40s. multicoloured . . . 15 15
1801 60s. multicoloured . . . 15 15

581 Dona Concha Felix de Calderon
583 Manila

1984. Birth Centenary of Dona Concha Felix de Calderon.
1802 **581** 60s. green and black . . 10 10
1803 3p.60 green and red . . 50 15

1984. Various stamps surch.
1804 **545** 60s. on 40s. multicoloured 15 15
1805 **558** 60s. on 40s. multicoloured 15 15
1806 – 3p.60 on 3p.20 blue (No. 1704) 95 30

1984. As Nos. 1700/4 but values changed, and new designs as T **526**.
1807 60s. brown and black . . . 15 10
1808 60s. violet and black . . . 15 10
1809 60s. black 15 10
1913 60s. blue 20 10
1889 60s. brown 20 10
1914 60s. red 20 15
1811 1p.80 blue 20 15
1812 2p.40 purple 35 15
1813 3p. brown 35 15
1814 3p.60 red 50 15
1815 4p.20 purple 60 20
DESIGNS: No. 1807, General Artemio Ricarte; 1808, Teodoro M. Kalaw (politician); 1809, Carlos P. Garcia (4th President); 1913, Quintin Paredes (senator); 1889, Dr. Deogracias V. Villadolid; 1914, Santiago Fonacier (former Senator and army chaplain); 1811, General Vicente Lim; 1812, Professor Nicanor Abelardo; 1813, Francisco Dagohoy; 1814, Aurora Aragon Quezon; 1815, Juan Sumulong.

1984. 150th Anniv of Ayala Corporation.
1818 **583** 70s. multicoloured . . . 15 10
1819 3p.60 multicoloured . . . 35 15

584 "Lady of the Most Holy Rosary with St. Dominic" (C. Francisco)

1984. "Espana 84" International Stamp Exhibition, Madrid. Multicoloured.
1820 2p.50 Type **584** 35 15
1821 5p. "Spoliarum" (Juan Luna) 80 35
MS1822 99 × 73 mm. 7p.50, As No. 1821; 7p.50, Virgin of Manila and Spanish galleon; 7p.50, Illustrations from Rizal's "The Monkey and the Turtle"; 7p.50, As No. 1820. Perf or imperf 8·00 8·00

585 Maria Paz Mendoza Guazon

589 Running

586 "Adolias amlana"

1984. Birth Centenary of Dr. Maria Paz Mendoza Guazon.
1823 **585** 60s. red and blue 15 10
1824 65s. red, black and blue 15 10

1984. Butterflies. Multicoloured.
1825 60s. Type **586** 15 10
1826 2p.40 "Papilio daedalus" . . 50 20
1827 3p. "Prothoe franckii semperi" 65 30
1828 3p.60 Philippine birdwing 80 30
1829 4p.20 Lurcher 95 45
1830 5p. "Chilasa idaeoides" . . 1·30 50

1984. National Children's Book Day. Stamp from miniature sheet ("The Monkey and the Turtle") surch **7-17-84 NATIONAL CHILDREN'S BOOK DAY 20**. Perf or imperf.
1831 7p.20 on 7p.50 multicoloured . . . . . . 15·00 8·75

1984. 420th Anniv of Philippine–Mexican Friendship. Stamp from miniature sheet (Virgin of Manila) surch **420TH PHIL-MEXICAN FRIENDSHIP 8-3-84 20**. Perf or imperf.
1832 7p.20 on 7p.50 multicoloured . . . . . . 15·00 8·75

1984. Olympic Games, Los Angeles. Multicoloured.
1833 60s. Type **589** 10 10
1834 2p.40 Boxing 45 20
1835 6p. Swimming . . . . . . 1·20 60
1836 7p.20 Windsurfing . . . . . 1·50 80
1837 8p.40 Cycling . . . . 1·80 90
1838 20p. Running (woman athlete) . . . . 4·00 2·20
MS1839 87 × 129 mm. 6p. × 4, As Nos. 1834 and 1836/8 . . . . 4·75 4·75

590 The Mansion

1984. 75th Anniv of Baguio City.
1840 **590** 1p.20 multicoloured . . 20 15

1984. 300th Anniv of Our Lady of Holy Rosary Parish. Stamp from miniature sheet ("Lady of the Most Holy Rosary") surch **9-1-84 300TH YR O.L. HOLY ROSARY PARISH 20**. Perf or imperf.
1841 7p.20 on 7p.50 multicoloured . . . . . . 30·00 26·00

592 Electric Train on Viaduct

1984. Light Railway Transit.
1842 **592** 1p.20 multicoloured . . 45 15

593 Australian and Philippine Stamps and Koalas

1984. "Ausipex 84" International Stamp Exhibition, Melbourne.
1843 **593** 3p. multicoloured . . . 60 30
1844 3p.60 multicoloured . . 75 30
MS1845 75 × 90 mm. **593** 20p. × 3, multicoloured . . . . 24·00 24·00

1984. National Museum Week. Stamp from miniature sheet (as No. 1821) surch **NATIONAL MUSEUM WEEK 10-5-84 20**. Perf or imperf.
1846 7p.20 on 7p.50 multicoloured . . . . . . 15·00 8·75

1984. Asia Regional Conference of Rotary International. No. 1728 surch **14-17 NOV. 84 R.I. ASIA REGIONAL CONFERENCE P1.20.**
1847 **551** 1p.20 on 2p.30 mult . . 20 15

596 Gold Award

1984. Philatelic Week. Gold Award at "Ausipex 84" to Mario Que. Multicoloured.
1848 1p.20 Type **596** 20 15
1849 3p. Page of Que's exhibit . . 45 15

597 Caracao

1984. Water Transport. Multicoloured.
1850 60s. Type **597** 20 15
1851 1p.20 Chinese junk 20 15
1852 6p. Spanish galleon . . . . 1·30 60
1853 7p.20 Casco (Filipino cargo prau) . . . . 1·50 75
1854 8p.40 Early paddle-steamer 1·60 90
1855 20p. Modern liner . . . . . 4·00 1·90

1984. No. **MS**1666 surch **3 00** with T **598**.
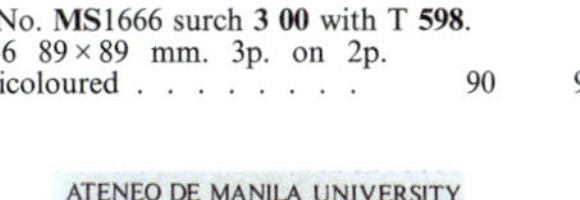
MS1856 89 × 89 mm. 3p. on 2p. multicoloured 90 90

599 Anniversary Emblem

1984. 125th Anniv of Ateneo de Manila University.
1857 **599** 60s. blue and gold . . . 20 15
1858 1p.20 blue and silver . . 35 20

600 Virgin and Child

602 Abstract

601 Manila–Dagupan Steam Locomotive, 1892

1984. Christmas. Multicoloured.
1859 60s. Type **600** 15 10
1860 1p.20 Holy Family 35 20

1984. Rail Transport. Multicoloured.
1861 60s. Type **601** 20 15
1862 1p.20 Light Rail Transit eletric train, 1984 . . . . 20 15
1863 6p. Bicol express, 1955 . . 1·30 60
1864 7p.20 Electric tram, 1905 . . 1·50 75
1865 8p.40 Diesel commuter railcar, 1972 . . . . . . 1·60 90
1866 20p. Horse tram, 1898 . . . 4·00 1·90

1984. 10th Anniv of Philippine Jaycees' Ten Outstanding Young Men Awards. Abstracts by Raul Isidro. Multicoloured.
1867 60s. brown background in circle 15 10
1868 60s. Type **602** 15 10
1869 60s. red background 15 10
1870 60s. blue and purple background 15 10
1871 60s. orange and brown background 15 10
1872 3p. As No. 1867 . . . . . 45 30
1873 3p. Type **602** 45 30
1874 3p. As No. 1869 . . . . . 45 30
1875 3p. As No. 1870 . . . . . 45 30
1876 3p. As No. 1871 . . . . . 45 30

603 Tobacco Plant and Dried Leaf

1985. 25th Anniv of Philippine Virginia Tobacco Administration.
1877 **603** 60s. multicoloured . . . 15 10
1878 3p. multicoloured . . . 60 30

1985. Philatelic Week, 1984. Nos. 1848/9 optd **Philatelic Week 1984.**
1879 **596** 1p.20 multicoloured . . 20 15
1880 – 3p. multicoloured . . . 50 35

605 National Research Council Emblem

1985. 5th Pacific Science Association Congress.
1881 **605** 60s. black, blue and light blue 15 10
1882 1p.20 black, blue and orange 45 20

606 "Carmona retusa"

1985. Medicinal Plants. Multicoloured.
1883a 60s. Type **606** 20 10
1884 1p.20 "Orthosiphon aristatus" 20 15
1885 2p.40 "Vitex negundo" . . 45 30
1886 3p. "Aloe barbadensis" . . 60 35
1887 3p.60 "Quisqualis indica" 1·30 45
1888 4p.20 "Blumea balsamifera" 90 50

607 "Early Bird" Satellite

1985. 20th Anniv of International Telecommunications Satellite Organization.
1896 **607** 60s. multicoloured . . . 15 10
1897 3p. multicoloured . . . 60 30

608 Piebalds

1985. Horses. Multicoloured.
1898 60s. Type **608** 20 15
1899 1p.20 Palominos 20 15
1900 6p. Bays . . . . 1·30 60
1901 7p.20 Browns . . . . 1·50 75
1902 8p.40 Greys . . . . 1·60 90
1903 20p. Chestnuts . . . . . . 4·00 1·90
MS1904 123 × 84 mm. 8p.40 × 4, As Nos. 1899/1901 and 1903 . . . 8·75 8·75

609 Emblem

1985. 25th Anniv of National Tax Research Centre.
1905 **609** 60s. multicoloured . . . 15 10

610 Transplanting Rice

1985. 25th Anniv of International Rice Research Institute, Los Banos. Multicoloured.
1906 60s. Type **610** 15 10
1907 3p. Paddy fields 35 20

611 Image of Holy Child of Cebu

1985. 420th Anniv of Filipino–Spanish Treaty. Mult.
1908 1p.20 Type **611** 20 15
1909 3p.60 Rajah Tupas and Miguel Lopez de Lagazpi signing treaty 45 15

1985. 10th Anniv of Diplomatic Relations with Chinese People's Republic. No. **MS**1661 optd **10th ANNIVERSARY PHILIPPINES AND PEOPLE'S REPUBLIC OF CHINA DIPLOMATIC RELATIONS 1975–1985**.
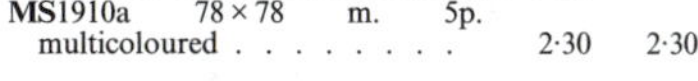
MS1910a 78 × 78 m. 5p. multicoloured . . . . 2·30 2·30

613 Early Anti-TB Label

1985. 75th Anniv of Philippine Tuberculosis Society. Multicoloured.
1911 60s. Screening for TB, laboratory work, health education and inoculation 15 10
1912 1p.20 Type **613** 30 20

1985. 45th Anniv of Girl Scout Charter. No. 1409 surch **45th ANNIVERSARY GIRL SCOUT CHARTER**, emblem and new value.
1917 **348** 2p.40 on 15s. on 10s. multicoloured 30 20
1918 4p.20 on 15s. on 10s. multicoloured 60 30
1919 7p.20 on 15s. on 10s. multicoloured 95 45

616 "Our Lady of Fatima"   **617** Family planting Tree

1985. Marian Year. 2000th Birth Anniversary of Virgin Mary. Multicoloured.
1920 1p.20 Type **616** 20 15
1921 2p.40 "Our Lady of Beaterio" (Juan Bueno Silva) 30 15
1922 3p. "Our Lady of Penafrancia" 35 20
1923 3p.60 "Our Lady of Guadalupe" 60 30

1985. Tree Week. International Year of the Forest.
1924 **617** 1p.20 multicoloured . . 20 15

618 Battle of Bessang Pass   **619** Vicente Orestes Romualdez

1985. 40th Anniv of Bessang Pass Campaign.
1925 **618** 1p.20 multicoloured . . 20 15

1985. Birth Centenary of Vicente Orestes Romualdez (lawyer).
1926a **619** 60s. blue 90 15
1927a 2p. mauve . . . . . . 1·20 35

620 Fishing

1985. International Youth Year. Children's Paintings. Multicoloured.
1928 2p.40 Type **620** 30 15
1929 3p.60 Picnic 50 15

621 Banawe Rice Terraces

1985. World Tourism Organization Congress, Sofia, Bulgaria.
1930 **621** 2p.40 multicoloured . . 30 20

622 Export Graph and Crane lifting Crate   **624** Emblem and Dove with Olive Branch

1985. Export Promotion Year.
1931 **622** 1p.20 multicoloured . . 20 15

1985. No. 1815 surch **P360.**
1932 3p.60 on 4p.20 purple . . . 75 35

1985. 40th Anniv of U.N.O.
1933 **624** 3p.60 multicoloured . . 45 20

625 Martin M-130 Flying Boat "China Clipper"

1985. 50th Anniv of First Trans-Pacific Commercial Flight (San Francisco–Manila). Multicoloured.
1934 3p. Type **625** 35 20
1935 3p.60 Route map, "China Clipper" and anniversary emblem 50 20

1985. Philatelic Week. Nos. 1863/4 surch **PHILATELIC WEEK 1985**, No. 1937 further optd **AIRMAIL.**
1936 60s. on 6p. mult (postage) 15 10
1937 3p. on 7p.20 mult (air) . . . 60 30

627 Bible and Churches

1985. National Bible Week.
1938 **627** 60s. multicoloured . . . 15 10
1939 3p. multicoloured . . . 60 30

628 Panuluyan (enactment of search for an inn)

1985. Christmas. Multicoloured.
1940 60s. Type **628** 15 10
1941 3p. Pagdalaw (nativity) . . 60 30

629 Justice holding Scales   **630** Rizal and "Noli Me Tangere"

1986. 75th Anniv of College of Law.
1942 **629** 60s. mauve and black . . 15 10
1943 3p. green, purple & black 60 30
See also No. 2009.

1986. Centenary of Publication of "Noli Me Tangere" (Jose Rizal's first book).
1944 **630** 60s. violet 10 10
1945 – 1p.20 green 30 20
1946 – 3p.60 brown 65 30
DESIGNS: 1p.20, 3p.60, Rizal, "To the Flowers of Heidelberg" (poem) and Heidelberg University.

631 Douglas DC-3, 1946   **632** Oil Refinery, Manila Bay

1986. 45th Anniv of Philippine Airlines. Each red, black and blue.
1947 60s. Type **631** 15 15
1948 60s. Douglas DC-4 Skymaster, 1946 . . . . 15 15
1949 60s. Douglas DC-6, 1948 . . 15 15
1950 60s. Vickers Viscount 784, 1957 . . . . 15 15
1951 2p.40 Fokker F.27 Friendship, 1960 . . . . 50 20
1952 2p.40 Douglas DC-8-50, 1962 . . . . 80 35
1953 2p.40 B.A.C. One Eleven 500, 1964 . . . . . . 50 20
1954 2p.40 Douglas DC-10-30, 1974 . . . . 50 20
1955 3p.60 Beech 18, 1941 . . . 75 35
1956 3p.60 Boeing 747-200, 1980 75 35
See also No. 2013.

1986. 25th Anniv of Bataan Refinery Corporation.
1957 **632** 60s. silver and green . . 15 10
1958 – 3p. silver and blue . . . 50 20
DESIGN—HORIZ: 3p. Refinery (different).

633 Emblem

1986. "Expo 86" World's Fair, Vancouver.
1959 **633** 60s. multicoloured . . . 15 10
1960 3p. multicoloured . . . 60 30

634 Emblem and Industrial and Agricultural Symbols

1986. 25th Anniv of Asian Productivity Organization.
1961 **634** 60s. black, green & orge 15 10
1962 3p. black, green & orange 60 30
1963 3p. brown (30 × 22 mm) 65 30

635 1906 2c. Stamp   **637** Corazon Aquino, Salvador Laurel and Hands

1986. "Ameripex 86" Int Stamp Exhibition, Chicago.
1964 **635** 60s. green, black & yellow 15 10
1965 – 3p. bistre, black and green 60 30
DESIGN: 3p. 1935 20c. stamp.
See also No. 2006.

1986. "People Power". Multicoloured.
1966 60s. Type **637** 15 10
1967 1p.20 Radio antennae, helicopter and people . . 20 15
1968 2p.40 Religious procession 45 20
1969 3p. Crowds around soldiers in tanks 50 20
MS1970 76 × 76 mm. 7p.20, Crowd, Pres. Aquino and Vice-Pres. Laurel (42 × 32 mm). Imperf 2·20 2·20

638 Monument and Paco and Taft Schools

1986. 75th Anniv of First La Salle School in Philippines.
1971 **638** 60s. black, lilac and green 15 15
1972 – 2p.40 black, blue & grn 45 20
1973 – 3p. black, yellow & green 50 20
MS1974 75 × 75 mm. 7p.20, black and emerald. Imperf . . . . . 4·50 4·50
DESIGNS: 2p.40, St. Miguel Febres Cordero and Paco school; 3p. St. Benilde and Taft school; 7p.20, Founding brothers of Paco school.

639 Aquino praying   **640** "Vanda sanderiana"

1986. 3rd Death Anniv of Benigno S. Aquino, jun.
1975 – 60s. green 15 15
1976 **639** 2p. multicoloured . . . 30 15
1977 – 3p.60 multicoloured . . 65 30
MS1978 75 × 75 mm. 10p. multicoloured. Imperf . . . . 2·50 2·50
DESIGNS: 27 × 36 mm (as T **526**—60s. Aquino. HORIZ (as T **639**)—3p.60 Aquino (different); 10p. Crowd and Aquino.
See also No. 2007.

1986. Orchids. Multicoloured.
1979 60s. Type **640** 15 10
1980 1p.20 "Epigeneium lyonii" 50 15
1981 2p.40 "Paphiopedilum philippinense" 90 20
1982 3p. "Amesiella philippinense" . . . . . 1·10 20

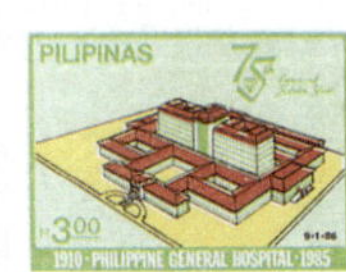

641 "Christ carrying the Cross"   **642** Hospital

1986. 400th Anniv of Quiapo District.
1983 **641** 60s. red, black and mauve 15 10
1984 – 3p.60 blue, black & grn 60 30
DESIGN—HORIZ: 3p.60, Quiapo Church.

1986. 75th Anniv of Philippine General Hospital.
1985 **642** 60s. multicoloured . . . 15 15
1986 3p. multicoloured . . . 50 20
2012 5p. brown . . . . 1·10 15

643 Comet and Earth

1986. Appearance of Halley's Comet. Multicoloured.
1987 60s. Type **643** 10 10
1988 2p.40 Comet, Moon and Earth 45 30

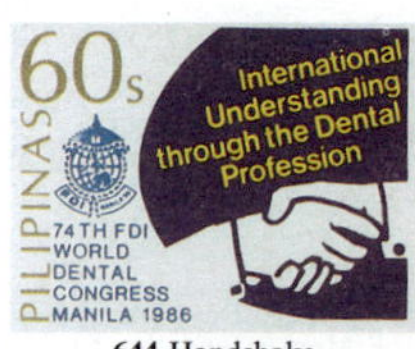

644 Handshake   **645** Emblem

1986. 74th International Dental Federation Congress, Manila. Multicoloured.
1989 60s. Type **644** 15 10
1990 3p. Jeepney, Manila 75 35
See also Nos. 2008 and 2011.

1986. 75th Anniv of Manila Young Men's Christian Association.
1991 **645** 2p. blue 45 15
1992 3p.60 red 65 35
2058 4p. blue 70 45

646 Old and New Buildings

1986. 85th Anniv of Philippine Normal College.
1993 – 60s. multicoloured . . . 15 10
1994 **646** 3p.60 yellow, brown & bl 90 45
DESIGN: 60s. Old and new buildings (different).

647 Butterfly and Beetles

1986. Philatelic Week and International Peace Year.
1995 **647** 60s. multicoloured . . . 15 10
1996 – 1p. blue and black . . . 20 15
1997 – 3p. multicoloured . . . 75 35
DESIGNS—VERT: 1p. Peace Year emblem. HORIZ: 3p. Dragonflies.

648 Mother and Child

651 Emblem

650 Manila Hotel, 1912

1986. Christmas. Multicoloured.
1998 60s. Type **648** 15 10
1999 60s. Couple with child and cow 15 10
2000 60s. Mother and child with doves 15 10
2001 1p. Mother and child receiving gifts (horiz) . . 30 15
2002 1p. Mother and child beneath arch (horiz) . . . 30 15
2003 1p. Madonna and shepherd adoring child (horiz) . . . 30 15
2004 1p. Shepherds and animals around child in manger (horiz) 30 15

1987. No. 1944 surch **P100**.
2005 **630** 1p. on 60s. violet 15 10

1987. As previous issues but smaller, 22 × 30 mm, 30 × 22 mm or 32 × 22 mm (5p.50), and values and colours changed.
2006 – 75s. green (As No. 1965) 15 10
2007 – 1p. blue (As No. 1975) 20 15
2008 **644** 3p.25 green 75 15
2009 **629** 3p.50 brown 80 15
2011 – 4p.75 green (As No. 1990) . . . . . . 1·10 15
2013 – 5p.50 blue (As No. 1956) 1·10 20

1987. 75th Anniv of Manila Hotel.
2014 **650** 1p. bistre and black . . 20 15
2015 – 4p. multicoloured . . . 75 35
2016 – 4p.75 multicoloured . . 90 45
2017 – 5p.50 multicoloured . . 1·10 50
DESIGNS: 4p. Hotel; 4p.75, Lobby; 5p.50, Staff in ante-lobby.

1987. 50th Anniv of International Eucharistic Congress, Manila. Multicoloured.
2018 75s. Type **651** 15 10
2019 1p. Emblem (different) (horiz) 30 15

652 Pres. Cory Aquino taking Oath

1987. Ratification of New Constitution.
2020 **652** 1p. multicoloured . . . 20 15
2021 – 5p.50 blue and brown . . 1·20 60
2060 – 5p.50 green and brown (22 × 31 mm) 80 15
DESIGN: 5p.50, Constitution on open book and dove.

653 Dr. Jose P. Laurel (founder) and Tower

1987. 35th Anniv of Lyceum.
2022 **653** 1p. multicoloured . . . 20 10
2023 2p. multicoloured . . . 60 15

654 City Seal, Man with Philippine Eagle and Woman with Fruit

1987. 50th Anniv of Davao City.
2024 **654** 1p. multicoloured . . . 15 10

655 Salary and Policy Loans

656 Emblem and People in Hand

1987. 50th Anniv of Government Service Insurance System. Multicoloured.
2025 1p. Type **655** 20 15
2026 1p.25 Disability and medicare 20 15
2027 2p. Retirement benefits . . . 35 20
2028 3p.50 Survivorship benefits 65 35

1987. 50th Anniv of Salvation Army in Philippines.
2029 **656** 1p. multicoloured . . . 30 10

657 Woman, Ballot Box and Map

659 Man with Outstretched Arm

658 Map and Flags as Leaves

1987. 50th Anniv of League of Women Voters.
2030 **657** 1p. blue and mauve . . 15 10

1987. As T **526**.
2031 1p. green 15 10
2032 1p. blue 15 10
2033 1p. red 15 10
2034 1p. purple and red 15 10
DESIGNS: No. 2031, Gen. Vicente Lukban; 2032, Wenceslao Q. Vinzons; 2033, Brigadier-General Mateo M. Capinpin; 2034, Jesus Balmori.

1987. 20th Anniv of Association of South-East Asian Nations.
2035 **658** 1p. multicoloured . . . 30 10

1987. Exports.
2036 **659** 1p. multicoloured . . . 15 10
2037 – 2p. green, yellow & brn 30 15
2059 – 4p.75 blue and black . . 65 15
DESIGN: 2p., 4p.75, Man, cogwheel and factory.

660 Nuns, People and Crucifix within Flaming Heart

661 Statue and Stained Glass Window

1967. 125th Anniv of Daughters of Charity in the Philippines.
2038 **660** 1p. blue, red and black 20 10

1987. Canonization of Blessed Lorenzo Ruiz de Manila (first Filipino saint). Multicoloured.
2039 1p. Type **661** 20 15
2040 5p.50 Lorenzo Ruiz praying before execution . . . . 1·30 35
MS2041 56 × 56 mm. 8p. As No. 2040. Imperf . . . . . . 1·80 1·80

1987. No. 2012 surch **P4.75**.
2042 **642** 4p.75 on 5p. brown . . 95 15

663 Nun and Emblem

1987. 75th Anniv of Good Shepherd Sisters in Philippines.
2043 **663** 1p. multicoloured . . . 20 10

664 Founders

1987. 50th Anniv of Philippines Boy Scouts.
2044 **664** 1p. multicoloured . . . 20 10

665 Family with Stamp Album

1987. 50th Anniv of Philippine Philatelic Club.
2045 **665** 1p. multicoloured . . . 20 10

666 Monks, Church and Wrecked Galleon

668 Dove with Letter

667 Flags

1987. 400th Anniv of Dominican Order in Philippines.
2046 **666** 1p. black, blue and orange 15 15
2047 – 4p.75 multicoloured . . 80 30
2048 – 5p.50 multicoloured . . 1·30 45
DESIGNS: 4p.75, J. A. Jeronimo Guerrero, Diego de Sta. Maria and Letran Dominican college; 5p.50, Pope and monks.

1987. 3rd Association of South-east Asian Nations Summit Meeting.
2049 **667** 4p. multicoloured . . . 95 10

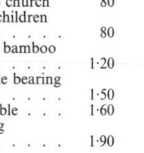

1987. Christmas. Multicoloured.
2050 1p. Type **668** 15 15
2051 1p. People and star decoration 15 15
2052 4p. Crowd going to church 80 20
2053 4p.75 Mother and children exchanging gifts 80 30
2054 5p.50 Children and bamboo cannons . . . . 1·20 30
2055 8p. Children at table bearing festive fare . . . . 1·50 50
2056 9p.50 Woman at table . . . 1·60 65
2057 11p. Woman having Christmas meal . . . . . 1·90 65

669 Emblem, Headquarters and Dr. Rizal

1987. 75th Anniv of Grand Lodge of Philippine Masons.
2061 **669** 1p. multicoloured . . . 30 10

670 Foodstuffs in Split Globe

1987. 40th Anniv of U.N.O. Multicoloured.
2062 1p. Type **670** (International Fund for Agricultural Development) 20 15
2063 1p. Means of transport and communications (Asian and Pacific Transport and Communications Decade) 20 15
2064 1p. People and hands holding houses (International Year of Shelter for the Homeless) 20 15
2065 1p. Happy children playing musical instruments (World Health Day: UNICEF child vaccination campaign) . . 20 15

671 Official Seals and Gavel

1988. Opening Session of 1987 Congress. Mult.
2066 1p. Type **671** 20 10
2067 5p.50 Congress in session and gavel (horiz) . . . . 1·40 45

672 Children and Bosco

1988. Death Centenary of St. John Bosco (founder of Salesian Brothers).
2068 **672** 1p. multicoloured . . . 15 10
2069 5p.50 multicoloured . . 1·20 45

673 Emblem

675 Envelope with Coded Addresses

1988. Buy Philippine-Made Movement Month.
2070 **673** 1p. multicoloured . . . 15 15

1988. Various stamps surch **P 3.00**.
2071 – 3p. on 3p.60 brown (No. 1946) 50 20
2072 **645** 3p. on 3p.60 red 60 20
2073 – 3p. on 3p.60 mult (No. 1977) 75 30
2074 – 3p. on 3p.60 blue, black and green (No. 1984) 50 20
2075 **646** 3p. on 3p.60 yellow, brown and blue . . . 75 30

1988. Postal Codes.
2076 **675** 60s. multicoloured . . . 15 10
2077 1p. multicoloured . . . 20 15

676 "Vesbius purpureus" (soldier bug)

677 Solar Eclipse

1988. Insect Predators. Multicoloured.
2078 1p. Type **676** 15 10
2079 5p.50 "Campsomeris aurulenta" (dagger wasp) 1·10 45

1988.
2080 **677** 1p. multicoloured . . . 15 10
2081 5p.50 multicoloured . . 1·20 45

678 Teodoro

679 Emblem

1988. 101st Birth Anniv of Toribio Teodoro (industrialist).
2082 **678** 1p. cinnamon, brn & red 15 10
2083 1p.20 blue, brown & red 20 15

1988. 75th Anniv of College of Holy Spirit.
2084 **679** 1p. brown, gold & black 15 10
2085 – 4p. brown, green & black 80 30
DESIGN: 4p. Arnold Janssen (founder) and Sister Edelwina (director, 1920–47).

680 Emblem
681 Luna and Hidalgo

1988. Newly Restored Democracies International Conference.
2086 **680** 4p. blue, ultram & blk 95 30

1988. National Juan Luna and Felix Resurreccion Hidalgo Memorial Exhibition.
2087 **681** 1p. black, yellow & brn 15 10
2088 5p.50 black, cinnamon and brown . . . . . 1·00 35

682 Magat Dam, Ramon, Isabela

1988. 25th Anniv of National Irrigation Administration.
2089 **682** 1p. multicoloured . . . 1·10 1·10
2090 5p.50 multicoloured . . 1·20 50

683 Scuba Diving, Siquijor

1988. Olympic Games, Seoul (1st issue). Multicoloured. Perf or imperf.
2091 1p. Type **683** 15 15
2092 1p.20 Big game fishing, Aparri, Cagayan 20 15
2093 4p. Yachting, Manila Central 75 45
2094 5p.50 Mountain climbing, Mt. Apo, Davao . . . . 1·10 65
2095 8p. Golfing, Cebu City . . . 1·50 95
2096 11p. Cycling (Tour of Mindanao), Marawi City 2·20 1·30
See also Nos. 2113/18.

684 Headquarters, Plaza Santa Cruz, Manila
686 Balagtas

1988. Banking Anniversaries. Multicoloured.
2097 1p. Type **684** (50th anniv of Philippine International Commercial Bank) . . . 15 15
2098 1p. Family looking at factory and countryside (25th anniv of Land Bank) 15 15
2099 5p.50 Type **684** 95 50
2100 5p.50 As No. 2098 . . . . 95 50

1988. Various stamps surch.
2101 1p.90 on 2p.40 mult (No. 1968) 45 15
2102 1p.90 on 2p.40 black, blue and green (No. 1972) . . 45 15
2103 1p.90 on 2p.40 mult (No. 1981) 45 15
2104 1p.90 on 2p.40 mult (No. 1988) 45 15

1988. Birth Bicentenary of Francisco Balagtas Baltasco (writer). Each green, brown and yellow.
2105 1p. Type **686** 15 10
2106 1p. As Type **686** but details reversed 15 10

687 Hospital
688 Brown Mushroom

1988. 50th Anniv of Quezon Institute (tuberculosis hospital).
2107 **687** 1p. multicoloured . . . 15 15
2108 5p.50 multicoloured . . 1·00 60

1988. Fungi. Multicoloured.
2109 60s. Type **688** 15 10
2110 1p. Rat's ear fungus 20 15
2111 2p. Abalone mushroom . . 35 20
2112 4p. Straw mushroom . . . 90 45

689 Archery
691 Red Cross Work
690 Department of Justice

1988. Olympic Games, Seoul (2nd issue). Multicoloured. Perf or imperf.
2113 1p. Type **689** 20 15
2114 1p.20 Tennis 20 15
2115 4p. Boxing 60 30
2116 5p.50 Athletics 90 45
2117 8p. Swimming . . . . . . 1·30 60
2118 11p. Cycling . . . . 1·80 95
MS2119 101 × 76 mm. 5p.50, Weightlifting; 5p.50, Basketball; 5p.50, Judo; 5p.50, Shooting. Imperf . . . . 4·50 4·50

1988. Law and Justice Week.
2120 **690** 1p. multicoloured . . . 15 10

1988. 125th Anniv of Red Cross.
2121 **691** 1p. multicoloured . . . 15 15
2122 5p.50 multicoloured . . 1·00 50

692 Girl and Boy
693 Map and Shrimps

1988. 50th Anniv of Christian Children's Fund.
2123 **692** 1p. multicoloured . . . 15 10

1988. 50th Anniv of Bacolod City Charter.
2124 **693** 1p. multicoloured . . . 15 10

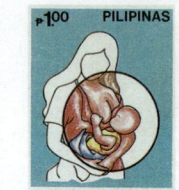

694 Breastfeeding
695 A. Aragon Quezon

1988. Child Survival Campaign. Multicoloured.
2125 1p. Type **694** 15 10
2126 1p. Growth monitoring . . 15 10
2127 1p. Immunization 15 10
2128 1p. Oral rehydration 15 10
2129 1p. Access for the disabled (U.N. Decade of Disabled Persons) 15 10

1988. Birth Centenary of Aurora Aragon Quezon.
2130 **695** 1p. multicoloured . . . 15 10
2131 5p.50 multicoloured . . 90 60

696 Post Office
697 Sampaloc Branch Transmitter

1988. Philatelic Week. Multicoloured.
2132 1p. Type **696** (inscr "1938") 20 15
2132b 1p. Type **696** (inscr "1988") 35 15
2133 1p. Stamp counter 20 15
2134 1p. Fern and stamp displays 20 15
2135 1p. People looking at stamp displays 20 15

1988. 10 Years of Technological Improvements by Philippine Long Distance Telephone Company.
2136 **697** 1p. multicoloured . . . 15 10

698 Clasped Hands and Dove
699 Crowd with Banners

1988. Christmas. Multicoloured.
2137 75s. Type **698** 15 15
2138 1p. Children making decorations (horiz) . . . 15 15
2139 2p. Man carrying decorations on yoke (horiz) 30 20
2140 3p.50 Christmas tree 60 30
2141 4p.75 Candle and stars . . . 80 35
2142 5p.50 Reflection of star forming heart (horiz) . . 95 45

1988. Commission on Human Rights (2143) and 40th Anniv of Universal Declaration of Human Rights (2144). Multicoloured.
2143 1p. Type **699** 15 10
2144 1p. Doves escaping from cage 15 10

700 Church, 1776
701 Statue and School

1988. 400th Anniv of Malate. Multicoloured.
2145 1p. Type **700** 15 10
2146 1p. Our Lady of Remedies Church anniversary emblem and statue of Virgin (Eduardo Castrillo) 15 10
2147 1p. Church, 1880 . . . . . 15 10
2148 1p. Church, 1988 . . . . . 15 10

1988. 50th Anniv of University of Santo Tomas Graduate School.
2149 **701** 1p. multicoloured . . . 15 10

702 Order's Activities
703 Miguel Ver (first leader)

1989. 50th Anniv of Oblates of Mary Immaculate.
2150 **702** 1p. multicoloured . . . 15 10

1989. 47th Anniv of Recognition of Hunters ROTC Guerrilla Unit (formed by Military Academy and University students). Mult.
2151 1p. Type **703** 15 10
2152 1p. Eleuterio Adevoso (leader after Ver's death) 15 10

704 Foodstuffs and Paulino Santos
705 Sinulog

1989. 50th Anniv of General Santos City.
2153 **704** 1p. multicoloured . . . 15 10

1989. "Fiesta Islands '89" (1st series). Mult.
2154 4p.75 Type **705** 95 35
2155 5p.50 Cenaculo (Lenten festival) 95 45
2156 6p.25 Iloilo Paraw Regatta 95 65
See also Nos. 2169/71, 2177/9, 2194/6 and 2210.

706 Tomas Mapua
707 Adventure Pool

1989. Birth Centenaries. Multicoloured.
2157 1p. Type **706** 15 10
2158 1p. Camilo Osias 15 10
2159 1p. Dr. Olivia Salamanca 15 10
2160 1p. Dr. Francisco Santiago 15 10
2161 1p. Leandro Fernandez . . 15 10

1989. 26th International Federation of Landscape Architects World Congress, Manila. Mult.
2162 1p. Type **707** 15 10
2163 1p. Paco Park 15 10
2164 1p. Street improvements in Malacanang area 15 10
2165 1p. Erosion control on upland farm 15 10

708 Palawan Peacock- Pheasant
709 Entrance and Statue of Justice

1989. Environment Month. Multicoloured.
2166 1p. Type **708** 15 10
2167 1p. Palawan bear cat . . . 15 10

1989. Supreme Court.
2168 **709** 1p. multicoloured . . . 30 15

1989. "Fiesta Islands '89" (2nd series). As T **705**. Multicoloured.
2169 60s. Turumba 15 10
2170 75s. Pahiyas 15 15
2171 3p.50 Independence Day . . 50 30

710 Birds, Quill, "Noli Me Tangere" and Flags

1989. Bicentenary of French Revolution and Decade of Philippine Nationalism.
2172 **710** 1p. multicoloured . . . 15 15
2173 5p.50 multicoloured . . 90 60

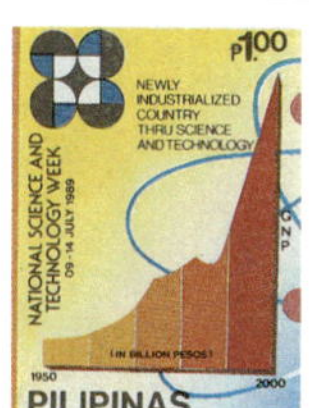

711 Graph

713 Monument, Flag, Civilian and Soldier

1989. National Science and Technology Week. Multicoloured.

2174 1p. Type **711** 15 10
2175 1p. "Man" (Leonardo da Vinci) and emblem of Philippine Science High School) 15 10

1989. New Constitution stamp of 1987 surch **P4 75**.

2176 4p.75 on 5p.50 green and brown (2060) 75 50

1989. "Fiesta Island 89" (3rd series). As T **705**.

2177 1p. Pagoda Sa Wawa (carnival float) 15 15
2178 4p.75 Cagayan de Oro Fiesta 80 35
2179 5p.50 Penafrancia Festival 95 45

1989. 50th Anniv of National Defence Department.

2180 **713** 1p. multicoloured . . . 20 10

714 Map and Satellite

715 Annunciation

1989. 10th Anniv of Asia–Pacific Telecommunity.

2181 **714** 1p. multicoloured . . . 30 15

1989. Christmas. Multicoloured.

2182 60s. Type **715** 10 10
2183 75s. Mary and Elizabeth . . 15 10
2184 1p. Mary and Joseph travelling to Bethlehem 15 10
2185 2p. Search for an inn . . . 30 20
2186 4p. Magi and star 65 45
2187 4p.75 Adoration of shepherds 75 50

716 Lighthouse, Liner and Lifebelt

1989. International Maritime Organization.

2188 **716** 1p. multicoloured . . . 20 10

717 Spanish Philippines 1854 5c. and Revolutionary Govt 1898 2c. Stamps

1989. "World Stamp Expo '89" International Stamp Exhibition, Washington D.C. Multicoloured.

2189 1p. Type **717** 15 10
2190 4p. U.S. Administration 1899 50c. and Commonwealth 1935 6c. stamps 75 50
2191 5p.50 Japanese Occupation 1942 2c. and Republic 1946 6c. stamps 90 60

718 Teacher using Stamp as Teaching Aid

1989. Philatelic Week. Philately in the Classroom. Multicoloured.

2192 1p. Type **718** 15 10
2193 1p. Children working with stamps 15 10

1989. "Fiesta Islands '89" (4th series). As T **705**.

2194 1p. Masked festival, Negros 15 15
2195 4p.75 Grand Canao, Baguio 80 35
2196 5p.50 Fireworks 95 45

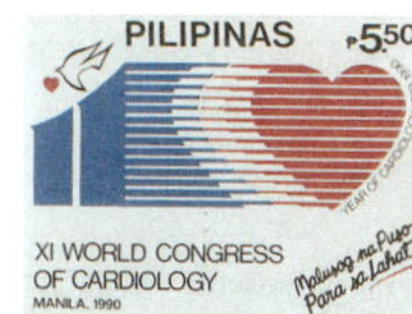

719 Heart

1990. 11th World Cardiology Congress, Manila.

2197 **719** 5p.50 red, blue and black 95 45

720 Glasses of Beer

1990. Centenary of San Miguel Brewery.

2198 **720** 1p. multicoloured . . . 15 15
2199 5p.50 multicoloured . . 95 45

721 Houses and Family

1990. Population and Housing Census. Multicoloured, colours of houses given.

2200 **721** 1p. blue 15 10
2201 1p. pink 15 10

722 Scouts

723 Claro Recto (politician)

1990. 50th Anniv of Philippine Girl Scouts.

2202 **722** 1p. multicoloured . . . 35 10
2203 1p.20 multicoloured . . 35 15

1990. Birth Centenaries. Multicoloured.

2204 1p. Type **723** 15 10
2205 1p. Manuel Bernabe (poet) 15 10
2206 1p. Guillermo Tolentino (sculptor) 15 10
2207 1p. Elpidio Quirino (President 1948–53) . . . 15 10
2208 1p. Dr. Bienvenido Gonzalez (University President, 1937–51) . . . 15 10

724 Badge and Globe

1990. 50th Anniv of Legion of Mary.

2209 **724** 1p. multicoloured . . . 15 10

1990. "Fiesta Islands '89" (5th series). As No. 2179 but new value.

2210 4p. multicoloured 95 35

725 Torch

1990. 20th Anniv of Asian–Pacific Postal Training Centre.

2211 **725** 1p. multicoloured . . . 15 15
2212 4p. multicoloured . . . 65 35

726 Catechism Class

727 Waling Waling Flowers

1990. National Catechetical Year.

2213 **726** 1p. multicoloured . . . 15 10
2214 3p.50 multicoloured . . 60 35

1990. 29th Orient and South-East Asian Lions Forum, Manila. Multicoloured.

2215 1p. Type **727** 20 15
2216 4p. Sampaguita flowers . . 65 30

728 Areas for Improvement

1990. 40th Anniv of United Nations Development Programme.

2217 **728** 1p. multicoloured . . . 15 10
2218 5p.50 multicoloured . . 90 60

729 Letters of Alphabet

1990. International Literacy Year.

2219 **729** 1p. green, orange & black 15 10
2220 5p.50 green, yellow & blk 90 60

730 "Laughter" (A. Magsaysay-Ho)

1990. Philatelic Week. Multicoloured.

2221 1p. "Family" (F. Amorsolo) (horiz) 20 15
2222 4p.75 "The Builders" (V. Edades) . . . . . . 1·20 60
2223 5p.50 Type **730** . . . . . 1·40 75

731 Star

1990. Christmas. Multicoloured.

2224 1p. Type **731** 15 10
2225 1p. Stars within stars (blue background) 15 10
2226 1p. Red and white star . . . 15 10
2227 1p. Gold and red star (green background) 15 10
2228 5p.50 Geometric star (Paskuhan Village, San Fernando) 15 10

732 Figures

1990. International White Cane Safety Day.

2229 **732** 1p. black, yellow and blue 20 15

733 La Solidaridad in 1990 and 1890 and Statue of Rizal

1990. Centenary of Publication of "Filipinas Dentro de Cien Anos" by Jose Rizal.

2230 **733** 1p. multicoloured . . . 20 15

734 Crowd before Figure of Christ

735 Tailplane and Stewardess

1991. 2nd Plenary Council of the Philippines.

2231 **734** 1p. multicoloured . . . 20 15

1991. 50th Anniv of Philippine Airlines.

2232 **735** 1p. mult (postage) . . . 15 15
2233 5p.50 multicoloured (air) 95 60

736 Gardenia **737** Sheepshank

1991. Flowers. Multicoloured.

2234 60s. Type **736** 10 10
2235 75s. Yellow bell 10 10
2475 1p. Yellow bell 10 10
2236 1p. Yellow plumeria 15 15
2237 1p. Red plumeria 15 15
2238 1p. Pink plumeria 15 15
2239 1p. White plumeria 15 15
2240 1p.20 Nerium 15 10
2241 3p.25 Ylang-ylang 60 35
2242 4p. Pink ixora 60 35
2243 4p. White ixora 60 35
2244 4p. Yellow ixora 60 35
2245 4p. Red ixora 60 35
2246 4p.75 Orange bougainvillea 65 45
2247 4p.75 Purple bougainvillea 65 45
2248 4p.75 White bougainvillea 65 45
2249 4p.75 Red bougainvillea . . 65 45
2250 5p. Canna 75 45
2251 5p.50 Red hibiscus 95 65
2252 5p.50 Yellow hibiscus . . . 95 65
2253 5p.50 White hibiscus 95 65
2254 5p.50 Pink hibiscus 95 65

See also Nos. 2322/41.

1991. 12th Asia–Pacific and 9th National Boy Scouts Jamboree. Multicoloured.

2255 1p. Reef knot 20 15
2256 4p. Type **737** 60 30
2257 4p.75 Granny knot 65 30
MS2258 88 × 82 mm. Nos. 2255/7. Imperf (sold at 16p.50) . . . . 3·00 3·00

738 Jorge Vargas

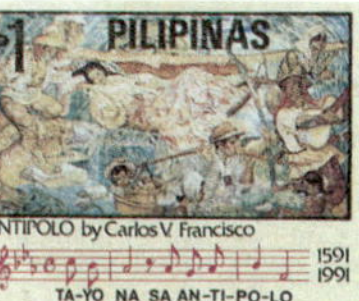

739 "Antipolo" (Carlos Francisco) and Score

1991. Birth Centenaries. Multicoloured.

2259 1p. Type **738** 15 10
2260 1p. Ricardo Paras 15 10
2261 1p. Jose Laurel 15 10
2262 1p. Vicente Fabella 15 10
2263 1p. Maximo Kalaw 15 10

1991. 400th Anniv of Antipolo.

2264 **739** 1p. multicoloured . . . 20 15

740 Philippine Eagle

1991. Endangered Species. The Philippine Eagle. Multicoloured.

2265	1p. Type **740**	45	30
2266	4p.75 Eagle on branch	1·90	1·30
2267	5p.50 Eagle in flight	2·20	1·50
2268	8p. Eagle feeding chick	3·25	2·20

741 Emblem

1991. Centenary of Founding of Society of Lawyers (from 1904 Philippine Bar Association).

2269	**741** 1p. multicoloured	20	15

742 Flags and Induction Ceremony

743 First Regular Division Emblem

1991. 50th Anniv of Induction of Philippine Reservists into United States Army Forces in the Far East. Background colours given where necessary in brackets. (a) T**742**.

2270	**742** 1p. multicoloured	20	15
MS2271	82 × 88 mm. **742** 16p. multicoloured. Imperf	2·75	2·75

(b) Showing Division emblems.

2272	**743** 2p. red, black and yellow	20	15
2273	– 2p. multicoloured (yellow) (2nd Regular)	20	15
2274	– 2p. multicoloured (yellow) (11th)	20	15
2275	– 2p. blue, yellow and black (yellow) (21st)	20	15
2276	**743** 2p. red and black	20	15
2277	– 2p. black, blue and red (2nd Regular)	20	15
2278	– 2p. multicoloured (white) (11th)	20	15
2279	– 2p. blue, yellow and black (white) (21st)	20	15
2280	– 2p. multicoloured (yellow) (31st)	20	15
2281	– 2p. multicoloured (yellow) (41st)	20	15
2282	– 2p. multicoloured (yellow) (51st)	20	15
2283	– 2p. multicoloured (yellow) (61st)	20	15
2284	– 2p. red, blue and black (31st)	20	15
2285	– 2p. multicoloured (white) (41st)	20	15
2286	– 2p. blue, black and red (51st)	20	15
2287	– 2p. multicoloured (white) (61st)	20	15
2288	– 2p. multicoloured (yellow) (71st)	20	15
2289	– 2p. multicoloured (yellow) (81st)	20	15
2290	– 2p. multicoloured (yellow) (91st)	20	15
2291	– 2p. multicoloured (yellow) (101st)	20	15
2292	– 2p. multicoloured (white) (71st)	20	15
2293	– 2p. multicoloured (white) (81st)	20	15
2294	– 2p. multicoloured (white) (91st)	20	15
2295	– 2p. multicoloured (white) (101st)	20	15
2296	– 2p. blue, black and yellow (Bataan Force)	20	15
2297	– 2p. yellow, red and black (yellow) (Philippine)	20	15
2298	– 2p. multicoloured (yellow) (Air Corps)	20	15
2299	– 2p. black, blue and yellow (Offshore Patrol)	20	15
2300	– 2p. blue and black (Bataan Force)	20	15
2301	– 2p. yellow, red and black (white) (Philippine)	20	15
2302	– 2p. multicoloured (white) (Air Corps)	20	15
2303	– 2p. black and blue (Offshore Patrol)	20	15

Nos. 2272/2303 (all as T **743**) show divisional emblems.

744 Basilio

745 St. John of the Cross

1991. Centenary of Publication of "El Filibusterismo" by Jose Rizal. Characters from the novel. Each red, blue and black.

2304	1p. Type **744**	15	15
2305	1p. Simoun	15	15
2306	1p. Father Florentino	15	15
2307	1p. Juli	15	15

1991. 400th Death of St. John of the Cross. Multicoloured.

2308	Type **745**	20	15
MS2309	59 × 59 mm. 16p. St. John praying, signature and Type **745**. Imperf	4·50	4·50

746 Faces (Children's Fund)

1991. United Nations Agencies.

2310	**746** 1p. multicoloured	15	15
2311	– 4p. multicoloured	60	20
2312	– 5p.50 black, red and blue	80	35

DESIGNS: 4p. Hands supporting boatload of people (High Commissioner for Refugees); 5p.50, 1951 15c. and 1954 3c. U.N. stamps (40th anniv of Postal Administration).

747 "Bayanihan" (Carlos "Botong" Francisco)

1991. Philatelic Week. Multicoloured.

2313	2p. Type **747**	30	15
2314	7p. "Sari-Sari Vendor" (Mauro Malang Santos)	1·00	50
2315	8p. "Give Us This Day" (Vicente Manansala)	1·20	60

748 Gymnastics

1991. 16th South-East Asian Games, Manila. Multicoloured.

2316	2p. Type **748**	30	15
2317	2p. Gymnastics (emblem at bottom)	30	15
2318	6p. Arnis (martial arts) (emblem at left) (vert)	65	15
2319	6p. Arnis (emblem at right) (vert)	65	15
MS2320	Two sheets. (a) 90 × 60 mm. Nos. 2318/19. Imperf; (b) 65 × 98 mm. Nos. 2316/19	3·00	3·00

Designs of the same value were issued together, se-tenant, each pair forming a composite design.

1991. 1st Philippine Philatelic Convention, Manila. No. **MS**1698 surch **p4**.

MS2321	4p. on 3p.20 purple and black	1·10	1·10

1991. Flowers. As T **736**. Multicoloured.

2322	1p.50 Type **736**	15	15
2323	2p. Yellow plumeria	20	20
2324	2p. Red plumeria	20	20
2325	2p. Pink plumeria	20	20
2326	2p. White plumeria	20	20
2327	3p. Nerium	30	30
2328	5p. Ylang-ylang	50	50
2329	6p. Pink ixora	60	60
2330	6p. White ixora	60	60
2331	6p. Yellow ixora	60	60
2332	6p. Red ixora	75	75
2333	7p. Orange bougainvillea	75	75
2334	7p. Purple bougainvillea	75	75
2335	7p. White bougainvillea	75	75
2336	7p. Red bougainvillea	80	80
2337	8p. Red hibiscus	80	80
2338	8p. Yellow hibiscus	80	80
2339	8p. White hibiscus	80	75
2340	8p. Pink hibiscus	80	80
2341	10p. Canna	1·00	1·00

750 Church

751 Player

1991. Christmas. Children's Paintings. Mult.

2342	2p. Type **750**	20	15
2343	6p. Christmas present	65	45
2344	7p. Santa Claus and tree	75	50
2345	8p. Christmas tree and star	90	60

1991. Centenary of Basketball. Multicoloured.

2346	2p. Type **751**	35	15
2347	6p. Basketball player and map (issue of first basketball stamp, 1934) (horiz)	90	30
2348	7p. Girls playing basketball (introduction of basketball in Philippines, 1904) (horiz)	1·00	35
2349	8p. Players	1·30	50
MS2350	Two sheets (a) 60 × 60 mm. Match scene. Imperf; (b) 73 × 101 mm. Nos. 2346/9	4·00	4·00

752 Monkey firing Cannon

1991. New Year. Year of the Monkey.

2351	**752** 2p. multicoloured	45	15
2352	6p. multicoloured	1·30	30

753 Pres. Aquino and Mailing Centre Emblem

1992. Kabisig Community Projects Organization. Multicoloured.

2353	2p. Type **753**	20	20
2354	6p. Housing	65	30
2355	7p. Livestock	80	35
2356	8p. Handicrafts	95	45

754 "Curcuma longa"

1992. Asian Medicinal Plants Symposium, Los Banos, Laguna. Multicoloured.

2357	2p. Type **754**	35	20
2358	6p. "Centella asiatica"	75	30
2359	7p. "Cassia alata"	90	35
2360	8p. "Ervatamia pandacaqui"	1·00	45

755 "Mahal Kita", Envelopes and Map

1992. Greetings Stamps. Multicoloured.

2361	2p. Type **755**	20	15
2362	2p. As No. 2361 but inscr "I Love You"	20	15
2363	6p. Heart and doves ("Mahal Kita")	75	35
2364	6p. As No. 2363 but inscr "I Love You"	75	35
2365	7p. Basket of flowers ("Mahal Kita")	80	35
2366	7p. As No. 2365 but inscr "I Love You"	80	35
2367	8p. Cupid ("Mahal Kita")	1·60	45
2368	8p. As No. 2367 but inscr "I Love You"	1·60	45

756 Philippine Pavilion and Couple Dancing

757 "Our Lady of the Sun" (icon)

1992. "Expo '92" World's Fair, Seville. Mult.

2369	2p. Type **756**	20	15
2370	8p. Pavilion, preacher and conquistador holding globe	95	45
MS2371	63 × 76 mm. 16p. Pavilion (horiz). Imperf	1·90	1·90

1992. 300th Anniv of Apparition of Our Lady of the Sun at Gate, Vaga Cavite.

2372	**757** 2p. multicoloured	20	15
2373	8p. multicoloured	95	45

758 Fish Farming

1992. 75th Anniv of Department of Agriculture. Multicoloured.

2374	2p. Type **758**	20	15
2375	2p. Pig farming	20	15
2376	2p. Sowing seeds	20	15

759 Race Horses and Emblem

760 Manuel Roxas (President, 1946–48)

1992. 125th Anniv of Manila Jockey Club.

2377	**759** 2p. multicoloured	20	15
MS2378	74 × 63 mm. **759** 8p. multicoloured. Imperf	95	95

1992. Birth Centenaries. Multicoloured.

2379	2p. Type **760**	20	15
2380	2p. Natividad Almeda-Lopez (judge)	20	15
2381	2p. Roman Ozaeta (judge)	20	15
2382	2p. Engracia Cruz-Reyes (women's rights campaigner and environmentalist)	20	15
2383	2p. Fernando Amorsolo (artist)	20	15

761 Queen, Bishop and 1978 30s. Stamp

1992. 30th Chess Olympiad, Manila. Mult.

2384	2p. Type **761**	20	15
2385	6p. King, queen and 1962 6s.+4s. stamp	65	45
MS2386	89 × 63 mm. 8p. Type **761**; 8p. As No. 2385. Imperf	1·80	1·80

762 Bataan Cross

1992. 50th Anniv of Pacific Theatre in Second World War. Multicoloured.

2387	2p. Type **762**	20	15
2388	6p. Map inside "W"	65	45
2389	8p. Corregidor eternal flame	95	65
MS2390	Two sheets. (a) 63 × 75 mm. 16p. Map of Bataan and cross; (b) 76 × 63 mm. 16p. Map of Corregidor and Eternal flame	3·00	3·00

763 President Aquino and President-elect Ramos

1992. Election of Fidel Ramos to Presidency.
2391 **763** 2p. multicoloured . . . 30 15

764 "Dapitan Shrine" (Cesar Legaspi)

1992. Centenary of Dr. Jose Rizal's Exile to Dapitan. Multicoloured.
2392 2p. Type **764** 20 15
2393 2p. Portrait (after Juan Luna) (vert) 20 15

765 "Spirit of ASEAN" (Visit Asean Year) **766** Member of the Katipunan

1992. 25th Anniv of Association of South-East Asian Nations. Multicoloured.
2394 2p. Type **765** 20 15
2395 2p. "ASEAN Sea" (25th Ministerial Meeting and Postal Ministers' Conf) 20 15
2396 6p. Type **765** 65 45
2397 6p. As No. 2395 . . . . . 65 45

1992. Centenary of Katipunan ("KKK") (revolutionary organization). Multicoloured.
2398 2p. Type **766** 20 15
2399 2p. Revolutionaries 20 15
2400 2p. Plotting (horiz) 20 15
2401 2p. Attacking (horiz) . . . 20 15

767 Dr. Jose Rizal, Text and Quill

1992. Centenary of La Liga Filipina.
2402 **767** 2p. multicoloured . . . 20 15

768 Swimming

1992. Olympic Games, Barcelona. Multicoloured.
2403 2p. Type **768** 20 15
2404 7p. Boxing 75 50
2405 8p. Hurdling 90 60
MS2406 87 × 85 mm. 1p. Type **768**; 7p. No. 2404; 8p. No. 2405. Imperf . . . . 4·50 4·50

769 School, Emblem and Students

1992. Centenaries. Multicoloured.
2407 2p. Type **769** (Sisters of the Assumption in the Philippines) 20 15
2408 2p. San Sebastian's Basilica, Manila (centenary (1991) of blessing of fifth construction) (vert) . . . 20 15

770 Masonic Symbols

1992. Centenary of Nilad Lodge (first Filipino Masonic Lodge).
2409 **770** 2p. black and green . . 20 15
2410 – 6p. multicoloured . . . 65 45
2411 – 8p. multicoloured . . . 90 60
DESIGNS: 6p. Antonio Luna and symbols; 8p. Marcelo del Pilar ("Father of Philippine Masonry") and symbols.

771 Ramos taking Oath

1992. Swearing in of President Fidel Ramos. Mult.
2412 2p. Type **771** 20 15
2413 8p. President taking oath in front of flag 95 45

772 Flamingo Guppy

1992. Freshwater Aquarium Fishes (1st series). Multicoloured.
2414 1p.50 Type **772** 15 10
2415 1p.50 Neon tuxedo guppy 15 10
2416 1p.50 King cobra guppy . . 15 10
2417 1p.50 Red-tailed guppy . . 15 10
2418 1p.50 Tiger lace-tailed guppy 15 10
2419 2p. Pearl-scaled goldfish . . 30 15
2420 2p. Red-capped goldfish . . 30 15
2421 2p. Lion-headed goldfish . . 30 15
2422 2p. Black moor goldfish . . 30 15
2423 2p. Bubble-eyed goldfish . . 30 15
2424 4p. Delta topsail platy ("Variatus") 60 60
2425 4p. Orange-spotted hi-fin platy 60 60
2426 4p. Red lyre-tailed swordtail 60 60
2427 4p. Bleeding heart hi-fin platy 60 60
MS2428 Two sheets. (a) 132 × 78 mm. 6p. Green discus; 6p. Brown discus; 7p. Red discus; 7p. Harald's blue discus; (b) 88 × 61 mm. 8p. Golden arowana. Imperf . . . . 2·50 2·50
See also Nos. 2543/**MS**2557.

1992. Philippines Stamp Exhibition, Taipeh, Taiwan. No. **MS**2428 optd **PHILIPPINE STAMP EXHIBITION 1992 – TAIPEI.**
MS2429 Two sheets. (a) 132 × 79 mm. 6p. × 2, 7p. × 2, multicoloured; (b) 88 × 61 mm. 8p. multicoloured . . . . 4·50 4·50

774 Couple

1992. Greetings Stamps. "Happy Birthday". Multicoloured.
2430 2p. Type **774** 20 15
2431 6p. Type **774** 65 45
2432 7p. Balloons and candles on birthday cake 75 50
2433 8p. As No. 2432 . . . . . 95 60

775 Melon, Beans, Tomatoes and Potatoes

1992. 500th Anniv of Discovery of America by Columbus. Multicoloured.
2434 2p. Type **775** 20 15
2435 6p. Maize and sweet potatoes 65 45
2436 8p. Pineapple, cashews, avocado and water melon 90 60

1992. Second National Philatelic Convention. No.**MS**2271 optd **Second National Philatelic Convention Cebu, Philippines, Oct 22—24, 1992.**
MS2437 **742** 16p. multicoloured 3·00 3·00

777 Figures around World Map

1992. International Nutrition Conference, Rome.
2438 **777** 2p. multicoloured . . . 20 15

778 Mother and Child **780** Family and Canoe

1992. Christmas.
2439 **778** 2p. multicoloured . . . 20 15
2440 – 6p. multicoloured . . . 65 45
2441 – 7p. multicoloured . . . 75 50
2442 – 8p. multicoloured . . . 95 60
DESIGNS: 6p. to 8p. Various designs showing mothers and children.

1992. Inauguration of Postal Museum and Philatelic Library. No. **MS**1566 optd **INAUGURATION OF THE PHILIPPINE POSTAL MUSEUM AND PHILTATELIC LIBRARY NOVEMBER 10 1992**
MS2443 76 × 76 mm. 5p. multicoloured . . . . 1·80 1·80

1992. Anti-drugs Campaign. Multicoloured.
2444 2p. Type **780** 20 15
2445 8p. Man carrying paddle, children and canoe . . . 90 60

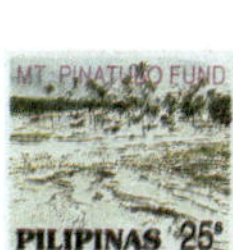

781 Damaged Trees **782** Red Junglefowl

1992. Mt. Pinatubo Fund (for victims of volcanic eruption). Multicoloured.
2446 25s. Type **781** 10 10
2447 1p. Mt. Pinatubo erupting 10 10
2448 1p. Cattle in ash-covered field 10 10
2449 1p. Refugee settlement . . . 10 10
2450 1p. People shovelling ash . . 10 10

1992. New Year. Year of the Cock. Mult.
2451 2p. Type **782** 20 15
2452 6p. Maranao Sarimanok (mythical bird) 65 45
MS2453 98 × 87 mm. Nos. 2451/2 plus two labels. Perf or Imperf 90 90

1992. Philippine Stamp Exhibition, Taipeh. No. **MS**2453 optd **PHILIPPPINE STAMP EHXIBIT TAIPEI DECEMBER 1—3 1992.**
MS2454 98 × 87 mm. 2, 6p. multicoloured . . . . 1·80 1·80

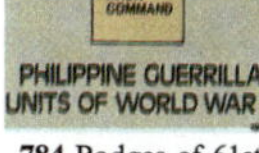

784 Badges of 61st and 71st Divisions, Cebu Area Command **785** "Family" (Cesar Legaspi) (family ties)

1992. Philippine Guerrilla Units of Second World War (1st series). Multicoloured.
2455 2p. Type **784** 20 15
2456 2p. Vinzon's Guerrillas and badges of 48th Chinese Guerrilla Squadron and 101st Division 20 15
2457 2p. Anderson's Command, Luzon Guerrilla Army Forces and badge of Bulacan Military Area . . 20 15
2458 2p. President Quezon's Own Guerrillas and badges of Marking's Fil-American Troops and Hunters ROTC Guerrillas 20 15
See also Nos. 2594/7, 2712/15 and 2809/12.

1992. Philatelic Week. Multicoloured.
2459 2p. Type **785** 20 15
2460 6p. "Pounding Rice" (Nena Saguil) (hard work and industry) 65 45
2461 7p. "Fish Vendors" (Romeo Tabuena) (flexibility and adaptability) 75 50

786 Black Shama

1992. Endangered Birds. Multicoloured. (a) As T **786**.
2462 2p. Type **786** 20 15
2463 2p. Blue-headed fantail . . . 20 15
2464 2p. Mindoro zone-tailed (inscr "Imperial") pigeon 20 15
2465 2p. Sulu hornbill 20 15
2466 2p. Red-vented (inscr "Philippine") cockatoo . . 20 15

(b) Size 29 × 39 mm.
2467 2p. Philippine trogon . . . 20 20
2468 2p. Rufous hornbill 20 20
2469 2p. White-bellied black woodpecker 20 20
2470 2p. Spotted wood kingfisher 20 20

(c) Size 36 × 26½ mm.
2471 2p. Brahminy kite 20 20
2472 2p. Philippine falconet . . . 20 20
2473 2p. Reef heron 20 20
2474 2p. Philippine duck (inscr "Mallard") 20 20

787 Flower (Jasmine) **788** Flower (Jasmine)

1993. National Symbols. Multicoloured. (a) As T **787**. "Pilipinas" in brown at top.
2476 1p. Type **787** 15 10
2571 2p. Flag 20 15
2478 6p. Leaf (palm) 65 45
2479 7p. Costume 75 50
2480 8p. Fruit (mango) 90 60

(b) As T **788**. "Pilipinas" in red at foot.
2481 60s. Tree 15 10
2512 1p. Flag 10 10
2513 1p. House 10 10
2514 1p. Costume 10 10
2515 1p. As No. 2481 . . . . . 10 10
2516 1p. Type **788** 10 10
2517 1p. Fruit 10 10
2518 1p. Leaf 10 10
2519 1p. Fish (milkfish) 10 10
2520 1p. Animal (water buffalo) 10 10
2521 1p. Bird (Philippine trogons) 10 10
2482 1p.50 As No. 2519 . . . . 15 10
2565 2p. Hero (Dr. Jose Rizal) 20 15
2566 2p. As No. 2513 . . . . . 20 15
2567 2p. As No. 2514 . . . . . 20 15
2568 2p. Dance ("Tinikling") . . 20 15
2569 2p. Sport (Sipa) 20 15
2570 2p. As No. 2521 . . . . . 20 15
2572 2p. As No. 2520 . . . . . 20 15
2573 2p. Type **788** 20 15
2574 2p. As No. 2481 . . . . . 20 15
2575 2p. As No. 2517 . . . . . 20 15
2576 2p. As No. 2518 . . . . . 20 15
2577 2p. As No. 2519 . . . . . 20 15
2578 2p. As No. 2512 . . . . . 20 15
2644 3p. As No. 2520 . . . . . 15 15
2645 5p. As No. 2521 . . . . . 30 20
2646 6p. As No. 2518 . . . . . 35 15
2647 7p. As No. 2514 . . . . . 40 25
2486 8p. As No. 2517 . . . . . 1·00 60
2649 10p. As No. 2513 . . . . . 55 30
See also Nos. **MS**2663, 2717/19, **MS**2753, 2818/20, **MS**2906, 2973/5, **MS**3010, 3017/19, 3089/3092, 3093/7, 3103/5, **MS**3106, 3107/21, **MS**3178 and 3200/9.

789 "Euploea mulciber dufresne"

1993. Butterflies. Multicoloured. (a) As T **789**.
2488 2p. Type **789** 20 15
2489 2p. "Cheritra orpheus" . . 20 15
2490 2p. "Delias henningia" . . . 20 15

2491 2p. "Mycalesis ita" 20 15
2492 2p. "Delias diaphana" . . . 20 15

(b) Size 28 × 35 mm.

2493 2p. "Papilio rumanzobia" 20 20
2494 2p. "Papilio palinurus" . . 20 20
2495 2p. "Trogonoptera trojana" 20 20
2496 2p. Tailed jay ("Graphium agamemnon") 20 20
MS2497 10p. "Papilio iowi", "Valeria boebera" and "Delias themis" . . . . 1·50 1·50

1993. Indopex 93 International Stamp Exhibition, Surabaya. No. **MS**2497 optd **INDOPEX 93 INDONESIA PHILATELIC EXHIBITION 1993, 6th ASIAN INTERNATIONAL PHILATELIC EXHIBITION 29th MAY – 4th JUNE 1993 SURABAYA – INDONESIA.**

MS2498 140 × 70 mm. 10p. multicoloured . . . . 2·20 2·20

791 Nicanor Abelardo

792 Boxing and Judo

1993. Birth Centenaries. Multicoloured.

2499 2p. Type **791** 20 15
2500 2p. Pilar Hidalgo-Lim . . . 20 15
2501 2p. Manuel Viola Gallego 20 15
2502 2p. Maria Ylagan-Orosa . . 20 15
2503 2p. Eulogio B. Rodriguez 20 15

1993. 17th South-East Asian Games, Singapore. Multicoloured.

2504 2p. Weightlifting, archery, fencing and shooting (79 × 29 mm) 20 15
2505 2p. Type **792** 20 15
2506 2p. Athletics, cycling, gymnastics and golf (79 × 29 mm) 20 15
2507 6p. Table tennis, football, volleyball and badminton (79 × 29 mm) 65 45
2508 6p. Billiards and bowling . . 65 45
2509 6p. Swimming, water polo, yachting and diving (79 × 29 mm) 65 45
MS2510 84 × 96 mm. 10p. Basketball (vert) . . . . 3·00 3·00

1993. 46th Anniv of Philippine Air Force. No. **MS**2497 optd **Towards the Year 2000, 46th PAF Anniversary 1 July 1993.**

MS2511 140 × 70 mm. 10p. multicoloured . . . . 7·50 7·50

794 "Spathoglottis chrysantha"

1993. Orchids. Multicoloured.

2522 2p. Type **794** 20 15
2523 2p. "Arachnis longicaulis" 20 15
2524 2p. "Phalaenopsis mariae" 20 15
2525 2p. "Coelogyne marmorata" 20 15
2526 2p. "Dendrobium sanderae" 20 15
2527 3p. "Dendrobium serratilabium" 30 20
2528 3p. "Phalaenopsis equestris" 30 20
2529 3p. "Vanda merrillii" . . . 30 20
2530 3p. "Vanda luzonica" . . . 30 20
2531 3p. "Grammatophyllum martae" 30 20
MS2532 Two sheets, each 58 × 99 mm. (a) 8p. "Aerides quinquevulnera" (27 × 77 mm); (b) 8p. "Vanda lamellate" (27 × 77 mm). Imperf 90 90

1993. "Taipei '93" Asian Stamp Exhibition. No. **MS**2532 optd **ASIAN INTERNATIONAL INVITATION STAMP EXHIBITION TAIPEI '93.**

MS2533 Two sheets, each 58 × 99 mm. Perf. (a) 8p. multicoloured; (b) 8p. multicoloured. Imperf 90 90

796 Dog in Window ("Thinking of You")

1993. Greetings Stamps. Multicoloured.

2534 2p. Type **796** 20 15
2535 2p. As No. 2534 but inscr "Naaalala Kita" 20 15
2536 6p. Dog looking at clock ("Thinking of You") . . 65 45
2537 6p. As No. 2536 but inscr "Naaalala Kita" 65 45
2538 7p. Dog looking at calendar ("Thinking of You") . . 75 50
2539 7p. As No. 2538 but inscr "Naaalala Kita" 75 50
2540 8p. Dog with pair of slippers ("Thinking of You") 90 60
2541 8p. As No. 2540 but inscr "Naaalala Kita" 90 60

797 Palms and Coconuts

799 Map and Emblem

798 Albino Ryukin Goldfish

1993. "Tree of Life".

2542 **797** 2p. multicoloured . . . 20 15

1993. Freshwater Aquarium Fishes (2nd series). Multicoloured. (a) As T **798**.

2543 2p. Type **798** 20 15
2544 2p. Black oranda goldfish 20 15
2545 2p. Lion-headed goldfish . . 20 15
2546 2p. Celestial goldfish 20 15
2547 2p. Pompon goldfish 20 15
2548 2p. Paradise fish 20 15
2549 2p. Pearl gourami 20 15
2550 2p. Red-tailed black shark (carp) 20 15
2551 2p. Tiger barb 20 15
2552 2p. Cardinal tetra 20 15

(b) Size 29 × 39 mm.

2553 2p. Pearl-scaled freshwater angelfish 20 15
2554 2p. Zebra freshwater angelfish 20 20
2555 2p. Marble freshwater angelfish 20 20
2556 2p. Black freshwater angelfish 20 20
MS2557 Two sheets. (a) 138 × 78 mm. 3p. Neon Siamese fighting fish; 3p. Libby Siamese fighting fish; 3p. Split-tailed Siamese fighting fish; 3p. Butterfly Siamese fighting fish. Perf. (b) 87 × 60 mm. 6p. Albino oscar. Imperf . . . . 3·75 3·50

1993. Basic Petroleum and Minerals Inc. "Towards Self-sufficiency in Energy".

2558 **799** 2p. multicoloured . . . 20 15

1993. "Bangkok '93" International Stamp Exhibition, Thailand. No. **MS**2557 optd **QUEEN SIRIKIT NATIONAL CONVENTION CENTRE 1-10 OCTOBER 1993, BANGKOK WORLD PHILATELIC EXHIBITION 1993.**

MS2559 Two sheets. (a) 3p. × 4, multicoloured; (b) 6p. multicoloured . . . . 7·50 7·50

801 Globe, Scales, Book and Gavel

1993. 16th Int Law Conference, Manila. Mult.

2560 2p. Type **801** 20 15
2561 6p. Globe, scales, gavel and conference emblem on flag of Philippines (vert) . . . 65 45
2562 7p. Woman holding scales, conference building and globe 80 50
2563 8p. Fisherman pulling in nets and emblem (vert) . . 95 65

802 Our Lady of La Naval (statue) and Galleon

1993. 400th Anniv of Our Lady of La Naval.

2564 **802** 2p. multicoloured . . . 20 15

803 Woman and Terraced Hillside

1993. International Year of Indigenous Peoples. Women in traditional costumes. Multicoloured.

2579 2p. Type **803** 20 15
2580 6p. Woman, plantation and mountain 65 45
2581 7p. Woman and mosque . . 80 50
2582 8p. Woman and Filipino vintas (sail canoes) . . . 95 65

804 Trees

1993. Philatelic Week. "Save the Earth". Mult.

2583 2p. Type **804** 20 15
2584 6p. Marine flora and fauna 65 45
2585 7p. Dove and irrigation system 80 50
2586 8p. Effects of industrial pollution 95 65

805 1949 6c.+4c. Stamp and Symbols

806 Moon-buggy and Society Emblem

1993. 400th Anniv of Publication of "Doctrina Christiana" (first book published in Philippines).

2587 **805** 2p. multicoloured . . . 20 15

1993. 50th Anniv of Filipino Inventors Society. Multicoloured.

2588 2p. Type **806** 20 15
2589 2p. Rice-harvesting machine 20 15

Nos. 2588/9 were issued together, se-tenant, forming a composite design.

807 Holy Family

808 Northern Luzon

1993. Christmas. Multicoloured.

2590 2p. Type **807** 20 15
2591 6p. Church goers 65 45
2592 7p. Cattle and baskets of food 80 50
2593 8p. Carol-singers 95 65

1993. Philippine Guerrilla Units of Second World War (2nd series). Multicoloured.

2594 2p. Type **808** 20 15
2595 2p. Bohol Area Command 20 15
2596 2p. Leyte Area Command 20 15
2597 2p. Palawan Special Battalion and Sulu Area Command 20 15

809 Dove over City (peace and order)

1993. "Philippines 2000" (development plan). Multicoloured.

2598 2p. Type **809** 20 15
2599 6p. Means of transport and communications 65 45
2600 7p. Offices, roads and factories (infrastructure and industry) 80 50
2601 8p. People from different walks of life (people empowerment) 95 65
MS2602 110 × 85 mm. 8p. Various motifs on themes of peace, transport and communication, infrastructure and industry and people power. Imperf . . . . 2·20 2·20

810 Shih Tzu

1993. New Year. Year of the Dog. Multicoloured.

2603 2p. Type **810** 20 15
2604 6p. Chow 65 45
MS2605 98 × 88 mm. Nos. 2603/4 plus two labels. Perf or imperf 1·50 1·50

811 Jamboree Emblem and Flags

1993. 1st Association of South-East Asian Nations Scout Jamboree, Makiling. Multicoloured.

2606 2p. Type **811** 20 15
2607 6p. Scout at camp-site, flags and emblem 65 45
MS2608 86 × 86 mm. Nos. 2606/7 1·80 1·80

812 Club Emblem on Diamond

1994. 75th Anniv of Manila Rotary Club.

2609 **812** 2p. multicoloured . . . 20 15

813 Teeth and Dental Hygiene Products

1994. 17th Asian–Pacific Dental Congress, Manila. Multicoloured.

2610 2p. Type **813** 20 15
2611 6p. Teeth, flags of participating countries and teeth over globe with Philippines circled (vert) 65 45

814 "Acropora micropthalma"

1994. Corals. Multicoloured.

2612 2p. Type **814** 20 15
2613 2p. "Seriatopora hystrix" . . 20 15
2614 2p. "Acropora latistella" . . 20 15
2615 2p. "Millepora tenella" . . 20 15
2616 2p. "Millepora tenella" (different) 20 15

2617 2p. "Pachyseris valenciennesi" 20 15
2618 2p. "Pavona decussata" 20 15
2619 2p. "Galaxea fascicularis" 20 15
2620 2p. "Acropora formosa" 20 15
2621 2p. "Acropora humilis" 20 15
2622 2p. "Isis sp." (vert) 20 20
2623 2p. "Plexaura sp." (vert) 20 20
2624 2p. "Dendronepthya sp." (vert) 20 20
2625 2p. "Heteroxenia sp." (vert) 20 20
MS2626 135 × 78 mm. 3p. "Xenia puertogalerae"; 3p. "Plexaura" sp. (different); 3p. "Dendrophyllia gracilis"; 3p. "Plerogyra sinuosa" 95 95

815 New Year Stamps of 1991 and 1992 bearing Exhibition Emblem

1994. "Hong Kong '94" Stamp Exhibition. Multicoloured.
2627 2p. Type **815** 20 15
2628 6p. 1993 New Year stamps 65 45
MS2629 Two sheets, each 98 × 72 mm. (a) Nos. 2627/8 (blue margin); (b) Nos. 2627/8 (green margin) 90 90

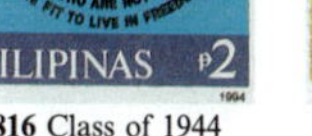

816 Class of 1944 Emblem

817 Airplane over Harbour, Man and Cogwheel and Emblem

1994. 50th Anniv of Philippine Military Academy Class of 1944.
2630 **816** 2p. multicoloured 20 15

1994. Naphilcon 94 First National Philatelic Congress. As No. **MS**2626 but with additional inscription in the central gutter.
MS2631 135 × 78 mm. 3p. × 4 multicoloured 1·40 1·40

1994. Federation of Filipino–Chinese Chambers of Commerce and Industry.
2632 **817** 2p. multicoloured 20 15

818 Stork carrying Baby ("Binabati Kita")

819 Gloria Diaz (Miss Universe 1969)

1994. Greetings Stamps. Multicoloured.
2633 2p. Type **818** 20 15
2634 2p. As No. 2633 but inscr "Congratulations" 20 15
2635 2p. Bouquet ("Binabati Kita") 20 15
2636 2p. As No. 2635 but inscr "Congratulations" 20 15
2637 2p. Mortar board, scroll and books ("Binabati Kita") 20 15
2638 2p. As No. 2637 but inscr "Congratulations" 20 15
2639 2p. Bouquet, doves and heads inside heart ("Binabati Kita") 20 15
2640 2p. As No. 2639 but inscr "Congratulations" 20 15

1994. Miss Universe Beauty Contest. Multicoloured.
2653 2p. Type **819** 20 15
2654 2p. Margie Moran (Miss Universe 1973) 20 15
2655 6p. Crown 65 45
2656 7p. Contestant 80 60
MS2657 90 × 80 mm. 8p. As No. 2653; 8p. As No. 2654 1·80 1·80

820 Antonio Molina (composer)

821 Map, Forest and Emblem (Baguio City)

1994. Birth Centenaries. Multicoloured.
2658 2p. Type **820** 20 15
2659 2p. Jose Yulo (Secretary of Justice) 20 15
2660 2p. Josefa Jara-Martinez (social worker) 20 15
2661 2p. Nicanor Reyes (accountant) 20 15
2662 2p. Sabino Padilla (judge) 20 15

1994. Centenary of Declaration of Philippine Independence (2nd issue). National Landmarks. Sheet 100 × 80 mm containing vert designs as T **788**. Multicoloured.
MS2663 2p. Aguinaldo Shrine; 2p. Barasoain Shrine; 3p. Rizal Shrine; 3p. Mabini Shrine 1·20 1·20

1994. Export Processing Zones. Multicoloured.
2664 2p. Type **821** 20 15
2665 2p. Cross on hilltop (Bataan) 20 15
2666 2p. Octagonal building (Mactan) 20 15
2667 2p. Aguinaldo Shrine (Cavite) 20 15
2668 7p. Map and products 80 50
2669 8p. Globe and products 95 65
Nos. 2264/7 and 2668/9 respectively were issued together, se-tenant, forming composite designs.

822 Cross through "ILLEGAL RECRUITMENT"

1994. Anti-illegal Recruitment Campaign.
2670 **822** 2p. multicoloured 20 15

823 Palawan Bearcat

1994. Mammals. Multicoloured.
2671 6p. Type **823** 75 45
2672 6p. Philippine tarsier 75 45
2673 6p. Malayan pangolin (inscr "Scaly Anteater") 75 45
2674 6p. Indonesian ("Palawan") porcupine 75 45
MS2675 96 × 67 mm. 12p. Visayan spotted deer (79 × 29 mm) 1·50 1·50

824 Glory of the Sea Cone ("Conus gloriamaris")

1994. "Philakorea 1994" International Stamp Exhibition, Seoul. Shells. Multicoloured.
2676 2p. Type **824** 20 15
2677 2p. Striate cone ("Conus striatus") 20 15
2678 2p. Geography cone ("Conus geographus") 20 15
2679 2p. Textile cone ("Conus textile") 20 15
MS2680 Two sheets, each 88 × 78 mm. (a) 6p. Striate cone; 6p. "Conus marmoreus" (Marble cone); (b) 6p. Marble cone; 6p. Geography cone 1·50 1·50

1994. "Singpex '94" National Stamp Exhibition, Singapore. As No. **MS**2675 but additionally inscribed "Singpex '94 31 August–3 September 1994" and emblem.
MS2681 96 × 67 mm. 12p. multicoloured 1·50 1·50

825 Sergio Osmena, Snr.

1994. 50th Anniv of Leyte Gulf Landings. Multicoloured.
2682 2p. Type **825** 20 15
2683 2p. Soldiers landing at Palo 20 15
2684 2p. "Peace – A Better World" emblem 20 15
2685 2p. Carlos Romulo 20 15
Nos. 2682/5 were issued together, se-tenant, forming a composite design.

826 Family (International Year of the Family)

1994. Anniversaries and Event. Multicoloured.
2686 2p. Type **826** 20 15
2687 6p. Workers (75th anniv of I.L.O.) 75 45
2688 7p. Aircraft and symbols of flight (50th anniv of I.C.A.O.) 90 60

827 Blue-naped Parrot

1994. "Aseanpex '94" Stamp Exhibition, Penang, Malaysia. Birds. Muilticoloured.
2689 2p. Type **827** 20 15
2690 2p. Luzon bleeding heart ("Bleeding Heart Pigeon") 20 15
2691 2p. Palawan peacock-pheasant 20 15
2692 2p. Koch's pitta 20 15
MS2693 69 × 55 mm. 12p. Philippine eagle (vert) 1·50 1·50

828 Presidents Fidel Ramos and W. Clinton

1994. Visit of United States President William Clinton to Philippines.
2694 **828** 2p. multicoloured 20 15
2695 8p. multicoloured 1·00 65

829 Convention Emblem

830 "Soteranna Puson y Quintos de Ventenilla" (Dionisio de Castro)

1994. Association of South-East Asian Nations Eastern Business Convention, Davao City.
2696 **829** 2p. multicoloured 30 15
2697 6p. multicoloured 75 50

1994. Philatelic Week. Portraits. Multicoloured.
2698 2p. Type **830** 30 1·70
2699 6p. "Quintina Castor de Sadie" (Simon Flores y de la Rosa) 75 50
2700 7p. "Portrait of the Artist's Mother" (Felix Hidalgo y Padilla) 90 60
2701 8p. "Una Bulaquena" (Juan Luna y Novicio) 1·00 65
MS2702 60 × 100 mm. 12p. "Cirilo and Severina Quaison Family" (Simon Flores y de la Rosa) ($28\frac{1}{2}$ × 79 mm) 1·50 1·50

831 Wreath

1994. Christmas. Multicoloured.
2703 2p. Type **831** 75 50
2704 6p. Angels 90 60
2705 7p. Bells 1·00 65
2706 8p. Christmas basket 1·00 65

832 Piggy Bank

1994. New Year. Year of the Pig. Multicoloured.
2707 2p. Type **832** 30 15
2708 6p. Pig couple 75 50
MS2709 98 × 88 mm. Nos. 2707/8 plus two labels. Perf or imperf 1·10 1·10

833 Raid on Prison

1994. 50th Anniversaries of Raid by Hunters ROTC Guerrillas on Psew Bilibi Prison and of Mass Escape by Inmates. Multicoloured.
2710 2p. Type **833** 20 15
2711 2p. Inmates fleeing 20 15
Nos. 2710/11 were issued together, se-tenant, forming a composite design.

834 East Central Luzon Guerrilla Area

835 Ribbon on Globe

1994. Philippine Guerrilla Units of Second World War (3rd series). Multicoloured.
2712 2p. Type **834** 20 15
2713 2p. Mindoro Provincial Battalion and Marinduque Guerrilla Force 20 15
2714 2p. Zambales Military District and Masbate Guerrilla Regiment 20 15
2715 2p. Samar Area Command 50 35

1994. National AIDS Awareness Campaign.
2716 **835** 2p. multicoloured 20 15

836 Flag

1994. Centenary of Declaration of Philippine Independence. Multicoloured.
2717 2p. Type **836** 20 15
2718 2p. Present state flag 20 15
2719 2p. Anniversary emblem 20 15
Nos. 2717/19 were issued together, se-tenant, forming a composite design.

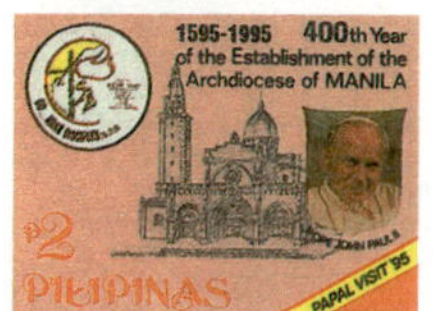

837 Pope John Paul II and Manila Cathedral

1995. Papal Visit. Multicoloured.
2720 2p. Type **837** (400th anniv of Manila Archdiocese) . . . 20 15
2721 2p. Pope and Cebu Cathedral (400th anniv of Diocese) 20 15
2722 2p. Pope and Caceres Cathedral (400th anniv of Diocese) 20 15
2723 2p. Pope and Nueva Segovia Cathedral (400th anniv of Diocese) 20 15
2724 2p. Pope, globe and Pope's arms 30 20
2725 6p. Pope and Federation of Asian Bishops emblem (6th Conference, Manila) 75 50
2726 8p. Pope, youths and emblem (10th World Youth Day) . . . . . . 1·00 65
MS2727 81 × 60 mm. 8p. Pope and President Fidel Ramos . . . . 1·00 1·00

1995. "Christypex '95" Philatelic Exhibition, Manila. No. MS2727 optd **CHRISTYPEX '95 JANUARY 4-16, 1995 University of Santo Tomas, Manila PHILIPPINE PHILATELIC FEDERATION**.
MS2728 81 × 60 mm. 8p. multicoloured . . . . 1·00 1·00

839 Landing Craft and Map

1995. 50th Anniv of Lingayen Gulf Landings. Multicoloured.
2729 2p. Type **839** 20 15
2730 2p. Map and emblems of 6th, 37th, 40th and 43rd army divisions 20 15
Nos. 2729/30 were issued together, se-tenant, forming a composite design.

840 Monument (Peter de Guzman) and Ruins of Intramuros (½-size illustration)

1995. 50th Anniv of Battle for the Liberation of Manila. Multicoloured.
2731 2p. Type **840** 10 10
2732 8p. Monument and ruins of Legislative Building and Department of Agriculture 40 20

841 Diokno

1995. 8th Death Anniv of Jose Diokno (politician).
2733 **841** 2p. multicoloured . . . 20 15

842 Anniversary Emblem and Ethnic Groups

1995. 75th Anniv of International School, Manila. Multicoloured.
2734 2p. Type **842** 20 15
2735 8p. Globe and cut-outs of children . . . . 1·00 65

843 Greater Malay Mouse Deer

1995. Mammals. Multicoloured.
2736 2p. Type **843** 20 15
2737 2p. Tamarau 20 15
2738 2p. Visayan warty pig . . . 20 15
2739 2p. Palm civet 20 15
MS2740 89 × 80 mm. 8p. Flying lemur; 8p. Philippine deer . . . 2·10 2·10

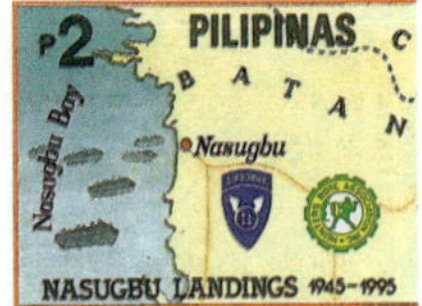

844 Nasugbu Landings

1995. 50th Anniversaries. Multicoloured.
2741 2p. Type **844** 20 15
2742 2p. Tagaytay Landings . . . 20 15
2743 2p. Battle of Nichols Airbase and Fort McKinley 20 15
Nos. 2741/2 were issued together, se-tenant, forming a composite design.

845 Memorial

1995. 50th Anniv of Liberation of Baguio.
2744 **845** 2p. multicoloured . . . 20 15

846 Cabanatuan Camp

847 Victorio Edades (artist)

1995. 50th Anniv of Liberation of Internment and Prisoner of War Camps. Multicoloured.
2745 2p. Type **846** 20 15
2746 2p. Entrance to U.S.T. camp 20 15
2747 2p. Los Banos camp 20 15
Nos. 2746/7 are wrongly inscribed "Interment".

1995. Birth Centenaries. Multicoloured.
2748 2p. Type **847** 20 15
2749 2p. Jovita Fuentes (opera singer) 20 15
2750 2p. Candido Africa (medical researcher) 20 15
2751 2p. Asuncion Arriola-Perez (politician) 20 15
2752 2p. Eduardo Quisumbing (botanist) 20 15

1995. Centenary of Declaration of Philippine Independence (3rd issue). 123rd Anniv of Cavite Mutiny. Sheet 100 × 80 mm. containing vert designs as T**788**.
MS2753 2p. Cavite shipyard; 2p. Centenary memorial; 3p. San Filipe fortress; 3p. Crisanto de los Reyes y Mendoza (death centenary) . . . . 1·30 80

848 Emblems and Bible

1995. 50th Anniv of Philippine Catholic Bishops' Conference, Manila.
2754 **848** 2p. multicoloured . . . 20 15

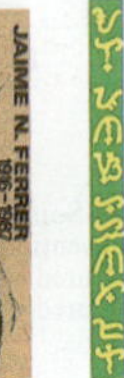

849 Ferrer

850 Neolithic Burial Jar, Manunggul

1995. 8th Death Anniv of Jaime Ferrer (administrator).
2755 **849** 2p. multicoloured . . . 20 15

1995. Archaeology. Multicoloured.
2756 2p. Type **850** 20 15
2757 2p. Iron age secondary burial jar, Ayub Cave, Mindanao 20 15
2758 2p. Iron age secondary burial jar (different), Ayub Cave 20 15
2759 2p. Neolithic ritual drinking vessel, Leta-Leta Cave, Palawan 20 15
MS2760 100 × 70 mm. 12p. 14th–15th century double-spouted vessel and presentation tray, Laurel, Batangas (80 × 30 mm) . . . . 1·60 1·60
See also No. **MS**2767.

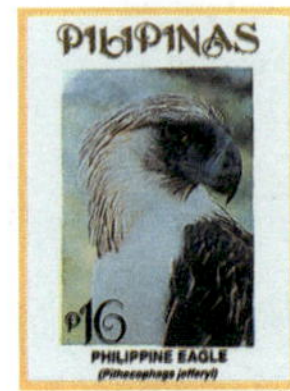

851 Philippine Eagle

852 Right Hand supporting Wildlife

1995. Adoption of the Philippine Eagle as National Bird. Sheet 69 × 55 mm.
MS2761 **851** 16p. multicoloured 2·20 2·20

1995. Association of South-East Asian Nations Environment Year. Multicoloured.
2762 2p. Type **852** 20 15
2763 2p. Left hand supporting wildlife 20 15
MS2764 89 × 78 mm. 6p. Type **852**; 6p. As No. 2766 . . . . 1·60 1·60
Nos. 2762/3 were issued together, se-tenant, forming a composite design.

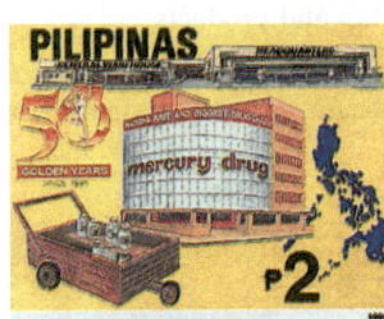

853 Anniversary Emblem, Buildings and Trolley

1995. 50th Anniv of Mercury Drug Corporation.
2765 **853** 2p. multicoloured . . . 20 15

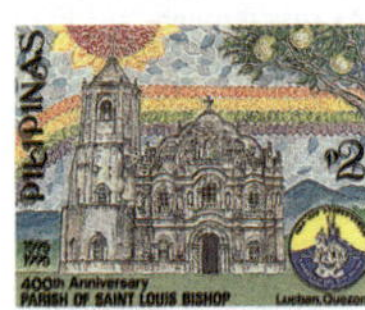

854 Parish Church

1995. 400th Anniv of Parish of Saint Louis Bishop, Lucban.
2766 **854** 2p. multicoloured . . . 20 15

1995. "Jakarta 95" Asian Stamp Exhibition. As No.**MS**2760 but with additional inscription at foot.
MS2767 100 × 70 mm. 12p. multicoloured . . . . 1·60 1·60

855 Instructor and Pupils

1995. 25th Anniv of Asian-Pacific Postal Training Centre, Bangkok.
2768 **855** 6p. multicoloured . . . 80 50

856 Crops and Child drinking from Well

857 Carlos Romulo

1995. 50th Anniv of F.A.O.
2769 **856** 8p. multicoloured . . . 1·10 75

1995. 50th Anniv of U.N.O. Multicoloured.
2770 2p. Jose Bengzon (inscr "Cesar Bengzon") 55 55
2771 2p. Rafael Salas (Assistant Secretary General) 55 55
2772 2p. Salvador Lopez (Secretary) 55 55
2773 2p. Jose Ingles (Under-secretary) 55 55
2775 2p. Type **857** 20 15
MS2774 71 × 57 mm. 16p. Carlos Romulo (President of General Assembly) . . . . 2·20 2·20
No. 2770 depicts Jose Bengzon in error for his brother Cesar.

858 Anniversary Emblem

859 Eclipse

1995. 50th Anniv of Manila Overseas Press Club.
2779 **858** 2p. multicoloured . . . 20 15

1995. Total Solar Eclipse.
2780 **859** 2p. multicoloured . . . 20 15

860 Flag

861 "Two Igorot Women" (Victorio Edades)

1995. National Symbols. With blue barcode at top. "Pilipinas" in red. Variously dated. Multicoloured.
2781 2p. Flag ("Pillipinas" at top) 20 15
2782 2p. Hero (Jose Rizal) . . . 20 15
2783 2p. House 20 15
2784 2p. Costume 20 15
2785 2p. Dance 20 15
2786 2p. Sport 20 15
2787 2p. Bird (Philippine eagle) 20 15
2788 2p. Type **860** 20 15
2789 2p. Animal (water buffalo) 20 15
2790 2p. Flower (jasmine) 20 15
2791 2p. Tree 20 15
2792 2p. Fruit (mango) 20 15
2793 2p. Leaf (palm) 20 15
2794 2p. Fish (milkfish) 20 15
For designs with barcode but "Pilipinas" in blue, see Nos. 2822/44.

1995. National Stamp Collecting Month (1st issue). Paintings by Filipino artists. Multicoloured.
2795 2p. Type **861** 30 15
2796 6p. "Serenade" (Carlos Francisco) 90 50
2797 7p. "Tuba Drinkers" (Vicente Manansala) . . . 95 65
2798 8p. "Genesis" (Hernando Ocampo) . . . . 1·00 80
MS2799 99 × 70 mm. "The Builders" (Victorio Edades) (79 × 29 mm) 1·60 1·60
See also No. **MS**2805.

862 Tambourine

863 Abacus and Anniversary Emblem

1995. Christmas. Musical instruments and Lines from Carols. Multicoloured.
2800 2p. Type **862** 20 15
2801 6p. Maracas 75 50
2802 7p. Guitar 95 65
2803 8p. Drum . . . . 1·20 80

1995. 50th Anniv of Sycip Gorres Velayo & Co. (accountants).
2804 **863** 2p. multicoloured . . . 20 15

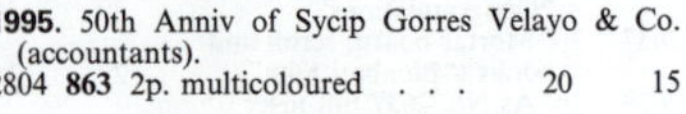

864 Pres. Ramos signing Stamp Month Proclamation

1995. National Stamp Collecting Month (2nd issue). Sheet 80 × 60 mm.
MS2805 **864** 8p. multicoloured . . . 1·10 1·10

865 Rat and Fireworks

1995. New Year. Year of the Rat. Multicoloured.
2806 2p. Type **865** 30 20
2807 6p. Model of rat 80 50
MS2808 98 × 88 mm. Nos. 2806/7 plus two greetings labels. Perf or imperf 1·20 1·20

866 Badge of Fil-American Irregular Troops Veterans Legion

1995. Philippine Guerrilla Units of Second World War (4th series). Multicoloured.
2809 2p. Type **866** 20 15
2810 2p. Badge of Bicol Brigade Veterans 20 15
2811 2p. Map of Fil-American Guerrilla forces (Cavite) and Hukbalahap unit (Pampanga) 20 15
2812 2p. Map of South Tarlac military district and Northwest Pampanga 20 15

867 Liberation of Panay and Romblon

1995. 50th Anniversaries. Multicoloured.
2813 2p. Type **867** 20 15
2814 2p. Liberation of Cebu 20 15
2815 2p. Battle of Ipo Dam 20 15
2816 2p. Battle of Bessang Pass 20 15
2817 2p. Surrender of General Yamashita 20 15

868 Jose Rizal

870 "Treating Patient" (Manuel Baldemor)

869 Top detail of Map of Islands (½-size illustration)

1995. Centenary of Declaration of Philippine Independence Revolutionaries. Multicoloured.
2818 2p. Type **868** 20 15
2819 2p. Andres Bonifacio 20 15
2820 2p. Apolinario Mabini 20 15

1995. 50th Anniv of End of Second World War. Dated "1995". Two sheets containing new designs as T **869** and previous designs. Multicoloured.
MS2821 Two sheets. (a) 177 × 139 mm. 2p. × 8, Nos. 2682/5, 2729/30 and 2741/2; 2p. × 4, As T **869** forming composite design of map of Philippine Islands (blue background). (b) 179 × 199 mm. 2p. × 13, Nos. 2710/11, 2731, 2743/7 and 2813/17; 2p. × 4 As T **869** forming composite design of map of Philippine Islands (green background); 2p. As No. 2732 8·00 8·00

1996. National Symbols. As T **860**, with blue barcode at top. "Pilipinas" in blue. Variously dated. Multicoloured.
2822 1p. Flower (jasmine) 15 10
2823 1p.50 Fish (milkfish) 20 15
2823a 2p. Flower (jasmine) 30 30
2824 3p. Animal (water buffalo) 35 30
2825 4p. Flag ("Pilipinas" at top) 50 35
2826 4p. Hero (Jose Rizal) 50 35
2827 4p. House 50 35
2828 4p. Costume 50 35
2829 4p. Dance 50 35
2830 4p. Sport 50 35
2831 4p. Bird (Philippine eagle) 50 35
2832 4p. Type **860** 50 35
2833 4p. Animal (head of water buffalo) (dated "1995") 50 35
2834 4p. Flower (jasmine) 50 35
2835 4p. Tree 50 35
2836 4p. Fruit (mango) 50 35
2837 4p. Leaf (palm) 50 35
2838 4p. Fish (milkfish) 50 35
2839 4p. Animal (water buffalo) (dated "1996") 50 35
2840 5p. Bird (Philippine eagle) 75 1·20
2841 6p. Leaf (palm) 80 50
2842 7p. Costume 90 60
2843 8p. Fruit (mango) 1·10 75
2844 10p. House 1·40 90

1996. 23rd International Congress of Internal Medicine, Manila.
2856 **870** 2p. multicoloured 20 15

871 Walled City of Intramuros

1996. Centenary of Sun Life of Canada (insurance company). Multicoloured.
2857 2p. Type **871** 20 15
2858 8p. Manila Bay sunset 1·10 75

872 Pair of Eastern Rosella (birds) on Branch ("I Love You")

873 University Building and Map of Islands on Grid

1996. Greetings Stamps. Multicoloured.
2859 2p. Type **872** 20 15
2860 2p. Eastern rosella (birds) ("Happy Valentine") 20 15
2861 6p. Cupid holding banner ("I Love You") 75 50
2862 6p. Cupid holding banner ("Happy Valentine") 75 50
2863 7p. Box of chocolates ("I Love You") 95 65
2864 7p. Box of chocolates ("Happy Valentine") 95 65
2865 8p. Butterfly and roses ("I Love You") 1·20 80
2866 8p. Butterfly and roses ("Happy Valentine") 1·20 80
Nos. 2861/2 were issued together, se-tenant, forming a composite design.

1996. 50th Anniv of Gregorio Araneta University Foundation.
2867 **873** 2p. multicoloured 20 15

874 Hospital

1996. 50th Anniv of Santo Tomas University Hospital.
2868 **874** 2p. multicoloured 20 15

875 Racoon Butterflyfish

1996. Fishes (1st series). Multicoloured.
2869 4p. Type **875** 50 35
2870 4p. Clown triggerfish 50 35
2871 4p. Regal angelfish 50 35
2872 4p. Mandarin fish 50 35
2873 4p. Emperor angelfish 50 35
2874 4p. Japan surgeonfish ("Powder Brown Tang") 50 35
2875 4p. Blue-girdled ("Majestic") angelfish 50 35
2876 4p. Palette surgeonfish ("Blue tang") 50 35
2877 4p. Moorish idol 50 35
2878 4p. Yellow-tailed ("Two-banded") anemonefish 50 35
MS2879 Two sheets (a) 140 × 81 mm. 4p. Clown triggerfish; 4p. Blue and red angelfish; 4p. Regal angelfish; 4p. Yellow-tailed anemonefish. (b) 82 × 61 mm. 12p. Lionfish 1·60 1·60
See also Nos. 2885/**MS**95.
MS2880 Two sheets. No. **MS**2879 additionally inscr in right margin for "Indonesia 96" World Youth Stamp Exhibition, Bandung 1·60 1·60
No **MS**2879 commemorates "ASENPEX '96".
See also Nos. 2885/**MS**2895.

1996. Basketball Championship. No. **MS**2510 trimmed to 85 × 85 mm (to remove inscr at foot) and optd in bottom margin with **PALARONG '96 PAMBANSA SOCSARGEN (SOUTH COTABATO, SARAGANI & GENERAL SANTOS CITY) APRIL 14-21, 1996.**
MS2881 10p. multicoloured 1·30 1·30

877 Francisco Ortigas

1996.
2882 **877** 4p. multicoloured 50 35

878 Mother Francisca and Convent

1996. 300th Anniv of Dominican Sisters of St. Catherine of Siena.
2883 **878** 4p. multicoloured 50 35

879 Nuclear Reactor (**880**)

1996. Centenary of Discovery of Radioactivity by Antoine Henri Becquerel.
2884 **879** 4p. multicoloured 50 35

1996. Fishes (2nd series). As T **875**. Multicoloured.
2885 4p. Spotted boxfish 50 35
2886 4p. Saddle ("Saddleback") butterflyfish 50 35
2887 4p. Sail-finned tang 50 35
2888 4p. Harlequin tuskfish 50 35
2889 4p. Clown wrasse 50 35
2890 4p. Yellow-faced ("Blue-faced") angelfish 50 35
2891 4p. Long-horned cowfish 50 35
2892 4p. Queen angelfish 50 35
2893 4p. Forceps ("Long-nosed") butterflyfish 50 35
2894 4p. Yellow tang 50 35
MS2895 Two sheets. (a) 133 × 80 mm. Nos. 2888, 2890 and 2892/3; (b) 136 × 74 mm. 4p. Purple fire goby; 4p. Yellow seahorse; 4p. Dusky batfish; 4p. Long-nosed hawkfish 4·50 4·50

1996. No. **MS**2895 additionally inscr in margin "CHINA 96–9th Asian International Exhibition" in English and Chinese and with exhibition emblem.
MS2896 Two sheets. (a) 133 × 80 mm. 4p. × 4 multicoloured. (b) 136 × 74 mm. 4p. × 4, multicoloured 4·50 4·50

1996. 10th Anniv of Young Philatelists' Society. Nos. 2471/4 optd with T **880**.
2897 2p. multicoloured 20 20
2898 2p. multicoloured 20 20
2899 2p. multicoloured 20 20
2900 2p. multicoloured 20 20

881 Carlos Garcia (President, 1957–61)

882 Satellite, Dish Aerial, Cock and Map

1996. Birth Centenaries. Multicoloured.
2901 4p. Type **881** 50 35
2902 4p. Casimiro del Rosario (physicist) 50 35
2903 4p. Geronima Pecson (first woman senator) 50 35
2904 4p. Cesar Bengson (mcmber of International Court of Justice) 50 35
2905 4p. Jose Corazon de Jesus (writer) 50 35

1996. Centenary of Declaration of Philippine Independence (6th issue). Centenary of Philippine Revolution. Sheet 100 × 80 mm containing vert designs as T **860** but with bar code sideways at right.
MS2906 4p. Cry of Pugadlawin; 4p. Battle of Pinaglabanan; 4p. Cry of Nueva Ecija; 4p. Battle of Binakayan 2·20 2·20

1996. 50th Anniv of ABS–CBN Broadcasting Services in Philippines. Multicoloured.
2907 4p. Type **882** 50 35
2908 8p. Cock, satellite and hemispheres 1·10 75

883 "M" and Heart

1996. "Convention City Manila".
2909 **883** 4p. multicoloured 50 35

884 Cojuangco

1996. Birth Centenary of Jose Cojuangco (entrepreneur and Corazon Aquino's father).
2910 **884** 4p. multicoloured 50 35

885 Brass Helmet and Top Hat

1996. 50th Anniv of Republic Day. Philippine–American Friendship Day. Multicoloured.
2911 4p. Type **885** 50 35
2912 8p. Philippine eagle and American bald eagle 1·10 75
MS2913 60 × 80 mm. 16p. American and Philippine flags (27 × 37 mm) 2·20 2·20

886 Boxing

1996. Centenary of Modern Olympic Games. Mult.
2914 4p. Type **886** 50 35
2915 6p. Athletics 80 50
2916 7p. Swimming 95 65
2917 8p. Equestrian 1·10 75
MS2918 119 × 80 mm. 4p. × 4, Motifs as in Nos. 2914/17 but with different backgrounds and inscriptions differently arranged 2·20 2·20

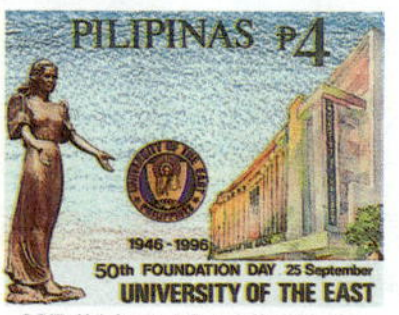

887 "Alma Mater" (statue, Guillermo Tolentino) and Manila Campus (after Florentino Concepcion)

1996. 50th Anniv of University of the East, Manila and Kalookan City.
2919 **887** 4p. multicoloured 50 35

888 "Dendrobium anosmum"

1996. Orchids. Multicoloured.
2920 4p. Type **888** 50 35
2921 4p. "Phalaenopsis equestris-alba" 50 35
2922 4p. "Aerides lawrenceae" . . 50 35
2923 4p. "Vanda javierii" 50 35
2924 4p. "Renanthera philippinensis" 50 35
2925 4p. "Dendrobium schuetzei" 50 35
2926 4p. "Dendrobium taurinum" 50 35
2927 4p. "Vanda lamellata" . . . 50 35
MS2928 141 × 64 mm. 4p. "Coelogyne pandurata"; 4p. "Vanda merrilii" (vert); 4p. "Cymbidium aliciae" (vert); 4p. "Dendrobium topaziacum" (vert) 2·20 2·20

889 Emblem and Globe

1996. 6th Asia–Pacific International Trade Fair, Manila.
2929 **889** 4p. multicoloured . . . 50 35

890 Children's Activities

891 Fran's Fantasy "Aiea"

1996. 50th Anniv of UNICEF. Multicoloured.
2930 4p. Type **890** 50 35
2931 4p. Windmills, factories, generator, boy with radio and children laughing . . 50 35
2932 4p. Mother holding "sun" baby and children gardening 50 35
2933 4p. Wind blowing toy windmills, boy with electrical fan and children playing 50 35
MS2934 91 × 58 mm. 16p. Boy with anemometer, girl with testubes, boy with magnifying glass and girl with windmill (39 × 29 mm) . . 2·20 2·20

1996. "Taipeh 96" Asian Stamp Exhibition. Orchids. Multicoloured.
2935 4p. Type **891** 50 35
2936 4p. Malvarosa Green Goddess "Nani" 50 35
2937 4p. Ports of Paradise "Emerald Isle" 50 35
2938 4p. Mem. Conrada Perez "Nani" 50 35
2939 4p. Pokai Tangerine "Lea" 50 35
2940 4p. Mem. Roselyn Reisman "Diana" 50 35
2941 4p. C. Moscombe x Toshie Aoki 50 35
2942 4p. Mem. Benigno Aquino "Flying Aces" 50 35
MS2943 97 × 65 mm. 12p. Pamela Hetherington "Coronation", Living Gold "Erin Treasure" and Eleanor Spicer "White Bouquet"(79 × 29 mm) . . . . 1·60 1·60

892 Communications

893 Philippine Nativity (Gilbert Miraflor)

1996. 4th Asia–Pacific Economic Co-operation Summit Conference, Subic. Multicoloured.
2944 4p. Type **892** 50 35
2945 6p. Open hands reaching towards sun (horiz) . . . 80 50
2946 7p. Grass and buildings (horiz) 95 65
2947 8p. Members' flags lining path leading to emblem, city and sun . . . . . . 1·10 75

1996. Christmas. Stamp design competition winning entries. Multicoloured.
2948 4p. Type **893** 50 35
2949 6p. Church (Stephanie Miljares) (horiz) 80 50
2950 7p. Carol singer with guitars (Mark Sales) (horiz) . . . 95 65
2951 8p. Carol singers and statue of buffalo (Lecester Glaraga) . . . . 1·10 75

894 Perez

1996. Birth Centenary of Eugenio Perez (politician).
2952 **894** 4p. multicoloured . . . 50 35

895 Carabao

1996. New Year. Year of the Ox. Multicoloured.
2953 4p. Type **895** 50 35
2954 6p. Tamaraw 80 50
MS2955 97 × 88 mm. Nos. 2953/4. Perf or imperf . . . . 1·30 1·30

896 Rizal aged 14

897 Father Mariano Gomez

1996. "Aseanpex '96" Association of South-East Asian Nations Stamp Exhibition, Manila. Death Centenary of Dr. Jose Rizal (1st issue). Mult.
2956 4p. Type **896** 50 35
2957 4p. Rizal aged 18 . . . . . 50 35
2958 4p. Rizal aged 25 . . . . . 50 35
2959 4p. Rizal aged 31 . . . . . 50 35
2960 4p. Title page of "Noli Me Tangere" (first novel) . . 50 35
2961 4p. Gomburza and associates 50 35
2962 4p. "Oyang Dapitana" (sculpture by Rizal) . . . 50 35
2963 4p. Bust by Rizal of Ricardo Carnicero (commandant of Dapitan) 50 35
2964 4p. Rizal's house at Calamba (horiz) 50 35
2965 4p. University of Santo Tomas, Manila (horiz) . . 50 35
2966 4p. Hotel de Oriente, Manila (horiz) 50 35
2967 4p. Dapitan during Rizal's exile (horiz) 50 35
2968 4p. Central University, Madrid (horiz) 50 35
2969 4p. British Museum, London (horiz) 50 35
2970 4p. Botanical Garden, Madrid (horiz) 50 35
2971 4p. Heidelberg, Germany (horiz) 50 35
MS2972 Four sheets, each 97 × 70 mm. (a) 12p. Cooking equipment and portrait as in T **896**; (b) 12p. Cooking equipment and portrait as in No. 2957; (c) 12p. No. 2958; (d) 12p. Cooking equipment and portrait as in No. 2959 . . . . 6·50 6·50
See also No. 2976.

1996. Centenary of Declaration of Philippine Independence. Execution of Secularist Priests, 1872. Multicoloured.
2973 4p. Type **897** 50 35
2974 4p. Father Jose Burgos . . 50 35
2975 4p. Father Jacinto Zamora 50 35

1997. "Hong Kong 97" Stamp Exhibition. Chinese Zodiac. Two sheets 161 × 100 mm containing previous New Year issues (some with changed face values). Multicoloured.
MS2977 Two sheets (a) 4p. × 5, As Nos. 2351, 2452, 2603, 2806 and 2953; (b) 6p. × 6, As Nos. 2352, 2451, 2604, 2708 and 2954 . . 8·00 8·00

898 Rizal (poster)

1996. Death Centenary of Dr. Jose Rizal (2nd issue).
2976 **898** 4p. multicoloured . . . 50 35

899 Soldier, Dove and National Colours

1997. Centenary of Philippine Army.
2978 **899** 4p. multicoloured . . . 50 45

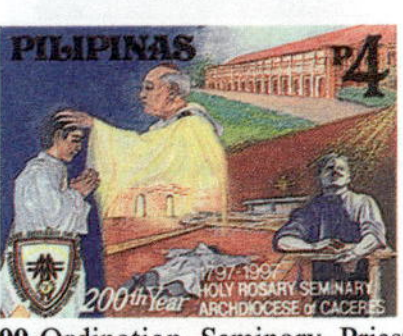
900 Ordination, Seminary, Priest prostrate before Altar and Priest at Devotions

1997. Bicentenary of Holy Rosary Seminary, Naga City.
2979 **900** 4p. multicoloured . . . 50 45

1997. National Symbols. As T **788** (no bar code). "Pilipinas" in blue. Multicoloured.
2980 1p. Flower (jasmine) 30 15
2981 5p. Bird (Philippine eagle) 1·30 45
2982 6p. Leaf (palm) . . . . . . 1·50 60
2983 7p. Costume . . . . 1·80 65
2984 8p. Fruit (mango) . . . . . 2·10 80
2985 10p. House . . . . 2·50 1·00

901 Volunteers attending Patient

1997. 50th Anniv of Philippine National Red Cross.
2986 **901** 4p. multicoloured . . . 50 45

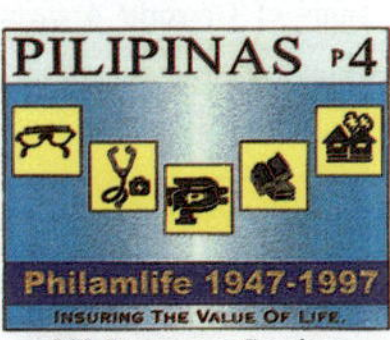
902 Insurance Services

1997. 50th Anniv of Philippine American Life Insurance Company.
2987 **902** 4p. multicoloured . . . 50 45

903 Columns

1997. Centenary of Department of Finance.
2988 **903** 4p. multicoloured . . . 50 45

904 Signatures and Globe

1997. 50th Anniv of J. Walter Thompson (Philippines) Inc. (advertising agency).
2989 **904** 4p. multicoloured . . . 50 45

1997. "Pacific 97" International Stamp Exhibition, San Francisco. No. **MS**2913 optd **World Philatelic Exhibition May 29 – June 8, 1997 San Francisco, California U.S.A.** in the right margin and with exhibition emblem in the left margin.
MS2990 16p. multicoloured . . . 3·00 3·00

1997. National Symbol. As T **860** (with bar code). "Pilipinas" in black at foot. Multicoloured.
2991 4p. Gem (South Sea pearls) 50 45

906 Visayan Warty Pig

1997. Endangered Animals. Multicoloured.
2992 4p. Type **906** 60 50
2993 4p. Sow and young Visayan warty pig 60 50
2994 4p. Visayan spotted deer buck 60 50
2995 4p. Roe and young Visayan spotted deer 60 50

907 Founding Signatories

1997. 30th Anniv of Association of South-East Asian Nations. Multicoloured.
2996 4p. Type **907** 60 50
2997 4p. Flags of founding member nations 60 50
2998 6p. Members' flags as figures forming circle around ASEAN emblem 90 75
2999 6p. Members' flags encircling globe 90 75

908 Symbols of Education and Law, University Building and Graduate

1997. 50th Anniv of Manuel L. Quezon University.
3000 **908** 4p. multicoloured . . . 50 4·50

909 Assembly Emblem

910 Isabelo Abaya

1997. 2nd World Scout Parliamentary Union General Assembly, Manila.
3001 **909** 4p. multicoloured . . . 50 45

1997. Battle of Candon. Multicoloured.
3002 4p. Type **910** 50 45
3003 6p. Abaya rallying revolutionaries (horiz) . . 75 65

911 Roberto Regala (diplomat and lawyer)

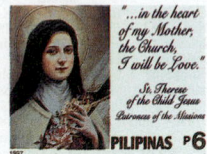

912 St. Theresa

1997. Birth Centenaries. Multicoloured.
3004 4p. Type **911** 50 45
3005 4p. Doroteo Espiritu (dentist) 50 45
3006 4p. Elisa Ochoa (nurse, first Congresswoman and 1930s' national tennis champion) 50 45

3007 4p. Mariano Marcos (politician) 50 45
3008 4p. Jose Romero (politician) 50 45

1997. Death Centenary of St. Theresa of Lisieux.
3009 **912** 6p. multicoloured 75 65

1997. Centenary of Declaration of Phillipine Independence (8th issue). Revolutionaries. Sheet 100 × 80 mm containing vert designs as T **860** but with barcode sideways at right.
MS3010 4p. Edilberto Evangelista and battle of Zapota Bride; 4p. Vicente Alvarez; 4p. Fracisco del Castillo; 4p. Pantaleon Villegas 2·20 2·20

913 "Homage to the Heroes of Bessang Pass" (Hernando Ruiz Ocampo)

1997. 50th Anniv of Stamp and Philatelic Division. Modern Art. Multicoloured.
3011 4p. Type **913** 45 45
3012 6p. "Jardin III" (Fernando Zobel) 75 65
3013 7p. "Abstraction" (Nena Saguil) (vert) 80 75
3014 8p. "House of Life" (Jose Joya) (vert) 95 90
MS3015 120 × 69 mm. 16p. "Dimension of Fear" (Jose Joya) (79 × 30 mm) 1·90 1·90

914 Man Painting with Feet

1997. Asian and Pacific Decade of Disabled Persons.
3016 **914** 6p. multicoloured 75 75

915 Bonifacio writing

1997. Centenary of Declaration of Philippine Independence. Statues of Andres Bonifacio. Multicoloured.
3017 4p. Type **915** 45 45
3018 4p. Bonifacio holding flag 45 45
3019 4p. Bonifacio holding sword 45 45

916 Von Stephan

1997. Death Centenary of Heinrich von Stephan (founder of U.P.U.).
3020 **916** 4p. multicoloured 50 50

917 Underwater Scene (½-size illustration)

1997. International Year of the Reef.
3021 **917** 8p. multicoloured 1·00 1·00
MS3022 100 × 69 mm. **917** 16p. multicoloured 2·10 2·10

918 "Adoration of the Magi"

920 "Dalagang Bukid" (Fernando Amorsolo)

919 Tiger

1997. Christmas. Stained Glass Windows. Mult.
3023 4p. Type **918** 45 45
3024 6p. Mary, Jesus and Wise Men 75 75
3025 7p. Mary on donkey and Nativity 80 80
3026 8p. "Nativity" 95 95

1997. New Year. Year of the Tiger. Multicoloured.
3027 4p. Type **919** 45 45
3028 6p. Head of tiger and tiger climbing rockface 65 65
MS3029 98 × 90 mm. Nos. 3027/8 plus two labels 1·10 1·10

1997. Stamp Collecting Month. Paintings. Multicoloured.
3030 4p. Type **920** 45 45
3031 6p. "Bagong Taon" (Arturo Luz) 75 75
3032 7p. "Jeepneys" (Vicente Manansala) (horiz) 80 80
3033 8p. "Encounter of the 'Nuestra Senora de Cavadonga' and the 'Centurion' " (Alfredo Carmelo) (horiz) 95 95
MS3034 102 × 60 mm. 16p. "Pista sa Nayon" (Carlos Francisco) (77 × 27 mm) 2·10 2·10

921 Hatch Grey

1997. Gamecocks. Multicoloured.
3035 4p. Type **921** 30 30
3036 4p. Spangled roundhead 30 30
3037 4p. Racey mug 30 30
3038 4p. Silver grey 30 30
3039 4p. Grey (vert) 30 30
3040 4p. Kelso (vert) 30 30
3041 4p. Bruner roundhead (vert) 30 30
3042 4p. Democrat (vert) 30 30
MS3043 Two sheets. (a) 55 × 69 mm. 12p. Cocks fighting (vert); (b) 99 × 59 mm. 16p. Cocks preparing to fight (79 × 29 mm) 2·10 2·10

922 Philippine Eagle

1997. National Symbols. Multicoloured.
3044 20p. Type **922** 1·50 1·50
3045 30p. Philippine eagle (different) 2·20 2·20
3046 50p. Philippine eagle (different) 3·75 3·75

923 Flag and Stars

1998. 50th Anniv of Art Association of the Philippines. Multicoloured.
3047 4p. Type **923** 45 45
3048 4p. Hand clasping paintbrushes 50 50

924 Mother Philippines, Club Building and Emblem

925 Marie Eugenie

1998. Centenary of Club Filipino (social club).
3049 **924** 4p. multicoloured 45 45

1998. Death Centenary of Blessed Marie Eugenie (founder of the Sisters of the Assumption).
3050 **925** 4p. multicoloured 45 45

926 Philippine and United States Flags

927 Emilio Jacinto

1998. 50th Anniv of Fulbright (student exchange) Program.
3051 **926** 4p. multicoloured 45 45

1998. Heroes of the Revolution. Multicoloured. White backgrounds. Blue barcode at foot.
3052 2p. Type **927** 20 15
3054 4p. Melchora Aquino 45 35
3055 4p. Jose Rizal 35 30
3056 5p. Antonio Luna 45 35
3057 8p. Marcelo del Pilar 60 50
3058 10p. Gregorio del Pilar 75 65
3059 11p. Andres Bonifacio 80 75
3060 13p. Apolinario Mabini 95 90
3061 15p. Emilio Aguinaldo 1·10 1·00
3062 18p. Juan Luna 1·30 1·20
See also Nos. 3179/88 and 3189/98.

928 Mt. Apo, Bagobo Woman, Orchids and Fruit

929 School and Emblem

1998. 50th Anniv of Apo View Hotel, Davao City.
3070 **928** 4p. multicoloured 45 45

1998. 75th Anniv of Philippine Cultural High School.
3071 **929** 4p. multicoloured 35 35

930 Old and Present School Buildings

1998. 75th Anniv of Victorino Mapa High School, San Rafael.
3072 **930** 4p. multicoloured 35 35

931 Lighthouse, Warship and Past and Present Uniforms

1998. Centenary of Philippine Navy.
3073 **931** 4p. multicoloured 35 35

932 University and Igorot Dancer

1998. 50th Anniv of University of Baguio.
3074 **932** 4p. multicoloured 35 35

933 Training Ship and Emblem

1998. 50th Anniv of Philippine Maritime Institute.
3075 **933** 4p. multicoloured 35 35

934 Forest, Palawan

1998. "EXPO '98" World's Fair, Lisbon. Mult.
3076 4p. Type **934** 35 35
3077 15p. Filipino vinta (sail canoe), Zamboanga (horiz) 1·10 1·10
MS3078 102 × 81 mm. 15p. Main Lobby of Philippine Pavilion (79 × 29 mm) 1·10 1·10

935 Climbing Ilang-ilang

1998. "Florikultura'98" International Garden Festival, San Fernando, Pampanga. Illustrations from "Flowers of the Philippines" by Manuel Blanco. Multicoloured.
3079 4p. Type **935** 30 30
3080 4p. "Hibiscus rosa-sinensis" 30 30
3081 4p. "Nerium oleander" 30 30
3082 4p. Arabian jasmine ("Jasminum sambac") 30 30
3083 4p. "Gardenia jasminoides" (vert) 30 30
3084 4p. Flame-of-the-forest ("Ixora coccinea") (vert) 30 30
3085 4p. Indian coral bean ("Erythrina indica") (vert) 30 30
3086 4p. "Abelmoschus moschatus" (vert) 30 30
MS3087 61 × 70 mm. 15p. "Medinilla magnifica" (vert) 3·00 3·00

936 City and Clark International Airport (½-size illustration)

1998. Clark Special Economic Zone.
3088 **936** 15p. multicoloured 1·10 1·10

937 Manila Galleon

1998. Centenary of Declaration of Philippine Independence. Philippines–Mexico–Spain Friendship. Multicoloured.
3089 15p. Type **937** 65 50
3090 15p. Philippine woman with flag, Legaspi-Urdaneta Monument and galleon 1·10 1·10
3091 15p. Spanish and Philippine flags, Cebu Basilica (after M. Miguel) and "Holy Child" (statuette) 1·10 1·10
MS3092 145 × 90 mm. Nos. 3089/91 plus three labels 3·25 3·25

938 "Spoliarium" (Juan Luna)

939 Andres Soriano (accountant)

1998. Centenary of Declaration of Philippine Independence. Multicoloured.
3093 4p. Type **938** 20 20
3094 8p. General Emilio Aguinaldo introducing Philippine national flag at Cavite 35 35
3095 16p. Execution of Jose Rizal, 1896 2·75 2·75
3096 16p. Andres Bonifacio and Katipunan monument 2·75 2·75
3097 20p. Barasoain Church (venue of first Philippine Congress, 1898) 3·25 3·25

1998. Birth Centenaries. Multicoloured.
3098 4p. Type **939** 35 35
3099 4p. Tomas Fonacier (University dean and historian) 35 35

3100 4p. Josefa Escoda (founder of Filipino Girl Scouts and social reformer) . . . 35 35
3101 4p. Lorenzo Tanada (politician) 35 35
3102 4p. Lazaro Francisco (writer) 35 35

940 Melchora Aquino

1998. Centenary of Declaration of Philippine Independence Women Revolutionaries. Mult.
3103 4p. Type **940** 20 20
3104 4p. Nazaria Lagos 20 20
3105 4p. Agueda Kahabagan . . 20 20

1998. Centenary of Philippine Independence (13th issue). Events of 1898. Sheet 100 × 80 mm containing vert designs as T **860** but with barcode sideways at right.
MS3106 4p. Cebu uprising; 4p. Negros uprising; 4p. Iligan uprising; 4p. Centenary emblem 1·20 1·20

1998. Centenary of Declaration of Philippine Independence (14th issue). Nos. 2644 (1993), 2825/32 and 2834/9 optd **1898 1998 KALAYAAN** and emblem.
3107 3p. Animal (head of water buffalo) 30 30
3108 4p. Flag ("Pilipinas" at top) 30 30
3109 4p. Hero (Jose Rizal) . . . 30 30
3110 4p. House 30 30
3111 4p. Costume 30 30
3112 4p. Dance 30 30
3113 4p. Sport 30 30
3114 4p. Bird (Philippine eagle) 30 30
3115 4p. Type **860** 30 30
3116 4p. Flower (jasmine) 30 30
3117 4p. Tree 30 30
3118 4p. Fruit (mango) 30 30
3119 4p. Leaf (palm) 30 30
3120 4p. Fish 30 30
3121 4p. Animal (water buffalo) 30 30

942 River Pasig

1998. River Pasig Environmental Campaign.
3122 **942** 4p. multicoloured . . . 35 35

943 Bottle-nosed ("Bottlenose") Dolphin

1998. Marine Mammals. Multicoloured.
3123 4p. Type **943** 30 30
3124 4p. Humpback whale . . . 30 30
3125 4p. Fraser's dolphin 30 30
3126 4p. Melon-headed whale . . 30 30
3127 4p. Minke whale 30 30
3128 4p. Striped dolphin 30 30
3129 4p. Sperm whale 30 30
3130 4p. Pygmy killer whale . . . 30 30
3131 4p. Cuvier's beaked whale 30 30
3132 4p. Killer whale 30 30
3133 4p. Bottle-nosed ("Bottlenose") dolphin (different) 30 30
3134 4p. Spinner dolphin ("Long-snouted spinner dolphin") 30 30
3135 4p. Risso's dolphin 30 30
3136 4p. Finless porpoise 30 30
3137 4p. Pygmy sperm whale . . 30 30
3138 4p. Pantropical spotted dolphin 30 30
3139 4p. False killer whale . . . 30 30
3140 4p. Blainville's beaked whale 30 30
3141 4p. Rough-toothed dolphin 30 30
3142 4p. Bryde's whale 30 30
MS3143 83 × 60 mm. 15p. Dugong 1·80 1·80

944 Coconuts and Products

1998. Centenary of Philippine Coconut Industry.
3144 **944** 4p. multicoloured . . . 30 30

945 Grapes, Emblem and Nun

1998. 75th Anniv of Holy Spirit Adoration Sisters in the Philippines.
3145 **945** 4p. multicoloured . . . 30 30

946 Child posting Letter **947** Holly Wreath

1998. Centenary of Postal Service. Multicoloured.
3146 6p. Type **946** 45 45
3147 6p. Globe and handshake 45 45
3148 6p. Philippine stamps, globe, airplane, galleon and building 45 45
3149 6p. Flags, dove and letters floating down to girl . . . 45 45
MS3150 102 × 60 mm. 15p. Boy holding letter and letters encircling globe . . . . 1·00 1·00

1998. Christmas. Multicoloured.
3151 6p. Type **947** 45 45
3152 11p. Star wreath 75 75
3153 13p. Flower wreath 90 90
3154 15p. Bell wreath . . . . . 1·00 1·00

948 2c. Postage Stamps (½-size illustration)

1998. "Philipinas 98" International Stamp Exhibition, Mandaluyong City. Six sheets each 121 × 60 mm containing horiz designs as T **948** showing 1898 Filipino Revolutionary Government Stamps. Multicoloured.
MS3155 Six sheets (a) 15p. Type **948** (blue background); (b) 15p. 2c. Postage and 1m. imperforate and perforate Printed Matter ("IMPRESOS") stamps; (c) 15p. 2 and 5c. Telegraph stamps; (d) 15p. 8c. Registered Letter ("CERTIFICADO") and 10c. Revenue ("RECIBOS") stamps; (e) 15p. Local issue and 5p. "LIBERTAD" stamp; (f) 15p. As No. **MS**3154a but imperforate and with green background . . . . 13·50 13·50

949 Person gagged with Barbed Wire

1998. 50th Anniv of Universal Declaration of Human Rights.
3156 **949** 4p. multicoloured . . . 10 10

950 Papal Mitre

1998. Shells. Multicoloured.
3157 4p. Type **950** 30 30
3158 4p. "Vexillum citrinum" . . 30 30
3159 4p. "Rugose mitre" ("Vexillum rugosum") . . 30 30
3160 4p. "Volema carinifera" . . 30 30
3161 4p. "Teramachia dalli" . . 30 30
3162 4p. "Nassarius vitiensis" . . 30 30
3163 4p. "Cymbiola imperialis" 30 30
3164 4p. "Cymbiola aulica" . . . 30 30
MS3165 97 × 70 mm. 8p. "Nassarius papillosus"; 8p. Trapezium horse conch ("Fasciolaria trapezium") 2·10 2·10

951 Sea Creatures (½-size illustration)

1998. International Year of the Ocean.
3166 **951** 15p. multicoloured . . . 45 35
MS3167 101 × 71 mm. No. 3166 1·80 1·80

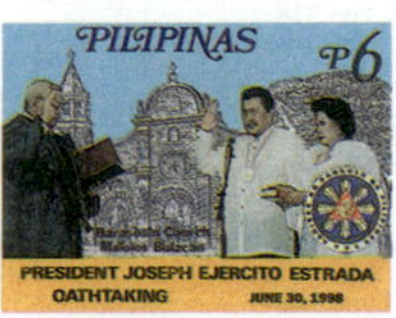

952 Taking Oath

1998. Inauguration of President Joseph Ejercito Estrada. Multicoloured.
3168 6p. Type **952** 45 45
3169 15p. Inaugural speech . . . 1·00 1·00

953 Rabbit

1998. New Year. Year of the Rabbit. Multicoloured.
3170 4p. Type **953** 30 30
3171 11p. Two rabbits 75 75
MS3172 97 × 89 mm. Nos. 3170/1 plus two labels. Perf or Imperf 2·00 2·00

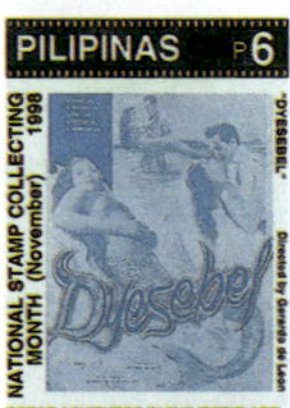

954 "Dyesebel"

1998. National Stamp Collecting Month. Film Posters.
3173 **954** 6p. blue and black . . . 45 45
3174 – 11p. brown and black . . 75 75
3175 – 13p. mauve and black . . 90 90
3176 – 15p. green and black . . 1·00 1·00
MS3177 58 × 101 mm. 15p. black 1·80 1·80
DESIGNS—As T **954** 11p. "Ang Sawa sa Lumang Simboryo"; 13p. "Prinsipe Amante"; 10p. (3176) "Anak Dalita". 26 × 76 mm—15p. (**MS**3177) "Siete Infantes de Lara".

955 "Noli Me Tangere" (Jose Rizal) (Pride in the Citizenry)

1998. Centenary of Declaration of Independence of Philippine Independence (15th issue). The Six Prides. Six sheets, each 84 × 90 mm containing vert designs as T **955**. Multicoloured.
MS3178 Six sheets. (a) 15p. Type **955**; (b) 15p. Banaue Rice Terraces (engineering); (c) 15p. Monument and woman holding national flag (Filipino people); (d) 15p. Malay woman in traditional costume (heritage); (e) 15p. Woman decorating pot and scripts (literature); (f) 15p. Woman with eagle on arm (resources) . . . 6·00 6·00

1998. Heroes of the Revolution. As Nos. 3052/62. Multicoloured. Blue barcode at foot. (a) Yellow backgrounds.
3179 6p. Type **927** 50 50
3180 6p. Melchora Aquino . . . 50 50
3181 6p. Jose Rizal 50 50
3182 6p. Antonio Luna 50 50
3183 6p. Marcelo del Pilar . . . 50 50
3184 6p. Gregorio del Pilar . . . 50 50
3185 6p. Andres Bonifacio . . . 50 50
3186 6p. Apolinario Mabini . . . 50 50
3187 6p. Emilio Aguinaldo . . . 50 50
3188 6p. Juan Luna 50 50

(b) Green backgrounds.
3189 15p. Type **927** . . . . . 1·10 1·10
3190 15p. Melchora Aquino . . . 1·10 1·10
3191 15p. Jose Rizal . . . . . . 1·10 1·10
3192 15p. Antonio Luna . . . . 1·10 1·10
3193 15p. Marcelo del Pilar . . 1·10 1·10
3194 15p. Gregorio del Pilar . . 1·10 1·10
3195 15p. Andres Bonifacio . . 1·10 1·10
3196 15p. Apolinario Mabini . . 1·10 1·10
3197 15p. Emilio Aguinaldo . . . 1·10 1·10
3198 15p. Juan Luna . . . . . . 1·10 1·10

(c) Pink background.
3229 5p. Jose Rizal 35 35

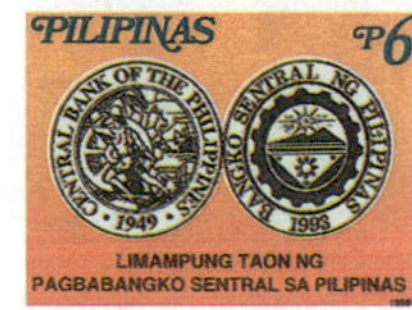

956 Old and New Bank Emblems

1999. 50th Anniv of Central Bank of the Philippines.
3199 **956** 6p. multicoloured . . . 35 35

957 Anniversary Emblem **958** Scouts and Guides

1999. Centenary of Declaration of Philippine Independence. Multicoloured.
3200 6p. Type **957** 35 35
3201 6p. General Emilio Aguinaldo's house (site of declaration, June 1898) . . 35 35
3202 6p. Malolos Congress, Barasoain Church, Bulacan (ratification by regions of declaration, September 1898) 35 35
3203 6p. House in Western Negros (uprising of 5 November 1898) 35 35
3204 6p. Cry of Santa Barbara, Iloilo (inauguration of government, 17 November 1898) 35 35
3205 6p. Cebu City (Victory over Colonial Forces of Spain, December 1898) 35 35
3206 6p. Philippine flag and emblem (declaration in Butaan City of sovereignty over Mindanao, 17 January 1899) 35 35
3207 6p. Facade of Church (Ratification of Constitution, 22 January 1899) 35 35
3208 6p. Carnival procession, Malolos (Inauguration of Republic, 23 January 1899) 35 35
3209 6p. Barosoain Church and anniversary emblem . . . 35 35

1999.
3210 5p. Type **958** . . . . . . 1·10 1·10
3211 5p. Children gardening . . . 1·10 1·10
Nos. 3210/11 were originally issued as Savings Bank stamps in 1995, but were authorized for postal use from 16 January 1999.

959 Cruise Liner

1999. Centenary of Department of Transportation and Communication. Multicoloured.
3212 6p. Type **959** 35 35
3213 6p. Airplane 35 35
3214 6p. Air traffic control tower 35 35
3215 6p. Satellite dish aerial and bus 35 35
MS3216 114 × 70 mm. 15p. Globe, stamps, Philpost headquarters and letters (79 × 27 mm) . . . . . 1·80 1·80
Nos. 3212/15 were issued together, se-tenant, forming a composite design.

960 San Juan del Monte Bridge

1999. Centenary of American–Filipino War.
3217 **960** 5p. multicoloured . . . 35 35

961 General Emilio Aguinaldo and Academy Arms

1999. Centenary (1998) of Philippine Military Academy.
3218 **961** 5p. multicoloured . . . 35 35

962 Green-backed Heron

1999. Birds. Multicoloured.
3219 5p. Type **962** 35 35
3220 5p. Common tern 35 35
3221 5p. Greater crested tern . . 35 35
3222 5p. Ruddy Turnstone . . . 35 35
3223 5p. Black-winged stilt . . . 35 35
3224 5p. Asiatic Dowitcher . . . 35 35
3225 5p. Whimbrel 35 35
3226 5p. Reef heron 35 35
MS3227 84 × 71 mm. 8p, Spotted greenshank; 8p. Tufted duck 3·00 3·00
MS3228 84 × 71 mm. As No. **MS**3227 but with different margin and emblem and inscription for "Australia 99" World Stamp Exhibition, Melbourne . . . . 80 1·20

963 Man holding Crutches

1999. 50th Anniv of Philippine Orthopaedic Association.
3230 **963** 5p. multicoloured . . . 35 35

964 Francisco Ortigas and Emblem

1999. 50th Anniv of Manila Lions Club.
3231 **964** 5p. multicoloured . . . 35 35

965 Entrance to Garden

1999. La Union Botanical Garden, San Fernando.
3232 5p. Type **965** 35 35
3233 5p. Kiosk 35 35
Nos. 3232/3 were issued together, se-tenant, forming a composite design.

966 Gliding Tree Frog

1999. Frogs. Multicoloured.
3234 5p. Type **966** 35 35
3235 5p. Common forest frog . . 35 35
3236 5p. Woodworth's frog . . . 35 35
3237 5p. Giant Philippine frog . . 35 35
MS3238 108 × 86 mm. 5p. Spiny tree frog; 5p. Truncate-toed chorus frog; 5p. Variable-backed frog 3·00 3·00

967 Manta Ray

1999. Marine Life. Multicoloured.
3239 5p. Type **967** 35 35
3240 5p. Painted rock lobster . . 35 35
3241 5p. Sea squirt 35 35
3242 5p. Banded sea snake . . . 35 35
MS3243 111 × 88 mm. 5p. Sea grapes; 5p. Branching coral; 5p. Sea urchin . . . . 4·00 4·00

968 Nakpil

1999. Birth Centenary of Juan Nakpil (architect).
3244 **968** 5p. multicoloured . . . 35 35

969 Child writing Letter and Globe

1999. 125th Anniv of Universal Postal Union. Multicoloured.
3245 5p. Type **969** 35 35
3246 15p. Girl with stamp album 1·10 1·10

970 Waling-Waling and Cattleya "Queen Sirikit'
971 Child writing

1999. 50 Years of Philippines–Thailand Diplomatic Relations. Multicoloured.
3247 5p. Type **970** 35 35
3248 11p. As Type **970** but with flowers transposed 80 80

1999. 150th Anniv of Mongol Pencils.
3249 **971** 5p. multicoloured . . . 35 35

972 Emblem and Handicapped Children

1999. 75th Anniv of Masonic Charities for Handicapped Children.
3250 **972** 5p. multicoloured . . . 35 35

973 Sampaguita and Rose of Sharon
975 Dove, Fishes, Bread and Quotation from Isaiah

974 Teachers, Nurses and Machinists

1999. 50 Years of Philippines–South Korea Diplomatic Relations. Multicoloured.
3251 5p. Type **973** 35 35
3252 11p. As Type **973** but with flowers transposed 80 80

1999. 50th Anniv of Community Chest Foundation.
3253 **974** 5p. multicoloured . . . 35 35

1999. Centenary of Philippine Bible Society.
3254 **975** 5p. multicoloured . . . 35 35

976 Score, Jose Palma (lyricist) and Julian Felipe (composer)

1999. Centenary of National Anthem.
3255 **976** 5p. multicoloured . . . 35 35

977 St. Francis of Assisi and Parish Church
979 Flags and Official Seal

1999. 400th Anniv of St. Francis of Assisi Parish, Sariaya, Quezon.
3256 **977** 5p. multicoloured . . . 35 35

1999. 25th Anniv of International Philippine Philatelic Society. No. **MS**3092 optd **25th ANNIVERSARY IPPS** on each stamp and in the margins with anniversary inscr and emblems in silver.
MS3257 145 × 90 mm. Nos. 3089/91 plus three labels . . . . 3·50 3·50

1999. The Senate.
3258 **979** 5p. multicoloured . . . 35 35

980 New Business, Arts and Sciences Faculty Building

1999. 60th Anniv of Chiang Kai Shek College, Manila.
3259 **980** 5p. multicoloured . . . 45 45

981 School Building

1999. 50th Anniv of Tanza National High School.
3260 **981** 5p. multicoloured . . . 45 45

982 St. Agustin Church, Paoay (World Heritage Day)

1999. United Nations Day. Multicoloured.
3261 5p. Type **982** 45 45
3262 11p. Elderly couple (International Year of the Older Person) 90 90
3263 15p. "Rizal Learns the Alphabet and Prayers from his Mother" (Miguel Galvez) (World Teachers' Day) . . . . 1·20 1·20

983 Angel
984 Tamaraw and Polar Bear

1999. Christmas. Multicoloured.
3264 5p. Type **983** 45 45
3265 11p. Angel holding star . . 90 90
3266 13p. Angel holding ribbon 1·10 1·10
3267 15p. Angel holding flowers 1·30 1·30
MS3268 141 × 95 mm. Nos. 3264/7 35 35

1999. 50 Years of Philippines–Canada Diplomatic Relations. Multicoloured.
3269 5p. Type **984** 45 45
3270 15p. As Type **984** but with animals transposed . . . 1·30 1·30

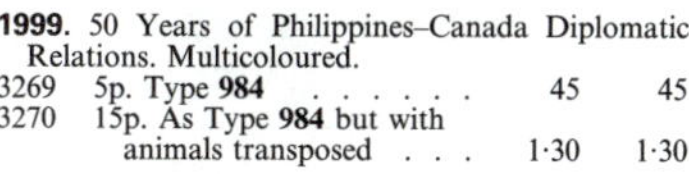
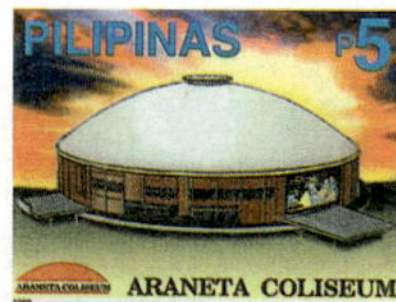

985 Coliseum

1999. Renovation of Araneta Coliseum.
3271 **985** 5p. multicoloured . . . 45 45

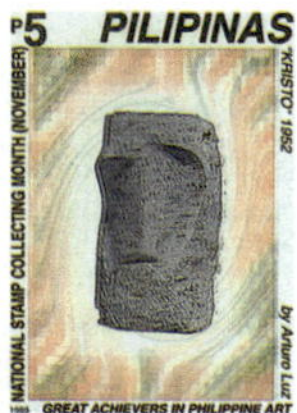

986 Sunrise
987 "Kristo" (Arturo Luz)

1999. 3rd Informal Summit of Association of South-east Asian Nations, Manila.
3272 **986** 5p. multicoloured . . . 45 45
3273 11p. multicoloured . . . 95 95

1999. National Stamp Collecting Month. Modern Sculptures. Multicoloured.
3274 5p. Type **987** 45 45
3275 11p. "Homage to Dodgie Laurel" (J. Elizalde Navarro) 90 90
3276 13p. "Hilojan" (Napoleon Abueva) . . . . 1·10 1·10
3277 15p. "Mother and Child" (Napoleon Abueva) . . . 1·30 1·30
MS3278 100 × 90 mm. 5p. "Mother's Revenge" (Jose Rival); 15p. "El Ermitano" (Jose Rival) (horiz) 2·50 2·50

988 Dragon

1999. New Year. Year of the Dragon. Multicoloured.
3279 5p. Type **988** 45 45
3280 15p. Dragon amongst clouds 90 90
MS3281 98 × 88 mm. Nos. 3279/80 plus two labels. Perf or imperf 1·50 1·50

989 Gen. Gregorio H. del Pilar

1999. Centenary of the Battle of Tirad Pass.
3282 **989** 5p. multicoloured . . . 45 45

990 *Paphiopedilum urbanianum*

1999. Orchids. Multicoloured.
3283 5p. Type **990** 45 45
3284 5p. *Phalaenopsis schilleriana* 45 45
3285 5p. *Dendrobium amethystoglossum* 45 45
3286 5p. *Paphiopedilum barbatum* 45 45
MS3287 132 × 83 mm. 5p. "Paphiopedilum haynaldianum" (horiz); 5p. "Phalaenopsis stuartiana" (horiz); 5p. "Trichoglottis brachiata" (horiz); 5p. "Ceratostylis rubra" (horiz) 1·80 1·80

991 General Licerio Geronimo

1999. Centenary of Battle of San Mateo.
3288 **991** 5p. multicoloured . . . 45 45

992 Crowds around Soldiers in Tanks

1999. New Millennium (1st series). "People Power". Multicoloured.
3289 5p. Type **992** 45 45
3290 5p. Radio antennae, helicopters and people . . 45 45
3291 5p. Religious procession . . 45 45
Nos. 3289/91 were issued together, se-tenant, forming a composite design.
See also Nos. 3311/13, 3357/9 and 3394/6.

993 Woman holding Gender Signs

2000. 25th Anniv of National Commission on Role of Filipino Women.
3292 **993** 5p. multicoloured . . . 45 45

994 Newspaper Headline and Headquarters **995** Manuel Roxas (1946–48)

2000. Centenary of the Manila Bulletin (newspaper).
3293 **994** 5p. multicoloured . . . 45 45

2000. Presidential Office. Multicoloured.
3294 5p. Type **995** 45 45
3295 5p. Elpidio Quirino (1948–53) 45 45

996 Golfer, Sailing Boat and Swimmers **997** Joseph Ejercito Estrada (1998–2000)

2000. 150th Anniv of La Union Province. Mult.
3296 5p. Type **996** 45 45
3297 5p. Tractor, building and worker 45 45
3298 5p. Government building . . 45 45
3299 5p. Airplane, bus, satellite dish, workers and bus . . 45 45

2000. Presidential Office. Multicoloured.
3300 5p. Presidential seal (face value at top left) 35 35
3301 5p. Type **997** 35 35
3302 5p. Fidel V. Ramos (1992–98) 35 35
3303 5p. Corazon C. Aquino (1986–92) 35 35
3304 5p. Ferdinand E. Marcos (1965–86) 35 35
3305 5p. Diosdado Macapagal (1961–65) 35 35
3306 5p. Carlos P. Garcia (1957–61) 35 35
3307 5p. Ramon Magsaysay (1953–57) 35 35
3308 5p. Elpidio Quirino (1948–53) 35 35
3309 5p. Manuel Roxas (1946–48) 35 35

998 Workers and Emblem

2000. Centenary of the Civil Service Commission.
3310 **998** 5p. multicoloured . . . 45 45

999 Golden Garuda, Palawan

2000. New Millennium (2nd series). Artefacts. Mult.
3311 5p. Type **999** 75 75
3312 5p. Sunrise at Pusan Point, Davao Oriental 75 75
3313 5p. Golden Tara, Agusan 75 75

1000 Outrigger Canoe, Boracay Island

2000. Tourist Sites. Multicoloured.
3314 5p. Type **1000** 35 35
3315 5p. Chocolate Hills, Bohol 35 35
3316 5p. El Nido Forest, Palawan 35 35
3317 5p. Vigan House, Ilocos Sur 35 35
MS3318 99 × 59 mm. 15p. Bananue rice terraces, Ifugao (79 × 29 mm) 1·80 1·80

1001 Great Wall of China and Chinese Phoenix

2000. 25th Anniv of Diplomatic Relations with Republic of China. Multicoloured.
3319 5p. Type **1001** 35 35
3320 11p. Banaue rice terraces and Philippine Sarimanok 80 80
MS3321 98 × 60 mm. 5p. Great Wall of China (39 × 29 mm); 11p. Banaue rice terraces (39 × 29 mm) 1·20 1·20

1002 Television and Emblem

2000. 50th Anniv of GMA Television and Radio Network.
3322 **1002** 5p. multicoloured . . . 45 45

1003 Church Building **1004** Carlos P. Garcia

2000. 400th Anniv of St. Thomas de Aquinas Parish, Mangaldan.
3323 **1003** 5p. multicoloured . . . 45 45

2000. Presidential Office. Multicoloured.
3324 10p. Type **1004** 90 90
3325 10p. Ramon Magsaysay . . 90 90
3326 11p. Ferdinand E. Marcos 95 95
3327 11p. Diosdado Macapagal 95 95
3328 13p. Corazon C. Aquino . . 1·00 1·00
3329 13p. Fidel V. Ramos . . . 1·00 1·00
3330 15p. Joseph Ejercito Estrada 1·20 1·20
3331 15p. Presidential seal (face value at top right) . . . . 1·20 1·20
See also Nos. 3489/98.

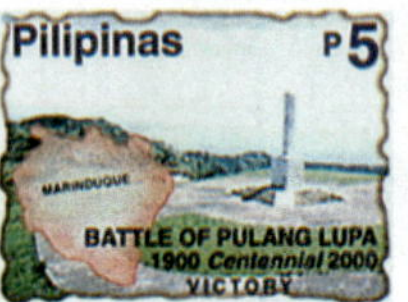

1005 Memorial and Map **1006** Joseph Ejercito Estrada

2000. Battle Centenaries. Multicoloured.
3332 5p. Type **1005** (Battle of Pulang Lupa) 45 45
3333 5p. Memorial and soldiers (Battle of Mabitac) . . . 45 45
3334 5p. Sun and soldiers (Battles of Cagayan, Agusan Hill and Makahambus Hill) (vert) 45 45
3335 5p. Map, memorial and bamboo signalling device (Battle of Paye) (vert) . . 45 45

2000. Presidential Office. Multicoloured.
3336 5p. Presidential seal 45 45
3337 5p. Type **1006** 45 45
3338 5p. Fidel V. Ramos 45 45
3339 5p. Corazon C. Aquino . . . 45 45
3340 5p. Ferdinand E. Marcos . . 45 45
3341 5p. Diosdado Macapagal . . 45 45
3342 5p. Carlos P. Garcia 45 45
3343 5p. Ramon Magsaysay . . . 45 45
3344 5p. Elpidio Quirino 45 45
3345 5p. Manuel Roxas 45 45

1007 Ornate Chequered Beetle

2000. Insects. Multicoloured.
3346 5p. Type **1007** 35 35
3347 5p. Sharpshooter bug . . . 35 35
3348 5p. Milkweed bug 35 35
3349 5p. Spotted cucumber beetle 35 35
3350 5p. Green June beetle . . . 35 35
3351 5p. Convergent ladybird beetle 35 35
3352 5p. Eastern hercules beetle 35 35
3353 5p. Harlequin cabbage bug 35 35
MS3354 Two sheets, each 99 × 19 mm. (a) Nos. 3346/9; (b) Nos. 3350/3 . . . . 4·50 4·50

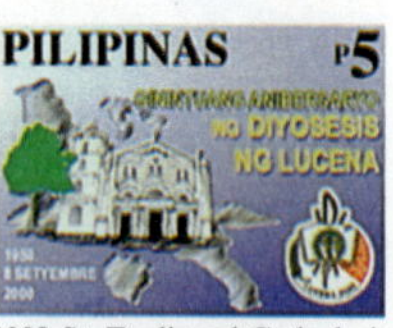

1008 St. Ferdinand Cathedral, Map and Emblem

2000. 50th Anniv of Lucena Diocese.
3355 **1008** 5p. multicoloured . . . 50 50

1009 Nurses and Patients

2000. 50th Anniv of Occupational Health Nurses' Association.
3356 **1009** 5p. multicoloured . . . 50 50

1010 Balanghai

2000. New Millennium (3rd series). Traditional Sea Craft. Multicoloured.
3357 5p. Type **1010** 45 45
3358 5p. Vinta 45 45
3359 5p. Caracoa 45 45

1011 Jars, Bank Note, Circuit Board, Computer Mouse and Emblem

2000. 50th Anniv of Equitable PCI Bank.
3360 **1011** 5p. multicoloured . . . 50 50

1012 Ship, Globe, Airplane and Workers

2000. Year of Overseas Filipino Workers.
3361 **1012** 5p. multicoloured . . . 50 50

1013 Pedro Poveda (founder), Buildings and Emblem

2000. 50th Anniv of the Teresian Association (international lay preacher association) in the Philippines.
3362 **1013** 5p. multicoloured . . . 50 50

1014 Congress in Session **1016** Running

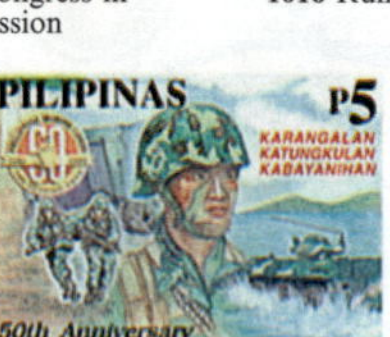

1015 Soldiers, Tank and Emblem

2000. House of Representatives.
3363 **1014** 5p. multicoloured . . . 45 45

2000. 50th Anniv of Philippine Marine Corps.
3364 **1015** 5p. multicoloured . . . 45 45

2000. Olympic Games, Sydney. Multicoloured.
3365 5p. Type **1016** 45 45
3366 5p. Archery 45 45
3367 5p. Rifle shooting 45 45
3368 5p. Diving 45 45
MS3369 100 × 85 mm. 5p. Boxing (horiz); 5p. Show jumping (horiz); 5p. Rowing (horiz); 5p. Taekwondo (horiz) . . . . . 3·00 3·00

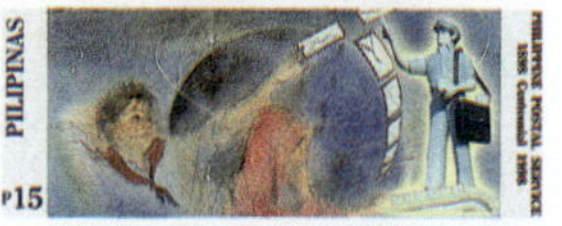

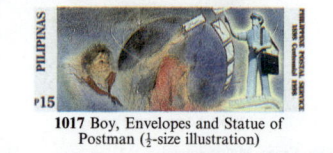

1017 Boy, Envelopes and Statue of Postman (½-size illustration)

2000. Postal Service. Sheet 100 × 60 mm.
MS3370 **1017** 15p. multicoloured 1·20 1·20

1018 B'laan Woman's Blouse, Davao del Sur

2000. "Sheer Realities: Clothing and Power in 19th-century Philippines" Exhibition, Manila. Multicoloured.

3371 5p. Type **1018** 45 45
3372 5p. T'boli T'nalak abaca cloth, South Cotabato . . 45 45
3373 5p. Kalinga/Gaddang cotton loincloth, Cordilleras (vert) 45 45
3374 5p. Portrait of Leticia Jimenez (anon) (vert) . . 45 45
MS3375 101 × 70 mm. 5p. Portrait of Teodora Devera Ygnacio (Justiniano Asuncion); 15p. Tawsug silk sash, Sulu Archipelago . . . . 2·50 2·50

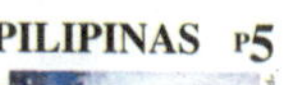

1019 Angel cradling Sunflowers

1020 1955 5c. Labour Management Congress Stamp

2000. Christmas. Multicoloured.

3376 5p. Type **1019** 45 45
3377 5p. As No. 3376 but inscribed "CHRISTMAS JUBILEUM" 45 45
3378 11p. Angel with basket of fruit and swag of leaves 90 90
3379 13p. Angel with basket of fruit on shoulder . . . . 1·00 1·00
3380 15p. Angel with garland of flowers . . . . 1·30 1·30

2000. 50th Anniv of Amateur Philatelists Organization Philatelic Society. Multicoloured.

3381 5p. Type **1020** 35 35
3382 5p. 1957 5c. Juan Luna birth centenary stamp (horiz) 35 35
3383 5p. 1962 5c. orchid stamp 35 35
3384 5p. 1962 6 + 4c. Rizal Foundation Fund stamp (horiz) 35 35

2000. No. 1977 surch **P5.00**.

3385 5p on 3p.60 multicoloured 35 35

1022 "Portrait of an Unknown Lady" (Juan Novicio Luna)

2000. Modern Art. Multicoloured.

3386 5p. Type **1022** 35 35
3387 11p. "Nude" (Jose Joya) (horiz) 80 80
3388 13p. "Lotus Odalisque" (Rodolfo Paras-Perez) (horiz) 90 90
3389 15p. "Untitled (Nude)" (Fernando Amorsolo) (horiz) . . . . 1·00 1·00
MS3390 100 × 80 mm. 15p. "The Memorial" (Cesar Legaspi) (79 × 29 mm) . . . . 2·50 2·50

1023 Snake

2000. New Year. Year of the Snake. Multicoloured.

3391 5p. Type **1023** 35 35
3392 11p. Snake 80 80
MS3393 98 × 88 mm. Nos. 3391/2. Perf or imperf . . . . 2·20 2·20

1024 Ships in Port (Trade and Industry)

2000. New Millennium (4th series). Multicoloured.

3394 5p. Type **1024** 35 35
3395 5p. Pupils and teacher (Education and Knowledge) 35 35
3396 5p. Globe, satellite, family using computer and woman using telephone (Communications and Technology) 35 35

1025 Pesos Fuertes (1st Philippines Banknote)

2001. 150th Anniv of Philippines Bank.

3397 **1025** 5p. multicoloured . . . 35 35

1026 Eagle

2001. "Hong Kong 2001" International Stamp Exhibition. Flora and Fauna. Multicoloured.

3398 5p. Type **1026** 35 35
3399 5p. Philippine tarsier 35 35
3400 5p. "Talisman Cove" (flower) 35 35
3401 5p. Turtle 35 35
3402 5p. Tamaraw 35 35
MS3403 Five sheets, each 80 × 71 mm. (a) 11p. As Type **1026**. (b) 11p. As No. 3399. (c) 11p. As No. 3400. (d) 11p. As No. 3401. (e) 11p. As No. 3402 7·50 7·50

1027 Rizal

2001. 150th Birth Anniv of General Paciano Rizal.

3404 **1027** 5p. multicoloured . . . 35 35

1028 Facade

2001. Centenary of San Beda College.

3405 **1028** 5p. multicoloured . . . 35 35

1029 High Altar, St. Peter's Basilica, Rome

1030 Presidential Seal

2001. 50th Anniv of Diplomatic Relations with Vatican City. Multicoloured.

3406 5p. Type **1029** 35 35
3407 15p. High altar, San Agustin Church, Manila . . . . . 1·10 1·10
MS3408 90 × 71 mm. 15p. Adam; 15p. God . . . . 2·20 2·20

The two stamps in No. **MS**3408 form the composite design of "Creation of Adam" (Michaelangelo).

2001. Multicoloured, background colour given.

3409 **1030** 5p. yellow 35 35
3410 10p. green 80 80
3411 11p. red 90 90
3412 13p. black . . . . . . 1·10 1·10
3413 15p. blue . . . . 1·30 1·30

1031 Our Lady of Manaoag

1032 Pres. Macapagal-Arroyo taking Presidential Oath

2001. 75th Anniv of Canonical Coronation of Our Lady of the Rosary of Manaoag.

3414 **1031** 5p. multicoloured . . . 35 35

2001. President Gloria Macapagal-Arroyo. Multicoloured.

3415 5p. Type **1032** 35 35
3416 5p. Pres. Macapagal-Arroyo waving 35 35

1033 Sydney Opera House and Philippines Cultural Centre

2001. Philippine-Australia Diplomatic Relations. Multicoloured.

3417 5p. Type **1033** 35 35
3418 13p. As Type **1033** but with subjects transposed . . . 1·10 1·10
MS3419 96 × 60 mm. 13p. Philippines Cultural Centre and Sydney Opera House (79 × 29 mm) 1·10 1·10

1034 Philippine Normal University

2001. University Centenaries. Multicoloured.

3420 5p. Type **1034** 35 35
3421 5p. Facade of Silliman University 35 35

1035 Scales of Justice and Court Building

2001. Centenary of Supreme Court.

3422 **1035** 5p. multicoloured . . . 35 35

1036 Joaquin J. Ortega

1037 Visayan Couple

2001. Anniversaries. Multicoloured.

3423 5p. Type **1036** (centenary of appointment as first Civil Governor of the Province of La Union) 35 35
3424 5p. Eugenio H. Lopez (businessman, birth centenary) 35 35

2001. "PHILANIPPON '01" International Stamp Exhibition, Japan. Boxer Codex (manuscript depicting Philippine lifestyle during first century of Spanish contact). Multicoloured.

3425 5p. Type **1037** 45 45
3426 5p. Tagalog couple 45 45
3427 5p. Moros of Luzon (man wearing red tunic) 45 45
3428 5p. Moros of Luzon (woman wearing blue dress) 45 45
MS3429 82 × 107 mm. 5p. Tattooed Pintados; 5p. Pintados wearing costumes; 5p. Cagayan woman; 5p. Zambal . . . . 1·80 1·80

1038 Teachers and Thomas (transport)

2001. Centenary of Arrival of American Teachers. Multicoloured.

3430 5p. Type **1038** 45 45
3431 15p. Pupils and school building . . . . 1·30 1·30

1039 Emblem

2001. Centenary of Technology University, Manila.

3432 **1039** 5p. multicoloured . . . 45 45

1040 Museum Artefacts

2001. Centenary of National Museum.

3433 **1040** 5p. multicoloured . . . 45 45

1041 1901 Lands Management Charter, Modern Surveyors and Emblems

2001. Centenary of Lands Management Bureau.

3434 **1041** 5p. multicoloured . . . 45 45

1042 Statue of St. Joseph and Seminary Building

2001. 400th Anniv of San Jose Seminary.

3435 **1042** 5p. multicoloured . . . 45 45

1043 Makati City Financial District

2001.

3436 **1043** 5p. multicoloured . . . 45 45

1044 Trumpet

2001. Musical Instruments. Multicoloured.

3437 5p. Type **1044** 45 45
3438 5p. Tuba 45 45
3439 5p. French horn 45 45
3440 5p. Trombone 45 45
MS3441 81 × 106 mm. VERT:—5p. × 4 Bass drum; Clarinet and oboe; Xylophone; Sousaphone . . . 1·80 1·80

1045 Off Shore Production Platform

2001. Malampaya Deep Water Gas to Power Project. Multicoloured.

3442 5p. Type **1045** 45 45
3443 15p. As No. 3442 but with gold border . . . . . . 1·30 1·30

1046 Two Stylized Figures

2001. International Year of Volunteers.

3444 **1046** 5p. multicoloured . . . 45 45

1047 Children surrounding globe

2001. United Nations Year of Dialogue among Civilizations.

3445 **1047** 15p. multicoloured . . 1·30 1·30

1048 Girls and Singers ("Herald Angels")

2001. Christmas.

3446 5p. Type **1048** 45 45
3447 11p. Boy and Christmas baubles ("Kumukutikutitap") . . 90 90
3448 13p. Children and lanterns ("Pasko ni Bitoy") . . . 1·00 1·00
3449 15p. Children blowing trumpets ("Pasko na naman") . . . . 1·30 1·30

1049 William Tell Monument

1050 St. George and Dragon

2001. 150th Anniv of Philippines–Switzerland Diplomatic Relations. Multicoloured.

3450 5p. Type **1049** 45 45
3451 15p. Jose P. Rizal Monument . . . . 1·30 1·30
MS3452 98 × 62 mm. 15p. Mayon volcano and Matterhorn (horiz) (80 × 30 mm) . . . . 1·30 1·30

2001. Centenary of Solicitor General's Office.

3453 **1050** 5p. multicoloured . . . 45 45

1051 "Puj" (Antonio Austria)

2001. National Stamp Collecting Month. Art. Multicoloured.

3454 5p. Type **1051** 45 45
3455 17p. "Hesus Nazereno" (Angelito Antonio) . . . 1·40 1·40
3456 21p. "Three Women with Basket" (Anita Magsaysay-Ho) (vert) . . 1·60 1·60
3457 22p. "Church with Yellow background" (Mauro Santos) . . . . 1·80 1·80
MS3458 102 × 74 mm. 22p. "Komedya ng Pakil" (Danilo Dalena) (80 × 30 mm) . . . . 1·80 1·80

1052 Couple (woman wearing brown apron)

2001. Inhabitants of Manila drawn by Jean Mallet. Multicoloured.

3462 5p. Couple in riding dress 45 45
3468 17p. Type **1052** . . . . . 1·40 1·40
3469 21p. Couple (woman wearing blue apron) . . . 1·60 1·60
3470 22p. Couple using pestles and mortar . . . . 1·80 1·80

1053 Red Horse

2001. New Year. Year of the Horse. Multicoloured.

3471 5p. Type **1053** 45 45
3472 17p. White horse . . . . . 1·40 1·40
MS3473 100 × 89 mm. As Nos. 3471/2 plus 2 labels . . . 1·80 1·80

No. **MS**3473 also exists imperforate.

1054 "Sanctification in Ordinary Life" (Godofredo F. Zapanta)

2002. Birth Centenary of Josemaria Escriva de Balaguer (founder of Opus Dei religious order).

3474 **1054** 5p. multicoloured . . . 45 45

1055 St. Paul's Metropolitan Cathedral

2002. UNESCO World Heritage Sites, Vigan City, Ilocos Sur Province. Multicoloured.

3475 5p. Type **1055** 45 45
3476 22p. Calee Crisologo . . . 1·90 1·90

1056 Salvador Araneta

1058 Envelope and "I Love You"

1057 "Manila Customs" (painting, Auguste Nicolas Vaillant)

2002. Birth Centenary of Salvador Araneta (nationalist politician and philanthropist).

3477 **1056** 5p. multicoloured . . . 45 45

2002. Centenary of Customs Bureau.

3478 **1057** 5p. multicoloured . . . 45 45

2002. St. Valentine's Day. Multicoloured.

3479 5p. Type **1058** 45 45
3480 5p. Couple enclosed in heart 45 45
3481 5p. Cat and dog 45 45
3482 5p. Air balloon 45 45

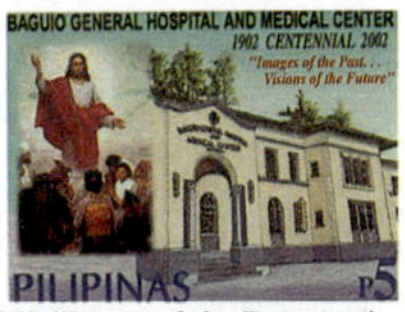

1059 "Image of the Resurrection" (detail, Fernando Amorsolo) and Hospital Faade

2002. Centenary of Baguio General Hospital and Medical Centre.

3483 **1059** 5p. multicoloured . . . 45 45

1060 Pedro Calungsod

1061 Virgin and Child (painting) and School Faade

2002. 330th Death Anniv of Pedro Calungsod. Multicoloured.

3484 5p. Type **1060** 45 45
MS3485 102 × 72 mm. 22p. Pedro Calungsod holding crucifix. Imperf . . . . 1·80 1·80

2002. Centenary of Negros Occidental High School.

3486 **1061** 5p. multicoloured . . . 45 45

1062 College Facade

2002. Centenary of La Consolacion College, Manila.

3487 **1062** 5p. multicoloured . . . 45 45

1063 Stupa, Buddha and Lotus Blossom

1064 Gloria Macapagal-Arroyo (2001–)

2002. Vesak Day.

3488 **1063** 5p. multicoloured . . . 45 45

2002. Presidential Office (2nd series). With blue barcode at foot. Multicoloured.

3489 5p. Type **1064** 45 45
3490 5p. Joseph Ejercito Estrada (1998–2000) 45 45
3491 5p. Fidel V. Ramos (1992–98) 45 45
3492 5p. Corazon C. Aquino (1986–92) 45 45
3493 5p. Ferdinand E. Marcos (1965–86) 45 45
3494 5p. Diosdado Macapagal (1961–65) 45 45
3495 5p. Carlos P. Garcia (1957–61) 45 45
3496 5p. Ramon Magsaysay (1953–57) 45 45
3497 5p. Elpidio Quirino (1948–1953) 45 45
3498 5p. Manuel Roxas (1946–1948) 45 45

1065 National Flag and School Faade

2002. Centenary of Cavite National High School.

3499 **1065** 5p. multicoloured . . . 45 45

1066 Emblem and Cathedral Faade

2002. Centenary Iglesia Filipina Independiente (religious movement).

3500 **1066** 5p. multicoloured . . . 45 45

1067 Fish

2002. Marine Conservation. Multicoloured.

3501 5p. Type **1067** 45 45
3502 5p. Fish laid head to head 45 45
3503 5p. Edge of mangrove swamp 45 45
3504 5p. Hands holding minnows 45 45
MS3505 90 × 77 mm. 5p. × 4, Man using binoculars from catamaran (no fishing); Mangrove swamp (reforestation of mangroves); Divers (reef monitoring); Rows of seaweed (seaweed farming) . . 1·80 1·80

No. **MS**3505 has a brief description of each stamp in the lower margin.

1068 Edge of Mangrove Swamp

1070 Participating Countries' Flags surrounding Communication Mast

2002. Philakorea 2002 International Stamp Exhibition, Seoul. Two sheets, each 97 × 86 mm containing T **1068** and similar vert design. Multicoloured.

MS3506 (a) 5p. Type **1068**; 17p. As No. 3488 (b) As No. **MS**3506a but with gold horizontal band . . 1·60 1·60

2002. No. 2476 optd **3p.**

3507 3p. on 60s. multicoloured 35 35

2002. TELMIN, TELSOM and ATRC Telecommunications Meetings held in Manila.

3508 **1070** 5p. multicoloured . . . 45 45

1071 Kapitan Moy Building and Giant Shoe

2002. Shoe Manufacture in Marikina City.
3509 **1071** 5p. multicoloured . . . 45 45

1072 Gerardo de Leon

2002. National Stamp Collecting Month. Multicoloured.
3510 5p. Type **1072** (filmmaker) 45 45
3511 17p. Francisca Reyes Aquino (folk dance researcher) . . . . . . 1·40 1·40
3512 21p. Pablo Antonio (architect) . . . . 1·60 1·60
3513 22p. Jose Garcia Villa (writer) . . . . 1·80 1·80
MS3514 100 × 74 mm. 22p. Honorata de la Rama (singer and actress) Imperf . . . . 1·80 1·80

1073 Kutsinta (rice cakes) **1074** Dove, Family and Crucifix

2002. Christmas. Multicoloured.
3515 5p. Type **1073** 45 45
3516 17p. Sapin-sapin (multilayered cake) . . . 1·40 1·40
3517 21p. Bibingka (rice and coconut cake) . . . . . . 1·60 1·60
3518 22p. Puto bumbong (cylindrical rice cakes) . . 1·80 1·80

2002. 4th World Meeting of Families (papal initiative), Manila (1st issue).
3519 **1074** 11p. multicoloured . . 90 90
See also No. 3528.

1075 Antonio Pigafetta

2002. 480th Anniv of First Circumnavigation of the Globe (1st issue). Multicoloured.
3520 5p. Type **1075** 45 45
3521 5p. Ferdinand Magellan . . 45 45
3522 5p. Charles I coin and *Vitoria* 45 45
3523 5p. Sebastian *Eleano* and *Vitoria* 45 45
See also No. **MS**3530.

1076 Female Goat

2002. Year of the Goat. Multicoloured.
3524 5p. Type **1076** 45 45
3525 17p. Male goat . . . . . 1·40 1·40
MS3526 99 × 88 mm. Nos. 3524/5. Perf or imperf . . . . 1·80 1·80

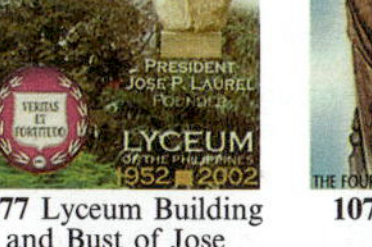

1077 Lyceum Building and Bust of Jose Laurel (founder) **1078** Holy Family

2002. 50th Anniv of Philippines Lyceum.
3527 **1077** 5p. multicoloured . . . 45 45

2002. 4th World Meeting of Families, Manila (2nd issue).
3528 **1078** 5p. multicoloured . . . 45 45

1079 Mt. Guiting (½-size illustration)

2002. International Year of Mountains. Sheet 96 × 70 mm.
MS3529 **1079** 22p. multicoloured 1·80 1·80

1080 Charles I Coin and 16th-century Map (½-size illustration)

2002. 480th Anniv of First Circumnavigation of the Globe (2nd issue). Sheet 104 × 85 mm. Imperf.
MS3530 **1080** 22p. multicoloured 1·80 1·80

1081 *Geodorum densiflorum*

2002. Orchids. (1st series). Multicoloured.
3531 5p. Type **1081** 45 45
3532 5p. *Nervilia plicata* 45 45
3533 5p. *Luisia teretifolia* 45 45
3534 5p. *Dendrobium Victoria-reginae* 45 45
MS3535 101 × 87 mm. 22p. *Grammatophylum scriptum*. Imperf 1·80 1·80
See also Nos. 3596/9.

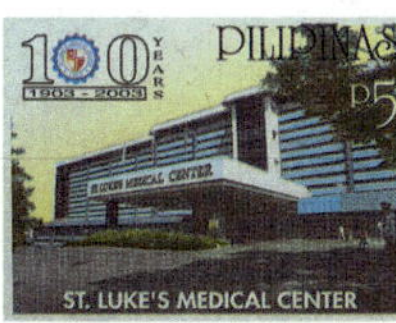

1082 Centre Buildings

2002. Centenary of St. Luke's Medical Centre, Manila.
3536 **1082** 5p. multicoloured . . . 15 15

1083 University Facade and Emblem

2003. 75th Anniv of Far Eastern University.
3537 **1083** 5p. multicoloured . . . 15 15

1084 20th-century Tram

2003. Centenary of Meralco (electric tram company).
3538 **1084** 5p. multicoloured . . . 15 15

1085 Heart-shaped Strawberry and Postman

2003. St. Valentine's Day. Multicoloured.
3539 5p. Type **1085** 15 15
3540 17p. Three hearts 45 45
3541 21p. Heart-shaped rainbow 55 55
3542 22p. Butterflies and heart-shaped flowers 60 60

1086 Kennon Mountain Road

2003. Centenary of Japanese Construction Workers Arrival.
3543 **1086** 23p. multicoloured . . 60 60

1087 Emblem and School Building

2003. Centenary of La Union National High School.
3544 **1087** 5p. multicoloured . . . 15 15

1088 Yakan Weaving

2003. Traditional Weaving (**MS**3544a/b) or Crafts (**MS**3544c). 50th Anniv of Summer Linguistics Institute. Three sheets, each 98 × 83 mm containing T **1087** and similar horiz designs. Multicoloured.
MS3545 (a) 15p. × 4, Type **1088**; Ifugao; Kagayanen; Bagbo Abaca; (b) 5p. × 2, Kalinga; Aklanon Pina; 17p. × 2, Tboli cross-stitch; Manobo beadwork (c) 11p. × 4, Ayta bow and arrows; Ibatan baskets; Palawano gong; Mindanao musical instruments. Set of 3 sheets . . . . 3·75 3·75

1089 Our Lady of Guadelupe (statue) **1091** *Dendrobium uniflorum*

1090 Apolinario Mabini carried in Litter

2003. 50th Anniv of Philippine—Mexico Diplomatic Relations. Multicoloured.
3546 5p. Type **1089** 15 15
3547 22p. Black Nazarene, Quiapo (statue) 60 60
MS3548 97 × 61 mm. 22p. Procession (80 × 30 mm) . . . 60 60

2003. Revolutionaries' Death Centenaries. Multicoloured.
3549 6p. Type **1090** 15 15
3550 6p. Luciano San Miguel . . 15 15

2003. Orchids. Multicoloured. (a) Without Latin inscription.
3551 6p. Type **1091** 15 15
3552 9p. *Paphiopedilum urbanianum* 25 25
3553 17p. *Epigeneium lyonii* . . . 45 45
3554 21p. *Thrixspermum subulatum* 55 55

(b) With Latin inscription.
3555 1p. *Liparis latifolia* 10 10
3556 2p. *Cymbidium finlaysonianum* 10 10
3557 3p. *Phalaenopsis philippinensis* 10 10
3558 4p. *Phalaenopsis fasiata* . . 10 10
3559 5p. *Spathoglotis plicata* . . . 10 10
3560 6p. As No. 3551 . . . . . 15 15
3561 6p. *Phalaenopsis fuscata* . . 15 15
3562 6p. *Phalaenopsis stuartiana* 15 15
3563 6p. *Renanthera monachia* . . 15 15
3564 6p. *Aerides quinquevulnera* 15 15
3565 8p. *Phalaenopsis schilleriana* 20 20
3566 9p. *Phalaenopsis pulchra* . . 25 25
3567 10p. *Kingidium philippinennse* 25 25
3568 17p. As. No. 3551 . . . . . 45 45
3569 20p. *Phaius tankervillae* . . 50 50
3570 21p. As. No. 3554 . . . . . 55 55
3571 22p. *Trichoglottis philippinensis* 55 55

2003. No. 3409 surch.
3581 1p. on 5p. multicoloured . . 10 10
3582 6p. on 5p. multicoloured . . 15 15

1093 Flag, Doctors and Patient **1094** Woman carrying Corn

2003. Centenary of Philippine Medical Association.
3583 **1093** 6p. multicoloured . . . 15 15

2003. 50th Anniv of Rural Banking.
3584 **1094** 6p. multicoloured . . . 15 15

1095 Rizal Monument, Rizal Park, Fujian,People's Republic of China **1096** Madoura Ceramics Exhibition Poster (Pablo Picasso)

2003. Jose Rizal (writer and reformer) Commemoration. Multicoloured.
3585 6p. Type **1095** 15 15
3586 17p. Pagoda and Jose Rizal (horiz) 45 45

2003. Philippines—Spain Friendship Day. Multicoloured.
3587 6p. Type **1096** 15 15
3588 22p. "Flashback" (Jose Joya) 60 60

1097 "Early Traders" (Cesar Amorsolo)

2003. Centenary of Chamber of Commerce.
3589 **1097** 6p. multicoloured . . . 15 15

1098 Mt. Makiling, Laguna

2003. Mountains. Multicoloured.
3590 6p. Type **1098** 15 15
3591 6p. Mt. Kanlaon 15 15
3592 6p. Mt. Kitangland 15 15
3593 6p. Mt. Mating-oy 15 15
MS3594 92 × 82 mm. 6p. × 4, Mt. Iraya; Mt. Hibok-Hibok; Mt. Apo; Mt. Sto Tomas 60 60

1099 Miners

2003. Centenary of Benguet Corporation.
3595 **1099** 6p. multicoloured . . . 15 15

1100 Mariposa 1102 Our Lady of Caysasay (statue)

2003. Orchids (2nd series). Multicoloured.
3596 30p. Type **1100** 80 80
3597 50p. Sanggumay . . . . . 1·30 1·30
3598 75p. Lady's slipper . . . . 2·00 2·00
3599 100p. Waling-waling . . . . 2·60 2·75

2003. 400th Anniv of Blessed Virgin of the Immaculate Conception (Our Lady of Caysasay), found by Juan Maningcad.
3605 **1102** 6p. multicoloured . . . 15 15

1103 Cornelio Villareal 1104 Teacher and Pupil (statue)

2003. Birth Centenary of Cornelio Villareal (Speaker of the House).
3606 **1103** 6p. multicoloured . . . 15 15

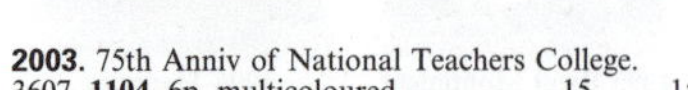

2003. 75th Anniv of National Teachers College.
3607 **1104** 6p. multicoloured . . . 15 15

1105 St. Francis and Parish Church 1107 Anniversary Emblem

2003. 50th Anniv of Santurio de San Antonio Parish Church.
3608 **1105** 6p. multicoloured . . . 15 15

2003. "No to Drugs" Campaign. Nos. 3409 and 3413 optd **No To Drugs**.
3609 6p. multicoloured (3409) . . 15 15
3610 15p. multicoloured (3413) 40 40

2003. 50th Anniv of Federation of Free Farmers.
3611 **1107** 6p. multicoloured . . . 15 15

1108 Boy sweeping away Drug Symbols (Nicole Caminian)

2003. "Youth against Drugs" Campaign. Winning Entries in Design a Stamp Competition. Multicoloured.
3612 6p. Type **1108** 15 15
3613 6p. Drug symbols behind "Stop" sign and children (Jarius Cabajar) 15 15
3614 6p. Children pasting over "Drug addiction" poster (Genevieve Lazarte) . . . 15 15
3615 6p. Boy cutting down tree inscribed "Drugs" 15 15

1109 "Mano Po Ninong II" (Jes Pelino)

2003. Christmas. Multicoloured.
3616 6p. Type **1109** 15 15
3617 17p. "Himig at Kulay Ng Pasko" (Jes Pelino) (vert) 45 45
3618 21p. "Noche Buena" (Mamerto Ynigo) (vert) 55 55
3619 22p. "Karoling Sa" Jeepney" (Jes Pelino) . . 60 60

2003. No. 3409 surch **1p**.
3620 1p. on 5p. multicoloured . . 10 10

2003. Nos. 3093/6 surch.
3621 17p. on 8p. multicoloured (3093) 45 45
3622 17p. on 8p. multicoloured (3094) 45 45
3623 22p. on 16p. multicoloured (3905) 60 60
3624 22p. on 16p. multicoloured (3906) 60 60

1112 Lake Buhi, Camarines Sur (½-size illustration)

2003. International Year of Freshwater. Sheet 109 × 88 mm.
MS3625 **1112** 22p. multicoloured 60 60

1113 Kenkoy (Tony Velasquez)

2003. National Stamp Collecting Month. Cartoon Characters. Multicoloured.
3626 6p. Type **1113** 15 15
3627 17p. Ikabod (Nonoy Marcelo) 45 45
3628 21p. Sakay N'Moy (Hugo Yonzon) (horiz) 55 55
3629 22p. Kalabog en Bosyo (Larry Alcaa) (horiz) . . 60 60
MS3630 101 × 70 mm. 22p. Hugo the sidewalk vendor (Rudolfo Ragodon) (80 × 30 mm) . . . 60 60

1114 Shoreline at Sunset

2003. 75th Anniv of Philippines Camera Club.
3631 **1114** 6p. multicoloured . . . 15 15

1115 First Philippines Stamps (⅗-size illustration)

2003. Filipinas 2004 Stamp Exhibition. Six sheets, each 142 × 82 mm and with different background colours. Multicoloured.
MS3632 (a) 22p. Type **1115** (yellow background). (b) 22p. Type **1115** (green background). (c) 22p. Type **1115** (flesh). (d) 22p. Type **1115** (lavender). (e) 22p. Type **1115** (azure). (f) 22p. Type **1115** (pink) Set of 6 sheets 3·00 3·00

1116 Capuchin Monkey

2003. New Year. "Year of the Monkey". Multicoloured.
3633 6p. Type **1116** 15 15
3634 17p. Orangutan 45 45
MS3635 98 × 90 mm. Nos. 3632/3. Perf or imperf 60 60

1117 *Rebutia spinosissima* 1118 Luneta Hotel

2003. Cacti. Multicoloured .2003.
3636 6p. Type **1117** 15 15
3637 6p. *Turbinicarpus alonsoi* . . 15 15
3638 6p. *Mammilaria spinosissima* 15 15
3639 6p. *Epithelantha bokei* . . . 15 15
MS3640 100 × 100 mm. 6p. × 4, *Aloe humilis* (horiz); Inscr "Euphorbia golisana" (horiz); Inscr "Gymnocalycium spinosissima" (horiz); *Mammilaria spinosissima* (horiz) (different) 60 60

2003. Architectural Heritage. Multicoloured.
3641 6p. Type **1118** 15 15
3642 6p. Hong Kong—Shanghai bank 15 15
3643 6p. El Hogar 15 15
3644 6p. Regina building 15 15
MS3645 101 × 101 mm. 6p. × 4, Pangasinan Capitol (horiz); Metropolitan theatre (horiz); Philtrust (horiz); University of Manila (horiz) 60 60

1119 First Sisters

2004. Centenary of Sisters of St. Paul of Chartres.
3646 **1119** 6p. multicoloured . . . 15 15

1120 Building Facade, Flag and Emblem

2004. 50th Anniv of Grepalife (Great Pacific Life Assurance Corporation).
3647 **1120** 6p. multicoloured . . . 15 15

1121 University Facade and Anniversary Emblem

2004. Centenary of Polytechnic University, Manila.
3648 **1121** 6p. multicoloured . . . 15 15

1122 1854 5 cuartos Stamp

2004. 150th Anniv of First Philippine Stamps. Designs showing 1854 stamps. Multicoloured.
3649 6p. Type **1122** 15 15
3650 6p.10 cuartos stamp 15 15
3651 6p. 1 real stamp 15 15
3652 6p. 2 reales stamp 15 15
MS3653 114 × 74 mm. 22p. First Stamps (80 × 30 mm) 50 50

1123 Brewer

2004. 150th Anniv of Tanduay Distillers.
3654 **1123** 6p. multicoloured . . . 15 15

1124 Dornier DO-24TT Seaplane

2004. Centenary of Powered Flight (2003).
3655 **1124** 6p. multicoloured . . . 15 15
3656 6p. multicoloured . . . 15 15

1125 President George W. Bush

2004. Visit of USA President George W. Bush to Philippines (18 October 2003). Multicoloured.
3657 6p. Type **1125** 15 15
3658 22p. Presidents George W. Bush and Gloria Macapagal-Arroyo . . . 50 50

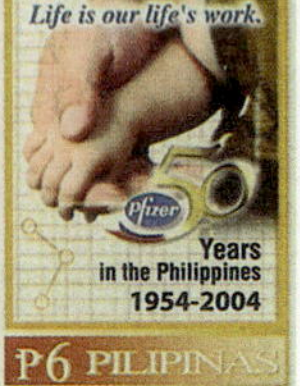

1126 Hands 1127 Our Lady of Piat (statue)

2004. 50th Anniv of Pfizer (pharmaceutical company).
3659 **1126** 6p. multicoloured . . . 15 15

2004. 400th Anniv of the Arrival of Our Lady of Piat.
3660 **1127** 6p. multicoloured . . . 15 15

1128 Inscr "Bantigue"

2004. Bonsai Trees. Multicoloured designs showing trees inscription given.
3661 6p. Type **1128** 15 15
3662 6p. Chinese elm 15 15
3663 6p. Bantigue with two stems in black tray 15 15
3664 6p. Bantigue in white pot 15 15
3665 6p. Balete sweeping down left 15 15
3666 6p. Balete leafless 15 15
3667 6p. Bantigue with large stem in orange pot 15 15
3668 6p. Mansanita 15 15
3669 6p. Bantigue (vert) 15 15
3670 6p. Kamuning Binangonan (vert) 15 15
3671 6p. Balete (vert) 15 15
3672 6p. Mulawinaso (vert) . . . 15 15
3673 6p. Kamuning Binangonan multi-stemmed (vert) . . . 15 15
3674 6p. Logwood (vert) 15 15
3675 6p. Kamuning Binangonan octagonal pot Bantolinao (vert) 15 15
MS3676 146 × 95 mm. 6p. × 4, Lemonsito; Bougainvillea on stand; Bougainvillea in flower; Kalyos 60 60

1129 Rifle Shooting

2004. Olympic Games, Athens. Multicoloured.
3677 6p. Type **1129** 15 15
3678 17p. Taekwondo 35 35
3679 21p. Swimming 45 45
3680 22p. Archery 50 50
MS3681 60 × 61 mm. 22p. Boxing 50 50

1130 Tomas Cloma

2004. Birth Centenary of Tomas Cloma (maritime educationalist).
3682 **1130** 6p. multicoloured . . . 15 15

1131 "Sandugo" (Carlos Francisco)

2004. 600th Birth Anniv of Miguel Lopez De Legazpi (first Governor General of Philippines).
3683 **1131** 6p. multicoloured . . . 15 15

1132 Rat

2004. Lunar New Year. Multicoloured.
3684 6p. Type **1132** 15 15
3685 6p. Ox 15 15
3686 6p. Tiger 15 15
3687 6p. Pig 15 15
3688 6p. Rabbit 15 15
3689 6p. Dog 15 15
3690 6p. Dragon 15 15
3691 6p. Rooster 15 15
3692 6p. Snake 15 15
3693 6p. Monkey 15 15
3694 6p. Goat 15 15
3695 6p. Horse 15 15

1133 Building Facade

2004. Centenary of Manila University.
3696 **1133** 6p. multicoloured . . . 15 15

1134 Decorated Tree

1136 People enclosed in Rice Grain (Maria Enna T. Alegre)

1135 Intamuros, Manila

2004. Christmas. Decorated trees. Multicoloured.
3697 6p. Type **1134** 15 15
3698 17p. With red ribbons and bells 35 35
3699 21p. With poinsettia flowers 45 45
3700 22p. With white stems . . . 50 50

2004. Centenary of Filipino—Chinese Chamber of Commerce. Multicoloured.
3701 6p. Type **1135** 15 15
3702 6p. Great Wall, China . . . 15 15
Nos. 3701/2 were issued together, se-tenant, forming a composite design.

2004. International Year of Rice. Winning Entries in Design a Stamp Competition. Multicoloured.
3703 6p. Type **1136** 15 15
3704 6p. Woman, rice and family (Lady Fatima Velasco) . . 15 15
3705 6p. Boy amongst plants (Gary Manalo) 15 15
3706 6p. Dove, rice stalk and family (Michael Villadolid) 15 15
3707 6p. Rice grains (Ljian Delgado) 15 15
3708 6p. Doves and man cradling rice plant (Sean Pajaron) 15 15

1137 19th-century Facade

1138 Lapu-Lapu (Francisco Coching)

2004. 400th Anniv of San Augustin Church. Multicoloured.
3709 6p. Type **1137** 15 15
3710 6p. Modern facade 15 15

2004. Stamp Collecting Month. Comics. Multicoloured.
3711 6p. Type **1138** 15 15
3712 6p. El Vibora (Frederico Javinal) 15 15
3713 6p. Kulafu (Francisco Reyes) (horiz) 15 15
3714 6p. Darna (Nestor Redondo) (horiz) 15 15
MS3715 68 × 95 mm. 22p. Darna (Mats Revelo) (30 × 80 mm) . . 50 50

1139 Rooster

2004. New Year. Year of the Rooster. Multicoloured.
3716 6p. Type **1139** 15 15
3717 17p. Rooster (different) . . 35 35
MS3718 138 × 80 mm. Nos. 3416/17 each × 2 . . . . 1·00 1·00

1140 *Otus megalottis nigrorum*

2004. Owls. Multicoloured.
3719 6p. Type **1140** 15 15
3720 6p. *Ninox philippensis centralis* 15 15
3721 6p. *Mimizuku gurneyi* . . . 15 15
3722 6p. *Bubo philippensis* 15 15

OFFICIAL STAMPS

1926. Commemorative issue of 1926 optd **OFFICIAL**.
O391 **49** 2c. black and green . . . 2·10 85
O392 4c. black and red . . . . 2·10 1·00
O393 18c. black and brown . . 6·50 3·25
O394 20c. black and orange . . 5·75 1·50

1931. Stamps of 1906 optd **O.B.**
O413 2c. green (No. 337) 15 15
O414 4c. red (No. 338) 15 15
O415 6c. violet (No. 339) 15 15
O416 8c. brown (No. 340) . . . 15 15
O417 10c. blue (No. 341) 15 15
O418 12c. orange (No. 342) . . . 25 15
O419 16c. olive (No. 344) 25 15
O420 20c. orange (No. 345) . . . 25 15
O421 26c. green (No. 346) . . . 35 25
O422 30c. grey (No. 347) 25 25

1935. Nos. 459/68 optd **O.B.**
O473 2c. red 15 15
O474 4c. green 15 15
O475 6c. brown 15 15
O476 8c. violet 15 15
O477 10c. red 15 15
O478 12c. black 15 15
O479 16c. blue 15 15
O480 20c. bistre 15 15
O481 26c. blue 25 25
O482 30c. red 35 35

1936. Stamps of 1935 Nos. 459/68 optd **O. B. COMMON-WEALTH** (2, 6, 20c.) or **O. B. COMMONWEALTH** (others).
O538 2c. red 15 15
O539 4c. green 15 15
O540 6c. brown 15 15
O541 8c. violet 15 15
O542 10c. red 15 15
O543 12c. black 15 15
O544 16c. blue 15 15
O545 20c. bistre 25 25
O546 26c. blue 35 35
O547 30c. red 25 25

1941. Nos. 563 and 623 optd **O. B.**
O565 **104** 2c. green 15 15
O624 – 2c. brown 15 15

1948. Various stamps optd **O.B.**
O738 **147** 1c. brown 15 10
O668 **125** 2c. green 50 10
O659 – 4c. brown (No. 629) . . 15 10
O739 – 5c. red (No. 731) . . . 15 10
O843 – 6c. blue (No. 842) . . 15 10
O660 **113** 10c. red 20 10
O740 – 10c. blue (No. 732) . . 20 15
O661 – 16c. grey (No. 632) . . 2·20 80
O669 – 20c. brown (No. 633) . . 15 15
O741 – 20c. red (No. 733) . . . 50 15
O670 – 50c. green (No. 634) . . 75 45

1950. Surch **ONE CENTAVO.**
O700 **125** 1c. on 2c. green (No. O668) 10 10

1959. No. 810 optd **O B.**
O811 1c. on 5c. red 15 10

1962. Nos. 898/904 optd **G. O.**
O908 5s. red 10 10
O909 6s. brown 15 10
O910 6s. blue 15 10
O911 10s. purple 20 15
O912 20s. blue 30 15
O913 30s. red 35 30
O914 50s. violet 45 35

1970. Optd **G.O.**
O1182 **318** 10s. red 15 10

OFFICIAL SPECIAL DELIVERY STAMP

1931. No. E353b optd **O.B.**
EO423 **E 47** 20c. violet 85 55

POSTAGE DUE STAMPS

1899. Postage Due stamps of United States of 1894 optd **PHILIPPINES.**
D268 **D 87** 1c. red . . . . 5·50 1·20
D269 2c. red . . . . 5·50 1·00
D270 3c. red . . . . 15·00 5·75
D271 5c. red . . . . 12·50 2·10
D272 10c. red . . . . 17·00 4·50
D273 30c. red . . . . £200 90·00
D274 50c. red . . . . £170 85·00

D 51 Post Office Clerk

D 118

1928.
D395 **D 51** 4c. red 15 15
D396 6c. red 15 15
D397 8c. red 15 15
D398 10c. red 15 15
D399 12c. red 15 15
D400 16c. red 25 25
D401 20c. red 15 15

1937. Surch **3 CVOS. 3.**
D521 **D 51** 3c. on 4c. red 15 15

1947.
D644 **D 118** 3c. red 15 15
D645 4c. blue 35 30
D646 6c. green 50 45
D647 10c. orange 80 60

SPECIAL DELIVERY STAMPS

1901. Special Delivery stamp of United States of 1888 optd **PHILIPPINES.**
E268 **46** 10c. blue (No. E283) . . £100 85·00

1907. Special Delivery stamp of United States optd **PHILIPPINES.**
E298 **E 117** 10c. blue £1500

E 47 Messenger running

1919. Perf (E353), perf or imperf (E353b).
E353 **E 47** 20c. blue 50 25
E353b 20c. violet 50 25

1939. Optd **COMMONWEALTH.** Perf.
E550 **E 47** 20c. violet 25 25

1945. Optd **VICTORY.**
E622 **E 47** 20c. violet (No. E550) 85 50

E 120 Cyclist Messenger and Post Office

1947.
E651 **E 120** 20c. purple 60 45

20¢
PHILIPPINES
E 219 G.P.O., Manila

E891 **E 219** 20c. mauve 35 30

PITCAIRN ISLANDS Pt. 1

An island group in the Pacific Ocean, nearly midway between Australia and America.

1940. 12 pence = 1 shilling;
20 shillings = 1 pound.
1967. 100 cents = 1 New Zealand dollar.

4 Lt. Bligh and the "Bounty"

1940.
1 – ½d. orange and green 40 60
2 – 1d. mauve and magenta . . . 55 80
3 – 1½d. grey and red 55 50
4 **4** 2d. green and brown . . . . 2·00 1·40
5 – 3d. green and blue . . . . . 1·25 1·40
5b – 4d. black and green . . . . 16·00 11·00
6 – 6d. brown and blue . . . . 5·00 1·50
6a – 8d. green and mauve . . . . 19·00 7·00
7 – 1s. violet and grey . . . . . 3·50 2·25
8 – 2s.6d. green and brown . . . 8·50 3·75

DESIGNS—HORIZ: ½d. Oranges; 1d. Fletcher Christian, crew and Pitcairn Is.; 1½d. John Adams and house; 3d. Map of Pitcairn Is. and Pacific; 4d. Bounty Bible; 6d. H.M.S. "Bounty"; 8d. School, 1949; 1s. Christian and Pitcairn Is.; 2s.6d. Christian, crew and Pitcairn coast.

4a Houses of Parliament, London

1946. Victory.
9 **4a** 2d. brown 70 30
10 3d. blue 70 30

4b King George VI and Queen Elizabeth

4c King George VI and Queen Elizabeth

1949. Silver Wedding.
11 **4b** 1½d. red 2·00 1·50
12 **4c** 10s. mauve 38·00 50·00

4d Hermes, Globe and Forms of Transport

4e Hemispheres, Jet-powered Vickers Viking Airliner and Steamer

4f Hermes and Globe

4g U.P.U. Monument

1949. U.P.U.
13 **4d** 2½d. brown 1·00 4·25
14 **4e** 3d. blue 8·00 4·25
15 **4f** 6d. green 4·00 4·25
16 **4g** 1s. purple 4·00 4·25

4h Queen Elizabeth II

1953. Coronation.
17 **4h** 4d. black and green 2·00 3·50

12 Handicrafts: Bird Model

1957.
33 – ½d. green and mauve 65 60
19 – 1d. black and green 3·50 1·75
20 – 2d. brown and blue 1·75 60
21 **12** 2½d. brown and orange 50 40
22 – 3d. green and blue 80 40
23 – 4d. red and blue (I) 90 40
23a – 4d. red and blue (II) 3·50 1·50
24 **12** 6d. buff and blue 1·75 55
25 – 8d. green and red 60 40
26 – 1s. black and brown 2·25 40
27 – 2s. green and orange 11·00 10·00
28 – 2s.6d. blue and red 23·00 9·00

DESIGNS—HORIZ: ½d. "Cordyline terminalis"; 3d. Bounty Bay; 4d. Pitcairn School; 6d. Map of Pacific; 8d. Inland scene; 1s. Model of the "Bounty"; 2s.6d. Launching new whaleboat. VERT: 1d. Map of Pitcairn; 2d. John Adams and "Bounty" Bible; 2s. Island wheelbarrow.

The 4d. Type I is inscr "PITCAIRN SCHOOL"; Type II is inscr "SCHOOL TEACHER'S HOUSE".

20 Pitcairn Island and Simon Young

1961. Cent of Return of Pitcairn Islanders.
29 **20** 3d. black and yellow 50 45
30 – 6d. brown and blue 1·00 75
31 – 1s. orange and green 1·00 75

DESIGNS: 6d. Maps of Norfolk and Pitcairn Islands; 1s. Migrant brigantine "Mary Ann".

20a Protein Foods

1963. Freedom from Hunger.
32 **20a** 2s.6d. blue 6·00 2·50

20b Red Cross Emblem

1963. Cent of Red Cross.
34 **20b** 2d. red and black 1·00 1·00
35 2s.6d. red and blue 2·25 4·00

23 Pitcairn Is. Longboat

24 Queen Elizabeth II (after Anthony Buckley)

1964. Multicoloured.
36 ½d. Type **23** 10 30
37 1d. H.M.S. "Bounty" 30 30
38 2d. "Out from Bounty Bay" 30 30
39 3d. Great frigate bird 75 30
40 4d. White tern 75 30
41 6d. Pitcairn warbler 75 30
42 8d. Red-footed booby 75 30
43 10d. Red-tailed tropic birds 60 30
44 1s. Henderson Island crake 60 30
45 1s.6d. Stephen's lory 3·00 1·25
46 2s.6d. Murphy's petrel 3·00 1·50
47 4s. Henderson Island fruit dove 4·00 1·75
48 8s. Type **24** 2·25 1·75

24a I.T.U. Emblem

1965. Centenary of I.T.U.
49 **24a** 1d. mauve and brown 75 40
50 2s.6d. turquoise and blue 4·00 3·50

24b I.C.Y. Emblem

1965. International Co-operation Year.
51 **24b** 1d. purple and turquoise 75 40
52 2s.6d. green and lavender 3·00 3·00

24c Sir Winston Churchill and St. Paul's Cathedral in Wartime

1966. Churchill Commemoration.
53 **24c** 2d. blue 1·00 85
54 3d. green 2·25 1·00
55 6d. brown 2·50 1·75
56 1s. violet 3·00 2·50

25 Footballer's Legs, Ball and Jules Rimet Cup

1966. World Cup Football Championship.
57 **25** 4d. multicoloured 1·00 1·00
58 2s.6d. multicoloured 1·50 1·75

25a W.H.O. Building.

1966. Inauguration of W.H.O. Headquarters, Geneva.
59 **25a** 8d. black, green and blue 3·00 3·25
60 1s.6d. black, purple and ochre 4·50 3·75

25b "Education"

25c "Science"

25d "Culture"

1966. 20th Anniv of UNESCO.
61 **25b** ½d. multicoloured 20 1·00
62 **25c** 10d. yellow, violet and olive 2·25 2·75
63 **25d** 2s. black, purple and orange 4·25 4·25

36 Mangarevan Canoe, c. 1325

1967. Bicentenary of Discovery of Pitcairn Islands'. Multicoloured.
64 ½d. Type **36** 10 20
65 1d. P. F. de Quiros and "San Pedro y San Pablo", 1606 20 20
66 8d. "San Pedro y San Pablo" and "Los Tres Reyes", 1606 25 20
67 1s. Carteret and H.M.S. "Swallow", 1767 25 25
68 1s.6d. "Hercules", 1819 25 25

1967. Decimal Currency. Nos. 36/48 surch with "Bounty" anchor and value.
69 **23** ½c. on ½d. multicoloured 10 10
70 – 1c. on 1d. multicoloured 30 1·25
71 – 2c. on 2d. multicoloured 25 1·25
72 – 2½c. on 3d. multicoloured 25 1·25
73 – 3c. on 4d. multicoloured 25 20
74 – 5c. on 6d. multicoloured 30 1·25
75 – 10c. on 8d. multicoloured 30 30
76 – 15c. on 10d. multicoloured 1·25 40
77 – 20c. on 1s. multicoloured 1·25 55
78 – 25c. on 1s.6d. multicoloured 1·50 1·25
79 – 30c. on 2s.6d. multicoloured 1·75 1·25
80 – 40c. on 4s. multicoloured 1·75 1·25
81 **24** 45c. on 8s. multicoloured 1·50 1·50

42 Bligh and "Bounty's" Launch

1967. 150th Death Anniv of Admiral Bligh.
82 **42** 1c. black, ultramarine & blue 10 10
83 – 8c. black, yellow and mauve 25 65
84 – 20c. black, brown and buff 25 70

DESIGNS: 8c. Bligh and followers cast adrift; 20c. Bligh's tomb.

45 Human Rights Emblem

1968. International Human Rights Year.
85 **45** 1c. multicoloured 10 10
86 2c. multicoloured 10 10
87 25c. multicoloured 35 35

46 Moro Wood and Flower

1968. Handicrafts (1st series).
88 **46** 5c. multicoloured 20 30
89 – 10c. green, brown and orange 20 40
90 – 15c. violet, brown & salmon 25 40
91 – 20c. multicoloured 25 45

DESIGNS—HORIZ: 10c. flying fish model. VERT: 15c. "Hand" vases; 20c. Woven baskets.

See also Nos. 207/10.

50 Microscope and Slides

1968. 20th Anniv of World Health Organization.
92 **50** 2c. black, turquoise and blue 10 20
93 – 20c. black, orange and purple 40 50

DESIGN: 20c. Hypodermic syringe and jars of tablets.

52 Pitcairn Island

64b Queen Elizabeth II

65 Lantana

1969. Multicoloured.
94 1c. Type **52** 1·50 1·00
95 2c. Captain Bligh and "Bounty" chronometer 25 15
96 3c. "Bounty" anchor (vert) 25 15
97 4c. Plans and drawing of "Bounty" 1·50 15
98 5c. Breadfruit containers and plant 60 15
99 6c. Bounty Bay 30 20
100 8c. Pitcairn longboat 1·50 20
101 10c. Ship landing point 2·50 85
102 15c. Fletcher Christian's Cave 1·75 50
103 20c. Thursday October Christian's house 60 40
104 25c. "Flying fox" cable system (vert) 70 40
105 30c. Radio Station, Taro Ground 55 45
106 40c. "Bounty" Bible 75 60
106a 50c. Pitcairn Coat-of-Arms 2·00 11·00
106b $1 Type **64b** 5·50 17·00

1970. Flowers. Multicoloured.
107 1c. Type **65** 15 50
108 2c. "Indian Shot" 20 65
109 5c. Pulau 25 75
110 25c. Wild gladiolus 60 2·00

69 Band-tailed Hind

1970. Fishes. Multicoloured.
111 5c. Type **69** 2·00 70
112 10c. High-finned rudderfish 2·00 85
113 15c. Elwyn's wrasse 2·50 1·00
114 20c. Yellow wrasse ("Whistling daughter") 3·00 1·25

1971. Royal Visit. No. 101 optd **ROYAL VISIT 1971**.
115 10c. multicoloured 1·00 1·50

71 Polynesian Rock Carvings

1971. Polynesian Pitcairn. Multicoloured.
116 5c. Type **71** 75 75
117 10c. Polynesian artefacts (horiz) 1·00 1·00
118 15c. Polynesian stone fish-hook (horiz) 1·00 1·00
119 20c. Polynesian stone deity 1·25 1·25

72 Commission Flag

74 Rose-apple

73 Red-tailed Tropic Birds and Longboat

1972. 25th Anniv of South Pacific Commission. Multicoloured.
120 4c. Type **72** 40 70
121 8c. Young and elderly (Health) 40 70
122 18c. Junior school (Education) 50 90
123 20c. Goods store (Economy) 60 1·60

1972. Royal Silver Wedding. Multicoloured, background colour given.
124 **73** 4c. green 30 60
125 20c. blue 45 90

1973. Flowers. Multicoloured.
126 4c. Type **74** 65 55
127 8c. Mountain-apple 75 75
128 15c. "Lata" 1·00 1·00
129 20c. "Dorcas-flower" 1·00 1·25
130 35c. Guava 1·00 1·75

74a Princess Anne and Captain Mark Phillips

1973. Royal Wedding. Multicoloured, background colours given.
131 **74a** 10c. mauve 20 15
132 25c. green 25 30

75 Obelisk Vertagus and Episcopal Mitre Shells

1974. Shells. Multicoloured.
147 4c. Type **75** 50 80
148 10c. Turtle dove-shell 60 1·00
149 18c. Indo-Pacific limpet, fringed false limpet and "Siphonaria normalis" 70 1·40
150 50c. "Ctena divergens" 1·00 2·00
MS151 130×121 mm. Nos. 147/50 2·75 14·00

76 Island Post Office

1974. Centenary of U.P.U.
152 **76** 4c. multicoloured 20 35
153 – 20c. purple, brown & black 25 60
154 – 35c. multicoloured 35 70
DESIGNS: 20c. Pre-stamp letter, 1922; 35c. Mailship and Pitcairn longboat.

77 Churchill and Text "Lift up your Hearts ..."

1974. Birth Cent of Sir Winston Churchill.
155 **77** 20c. olive, green and grey 30 65
156 – 35c. brown, green and grey 40 75
DESIGN: 35c. Text "Give us the tools ...".

78 H.M.S. "Seringapatam" (frigate), 1830

1975. Mailboats. Multicoloured.
157 4c. Type **78** 25 50
158 10c. "Pitcairn" (missionary schooner), 1890 30 75
159 18c. "Athenic" (liner), 1904 35 1·10
160 50c. "Gothic" (liner), 1948 60 1·75
MS161 145×110mm. Nos. 157/60 11·00 16·00

79 "Polistes jadwigae" (wasp)

1975. Pitcairn Insects. Multicoloured.
162 4c. Type **79** 25 45
163 6c. "Euconocephalus sp." (grasshopper) 25 55
164 10c. "Anomis flavia" and "Chasmina tibialis" (moth) 30 70
165 15c. "Pantala flavescens" (skimmer) 40 1·00
166 20c. "Gnathothlibus erotus" (banana moth) 50 1·25

80 Fletcher Christian

81 Chair of Homage

1976. Bicent of American Revolution. Mult.
167 5c. Type **80** 20 65
168 10c. H.M.S. "Bounty" 25 80
169 30c. George Washington 25 95
170 50c. "Mayflower", 1620 35 1·50

1977. Silver Jubilee. Multicoloured.
171 8c. Prince Philip's visit, 1971 10 15
172 20c. Type **81** 20 25
173 50c. Enthronement 40 50

82 The Island's Bell

84 Coronation Ceremony

83 Building a "Bounty" Model

1977. Multicoloured.
174 1c. Type **82** 10 50
175 2c. Building a longboat (horiz) 10 50
176 5c. Landing cargo (horiz) 10 50
177 6c. Sorting supplies (horiz) 10 50
178 9c. Cleaning wahoo (fish) 10 50
179 10c. Cultivation (horiz) 10 50
179a 15c. Sugar Mill (horiz) 50 1·00
180 20c. Grating coconut and bananas (horiz) 15 50
181 35c. The Island church (horiz) 15 70
182 50c. Fetching miro logs, Henderson Is. (horiz) 20 1·00
182b 70c. Burning obsolete stamp issues 50 1·25
183 $1 Prince Philip, Bounty Bay and Royal Yacht "Britannia" (horiz) 40 1·10
184 $2 Queen Elizabeth II (photograph by Reginald Davis) 50 1·75

1978. "Bounty" Day. Multicoloured.
185 6c. Type **83** 20 20
186 20c. The model at sea 25 25
187 35c. Burning the model 35 35
MS188 166×122 mm. Nos. 185/7 5·00 9·50

1978. 25th Anniv of Coronation. Sheet 94×78 mm.
MS189 **84** $1.20 multicoloured 80 1·75

85 Harbour before Development

1978. "Operation Pallium" (Harbour Development Project). Multicoloured.
190 15c. Type **85** 25 50
191 20c. Unloading R.F.A. "Sir Geraint" 30 60
192 30c. Work on the jetty 35 70
193 35c. Harbour after development 40 80

86 John Adams and Diary Extract

1979. 150th Death Anniv of John Adams ("Bounty" mutineer). Multicoloured.
194 35c. Type **86** 30 70
195 70c. John Adams' grave and diary extract 45 90

87 Pitcairn's Island sketched from H.M.S. "Amphitrite"

1979. 19th-century Engravings.
196 **87** 6c. black, brown and stone 15 20
197 – 9c. black, violet & lt violet 15 25
198 – 20c. black, green and yellow 15 40
199 – 70c. black, scarlet and red 30 1·00
DESIGNS: 9c. Bounty Bay and Village of Pitcairn; 20c. Lookout Ridge; 70c. Church and School House.

88 Taking Presents to the Square

1979. Christmas. Int Year of the Child. Mult.
200 6c. Type **88** 10 20
201 9c. Decorating trees with presents 10 25
202 20c. Chosen men distributing gifts 15 40
203 35c. Carrying presents home 20 50
MS204 198×73 mm. Nos. 200/3 75 1·40

89 Loading Mail from Supply Ship to Longboats

1980. "London 1980" International Stamp Exhibition. Sheet 120×135 mm containing T **89** and similar horiz designs. Multicoloured.
MS205 35c. Type **89**; 35c. Mail being conveyed by "Flying Fox" (hoisting mechanism) to the Edge; 35c. Tractor transporting mail from the Edge to Adamstown; 35c. Mail being off-loaded at Post Office 75 1·50

90 Queen Elizabeth the Queen Mother at Henley Regatta

1980. 80th Birthday of The Queen Mother.
206 **90** 50c. multicoloured 40 70

1980. Handicrafts (2nd series). As T **46**. Multicoloured.
207 9c. Turtles (wood carvings) 10 10
208 20c. Pitcairn wheelbarrow (wood carving) 10 15
209 35c. Gamet (wood carving) (vert) 15 25
210 40c. Woven bonnet and fan (vert) 15 25

91 Part of Adamstown

1981. Landscapes. Multicoloured.
211 6c. Type **91** 10 10
212 9c. Big George 10 15
213 20c. Christian's Cave, Gannets Ridge 15 20
214 35c. Radio Station from Pawala Valley Ridge 20 30
215 70c. Tatrimoa 30 45

92 Islanders preparing for Departure

1981. 125th Anniv of Pitcairn Islanders' Migration to Norfolk Island. Multicoloured.
216 9c. Type **92** 15 30
217 35c. View of Pitcairn Island from "Morayshire" 25 50
218 70c. "Morayshire" 40 90

93 Prince Charles as Colonel-in-Chief, Cheshire Regiment
95 Pitcairn Islands Coat of Arms

94 Lemon

1981. Royal Wedding. Multicoloured.
219 20c. Wedding bouquet from Pitcairn Islands 20 20
220 35c. Type **93** 25 20
221 $1.20 Prince Charles and Lady Diana Spencer 75 60

1982. Fruit. Multicoloured.
222 9c. Type **94** 10 10
223 20c. Pomegranate 15 20
224 35c. Avocado 20 30
225 70c. Pawpaw 40 65

1982. 21st Birthday of Princess of Wales. Multicoloured.
226 6c. Type **95** 10 20
227 9c. Princess at Royal Opera House, Covent Garden, December 1981 45 20
228 70c. Balcony Kiss 55 60
229 $1.20 Formal portrait 1·00 80

96 Raphael's Angels

1982. Christmas. Raphael's Angels.
230 **96** 15c. black, silver and pink 20 20
231 – 20c. black, silver and yellow 20 20
232 – 50c. brown, silver and stone 30 30
233 – $1 black, silver and blue 40 40
DESIGNS: 20c. to $1 Different details, the 50c. and $1 being vertical.

97 Radio Operator

1983. Commonwealth Day. Multicoloured.
234 6c. Type **97** 10 10
235 9c. Postal clerk 10 10
236 70c. Fisherman 35 65
237 $1.20 Artist 60 1·10

98 "Topaz" sights Smoke on Pitcairn

1983. 175th Anniv of Folger's Discovery of the Settlers. Multicoloured.
238 6c. Type **98** 30 20
239 20c. Three islanders approach the "Topaz" 35 30
240 70c. Capt. Mayhew Folger welcomed by John Adams 60 75
241 $1.20 Folger presented with "Bounty" chronometer 75 1·10

99 Hattie-Tree

1983. Trees of Pitcairn Islands (1st series). Multicoloured.
242 35c. Type **99** 25 55
243 35c. Leaves from Hattie-Tree 25 55
244 70c. Pandanus 40 90
245 70c. Pandanus and basket weaving 40 90
See also Nos. 304/7.

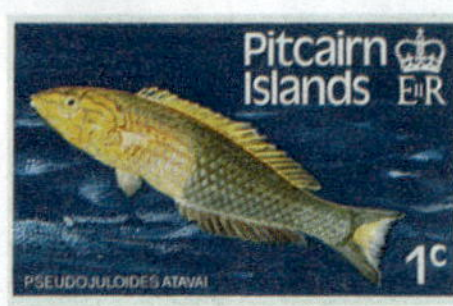

100 Atava wrasse

1984. Fishes. Multicoloured.
246 1c. Type **100** 20 30
247 4c. Black-eared wrasse 30 35
248 6c. Long-finned parrotfish 30 35
249 9c. Yellow-edged lyretail 30 35
250 10c. Black-eared angelfish 30 40
251 15c. Emery's damselfish 30 40
252 20c. Smith's butterflyfish 40 50
253 35c. Crosshatched triggerfish 50 60
254 50c. Yellow damselfish 50 75
255 70c. Pitcairn angelfish 70 95
312 90c. As 9c. 4·00 5·00
256 $1 Easter Island soldierfish 70 1·25
257 $1.20 Long-finned anthias 75 2·00
258 $2 White trevally 1·25 2·50
313 $3 Wakanoura moray 5·50 7·50

101 "Southern Cross"

1984. Night Sky.
259 **101** 15c. blue, lilac and gold 20 20
260 – 20c. blue, green and gold 30 30
261 – 70c. blue, brown and gold 75 75
262 – $1 blue, light blue and gold 1·00 1·00
DESIGNS: 20c. "Southern Fish"; 70c. "Lesser Dog"; $1 "The Virgin".

102 Aluminium Longboat

1984. "Ausipex" International Stamp Exhibition, Melbourne. Sheet 134 × 86 mm containing T **102** and similar horiz design. Multicoloured.
MS263 50c. Type **102**; $2 Traditional-style wooden longboat 1·50 2·00

103 "H.M.S. "Portland" standing off Bounty Bay" (J. Linton Palmer)
104 The Queen Mother with the Queen and Princess Margaret, 1980

1985. 19th-century Paintings (1st series). Mult.
264 6c. Type **103** 40 40
265 9c. "Christian's Look Out" (J. Linton Palmer) 40 40
266 35c. "The Golden Age" (J. Linton Palmer) 75 60
267 $2 "A View of the Village, 1825" (William Smyth) (48 × 31 mm) 1·75 2·25
See also Nos. 308/11.

1985. Life and Times of Queen Elizabeth the Queen Mother. Multicoloured.
268 6c. Receiving the Freedom of Dundee, 1964 10 25
269 35c. Type **104** 30 55
270 70c. The Queen Mother in 1983 50 85
271 $1.20 With Prince Henry at his christening (from photo by Lord Snowdon) 70 1·50
MS272 91 × 73 mm. $2 In coach at Ascot Races 2·75 2·00

105 "Act 6" (container ship)

1985. Ships (1st issue). Multicoloured.
273 50c. Type **105** 95 1·75
274 50c. "Columbus Louisiana" (container ship) 95 1·75
275 50c. "Essi Gina" (tanker) (48 × 35 mm) 95 1·75
276 50c. "Stolt Spirit" tanker (48 × 35 mm) 95 1·75
See also Nos. 296/9.

106 "Madonna and Child" (Raphael)
107a Prince Andrew and Miss Sarah Ferguson

107 Green Turtle

1985. Christmas. Designs showing "Madonna and Child" paintings. Multicoloured.
277 6c. Type **106** 70 50
278 9c. Krause (after Raphael) 70 50
279 35c. Andreas Mayer 1·25 70
280 $2 Unknown Austrian master 3·00 4·00

1986. Turtles. Multicoloured.
281 9c. Type **107** 75 90
282 20c. Green turtle and Pitcairn Island 1·25 1·25
283 70c. Hawksbill turtle 2·25 3·75
284 $1.20 Hawksbill turtle and Pitcairn Island 2·75 4·25

1986. 60th Birthday of Queen Elizabeth II. As T **246b** of Papua New Guinea.
285 6c. Princess Elizabeth at Royal Lodge, Windsor, 1946 15 20
286 9c. Wedding of Princess Anne, 1973 15 20
287 20c. At Order of St. Michael and St. George service, St. Paul's Cathedral, 1961 25 30
288 $1.20 At Electrical Engineering Concert, Royal Festival Hall, 1971 60 1·25
289 $2 At Crown Agents Head Office, London 1983 75 2·00

1986. Royal Wedding. Multicoloured.
290 20c. Type **107a** 50 50
291 $1.20 Prince Andrew aboard "Bluenose II" off Halifax, Canada, 1985 2·25 2·75

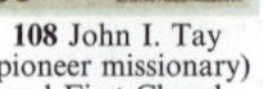

108 John I. Tay (pioneer missionary) and First Church
110 *Bounty* (replica)

109 Pitcairn Island Home

1986. Centenary of Seventh-Day Adventist Church on Pitcairn. Multicoloured.
292 6c. Type **108** 50 50
293 20c. "Pitcairn" (missionary schooner) and second church (1907) 1·25 1·00
294 35c. Baptism at Down Isaac and third church (1945) 1·75 1·50
295 $2 Islanders singing farewell hymn and present church (1954) 3·75 4·25

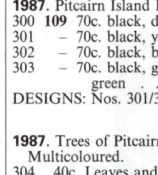

1987. Ships (2nd series). As T **105**. Multicoloured.
296 50c. "Samoan Reefer" (freighter) 1·00 2·25
297 50c. "Brussel" (container ship) 1·00 2·25
298 50c. "Australian Exporter" (container ship) (48 × 35 mm) 1·00 2·25
299 50c. "Taupo" (cargo liner) (48 × 35 mm) 1·00 2·25

1987. Pitcairn Island Homes.
300 **109** 70c. black, dp violet & vio 60 60
301 – 70c. black, yellow & brn 60 60
302 – 70c. black, blue & dp blue 60 60
303 – 70c. black, green and deep green 60 60
DESIGNS: Nos. 301/3, different houses.

1987. Trees of Pitcairn Islands (2nd series). As T **99**. Multicoloured.
304 40c. Leaves and flowers from "Erythrina variegata" 1·25 1·75
305 40c. "Erythrina variegata" tree 1·25 1·75
306 $1.80 Leaves from "Aleurites moluccana" and nut torch 2·00 3·00
307 $1.80 "Aleurites moluccana" tree 2·00 3·00

1987. 19th-century Paintings (2nd series). Paintings by Lt. Conway Shipley in 1848. As T **103**. Multicoloured.
308 20c. "House and Tomb of John Adams" 65 60
309 40c. "Bounty Bay" 1·00 85
310 90c. "School House and Chapel" 1·75 2·00
311 $1.80 "Pitcairn Island" (48 × 31 mm) 2·75 5·00

1988. Bicentenary of Australian Settlement. Sheet 112 × 76 mm.
MS314 **110** $3 multicoloured 4·25 2·75

111 H.M.S. "Swallow" (survey ship), 1767

1988. Ships. Multicoloured.
315 5c. Type **111** 50 80
316 10c. H.M.S. "Pandora" (frigate), 1791 50 80
317 15c. H.M.S. "Briton" and H.M.S. "Tagus" (frigates), 1814 55 90
318 20c. H.M.S. "Blossom" (survey ship), 1825 60 85

319 30c. "Lucy Anne" (barque), 1831 . . . 70 90
320 35c. "Charles Doggett" (whaling brig), 1831 . . . 70 90
321 40c. H.M.S. "Fly" (sloop), 1838 . . . 75 95
322 60c. "Camden" (missionary brig.), 1840 . . . 1·00 1·40
323 90c. H.M.S. "Virago" (paddle-sloop), 1853 . . . 1·00 1·75
324 $1.20 "Rakaia" (screw-steamer), 1867 . . . 1·25 2·00
325 $1.80 H.M.S. "Sappho" (screw-sloop), 1882 . . . 1·50 2·50
326 $5 H.M.S. "Champion" (corvette), 1893 . . . 3·00 5·50

112 Raising the Union Jack, 1838 **113** Angel

1988. 150th Anniv of Pitcairn Island Constitution. Each showing different extract from original Constitution. Multicoloured.
327 20c. Type **112** . . . 15 20
328 40c. Signing Constitution on board H.M.S. "Fly", 1838 30 35
329 $1.05 Voters at modern polling station . . . 75 80
330 $1.80 Modern classroom . . 1·25 1·40

1988. Christmas. Multicoloured.
331 90c. Type **113** . . . 65 70
332 90c. Holy Family . . . 65 70
333 90c. Two Polynesian Wise Men . . . 65 70
334 90c. Polynesian Wise Man and shepherd . . . 65 70

114 Loading Stores, Deptford

1989. Bicentenary of Pitcairn Island Settlement (1st issue). Multicoloured.
335 20c. Type **114** . . . 1·50 1·50
336 20c. H.M.S. "Bounty" leaving Spithead . . . 1·50 1·50
337 20c. H.M.S. "Bounty" at Cape Horn . . . 1·50 1·50
338 20c. Anchored in Adventure Bay, Tasmania . . . 1·50 1·50
339 20c. Crew collecting breadfruit . . . 1·50 1·50
340 20c. Breadfruit in cabin . . . 1·50 1·50
See also Nos. 341/7, 356/61 and 389/94.

1989. Bicentenary of Pitcairn Island Settlement (2nd issue). As T **114**. Multicoloured.
341 90c. H.M.S. "Bounty" leaving Tahiti . . . 3·00 3·00
342 90c. Bligh awoken by mutineers . . . 3·00 3·00
343 90c. Bligh before Fletcher Christian . . . 3·00 3·00
344 90c. Provisioning "Bounty's" launch . . . 3·00 3·00
345 90c. "Mutineers casting Bligh adrift" (Robert Dodd) . . 3·00 3·00
346 90c. Mutineers discarding breadfruit plants . . . 3·00 3·00
MS347 110 × 85 mm. 90c. No. 345; 90c. Isle of Man 1989 35p. Mutiny stamp; 90c. Norfolk Island 39c. Mutiny stamp . . . 3·75 4·50

115 R.N.Z.A.F. Lockheed Orion making Mail Drop, 1985

1989. Aircraft. Multicoloured.
348 20c. Type **115** . . . 1·50 60
349 80c. Beech 80 Queen Air on photo-mission, 1983 . . . 2·75 1·25
350 $1.05 Boeing-Vertol Chinook helicopter landing diesel fuel from U.S.S. "Breton", 1969 . . . 3·00 1·50
351 $1.30 R.N.Z.A.F. Lockheed Hercules dropping bulldozer, 1983 . . . 3·00 1·75

116 Ducie Island

1989. Islands of Pitcairn Group. Mult.
352 15c. Type **116** . . . 60 50
353 90c. Henderson Island . . . 1·75 1·25
354 $1.05 Oeno Island . . . 1·90 1·75
355 $1.30 Pitcairn Island . . . 1·90 1·75

1990. Bicentenary of Pitcairn Island Settlement (3rd issue). As T **114**. Multicoloured.
356 40c. Mutineers sighting Pitcairn Island . . . 1·50 1·50
357 40c. Ship's boat approaching landing . . . 1·50 1·50
358 40c. Exploring island . . . 1·50 1·50
359 40c. Ferrying goods ashore 1·50 1·50
360 40c. Burning of H.M.S. "Bounty" . . . 1·50 1·50
361 40c. Pitcairn Island village . . 1·50 1·50

117 Ennerdale, Cumbria, and Peter Heywood

1990. "Stamp World London '90" International Stamp Exhibition, London. Designs showing English landmarks and "Bounty" crew members. Multicoloured.
362 80c. Type **117** . . . 75 80
363 90c. St. Augustine's Tower, Hackney, and John Adams 85 90
364 $1.05 Citadel Gateway, Plymouth, and William Bligh . . . 1·00 1·25
365 $1.30 Moorland Close, Cockermouth, and Fletcher Christian . . . 1·25 1·40

117a Queen Elizabeth, 1937 **119** Stephen's Lory ("Redbreast")

118 "Bounty" Chronometer and 1940 1d. Definitive

1990. 90th Birthday of Queen Elizabeth the Queen Mother.
378 **117a** 40c. multicoloured . . . 75 85
379 – $3 black and red . . . 3·00 3·75
DESIGN—29 × 37 mm: $3 King George VI and Queen Elizabeth on way to Silver Wedding Service, 1948.

1990. 50th Anniv of Pitcairn Islands Stamps. Multicoloured.
380 20c. Type **118** . . . 80 80
381 80c. "Bounty" Bible and 1958 4d. definitive . . . 1·60 1·75
382 90c. "Bounty" Bell and 1969 30c. definitive . . . 1·75 1·90
383 $1.05 Mutiny on the "Bounty" and 1977 $1 definitive . . . 2·00 2·50
384 $1.30 Penny Black and 1988 15c. definitive . . . 2·25 2·75

1990. "Birdpex '90" International Stamp Exhibition, Christchurch, New Zealand. Multicoloured.
385 20c. Type **119** . . . 75 75
386 90c. Henderson Island fruit dove ("Wood Pigeon") . . 1·50 1·60
387 $1.30 Pitcairn warbler ("Sparrow") . . . 1·75 2·75
388 $1.80 Henderson Island crake ("Chicken Bird") . . . 2·00 3·00

1991. Bicent of Pitcairn Island Settlement (4th issue). Celebrations. As T **114**. Multicoloured.
389 80c. Re-enacting landing of mutineers . . . 2·50 2·75
390 80c. Commemorative plaque 2·50 2·75
391 80c. Memorial church service 2·50 2·75
392 80c. Cricket match . . . 2·50 2·75
393 80c. Burning model of "Bounty" . . . 2·50 2·75
394 80c. Firework display . . . 2·50 2·75

120 "Europa"

1991. Cruise Liners. Multicoloured.
395 15c. Type **120** . . . 1·00 60
396 80c. "Royal Viking Star" . . 2·00 1·75
397 $1.30 "World Discoverer" . . 2·50 2·75
398 $1.80 "Sagafjord" . . . 3·00 3·50

1991. 65th Birthday of Queen Elizabeth II and 70th Birthday of Prince Philip. As T **120a** of Pitcairn Islands. Multicoloured.
399 20c. Prince Philip (vert) . . . 75 30
400 $1.30 Queen in robes of the Order of St. Michael and St. George (vert) . . . 1·75 1·25

121 Bulldozer

1991. Island Transport. Multicoloured.
401 20c. Type **121** . . . 40 30
402 80c. Two-wheeled motorcycle 1·25 1·00
403 $1.30 Tractor . . . 1·25 1·40
404 $1.80 Three-wheeled motorcycle . . . 2·00 2·25

122 The Annunciation

1991. Christmas. Multicoloured.
405 20c. Type **122** . . . 30 30
406 80c. Shepherds and lamb . . 90 90
407 $1.30 Holy Family . . . 1·25 1·25
408 $1.80 Three Wise Men . . . 1·75 1·75

122c Bounty Bay

1992. 40th Anniv of Queen Elizabeth II's Accession. Multicoloured.
409 20c. Type **122c** . . . 25 25
410 60c. Sunset over Pitcairn . . 70 70
411 90c. Pitcairn coastline . . . 90 90
412 $1 Three portraits of Queen Elizabeth . . . 95 95
413 $1.80 Queen Elizabeth II . . 1·60 1·60

123 Insular Shark

1992. Sharks. Multicoloured.
414 20c. Type **123** . . . 80 50
415 $1 Sand tiger . . . 2·00 1·50
416 $1.50 Black-finned reef shark 2·25 2·00
417 $1.80 Grey reef shark . . . 2·50 2·00

124 "Montastrea sp." and "Acropora spp." (corals)

1992. The Sir Peter Scott Memorial Expedition to Henderson Island. Multicoloured.
418 20c. Type **124** . . . 80 60
419 $1 Henderson sandalwood . . 1·75 1·50
420 $1.50 Murphy's petrel . . . 3·00 2·75
421 $1.80 Henderson hawkmoth 3·00 3·00

125 Bligh's Birthplace at St. Tudy, Cornwall

1992. 175th Death Anniv of William Bligh. Multicoloured.
422 20c. Type **125** . . . 50 60
423 $1 Bligh on "Bounty" . . . 1·50 1·50
424 $1.50 Voyage in "Bounty's" launch . . . 2·00 2·75
425 $1.80 "William Bligh" (R. Combe) and epitaph 2·25 3·00

126 H.M.S. "Chichester" (frigate)

1993. Modern Royal Navy Vessels. Mult.
426 15c. Type **126** . . . 75 50
427 20c. H.M.S. "Jaguar" (frigate) . . . 75 50
428 $1.80 H.M.S. "Andrew" (submarine) . . . 3·25 3·25
429 $3 H.M.S. "Warrior" (aircraft carrier) and Westland Dragonfly helicopter . . . 5·75 5·50

127 Queen Elizabeth II in Coronation Robes

1993. 40th Anniv of Coronation.
430 **127** $5 multicoloured . . . 6·00 7·00

128 Pawala Valley Ridge

1993. Island Views. Multicoloured.
431 10c. Type **128** . . . 20 20
432 90c. St. Pauls . . . 90 90
433 $1.20 Matt's Rocks from Water Valley . . . 1·25 1·50
434 $1.50 Ridge Rope to St. Paul's Pool . . . 1·50 1·75
435 $1.80 Ship Landing Point . . 1·75 2·25

129 Indo-Pacific Tree Gecko

1993. Lizards. Multicoloured.
436 20c. Type **129** . . . 80 50
437 45c. Stump-toed gecko . . . 1·00 1·25
438 45c. Mourning gecko . . . 1·00 1·25
439 $1 Moth skink . . . 2·00 1·50

440 $1.50 Snake-eyed skink . . . 2·50 2·75
441 $1.50 White-bellied skink . . 2·50 2·75

1994. "Hong Kong '94" International Stamp Exhibition. Nos. 437/8 and 440/1 optd **HONG KONG '94** and emblem.

442 45c. Stump-toed gecko . . . 80 90
443 45c. Mourning gecko 80 90
444 $1.50 Snake-eyed skink . . . 2·25 2·75
445 $1.50 White-bellied skink . . 2·25 2·75

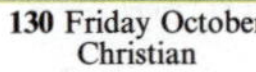

130 Friday October Christian

131 Landing Stores from Wreck of "Wildwave", Oeno Island, 1858

1994. Early Pitcairners. Multicoloured.

446 5c. Type **130** 20 30
447 20c. Moses Young 50 40
448 $1.80 James Russell McCoy 2·25 2·75
449 $3 Rosalind Amelia Young 3·75 5·00

1994. Shipwrecks. Multicoloured.

450 20c. Type **131** 65 60
451 90c. Longboat trying to reach "Cornwallis", Pitcairn Island, 1875 . . . . 1·75 1·75
452 $1.80 "Acadia" aground, Ducie Island, 1881 . . . . 3·00 3·50
453 $3 Rescuing survivors from "Oregon", Oeno Island, 1883 . . . . 4·25 4·50

132 Fire Coral

133 Angel and "Ipomoea acuminata"

1994. Corals. Multicoloured.

454 20c. Type **132** 80 70
455 90c. Cauliflower coral and arc-eyed hawkfish (horiz) 2·00 2·00
456 $1 Lobe coral and high-finned rudderfish . . . . 2·00 2·00
MS457 100 × 70 mm. $3 Coral garden and mailed butterflyfish 4·00 5·00

1994. Christmas. Flowers. Multicoloured.

458 20c. Type **133** 35 25
459 90c. Shepherds and "Hibiscus rosa-sinensis" (vert) . . . 1·25 1·40
460 $1 Star and "Plumeria rubra" 1·25 1·40
461 $3 Holy Family and "Alpinia speciosa" (vert) . . . . . 3·00 3·25

134 White ("Fairy") Tern on Egg

1995. Birds. Multicoloured.

462 5c. Type **134** 30 60
463 10c. Red-tailed tropic bird chick (vert) 30 60
464 15c. Henderson Island crake with chick 40 70
465 20c. Red-footed booby feeding chick (vert) 40 70
466 45c. Blue-grey noddy 60 80
467 50c. Pitcairn ("Henderson Reed") warbler in nest . . 65 90
468 90c. Common noddy . . . . 1·00 1·00
469 $1 Blue-faced ("Masked") booby and chick (vert) . . 1·10 1·10
470 $1.80 Henderson Island fruit dove . . . . 1·50 1·75
471 $2 Murphy's petrel . . . . . 1·75 2·25
472 $3 Christmas Island shearwater . . . . 2·25 3·00
473 $5 Red-tailed tropic bird juvenile . . . . 3·50 4·50

135 Islanders in Longboats

1995. Oeno Island Holiday. Multicoloured.

474 20c. Type **135** 40 60
475 90c. Playing volleyball on beach . . . . 1·25 1·25
476 $1.80 Preparing picnic . . . 2·25 3·25
477 $3 Singsong . . . . 3·50 5·00

136 Queen Elizabeth the Queen Mother

1995. 95th Birthday of Queen Elizabeth the Queen Mother. Sheet 75 × 90 mm.

MS478 **136** $5 multicoloured . . 5·50 5·00

137 Guglielmo Marconi and Early Wireless, 1901

1995. Centenary of First Radio Transmission. Multicoloured.

479 20c. Type **137** 40 60
480 $1 Pitcairn radio transmitter, c. 1938 . . . . 1·10 1·25
481 $1.50 Satellite Earth Station equipment, 1994 . . . . . 1·75 2·75
482 $3 Communications satellite in orbit, 1992 . . . . . . 3·25 5·00

137a United Nations Float, Lord Mayor's Show

1995. 50th Anniv of United Nations. Multicoloured.

483 20c. Type **137a** 30 30
484 $1 R.F.A. "Brambleleaf" (tanker) . . . . 1·40 1·25
485 $1.50 U.N. Ambulance . . . 2·00 2·25
486 $3 R.A.F. Lockheed L-1011 TriStar . . . . 3·50 3·75

138 Early Morning at the Jetty

1996. Supply Ship Day. Multicoloured.

487 20c. Type **138** 25 30
488 40c. Longboat meeting "America Star" (freighter) 45 55
489 90c. Loading supplies into longboats . . . . 1·00 1·10
490 $1 Landing supplies on jetty 1·10 1·25
491 $1.50 Sorting supplies at the Co-op . . . . 1·75 2·25
492 $1.80 Tractor towing supplies 1·90 2·25

1996. 70th Birthday of Queen Elizabeth II. As T **55** of Tokelau, each incorporating a different photograph of the Queen. Multicoloured.

493 20c. Bounty Bay 45 45
494 90c. Jetty and landing point, Bounty Bay . . . . 1·40 1·40
495 $1.80 Matt's Rocks . . . . . 2·25 2·50
496 $3 St. Pauls . . . . 4·00 4·50

139 Chinese junk

1996. "CHINA '96" 9th Asian International Stamp Exhibition, Peking. Multicoloured.

497 $1.80 Type **139** . . . . . 2·25 2·50
498 $1.80 H.M.S. "Bounty" . . . 2·25 2·50
MS499 80 × 79 mm. 90c. China 1984 8f. Year of the Rat stamp; 90c. Polynesian rat eating banana 2·00 2·00

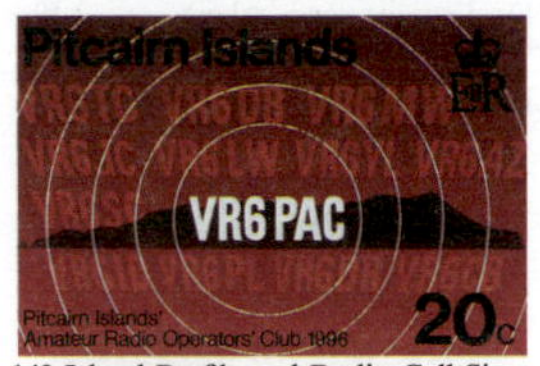

140 Island Profile and Radio Call Signs

1996. Amateur Radio Operations from Pitcairn Islands. Multicoloured.

500 20c. Type **140** 45 45
501 $1.50 Radio operator calling for medical assistance . . . 2·00 2·25
502 $1.50 Doctors giving medical advice by radio . . . . . 2·00 2·25
503 $2.50 Andrew Young (first radio operator), 1938 . . . 2·75 3·00

141 Pitcairn Warbler ("Henderson Island Reed Warbler")

142 Coat of Arms

1996. Endangered Species. Local Birds. Mult.

504 5c. Type **141** 30 30
505 10c. Stephen's lory ("Stephen's Lorikeet") . . 30 30
506 20c. Henderson Island crake ("Henderson Island Rail") 50 50
507 90c. Henderson Island fruit dove . . . . 1·25 1·25
508 $2 White tern (horiz) . . . . 2·00 2·25
509 $2 Blue-faced booby ("Masked Booby") (horiz) 2·00 2·25

1997. "HONG KONG '97" International Stamp Exhibition. Chinese New Year ("Year of the Ox"). Sheet 82 × 87 mm.

MS510 **142** $5 multicoloured . . 5·00 5·50

143 "David Barker" (supply ship)

1997. 50th Anniv of South Pacific Commission. Sheet 115 × 56 mm, containing T **143** and similar horiz design. Multicoloured.

MS511 $2.50 Type **143**; $2.50 "McLachlan" (fishing boat) . . 8·50 8·50

144 Health Centre

1997. Island Health Care. Multicoloured.

512 20c. Type **144** 30 25
513 $1 Nurse treating patient . . 1·00 1·00
514 $1.70 Dentist treating woman 1·75 1·90
515 $3 Evacuating patient by longboat . . . . 3·00 3·25

1997. Golden Wedding of Queen Elizabeth and Prince Philip. As T **316a** of Papua New Guinea. Multicoloured.

516 20c. Prince Philip driving carriage 30 40
517 20c. Queen Elizabeth 30 40
518 $1 Prince Philip at Royal Windsor Horse Show, 1996 1·00 1·25
519 $1 Queen Elizabeth with horse . . . . 1·00 1·25
520 $1.70 Queen Elizabeth and Prince Philip at the Derby, 1991 . . . . 1·50 1·75
521 $1.70 Prince Charles hunting, 1995 . . . . 1·50 1·75

Nos. 516/17, 518/19 and 520/21 respectively were printed together, se-tenant, with the backgrounds forming composite designs.

145 Island and Star

1997. Christmas. Multicoloured.

522 20c. Type **145** 35 25
523 80c. Hand ringing bell . . . 1·00 80
524 $1.20 Presents in baskets . . 1·40 1·50
525 $3 Families outside church 2·75 3·00

146 Christian's Cave

1997. Christian's Cave. Multicoloured.

526 5c. Type **146** 15 20
527 20c. View from the beach . . 35 35
528 35c. Cave entrance (vert) . . 50 50
529 $5 Pathway through forest (vert) . . . . 3·75 5·00

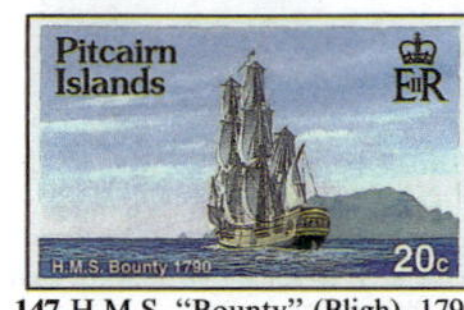

147 H.M.S. "Bounty" (Bligh), 1790

1998. Millennium Commemoration (1st issue). Sailing Ships. Multicoloured.

530 20c. Type **147** 40 40
531 90c. H.M.S. "Swallow" (Carteret), 1767 . . . . . 1·00 1·00
532 $1.80 H.M.S. "Briton" and H.M.S. "Tagus" (frigates), 1814 . . . . 1·50 1·60
533 $3 H.M.S. "Fly" (sloop), 1838 . . . . 2·50 2·75

See also Nos. 549/52 and 577/80.

1998. Diana, Princess of Wales Commemoration. Sheet, 145 × 70 mm, containing vert designs as T **91** of Kiribati. Multicoloured.

MS534 90c. Wearing pearl choker and red evening dress; 90c. Wearing white hat and pearl necklace; 90c. Carrying bouquet; 90c. Wearing white dress and hat (*sold at* $3.60+40c. *charity premium*) . . . . 3·50 3·75

148 "Bidens mathewsii"

1998. Flowers. Multicoloured.

535 20c. Type **148** 80 70
536 90c. "Hibiscus" sp. . . . . . 1·75 1·40
537 $1.80 "Osteomeles anthyllidifolia" . . . . . . 2·75 2·75
538 $3 "Ipomoea littoralis" . . . 3·75 5·50

149 Fishing

1998. International Year of the Ocean. Multicoloured.
539 20c. Type **149** 80 70
540 90c. Diver at wreck of "Cornwallis" (vert) . . . . 1·75 1·40
541 $1.80 Reef fish . . . . 2·50 2·50
542 $3 Murphy's petrel and great frigate bird (vert) . . . . . 4·00 4·25
MS543 86 × 86 mm. Nos. 539/42 8·50 9·00

150 George Nobbs and Class, 1838

1999. Development of Local Education. Mult.
544 20c. Type **150** 75 60
545 90c. Children outside thatched school, 1893 . . . 1·60 1·40
546 $1.80 Boy in wheelbarrow outside wooden school, 1932 . . . . 2·50 2·75
547 $3 Modern classroom with computer . . . . 3·50 4·25

151 H.M.S. "Bounty" and Anchor

1999. "Australia '99" World Stamp Exhibition, Melbourne. Pitcairn Archaeology Project. Sheet, 190 × 80 mm, containing T **151** and similar diamond-shaped designs. Multicoloured.
MS548 50c. Type **151**; $1 "Bounty" approaching Pitcairn and cannon; $1.50, "Bounty" on fire and chronometer; $2 "Bounty" sinking and metal bucket . . . . . . 5·50 5·50

152 John Adams (survivor of "Bounty" crew) and Bounty Bay

1999. Millennium Commemoration (2nd issue). Multicoloured.
549 20c. Type **152** 75 60
550 90c. "Topaz" (sealer), 1808 1·60 1·10
551 $1.80 George Hunn Nobbs and Norfolk Island . . . . 2·25 3·00
552 $3 H.M.S "Champion" (corvette), 1893 . . . . . 3·75 4·50

153 Prince Edward and Miss Sophie Rhys-Jones

1999. Royal Wedding. Multicoloured.
553 $2.50 Type **153** . . . . . . 2·25 2·75
554 $2.50 Engagement photograph . . . . 2·25 2·75

154 Bee-keepers at Work

1999. Bee-keeping. Multicoloured. Self-adhesive.
555 20c. Type **154** 75 65
556 $1 Bee on passion flower . . 1·60 1·40
557 $1.80 Bees in honeycomb . . 2·50 2·75
558 $3 Bee on flower and jar of "Mutineer's Dream" honey 3·50 4·25
MS559 74 × 100 mm. No. 556 . . 2·50 2·75
No. **MS**559 includes the "China '99" International Stamp Exhibition emblem on the sheet margin.

155 Arrival of "Yankee" (schooner), 1937

2000. Protection of "Mr. Turpen" (Galapagos Tortoise on Pitcairn). Multicoloured.
560 5c. Type **155** . . . . 1·25 1·50
561 20c. Off-loading Mr. Turpen at Bounty Bay . . . . . . 1·50 1·75
562 35c. Mr. Turpen . . . . . . 1·60 1·90
563 $5 Head of Mr. Turpen . . . 4·75 5·50
Nos. 560/3 were printed together, se-tenant, with the background forming a composite design.

156 *Guettarda speciosa* (flower)

2000. Flowers of Pitcairn Islands. Multicoloured.
564 10c. Type **156** 10 10
565 15c. *Hibiscus tiliaceus* 10 15
566 20c. *Selenicereus grandiflorus* 15 20
567 30c. *Metrosideros collina* . . 20 25
568 50c. *Alpinia zerumbet* . . . 35 40
569 $1 *Syzygium jambos* 75 80
570 $1.50 *Commelina diffusa* . . 1·10 1·20
571 $1.80 *Canna indica* . . . . . 1·20 1·30
572 $2 *Allamanda cathartica* . . 1·50 1·60
573 $3 *Calophyllum inophyllum* 2·20 2·30
574 $5 *Ipomea indica* . . . . . 3·75 4·00
575 $10 *Bauhinia monandra* (40 × 40 mm) . . . . . . 7·25 7·50

2000. "The Stamp Show 2000" International Stamp Exhibition, London. Sheet, 120 × 80 mm, containing Nos. 570 and 572.
MS576 $1.50 Commelina diffusa; $2 Allamanda cathartica . . . . 4·50 5·00

157 Longboat

2000. Millennium Commemoration (3rd issue). Communications. Multicoloured.
577 20c. Type **157** 80 70
578 90c. Landing and Longboat House . . . . 1·75 1·10
579 $1.80 Honda quad with trailer of watermelons . . . 2·75 3·00
580 $3 Woman with printer at Satellite Station . . . . . 3·50 4·00

158 Surveyor and Helicopter

2000. "EXPO 2000" World Stamp Exhibition, Anaheim, U.S.A. Anglo-American Joint Satellite Recovery Survey Mission, Henderson Island, 1966. Sheet, 120 × 180 mm, containing T **158** and similar vert design. Multicoloured.
MS581 $2.50 Type **158**; $2.50 Survey team and U.S.S. *Sunnyvale* (satellite recovery vessel) . . . 7·00 7·50
No. **MS**581 was issued folded in half horizontally with the issue title, "CLASSIFIED INFORMATION" and seal printed on the gum of the top panel. Details of the survey appear on the other side of this section.

159 Queen Elizabeth the Queen Mother

2000. Queen Elizabeth the Queen Mother's 100th Birthday. Sheet, 127 × 95 mm (oval-shaped), containing T **159** and similar vert design. Multicoloured.
MS582 $2 Type **159**; $3 Queen Mother wearing plum outfit . . 4·50 5·50

160 Wrapping Presents

2000. Christmas. Multicoloured.
583 20c. Type **160** 75 50
584 80c. Ringing island bell . . . 1·75 90
585 $1.50 Making decorations . . 2·50 2·50
586 $3 Opening presents . . . . 3·50 4·50

161 *Europa* (liner)

2001. Cruise Ships. Multicoloured.
587 $1.50 Type **161** . . . . . . 2·25 2·50
588 $1.50 *Rotterdam VI* . . . . 2·25 2·50
589 $1.50 *Saga Rose* . . . . . . 2·25 2·50
590 $1.50 *Bremen* . . . . 2·25 2·50

162 Coconut

2001. Tropical Fruits. Multicoloured.
591 20c. Type **162** 30 30
592 80c. Pomegranate 75 75
593 $1 Passion fruit 90 90
594 $3 Pineapple . . . . 2·25 3·00
MS595 103 × 70mm. Nos. 592 and 594 . . . . 3·25 3·75

163 Keyboard

2001. Introduction of Pitcairn Islands Internet Domain Name. Multicoloured. Self-adhesive.
596 20c. Type **163** 70 55
597 50c. Circuit board . . . . . 1·25 80
598 $1 Microchip . . . . 1·75 1·25
599 $5 Mouse . . . . 5·50 7·50

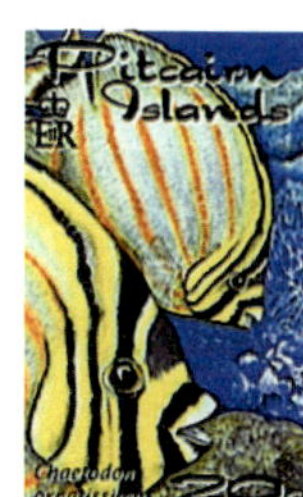

164 Ornate Butterflyfish (*Chaetodon ornatissimus*)

165 Man carrying Driftwood

2001. Reef Fish. Multicoloured.
600 20c. Type **164** 75 55
601 80c. Mailed butterflyfish (*Chaetodon reticulatus*) . . 1·25 80
602 $1.50 Racoon butterflyfish (*Chaetodon lunula*) . . . . 2·00 2·25
603 $2 *Henochus chrysostomus* . . 2·50 2·75
MS604 87 × 120 mm. Nos. 600 and 603 . . . . 2·50 3·00
No. **MS**604 has the paper around the outlines of fish along the upper edge of the sheet cut away.

2001. Woodcarving. Multicoloured.
605 20c. Type **165** 80 95
606 50c. Carver at work . . . . 1·25 1·50
607 $1.50 Working on wood lathe 2·00 2·25
608 $3 Taking carvings to *World Discoverer* (cruise liner) for sale . . . . 3·00 3·25
Nos. 605/8 were printed together, se-tenant, with the backgrounds forming a composite design.

166 *Cypraea argus* Shell

2001. Cowrie Shells. Multicoloured.
609 20c. Type **166** 75 55
610 80c. *Cypraea isabella* . . . . 1·25 80
611 $1 *Cypraea mappa* . . . . . 1·50 1·25
612 $3 *Cypraea mauritiana* . . . 3·25 4·25

2002. Golden Jubilee. Sheet, 162 × 95 mm, containing designs as T **153** of Nauru.
MS613 50c. black, violet and gold; $1 multicoloured; $1.20 black, violet and gold; $1.50 multicoloured; $2 multicoloured 6·00 7·00
DESIGNS—HORIZ: 50c. Queen Elizabeth with Princesses Elizabeth and Margaret; $1 Queen Elizabeth in evening dress; $1.20 Princess Elizabeth in evening dress; $1.50 Queen Elizabeth in blue hat and coat. VERT (38 × 51 mm)—$2 Queen Elizabeth after Annigoni.

167 James McCoy (President of Island Council)

2002. Pitcairn Islands Celebrities. Multicoloured.
614 $1.50 Type **167** . . . . . . 2·00 2·25
615 $1.50 Admiral Sir Fairfax Moresby . . . . 2·00 2·25
616 $1.50 Gerald DeLeo Bliss (postmaster, Cristobal, Panama Canal Zone) . . . 2·00 2·25
617 $1.50 Captain Arthur Jones of Shaw Savill Line . . . . 2·00 2·25

168 "Simba Christian" (cat)

2002. Pitcairn Cats. Multicoloured.
618 20c. Type **168** 70 50
619 $1 "Miti Christian" . . . . 1·50 80

620 $1.50 "Nala Brown" . . . . 2·00 2·25
621 $3 "Alicat Palau" . . . . . 3·25 3·75
MS622 92 × 86 mm. Nos. 618 and 621 . . . . 3·75 4·25

2002. Queen Elizabeth the Queen Mother Commemoration. As T **156** of Nauru.
623 40c. black, gold and purple 80 55
624 $1 brown, gold and purple 1·50 1·00
625 $1.50 multicoloured . . . . 2·00 2·00
626 $2 multicoloured . . . . . . 2·50 3·00
MS627 145 × 70 mm. Nos. 624 and 626 . . . . 4·00 4·50

DESIGNS: 40c. Lady Elizabeth Bowes-Lyon, 1910; $1 Lady Elizabeth Bowes-Lyon, 1923; $1.50, Queen Mother at Leatherhead, 1970; $2 Queen Mother at Scrabster. Designs as Nos. 624 and 626 in No. **MS**627 omit the "1900-2002" inscription and the coloured frame.

169 Woman cutting Palm Fronds and Fan

2002. Weaving. Multicoloured.
628 40c. Type **169** . . . . 1·00 1·25
629 80c. Woman preparing leaves and woven bag . . . . . 1·25 1·50
630 $1.50 Millie Christian weaving basket . . . . . 1·75 2·00
631 $2.50 Thelma Brown at basket stall in the Square 2·50 3·00

Nos. 628/31 were printed together, se-tenant, with the backgrounds forming a composite design.

170 Dudwi Nut Tree (*Aleurites moluccana*)

2002. Trees. Multicoloured.
632 40c. Type **170** 80 60
633 $1 Toa (*Cordia subcordata*) 1·50 1·00
634 $1.50 Miro (*Thespesia populnea*) . . . . 2·00 2·00
635 $3 Hulianda (*Cerbera manghas*) . . . . 3·50 4·00

171 *America Star* (container ship) and Island Longboat

2003. 21 Years of Blue Star Line Service to Pitcairn Islands. Sheet 158 × 75 mm.
MS636 **171** $5 multicoloured . . 6·50 7·50

172 *Conus geographus* Shell

2003. Conus Shells. Multicoloured.
637 40c. Type **172** 85 60
638 80c. *Conus textile* . . . . . 1·25 75
639 $1 *Conus striatus* . . . . . . 1·50 1·00
640 $1.20 *Conus marmoreus* . . . 1·60 1·50
641 $3 *Conus litoglyphus* . . . . 3·75 4·25

2003. 50th Anniv of Coronation. As T **114** of Kiribati. Multicoloured.
642 40c. Queen Elizabeth II wearing tiara 80 55
643 80c. Coronation Coach drawn by eight horses . . 1·25 75
644 $1.50 Queen wearing tiara and white gown . . . . . 2·00 2·00
645 $3 Queen with bishops and Maids of Honour . . . . 3·75 4·25
MS646 95 × 115 mm. 40c. As No. 642; $3 As No. 645 . . . 4·25 4·50

173 Women Storing Leaves in Earthenware Jars and *Bauhinia monandra*

174 Diadem Squirrel Fish

2003. Art of Pitcairn (3rd series). Painted Leaves. Multicoloured.
647 40c. Type **173** 85 90
648 80c. Woman washing soaked leaves and *Bauhinia monandra* . . . . 1·40 1·50
649 $1.50 Bernice Christian with dried leaf and paints and *Sapindrus saponaria* plant 2·00 2·25
650 $3 Charlotte Christian painting leaf, Bauhinia leaf and *Bounty* . . . . 3·00 3·25

Nos. 647/50 were printed together, se-tenant with the backgrounds forming a composite design.

2003. Squirrel Fish. Multicoloured.
651 40c. Type **174** 80 55
652 80c. Scarlet-finned squirrel fish . . . . 1·25 75
653 $1.50 Silver-spotted squirrel fish . . . . 2·25 2·00
654 $3 Bloodspot squirrel fish . . 4·00 4·50
MS655 100 × 80 mm. No. 654 . . 4·50 5·00

175 "Holy Virgin in a Wreath of Flowers" (detail) (Rubens and Jan Brueghel)

2003. Christmas. Multicoloured.
656 40c. Type **175** 80 50
657 $1 "Madonna della Rosa" (detail) (Raphael) . . . . 1·40 90
658 $1.50 "Stuppacher Madonna" (detail) (Matthias Grunewald) . . . . 2·25 1·90
659 $3 "Madonna with Cherries" (detail) (Titian) 4·00 4·50

176 *Terebra maculate*

2004. Terebra Shells. Multicoloured.
660 40c. Type **176** 75 55
661 80c. *Terebra subulata* . . . . 1·25 75
662 $1.20 *Terebra crenulata* . . . 1·75 1·50
663 $3 *Terebra dimidiatai* . . . . 4·00 4·50

177 Bounty Bay and Hill of Difficulty

2004. Scenic Views. Multicoloured.
664 50c. Type **177** 85 60
665 $1 Christian's Cave on rock face (horiz) . . . . 1·60 1·10
666 $1.50 St. Paul's Pool . . . . 2·25 2·50
667 $2.50 Ridge Rope towards St. Paul's Point (horiz) . . 3·00 3·50

178 HMS *Pitcairn*

2004. 60th Anniv of Commission of HMS *Pitcairn*. Sheet 135 × 80 mm.
MS668 **178** $5.50 multicoloured. 6·75 7·25

179 HMAV *Bounty* Replica

2004. HMAV *Bounty* Replica (three masted ship). Mulicoloured.
669 60c. Type **179** . . . . 1·00 70
670 80c. Stern of ship . . . . . 1·25 90
671 $1 Figurehead . . . . 1·40 1·25
672 $3.50 Ropes and HMAV *Bounty* replica sailing . . . 4·50 5·00
MS673 103 × 72 mm. $3.50 As No. 672 . . . . 4·50 5·00

180 Murphy's Petrels

2004. Murphy's Petrel. Multicoloured.
674 40c. Type **180** 75 55
675 50c. Murphy's petrel and young in nest 85 60
676 $1 Murphy's petrel from side (vert) . . . . 1·40 1·10
677 $2 Head of Murphy's petrel (vert) . . . . 2·50 3·00
678 $2.50 Murphy's petrel in flight . . . . 3·00 3·50
MS679 154 × 86 mm. Nos. 674/8 7·50 8·00

181 Beach, Ducie Island

2005. Scenery (1st issue). Ducie and Oeno Islands. Photographs by Dr. Michael Brooke, Cambridge, and Brian Bell, Blenheim. Multicoloured.
680 50c. Type **181** 75 55
681 60c. Coral reef, Ducie Island 90 70
682 80c. Low sun, Ducie Island 1·25 90
683 $1 Boat moored off beach, Oeno . . . . 1·40 1·25
684 $1.50 Palm trees on beach, Oeno . . . . 2·25 2·50
685 $2.50 View of Oeno from sea 3·00 3·50

See also Nos. 704/9.

182 Corona

2005. Solar Eclipse, Oeno. Sheet 144 × 48 mm containing T **182** and similar circular designs. Multicoloured.
MS686 $1 Type **182**; $2 Chromosphere; $3 Photosphere 7·25 7·50

183 *Hypolimnas bolina* (male)

2005. Blue Moon Butterfly. Sheet 135 × 51 mm containing T **183** and similar square design. Multicoloured.
MS687 $1.50 Type **183**; $4 *Hypolimnas bolina* (female) . . 6·75 7·25

184 Prince Charles and Mrs. Camilla Parker-Bowles

2005. Royal Wedding.
688 **184** $5 multicoloured . . . . 6·50 6·75

185 HMS *Bounty* (Replica)

2005. HMS *Bounty* (Replica). Multicoloured.
689 40c. Type **185** 70 50
690 $1 Port side of ship . . . . 1·40 1·10
691 $1.20 Sailing off coast . . . 1·75 1·75
692 $3 Bowsprit and in full sail 4·00 4·50
MS693 122 × 87 mm. $3 As No. 692 4·00 4·50

186 Bristle-thighed Curlews

2005. Bristle-thighed Curlew (*Numenius tahitiensis*). Multicoloured.
694 60c. Type **186** . . . . 1·00 75
695 $1 Back of bird . . . . . . 1·40 1·10
696 $1.50 Beak open (vert) . . . 2·00 2·00
697 $1.80 Beak closed (vert) . . . 2·00 2·50
698 $2 Perched on rock . . . . . 2·50 2·75
MS699 156 × 86 mm. Nos. 694/8 8·25 8·50

187 Hibiscus Flower in Bauble

2005. Christmas. Designs showing baubles. Multicoloured.
700 40c. Type **187** 75 55
701 80c. Red-tailed tropic bird . . 1·40 1·00
702 $1.80 Arms . . . . 2·00 2·50
703 $2.50 Sailing ship . . . . . 3·50 3·75

2005. Scenery (2nd issue). Henderson Island. As T **181** showing coastal views and line drawings of fauna. Multicoloured.
704 50c. Flying insects and misty shoreline 70 50
705 60c. Parrots and sandy beach 1·00 75
706 $1 Tropic birds and sandy bay . . . . 1·40 1·10
707 $1.20 Lobsters and shore with overhanging rock ledge . . . . 1·75 1·75
708 $1.50 Octopus and cliffs . . . 2·00 2·00
709 $2 Turtles and sandy beach 2·50 2·75

POLAND Pt. 5

A country lying between Russia and Germany, originally independent, but divided between Prussia, Austria and Russia in 1772/95. An independent republic since 1918. Occupied by Germany from 1939 to 1945.

1860. 100 kopeks = 1 rouble.
1918. 100 pfennig = 1 mark.
1918. 100 halerzy = 1 korona.
100 fenigow = 1 marka.
1924. 100 groszy = 1 zloty.

1 Russian Arms

2 Sigismund III Vasa Column, Warsaw

1860.
1b 1 10k. blue and red . . . . . £675 80·00

1918. Surch **POCZTA POLSKA** and value in fen. as in T **2**.
2 **2** 5f. on 2g. brown 45 70
3 – 10f. on 6g. green 45 65
4 – 25f. on 10g. red . . . . . . 1·60 1·40
5 – 50f. on 20g. blue . . . . . . 3·50 4·00
DESIGNS: 6g. Arms of Warsaw; 10g. Polish eagle; 20g. Jan III Sobieski Monument, Warsaw.

1918. Stamps of German Occupation of Poland optd **Poczta Polska** or surch also.
9 **10** 3pf. brown . . . . 10·00 7·00
10 5pf. green 50 35
6 **24** 5 on 2½pf. grey 30 20
7 **10** 5 on 3pf. brown . . . . . 1·75 1·25
11 10pf. red 20 20
12 **24** 15pf. violet 25 25
13 **10** 20pf. blue 25 25
8 **24** 25 on 7½pf. orange 30 20
14 **10** 30pf. black & orange on buff 20 20
15 40pf. black and red . . . . 1·00 50
16 60pf. mauve 40 40

1918. Stamps of Austro-Hungarian Military Post (Nos. 69/71) optd **POLSKA POCZTA** and Polish eagle.
17 10h. green . . . . 4·75 6·25
18 20h. red . . . . 4·75 6·25
19 45h. blue . . . . 4·75 6·25

1918. As stamps of Austro-Hungarian Military Post of 1917 optd **POLSKA POCZTA** and Polish eagle or surch also.
20b 3h. on 3h. olive . . . . . . 19·00 13·00
21 3h. on 15h. red . . . . . . 3·50 2·25
22 10h. on 30h. green . . . . . 3·75 2·75
23 25h. on 40h. olive . . . . . 5·00 2·75
24 45h. on 60h. red . . . . . . 3·50 3·50
25 45h. on 80h. blue . . . . . 6·00 5·00
28 50h. green . . . . 28·00 21·00
26 50h. on 60h. red . . . . . . 3·50 4·00
29 90h. violet . . . . 4·75 3·50

1919. Stamps of Austria optd **POCZTA POLSKA**, No. 49 also surch **25**.
30 **49** 3h. violet £200 £190
31 5h. green £200 £190
32 6h. orange . . . . 15·00 16·00
33 10h. purple £200 £190
34 12h. blue . . . . 18·00 21·00
35 **60** 15h. red . . . . 10·00 6·75
36 20h. green . . . . 80·00 70·00
37 25h. blue £650 £600
49 **51** 25 on 80h. brown . . . . 2·25 3·00
38 **60** 30h. violet £140 £110
39 **51** 40h. green . . . . 13·50 10·00
40 50h. green . . . . 4·50 5·25
41 60h. blue . . . . 2·75 5·75
42 80h. brown . . . . 3·75 5·00
43 90h. purple £550 £600
44 1k. red on yellow . . . . 6·75 10·50
45 **52** 2k. blue . . . . 4·25 4·75
46 3k. red . . . . 45·00 60·00
47 4k. green . . . . 75·00 85·00
48a 10k. violet £3500 £3750

11

15

16

17 Agriculture

18 Ploughing in peace

19 Polish Uhlan

1919. Imperf.
50 **11** 2h. grey 35 60
51 3h. violet 35 60
52 5h. green 15 35
53 6h. orange . . . . 12·50 22·00
54 10h. red 15 35
55 15h. brown 15 15
56 20h. olive 35 55
57 25h. red 15 15
58 50h. blue 25 35
59 70h. blue 35 60
60 1k. red and grey 60 85

1919. For Southern Poland. Value in halerzy or korony. Imperf or perf.
68 **15** 3h. brown 10 10
69 5h. green 10 10
70 10h. orange 10 10
71 15h. red 10 10
72 **16** 20h. brown 10 10
85 25h. blue 10 10
86 50h. brown 10 10
75 **17** 1k. green 20 10
88 1k.50 brown 70 10
89 2k. blue 90 10
90 **18** 2k.50 purple 90 35
91 **19** 5k. blue . . . . 1·40 45

1919. For Northern Poland. Value in fenigow or marki. Imperf or perf.
104 **15** 3f. brown 10 10
105 5f. green 10 10
179 5f. blue 30 60
106 10f. purple 10 10
129 10f. brown 10 10
107 15f. red 10 10
108 **16** 20f. blue 10 10
181 20f. red 30 60
109 25f. green 10 10
110 50f. green 10 10
183 50f. orange 30 60
137 **17** 1m. violet 20 10
112 1m.50 green 50 25
138 2m. brown 20 10
114 **18** 2m.50 brown 90 55
139 3m. brown 30 10
140 **19** 5m. purple 10 10
141 6m. red 10 10
142 10m. red 25 15
143 20m. green 60 35

1919. 1st Polish Philatelic Exhibition and Polish White Cross Fund. Surch **I POLSKA WYSTAWA MAREK**, cross and new value. Imperf or perf.
116 **15** 5+5f. green 20 20
117 10+5f. purple 50 20
118 15+5f. red 20 20
119 **16** 25+5f. olive 30 20
120 50+5f. green 75 55

20

21 Prime Minster Paderewski

22 A. Trampezynski

23 Eagle and Sailing Ship

24

1919. 1st Session of Parliament in Liberated Poland. Dated "1919".
121 **20** 10f. mauve 25 15
122 **21** 15f. red 25 15
123 **22** 20f. brown (21 × 25 mm) 65 30
124 20f. brown (17 × 20 mm) 1·25 1·25
125 – 25f. green 40 15
126 **23** 50f. blue 40 25
127 – 1m. violet 65 55
DESIGN—As Type **21**: 25f. Gen. Pilsudski. As Type **23**: 1m. Griffin and fasces.

1920.
146 **24** 40f. violet 10 10
182 40f. brown 30 60
184 75f. green 30 60

1920. As T **15**, but value in marks ("Mk").
147 **15** 1m. red 10 10
148 2m. green 10 10
149 3m. blue 10 10
150 4m. red 10 10
151 5m. purple 10 10
152 8m. brown 65 20

1921. Surch **3 Mk** and bars.
153 **24** 3m. on 40f. violet 20 10

1921. Red Cross Fund. Surch with cross and **30MK**.
154 **19** 5m.+30m. purple . . . . . 3·50 7·50
155 6m.+30m. red . . . . . . 3·50 7·50
156 10m.+30m. red . . . . . 7·00 15·00
157 20m.+30m. green . . . . . 28·00 70·00

28 Sun of Peace

29 Agriculture

1921. New Constitution.
158 **28** 2m. green . . . . 1·10 1·90
159 3m. blue . . . . 1·10 1·90
160 4m. red 55 55
161 **29** 6m. red 55 65
162 10m. green 90 65
163 – 25m. violet . . . . 2·40 2·00
164 – 50m. green and buff . . . 1·60 1·00
DESIGN: 25, 50m. "Peace" (Seated women).

31 Sower

32

1921. Peace Treaty with Russia.
165 **31** 10m. blue 10 10
166 15m. brown 10 10
167 20m. red 10 10

1921.
170 **32** 25m. violet and buff . . . 10 10
171 50m. red and buff 10 10
172 100m. brown and orange . . 10 10
173 200m. pink and black . . . 10 10
174 300m. green 10 10
175 400m. brown 10 10
176 500m. purple 10 10
177 1000m. orange 10 10
178 2000m. violet 10 10

33 Silesian Miner

1922.
185 **33** 1m. black 30 60
186 1m.25 green 30 60
187 2m. red 30 60
188 3m. green 30 60
189 4m. blue 30 60
190 5m. brown 30 60
191 6m. orange . . . . 30 1·50
192 10m. brown 30 60
193 20m. purple 30 60
194 50m. olive . . . . 30 3·75
195 80m. red . . . . 95 4·50
196 100m. violet . . . . 95 4·50
197 200m. orange . . . . . . 1·90 7·50
198 300m. blue . . . . 5·00 15·00

34 Copernicus

39

1923. 450th Birth Anniv of Copernicus (astronomer) and 150th Death Anniv of Konarski (educationist).
199 **34** 1,000m. slate 55 45
200 – 3,000m. brown 25 45
201 **34** 5,000m. red 55 55
DESIGN: 3,000m. Konarski.

1923. Surch.
202 **32** 10 TYSIECY (=10000) on 25m. violet and buff . . 10 10
206 **15** 20,000m. on 2m. green (No. 148) 35 40
204 **31** 25,000m. on 20m. red . . . 10 10
205 50,000m. on 10m. blue . . 20 20
207 **15** 100,000m. on 5m. purple (No. 151) 10 10

1924.
208 **39** 10,000m. purple 30 30
209 20,000m. green 10 25
210 30,000m. red 70 35
211 50,000m. green 70 35
212 100,000m. brown 55 30
213 200,000m. blue 55 25
214 300,000m. mauve 55 45
215 500,000m. brown . . . . . 55 1·90
216 1,000,000m. pink . . . . . 55 5·25
217 2,000,000m. green . . . . 90 23·00

40

41 President Wojciechowski

1924. New Currency.
218 **40** 1g. brown 45 40
219 2g. brown 45 10
220 3g. orange 55 10
221 5g. green 70 10
222 10g. green 70 10
223 15g. red 70 10
224 20g. blue . . . . 2·75 10
225 25g. red . . . . 3·50 10
226 30g. violet . . . . 17·50 20
227 40g. blue . . . . 4·00 30
228 50g. purple . . . . 2·75 25
229 **41** 1z. red . . . . 22·00 2·40

42

43 Holy Gate, Vilna

44 Town Hall, Pozan

48 Galleon

1925. National Fund.
230 **42** 1g.+50g. brown . . . . . 15·00 22·00
231 2g.+50g. brown . . . . . 15·00 22·00
232 3g.+50g. orange . . . . . 15·00 22·00
233 5g.+50g. green . . . . . 15·00 22·00
234 10g.+50g. green . . . . . 15·00 22·00
235 15g.+50g. red . . . . . . 15·00 22·00
236 20g.+50g. blue . . . . . 15·00 22·00
237 25g.+50g. red . . . . . . 15·00 22·00
238 30g.+50g. violet . . . . . 15·00 22·00
239 40g.+50g. blue . . . . . 15·00 22·00
240 50g.+50g. purple . . . . . 15·00 22·00

1925.
241 **43** 1g. brown 30 10
242 – 2g. olive 45 35
243a – 3g. blue . . . . 1·40 10
244a **44** 5g. green . . . . 1·10 10
245a – 10g. violet . . . . 1·10 10
246 – 15g. red . . . . 1·10 10
247 **48** 20g. red . . . . 6·50 10
248 **43** 24g. blue . . . . 7·00 70
249 – 30g. blue . . . . 3·75 10
250 – 40g. blue . . . . 3·00 10
251 **48** 45g. mauve . . . . 13·00 1·10
DESIGNS—As Type **43**: VERT: 2, 30g. Jan III Sobieski Statue, Lwow. As Type **44**: 3, 10g. King Sigismund Vasa Column, Warsaw. HORIZ: 15, 40g. Wawel Castle, Cracow.

49 LVG Schneider Biplane

50 Chopin

1925. Air.
252 **49** 1g. blue . . . . 45 4·75
253 2g. orange . . . . 45 4·75
254 3g. brown . . . . 45 4·75
255 5g. brown 45 55
256 10g. green . . . . 1·40 65
257 15g. mauve . . . . 1·60 75
258 20g. olive . . . . 12·50 4·75
259 30g. red . . . . 6·50 1·75
260 45g. lilac . . . . 8·50 3·50

1927.
261 **50** 40g. blue . . . . 12·00 2·40

51 Marshal Pilsudski

52 Pres. Moscicki

1927.
262 **51** 20g. red . . . . 2·00 25
262a 25g. brown . . . . 2·00 25

1927.
263 **52** 20g. red . . . . 6·00 70

53

54 Dr. Karl Kaczkowski

1927. Educational Funds.
264 **53** 10g.+5g. purple on green 7·50 10·00
265 20g.+5g. blue on yellow . . 7·50 10·00

1927. 4th Int Military Medical Congress, Warsaw.
266 **54** 10g. green . . . . 2·75 2·10
267 25g. red . . . . 5·25 4·00
268 40g. blue . . . . 7·00 3·00

55 J. Slowacki (poet)

56 Marshal Pilsudski

57 Pres. Moscicki

58 Gen. Joseph Bem

1927. Transfer of Slowacki's remains to Cracow.
269 **55** 20g. red . . . . 4·50 75

1928. Warsaw Philatelic Exhibition. Sheet 117 × 88 mm. T **56/7** in deep sepia.
MS270 50g. and 1z. (+1z.50) . . £325 £250
See also Nos. 272/3, 328 and **MS**332a/c.

1928.
272 **56** 50g. grey . . . . 2·75 20
272a 50g. green . . . . 6·50 25
273 **57** 1z. black on cream . . . 8·50 20

1928.
271 **58** 25g. red . . . . 2·25 25

59 H. Sienkiewicz

60 Slav God, "Swiatowit"

1928. Henryk Sienkiewicz (author).
274 **59** 15g. blue . . . . 1·75 25

1929. National Exhibition, Poznan.
275 **60** 25g. brown . . . . 1·75 25

61

62 King Jan III Sobieski

63

1929.
276 **61** 5g. violet 20 20
277 10g. green 55 20
278 25g. brown 35 25

1930. Birth Tercentenary of Jan III Sobieski.
279 **62** 75g. purple . . . . 5·00 25

1930. Centenary of "November Rising" (29 November 1830).
280 **63** 5g. purple 55 20
281 15g. blue . . . . 2·40 35
282 25g. lake . . . . 1·50 20
283 30g. red . . . . 8·00 3·50

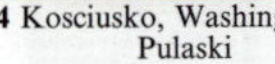
64 Kosciusko, Washington and Pulaski

65

1932. Birth Bicentenary of George Washington.
284 **64** 30g. brown on cream . . . 2·25 35

1932.
284a **65** 5g. violet 20 20
285 10g. green 20 20
285a 15g. red 20 20
286 20g. grey 45 20
287 25g. bistre 45 20
288 30g. red . . . . 1·90 20
289 60g. blue . . . . 20·00 20

67 Town Hall, Torun

68 Franciszek Zwirko (airman) and Stanislaw Wigura (aircraft designer)

1933. 700th Anniv of Torun.
290 **67** 60g. blue on cream . . . . 28·00 1·10

1933. Victory in Flight round Europe Air Race, 1932.
292 **68** 30g. green . . . . 16·00 1·75

1933. Torun Philatelic Exhibition.
293 **67** 60g. red on cream . . . . 18·00 15·00

69 Altar-piece, St. Mary's Church, Cracow

1933. 4th Death Centenary of Veit Stoss (sculptor).
294 **69** 80g. brown on cream . . . 14·00 2·00

70 "Liberation of Vienna" by J. Matejko

1933. 250th Anniv of Relief of Vienna.
295 **70** 1z.20 blue on cream . . . 35·00 12·50

71 Cross of Independence

73 Marshal Pilsudski and Legion of Fusiliers Badge

1933. 15th Anniv of Proclamation of Republic.
296 **71** 30g. red . . . . 8·00 40

1934. Katowice Philatelic Exhibition. Optd **Wyst. Filat. 1934 Katowice**.
297 **65** 20g. grey . . . . 35·00 29·00
298 30g. red . . . . 35·00 29·00

1934. 20th Anniv of Formation of Polish Legion.
299 **73** 25g. blue 70 35
300 30g. brown . . . . 2·00 40

1934. Int Air Tournament. Optd **Challenge 1934**.
301 **49** 20g. olive . . . . 12·00 10·00
302 **68** 30g. green . . . . 7·50 2·50

1934. Surch in figures.
303 **69** 25g. on 80g. brown on cream . . . . 5·00 60
304 **65** 55g. on 60g. blue . . . . . 4·50 35
305 **70** 1z. on 1z.20 blue on cream 18·00 4·75

77 Marshal Pilsudski

1935. Mourning Issue.
306 **77** 5g. black 75 25
307 15g. black 75 30
308 25g. black . . . . 1·25 25
309 45g. black . . . . 4·00 2·00
310 1z. black . . . . 7·00 4·25

1935. Optd **Kopiec Marszalka Pilsudskiego**.
311 **65** 15g. red 80 65
312 **73** 25g. blue . . . . 2·75 2·00

79 Pieskowa Skala (Dog's Rock)

80 Pres. Moscicki

1935.
313 **79** 5g. blue 50 10
317 – 5g. violet 25 10
314 – 10g. green 50 10
318 – 10g. green 65 10
315 – 15g. blue . . . . 2·75 10
319 – 15g. lake 35 10
316 – 20g. black . . . . 1·00 10
320 – 20g. orange 55 10
321a – 25g. green 80 10
322 – 30g. red . . . . 1·75 10
323a – 45g. mauve . . . . 1·60 10
324a – 50g. black . . . . 2·50 10
325 – 55g. blue . . . . 6·25 40
326 – 1z. brown . . . . 3·50 70
327 **80** 3z. brown . . . . 2·50 3·50
DESIGNS: 5g. (No. 317) Monastery of Jasna Gora, Czestochowa; 10g. (314) Lake Morskie Oko; 10g. (318) "Batory" (liner) at sea passenger terminal, Gdynia; 15g. (315) "Pilsudski" (liner); 15g. (319) University, Lwow; 20g. (316) Pieniny-Czorsztyn; 20g. (320) Administrative Buildings, Katowice; 25g. Belvedere Palace, Warsaw; 30g. Castle at Mir; 45g. Castle at Podhorce; 50g. Cloth Hall, Cracow; 55g. Raczynski Library, Poznan; 1z. Vilna Cathedral.

1936. 10th Anniv of Moscicki Presidency. As T **57** but inscr "1926. 3. VI. 1936" below design.
328 **57** 1z. blue . . . . 5·00 6·00

1936. Gordon-Bennett Balloon Race. Optd **GORDON-BENNETT 30. VIII. 1936.**
329 30g. red (No. 322) . . . . . 11·00 5·75
330 55g. blue (No. 325) . . . . . 11·00 5·75

82 Marshal Smigly-Rydz

83 Pres. Moscicki

1937.
331 **82** 25g. blue 35 10
332 55g. blue 50 10

1937. Visit of King of Rumania. Three sheets each 102 × 125 mm each containing a block of four of earlier types in new colours.
MS332a **82** 25g. sepia . . . . . 21·00 32·00
MS332b **56** 50g. blue . . . . . 21·00 32·00
MS332c **57** 1z. black . . . . . . 21·00 32·00

1938. President's 70th Birthday.
333 **83** 15g. grey 40 10
334 30g. purple 60 10

84 Kosciuszko, Paine and Washington

1938. 150th Anniv of U.S. Constitution.
335 **84** 1z. blue . . . . 1·10 1·40

84a Postal Coach

1938. 5th Philatelic Exhibition, Warsaw. Sheet 130 × 103 mm.
MS335a **84a** 45g. (× 2) green; 55g. (× 2) blue . . . . £110 85·00

84b Stratosphere Balloon

1938. Proposed Polish Stratosphere Flight. Sheet 75 × 125 mm.
MS335b **84b** 75g. (+1z.25) violet 90·00 70·00

85a

86 Marshal Pilsudski

1938. 20th Anniv of Independence. (a) As T **85a** and **86**.
336 – 5g. orange 10 10
337 – 10g. green 10 10
338 **85a** 15g. brown (A) 15 15
357 15g. brown (B) 35 25
339 – 20g. blue 40 10
340 – 25g. purple 10 10
341 – 30g. red 50 10
342 – 45g. black 90 65
343 – 50g. mauve . . . . 1·75 10
344 – 55g. blue 50 10
345 – 75g. green . . . . 2·25 1·90
346 – 1z. orange . . . . 2·25 1·90
347 – 2z. red . . . . 8·50 11·00
348 **86** 3z. blue . . . . 8·50 14·00

(b) 102 × 105 mm, containing four portraits as T **83** but with value and inscr transposed, all in purple.
MS348a 25g. Marshal Pilsudski; 25g. Pres. Narutowicz; 25g. Pres. Moscicki; 25g. Marshal Smigly-Rydz . . . . 12·00 20·00
DESIGNS—VERT: 5g. Boleslaw the Brave; 10g. Casimir the Great; 20g. Casimir Jagiellon; 25g. Sigismund August; 30g. Stefan Batory; 45g. Chodkiewicz and Zolkiewski; 50g. Jan III Sobieski; 55g. Symbol of Constitution of May 3rd, 1791; 75g. Kosciuszko, Poniatowski and Dabrowski; 1z. November Uprising 1830–31; 2z. Romuald Traugutt.
(A) Type **85a**. (B) as Type **85a** but crossed swords omitted.

87 Teschen comes to Poland

88 "Warmth"

1938. Acquisition of Teschen.
349 **87** 25g. purple . . . . 1·50 35

1938. Winter Relief Fund.
350 **88** 5g.+5g. orange . . . . . . 40 1·40
351 25g.+10g. purple . . . . . 85 3·25
352 55g.+15g. blue . . . . . . 1·40 3·50

89 Tatra Mountaineer

1939. International Ski Championship, Zakopane.
353 **89** 15g. brown . . . . 1·10 80
354 25g. purple . . . . 1·40 1·10
355 30g. red . . . . 1·90 1·50
356 55g. blue . . . . 7·50 5·00

90 Pilsudski and Polish Legionaries

1939. 25th Anniv of 1st Battles of Polish Legions.
358 **90** 25g. purple . . . . 1·10 45
MS358a 103 × 125 mm. 25g. T **90**; 25g. T **77**; 25g. T **82** . . . . . 24·00 32·00

1939–1945. GERMAN OCCUPATION.

1939. T **94** of Germany surch **Deutsche Post OSTEN** and value.
359 **94** 6g. on 3pf. brown 20 40
360 8g. on 4pf. blue 20 40
361 12g. on 6pf. green 20 40
362 16g. on 8pf. red 65 75
363 20g. on 10pf. brown . . . 20 40
364 24g. on 12pf. red 20 40
365 30g. on 15pf. purple . . . 65 65
366 40g. on 20pf. blue 65 40
367 50g. on 25pf. blue 65 65
368 60g. on 30pf. green 80 40
369 80g. on 40pf. mauve . . . 80 65
370 1z. on 50pf. black & green 1·90 1·00
371 2z. on 100pf. black & yell 3·50 2·50

1940. Surch **General-Gouvernement**, Nazi emblem and value.
372 – 2g. on 5g. orge (No. 336) 30 35
373 – 4g. on 5g. orge (No. 336) 30 35
374 – 6g. on 10g. grn (No. 337) 30 35
375 – 8g. on 10g. grn (No. 337) 30 35
376 – 10g. on 10g. green (No. 337) 30 35
377 **107** 12g. on 15g. brown (No. 338) 30 35
378 16g. on 15g. brown (No. 338) 30 35
379 **104** 24g. on 25g. blue . . . 2·50 2·50
380 – 24g. on 25g. purple (No. 340) 30 35
381 – 30g. on 30g. red (No. 341) 45 30
382 **110** 30g. on 5g.+5g. orange 45 30
383 **105** 40g. on 30g. purple . . 65 1·00
384 **110** 40g. on 25g.+10g. pur 65 50
385 – 50g. on 50g. mauve (No. 343) 65 50
386 **104** 50g. on 55g. blue . . . 30 50
386a D **88** 50g. on 20g. green . . 1·90 1·90
386b 50g. on 25g. green . . 12·50 11·50
386c 50g. on 30g. green . . 25·00 28·00
386d 50g. on 50g. green . . 1·90 1·60
386e 50g. on 1z. green . . . 1·90 1·60
387 – 60g. on 55g. blue (No. 344) . . . . . 9·50 6·25
388 – 80g. on 75g. green (No. 345) . . . . . 9·50 7·25
388a **110** 1z. on 55g.+15g. blue 7·50 8·25
389 – 1z. on 1z. orge (No. 346) . . . . . 9·50 6·25
390 – 2z. on 2z. red (No. 347) . . . . . 6·25 3·75
391 **108** 3z. on 3z. blue . . . . 6·25 3·75
Nos. 386a/e are postage stamps.

93 Copernicus Memorial, Cracow

95

1940.
392 – 6g. brown 25 55
393 – 8g. brown 25 55
394 – 8g. black 25 30
395 – 10g. green 25 20
396 **93** 12g. green . . . . 2·50 25
397 12g. violet 25 25
398 – 20g. brown 20 10
399 – 24g. red 20 10
400 – 30g. violet 20 10
401 – 30g. purple 20 30
402 – 40g. black 20 15
403 – 48g. brown . . . . 65 1·10
404 – 50g. blue 20 15
405 – 60g. green 20 20
406 – 80g. violet 45 25
407 – 1z. purple . . . . 1·90 80
408 – 1z. green 65 65
DESIGNS: 6g. Florian gate, Cracow; 8g. Castle Keep, Cracow; 10g. Cracow Gate, Lublin; 20g. Church of the Dominicans, Cracow; 24g. Wawel Castle, Cracow; 30g. Old Church in Lublin; 40g. Arcade, Cloth Hall, Cracow; 48g. Town Hall, Sandomir; 50g. Town Hall, Cracow; 60g. Court-yard of Wawel Castle, Cracow; 80g. St. Mary's Church, Cracow; 1z. Bruhl Palace, Warsaw.

1940. Red Cross Fund. As last, new colours, surch with Cross and premium in figures.
409 12g.+8g. green . . . . . . 2·40 3·25
410 24g.+16g. green . . . . . 2·40 3·25
411 50g.+50g. green . . . . . 3·50 4·50
412 80g.+80g. green . . . . . 3·50 4·50

1940. 1st Anniv of German Occupation.
413 **95** 12g.+38g. green on yellow 2·00 2·50
414 – 24g.+26g. red on yellow . . 2·00 2·50
415 – 30g.+20g. violet on yellow 3·00 3·50
DESIGNS: 24g. Woman with scarf; 30g. Fur-capped peasant as Type **96**.

96

1940. Winter Relief Fund.
416 **96** 12g.+8g. green . . . . . . 1·00 75
417 24g.+16g. red . . . . . . 1·40 1·25
418 30g.+30g. brown . . . . . 1·40 1·90
419 50g.+50g. blue . . . . . . 2·40 2·50

97 Cracow

1941.
420 **97** 10z. grey and red . . . . 1·25 1·90

98 The Barbican, Cracow

99 Adolf Hitler

1941.
421 **98** 2z. blue 25 60
422 – 4z. green 50 95
DESIGN: 4z. Tyniec Monastery.
See also Nos. 465/8.

1941.
423 **99** 2g. grey 20 25
424 6g. brown 20 25
425 8g. blue 20 25
426 10g. green 20 10
427 12g. violet 20 25
428 16g. orange 25 15
429 20g. brown 20 20
430 24g. red 20 20
431 30g. purple 20 10
432 32g. green 20 35
433 40g. blue 20 20
434 48g. brown 35 40
435 50g. blue 15 55
436 60g. green 15 55
437 80g. purple 15 55
441 1z. green 45 50
442 1z.20 brown 45 75
443 1z.60 blue 40 90

1942. Hitler's 53rd Birthday. As T **99**, but premium inserted in design.
444 30g.+1z. purple on yellow . . 25 50
445 50g.+1z. blue on yellow . . . 25 50
446 1z.20+1z. brown on yellow 25 50

100 Modern Lublin

1942. 600th Anniv of Lublin.
447 – 12g.+8g. purple 10 25
448 **100** 24g.+6g. brown 10 25
449 – 50g.+50g. blue 15 35
450 **100** 1z.+1z. green 30 65
DESIGN: 12, 50g. Lublin, after an ancient engraving.

101 Copernicus

102 Adolf Hitler

1942. 3rd Anniv of German Occupation.
451 – 12g.+18g. violet 10 30
452 – 24g.+26g. red 10 30
453 – 30g.+30g. purple 10 30
454 – 50g.+50g. blue 10 30
455 **101** 1z.+1z. green 40 70
DESIGNS: 12g. Veit Stoss (Vit Stvosz); 24g. Hans Durer; 30g. J. Schuch; 50g. J. Elsner.

1943. Hitler's 54th Birthday.
456 **102** 12g.+1z. violet 20 50
457 24g.+1z. red 20 50
458 84g.+1z. green 20 50

1943. 400th Death Anniv of Nicolas Copernicus (astronomer). As No. 455, colour changed, optd **24. MAI 1543 24. MAI 1943.**
459 **101** 1z.+1z. purple 60 75

103 Cracow Gate, Lublin

103a Lwow

1943. 3rd Anniv of Nazi Party in German-occupied Poland.
460 **103** 12g.+38g. green 15 10
461 – 24g.+76g. red 15 10
462 – 30g.+70g. purple 15 10
463 – 50g.+1z. blue 15 10
464 – 1z.+2z. grey 60 25
DESIGNS: 24g. Cloth Hall, Cracow; 30g. Administrative Building, Radom; 50g. Bruhl Palace, Warsaw; 1z. Town Hall, Lwow.

1943.
465 – 2z. green 20 10
466 – 4z. violet 25 35
467 **103a** 6z. brown 35 40
468 – 10z. grey and brown . . 50 40
DESIGNS: 2z. The Barbican, Cracow; 4z. Tyniec Monastery; 10z. Cracow.

104 Adolf Hitler

105 Konrad Celtis

1944. Hitler's 55th Birthday.
469 **104** 12z.+1z. green 10 15
470 24z.+1z. brown 10 15
471 84z.+1z. violet 20 15

1944. Culture Funds.
472 **105** 12g.+18g. green 10 10
473 – 24g.+26g. red 10 10
474 – 30g.+30g. purple 10 10
475 – 50g.+50g. blue 25 25
476 – 1z.+1z. brown 25 25
PORTRAITS: 24g. Andreas Schluter; 30g. Hans Boner; 50g. Augustus the Strong; 1z. Gottlieb Pusch.

105a Cracow Castle

1944. 5th Anniv of German Occupation.
477a **105a** 10z.+10z. black and red 6·00 10·00

1941–45. ISSUES OF EXILED GOVERNMENT IN LONDON.

For correspondence on Polish sea-going vessels and, on certain days, from Polish Military camps in Great Britain.

106 Ruins of Ministry of Finance, Warsaw

107 Vickers-Armstrong Wellington and Hawker Hurricanes used by Poles in Great Britain

1941.
478 – 5g. violet . . . . 1·00 1·40
479 **106** 10g. green . . . . 1·50 1·50
480 – 25g. grey . . . . 1·75 2·00
481 – 55g. blue . . . . 2·25 2·00
482 – 75g. olive . . . . 5·75 6·50
483 – 80g. red . . . . 5·75 6·50
484 **107** 1z. blue . . . . 5·75 6·50
485 – 1z.50 brown . . . . . . 5·75 6·50
DESIGNS—VERT: 5g. Ruins of U.S. Embassy, Warsaw; 25g. Destruction of Mickiewicz Monument, Cracow; 1z.50, Polish submarine "Orzel". HORIZ: 55g. Ruins of Warsaw; 75g. Polish machine-gunners in Great Britain; 80g. Polish tank in Great Britain.

108 Vickers-Armstrong Wellington and U-boat

109 Merchant Navy

1943.
486 **108** 5g. red . . . . 85 1·10
487 **109** 10g. green . . . . 1·10 1·40
488 – 25g. violet . . . . 1·10 1·40
489 – 55g. blue . . . . 1·50 1·90
490 – 75g. brown . . . . 3·00 3·25
491 – 80g. red . . . . 3·00 3·25
492 – 1z. olive . . . . 3·00 3·25
493 – 1z.50 black . . . . 3·75 6·75
DESIGNS—VERT: 25g. Anti-tank gun in France; 55g. Poles at Narvik; 1z. Saboteurs damaging railway line. HORIZ: 75g. The Tobruk road; 80g. Gen. Sikorski visiting Polish troops in Middle East; 1z.50, Underground newspaper office.

1944. Capture of Monte Casino. Nos. 482/5 surch **MONTE CASSINO 18 V 1944** and value and bars.
494 – 45g. on 75g. olive . . . . 13·00 16·00
495 – 55g. on 80g. red . . . . . 13·00 16·00
496 **107** 80g. on 1z. blue . . . . . 13·00 16·00
497 – 1z.20 on 1z.50 brown . . 13·00 16·00

111 Polish Partisans

112 Romuald Traugutt

1945. Relief Fund for Survivors of Warsaw Rising.
498 **111** 1z.+2z. green . . . . . . 7·00 9·25

1944. INDEPENDENT REPUBLIC.

1944. National Heroes.
499 **112** 25g. red . . . . 48·00 65·00
500 – 50g. green . . . . 48·00 65·00
501 – 1z. blue . . . . 48·00 80·00
PORTRAITS: 50g. Kosciuszko; 1z. H. Dabrowski.

113 White Eagle

114 Grunwald Memorial, Cracow

1944.
502 **113** 25g. red . . . . 1·40 1·10
503 **114** 50g. green . . . . 1·40 75

1944. No. 502 surch with value **31.XII., 1943** or **1944** and **K.R.N., P.K.W.N.** or **R.T.R.P.**
504 **113** 1z. on 25g. red . . . . . 2·50 3·50
505 2z. on 25g. red . . . . . 2·50 3·50
506 3z. on 25g. red . . . . . 2·50 3·50

1945. 82nd Anniv of 1863 Revolt against Russia. Surch with value and **22.I.1863.**
507 **112** 5z. on 25g. brown . . . . 42·00 65·00

1945. Liberation. No. 502 surch **3zl**, with town names and dates as indicated.
508 3z. on 25g. Bydgoszcz 23.1.1945 . . . . 5·75 9·75
509 3z. on 25g. Czestochowa 17.1.1945 . . . . 5·75 9·75
510 3z. on 25g. Gniezno 22.1.1945 . . . . 5·75 9·75
511 3z. on 25g. Kalisz 24.1.1945 5·75 9·75
512 3z. on 25g. Kielce 15.1.1945 5·75 9·75
513 3z. on 25g. Krakow 19.1.1945 5·75 9·75
514 3z. on 25g. Lodz 19.1.1945 5·75 9·75
515 3z. on 25g. Radom 16.1.1945 5·75 9·75
516 3z. on 25g. Warszawa 17.1.1945 . . . . 14·50 20·00
517 3z. on 25g. Zakopane 29.1.1945 . . . . 8·00 13·50

120 Flag-bearer and War Victim

121 Lodz Factories

1945. Liberation of Warsaw.
518 **120** 5z. red . . . . 2·25 2·25

1945. Liberation of Lodz.
519 **121** 1z. blue 80 40

1945. 151st Anniv of Kosciuszko's Oath of Allegiance. No. 500 surch **5zl. 24.III.1794.**
520 5z. on 50g. green . . . . . 11·50 17·00

123 Grunwald Memorial, Cracow

125 H.M.S. "Dragon" (cruiser)

1945. Cracow Monuments. Inscr "19.1.1945".
521 **123** 50g. purple 25 15
522 – 1z. brown 30 15
523 – 2z. blue . . . . 1·10 15
524 – 3z. violet 95 40
525 – 5z. green . . . . 6·00 6·75
DESIGNS—VERT: 1z. Kosciuszko Statue; 3z. Copernicus Memorial. HORIZ: 2z. Cloth Hall; 5z. Wawel Castle.

1945. 25th Anniv of Polish Maritime League.
526 **125** 50g.+2z. orange . . . . . 7·00 10·50
527 – 1z.+3z. blue . . . . . . 4·00 7·50
528 – 2z.+4z. red . . . . . . 2·75 7·00
529 – 3z.+5z. olive . . . . . . 2·75 7·00
DESIGNS—VERT: 1z. "Dar Pomorza" (full-rigged cadet ship); 2z. Naval ensigns. HORIZ: 3z. Crane and tower, Gdansk.

126 Town Hall, Poznan

1945. Postal Employees Congress.
530 **126** 1z.+5z. green . . . . . . 19·00 32·00

127 Kosciuszko Memorial, Lodz

128 Grunwald, 1410

1945.
531 **127** 3z. purple 70 25

1945. 535th Anniv of Battle of Grunwald.
532 **128** 5z. blue . . . . 6·75 6·25

129 Eagle and Manifesto

133 Crane Tower, Gdansk

130 Westerplatte

1945. 1st Anniv of Liberation.
533 **129** 3z. red . . . . 10·00 16·00

1945. 6th Anniv of Defence of Westerplatte.
534 **130** 1z.+9z. slate . . . . . . 21·00 27·00

1945. Surch with new value and heavy bars.
535 **114** 1z. on 50g. green 55 30
536a **113** 1z.50 on 25g. red 55 30

1945. Liberation of Gdansk (Danzig). Perf or imperf.
537 **133** 1z. olive 20 20
538 – 2z. blue 30 20
539 – 3z. purple 90 20
DESIGNS—VERT: 2z. Stock Exchange, Gdansk. HORIZ: 3z. High Gate, Gdansk.

135 St. John's Cathedral

1945. "Warsaw, 1939–1945". Warsaw before and after destruction. Imperf.
540 – 1z.50 red 20 10
541 **135** 3z. blue 20 10
542 – 3z.50 green . . . . 1·25 45
543 – 6z. grey 25 20
544 – 8z. brown . . . . 2·75 55
545 – 10z. purple 55 55
DESIGNS: 1z.50, Royal Castle; 3z.50, City Hall; 6z. G.P.O.; 8z. War Ministry; 10z. Church of the Holy Cross.

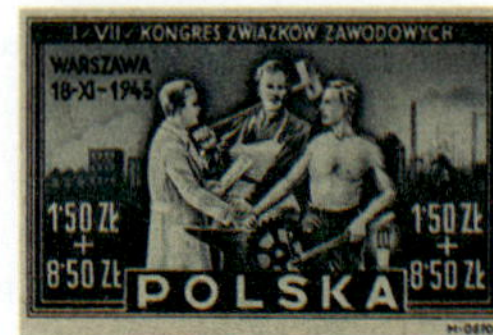

136 United Workers

1945. Trades' Union Congress.
546 **136** 1z.50+8z.50 grey . . . . 6·75 8·75

137 Soldiers of 1830 and Jan III Sobieski Statue

1945. 115th Anniv of 1830 Revolt against Russia.
547 **137** 10z. grey . . . . 8·50 12·50

1946. 1st Anniv of Warsaw Liberation. Nos. 540/5 optd **WARSZAWA WOLNA 17 Styczen 1945–1946**. Imperf.
548 1z.50 red . . . . 1·90 4·25
549 3z. blue . . . . 1·90 4·25
550 3z.50 green . . . . 1·90 4·25
551 6z. grey . . . . 1·90 4·25
552 8z. brown . . . . 1·90 4·25
553 10z. purple . . . . 1·90 4·25

139 Insurgent

140 Lisunov Li-2 over Ruins of Warsaw

1946. 83rd Anniv of 1863 Revolt.
554 **139** 6z. blue . . . . 7·50 10·50

1946. Air.
555 **140** 5z. grey 35 10
556 10z. purple 45 25
557 15z. blue . . . . 2·75 25
558 20z. purple . . . . 1·10 25
559 25z. green . . . . 2·10 35
560 30z. red . . . . 3·50 50

141 Fighting in Spain

1946. Polish Legion in the Spanish Civil War.
561 **141** 3z.+5z. red . . . . 6·00 8·75

142 Bydgoszcz

143 "Death" over Majdanek Concentration Camp

1946. 600th Anniv of City of Bydgoszcz.
562 **142** 3z.+2z. grey . . . . . . 7·25 13·00

1946. Majdanek Concentration Camp.
563 **143** 3z.+5z. green . . . . . . 2·75 4·00

144 Shield and Soldiers

145 Infantry

1946. Uprisings in Upper Silesia (1919–23) and Silesian Campaign against the Germans (1939–45).
564 **144** 3z.+7z. brown . . . . . 95 1·10

1946. 1st Anniv of Peace.
565 **145** 3z. brown 45 35

146 Polish Coastline

148 Bedzin Castle

147 Pres. Bierut, Premier O. Morawski and Marshal Zymierski

1946. Maritime Festival.
566 **146** 3z.+7z. blue . . . . . . 2·50 3·75

1946. 2nd Anniv of Polish Committee of National Liberation Manifesto.
567 **147** 3z. violet . . . . 3·50 6·00

1946. Imperf (5z., 10z.) or perf (6z.).
568 **148** 5z. olive 25 15
568a 5z. brown 45 15
569 – 6z. black 35 10
570 – 10z. blue 80 25
DESIGNS—VERT: 6z. Tombstone of Henry IV. HORIZ: 10z. Castle at Lanckorona.

149 Crane, Monument and Crane Tower, Gdansk

1946. The Fallen in Gdansk.
571 **149** 3z.+12z. grey . . . . . . 2·25 3·00

150 Schoolchildren at Desk

1946. Polish Work for Education and Fund for International Bureau of Education.
571a **150** 3z.+22z. red . . . . . 30·00 55·00
571b – 6z.+24z. blue . . . . . 30·00 55·00
571c – 11z.+19z. green . . . . 30·00 55·00
MS571d 128 × 80 mm. Nos. 571a/c colours slightly changed (sold at 25+75z.) £450 £900
DESIGNS: 6z. Court of Jagiellonian University, Cracow; 11z. Gregory Piramowicz (1735–1801), founder of the Education Commission.

152 Stojalowski, Bojko, Stapinski and Witos

1946. 50th Anniv of Peasant Movement and Relief Fund.
572 **152** 5z.+10z. green . . . . . 2·25 3·00
573 5z.+10z. blue . . . . . . 2·25 3·00
574 5z.+10z. olive . . . . . . 2·25 3·00

1947. Opening of Polish Parliament. Surch **+7 SEJM USTAWODAWCZY 19.1.1947**.
575 **147** 3z.+7z. violet . . . . . . 7·50 12·00

1947. 22nd National Ski Championships, Zakopane. Surch **5+15 zl XXII MISTRZOSTWA NARCIARSKIE POLSKI 1947**.
576 **113** 5+15z. on 25g. red . . . 3·25 5·00

1947. No. 569 surch **5 ZL** in outlined figure and capital letters between stars.
577 5z. on 6z. black 65 25

156 Home of Emil Zegadlowicz

157 Frederic Chopin (musician)

158 Boguslawski, Modrzejewska and Jaracz (actors)

159 Wounded Soldier, Nurse and Child

1947. Emil Zegadlowicz Commemoration.
578 **156** 5z.+15z. green . . . . . 2·25 3·25

1947. Polish Culture. Imperf or perf.
579 – 1z. blue 20 25
580 – 1z. grey 20 10
581 – 2z. brown 25 10
582 – 2z. orange 15 10
583 **157** 3z. green 60 25
584 3z. olive . . . . 1·90 25
585 **158** 5z. black 60 10
586 5z. brown 20 10
587 – 6z. grey . . . . 1·00 10
588 – 6z. red 35 10
589 – 10z. grey . . . . 1·25 10
590 – 10z. blue . . . . 1·50 30
591 – 15z. violet . . . . 1·60 30
592 – 15z. brown 35 70
593 – 20z. black . . . . 2·50 50
594 – 20z. purple . . . . . . 1·10 50
MS594a 210 × 128 mm in shades similar to second issue of colours listed above (sold at 62+438z.) £190 £250
PORTRAITS—HORIZ: 1z. Matejko, Malczewski and Chelmonski (painters); 6z. Swietochowski, Zeromski and Prus (writers); 15z. Wyspianski, Slowacki and Kasprowicz (poets). VERT: 2z. Brother Albert of Cracow; 10z. Marie Curie (scientist); 20z. Mickiewicz (poet).

1947. Red Cross Fund.
595 **159** 5z.+5z. grey and red . . . 3·00 5·00

161 Steelworker

163 Brother Albert of Cracow

1947. Occupations.
596 **161** 5z. lake . . . . 1·40 35
597 – 10z. green 45 20
598 – 15z. blue 90 30
599 – 20z. black . . . . 1·40 30

DESIGNS: 10z. Harvester; 15z. Fisherman; 20z. Miner.

1947. Air. Surch **LOTNICZA**, bars and value.
600 **114** 40z. on 50g. green . . . . 2·10 65
602 **113** 50z. on 25g. red . . . . . 3·25 1·60

1947. Winter Relief Fund.
603 **163** 2z.+18z. violet . . . . . 1·25 4·50

164 Sagittarius
165 Chainbreaker

1948. Air.
604 **164** 15z. violet . . . . 1·60 25
605 25z. blue . . . . 1·10 20
606 30z. brown . . . . 1·10 45
607 50z. green . . . . 2·25 45
608 75z. black . . . . 2·25 55
609 100z. orange . . . . . . 2·25 55

1948. Revolution Centenaries.
610 **165** 15z. brown 45 10
611 – 30z. brown . . . . 1·50 25
612 – 35z. green . . . . 3·25 55
613 – 60z. red . . . . 1·75 65
PORTRAITS—HORIZ: 30z. Generals H. Dembinski and J. Bem; 35z. S. Worcell, P. Sciegienny and E. Dembowski; 60z. F. Engels and K. Marx.

167 Insurgents
168 Wheel and Streamers

1948. 5th Anniv of Warsaw Ghetto Revolt.
614 **167** 15z. black . . . . 2·00 3·50

1948. Warsaw–Prague Cycle Race.
615 **168** 15z. red and blue . . . . 3·25 45

169 Cycle Race
170 "Oliwa" under Construction

1948. 7th Circuit of Poland Cycle Race.
616 **169** 3z. black . . . . 1·75 4·00
617 6z. brown . . . . 1·75 4·25
618 15z. green . . . . 2·50 5·50

1948. Merchant Marine.
619 **170** 6z. violet . . . . 1·40 2·00
620 – 15z. red . . . . 1·75 3·00
621 – 35z. grey . . . . 2·00 5·00
DESIGNS—HORIZ: 15z. Freighter at wharf; 35z. "General M. Zaruski" (cadet ketch).

173 Firework Display
174 "Youth"

1948. Wroclaw Exhibition.
622 **173** 6z. blue 55 30
623 15z. red 90 25
624 18z. red . . . . 1·40 45
625 35z. brown . . . . 1·40 45

1948. International Youth Conf, Warsaw.
626 **174** 15z. blue 65 25

175 Roadway, St. Anne's Church and Palace
176 Torun Ramparts and Mail Coach

1948. Warsaw Reconstruction Fund.
627 **175** 15z.+5z. green 25 25

1948. Philatelic Congress, Torun.
628 **176** 15z. brown . . . . 1·00 25

177 Streamlined Steam Locomotive No. Pm36-1 (1936), Clock and Winged Wheel
178 President Bierut

1948. European Railway Conference.
629 **177** 18z. blue . . . . 6·00 18·00

1948.
629a **178** 2z. orange 15 10
629b 3z. green 15 10
630 5z. brown 15 10
631 6z. black 95 10
631a 10z. violet 25 10
632 15z. red 80 10
633 18z. green . . . . 1·10 10
634 30z. blue . . . . 1·90 25
635 35z. purple . . . . . . 3·00 50

179 Workers and Flag

1948. Workers' Class Unity Congress. (a) Dated "8 XII 1948".
636 **179** 5z. red 85 65
637 – 15z. violet 85 65
638 – 25z. brown 85 65

(b) Dated "XII 1948".
639 **179** 5z. plum . . . . 2·00 1·60
640 – 15z. blue . . . . 2·00 1·60
641 – 25z. green . . . . 2·75 2·25
DESIGNS: 15z. Flags and portraits of Engels, Marx, Lenin and Stalin; 25z. Workers marching and portrait of L. Warynski.

180 Baby
180a Pres. Franklin D. Roosevelt

1948. Anti-tuberculosis Fund. Portraits of babies as T **180**.
642 **180** 3z.+2z. green . . . . . 4·00 4·75
643 – 5z.+5z. brown . . . . . 4·00 4·75
644 – 6z.+4z. purple . . . . . 2·25 4·75
645 – 15z.+10z. red . . . . . 2·00 3·00

1948. Air. Honouring Presidents Roosevelt, Pulaski and Kosciuszko.
645a **180a** 80z. violet . . . . . . 21·00 21·00
645b – 100z. purple (Pulaski) 21·00 21·00
645c – 120z. blue (Kosciuszko) 21·00 21·00
MS645d 160 × 95 mm. Nos. 645a/c 300+200z. colours changed . . £250 £375

181 Workers

1949. Trades' Union Congress, Warsaw.
646 **181** 3z. red . . . . 1·10 1·25
647 – 5z. blue . . . . 1·10 1·25
648 – 15z. green . . . . 1·50 1·50
DESIGNS: 5z. inscr "PRACA" (Labour), Labourer and tractor; 15z. inscr "POKOJ" (Peace), Three labourers.

182 Banks of R. Vistula
183 Pres. Bierut

1949. 5th Anniv of National Liberation Committee.
649 **182** 10z. black . . . . 2·10 2·00
650 **183** 15z. mauve . . . . 2·10 2·00
651 – 35z. blue . . . . 2·10 2·00
DESIGN—VERT: 35z. Radio station, Rasyn.

184 Mail Coach and Map
185 Worker and Tractor

1949. 75th Anniv of U.P.U.
652 **184** 6z. violet . . . . 1·25 2·00
653 – 30z. blue (liner) . . . . 2·25 2·00
654 – 80z. green (airplane) . . . 4·25 4·75

1949. Congress of Peasant Movement.
655 **185** 5z. red 95 25
656 10z. red 25 10
657 15z. green 25 10
658 35z. brown . . . . 1·25 1·25

186 Frederic Chopin
187 Mickiewicz and Pushkin

1949. National Celebrities.
659 – 10z. purple . . . . 2·40 2·10
660 **186** 15z. red . . . . 3·25 2·40
661 – 35z. blue . . . . 2·40 2·40
PORTRAITS: 10z. Adam Mickiewicz; 35z. Julius Slowacki.

1949. Polish–Russian Friendship Month.
662 **187** 15z. violet . . . . 3·50 4·25

188 Postman
189 Mechanic, Hangar and Aeroplane

1950. 3rd Congress of Postal Workers.
663 **188** 15z. purple . . . . 2·10 2·75

1950. Air.
664 **189** 500z. lake . . . . 4·50 6·50

190
195a

1950. (a) With frame.
665 **190** 15z. red 60 10

(b) Without frame. Values in "zloty".
673 **195a** 5z. green 15 10
674 10z. red 15 10
675 15z. blue 95 50
676 20z. violet 45 35
677 25z. brown 45 35
678 30z. red 65 40
679 40z. brown 80 50
680 50z. olive . . . . 1·60 1·00
For values in "groszy" see Nos. 687/94.

191 J. Marchlewski
192 Workers

1950. 25th Death Anniv of Julian Marchlewski (patriot).
666 **191** 15z. black 70 35

1950. Reconstruction of Warsaw.
667 **192** 5z. brown 15 15
See also No. 695.

193 Worker and Flag
194 Statue

1950. 60th Anniv of May Day Manifesto.
668 **193** 10z. mauve . . . . 1·75 40
669 – 15z. olive . . . . 1·75 25
DESIGN—VERT: 15z. Three workers and flag.

1950. 23rd International Fair, Poznan.
670 **194** 15z. brown 35 10

195 Dove and Globe
196 Industrial and Agricultural Workers

1950. International Peace Conference.
671 **195** 10z. green 85 25
672 15z. brown 35 15

1950. Six Year Reconstruction Plan.
681 **196** 15z. blue 25 10
See also Nos. 696/e.

197 Hibner, Kniewski and Rutkowski
198 Worker and Dove

1950. 25th Anniv of Revolutionaries' Execution.
682 **197** 15z. grey . . . . 2·50 65

1950. 1st Polish Peace Congress.
683 **198** 15z. green 50 25

REVALUATION SURCHARGES. Following a revaluation of the Polish currency, a large number of definitive and commemorative stamps were locally overprinted "Groszy" or "gr". There are 37 known types of overprint and various colours of overprint. We do not list them as they had only local use, but the following is a list of the stamps which were duly authorised for overprinting: Nos. 579/94, 596/615 and 619/58. Overprints on other stamps are not authorized.

Currency Revalued: 100 old zlotys = 1 new zloty.

199 Dove (after Picasso)

1950. 2nd World Peace Congress, Warsaw.
684 **199** 40g. blue . . . . 1·75 35
685 45g. red 35 15

200 General Bem and Battle of Piski

1950. Death Centenary of General Bem.
686 **200** 45g. blue . . . . 2·50 2·00

1950. As T **195a**. Values in "groszy".
687 **195a** 5g. violet 10 10
688 10g. green 10 10
689 15g. olive 10 10
690 25g. red 10 10
691 30g. red 15 10
692 40g. orange 15 10
693 45g. blue . . . . 1·25 10
694 75g. brown 70 10

1950. As No. 667 but value in "groszy".
695 **192** 15g. green 10 10

1950. As No. 681 but values in "groszy" or "zlotys".
696 **196** 45g. blue 15 10
696b 75g. brown 30 10
696d 1z.15 green 95 10
696e 1z.20 red 70 10

201 Woman and Doves
202 Battle Scene and J. Dabrowski

1951. Women's League Congress.
697 **201** 45g. red 45 35

1951. 80th Anniv of Paris Commune.
698 **202** 45g. green 30 10

1951. Surch **45 gr.**
699 **199** 45g. on 15z. red 55 15

204 Worker with Flag

205 Smelting Works

1951. Labour Day.
700 **204** 45g. red 45 15

1951.
701 **205** 40g. blue 25 10
702 45g. black 25 10
702a 60g. brown 25 10
702c 90g. lake 85 10

206 Pioneer and Badge

207 St. Staszic

1951. Int Children's Day. Inscr "I-VI-51".
703 **206** 30g. olive . . . . 1·10 65
704 – 45g. blue (Boy, girl and map) . . . . 6·25 65

1951. 1st Polish Scientific Congress. Inscr "KONGRES NAUKI POLSKIEJ".
705 **207** 25g. red . . . . 3·75 2·75
706 – 40g. blue 60 20
707 – 45g. violet . . . . 8·00 1·60
708 – 60g. green 60 20
709 – 1z.15 purple . . . . . . 1·00 55
710 – 1z.20 grey . . . . 1·75 20
DESIGNS—As Type **207**: 40g. Marie Curie; 60g. M. Nencki; 1z.15, Copernicus; 1z.20, Dove and book. HORIZ—36×21 mm: 45g. Z. Wroblewski and Olszewski.

209 F. Dzerzhinsky

211 Young People and Globe

210 Pres. Bierut, Industry and Agriculture

1951. 25th Death Anniv of Dzerzhinsky (Russian politician).
711 **209** 45g. brown 30 25

1951. 7th Anniv of People's Republic.
712 **210** 45g. red . . . . 1·10 15
713 60g. green . . . . 16·00 5·25
714 90g. blue . . . . 3·50 65

1951. 3rd World Youth Festival, Berlin.
715 **211** 40g. blue . . . . 1·10 25

1951. Surch **45 gr.**
716 **195a** 45g. on 30z. claret . . . 30 25

213 Sports Badge

214 Stalin

1951. Spartacist Games.
717 **213** 45g. green . . . . 1·25 1·10

1951. Polish–Soviet Friendship.
718 **214** 45g. red 15 10
719 90g. black . . . . 1·10 60

215 Chopin and Moniuszko

216 Mining Machinery

1951. Polish Musical Festival.
720 **215** 45g. black 40 20
721 90g. red . . . . 1·50 55

1951. Warsaw Stamp Day. Sheet 90×120 mm comprising Nos. 696a/e printed in brown.
MS721a **196** Sold at 5z. . . . . 13·50 13·50

1951. Six Year Plan (Mining).
722 **216** 90g. brown 30 15
723 1z.20 blue 30 15
724 1z.20+15g. orange 45 20

217 Building Modern Flats

218 Installing Electric Cables

1951. Six Year Plan (Reconstruction).
725 **217** 30g. green 10 10
726 30g.+15g. red 25 10
727 1z.15 purple 25 10

1951. Six Year Plan (Electrification).
728 **218** 30g. black 10 10
729 45g. red 20 10
730 45g.+15g. brown 55 10

219 M. Nowotko

220 Women and Banner

1952. 10th Anniv of Polish Workers' Coalition.
731 **219** 45g.+15g. lake 20 10
732 – 90g. brown 45 30
733 – 1z.15 orange 45 65
PORTRAITS: 90g. P. Finder; 1z.15, M. Fornalska.

1952. International Women's Day.
734 **220** 45g.+15g. brown 45 10
735 1z.20 red 50 35

221 Gen. Swierczewski

222 Ilyushin Il-12 over Farm

1952. 5th Death Anniv of Gen. Swierczewski.
736 **221** 45g.+15g. brown 45 10
737 90g. blue 50 30

1952. Air. Aeroplanes and views.
738 – 55g. blue (Tug and freighters) 35 30
739 **222** 90g. green 35 30
740 – 1z.40 purple (Warsaw) . . 45 45
741 – 5z. black (Steelworks) . . 1·40 55

223 President Bierut

224 Cyclists and City Arms

1952. Pres. Bierut's 60th Birthday.
742 **223** 45g.+15g. red 45 35
743 90g. green 80 80
744 1z.20+15g. blue . . . . . 1·00 35

1952. 5th Warsaw–Berlin–Prague Peace Cycle Race.
745 **224** 40g. blue . . . . 1·50 90

225 Workers and Banner

226 Kraszewski

1952. Labour Day.
746 **225** 45g.+15g. red 20 15
747 75g. green 55 35

1952. 140th Birth Anniv of Jozef Ignacy Kraszewski (writer).
748 **226** 25g. purple 50 25

227 Maria Konopnicka

228 H. Kollataj

1952. 110th Birth Anniv of Maria Konopnicka (poet).
749 **227** 30g.+15g. green 50 15
750 1z.15 brown 80 55

1952. 140th Death Anniv of Hugo Kollataj (educationist and politician).
751 **228** 45g.+15g. brown 35 15
752 1z. green 50 35

229 Leonardo da Vinci

231 N. V. Gogol

230 President Bierut and Children

1952. 500th Birth Anniv of Leonardo da Vinci (artist).
753 **229** 30g.+15g. blue 70 50

1952. International Children's Day.
754 **230** 45g.+15g. blue . . . . . 2·50 70

1952. Death Centenary of Nikolai Gogol (Russian writer).
755 **231** 25g. green 85 60

232 Cement Works

233 Swimmers

1952. Construction of Concrete Works, Wierzbica.
756 **232** 3z. black . . . . 2·10 35
757 10z. red . . . . 2·50 35

1952. Sports Day.
758 **233** 30g.+15g. blue . . . . . 4·25 1·10
759 – 45g.+15g. violet . . . . . 1·50 20
760 – 1z.15 green . . . . 1·40 1·50
761 – 1z.20 red 80 80
DESIGNS: 45g. Footballers; 1z.15, Runners; 1z.20, High jumper.

234 Yachts

235 Young Workers

1952. Shipbuilders' Day.
762 **234** 30g.+15g. green . . . . . 3·25 70
763 – 45g.+15g. blue 70 25
764 – 90g. plum . . . . 70 1·25
DESIGNS—VERT: 45g. Full-rigged cadet ship "Dar Pomorza"; 90g. "Brygada Makowskiego" (freighter) under construction.

1952. Youth Festival, Warsaw.
765 **235** 30g.+15g. green 40 25
766 – 45g.+15g. red 70 15
767 – 90g. brown 40 35
DESIGNS—HORIZ: 45g. Girl and boy students; 90g. Boy bugler.

236 "New Constitution"

237 L. Warynski

1952. Adoption of New Constitution.
768 **236** 45g.+15g. green & brown 1·10 15
769 3z. violet and brown . . . 40 35

1952. 70th Anniv of Party "Proletariat".
770 **237** 30g.+15g. red 55 15
771 45g.+15g. brown 55 15

238 Jaworzno Power Station

239 Frydman

1952. Electricity Power Station, Jaworzno.
772 **238** 45g.+15g. red 70 10
773 1z. black 65 50
774 1z.50 green 65 20

1952. Pleniny Mountain Resorts.
775 **239** 45g.+15g. purple 55 10
776 – 60g. green (Grywald) . . 35 45
777 – 1z. red (Niedzica) . . . . 1·00 15

240 Pilot and Glider

241 Avicenna

1952. Aviation Day.
778 **240** 30g.+15g. green . . . . . 1·25 10
779 – 45g.+15g. red . . . . . . 2·00 70
780 – 90g. blue 35 35
DESIGNS: 45g. Pilot and Yakovlev Yak-18U; 90g. Parachutists descending.

1952. Birth Millenary of Avicenna (Arab physician).
781 **241** 75g. red 35 25

242 Victor Hugo

243 Shipbuilding

1952. 150th Birth Anniv of Victor Hugo (French author).
782 **242** 90g. brown 35 25

1952. Gdansk Shipyards.
783 **243** 5g. green 15 10
784 15g. red 15 10

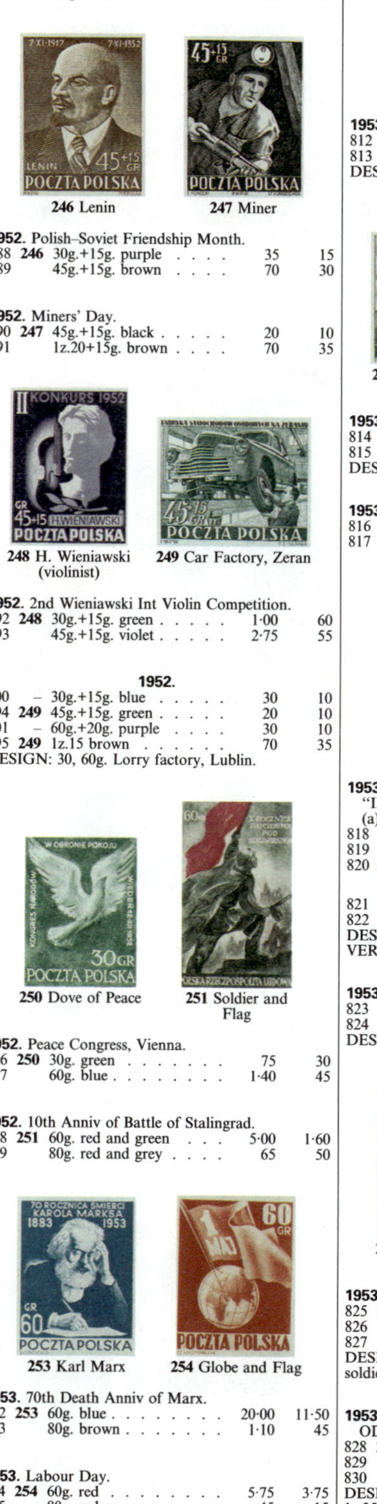

244 H. Sienkiewicz (author)

245 Assault on Winter Palace, Petrograd

1952.
785 **244** 45g.+15g. brown 35 15

1952. 35th Anniv of Russian Revolution. Perf or Imperf.
786 **245** 45g.+15g. red 90 20
787 60g. brown 35 30

246 Lenin

247 Miner

1952. Polish–Soviet Friendship Month.
788 **246** 30g.+15g. purple 35 15
789 45g.+15g. brown 70 30

1952. Miners' Day.
790 **247** 45g.+15g. black 20 10
791 1z.20+15g. brown 70 35

248 H. Wieniawski (violinist)

249 Car Factory, Zeran

1952. 2nd Wieniawski Int Violin Competition.
792 **248** 30g.+15g. green . . . . . 1·00 60
793 45g.+15g. violet . . . . . 2·75 55

1952.
800 – 30g.+15g. blue 30 10
794 **249** 45g.+15g. green 20 10
801 – 60g.+20g. purple 30 10
795 **249** 1z.15 brown 70 35
DESIGN: 30, 60g. Lorry factory, Lublin.

250 Dove of Peace

251 Soldier and Flag

1952. Peace Congress, Vienna.
796 **250** 30g. green 75 30
797 60g. blue . . . . 1·40 45

1952. 10th Anniv of Battle of Stalingrad.
798 **251** 60g. red and green . . . 5·00 1·60
799 80g. red and grey 65 50

253 Karl Marx

254 Globe and Flag

1953. 70th Death Anniv of Marx.
802 **253** 60g. blue . . . . 20·00 11·50
803 80g. brown . . . . 1·10 45

1953. Labour Day.
804 **254** 60g. red . . . . 5·75 3·75
805 80g. red 45 15

255 Cyclists and Arms of Warsaw

256 Boxer

1953. 6th International Peace Cycle Race.
806 – 80g. green 85 40
807 **255** 80g. brown 85 40
808 – 80g. red . . . . 13·50 9·25
DESIGNS: As Type **255**, but Arms of Berlin (No. 806) or Prague (No. 808).

1953. European Boxing Championship, Warsaw. Inscr "17-24. V. 1953".
809 **256** 40g. lake . . . . 1·00 45
810 80g. orange . . . . . . 10·00 4·75
811 – 95g. purple 85 60
DESIGN: 95g. Boxers in ring.

257 Copernicus (after Matejko)

1953. 480th Birth Anniv of Copernicus (astronomer).
812 **257** 20g. brown . . . . 1·75 40
813 – 80g. blue . . . . 13·50 13·50
DESIGN—VERT: 80g. Copernicus and diagram.

258 "Dalmor" (trawler)

259 Warsaw Market-place

1953. Merchant Navy Day.
814 **258** 80g. green . . . . 1·60 10
815 – 1z.35 blue . . . . 1·60 3·25
DESIGN: 1z.35, "Czech" (freighter).

1953. Polish National Day.
816 **259** 20g. lake 25 20
817 2z.35 blue . . . . 4·25 3·25

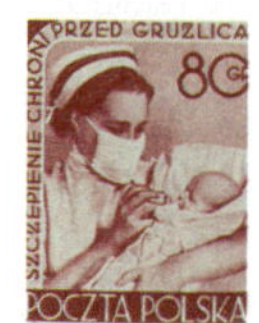

260 Students' Badge

261 Nurse Feeding Baby

1953. 3rd World Students' Congress, Warsaw. Inscr "III SWIATOWY KONGRESS STUDENTOW".
(a) Postage. Perf.
818 – 40g. brown 15 15
819 **260** 1z.35 green 70 15
820 – 1z.50 blue . . . . 2·50 2·75

(b) Air. Imperf.
821 **260** 55g. plum . . . . 1·75 60
822 75g. red . . . . 90 1·60
DESIGNS—HORIZ: 40g. Students and globe. VERT: 1z.50, Woman and dove.

1953. Social Health Service.
823 **261** 80g. red . . . . 8·75 5·25
824 – 1z.75 green 40 40
DESIGN: 1z.75, Nurse, mother and baby.

262 M. Kalinowski

263 Jan Kochanowski (poet)

1953. 10th Anniv of Polish People's Army.
825 **262** 45g. brown . . . . 3·75 3·00
826 – 80g. red 80 10
827 – 1z.75 olive 80 10
DESIGNS—HORIZ: 80g. Russian and Polish soldiers. VERT: 1z.75, R. Pazinski.

1953. "Renaissance" Commemoration. Inscr "ROK ODRODZENIA".
828 **263** 20g. brown 15 10
829 – 80g. purple 60 10
830 – 1z.35 blue . . . . 2·75 1·75
DESIGNS—HORIZ: 80g. Wawel Castle. VERT: 1z.35, Mikolaj Rej (writer).

264 Palace of Science and Culture

265 Dunajec Canyon, Pieniny Mountains

1953. Reconstruction of Warsaw. Inscr "WARSZAWA".
831 **264** 80g. red . . . . 9·75 1·50
832 – 1z.75 blue . . . . 1·90 45
833 – 2z. purple . . . . 5·00 3·50
DESIGNS: 1z.75, Constitution Square; 2z. Old City Market, Warsaw.

1953. Tourist Series.
834 – 20g. lake and blue 10 10
835 – 80g. lilac and green . . . 3·25 1·25
836 **265** 1z.75 green and brown . . 70 10
837 – 2z. black and red . . . . 1·10 10
DESIGNS—HORIZ: 20g. Krynica Spa; 2z. Clechocinek Spa. VERT: 80g. Morskie Oko Lake, Tatra Mountains.

266 Skiing

267 Infants playing

1953. Winter Sports.
838 – 80g. blue . . . . 1·50 40
839 **266** 95g. green . . . . 1·25 40
840 – 2z.85 red . . . . 4·00 2·10
DESIGNS—VERT: 80g. Ice-skating; 2z.85, Ice-hockey.

1953. Children's Education.
841 **267** 10g. violet 60 15
842 – 80g. red 90 30
843 – 1z.50 green . . . . 6·00 2·25
DESIGNS: 80g. Girls and school; 1z.50, Two Schoolgirls writing.

268 Class EP 02 Electric Locomotive

269 Mill Girl

1954. Electrification of Railways.
844 – 60g. blue . . . . 8·00 4·75
845 **268** 80g. brown 90 25
DESIGN: 60g. Class EW54 electric commuter train.

1954. International Women's Day.
846 **269** 20g. green . . . . 2·45 1·50
847 – 40g. blue 60 10
848 – 80g. brown 60 10
DESIGNS: 40g. Postwoman; 80g. Woman driving tractor.

270 Flags and Mayflowers

271 "Warsaw–Berlin–Prague"

1954. Labour Day.
849 **270** 40g. brown 70 40
850 60g. blue 70 25
851 80g. red 70 25

1954. 7th International Peace Cycle Race. Inscr "2-17 MAJ 1954".
852 **271** 80g. brown 80 25
853 – 80g. blue (Dove and cycle wheel) 80 25

272 Symbols of Labour

1954. 3rd Trades' Union Congress, Warsaw.
854 **272** 25g. blue . . . . 1·25 1·10
855 80g. lake 40 25

272a Postal Coach and Plane

1954. Air. 3rd Polish Philatelic Society Congress. Sheet 57 × 76 mm.
MS855a **272a** 5z.+(2z.50) green 26·00 21·00

273 Glider and Flags

1954. International Gliding Competition.
856 – 45g. green 65 15
857 **273** 60g. violet . . . . 1·90 70
858 60g. brown . . . . . . 1·25 15
859a – 1z.35 blue . . . . 2·40 25
DESIGNS: 45g. Glider and clouds in frame; 1z.35, Glider and sky.

274 Paczkow

275 Fencing

1954. Air. Inscr "POCZTA LOTNICZA".
860 **274** 60g. green 25 10
861 – 80g. red 35 10
862 – 1z.15 black . . . . 1·75 1·60
863 – 1z.50 red 80 10
864 – 1z.55 blue 80 10
865 – 1z.95 brown . . . . . . 1·00 10
DESIGNS—Ilyushin Il-12 airplane over: 80g. Market-place, Kazimierz Dolny; 1z.15, Wawel Castle, Cracow; 1z.50, Town Hall, Wroclaw; 1z.55, Lazienki Palace, Warsaw; 1z.95, Cracow Tower, Lublin.

1954. 2nd Spartacist Games (1st issue). Inscr "II OGOLNOPOLSKA SPARTAKIADA".
866 **275** 25g. purple . . . . 1·25 50
867 – 60g. turquoise . . . . . . 1·25 35
868 – 1z. blue . . . . 2·40 70
DESIGNS—VERT: 60g. Gymnastics. HORIZ: 1z. Running.

276 Spartacist Games Badge

277 Battlefield

1954. 2nd Spartacist Games (2nd issue).
869 **276** 60g. brown . . . . 1·10 35
870 1z.55 grey . . . . 1·10 60

1954. 10th Anniv of Liberation and Battle of Studzianki.
871 **277** 60g. green . . . . 1·60 40
872 – 1z. blue . . . . 5·50 3·00
DESIGN—HORIZ: 1z. Soldier, airman and tank.

278 Steel Works

1954. 10th Anniv of Second Republic.
873 – 10g. sepia and brown . . 65 10
874 – 20g. green and red . . . 35 10
876 **278** 25g. black and buff . . . 1·00 45
877 – 40g. brown and yellow . . 45 15
878 – 45g. purple and mauve . . 45 15
880 – 60g. purple and green . . 40 25
881 – 1z.15 black and turquoise 6·00 15
882 – 1z.40 brown and orange 12·50 2·50
883 – 1z.55 blue and indigo . . 2·50 65
884 – 2z.10 blue and cobalt . . 3·50 1·25
DESIGNS: 10g. Coal mine; 20g. Soldier and flag; 40g. Worker on holiday; 45g. House-builders; 60g. Tractor and binder; 1z.15, Lublin Castle; 1z.40, Customers in bookshop; 1z.55, "Soldek" (freighter) alongside wharf; 2z.10, Battle of Lenino.

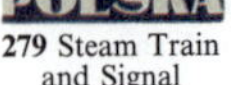

279 Steam Train and Signal

280 Picking Apples

1954. Railway Workers' Day.
885 **279** 40g. blue . . . . 3·00 60
886 – 60g. black . . . . 2·50 75
DESIGN: 60g. Steam night express.

1954. Polish–Russian Friendship.
887 **280** 40g. violet . . . . 1·60 1·10
888 60g. black 70 25

281 Elblag

282 Chopin and Grand Piano

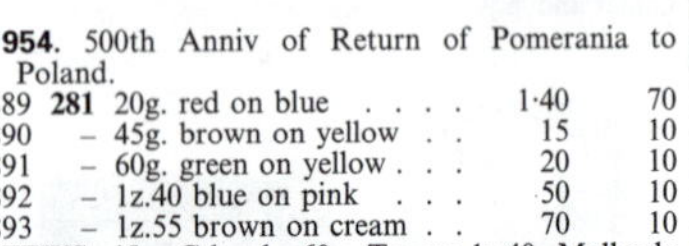

1954. 500th Anniv of Return of Pomerania to Poland.
889 **281** 20g. red on blue . . . . 1·40 70
890 – 45g. brown on yellow . . 15 10
891 – 60g. green on yellow . . . 20 10
892 – 1z.40 blue on pink . . . 50 10
893 – 1z.55 brown on cream . . 70 10
VIEWS: 45g. Gdansk; 60g. Torun; 1z.40, Malbork; 1z.55, Olsztyn.

1954. 5th International Chopin Piano Competition, Warsaw (1st issue).
894 **282** 45g. brown 25 10
895 60g. green 60 10
896 1z. blue . . . . 1·75 80
See also Nos. 906/7.

283 Battle Scene

1954. 160th Anniv of Kosciuszko's Insurrection.
897 **283** 40g. olive 45 10
898 – 60g. brown 60 10
899 – 1z.40 black . . . . 1·50 95
DESIGNS: 60g. Kosciuszko on horseback, with insurgents; 1z.40, Street battle.

284 European Bison

285 "The Liberator"

1954. Protected Animals.
900 **284** 45g. brown and green . . 35 10
901 – 60g. brown and green . . 35 10
902 – 1z.90 brown and blue . . 70 10
903 – 3z. brown and turquoise 1·10 55
ANIMALS: 60g. Elk; 1z.90, Chamois; 3z. Eurasian beaver.

1955. 10th Anniv of Liberation of Warsaw.
904 **285** 40g. brown . . . . 1·60 70
905 – 60g. blue . . . . 1·60 45
DESIGN: 60g. "Spirit of Poland".

286 Bust of Chopin (after L. Isler)

287 Mickiewicz Monument

1955. 5th International Chopin Piano Competition (2nd issue).
906 **286** 40g. brown 55 25
907 60g. blue . . . . 1·60 80

1955. Warsaw Monuments.
908 – 5g. green on yellow . . . 20 10
909 – 10g. purple on yellow . . 20 10
910 – 15g. black on green . . . 20 10
911 – 20g. blue on pink . . . 20 10
912 – 40g. violet on lilac . . . 60 10
913 – 45g. brown on orange . . 1·25 25
914 **287** 60g. blue on grey 20 10
915 – 1z.55 green on grey . . . 1·90 25
MONUMENTS: 5g. "Siren"; 10g. Dzerzhinski Statue; 15g. King Sigismund III Statue; 20g. "Brotherhood in Arms"; 40g. Copernicus; 45g. Marie Curie Statue; 1z.55, Kilinski Statue.

288 Flags and Tower

289

1955. 10th Anniv of Russo-Polish Treaty of Friendship.
916 **288** 40g. red 35 10
917 40g. brown 85 55
918 – 60g. brown 35 10
919 – 60g. turquoise 35 10
DESIGN: 60g. Statue of "Friendship".

1955. 8th International Peace Cycle Race.
920 **289** 40g. brown 45 25
921 – 60g. blue 25 10
DESIGN: 60g. "VIII" and doves.

290 Town Hall, Poznan

291 Festival Emblem

1955. 24th International Fair, Poznan.
922 **290** 40g. blue 25 25
923 60g. red 10 10

1955. Cracow Festival.
924 **291** 20g. multicoloured . . . 35 10
925 – 40g. multicoloured . . . 10 10
926 **291** 60g. multicoloured . . . 70 25
No. 925 is as T **291** but horiz and inscr "FESTIWAL SZTUKI", etc.

1955. 6th Polish Philatelic Exhibition, Poznan. Two sheets 50 × 70 mm as T **290**.
MS926a 2z.+(1z.) black and green 4·25 2·40
MS926b 3z.+(1z.50) black and red 21·00 12·50

292 "Peace"

293 Motor Cyclists

1955. 5th International Youth Festival, Warsaw.
927 – 25g. brown, pink & yellow 25 10
928 – 40g. grey and blue . . . 25 10
929 – 45g. red, mauve and yellow 45 10
930 **292** 60g. ultramarine and blue 35 10
931 – 60g. black and orange . . 35 10
932 **292** 1z. purple and blue . . . 80 80
DESIGNS: 25, 45g. Pansies and dove; 40, 60g. (No. 931) Dove and tower.

1955. 13th International Tatra Mountains Motor Cycle Race.
933 **293** 40g. brown 25 25
934 60g. green 10 10

294 Stalin Palace of Culture and Science, Warsaw

295 Athletes

1955. Polish National Day.
935 **294** 60g. blue 10 10
936 60g. grey 10 10
937 75g. green 55 25
938 75g. brown 55 25

1955. 2nd International Games. Imperf or perf.
939 **295** 20g. brown 10 10
940 – 40g. purple 15 10
941 – 60g. blue 25 10
942 – 1z. red 45 10
943 – 1z.35 lilac 55 10
944 – 1z.55 green . . . . 1·10 80
DESIGNS—VERT: 40g. Throwing the hammer; 1z. Netball; 1z.35, Sculling; 1z.55, Swimming. HORIZ: 60g. Stadium.

1955. International Philatelic Exhibition, Warsaw. Two sheets 61 × 84 mm. Imperf.
MS944a 1z.+(1z.) As No. 929 . . 4·50 3·25
MS944b 2z.+(1z.) As No. 932 . . 23·00 20·00

296 Szczecin

297 Peasants and Flag

1955. 10th Anniv of Return of Western Territories.
945 **296** 25g. green 10 10
946 – 40g. red (Wroclaw) . . . 25 10
947 – 60g. blue (Zielona Gora) 55 10
948 – 95g. black (Opole) . . . . 1·50 60

1955. 50th Anniv of 1905 Revolution.
949 **297** 40g. brown 55 45
950 60g. red 25 25

298 Mickiewicz

299 Statue

1955. Death Cent of Adam Mickiewicz (poet).
951 **298** 20g. brown 20 10
952 **299** 40g. brown and orange 20 10
953 – 60g. brown and green . . 25 10
954 – 95g. black and red . . . 1·40 45
DESIGNS—As Type **299**: 60g. Sculptured head; 95g. Statue.

300 Teacher and Pupil

301 Rook and Hands

1955. 50th Anniv of Polish Teachers' Union.
955 **300** 40g. brown . . . . 1·60 35
956 – 60g. blue . . . . 2·75 80
DESIGN: 60g. Open book and lamp.

1956. 1st World Chess Championship for the Deaf and Dumb, Zakopane.
957 **301** 40g. red . . . . 2·25 80
958 – 60g. blue . . . . 1·40 10
DESIGN: 60g. Knight and hands.

302 Ice Skates

304 Racing Cyclist

303 Officer and "Kilinski" (freighter)

1956. 11th World Students' Winter Sports Championship.
959 **302** 20g. black and blue . . . 3·25 1·60
960 – 40g. blue and green . . . 80 10
961 – 60g. red and mauve . . . 80 10
DESIGNS: 40g. Ice-hockey sticks and puck; 60g. Skis and ski sticks.

1956. Merchant Navy.
962 **303** 5g. green 15 10
963 – 10g. red 20 10
964 – 20g. blue 25 10
965 – 45g. brown 90 55
966 – 60g. blue 20 55
DESIGNS: 10g. Tug and barges; 20g. "Pokoj" (freighter) in dock; 45g. Building "Marceli Nowatka" (freighter); 60g. "Fryderyk Chopin" (freighter) and "Radunia" (trawler).

1956. 9th International Peace Cycle Race.
967 **304** 40g. blue . . . . 1·10 70
968 60g. green 20 10

305 Lodge, Tatra Mountains

307 Ghetto Heroes' Monument

1956. Tourist Propaganda.
969 **305** 30g. green 10 10
970 – 40g. brown 10 10
971 – 60g. blue . . . . 1·60 60
972 – 1z.15 purple 55 10
DESIGNS: 40g. Compass, rucksack and map; 60g. Canoe and map; 1z.15, Skis and mountains.

1956. No. 829 surch.
973 10g. on 80g. purple 70 35
974 40g. on 80g. purple 45 10
975 60g. on 80g. purple 45 10
976 1z.35 on 80g. purple . . . . 2·25 1·00

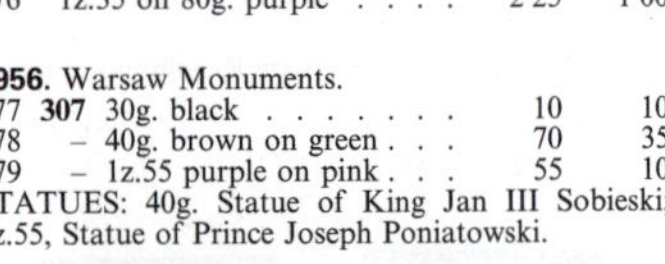

1956. Warsaw Monuments.
977 **307** 30g. black 10 10
978 – 40g. brown on green . . . 70 35
979 – 1z.55 purple on pink . . . 55 10
STATUES: 40g. Statue of King Jan III Sobieski; 1z.55, Statue of Prince Joseph Poniatowski.

308 "Economic Co-operation"

309 Ludwika Wawrzynska (teacher)

1956. Russo-Polish Friendship Month.
980 – 40g. brown and pink . . 45 35
981 **308** 60g. red and bistre . . . 25 10
DESIGN: 40g. Polish and Russian dancers.

1956. Ludwika Wawrzynska Commemoration.
982 **309** 40g. brown . . . . 95 1·50
983 60g. blue 35 10

310 "Lady with a Weasel" (Leonardo da Vinci)

311 Honey Bee and Hive

310a Music Quotation and Profiles of Chopin and Liszt

1956. International Campaign for Museums.
984 – 40g. green . . . . 2·25 1·40
985 – 60g. violet 95 10
986 **310** 1z.55 brown . . . . . . 1·90 25
DESIGNS: 40g. Niobe (bust); 60g. Madonna (Vit Stvosz).

1956. Stamp Day. Sheet 55 × 75 mm.
MS986a **310a** 4z. (+2z.) green . . 18·00 18·00

1956. 50th Death Anniv of Jan Dzierzon (apiarist).
987 **311** 40g. brown on yellow . . 1·10 25
988 – 60g. brown on yellow . . 25 10
DESIGN: 60g. Dr. J. Dzierzon.

312 Fencing

313 15th-century Postman

1956. Olympic Games. Inscr "MELBOURNE 1956".
989 **312** 10g. brown and grey . . . 20 10
990 – 20g. lilac and brown . . . 25 10
991 – 25g. black and blue . . . 70 25

992 – 40g. brown and green . . 35 10
993 – 60g. brown and red . . . 60 10
994 – 1z.55 brown and violet . . 2·75 1·10
995 – 1z.55 brown and orange 1·25 35
DESIGNS: No. 990, Boxing; 991, Rowing; 992, Steeplechase; 993, Javelin throwing; 994, Gymnastics; 995, Long jumping (Elizabeth Dunska-krzesinska's gold medal).

1956. Re-opening of Postal Museum, Wroclaw.
996 **313** 60g. black on blue . . . . 3·00 2·75

314 Snow Crystals and Skier of 1907 — 315 Apple Tree and Globe

1957. 50 Years of Skiing in Poland.
997 **314** 40g. blue 20 10
998 – 60g. green 20 10
999 – 1z. purple 45 35
DESIGNS (with snow crystals)—VERT: 60g. Skier jumping. HORIZ: 1z. Skier standing.

1957. U.N.O. Commemoration.
1000 **315** 5g. red and turquoise . . 25 10
1001 – 15g. blue and grey . . . 45 10
1002 – 40g. green and grey . . 80 60
MS1002a 55 × 70 mm. 1z.50 blue and green . . . . 15·00 15·00
DESIGNS—VERT: 15g. U.N.O. emblem; 40g. 1z.50, U.N.O. Headquarters, New York.

316 Skier — 317 Winged Letter

1957. 12th Death Annivs of Bronislaw Czech and Hanna Marusarzowna (skiers).
1003 **316** 60g. brown 90 35
1004 60g. blue 45 10

1957. Air. 7th Polish National Philatelic Exhibition, Warsaw.
1005 **317** 4z.+2z. blue . . . . . . 3·00 3·00
MS1005a 55 × 75 mm. 4z.+2z. blue (T **317**) . . . . 7·00 6·25

318 Foil, Sword and Sabre on Map — 319 Dr. S. Petrycy (philosopher)

1957. World Youth Fencing Championships, Warsaw.
1006 **318** 40g. purple 45 10
1007 – 60g. red 20 10
1008 – 60g. blue 20 10
DESIGNS: Nos. 1007/8 are arranged in se-tenant pairs in the sheet and together show two fencers duelling.

1957. Polish Doctors.
1009 **319** 10g. brown and blue . . 10 10
1010 – 20g. lake and green . . . 10 10
1011 – 40g. black and red . . . 10 10
1012 – 60g. purple and blue . . 45 25
1013 – 1z. blue and yellow . . . 20 10
1014 – 1z.35 brown and green 15 10
1015 – 2z.50 violet and red . . 35 10
1016 – 3z. brown and violet . . 45 10
PORTRAITS: 20g. Dr. W. Oczko; 40g. Dr. J. Sniadecki; 60g. Dr. T. Chalubinski; 1z. Dr. W. Bieganski; 1z.35, Dr. J. Dietl; 2z.50, Dr. B. Dybowski; 3z. Dr. H. Jordan.

320 Cycle Wheel and Flower — 321 Fair Emblem

1957. 10th International Peace Cycle Race.
1017 **320** 60g. blue 25 10
1018 – 1z.50 red (Cyclist) . . . 45 25

1957. 26th International Fair, Poznan.
1019 **321** 60g. blue 25 25
1020 2z.50 green 25 25

322 Carline Thistle — 323 Fireman

1957. Wild Flowers.
1021 **322** 60g. yellow, green & grey 35 10
1022 – 60g. green and blue . . . 35 10
1023 – 60g. olive and grey . . . 35 10
1024 – 60g. purple and green . . 60 35
1025 – 60g. purple and green . . 35 10
FLOWERS—VERT: No. 1022, Sea holly; 1023, Edelweiss; 1024, Lady's slipper orchid; 1025, Turk's cap lily.

1957. International Fire Brigades Conference, Warsaw. Inscr "KONGRES C.T.I.F. WARSZAWA 1957".
1026 **323** 40g. black and red . . . 10 10
1027 – 60g. green and red . . . 10 10
1028 – 2z.50 violet and red . . 25 10
DESIGNS: 60g. Flames enveloping child; 2z.50, Ear of corn in flames.

324 Town Hall, Leipzig — 325 "The Letter" (after Fragonard)

1957. 4th Int Trade Union Congress, Leipzig.
1029 **324** 60g. violet 25 10

1957. Stamp Day.
1030 **325** 2z.50 green 60 10

326 Red Banner — 327 Karol Libelt (founder)

1957. 40th Anniv of Russian Revolution.
1031 **326** 60g. red and blue . . . 10 10
1032 – 2z.50 brown and black 25 10
DESIGN: 2z.50, Lenin Monument, Poronin.

1957. Centenary of Poznan Scientific Society.
1033 **327** 60g. red 25 10

328 H. Wieniawski (violinist) — 329 Ilyushin Il-14P over Steel Works

1957. 3rd Wieniawski Int Violin Competition.
1034 **328** 2z.50 blue 35 15

1957. Air.
1035 **329** 90g. black and pink . . 15 10
1036 – 1z.50 brown and salmon 15 10
1037 – 3z.40 sepia and buff . . 45 10
1038 – 3z.90 brown and yellow 90 60
1039 – 4z. blue and green . . . 45 10
1039a – 5z. lake and lavender 55 10
1039b – 10z. brown and turquoise 90 35
1040 – 15z. violet and blue . . 1·50 45
1040a – 20z. violet and yellow 1·60 80
1040b – 30z. olive and buff . . 2·75 1·10
1040c – 50z. blue and drab . . 8·25 1·10
DESIGNS—Ilyushin Il-14P over: 1z.50, Castle Square, Warsaw; 3z.40, Market, Cracow; 3z.90, Szczecin; 4z. Karkonosze Mountains; 5z. Old Market, Gdansk; 10z. Liw Castle; 15z. Lublin; 20z. Cable railway, Kasprowy Wierch; 30z. Porabka Dam; 50z. "Batory" (liner).
For stamp as No. 1039b, but printed in purple only, see No. 1095.

330a J. A. Komensky (Comenius) — 331 A. Strug

1957. 300th Anniv of Publication of Komensky's "Opera Didactica Omnia".
1041 **330a** 2z.50 red 35 10

1957. 20th Death Anniv of Andrzej Strug (writer).
1042 **331** 2z.50 brown 25 10

332 Joseph Conrad and Full-rigged Sailing Ship "Torrens"

1957. Birth Centenary of Joseph Conrad (Korzeniowski) (author).
1043 **332** 60g. brown on green . . 10 10
1044 2z.50 blue on pink . . . 50 10

333 Postman of 1558 — 334 Town Hall, Biecz

1958. 400th Anniv of Polish Postal Service (1st issue).
1045 **333** 2z.50 purple and blue . . 35 10
For similar stamps see Nos. 1063/7.

1958. Ancient Polish Town Halls.
1046 **334** 20g. green 10 10
1047 – 40g. brown (Wroclaw) 10 10
1048 – 60g. blue (Tarnow) (horiz) 10 10
1049 – 2z.10 lake (Gdansk) . . 15 10
1050 – 2z.50 violet (Zamosc) . . 55 35

335 Zander — 336 Warsaw University

1958. Fishes.
1051 **335** 40g. yellow, black & blue 15 10
1052 – 60g. blue, indigo & green 25 10
1053 – 2z.10 multicoloured . . . 45 10
1054 – 2z.50 green, black & violet . . . . 1·50 45
1055 – 6z.40 multicoloured 45 45
DESIGNS—VERT: 60g. Atlantic salmon; 2z.10, Northern pike; 2z.50, Brown trout. HORIZ 6z.40, European grayling.

1958. 140th Anniv of Warsaw University.
1056 **336** 2z.50 blue 35 10

337 Fair Emblem — 338

1958. 27th International Fair, Poznan.
1057 **337** 2z.50 red and black . . . 35 10

1958. 7th International Gliding Championships.
1058 **338** 60g. black and blue . . . 10 10
1059 – 2z.50 black and grey . . 25 10
DESIGN: 2z.50, As Type **338** but design in reverse.

339 Armed Postman — 340 Polar Bear on Iceberg

1958. 19th Anniv of Defence of Gdansk Post Office.
1060 **339** 60g. blue 10 10

1958. I.G.Y. Inscr as in T **340**.
1061 **340** 60g. black 15 10
1062 – 2z.50 blue 70 10
DESIGN: 2z.50, Sputnik and track of rocket.

341 Tomb of Prosper Prowano (First Polish Postmaster) — 342 Envelope, Quill and Postmark

1958. 400th Anniv of Polish Postal Service (2nd issue).
1063 **341** 40g. purple and blue . . 55 10
1064 – 60g. black and lilac . . . 15 10
1065 – 95g. violet and yellow . . 15 10
1066 – 2z.10 blue and grey . . . 80 45
1067 – 3z.40 brown & turquoise 55 35
DESIGNS: 60g. Mail coach and Church of Our Lady, Cracow; 95g. Mail coach (rear view); 2z.10, 16th-century postman; 3z.40, Kogge.
Nos. 1064/7 show various forms of modern transport in clear silhouette in the background.

1958. Stamp Day.
1068 **342** 60g. green, red and black 55 55

343 Partisans' Cross — 345 Galleon

344 "Mail Coach in the Kielce District" (after painting by A. Kedzierskiego)

1958. 15th Anniv of Polish People's Army. Polish decorations.
1069 **343** 40g. buff, black and green 15 10
1070 – 60g. multicoloured . . . 15 10
1071 – 2z.50 multicoloured . . . 55 25
DESIGNS: 60g. Virtuti Military Cross; 2z.50, Grunwald Cross.

1958. Polish Postal Service 400th Anniv Exhibition.
1072 **344** 2z.50 black on buff . . . 90 1·10

1958. 350th Anniv of Polish Emigration to America.
1073 **345** 60g. green 25 10
1074 – 2z.50 red (Polish emigrants) 45 55

346 UNESCO Headquarters, Paris — 347 S. Wyspianski (dramatist and painter)

1958. Inauguration of UNESCO Headquarters Building, Paris.
1075 **346** 2z.50 black and green . . 70 55

1958. Famous Poles.
1076 **347** 60g. violet 10 10
1077 – 2z.50 green 25 35
PORTRAIT: 2z.50, S. Moniuszko (composer).

348 "Human Rights"

349 Party Flag

348a Coach and Horses (after A. Kedzierski)

1958. 10th Anniv of Declaration of Human Rights.
1078 **348** 2z.50 lake and brown . . 60 10

1958. 400th Anniv of Polish Postal Service. Sheet 86 × 76 mm.
MS1078a **348a** 50z. blue . . . . 18·00 20·00

1958. 40th Anniv of Polish Communist Party.
1079 **349** 60g. red and purple . . . 10 10

350 Yacht

351 The "Guiding Hand"

1959. Sports.
1080 **350** 40g. ultramarine and blue 35 10
1081 – 60g. purple and salmon 35 10
1082 – 95g. purple and green . . 70 25
1083 – 2z. blue and green . . . 35 10
DESIGNS: 60g. Archer; 95g. Footballers; 2z. Horseman.

1959. 3rd Polish United Workers' Party Congress.
1084 **351** 40g. black, brown and red 10 10
1085 – 60g. multicoloured . . . 10 10
1086 – 1z.55 multicoloured . . . 45 25
DESIGNS—HORIZ: 60g. Hammer and ears of corn. VERT: 1z.55, Nowa Huta foundry.

352 Death Cap

1959. Mushrooms.
1087 **352** 20g. yellow, brown & green . . . . 2·25 10
1088 – 30g. multicoloured . . . 25 10
1089 – 40g. multicoloured . . . 55 10
1090 – 60g. multicoloured . . . 55 10
1091 – 1z. multicoloured . . . 80 10
1092 – 2z.50 brown, green & bl 1·10 25
1093 – 3z.40 multicoloured . . . 1·25 35
1094 – 5z.60 brown, grn & yell 3·50 1·10
MUSHROOMS: 30g. Butter mushroom; 40g. Cep; 60g. Saffron milk cap; 1z. Chanterelle; 2z.50, Field mushroom; 3z.40, Fly agaric; 5z.60, Brown beech bolete.

1959. Air. 65 Years of Philately in Poland and 6th Polish Philatelic Assn Congress, Warsaw. As No. 1039b but in one colour only.
1095 10z. purple . . . . 3·25 3·75

353 "Storks" (after Chelmonski)

354 Miner

1959. Polish Paintings.
1096 **353** 40g. green 15 10
1097 – 60g. purple 35 10
1098 – 1z. black 35 10
1099 – 1z.50 brown 70 25
1100 – 6z.40 blue . . . . 3·25 1·10
PAINTINGS—VERT: 60g. "Motherhood" (Wyspianski); 1z. "Madame de Romanet" (Rodakowski); 1z.50, "Death" (Maiczewski). HORIZ: 6z.40, "The Sandmen" (Gierymski).

1959. 3rd Int Miners' Congress, Katowice.
1101 **354** 2z.50 multicoloured . . . 60 25

355 Sheaf of Wheat ("Agriculture")

356 Dr. L. Zamenhof

1959. 15th Anniv of People's Republic.
1102 **355** 40g. green and black . . 10 10
1103 – 60g. red and black . . . 10 10
1104 – 1z.50 blue and black . . 20 10
DESIGNS: 60g. Crane ("Building"); 1z.50, Corinthian column, and book ("Culture and Science").

1959. International Esperanto Congress, Warsaw and Birth Centenary of Dr. Ludwig Zamenhof (inventor of Esperanto).
1105 **356** 60g. black & green on green 15 10
1106 – 1z.50 green, red and violet on grey 80 35
DESIGN: 1z.50, Esperanto Star and globe.

357 "Flowering Pink" (Map of Austria)

358

1959. 7th World Youth Festival, Vienna.
1107 **357** 60g. multicoloured . . . 10 10
1108 2z.50 multicoloured . . . 45 45

1959. 30th Anniv of Polish Airlines "LOT".
1109 **358** 60g. blue, violet and black 15 10

359 Parliament House, Warsaw

1959. 48th Inter-Parliamentary Union Conf, Warsaw.
1110 **359** 60g. green, red and black 10 10
1111 2z.50 purple, red & black 55 35

1959. Baltic States' International Philatelic Exhibition, Gdansk. No. 890 optd **BALPEX I - GDANSK 1959.**
1112 45g. brown on lemon . . . 70 70

361 Dove and Globe

362 Nurse with Bag

1959. 10th Anniv of World Peace Movement.
1113 **361** 60g. grey and blue . . . 20 10

1959. 40th Anniv of Polish Red Cross. Cross in red.
1114 **362** 40g. black and green . . 20 10
1115 – 60g. brown 20 10
1116 – 2z.50 black and red . . . 90 45
DESIGNS—VERT: 60g. Nurse with bottle and bandages. SQUARE—23 × 23 mm: 2z.50, J. H. Dunant.

363 Emblem of Polish–Chinese Friendship Society

364

1959. Polish–Chinese Friendship.
1117 **363** 60g. multicoloured . . . 45 10
1118 2z.50 multicoloured . . . 25 10

1959. Stamp Day.
1119 **364** 60g. red, green & turq 15 10
1120 2z.50 blue, green and red 25 10

365 Sputnik "3"

1959. Cosmic Flights.
1121 **365** 40g. black and blue . . . 15 10
1122 – 60g. black and lake . . . 25 10
1123 – 2z.50 blue and green . . 1·10 60
DESIGNS: 60g. Rocket "Mieczta" encircling Sun; 2z.50, Moon rocket "Lunik 2".

366 Schoolgirl

367 Darwin

1959. "1000 Schools for Polish Millennium". Inscr as in T **366**.
1124 **366** 40g. brown and green . . 15 10
1125 – 60g. red, black and blue 15 10
DESIGN: 60g. Children going to school.

1959. Famous Scientists.
1126 **367** 20g. blue 10 10
1127 – 40g. olive (Mendeleev) 10 10
1128 – 60g. purple (Einstein) . . 15 10
1129 – 1z.50 brown (Pasteur) . . 25 10
1130 – 1z.55 green (Newton) . . 55 10
1131 – 2z.50 violet (Copernicus) 90 70

368 Costumes of Rzeszow

369 Costumes of Rzeszow

1959. Provincial Costumes (1st series).
1132 **368** 20g. black and green . . 10 10
1133 **369** 20g. black and green . . 10 10
1134 – 60g. brown and pink . . 15 10
1135 – 60g. brown and pink . . 15 10
1136 – 1z. red and blue 15 10
1137 – 1z. red and blue 15 10
1138 – 2z.50 green and grey . . 35 10
1139 – 2z.50 green and grey . . 35 10
1140 – 5z.60 blue and yellow . . 1·40 55
1141 – 5z.60 blue and yellow . . 1·40 55
DESIGNS—Male and female costumes of: Nos. 1134/5, Kurpic; 1136/7, Silesia; 1138/9, Mountain regions; 1140/1, Szamotuly.
See also Nos. 1150/9.

370 Piano

371 Polish 10k. Stamp of 1860 and Postmark

1960. 150th Birth Anniv of Chopin and Chopin Music Competition, Warsaw.
1142 **370** 60g. black and violet . . 45 10
1143 – 1z.50 black, red and blue 70 10
1144 – 2z.50 brown . . . . . . 2·25 1·50
DESIGNS—As Type **370**: 1z.50, Portion of Chopin's music. 25 × 39½ mm: 2z.50, Portrait of Chopin.

1960. Stamp Centenary.
1145 **371** 40g. red, blue and black 15 10
1146 – 60g. blue, black and violet 25 10
1147 – 1z.35 blue, red and grey 70 45
1148 – 1z.55 red, black & green 80 35
1149 – 2z.50 green, black & ol 1·40 70
DESIGNS: 1z.35, Emblem inscr "1860 1960". Reproductions of Polish stamps: 60g. No. 356; 1z.55, No. 533; 2z.50, No. 1030. With appropriate postmarks.

1960. Provincial Costumes (2nd series). As T **368/69**.
1150 40g. red and blue 10 10
1151 40g. red and blue 10 10
1152 2z. blue and yellow 15 10
1153 2z. blue and yellow 15 10
1154 3z.10 turquoise and green 25 10
1155 3z.10 turquoise and green 25 10
1156 3z.40 brown and turquoise 35 25
1157 3z.40 brown and turquoise 35 25
1158 6z.50 violet and green . . . 1·10 45
1159 6z.50 violet and green . . . 1·10 45
DESIGNS—Male and female costumes of: Nos. 1150/1, Cracow; 1152/3, Lowicz; 1154/5, Kujawy; 1156/7, Lublin; 1158/9, Lubusz.

372 Throwing the Discus

373 King Wladislaw Jagiello's Tomb, Wawel Castle

1960. Olympic Games, Rome. Rings and inscr in black.
1160 60g. blue (T **372**) 15 10
1161 60g. mauve (Running) . . . 15 10
1162 60g. violet (Cycling) 15 10
1163 60g. turq (Show jumping) 15 10
1164 2z.50 blue (Trumpeters) . . 70 35
1165 2z.50 brown (Boxing) . . . 70 35
1166 2z.50 red (Olympic flame) 70 35
1167 2z.50 green (Long jump) . . 70 35
Stamps of the same value were issued together, se-tenant, forming composite designs illustrating a complete circuit of the stadium track.

1960. 550th Anniv of Battle of Grunwald.
1168 **373** 60g. brown 25 10
1169 – 90g. green 60 35
1170 – 2z.50 black . . . . . . 2·75 1·50
DESIGNS—As Type **373**: 90g. Proposed Grunwald Monument. HORIZ: 78 × 35½ mm: 2z.50, "Battle of Grunwald" (after Jan Matejko).

374 1860 Stamp and Postmark

375 Lukasiewicz (inventor of petrol lamp)

1960. International Philatelic Exhn, Warsaw.
1171 **374** 10z.+10z. red, black and blue . . . . 6·25 8·00

1960. Lukasiewicz Commemoration and 5th Pharmaceutical Congress. Poznan.
1172 **375** 60g. black and yellow . . 15 10

376 "The Annunciation"

377 Paderewski

1960. Altar Wood Carvings of St. Mary's Church, Cracow, by Veit Stoss.
1173 **376** 20g. blue 25 10
1174 – 30g. brown 15 10
1175 – 40g. violet 25 10
1176 – 60g. green 25 10
1177 – 2z.50 red . . . . 1·10 25
1178 – 5z.60 brown . . . . . . 4·25 4·75
MS1178a 86 × 107 mm. 10z. black 8·00 6·50
DESIGNS: 30g. "The Nativity"; 40g. "Homage of the Three Kings"; 60g. "The Resurrection"; 2z.50, "The Ascension"; 5z.60, "The Descent of the Holy Ghost". VERT: (72 × 95 mm). 10z. The Assumption of the Virgin.

1960. Birth Centenary of Paderewski.
1179 **377** 2z.50 black 35 35

1960. Stamp Day. Optd **DZIEN ZNACZKA 1960.**
1180 **371** 40g. red, blue and black 1·25 70

379 Gniezno

380 Great Bustard

1960. Old Polish Towns as T **379**.
1181 5g. brown 10 10
1182 10g. green 10 10
1183 20g. brown 10 10
1184 40g. red 10 10
1185 50g. violet 10 10
1186 60g. lilac 10 10
1187 60g. blue 10 10
1188 80g. blue 15 10
1189 90g. brown 15 10
1190 95g. green 35 10
1191 1z. red and lilac 15 10
1192 1z.15 green and orange 35 10
1193 1z.35 mauve and green 15 10
1194 1z.50 brown and blue 35 10
1195 1z.55 lilac and yellow 35 10
1196 2z. blue and lilac 20 10
1197 2z.10 brown and yellow 20 10
1198 2z.50 violet and green 25 10
1199 3z.10 red and grey 35 35
1200 5z.60 grey and green 60 35
TOWNS: 10g. Cracow; 20g. Warsaw; 40g. Poznan; 50g. Plock; 60g. mauve, Kalisz; 60g. blue, Tczew; 80g. Frombork; 90g. Torum; 95g. Puck; 1z. Slupsk; 1z.15, Gdansk; 1z.35, Wroclaw; 1z.50, Szczecin; 1z.55, Opole; 2z. Kolobrzeg; 2z.10, Legnica; 2z.50, Katowice; 3z.10, Lodz; 5z.60, Walbrzych.

1960. Birds. Multicoloured.
1201 10g. Type **380** 10 10
1202 20g. Common Raven 10 10
1203 30g. Great cormorant 10 10
1204 40g. Black stork 25 10
1205 50g. Eagle owl 55 10
1206 60g. White-tailed sea eagle 55 10
1207 75g. Golden eagle 55 10
1208 90g. Short-toed eagle 60 35
1209 2z.50 Rock thrush 3·25 1·75
1210 4z. River kingfisher 2·75 1·25
1211 5z.60 Wallcreeper 4·50 1·40
1212 6z.50 European roller 6·50 3·25

381 Front page of Newspaper "Proletaryat" (1883)

382 Ice Hockey

1961. 300th Anniv of Polish Newspaper Press.
1213 – 40g. green, blue and black 55 25
1214 **381** 60g. yellow, red and black 55 25
1215 – 2z.50 blue, violet & black 3·25 2·75
DESIGNS—Newspaper front page: 40g. "Mercuriusz" (first issue, 1661); 2z.50, "Rzeczpospolita" (1944).

1961. 1st Winter Military Spartakiad.
1216 **382** 40g. black, yellow & lilac 35 10
1217 – 60g. multicoloured 95 15
1218 – 1z. multicoloured 5·25 2·75
1219 – 1z.50 black, yell & turq 90 35
DESIGNS: 60g. Ski jumping; 1z. Rifle-shooting; 1z.50, Slalom.

383 Congress Emblem

384 Yuri Gagarin

1961. 4th Polish Engineers' Conference.
1220 **383** 60g. black and red 15 10

1961. World's 1st Manned Space Flight.
1221 **384** 40g. black, red and brown 60 10
1222 – 60g. red, black and blue 60 35
DESIGN: 60g. Globe and star.

385 Fair Emblem

1961. 30th International Fair, Poznan.
1223 **385** 40g. black, red and blue 10 10
1224 1z.50 black, blue and red 25 10
See also No. **MS**1245a.

386 King Mieszko I

1961. Famous Poles (1st issue).
1225 **386** 60g. black and blue 10 10
1226 – 60g. black and red 10 10
1227 – 60g. black and green 10 10
1228 – 60g. black and violet 80 25
1229 – 60g. black and brown 10 10
1230 – 60g. black and olive 10 10
PORTRAITS: No. 1226, King Casimire the Great; 1227, King Casmir Jagiellon; 1228, Copernicus; 1229, A. F. Modrzewski; 1230, Kosciuszko.
See also Nos. 1301/6 and 1398/1401.

387 "Leskov" (trawler support ship)

1961. Shipbuilding Industry. Multicoloured.
1231 60g. Type **387** 25 10
1232 1z.55 "Severodvinsk" (depot ship) 35 10
1233 2z.50 "Rambutan" (coaster) 60 35
1234 3z.40 "Krynica" (freighter) 90 45
1235 4z. "B 54" freighter 1·25 70
1236 5z.60 "Bavsk" (tanker) 4·25 1·90
SIZES: 2z.50, As Type **387**; 5z.60, 108 × 21 mm; Rest, 81 × 21 mm.

388 Posthorn and Telephone Dial

389 Opole Seal

1961. Communications Ministers' Conference, Warsaw.
1237 **388** 40g. red, green and blue 10 10
1238 – 60g. violet, yellow & purple 15 10
1239 – 2z.50 ultram, blue & bis 55 10
MS1239a 108 × 66 mm. Nos. 1237/9 (sold at 5z.) 5·25 3·25
DESIGNS: 60g. Posthorn and radar screen; 2z.50, Posthorn and conference emblem.

1961. Polish Western Provinces.
1240 40g. brown on buff 15 10
1241 40g. brown on buff 15 10
1242 60g. violet on pink 15 10
1243 60g. violet on pink 15 10
1243a 95g. green on blue 25 25
1243b 95g. green on blue 25 25
1244 2z.50 sage on green 45 25
1245 2z.50 sage on green 45 25
DESIGNS—VERT: No. 1240, Type **389**; 1242, Henry IV's tomb; 1243a, Seal of Conrad II; 1244, Prince Barnim's seal. HORIZ: No. 1241, Opole cement works; 1243, Wroclaw apartment-house; 1243b, Factory interior, Zielona Gora; 1245, Szczecin harbour.
See also Nos. 1308/13.

1961. "Intermess II" Stamp Exhibition. Sheet 121 × 51 mm containing pair of No. 1224 but imperf.
MS1245a 1z.50 (×2) (sold at 4z.50+2z.50) 5·50 3·50

390 Beribboned Paddle

391 Titov and Orbit within Star

1961. 6th European Canoeing Championships. Multicoloured.
1246 40g. Two canoes within letter "E" (horiz) 15 10
1247 60g. Two four-seater canoes at finishing post (horiz) 15 10
1248 2z.50 Type **390** 1·25 60

1961. 2nd Russian Manned Space Flight.
1249 **391** 40g. black, red and pink 45 10
1250 – 60g. blue and black 45 10
DESIGN: 60g. Dove and spaceman's orbit around globe.

392 Monument

393 P.K.O. Emblem and Ant

1961. 40th Anniv of 3rd Silesian Uprising.
1251 **392** 60g. grey and green 10 10
1252 – 1z.55 grey and blue 25 10
DESIGN: 1z.55, Cross of Silesian uprisers.

1961. Savings Month.
1253 – 40g. red, yellow and black 15 10
1254 **393** 60g. brown, yellow & black 15 10
1255 – 60g. blue, violet and pink 15 10
1256 – 60g. green, red and black 15 10
1257 – 2z.50 mauve, grey & black 2·25 1·25
DESIGNS: No. 1253, Savings Bank motif; 1255, Bee; 1256, Squirrel; 1257, Savings Bank book.

394 "Mail Cart" (after J. Chelmonski)

1961. Stamp Day and 40th Anniv of Postal Museum.
1258 **394** 60g. brown 25 10
1259 60g. green 25 10

395 Congress Emblem

396 Emblem of Kopasyni Mining Family, 1284

1961. 5th W.F.T.U. Congress, Moscow.
1260 **395** 60g. black 15 10

1961. Millenary of Polish Mining Industry.
1261 **396** 40g. purple and orange 15 10
1262 – 60g. grey and blue 15 10
1263 – 2z.50 green and black 55 25
DESIGNS: 60g. 14th-century seal of Bytom; 2z.50, Emblem of Int Mine Constructors' Congress, Warsaw, 1958.

397 Child and Syringe

398 Cogwheel and Wheat

1961. 15th Anniv of UNICEF.
1264 **397** 40g. black and blue 10 10
1265 – 60g. black and orange 10 10
1266 – 2z.50 black and turquoise 60 25
DESIGNS—HORIZ: 60g. Children of three races. VERT: 2z.50, Mother and child, and feeding bottle.

1961. 15th Economic Co-operative Council Meeting, Warsaw.
1267 **398** 40g. red, yellow and blue 15 10
1268 – 60g. red, blue & ultram 15 10
DESIGN: 60g. Oil pipeline map, E. Europe.

399 Caterpillar-hunter

400 Worker with Flag and Dove

1961. Insects. Multicoloured.
1269 20g. Type **399** 15 10
1270 30g. Violet ground beetle 15 10
1271 40g. Alpine longhorn beetle 15 10
1272 50g. "Cerambyx cerdo" (longhorn beetle) 15 10
1273 60g. "Carabus auronitens" (ground beetle) 15 10
1274 80g. Stag beetle 25 10
1275 1z.15 Clouded apollo (butterfly) 55 10
1276 1z.35 Death's-head hawk moth 35 10
1277 1z.50 Scarce swallowtail (butterfly) 60 10
1278 1z.55 Apollo (butterfly) 60 10
1279 2z.50 Red wood ant 1·10 45
1280 5z.60 White-tailed bumble bee 5·75 3·50
Nos. 1275/80 are square, 36½ × 36½ mm.

1962. 20th Anniv of Polish Workers' Coalition.
1281 **400** 60g. brown, black and red 10 10
1282 – 60g. bistre, black and red 10 10
1283 – 60g. blue, black and red 10 10
1284 – 60g. grey, black and red 10 10
1285 – 60g. blue, black and red 10 10
DESIGNS: No. 1282, Steersman; 1283, Worker with hammer; 1284, Soldier with weapon; 1285, Worker with trowel and rifle.

401 Two Skiers Racing

1962. F.I.S. Int Ski Championships, Zakopane.
1286 **401** 40g. blue, grey and red 10 10
1287 40g. blue, brown and red 90 25
1288 – 60g. blue, grey and red 20 10
1289 – 60g. blue, brown and red 1·10 60
1290 – 1z.50 blue, grey and red 35 10
1291 – 1z.50 violet, grey and red 1·75 60
MS1291a 67 × 80 mm. 10z. (+5z.) blue, grey and red 4·25 4·00
DESIGNS—HORIZ: 60g. Skier racing. VERT: 1z.50, Ski jumper; 10z. F.I.S. emblem.

402 Majdanek Monument

1962. Concentration Camp Monuments.
1292 – 40g. blue 10 10
1293 **402** 60g. black 25 10
1294 – 1z.50 violet 35 15
DESIGNS—VERT: (20 × 31 mm): 40g. Broken carnations and portion of prison clothing (Auschwitz camp); 1z.50, Treblinka monument.

403 Racing Cyclist

1962. 15th International Peace Cycle Race.
1295 **403** 60g. black and blue 25 10
1296 – 2z.50 black and yellow 55 10
1297 – 3z.40 black and violet 90 45
DESIGNS—74½ × 22 mm: 2z.50, Cyclists & "XV". As Type **403**: 3z.40, Arms of Berlin, Prague and Warsaw, and cycle wheel.

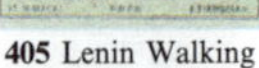

405 Lenin Walking

406 Gen. K. Swierczewski-Walter (monument)

1962. 50th Anniv of Lenin's Sojourn in Poland.
1298 **405** 40g. green and light green 45 10
1299 – 60g. lake and pink . . . 15 10
1300 – 2z.50 brown and yellow 45 10
DESIGNS: 60g. Lenin; 2z.50, Lenin wearing cap, and St. Mary's Church, Cracow.

1962. Famous Poles (2nd issue). As T **386**.
1301 60g. black and green 10 10
1302 60g. black and brown . . . 10 10
1303 60g. black and blue 40 10
1304 60g. black and bistre . . . 10 10
1305 60g. black and purple . . . 10 10
1306 60g. black and turquoise . . 10 10
PORTRAITS: No. 1301, A. Mickiewicz (poet); 1302, J. Slowacki (poet); 1303, F. Chopin (composer); 1304, R. Traugutt (patriot); 1305, J. Dabrowski (revolutionary); 1306, Maria Konopnicka (poet).

1962. 15th Death Anniv of Gen. K. Swierczewski-Walter (patriot).
1307 **406** 60g. black 15 10

1962. Polish Northern Provinces. As T **389**.
1308 60g. blue and grey 10 10
1309 60g. blue and grey 10 10
1310 1z.55 brown and yellow . . 20 10
1311 1z.55 brown and yellow . . 20 10
1312 2z.50 slate and grey 55 35
1313 2z.50 slate and grey 55 35
DESIGNS—VERT: No. 1308, Princess Elizabeth's seal; 1310, Gdansk Governor's seal; 1312, Frombork Cathedral. HORIZ: No. 1309, Insulators factory, Szczecinek; 1311, Gdansk shipyard; 1313, Laboratory of Agricultural College, Kortowo.

407 "Crocus scepusiensis" (Borb)

408 "The Poison Well", after J. Malczewski

1962. Polish Protected Plants. Plants in natural colours.
1314 **407** 60g. yellow 15 10
1315 A 60g. brown 70 35
1316 B 60g. pink 15 10
1317 C 90g. green 25 10
1318 D 90g. olive 25 10
1319 E 90g. green 25 10
1320 F 1z.50 blue 35 10
1321 G 1z.50 green 45 10
1322 H 1z.50 turquoise 35 10
1323 I 2z.50 green 80 55
1324 J 2z.50 turquoise 80 55
1325 K 2z.50 blue . . . . . . 1·10 55
PLANTS: A, "Platanthera bifolia" (Rich); B, "Aconitum callibotryon" (Rchb.); C, "Gentiana clusii" (Perr. et Song); D, "Dictamnus albus" (L.); E, "Nymphaca alba" (L.); F, "Daphne mezereum" (L.); G, "Pulsatilla vulgaris" (Mill.); H, "Anemone silvestris" (L.); I, "Trollius europaeus" (L.); J, "Galanthus nivalis" (L.); K, "Adonis vernalis" (L.).

1962. F.I.P. Day ("Federation Internationale de Philatelie").
1326 **408** 60g. black on cream . . 25 25

409 Pole Vault

1962. 7th European Athletic Championships, Belgrade. Multicoloured.
1327 40g. Type **409** 10 10
1328 60g. 400 m relay 10 10
1329 90g. Throwing the javelin 10 10
1330 1z. Hurdling 10 10
1331 1z.50 High-jumping 10 10
1332 1z.55 Throwing the discus 10 10
1333 2z.50 100 m final 45 15
1334 3z.40 Throwing the hammer 95 35

410 "Anopheles sp."

411 Cosmonauts "in flight"

1962. Malaria Eradication.
1335 **410** 60g. brown and turquoise 10 10
1336 – 1z.50 multicoloured 15 10
1337 – 2z.50 multicoloured . . . 60 25
MS1337a 60 × 81 mm. 3z. multicoloured . . . . 1·25 45
DESIGNS: 1z.50, Malaria parasites in blood; 2z.50, Cinchona plant; 3z. Anopheles mosquito.

1962. 1st "Team" Manned Space Flight.
1338 **411** 60g. green, black & violet 15 10
1339 – 2z.50 red, black and turquoise 45 25
MS1339a 70 × 94 mm. 10z. red, black and blue . . . . 2·75 2·00
DESIGN: 2z.50, Two stars (representing space-ships) in orbit.

412 "A Moment of Determination" (after painting by A. Kamienski)

413 Mazovian Princes' Mansion, Warsaw

1962. Stamp Day.
1340 **412** 60g. black 10 10
1341 2z.50 brown 45 20

1962. 25th Anniv of Polish Democratic Party.
1342 **413** 60g. black on red . . . 15 10

414 Cruiser "Aurora"

1962. 45th Anniv of Russian Revolution.
1343 **414** 60g. blue and red . . . 15 10

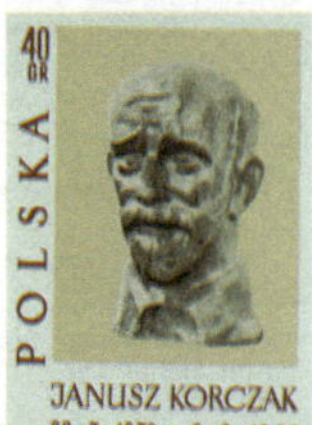

415 J. Korczak (bust after Dunikowski)

1962. 20th Death Anniv of Janusz Korczak (child educator).
1344 **415** 40g. sepia, bistre & brn 15 10
1345 – 60g. multicoloured . . . 35 10
1346 – 90g. multicoloured . . . 35 10
1347 – 1z. multicoloured 35 10
1348 – 2z.50 multicoloured . . . 70 10
1349 – 5z.60 multicoloured . . . 2·40 40
DESIGNS: 60g. to 5z.60, Illustrations from Korczak's children's books.

416 Old Town, Warsaw

1962. 5th T.U. Congress, Warsaw.
1350 **416** 3z.40 multicoloured . . . 70 25

417 Master Buncombe

419 Tractor and Wheat

418 R. Traugutt (insurgent leader)

1962. Maria Konopnicka's Fairy Tale "The Dwarfs and Orphan Mary". Multicoloured.
1351 40g. Type **417** 45 10
1352 60g. Lardie the Fox and Master Buncombe . . . . 1·40 1·00
1353 1z.50 Bluey the Frog making music 55 10
1354 1z.55 Peter's kitchen 55 25
1355 2z.50 Saraband's concert in Nightingale Valley 70 70
1356 3z.40 Orphan Mary and Subearthy . . . . 2·25 1·60

1963. Centenary of January (1863) Rising.
1357 **418** 60g. black, pink & turq 15 10

1963. Freedom from Hunger. Multicoloured.
1358 40g. Type **419** 15 10
1359 60g. Millet and hoeing . . . 80 25
1360 2z.50 Rice and mechanical harvester 70 35

420 Cocker Spaniel

1963. Dogs.
1361 **420** 20g. red, black and lilac 10 10
1362 – 30g. black and red . . . 10 10
1363 – 40g. ochre, black and lilac 25 10
1364 – 50g. ochre, black and blue 25 10
1365 – 60g. black and blue . . . 25 10
1366 – 1z. black and green . . . 70 25
1367 – 2z.50 brown, yell & blk 1·10 45
1368 – 3z.40 black and red . . . 3·00 1·40
1369 – 6z.50 black and yellow 6·00 3·75
DOGS—HORIZ: 30g. Sheep-dog; 40g. Boxer; 2z.50, Gun-dog "Ogar"; 6z.50, Great Dane. VERT: 50g. Airedale terrier; 60g. French bulldog; 1z. French poodle; 3z.40, Podhale sheep-dog.

421 Egyptian Galley (15th century B.C.)

422 Insurgent

1963. Sailing Ships (1st series).
1370 **421** 5g. brown on bistre . . . 10 10
1371 – 10g. turquoise on green 15 10
1372 – 20g. blue on grey . . . 15 10
1373 – 30g. black on olive . . . 20 10
1374 – 40g. blue on blue 20 10
1375 – 60g. purple on brown . . 35 10
1376 – 1z. black on blue 40 10
1377 – 1z.15 green on pink . . . 65 10
SHIPS: 10g. Phoenician merchantman (15th cent B.C.); 20g. Greek trireme (5th cent B.C.); 30g. Roman merchantman (3rd cent A.D.); 40g. "Mora" (Norman ship, 1066); 60g. Hanse kogge (14th cent); 1z. Hulk (16th cent); 1z.15, Carrack (15th cent).
See also Nos. 1451/66.

1963. 20th Anniv of Warsaw Ghetto Uprising.
1378 **422** 2z.50 brown and blue . . 30 10

423 Centenary Emblem

424 Lizard

1963. Red Cross Centenary.
1379 **423** 2z.50 red, blue and yellow 65 20

1963. Protected Reptiles and Amphibians. Reptiles in natural colours: inscr in black: background colours given.
1380 **424** 30g. green 10 10
1381 – 40g. olive 10 10
1382 – 50g. brown 10 10
1383 – 60g. grey 10 10
1384 – 90g. green 10 10
1385 – 1z.15 grey 10 10
1386 – 1z.35 blue 10 10
1387 – 1z.50 turquoise 30 15
1388 – 1z.55 pale blue 30 10
1389 – 2z.50 lavender 30 20
1390 – 3z. green 75 20
1391 – 3z.40 purple . . . . . 1·90 1·90
DESIGNS: 40g. Copperhead (snake); 50g. Marsh tortoise; 60g. Grass snake; 90g. Blindworm; 1z.15, Tree toad; 1z.35, Mountain newt; 1z.50, Crested newt; 1z.55, Green toad; 2z.50, "Bombina" toad; 3z. Salamander; 3z.40, "Natterjack" (toad).

425 Epee, Foil, Sabre and Knight's Helmet

1963. World Fencing Championships, Gdansk.
1392 **425** 20g. yellow and brown 10 10
1393 – 40g. light blue and blue 10 10
1394 – 60g. vermilion and red 10 10
1395 – 1z.15 light green & green 10 10
1396 – 1z.55 red and violet . . 35 10
1397 – 6z.50 yellow, pur & bis 1·25 60
MS1397a 110 × 93 mm. Nos. 1393/6 30·00 30·00
DESIGNS—HORIZ: Fencers with background of: 40g. Knights jousting; 60g. Dragoons in sword-fight; 1z.15, 18th-century duellists; 1z.55, Old Gdansk. VERT: 6z.50, Inscription and Arms of Gdansk.

1963. Famous Poles (3rd issue). As T **386**.
1398 60g. black and brown . . . 10 10
1399 60g. black and brown . . . 10 10
1400 60g. black and turquoise . . 10 10
1401 60g. black and green 10 10
PORTRAITS: No. 1398, L. Warynski (patriot); 1399, L. Krzywicki (economist); 1400, M. Sklodowska-Curie (scientist); 1401, K. Swierczewski (patriot).

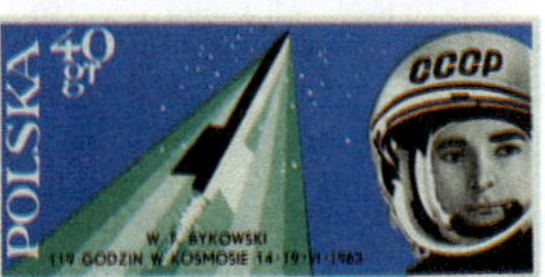

426 Bykovsky and "Vostok 5"

1963. 2nd "Team" Manned Space Flights.
1402 **426** 40g. black, green and blue 10 10
1403 – 60g. black, blue and green 10 10
1404 – 6z.50 multicoloured . . . 90 30
DESIGNS: 60g. Tereshkova and "Vostok 6"; 6z.50, "Vostoks 5 and 6" in orbit.

427 Basketball

1963. 13th European (Men's) Basketball Championships, Wroclaw.
1405 **427** 40g. multicoloured . . . 10 10
1406 – 50g. green, black and pink 10 10
1407 – 60g. black, green and red 10 10
1408 – 90g. multicoloured . . . 10 10
1409 – 2z.50 multicoloured . . . 20 10
1410 – 5z.60 multicoloured . . . 1·50 40
MS1410a 76 × 86 mm. 10z. (+5z.) multicoloured . . . . 2·25 1·10

DESIGNS: 50g. to 2z.50, As Type **427** but with ball, players and hands in various positions; 5z.60, Hands placing ball in net; 10z. Town Hall, People's Hall and Arms of Wroclaw.

428 Missile

1963. 20th Anniv of Polish People's Army. Multicoloured.

1411 20g. Type **428** 10 10
1412 40g. "Błyskawica" (destroyer) 10 10
1413 60g. PZL-106 Kruk (airplane) 10 10
1414 1z.15 Radar scanner 10 10
1415 1z.35 Tank 10 10
1416 1z.55 Missile carrier 10 10
1417 2z.50 Amphibious troop carrier 10 10
1418 3z. Ancient warrior, modern soldier and two swords 30 20

429 "A Love Letter" (after Czachorski)

1963. Stamp Day.

1419 **429** 60g. brown 20 10

1963. Visit of Soviet Cosmonauts to Poland. Nos. 1402/4 optd **23-28. X. 1963** and **w Polsce** together with Cosmonauts' names.

1420 **426** 40g. black, green and blue 20 10
1421 – 60g. black, blue and green 30 10
1422 – 6z.50 multicoloured 1·40 75

431 Tsiolkovsky's Rocket and Formula

432 Mazurian Horses

1963. "The Conquest of Space". Inscr in black.

1423 **431** 30g. turquoise 10 10
1424 – 40g. olive 10 10
1425 – 50g. violet 10 10
1426 – 60g. brown 10 10
1427 – 1z. turquoise 10 10
1428 – 1z.50 red 10 10
1429 – 1z.55 blue 10 10
1430 – 2z.50 purple 10 10
1431 – 5z.60 green 65 30
1432 – 6z.50 turquoise 1·10 30
MS1432a 78×106 mm. Nos. 1431/2 (two of each) 30·00 30·00

DESIGNS: 40g. "Sputnik 1"; 50g. "Explorer 1"; 60g. Banner carried by "Lunik 2"; 1z. "Lunik 3"; 1z.50, "Vostok 1"; 1z.55, "Friendship 7"; 2z.50, "Vostoks 3 and 4"; 5z.60, "Mariner 2"; 6z.50, "Mars 1".

1963. Polish Horse-breeding. Multicoloured.

1433 20g. Arab stallion "Comet" 15 10
1434 30g. Wild horses 15 10
1435 40g. Sokolski horse 20 10
1436 50g. Arab mares and foals 20 10
1437 60g. Type **432** 20 10
1438 90g. Steeplechasers 45 10
1439 1z.55 Arab stallion "Witez II" 80 10
1440 2z.50 Head of Arab horse (facing right) 1·50 10
1441 4z. Mixed breeds 3·75 60
1442 6z.50 Head of Arab horse (facing left) 5·25 2·40

SIZES—TRIANGULAR (55×27½ mm): 20, 30, 40g. HORIZ: (75×26 mm): 50, 90g., 4z. VERT: as Type **432**: 1z.55, 2z.50, 6z.50.

433 Ice Hockey

1964. Winter Olympic Games, Innsbruck. Mult.

1443 20g. Type **433** 10 10
1444 30g. Slalom 10 10
1445 40g. Downhill skiing 10 10
1446 60g. Speed skating 10 10
1447 1z. Ski-jumping 10 10
1448 2z.50 Tobogganing 10 10
1449 5z.60 Cross-country skiing 75 60
1450 6z.50 Pairs, figure skating 1·50 80
MS1450a 110×94 mm. Nos. 1448 and 1450 (two of each) 23·00 23·00

1964. Sailing Ships (2nd series). As T **421** but without coloured backgrounds. Some new designs.

1451 **421** 5g. brown 10 10
1452 – 10g. green 10 10
1453 – 20g. blue 10 10
1454 – 30g. bronze 10 10
1455 – 40g. blue 10 10
1456 – 60g. purple 10 10
1457 – 1z. brown 15 10
1458 – 1z.15 brown 15 10
1459 – 1z.35 blue 15 10
1460 – 1z.50 purple 15 10
1461 – 1z.55 black 15 10
1462 – 2z. violet 15 10
1463 – 2z.10 green 15 10
1464 – 2z.50 mauve 20 10
1465 – 3z. olive 30 10
1466 – 3z.40 brown 30 10

SHIPS—HORIZ: 10g. to 1z.15, As Nos. 1370/7; 1z.50, "Ark Royal" (English galleon, 1587); 2z.10, Ship of the line (18th cent); 2z.50, Sail frigate (19th cent); 3z. "Flying Cloud" (clipper, 19th cent). VERT: 1z.35, Columbus's "Santa Maria"; 1z.55, "Wodnik" (Polish warship, 17th cent); 2z. Dutch fleute (17th cent); 3z.40, "Dar Pomorza" (cadet ship).

434 "Flourishing Tree"

1964. 20th Anniv of People's Republic (1st issue).

1467 **434** 60g. multicoloured 10 10
1468 – 60g. black, yellow and red 10 10

DESIGN: No. 1468, Emblem composed of symbols of agriculture and industry.
See also Nos. 1497/1506.

435 European Cat

436 Casimir the Great (founder)

1964. Domestic Cats. As T **435**.

1469 30g. black and yellow 15 10
1470 40g. multicoloured 15 10
1471 50g. black, turquoise & yellow 15 10
1472 60g. multicoloured 35 10
1473 90g. multicoloured 30 10
1474 1z.35 multicoloured 30 10
1475 1z.55 multicoloured 50 10
1476 2z.50 yellow, black and violet 80 45
1477 3z.40 multicoloured 1·90 80
1478 6z.50 multicoloured 3·75 1·90

CATS—European: 30, 40, 60g., 1z.55, 2z.50, 6z.50. Siamese: 50g. Persian: 90g., 1z.35, 3z.40.
Nos. 1472/5 are horiz.

1964. 600th Anniv of Jagiellonian University, Cracow.

1479 **436** 40g. purple 10 10
1480 – 40g. green 10 10
1481 – 60g. violet 10 10
1482 – 60g. blue 10 10
1483 – 2z.50 sepia 65 10

PORTRAITS: No. 1480, Hugo Kollataj (educationist and politician); 1481, Jan Dlugosz (geographer and historian); 1482, Copernicus (astronomer); 1483 (36×37 mm), King Wladislaw Jagiello and Queen Jadwiga.

437 Northern Lapwing

1964. Birds. Multicoloured.

1484 30g. Type **437** 15 10
1485 40g. Bluethroat 15 10
1486 50g. Black-tailed godwit 15 10
1487 60g. Osprey (vert) 20 10
1488 90g. Grey heron (vert) 30 10
1489 1z.35 Little gull (vert) 45 10
1490 1z.55 Common shoveler 45 10
1491 5z.60 Black-throated diver 1·00 30
1492 6z.50 Great crested grebe 1·40 65

438 Red Flag on Brick Wall

1964. 4th Polish United Workers' Party Congress, Warsaw. Inscr "PZPR". Multicoloured.

1493 60g. Type **438** 10 10
1494 60g. Beribboned hammer 10 10
1495 60g. Hands reaching for Red Flag 10 10
1496 60g. Hammer and corn emblems 10 10

439 Factory and Cogwheel

441 Battle Scene

440 Gdansk Shipyard

1964. 20th Anniv of People's Republic (2nd issue).

1497 **439** 60g. black and blue 10 10
1498 – 60g. black and green 10 10
1499 – 60g. red and orange 10 10
1500 – 60g. blue and grey 10 10
1501 **440** 60g. blue and green 10 10
1502 – 60g. violet and mauve 10 10
1503 – 60g. brown and violet 10 10
1504 – 60g. bronze and green 10 10
1505 – 60g. purple and red 10 10
1506 – 60g. brown and yellow 10 10

DESIGNS—As Type **439**: No. 1498, Tractor and ear of wheat; 1499, Mask and symbols of the arts; 1500, Atomic symbol and book. As Type **440**: No. 1502, Lenin Foundry, Nowa Huta; 1503, Cement Works, Chelm; 1504, Turoszow power station; 1505, Petro-chemical plant, Plock; 1506, Tarnobrzeg sulphur mine.

1964. 20th Anniv of Warsaw Insurrection.

1507 **441** 60g. multicoloured 10 10

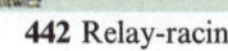
442 Relay-racing

443 Congress Emblem

1964. Olympic Games, Tokyo. Multicoloured.

1508 20g. Triple-jumping 10 10
1509 40g. Rowing 10 10
1510 60g. Weightlifting 10 10
1511 90g. Type **442** 10 10
1512 1z. Boxing 10 10
1513 2z.50 Football 30 10
1514 5z.60 High jumping (women) 90 30
1515 6z.50 High-diving 1·40 45
MS1515a 83×111 mm. Nos. 1514/15 (two of each) 30·00 23·00

SIZES: DIAMOND—20g. to 60g. SQUARE—90g. to 2z.50. VERT: (23½×36 mm)—5z.60, 6z.50.

MS1515b 79×106 mm. 2z.50 Rifle-shooting, 2z.50 Canoeing, 5z. Fencing, 5z. Basketball 3·50 1·50

1964. 15th Int Astronautical Congress, Warsaw.

1516 **443** 2z.50 black and violet 35 10

444 Hand holding Hammer

445 S. Zeromski

1964. 3rd Congress of Fighters for Freedom and Democracy Association, Warsaw.

1517 **444** 60g. red, black and green 10 10

1964. Birth Cent of Stefan Zeromski (writer).

1518 **445** 60g. brown 10 10

446 Globe and Red Flag

448 Eleanor Roosevelt

447 18th-century Stage Coach (after Brodowski)

1964. Centenary of "First International".

1519 **446** 60g. black and red 10 10

1964. Stamp Day.

1520 **447** 60g. green 20 10
1521 60g. brown 20 10

1964. 80th Birth Anniv of Eleanor Roosevelt.

1522 **448** 2z.50 brown 20 10

449 Battle of Studzianki (after S. Zoltowski)

1964. "Poland's Struggle" (World War II) (1st issue).

1523 – 40g. black 10 10
1524 – 40g. violet 10 10
1525 – 60g. blue 10 10
1526 – 60g. green 10 10
1527 **449** 60g. bronze 10 10

DESIGNS—VERT: No. 1523, Virtuti Militari Cross; 1524, Westerplatte Memorial, Gdansk; 1525, Bydogoszez Memorial. HORIZ: No. 1526, Soldiers crossing the Oder (after S. Zoltowski).
See also Nos. 1610/12.

449a W. Komarov

1964. Russian Three-manned Space Flight. Sheet 114×63 mm depicting crew.

MS1527a 60g. black and red (T **449a**); 60g. black and green (Feoktistov); 60g. black and blue (Yegorov) 95 50

450 Cyclamen
451 Spacecraft of the Future

1964. Garden Flowers. Multicoloured.
1528 20g. Type **450** 10 10
1529 30g. Freesia 10 10
1530 40g. Rose 10 10
1531 50g. Peony 10 10
1532 60g. Lily 10 10
1533 90g. Poppy 10 10
1534 1z.35 Tulip 10 10
1535 1z.50 Narcissus 65 30
1536 1z.55 Begonia 20 10
1537 2z.50 Carnation 45 10
1538 3z.40 Iris 75 30
1539 5z.60 Japanese camelia . . . 1·25 60
Nos. 1534/9 are smaller, 26½ × 37 mm.

1964. Space Research. Multicoloured.
1540 20g. Type **451** 10 10
1541 30g. Launching rocket . . . 10 10
1542 40g. Dog "Laika" and rocket 10 10
1543 60g. "Lunik 3" and Moon 10 10
1544 1z.55 Satelite 10 10
1545 2z.50 "Elektron 2" 35 10
1546 5z.60 "Mars 1" 50 10
1547 6z.50+2z. Gagarin seated in capsule . . . . 3·50 30

452 "Siren of Warsaw"

1965. 20th Anniv of Liberation of Warsaw.
1548 **452** 60g. green 10 10

453 Edaphosaurus

1965. Prehistoric Animals (1st series). Mult.
1549 20g. Type **453** 10 10
1550 30g. Cryptocleidus (vert) . . 10 10
1551 40g. Brontosaurus 10 10
1552 60g. Mesosaurus (vert) . . . 10 10
1553 90g. Stegosaurus 10 10
1554 1z.15 Brachiosaurus (vert) 10 10
1555 1z.35 Styracosaurus 20 10
1556 3z.40 Corythosaurus (vert) 50 10
1557 5z.60 Rhamphorhynchus (vert) . . . . 1·40 45
1558 6z.50 Tyrannosaurus . . . . 1·90 1·10
See also Nos. 1639/47.

454 Petro-chemical Works, Plock, and Polish and Soviet Flags

1965. 20th Anniv of Polish–Soviet Friendship Treaty. Multicoloured.
1559 60g. Seal (vert, 27 × 38½ mm) 10 10
1560 60g. Type **454** 10 10

455 Polish Eagle and Civic Arms

1965. 20th Anniv of Return of Western and Northern Territories to Poland.
1561 **455** 60g. red 10 10

456 Dove of Peace
457 I.T.U. Emblem

1965. 20th Anniv of Victory.
1562 **456** 60g. red and black . . . 10 10

1965. Centenary of I.T.U.
1563 **457** 2z.50 black, violet & blue 45 10

458 Clover-leaf Emblem and "The Friend of the People" (journal)
459 "Dragon" Dinghies

1965. 70th Anniv of Peasant Movement. Mult.
1564 40g. Type **458** 10 10
1565 60g. Ears of corn and industrial plant (horiz) . . 10 10

1965. World Finn Sailing Championships, Gdynia. Multicoloured.
1566 30g. Type **459** 10 10
1567 40g. "5.5 m." dinghies . . . 10 10
1568 50g. "Finn" dinghies (horiz) 10 10
1569 60g. "V" dinghies 10 10
1570 1z.35 "Cadet" dinghies (horiz) 20 10
1571 4z. "Star" yachts (horiz) . . 65 35
1572 5z.60 "Flying Dutchman" dinghies . . . . 1·25 60
1573 6z.50 "Amethyst" dinghies (horiz) . . . . 1·90 1·90
MS1573a 79 × 59 mm. 15z. Finn dinghies . . . . 1·75 1·10

460 Marx and Lenin
461 17th-cent Arms of Warsaw

1965. Postal Ministers' Congress, Peking.
1574 **460** 60g. black on red . . . 10 10

1965. 700th Anniv of Warsaw.
1575 **461** 5g. red 10 10
1576 – 10g. green 10 10
1577 – 20g. blue 10 10
1578 – 40g. brown 10 10
1579 – 60g. orange 10 10
1580 – 1z.50 black 10 10
1581 – 1z.55 blue 10 10
1582 – 2z.50 purple 10 10
MS1583 51 × 62 mm. 3z.40 black and bistre 75 50
DESIGNS—VERT: 10g. 13th-cent antiquities. HORIZ: 20g. Tombstone of last Masovian dukes; 40g. Old Town Hall; 60g. Barbican; 1z.50, Arsenal; 1z.55, National Theatre; 2z.50, Staszic Palace; 3z.40, T **462**.

463 I.Q.S.Y. Emblem

1965. International Quiet Sun Year. Multicoloured. Background colours given.
1584 **463** 60g. blue 10 10
1585 60g. violet 10 10
1586 – 2z.50 red 30 10
1587 – 2z.50 brown 30 10
1588 – 3z.40 orange 45 10
1589 – 3z.40 olive 45 10
DESIGNS: 2z.50, Solar scanner; 3z.40, Solar System.

464 "Odontoglossum grande"
465 Weightlifting

1965. Orchids. Multicoloured.
1590 20g. Type **464** 10 10
1591 30g. "Cypripedium hibridum" 10 10
1592 40g. "Lycaste skinneri" . . 10 10
1593 50g. "Cattleya warzewicza" 10 10
1594 60g. "Vanda sanderiana" . . 10 10
1595 1z.35 "Cypripedium hibridum" (different) . . 30 10
1596 4z. "Sobralia" 45 30
1597 5z.60 "Disa grandiflora" . . 1·25 45
1598 6z.50 "Cattleya labiata" . . 1·90 50

1965. Olympic Games, Tokyo. Polish Medal Winners. Multicoloured.
1599 30g. Type **465** 10 10
1600 40g. Boxing 10 10
1601 50g. Relay-racing 10 10
1602 60g. Fencing 10 10
1603 90g. Hurdling (women's 80 m) 10 10
1604 3z.40 Relay-racing (women's) 45 10
1605 6z.50 "Hop, step and jump" 90 60
1606 7z.10 Volleyball (women's) 1·25 45

466 "The Post Coach" (after P. Michalowski)

1965. Stamp Day.
1607 **466** 60g. brown 20 10
1608 – 2z.50 green 30 10
DESIGN: 2z.50, "Coach about to leave" (after P. Michalowski).

467 U.N. Emblem
468 Memorial, Holy Cross Mountains

1965. 20th Anniv of U.N.O.
1609 **467** 2z.50 blue 30 10

1965. "Poland's Struggle" (World War II) (2nd issue).
1610 **468** 60g. brown 10 10
1611 – 60g. green 10 10
1612 – 60g. brown 10 10
DESIGNS—VERT: No. 1611, Memorial Plaszow. HORIZ: No. 1612, Memorial, Chelm-on-Ner.

469 Wolf

1965. Forest Animals. Multicoloured.
1613 20g. Type **469** 10 10
1614 30g. Lynx 10 10
1615 40g. Red fox 10 10
1616 50g. Eurasian badger . . . 10 10
1617 60g. Brown bear 10 10
1618 1z.50 Wild boar 35 10
1619 2z.50 Red deer 35 10
1620 5z.60 European bison . . . 90 30
1621 7z.10 Elk . . . . 1·50 50

470 Gig

1965. Horse-drawn Carriages in Lancut Museum. Multicoloured.
1622 20g. Type **470** 10 10
1623 40g. Coupe 10 10
1624 50g. Ladies' "basket" (trap) 10 10
1625 60g. "Vis-a-vis" 10 10
1626 90g. Cab 10 10
1627 1z.15 Berlinka 15 10
1628 2z.50 Hunting brake 45 10
1629 6z.50 Barouche . . . . . . 1·25 30
1630 7z.10 English brake . . . . 1·75 50
Nos. 1627/9 are 77 × 22 mm and No. 1630 is 104 × 22 mm.

471 Congress Emblem and Industrial Products

1966. 5th Polish Technicians' Congress, Katowice.
1631 **471** 60g. multicoloured . . . 10 10

1966. 20th Anniv of Industrial Nationalization. Designs similar to T **471**. Multicoloured.
1632 60g. Pithead gear (vert) . . 10 10
1633 60g. "Henryk Jedza" (freighter) 10 10
1634 60g. Petro-chemical works, Plock 10 10
1635 60g. Combine-harvester . . 10 10
1636 60g. Class EN 57 electric train 10 10
1637 60g. Exhibition Hall, 35th Poznan Fair 10 10
1638 60g. Crane (vert) 10 10

1966. Prehistoric Animals (2nd series). As T **453**. Multicoloured.
1639 20g. Terror fish 10 10
1640 30g. Lobefin 10 10
1641 40g. Ichthyostega 10 10
1642 50g. Mastodonsaurus . . . 10 10
1643 60g. Cynognathus 10 10
1644 2z.50 Archaeopteryx (vert) 10 10
1645 3z.40 Brontotherium 60 10
1646 6z.50 Machairodus 90 45
1647 7z.10 Mammuthus . . . . 2·10 50

472 H. Sienkiewicz (novelist)
473 Footballers (Montevideo, 1930)

1966. 50th Death Anniv of Henryk Sienkiewicz.
1648 **472** 60g. black on buff . . . 10 10

1966. World Cup Football Championship.
(a) Football scenes representing World Cup finals.
1649 20g. Type **473** 10 10
1650 40g. Rome, 1934 . . . . . 10 10
1651 60g. Paris, 1938 . . . . . . 10 10
1652 90g. Rio de Janeiro, 1950 10 10
1653 1z.50 Berne, 1954 . . . . . 60 10
1654 3z.40 Stockholm, 1958 . . . 60 10
1655 6z.50 Santiago, 1962 . . . . 1·25 10
1656 7z.10 "London", 1966 (elimination match, Glasgow, 1965) . . . . . 1·75 35

(b) 61 × 81 mm.
MS1657 **474** 13z.50+1z.50 . . . 2·40 1·40

475 Soldier with Flag, and Dove of Peace
476 Women's Relay-racing

477

1966. 21st Anniv of Victory Day.
1658 **475** 60g. red and black on silver 10 10

1966. 8th European Athletic Championships, Budapest. Multicoloured.
1659 20g. Runner starting race (vert) 10 10
1660 40g. Type **476** 10 10
1661 60g. Throwing the javelin (vert) 10 10
1662 90g. Women's hurdles . . . 10 10
1663 1z.35 Throwing the discus (vert) 10 10
1664 3z.40 Finish of race 45 10
1665 6z.50 Throwing the hammer (vert) 75 35
1666 7z.10 High-jumping . . . . 1·10 60
MS1667 **477** 110 × 66 mm. 5z. Imperf . . . . 2·40 1·25

478 White Eagle

479 Flowers and Produce

1966. Polish Millenary (1st issue). Each red and black on gold.
1668 60g. Type **478** 10 10
1669 60g. Polish flag 10 10
1670 2z.50 Type **478** 10 10
1671 2z.50 Polish flag 10 10
See also Nos. 1717/18.

1966. Harvest Festival. Multicoloured.
1672 40g. Type **479** 20 10
1673 60g. Woman and loaf . . . 20 10
1674 3z.40 Festival bouquet . . . 50 35
The 3z.40 is 49 × 48 mm.

480 Chrysanthemum

481 Tourist Map

1966. Flowers. Multicoloured.
1675 10g. Type **480** 10 10
1676 20g. Poinsettia 10 10
1677 30g. Centaury 10 10
1678 40g. Rose 10 10
1679 60g. Zinnia 10 10
1680 90g. Nasturtium 10 10
1681 5z.60 Dahlia 90 30
1682 6z.50 Sunflower 80 45
1683 7z.10 Magnolia . . . . . . 1·90 50

1966. Tourism.
1684 **481** 10g. red 10 10
1685 – 20g. olive 10 10
1686 – 40g. blue 10 10
1687 – 60g. brown 10 10
1688 – 60g. black 10 10
1689 – 1z.15 green 15 10
1690 – 1z.35 red 10 10
1691 – 1z.55 violet 10 10
1692 – 2z. green 40 10
DESIGNS: 20g. Hela Lighthouse; 40g. Yacht; 60g. (No. 1687), Poniatowski Bridge, Warsaw; 60g. (No. 1688), Mining Academy, Kielce; 1z.15, Dunajec Gorge; 1z.35, Old oaks, Rogalin; 1z.55, Silesian Planetarium; 2z. "Batory" (liner).

482 Roman Capital

1966. Polish Culture Congress.
1693 **482** 60g. red and brown . . 10 10

483 Stable-man with Percherons

1966. Stamp Day.
1694 **483** 60g. brown 10 10
1695 – 2z.50 green 10 10
DESIGN: 2z.50, Stablemen with horses and dogs.

484 Soldier in Action

1966. 30th Anniv of Jaroslav Dabrowski Brigade.
1696 **484** 60g. black, green and red 10 10

485 Woodland Birds

1966. Woodland Birds. Multicoloured.
1697 10g. Type **485** 15 10
1698 20g. Green woodpecker . . 15 10
1699 30g. Jay 20 10
1700 40g. Golden oriole 20 10
1701 60g. Hoopoe 20 10
1702 2z.50 Common redstart . . 45 35
1703 4z. Spruce siskin . . . . . 1·50 35
1704 6z.50 Chaffinch . . . . . . 1·50 60
1705 7z.10 Great tit . . . . . . 1·50 60

486 Ram (ritual statuette)

487 "Vostok 1"

1966. Polish Archaeological Research.
1706 **486** 60g. blue 10 10
1707 – 60g. green 10 10
1708 – 60g. brown 10 10
DESIGNS—VERT: No. 1707, Plan of Biskupin settlement. HORIZ: No. 1708, Brass implements and ornaments.

1966. Space Research. Multicoloured.
1709 20g. Type **487** 10 10
1710 40g. "Gemini" 10 10
1711 60g. "Ariel 2" 10 10
1712 1z.35 "Proton 1" 10 10
1713 1z.50 "FR 1" 20 10
1714 3z.40 "Alouette" 35 10
1715 6z.50 "San Marco 1" . . . 1·25 10
1716 7z.10 "Luna 9" . . . . . . 1·50 30

488 Polish Eagle and Hammer

1966. Polish Millenary (2nd issue).
1717 **488** 40g. purple, lilac and red 10 10
1718 – 60g. purple, green and red 10 10
DESIGN: 60g. Polish eagle and agricultural and industrial symbols.

489 Dressage

1967. 150th Anniv of Racehorse Breeding in Poland. Multicoloured.
1719 10g. Type **489** 15 10
1720 20g. Cross-country racing 15 10
1721 40g. Horse-jumping 15 10
1722 60g. Jumping fence in open country 30 10
1723 90g. Horse-trotting 30 10
1724 5z.90 Playing polo 90 10
1725 6z.60 Stallion "Ofir" . . . . 1·40 45
1726 7z. Stallion "Skowronek" . . 2·10 45

490 Black-wedged Butterflyfish

1967. Exotic Fishes. Multicoloured.
1727 5g. Type **490** 10 10
1728 10g. Emperor angelfish . . . 10 10
1729 40g. Racoon butterflyfish . . 10 10
1730 60g. Clown triggerfish . . . 10 10
1731 90g. Undulate triggerfish . . 10 10
1732 1z.50 Picasso triggerfish . . 20 10
1733 4z.50 Black-finned melon butterflyfish 75 10
1734 6z.60 Semicircle angelfish . . 95 45
1735 7z. Saddle butterflyfish . . . 1·25 75

491 Auschwitz Memorial

1967. Polish Martyrdom and Resistance, 1939–45.
1736 **491** 40g. brown 10 10
1737 – 40g. black 10 10
1738 – 40g. violet 10 10
DESIGNS—VERT: No. 1737, Auschwitz-Monowitz Memorial; 1738, Memorial guide's emblem.
See also Nos. 1770/2, 1798/9 and 1865/9.

492 Cyclists

1967. 20th International Peace Cycle Race.
1739 **492** 60g. multicoloured . . . 10 10

493 Running

1967. Olympic Games (1968). Multicoloured.
1740 20g. Type **493** 10 10
1741 40g. Horse-jumping 10 10
1742 60g. Relay-running 10 10
1743 90g. Weight-lifting 10 10
1744 1z.35 Hurdling 10 10
1745 3z.40 Gymnastics 45 15
1746 6z.60 High-jumping 60 35
1747 7z. Boxing . . . . 1·10 65
MS1748 65 × 86 mm. 10z.+5z. multicoloured . . . . 1·90 1·25
DESIGN: (30 × 30 mm.)—10z. Kusocinski winning 10,000 meters race at Olympic Games, Los Angeles, 1932.

494 Socialist Symbols

1967. Polish Trade Unions Congress, Warsaw.
1749 **494** 60g. multicoloured . . . 10 10

495 "Arnica montana"

1967. Protected Plants. Multicoloured.
1750 40g. Type **495** 10 10
1751 60g. "Aquilegia vulgaris" . . 10 10
1752 3z.40 "Gentiana punctata" 35 10
1753 4z.50 "Lycopodium clavatum" 35 10
1754 5z. "Iris sibirica" 60 10
1755 10z. "Azalea pontica" . . . 1·10 30

496 Katowice Memorial

497 Marie Curie

1967. Inauguration of Katowice Memorial.
1756 **496** 60g. multicoloured . . . 10 10

1967. Birth Centenary of Marie Curie.
1757 **497** 60g. lake 10 10
1758 – 60g. brown 10 10
1759 – 60g. violet 10 10
DESIGNS: No. 1758, Marie Curie's Nobel Prize diploma; 1759, Statue of Marie Curie, Warsaw.

498 "Fifth Congress of the Deaf" (sign language)

1967. 5th World Federation of the Deaf Congress, Warsaw.
1760 **498** 60g. black and blue . . . 10 10

499 Bouquet

1967. "Flowers of the Meadow". Multicoloured.
1761 20g. Type **499** 10 10
1762 40g. Red poppy 10 10
1763 60g. Field bindweed 10 10
1764 90g. Wild pansy 10 10
1765 1z.15 Tansy 10 10
1766 2z.50 Corn cockle 20 10
1767 3z.40 Field scabious 45 30
1768 4z.50 Scarlet pimpernel . . 1·40 35
1769 7z.90 Chicory . . . . 1·50 30

1967. Polish Martyrdom and Resistance, 1939–45 (2nd series). As T **491**.
1770 40g. blue 10 10
1771 40g. green 10 10
1772 40g. black 10 10
DESIGNS—HORIZ: No. 1770, Stutthof Memorial. VERT: No. 1771, Walez Memorial; 1772, Lodz-Radogoszez Memorial.

500 "Wilanow Palace" (from painting by W. Kasprzycki)

1967. Stamp Day.
1773 **500** 60g. brown and blue . . 10 10

501 Cruiser "Aurora"

1967. 50th Anniv of October Revolution. Each black, grey and red.
1774 60g. Type **501** 10 10
1775 60g. Lenin 10 10
1776 60g. "Luna 10" 10 10

502 Peacock   503 Kosciuszko

1967. Butterflies. Multicoloured.
1777 10g. Type **502** 10 10
1778 20g. Swallowtail 10 10
1779 40g. Small tortoiseshell . . . 10 10
1780 60g. Camberwell beauty . . 15 10
1781 2z. Purple emperor 30 10
1782 2z.50 Red admiral 35 10
1783 3z.40 Pale clouded yellow 35 10
1784 4z.50 Marbled white . . . . 1·75 80
1785 7z.90 Large blue . . . . . 1·90 80

1967. 150th Death Anniv of Tadeusz Kosciuszko (national hero).
1786 **503** 60g. chocolate and brown 10 10
1787 2z.50 green and red . . . 20 10

504 "The Lobster" (Jean de Heem)

1967. Famous Paintings.
1788 – 20g. multicoloured . . . 20 10
1789 – 40g. multicoloured . . . 10 10
1790 – 60g. multicoloured . . . 10 10
1791 – 2z. multicoloured 30 20
1792 – 2z.50 multicoloured . . . 30 20
1793 – 3z.40 multicoloured . . . 60 20
1794 **504** 4z.50 multicoloured . . . 1·10 60
1795 – 6z.60 multicoloured . . . 1·40 75
DESIGNS (Paintings from the National Museums, Warsaw and Cracow). VERT: 20g. "Lady with a Weasel" (Leonardo da Vinci); 40g. "The Polish Lady" (Watteau); 60g. "Dog fighting Heron" (A. Hondius); 2z. "Fowler tuning Guitar" (J. B. Greuze); 2z.50, "The Tax Collectors" (M. van Reymerswaele); 3z.40, "Daria Fiodorowna" (F. S. Rokotov). HORIZ: 6z.60, "Parable of the Good Samaritan" (landscape, Rembrandt).

505 W. S. Reymont

1967. Birth Centenary of W. S. Reymont (novelist).
1796 **505** 60g. brown, red and ochre 10 10

506 J. M. Ossolinski (medallion), Book and Flag

1967. 150th Anniv of Ossolineum Foundation.
1797 **506** 60g. brown, red and blue 10 10

1967. Polish Martyrdom and Resistance, 1939–45 (3rd series). As T **491**.
1798 40g. red 10 10
1799 40g. brown 10 10
DESIGNS—VERT: No. 1798, Zagan Memorial. HORIZ: No. 1799, Lambinowice Memorial.

507 Ice Hockey

1968. Winter Olympic Games, Grenoble. Mult.
1800 40g. Type **507** 10 10
1801 60g. Downhill 10 10
1802 90g. Slalom 10 10
1803 1z.35 Speed-skating 10 10
1804 1z.55 Ski-walking 10 10
1805 2z. Tobogganing 20 20
1806 7z. Rifle-shooting on skis . . 50 45
1807 7z.90 Ski-jumping (different) 95 60

508 "Puss in Boots"   510 "Peace" (poster by H. Tomaszewski)

509 "Passiflora quadrangularis"

1968. Fairy Tales. Multicoloured.
1808 20g. Type **508** 10 10
1809 40g. "The Raven and the Fox" 10 10
1810 60g. "Mr. Twardowski" . . 10 10
1811 2z. "The Fisherman and the Fish" 20 10
1812 2z.50 "Little Red Riding Hood" 30 10
1813 3z.40 "Cinderella" 45 10
1814 5z.50 "The Waif" . . . . . 1·25 45
1815 7z. "Snow White" . . . . . 1·50 60

1968. Flowers. Multicoloured.
1816 10g. "Clianthus dampieri" 10 10
1817 20g. Type **509** 10 10
1818 30g. "Strelitzia reginae" . . 10 10
1819 40g. "Coryphanta vivipara" 10 10
1820 60g. "Odontonia" 10 10
1821 90g. "Protea cyneroides" . . 10 10
1822 4z.+2z. "Abutilon" 20 10
1823 8z.+4z. "Rosa polyantha" 1·90 30

1968. 2nd Int Poster Biennale, Warsaw. Mult.
1824 60g. Type **510** 10 10
1825 2z.50 Gounod's "Faust" (poster by Jan Lenica) . . 10 10

511 Zephyr Glider

1968. 11th World Gliding Championships, Leszno. Gliders. Multicoloured.
1826 60g. Type **511** 10 10
1827 90g. Stork 10 10
1828 1z.50 Swallow 15 10
1829 3z.40 Fly 35 20
1830 4z. Seal 80 30
1831 5z.50 Pirate 95 30

512 Child with "Stamp"   513 Part of Monument

1968. "75 years of Polish Philately". Multicoloured.
1832 60g. Type **512** 10 10
1833 60g. Balloon over Poznan 10 10

1968. Silesian Insurrection Monument, Sosnowiec.
1834 **513** 60g. black and purple . . 10 10

514 Relay-racing

1968. Olympic Games, Mexico. Multicoloured.
1835 30g. Type **514** 10 10
1836 40g. Boxing 10 10
1837 60g. Basketball 10 10
1838 90g. Long-jumping 10 10
1839 2z.50 Throwing the javelin 15 10
1840 3z.40 Gymnastics 30 10
1841 4z. Cycling 35 10
1842 7z.90 Fencing 65 10
1843 10z.+5z. Torch runner and Aztec bas-relief (56 × 45 mm) . . . . . . 1·75 30

515 "Knight on a Bay Horse" (P. Michalowski)

1968. Polish Paintings. Multicoloured.
1844 40g. Type **515** 10 10
1845 60g. "Fisherman" (L. Wyczolkowski) . . . 10 10
1846 1z.15 "Jewish Woman with Lemons" (A. Gierymski) 10 10
1847 1z.35 "Eliza Parenska" (S. Wyspianski) 15 10
1848 1z.50 "Manifesto" (W. Weiss) 20 10
1849 4z.50 "Stanczyk" (Jan Matejko) (horiz) 50 10
1850 5z. "Children's Band" (T. Makowski) (horiz) . . 80 10
1851 7z. "Feast II" (Z. Waliszewski) (horiz) 90 35

516 "September, 1939" (Bylina)

1968. 25th Anniv of Polish People's Army. Designs show paintings.
1852 40g. violet and olive on yellow 10 10
1853 40g. blue and violet on lilac 10 10
1854 40g. green and blue on grey 10 10
1855 40g. black and brown on orange 10 10
1856 40g. purple & green on green 10 10
1857 60g. brown & ultram on bl 10 10
1858 60g. purple & green on green 10 10
1859 60g. olive and red on pink 10 10
1860 60g. green and brown on red 20 10
1861 60g. blue & turquoise on blue 30 10
PAINTINGS AND PAINTERS: No. 1852, Type **516**; 1853, "Partisans" (Maciag); 1854, "Lenino" (Bylina); 1855, "Monte Cassino" (Boratynski); 1856, "Tanks before Warsaw" (Garwatowski); 1857, "Neisse River" (Bylina); 1858, "On the Oder" (Mackiewicz); 1859, "In Berlin" (Bylina); 1860, "Blyskawica" (destroyer) (Mokwa); 1861, "Pursuit" (Mikoyan Gurevich MiG-17 aircraft) (Kulisiewicz).

517 "Party Members" (F. Kowarski)

1968. 5th Polish United Workers' Party Congress, Warsaw. Multicoloured designs showing paintings.
1862 60g. Type **517** 10 10
1863 60g. "Strike" (S. Lentz) (vert) 10 10
1864 60g. "Manifesto" (W. Weiss) (vert) 10 10

1968. Polish Martyrdom and Resistance, 1939–45 (4th series). As T **491**.
1865 40g. grey 10 10
1866 40g. brown 10 10
1867 40g. brown 10 10
1868 40g. blue 10 10
1869 40g. brown 10 10
DESIGNS—HORIZ: No. 1865, Tomb of Unknown Soldier, Warsaw; 1866, Guerillas' Monument, Kartuzy. VERT: No. 1867, Insurgents' Monument, Poznan; 1868, People's Guard Insurgents' Monument, Polichno; 1869, Rotunda, Zamosc.

518 "Start of Hunt" (W. Kossak)

1968. Paintings. Hunting Scenes. Multicoloured.
1870 20g. Type **518** 10 10
1871 40g. "Hunting with Falcon" (J. Kossak) 10 10
1872 60g. "Wolves' Raid" (A. Wierusz-Kowalski) . . 10 10
1873 1z.50 "Home-coming with a Bear" (J. Falat) 30 10
1874 2z.50 "The Fox-hunt" (T. Sutherland) 20 10
1875 3z.40 "The Boar-hunt" (F. Snyders) 30 10
1876 4z.50 "Hunters' Rest" (W. G. Pierow) . . . . . 1·25 45
1877 8z.50 "Hunting a Lion in Morocco" (Delacroix) . . 1·25 90

519 Maltese Terrier   520 House Sign

1969. Pedigree Dogs. Multicoloured.
1878 20g. Type **519** 10 10
1879 40g. Wire-haired fox-terrier (vert) 20 10
1880 60g. Afghan hound 20 20
1881 1z.50 Rough-haired terrier 20 10
1882 2z.50 English setter 45 10
1883 3z.40 Pekinese 50 20
1884 4z.50 Alsatian (vert) . . . . 1·10 30
1885 8z.50 Pointer (vert) . . . . 2·25 65

1969. 9th Polish Democratic Party Congress.
1886 **520** 60g. red, black and grey 10 10

521 "Dove" and Wheat-ears   522 Running

1969. 5th Congress of United Peasant's Party.
1887 **521** 60g. multicoloured . . . 10 10

1969. 75th Anniv of International Olympic Committee and 50th Anniv of Polish Olympic Committee. Multicoloured.
1888 10g. Type **522** 10 10
1889 20g. Gymnastics 10 10
1890 40g. Weightlifting 10 10
1891 60g. Throwing the javelin 10 10
1892 2z.50+50g. Throwing the discus 10 10
1893 3z.40+1z. Running 20 10
1894 4z.+1z.50 Wrestling 60 30
1895 7z.+2z. Fencing . . . . . . 1·10 35

523 Pictorial Map of Swietokrzyski National Park

1969. Tourism (1st series). Multicoloured.

1896	40g. Type **523**	10	10
1897	60g. Niedzica Castle (vert)	10	10
1898	1z.35 Kolobrzeg Lighthouse and yacht	20	10
1899	1z.50 Szczecin Castle and Harbour	20	10
1900	2z.50 Torun and Vistula River	15	10
1901	3z.40 Klodzko, Silesia (vert)	20	20
1902	4z. Sulejow	35	30
1903	4z.50 Kazimierz Dolny market-place (vert)	35	30

See also Nos. 1981/5.

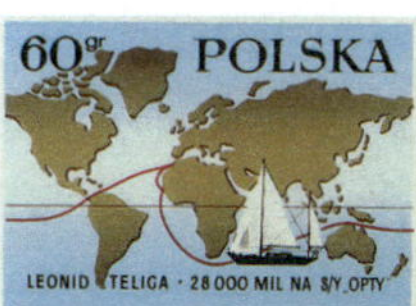

524 Route Map and "Opty"

1969. Leonid Teliga's World Voyage in Yacht "Opty".

1904 **524**	60g. multicoloured	10	10

525 Copernicus (after woodcut by T. Stimer) and Inscription

526 "Memory" Flame and Badge

1969. 500th Birth Anniv (1973) of Copernicus (1st issue).

1905 **525**	40g. brown, red & yellow	10	10
1906 –	60g. blue, red and green	10	10
1907 –	2z.50 olive, red & purple	35	30

DESIGNS: 60g. Copernicus (after J. Falck) and 15th-century globe; 2z.50, Copernicus (after painting by J. Matejko) and diagram of heliocentric system.

See also Nos. 1995/7, 2069/72, 2167/70, 2213/14 and 2217/21.

1969. 5th National Alert of Polish Boy Scout Association.

1908 **526**	60g. black, red and blue	10	10
1909 –	60g. red, black and green	10	10
1910 –	60g. black, green and red	10	10

DESIGN: No. 1909, "Defence" eagle and badge; 1910, "Labour" map and badge.

528 Coal-miner

1969. 25th Anniv of Polish People's Republic. Multicoloured.

1911	60g. Frontier guard and arms	10	10
1912	60g. Plock petro-chemical plant	10	10
1913	60g. Combine-harvester	10	10
1914	60g. Grand Theatre, Warsaw	10	10
1915	60g. Curie statue and University, Lublin	10	10
1916	60g. Type **528**	10	10
1917	60g. Sulphur-worker	10	10
1918	60g. Steel-worker	10	10
1919	60g. Shipbuilder	10	10

Nos. 1911/5 are vert and have white arms embossed in the top portion of the stamps.

529 Astronauts and Module on Moon

1969. 1st Man on the Moon.

1920 **529**	2z.50 multicoloured	60	45

530 "Motherhood" (S. Wyspianski)

1969. Polish Paintings. Multicoloured.

1921	20g. Type **530**	10	10
1922	40g. "Hamlet" (J. Malczewski)	10	10
1923	60g. "Indian Summer" (J. Chelmonski)	10	10
1924	2z. "Two Girls" (Olga Boznanska) (vert)	20	10
1925	2z.50 "The Sun of May" (J. Mehoffer) (vert)	10	10
1926	3z.40 "Woman combing her Hair" (W. Slewinski)	30	30
1927	5z.50 "Still Life" (J. Pankiewicz)	60	30
1928	7z. "Abduction of the King's Daughter" (W. Wojtkiewicz)	1·25	45

531 "Nike" statue

533 Krzczonow (Lublin) Costumes

532 Majdanek Memorial

1969. 4th Congress of Fighters for Freedom and Democracy Association.

1929 **531**	60g. red, black and brown	10	10

1969. Inauguration of Majdanek Memorial.

1930 **532**	40g. black and mauve	10	10

1969. Provincial Costumes. Multicoloured.

1931	40g. Type **533**	10	10
1932	60g. Lowicz (Lodz)	10	10
1933	1z.15 Rozbasrk (Katowice)	10	10
1934	1z.35 Lower Silesia (Wroclaw)	10	10
1935	1z.50 Opoczno (Lodz)	30	10
1936	4z.50 Sacz (Cracow)	60	15
1937	5z. Highlanders, Cracow	45	30
1938	7z. Kurpie (Warsaw)	65	35

534 "Pedestrians Keep Left"

535 "Welding" and I.L.O. Emblem

1969. Road Safety. Multicoloured.

1939	40g. Type **534**	10	10
1940	60g. "Drive Carefully" (horses on road)	10	10
1941	2z.50 "Do Not Dazzle" (cars on road at night)	15	10

1969. 50th Anniv of I.L.O.

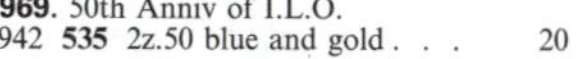

1942 **535**	2z.50 blue and gold	20	10

536 "The Bell-founder"

537 "Angel" (19th-century)

1969. Miniatures from Behem's Code of 1505. Multicoloured.

1943	40g. Type **536**	10	10
1944	60g. "The Painter"	10	10
1945	1z.35 "The Woodcarver"	10	10
1946	1z.55 "The Shoemaker"	20	10
1947	2z.50 "The Cooper"	20	10
1948	3z.40 "The Baker"	20	20
1949	4z.50 "The Tailor"	60	30
1950	7z. "The Bowyer"	1·00	60

1969. Polish Folk Sculpture. Multicoloured.

1951	20g. Type **537**	10	10
1952	40g. "Sorrowful Christ" (19th-century)	10	10
1953	60g. "Sorrowful Christ" (19th-cent) (different)	10	10
1954	2z. "Weeping Woman" (19th-century)	20	10
1955	2z.50 "Adam and Eve" (F. Czajkowski)	20	10
1956	3z.40 "Girl with Birds" (L. Kudla)	30	10
1957	5z.50+1z.50 "Choir" (A. Zegadlo)	75	35
1958	7z.+1z. "Organ-grinder" (Z. Skretowicz)	80	50

Nos. 1957/8 are larger, size 25 × 35 mm.

538 Leopold Staff

1969. Modern Polish Writers.

1959 **538**	40g. black, olive & green	10	10
1960 –	60g. black, red and pink	10	10
1961 –	1z.35 black, deep blue and blue	10	10
1962 –	1z.50 black, violet & lilac	10	10
1963 –	1z.55 black, deep green and green	10	10
1964 –	2z.50 black, deep blue and blue	20	10
1965 –	3z.40 black, brn & flesh	30	25

DESIGNS: 60g. Wladyslaw Broniewski; 1z.35, Leon Kruczkowski; 1z.50, Julian Tuwim; 1z.55, Konstanty Ildefons Galczynski; 2z.50, Maria Dabrowska; 3z.40, Zofia Nalkowska.

539 Nike Monument

1970. 25th Anniv of Liberation of Warsaw.

1966 **539**	60g. multicoloured	20	10

540 Early Printing Works and Colour Dots

1970. Centenary of Printers' Trade Union.

1967 **540**	60g. multicoloured	10	10

541 Mallard

1970. Game Birds. Multicoloured.

1968	40g. Type **541**	10	10
1969	60g. Common pheasant	30	10
1970	1z.15 Eurasian woodcock	20	10
1971	1z.35 Ruff	30	10
1972	1z.50 Wood pigeon	30	10
1973	3z.40 Black grouse	35	10
1974	7z. Grey partridge	1·90	45
1975	8z.50 Western capercaillie	2·75	50

542 Lenin at Desk

1970. Birth Centenary of Lenin.

1976 **542**	40g. grey and red	10	10
1977 –	60g. brown and red	10	10
1978 –	2z.50 black and red	10	10
MS1979	134 × 81 mm. No. 1977 × 4	2·10	45

DESIGNS: 60g. Lenin addressing meeting; 2z.50, Lenin at Party conference.

543 Polish and Russian Soldiers in Berlin

1970. 25th Anniv of Liberation.

1980 **543**	60g. multicoloured	10	10

1970. Tourism (2nd series). As T **523**, but with imprint "PWPW 70". Multicoloured.

1981	60g. Town Hall, Wroclaw (vert)	10	10
1982	60g. View of Opol	10	10
1983	60g. Legnica Castle	10	10
1984	60g. Bolkow Castle	10	10
1985	60g. Town Hall, Brzeg	10	10

544 Polish "Flower"

1970. 25th Anniv of Return of Western Territories.

1986 **544**	60g. red, silver and green	10	10

545 Movement Flag

546 U.P.U. Emblem and New Headquarters

1970. 75th Anniv of Peasant Movement.

1987 **545**	60g. multicoloured	10	10

1970. New U.P.U. Headquarters Building, Berne.

1988 **546**	2z.50 blue and turquoise	20	10

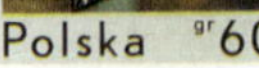

547 Footballers

548 Hand with "Lamp of Learning"

1970. Gornik Zabrze v. Manchester City, Final of European Cup-winners Cup Championship.
1989 **547** 60g. multicoloured . . . 20 10

1970. 150th Anniv of Plock Scientific Society.
1990 **548** 60g. olive, red and black 10 10

549 "Olympic Runners" (from Greek amphora)

1970. 10th Session of Int Olympic Academy.
1991 **549** 60g. red, yellow and black 10 10
1992 – 60g. violet, blue and black 10 10
1993 – 60g. multicoloured . . . 10 10
MS1994 71 × 101 mm. 10z.+5z. multicoloured . . . . 1·90 1·00
DESIGNS: No. 1992, "The Archer"; 1993, Modern runners; **MS**1994, "Horse of Fame" emblem of Polish Olympic Committee.

550 Copernicus (after miniature by Bacciarelli) and Bologna

1970. 500th Birth Anniv (1973) of Copernicus (2nd issue).
1995 **550** 40g. green, orange & lilac 10 10
1996 – 60g. lilac, green & yellow 10 10
1997 – 2z.50 brown, blue & green 35 10
DESIGNS: 60g. Copernicus (after miniature by Lesseur) and Padua; 2z.50, Copernicus (by N. Zinck, after lost Goluchowska portrait) and Ferrara.

551 "Aleksander Orlowski" (self-portrait)

1970. Polish Miniatures. Multicoloured.
1998 20g. Type **551** 10 10
1999 40g. "Jan Matejko" (self-portrait) 10 10
2000 60g. "Stefan Batory" (unknown artist) 10 10
2001 2z. "Maria Leszczynska" (unknown artist) 10 10
2002 2z.50 "Maria Walewska" (Marie-Victorie Jacquetot) 20 10
2003 3z.40 "Tadeusz Kosciuszko" (Jan Rustem) 20 10
2004 5z.50 "Samuel Linde" (G. Landolfi) 65 40
2005 7z. "Michal Oginski" (Nanette Windisch) . . . 1·40 20

552 U.N. Emblem within "Eye"

1970. 25th Anniv of United Nations.
2006 **552** 2z.50 multicoloured . . . 20 10

553 Piano Keyboard and Chopin's Signature

554 Population Pictograph

1970. 8th International Chopin Piano Competition.
2007 **553** 2z.50 black and violet . . 20 10

1970. National Census. Multicoloured.
2008 40g. Type **554** 10 10
2009 60g. Family in "house" . . 10 10

555 Destroyer "Piorun" (½-size illustration)

1970. Polish Warships, World War II.
2010 **555** 40g. brown 10 10
2011 – 60g. black 10 10
2012 – 2z.50 brown 35 10
DESIGNS: 60g. "Orzel" (submarine); 2z.50, H.M.S. "Garland" (destroyer loaned to Polish Navy).

556 "Expressions" (Maria Jarema)

1970. Stamp Day. Contemporary Polish Paintings. Multicoloured.
2013 20g. "The Violin-cellist" (J. Nowosielski) (vert) . . 10 10
2014 40g. "View of Lodz" (B. Liberski) (vert) . . . 10 10
2015 60g. "Studio Concert" (W. Taranczewski) (vert) 10 10
2016 1z.50 "Still Life" (Z. Pronaszko) (vert) . . 10 10
2017 2z. "Hanging-up Washing" (A. Wroblewski) (vert) . . 10 10
2018 3z.40 Type **556** 20 10
2019 4z. "Canal in the Forest" (P. Potworowski) 45 10
2020 8z.50 "The Sun" (W. Strzeminski) 95 10

557 "Luna 16" landing on Moon

558 "Stag" (detail from "Daniel" tapestry)

1970. Moon Landing of "Luna 16".
2021 **557** 2z.50 multicoloured . . . 30 10

1970. Tapestries in Wawel Castle. Multicoloured.
2022 60g. Type **558** 10 10
2023 1z.15 "White Stork" (detail) 30 10
2024 1z.35 "Panther fighting Dragon" 10 10
2025 2z. "Man's Head" (detail, "Deluge" tapestry) . . . 20 10
2026 2z.50 "Child with Bird" (detail, "Adam Tilling the Soil" tapestry) 25 10
2027 4z. "God, Adam and Eve" (detail, "Happiness in Paradise" tapestry) . . . 45 30
2028 4z.50 Royal Monogram tapestry 75 30
MS2029 Two sheets, each 62 × 89 mm. (a) 5z.50 Polish coat-of-arms; (b) 7z.+3z. Monogram and satyrs. Imperf. Set of 2 sheets 2·10 1·25

559 Cadet ship "Dar Pomorza"

1971. Polish Ships. Multicoloured.
2030 40g. Type **559** 10 10
2031 60g. Liner "Stefan Batory" 10 10
2032 1z.15 Ice-breaker "Perkun" 15 10
2033 1z.35 Lifeboat "R-1" . . . 20 10
2034 1z.50 Bulk carrier "Ziemia Szczecinska" 30 10
2035 2z.50 Tanker "Beskidy" . . 30 10
2036 5z. Freighter "Hel" 65 20
2037 8z.50 Ferry "Gryf" . . . . 1·40 50

560 Checiny Castle

1971. Polish Castles. Multicoloured.
2038 20g. Type **560** 10 10
2039 40g. Wisnicz 10 10
2040 60g. Bedzin 10 10
2041 2z. Ogrodzieniec 15 10
2042 2z.50 Niedzica 15 10
2043 3z.40 Kwidzyn 35 10
2044 4z. Pieskowa Skala 35 10
2045 8z.50 Lidzbark Warminski 90 30

561 Battle of Pouilly, J. Dabrowski and W. Wroblewski

1971. Centenary of Paris Commune.
2046 **561** 60g. brown, blue and red 10 10

562 Plantation

563 "Bishop Marianos"

1971. Forestry Management. Multicoloured.
2047 40g. Type **562** 10 10
2048 60g. Forest (27 × 47 mm) . . 10 10
2049 1z.50 Tree-felling 20 10

1971. Fresco. Discoveries made by Polish Expedition at Faras, Nubia. Multicoloured.
2050 40g. Type **563** 10 10
2051 60g. "St. Anne" 10 10
2052 1z.15 "Archangel Michael" 10 10
2053 1z.35 "The Hermit, Anamon" 10 10
2054 1z.50 "Head of Archangel Michael" 10 10
2055 4z.50 "Evangelists' Cross" 35 10
2056 5z. "Christ protecting a nobleman" 60 20
2057 7z. "Archangel Michael" (half-length) 75 45

564 Revolutionaries

1971. 50th Anniv of Silesian Insurrection.
2058 **564** 60g. brown and gold . . . 10 10
MS2059 108 × 106 mm. No. 2058 × 3 . . . . 2·10 95

565 "Soldiers"

1971. 25th Anniv of UNICEF Children's Drawings. Multicoloured.
2060 20g. "Peacock" (vert) . . . 10 10
2061 40g. Type **565** 10 10
2062 60g. "Lady Spring" (vert) 10 10
2063 2z. "Cat and Ball" 10 10
2064 2z.50 "Flowers in Jug" (vert) 20 10
2065 3z.40 "Friendship" 30 10
2066 5z.50 "Clown" (vert) . . . 70 30
2067 7z. "Strange Planet" 80 35

566 Fair Emblem

567 Copernicus's House, Torun

1971. 40th International Fair, Poznan.
2068 **566** 60g. multicoloured . . . 10 10

1971. 500th Birth Anniv (1973) of Copernicus (3rd issue). Multicoloured.
2069 40g. Type **567** 10 10
2070 60g. Collegium Naius, Jagiellonian University, Cracow (horiz) 10 10
2071 2z.50 Olsztyn Castle (horiz) 20 10
2072 4z. Frombork Cathedral . . 70 20

568 Folk Art Pattern

569 "Head of Worker" (X. Dunikowski)

1971. Folk Art. "Paper Cut-outs" showing various patterns.
2073 **568** 20g. black, green and blue 10 10
2074 – 40g. blue, green & cream 10 10
2075 – 60g. brown, blue and grey 10 10
2076 – 1z.15 purple, brn & buff 10 10
2077 – 1z.35 green, red & yellow 10 10

1971. Modern Polish Sculpture. Multicoloured.
2078 40g. Type **569** 10 10
2079 40g. "Foundryman" (X. Dunikowski) 10 10
2080 60g. "Miners" (M. Wiecek) 10 10
2081 60g. "Harvester" (S. Horno-Poplawski) 10 10
MS2082 158 × 85 mm. Nos. 2078/81 2·40 1·25

570 Congress Emblem and Computer Tapes

1971. 6th Polish Technical Congress, Warsaw.
2083 **570** 60g. violet and red . . . 10 10

571 "Angel" (J. Mehoffer)

573 PZL P-11C Fighters

572 "Mrs. Fedorowicz" (W. Pruszkowski)

1971. Stained Glass Windows. Multicoloured.
2084 20g. Type **571** 10 10
2085 40g. "Lillies" (S. Wyspianski) 10 10
2086 60g. "Iris" (S. Wyspianski) 10 10
2087 1z.35 "Apollo" (S. Wyspianski) 10 10
2088 1z.55 "Two Wise Men" (14th-century) 10 10
2089 3z.40 "The Flight into Egypt" (14th-century) . . 30 10
2090 5z.50 "Jacob" (14th-century) 50 10
2091 8z.50+4z. "Madonna" (15th-century) 80 10

1971. Contemporary Art from National Museum, Cracow. Multicoloured.
2092 40g. Type **572** 10 10
2093 50g. "Woman with Book" (T. Czyzeski) 10 10
2094 60g. "Girl with Chrysanthemums" (O. Boznanska) 10 10
2095 2z.50 "Girl in Red Dress" (J. Pankiewicz) (horiz) . . 10 10
2096 3z.40 "Reclining Nude" (L. Chwistek) (horiz) . . 20 10
2097 4z.50 "Strange Garden" (J. Mehoffer) 35 10
2098 5z. "Wife in White Hat" (Z. Pronaszko) 45 10
2099 7z.+1z. "Seated Nude" (W. Weiss) 65 45

1971. Polish Aircraft of World War II. Mult.
2100 90g. Type **573** 10 10
2101 1z.50 PZL 23A Karas fighters 20 10
2102 3z.40 PZL P-37 Los bomber 30 20

574 Royal Castle, Warsaw (pre-1939)

1971. Reconstruction of Royal Castle, Warsaw.
2103 **574** 60g. black, red and gold 10 10

575 Astronauts in Moon Rover

576 "Lunokhod 1"

1971. Moon Flight of "Apollo 15".
2104 **575** 2z.50 multicoloured . . . 45 10
MS2105 122×157 mm. No. 2104 ×6 plus 2 stamp-size se-tenant labels, showing Space scenes 3·75 2·75

1971. Moon Flight of "Lunik 17" and "Lunokhod 1".
2106 **576** 2z.50 multicoloured . . . 45 10
MS2107 158×118 mm. No. 2106 ×6 plus 2 stamp-size se-tenant labels, showing Space scenes 3·75 1·90

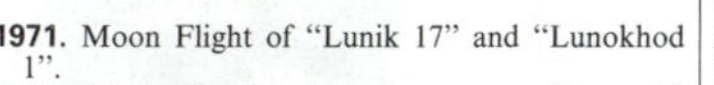

577 Worker at Wheel

578 Ship-building

1971. 6th Polish United Workers' Party Congress.
(a) Party Posters.
2108 **577** 60g. red, blue and grey 10 10
2109 60g. red and grey (Worker's head) . . . 10 10
(b) Industrial Development. Each in gold and red.
2110 60g. Type **578** 10 10
2111 60g. Building construction 10 10
2112 60g. Combine-harvester . . 10 10
2113 60g. Motor-car production 10 10
2114 60g. Pit-head 10 10
2115 60g. Petro-chemical plant . . 10 10
MS2116 102×115 mm. Nos. 2110/15 1·10 80

579 "Prunus cerasus"

1971. Flowers of Trees and Shrubs. Multicoloured.
2117 10g. Type **579** 10 10
2118 20g. "Malusniedzwetzskyana" 10 10
2119 40g. "Pyrus L." 10 10
2120 60g. "Prunus persica" . . . 10 10
2121 1z.15 "Magnolia kobus" . . 10 10
2122 1z.35 "Crategus oxyacantha" 10 10
2123 2z.50 "Malus M." 10 10
2124 3z.40 "Aesculus carnea" . . 20 10
2125 5z. "Robinia pseudacacia" 75 20
2126 8z.50 "Prunus avium" . . . 1·40 50

580 "Worker" (sculpture, J. Januszkiewicz)

1972. 30th Anniv of Polish Workers' Coalition.
2127 **580** 60g. black and red . . . 10 10

581 Luge

1972. Winter Olympic Games, Sapporo, Japan. Multicoloured.
2128 40g. Type **581** 10 10
2129 60g. Slalom (vert) 10 10
2130 1z.65 Biathlon (vert) 20 10
2131 2z.50 Ski jumping 35 25
MS2132 85×68 mm. 10z.+5z. Downhill skiing . . . . 2·10 1·25

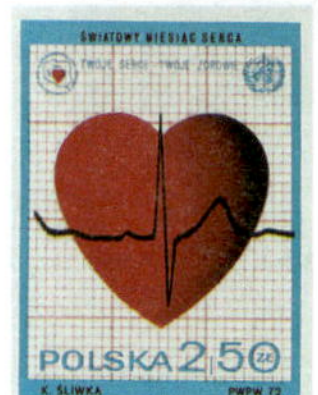

582 "Heart" and Cardiogram Trace

583 Running

1972. World Heart Month.
2133 **582** 2z.50 multicoloured . . . 20 10

1972. Olympic Games, Munich. Multicoloured.
2134 20g. Type **583** 10 10
2135 30g. Archery 10 10
2136 40g. Boxing 10 10
2137 60g. Fencing 10 10
2138 2z.50 Wrestling 10 10
2139 3z.40 Weightlifting 10 10
2140 5z. Cycling 60 10
2141 8z.50 Shooting 95 20
MS2142 70×80 mm. 10z.+5z. As 30g. . . . . 1·40 75

584 Cyclists

585 Polish War Memorial, Berlin

1972. 25th International Peace Cycle Race.
2143 **584** 60g. multicoloured . . . 10 10

1972. "Victory Day, 1945".
2144 **585** 60g. green 10 10

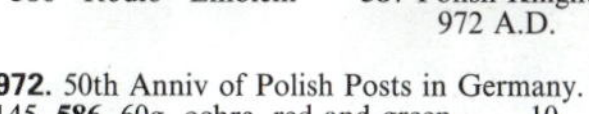
586 "Rodlo" Emblem

587 Polish Knight of 972 A.D.

1972. 50th Anniv of Polish Posts in Germany.
2145 **586** 60g. ochre, red and green 10 10

1972. Millenary of Battle of Cedynia.
2146 **587** 60g. multicoloured . . . 10 10

588 Cheetah

1972. Zoo Animals. Multicoloured.
2147 20g. Type **588** 10 10
2148 40g. Giraffe (vert) 20 10
2149 60g. Toco toucan 30 10
2150 1z.35 Chimpanzee 20 10
2151 1z.65 Common gibbon . . . 30 10
2152 3z.40 Crocodile 35 10
2153 4z. Red kangaroo 65 10
2154 4z.50 Tiger (vert) . . . . . 2·75 60
2155 7z. Mountain zebra . . . . 3·00 1·25

589 L. Warynski. (founder)

590 F. Dzerzhinsky

1972. 90th Anniv of Proletarian Party.
2156 **589** 60g. multicoloured . . . 10 10

1972. 95th Birth Anniv of Feliks Dzerzhinsky (Russian politician).
2157 **590** 60g. black and red . . . 10 10

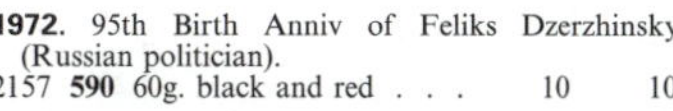

591 Global Emblem

592 Scene from "In Barracks" (ballet)

1972. 25th Int Co-operative Federation Congress.
2158 **591** 60g. multicoloured . . . 10 10

1972. Death Centenary of Stanislaus Moniuszko (composer). Scenes from Works.
2159 **592** 10g. violet and gold . . 10 10
2160 – 20g. black and gold . . 10 10
2161 – 40g. green and gold . . 10 10
2162 – 60g. blue and gold . . . 10 10
2163 – 1z.15 blue and gold . . . 10 10
2164 – 1z.35 blue and gold . . . 10 10
2165 – 1z.55 green and gold . . 20 10
2166 – 2z.50 brown and gold . . 20 10
DESIGNS: 20g. "The Countess" (opera); 40g. "The Haunted Manor" (opera); 60g. "Halka" (opera); 1z.15, "New Don Quixote" (ballet); 1z.35, "Verbum Nobile"; 1z.55, "Ideal" (operetta); 2z.50, "Pariah" (opera).

593 "Copernicus the Astronomer"

1972. 500th Birth Anniv (1973) of Nicolas Copernicus. (4th issue).
2167 **593** 40g. black and blue . . . 10 10
2168 – 60g. black and orange 10 10
2169 – 2z.50 black and red . . . 10 10
2170 – 3z.40 black and green . . 15 10
MS2171 62×102 mm. 10z.+5z. multicoloured . . . . 2·75 1·40
DESIGNS: 60g. Copernicus and Polish eagle; 2z.50, Copernicus and Medal; 3z.40, Copernicus and page of book; VERT: (29×48 mm)—10z.+5z. Copernicus charting the planets.

594 "The Amazon" (P. Michalowski)

1972. Stamp Day. Polish Paintings. Multicoloured.
2172 30g. Type **594** 10 10
2173 40g. "Ostafi Laskiewicz" (J. Metejko) 10 10
2174 60g. "Summer Idyll" (W. Gerson) 10 10
2175 2z. "The Neapolitan Woman" (A. Kotsis) . . 10 10
2176 2z.50 "Girl Bathing" (P. Szyndler) 10 10
2177 3z.40 "The Princess of Thum" (A. Grottger) . . 10 10
2178 4z. "Rhapsody" (S. Wyspianski) 15 30
2179 8z.50+4z. "Young Woman" (J. Malczewski) (horiz) . . 35 35

1972. Nos. 1578/9 surch.
2180 50g. on 40g. brown 10 10
2181 90g. on 40g. brown 10 10
2182 1z. on 40g. brown 10 10
2183 1z.50 on 60g. orange . . . 10 10
2184 2z.70 on 40g. brown 15 10
2185 4z. on 60g. orange 30 10
2186 4z.50 on 60g. orange . . . 30 10
2187 4z.90 on 60g. orange . . . 45 10

596 "The Little Soldier" (E. Piwowarski)

1972. Children's Health Centre.
2188 **596** 60g. black and pink . . 10 10

597 "Royal Castle, Warsaw". (E. J. Dahlberg, 1656)

598 Chalet, Chocholowska Valley

1972. Restoration of Royal Castle, Warsaw.
2189 **597** 60g. black, violet and blue 10 10

1972. Tourism. Mountain Chalets. Multicoloured.
2190 40g. Type **598** 10 10
2191 60g. Hala Ornak (horiz) . . 10 10
2192 1z.55 Hala Gasienicowa . . 10 10
2193 1z.65 Valley of Five Lakes (horiz) 15 10
2194 2z.50 Morskie Oko 30 10

599 Trade Union Banners

600 Congress Emblem

1972. 7th Polish Trade Union Congresses.
2195 **599** 60g. multicoloured . . . 10 10

1972. 5th Socialist Youth Union Congress.
2196 **600** 60g. multicoloured . . . 10 10

601 Japanese Azalea

1972. Flowering Shrubs. Multicoloured.
2197 40g. Type **601** 10 10
2198 50g. Alpine rose 10 10
2199 60g. Pomeranian honeysuckle 10 10
2200 1z.65 Chinese quince 10 10
2201 2z.50 Korean cranberry . . 25 10
2202 3z.40 Pontic azalea 35 10
2203 4z. Delavay's white syringa 75 20
2204 8z.50 Common lilac ("Massena") . . . . . . 1·60 65

602 Piast Knight (10th-century)

603 Copernicus

1972. Polish Cavalry Through the Ages. Mult.
2205 20g. Type **602** 10 10
2206 40g. 13th-century knight . . 10 10
2207 60g. Knight of Wladyslaw Jagiello's Army (15th-century) (horiz) . . 10 10
2208 1z.35 17th-century hussar . . 10 10
2209 4z. Lancer of National Guard (18th-century) . . 50 10
2210 4z.50 "Congress Kingdom" cavalry officer 50 10
2211 5z. Trooper of Light Cavalry (1939) (horiz) . . 1·10 10
2212 7z. Trooper of People's Army (1945) . . . . . . 1·10 60

1972. 500th Birth Anniv (1973) of Copernicus (5th issue).
2213 **603** 1z. brown 15 10
2214 1z.50 ochre 20 10

604 Couple with Hammer and Sickle

605 "Copernicus as Young Man" (Bacciarelli)

1972. 50th Anniv of U.S.S.R. Multicoloured.
2215 40g. Type **604** 10 10
2216 60g. Red star and globe . . 10 10

1973. 500th Birth Anniv of Copernicus (6th issue). Multicoloured.
2217 1z. Type **605** 10 10
2218 1z.50 "Copernicus" (anon) 10 10
2219 2z.70 "Copernicus" (Zinck Nor) 20 10
2220 4z. "Copernicus" (from Strasbourg clock) 45 30
2221 4z.90 "Copernicus" (Jan Matejko) (horiz) 60 30

606 Coronation Sword

607 Statue of Lenin

1973. Polish Art. Multicoloured.
2222 50g. Type **606** 10 10
2223 1z. Kruzlowa Madonna (detail) 10 10
2224 1z. Armour of hussar . . . 10 10
2225 1z.50 Carved head from Wavel Castle 10 10
2226 1z.50 Silver cockerel 10 10
2227 2z.70 Armorial eagle 30 10
2228 4z.90 Skarbimierz Madonna 60 35
2229 8z.50 "Portrait of Tenczynski" (anon) . . . 95 60

1973. Unveiling of Lenin's Statue, Nowa Huta.
2230 **607** 1z. multicoloured 10 10

608 Coded Letter

1973. Introduction of Postal Codes.
2231 **608** 1z. multicoloured 10 10

609 Wolf

1973. International Hunting Council Congress and 50th Anniv of Polish Hunting Association. Game Animals. Multicoloured.
2232 50g. Type **609** 10 10
2233 1z. Mouflon 10 10
2234 1z.50 Elk 10 10
2235 2z.70 Western capercaillie 10 10
2236 3z. Roe deer 10 10
2237 4z.50 Lynx 55 10
2238 4z.90 Red deer . . . . . . 1·10 35
2239 5z. Wild boar . . . . . . 1·25 45

610 "Salyut"

611 Open Book and Flame

1973. Cosmic Research. Multicoloured.
2240 4z.90 Type **610** 35 30
2241 4z.90 "Copernicus" (U.S. satellite) 35 30

1973. 2nd Polish Science Congress, Warsaw.
2242 **611** 1z.50 multicoloured . . . 10 10

612 Ancient Seal of Poznan

613 M. Nowotko

1973. "Polska 73" Philatelic Exhibition, Poznan. Multicoloured.
2243 1z. Type **612** 10 10
2244 1z.50 Tombstone of N. Tomicki 10 10
2245 2z.70 Kalisz paten 20 10
2246 4z. Bronze gates, Gniezno Cathedral (horiz) 30 10
MS2247 91 × 66 mm. 10z.+5z. purple and olive . . . . 1·50 95
MS2248 91 × 66 mm. 10z.+5z. purple and lilac . . . . 6·00 1·10

1973. 80th Birth Anniv of Marceli Nowotko (party leader).
2249 **613** 1z.50 black and red . . . 10 10

614 Cherry Blossom

1973. Protection of the Environment. Mult.
2250 50g. Type **614** 10 10
2251 90g. Cattle in meadow . . . 10 10
2252 1z. White stork on nest . . 30 10
2253 1z.50 Pond life 10 10
2254 2z.70 Meadow flora 15 10
2255 4z.90 Ocean fauna 35 10
2256 5z. Forest life . . . . 1·90 30
2257 6z.50 Agricultural produce 1·25 50

615 Motor-cyclist

1973. World Speedway Race Championships, Chorzow.
2258 **615** 1z.50 multicoloured . . . 10 10

616 "Copernicus" (M. Bacciarelli)

1973. Stamp Day.
2259 **616** 4z.+2z. multicoloured . . 45 30

617 Tank

1973. 30th Anniv of Polish People's Army. Mult.
2260 1z. Type **617** 10 10
2261 1z. Mikoyan Gurevich MiG-21D airplane 10 10
2262 1z.50 Guided missile 10 10
2263 1z.50 "Puck" (missile boat) 15 10

618 G. Piramowicz and Title Page

1973. Bicent of Nat Educational Commission.
2264 **618** 1z. brown and yellow . . 10 10
2265 – 1z.50 green, & light green 10 10
DESIGN: 1z.50, J. Sniadecki, H. Kollataj and J. U. Niemcewicz.

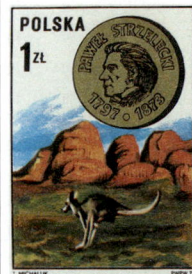

619 Pawel Strzelecki (explorer) and Red Kangaroo

620 Polish Flag

1973. Polish Scientists. Multicoloured.
2266 1z. Type **619** 10 10
2267 1z. Henryk Arctowski (Polar explorer) and Adelie penguins 20 10
2268 1z.50 Stefan Rogozinkski (explorer) and "Lucy-Margaret" (schooner) . . 15 10
2269 1z.50 Benedykt Dybowski (zoologist) and sable, Lake Baikal 10 10
2270 2z. Bronislaw Malinowski (anthropologist) and New Guinea dancers 10 10
2271 2z.70 Stefan Drzewiecki (oceanographer) and submarine 20 10
2272 3z. Edward Strasburger (botanist) and classified plants 20 10
2273 8z. Ignacy Domeyko (geologist) and Chilean desert landscape 80 30

1973. 25th Anniv of Polish United Workers' Party.
2274 **620** 1z.40 red, blue and gold 10 10

621 Jelcz-Berliet Coach

1973. Polish Motor Vehicles. Multicoloured.
2275 50g. Type **621** 10 10
2276 90g. Jelcz "316" truck . . . 10 10
2277 1z. Polski-Fiat "126p" saloon 10 10
2278 1z.50 Polski-Fiat "125p" saloon and mileage records 10 10
2279 4z. Nysa "M-521" utility van 30 25
2280 4z.50 Star "660" truck . . . 60 30

622 Iris

623 Cottage, Kurpie

1974. Flowers. Drawings by S. Wyspianski.
2281 **622** 50g. purple 10 10
2282 – 1z. green 10 10
2283 – 1z.50 red 10 10
2284 – 3z. violet 30 10
2285 – 4z. blue 30 10
2286 – 4z.50 green 45 10
FLOWERS: 1z. Dandelion; 1z.50, Rose; 3z. Thistle; 4z. Cornflower; 4z.50, Clover.

1974. Wooden Architecture. Multicoloured.
2287 1z. Type **623** 10 10
2288 1z.50 Church, Sekowa . . . 10 10
2289 4z. Town Hall, Sulmierzycc 20 10
2290 4z.50 Church, Lachowice . . 30 10
2291 4z.90 Windmill, Sobienie Jeziory 45 20
2292 5z. Orthodox Church, Ulucz 50 20

624 19th-century Mail Coach
625 Cracow Motif

1974. Centenary of Universal Postal Union.
2293 **624** 1z.50 multicoloured . . . 10 10

1974. "SOCPHILEX IV" Int Stamp Exn, Katowice. Regional Floral Embroideries. Multicoloured.
2294 50g. Type **625** 10 10
2295 1z.50 Lowicz motif 10 10
2296 4z. Silesian motif 20 10
MS2297 69 × 71 mm. No. 2296 × 3 1·10 30

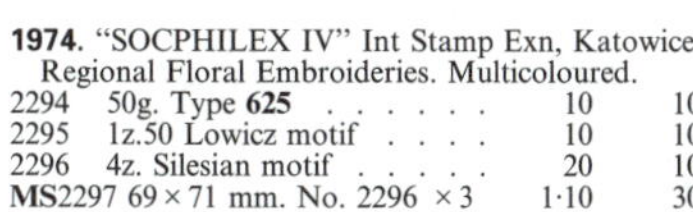

626 Association Emblem
627 Soldier and Dove

1974. 5th Congress of Fighters for Freedom and Democracy Association, Warsaw.
2298 **626** 1z.50 red 10 10

1974. 29th Anniv of Victory over Fascism in Second World War.
2299 **627** 1z.50 multicoloured . . . 10 10

628 "Comecon" Headquarters, Moscow

1974. 25th Anniv of Council for Mutual Economic Aid.
2300 **628** 1z.50 brown, red & blue 10 10

629 World Cup Emblem

1974. World Cup Football Championship, West Germany. Multicoloured.
2301 4z.90 Type **629** 25 15
2302 4z.90 Players and Olympic Gold Medal of 1972 . . . 25 15
MS2303 116 × 83 mm. Nos. 2301/2 10·50 9·00
See also No. MS2315.

630 Model of 16th-century Galleon
631 Title page of "Chess" by J. Kochanowski

1974. Sailing Ships. Multicoloured.
2304 1z. Type **630** 10 10
2305 1z.50 Sloop "Dal" (1934) 10 10
2306 2z.70 Yacht "Opty" (Teliga's circumnavigation, 1969) 10 10
2307 4z. Cadet ship "Dar Pomorza", 1972 . . . . . 40 10
2308 4z.90 Yacht "Polonez" (Baranowski's circumnavigation, 1973) 55 25

1974. 10th Inter-Chess Festival, Lublin. Mult.
2309 1z. Type **631** 10 15
2310 1z.50 "Education" (18th-century engraving, D. Chodowiecki) 20 15

632 Lazienkowska Road Junction

1974. Opening of Lazienkowska Flyover.
2311 **632** 1z.50 multicoloured . . . 15 15

633 Face and Map of Poland
634 Strawberries

1974. 30th Anniv of Polish People's Republic.
2312 **633** 1z.50 black, gold and red 15 10
2313 – 1z.50 multicoloured (silver background) . . 15 10
2314 – 1z.50 multicoloured (red background) 15 10
DESIGN—31 × 43 mm: Nos. 2313/14, Polish "Eagle".

1974. Poland–Third Place in World Cup Football Championship. Sheet 107 × 121 mm containing four stamps as No. 2301, but with inscr in silver instead of black, and two labels.
MS2315 **629** 4z.90 × 4 multicoloured 3·00 1·90

1974. 19th International Horticultural Congress, Warsaw. Fruits, Vegetables and Flowers. Mult.
2316 50g. Type **634** 10 10
2317 90g. Blackcurrants 10 10
2318 1z. Apples 10 10
2319 1z.50 Cucumbers 20 10
2320 2z.70 Tomatoes 30 10
2321 4z.50 Green peas 75 10
2322 4z.90 Pansies . . . . 1·10 20
2323 5z. Nasturtiums . . . . . . 1·50 30

635 Civic Militia and Security Service Emblem

636 "Child in Polish Costume" (L. Orlowski)

1974. 30th Anniv of Polish Civic Militia and Security Service.
2324 **635** 1z.50 multicoloured . . . 10 10

1974. Stamp Day. "The Child in Polish Costume" Painting. Multicoloured.
2325 50g. Type **636** 10 10
2326 90g. "Girl with Pigeon" (anon) 10 10
2327 1z. "Portrait of a Girl" (S. Wyspianski) 10 10
2328 1z.50 "The Orphan from Poronin" (W. Slewinski) 10 10
2329 3z. "Peasant Boy" (K. Sichulski) 20 10
2330 4z.50 "Florence Page" (A. Gierymski) 35 10
2331 4z.90 "Tadeusz and Dog" (P. Michalowski) 45 30
2332 6z.50 "Boy with Doe" (A. Kotsis) 60 35

637 "The Crib", Cracow

1974. Polish Art. Multicoloured.
2333 1z. Type **637** 10 10
2334 1z.50 "The Flight to Egypt" (15th-century polyptych) 10 10
2335 2z. "King Sigismund III Vasa" (16th-century miniature) 20 10
2336 4z. "King Jan Olbracht" (16th-century title-page) 75 30

638 Angler and Fish
639 "Pablo Neruda" (O. Guayasamin)

1974. Polish Folklore. 16th-century Woodcuts (1st series).
2337 **638** 1z. black 10 10
2338 – 1z.50 blue 10 10
DESIGN: 1z.50, Hunter and wild animals.
See also Nos. 2525/6.

1974. 70th Birth Anniv of Pablo Neruda (Chilean poet).
2339 **639** 1z.50 multicoloured . . . 10 10

640 "Nike" Memorial and National Opera House

1975. 30th Anniv of Warsaw Liberation.
2340 **640** 1z.50 multicoloured . . . 10 10

641 Male Lesser Kestrel
642 Broken Barbed Wire

1975. Birds of Prey. Multicoloured.
2341 1z. Type **641** 25 10
2342 1z. Lesser kestrel (female) 25 10
2343 1z.50 Western red-footed falcon (male) 25 10
2344 1z.50 Western red-footed falcon (female) 25 10
2345 2z. Northern hobby 30 10
2346 3z. Common kestrel 55 10
2347 4z. Merlin . . . . 1·40 75
2348 8z. Peregrine falcon . . . . 2·10 1·50

1975. 30th Anniv of Auschwitz Concentration Camp Liberation.
2349 **642** 1z.50 black and red . . . 10 10

643 Hurdling

1975. 6th European Indoor Athletic Championships, Katowice. Multicoloured.
2350 1z. Type **643** 10 10
2351 1z.50 Pole vault 10 10
2352 4z. Triple jump 30 10
2353 4z.90 Running 30 10
MS2354 72 × 63 mm. 10z.+5z. green and silver (Montreal Olympics emblem) (26 × 31 mm) . . . . 1·90 90

644 "St. Anne" (Veit Stoss)

1975. "Arphila 1975" International Stamp Exhibition, Paris.
2355 **644** 1z.50 multicoloured . . . 10 10

645 Globe and "Radio Waves"

1975. International Amateur Radio Union Conference, Warsaw.
2356 **645** 1z.50 multicoloured . . . 10 10

646 Stone, Pine and Tatra Mountains

647 Hands holding Tulips and Rifle

1975. Centenary of Mountain Guides' Association. Multicoloured.
2357 1z. Type **646** 10 10
2358 1z. Gentians and Tatra Mountains 10 10
2359 1z.50 Sudety Mountains (horiz) 10 10
2360 1z.50 Branch of yew (horiz) 10 10
2361 4z. Beskidy Mountains . . . 30 15
2362 4z. Arnica blossoms 30 10

1975. 30th Anniv of Victory over Fascism.
2363 **647** 1z.50 multicoloured . . . 15 10

648 Flags of Member Countries

1975. 20th Anniv of Warsaw Treaty Organization.
2364 **648** 1z.50 multicoloured . . . 10 10

649 Hens

1975. 26th European Zoo-technical Federation Congress, Warsaw. Multicoloured.

2365	50g. Type **649**	10	10
2366	1z. Geese	10	10
2367	1z.50 Cattle	10	10
2368	2z. Cow	10	10
2369	3z. Wielkopolska horse	30	20
2370	4z. Pure-bred Arab horses	30	20
2371	4z.50 Pigs	1·10	80
2372	5z. Sheep	1·75	1·10

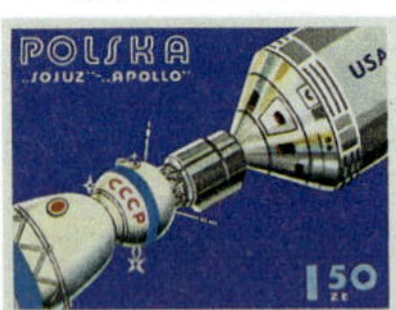

650 "Apollo" and "Soyuz" Spacecraft linked

1975. "Apollo–Soyuz" Space Project. Mult.

2373	1z.50 Type **650**	10	10
2374	4z.90 "Apollo" spacecraft	45	10
2375	4z.90 "Soyuz" spacecraft	45	25
MS2376	119 × 156 mm. Nos. 2373 × 2, 2374 × 2 and 2375 × 2	5·25	3·25

651 Organization Emblem

1975. National Health Protection Fund.

2377	**651** 1z.50 blue, black & silver	10	10

652 U.N. Emblem

1975. 30th Anniv of U.N.O.

2378	**652** 4z. multicoloured	30	10

653 Polish Flag within "E" for Europe

1975. European Security and Co-operation Conference, Helsinki.

2379	**653** 4z. red, blue and black	30	25

654 "Bolek and Lolek"

1975. Children's Television Characters. Mult.

2380	50g. Type **654**	10	15
2381	1z. "Jacek" and "Agatka"	10	15
2382	1z.50 "Reksio" (dog)	10	15
2383	4z. "Telesfor" (dragon)	45	15

655 Institute Emblem

656 Women's Faces

1975. 40th Session of International Statistics Institute.

2384	**655** 1z.50 multicoloured	10	10

1975. International Women's Year.

2385	**656** 1z.50 multicoloured	10	10

657 Albatros Biplane

1975. 50th Anniv of First Polish Airmail Stamps. Multicoloured.

2386	2z.40 Type **657**	15	15
2387	4z.90 Ilyushin Il-62 airplane	40	15

658 "Mary and Margaret" and Polish Settlers

659 Frederic Chopin

1975. Bicentenary of American Revolution. Poles in American Life. Multicoloured.

2388	1z. Type **658**	15	10
2389	1z.50 Polish glass-works, Jamestown	10	10
2390	2z.70 Helena Modrzejewska (actress)	10	10
2391	4z. K. Pulaski (soldier)	25	10
2392	6z.40 T. Kosciuzko (soldier)	60	30
MS2393	117 × 102 mm. 4z.90 Washington; 4z.90 Kosciuszko; 4z.90 Pulaski	1·10	70

1975. 9th International Chopin Piano Competition.

2394	**659** 1z.50 black, lilac & gold	10	20

660 "Self-portrait"

661 Market Place, Kazimierz Dolny

1975. Stamp Day. Birth Centenary of Xawery Dunikowski (sculptor). Multicoloured.

2395	50g. Type **660**	10	10
2396	1z. "Breath"	10	10
2397	1z.50 "Maternity"	15	10
2398	8z.+4z. "Silesian Insurrectionists"	90	35

1975. European Architectural Heritage Year.

2399	**661** 1z. green	10	10
2400	– 1z.50 brown	10	10

DESIGN—VERT: 1z.50, Town Hall, Zamosc.

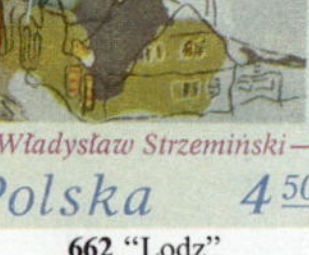

662 "Lodz" (W. Strzeminski)

664 Symbolized Figure "7"

663 Henry IV's Eagle Gravestone Head (14th-century)

1975. "Lodz 75" National Stamp Exhibition.

2401	**662** 4z.50 multicoloured	30	20
MS2402	80 × 101 mm. No. 2401	95	65

1975. Piast Dynasty of Silesia.

2403	**663** 1z. green	10	10
2404	– 1z.50 brown	10	10
2405	– 4z. violet	25	10

DESIGNS: 1z.50, Seal of Prince Boleslaw of Legnica; 4z. Coin of last Prince, Jerzy Wilhelm.

1975. 7th Congress of Polish United Workers Party.

2406	**664** 1z. multicoloured	10	10
2407	– 1z.50 red, blue and silver	10	10

DESIGN: 1z.50, Party initials "PZPR".

665 Ski Jumping

1976. Winter Olympic Games, Innsbruck. Mult.

2408	50g. Type **665**	10	10
2409	1z. Ice hockey	10	10
2410	1z.50 Skiing	10	10
2411	2z. Skating	10	10
2412	4z. Tobogganing	30	10
2413	6z.40 Biathlon	40	30

666 Richard Trevithick and his Locomotive, 1803

1976. History of the Railway Locomotive. Mult.

2414	50g. Type **666**	10	10
2415	1z. Murray and Blenkinsop's steam locomotive and carriage, 1810	10	10
2416	1z.50 George Stephenson and his locomotive "Rocket", 1829	10	10
2417	1z.50 Polish "Universal" electric locomotive No. ET22-001, 1969	10	10
2418	2z.70 Robert Stephenson and his locomotive "North Star", 1837	10	10
2419	3z. Joseph Harrison and his locomotive, 1840	15	10
2420	4z.50 Locomotive "Thomas Rogers", 1855, U.S.A.	75	45
2421	4z.90 A. Xiezopolski and Series Ok22 steam locomotive, 1922	75	45

667 Flags of Member Countries

1976. 20th Anniv of Institute for Nuclear Research (C.M.E.A.).

2422	**667** 1z.50 multicoloured	15	10

668 Early Telephone, Satellite and Radar

1976. Telephone Centenary.

2423	**668** 1z.50 multicoloured	10	10

669 Jantar Glider

670 Player

1976. Air. Contemporary Aviation.

2424	**669** 5z. blue	35	10
2425	– 10z. brown	75	10
2425a	– 20z. olive	1·50	10
2425b	– 50z. lake	3·50	60

DESIGN: 10z. Mil Mi-6 helicopter; 20z. PZL-106A agricultural airplane; 50z. PZL-Mielec TS-11 Iskra jet trainer over Warsaw Castle.

1976. World Ice Hockey Championships, Katowice. Multicoloured.

2426	1z. Type **670**	10	10
2427	1z.50 Player (different)	10	10

671 Polish U.N. Soldier

1976. Polish Troops in U.N. Sinai Force.

2428	**671** 1z.50 multicoloured	10	10

672 "Glory to the Sappers" (S. Kulon)

673 "Interphil 76"

1976. War Memorials. Multicoloured.

2429	1z. Type **672**	10	10
2430	1z. 1st Polish Army Monument, Sandau, Laba (B. Koniuszy)	10	10

1976. "Interphil '76" Int Stamp Exn, Philadelphia.

2431	**673** 8z.40 multicoloured	55	30

674 Wielkopolski Park and Tawny Owl

1976. National Parks. Multicoloured.

2432	90g. Type **674**	30	10
2433	1z. Wolinski Park and white-tailed sea eagle	30	10
2434	1z.50 Slowinski Park and seagull	35	10
2435	4z.50 Bieszczadzki Park and lynx	30	10
2436	5z. Ojcowski Park and bat	30	20
2437	6z. Kampinoski Park and elk	35	30

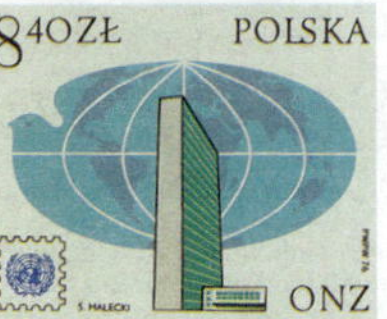

675 Peace Dove within Globe

1976. 25th Anniv of U.N. Postal Administration.

2438	**675** 8z.40 multicoloured	60	25

676 Fencing

677 National Theatre

1976. Olympic Games, Montreal. Multicoloured.

2439	50g. Type **676**	10	10
2440	1z. Cycling	10	10
2441	1z.50 Football	10	10
2442	4z.20 Boxing	30	10
2443	6z.90 Weightlifting	55	15
2444	8z.40 Athletics	60	25
MS2445	78 × 94 mm. 10z.+5z. black and red (Volleyball) (23 × 29 mm)	1·50	85

1976. Cent of National Theatre, Poznan.

2446	**677** 1z.50 green and orange	15	10

678 Aleksander Czekanowski and Baikal Landscape

679 "Sphinx"

1976. Death Centenary of Aleksander Czekanowski (geologist).

2447	**678** 1z.50 multicoloured	15	15

1976. Stamp Day. Corinthian Vase Paintings (7th century B.C.). Multicoloured.

2448	1z. Type **679**	10	10
2449	1z.50 "Siren" (horiz)	10	10
2450	2z. "Lion" (horiz)	15	10
2451	4z.20 "Bull" (horiz)	30	10
2452	4z.50 "Goat" (horiz)	30	25
2453	8z.+4z. "Sphinx" (different)	1·00	45

680 Warszawa "M 20"

1976. 25th Anniv of Zeran Motor-car Factory, Warsaw. Multicoloured.

2454	1z. Type **680**	10	10
2455	1z.50 Warszawa "223"	10	10
2456	2z. Syrena "104"	15	10
2457	4z.90 Polski - Fiat "125P"	40	15
MS2458	137 × 109 mm. Nos. 2454/7	1·90	1·10

681 Molten Steel Ladle

1976. Huta Katowice Steel Works.

2459	**681** 1z.50 multicoloured	15	15

682 Congress Emblem

683 "Wirzbieto Epitaph" (painting on wood, 1425)

1976. 8th Polish Trade Unions Congress.

2460	**682** 1z.50 orange, bistre and brown	15	15

1976. Polish Art. Multicoloured.

2461	1z. Type **683**	10	15
2462	6z. "Madonna and Child" (painted carving, c.1410)	40	15

684 Tanker "Zawrat" at Oil Terminal, Gdansk

1976. Polish Ports. Multicoloured.

2463	1z. Type **684**	10	10
2464	1z. Ferry "Gryf" at Gdansk	10	10
2465	1z.50 Loading container ship "General Bem", Gdynia	20	10
2466	1z.50 Liner "Stefan Batory" leaving Gdynia	20	10
2467	2z. Bulk carrier "Ziemia Szczecinska" loading at Szczecin	25	10
2468	4z.20 Loading coal, Swinoujscie	30	10
2469	6z.90 Pleasure craft, Kolobrzeg	40	30
2470	8z.40 Coastal map	60	30

685 Nurse and Patient

686 Order of Civil Defence Service

1977. Polish Red Cross.

2471	**685** 1z.50 multicoloured	10	10

1977. Polish Civil Defence.

2472	**686** 1z.50 multicoloured	10	10

687 Ball in Road

1977. Child Road Safety Campaign.

2473	**687** 1z.50 multicoloured	10	10

688 Dewberries

689 Computer Tape

1977. Wild Fruits. Multicoloured.

2474	50g. Type **688**	10	10
2475	90g. Cowberries	10	10
2476	1z. Wild strawberries	10	10
2477	1z.50 Bilberries	15	10
2478	2z. Raspberries	15	10
2479	4z.50 Sloes	30	10
2480	6z. Rose hips	40	10
2481	6z.90 Hazelnuts	45	30

1977. 30th Anniv of Russian–Polish Technical Co-operation.

2482	**689** 1z.50 multicoloured	10	10

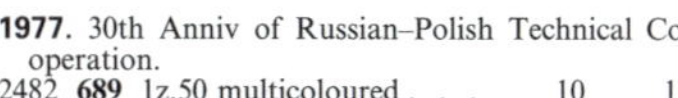

690 Pendulum Traces and Emblem

1977. 7th Polish Congress of Technology.

2483	**690** 1z.50 multicoloured	10	10

691 "Toilet of Venus"

1977. 400th Birth Anniv of Peter Paul Rubens. Multicoloured.

2484	1z. Type **691**	10	10
2485	1z.50 "Bathsheba at the Fountain"	10	10
2486	5z. "Helena Fourment with Fur Coat"	30	10
2487	6z. "Self-portrait"	45	30
MS2488	76 × 62 mm. 8z.+4z. sepia ("The Stoning of St. Stephan") (21 × 26 mm)	1·40	85

692 Dove

694 Wolf

693 Cyclist

1977. World Council of Peace Congress.

2489	**692** 1z.50 blue, yellow & black	10	10

1977. 30th International Peace Cycle Race.

2490	**693** 1z.50 multicoloured	10	10

1977. Endangered Animals. Multicoloured.

2491	1z. Type **694**	10	10
2492	1z.50 Great bustard	30	15
2493	1z.50 Common kestrel	30	15
2494	6z. European otter	40	25

695 "The Violinist" (J. Toorenvliet)

697 H. Wieniawski and Music Clef

696 Midsummer's Day Bonfire

1977. "Amphilex 77" Stamp Exhibition, Amsterdam.

2495	**695** 6z. multicoloured	40	30

1977. Folk Customs. 19th-century Wood Engravings. Multicoloured.

2496	90g. Type **696**	10	10
2497	1z. Easter cock (vert)	10	10
2498	1z.50 "Smigus" (dousing of women on Easter Monday, Miechow district) (vert)	10	10
2499	3z. Harvest Festival, Sandomierz district (vert)	25	10
2500	6z. Children with Christmas crib (vert)	40	10
2501	8z.40 Mountain wedding dance	55	25

1977. Wieniawski International Music Competitions, Poznan.

2502	**697** 1z.50 black, red and gold	25	10

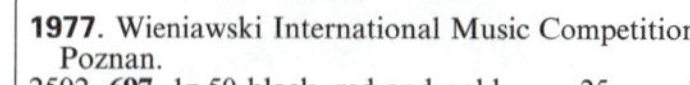

698 Apollo ("Parnassius apollo")

1977. Butterflies. Multicoloured.

2503	1z. Type **698**	30	10
2504	1z. Large tortoiseshell ("Nymphalis polychloros")	30	10
2505	1z.50 Camberwell beauty ("Nymphalis antiopa")	40	10
2506	1z.50 Swallowtail ("Papilio machaon")	40	10
2507	5z. High brown fritillary	1·10	10
2508	6z.90 Silver-washed fritillary	1·90	45

699 Keyboard and Arms of Slupsk

700 Feliks Dzerzhinsky

1977. Piano Festival, Slupsk.

2509	**699** 1z.50 mauve, blk & grn	15	10

1977. Birth Centenary of Feliks Dzerzhinsky (Russian politician).

2510	**700** 1z.50 brown and ochre	15	15

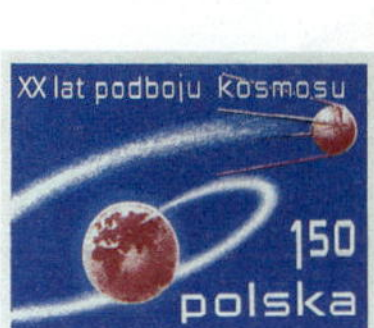

701 "Sputnik" circling Earth

702 Silver Dinar (11th century)

1977. 60th Anniv of Russian Revolution and 20th Anniv of 1st Artificial Satellite (1st issue).

2511	**701** 1z.50 red and blue	15	15
MS2512	99 × 125 mm. No. 2511 × 3 plus three labels	75	75

See also No. 2527.

1977. Stamp Day. Polish Coins. Multicoloured.

2513	50g. Type **702**	10	10
2514	1z. Cracow grosz, 14th-century	10	10
2515	1z.50 Legnica thaler, 17th-century	10	10
2516	4z.20 Gdansk guilder, 18th-century	30	10
2517	4z.50 Silver 5z. coin, 1936	30	10
2518	6z. Millenary 100z. coin, 1966	55	25

703 Wolin Gate, Kamien Pomorski

704 "Sputnik 1" and "Mercury" Capsule

1977. Architectural Monuments. Multicoloured.

2519	1z. Type **703**	10	10
2520	1z. Larch church, Debno	10	10
2521	1z.50 Monastery, Przasnysz (horiz)	10	10
2522	1z.50 Plock cathedral (horiz)	10	10
2523	6z. Kornik castle (horiz)	45	10
2524	6z.90 Palace and garden, Wilanow (horiz)	55	30

1977. Polish Folklore. 16th-century woodcuts (2nd series). As T **638**.

2525	4z. sepia	25	30
2526	4z.50 brown	30	10

DESIGNS: 4z. Bird snaring; 4z.50, Bee-keeper and hives.

1977. 20th Anniv of 1st Space Satellite (2nd issue).

2527	**704** 6z.90 multicoloured	45	40

705 DN Category Iceboats

1978. 6th World Ice Sailing Championships.
2528 **705** 1z.50 black, grey & blue 15 10
2529 – 1z.50 black, grey & blue 25 10
DESIGN: No. 2529, Close-up of DN iceboat.

706 Electric Locomotive and Katowice Station

1978. Railway Engines. Multicoloured.
2530 50g. Type **706** 10 10
2531 1z. Steam locomotive No. Py27 and tender No. 721, Znin-Gasawa railway 10 10
2532 1z. Streamlined steam locomotive No. Pm36-1 (1936) and Cegielski's factory, Poznan 10 10
2533 1z.50 Electric locomotive and Otwock station 10 10
2534 1z.50 Steam locomotive No. 17 KDM and Warsaw Stalowa station 10 10
2535 4z.50 Steam locomotive No. Ty51 and Gdynia station 30 10
2536 5z. Steam locomotive No. Tr21 and locomotive works, Chrzanow 40 10
2537 6z. Cockerill steam locomotive and Vienna station 55 30

707 Czeslaw Tanski and Glider

1978. Aviation History and 50th Anniv of Polish Aero Club. Multicoloured.
2538 50g. Type **707** 10 10
2539 1z. Franciszek Zwirko and Stanislaw Wigura with RWD-6 aircraft (vert) 10 10
2540 1z.50 Stanislaw Skarzynski and RWD-5 bis monoplane (vert) 10 10
2541 4z.20 Mil Mi-2 helicopter (vert) 25 10
2542 6z.90 PZL-104 Wilga 35 monoplane 75 25
2543 8z.40 SZD-45 Ogar powered glider 60 25

708 Tackle

1978. World Cup Football Championship, Argentina. Multicoloured.
2544 1z.50 Type **708** 10 10
2545 6z.90 Ball on field (horiz) 45 30

709 Biennale Emblem
710 Kazimierz Stanislaw Gzowski (bridge engineer)

1978. 7th International Poster Biennale, Warsaw.
2546 **709** 1z.50 mauve, yell & vio 15 15

1978. "Capex 78" International Stamp Exhibition, Toronto. Sheet 68 × 79 mm.
MS2547 **710** 8z.40+4z. multicoloured 1·10 70

711 Polonez Saloon Car

1978. Car Production.
2548 **711** 1z.50 multicoloured 10 10

712 Fair Emblem
713 Miroslaw Hermaszewski

1978. 50th International Fair, Poznan.
2549 **712** 1z.50 multicoloured 10 10

1978. 1st Pole in Space. Multicoloured. With or without date.
2550 1z.50 Type **713** 10 10
2551 6z.90 M. Hermaszewski and globe 55 25

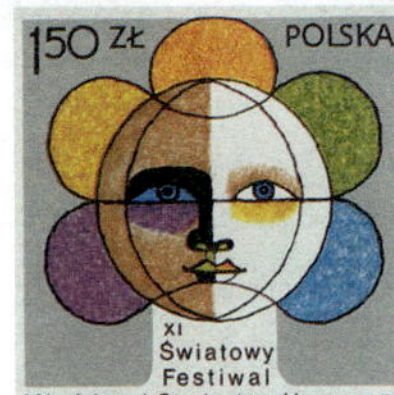

714 Globe containing Face

1978. 11th World Youth and Students Festival, Havana.
2552 **714** 1z.50 multicoloured 10 10

715 Flowers

1978. 30th Anniv Polish Youth Union. Sheet 69 × 79 mm.
MS2553 **715** 1z.50 multicoloured 40 40

716 Mosquito and Malaria Organisms
717 Pedunculate Oak

1978. 4th International Congress of Parasitologists, Warsaw and Cracow. Multicoloured.
2554 1z.50 Type **716** 10 10
2555 6z. Tsetse fly and sleeping sickness organism 40 40

1978. Environment Protection. Trees. Mult.
2556 50g. Norway Maple 10 10
2557 1z. Type **717** 10 10
2558 1z.50 White Poplar 10 10
2559 4z.20 Scots Pine 25 10
2560 4z.50 White Willow 25 10
2561 6z. Birch 40 15

718

1978. "PRAGA 1978" International Stamp Exhibition. Sheet 69 × 79 mm.
MS2562 **718** 6z. multicoloured 1·10 60

719 Communications

1978. 20th Anniv of Socialist Countries Communications Organization.
2563 **719** 1z.50 red, lt blue & blue 10 10

720 "Peace" (Andre Le Brun)

1978.
2564 **720** 1z. violet 10 10
2565 1z.50 turquoise 10 10
2565a 2z. brown 10 10
2565b 2z.50 blue 25 10

721 Polish Unit of U.N. Middle East Force

1978. 35th Anniv of Polish People's Army. Mult.
2566 1z.50 Colour party of Tadeusz Kosciuszko 1st Warsaw Infantry Division 10 10
2567 1z.50 Mechanized Unit colour party 10 10
2568 1z.50 Type **721** 10 10

722 "Portrait of a Young Man" (Raphael)

1978. Stamp Day.
2569 **722** 6z. multicoloured 40 30

723 Janusz Korczak with Children

1978. Birth Centenary of Janusz Korczak (pioneer of children's education).
2570 **723** 1z.50 multicoloured 25 10

724 Wojciech Boguslawski

1978. Polish Dramatists. Multicoloured.
2571 50g. Type **724** 10 10
2572 1z. Aleksander Fredro 10 10
2573 1z.50 Juliusz Slowacki 10 10
2574 2z. Adam Mickiewicz 10 10
2575 4z.50 Stanislaw Wyspianski 30 10
2576 6z. Gabriela Zapolska 45 25

725 Polish Combatants' Monument and Eiffel Tower

1978. Monument to Polish Combatants in France, Paris.
2577 **725** 1z.50 brown, blue & red 20 10

726 Przewalski Horses

1978. 50th Anniv of Warsaw Zoo. Multicoloured.
2578 50g. Type **726** 10 10
2579 1z. Polar bears 10 10
2580 1z.50 Indian elephants 25 10
2581 2z. Jaguars 30 10
2582 4z.20 Grey seals 30 10
2583 4z.50 Hartebeests 30 10
2584 6z. Mandrills 45 30

727 Party Flag

1978. 30th Anniv of Polish Workers' United Party.
2585 **727** 1z.50 red, gold and black 10 10

728 Stanislaw Dubois

1978. Leaders of Polish Workers' Movement.
2586 **728** 1z.50 blue and red 10 10
2587 – 1z.50 lilac and red 10 10
2588 – 1z.50 olive and red 10 10
2589 – 1z.50 brown and red 10 10
DESIGNS: No. 2587, Aleksander Zawadzki; 2588, Julian Lenski; 2589, Aldolf Warski.

729 Ilyushin Il-62M and Fokker F.VIIb/3m

1979. 50th Anniv of LOT Polish Airlines.
2590 **729** 6z.90 multicoloured 55 25

730 Steam Train

1979. International Year of the Child. Children's Paintings. Multicoloured.
2591 50g. Type **730** 10 10
2592 1z. "Mother with Children" 10 10
2593 1z.50 Children playing 10 10
2594 6z. Family Group 40 25

731 "Portrait of Artist's Wife with Foxgloves" (Karol Mondrala)

1979. Contemporary Graphics.
2595 – 50g. lilac 10 10
2596 **731** 1z. green 10 10
2597 – 1z.50 blue 10 10
2598 – 4z.50 brown 30 10
DESIGNS—HORIZ: 50g. "Lightning" (Edmund Bartlomiejezyk). VERT: 1z.50, "The Musicians" (Tadeusz Kulisiewicz); 4z.50, "Head of a Young Man" (Wladyslaw Skoczylas).

732 A. Frycz Modrzewski (political writer), King Stefan Batory and Jan Zamoyski (chancellor)

1979. 400th Anniv (1978) of Royal Tribunal in Piotrkow Trybunalski.
2599 **732** 1z.50 brown and deep brown 10 10

733 Pole Vaulting

1979. 60th Anniv of Polish Olympic Committee.
2600 **733** 1z. Lilac, brown and red 10 10
2601 – 1z.50 lilac, brown and red 10 10
2602 – 6z. lilac, brown and red 40 10
2603 – 8z.40 lilac, brown and red 60 25
MS2604 102 × 61 mm. 10z.+5z. brown 90 75
DESIGNS: 1z.50, High jump; 6z. Skiing; 8z.40, Horse riding; 10z. Olympic rings.

734 European Flounder

1979. Centenary of Polish Angling. Multicoloured.
2605 50g. Type **734** 10 10
2606 90g. Eurasian perch 10 10
2607 1z. European grayling . . . 10 10
2608 1z.50 Atlantic salmon . . . 10 10
2609 2z. Brown trout 15 10
2610 4z.50 Northern pike 30 10
2611 5z. Common carp 45 10
2612 6z. Wels 45 20

735 "30 Years of RWPG"

1979. 30th Anniv of Council of Mutual Economic Aid.
2613 **735** 1z.50 red, ultram & blue 10 10

736 Soldier, Civilian and Congress Emblem
738 Pope and Auschwitz Concentration Camp Memorial

737 St. George's Church, Sofia

1979. 6th Congress of Association of Fighters for Liberty and Democracy.
2614 **736** 1z.50 red and black . . . 10 10

1979. "Philaserdica 79" International Stamp Exhibition, Sofia, Bulgaria.
2615 **737** 1z.50 orange, brn & red 10 10

1979. Visit of Pope John Paul II. Multicoloured.
2616 1z.50 Pope and St. Mary's Church, Cracow 25 10
2617 8z.40 Type **738** 70 30
MS2618 68 × 79 mm. 50z. Framed portrait of Pope (26 × 35 mm) 7·00 5·25

739 River Paddle-steamer "Ksiaze Ksawery" and Old Warsaw

1979. 150th Anniv of Vistula River Navigation. Multicoloured.
2619 1z. Type **739** 10 10
2620 1z.50 River paddle-steamer "General Swierczewski" and Gdansk 10 10
2621 4z.50 River tug "Zubr" and Plock 25 10
2622 6z. Passenger launch "Syrena" and modern Warsaw 45 25

740 Statue of Tadeusz Kosciuszko (Marian Konieczny)
741 Mining Machinery

1979. Monument to Tadeusz Kosciuszko in Philadelphia.
2623 **740** 8z.40 multicoloured . . . 40 25

1979. Wieliczka Salt Mine.
2624 **741** 1z. brown and black . . 10 10
2625 – 1z.50 turquoise and black 10 10
DESIGN: 1z.50, Salt crystals.

742 Heraldic Eagle
743 Rowland Hill and 1860 Stamp

1979. 35th Anniv of Polish People's Republic.
2626 – 1z.50 red, silver and black 15 10
2627 **742** 1z.50 red, silver and blue 15 10
MS2628 120 × 84 mm. Nos. 2626/7 plus label 40 45
DESIGN: No. 2626, Girl and stylized flag.

1979. Death Centenary of Sir Rowland Hill.
2629 **743** 6z. blue, black and orange 40 10

744 "The Rape of Europa" (Bernardo Stozzi)

1979. International Stamp Exhibition. Sheet 86 × 63 mm.
MS2630 **744** 10z. multicoloured 75 60

745 Wojciech Jastrzebowski

1979. 7th Congress of International Ergonomic Association, Warsaw.
2631 **745** 1z.50 multicoloured . . . 15 10

746 Monument (Wincenty Kucma)

1979. Unveiling of Monument to Defenders of Polish Post, Gdansk, and 40th Anniv of German Occupation.
2632 **746** 1z.50 grey, sepia and red 15 10
MS2633 79 × 69 mm. **746** 10z.+5z. grey, sepia and red. Imperf . . 1·00 85

747 Radio Mast and Telecommunications Emblem

1979. 50th Anniv of International Radio Communication Advisory Committee.
2634 **747** 1z.50 multicoloured . . . 15 10

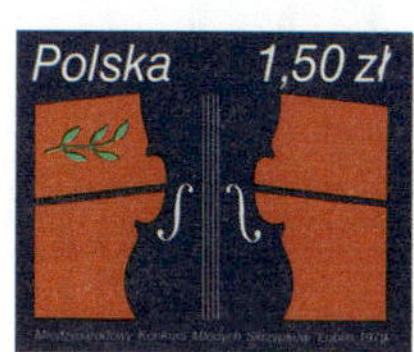

748 Violin

1979. Wieniawski Young Violinists' Competition, Lublin.
2635 **748** 1z.50 blue, orange & green 15 10

749 Statue of Kazimierz Pulaski, Buffalo (K. Danilewicz)
750 Franciszek Jozwiak (first Commander)

1979. Death Bicentenary of Kazimierz Pulaski (American Revolution Hero).
2636 **749** 8z.40 multicoloured . . . 60 30

1979. 35th Anniv of Civic Militia and Security Force.
2637 **750** 1z.50 blue and gold . . . 15 10

751 Post Office in Rural Area

1979. Stamp Day. Multicoloured.
2638 1z. Type **751** 10 10
2639 1z.50 Parcel sorting machinery 10 10
2640 4z.50 Loading containers on train 45 10
2641 6z. Mobile post office . . . 60 25

752 "The Holy Family" (Ewelina Peksowa)
753 "Soyuz 30-Salyut 6" Complex and Crystal

1979. Polish Folk Art. Glass Paintings. Mult.
2642 2z. Type **752** 10 10
2643 6z.90 "The Nativity" (Zdzislaw Walczak) . . . 45 25

1979. Space Achievements. Multicoloured.
2644 1z. Type **753** (1st anniv of 1st Pole in space) 10 10
2645 1z.50 "Kopernik" and "Copernicus" satellites . . 10 10
2646 2z. "Lunik 2" and "Ranger 7" spacecraft (20th anniv of 1st unmanned Moon landing) 10 10
2647 4z.50 Yuri Gagarin and "Vostok 1" 10 10
2648 6z.90 Neil Armstrong, lunar module and "Apollo 11" (10th anniv of first man on Moon) 25 30
MS2649 120 × 103 mm. Nos. 2644/8 plus label (sold at 20z.90) . . . 1·25 1·25

754 Coach and Four
755 Slogan on Map of Poland

1980. 150th Anniv of Sierakow Stud Farm. Mult.
2650 1z. Type **754** 10 10
2651 2z. Horse and groom . . . 10 10
2652 2z.50 Sulky racing 10 10
2653 3z. Hunting 25 10
2654 4z. Horse-drawn sledge . . 30 10
2655 6z. Haywain 45 10
2656 6z.50 Grooms exercising horses 55 25
2657 6z.90 Show jumping 60 30

1980. 8th Polish United Workers' Party Congress. Multicoloured.
2658 2z.50 Type **755** 25 10
2659 2z.50 Janusz Stann (26 × 46 mm) 25 10

756 Horse Jumping

1980. Olympic Games, Moscow, and Winter Olympic Games, Lake Placid. Multicoloured.
2660 2z. Type **756** 10 10
2661 2z.50 Archery 25 10
2662 6z.50 Skiing 45 10
2663 8z.40 Volleyball 60 30

757 Town Plan and Old Town Hall

1980. 400th Anniv of Zamosc.
2665 **757** 2z.50 buff, green & brn 15 10

758 Satellite orbiting Earth

1980. "Intercosmos" Space Programme. Sheet 63×79 mm.
MS2666 **758** 6z.90+3z. multicoloured . . . 60 70

759 Seals of Poland and Russia

1980. 35th Anniv of Soviet–Polish Friendship Treaty.
2667 **759** 2z.50 multicoloured . . . 25 10

760 "Lenin in Cracow" (Zbigniew Pronaszko)

1980. 110th Birth Anniv of Lenin.
2668 **760** 2z.50 multicoloured . . . 25 10

761 Workers with Red Flag

1980. 75th Anniv of Revolution of 1905.
2669 **761** 2z.50 red, black & yellow 25 10

762 Dove

763 Shield with Crests of Member Nations

1980. 35th Anniv of Liberation.
2670 **762** 2z.50 multicoloured . . . 25 10

1980. 25th Anniv of Warsaw Pact.
2671 **763** 2z. grey and red 25 10

764 Speleological Expedition, Cuba

1980. Polish Scientific Expeditions. Multicoloured.
2672 2z. Type **764** 10 10
2673 2z. Antarctic 30 10
2674 2z.50 Archaeology, Syria . . 25 10
2675 2z.50 Ethnology, Mongolia 25 10
2676 6z.50 Mountaineering, Nepal 40 10
2677 8z.40 Paleontology, Mongolia 55 25

765 School and Arms

766 "Clathrus ruber"

1980. 800th Anniv of Malachowski School, Plock.
2678 **765** 2z. green and black . . . 15 10

1980. Fungi. Multicoloured.
2679 2z. Type **766** 20 10
2680 2z. "Xerocomus parasiticus" 20 10
2681 2z.50 Old man of the woods ("Strobilomyces floccopus") 25 10
2682 2z.50 "Phallus hadriani" . . 25 10
2683 8z. Cauliflower fungus . . . 40 20
2684 10z.50 Giant puff-ball . . . 40 45

767 T. Ziolowski and "Lwow"

1980. Polish Merchant Navy School. Cadet Ships and their Captains.
2685 **767** 2z. black, mauve and violet 20 10
2686 – 2z.50 black, light blue and blue 25 10
2687 – 6z. black, pale green and green 30 10
2688 – 6z.50 black, yellow and grey 40 10
2689 – 6z.90 black, grey and green 45 25
2690 – 8z.40 black, blue and green 55 25

DESIGNS: 2z.50, A. Garnuszewski and "Antoni Garnuszewski"; 6z. A. Ledochowski and "Zenit"; 6z.50, K. Porebski and "Jan Turleski"; 6z.90, G. Kanski and "Horyzont"; 8z.40, Maciejewicz and "Dar Pomorza".

768 Town Hall

769 "Atropa belladonna"

1980. Millenary of Sandomir.
2691 **768** 2z.50 brown and black 15 10

1980. Medicinal Plants. Multicoloured.
2692 2z. Type **769** 15 10
2693 2z.50 "Datura innoxia" . . 20 10
2694 3z.40 "Valeriana officinalis" 25 10
2695 5z. "Menta piperita" . . . 30 10
2696 6z.50 "Calendula officinalis" 40 25
2697 8z. "Salvia officinalis" . . . 55 30

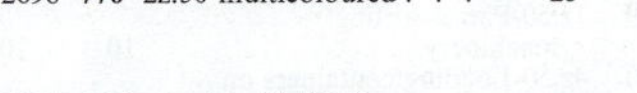

770 Jan Kochanowski

771 U.N. General Assembly

1980. 450th Birth Anniv of Jan Kochanowski (poet).
2698 **770** 2z.50 multicoloured . . . 25 15

1980. 35th Anniv of U.N.O.
2703 **771** 8z.40 brown, blue & red 60 30

772 Chopin and Trees

1980. 10th International Chopin Piano Competition, Warsaw.
2704 **772** 6z.90 multicoloured . . . 45 30

773 Postman emptying Post Box

1980. Stamp Day. Multicoloured.
2705 2z. Type **773** 20 10
2706 2z.50 Mail sorting 20 10
2707 6z. Loading mail onto aircraft 45 10
2708 6z.50 Letter boxes 55 25
MS2709 12×94 mm. Nos. 2705/8 3·50 1·75

774 Child embracing Dove

1980. United Nations Declaration on the Preparation of Societies for Life in Peace.
2710 **774** 8z.40 multicoloured . . . 60 30

775 "Battle of Olszynka Grochowska" (Wojciech Kossak)

1980. 150th Anniv of Battle of Olszynka Grochowska.
2711 **775** 2z.50 multicoloured . . . 25 15

776 Fire Engine

1980. Warsaw Horse-drawn Vehicles. Mult.
2712 2z. Type **776** 15 10
2713 2z.50 Omnibus 20 10
2714 3z. Brewery dray 25 10
2715 5z. Sledge-cab 30 10
2716 6z. Horse tram 40 30
2717 6z.50 Droshky cab 50 45

777 "Honour to the Silesian Rebels" (statue by Jan Borowczak)

778 Picasso

1981. 60th Anniv of Silesian Rising.
2718 **777** 2z.50 green 15 10

1981. Birth Centenary of Pablo Picasso (artist).
2719 **778** 8z.40 multicoloured . . . 60 30
MS2720 95×130 mm. No. 2719 ×2 plus labels (sold at 20z.80) . . 2·50 1·40

779 Balloon of Pilatre de Rozier and Romain, 1785

780 "Iphigenia" (Anton Maulbertsch)

1981. Balloons. Multicoloured.
2721 2z. Type **779** 20 10
2722 2z. Balloon of J. Blanchard and J. Jeffries, 1785 . . . 20 10
2723 2z.50 Eugene Godard's quiintuple "acrobatic" balloon, 1850 . . . . . 25 10
2724 3z. F. Hynek and Z. Burzynski's "Kosciuszko", 1933 . . . 25 10
2725 6z. Z. Burzynski and N. Wyescki's "Polonia II", 1935 . . . . 45 25
2726 6z.50 Ben Abruzzo, Max Anderson and Larry Newman's "Double Eagle II", 1978 . . . . 45 25
MS2727 59×98 mm. 10z.50 Balloon SP-BCU *L.O.P.P.* and Gordon Bennett statuette 80 95

1981. "WIPA 1981" International Stamp Exhibition, Vienna.
2728 **780** 10z.50 multicoloured . . 85 30

781 Wroclaw, 1493

782 Sikorski

1981. Towns.
2729 – 4z. violet 30 15
2730 – 5z. green 55 15
2731 – 6z. orange 60 15
2732 **781** 6z.50 brown 55 25
2733 – 8z. blue 70 30

DESIGNS—VERT: 4z. Gdansk, 1652; 5z. Cracow, 1493. HORIZ: 6z. Legnica, 1744; 8z. Warsaw, 1618.

1981. Birth Centenary of General Wladyslaw Sikorski (statesman).
2744 **782** 6z.50 multicoloured . . . 55 25

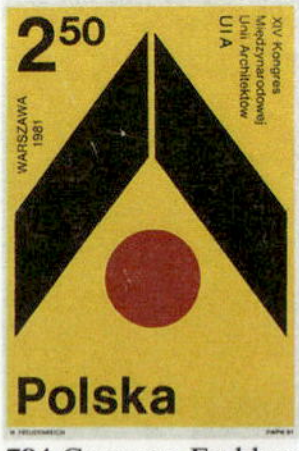

783 Faience Vase

784 Congress Emblem

1981. Pottery. Multicoloured.
2745 1z. Type **783** 15 10
2746 2z. Porcelain cup and saucer in "Baranowka" design 25 10
2747 2z.50 Porcelain jug, Korzec manufacture 25 10
2748 5z. Faience plate with portrait of King Jan III Sobieski by Thiele 45 25
2749 6z.50 Faience "Secession" vase 60 25
2750 8z.40 Porcelain dish, Cmielow manufacture . . 75 30

1981. 14th International Architects' Union Congress, Warsaw.
2751 **784** 2z. yellow, black and red 25 10

785 Wild Boar, Rifle and Oak Leaves **786** European Bison

1981. Game Shooting. Multicoloured.
2752 2z. Type **785** 15 10
2753 2z. Elk, rifle and fir twigs 15 10
2754 2z.50 Red fox, shotgun, cartridges and fir branches 25 10
2755 2z.50 Roe deer, feeding rack, rifle and fir branches 25 10
2756 6z.50 Mallard, shotgun, basket and reeds 70 55
2757 6z.50 Barnacle goose, shotgun and reeds (horiz) 70 55

1981. Protection of European Bison. Mult.
2758 6z.50 Type **786** 70 30
2759 6z.50 Two bison, one grazing 70 30
2760 6z.50 Bison with calf . . . 70 30
2761 6z.50 Calf Feeding 70 30
2762 6z.50 Two bison, both looking towards right . . 70 30

787 Tennis Player

1981. 60th Anniv of Polish Tennis Federation.
2763 **787** 6z.50 multicoloured . . . 55 30

788 Boy with Model Airplane

1981. Model Making. Multicoloured.
2764 1z. Type **788** 15 10
2765 2z. Model of "Atlas 2" tug 30 10
2766 2z.50 Cars 30 10
2767 4z.20 Man with gliders . . . 30 10
2768 6z.50 Racing cars 60 20
2769 8z. Boy with yacht 70 20

789 Disabled Pictogram **791** H. Wieniawski and Violin Head

790 17th-cent Flint-lock Pistol

1981. International Year of Disabled Persons.
2770 **789** 8z.40 green, light green and black 70 30

1981. Stamp Day. Antique Weapons. Mult.
2771 2z.50 Type **790** 25 10
2772 8z.40 17th-century gala sabre 70 25

1981. Wieniawski Young Violinists' Competition.
2773 **791** 2z.50 multicoloured . . . 25 15

792 Bronislaw Wesolowski **793** F.A.O. Emblem and Globe

1981. Activists of Polish Workers' Movement.
2774 **792** 50g. green and black . . 10 10
2775 – 2z. blue and black . . . 15 10
2776 – 2z.50 brown and black 20 10
2777 – 6z.50 mauve and black 70 25
DESIGNS: 2z. Malgorzata Fornalska; 2z.50, Maria Koszutska; 6z.50, Marcin Kasprzak.

1981. World Food Day.
2778 **793** 6z.90 brown, orange & yellow 55 25

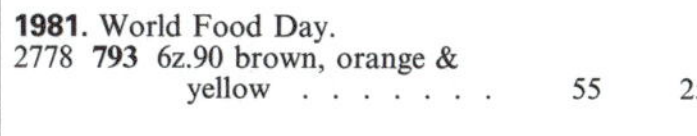

794 Helena Modrzejewska (actress)

1981. Bicentenary of Cracow Old Theatre.
2779 **794** 2z. purple, grey and violet 15 10
2780 – 2z.50 blue, stone & brn 25 10
2781 – 6z.50 violet, blue & grn 55 25
2782 – 8z. brown, green and red 85 25
DESIGNS: 2z.50, Stanislaw Kozmian (politician, writer and theatre director); 6z.50, Konrad Swinarski (stage manager and scenographer); 8z. Old Theatre building.

795 Cracow and Vistula River **796** Gdansk Memorial

1981. Vistula River Project. Sheet 62 × 51 mm.
MS2783 **795** 10z.50 multicoloured 1·25 1·10

1981. Memorials to the Victims of the 1970 Uprisings.
2784 **796** 2z.50+1z. grey, black and red 30 10
2785 – 6z.50+1z. grey, black and blue 75 30
DESIGN: 6z.50, Gdynia Memorial.

797 "Epiphyllopsis gaertneri"

1981. Succulent Plants. Multicoloured.
2786 90g. Type **797** 15 10
2787 1z. "Cereus tonduzii" . . . 15 10
2788 2z. "Cylindropuntia leptocaulis" 15 10
2789 2z.50 "Cylindropuntia fulgida" 25 10
2790 2z.50 "Coralluma lugardi" 25 10
2791 6z.50 "Nopalea cochenillifera" . . . . . 1·60 30
2792 6z.50 "Lithops helmutii" . . 60 30
2793 10z.50 "Cylindropuntia spinosior" . . . . . . 1·00 40

798 Writing on Wall **799** Faience Plate

1982. 40th Anniv of Polish Workers' Coalition.
2794 **798** 2z.50 pink, red and black 25 15

1982. Polish Ceramics. Multicoloured.
2795 1z. Type **799** 15 15
2796 2z. Porcelain cup and saucer, Korzec 25 15
2797 2z.50 Porcelain tureen and sauce-boat, Barnowka . . 25 15
2798 6z. Porcelain inkpot, Horodnica 55 30
2799 8z. Faience "Hunter's Tumbler", Lubartow . . 65 30
2800 10z.50 Faience figurine of nobleman, Biala Podlaska 1·10 45

800 Ignacy Lukasiewicz and Lamp **801** Karol Szymanowski

1982. Death Centenary of Ignacy Lukasiewicz (inventor of petroleum lamp).
2801 **800** 1z. multicoloured 15 10
2802 – 2z. multicoloured 25 10
2803 – 2z.50 multicoloured . . . 30 10
2804 – 3z.50 multicoloured . . . 30 10
2805 – 9z. multicoloured 85 30
2806 – 10z. multicoloured . . . 90 35
DESIGNS: 2z. to 10z. Different designs showing lamps.

1982. Birth Centenary of Karol Szymanowski (composer).
2807 **801** 2z.50 brown and gold . . 25 25

802 RWD 6, 1932

1982. 50th Anniv of Polish Victory in Tourist Aircraft Challenge Competition. Multicoloured.
2808 27z. Type **802** 75 25
2809 31z. RWD 9 (winner of 1934 Challenge) . . . . . 1·00 30
MS2810 89 × 101 mm. Nos. 2808/9 2·25 1·60

803 Henryk Sienkiewicz (literature, 1905) **804** Football as Globe

1982. Polish Nobel Prize Winners.
2811 **803** 3z. green and black . . . 10 10
2812 – 15z. brown and black . . 40 15
2813 – 25z. blue 90 25
2814 – 31z. grey and black . . . 75 45
DESIGNS: 15z. Wladyslaw Reymont (literature, 1924); 25z. Marie Curie (physics, 1903, and chemistry, 1911); 31z. Czeslaw Milosz (literature, 1980).

1982. World Cup Football Championship, Spain. Multicoloured.
2815 25z. Type **804** 75 30
2816 27z. Bull and football (35 × 28 mm) 85 55

805 "Maria kazimiera Sobieska"

1982. "Philexfrance 82" International Stamp Exhibition, Paris. Sheet 69 × 86 mm.
MS2817 **805** 65z. multicoloured 2·40 2·40

806 Stanislaw Sierakowski and Boleslaw Domanski (former Association presidents) **807** Text around Globe

1982. 60th Anniv of Association of Poles in Germany.
2818 **806** 4z.50 red and green . . . 40 15

1982. 2nd U.N. Conference on the Exploration and Peaceful Uses of Outer Space, Vienna.
2819 **807** 31z. multicoloured . . . 75 40

1982. No. 2732 surch **10 °°**.
2820 10z. on 6z.50 brown 30 10

809 Father Augustyn Kordecki (prior) **810** Marchers with Banner

1982. 600th Anniv of "Black Madonna" (icon) of Jasna Gora. Multicoloured.
2821 2z.50 Type **809** 10 10
2822 25z. "Siege of Jasna Gora by Swedes, 1655" (detail) (horiz) 40 10
2823 65z. "Black Madonna" . . 1·10 45
MS2824 122 × 108 mm. No. 2823 × 2 (sold at 140z.) . . . . . . 10·50 12·50
The premium on No. **MS**2824 was for the benefit of the Polish Philatelic Federation.

1982. Centenary of Proletarian Party.
2825 **810** 6z. multicoloured 30 15

811 Norbert Barlicki **812** Dr. Robert Koch

1982. Activists of Polish Workers' Movement.
2826 **811** 5z. light blue, blue and black 10 15
2827 – 6z. deep green, green and black 10 15
2828 – 15z. pink, red and black 25 15
2829 – 20z. mauve, violet and black 40 15
2830 – 29z. light brown, brown and black 45 15
DESIGNS: 6z. Pawel Finder; 15z. Marian Buczek; 20z. Cezaryna Wojnarowska; 29z. Ignacy Daszynski.

1982. Centenary of Discovery of Tubercle Bacillus. Multicoloured.
2831 10z. Type **812** 25 15
2832 25z. Dr. Odo Bujwid . . . 85 30

813 Carved Head of Woman **813a** Head of Ruler

1982. Carved Heads from Wawel Castle.
2835 **813a** 3z.50 brown 15 10
2836 – 5z. green 15 10
2837 – 5z. red 10 10
2838 – 10z. blue 15 10
2839 – 15z. brown 15 10
2840 – 20z. grey 45 10
2841 **813a** 20z. blue 15 10
2842 – 40z. brown 75 10
2833 **813** 60z. orange and brown 1·25 25
2843 – 60z. green 15 10
2834 – 100z. ochre and brown 2·75 40
2843a – 200z. black . . . . . 2·25 30
DESIGNS—As T **813**: 100z. Man. As T **813a**: 5z. (2836), Warrior; 5z. (2837), 15z. Woman wearing chaplet; 10z. Man in cap; 20z. (2840), Thinker; 40z. Man in beret; 60z. Young man; 200z. Man.

814 Maximilian Kolbe (after M. Koscielniak)

1982. Sanctification of Maximilian Kolbe (Franciscan concentration camp victim).
2844 **814** 27z. multicoloured . . . 1·00 40

815 Polar Research Station

1982. 50th Anniv of Polish Polar Research.
2845 **815** 27z. multicoloured . . . 1·10 40

816 "Log Floats on Vistula River" (drawing by J. Telakowski) **817** Stanislaw Zaremba

1982. Views of the Vistula River.
2846 **816** 12z. blue 25 10
2847 – 17z. blue 30 10
2848 – 25z. blue 40 25
DESIGNS: 17z. "Kazimierz Dolny" (engraving by Andriollo); 25z. "Danzig" (18th-cent engraving).

1982. Mathematicians.
2849 **817** 5z. lilac, blue and black 25 15
2850 – 6z. orange, violet and black 25 15
2851 – 12z. blue, brown and black 40 15
2852 – 15z. yellow, brown and black 60 25
DESIGNS: 6z. Waclaw Sierpinski; 12z. Zygmunt Janiszewski; 15z. Stefan Banach.

818 Military Council Medal

1982. 1st Anniv of Military Council.
2853 **818** 2z.50 multicoloured . . . 25 15

819 Deanery Gate

1982. Renovation of Cracow Monuments (1st series).
2854 **819** 15z. black, olive & green 45 15
2855 – 25z. black, purple & mauve 55 25
MS2856 75 × 93 mm. 65z. green, purple and sepia (22 × 27 mm) 1·25 90
DESIGNS: 25z. Gateway of Collegium Iuridicum; 65z. Street plan of Old Cracow.
See also Nos. 2904/5, 2968/9; 3029/3, 3116 and 3153.

820 Bernard Wapowski Map, 1526

1982. Polish Maps.
2857 **820** 5z. multicoloured 10 10
2858 – 6z. brown, black and red 15 10
2859 – 8z. multicoloured 20 10
2860 – 25z. multicoloured . . . 55 30
DESIGNS: 6z. Map of Prague, 1839; 8z. Map of Poland from Eugen Romer's Atlas, 1908; 25z. Plan of Cracow by A. Buchowiecki, 1703, and Astrolabe.

821 "The Last of the Resistance" (Artur Grottger)

1983. 120th Anniv of January Uprising.
2861 **821** 6z. brown 15 10

822 "Grand Theatre, Warsaw, 1838" (Maciej Zaleski)

1983. 150th Anniv of Grand Theatre, Warsaw.
2862 **822** 6z. multicoloured 15 10

823 Wild Flowers

1983. Environmental Protection. Multicoloured.
2863 5z. Type **823** 15 10
2864 6z. Mute swan and river fishes 30 15
2865 17z. Hoopoe and trees . . . 90 35
2866 30z. Sea fishes 90 45
2867 31z. European bison and roe deer 90 45
2868 38z. Fruit 90 60

824 Karol Kurpinski (composer)

1983. Celebrities.
2869 **824** 5z. light brown and brown 25 10
2870 – 6z. purple and violet . . 25 10
2871 – 17z. light green and green 60 30
2872 – 25z. light brown and brown 65 30
2873 – 27z. light blue and blue 75 30
2874 – 31z. lilac and violet . . . 85 30
DESIGNS: 6z. Maria Jasnorzewska Pawlikowska (poetess); 17z. Stanislaw Szober (linguist); 25z. Tadeusz Banachiewicz (astronomer and mathematician); 27z. Jaroslaw Iwaskiewicz (writer); 31z. Wladyslaw Tatarkiewicz (philosopher and historian).

825 3000 Metres Steeplechase

1983. Sports Achievements.
2875 **825** 5z. pink and violet . . . 25 15
2876 – 6z. pink, brown and black 25 15
2877 – 15z. yellow and green . . 45 15
2878 – 27z.+5z. light blue, blue and black . . . . . . 1·00 30
DESIGNS: 6z. Show jumping; 1z. Football; 27z.+5z. Pole vault.

826 Ghetto Heroes Monument (Natan Rappaport) **827** Customs Officer and Suitcases

1983. 40th Anniv of Warsaw Ghetto Uprising.
2879 **826** 6z. light brown & brown 25 15

1983. 30th Anniv of Customs Co-operation Council.
2880 **827** 5z. multicoloured 15 15

828 John Paul II and Jasna Gora Sanctuary **829** Dragoons

1983. Papal Visit. Multicoloured.
2881 31z. Type **828** 85 40
2882 65z. Niepokalanow Church and John Paul holding crucifix . . . . 1·90 75
MS2883 107 × 81 mm. No. 2882 1·90 1·90

1983. 300th Anniv of Polish Relief of Vienna (1st issue). Troops of King Jan III Sobieski. Mult.
2884 5z. Type **829** 15 10
2885 5z. Armoured cavalryman 15 10
2886 6z. Infantry non-commissioned officer and musketeer 25 10
2887 15z. Light cavalry lieutenant 30 30
2888 27z. "Winged" hussar and trooper with carbine . . . 90 45
See also Nos. 2893/6.

830 Arrow piercing "E"

1983. 50th Anniv of Deciphering "Enigma" Machine Codes.
2889 **830** 5z. red, grey and black 15 15

831 Torun

1983. 750th Anniv of Torun.
2890 **831** 6z. multicoloured 25 15

832 Child's Painting

1983. "Order of the Smile" (Politeness Publicity Campaign).
2892 **832** 6z. multicoloured 25 15
MS2891 142 × 116 mm. No. 2890 × 4 . . . . 2·75 2·75

833 King Jan III Sobieski

1983. 300th Anniv of Relief of Vienna (2nd issue). Multicoloured.
2893 5z. Type **833** 25 15
2894 6z. King Jan III Sobieski (different) 25 15
2895 6z. "King Jan III Sobieski on Horseback" (Francesco Trevisani) . . 25 15
2896 25z. "King Jan III Sobieski" (Jerzy Eleuter) 90 30
MS2897 97 × 75 mm. 65z. +10z. "King Jan III Sobieski at Vienna" (Jan Matejko). Imperf . . . . 1·90 1·90

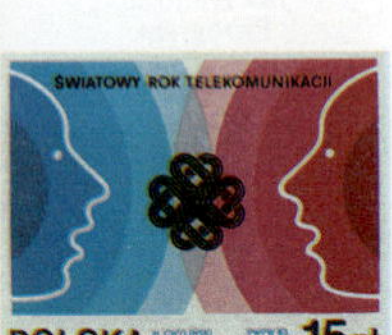

834 Wanda Wasilewska **835** Profiles and W.C.Y. Emblem

1983. 40th Anniv of Polish People's Army. Multicoloured.
2898 **834** 5z. multicoloured 10 10
2899 – 5z. deep green, green and black 10 10
2900 – 6z. multicoloured 25 10
2901 – 6z. multicoloured 25 10
DESIGNS—VERT: No. 2899, General Zygmunt Berling; 2900, "The Frontier Post" (S. Poznanski). HORIZ: No. 2901, "Taking the Oath" (S. Poznanski).

1983. World Communications Year.
2902 **835** 15z. multicoloured . . . 45 25

836 Boxing

1983. 60th Anniv of Polish Boxing Federation.
2903 **836** 6z. multicoloured 25 15

1983. Renovation of Cracow Monuments (2nd series). As T **819**.
2904 5z. brown, purple and black 15 10
2905 6z. black, green and blue . . 15 15
DESIGNS—HORIZ: 5z. Cloth Hall. VERT: 6z. Town Hall tower.

837 Biskupiec Costume **838** Hand with Sword (poster by Zakrzewski and Krolikowski, 1945)

1983. Women's Folk Costumes. Multicoloured.
2906 5z. Type **837** 15 10
2907 5z. Rozbark 15 10
2908 6z. Warmia & Mazuria . . 25 10
2909 6z. Cieszyn 25 10
2910 25z. Kurpie 90 30
2911 38z. Lubusk . . . . 1·25 55

1983. 40th Anniv of National People's Council.
2912 **838** 6z. multicoloured 25 10

839 Badge of "General Bem" Brigade **840** Dulcimer

1983. 40th Anniv of People's Army.
2913 **839** 5z. multicoloured 25 10

1984. Musical Instruments (1st series). Mult.
2914 5z. Type **840** 15 10
2915 6z. Kettle drum and tambourine 25 15
2916 10z. Accordion 40 30
2917 15z. Double bass 45 40
2918 17z. Bagpipe 55 45
2919 29z. Country band (wood carvings by Tadeusz Zak) 90 65

841 Wincenty Witos **842** "Clematis lanuginosa"

1984. 110th Birth Anniv of Wincenty Witos (leader of Peasants' Movement).
2920 **841** 6z. brown and green . . 25 10

1984. Clematis. Multicoloured.
2921 5z. Type **842** 20 10
2922 6z. "C. tangutica" 25 10
2923 10z. "C. texensis" 30 10
2924 17z. "C. alpina" 45 15
2925 25z. "C. vitalba" 90 30
2926 27z. "C. montana" . . . . 1·00 45

843 "The Ecstasy of St. Francis" (El Greco)

1984. "Espana 84" International Stamp Exhibition, Madrid.
2927 **843** 27z. multicoloured . . . 90 40

844 Handball

1984. Olympic Games, Los Angeles, and Winter Olympics, Sarajevo. Multicoloured.
2928 5z. Type **844** 10 10
2929 6z. Fencing 15 10
2930 15z. Cycling 45 25
2931 16z. Janusz Kusocinski winning 10,000 m race, 1932 Olympics, Los Angeles 60 30
2932 17z. Stanislawa Walasiewiczowna winning 100 m race, 1932 Olympics, Los Angeles . . 60 30
2933 31z. Women's slalom (Winter Olympics) . . . . 1·00 45
MS2934 129 × 78 mm. Nos. 2931/2 1·25 1·10
The 10z. premium on **MS**2934 was for the benefit of the Polish Olympic Committee.

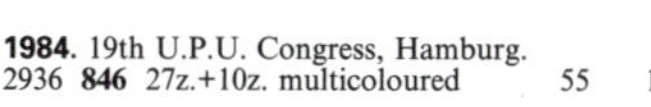
845 Monte Cassino Memorial Cross and Monastery **846** "German Princess" (Lucas Cranach)

1984. 40th Anniv of Battle of Monte Cassino.
2935 **845** 15z. olive and red . . . 55 25

1984. 19th U.P.U. Congress, Hamburg.
2936 **846** 27z.+10z. multicoloured 55 1·90

847 "Warsaw from the Praga Bank" (Canaletto)

1984. Paintings of Vistula River. Multicoloured.
2937 5z. Type **847** 25 25
2938 6z. "Trumpet Festivity" (A. Gierymski) 25 25
2939 25z. "The Vistula near Bielany District" (J. Rapacki) 90 65
2940 27z. "Steamship Harbour in the Powisle District" (F. Kostrzewski) . . . . 1·00 75

848 Order of Grunwald Cross **849** Group of Insurgents

1984. 40th Anniv of Polish People's Republic. Multicoloured.
2941 5z. Type **848** 25 10
2942 6z. Order of Revival of Poland 25 10
2943 10z. Order of Banner of Labour, First Class . . . 30 10
2944 16z. Order of Builders of People's Poland 60 30
MS2945 156 × 101 mm. Nos. 2941/4 4·25 6·00

1984. 40th Anniv of Warsaw Uprising. Mult.
2946 4z. Type **849** 25 10
2947 5z. Insurgent on postal duty 25 10
2948 6z. Insurgents fighting . . . 25 10
2949 25z. Tending wounded . . . 95 30

850 Defence of Oksywie Holm and Col. Stanislaw Dabek

1984. 45th Anniv of German Invasion. Mult.
2950 5z. Type **850** 25 10
2951 6z. Battle of Bzura River and Gen. Tadeusz Kutrzeba 25 10
See also Nos. 3004/5, 3062, 3126/8, 3172/4 and 3240/3.

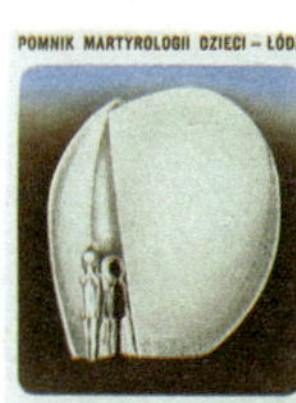

851 "Broken Heart" (monument, Lodz Concentration Camp)

1984. Child Martyrs.
2952 **851** 16z. brown, blue and deep brown 45 25

852 Militiaman and Ruins

1984. 40th Anniv of Security Force and Civil Militia. Multicoloured.
2953 5z. Type **852** 15 10
2954 6z. Militiaman in control centre 25 10

853 First Balloon Flight, 1784 (after Chostovski)

1984. Polish Aviation.
2955 **853** 5z. black, green & mauve 25 10
2956 – 5z. multicoloured 25 10
2957 – 6z. multicoloured 25 10
2958 – 10z. multicoloured . . . 30 10
2959 – 16z. multicoloured . . . 40 15
2960 – 27z. multicoloured . . . 90 30
2961 – 31z. multicoloured . . . 1·10 50

DESIGNS: No. 2956, Michal Scipio del Campo and biplane (1st flight over Warsaw, 1911); 2957, Balloon "Polonez" (winner, Gordon Bennett Cup, 1983); 2958, PWS 101 and Jantar gliders (Lilienthal Medal winners); 2959, PZL-104 Wilga airplane (world precise flight champion, 1983); 2960, Jan Nagorski and Farman M.F.7 floatplane (Arctic zone flights, 1914); 2961, PZL P-37 Los and PZL P-7 aircraft.

854 Weasel

1984. Fur-bearing Animals. Multicoloured.
2962 4z. Type **854** 15 10
2963 5z. Stoat 15 10
2964 5z. Beech marten 25 10
2965 10z. Eurasian beaver 25 10
2966 10z. Eurasian otter 25 10
2967 65z. Alpine marmot . . . . 1·90 60

1984. Renovation of Cracow Monuments (3rd series). As T **819**.
2968 5z. brown, black and green 15 10
2969 15z. blue, brown and black 30 15
DESIGNS—VERT: 5z. Wawel cathedral. HORIZ: 15z. Wawel castle (royal residence).

855 Protestant Church, Warsaw

1984. Religious Architecture. Multicoloured.
2970 5z. Type **855** 10 10
2971 10z. Saint Andrew's Roman Catholic church, Krakow 25 10
2972 15z. Greek Catholic church, Rychwald 40 10
2973 20z. St. Maria Magdalena Orthodox church, Warsaw 55 10
2974 25z. Tykocin synagogue, Kaczorow (horiz) 60 30
2975 31z. Tatar mosque, Kruszyiany (horiz) . . . 75 30

856 Steam Fire Hose (late 19th century)

1985. Fire Engines. Multicoloured.
2976 4z. Type **856** 10 10
2977 10z. "Polski Fiat", 1930s . . 25 10
2978 12z. "Jelcz 315" fire engine 30 10
2979 15z. Manual fire hose, 1899 40 10
2980 20z. "Magirus" fire ladder on "Jelcz" chassis 55 30
2981 30z. Manual fire hose (early 18th century) 85 40

857 "Battle of Raclawice" (Jan Styka and Wojciech Kossak)

1985.
2982 **857** 27z. multicoloured . . . 60 30

858 Wincenty Rzymowski

859 Badge on Denim

1985. 35th Death Anniv of Wincenty Rzymowski (founder of Polish Democratic Party).
2983 **858** 10z. violet and red . . . 30 15

1985. International Youth Year.
2984 **859** 15z. multicoloured . . . 40 15

860 Boleslaw III, the Wry-mouthed, and Map

1985. 40th Anniv of Return of Western and Northern Territories to Poland. Multicoloured.
2985 5z. Type **860** 10 10
2986 10z. Wladyslaw Gomulka (vice-president of first postwar government) and map 30 15
2987 20z. Piotr Zaremba (Governor of Szczecin) and map 60 25

861 "Victory, Berlin 1945" (Joesf Mlynarski)

1985. 40th Anniv of Victory over Fascism.
2988 **861** 5z. multicoloured 15 15

862 Warsaw Arms and Flags of Member Countries

864 Cadet Ship "Iskra"

863 Wolves in Winter

1985. 30th Anniv of Warsaw Pact.
2989 **862** 5z. multicoloured 15 15

1985. Protected Animals. The Wolf. Mult.
2990 5z. Type **863** 15 10
2991 10z. She-wolf with cubs . . 30 25
2992 10z. Close-up of wolf . . . 30 25
2993 20z. Wolves in summer . . 60 45

1985. Musical Instruments (2nd series). As T **840**. Multicoloured.
2994 5z. Rattle and tarapata . . 15 10
2995 10z. Stick rattle and berlo . 30 10
2996 12z. Clay whistles 40 10
2997 20z. Stringed instruments . . 60 25
2998 25z. Cow bells 85 25
2999 31z. Wind instruments . . . 1·00 30

1985. 40th Anniv of Polish Navy.
3000 **864** 5z. blue and yellow . . . 15 10

865 Tomasz Nocznicki

1985. Leaders of Peasants' Movement.
3001 **865** 10z. green 25 10
3002 – 20z. brown 45 25
DESIGN: 20z. Maciej Rataj.

866 Hockey Players

1985. 60th Anniv (1986) of Polish Field Hockey Association.
3003 **866** 5z. multicoloured 15 10

1985. 46th Anniv of German Invasion. As T **850**. Multicoloured.
3004 5z. Defence of Wizna and Capt. Wladyslaw Raginis 15 10
3005 10z. Battle of Mlawa and Col. Wilhelm Liszka-Lawicz 30 10

867 Type 20k Goods Wagon

1985. PAFAWAG Railway Rolling Stock. Mult.
3006 5z. Type **867** 15 10
3007 10z. Electric locomotive No. ET22-001, 1969 . . . . . 25 10
3008 17z. Type OMMK wagon 40 25
3009 20z. Type 111A passenger carriage 55 30

868 "Madonna with Child St. John and Angel" (Sandro Botticelli)

1985. "Italia '85" International Stamp Exhibition, Rome. Sheet 81 × 108 mm.
MS3010 **868** 65z.+15z. multicoloured . . . . 1·90 1·90

869 Green-winged Teal

1985. Wild Ducks. Multicoloured.
3011 5z. Type **869** 15 10
3012 5z. Garganey 15 10
3013 10z. Tufted duck 30 10
3014 15z. Common goldeneye . . 40 10
3015 25z. Eider 65 30
3016 29z. Red-crested pochard . . 1·00 30

870 U.N. Emblem and "Flags"

1985. 40th Anniv of U.N.O.
3017 **870** 27z. multicoloured . . . 60 30

871 Ballerina

872 "Marysia and Burek in Ceylon"

1985. Bicentenary of Polish Ballet.
3018 **871** 5z. green, orange and red 15 10
3019 – 15z. brown, violet & orange 45 10
DESIGN: 15z. Male dancer.

1985. Birth Centenary of Stanislaw Ignacy Witkiewicz (artist). Multicoloured.
3020 5z. Type **872** 15 10
3021 10z. "Woman with Fox" (horiz) 30 10
3022 10z. "Self-portrait" 30 10
3023 20z. "Compositions (1917–20)" 55 30
3024 25z. "Nena Stachurska" . . 65 30

873 Oliwa Church Organ and Bach

874 Human Profile

1985. 300th Birth Anniv of Johann Sebastian Bach (composer). Sheet 67 × 79 mm.
MS3025 **873** 65z. multicoloured 1·50 1·25

1986. Congress of Intellectuals for Defence of Peaceful Future of the World, Warsaw.
3026 **874** 10z. ultramarine, violet and blue 30 10

875 Michal Kamienski and Planetary and Comet's Orbits

1985. Appearance of Halley's Comet.
3027 **875** 25z. blue and brown . . 60 30
3028 – 25z. deep blue, blue and brown 60 30
DESIGN: No. 3028, "Vega", "Planet A", "Giotto" and "Ice" space probes and comet.

1986. Renovation of Cracow Monuments (4th series). As T **819**.
3029 5z. dp brown, brown & black 10 10
3030 10z. green, brown and black 25 10
DESIGNS: 5z. Collegium Maius (Jagiellonian University Museum); 10z. Kazimierz Town Hall.

876 Sun

877 Grey Partridge

1986. International Peace Year.
3031 **876** 25z. yellow, light blue and blue 45 25

1986. Game. Multicoloured.
3032 5z. Type **877** 30 30
3033 5z. Common rabbit 10 10
3034 10z. Common pheasants (horiz) 55 55
3035 10z. Fallow deer (horiz) . . 15 10
3036 20z. Hare 30 30
3037 40z. Argali 65 65

878 Kulczynski

880 Paderewski (composer)

879 "Warsaw Fire Brigade, 1871" (detail, Jozef Brodowski)

1986. 10th Death Anniv (1985) of Stanislaw Kulczynski (politician).
3038 **878** 10z. light brown and brown 25 10

1986. 150th Anniv of Warsaw Fire Brigade.
3039 **879** 10z. dp brown & brown 25 10

1986. "Ameripex '86" International Stamp Exhibition, Chicago.
3040 **880** 65z. blue, black and grey 1·40 45

881 Footballers

1986. World Cup Football Championship, Mexico.
3041 **881** 25z. multicoloured . . . 45 30

882 "Wilanow"

1986. Passenger Ferries. Multicoloured.
3042 10z. Type **882** 25 15
3043 10z. "Wawel" 25 15
3044 15z. "Pomerania" 30 15
3045 25z. "Rogalin" 55 25
MS3046 Two sheets, each 116 × 98 mm. (a) Nos. 3042/3 (sold at 30z.); (b) Nos. 3044/5 (sold at 55z.) . . . . 6·00 2·40

883 A. B. Dobrowolski, Map and Research Vessel "Kopernik"

885 "The Paulinite Church on Skalka in Cracow" (detail), 1627

884 Workers and Emblem

1986. 25th Anniv of Antarctic Agreement.
3047 **883** 5z. green, black and red 10 15
3048 – 40z. lavender, violet and orange . . . . 1·90 30

DESIGN: 40z. H. Arctowski, map and research vessel "Profesor Siedlecki".

1986. 10th Polish United Workers' Party Congress, Warsaw.
3049 **884** 10z. blue and red 25 10

1986. Treasures of Jasna Gora Monastery. Mult.
3050 5z. Type **885** 15 10
3051 5z. "Tree of Jesse", 17th-century 15 10
3052 20z. Chalice, 18th-century 40 25
3053 40z. "Virgin Mary" (detail, chasuble column), 15th-century . . . . . . 1·10 30

886 Precision Flying (Waclaw Nycz)

1986. 1985 Polish World Championship Successes. Multicoloured.
3054 5z. Type **886** 15 10
3055 10z. Windsurfing (Malgorzata Palasz-Piasecka) 40 10
3056 10z. Glider areobatics (Jerzy Makula) 30 10
3057 15z. Wrestling (Bogdan Daras) 30 10
3058 20z. Individual road cycling (Lech Piasecki) 45 25
3059 30z. Women's modern pentathlon (Barbara Kotowska) 75 30

887 "Bird" in National Costume carrying Stamp

888 Schweitzer

1986. "Stockholmia '86" International Stamp Exhibition.
3060 **887** 65z. multicoloured . . . 1·40 45
MS3061 94 × 80 mm. No. 3060 1·60 1·60

1986. 47th Anniv of German Invasion. As T **850**. Multicoloured.
3062 10z. Battle of Jordanow and Col. Stanislaw Maczek . . 25 10

1986. 10th Death Anniv (1985) of Albert Schweitzer (medical missionary).
3063 **888** 5z. brown, lt brown & blue 15 10

889 Airliner and Postal Messenger

890 Basilisk

1986. World Post Day.
3064 **889** 40z. brown, blue and red 75 30
MS3065 81 × 81 mm. No. 3064 × 2 (sold at 120z.) . . . . 10·50 9·00

1986. Folk Tales. Multicoloured.
3066 5z. Type **890** 15 15
3067 5z. Duke Popiel (vert) . . . 15 15
3068 10z. Golden Duck 25 15
3069 10z. Boruta the Devil (vert) 25 15
3070 20z. Janosik the Robber (vert) 40 15
3071 50z. Lajkonik (vert) . . . . 1·10 40

891 Kotarbinski

892 20th-century Windmill, Zygmuntow

1986. Birth Centenary of Tadeusz Kotarbinski (philosopher).
3072 **891** 10z. deep brown and brown 25 30

1986. Wooden Architecture. Multicoloured.
3073 5z. Type **892** 15 10
3074 5z. 17th-century church, Baczal Dolny 15 10
3075 10z. 19th-century Oravian cottage, Zubrzyca Gorna 25 10
3076 15z. 18th-century Kashubian arcade cottage, Wdzydze 25 15
3077 25z. 19th-century barn, Grzawa 55 25
3078 30z. 19th-century watermill, Siolkowice Stare 75 30

893 Mieszko (Mieczyslaw) I

1986. Polish Rulers (1st series). Drawings by Jan Matejko.
3079 **893** 10z. brown and green . . 30 30
3080 – 25z. black and purple . . 75 45
DESIGN: 25z. Queen Dobrawa (wife of Mieszko I).
See also Nos. 3144/5, 3193/4, 3251/2, 3341/2, 3351/2, 3387/8, 3461/4, 3511/12, 3548/51, 3641/4, 3705/8, 3732/5, 3819/22 and 3887/91.

894 Star

1986. New Year.
3081 **894** 25z. multicoloured . . . 45 30

895 Trip to Bielany, 1887

1986. Centenary of Warsaw Cyclists' Society.
3082 **895** 5z. multicoloured 10 15
3083 – 5z. brown, light brown and black 10 15
3084 – 10z. multicoloured . . . 25 15
3085 – 10z. multicoloured . . . 25 15
3086 – 30z. multicoloured . . . 60 30
3087 – 50z. multicoloured . . . 1·10 45
DESIGNS: No. 3083, Jan Stanislaw Skrodaki (1895 touring record holder); 3084, Dynasy (Society's headquarters, 1892–1937); 3085, Mieczyslaw Baranski (1896 Kingdom of Poland road cycling champion); 3086, Karolina Kociecka; 3087, Henryk Weiss (Race champion).

896 Lelewel

1986. Birth Bicentenary of Joachim Lelewel (historian).
3088 **896** 10z.+5z. multicoloured 30 15

897 Krill and "Antoni Garnuszewski" (cadet freighter)

1987. 10th Anniv of Henryk Arctowski Antarctic Station, King George Island, South Shetlands. Multicoloured.
3089 5z. Type **897** 10 10
3090 5z. Antarctic toothfish, marbled rockfish and "Zulawy" (supply ship) 10 10
3091 10z. Southern fulmar and "Pogoria" (cadet brigantine) 30 10
3092 10z. Adelie penguin and "Gedania" (yacht) 30 10
3093 30z. Fur seal and "Dziunia" (research vessel) 40 10
3094 40z. Leopard seals and "Kapitan Ledochowski" (research vessel) 45 30

898 "Portrait of a Woman"

1987. 50th Death Anniv (1986) of Leon Wyczolkowski (artist). Multicoloured.
3095 5z. "Cineraria Flowers" (horiz) 10 10
3096 10z. Type **898** 15 10
3097 10z. "Wooden Church" (horiz) 15 10
3098 25z. "Beetroot Lifting" . . 40 10
3099 30z. "Wading Fishermen" (horiz) 45 15
3100 40z. "Self-portrait" (horiz) 60 40

899 "Ravage" (from "War Cycle") and Artur Grottger

1987. 150th Birth Anniv of Artur Grottger (artist).
3101 **899** 15z. brown and stone . . 25 10

900 Swierczewski

901 Strzelecki

1987. 90th Birth Anniv of General Karol Swierczewski.
3102 **900** 15z. green and olive . . 25 10

1987. 190th Birth Anniv of Pawel Edmund Strzelecki (scientist and explorer of Tasmania).
3103 **901** 65z. green 60 30

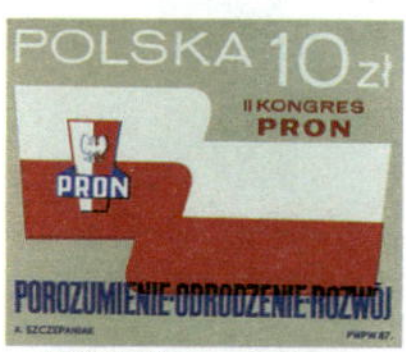

902 Emblem and Banner

1987. 2nd Patriotic Movement for National Revival Congress.
3104 **902** 10z. red, blue and brown 15 10

903 CWS "T-1" Motor Car, 1928

1987. Polish Motor Vehicles. Multicoloured.
3105 10z. Type **903** 10 10
3106 10z. Saurer-Zawrat bus, 1936 . . . . 10 10
3107 15z. Ursus-A lorry, 1928 . . 25 10
3108 15z. Lux-Sport motor car, 1936 . . . . 25 10
3109 25z. Podkowa "100" motor cycle, 1939 . . . . . . 30 10
3110 45z. Sokol "600 RT" motor cycle, 1935 . . . . 55 55

904 Royal Palace, Warsaw

1987.
3111 **904** 50z. multicoloured . . . 60 30

905 Pope John Paul II

1987. 3rd Papal Visit. Multicoloured.
3112 15z. Type **905** 25 15
3113 45z. Pope and signature . . 45 30
MS3114 77 × 66 mm. 50z. Profile of Pope (21 × 27 mm) 60 60

906 Polish Settler at Kasubia, Ontario

1987. "Capex '87" International Stamp Exhibition, Toronto.
3115 **906** 50z.+20z. multicoloured 75 40

1987. Renovation of Cracow Monuments (5th series). As T **819**.
3116 10z. lilac, black and green 15 10
DESIGN: 10z. Barbican.

907 Ludwig Zamenhof (inventor) and Star

1987. Cent of Esperanto (invented language).
3117 **907** 5z. brown, green & black 60 25

908 "Poznan Town Hall" (Stanislaw Wyspianski)

909 Queen Bee

1987. "Poznan 87" National Stamp Exhibition.
3118 **908** 15z. brown and orange 25 15

1987. "Apimondia 87" International Bee Keeping Congress, Warsaw. Multicoloured.
3119 10z. Type **909** 15 10
3120 10z. Worker bee 15 10
3121 15z. Drone 25 10
3122 15z. Hive in orchard 25 10
3123 40z. Worker bee on clover flower 60 25
3124 50z. Forest bee keeper collecting honey 75 30

910 1984 Olympic Stamp and Laurel Wreath

1987. "Olymphilex '87" Olympic Stamps Exhibition, Rome. Sheet 83 × 57 mm.
MS3125 **910** 45z.+10z. multicoloured 75 85
The premium was for the benefit of the Polish Olympic Committee's fund.

1987. 48th Anniv of German Invasion. As T **850**. Multicoloured.
3126 10z. Battle of Mokra and Col. Julian Filipowicz . . 15 10
3127 10z. Fighting at Oleszyce and Brig.-Gen. Jozef Rudolf Kustron 15 10
3128 15z. PZL P-7 aircraft over Warsaw and Col. Stefan Pawlikowsi 30 10

911 Hevelius and Sextant

912 High Jump (World Acrobatics Championships, France)

1987. 300th Death Anniv of Jan Hevelius (astronomer). Multicoloured.
3129 15z. Type **911** 25 10
3130 40z. Hevelius and map of constellations (horiz) . . . 55 25

1987. 1986 Polish World Championship Successes. Multicoloured.
3131 10z. Type **912** 15 10
3132 15z. Two-man canoe (World Canoeing Championships, Canada) 25 10
3133 20z. Marksman (Free pistol event, World Marksmanship Championships, East Germany) 30 15
3134 25z. Wrestlers (World Wrestling Championships, Hungary) 45 15

913 "Stacionar 4" Telecommunications Satellite

1987. 30th Anniv of launch of "Sputnik 1" (first artificial satellite). Sheet 67 × 82 mm.
MS3135 **913** 40z. multicoloured 55 60

914 Warsaw Post Office and Ignacy Franciszek Przebendowski (Postmaster General)

1987. World Post Day.
3136 **914** 15z. green and red . . . 25 10

915 "The Little Mermaid"

916 Col. Stanislaw Wieckowski (founder)

1987. "Hafnia 87" International Stamp Exhibition, Copenhagen. Hans Christain Andersen's Fairy Tales. Multicoloured.
3137 10z. Type **915** 15 10
3138 10z. "The Nightingale" . . 15 10
3139 20z. "The Wild Swans" . . 25 15
3140 20z. "The Little Match Girl" 25 15
3141 30z. "The Snow Queen" . . 40 30
3142 40z. "The Tin Soldier" . . . 55 15

1987. 50th Anniv of Democratic Clubs.
3143 **916** 15z. black and blue . . . 25 10

1987. Polish Rulers (2nd series). As T **893**. Drawings by Jan Matejko.
3144 10z. green and blue 15 15
3145 15z. blue and ultramarine 40 30
DESIGNS: 10z. Boleslaw I, the Brave; 15z. Mieszko (Mieczyslaw) II.

917 Santa Claus with Christmas Trees

1987. New Year.
3146 **917** 15z. multicoloured . . . 15 15

918 Emperor Dragonfly

1988. Dragonflies. Multicoloured.
3147 10z. Type **918** 15 10
3148 15z. Four-spotted libellula ("Libellula quadrimaculata") (vert) 30 10
3149 15z. Banded agrion ("Calopteryx splendens") 30 10
3150 20z. "Cordulegaster annulatus" (vert) 30 10
3151 30z. "Sympetrum pedemontanum" 40 25
3152 50z. "Aeschna viridis" (vert) 65 30

1988. Renovation of Cracow Monuments (6th series). As T **819**.
3153 15z. yellow, brown and black 15 10
DESIGN: 15z. Florianska Gate.

919 Composition

1988. International Year of Graphic Design.
3154 **919** 40z. multicoloured . . . 40 40

920 17th-century Friesian Wall Clock with Bracket Case

1988. Clocks and Watches. Multicoloured.
3155 10z. Type **920** 15 10
3156 10z. 20th-century annual clock (horiz) 15 10
3157 15z. 18th-century carriage clock 15 10
3158 15z. 18th-century French rococo bracket clock . . 15 10
3159 20z. 19th-century pocket watch (horiz) 25 10
3160 40z. 17th-cent tile-case clock from Gdansk by Benjamin Zoll (horiz) . . 40 15

921 Atlantic Salmon and Reindeer

1988. "Finlandia 88" International Stamp Exhibition, Helsinki.
3161 **921** 45z.+30z. multicoloured 60 30

922 Triple Jump

924 Wheat as Graph on VDU

923 Kukuczka

1988. Olympic Games, Seoul. Multicoloured.
3162 15z. Type **922** 25 10
3163 20z. Wrestling 25 10
3164 20z. Canoeing 25 10
3165 25z. Judo 25 10
3166 40z. Shooting 40 15
3167 55z. Swimming 55 30

1988. Award of Special Olympic Silver Medal to Jerzy Kukuczka for Mountaineering Achievements. Sheet 84 × 66 mm.
MS3168 **923** 70z.+10z. multicoloured 75 75

1988. 16th European Conference of Food and Agriculture Organization, Cracow. Multicoloured.
3169 15z. Type **924** 15 10
3170 40z. Factory in forest . . . 30 10

925 PZL P-37 Los Bomber

1988. 70th Anniv of Polish Republic (1st issue). 60th Anniv of Polish State Aircraft Works.
3171 **925** 45z. multicoloured . . . 30 10
See also Nos. 3175, 3177, 3181/88 and 3190/2.

1988. 49th Anniv of German Invasion. As T **850**. Multicoloured.
3172 15z. Battle of Modlin and Brig.-Gen. Wiktor Thommee 25 10
3173 20z. Battle of Warsaw and Brig.-Gen. Walerian Czuma 25 10
3174 20z. Battle of Tomaszow Lubelski and Brig.-Gen. Antoni Szylling 25 10

1988. 70th Anniv of Polish Republic (2nd issue). 50th Anniv of Stalowa Wola Ironworks. As T **925**. Multicoloured.
3175 15z. View of plant 15 10

926 Postal Emblem and Tomasz Arciszewski (Postal Minister, 1918–19)

1988. World Post Day.
3176 **926** 20z. multicoloured . . . 15 10

1988. 70th Anniv of Polish Republic (3rd issue). 60th Anniv of Military Institute for Aviation Medicine. As T **925**. Multicoloured.
3177 20z. Hanriot XIV hospital aircraft (38 × 28 mm) . . 15 10

927 On the Field of Glory Medal

1988. Polish People's Army Battle Medals (1st series). Multicoloured.
3178 20z. Type **927** 15 10
3179 20z. Battle of Lenino Cross 15 10
See also Nos. 3249/50.

928 "Stanislaw Malachowski" and "Kazimierz Nestor Sapieha"

1988. Bicentenary of Four Years Diet (political and social reforms). Paintings of Diet Presidents by Jozef Peszko.
3180 **928** 20z. multicoloured . . . 15 10

929 Ignacy Daszynski (politician)

1988. 70th Anniv of Polish Republic (4th issue). Personalities.
3181 **929** 15z. green, red and black 10 10
3182 – 15z. green, red and black 10 10
3183 – 20z. brown, red and black 15 10
3184 – 20z. brown, red and black 15 10
3185 – 20z. brown, red and black 15 10
3186 – 200z. purple, red & black 1·40 55
3187 – 200z. purple, red & black 1·40 55
3188 – 200z. purple, red & black 1·40 55
MS3189 102 × 60 mm. Nos. 3186/8 13·50 13·50
DESIGNS: No. 3182, Wincenty Witos (politician); 3183, Julian Marchlewski (trade unionist and economist); 3184, Stanislaw Wojciechowski (politician); 3185, Wojciech Korfanty (politician); 3186, Ignacy Paderewski (musician and politician); 3187; Marshal Jozef Pilsudski; 3188, Gabriel Narutowicz (President, 1922).

1988. 70th Anniv of Polish Republic (5th issue). As T **925**. Multicoloured.
3190 15z. Coal wharf, Gdynia Port (65th anniv) (38 × 28 mm) 10 10
3191 20z. Hipolit Cegielski (founder) and steam locomotive (142nd anniv of H. Cegielski Metal Works, Poznan) (38 × 28 mm) 15 10
3192 40z. Upper Silesia Tower (main entrance) (60th anniv of International Poznan Fair) 30 10

1988. Polish Rulers (3rd series). Drawings by Jan Matejko. As T **893**.
3193 10z. deep brown and brown 30 10
3194 15z. deep brown and brown 45 10
DESIGNS: 10z. Queen Rycheza; 15z. Kazimierz (Karol Odnowiciel) I.

930 Snowman

1988. New Year.
3195 **930** 20z. multicoloured . . . 15 10

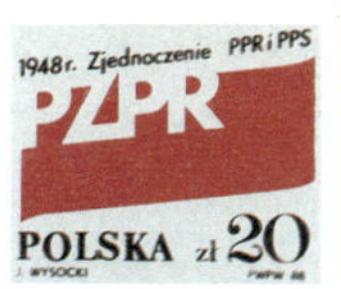

931 Flag **932** "Blysk"

1988. 40th Anniv of Polish United Workers' Party.
3196 **931** 20z. red and black . . . 15 10

1988. Fire Boats. Multicoloured.
3197 10z. Type **932** 10 10
3198 15z. "Plomien" 10 10
3199 15z. "Zar" 10 10
3200 20z. "Strazak II" 25 10
3201 20z. "Strazak 4" 25 10
3202 45z. "Strazak 25" 40 30

933 Ardennes

1989. Horses. Multicoloured.
3203 15z. Lippizaner (horiz) . . . 10 10
3204 15z. Type **933** 10 10
3205 20z. English thoroughbred (horiz) 25 10
3206 20z. Arab 25 10
3207 30z. Great Poland race-horse (horiz) 40 10
3208 70z. Polish horse 75 30

934 Wire-haired Dachshund

1989. Hunting Dogs. Multicoloured.
3209 15z. Type **934** 10 10
3210 15z. Cocker spaniel 10 10
3211 20z. Czech fousek pointer 10 10
3212 20z. Welsh terrier 10 10
3213 25z. English setter 15 10
3214 45z. Pointer 30 30

935 Gen. Wladyslaw Anders and Plan of Battle **936** Marianne

1989. 45th Anniv of Battle of Monte Cassino.
3215 **935** 80z. multicoloured . . . 40 30
See also Nos. 3227, 3247, 3287 and 3327.

1989. Bicentenary of French Revolution.
3216 **936** 100z. black, red and blue 40 25
MS3217 93 × 118 mm. No. 3216 × 2 plus two labels (sold at 270z.) 90 1·10

937 Polonia House

1989. Opening of Polonia House (cultural centre), Pultusk.
3218 **937** 100z. multicoloured . . . 45 25

938 Monument (Bohdan Chmielewski)

1989. 45th Anniv of Civic Militia and Security Force.
3219 **938** 35z. blue and brown . . 25 15

939 Xaweri Dunikowski (artist) **941** Firemen

940 Astronaut

1989. Recipients of Order of Builders of the Republic of Poland. Multicoloured.
3220 35z. Type **939** 15 10
3221 35z. Stanislaw Mazur (farmer) 15 10
3222 35z. Natalia Gasiorowska (historian) 15 10
3223 35z. Wincenti Pstrowski (initiator of worker performance contests) . . 15 10

1989. 20th Anniv of First Manned Landing on Moon.
3224 **940** 100z. multicoloured . . . 45 25
MS3225 85 × 85 mm. No. 3224 2·10 1·40

1989. World Fire Fighting Congress, Warsaw.
3226 **941** 80z. multicoloured . . . 30 10

1989. 45th Anniv of Battle of Falaise. As T **935**. Multicoloured.
3227 165z. Plan of battle and Gen. Stanislaw Maczek (horiz) 60 30

942 Daisy **943** Museum Emblem

1989. Plants. (a) Perf.
3229 **942** 40z. green 15 10
3230 – 60z. violet 15 10
3231 **942** 150z. red 30 10
3232 – 500z. mauve 30 10
3233 – 700z. green 15 10
3234 – 1000z. blue 90 30

(b) Self-adhesive. Imperf.
3297 – 2000z. green 40 25
3298 – 5000z. violet 85 40
DESIGNS: 60z. Juniper; 500z. Wild rose; 700z. Lily of the valley; 1000z. Blue cornflower; 2000z. Water lily; 5000z. Iris.

1989. 50th Anniv of German Invasion. As T **850**.
3240 25z. grey, orange and black 25 10
3241 25z. multicoloured 25 10
3242 35z. multicoloured 40 30
3243 35z. multicoloured 40 30
DESIGNS: No. 3240, Defence of Westerplatte and Captain Franciszek Dabrowski; 3241, Defence of Hel and Captain B. Przybyszewski; 3242, Battle of Kock and Brig.-Gen. Franciszek Kleeberg; 3243, Defence of Lwow and Brig.-Gen. Wladyslaw Langner.

1989. Caricature Museum.
3244 **943** 40z. multicoloured . . . 15 10

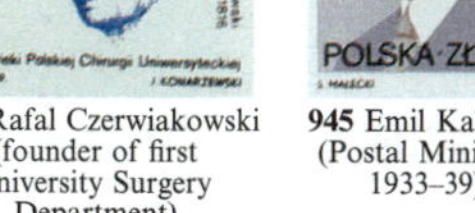

944 Rafal Czerwiakowski (founder of first university Surgery Department) **945** Emil Kalinski (Postal Minister, 1933–39)

1989. Polish Surgeons' Society Centenary Congress, Cracow.
3245 **944** 40z. blue and black . . . 25 10
3246 – 60z. green and black . . 25 10
DESIGN: 60z. Ludwik Rydygier (founder of Polish Surgeons' Society).

1989. 45th Anniv of Landing at Arnhem. As T **935**. Multicoloured.
3247 210z. Gen. Stanislaw Sosabowski and plan of battle 75 45

1989. World Post Day.
3248 **945** 60z. multicoloured . . . 25 25

1989. Polish People's Army Battle Medals (2nd series). As T **927**. Multicoloured.
3249 60z. "For Participation in the Struggle for the Rule of the People" 25 15
3250 60z. Warsaw 1939–45 Medal 25 15

1989. Polish Rulers (4th series). As T **893**. Drawings by Jan Matejko.
3251 20z. black and grey 30 10
3252 30z. sepia and brown . . . 30 30
DESIGNS: 20z. Boleslaw II, the Bold; 30z. Wladyslaw I Herman.

946 Stamps

1989. "World Stamp Expo '89" International Stamp Exhibition, Washington D.C.
3253 **946** 500z. multicoloured . . . 1·10 65

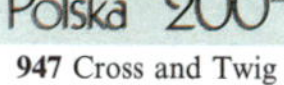

947 Cross and Twig **949** Photographer and Medal depicting Maksymilian Strasz

948 Ignacy Paderewski and Roman Dmowski (Polish signatories)

1989. 70th Anniv of Polish Red Cross.
3254 **947** 200z. red, green and black 45 25

1989. 70th Anniv of Treaty of Versailles.
3255 **948** 350z. multicoloured . . . 60 60

1989. 150th Anniv of Photography. Multicoloured.
3256 40z. Type **949** 15 10
3257 60z. Lens shutter as pupil of eye (horiz) 15 10

1989. No. 2729 surch **500**.
3258 500z. on 4z. violet 90 45

951 Painting by Jan Ciaglinski

1989. Flower Paintings by Artists Named. Mult.
3259 25z. Type **951** 10 10
3260 30z. Wojciech Weiss 10 10
3261 35z. Antoni Kolasinski . . . 15 10
3262 50z. Stefan Nacht-Samborski 15 10
3263 60z. Jozef Pankiewicz . . . 15 10
3264 85z. Henryka Beyer 25 25
3265 110z. Wladyslaw Slewinski 30 30
3266 190z. Czeslaw Wdowiszewski 40 40

952 Christ

1989. Icons (1st series). Multicoloured.
3267 50z. Type **952** 15 10
3268 60z. Two saints with books 15 10
3269 90z. Three saints with books 25 15
3270 150z. Displaying scriptures (vert) 40 40
3271 200z. Madonna and child (vert) 45 45
3272 350z. Christ with saints and angels (vert) 45 45
See also Nos. 3345/50.

1990. No. 2839 surch **350 zl.**
3273 350z. on 15z. brown 60 30

954 Krystyna Jamroz **955** High Jumping

1990. Singers. Multicoloured.
3274 100z. Type **954** 25 25
3275 150z. Wanda Werminska . . 25 25
3276 350z. Ada Sari 40 40
3277 500z. Jan Kiepura 45 45

1990. Sports. Multicoloured.
3278 100z. Yachting 15 25
3279 200z. Rugby 15 30
3280 400z. Type **955** 15 30
3281 500z. Ice skating 15 40
3282 500z. Diving 15 45
3283 1000z. Gymnastics 25 30

956 Kozlowski

1990. Birth Centenary (1989) of Roman Kozlowski (palaeontologist).
3284 **956** 500z. brown and red . . 15 25

957 John Paul II

1990. 70th Birthday of Pope John Paul II.
3285 **957** 1000z. multicoloured . . 30 30

958 1860 10k. Stamp and Anniversary Stamp

1990. 130th Anniv of First Polish Postage Stamp. Sheet 65 × 68 mm.
MS3286 **958** 1000z. orange and blue . . . 60 30

1990. 50th Anniv of Battle of Narvik. As T **935**. Multicoloured.
3287 1500z. Gen. Zygmunt Bohusz-Szyszko and plan of battle 30 25

959 Ball and Colosseum

1990. World Cup Football Championship, Italy.
3288 **959** 1000z. multicoloured . . 15 25

1990. No. 3230 surch **700 zł.**
3289 700z. on 60z. violet 15 15

961 Memorial

963 Stagnant Pond Snail

962 People and "ZUS"

1990. 34th Anniv of 1956 Poznan Uprising.
3290 **961** 1500z. multicoloured . . 25 15

1990. 70th Anniv of Social Insurance.
3291 **962** 1500z. blue, mauve & yellow 30 25

1990. Shells. No value expressed.
3292 – B (500z.) lilac 25 10
3293 **963** A (700z.) green 45 10
DESIGN: B, River snail.

964 Cross

1990. 50th Anniv of Katyn Massacre.
3294 **964** 1500z. black and red . . 25 10

965 Weather Balloon

1990. Polish Hydrology and Meteorology Service. Multicoloured.
3295 500z. Type **965** 10 10
3296 700z. Water-height gauge . . 25 10

966 Women's Kayak Pairs

1990. 23rd World Canoeing Championships. Mult.
3305 700z. Type **966** 25 10
3306 1000z. Men's kayak singles 30 30

967 Victory Sign

968 Jacob's Ladder

1990. 10th Anniv of Solidarity Trade Union.
3307 **967** 1500z. grey, black and red 25 30

1990. Flowers. Multicoloured.
3308 200z. Type **968** 10 10
3309 700z. Floating heart water fringe ("Nymphoides peltata") 15 10
3310 700z. Dragonhead ("Dracocephalum ruyschiana") 15 10
3311 1000z. "Helleborus purpurascens" 25 10
3312 1500z. Daphne cneorum . . 45 40
3313 1700z. Campion 65 45

969 Serving Dish, 1870–87

1990. Bicentenary of Cmieow Porcelain Works. Multicoloured.
3314 700z. Type **969** 15 10
3315 800z. Plate, 1887–90 (vert) 25 10
3316 1000z. Cup and saucer, 1887 30 10
3317 1000z. Figurine of dancer, 1941–44 (vert) 30 10
3318 1500z. Chocolate box, 1930–90 . . . . 55 25
3319 2000z. Vase, 1979 (vert) . . 60 40

970 Little Owl

972 Collegiate Church, Tum (12th century)

971 Walesa

1990. Owls. Multicoloured.
3320 200z. Type **970** 15 10
3321 500z. Tawny owl (value at left) 35 10
3322 500z. Tawny owl (value at right) 35 10
3323 1000z. Short-eared owl . . . 50 25
3324 1500z. Long-eared owl . . . 80 30
3325 2000z. Barn owl . . . . . 1·10 40

1990. Lech Walesa, 1984 Nobel Peace Prize Winner and new President.
3326 **971** 1700z. multicoloured . . 40 25

1990. 50th Anniv of Battle of Britain. As T **935**. Multicoloured.
3327 1500z. Emblem of 303 Squadron, Polish Fighter Wing R.A.F. and Hawker Hurricane 45 45

1990. Historic Architecture. Multicoloured.
3328 700z. Type **972** 25 20
3329 800z. Reszel Castle (11th century) 25 25
3330 1500z. Chelmno Town Hall (16th century) 60 60
3331 1700z. Church of the Nuns of the Visitation, Warsaw (18th century) 60 60

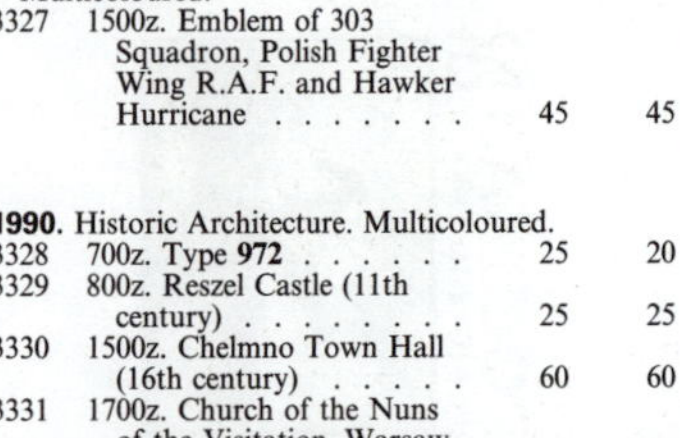

973 "King Zygmunt II August" (anon)

974 Silver Fir

1991. Paintings. Multicoloured.
3332 500z. Type **973** 15 10
3333 700z. "Adoration of the Magi" (Pultusk Codex) 25 10
3334 1000z. "St Matthew" (Pultusk Codex) 30 10
3335 1500z. "Expelling of Merchants from Temple" (Nikolai Haberschrack) 45 30
3336 1700z. "The Annunciation" (miniature) 55 30
3337 2000z. "Three Marys" (Nikolai Haberschrack) 60 40

1991. Cones. Multicoloured.
3338 700z. Type **974** 15 10
3339 1500z. Weymouth pine . . . 25 25
See also Nos. 3483/4.

975 Radziwill Palace

977 Chmielowski

1991. Admission of Poland into European Postal and Telecommunications Conference.
3340 **975** 1500z. multicoloured . . 30 25

1991. Polish Rulers (5th series). Drawings by Jan Matejko. As T **893** but surch.
3341 1000z. on 40z. black & green 40 25
3342 1500z. on 50z. black and red 55 30
DESIGNS: 1000z. Boleslaw III, the Wry Mouthed; 1500z. Wladyslaw II, the Exile.
Nos. 3341/2 were not issued unsurcharged.

1991. 75th Death Anniv of Adam Chmielowski ("Brother Albert") (founder of Albertine Sisters).
3343 **977** 2000z. multicoloured . . 40 25

978 Battle (detail of miniature, Schlackenwerth Codex, 1350)

1991. 750th Anniv of Battle of Legnica.
3344 **978** 1500z. multicoloured . . 30 25

1991. Icons (2nd series). As T **952**. Mult.
3345 500z. "Madonna of Nazareth" 10 10
3346 700z. "Christ the Acheirophyte" 15 10
3347 1000z. "Madonna of Vladimir" 25 10
3348 1500z. "Madonna of Kazan" 40 15
3349 2000z. "St. John the Baptist" 55 25
3350 2200z. "Christ the Pentocrator" 85 30

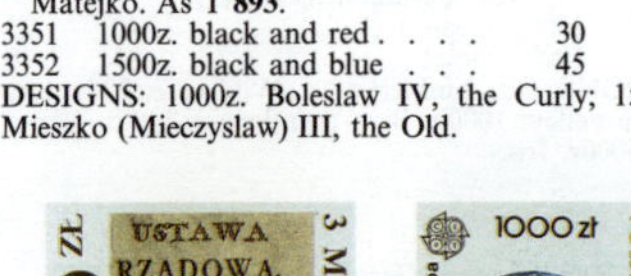

1991. Polish Rulers (6th series). Drawings by Jan Matejko. As T **893**.
3351 1000z. black and red 30 25
3352 1500z. black and blue . . . 45 25
DESIGNS: 1000z. Boleslaw IV, the Curly; 1500z. Mieszko (Mieczyslaw) III, the Old.

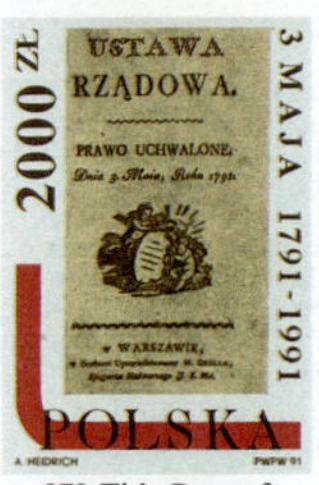

979 Title Page of Constitution

980 Satellite in Earth Orbit

1991. Bicentenary of 3rd May Constitution.
3353 **979** 2000z. brown, buff & red 40 30
3354 – 2500z. brown, stone & red 55 40
MS3355 85 × 85 mm. 3000z. multicoloured 75 75
DESIGNS: 2500z. "Administration of Oath by Gustav Taubert" (detail, Johann Friedrich Bolt); 3000z. "Constitution, 3 May 1791" (Jan Matejko).

1991. Europa. Europe in Space.
3356 **980** 1000z. multicoloured . . 25 25

981 Map and Battle Scene

1991. 50th Anniv of Participation of "Piorun" (destroyer) in Operation against "Bismarck" (German battleship).
3357 **981** 2000z. multicoloured . . 45 30

982 Arms of Cracow

983 Pope John Paul II

1991. European Security and Co-operation Conference Cultural Heritage Symposium, Cracow.
3358 **982** 2000z. purple and blue 40 30

1991. Papal Visit. Multicoloured.
3359 1000z. Type **983** 25 10
3360 2000z. Pope in white robes 40 30

984 Bearded Penguin

985 Making Paper

1991. 30th Anniv of Antarctic Treaty.
3361 **984** 2000z. multicoloured . . 40 30

1991. 500th Anniv of Paper Making in Poland.
3362 **985** 2500z. blue and red . . . 40 30

986 Prisoner

1991. Commemoration of Victims of Stalin's Purges.
3363 **986** 2500z. red and black . . 40 30

987 Pope John Paul II

1991. 6th World Youth Day, Czestochowa. Sheet 70 × 87 mm.
MS3364 **987** 3500z. multicoloured 75 85

988 Ball and Basket

1991. Centenary of Basketball.
3365 **988** 2500z. multicoloured . . 55 30

989 "Self-portrait" (Leon Wyczolkowski)

1991. "Bydgoszcz '91" National Stamp Exn.
3366 **989** 3000z. green and brown 55 40
MS3367 155 × 92 mm. No. 3366 × 4 2·25 2·40

990 Twardowski

1991. 125th Birth Anniv of Kazimierz Twardowski (philosopher).
3368 **990** 2500z. black and grey . . 60 40

991 Swallowtail

1991. Butterflies and Moths. Multicoloured.
3369 1000z. Type **991** 25 25
3370 1000z. Dark crimson underwing ("Mormonia sponsa") 25 25
3371 1500z. Painted lady ("Vanessa cardui") . . . 30 25
3372 1500z. Scarce swallowtail ("Iphiclides podalirius") 30 25
3373 2500z. Scarlet tiger moth ("Panaxia dominula") . . 55 40
3374 2500z. Peacock ("Nymphalis io") 55 40
MS3375 127 × 63 mm. 15000z. Black-veined white (*Aporia crataegi*) (46 × 33 mm) plus label for "Phila Nippon '91" International Stamp Exhibition 1·90 2·25

992 "The Shepherd's Bow" (Francesco Solimena)

1991. Christmas.
3376 **992** 1000z. multicoloured . . 30 25

993 Gen. Stanislaw Kopanski and Battle Map

1991. 50th Anniv of Participation of Polish Troops in Battle of Tobruk.
3377 **993** 2000z. multicoloured . . 40 45

994 Brig.-Gen. Michal Tokarzewski-Karaszewicz

995 Lord Baden-Powell (founder)

1991. World War II Polish Underground Army Commanders.
3378 **994** 2000z. black and red . . 40 25
3379 – 2500z. red and violet . . 45 30
3380 – 3000z. violet and mauve 55 40
3381 – 5000z. brown and green 90 60
3382 – 6500z. dp brown & brn 1·10 75
DESIGNS: 2500z. Gen. Broni Kazimierz Sosnkowski; 3000z. Lt.-Gen. Stefan Rowecki; 5000z. Lt.-Gen. Tadeusz Komorowski; 6500z. Brig.-Gen. Leopold Okulicki.

1991. 80th Anniv of Scout Movement in Poland.
3383 **995** 1500z. yellow and green 30 10
3384 – 2000z. blue and yellow 45 30
3385 – 2500z. violet and yellow 55 30
3386 – 3500z. brown and yellow 65 45
DESIGNS: 2000z. Andrzej Malkowski (Polish founder); 2500z. "Watch on the Vistula" (Wojciech Kossak); 3500z. Polish scout in Warsaw Uprising, 1944.

1992. Polish Rulers (7th series). As T **893**.
3387 1500z. brown and green . . 40 25
3388 2000z. black and blue . . . 55 40
DESIGNS: 1500z. Kazimierz II, the Just; 2000z. Leszek I, the White.

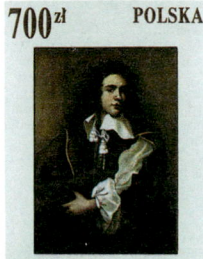

996 Sebastien Bourdon

1992. Self-portraits. Multicoloured.
3389 700z. Type **996** 15 10
3390 1000z. Sir Joshua Reynolds 25 10
3391 1500z. Sir Godfrey Kneller 25 10
3392 2000z. Bartolome Esteban Murillo 40 25
3393 2200z. Peter Paul Rubens 45 25
3394 3000z. Diego de Silva y Velazquez 60 45

997 Skiing

1992. Winter Olympic Games, Albertville. Mult.
3395 1500z. Type **997** 25 25
3396 2500z. Ice hockey 45 30

998 Manteuffel

1992. 90th Birth Anniv of Tadeusz Manteuffel (historian).
3397 **998** 2500z. brown 45 30

999 Nicolas Copernicus (astronomer)

1992. Famous Poles. Multicoloured.
3398 1500z. Type **999** 25 10
3399 2000z. Frederic Chopin (composer) 40 25
3400 2500z. Henryk Sienkiewicz (writer) 45 25
3401 3500z. Marie Curie (physicist) 60 30
MS3402 80 × 81 mm. 5000z. Kazimierz Funk (biochemist) 75 75

1000 Columbus and Left-hand Detail of Map

1992. Europa. 500th Anniv of Discovery of America by Columbus. Multicoloured.
3403 1500z. Type **1000** 25 25
3404 3000z. "Santa Maria" and right-hand detail of Juan de la Costa map, 1500 . . 55 45
Nos. 3403/4 were issued together, se-tenant, forming a composite design.

1001 River Czarna Wiselka

1003 Family and Heart

1002 Prince Jozef Poniatowski

1992. Environmental Protection. River Cascades. Multicoloured.
3405 2000z. Type **1001** 45 15
3406 2500z. River Swider 60 40
3407 3000z. River Tanew 60 30
3408 3500z. Mickiewicz waterfall 60 40

1992. Bicentenary of Order of Military Virtue. Multicoloured.
3409 1500z. Type **1002** 25 25
3410 3000z. Marshal Jozef Pilsudski 40 30
MS3411 108 × 93 mm. 20000z. "Virgin Mary of Czestochowa" (icon) (36 × 57 mm) . . . . . 3·00 3·50

1992. Children's Drawings. Multicoloured.
3412 1500z. Type **1003** 25 10
3413 3000z. Butterfly, sun, bird and dog 60 30

1004 Fencing

1992. Olympic Games, Barcelona. Multicoloured.
3414 1500z. Type **1004** 25 10
3415 2000z. Boxing 40 30
3416 2500z. Running 45 30
3417 3000z. Cycling 55 40

1005 Runners

1992. "Olymphilex '92" Olympic Stamps Exhibition, Barcelona. Sheet 86 × 81 mm.
MS3418 **1005** 20000z. multicoloured 3·50 3·25

1006 Statue of Korczak

1992. 50th Death Anniv of Janusz Korczak (educationist).
3419 **1006** 1500z. black, brown & yellow 30 30

1007 Flag and "V"

1008 Wyszinski

1992. 5th Polish Veterans World Meeting.
3420 **1007** 3000z. multicoloured . . 55 55

1992. 11th Death Anniv of Stefan Wyszinski (Primate of Poland) (3421) and 1st Anniv of World Youth Day (3422). Multicoloured.
3421 1500z. Type **1008** 30 15
3422 3000z. Pope John Paul II embracing youth 60 45

1009 National Colours encircling World Map

1992. World Meeting of Expatriate Poles, Cracow.
3423 **1009** 3000z. multicoloured . . 60 45

1010 Polish Museum, Adampol

1992. 150th Anniv of Polish Settlement at Adampol, Turkey.
3424 **1010** 3500z. multicoloured . . 60 45

1011 18th-century Post Office Sign, Slonim

1992. World Post Day.
3425 **1011** 3500z. multicoloured . . 60 45

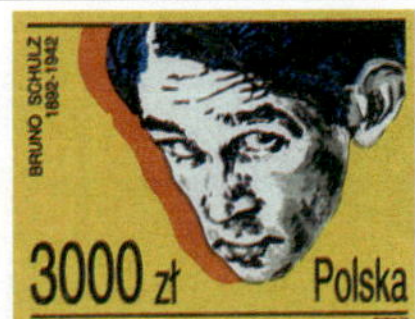

1012 "Dedication" (self-portrait)

1992. Birth Centenary of Bruno Schulz (writer and artist).

3426 **1012** 3000z. multicoloured . . 55 45

1013 "Seated Girl" (Henryk Wicinski)

1992. Polish Sculptures. Multicoloured.

3427 2000z. Type **1013** 40 15
3428 2500z. "Portrait of Tytus Czyzewski" (Zbigniew Pronaszko) 45 30
3429 3000z. "Polish Nike" (Edward Wittig) 60 45
3430 3500z. "The Nude" (August Zamoyski) 60 45
MS3431 107 × 90 mm. Nos. 3427/30 1·60 1·60

1014 "10th Theatrical Summer in Zamosc" (Jan Mlodozeniec)

1992. Poster Art (1st series). Multicoloured.

3432 1500z. Type **1014** 25 10
3433 2000z. "Red Art" (Franciszek Starowieyski) 45 30
3434 2500z. "Circus" (Waldemar Swierzy) 50 45
3435 3500z. "Mannequins" (Henryk Tomaszewski) . . 65 55

See also Nos. 3502/3, 3523/4, 3585/6 and 3712/15.

1015 Girl skipping with Snake

1992. "Polska '93" International Stamp Exn, Poznan (1st issue). Multicoloured.

3436 1500z. Type **1015** 25 10
3437 2000z. Boy on rocking horse with upside-down runners 45 25
3438 2500z. Boy firing bird from bow 45 30
3439 3500z. Girl placing ladder against clockwork giraffe 65 55

See also Nos. 3452, 3453/6 and 3466/9.

1016 Medal and Soldiers

1992. 50th Anniv of Formation of Polish Underground Army. Multicoloured.

3440 1500z. Type **1016** 25 25
3441 3500z. Soldiers 60 55
MS3442 75 × 95 mm. 20000z.+500z. "WP AK" (26 × 32 mm) . . . 3·00 3·00

1017 Church and Star **1018** Wheat

1992. Christmas.

3443 **1017** 1000z. multicoloured . . 15 10

1992. International Nutrition Conference, Rome. Multicoloured.

3444 1500z. Type **1018** 25 10
3445 3500z. Glass, bread, vegetables and jug on table 55 45

1019 Arms of Sovereign Military Order **1020** Arms, 1295

1992. Postal Agreement with Sovereign Military Order of Malta.

3446 **1019** 3000z. multicoloured . . 55 45

1992. History of the White Eagle (Poland's arms). Each black, red and yellow.

3447 2000z. Type **1020** 40 10
3448 2500z. 15th-century arms . . 45 30
3449 3000z. 18th-century arms . . 60 30
3450 3500z. Arms, 1919 . . . . 65 40
3451 5000z. Arms, 1990 . . . . 90 55

1021 Exhibition Emblem and Stylized Stamp

1992. Centenary of Polish Philately and "Polska '93" International Stamp Exhibition, Poznan (2nd issue).

3452 **1021** 1500z. multicoloured . . 25 10

1022 Amber

1993. "Polska '93" International Stamp Exhibition, Poznan (3rd issue). Amber. Multicoloured.

3453 1500z. Type **1022** 25 10
3454 2000z. Pinkish amber . . . 40 25
3455 2500z. Amber in stone . . . 45 45
3456 3000z. Amber containing wasp 60 55
MS3457 82 × 88 mm. 20000z. Detail of map with necklace representing amber route (44 × 29 mm) . . 2·40 2·75

1023 Downhill Skier **1024** Flower-filled Heart

1993. Winter University Games, Zakopane.

3458 **1023** 3000z. multicoloured . . 45 45

1993. St. Valentine's Day. Multicoloured.

3459 1500z. Type **1024** 25 25
3460 3000z. Heart in envelope . . 55 45

1993. Polish Rulers (8th series). As T **983** showing drawings by Jan Matejko.

3461 1500z. brown and green . . 30 25
3462 2000z. black and mauve . . 55 30
3463 2500z. black and green . . . 65 40
3464 3000z. deep brown and brown 85 55

DESIGNS: 1500z. Wladyslaw Laskonogi; 2000z. Henryk I; 2500z. Konrad I of Masovia; 3000z. Boleslaw V, the Chaste.

1025 Arsenal

1993. 50th Anniv of Attack by Szare Szeregi (formation of Polish Scouts in the resistance forces) on Warsaw Arsenal.

3465 **1025** 1500z. multicoloured . . 30 30

1026 Jousters with Lances

1993. "Polska '93" International Stamp Exhibition, Poznan (4th issue). Jousting at Golub Dobrzyn. Designs showing a modern and a medieval jouster. Multicoloured.

3466 1500z. Type **1026** 25 10
3467 2000z. Jousters 30 30
3468 2500z. Jousters with swords 75 40
3469 3500z. Officials 65 40

1027 Szczecin **1028** Jew and Ruins

1993. 750th Anniv of Granting of Town Charter to Szczecin.

3470 **1027** 1500z. multicoloured . . 30 30

1993. 50th Anniv of Warsaw Ghetto Uprising.

3471 **1028** 4000z. black, yellow & blue 90 60

1029 Works by A. Szapocznikow and J. Lebenstein

1993. Europa. Contemporary Art. Multicoloured.

3472 1500z. Type **1029** 25 25
3473 4000z. "CXCIX" (S. Gierawski) and "Red Head" (B. Linke) 65 55

1030 "King Alexander Jagiellonczyk in the Sejm" (Jan Laski, 1505)

1993. 500th Anniv of Parliament.

3474 **1030** 2000z. multicoloured . . 30 30

1031 Nullo

1993. 130th Death Anniv of Francesco Nullo (Italian volunteer in January 1863 Rising).

3475 **1031** 2500z. multicoloured . . 45 45

1032 Lech's Encounter with the White Eagle after Battle of Gniezno

1993. "Polska'93" International Stamp Exhibition, Poznan (5th issue). Sheet 103 × 86 mm.

MS3476 **1032** 50000z. brown . . 6·75 6·75

1033 Cap **1034** Copernicus and Solar System

1993. 3rd World Congress of Cadets of the Second Republic.

3477 **1033** 2000z. multicoloured . . 30 30

1993. 450th Death Anniv of Nicolas Copernicus (astronomer).

3478 **1034** 2000z. multicoloured . . 40 40

1035 Fiki Miki and Lion

1993. 40th Death Anniv of Kornel Makuszynski (writer of children's books). Multicoloured.

3479 1500z. Type **1035** 30 25
3480 2000z. Billy goat 45 30
3481 3000z. Fiki Miki 60 45
3482 5000z. Billy goat riding ostrich . . . . 1·00 60

1993. Cones. As T **974**. Multicoloured.

3483 10000z. Arolla pine . . . . 1·40 85
3484 20000z. Scots pine . . . . . 3·00 1·50

1036 Eurasian Tree Sparrow

1993. Birds. Multicoloured.

3485 1500z. Type **1036** 30 15
3486 2000z. Pied wagtail 40 25
3487 3000z. Syrian woodpecker . . 60 45
3488 4000z. Eurasian goldfinch . . 85 65
3489 5000z. Common starling . . 90 85
3490 6000z. Northern bullfinch . . 1·25 90

1037 Soldiers Marching

1993. Bicentenary of Dabrowski's "Mazurka" (national anthem) (1st issue).

3491 **1037** 1500z. multicoloured . . 30 30

See also Nos. 3526, 3575, 3639 and 3700.

1038 "Madonna and Child" (St. Mary's Basilica, Lesna Podlaska)

1993. Sanctuaries to St. Mary. Multicoloured.
3492 1500z. Type **1038** 25 25
3493 2000z. "Madonna and Child" (St. Mary's Church, Swieta Lipka) . . 40 30

1039 Handley Page Halifax and Parachutes

1993. The Polish Rangers (Second World War air troop).
3494 **1039** 1500z. multicoloured . . 30 30

1040 Trumpet Player

1993. "Jazz Jamboree '93" International Jazz Festival, Warsaw.
3495 **1040** 2000z. multicoloured . . 40 30

1041 Postman

1042 St. Jadwiga (miniature, Schlackenwerther Codex)

1993. World Post Day.
3496 **1041** 2500z. brown, grey and blue 40 40

1993. 750th Death Anniv of St. Jadwiga of Silesia.
3497 **1042** 2500z. multicoloured . . 45 45

1043 Pope John Paul II

1993. 15th Anniv of Pope John Paul II. Sheet 70 × 92 mm.
MS3498 **1043** 20000z. multicoloured 3·00 3·00

1044 Golden Eagle and Crown

1045 St. Nicholas

1993. 75th Anniv of Republic. Multicoloured.
3499 4000z. Type **1044** 65 55
MS3500 66 × 89 mm. 20000z. Silhouette and shadow of flying eagle (31 × 38 mm) . . . . . . 3·75 3·75

1993. Christmas.
3501 **1045** 1500z. multicoloured . . 30 30

1993. Poster Art (2nd series). As T **1014**. Mult.
3502 2000z. "Come and see Polish Mountains" (M. Urbaniec) 30 30
3503 5000z. Production of Alban Berg's "Wozzeck" (J. Lenica) 75 60

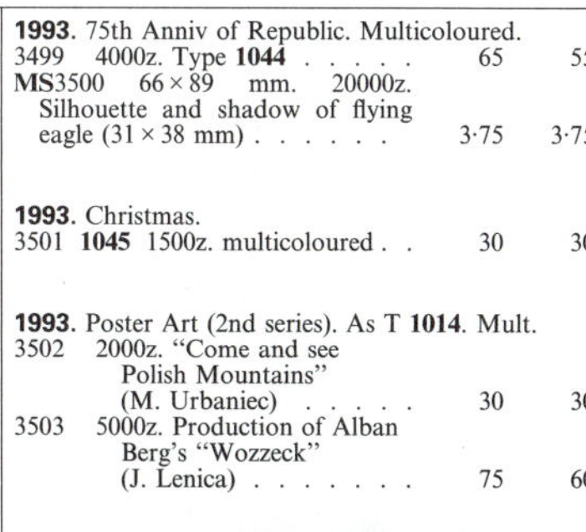

1046 Daisy shedding Petals

1047 Cross-country Skiing

1994. Greetings Stamp.
3504 **1046** 1500z. multicoloured . . 40 40

1994. Winter Olympic Games, Lillehammer, Norway. Multicoloured.
3505 2500z. Type **1047** 45 45
3506 5000z. Ski jumping 85 75
MS3507 81 × 80 mm. 10000z. Downhill skiing . . . . 1·00 60

1048 Bem and Cannon

1994. Birth Bicentenary of General Jozef Bem.
3508 **1048** 5000z. multicoloured . . 75 75

1049 Jan Zamojski (founder)

1050 Cracow Battalion Flag and Scythes

1994. 400th Anniv of Zamojski Academy, Zamosc.
3509 **1049** 5000z. grey, black and brown 75 60

1994. Bicentenary of Tadeusz Kosciuszko's Insurrection.
3510 **1050** 2000z. multicoloured . . 40 40

1994. Polish Rulers (9th series). Drawings by Jan Matejko. As T **893**.
3511 2500z. black and blue . . . 45 25
3512 5000z. black, deep violet and violet 85 90
DESIGN: 2500z. Leszek II, the Black; 5000a. Przemysl II.

1051 Oil Lamp, Open Book and Spectacles

1052 "Madonna and Child"

1994. Europa. Inventions and Discoveries. Mult.
3513 2500z. Type **1051** (invention of modern oil lamp by Ignacy Lukasiewicz) . . . 45 40
3514 6000z. Illuminated filament forming "man in the moon" (astronomy) . . . 1·10 85

1994. St. Mary's Sanctuary, Kalwaria Zebrzydowska.
3515 **1052** 4000z. multicoloured . . 60 45

1053 Abbey Ruins and Poppies

1994. 50th Anniv of Battle of Monte Cassino.
3516 **1053** 6000z. multicoloured . . 75 60

1054 Mazurka

1994. Traditional Dances. Multicoloured.
3517 3000z. Type **1054** 30 30
3518 4000z. Coralski 40 40
3519 9000z. Krakowiak 85 75

1055 Cogwheels

1994. 75th Anniv of International Labour Organization.
3520 **1055** 6000z. deep blue, blue and black 60 55

1056 Optic Fibre Cable

1994. 75th Anniv of Polish Electricians Association.
3521 **1056** 4000z. multicoloured . . 55 40

1057 Map of Americas on Football

1994. World Cup Football Championship, U.S.A.
3522 **1057** 6000z. multicoloured . . 75 75

1994. Poster Art (3rd series). As T **1014**. Mult.
3523 4000z. "Monsieur Fabre" (Wiktor Gorka) 45 55
3524 6000z. "8th OISTAT Congress" (Hurbert Hilscher) (horiz) 75 75

1058 Znaniecki

1059 Polish Eagle and Ribbon

1994. 36th Death Anniv of Professor Florian Znaniecki.
3525 **1058** 9000z. green, bistre & yellow . . . . 1·25 85

1994. Bicentenary of Dabrowski's Mazurka (2nd issue). As T **1037**. Multicoloured.
3526 2500z. Troops preparing to charge 45 40

1994. 50th Anniv of Warsaw Uprising.
3527 **1059** 2500z. multicoloured . . 45 35

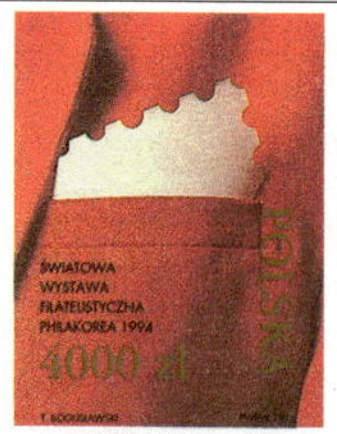

1060 "Stamp" protruding from Pocket

1061 Basilica of St. Brigida, Gdansk

1994. "Philakorea 1994" International Stamp Exhibition, Seoul.
3528 **1060** 4000z. multicoloured . . 60 45

1994. Sanctuaries.
3529 **1061** 4000z. multicoloured . . 60 40

1062 "Nike" (goddess of Victory)

1994. Centenary of International Olympic Committee.
3530 **1062** 4000z. multicoloured . . 60 40

1063 Komeda and Piano Keys

1994. 25th Death Anniv of Krzysztof Komeda (jazz musician).
3531 **1063** 6000z. multicoloured . . 60 50

1064 Long-finned Bristle-mouthed Catfish

1065 Arms of Polish Post, 1858

1994. Fishes. Multicoloured.
3532 4000z. Type **1064** 60 45
3533 4000z. Freshwater angelfish ("Pterophyllum scalare") 60 45
3534 4000z. Red swordtail ("Xiphophorus helleri"), neon tetra ("Paracheirodon innesi") and Berlin platy 60 45
3535 4000z. Neon tetra ("Poecilia reticulata") and guppies 60 45
Nos. 3532/5 were issued together, se-tenant, forming a composite design.

1994. World Post Day.
3536 **1065** 4000z. multicoloured . . 45 40

1066 Kolbe

1994. Maximilian Kolbe (concentration camp victim) Year.
3537 **1066** 2500z. multicoloured . . 45 40

1067 Pigeon

1994. Pigeons. Multicoloured.
3538 4000z. Type **1067** 25 30
3539 4000z. Friar pigeon 25 30
3540 6000z. Silver magpie pigeon 40 50
3541 6000z. Danzig pigeon (black) 40 50
MS3542 79 × 94 mm. 10000z. Short-tail pigeon . . . . 1·25 1·40

1068 Musicians playing Carols

1994. Christmas.
3543 **1068** 2500z. multicoloured . . 35 30

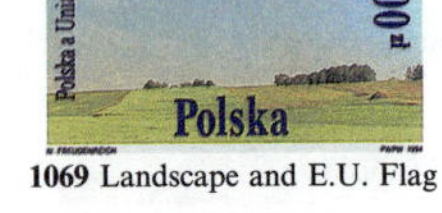

1069 Landscape and E.U. Flag

1994. Application by Poland for Membership of European Union.
3544 **1069** 6000z. multicoloured . . 90 70

Currency reform. 10000 (old) zlotys = 1 (new) zloty

1070 "I Love You" on Pierced Heart

1995. Greetings Stamp.
3545 **1070** 35g. red and blue . . . 25 30

1071 Rain, Sun and Water

1995. 75th Anniv of Hydrological-Meteorological Service.
3546 **1071** 60g. multicoloured . . 50 40

1072 Flag and Sea **1073** St. John

1995. 75th Anniv of Poland's "Marriage to the Sea" (symbolic ceremony commemorating renewal of access to sea).
3547 **1072** 45g. multicoloured . . 40 30

1995. Polish Rulers (10th series). As T **893** showing drawings by Jan Matejko.
3548 35g. deep brown, brown and light brown 25 25
3549 45g. olive, deep green and green 35 30
3550 60g. brown and ochre . . . 45 40
3551 80g. black and blue 60 60
DESIGNS: 35g. Waclaw II; 45g. Wladyslaw I; 60g. Kazimierz III, the Great; 80g. Ludwik Wegierski.

1995. 500th Birth Anniv of St. John of God (founder of Order of Hospitallers).
3552 **1073** 60g. multicoloured . . 45 30

1074 Eggs

1995. Easter. Decorated Easter eggs. Mult, background colours given.
3553 **1074** 35g. red 25 25
3554 – 35g. lilac 25 25
3555 – 45g. blue 35 40
3556 – 45g. green 35 40

1995. Cones. As T **974**. Multicoloured.
3557 45g. European larch 30 35
3558 80g. Mountain pine 60 60

1075 Polish Officer's Button and Leaf

1995. Katyn Commemoration Year.
3559 **1075** 80g. multicoloured . . 60 50

1076 Rose and Barbed Wire

1995. Europa. Peace and Freedom. Multicoloured.
3560 35g. Type **1076** (liberation of concentration camps) 30 35
3561 80g. Flowers in helmet . . . 60 55

1077 Commom Cranes

1995. 50th Anniv of Return of Western Territories.
3562 **1077** 45g. multicoloured . . 60 40

1078 Pope and Wadowice Church Font

1995. 75th Birthday of Pope John Paul II.
3563 **1078** 80g. multicoloured . . 40 45

1079 Puppets under Spotlight ("Miromagia")

1995. 50th Anniv of Groteska Fairy Tale Theatre. Multicoloured.
3564 35g. Type **1079** 30 25
3565 35g. Puppets in scene from play 30 25
3566 45g. Puppet leaning on barrel ("Thomas Fingerchen") (vert) . . . 40 30
3567 45g. Clown ("Bumstara Circus") 40 30

1080 Cockerill Steam Locomotive and Train, 1845, Warsaw–Vienna

1995. 150th Anniv of Polish Railways. Mult.
3568 35g. Type **1080** 30 20
3569 60g. "Lux-Torpedo" diesel railcar, 1927 . . . . . . 50 35
3570 80g. Electric freight train . . 70 45
3571 1z. Eurocity "Sobieski" express, 1992, Warsaw–Vienna 85 55

1081 Symbols of Nations

1995. 50th Anniv of U.N.O.
3572 **1081** 80g. multicoloured . . 60 50

1082 Bank

1995. 125th Anniv of Warsaw Commercial Bank.
3573 **1082** 45g. multicoloured . . 40 40

1083 Loaf and Four-leaved Clover

1995. Centenary of Peasant Movement.
3574 **1083** 45g. multicoloured . . 40 40

1995. Bicentenary of Dabrowski's "Mazurka" (3rd issue). As T **1037**. Multicoloured.
3575 35g. Mounted troops . . . 30 40

1084 Rowan Berries **1085** Madonna and Child

1995. Fruits of Trees. No value expressed. Mult.
3576 A (35g.) Type **1084** 30 25
3577 B (45g.) Acorns and sessile oak leaves 30 35

1995. Basilica of the Holy Trinity, Lezajsk.
3578 **1085** 45g. multicoloured . . 40 35

1086 Marshal Josef Pilsudski

1995. 75th Anniv of Defence of Warsaw and of Riga Peace Conference.
3579 **1086** 45g. multicoloured . . 40 40

1087 Dressage

1995. World Carriage Driving Championships, Poznan. Multicoloured.
3580 60g. Type **1087** 40 40
3581 80g. Cross-country event . . 55 55

1088 Warsaw Technical University **1089** Russian Space Station and U.S. Spacecraft

1995. "Warsaw '95" National Stamp Exhibition. Multicoloured.
3582 35g. Type **1088** 30 40
MS3583 94×71 mm. 1z. Castle Place, Warsaw (horiz) 75 85

1995. 11th World Cosmonauts Congress, Warsaw.
3584 **1089** 80g. multicoloured . . 60 50

1995. Poster Art (4th series). As T **1014**. Mult.
3585 35g. "The Crazy Locomotive" (Jan Sawka) 25 25
3586 45g. "The Wedding" (Eugeniusz Get Stankiewicz) 40 40

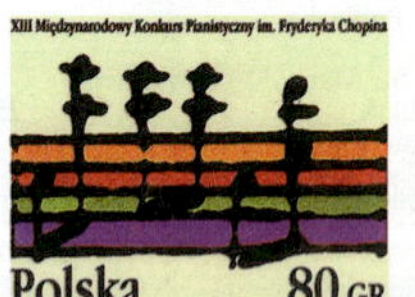

1090 Bar from Polonaise (Frederic Chopin) **1091** Postman

1995. 13th International Chopin Piano Competition.
3587 **1090** 80g. multicoloured . . 60 50

1995. Post Day. Multicoloured.
3588 45g. Type **1091** 40 25
3589 80g. Feather fixed to envelope by seal 60 55

1092 Acrobatic Pyramid **1094** Crib

1093 Groszkowski and Formula

1995. World Acrobatic Sports Championships, Wroclaw.
3590 **1092** 45g. multicoloured . . 40 40

1995. 11th Death Anniv of Professor Janusz Groszkowski (radio-electronic scientist).
3591 **1093** 45g. multicoloured . . 40 40

1995. Christmas. Multicoloured.
3592 35g. Type **1094** 40 25
3593 45g. Wise men, Christmas tree and star of Bethlehem 40 25
Nos. 3592/3 were issued together, se-tenant, forming a composite design.

1095 Blue Tit

1995. Song Birds. Multicoloured.
3594 35g. Type **1095** 25 20
3595 45g. Long-tailed tit 35 25
3596 60g. Great grey shrike . . . 45 35
3597 80g. Hawfinch 60 45

1096 Extract from Poem and Bow

1996. 75th Birth Anniv of Krzysztof Kamil Baczynski (poet).
3598 **1096** 35g. multicoloured . . 30 40

1097 Cherries and "I love you"

1098 Romanesque-style Inowlodz Church

1996. Greetings Stamp.
3599 **1097** 40g. multicoloured . . 40 30

1996. Architectural Styles. Multicoloured.
3600 40g. Type **1098** 40 30
3601 55g. Gothic-style St. Mary the Virgin's Church, Cracow 45 35
3602 70g. Renaissance-style St. Sigismund's Chapel, Wawel Castle 60 50
3603 1z. Baroque-style Church of the Order of the Holy Sacrament, Warsaw . . . 90 75

1099 "Oceania"

1996. Sailing Ships. Multicoloured.
3604 40g. Type **1099** 30 30
3605 55g. "Zawisza Czarny" (cadet schooner) 45 40
3606 70g. "General Zaruski" (cadet ketch) 55 55
3607 75g. "Fryderyk Chopin" (cadet brig) 60 55

1100 16th-century Warsaw

1101 Bull (Taurus)

1996. 400th Anniv of Warsaw.
3608 **1100** 55g. multicoloured . . 45 35

1996. Signs of the Zodiac. Multicoloured.
3609 5g. Workman in water (Aquarius) 15 15
3610 10g. "Fish-person" holding fish (Pisces) 15 15
3611 20g. Type **1101** 10 10
3612 25g. Twins looking through keyhole (Gemini) 15 15
3613 30g. Crab smoking pipe (Cancer) 15 15
3614 40g. Maid and cogwheels (Virgo) 25 25
3615 50g. Lion in military uniform (Leo) 30 25
3616 55g. Couple with head and shoulders as scales (Libra) 30 30
3617 70g. Ram with ram-head (Aries) 45 25
3618 1z. Woman with scorpion's tail hat (Scorpio) 70 35
3619 2z. Archer on motor cycle (Sagittarius) . . . . . 1·40 75
3620 5z. Office worker shielding face with paper mask (Capricorn) . . . . 3·25 1·60

1102 Hanka Ordonowna (singer)

1996. Europa. Famous Women. Multicoloured.
3621 40g. Type **1102** 30 25
3622 1z. Pola Negri (actress) . . 70 65

1103 Flag of Osiek and Old Photographs forming "1921"

1996. 75th Anniv of Silesian Uprising.
3623 **1103** 55g. red, green and black 40 40

1104 "On Bergamuty Islands"

1996. 50th Anniv of UNICEF. Scenes from Fairy Tales by Jan Brzechwa. Multicoloured.
3624 40g. Type **1104** 35 30
3625 40g. Waiters carrying trays of apples (nursery rhyme) 35 30
3626 55g. Vegetable characters ("At the Market Stall") 55 40
3627 55g. Chef holding duck ("Wacky Duck") 55 40
3628 70g. Woman and birdchild ("The Fibber") 60 60
3629 70g. Red fox ("The Impishness of Witalis Fox") 60 60

1105 "City Walls and Building"

1996. Paintings by Stanislaw Noakowski. Mult.
3630 40g. Type **1105** 30 25
3631 55g. "Renaissance Bedroom" 40 35
3632 70g. "Rural Gothic Church" 50 50
3633 1z. "Renaissance Library" 70 65

1106 Discus on Ribbon

1108 St. Mary of Przeczycka

1107 Tweezers holding Stamp showing Emblem

1996. Olympic Games, Atlanta, and Centenary of Modern Olympic Games. Multicoloured.
3634 40g. Type **1106** (gold medal, Halina Konopacka, 1928) 25 25
3635 55g. Tennis ball (horiz) . . 40 35
3636 70g. Polish Olympic Committee emblem (horiz) 50 45
3637 1z. Bicycle wheel 70 50

1996. "Olymphilex '96" International Sports Stamp Exhibition, Atlanta.
3638 **1107** 1z. multicoloured . . . 70 65

1996. Bicentenary of Dabrowski's Mazurka (4th issue). As T **1037**. Multicoloured.
3639 40g. Charge of Polish cavalry at Somosierra . . 45 30

1996. St. Mary's Church, Przeczycka.
3640 **1108** 40g. multicoloured . . 45 35

1996. Polish Rulers (11th series). As T **893**.
3641 40g. brown and bistre . . . 30 25
3642 55g. lilac and mauve 45 35
3643 70g. deep grey and grey . . 55 50
3644 1z. deep green, green and yellow 80 65

DESIGNS: 40g. Queen Jadwiga (wife of Wladyslaw II); 55g. Wladyslaw II Jagiello; 70g. Wladyslaw III Warnenczyk; 1z. Kazimierz IV Jagiellonczyk.

1109 Mt. Giewont and Edelweiss

1996. The Tatra Mountains. Multicoloured.
3645 40g. Type **1109** 30 20
3646 40g. Mt. Krzesanica and spring gentian 30 20
3647 55g. Mt. Koscielec and leopard's bane 45 25
3648 55g. Mt. Swinica and clusius gentian 45 25
3649 70g. Mt. Rysy and ragwort 55 30
3650 70g. Mieguszowieckie peaks and pine trees 55 30

1110 Seifert

1996. 50th Birth Anniv of Zbigniew Seifert (jazz musician).
3651 **1110** 70g. multicoloured . . 75 45

1111 "Changing of Horses at Post Station" (detail, Mieczyslaw Watorski)

1996. World Post Day. 75th Anniv of Post and Telecommunications Museum, Wroclaw. Paintings. Multicoloured.
3652 40g. Type **1111** 30 25
MS3653 102 × 81 mm. 1z.+20g. "Mail Coach at Jagniatkowo with View over Karkonosze" (Professor Tager) (42 × 30 mm) 90 85

1112 Father Christmas on Horse-drawn Sleigh

1113 Head of Male

1996. Christmas. Multicoloured.
3654 40g. Type **1112** 25 10
3655 55g. Carol singers with star lantern 35 25

1996. The European Bison. Multicoloured.
3656 55g. Type **1113** 40 40
3657 55g. Head of female 40 40
3658 55g. Pair of bison 40 40
3659 55g. Male 40 40

1114 Wislawa Szymborska

1996. Award of Nobel Prize for Literature to Wislawa Szymborska (poet).
3660 **1114** 1z. multicoloured . . . 75 65

1115 "I Love You" on King of Hearts Playing Card

1997. Greetings Stamps. Multicoloured.
3661 B (40g.) Type **1115** 30 25
3662 A (55g.) Queen of hearts playing card . . . . . . 45 1·00

Nos. 3661/2 were issued together, se-tenant, forming a composite design.

No. 3661 was sold at the rate for postcards and No. 3662 for letters up to 20 grams.

1116 Blessing the Palms

1997. Easter. Traditional Customs. Multicoloured.
3663 50g. Type **1116** 30 25
3664 60g. Woman and child painting Easter eggs . . . 40 35
3665 80g. Priest blessing the food 55 45
3666 1z.10 Man throwing water over woman's skirts on Easter Monday 65 45

1117 Long Market and Town Hall (after Mateusz Deisch)

1997. Millenary of Gdansk. Each brown, cinnamon and red.
3667 50g. Type **1117** 60 40
MS3668 94 × 71 mm. 1z.10 St. Mary's Church and Hall of the Main Town (after Mateusz Merian) (horiz) 75 85

1118 St. Adalbert and Monks addressing Pagans

1997. Death Millenary of St. Adalbert (Bishop of Prague).
3669 **1118** 50g. brown 30 25
3670 – 60g. green 40 35
3671 – 1z.10 lilac 70 40

DESIGNS—VERT: 60g. St. Adalbert and anniversary emblem; 1z.10, St. Adalbert.

1119 Mansion House, Lopuszna

1120 The Crock of Gold

1997. Polish Manor Houses. Multicoloured.
3671a 10g Lipkowie, Warsaw . . 10 10
3672 50g. Type **1119** 20 10
3673 55g. Henryk Sienkewicz Museum, Oblegorek . . 35 20
3674 60g. Zyrzyn 50 20
3675 65g. Stanislaw Wyspianski Museum, Bronowice, near Cracow 60 20
3675a 70g. Modlnica 65 35
3675b 80g. Grabonog, Gostyn . . 75 35
3676 90g. Obory, near Warsaw 90 60
3676a 1z. Krzelawice 95 45
3677 1z.10 Ozarow . . . . . . 1·00 35
3678 1z.20 Jozef Krasnewski Museum, Biala 65 35
3678a 1z.40 Winna Gora 75 80
3678b 1z.50 Sulejowku, Warsaw 45 15
3678c 1z.55 Zelazowa Wola . . 80 80
3678d 1z.60 Potok Zloty . . . 80 95
3678e 1z.65 Sucha, Wegrow . . . 90 95
3679 1z.70 Tulowice . . . . . . 95 1·00
3679a 1z.85 Kasna Dolna 90 80
3679b 1z.90 Petrykozach Mszczonowa 60 20
3680 2z.20 Kuznocin . . . . . 1·10 95
3681 2z.65 Liwia, Wegrow . . . 1·50 1·10

3682 3z. Janowcu, Pulaw 90 30
3683 10z. Koszuty 5·50 4·00
See also Nos. 3727/8.

1997. Europa. Tales and Legends. Multicoloured.
3685 50g. Type **1120** 30 35
3686 1z.10 Wars, Sawa and mermaid-siren 70 80

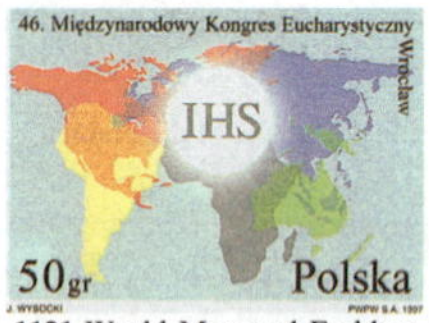

1121 World Map and Emblem

1997. 46th International Eucharistic Congress, Wroclaw.
3687 **1121** 50g. multicoloured 30 35

1122 San Francisco–Oakland Bay Bridge

1997. "Pacific 97" International Stamp Exhibition, San Francisco.
3688 **1122** 1z.30 multicoloured 75 75

1123 Pope John Paul II

1997. 5th Papal Visit. Sheet 76 × 90 mm.
MS3689 **1123** 1z.10 multicoloured 75 85

1124 European Long-eared Bat

1997. Bats. Multicoloured.
3690 50g. Type **1124** 30 20
3691 60g. Common noctule 40 25
3692 80g. Brown bat 50 35
3693 1z.30 Red bat 85 55

1125 "Founding of the Main School" (Jan Matejko)

1997. 600th Anniv of Faculty of Theology, Jagiellonian University, Cracow.
3694 **1125** 80g. multicoloured 60 55

1126 Map highlighting Settled Area

1997. Centenary of Polish Migration to Argentina.
3695 **1126** 1z.40 multicoloured 80 75

1127 "Return from War to the Village"

1997. Paintings by Juliusz Kossak. Multicoloured.
3696 50g. Type **1127** 30 25
3697 60g. "Cracowian Wedding" 35 35
3698 80g. "In the Stable" 50 45
3699 1z.10 "Stablehand with Pair of Horses" 65 60

1997. Bicentenary of Dabrowski's "Mazurka" (5th issue). As T **1037**.
3700 50g. Dabrowski and Wybicki's arrival in Poznan, 1806 35 35
MS3701 85 × 77 mm. 1z.10 Manuscript of lyrics and Jozef Wybicki (composer) 75 65

1128 Strzelecki and Route Map around Australia

1997. Birth Bicentenary of Pawel Strzelecki (explorer).
3702 **1128** 1z.50 multicoloured 90 90

1129 Flooded Houses

1130 "Holy Mother of Consolation" (icon)

1997. Flood Relief Fund.
3703 **1129** 60g.+30g. multicoloured 75 65

1997. Church of the Holy Mother of Consolation and St. Michael the Archangel, Gorka Duchowa.
3704 **1130** 50g. multicoloured 30 40

1997. Polish Rulers (12th series). As T **893**.
3705 50g. agate, brown and bistre 35 30
3706 60g. purple and blue 45 40
3707 80g. green, deep green and olive 60 50
3708 1z.10 purple and lilac 80 65
DESIGNS: 50g. Jan I Olbracht; 60g. Aleksander Jagiellonczyk; 80g. Zygmunt I, the Old; 1z.10, Zygmunt II August.

1131 Kosz

1132 Globe and posthorn

1997. 24th Death Anniv of Mieczyslaw Kosz (jazz musician).
3709 **1131** 80g. multicoloured 60 50

1997. World Post Day.
3710 **1132** 50g. multicoloured 35 35

1133 St. Basil's Cathedral, Moscow

1997. "Moskva 97" International Stamp Exhibition, Moscow.
3711 **1133** 80g. multicoloured 60 70

1997. Poster Art (5th series). As T **1014**.
3712 50g. multicoloured 35 25
3713 50g. black 35 25
3714 60g. multicoloured 40 45
3715 60g. multicoloured 40 45
POSTERS—HORIZ: No. 3712, Advertisement for Radion washing powder (Tadeusz Gronowski). VERT: No. 3713, Production of Stanislaw Witkiewicz's play "Shoemakers" (Roman Cieslewicz); 3714, Production of Aleksander Fredro's play "A Husband and a Wife" (Andrzej Pagowski); 3715, Production of ballet "Goya" (Wiktor Sadowski).

1134 Nativity

1997. Christmas. Multicoloured.
3716 50g. Type **1134** 25 20
3717 60g. Christmas Eve feast (horiz) 35 25
3718 80g. Family going to church for Midnight Mass (horiz) 45 30
3719 1z.10 Waits (carol singers representing animals) 60 40

1135 Common Shelducks

1997. Praecocial Chicks. Multicoloured.
3720 50g. Type **1135** 35 35
3721 50g. Goosanders ("Mergus merganser") 35 35
3722 50g. Common snipes ("Gallinago gallinago") 35 35
3723 50g. Moorhens ("Gallinula chloropus") 35 35

1136 Ski Jumping

1137 Dog wearing Cat T-shirt inscr "I Love You"

1998. Winter Olympic Games, Nagano, Japan.
3724 **1136** 1z.40 multicoloured 80 75

1998. Greetings Stamps. No value expressed. Multicoloured.
3725 B (55g.) Type **1137** 35 25
3726 A (65g.) Cat wearing dog T-shirt 35 35

1998. Polish Manor Houses. No value expressed. As T **1119**. Multicoloured.
3727 B (55g.) Gluchy 35 25
3728 A (65g.) Jan Kochanwoski Museum, Czarnolas 35 35

1138 Paschal Lamb

1140 Grey Seal

1139 Polish National Guard and Civilians at Lvov Barricades

1998. Easter. Multicoloured.
3729 55g. Type **1138** 35 20
3730 65g. The Resurrected Christ 35 20

1998. 150th Anniv of 1848 Revolutions.
3731 **1139** 55g. brown 45 25

1998. Polish Rulers (13th series). As T **893**.
3732 55g. brown and light brown 35 20
3733 65g. purple, deep purple and mauve 40 35
3734 80g. deep green and green 50 45
3735 90g. lilac, purple and mauve 60 45
DESIGNS: 55g. Henryk Walezy; 65g. Queen Anna Jagiellonka (wife of Stefan I); 80g. Stefan I Batory; 90g. Zygmunt III Wasa.

1998. Protection of Baltic Sea. Marine Life. Mult.
3736 65g. Type **1140** 45 35
3737 65g. "Patoschistus microps" (fish), jellyfish and shells 45 35
3738 65g. Twaite shad ("Alosa fallax") and pipefish ("Syngnathus typhle") 45 35
3739 65g. Common sturgeon ("Acipenser sturio") 45 35
3740 65g. Atlantic salmon ("Salmo salar") 45 35
3741 65g. Common porpoise 45 35
MS3742 76 × 70 mm. 1z.20 Grey seal 1·60 1·40
Nos. 3736/41 were issued together, se-tenant, forming a composite design.

1141 Exhibition Emblem and 1948 Israeli 500 m. Stamp

1998. "Israel '98" International Stamp Exhibition, Tel Aviv.
3743 **1141** 90g. multicoloured 75 80

1142 Festival Emblem

1998. Europa. National Festivals.
3744 **1142** 55g. multicoloured 55 50
3745 – 1z.20 black, red and blue 90 95
DESIGNS: 55g. Type **1142** ("Warsaw Autumn" International Festival of Music); 1z.20, State flag and opening bars of "Welcome the May Dawn" (3rd of May Constitution Day).

1144 "Longing Holy Mother"

1145 "Triple Self-portrait"

1998. Coronation of "Longing Holy Mother" (icon in Powsin Church).
3752 **1144** 55g. multicoloured 45 75

1998. 30th Death Anniv of Nikifor (Epifan Drowniak) (artist). Multicoloured.
3753 55g. Type **1145** 35 40
3754 65g. "Cracow Office" 40 50
3755 1z.20 "Orthodox Church" 75 80
3756 2z.35 "Ucrybow Station" 1·50 1·60

1146 Anniversary Inscription

1998. 80th Anniv of Main Board of Statistics.
3757 **1146** 55g. multicoloured 45 40

1147 "Madonna and Child"

1998. Basilica of the Visitation of St. Mary the Virgin, Sejny.
3758 **1147** 55g. multicoloured . . 45 40

1148 Jesus (stained glass window)

1998. Bicentenary of Diocese of Warsaw.
3759 **1148** 65g. multicoloured . . 45 50

1998. 17th Congress of Polish Union of Stamp Collectors. Sheet 114 × 77 mm containing T **1141** and similar horiz design. Each blue and cream.
MS3760 65g. × 2 Composite design showing 17th-century engraving of Szczecin from Descriptio Urbis Stettinensis by Paul Feideborn 85 95

1150 Pierre and Marie Curie (physicists)

1998. Centenary of Discovery of Polonium and Radium.
3761 **1150** 1z.20 multicoloured . . 70 80

1151 Mazowsze Dancers

1998. 50th Anniv of Mazowsze Song and Dance Group. Multicoloured.
3762 65g. Type **1151** 40 50
3763 65g. Dancers (different) . . 40 50
Nos. 3762/3 were issued together, se-tenant, forming a composite design.

1152 Mniszchow Palace

1998. Belgium Embassy, Warsaw.
3764 **1152** 1z.20 multicoloured . . 70 75

1153 "King Sigismund" (Studio of Rubens)

1154 Coloured Envelopes

1998. 400th Anniv of Battle of Stangebro.
3765 **1153** 1z.20 brown . . . . . 70 1·00

1998. World Post Day.
3766 **1154** 65g. multicoloured . . 45 50

1155 Pope John Paul II and People of Different Races

1157 "Nativity"

1156 State Flags and 1919 Seal

1998. 20th Anniv of Selection of Karol Wojtyla to Papacy.
3767 **1155** 65g. multicoloured . . 45 50

1998. 80th Anniv of Independence.
3768 **1156** 65g. black, red and gold 45 50

1998. Christmas. Polyptych, Grudziadz. Mult.
3769 55g. Type **1157** 40 40
3770 65g. "Adoration of the Wise Men" 40 50

1158 Anniversary Emblem

1998. 50th Anniv of Universal Declaration of Human Rights.
3771 **1158** 1z.20 blue and ultramarine 75 80

1159 Maryla Wereszczakowna and Moonlit Night

1998. Birth Bicentenary of Adam Mickiewicz (poet). Multicoloured.
3772 55g. Type **1159** 30 35
3773 65g. Cranes flying over tomb of Maria Potocka 40 45
3774 90g. Burning candles and cross 45 60
3775 1z.20 House, field of flowers and uhlan's shako 60 75
MS3776 61 × 76 mm. 2z.45 Mickiewicz (bust by Jean David d'Angers) (30 × 38 mm) . . . . 1·60 2·00

1160 "Piorun" (destroyer), 1942–46

1999. 80th Anniv (1998) of Polish Navy. Mult.
3777 55g. Type **1160** 40 35
3778 55g. "Piorun" (missile corvette), 1994 . . . . . 40 35

1161 Dominoes

1999. Greetings stamps. Value expressed by letter. Multicoloured.
3779 B (60g.) Type **1161** 40 35
3780 A (65g.) Dominoes (different) 40 45

1162 Ernest Malinowski and Railway Bridge over Varrugas Canyon

1999. Polish Engineers. Multicoloured.
3781 1z. Type **1162** (death cent) 55 60
3782 1z.60 Rudolf Modrzejewski and Benjamin Franklin Bridge over Delaware River, Philadelphia . . . 85 95

1163 "Prayer in Ogrojec"

1165 "Victorious St. Mary of Kozielsk" (sculpture)

1164 Chinese Ideograms

1999. Easter. Multicoloured.
3783 60g. Type **1163** 30 35
3784 65g. "Carrying the Cross" 30 35
3785 1z. "Pieta" 50 55
3786 1z.40 "Resurrection" . . . 75 70
Nos. 3783/4 and 3786 show details of the Grudzic polyptych.

1999. "China '99" International Stamp Exhibition, Peking. Sheet 80 × 96 mm.
MS3787 **1164** 1z.70 multicoloured 90 1·10

1999. Images of Virgin Mary made by Polish Prisoners of War. Multicoloured.
3788 60g. Type **1165** 30 35
3789 70g. "St. Mary of Katyn" (bas-relief, Stanislaw Balos) 40 35

1166 Jan Skrzetuski passing Zbara Fortress ("With Fire and Sword")

1999. "Heroes of the Trilogy " (novels) by Henryk Sienkiewicz. Multicoloured.
3790 70g. Type **1166** 35 35
3791 70g. Onufry Zagloba and 17th-century map of Poland (all three parts) 35 35
3792 70g. Longinus Podbipieta defending Zbara and three Tartars ("With Fire and Sword") 35 35
3793 70g. Bohun with Helena Kuncewiczowna on way to Czarci Jar ("With Fire and Sword") 35 35
3794 70g. Andrzej Kmicic and cannon at Jasna Gora Monastery ("The Deluge") 35 35
3795 70g. Michal Jerzy Wolodyjowski and Basia Jeziorkowska fencing ("Pan Michael") 35 35

1167 Polish Flag and N.A.T.O. Emblem

1999. 50th Anniv of North Atlantic Treaty Organization and Accession of Poland.
3796 **1167** 70g. multicoloured . . 45 35

1168 Anniversary Emblem and Headquarters, Strasbourg

1999. 50th Anniv of Council of Europe.
3797 **1168** 1z. multicoloured . . . 55 60

1169 Three-toed Woodpecker

1999. Europa. Parks and Gardens. Bialowieski National Park.
3798 **1169** 1z.40 multicoloured . . 75 90

1170 Mountain Biking

1999. Youth Sports. Multicoloured.
3799 60g. Type **1170** 40 35
3800 70g. Snowboarding 40 50
3801 1z. Skateboarding 60 60
3802 1z.40 Rollerblading . . . . 85 1·00

1171 St. Mary's Church, Cracow, Pope John Paul II and Crowd

1999. 6th Papal Visit to Poland. Multicoloured.
3803 60g. Type **1171** 35 30
3804 70g. Pope and crowd with crosses 40 40
3805 1z. Pope and cheering teenagers 60 50
3806 1z.40 Eiffel Tower (Paris), "Christ the Saviour" (statue, Rio de Janeiro), Pope and church at Fatima, Portugal 80 65

1172 Ignacy Paderewski and Roman Dmowski (signatories)

1999. 80th Anniv of Treaty of Versailles.
3807 **1172** 1z.40 multicoloured . . 85 1·00

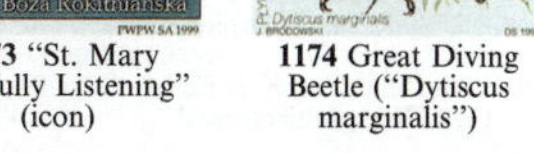

1173 "St. Mary Carefully Listening" (icon)

1174 Great Diving Beetle ("Dytiscus marginalis")

1999. St. Mary's Sanctuaries. Multicoloured.
3808 60g. Type **1173** (church of St. Mary Queen of Poland, Rokitno) 40 40
3809 70g. "Mary" (statue, Ms. Jazlowiecka), Convent of Order of the Immaculate Conception, Szymanow 40 50

1999. Insects. Multicoloured.
3810 60g. Type **1174** 30 35
3811 60g. "Corixa punctata" . . 30 35
3812 70g. "Limnophilus" 40 45
3813 70g. "Perla marginata" . . 40 45
3814 1z.40 Emperor dragonfly ("Anax imperator") . . . 80 95
3815 1z.40 "Ephemera vulgata" 80 95

1175 Ksiaz Castle

1999. "Walbrzych '99" 18th National Stamp Exhibition. Sheet 74 × 105 mm.
MS3816 **1175** 1z. blue 75 85

1176 Red Deer

1999. Eastern Carpathian Mountains International Biosphere Reserve (covering Polish, Ukrainian and Slovakian National Parks). Multicoloured.
3817 1z.40 Type **1176** 70 90
3818 1z.40 Wild cat 70 90

1999. Polish Rulers (14th series). As T **893**.
3819 60g. black and green 35 20
3820 70g. brown and light brown 40 35
3821 1z. black and blue 60 40
3822 1z.40 deep purple and purple 80 45
DESIGNS: 60g. Wladyslaw IV Waza; 70g. Jan II Kazimierz; 1z. Michal Korybut Wisniowiecki; 1z.40, Jan III Sobieski.

1177 U.P.U. Emblem

1999. 125th Anniv of Universal Postal Union.
3823 **1177** 1z.40 multicoloured . . 70 85

1178 Chopin and Academy of Fine Arts, Warsaw

1999. 150th Death Anniv of Frederic Chopin (composer).
3824 **1178** 1z.40 green 70 85

1179 Popieluszko

1999. 15th Death Anniv of Father Jerzy Popieluszko.
3825 **1179** 70g. multicoloured . . 40 50

1180 Barbed Wire

1999. Homage to 20th-century Heroes of Poland. Sheet 93 × 70 mm.
MS3826 **1180** 1z. multicoloured 60 70

1181 Angel ("Silent Night")

1999. Christmas. Inscr in Polish with the opening lines of carols. Multicoloured.
3827 60g. Type **1181** 35 25
3828 70g. Angel ("Sleep, Jesus Baby") 40 25
3829 1z. Angel ("Let's Go Everybody to the Stable") 55 40
3830 1z.40 Angel ("The God is Born") 80 60

1182 Polish Museum, Rapperswil Castle, Switzerland

1999. Polish Overseas Cultural Buildings. Mult.
3831 1z. Type **1182** 60 40
3832 1z.40 Marian Priests' Museum, Fawley Court, England 80 60
3833 1z.60 Polish Library, Paris, France 95 65
3834 1z.80 Polish Institute and Gen. Sikorski Museum, London, England . . . . 1·10 75

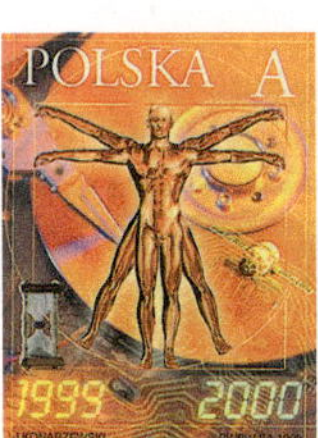

1183 "Proportions of Man" (Da Vinci)

1185 Otto III granting Crown to Boleslaw I

1184 Bronislaw Malinowski (sociologist)

2000. New Year 2000.
3835 **1183** A (70g.) multicoloured 55 50

2000. Polish Personalities. Multicoloured.
3836 1z.55 Type **1184** 75 75
3837 1z.95 Jozef Zwierzycki (geologist) . . . . 1·10 1·00

2000. 1000th Anniv of the Gniezno Summit and the Catholic Church in Poland. Multicoloured.
3838 70g. Type **1185** 45 45
3839 80g. Archbishop of Gnesna, and Bishops of Cracovina, Wratislavia and Colberga 45 45
MS3840 77 × 65 mm. 1z.55 Provincial representatives presenting gifts to Otto III as Roman Emperor (horiz) . . . 90 80

1186 Jesus in Tomb

2000. Easter. Multicoloured.
3841 70g. Type **1186** 45 45
3842 80g. Resurrected Christ . . 45 45

1187 Saurolophus

2000. Prehistoric Animals. Multicoloured.
3843 70g. Type **1187** 40 45
3844 70g. Gallimimus 40 45
3845 80g. Saichania 45 50
3846 80g. Protoceratops 45 50
3847 1z.55 Prenocephale . . . . 85 1·00
3848 1z.55 Velociraptor . . . . . 85 1·00

1188 Wajda

2000. Presentation of American Film Academy Award to Andrzej Wajda (film director).
3849 **1188** 1z.10 black 60 95

1189 Pope John Paul kneeling, St. Peter's Basilica, Rome

2000. Holy Year 2000 Opening of Holy Door, St. Peter's Basilica, Rome.
3850 **1189** 80g. multicoloured . . 45 45

1190 Artist and Model, Poster for *Wesele* (play), and Building

2000. Crakow, European City of Culture.
3851 **1190** 70g. multicoloured . . 40 45
3852 – 1z.55 multicoloured . . 95 90
MS3853 110 × 77 mm. 1z.75 blue (39 × 30 mm) 95 90
DESIGNS: No. 3852, Jagiellonian University, Pope John Paul II, Queen Jadwiga and Krzysztof Penderecki (composer). 38 × 30 mm—**MS**3853, View of Crakow (wood carving), 1489.

1191 Dying Rose

2000. "Stop Drug Addiction" Campaign.
3854 **1191** 70g. multicoloured . . 40 45

1192 "Building Europe"

1193 Pope John Paul II

2000. Europa.
3855 **1192** 1z.55 multicoloured . . 90 75

2000. 80th Birthday of Pope John Paul II.
3856 **1193** 80g. violet 45 45
3857 – 1z.10 multicoloured . . 60 60
3858 – 1z.55 green 75 90
DESIGNS: No. 3857, Holy Mother, Czestochowa; 3858, Pastoral Staff.

1194 Woman's Face and Fan

2000. "Espana 2000" International Stamp Exhibition, Madrid.
3859 **1194** 1z.55 multicoloured . . 90 85

1195 Family

2000. Parenthood.
3860 **1195** 70g. multicoloured . . 40 45

1196 Cathedral, Faade

2000. Millenary of Wroclaw. Sheet 70 × 90 mm.
MS3861 **1196** 1z.55 multicoloured 85 55

1197 Karol Marcinkowski

2000. Personalities. Multicoloured.
3862 70g. Type **1197** (founder of Scientific Assistance Association) 35 20
3863 80g. Josemaria Escriva de Balaguer (founder of Priests' Association of St. Cross, 1943) 35 30

1198 Gerwazy and the Count

2000. *Pan Tadeusz* (poem by Adam Mickiewicz). Illustrations by Michal Elwiro Andriolli from the 1882 edition.

3864	**1198**	70g. brown	40	15
3865	–	70g. brown	40	15
3866	–	80g. green	45	20
3867	–	80g. green	45	20
3868	–	1z.10 purple	60	30
3869	–	1z.10 purple	60	30

DESIGNS: No. 3865, Telimenta reclining and the Judge; 3866, Father Robak, Judge and Gerwazy; 3867, Gathering in forest; 3868, Jankiel playing musical instrument; 3869, Zosia and Tadeusz.

1199 Pope John Paul II and St. Peter's Basilica, Rome

1200 "Self-portrait"

2000. National Pilgrimage to Rome. Multicoloured.

3870	80g. Type **1199**	45	30
3871	1z.55 Cross and Colosseum	85	60

2000. Birth Bicentenary of Piotr Michalowski (artist). Multicoloured.

3872	70g. Type **1200**	70	25
3873	80g. "Portrait of a Boy in a Hat"	80	30
3874	1z.10 "Stable-boy Bridling Percherons" (horiz) . . .	1·10	40
3875	1z.55 "Horses with Cart" (horiz)	1·50	55

1201 Mary and Jesus (painting), Rozanystok

2000. St. Mary's Sanctuaries. Multicoloured.

3876	70g. Type **1201**	25	10
3877	1z.55 Mary with crown supported by angels, Lichen	55	20

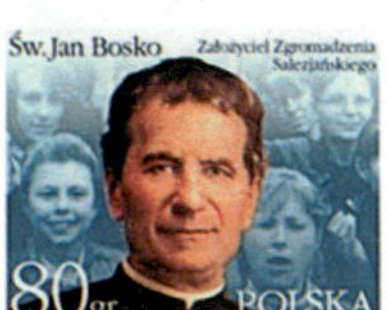
1202 John Bosco (founder of movement)

2000. Salesian Society (religious educational institution) in Poland.

3878 **1202** 80g. multicoloured . . 45 30

1203 Victory Sign

2000. 20th Anniv of Solidarity Trade Union. Sheet 60 × 78 mm.

MS3879 **1203** 1z.65 multicoloured 95 60

1204 Running

2000. Olympic Games, Sydney. Multicoloured.

3880	70g. Type **1204**	35	25
3881	80g. Diving, wind-surfing, sailing and kayaking . . .	40	30
3882	1z.10 Weight lifting, high jumping and fencing . . .	55	40
3883	1z.55 Athletics, basketball and judo	80	55

1205 Postman (Tomasz Wistuba)

1207 Priest and Cross

1206 Man with Postage Stamp Wings

2000. World Post Day. Winning Entries in Children's Painting Competition. Multicoloured.

3884	70g. Type **1205**	40	30
3885	80g. Customers and flying stork in Post Office (Katarzyna Chrzanowska) (horiz)	45	30
3886	1z.10 Post Office on "stamp" (Joanna Zbik) (horiz)	60	40
3887	1z.55 Woman at Post Office counter (Katarzyna Lonak) (horiz)	85	55

2000. 50th Anniv of Polish Philatelic Union. Sheet 75 × 60 mm.

MS3888 **1206** 1z.55 multicoloured 90 50

2000. Polish Rulers (15th series). As T **893**.

3889	70g. black, green and olive	40	30
3890	80g. black and purple . . .	45	30
3891	1z.10 black, blue and cobalt	60	40
3892	1z.55 black and brown . . .	85	55

DESIGNS; 70g. August II; 80g. Stanislaw Leszczynski; 1z.10, August III; 1z.55, Stanislaw August Poniatowski.

2000. 60th Anniv of Katyn Massacre. Mult.

3893	70g. Type **1207**	35	20
3894	80g. Pope John Paul II kneeling at monument, Muranow	40	30

1208 Nativity

2000. Christmas. Multicoloured.

3895	70g. Type **1208**	35	30
3896	80g. Wedding at Cana . . .	40	35
3897	1z.10 The Last Supper . . .	55	45
3898	1z.55 The Ascension	80	85

1209 Building Facade

1210 Privately Issued Stamp

2000. Centenary of Warsaw Art Gallery.

3899 **1209** 70g. multicoloured . . 45 40

2000. Underground Post during Martial Law, 1982–89.

3900 **1210** 80g. multicoloured . . 45 35

1211 Pope John Paul II, Emblem and Crowd

2001. End of Holy Year 2000. Value expressed by letter.

3901 **1211** A (1z.10) mult 40 15

1212 Mountains reflected in Ski Goggles

2001. 20th University Games, Zakopane.

3902 **1212** 1z. multicoloured . . . 35 10

1213 Computer Mouse

2001. The Internet.

3903 **1213** 1z. multicoloured . . . 35 10

1214 Adam Malysz (ski jumper)

2001. World Classic Seniors Championships. Multicoloured.

3904	1z. Type **1214**	35	10
3905	1z. As Type **1214** but additionally inscribed "Adam Malysz"	35	10
3906	1z. As No. 3905 but additionally inscribed "Mistrzem Swiata" . . .	35	10

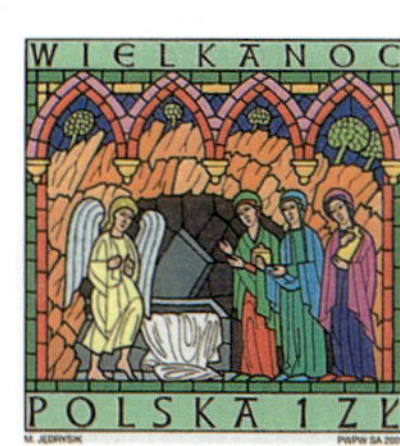
1215 Tomb of the Resurrected Christ

2001. Easter. Multicoloured.

3907	1z. Type **1215**	35	10
3908	1z.90 Resurrected Christ and Apostles	35	10

1216 Emblem and Basketball Players

2001. 12th Salesian Youth World Championships, Warsaw.

3909 **1216** 1z. multicoloured . . . 35 10

1217 Water Droplet

2001. Europa. Water Resources.

3910 **1217** 1z.90 multicoloured . . 65 20

1218 Man and Mermaid on Beach ("Holiday Greetings")

2001. Greetings Stamps. Multicoloured.

3911	1z. Type **1218**	35	10
3912	1z. Man presenting bouquet to woman ("Best Wishes")	35	10

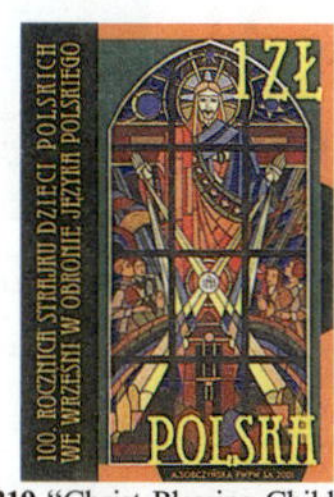
1219 "Christ Blessing Children of Wrzesnia" (Marian Turwid) (stained-glass window), Parish Church, Wrzesnia

2001. Centenary of Support of Wrzesnia Schoolchildren for the Language.

3913 **1219** 1z. multicoloured . . . 35 10

1220 Polish Scientific Institute and Wanda Stachiewicz Library,Montreal, Canada

2001. Polish Institutions Abroad. Multicoloured.

3914	1z. Type **1220**	35	10
3915	1z.90 Bust of Josef Pilsudski, Josef Pilsudski Institute, New York . . .	65	20
3916	2z.10 Polonia Museum, Archives and Library, Orchard Lake, Michigan	75	25
3917	2z.20 Polish Museum, Chicago	75	25

1221 Snowdrop (*Galanthus nivalis*) and European Lynx (*Lynx lynx*)

2001. Convention on International Trade of Wild Animals and Plants Threatened with Extinction (C.I.T.E.S.). Multicoloured.

3918	1z. Type **1221**	35	10
3919	1z. Apollo butterfly (*Parnassius apollo*) and orchid (*Orchis sambucina*)	35	10
3920	1z. Northern eagle owl (*Bubo bubo*) and *Adonis vernalis* (plant)	35	10
3921	1z.90 Lady's slipper orchid (*Cypripedium calceolus*) and brown bear (*Ursus arctos*)	65	20
3922	1z.90 Peregrine falcon (*Falco peregrinus*) and *Orchis pallens*	65	20
3923	1z.90 Wide leaf orchid (*Orchis latifolia*) and European otter (*Lutra lutra*)	65	20

MS3924 90 × 70 mm. 2z. World map and emblem (35 × 28 mm) . . . 1·25 80

1222 Cardinal Wyszynski and Text

2001. Birth Centenary of Cardinal Stefan Wyszynski (Primate of Poland, 1948–81).
3925 **1222** 1z. multicoloured . . . 35 10

1223 Father Kolbe and Handwriting

2001. 60th Death Anniv of Maksymilian Maria Kolbe (founder of Knighthood of the Immaculate, and concentration camp victim).
3926 **1223** 1z. multicoloured . . . 35 10

1224 "St. Mary of the Beautiful Love" (icon)
1225 Model of Sanctuary

2001. St. Mary's Sanctuaries. Multicoloured.
3927 1z. Type **1224** (Cathedral of St. Martin and St. Nicolas, Bydgoszcz) 35 10
3928 1z. St. Mary of Ludzmierz, Basilica of the Assumption of St. Mary, Ludzmierz 35 10
3929 1z.90 St. Mary the Winner, Church of St. Mary in Piasek, Wroclaw 65 20

2001. Completion of Section of God's Mercy Sanctuary at Cracow-Lagiewniki.
3930 **1225** 1z. multicoloured . . . 35 10

1226 Ligia, Vinius and Petrinius

2001. *Quo Vadis* (film directed by Jerzy Kawalerowicz). Depicting scenes from the film. Multicoloured.
3931 1z. Type **1226** 35 10
3932 1z. Nero singing at feast . . 35 10
3933 1z. St. Peter in the catacombs and the baptism of Chilon Chilonides 35 10
3934 1z. Chilon Chilonides and crowd fleeing 35 10
3935 1z. Liga tied to the back of a bull and in the arms of Ursus 35 10
3936 1z. St. Peter blessing Vincius and Liga 35 10

1227 Copper Furnace

2001. "Euro Cuprum 2001" European Stamp Exhibition, Lubin. Multicoloured.
3937 1z. Type **1227** 35 10
3938 1z.90 Engraver at work and men dredging copper sheets 65 20
3939 2z. Inking plates and engraving press 70 20
MS3940 88 × 76 mm. 3z. 18th-century engraving of Lubin and burin (50 × 39 mm) 90 30

1228 "Battle of Chocim" (detail, Stanislaw Batowski-Kaczor) and Breast-plate of Stanislaw Skorkowski's Armour

2001. "One Century Passes it Over to Another Century" Exhibition, Polish Military Museum, Warsaw.
3941 **1228** 1z. multicoloured . . . 35 10

1229 Steam and Electric Locomotives

2001. 75th Anniv of Polish State Railways.
3942 **1229** 1z. multicoloured . . . 35 10

1230 Street Scene (Marcin Kuron)

2001. Winners of "Poland in 21st Century" (children's painting competition). Multicoloured.
3943 1z. Type **1230** 35 10
3944 1z.90 Rockets behind girl and boy (Agata Grzyb) 65 20
3945 2z. Futuristic car and house on wheels (Joanna Sadrakula) 70 25

1231 Football and Players
1232 Children encircling Globe

2001. Qualification of Poland for World Cup Football Championship, Japan and South Korea.
3946 **1231** 1z. multicoloured . . . 35 10

2001. World Post Day. United Nations Year of Dialogue among Civilizations.
3947 **1232** 1z.90 multicoloured . . 65 20

1233 "100 Years Ago" (detail, Wlodzimierz Kugler)

2001. 80th Anniv of Post and Telecommunication Museum, Wroclaw. Sheet 87 × 70 mm.
MS3948 **1233** 3z.+75g. multicoloured . . . . 1·10 35

1234 Violin Peg Box and Scroll

2001. 12th Henryk Wieniawski International Violin Competition, Poznan.
3949 **1234** 1z. multicoloured . . . 35 10

1235 Pope John Paul II

2001. Papal Day.
3950 **1235** 1z. multicoloured . . . 35 10

1236 Building Facade

2001. Centenary of National Philharmonic Orchestra.
3951 **1236** 1z. multicoloured . . . 35 10

1237 Pope John Paul II

2001. New Millennium. Multicoloured.
3952 1z. Type **1237** 35 10
3953 1z. President Lech Walesa and cover of 1791 constitution 35 10
3954 1z. Covers of *Glos Wolny Wolnosc Ubespieczaiacy, Kultura, Zniewolony umysl* and *O skutecznym rad sposobie* (magazines) . . . 35 10
3955 1z. Wojciech Boguslawski (actor and dramatist) and Jerzy Grotowski (director) 35 10
3956 1z. General Jozef Pilsudski (soldier and President 1918–22) and posters (1989) 35 10
3957 1z. N.A.T.O. emblem and General Kazimierz Pulaski (soldier) 35 10
3958 1z. Nicolaus Copernicus and Aleksander Wolszczan (astronomers) 35 10
3959 1z. Jan of Glogow (wood engraving) (mathematician and astronomer) and Tadeusz Kotarbinski (physicist) 35 10
3960 1z. "Do Broni" (poster, 1920) and "Bitwa pod Grunwaldem" (detail) (painting, Jan Matejko) 35 10
3961 1z. Leaders of November Uprising, 1830 . . . . . 35 10
3962 1z. Head of John the Apostle (detail) (wooden altarpiece, Wit Stwosz) and sculpture by Magdalena Abakanowicz 35 10
3963 1z. Frederik Chopin, Krzysztof Penderecki (composers) and score of *Mazurka No. 10* by Karol Szymanowski 35 10
3964 1z. Royal Castle, Warsaw and view of Cracow (wood engraving) 35 10
3965 1z. Jan III Sobieski (painting) and emblem of European Union 35 10
3966 1z. Wislawa Szymborska (Nobel Prizewinner for Literature) and Mikolaj Rej (poet) 35 10
3967 1z. Janusz Kusocinski and Robert Korzeniowski (athletes) 35 10

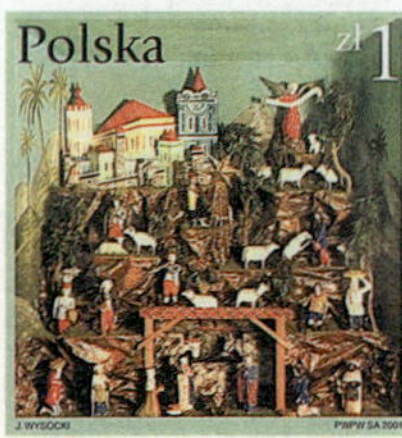

1238 Lower Silesian Crib

2001. Christmas. Multicoloured.
3968 1z. Type **1238** 35 10
3969 1z.90 Lower Silesian Crib (different) 35 10

1239 Radio Station Building and Virgin Mary (statue)

2001. 10th Anniv of "Radio Maryia" (religious broadcasting station). Multicoloured.
3970 1z. Type **MS**1239 . . . . . 30 10
MS3971 176 × 78 mm. 1z. Virgin Mary (statue) and crowd; 1z. Type **1239**; 1z. Crowd and crowned Virgin Mary (statue) 90 30

1240 Pear and Apple

2002. Valentine's Day.
3972 **1240** 1z.10 multicoloured . . 25 10

1241 Downhill, Biathlon, Ice-skating, and Ski Jumping

2002. Winter Olympic Games, Salt Lake City, U.S.A.
3973 **1241** 1z.10 multicoloured . . 25 10

1242 Jan Czerski

2002. Explorers. Multicoloured.
3974 2z. Type **1242** 50 15
3975 2z. Bronislaw Pilsudski . . . 50 15

1243 Gniezno
1244 Flowers

2002. Polish Cities.
3975a – 5g. multicoloured . . 10 10
3975b – 20g. multicoloured 10 10
3975c – 30g. multicoloured 10 10
3975d – 1z.20 multicoloured 25 10
3975e – 1z.25 multicoloured 25 10
3975ea – 1z.30 multicoloured 25 10
3975h – 1z.80 multicoloured 40 10
3975i – 1z.90 multicoloured 50 15
3976 **1243** 2z. multicoloured . . 50 15
3977 – 2z.10 multicoloured 50 15
3977a – 2z.20 multicoloured 80 25
3977c – 2z.60 multicoloured 60 20
3977d – 2z.80 multicoloured 1·00 35
3978 – 3z.20 multicoloured 75 25
3978a – 3z.40 multicoloured 80 30
3978bb – 3z.45 multicoloured 80 30
3978ba – 3z.50 green and deep green . . . . . . 1·20 40

DESIGNS: No. 3975a, Sandomierz (horiz); 3975b, Sieradz; 3975c, Katowice (horiz); 3975d, Torun; 3975e, Gdansk; 3975ea, Poznan (horiz); 3975h, Kalisz (horiz); 3975i, Lodz (horiz); 3977, Krakow; 3977a, Sopot (horiz); 3977c, Pfock (horiz); 3977d, Szczecin (horiz); 3978, Warsaw; 3978a, Kazimierz Dolny; 3978b, Lublin (horiz); 3978ba, (Przemysl).

2002. Easter. Multicoloured.
3979 1z.10 Type **1244** 25 10
3980 2z. Chicks 50 15

1245 Labrador Retriever and Puppies

2002. Domestic and Wild Animals. Multicoloured.
3981 1z.10 Type **1245** 25 10
3982 1z.10 Cat and kittens 25 10
3983 1z.10 Wolf and cubs 25 10
3984 1z.10 Lynx and kittens . . . 25 10

1246 Soldiers marching

2002. 60th Anniv of Evacuation of General Wladislaw Ander's Army from U.S.S.R.
3985 **1246** 1z.10 multicoloured . . 25 10

1247 Trees (Amanda Zejmis)

1249 Radio Microphone

1248 Stylized Figures

2002. Paintings. Multicoloured.
3986 1z.10 Type **1257** 25 10
3987 1z.10 Vase and ornaments (Henryk Paraszczuk) . . . 25 10
3988 2z. Landscape (Lucjan Matula) (horiz) 50 15
3989 3z.20 Basket of flowers (Jozefa Laciak) (horiz) . . 75 25

2002. National Census.
3990 **1248** 1z.10 multicoloured . . 25 10

2002. 50th Anniv of "Radio Free Europe".
3991 **1249** 2z. multicoloured . . . 50 15

1250 Fireman

2002. 10th Anniv of State Fire Brigade.
3992 **1250** 1z.10 multicoloured . . 25 10

1251 Circus Artist

2002. Europa. Circus.
3993 **1251** 2z. multicoloured . . . 50 15

1252 "Madonna with the Child, St. John the Baptist and the Angel" (Sandro Botticelli)

2002. 140th Anniv of the National Gallery, Warsaw.
3994 **1252** 1z.10 multicoloured . . 25 10

1253 Maria Konopnicka

1254 Scooter

2002. 160th Birth Anniv of Maria Konopnicka (poet and writer).
3995 **1253** 1z.10 brown, ochre and green 25 10

2002. Children's Games. Multicoloured.
3996 1z.10 Type **1254** 25 10
3997 1z.10 Flying kite 25 10
3998 1z.10 Badminton 25 10

1255 Football and Globe

2002. World Cup Football Championship, Japan and South Korea. Multicoloured.
3999 1z.10 Type **1255** 25 10
4000 2z. Player chasing ball . . . 50 15

1256 Domeyko and Santiago University, Chile

2002. Birth Bicentenary of Ignacego Domeyki (scientist).
4015 **1256** 2z.60 multicoloured . . 60 20

1257 Hibiscus and Tulips

2002. "Philakorea 2002" International Philatelic Exhibition, Seoul and "Amphilex 2002" International Philatelic Exhibition, Amsterdam.
4016 **1257** 2z. multicoloured . . . 50 15

1258 Pope John Paul II and Basilica of Virgin Mary of the Angel, Kalwaria Zebrzydowska

2002. 7th Papal Visit To Poland (1st issue). Multicoloured.
4017 1z.10 Type **1258** 25 10
4018 1z.80 Pope John Paul II and Sanctuary of God's Mercy, Sisters of Virgin Mary's Convent, Lagiewniki 40 10
See also No. **MS**4022.

1259 "Holy Lady of Assistance"

2002. St. Mary's Sanctuaries. Multicoloured.
4019 1z.10 Type **1259** (Church of the Holy Lady of Assistance, Jaworzno) . . 25 10
4020 1z.10 "Holy Virgin of Opole" (Cathedral of Holy Cross, Opole) . . . 25 10
4021 2z. "Holy Virgin of Trabki" (Church of the Assumption of the Holy Lady, Trabki Wielkie) . . 50 15

1260 Pope John Paul II and Wawel Castle, Cracow

2002. 7th Papal Visit To Poland (2nd issue). Sheet 73 × 57 mm.
MS4022 **1260** 3z.20 black 75 75

1261 Spa Building, Ciechocinku

2002. 18th Polish Philatelic Association Convention, Ciechocinku. Sheet 74 × 105 mm.
MS4023 **1261** 3z.20 brown . . . 75 75

1262 Czesnik Raptusiewicz and Dyndalski

2002. "Zemsta" (Revenge) (film directed by Andrzej Wajda). Sheet 177 × 137 mm containing T **1262**, Showing scenes from the film. Multicoloured.
MS4024 1z.10 Type **1262**; 1z.10 Klara and Waclaw; 1z.10 Papkin; 1z.10 Regent Milczek and Papkin; 1z.10 Regent Milczek and Czesnik Raptusiewicz; 1z.10 Podstolina and Klara . . . . 1·60 1·60

1263 Schwarzkopf Okl-359

2002. Steam Locomotives. Showing locomotives from Wolsztyn Railway Museum. Multicoloured.
4025 1z.10 Type **1263** 25 10
4026 1z.10 Fablok 0149-7 . . . . 25 10
4027 2z. Krolewiec Tki3-87 . . . 50 15
4028 2z. Express locomotive Pm 36-2 . . . . 50 15

1264 Hands holding Pens

2002. World Post Day.
4029 **1264** 2z. multicoloured . . . 50 15

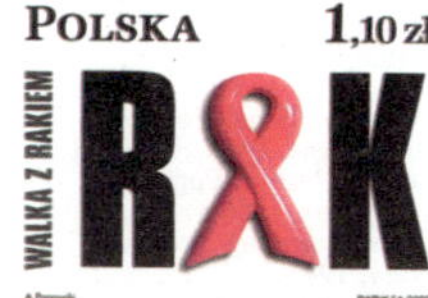
1265 Emblem

2002. Anti-Cancer Campaign.
4030 **1265** 1z.10 multicoloured . . 25 10

1266 Emblem

2002. 50th Anniv of Polish Television. Sheet 185 × 115 mm containing T **1266** Showing emblems of television programmes. Multicoloured.
MS4031 1z.10 Type **1266** (TV News); 1z.10 TV Theatre; 1z.10 "Pegaz" (cultural programme); 1z.10 "Teleranek" (children's programme) . . . . 1·00 1·00

1267 St. Stanislaw

2002. Saints. Sheet 136 × 165 mm containing T **1267** and similar vert designs. Multicoloured.
MS4032 1z.10 Type **1267**; 1z.10 St. Kazimierz; 1z.10 St. Faustyna Kowalska; 1z.10 St. Benedict; 1z.10 St. Cyril and St. Methody; 1z.10 St. Catherine of Siena . . 1·60 1·60

1268 Christmas Tree Baubles

2002. Christmas. Multicoloured.
4033 1z.10 Type **1268** 25 10
4034 2z. Small purple and large yellow baubles 50 15

1269 "POLSKA" superimposed on "EUROPA"

2003. Poland's Accession to European Union (1st issue). Negotiations.
4035 **1269** 1z.20 multicoloured . . 35 10
See also No. 4067, 4069 and 4120.

1270 Pope John Paul II

1271 Pope John Paul II on Balcony of St. Peter's Basilica, 1978

2003. 25th Anniv of the Pontificate of Pope John Paul II (1st issue). Multicoloured.

4036 1z.20 Type **1270** 35 10
4037 1z.20 Celebrating mass, Victory Square, Warsaw, 1979 . . . . 35 10
4038 1z.20 Addressing young people, Parc des Princes Stadium, Paris, 1980 . . . 35 10
4039 1z.20 Assassination attempt, St. Peter Square, 1981 . . 35 10
4040 1z.20 Giving homily surrounded by flowers, Portugal, 1982 . . . . . 35 10
4041 1z.20 Kneeling in front of Holy Doors, start of Holy Year of Redemption, 1983 35 10
4042 1z.20 Meeting Sandro Pertini, Pres. of Italy, 1984 . . . . 35 10
4043 1z.20 International Youth Day, Rome, 1985 . . . . 35 10
4044 1z.20 First visit of Pope to Synagogue, 1986 . . . . 35 10
4045 1z.20 Inaugurating Year of Mary, 1987 . . . . 35 10
4046 1z.20 Visiting European Parliament, Strasbourg, 1988 . . . . 35 10
4047 1z.20 Meeting Mikhail Gorbachev, Pres. Soviet Union, 1989 . . . . . . 35 10
4048 1z.20 Visiting lepers in Guinea-Bissau, 1990 . . . 35 10
4049 1z20 Addressing Bishop's Synod, 1991 . . . . . . 35 10
4050 1z.20 Pronouncing the Catechism, 1992 . . . . 35 10
4051 1z.20 Enthroned, Assissi, 1993 . . . . 35 10
4052 1z.20 Celebrating Mass in the Sistine Chapel, 1994 35 10
4053 1z.20 Addressing the United Nations, 1995 . . . . . 35 10
4054 1z.20 Walking through the Brandenburg Gate with Chancellor Helmut Kohl, 1996 . . . . 35 10
4055 1z.20 Celebrating Mass in Sarajevo, 1997 . . . . . 35 10
4056 1z.20 With Fidel Castro, Cuba, 1998 . . . . 35 10
4057 1z.20 Opening door, Christmas, 1999 . . . . . 35 10
4058 1z.20 With young people, World Youth Day, Rome, 2000 . . . . 35 10
4059 1z.20 Closing door of St. Peter's Basilica, 2001 35 10
4060 1z.20 Visiting the Italian Parliament, 2002 . . . . 35 10

2003. 25th Anniv of the Pontificate of Pope John Paul II (2nd issue).

4061 **1271** 10z. silver . . . . . . 3·00 90

1272 "Christ Anxious" **1273** Andrzej Modrzewski

2003. 500th Birth Anniv of Andrzej Frycz Modrzewski (writer).

4062 **1272** 1z.20 black 35 10

2003. Easter. Folk Sculpture. Multicoloured.

4063 1z.20 Type **1273** 35 10
4064 2z.10 "Christ Vanquisher" 60 15

1274 Poznan Ancient and Modern

2003. 750th Anniv of Poznan.

4065 **1274** 1z.20 multicoloured . . 35 10
MS4066 95 × 72 mm 3z.40 cinnamon and black (40 × 31 mm) . . . . 1·00 1·00

DESIGN: 3z.40 Ancient view of city and city arms.

1275 Portico and Clouds

2003. Poland's Accession to European Union (2nd issue).

4067 **1275** 1z.20 multicoloured . . 35 10

1276 Poster for "Vanitas" Exhibition (Wieslaw Walkuski)

2003. Europa. Poster Art.

4068 **1276** 2z.10 multicoloured . . 60 15

1277 "POLSKA" superimposed on "EUROPA"

2003. Poland's Accession to European Union (3rd issue). Referendum.

4069 **1277** 1z.20 multicoloured . . 35 10

1278 Island Palace (south view)

2003. Royal Baths, Lazienki Park, Warsaw. Multicoloured.

4070 1z.20 Type **1278** 35 10
4071 1z.80 Island Palace (north view) 55 15
4072 2z.10 Myslewicki Palace . . 60 15
4073 2z.60 Amphitheatre 75 20

1279 Pyramids and Camel (Anna Golebiewska)

2003. Children's Paintings. Stamp Design Competition Winners. Designs on theme "My Dream Vacation". Multicoloured.

4074 1z.20 Type **1279** 35 10
4075 1z.80 Girl windsurfing (Marlena Krejpcio) (vert) 55 15
4076 2z.10 Wind-surfer and fish (Michal Korze) 60 15
4077 2z.60 Girl and hens (Ewa Zadjdler) 75 20

1280 "Krak" (anonymous)

2003. Fairy Tales. Multicoloured.

4078 1z.20 Type **1280** 35 10
4079 1z.80 "Stupid Mateo" (Josef Kraszewski) 55 15
4080 2z.10 "Frog Princess" (Antoni Glinski) 60 15
4081 2z.60 "Crock of Gold" (Josef Kraszewski) 75 20

1281 Katowice Cathedral

2003. Katowice 2003 National Stamp Exhibition. Sheet 94 × 71 mm.

MS4082 **1281** 3z.40 black, brown and ochre . . . . 1·00 1·00

No. **MS**4082 also exists imperforate.

1282 "Self Portrait" **1283** Post Horn

2003. Birth Centenary of Julian Falat (artist). Multicoloured.

4083 1z.20 Type **1282** 40 10
4084 1z.80 "Spear Men" 60 20
4085 2z.10 "Winter Landscape with River and Bird" (horiz) 70 20
4086 2z.60 "Aboard Ship-Merchants of Ceylon" (horiz) 85 25

2003. World Post Day.

4087 **1283** 2z.20 multicoloured . . 75 25

1284 "Holy Virgin of Czestochowa" **1286** Dancers wearing Traditional Costume

1285 Motor Cycle (1903)

2003. St. Mary's Sanctuaries. Multicoloured.

4088 1z.20 Type **1284** (Church of the Holy Redeemer, Warsaw) 40 10
4089 1z.80 "Holy Mother Benevolent" (Basilica of Assumption of Holy Virgin, Krzeszowice) . . . 60 20
4090 2z.10 "Holy Virgin" (Church of the Holy Virgin, Zieleniec) 70 20

2003. Centenary of Motor Cycle Racing in Poland. Multicoloured.

4091 1z.20 Type **1285** 40 20
4092 1z.20 Rudge (c. 1930) . . . 40 10
4093 1z.20 NSU (c. 1940) 40 10

2003. 50th Anniv of Folk Dance Troup "Slask". Multicoloured.

4094 1z.20 Type **1286** 40 10
4095 1z.20 Dancers (different) . . 40 10

Nos. 4094/5 were issued together, se-tenant, forming a composite design.

1287 Perching Adult holding Fish

2003. Endangered Species. Osprey (*Pandion haliaetus*). Multicoloured.

4096 1z.20 Type **1287** 40 10
4097 1z.20 Adult and chicks on nest 40 10
4098 1z.20 Adult catching fish (one wing visible) 40 10
4099 1z.20 Adult carrying fish (both wings visible) . . . 40 10

Nos. 4096/9 were issued together, se-tenant, forming a composite design.

1288 Two White Storks

2003. *www.poland.gov.pl* (Poland on the internet).

4100 **1288** 2z.10 multicoloured . . 70 20

1289 The Nativity

2003. Christmas. Multicoloured.

4101 1z.20 Type **1289** 40 10
4102 1z.80 Three Kings 60 20
4103 2z.10 Angel appearing to Mary (vert) 70 20
4104 2z.60 Holy Family (vert) . . 85 25

1290 Wislawa Szymborska

2003. Polish Influence Abroad (1st series). Showing designs from other countries' stamps.

4105 **1290** 1z.20 purple, green and black 40 10
4106 – 1z.80 ultramarine, blue and black (horiz) . . 60 20
4107 – 2z.10 purple, azure and black 70 20
4108 – 2z.60 slate and black (horiz) 85 25

DESIGNS: 1z.20, Wislawa Szymborska (writer) (as Sweden No. 2120); 1z.80, Marie Sklodowska-Curie (physicist) (as France No. 1765); 2z.10, Czeslaw Milosz (writer) (as Sweden No. 1299); 2z.60, "Holy Virgin of Czestochowa" (as Vatican City No. 481).

See also Nos. 4112/13.

1291 Heart

2004. Orchestra of Holy Day Assistance (fund raising charity).

4109 **1291** 1z.25 multicoloured . . 40 10

1292 Airliner

2004. 75th Anniv of LOT (Polish airlines).

4110 **1292** 1z.25 multicoloured . . 40 10

1293 Boy and Girl with Heart-shaped Balloon

2003. St. Valentine.
4111 **1293** 1z.25 multicoloured . . 40 10

1294 Helena Paderewska

2004. Polish Influence Abroad (2nd series). Multicoloured.
4112 2z.10 Type **1294** co-founder of USA Polish White Cross (humanitarian organization) 70 20
4113 2z.10 Lucjan Bojnowski (New Britain, USA church pioneer) 70 20

1295 Chocolate Rabbit

2004. Easter. Multicoloured.
4114 1z.25 Type **1295** 40 10
4115 2z.10 Ceramic lamb 70 20

1296 Beaver and Frog

2004. Fauna. Multicoloured.
4116 1z.25 Type **1296** 40 10
4117 1z.25 Kingfisher, crayfish, roach and water beetle . . 40 10
4118 1z.25 Grayling, leech and water snail 40 10
4119 1z.25 Pike, grebe and roach 40 10
Nos. 4116/19 were issued together, se-tenant, forming a composite design.

1297 Map of Europe and New Members' Flags
1298 Rucksack as Landscape

2004. Poland's Accession to European Union (4th issue).
4120 **1297** 2z.10 multicoloured . . 70 20

2004. Europa. Holidays.
4121 **1298** 2z.10 multicoloured . . 70 20

1299 Figure (sculpture, St. Mariacki Square, Krakow)
1300 Pope John Paul II

2004. 10th Government Postage Stamp Printers' Conference, Krakow.
4122 **1299** 3z.45 multicoloured . . 1·10 35

2004. Pope John Paul II visits to Poland, 1970–2002. Two sheets, each 115 × 185 mm containing T **1300** and similar vert designs. Multicoloured.
MS4123 (a) 1z.25 × 4, Type **1300** (1979); At prayer (1983); Holding reliquary (1987); Resting head against staff (1991). (b) 1z.25 × 4, Holding staff (1991); With raised hand (1997); Seated facing right (1999); Seated facing left (2002). Set of 2 sheets . . . . 3·50 3·50

1301 Crimson Rosella (*Platycercus elegans*)
1302 "Self-portrait wearing White"

2004. Birds. Multicoloured.
4124 1z.25 Type **1301** 40 10
4125 1z.25 Cockatiel (*Nymphicus hollandicus*) 40 10
4126 1z.25 Budgerigar (*Melopsittacus undulates*) 40 10
4127 1z.25 Spotted-side finch (*Poephila guttata*), Gouldian finch (*Chloebia gouldiae*) and Java sparrow (*Padda oryzivora*) 40 10

2004. 150th Birth Anniv of Jacek Malczewski (artist). Multicoloured.
4128 1z.25 Type **1302** 40 10
4129 1z.90 "Ellenai" 65 20
4130 2z.10 "Tobias with Harpy" (horiz) 70 20
4131 2z.60 "The Unknown Note" (horiz) 85 25

1303 Sun Wu-Kung (monkey king)

2004. Singapore International Stamp Exhibition. Sheet 90 × 70 mm.
MS4132 **1303** 3z.45 multicoloured 1·10 1·10

1304 Boxer

2004. Olympic Games, Athens. Sheet 198 × 117 mm containing T **1304** and similar horiz designs. Multicoloured.
MS4133 1z.25 × 4, Type **1304**; Hurdler; Show jumper; Wrestler 1·60 1·60
The stamps and margin of **MS**4133 form a composite design.

1305 Witold Gombrowicz

2004. Birth Centenary of Witold Gombrowicz (writer).
4134 **1305** 1z.25 ultramarine . . . 40 10

1306 "Holy Mother of Miedzna"

2004. St. Mary's Sanctuaries. Multicoloured.
4135 1z.25 Type **1306** (Church of the Annunciation of Our Lady of Miedzna) 40 10
4136 1z.25 "Holy Mary and Family" (John the Baptist Basilica, Studiazianna) . . 40 10
4137 1z.25 "Holy Virgin of Sianow" (Church of the Nativity of Our Lady of Sianow) 40 10
4138 1z.25 "Holy Mary of Rywald" (St. Sebastian and Nativity of Our Lady, Rywald) 40 10
4139 1z.25 "Holy Mary of Piekary" (Name of Our Lady and St. Bartholome Basilica,Piekary Slaskie) 40 10
4140 1z.25 "Holy Mary of Ruda" (Assumption of Our Lady Church, Ruda) 40 10
4141 1z.25 "Holy Mary of Lomza" (Archangel St. Michael Cathedral, Lomza) 40 10
4142 1z.25 "Holy Mary of Perpetual Assistance" (Barefoot Carmelite Convent,Niedzwiady) . . 40 10
4143 1z.25 "Holy Mary of Rychwald" (St. Nicholas and Our Lady of Scapular, Rychwald) . . . 40 10
4144 1z.25 "Crying Holy Mary" (St. John the Baptist and Evangelist, Lublin) . . . 40 10
4145 1z.25 "Holy Mary of Dzikow" (Assumption of Our Lady Convent, Tarnobrzeg) 40 10
4146 1z.25 "Holy Mary of Rzeszow" (Assumption of Our Lady Church, Rzeszow) 40 10
4147 1z.25 "Gracious Holy Mary" (St. Stanislaw, St. Peter and St. Paul, Lubaczow) 40 10
4148 1z.25 "Holy Mother of Fatima" (Immaculate Heart of Our Lady of Fatima,Szczecin) 40 10
4149 1z.25 "Pieta of Skrzatusz" (Assumption of Our lady Church, Skrzatusz) . . . 40 10
4150 1z.25 "Pieta of Obory" (Visitation of Our Lady Church, Obory) 40 10
4151 1z.25 "Holy Mary of Jasnagora" (Queen of Poland Sanctuary, Jasnagora) 40 10

1307 Czeslaw Niemen

2004. Czeslaw Wydrzycki (Niemen) (musician) Commemoration.
4152 **1307** 1z.25 black 40 10

1308 Raft on River Dunajec

2004. Raft Men working on River Dunajec (bordering Slovakia and Poland).
4153 **1308** 2z.10 multicoloured . . 70 20
A stamp of the same design was issued by Slovakia.

1309 Motor Cyclists

2004. Motor Sports. Multicoloured.
4154 1z.25 Type **1309** 40 10
4155 1z.25 Race car 40 10
4156 1z.25 Kart racing 40 10
4157 1z.25 Motor cyclist (2004 International Six Day's Enduro) 40 10
Nos. 4154/7 were issued together, se-tenant, forming a composite design.

1310 Binary Codes forming Postman

2004. World Post Day.
4158 **1310** 2z.10 multicoloured . . 70 20

1311 Holy Mary Church, Krakow
1312 People entering Church

2004. World Heritage Sites. Multicoloured.
4159 1z.25 Type **1311** 40 10
4160 1z.25 Tower, St. John the Baptist and Evangelist Cathedral, Torun 40 10
4161 1z.25 Town Hall, Zamosc 40 10
4162 1z.25 Riverside, Warsaw (horiz) 40 10
4163 1z.25 Castle, Malbork (horiz) 40 10

2004. Christmas. Multicoloured.
4164 1z.25 Type **1312** 40 10
4165 1z.25 Decorated window (horiz) 40 10

1313 Protoplanet circling Sun

2004. History of Earth. Multicoloured.
4166 1z.25 Type **1313** 40 10
4167 1z.25 Asteroids bombarding earth 40 10
4168 1z.25 Dinosaurs 40 10
4169 1z.25 International space station in orbit 40 10

1314 "13"

2005. Orchestra of Holy Day Assistance (fund raising charity).
4170 **1314** 1z.30 multicoloured . . 45 15

1315 Konstanty Galczynski

2005. Birth Centenary of Konstanty Ildefons Galczynski (writer).
4171 **1315** 1z.30 multicoloured . . 45 15

1316 Mikolaj Rej

2005. 500th Birth Anniv of Mikolaj Rej (writer).
4172 **1316** 1z.30 black and vermilion 45 15

1317 Masked Swordsman and Carved Heart on Tree

2005. Greetings Stamp.
4173 **1317** 1z.30 multicoloured . . 45 15

1318 Rabbit

1319 "The Little Mermaid"

2005. Easter. Multicoloured.
4174 1z.30 Type **1318** 45 15
4175 2z.30 Chick 80 25

2005. Birth Bicentenary of Hans Christian Andersen (writer). Multicoloured.
4176 1z.30 Type **1319** 45 15
4177 1z.30 "The Snow Queen" 45 15

1320 Pope John Paul II

2005. Pope John Paul II Commemoration (1st issue).
4178 **1320** 1z.30 multicoloured . . 45 15
See also No. **MS**4184.

1321 Sky Diving

2005. Extreme Sports. Multicoloured.
4179 1z.30 Type **1321** 45 15
4180 1z.30 Bungee jumping . . . 45 15
4181 1z.30 Rock climbing . . . 45 15
4182 1z.30 White water rafting . . 45 15

1322 Shell

2005. Pacific Explorer International Stamp Exhibition, Sydney. Sheet 90 × 70 mm. Perf or imperf.
MS4183 **1322** 3z.50 multicoloured 1·20 1·20

1323 Pope John Paul II

2005. Pope John Paul II Commemoration (2nd issue). Sheet 70 × 83 mm.
MS4184 **1323** 1z.30 multicoloured 45 15

1324 Bread

2005. Europa. Gastronomy.
4185 **1324** 2z.20 multicoloured . . 80 25

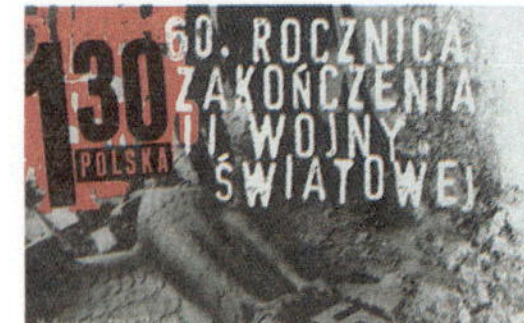

1325 Rubble

2005. 60th Anniv of End of World War II.
4186 **1325** 1z.30 black and vermilion 45 15

1326 "The Hour of the Crimson Rose" (M. Kruger)

2005. Stories. Sheet 124 × 124 mm containing T **1326** and similar square designs. Multicoloured.
MS4187 1z.30 Type **1326**; 2z. "The Little Prince" (Antoine de Saint-Exupery); 2z.20 "2000 Leagues under the Sea" (Jules Verne); 2z.80 "In the Desert and the Forest" (H. Sienkiewicz) . . . . 3·00 3·00

1327 "Stanislaw Kostka Potocki" (Jacques-Louis David)

1328 Embroidered Rose (Podhale)

2005. Bicentenary of National Museum, Wilanow. Sheet 95 × 130 mm containing T **1327** and similar vert designs. Multicoloured.
MS4188 1z.30 Type **1327**; 2z.17th-century Nautilus wine cup; 2z.20 Flower girl (18th-century porcelain); 2z.80 19th-century clock . . . . 3·00 3·00

2005. Embroidery. Designs showing embroidered roses. Multicoloured.
4189 1z.30 Type **1328** 45 15
4190 2z. Rose (Lowicz) 70 20
4191 2z.20 Rose (Podhale) (different) 80 25
4192 2z.80 Rose (Lowicz) (different) . . . . 1·00 35

1329 Hurdling

2005. International Athletics Championship, Helsinki. Sheet 200 × 115 mm containing T **1329** and similar horiz designs. Multicoloured.
MS4193 1z.30 Type **1329**; 1z.30 Shot put; 2z. Triple jump; 2z. Pole vault 2·30 2·30

1330 Jozef Pilsudski (Commander in Chief)

2005. 85th Anniv of Battle of Warsaw ("Miracle on the Vistula"). Sheet 70 × 90 mm.
MS4194 **1330** 3z.50 multicoloured 1·20 40

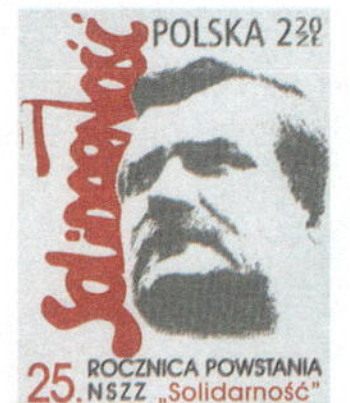

1331 Lech Walesa (founder)

2005. 25th Anniv of Solidarity (trade union).
4195 **1331** 2z.20 vermilion, grey and black 80 25

1332 "80"

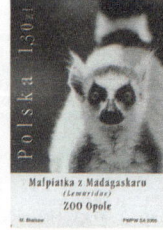

1334 Lemur (Opole)

1333 Music Score and Frederick Chopin

2005. 80th Anniv of Radio.
4196 **1332** 1z.30 rosine and black 45 15

2005. Frederick Chopin International Piano Competition.
4197 **1333** 2z.20 green, vermilion and black 80 25

2005. Zoological Gardens. Each black.
4198 1z.30 Type **1334** 45 15
4199 2z. Siberian tiger (*Panthera tigris altaica*) (Wroclaw) 70 20
4200 2z.20 White rhinoceros (*Ceratotherium simum*) (Poznan) 80 25
4201 2z.80 Anteater (Warsaw) . . 1·00 35

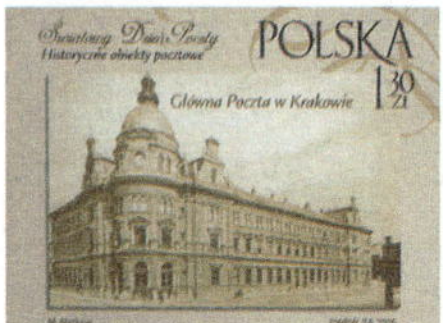

1335 Post Office Building, Cracow

2005. Post Day. Architecture.
4202 **1335** 1z.30 multicoloured . . 45 15

1336 Gingerbread Men

2005. 60th Anniv of United Nations.
4203 **1336** 2z.20 multicoloured . . 80 25

1337 St. Maciej's Church and St. Stefan's Statue, Budapest

2005. European Capitals. Multicoloured.
4204 1z.30 Type **1337** 45 15
4205 1z.30 Vilnius Cathedral . . 45 15
4206 2z.20 Arc de Triomphe, Paris 80 25
4207 2z.20 Monument to the Discoverers Belem, Lisbon 80 25
4208 2z.80 Government building, Dublin . . . . 1·00 40

1338 "Ploughing in the Ukraine" (L. J. Wyczolkowski)

2005. Art. Polish Impressionists. Sheet 94 × 130 mm containing T **1338** and similar horiz designs. Multicoloured.
MS4209 1z.30 × 2, Type **1338**; "Still Life" (J. Panekiewicz); 2z. × 2, "Flower Sellers" (O. Boznanska); "The Garden" (W. Podkowinski) 2·30 2·30

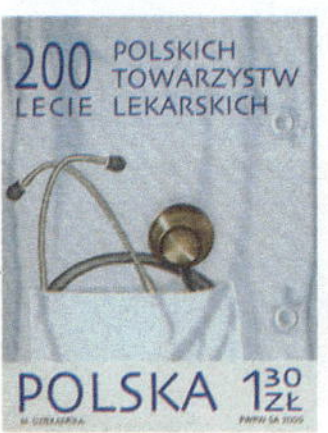

1339 Stethoscope in Pocket

1340 Trees and Angel

2005. Bicentenary of Doctors' Association.
4210 **1339** 1z.30 multicoloured . . 45 15

2005. Christmas. Multicoloured.
4211 1z.30 Type **1340** 45 15
4212 2z.20 Angel facing right . . 80 25

MILITARY POST

I. Polish Corps in Russia, 1918.

1918. Stamps of Russia optd **POCZTA Pol. Korp.** and eagle. Perf or imperf. (70k.).
M 1 **22** 3k. red . . . . 55·00 55·00
M 2 **23** 4k. red . . . . 55·00 55·00
M 3 **22** 5k. red . . . . 17·00 13·50
M 4 **23** 10k. blue . . . . 17·00 13·50
M 5 **22** 10k. on 7k. blue (No. 151) £425 £500
M 6 **10** 15k. blue and purple . . . 3·75 3·75
M 7 **14** 20k. red and blue . . . . 6·75 5·50
M 8 **10** 25k. mauve and green . . 85·00 70·00
M 9 35k. green and purple . . 3·75 3·75
M10 **14** 40k. green and purple . . 13·50 9·75
M11 **10** 70k. orge & brn (No. 166) £275 £225

1918. Stamps of Russia surch **Pol. Korp.**, eagle and value. (a) Perf on Nos. 92/4.
M12A **22** 10k. on 3k. red . . . . 3·50 3·50
M13A 35k. on 1k. orange . . . 50·00 50·00
M14A 50k. on 2k. green . . . 3·50 3·50
M15A 1r. on 3k. red . . . . . 70·00 65·00

(b) Imperf on Nos. 155/7.
M12B **22** 10k. on 3k. red . . . . 1·40 1·40
M13B 35k. on 1k. orange . . . 55 55
M14B 50k. on 2k. green . . . 1·40 1·40
M15B 1r. on 3k. red . . . . . 3·25 2·40

II. Polish Army in Russia, 1942.

M 3 "We Shall Return"

1942.
M16 M **3** 50k. brown £170 £425

NEWSPAPER STAMPS

1919. Newspaper stamps of Austria optd **POCZTA POLSKA**. Imperf.
N50 N **53** 2h. brown . . . . . . 8·75 10·50
N51 4h. green . . . . 1·75 2·25
N52 6h. blue . . . . 1·75 2·25
N53 10h. orange . . . . . 35·00 42·00
N54 30h. red . . . . 3·75 5·50

OFFICIAL STAMPS

O **24**

O **70**

1920.
O128 O **24** 3f. red 10 25
O129 5f. red 10 10
O130 10f. red 10 10
O131 15f. red 10 10
O132 25f. red 10 10
O133 50f. red 10 10
O134 100f. red 25 25
O135 150f. red 30 30

O136 200f. red 30 35
O137 300f. red 30 35
O138 600f. red 40 50

1933. (a) Inscr "ZWYCZAJNA".
O295 **O 70** (No value) mauve . . 15 15
O306 (No value) blue . . . 20 20
(b) Inscr "POLECONA".
O307 **O 70** (No value) red 20 20

O 93

1940. (a) Size 31 × 23 mm.
O392 **O 93** 6g. brown . . . . . . 1·25 1·60
O393 8g. grey . . . . . . 1·25 1·60
O394 10g. green . . . . . 1·25 1·60
O395 12g. green . . . . . 1·25 1·60
O396 20g. brown . . . . . 1·25 2·25
O397 24g. red . . . . . . 9·50 45
O398 30g. red . . . . . . 1·60 2·25
O399 40g. violet . . . . . 1·60 3·75
O400 48g. green . . . . . 5·00 3·75
O401 50g. blue . . . . . 1·25 2·25
O402 60g. green . . . . . 1·25 1·75
O403 80g. purple . . . . . 1·25 1·75
(b) Size 35 × 26 mm.
O404 **O 93** 1z. purple and grey . . 3·75 4·50
O405 3z. brown and grey . . 3·75 4·50
O406 5z. orange and grey . . 5·00 5·75
(c) Size 21 × 16 mm.
O407 **O 93** 6g. brown . . . . . . 65 1·00
O408 8g. grey . . . . . . 1·25 1·75
O409 10g. green . . . . . 1·90 1·90
O410 12g. green . . . . . 1·90 1·60
O411 20g. brown . . . . . 95 1·00
O412 24g. red 95 85
O413 30g. red . . . . . . 1·25 2·25
O414 40g. violet . . . . . 1·90 2·00
O415 50g. blue . . . . . 1·90 2·00

O 102 O 128 O 277

1943.
O456 **O 102** 6g. brown 30 60
O457 8g. blue 30 60
O458 10g. green 30 60
O459 12g. violet 30 60
O460 16g. orange 30 60
O461 20g. green 30 60
O462 24g. red 30 60
O463 30g. purple 30 60
O464 40g. blue 30 60
O465 60g. green 30 60
O466 80g. purple 30 60
O467 100g. grey 30 95

1945. No value. (a) With control number below design. Perf or imperf.
O534 **O 128** (5z.) blue 45 25
O535 (10z.) red 45 25
(b) Without control number below design. Perf.
O748 **O 128** (60g.) pale blue . . . 35 25
O805 (60g.) indigo 55 25
O806 (1.55z.) red 55 25
The blue and indigo stamps are inscr "ZWYKLA" (Ordinary) and the red stamps "POLECONA" (Registered).

1954. No value.
O871 **O 277** (60g.) blue 20 15
O872 (1.55z.) red ("POLECONA") 40 15

POSTAGE DUE STAMPS

1919. Postage Due Stamps of Austria optd **POCZTA POLSKA**.
D50 **D 55** 5h. red . . . . 5·50 5·00
D51 10h. red £1750 £2750
D52 15h. red . . . . 3·25 2·50
D53 20h. red £550 £550
D54 25h. red . . . . 19·00 17·00
D55 30h. red £950 £950
D56 40h. red £220 £220
D57 **D 56** 1k. blue £2000 £2500
D58 5k. blue £2000 £2500
D59 10k. blue £9750 £9000

1919. Postage Due Provisionals of Austria optd **POCZTA POLSKA**.
D60 **50** 15 on 36h. (No. D287) . . £300 £325
D61 50 on 42h. (No. D289) . . 30·00 25·00

D 20 D 28 D 63

1919. Sold in halerzy or fenigow.
D 92 **D 20** 2h. blue 10 10
D 93 4h. blue 10 10
D 94 5h. blue 10 10
D 95 10h. blue 10 10
D 96 20h. blue 10 10
D 97 30h. blue 10 10
D 98 50h. blue 10 10
D145 100h. blue 20 10
D146 200f. blue 75 10
D147 500h. blue 75 10
The 20, 100 and 500 values were sold in both currencies.

1919. Sold in fenigow.
D128 **D 20** 2f. red 10 25
D129 4f. red 10 10
D130 5f. red 10 10
D131 10f. red 10 10
D132 20f. red 10 10
D133 30f. red 10 10
D134 50f. red 25 25
D135 100f. red 30 30
D136 200f. red 30 35

1921. Stamps of 1919 surch with new value and **doplata**. Imperf.
D154 **11** 6m. on 15h. brown . . . 70 90
D155 6m. on 25h. red 50 55
D156 20m. on 10h. red . . . 1·90 2·10
D157 20m. on 50h. blue . . . 1·00 1·75
D158 35m. on 70h. blue . . . 8·75 12·50

1921. Value in marks. (a) Size 17 × 22 mm.
D159 **D 28** 1m. blue 20 10
D160 2m. blue 20 10
D161 4m. blue 20 10
D162 6m. blue 20 10
D163 8m. blue 20 10
D164 20m. blue 20 10
D165 50m. blue 20 10
D166 100m. blue 20 10
(b) Size 19 × 24 mm.
D199 **D 28** 50m. blue 10 10
D200 100m. blue 10 10
D201 200m. blue 10 10
D202 500m. blue 10 10
D203 1000m. blue 10 10
D204 2000m. blue 10 10
D205 10,000m. blue 10 10
D206 20,000m. blue 10 10
D207 30,000m. blue 10 10
D208 50,000m. blue 10 10
D209 100,000m. blue 10 10
D210 200,000m. blue 10 10
D211 300,000m. blue 30 20
D212 500,000m. blue 40 40
D213 1,000,000m. blue . . . 75 55
D214 2,000,000m. blue . . . 1·10 90
D215 3,000,000m. blue . . . 1·40 1·10

1923. Surch.
D216 **D 28** 10,000 on 8m. blue . . 10 15
D217 20,000 on 20m. blue . 10 35
D218 50,000 on 2m. blue . . 1·25 60

1924. As Type **D 28** but value in "groszy" or "zloty".
(a) Size 20 × 25½ mm.
D229 **D 28** 1g. brown 10 10
D230 2g. brown 20 10
D231 4g. brown 20 10
D232 6g. brown 20 10
D233 10g. brown . . . . . 3·25 10
D234 15g. brown . . . . . 3·25 10
D235 20g. brown . . . . . 6·75 10
D236 25g. brown . . . . . 4·75 10
D237 30g. brown 95 10
D238 40g. brown . . . . . 1·40 10
D239 50g. brown . . . . . 1·40 10
D240 1z. brown 90 10
D241 2z. brown 90 25
D242 3z. brown . . . . . 1·40 45
D243 5z. brown . . . . . 1·40 30
(b) Size 19 × 24 mm.
D290 **D 28** 1g. brown 20 10
D291 2g. brown 20 10
D292 10g. brown 90 10
D293 15g. brown . . . . . 1·40 10
D294 20g. brown . . . . . 3·25 10
D295 25g. brown . . . . . 30·00 10

1930.
D280 **D 63** 5g. brown 35 20

1934. Nos. D79/84 surch.
D301 **D 28** 10g. on 2z. brown . . 20 15
D302 15g. on 2z. brown . . 20 15
D303 20g. on 1z. brown . . 20 15
D304 20g. on 5z. brown . . 1·75 35
D305 25g. on 40g. brown . . 60 35
D306 30g. on 40g. brown . . 65 45
D307 50g. on 40g. brown . . 65 45
D308 50g. on 3z. brown . . 2·10 60

1934. No. 273 surch **DOPLATA** and value.
D309 10g. on 1z. black on cream 70 20
D310 20g. on 1z. black on cream 1·50 55
D311 25g. on 1z. black on cream 70 20

D 88 D 97

1938.
D350 **D 88** 5g. green 15 10
D351 10g. green 15 10
D352 15g. green 15 10
D353 20g. green 40 10
D354 25g. green 10 10
D355 30g. green 10 10
D356 50g. green 45 50
D357 1z. green . . . . . 2·25 1·75

1940. German Occupation.
D420 **D 97** 10g. orange 25 75
D421 20g. orange . . . . . 25 1·00
D422 30g. orange . . . . . 25 1·00
D423 50g. orange . . . . . 70 2·00

D 126 D 190

1945. Size 26 × 19½ mm. Perf.
D530 **D 126** 1z. brown 10 10
D531 2z. brown 20 10
D532 3z. brown 25 20
D533 5z. brown 40 25

1946. Size 29 × 21½ mm. Perf or imperf.
D646 **D 126** 1z. brown 10 10
D647 2z. brown 10 10
D572 3z. brown 10 10
D573 5z. brown 10 10
D574 6z. brown 10 10
D575 10z. brown 10 10
D649 15z. brown 10 10
D577 25z. brown 50 20
D651 100z. brown 55 35
D652 150z. brown 80 45

1950.
D665 **D 190** 5z. red 15 15
D666 10z. red 15 15
D667 15z. red 15 15
D668 20z. red 15 15
D669 25z. red 30 15
D670 50z. red 45 15
D671 100z. red 55 30

1951. Value in "groszy" or "zloty".
D701 **D 190** 5g. red 10 10
D702 10g. red 10 10
D703 15g. red 10 10
D704 20g. red 10 10
D705 25g. red 10 10
D706 30g. red 10 10
D707 50g. red 10 10
D708 60g. red 10 10
D709 90g. red 25 10
D710 1z. red 25 10
D711 2z. red 45 25
D712 5z. purple 95 30

1953. As last but with larger figures of value and no imprint below design.
D804 **D 190** 5g. brown 10 10
D805 10g. brown 10 10
D806 15g. brown 10 10
D807 20g. brown 10 10
D808 25g. brown 10 10
D809 30g. brown 10 10
D810 50g. brown 10 10
D811 60g. brown 10 10
D812 90g. brown 25 10
D813 1z. brown 25 10
D814 2z. brown 45 10

1980. As Type **D 190** but redrawn without imprint.
D2699 1z. red 10 10
D2700 2z. drab 10 10
D2701 3z. violet 30 10
D2702 5z. brown 50 30

D 1143

1998.
D3746 **D 1143** 5g. blue, vio & yell 10 10
D3747 10g. blue, turq & yell 10 10
D3748 20g. bl, grn & yell 10 10
D3749 50g. black & yell 15 10
D3750 80g. bl, orge & yell 25 10
D3751 1z. blue, red & yell 35 15

POLISH POST IN DANZIG Pt. 5

For Polish post in Danzig, the port through which Poland had access to the sea between the two Great Wars.

100 groszy = 1 zloty.

Stamps of Poland optd **PORT GDANSK**.

1925. Issue of 1924.
R 1 **40** 1g. brown . . . . 30 1·50
R 2 2g. brown . . . . 30 3·50
R 3 3g. orange . . . . . . 30 1·50
R 4 5g. green . . . . 9·50 6·50
R 5 10g. green . . . . . . 3·50 3·25
R 6 15g. red . . . . 19·00 5·00
R 7 20g. blue . . . . 1·50 1·50
R 8 25g. red . . . . 1·00 1·50
R 9 30g. violet . . . . . . 1·00 1·50
R10 40g. blue . . . . 1·00 1·50
R11 50g. purple . . . . . . 2·75 1·75

1926. Issues of 1925–28.
R14 **44** 5g. green . . . . 70 3·00
R15 – 10g. violet (No. 245a) . . 70 3·00
R16 – 15g. red (No. 246) . . . . 2·10 3·50
R17 **48** 20g. red . . . . 1·75 1·75
R18 **51** 25g. brown . . . . . . 2·75 1·75
R19 **57** 1z. black and cream . . . 19·00 23·00

1929. Issues of 1928/9.
R21 **61** 5g. violet . . . . 1·00 1·50
R22 10g. green . . . . . . 1·00 1·50
R23 **59** 15g. blue . . . . 2·45 4·50
R24 **61** 25g. brown . . . . . . 2·10 1·50

1933. Stamp of 1928 with vert opt.
R25 **57** 1z. black on cream . . . . 60·00 90·00

1934. Issue of 1932.
R26 **65** 5g. violet . . . . 2·40 3·50
R27 10g. green . . . . . . 23·00 90·00
R28 15g. red . . . . 2·40 3·50

1936. Issue of 1935.
R29 **79** 5g. blue (No. 313) . . . . 2·10 3·50
R31 – 5g. violet (No. 317) . . . 70 1·75
R30 – 15g. blue (No. 315) . . . 2·10 5·00
R32 – 15g. lake (No. 319) . . . 70 1·75
R33 – 25g. green (No. 321a) . . 2·10 3·50

R 6 Port of Danzig

1938. 20th Anniv of Polish Independence.
R34 **R 6** 5g. orange . . . . 40 1·50
R35 15g. brown . . . . . . 40 1·50
R36 25g. purple . . . . . . 40 1·50
R37 55g. blue . . . . 70 2·75

POLISH POST OFFICE IN TURKEY Pt. 5

Stamps used for a short period for franking correspondence handed in at the Polish Consulate, Constantinople.

100 fenigow = 1 marka.

1919. Stamps of Poland of 1919 optd **LEVANT**. Perf.
1 **15** 3f. brown . . . . 35·00
2 5f. green . . . . 35·00
3 10f. purple . . . . 35·00
4 15f. red . . . . 35·00
5 20f. blue . . . . 35·00
6 25f. olive . . . . 35·00
7 50f. green . . . . 35·00
8 **17** 1m. violet . . . . 40·00
9 1m.50 green . . . . . . 40·00
10 2m. brown . . . . 40·00
11 **18** 2m.50 brown . . . . . . 40·00
12 **19** 5m. purple . . . . 40·00

PONTA DELGADA Pt. 9

A district of the Azores, whose stamps were used from 1868, and again after 1905.

1000 reis = 1 milreis.

1892. As T **26** of Portugal but inscr "PONTA DELGADA".
6 5r. yellow . . . . 2·50 1·80
7 10r. mauve . . . . 2·50 1·70
8 15r. brown . . . . 3·50 2·50
9 20r. lilac . . . . 3·50 2·50
3 25r. green . . . . 7·25 1·50
12 50r. blue . . . . 7·50 3·75
25 75r. pink . . . . 7·25 6·00
14 80r. green . . . . 12·00 9·00
15 100r. brown on yellow . . . 12·00 7·25
28 150r. red on pink . . . . . 55·00 34·00
16 200r. blue on blue . . . . 55·00 50·00
17 300r. blue on brown . . . . 55·00 50·00

1897. "King Carlos" key-types inscr "PONTA DELGADA".
29 **S** 2½r. grey 50 35
30 5r. orange 50 35
31 10r. green 50 35
32 15r. brown . . . . 3·25 3·00
45 15r. green . . . . 1·70 1·20
33 20r. lilac . . . . 1·70 1·30
34 25r. green . . . . 2·50 1·30
46 25r. red . . . . 1·50 45
35 50r. blue . . . . 2·50 1·30
48 65r. blue . . . . 1·20 50
36 75r. pink . . . . 5·50 1·30
49 75r. brown on yellow . . . . 11·50 7·00
37 80r. mauve . . . . 1·50 1·30
38 100r. blue on blue . . . . . 3·50 1·30
50 115r. brown on pink . . . . 2·75 1·40
51 130r. brown on cream . . . 1·90 1·40
39 150r. brown on yellow . . . 1·90 1·50

52 180r. grey on pink . . . . . 1·90 1·40
40 200r. purple on pink . . . . 6·50 5·75
41 300r. blue on pink . . . . . 6·50 5·75
42 500r. black on blue . . . . . 14·00 11·00

POONCH Pt. 1

A state in Kashmir, India. Now uses Indian stamps.

12 pies = 1 anna;
16 annas = 1 rupee

1 4

1876. Imperf.
1 1 6p. red £11000 £150
2 ½a. red . . . . — £4500

1880. Imperf.
53 1 1p. red . . . . 2·75 2·50
12 4 ½a. red . . . . 2·75 3·50
50 1a. red . . . . 2·50 3·75
52 2a. red (22 × 22 mm) . . . . . 2·75 3·75
31 4a. red (28 × 27 mm) . . . . 4·75 4·75
These stamps were printed on various coloured papers.

OFFICIAL STAMPS

1888. Imperf.
O1 1 1p. black . . . . 2·50 2·75
O7 4 ½a. black . . . . 3·00 3·50
O3 1a. black . . . . 2·75 3·00
O4 2a. black . . . . 4·75 4·75
O5 4a. black . . . . 7·50 11·00

PORT LAGOS Pt. 6

French Post Office in the Turkish Empire. Closed in 1898.

25 centimes = 1 piastre.

1893. Stamps of France optd **Port-Lagos** and the three higher values surch also in figures and words.
75 10 5c. green . . . . 18·00 11·00
76 10c. black on lilac . . . . . 40·00 30·00
77 15c. blue . . . . 40·00 60·00
78 1p. on 25c. black on pink 30·00 32·00
79 2p. on 50c. red . . . . 75·00 70·00
80 4p. on 1f. green . . . . . . 48·00 75·00

PORT SAID Pt. 6

French Post Office in Egypt. Closed 1931.

1902. 100 centimes = 1 franc.
1921. 10 milliemes = 1 piastre.

1899. Stamps of France optd **PORT SAID**.
101 10 1c. black on blue . . . . . 95 1·50
102 2c. brown on buff . . . . 1·20 2·50
103 3c. grey . . . . 1·00 2·50
104 4c. brown on grey . . . . 80 3·50
105 5c. green . . . . 1·30 3·50
107 10c. black on lilac . . . . 4·25 6·00
109 15c. blue . . . . 4·50 10·00
110 20c. red on green . . . . 4·25 13·50
111 25c. black on pink . . . . 3·00 30
112 30c. brown . . . . 8·25 14·00
113 40c. red on yellow . . . . 9·50 12·50
115 50c. red . . . . 13·00 14·00
116 1f. green . . . . 22·00 20·00
117 2f. brown on blue . . . . 50·00 70·00
118 5f. mauve on lilac . . . . 60·00 £110

1899. No. 107 surch. (a) **25c VINGT-CINQ.**
119 10 25c. on 10c. black on lilac £325 £110

(b) **VINGT-CINQ** only.
121 10 25c. on 10c. black on lilac £120 26·00

1902. "Blanc", "Mouchon" and "Merson" key-types inscr "PORT SAID".
122 A 1c. grey 10 80
123 2c. purple . . . . 25 1·80
124 3c. red . . . . 45 2·75
125 4c. brown . . . . 20 2·30
126a 5c. green . . . . 1·40 2·00
127 B 10c. red . . . . 1·40 25
128 15c. red . . . . 2·30 3·25
128a 15c. orange . . . . 5·75 6·25
129 20c. brown . . . . 1·30 3·50
130 25c. blue . . . . 1·00 10
131 30c. mauve . . . . 3·75 3·00
132 C 40c. red and blue . . . . 2·75 4·75
133 50c. brown and lilac . . . 2·75 2·75
134 1f. red and green . . . . 8·00 11·50
135 2f. lilac and buff . . . . . 7·75 21·00
136 5f. blue and buff . . . . 25·00 50·00

1915. Red Cross. Surch **5c** and red cross.
137 B 10c.+5c. red . . . . 95 4·25

1921. Surch with value in figures and words (without bars).
151a A 1m. on 1c. grey . . . . . 3·75 4·75
152 2m. on 5c. green . . . . . 2·75 4·75
153 B 4m. on 10c. red . . . . . 2·00 4·50
166a A 5m. on 1c. grey . . . . . 25·00 38·00
167 5m. on 2c. purple . . . . 18·00 26·00
154 5m. on 3c. red . . . . . . 10·00 17·00
141 5m. on 4c. brown . . . . 11·50 19·00
155 B 6m. on 15c. orange . . . 2·30 5·75
156 6m. on 15c. red . . . . . 20·00 24·00
157 8m. on 20c. brown . . . . 3·00 5·75
168 A 10m. on 2c. purple . . . . 9·75 24·00
142 10m. on 4c. brown . . . . 29·00 40·00
158 B 10m. on 25c. blue . . . . 3·00 2·50
159 10m. on 30c. mauve . . . 5·50 12·00
144 12m. on 30c. mauve . . . 40·00 60·00
145 A 15m. on 4c. brown . . . . 11·50 15·50
169 B 15m. on 15c. red . . . . 38·00 65·00
170 15m. on 20c. brown . . . 50·00 70·00
146 C 15m. on 40c. red and blue 55·00 85·00
160 15m. on 50c. brown and lilac . . . . 4·50 8·00
161 B 15m. on 50c. blue . . . . 6·00 4·75
162 30m. on 1f. red and green 4·25 9·00
171 C 30m. on 50c. brown & lilac £225 £200
172 60m. on 50c. brown and lilac . . . . £225 60·00
149 60m. on 2f. lilac and buff 95·00 £110
164 60m. on 2f. red and green 6·75 17·00
173 150m. on 50c. brown and lilac £250 £250
165 150m. on 5f. blue and buff 9·00 18·00

1925. Surch with value in figures and words and bars over old value.
174 A 1m. on 1c. grey . . . . . 50 4·75
175 2m. on 5c. green . . . . . 2·50 5·00
176 B 4m. on 10c. red . . . . . 1·10 4·75
177 A 5m. on 3c. red . . . . . . 1·30 3·25
178 B 6m. on 15c. orange . . . 2·00 5·50
179 8m. on 20c. brown . . . . 2·00 5·50
180 10m. on 25c. blue . . . . 2·30 2·75
181 15m. on 50c. blue . . . . 3·00 3·00
182 C 30m. on 1f. red and green 1·70 4·00
183 60m. on 2f. red and green 2·50 5·50
184 150m. on 5f. blue and buff 3·75 7·25

1927. Altered key-types. Inscr "Mm" below value.
185 A 3m. orange . . . . 3·25 5·50
186 B 15m. blue . . . . 3·25 5·50
187 20m. mauve . . . . 2·75 5·75
188 C 50m. red and green . . . . 4·50 8·25
189 100m. blue and yellow . . 2·50 9·75
190 250m. green and red . . . 10·50 16·00

1927. "French Sinking Fund" issue. As No. 186 (colour changed) surch **+5 Mm Caisse d'Amortissement**.
191 B 15m.+5m. orange . . . . . 1·80 7·75
192 15m.+5m. mauve . . . . . 3·00 7·75
193 15m.+5m. brown . . . . . 2·50 7·75
194 15m.+5m. lilac . . . . . . 5·00 11·50

POSTAGE DUE STAMPS

1921. Postage Due stamps of France surch in figures and words.
D174 D 11 2m. on 5c. blue . . . 55·00 60·00
D175 4m. on 10c. brown . . 60·00 65·00
D176 10m. on 30c. red . . . 60·00 60·00
D166 12m. on 10c. brown 48·00 60·00
D167 15m. on 5c. blue . . . 50·00 75·00
D177 15m. on 50c. purple 75·00 75·00
D168 30m. on 20c. olive . . 60·00 75·00
D169 30m. on 50c. purple £2250 £2500
For 1928 issues, see Alexandria.

PORTUGAL Pt. 9

A country on the S.W. coast of Europe, a kingdom until 1910, when it became a republic.

1853. 1000 reis = 1 milreis.
1912. 100 centavos = 1 escudo.
2002. 100 cents = 1 euro.

1 Queen Maria II 5 King Pedro V 9 King Luis

1853. Various frames. Imperf.
1 1 5r. brown £3000 £900
4 25r. blue . . . . £1000 20·00
6 50r. green £3500 £950
8 100r. lilac £33000 £2000

1855. Various frames. Imperf.
18a 5 5r. brown . . . . £400 75·00
21 25r. blue . . . . £400 14·00
22 25r. pink . . . . £300 7·00
13 50r. green . . . . £500 75·00
15 100r. lilac . . . . £800 95·00

1862. Various frames. Imperf.
24 9 5r. brown . . . . £130 28·00
28 10r. yellow . . . . £150 49·00
30 25r. pink . . . . £110 5·00
32 50r. green . . . . £750 80·00
34 100r. lilac . . . . £850 95·00

14 King Luis 15

1866. With curved value labels. Imperf.
35 14 5r. black . . . . £110 10·50
36 10r. yellow £250 £150
37 20r. bistre . . . . £200 70·00
38 25r. pink . . . . £250 8·50
39 50r. green . . . . £250 70·00
41 80r. orange . . . . £250 70·00
43 100r. purple £325 £120
45 120r. blue . . . . £325 75·00

1867. With curved value labels. Perf.
52 14 5r. black . . . . £120 46·00
54 10r. yellow £250 £110
56 20r. bistre £300 £110
57 25r. pink . . . . 65·00 7·00
60 50r. green £250 £110
61 80r. orange £350 £110
62 100r. lilac £250 £110
64 120r. blue . . . . £300 70·00
67 240r. lilac £1000 £500

1870. With straight value labels. Perf.
69 15 5r. black . . . . 55·00 5·50
70 10r. yellow . . . . 75·00 28·00
158 10r. green . . . . 95·00 39·00
74 15r. brown . . . . £110 30·00
76 20r. bistre . . . . 75·00 26·00
143 20r. red . . . . £350 55·00
80 25r. red . . . . 44·00 3·75
115 50r. green . . . . £150 44·00
117 50r. blue . . . . £325 55·00
148 80r. orange . . . . £120 19·00
153 100r. mauve . . . . 70·00 14·00
93 120r. blue . . . . £275 75·00
95 150r. blue £350 £120
155 150r. yellow . . . . £130 14·00
99 240r. lilac £1500 £1100
156 300r. mauve . . . . £120 32·00
128 1000r. black . . . . £275 85·00

16 King Luis 17

1880. Various frames for T **16**.
185 16 5r. black . . . . 28·00 4·25
188 25r. grey . . . . 30·00 3·75
190 25r. brown . . . . 30·00 3·75
180 17 25r. grey . . . . £325 30·00
184 16 50r. blue . . . . £325 16·00

19 King Luis 26 King Carlos

1882. Various frames.
229 19 5r. black . . . . 14·50 1·40
231 10r. green . . . . 37·00 4·25
232 20r. red . . . . 44·00 18·00
212 25r. brown . . . . 30·00 2·50
234 25r. mauve . . . . 29·00 3·25
236 50r. blue . . . . 46·00 3·25
216 500r. black £500 £325
217 500r. mauve . . . . £275 55·00

1892.
271 26 5r. orange . . . . 12·50 2·10
239 10r. mauve . . . . 29·00 5·50
256 15r. brown . . . . 35·00 9·00
242 20r. lilac . . . . 55·00 12·50
275 25r. green . . . . 40·00 2·75
244 50r. blue . . . . 35·00 9·75
245 75r. red . . . . 65·00 8·50
262 80r. green . . . . 90·00 55·00
248 100r. brown on buff . . . 65·00 6·75
265 150r. red on pink . . . . £160 55·00
252 200r. blue on blue . . . . £160 46·00
267 300r. blue on brown . . . £180 70·00

1892. Optd **PROVISORIO**.
284 19 5r. black . . . . 17·00 9·00
283 10r. green . . . . 17·00 9·00
297 15 15r. brown . . . . 17·00 14·50
290 19 20r. red . . . . 41·00 23·00
291 25r. mauve . . . . 14·50 5·50
292 50r. blue . . . . 75·00 65·00
293 15 80r. orange . . . . £110 95·00

1893. Optd **1893 PROVISORIO** or surch also.
302 19 5r. black . . . . 14·50 7·25
303 10r. green . . . . 17·00 9·75
304 20r. red . . . . 41·00 23·00
309 20r. on 25r. mauve . . . . 55·00 50·00
305 25r. mauve £110 £100
306 50r. blue £110 £110
310 15 50r. on 80r. orange . . . £130 £110
312 75r. on 80r. orange . . . 75·00 75·00
308 80r. orange £110 £110

32 Prince Henry in his Caravel and Family Motto

1894. 500th Birth Anniv of Prince Henry the Navigator.
314 32 5r. orange . . . . 3·75 70
315 10r. red . . . . 3·75 70
316 15r. brown . . . . 11·50 3·50
317 20r. lilac . . . . 11·50 4·25
318 – 25r. green . . . . 10·00 1·40
319 – 50r. blue . . . . 29·00 6·25
320 – 75r. red . . . . 55·00 12·00
321 – 80r. green . . . . 55·00 14·50
322 – 100r. brown on buff . . . 42·00 10·50
323 – 150r. red . . . . £140 34·00
324 – 300r. blue on buff . . . . £150 39·00
325 – 500r. purple . . . . £325 80·00
326 – 1000r. black on buff . . . £600 £120
DESIGNS: 25r. to 100r. Prince Henry directing movements of his fleet; 150r. to 1000r. Prince Henry's studies.

35 St. Anthony's Vision 37 St. Anthony ascending into Heaven

1895. 700th Birth Anniv of St. Anthony (Patron Saint). With a prayer in Latin printed on back.
327 35 2½r. black . . . . 4·25 1·10
328 – 5r. orange . . . . 4·25 1·10
329 – 10r. mauve . . . . 14·00 8·50
330 – 15r. brown . . . . 15·00 8·50
331 – 20r. lilac . . . . 15·00 9·00
332 – 25r. purple and green . . 13·50 1·10
333 37 50r. brown and blue . . . 33·00 23·00
334 75r. brown and red . . . . 50·00 41·00
335 80r. brown and green . . 65·00 65·00
336 100r. black and brown . . 60·00 31·00
337 – 150r. red and bistre . . . £170 £110
338 – 200r. blue and bistre . . £160 £120
339 – 300r. grey and bistre . . £225 £140
340 – 500r. brown and green . . £400 £325
341 – 1000r. lilac and green . . £650 £400
DESIGNS—HORIZ: 5r. to 25r. St. Anthony preaching to fishes. VERT: 150r. to 1000r. St. Anthony from picture in Academy of Fine Arts, Paris.

39 King Carlos

1895. Numerals of value in red (Nos. 354 and 363) or black (others).
342 39 2½r. grey 25 15
343 5r. orange 25 15
344 10r. green 55 25
345 15r. green . . . . 49·00 2·50
346 15r. brown . . . . 95·00 3·75
347 20r. lilac 90 35
348 25r. green . . . . 65·00 25
349 25r. red 40 15
351 50r. blue 55 25
352 65r. blue 55 25
353 75r. red . . . . £120 4·50
354 75r. brown on yellow . . . 1·80 75
355 80r. mauve . . . . 2·30 1·10
356 100r. blue on blue . . . . 1·10 40
357 115r. brown on pink . . . 5·00 2·75
358 130r. brown on cream . . 4·00 1·40
359 150r. brown on yellow . . £150 24·00
360 180r. grey on pink . . . . 16·00 9·50
361 200r. puple on pink . . . 17·00 2·30
362 300r. blue on pink . . . . 3·75 2·10
363 500r. black on blue . . . . 10·00 4·75

40 Departure of Fleet

43 Muse of History

44 Da Gama and Camoens and "Sao Gabriel" (flagship)

1898. 4th Centenary of Discovery of Route to India by Vasco da Gama.
378 **40** 2½r. green . . . 1·40 35
379 – 5r. red . . . 1·40 35
380 – 10r. purple . . . 9·00 1·60
381 **43** 25r. green . . . 5·25 55
382 **44** 50r. blue . . . 11·00 3·25
383 – 75r. brown . . . 46·00 11·00
384 – 100r. brown . . . 32·00 11·00
385 – 150r. brown . . . 70·00 29·00
DESIGNS—HORIZ: 5r. Arrival at Calicut; 10r. Embarkation at Rastello; 100r. Flagship "Sao Gabriel"; 150r. Vasco da Gama. VERT: 75r. Archangel Gabriel, Patron Saint of the Expedition.

48 King Manoel II **49**

1910.
390 **48** 2½r. lilac . . . 20 15
391 5r. black . . . 20 15
392 10r. green . . . 30 20
393 15r. brown . . . 2·75 1·40
394 20r. red . . . 85 70
395 25r. brown . . . 65 20
396 50r. blue . . . 1·50 70
397 75r. brown . . . 9·75 5·25
398 80r. grey . . . 2·75 2·30
399 100r. brown on green . . . 10·50 3·25
400 200r. green on orange . . . 6·25 4·50
401 300r. black on blue . . . 7·00 5·25
402 **49** 500r. brown and green . . . 14·00 12·50
403 1000r. black and blue . . . 32·00 25·00

1910. Optd **REPUBLICA.**
404 **48** 2½r. lilac . . . 30 10
405 5r. black . . . 30 10
406 10r. green . . . 3·75 1·20
407 15r. brown . . . 1·20 90
408 20r. red . . . 4·50 1·60
409 25r. brown . . . 85 25
410 50r. blue . . . 6·25 2·10
411 75r. brown . . . 9·50 4·00
412 80r. grey . . . 3·50 2·50
413 100r. brown on green . . . 2·10 75
414 200r. green on orange . . . 2·50 1·80
415 300r. black on blue . . . 4·00 3·00
416 **49** 500r. brown and green . . . 10·00 8·75
417 1000r. black and blue . . . 25·00 21·00

1911. Optd **REPUBLICA** or surch also.
441 **40** 2½r. green . . . 45 10
442a D **48** 5r. black . . . 90 35
443a 10r. mauve . . . 1·50 70
444 – 15r. on 5r. red (No. 379) . . . 85 35
445a D **48** 20r. orange . . . 6·00 3·25
446 **43** 25r. green . . . 45 20
447 **44** 50r. blue . . . 3·50 1·60
448 – 75r. brown (No. 383) 46·00 33·00
449 – 80r. on 150r. (No. 385) 7·00 5·00
450 – 100r. brown (No. 384) 7·00 3·25
451 D **48** 200r. brown on buff . £130 70·00
452 300r. on 50r. grey . . 95·00 44·00
453 500r. on 100r. red on pink . . . 49·00 25·00
454 – 1000r. on 10r. (No. 380) . . . 65·00 39·00

1911. Vasco da Gama stamps of Madeira optd **REPUBLICA** or surch also.
455 2½r. green . . . 12·50 8·75
456 15r. on 5r. red . . . 2·75 2·10
457 25r. green . . . 6·25 5·00
458 50r. blue . . . 11·50 8·75
459 75r. brown . . . 11·50 5·75
460 80r. on 150r. brown . . . 13·50 11·50
461 100r. brown . . . 39·00 8·75
462 1000r. on 10r. purple . . . 39·00 26·00

56 Ceres

60 Presidents of Portugal and Brazil and Airmen Gago Coutinho and Sacadura Cabral

1912.
484 **56** ¼c. brown . . . 60 30
485 ½c. black . . . 1·80 90
486 1c. green . . . 1·30 40
515 1c. brown . . . 25 20
488 1½c. brown . . . 7·25 3·00
516 1½c. green . . . 30 20
490 2c. red . . . 7·25 1·80
517 2c. yellow . . . 25 20
702 2c. brown . . . 15 15
492 2½c. lilac . . . 50 20
521 3c. red . . . 30 20
703 3c. blue . . . 15 15
495 3½c. green . . . 35 20
523 4c. green . . . 1·80 25
704 4c. orange . . . 15 15
497 5c. blue . . . 7·25 70
705 5c. brown . . . 15 15
527 6c. purple . . . 35 20
706 6c. brown . . . 15 15
815 6c. red . . . 35 20
500 7½c. brown . . . 9·00 2·10
529 7½c. blue . . . 35 20
530 8c. grey . . . 50 35
531 8c. green . . . 70 55
532 8c. orange . . . 60 45
503 10c. brown . . . 17·00 1·10
707 10c. red . . . 15 15
504 12c. blue . . . 1·10 55
534 12c. green . . . 60 40
535 13½c. blue . . . 1·50 1·10
481 14c. blue on yellow . . . 2·50 1·60
536 14c. purple . . . 70 55
505 15c. brown . . . 1·10 55
708 15c. black . . . 25 15
709 16c. blue . . . 25 15
474 20c. brown on green . . . 18·00 1·80
475 20c. brown on buff . . . 18·00 5·00
539 20c. brown . . . 70 40
540 20c. green . . . 55 45
541 20c. grey . . . 55 45
542 24c. blue . . . 70 40
543 25c. pink . . . 60 30
710 25c. grey . . . 25 15
819 25c. green . . . 55 30
476 30c. brown on pink . . . £130 11·50
477 30c. brown on yellow . . . 12·00 2·30
545 30c. brown . . . 60 35
820 32c. green . . . 55 30
548 36c. red . . . 2·00 45
549 40c. blue . . . 1·20 85
550 40c. brown . . . 70 40
712 40c. green . . . 35 15
713 48c. pink . . . 1·20 90
478 50c. orange on orange . . . 16·00 1·40
553 50c. yellow . . . 1·40 70
824 50c. red . . . 1·80 90
554 60c. blue . . . 1·80 70
715 64c. blue . . . 2·10 1·80
826 75c. red . . . 1·90 95
510 80c. pink . . . 1·80 1·10
558 80c. lilac . . . 1·20 60
827 80c. green . . . 1·90 95
559 90c. blue . . . 2·10 75
717 96c. red . . . 2·30 1·20
480 1e. green on blue . . . 21·00 1·40
561 1e. lilac . . . 4·50 2·30
565 1e. blue . . . 6·00 2·50
566 1e. purple . . . 2·10 90
829 1e. red . . . 4·25 1·00
562 1e.10 brown . . . 4·50 2·00
563 1e.20 green . . . 2·75 1·40
830 1e.20 brown . . . 3·25 1·10
831 1e.25 blue . . . 2·75 1·10
568 1e.50 lilac . . . 18·00 4·25
720 1e.60 blue . . . 2·50 60
721 2e. green . . . 15·00 1·10
833 2e. mauve . . . 20·00 6·75
572 2e.40 green . . . £225 £160
573 3e. pink . . . £225 £140
722 3e.20 green . . . 5·75 1·10
723 4e.50 yellow . . . 5·75 1·10
575 5e. green . . . 46·00 10·50
724 5e. brown . . . 80·00 3·75
725 10e. red . . . 9·00 2·10
577 20e. blue . . . £350 £200

1923. Portugal–Brazil Trans-Atlantic Flight.
578 **60** 1c. brown . . . 15 70
579 2c. orange . . . 15 70
580 3c. blue . . . 15 70
581 4c. green . . . 15 70
582 5c. brown . . . 15 70
583 10c. brown . . . 15 70
584 15c. black . . . 15 70
585 20c. green . . . 15 70
586 25c. red . . . 15 70
587 30c. brown . . . 65 2·00
588 40c. brown . . . 15 70
589 50c. yellow . . . 35 90
590 75c. purple . . . 35 1·10
591 1e. blue . . . 35 2·10
592 1e.50 grey . . . 70 2·40
593 2e. green . . . 70 6·25

62 Camoens at Ceuta

63 Saving the "Lusiad"

1924. 400th Birth Anniv of Camoens (poet). Value in black.
600 **62** 2c. blue . . . 15 15
601 3c. orange . . . 15 15
602 4c. grey . . . 15 15
603 5c. green . . . 15 15
604 6c. red . . . 15 15
605 **63** 8c. brown . . . 15 15
606 10c. violet . . . 15 15
607 15c. green . . . 15 15
608 16c. purple . . . 20 20
609 20c. orange . . . 35 20
610 – 25c. violet . . . 35 20
611 – 30c. brown . . . 35 20
612 – 32c. green . . . 85 1·10
613 – 40c. blue . . . 30 25
614 – 48c. red . . . 1·30 1·30
615 – 50c. red . . . 1·40 95
616 – 64c. green . . . 1·40 95
617 – 75c. lilac . . . 1·50 95
618 – 80c. brown . . . 1·10 95
619 – 96c. red . . . 1·10 95
620 – 1e. turquoise . . . 1·10 85
621 – 1e.20 brown . . . 5·50 5·00
622 – 1e.50 red . . . 1·30 90
623 – 1e.60 blue . . . 1·30 90
624 – 2e. green . . . 5·50 5·00
625 – 2e.40 green on green . . . 3·75 2·75
626 – 3e. blue on blue . . . 1·60 1·10
627 – 3e.20 black on turquoise . . . 1·60 1·00
628 – 4e.50 black on yellow . . . 4·25 3·00
629 – 10e. brown on pink . . . 9·50 8·50
630 – 20e. violet on mauve . . . 9·50 7·25
DESIGNS—VERT: 25c. to 48c. Luis de Camoens; 50c. to 96c. 1st Edition of "Lusiad"; 20e. Monument to Camoens. HORIZ: 1e. to 2e. Death of Camoens; 2e.40 to 10e. Tomb of Camoens.

65 Branco's House at S. Miguel de Seide

67 Camilo Castelo Branco

1925. Birth Centenary of Camilo Castelo Branco (novelist). Value in black.
631 **65** 2c. orange . . . 20 15
632 3c. green . . . 20 15
633 4c. blue . . . 20 15
634 5c. red . . . 20 15
635 6c. purple . . . 20 15
636 8c. brown . . . 20 15
637 A 10c. blue . . . 20 15
638 **67** 15c. green . . . 20 15
639 A 16c. orange . . . 30 30
640 20c. violet . . . 30 30
641 **67** 25c. red . . . 30 30
642 A 30c. bistre . . . 30 30
643 32c. green . . . 1·10 1·10
644 **67** 40c. black and green . . . 70 70
645 A 48c. red . . . 3·25 3·25
646 B 50c. green . . . 70 70
647 64c. brown . . . 3·25 3·25
648 75c. grey . . . 65 65
649 **67** 80c. brown . . . 65 65
650 B 96c. red . . . 1·50 1·50
651 1e. lilac . . . 1·50 1·50
652 1e.20 green . . . 1·50 1·50
653 C 1e.50 blue on blue . . . 27·00 14·00
654 **67** 1e.60 blue . . . 5·25 4·00
655 C 2e. green on green . . . 6·50 4·50
656 2e.40 red on orange . . . 55·00 33·00
657 3e. red on blue . . . 70·00 43·00
658 3e.20 black on green . . . 33·00 33·00
659 **67** 4e.50 black and red . . . 13·00 4·00
660 C 10e. brown on buff . . . 13·50 4·50
661 D 20e. black on orange . . . 14·50 4·50
DESIGNS—HORIZ: A, Branco's study. VERT: B, Teresa de Albuquerque; C, Mariana and Joao da Cruz; D, Simao de Botelho. Types B/D shows characters from Branco's "Amor de Peredicao".

76 Afonso I, first King of Portugal, 1140

80 Goncalo Mendes da Maia

77 Battle of Aljubarrota

1926. 1st Independence issue. Dated 1926. Centres in black.
671 **76** 2c. orange . . . 20 20
672 – 3c. blue . . . 20 20
673 **76** 4c. green . . . 20 20
674 – 5c. brown . . . 20 20
675 **76** 6c. orange . . . 20 20
676 – 15c. green . . . 20 20
677 **76** 16c. blue . . . 70 70
678 **77** 20c. violet . . . 70 70
679 – 25c. red . . . 75 75
680 **77** 32c. green . . . 95 95
681 – 40c. brown . . . 55 55
682 – 46c. red . . . 3·50 3·50
683 – 50c. bistre . . . 3·50 3·50
684 – 64c. green . . . 4·75 4·75
685 – 75c. brown . . . 4·75 4·75
686 – 96c. red . . . 7·25 7·25
687 – 1e. violet . . . 7·25 7·25
688 **77** 1e.60 blue . . . 9·75 9·75
689 – 3e. purple . . . 29·00 29·00
690 – 4e.50 green . . . 36·00 36·00
691 **77** 10e. red . . . 60·00 60·00
DESIGNS—VERT: 25, 40, 50, 75c. Philippa de Vilhena arms her sons; 64c., 1e. Don Joao IV, 1640; 96c., 3e., 4e.50, Independence Monument, Lisbon. HORIZ: 3, 5, 15, 46c. Monastery of D. Joao I.

1926. 1st Independence issue surch. Centres in black.
692 2c. on 5c. brown . . . 1·20 1·20
693 2c. on 46c. red . . . 1·20 1·20
694 2c. on 64c. green . . . 1·60 1·60
695 3c. on 75c. brown . . . 1·60 1·60
696 3c. on 96c. red . . . 2·10 2·10
697 3c. on 1e. violet . . . 1·80 1·80
698 4c. on 1e.60 blue . . . 12·00 12·00
699 4c. on 3e. purple . . . 4·25 4·25
700 6c. on 4e.50 green . . . 4·25 4·25
701 6c. on 10e. red . . . 4·25 4·25

1927. 2nd Independence issue. Dated 1927. Centres in black.
726 **80** 2c. brown . . . 20 15
727 – 3c. blue . . . 20 15
728 **80** 4c. orange . . . 20 15
729 – 5c. brown . . . 20 15
730 – 6c. brown . . . 20 15
731 – 15c. brown . . . 50 40
732 – 16c. blue . . . 1·10 40
733 **80** 25c. grey . . . 1·30 1·20
734 – 32c. green . . . 2·75 1·70
735 – 40c. green . . . 70 55
736 **80** 48c. red . . . 12·00 10·50
737 – 80c. violet . . . 8·50 7·25
738 – 96c. red . . . 15·00 14·00
739 – 1e.60 blue . . . 16·00 15·00
740 – 4e.50 brown . . . 24·00 23·00
DESIGNS—HORIZ: 3, 15, 80c. Gulmaraes Castle; 6, 32c. Battle of Montijo. VERT: 5, 16c., 1e.50, Joao das Regras; 40, 96c. Brites de Aimelda; 4e.50, J. P. Ribeiro.

1928. Surch.
742 **56** 4c. on 8c. orange . . . 45 35
743 4c. on 30c. brown . . . 45 35
744 10c. on ¼c. brown . . . 45 20
745 10c. on ½c. black . . . 60 45
746 10c. on 1c. brown . . . 60 45
747 10c. on 4c. green . . . 45 40
748 10c. on 4c. orange . . . 45 40
749 10c. on 5c. brown . . . 45 40
751 15c. on 16c. blue . . . 1·10 85
752 15c. on 20c. brown . . . 35·00 35·00
753 15c. on 20c. grey . . . 45 35
754 15c. on 24c. blue . . . 2·30 1·70
755 15c. on 25c. pink . . . 45 35
756 15c. on 25c. grey . . . 45 35
757 16c. on 32c. green . . . 95 85
758 40c. on 2c. yellow . . . 45 35
760 40c. on 2c. brown . . . 40 35
761 40c. on 3c. blue . . . 45 40
762 40c. on 50c. yellow . . . 40 30
763 40c. on 60c. blue . . . 95 70
764 40c. on 64c. blue . . . 95 85
765 40c. on 75c. pink . . . 95 95
766 40c. on 80c. lilac . . . 70 55
767 40c. on 90c. blue . . . 4·50 3·50
768 40c. on 1e. grey . . . 90 90
769 40c. on 1e.10 brown . . . 95 85
770 80c. on 6c. purple . . . 90 75
771 80c. on 6c. brown . . . 90 75
772 80c. on 48c. pink . . . 1·30 1·10
773 80c. on 1e.50 lilac . . . 2·00 1·30
774 96c. on 1e.20 green . . . 3·75 2·50
775 96c. on 1e.20 buff . . . 3·75 3·00
777 1e.60 on 2e. green . . . 38·00 29·00
778 1e.60 on 3e.20 green . . . 10·50 7·75
779 1e.60 on 20e. blue . . . 14·50 10·50

84 Storming of Santarem

1928. 3rd Independence issue. Dated 1928. Centres in black.
780 – 2c. blue . . . 15 15
781 **84** 3c. green . . . 15 15
782 – 4c. red . . . 15 15
783 – 5c. green . . . 15 15
784 – 6c. brown . . . 15 15
785 **84** 15c. grey . . . 75 75
786 – 16c. purple . . . 75 75
787 – 25c. blue . . . 75 75
788 – 32c. green . . . 4·00 4·00
789 – 40c. brown . . . 80 75
790 – 50c. red . . . 9·75 6·00
791 **84** 80c. grey . . . 10·50 7·50
792 – 96c. red . . . 18·00 16·00
793 – 1e. mauve . . . 29·00 29·00
794 – 1e.60 blue . . . 13·50 12·00
795 – 4e.50 yellow . . . 14·50 14·00
DESIGNS—VERT: 2, 25c., 1e.60, G. Paes; 6, 32, 96c. Joana de Gouveia; 4e.50, Matias de Albuquerque. HORIZ: 4, 16, 50c. Battle of Rolica; 5, 40c., 1e. Battle of Atoleiros.

1929. Optd **Revalidado.**
805 **56** 10c. red . . . 45 35
806 15c. black . . . 40 35
807 40c. brown . . . 70 55
808 40c. green . . . 60 45
810 96c. red . . . 6·00 4·75
811 1e.60 blue . . . 23·00 18·00

1929. Telegraph stamp surch **CORREIO 1$60** and bars.
812 – 1e.60 on 5c. brown . . . 15·00 11·00

88 Camoens' Poem "Lusiad"

89 St. Anthony's Birthplace

1931.

835 **88** 4c. brown 25 15
836 5c. brown 25 15
837 6c. grey 25 15
838 10c. mauve 25 20
839 15c. black 25 20
840 16c. blue . . . . 1·30 70
841 25c. green . . . . 3·25 40
841a 25c. blue . . . . 3·75 40
841b 30c. green . . . . 2·00 40
842 40c. red . . . . 6·75 15
843 48c. brown . . . . 1·30 1·00
844 50c. brown 30 15
845 75c. red . . . . 5·25 1·20
846 80c. green 40 20
846a 95c. red . . . . 17·00 7·00
847 1e. purple . . . . 32·00 15
848 1e.20 green . . . . 2·30 1·00
849 1e.25 blue . . . . 2·00 20
849a 1e.60 blue . . . . 33·00 4·50
849b 1e.75 blue 70 30
850 2e. mauve 55 30
851 4e.50 orange . . . . 1·60 25
852 5e. green . . . . 1·60 25

1931. 700th Death Anniv of St. Anthony.
853 **89** 15c. purple 70 30
854 – 25c. myrtle and green . . . 1·10 30
855 – 40c. brown and buff . . . 40 30
856 – 75c. pink . . . . 23·00 14·50
857 – 1e.25 grey and blue . . . . 55·00 32·00
858 – 4e.50 purple and mauve . . 27·00 3·75
DESIGNS—VERT: 25c. Saint's baptismal font; 40c. Lisbon Cathedral; 75c. St. Anthony; 1e.25, Santa Cruz Cathedral, Coimbra. HORIZ: 4e.50, Saint's tomb, Padua.

90 Don Nuno Alvares Pereira

94 President Carmona

1931. 5th Death Centenary of Pereira.
859 **90** 15c. black . . . . 1·10 1·10
860 25c. green and black . . . 11·00 1·20
861 40c. orange . . . . 2·75 55
862 75c. red . . . . 22·00 22·00
863 1e.25 light blue and blue . . 27·00 22·00
864 4e.50 green and brown . . £130 55·00

1933. Pereira issue of 1931 surch.
865 **90** 15c. on 40c. orange 70 35
866 40c. on 15c. black . . . . 3·75 2·50
867 40c. on 25c. green & black . 1·10 90
868 40c. on 75c. red . . . . . 8·50 4·25
869 40c. on 1e.25 light blue and blue . . . . 8·50 4·25
870 40c. on 4e.50 green and brown . . . . 8·50 4·25

1933. St. Anthony issue of 1931 surch.
871 – 15c. on 40c. brown and buff 85 35
872 **89** 40c. on 15c. purple . . . . 2·50 1·30
873 – 40c. on 25c. myrtle and green . . . . 2·00 35
874 – 40c. on 75c. pink . . . . . . 8·50 5·50
875 – 40c. on 1e.25 grey and blue 8·50 5·50
876 – 40c. on 4e.50 purple and mauve . . . . 8·50 5·50

1934.
877 **94** 40c. violet . . . . 19·00 35

95

96 Queen Maria

1934. Colonial Exhibition.
878 **95** 25c. brown . . . . 3·25 1·70
879 40c. red . . . . 20·00 40
880 1e.60 blue . . . . 31·00 13·50

1935. 1st Portuguese Philatelic Exhibition.
881 **96** 40c. red . . . . 1·50 30

97 Temple of Diana at Evora

98 Prince Henry the Navigator

99 "All for the Nation"

100 Coimbra Cathedral

1935.
882 **97** 4c. black 45 20
883 5c. blue 55 20
884 6c. brown 80 35
885 **98** 10c. green . . . . 7·75 20
886 15c. red 35 20
887 **99** 25c. blue . . . . 6·25 45
888 40c. brown . . . . 2·10 10
889 1e. red . . . . 9·75 50
890 **100** 1e.75 blue . . . . 80·00 1·30
890a **99** 10e. grey . . . . 23·00 2·50
890b 20e. blue . . . . 31·00 2·20

102 Shield and Propeller

103 Symbol of Medicine

1937. Air.
891 **102** 1e.50 blue 45 30
892 1e.75 red 75 35
893 2e.50 red 90 35
893a 3e. blue . . . . 14·50 12·50
893b 4e. green . . . . 19·00 19·00
894 5e. red . . . . 1·80 1·30
895 10e. purple . . . . 3·25 1·40
895a 15e. orange . . . . 12·50 7·50
896 20e. brown . . . . 8·75 2·75
896a 50e. purple . . . . £170 80·00

1937. Centenary of Medical and Surgical Colleges at Lisbon and Oporto.
897 **103** 25c. blue . . . . 11·00 95

104 Gil Vicente

106 Grapes

107 Cross of Avis

1937. 400th Death Anniv of Gil Vicente (poet).
898 **104** 40c. brown . . . . 20·00 20
899 1e. red . . . . 2·75 20

1938. Wine and Raisin Congress.
900 **106** 15c. violet . . . . 1·40 55
901 25c. brown . . . . 3·25 1·80
902 40c. mauve . . . . 10·50 35
903 1e.75 blue . . . . 31·00 27·00

1940. Portuguese Legion.
904 **107** 5c. buff 35 10
905 10c. violet 35 10
906 15c. blue 35 10
907 25c. brown . . . . 23·00 1·20
908 40c. green . . . . 40·00 40
909 80c. green . . . . 2·50 55
910 1e. red . . . . 60·00 3·75
911 1e.75 blue . . . . 8·50 2·75
MS911a 155 × 170 mm. Nos. 904/11 (sold at 5e.50) £550 £850

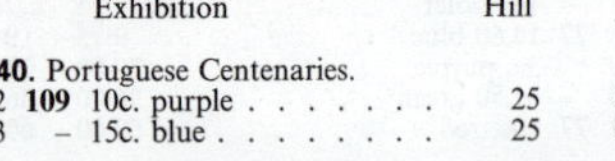
109 Portuguese World Exhibition

113 Sir Rowland Hill

1940. Portuguese Centenaries.
912 **109** 10c. purple 25 20
913 – 15c. blue 25 25
914 – 25c. green . . . . 1·40 25
915 – 35c. green . . . . 1·20 35
916 – 40c. brown . . . . 2·75 20
917 **109** 80c. purple . . . . 5·50 35
918 – 1e. red . . . . 12·50 1·60
919 – 1e.75 blue . . . . 7·25 2·75
MS919a 160 × 229 mm. Nos. 912/9 (sold at 10e.) £275 £350
DESIGNS—VERT: 15, 35c. Statue of King Joao IV; 25c., 1e. Monument of Discoveries, Belem; 40c., 1e.75, King Afonso Henriques.

1940. Centenary of First Adhesive Postage Stamps.
920 **113** 15c. purple 30 10
921 25c. red 30 10
922 35c. green 35 15
923 40c. purple 50 15
924 50c. green . . . . 19·00 4·50
925 80c. blue . . . . 2·30 1·20
926 1e. red . . . . 22·00 3·75
927 1e.75 blue . . . . 7·00 3·75
MS928 160 × 152 mm. Nos. 920/7 (sold at 10e.) £110 £200

114 Fish-woman of Nazare

115 Caravel

1941. Costumes.
932 **114** 4c. green 20 20
933 – 5c. brown 20 20
934 – 10c. purple . . . . 3·75 1·30
935 – 15c. green 20 20
936 – 25c. purple . . . . 2·50 75
937 – 40c. green 20 20
938 – 80c. blue . . . . 3·75 2·40
939 – 1e. red . . . . 10·50 1·80
940 – 1e.75 blue . . . . 11·50 5·00
941 – 2e. orange . . . . 44·00 25·00
MS941a 163 × 146 mm. Nos. 932/41 (sold at 10e.) £200 £180
DESIGNS: 5c. Woman from Coimbra; 10c. Vine-grower of Saloio; 15c. Fish-woman of Lisbon; 25c. Woman of Olhao; 40c. Woman of Aveiro; 80c. Shepherdess of Madeira; 1e. Spinner of Viana do Castelo; 1e.75, Horsebreeder of Ribatejo; 2e. Reaper of Alentejo.

1943.
942 **115** 5c. black 10 10
943 10c. brown 10 10
944 15c. grey 10 10
945 20c. violet 10 10
946 30c. purple 10 10
947 35c. green 20 10
948 50c. purple 20 10
948a 80c. green . . . . 3·25 45
949 1e. red . . . . 7·75 10
949a 1e. lilac . . . . 2·30 20
949b 1e.20 red . . . . 3·25 25
949c 1e.50 green . . . . 37·00 40
950 1e.75 blue . . . . 24·00 10
950a 1e.80 orange . . . . 34·00 3·25
951 2e. brown . . . . 1·80 10
951a 2e. blue . . . . 4·75 50
952 2e.50 red . . . . 2·75 10
953 3e.50 blue . . . . 11·50 50
953a 4e. orange . . . . 50·00 2·75
954 5e. red . . . . 1·40 25
954a 6e. green . . . . 95·00 4·00
954b 7e.50 green . . . . 29·00 3·75
955 10e. grey . . . . 3·25 30
956 15e. green . . . . 29·00 1·10
957 20e. green . . . . 90·00 65
958 50e. red . . . . £250 1·10

116 Labourer

117 Mounted Postal Courier

1943. 1st Agricultural Science Congress.
959 **116** 10c. blue 85 30
960 50c. red . . . . 1·30 35

1944. 3rd National Philatelic Exhibition, Lisbon.
961 **117** 10c. brown 30 10
962 50c. violet 30 10
963 1e. red . . . . 3·75 70
964 1e.75 blue . . . . 3·75 2·30
MS964a 82 × 121 mm. Nos. 961/4 (sold at 7e.50) . . . . 49·00 £250

118 Felix Avellar Brotero

120 Vasco da Gama

1944. Birth Bicentenary of Avellar Brotero (botanist).
965 **118** 10c. brown 25 15
966 – 50c. green . . . . 1·40 15
967 – 1e. red . . . . 8·00 1·70
968 **118** 1e.75 blue . . . . 7·00 2·75
MS968a 144 × 195 mm. Nos. 965/8 (sold at 7e.50) . . . . 55·00 £110
DESIGN: 50c., 1e. Brotero's statue, Coimbra.

1945. Portuguese Navigators.
969 – 10c. brown 20 10
970 – 30c. orange 20 10
971 – 35c. green 35 20
972 **120** 50c. green . . . . 1·30 25
973 – 1e. red . . . . 3·25 70
974 – 1e.75 blue . . . . 4·00 2·20
975 – 2e. black . . . . 5·00 2·50
976 – 3e.50 red . . . . 9·00 4·50
MS976a 167 × 173 mm. Nos. 969/76 (sold at 15e.) . . . . 39·00 £140
PORTRAITS: 10c. Gil Eanes; 30c. Joao Goncalves Zarco; 35c. Bartolomeu Dias; 1e. Pedro Alvares Cabral; 1e.75, Fernao de Magalhaes (Magellan); 2e. Frey Goncalo Velho; 3e.50, Diogo Cao.

121 President Carmona

122

1945.
977 **121** 10c. violet 25 20
978 30c. brown 25 20
979 35c. green 30 20
980 50c. green 40 20
981 1e. red . . . . 10·50 1·40
982 1e.75 blue . . . . 8·50 4·25
983 2e. purple . . . . 47·00 5·50
984 3e.50 grey . . . . 34·00 8·00
MS984a 136 × 98 mm. Nos. 977/84 (sold at 15e.) £200 £250

1945. Naval School Centenary.
985 **122** 10c. brown 15 10
986 50c. green 20 15
987 1e. red . . . . 3·25 80
988 1e.75 blue . . . . 3·50 2·75
MS988a 115 × 134 mm. Nos. 985/8 (sold at 7e.50) . . . . 42·00 £140

123 Almourol Castle

1946. Portuguese Castles.
989 – 10c. purple 10 10
990 – 30c. brown 10 10
991 – 35c. green 15 10
992 – 50c. grey 35 10
993 **123** 1e. red . . . . 23·00 1·10
994 – 1e.75 blue . . . . 13·00 2·50
995 – 2e. green . . . . 42·00 4·75
996 – 3e.50 brown . . . . 19·00 6·00
MS996a 135 × 102 mm. 1e.75 grey-blue on buff (block of 4) (sold at 12e.50) £170 £325
DESIGNS: Castles at Silves (10c.); Leiria (30c.); Feira (35c.); Guimaraes (50c.); Lisbon (1e.75); Braganza (2e.) and Ourem (3e.50).

124 "Decree Founding National Bank"

125 Madonna and Child

1946. Centenary of Bank of Portugal.
997 **124** 50c. blue 55 30
MS997a 156 × 144 mm. No. 997 (block of four) (sold at 7e.50) £130 £200

1946. Tercentenary of Proclamation of St. Mary of Castile as Patron Saint of Portugal.
998 **125** 30c. grey 20 15
999 50c. green 20 15
1000 1e. red . . . . 2·30 1·10
1001 1e.75 blue . . . . 4·50 2·40
MS1001a 108 × 158 mm. Nos. 998/1001 on grey paper (sold at 7e.50) . . . . 65·00 £140

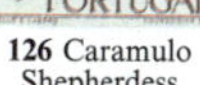

126 Caramulo Shepherdess

127 Surrender of the Keys of Lisbon

1947. Regional Costumes.

No.	Type	Description	Mint	Used
1002	126	10c. mauve	20	15
1003	–	30c. red	20	15
1004	–	35c. green	20	15
1005	–	50c. brown	35	15
1006	–	1e. red	13·00	55
1007	–	1e.75 blue	13·50	4·25
1008	–	2e. blue	45·00	5·00
1009	–	3e.50 green	33·00	7·75
MS1009a		135 × 98 mm. Nos. 1002/9 (sold at 15e.)	£250	£275

COSTUMES: 30c. Malpique timbrel player; 35c. Monsanto flautist; 50c. Woman of Avintes; 1e. Maia field labourer; 1e.75, Woman of Algarve; 2e. Miranda do Douro bastonet player; 3e.50, Woman of the Azores.

1947. 800th Anniv of Recapture of Lisbon from the Moors.

No.	Type	Description	Mint	Used
1010	127	5c. green	15	10
1011		20c. red	15	10
1012		50c. violet	15	15
1013		1e.75 blue	5·00	5·25
1014		2e.50 brown	8·00	6·75
1015		3e.50 black	14·00	11·00

128 St. Joao de Brito

1948. Birth Tercentenary of St. Joao de Brito.

No.	Type	Description	Mint	Used
1016	128	30c. green	15	10
1017	–	50c. brown	15	10
1018	128	1e. red	7·75	1·80
1019	–	1e.75 blue	9·00	3·00

DESIGN: 50c., 1e.75, St. Joao de Brito (different).

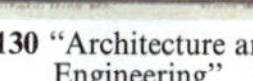

130 "Architecture and Engineering"

131 King Joao I

1948. Exhibition of Public Works and National Congress of Engineering and Architecture.

No.	Type	Description	Mint	Used
1020	130	50c. purple	55	30

1949. Portraits.

No.	Type	Description	Mint	Used
1021	131	10c. violet and buff	20	10
1022	–	30c. green and buff	20	10
1023	–	35c. green and olive	40	10
1024	–	50c. blue and light blue	1·00	10
1025	–	1e. lake and red	1·00	10
1026	–	1e.75 black and grey	20·00	16·00
1027	–	2e. blue and light blue	11·00	2·20
1028	–	3e.50 chocolate & brown	40·00	19·00
MS1028a		136 × 98 mm. Nos. 1021/8 (sold for 15e.)	70·00	85·00

PORTRAITS: 30c. Queen Philippa; 35c. Prince Fernando; 50c. Prince Henry the Navigator; 1e. Nun Alvares; 1e.75, Joao da Regras; 2e. Fernao Lopes; 3e.50, Afonso Domingues.

132 Statue of Angel

133 Hands and Letter

1949. 16th Congress of the History of Art.

No.	Type	Description	Mint	Used
1029	132	1e. red	8·75	15
1030		5e. brown	1·90	30

1949. 75th Anniv of U.P.U.

No.	Type	Description	Mint	Used
1031	133	1e. lilac	30	10
1032		2e. blue	75	25
1033		2e.50 green	4·25	1·30
1034		4e. brown	11·50	3·75

134 Our Lady of Fatima

135 Saint and Invalid

1950. Holy Year.

No.	Type	Description	Mint	Used
1035	134	50c. green	40	20
1036		1e. brown	2·30	25
1037		2e. blue	5·00	1·60
1038		5e. lilac	70·00	30·00

1950. 400th Death Anniv of San Juan de Dios.

No.	Type	Description	Mint	Used
1039	135	20c. violet	20	10
1040		50c. red	30	25
1041		1e. green	3·50	45
1042		1e.50 orange	11·50	3·25
1043		2e. blue	9·75	2·40
1044		4e. brown	40·00	9·00

136 G. Junqueiro

137 Fisherman with Meagre

1951. Birth Centenary of Junqueiro (poet).

No.	Type	Description	Mint	Used
1045	136	50c. brown	3·75	40
1046		1e. blue	1·10	30

1951. Fisheries Congress.

No.	Type	Description	Mint	Used
1047	137	50c. green on buff	3·00	50
1048		1e. purple on buff	80	15

138 Dove and Olive Branch

139 15th century Colonists

1951. Termination of Holy Year.

No.	Type	Description	Mint	Used
1049	138	20c. brown and buff	20	20
1050		90c. green and yellow	6·25	1·80
1051	–	1e. purple and pink	6·25	25
1052	–	2e.30 green and blue	9·00	2·30

PORTRAIT: 1e., 2e.30, Pope Pius XII.

1951. 500th Anniv of Colonization of Terceira, Azores.

No.	Type	Description	Mint	Used
1053	139	50c. blue on flesh	1·80	45
1054		1e. brown on buff	1·10	40

140 Revolutionaries

1951. 25th Anniv of National Revolution.

No.	Type	Description	Mint	Used
1055	140	1e. brown	6·50	20
1056		2e.30 blue	4·50	1·50

141 Coach of King Joao VI

1952. National Coach Museum.

No.	Type	Description	Mint	Used
1057	–	10c. purple	10	10
1058	141	20c. green	10	10
1059	–	50c. green	45	10
1060	–	90c. green	2·20	1·60
1061	–	1e. orange	90	10
1062	–	1e.40 pink	5·25	4·50
1063	141	1e.50 brown	5·00	2·50
1064	–	2e.30 blue	2·75	2·10

DESIGNS (coaches of): 10, 90c. King Felippe II; 50c., 1e.40, Papal Nuncio to Joao V; 1e., 2e.30, King José.

142 "N.A.T.O."

143 Hockey Players

1952. 3rd Anniv of N.A.T.O.

No.	Type	Description	Mint	Used
1065	142	1e. green and deep green	7·75	20
1066		3e.50 grey and blue	£200	23·00

1952. 8th World Roller-skating Hockey Championship.

No.	Type	Description	Mint	Used
1067	143	1e. black and blue	2·75	10
1068		3e.50 black and brown	4·50	2·50

144 Teixeira

145 Marshal Carmona Bridge

1952. Birth Centenary of Prof. Gomes Teixeira (mathematician).

No.	Type	Description	Mint	Used
1069	144	1e. mauve and pink	70	10
1070		2e.30 deep blue and blue	6·00	4·50

1952. Centenary of Ministry of Public Works.

No.	Type	Description	Mint	Used
1071	145	1e. brown on stone	40	20
1072	–	1e.40 lilac on stone	9·75	5·50
1073	–	2e. green on stone	5·00	2·50
1074	–	3e.50 blue on stone	9·50	4·25

DESIGNS: 1e.40, 28th May Stadium, Braga; 2e. Coimbra University; 3e.50, Salazar Barrage.

146 St. Francis Xavier

147 Medieval Knight

1952. 4th Death Centenary of St. Francis Xavier.

No.	Type	Description	Mint	Used
1075	146	1e. blue	40	20
1076		2e. purple	1·50	40
1077		3e.50 blue	18·00	12·00
1078		5e. lilac	33·00	4·25

1953.

No.	Type	Description	Mint	Used
1079	147	5c. green on yellow	15	10
1080		10c. grey on pink	15	10
1081		20c. orange on yellow	15	10
1081a		30c. purple on buff	20	10
1082		50c. black	15	10
1083		90c. green on yellow	13·50	65
1084		1e. brown on pink	30	10
1085		1e.40 red	12·50	1·30
1086		1e.50 red on yellow	40	10
1087		2e. black	40	10
1088		2e.30 blue	15·00	90
1089		2e.50 black on pink	90	15
1089a		2e.50 green on yellow	90	15
1090		5e. purple on yellow	90	15
1091		10e. blue on yellow	4·00	25
1092		20e. brown on yellow	14·00	30
1093		50e. lilac	4·00	50

148 St. Martin of Dume

149 G. Gomes Fernandes

1953. 14th Centenary of Landing of St. Martin of Dume on Iberian Peninsula.

No.	Type	Description	Mint	Used
1094	148	1e. black and grey	95	10
1095		3e.50 brown and yellow	10·50	5·75

1953. Birth Centenary of Fernandes (fire-brigade chief).

No.	Type	Description	Mint	Used
1096	149	1e. purple and cream	55	15
1097		2e.30 blue and cream	9·00	6·00

150 Club Emblems, 1903 and 1953

151 Princess St. Joan

1953. 50th Anniv of Portuguese Automobile Club.

No.	Type	Description	Mint	Used
1098	150	1e. deep green and green	55	20
1099		3e.50 brown and buff	11·00	5·75

1953. 5th Centenary of Birth of Princess St. Joan.

No.	Type	Description	Mint	Used
1100	151	1e. black and green	2·10	15
1101		3e.50 deep blue and blue	10·50	6·75

152 Queen Maria II

1953. Centenary of First Portuguese Stamps. Bottom panel in gold.

No.	Type	Description	Mint	Used
1102	152	50c. red	15	10
1103		1e. brown	15	10
1104		1e.40 purple	1·40	70
1105		2e.30 blue	3·50	2·10
1106		3e.50 blue	3·50	2·20
1107		4e.50 green	2·20	1·60
1108		5e. green	5·50	1·60
1109		20e. violet	49·00	8·75

153

154

1954. 150th Anniv of Trade Secretariat.

No.	Type	Description	Mint	Used
1110	153	1e. blue and light blue	50	15
1111		1e.50 brown and buff	2·50	75

1954. People's Education Plan.

No.	Type	Description	Mint	Used
1112	154	50c. blue and light blue	20	10
1113		1e. red and pink	20	10
1114		2e. deep green and green	23·00	1·40
1115		2e.50 brown and light brown	20·00	1·30

155 Cadet and College Banner

156 Father Manuel da Nobrega

1954. 150th Anniv of Military College.

No.	Type	Description	Mint	Used
1116	155	1e. brown and green	1·20	15
1117		3e.50 blue and green	5·25	3·00

1954. 400th Anniv of Sao Paulo.

No.	Type	Description	Mint	Used
1118	156	1e. brown	40	20
1119		2e.30 blue	42·00	25·00
1120		3e.50 green	11·50	3·25
1121		5e. green	33·00	5·00

157 King Sancho I, 1154–1211

158 Telegraph Poles

1955. Portuguese Kings.

No.	Type	Description	Mint	Used
1122	–	10c. purple	20	15
1123	157	20c. green	20	15
1124	–	50c. blue	30	15
1125	–	90c. green	2·50	1·40
1126	–	1e. brown	1·10	20
1127	–	1e.40 red	6·50	3·75
1128	–	1e.50 green	3·00	1·20
1129	–	2e. red	8·00	3·25
1130	–	2e.30 blue	7·25	2·75

KINGS: 10c. Afonso I; 50c. Afonso II; 90c. Sancho II; 1e. Afonso III; 1e.40, Diniz; 1e.50, Afonso IV; 2e. Pedro I; 2e.30, Fernando.

1955. Centenary of Electric Telegraph System in Portugal.
1131 **158** 1e. red and brown . . . 40 15
1132 2e.30 blue and green . . 18·00 4·00
1133 3e.50 green and yellow 17·00 3·50

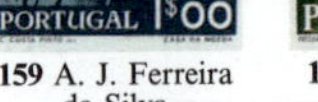

159 A. J. Ferreira da Silva **160** Steam Locomotive, 1856

1956. Birth Centenary of Ferreira da Silva (teacher).
1134 **159** 1e. deep blue, blue and azure 25 15
1135 2e.30 deep green, emerald and green . . 11·00 5·25

1956. Centenary of Portuguese Railways.
1136 **160** 1e. olive and green . . . 40 10
1137 – 1e.50 blue and green . . 2·75 40
1138 – 2e. brown and bistre . . 24·00 1·40
1139 **160** 2e.50 brown and deep brown . . . . 33·00 2·40
DESIGN: 1e.50, 2e. Class 2500 electric locomotive, 1956.

161 Madonna and Child **162** Almeida Garrett (after Barata Feyo)

1956. Mothers' Day.
1140 **161** 1e. sage and green . . . 25 10
1141 1e.50 lt brown and brown 85 30

1957. Almeida Garrett (writer) Commem.
1142 **162** 1e. brown 40 15
1143 2e.30 lilac . . . . 32·00 12·00
1144 3e.50 green . . . . . . 7·25 1·30
1145 5e. red . . . . 55·00 11·00

163 Cesario Verde **164** Exhibition Emblem

1957. Cesario Verde (poet) Commem.
1146 **163** 1e. brown, buff and green 40 10
1147 3e.30 black, olive and green . . . . 1·50 1·20

1958. Brussels International Exhibition.
1148 **164** 1e. multicoloured 40 10
1149 3e.30 multicoloured . . . 1·80 1·40

165 St. Elizabeth **166** Institute of Tropical Medicine, Lisbon

1958. St. Elizabeth and St. Teotonio Commem.
1150 **165** 1e. red and cream . . . 25 10
1151 – 2e. green and cream . . 70 40
1152 **165** 2e.50 violet and cream 5·75 90
1153 – 5e. brown and cream . . 7·25 1·10
PORTRAIT: 2, 5e. St. Teotonio.

1958. 6th Int Congress of Tropical Medicine.
1154 **166** 1e. green and grey . . . 2·75 20
1155 2e.50 blue and grey . . . 8·25 1·50

167 Liner **168** Queen Leonora

1958. 2nd National Merchant Navy Congress.
1156 **167** 1e. brown, ochre & sepia 7·00 20
1157 4e.50 violet, lilac and blue . . . . 5·25 2·40

1958. 500th Birth Anniv of Queen Leonora. Frames and ornaments in bistre, inscriptions and value tablet in black.
1158 **168** 1e. blue and brown . . . 20 10
1159 1e.50 turquoise and blue 4·25 75
1160 2e.30 blue and green . . 4·00 1·30
1161 4e.10 blue and grey . . . 4·00 1·70

169 Arms of Aveiro **170**

1959. Millenary of Aveiro.
1162 **169** 1e. multicoloured . . . . 1·90 20
1163 5e. multicoloured . . . . 14·50 2·00

1960. 10th Anniv of N.A.T.O.
1164 **170** 1e. black and lilac . . . 35 15
1165 3e.50 green and grey . . 3·50 1·80

171 "Doorway to Peace" **172** Glider

1960. World Refugee Year. Symbol in black.
1166 **171** 20c. yellow, lemon & brn 15 10
1167 1e. yellow, green and blue 55 10
1168 1e.80 yellow and green 1·20 1·00

1960. 50th Anniv of Portuguese Aero Club. Multicoloured.
1169 1e. Type **172** 20 10
1170 1e.50 Light monoplane . . . 70 25
1171 2e. Airplane and parachutes 1·40 65
1172 2e.50 Model glider . . . . 2·75 1·30

173 Padre Cruz (after M. Barata) **174** University Seal

1960. Death Centenary of Padre Cruz.
1173 **173** 1e. brown 25 15
1174 4e.30 blue . . . . 9·25 6·75

1960. 400th Anniv of Evora University.
1175 **174** 50c. blue 20 10
1176 1e. brown and yellow . . 40 10
1177 1e.40 purple . . . . . . 3·00 1·60

175 Prince Henry's Arms **175a** Conference Emblem

1960. 5th Death Centenary of Prince Henry the Navigator. Multicoloured.
1178 1e. Type **175** 35 10
1179 2e.50 Caravel . . . . 3·75 30
1180 3e.50 Prince Henry the Navigator . . . . 5·25 1·50
1181 5e. Motto . . . . 8·75 85
1182 8e. Barketta . . . . 2·10 75
1183 10e. Map showing Sagres 15·00 2·00

1960. Europa.
1184 **175a** 1e. light blue and blue 20 15
1185 3e.50 red and lake . . . 3·75 2·00

176 Emblems of Prince Henry and Lisbon

1960. 5th National Philatelic Exhibition, Lisbon.
1186 **176** 1e. blue, black and green 40 15
1187 3e.30 blue, black and light blue . . . . . . 5·75 3·75

177 Portuguese Flag **178** King Pedro V

1960. 50th Anniv of Republic.
1188 **177** 1e. multicoloured 30 10

1961. Cent of Lisbon University Faculty of Letters.
1189 **178** 1e. green and brown . . 30 10
1190 6e.50 brown and blue . . 3·75 95

179 Arms of Setubal **180**

1961. Centenary of Setubal City.
1191 **179** 1e. multicoloured 35 10
1192 4e.30 multicoloured . . . 20·00 6·00

1961. Europa.
1193 **180** 1e. light blue, blue and deep blue 10 10
1194 1e.50 light green, green and deep green . . . 1·50 1·40
1195 3e.50 pink, red and lake 1·70 1·70

181 Tomar Gateway **182** National Guardsman

1961. 800th Anniv of Tomar.
1196 – 1e. multicoloured 15 10
1197 **181** 3e.50 multicoloured . . . 1·50 1·20
DESIGN: 1e. As Type **181** but without ornamental background.

1962. 50th Anniv of National Republican Guard.
1198 **182** 1e. multicoloured 15 10
1199 2e. multicoloured . . . . 2·20 85
1200 2e.50 multicoloured . . . 2·20 65

183 St. Gabriel (Patron Saint of Telecommunications) **184** Scout Badge and Tents

1962. St. Gabriel Commemoration.
1201 **183** 1e. brown, green and olive 75 10
1202 3e.50 green, brown & ol 55 45

1962. 18th International Scout Conference (1961).
1203 **184** 20c. multicoloured . . . 10 10
1204 50c. multicoloured . . . 20 10
1205 1e. multicoloured 70 10
1206 2e.50 multicoloured . . . 4·50 55
1207 3e.50 multicoloured . . . 1·00 55
1208 6e.50 multicoloured . . . 1·30 90

185 Children with Ball **186** Europa "Honeycomb"

1962. 10th International Paediatrics Congress, Lisbon. Centres in black.
1209 – 50c. yellow and green . . 15 10
1210 – 1e. yellow and grey . . . 1·00 15
1211 **185** 2e.80 yellow and brown 2·50 1·20
1212 – 3e.50 yellow and purple 5·50 2·00
DESIGNS: 50c. Children with book; 1e. Inoculating child; 3e.50, Weighing baby.

1962. Europa. "EUROPA" in gold.
1213 **186** 1e. ultramarine, light blue and blue 20 10
1214 1e.50 deep green, light green and green . . . 1·40 75
1215 3e.50 purple, pink and claret . . . . 1·80 1·60

187 St. Zenon (the Courier) **188** Benfica Emblem and European Cup

1962. Stamp Day. Saint in yellow and pink.
1216 **187** 1e. black and purple . . 15 10
1217 2e. black and green . . . 1·10 75
1218 2e.80 black and bistre . . 2·00 1·90

1963. Benfica Club's Double Victory in European Football Cup Championship (1961–62).
1219 **188** 1e. multicoloured 85 10
1220 4e.30 multicoloured . . . 1·30 1·40

189 Campaign Emblem

1963. Freedom from Hunger.
1221 **189** 1e. multicoloured 10 10
1222 3e.30 multicoloured . . . 1·50 1·10
1223 3e.50 multicoloured . . . 1·40 1·10

190 Mail Coach **191** St. Vincent de Paul

1963. Centenary of Paris Postal Conference.
1224 **190** 1e. blue, light blue and grey 10 10
1225 1e.50 multicoloured . . . 2·20 55
1226 5e. brown, lilac & lt brown 70 40

1963. 300th Death Anniv of St. Vincent de Paul. Inscr in gold.
1227 **191** 20c. ultramarine and blue 10 10
1228 1e. blue and grey 40 10
1229 2e.80 black and green . . 4·75 1·90
1230 5e. grey and mauve . . . 3·75 1·40

192 Medieval Knight

1963. 800th Anniv of Military Order of Avis.
1231 **192** 1e. multicoloured 15 10
1232 1e.50 multicoloured . . . 60 25
1233 2e.50 mulitcoloured . . . 1·50 1·00

193 Europa "Dove"

1963. Europa.
1234 **193** 1e. grey, blue and black 30 10
1235 2e.50 grey, green & black 2·75 1·30
1236 3e.50 grey, red and black 4·75 2·40

194 Supersonic Flight **195** Pharmacist's Jar

1963. 10th Anniv of T.A.P. Airline.
1237 **194** 1e. blue and deep blue 15 10
1238 2e.50 light green & green 1·30 65
1239 3e.50 orange and red 1·80 1·20

1964. 400th Anniv of Publication of "Coloquios dos Simples" (Dissertation on Indian herbs and drugs) by Dr. G. d'Orta.
1240 **195** 50c. brown, black & bis 35 10
1241 1e. purple, black and red 35 15
1242 4e.30 blue, black & grey 4·75 4·00

196 Bank Emblem **197** Sameiro Shrine (Braga)

1964. Centenary of National Overseas Bank.
1243 **196** 1e. yellow, green and blue 10 10
1244 2e.50 yellow, olive & grn 2·75 1·10
1245 3e.50 yellow, green & brn 2·10 1·20

1964. Centenary of Sameiro Shrine.
1246 **197** 1e. yellow, brown and red 15 10
1247 2e. yellow, light brown and brown 1·90 85
1248 5e. yellow, green and blue 2·40 1·10

198 Europa "Flower" **199** Sun and Globe

1964. Europa.
1249 **198** 1e. deep blue, light blue and blue 45 10
1250 3e.50 brown, light brown and purple 4·00 1·20
1251 4e.30 deep green, light green and green 5·25 3·50

1964. International Quiet Sun Years.
1252 **199** 1e. mulitcoloured 25 10
1253 8e. multicoloured 1·50 1·20

200 Olympic "Rings" **201** E. Coelho (founder)

1964. Olympic Games, Tokyo.
1254 **200** 20c. multicoloured 15 10
1255 1e. multicoloured 20 20
1256 1e.50 multicoloured 1·80 1·10
1257 6e.50 multicoloured 3·00 2·00

1964. Centenary of "Diario de Noticias" (newspaper).
1258 **201** 1e. multicoloured 55 15
1259 5e. mutlicoloured 7·50 1·10

202 Traffic Signals **203** Dom Fernando (second Duke of Braganza)

1965. 1st National Traffic Congress Lisbon.
1260 **202** 1e. yellow, red and green 20 10
1261 3e.30 green, red & yellow 6·50 3·75
1262 3e.50 red, yellow & green 4·00 1·50

1965. 500th Anniv of Braganza.
1263 **203** 1e. red and black 20 15
1264 10e. green and black 2·75 90

204 Angel and Gateway **205** I.T.U. Emblem

1965. 900th Anniv of Capture of Coimbra from the Moors.
1265 **204** 1e. multicoloured 10 10
1266 2e.50 multicoloured 2·20 1·50
1267 5e. multicoloured 2·30 2·00

1965. Centenary of I.T.U.
1268 **205** 1e. green and brown 15 10
1269 3e.50 purple and green 1·80 1·40
1270 6e.50 blue and green 1·50 1·20

206 C. Gulbenkian **207** Red Cross Emblem

1965. 10th Death Anniv of Calouste Gulbenkian (oil industry pioneer and philanthropist).
1271 **206** 1e. multicoloured 65 10
1272 8e. multicoloured 60 55

1965. Centenary of Portuguese Red Cross.
1273 **207** 1e. red, green and black 20 10
1274 4e. red, green and black 2·75 1·30
1275 4e.30 red, light red & black 13·50 8·50

208 Europa "Sprig" **209** North American F-86 Sabre Jet Fighter

1965. Europa.
1276 **208** 1e. lt blue, black and blue 25 10
1277 3e.50 flesh, brown & red 6·25 1·50
1278 4e.30 light green, black and green 16·00 7·50

1965. 50th Anniv of Portuguese Air Force.
1279 **209** 1e. red, green and olive 20 10
1280 2e. red, green and brown 1·50 75
1281 5e. red, green and blue 2·75 1·70

210 **211** Monogram of Christ

1965. 500th Birth Anniv of Gil Vicente (poet and dramatist). Designs depicting characters from Vicente's poems.
1282 **210** 20c. multicoloured 15 10
1283 – 1e. multicoloured 40 15
1284 – 2e.50 multicoloured 3·25 60
1285 – 6e.50 multicoloured 1·20 75

1966. International Committee for the Defence of Christian Civilisation Congress, Lisbon.
1286 **211** 1e. violet, gold and bistre 10 10
1287 3e.30 black, gold & pur 6·75 4·00
1288 5e. black, gold and red 4·25 1·30

212 Emblems of Agriculture, Construction and Industry **213** Giraldo the "Fearless"

1966. 40th Anniv of National Revolution.
1289 **212** 1e. black, blue and grey 20 10
1290 3e.50 brown, light brown and bistre 3·00 1·60
1291 4e. purple, red and pink 3·00 1·10

1966. 800th Anniv of Reconquest of Evora.
1292 **213** 1e. multicoloured 35 10
1293 8e. multicoloured 1·20 75

214 Salazar Bridge **215** Europa "Ship"

1966. Inauguration of Salazar Bridge, Lisbon.
1294 **214** 1e. red and gold 20 10
1295 2e.50 blue and gold 1·40 75
1296 – 2e.80 blue and silver 2·20 1·60
1297 – 4e.30 green and silver 2·50 1·80
DESIGN—VERT: 2e.80, 4e.30, Salazar Bridge (different view).

1966. Europa.
1298 **215** 1e. multicoloured 30 10
1299 3e.50 multicoloured 11·00 2·00
1300 4e.50 multicoloured 11·50 3·25

216 C. Pestana (bacteriologist) **217** Bocage

1966. Portuguese Scientists. Portraits in brown and bistre; background colours given.
1301 **216** 20c. green 10 10
1302 – 50c. orange 10 10
1303 – 1e. yellow 20 10
1304 – 1e.50 brown 40 10
1305 – 2e. brown 1·90 20
1306 – 2e.50 green 2·10 55
1307 – 2e.80 orange 2·40 1·80
1308 – 4e.30 blue 4·00 3·00
SCIENTISTS: 50c. E. Moniz (neurologist); 1e. E. A. P. Coutinho (botanist); 1e.50, J. C. da Serra (botanist); 2e. R. Jorge (hygienist and anthropologist); 2e.50, J. L. de Vasconcelos (ethnologist); 2e.80, M. Lemos (medical historian); 4e.30, J. A. Serrano (anatomist).

1966. Birth Bicentenary (1965) of Manuel M. B. du Bocage (poet).
1309 **217** 1e. black, green and bistre 10 10
1310 2e. black, green & brown 95 45
1311 6e. black, green and grey 1·50 90

218 Cogwheels **219** Adoration of the Virgin

1967. Europa.
1312 **218** 1e. blue, black & lt blue 30 10
1313 3e.50 brown, black and orange 7·75 1·30
1314 4e.30 green, black and light green 12·50 2·50

1967. 50th Anniv of Fatima Apparitions. Mult.
1315 1e. Type **219** 10 10
1316 2e.80 Fatima Church 60 55
1317 3e.50 Virgin of Fatima 40 30
1318 4e. Chapel of the Apparitions 55 35

220 Roman Senators **221** Lisnave Shipyard

1967. New Civil Law Code.
1319 **220** 1e. red and gold 10 10
1320 2e.50 blue and gold 2·20 1·20
1321 4e.30 green and gold 1·60 1·20

1967. Inauguration of Lisnave Shipyard, Lisbon.
1322 **221** 1e. multicoloured 15 10
1323 – 2e.80 multicoloured 2·75 1·30
1324 **221** 3e.50 multicoloured 1·70 1·20
1325 – 4e.30 multicoloured 2·50 1·30
DESIGN: 2e.80, 4e.30, Section of ship's hull and location map.

222 Serpent Symbol **223** Flags of EFTA Countries

1967. 6th European Rheumatological Congress, Lisbon.
1326 **222** 1e. multicoloured 15 10
1327 2e. multicoloured 1·30 65
1328 5e. multicoloured 1·80 1·30

1967. European Free Trade Association.
1329 **223** 1e. multicoloured 10 10
1330 3e.50 multicoloured 1·30 1·20
1331 4e.30 multicoloured 3·25 3·25

224 Tombstones **225** Bento de Goes

1967. Centenary of Abolition of Death Penalty in Portugal.
1332 **224** 1e. green 10 10
1333 2e. brown 1·40 90
1334 5e. green 2·40 1·90

1968. Bento de Goes Commemoration.
1335 **225** 1e. blue, brown and green 75 10
1336 8e. purple, green & brown 1·50 75

226 Europa "Key" **227** "Maternal Love"

1968. Europa.
1337 **226** 1e. multicoloured 35 10
1338 3e.50 multicoloured 8·75 1·80
1339 4e.30 multicoloured 16·00 3·50

1968. 30th Anniv of Organization of Mothers for National Education (O.M.E.N.).
1340 **227** 1e. black, orange and grey 10 10
1341 2e. black, orange and pink 1·80 75
1342 5e. black, orange and blue 2·00 1·70

228 "Victory over Disease"

1968. 20th Anniv of W.H.O.

1343	228	1e. multicoloured	15	10
1344		3e.50 multicoloured	1·50	65
1345		4e.30 multicoloured	7·75	5·75

229 Vineyard, Girao

1968. "Lubrapex 1968" Stamp Exhibition. Madeira—"Pearl of the Atlantic". Multicoloured.

1346	50c. Type **229**	15	10
1347	1e. Firework display	20	10
1348	1e.50 Landscape	40	15
1349	2e.80 J. Fernandes Vieira (liberator of Pernambuco) (vert)	2·50	1·80
1350	3e.50 Embroidery (vert)	1·60	1·20
1351	4e.30 J. Goncalves Zarco (navigator) (vert)	8·75	7·25
1352	20e. "Muschia aurea" (vert)	4·25	1·30

230 Pedro Alvares Cabral (from medallion)

1969. 500th Birth Anniv of Pedro Alvares Cabral (explorer).

1353	230	1e. blue	20	10
1354	–	3e.50 purple	4·50	2·40
1355	–	6e.50 multicoloured	2·75	2·20

DESIGNS—VERT: 3e.50, Cabral's arms. HORIZ: 6e.50, Cabral's fleet (from contemporary docu-ments).

231 Colonnade

232 King Joseph I

1969. Europa.

1356	231	1e. multicoloured	40	10
1357		3e.50 multicoloured	9·25	2·00
1358		4e.30 multicoloured	18·00	4·25

1969. Centenary of National Press.

1359	232	1e. multicoloured	15	10
1360		2e. multicoloured	1·20	65
1361		8e. multicoloured	1·10	90

233 I.L.O. Emblem

234 J. R. Cabrilho (navigator and colonizer)

1969. 50th Anniv of I.L.O.

1362	233	1e. multicoloured	10	10
1363		3e.50 multicoloured	1·70	80
1364		4e.30 multicoloured	2·75	2·00

1969. Bicentenary of San Diego, California.

1365	234	1e. dp green, yellow & grn	10	10
1366		2e.50 brown, light brown and blue	1·80	65
1367		6e.50 deep brown, green and brown	2·00	1·30

235 Vianna da Motta (from painting by C. B. Pinheiro)

1969. Birth Centenary (1968) of Jose Vianna da Motta (concert pianist).

1368	235	1e. multicoloured	1·00	10
1369		9e. multicoloured	1·00	90

236 Coutinho and Fairey IIID Seaplane

1969. Birth Centenary of Gago Coutinho (aviator). Multicoloured.

1370	1e. Type **236**	15	10
1371	2e.80 Coutinho and sextant	2·75	1·40
1372	3e.30 Type **236**	2·50	1·90
1373	4e.30 As No. 1371	2·50	2·00

237 Vasco da Gama

1969. 500th Birth Anniv of Vasco da Gama. Multicoloured.

1374	1e. Type **237**	25	15
1375	2e.50 Arms of Vasco da Gama	3·25	2·50
1376	3e.50 Route map (horiz)	2·40	1·10
1377	4e. Vasca da Gama's fleet (horiz)	2·20	90

238 "Flaming Sun"

239 Distillation Plant and Pipelines

1970. Europa.

1378	238	1e. cream and blue	35	10
1379		3e.50 cream and brown	7·75	1·40
1380		4e.30 cream and green	13·50	4·25

1970. Inauguration of Porto Oil Refinery.

1381	239	1e. blue and light blue	10	10
1382	–	2e.80 black and green	2·75	2·00
1383	239	3e.30 green and olive	1·80	1·40
1384	–	6e. brown and light brown	1·50	1·20

DESIGN: 2e.80, 6e. Catalytic cracking plant and pipelines.

240 Marshal Carmona (from sculpture by L. de Almeida)

1970. Birth Centenary of Marshal Carmona.

1385	240	1e. green and black	20	10
1386		2e.50 blue, red and black	2·00	80
1387		7e. blue and black	1·80	1·30

241 Station Badge

1970. 25th Anniv of Plant-breeding Station.

1388	241	1e. multicoloured	10	10
1389		2e.50 multicoloured	1·40	55
1390		5e. multicoloured	1·90	75

242 Emblem within Cultural Symbol

1970. Expo 70. Multicoloured.

1391	1e. Compass (postage)	20	10
1392	5e. Christian symbol	1·60	1·30
1393	6e.50 Symbolic initials	4·00	3·25
1394	3e.50 Type **242** (air)	75	40

243 Wheel and Star

1970. Centenaries of Covilha (Nos. 1395/6) and Santarem (Nos. 1397/8). Multicoloured.

1395	1e. Type **243**	15	10
1397	1e. Castle	3·00	1·70
1396	2e.80 Ram and weaving frame	15	10
1398	4e. Two knights	1·80	1·00

244 "Great Eastern" laying Cable

1970. Centenary of Portugal–England Submarine Telegraph Cable.

1399	244	1e. black, blue and green	10	10
1400		2e.50 black, green & buff	1·90	55
1401	–	2e.80 multicoloured	3·75	2·75
1402	–	4e. multicoloured	1·80	90

DESIGN: 2e.80, 4e. Cable cross-section.

245 Harvesting Grapes

246 Mountain Windmill, Bussaco Hills

1970. Port Wine Industry. Multicoloured.

1403	50c. Type **245**	10	10
1404	1e. Harvester and jug	20	10
1405	3e.50 Wine-glass and wine barge	1·10	20
1406	7e. Wine-bottle and casks	1·10	75

1971. Portuguese Windmills.

1407	246	20c. brown, black & sepia	10	10
1408	–	50c. brown, black & blue	10	10
1409	–	1e. purple, black and grey	25	10
1410	–	2e. red, black and mauve	90	20
1411	–	3e.30 chocolate, black and brown	2·75	2·30
1412	–	5e. brown, black & green	2·50	75

WINDMILLS: 50c. Beira Litoral Province; 1e. "Saloio" type Estremadura Province; 2e. St. Miguel Azores; 3e.30, Porto Santo, Madeira; 5e. Pico, Azores.

247 Europa Chain

1971. Europa.

1413	247	1e. green, blue and black	30	15
1414		3e.50 yellow, brn & blk	6·00	65
1415		7e.50 brown, green & blk	11·00	2·10

248 F. Franco

249 Pres. Salazar

1971. Portuguese Sculptors.

1416	248	20c. black	10	10
1417	–	1e. red	30	10
1418	–	1e.50 brown	65	55
1419a	–	2e.50 blue	1·10	40
1420	–	3e.50 mauve	1·50	65
1421	–	4e. green	2·75	2·10

DESIGNS: 1e. A. Lopes; 1e.50, A. de Costa Mota; 2e.50, R. Gameiro; 3e.50, J. Simoes de Almeida (the Younger); 4e. F. dos Santos.

1971. Pres. Antonio Salazar Commemoration.

1422	249	1e. brown, green & orge	20	10
1423		5e. brown, purple & orge	1·80	50
1424		10e. brown, blue & orge	3·00	1·30

250 Wolframite

1971. 1st Spanish–Portuguese–American Congress of Economic Geology. Multicoloured.

1425	1e. Type **250**	10	10
1426	2e.50 Arsenopyrite	2·10	55
1427	3e.50 Beryllium	70	40
1428	6e.50 Chalcopyrite	1·30	60

251 Town Gate

252 Weather Equipment

1971. Bicentenary of Castelo Branco. Mult.

1429	1e. Type **251**	10	10
1430	3e. Town square and monument	1·50	70
1431	12e.50 Arms of Castelo Branco (horiz)	1·30	70

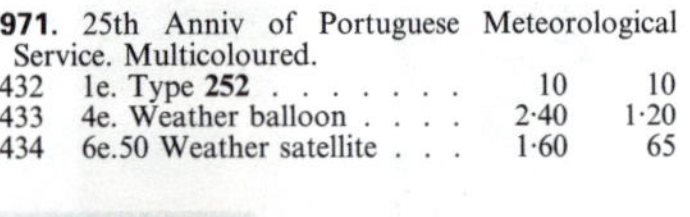

1971. 25th Anniv of Portuguese Meteorological Service. Multicoloured.

1432	1e. Type **252**	10	10
1433	4e. Weather balloon	2·40	1·20
1434	6e.50 Weather satellite	1·60	65

253 Drowning Missionaries

254 Man and his Habitat

1971. 400th Anniv of Martyrdom of Brazil Missionaries.

1435	253	1e. black, blue and grey	10	10
1436		3e.30 black, purple & brn	2·10	1·50
1437		4e.80 black, grn & olive	2·20	1·50

1971. Nature Conservation. Multicoloured.

1438	1e. Type **254**	10	10
1439	3e.30 Horses and trees ("Earth")	65	40
1440	3e.50 Birds ("The Atmosphere")	75	35
1441	4e.50 Fishes ("Water")	2·75	1·80

255 Clerigos Tower, Oporto

1972. Buildings and Views.

1442	–	5c. grey, black and green	15	10
1443	–	10c. black, green & blue	15	10
1444	–	30c. sepia, brown & yell	15	10
1445	–	50c. blue, orange & blk	20	10
1446p	255	1e. black, brown & grn	55	10
1447	–	1e.50 brown, blue & blk	50	10
1448p	–	2e. black, brown & pur	2·10	10

1449p – 2e.50 brown, light brown and grey . . . 90 10
1450 – 3e. yellow, black & brn 60 10
1451p – 3e.50 green, orge & brn 1·50 10
1452 – 4e. black, yellow & blue 60 10
1453 – 4e.50 black, brn & grn 90 10
1454 – 5e. green, brown & black . . . . 6·00 10
1455 – 6e. bistre, green & black . . . . 2·20 20
1456 – 7e.50 black, orge & grn 1·20 10
1457 – 8e. bistre, black & green . . . . 1·50 10
1458 – 10e. multicoloured . . 60 10
1459 – 20e. multicoloured . . 5·25 15
1460 – 50e. multicoloured . . 5·00 25
1461 – 100e. multicoloured . . 90 65

DESIGNS—As T **255**: 5c. Aguas Livres aqueduct, Lisbon; 10c. Lima Bridge; 30c. Monastery interior, Alcobaca; 50c. Coimbra University; 1e.50, Belem Tower, Lisbon; 2e. Domus Municipalis, Braganza; 2e.50, Castle, Vila de Feira; 3e. Misericord House, Viana do Castelo; 3e.50, Window, Tomar Convent; 4e. Gateway, Braga; 4e.50, Dolmen of Carrazeda; 5e. Roman Temple, Evora; 6e. Monastery, Leca do Balio; 7e.50, Almourol Castle; 8e. Ducal Palace, Guimaraes. 31 × 22 mm: 10e. Cape Girao, Madeira; 20e. Episcopal Garden, Castelo Branco; 50e. Town Hall, Sintra; 100e. Seven Cities' Lake, Sao Miguel, Azores.

256 Arms of Pinhel

257 Heart and Pendulum

1972. Bicentenary of Pinhel's Status as a City. Multicoloured.
1464 1e. Type **256** 15 10
1465 2e.50 Balustrade (vert) . . . 1·80 40
1466 7e.50 Lantern on pedestal (vert) . . . . 1·50 70

1972. World Heart Month.
1467 **257** 1e. red and lilac 15 10
1468 – 4e. red and green . . . . 3·25 1·30
1469 – 9e. red and brown . . . 1·70 80

DESIGNS: 4e. Heart in spiral; 9e. Heart and cardiogram trace.

258 "Communications"

259 Container Truck

1972. Europa.
1470 **258** 1e. multicoloured 35 10
1471 3e.50 multicoloured . . . 3·75 40
1472 6e. multicoloured . . . . 10·00 1·80

1972. 13th International Road Transport Union Congress, Estoril. Multicoloured.
1473 1e. Type **259** 15 10
1474 4e.50 Roof of taxi-cab . . . 2·20 1·30
1475 8e. Motor-coach . . . . . 1·80 1·00

260 Football

1972. Olympic Games, Munich. Multicoloured.
1476 50c. Type **260** 10 10
1477 1e. Running 15 10
1478 1e.50 Show jumping 50 20
1479 3e.50 Swimming . . . . . 1·20 40
1480 4e.50 Yachting . . . . . . 1·60 1·20
1481 5e. Gymnastics . . . . . . 3·00 1·10

261 Marquis de Pombal

262 Tome de Sousa

1972. Pombaline University Reforms. Multicoloured.
1482 1e. Type **261** 15 10
1483 2e.50 "The Sciences" (emblems) . . . . 1·70 85
1484 8e. Arms of Coimbra University. . . . . 1·80 1·30

1972. 150th Anniv of Brazilian Independence. Mult.
1485 1e. Type **262** 15 10
1486 2e.50 Jose Bonifacio 80 30
1487 3e.50 Dom Pedro IV . . . 80 30
1488 6e. Dove and globe . . . . 1·80 90

263 Sacadura, Cabral, Gago, Coutinho and Fairey III D Seaplane

1972. 50th Anniv of 1st Lisbon–Rio de Janeiro Flight. Multicoloured.
1489 1e. Type **263** 10 10
1490 2e.50 Route map 85 40
1491 2e.80 Type **263** . . . . . 1·10 90
1492 3e.80 As 2e.50 . . . . . . 1·80 1·40

264 Camoens

1972. 400th Anniv of Camoens' "Lusiads" (epic poem).
1493 **264** 1e. yellow, brown & black 15 10
1494 – 3e. blue, green and black 1·40 75
1495 – 10e. brown, purple & blk 1·80 90

DESIGNS: 3e. "Saved from the Sea"; 10e. "Encounter with Adamastor".

265 Graph and Computer Tapes

1973. Portuguese Productivity Conference, Lisbon. Multicoloured.
1496 1e. Type **265** 10 10
1497 4e. Computer scale . . . . 1·40 75
1498 9e. Graphs . . . . 1·30 65

266 Europa "Posthorn"

268 Child Running

267 Pres. Medici and Arms

1973. Europa.
1499 **266** 1e. multicoloured 40 10
1500 4e. multicoloured . . . . 11·00 1·10
1501 6e. multicoloured . . . . 12·50 2·10

1973. Visit of Pres. Medici of Brazil. Mult.
1502 1e. Type **267** 15 10
1503 2e.80 Pres. Medici and globe 80 70
1504 3e.50 Type **267** 90 65
1505 4e.80 As No. 1503 . . . . 95 70

1973. "For the Child".
1506 **268** 1e. dp blue, blue & brown 15 10
1507 – 4e. purple, mauve & brn 1·60 70
1508 – 7e.50 orange, ochre and brown . . . . 1·70 1·10

DESIGNS: 4e. Child running (to right); 7e.50, Child jumping.

269 Transport and Weather Map

1973. 25th Anniv of Ministry of Communications. Multicoloured.
1509 1e. Type **269** 10 10
1510 3e.80 "Telecommunications" 50 40
1511 6e. "Postal Services" . . . . 1·20 70

270 Child and Written Text

1973. Bicentenary of Primary State School Education. Multicoloured.
1512 1e. Type **270** 15 10
1513 4e.50 Page of children's primer . . . . 1·80 55
1514 5e.30 "Schooldays" (child's drawing) (horiz) . . . . . 1·40 75
1515 8e. "Teacher and children" (horiz) . . . . 3·75 1·50

271 Electric Tramcar

272 League Badge

1973. Centenary of Oporto's Public Transport System. Multicoloured.
1516 1e. Horse tram 15 10
1517 3e.50 Modern bus . . . . . 2·30 1·50
1518 7e.50 Type **271** . . . . . . 2·50 1·30
Nos. 1516/17 are $31\frac{1}{2} \times 31\frac{1}{2}$ mm.

1973. 50th Anniv of Servicemen's League. Multicoloured.
1519 1e. Type **272** 10 10
1520 2e.50 Servicemen . . . . . 2·30 75
1521 11e. Awards and medals . . 1·90 65

273 Death of Nuno Goncalves

274 Damiao de Gois (after Durer)

1973. 600th Anniv of Defence of Faria Castle by the Alcaide, Nuno Goncalves.
1522 **273** 1e. green and yellow . . 30 10
1523 10e. purple and yellow 2·30 1·20

1974. 400th Death Anniv of Damiao de Gois (scholar and diplomat). Multicoloured.
1524 1e. Type **274** 10 10
1525 4e.50 Title-page of "Chronicles of Prince Dom Joao" . . . . 2·50 65
1526 7e.50 Lute and "Dodecahordon" score 1·40 60

275 "The Exile" (A. Soares dos Reis)

276 Light Emission

1974. Europa.
1527 **275** 1e. green, blue and olive 55 15
1528 4e. green, red and yellow 13·50 75
1529 6e. dp green, green & blue . . . . 17·00 1·40

1974. Inauguration of Satellite Communications Station Network.
1530 **276** 1e.50 green 15 10
1531 – 4e.50 blue . . . . 1·30 70
1532 – 5e.30 purple . . . . . . 2·20 1·10

DESIGNS: 4e.50, Spiral Waves; 5e.30, Satellite and Earth.

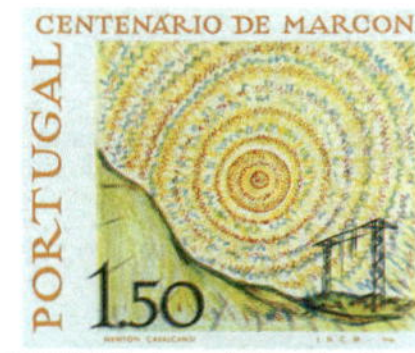

277 "Diffusion of Hertzian Radio Waves"

1974. Birth Centenary of Guglielmo Marconi (radio pioneer). Multicoloured.
1533 1e.50 Type **277** 15 10
1534 3e.30 "Radio waves across Space" . . . . 2·20 90
1535 10e. "Radio waves for Navigation" . . . . . . 1·40 60

278 Early Post-boy and Modern Mail Van

1974. Centenary of U.P.U. Multicoloured.
1536 1e.50 Type **278** 10 10
1537 2e. Hand with letters . . . 80 10
1538 3e.30 Sailing packet and modern liner 40 20
1539 4e.50 Dove and airliner . . 1·40 60
1540 5e.30 Hand with letter . . . 55 40
1541 20e. Steam and electric locomotives . . . . . . 2·75 1·30
MS1542 106 × 147 mm. Nos. 1536/41 (sold at 50e.) . . . . 6·25 6·25

279 Luisa Todi

280 Arms of Beja

1974. Portuguese Musicians.
1543 **279** 1e.50 purple 10 10
1544 – 2e. red . . . . 1·30 30
1545 – 2e.50 brown 80 20
1546 – 3e. blue . . . . 1·30 40
1547 – 5e.30 green 80 55
1548 – 11e. red . . . . 1·00 65

PORTRAITS: 2e. Joao Domingos Bomtempo; 2e.50,Carlos Seixas; 3e. Duarte Lobo; 5e.30, Joaode Sousa Carvalho; 11e. Marcos Portugal.

1974. Bimillenary of Beja. Multicoloured.
1549 1e.50 Type **280** 15 10
1550 3e.50 Beja's inhabitants through the ages . . . . 2·50 1·10
1551 7e. Moorish arches . . . . 2·75 1·30

281 "The Annunciation"

282 Rainbow and Dove

1974. Christmas. Multicoloured.
1552 1e.50 Type **281** 10 10
1553 4e.50 "The Nativity" . . . 3·25 65
1554 10e. "The Flight into Egypt" . . . . 2·50 90

1974. Portuguese Armed Forces Movement of 25 April.
1555 **282** 1e.50 multicoloured . . . 10 10
1556 3e.50 multicoloured . . . 3·50 1·60
1557 5e. multicoloured . . . . 2·00 75

283 Egas Moniz **284** Farmer and Soldier

1974. Birth Centenary of Professor Egas Moniz (brain surgeon).
1558 **283** 1e.50 brown and orange . . . 30 10
1559 – 3e.30 orange and brown 1·50 55
1560 – 10e. grey and blue . . . 5·50 85
DESIGNS: 3e.30, Nobel Medicine and Physiology Prize medal, 1949; 10e. Cerebral angiograph, 1927.

1975. Portuguese Cultural Progress and Citizens' Guidance Campaign.
1561 **284** 1e.50 multicoloured . . . 10 10
1562 3e. multicoloured . . . . 2·00 70
1563 4e.50 multicoloured . . . 2·75 1·10

285 Hands and Dove of Peace **286** "The Hand of God"

1975. 1st Anniv of Portuguese Revolution. Multicoloured.
1564 1e.50 Type **285** 15 10
1565 4e.50 Hands and peace dove 2·75 75
1566 10e. Peace dove and emblem 3·50 1·10

1975. Holy Year. Multicoloured.
1567 1e.50 Type **286** 15 10
1568 4e.50 Hand with cross . . . 3·50 1·10
1569 10e. Peace dove . . . . . . 4·50 1·20

287 "The Horseman of the Apocalypse" (detail of 12th-cent manuscript)

1975. Europa. Multicoloured.
1570 1e.50 Type **287** 80 10
1571 10e. "Fernando Pessoa" (poet) (A. Negreiros) . . 28·00 1·10

288 Assembly Building

1975. Opening of Portuguese Constituent Assembly.
1572 **288** 2e. black, red and yellow 30 10
1573 20e. black, green & yellow . . . . 6·00 1·50

289 Hiking

1975. 36th International Camping and Caravanning Federation Rally. Multicoloured.
1574 2e. Type **289** . . . . 1·00 10
1575 4e.50 Boating and swimming 3·00 1·10
1576 5e.30 Caravanning . . . . 1·60 1·10

290 Planting Tree

1975. 30th Anniv of U.N.O. Multicoloured.
1577 2e. Type **290** 50 10
1578 4e.50 Releasing peace dove 1·70 55
1579 20c. Harvesting corn . . . . 3·75 1·40

291 Lilienthal Glider and Modern Space Rocket

1975. 26th International Astronautical Federation Congress, Lisbon. Multicoloured.
1580 2e. Type **291** 45 10
1581 4e.50 "Apollo"–"Soyuz" space link . . . . 2·10 85
1582 5e.30 R. H. Goddard, R. E. Pelterie, H. Oberth and K. E. Tsiolkovsky (space pioneers) . . . . 1·00 85
1583 10e. Astronaut and spaceships (70 × 32 mm) 4·50 1·40

292 Surveying the Land

1975. Centenary of National Geographical Society, Lisbon. Multicoloured.
1584 2e. Type **292** 20 10
1585 8e. Surveying the sea . . . 1·50 75
1586 10e. Globe and people . . . 3·25 1·20

293 Symbolic Arch **294** Nurse in Hospital Ward

1975. European Architectural Heritage Year.
1587 **293** 2e. grey, blue & deep blue 30 10
1588 – 8e. grey and red . . . . 3·50 75
1589 – 10e. multicoloured . . . 3·50 1·00
DESIGNS: 8e. Stylized building plan; 10e. Historical building being protected from development.

1975. International Women's Year. Multicoloured.
1590 50c. Type **294** 10 10
1591 2e. Woman farm worker . . 1·10 35
1592 3e.50 Woman office worker 1·10 65
1593 8e. Woman factory worker 1·80 1·30
MS1594 104 × 115 mm. Nos. 1590/3 (sold at 25e.) . . . . 3·75 3·75

295 Pen-nib as Plough Blade

1976. 50th Anniv of National Writers Society.
1595 **295** 3e. blue and red 45 10
1596 20e. red and blue . . . . 4·25 1·30

296 First Telephone Set

1976. Telephone Centenary.
1597 **296** 3e. black, green & dp grn 95 10
1598 – 10e.50 black, red and pink . . . . 3·25 90
DESIGNS: 10e.50, Alexander Graham Bell.

297 "Industrial Progress" **298** Carved Olive-wood Spoons

1976. National Production Campaign.
1599 **297** 50c. red 20 10
1600 – 1e. green 50 15
DESIGN: 1e. Consumer goods.

1976. Europa. Multicoloured.
1601 3e. Type **298** . . . . 3·25 10
1602 20e. Gold ornaments . . . 47·00 6·25

299 Stamp Designing

1976. "Interphil 76" International Stamp Exhibition, Philadelphia. Multicoloured.
1603 3e. Type **299** 20 10
1604 7e.50 Stamp being hand-cancelled . . . . 1·20 65
1605 10e. Stamp printing . . . . 1·70 75

300 King Fernando promulgating Law

1976. 600th Anniv of Law of "Sesmarias" (uncultivated land). Multicoloured.
1606 3e. Type **300** 15 10
1607 5e. Plough and farmers repelling hunters . . . . 1·80 45
1608 10e. Corn harvesting . . . . 2·00 85
MS1609 230 × 150 mm. Nos. 1606/8 (sold at 30e.) . . . . 4·25 85·00

301 Athlete with Olympic Torch

1976. Olympic Games, Montreal. Multicoloured.
1610 3e. Type **301** 20 10
1611 7e. Women's relay . . . . . 1·60 1·30
1612 10e.50 Olympic flame . . . 2·20 1·20

302 "Speaking in the Country"

1976. Literacy Campaign. Multicoloured.
1613A 3e. Type **302** 60 10
1614A 3e. "Speaking at Sea" . . 60 10
1615A 3e. "Speaking in Town" 60 10
1616B 3e. "Speaking at Work" 85 10
MS1617 145 × 104 mm. Nos. 1613/16 (sold at 25e.) . . . . 12·00 12·00

303 Azure-winged Magpie **304** "Lubrapex" Emblem and Exhibition Hall

1976. "Portucale 77" Thematic Stamp Exhibition, Oporto (1st issue). Flora and Fauna. Mult.
1618 3e. Type **303** 20 10
1619 5e. Lynx . . . . 1·20 25
1620 7e. Portuguese laurel cherry and blue tit . . . . 1·30 90
1621 10e.50 Little wild carnation and lizard . . . . 1·40 1·20
See also Nos 1673/8.

1976. "Lubrapex 1976" Luso–Brazilian Stamp Exhibition. Multicoloured.
1622 3e. Type **304** 35 10
1623 20e. "Lubrapex" emblem and "stamp" . . . . . 2·50 1·50
MS1624 180 × 142 mm. Nos. 1622/3 (sold at 30e.) . . . . 3·50 4·25

305 Bank Emblem

1976. Centenary of National Trust Fund Bank.
1625 **305** 3e. multicoloured 10 10
1626 7e. multicoloured . . . . 2·20 90
1627 15e. multicoloured . . . 3·50 1·20

306 Sheep Grazing **307** "Liberty"

1976. Water Conservation. Protection of Humid Zones. Multicoloured.
1628 1e. Type **306** 20 10
1629 3e. Marshland . . . . . . 1·00 20
1630 5e. Sea trout . . . . 2·10 35
1631 10e. Mallards . . . . 4·00 1·10

1976. Consolidation of Democratic Institutions.
1632 **307** 3e. grey, green and red 70 15

308 Examining Child's Eyes

1976. World Health Day. Detection and Prevention of Blindness. Multicoloured.
1633 3e. Type **308** 20 10
1634 5e. Welder wearing protective goggles . . . . 2·20 30
1635 10e.50 Blind person reading Braille . . . . 1·80 1·10

309 Hydro-electric Power

1976. Uses of Natural Energy. Multicoloured.
1636 1e. Type **309** 10 10
1637 4e. Fossil fuel (oil) 60 15
1638 5e. Geo-thermic sources . . 80 25
1639 10e. Wind power . . . . . 1·60 80
1640 15e. Solar energy . . . . . 2·75 1·50

310 Map of Member Countries

1977. Admission of Portugal to the Council of Europe.
1641 **310** 8e.50 multicoloured . . . 1·30 1·30
1642 10e. multicoloured . . . 1·30 1·20

311 Bottle inside Human Body

1977. 10th Anniv of Portuguese Anti-Alcoholic Society. Multicoloured.
1643 3e. Type **311** 15 10
1644 5e. Broken body and bottle 1·00 40
1645 15e. Sun behind prison bars and bottle . . . . 2·40 1·40

312 Forest

1977. Natural Resources. Forests. Multicoloured.
1646 1e. Type **312** 10 10
1647 4e. Cork oaks 75 25
1648 7e. Logs and trees . . . . 1·60 1·30
1649 15e. Trees by the sea . . . 1·60 1·30

313 Exercising **315** John XXI Enthroned

314 Southern Plains

1977. International Rheumatism Year.
1650 – 4e. orange, brown & blk 20 10
1651 **313** 6e. ultramarine, blue and black . . . . 1·20 1·00
1652 – 10e. red, mauve and black . . . . 1·10 70
DESIGNS: 4e. Rheumatism victim; 10e. Group exercising.

1977. Europa. Multicoloured.
1653 4e. Type **314** 30 10
1654 8e.50 Northern terraced mountains . . . . . . 1·80 75
MS1655 148 × 95 mm. Nos. 1653/4 each × 3 . . . . 75·00 25·00

1977. 7th Death Centenary of Pope John XXI. Multicoloured.
1656 4e. Type **315** 20 10
1657 15e. Pope as doctor 70 45

316 Compass

1977. Camoes Day.
1658 **316** 4e. multicoloured 20 10
1659 8e.50 multicoloured . . . 1·20 1·10

317 Child and Computer

1977. Permanent Education. Multicoloured.
1660 4e. Type **317** 40 15
1661 4e. Flautist and dancers . . 40 15
1662 4e. Farmer and tractor . . . 40 15
1663 4e. Students and atomic construction 40 15
MS1664 148 × 96 mm. Nos. 1660/3 (sold at 20e.) . . . . 4·25 5·50

318 Pyrite

1977. Natural Resources. The Subsoil. Mult.
1665 4e. Type **318** 20 10
1666 5e. Marble . . . . 1·00 30
1667 10e. Iron ore . . . . 1·10 55
1668 20e. Uranium . . . . 2·50 1·30

319 Alexandre Herculano

1977. Death Centenary of Alexandre Herculano (writer and politician).
1669 **319** 4e. multicoloured 25 10
1670 15e. multicoloured . . . 1·80 55

320 Early Steam Locomotive and Peasant Cart (ceramic panel, J. Colaco)

1977. Centenary of Railway Bridge over River Douro. Multicoloured.
1671 4e. Type **320** 30 10
1672 10e. Maria Pia bridge (Eiffel) . . . . 2·30 1·80

321 Poviero (Northern coast)

1977. "Portucale 77" Thematic Stamp Exhibition, Oporto (2nd issue). Coastal Fishing Boats. Multicoloured.
1673 2e. Type **321** 45 10
1674 3e. Sea-going rowing boat, Furadouro 30 10
1675 4e. Rowing boat from Nazare 30 10
1676 7e. Caicque from Algarve 55 25
1677 10e. Tunny fishing boat, Algarve 85 60
1678 15e. Boat from Buarcos . . 1·30 95
MS1679 148 × 104 mm. Nos. 1673/8 (sold at 60e.) . . . . 4·25 4·25

322 "The Adoration" (Maria do Sameiro A. Santos)

1977. Christmas. Children's Paintings. Mult.
1680 4e. Type **322** 25 10
1681 7e. "Star over Bethlehem" (Paula Maria L. David) 1·20 45
1682 10e. "The Holy Family" (Carla Maria M. Cruz) (vert) . . . . 1·30 65
1683 20e. "Children following the Star" (Rosa Maria M. Cardoso) (vert) . . . 2·75 1·10

323 Medical Equipment and Operating Theatre

1978. (a) Size 22 × 17 mm.
1684 **323** 50c. green, black and red 10 10
1685 – 1e. blue, orange and black 10 10
1686 – 2e. blue, green & brown 10 10
1687 – 3e. brown, green and black 15 10
1688 – 4e. green, blue & brown 15 10
1689 – 5e. blue, green & brown 15 10
1690 – 5e.50 brown, buff and green 20 10
1691 – 6e. brown, yellow & grn 20 10
1692 – 6e.50 blue, deep blue and green 20 10
1693 – 7e. black, grey and blue 20 10
1694 – 8e. ochre, brown and grey 20 10
1694a – 8e.50 brn, blk & lt brn 30 10
1695 – 9e. yellow, brown & blk 30 10
1696 – 10e. brown, black & grn 30 10
1697 – 12e.50 blue, red and black 30 10
1698 – 16e. brown, black and violet 30 10

(b) Size 30 × 21 mm.
1699 – 20e. multicoloured 55 10
1700a – 30e. multicoloured 65 20
1701 – 40e. multicoloured 65 30
1702 – 50e. multicoloured . . . 1·10 20
1703 – 100e. multicoloured . . . 1·80 40
1703a – 250e. multicoloured . . . 4·50 75
DESIGNS: 1e. Old and modern kitchen equipment; 2e. Telegraph key and masts, microwaves and dish aerial; 3e. Dressmaking and ready-to-wear clothes; 4e. Writing desk and computer; 5e. Tunny fishing boats and modern trawler; 5e.50, Manual and mechanical weaver's looms; 6e. Plough and tractor; 6e.50, Monoplane and B.A.C. One Eleven airliner; 7e. Hand press and modern printing press; 8e. Carpenter's hand tools and mechanical tool; 8e.50, Potter's wheel and modern ceramic machinery; 9e. Old cameras and modern cine and photo cameras; 10e. Axe, saw and mechanical saw; 12e.50, Navigation and radar instruments; 16e. Manual and automatic mail sorting; 20e. Hand tools and building site; 30e. Hammer, anvil, bellows and industrial complex; 40e. Peasant cart and lorry; 50e. Alembic, retorts and modern chemical plant; 100e. Carpenter's shipyard, modern shipyard and tanker; 250e. Survey instruments.

324 Mediterranean Soil

1978. Natural Resources. The Soil. Mult.
1704 4e. Type **324** 30 10
1705 5e. Rock formation 55 15
1706 10e. Alluvial soil . . . . . 1·10 65
1707 20e. Black soil . . . . . . 2·75 90

325 Pedestrian on Zebra Crossing

1978. Road Safety.
1708 **325** 1e. blue, black and orange 15 10
1709 – 2e. blue, black and green 30 10
1710 – 2e.50 blue, black & lt bl 75 10
1711 – 5e. blue, black and red 1·40 20
1712 – 9e. blue, black & ultram 2·50 75
1713 – 12e.50 blue and black . . 3·75 1·90
DESIGNS: 2e. Motor cyclist; 2e.50, Children in back of car; 5e. Driver in car; 9e. View of road from driver's seat; 12e.50, Road victim ("Don't drink and drive").

326 Roman Tower of Centum Cellas, Belmonte **327** Roman Bridge, Chaves

1978. Europa. Multicoloured.
1714 10e. Type **326** . . . . . . 1·30 20
1715 40e. Belem Monastery, Lisbon . . . . 3·50 1·30
MS1716 111 × 96 mm. Nos. 1714/15 each × 2 (sold at 120e.) . . . 55·00 14·00

1978. 19th Century of Chaves (Aquae Flaviae). Multicoloured.
1717 5e. Type **327** 45 15
1718 20e. Inscribed tablet from bridge . . . . 2·50 1·10

328 Running

1978. Sport for All. Multicoloured.
1719 5e. Type **328** 20 10
1720 10e. Cycling 40 30
1721 12e.50 Swimming 95 75
1722 15e. Football 95 95

329 Pedro Nunes

1978. 400th Death Anniv of Pedro Nunes (cosmographer). Multicoloured.
1723 5e. Type **329** 15 10
1724 20e. Nonio (navigation instrument) and diagram 1·50 45

330 Trawler, Crates of Fish and Lorry

1978. Natural Resources. Fishes. Multicoloured.
1725 5e. Type **330** 20 10
1726 9e. Trawler and dockside cranes 70 20
1727 12e.50 Trawler, radar and lecture . . . . 1·30 1·00
1728 15e. Trawler with echo-sounding equipment and laboratory . . . . 2·00 1·30

331 Post Rider

1978. Introduction of Post Code. Multicoloured.
1729 5e. Type **331** 35 20
1730 5e. Pigeon with letter . . . 35 20
1731 5e. Sorting letters 35 20
1732 5e. Pen nib and post codes 35 20

332 Symbolic Figure

1978. 30th Anniv of Declaration of Human Rights. Multicoloured.
1733 14e. Type **332** 70 40
1734 40e. Similar symbolic figure, but facing right . . . . . 1·90 1·10
MS1735 120 × 100 mm. Nos. 1733/4 each × 2 . . . . 4·50 4·50

333 Sebastiao Magalhaes Lima

1978. 50th Death Anniv of Magalhaes Lima (journalist and pacifist).
1736 **333** 5e. multicoloured 30 10

334 Portable Post Boxes and Letter Balance

1978. Centenary of Post Museum. Multicoloured.
1737 4e. Type **334** 30 10
1738 5e. Morse equipment . . . 30 10
1739 10e. Printing press and Portuguese stamps of 1853 (125th anniv) . . . 1·20 25
1740 14e. Books, bookcase and entrance to Postal Library (centenary) . . . . 2·75 1·80
MS1741 120 × 99 mm. Nos. 1737/40 (sold at 40e.) . . . . 5·00 5·00

335 Emigrant at Railway Station

1979. Portuguese Emigrants. Multicoloured.
1742 5e. Type **335** 20 10
1743 14e. Emigrants at airport . . 75 55
1744 17e. Man greeting child at railway station . . . . . 1·10 1·10

336 Traffic

1979. Fight Against Noise. Multicoloured.

1745	4e. Type **336**	20	10
1746	5e. Pneumatic drill	75	15
1747	14e. Loud hailer	1·70	70

337 N.A.T.O. Emblem

1979. 30th Anniv of N.A.T.O.

1748 **337**	5e. blue, red and brown	30	10
1749	50e. blue, yellow and red	3·00	2·40
MS1750	120 × 100 mm. Nos. 1748/9 each × 2	4·50	4·50

338 Door-to-door Delivery

1979. Europa. Multicoloured.

1751	14e. Postal messenger delivering letter in cleft stick	60	35
1752	40e. Type **338**	1·40	1·00
MS1753	119 × 103 mm. Nos. 1751/2 each × 2	28·00	5·50

339 Children playing Ball

1979. International Year of the Child. Multicoloured.

1754	5e.50 Type **339**	20	10
1755	6e.50 Mother, baby and dove	30	10
1756	10e. Child eating	50	35
1757	14e. Children of different races	1·10	95
MS1758	110 × 104 mm. Nos. 1754/7 (sold at 40e.)	3·50	3·50

340 Saluting the Flag

1979. Camoes Day.

1759 **340**	6e.50 multicoloured	40	10
MS1760	148 × 125 mm. No. 1759 × 9	4·25	3·75

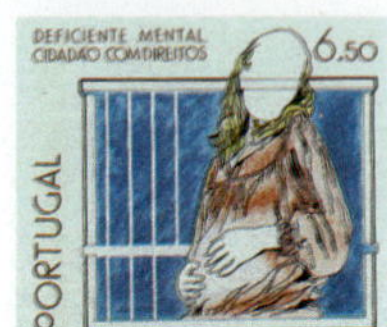

341 Pregnant Woman

1979. The Mentally Handicapped. Multicoloured.

1761	6e.50 Type **341**	35	10
1762	17e. Boy sitting in cage	90	55
1763	20e. Face, and hands holding hammer and chisel	1·20	85

342 Children reading Book

1979. 50th Anniv of International Bureau of Education. Multicoloured.

1764	6e.50 Type **342**	40	10
1765	17e. Teaching a deaf child	1·90	1·00

343 Water Cart, Caldas de Monchique

1979. "Brasiliana 79" International Stamp Exhibition. Portuguese Country Carts. Mult.

1766	2e.50 Type **343**	15	15
1767	5e.50 Wine sledge, Madeira	20	15
1768	6e.50 Wine cart, Upper Douro	40	10
1769	16e. Covered cart, Alentejo	90	80
1770	19e. Cart, Mogadouro	1·30	1·10
1771	20e. Sand cart, Murtosa	1·30	40

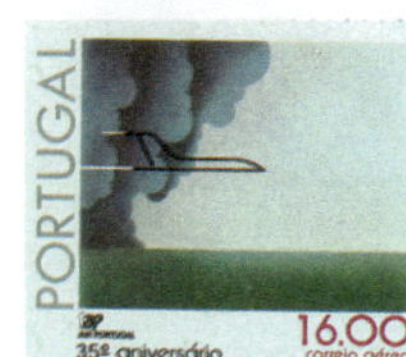

344 Aircraft flying through Storm Cloud

1979. 35th Anniv of TAP National Airline. Multicoloured.

1772	16e. Type **344**	1·20	60
1773	19e. Aircraft and sunset	1·30	85

345 Antonio Jose de Almeida

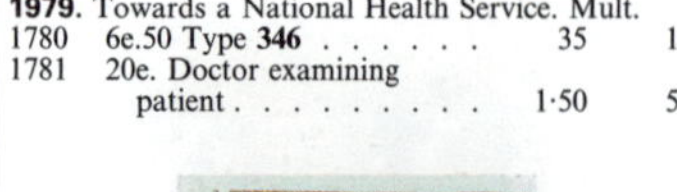

346 Family Group

1979. Republican Personalities (1st series).

1774 **345**	5e.50 mauve, grey and red	35	10
1775 –	6e.50 red, grey and carmine	35	10
1776 –	10e. brown, grey and red	60	10
1777 –	16e. blue, grey and red	1·00	65
1778 –	19e.50 green, grey and red	1·70	1·10
1779 –	20e. purple, grey and red	1·40	45

DESIGNS: 6e. Afonso Costa; 10e. Teofilo Braga; 16e. Bernardino Machado; 19e.50, Joao Chagas; 20e. Elias Garcia.

See also Nos. 1787/92.

1979. Towards a National Health Service. Mult.

1780	6e.50 Type **346**	35	10
1781	20e. Doctor examining patient	1·50	55

347 "The Holy Family"

1979. Christmas. Tile Pictures. Multicoloured.

1782	5e.50 Type **347**	40	25
1783	6e.50 "Adoration of the Shepherds"	40	20
1784	16e. "Flight into Egypt"	1·20	1·00

348 Rotary Emblem and Globe

1980. 75th Anniv of Rotary International. Mult.

1785	16e. Type **348**	1·10	65
1786	50e. Rotary emblem and torch	3·00	1·80

349 Jaime Cortesao

1980. Republican Personalities (2nd series).

1787 –	3e.50 orange and brown	20	10
1788 –	5e.50 green, olive and deep olive	30	15
1789 –	6e.50 lilac and violet	30	15
1790 **349**	11e. multicoloured	1·60	1·10
1791 –	16e. ochre and brown	1·10	70
1792 –	20e. green, blue & lt blue	1·10	40

DESIGNS: 3e.50, Alvaro de Castro; 5e.50, Antonio Sergio; 6e.50, Norton de Matos; 16e. Teixeira Gomes; 20e. Jose Domingues dos Santos.

350 Serpa Pinto

352 Luis Vaz de Camoes

351 Barn Owl

1980. Europa, Multicoloured.

1793	16e. Type **350**	75	40
1794	60e. Vasco da Gama	2·30	1·10
MS1795	107 × 110 mm. Nos. 1793/4 each × 2	15·00	2·75

1980. Protection of Species. Animals in Lisbon Zoo. Multicoloured.

1796	6e.50 Type **351**	30	10
1797	16e. Red fox	85	40
1798	19e.50 Wolf	1·20	55
1799	20e. Golden eagle	1·20	45
MS1800	109 × 107 mm. Nos. 1796/9	3·50	3·50

1980. 400th Death Anniv of Luis Vaz de Camoes (poet).

1801 **352**	6e.50 multicoloured	55	10
1802	20e. multicoloured	1·30	65

353 Pinto in Japan

1980. 400th Anniv of Fernao Mendes Pinto's "A Peregrinacao" (The Pilgrimage). Multicoloured.

1803	6e.50 Type **353**	35	10
1804	10e. Sea battle	1·10	55

354 Lisbon and Statue of St. Vincent (Jeronimos Monastery)

1980. World Tourism Conference, Manila, Philippines. Multicoloured.

1805	6e.50 Type **354**	35	10
1806	8e. Lantern Tower, Evora Cathedral	40	25
1807	11e. Mountain village and "Jesus with Top-hat" (Mirando do Douro Cathedral)	85	50
1808	16e. Canicada dam and "Lady of the Milk" (Braga Cathedral)	1·50	80
1809	19e.50 Aveiro River and pulpit from Santa Cruz Monastery, Coimbra	1·90	90
1810	20e. Rocha beach and ornamental chimney, Algarve	1·80	55

355 Caravel

1980. "Lubrapex 80" Portuguese–Brazilian Stamp Exhibition, Lisbon. Multicoloured.

1811	6e.50 Type **355**	35	10
1812	8e. Nau	75	40
1813	16e. Galleon	1·40	60
1814	19e.50 Early paddle-steamer with sails	2·00	70
MS1815	132 × 88 mm. Nos. 1811/14 (sold at 60e.)	6·25	6·25

356 Lightbulbs

1980. Energy Conservation. Multicoloured.

1816	6e.50 Type **356**	30	10
1817	16e. Speeding car	2·10	75

357 Duke of Braganza and Open Book

1980. Bicentenary of Academy of Sciences, Lisbon. Multicoloured.

1818	6e.50 Type **357**	30	10
1819	19e.50 Uniformed academician, Academy and sextant	1·50	75

358 Cigarette contaminating Lungs

1980. Anti-Smoking Campaign. Multicoloured.

1820	6e.50 Type **358**	30	10
1821	19e.50 Healthy figure pushing away hand with cigarette	2·00	1·10

359 Head and Computer Punch-card

1981. National Census. Multicoloured.

1822	6e.50 Type **359**	30	10
1823	16e. Houses and punch-card	1·50	1·00

360 Fragata, River Tejo

1981. River Boats. Multicoloured.

1824	8e. Type **360**	30	20
1825	8e.50 Rabelo, River Douro	30	20
1826	10e. Moliceiro, Aveiro River	55	20
1827	16e. Barco, River Lima	75	50
1828	19e.50 Carocho, River Minho	90	50
1829	20e. Varino, River Tejo	90	40

361 "Rajola" Tile from Setubal Peninsula (15th century)

1981. Tiles (1st series).
1830 **361** 8e.50 multicoloured . . . 75 10
MS1831 146 × 102 mm. No. 1830 × 6 . . . . 4·50 5·00

See also Nos. 1483/**MS**1844, 1847/**MS**1848, 1862/**MS**1864, 1871/**MS**1872, 1885/**MS**1886, 1893/**MS**1894, 1902/**MS**1904, 1914/**MS**1915, 1926/**MS**1927, 1935/**MS**1936, 1941/**MS**1943, 1952/**MS**1953, 1970/**MS**1971, 1972/**MS**1973, 1976/**MS**1978, 1983/**MS**1984, 1993/**MS**1994, 2020/**MS**2021 and 2031/**MS**2033.

362 Agua Dog

1981. 50th Anniv of Kennel Club of Portugal. Multicoloured.
1832 7e. Type **362** 45 15
1833 8e.50 Serra de Aires 45 20
1834 15e. Perdigueiro 85 20
1835 22e. Podengo . . . . 1·20 70
1836 25e.50 Castro Laboreiro . . 1·90 1·10
1837 33e.50 Serra de Estrela . . . 2·50 70

363 "Agriculture" **364** Dancer and Tapestry

1981. May Day. Multicoloured.
1838 8e.50 Type **363** 30 10
1839 25e.50 "Industry" . . . . . 1·50 90

1981. Europa. Multicoloured.
1840 22e. Type **364** . . . . . . 1·40 55
1841 48e. Painted boat prow, painted plate and shipwright with model boat . . . . 3·00 1·30
MS1842 108 × 109 mm. Nos. 1840/1 each × 2 . . . . 22·00 4·50

1981. Tiles (2nd series). Horiz design as T **361**.
1843 8e.50 multicoloured 75 10
MS1844 146 × 102 mm. No. 1843 × 6 . . . . 4·50 4·75
DESIGN: 8e.50, Tracery-pattern tile from Seville (16th century).

365 St. Anthony Writing

1981. 750th Death Anniv of St. Anthony of Lisbon. Multicoloured.
1845 8e.50 Type **365** 45 10
1846 70e. St. Anthony giving blessing . . . . 3·75 1·90

1981. Tiles (3rd series). As T **361**. Mult.
1847 8e.50 Arms of Jaime, Duke of Braganca (Seville, 1510) 75 10
MS1848 146 × 102 mm. No. 1847 × 6 . . . . 3·75 4·50

366 King Joao II and Caravels

1981. 500th Anniv of King Joao II's Accession. Multicoloured.
1849 8e.50 Type **366** 50 10
1850 27e. King Joao II on horseback . . . . 2·50 90

367 "Dom Luiz", 1862

1981. 125th Anniv of Portuguese Railways. Multicoloured.
1851 8e.50 Type **367** 70 10
1852 19e. Pacific steam locomotive, 1925 . . . . 2·10 1·00
1853 27e. Alco 1500 diesel locomotive, 1948 . . . . 2·20 1·10
1854 33e.50 Alsthom BB 2600 electric locomotive, 1974 3·00 90

368 "Perrier" Pump, 1856

1981. Portuguese Fire Engines. Multicoloured.
1855 7e. Type **368** 45 15
1856 8e.50 Ford fire engine, 1927 65 15
1857 27e. Renault fire pump, 1914 . . . . 2·50 1·00
1858 33e.50 Ford "Snorkel" combined hoist and pump, 1978 . . . . . . 3·00 95

369 "Virgin and Child"

1981. Christmas. Crib Figures. Multicoloured.
1859 7e. Type **369** 55 35
1860 8e.50 "Nativity" 75 20
1861 27e. "Flight into Egypt" . . 2·50 1·50

1981. Tiles (4th series). As T **361**. Multicoloured.
1862 8e.50 "Pisana" tile, Lisbon (16th century) 75 15
MS1863 146 × 102 mm. No. 1862 × 6 . . . . 5·00 5·00
MS1864 120 × 102 mm. Nos. 1830, 1843, 1847 and 1862 . . . . . 5·00 5·00

370 St. Francis with Animals **371** Flags of E.E.C. Members

1982. 800th Birth Anniv of St. Francis of Assisi. Multicoloured.
1865 8e.50 Type **370** 40 10
1866 27e. St. Francis helping to build church . . . . . . 2·10 1·50

1982. 25th Anniv of European Economic Community.
1867 **371** 27e. multicoloured . . . 1·30 70
MS1868 155 × 88 mm. No. 1867 × 4 5·00 5·00

372 Fort St. Catherina, Lighthouse and Memorial Column

1982. Centenary of Figueira da Foz City. Mult.
1869 10e. Type **372** 55 10
1870 19e. Tagus Bridge, shipbuilding yard and trawler . . . . 1·80 90

1982. Tiles (5th series). As T **361**. Multicoloured.
1871 10e. Italo-Flemish pattern tile (17th century) 75 15
MS1872 146 × 102 mm. No. 1871 × 6 . . . . 3·75 4·50

373 "Sagres I" (cadet barque) **374** Edison Gower Bell Telephone, 1883

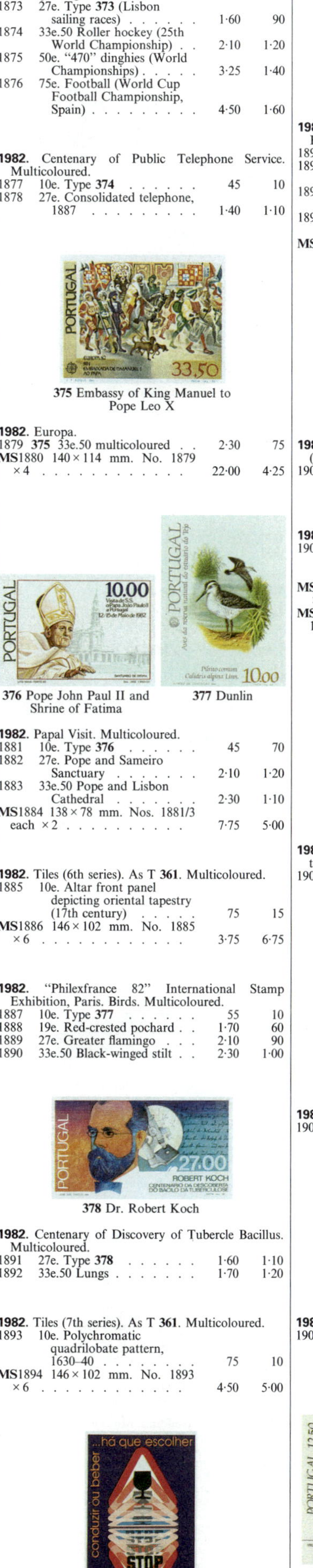

1982. Sporting Events. Multicoloured.
1873 27e. Type **373** (Lisbon sailing races) . . . . . . 1·60 90
1874 33e.50 Roller hockey (25th World Championship) . . 2·10 1·20
1875 50e. "470" dinghies (World Championships) . . . . . 3·25 1·40
1876 75e. Football (World Cup Football Championship, Spain) . . . . 4·50 1·60

1982. Centenary of Public Telephone Service. Multicoloured.
1877 10e. Type **374** 45 10
1878 27e. Consolidated telephone, 1887 . . . . 1·40 1·10

375 Embassy of King Manuel to Pope Leo X

1982. Europa.
1879 **375** 33e.50 multicoloured . . 2·30 75
MS1880 140 × 114 mm. No. 1879 × 4 . . . . 22·00 4·25

376 Pope John Paul II and Shrine of Fatima **377** Dunlin

1982. Papal Visit. Multicoloured.
1881 10e. Type **376** 45 70
1882 27e. Pope and Sameiro Sanctuary . . . . 2·10 1·20
1883 33e.50 Pope and Lisbon Cathedral . . . . 2·30 1·10
MS1884 138 × 78 mm. Nos. 1881/3 each × 2 . . . . 7·75 5·00

1982. Tiles (6th series). As T **361**. Multicoloured.
1885 10e. Altar front panel depicting oriental tapestry (17th century) 75 15
MS1886 146 × 102 mm. No. 1885 × 6 . . . . 3·75 6·75

1982. "Philexfrance 82" International Stamp Exhibition, Paris. Birds. Multicoloured.
1887 10e. Type **377** 55 10
1888 19e. Red-crested pochard . . 1·70 60
1889 27e. Greater flamingo . . . 2·10 90
1890 33e.50 Black-winged stilt . . 2·30 1·00

378 Dr. Robert Koch

1982. Centenary of Discovery of Tubercle Bacillus. Multicoloured.
1891 27e. Type **378** . . . . . . 1·60 1·10
1892 33e.50 Lungs . . . . 1·70 1·20

1982. Tiles (7th series). As T **361**. Multicoloured.
1893 10e. Polychromatic quadrilobate pattern, 1630–40 . . . . 75 10
MS1894 146 × 102 mm. No. 1893 × 6 . . . . 4·50 5·00

379 Wine Glass and Stop Sign

1982. "Don't Drink and Drive".
1895 **379** 10e. multicoloured . . . 55 10

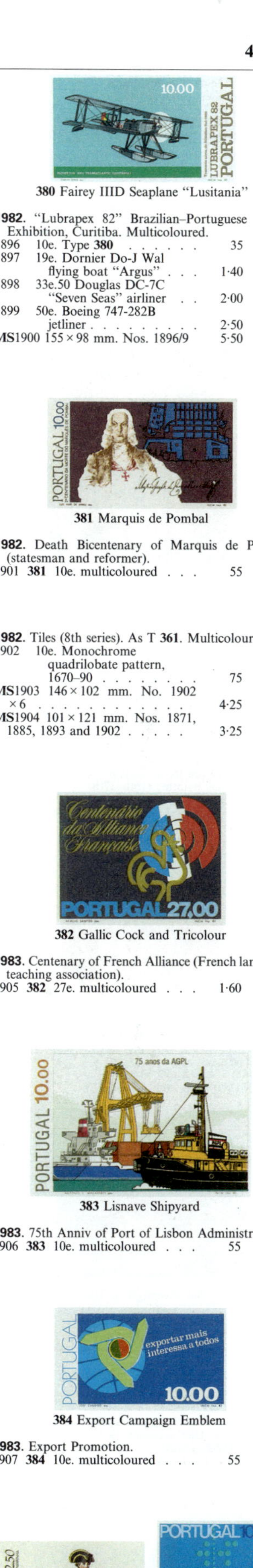

380 Fairey IIID Seaplane "Lusitania"

1982. "Lubrapex 82" Brazilian–Portuguese Stamp Exhibition, Curitiba. Multicoloured.
1896 10e. Type **380** 35 10
1897 19e. Dornier Do-J Wal flying boat "Argus" . . . 1·40 75
1898 33e.50 Douglas DC-7C "Seven Seas" airliner . . 2·00 75
1899 50e. Boeing 747-282B jetliner . . . . 2·50 1·10
MS1900 155 × 98 mm. Nos. 1896/9 5·50 5·50

381 Marquis de Pombal

1982. Death Bicentenary of Marquis de Pombal (statesman and reformer).
1901 **381** 10e. multicoloured . . . 55 10

1982. Tiles (8th series). As T **361**. Multicoloured.
1902 10e. Monochrome quadrilobate pattern, 1670–90 . . . . 75 10
MS1903 146 × 102 mm. No. 1902 × 6 . . . . 4·25 4·25
MS1904 101 × 121 mm. Nos. 1871, 1885, 1893 and 1902 . . . . . 3·25 3·25

382 Gallic Cock and Tricolour

1983. Centenary of French Alliance (French language teaching association).
1905 **382** 27e. multicoloured . . . 1·60 75

383 Lisnave Shipyard

1983. 75th Anniv of Port of Lisbon Administration.
1906 **383** 10e. multicoloured . . . 55 10

384 Export Campaign Emblem

1983. Export Promotion.
1907 **384** 10e. multicoloured . . . 55 10

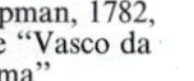

385 Midshipman, 1782, and Frigate "Vasco da Gama" **386** W.C.Y. Emblem

1983. Naval Uniforms. Multicoloured.
1908 12e.50 Type **385** 55 10
1909 25e. Seaman and steam corvette "Estefania", 1845 1·50 40

1910 30e. Marine sergeant and cruiser "Adamastor", 1900 . . . . 1·80 55
1911 37e.50 Midshipman and frigate "Joao Belo", 1982 2·20 75

1983. World Cummunications Year. Mult.
1912 10e. Type **386** 55 20
1913 33e.50 W.C.Y. emblem (diff) 1·80 1·10

1983. Tiles (9th series). As T **361**. Multicoloured.
1914 12e.50 Hunter killing white bull (tile from Saldanha Palace, Lisbon, 17/18th century) 90 15
MS1915 146 × 102 mm. No. 1914 × 6 . . . . 4·00 4·50

387 Portuguese Helmet (16th century)

1983. "Expo XVII" Council of Europe Exhibition. Multicoloured.
1916 11e. Type **387** 55 20
1917 12e.50 Astrolabe (16th century) 75 20
1918 25e. Portuguese caravels (from 16th-century Flemish tapestry) . . . . 1·60 55
1919 30e. Carved capital (12th century) . . . . 2·10 60
1920 37e.50 Hour glass (16th century) . . . . 2·30 90
1921 40e. Detail from Chinese panel painting (16th–17th century) . . . . 2·40 85
MS1922 115 × 120 mm. Nos. 1916/21 8·50 8·50

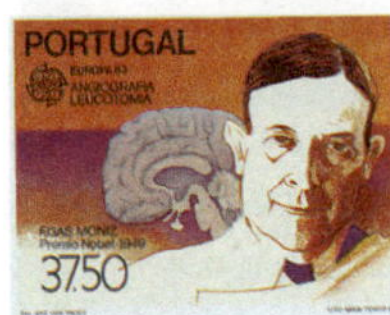

388 Egas Moniz (Nobel Prize winner and brain surgeon)

1983. Europa.
1923 **388** 37e.50 multicoloured . . 2·40 70
MS1924 140 × 114 mm. No. 1923 × 4 . . . . 22·00 3·50

389 Passenger in Train

1983. European Ministers of Transport Conference.
1925 **389** 30e. blue, deep blue and silver . . . . 2·50 70

1983. Tiles (10th series). As T **361**. Multicoloured.
1926 12e.50 Tiles depicting birds (18th century) 90 15
MS1927 146 × 102 mm. No. 1926 × 6 . . . . 4·00 4·50

390 Mediterranean Monk Seal

1983. "Brasiliana 83" International Stamp Exhibition, Rio de Janeiro. Marine Mammals. Multicoloured.
1928 12e.50 Type **390** 90 15
1929 30e. Common dolphin . . . 2·20 50
1930 37e.50 Killer whale . . . . 3·00 1·20
1931 80e. Humpback whale . . . 5·00 1·10
MS1932 133 × 81 mm. Nos. 1928/31 9·75 2·75

391 Assassination of Spanish Administrator by Prince John

393 "Adoration of the Magi"

392 Bartolomeu de Gusmao and Model Balloon, 1709

1983. 600th Anniv of Independence. Mult.
1933 12e.50 Type **391** 80 15
1934 30e. Prince John proclaimed King of Portugal . . . . 2·75 1·20

1983. Tiles (11th series). As T **361**. Multicoloured.
1935 12e.50 Flower pot by Gabriel del Barco (18th century) 90 15
MS1936 146 × 102 mm. No. 1935 × 6 . . . . 4·50 5·00

1983. Bicentenary of Manned Flight. Mult.
1937 16e. Type **392** 75 10
1938 51e. Montgolfier balloon, 1783 . . . . 2·00 90

1983. Christmas. Stained Glass Windows from Monastery of Our Lady of Victory, Batalha. Multicoloured.
1939 12e.50 Type **393** 70 15
1940 30e. "The Flight into Egypt" . . . . 2·30 90

1983. Tiles (12th series). As T **361**. Multicoloured.
1941 12e.50 Turkish horseman (18th century) 90 15
MS1942 146 × 102 mm. No. 1941 × 6 . . . . 4·50 5·25
MS1943 120 × 102 mm. Nos. 1914, 1926, 1935 and 1941 . . . . . 4·25 4·25

394 Siberian Tiger

1983. Centenary of Lisbon Zoo. Multicoloured.
1944 16e. Type **394** . . . . . . 1·70 20
1945 16e. Cheetah . . . . 1·70 20
1946 16e. Blesbok . . . . 1·70 20
1947 16e. White rhino . . . . . 1·70 20

395 Fighter Pilot and Hawker Hurricane Mk II, 1954

1983. Air Force Uniforms. Multicoloured.
1948 16e. Type **395** 55 10
1949 35e. Pilot in summer uniform and Republic F-84G Thunderjet, 1960 2·10 55
1950 40e. Paratrooper in walking-out uniform and Nord 2501D Noratlas military transport plane, 1966 . . 2·00 65
1951 51e. Pilot in normal uniform and Vought A-70 Corsair II bomber, 1966 . . . . 2·50 90

1984. Tiles (13th series). As T **361**. Multicoloured.
1952 16e. Coat of arms of King Jose I (late 18th century) 90 15
MS1953 146 × 102 mm. No. 1952 × 6 . . . . 4·50 4·50

396 "25" on Crate (25th Lisbon International Fair)

1984. Events.
1954 35e. Type **396** . . . . . . 1·80 55
1955 40e. Wheat rainbow and globe (World Food Day) 1·90 65
1956 51e. Hand holding stylized flower (15th World Congress of International Rehabilitation) (vert) . . 2·40 90

397 National Flag

1984. 10th Anniv of Revolution.
1957 **397** 16e. multicoloured . . . 1·20 10

398 Bridge

1984. Europa.
1958 **398** 51e. multicoloured . . . 2·50 1·10
MS1959 140 × 114 mm. No. 1958 × 4 . . . . 9·00 9·00

399 "Panel of St. Vincent"

1984. "Lubrapex 84" Portuguese–Brazilian Stamp Exhibition. Multicoloured.
1960 16e. Type **399** 70 10
1961 40e. "St. James" (altar panel) . . . . 2·30 60
1962 51e. "View of Lisbon" (painting) . . . . 3·50 95
1963 66e. "Head of Youth" (Domingos Sequeira) . . 3·50 1·20
MS1964 110 × 111 mm. Nos. 1960/3 8·50 8·50

400 Fencing

1984. Olympic Games, Los Angeles, and 75th Anniv of Portuguese Olympic Committee. Multicoloured.
1965 35e. Type **400** . . . . . . 1·60 30
1966 40e. Gymnastics . . . . . 2·10 60
1967 51e. Running . . . . 3·00 1·00
1968 80e. Pole vaulting . . . . . 3·25 1·10
MS1969 90 × 92 mm. 100e. Hurdling 7·00 7·00

1984. Tiles (14th series). As T **361**. Multicoloured.
1970 16e. Pictorial tile from Pombal Palace, Lisbon (late 18th century) 90 15
MS1971 146 × 102 mm. No. 1970 × 6 . . . . 4·25 4·50

1984. Tiles (15th series). As T **361**. Multicoloured.
1972 16e. Four art nouveau tiles (late 19th century) 90 15
MS1973 146 × 102 mm. No. 1972 × 6 . . . . 4·00 4·00

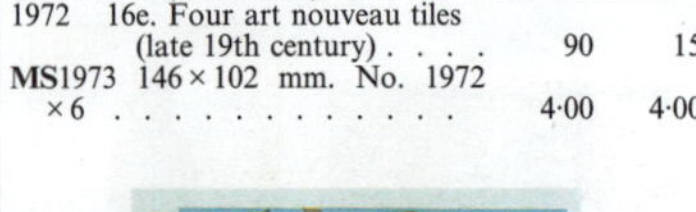

401 Gil Eanes

1984. Anniversaries. Multicoloured.
1974 16e. Type **401** (550th anniv of rounding of Cape Bojador) 50 10
1975 51e. King Pedro IV of Portugal and I of Brazil (150th death anniv) . . . 2·50 1·00

1984. Tiles (16th series). As T **361**. Multicoloured.
1976 16e. Grasshoppers and wheat (R. Bordalo Pinheiro, 19th century) . . 90 15
MS1977 146 × 102 mm. No. 1976 × 6 . . . . 3·00 3·00
MS1978 120 × 102 mm. Nos. 1952, 1970, 1972 and 1976 . . . . . 4·25 4·25

402 Infantry Grenadier, 1740, and Regiment in Formation

1985. Army Uniforms. Multicoloured.
1979 20e. Type **402** 55 10
1980 46e. Officer, Fifth Cavalry, 1810, and cavalry charge 2·50 55
1981 60e. Artillery corporal, 1891, and Krupp 9 mm gun and crew . . . . 2·75 75
1982 100e. Engineer in chemical protection suit, 1985, and bridge-laying armoured car . . . . 3·25 1·20

1985. Tiles (17th series). As T **361**. Multicoloured.
1983 20e. Detail of panel by Jorge Barrados in Lisbon Faculty of Letters (20th century) 85 15
MS1984 146 × 102 mm. No. 1983 × 6 . . . . 4·25 5·00

403 Calcada R. dos Santos Kiosk

1985. Lisbon Kiosks. Multicoloured.
1985 20e. Type **403** . . . . . . 1·20 15
1986 20e. Tivoli kiosk, Avenida da Liberdade . . . . . . 1·20 15
1987 20e. Porto de Lisboa kiosk 1·20 15
1988 20e. Rua de Artilharia Um kiosk . . . . 1·20 15

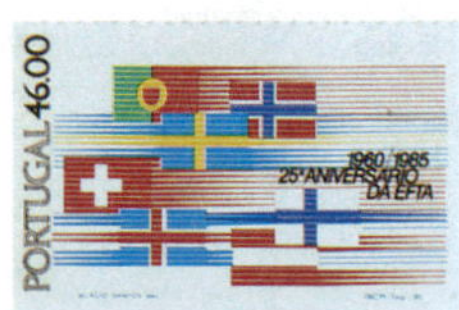

404 Flags of Member Countries

1985. 25th Anniv of European Free Trade Assn.
1989 **404** 46e. multicoloured . . . 1·50 60

405 Profiles

1985. International Youth Year.
1990 **405** 60e. multicoloured . . . 1·90 85

406 Woman holding Adufe (tambourine)

1985. Europa.
1991 **406** 60e. multicoloured . . . 3·50 1·10
MS1992 140 × 114 mm. No. 1991 × 4 . . . . 27·00 5·00

1985. Tiles (18th series). As T **361**. Multicoloured.
1993 20e. Detail of panel by Maria Keil on Avenida Infante Santo (20th century) 90 15
MS1994 146 × 102 mm. No. 1993 × 6 . . . . 4·25 5·00

407 Knight on Horseback

1985. Anniversaries. Multicoloured.
1995 20e. Type **407** (600th anniv of Battle of Aljubarrota) 70 10
1996 46e. Queen Leonor and hospital (500th anniv of Caldas da Rainha thermal hospital) . . . . 2·20 75
1997 60e. Pedro Reinel (500th anniversary of first Portuguese sea-chart) . . 2·40 1·00

408 Farmhouse, Minho **409** Aquilino Ribeiro (writer)

1985. Architecture.
1998 – 50c. black, bistre and blue 10 10
1999 – 1e. black, yellow & green 10 10
2000 – 1e.50 black, green and emerald 10 10
2001 – 2e.50 brown, orange & bl 10 10
2002 – 10e. black, purple & pink 20 10
2003 **408** 20e. brn, yell & dp yell 30 10
2004 – 22e.50 brown, blue and ochre 30 10
2005 – 25e. brown, yellow & grn 40 10
2006 – 27e. black, grn & yell . . 50 10
2007 – 29e. black, yellow & orge 50 10
2008 – 30e. black, blue & brown 50 10
2009 – 40e. black, yellow & grn 65 15
2010 – 50e. black, blue & brown 80 15
2011 – 55e. black, yellow & grn 80 15
2012 – 60e. black, orange & blue . . . . 1·10 25
2013 – 70e. black, yellow & orge 1·10 25
2014 – 80e. brown, green and red . . . . 1·10 35
2015 – 90e. brown, yellow & grn 1·30 35
2016 – 100e. brown, yellow & bl 1·60 40
2017 – 500e. black, grey and blue . . . . 6·50 75
DESIGNS: 50e. Saloia house, Estremadura; 1e. Beira inland house; 1e.50, Ribatejo house; 2e.50, Tras-os-montes houses; 10e. Minho and Douro coast house; 22e.50, Alentejo houses; 25e. Sitio house, Algarve; 27e. Beira inland house (different); 29e. Tras-os-montes house; 30e. Algarve house; 40e. Beira inland house (different); 50e. Beira coasthouse; 55e. Tras-os-montes house (different); 60e. Beira coast house (different); 70e. South Estramadura and Alentejo house; 80e. Estremadura house; 90e. Minho house; 100e. Monte house, Alentejo; 500e. Terraced houses, East Algarve.

1985. Tiles (19th series). As T **361**. Multicoloured.
2020 20e. Head of woman by Querubim Lapa (20th century) 90 15
MS2021 147 × 101 mm. No. 2020 × 6 . . . . 4·25 5·00

1985. Anniversaries. Multicoloured.
2022 20e. Type **409** (birth centenary) 65 10
2023 46e. Fernando Pessoa (poet 50th death anniv) . . . 1·80 65

410 Berlenga National Reserve

1985. National Parks and Reserves. Multicoloured.
2024 20e. Type **410** 50 10
2025 40e. Estrela Mountains National Park . . . . . 1·70 60
2026 46e. Boquilobo Marsh National Reserve . . . . 2·50 90
2027 80e. Formosa Lagoon National Reserve . . . . 2·75 90
MS2028 100 × 68 mm. 100e. Jacinto Dunes National Reserve . . . 5·50 5·50

411 "Nativity" **412** Post Rider

1985. Christmas. Illustrations from "Book of Hours of King Manoel I". Multicoloured.
2029 20e. Type **411** 55 10
2030 46e. "Adoration of the Three Wise Men" . . . . 1·90 70

1985. Tiles (20th series). As T **361**. Multicoloured.
2031 20e. Detail of panel by Manuel Cargaleiro (20th century) 90 15
MS2032 146 × 102 mm. No. 2031 × 6 . . . . 5·00 5·00
MS2033 120 × 102 mm. Nos. 1983, 1993, 2020 and 2031 . . . . . 5·00 5·00

1985. No value expressed.
2034 **412** (–) green and deep green 85 15

413 Map and Flags of Member Countries

1985. Admission of Portugal and Spain to European Economic Community. Multicoloured.
2035 20e. Flags of Portugal and Spain uniting with flags of other members 65 10
2036 57e.50 Type **413** . . . . . 2·40 90
See also No. **MS**2056.

414 Feira Castle

1986. Castles (1st series). Multicoloured.
2037 22e.50 Type **414** 90 15
2038 22e.50 Beja Castle 90 15
See also Nos. 2040/1, 2054/5, 2065/6, 2073/4, 2086/7 2093/4, 2102/3 and 2108/9.

415 Globe and Dove

1986. International Peace Year.
2039 **415** 75e. multicoloured . . . 2·75 1·10

1986. Castles (2nd series). As T **414**. Multicoloured.
2040 22e.50 Braganca Castle . . 90 15
2041 22e.50 Guimaraes Castle . . 90 15

416 Benz Motor Tricycle, 1886

1986. Centenary of Motor Car. Multicoloured.
2042 22e.50 Type **416** . . . . . 1·30 10
2043 22e.50 Daimler motor car, 1886 . . . . 1·30 10

417 Allis Shad

1986. Europa.
2044 **417** 68e.50 multicoloured . . 2·75 95
MS2045 140 × 114 mm. No. 2044 × 4 . . . . 25·00 5·00

418 Alter

1986. "Ameripex 86" International Stamp Exn, Chicago. Thoroughbred Horses. Multicoloured.
2046 22e.50 Type **418** 55 10
2047 47e.50 Lusitano . . . . . . 1·90 75
2048 52e.50 Garrano . . . . . . 2·40 95
2049 68e.50 Sorraia . . . . . . 2·75 1·00

419 Comet

1986. Appearance of Halley's Comet. Sheet 100 × 68 mm.
MS2050 **419** 100e. multicoloured 10·50 10·50

420 Diogo Cao (navigator) and Monument

1986. Anniversaries. Multicoloured.
2051 22e.50 Type **420** (500th anniv of 2nd expedition to Africa) 55 10
2052 52e.50 Passos Manuel (Director) and capital (150th anniv of National Academy of Fine Arts, Lisbon) . . . . 1·80 75
2053 52e.50 Joao Baptista Ribeiro (painter and Oporto Academy Director) and drawing (150th anniv of Portuguese Academy of Fine Arts, Oporto) . . . 1·80 75

1986. Castles (3rd series). As T **414**. Multicoloured.
2054 22e.50 Belmonte Castle . . 55 15
2055 22e.50 Montemor-o-Velho Castle . . . . 1·60 75

1986. "Europex 86" Stamp Exhibition, Lisbon. Sheet 127 × 91 mm.
MS2056 Nos. 2035/6 each × 2 . . 5·50 5·50

421 Hand writing on Postcard

1986. Anniversaries. Multicoloured.
2057 22e.50 Type **421** (centenary of first Portuguese postcards) 90 15
2058 47e.50 Guardsman and houses (75th anniv of National Republican Guard) . . . . 1·60 70
2059 52e.50 Calipers, globe and banner (50th anniv of Order of Engineers) . . . 1·70 75

422 Seasonal Mill, Douro

1986. "Luprapex 86" Portuguese–Brazilian Stamp Exhibition, Rio de Janeiro. Multicoloured.
2060 22e.50 Type **422** 55 10
2061 47e.50 Seasonal mill, Coimbra . . . . 1·40 90
2062 52e.50 Overshot bucket mill, Gerez . . . . 1·80 1·00
2063 90e. Permanent stream mill, Braga . . . . 2·75 85
MS2064 140 × 114 mm. Nos. 2060/3 8·50 7·00

1987. Castles (4th series). As T **414**. Mult.
2065 25e. Silves Castle 90 15
2066 25e. Evora-Monte Castle . . 90 15

423 Houses on Stilts, Tocha

1987. 75th Anniv (1986) of Organized Tourism. Multicoloured.
2067 25e. Type **423** 55 10
2068 57e. Fishing boats, Espinho 2·30 1·00
2069 98e. Fountain, Arraiolos . . 3·00 90

424 Hand, Sun and Trees

1987. European Environment Year. Multicoloured.
2070 25e. Type **424** 55 10
2071 57e. Hands and flower on map of Europe . . . . . 1·60 80
2072 74e.50 Hand, sea, purple dye murex shell, moon and rainbow . . . . . . 2·75 90

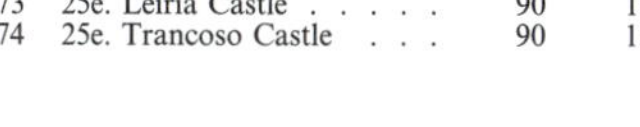

1987. Castles (5th series). As T **414**. Multicoloured.
2073 25e. Leiria Castle 90 15
2074 25e. Trancoso Castle . . . 90 15

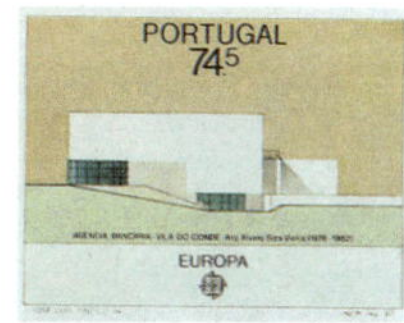

425 Bank Borges and Irmao Agency, Vila do Conde (Alvaro Siza)

1987. Europa. Architecture.
2075 **425** 74e.50 multicoloured . . 2·50 1·00
MS2076 140 × 114 mm. No. 2075 × 4 . . . . 24·00 5·50

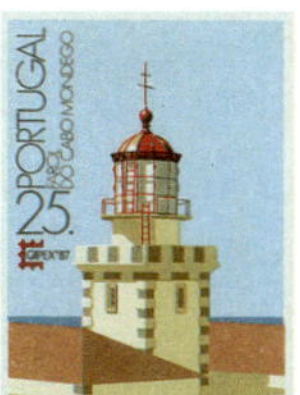

426 Cape Mondego **427** Souza-Cardoso (self-portrait)

1987. "Capex '87" International Stamp Exhibition Toronto. Portuguese Lighthouses. Multicoloured.
2077 25e. Type **426** 90 15
2078 25e. Berlenga 90 15
2079 25e. Aveiro 90 15
2080 25e. Cape St. Vincent . . . 90 15

1987. Birth Centenary of Amadeo de Souza-Cardoso (painter).
2081 **427** 74e.50 multicoloured . . 1·90 80

428 Clipped 400 Reis Silver Coin

1987. 300th Anniv of Portuguese Paper Currency.
2082 **428** 100e. multicoloured . . . 2·50 75

429 Dias's Fleet leaving Lisbon

1987. 500th Anniv of Bartolomeu Dias's Voyages (1st issue). Multicoloured.
2083 25e. Type **429** 95 15
2084 25e. Ships off coast of Africa 95 15
Nos. 2083/4 were printed together, se-tenant, each pair forming a composite design.
See also Nos. 2099/2100.

430 Library

1987. 150th Anniv of Portuguese Royal Library, Rio de Janeiro.
2085 **430** 125e. multicoloured . . . 3·25 1·20

1987. Castles (6th series). As T **414**. Multicoloured.
2086 25e. Marvao Castle 95 15
2087 25e. St. George's Castle, Lisbon 95 15

431 Records and Compact Disc Player

1987. Centenary of Gramophone Record. Sheet 140 × 114 mm containing T **431** and similar horiz design. Multicoloured.
MS2088 75e. Type **431**; 125e. Early gramophone . . . . 8·50 8·50

432 Angels around Baby Jesus, Tree and Kings (Jose Manuel Coutinho)

1987. Christmas. Children's Paintings. Mult.
2089 25e. Type **432** 65 10
2090 57e. Children dancing around sunburst (Rosa J. Leitao) . . . . 1·80 75
2091 74e.50 Santa Claus flying on dove (Sonya Alexandra Hilario) . . . . 2·10 1·10
MS2092 140 × 114 mm. Nos. 2089/91 4·50 4·50

1988. Castles (7th series). As T **414**. Multicoloured.
2093 27e. Fernandine Walls, Oporto 90 15
2094 27e. Almourol Castle . . . 90 15

433 Lynx

1988. Iberian Lynx. Multicoloured.
2095 27e. Type **433** . . . . . . 1·00 15
2096 27e. Lynx carrying rabbit 1·00 15
2097 27e. Pair of lynxes . . . . 1·00 15
2098 27e. Mother with young . . 1·00 15

434 King Joao II sending Pero da Covilha on Expedition

1988. 500th Anniv of Voyages of Bartolomeu Dias (2nd issue) (2099/2100) and Pero da Covilha (2101). Multicoloured.
2099 27e. Dias's ships in storm off Cape of Good Hope 2·50 1·00
2100 27e. Contemporary map . . 2·20 80
2101 105e. Type **434** . . . . . . 2·50 1·00
Nos. 2099/2100 are as T **429**.

1988. Castles (8th series). As T **414**. Multicoloured.
2102 27e. Palmela Castle 90 15
2103 27e. Vila Nova da Cerveira Castle 90 15

435 19th-century Mail Coach

1988. Europa. Transport and Communications.
2104 **435** 80e. multicoloured . . . 2·20 80
MS2105 139 × 112 mm. As No. 2104 × 4 but with cream background 24·00 5·25

436 Map of Europe and Monnet

1988. Birth Centenary of Jean Monnet (statesman). "Europex 88" Stamp Exhibition.
2106 **436** 60e. multicoloured . . . 1·50 60

437 Window reflecting Cordovil House and Fountain

1988. UNESCO World Heritage Site, Evora. "Lubrapex 88" Stamp Exhibition. Sheet 112 × 139 mm.
MS2107 **437** 150e. multicoloured 7·75 7·75

1988. Castles (9th series). As T **414**. Multicoloured.
2108 27e. Chaves Castle 90 15
2109 27e. Penedono Castle . . . 90 15

438 "Part of a Viola" (Amadeo de Souza-Cardoso)

1988. 20th-century Portuguese Paintings (1st series). Multicoloured.
2110 27e. Type **438** 55 10
2111 60e. "Acrobats" (Almada Negreiros) . . . . 1·60 75
2112 80e. "Still Life with Viola" (Eduardo Viana) . . . . 1·90 90
MS2113 138 × 112 mm. Nos. 2110/12 5·25 5·25
See also Nos. 2121/MS2125, 2131/MS2134, 2148/MS2152, 2166/MS2169 and 2206/MS2210.

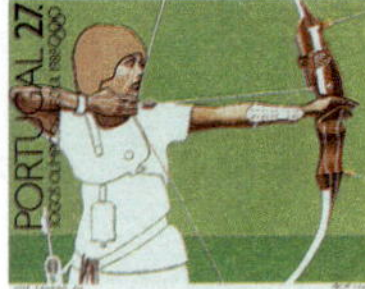

439 Archery

1988. Olympic Games, Seoul. Multicoloured.
2114 27e. Type **439** 50 10
2115 55e. Weightlifting . . . . . 1·50 80
2116 60e. Judo . . . . 1·60 85
2117 80e. Tennis . . . . 2·40 90
MS2118 114 × 67 mm. 200e. Yachting (39 × 30 mm) . . . . 9·00 9·00

440 "Winter" (House of the Fountains, Coimbra)

1988. Roman Mosaics of 3rd Century. Mult.
2119 27e. Type **440** 60 10
2120 80e. "Fish" (Baths, Faro) 1·90 75

1988. 20th Century Portuguese Paintings (2nd series). As T **438**. Multicoloured.
2121 27e. "Internment" (Mario Eloy) 10 10
2122 60e. "Lisbon Houses" (Carlos Botelho) . . . . 1·30 65
2123 80e. "Avejao Lirico" (Antonio Pedro) . . . . 1·90 75
MS2124 140 × 114 mm. Nos. 2121/3 5·25 5·25
MS2125 139 × 144 mm. Nos. 2110/12 and 2121/3 . . . . 9·00 9·00

441 Braga Cathedral

1989. Anniversaries. Multicoloured.
2126 30e. Type **441** (900th anniv) 75 30
2127 55e. Caravel, Fischer's lovebird and S. Jorge da Mina Castle (505th anniv) 1·40 65
2128 60e. Sailor using astrolabe (500th anniv of South Atlantic voyages) . . . . 1·90 85
Nos. 2127/8 also have the "India 89" Stamp Exhibition, New Delhi, emblem.

442 "Greetings" **443** Flags in Ballot Box

1989. Greetings Stamps. Multicoloured.
2129 29e. Type **442** 55 10
2130 60e. Airplane distributing envelopes inscribed "with Love" . . . . 1·10 55

1989. 20th-Century Portuguese Paintings (3rd series). As T **438**. Multicoloured.
2131 29e. "Antithesis of Calm" (Antonio Dacosta) . . . 50 10
2132 60e. "Unskilled Mason's Lunch" (Julio Pomar) . . 1·50 65
2133 87e. "Simumis" (Vespeira) 1·90 1·00
MS2134 139 × 111 mm. Nos. 2131/3 5·25 5·25

1989. 3rd Direct Elections to European Parliament.
2135 **443** 60e. multicoloured . . . 1·40 65

444 Boy with Spinning Top

1989. Europa. Children's Games and Toys. Multicoloured.
2136 80e. Type **444** . . . . . . 1·90 85
MS2137 138 × 112 mm. 80e. × 2 Type **444**; 80e. × 2 Spinning tops 32·00 9·75

445 Cable Railway

1989. Lisbon Transport. Multicoloured.
2138 29e. Type **445** 55 15
2139 65e. Electric tramcar . . . . 1·70 80
2140 87e. Santa Justa lift . . . . 1·90 1·10
2141 100e. Bus . . . . 2·30 80
MS2142 100 × 50 mm. 250e. River ferry (39 × 29 mm) . . . . . . 7·75 7·75

446 Gyratory Mill, Ansiao

1989. Windmills. Multicoloured.
2143 29e. Type **446** 55 20
2144 60e. Stone mill, Santiago do Cacem . . . . 1·70 80
2145 87e. Post mill, Afife . . . . 1·90 1·00
2146 100e. Wooden mill, Caldas da Rainha . . . . 2·30 90

447 Drummer Boy

1989. Bicentenary of French Revolution and "Philexfrance 89" International Stamp Exhibition, Paris. Sheet 111 × 139 mm.
MS2147 **447** 250e. multicoloured 7·75 7·75

1989. 20th-Century Portuguese Paintings (4th series). As T **438**.
2148 29e. blue, green and black 45 10
2149 60e. multicoloured . . . . . 1·50 60
2150 87e. multicoloured . . . . . 2·00 95
MS2151 139 × 111 mm. Nos. 2148/50 5·25 5·25
MS2152 138 × 144 mm. Nos. 231/3 and 2148/50 . . . . 9·00 9·00
DESIGNS: 29e. "046-72" (Fernando Lanhas); 60e. "Spirals" (Nadir Afonso); 87e. "Sim" (Carlos Calvet).

448 Luis I (death centenary) and Ajuda Palace, Lisbon

1989. National Palaces (1st series). Multicoloured.
2153 29e. Type **448** 40 15
2154 60e. Queluz Palace . . . . 1·40 85
See also Nos. 2211/14.

449 "Armeria pseudarmeria"

1989. Wild Flowers. Multicoloured.
2155 29e. Type **449** 40 10
2156 60e. "Santolina impressa" 1·20 65
2157 87e. "Linaria lamarckii" . . 1·70 90
2158 100e. "Limonium multiflorum" . . . . . . 2·30 1·20

450 Blue and White Plate

1990. Portuguese Faience (1st series). Mult.
2159 33e. Type **450** 55 20
2160 33e. Blue and white plate with man in centre . . . 55 20
2161 35e. Vase decorated with flowers 75 20
2162 60e. Fish-shaped jug . . . . 1·30 75
2163 60e. Blue and white plate with arms in centre . . . 1·30 75
2164 60e. Blue and white dish with lid . . . . 1·30 75
MS2165 112 × 140 mm. 250e. Plate with crown in centre . . . . . 5·50 5·50
See also Nos. 2221/**MS**2227 and 2262/**MS**2268.

1990. 20th-Century Portuguese Paintings (5th series). As T **438**. Multicoloured.
2166 32e. "Aluenda-Tordesillas" (Joaquim Rodrigo) . . . 45 10
2167 60e. "Painting" (Luis Noronha da Costa) . . . 1·20 55
2168 95e. "Painting" (Vasco Costa) . . . . 2·00 90
MS2169 138 × 111 mm. Nos. 2166/8 5·25 5·25

451 Joao Goncalves Zarco

1990. Portuguese Navigators.
2170 **451** 2e. red, pink and black 10 10
2171 – 3e. green, blue and black 10 10
2172 – 4e. purple, red and black 10 10
2173 – 5e. brown, grey & black 10 10
2174 – 6e. deep green, green and black 10 10
2175 – 10e. dp red, red & black 10 10
2176 – 32e. green, brown & blk 50 10
2177 – 35e. red, pink and black 40 10
2178 – 38e. blue, lt blue & black 40 15
2179 – 42e. green, grey & black 50 10
2180 – 45e. green, yellow & blk 45 20
2181 – 60e. yellow, purple & blk 1·00 30
2182 – 65e. brown, green & blk 95 20
2183 – 70e. violet, mauve & blk 95 20
2184 – 75e. olive, green & black 90 45
2185 – 80e. orange, brn & blk 1·30 55
2186 – 100e. red, orange & blk 1·90 65
2187 – 200e. green, yellow & blk 2·75 65
2188 – 250e. blue, green & black 4·25 1·40
2189 – 350e. red, pink and black 5·00 1·60
DESIGNS: 3e. Pedro Lopes de Sousa; 4e. Duarte Pacheco Pereira; 5e. Tristao Vaz Teixeira; 6e. Pedro Alvares Cabral; 10e. Joao de Castro; 32e. Bartolomeu Perestrelo; 35e. Gil Eanes: 38e. Vasco da Gama; 42e. Joao de Lisboa; 45e. Joao Rodrigues Cabrilho; 60e. Nuno Tristao; 65e. Joaoda Nova; 70e. Fernao de Magalhaes (Magellan); 75e. Pedro Fernandes de Queiros; 80e. Diogo Gomes; 100e. Diogo de Silves; 200e. Estevao Gomes; 250e. Diogo Cao; 350e. Bartolomeu Dias.

452 Score and Singers

1990. Anniversaries. Multicoloured.
2191 32e. Type **452** (centenary of "A Portuguesa" (national anthem)) 50 15
2192 70e. Students and teacher (700th anniv of granting of charter to Lisbon University) (vert) . . . . 1·70 75

453 Santo Tirso Post Office

1990. Europa. Post Office Buildings. Multicoloured.
2193 80e. Type **453** . . . . . . 1·40 75
MS2194 139 × 111 mm. 80e. × 2 Type **453**; 80e. × 2 19th-century Mail Coach Office . . . . . . 22·00 5·50

454 Stamping Letter

1990. "Stamp World London 90" International Stamp Exhibition and 150th Anniv of the Penny Black. Sheet 111 × 140 mm.
MS2195 **454** 250e. multicoloured 7·75 7·75

455 Street with Chairs under Trees

1990. Greetings Stamps. Multicoloured.
2196 60e. Type **455** . . . . . . 1·10 50
2197 60e. Hand holding bouquet out of car window . . . . 1·10 50
2198 60e. Man with bouquet crossing street . . . . . 1·10 50
2199 60e. Women with bouquet behind pillar box . . . . 1·10 50

456 Camilo Castelo Branco (writer)

1990. Death Anniversaries. Multicoloured.
2200 65e. Type **456** (centenary) 1·20 65
2201 70e. Brother Bartolomeu dos Martires (Bishop of Braga, 400th anniv) . . . 1·40 75

457 Barketta

1990. 15th-Century Explorers' Ships. Mult.
2202 32e. Type **457** 45 10
2203 60e. Carvel-built fishing boat 1·20 55
2204 70e. Nau . . . . 1·40 80
2205 95e. Caravel . . . . 1·90 1·10

1990. 20th-Century Portuguese Paintings (6th series). As T **438**. Multicoloured.
2206 32e. "Dom Sebastiao" (Costa Pinheiro) 45 10
2207 60e. "Domestic Scene with Green Dog" (Paula Rego) 1·10 60
2208 95e. "Homage to Magritte" (Jose de Guimaraes) . . . 2·00 95
MS2209 138 × 112 mm. Nos. 2206/8 5·25 5·25
MS2210 138 × 145 mm. Nos. 2166/8 and 2206/8 . . . . 9·00 9·00

458 Pena Palace

1990. National Palaces (2nd series). Mult.
2211 32e. Type **458** 45 10
2212 60e. Vila Palace . . . . . . 1·20 55
2213 70e. Mafra Palace . . . . . 1·40 75
2214 120e. Guimaraes Palace . . 1·90 1·10

459 Carneiro

1990. 10th Death Anniv of Francisco Sa Carneiro (founder of Popular Democratic Party and Prime Minister, 1980).
2215 **459** 32e. black and brown . . 55 20

460 Steam Locomotive No. 02, 1887

1990. Centenary of Rossio Railway Station, Lisbon, Multicoloured.
2216 32e. Type **460** 45 10
2217 60e. Steam locomotive No. 010, 1891 . . . . . 1·20 55
2218 70e. Steam locomotive No. 071, 1916 . . . . . 1·40 75
2219 95e. Electric train, 1956 . . 1·90 1·00
MS2220 112 × 80 mm. 200e. Station clock (39 × 29 mm) . . . . . . 5·25 5·25

1991. Portuguese Faience (2nd series). As T **450**. Multicoloured.
2221 35e. Barrel of fish and plate (Rato factory Lisbon) . . 55 20
2222 35e. Floral vase (Bica do Sapato factory) 55 20
2223 35e. Gargoyle (Costa Briozo factory, Coimbra) 55 20
2224 60e. Dish with leaf pattern (Juncal factory) . . . . . 1·10 55
2225 60e. Coffee pot (Cavaquinho factory, Oporto) . . . . 1·10 55
2226 60e. Mug (Massarelos factory, Oporto) . . . . 1·10 55
MS2227 114 × 140 mm. 250e. Plate with portrait in centre (Miragaia factory, Oporto) . . . . 5·00 5·00

461 Greater Flamingoes

1991. European Tourism Year. Multicoloured.
2228 60e. Type **461** . . . . . . 1·10 55
2229 110e. European chameleon 1·80 75
MS2230 112 × 104 mm. 250e. Red deer (39 × 31 mm) . . . . 4·50 4·50

462 "Eutelsat II" Satellite

1991. Europa. Europe in Space. Multicoloured.
2231 80e. Type **462** . . . . . . 1·40 80
MS2232 140 × 112 mm. 80e. × 2, Type **462**; 80e. × 2, "Olympus I" satellite . . . . 22·00 6·25

463 Caravel

1991. 16th-Century Explorers' Ships. Mult.
2233 35e. Type **463** 45 10
2234 75e. Port view of nau . . . 1·30 55
2235 80e. Stern view of nau . . . 1·40 70
2236 110e. Galleon . . . . 1·80 75

464 "Isabella of Portugal and Philip the Good" (anon)

1991. "Europhalia 91 Portugal" Festival, Belgium. Sheet 140 × 112 mm.
MS2237 **464** 300e. multicoloured 7·75 7·75

465 Emerald and Diamond Bow

1991. "Royal Treasures" Exhibition, Ajuda Palace (1st issue). Multicoloured.
2238 35e. Type **465** 45 15
2239 60e. Royal sceptre . . . . . 1·10 55
2240 70e. Sash of the Grand Cross . . . . 1·40 65
2241 80e. Hilt of sabre . . . . . 2·20 90
2242 140e. Crown . . . . 1·30 60
See also Nos. 2270/4.

466 Antero de Quental (writer)

1991. Anniversaries. Multicoloured.
2243 35e. Type **466** (death centenary) 45 15
2244 110e. Arrival of expedition and baptism of Sonyo prince (500th anniv of first Portuguese missionary expedition to the Congo) . . . . 1·90 85

467 Faculty of Architecture, Oporto University (Siza Vieira)

1991. Architecture. Multicoloured.
2245 35e. Type **467** 45 10
2246 60e. Torre do Tombo (Arsenio Cordeiro Associates) 90 40
2247 80e. Maria Pia bridge over River Douro (Edgar Cardoso) and Donna Maria bridge . . . . . . 1·40 65
2248 110e. Setubal–Braga highway . . . . 1·80 75

468 King Manoel I creating Public Post, 1520

1991. History of Communications in Portugal. Mult.
2249 35e. Type **468** 45 10
2250 60e. Woman posting letter and telegraph operator (merging of posts and telegraph operations, 1881) 90 45
2251 80e. Postman, mail van and switchboard operator (creation of Posts and Telecommunications administration, 1911) . . 1·30 65
MS2252 140 × 111 mm. 110e. Modern means of communications (introduction of priority mail service, 1991) . . . . 1·80 1·80

469 Show Jumping

1991. Olympic Games, Barcelona (1992) (1st issue). Multicoloured.
2253 35e. Type **469** 45 10
2254 60e. Fencing 90 40
2255 80e. Shooting . . . . 1·40 65
2256 110e. Yachting . . . . . . 1·80 75
See also Nos. 2295/8.

470 Peugeot "19", 1899

1991. Caramulo Automobile Museum. Mult.
2257 35e. Type **470** 45 10
2258 60e. Rolls Royce "Silver Ghost", 1911 . . . . . . 90 40

2259 80e. Bugatti "35B", 1930 . . 1·40 70
2260 110e. Ferrari "1965 Inter", 1950 . . . . 1·60 75
MS2261 140 × 111 mm. 70e. × 2 Mercedes Benz 380K (1934); 70e × 2 Hispano-Suiza H6b (1924) 3·75 3·75
See also Nos. 2275/**MS**2279.

1992. Portuguese Faience (3rd series). As T **450**. Multicoloured.
2262 40e. Jug (Viana do Castelo factory) 55 30
2263 40e. Plate with flower design ("Ratinho" faience, Coimbra) 55 30
2264 40e. Dish with lid (Estremoz factory) 55 30
2265 65e. Decorated violin by Wescislau Cifka (Constancia factory, Lisbon) . . . . 1·00 45
2266 65e. Figure of man seated on barrel (Calvaquinho factory, Oporto) . . . . 1·00 45
2267 65e. Figure of woman (Fervenca factory, Oporto) . . . . 1·00 45
MS2268 112 × 140 mm. 260e. Political figures by Rafael Bordalo Pinheiro (Caldas da Rainha factory) (44 × 38 mm) . . . . 3·50 3·50

471 Astrolabe (Presidency emblem)

1992. Portuguese Presidency of European Community.
2269 **471** 65e. multicoloured . . . 95 45

1992. "Royal Treasures" Exhibition, Ajuda Palace (2nd issue). As T **465**. Multicoloured.
2270 38e. Coral diadem 45 15
2271 65e. Faberge clock 90 45
2272 70e. Gold tobacco box studded with diamonds and emeralds by Jacquemin 1·20 65
2273 85e. Royal sceptre with dragon supporting crown 1·50 80
2274 125e. Necklace of diamond stars by Estevao de Sousa 1·10 55

1992. Oeiras Automobile Museum. As T **470**. Multicoloured.
2275 38e. Citroen "Torpedo", 1922 . . . . 45 10
2276 65e. Robert Schneider, 1914 1·10 45
2277 85e. Austin "Seven", 1933 1·30 65
2278 120e. Mercedes Benz armoured "770", 1938 . . 1·60 75
MS2279 140 × 111 mm. 70e. × 2 Renault 10/14 (1911); 70e. × 2 Ford Model T (1927) . . . . 3·75 3·75

472 Portuguese Traders

1992. 450th Anniv of First Portuguese Contacts with Japan (1st issue). Details of painting attributed to Kano Domi. Multicoloured.
2280 38e. Type **472** 45 10
2281 120e. Portuguese visitors with gifts . . . . 1·60 75
See also Nos. 2342/4.

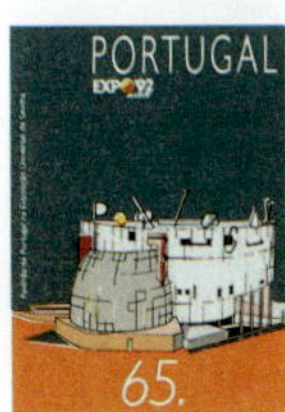

473 Portuguese Pavilion

474 Cross-staff

1992. "Expo '92" World's Fair, Seville.
2282 **473** 65e. multicoloured . . . 85 40

1992. Nautical Instruments (1st series). Mult.
2283 60e. Type **474** 75 30
2284 70e. Quadrant 95 55
2285 100e. Astrolabe 95 55
2286 120e. Compass . . . . . . 1·60 75
MS2287 140 × 112 mm. Nos. 2283/6 4·25 4·25
See also Nos. 2318/21.

475 Royal All Saints Hospital, Lisbon

1992. Anniversaries. Multicoloured.
2288 38e. Type **475** (500th anniv of foundation) 55 25
2289 70e. Lucia, Francisco and Jacinta (75th anniv of apparition of Our Lady at Fatima) 90 40
2290 120e. Crane and docks (centenary of Port of Leixoes) . . . . 1·60 70

476 Columbus with King Joao II

1992. Europa. 500th Anniv of Discovery of America. Multicoloured.
2291 85e. Type **476** . . . . . . 1·30 60
MS2292 Six sheets (a) 260e. brown and black (Type **479**); (b) 260e. blue and black (Columbus sighting land); (c) 260e. purple and black (Landing of Columbus); (d) 260e. lilac and black (Columbus welcomed at Barcelona); (e) 260e. black (Columbus presenting natives); (f) 260e. black ("America", Columbus and "Liberty") . . . . 49·00 25·00

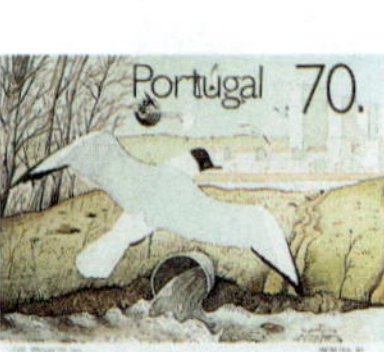

478 Black-headed Gull flying over contaminated River **479** Running

1992. 2nd United Nations Conference on Environment and Development, Rio de Janeiro. Multicoloured.
2293 70e. Type **478** 95 40
2294 120e. River kingfisher and butterfly beside clean river 1·50 80
Nos. 2293/4 were issued together, se-tenant, forming a composite design.

1992. Olympic Games, Barcelona (2nd issue). Mult.
2295 38e. Type **479** 45 15
2296 70e. Football . . . . 1·00 50
2297 85e. Hurdling . . . . 1·20 60
2298 120e. Roller hockey . . . . 1·50 65
MS2299 140 × 112 mm. 250e. Basketball . . . . 3·25 3·25

480 Bullfighter on Horse

1992. Centenary of Campo Pequeno Bull Ring, Lisbon. Multicoloured.
2300 38e. Type **480** 45 15
2301 65e. Bull charging at horse 90 40
2302 70e. Bullfighter attacking bull . . . . 1·10 60
2303 155e. Bullfighter flourishing hat . . . . 1·80 90
MS2304 140 × 113 mm. 250e. Entrance to ring (35 × 50 mm) 3·25 3·25

482 Star

1992. European Single Market.
2313 **482** 65e. multicoloured . . . 85 40

483 Industrial Safety Equipment

1992. European Year of Health, Hygiene and Safety in the Workplace.
2314 **483** 120e. multicoloured . . . 1·60 70

484 Post Office Emblem

1993. No value expressed.
2315 **484** (–) red and black 55 25
No. 2315 was sold at the current first class inland letter rate. This was 42e. at time of issue.

485 Graphic Poem

1993. Birth Centenary of Jose de Almada Negreiros (artist and poet). Multicoloured.
2316 40e. Type **485** 45 20
2317 65e. Trawlers (painting) . . 90 45

486 Sand Clock

1993. Nautical Instruments (2nd series). Mult.
2318 42e. Type **486** 45 20
2319 70e. Nocturlabio . . . . . 1·00 45
2320 90e. Kamal . . . . 1·20 65
2321 130e. Back-staff . . . . . . 1·70 75

487 View from Window

1993. Europa. Contemporary Art. Untitled paintings by Jose Escada. Multicoloured.
2322 90e. Type **487** . . . . . . 1·30 60
MS2323 140 × 112 mm. 90e. × 2 Type **487**; 90e. × 2 Body parts 5·50 5·50

488 Rossini and "The Barber of Seville"

1993. Bicentenary of San Carlos National Theatre, Lisbon. Multicoloured.
2324 42e. Type **488** 45 20
2325 70e. Verdi and "Rigoletto" 1·00 45
2326 90e. Wagner and "Tristan and Isolde" . . . . 1·20 65
2327 130e. Mozart and "The Magic Flute" . . . . . . 1·70 70
MS2328 140 × 112 mm. 300e. Exterior of theatre (39 × 29 mm) 3·50 3·50

489 Fireman's Helmet

1993. 125th Anniv of Association of Volunteer Firemen of Lisbon.
2329 **489** 70e. multicoloured . . . 90 40

490 Santos-o-Velho, Lisbon

491 "Angel of the Annunciation" (from Oporto Cathedral)

1993. Union of Portuguese-speaking Capital Cities.
2330 **490** 130e. multicoloured . . . 1·70 75
MS2331 140 × 112 mm. No. 2330 × 4 . . . . 5·25 5·25

1993. Sculptures (1st series). Multicoloured.
2332 42e. Type **491** 45 15
2333 70e. "St Mark" (Cornelius de Holanda) (horiz) . . . 95 45
2334 75e. "Madonna and Child" 1·10 45
2335 90e. "Archangel St. Michael" . . . . . . 1·20 55
2336 130e. "Count of Ferreira" (Soares dos Reis) . . . . 1·70 80
2337 170e. "Construction" (Heldar Batista) . . . . . 2·10 95
MS2338 112 × 140 mm. 75e. Marble bust of Agrippina the Elder; 75e. "Virgin of the Annunciation" (Master of the Royal Tombs); 75e. "The Widow" (Teixeira Lopes); 75e. "Love Ode" (Canto da Maya) 3·50 3·50
See also Nos. 2380/**MS**2386 and 2466/**MS**2472.

492 Road Tanker and Electric Tanker Train

1993. Int Railways Congress, Lisbon. Mult.
2339 90e. Type **492** . . . . . . 1·00 45
2340 130e. Electric train and traffic jam . . . . 1·60 75
MS2341 140 × 112 mm. 300e. Train 3·25 3·25

493 Japanese Man with Musket

1993. 450th Anniv of First Portuguese Visit to Japan (2nd issue). Multicoloured.
2342 42e. Type **493** 45 20
2343 130e. Portuguese missionaries . . . . . . 1·70 75
2344 350e. Traders carrying goods . . . . 4·00 1·80

494 Peniche Trawler

1993. Trawlers (1st series). Multicoloured.
2345 42e. Type **494** 45 20
2346 70e. Peniche type trawler . . 85 40
2347 90e. "Germano 3" (steam trawler) . . . . 1·10 55
2348 130e. "Estrela 1" (steam trawler) . . . . 1·50 65
See also Nos. 2392/5.

495 Rural Post Bag, 1800

1993. Post Boxes. Multicoloured.
2349 42e. Type **495** 45 20
2350 70e. 19th-century wall-mounted box for railway travelling post office . . . 85 40
2351 90e. 19th-century pillar box 1·10 55
2352 130e. Modern multi-function post box . . . . 1·50 65
MS2353 140 × 112 mm. 300e. 19th-century box for animal-drawn post wagons . . . . . 3·25 3·25

496 Imperial Eagle

1993. Endangered Birds of Prey. Multicoloured.
2354 42e. Type **496** 45 20
2355 70e. Eagle owl . . . . . . 1·10 45
2356 130e. Peregrine falcon . . . 1·60 80
2357 350e. Hen harrier . . . . . 3·75 1·70

497 Knot

1993. 40th Anniv of Brazil–Portugal Consultation and Friendship Treaty.
2358 **497** 130e. multicoloured . . . 1·50 70

498 Arms

1993. 850th Anniv of Zamora Conference (recognizing Afonso I as King of Portugal). Sheet 106 × 114 mm.
MS2359 **498** 150e. multicoloured 1·80 1·80

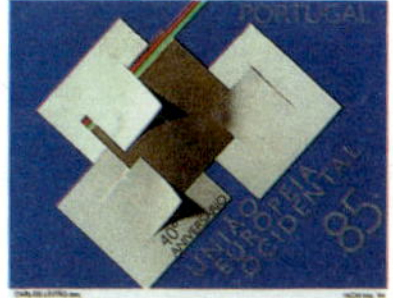
499 Stylized Map of Member Nations

1994. 40th Anniv of Western European Union.
2360 **499** 85e. multicoloured . . . 90 45

500 Olympic Rings as Torch Flame

1994. Centenary of Int Olympic Committee. Mult.
2361 100e. Type **500** . . . . . . 1·10 55
2362 100e. "100" and rings . . . 1·10 55

501 Oliveira Martins (historian)

1994. Centenaries. Multicoloured.
2363 45e. Type **501** (death) . . . 45 20
2364 100e. Florbela Espanca (poet, birth) . . . . . . 1·10 60

502 Map and Prince Henry (½-size illustration)

1994. 600th Birth Anniv of Prince Henry the Navigator.
2365 **502** 140e. multicoloured . . . 1·50 75

503 Dove

1994. 20th Anniv of Revolution.
2366 **503** 75e. multicoloured . . . 85 40

504 Mounted Knight and Explorer with Model Caravel

1994. Europa. Discoveries. Multicoloured.
2367 100e. Type MS504 . . . . 1·10 55
MS2368 140 × 112 mm. 100e. × 2 Type **504**; 100e. × 2 Millet and explorer with model caravel . . 3·75 3·75

505 Emblem

1994. International Year of the Family.
2369 **505** 45e. red, black and lake 45 20
2370 140e. red, black and green . . . . 1·60 80

506 Footballer kicking Ball and World Map

1994. World Cup Football Championship, U.S.A. Multicoloured.
2371 100e. Type **506** . . . . . . 1·10 55
2372 140e. Ball and footballers' legs . . . . 1·50 75

507 King Joao II of Portugal and King Fernando of Spain (½-size illustration)

1994. 500th Anniv of Treaty of Tordesillas (defining Portuguese and Spanish spheres of influence).
2373 **507** 140e. multicoloured . . . 1·50 75

508 Music

1994. Lisbon, European Capital of Culture. Multicoloured.
2374 45e. Type **508** 40 20
2375 75e. Photography and cinema 80 30
2376 100e. Theatre and dance . . 95 55
2377 140e. Art . . . . 1·40 75
MS2378 140 × 112 mm. Nos. 2374/7 4·25 4·25

509 Emblem

1994. Portuguese Road Safety Year.
2379 **509** 45e. red, green and black 45 15

1994. Sculptures (2nd series). As T **491**. Mult.
2380 45e. Carved stonework from Citania de Briteiros (1st century) (horiz) 40 20
2381 75e. Visigothic pilaster (7th century) 55 30
2382 80e. Capital from Amorim Church (horiz) 85 45
2383 100e. Laying Christ's body in tomb (attr Joao de Ruao) (Monastery Church of Santa Cruz de Coimbra) (horiz) . . . . 1·00 50
2384 140e. Carved wood reliquary (Santa Maria Monastery, Alcobaca) (horiz) . . . . 1·40 75
2385 180e. Relief of Writers (Leopoldo de Almeida) (Lisbon National Library) (horiz) . . . . 2·00 90
MS2386 112 × 140 mm. 75e. Queen Urraca's tomb (Santa Maria Monastery, Alcobaca); 75e. Count of Ourem tomb (Colegiada de Ourem Church); 75e. Joao de Noronha and Isabel de Sousa's tomb (Santa Maria Church, Obidos); 75e. Mausoleum of Admiral Machado dos Santos (Alto de Sao Joao Cemetery, Lisbon) . . . . 2·75 2·75

510 Falconer, Peregrine Falcon and Dog

1994. Falconry. Designs showing a peregrine falcon in various hunting scenes. Multicoloured.
2387 45e. Type **510** 40 20
2388 75e. Falcon chasing duck . . 80 35
2389 100e. Falconer approaching falcon with dead duck . . 1·00 55
2390 140e. Falcons . . . . 1·40 75
MS2391 97 × 121 mm. 250e. Hooded falcon on falconer's arm . . . 2·50 2·50

511 "Maria Arminda"

1994. Trawlers (2nd series). Multicoloured.
2392 45e. Type **511** 40 20
2393 75e. "Bom Pastor" 80 35
2394 100e. Aladores trawler with triplex haulers . . . . . 1·00 55
2395 140e. "Sueste" . . . . . . 1·40 75

512 19th-century Horse-drawn Wagon

1994. Postal Transport. Multicoloured.
2396 45e. Type **512** 40 20
2397 75e. Travelling Post Office sorting carriage No. C7, 1910 . . . . 80 40
2398 100e. Mercedes mail van, 1910 . . . . 1·00 45
2399 140e. Volkswagen mail van, 1950 . . . . 1·40 75
MS2400 140 × 112 mm. 250e. Daf truck, 1983A . . . . 2·75 2·75

513 Multiple Unit Set, Sintra Suburban Railway (½-size illustration)

1994. Modern Electric Locomotives (1st series). Multicoloured.
2401 45e. Type **513** 40 20
2402 75e. Locomotive No. 5611-7 (national network) 75 40
2403 140e. Lisbon Underground train . . . . 1·40 70
See also No. 2465.

514 Medal

1994. 150th Anniv of Montepio Geral Savings Bank (45e.) and World Savings Day (100e.). Mult.
2404 45e. Type **514** 45 20
2405 100e. Coins and bee . . . . 1·00 50

515 St. Philip's Fort, Setubal

1994. Pousadas (hotels) in Historic Buildings. Multicoloured.
2406 45e. Type **515** 40 20
2407 75e. Obidos Castle 80 40
2408 100e. Convent of Loios, Evora . . . . 1·00 45
2409 140e. Santa Marinha Monastery, Guimaraes . . 1·40 75

516 Businessman and Tourist

1994. American Society of Travel Agents World Congress, Lisbon.
2410 **516** 140e. multicoloured . . . 90 70

517 Statuette of Missionary, Mozambique

1994. Evangelization by Portuguese Missionaries. Multicoloured.
2411 45e. Type **517** 40 20
2412 75e. "Child Jesus the Good Shepherd" (carving), India 80 40
2413 100e. Chalice, Macao . . . 1·00 45
2414 140e. Carving of man in frame, Angola (horiz) . . 1·40 75

518 Africans greeting Portuguese

1994. 550th Anniv of First Portuguese Landing in Senegal.
2415 **518** 140e. multicoloured . . . 90 70

519 Battle Scene (detail of the panel, Hall of Battles, Fronteira Palace, Lisbon)

1994. 350th Anniv of Battle of Montijo. Sheet 63 × 83 mm.
MS2416 **519** 150e. multicoloured 1·40 1·40

520 Adoration of the Wise Men

1994. Christmas. Sheet 140 × 111 mm.
MS2417 **520** 150e. multicoloured . . . 1·40 1·40

521 Great Bustard

1995. European Nature Conservation Year. Multicoloured.
2418 42e. Type **521** 40 20
2419 90e. Osprey 90 50
2420 130e. Schreiber's green lizard . . . . 1·30 60
MS2421 140 × 112 mm. Nos. 2418/20 3·25 3·25

522 St. John and Sick Man

1995. 500th Birth Anniv of St. John of God (founder of Order of Hospitallers).
2422 **522** 45e. multicoloured . . . 40 20

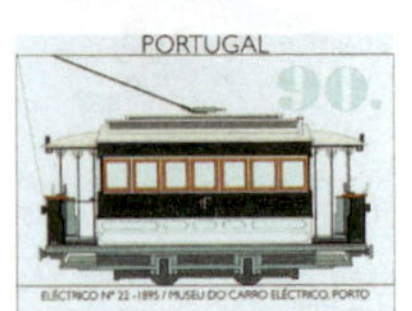

523 Electric Tramcar No. 22, 1895

1995. Centenaries of Trams and Motor Cars in Portugal. Multicoloured.
2423 90e. Type **523** 85 40
2424 130e. Panhard and Levassor motor car . . . . 1·20 65

524 Bread Seller

1995. 19th-century Itinerant Trades. Multicoloured.
2425 1e. Type **524** 10 10
2426 2e. Laundrywoman 10 10
2427 3e. Broker 10 10
2428 5e. Broom seller 10 10
2429 10e. Fish seller 10 10
2431 20e. Spinning-wheel and spoon seller 20 10
2432 30e. Olive oil and vinegar seller 25 10
2433 40e. Seller of indulgences 30 15
2434 45e. General street trader 40 20
2435 47e. Hot chestnut seller . . 40 20
2436 49e. Clothes mender . . . 40 20
2437 50e. Fruit seller 50 25
2437a 50e. Pottery seller 50 25
2438 51e. Knife grinder 35 20
2439 75e. Whitewasher 80 40
2440 78e. Cloth seller 70 35
2440b 80e. Carrier/messenger boy 80 40
2440c 85e. Goose seller 75 40
2440d 86e. Bread seller 65 30
2440e 95e. Coachman 75 40
2441 100e. Mussels seller 90 50
2441a 100e. Milk seller 80 40
2442 210e. Basket seller . . . . 1·80 90
2443 250e. Water seller . . . . 2·20 1·10
2447 250e. Pastry seller . . . . 2·20 1·10

526 Emblem

1995. 50th Anniv of U.N.O. Multicoloured.
2449 75e. Type **526** 65 35
2450 135e. Clouds and emblem 1·30 65
MS2451 140 × 111 mm. No. 2449/50 each × 2 . . . . 4·25 4·25

527 Evacuees from Gibraltar arriving at Madeira (½-size illustration)

1995. Europa. Peace and Freedom. Portuguese Neutrality during Second World War. Mult.
2452 95e. Type **527** 90 45
2453 95e. Refugees waiting at Lisbon for transatlantic liner and Aristides de Sousa Mendes (Portuguese Consul in Bordeaux) 90 45

528 "St. Antony holding Child Jesus" (painting)

1995. 800th Birth Anniv of St. Antony of Padua (Franciscan preacher). Multicoloured.
2454 45e. Type **528** 40 20
2455 75e. St. Antony with flowers (vert) 75 35
2456 135e. "St. Antony holding Child Jesus" (statue) . . . 1·30 65
MS2457 96 × 110 mm. 250e. "St. Anthony holding Baby Jesus" (18th-century Madeiran statue) 5·00 5·00

529 Carpenters with Axes and Women with Water, 1395

1995. 600th Anniv of Fire Service in Portugal. Multicoloured.
2458 45e. Type **529** 40 20
2459 80e. Fire cart and men carrying barrels of water, 1834 . . . . 80 35
2460 95e. Merryweather steam-powered fire engine, 1867 90 55
2461 135e. Zoost fire engine No. 1, 1908 . . . . . . 1·20 65
MS2462 Two sheets, each 120 × 100 mm. (a) 4 × 45e. Dutch fire engine, 1701; (b) 4 × 75e. Picota fire engine, 1780 and Portuguese fire cart, 1782 . . . 4·00 4·00

530 Coronation

1995. 500th Anniv of Accession of King Manoel I.
2463 **530** 45e. brown, yellow and red 40 20
MS2464 112 × 140 mm. No. 2463 × 4 . . . . 2·10 2·10

1995. Modern Electric Locomotives (2nd series). As T **513**.
2465 80e. multicoloured 70 35
DESIGN: 80e. Articulated trams.

1995. Sculptures (3rd series). As T **491**. Multicoloured.
2466 45e. "Warrior" (castle statue) 40 20
2467 75e. Double-headed fountain 75 35
2468 80e. "Truth" (monument to Eca de Queiros by Antonio Teixeira Lopes) 75 40
2469 95e. First World War memorial, Abrantes (Ruy Gameiro) 85 50
2470 135e. "Fernao Lopes" (Martins Correia) . . . . 1·20 65
2471 190e. "Fernando Pessoa" (Lagoa Henriques) . . . 1·80 85
MS2472 112 × 140 mm. 75e. "Knight" (from Chapel of the Ferreiros); 75e. "King Jose I" (J. Machado de Castro), Commerce Square, Lisbon; 75e. "King Joao IV" (Francisco Franco), Vila Vicosa; 75e. "Vimara Peres" (Barata Feyo), Oporto Cathedral Square . . . 2·50 2·50

531 "Portugal's Guardian Angel" (sculpture, Diogo Pires)

533 Archangel Gabriel

532 Queiroz

1995. Art of the Period of Discoveries (15th–16th centuries). Multicoloured.
2473 45e. Type **531** 40 20
2474 75e. Reliquary of Queen Leonor (Master Joao) . . 75 35
2475 80e. "Don Manuel" (sculpture, Nicolas Chanterenne) 75 40
2476 95e. "St. Anthony" (painting, Nuno Goncalves) 85 50
2477 135e. "Adoration of the Three Wise Men" (painting, Grao Vasco) . . 1·20 65
2478 190e. "Christ on the Way to Calvary" (painting, Jorge Afonso) . . . . 1·80 85
MS2479 140 × 112 mm. 200e. "St. Vincent" (polyptych, Nuno Goncalves) . . . . 2·10 2·10

1995. 150th Birth Anniv of Eca de Queiroz (writer).
2480 **532** 135e. multicoloured . . . 1·20 65

1995. Christmas. Multicoloured. (a) With country name at foot.
2481 80e. Type **533** . . . . . . 1·10 90
MS2482 112 × 140 mm. No. 2481 × 4 4·25 4·25

(b) With country name omitted.
2483 80e. Type **533** 75 70
MS2484 112 × 140 mm. No. 2483 × 4 . . . . 5·25 5·25

534 Airbus Industrie A340/300

1995. 50th Anniv of TAP Air Portugal.
2485 **534** 135e. multicoloured . . . 1·20 65

535 King Carlos I of Portugal (½-size illustration)

1996. Centenary of Oceanographic Expeditions. Multicoloured.
2486 95e. Type **535** 85 50
2487 135e. Prince Albert I of Monaco . . . . 1·30 60

536 Books

1996. Anniversaries. Multicoloured.
2488 80e. Type **536** (bicentenary of National Library) . . . 75 35
2489 200e. Hand writing with quill pen (700th anniv of adoption of Portuguese as official language) . . . . 1·80 90

537 Joao de Deus (poet and author of reading primer)

1996. Writers' Anniversaries. Multicoloured.
2490 78e. Type **537** (death centenary) 75 35
2491 140e. Joao de Barros (historian, philosopher and grammarian, 500th birth) . . . . 1·30 65

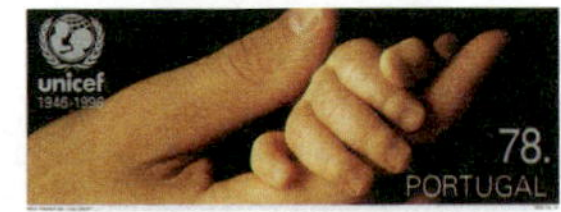

538 Holding Child's Hand (½-size illustration)

1996. 50th Anniv of UNICEF. Multicoloured.
2492 78e. Type **538** 75 40
2493 140e. Children of different races . . . . 1·20 60

539 Helena Vieira da Silva (artist, self-portrait)

1996. Europa. Famous Women.
2494 **539** 98e. multicoloured . . . 90 45
MS2495 140 × 112 mm. No. 2494 × 3 . . . . 2·75 2·75

540 Match Scene

1996. European Football Championship, England. Multicoloured.
2496 78e. Type **540** 70 40
2497 140e. Match scene (different) 1·30 60
MS2498 140 × 112 mm. Nos. 2496/7 2·10 2·10

541 Caravel and Arms (½-size illustration)

1996. 500th Death Anniv of Joao Vaz Corte-Real (explorer). Multicoloured.
2499 140e. Type **541** . . . . . . 1·30 70
MS2500 90 × 127 mm. 315e. Close-up of caravel in Type **541** (39 × 30 mm) . . . . 2·75 2·75

542 Wrestling

1996. Olympic Games, Atlanta. Multicoloured.
2501 47e. Type **542** 40 20
2502 78e. Show jumping 75 35
2503 98e. Boxing 90 50
2504 140e. Running . . . . . . 1·20 70
MS2505 96 × 110 mm. 300e. Athletes at starting blocks . . . . . . 2·50 2·50

543 Hilario and Guitar

1996. Death Centenary of Augusto Hilario (fado singer).
2506 **543** 80e. multicoloured . . . 75 35

544 Antonio Silva (actor)

1996. Centenary of Motion Pictures. Multicoloured.
2507 47e. Type **544** 40 20
2508 78e. Vasco Santana (actor) 65 35
2509 80e. Laura Alves (actress) 65 35
2510 98e. Auelio Pais dos Reis (director) 85 40
2511 100e. Leitao de Barros (director) 90 50
2512 140e. Antonio Lopes Ribeiro (director) . . . . 1·30 65
MS2513 Two sheets, each 112 × 140 mm. (a) Nos. 2507/9; (b) Nos. 2510/12 . . . . 4·75 4·75
MS2514 141 × 111 mm. Nos. 2507/12 5·00 5·00

545 King Afonso V

1996. 550th Anniv of Alphonsine Collection of Statutes.
2515 **545** 350e. multicoloured . . . 3·00 1·50

546 Perdigao

1996. Birth Centenary of Jose de Azeredo Perdigao (lawyer and Council of State member).
2516 **546** 47e. multicoloured . . . 45 20

547 Aveiro

1996. District Arms (1st series). Multicoloured.
2517 47e. Type **547** 40 20
2518 78e. Beja 65 35
2519 80e. Braga 70 35
2520 98e. Braganca 85 40
2521 100e. Castelo Branco . . . 90 50
2522 140e. Coimbra . . . . . . 1·30 65
MS2523 Two sheets, each 140 × 112 mm. (a) Nos. 2517/19; (b) Nos. 2520/2 . . . . 4·50 4·50
See also Nos. 2579/**MS**85 and 2648/**MS**54.

548 Henry of Burgundy (governor of Portucale) and his Wife Theresa

1996. 900th Anniv of Foundation of County of Portucale by King Afonso VI of Leon and Castille.
2524 **548** 47e. multicoloured . . . 45 20

549 Rojoes (Pork dish)

1996. Traditional Portuguese Dishes (1st series). Multicoloured.
2525 47e. Type **549** 40 20
2526 78e. Boticas trout 65 30
2527 80e. Oporto tripe 70 30
2528 98e. Baked cod with jacket potatoes 85 40
2529 100e. Aveiro eel 90 55
2530 140e. Peniche lobster . . . 1·30 65
See also Nos. 2569/74.

550 Lisbon Postman, 1821

1996. 175th Anniv of Home Delivery Postal Service. Multicoloured.
2531 47e. Type **550** 40 20
2532 78e. Postman, 1854 . . . . 65 35
2533 98e. Rural postman, 1893 85 40
2534 100e. Postman, 1939 . . . . 90 50
2535 140e. Modern postman, 1992 . . . . 1·30 65

551 King Manoel I in Shipyard

1996. 500th Anniv (1997) of Discovery of Sea-route to India by Vasco da Gama (1st issue). Multicoloured.
2536 47e. Type **551** 40 20
2537 78e. Departure from Lisbon 65 30
2538 98e. Fleet in Atlantic Ocean 90 50
2539 140e. Sailing around Cape of Good Hope . . . . . 1·20 65
MS2540 141 × 113 mm. 315e. "Dream of King Manuel I" (illustration from Poem IV of *The Lusiads* by Luis de Camoes) . . 2·50 2·50
See also Nos. 2592/**MS**96 and 2665/**MS**80.

552 "Banknote"

1996. 150th Anniv of Bank of Portugal.
2541 **552** 78e. multicoloured . . . 70 35

553 East Timorese Couple

1996. Rights of People of East Timor. Award of 1996 Nobel Peace Prize to Don Carlos Ximenes Belo and Jose Ramos Horton.
2542 **553** 140e. multicoloured . . . 1·20 65

554 Clouds forming Map of Europe

1996. Organization for Security and Co-operation in Europe Summit Meeting, Lisbon. Sheet 95 × 110 mm.
MS2543 **554** 200e. multicoloured 1·80 1·80

555 Portuguese Galleon

1997. Sailing Ships of the India Shipping Line. Multicoloured.
2544 49e. Type **555** 40 20
2545 80e. "Principe da Beira" (nau) 75 30
2546 100e. Bow view of "Don Fernando II e Gloria" (sail frigate) 85 50
2547 140e. Stern view of "Don Fernando II e Gloria" . . 1·30 65

556 Youth with Flower

1997. "No to Drugs – Yes to Life" (anti-drugs campaign).
2548 **556** 80e. multicoloured . . . 70 35

557 Arms

1997. Bicent of Managing Institute of Public Credit.
2549 **557** 49e. multicoloured . . . 45 20

558 Desman eating Worm

559 Moorish Girl guarding Hidden Treasure

1997. The Pyrenean Desman. Multicoloured.
2550 49e. Type **558** 45 25
2551 49e. Diving 45 25
2552 49e. With wet fur 45 25
2553 49e. Cleaning snout 45 25

1997. Europa. Tales and Legends.
2554 **559** 100e. multicoloured . . . 95 45
MS2555 140 × 107 mm. No. 2554 × 3 . . . . 2·75 2·75

560 Surfing

1997. Adventure Sports. Multicoloured.
2556 49e. Type **560** 40 20
2557 80e. Skateboarding 75 30
2558 100e. In-line skating 85 50
2559 140e. Paragliding . . . . . 1·30 65
MS2560 134 × 113 mm. 150e. B.M.X. cycling; 150e. Hang-gliding . . . . 2·50 2·50

561 Night Attack on Santarem Fortress

562 Frois with Japanese Man

563 Indian Children and Jose de Anchieta

1997. 850th Anniv of Capture from the Moors of Santarem and Lisbon. Multicoloured.
2561 80e. Type **561** 70 35
2562 80e. Victorious King Afonso riding past Lisbon city walls 70 35
MS2563 140 × 113 mm. Nos. 2561/2 each × 2 . . . . 3·00 3·00

1997. 400th Death Anniv of Father Luis Frois (author of "The History of Japan"). Multicoloured.
2564 80e. Type **562** 65 30
2565 140e. Father Frois and church (vert) . . . . . . 1·30 65
2566 140e. Father Frois and flowers (vert) . . . . . . 1·30 65

1997. Death Anniversaries of Missionaries to Brazil. Multicoloured.
2567 140e. Type **563** (400th) . . . 1·20 65
2568 350e. Antonio Vieira in pulpit (300th) . . . . . . 3·00 1·50

1997. Traditional Portuguese Dishes (2nd series). As T **549**. Multicoloured.
2569 10e. Scalded kid, Beira Baixa 10 10
2570 49e. Fried shad with bread-pap, Ribatejo 40 20
2571 80e. Lamb stew, Alentejo . . 65 35
2572 100e. Rich fish chowder, Algarve 85 40
2573 140e. Black scabbardfish fillets with maize, Madeira 1·20 65
2574 200e. Stewed octopus, Azores . . . . 1·70 90

564 Centre of Oporto

1997. "Lubrapex 97" Portuguese–Brazilian Stamp Exhibition, Oporto. UNESCO World Heritage Site. Sheet 121 × 85 mm.
MS2575 **564** 350e. multicoloured 3·25 3·25

565 Couple before Clerk

566 Laboratory, Lisbon

1997. 700th Anniv of Mutual Assurance in Portugal.
2576 **565** 100e. multicoloured . . . 85 40

1997. 50th Anniv of National Laboratory of Civil Engineering.
2577 **566** 80e. multicoloured . . . 65 35

567 King Dinis and Arms of Portugal and King Fernando IV and Arms of Castile and Leon

1997. 700th Anniv of Treaty of Alcanices (defining national frontiers).
2578 **567** 80e. multicoloured . . . 65 35

568 Evora

1997. District Arms (2nd series). Multicoloured.
2579 10e. Type **568** 10 10
2580 49e. Faro 40 20
2581 80e. Guarda 65 35
2582 100e. Leiria 85 40
2583 140e. Lisbon . . . . 1·20 65
2584 200e. Portalegre . . . . . . 1·70 90
MS2585 Two sheets, each 140 × 112 mm. (a) Nos. 2579, 2581 and 2583; (b) Nos. 2480, 2582 and 2584 . . . . 4·50 4·50

569 Chart by Lopo Homem-Reineis, 1519

1997. Portuguese Charts. Multicoloured.
2586 49e. Type **569** 40 20
2587 80e. Chart by Joao Freire, 1546 . . . . 65 30
2588 100e. Planisphere by Diogo Ribeiro, 1529 . . . . . . 90 40
2589 140e. Chart showing Tropic of Capricorn (anon), 1630 1·20 65
MS2590 139 × 112 mm. Nos. 2586/9 2·75 2·75

570 Queen Maria I and Mail Coach

1997. Bicentenary of State Postal Service.
2591 **570** 80e. multicoloured . . . 65 35

571 Erecting Landmark Monument, Quelimane

1997. 500th Anniv of Discovery of Portugal–India Sea Route (2nd issue). Multicoloured.
2592 49e. Type **571** 40 20
2593 80e. Arrival of fleet at Mozambique 65 30
2594 100e. Arrival of fleet in Mombasa 90 40
2595 140e. King of Melinde greeting Vasco da Gama 1·20 65
MS2596 140 × 113 mm. 315e. Vasco da Gama on beach at Natal . . 2·50 2·50

572 Squid

1997. "Expo'98" World Fair, Lisbon. Ocean Life (1st issue). Multicoloured.
2597 49e. Type **572** 40 20
2598 80e. Rock lobster larva . . 65 30
2599 100e. Adult "Pontellina plumata" (crustacean) . . 90 40
2600 140e. Senegal sole (pastlarva) . . . . 1·20 65
MS2601 110 × 150 mm. 100e. *Calcidiscus leptoporus*; 100e. *Tabellaria sp.* colonies . . . . 1·40 1·40
See also Nos. 2611/**MS**2615, 2621/**MS**2629 and 2630/41.

573 Sintra

1997. UNESCO World Heritage Site, Sintra. "Indepex 97" International Stamp Exhibition, New Delhi. Sheet 112 × 140 mm.
MS2602 **573** 350e. multicoloured 2·75 2·75

574 Officer and Plan of Almeida Fortress, 1848

1998. 350th Anniv of Portuguese Military Engineering. Multicoloured.
2603 50e. Type **574** 40 20
2604 80e. Officer and plan of Miranda do Oduro Fortress, 1834 . . . . . 65 30
2605 100e. Officer and plan of Moncao Fortress, 1797 90 40
2606 140e. Officer and plan of Elvas Fortress, 1806 . . . 1·20 65

575 Ivens and African Scene **576** Adoration of the Madonna (carving)

1998. Death Centenary of Roberto Ivens (explorer).
2607 **575** 140e. multicoloured . . . 1·20 60

1998. 500th Anniv of Holy Houses Misericordia (religious social relief order).
2608 80e. Type **576** 65 30
2609 100e. Attending patient (tile mural) 85 45

577 Aqueduct ocer Alcantra

1998. 250th Anniv of Aqueduct of the Free Waters (from Sintra to Lisbon). Sheet 155 × 110 mm.
MS2610 **577** 350e. multicoloured 2·75 2·75

1998. "Expo '98" World's Fair, Lisbon (2nd issue). Ocean Life. As T **572**. Multicoloured.
2611 50e. Crab ("Pilumnus" sp.) larva 40 20
2612 85e. Monkfish ("Lophius piscatonis") larva 70 40
2613 100e. Gilthead sea bream ("Sparus aurata") larva 90 45
2614 140e. Medusa ("Cladonema radiatum") . . . . 1·20 65
MS2615 112 × 140 mm. 110e. Bioluminescent protozoan (*Noctiluca miliaris*); 110e. Dinoflagellate (*Dinophysis acuta*) 1·40 1·40

578 Vasco da Gama Bridge

1998. Opening of Vasco da Gama Bridge (from Sacavem to Montijo).
2616 **578** 200e. multicoloured . . . 1·70 85
MS2617 125 × 85 mm. As No. 2616 but with background extended to edges . . . . 1·40 1·40

579 Coloured Balls

1998. 150th Anniv of Oporto Industrial Association.
2618 **579** 80e. multicoloured . . . 70 35

580 Seahorse

1998. International Year of the Ocean. Centenary of Vasco da Gama Aquarium. Multicoloured.
2619 50e. Type **580** 40 20
2620 80e. Angelfish and shoal . . 70 40

581 Diver and Astrolabe

1998. "Expo '98" World's Fair, Lisbon (3rd issue). (a) The Ocean. Multicoloured.
2621 50e. Type **581** 40 20
2622 50e. Caravel 40 20
2623 85e. Fishes and coral reef (inscr "oceanario") . . . 70 35
2624 85e. Underwater exploration equipment observing fishes 70 35
2625 140e. Mermaid and sea anemones . . . . . . 1·20 65
2626 140e. Children with hands on globe . . . . 1·20 65

(b) Miniature Sheets. Designs as T **581**.
MS2627 154 × 116 mm. 50e. Portuguese Pavilion; 85e. Pavilion of the Future; 85e. Oceanarium; 140e. Knowledge of the Seas Pavilion; 140e. Pavilion of Utopia 2·10 2·10
MS2628 Two sheets, each 147 × 90 mm. (a) Nos. 2621/6; (b) 80e. Postal mascot; stamps as in No. **MS**2627 . . . . 2·10 2·10
MS2629 148 × 151 mm. Nos. 2597/ **MS**2601 and 2611/**MS**2615 . . 2·10 2·10

(c) As Nos. 2611/14 (but with Latin names removed) and 2621/6. Size 29 × 23 mm. Self-adhesive.
2630 50e. As No. 2612 . . . . . 40 20
2631 50e. Bioluminescent protozoan 40 20
2632 50e. As No. 2611 . . . . . 40 20
2633 50e. As No. 2613 . . . . . 40 20
2634 50e. Dinoflagellate 40 20
2635 50e. As No. 2614 . . . . . 40 20
2636 85e. Type **581** 75 35
2637 85e. As No. 2624 . . . . . 75 35
2638 85e. As No. 2626 . . . . . 75 35
2639 85e. As No. 2622 . . . . . 75 35
2640 85e. As No. 2623 but inscr "Portugal e os Oceanos" 75 35
2641 85e. As No. 2625 . . . . . 75 35
The designers' names and printer's imprints have been removed from Nos. 2630/41.

582 Revellers before Statues of St. Antony of Padua, St. John and St. Peter

1998. Europa. National Festivals.
2642 **582** 100e. multicoloured . . . 85 40
MS2643 140 × 108 mm. No. 2642 × 3 . . . . 2·10 2·10

583 Marie Curie

1998. Centenary of Discovery of Radium.
2644 **583** 140e. multicoloured . . . 1·20 55

584 Ferreira de Castro and Illustration to "The Jungle"

1998. Birth Centenary of Jose Ferreira de Castro (writer).
2645 **584** 50e. multicoloured . . . 40 20

585 Untitled Painting

1998. Death Centenary of Bernardo Marques (artist).
2646 **585** 85e. multicoloured . . . 70 35

586 Adam (Michelangelo) (detail from Sistine Chapel ceiling)

1998. "Juvalex '98" Stamp Exhibition. 50th Anniv of Universal Declaration of Human Rights. Sheet 90 × 55 mm.
MS2647 **586** 315e. multicoloured 2·50 2·50

1998. District Arms (3rd series). As T **568**. Multicoloured.
2648 50e. Vila Real 40 20
2649 85e. Setubal 70 35
2650 85e. Viana do Castelo (150th anniv of elevation to city) 70 35
2651 100e. Santarem 85 40
2652 100e. Viseu 85 40
2653 200e. Oporto . . . . 1·60 80
MS2654 Two sheets, each 140 × 113 mm. (a) Nos. 2648, 2650 and 2653; (b) Nos. 2649 and 2651/2 . . . . 4·50 4·50

587 Glass Production

1998. 250th Anniv of Glass Production in Marinha Grande. Multicoloured.
2655 50e. Type **587** 40 20
2656 80e. Heating glass and finished product 75 30
2657 100e. Bottles and factory . . 90 40
2658 140e. Blue bottles and glass-maker . . . . 1·50 60

588 "Sagres II" (cadet barque), Portugal

1998. Vasco da Gama Regatta. Multicoloured.
2659 50e. Type **588** 40 20
2660 85e. "Asgard II" (Irish cadet brigantine) 75 30
2661 85e. "Rose" (American replica) 75 30
2662 100e. "Amerigo Vespucci" (Italian cadet ship) . . . 85 40
2663 100e. "Kruzenshtern" (Russian cadet barque) . . 85 40
2664 140e. "Creoula" (Portuguese cadet schooner) . . . . . 1·10 65

589 Da Gama with Pilot Ibn Madjid

1998. 500th Anniv (1997) of Discovery of Sea-route to India by Vasco da Gama (3rd issue). Mult.
2665 50e. Type **551** 40 20
2666 50e. As No. 2537 . . . . . 40 20
2667 50e. As No. 2538 . . . . . 40 20
2668 50e. As No. 2539 . . . . . 40 20
2669 50e. Type **571** 40 20
2670 50e. As No. 2593 . . . . . 40 20

2671 50e. As No. 2594 . . . . . 40 20
2672 50e. As No. 2595 . . . . . 40 20
2673 50e. Type **589** 40 20
2674 50e. "Sao Gabriel" (flagship) in storm 40 20
2675 50e. Fleet arriving at Calicut 40 20
2676 50e. Audience with the Samorin of Calicut . . . 40 20
2677 80e. As No. 2674 . . . . . 65 30
2678 100e. As No. 2675 . . . . 85 40
2679 140e. As No. 2676 . . . . 1·20 60
MS2680 140 × 112 mm. 315e. King of Melinde listening to Vasco da Gama . . . . 2·50 2·50

590 Modern Mail Van

1998. Bicentenaries of Inauguration of Lisbon–Coimbra Mail Coach Service and of Re-organization of Maritime Mail Service to Brazil. Mult.
2681 50e. Type **590** 40 20
2682 140e. Mail coach and "Postilhao da America" (brigantine) . . . . 1·10 60

591 Globe and Flags of participating Countries

1998. 8th Iberian-American Summit of State Leaders and Govenors, Oporto. Sheet 90 × 55 mm.
MS2683 **591** 140e. multicoloured 1·10 1·10

592 Cave paintings

1998. Archeological Park, Coa Valley. Sheet 140 × 113 mm.
MS2684 **592** 350e. multicoloured 2·50 2·50

593 Male and Female Figures

595 Knife Grinder

594 Saramago

1998. Health Awareness.
2685 **593** 100e. multicoloured . . . 85 40

1998. Jose Saramago (winner of Nobel prize for Literature, 1998). Sheet 140 × 114 mm.
MS2686 **594** 200e. multicoloured 1·40 1·40

DENOMINATION. From No. 2687 Portugal stamps are denominated both in escudos and in euros. As no cash for this latter is in circulation, the catalogue continues to use the escudo value.

1999. 19th-Century Itinerant Trades. Multicoloured. Self-adhesive.
2687 51e. Type **595** 75 40
2688 95e. Coachman . . . . . . 1·20 55

596 Flags of European Union Members and Euro Emblem

1999. Introduction of the Euro (European currency).
2696 **596** 95e. multicoloured . . . 1·20 55

597 Galleon and Aborigines

1999. "Australia 99" International Stamp Exhibition, Melbourne. The Portuguese in Australia. Multicoloured.
2697 140e. Kangaroos and galleon . . . . 1·20 55
2698 140e. Type **597** . . . . . . 1·20 55
MS2699 137 × 104 mm. 350e. Motifs of Nos. 2697/8 (79 × 30 mm) 2·50 2·50
Nos. 2697/8 were issued together, se-tenant, forming a composite design.

598 Norton de Matos

1999. 50th Anniv of Candidature of General Jose Norton de Matos to Presidency of the Republic.
2700 **598** 80e. multicoloured . . . 65 35

599 Almeida Garrett

1999. Birth Bicentenary of Joao Bapista Almeida Garrett (writer).
2701 **599** 95e. multicoloured . . . 75 40
MS2702 130 × 105 mm. **599** 210e. multicoloured . . . . 1·40 1·40

600 Breguet 16 Bn2 Patria

1999. 25th Anniv of Sarmento de Beires and Brito Pais's Portugal–Macao Flight. Multicoloured.
2703 140e. Type **600** . . . . . . 1·20 55
2704 140e. De Havilland D.H.9 biplane . . . . 1·20 55
MS2705 137 × 104 mm. Nos. 2703/4 2·10 2·10

601 Carnation

1999. 25th Anniv of Revolution. Multicoloured.
2706 51e. Type **601** 40 20
2707 80e. National Assembly building (78 × 29 mm) . . 65 40
MS2708 140 × 108 mm. Nos. 2706/7 85 85

602 Council Emblem

1999. 50th Anniv of Council of Europe.
2709 **602** 100e. multicoloured . . . 80 40

603 Wolf and Iris (Peneda-Geres National Park)

1999. Europa. Parks and Gardens.
2710 **603** 100e. multicoloured . . . 80 40
MS2711 154 × 109 mm. No. 2710 × 3 70 70

604 Marquis de Pombal

1993. 300th Birth Anniv of Marquis de Pombal (statesman and reformer). Multicoloured.
2712 80e. Type **604** 65 35
MS2713 170 × 135 mm. 80e. Head of Marquis and part of statue; 210e. Hand holding quill . . . . . 2·10 2·10

605 Harbour

1999. "Meeting of Cultures". Return of Macao to China. Multicoloured.
2714 51e. Type **605** 40 20
2715 80e. Dancers 65 30
2716 95e. Procession of the Madonna 75 40
2717 100e. Ruins of St. Paul's Basilica 85 40
2718 140e. Garden with bust of Luis Camoes (horiz) . . . 1·10 60

606 De Havilland D.H.82A Tiger Moth

1999. 75th Anniv of Military Aeronautics. Multicoloured.
2719 51e. Type **606** 40 20
2720 51e. Supermarine Spitfire V6 fighter 40 20
2721 85e. Breguet Bre XIV A2 . . 70 35
2722 85e. SPAD VII-C1 . . . . 70 35
2723 95e. Caudron G-3 . . . . . 85 45
2724 95e. Junkers Ju 52/3m . . . 85 45
MS2725 150 × 117mm. Nos. 2719/24 4·00 4·00

607 Portion by Antonio Pedro

1999. 50th Anniv of Surrealism (modern art movement) in Portugal. Designs showing details by artist named of collective painting "Cadavre Exquis". Multicoloured.
2726 51e. Type **607** 40 20
2727 80e. Vespeira 65 30
2728 95e. Moniz Pereira 75 40
2729 100e. Fernando de Azevedo 85 40
2730 140e. Antonio Domingues 1·20 60
MS2731 175 × 153 mm. Nos. 2726/30 forming a composite design of complete picture . . . . 3·25 3·25

608 Passenger Train on Bridge

1999. Inauguration of Railway Section of the 25th of April Bridge over River Tagus, Lisbon. Mult.
2732 51e. Type **608** 40 20
2733 95e. Passenger train on bridge (different) 75 45
MS2734 Two sheets, each 140 × 110 mm. (a) 350e. Close-up of part of Type **608** (79 × 30 mm); (b) 350e. Close-up of part of No. 2733 (79 × 30 mm) . . . . 5·00 5·00

609 Heinrich von Stephan (founder)

1999. 125th Anniv of Universal Postal Union. Multicoloured.
2735 95e. Type **609** 75 40
2736 140e. Globe, letter and keyboard . . . . 1·10 55
MS2737 140 × 98 mm. 315e. Combination of motifs in Nos. 2735/6 (79 × 29 mm) . . . 2·50 2·50

610 Egg Packs

1999. Convent Sweets (1st series). Multicoloured.
2738 51e. Type **610** 40 20
2739 80e. Egg pudding 65 30
2740 95e. Angel's purses 75 40
2741 100e. Abrantes straw . . . 80 40
2742 140e. Viseu chestnuts . . . 1·10 55
2743 210e. Honey cake . . . . . 1·60 90
See also Nos. 2785/90.

611 Portuguese Troops and Moslem Ships

1999. 750th Anniv of King Afonso III's Conquest of the Algarve.
2744 **611** 100e. multicoloured . . . 80 40

612 Camara Pestana (bacteriologist)

1999. Medical Anniversaries. Multicoloured.
2745 51e. Type **612** (death centenary) 40 20
2746 51e. Ricardo Jorge (founder of National Health Institute, 60th death anniv) 40 20
2747 80e. Francisco Gentil (oncologist, 35th death anniv) 65 30
2748 80e. Egas Moniz (neurosurgeon, 125th birth anniv) 65 30
2749 95e. Joao Cid dos Santos (surgeon, 23rd death anniv) 75 40
2750 95e. Reynaldo dos Santos (arteriography researcher, 30th death anniv (2000)) 75 40

613 Jose Diogo de Mascarenhas Neto (first General Mail Lieutenant)

1999. Bicentenary of the Provisional Mail Rules (re-organization of postal system).
2751 **613** 80e. multicoloured . . . 65 30

614 Barata, Stamps and Mural

1999. Birth Centenary of Jaime Martins Barata (artist and stamp designer).
2752 **614** 80e. multicoloured . . . 65 30

615 Wise Men following Star (Maria Goncalves)

1999. Christmas. National Association of Art and Creativity for and by Handicapped Persons. Designs with artists name in brackets. Multicoloured.
2753 51e. Type **615** 40 20
2754 95e. Father Christmas delivering presents (Marta Silva) 75 40
2755 140e. Father Christmas (Luis Farinha) . . . . . 1·10 60
2756 210e. The Nativity (Maria Goncalves) . . . . 1·60 80

616 Macanese Architcture

1999. Portuguese–Chinese Cultural Mix in Macao. Sheet 138 × 90 mm.
MS2757 **616** 140e. black and red 2·50 2·50

618 "Madonna and Child" (Alvaro Pires of Evora) Maia, Oporto)

620 Golden Eagle

619 Astronaut and Space Craft

2000. 2000th Birth Anniv of Jesus Christ.
2759 **618** 52e. multicoloured . . . 40 20

2000. The Twentieth Century. Conquest of Space.
2760 **619** 86e. multicoloured . . . 65 35

2000. Birds. (1st series). Multicoloured. (a) Ordinary gum. Size 30 × 27 mm.
2761 52e. Type **620** 40 20
2762 85e. Great crested grebe . . 65 30
2763 90e. Greater flamingo . . . 70 40
2764 100e. Northern gannet . . . 80 40
2765 215e. Green-winged teal . . 1·60 90

(b) Self-adhesive gum. Size 28 × 25 mm.
2766 52e. As No. 2761 . . . . . 40 20
2767 100e. As No. 2764 . . . . 65 35

See also Nos. 2832/9.

621 Crowd and Suffragetts

2000. The Twentieth Century (2nd issue). Three sheets, each 190 × 220 mm, containing T **621** and similar multicoloured designs.
MS2768 (a) 52e. Type **621** (human Rights); 52e. Fashion through the century (59 × 29 mm); 52e. Windmills, electricity pylon and birds (ecology) (59 × 39 mm); 52e. Early airplanes, car, stylised steamlined high speed train and ship (transport); 52e. As No. 2760; 52e. Space shuttle on launch pad (conquest of Space). (b) 52e. Marcel Proust and Thomas Marin (novelists), James Joyce (writer), Franz Kafka (novelist), Fernando Pessoa (poet), Jorge Luis Borges and Samuel Beckett (writers) (literature) (49 × 29 mm); 52e. Achille-Claude Debussy, Igor Stravinsky, Arnold Schoenberg, Bela Bartok, George Gershwin (composers), Charlie Parker (saxophonist) and William (Bill) Evans (pianist) (music) (49 × 29 mm); 52e. Performers (theatre); 52e. Auditorium and performers (theatre) (59 × 29 mm); 52e. Sculptures and paintings (art) (49 × 29 mm); 52e. Abstract art (29 × 29 mm); 52e. Charlie Chaplin on left (cinema) (49 × 29 mm); 52e. Woody Allen on left (cinema and television) (29 × 29 mm); 52e. Old and modern buildings (architecture); 52e. Modern buildings (architecture); 52e. Front and aerial views of modern buildings (architecture). (c) 52e. Edmund Husser, Ludwig Wittgenstein and Martin Heidegger (philosophy); 52e. Jules Poincare, Kurt Godel and Andrei Kolmogorov (mathematics); 52e. Max Planck, Albert Einstein and Niels Bohr (physics) (49 × 29 mm); 52e. Franz Boas (anthropologist), Levi Strauss (clothing manufacturer) and Margaret Mead (anthropologist) (social science and medicine); 52e. Sigmund Freud (neurologist) and Alexander Fleming (bacteriologist) (social science and medicine) (29 × 29 mm); 52e. Christiaan Barnard performing operation (organ transplant surgeon) (medicine); 52e. Office workers, Joseph Schumpeter and John Keynes (economics); 52e. Circuit boards (technology); 52e. Fibre optics (technology) (29 × 29 mm); 52e. Binary code, Alan Tuning (mathematician) and John von Neuman (mathematician) (information technology and telecommunications); 52e. Guglielmo Marconi (physicist) and satellite aerials (information technology and telecommunications); 52e. Binary code and satellite (information technology and telecommunications) (29 × 29 mm) 10·50 10·50

622 Members' Flags forming Stars

2000. Portuguese Presidency of European Union Council.
2769 **622** 100e. multicoloured . . . 80 40

623 Native Indians

2000. 500th Anniv of Discovery of Brazil. Multicoloured.
2770 52e. Type **623** 40 20
2771 85e. Native Indians watching Pedro Alvares Cabral's fleet 65 30
2772 100e. Ship's crew and sails 80 40
2773 140e. Native Indians and Portuguese sailors meeting 1·10 60
MS2774 140 × 140 mm. Nos. 2770/3 2·50 2·50

624 "Building Europe"

2000. Europa.
2775 **624** 100e. multicoloured . . . 80 40
MS2776 154 × 109 mm. No. 2775 × 3 . . . . 2·10 2·10

625 Pope John Paul II and Children

2000. Papal Visit to Portugal. Beatification of Jacinta and Francisco Marto (Children of Fatima).
2777 **625** 52e. multicoloured . . . 40 20

626 Draisienne Bicycle, 1817

2000. "The Stamp Show 2000" International Stamp Exhibition, London. Centenary of International Cycling Union. Bicycles. Mult.
2778 52e. Type **626** 40 20
2779 85e. Michaux, 1868 . . . . 65 30
2780 100e. Ariel, 1871 . . . . . 85 40
2781 140e. Rover, 1888 . . . . . 1·10 55
2782 215e. BTX, 2000 . . . . . 1·70 85
2783 350e. GT, 2000 . . . . . . 2·75 1·40
MS2784 140 × 112 mm. Nos. 2778/83 2·50 2·50

627 Slices of Tomar

2000. Convent Sweets (2nd series). Multicoloured.
2785 52e. Type **627** 40 20
2786 85e. Rodrigo's present . . . 70 30
2787 100e. Sericaia 95 40
2788 140e. Lo bread . . . . . . 1·10 55
2789 215e. Grated bread . . . . 1·30 85
2790 350e. Royal paraiso cake . . 3·00 1·40

628 Fishing Boat and Fishes

2000. Fishermen's Day.
2791 **628** 52e. multicoloured . . . 40 20

629 Portuguese Landscapes (½-size illustration)

2000. "EXPO 2000" World's Fair, Hanover, Germany. Humanity–Nature–Technology. Mult.
2792 100e. Type **629** 75 40
MS2793 140 × 113 mm. 350e. Portuguese Pavilion, Hanover (39 × 30 mm) . . . . 2·50 2·50

630 Statue and Assembly Hall

2000. 25th Anniv of Constituent Assembly.
2794 **630** 85e. multicoloured . . . 65 30

631 Fishermen and Boat

2000. Cod Fishing. Multicoloured.
2795 52e. Type **631** 40 20
2796 85e. Fishing barquentine and fisherman at ship's wheel 65 30
2797 100e. Three fishermen and boat 75 40
2798 100e. Fisherman and dories on fishing schooner . . . 75 40
2799 140e. Fisherman rowing and fishing barquentine . . . 1·10 55
2800 215e. Fisherman and fishing schooner . . . . 1·60 85
MS2801 140 × 112 mm. Nos. 2795/2800 . . . . 4·50 4·50

632 De Queiroz

2000. Death Centenary of Eca de Queiroz (author).
2802 **632** 85e. multicoloured . . . 65 30

633 Running

2000. Olympic Games, Sydney. Multicoloured.
2803 52e. Type **633** 40 20
2804 85e. Show jumping 65 30
2805 100e. Dinghy racing 75 40
2806 140e. Diving . . . . 1·10 55
MS2807 140 × 112 mm. 85e. Fencing; 215e. Beach volleyball 2·10 2·10
Nos. 2803/6 are wrongly inscribed "Sidney".

634 Airplane and Runway

2000. Inauguration of Madeira Airport Second Runway Extension.
2808 **634** 140e. multicoloured . . . 1·10 55
MS2809 110 × 80 mm. 140e. multicoloured . . . . 2·50 2·50

635 Writing Letter on Computer

2000. 50th Anniv of Snoopy (cartoon character created by Charles Schulz). Postal Service. Mult.
2810 52e. Type **635** 40 20
2811 52e. Posting letter 40 20
2812 85e. Driving post van . . . 65 30
2813 100e. Sorting post 75 40
2814 140e. Delivering post . . . 1·10 55
2815 215e. Reading letter . . . . 1·60 85
MS2816 140 × 112 mm. Nos. 2810/15 4·25 4·25

636 Drawing, Telescope and Sextant

2000. 125th Anniv of Lisbon Geographic Society. Multicoloured.
2817 85e. Type **636** 65 30
2818 100e. Sextant and drawing 75 40
Nos. 2817/18 were issued together, se-tenant, forming a composite design.

637 Carolina Michaelis de Vasconcellos (teacher)

2001. The Twentieth Century. History and Culture. Multicoloured.
2819 85e. Type **637** 70 35
2820 85e. Miguel Bombarda (doctor and politician) . . 70 35
2821 85e. Bernardino Machado (politician) 70 35
2822 85e. Tomas Alcaide (lyricist) 70 35
2823 85e. Jose Regio (writer) . . 70 35
2824 85e. Jose Rodrigues Migueis (writer) 70 35
2825 85e. Vitorino Nemesio (scholar) 70 35
2826 85e. Bento de Jesus Caraca (scholar) 70 35

638 Athletics

2001. World Indoor Athletics Championship, Lisbon. Multicoloured.
2827 85e. Type **638** 65 30
2828 90e. Pole vault 70 35
2829 105e. Shot put 80 40
2830 250e. High jump . . . . . 1·90 90
MS2831 122 × 100 mm. 350e. hurdles . . . . 2·50 2·50

2001. Birds (2nd series). As T **620**. Multicoloured.
(a) Ordinary gum. Size 27 × 25 mm.
2832 53e. Little bustard 40 20
2833 85e. Purple swamphen . . . 65 30
2834 105e. Collared Pratincole . . 80 40
2835 140e. Black-shouldered kite 1·10 55
2836 225e. Egyptian vulture . . . 1·70 90
(b) Self-adhesive gum. (i) Size 25 × 21 mm.
2837 53e. As No. 2832 . . . . . 40 20
2838 105e. As No. 2834 . . . . 80 40
(ii) Size 48 × 22 mm.
2839 85e. Purple swamphen . . . 65 30
No. 2839 is inscribed "CorreioAzul".

639 Decorated Dish

2001. Arab Artefacts. Multicoloured.
2840 53e. Type **639** 40 20
2841 90e. Painted tile 70 30
2842 105e. Carved stone tablet and fortress 80 40
2843 140e. Coin . . . . 1·10 55
2844 225e. Carved container . . . 1·70 85
2845 350e. Jug . . . . 2·75 1·40

640 Coastal Environment (Angela M. Lopes)

2001. "Stampin' the Future". Winning Entries in Children's International Painting Competition. Multicoloured.
2846 85e. Type **640** 65 30
2847 90e. Earth, Sun and watering can (Maria G. Silva) (vert) 70 35
2848 105e. Marine life (Joao A. Ferreira) 80 40

641 Statue, Building Facade and Stained Glass Window

2001. Centenary of National Fine Arts Society. Multicoloured.
2849 85e. Type **641** 65 30
2850 105e. Painting and woman holding palette and brush 80 40
MS2851 105 × 80 mm. 350e. "Hen with Chicks" (detail) (Girao) 2·50 2·50

642 Congress in Session

2001. 25th Anniv of Portuguese Republic Constitution.
2852 **642** 85e. multicoloured . . . 65 35

643 Fishes

2001. Europa. Water Resources.
2853 **643** 105e. multicoloured . . . 80 40
MS2854 140 × 110 mm. No. 2853 × 3 . . . . 2·20 2·20

644 Couple and Heart

2001. Greetings Stamps. Multicoloured.
2855 85e. Type **644** 65 35
2856 85e. Birthday cake 65 35
2857 85e. Glasses 65 35
2858 85e. Bunch of flowers . . . 65 35
MS2859 91 × 110 mm. Nos. 2855/8 2·40 2·40

645 Open Book

2001. Porto, European City of Culture. Multicoloured.
2860 53e. Type **645** 40 20
2861 85e. Bridge and Globe . . . 65 30
2862 105e. Grand piano 80 40
2863 140e. Stage curtain . . . . 1·10 55
2864 225e. Picture frame . . . . 1·70 85
2865 350e. Firework display . . . 2·75 1·40
MS2866 140 × 110 mm. Nos. 2861/6 6·75 6·75

646 Campaign Cannon, 1773

2001. 150th Anniv of Military Museum, Lisbon. Multicoloured.
2867 85e. Type **646** 65 30
2868 105e. 16th-century armour 80 45
MS2869 140 × 112 mm. 53e. Pistol of King Jose I, 1757; 53e. Cannon on carriage, 1797; 140e. Cannon "Tigre", 1533; 140e. 15th-century helmet . . . . 2·75 2·75

647 Brown Bear

2001. Lisbon Zoo. Multicoloured.
2870 53e. Type **647** 40 20
2871 85e. Emperor tamarin . . . 65 30
2872 90e. Green iguana 70 40
2873 105e. Humboldt penguin . . 85 40
2874 225e. Toco toucan . . . . . 1·70 85
2875 350e. Giraffe . . . . 2·75 1·30
MS2876 140 × 112 mm. 85e. Indian elephant (29 × 38 mm); 85e. Grevy's zebra (29 × 39 mm); Lion (29 × 38 mm); White rhinoceros (29 × 38 mm) . . . . 4·50 4·50

648 Emblem

2001. 47th Lion's European Forum, Oporto.
2877 **648** 85e. multicoloured . . . 65 30

649 Azinhoso Pillory

2001. Pillories. Multicoloured.
2878 53e. Type **649** 40 20
2879 53e. Soajo 40 20
2880 53e. Braganca 40 20
2881 53e. Linhares 40 20
2882 53e. Arcos de Valdevez . . 40 20
2883 53e. Vila de Rua 40 20
2884 53e. Sernancelhe 40 20
2885 53e. Frechas 40 20

650 Faces

2001. United Nations Year of Dialogue among Civilizations.
2886 **650** 140e. multicoloured . . . 1·00 55

651 Disney

2001. Birth Centenary of Walt Disney (artist and film producer).
2887 53e. Type **651** 40 20
MS2888 160 × 132 mm. 53e. Huey, Dewey and Louie, and 15th-century Mudejares tiles; 53e. Mickey Mouse and 16th-century tiles forming coat of arms; 53e. Minnie Mouse and 17th-century religious allegory tiles; 53e. Goofy and 18th-century tiles of birds; 53e. Type **651**; 53e. Pluto and 19th-century tile design by Rafael Bordalo Pinheiro; 53e. Donald Duck and 19th-century tiles; 53e. Scrooge McDuck and 20th-century "Querubim Lapa" tiles; 53e. Daisy Duck and 20th-century tile designs by Manuel Cargaleiro . . . . . . 3·75 3·75

652 Royal Police Guard, 1801

2001. Bicentenary of National Guard. Multicoloured.
2889 53e. Type **652** 40 20
2890 85e. Lisbon Municipal Guard bandsman, 1834 65 30
2891 90e. Infantry helmet, 1911 and modern guardsman 65 35
2892 105e. Mounted division helmet of 1911 and modern guardsmen . . . 75 40
2893 140e. Guardsmen with motorcycle and car . . . 1·10 50
2894 350e. Customs and Excise officer and boat . . . . . 2·50 1·30
MS2895 117 × 90 mm. 225e. Mounted division helmet and guardsman of 1911 . . . . . 1·60 1·60

653 Chinese Junk

2001. Ships. Multicoloured.
2896 53e. Type **653** 40 20
2897 53e. Portuguese caravel . . 40 20

654 1c. Coin

2002. New Currency. Multicoloured.
2898 1c. Type **654** 10 10
2899 2c. 2c. coin 10 10
2900 5c. 5c. coin 10 10
2901 10c. 10c. coin 15 10
2902 20c. 20c. coin 30 20
2903 50c. 50c. coin 75 40
2904 €1 €1 coin . . . . 1·50 75
2905 €2 €2 coin . . . . 3·00 1·50

655 Horse-rider

2002. No value expressed.
2906 **655** A (28c.) multicoloured 40 20
No. 2906 was sold at the current first class inland letter rate.

657 European Bee-eater

2002. Birds (1st series). Multicoloured. (i) Ordinary gum. Size 30 × 26 mm.
2914 2c. Type **657** 10 20
2915 28c. Little tern 40 30
2916 43c. Eagle owl 65 40
2917 54c. Pin-tailed sandgrouse 80 45
2918 60c. Red-necked nightjar . . 90 55
2919 70c. Greater spotted cuckoo 1·10 30
(ii) Self-adhesive gum. Size 49 × 23 mm.
2920 43c. Little tern (different) . . 65 30
(iii) Self-adhesive gum. Size 29 × 24 mm.
2921 28c. As No. 2919 . . . . . 40 20
2922 54c. As No. 2916 . . . . . 80 40
(iiii) Self-adhesive gum. Size 27 × 23 mm.
2923 28c. As No. 2919 . . . . . 40 20
2924 54c. As No. 2916 . . . . . 80 40
See also Nos. 2988/92.

658 De Gois

2002. 500th Birth Anniv of Damiao de Gois (writer).
2925 **658** 45c. multicoloured . . . 65 30

659 Loxodromic Curve, Ship and Globe

2002. 500th Birth Anniv of Pedro Nunes (mathematician). Multicoloured.
2926 28c. Type **659** 40 20
2927 28c. Nonius (navigational instrument) 40 20
2928 €1.15 Portrait of Nunes . . 1·70 85
MS2929 140 × 105 mm Nos. 2926/8 2·50 2·50

660 Children and Flower

2002. America. Youth, Education and Literacy. Multicoloured.
2930 70c. Type **660** . . . . . . 1·10 55
2931 70c. Children, book and letters . . . . 1·10 55
2932 70c. Children and pencil . . 1·10 55

661 Refracting Telescope and Polytechnic School Observatory, Lisbon

2002. Astronomy. Multicoloured.
2933 28c. Type **661** 40 20
2934 28c. 16th-century astrolabe and Colegio dos Nobres, Lisbon 40 20
2935 43c. Quadrant and Solar Observatory, Coimbra . . 65 30
2936 45c. Terrestrial telescope and King Pedro V 45 30
2937 45c. Cassegrain telescope and King Luis 45 30
2938 54c. Earth, refracting telescope and Observatory, Ajuda . . . 80 40
*2939 €1.15 Cassegrain telescope and Saturn . . . . 1·70 85
2940 €1.75 Zeiss projector and planets . . . . 2·50 1·30
MS2941 140 × 111 mm. 70c. 18th-century armillary sphere; 70c. 19th-century theodolite . . . . 2·00 2·00

662 Square and Compass

2002. Bicentenary of Grande Oriente Lusitano (Masonic Grand Lodge).
2942 **662** 43c. multicoloured . . . 65 30

663 Clown

2002. Europa. Circus.
2943 **663** 54c. multicoloured . . . 80 40
MS2944 140 × 110 mm No. 2943 × 3 2·40 2·40

664 *Scabiosa nitens*

2002. Flowers of Azores. Multicoloured.
2945 28c. Type **664** 40 20
2946 45c. *Viburnum tinus subcordatum* 65 30
2947 54c. *Euphorbia azorica* . . . 80 40
2948 70c. *Lysimachia nemorum azorica* . . . . 1·00 55
2949 €1.15 *Bellis azorica* . . . . 1·70 85
2950 €1.75 *Spergularia azorica* 2·50 1·30
MS2951 120 × 121 mm €1.15 *Azorina vidalii*; €1.75 *Senecio malvifolius* . . . . 4·50 4·50

665 General Dynamics F-16 Fighting Falcon

2002. 50th Anniv of Portuguese Air Force. Multicoloured.
2952 28c. Type **665** 40 20
2953 43c. Sud Aviation SA 300 Puma helicopter 65 30
2954 54c. Dassault Dornier Alpha Jet A 80 40
2955 70c. Lockheed C-130 Hercules transport aircraft 1·00 55
2956 €1.25 Lockheed P-3P Orion reconnaissance aircraft . . 1·80 90
2957 €1.75 Fiat G-91 fighter aircraft . . . . 2·50 1·30
MS2958 140 × 112 mm €1.15 Four airplanes; €1.75 Aerospatiale Epsilon TB 30 . . . . 4·25 4·25

666 Gymnastics

2002. Sports and Sports Anniversaries. Multicoloured.
2959 28c. Type **666** (50th anniv of Portuguese Gymnastic Federation) 40 20
2960 28c. Walking race 40 20
2961 45c. Basketball 65 30
2962 45c. Handball 65 30
2963 54c. Roller hockey (sixth Women's World Roller Hockey Championship, Pacos de Ferriera) 75 40
2964 54c. Fencing (World Fencing Championship, Lisbon) 75 40
2965 €1.75 Footballers (World Cup Football Championship, Japan and South Korea) . . . . . . 2·50 1·20
2966 €1.75 Golf . . . . . . 2·50 1·20
MS2967 140 × 110 mm. €1 Footballer and part of football; €2 Torsos and legs of two players 4·25 4·25
Nos. **MS**2967 was inscribed for "PHILAKOREA 2002" International Stamp Exhibition, Seoul, in the margin.

667 Globe and Emblem

2002. 13th World International Economic Association Congress.
2968 **667** 70c. multicoloured . . . 1·00 50

668 Anniversary Emblem

2002. 150th Anniv of Ministry of Public Works, Transport and Housing. Multicoloured.
2969 43c. Type **668** 60 30
MS2970 144 × 123 mm. 43c. × 6, Ship and oil terminal; Locomotive; Aeroplane; Bridge and city skyline; Factories; Houses . . . 3·75 3·75

669 Portrait and Symbols of Industry and Agriculture

2002. 150th Anniv of Technical Education.
2971 **669** 43c. multicoloured . . . 60 30

670 Virgin and Child (statue) and Window, Alcobaca Monastery

671 1870 Dress Uniform

2002. UNESCO World Heritage Sites. Multicoloured.
2972 28c. Type **670** 40 20
2973 28c. Lion (statue) and embossed ceiling, Jeronimos Monastery . . 40 20
2974 43c. Column capitals, Guimaraes 60 30
2975 43c. Cherub (statue) and vineyards, Alto Douro . . 60 30
2976 54c. Corbel, lake and vineyards, Alto Douro (horiz) (80 × 30 mm) . . . 75 40
2977 54c. Houses and statues, Guimaraes (horiz) (80 × 30 mm) 75 40
2978 70c. Carved arch and statue, Jeronimos Monastery (horiz) (80 × 30 mm) . . . 1·00 50
2979 70c. Nave and tomb, Alcobaca Monastery (horiz) (80 × 30 mm) . . . 1·00 50
MS2980 Four sheets, each 141 × 114 mm. (a) €1.25 Door and statue, Alcobaca Monastery; (b) €1.25 Double doors, Jeronimos Monastery; (c) €1.25 Arches, Guimaraes; (d) €1.25 Grapes, Alto Douro . . . . . 7·00 7·00

2003. Bicentenary of Military College, Luz. Multicoloured.
2981 20c. Type **671** 30 15
2982 30c. 1806 uniform 40 20
2983 43c. 1837 parade uniform 60 30
2984 55c. 1861 uniform (rear view) 75 40
2985 70c. 1866 dress uniform . . 1·00 50
2986 €2 1912 cavalry cadet uniform . . . . 2·75 1·40
MS2987 141 × 114 mm. €1 1802 uniform; €1 1948 Porta Guiao dress uniform . . . . 2·75 2·75

2003. Birds (2nd series). As T **657**. Multicoloured.
(a) Ordinary gum.
2988 1c. Green woodpecker . . . 10 10
2989 30c. Rock dove 40 20
2990 43c. Blue thrush 60 30
2991 55c. Sub-alpine warbler . . 75 40
2992 70c. Black-eared wheatear 1·00 50

(b) Self-adhesive gum. Size 27 × 23 mm.
2989a 30c. No. 2989 . . . . . .
2990a 43c. No. 2990 (50 × 23 mm)
2991a 55c. No. 2991 . . . . . .
No. 2990a is inscribed "CorreioAzul".

672 People forming Mobility Symbol

2003. European Year of the Disabled. Multicoloured.
2993 30c. Type **672** 40 20
2994 55c. People forming head shape 75 40
2995 70c. As No. 2994 but with eyes, ears and mouth pink 1·00 50

673 1853 5r. Stamp and Queen Donna Maria II

2003. 150th Anniv of First Postage Stamp (1st issue). Designs showing 1853 stamps. Multicoloured.
2996 30c. Type **673** 40 20
2997 43c. 25r. stamp and coin . . 60 30
2998 55c. 50r. stamp and portrait 75 40
2999 70c. 100r. stamp and arms 1·00 50
See also Nos. 3011 and **MS**3047.

674 *Orchis italica*

2003. Orchids. Multicoloured.
3000 46c. *Aceras anthropophorum* 65 30
3001 46c. *Dactylorhiza maculate* 65 30
MS3002 Two sheets, each 113 × 140 mm. (a) 30c. Type **674**; 30c. *Ophrys tenthredinifera*; 30c. *Ophrys fusca fusca*; 30c. *Orchis papilionacea*; 30c. *Barlia robertiana*; 30c. *Ophrys lutea*; 30c. *Ophrys fusca*; 30c. *Ophrys apifera*; 30c. *Dactylorhiza ericetorum*. (b) 30c. *Orchis champagneuxii*; 30c. *Orchis morio*; 30c. *Serapias cordigera*; 30c. *Orchis coriophora*; 30c. *Ophrys bombyliflora*; 30c. *Ophrys vernixia*; 30c. *Ophrys speculum*; 30c. *Ophrys scoplopax*; 30c. *Anacamptis pyramidalis* 7·50 7·50

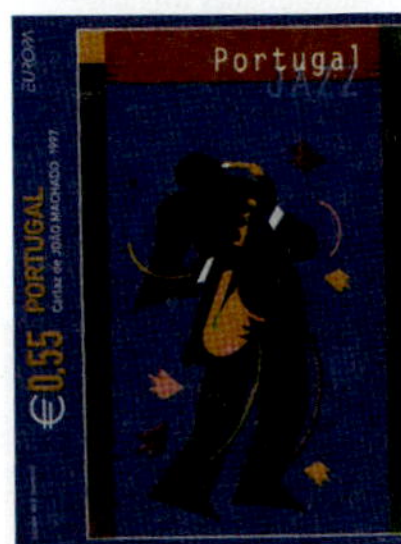

675 Jazz Festival (Joao Machado)

2003. Europa. Poster Art. Multicoloured.
3003 55c. Type **675** 75 40
3004 55c. Woman wearing swimsuit ("Espimho") (Fred Kradolfer) 75 40
MS3005 140 × 113 mm. Nos. 3004/5 1·50 1·50

676 Lawyer and Union Seal

2003. International Lawyer's Congress, Lisbon. Multicoloured.
3006 30c. Type **676** 40 20
3007 43c. Lawyers, arms and Court building 60 30
3008 55c. Medieval lawyer, Bishop and legal document 75 40
3009 70c. Lawyer's union presidential medal and female lawyer . . . . . . 1·00 50
MS3010 140 × 113 mm. €1 Lawyer wearing red robe and seal; €2 Seal, painted plaque and bishop 4·25 4·25

677 "150" and Stamp (Viseu)

2003. 150th Anniv of Portuguese First Stamp (2nd issue). Itinerant Exhibition.
3011 **677** 30c. multicoloured . . . 40 20
3012 30c. multicoloured . . . 40 20
3013 30c. multicoloured . . . 40 20

678 Championship Emblem

2003. Euro 2004 Football Championship, Portugal (1st issue).
3014 **678** 30c. multicoloured . . . 40 20
3015 43c. multicoloured . . . 60 30
3016 47c. multicoloured . . . 65 35
3017 55c. multicoloured . . . 75 40
3018 70c. multicoloured . . . 1·00 50
MS3019 (a) 140 × 109 mm. 55c. × 4, Parts of championship emblem. (b) 190 × 200 mm. Nos. 3014/18 and **MS**3019a . . . . 3·00 3·00
See also Nos. **MS**3072, 3073/4, 3084/**MS**88, 3110/17, 3119/28 and **MS**3147.

679 Open-topped Car

2003. Centenary of Portuguese Automobile Club. Multicoloured.
3020 30c. Type **679** 40 20
3021 43c. Club engineer riding motorcycle 60 30
3022 €2 Racing cars . . . . . . 2·75 1·40

680 Ricardo do Espirito Santo Silva

2003. 50th Anniv of Ricardo do Espirito Santo Silva Foundation. Multicoloured.
3023 30c. Type **680** 40 20
3024 30c. 18th-century inlaid chess table 40 20
3025 43c. Cutlery box, 1720–1750 60 30
3026 43c. 15th-century silver tray 60 30
3027 55c. 18th-century wooden container 75 40
3028 55c. Ming dynasty ceramic box 75 40
MS3029 140 × 112 mm. €1 17th-century cupboard; €1 18th-century tapestry . . . . . 2·75 2·75

681 "Bay of Funchal" (W. G. James) (1839)

2003. Museums of Madeira. Black (No. **MS**3034) or multicoloured (others).
3030 30c. Type **681** 40 20
3031 43c. Nativity (straw sculpture, Manuel Orlando Noronha Gois) 60 30
3032 55c. "O Largo da Fonte" (Andrew Picken) (1840) 75 40
3033 70c. "Le Depart" (Martha Teles) (1983) . . . . . . 1·00 50
MS3034 140 × 112 mm. €1 Vicente Gomes da Silva (photograph); €2 Jorge Bettencourt (photograph) 4·25 4·25

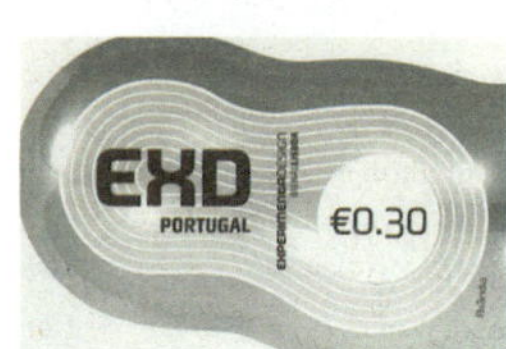

682 Curved Shape containing "EXD"

2003. ExperimentaDesign2003 (design exhibition). Sheet containing T **682** and similar curved designs. Either black (30c.) or black and red (others). Self-adhesive.
3035 30c. Type **682** 40 20
3036 30c. "EXD" centrally . . . 40 20
3037 30c. "EXD" bottom 40 20
3038 30c. "EXD" left 40 20
3039 43c. As No. 3038 but design reversed 60 30
3040 43c. As No. 3037 but design reversed 60 30
3041 43c. As No. 3036 but design reversed 60 30
3042 43c. As No. 3035 but design reversed 60 30
3043 55c. As No. 3035 . . . . . 75 40
3044 55c. As No. 3036 . . . . . 75 40
3045 55c. As No. 3037 . . . . . 75 40
3046 55c. As No. 3038 . . . . . 75 40

683 Queen Maria II

2003. 150th Anniv of First Portuguese Stamp (3rd issue). Four sheets, each 140 × 112 mm containing T **683** and similar multicoloured designs. **MS**3047 (a) 30c. Type **683**; 30c. × 4 No. 2996 × 4 (25.9); (b) €1 Queen Maria II and euro coins (90 × 40 mm) (12.12); (c) €2.50 Seal and postal marks (80 × 30 mm) (23.9); (d) €3 King Pedro V, 1853 25r. stamp and Queen Maria II (80 × 30 mm) 11·00 11·00

684 St. John's Well, Vila Real

2003. America. Fountains. Multicoloured.
3048 30c. Type **684** 40 20
3049 43c. Fountain of Virtues, Porto 60 30
3050 55c. Fountain, Giraldo Square, Evora 75 40
3051 70c. Senora da Saude fountain, St. Marcos de Tavira . . . . 1·00 50
3052 €1 Town fountain, Castelo de Vide . . . . 1·40 70
3053 €2 St. Andreas fountain, Guarda . . . . 2·75 1·40

685 Jose I engraved Glass Tumbler (18th-century)

2003. Glass Production. Multicoloured.
3054 30c. Type **685** 40 20
3055 55c. Maria II engraved tumbler (19th-century) . . 75 40
3056 70c. Blue glass vase (Carmo Valente) (20th-century) . . 1·00 50
3057 €2 Bulbous vase (Helena Matos) (20th-century) . . 2·75 1·40
MS3058 140 × 112 mm. €1.50 Stained glass window (detail) (Fernando Santos) (19th-century) 2·10 2·10

686 Persian Medicine Jar and Roman Dropper

2003. Medicine and Pharmacy. Multicoloured.
3059 30c. Type **686** 40 20
3060 43c. Ceramic bottle and jar 60 30
3061 55c. Pestle and mortar . . 75 40
3062 70c. Still and glass bottle . . 1·00 50

687 Drawing Board and Chair (Jose Espinho)

2003. Contemporary Design. Multicoloured.
3063 43c. Type **687** 60 30
3064 43c. Telephone point (Pedro Silva Dias) (vert) 60 30
3065 43c. Tea trolley (Cruz de Carvlho) 60 30
3066 43c. Tap (Carlos Aguiar) . . 60 30
3067 43c. Desk (Daciano da Costa) 60 30
3068 43c. Knives (Eduardo Afonso Dias) 60 30
3069 43c. Stacking chairs (Leonor and Antonio Sena da Silva) 60 30
3070 43c. Flask (Carlos Rocha) (vert) 60 30
3071 43c. Chair (Antonio Garcia) (vert) 60 30

688 Championship Emblem

2003. Euro 2004 Football Championship, Portugal (2nd issue). Stadiums (2nd issue). Sheet 150 × 165 mm containing T **688** and similar horiz designs. Multicoloured.
MS3072 30c. × 10 Type **688**; Municipal stadium, Aveiro; Dr. Magalhaes Pessoa stadium, Leiria; Luz stadium, Lisbon; D. Afonso Henriques stadium, Guimaraes; Municipal stadium, Coimbra; Bessa stadium, Porto; Dragao stadium, Porto; Algarve stadium, Faro-Loule; Jose Alvalade stadium, Lisbon . . . 4·25 4·25

689 Kinas

2004. European Football Championship 2004, Portugal (3rd series). Mascot. Multicoloured. Self adhesive.
3073 45c. Type **689** (postage) . . 60 30
3074 €1.75 Kinas and football (air) . . . . 2·40 1·20
No. 3073 was inscribed "CorreioAzul". No. 3074 was inscribed "Airmail Priority".

690 King Joao IV and Vila Vicosa

2004. 400th Birth Anniv of King Joao IV. Multicoloured.
3075 45c. Type **690** 60 30
3076 €1 King Joao standing . . 1·40 70
Nos. 3075/6 were issued together, se-tenant, forming a composite design.

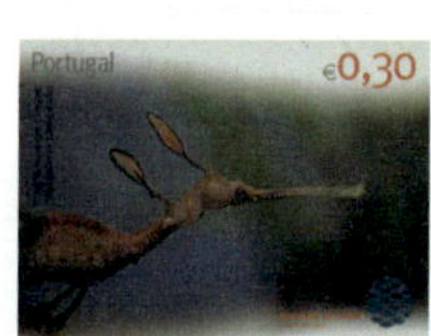

691 Seadragon (*Phyllopteryx taeniolatus*)

2004. Lisbon Oceanarium. Multicoloured.
3077 30c. Type **691** 40 20
3078 45c. Magellanic penguin (*Spheniscus magellanicus*) 60 30
3079 56c. *Hypsypops rubicundus* 75 40
3080 72c. Sea otter (*Enhydra lutris*) . . . . 1·00 50
3081 €1 Grey nurse shark (*Carcharias Taurus*) . . . 1·40 70
3082 €2 Atlantic puffin (*Fratercula artica*) . . . . 2·75 1·40
MS3083 140 × 112 mm. €1.50 Macaroni penguin (*Eudyptes Chrysolophus*) (80 × 30 mm) . . 2·10 2·10

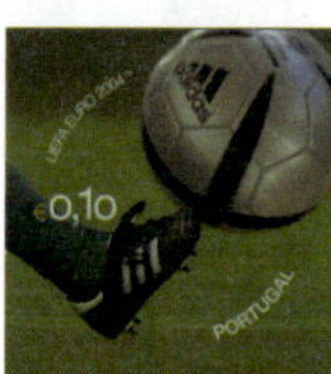

692 Foot kicking Ball

2004. European Football Championship 2004, Portugal (4th series). Official Match Ball. Multicoloured. Self-adhesive.
3084 10c. Type **692** 10 10
3085 20c. Ball right 30 15
3086 30c. Ball and line 40 20
3087 50c. Ball and goal post . . 75 40
MS3088 140 × 104mm. Nos. 3084/7. 1·50 1·50

693 Portugal

2004. European Football Championship 2004, Portugal (5th series). Participating Teams. Designs showing Kinas (mascot) and country flags. Multicoloured.
3089 30c. Type **693** 40 20
3090 30c. France 40 20
3091 30c. Sweden 40 20
3092 30c. Czech Republic 40 20
3093 30c. Greece 40 20
3094 30c. UK 40 20
3095 30c. Bulgaria 40 20
3096 30c. Latvia 40 20
3097 30c. Spain 40 20
3098 30c. Switzerland 40 20
3099 30c. Denmark 40 20
3100 30c. Germany 40 20
3101 30c. Russia 40 20
3102 30c. Croatia 40 20
3103 30c. Italy 40 20
3104 30c. Netherlands 40 20

2004. Birds (3rd series). As T **657**. Multicoloured.
3105 30c. Red crossbill 40 20
3106 45c. Red-rumped swallow 60 30
3107 56c. Golden oriole 75 40
3108 58c. Crested lark 75 40
3109 72c. Crested tit . . . . . . 1·00 50

694 "Moliceiros" Boat (Aveiro)

2004. European Football Championship 2004, Portugal (6th series). Host Cities. Multicoloured.
3110 30c. Type **694** 40 20
3111 30c. University tower (Coimbra) 40 20
3112 30c. Don Afonso Henriques (statue) (Guimaraes) . . . 40 20
3113 30c. Castle (Leiria) 40 20
3114 30c. Tower (Faro/Loule) . . 40 20
3115 30c. Bom Jesus (Braga) . . 40 20
3116 30c. Torre di Belem (Lisbon) 40 20
3117 30c. D. Luís I Bridge (Porto) 40 20

695 Carnations

2004. 30th Anniv of 25 April (Carnation revolution).
3118 **695** 45c. multicoloured . . . 60 30

696 Dr. Magalhaes Pessoa Stadium, Leiria

2004. European Football Championship 2004, Portugal (7th series). Stadiums (2nd issue). Multicoloured.
3119 30c. Type **696** 40 20
3120 30c. Municipal stadium, Coimbra 40 20
3121 30c. Municipal stadium, Braga 40 20
3122 30c. Bessa stadium, Porto 40 20
3123 30c. Luz stadium, Lisbon 40 20
3124 30c. D. Afonso Henriques stadium, Guimaraes . . . 40 20
3125 30c. Algarve stadium, Faro-Loule 40 20
3126 30c. Jose Alvalade stadium, Lisbon 40 20
3127 30c. Dragao stadium, Porto 40 20
3128 30c. Municipal stadium, Aveiro 40 20

697 Stylized Figures

2004. European Union. Multicoloured.
3129 30c. Type **697** (EU parliamentary elections) . . 40 20
3130 56c. EU emblem and new members' flags (80 × 30 mm) (new members) 40 20
MS3131 140 × 111 mm × 2 Original members' flags (80 30 mm) . . 2·75 2·75

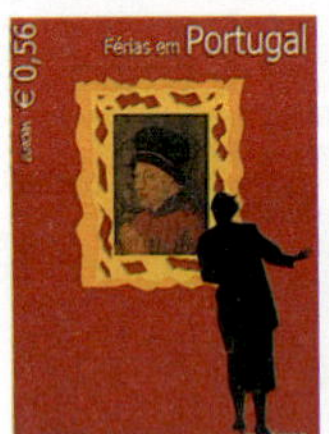

698 Picture Gallery

699 Bells of Early Telephone

2004. Europa. Holidays. Multicoloured.
3132 56c. Type **698** 80 40
3133 56c. Beach 80 40
MS3134 141 × 112 mm. Nos. 3132/3 1·60 1·60

2004. Centenary of Telephone Line from Porto to Lisbon. Multicoloured.
3135 30c. Type **699** 40 20
3136 45c. Insulator 60 30
3137 56c. Fibre optic cable . . . 80 40
3138 72c. Video telephone . . . . 1·00 50
MS3139 140 × 112 mm. €1. × 2, No. 3135; No. 3138 . . . . . 2·75 2·75

700 Flower (illustration, Maimonides' Mishneh Torah)

2004. Jewish Heritage. Multicoloured.
3140 30c. Type **700** 40 20
3141 45c. Star of David (illustration, Cervera Bible) 60 30
3142 56c. Menorah (illustration, Cervera Bible) 80 40
3143 72c. Menorah (carved tablet) 1·00 50
3144 €1 Illustration, Abravanel Bible . . . . 1·40 70
3145 €2 Prophet (statue, de Cristo Convent, Tomar) 2·75 1·40
MS3146 140 × 112 mm. €1.50 Shaare Tikva Synagogue (centenary) . . . . 2·00 2·00

701 Henri Delaunay Trophy

2004. European Football Championship 2004, Portugal (8th series). Sheet 140 × 112 mm. Multicoloured.
MS3147 **701** €1 multicoloured 1·40 1·40

702 Stamps

2004. 50th Anniv of Portuguese Philatelic Federation. Multicoloured.
3148 30c. Type **702** 40 20
MS3149 111 × 79 mm €1.50 Seal 2·00 2·00

703 Footballers Past and Present (½ size illustration)

2004. 50th Anniv of Union of European Football Associations (UEFA). Sheet 141 × 85 mm.
MS3150 **703** €1 multicoloured 1·40 1·40

704 Hurdler

2004. Olympic Games, Athens 2004. Multicoloured.
3151 30c. Type **704** 40 20
3152 45c. High jump 60 30

705 Swimmer

2004. Paralymic Games, Athens 2004. Multicoloured.
3153 30c. Type **705** 40 20
3154 45c. Wheelchair racer . . . 60 30
3155 56c. Cyclist 75 40
3156 72c. Runner . . . . 1·00 50

706 Pedro Homem de Melo

2004. Birth Centenary of Pedro Homem de Melo (folklorist). Sheet 140 × 112 mm.
MS3157 **706** €2 multicoloured 2·75 25

707 Museum Facade (½-size illustration)

2004. Inauguration of Belem Palace Museum (President of the Republic's Museum). Multicoloured.
3158 45c. Type **708** 60 30
MS3159 140 × 112 mm. €1 Museum interior . . . . 1·40 1·40

708 Quim and Manecas (Jose Stuart Carvalhais)

2004. Comic Strips. Multicoloured.
3160 30c. Type **708** 40 20
3161 45c. Guarda Abila (Julio Pinto and Nuno Saraiva) 60 30
3162 56c. Simao Infante (Raul Correia and Eduardo Teixeira Coelho) 75 35
3163 72c. APior Banda du Mondo (Jose Carlos Fernandes) . . . . 1·00 50
MS3164 141 × 111 mm. 50c. × 4, Oespiao Acacio (Relvas); Jim del Monaco (Louro and Simoes); Tomahawk Tom (Vitor Peon); Pitanga (Arlndo Fagundes) . . 2·75 2·75

709 Third-century Sarcophagus and Mosaic

2004. Viticulture. Multicoloured.
3165 30c. Type **709** 40 20
3166 45c. Mosaic and 12th-century tapestry . . 60 30
3167 56c. Man carrying grapes (14th-century missal) and grape harvesting (15th-century Book of Hours) 75 35
3168 72c. Grape harvesting and "Grupo de Leao" (Columbano Bordalo Pine) . . . . 1·00 50
3169 €1 "Grupo de Leo" and 20th-century stained glass window . . . . 1·40 70
MS3170 140 × 115 mm. 50c. × 4, Fields, grapes and mechanical harvester; Harvester and amphora; Barrels in cellar, steel vats and barrels; Barrels, bottling and glass of wine . . . . 2·75 2·75
Nos. 3165/6 were issued together, se-tenant, forming a composite design.

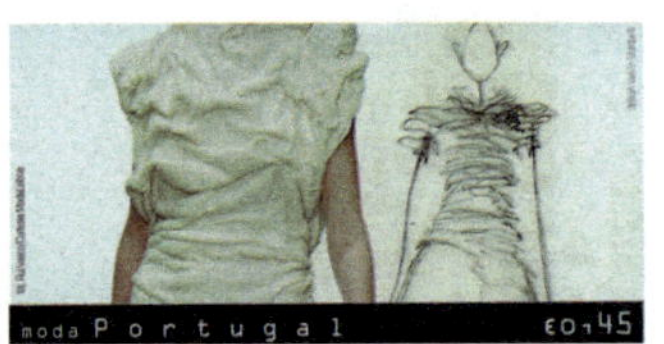

710 Ruched Dress (Alexandra Moura) (⅔-size illustration)

2004. Fashion. Sheet 190 × 200 mm containing T **710** and similar horiz designs. Multicoloured.
MS3171 45c. × 10, Type **710**; Poncho (Ana Salazar); Boned and laced dress (Filipe Faisca); Ribboned skirt (J. Branco and L. Sanchez); Wrap-over dress Antonio Tenente); Frilled front (Luis Buchinho); White top and skirted pants (Osvaldo Martins); Magenta dress with red attachments (Dino Alves); Silk-edged coat (Alves and Goncalves); Sequinned halter necked dress (Fatima Lopes) . . . . 6·00 6·00

711 "Adoration of the Magi" (Jorge Afonso)

2004. Christmas. Multicoloured.
3172 30c. Type **711** 40 20
3173 45c. "Adoration of the Magi" (16th-century Flamenga school) 60 30
3174 56c. "Escape into Egypt" (Francisco Vieira) 75 35
3175 72c. "Nativity" (Portuguese school) . . . . 1·00 50
MS3176 140 × 112 mm. €3 "Nativity" (detail) (Josefa de Obidos) (50 × 35 mm) . . . . 4·00 4·00

712 "Entrudo", Lazarim, Lamego

2005. Masks. Multicoloured. (a) Ordinary gum.
3177 10c. Type **712** 15 10
3178 30c. "Festa dos Rapazes", Salsas, Braganca 40 20
3179 45c. "Festa do Chocalheiro" Mougadouro, Braganca 60 30
3180 57c. "Cardador", Vale de Ilhavo 80 40
3181 74c. "Festa dos Rapazes", Avelada, Braganca . . . 1·00 50

(b) Self-adhesive gum.
3182 30c. As No. 3178 (29 × 24 mm) 40 20
3183 45c. As No. 3179 (48 × 23 mm) 60 30
3184 57c. As No. 3180 (29 × 24 mm) 80 40
No. 3183 is inscribed "Correio Azul".
See also No. 3319/21.

713 Subway Train and Tram

2005. Public Transport. Multicoloured.
3185 30c. Type **713** 40 20
3186 50c. Locomotive and tram 70 35
3187 57c. Hovercraft 80 40
3188 €1 Coach . . . . 1·40 70
3189 €2 Train . . . . 2·70 1·40
Nos. 3185/9 were issued together, se-tenant, forming a composite design.

714 Sortelha

2005. Historic Villages (1st issue). Multicoloured.
3190 30c. Type **714** 40 20
3191 30c. Idanha-a-Velha 40 20
3192 30c. Castelo Novo 40 20
3193 30c. Castelo Rodrigo . . . 40 20
3194 30c. Piodao 40 20
3195 30c. Linhares 40 20
3196 30c. Transcoso 40 20
3197 30c. Monsanto 40 20
3198 30c. Almeida 40 20
3199 30c. Belmonte 40 20
3200 30c. Marialva 40 20
3201 30c. Castelo Mendo 40 20
3202 30c. Buildings and coast, Linhares 40 20
3203 30c. Roof tops, Transcoso 40 20
3204 30c. Church, Marialva . . . 40 20
3205 30c. Castle and houses, Castelo Rodrigo 40 20
3206 30c. Buildings and terrace, Almeida 40 20
3207 30c. Houses, Castelo Mendo 40 20
3208 30c. Rooftops, Sortelha . . 40 20
3209 30c. Balcony, Belmonte . . 40 20
3210 30c. Rooftops, Monsanto 40 20
3211 30c. Ruins, Idanha-a-Velha 40 20
3212 30c. Tower, Castelo Novo 40 20
3213 30c. Rooftops, Piodao . . . 40 20
3214 57c. Castle, Linhares . . . 80 40
3215 57c. Castle walls, Transcoso 80 40
3216 57c. Bells, Mariavla 80 40
3217 57c. Church, Castelo Rodrigo 80 40
3218 57c. Walls, Almeida 80 40
3219 57c. Rooftops, Castelo Mendo 80 40
3220 57c. Column, Sortelha . . . 80 40
3221 57c. Castle walls, Belmonte 80 40
3222 57c. Tower, Monsanto . . . 80 40
3223 57c. Doorway, Idanha-a-Velha 80 40
3224 57c. Rooftops, Castelo Novo 80 40
3225 57c. Building facade, Piodao 80 40
See also No. **MS**3247.

715 "A Beira-Mar"

2005. 150th Birth Anniv of Jose Malhoa (artist). Multicoloured.
3226 30c. Type **715** 40 20
3227 45c. "As Promessas" . . . 60 30
MS3228 93 × 117 mm. €1.77 "Conversa com o Vizinho" . . 2·40 2·40

716 Cozido a Portuguesa (stew)

2005. Europa. Gastronomy. Multicoloured.
3229 57c. Type **716** 80 40
MS3230 125 × 95 mm. 57c. × 2, Bacalhau assado com batatas a murro (cod and potatoes) × 2 1·60 1·60

717 Paul Harris (founder)

2005. Centenary of Rotary International.
3231 **717** 74c. Multicoloured . . . 1·00 50
MS3232 125 × 95 mm. **717** €1.75 multicoloured . . . . 2·40 2·40

718 19th-century Open Carriage (Carrinho de Passeio)

2005. Centenary of National Coach Museum, Lisbon. Multicoloured.
3233 30c. Type **718** 40 20
3234 30c. 19th-century closed carriage (Carruagem de Porto Covo) 40 20
3235 45c. 17th-century carriage (Coche Francisca Saboia) 60 30
3236 45c. 18th-century small carriage ("Das Plumas") 60 30
3237 57c. 18th-century sedan chair 80 30
3238 74c. 18th-century coach (Coches dos oceanos) . . 1·00 50
MS3239 125 × 100 mm. €1.75 Queen Amelia . . . . 2·40 2·40

719 Pegoes Aqueduct, Tomar

720 Man and Cat (Raphael Bordallo Pinheiro)

2005. Cultural Heritage. Multicoloured.
3240 5c. Type **719** 10 10
3241 30c. Chalice (1581) 40 20
3242 45c. Stained glass, De Christo convent, Tomar 60 30
3243 57c. Turret, Angra, Azores 80 80
3244 €1 Ship . . . . 1·40 70
3245 €2 St. Vincente de Fora church, Lisbon . . . . . 2·70 1·40
MS3246 112 × 140 mm. €1.20 Crucifix, Tesauro da Se, Lisbon 1·60 1·60

2005. Historic Villages (2nd issue). 12 sheets, each 60 × 150 mm containing horiz designs as T **714**.
MS3247 (a) Nos. 3202 and 3214 (b) Nos. 3203 and 3215 (c) Nos. 3204 and 3216 (d) Nos. 3205 and 3217 (e) Nos. 3206 and 3218 (f) Nos. 3207 and 3219 (g) Nos. 3208 and 3220 (h) Nos. 3209 and 3221 (i) Nos. 3210 and 3222 (j) Nos. 3211 and 3223 (k) Nos. 3212 and 3224 (l) Nos. 3213 and 3225 14·50 14·50

2005. Caricaturists. Multicoloured.
3248 30c. Type **720** 40 20
3249 30c. Bearded man (Sebastiao Sanhudo) 40 20
3250 30c. Soldier (Celso Herminio) 40 20
3251 30c. Man wearing glasses (Leal da Camara) 40 20
3252 30c. Man holding broken pencil (Francisco Valenca) 40 20
3253 30c. Man smoking (Stuart Carvalhais) 40 20
3254 30c. Guarda Ricardo (Sam (Samuel Torres de Carvalho)) 40 20
3255 30c. Almada Negreios (Joao Abel Manta) 40 20
3256 30c. Man tie (Augusto Cid) 40 20
3257 30c. Head and pencil (Antonio Atunes) 40 20
3258 30c. Ze Povinho (Raphael Bordallo Pinheiro) . . . 40 20

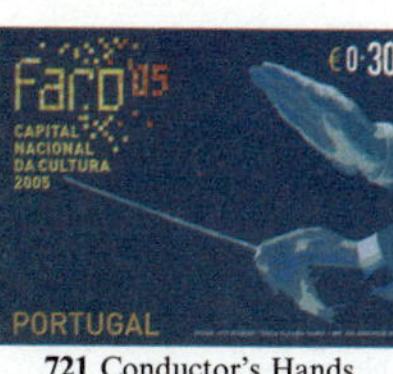

721 Conductor's Hands

2005. Faro—National Cultural Capital 2005. Multicoloured.
3259 30c. Type **721** 40 20
3260 45c. Ancient pot 60 30
3261 57c. Shell 80 40
3262 74c. Hands . . . . 1·00 50

722 Coastline and Bell

2005. Tourism. Multicoloured. (a) Lisbon.
3263 45c. Type **722** 60 30
3264 48c. Monument and tram 65 35
3265 57c. Tram, rooftops and cupola 80 40

(b) Porto e Norte.
3266 45c. Ceramic rooster, valley and church 60 30
3267 48c. Church, bay and wine glass 65 35
3268 57c. Wine glass, seafront and yachts 80 40
Nos. 3263/5 and 3266/8, respectively were printed together, se-tenant, each forming a composite design.

723 Harvesting Bark from protected Cork Trees

2005. Environmental Protection. Multicoloured.
3269 30c. Type **723** 40 20
3270 45c. Fire prevention officers 60 30
3271 57c. Bucaco Forest 80 40
MS3272 95 × 95 mm. €2 Chestnut trees (Serra de S. Mamede) . . 2·70 2·70

724 "50" and UN Emblem

2005. 50th Anniv of United Nations Membership. Multicoloured.
3273 30c. Type **724** 40 20
3274 45c. Dove (International Day of Peace) 60 30
3275 57c. Child (UNESCO—Children at Risk) 80 80
3276 74c. Albert Einstein (International Year of Physics) . . . . 1·00 50

725 Sundial, St John the Baptist Church, Sao Joao das Lampas

2005. Annular Solar Eclipse—3rd October. Multicoloured.
3277 45c. Type **725** 60 30
3278 €1 Portable sundial, 1770 1·40 70
MS3279 125 × 135 mm. €1.20 × 3, Partial eclipse, Lisbon; Annulus, Braganca; Partial eclipse, Faro 2·80 2·80

726 Pen Nib

2005. Communications. Multicoloured.
3280 30c. Type **726** 40 20
3281 45c. Radio microphone . . 60 30
3282 57c. Television camera . . . 80 40
3283 74c. Globe and (internet) . . . . 1·00 50
MS3284 Two sheets, each 125 × 90 mm. (a) €1.10 Newspaper; €1.55 Radio studio. (b) €1.10 Television studio; €1.55 "http://www" (internet) 6·50 6·50

727 Fisherman and Boats, Aldeia da Carrasqueira

2005. Fishing Villages. Multicoloured.
3285 30c. Type **727** 40 20
3286 30c. Moorings and pier, Aldeia da Carrasqueira 40 20
3287 30c. Boat, Tai O, Hong Kong 40 20
3288 30c. Wrapped fish, Tai O . . 40 20
Nos. 3285/6 and 3287/8 respectively were issued together, se-tenant, forming a composite design.
Stamps of the same design were issued by Hong Kong.

728 Multipurpose Ship

2005. Modernisation of the Navy. Black.
3289 45c. Type **728** 60 30
3290 57c. Hydro-oceanographic ship 80 40
3291 74c. Patrol vessel . . . . . 1·00 50
3292 €2 Submarine . . . . . . 2·70 1·40

729 Alvaro Cunhal, Women and Children

2005. Alvaro Barreirinhas Cunhal (politician and writer) Commemoration. Multicoloured.
3293 30c. Type **729** 40 20
MS3294 112 × 104 mm. €1 Alvaro Cunhal and girl . . . . 1·40 1·40

730 Building

2005. Serralves Foundation. Multicoloured.
3295 30c. Type **730** 40 20
3296 45c. "Projected Shadow of Adami" (Lourdes de Castro) 60 30
3297 48c. Building facade 65 35
3298 57c. Trowel (Claes Oldenburg Cooseje van Bruggen) 80 40
3299 74c. Hand and painting . . 1·00 50
3300 €1 Path, hedges and lawn 1·40 70
MS3301 Two sheets, each 125 × 150 mm. (a) 30c. As No. 3297 (horiz); 45c. Path; 45c. Columns and balustrade; 45c. Tower; 45c. Canal and evergreens (b) €1 Museum building (80 × 30 mm); €1 Museum displays (80 × 30 mm); €1 Parkland . . . . 6·75 6·75

731 Futebol Clube do Porto Emblem and Player (1993)

2005. Football Clubs' Centenaries. Showing emblem and player. Multicoloured.
3302 N (30c.) Type **731** 40 20
3303 N (30c.) Sport Lisboa e Benefica (2004) 40 20
3304 N (30c.) Sporting Clube de Portugal (2006) 40 20
MS3305 Three sheets, each 125 × 96 mm. (a) €1 Porto Football Club emblem and trophy; (b) €1 Sport Lisboa e Benefica emblem, player, stadium and trophy; (c) €1 Anniversary emblem . . . . 4·00 4·00
Nos. 3302/4 were for use on letters weighing 20 grams or less.

732 Scenes of Devastation (½-size illustration)

2005. 250th Anniv of Earthquake—31 October 1755. Multicoloured.
3306 45c. Type **732** 60 30
3307 €2 Aftermath . . . . . . 2·80 1·40
MS3308 80 × 80 mm. €2.65 Survivors (40 × 30 mm) . . . . 3·50 3·50

733 Children's Party

2006. Greetings Stamps. Multicoloured. (a) Sheet stamps.
3309 N. Type **733** 40 20
3310 N. Girl and couples 40 20
3311 N. Mother, father and baby 40 20
3312 N. Conductor 40 20
3313 N. Couple about to kiss . . 40 20

(b) Size 40 × 29 mm.
3314 N. As No. 3309 . . . . . . 40 20
3315 N. As No. 3310 . . . . . . 40 20
3316 N. As No. 3311 . . . . . . 40 20
3317 N. As No. 3312 . . . . . . 40 20
3318 N. As No. 3313 . . . . . . 40 20
Nos. 3314/18 were issued together, se-tenant, forming a composite design.

2006. Masks (2nd series). As T **712**. Multicoloured. Self-adhesive gum.
3319 N. "Festa dos Rapazes", Salsas, Bragana (29 × 24 mm) 40 20
3320 A. Lazarim carnival, Bragana (29 × 24 mm) . . 60 30
3321 E. "Dia de Ano Novo", Mogadouro, Bragana (29 × 24 mm) 80 40
No. 3320 is inscribed "Correio Azul".
No. 3319 was for use on normal domestic mail, up to 20 grams, 3320 was for domestic first class(blue) mail and 3321 was for European mail.

734 Rain Clouds

2006. Water. Multicoloured.
3322 N. Type **734** 40 20
3323 N. Glass of water 40 20
3324 A. Water from tap 60 30
3325 A. Water turbines 60 30
3326 E. Yacht 80 40
3327 E. Flower 80 40
Nos. 3322/3 was for use on normal domestic mail, up to 20 grams, 3324/5 was for domestic first class(blue) mail and, 3326/7 was for European mail.

735 Baptising

2006. 500th Birth Anniv of Saint Francis Xavier. Multicoloured.
3328 45c. Type **735** 60 30
3329 €1 Preaching . . . . . . 1·40 70
MS3330 85 × 125 mm. €2.75 Saint Francis Xavier (painting) . . . 3·75 3·75

CHARITY TAX STAMPS

Used on certain days of the year as an additional postal tax on internal letters. Other values in some of the types were for use on telegrams only. The proceeds were devoted to public charities. If one was not affixed in addition to the ordinary postage, postage due stamps were used to collect the deficiency and the fine.

1911. Optd **ASSISTENCIA**.
C455 **48** 10r. green (No. 406) . . . 9·00 2·40
C484 **56** 1c. green (No. 486) . . . 6·25 1·90

C 57 "Lisbon"

C 58 "Charity"

1913. Lisbon Festival.

C485	C 57	1c. green	1·00	75

1915. For the Poor.

C486	C 58	1c. red	35	30
C669		15c. red	55	55

1924. Surch **15 ctvs.**

C594	C 58	15c. on 1c. red	1·30	75

C 71 Muse of History

C 81 Hurdler

C 73 Monument to De Pombal

C 75 Marquis de Pombal

1925. Portuguese Army in Flanders, 1484 and 1918.

C662	C 71	10c. red	1·20	1·20
C663		10c. green	1·20	1·20
C664		10c. blue	1·20	1·20
C665		10c. brown	1·20	1·20

1925. Marquis de Pombal Commemoration.

C666	C 73	15c. blue and black	1·10	80
C667	–	15c. blue and black	55	40
C668	C 75	15c. blue and black	1·10	80

DESIGN: No. C677, Planning reconstruction of Lisbon.

1928. Olympic Games.

C741	C 81	15c. black and red	4·00	2·75

NEWSPAPER STAMPS

N 16

N 17

1876.

N180	N 16	2r. black	22·00	14·50
N178	N 17	2½r. green	14·50	1·40
N187		2½r. brown	14·50	1·40

OFFICIAL STAMPS

1938. Optd **OFICIAL**.

O900	99	40c. brown	55	15

O 144

1952. No value.

O1069	O 144	(1e.) black and stone	55	10
O1070		(1e.) black and stone	70	15

On No. O1069 "CORREIO DE PORTUGAL" is in stone on a black background, on No. O1070 it is in black on the stone background.

PARCEL POST STAMPS

P 59

1920.

P578	P 59	1c. brown	30	30
P579		2c. orange	30	30
P580		5c. brown	30	30
P581		10c. brown	30	30
P582		20c. blue	35	30
P583		40c. red	40	30
P584		50c. black	70	60
P585		60c. blue	60	55
P586		70c. brown	3·75	2·40
P587		80c. blue	4·25	4·00
P588		90c. violet	4·25	2·75
P589		1e. green	4·50	4·00
P591		2e. lilac	13·00	4·25
P592		3e. green	25·00	5·00
P593		4e. blue	50·00	8·50
P594		5e. lilac	70·00	6·00
P595		10e. brown	£100	11·00

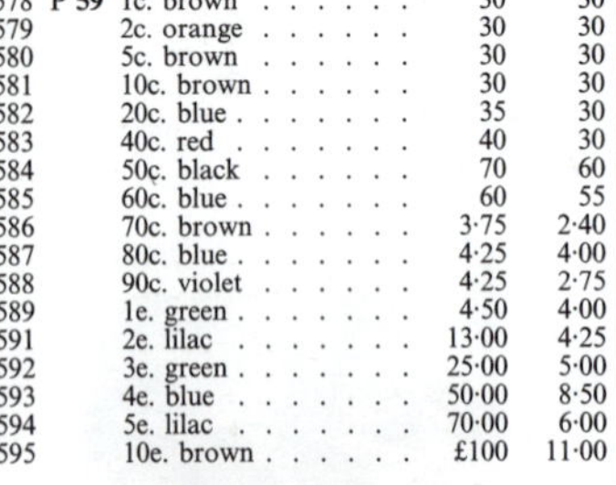
P 101

1936.

P891	P 101	50c. grey	80	65
P892		1e. brown	80	65
P893		1e.50 violet	80	65
P894		2e. purple	3·25	70
P895		2e.50 green	3·25	70
P896		4e.50 purple	7·00	75
P897		5e. violet	11·00	90
P898		10e. orange	15·00	2·20

POSTAGE DUE STAMPS

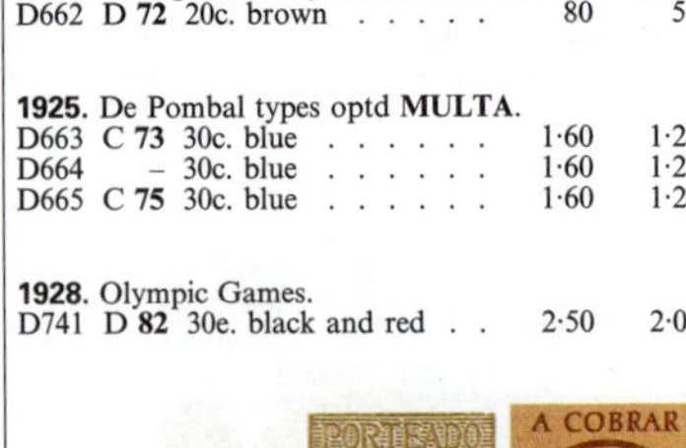
D 48 Da Gama received by the Zamorin of Calicut

D 49

1898.

D386	D 48	5r. black	4·75	4·00
D387		10r. mauve	4·75	4·00
D388		20r. orange	8·00	4·00
D389		50r. grey	65·00	12·00
D390		100r. red on pink	90·00	48·00
D391		200r. brown on buff	90·00	65·00

1904.

D392	D 49	5r. brown	50	45
D393		10r. orange	3·25	1·10
D394		20r. mauve	9·75	4·75
D395		30r. green	6·25	3·25
D396		40r. lilac	8·25	3·25
D397		50r. red	60·00	5·50
D398		100r. blue	9·75	7·75

1911. Optd **REPUBLICA**.

D418	D 49	5r. brown	45	30
D419		10r. orange	45	30
D420		20r. mauve	1·60	1·20
D421		30r. green	1·50	30
D422		40r. lilac	1·60	30
D423		50r. red	6·75	5·50
D424		100r. blue	7·50	6·25

1915. As Type **D 49** but value in centavos.

D491	D 49	½c. brown	80	75
D498		1c. orange	80	75
D493		2c. purple	80	75
D499		3c. green	80	75
D500		4c. lilac	80	75
D501		5c. red	80	75
D497		10c. blue	80	75

1921.

D578	D 49	½c. green	45	45
D579		4c. green	45	45
D580		8c. green	45	45
D581		10c. green	45	45
D582		12c. green	60	60
D583		16c. green	60	60
D584		20c. green	60	60
D585		24c. green	60	60
D586		32c. green	60	60
D587		36c. green	1·60	1·60
D588		40c. green	1·60	1·60
D589		48c. green	80	80
D590		50c. green	80	80
D591		60c. green	80	80
D592		72c. green	80	80
D593		80c. green	8·75	8·75
D594		1e.20 green	3·75	3·75

D 72

D 82

1925. Portuguese Army in Flanders, 1484 and 1918.

D662	D 72	20c. brown	80	55

1925. De Pombal types optd **MULTA**.

D663	C 73	30c. blue	1·60	1·20
D664	–	30c. blue	1·60	1·20
D665	C 75	30c. blue	1·60	1·20

1928. Olympic Games.

D741	D 82	30e. black and red	2·50	2·00

D 91

D 108

D 218

1932.

D865	D 91	5e. buff	60	55
D866		10e. blue	60	55
D867		20e. pink	1·50	1·20
D868		30e. blue	1·80	1·20
D869		40e. green	1·80	1·20
D870		50e. grey	2·00	1·20
D871		60e. pink	5·00	2·20
D872		80e. purple	9·50	4·75
D873		1e.20 green	16·00	15·00

1940.

D912	D 108	5c. brown	65	50
D923		10c. lilac	35	20
D924		20c. red	35	20
D925		30c. violet	35	20
D926		40c. mauve	35	20
D927		50c. blue	35	20
D928		60c. green	35	20
D929		80c. red	35	20
D930		1e. brown	35	20
D931		2e. mauve	70	50
D922		5e. orange	13·50	11·00

1967.

D1312	D 218	10c. brown, yellow and orange	10	10
D1313		20e. purple, yellow and brown	10	10
D1314		30e. brown, light yellow and yellow	10	10
D1315		40e. purple, yellow and bistre	10	10
D1316		50e. indigo, blue and light blue	15	10
D1317		60e. olive, blue and turquoise	15	10
D1318		80e. indigo, blue and light blue	15	10
D1319		1e. indigo, bl & ultram	15	10
D1320		2e. olive, light green and green	15	10
D1321		3e. deep green, light green and green	20	10
D1322		4e. deep green, green and turquoise	20	15
D1323		5e. brown, mauve and purple	20	15
D1324		9e. deep lilac, lilac and violet	20	15
D1325		10e. deep purple, grey and purple	20	15
D1326		20e. maroon, grey and purple	65	15
D1327		40e. lilac, grey and mauve	1·40	65
D1328		50e. maroon, grey and purple	1·60	95

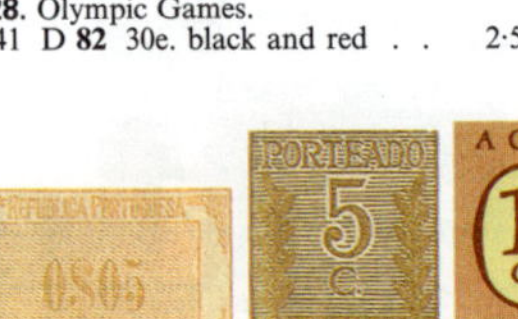
D 481

1992. Inscr "CORREIOS DE PORTUGAL".

D2305	D 481	1e. blue, deep blue and black	10	10
D2306		2e. light green, green and black	10	10
D2307		5e. yellow, brown and black	10	10
D2308		10e. red, orange and black	15	10
D2309		20e. green, violet and black	30	10
D2310		50e. yellow, green and black	70	30
D2311		100e. orange, red and black	1·20	65
D2312		200e. mauve, violet and black	2·40	1·40

1995. Inscr "CTT CORREIOS".

D2445	D 481	3e. multicoloured	10	10
D2446		4e. multicoloured	10	10
D2446a		5e. multicoloured	10	10
D2447		9e. multicoloured	10	10
D2447a		10e. red, orange and black	10	10
D2447b		20e. multicoloured	20	10
D2448		40e. multicoloured	40	20
D2449		50e. multicoloured	70	30
D2450		100e. orange, red and black	1·00	50

D 656 "0.01"

2002. Multicoloured.

D2907	1c. Type D 656	10	10
D2908	2c. "0.02"	10	10
D2909	5c. "0.05"	10	10
D2910	10c. "0.10"	20	10
D2911	25c. "0.25"	45	20
D2912	50c. "0.50"	85	45
D2913	€1 "1"	1·70	85

PORTUGUESE COLONIES Pt. 9

General issues for the Portuguese possessions in Africa: Angola, Cape Verde Islands, Guinea, Lourenco Marques, Mozambique, Congo, St. Thomas and Prince Islands, and Zambezia.

1898. 1000 reis = 1 milreis.
1919. 100 centavos = 1 escudo.

1898. 400th Anniv of Vasco da Gama's Discovery of Route to India. As Nos. 378/85 of Portugal but inscr "AFRICA".

1	2½r. green	60	50
2	5r. red	60	50
3	10r. purple	60	50
4	25r. green	60	50
5	50r. blue	60	50
6	75r. brown	5·00	4·25
7	100r. brown	5·00	3·50
8	150r. brown	7·25	3·50

CHARITY TAX STAMPS

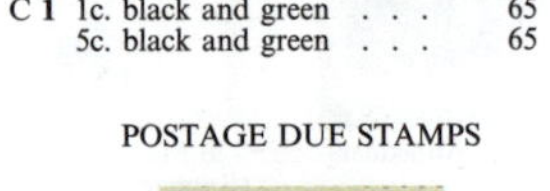
C 1

1919. Fiscal stamps optd **TAXA DE GUERRA**.

C1	C 1	1c. black and green	65	65
C2		5c. black and green	65	65

POSTAGE DUE STAMPS

D 1

1945. Value in black.

D1	D 1	10c. purple	25	25
D2		20c. purple	25	25
D3		30c. blue	25	25
D4		40c. brown	25	25
D5		50c. lilac	25	25
D6		1e. brown	1·20	1·20
D7		2e. green	2·00	2·00
D8		3e. red	3·25	3·25
D9		5e. yellow	5·00	5·00

PORTUGUESE CONGO Pt. 9

The area known as Portuguese Congo, now called Cabinda, was the part of Angola north of the River Congo. It issued its own stamps from 1894 until 1920

1894. 1000 reis = 1 milreis.
1913. 100 centavos = 1 escudo.

1894. "Figures" key-type inscr " CONGO".

8	R	5r. orange	95	85
9		10r. mauve	1·40	90
10		15r. brown	2·40	1·90
12		20r. lilac	2·40	1·90
13		25r. green	1·50	55
22		50r. blue	2·75	1·70
5		75r. pink	5·00	3·00
6		80r. green	6·25	4·50
7		100r. brown on yellow	5·50	3·75
17		150r. red on pink	10·50	8·75
18		200r. blue on blue	10·50	8·75
19		300r. blue on brown	13·50	11·00

1898. "King Carlos" key-type inscr "CONGO".

24	S	2½r. grey	35	30
25		5r. red	35	30
26		10r. green	60	30
27		15r. brown	1·20	1·20
66		15r. green	95	15
28		20r. lilac	95	70
29		25r. green	1·20	70
67		25r. red	95	15
30		50r. blue	1·70	1·20
68		50r. brown	2·20	1·40
69		65r. blue	6·75	5·50
31		75r. pink	3·00	1·30
70		75r. purple	2·75	2·30
32		80r. mauve	3·00	2·00
33		100r. blue on blue	2·40	1·80

71	115r. brown on pink	6·75	4·75
72	130r. brown on yellow	8·00	6·75
34	150r. brown on yellow	3·25	2·50
35	200r. purple on pink	4·75	3·00
36	300r. blue on pink	4·00	2·75
73	400r. blue on cream	7·75	6·50
37	500r. black on blue	14·00	8·00
38	700r. mauve on yellow	26·00	16·00

1902. Surch.

74 S	50r. on 65r. blue	4·00	2·50
40 R	65r. on 15r. brown	3·75	2·50
41	65r. on 20r. lilac	1·80	1·40
44	65r. on 25r. green	3·75	2·50
46	65r. on 300r. blue on brn	4·75	4·50
50 V	115r. on 2½r. brown	3·75	2·50
47 R	115r. on 10r. mauve	3·75	2·50
48	115r. on 50r. blue	3·50	2·50
53	130r. on 5r. orange	3·75	2·75
54	130r. on 75r. pink	3·75	2·50
57	130r. on 100r. brn on yell	3·75	2·75
58	400r. on 80r. green	1·60	1·20
60	400r. on 150r. red on pink	2·30	1·90
61	400r. on 200r. blue on blue	2·30	1·90

1902. "King Carlos" key-type of Portuguese Congo optd **PROVISORIO**.

62 S	15r. brown	1·70	1·20
63	25r. green	1·70	1·20
64	50r. blue	1·70	1·20
65	75r. pink	4·00	4·00

1911. "King Carlos" key-type of Angola, optd **REPUBLICA** and **CONGO** with bar (200r. also surch).

75 S	2½r. grey	1·20	80
76	5r. red	1·70	1·20
77	10r. green	1·70	1·20
78	15r. green	1·70	1·20
79	25r. on 200r. purple on pink	2·50	1·70

1911. "King Carlos" key-type of Portuguese Congo optd **REPUBLICA**.

80 S	2½r. grey	20	20
81	5r. orange	30	30
82	10r. green	30	30
83	15r. green	30	30
84	20r. lilac	30	30
85	25r. red	30	30
86	50r. brown	40	30
87	75r. purple	65	55
88	100r. blue on blue	80	55
89	115r. brown on pink	1·20	95
90	130r. brown on yellow	1·20	95
143	200r. purple on pink	2·10	1·50
92	400r. blue on cream	4·75	3·00
93	500r. black on blue	4·75	3·00
94	700r. mauve on yellow	5·75	3·50

1913. Surch **REPUBLICA CONGO** and value on "Vasco da Gama" stamps of (a) Portuguese Colonies.

95	¼c. on 2½r. green	90	75
96	½c. on 5r. red	90	75
97	1c. on 10r. purple	90	75
98	2½c. on 25r. green	90	75
99	5c. on 50r. blue	1·10	1·00
100	7½c. on 75r. brown	1·90	1·70
101	10c. on 100r. brown	1·40	1·00
102	15c. on 150r. brown	1·00	1·00

(b) Macao.

103	¼c. on ½a. green	1·20	1·10
104	½c. on 1a. red	1·20	1·10
105	1c. on 2a. purple	1·20	1·10
106	2½c. on 4a. green	1·20	1·10
107	5c. on 8a. blue	1·20	1·10
108	7½c. on 12a. brown	2·40	1·60
109	10c. on 16a. brown	1·50	1·10
110	15c. on 24a. brown	1·50	1·10

(c) Portuguese Timor.

111	¼c. on ½a. green	1·20	1·10
112	½c. on 1a. red	1·20	1·10
113	1c. on 2a. purple	1·20	1·10
114	2½c. on 4a. green	1·20	1·10
115	5c. on 8a. blue	1·20	1·10
116	7½c. on 12a. brown	2·40	1·60
117	10c. on 16a. brown	1·50	1·10
118	15c. on 24a. brown	1·50	1·10

1914. "Ceres" key-type inscr "CONGO".

135 U	¼c. green	45	35
120	½c. black	55	35
121	1c. green	1·90	1·20
122	1½c. brown	1·20	75
136	2c. red	45	35
124	2½c. violet	40	35
125	5c. blue	55	55
126	7½c. brown	90	75
127	8c. grey	1·10	90
128	10c. red	1·10	90
129	15c. purple	1·20	90
130	20c. green	1·20	90
131	30c. brown on green	2·50	1·50
132	40c. brown on pink	2·50	1·70
133	50c. orange on orange	3·00	1·70
134	1c. green on blue	3·75	2·75

1914. "King Carlos" key-type of Portuguese Congo optd **PROVISORIO** and **REPUBLICA**.

146 S	15r. brown (No. 62)	85	55
147	50r. blue (No. 64)	85	55
140	75r. pink (No. 65)	1·30	1·10

1914. Provisional stamps of 1902 optd **REPUBLICA**.

148 S	50r. on 65r. blue	85	55
150 V	115r. on 2½r. brown	55	30
151 R	115r. on 10r. mauve	50	35
154	115r. on 50r. blue	1·30	75
156	130r. on 5r. orange	1·30	75
157	130r. on 75r. pink	85	55
160	130r. on 100r. brown on yellow	60	35

NEWSPAPER STAMP

1894. "Newspaper" key-type inscr "CONGO".

N24 V	2½r. brown	95	80

PORTUGUESE GUINEA Pt. 9

A former Portuguese territory, on the west coast of Africa, with adjacent islands. Used stamps of Cape Verde Islands from 1877 until 1881. In September 1974 the territory became independent and was renamed Guinea-Bissau.

1881. 1000 reis = 1 milreis.
1913. 100 centavos = 1 escudo.

1881. "Crown" key-type inscr "CABO VERDE" and optd **GUINE**.

19 P	5r. black	4·00	3·00
20	10r. yellow	£160	£160
31	10r. green	6·75	4·75
21	20r. bistre	3·25	2·20
32	20r. red	6·75	5·00
13	25r. pink	2·40	1·70
28	25r. lilac	3·00	1·90
23	40r. blue	£180	£110
29	40r. yellow	1·90	1·50
24	50r. green	£180	£110
30	50r. blue	5·75	2·50
16	100r. lilac	8·00	6·25
17	200r. orange	11·50	8·00
18	300r. brown	14·00	11·00

3 24 Ceres

1886.

35 3	5r. black	6·00	5·50
36	10r. green	7·25	4·00
37	20r. red	10·50	4·00
38	25r. purple	10·50	6·25
46	40r. brown	8·75	6·25
40	50r. blue	17·00	6·25
47	80r. grey	16·00	11·00
48	100r. brown	16·00	11·00
43	200r. lilac	38·00	22·00
44	300r. orange	48·00	36·00

1893. "Figures" key-type inscr "GUINE".

50 R	5r. yellow	1·90	1·10
51	10r. mauve	1·90	1·10
52	15r. brown	2·40	1·50
53	20r. lilac	2·40	1·50
54	25r. green	2·40	1·50
55	50r. blue	4·25	2·20
57	75r. pink	11·50	7·00
58	80r. green	11·50	7·00
59	100r. brown on buff	11·50	7·00
60	150r. red on pink	11·50	7·00
61	200r. blue on blue	19·00	15·00
62	300r. blue on brown	18·00	15·00

1898. "King Carlos" key-type inscr "GUINE".

65 S	2½r. grey	35	30
66	5r. red	35	30
67	10r. green	35	30
68	15r. brown	3·00	2·20
114	15r. green	1·80	95
69	20r. lilac	1·40	95
70	25r. green	1·70	1·10
115	25r. red	95	55
71	50r. blue	2·20	1·20
116	50r. brown	2·40	1·80
117	65r. blue	7·50	6·00
72	75r. pink	12·50	8·25
118	75r. purple	3·25	3·00
73	80r. mauve	3·00	1·90
74	100r. blue on blue	2·75	1·90
119	115r. brown on pink	8·50	6·25
120	130r. brown on yellow	8·75	6·25
75	150r. brown on yellow	9·00	3·75
76	200r. purple on pink	9·00	3·75
77	300r. blue on pink	8·00	4·75
121	400r. blue on yellow	9·50	7·00
78	500r. black on blue	12·50	7·25
79	700r. mauve on yellow	17·00	12·00

1902. Surch.

122 S	50r. on 65r. blue	4·75	3·00
81 3	65r. on 10r. green	6·75	3·75
84 R	65r. on 10r. mauve	5·75	3·00
85	65r. on 15r. brown	5·75	3·00
82 3	65r. on 20r. red	6·75	3·75
86 R	65r. on 20r. lilac	5·75	3·00
83 3	65r. on 25r. purple	6·75	3·75
88 R	65r. on 50r. blue	2·75	2·50
97 V	115r. on 2½r. brown	4·00	2·75
93 R	115r. on 5r. yellow	5·25	2·75
95	115r. on 25r. green	6·00	3·00
89 3	115r. on 40r. brown	5·75	3·50
91	115r. on 50r. blue	5·75	3·50
92	115r. on 300r. orange	7·25	4·75
98	130r. on 80r. grey	7·25	5·25
100	130r. on 100r. brown	7·75	5·25
102 R	130r. on 150r. red on pink	6·00	3·00
103	130r. on 200r. blue on blue	6·75	3·50
104	130r. on 300r. blue on brn	6·75	4·00
105 3	400r. on 5r. black	33·00	31·00
107 R	400r. on 75r. pink	4·25	4·00
108	400r. on 80r. green	2·75	1·70
109	400r. on 100r. brn on buff	3·75	1·70
106 3	400r. on 200r. lilac	12·50	7·00

1902. "King Carlos" key-type of Portuguese Guinea optd **PROVISORIO**.

110 S	15r. brown	2·40	1·50
111	25r. green	2·40	1·50
112	50r. blue	2·75	1·70
113	75r. pink	5·75	4·75

1911. "King Carlos" key-type of Portuguese Guinea optd **REPUBLICA**.

123 S	2½r. grey	45	35
124	5r. red	55	35
125	10r. green	65	35
126	15r. green	65	50
127	20r. lilac	65	50
128	25r. red	65	50
129	50r. brown	5·50	3·00
130	75r. purple	65	50
131	100r. blue on blue	65	50
132	115r. brown on pink	1·50	60
133	130r. brown on yellow	1·50	70
134	200r. purple on pink	1·50	70
135	400r. blue on yellow	7·00	2·75
136	500r. black on blue	2·30	1·70
137	700r. mauve on yellow	2·30	1·70

1913. Surch **REPUBLICA GUINE** and value on "Vasco da Gama" stamps. (a) Portuguese Colonies.

138	¼c. on 2½r. green	3·50	4·00
139	½c. on 5r. red	1·50	1·30
140	1c. on 10r. purple	1·50	1·30
141	2½c. on 25r. green	1·50	1·30
142	5c. on 50r. blue	1·50	1·30
143	7½c. on 75r. brown	3·50	2·75
144	10c. on 100r. brown	1·50	1·00
145	15c. on 150r. brown	4·25	3·50

(b) Macao.

146	¼c. on ½a. green	1·70	1·30
147	½c. on 1a. red	1·70	1·30
148	1c. on 2a. purple	1·70	1·30
149	2½c. on 4a. green	1·70	1·30
150	5c. on 8a. blue	1·70	1·30
151	7½c. on 12a. brown	3·00	2·10
152	10c. on 16a. brown	2·50	2·10
153	15c. on 24a. brown	3·25	2·20

(c) Portuguese Timor.

154	¼c. on ½a. green	1·70	1·30
155	½c. on 1a. red	1·70	1·30
156	1c. on 2a. purple	1·70	1·30
157	2½c. on 4a. green	1·70	1·30
158	5c. on 8a. blue	1·70	1·30
159	7½c. on 12a. brown	3·00	2·10
160	10c. on 16a. brown	2·50	2·10
161	15c. on 24a. brown	3·25	2·20

1913. "King Carlos" key-type of Portuguese Guinea optd **PROVISORIO** and **REPUBLICA**.

184 S	15r. brown	13·50	9·25
185	50r. blue	1·10	90
164	75r. pink	13·50	9·25

1914. "Ceres" key-type inscr "GUINE". Name and value in black.

204 U	¼c. green	75	50
209	½c. black	50	35
210	1c. green	1·10	55
211	1½c. brown	70	45
212	2c. red	75	40
213	2c. grey	30	25
214	2½c. violet	30	25
215	3c. orange	30	25
216	4c. red	30	25
217	4½c. grey	30	25
218	5c. blue	30	25
219	6c. mauve	30	30
220	7c. blue	45	25
221	7½c. brown	30	25
222	8c. grey	30	25
223	10c. red	30	25
224	12c. green	75	45
225	15c. red	30	25
226	20c. green	30	30
227	24c. blue	1·90	1·30
228	25c. brown	1·90	1·30
180	30c. brown on green	5·25	3·50
229	30c. green	90	45
181	40c. brown on pink	3·50	70
230	40c. turquoise	90	50
182	50c. orange on orange	3·50	70
231	50c. mauve	1·90	85
232	60c. blue	1·50	1·30
233	60c. red	2·10	90
234	80c. red	1·50	85
183	1e. green on blue	4·75	2·30
235	1e. blue	3·25	1·90
236	1e. pink	3·00	1·40
237	2e. purple	5·75	4·00
238	5e. bistre	14·50	7·50
239	10e. pink	27·00	10·00
240	20e. green	55·00	30·00

1915. Provisional stamps of 1902 optd **REPUBLICA**.

186 S	50r. on 65r. blue	1·10	90
187 V	115r. on 2½r. brown	1·70	1·00
190 R	115r. on 5r. yellow	1·20	75
191	115r. on 25r. green	1·10	90
192 3	115r. on 40r. brown	6·00	3·75
194	115r. on 50r. blue	1·00	90
196	130r. on 80r. grey	3·25	2·00
197	130r. on 100r. brown	2·75	2·20
199 R	130r. on 150r. red on pink	1·10	90
200	130r. on 200r. blue on blue	1·10	90
201	130r. on 300r. blue on brn	1·10	90

1920. Surch.

241 U	4c. on ½c. green	4·00	2·75
242	6c. on ½c. black	4·00	2·75
243 S	12c. on 115r. brown on pink (No. 132)	10·00	6·25

1925. Stamps of 1902 (Nos. 107/9) surch **Republica** and new value.

244 R	40c. on 400r. on 75r. pink	1·10	85
245	40c. on 400r. on 80r. green	1·10	85
246	40c. on 400r. on 100r. brown on buff	1·10	85

1931. "Ceres" key-type of Portuguese Guinea surch.

247 U	50c. on 60c. red	2·30	1·70
248	70c. on 80c. red	2·40	2·20
249	1e.40 on 2e. purple	5·75	4·00

1933.

251 24	1c. brown	20	15
252	5c. brown	20	15
253	10c. mauve	20	15
254	15c. black	35	30
255	20c. grey	35	30
256	30c. green	35	30
257	40c. red	85	35
258	45c. turquoise	85	35
259	50c. brown	85	55
260	60c. green	90	55
261	70c. brown	90	55
262	80c. green	1·60	60
263	85c. red	2·75	1·30
264	1e. purple	1·30	85
265	1e.40 blue	4·75	2·75
266	2e. mauve	2·50	1·40
267	5e. green	8·50	5·25
268	10e. brown	15·00	7·00
269	20e. orange	48·00	23·00

27 Vasco da Gama 28 Airplane over Globe

1938.

270 27	1c. green (postage)	15	15
271	5c. brown	15	15
272	10c. red	20	20
273	15c. purple	20	20
274	20c. grey	50	20
275 –	30c. purple	50	35
276 –	35c. green	50	35
277 –	40c. brown	50	35
278 –	50c. mauve	50	35
279 –	60c. black	50	35
280 –	70c. violet	50	35
281 –	80c. orange	85	45
282 –	1e. red	1·20	45
283 –	1e.75 blue	1·50	90
284 –	2e. red	4·00	1·40
285 –	5e. green	5·75	2·75
286 –	10e. blue	7·75	3·50
287 –	20e. brown	26·00	5·50
288 28	10c. red (air)	85	60
289	20c. violet	85	60
290	50c. orange	85	60
291	1e. blue	85	60
292	2e. red	7·25	3·75
293	3e. green	2·40	1·20
294	5e. brown	5·25	1·60
295	9e. red	7·50	4·00
296	10e. mauve	13·00	4·50

DESIGNS (postage): 30c. to 50c. Mousinho de Albuquerque; 60c. to 1e. Dam; 1e.75 to 5e. Prince Henry the Navigator; 10, 20e. Afonso de Albuquerque.

31 Cacheu Castle 32 Native Huts

1946. 500th Anniv of Discovery of Portuguese Guinea.

297 31	30c. black and grey	85	60
298 –	50c. green and light green	45	45
299 –	50c. purple and claret	45	45
300 –	1e.75 blue and light blue	2·75	1·10
301 –	3e.50 red and pink	4·75	1·70
302 –	5e. brown and chocolate	13·50	5·50
303 –	20e. violet and mauve	23·00	9·25
MS303a	175 × 221 mm. Nos. 297/303 (sold at 40e.)	75·00	

DESIGNS—VERT: 50c. Nuno Tristao; 1e.75, President Grant; 3e.50, Teixeiro Pinto; 5e. Honorio Barreto. HORIZ: 20e. Church at Bissau.

1948.

304 32	5c. brown	15	10
305 –	10c. purple	2·75	1·50
306 –	20c. mauve	65	45
307 –	35c. green	85	45
308 –	50c. red	45	15

309 – 70c. blue 65 45
310 – 80c. green . . . . 1·00 45
311 – 1e. red . . . . 1·00 45
312 – 1e.75 blue . . . . 12·00 5·25
313 – 2e. blue . . . . 13·50 1·50
314 – 3e.50 brown . . . . 2·75 1·40
315 – 5e. grey . . . . 4·75 2·75
316 – 20e. violet . . . . 22·00 7·00
MS316a 176 × 158 mm. Nos. 304/16 (sold at 40e.) . . . . 90·00
DESIGNS: 10c. Crowned crane; 20c., 3e.50, Youth; 35c., 5e. Woman; 50c. Musician; 70c. Man; 80c., 20e. Girl; 1, 2e. Drummer; 1e.75, Bushbuck.

33 Our Lady of Fatima
34 Letter and Globe

1948. Statue of Our Lady of Fatima.
317 **33** 50c. green . . . . 4·25 3·50

1949. 75th Anniv of U.P.U.
318 **34** 2e. orange . . . . 5·25 2·40

1950. Holy Year. As Nos. 425/6 of Macao.
319 1e. purple . . . . 2·10 1·20
320 3e. green . . . . 3·25 1·70

36 Our Lady of Fatima
37 Doctor examining Patient

1951. Termination of Holy Year.
321 **36** 1e. brown and buff 95 55

1952. 1st Tropical Medicine Congress, Lisbon.
322 **37** 50c. brown and purple . . 45 45

39 Exhibition Entrance
40 "Analeptes Trifasciata" (longhorn beetle)

1953. Missionary Art Exhibition.
323 **39** 10c. red and green 10 10
324 50c. blue and brown . . . 1·00 35
325 3e. black and orange . . . 2·40 1·10

1953. Bugs and Beetles. Multicoloured.
326 5c. Type **40** 15 10
327 10c. "Callidea panaethiopica kirk" (shieldbug) 15 15
328 30c. "Craspedophorus brevicollis" (ground beetle) 15 10
329 50c. "Anthia nimrod" (ground beetle) 20 10
330 70c. "Platypria luctuosa" (leaf beetle) 45 25
331 1e. "Acanthophorus maculatus" (longhorn beetle) 45 15
332 2e. "Cordylomera nitidipennis" (longhorn beetle) . . . . 1·00 20
333 3e. "Lycus latissimus" (powder-post beetle) . . . 2·30 30
334 5e. "Cicindeia brunet" (tiger beetle) . . . . 2·40 85
335 10e. "Colliurus dimidiata" (ground beetle) . . . . . 5·75 2·75

41 Portuguese Stamp of 1853 and Arms of Portuguese Overseas Provinces
43 Arms of Cape Verde Islands and Portuguese Guinea

42 Father M. de Nobrega and View of Sao Paulo

1953. Portuguese Stamp Centenary.
336 **41** 50c. multicoloured . . . . 1·00 85

1954. 4th Centenary of Sao Paulo.
337 **42** 1e. multicoloured 30 20

1955. Presidential Visit.
338 **43** 1e. multicoloured 30 20
339 2e.50 mulitcoloured 60 40

44 Exhibition Emblem Globe and Arms
46 Statue of Barreto at Bissau

45 "Matenus stenegalenis"

1958. Brussels International Exhibition.
340 **44** 2e.50 green 65 45

1958. 6th Int Congress of Tropical Medicine.
341 **45** 5e. multicoloured . . . . . 3·00 1·30

1959. Death Centenary of Honorio Barreto (statesman).
342 **46** 2e.50 multicoloured 30 25

47 Astrolabe
48 "Medical Service"

1960. 500th Death Anniv of Prince Henry the Navigator.
343 **47** 2e.50 multicoloured 35 30

1960. 10th Anniv of African Technical Co-operation Commission.
344 **48** 1e.50 multicoloured 30 25

49 Motor Racing
50 "Anopheles gambiae"

1962. Sports. Multicoloured.
345 50c. Type **49** 40 10
346 1e. Tennis 65 25
347 1e.50 Putting the shot 45 25
348 2e.50 Wrestling 55 30
349 3e.50 Shooting 60 30
350 15e. Volleyball . . . . 1·60 85

1962. Malaria Eradication.
351 **50** 2e.50 multicoloured 60 40

51 Common Spitting Cobra
52 Map of Africa, Boeing 707 and Lockheed L.1049G Super Constellation

1963. Snakes. Multicoloured.
352 20c. Type **51** 15 10
353 35c. African rock python . . 15 10
354 70c. Boomslang 55 30
355 80c. West African mamba . . 55 25
356 1e.50 Symthe's watersnake . . 55 15
357 2e. Common night adder . . 25 10
358 2e.50 Green swampsnake . . 2·10 30
359 3e.50 Brown house snake . . 35 20
360 4e. Spotted wolfsnake 50 20
361 5e. Common puff adder . . . 60 30
362 15e. Striped beauty snake . . 1·40 1·00
363 20e. African egg-eating snake 1·90 1·50
The 2e. and 20e. are horiz.

1963. 10th Anniv of Transportes Aereos Portugueses (airline).
364 **52** 2e.50 multicoloured 60 25

53 J. de A. Corvo
54 I.T.U. Emblem and St. Gabriel

1964. Centenary of National Overseas Bank.
365 **53** 2e.50 multicoloured 65 40

1965. Centenary of I.T.U.
366 **54** 2e.50 multicoloured . . . . 1·70 70

55 Soldier, 1548

1966. Portuguese Military Uniforms. Multicoloured.
367 25c. Type **55** 15 10
368 40c. Arquebusier, 1578 . . . 25 10
369 60c. Arquebusier, 1640 . . . 35 10
370 1e. Grenadier, 1721 . . . . . 40 10
371 2e.50 Captain of Fusiliers, 1740 . . . . 70 10
372 4e.50 Infantryman, 1740 . . 1·70 30
373 7e.50 Sergeant-major, 1762 3·25 1·40
374 10e. Engineers' officer, 1806 3·25 1·40

56 B. C. Lopes School and Bissau Hospital

1966. 40th Anniv of Portuguese National Revolution.
375 **56** 2e.50 multicoloured 60 40

57 O. Muzanty and Cruiser "Republica"

1967. Centenary of Military Naval Assn. Mult.
376 50c. Type **57** 25 15
377 1e. A. de Cerqueira and destroyer "Guadiana" . . 90 40

58 Chapel of the Apparitions and Monument of the Holy Spirit
63 Pres. Tomas

1967. 50th Anniv of Fatima Apparitions.
378 **58** 50c. multicoloured 20 10

1968. Visit of President Tomas of Portugal.
396 **63** 1e. multicoloured 25 15

64 Cabral's Arms
66 Admiral Coutinho's Astrolabe

1968. 500th Birth Anniv of Pedro Cabral (explorer).
397 **64** 2e.50 multicoloured 55 20

1969. Birth Centenary of Admiral Gago Coutinho.
409 **66** 1e. multicoloured 25 15

67 Arms of Vasco da Gama
68 L. A. Rebello da Silva

1969. 500th Birth Anniv of Vasco da Gama (explorer).
410 **67** 2e.50 multicoloured 30 10

1969. Centenary of Overseas Administrative Reforms.
411 **68** 50c. multicoloured 25 10

69 Arms of King Manoel I
70 Ulysses Grant and Square, Bolama

1969. 500th Birth Anniv of Manoel I.
412 **69** 2e. multicoloured 30 10

1970. Centenary of Arbitral Judgment on Sovereignty of Bolama.
413 **70** 2e.50 multicoloured 35 20

71 Marshal Carmona
73 Camoens

1970. Birth Centenary of Marshal Carmona.
414 **71** 1e.50 multicoloured 30 15

1972. 400th Anniv of Camoens' "The Lusiads" (epic poem).
422 **73** 50c. multicoloured 25 20

74 Weightlifting and Hammer-throwing

1972. Olympic Games, Munich.
423 **74** 2e.50 multicoloured 30 10

75 Fairey IIID Seaplane "Lusitania" taking-off from Lisbon

1972. 50th Anniv of 1st Lisbon–Rio de Janeiro Flight.
424 **75** 1e. multicoloured 20 10

76 W.M.O. Emblem

1973. Centenary of I.M.O./W.M.O.
425 **76** 2e. multicoloured 25 15

CHARITY TAX STAMPS

The notes under this heading in Portugal also apply here.

C **16** C **29a** Arms

C **26**

1919. Fiscal stamp optd **REPUBLICA TAXA DE GUERRA**.
C241 C **16** 10r. brown, buff & blk 50·00 37·00

1925. Marquis de Pombal Commem stamps of Portugal but inscr "GUINE".
C247 C **73** 15c. black and red 65 55
C248 – 15c. black and red 65 55
C249 C **75** 15c. black and red 65 55

1934.
C270 C **26** 50c. purple and green 10·00 5·50

1938.
C297 C **29a** 50c. yellow 9·25 4·75
C298 50c. brown and green 9·25 4·75

1942. As Type **C 29a** but smaller, 20½ × 25 mm.
C299 C **29a** 50c. black and brown 20 20
C300 50c. black and yellow 2·30 1·30
C301 50c. brown and yellow 2·20 90
C302 2e.50 black and blue 30 35
C303 5e. black and green 35 20
C304 10e. black and blue 1·00 45

Nos. C302/4 were used at several small post offices as ordinary postage stamps during a temporary shortage.

C **59** C **60**

1967. National Defence. No gum.
C379 C **59** 50c. red, pink and black 1·30 60
C380 1e. red, green and black 75 55
C381 5e. red, grey and black 1·70 1·80
C382 10e. red, blue and black 3·75 3·75

A 50e. in the same design was for fiscal use only.

1967. National Defence. No gum.
C383 C **60** 50c. red, pink and black 30 30
C384 1e. red, green and black 30 30
C385 5e. red, grey and black 70 60
C386 10e. red, blue and black 1·40 80

C **61** Carved Statuette of Woman

C **65** Hands grasping Sword

1967. Guinean Artifacts from Bissau Museum. Multicoloured.
C387 50c. Type C **61** 25 20
C388 1e. "Tree of life" (carving) (horiz) 25 20
C389 2e. Cow-headed statuette 30 20
C390 2e.50 "The Magistrate" (statuette) 45 50
C391 5e. "Kneeling Servant" (statuette) 60 50
C392 10e. Stylized pelican (carving) 1·10 1·10
MSC393 149 × 199 mm. Nos. C387/92. Imperf. No gold (sold at 25e.) 5·25 5·25

1968. No. C389 but inscr "TOCADOR DE BOMBOLON" surch.
C394 50c. on 2e. multicoloured 35 35
C395 1e. on 2e. multicoloured 35 35

1969. National Defence.
C398 C **65** 50c. multicoloured 35 35
C399 1e. multicoloured 35 35
C400 2e. multicoloured 35 35
C401 2e.50 multicoloured 35 35
C402 3e. multicoloured 35 35
C403 4e. multicoloured 40 35
C404 5e. multicoloured 55 50
C405 8e. multicoloured 90 90
C406 9e. multicoloured 1·20 1·20
C407 10e. multicoloured 1·00 1·00
C408 15e. multicoloured 1·50 1·50

NOTE—30, 50 and 100e. stamps in the same design were for fiscal use only.

C **72** Mother and Children

1971.
C415 C **72** 50c. multicoloured 20 20
C416 1e. multicoloured 20 20
C417 2e. multicoloured 20 20
C418 3e. multicoloured 20 20
C419 4e. multicoloured 20 20
C420 5e. multicoloured 30 20
C421 10e. multicoloured 60 35

Higher values were intended for fiscal use.

NEWSPAPER STAMP

1983. "Newspaper" key-type inscr "GUINE".
N50 V 2½r. brown 1·30 80

POSTAGE DUE STAMPS

1904. "Due" key-type inscr "GUINE". Name and value in black.
D122 W 5r. green 85 45
D123 10r. grey 85 45
D124 20r. brown 85 45
D125 30r. orange 1·40 1·10
D126 50r. brown 1·40 1·10
D127 60r. brown 3·75 2·75
D128 100r. mauve 3·75 2·75
D129 130r. blue 3·75 2·75
D130 200r. red 5·75 5·25
D131 500r. lilac 13·50 5·25

1911. "Due" key-type of Portuguese Guinea optd **REPUBLICA**.
D138 W 5r. green 20 15
D139 10r. grey 25 20
D140 20r. brown 35 25
D141 30r. orange 35 25
D142 50r. brown 45 25
D143 60r. brown 1·10 85
D208 100r. mauve 2·00 1·70
D145 130r. blue 2·20 1·70
D146 200r. red 2·20 1·70
D147 500r. lilac 1·70 1·40

1921. "Due" key-type of Portuguese Guinea. Currency changed.
D244 W ½c. green 30 25
D245 1c. grey 30 25
D246 2c. brown 30 20
D247 3c. orange 30 25
D248 5c. brown 30 25
D249 6c. brown 75 70
D250 10c. mauve 75 70
D251 13c. blue 75 70
D252 20c. red 75 70
D253 50c. grey 75 70

1925. Marquis de Pombal stamps, as Nos. C247/9 optd **MULTA**.
D254 C **73** 30c. black and red 65 60
D255 – 30c. black and red 65 60
D256 C **75** 30c. black and red 65 60

1952. As Type D **70** of Macao, but inscr "GUINE PORTUGUESA". Numerals in red, name in black (except 2e. in blue).
D323 10c. green and pink 15 15
D324 30c. violet and grey 15 15
D325 50c. green and lemon 15 15
D326 1e. blue and grey 15 15
D327 2e. black and olive 25 25
D328 5e. brown and orange 55 50

PORTUGUESE INDIA Pt. 9

Portuguese territories on the west coast of India, consisting of Goa, Damao and Diu. Became part of India in December 1961.

1871. 1000 reis = 1 milreis.
1882. 12 reis = 1 tanga; 16 tangas = 1 rupia
1959. 100 centavos = 1 escudo.

1 9

1871. Perf.
35 **1** 10r. black 5·25 4·50
33a 15r. pink 12·00 8·75
26 20r. red 18·00 12·00
21 40r. blue 75·00 60·00
22 100r. green 65·00 47·00
23 200r. yellow £180 £160
27 300r. purple 85·00 90·00
28 600r. purple £150 £100
29 900r. purple £150 £100

1877. Star above value. Imperf (241/3) or perf (others).
241 **9** 1½r. black 1·60 1·20
242 4½r. green 16·00 13·00
243 6r. green 13·00 9·50
48 10r. black 29·00 25·00
49 15r. pink 32·00 28·00
50 20r. red 8·75 8·25
51 40r. blue 18·00 16·00
52 100r. green 75·00 60·00
53 200r. yellow 75·00 75·00
54 300r. purple £110 90·00
55 600r. purple £110 90·00
56 900r. purple £110 90·00

1877. "Crown" key-type inscr "INDIA PORTUGUEZA". Perf.
65 P 5r. black 5·25 3·50
58 10r. buff 8·75 7·25
78 10r. green 10·50 8·75
67 20r. bistre 7·25 5·50
68 25r. pink 8·75 7·25
79 25r. grey 38·00 29·00
80 25r. purple 28·00 21·00
69 40r. blue 14·50 8·75
81 40r. yellow 34·00 27·00
70b 50r. green 27·00 18·00
82 50r. blue 18·00 16·00
71 100r. lilac 12·00 10·50
64 200r. orange 24·00 18·00
73 300r. brown 25·00 24·00

See also Nos. 204/10.

1881. Surch in figures.
213 **1** 1½ on 10r. black — £275
215 **9** 1½ on 10r. black — £300
90 **1** 1½ on 20r. red 70·00 65·00
91 **9** 1½ on 20r. red £160 £120
217 **1** 4½ on 40r. blue 31·00 31·00
223 4½ on 100r. green 23·00 19·00
96 5 on 10r. black 7·25 6·00
98 **9** 5 on 10r. black 65·00 27·00
101 **1** 5 on 15r. pink 2·40 2·40
106 5 on 20r. red 2·40 2·40
108 **9** 5 on 20r. red 2·40 2·40
224 **1** 6 on 20r. red
228 6 on 100r. green £200 £150
231 6 on 200r. yellow — £130
233 **9** 6 on 200r. yellow £375 £300

1881. "Crown" key-type of Portuguese India surch in figures.
199 P 1½ on 4½ on 5r. black 50·00 42·00
109 1½ on 5r. black 1·70 80
200 1½ on 6 on 10r. green 70·00 65·00
110 1½ on 10r. green 1·50 1·30
111 1½ on 20r. bistre 16·00 12·50
157 1½ on 25r. grey 38·00 31·00
158 1½ on 100r. lilac 60·00 55·00
200a 1½ on 1t. on 20r. bistre — £130
201 2 on 4t. on 50r. green £300 £250
114 4½ on 5r. black 7·75 7·75
115 4½ on 10r. green £160 £160
116 4½ on 20r. bistre 3·50 3·25
162 4½ on 25r. purple 15·00 13·00
118 4½ on 100r. lilac £110 £110
119a 6 on 10r. buff 60·00 55·00
120 6 on 10r. green 12·50 9·75
121 6 on 20r. bistre 18·00 13·00
167 6 on 25r. grey 38·00 23·00
168 6 on 25r. purple 3·00 2·20
169 6 on 40r. blue 75·00 55·00
170 6 on 40r. yellow 55·00 48·00
171 6 on 50r. green 55·00 48·00
127 6 on 50r. blue 65·00 55·00
202 6 on 1t. on 10r. green £140
128 1t. on 10r. green £130 £120
129 1t. on 20r. bistre 55·00 41·00
175 1t. on 25r. grey 35·00 29·00
176 1t. on 25r. purple 15·00 11·50
132 1t. on 40r. blue 19·00 15·00
178 1t. on 50r. green 60·00 55·00
134 1t. on 50r. blue 29·00 19·00
136 1t. on 100r. lilac 23·00 14·50
137 1t. on 200r. orange 41·00 35·00
139 2t. on 25r. purple 15·00 10·00
182 2t. on 25r. grey 38·00 31·00
184 2t. on 40r. blue 35·00 31·00
141 2t. on 40r. yellow 35·00 29·00
142a 2t. on 50r. green 27·00 37·00
143 2t. on 50r. blue 90·00 75·00
144 2t. on 100r. lilac 13·00 10·00
188 2t. on 200r. orange 41·00 31·00
189 2t. on 300r. brown 38·00 35·00
190 4t. on 10r. green 11·50 9·50
191 4t. on 50r. green 11·50 9·50
148 4t. on 200r. orange 50·00 35·00
193 8t. on 20r. bistre 48·00 35·00
194 8t. on 25r. pink £225 £200
151 8t. on 40r. blue 48·00 38·00
196 8t. on 100r. lilac 41·00 35·00
197 8t. on 200r. orange 35·00 31·00
198 8t. on 300r. brown 41·00 35·00

1882. "Crown" key-type of Portuguese India.
204 P 1½r. black 70 65
205 4½r. green 1·20 60
206 6r. green 95 75
207 1t. pink 95 60
208 2t. blue 95 55
209 4t. purple 3·50 2·30
210 8t. orange 3·50 3·00

1886. "Embossed" key-type inscr "INDIA PORTUGUEZA".
244 Q 1½r. black 2·50 1·30
245 4½r. olive 3·00 1·40
246 6r. green 3·25 1·80
247 1t. red 5·00 2·75
248 2t. blue 9·25 4·50
249 4t. lilac 9·25 4·50
257 8t. orange 8·25 4·50

1895. "Figures" key-type inscr "INDIA".
271 R 1½r. black 1·20 65
259 4½r. orange 1·20 75
273 6r. green 1·20 65
274 9r. lilac 5·00 3·50
260 1t. blue 1·70 1·20
261 2t. red 1·70 75
262 4t. blue 2·10 1·20
270 8t. lilac 3·75 2·30

1898. As Vasco da Gama stamps of Portugal T **40** etc, but inscr "INDIA".
275 1½r. green 1·00 45
276 4½r. red 1·00 45
277 6r. purple 1·00 65
278 9r. green 1·50 65
279 1t. blue 2·10 1·50
280 2t. brown 2·50 1·50
281 4t. brown 2·50 2·00
282 8t. brown 5·25 3·50

DESIGNS—HORIZ: 1½r. Departure of fleet; 4½r. Arrival at Calicut; 6r. Embarkation at Rastello; 4t. Flagship "Sao Gabriel"; 8t. Vasco da Gama. VERT: 9r. Muse of History; 1t. Flagship "Sao Gabriel" and portraits of Da Gama and Camoens; 2t. Archangel Gabriel, patron saint of the expedition.

1898. "King Carlos" key-type inscr "INDIA". Value in red (No. 292) or black (others).
323 S 1r. grey 35 30
283 1½r. orange 35 25
324 1½r. grey 45 25
325 2r. orange 35 25
326 2½r. brown 45 25
327 3r. blue 45 25
284 4½r. green 1·00 65
285 6r. brown 1·00 65
328 6r. green 45 25
286 9r. lilac 1·00 65
287 1t. green 1·00 45
329 1t. red 55 25
288 2t. blue 1·20 45
330 2t. brown 2·10 1·00
331 2½t. blue 7·50 3·75
289 4t. blue on blue 2·50 1·10
332 5t. brown on yellow 2·50 1·40
290 8t. purple on pink 5·00 2·30
291 12t. blue on pink 3·75 2·30
334 12t. green on pink 5·00 2·30
292 1rp. black on blue 7·50 3·25
335 1rp. blue on yellow 10·50 9·75
293 2rp. mauve on yellow 10·50 6·25
336 2rp. black on yellow 20·00 20·00

1900. No. 288 surch **1½ Reis**.
295 S 1½r. on 2t. blue 2·10 1·20

1902. Surch.
299 R 1r. on 6r. green 60 40
298 Q 1r. on 2t. blue 70 45
300 2r. on 4½r. olive 50 40
301 R 2r. on 8t. lilac 60 40
302 Q 2½r. on 6r. green 60 40
303 R 2½r. on 9r. lilac 60 40
305 3r. on 4½r. orange 1·40 95
304 Q 3r. on 1t. red 50 40
306 R 3r. on 1t. blue 1·20 1·20
337 S 2t. on 2½t. blue and black 2·20 1·90
307 Q 2½t. on 1½r. black 1·70 1·30
310 R 2½t. on 1½r. black 1·70 1·20
309 Q 2½t. on 4t. lilac 1·70 1·20
315 R 5t. on 2t. red 1·70 1·20

317 5t. on 4t. blue 1·70 1·20
314 Q 5t. on 8t. orange 1·00 65

1902. 1898 "King Carlos" stamps optd **PROVISORIO**.
319 S 6r. brown and black 1·70 1·20
320 1t. green and black 1·70 1·20
321 2t. blue and black 1·70 1·20

1911. 1898 "King Carlos" stamps optd **REPUBLICA**. Value in black.
338 S 1r. grey 25 20
339 1½r. grey 25 20
340 2r. orange 25 20
341 2½r. brown 45 20
342 3r. blue 45 20
343 4½r. green 45 20
344 6r. green 35 20
345 9r. lilac 45 20
346 1t. red 65 20
347 2t. brown 75 20
348 4t. blue on blue 1·30 1·10
349 5t. brown on yellow 1·60 1·10
350 8t. purple on pink 4·75 2·75
402 12t. green on pink 3·00 2·30
352 1rp. blue on yellow 7·50 6·50
405 2rp. black on yellow 10·50 7·00
404 2rp. mauve on yellow 10·50 7·00

Both unused and used prices for the following issue (Nos. 371 etc.) are for entire stamps showing both halves.

1911. Various stamps bisected by vertical perforation, and each half surch. (a) On 1898 "King Carlos" key-type.
371 S 1r. on 2r. orange and black 40 40
372 1r. on 1t. red and black 40 40
378 1r. on 5t. brown and black on yellow 60 45
374 1½r. on 2½r. brown and black 70 60
354 1½r. on 4½r. green and black 15·00 7·00
355 1½r. on 9r. lilac and black 60 45
356 1½r. on 4t. blue and black on blue 60 45
375 2r. on 2½r. brown and black 60 45
357 2r. on 4t. blue and black on blue 1·00 60
376 3r. on 2½r. brown and black 60 45
377 3r. on 2t. brown and black 70 60
358 6r. on 4½r. green and black 80 65
359d 6r. on 9r. lilac and black 80 65
379 6r. on 8t. purple and black on pink 2·75 2·20

(b) On 1902 Provisional issue.
360 R 1r. on 5t. on 2t. red 7·50 6·00
361 1r. on 5t. on 4t. blue 6·25 4·50
363 Q 1r. on 5t. on 8t. orange 2·75 1·90
364 2r. on 2½r. on 6r. green 2·50 2·30
365 R 2r. on 2½r. on 9r. lilac 17·00 13·50
366 3r. on 5t. on 2t. red 7·50 4·50
367 3r. on 5t. on 4t. blue 7·50 4·50
370 Q 3r. on 5t. on 8t. orange 2·10 1·40

(c) On 1911 issue (optd **REPUBLICA**).
380 S 1r. on 1r. grey and black 40 35
381 1r. on 2r. orange and black 40 35
382 1r. on 1t. red and black 40 35
383 1r. on 5t. brown and black on yellow 40 35
384 1½r. on 4½r. green and black 60 35
419 3r. on 2t. brown and black 3·00 2·00
420 6r. on 4½r. green and black 1·40 65
386 6r. on 9r. lilac and black 60 35
422 6r. on 8t. purple and black on pink 1·50 1·20

1913. Nos. 275/82 optd **REPUBLICA**.
389 1½r. green 40 25
390 4½r. red 40 25
391 6r. purple 45 35
392 9r. green 55 35
393 1t. blue 95 35
394 2t. brown 1·30 1·40
395 4t. brown 1·10 35
396 8t. brown 1·90 1·10

1914. Stamps of 1902 optd **REPUBLICA**.
406 R 2r. on 8t. lilac 6·25 4·00
407 Q 2½r. on 6r. green 1·00 75
415 S 1t. green and black (No. 320) 7·50 4·50
458 2t. blue and black (No. 321) 1·20 1·10
459 2t. on 2½t. blue and black 1·40 1·10
408 R 5t. on 2t. red 3·00 2·20
410 5t. on 4t. blue 3·00 2·30
460 Q 5t. on 8t. orange 1·70 1·30

1914. "King Carlos" key-type of Portuguese India optd **REPUBLICA** and surch.
423 S 1½r. on 4½r. green and black 50 45
424 1½r. on 9r. lilac and black 50 45
425 1½r. on 12t. green and black on pink 80 75
426 3r. on 1t. red and black 55 45
427 3r. on 2t. brown and black 95 75
428 3r. on 8t. purple and black on pink 2·10 1·60
429 3r. on 1rp. blue and black on yellow 75 50
430 3r. on 2rp. black on yellow 95 65

1914. Nos. 390 and 392/6 surch.
433 1½ on 4½r. red 50 40
434 1½r. on 9r. green 50 40
435 3r. on 1t. blue 50 40
436 3r. on 2t. brown 80 50
437 3r. on 4t. brown 50 40
438 3r. on 8t. brown 2·20 1·20

1914. "Ceres" key-type inscr "INDIA". Name and value in black.
439 U 1r. green 50 40
440 1½r. green 50 40
441 2r. black 65 40
442 2½r. green 65 40
443 3r. lilac 75 40
474 4r. blue 1·40 1·00
444 4½r. red 75 40
445 5r. green 75 40
446 6r. brown 75 40
447 9r. blue 80 45
448 10r. red 1·00 60
449 1t. violet 1·70 60
481 1½t. green 1·40 1·00
450 2t. blue 1·70 75
483 2½t. turquoise 1·40 1·00
451 3t. brown 2·50 95
484 3t. 4 brown 5·00 2·30
452 4t. grey 1·70 1·20
453 8t. purple 6·25 4·50
454 12t. brown on green 4·50 3·50
455 1rp. brown on pink 21·00 11·50
487 1rp. brown 18·00 14·00
456 2rp. orange on orange 12·50 9·50
488 2rp. yellow 19·00 14·00
457 3rp. green on blue 14·50 9·75
489 3rp. green 29·00 23·00
490 5rp. red 33·00 26·00

1922. "Ceres" key-type of Portuguese India surch with new value.
496 U 1½r. on 8t. purple and black 1·40 95
492 1½r. on 2r. black 70 50
497 2½t. on 3t. 4 brown and black 43·00 32·00

34 Vasco da Gama and Flagship "Sao Gabriel"

1925. 400th Death Anniv of Vasco da Gama. No gum.
493 **34** 6r. brown 4·50 2·75
494 1t. purple 6·25 3·00

36 The Signature of Francis

40 "Portugal" and Galeasse

1931. St. Francis Xavier Exhibition.
498 – 1r. green 75 70
499 **36** 2r. brown 85 70
500 – 6r. purple 1·60 1·75
501 – 1½t. brown 5·75 3·75
502 – 2t. blue 9·50 5·50
503 – 2½t. red 13·50 5·50
DESIGNS—VERT: 1r. Monument to St. Francis; 6r. St. Francis in surplice and cassock; 1½t. St. Francis and Cross; 2½t. St. Francis's Tomb. HORIZ: 2t. Bom Jesus Church, Goa.

1933.
504 **40** 1r. brown 20 15
505 2r. brown 20 15
506 4r. mauve 20 15
507 6r. green 20 15
508 8r. black 45 35
509 1t. grey 45 35
510 1½t. red 45 35
511 2t. brown 45 35
512 2½t. blue 1·40 55
513 3t. turquoise 1·60 55
514 5t. red 2·30 55
515 1rp. green 5·75 2·20
516 2rp. purple 11·50 5·75
517 3rp. orange 15·00 8·75
518 5rp. green 32·00 21·00

1938. As T **27** and **28** of Portuguese Guinea, but inscr "ESTADO DA INDIA".
519 **27** 1r. green (postage) 20 15
520 2r. brown 20 15
521 3r. violet 20 15
522 6r. green 20 15
523 – 10r. red 45 30
524 – 1t. mauve 45 30
525 – 1½t. red 45 30
526 – 2t. orange 45 30
527 – 2½t. blue 45 30
528 – 3t. grey 1·00 35
529 – 5t. purple 1·60 45
530 – 1rp. red 4·50 90
531 – 2rp. green 6·75 2·50
532 – 3rp. blue 13·00 6·00
533 – 5rp. brown 28·00 7·25
DESIGNS: 10r. to 1½t. Mousinho de Albuquerque; 2t. to 3t. Prince Henry the Navigator; 5t. to 2rp. Dam; 3, 5rp. Afonso de Albuquerque.

534 **28** 1t. red (air) 1·40 65
535 2½t. violet 1·40 65
536 3½t. orange 1·40 65
537 4½t. blue 1·40 65
538 7t. red 1·60 65
539 7½t. green 1·80 65
540 9t. brown 6·25 1·90
541 11t. mauve 6·75 1·90

1942. Surch.
549 **40** 1r. on 8r. black 85 70
546 1r. on 5t. red 85 70
550 2r. on 8r. black 85 70
547 3r. on 1½t. red 90 75
551 3r. on 2t. brown 90 75
552 3r. on 3rp. orange 2·10 1·60
553 6r. on 2½t. blue 2·10 1·60
554 6r. on 3t. turquoise 2·10 1·60
542 1t. on 1½t. red 2·50 1·90
548 1t. on 2t. brown 2·10 1·60
543 1t. on 1rp. green 2·50 1·90
544 1t. on 2rp. purple 2·50 1·90
545 1t. on 5rp. green 2·50 1·90

48 St. Francis Xavier

50 D. Joao de Castro

1946. Portraits and View.
555 **48** 1r. black and grey 65 30
556 – 2r. purple and pink 65 30
557 – 6r. bistre and buff 65 30
558 – 7r. violet and mauve 2·75 90
559 – 9r. brown and buff 2·75 90
560 – 1t. green and light green 2·20 90
561 – 3½t. blue and light blue 2·30 1·20
562 – 1rp. purple and bistre 6·00 1·50
MS563 169×280 mm. Nos. 555/62 (sold at 1½rp.) 38·00 33·00
DESIGNS: 2r. Luis de Camoens; 6r. Garcia de Orta; 7r. Beato Joao Brito; 9r. Vice-regal Archway; 1t. Afonso de Albuquerque; 3½t. Vasco da Gama; 1rp. D. Francisco de Almeida.

1948. Portraits.
564 **50** 3r. blue and light blue 1·60 60
565 – 1t. green and light green 1·60 70
566 – 1½t. purple and mauve 2·75 1·40
567 – 2½t. red and orange 3·50 1·60
568 – 7½t. purple and brown 5·00 2·20
MS569 108×149 mm. Nos. 564/8 (sold at 1rp.) 38·00 36·00
PORTRAITS: 1t. St. Francis Xavier; 1½t. P. Jose Vaz; 2½t. D. Luis de Ataide; 7½t. Duarte Pacheco Pereira.

1948. Statue of Our Lady of Fatima. As T **33** of Portuguese Guinea.
570 1t. green 5·25 3·00

53 Our Lady of Fatima

59 Father Jose Vaz

1949. Statue of Our Lady of Fatima.
571 **53** 1r. light blue and blue 1·30 65
572 3r. yellow, orange and lemon 1·30 65
573 9r. red and mauve 1·90 80
574 2t. green and light green 6·75 1·30
575 9t. red and vermilion 6·00 2·10
576 2rp. brown and purple 11·50 2·50
577 5rp. black and green 21·00 6·25
578 8rp. blue and violet 46·00 11·50

1949. 75th Anniv of U.P.U. As T **34** of Portuguese Guinea.
579 2½t. red 3·50 1·70

1950. Holy Year. As Nos. 425/6 of Macao.
580 **65** 1r. bistre 90 35
588 1r. red 30 25
589 2r. green 30 25
590 – 3r. brown 30 25
591 **65** 6r. grey 30 65
592 – 9r. mauve 90 65
593 **65** 1t. blue 90 65
581 – 2t. green 95 55
594 – 2t. yellow 90 65
595 **65** 4t. brown 75 65

1950. Nos. 523 and 527 surch.
582 1real on 10r. red 35 30
583 1real on 2½t. blue 35 30
584 2reis on 10r. red 35 30
585 3reis on 2½t. blue 35 30
586 6reis on 2½t. blue 35 30
587 1tanga on 2½t. blue 35 30

1951. Termination of Holy Year. As T **36** of Portuguese Guinea.
596 1rp. blue and grey 1·50 1·00

1951. 300th Birth Anniv of Jose Vaz.
597 **59** 1r. grey and slate 15 10
598 – 2r. orange and brown 15 10
599 **59** 3r. grey and black 45 25
600 – 1t. blue and indigo 20 20
601 **59** 2t. purple and maroon 20 20
602 – 3t. green and black 40 25
603 **59** 9t. violet and blue 40 25
604 – 10t. violet and mauve 95 55
605 – 12t. brown and black 3·25 75
DESIGNS: 2r., 1, 3, 10t. Sancoale Church Ruins; 12t. Veneravel Altar.

60 Goa Medical School

1952. 1st Tropical Medicine Congress, Lisbon.
606 **60** 4½t. turquoise and black 4·75 1·80

1952. 4th Death Cent of St. Francis Xavier. As Nos. 452/4 of Macao but without lined background.
607 6r. multicoloured 30 20
608 2t. multicoloured 2·10 50
609 5t. green, silver and mauve 4·25 1·00
MS610 76×65 mm. 4t. green, silver and ochre (as No. 609 but smaller); 8t. slate (T **62**) 16·00 16·00
MS611 90×100 mm. 9t. sepia and brown (T **62**) 16·00 16·00

62 St. Francis Xavier

63 Stamp of 1871

64 The Virgin

1952. Philatelic Exhibition, Goa.
612 **63** 3t. black 13·00 9·75
613 **62** 5t. black and lilac 13·00 9·75

1953. Missionary Art Exhibition.
614 **64** 6r. black and blue 25 15
615 1t. brown and buff 90 65
616 3t. lilac and yellow 2·75 1·30

1953. Portuguese Postage Stamp Centenary. As T **41** of Portuguese Guinea.
617 1t. multicoloured 95 75

66 Dr. Gama Pinto

67 Academy Buildings

1954. Birth Centenary of Dr. Gama Pinto.
618 **66** 3r. green and grey 20 15
619 2t. black and blue 35 30

1954. 4th Centenary of Sao Paulo. As T **42** of Portuguese Guinea.
620 2t. multicoloured 40 35

1954. Centenary of Afonso de Albuquerque National Academy.
621 **67** 9t. multicoloured 95 45

68 Mgr. Dalgado

71 M. A. de Sousa

72 F. de Almeida

73 Map of Bacaim

1955. Birth Centenary of Mgr. Dalgado.
622 **68** 1r. multicoloured 10 10
623 1t. multicoloured 30 20

1956. 450th Anniv of Portuguese Settlements in India. Multicoloured. (a) Famous Men. As T **71**.
624 6r. Type **71** 15 15
625 1½t. F. N. Xavier 20 15
626 4t. A. V. Lourenco 20 15
627 8t. Father Jose Vaz 45 25

628 9t. M. G. de Heredia 45 25
629 2rp. A. C. Pacheco . . . . . 1·70 1·10

(b) Viceroys. As T **72**.

630 3r. Type **72** 15 15
631 9r. A. de Albuquerque . . . 15 15
632 1t. Vasco da Gama 25 20
633 3t. N. da Cunha 35 20
634 10t. J. de Castro 50 20
635 3rp. C. de Braganca . . . . 2·40 1·30

(c) Settlements. As T **73**.

636 2t. Type **73** . . . . 2·75 1·80
637 2½t. Mombaim . . . . 1·30 1·00
638 3½t. Damao . . . . 1·30 1·00
639 5t. Diu 65 50
640 12t. Cochim . . . . 1·00 90
641 1rp. Goa . . . . 2·20 1·60

74 Map of Damao. Dadra and Nagar Aveli Districts

75 Arms of Vasco da Gama

1957. Centres multicoloured.

642 **74** 3r. grey 10 10
643 6r. green 10 10
644 3t. pink 20 15
645 6t. blue 20 15
646 11t. bistre 65 20
647 2rp. lilac . . . . 1·20 75
648 3rp. yellow . . . . 1·70 1·60
649 5rp. red . . . . 3·00 2·00

1958. Heraldic Arms of Famous Men. Multicoloured.

650 2r. Type **75** 10 10
651 6r. Lopo Soares de Albergaria 10 10
652 9r. D. Francisco de Almeida 10 10
653 1t. Garcia de Noronha . . . 15 15
654 4t. D. Afonso de Albuquerque 20 15
655 5t. D. Joao de Castro . . . 35 15
656 11t. D. Luis de Ataide . . . 55 50
657 1rp. Nuno da Cunha 85 55

1958. 6th International Congress of Tropical Medicine. As T **45** of Portuguese Guinea.

658 5t. multicoloured 80 60

DESIGN: 5t. "Holarrhena antidysenterica" (plant).

1958. Brussels Int Exn. As T **44** of Portuguese Guinea.

659 1rp. multicoloured 55 50

1959. Surch in new currency.

660 – 5c. on 2r. (No. 650) . . . 15 15
661 **74** 10c. on 3r. grey 15 15
662 – 15c. on 6r. (No. 651) . . . 15 15
663 – 20c. on 9r. (No. 652) . . . 15 15
664 – 30c. on 1t. (No. 653) . . . 15 15
681 – 40c. on 1½t. (No. 566) . . 15 15
682 – 40c. on 1½t. (No. 625) . . 15 15
683 – 40c. on 2t. (No. 620) . . . 15 15
665 **73** 40c. on 2t.30 . . . . . . 15 15
666 – 40c. on 2½t. (No. 637) . . 15 35
667 – 40c. on 3½t. (No. 638) . . 15 15
668 **74** 50c. on 3t. pink 15 15
684 **64** 80c. on 3t. lilac and yellow 15 15
669 – 80c. on 3t. (No. 633) . . . 15 15
685 – 80c. on 3½t. (No. 561) . . 15 15
686 – 80c. on 5t. (No. 658) . . . 65 25
670 – 80c. on 10t. (No. 634) . . 40 35
687 – 80c. on 1rp. (No. 659) . . 1·30 85
671 – 80c. on 3rp. (No. 635) . . 65 35
672 – 1e. on 4t. (No. 654) . . . 15 15
673 – 1e.50 on 5t. (No. 655) . . 25 15
674 **74** 2e. on 6t. blue 15 15
675 2e.50 on 11t. bistre . . . 40 15
676 – 4e. on 11t. (No. 656) . . . 50 35
677 – 4e.50 on 1rp. (No. 657) . . 65 50
678 **74** 5e. on 2rp. lilac 65 35
679 10e. on 3rp. yellow . . . . 1·00 85
680 30e. on 5rp. red . . . . . 3·00 85

78 Coin of Manoel I

79 Prince Henry's Arms

1959. Portuguese Indian Coins. Designs showing both sides of coins of various rulers. Multicoloured.

688 5c. Type **78** 10 10
689 10c. Joao III 10 10
690 15c. Sebastiao 10 10
691 30c. Filipe I 25 20
692 40c. Filipe II 25 20
693 50c. Filipe III 30 10
694 60c. Joao IV 30 10
695 80c. Afonso VI 30 10
696 1e. Pedro II 30 10
697 1e.50 Joao V 30 10
698 2e. Jose I 45 30
699 2e.50 Maria I 50 25
700 3e. Prince Regent Joao . . . 50 30
701 4e. Pedro IV 50 35
702 4e.40 Miguel 65 50
703 5e. Maria II 65 50
704 10e. Pedro V . . . . 1·00 1·00
705 20e. Luis . . . . 2·20 2·00
706 30e. Carlos . . . . 3·25 2·50
707 50e. Portuguese Republic . . 5·25 3·25

1960. 500th Death Anniv of Prince Henry the Navigator.

708 **79** 3e. multicoloured . . . . . 1·30 60

The 1962 sports set and malaria eradication stamp similar to those for the other territories were ready for issue when Portuguese India was occupied, but they were not put on sale there.

CHARITY TAX STAMPS.

The notes under this heading in Portugal also apply here.

1919. Fiscal stamp. Type C **1** of Portuguese Africa optd **TAXA DE GUERRA**.

C491 Rps. 0:00:05, 48 green . . . 2·20 1·70
C492 Rps. 0:02:03, 43 green . . . 4·75 3·00

1925. Marquis de Pombal Commem stamps of Portugal, but inscr "INDIA".

C495 C **73** 6r. pink 50 45
C496 – 6r. pink 50 45
C497 C **75** 6r. pink 50 45

C **52** Mother and Child

C **69** Mother and Child

1948. (a) Inscr "ASSISTENCIA PUBLICA".

C571 C **52** 6r. green . . . . . . 3·50 2·10
C572 6r. yellow . . . . . . 2·50 1·60
C573 1t. red . . . . 3·50 2·10
C574 1t. orange . . . . . . 2·50 1·60
C575 1t. green . . . . . . 3·75 2·30

(b) Inscr "PROVEDORIA DE ASSISTENCIA PUBLICA".

C607 C **52** 1t. grey . . . . 3·25 2·00

1951. Surch **1 tanga**.

C606 C **52** 1t. on 6r. red . . . . 2·50 1·60

1953. Optd **"Revalidado" P. A. P.** and dotted line.

C617 C **52** 1t. red . . . . 7·75 4·50

1953. Surch as in Type C **69**.

C624 C **69** 1t. on 4t. blue . . . . 9·50 6·75

C **70** Mother and Child

C **80** Arms and People

1956.

C625 C **70** 1t. black, green and red 65 40
C626 1t. blue, orange & grn 55 40

1957. Surch **6 reis**.

C650 C **70** 6r. on 1t. black, green and red 90 55

1959. Surch.

C688 C **70** 20c. on 1t. blue, orange and green 45 45
C689 40c. on 1t. blue, orange and green 45 45

1960.

C709 C **80** 20e. brown and red . . 45 45

POSTAGE DUE STAMPS

1904. "Due" key-type inscr "INDIA".

D337 W 2r. green 35 35
D338 3r. green 35 30
D339 4r. orange 35 30
D340 5r. grey 35 30
D341 6r. grey 35 30
D342 9r. brown 55 50
D343 1t. red 55 50
D344 2t. brown . . . . 1·00 60
D345 5t. blue . . . . 2·50 2·10
D346 10t. red . . . . 2·75 2·50
D347 1rp. lilac . . . . 11·50 5·50

1911. Nos. D337/47 optd **REPUBLICA**.

D354 W 2r. green 25 15
D355 3r. green 25 15
D356 4r. orange 25 15
D357 5r. grey 25 15
D358 6r. grey 30 15
D359 9r. brown 40 15
D360 1t. red 40 15
D361 2t. brown 65 35
D362 5t. blue . . . . 1·40 1·20
D363 10t. red . . . . 4·25 2·50
D364 1rp. lilac . . . . 4·25 2·50

1925. Marquis de Pombal stamps, as Nos. C495/7 optd **MULTA**.

D495 C **73** 1t. pink 35 35
D496 – 1t. pink 35 35
D497 C **75** 1t. pink 35 35

1943. Stamps of 1933 surch **Porteado** and new value.

D549 **40** 3r. on 2½t. blue 45 40
D550 6r. on 3t. turquoise . . . 1·00 60
D551 1t. on 5t. red . . . . . 1·80 1·50

1945. As Type D **1** of Portuguese Colonies, but optd **ESTADO DA INDIA**.

D555 2r. black and red 75 70
D556 3r. black and blue 75 70
D557 4r. black and yellow . . . 75 70
D558 6r. black and green 75 70
D559 1t. black and brown . . . 1·00 85
D560 2t. black and brown . . . 1·00 85

1951. Surch **Porteado** and new value and bar.

D588 2rs. on 7r. (No. 558) . . . 45 40
D589 3rs. on 7r. (No. 558) . . . 45 40
D590 1t. on 1rp. (No. 562) . . . 45 40
D591 2t. on 1rp. (No. 562) . . . 45 40

1952. As Type D **70** of Macao, but inscr "INDIA PORTUGUESA". Numerals in red, name in black.

D606 2r. olive and brown 15 15
D607 3r. black and green 15 15
D608 6r. blue and turquoise . . . 20 15
D609 1t. red and grey 25 20
D610 2t. orange, green and grey 60 50
D611 10t. blue, green and yellow 2·20 2·10

1959. Nos. D606/8 and D610/11 surch in new currency.

D688 5c. on 2r. multicoloured . . 20 15
D689 10c. on 3r. multicoloured 20 15
D690 15c. on 6r. multicoloured 30 30
D691 60c. on 2t. multicoloured 95 90
D692 60c. on 10t. multicoloured 2·75 2·40

PORTUGUESE TIMOR Pt. 9

The eastern part of Timor in the Indonesian Archipelago. Administered as part of Macao until 1896, then as a separate Portuguese Overseas Province until 1975.

Following a civil war and the intervention of Indonesian forces the territory was incorporated into Indonesia on 17 July 1976.

1885. 1000 reis = 1 milreis.
1894. 100 avos = 1 pataca.
1960. 100 centavos = 1 escudo.

1885. "Crown" key-type inscr "MACAU" optd **TIMOR**.

1 P 5r. black 95 80
12 10r. green . . . . 2·40 2·10
3 20r. red . . . . 4·50 2·50
4 25r. lilac 80 60
5 40r. yellow . . . . 2·10 1·80
6 50r. blue 95 75
7 80r. grey . . . . 2·50 1·80
8 100r. purple 95 80
19 200r. orange . . . . 2·10 1·80
20 300r. brown . . . . 2·10 1·80

1887. "Embossed" key-type inscr "CORREIO DE TIMOR".

21 Q 5r. black . . . . 1·50 95
22 10r. green . . . . 1·60 1·30
23 20r. red . . . . 2·40 1·30
24 25r. mauve . . . . 3·00 1·50
25 40r. brown . . . . 5·25 2·20
26 50r. blue . . . . 5·25 2·40
27 80r. grey . . . . 6·25 2·50
28 100r. brown . . . . 6·75 3·25
29 200r. lilac . . . . 13·50 6·75
30 300r. orange . . . . 15·00 8·00

1892. "Embossed" key-type inscr "PROVINCIA DE MACAU" surch **TIMOR 30 30**. No gum.

32 Q 30 on 300r. orange . . . . . 3·00 1·80

1894. "Figures" key-type inscr "TIMOR".

33 R 5r. orange 90 50
34 10r. mauve 90 60
35 15r. brown . . . . 1·30 60
36 20r. lilac . . . . 1·30 60
37 25r. green . . . . 1·50 90
38 50r. blue . . . . 2·20 1·60
39 75r. pink . . . . 3·00 2·20
40 80r. green . . . . 3·00 2·20
41 100r. brown on buff . . . . 2·20 1·90
42 150r. red on pink . . . . . 9·50 4·75
43 200r. blue on blue . . . . 9·50 5·25
44 300r. blue on brown . . . . 12·00 6·00

1894. Nos. 21/30 surch **PROVISORIO** and value in European and Chinese. No gum.

46 Q 1a. on 5r. black 90 55
47 2a. on 10r. green 90 50
48 3a. on 20r. red . . . . . . 1·10 90
49 4a. on 25r. purple . . . . . 1·50 90
50 6a. on 40r. brown . . . . . 1·50 90
51 8a. on 50r. blue . . . . . . 2·20 1·20
52 13a. on 80r. grey . . . . . 3·00 1·80
53 16a. on 100r. brown . . . . 5·25 5·25
54 31a. on 200r. lilac . . . . . 5·25 5·25
55 47a. on 300r. orange . . . . 15·00 12·00

1895. No. 32 further surch **5 avos PROVISORIO** and Chinese characters with bars over the original surch.

56 Q 5a. on 30 on 300r. orange 16·00 12·50

1898. 400th Anniv of Vasco da Gama's Discovery of Route to India. As Nos. 1/8 of Portuguese Colonies, but inscr "TIMOR" and value in local currency.

58 ½a. green . . . . 1·20 80
59 1a. red . . . . 1·20 80
60 2a. purple . . . . 1·20 80
61 4a. green . . . . 1·20 80
62 8a. blue . . . . 1·60 1·20
63 12a. brown . . . . 2·20 1·50
64 16a. brown . . . . 2·20 1·80
65 24a. brown . . . . 3·50 2·40

1898. "King Carlos" key-type inscr "TIMOR". Name and value in red (78a.) or black (others). With or without gum.

68 S ½a. grey . . . . 1·60 1·50
69 1a. red . . . . 1·60 1·50
70 2a. green 30 30
71 2½a. brown 80 65
72 3a. lilac 80 65
112 3a. green . . . . 1·40 80
73 4a. green 80 65
113 5a. red . . . . 1·20 80
114 6a. brown . . . . 1·20 80
74 8a. blue 80 65
115 9a. brown . . . . 1·20 80
75 10a. blue 80 65
116 10a. brown . . . . 1·20 80
76 12a. pink . . . . 2·40 2·20
117 12a. blue . . . . 6·00 5·25
118 13a. mauve . . . . 1·50 95
119 15a. lilac . . . . 2·50 1·80
78 16a. blue on blue . . . . . 2·40 2·20
79 20a. brown on yellow . . . 2·40 2·20
120 22a. brown on pink . . . . 2·50 2·20
80 24a. brown on buff . . . . 2·40 2·20
81 31a. purple on pink . . . . 2·40 2·20
121 31a. brown on cream . . . 2·50 2·20
82 47a. blue on pink . . . . . 4·50 3·50
122 47a. purple on pink . . . . 2·75 2·20
83 78a. black on blue . . . . 6·00 4·50
123 78a. blue on yellow . . . . 6·25 4·50

1899. Nos. 78 and 81 surch **PROVISORIO** and value in figures and bars.

84 S 10 on 16a. blue on blue . . . 1·60 1·50
85 20 on 31a. purple on pink . . 1·60 1·50

1902. Surch.

88 R 5a. on 5r. orange 80 65
86 Q 5a. on 25r. mauve . . . . 1·50 80
89 R 5a. on 25r. green 80 65
90 5a. on 50r. blue 95 80
87 Q 5a. on 200r. lilac . . . . . 2·20 1·50
95 V 6a. on 2½r. brown 60 50
92 Q 6a. on 10r. green . . . . . 95·00 75·00
94 R 6a. on 20r. lilac 95 80
93 Q 6a. on 300r. orange . . . . 2·20 2·20
100 R 9a. on 15r. brown 95 80
98 Q 9a. on 40r. brown . . . . 2·50 2·20
101 R 9a. on 75r. pink 95 80
99 Q 9a. on 100r. brown . . . . 2·50 2·20
124 S 10a. on 12a. blue . . . . . 1·60 1·50
104 R 15a. on 10r. mauve . . . . 1·50 1·30
102 Q 15a. on 20r. red . . . . . 2·50 2·20
103 15a. on 50r. blue . . . . . 75·00 65·00
105 R 15a. on 100r. brn on buff 1·50 1·30
106 15a. on 300r. blue on brn 1·50 1·30
107 Q 22a. on 80r. grey . . . . . 5·25 4·50
108 R 22a. on 80r. green . . . . 2·50 2·40
109 22a. on 200r. blue on blue 2·50 2·40

1902. Nos. 72 and 76 optd **PROVISORIO**.

110 S 3a. lilac . . . . 1·20 80
111 12a. pink . . . . 3·00 2·20

1911. Nos. 68, etc, optd **REPUBLICA**.

125 S ½a. grey 30 30
126 1a. red 30 30
127 2a. green 30 30
128 3a. green 30 30
129 5a. red 60 30
130 6a. brown 60 30
131 9a. brown 60 30
132 10a. brown 80 75
133 13a. purple 80 75
134 15a. lilac 80 75
135 22a. brown on pink 80 75
136 31a. brown on cream . . . 80 75
163 31a. purple on pink . . . . 1·50 1·20
137 47a. purple on pink . . . . 1·80 1·50
165 47a. blue on pink . . . . . 2·40 1·90
167 78a. blue on yellow . . . . 3·00 2·20
168 78a. black on blue . . . . 3·00 3·00

1911. No. 112 and provisional stamps of 1902 optd **Republica**.

139 S 3a. green . . . . 1·00 90
140 R 5a. on 5r. orange 75 75
141 5a. on 25r. green 75 75
142 5a. on 50r. blue . . . . . 1·80 1·50
144 V 6a. on 2½r. brown . . . . 1·50 95
146 R 6a. on 20r. lilac 90 75
147 9a. on 15r. brown 90 75
148 S 10a. on 12a. blue 90 75
149 R 15a. on 100r. brown on buff . . . . 1·00 1·00
150 22a. on 80r. green . . . . 1·90 1·50
151 22a. on 200r. blue on blue 1·90 1·50

1913. Provisional stamps of 1902 optd **REPUBLICA**.

192 S 3a. lilac (No. 110) 45 35
194 R 5a. on 5r. orange 45 30
195 5a. on 25r. green 45 30
196 5a. on 50r. blue 45 65
200 V 6a. on 2½r. brown 45 30

201 R 6a. on 20r. lilac 45 30
202 9a. on 15r. brown 45 30
203 9a. on 75r. pink 50 30
193 S 10a. on 10a. blue 45 35
204 R 15a. on 10r. mauve 50 30
205 15a. on 100r. brown on buff 60 30
206 15a. on 300r. blue on brn 60 30
207 22a. on 80r. green . . . . 1·50 95
208 22a. on 200r. blue on blue 2·20 1·60

1913. Vasco da Gama stamps of Timor optd **REPUBLICA** or surch also.
169 ½a. green 45 35
170 1a. red 45 35
171 2a. purple 45 35
172 4a. green 45 35
173 8a. blue 80 60
174 10a. on 12a. brown . . . . . 1·50 1·20
175 16a. brown . . . . 1·20 80
176 24a. brown . . . . 1·50 1·30

1914. "Ceres" key-type inscr "TIMOR". Name and value in black.
211 U ½a. green 60 60
212 1a. black 60 60
213 1½a. green 60 60
214 2a. green 60 60
180 3a. brown 60 45
181 4a. red 60 45
182 6a. violet 65 45
216 7a. green 95 90
217 7½a. blue 95 90
218 9a. blue . . . . 1·10 90
183 10a. blue 65 45
219 11a. grey . . . . 1·50 1·20
184 12a. brown 95 75
221 15a. mauve . . . . 4·50 2·75
185 16a. grey 95 75
222 18a. blue . . . . 4·50 2·75
223 19a. green . . . . 4·50 2·75
186 20a. red . . . . 9·50 3·00
224 36a. turquoise . . . . 4·50 2·75
187 40a. purple . . . . 5·25 3·00
225 54a. brown . . . . 4·50 2·75
188 58a. brown on green . . . 5·25 2·50
226 72a. red . . . . 8·75 5·50
189 76a. brown on pink . . . . 5·25 4·50
190 1p. orange on orange . . . 8·00 6·75
191 3p. green on blue . . . . . 22·00 13·50
227 5p. red . . . . 37·00 16·00

1920. No. 196 surch ½ **Avo P. P. n.° 68 19-3-1920** and bars.
229 R ½a. on 5a. on 50r. blue . . 8·00 7·50

1932. Nos. 226 and 221 surch with new value and bars.
230 U 6a. on 72a. red 90 75
231 12a. on 15a. mauve 90 75

25a "Portugal" and Galeasse

1935.
232 **25a** ½a. brown 20 15
233 1a. brown 20 15
234 2a. green 20 15
235 3a. mauve 35 15
236 4a. black 35 20
237 5a. grey 35 30
238 6a. brown 35 30
239 7a. red 35 30
240 8a. turquoise 60 30
241 10a. red 60 30
242 12a. blue 60 30
243 14a. green 60 30
244 15a. purple 60 30
245 20a. orange 75 30
246 30a. green 75 45
247 40a. violet . . . . 2·40 1·20
248 50a. brown . . . . 2·40 1·20
249 1p. blue . . . . 5·50 3·50
250 2p. brown . . . . 14·00 5·50
251 3p. green . . . . 19·00 7·50
252 5p. mauve . . . . 31·00 15·00

26a Vasco da Gama

26b Airplane over globe

1938.
253 **26a** 1a. green (postage) . . . 20 20
254 2a. brown 20 20
255 3a. violet 20 20
256 4a. green 20 20
257 – 5a. red 20 20
258 – 6a. grey 20 20
259 – 8a. purple 20 20
260 – 10a. mauve 20 20
261 – 12a. red 30 30
262 – 15a. orange 60 45
263 – 20a. blue 60 45
264 – 40a. black 90 60
265 – 50a. brown . . . . 1·30 90
266 – 1p. red . . . . 4·50 2·75
267 – 2p. olive . . . . 12·00 3·00
268 – 3p. blue . . . . 13·50 6·75
269 – 5p. brown . . . . 30·00 13·50
270 **26b** 1a. red (air) 45 45
271 2a. violet 50 45
272 3a. orange 50 45
273 5a. blue 60 60
274 10a. red 75 75
275 20a. green . . . . 1·60 95
276 50a. brown . . . . 3·25 2·75
277 70a. red . . . . 4·00 3·50
278 1p. mauve . . . . 8·75 4·00
DESIGNS—POSTAGE: 5a. to 8a. Mousinho de Albuquerque; 10a. to 15a. Prince Henry the Navigator; 20a. to 50a. Dam; 1p. to 5p. Afonso de Albuquerque.

1946. Stamps as above but inscr "MOCAMBIQUE" surch **TIMOR** and new value.
279 **26a** 1a. on 15c. purple (post) 3·25 2·75
280 – 4a. on 35c. green . . . . 3·25 2·75
281 – 8a. on 50c. mauve . . . . 3·25 2·75
282 – 10a. on 70c. violet . . . . 3·25 2·75
283 – 12a. on 1e. red . . . . . 3·25 2·75
284 – 20a. on 1e.75 blue . . . . 3·25 2·75
285 **26b** 8a. on 50c. orange (air) 3·25 2·75
286 12a. on 1e. blue . . . . . 3·25 2·75
287 40a. on 3e. green . . . . 3·25 2·75
288 50a. on 5e. brown . . . . 3·25 2·75
289 1p. on 10e. mauve . . . . 3·75 2·75

1947. Nos. 253/64 and 270/78 optd **LIBERTACAO**.
290 **26a** 1a. green (postage) . . . 9·50 6·25
291 2a. brown . . . . 22·00 12·00
292 3a. violet . . . . 8·75 3·75
293 4a. green . . . . 8·75 3·75
294 – 5a. red . . . . 3·75 1·50
295 – 8a. purple 95 45
296 – 10a. mauve . . . . . . 3·75 1·60
297 – 12a. red . . . . 3·75 1·60
298 – 15a. orange . . . . . . 3·75 1·60
299 – 20a. blue . . . . 48·00 27·00
300 – 40a. black . . . . 9·50 7·50
301 **26b** 1a. red (air) . . . . . . 15·00 4·00
302 2a. violet . . . . 15·00 4·00
303 3a. orange . . . . 15·00 4·00
304 5a. blue . . . . 15·00 4·00
305 10a. red . . . . 3·75 1·30
306 20a. green . . . . 3·75 1·30
307 50a. brown . . . . 3·75 1·30
308 70a. red . . . . 15·00 3·75
309 1p. mauve . . . . 6·25 1·50

30 Girl with Gong

31 Pottery-making

1948.
310 – 1a. brown and turquoise 60 30
311 **30** 3a. brown and grey . . . . 1·30 65
312 – 4a. green and mauve . . . 1·60 1·30
313 – 8a. grey and red 95 35
314 – 10a. green and brown . . . 95 35
315 – 20a. ultramarine and blue 95 60
316 – 1p. blue and orange . . . 19·00 4·50
317 – 3p. brown and violet . . . 19·00 8·00
MS317a 130 × 99 mm. Nos. 310/17 (sold at 5p.) . . . .
DESIGNS: 1a. Native woman; 4a. Girl with baskets; 8a. Chief of Aleixo de Ainaro; 10a. Timor chief; 20a. Warrior and horse; 1, 3p. Tribal chieftains.

1948. Honouring the Statue of Our Lady of Fatima. As T **33** of Portuguese Guinea.
318 8a. grey . . . . 5·50 5·50

1949. 75th Anniv of U.P.U. As T **34** of Portuguese Guinea.
319 16a. brown . . . . 13·50 8·00

1950.
320 **31** 20a. blue 60 60
321 – 50a. brown (Young girl) 1·80 80

1950. Holy Year. As Nos. 425/6 of Macao.
322 40a. green . . . . 1·30 90
323 70a. brown . . . . 1·90 1·30

32 "Belamcanda chinensis"

34 Statue of The Virgin

1950.
324 **32** 1a. red, green and grey . . 45 30
325 – 3a. yellow, green and brown . . . . 1·90 1·50
326 – 10a. pink, green and blue 2·20 1·60
327 – 16a. multicoloured . . . . 4·50 2·20
328 – 20a. yellow, green and turquoise . . . . 1·90 1·60
329 – 30a. yellow, green and blue 2·20 1·60
330 – 70a. multicoloured . . . . 3·00 1·80
331 – 1p. red, yellow and green 5·25 3·75
332 – 2p. green, yellow and red 7·50 6·00
333 – 5p. pink, green and black 12·50 9·50

FLOWERS: 3a. "Caesalpinia pulcherrima"; 10a. "Calotropis gigantea"; 16a. "Delonix regia"; 20a. "Plumeria rubra"; 30a. "Allamanda cathartica"; 70a. "Haemanthus multiflorus"; 1p. "Bauhinia"; 2p. "Eurycles amboiniensis"; 5p. "Crinum longiflorum".

1951. Termination of Holy Year. As T **36** of Portuguese Guinea .
334 86a. blue and turquoise . . . 1·50 1·30

1952. 1st Tropical Medicine Congress, Lisbon. As T **37** of Portuguese Guinea.
335 10a. brown and green 80 65
DESIGN: Nurse weighing baby.

1952. 400th Death Anniv of St. Francis Xavier. Designs as No. 452/4 of Macao.
336 1a. black and grey 15 15
337 16a. brown and buff 65 50
338 1p. red and grey . . . . . . 3·00 1·60

1953. Missionary Art Exhibition.
339 **34** 3a. brown and light brown 15 10
340 16a. brown and stone . . . 45 35
341 50a. blue and brown . . . 1·30 1·20

1954. Portuguese Stamp Centenary. As T **41** of Portuguese Guinea.
342 10a. multicoloured 90 80

1954. 400th Anniv of Sao Paulo. As T **42** of Portuguese Guinea.
343 16a. multicoloured 75 45

35 Map of Timor

38 Elephant Jar

1956.
344 **35** 1a. multicoloured 10 10
345 3a. multicoloured 10 10
346 8a. multicoloured 30 20
347 24a. multicoloured 35 20
348 32a. multicoloured 45 20
349 40a. multicoloured 65 35
350 1p. multicoloured . . . . 1·90 45
351 3p. multicoloured . . . . 5·50 2·75

1958. 6th International Congress of Tropical Medicine. As T **45** of Portuguese Guinea.
352 32a. multicoloured . . . . . 2·75 1·90
DESIGN: 32a. "Calophyllum inophyllum" (plant).

1958. Brussels International Exhibition. As T **44** of Portuguese Guinea.
353 40a. multicoloured 45 35

1960. New currency. Nos. 344/51 surch thus: **$05** and bars.
354 **35** 5c. on 1a. multicoloured 15 10
355 10c. on 3a. multicoloured 15 10
356 20c. on 8a. multicoloured 15 10
357 30c. on 24a. multicoloured 15 10
358 50c. on 32s. multicoloured 15 10
359 1e. on 40a. multicoloured 15 15
360 2e. on 40a. multicoloured 30 20
361 5e. on 1p. multicoloured 65 45
362 10e. on 3p. multicoloured 2·20 1·10
363 15e. on 3p. multicoloured 2·20 1·30

1960. 500th Death Anniv of Prince Henry the Navigator. As T **47** of Portuguese Guinea. Multicoloured.
364 4e.50 Prince Henry's motto (horiz) 45 20

1962. Timor Art. Multicoloured.
365 5c. Type **38** 10 10
366 10c. House on stilts 10 10
367 20c. Idol 20 20
368 30c. Rosary 20 20
369 50c. Model of outrigger canoe (horiz) 45 35
370 1e. Casket 35 35
371 2e.50 Archer 60 35
372 4e. Elephant 75 35
373 5e. Native climbing palm tree 95 35
374 10e. Statuette of woman . . 3·00 95
375 20e. Model of cockfight (horiz) . . . . 7·50 2·40
376 50e. House, bird and cat . . 7·25 2·40

1962. Sports. As T **49** of Portuguese Guinea. Multicoloured.
377 50c. Game shooting 10 10
378 1e. Horse-riding 65 20
379 1e.50 Swimming 50 30
380 2e. Athletes 35 35
381 2e.50 Football 65 50
382 15e. Big-game hunting . . . 1·90 1·30

1962. Malaria Eradication. Mosquito design as T **50** of Portuguese Guinea. Multicoloured.
383 2e.50 "Anopheles sundaicus" 50 45

1964. Centenary of National Overseas Bank. As T **53** of Portuguese Guinea, but portrait of M. P. Chagas.
384 2e.50 multicoloured 60 45

1965. I.T.U. Centenary. As T **54** of Portuguese Guinea.
385 1e.50 multicoloured 90 60

1966. 40th Anniv of National Revolution. As T **56** of Portuguese Guinea, but showing different buildings. Multicoloured.
386 4e.50 Dr V. Machado's College and Health Centre, Dili 80 50

1967. Centenary of Military Naval Assn. As T **57** of Portuguese Guinea. Multicoloured.
387 10c. Gago Coutinho and gunboat "Patria" 20 20
388 4e.50 Sacadura Cabral and Fairey IIID seaplane "Lusitania" . . . . 1·50 80

39 Sepoy Officer, 1792

40 Pictorial Map of 1834, and Arms

1967. Portuguese Military Uniforms. Mult.
389 35c. Type **39** 15 15
390 1e. Infantry officer, 1815 . . 1·30 30
391 1e.50 Infantryman 1879 . . . 20 15
392 2e. Infantryman, 1890 . . . 20 15
393 2e.50 Infantry officer, 1903 30 15
394 3e. Sapper, 1918 . . . . . . 50 30
395 4e.50 Commando, 1964 . . . 90 30
396 10e. Parachutist, 1964 . . . 1·30 65

1967. 50th Anniv of Fatima Apparitions. As T **58** of Portuguese Guinea.
397 3e. Virgin of the Pilgrims . . 35 15

1968. 500th Birth Anniv of Pedro Cabral (explorer). As T **64** of Portuguese Guinea. Mult.
398 4e.50 Lopo Homen-Reineis' map, 1519 (horiz) 80 35

1969. Birth Centenary of Admiral Gago Coutinho. As T **66** of Portuguese Guinea. Mult.
399 4e.50 Frigate "Almirante Gago Coutinho" (horiz) . . 95 65

1969. Bicentenary of Dili (capital of Timor).
400 **40** 1e. multicoloured 35 20

1969. 500th Anniv of Vasco da Gama (explorer). As T **67** of Portuguese Guinea. Mult.
401 5e. Convert Medallion . . . 35 20

1969. Centenary of Overseas Administrative Reforms. As T **68** of Portuguese Guinea.
402 5e. multicoloured 35 15

1969. 500th Birth Anniv of King Manoel I. As T **69** of Portuguese Guinea. Multicoloured.
403 4e. Emblem of Manoel I in Jeronimos Monastery . . . 35 15

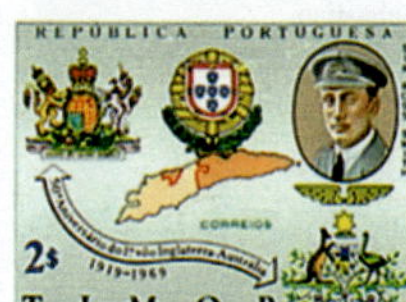

41 Map, Sir Ross Smith, and Arms of Britain, Timor and Australia

1969. 50th Anniv of 1st England–Australia Flight.
404 41 2e. multicoloured 45 30

1970. Birth Centenary of Marshal Carmona. As T **71** of Portuguese Guinea. Multicoloured.
414 1e. Portrait in civilian dress 15 15

1972. 400th Anniv of Camoens' "The Lusiads" (epic poem). As T **73** of Portuguese Guinea. Multicoloured.
415 1e. Missionaries, natives and galleon 20 15

1972. Olympic Games, Munich. As T **74** of Portuguese Guinea. Multicoloured.
416 4e.50 Football 45 20

1972. 50th Anniv of 1st Flight from Lisbon to Rio de Janeiro. As T **75** of Portuguese Guinea. Multicoloured.
417 1e. Aviators Gago Coutinho and Sacadura Cabral in Fairey IIID seaplane . . . 35 30

1973. W.M.O. Centenary. As T **76** of Portuguese Guinea.
418 20e. multicoloured . . . . . 1·50 1·10

CHARITY TAX STAMPS

The notes under this heading in Portugal also apply here.

1919. No. 211 surch **2 AVOS TAXA DA GUERRA**. With or without gum.
C228 U 2a. on ½a. green . . . . 5·25 4·50

1919. No. 196 surch **2 TAXA DE GUERRA** and bars.
C230 R 2 on 5a. on 50r. blue . . 30·00 18·00

1925. Marquis de Pombal Commem. As Nos. 666/8 of Portugal, but inscr "TIMOR".
C231 C 73 2a. red 30 20
C232 – 2a. red 30 20
C233 C 75 2a. red 30 20

1934. Educational Tax. Fiscal stamps as Type C **1** of Portuguese Colonies, with values in black, optd **Instrucao D. L. n.° 7 de 3-2-1934** or surch also. With or without gum.
C234 2a. green . . . . 1·90 1·50
C235 5a. green . . . . 3·00 1·60
C236 7a. on ½a. pink . . . . . . 3·50 2·20

1936. Fiscal stamps as Type C **1** of Portuguese Colonies, with value in black, optd **Assistencia D. L. n.° 72**. With or without gum.
C253 10a. pink . . . . 2·20 1·60
C254 10a. green . . . . 1·60 1·50

C 29

C 42 Woman and Star

1948. No gum.
C310 C 29 10a. blue . . . . . . 1·60 1·30
C311 20a. green . . . . . . 2·20 1·50
The 20a. has a different emblem.

1960. Similar design. New currency. No gum.
C364 70c. blue 65 65
C400 1e.30 green . . . . 1·20 1·20

1969.
C405 C 42 30c. blue and light blue 20 20
C406 50c. purple and orange 20 20
C407 1e. brown and yellow 20 20

1970. Nos. C364 and C400 surch **D. L. n.° 776** and value.
C408 30c. on 70c. blue . . . . . 7·00 7·00
C409 30c. on 1e.30 green . . . . 7·00 7·00
C410 50c. on 70c. blue . . . . . 12·00 12·00
C411 50c. on 1e.30 green . . . . 7·00 7·00
C412 1e. on 70c. blue . . . . . 7·00 7·00
C413 1e. on 1e.30 green . . . . 7·00 7·00

NEWSPAPER STAMPS

1892. "Embossed" key-type inscr "PROVINCIA DE MACAU" surch **JORNAES TIMOR 2½ 2½**. No gum.
N31 Q 2½ on 20r. red . . . . . . 3·75 1·90
N32 2½ on 40r. brown . . . . 1·10 75
N33 2½ on 80r. grey . . . . . 1·10 75

1893. "Newspaper" key-type inscr "TIMOR".
N36 V 2½r. brown 50 45

1894. No. N36 surch **½ avo PROVISORIO** and Chinese characters.
N58 V ½a. on 2½r. brown . . . . 1·20 1·20

POSTAGE DUE STAMPS

1904. "Due" key-type inscr "TIMOR". Name and value in black. With or without gum (1, 2a.), no gum (others).
D124 W 1a. green 35 35
D125 2a. grey 35 35
D126 5a. brown 95 80
D127 6a. orange 95 80
D128 10a. brown 95 80
D129 15a. brown . . . . . . 1·60 1·30
D130 24a. blue . . . . 4·00 2·75
D131 40a. red . . . . 4·00 2·75
D132 50a. orange . . . . . . 5·50 3·25
D133 1p. lilac . . . . 12·00 7·00

1911. "Due" key-type of Timor optd **REPUBLICA**.
D139 W 1a. green 30 35
D140 2a. grey 30 35
D141 5a. brown 30 80
D142 6a. orange 35 80
D143 10a. brown . . . . . . 1·80 1·50
D144 15a. brown . . . . . . 90 1·30
D145 24a. blue . . . . 1·50 95
D146 40a. red . . . . 1·60 2·75
D147 50a. orange . . . . . . 2·20 3·25
D178 1p. lilac 35 35

1925. Marquis de Pombal tax stamps. As Nos. C231/3 of Timor, optd **MULTA**.
D231 C 73 4a. red 30 20
D232 – 4a. red 30 20
D233 C 75 4a. red 30 20

1952. As Type D **70** of Macao, but inscr "TIMOR PORTUGUES". Numerals in red; name in black.
D336 1a. sepia and brown . . . 15 15
D337 3a. brown and orange . . . 15 15
D338 5a. green and turquoise . . 15 15
D339 10a. green and light green 15 15
D340 30a. violet and light violet 20 15
D341 1p. red and orange 60 35

For subsequent issues see **EAST TIMOR**.

PRINCE EDWARD ISLAND Pt. 1

An island off the East coast of Canada, now a province of that Dominion, whose stamps it uses.

1861. 12 pence = 1 shilling.
1872. 100 cents = 1 dollar.

1

7

1861. Queen's portrait in various frames. Values in pence.
9 1 1d. orange . . . . 35·00 45·00
28 2d. red . . . . 7·50 10·00
30 3d. blue . . . . 10·00 14·00
31 4d. black . . . . 5·00 28·00
18 6d. green £100 £100
20 9d. mauve . . . . 85·00 85·00

1870.
32 7 4½d. (3d. stg.) brown . . . . 48·00 60·00

8

1872. Queen's portrait in various frames. Values in cents.
44 8 1c. orange . . . . 6·50 21·00
38 2c. blue . . . . 20·00 42·00
37 3c. red . . . . 18·00 27·00
40 4c. green . . . . 7·00 20·00
41 6c. black . . . . 5·00 21·00
42 12c. mauve . . . . 5·00 38·00

PRUSSIA Pt. 7

Formerly a kingdom in the N. of Germany. In 1867 it became part of the North German Confederation.

1850. 12 pfennig = 1 silbergroschen; 30 silbergroschen = 1 thaler.
1867. 60 kreuzer = 1 gulden.

1 Friedrich Wilhelm IV

3

4

1850. Imperf.
14 1 4pf. green . . . . 70·00 33·00
4 6pf. red . . . . 80·00 47·00
22 ½sgr. (=6pf.) red £200 £150
5 1sgr. black on pink . . . . . 80·00 8·50
16 1sgr. pink . . . . 32·00 2·50
6 2sgr. black on blue . . . . . £110 17·00
18 2sgr. blue . . . . £110 17·00
8 3sgr. black on yellow . . . . £110 13·00
21 3sgr. yellow . . . . £100 15·00

1861. Roul.
24 3 3pf. lilac . . . . 30·00 38·00
26 4pf. green . . . . 10·50 8·50
28 6pf. orange . . . . 10·50 13·00
31 4 1sgr. pink . . . . 3·75 85
35 2sgr. blue . . . . 10·50 1·70
36 3sgr. yellow . . . . 8·50 2·10

5

7

1866. Printed in reverse on back of specially treated transparent paper. Roul.
38 5 10sgr. pink . . . . 70·00 70·00
39 – 30sgr. blue . . . . 95·00 £190
The 30 sgr. has the value in a square.

1867. Roul.
40 7 1k. green . . . . 26·00 43·00
42 2k. orange . . . . 43·00 85·00
43 3k. pink . . . . 21·00 26·00
45 6k. blue . . . . 21·00 43·00
46 9k. bistre . . . . 30·00 43·00

PUERTO RICO Pt. 9, Pt. 22

A West Indian island ceded by Spain to the United States after the war of 1898. Until 1873 stamps of Cuba were in use. Now uses stamps of the U.S.A.

1873. 100 centimos = 1 peseta.
1881. 1000 milesimas = 100 centavos = 1 peso.
1898. 100 cents = 1 dollar.

A. SPANISH OCCUPATION

(2)

1873. Nos. 53/5 of Cuba optd with T **2**.
1 25c. de p. lilac . . . . 36·00 95
3 50c. de p. brown . . . . . . 95·00 4·75
4 1p. brown . . . . £225 19·00

1874. No. 57 of Cuba with opt similar to T **2** (two separate characters).
5 25c. de p. blue . . . . 31·00 2·20

1875. Nos. 61/3 of Cuba with opt similar to T **2** (two separate characters).
6 25c. de p. blue . . . . 22·00 2·20
7 50c. de p. green . . . . . . 31·00 2·50
8 1p. brown . . . . £120 13·50

1876. Nos. 65a and 67 of Cuba with opt similar to T **2** (two separate characters).
9 25c. de p. lilac . . . . 3·50 1·80
10 50c. de p. blue . . . . 8·25 3·00
11 1p. black . . . . 38·00 10·50

1876. Nos. 65a and 67 of Cuba with opt as last, but characters joined.
12 25c. de p. lilac . . . . 30·00 85
13 1p. black . . . . 65·00 10·00

1877. As T **9** of Philippines, but inscr "PTO-RICO 1877".
14 5c. brown . . . . 6·25 2·20
15 10c. red . . . . 19·00 2·50
16 15c. green . . . . 29·00 11·00
17 25c. blue . . . . 11·00 1·80
18 50c. bistre . . . . 19·00 4·25

1878. As T **9** of Philippines, but inscr "PTO-RICO 1878".
19 5c. grey . . . . 14·00 14·00
20 10c. brown . . . . £225 80·00
21 25c. green . . . . 1·80 1·10
22 50c. blue . . . . 6·00 2·40
23a 1p. bistre . . . . 11·00 5·25

1879. As T **9** of Philippines, but inscr "PTO-RICO 1879".
24 5c. red . . . . 12·00 5·25
25 10c. brown . . . . 12·00 5·25
26 15c. grey . . . . 12·00 5·25
27 25c. blue . . . . 4·25 1·80
28 50c. green . . . . 12·00 5·25
29 1p. lilac . . . . 55·00 23·00

1880. "Alfonso XII" key-type inscr "PUERTO-RICO 1880".
30 X ½c. green . . . . 24·00 18·00
31 ½c. red . . . . 6·50 2·40
32 1c. purple . . . . 11·00 9·50
33 2c. grey . . . . 6·50 4·25
34 3c. buff . . . . 6·50 4·25
35 4c. black . . . . 6·50 4·25
36 5c. green . . . . 3·25 1·80
37 10c. red . . . . 3·50 2·20
38 15c. brown . . . . 6·50 3·25
39 25c. lilac . . . . 3·25 1·60
40 40c. grey . . . . 12·00 1·60
41 50c. brown . . . . 25·00 16·00
42 1p. bistre . . . . 90·00 19·00

1881. "Alfonso XIII" key-type inscr "PUERTO-RICO 1881".
43 X ½m. red 25 15
45 1m. violet 25 15
46 2m. red 45 30
47 4m. green 85 25
48 6m. purple 85 50
49 8m. blue . . . . 1·90 1·20
50 1c. green . . . . 3·25 1·20
51 2c. red . . . . 4·00 3·25
52 3c. brown . . . . 9·00 5·25
53 5c. lilac . . . . 3·00 30
54 8c. brown . . . . 3·00 1·40
55 10c. grey . . . . 26·00 8·25
56 20c. bistre . . . . 34·00 16·00

1882. "Alfonso XII" key-type inscr "PUERTO-RICO".
57 X ½m. red 20 15
74 1m. red 20 15
75 1m. orange 20 20
59 2m. mauve 20 15
60 4m. purple 20 15
61 6m. brown 40 15
62 8m. green 40 15
63 1c. green 20 15
64 2c. red . . . . 1·20 15
65 3c. yellow . . . . 4·00 2·40
76 3c. brown . . . . 2·75 50
77 5c. lilac . . . . 16·00 1·20
67 8c. brown . . . . 3·50 15
68 10c. green . . . . 3·50 30
69 20c. grey . . . . 5·75 30
70 40c. blue . . . . 40·00 16·00
71 80c. bistre . . . . 60·00 22·00

1890. "Baby" key-type inscr "PUERTO-RICO".
80 Y ½m. black 20 15
95 ½m. grey 15 15
111 ½m. brown 15 15
124 ½m. purple 20 15
81 1m. green 30 15
96 1m. purple 15 15
112 1m. blue 15 15
125 1m. brown 20 15
82 2m. red 20 15
97 2m. purple 15 15
126 2m. green 20 15
83 4m. black . . . . 11·50 6·25
98 4m. blue 15 15
114 4m. brown 15 15
127 4m. green . . . . 1·00 30
84 6m. brown . . . . 40·00 16·00
99 6m. red 15 15
85 8m. bistre . . . . 29·00 23·00
100 8m. green 15 15
86 1c. brown 20 15
101 1c. green 60 15
115 1c. purple . . . . 6·00 50
128 1c. red 70 15
87 2c. purple . . . . 1·00 95
102 2c. pink 95 15
116 2c. lilac . . . . 2·40 50
129 2c. brown 70 15
88 3c. blue . . . . 6·00 50
103 3c. orange 95 15
117 3c. grey . . . . 6·00 50
131 3c. brown 25 15
118 4c. blue . . . . 1·50 50
132 4c. brown 80 15
89 5c. purple . . . . 12·50 45
104 5c. green 95 15
133 5c. blue 25 15
120 6c. orange 50 15
134 6c. lilac 25 15
90 8c. blue . . . . 16·00 1·90
105 8c. brown 15 15
121 8c. purple . . . . 13·00 5·25
135 8c. red . . . . 3·00 1·50
106 10c. red . . . . 1·40 35
122 20c. red . . . . 1·60 50
107 20c. lilac . . . . 2·30 50
136 20c. grey . . . . 7·25 1·50
93 40c. orange . . . . £120 50·00
108 40c. blue . . . . 5·75 3·75
137 40c. red . . . . 7·25 1·50
94 80c. green £475 £170
109 80c. red . . . . 14·50 11·50
138 80c. black . . . . 29·00 23·00

13 Landing of Columbus

1893. 400th Anniv of Discovery of America by Columbus.
110 13 3c. green . . . . £190 47·00

1898. "Curly Head" key-type inscr "PTO RICO 1898 y 99".
139 Z 1m. brown 15 15
140 2m. brown 15 15
141 3m. brown 15 15
142 4m. brown . . . . 1·50 60
143 5m. brown 15 15
144 1c. purple 15 15
145 2c. green 15 15
146 3c. brown 15 15

147 4c. orange . . . . 1·50 1·10
148 5c. pink 15 15
149 6c. blue 15 15
150 8c. brown 15 15
151 10c. red 15 15
152 15c. grey 15 15
153 20c. purple . . . . 1·80 60
154 40c. lilac . . . . 1·30 1·40
155 60c. black . . . . 1·30 1·40
156 80c. brown . . . . 4·75 5·25
157 1p. green . . . . 10·50 10·50
158 2p. blue . . . . 25·00 14·00

1898. "Baby" key-type inscr "PUERTO RICO" and optd **Habilitado PARA 1898 y '99**.
159 Y ¼m. purple . . . . . . 10·50 6·00
160 1m. brown 45 25
161 2m. green 25 25
162 4m. green 25 25
163 1c. purple . . . . 1·20 1·20
164 2c. brown 25 25
165 3c. blue . . . . 21·00 9·50
166 3c. brown . . . . 1·80 1·80
167 4c. brown 45 45
168 4c. blue . . . . 12·50 8·25
169 5c. blue 45 45
170 5c. green . . . . 6·00 4·50
172 6c. lilac 45 30
173a 8c. red 70 30
174 20c. grey 70 70
175 40c. red . . . . 1·00 70
176 80c. black . . . . 21·00 14·00

WAR TAX STAMPS

1898. 1890 and 1898 stamps optd **IMPUESTO DE GUERRA** or surch also.
W177 Y 1m. blue . . . . . . 2·75 1·90
W178 1m. brown . . . . . . 7·25 5·25
W179 2m. red . . . . . . 14·00 9·00
W180 2m. green . . . . . . 7·25 5·25
W181 4m. green . . . . . . 8·00 8·00
W182a 1c. brown . . . . . . 7·25 4·50
W183 1c. purple . . . . . . 12·00 11·50
W184 2c. purple 95 95
W185 2c. pink 45 30
W186 2c. lilac 45 30
W187 2c. brown 40 35
W192 2c. on 2m. red 45 30
W193c 2c. on 5c. green . . . . 2·75 1·80
W188 3c. orange . . . . . . 14·00 11·50
W194 3c. on 10c. red . . . . 2·40 1·80
W195 4c. on 20c. red . . . . 14·00 10·50
W189 5c. green . . . . . . 1·90 1·90
W196a 5c. on ½m. brown . . . 3·00 3·00
W197 5c. on 1m. purple . . . 30 30
W198 5c. on 1m. blue . . . . 7·25 5·25
W199 Z 5c. on 1m. brown . . . 7·25 5·25
W200 Y 5c. on 5c. green . . . . 7·25 4·75
W191 8c. purple . . . . . . 21·00 18·00

B. UNITED STATES OCCUPATION

1899. 1894 stamps of United States (No. 267 etc) optd **PORTO RICO**.
202 1c. green . . . . 4·50 1·40
203 2c. red . . . . 4·00 1·10
204 5c. blue . . . . 7·25 2·20
205 8c. brown . . . . 23·00 16·00
206 10c. brown . . . . 14·50 4·75

1900. 1894 stamps of United States (No. 267 etc) optd **PUERTO RICO**.
210 1c. green . . . . 5·25 1·20
212 2c. red . . . . 4·50 1·40

POSTAGE DUE STAMPS

1899. Postage Due stamps of United States of 1894 optd **PORTO RICO**.
D207 D 87 1c. red . . . . . . 19·00 6·75
D208 2c. red . . . . . . 14·50 4·75
D209 10c. red . . . . . . £140 48·00

QATAR Pt. 1, Pt. 19

An independent Arab Shaikhdom with British postal administration until 23 May 1963. The stamps of Muscat were formerly used at Doha and Urm Said. Later issues by the Qatar Post Department.

1966. 100 dirhams = 1 riyal.
1967. 100 naye paise = 1 rupee.

Stamps of Great Britain surcharged **QATAR** and value in Indian currency.

1957. Queen Elizabeth II and pictorials.
1 **157** 1n.p. on 5d. brown 10 10
2 **154** 3n.p. on ½d. orange 15 15
3 6n.p. on 1d. blue 15 15
4 9n.p. on 1½d. green 15 10
5 12n.p. on 2d. brown . . . . 20 2·25
6 **155** 15n.p. on 2½d. red 15 10
7 20n.p. on 3d. lilac 15 10
8 25n.p. on 4d. blue . . . . 40 1·50
9 **157** 40n.p. on 6d. purple . . . 15 10
10 **158** 50n.p. on 9d. olive . . . 40 75
11 **159** 75n.p. on 1s.3d. green . . 50 3·00
12 1r. on 1s.6d. blue . . . 10·00 10
13 **166** 2r. on 2s.6d. brown . . . 3·50 4·25
14 – 5r. on 5s. red . . . . 5·00 4·25
15 – 10r. on 10s. blue . . . 5·50 16·00

1957. World Scout Jubilee Jamboree.
16 **170** 15n.p. on 2½d. red 35 35
17 **171** 25n.p. on 4d. blue 35 35
18 – 75n.p. on 1s.3d. green . . 40 40

8 Shaikh Ahmad bin All al Thani

9 Peregrine Falcon

11 Oil Derrick

1961.
27 **8** 5n.p. red 15 15
28 15n.p. black 30 15
29 20n.p. purple 30 15
30 30n.p. green 35 30
31 **9** 40n.p. red . . . . 2·40 30
32 50n.p. brown . . . . 3·25 30
33 – 75n.p. blue . . . . 1·60 1·60
34 **11** 1r. red . . . . 1·90 35
35 2r. blue . . . . 3·50 1·00
36 – 5r. green . . . . 19·00 4·25
37 – 10r. black . . . . 45·00 7·50
DESIGNS—As Type **9**: 75n.p. Dhow. As Type **11**: 5r., 10r. Mosque.

1964. Olympic Games, Tokyo. Optd **1964**, Olympic rings and Arabic inscr or surch also.
38 **9** 50n.p. brown . . . . . . 2·40 1·75
39 – 75n.p. blue (No. 33) . . . . 2·50 1·75
40 – 1r. on 10r. black (No. 37) . . 2·50 1·10
41 **11** 2r. blue . . . . 4·75 1·90
42 5r. green (No. 36) . . . . 10·50 5·75

1964. Pres. Kennedy Commem. Optd **John F Kennedy 1917–1963** in English and Arabic or surch also.
43 **9** 50n.p. brown . . . . . . 7·75 2·20
44 – 75n.p. blue (No. 33) . . . . 3·00 1·60
45 – 1r. on 10r. black (No. 37) . . 3·50 1·50
46 **11** 2r. blue . . . . 4·50 3·25
47 – 5r. green (No. 36) . . . . 11·50 6·50

15 Colonnade, Temple of Isis

16 Scouts on Parade

1965. Nubian Monuments Preservation. Mult.
48 1n.p. Type **15** 40 20
49 2n.p. Temple of Isis, Philac . . 40 20
50 3n.p. Trajan's Kiosk, Philac . . 45 20
51 1r. As 3n.p. . . . . 1·60 75
52 1r.50 As 2n.p. . . . . . . 3·25 90
53 2r. Type **15** . . . . 2·40 90

1965. Qatar Scouts.
54 – 1n.p. brown and green . . . 20 10
55 – 2n.p. blue and brown . . . 20 10
56 – 3n.p. blue and green . . . 20 10
57 – 4n.p. brown and blue . . . 20 10
58 – 5n.p. blue and turquoise . . 20 10
59 **16** 30n.p. multicoloured . . . . 1·40 60
60 40n.p. multicoloured . . . . 1·60 90
61 1r. multicoloured . . . . 3·50 1·80
MS61a 108 × 76 mm. Nos. 59/61 . . 9·50 6·25
DESIGNS—TRIANGULAR (60 × 30 mm): 1, 4n.p. Qatar Scout badge; 2, 3, 5n.p. Ruler, badge, palms and camp.

17 "Telstar" and Eiffel Tower

1965. I.T.U. Centenary.
62 **17** 1n.p. brown and blue 20 10
63 – 2n.p. brown and blue . . . 20 10
64 – 3n.p. violet and green . . . 20 10
65 – 4n.p. blue and brown . . . 20 10
66 **17** 5n.p. brown and violet . . . 20 10
67 – 40n.p. black and red . . . 1·90 60
68 – 50n.p. brown and green . . 2·40 75
69 – 1r. red and green . . . . 3·25 1·10
MS69a 89 × 89 mm. Nos. 68/9 . . 18·00 7·50
DESIGNS: 2n.p., 1r. "Syncom 3" and pagoda; 3, 40n.p. "Relay" and radar scanner; 4, 50n.p. Post Office Tower (London), globe and satellites.

18 Jigsaw Triggerfish

1965. Fish of the Arabian Gulf. Multicoloured.
70 1n.p. Type **18** 15 15
71 2n.p. Harlequin sweetlips . . . 15 15
72 3n.p. Saddle butterflyfish . . . 15 15
73 4n.p. Thread-finned butterflyfish 15 15
74 5n.p. Masked unicornfish . . . 15 15
75 15n.p. Paradise fish 15 15
76 20n.p. White-spotted surgeonfish 20 20
77 30n.p. Rio Grande cichlid . . 45 20
78 40n.p. Convict cichlid 60 45
79 50n.p. As 2n.p. 90 60
80 75n.p. Type **18** . . . . . . 1·50 75
81 1r. As 30n.p. . . . . 2·40 90
82 2r. As 20n.p. . . . . 5·50 2·50
83 3r. As 15n.p. . . . . 6·75 3·00
84 4r. As 5n.p. . . . . 8·75 3·75
85 5r. As 4n.p. . . . . 12·50 4·00
86 10r. As 3n.p. . . . . 20·00 8·00

19 Basketball

1966. Pan-Arab Games, Cairo (1965).
87 **19** 1r. black, grey and red . . . 90 60
88 – 1r. brown and green 90 60
89 – 1r. red and blue 90 60
90 – 1r. green and blue 90 60
91 – 1r. blue and brown 90 60
SPORTS: No. 88, Horse-jumping; No. 89, Running; No. 90, Football; No. 91, Weightlifting.

1966. Space Rendezvous. Nos. 62/9 optd with two space capsules and **SPACE RENDEZVOUS 15th. DECEMBER 1965** in English and Arabic.
92 **17** 1n.p. brown and blue . . . 65 10
93 – 2n.p. brown and blue . . . 65 10
94 – 3n.p. violet and green . . . 65 10
95 – 4n.p. blue and brown . . . 65 10
96 **17** 5n.p. brown and violet . . . 65 10
97 – 40n.p. black and red . . . 2·40 30
98 – 50n.p. brown and green . . 2·40 35
99 – 1r. red and green . . . . 4·25 65
MS100 89 × 89 mm. Nos. 98/9 . . 22·00 11·00

21 Shaikh Ahmed

1966. Gold and Silver Coinage. Circular designs embossed on gold (G) or silver (S) foil, backed with "Walsall Security Paper" inscr in English and Arabic. Imperf. (a) Diameter 42 mm.
101 **21** 1n.p. bistre and purple (S) . . 20 15
102 – 3n.p. black and orange (S) . . 20 15
103 **21** 4n.p. violet and red (G) . . . 20 15
104 – 5n.p. green and mauve (G) . . 20 15

(b) Diameter 55 mm.
105 **21** 10n.p. brown and violet (S) . . 45 15
106 – 40n.p. red and blue (S) . . 1·20 30
107 **21** 70n.p. blue & ultram (G) . . 1·90 75
108 – 80n.p. mauve and green (G) . . . . 1·90 75

(c) Diameter 64 mm.
109 **21** 1r. mauve and black (S) . . 2·25 90
110 – 2r. green and purple (S) . . 4·75 1·80
111 **21** 5r. purple and orange (G) . . 10·50 4·00
112 – 10r. blue and red (G) . . . 21·00 9·50
The 1, 4, 10, 70n.p. and 1 and 5r. each show the obverse side of the coins as Type **21**. The remainder show the reverse side of the coins (Shaikh's seal).

22 I.C.Y. and U.N. Emblem

1966. International Co-operation Year.
113 **22** 40n.p. brown, violet & bl . . 1·50 90
114 A 40n.p. violet, brn & turq . . 1·50 90
115 B 40n.p. blue, brown & vio . . 1·50 90
116 C 40n.p. turquoise, vio & bl . . 1·50 90
MS117 140 × 87½ mm. Nos. 113/16. Imperf . . . . 24·00 15·00
DESIGNS: A, Pres. Kennedy, I.C.Y. emblem and U.N. Headquarters; B, Dag Hammarskjold and U.N. General Assembly; C, Nehru and dove.
Nos. 113/16 were issued together in blocks of four, each sheet containing four blocks separated by gutter margins. Subsequently the sheets were reissued perf and imperf with the opt **U.N. 20TH ANNIVERSARY** on the stamps. The gutter margins were also printed in various designs, face values and overprints.

23 Pres. Kennedy and New York Skyline

1966. Pres. Kennedy Commemoration. Multicoloured.
118 10n.p. Type **23** 20 15
119 30n.p. Pres. Kennedy and Cape Kennedy 45 20
120 60n.p. Pres. Kennedy and Statue of Liberty 75 45
121 70n.p. Type **23** 90 65
122 80n.p. As 30n.p. . . . . . . 1·10 75
123 1r. As 60n.p. . . . . 1·50 1·10
MS124 105 × 70 mm. 50n.p. (As 60n.p.). Imperf . . . . 10·50 8·00

24 Horse-jumping

1966. Olympic Games Preparation (Mexico). Multicoloured.
125 1n.p. Type **24** 15 15
126 4n.p. Running 15 15
127 5n.p. Throwing the javelin . . 15 15
128 70n.p. Type **24** 95 50
129 80n.p. Running . . . . . . 1·00 60
130 90n.p. Throwing the javelin . . 1·10 80
MS131 105 × 70 mm. 50n.p. (As Type **24**) . . . . 18·00 15·00

25 J. A. Lovell and Capsule

1966. American Astronauts. Each design showing spacecraft and astronaut. Multicoloured.
132 5n.p. Type **25** 15 15
133 10n.p. T. P. Stafford 15 15
134 15n.p. A. B. Shepard 15 15
135 20n.p. J. H. Glenn 20 15
136 30n.p. M. Scott Carpenter . . 35 20
137 40n.p. W. M. Schirra 45 30
138 50n.p. V. I. Grissom 60 45
139 60n.p. L. G. Cooper 90 65
MS140 116 × 75 mm. **26** 50n.p. multicoloured. Imperf . . . . 15·00 8·75
Nos. 132/4 are diamond-shaped as Type **25**, the remainder are horiz designs (56 × 25 mm).

1966. Various stamps with currency names changed to dirhams and riyals by overprinting in English and Arabic. (i) Nos. 27/37 (Definitives).
141 **8** 5d. on 5n.p. red . . . . . 3·00 2·00
142 15d. on 15n.p. black . . . . 3·00 2·00
143 20d. on 20n.p. purple . . . 3·00 2·00
144 30d. on 30n.p. green . . . . 9·00 4·00
145 **9** 40d. on 40n.p. red . . . . 20·00 10·00
146 50d. on 50n.p. brown . . . 32·00 15·00
147 – 75d. on 75n.p. blue . . . . 55·00 20·00
148 **11** 1r. on 1r. red . . . . . . 70·00 28·00
149 2r. on 2r. blue . . . . . 90·00 62·00
150 – 5r. on 5r. green . . . . £110 80·00
151 – 10r. on 10r. black £170 £110

(ii) Nos. 70/86 (Fish). Multicoloured.
152 1d. on 1n.p. . . . . 1·00 80
153 2d. on 2n.p. . . . . 1·00 80
154 3d. on 3n.p. . . . . 1·00 80
155 4d. on 4n.p. . . . . 1·00 80
156 5d. on 5n.p. . . . . 1·00 80
157 15d. on 15n.p. . . . . . . 1·10 80
158 20d. on 20n.p. . . . . . . 1·20 80
159 30d. on 30n.p. . . . . . . 1·30 80
160 40d. on 40n.p. . . . . . . 1·50 2·00
161 50d. on 50n.p. . . . . . . 2·00 3·00
162 75d. on 75n.p. . . . . . . 2·40 10·00
163 1r. on 1r. . . . . 23·00 16·00
164 2r. on 2r. . . . . 35·00 20·00

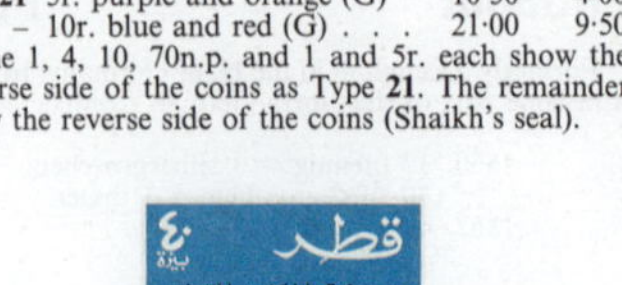

165 3r. on 3r. . . . . 40·00 25·00
166 4r. on 4r. . . . . 65·00 35·00
167 5r. on 5r. . . . . 70·00 45·00
168 10r. on 10r. . . . . 90·00 60·00

27 National Library, Doha

1966. Education Day. Multicoloured.
169 2n.p. Type **27** . . . . 1·90 30
170 3n.p. School and playing field 1·90 30
171 5n.p. School and gardens . . 1·90 30
172 1r. Type **27** . . . . 4·50 2·40
173 2r. As 3n.p . . . . 6·50 3·75
174 3r. As 5n.p . . . . 11·50 3·75

28 Palace, Doha

1966. Currency expressed in naye paise and rupees. Multicoloured.
175 2n.p. Type **28** 30 15
176 3n.p. Gulf Street, Shahra Al-Khalij 30 15
177 10n.p. Doha airport 65 15
178 15n.p. Garden, Rayan . . . 65 15
179 20n.p. Head Post Office, Doha 80 15
180 30n.p. Mosque Doha (vert) 1·30 20
181 40n.p. Shaikh Ahmad . . . . 1·60 35
182 50n.p. Type **28** . . . . . . 1·80 60
183 60n.p. As 3n.p. . . . . . . 3·25 90
184 70n.p. As 10n.p. . . . . . . 3·75 1·30
185 80n.p. As 15n.p. . . . . . . 3·00 1·50
186 90n.p. As 20n.p. . . . . . . 3·50 2·50
187 1r. As 30n.p. (vert) . . . . . 4·25 2·75
188 2r. As 40n.p. . . . . 7·75 6·50

29 Hands holding Jules Rimet Trophy

1966. World Cup Football Championship, England.
189 **29** 60n.p. mult (postage) . . . 1·20 90
190 – 70n.p. multicoloured . . . 1·40 1·00
191 – 80n.p. multicoloured . . . 1·80 1·30
192 – 90n.p. multicoloured . . . 1·90 1·50
193 – 1n.p. blue (air) 15 15
194 – 2n.p. blue 20 15
195 – 3n.p. blue 30 20
196 – 4n.p. blue 35 30
MS197 Four sheets each 105 × 70 mm. Each sheet contains one design as Nos. 189/192 with face value of 25n.p. Imperf . . 31·00 15·00
DESIGNS: No. 190, Jules Rimet Trophy and "football" globe; No. 191, Footballers and globe; No. 192, Wembley stadium; Nos. 193/6, Jules Rimet Trophy.

30 A.P.U. Emblem

32 Traffic Lights

31 Astronauts on Moon

1967. Admission of Qatar to Arab Postal Union.
198 **30** 70d. brown and violet . . 1·50 75
199 80d. brown and blue . . . 1·80 75

1967. U.S. "Apollo" Space Missions. Mult.
200 5d. Type **31** 10 10
201 10d. "Apollo" spacecraft . . 10 10
202 20d. Landing module on Moon 15 10
203 30d. Blast-off from Moon . . 30 15
204 40d. "Saturn 5" rocket . . . 45 20
205 70d. Type **31** 95 60
206 80d. As 10d. . . . . 1·10 80
207 1r. As 20d. . . . . 1·20 95
208 1r.20 As 30d. . . . . . . 1·50 1·10
209 2r. As 40d. . . . . 2·00 1·50
MS210 100 × 70 mm. No. 209. Imperf . . . . 9·50 7·50

1967. Traffic Day.
211 **32** 20d. multicoloured 35 15
212 30d. multicoloured 75 35
213 50d. multicoloured . . . . 1·10 60
214 1r. multicoloured . . . . . 3·25 1·30

33 Brownsea Island and Jamboree Camp, Idaho

1967. Diamond Jubilee of Scout Movement and World Scout Jamboree, Idaho. Multicoloured.
215 1d. Type **33** 20 10
216 2d. Lord Baden-Powell . . . 20 10
217 3d. Pony-trekking 20 10
218 5d. Canoeing 35 10
219 15d. Swimming . . . . . . 1·10 30
220 75d. Rock-climbing . . . . 2·50 90
221 2r. World Jamboree emblem 6·75 3·00

34 Norman Ship (from Bayeux Tapestry)

1967. Famous Navigators' Ships. Multicoloured.
222 1d. Type **34** 30 10
223 2d. "Santa Maria" (Columbus) 35 10
224 3d. "Sao Gabriel" (Vasco da Gama) 50 10
225 75d. "Vitoria" (Magellan) . . 3·00 1·10
226 1r. "Golden Hind" (Drake) 4·00 1·50
227 2r. "Gipsy Moth IV" (Chichester) . . . . 6·75 2·10

35 Arab Scribe

1968. 10th Anniv of Qatar Postage Stamps. Multicoloured.
228 1d. Type **35** 30 10
229 2d. Pigeon post (vert) 30 10
230 3d. Mounted postman . . . 35 10
231 60d. Rowing boat postman (vert) . . . . 2·10 90
232 1r.25 Camel postman . . . . 4·00 1·50
233 2r. Letter-writing and Qatar 1n.p. stamp of 1957 . . . 6·75 2·20

36 Human Rights Emblem and Barbed Wire

1968. Human Rights Year. Multicoloured designs embodying Human Rights emblem.
234 1d. Type **36** 15 10
235 2d. Arab refugees 15 10
236 3d. Scales of justice 20 10
237 60d. Opening doors . . . . 1·30 75
238 1r.25 Family (vert) . . . . . 1·80 1·60
239 2r. Human figures . . . . . 3·75 2·20

37 Shaikh Ahmad

39 Shaikh Ahmad

38 Dhow

1968.
240 **37** 5d. green and blue 15 10
241 10d. brown and blue . . . 30 10
242 20d. red and black 50 10
243 25d. green and purple . . . 1·30 15
244 **38** 35d. green, blue and pink 2·10 15
245 – 40d. purple, blue & orange 2·75 20
246 – 60d. brown, blue and violet 3·50 45
247 – 70d. black, blue and green 4·00 60
248 – 1r. blue, yellow and green 4·75 75
249 – 1r.25 blue, pink and light blue . . . . 5·50 90
250 – 1r.50 green, blue & purple 6·25 1·10
251 **39** 2r. blue, brown and cinnamon . . . . 8·75 1·50
252 5r. purple, green and light green . . . . 16·00 4·50
253 10r. brown, ultram & blue 28·00 7·00
DESIGNS—As Type **38**: 40d. Water purification plant; 60d. Oil jetty; 70d. Qatar mosque; 1r. Palace Doha; 1r.25, Doha fort; 1r.50, Peregrine falcon.

41 Maternity Ward

1968. 20th Anniv of W.H.O. Multicoloured.
258 1d. Type **41** 35 10
259 2d. Operating theatre 35 10
260 3d. Dental surgery 35 10
261 60d. X-ray examination table 1·90 35
262 1r.25 Laboratory . . . . . . 3·25 90
263 2r. State Hospital Qatar . . . 4·75 1·50

42 Throwing the Discus

1968. Olympic Games, Mexico. Multicoloured.
264 1d. Type **42** 20 10
265 2d. Olympic Flame and runner 20 10
266 3d. "68", rings and gymnast 35 10
267 60d. Weightlifting and Flame 1·80 75
268 1r.25 "Flame" in mosaic pattern (vert) . . . . . . 3·50 1·10
269 2r. "Cock" emblem . . . . . 4·75 1·60

43 U.N. Emblem and Flags

1968. United Nations Day. Multicoloured.
270 1d. Type **43** 15 10
271 4d. Dove of Peace and world map 35 10
272 5d. U.N. Headquarters and flags 35 10
273 60d. Teacher and class . . . 2·75 75
274 1r.50 Agricultural workers . . 4·50 1·10
275 2r. U. Thant and U.N. Assembly . . . . 5·25 1·30

44 Trawler "Ross Rayyan"

1969. Progress in Qatar. Multicoloured.
276 1d. Type **44** 15 10
277 4d. Primary school 15 10
278 5d. Doha International Airport 35 10
279 60d. Cement factory and road-making . . . . 2·10 50
280 1r.50 Power station and pylon . . . . 5·25 1·30
281 2r. Housing estate . . . . . 7·00 1·60

45 Armoured Cars

1969. Qatar Security Forces. Multicoloured.
282 1d. Type **45** 30 10
283 2d. Traffic control 30 10
284 3d. Military helicopter . . . 35 15
285 60d. Section of military band 2·10 65
286 1r.25 Field gun . . . . . . 4·00 90
287 2r. Mounted police . . . . . 6·75 1·80

46 Tanker "Sivella" at Mooring

1969. Qatar's Oil Industry. Multicoloured.
288 1d. Type **46** 30 10
289 2d. Training school 30 10
290 3d. "Sea Shell" (oil rig) and "Shell Dolphin" (supply vessel) 50 10
291 60d. Storage tanks, Halul . . 2·40 75
292 1r.50 Topping plant . . . . 6·25 1·60
293 2r. Various tankers, 1890–1968 . . . . 9·50 2·20

47 "Guest-house" and Dhow-building

1969. 10th Scout Jamboree, Qatar. Multicoloured.
294 1d. Type **47** 15 10
295 2d. Scouts at work 15 10
296 3d. Review and March Past 30 10
297 60d. Interior gateway . . . . 3·00 75
298 1r.25 Camp entrance . . . . 4·75 1·10
299 2r. Hoisting flag, and Shaikh Ahmad . . . . 6·75 1·60
MS300 128 × 110m. Nos. 294/7. Imperf . . . . 11·00 5·50

48 Neil Armstrong

1969. 1st Man on the Moon. Multicoloured.
301 1d. Type **48** 15 10
302 2d. Edward Aldrin 15 10
303 3d. Michael Collins 15 10
304 60d. Astronaut on Moon . . 1·20 45
305 1r.25 Take-off from Moon . 2·50 1·20
306 2r. Splashdown (horiz) . . . 4·75 1·80

49 Douglas DC-8 and Mail Van

1970. Admission to U.P.U. Multicoloured.
307 1d. Type **49** 15 15
308 2d. Liner "Oriental Empress" 15 15
309 3d. Loading mail-van 30 15
310 60d. G.P.O., Doha . . . . 1·60 75
311 1r.25 U.P.U. Building, Berne 3·50 1·10
312 2r. U.P.U. Monument, Berne 5·50 1·50

50 League Emblem, Flag and Map

1970. Silver Jubilee of Arab League.
313 **50** 35d. multicoloured 90 30
314 60d. multicoloured . . . . 1·50 50
315 1r.25 multicoloured . . . . 3·00 90
316 1r.50 multicoloured . . . . 3·75 1·50

51 Vickers VC-10 on Runway

1970. 1st Gulf Aviation Vickers VC-10 Flight, Doha–London. Multicoloured.
317 1d. Type **51** 20 10
318 2d. Peregrine falcon and VC-10 . . . . 45 10
319 3d. Tail view of VC-10 . . . 45 10
320 60d. Gulf Aviation emblem on map . . . . 2·75 75
321 1r.25 VC-10 over Doha . . . 6·00 1·10
322 2r. Tail assembly of VC-10 9·50 3·75

52 "Space Achievements"

1970. International Education Year.
323 **52** 35d. multicoloured 75 30
324 60d. multicoloured . . . . 1·50 60

53 Freesias

55 Globe, "25" and U.N. Emblem

54 Toyahama Fishermen with Giant "Fish"

1970. Qatar Flowers. Multicoloured.
325 1d. Type **53** 15 10
326 2d. Azalieas 15 10
327 3d. Ixias 15 10
328 60d. Amaryllises . . . . . . 2·75 60
329 1r.25 Cinerarias . . . . . . 4·50 1·30
330 2r. Roses . . . . 6·00 1·80

1970. "EXPO 70" World Fair, Osaka. Multicoloured.
331 1d. Type **54** 15 10
332 2d. Expo emblem and map of Japan 15 10
333 3d. Fisherman on Shikoku beach 35 10
334 60d. Expo emblem and Mt. Fuji . . . . 2·10 60
335 1r.50 Gateway to Shinto Shrine . . . . 4·50 1·10
336 2r. Expo Tower and Mt. Fuji 6·25 2·40
MS336a 126 × 111 mm. Nos. 331/4. Imperf . . . . 10·50 5·25
Nos. 333, 334 and 336 are vert.

1970. 25th Anniv of U.N.O. Multicoloured.
337 1d. Type **55** 20 10
338 2d. Flowers in gun-barrel . . 20 10
339 3d. Anniversary cake 35 10
340 35d. "The U.N. Agencies" . . 1·20 35
341 1r.50 "Trumpet fanfare" . . 3·00 90
342 2r. "World friendship" . . . 3·50 1·50

56 Al Jahiz (philosopher) and Ancient Globe

1971. Famous Men of Islam. Multicoloured.
343 1d. Type **56** 30 15
344 2d. Saladin (soldier), palace and weapons 30 15
345 3d. Al Farabi (philosopher and musician), felucca and instruments 50 15
346 35d. Ibn Al Haithum (scientist), palace and emblems . . . . 2·10 30
347 1r.50 Al Motanabbi (poet), symbols and desert . . . . 6·50 1·80
348 2r. Ibn Sina (Avicenna) (physician and philosopher), medical instruments and ancient globe . . . . 7·75 2·10

57 Great Cormorant and Water Plants

1971. Qatar Fauna and Flora. Multicoloured.
349 1d. Type **57** 75 15
350 2d. Lizard and prickly pear 75 15
351 3d. Greater flamingos and palms 75 15
352 60d. Arabian oryx and yucca 3·75 75
353 1r.25 Mountain gazelle and desert dandelion . . . . . 6·50 1·80
354 2r. Dromedary, palm and bronzed chenopod . . . . 7·50 2·50

58 Satellite Earth Station, Goonhilly

1971. World Telecommunications Day. Mult.
355 1d. Type **58** 15 10
356 2d. Cable ship "Ariel" . . . 15 10
357 3d. Post Office Tower and T.V. control-room 15 10
358 4d. Modern telephones . . . 15 10
359 5d. Video-phone equipment 15 10
360 35d. As 3d. . . . . 1·50 35
361 75d. As 5d. . . . . 2·20 60
362 3r. Telex machine . . . . . 8·75 3·00

59 Arab Child reading Book

60 A.P.U. Emblem

1971. 10th Anniv of Education Day.
363 **59** 35d. multicoloured 75 20
364 55d. multicoloured . . . . 1·50 35
365 75d. multicoloured . . . . 3·00 75

1971. 25th Anniv of Arab Postal Union.
366 **60** 35d. multicoloured 90 20
367 55d. multicoloured . . . . 1·30 45
368 75d. multicoloured . . . . 1·80 75
369 1r.25 multicoloured . . . . 2·75 1·20

61 "Hammering Racism"

1971. Racial Equality Year. Multicoloured.
370 1d. Type **61** 20 10
371 2d. "Pushing back racism" 20 10
372 3d. War-wounded 20 10
373 4d. Working together (vert) 20 10
374 5d. Playing together (vert) . . 20 10
375 35d. Racial "tidal-wave" . . 1·50 35
376 75d. Type **61** . . . . 3·50 75
377 3r. As 2d. . . . . 7·50 3·00

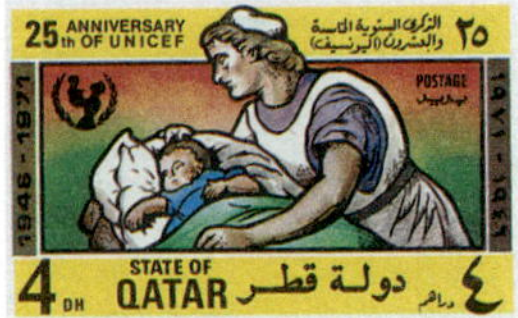
62 Nurse and Child

1971. 25th Anniv of UNICEF. Multicoloured.
378 1d. Mother and child (vert) 20 10
379 2d. Child's face 20 10
380 3d. Child with book (vert) . . 20 10
381 4d. Type **62** 20 10
382 5d. Mother and baby 20 10
383 35d. Child with daffodil (vert) 1·10 20
384 75d. As 3d. . . . . 3·25 75
385 3r. As 1d. . . . . 7·25 3·00

63 Shaikh Ahmad, and Flags of Arab League and Qatar

1971. Independence.
386 **63** 35d. multicoloured 75 15
387 – 75d. multicoloured . . . . 1·50 35
388 – 1r.25 black, pink & brown 2·20 60
389 – 3r. multicoloured . . . . 6·75 2·50
MS390 80 × 128 mm. No. 389. Imperf . . . . 14·00 9·50
DESIGNS—HORIZ: 75d. As Type **63**, but with U.N. flag in place of Arab League flag. VERT: 1r.25, Shaikh Ahmad; 3r. Handclasp.

64 European Roller

66 Shaikh Khalifa bin Hamad al-Thani

1972. Birds. Multicoloured.
391 1d. Type **64** 20 20
392 2d. River kingfisher 20 20
393 3d. Rock thrush 20 20
394 4d. Caspian tern 30 20
395 5d. Hoopoe 30 20
396 35d. European bee eater . . 3·50 1·00
397 75d. Golden oriole . . . . . 8·50 3·50
398 3r. Peregrine falcon . . . . 26·00 12·50

1972. Nos. 328/30 surch with value in English and Arabic.
399 10d. on 60d. multicoloured 1·40 30
400 1r. on 1r.25 multicoloured . . 7·00 1·50
401 5r. on 2r. multicoloured . . . 13·50 6·00

1972.
402 **66** 5d. blue and violet 35 15
403 10d. red and brown . . . 35 30
404 35d. green and orange . . 95 30
405 55d. mauve and green . . 1·90 75
406 75d. mauve and blue . . . 3·00 1·20
407 – 1r. black and brown . . . 4·00 1·20
408 – 1r.25 black and green . . . 4·75 1·50
409 – 5r. black and blue . . . . 16·00 5·25
410 – 10r. black and red . . . . 27·00 10·50
The rupee values are larger, 27 × 32 mm.
For similar design but with Shaikh's head turned slightly to right, see Nos. 444a/b.

67 Book Year Emblem

1972. International Book Year.
411 **67** 35d. black and blue . . . 1·10 20
412 55d. black and brown . . . 1·80 30
413 75d. black and green . . . 2·75 45
414 1r.25 black and lilac . . . 4·50 75

68 Football

1972. Olympic Games, Munich. Designs depicting sportsmen's hands or feet. Multicoloured.
415 1d. Type **68** 15 15
416 2d. Running (foot on starting block) 15 15
417 3d. Cycling (hand) 15 15
418 4d. Gymnastics (hand) . . . 15 15
419 5d. Basketball (hand) 20 15
420 35d. Discus (hand) 55 60
421 75d. Type **68** . . . . 1·10 1·10
422 3r. As 2d. . . . . 4·50 2·10
MS423 150 × 108 mm. Nos. 415/20. Imperf . . . . 35 2·20

69 Underwater Pipeline Construction

1972. "Oil from the Sea". Multicoloured.
424 1d. Drilling (vert) 20 15
425 4d. Type **69** 20 15
426 5d. Offshore rig "Sea Shell" 20 15
427 35d. Underwater "prospecting" for oil . . . 1·10 20
428 75d. As 1d. . . . . 2·20 45
429 3r. As 5d. . . . . 11·00 2·20

70 Administrative Building

1972. Independence Day. Multicoloured.
430 10d. Type **70** 65 10
431 35d. Handclasp and Arab League flag . . . . 1·60 20
432 75d. Handclasp and U.N. flag . . . . 3·25 50
433 1r.25 Shaikh Khalifa . . . . 5·50 80
MS434 129 × 103 mm. No. 433. Imperf . . . . 1·50 4·75

71 Dish Aerial, Satellite and Telephone (I.T.U.)

1972. United Nations Day. Multicoloured.
435 1d. Type **71** 75 15
436 2d. Archaeological team (UNESCO) 75 15
437 3d. Tractor, produce and helicopter (F.A.O.) 75 15
438 4d. Children with books (UNICEF) 75 15
439 5d. Weather satellite (W.M.O.) 75 15
440 25d. Construction workers (I.L.O.) . . . . 3·75 45
441 55d. Child care (W.H.O.) . . 7·50 1·00
442 1r. Airliner and van (U.P.U.) 13·50 1·80

72 Emblem and Flags
72a Shaikh Khalifa

1972. 10th Session of Arab States Civil Aviation Council, Qatar.
443 72 25d. multicoloured . . . . 1·50 35
444 30d. multicoloured . . . . 2·20 50

1972.
444a 72a 10d. red and brown . . 23·00 23·00
444b 25d. green and purple 23·00 23·00

73 Shaikh Khalifa

74 Clock Tower, Doha

1973.
445 73 5d. multicoloured 45 15
446 10d. multicoloured 65 15
447 20d. multicoloured 90 15
448 25d. multicoloured . . . . 1·10 15
449 35d. multicoloured . . . . 1·30 20
450 55d. multicoloured . . . . 2·20 35
451 74 75d. purple, green and blue 3·25 75
452 73 1r. multicoloured . . . . . 8·75 2·20
453 5r. multicoloured . . . . . 26·00 9·50
454 10r. multicoloured . . . . 35·00 25·00
Nos. 452/4 are larger, 27 × 32 mm.

75 Housing Development

1973. 1st Anniv of Shaikh Khalifa's Accession. Multicoloured.
455 2d. Road construction . . . 15 10
456 3d. Type 75 . . . . 15 10
457 4d. Hospital operating theatre 15 10
458 5d. Telephone exchange . . . 15 10
459 15d. School classroom . . . 60 10
460 20d. Television studio . . . 75 15
461 35d. Shaikh Khalifa . . . . 1·20 20
462 55d. Gulf Hotel, Doha . . . 1·50 35
463 1r. Industrial plant . . . . . 1·80 45
464 1r.35 Flour mills . . . . . . 2·50 65

76 Aerial Crop-spraying

1973. 25th Anniv of W.H.O. Multicoloured.
465 2d. Type 76 . . . . 30 15
466 3d. Drugs and syringe . . . 30 15
467 4d. Woman in wheelchair (Prevention of polio) . . . 30 15
468 5d. Mosquito (Malaria control) 60 15
469 55d. Mental patient (Mental Health Research) . . . 4·50 75
470 1r. Dead trees (Anti-pollution) . . . . 8·75 1·50

77 Weather Ship

1973. Centenary of World Meteorological Organization. Multicoloured.
471 2d. Type 77 . . . . 30 15
472 3d. Launching radio-sonde balloon 30 15
473 4d. Hawker Siddeley H.S.125 weather plane 30 15
474 5d. Meteorological station . . 30 15
475 10d. Met airplane taking-off 95 20
476 1r. "Nimbus 1" . . . . . . 7·00 75
477 1r.55 Rocket on launch-pad 10·50 1·40

78 Handclasp

1973. Independence Day. Multicoloured.
478 15d. Type 78 . . . . 15 10
479 35d. Agriculture 35 15
480 55d. Government building . . 95 30
481 1r.35 View of Doha . . . . 2·10 65
482 1r.55 Illuminated fountain . . 2·40 75

79 Child planting Sapling (UNESCO)

1973. United Nations Day. Multicoloured.
483 2d. Type 79 . . . . 30 10
484 4d. U.N. Headquarters, New York, and flags 30 10
485 5d. Building construction (I.L.O.) 30 10
486 35d. Nurses in dispensary (W.H.O.) 75 20
487 1r.35 Radar control (I.T.U.) 3·00 75
488 3r. Inspection of wheat and cattle (F.A.O.) . . . . . . 7·50 2·20

80 "Open Gates"

1973. 25th Anniv of Declaration of Human Rights. Multicoloured.
489 2d. Type 80 . . . . 15 15
490 4d. Freedom marchers . . . 15 15
491 5d. "Equality of Man" . . . 30 15
492 35d. Primary education . . . 90 20
493 1r.35 General Assembly, U.N. . . . . 3·00 75
494 3r. Flame emblem (vert) . . . 5·25 1·20

81 New Flyover, Doha

1974. 2nd Anniv of Shaikh Khalifa's Accession. Mult.
495 2d. Type 81 . . . . 15 10
496 3d. Education symbol 15 10
497 5d. Gas plant 15 10
498 35d. Gulf Hotel, Doha . . . 75 20
499 1r.55 Space communications station . . . . 3·25 1·10
500 2r.25 Shaikh Khalifa . . . . 4·50 1·50

82 Camel Caravan and Articulated Mail Van

1974. Centenary of U.P.U. Multicoloured.
501 2d. Type 82 . . . . 20 10
502 3d. Early mail wagon and Japanese "Hikari" express train 20 10
503 10d. "Hindoostan" (paddle-steamer) and "Iberia" (liner) 75 20
504 35d. Early (Handley Page H.P.42) and modern (Vickers VC-10) mail planes . . . . 1·30 30
505 75d. Manual and mechanized mail-sorting . . . . 1·50 45
506 1r.25 Early and modern P.O. sales counters . . . . . . 2·50 75

83 Doha Hospital

1974. World Population Year. Multicoloured.
507 5d. Type 83 . . . . 10 10
508 10d. W.P.Y. emblem 20 10
509 15d. Emblem within wreath 20 10
510 35d. World population map 45 20
511 1r.75 New-born infants and clock ("a birth every minute") . . . . 2·40 1·10
512 2r.25 "Ideal Family" group 3·25 1·10

84 Television Station

1974. Independence Day. Multicoloured.
513 5d. Type 84 . . . . 30 15
514 10d. Doha palace 60 15
515 15d. Teachers' College . . . 90 15
516 75d. Clock tower and mosque 2·40 30
517 1r.55 Roundabout and surroundings . . . . 4·50 60
518 2r.25 Shaikh Khalifa . . . . 6·75 90

85 Operating Theatre (W.H.O.)

1974. United Nations Day.
519 85 5d. orange, purple & black 30 15
520 – 10d. orange, red and black 60 15
521 – 20d. blue, green and black 1·20 15
522 – 25d. blue, brown and black 1·80 20
523 – 1r.75 blue, mauve & black 6·75 75
524 – 2r. blue, orange and black 7·50 90
DESIGNS: 10d. Satellite earth station (I.T.U.); 20d. Tractor (F.A.O.); 25d. Classroom (UNESCO); 1r.75, African open-air court (Human Rights); 2r. U.P.U. and U.N. emblems (U.P.U.).

86 Vickers VC-10 Airliner

1974. Arab Civil Aviation Day.
525 86 20d. multicoloured . . . . 1·20 20
526 – 25d. blue, green and yellow 1·80 20
527 – 30d. multicoloured . . . . 2·40 30
528 – 50d. red, green and purple 3·00 35
DESIGNS: 25d. Doha airport; 30, 50d. Flags of Qatar and the Arab League.

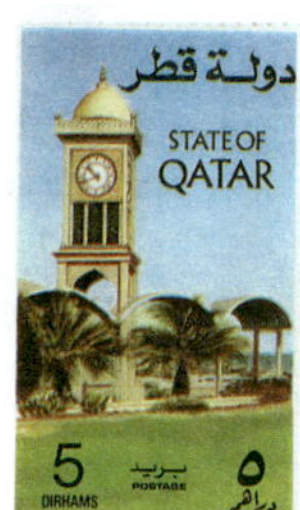
87 Clock Tower, Doha

1974. Tourism. Multicoloured.
529 5d. Type 87 . . . . 65 10
530 10d. White-cheeked terns, hoopoes and Shara'o Island (horiz) 90 10
531 15d. Fort Zubara (horiz) . . 1·10 10
532 35d. Dinghies and Gulf Hotel (horiz) . . . . 1·80 20
533 55d. Qatar by night (horiz) 2·20 35
534 75d. Arabian oryx (horiz) . . 3·50 60
535 1r.25 Khor-al-Udeid (horiz) 4·75 75
536 1r.75 Ruins Wakrah (horiz) 7·00 90

88 Traffic Roundabout, Doha

1975. 3rd Anniv of Shaikh Khalifa's Accession. Multicoloured.
537 10d. Type 88 . . . . 65 10
538 35d. Oil pipelines . . . . . 1·10 20
539 55d. Laying offshore pipelines 1·80 25
540 1r. Oil refinery . . . . 3·50 75
541 1r.35 Shaikh Khalifa (vert) 4·50 1·10
542 1r.55 As 1r.35 . . . . 5·50 1·50

89 Flintlock Pistol

1975. Opening of National Museum. Multicoloured.
543 2d. Type 89 . . . . 30 10
544 3d. Arabesque-pattern mosaic 60 10
545 35d. Museum buildings . . . 1·50 20
546 75d. Museum archway (vert) 3·00 35
547 1r.25 Flint tools . . . . . . 4·75 75
548 3r. Gold necklace and pendant (vert) . . . . . . 7·75 1·50

90 Policeman and Road Signs

1975. Traffic Week. Multicoloured.
549 5d. Type 90 . . . . 90 15
550 15d. Traffic arrows and signal lights . . . . 2·40 30
551 35d. Type 90 . . . . 3·50 45
552 55d. As 15d. . . . . 6·00 75

91 Flag and Emblem

1975. 10th Anniv of Arab Labour Charter.
553 91 10d. multicoloured 65 15
554 35d. multicoloured . . . . 1·50 25
555 1r. multicoloured . . . . . 4·50 75

92 Government Building, Doha

1975. 4th Anniv of Independence. Multicoloured.
556 5d. Type 92 . . . . 60 10
557 15d. Museum and clock tower, Doha . . . . 1·20 10
558 35d. Constitution – Arabic text (vert) . . . . 1·50 20
559 55d. Ruler and flag (vert) . . 2·40 30
560 75d. Constitution – English text (vert) . . . . 3·00 45
561 1r.25 As 55d. . . . . 4·75 75

93 Telecommunications Satellite (I.T.U.)

1975. 30th Anniv of U.N.O. Multicoloured.
562 5d. Type 93 . . . . 15 10
563 15d. U.N. Headquarters, New York 30 10
564 35d. U.P.U. emblem and map 75 15
565 1r. Doctors tending child (UNICEF) . . . . 1·80 60
566 1r.25 Bulldozer (I.L.O.) . . . 3·25 90
567 2r. Students in class (UNESCO) . . . . 5·25 1·20

94 Fertilizer Plant

1975. Qatar Industry. Multicoloured.

568	5d. Type **94**	35	10
569	10d. Flour mills (vert)	65	10
570	35d. Natural gas plant	1·30	20
571	75d. Oil refinery	3·00	80
572	1r.25 Cement works	3·75	1·10
573	1r.55 Steel mills	5·50	1·50

95 Modern Building, Doha

1976. 4th Anniv of Shaikh Khalifa's Accession.

574 **95**	5d. multicoloured	20	15
575 –	10d. multicoloured	20	15
576 –	35d. multicoloured	1·10	20
577 –	55d. multicoloured	1·80	35
578 –	75d. multicoloured	2·20	60
579 –	1r.55 multicoloured	5·50	1·50

DESIGNS: Nos. 575/6 and 579 show public buildings; Nos. 577/8 show Shaikh Khalifa with flag.

96 Tracking Aerial

97 Early and Modern Telephones

1976. Opening of Satellite Earth Station. Mult.

580	35d. Type **96**	90	20
581	55d. "Intelsat" satellite	1·10	35
582	75d. Type **96**	1·60	60
583	1r. As 55d.	2·40	75

1976. Telephone Centenary.

584 **97**	1r. multicoloured	2·20	90
585	1r.35 multicoloured	3·00	1·20

98 Tournament Emblem

100 Football

99 Qatar Dhow

1976. 4th Arabian Gulf Football Cup Tournament. Multicoloured.

586	5d. Type **98**	15	15
587	10d. Qatar Stadium	35	15
588	35d. Type **98**	1·80	20
589	55d. Two players with ball	2·75	45
590	75d. Player with ball	3·25	75
591	1r.25 As 10d.	4·50	95

1976. Dhows.

592 **99**	10d. multicoloured	1·10	10
593 –	35d. multicoloured	2·20	15
594 –	80d. multicoloured	4·50	50
595 –	1r.25 multicoloured	6·00	90
596 –	1r.50 multicoloured	6·75	1·10
597 –	2r. multicoloured	9·50	1·80

DESIGNS: 35d. to 2r. Various craft.

1976. Olympic Games, Montreal, Multicoloured.

598	5d. Type **100**	20	10
599	10d. Yachting	60	10
600	35d. Show jumping	1·50	15
601	80d. Boxing	2·20	45
602	1r.25 Weightlifting	3·00	75
603	1r.50 Basketball	4·00	1·10

101 Urban Housing Development

1976. United Nations Conference on Human Settlements. Multicoloured.

604	10d. Type **101**	15	15
605	35d. U.N. and conference emblems	65	15
606	80d. Communal housing development	1·60	35
607	1r.25 Shaikh Khalifa	3·50	80

102 Kentish Plover

1976. Birds. Multicoloured.

608	5d. Type **102**	60	15
609	10d. Great cormorant	1·30	15
610	35d. Osprey	3·75	35
611	80d. Greater flamingo (vert)	7·50	75
612	1r.25 Rock thrush (vert)	11·00	1·20
613	2r. Saker falcon (vert)	13·50	1·50

103 Shaikh Khalifa and Flag

105 Shaikh Khalifa

104 U.N. Emblem

1976. 5th Anniv of Independence. Multicoloured.

614	5d. Type **103**	15	10
615	10d. Type **103**	50	15
616	40d. Doha buildings (horiz)	95	20
617	80d. As 40d.	1·30	45
618	1r.25 "Dana" (oil rig) (horiz)	2·20	60
619	1r.50 United Nations and Qatar emblems (horiz)	3·00	75

1976. United Nations Day.

620 **104**	2r. multicoloured	3·00	75
621	3r. multicoloured	4·50	1·20

1977. 5th Anniv of Amir's Accession.

622 **105**	20d. multicoloured	90	20
623	1r.80 multicoloured	6·00	1·30

106 Shaikh Khalifa

107 Envelope and A.P.U. Emblem

1977.

624 **106**	5d. multicoloured	30	10
625	10d. multicoloured	35	10
626	35d. multicoloured	65	20
627	80d. multicoloured	1·30	30
628	1r. multicoloured	2·75	45
629	5r. multicoloured	8·00	1·60
630	10r. multicoloured	18·00	3·25

Nos. 628/30 are larger, size 25 × 31 mm.

1977. 25th Anniv of Arab Postal Union.

631 **107**	35d. multicoloured	90	20
632	1r.35 multicoloured	3·00	90

108 Shaikh Khalifa and Sound Waves

1977. International Telecommunications Day.

633 **108**	35d. multicoloured	60	20
634	1r.80 multicoloured	3·75	1·30

108a Shaikh Khalifa

109 Parliament Building, Doha

1977.

634a **108a**	5d. multicoloured	30	30
634c	10d. multicoloured	45	45
634d	35d. multicoloured	60	60
634e	80d. multicoloured	1·50	1·50

1977. 6th Anniv of Independence. Multicoloured.

635	80d. Type **109**	2·20	75
636	80d. Main business district, Doha	2·20	75
637	80d. Motorway, Doha	2·20	75

110 U.N. Emblem

1977. United Nations Day.

638 **110**	20d. multicoloured	50	20
639	1r. multicoloured	2·50	90

111 Steel Mill

1978. 6th Anniv of Amir's Accession. Mult.

640	20d. Type **111**	80	10
641	80d. Operating theatre	1·60	20
642	1r. Children's classroom	2·75	35
643	5r. Shaikh Khalifa	8·00	1·20

112 Oil Refinery

1978. 7th Anniv of Independence. Multicoloured.

644	35d. Type **112**	60	20
645	80d. Apartment buildings	1·20	35
646	1r.35 Town centre, Doha	2·20	75
647	1r.80 Shaikh Khalifa	3·00	90

113 Man reading Alphabet

1978. International Literacy Day.

648 **113**	35d. multicoloured	75	20
649	80d. multicoloured	2·20	50

114 U.N. Emblem and Qatar Flag

1978. United Nations Day.

650 **114**	35d. multicoloured	60	20
651	80d. multicoloured	1·80	50

115 "Human Rights Flame"

116 I.Y.C. Emblem

1978. 30th Anniv of Declaration of Human Rights. Multicoloured.

652	35d. Type **115**	45	15
653	80d. Type **115**	1·00	45
654	1r.25 Flame and scales of justice	1·50	60
655	1r.80 As 1r.25	2·20	90

1979. International Year of the Child.

656 **116**	35d. mauve, blue and black	35	20
657	1r.80 green, blue & black	1·10	90

117 Shaikh Khalifa

118 Shaikh Khalifa and Laurel Wreath

1979.

658 **117**	5d. multicoloured	15	10
659	10d. multicoloured	20	10
660	20d. multicoloured	45	10
661	25d. multicoloured	60	10
662	35d. multicoloured	90	30
663	60d. multicoloured	1·10	35
664	80d. multicoloured	1·50	45
665	1r. multicoloured	1·60	50
666	1r.25 multicoloured	1·00	60
667	1r.35 multicoloured	2·10	75
668	1r.80 multicoloured	3·00	90
669	5r. multicoloured	6·75	1·60
670	10r. multicoloured	13·50	3·25

Nos. 665/70 are larger, size 27 × 32½ mm.

1979. 7th Anniv of Amir's Accession.

671 **118**	35d. multicoloured	75	20
672	80d. multicoloured	1·00	30
673	1r. multicoloured	1·20	35
674	1r.25 multicoloured	1·50	45

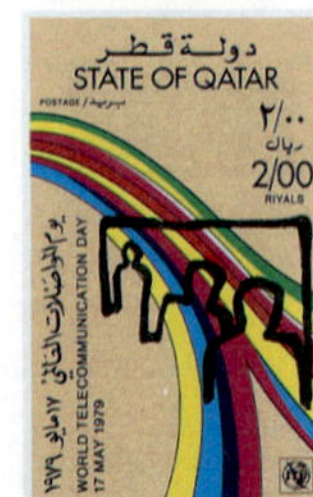

119 Wave Pattern and Television Screen

1979. World Telecommunications Day.

675 **119**	2r. multicoloured	1·90	75
676	2r.80 multicoloured	2·50	1·10

120 Two Children supporting Globe

1979. 50th Anniv of Int Bureau of Education.

677 **120**	35d. multicoloured	45	15
678	80d. multicoloured	1·80	45

121 Rolling Mill

122 U.N. Emblem and Flag of Qatar

1979. 8th Anniv of Independence. Multicoloured.
679 5d. Type **121** 45 10
680 10d. Aerial view of Doha . . 65 15
681 1r.25 Qatar flag . . . . . . 2·20 60
682 2r. Shaikh Khalifa . . . . . 3·25 75

1979. United Nations Day.
683 **122** 1r.25 multicoloured . . . 2·75 60
684 2r. multicoloured . . . . 4·00 90

123 Mosque Minaret and Crescent Moon

1979. 3rd World Conference on the Prophet's Seera and Sunna.
685 **123** 35d. multicoloured . . . 1·80 45
686 1r.80 multicoloured . . . 5·25 1·00

124 Shaikh Khalifa

1980. 8th Anniv of Amir's Accession.
687 **124** 20d. multicoloured . . . 65 15
688 60d. multicoloured . . . 1·80 35
689 1r.25 multicoloured . . . 2·75 60
690 2r. multicoloured . . . 5·50 1·10

125 Emblem

1980. 6th Congress of Arab Towns Organization, Doha.
691 **125** 2r.35 multicoloured . . . 4·50 90
692 2r.80 multicoloured . . . 6·75 1·20

126 Oil Refinery

1980. 9th Anniv of Independence. Multicoloured.
693 10d. Type **126** 35 10
694 35d. Doha . . . . 1·10 20
695 2r. Oil Rig . . . . 4·75 1·20
696 2r.35 Hospital . . . . 6·00 1·50

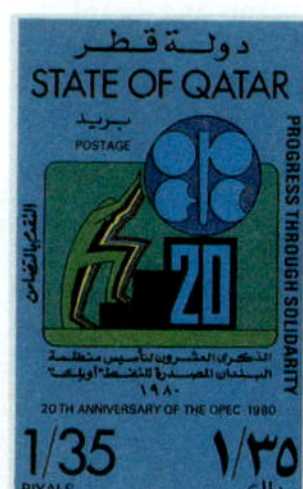

127 Figures supporting O.P.E.C. Emblem

1980. 20th Anniv of Organization of Petroleum Exporting Countries.
697 **127** 1r.35 multicoloured . . . 2·10 60
698 2r. multicoloured . . . . 3·50 90

128 U.N.Emblem

129 Mosque and Kaaba, Mecca

1980. United Nations Day.
699 **128** 1r.35 blue, light blue and purple . . . . 1·60 60
700 1r.80 turquoise, green and black . . . . 2·20 75

1980. 1400th Anniv of Hegira.
701 **129** 10d. multicoloured . . . 20 10
702 35d. multicoloured . . . 60 20
703 1r.25 multicoloured . . . 1·10 60
704 2r.80 multicoloured . . . 2·75 1·50

130 I.Y.D.P. Emblem

1981. International Year of Disabled Persons.
705 **130** 2r. multicoloured . . . . 2·40 1·10
706 3r. multicoloured . . . . 3·50 1·50

131 Student

132 Shaikh Khalifa

1981. 20th Anniv of Education Day.
707 **131** 2r. multicoloured . . . . 2·20 75
708 3r. multicoloured . . . . 3·00 1·10

1981. 9th Anniv of Amir's Accession.
709 **132** 10d. multicoloured . . . 30 10
710 35d. multicoloured . . . 75 15
711 80d. multicoloured . . . 1·50 35
712 5r. multicoloured . . . . 7·50 1·80

133 I.T.U. and W.H.O. Emblems and Ribbons forming Caduceus

134 Torch

1981. World Telecommunications Day.
713 **133** 2r. multicoloured . . . . 2·40 75
714 2r.80 multicoloured . . . 3·50 1·10

1981. 30th International Military Football Championship.
715 **134** 1r.25 multicoloured . . . 2·50 75
716 2r.80 multicoloured . . . 4·75 1·50

135 Qatar Flag

1981. 10th Anniv of Independence.
717 **135** 5d. multicoloured 35 10
718 60d. multicoloured . . . 1·10 30
719 80d. multicoloured . . . 1·50 35
720 5r. multicoloured . . . . 8·75 2·20

136 Tractor gathering Crops

1981. World Food Day.
721 **136** 2r. multicoloured . . . . 3·25 1·50
722 2r.80 multicoloured . . . 4·50 1·80

137 Red Crescent

1982. Qatar Red Crescent.
723 **137** 20d. multicoloured . . . 50 15
724 2r.80 multicoloured . . . 4·50 1·50

138 Shaikh Khalifa

1982. 10th Anniv of Amir's Accession.
725 **138** 10d. multicoloured . . . 45 10
726 20d. multicoloured . . . 90 15
727 1r.25 multicoloured . . . 3·25 65
728 2r.80 multicoloured . . . 7·50 1·30

139 Hamad General Hospital

1982. Hamad General Hospital.
729 **139** 10d. multicoloured . . . 35 15
730 2r.35 multicoloured . . . 3·50 1·30

140 Shaikh Khalifa

1982.
731 **140** 5d. multicoloured 15 10
732 10d. multicoloured . . . 15 10
733 15d. multicoloured . . . 20 10
734 20d. multicoloured . . . 20 10
735 25d. multicoloured . . . 30 15
736 35d. multicoloured . . . 45 15
737 60d. multicoloured . . . 60 15
738 80d. multicoloured . . . 80 15
739 – 1r. multicoloured . . . . 1·00 30
740 – 1r.25 multicoloured . . . 1·30 30
741 – 2r. multicoloured . . . . 2·10 75
742 – 5r. multicoloured . . . . 5·25 1·80
743 – 10r. multicoloured . . . . 10·50 3·75
744 – 15r. multicoloured . . . . 15·00 6·00

DESIGNS—25 × 32 mm: 1r. to 2r. Oil refinery; 5r. to 15r. Doha clock tower.

142 "Bar'zan" Container Ship

1982. 6th Anniv of United Arab Shipping Company.
745 **142** 20d. multicoloured . . . 60 15
746 2r.35 multicoloured . . . 5·25 1·30

143 A.P.U. Emblem

144 National Flag

1982. 30th Anniv of Arab Postal Union.
747 **143** 35d. multicoloured . . . 75 20
748 2r.80 multicoloured . . . 4·50 1·10

1982. 11th Anniv of Independence.
749 **144** 10d. multicoloured . . . 45 15
750 80d. multicoloured . . . 1·20 30
751 1r.25 multicoloured . . . 2·20 75
752 2r.80 multicoloured . . . 4·50 1·10

145 W.C.Y. Emblem

147 Arabic Script

146 Conference Emblem

1983. World Communications Year.
753 **145** 35d. multicoloured . . . 60 20
754 2r.80 multicoloured . . . 3·25 1·10

1983. 2nd Gulf Postal Organization Conference.
755 **146** 1r. multicoloured . . . . 1·30 60
756 1r.35 multicoloured . . . 2·10 90

1983. 12th Anniv of Independence.
757 **147** 10d. multicoloured . . . 20 15
758 35d. multicoloured . . . 45 20
759 80d. multicoloured . . . 90 35
760 2r.80 multicoloured . . . 3·25 1·10

148 Council Emblem

1983. 4th Session of Gulf Co-operation Council Supreme Council.
761 **148** 35d. multicoloured . . . 75 20
762 2r.80 multicoloured . . . 4·00 1·10

149 Globe and Human Rights Emblem

1983. 35th Anniv of Declaration of Human Rights. Multicoloured.
763 1r.25 Type **149** . . . . . . 1·80 75
764 2r.80 Globe and emblem in balance . . . . 4·00 1·10

150 Harbour 151 Shaikh Khalifa

1984.
765 **150** 15d. multicoloured . . . 20 10
765a **151** 25d. mult (22 × 27 mm) 30 15
766 **150** 40d. multicoloured . . . 45 15
767 50d. multicoloured . . . 50 20
767a **151** 75d. mult (22 × 27 mm) 75 35
768 1r. multicoloured . . . . 1·10 45
769 1r.50 multicoloured . . . 1·60 65
769a 2r. multicoloured . . . . 1·90 1·10
770 2r.50 multicoloured . . . 2·75 1·10
771 3r. multicoloured . . . . 3·25 1·30
772 5r. multicoloured . . . . 5·50 2·20
773 10r. multicoloured . . . 11·00 4·50

152 Flag and Shaikh Khalifa

1984. 13th Anniv of Independence.
774 **152** 15d. multicoloured . . . 45 15
775 1r. multicoloured . . . . 1·50 45
776 2r.50 multicoloured . . . 3·25 1·10
777 3r.50 multicoloured . . . 4·50 1·50

153 Teacher and Blackboard 154 I.C.A.O. Emblem

1984. International Literacy Day. Multicoloured, background colour behind board given.
778 **153** 1r. mauve . . . . 2·20 45
779 1r. orange . . . . 2·20 45

1984. 40th Anniv of I.C.A.O.
780 **154** 20d. multicoloured . . . 35 15
781 3r.50 multicoloured . . . 4·75 1·50

155 I.Y.Y. Emblem 156 Crossing the Road

1985. International Youth Year.
782 **155** 50d. multicoloured . . . 75 20
783 1r. multicoloured . . . . 1·60 50

1985. Traffic Week. Multicoloured, frame colour given.
784 **156** 1r. red . . . . 1·80 50
785 1r. blue . . . . 1·80 50

157 Emblem

1985. 40th Anniv of League of Arab States.
786 **157** 50d. multicoloured . . . 1·00 20
787 4r. multicoloured . . . . 5·25 1·60

158 Doha

1985. 14th Anniv of Independence. Multicoloured.
788 40d. Type **158** 60 15
789 50d. Dish aerials and microwave tower 75 20
790 1r.50 Oil refinery . . . . . . 2·40 60
791 4r. Cement works . . . . . 6·00 1·80

159 O.P.E.C. Emblem in "25"

1985. 25th Anniv of Organization of Petroleum Exporting Countries. Multicoloured, background colours given.
792 **159** 1r. red . . . . 2·20 60
793 1r. green . . . . 2·20 60

160 U.N. Emblem

1985. 40th Anniv of U.N.O.
794 **160** 1r. multicoloured 75 60
795 3r. multicoloured . . . . 2·20 1·60

161 Emblem

1986. Population and Housing Census.
796 **161** 1r. multicoloured . . . . 1·10 60
797 3r. multicoloured . . . . 3·25 1·60

162 "Qatari ibn al-Fuja'a" (container ship)

1986. 10th Anniv of United Arab Shipping Company. Multicoloured.
798 1r.50 Type **162** . . . . . . 1·10 75
799 4r. "Al Wajda" (container ship) . . . . 3·00 1·80

163 Flag and Shaikh Khalifa

1986. 15th Anniv of Independence.
800 **163** 40d. multicoloured . . . 35 20
801 50d. multicoloured . . . 50 30
802 1r. multicoloured . . . . 1·00 60
803 4r. multicoloured . . . . 3·75 2·20

164 Shaikh Khalifa 165 Palace

1987.
804 **164** 15r. multicoloured . . . . 9·50 6·00
805 20r. multicoloured . . . . 12·50 7·50
806 30r. multicoloured . . . . 22·00 12·00

1987. 15th Anniv of Amir's Accession.
807 **165** 50d. multicoloured . . . 45 20
808 1r. multicoloured . . . . 1·00 45
809 1r.50 multicoloured . . . 1·30 60
810 4r. multicoloured . . . . 3·25 1·80

166 Emblem 167 Emblem

1987. 35th Anniv of Arab Postal Union.
811 **166** 1r. yellow, green and black . . . . 1·20 45
812 1r.50 multicoloured . . . 1·80 75

1987. Gulf Environment Day.
813 **167** 1r. multicoloured . . . . 95 6·00
814 4r. multicoloured . . . . 3·75 2·20

168 Modern Complex

1987. 16th Anniv of Independence.
815 25d. Type **168** 45 15
816 75d. Aerial view of city . . . 1·20 35
817 2r. Modern building . . . . 2·20 90
818 4r. Oil refinery . . . . 4·50 1·80

169 Pens in Fist 170 Anniversary Emblem

1987. International Literacy Day.
819 **169** 1r.50 multicoloured . . . 1·10 75
820 4r. multicoloured . . . . 2·50 1·80

1988. 40th Anniv of W.H.O.
821 **170** 1r.50 yellow, black and blue . . . . 1·00 95
822 2r. yellow, black and pink 1·30 1·10

171 State Arms, Shaikh Khalifa and Flag

1988. 17th Anniv of Independence.
823 **171** 50d. multicoloured . . . 60 30
824 75d. multicoloured . . . 80 35
825 1r.50 multicoloured . . . 1·30 80
826 2r. multicoloured . . . . 1·80 1·00

172 Post Office

1988. Opening of New Doha General Post Office.
827 **172** 1r.50 multicoloured . . . 90 75
828 4r. multicoloured . . . . 2·20 1·80

173 Housing Development

1988. Arab Housing Day.
829 **173** 1r.50 multicoloured . . . 1·30 75
830 4r. multicoloured . . . . 3·50 1·80

174 Hands shielding Flame 175 Dish Aerials and Arrows

1988. 40th Anniv of Declaration of Human Rights.
831 **174** 1r.50 multicoloured . . . 90 75
832 2r. multicoloured . . . . 1·20 1·00

1989. World Telecommunications Day.
833 **175** 2r. multicoloured 60 95
834 4r. multicoloured . . . . 2·20 1·80

176 Headquarters

1989. 10th Anniv of Qatar Red Crescent Society.
835 **176** 4r. multicoloured . . . . 5·25 2·20

177 Palace

1989. 18th Anniv of Independence.
836 **177** 75d. multicoloured . . . 45 35
837 1r. multicoloured 80 65
838 1r.50 multicoloured . . . 1·00 75
839 2r. multicoloured . . . . 1·50 90

178 Anniversary Emblem

1990. 40th Anniv of Gulf Air.
840 **178** 50d. multicoloured . . . 60 20
841 75d. multicoloured . . . 90 35
842 4r. multicoloured . . . . 4·50 1·80

179 Map and Rising Sun

1990. 19th Anniv of Independence. Multicoloured.
843 50d. Type **179** 60 20
844 75d. Map and sunburst . . . 90 35
845 1r.50 Musicians and sword dancer . . . . 1·80 75
846 2r. As No. 845 . . . . 2·75 1·20

180 Anniversary Emblem 181 Emblem and Dhow

1990. 30th Anniv of Organization of Petroleum Exporting Countries. Multicoloured.
847 50d. Type **180** 75 20
848 1r.50 Flags of member nations . . . . 2·20 75

1990. 11th Session of Supreme Council of Gulf Co-operation Council. Multicoloured.
849 50d. Type **181** 60 60
850 1r. Council heads of state and emblem . . . . 1·20 45
851 1r.50 State flag and Council emblem . . . . 1·10 75
852 2r. State and Council emblems . . . . 2·20 90

182 "Glossonema edule"

183 Emblem

1991. Plants. Multicoloured.
853 10d. Type **182** 20 10
854 25d. "Lycium shawii" 20 10
855 50d. "Acacia tortilis" 30 20
856 75d. "Acacia ehrenbergiana" 45 30
857 1r. "Capparis spinosa" . . . 60 50
858 4r. "Cymbopogon parkeri" 2·75 2·20
No. 858 is wrongly inscribed "Cymhopogon".

1991. 20th Anniv of Independence. Multicoloured.
859 25d. Type **183** 45 15
860 75d. As Type **183** but different Arabic inscription 65 30
861 1r. View of Doha (35 × 32 mm) 90 45
862 1r.50 Palace (35 × 32 mm) . . 1·30 75

184 Seabream

1991. Fishes. Multicoloured.
863 10d. Type **184** 15 10
864 15d. Pennant coralfish . . . 15 10
865 25d. Scarlet-finned squirrelfish 30 15
866 50d. Smooth houndshark . . 50 30
867 75d. Seabream 75 45
868 1r. Golden trevally 90 65
869 1r.50 Rabbitfish . . . . 1·50 1·00
870 2r. Yellow-banded angelfish 1·80 1·30

185 Shaikh Khalifa

1992. Multicoloured. (a) Size 22 × 28 or 28 × 22 mm.
871 10d. Type **185** 10 10
872 25d. North Field gas project 15 10
873 50d. Map of Qatar 30 20
874 75d. Petrochemical factory (horiz) 50 30
875 1r. Oil refinery (horiz) . . . 60 35

(b) Size 25 × 32 or 32 × 25 mm.
876 1r.50 As No. 872 . . . . . . 75 60
877 2r. As No. 873 . . . . 95 75
878 3r. As No. 874 . . . . 2·20 1·50
879 4r. As No. 875 . . . . 2·50 1·60
880 5r. As No. 873 . . . . 2·50 1·80
881 10r. As No. 875 . . . . . . 6·75 3·75
882 15r. Shaikh Khalifa (different frame) . . . . 7·50 5·50
883 20r. As No. 882 . . . . . . 13·50 7·50
884 30r. As No. 882 . . . . . . 15·00 11·00

186 Shaikh Khalifa and Gateway

187 Heart in Centre of Flower

1992. 20th Anniv of Amir's Accession. Mult.
885 25d. Type **186** 30 15
886 50d. Type **186** 60 20
887 75d. Archway and "20" . . . 90 35
888 1r.50 As No 887 . . . . . . 1·80 75

1992. World Health Day. "Heartbeat, the Rhythm of Health". Multicoloured.
889 50d. Type **187** 35 20
890 1r.50 Heart on clockface and cardiograph (horiz) . . . . 1·10 75

188 Women dancing

1992. Children's Paintings. Multicoloured.
891 25d. Type **188** 35 10
892 50d. Children's playground 75 20
893 75d. Boat race . . . . 1·30 30
894 1r.50 Fishing fleet . . . . . 2·20 45
MS895 122 × 102 mm. Nos. 891/4 £150 £150

189 Runner and Emblems

1992. Olympic Games, Barcelona. Multicoloured.
896 50d. Type **189** 60 15
897 1r.50 Footballer and emblems 1·30 45

190 Shaikh Khalifa and Script

1992. 21st Anniv of Independence. Multicoloured.
898 50d. Type **190** 35 20
899 50d. Shaikh Kalifa and "21" in English and Arabic . . 35 20
900 1r. Oil well, pen and dhow (42 × 42 mm) 75 50
901 1r. Dhow in harbour (42 × 42 mm) 75 50

191 Ball, Flag and Emblem

1992. 11th Arabian Gulf Football Championship. Multicoloured.
902 50d. Type **191** 45 20
903 1r. Ball bursting goal net (vert) 90 50

192 Emblems and Globe

1992. International Nutrition Conference, Rome. Multicoloured.
904 50d. Type **192** . . . . . . 1·10 20
905 1r. Cornucopia (horiz) . . . 1·80 35

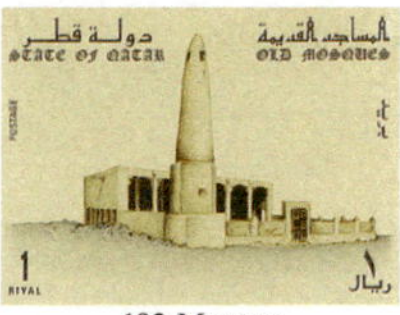

193 Mosque

1993. Old Mosques. Each sepia, yellow and brown.
906 1r. Type **193** 65 50
907 1r. Mosque (minaret without balcony) 65 50
908 1r. Mosque (minaret with wide balcony) 65 50
909 1r. Mosque (minaret with narrow balcony) 65 50

194 Presenter and Dish Aerial

1993. 25th Anniv of Qatar Broadcasting. Mult.
910 25d. Type **194** 35 10
911 50d. Rocket and satellite . . . 90 30
912 75d. Broadcasting House . . 1·10 45
913 1r. Journalists . . . . 1·80 50
MS914 123 × 114 mm. Nos. 910/13 forming a composite design . . 90·00 90·00

195 Oil Refinery and Sea

196 Scroll, Quill and Paper

1993. 22nd Anniv of Independence. Multicoloured.
915 25d. Type **195** 15 10
916 50d. Flag and clock tower, Doha 30 20
917 75d. "22" in English and Arabic 45 35
918 1r.50 Flag and fort 95 80

1993. International Literacy Day. Multicoloured.
919 25d. Type **196** 15 10
920 50d. Fountain pen and flags spelling "Qatar" 30 20
921 75d. Fountain pen and Arabic characters 45 35
922 1r.50 Arabic text on scroll and fountain pen 95 80

197 Girls playing

1993. Children's Games. Multicoloured.
923 25d. Type **197** 35 10
924 50d. Boys playing with propeller (vert) 75 20
925 75d. Wheel and stick race (vert) . . . . 1·10 35
926 1r.50 Skipping . . . . 2·20 80
MS927 Two sheets (a) 114 × 93 mm. Nos. 923 × 2 and 926 × 2; (b) 93 × 114 mm. Nos. 924 × 2 and 925 × 2 . . . . 65·00 65·00

198 Lanner Falcon

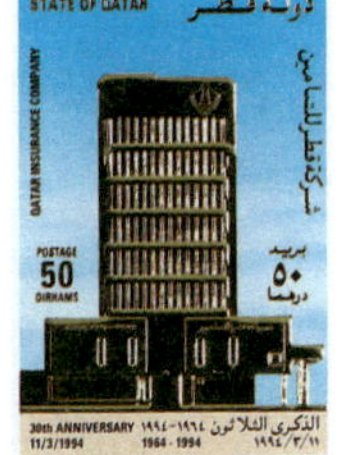

199 Headquarters

1993. Falcons. Multicoloured.
928 25d. Type **198** 30 15
929 50d. Saker falcon 60 20
930 75d. Barbary falcon 90 35
931 1r.50 Peregrine falcon . . . . 1·90 80
MS932 122 × 104 mm. Nos. 928/31 £100 £120

1994. 30th Anniv of Qatar Insurance Company. Multicoloured.
933 50d. Type **199** 60 20
934 1r.50 Company emblem and international landmarks . . 1·90 75

200 Hands catching Drops from Tap

201 Gavel, Scales and National Flag

1994. World Water Day. Mulicoloured.
935 25d. Type **200** 35 15
936 1r. Hands catching raindrop, water tower, crops and United Nations emblem . . 90 50

1994. Qatar International Law Conference. Multicoloured.
937 75d. Type **201** 45 35
938 2r. Gavel and scales suspended from flag . . . 1·20 1·10

202 Society Emblem

203 Anniversary Emblem

1994. Qatar Society for Welfare and Rehabilitation of the Handicapped. Multicoloured.
939 25d. Type **202** 30 15
940 75d. Handicapped symbol and hands 90 30

1994. 75th Anniv of I.L.O. Multicoloured.
941 25d. Type **203** 30 15
942 2r. Anniversary emblem and cogwheel . . . . 2·20 75

204 Family and Emblem

205 Scroll

1994. International Year of the Family.
943 **204** 25d. blue and black . . . 30 15
944 – 1r. multicoloured 95 45
DESIGN: 1r. I.Y.F. emblem and stylized family standing on U.N. emblem.

1994. 23rd Anniv of Independence. Multicoloured.
945 25d. Type **205** 20 15
946 75d. Oasis 65 35
947 1r. Industry 90 50
948 2r. Scroll (different) . . . . 2·10 1·20

206 Map, Airplane and Emblem

1994. 50th Anniv of I.C.A.O. Multicoloured.
949 25d. Type **206** 65 15
950 75d. Anniversary emblem . . 1·60 35

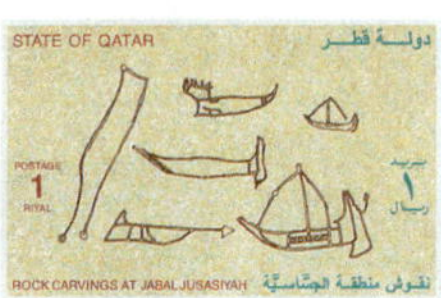

207 Ship-like Carvings

1995. Rock Carvings, Jabal Jusasiyah. Multicoloured.
951 1r. Type **207** 45 30
952 1r. Circular and geometric patterns 45 30
953 1r. Six irregular-shaped carvings 45 30
954 1r. Carvings including three multi-limbed creatures . . 45 30
955 1r. Nine multi-limbed creatures 45 30
956 1r. Fishes 45 30

208 Precious Wentletrap ("Epitonium scalare")

1995. Gulf Environment Day. Sea Shells. Multicoloured.

957 75d. Type **208** 35 30
958 75d. Feathered cone ("Conus pennaceus") 35 30
959 75d. "Cerithidea cingulata" 35 30
960 75d. "Hexaplex kuesterianus" 35 30
961 1r. Giant spider conch ("Lambis truncata sebae") 45 35
962 1r. Woodcock murex ("Murex scolopax") . . . 45 35
963 1r. "Thais mutabilis" 45 35
964 1r. Spindle shell ("Fusinus arabicus") 45 35

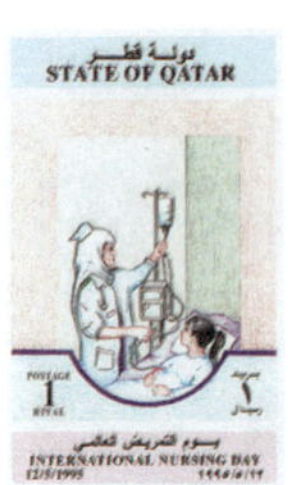

209 Nursing Patient

211 Anniversary Emblem

210 Schoolchildren

1995. International Nursing Day. Multicoloured.

965 1r. Type **209** 90 45
966 1r.50 Vaccinating child . . . 1·30 75

1995. 24th Anniv of Independence. Multicoloured.

967 1r. Type **210** 45 35
968 1r. Palm trees 45 35
969 1r.50 Port 75 60
970 1r.50 Doha 75 60

Nos. 967/70 were issued together, se-tenant, forming a composite design.

1995. 50th Anniv of U.N.O.

971 **211** 1r.50 multicoloured . . . 1·10 60

212 Addra Gazelle

1996. Mammals. Multicoloured.

972 25d. Type **212** 10 10
973 50d. Beira antelope 20 15
974 75d. "Gazella dorcas pelzelni" 35 30
975 1r. Dorcas gazelle 45 35
976 1r.50 Speke's gazelle 75 60
977 2r. Soemmering's gazelle . . . 1·10 95
MS978 121 × 81 mm. 3r. Speke's gazelle, *Gazella dorcas pelzelni* and Soemmering's gazelle. Imperf 22·00 18·00

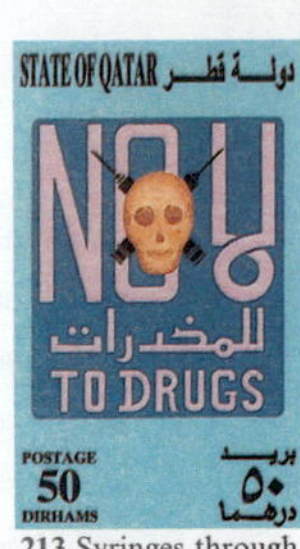

213 Syringes through Skull

214 Map of Qatar and Games Emblem

1996. International Day against Drug Abuse. Multicoloured.

979 50d. Type **213** 35 20
980 1r. "No entry" sign over syringes in hand 65 30

1996. Olympic Games, Atlanta. Multicoloured.

981 10d. Type **214** 10 10
982 15d. Rifle shooting 10 10
983 25d. Bowling 10 10
984 50d. Table tennis 20 15
985 1r. Running 45 35
986 1r.50 Yachting 75 60

Nos. 981/6 were issued together, se-tenant, forming a composite design.

215 Map, National Flag and Shaikh Hamad

1996. 25th Anniv of Independence.

987 **215** 1r.50 multicoloured . . . 1·00 60
988 2r. multicoloured . . . . 1·30 75

216 Shaikh Hamad

217 Shaikh Hamad

1996.

990 **216** 25d. multicoloured . . . 10 10
991 50d. multicoloured . . . 20 15
992 75d. multicoloured . . . 35 20
993 1r. multicoloured 45 30
994 **217** 1r.50 multicoloured . . . 75 45
995 2r. multicoloured 95 50
997 4r. multicoloured . . . . 1·80 1·20
998 5r. multicoloured . . . . 2·20 2·40
999 10r. multicoloured . . . 4·50 3·00
1001 20r. multicoloured . . . 8·75 6·00
1002 30r. multicoloured . . . 13·50 8·75

218 Doha Clock Tower, Dove and Heads of State

219 Children and UNICEF Emblem

1996. 17th Session of Gulf Co-operation Council Supreme Council, Doha. Multicoloured.

1004 1r. Type **218** 45 30
1005 1r.50 Council emblem, dove and national flag 75 60

1996. 50th Anniv of UNICEF. Multicoloured.

1006 75d. Type **219** 35 20
1007 75d. Children and emblem 35 20

220 Al-Wajbah

1997. Forts. Multicoloured.

1008 25d. Type **220** 15 10
1009 75d. Al-Zubarah (horiz) . . 35 30
1010 1r. Al-Kout Fort, Doha (horiz) 45 35
1011 3r. Umm Salal Mohammed (horiz) . . . . 1·50 1·30

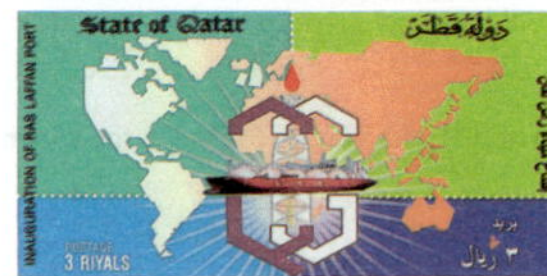

221 World Map and Liquid Gas Containers (½-size illustration)

1997. Inauguration of Ras Laffan Port.

1012 **221** 3r. multicoloured . . . . 2·20 1·10

222 Palomino

1997. Arab Horses. Multicoloured.

1013 25d. Type **222** 15 10
1014 75d. Black horse 45 30
1015 1r. Grey 60 35
1016 1r.50 Bay 90 60
MS1017 121 × 81 mm. 3r. Mares and foals . . . . 48·00 18·00

223 Arabic Script within Wreath, Flag and Shaikh Hamad

1997. 26th Anniv of Independence. Multicoloured.

1018 1r. Type **223** 50 35
1019 1r.50 Amir, oil refinery and Government Palace . . . 75 60

224 Graph

1997. Middle East and Northern Africa Economic Conference, Doha.

1020 **224** 2r. multicoloured 95 75

225 Nubian Flower Bee

1998. Insects. Multicoloured.

1021 2r. Type **225** 95 60
1022 2r. Domino beetle 95 60
1023 2r. Seven-spotted ladybird 95 60
1024 2r. Desert giant ant 95 60
1025 2r. Eastern death's-head hawk moth 95 60
1026 2r. Arabian darkling beetle 95 60
1027 2r. Yellow digger 95 60
1028 2r. Mole cricket 95 60
1029 2r. Migratory locust 95 60
1030 2r. Elegant rhinoceros beetle 95 60
1031 2r. Oleander hawk moth . . 95 60
1032 2r. American cockroach . . 95 60
1033 2r. Girdled skimmer 95 60
1034 2r. Sabre-toothed beetle . . 95 60
1035 2r. Arabian cicada 95 60
1036 2r. Pin-striped ground weevil 95 60
1037 2r. Praying mantis 95 60
1038 2r. Rufous bombardier beetle 95 60
1039 2r. Diadem 95 60
1040 2r. Shore earwig (inscr "Earwing") 95 60
MS1041 Two sheets, each 91 × 59 mm. (a) No. 1029; (b) No. 1039 . . . . 22·00 15·00

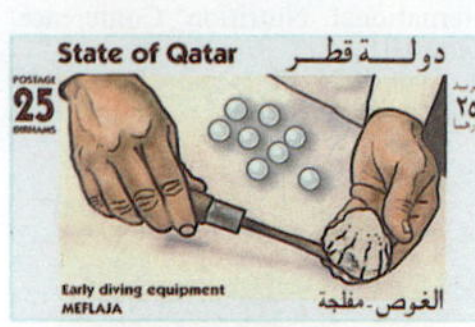

226 Opening Oysters

1998. Early Pearl-diving Equipment. Multicoloured.

1042 25d. Type **226** 15 10
1043 75d. Opened oyster with pearl 35 20
1044 1r. Scales for weighing pearls 45 30
1045 1r.50 Basket for keeping oysters (vert) 75 60
MS1046 106 × 83 mm. 2r. Pearl diver 6·75 4·60

227 Shaikh Hamad

228 Anniversary Emblem

1998. 27th Anniv of Independence. Multicoloured.

1047 1r. Type **227** 45 30
1048 1r.50 Shaikh Hamad (horiz) 75 60

1998. 25th Anniv of University of Qatar.

1049 **228** 1r. multicoloured 45 30
1050 1r.50 multicoloured . . . 75 60

229 Dromedaries

1999. Dromedaries. Multicoloured.

1051 25d. Type **229** 10 10
1052 75d. One dromedary 35 30
1053 1r. Three dromedaries . . . 45 35
1054 1r.50 Four young dromedaries with herd . . 75 60
MS1055 106 × 83 mm. 2r. Adult and young . . . . 10·50 7·50

230 Emblem

1999. General Assembly of International Equestrian Federation, Doha.

1056 **230** 1r.50 multicoloured . . . 75 60

231 Umayyad Dirham

1999. Coins. Multicoloured.

1057 1r. Type **231** 45 30
1058 1r. Umayyad dirham (four small circles around edge of right-hand coin) . . . 45 30
1059 1r. Abbasid dirham (three lines of inscr on left-hand coin) 45 30
1060 1r. Abbasid dirham (six lines of inscr on left-hand coin) 45 30
1061 1r. Umayyad dirham (five small circles around edge of right-hand coin) . . . 45 30
1062 2r. Abbasid dirham (three lines on inscr on left-hand coin) 90 75
1063 2r. Umayyad dinar 90 75
1064 2r. Abbasid dinar (five lines of inscr on left-hand coin) 90 75
1065 2r. Murabitid dinar 90 75
1066 2r. Fatimid dinar 90 75
MS1067 Two sheets, each 112 × 70 mm. (a) 2r. Arab Sasanian dirham; (b) 3r. Umayyad dirham . . . . 13·50 10·50

232 Shaikh Hamad

1999. 28th Anniv of Independence.

1068 **232** 1r. multicoloured 45 35
1069 1r.50 multicoloured . . . 75 60

233 Tree of Letters **234** Postal Emblems on "Stamps"

1999. 125th Anniv of Universal Postal Union. Multicoloured.

1070 1r. Type **233** 45 35
1071 1r.50 General Post Office, Doha (horiz) 75 60

1999. 5th Arab Gulf Countries Stamp Exhibition, Doha. Multicoloured.

1072 1r. Type **234** 45 35
1073 1r.50 Exhibition emblem (horiz) 75 60

235 Flower and Emblem

1999. National Committee for Children with Special Needs.

1074 **235** 1r.50 multicoloured . . . 75 60

236 Clock Tower

2000. New Millennium.

1075 **236** 1r.50 gold and red . . . 75 75
1076 2r. gold and blue . . . . 1·10 1·10

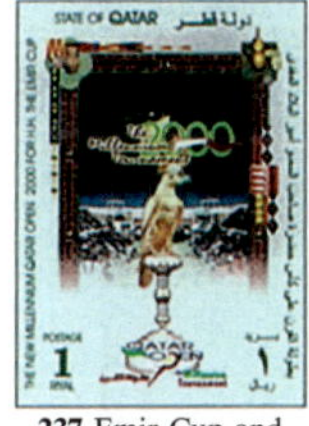
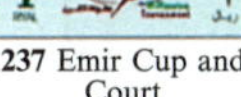

237 Emir Cup and Court **238** Map and Water Droplet

2000. New Millennium Open Tennis Championships, Qatar. Multicoloured.

1077 1r. Type **237** 60 60
1078 1r.50 Emir Cup and racquet 90 90

2000. Gulf Co-operation Council Water Week. Mult.

1079 1r. Type **238** 60 60
1080 1r.50 Dried earth and water droplet 90 90

239 Bat and Ball

2000. 15th Asian Table Tennis Championship, Doha.

1081 **239** 1r.50 multicoloured . . . 75 75

240 Shaikh Hamad, Fort and Emblem

2000. 29th Anniv of Independence. Multicoloured.

1082 1r. Type **240** 75 75
1083 1r.50 Shaikh Hamad, city and oil drilling platform 1·10 1·10

241 Emblem and Dove carrying Letter

2000. 50th Anniv of Qatar Post Office. Multicoloured.

1084 1r.50 Type **241** . . . . . . 1·10 1·10
1085 2r. Emblem, magnifying glass and building facade 1·50 1·50

242 Emblem

2000. 9th Islamic Summit Conference, Doha. Multicoloured.

1086 1r. Type **242** 75 75
1087 1r.50 Emblem and olive branch (47 × 30 mm) . . . 1·10 1·10

243 Gas Terminal

2001. "Clean Environment". Multicoloured.

1088 1r. Type **243** 65 65
1089 1r.50 Oryx and gas installation 95 95
1090 2r. Flamingoes and Ras Laffan city skyline . . . 1·50 1·50
1091 3r. Earth viewed from space 1·90 1·90

244 Castle, Koran and Ship

2001. 30th Anniv of Independence.

1092 **244** 1r. multicoloured 75 75
1093 1r.50 multicoloured . . . 1·10 1·10

245 Children encircling Globe

2001. United Nations Year of Dialogue among Civilizations. Multicoloured.

1094 1r.50 Type **245** . . . . . . 1·10 1·10
1095 2r. Leaves . . . . 1·60 1·60

246 Building and Emblem

2001. 4th World Trade Organization Ministerial Conference, Doho, Qatar.

1096 **246** 1r. multicoloured 50 50
1097 1r.50 multicoloured . . . 75 75

247 Door

2001. Traditional Wooden Doors. Multicoloured.

1098 25d. Type **247** 20 20
1099 75d. Small door in left-hand panel and large bolt at right 50 50
1110 1r.50 Plain doors . . . . . 1·30 1·30
1101 2r. Knocker at left and smaller door in right-hand panel . . . . 1·50 1·50
MS1102 100 × 70 mm. 3r. As No. 1101 . . . . 7·50 7·50

248 Uruguay, 1930 **249** Championship Emblem

2002. World Cup Football Championship, Japan and South Korea. Multicoloured.

1103 2r. Type **248** . . . . . . 1·30 1·30
1104 2r. Italy, 1934 . . . . . . 1·30 1·30
1105 2r. France, 1938 . . . . . 1·30 1·30
1106 2r. Brasil, 1950 . . . . . 1·30 1·30
1107 2r. Switzerland, 1954 . . . 1·30 1·30
1108 2r. Sweden, 1958 . . . . . 1·30 1·30
1109 2r. Chile, 1962 . . . . . . 1·30 1·30
1110 2r. England, 1966 . . . . . 60 50
1111 2r. Mexico, 1970 . . . . . 1·30 1·30
1112 2r. West Germany, 1974 . . 1·30 1·30
1113 2r. Argentina, 1978 . . . . 1·30 1·30
1114 2r. Spain, 1982 . . . . . . 1·30 1·30
1115 2r. Mexico, 1986 . . . . . 1·30 1·30
1116 2r. Italy, 1990 . . . . . . 1·30 1·30
1117 2r. USA, 1994 . . . . . . 1·30 1·30
1118 2r. France, 1998 . . . . . 1·30 1·30
1119 2r. 2002 Championship emblem . . . . 1·30 1·30
1120 2r. World Cup trophy . . . 1·30 1·30
MS1121 133 × 78 mm. Nos. 2019/20 2·75 2·75

2002. 14th Asian Games, Busan. Sheet 133 × 73 mm containing T **249** and similar vert design. Multicoloured.

MS1122 1r. Type **249**; 1r. 15th (2006) Asian Games championship emblem . . . . 2·75 2·75

250 Emblem

2002. 1st Anniv of Global Post Code. Multicoloured.

1123 **250** 1r. multicoloured 65 65
1124 3r. multicoloured . . . . 2·00 2·00

251 Runner, Heart and No-Smoking Sign

2003. World No-Smoking Day.

1125 **251** 1r.50 multicoloured . . . 95 95

No. 1125 was printed using thermochromatic (heat sensitive) ink. When the image is pressed parts of the design disappear leaving only the runner visible.

252 Boy and Crescent

2003. 25th Anniv of Qatar Red Crescent (humanitarian organization). Multicoloured.

1126 75d. Type **252** 50 50
1127 75d. Building facade 50 50

253 Al Mashmoom (earrings)

2003. Jewellery. Multicoloured.

1128 25d. Type **253** 10 10
1129 25d. Al Mertash (necklace) 10 10
1130 50d. Khatim (ring) 15 15
1131 50d. Ishqab (earrings) . . . 15 15
1132 1r.50 Shmailat (bangle) . . 45 35
1133 1r.50 Tassa (headdress) . . 45 35

254 *Wright Flyer*

2003. Centenary of Powered Flight. Sheet 110 × 76 mm containing T **254** and similar horiz designs. Multicoloured. P 14½.

MS1134 50d. × 4 Type **254**; Otto Lilienthal's glider; Qatar Airways Boeing A330; Airplane . . . . 1·00 80

255 Family and Emblems

2004. 10th Anniv of International Year of the Family.

1135 **255** 2r.50 blue and light blue 75 65

256 FIFA Emblem

2004. Centenary of FIFA (Federation Internationale de Football Association).

1136 **256** 50d. multicoloured . . . 15 10

257 Flag, Shaikh Hamad and Book

2004. Establishment of Permanent Constitution.

1137 **257** 50d. multicoloured . . . 15 10

258 Athens 2004 and Olympic Emblems

2004. Olympic Games, Athens 2004. Sheet 72 × 72 mm containing T **258** and similar vert design. Multicoloured.

MS1138 3r. × 2, Type **258**; As Type **258** but with colours and face value reversed . . . . . . 1·10 1·00

259 Motorcyclist **260** Emblem

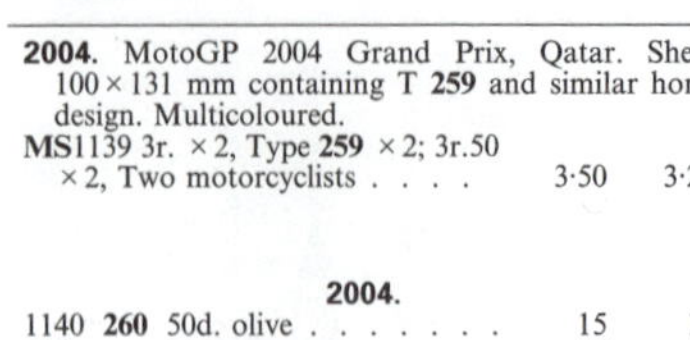

2004. MotoGP 2004 Grand Prix, Qatar. Sheet 100 × 131 mm containing T **259** and similar horiz design. Multicoloured.
MS1139 3r. × 2, Type **259** × 2; 3r.50 × 2, Two motorcyclists . . . . 3·50 3·25

2004.

1140 **260**	50d. olive	15	10
1141	50d. green	15	10
1142	50d. brown	15	10
1143	50d. purple	15	10
1144	50d. blue	15	10

261 Hand holding Olive Branch

2004. National Human Rights Committee.
1145 **261** 50d. multicoloured . . . 15 10

262 Al Sadd Sports Club

2004. 17th Arabian Gulf Cup. Sheet 100 × 100 mm containing T **262** and similar multicoloured designs.
MS1146 1r.50 × 5, Type **262**; Ball and player's legs (vert); Games emblem (35 × 35 mm); Goalkeeper (vert); Sudaifi (games mascot) 75 75

263 Orry

2004. 15th Asian Games, 2006, Doha. Official Mascot. Showing Orry (official mascot). Multicoloured. (a) Ordinary gum.

1147	50d. Type **263**	15	10
1148	1r. Sitting in dhow (horiz)	30	20
1149	1r.50 Marking off calender (horiz)	45	35
1150	2r. Carrying flaming torch	60	40
1151	3r. Lighting flame	90	70
1152	3r.50 Waving flag at Khalifa stadium	1·00	80

(b) Self-adhesive.

1153	50d. Type **263**	15	10
1154	1r. No. 1148 (horiz) . . .	30	20
1155	1r.50 No. 1149 (horiz) . . .	45	35
1156	2r. No. 1150	60	40
1157	3r. No. 1151	90	70
1158	3r.50 No. 1152	1·00	80

264 De Soto (1950)

2005. Classic Cars. Sheet 110 × 130 mm containing T **264** and similar horiz designs. Multicoloured.
MS1159 50d. × 8, Type **264**; Chevrolet (1958); Dodge Sedan (1938); Chrysler (1947); Dodge Power Wagon; Orange Chevrolet truck; Green Dodge truck; Two-tone Dodge truck . . . . . . 1·20 1·20

265 *Team Daedalus* Catamaran

2005. Oryx Quest 2005 (round the world sail race). Catamarans. Multicoloured.

1160	50d. Type **265**	15	10
1161	50d. With Qatar flag as sail	15	10
1162	50d. *Team Cheyenne* (vert)	15	10
1163	50d. *Team Geronimo* (vert)	15	10

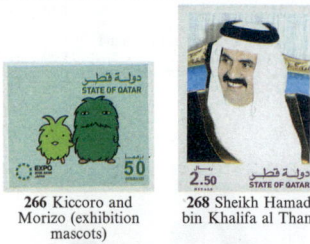

266 Kiccoro and Morizo (exhibition mascots)

268 Sheikh Hamad bin Khalifa al Thani

267 Emblem

2005. Expo 2005 World Exposition, Aichi. Multicoloured.

1164	50d. Type **266**	15	10
1165	50d. Qatar flag	15	10

2005. Doha Development Forum. Sheet 95 × 75 mm containing T **267** and similar horiz design. Multicoloured.
MS1166 6r. × 2, Type **267**; Emblem (different) . . . . 2·00 2·00

2005. 10th Anniv of Accession of Emir Sheikh Hamad bin Khalifa al Thani. Sheet 160 × 53 mm.
MS1167 **268** 2r.50 multicoloured 80 80

269 Sarajevo and Doha

2005.
1168 **269** 2r.50 multicoloured . . . 80 50

270 Flag

2005. Self-adhesive.

1169 **270**	50d. purple	15	10
1170	1r. purple	35	20
1171	1r.50 purple	50	30
1172	2r.50 purple	80	50
1173	3r. purple	95	60
1174	3r.50 purple	1·10	65

POSTAGE DUE STAMPS

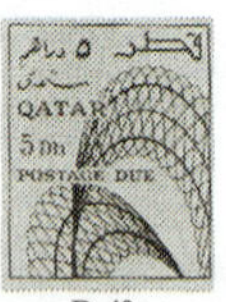

D 40

1968.

D254 D **40**	5d. blue	26·00	26·00
D255	10d. red	30·00	30·00
D256	20d. green	37·00	37·00
D257	30d. lilac	41·00	41·00

QU'AITI STATE IN HADHRAMAUT Pt. 1

The stamps of Aden were used in Qu'aiti State in Hadhramaut from 22 April 1937 until 1942.

1937. 16 annas = 1 rupee.
1951. 100 cents = 1 shilling.
1966. 1000 fils = 1 dinar.

(I) Issues inscribed "SHIHR and MUKALLA"

1 Sultan of Shihr and Mukalla

2 Mukalla Harbour

1942.

1 **1**	$\frac{1}{2}$a. green	1·00	50
2	$\frac{3}{4}$a. brown	1·75	30
3	1a. blue	1·00	1·00
4 **2**	1$\frac{1}{2}$a. red	1·50	50
5 –	2a. brown	1·50	1·75
6 –	2$\frac{1}{2}$a. blue	50	30
7 –	3a. brown and red	1·00	75
8 –	8a. red	50	40
9 –	1r. green	4·50	3·75
10 –	2r. blue and purple	12·00	8·50
11 –	5r. brown and green	16·00	11·00

DESIGNS—VERT: 2a. Gateway of Shihr; 3a. Outpost of Mukalla; 1r. Du'an. HORIZ: 2$\frac{1}{2}$a. Shibam; 8a. 'Einat; 2r. Mosque in Hureidha; 5r. Meshhed.

1946. Victory. Optd **VICTORY ISSUE 8TH JUNE 1946.**

12 **2**	1$\frac{1}{2}$a. red	15	1·00
13 –	2$\frac{1}{2}$a. blue	15	15

1949. Royal Silver Wedding. As T **4b/c** of Pitcairn Islands.

14	1$\frac{1}{2}$a. red	50	3·75
15	5r. green	16·00	9·50

1949. U.P.U. As T **4d/g** of Pitcairn Islands surch.

16	2$\frac{1}{2}$a. on 20c. blue	15	20
17	3a. on 30c. red	1·10	50
18	8a. on 50c. orange	25	60
19	1r. on 1s. blue	30	50

1951. Stamps of 1942 surch in cents or shillings.

20	5c. on 1a. blue	15	20
21	10c. on 2a. sepia	15	20
22	15c. on 2$\frac{1}{2}$a. blue	15	20
23	20c. on 3a. sepia and red . .	30	60
24	50c. on 8a. red	50	2·00
25	1s. on 1r. green	2·00	40
26	2s. on 2r. blue and purple . .	8·00	16·00
27	5s. on 5r. brown and green . .	13·00	26·00

1953. Coronation. As T **4h** of Pitcairn Islands.
28 15c. black and blue . . . . . 1·00 55

(II) Issues inscribed "HADHRAMAUT"

11 Metal Work

22 Metal Work

1955. Occupations. Portrait as in T **11**.

29 **11**	5c. blue	30	10
30 –	10c. black (Mat-making) . .	75	10
31 –	15c. green (Weaving) . . .	50	10
32 –	25c. red (Pottery)	40	10
33 –	35c. blue (Building)	70	10
34 –	50c. orange (Date cultivation)	40	10
35 –	90c. brown (Agriculture) . .	50	15
36 –	1s. black and orange (Fisheries) (horiz)	50	10
37 –	1s.25 black and orange (Lime-burning) (horiz) . .	55	55
38 –	2s. black and blue (Dhow building) (horiz)	4·00	60
39 –	5s. black and green (Agriculture) (horiz) . .	5·00	1·75
40 –	10s. black and red (as No. 37) (horiz)	5·50	7·50

1963. Occupations. As Nos. 29/40 but with inset portrait of Sultan Awadh bin Saleh el Qu'aiti, as in T **22**.

41 **22**	5c. blue	10	1·50
42 –	10c. black	10	1·25
43 –	15c. green	10	1·50
44 –	25c. red	10	50
45 –	35c. blue	10	1·75
46 –	50c. orange	10	1·00
47 –	70c. brown (As No. 35) . .	15	75
48 –	1s. black and lilac	20	30
49 –	1s.25 black and orange . . .	45	4·25
50 –	2s. black and blue	3·25	1·75
51 –	5s. black and green	13·00	27·00
52 –	10s. black and red	17·00	27·00

1966. Nos. 41/52 surch **SOUTH ARABIA** in English and Arabic, with value and bar.

53 **5**	5f. on 5c.	10	60
54 –	5f. on 10c.	20	60
55 –	10f. on 15c.	10	30
56 –	15f. on 25c.	10	60
57 –	20f. on 35c.	10	1·50
58 –	25f. on 50c.	10	60
59 –	35f. on 70c.	10	60
60 –	50f. on 1s.	10	30
61 –	65f. on 1s.25	1·00	30
62 –	100f. on 2s.	1·75	75
63 –	250f. on 5s.	1·50	1·50
64 –	500f. on 10s.	19·00	3·00

1966. Churchill Commemoration. Nos. 54/6 optd **1874–1965 WINSTON CHURCHILL.**

65	5f. on 10c.	5·50	11·00
66	10f. on 15c.	6·50	12·00
67	15f. on 25c.	8·50	13·00

1966. President Kennedy Commemoration. Nos. 57/9 optd **1917–63 JOHN F. KENNEDY.**

68	20f. on 35c.	1·50	6·00
69	25f. on 50c.	1·50	6·50
70	35f. on 70c.	1·50	7·50

25 World Cup Emblem

1966. World Cup Football Championship.

71 **25**	5f. purple and orange . . .	1·75	25
72 –	10f. violet and green	2·00	25
73 –	15f. purple and orange . . .	2·25	30
74 –	20f. violet and green	2·50	30
75 **25**	25f. green and red	2·75	30
76 –	35f. blue and yellow	3·25	35
77 –	50f. green and red	3·75	40
78 **25**	65f. blue and yellow	4·50	40
MS78a	110 × 110 mm. Nos. 77/8	20·00	7·50

DESIGNS: 10, 35f. Wembley Stadium; 15, 50f. Footballers; 20f. Jules Rimet Cup and football.

29 Mexican Hat and Basket

1966. Pre-Olympic Games, Mexico (1968).
79 **29** 75f. sepia and green . . . . 1·25 75

30 Telecommunications Satellite

1966. International Co-operation Year.

80 **30**	5f. mauve, purple and green	2·50	35
81 –	10f. multicoloured	2·75	35
82 –	15f. purple, blue and red . .	3·00	40
83 **30**	20f. blue, purple and red . .	3·25	45
84 –	25f. multicoloured	3·25	50
85 **30**	35f. purple, red and blue . .	3·75	60
86 –	50f. purple, green and red	4·50	75
87 **30**	65f. brown, violet and red	5·00	80

DESIGNS: 10f. Olympic runner (inscr "ROME 1960"); 15f. Fishes; 25f. Olympic runner (inscr "TOKIO 1964"); 50f. Tobacco plant.

APPENDIX

The following stamps have either been issued in excess to postal needs or have not been made available to the public in reasonable quantities at face value.

1967.

Stampex, London. Postage 5, 10, 15, 20, 25f.; Air 50, 65f.

Amphilex International Stamp Exhibition, Amsterdam. Air 75f.

Olympic Games, Mexico (1968). 75f.

Paintings. Postage 5, 10, 15, 20, 25f.; Air 50, 65f.

Scout Jamboree, Idaho. Air 35f.

Space Research. Postage 10, 25, 35, 50, 75f.; Air 100, 250f.

The National Liberation Front is said to have taken control of Qu'aiti State in Hadhramaut on 17 September 1967.

QUEENSLAND Pt. 1

The north eastern state of the Commonwealth of Australia whose stamps it now uses.

12 pence = 1 shilling;
20 shillings = 1 pound.

1

7

1860. Imperf.
1 **1** 1d. red £2750 £800
2 2d. blue £7000 £1700
3 6d. green £4250 £800

1860. Perf.
94 **1** 1d. red . . . . 38·00 5·00
99 2d. blue . . . . 38·00 1·00
101 3d. brown . . . . 75·00 9·00
65 3d. green . . . . 85·00 6·00
54 4d. grey . . . . £200 20·00
55 4d. lilac . . . . £160 18·00
103 4d. yellow . . . . £700 24·00
27 6d. green . . . . £110 12·00
108 1s. purple . . . . 50·00 9·00
29 1s. grey . . . . £180 22·00
119 2s. blue . . . . £100 32·00
121 2s.6d. red . . . . £160 60·00
58 5s. red . . . . £375 85·00
123 5s. yellow . . . . £225 90·00
125 10s. brown £450 £160
127 20s. red £1100 £190

1879.
134 **7** 1d. brown . . . . 45·00 6·00
135 1d. orange . . . . 26·00 4·50
136 1d. red . . . . 23·00 2·75
138 2d. blue . . . . 40·00 1·25
141 4d. yellow . . . . £160 10·00
142 6d. green . . . . 85·00 4·50
145 1s. mauve . . . . 75·00 6·50

1880. Nos. 136 surch **Half-penny**.
151 **7** ½d. on 1d. brown £250 £150

9

13

12 14

1882.
152 **9** 2s. blue . . . . £120 32·00
158 2s.6d. orange . . . . 45·00 23·00
159 5s. red . . . . 42·00 32·00
160 10s. brown . . . . £100 45·00
161 £1 green . . . . £225 65·00

1882. Shaded background around head.
185 **13** ½d. green . . . . 5·00 1·50
206 **12** 1d. orange . . . . 2·50 40
204 2d. blue . . . . 4·00 30
191 **14** 2½d. red . . . . 13·00 1·50
192 **12** 3d. brown . . . . 9·00 3·25
193 4d. yellow . . . . 13·00 2·50
196 6d. green . . . . 11·00 1·50
173 1s. mauve . . . . 11·00 3·00
197 2s. brown . . . . 42·00 22·00

15

16

17

1895. Head on white background.
208 **15** ½d. green . . . . 1·90 75
210 **16** 1d. red . . . . 3·50 20
212 2d. blue . . . . 13·00 45
213 **17** 2½d. red . . . . 16·00 3·75
215 5d. brown . . . . 20·00 3·75

19 21

1896.
229 **19** 1d. red . . . . 12·00 50

1897. Same designs, but figures in all four corners, as T **21**.
286 ½d. green . . . . 1·75 2·75
232 1d. red . . . . 2·50 25
234 2d. blue . . . . 3·25 25
236 2½d. red . . . . 17·00 22·00
238 2½d. purple on blue . . . . 9·50 2·50
241 3d. brown . . . . 8·00 2·50
244 4d. yellow . . . . 9·00 2·25
294 4d. black . . . . 19·00 4·50
246 5d. brown . . . . 8·50 2·50
250 6d. green . . . . 7·00 2·50
298 1s. mauve . . . . 14·00 3·00
254 2s. green . . . . 30·00 25·00

26 27

1899.
262a **26** ½d. green . . . . 2·50 1·75

1900. S. African War Charity. Inscr "PATRIOTIC FUND 1900".
264a **27** 1d. (1s.) mauve £120 £110
264b – 2d. (2s.) violet (horiz) . . £300 £275

28

1903.
265 **28** 9d. brown and blue . . . . 23·00 2·75

REGISTRATION STAMP

1861. Inscr "REGISTERED".
20 **1** (No value) yellow . . . . . 75·00 38·00

QUELIMANE Pt. 9

A district of Portuguese E. Africa, now part of Mozambique, whose stamps it now uses.

100 centavos = 1 escudo.

1913. Surch **REPUBLICA QUELIMANE** and new value on "Vasco da Gama" stamps of
(a) Portuguese Colonies.
1 ¼c. on 2½r. green . . . . . . 1·50 1·10
2 ½c. on 5r. red . . . . 1·50 1·10
3 1c. on 10r. purple . . . . . . 1·50 1·10
4 2½c. on 25r. green . . . . . . 1·50 1·10
5 5c. on 50r. blue . . . . 1·50 1·10
6 7½c. on 75r. brown . . . . . . 2·75 1·50
7 10c. on 100r. brown . . . . . 1·70 85
8 15c. on 150r. brown . . . . . 1·70 85

(b) Macao.
9 ¼c. on ½a. green . . . . 1·50 1·10
10 ½c. on 1a. red . . . . 1·50 1·10
11 1c. on 2a. purple . . . . . . 1·50 1·10
12 2½c. on 4a. green . . . . . . 1·50 1·10
13 5c. on 8a. blue . . . . 1·50 1·10
14 7½c. on 12a. brown . . . . . 2·75 1·50
15 10c. on 16a. brown . . . . . 1·70 85
16 15c. on 24a. brown . . . . . 1·70 85

(c) Portuguese Timor.
17 ¼c. on ½a. green . . . . 1·50 1·10
18 ½c. on 1a. red . . . . 1·50 1·10
19 1c. on 2a. purple . . . . . . 1·50 1·10
20 2½c. on 2a. green . . . . . . 1·50 1·10
21 5c. on 8a. blue . . . . 1·50 1·10
22 7½c. on 12a. brown . . . . . 2·75 1·50
23 10c. on 16a. brown . . . . . 1·70 85
24 15c. on 24a. brown . . . . . 1·70 85

1914. "Ceres" key-type inscr "QUELIMANE".
25 U ¼c. green 65 60
26 ½c. black . . . . 1·30 85
42 1c. green . . . . 1·30 85
28 1½c. brown . . . . 1·60 1·10
29 2c. red . . . . 1·30 1·30
30 2½c. violet 65 50
31 5c. blue . . . . 1·20 90
43 7½c. brown . . . . 1·40 1·10
33 8c. grey . . . . 1·40 1·10
44 10c. red . . . . 1·40 1·10
35 15c. purple . . . . 1·90 1·60
45 20c. green . . . . 1·40 1·40
37 30c. brown on green . . . . 3·00 2·10
38 40c. brown on pink . . . . . 3·25 2·10
39 50c. orange on orange . . . 3·25 2·10
40 1e. green on blue . . . . . 3·50 2·50

RAJASTHAN Pt. 1

Formed in 1948 from states in Rajputana, India, which included Bundi, Jaipur and Kishangarh whose separate posts functioned until 1 April 1950. Now uses Indian stamps.

12 pies = 1 anna;
16 annas = 1 rupee.

BUNDI

(1)

1949. Nos. 86/92 of Bundi or optd with T **1**.
1 **21** ¼a. green . . . . 5·50
2 ½a. violet . . . . 4·50
3 1a. green . . . . 4·75
11 – 2a. red . . . . 7·50 70·00
12 – 4a. orange . . . . 3·50 70·00
6 – 8a. blue . . . . 7·00
14 – 1r. brown . . . . 7·50
Nos. 1, 2, 3 and 6 used are worth about six times the unused prices.

JAIPUR

राजस्थान

RAJASTHAN
(2)

1949. Stamps of Jaipur optd with T **2**.
15 **7** ¼a. black and purple . . . . 6·50 19·00
16 ½a. black and violet . . . . 5·00 20·00
17 ¾a. black and orange . . . . 9·00 24·00
18 1a. black and blue . . . . . 6·00 42·00
19 2a. black and orange . . . . 8·00 55·00
20 2½a. black and red . . . . . 8·50 27·00
21 3a. black and green . . . . 10·00 65·00
22 4a. black and green . . . . 9·00 75·00
23 6a. black and blue . . . . . 9·50 £100
24 8a. black and brown . . . . 16·00 £150
25 1r. black and bistre . . . . . 20·00 £200

KISHANGARH

1949. Stamps of Kishangarh handstamped with T **1**.
(a) On stamps of 1899.
26a **2** ¼a. pink . . . . — £200
27 ½a. blue £450
29 1a. lilac . . . . 14·00 40·00
30 4a. brown . . . . 75·00 £100
31 1r. green £275 £300
31a 2r. red £350
32 5r. mauve £325 £325

(b) On stamps of 1904.
33 **13** ½a. brown . . . . — £160
33a 1a. blue . . . . — £225
34 4a. brown . . . . 13·00
35 **2** 8a. grey £100 £160
36 **13** 8a. violet . . . . 11·00
37 1r. green . . . . 12·00
38 2r. yellow . . . . 19·00
39 5r. brown . . . . 27·00

(c) On stamps of 1912.
40 **14** ½a. green . . . . — £200
41 1a. red . . . . — £200
43 2a. purple . . . . 3·00 8·00
44 4a. blue . . . . — £475
45 8a. brown . . . . 5·00
46 1r. mauve . . . . 10·00
47 2r. green . . . . 10·00
48 5r. brown £375

(d) On stamps of 1928.
56 **16** ¼a. blue . . . . 48·00 48·00
57 ½a. green . . . . 30·00 30·00
58 – 1a. red . . . . 60·00 60·00
59 – 2a. purple £170 £170
61 **16** 4a. brown . . . . 2·50 8·00
51 8a. violet . . . . 6·00 55·00
63 1r. green . . . . 6·50
53 2r. yellow . . . . 16·00
54 5r. red . . . . 16·00

RAJPIPLA Pt. 1

A state of Bombay, India. Now uses Indian stamps.

12 pies = 1 anna;
12 annas = 1 rupee.

1 (1 pice)

2 (2a.)

1880.
1 **1** 1p. blue . . . . 3·25 35·00
2 **2** 2a. green . . . . 28·00 £100
3 4a. red . . . . 15·00 65·00

RAS AL KHAIMA Pt. 19

Arab Shaikhdom in the Arabian Gulf. Ras al Khaima joined the United Arab Emirates in February 1972 and U.A.E. stamps were used in the shaikhdom from 1 January 1973.

1964. 100 naye paise = 1 rupee.
1966. 100 dirhams = 1 riyal.

1 Shaikh Saqr bin Mohamed al-Qasimi

3 Dhow

1964.
1 **1** 5n.p. brown and black 10 10
2 15n.p. blue and black 10 10
3 – 30n.p. brown and black . . . 15 15
4 – 40n.p. blue and black 25 25
5 – 75n.p. red and black 65 55
6 **3** 1r. brown and green . . . . 1·80 90
7 2r. brown and violet . . . . 2·75 2·00
8 5r. brown and blue . . . . . 6·00 5·75
DESIGNS—As Type **1**: 30n.p. to 75n.p. Seven palms.

3a Pres. Kennedy inspecting "Friendship 7"

1965. Pres. Kennedy Commemoration.
9 **3a** 2r. blue and brown 95 95
10 – 3r. blue and brown . . . . 1·60 1·60
11 – 4r. blue and brown . . . . 2·30 2·30
MS11a Three sheets 140×108 or 108×140 mm. 1r. stamps in block of four as Nos. 9/11 . . . . . . 10·00 8·50
DESIGNS—HORIZ: 3r. Kennedy and wife. VERT: 4r. Kennedy and flame of remembrance.

4 Sir Winston Churchill and Houses of Parliament

1965. Churchill Commemoration.
12 **4** 2r. blue and brown 95 95
13 – 3r. blue and brown . . . . . 1·60 1·60
14 – 4r. blue and brown . . . . . 2·30 2·30
MS14a Three sheets 140×108 or 108×140 mm. 1r. stamps in blocks of four as Nos. 12/14 . . . . 8·75 4·25
DESIGNS—HORIZ: 3r. Churchill and Pres. Roosevelt; 4r. Churchill, and Heads of State at his funeral.

1965. Olympic Games, Tokyo (1964). Optd **OLYMPIC TOKYO 1964** in English and Arabic and Olympic "rings".
15 **3** 1r. brown and green 55 55
16 2r. brown and violet . . . . 1·20 1·20
17 5r. brown and blue . . . . . 3·00 2·40

1965. Death Centenary of Abraham Lincoln. Optd **ABRAHAM LINCOLN 1809-1865** in English and Arabic.
18 **3** 1r. brown and green 55 55
19 2r. brown and violet . . . . 1·20 1·20
20 5r. brown and blue . . . . . 3·00 3·00

1965. 20th Death Anniv of Pres. Roosevelt. Optd **FRANKLIN D. ROOSEVELT 1882-1945** in English and Arabic.
21 **3** 1r. brown and green 55 55
22 2r. brown and violet . . . . 1·20 1·20
23 5r. brown and blue . . . . . 3·00 3·00

8 Satellite and Tracking Station

1966. I.T.U. Centenary. Multicoloured.

24 15n.p. Type **8** 25 15
25 50n.p. Post Office Tower, London, "Telstar" and tracking gantry 40 25
26 85n.p. Rocket on launching-pad and "Relay" 90 25
27 1r. Type **8** . . . . 1·00 40
28 2r. As 50n.p. . . . . 1·80 50
29 3r. As 85n.p. . . . . 2·10 95
MS30 110 × 80 mm. 5r. Globe and satellites (53 × 33 mm). Imperf 3·50 1·90

9 Swimming **10** Carpenter

1966. Pan-Arab Games, Cairo (1965).

31 A 1n.p. brown, pink and green 10 10
32 B 2n.p. black, grey and green 10 10
33 C 3n.p. brown, pink and green 10 10
34 D 4n.p. brown, pink and purple 10 10
35 A 5n.p. black, grey and orange 10 10
36 **9** 10n.p. brown, pink and blue 15 10
37 B 25n.p. brown, pink and cinnamon 40 15
38 C 50n.p. black, grey and violet 80 40
39 D 75n.p. black, grey and blue 1·30 55
40 **9** 1r. black, grey and green . . 1·80 70
MS41 D 100 × 85 mm. 5r. violet, blue and yellow. Imperf . . . 4·75 3·00

DESIGNS: A, Running; B, Boxing; C, Football; D, Fencing.

1966. American Astronauts.

42 **10** 25n.p. black, gold and purple 15 10
43 – 50n.p. black, silver & brown 25 15
44 – 75n.p. black, silver and blue 40 15
45 – 1r. black, silver and bistre 55 25
46 – 2r. black, silver and mauve 1·20 65
47 – 3r. black, gold and green . . 1·80 90
48 – 4r. black, gold and red . . . 2·40 1·30
49 – 5r. black, gold and blue . . 3·00 1·50
MS50 Two sheets each 156 × 106 mm containing stamps as Nos. 42/5 and 46/9 but without face values. Imperf (sold at 4r. each) . . . . 6·75 2·75

ASTRONAUTS: 50n.p. Glenn; 75n.p. Shepard; 1r. Cooper; 2r. Grissom; 3r. Schirra; 4r. Stafford; 5r. Lovell.

11 Shaikh Sabah of Kuwait and Shaikh Saqr of Ras al Khaima

1966. International Co-operation Year.

51 **11** 1r. black and red 65 30
52 A 1r. black and lilac 65 30
53 B 1r. black and pink 65 30
54 C 1r. black and green 65 30
55 D 1r. black and green 65 30
56 E 1r. black and yellow 65 30
57 F 1r. black and orange 65 30
58 G 1r. black and blue 65 30
MS59 Two sheets each 127 × 115 mm. Nos. 51/4 and 55/8. Imperf . . . . 5·75 3·00

SHAIKH SAQR AND WORLD LEADERS: A, Shaikh Ahmad of Qatar; B, Pres. Nasser; C, King Hussein; D, Pres. Johnson; E, Pres. De Gaulle; F, Pope Paul VI; G, Prime Minister Harold Wilson.

NEW CURRENCY SURCHARGES. During the latter half of 1966 various issues appeared surcharged in dirhams and riyals. The 1964 definitives with this surcharge are listed below as there is considerable evidence of their postal use. Nos. 24/58 also exist with these surcharges.

In August 1966 Nos. 1/14, 24/9 and 51/8 appeared surcharged in fils and rupees. As Ras Al Khaima did not adopt this currency their status is uncertain.

1966. Nos. 1/8 with currency names changed to dirhams and riyals by overprinting in English and Arabic.

60 **1** 5d. on 5n.p. brown and black 10 10
60a – 5d. on 75n.p. red and black 30 20
64b **3** 5d. on 5r. brown and blue 30 20
61 **1** 15d. on 15n.p. blue & black 30 25
62 – 30d. on 30n.p. brown and black 65 50
63 – 40d. on 40n.p. blue & black 90 65
64 – 75d. on 75n.p. red and black . . . . 1·60 80
65 **3** 1r. on 1r. brown and green 1·40 90
66 2r. on 2r. brown and violet 3·25 2·40
67 5r. on 5r. brown and blue 6·50 4·75

15 W.H.O. Building and Flowers

1966. Inauguration of W.H.O. Headquarters, Geneva.

68 **15** 15d. multicoloured (postage) 15 10
69 – 35d. multicoloured 50 15
70 **15** 50d. multicoloured (air) . . 55 30
71 – 3r. multicoloured . . . . 1·90 80
MS72 79 × 72 mm. No. 71. Imperf 2·75 1·20

DESIGN: 35d., 3r. As Type **15** but with red instead of yellow flowers at left.

16 Queen Elizabeth II presenting Jules Rimet Cup to Bobby Moore, Captain of England Team

1966. Air. England's Victory in World Cup Football Championship. Multicoloured.

73 1r. Wembley Stadium 80 30
74 2r. Goalkeeper saving ball . . 1·70 65
75 3r. Footballers with ball . . 2·00 95
76 4r. Type **16** . . . . 2·75 1·80
MS77 Two sheets each 90 × 80 mm. Nos. 73 and 76. Imperf . . . . 7·00 4·25

17 Shaikh Saqr

18 Oil Rig

1971.

78 **17** 5d. multicoloured . . . .
79 **18** 20d. multicoloured . . . .
80 **17** 30d. multicoloured . . . .

For later issues see **UNITED ARAB EMIRATES**.

APPENDIX

The following stamps have either been issued in excess of postal needs or have not been available to the public in reasonable quantities at face value. Such stamps may later be given full listing if there is evidence of regular postal use.

1967.

"The Arabian Nights". Paintings. Air 30, 70d., 1, 2, 3r.

Cats. Postage 1, 2, 3, 4, 5d.; Air 3r.

Arab Paintings. 1, 2, 3, 4, 10, 20, 30d.

European Paintings. Air 60, 70d., 1, 2, 3, 5, 10r.

50th Birth Anniv of Pres. John F. Kennedy. Optd on 1965 Pres. Kennedy Commem. 2, 3, 4r.

World Scout Jamboree, Idaho. Postage 1, 2, 3, 4d.; Air 35, 75d., 1r.

U.S. "Apollo" Disaster. Optd on 1966 American Astronauts issue. 25d. on 25n.p., 50d. on 50n.p., 75d. on 75n.p., 1, 2, 3, 4, 5r.

Summer Olympics Preparation, Mexico 1968. Postage 10, 20, 30, 40d.; Air 1, 2r.

Winter Olympics Preparation, Grenoble 1968. Postage 1, 2, 3, 4, 5d.; Air 85d., 2, 3r.

1968.

Mothers' Day. Paintings. Postage 20, 30, 40, 50d.; Air 1, 2, 3, 4r.

International Human Rights Year. 2r. × 3.

International Museum Campaign. Paintings. 15, 15, 20, 25, 35, 40, 45, 60, 70, 80, 90d.; 1, 1r.25, 1r.50, 2r.50, 2r.75.

Winter Olympic Medal Winners, Grenoble. 50d., 1, 1r.50, 2, 2r.50, 3r.

Olympic Games, Mexico. Air 1, 2, 2, 3, 3, 4r. 5th Death Anniv of Pres. John F. Kennedy. Air. 2, 3r.

Christmas. Religious Paintings. Postage 20, 30, 40, 50, 60d., 1r.; Air 2, 3, 4r.

1969.

Famous Composers (1st series). Paintings. 25, 50, 75d., 1r.50, 2r.50.

Famous Operas. 20, 40, 60, 80d., 1, 2r.

Famous Men. Postage 20, 30, 50d.; Air 1r.50, 2, 3, 4, 5r.

International Philatelic Exhibition, Mexico 1968 (EFIMEX). Postage 10, 10, 25, 35, 40, 50, 60, 70d.; Air 1, 2, 3, 5, 5r.

Int Co-operation in Olympics. 1, 2, 3, 4r.

International Co-operation in Space. Air 1r.50, 2r.50, 3r.50, 4r.50.

Birth Bicentenary of Napoleon. Paintings. Postage 1r.75, 2r.75, 3r.75; Air 75d.

"Apollo" Moon Missions. Air 2, 2r.50, 3, 3r.50, 4, 4r.50, 5, 5r.50.

"Apollo 11" Astronauts. Air 2r.25, 3r.25, 4r.25, 5r.25.

"Apollo 12" Astronauts. Air 60d., 2r.60, 3r.60, 4r.60, 5r.60.

1970.

Christmas 1969. Religious Paintings. Postage 50d.; Air 3, 3r.50.

World Cup, Mexico. Air 1, 2, 3, 4, 5, 6r.

Easter. Religious Paintings. Postage 50d.; Air 3, 3r.50.

Paintings by Titian and Tiepolo. Postage 50, 50d.; Air 3, 3, 3r.50, 3r.50.

Winter Olympics, Sapporo 1972. Air 1, 2, 3, 4, 5, 6r.

Olympic Games, Munich 1972. Air 1, 2, 3, 4, 5, 6r.

Paul Gauguin's Paintings. Postage 50d.; Air 3, 3r.50.

Christmas. Religious Paintings. Postage 50d.; Air 3, 3r.50.

"World Cup Champions, Brazil". Optd on Mexico World Cup issue. Air 1, 2, 3, 4, 5, 6r.

"EXPO 70" World Fair, Osaka, Japan (1st issue). Postage 40, 45, 50, 55, 60, 65, 70, 75d.; Air 80, 85, 90, 95d., 1r.60, 1r.65, 1r.85, 2r.

"EXPO 70" World Fair, Osaka, Japan (2nd issue). Postage 55, 65, 75d.; Air 25, 85, 95d., 1r.50, 1r.75.

Space Programmes. Air 1r. × 6, 2r. × 6, 4r. × 6.

Famous Frenchmen. Air 1r. × 4, 2r. × 4, 2r.50 × 2, 3r. × 2, 4r. × 4, 5r.50 × 2.

Int Philatelic Exn (Philympia '70). Air 1r. × 4, 1r.50 × 4, 2r.50 × 4, 3r. × 4, 4r. × 4.

Events in the Life of Christ. Religious Paintings. 5, 10, 25, 50d., 1, 2, 5r.

"Stages of the Cross". Religious Paintings. 10, 20, 30, 40, 50, 60, 70, 80d., 1, 1r.50, 2, 2r.50, 3, 3r.50.

The Life of Mary. Religious Paintings. 10, 15, 30, 60, 75d., 3, 4r.

1971.

Easter. "Stages of the Cross" (1970) but with additional inscr "EASTER". 10, 20, 30, 40, 50, 60, 70, 80d., 1, 1r.50, 2, 2r.50, 3, 3r.50.

Charles de Gaulle Memorial. Postage 50d.; Air 1, 1r.50, 2, 3, 4r.

Safe Return of "Apollo 14". Postage 50d.; Air 1, 1r.50, 2, 3, 4r.

U.S.A.–Japan Baseball Friendship. Postage 10, 25, 30, 80d.; Air 50, 70d., 1, 1r.50.

Munich Olympics, 1972. Postage 50d.; Air 1, 1r.50, 2, 3, 4r.

Cats. 35, 60, 65, 110, 120, 160d.

13th World Jamboree, Japan. Postage 30, 50, 60, 75d.; Air 1, 1r.50, 3, 4r.

Sapporo Olympic Gold Medal Winners. Optd on 1970 Winter Olympics, Sapporo 1972, issue. Air 1, 2, 3, 4, 5, 6r.

Munich Olympic Medal Winners, Optd on 1970 Summer Olympics, Munich 1972, issue. Air 1, 2, 3, 4, 5, 6r.

Japanese Locomotives. Postage 30, 35, 75d.; Air 90d., 1, 1r.75.

"Soyuz 11" Russian Cosmonauts Memorial. Air 1, 2, 3, 4r.

"Apollo 15". Postage 50d.; Air 1, 1r.50, 2, 3, 4r.

Dogs. 5, 20, 75, 85, 185, 200d.

Durer's Paintings. Postage 50d.; Air 1, 1r.50 2, 3, 4r.

Famous Composers (2nd series). Postage 50d.; Air 1, 1r.50, 2, 3, 4r.

"Soyuz 11" and "Salyut" Space Projects. Postage 50 d.; Air 1, 1r.50, 2, 3, 4r.

Butterflies. Postage 15, 20, 70d.; Air 1r.25, 1r.50, 1r.70.

Wild Animals. 10, 40, 80 d.; 1r.15, 1r.30, 1r.65.

Fishes. 30, 50, 60, 90d., 1r.45, 1r.55.

Ludwig van Beethoven. Portraits. Postage 50d.; Air 1, 1r.50, 2, 3, 4r.

1972.

Birds. 50, 55, 80, 100, 105, 190d.

Winter Olympics, Sapporo (1st issue). Postage 20, 30, 50d., Air 70, 90d., 2r.50

Winter Olympics, Sapporo (2nd issue). Postage 5, 60, 80, 90d.; Air 1r.10, 1r.75

Mozart. Portraits. Postage 50d.; Air 1, 1r.50, 2, 3, 4r.

Olympic Games, Munich. Postage 50d.; Air 1, 1r.50, 2, 3, 4r.

"In Memory of Charles de Gaulle". Optd on 1971 Charles de Gaulle memorial issue. Postage 50d.; Air 1, 1r.50, 2, 3, 4r.

Winter Olympics, Sapporo (3rd issue). Postage 15, 45d.; Air 65, 75d., 1r.20, 1r.25.

Horses. Postage 10, 25, 30d.; Air 1r.40, 1r.80, 1r.95.

Parrots. 40, 45, 70, 95d., 1r.35, 1r.75.

"Apollo 16". Postage 50d.; Air 1, 1r.50, 2, 3, 4r.

European Footballers. Postage 50d.; Air 1, 1r.50, 2, 3, 4r.

A number of issues on gold or silver foil also exist, but it is understood that these were mainly for presentation purposes, although valid for postage.

In common with the other states of the United Arab Emirates the Ras al Khaima stamp contract was terminated on 1st August 1972, and any further new issues released after that date were unauthorized.

REDONDA Pt. 1

A dependency of Antigua.

The following stamps were issued in anticipation of commercial and tourist development, philatelic mail being handled by a bureau in Antigua. Since at the present time the island is uninhabited, we do not list or stock these items. It is understood that the stamps are valid for the prepayment of postage in Antigua. Miniature sheets, imperforate stamps etc, are excluded from this section.

1979.

Antigua 1976 definitive issue optd **REDONDA**. 3, 5, 10, 25, 35, 50, 75c., $1, $2.50, $5, $10.

Antigua Coronation Anniversary issue optd **REDONDA**. 10, 30, 50, 90c., $2.50.

Antigua World Cup Football Championship issue optd **REDONDA**. 10, 15c., $3.

Death Centenary of Sir Rowland Hill. 50, 90c., $2.50, $3.

International Year of the Child 25, 50c., $1, $2.

Christmas. Paintings. 8, 50, 90c., $3.

1980.

Marine Life. 8, 25, 50c., $4.

75th Anniv of Rotary International. 25, 50c., $1, $2.

Birds of Redonda. 8, 10, 15, 25, 30, 50c., $1, $2, $5.

Olympic Medal Winners, Lake Placid and Moscow. 8, 25, 50c., $3.

80th Birthday of Queen Elizabeth the Queen Mother. 10c., $2.50.

Christmas Paintings. 8, 25, 50c., $4.

1981.

Royal Wedding. 25, 55c., $4.

Christmas. Walt Disney Cartoon Characters. ½, 1, 2, 3, 4, 5, 10c., $2.50, $3.

World Cup Football Championship, Spain (1982). 30c. × 2, 50c. × 2, $1 × 2, $2 × 2.

1982.

Boy Scout Annivs. 8, 25, 50c., $3, $5.

Butterflies. 8, 30, 50c., $2.

21st Birthday of Princess of Wales. $2, $4.

Birth of Prince William of Wales. Optd on Princess of Wales 21st Birthday issue. $2, $4.

Christmas. Walt Disney's "One Hundred and One Dalmatians". ½, 1, 2, 3, 4, 5, 10c., $2.50, $3.

1983.

Easter. 500th Birth Anniv of Raphael. 10, 50, 90c., $5.

Bicent of Manned Flight. 10, 50, 90c., $2.50.

Christmas. Walt Disney Cartoon Characters. "Deck the Halls". ½, 1, 2, 3, 4, 5, 10c., $2.50, $3.

1984.

Easter. Walt Disney Cartoon Characters. ½, 1, 2, 3, 4, 5, 10c., $2, $4.

Olympic Games, Los Angeles. 10, 50, 90c., $2.50.

Christmas. 50th Birthday of Donald Duck. 45, 60, 90c., $2, $4.

1985.

Birth Bicentenary of John J. Audubon (ornithologist) (1st issue). 60, 90c., $1, $3.

Life and Times of Queen Elizabeth the Queen Mother. $1, $1.50, $2.50.

Royal Visit. 45c., $1, $4.

150th Birth Anniv of Mark Twain (author). 25, 50c., $1.50, $3.

Birth Bicentenaries of Grimm Brothers (folklorists). Walt Disney cartoon characters. 30, 60, 70c., $4.

1986.

Birth Bicentenary of John J. Audubon (ornith-ologist) (2nd issue). 90c., $1, $1.50, $3.

Appearance of Halley's Comet. 5, 15, 55c., $4.

Centenary of Statue of Liberty (1st issue). 20, 25, 30c., $4.

60th Birthday of Queen Elizabeth II. 50, 60c., $4.

Royal Wedding. 60c., $1, $4.

Christmas (1st issue). Disney characters in Hans Andersen Stories. 30, 60, 70c., $4.

Christmas (2nd issue). "Wind in the Willows" (by Kenneth Grahame). 25, 50c., $1.50, $3.

1987.

"Capex '87" International Stamp Exhibition, Toronto. Disney characters illustrating Art of Animation. 25, 30, 50, 60, 70c., $1.50, $3, $4.

Birth Centenary of Marc Chagall (artist). 10, 30, 40, 60, 90c., $1, $3, $4.

Centenary of Statue of Liberty (2nd issue). 10, 15, 25, 30, 40, 60, 70, 90c., $1, $2, $3, $4.

250th Death Anniv of Sir Isaac Newton (scientist). 20c., $2.50.

750th Anniv of Berlin. $1, $4.

Bicentenary of U.S. Constitution. 30c., $3.

16th World Scout Jamboree, Australia. 10c., $4.

1988.

500th Anniv (1992) of Discovery of America by Columbus. 15, 30, 45, 60, 90c., $1, $2, $3.

"Finlandia '88" International Stamp Exhibition, Helsinki. Disney characters in Finnish scenes. 1, 2, 3, 4, 5, 6c., $5, $6.

Olympic Games, Seoul. 25, 60c., $1.25, $3.

500th Birth Anniv of Titian. 10, 25, 40, 70, 90c., $2, $3, $4.

1989.

20th Anniv of First Manned Landing on Moon. Disney characters on Moon. ½, 1, 2, 3, 4, 5c., $5, $6.

500th Anniv (1992) of Discovery of America by Columbus (2nd issue). Pre-Columbian Societies. 15, 45, 45, 50c., $2, $2, $3, $3.

Christmas. Disney Characters and Cars of 1950s. 25, 35, 45, 60c., $1, $2, $3, $4.

1990.

Christmas. Disney Characters and Hollywood cars. 25, 35, 40, 60c., $2, $3, $4, $5.

1991.

Nobel Prize Winners. 5, 15, 25, 40, 50c., $1, $2, $4.

REUNION Pt. 6

An island in the Indian Ocean, E. of Madagascar, now an overseas department of France.

100 centimes = 1 franc.

1

1852. Imperf. No gum.
1 1 15c. black on blue £31000 £19000
2 30c. black on blue £30000 £18000

1885. Stamps of French Colonies surch **R** and value in figures. Imperf.
5 D 5c. on 30c. brown . . . . . 50·00 48·00
7 H 5c. on 30c. brown . . . . . 3·50 5·25
3 A 5c. on 40c. orange £250 £225
6 F 5c. on 40c. orange . . . . . 50·00 55·00
8 H 5c. on 40c. red on yellow . . 65·00 £110
9 10c. on 40c. red on yellow 9·75 3·75
10 20c. on 30c. brown . . . . . 60·00 50·00
4 A 25c. on 40c. orange . . . . 60·00 42·00

1891. Stamps of French Colonies optd **REUNION**. Imperf (Types F and H) or perf (Type J).
17 A J 1c. black on blue . . . . 55 2·50
18 B 2c. brown on buff 65 75
19 A 4c. brown on grey . . . 3·00 4·25
20 A 5c. green on green . . . 5·00 1·20
21 A 10c. black on lilac . . . 26·00 1·70
22 B 15c. blue on blue . . . . 60·00 1·40
23 A 20c. red on green . . . 11·00 10·50
24 A 25c. black on pink . . . 55·00 1·40
13 A H 30c. brown . . . . 44·00 55·00
25Aa J 35c. black on yellow . . . 14·00 16·00
11 B F 40c. orange £350 £350
14 A H 40c. red on yellow . . . 34·00 21·00
26 A J 40c. red on buff . . . . 85·00 75·00
15 A H 75c. red £275 £275
27 A J 75c. red on pink £475 £400
12 B F 80c. pink . . . . 75·00 55·00
16 A H 1f. green . . . . 65·00 50·00
28 B J 1f. green £375 £350

1891. Stamps of French Colonies surch **REUNION** and new value.
29 J 02c. on 20c. red on green . . 3·75 6·25
30 15c. on 20c. red on green . . 7·50 3·75
31 2 on 20c. red on green . . . 3·00 2·50

1892. "Tablet" key-type inscr "REUNION".
34 D 1c. black and red on blue . . 20 20
35 2c. brown and blue on buff 1·30 35
36 4c. brown and blue on grey 2·75 20
50 5c. green and red . . . . . 1·90 10
38 10c. black and blue on lilac 4·00 1·20
51 10c. red and blue . . . . . 2·30 15
39 15c. blue and red . . . . . 48·00 30
52 15c. grey and red . . . . . 8·25 10
40 20c. red and blue on green 14·00 10·00
41 25c. black and red on pink 17·00 2·00
53 25c. blue and red . . . . . 19·00 25·00
42 30c. brown and blue on drab 19·00 7·25
43 40c. red and blue on yellow 50·00 10·50
44 50c. red and blue on pink 90·00 16·00
54 50c. brown and red on blue 55·00 55·00
55 50c. brown and blue on blue 50·00 55·00
45 75c. brown and red on orange . . . . 60·00 50·00
46 1f. green and red . . . . . 42·00 44·00

1893. Stamp of French Colonies, "Commerce" type, surch **2 c.**
47 J 2c. on 20c. red on green . . . 2·50 1·70

1901. "Tablet" key-type surch in figures.
56 D 5c. on 40c. red and blue on yellow . . . . 2·30 6·25
57 5c. on 50c. red and blue on pink . . . . 3·75 6·00
58 15c. on 75c. brown and red on orange . . . . 19·00 24·00
59 15c. on 1f. green and red . . 12·50 8·50

16 Map of Reunion

17 View of Saint-Denis and Arms of the Colony

18 View of St. Pierre and Crater Dolomieu

1907.
60 16 1c. red and lilac 45 10
61 2c. blue and brown 70 60
62 4c. red and green . . . . 95 1·20
63 5c. red and green . . . . 2·50 10
92 5c. violet and yellow . . . 35 10
64 10c. green and red . . . . 5·50 10
93 10c. turquoise and green 50 10
94 10c. red and lake on blue 1·00 10
65 15c. blue and black . . . . 3·00 1·20
95 15c. turquoise and green 60 50
96 15c. red and blue . . . . 2·30 1·50
66 17 20c. green and olive . . . 3·25 1·40
67 25c. brown and blue . . . 5·75 85
97 25c. blue and brown . . . 1·50 10
68 30c. green and brown . . . 1·10 1·00
98 30c. pink and red . . . . 3·25 2·75
99 30c. red and grey . . . . 2·30 1·70
100 30c. light green and green 3·25 4·50
69 35c. blue and brown . . . 2·75 1·40
101 40c. brown and green . . . 2·50 25
70 45c. pink and violet . . . 2·50 3·75
102 45c. red and purple . . . . 2·30 3·75
103 45c. red and mauve . . . . 3·50 6·75
71 50c. blue and brown . . . 3·25 2·50
104 50c. ultramarine and blue 2·00 2·30
105 50c. violet and yellow . . . 1·90 10
106 60c. brown and blue . . . 2·00 4·50
107 65c. blue and violet . . . . 3·75 4·00
72 75c. pink and red . . . . 2·50 1·10
108 75c. purple and brown . . 3·75 4·50
109 90c. pink and red . . . . 10·00 14·00
73 18 1f. blue and brown . . . . 2·75 2·30
110 1f. blue . . . . 3·00 2·50
111 1f. lilac and brown . . . . 3·75 1·60
112 1f.10 mauve and brown . . 3·50 3·25
113 1f.50 lt blue & blue on bl 19·00 19·00
74 2f. green and red . . . . . 5·50 1·10
114 3f. mauve on pink . . . . 12·50 10·00
75 5f. brown and pink . . . . 9·00 7·00

1912. "Tablet" key-type surch.
76A D 05 on 2c. brown and red on buff 50 15
77A 05 on 15c. grey and red . . 45 30
78A 05 on 20c. red and blue on green . . . . 3·25 4·75
79A 05 on 25c. black and red on pink . . . . 85 4·25
80A 05 on 30c. brown and blue on drab . . . . 35 2·30
81A 10 on 40c. red and blue on yellow . . . . 45 3·75
82A 10 on 50c. brown and blue on blue . . . . 1·90 3·50
83 10 on 75c. brown and red on orange . . . . 1·90 16·00

1915. Red Cross Surch **5c** and red cross.
90 16 10c.+5c. green and red . . . 95 4·25

1917. Surch **0,01**.
91 16 0,01 on 4c. chestnut and brown . . . . 3·75 2·75

1922. Surch in figures only.
115 17 40 on 20c. yellow and green . . . . 65 1·30
116 50 on 45c. red and purple 4·00 2·00
117 50 on 45c. red and mauve £200 £200
118 50 on 65c. blue and violet 3·75 3·25
119 60 on 75c. carmine and red 75 45
120 16 65 on 15c. blue and black 2·75 5·75
121 85 on 15c. blue and black 2·00 5·50
122 17 85 on 75c. pink and red . . 2·30 5·75
123 90 on 75c. pink and red . . 2·75 3·25

1924. Surch in cents and francs.
124 18 25c. on 5f. brown and pink 1·70 3·00
125 1f.25 on 1f. blue . . . . . 1·80 2·75
126 1f.50 on 1f. light blue and blue on blue . . . . . 1·50 40
127 3f. on 5f. blue and red . . 4·50 3·50
128 10f. on 5f. red and green 18·00 30·00
129 20f. on 5f. pink and brown 24·00 30·00

1931. "Colonial Exhibition" key-types inscr "REUNION".
130 E 40c. green and black . . . 5·50 5·00
131 F 50c. mauve and black . . . 6·00 4·50
132 G 90c. red and black . . . . 4·25 6·00
133 H 1f.50 blue and black . . . 6·75 8·00

30 Cascade, Salazie

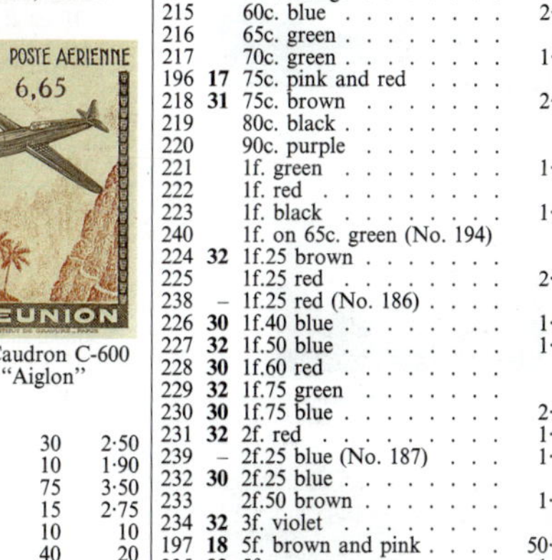

31 Anchain Peak, Salazie

32 Leon Dierx Museum

34 Caudron C-600 "Aiglon"

1933.
134 30 1c. purple . . . . 30 2·50
135 2c. brown . . . . 10 1·90
136 3c. mauve . . . . 75 3·50
137 4c. olive . . . . 15 2·75
138 5c. orange 10 10
139 10c. blue 40 20
140 15c. black 15 10
141 20c. blue . . . . 40 2·30
142 25c. brown 70 25
143 30c. green 80 60
144 31 35c. green . . . . 1·90 4·25
145 40c. blue . . . . 2·75 1·10
146 40c. brown . . . . 60 4·50
147 45c. mauve . . . . 1·70 5·00
148 45c. green . . . . 1·80 4·75
149 50c. red 65 10
150 55c. orange . . . . 3·00 4·25
151 60c. blue . . . . 70 4·50
152 65c. olive . . . . 4·25 2·30
153 70c. olive . . . . 3·25 4·75
154 75c. brown . . . . 7·00 9·50
155 80c. black . . . . 2·00 5·00
156 90c. red . . . . 5·50 5·25
157 90c. purple . . . . 1·70 2·00
158 1f. green . . . . 5·25 45
159 1f. red . . . . 2·30 4·75
160 1f. black . . . . 1·30 4·50
161 32 1f.25 brown . . . . 1·20 4·50
162 1f.25 red . . . . 2·75 5·00
163 30 1f.40 blue . . . . 2·50 4·75
164 32 1f.50 blue 80 10
165 30 1f.60 red . . . . 3·25 4·75
166 32 1f.75 olive . . . . 2·50 1·00
167 30 1f.75 blue . . . . 2·50 5·00
168 32 2f. red . . . . 90 2·30
169 30 2f.25 blue . . . . 4·75 5·75
170 2f.50 brown . . . . 2·30 3·25
171 32 3f. violet . . . . 1·70 1·00
172 5f. mauve . . . . 1·70 4·25
173 10f. blue . . . . 2·30 4·75
174 20f. brown . . . . 3·00 5·75

1937. Air. Pioneer Flight from Reunion to France by Laurent, Lenier and Touge. Optd **REUNION – FRANCE par avion "ROLAND GARROS"**.
174a 31 50c. red £700 £200

1937. International Exhibition, Paris. As Nos. 168/73 of St.-Pierre et Miquelon.
175 20c. violet . . . . 1·40 5·00
176 30c. green . . . . 1·70 5·00
177 40c. red . . . . 70 4·00
178 50c. brown and agate . . . . 95 2·75
179 90c. red . . . . 1·30 4·00
180 1f.50 blue . . . . 1·70 5·00

1938. Air.
181 34 3f.65 blue and red 95 95
182 6f.65 brown and red . . . 1·10 4·75
183 9f.65 red and blue . . . . 65 5·00
184 12f.65 brown and green . . 1·40 6·00

1938. International Anti-cancer Fund. As T **17a** of Oceanic Settlements.
185 1f.75+50c. blue . . . . . . 5·50 25·00

1939. New York World's Fair. As T **17b** of Oceanic Settlements.
186 1f.25 red . . . . 2·30 5·25
187 2f.25 blue . . . . 1·90 5·25

1939. 150th Anniv of French Revolution. As T **17c** of Oceanic Settlements.
188 45c.+25c. green and black (postage) . . . . 6·50 16·00
189 70c.+30c. brown and black 5·25 16·00
190 90c.+35c. orange and black 4·00 22·00
191 1f.25+1f. red and black . . . 4·00 22·00
192 2f.25+2f. blue and black . . 4·75 22·00
193 3f.65+4f. blk & orge (air) . . 8·25 36·00

1943. Surch **1f.**
194 31 1f. on 65c. green . . . . . 1·60 1·30

1943. Optd **France Libre**.
198 30 1c. purple (postage) . . . 65 5·25
199 2c. brown . . . . 75 4·25
200 3c. purple . . . . 65 5·25
195 16 4c. red and green . . . . 1·40 7·50
201 30 4c. green . . . . 40 5·25
202 5c. red . . . . 1·20 5·25
203 10c. blue . . . . 20 3·75
204 15c. black . . . . 20 5·00
205 20c. blue . . . . 1·10 5·25
206 25c. brown . . . . 1·10 4·50
207 30c. green . . . . 85 4·25
208 31 35c. green . . . . 40 4·50
209 40c. blue . . . . 50 4·50
210 40c. brown . . . . 80 4·25
211 45c. mauve . . . . 45 4·75
212 45c. green . . . . 80 4·25
213 50c. red . . . . 80 3·50
214 55c. orange . . . . 40 4·75
215 60c. blue . . . . 2·30 4·25
216 65c. green . . . . 95 4·75
217 70c. green . . . . 1·70 5·00
196 17 75c. pink and red . . . . 60 5·25
218 31 75c. brown . . . . 2·50 7·00
219 80c. black . . . . 25 4·75
220 90c. purple . . . . 20 4·75
221 1f. green . . . . 1·20 4·25
222 1f. red . . . . 40 2·75
223 1f. black . . . . 1·50 5·75
240 1f. on 65c. green (No. 194) 65 2·50
224 32 1f.25 brown . . . . 90 5·25
225 1f.25 red . . . . 2·30 4·75
238 – 1f.25 red (No. 186) . . . . 70 6·25
226 30 1f.40 blue . . . . 1·20 5·00
227 32 1f.50 blue . . . . 1·00 4·50
228 30 1f.60 red . . . . 90 5·25
229 32 1f.75 green . . . . 65 4·50
230 30 1f.75 blue . . . . 2·30 8·00
231 32 2f. red . . . . 1·20 3·25
239 – 2f.25 blue (No. 187) . . . 1·50 6·25
232 30 2f.25 blue . . . . 65 5·00
233 2f.50 brown . . . . 1·90 10·50
234 32 3f. violet . . . . 60 4·00
197 18 5f. brown and pink . . . . 50·00 60·00
235 32 5f. mauve . . . . 1·10 2·50
236 10f. blue . . . . 2·00 10·50
237 20f. brown . . . . 5·25 18·00
241 34 3f.65 blue and red (air) . . 2·30 8·25
242 6f.65 brown and red . . . 2·30 7·75
243 9f.65 red and blue . . . . 1·60 7·75
244 12f.65 brown and green . . 2·50 8·25

37 Chief Products

1943. Free French Issue.
245 37 5c. brown . . . . 10 2·75
246a 10c. blue . . . . 1·10 1·50
247 25c. green . . . . 25 3·50
248 30c. red . . . . 70 3·50
249 40c. green . . . . 25 3·50
250 80c. mauve . . . . 85 3·50
251 1f. purple 80 30
252 1f.50 red 95 90
253 2f. black . . . . 55 2·30
254 2f.50 blue . . . . 1·10 3·25
255 4f. violet . . . . 1·10 1·00
256 5f. yellow . . . . 1·00 20

257 10f. brown . . . . 1·20 50
258 20f. green . . . . 1·40 1·40

1944. Air. Free French Administration. As T **19a** of Oceanic Settlements.
259 1f. orange 35 55
260 1f.50 red 45 35
261 5f. purple . . . . 70 1·10
262 10f. black . . . . 1·40 4·00
263 25f. blue . . . . 2·00 3·50
264 50f. green . . . . 1·90 1·50
265 100f. red . . . . 2·25 3·25

1944. Mutual Air and Red Cross Funds. As T **19b** of Oceanic Settlements.
266 5f.+20f. black . . . . 90 5·75

1945. Eboue. As T **20a** of Oceanic Settlements.
267 2f. black 25 80
268 25f. green . . . . 60 4·25

1945. Surch.
269 **37** 50c. on 5c. brown . . . . 1·00 4·75
270 60c. on 5c. brown . . . . 1·10 2·75
271 70c. on 5c. brown . . . . 55 4·75
272 1f.20 on 5c. brown . . . . 1·00 4·00
273 2f.40 on 25c. green . . . . 1·60 3·75
274 3f. on 25c. green . . . . . 95 1·80
275 4f.50 on 25c. green . . . . 1·00 2·50
276 15f. on 2f.50 blue 75 75

1946. Air. Victory. As T **20b** of Oceanic Settlements.
277 8f. grey . . . . 20 1·70

1946. Air. From Chad to the Rhine. As T **20c** of Oceanic Settlements.
278 5f. red . . . . 1·70 5·25
279 10f. violet . . . . 1·20 5·00
280 15f. black . . . . 1·50 4·75
281 20f. red . . . . 1·70 4·00
282 25f. blue . . . . 1·40 5·00
283 50f. green . . . . 2·00 5·75

39 Cliffs

40 Banana Tree and Cliff

41 Mountain Landscape

42 Shadow of Airplane over Coast

1947.
284 **39** 10c. orange & grn (postage) . . . . 10 3·75
285 30c. orange and blue . . . 10 3·75
286 40c. orange and brown . . . 10 4·50
287 – 50c. brown and green . . . 10 3·75
288 – 60c. brown and blue . . . 10 4·75
289 – 80c. green and brown . . . 10 4·75
290 – 1f. purple and blue . . . 45 35
291 – 1f.20 grey and green . . . 80 4·50
292 – 1f.50 purple and orange . . 65 5·00
293 **40** 2f. blue and green . . . 80 10
294 3f. purple and green . . . 1·50 2·50
295 3f.60 pink and red . . . 1·30 5·25
296 4f. blue and brown . . . 1·70 2·30
297 **41** 5f. mauve and brown . . . 1·80 1·30
298 6f. blue and brown . . . 1·90 1·50
299 10f. orange and blue . . . 2·30 3·00
300 – 15f. purple and blue . . . 1·90 6·75
301 – 20f. blue and orange . . . 2·75 9·25
302 – 25f. brown and mauve . . . 2·00 5·25
303 **42** 50f. green and grey (air) . . 6·50 13·50
304 – 100f. orange and brown . . 10·50 24·00
305 – 200f. blue and orange . . . 7·75 30·00

DESIGNS—20 × 37 mm: 50c. to 80c. Cutting sugar cane; 1f. to 1f.50, Cascade. 28 × 50 mm: 100f. Douglas DC-4 airplane over Reunion. 37 × 20 mm: 15f. to 25f. "Ville de Strasbourg" (liner) approaching Reunion. 50 × 28 mm: 200f. Reunion from the air.

1949. Stamps of France surch **CFA** and value. (a) Postage. (i) Ceres.
306 **218** 50c. on 1f. red . . . . . 10 1·60
307 60c. on 2f. green . . . . . 90 6·75

(ii) Nos. 972/3 (Arms).
308 10c. on 30c. black, red and yellow (Alsace) . . . . . 40 4·50
309 30c. on 50c. brown, yellow and red (Lorraine) . . . . 20 5·00

(iii) Nos. 981, 979 and 982/a (Views).
310 5f. on 20f. blue (Finistere) . . 1·80 90
311 7f. on 12f. red (Luxembourg Palace) . . . . 1·10 2·30
312 8f. on 25f. blue (Nancy) . . . 3·00 90
313 10f. on 25f. brown (Nancy) 65 40

(iv) Marianne.
314 **219** 1f. on 3f. mauve 15 10
315 2f. on 4f. green 25 20
316 2f. on 5f. green . . . . 2·75 9·75
317 2f. on 5f. violet 60 20
318 2f.50 on 5f. blue . . . . 2·75 27·00
319 3f. on 6f. red 50 20
320 3f. on 6f. green 65 85
321 4f. on 10f. violet 45 20
322 6f. on 12f. blue . . . . 1·50 70
323 6f. on 12f. orange . . . . 1·80 1·00
324 9f. on 18f. red . . . . . 1·30 8·75

(v) Conques Abbey.
325 **263** 11f. on 18f. blue . . . . 90 2·50

(b) Air. (i) Nos. 967/70 (Mythology).
326 – 20f. on 40f. green 90 55
327 **236** 25f. on 50f. pink . . . . 1·60 30
328 **237** 50f. on 100f. blue . . . . 2·75 1·30
329 – 100f. on 200f. red . . . . 10·00 10·00

(ii) Nos. 1056 and 1058/9 (Cities).
330 100f. on 200f. green (Bordeaux) . . . . 40·00 36·00
331 200f. on 500f. red (Marseilles) 36·00 42·00
332 500f. on 1000f. purple and black on blue (Paris) . . . 95·00 £160

1950. Stamps of France surch **CFA** and value. (a) Nos. 1050 and 1052 (Arms).
342 10c. on 50c. yellow, red and blue (Guyenne) . . . . . 10 3·25
343 1f. on 2f. red, yellow and green (Auvergne) . . . . . 1·40 6·25

(b) On Nos. 1067/8 and 1068b (Views).
344 – 5f. on 20f. red (Comminges) . . . . . 1·10 50
345 **284** 8f. on 25f. blue (Wandrille) 70 25
346 – 15f. on 30f. blue (Arbois) 60 50

1951. Nos. 1123/4 of France (Arms) surch **CFA** and value.
347 50c. on 1f. red, yellow and blue (Bearn) 15 75
348 1f. on 2f. yellow, blue and red (Touraine) 10 15

1952. Nos. 1138 and 1144 of France surch **CFA** and value.
349 **323** 5f. on 20f. violet (Chambord) 55 20
350 **317** 8f. on 40f. violet (Bigorre) 1·00 10

1953. Stamps of France surch **CFA** and value. (a) Nos. 1162, 1168 and 1170 (Literary Figures and National Industries).
351 3f. on 6f. lake and red (Gargantua) 55 45
352 8f. on 40f. brown and chocolate (Porcelain) . . . 55 10
353 20f. on 75f. red and carmine (Flowers) 95 80

(b) Nos. 1181/2 (Arms).
354 50c. on 1f. yellow, red and black (Poitou) 35 75
355 1f. on 2f. yellow, blue and brown (Champagne) . . . 30 5·25

1954. Stamps of France surch **CFA** and value. (a) Postage. (i) Nos. 1188 and 1190 (Sports).
356 8f. on 40f. blue and brown (Canoeing) . . . . 3·75 2·75
357 20f. on 75f. red and orange (Horse jumping) . . . . . 12·50 50·00

(ii) Nos. 1205/8 and 1210/11 (Views).
358 2f. on 6f. indigo, blue and green (Lourdes) . . . . . 60 1·30
359 3f. on 8f. green and blue (Andelys) . . . . 90 5·00
360 4f. on 10f. brown and blue (Royan) 50 85
361 6f. on 12f. lilac and violet (Quimper) 75 90
362 9f. on 18f. indigo, blue and green (Cheverny) . . . . 1·00 8·00
363 10f. on 20f. brown, chestnut and blue (Ajaccio) . . . . 1·90 2·50

(iii) No. 1229 (Arms).
364 1f. on 2f. yellow, red and black (Angoumois) 10 10

(b) Air. Nos. 1194/7 (Aircraft).
365 50f. on 100f. brown and blue (Mystere IV) . . . . . 2·75 70
366 100f. on 200f. purple and blue (Noratlas) . . . . . 2·30 2·50
367 200f. on 500f. red and orange (Magister) . . . . 19·00 26·00
368 500f. on 1000f. indigo, purple and blue (Provence) . . . 10·00 30·00

1955. Stamps of France surch **CFA** and value. (a) Nos. 1262/5, 1266, 1268 and 1268b (Views).
369 2f. on 6f. red (Bordeaux) . . 60 1·10
370 3f. on 8f. blue (Marseilles) . . 80 60
371 4f. on 10f. blue (Nice) . . . 90 90
372 5f. on 12f. brown and grey (Cahors) 30 20
373 6f. on 18f. blue and green (Uzerche) 35 25
374 10f. on 25f. brown and chestnut (Brouage) 35 20
375 17f. on 70f. black and green (Cahors) . . . . 1·30 8·50

(b) No. 1273 (Arms).
376 50c. on 1f. yellow, red and blue (Comtat Venaissin) . . 10 10

1956. Nos. 1297/1300 of France (Sports) surch **CFA** and value.
377 8f. on 30f. black and grey (Basketball) 55 15
378 9f. on 40f. purple and brown (Pelota) . . . . 75 1·20
379 15f. on 50f. violet and purple (Rugby) . . . . 1·50 2·30
380 20f. on 75f. green, black and blue (Climbing) . . . . . 80 2·00

1957. Stamps of France surch **CFA** and value. (a) Postage. (i) Harvester.
381 **344** 2f. on 6f. brown 40 10
382 4f. on 12f. purple 80 65
383 5f. on 10f. green 75 40

(ii) France.
384 **362** 10f. on 20f. blue 30 10
385 12f. on 25f. red 70 15

(iii) No. 1335 (Le Quesnoy).
386 7f. on 15f. black and green 60 30

(iv) Nos. 1351, 1352/3, 1354/5 and 1356a (Tourist Publicity).
387 3f. on 10f. chocolate and brown (Elysee) 40 40
388 6f. on 18f. brown and blue (Beynac) . . . . 65 1·80
389 9f. on 25f. brown and grey (Valencay) . . . . 60 3·75
390 17f. on 35f. mauve and red (Rouen) . . . . 80 3·25
391 20f. on 50f. brown and green (St. Remy) 45 20
392 25f. on 85f. purple (Evian-les-Bains) . . . . 1·10 60

(b) Air. Nos. 1319/20 (Aircraft).
393 200f. on 500f. black and blue (Caravelle) . . . . 6·50 11·50
394 500f. on 1000f. black, violet and brown (Alouette II) . . 10·00 34·00

1960. Nos. 1461, 1464 and 1467 of France (Tourist Publicity) surch **CFA** and value.
395 7f. on 15c. indigo and blue (Laon) . . . . 1·50 45
396 20f. on 50c. purple and green (Tlemcen) . . . . 8·25 1·70
397 50f. on 1f. violet, green and blue (Cilaos) 80 50

1961. Harvester and Sower stamps of France (in new currency) surch **CFA** and value.
398 **344** 5f. on 10c. green . . . . 85 1·30
400 **453** 10f. on 20c. red and turquoise 75 25

1961. "Marianne" stamp of France surch **12f. CFA.**
401 **463** 12f. on 25c. grey & purple 45 30

1961. Nos. 1457, 1457b and 1459/60 of France (Aircraft) surch **CFA** and value.
402 100f. on 2f. purple and blue (Noratlas) . . . . 5·00 1·50
403 100f. on 2f. indigo and blue (Mystere Falcon 20) . . . 1·40 1·50
404 200f. on 5f. black and blue (Caravelle) . . . . 5·25 5·00
405 500f. on 10f. black, violet and brown (Alouette II) . . . 17·00 11·50

1962. Red Cross stamps of France (Nos. 1593/4) surch **CFA** and value.
409 10f.+5f. on 20c.+10c. . . . 1·20 3·50
410 12f.+5f. on 25c.+10c. . . . 1·20 5·50

1962. Satellite Link stamps of France surch **CFA** and value.
411 12f. on 25c. (No. 1587) . . . 35 2·75
412 25f. on 50c. (No. 1588) . . . 50 3·50

1963. Nos. 1541 and 1545 of France (Tourist Publicity) surch **CFA** and value.
413 7f. on 15c. grey, purple and blue (Saint-Paul) . . . . 1·20 3·50
414 20f. on 45c. brown, green and blue (Sully) 80 90

1963. Nos. 1498b/9b and 1499e/f of France (Arms) surch **CFA** and value.
415 1f. on 2c. yellow, green and blue (Gueret) 10 30
416 2f. on 5c. mult (Oran) . . . 15 30
417 2f. on 5c. red, yellow and blue (Armiens) 30 30
418 5f. on 10c. blue, yellow and red (Troyes) 35 30
419 6f. on 18c. multicoloured (St. Denis) 10 50
420 15f. on 30c. red and blue (Paris) 40 30

1963. Red Cross stamps of France Nos. 1627/8 surch **CFA** and value.
421 10f.+5f. on 20c.+10c. . . . 1·80 7·00
422 12f.+5f. on 25c.+10c. . . . 1·70 7·00

1964. 'PHILATEC 1964' International Stamp Exhibition stamp of France surch **CFA** and value.
423 12f. on 25c. (No. 1629) . . . 90 45

1964. Nos. 1654/5 of France (Tourist Publicity) surch **CFA** and value.
431 20f. on 40c. chocolate, green and brown (Ronchamp) . . 95 3·00
432 35f. on 70c. purple, green and blue (Provins) . . . . . . 60 1·70

1964. Red Cross stamps of France Nos. 1665/6 surch **CFA** and value.
433 10f.+5f. on 20c.+10c. . . . 2·00 4·00
434 12f.+5f. on 25c.+10c. . . . 2·00 4·50

1965. No. 1621 of France (Saint Flour) surch **3F CFA.**
435 30f. on 60c. red, green & blue 95 1·70

1965. Nos 1684/5 and 1688 of France (Tourist Publicity) surch **CFA** and value.
436 25f. on 50c. blue, green and bistre (St. Marie) . . . . . 1·00 1·90
437 30f. on 60c. brown and blue (Aix les Bains) . . . . . . 60 1·90
438 50f. on 1f. grey, green and brown (Carnac) . . . . . 2·00 1·70

1965. Tercent of Colonization of Reunion. As No. 1692 of France, but additionally inscr 'CFA'.
439 15f. blue and red . . . . . . 1·20 40

1965. Red Cross stamps of France Nos. 1698/9 surch **CFA** and value.
440 12f.+5f. on 25c.+10c. . . . 1·90 4·50
441 15f.+5f. on 30c.+ 10c. . . . 1·90 4·50

1966. "Marianne" stamp of France surch **10f CFA.**
442 **476** 10f. on 20c. red and blue 2·50 3·50

1966. Launching of 1st French Satellite. Nos. 1696/7 (plus se-tenant label) of France surch **CFA** and value.
443 15f. on 30c. blue, turquoise and light blue . . . . . . 1·80 2·50
444 30f. on 60c. blue, turquoise and light blue . . . . . . 2·30 2·50

1966. Red Cross stamps of France Nos. 1733/4 surch **CFA** and value.
445 12f.+5f. on 25c.+10c. . . . 1·50 4·00
446 15f.+5f. on 30c.+10c. . . . 1·50 4·00

1967. World Fair Montreal. No. 1747 of France surch **CFA** and value.
447 30f. on 60c. . . . . 95 4·00

1967. No. 1700 of France (Arms of Auch) surch **2fCFA.**
448 2f. on 5c. red and blue . . . 55 3·25

1967. 50th Anniv of Lions Int. No. 1766 of France surch **CFA** and value.
449 20f. on 40c. . . . . 1·50 3·75

1967. Red Cross. Nos. 1772/3 of France surch **CFA** and value.
450 12f.+5f. on 25c.+10c. . . . 2·30 7·50
451 15f.+5f. on 30c .+ 10c. . . . 2·30 7·50

1968. French Polar Exploration. No. 1806 of France surch **CFA** and value.
452 20f. on 40c. . . . . 2·30 3·75

1968. Red Cross stamps of France Nos. 1812/13 surch **CFA** and value.
453 12f.+5f. on 25c.+10c. . . . 2·30 4·75
454 15f.+5f. on 30c.+10c. . . . 2·30 4·75

1969. Stamp Day. No. 1824 of France surch **CFA** and value.
455 15f.+5f. on 30c.+10c. . . . 2·00 4·25

1969. "Republique" stamps of France surch **CFA** and value.
456 **604** 15f. on 30c. green . . . . 1·20 3·25
457 20f. on 40c. mauve . . . 85 80

1969. No. 1735 of France (Arms of Saint-Lo) surch **10F CFA**.
458 10f. on 20c. multicoloured . . 1·60 3·00

1969. Birth Bicent of Napoleon Bonaparte. No. 1845 of France surch **CFA** and value.
459 35f. on 70c. green, violet & bl 2·75 4·25

1969. Red Cross stamps of France Nos. 1853/4 surch **CFA** and value.
460 20f.+7f. on 40c.+15c. . . . 2·30 4·50
461 20f.+7f. on 40c.+15c. . . . 2·30 4·50

1970. Stamp Day. No. 1866 of France surch **CFA** and value.
462 20f.+5f. on 40c +.10c. . . . 2·30 4·00

1970. Red Cross. Nos. 1902/3 of France surch **CFA** and value.
463 20f.+7f. on 40c.+15c. . . . 4·00 5·75
464 20f.+7f. on 40c.+15c. . . . 4·00 5·75

1971. "Marianne" stamp of France surch **25f CFA**.
465 **668** 25f. on 50c. mauve . . . 90 65

1971. Stamp Day. No. 1919 of France surch **CFA** and value.
466 25f.+5f. on 50c.+10c. . . . 1·40 3·75

1971. "Antoinette". No. 1920 of France surch **CFA** and value.
467 40f. on 80c. . . . . 2·30 4·25

1971. No. 1928 of France (Rural Aid) surch **CFA** and value.
468 **678** 15f. on 40c. . . . . . . 1·80 3·50

1971. Nos. 1931/2 of France (Tourist Publicity) surch **CFA** and value.
469 45f. on 90c. brown, green and ochre (Riquewihr) . . . . 1·30 3·25
470 50f. on 1f.10 brown, blue and green (Sedan) . . . . . . 2·00 2·00

1971. 40th Anniv of 1st Meeting of Crafts Guilds Association. No. 1935 of France surch **CFA** and value.
471 **680** 45c. on 90c. purple & red 1·90 3·50

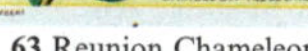
63 Reunion Chameleon

64 De Gaulle in Uniform (June 1940)

1971. Nature Protection.
472 **63** 25f. green, brown & yellow 2·50 2·30

1971. De Gaulle Commemoration.
473 **64** 25f. black . . . . 2·30 3·25
474 – 25f. blue . . . . 2·30 3·25
475 – 25f. red . . . . 2·30 3·25
476 – 25f. black . . . . 2·30 3·25
DESIGNS: No. 473, De Gaulle in uniform (June, 1940); No. 474, De Gaulle at Brazzaville, 1944; No. 475, De Gaulle in Paris, 1944; No. 476, De Gaulle as President of the French Republic, 1970 (T **64**).

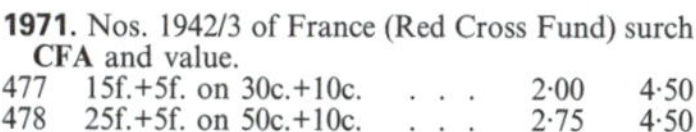
1971. Nos. 1942/3 of France (Red Cross Fund) surch **CFA** and value.
477 15f.+5f. on 30c.+10c. . . . 2·00 4·50
478 25f.+5f. on 50c.+10c. . . . 2·75 4·50

65 King Penguin, Map and Exploration Ships

1972. Bicentenary of Discovery of Crozet Islands and Kerguelen (French Southern and Antarctic Territories).
479 **65** 45f. black, blue and brown 6·25 9·50

1972. No. 1956 of France surch **CFA** and value.
480 **688** 25f.+5f. on 50c+10c. blue, drab and yellow . . . . 2·50 4·00

1972. No. 1966 of France (Blood Donors) surch **CFA** and value.
481 **692** 15f. on 40c. red . . . . . 2·30 3·25

1972. Air. No 1890 of France (Daurat and Vanier) surch **CFA** and value.
482 **662** 200f. on 5f. brn, grn & bl 4·25 4·25

1972. Postal Codes. Nos. 1969/70 of France surch **CFA** and value.
483 **695** 15f. on 30c. red, black and green . . . . . . 2·00 3·50
484 25f. on 50c. yell, blk & red . . . . 1·60 1·80

1972. Red Cross Fund. Nos. 1979/80 of France surch **CFA** and value.
485 **701** 15f.+5f. on 30c.+10c. . . 2·30 4·25
486 25f.+5f. on 50c.+10c. . . 2·50 4·25

1973. Stamp Day. No. 1996 of France surch **CFA** and value.
487 **707** 25f.+5f. on 50c.+10c. . . 3·50 4·50

1973. No. 2011 of France surch **CFA** and value.
488 **714** 45f. on 90c. green, violet and blue . . . . 2·75 4·50

1973. No. 2008 of France surch **CFA** and value.
489 50f. on 1f. green, brown & bl 2·00 2·00

1973. No. 1960 of France surch **CFA** and value.
490 100f. on 2f. purple and green 2·50 3·75

1973. No. 2021/2 of France surch **CFA** and value.
491 **721** 15f.+5f. on 30c.+10c. green and red . . . . . 2·75 4·50
492 25f.+5f. on 50c .+ 10c. red and black . . . . . 2·75 4·00

1973. No. 2026 of France surch **CFA** and value.
494 **725** 25f. on 50c. brown, blue and purple . . . . . . 2·30 3·25

1974. Stamp Day. No. 2031 surch **FCFA** and value.
495 **727** 25f.+5f. on 50c .+ 10c. 2·30 4·00

1974. French Art. No. 2033/6 surch **FCFA** and value.
496 100f. on 2f. multicoloured . . 2·50 4·75
497 100f. on 2f. multicoloured . . 2·00 5·50
498 100f. on 2f. brown and blue 3·00 5·25
499 100f. on 2f. multicoloured . . 2·30 5·25

1974. French Lifeboat Service. No. 2040 surch **FCFA** and value.
500 **731** 45f. on 90c. blue, red and brown . . . . 2·50 4·50

1974. Centenary of Universal Postal Union. No. 2057 surch **FCFA** and value.
501 **741** 60f. on 1f.20 green, red and blue . . . . 1·50 4·50

1974. "Marianne" stamps of France surch **FCFA** and value.
502 **668** 30f. on 60c. green . . . . 2·30 5·00
503 40f. on 80c. red . . . . . 2·50 5·00

1974. Red Cross Fund. "The Seasons". Nos. 2059/60 surch **FCFA** and value.
504 **743** 30f.+7f. on 60c.+15c. . . 2·50 4·50
505 – 40f.+7f . on 80c.+15c. . . 2·75 4·75

From 1 January 1975 the CFA franc was replaced by the French Metropolitan franc, and Reunion subsequently used unsurcharged stamps of France.

PARCEL POST STAMPS

P 5

P 20

1890.
P11 **P 5** 10c. black on yellow (black frame) £250 £150
P13 10c. black on yellow (blue frame) . . . . . . 30·00 25·00

1907. Receipt stamps surch as in Type **P 20**.
P76 **P 20** 10c. brown and black . . 29·00 22·00
P77 10c. brown and red . . 30·00 21·00

POSTAGE DUE STAMPS

D 4

D 19

1889. Imperf.
D11 **D 4** 5c. black . . . . 17·00 4·50
D12 10c. black . . . . 9·50 4·00
D13 15c. black . . . . 38·00 18·00
D14 20c. black . . . . 50·00 5·25
D15 30c. black . . . . 45·00 5·25

1907.
D76 **D 19** 5c. red on yellow . . . 20 15
D77 10c. blue on blue . . . 60 25
D78 15c. black on grey . . . 90 3·00
D79 20c. pink . . . . 1·30 35
D80 30c. green on green . . 60 4·25
D81 50c. red on green . . . 1·00 1·80
D82 60c. pink on blue . . . 1·40 4·00
D83 1f. lilac . . . . 1·20 4·00

1927. Surch.
D130 **D 19** 2f. on 1f. red . . . . 4·50 17·00
D131 3f. on 1f. brown . . . 4·75 17·00

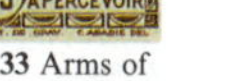
D 33 Arms of Reunion

D 43

1933.
D175 **D 33** 5c. purple . . . . . . 10 3·00
D176 10c. green . . . . . . 10 3·75
D177 15c. brown . . . . . . 10 3·00
D178 20c. orange . . . . . 10 3·50
D179 30c. olive . . . . . . 10 4·25
D180 50c. blue . . . . . . 10 5·00
D181 60c. brown . . . . . 10 5·00
D182 1f. violet . . . . . . 10 5·00
D183 2f. blue . . . . 10 5·00
D184 3f. red . . . . 10 5·00

1947.
D306 **D 43** 10c. mauve . . . . . . 10 3·75
D307 30c. brown . . . . . 10 3·75
D308 50c. green . . . . . . 10 4·00
D309 1f. brown . . . . . . 1·30 4·75
D310 2f. red . . . . 2·75 4·75
D311 3f. brown . . . . . . 1·70 5·00
D312 4f. blue . . . . 1·60 5·50
D313 5f. red . . . . 1·60 5·50
D314 10f. green . . . . . . 1·50 5·25
D315 20f. blue . . . . . . 2·75 5·75

1949. As Type D **250** of France, but inscr "TIMBRE TAXE" surch **CFA** and value.
D333 10c. on 1f. blue . . . . 10 4·75
D334 50c. on 2f. blue . . . . 10 4·75
D335 1f. on 3f. red . . . . . 35 5·00
D336 2f. on 4f. violet . . . . 75 5·75
D337 3f. on 5f. pink . . . . . 1·50 5·50
D338 5f. on 10f. red . . . . . 90 6·50
D339 10f. on 20f. brown . . . 1·10 7·25
D340 20f. on 50f. green . . . 3·00 11·50
D341 50f. on 100f. green . . . 8·75 40·00

1962. Wheat Sheaves Type of France surch **CFA** and value.
D406 **D 457** 1f. on 5c. mauve . . 85 4·25
D407 10f. on 20c. brown 2·50 5·25
D408 20f. on 50c. green . . 17·00 29·00

1964. Nos. D1650/4 and D1656/7 of France surch **CFA** and value.
D424 – 1f. on 5c. . . . . . 10 3·00
D425 – 5f. on 10c. . . . . . 20 3·00
D426 **D 539** 7f. on 15c. . . . . . 10 3·25
D427 – 10f. on 20c. . . . . 2·30 3·75
D428 – 15f. on 30c. . . . . 25 3·25
D429 – 20f. on 50c. . . . . 40 3·50
D430 – 50f. on 1f. . . . . . 65 4·00

RHODESIA Pt. 1

A British territory in central Africa, formerly administered by the British South Africa Co. In 1924 divided into the territories of Northern and Southern Rhodesia which issued their own stamps (q.v.). In 1964 Southern Rhodesia was renamed Rhodesia; on becoming independent in 1980 it was renamed Zimbabwe.

1890. 12 pence = 1 shilling;
20 shillings = 1 pound.
1970. 100 cents = 1 dollar.

1 Arms of the Company

1890. The pound values are larger.
18 **1** ½d. blue and red . . . . . . 2·50 3·50
1 1d. black . . . . 10·00 2·75
20 2d. green and red . . . . . 19·00 3·00
21 3d. black and green . . . . 13·00 4·50
22 4d. brown and black . . . . 25·00 3·00
3 6d. blue . . . . 29·00 3·75
23 8d. red and blue . . . . . . 13·00 13·00
4 1s. brown . . . . 40·00 9·00
5 2s. orange . . . . 48·00 27·00
6 2s.6d. purple . . . . 30·00 42·00
25 3s. brown and green . . . . £150 80·00
26 4s. black and red . . . . . 32·00 50·00
8 5s. yellow . . . . 65·00 50·00
9 10s. green . . . . 80·00 £100
10 – £1 blue £190 £130
11 – £2 red £425 £150
12 – £5 green £1600 £450
13 – £10 brown £2750 £700

1891. Surch in figures.
14 **1** ½d. on 6d. blue £110 £350
15 2d. on 6d. blue £130 £475
16 4d. on 6d. blue £160 £600
17 8d. on 1s. brown £160 £650

5

9

1896. The ends of ribbons containing motto cross the animals' legs.
41 **5** ½d. grey and mauve . . . . 3·00 3·25
42 1d. red and green . . . . . 4·50 3·75
43 2d. brown and mauve . . . 10·00 4·50
31 3d. brown and blue . . . . 5·00 1·75
44a 4d. blue and mauve . . . . 11·00 50
46 6d. mauve and red . . . . 9·00 75
34 8d. green and mauve on buff . . . . 7·00 60
35 1s. green and blue . . . . . 15·00 2·75
47 2s. blue and green on buff 26·00 8·50
48 2s.6d. brown & pur on yell 70·00 50·00
36 3s. green and mauve on blue 65·00 35·00
37 4s. red and blue on green 50·00 2·75
49 5s. brown and green . . . . 50·00 9·00
50 10s. grey and red on rose £100 65·00

1896. Surch in words.
51 **1** 1d. on 3d. black and green £475 £550
52 1d. on 4s. black and red . . £250 £275
53 3d. on 5s. yellow £170 £225

1896. Cape of Good Hope stamps optd **BRITISH SOUTH AFRICA COMPANY**.
58 **6** ½d. black (No. 48) . . . . . 13·00 19·00
59 **17** 1d. red (No. 58a) . . . . . 15·00 20·00
60 **6** 2d. brown (No. 60) . . . . 18·00 11·00
61 3d. red (No. 40) . . . . . 50·00 75·00
62 4d. blue (No. 51) . . . . . 20·00 20·00
63 **4** 6d. purple (No. 52a) . . . . 50·00 65·00
64 **6** 1s. yellow (No. 65) £140 £140

1897. The ends of motto ribbons do not cross the animals' legs.
66 **9** ½d. grey and mauve . . . . 3·25 5·50
67 1d. red and green . . . . . 3·50 5·00
68 2d. brown and mauve . . . . 9·00 2·25
69 3d. brown and blue . . . . 3·00 50
70 4d. blue and mauve . . . . 12·00 2·25
71 6d. mauve and red . . . . 7·50 3·50
72 8d. green and mauve on buff 13·00 50
73 £1 black and brown on green £350 £225

10

11

1898. Nos. 90/93a are larger (24 × 28½ mm).
75a **10** ½d. green . . . . 2·75 1·50
77 1d. red . . . . 4·50 50
79 2d. brown . . . . 3·25 60
80 2½d. blue . . . . 5·50 80
81 3d. red . . . . 5·00 80
82 4d. olive . . . . 4·75 30
83 6d. purple . . . . 12·00 1·75
84 **11** 1s. brown . . . . 17·00 2·75
85 2s.6d. grey . . . . 45·00 1·00
86 3s. violet . . . . 16·00 2·25
87 5s. orange . . . . 42·00 12·00
88 7s.6d. black . . . . 70·00 21·00
89 10s. green . . . . 29·00 1·00
90 – £1 purple . . . . £275 95·00
91 – £2 brown . . . . 85·00 6·50
92 – £5 blue £3250 £2500
93 – £10 lilac £3250 £2250
93a – £20 brown £14000

13 Victoria Falls

1905. Visit of British Assn. and Opening of Victoria Falls Bridge across Zambesi.

94 **13** 1d. red . . . . 4·50 5·00
95 2½d. blue . . . . 10·00 7·00
96 5d. red . . . . 42·00 60·00
97 1s. green . . . . 27·00 42·00
98 2s.6d. black £100 £150
99 5s. violet . . . . 90·00 40·00

1909. Optd **RHODESIA.** or surch also.

100 **10** ½d. green . . . . 2·25 1·25
101 1d. red . . . . 3·75 1·00
102 2d. brown . . . . 1·75 4·00
103 2½d. blue . . . . 1·25 70
104 3d. red . . . . 1·60 80
105 4d. olive . . . . 4·25 1·75
114 5d. on 6d. purple . . . . 7·00 12·00
106 6d. purple . . . . 5·00 4·75
116 **11** 7½d. on 2s.6d. grey . . . 3·50 3·75
117a 10d. on 2s. violet . . . . 4·25 3·75
107c 1s. brown . . . . 8·50 4·00
118 2s. on 5s. orange . . . . 12·00 7·50
108 2s.6d. grey . . . . 20·00 10·00
109 3s. violet . . . . 15·00 10·00
110 5s. orange . . . . 28·00 42·00
111 7s.6d. black . . . . 90·00 21·00
112 10s. green . . . . 35·00 14·00
113 – £1 purple . . . . £150 80·00
113d – £2 brown £3250 £275
113e – £5 blue £7000 £4250

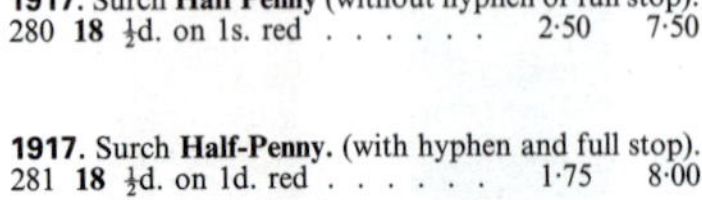

17 18

1910.

119 **17** ½d. green . . . . 12·00 1·75
123 1d. red . . . . 22·00 3·00
128 2d. black and grey . . . 55·00 7·00
131a 2½d. blue . . . . 22·00 7·00
135 3d. purple and yellow . . 40·00 14·00
140 4d. black and orange . . 40·00 15·00
141 5d. purple and olive . . . 29·00 48·00
145 6d. purple and mauve . . 35·00 16·00
148 8d. black and purple . . £140 90·00
149 10d. red and purple . . . 38·00 48·00
152 1s. black and green . . . 48·00 13·00
153 2s. black and blue . . . . 80·00 55·00
157 2s.6d. black and red . . . £300 £325
158 3s. green and violet . . . £170 £170
160a 5s. red and green £225 £190
160b 7s.6d. red and blue . . . £600 £425
164 10s. green and orange . . £375 £400
166 £1 red and black £1120 £375

1913.

187 **18** ½d. green . . . . 5·00 2·00
192 1d. red . . . . 4·00 2·00
198 1½d. brown . . . . 5·00 2·00
291 2d. black and grey . . . . 7·50 4·25
200 2½d. blue . . . . 5·50 26·00
259 3d. black and yellow . . . 11·00 2·50
261 4d. black and orange . . . 14·00 5·50
212 5d. black and green . . . 4·75 13·00
295 6d. black and mauve . . . 5·00 4·00
230 8d. violet and green . . . 14·00 55·00
247 10d. blue and red . . . . 9·00 29·00
272 1s. black and blue . . . . 9·00 7·00
273 2s. black and brown . . . 12·00 15·00
236 2s.6d. blue and brown . . 50·00 32·00
304 3s. brown and blue . . . . 90·00 £110
239 5s. blue and green . . . . 55·00 60·00
252 7s.6d. mauve and grey . . £140 £190
309 10s. red and green £180 £225
242 £1 black and purple . . . £400 £550

1917. Surch **Half Penny** (without hyphen or full stop).

280 **18** ½d. on 1s. red . . . . . . 2·50 7·50

1917. Surch **Half-Penny.** (with hyphen and full stop).

281 **18** ½d. on 1d. red . . . . . . 1·75 8·00

RHODESIA

The following stamps are for the former Southern Rhodesia, renamed Rhodesia.

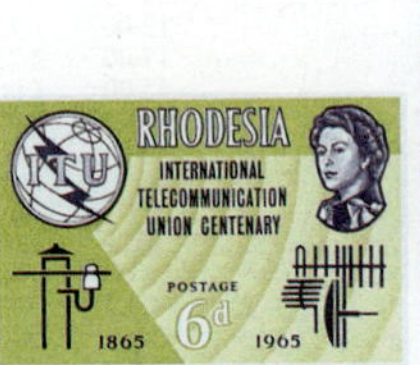

59 "Telecommunications" **60** Bangala Dam

1965. Centenary of I.T.U.

351 **59** 6d. violet and olive . . . . 1·25 40
352 1s.3d. violet and lilac . . . 1·50 40
353 2s.6d. violet and brown . . 2·25 4·50

1965. Water Conservation. Multicoloured.

354 3d. Type **60** 30 10
355 4d. Irrigation canal . . . . 1·00 1·00
356 2s.6d. Cutting sugar cane . . 2·25 3·50

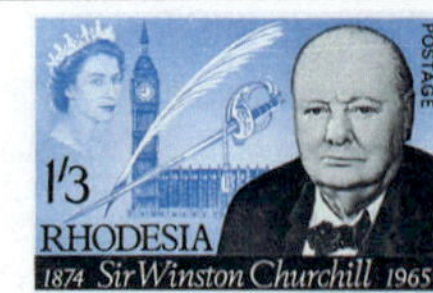

63 Sir Winston Churchill, Quill, Sword and Houses of Parliament

1965. Churchill Commemoration.

357 **63** 1s.3d. black and blue . . . 70 35

64 Coat of Arms **67** Emeralds

1965. "Independence".

358 **64** 2s.6d. multicoloured . . . 15 15

1966. Optd **INDEPENDENCE 11th November 1965**.

(a) On Nos. 92/105 of Southern Rhodesia.

359 **45** ½d. yellow, green and blue 10 10
360 – 1d. violet and ochre . . . 10 10
361 – 2d. yellow and violet . . . 10 10
362 – 3d. brown and blue 10 10
363 – 4d. orange and green . . . 15 10
364 **50** 6d. red, yellow and green 15 10
365 – 9d. brown, yellow and green 30 10
366 – 1s. green and ochre 40 10
367 – 1s.3d. red, violet and green 50 50
368 – 2s. blue and ochre . . . . 60 3·25
369 – 2s.6d. blue and red . . . . 60 1·00
370 **56** 5s. multicoloured . . . . . 1·25 5·50
371 – 10s. multicoloured . . . . 3·25 2·25
372 – £1 multicoloured . . . . . 1·25 2·25

(b) Surch on No. 357.

373 **63** 5s. on 1s.3d. black and blue . . . . 3·50 9·00

1966. As Nos. 92/105 of Southern Rhodesia, but inscr "RHODESIA" as in T **67**. Some designs and colours changed.

374 – 1d. violet and ochre . . . 10 10
375 – 2d. orange & grn (As No. 96) 10 10
376 – 3d. brown and blue 10 10
377 **67** 4d. green and brown . . . 1·25 10
378 **50** 6d. red, yellow and green 15 10
379 – 9d. yellow & vio (As No. 94) 15 20
380 **45** 1s. yellow, green and blue 15 10
381 – 1s.3d. bl & ochre (As No. 101) 25 15
382 – 1s.6d. brn, yell & grn (As No. 98) . . . . 2·25 25
383 – 2s. red, vio & grn (As No. 100) 40 80
384 – 2s.6d. blue, red & turquoise 1·50 20
385 **56** 5s. multicoloured 40 90
386 – 10s. multicoloured . . . . 2·50 3·50
387 – £1 multicoloured . . . . . 3·25 7·00

Nos. 379/80 are in larger format as Type **50** of Southern Rhodesia.

Stamps in these designs were later printed locally. These vary only slightly from the above in details and shade.

For Nos. 376, 380 and 382/4 in dual currency see Nos. 408/12.

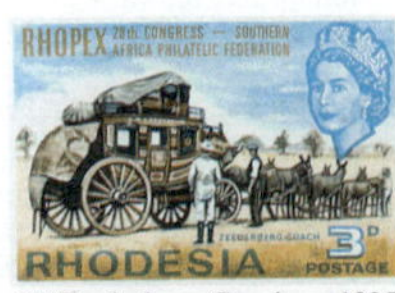

68 Zeederberg Coach, c. 1895

1966. 28th Congress of Southern Africa Philatelic Federation ("Rhopex").

388 **68** 3d. multicoloured 15 10
389 – 9d. multicoloured 15 20
390 – 1s.6d. blue and black . . . 25 30
391 – 2s.6d. pink, green and black 30 55
MS392 126 × 84 mm. Nos. 388/91 5·00 11·00

DESIGNS: 9d. Sir Rowland Hill; 1s.6d. The Penny Black; 2s.6d. Rhodesian stamp of 1892 (No. 12).

69 De Havilland Dragon Rapide (1946) **70** Kudu

1966. 20th Anniv of Central African Airways.

393 **69** 6d. multicoloured 75 35
394 – 1s.3d. multicoloured . . . 1·00 40
395 – 2s.6d. multicoloured . . . 1·50 1·50
396 – 5s. black and blue . . . . 2·25 4·50

AIRCRAFT: 1s.3d. Douglas DC-3 (1953); 2s.6d. Vickers Viscount 748 "Matopos" (1956); 5s. B.A.C. One Eleven.

1967. Dual Currency Issue. As Nos. 376, 380 and 382/4. but value in dual currency as T **70**.

408 **70** 3d./2½c. brown and blue . . 50 15
409 – 1s./10c. yellow, green and blue (No. 380) 50 25
410 – 1s.6d./15c. brown, yellow and green (No. 382) . . 3·50 70
411 – 2s./20c. red, violet and green (No. 383) . . . . 1·50 3·00
412 – 2s.6d./25c. ultramarine, red and blue (No. 384) . . . 16·00 25·00

71 Dr. Jameson (administrator)

1967. Famous Rhodesians (1st series) and 50th Death Anniv of Dr. Jameson.

413 **71** 1s.6d. multicoloured . . . 20 35

See also Nos. 426, 430, 457, 458, 469, 480, 488 and 513.

72 Soapstone Sculpture (Joram Mariga)

1967. 10th Anniv of Opening of Rhodes National Gallery.

414 **72** 3d. brown, green and black 10 10
415 – 9d. blue, brown and black 20 20
416 – 1s.3d. multicoloured . . . 20 25
417 – 2s.6d. multicoloured . . . 25 35

DESIGNS: 9d. "The Burgher of Calais" (detail, Rodin); 1s.3d. "The Knight" (stamp design wrongly inscr) (Roberto Crippa); 2s.6d. "John the Baptist" (Mossini).

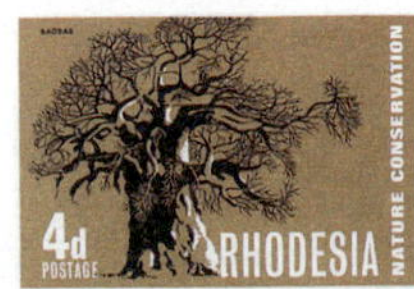

73 Baobab Tree

1967. Nature Conservation.

418 **73** 4d. brown and black . . . 10 20
419 – 4d. green and black . . . 25 20
420 – 4d. grey and black 25 20
421 – 4d. orange and black . . . 10 20

DESIGNS—HORIZ: No. 419, White rhinoceros; No. 420, African elephants. VERT: No. 421, Wild gladiolus.

74 Wooden Hand Plough

1968. 15th World Ploughing Contest, Norton, Rhodesia.

422 **74** 3d. orange, red and brown 10 10
423 – 9d. multicoloured 15 20
424 – 1s.6d. multicoloured . . . 20 55
425 – 2s.6d. multicoloured . . . 20 75

DESIGNS: 9d. Early wheel plough; 1s.6d. Steam powered tractor, and ploughs; 2s.6d. Modern tractor, and plough.

75 Alfred Beit (national benefactor)

1968. Famous Rhodesians (2nd issue).

426 **75** 1s.6d. orange, black & brn 20 30

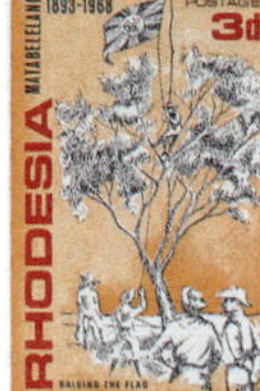

76 Raising the Flag, Bulawayo, 1893

1968. 75th Anniv of Matabeleland.

427 **76** 3d. orange, red and black 15 10
428 – 9d. multicoloured 15 20
429 – 1s.6d. green, emerald & blk 20 60

DESIGNS: 9d. View and coat of arms of Bulawayo; 1s.6d. Allan Wilson (combatant in the Matabele War).

77 Sir William Henry Milton (administrator)

1969. Famous Rhodesians (3rd issue).

430 **77** 1s.6d. multicoloured . . . 20 55

78 2ft. Gauge Locomotive No. 15, 1897

1969. 70th Anniv of Opening of Beira–Salisbury Railway. Multicoloured.

431 3d. Type **78** 50 10
432 9d. 7th Class steam locomotive No. 43, 1903 70 40
433 1s.6d. Beyer, Peacock 15th Class steam locomotive No. 413, 1951 . . . . . 1·00 1·50
434 2s.6d. Class DE2 diesel-electric locomotive No. 1203, 1955 . . . . . 1·50 4·00

79 Low Level Bridge

1969. Bridges of Rhodesia. Multicoloured.

435 3d. Type **79** 40 10
436 9d. Mpudzi bridge 60 25
437 1s.6d. Umniati bridge 90 75
438 2s.6d. Birchenough bridge . . 1·25 1·50

80 Harvesting Wheat **81** Devil's Cataract, Victoria Falls

1970. Decimal Currency.

439 **80** 1c. multicoloured 10 10
440 – 2c. multicoloured 10 10
441 – 2½c. multicoloured . . . 10 10
441c – 3c. multicoloured . . . . 1·25 10
442 – 3½c. multicoloured . . . 10 10
442b – 4c. multicoloured . . . . 1·75 60
443 – 5c. multicoloured 15 10
443b – 6c. multicoloured . . . . 4·00 3·75
443c **81** 7½c. multicoloured . . . 7·00 60
444 8c. multicoloured 75 20
445 – 10c. multicoloured . . . 60 10
446 – 12½c. multicoloured . . . 1·00 10
446a – 14c. multicoloured . . . 12·00 70
447 – 15c. multicoloured . . . 1·25 15
448 – 20c. multicoloured . . . 1·00 15
449 – 25c. multicoloured . . . 4·00 60
450 – 50c. turquoise and blue 1·25 55
451 – $1 multicoloured . . . . 2·75 1·25
452 – $2 multicoloured . . . . 6·00 15·00

DESIGNS—As Type **80**: 2c. Pouring molten metal; 2½c. Zimbabwe Ruins; 3c. Articulated lorry; 3½c., 4c. Statue of Cecil Rhodes; 5c. Mine headgear; 6c. Hydrofoil "Seaflight". As Type **81**: 10c. Yachting on Lake Mcllwaine; 12½c. Hippopotamus in river; 14c., 15c. Kariba Dam; 20c. Irrigation canal. 31 × 26 mm: 25c. Bateleurs; 50c. Radar antenna and Vickers Viscount 810; $1 "Air Rescue"; $2 Rhodesian flag.

82 Despatch Rider, c. 1890

1970. Inauguration of Posts and Telecommunications Corporation. Multicoloured.
453 2½c. Type **82** 30 10
454 3½c. Loading mail at Salisbury airport 40 50
455 15c. Constructing telegraph line, c. 1890 . . . . 45 1·25
456 25c. Telephone and modern telecommunications equipment . . . . 50 2·00

83 Mother Patrick (Dominican nurse and teacher)

1971. Famous Rhodesians (4th issue).
457 **83** 15c. multicoloured 60 50

84 Fredrick Courteney Selous (big-game hunter, explorer and pioneer)

1971. Famous Rhodesians (5th issue).
458 **84** 15c. multicoloured 40 70

85 Hoopoe

86 Porphyritic Granite

1971. Birds of Rhodesia (1st series). Multicoloured.
459 2c. Type **85** 50 20
460 2½c. Half-collared kingfisher (horiz) 50 10
461 5c. Golden-breasted bunting 70 20
462 7½c. Carmine bee eater . . . 80 20
463 8c. Red-eyed bulbul 80 30
464 25c. Senegal wattled plover (horiz) . . . . 1·50 1·50
See also Nos. 537/42.

1971. "Granite 71" Geological Symposium. Multicoloured.
465 2½c. Type **86** 35 10
466 7½c. Muscovite mica seen through microscope . . . 50 20
467 15c. Granite seen through microscope 90 55
468 25c. Geological map of Rhodesia . . . . 90 1·50

87 Dr. Robert Moffat (missionary)

1972. Famous Rhodesians (6th issue).
469 **87** 13c. multicoloured 50 75

88 Bird ("Be Airwise")

1972. "Prevent Pollution". Multicoloured.
470 2½c. Type **88** 15 10
471 3½c. Antelope ("Be Countrywise") 15 20
472 7c. Fish ("Be Waterwise") . . 15 30
473 13c. City ("Be Citywise") . . 20 55

1972. "Rhophil '72". Nos. 439, 441 and 442 with commemorative inscr in margins.
MS474 1c. multicoloured . . . . 1·10 2·00
MS475 2½c. multicoloured . . . 1·10 2·00
MS476 3½c. multicoloured . . . 1·10 2·00
MS474/6 Set of 3 sheets . . . . 3·00 5·50

89 "The Three Kings"

91 W.M.O. Emblem

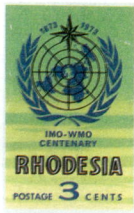

90 Dr. David Livingstone

1972. Christmas.
477 **89** 2c. multicoloured 10 10
478 5c. multicoloured 15 20
479 13c. multicoloured 30 55

1973. Famous Rhodesians (7th issue).
480 **90** 14c. multicoloured 50 75

1973. Centenary of I.M.O./W.M.O.
481 **91** 3c. multicoloured 10 10
482 14c. multicoloured 30 15
483 25c. multicoloured 40 75

92 Arms of Rhodesia

1973. 50th Anniv of Responsible Government.
484 **92** 2½c. multicoloured 10 10
485 4c. multicoloured 15 15
486 7½c. multicoloured 20 25
487 14c. multicoloured . . . . 35 1·25

93 George Pauling (construction engineer)

1974. Famous Rhodesians (8th issue).
488 **93** 14c. multicoloured . . . . 50 1·25

94 Greater Kudu

95 Thunbergia

96 "Charaxes varanes"

1974. Multicoloured. (a) Antelopes.
489 1c. Type **94** 10 10
490 2½c. Eland 75 10
491 3c. Roan antelope 10 10
492 4c. Reedbuck 20 10
493 5c. Bushbuck 20 60

(b) Wild Flowers.
494 6c. Type **95** 20 10
495 7½c. Flame lily 50 20
496 8c. As 7½c. 20 10
497 10c. Devil thorn 20 10
498 12c. Hibiscus . . . . 40 2·00
499 12½c. Pink sabi star . . . . 1·00 35
500 14c. Wild pimpernel . . . . 1·00 35
501 15c. As 12½c. 40 75
502 16c. As 14c. 40 30

(c) Butterflies.
503 20c. Type **96** . . . . 1·00 35
504 24c. "Precis hierta" 40 40
505 25c. As 24c. . . . . 1·50 1·50
506 50c. "Colotis regina" 40 60
507 $1 "Graphium antheus" . . . 40 60
508 $2 "Hamanumida daedalus" 40 75

97 Collecting Mail

1974. Centenary of U.P.U. Multicoloured.
509 3c. Type **97** 15 10
510 4c. Sorting mail 15 10
511 7½c. Mail delivery 20 20
512 14c. Weighing parcel 30 90

98 Thomas Baines (artist)

1975. Famous Rhodesians (9th issue).
513 **98** 14c. multicoloured 50 60

99 "Euphorbia confinalis"

100 Prevention of Head Injuries

1975. Int Succulent Congress, Salisbury ("Aloe '75"). Multicoloured.
514 2½c. Type **99** 10 10
515 3c. "Aloe excelsa" 10 10
516 4c. "Hoodia lugardii" 10 10
517 7½c. "Aloe orthlopha" . . . 15 10
518 14c. "Aloe musapana" . . . 30 10
519 25c. "Aloe saponaria" . . . 50 2·00

1975. Occupational Safety. Multicoloured.
520 2½c. Type **100** 10 10
521 4c. Bandaged hand and gloved hand 15 10
522 7½c. Broken glass and eye . . 15 15
523 14c. Blind man and welder with protective mask . . . 20 55

101 Telephones, 1876 and 1976

103 Roan Antelope

1976. Telephone Centenary.
524 **101** 3c. grey and blue 10 10
525 – 14c. black and brown . . 20 55
DESIGN: 14c. Alexander Graham Bell.

1976. Nos. 495, 500 and 505 surch.
526 8c. on 7½c. multicoloured . . 15 15
527 16c. on 14c. multicoloured . . 15 15
528 24c. on 25c. multicoloured . . 20 60

1976. Vulnerable Wildlife. Multicoloured.
529 4c. Type **103** 10 10
530 6c. Brown hyena 15 60
531 8c. Hunting dog 15 10
532 16c. Cheetah 20 35

104 Msasa

105 Garden Bulbul ("Blackeyed-Bulbul")

1976. Trees of Rhodesia. Multicoloured.
533 4c. Type **104** 10 10
534 6c. Red mahogany 10 10
535 8c. Mukwa 15 10
536 16c. Rhodesian teak 20 55

1977. Birds of Rhodesia (2nd series). Mult.
537 3c. Type **105** 15 10
538 4c. Yellow-mantled whydah ("Yellow-mantled Wydah") 15 10
539 6c. Cape longclaw ("Orange throated longclaw") . . . 20 60
540 8c. Magpie shrike ("Eastern Long-tailed Shrike") . . . 20 35
541 16c. Lesser blue-eared glossy starling ("Lesser Blue-eared Starling") 25 60
542 24c. Green wood hoopoe ("Red-billed Wood hoopoe") . . . . 30 1·10

106 "Lake Kyle" (Joan Evans)

107 Virgin and Child

1977. Landscape Paintings. Multicoloured.
543 3c. Type **106** 10 10
544 4c. "Chimanimani Mountains" (Joan Evans) 10 10
545 6c. "Rocks near Bonsor Reef" (Alice Balfour) . . . 10 30
546 8c. "A Dwala near Devil's Pass" (Alice Balfour) . . . 10 10
547 16c. "Zimbabwe" (Alice Balfour) 15 30
548 24c. "Victoria Falls" (Thomas Baines) 25 60

1977. Christmas.
549 **107** 3c. multicoloured 10 10
550 6c. multicoloured 10 20
551 8c. multicoloured 10 10
552 16c. multicoloured 15 30

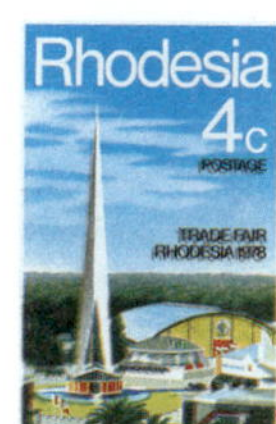

108 Fair Spire

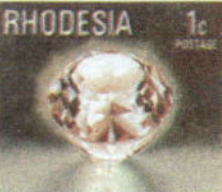

109 Morganite

1978. Trade Fair Rhodesia, Bulawayo. Multicoloured.
553 4c. Type **108** 10 10
554 8c. Fair Spire (different) . . . 15 25

1978. Gemstones, Wild Animals and Waterfalls. Multicoloured.
555 1c. Type **109** 10 10
556 3c. Amethyst 10 10
557 4c. Garnet 10 10
558 5c. Citrine 10 10
559 7c. Blue topaz 10 10
560 9c. White rhinoceros 15 10
561 11c. Lion 10 20
562 13c. Warthog . . . . 10 1·25
563 15c. Giraffe 15 30
564 17c. Common zebra 15 10
565 21c. Odzani Falls 15 40
566 25c. Goba Falls 15 15
567 30c. Inyangombi Falls . . . 15 15
568 $1 Bridal Veil Falls 20 35
569 $2 Victoria Falls 30 60
Nos. 560/4 are 26 × 23 mm, and Nos. 565/9 32 × 27 mm.

112 Wright Flyer I

1978. 75th Anniv of Powered Flight. Mult.
570 4c. Type **112** 10 10
571 5c. Bleriot XI 10 10
572 7c. Vickers Vimy "Silver Queen II" 10 10
573 9c. Armstrong Whitworth A.W.15 Atalanta 10 10
574 17c. Vickers Viking 1B "Zambezi" 10 10
575 25c. Boeing 720B 15 50

POSTAGE DUE STAMPS

D 2

D 3 Zimbabwe Bird (soapstone sculpture)

1965. Roul.

D 8 D 2 1d. red . . . 50 12·00
D 9 2d. blue . . . 40 8·00
D10 4d. green . . . 50 8·00
D11 6d. plum . . . 50 6·00

1966.

D12 D 3 1d. red . . . 60 3·25
D13 2d. blue . . . 75 1·50
D14 4d. green . . . 75 4·00
D15 6d. violet . . . 75 1·50
D16 1s. brown . . . 75 1·50
D17 2s. black . . . 1·00 4·75

1970. Decimal Currency. As Type D 3 but larger (26×22½ mm).

D18 D 3 1c. green . . . 75 1·25
D19 2c. blue . . . 75 60
D20 5c. violet . . . 1·75 1·75
D21 6c. yellow . . . 3·50 4·00
D22 10c. red . . . 1·75 4·00

RHODESIA AND NYASALAND Pt. 1

Stamps for the Central African Federation of Northern and Southern Rhodesia and Nyasaland Protectorate. The stamps of the Federation were withdrawn on 19 February 1964 when all three constituent territories had resumed issuing their own stamps.

12 pence = 1 shilling;
20 shillings = 1 pound.

1 Queen Elizabeth II

2 Queen Elizabeth II

1954.

1 1 ½d. orange . . . 15 10
2 1d. blue . . . 15 10
3 2d. green . . . 15 10
3a 2½d. ochre . . . 4·25 10
4 3d. red . . . 20 10
5 4d. brown . . . 60 20
6 4½d. green . . . 30 1·25
7 6d. purple . . . 2·25 10
8 9d. violet . . . 2·00 1·00
9 1s. grey . . . 2·00 10
10 2 1s.3d. red and blue . . . 3·00 25
11 2s. blue and brown . . . 7·50 3·00
12 2s.6d. black and red . . . 6·00 2·00
13 5s. violet and olive . . . 17·00 6·00
14 – 10s. turquoise and orange . . . 19·00 7·50
15 – £1 olive and lake . . . 30·00 26·00

The 10s. and £1 are as Type 2 but larger (31×17 mm) and have the name at top and foliage on either side of portrait.

4 De Havilland Comet 1 over Victoria Falls

5 Livingstone and Victoria Falls

1955. Cent of Discovery of Victoria Falls.

16 4 3d. blue and turquoise . . . 55 30
17 5 1s. purple and blue . . . 55 70

6 Tea Picking

11 Lake Bangweulu

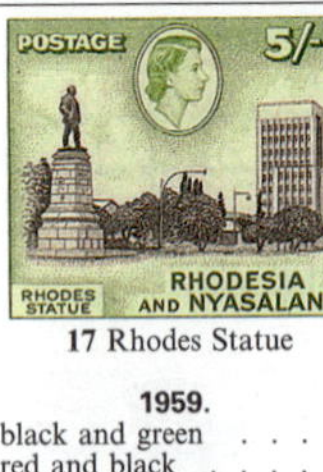

17 Rhodes Statue

1959.

18 6 ½d. black and green . . . 70 1·00
19 – 1d. red and black . . . 15 10
20 – 2d. violet and brown . . . 2·00 50
21 – 2½d. purple and blue . . . 1·75 50
22 – 3d. black and blue . . . 40 10
23 11 4d. purple and green . . . 1·25 10
24 – 6d. blue and green . . . 2·00 10
24a – 9d. brown and violet . . . 8·00 2·75
25 – 1s. green and blue . . . 1·25 10
26 – 1s.3d. green and brown . . . 3·00 10
27 – 2s. green and red . . . 3·25 60
28 – 2s.6d. blue and brown . . . 4·50 30
29 17 5s. brown and green . . . 9·00 2·25
30 – 10s. brown and red . . . 25·00 17·00
31 – £1 black and violet . . . 45·00 55·00

DESIGNS—VERT (as Type **6**): 1d. V.H.F. mast; 2d. Copper mining; 2½d. Fairbridge Memorial. (As Type **11**): 6d. Eastern Cataract, Victoria Falls. HORIZ (as Type **6**): 3d. Rhodes's grave. (As Type **11**): 9d. Rhodesian railway trains; 1s. Tobacco; 1s.3d. Lake Nyasa; 2s. Chirundu Bridge; 2s.6d. Salisbury Airport. (As Type **17**): 10s. Mlanje; £1 Federal Coat of Arms.

20 Kariba Gorge, 1955

1960. Opening of Kariba Hydro-electric Scheme.

32 20 3d. green and orange . . . 70 10
33 – 6d. brown and bistre . . . 70 20
34 – 1s. blue and green . . . 2·50 4·00
35 – 1s.3d. blue and brown . . . 2·50 2·75
36 – 2s.6d. purple and red . . . 3·50 8·00
37 – 5s. violet and turquoise . . . 8·00 11·00

DESIGNS: 6d. 330 k.V. power lines; 1s. Barrage wall; 1s.3d. Barrage and lake; 2s.6d. Interior of power station; 5s. Queen Mother and barrage wall (inscr "ROYAL OPENING").

26 Miner drilling

1961. 7th Commonwealth Mining and Metallurgical Congress.

38 26 6d. green and brown . . . 50 20
39 – 1s.3d. black and blue . . . 50 80

DESIGN: 1s.3d. Surface installations, Nchanga Mine.

28 De Havilland Hercules "City of Basra" on Rhodesian Airstrip

1962. 30th Anniv of 1st London–Rhodesian Airmail Service.

40 28 6d. green and red . . . 35 25
41 – 1s.3d. blue, black and yellow . . . 1·50 50
42 – 2s.6d. red and violet . . . 4·00 5·00

DESIGNS: 1s.3d. Short S.23 flying boat "Canopus" taking off from Zambesi; 2s.6d. Hawker Siddeley Comet 4 at Salisbury Airport.

31 Tobacco Plant

1963. World Tobacco Congress, Salisbury.

43 31 3d. green and olive . . . 30 10
44 – 6d. green, brown and blue . . . 40 35
45 – 1s.3d. brown and blue . . . 60 45
46 – 2s.6d. yellow and brown . . . 1·00 2·75

DESIGNS: 6d. Tobacco field; 1s.3d. Auction floor; 2s.6d. Cured tobacco.

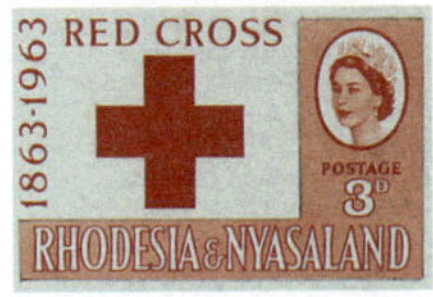

35

1963. Centenary of Red Cross.

47 35 3d. red . . . 1·00 10

36 African "Round Table" Emblem

1963. World Council of Young Men's Service Clubs, Salisbury.

48 36 6d. black, gold and green . . . 50 1·50
49 1s.3d. multicoloured . . . 50 1·00

POSTAGE DUE STAMPS

D 1

1961.

D1 D 1 1d. red . . . 3·75 5·50
D2 2d. blue . . . 3·00 3·00
D3 4d. green . . . 3·00 9·50
D4 6d. purple . . . 4·50 7·50

RIAU-LINGGA ARCHIPELAGO Pt. 21

A group of islands E of Sumatra and S of Singapore. Part of Indonesia.

100 cents or sen = 1 rupiah.

1954. Optd **RIAU**. (a) On stamps of Indonesia.

1 96 5s. red . . . 28·00 19·00
2 7½s. green . . . 20 35
3 10s. blue . . . 32·00 40·00
4 15s. violet . . . 80 80
5 20s. red . . . 95 1·10
6 25s. green . . . 65·00 22·00
7 97 30s. red . . . 2·40 1·60
8 35s. violet . . . 20 35
9 40s. green . . . 20 35
10 45s. purple . . . 25 35
11 50s. brown . . . £190 32·00
12 98 60s. brown . . . 20 35
13 98 70s. grey . . . 60 65
14 75s. blue . . . 3·25 1·60
15 80s. purple . . . 50 1·90
16 90s. green . . . 50 1·10

(b) On Netherlands Indies Nos. 566/71.

17 – 1r. violet . . . 6·25 1·60
18 – 2r. green . . . 65 1·90
19 – 3r. purple . . . 95 1·90
20 – 5r. brown . . . 95 1·90
21 – 10r. black . . . 1·25 2·40
22 – 25r. brown . . . 1·25 2·40

1958. Stamps of Indonesia optd **RIAU**.

26 115 5s. blue . . . 20 35
27 10s. brown (No. 714) . . . 40 35
28 15s. purple (No. 715) . . . 40 1·50
29 – 20s. green (No. 716) . . . 40 35
30 – 25s. brown (No. 717) . . . 40 35
31 – 30s. orange (No. 718) . . . 40 35
32 – 50s. brown (No. 722) . . . 40 35

1960. Stamps of Indonesia optd **RIAU**.

33 99 1r.25 orange . . . 95 3·25
34 1r.50 brown . . . 95 3·25
35 2r.50 brown . . . 1·25 4·75
36 4r. green . . . 25 4·75
37 6r. mauve . . . 25 4·75
38 15r. stone . . . 25 4·75
39 20r. purple . . . 25 6·25
40 40r. green . . . 25 7·00
41 50r. violet . . . 35 7·50

RIO DE ORO Pt. 9

A Spanish territory on the West Coast of North Africa, renamed Spanish Sahara in 1924.

100 centimos = 1 peseta.

1905. "Curly Head" key-type inscr "COLONIA DE RIO DE ORO".

1 Z 1c. green . . . 3·75 3·00
2 2c. red . . . 3·75 3·00
3 3c. black . . . 3·75 3·00
4 4c. brown . . . 3·75 3·00
5 5c. red . . . 3·75 3·00
6 10c. brown . . . 3·75 3·00
7 15c. brown . . . 3·75 3·00
8 25c. blue . . . 70·00 31·00
9 50c. green . . . 36·00 13·00
10 75c. violet . . . 36·00 18·00
11 1p. brown . . . 85·00 7·75
12 2p. orange . . . £110 48·00
13 3p. lilac . . . 50·00 18·00
14 4p. green . . . 50·00 18·00
15 5p. blue . . . 70·00 37·00
16 10p. red . . . £180 £120

1906. "Curly Head" key-type surch **HABILITADO PARA 15 CENTS** in circle.

17 Z 15c. on 25c. blue . . . £200 70·00

3

7

11

1907.

18 3 1c. purple . . . 3·00 2·40
19 2c. black . . . 3·00 2·40
20 3c. brown . . . 3·00 2·40
21 4c. red . . . 3·00 2·40
22 5c. brown . . . 3·00 2·40
23 10c. brown . . . 3·00 2·40
24 15c. blue . . . 3·00 2·40
25 25c. green . . . 7·50 2·40
26 50c. purple . . . 7·50 2·40
27 75c. brown . . . 7·50 2·40
28 1p. buff . . . 12·50 2·40
29 2p. lilac . . . 4·50 2·40
30 3p. green . . . 4·75 2·40
31 4p. blue . . . 7·00 4·50
32 5p. red . . . 7·00 4·50
33 10p. green . . . 7·00 11·00

1907. Nos. 9/10 surch **1907 10 Cens.**

34 Z 10c. on 50c. green . . . 75·00 29·00
35 10c. on 75c. violet . . . 55·00 29·00

1908. Nos. 12 and 26 surch **1908** and value.

36 Z 2c. on 2p. orange . . . 46·00 29·00
37 3 10c. on 50c. purple . . . 22·00 4·50

1908. Surch **HABILITADO PARA 15 CENTS** in circle.

38 3 15c. on 25c. green . . . 26·00 5·00
39 15c. on 75c. brown . . . 35·00 9·00
40 15c. on 1p. buff . . . 35·00 9·00
71 15c. on 3p. green . . . £140 25·00
72 15c. on 5p. red . . . 10·50 10·00

1908. Large Fiscal stamp inscr "TERRITORIOS ESPAÑOLES DEL AFRICA OCCIDENTAL" surch **HABILITADO PARA CORREOS RIO DE ORO 5 CENS.** Imperf.

45 5c. on 50c. green . . . 75·00 31·00

1909.

47 7 1c. orange . . . 65 50
48 2c. orange . . . 65 50
49 5c. green . . . 65 50
50 10c. red . . . 65 50
51 15c. green . . . 65 50
52 20c. purple . . . 1·90 85
53 25c. blue . . . 1·90 85
54 30c. red . . . 1·90 85
55 40c. brown . . . 1·90 85
56 50c. purple . . . 3·25 85
57 1p. brown . . . 4·50 4·00
58 4p. red . . . 5·50 5·75
59 10p. purple . . . 11·50 9·50

1910. Nos. 13/16 surch **1910** and value.

60 Z 10c. on 5p. blue . . . 15·00 13·50
62 10c. on 10p. red . . . 13·50 7·50
65 15c. on 3p. lilac . . . 13·50 7·50
66 15c. on 4p. green . . . 13·50 7·50

1911. Surch with value in figures and words.

67 3 2c. on 4p. blue . . . 10·50 9·00
68 5c. on 10p. green . . . 27·00 9·00
69 10c. on 2p. lilac . . . 14·00 9·50
70 10c. on 3p. green . . . £170 55·00

1912.

73 11 1c. pink . . . 25 15
74 2c. lilac . . . 25 15
75 5c. green . . . 25 15
76 10c. red . . . 25 15
77 15c. brown . . . 25 15
78 20c. brown . . . 25 15
79 25c. blue . . . 25 15
80 30c. lilac . . . 25 15
81 40c. green . . . 25 15
82 50c. purple . . . 25 15
83 1p. red . . . 2·50 65
84 4p. red . . . 5·50 3·25
85 10p. brown . . . 8·50 5·50

12

14

15

1914.

86 12 1c. brown . . . 30 15
87 2c. purple . . . 30 15
88 5c. green . . . 30 15
89 10c. red . . . 30 15
90 15c. red . . . 30 15
91 20c. red . . . 30 15

92		25c. blue	30	15
93		30c. green	30	15
94		40c. orange	30	15
95		50c. brown	30	15
96		1p. lilac	2·50	3·00
97		4p. red	7·00	3·00
98		10p. violet	8·75	8·75

1917. Nos. 73/85 optd **1917**.

99	11	1c. pink	11·00	1·30
100		2c. lilac	11·00	1·30
101		5c. green	2·50	1·30
102		10c. red	2·50	1·30
103		15c. brown	2·50	1·30
104		20c. brown	2·50	1·30
105		25c. blue	2·50	1·30
106		30c. lilac	2·50	1·30
107		40c. green	2·50	1·30
108		50c. purple	2·50	1·30
109		1p. red	14·00	6·25
110		4p. red	19·00	8·00
111		10p. brown	33·00	14·00

1919.

112	14	1c. brown	80	45
113		2c. purple	80	45
114		5c. green	80	45
115		10c. red	80	45
116		15c. red	80	45
117		20c. orange	80	45
118		25c. blue	80	45
119		30c. green	80	45
120		40c. orange	80	45
121		50c. brown	80	45
122		1p. lilac	5·50	3·75
123		4p. red	9·50	7·00
124		10p. violet	14·00	10·50

1920.

125	15	1c. purple	70	45
126		2c. pink	70	45
127		5c. red	70	45
128		10c. purple	70	45
129		15c. brown	70	45
130		20c. green	70	45
131		25c. orange	70	45
132		30c. blue	4·50	4·50
133		40c. orange	2·50	1·70
134		50c. purple	2·50	1·70
135		1p. green	2·50	1·70
136		4p. red	4·75	4·00
137		10p. brown	11·50	10·50

1921. As Nos. 14/26 of La Aguera but inscr "RIO DE ORO".

138		1c. yellow	70	45
139		2c. brown	70	45
140		5c. green	70	45
141		10c. red	70	45
142		15c. green	70	45
143		20c. blue	70	45
144		25c. blue	70	45
145		30c. pink	1·30	1·30
146		40c. violet	1·30	1·30
147		50c. orange	1·30	1·30
148		1p. mauve	4·50	2·20
149		4p. purple	7·00	5·00
150		10p. brown	12·00	11·50

For later issues see **SPANISH SAHARA**.

RIO MUNI Pt. 9

A coastal settlement between Cameroun and Gabon, formerly using the stamps of Spanish Guinea. On 12 October 1968 it became independent and joined Fernando Poo to become Equatorial Guinea.

100 centimos = 1 peseta.

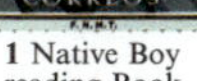

1 Native Boy reading Book

2 Cactus

1960.

1	1	25c. grey	15	15
2		50c. brown	15	15
3		75c. purple	15	15
4		1p. red	15	15
5		1p.50 green	15	15
6		2p. purple	15	15
7		3p. blue	30	15
8		5p. brown	80	20
9		10p. green	1·20	30

1960. Child Welfare Fund.

10	2	10c.+5c. purple	20	20
11	–	15c.+5c. brown	20	20
12	–	35c. green	20	20
13	2	80c. green	20	20

DESIGNS: 15c. Sprig with berries; 35c. Star-shaped flowers.

3 Bishop Juan de Ribera

4 Mandrill with Banana

1960. Stamp Day.

14	3	10c.+5c. red	20	20
15	–	20c.+5c. green	20	20
16	–	30c.+10c. brown	20	20
17	3	50c.+20c. brown	20	20

DESIGNS: 20c. Portrait of man (after Velazquez); 30c. Statue.

1961. Child Welfare. Inscr "PRO-INFANCIA 1961".

18	4	10c.+5c. red	20	20
19	–	25c.+10c. violet	20	20
20	4	80c.+20c. green	20	20

DESIGN—VERT: 25c. African elephant.

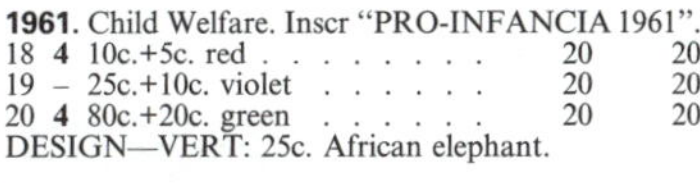

5

6 Statuette

1961. 25th Anniv of Gen. Franco as Head of State.

21	–	25c. grey	20	20
22	5	50c. brown	20	20
23	–	70c. green	20	20
24	5	1p. red	20	20

DESIGNS: 25c. Map; 70c. Government building.

1961. Stamp Day. Inscr "DIA DEL SELLO 1961".

25	6	10c.+5c. red	20	20
26	–	25c.+10c. purple	20	20
27	6	30c.+10c. brown	20	20
28	–	1p.+10c. orange	20	20

DESIGN: 25c., 1p. Figure holding offering.

7 Girl wearing Headdress

8 African Buffalo

1962. Child Welfare. Inscr "PRO-INFANCIA 1962".

29	7	25c. violet	20	20
30	–	50c. green	20	20
31	7	1p. brown	20	20

DESIGN: 50c. Native mask.

1962. Stamp Day. Inscr "DIA DEL SELLO 1962".

32	8	15c. green	20	20
33	–	35c. purple	20	20
34	8	1p. red	20	20

DESIGN—VERT: 35c. Gorilla.

9 Statuette

10 "Blessing"

1963. Seville Flood Relief.

35	9	50c. green	20	20
36		1p. brown	20	20

1963. Child Welfare. Inscr "PRO-INFANCIA 1963".

37	–	25c. violet	20	20
38	10	50c. green	20	20
39	–	1p. red	20	20

DESIGN: 25c., 1p. Priest.

11 Child at Prayer

12 Copal Flower

1963. "For Barcelona".

40	11	50c. green	20	20
41		1p. brown	20	20

1964. Stamp Day. Inscr "DIA DEL SELLO 1963".

42	12	25c. violet	20	20
43	–	50c. turquoise	20	20
44	12	1p. red	20	20

FLOWER—HORIZ: 50c. Cinchona blossom.

13 Giant Ground Pangolin

1964. Child Welfare. Inscr "PRO-INFANCIA 1964".

45	13	25c. violet	20	20
46	–	50c. green (Chameleon)	20	20
47	13	1p. brown	20	20

1964. Wild Life. As T **13** but without "PRO INFANCIA" inscription.

48		15c. brown	15	15
49		25c. violet	15	15
50		50c. green	15	15
51		70c. green	15	15
52		1p. brown	55	15
53		1p.50 green	55	15
54		3p. blue	1·20	20
55		5p. brown	3·00	35
56		10p. green	5·50	90

ANIMALS: 15, 70c., 3p. Crocodile; 25c., 1, 5p. Leopard; 50c., 1p.50, 10p. Black rhinoceros.

14 "Goliath" Frog

15 Woman

1964. Stamp Day.

57	14	50c. green	20	20
58	–	1p. red	20	20
59	14	1p.50 green	20	20

DESIGN—VERT: 1p. Helmeted guineafowl.

1965. 25th Anniv of End of Spanish Civil War.

60	15	50c. green	20	20
61	–	1p. red	20	20
62	–	1p.50 turquoise	20	20

DESIGNS: 1p. Nurse; 1p.50, Logging.

16 Goliath Beetle

1965. Child Welfare. Insects.

63	16	50c. green	20	20
64	–	1p. brown	20	20
65	16	1p.50 black	20	20

DESIGN: 1p. "Acridoxena hewaniana".

17 Leopard and Arms of Rio Muni

1965. Stamp Day.

66	–	50c. grey	20	20
67	17	1p. brown	25	25
68	–	2p.50 violet	1·70	1·00

DESIGN—VERT: 50c., 2p.50, Common pheasant.

18 African Elephant and Grey Parrot

1966. Child Welfare.

69	18	50c. brown	20	20
70		1p. lilac	20	20
71	–	1p.50 blue	20	20

DESIGN: 1p.50, African and lion.

19 Water Chevrotain

20 Floss Flowers

1966. Stamp Day.

72	19	10c. brown and ochre	20	20
73	–	40c. brown and yellow	20	20
74	19	1p.50 violet and red	20	20
75	–	4p. blue and green	20	20

DESIGN—VERT: 40c., 4p. Giant ground pangolin.

1967. Child Welfare.

76	20	10c. yellow, olive and green	20	20
77	–	40c. green, black and mauve	20	20
78	20	1p.50 red and blue	20	20
79	–	4p. black and green	20	20

DESIGNS: 40c., 4p. Ylang-ylang (flower).

21 Bush Pig

1967. Stamp Day.

80	21	1p. chestnut and brown	20	20
81	–	1p.50 brown and green	20	20
82	–	3p.50 brown and green	35	35

DESIGNS—VERT: 1p.50, Potto. HORIZ: 3p.50, African golden cat.

1968. Child Welfare. Signs of the Zodiac. As T **56a** of Spanish Sahara.

83		1p. mauve on yellow	20	20
84		1p.50 brown on pink	20	20
85		2p.50 violet on yellow	35	35

DESIGNS: 1p. Cancer (crab); 1p.50, Taurus (bull); 2p.50, Gemini (twins).

ROMAGNA Pt. 8

One of the Papal states, now part of Italy. Stamps issued prior to union with Sardinia in 1860.

100 bajocchi = 1 scudo.

1

1859. Imperf.

2	1	½b. black on buff	18·00	£225
3		1b. black on grey	18·00	£110
4		2b. black on buff	32·00	£120
5		3b. black on green	37·00	£250
6		4b. black on brown	£500	£120
7		5b. black on lilac	46·00	£300
8		6b. black on green	£250	£6000
9		8b. black on pink	£180	£1400
10		20b. black on green	£180	£2000

ROMANIA Pt. 3

A republic in S.E. Europe bordering on the Black Sea, originally a kingdom formed by the union of Moldavia and Wallachia.

1858. 40 parale = 1 piastre.
1867. 100 bani = 1 leu.
2005. 10000 leu (l.) = 1 new leu (l.)

MOLDAVIA

1

2

1858. Imperf.
1 **1** 27p. black on red £19000 £6000
2 54p. blue on green £8500 £2500
3 81p. blue on blue £19000 £21000
4 108p. blue on pink £11000 £6000

1858. Imperf.
12 **2** 5p. black £140
13 40p. blue £140 £150
14 80p. red £425 £225

ROMANIA

4

1862. Imperf.
29 **4** 3p. yellow . . . . 45·00 £140
30 6p. red . . . . 32·00 £110
31 30p. blue . . . . 37·00 40·00

5 Prince Alexander Cuza

6 Prince Carol

7 Prince Carol

1865. Imperf.
49a **5** 2p. orange . . . . 25·00 £160
46 5p. blue . . . . 25·00 £150
48 20p. red . . . . 19·00 24·00

1866. Imperf.
60 **6** 2p. black on yellow . . . . 15·00 50·00
61 5p. black on blue . . . . 30·00 £300
62 20p. black on red . . . . . 12·50 11·00

1868. Imperf.
71 **7** 2b. orange . . . . 24·00 17·00
72 3b. mauve . . . . 30·00 20·00
66c 4b. blue . . . . 35·00 24·00
67 18b. red . . . . £140 16·00

8

9

10

1869. Without beard. Imperf.
74 **8** 5b. orange . . . . 55·00 23·00
75 10b. blue . . . . 27·00 19·00
76 15b. red . . . . 27·00 17·00
77c 25b. blue and orange . . . 27·00 17·00
78 50b. red and blue . . . . . £120 25·00

1871. With beard. Imperf.
83 **9** 5b. red . . . . 27·00 18·00
84 10b. orange . . . . 37·00 20·00
99 10b. blue . . . . 35·00 25·00
86 15b. red . . . . £110 95·00
87 25b. brown . . . . 33·00 27·00
100 50b. red and blue £140 £160

1872. Perf.
93 **9** 5b. red . . . . 55·00 25·00
94 10b. blue . . . . 55·00 20·00
95 25b. brown . . . . 26·00 25·00

1872. Perf.
112 **10** 1½b. green . . . . 5·25 1·70
124 1½b. black . . . . 4·00 90
105 3b. green . . . . 21·00 2·20
125 3b. olive . . . . 9·50 5·00
106 5b. bistre . . . . 11·50 2·10
126 5b. green . . . . 3·25 1·00
107 10b. blue . . . . 10·00 2·40
127c 10b. red . . . . 8·50 1·00
115 15b. brown . . . . 45·00 5·00
128a 15b. red . . . . 30·00 7·00
110 25b. orange . . . . 70·00 9·00
130 25b. blue . . . . 95·00 8·75
116 30b. red . . . . £130 32·00
111 50b. red . . . . 65·00 24·00
131 50b. bistre . . . . 75·00 9·25

11 King Carol

12 King Carol

14 King Carol

1880.
146a **11** 15b. brown . . . . 9·50 95
147 25b. blue . . . . 12·50 1·20

1885. On white or coloured papers.
161 **12** 1½b. black . . . . 2·10 90
163 3b. green . . . . 3·00 90
165a 3b. violet . . . . 3·00 90
166 5b. green . . . . 3·00 90
168 10b. red . . . . 3·00 1·10
169 15b. brown . . . . 10·50 1·30
171 25b. blue . . . . 10·50 2·10
186 50b. brown . . . . 42·00 11·00

1890.
271 **14** 1½b. lake . . . . 1·10 45
272a 3b. mauve . . . . 1·20 80
273 5b. green . . . . 1·50 60
274 10b. red . . . . 7·25 65
255 15b. brown . . . . 11·50 1·90
306 25b. blue . . . . 7·50 3·50
307 50b. orange . . . . 19·00 9·25

15

17

19

1891. 25th Anniv of Reign.
300 **15** 1½b. lake . . . . 2·50 3·25
293 3b. mauve . . . . 2·50 3·25
294 5b. green . . . . 4·25 4·75
295 10b. red . . . . 4·25 4·75
303 15b. brown . . . . 4·25 4·00

1893. Various frames as T **17** and **19**.
316 1 BANI brown 80 60
426 1 BAN brown . . . . 1·10 55
317 1½b. black . . . . 1·10 40
533 3b. brown 85 30
319 5b. blue . . . . 1·10 60
534 5b. green . . . . 1·50 30
320 10b. green . . . . 1·50 60
535 10b. red . . . . 1·70 45
332 15b. pink . . . . 2·50 35
400 15b. black . . . . 1·60 50
430 15b. brown . . . . 1·60 45
545 15b. violet . . . . 2·10 50
322 25b. mauve . . . . 4·00 70
701 25b. blue 50 30
421 40b. green . . . . 9·00 85
324 50b. orange . . . . 10·50 90
325 1l. pink and brown . . . . 19·00 1·20
326 2l. brown and orange . . . . 19·00 2·00
See also Nos. 532 etc.

25 Four-in-hand Postal Coach

26 New Post Office, Bucharest

1903. Opening of New Post Office in 1901.
464 **25** 1b. brown . . . . 1·30 60
465 3b. red . . . . 2·10 95
466 5b. green . . . . 3·50 1·20
467 10b. red . . . . 3·75 1·60
468 15b. black . . . . 3·75 1·30
472 **26** 15b. black . . . . 2·40 2·00
469 **25** 25b. blue . . . . 11·00 7·00
473 **26** 25b. blue . . . . 6·25 3·50
470 **25** 40b. green . . . . 16·00 7·25
474 **26** 40b. green . . . . 8·75 5·00
471 **25** 50b. orange . . . . 21·00 9·25
475 **26** 50b. orange . . . . 8·75 5·00
476 1l. brown . . . . 8·75 5·00
477 2l. red . . . . 70·00 45·00
478 5l. lilac . . . . 90·00 50·00
See also No. 1275.

1905. Various frames as T **17** and **19**.
532 1 ban black 25 25
625b 1½b. yellow . . . . 1·40 1·10
703 40b. brown 90 55
705 50b. pink . . . . 1·00 60
432 1l. black and green . . . . 21·00 1·70
706 1l. green . . . . 1·50 40
433 2l. black and brown . . . . 16·00 2·10
707 2l. orange . . . . 2·30 60

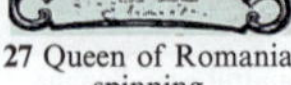
27 Queen of Romania spinning

28 Queen of Romania weaving

1906. Welfare Fund. Motto: "God guide our Hand".
481 **27** 3b.(+7) brown . . . . . . 2·50 2·50
482 5b.(+10) green . . . . . 2·50 2·50
483 10b.(+10) red . . . . . 9·50 7·75
484 15b.(+10) purple . . . . 9·00 4·50

1906. Welfare Fund. Motto: "Woman weaves the Future of the Country".
485 **28** 3b.(+7) brown . . . . . . 2·20 2·30
486 5b.(+10) green . . . . . 2·20 2·30
487 10b.(+10) red . . . . . 12·00 8·25
488 15b.(+10) lilac . . . . . 7·75 4·25

29 Queen of Romania nursing wounded Soldier

30

1906. Welfare Fund. Motto: "The Wounds dressed and the Tears wiped away".
489 **29** 3b.(+7) brown . . . . . . 2·20 2·30
490 5b.(+10) green . . . . . 2·20 2·30
491 10b.(+10) red . . . . . 12·00 9·00
492 15b.(+10) purple . . . . 7·75 5·75

1906. 25th Anniv of Kingdom.
493 **30** 1b. black and bistre . . . 30 30
494 3b. black and brown . . . 1·10 40
495 5b. black and green . . . 70 35
496 10b. black and red 70 35
497 15b. black and violet . . . 75 35
498 25b. black and blue . . . 9·00 4·75
499 40b. black and brown . . . 2·10 95
500 50b. black and brown . . . 2·10 95
501 1l. black and red . . . . 2·10 95
502 2l. black and orange . . . 2·10 95

31 Prince Carol at Battle of Calafat

32

1906. 40 Years' Rule of Prince and King. Dated "1906".
503 – 1b. black and bistre . . . 15 25
504 – 3b. black and brown . . . 30 25
505 **31** 5b. black and green . . . 65 25
506 – 10b. black and red . . . 30 45
507 – 15b. black and violet . . 30 45
508 – 25b. black and blue . . . 3·50 2·50
508a – 25b. black and green . . 4·50 5·50
509 – 40b. black and brown . . 50 65
510 – 50b. black and brown . . 60 65
511 – 1l. black and red 90 90
512 – 2l. black and orange . . . 1·20 1·30
DESIGNS—HORIZ: 1b. Prince Carol taking oath of allegiance in 1866; 3b. Prince in carriage; 10b. Meeting of Prince and Osman Pasha, 1878; 15b. Carol when Prince in 1866 and King in 1906; 25b. Romanian Army crossing Danube, 1877; 40b. Triumphal entry into Bucharest, 1878; 50b. Prince at head of Army in 1877; 1l. King Carol at Cathedral in 1896; 2l. King at shrine of S. Nicholas, 1904.

1906. Welfare Fund. Motto: "But Glory, Honour and Peace to All that do Good".
513 **32** 3b.(+7) brown, bistre and blue . . . . 1·40 1·30
514 5b.(+10) green, red and bistre . . . . 1·40 1·30
515 10b.(+10) red, bistre and blue . . . . 2·75 2·50
516 15b.(+10) violet, bistre and blue . . . . 8·50 4·00

33 Peasant ploughing and Angel

1906. Jubilee Exhibition, Bucharest.
517 **33** 5b. black and green . . . 2·75 85
518 10b. black and red . . . . 2·75 85
519 – 15b. black and violet . . . 4·00 1·40
520 – 25b. black and blue . . . 4·00 1·40
521 – 30b. brown and red . . . 4·75 1·40
522 – 40b. brown and green . . . 6·25 1·70
523 – 50b. black and orange . . 5·50 2·00
524 – 75b. sepia and brown . . . 5·50 2·00
525 – 1l.50 brown and mauve . . 50·00 25·00
526 – 2l.50 brown and yellow . . 21·00 14·50
527 – 3l. brown and orange . . . 16·00 14·00
DESIGNS—HORIZ: 15, 25b. Exhibition Building. VERT: 30, 40b. Farmhouse; 50, 75b. (different), Royal Family pavilion; 1l.50, 2l.50, King Carol on horseback; 3l. Queen Elizabeth (Carmen Sylva).

34 Princess Maria and her Children receiving Poor Family conducted by an Angel

1907. Welfare Fund.
528 **34** 3b.(+7) brown . . . . . . 4·75 2·75
529 5b.(+10) brown and green 2·75 1·40
530 10b.(+10) brown and red 2·30 1·40
531 15b.(+10) brown and blue 1·70 1·50

35

37

1908.
575 **35** 5b. green . . . . 1·40 30
562 10b. red 35 10
577 15b. violet . . . . 7·75 2·10
564 25b. blue 90 15
579 40b. green 55 15
702 40b. brown . . . . 3·50 1·60
566 50b. orange 55 15
705 50b. red 75 45
581 1l. brown . . . . 1·60 30
582 2l. red . . . . 7·75 2·40

1908.
583 **37** 1b. black 25 10
590 3b. brown 70 15
585 5b. green 25 15
592 10b. red 45 15
599 15b. violet . . . . 11·50 8·50
594 15b. olive 60 15
692 15b. brown 65 40

38

39 Troops crossing Danube

1913. Acquisition of Southern Dobruja.
626 – 1b. black 50 30
627 **38** 3b. brown and grey . . . 1·50 60
628 **39** 5b. black and green . . . 1·20 20
629 – 10b. black and orange . . 85 20
630 – 15b. violet and brown . . 1·10 55
631 – 25b. brown and blue . . . 1·50 85
632 **39** 40b. red and brown . . . 3·00 1·30
633 **38** 50b. blue and yellow . . . 3·75 3·00
634 1l. brown and blue . . . . 9·00 7·75
635 2l. red and red . . . . . 12·00 10·50
DESIGNS—VERT (As Type **38**): 1b. "Dobruja" holding flag. HORIZ (As Type **39**): 10b. Town of Constanza; 25b. Church and School in Dobruja. (24×16 mm): 15b. Mircea the Great and King Carol.

1918. Surch **25. BANI**.
657 **37** 25b. on 1b. black 80 80

1918. Optd **1918**.
662 **37** 5b. green 50 30
663 10b. red 50 35

TRANSYLVANIA

The Eastern portion of Hungary. Union with Romania proclaimed in December 1918 and the final frontiers settled by the Treaty of Trianon on 4 June 1920.

The following issues for Transylvania (Nos. 747/858) were valid throughout Romania.

(42)

(43)

(The "F" stands for King Ferdinand and "P.T.T." for Posts Telegraphs and Telephones).

The values "BANI", "LEU" or "LEI" appear above or below the monogram.

A. Issues for Cluj (Kolozsvar or Klausenburg).

1919. Various stamps of Hungary optd as T **42**.

(a) Flood Relief Charity stamps of 1913.

747 **7** 1l. on 1f. grey . . . . . . 20·00 18·00
748 1l. on 2f. yellow . . . . . . £100 80·00
749 1l. on 3f. orange . . . . . 48·00 42·00
750 1l. on 5f. green . . . . . . 2·10 1·60
751 1l. on 10f. red . . . . . . 2·10 1·60
752 1l. on 12f. lilac on yellow 7·75 5·75
753 1l. on 16f. green . . . . . 4·25 3·00
754 1l. on 25f. blue . . . . . . 48·00 42·00
755 1l. on 35f. purple . . . . . 4·25 3·00
756 **8** 1l. on 1k. red . . . . 55·00 50·00

(b) War Charity stamps of 1916.

757 **20** 10(+2) b. red 30 20
758 – 15(+2) b. violet 30 20
759 **22** 40(+2) b. lake 40 30

(c) Harvesters and Parliament Types.

760 **18** 2b. brown 15 20
761 3b. red 30 20
762 5b. green 30 20
763 6b. blue 30 20
764 10b. red £140 £100
765 15b. violet (No. 244) . . . 5·00 3·75
766 15b. violet 15 10
767 25b. blue 15 10
768 35b. brown 15 10
769 40b. olive 15 10
770 **19** 50b. purple 30 20
771 75b. blue 40 30
772 80b. green 40 30
773 1l. lake 40 30
774 2l. brown 55 40
775 3l. grey and violet . . . . 3·50 2·50
776 5l. brown . . . . 2·75 2·10
777 10l. lilac and brown . . . 3·50 2·50

(d) Charles and Zita stamps.

778 **27** 10b. red . . . . 28·00 21·00
779 15b. violet . . . . 10·50 7·75
780 20b. brown 15 10
781 25b. blue 70 50
782 **28** 40b. green 30 20

B. Issues for Oradea (Nagyvarad or Grosswardein).

1919. Various stamps of Hungary optd as T **43**. (a) "Turul" Type.

794 **7** 2b. yellow . . . . 5·50 4·25
795 3b. orange . . . . 9·75 7·25
796 6b. drab 70 50
797 16b. green . . . . 17·00 12·50
798 50b. lake on blue 95 75
799 70b. brown and green . . . 18·00 16·00

(b) Flood Relief Charity stamps of 1913.

800 **7** 1l. on 1f. grey 95 75
801 1l. on 2f. yellow . . . . . . 4·25 3·00
802 1l. on 3f. orange . . . . . 1·40 1·00
803 1l. on 5l. green 30 20
804 1l. on 6f. drab 95 75
805 1l. on 10f. red 30 20
806 1l. on 12f. lilac on yellow 49·00 45·00
807 1l. on 16f. green . . . . . 1·40 1·00
808 1l. on 20f. brown . . . . . 6·25 4·75
809 1l. on 25f. blue . . . . . . 4·25 3·00
810 1l. on 35f. purple . . . . . 4·25 3·00

(c) War Charity stamp of 1915.

811 **7** 5+2b. green (No. 173) . . . 7·50 7·75

(d) War Charity stamps of 1916.

812 **20** 10(+2) b. red 30 20
813 – 15(+2) b. violet 15 10
814 **22** 40(+2) b. lake 40 30

(e) Harvesters and Parliament Types.

815 **18** 2b. brown 15 10
816 3b. red 15 10
817 5b. green 30 20
818 6b. blue 85 60
819 10b. red . . . . 1·40 1·00
820 15b. violet (No. 244) . . . £120 £100
821 15b. violet 15 10
822 20b. brown . . . . 12·50 9·25
823 25b. blue 30 20
824 35b. brown 30 20
825 40b. olive 30 20
826 **19** 50b. purple 30 20
827 75b. blue 40 30
828 80b. green 40 30
829 1l. lake 40 30
830 2l. brown 55 40
831 3l. grey and violet . . . . 3·50 2·50
832 5l. brown . . . . 2·75 2·10
833 10l. lilac and brown . . . 3·50 2·50

(f) Charles and Zita stamps.

834 **27** 10b. red . . . . 2·75 2·10
835 20b. brown 15 10
836 25b. blue 40 30
837 40b. green 70 50

The following (Nos. 838/58) are also optd **KOZTARSASAG**.

(g) Harvesters and Parliament Types.

838 **18** 2b. brown . . . . 1·70 1·20
839 3b. red 40 30
840 4b. grey 30 20
841 5b. green 40 30
842 6b. blue . . . . 2·10 1·60
843 10b. red . . . . 15·00 12·50
844 20b. brown . . . . 1·70 1·20
845 40b. olive 40 30
846 **19** 1l. lake 30 20
847 3l. grey and violet . . . . 1·10 85
848 5l. brown . . . . 4·75 3·75

(h) Charles and Zita stamps.

849 **27** 10b. red £120 £130
850 20b. brown . . . . 2·75 2·10
851 25b. blue 55 40
852 **28** 50b. purple 30 20

(k) Harvesters and Parliament Types inscr "MAGYAR POSTA".

853 **18** 5b. green 15 10
854 20b. red 15 10
855 20b. brown 15 10
856 25b. blue 70 50
857 40b. olive 95 75
858 **19** 5l. brown . . . . 8·25 6·25

(**44**) King Ferdinand's Monogram — **45** King Ferdinand — **46** King Ferdinand

1919. Optd with T **44**.

873 **37** 1b. black 05 25
874 5b. green 35 50
878a 10b. red 10 15

1920.

891 **45** 1b. black 10 15
892 5b. green 10 15
893 10b. red 10 15
882 15b. brown 45 25
895 25b. blue 30 30
896 25b. brown 30 30
910 40b. brown 65 20
898 50b. pink 30 15
887 1l. green 65 20
900 1l. red 40 30
889 2l. orange 55 30
902 2l. blue 80 25
903 2l. red . . . . 2·20 1·30

1922.

923 **46** 3b. black 20 10
924 5b. black 10 10
925 10b. green 15 10
926 25b. brown 25 10
927 25b. red 30 10
928 30b. violet 30 10
929 50b. yellow 15 10
930 60b. green . . . . 1·40 50
931 1l. violet 35 10
932 2l. red . . . . 1·80 20
933a 2l. green . . . . 1·10 10
934 3l. blue . . . . 4·50 65
935a 3l. brown . . . . 4·50 60
937 3l. red . . . . 1·10 10
936a 3l. pink . . . . 7·00 1·30
938 5l. green . . . . 2·75 65
939b 5l. brown 75 10
940 6l. blue . . . . 4·50 85
941 6l. red . . . . 8·25 2·50
942 6l. olive . . . . 4·50 60
943 7l.50 blue . . . . 3·75 35
944 10l. blue . . . . 3·75 30

47 Cathedral of Alba Julia — **48** King Ferdinand

49 State Arms — **51** Michael the Brave and King Ferdinand

1922. Coronation.

1032 **47** 5b. black 40 25
1033 **48** 25b. brown 70 30
1034 **49** 50b. green 70 65
1035 – 1l. olive 70 45
1036 **51** 2l. red 80 50
1037 – 3l. blue . . . . 2·75 1·10
1050 – 6l. violet . . . . 9·25 5·75

DESIGNS—As Type **48**: 1l. Queen Marie as a nurse; 3l. Portrait of King but rectangular frame. Larger (21 × 33 mm): 6l. Queen Marie in coronation robes.

54 King Ferdinand — **55** Map of Romania

1926. King's 60th Birthday. Imperf or perf.

1051 **54** 10b. green 40 30
1052 25b. orange 40 30
1053 50b. brown 40 30
1054 1l. violet 40 30
1055 2l. green 40 30
1056 3l. red 40 30
1057 5l. brown 40 30
1058 6l. olive 40 30
1059 9l. grey 40 30
1060 10l. blue 40 30

1927. 50th Anniv of Romanian Geographical Society.

1061 **55** 1+9l. violet . . . . 2·75 1·10
1062 – 2+8l. green . . . . 2·75 1·10
1063 – 3+7l. red . . . . 2·75 1·10
1064 – 5+5l. blue . . . . 2·75 1·20
1065 – 6+4l. olive . . . . 6·00 1·90

DESIGNS: 2l. Stephen the Great; 3l. Michael the Brave; 5l. Carol and Ferdinand; 6l. Adam Clisi Monument.

60 King Carol and King Ferdinand

1927. 50th Anniv of Independence.

1066 **60** 25b. red 40 10
1067 – 30b. black 30 20
1068 – 50b. green 40 20
1069 **60** 1l. blue 30 20
1070 – 2l. green 30 20
1071 – 3l. purple 30 25
1072 – 4l. brown 70 30
1073 – 4l.50 brown . . . . . . 2·00 1·20
1074 – 5l. brown 50 25
1075 – 6l. red . . . . 1·30 65
1076 **60** 7l.50 blue 50 25
1077 – 10l. blue . . . . 2·00 45

DESIGNS—HORIZ: 30b., 2, 3, 5l. King Ferdinand. VERT: 50b., 4l., 4l.50, 6l. King Ferdinand as in Type **60**.

63 King Michael — **64** King Michael

1928.

1080 **63** 25b. black 35 15
1081 30b. pink 65 15
1082 50b. olive 35 15

1928. (a) Size $18\frac{1}{2} \times 24\frac{1}{2}$ mm.

1083 **64** 1l. purple 45 15
1084 2l. green . . . . 1·00 15
1085 3l. red . . . . 1·00 15
1086 5l. brown . . . . 1·60 15
1087 7l.50 blue . . . . 6·75 65
1088 10l. blue . . . . 6·00 25

(b) Size 18 × 23 mm.

1129 **64** 1l. purple 85 15
1130 2l. green . . . . 1·00 20
1131 3l. red . . . . 2·10 15
1132 7l.50 blue . . . . 4·25 1·20
1133 10l. blue . . . . 16·00 6·25

65 Bessarabian Parliament House

1928. 10th Anniv of Annexation of Bessarabia.

1092 **65** 1l. green . . . . 1·40 45
1093 2l. brown . . . . 1·40 45
1094 – 3l. sepia . . . . 1·40 45
1095 – 5l. lake . . . . 1·70 55
1096 – 7l.50 blue . . . . 2·10 70
1097 – 10l. blue . . . . 3·25 1·50
1098 – 20l. violet . . . . 5·25 2·50

DESIGNS: 3, 5, 20l. Hotin Fortress; 7l.50, 10l. Fortress Cetatea Alba.

66 Bleriot SPAD 33 Biplane

1928. Air.

1099 **66** 1l. brown . . . . 6·25 4·00
1100 2l. blue . . . . 6·25 4·00
1101 5l. red . . . . 6·25 4·00

67 King Carol and King Michael

1928. 50th Anniv of Acquisition of Northern Dobruja.

1102 **67** 1l. green 55 40
1103 – 2l. brown 75 40
1104 **67** 3l. grey 85 40
1105 – 5l. mauve 85 40
1106 – 7l.50 blue . . . . 1·00 45
1107 – 10l. blue . . . . 4·25 1·10
1108 – 20l. red . . . . 5·25 1·30

DESIGNS: 2l. Constanza Harbour and Carol Lighthouse; 5l., 7l.50, Adam Clisi Monument; 10, 20l. Saligny Bridge over River Danube, Cernavoda.

68

69 The Union

1929. 10th Anniv of Union of Romania and Transylvania.

1109 **68** 1l. purple . . . . 1·40 95
1110 **69** 2l. green . . . . 1·40 95
1111 – 3l. brown . . . . 1·50 95
1112 – 4l. red . . . . 1·40 1·00
1113 – 5l. orange . . . . 1·80 1·10
1114 – 10l. blue . . . . 3·75 2·00

DESIGNS—HORIZ: 1l. Ferdinand I, Stephen the Great, Michael the Brave, Hunyadi and Brancoveanu; 10l. Ferdinand I. VERT: 2l. Union; 3l. Avram Jancu; 4l. King Michael the Brave; 5l. Bran Castle.

1930. Stamps of King Michael optd **8 IUNIE 1930** (Accession of Carol II).

1134 **63** 25b. black (postage) . . . 35 15
1135 30b. pink 55 15
1136 50b. olive 55 15
1142 **64** 1l. purple (No. 1129) . . 45 15
1143 2l. green (No. 1130) . . . 45 15
1144 3l. red (No. 1131) 55 15
1137 5l. brown 80 15
1140 7l.50 blue (No. 1087) . . 3·25 90
1145 7l.50 blue (No. 1132) . . 2·20 40
1138 10l. blue (No. 1088) . . . 4·50 1·00
1146 10l. blue (No. 1133) . . . 1·40 55

1147 **66** 1l. brown (air) . . . . . 12·00 6·00
1148 2l. blue . . . . 12·00 6·00
1149 5l. red . . . . 12·00 6·00

72 King Carol II — **73** King Carol II — **76** King Carol II

1930.

1172 **72** 25b. black 30 10
1173 50b. brown 70 30
1174 1l. violet 35 10
1175 2l. green 55 10
1176 **73** 3l. red . . . . 1·30 10
1177 4l. orange . . . . 1·40 10
1178 6l. red . . . . 1·60 10
1179 7l.50 blue . . . . 1·80 15
1180 – 10l. blue . . . . 3·50 10
1181 – 16l. green . . . . 8·50 15
1182 – 20l. yellow . . . . 9·25 45

DESIGN: 10l. to 20l. Portrait as Type **72**, but in plain circle, with "ROMANIA" at top.

1930. Air.

1183 **76** 1l. violet on blue . . . . 2·30 1·30
1184 2l. green on blue . . . . 2·75 1·50
1185 5l. brown on blue . . . . 5·25 2·30
1186 10l. blue on blue . . . . 9·25 4·75

77 Map of Romania — **78** Woman with Census Paper — **79** King Carol II

1930. National Census.

1187 **77** 1l. violet . . . . 1·00 35
1188 **78** 2l. green . . . . 1·40 40
1189 4l. orange . . . . 2·00 20
1190 6l. red . . . . 5·00 40

1931.

1191 **79** 30l. blue and olive . . . . 1·10 55
1192 50l. blue and red . . . . 1·50 1·00
1193 100l. blue and green . . . 3·50 1·80

80 King Carol II

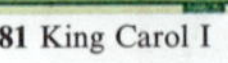

81 King Carol I   **82** Kings Carol II, Ferdinand I and Carol I

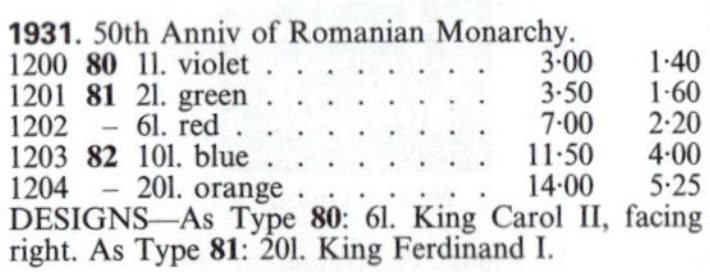

1931. 50th Anniv of Romanian Monarchy.
1200 **80** 1l. violet . . . . 3·00 1·40
1201 **81** 2l. green . . . . 3·50 1·60
1202 – 6l. red . . . . 7·00 2·20
1203 **82** 10l. blue . . . . 11·50 4·00
1204 – 20l. orange . . . . 14·00 5·25
DESIGNS—As Type **80**: 6l. King Carol II, facing right. As Type **81**: 20l. King Ferdinand I.

83 Naval Cadet Ship "Mircea"

1931. 50th Anniv of Romanian Navy.
1205 **83** 6l. red . . . . 4·75 2·75
1206 – 10l. blue . . . . 6·75 3·25
1207 – 12l. green . . . . 21·00 3·50
1208 – 20l. orange . . . . 10·50 6·75
DESIGNS: 10l. Monitors "Lascar Catargiu" and "Mihail Kogalniceaunu"; 16l. Monitor "Ardeal"; 20l. Destroyer "Regele Ferdinand".

84 Bayonet Attack

87 King Carol I

88 Infantry Attack   **89** King Ferdinand I

1931. Centenary of Romanian Army.
1209 **84** 25b. black . . . . 1·50 80
1210 – 50b. brown . . . . 2·20 1·10
1211 – 1l. violet . . . . 2·40 1·30
1212 **87** 2l. green . . . . 3·75 1·60
1213 **88** 3l. red . . . . 9·50 5·25
1214 **89** 7l.50 blue . . . . 10·00 11·00
1215 – 16l. green . . . . 12·00 4·50
DESIGNS: 50b. Infantryman, 1870, 20 × 33 mm: 1l. Infantry and drummer, 1830, 23 × 36 mm: 16l. King Carol II in uniform with plumed helmet, 21 × 34 mm.

91 Scouts' Encampment   **92a** Farman F.121 Jaribu

1931. Romanian Boy Scouts' Exhibition Fund.
1221 **91** 1l.+1l. red . . . . 3·00 2·50
1222 – 2l.+2l. green . . . . . . 3·50 3·50
1223 – 3l.+3l. blue . . . . 4·75 4·25
1224 – 4l.+4l. brown . . . . . . 6·75 5·25
1225 – 6l.+6l. brown . . . . . . 10·50 6·75
DESIGNS—VERT: As Type **91**: 3l. Recruiting, 22 × 37½ mm; 2l. Rescue work, 22 × 41½ mm; 4l. Prince Nicholas; 6l. King Carol II in scoutmaster's uniform.

1931. Air.
1226 **92a** 2l. green . . . . 1·30 65
1227 – 3l. red . . . . 1·60 1·00
1228 – 5l. brown . . . . 1·20 1·30
1229 – 10l. blue . . . . 4·25 2·75
1230 – 20l. violet . . . . 15·00 4·25
DESIGNS—As T **92a**: 3l. Farman F.300 and biplane; 5l. Farman F.60 Goliath; 10l. Fokker F.XII. 34 × 20 mm: 20l. Three aircraft flying in formation.

95 Kings Carol II, Ferdinand I and Carol I   **96** Alexander the Good

1931.
1231 **95** 16l. green . . . . 10·50 55

1932. 500th Death Centenary of Alexander I, Prince of Moldavia.
1232 **96** 6l. red . . . . 10·50 7·50

97 King Carol II

98 Semaphore Signaller

1932.
1248 **97** 10l. blue . . . . 11·00 35

1932. Boy Scouts' Jamboree Fund.
1256 – 25b.+25b. green . . . . . 3·25 1·90
1257 **98** 50b.+50b. blue . . . . . 3·25 2·75
1258 – 1l.+1l. green . . . . . . 4·00 3·50
1259 – 2l.+2l. red . . . . 7·25 5·25
1260 – 3l.+3l. blue . . . . 18·00 10·50
1261 – 6l.+6l. brown . . . . . . 19·00 15·00
DESIGNS—VERT: As Type **98**: 25b. Scouts in camp; 1l. On the trail; 3l. King Carol II; 6l. King Carol and King Michael when a Prince. HORIZ: 20 × 15 mm: 2l. Camp fire.

99 Cantacuzino and Gregory Chika

1932. 9th International Medical Congress.
1262 **99** 1l. red . . . . 4·75 5·25
1263 – 6l. orange . . . . 17·00 7·25
1264 – 10l. blue . . . . 30·00 12·50
DESIGNS: 6l. Congress in session; 10l. Hygeia and Aesculapius.

100 Tuberculosis Sanatorium

1932. Postal Employees' Fund.
1265 **100** 4l.+1l. green . . . . . 3·75 2·40
1266 – 6l.+1l. brown . . . . . . 5·25 2·75
1267 – 10l.+1l. blue . . . . . . 8·50 4·50
DESIGNS—VERT: 6l. War Memorial tablet. HORIZ: 10l. Convalescent home.

101 King Carol II

1932. International Philatelic Exhibition, Bucharest (EFIRO). Sheet 100 × 125 mm.
MS1267a **101** 6l.+5l. olive . . . 30·00 40·00

102 "Bull's head"   **103** Dolphins   **104** Arms

1932. 75th Anniv of First Moldavian Stamps. Imperf.
1268 **102** 25b. black 65 20
1269 – 1l. purple 80 40
1270 **103** 2l. green 95 50
1271 – 3l. red . . . . 1·20 65
1272 **104** 6l. red . . . . 1·30 85
1273 – 7l.50 blue . . . . 2·75 1·20
1274 – 10l. blue . . . . 5·75 2·00
DESIGNS—As Type **103**: 1l. Lion rampant and bridge; 3l. Eagle and castles; 7l.50, Eagle; 10l. Bull's head.

1932. 30th Anniv of Opening of G.P.O., Bucharest. As T **25** but smaller.
1275 16l. green . . . . 9·25 5·00

105 Ruins of Trajan's Bridge, Arms of Turnu-Severin and Towers of Severus

1933. Centenary of Founding of Turnu-Severin.
1279 **105** 25b. green 50 35
1280 – 50b. blue 80 45
1281 – 1l. brown . . . . 1·20 65
1282 – 2l. green . . . . 1·60 1·20
DESIGNS: 50b. Trajan at the completion of bridge over the Danube; 1l. Arrival of Prince Carol at Turnu-Severin; 2l. Trajan's Bridge.

107 Carmen Sylva and Carol I

1933. 50th Anniv of Construction of Pelesch Castle, Sinaia.
1283 **107** 1l. violet . . . . 1·60 1·20
1284 – 3l. brown . . . . 1·60 1·50
1285 – 6l. red . . . . 2·00 1·70
DESIGNS: 3l. Eagle and medallion portraits of Kings Carol I, Ferdinand I and Carol II; 6l. Pelesch Castle.

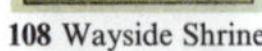

108 Wayside Shrine   **110** King Carol II

1934. Romanian Women's Exhibition. Inscr "L.N.F.R. MUNCA NOASTRA ROMANEASCA".
1286 **108** 1l.+1l. brown . . . . . 1·60 1·30
1287 – 2l.+1l. blue . . . . . . 2·20 1·70
1288 – 3l.+1l. green . . . . . . 2·50 2·20
DESIGNS—HORIZ: 2l. Weaver. VERT: 3l. Spinner.

1934. Mamaia Jamboree Fund. Nos. 1256/61 optd **MAMAIA 1934** and Arms of Constanza.
1289 – 26b.+25b. green . . . . . 3·50 3·00
1290 **98** 50b.+50b. blue . . . . . 4·00 3·25
1291 – 1l.+1l. green . . . . . . 5·25 4·75
1292 – 2l.+2l. red . . . . 7·50 6·50
1293 – 3l.+3l. blue . . . . 15·00 11·00
1294 – 6l.+6l. brown . . . . . . 17·00 14·00

1934.
1295 – 50b. brown 80 40
1296 **110** 2l. green 85 40
1297 4l. orange . . . . 2·10 45
1298 – 6l. lake . . . . 5·75 40
DESIGNS: 50b. Profile portrait of King Carol II in civilian clothes; 6l. King Carol in plumed helmet.

112 "Grapes for Health"

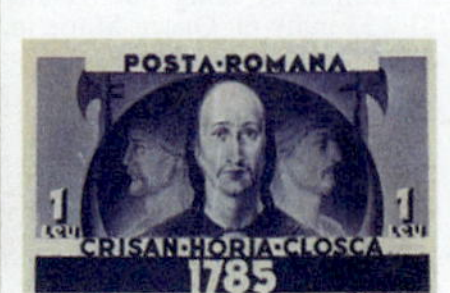

113 Crisan, Horia and Closca

1934. Bucharest Fruit Exhibition.
1299 **112** 1l. green . . . . 3·00 2·10
1300 – 2l. brown . . . . 3·00 2·10
DESIGN: 2l. Woman with fruit.

1935. 150th Anniv of Death of Three Romanian Martyrs. Portraits inscr "MARTIR AL NEAMULUI 1785".
1301 **113** 1l. violet 55 35
1302 – 2l. green (Crisan) 60 50
1303 – 6l. brown (Closca) . . . 1·60 1·00
1304 – 10l. blue (Horia) . . . . 2·40 2·10

114 Boy Scouts

1935. 5th Anniv of Accession of Carol II.
1305 – 25b. black . . . . 3·00 2·00
1306 – 1l. violet . . . . 4·50 3·50
1307 **114** 2l. green . . . . 5·75 5·25
1308 – 6l.+1l. brown . . . . . . 7·00 7·25
1309 – 10l.+2l. blue . . . . . . 14·50 17·00
DESIGNS—VERT: 25b. Scout saluting; 1l. Bugler; 6l. King Carol II. HORIZ: 10l. Colour party.

1935. Portraits as T **110** but additionally inscr "POSTA".
1310 – 25b. black 15 10
1311 – 50b. brown 15 10
1312 – 1l. violet 15 10
1313 **110** 2l. green 45 10
1315 – 3l. red 75 10
1316 – 3l. blue . . . . 1·10 20
1317 **110** 4l. orange . . . . 1·20 25
1318 – 5l. red . . . . 1·10 70
1319 – 6l. lake . . . . 1·50 25
1320 – 7l.50 blue . . . . 1·80 40
1321 – 8l. purple . . . . 2·10 50
1322 **110** 9l. blue . . . . 2·50 65
1323 – 10l. blue . . . . 1·10 20
1324 – 12l. blue . . . . 1·70 85
1325 – 15l. brown . . . . 1·70 60
1326 – 16l. green . . . . 2·30 35
1327 – 20l. orange . . . . 1·40 40
1328 – 24l. red . . . . 2·50 60
PORTRAITS—IN PROFILE: 25b., 15l. In naval uniform; 50b., 3, 8, 10l. In civilian clothes. THREE-QUARTER FACE: 1, 5, 7l.50, In civilian clothes. FULL FACE: 6, 12, 16, 20, 24l. In plumed helmet.

118 King Carol II

119 Oltenia Peasant Girl

1936. Bucharest Exhibition and 70th Anniv of Hohenzollern–Sigmaringen Dynasty.
1329 **118** 6l.+1l. red . . . . 1·00 65

1936. 6th Anniv of Accession of Carol II Inscr "O.E.T.R. 8 IUNIE 1936".
1330 **119** 50b.+50b. brown . . . . 1·10 55
1331 – 1l.+1l. violet 85 60
1332 – 2l.+1l. green 85 65
1333 – 3l.+1l. red . . . . 1·20 85
1334 – 4l.+2l. red . . . . 1·40 85
1335 – 6l.+3l. grey . . . . 1·70 1·00
1336 – 10l.+5l. blue . . . . . . 2·75 2·50
DESIGNS (costumes of following districts)—VERT: 1l. Banat; 4l. Gori; 6l. Neamz. HORIZ: 2l. Saliste; 3l. Hateg; 10l. Suceava (Bukovina).

120 Brasov Jamboree Badge

121 Liner "Transylvania"

1936. National Scout Jamboree, Brasov.
1337 – 1l.+1l. blue . . . . 3·00 3·25
1338 – 3l.+3l. grey . . . . 4·75 4·00
1339 **120** 6l.+6l. red . . . . 6·75 4·75
DESIGNS: 1l. National Scout Badge; 3l. Tenderfoot Badge.

1936. 1st Marine Exhibition, Bucharest.
1343 – 1l.+1l. violet . . . . . . 3·00 3·75
1344 – 3l.+2l. blue . . . . 4·50 3·00
1345 **121** 6l.+3l. red . . . . 5·50 4·25
DESIGNS: 1l. Submarine "Delfinul"; 3l. Naval cadet ship "Mircea".

1936. 18th Anniv of Annexation of Transylvania and 16th Anniv of Foundation of "Little Entente" Nos. 1320 and 1323 optd **CEHOSLOVACIA YUGOSLAVIA 1920-1936.**
1346 7l.50 blue . . . . 2·75 3·00
1347 10l. blue . . . . 2·30 3·00

123 Creanga's Birthplace

1937. Birth Centenary of Ion Creanga (poet).
1348 **123** 2l. green 80 55
1349 – 3l. red . . . . 1·10 65

1350 **123** 4l. violet . . . . 1·60 85
1351 – 6l. brown . . . . 2·75 1·70
DESIGN: 3, 6l. Portrait of Creanga, 37 × 22 mm.

124 Footballers

1937. 7th Anniv of Accession of Carol II.
1352 **124** 25b.+25b. olive 65 25
1353 – 50b.+50b. brown 65 30
1354 – 1l.+50b. violet . . . . 1·00 45
1355 – 2l.+1l. green . . . . . 1·00 55
1356 – 3l.+1l. red . . . . . . 1·50 60
1357 – 4l.+1l. red . . . . . . 2·50 70
1358 – 6l.+2l. brown . . . . . 3·25 1·10
1359 – 10l.+4l. blue . . . . . 4·00 1·60
DESIGNS—HORIZ: 50b. Swimmer; 3 l. King Carol II hunting; 10l. U.F.S.R. Inaugural Meeting. VERT: 1l. Javelin thrower; 2l. Skier; 4l. Rowing; 6l. Steeplechaser.
Premium in aid of the Federation of Romanian Sports Clubs (U.F.S.R.).

127 Curtea de Arges Cathedral

128 Hurdling

1937. "Little Entente".
1360 **127** 7l.50 blue . . . . 1·20 75
1361 10l. blue . . . . 1·80 50

1937. 8th Balkan Games, Bucharest. Inscr as in T **115**.
1362 – 1l.+1l. violet 90 70
1363 – 2l.+1l. green . . . . . 1·00 95
1364 **128** 4l.+1l. red . . . . . . 1·00 1·30
1365 – 6l.+1l. brown . . . . . 1·40 1·30
1366 – 10l.+1l. blue . . . . . 4·25 2·40
DESIGNS: 1l. Sprinting; 2l. Throwing the javelin; 6l. Breasting the tape; 10l. High jumping.

1937. 16th Birthday of Crown Prince Michael and his promotion to Rank of Sub-lieutenant. Sheet 125 × 152 mm containing four stamps of 1935–40 surch.
MS1367 2l. on 20l. (No. 1327); 6l. on 10l. (No. 1323); 10l. on 6l. (No. 1319); 20l. on 2l. (No. 1313) 4·00 6·00

129 Arms of Romania, Greece, Turkey and Yugoslavia

130 King Carol II

1938. Balkan Entente.
1368 **129** 7l.50 blue . . . . 1·00 70
1369 10l. blue . . . . 1·60 50

1938. New Constitution. Profile portraits of King inscr "27 FEBRUARIE 1938". 6l. shows Arms also.
1370 **130** 3l. red 55 45
1371 – 6l. brown 95 45
1372 – 10l. blue . . . . 1·30 85

131 King Carol II and Provincial Arms

132 Dimitrie Cantemir

1938. Fund for Bucharest Exhibition celebrating 20th Anniv of Union of Provinces.
1373 **131** 6l.+1l. mauve 70 45

1938. Boy Scouts' Fund. 8th Anniv of Accession of Carol II. Inscr "STRAJA TARII 8 IUNIE 1938".
1374 **132** 25b.+25b. olive 40 40
1375 – 50b.+50b. brown 45 40
1376 – 1l.+1l. violet 60 40
1377 – 2l.+2l. green 70 40
1378 – 3l.+2l. mauve 70 40
1379 – 4l.+2l. red 75 45
1380 – 6l.+2l. brown . . . . . 1·10 50
1381 – 7l.50 blue . . . . . . 1·00 50
1382 – 10l. blue 95 60
1383 – 16l. green . . . . . . 1·60 1·60
1384 – 20l. red . . . . 2·40 1·60
PORTRAITS: 50b. Maria Doamna; 1l. Mircea the Great; 2l. Constantin Brancoveanu; 3l. Stephen the Great; 4l. Prince Cuza; 6l. Michael the Brave; 7l.50, Queen Elisabeth; 10l. King Carol II; 16l. King Ferdinand I; 20l. King Carol I.

134 "The Spring"

135 Prince Carol in Royal Carriage

1938. Birth Centenary of Nicholas Grigorescu (painter).
1385 **134** 1l.+1l. blue 75 50
1386 – 2l.+1l. green . . . . . 1·10 80
1387 – 4l.+1l. red . . . . . . 1·10 85
1388 – 6l.+1l. red . . . . . . 1·20 1·10
1389 – 10l.+1l. blue . . . . . 2·00 1·80
DESIGNS—HORIZ: 2l. "Escorting Prisoners" (Russo-Turkish War 1877–78); 4l. "Returning from Market". VERT: 6l. "Rodica, the Water Carrier"; 10l. Self-portrait.

1939. Birth Centenary of King Carol I.
1390 **135** 25b. black 10 10
1391 – 50b. brown 10 10
1392 – 1l. violet 20 10
1393 – 1l.50 green 10 10
1394 – 2l. blue 10 10
1395 – 3l. red 10 10
1396 – 4l. red 10 10
1397 – 5l. black 10 10
1398 – 7l. black 10 10
1399 – 8l. blue 25 15
1400 – 10l. mauve 25 15
1401 – 12l. blue 30 20
1402 – 15l. blue 35 15
1403 – 16l. green 75 45
DESIGNS—HORIZ: 50b. Prince Carol at Battle of Calafat; 1l.50, Sigmaringen and Pelesch Castles; 5l. Carol I, Queen Elizabeth and Arms of Romania. VERT: 1l. Examining plans for restoring Curtea de Arges Monastery; 2l. Carol I and Queen Elizabeth; 3l. Carol I at age of 8; 4l. In 1866; 5l. In 1877; 7l. Equestrian statue; 8l. Leading troops in 1878; 10l. In General's uniform; 12l. Bust; 16l. Restored Monastery of Curtea de Arges.

1939. As last but in miniature sheet form. Perf or Imperf.
MS1404 141 × 116 mm. Nos. 1390/1 and 1393 (sold at 20l.) . . . . 1·25 1·50
MS1405 126 × 146 mm. Nos. 1394 and 1398/1400 . . . . 1·25 1·50
MS1406 126 × 146 mm. Nos. 1395/6 and 1401 (sold at 50l.) . . . . 1·25 1·50

136 Romanian Pavilion N.Y. World's Fair

137 Michael Eminescu, after painting by Joano Basarab

1939. New York World's Fair.
1407 **136** 6l. lake 45 45
1408 – 12l. blue 45 45
DESIGN: 12l. Another view of Pavilion.

1939. 50th Death Anniv of Michael Eminescu (poet).
1409 **137** 5l. black 45 40
1410 – 7l. red 45 40
DESIGN: 7l. Eminescu in later years.

138 St. George and Dragon

139 Diesel Railcar, Class 142 Steam Locomotive (1936) and Locomotive "Calugareni" (1869)

1939. 9th Anniv of Accession of Carol II and Boy Scouts' Fund.
1411 **138** 25b.+25b. grey 45 45
1412 50b.+50b. brown 45 45
1413 1l.+1l. blue 45 45
1414 2l.+2l. green 60 45
1415 3l.+2l. purple 65 45
1416 4l.+2l. orange . . . . . 1·10 65
1417 6l.+2l. red . . . . . . 1·10 65
1418 8l. grey . . . . 1·10 70
1419 10l. blue . . . . 1·20 75
1420 12l. blue . . . . 1·40 1·00
1421 16l. green . . . . 2·75 1·80

1939. 70th Anniv of Romanian Railways.
1422 **139** 1l. violet . . . . 1·10 60
1423 – 4l. red . . . . 1·20 65
1424 – 5l. grey . . . . 1·20 1·00
1425 – 7l. mauve . . . . 1·60 1·00
1426 – 12l. blue . . . . 2·30 1·40
1427 – 15l. green . . . . . . 3·50 2·00
DESIGNS—HORIZ: 4l. Class 142 steam train crossing bridge, 1936; 15l. Railway Headquarters, Budapest. VERT: 5, 7l. Locomotive "Calugareni" (1869) leaving station; 12l. Diesel-mechanical twin set (1937) crossing bridge.

1940. Balkan Entente. As T **103** of Yugoslavia, but with Arms rearranged.
1428 12l. blue 65 55
1429 16l. blue 65 55

141 King Carol II

142 King Carol II

1940. Aviation Fund.
1430 **141** 1l.+50b. green 30 25
1431 2l.50+50b. green 35 30
1432 3l.+1l. red 55 40
1433 3l.50+50b. brown . . . 55 45
1434 4l.+1l. orange 70 50
1435 6l.+1l. blue . . . . . . 1·00 30
1436 9l.+1l. blue . . . . . . 1·30 95
1437 14l.+1l. green . . . . . 1·60 1·20

1940. 10th Anniv of Accession and Aviation Fund. Portraits of King Carol II.
1438 **142** 1l.+50b. purple 75 30
1439 4l.+1l. brown 75 45
1440 – 6l.+1l. blue 75 60
1441 – 8l. red . . . . 1·00 85
1442 – 16l. blue . . . . 1·40 1·10
1443 – 32l. brown . . . . . . 2·10 1·90
PORTRAITS: 6, 16l. In steel helmet; 8l. In military uniform; 32l. In flying helmet.

144 The Iron Gates of the Danube

1940. Charity. 10th Anniv of Accession of Carol II and Boy Scouts' Fund. Inscr "STRAJA TARII 8 IUNIE 1940".
1444 **144** 1l.+1l. violet 50 50
1445 – 2l.+1l. brown 55 55
1446 – 3l.+1l. green 55 60
1447 – 4l.+1l. black 65 70
1448 – 5l.+1l. orange 80 80
1449 – 8l.+1l. red 80 85
1450 – 12l.+2l. blue 90 95
1451 – 16l.+2l. grey . . . . . 3·50 1·90
DESIGNS—HORIZ: 3l. Hotin Fortress; 4l. Hurez Monastery. VERT: 2l. Greco-Roman ruins; 5l. Church in Suceava; 8l. Alba Julia Cathedral; 12l. Village Church, Transylvania; 16l. Triumphal Arch, Bucharest.

1940. Armaments Fund. Nos. **MS**1404/6 optd **PRO PATRIA 1940**. Perf or Imperf.
MS1452 on No. **MS**1404 . . . . 10·00 8·50
MS1453 on No. **MS**1405 . . . . 18·00 20·00
MS1454 on No. **MS**1406 . . . . 10·00 8·50

145 King Michael

146 King Michael

1940.
1455 **145** 25b. green 10 10
1456 50b. olive 10 10
1457 1l. violet 10 10
1458 2l. orange 10 10
1608 3l. brown 10 10
1609 3l.50 brown 10 10
1459 4l. grey 10 10
1611 4l.50 brown 10 10
1460 5l. pink 10 10
1613 6l.50 violet 10 10
1461 7l. blue 10 10
1615 10l. mauve 10 10
1616 11l. blue 10 10
1463 12l. blue 10 10
1464 13l. purple 10 10
1618 15l. blue 10 10
1619 16l. blue 10 10
1620 20l. brown 10 10
1621 29l. blue 55 70
1467 30l. green 10 10
1468 50l. brown 10 10
1469 100l. brown 10 10

1940. Aviation Fund.
1470 **146** 1l.+50b. green 10 15
1471 2l.+50b. green 10 15
1472 2l.50+50b. green 10 15
1473 3l.+1l. violet 10 15
1474 3l.50+50b. pink 20 30
1475 4l.+50b. red 10 20
1476 4l.+1l. brown 10 20
1477 5l.+1l. red 55 45
1478 6l.+1l. blue 10 20
1479 7l.+1l. green 20 20
1480 8l.+1l. violet 20 20
1481 12l.+1l. brown 20 20
1482 14l.+1l. blue 20 20
1483 19l.+1l. mauve 95 30

147 Codreanu (founder)

148 Codreanu (founder)

1940. "Iron Guard" Fund.
1484 **147** 7l.+30l. grn (postage) . . 3·75 3·50
1485 **148** 20l.+5l. green (air) . . . 1·90 1·70

149 Ion Mota

150 Library

1941. Marin and Mota (legionaries killed in Spain).
1486 – 7l.+7l. red . . . . 1·50 2·75
1487 **149** 15l.+15l. blue . . . . . 5·25 5·50
MS1487a 89 × 35 mm. As Nos. 1486/7 both in green. Imperf. (sold at 300l.) . . . . 40·00 55·00
DESIGN: 7l. Vasile Marin.

1941. Carol I Endowment Fund. Inscr "1891 1941".
1488 – 1l.50+43l.50 violet . . . 1·30 1·40
1489 **150** 2l.+43l. red . . . . . . 1·30 1·40
1490 – 7l.+38l. red . . . . . . 1·30 1·40
1491 – 10l.+35l. green . . . . . 2·20 2·00
1492 – 16l.+29l. brown . . . . 3·00 2·30
DESIGNS: 1l.50, Ex-libris; 7l. Foundation building and equestrian statue; 10l. Foundation stone; 16l. King Michael and Carol I.

1941. Occupation of Cernauti. Nos. 1488/92 optd **CERNAUTI 5 Iulie 1941**.
1493 – 1l.50+43l.50 violet . . . 2·75 3·00
1494 **150** 2l.+43l. red . . . . . . 2·75 3·00
1495 – 7l.+38l. red . . . . . . 2·75 3·00
1496 – 10l.+35l. green . . . . . 2·75 3·00
1497 – 16l.+29l. brown . . . . 3·25 3·25

1941. Occupation of Chisinau. Nos. 1488/92 optd **CHISINAU 16 Iulie 1941**.
1498 – 1l.50+43l.50 violet . . . 2·75 3·25
1499 **150** 2l.+43l. red . . . . . . 2·75 3·25
1500 – 7l.+38l. red . . . . . . 2·75 3·25
1501 – 10l.+35l. green . . . . . 2·75 3·25
1502 – 16l.+29l. brown . . . . 3·25 3·25

153 "Charity"

154 Prince Voda

1941. Red Cross Fund. Cross in red.
1503 **153** 1l.50+38l.50 violet . . . 95 90
1504 2l.+38l. red 95 90
1505 5l.+35l. olive 95 90
1506 7l.+33l. brown 95 90
1507 10l.+30l. blue . . . . . 2·00 1·70
MS1508 105 × 73 mm. Nos. 1506/7. Imperf. (sold at 200l.) . . . . 14·00 18·00

1941. Conquest of Transdniestria.
1572 **154** 3l. orange 15 45
1509 6l. brown 35 40
1510 12l. violet 35 55
1511 24l. blue 75 90

155 King Michael and Stephen the Great

1941. Anti-Bolshevik Crusade. Inscr "RAZBOIUL SFANT CONTRA BOLSEVISMULUI".
1512 **155** 10l.+30l. blue . . . . . 75 1·90
1513 – 12l.+28l. red . . . . . 75 1·90
1514 – 16l.+24l. brown . . . . 1·10 2·40
1515 – 20l.+20l. violet . . . . 1·10 2·40
MS1516 105 × 73 mm. 16l. blue (emblems and angel with sword); 20l. red (helmeted soldiers and eagle). No gum. (sold at 200l.) 6·50 9·00
DESIGNS: 12l. Hotin and Akkerman Fortresses; 16l. Arms and helmeted soldiers; 20l. Bayonet charge and Arms of Romania.

1941. Fall of Odessa. Nos. 1512/15 optd **ODESA 16 Oct. 1941.**
1517 **155** 10l.+30l. blue 75 90
1518 – 12l.+28l. red 75 90
1519 – 16l.+24l. brown . . . . 1·10 2·50
1520 – 20l.+20l. violet . . . . 1·10 2·50
MS1521 (No. **MS**1516) . . . . . 10·00 14·00

157 Hotin

1941. Restoration of Bessarabia and Bukovina (Suceava). Inscr "BASARABIA" or "BUCOVINA".
1522 – 25b. red 10 10
1523 **157** 50b. brown 10 10
1524 – 1l. violet 10 10
1525 – 1l.50 green 10 10
1526 – 2l. brown 10 10
1527 – 3l. olive 15 10
1528 – 5l. olive 25 10
1529 – 5l.50 brown 25 15
1530 – 6l.50 mauve 75 50
1531 **157** 9l.50 grey 75 60
1532 – 10l. purple 50 15
1533 – 13l. blue 75 20
1534 – 17l. brown 90 20
1535 – 26l. green . . . . . . 1·00 40
1536 – 39l. blue . . . . . . 1·40 55
1537 – 130l. yellow . . . . . . 4·00 3·00
VIEWS—VERT: 25b., 5l. Paraclis Hotin; 3l. Dragomirna; 13l. Milisauti. HORIZ: 1, 17l. Sucevita; 1l.50, Soroca; 2, 5l.50, Tighina; 6l.50, Cetatea Alba; 10, 130l. Putna; 26l. St. Nicolae, Suceava; 39l. Monastery. Rughi.

1941. Winter Relief Fund. Inscr "BASARABIA" or "BUCOVINA".
1538 – 3l.+50b. red 25 30
1539 – 5l.50+50b. orange . . . 45 50
1540 – 5l.50+1l. black 45 50
1541 – 6l.50+1l. brown 55 65
1542 – 8l.+1l. blue 55 35
1543 – 9l.50+1l. blue 80 75
1544 – 10l.50+1l. blue 80 35
1545 – 16l.+1l. mauve 95 90
1546 **157** 25l.+1l. grey . . . . . . 1·20 95
VIEWS—HORIZ: 3l. Sucevita; 5l.50, (1539), Monastery, Rughi; 5l.50, (1540), Tighina; 6l.50, Soroca; 8l. St. Nicolae, Suceava; 10l.50, Putna; 16l. Cetatea Alba. VERT: 8l.50, Milisauti.

158 Titu Maiorescu

159 Coat-of-Arms of Bukovina

1942. Prisoners of War Relief Fund through International Education Office, Geneva.
1549 **158** 9l.+11l. violet . . . . . 70 1·10
1550 20l.+20l. brown . . . . 90 1·90
1551 20l.+30l. blue . . . . . 90 2·00
MS1552 128 × 81 mm. Nos. 1549/51. Imperf. No gum. (sold at 200l.) 5·00 6·00

1942. 1st Anniv of Liberation of Bukovina.
1553 **159** 9l.+4l. red . . . . 1·50 2·50
1554 – 18l.+32l. blue . . . . . 1·50 2·50
1555 – 20l.+30l. red . . . . . . 1·50 2·50
ARMORIAL DESIGNS: 18l. Castle; 20l. Mounds and crosses.

160 Map of Bessarabia, King Michael, Antonescu, Hitler and Mussolini

161 Statue of Miron Costin

1942. 1st Anniv of Liberation of Bessarabia.
1556 **160** 9l.+41l. brown . . . . . 1·50 2·30
1557 – 18l.+32l. olive . . . . . 1·50 2·30
1558 – 20l.+30l. blue . . . . . 1·50 2·30
DESIGNS—VERT: 18l. King Michael and Marshal Antonescu below miniature of King Stephen. HORIZ: 20l. Marching soldiers and miniature of Marshal Antonescu.

1942. 1st Anniv of Incorporation of Transdniestria.
1559 **161** 6l.+44l. brown . . . . . 1·00 1·70
1560 12l.+38l. violet . . . . . 1·00 1·70
1561 24l.+26l. blue . . . . . 1·00 1·70

162 Andrei Muresanu

163 Statue of Avram Iancu

1942. 80th Death Anniv of A. Muresanu (novelist).
1562 **162** 5l.+5l. violet 80 95

1943. Fund for Statue of Iancu (national hero).
1563 **163** 16l.+4l. brown . . . . . 85 1·10

164 Nurse and wounded Soldier

165 Sword and Shield

1943. Red Cross Charity. Cross in red.
1564 **164** 12l.+88l. red 65 60
1565 16l.+84l. blue 65 60
1566 20l.+80l. olive 65 60
MS1567 100 × 60 mm. Nos. 1565/6 (different shades). Imperf. No gum. (sold at 500l.) . . . . . 3·50 5·00

1943. Charity. 2nd Year of War. Inscr "22 JUNIE 1941 22 JUNIE 1943".
1568 **165** 36l.+164l. brown . . . . 1·10 2·00
1569 – 62l.+138l. blue . . . . . 1·10 2·00
1570 – 76l.+124l. red . . . . . 1·10 2·00
MS1571 90 × 65 mm. Nos. 1569/70 (different shades). Imperf. No gum. (sold at 600l.) . . . . . 10·00 12·00
DESIGNS—VERT: 62l. Sword severing chain; 76l. Angel protecting soldier and family.

167 P. Maior

1943. Transylvanian Refugees' Fund (1st issue).
1576 **167** 16l.+134l. red 40 55
1577 – 32l.+118l. blue 40 55
1578 – 36l.+114l. purple 40 55
1579 – 62l.+138l. red 40 55
1580 – 91l.+109l. brown 40 55
PORTRAITS—VERT: 32l. G. Sincai; 36l. T. Cipariu; 91l. G. Cosbuc. HORIZ: 62l. Horia, Closca and Crisan.
See also Nos. 1584/8.

169 King Michael and Marshal Antonescu

1943. 3rd Anniv of King Michael's Reign.
1581 **169** 16l.+24l. blue . . . . . 1·30 1·60

170 Sports Shield

171 Calafat, 1877

1943. Charity. Sports Week.
1582 **170** 16l.+24l. blue 55 45
1583 16l.+24l. brown 55 45

1943. Transylvanian Refugees' Fund (2nd issue) Portraits as T **167**.
1584 16l.+134l. mauve 45 45
1585 51l.+99l. orange 45 45
1586 56l.+144l. red 45 45
1587 76l.+124l. blue 45 45
1588 77l.+123l. brown 45 45
PORTRAITS—VERT: 16l. S. Micu; 51l. G. Lazar; 56l. O. Goga; 76l. S. Barnutiu; 77l. A. Saguna.

1943. Centenary of National Artillery.
1596 **171** 1l.+1l. brown 20 30
1597 – 2l.+2l. violet 20 30
1598 – 3l.50+3l.50 blue 20 30
1599 – 4l.+4l. mauve 20 30
1600 – 5l.+5l. orange 35 45
1601 – 6l.50+6l.50 blue 35 45
1602 – 7l.+7l. purple 50 65
1603 – 20l.+20l. red . . . . . . 90 1·10
DESIGNS—HORIZ: (1l. to 7l. inscr battle scenes): 2l. "1916–1918"; 3l.50, Stalingrad; 4l. Crossing R. Tisza; 5l. Odessa; 6l.50, Caucasus; 7l. Sevastopol; 20l. Bibescu and King Michael.

172 Association Insignia

1943. 25th Anniv of National Engineers' Assn.
1624 **172** 21l.+29l. brown 85 65

173 Motor-cycle and Delivery Van

1944. Postal Employees' Relief Fund and Bicentenary of National Postal Service. (a) Without opt.
1625 **173** 1l.+49l. red . . . . . . 90 1·40
1626 – 2l.+48l. mauve . . . . . 90 1·40
1627 – 4l.+46l. blue . . . . . . 90 1·40
1628 – 10l.+40l. purple . . . . 90 1·40
MS1629 143 × 86 mm. Nos. 1625/7 but in red (sold at 200l.) . . . . 2·75 4·00
MS1630 As last but in violet and imperf . . . . 2·75 4·00

(b) Optd **1744 1944.**
1631 **173** 1l+49l. red . . . . . . 2·40 3·00
1632 – 2l.+48l. mauve . . . . . 2·40 3·00
1633 – 4l.+46l. blue . . . . . . 2·40 3·00
1634 – 10l.+40l. purple . . . . 2·40 3·00
MS1635 (No. **MS**1629) . . . . . 5·50 8·00
MS1636 (No. **MS**1630) . . . . . 5·50 8·00
DESIGNS—HORIZ: 2l. Post motorcycle, post van and eight horses; 4l. Chariot. VERT: Horseman and globe.

174 Dr. Cretzulescu

175 Rugby Player

1944. Cent of Medical Teaching in Romania.
1637 **174** 35l.+65l. blue 80 70

1944. 30th Anniv of Foundation of National Rugby Football Association.
1638 **175** 16l.+184l. red . . . . . 2·40 3·00

176 Stefan Tomsa Church, Radaseni

177 Fruit Pickers

1944. Cultural Fund. Town of Radaseni. Inscr "RADASENI".
1639 **176** 5l.+145l. blue 55 55
1640 – 12l.+138l. red 55 55
1641 **177** 15l.+135l. orange 55 55
1642 – 32l.+118l. brown 55 55
DESIGNS—HORIZ: 12l. Agricultural Institution; 32l. School.

178 Queen Helen

179 King Michael and Carol I Foundation, Bucharest

1945. Red Cross Relief Fund. Portrait in black on yellow and Cross in red.
1643 **178** 4l.50+5l.50 violet 25 20
1644 10l.+40l. brown 45 25
1645 15l.+75l. blue 70 45
1646 20l.+80l. red 85 70

1945. King Carol I Foundation Fund.
1647 **179** 20l.+180l. orange 35 35
1648 25l.+175l. slate 35 35
1649 35l.+165l. brown 35 35
1650 76l.+125l. violet 35 35
MS1651 74 × 60 mm. 200l.+1000l. blue (as T **179** but portrait of King Carol I) Imperf. No gum . . . 6·00 6·00

180 A. Saguna

181 A. Muresanu

1945. Liberation of Northern Transylvania. Inscr "1944".
1652 **180** 25b. red 45 40
1653 **181** 50b. orange 20 20
1654 – 4l.50 brown 25 20
1655 – 11l. blue 25 20
1656 – 15l. green 25 20
1657 – 31l. violet 25 20
1658 – 35l. grey 25 20
1659 – 41l. olive 25 75
1660 – 55l. brown 25 20
1661 – 61l. mauve 25 20
1662 – 75l.+75l. brown 30 25
DESIGNS—HORIZ: 4l.50, Samuel Micu; 31l. George Lazar; 55l. Horia, Closca and Crisan; 61l. Petru Maior; 75l. King Ferdinand and King Michael. VERT: 11l. George Sincai; 15l. Michael the Brave; 35l. Avram Iancu; 41l. Simeon Barnutiu.

182 King Michael

183 King Michael

184 King Michael

185 King Michael

1945.
1663 **182** 50b. grey 10 10
1664 **183** 1l. brown 10 10
1665 2l. violet 10 10
1666 **182** 2l. brown 10 15
1667 **183** 4l. green 10 10
1668 **184** 5l. mauve 10 10
1669 **182** 10l. blue 10 10
1670 10l. brown 10 10
1671 **183** 10l. brown 10 10
1672 **182** 15l. mauve 10 10
1673 20l. blue 10 10
1674 20l. lilac 10 10
1675 **184** 20l. purple 10 10
1676 25l. red 10 10
1677 35l. brown 10 10
1678 40l. red 10 10
1679 **183** 50l. blue 10 15
1680 55l. red 15 15
1681 **184** 75l. green 20 10
1682 **185** 80l. orange 10 10
1683 80l. blue 10 10
1684 **182** 80l. blue 10 10
1685 **185** 100l. brown 10 10
1686 **182** 137l. green 20 10
1687 **185** 160l. green 10 10
1688 160l. violet 10 10
1689 200l. green 30 15
1690 200l. red 10 10
1691 **183** 200l. red 10 10
1692 **185** 300l. blue 10 10
1693 360l. brown 20 10
1694 400l. violet 10 10
1695 **183** 400l. red 10 10
1696 **185** 480l. brown 20 10
1697 **182** 500l. mauve 20 10
1698 **185** 600l. green 10 15
1699 **184** 860l. brown 10 10
1700 **185** 1000l. green 20 15
1701 **182** 1500l. green 20 10

1702 **185** 2400l. lilac 40 10
1703 **183** 2500l. blue 20 10
1704 **185** 3700l. blue 40 10
1705 **182** 5000l. grey 10 10
1706 8000l. green 35 15
1707 **185** 10000l. brown 55 35

186 N. Jorga

1945. War Victims' Relief Fund.
1708 – 12l.+188l. blue 25 40
1709 – 16l.+184l. brown 25 40
1710 **186** 20l.+180l. brown 25 40
1711 – 32l.+168l. red 25 40
1712 – 35l.+165l. blue 25 40
1713 – 36l.+164l. violet . . . . 1·80 1·10
MS1714 76×60 mm. Nos. 1711/12 but mauve. Imperf. (sold at 1000l.) 7·50 13·00
PORTRAITS: 12l. Ian Gheorghe Duca (Prime Minister, 1933); 16l. Virgil Madgearu (politician); 32l. Ilie Pintilie (communist); 35l. Bernath Andrei (communist); 36l. Filimon Sarbu (saboteur).

187 Books and Torch

188 Karl Marx

1945. Charity. 1st Romanian–Soviet Congress Fund. Inscr "ARLUS".
1715 **187** 20l.+80l. olive 25 35
1716 – 35l.+165l. red 25 35
1717 – 75l.+225l. blue 25 35
1718 – 80l.+420l. brown 25 35
MS1719 60×75 mm. As Nos. 1716/17 but in red. Imperf. (sold at 900l.) . . . . 5·00 6·50
DESIGNS: 35l. Soviet and Romanian flags; 75l. Drawn curtain revealing Kremlin; 80l. T. Vladimirescu and A. Nevsky.

189 Postman

1945. Trade Union Congress, Bucharest. Perf or imperf.
1720 **188** 75l.+425l. red . . . . . 1·40 2·00
1723 75l.+425l. blue . . . . . 3·25 5·75
1721 – 120l.+380l. blue . . . . 1·40 2·00
1724 – 120l.+380l. brown . . . 4·00 5·75
1722 – 155l.+445l. brown . . . 1·60 2·00
1725 – 155l.+445l. red . . . . 4·00 5·75
PORTRAITS: 120l. Engels; 155l. Lenin.

1945. Postal Employees. Inscr "MUNCA P.T.T.".
1726 **189** 100l. brown 60 45
1727 100l. olive 60 45
1728 – 150l. brown 90 70
1729 – 150l. red 90 70
1730 – 250l. olive . . . . 1·10 1·10
1731 – 250l. blue . . . . 1·10 1·10
1732 – 500l. mauve . . . . . . 6·25 9·25
DESIGNS: 150l. Telegraphist; 250l. Lineman; 500l. Post Office, Bucharest.

190 Throwing the Discus

192 Agricultural and Industrial Workers

1945. Charity. With shield inscr "O.S.P.". Perf or imperf.
1733 **190** 12l.+188l. olive (post) . . 1·60 1·80
1738 – 12l.+188l. orange . . . . 1·60 1·40
1734 – 16l.+184l. blue . . . . . 1·60 1·80
1739 – 16l.+184l. purple . . . . 1·60 1·40
1735 – 20l.+180l. green . . . . 1·60 1·80
1740 – 20l.+180l. violet . . . . 1·60 1·40
1736 – 32l.+168l. mauve . . . . 1·60 1·80
1741 – 32l.+168l. green . . . . 1·60 1·40
1737 – 35l.+165l. blue . . . . . 1·60 1·80
1742 – 35l.+165l. olive . . . . 1·60 1·40
1743 – 200l.+1000l. bl (air) . . 12·00 14·00

DESIGNS—As T **190**: 16l. Diving; 20l. Skiing; 32l. Volleyball; 35l. "Sport and work". 36×50 mm: 200l. Airplane and bird.

1945. 1st Anniv of Romanian Armistice with Russia.
1744 **192** 100l.+400l. red 40 50
1745 – 200l.+800l. blue 40 50
DESIGN: 200l. King Michael, "Agriculture" and "Industry".

193 T. Vladimirescu

194 Destitute Children

1945. Charity. Patriotic Defence Fund. Inscr "APARAREA PATRIOTICA".
1746 – 20l.+580l. brown . . . . 4·75 6·75
1747 – 20l.+580l. mauve . . . . 4·75 6·75
1748 – 40l.+560l. blue . . . . . 4·75 6·75
1749 – 40l.+560l. green . . . . 4·75 6·75
1750 – 55l.+545l. red . . . . . 4·75 6·75
1751 – 55l.+545l. brown . . . . 4·75 6·75
1752 **193** 60l.+540l. blue . . . . . 4·75 6·75
1753 60l.+540l. brown . . . . 4·75 6·75
1754 – 80l.+520l. red . . . . . 4·75 6·75
1755 – 80l.+520l. mauve . . . . 4·75 6·75
1756 – 100l.+500l. green . . . . 4·75 6·75
1757 – 100l.+500l. brown . . . 4·75 6·75
DESIGNS—HORIZ: 20l. "Political Amnesty"; 40l. "Military Amnesty"; 55l. "Agrarian Amnesty"; 100l. King Michael and "Recontruction". VERT: 80l. Nicholas Horia.

1945. Child Welfare Fund.
1758 **194** 40l. blue 30 25

195 I. Ionescu, G. Titeica, A. G. Idachimescu and V. Cristescu

1945. 50th Anniv of Founding of Journal of Mathematics.
1759 **195** 2l. brown 10 10
1760 – 80l. blue 60 65
DESIGN: 80l. Allegory of Learning.

196 Saligny Bridge

1945. 50th Anniv of Saligny Bridge over River Danube, Cernavoda.
1761 **196** 80l. black 30 30

197 Class E.18 Electric Locomotive, 1935, Germany

198

1945. Charity. 16th Congress of Romanian Engineers. Perf or imperf. (a) Postage.
1762 **197** 10l.+490l. olive . . . . 2·10 1·90
1767 10l.+490l. blue . . . . . 2·10 1·90
1763 – 20l.+480l. brown 30 45
1768 – 20l.+480l. violet 30 45
1764 – 25l.+475l. purple 30 45
1769 – 25l.+475l. green 30 45
1765 – 55l.+445l. blue 30 45
1770 – 55l.+445l. grey 30 45
1766 – 100l.+400l. brown . . . 30 45
1771 – 100l.+400l. mauve . . . 30 45

(b) Air. Symbolical design as T **198**. Imperf.
1772 **198** 80l.+420l. grey . . . . . 1·10 1·10
1773 – 200l.+800l. blue . . . . 1·20 1·10
MS1774 75×55 mm. 80l. purple (as 1772) . . . . 10·00 10·00
MS1775 75×55 mm. 80l. green (as 1773) . . . . 15·00 15·00

DESIGNS—As Type **197**: 20l. Coats of Arms; 25l. Arterial road; 55l. Oil wells; 100l. "Agriculture". As T **198**: 200l. Icarus and Lockheed 14 Super Electra airplane.

199 Globe and Clasped Hands

1945. Charity. World Trade Union Congress, Paris. Symbolical designs inscr "CONFERINTA MONDIAL LA SINDICALA DIN PARIS 25 SEPTEMVRE 1945".
1776 **199** 80l.+920l. mauve . . . . 9·00 9·75
1777 – 160l.+1840l. brown . . . 9·00 9·75
1778 – 320l.+1680l. violet . . . 9·00 9·75
1779 – 440l.+2560l. green . . . 9·00 9·75
DESIGNS: 160l. Globe and Dove of Peace; 320l. Hand and hammer; 440l. Scaffolding and flags.

1946. Nos 1444/5 surch in figures.
1780 10l.+90l. on 100l.+400l. . . 90 1·70
1781 10l.+90l. on 200l.+800l. . . 90 1·70
1782 20l.+80l. on 100l.+400l. . . 90 1·70
1783 20l.+80l. on 200l.+800l. . . 90 1·70
1784 80l.+120l. on 100l.+400l. 90 1·70
1785 80l.+120l. on 200l.+800l. 90 1·70
1786 100l.+150l. on 100l.+400l. 90 1·70
1787 100l.+150l. on 200l.+800l. 90 1·70

200 Sower

201 Distribution of Title Deeds

1946. Agrarian Reform. Inscr "REFORMA AGRARA".
1788 – 80l. blue 30 30
1789 **200** 50l.+450l. red 30 30
1790 **201** 100l.+900l. purple . . . 30 30
1791 – 200l.+800l. orange . . . 30 30
1792 – 400l.+1600l. green . . . 30 30
MS1793 75×60 mm. 80l. blue (as No. 1789 but larger) (sold at 100l.) (air) . . . . 12·00 13·50
DESIGNS—VERT: 80l Blacksmith and ploughman. HORIZ: 200l. Ox-drawn farm wagon; 400l. Plough and tractor.

202

1946. 25th Anniv of Bucharest Philharmonic Orchestra.
1794 **202** 10l. blue 10 10
1795 – 20l. brown 10 10
1796 – 55l. green 10 10
1797 – 80l. violet 20 20
1798 – 160l. orange 10 10
1799 **202** 200l.+800l. red 80 85
1800 – 350l.+1650l. blue . . . . 1·00 1·10
MS1801 No. 1799×12+4 labels 25·00 35·00
MS1802 No. 1800×12+4 labels 25·00 35·00
DESIGNS: 20l., 55l., 160l. "XXV" and musical score; 80l., 350l. G. Enescu.

203 Building Worker

205 Sower

204 Sky-writing

1946. Labour Day. Designs of workers inscr "ZIUA MUNCII".
1803 **203** 10l. red 10 50
1804 10l. green 50 45
1805 20l. blue 50 45
1806 20l. brown 10 50
1807 200l. red 20 20

1946. Air. Labour Day. Sheet 70×63 mm.
MS1808 **204** 200l. blue and vermilion (sold at 10,000l.) . . . . 10·00 11·00

1946. Youth Issue.
1809 **205** 10l.+100l. red & brn . . 10 10
1810 – 10l.+200l. pur & blue . . 1·20 1·10
1811 – 80l.+200l. brn & pur . . 10 10
1812 – 80l.+300l. mve & brn . . 10 10
1813 – 200l.+400l. red & grn . . 10 10
DESIGNS: No. 1810, Hurdling; 1811, Student; 1812, Worker and factory; 1813, Marching with flag.

206 Aviator and Aircraft

207 Football

1946. Air. Youth Issue.
1814 – 200l. blue and green . . 2·75 3·00
1815 **206** 500l. blue and orange . . 2·75 3·00
DESIGN: 200l. Airplane on ground.

1946. Sports, designs inscr "O.S.P." Perf or imperf.
1816 **207** 10l. blue (postage) . . . 30 35
1817 – 20l. red 30 35
1818 – 50l. violet 30 35
1819 – 80l. brown 30 35
1820 – 160l.+1340l. green . . . 30 35

1821 – 300l. red (air) . . . . . 1·00 1·30
1822 – 300l.+1200l. blue . . . . 1·00 1·30
MS1823 58×64 mm. 300l. crimson (as No. 1821 but larger). Imperf. (sold at 1300l.) . . . . 18·00 15·00
DESIGNS: 20l. Diving; 50l. Running; 80l. Mountaineering; 160l. Ski jumping; 300l. (both) Flying.

208 "Traditional Ties"

209 Banat Girl holding Distaff

1946. Romanian–Soviet Friendship Pact.
1824 **208** 80l. brown 10 20
1825 – 100l. blue 10 20
1826 – 300l. grey 10 20
1827 – 300l.+1200l. red 80 55
MS1828 70×65 mm. 1000l. scarlet (as No. 1827) (sold at 6000l.) 7·00 8·00
DESIGNS: 100l. "Cultural ties"; 300l. "Economic ties"; 300l.+1200l. Dove.
No. 1827 also exists imperf.

1946. Charity. Women's Democratic Federation.
1829 – 80l. olive 55 10
1830 **209** 80l.+320l. red 10 10
1831 – 140l.+360l. orange . . . 10 10
1832 – 300l.+450l. green . . . 20 20
1833 – 600l.+900l. blue 30 25
MS1834 80×65 mm. 500l.+9500l. vermilion and chocolate (air) 7·00 8·00
DESIGNS: 80l. Girl and handloom; 140l. Wallachian girl and wheatsheaf; 300l. Transylvanian horsewoman; 600l. Moldavian girl carrying water.

211 King Michael and Food Transport

1947. Social Relief Fund.
1845 – 300l. olive 10 20
1846 **211** 600l. mauve 30 25
1847 – 1500l.+3500l. orange . . 30 25
1848 – 3700l.+5300l. violet . . 30 25
MS1849 52×36 mm. **212** 5000l.+5000l. ultramarine. Imperf. No gum . . . . 7·00 8·00
DESIGNS—VERT: 300l. Loaf of bread and hungry child; 1500l. Angel bringing food and clothing to destitute people; 3700l. Loaf of bread and starving family.

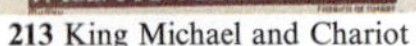

213 King Michael and Chariot

214 Symbols of Labour and Clasped Hands

1947. Peace.
1850 **213** 300l. purple 20 25
1851 – 600l. brown 20 25
1852 – 3000l. blue 20 25
1853 – 7200l. green 20 25
DESIGNS—VERT: 600l. Winged figure of Peace; 300l. Flags of four Allied Nations; 7200l. Dove of Peace.

1947. Trades Union Congress.
1854 **214** 200l. blue (postage) . . . 35 30
1855 300l. orange 35 30
1856 600l. red 35 30
1857 – 1100l. blue (air) 60 85
DESIGN—22 × 37 mm: 1100l. As Type **214** with Lockheed Super Electra airplane at top.

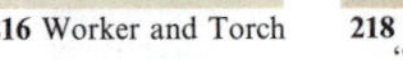

216 Worker and Torch

218 Symbolical of "Learning"

1947. Air. Trades Union Congress. Imperf.
1858 **216** 3000l.+7000l. brown . . 85 85

1947. Charity. People's Culture.
1859 – 200l.+200l. blue 15 20
1860 – 300l.+300l. brown . . . 15 20
1861 – 600l.+600l. green . . . 15 20
1862 – 1200l.+1200l. blue . . . 15 20
1863 **218** 1500l.+1500l. red . . . 15 20
MS1864 64 × 80 mm. 3700l.+3700l. blue and brown (as T **218**). Imperf 2·00 2·25
DESIGNS—HORIZ: 200l. Boys' reading class; 300l. Girls' school; 600l. Engineering classroom; 1200l. School building.

219 King Michael

1947.
1865 **219** 1000l. blue 10 15
1869 3000l. blue 10 15
1866 5500l. green 15 15
1870 7200l. mauve 10 15
1871 15000l. blue 15 15
1867 20000l. brown 25 25
1872 21000l. mauve 15 25
1873 36000l. violet 35 30
1868 50000l. orange 40 30
Nos. 1865/8 are size 18 × 21½ mm and Nos. 1869/73 are 25 × 30 mm.

220 N. Grigorescu

221 Lisunov Li-2 Airliner

1947. Charity. Institute of Romanian–Soviet Studies.
1874 – 1500l.+1500l. purple (postage) 25 20
1875 – 1500l.+1500l. orange . . 25 20
1876 – 1500l.+1500l. green . . 25 20
1877 **220** 1500l.+1500l. blue . . . 25 20
1878 – 1500l.+1500l. blue . . . 25 20
1879 – 1500l.+1500l. lake . . . 25 20
1880 – 1500l.+1500l. red . . . 25 20
1881 – 1500l.+1500l. brown . . 25 20
1882 **221** 15000l.+15000l. green (air) 75 65
PORTRAITS: No. 1874, Petru Movila; 1875, V. Babes; 1876, M. Eminescu; 1878, P. Tchaikovsky; 1879, M. Lomonosov; 1880, A. Pushkin; 1881, I. Y. Repin.
No. 1882 is imperf.

222 Miner

224 Douglas DC-4 Airliner over Black Sea

1947. Charity. Labour Day.
1883 **222** 1000l.+1000l. olive . . . 20 25
1884 – 1500l.+1500l. brown . . 15 20
1885 – 2000l.+2000l. blue . . . 15 20
1886 – 2500l.+2500l. mauve . . 15 20
1887 – 3000l.+3000l. red 20 25
DESIGNS: 1500l. Peasant; 2000l. Peasant woman; 2500l. Intellectual; 3000l. Factory worker.

1947. Air. Labour Day.
1888 – 3000l. red 25 25
1889 – 3000l. green 25 25
1890 – 3000l. brown 25 35
1891 **224** 3000l.+12,000l. blue . . 50 40
DESIGNS—24½ × 30 mm: No. 1888, Four parachutes; 1889, Air Force Monument; 1890, Douglas DC-4 over landscape.

(New currency 1 (new) leu = 100 (old) lei.)

225 King Michael and Timber Barges

227

1947. Designs with medallion portrait of King Michael.
1892 – 50b. orange 10 10
1893 **225** 1l. brown 10 10
1894 – 2l. blue 10 10
1895 – 3l. red 10 10
1896 – 5l. blue 10 10
1897 – 10l. blue 25 15
1898 – 12l. violet 60 30
1899 – 15l. blue . . . . 1·75 30
1900 – 20l. brown . . . . . . 1·00 20
1901 – 32l. brown . . . . . . 4·75 1·90
1902 – 36l. lake . . . . 6·25 1·50
DESIGNS: 50b. Harvesting; 2l. River Danube; 3l. Reshitza Industries; 5l. Curtea de Arges Cathedral; 10l. Royal Palace, Bucharest; 12, 36l. Saligny Bridge, Cernavoda; 15, 32l. Liner "Transylvania" in Port of Constantza; 20l. Oil Wells, Prahova.

1947. Balkan Games. Surch **2+3 LEI C.B.A. 1947** and bar.
1903 **219** 2+3l. on 36,000l. violet 55 70

1947. 17th Congress of General Assn of Romanian Engineers. With monogram as in T **227**.
1904 **227** 1l.+1l. red (postage) . . 10 10
1905 – 2l.+2l. brown 10 10
1906 – 3l.+3l. violet 25 25
1907 – 4l.+4l. olive 10 20
1908 – 5l.+5l. blue (air) 45 55
DESIGNS: 2l. Sawmill; 3l. Refinery; 4l. Steel mill; 5l. Gliders over mountains.

1947. Charity. Soviet–Romanian Amity. As No. 1896 surch **ARLUS 1-7-XI. 1947 +5.** Imperf.
1909 5l.+5l. blue 50 45

229 Beehive

230 Food Convoy

1947. Savings Day.
1910 **229** 12l. red 15 25

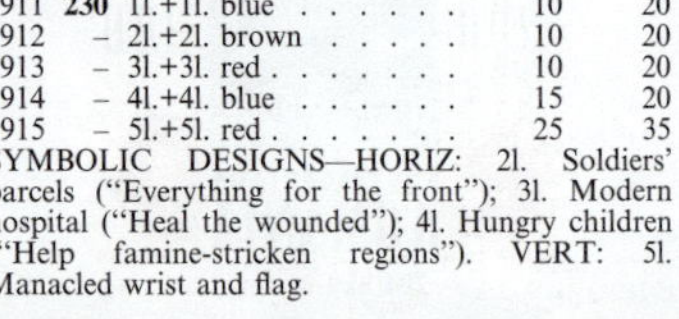

1947. Patriotic Defence.
1911 **230** 1l.+1l. blue 10 20
1912 – 2l.+2l. brown 10 20
1913 – 3l.+3l. red 10 20
1914 – 4l.+4l. blue 15 20
1915 – 5l.+5l. red 25 35
SYMBOLIC DESIGNS—HORIZ: 2l. Soldiers' parcels ("Everything for the front"); 3l. Modern hospital ("Heal the wounded"); 4l. Hungry children ("Help famine-stricken regions"). VERT: 5l. Manacled wrist and flag.

231 Allegory of work

1947. Charity. Trades Union Congress, Bucharest. Inscr "C.G.M. 1947".
1916 – 2l.+10l. red (postage) . . 15 20
1917 **231** 7l.+10l. black 20 25
1918 – 11l. red and blue (air) . . 35 45
DESIGNS—As T **231**: 2l. Industrial and agricultural workers. 23 × 18 mm: 11l. Lisunov Li-2 airliner over demonstration.

233 Map of Romania

1948. Census of 1948.
1925 **233** 12l. blue 30 20

234 Printing Works and Press

1948. 75th Anniv of Romanian State Stamp Printing Works.
1926 **234** 6l. red 95 70
1927 7l.50 green 45 10

235 Discus Thrower

237 Industrial Worker

1948. Balkan Games, 1947. Inscr as in T **235**. Imperf or perf.
1928 **235** 1l.+1l. brown (postage) 30 35
1929 – 2l.+2l. red 45 45
1930 – 5l.+5l. blue 70 70
1931 – 7l.+7l. violet (air) . . . 85 65
1932 – 10l.+10l. green . . . . 1·30 95
DESIGNS: 2l. Runner; 5l. Heads of two young athletes; 7, 10l. Airplane over running track.

1948. Nos. 1892/1902 optd **R.P.R.** (Republica Populara Romana).
1933 50b. orange 10 20
1934 1l. brown 10 15
1935 2l. blue 45 15
1936 3l. red 55 15
1937 5l. blue 90 15
1938 10l. blue . . . . 1·10 25
1939 12l. violet . . . . . . 2·10 30
1940 15l. blue . . . . 2·10 35
1941 20l. brown . . . . . . 1·30 35
1942 32l. brown . . . . . . 8·50 4·00
1943 36l. lake . . . . 6·50 2·40

1948. Young Workers' Union. Imperf or perf.
1954 **237** 2l.+2l. blue (postage) . . 25 30
1955 – 3l.+3l. green 25 25
1956 – 5l.+5l. brown 25 35
1957 – 8l.+8l. red 30 35
1958 – 12l.+12l. blue (air) . . . 1·10 1·00
DESIGNS—As Type **237**: 3l. Peasant girl and wheatsheaf; 5l. Student and book. TRIANGULAR: 8l. Youths bearing Filimon Sarbu banner. 36 × 23 mm: 12l. Airplane and barn swallows.

240 "Friendship"

241 "New Constitution"

1948. Romanian–Bulgarian Amity.
1959 **240** 32l. brown 70 45

1948. New Constitution.
1960 **241** 1l. red 15 20
1961 2l. orange 35 35
1962 12l. blue . . . . 1·60 60

242 Globe and Banner

243 Aviator and Heinkel He 116A

244 Barbed Wire Entanglement

1948. Labour Day.
1963 **242** 8l.+8l. red (postage) . . 1·10 2·00
1964 – 10l.+10l. green . . . . 1·90 2·50
1965 – 12l.+12l. brown . . . . 2·25 3·25
1966 **243** 20l.+20l. blue (air) . . . 4·25 5·00
DESIGNS—HORIZ: 10l. Peasants and mountains. VERT: 12l. Worker and factory.

1948. Army Day.
1967 – 1l.50+1l.50 red (postage) 20 30
1968 **244** 2l.+2l. purple 20 30
1969 – 4l.+4l. brown 50 55
1970 – 7l.50+7l.50 black . . . . 90 1·00
1971 – 8l.+8l. violet . . . . . . 1·00 1·10
1972 – 3l.+3l. blue (air) . . . . 3·75 4·50
1973 – 5l.+5l. blue . . . . . . 6·75 6·75
DESIGNS—VERT: 1l.50, Infantry; 3l. Ilyushin Stormovik fighter planes; 5l. Petlyakov Pe-2 dive bomber Il-2M3. HORIZ: 4l. Artillery; 7l.50, Tank; 8l. Destroyer.

245 Five Portraits

246 Proclamation of Islaz

1948. Cent of 1848 Revolution. Dated "1848 1948".
1974 – 2l.+2l. purple 20 30
1975 **245** 5l.+5l. violet 25 35
1976 **246** 11l. red 40 40
1977 – 10l.+10l. green 40 30
1978 – 36l.+18l. blue . . . . . 1·50 1·20
DESIGNS—22 × 38 mm. HORIZ: 10l. Balcescu, Petofi, Iancu, Barnutiu Baritiu and Murcu. VERT: 2l. Nicolas Balcescu; 36l. Balcescu, Kogalniceanu, Alecsandri and Cuza.

247 Emblem of Republic

1948.
2023 **247** 50b. red 70 30
1980 0.50l. red 15 10
1981 1l. brown 15 10
1982 2l. green 15 10
1983 3l. grey 25 10
1984 4l. brown 25 10
1985 5l. blue 25 10
2028 5l. violet . . . . 1·10 10
1986 10l. blue 65 10
No. 2023 is inscribed "BANI 0.50" (= ½ bani) and in No. 1980 this was corrected to "LEI 0.50".

248 Monimoa Gliders

249 Yachts

1948. Air Force and Navy Day. (a) Air Force (vert).
1987 **248** 2l.+2l. blue 75 95
1988 – 5l.+5l. violet 75 95
1989 – 8l.+8l. red . . . . 1·10 1·50
1990 – 10l.+10l. brown . . . . 1·90 1·90

(b) Navy (horiz).
1991 **249** 2l.+2l. green 75 95
1992 – 5l.+5l. grey 75 95
1993 – 8l.+8l. blue . . . . . . 1·10 1·50
1994 – 10l.+10l. red . . . . . . 1·90 2·00

DESIGNS—AIR FORCE: 5l. Aurel Vlaicu's No. 1 "Crazy Fly" airplane; 8l. Lisunov Li-2 airliner and tractor; 10l. Lisunov Li-2 airliner. NAVY: 5l. "Mircea" (cadet ship), 1882; 8l. "Romana Mare" (Danube river steamer); 10l. "Transylvania" (liner).

1948. Surch.

1995	**240**	31l. on 32l. brown	55	30

251 Newspapers and Torch

252 Soviet Soldiers' Monument

1948. Press Week. Imperf or perf.

1996	**251**	5l.+5l. red	10	10
1997		10l. brown	30	45
1998	–	10l.+10l. violet	65	60
1999	–	15l.+15l. blue	90	1·00

DESIGNS—HORIZ: 10l. (No. 1998), Flag, torch and ink-well. VERT: 15l. Alex Sahia (journalist).

1948. Romanian–Russian Amity.

2000	**252**	10l. red (postage)	35	45
2001	–	10l.+10l. green	2·10	2·10
2002	–	15l.+15l. blue	2·40	2·75
2003	–	20l.+20l. blue (air)	7·25	7·50

DESIGNS—VERT: 10l. (No. 2001), Badge of Arlus; 15l. Kremlin. HORIZ: 20l. Lisunov Li-2 airplane.

255 Emblem of Republic

1948. Air. Designs showing aircraft.

2004	**255**	30l. red	20	10
2005	–	50l. green	30	30
2006	–	100l. blue	3·75	2·10

DESIGNS: 50l. Workers in a field; 100l. Steam train, airplane and liner.

256 Lorry

1948. Work on Communications.

2007	–	1l.+1l. black and green	30	45
2008	**256**	3l.+3l. black & brown	30	50
2009	–	11l.+11l. black & blue	1·90	1·75
2010	–	15l.+15l. black and red	4·75	3·50
MS2011		110 × 85 mm. Nos. 2007/10 but in red, blue and red respectively. Imperf. No gum	24·00	25·00

DESIGNS: 1l. Dockers loading freighter; 11l. Lisunov Li-2 airliner on ground and in the air; 15l. Steam train.

257 Nicolas Balcescu

1948.

2012	**257**	20l. red	40	25

258 Hands Breaking Chain

1948. 1st Anniv of People's Republic.

2013	**258**	5l. red	30	25

259 Runners

260 Lenin

1948. National Sports Organization. Imperf or perf.

2014	**259**	5l.+5l. green (postage)	2·30	2·30
2017		5l.+5l. brown	2·30	2·30
2015	–	10l.+10l. violet	4·00	4·00
2018	–	10l.+10l. red	4·00	4·00
2016	–	20l.+20l. blue (air)	16·50	15·00
2019	–	20l.+20l. green	16·50	15·00

DESIGNS—HORIZ: 10l. Parade of athletes with flags. VERT: 20l. Boy flying model airplane.

1949. 25th Death Anniv of Lenin. Perf or imperf.

2020	**260**	20l. black	20	25

261 Dancers

263 Pushkin

262 I. C. Frimu and Revolutionaries

1949. 90th Anniv of Union of Romanian Principalities.

2021	**261**	10l. blue	30	25

1949. 30th Death Anniv of Ion Frimu (union leader and journalist). Perf or imperf.

2022	**262**	20l. red	30	25

1949. 150th Birth Anniv of A. S. Pushkin (Russian poet).

2030	**263**	11l. red	55	45
2031		30l. green	65	55

264 Globe and Posthorn

265 Forms of Transport

1949. 75th Anniv of U.P.U.

2032	**264**	20l. brown	1·20	1·00
2033	**265**	30l. blue	2·75	3·00

266 Russians entering Bucharest

1949. 5th Anniv of Russian Army's Entry into Bucharest. Perf or imperf.

2034	**266**	50l. brown on green	55	55

267 "Romanian–Soviet Amity"

1949. Romanian–Soviet Friendship Week. Perf or imperf.

2035	**267**	20l. red	40	40

268 Forms of Transport

269 Stalin

1949. International Congress of Transport Unions. Perf or imperf.

2036	**268**	11l. blue	65	65
2037		20l. red	1·10	90

1949. Stalin's 70th Birthday. Perf or imperf.

2038	**269**	31l. green	30	25

1950. Philatelic Exhibition, Bucharest. Sheet 110 × 80 mm comprising T **1** and **247**. Imperf. No gum.

MS2039	81 (p) blue and deep blue; 10l. carmine and rose (sold at 50l.)	5·00	4·00

270 "The Third Letter"

271 Michael Eminescu

1950. Birth Centenary of Eminescu (poet).

2040	**270**	11l. green	75	50
2041	–	11l. brown	1·10	45
2042	–	11l. mauve	75	35
2043	–	11l. violet	75	35
2044	**271**	11l. blue	70	35

DESIGNS (Scenes representing poems): No. 2041, "Angel and Demon"; 2042, "Ruler and Proletariat"; 2043, "Life".

272 "Dragaica Fair"

1950. Birth Centenary of Ion Andreescu (painter).

(a) Perf.

2045	**272**	5l. olive	70	50
2047	–	20l. brown	1·50	1·00

(b) Perf or imperf.

2046	–	11l. blue	1·10	60

DESIGNS—VERT: 11l. Andreescu. HORIZ: 20l. "The Village Well".

273 Factory and Graph

274 Worker and Flag

1950. State Plan, 1950 Inscr "PLANUL DU STAT 1950".

2048	**273**	11l. red	25	20
2049	–	31l. violet	85	35

DESIGN: 31l. Tractor and factories.

No. 2048 exists imperf.

1950. Labour Day. Perf or imperf.

2050	**274**	31l. orange	30	10

275 Emblem of Republic

276 Trumpeter and Drummer

1950.

2051	**275**	50b. black	25	20
2052		1l. red	20	10
2053		2l. grey	20	10
2054		3l. purple	25	10
2055		4l. mauve	20	10
2056		5l. brown	25	10
2057		6l. green	25	10
2058		7l. brown	25	10
2059		7l.50 blue	35	10
2060		10l. brown	45	10
2061		11l. red	45	10
2062		15l. blue	45	10
2063		20l. green	45	10
2064		31l. green	60	10
2065		36l. brown	1·00	45

For stamps as Type **275** but with inscriptions in white, see Nos. 2240, etc, and Nos. 2277/8.

1950. 1st Anniv of Romanian Pioneers Organization.

2074	**276**	8l. blue	85	45
2075	–	11l. purple	1·30	75
2076	–	31l. red	2·40	1·50

DESIGNS: 11l. Children reading; 31l. Youth parade.

277 Engineer

278 Aurel Vlaicu and his Airplane No. 1 "Crazy Fly"

1950. Industrial Nationalization.

2077	**277**	11l. red	25	25
2078		11l. blue	45	25
2079		11l. brown	45	25
2080		11l. olive	15	15

1950. 40th Anniv of 1st Flight by A. Vlaicu.

2081	**278**	3l. green	30	20
2082		6l. blue	30	25
2083		8l. blue	40	35

279 Mother and Child

1950. Peace Congress, Bucharest.

2084	**279**	11l. red	20	20
2085	–	20l. brown	30	20

DESIGN: 20l. Lathe operator and graph.

280 Statue and Flags

282 Young People and Badge

1950. Romanian–Soviet Amity.

2086	**280**	30l. brown	40	25

1950. Romanian–Hungarian Amity. Optd **TRAIASCA PRIETENIA ROMANO-MAGHIARA**.

2087	**275**	15l. blue	55	25

1950. GMA Complex Sports Facilities. Designs incorporating badge.

2088	–	3l. red	1·10	1·00
2089	**282**	5l. brown	75	70
2090		5l. blue	75	70
2091	–	11l. green	75	70
2092	–	31l. olive	1·60	1·60

DESIGNS: 3l. Agriculture and Industry; 11l. Runners; 31l. Gymnasts.

283

284 Ski-jumper

1950. 3rd Congress of "ARLUS".
2093 **283** 11l. orange on orange . . 30 25
2094 11l. blue on blue 30 25

1951. Winter Sports.
2095 **284** 4l. brown 45 65
2096 – 5l. red 55 55
2097 – 11l. blue . . . . 1·10 55
2098 – 20l. brown . . . . . . 1·10 90
2099 – 31l. green . . . . 2·75 1·60
DESIGNS: 5l. Skater; 11l. Skier; 20l. Ice hockey; 31l. Tobogganing.

286 Peasant and Tractor

1951. Agricultural and Industrial Exhibition.
2100 – 11l. brown 10 15
2101 **286** 31l. blue 45 25
DESIGN—VERT: 11l. Worker and machine.

287 Star of the Republic, Class I-II

288 Youth Camp

1951. Orders and Medals. Perf or imperf.
2102 – 2l. green 15 20
2103 – 4l. blue 20 25
2104 – 11l. red 30 35
2105 **287** 35l. brown 40 55
DESIGNS: 2l. Medal of Work; 4l. Star of the Republic, Class III–V; 11l. Order of Work.

1951. 2nd Anniv of Romanian Pioneers Organization.
2106 **288** 1l. green 65 45
2107 – 11l. blue 65 45
2108 – 35l. red 85 65
DESIGNS—VERT: 11l. Children meeting Stalin. HORIZ: 35l. Decorating boy on parade.

289 Woman and Flags

290 Ion Negulici

1951. International Women's Day. Perf or imperf.
2109 **289** 11l. brown 40 25

1951. Death Centenary of Negulici (painter).
2110 **290** 35l. red . . . . 2·25 1·75

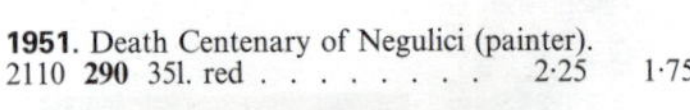

291 Cyclists

1951. Romanian Cycle Race.
2111 **291** 11l. brown . . . . . . 1·10 70

292 F. Sarbu

294 Students

293 "Revolutionary Romania"

1951. 10th Death Anniv of Sarbu (patriot).
2112 **292** 11l. brown 40 25

1951. Death Centenary of C. D. Rosenthal (painter).
2113 **293** 11l. green 95 55
2114 11l. orange 95 55
2115 – 11l. brown 95 55
2116 – 11l. violet 95 55
DESIGN—VERT: Nos. 2115/16, "Rumania calls to the Masses".

1951. 3rd World Youth Festival, Berlin.
2117 **294** 1l. red 30 35
2118 – 5l. blue 60 35
2119 – 11l. purple . . . . . . 1·00 75
DESIGNS: 5l. Girl, boy and flag; 11l. Young people around globe.

295 "Scanteia" Building

296 Soldier and Pithead

1951. 20th Anniv of "Scanteia" (Communist newspaper).
2120 **295** 11l. blue 40 25

1951. Miners' Day.
2121 **296** 5l. blue 30 25
2122 – 11l. mauve 45 25
DESIGN: 11l. Miner and pithead.

297 Order of Defence

298 Oil Refinery

1951. Liberation Day.
2123 **297** 10l. red 30 25

1951. Five-Year Plan. Dated "1951 1955".
2124 **298** 1l. olive (postage) . . . 25 20
2125 – 2l. red 90 20
2126 – 3l. red 50 40
2127 – 4l. brown 35 20
2128 – 5l. green 35 15
2129 – 6l. blue . . . . 1·30 90
2130 – 7l. green 85 45
2131 – 8l. brown 55 30
2132 – 11l. blue . . . . . . 1·10 40
2133 – 35l. violet 75 50

2134 – 30l. green (air) . . . . 3·00 2·00
2135 – 50l. brown . . . . . . 6·00 4·25
DESIGNS: 2l. Miner and pithead; 3l. Soldier and pylons; 4l. Steel furnace; 5l. Combine-harvester; 6l. Canal construction; 7l. Threshing machine; 8l. Sanatorium; 11l. Dam and pylons; 30l. Potato planting; 35l. Factory; 50l. Liner, steam locomotive and Lisunov Li-2 airliner.

299 Orchestra and Dancers

300 Soldier and Arms

1951. Music Festival.
2136 **299** 11l. brown 30 35
2137 – 11l. blue (Mixed choir) 40 25
2138 – 11l. mauve (Lyre and dove) (vert) . . . 30 25

1951. Army Day.
2139 **300** 11l. blue 30 25

301 Arms of U.S.S.R. and Romania

1951. Romanian–Soviet Friendship.
2140 **301** 4l. brown on buff . . . 20 20
2141 35l. orange 60 50

302 P. Tcancenco

304 I. L. Caragiale

303 Open Book "1907"

1951. 25th Death Anniv of Tcancenco (revolutionary).
2142 **302** 10l. olive 30 45

1952. Birth Centenary of Ion Caragiale (dramatist).
(a) Unissued values surch.
2143 **303** 20b. on 11l. red 55 40
2144 – 55b. on 11l. green . . . 80 45
2145 **304** 75b. on 11l. blue . . . . 1·10 55

(b) Without surch.
2146 **303** 55b. red . . . . 1·00 25
2147 – 55b. green . . . . 1·00 25
2148 **304** 55b. blue . . . . 1·00 25
2149 – 1l. brown . . . . 2·50 1·20
DESIGNS—HORIZ: Nos. 2144, 2147, Profile of Caragiale; 1l. Caragiale addressing assembly.

1952. Currency revalued. Surch.
2174 **275** 3b. on 1l. red . . . . . 1·30 4·50
2175 3b. on 2l. grey . . . . 1·50 90
2176 3b. on 4l. mauve . . . 1·30 85
2177 3b. on 5l. red . . . . . 1·50 90
2178 3b. on 7l.50 blue . . . 4·25 1·30
2179 3b. on 10l. brown . . . 1·50 90
2157a **255** 3b. on 30l. red . . . . 6·25 4·75
2158 – 3b. on 50l. (No. 2005) 1·80 1·40
2159 – 3b. on 100l. (No. 2006) 6·25 3·00
2191 **278** 10b. on 3l. green . . . 1·50 70
2218 **301** 10b. on 4l. brown on buff 80 70
2192 **278** 10b. on 6l. blue . . . . 1·60 70
2193 10b. on 8l. blue . . . . 1·60 70
2220 **302** 10b. on 10l. olive . . . 1·75 70
2160 **263** 10b. on 11l. red . . . . 2·40 1·80
2164 **270** 10b. on 11l. green . . . 2·40 1·80
2165 – 10b. on 11l. (No. 2041) 2·20 1·80
2166 – 10b. on 11l. (No. 2042) 2·20 1·80
2167 – 10b. on 11l. (No. 2043) 2·20 1·80
2168 **271** 10b. on 11l. blue . . . 2·20 1·80
2161 **263** 10b. on 30l. green . . . 2·50 1·80
2219 **301** 10b. on 35l. orange . . 2·00 1·20
2199 – 20b. on 2l. (No. 2102) 2·75 1·60
2200 – 20b. on 4l. (No. 2103) 2·75 1·60
2171 **273** 20b. on 11l. red . . . . 1·70 1·10
2201 – 20b. on 11l. (No. 2104) 2·75 1·60
2194 – 20b. on 20l. (No. 2085) 1·70 80
2172 – 20b. on 31l. (No. 2049) 1·70 1·10
2202 **287** 20b. on 35l. brown . . 2·75 1·60
2206 **298** 35b. on 1l. olive . . . . 2·75 95
2207 – 35b. on 2l. (No. 2125) 4·50 1·40
2208 – 35b. on 3l. (No. 2126) 3·25 1·40
2209 – 35b. on 4l. (No. 2127) 2·75 1·50
2210 – 35b. on 5l. (No. 2128) 2·75 2·30
2151 **241** 50b. on 12l. blue . . . 2·75 65
2180 **275** 55b. on 50b. black . . 4·50 1·20
2181 55b. on 3l. purple . . . 4·50 1·20
2195 – 55b. on 3l. (No. 2088) 19·00 12·00
2169 **272** 55b. on 5l. olive . . . . 7·00 3·75
2204 **295** 55b. on 5l. blue . . . . 5·75 2·75
2182 **275** 55b. on 6l. green . . . 4·50 1·20
2183 55b. on 7l. brown . . . 4·50 1·20
2188 **276** 55b. on 8l. blue . . . . 5·25 4·00
2205 **297** 55b. on 10l. red . . . . 3·00 2·40
2170 – 55b. on 11l. (No. 2046) 7·25 3·25
2189 – 55b. on 11l. (No. 2075) 4·00 3·00
2150 **233** 55b. on 12l. blue . . . 1·70 1·80
2184 **275** 55b. on 15l. blue . . . 4·00 1·20
2185 55b. on 20l. green . . . 4·25 1·80
2196 – 55b. on 20l. (No. 2098) 18·00 12·00
2186 **275** 55b. on 31l. green . . . 4·75 1·20
2173 **274** 55b. on 31l. orange . . 2·75 2·50
2190 – 55b. on 31l. (No. 2076) 4·00 4·00
2197 – 55b. on 31l. (No. 2099) 17·00 12·00
2198 **286** 55b. on 31l. blue . . . 3·00 2·75
2203 – 55b. on 35l. (No. 2108) 4·00 5·25
2187 **275** 55b. on 36l. brown . . 4·25 1·70
2211 – 1l. on 6l. (No. 2129) . . 6·00 3·75
2212 – 1l. on 7l. (No. 2130) . . 6·00 2·20
2213 – 1l. on 8l. (No. 2131) . . 4·50 2·75
2214 – 1l. on 11l. (No. 2132) 6·00 2·30
2216 – 1l. on 30l. (No. 2134) 6·75 2·10
2215 – 1l. on 35l. (No. 2133) 6·00 2·10
2217 – 1l. on 50l. (No. 2135) 13·50 4·25
2152 – 1l.75 on 2l.+2l. purple (No. 1974) . . . . . 7·00 3·00
2153 **245** 1l.75 on 5l.+5l. violet 7·00 3·00
2154 **246** 1l.75 on 11l. red . . . 7·00 3·00
2155 – 1l.75 on 10l.+10l. (No. 1977) . . . . . 7·00 3·00
2156 – 1l.75 on 36l.+18l. (No. 1978) . . . . . 7·00 3·00

1952. Air. Surch with airplane, **AERIANA** and value.
2162 **264** 3l. on 20l. brown . . . . 30·00 21·00
2163 **265** 5l. on 30l. blue . . . . 45·00 24·00

307 Railwayman

308 Gogol and character from "Taras Bulba"

1952. Railway Day.
2229 **307** 55b. brown . . . . . . 1·75 25

1952. Death Centenary of Nikolai Gogol (Russian writer).
2230 **308** 55b. blue 85 25
2231 – 1l.75 green . . . . . . 2·75 45
DESIGN—VERT: 1l.75, Gogol and open book.

309 Maternity Medal

310 I. P. Pavlov

1952. International Women's Day.
2232 **309** 20b. blue and purple . . 50 15
2233 – 55b. brown and chestnut 1·00 30
2234 – 1l.75 brown and red . . 2·50 45
MEDALS: 55b. "Glory of Maternity" medal; 1l.75, "Mother Heroine" medal.

1952. Romanian–Soviet Medical Congress.
2235 **310** 11l. red . . . . 1·90 25

311 Hammer and Sickle Medal

312 Boy and Girl Pioneers

1952. Labour Day.
2236 **311** 55b. brown . . . . . . 1·20 20

1952. 3rd Anniv of Romanian Pioneers Organization.
2237 **312** 20b. brown 80 15
2238 – 55b. green . . . . 1·80 25
2239 – 1l.75 blue . . . . 3·75 35
DESIGNS—VERT: 55b. Pioneer nature-study group. HORIZ: 1l.75, Worker and pioneers.

1952. As T **275** but with figures and inscriptions in white. Bani values size $20\frac{1}{4} \times 24\frac{1}{4}$ mm, lei values size $24\frac{1}{2} \times 29\frac{1}{2}$ mm.
2240 **275** 3b. orange 25 20
2241 5b. red 35 15
2242 7b. green 40 25
2243 10b. brown 50 15
2244 20b. blue . . . . 1·75 15
2245 35b. brown . . . . . . 1·20 15
2246 50b. green . . . . . . 1·60 15
2247 55b. violet . . . . . . 3·50 15
2248 1l.10 brown . . . . . . 3·25 20
2249 1l.75 violet . . . . . . 15·50 35
2250 2l. olive . . . . 3·25 40
2251 2l.35 brown . . . . . . 3·50 35
2252 2l.55 orange . . . . . 4·50 35
2253 3l. green . . . . 4·75 35
2254 5l. red . . . . 6·25 60
For similar stamps with star added at top of emblem, see Nos. 2277/8.

314 "Smirdan" (after Grigorescu)

315 Leonardo da Vinci

1952. 75th Anniv of Independence.
2255 **314** 50b. lake 55 10
2256 – 1l.10 blue 90 30

DESIGN—HORIZ: 1l.10, Romanian and Russian soldiers.

1952. 500th Anniv of Birth of Leonardo da Vinci.
2257 **315** 55b. violet . . . . . . 2·30 35

316 Miner **317** Students' Union Badge

1952. Miners' Day.
2258 **316** 20b. red . . . . 1·10 30
2259 55b. violet . . . . . . 1·00 25

1952. Int Students' Union Council, Bucharest.
2260 **317** 10b. blue 20 10
2261 – 20b. orange . . . . . . 1·50 25
2262 – 55b. green . . . . 1·50 30
2263 – 1l.75 red . . . . 2·75 75
DESIGNS—HORIZ: 20b. Student in laboratory (35½ × 22 mm); 1l.75, Six students dancing (30 × 24 mm). VERT: 55b. Students playing football (24 × 30 mm).

318 Soldier, Sailor and Airman

1952. Army Day.
2264 **318** 55b. blue 85 25

319 Statue and Flags **320** Workers and Views of Russia and Romania (after N. Parlius)

1952. Romanian–Soviet Friendship.
2265 **319** 55b. red 55 10
2266 **320** 1l.75 brown . . . . . . 1·50 30

321 Rowing **322** N. Balcescu (after C. Tattarescu)

1952. Physical Culture.
2267 **321** 20b. blue . . . . 1·90 20
2268 – 1l.75 red (Athletes) . . . 4·75 60

1952. Death Centenary of Balcescu (revolutionary).
2269 **322** 55b. grey . . . . 2·40 10
2270 1l.75 olive . . . . 6·00 75

323 Emblem and Flags **324**

1952. New Constitution.
2271 **323** 55b. green 95 25

1952. 5th Anniv of People's Republic.
2272 **324** 55b. multicoloured . . . 1·70 40

325 Millo, Caragiale and Mme. Romanescu **326** Foundry Worker

1953. Centenary of Caragiale National Theatre.
2273 **325** 55b. blue . . . . 1·70 25

1953. 3rd Industrial and Agricultural Congress.
2274 **326** 55b. green 60 10
2275 – 55b. orange 50 30
2276 – 55b. brown 65 10
DESIGNS—HORIZ: No. 2275, Farm workers and tractor; 2276, Workman, refinery and oil wells.

1953. As Nos. 2240, etc, but with star added at top of emblem.
2277 **275** 5b. red 35 15
2278 55b. purple . . . . . . 1·00 25

327 "The Strikers of Grivitsa" (after Nazarev)

1953. 20th Anniv of Grivitsa Strike.
2279 **327** 55b. brown . . . . . . 1·40 25

328

1953. 5th Anniv of Treaty of Friendship with Russia.
2280 **328** 55b. brown on blue . . . 1·40 25

329 Table Tennis Badge **330** Oltenian Carpet

1953. 20th World Table Tennis Championship, Bucharest.
2281 **329** 55b. green . . . . 5·00 1·00
2282 55b. brown . . . . . . 4·25 75

1953. Romanian Art.
2283 – 10b. green 35 10
2284 – 20b. brown 80 10
2285 – 35b. violet . . . . . . 1·40 10
2286 – 55b. blue . . . . 2·40 10
2287 **330** 1l. purple . . . . 4·25 20
DESIGNS—VERT: 10b. Pottery; 20b. Campulung peasant girl; 55b. Apuseni Mountains peasant girl. HORIZ: 35b. National dance.

331 Karl Marx **332** Pioneers planting Tree

1953. 70th Death Anniv of Karl Marx.
2288 **331** 1l.55 brown . . . . . . 1·70 35

1953. 4th Anniv of Romanian Pioneers Organization.
2289 **332** 35b. green 80 20
2290 – 55b. blue . . . . 1·30 20
2291 – 1l.75 brown . . . . . . 2·10 40
DESIGNS—VERT: 55b. Boy and girl flying model gliders. HORIZ: 1l.75, Pioneers and instructor.

333 Women and Flags **334**

1953. 3rd World Congress of Women.
2292 **333** 55b. brown . . . . . . 1·20 25

1953. 4th World Youth Festival.
2293 **334** 20b. orange 55 25
2294 – 55b. blue 70 40
2295 – 65b. red 95 65
2296 – 1l.75 purple . . . . . . 3·75 1·30
DESIGNS—VERT: 55b. Students releasing dove over globe. HORIZ: 65b. Girl presenting bouquet; 1l.75, Folk dancers.

335 Cornfield and Forest **336** V. V. Mayakovsky

1953. Forestry Month.
2297 – 20b. blue 65 55
2298 **335** 38b. green 60 80
2299 – 55b. brown . . . . . . 2·30 60
DESIGNS—VERT: 20b. Waterfall and trees; 55b. Forestry worker.

1953. 60th Birth Anniv of Vladimir Mayakovsky (Russian poet).
2300 **336** 55b. brown . . . . . . 1·20 35

337 Miner

1953. Miners' Day.
2301 **337** 1l.55 black . . . . . . 2·00 25

338 Telephonist, G.P.O. and P.O. Worker

1953. 50th Anniv of Construction of G.P.O.
2302 **338** 20b. brown 35 10
2303 – 55b. olive 60 10
2304 – 1l. blue . . . . 1·30 20
2305 – 1l.55 lake . . . . 2·00 45
DESIGNS: 55b. Postwoman and G.P.O.; 1l. G.P.O. radio transmitter and map; 1l.55, Telegraphist, G.P.O. and teletypist.

339 **340** Soldier and Flag

1953. 9th Anniv of Liberation.
2306 **339** 55b. brown 85 25

1953. Army Day.
2307 **340** 55b. olive 95 25

341 Girl and Model Glider

1953. Aerial Sports.
2308 **341** 10b. green and orange . . 1·90 35
2309 – 20b. olive and brown . . 2·75 20
2310 – 55b. purple and red . . 10·00 45
2311 – 1l.75 brown and purple 12·00 70
DESIGNS: 20b. Parachutists; 55b. Glider and pilot; 1l.75, Zlin Z-22 monoplane.

342 Workman, Girl and Flags

1953. Romanian–Soviet Friendship.
2312 **342** 55b. brown 60 10
2313 – 1l.55 lake . . . . 1·50 35
DESIGN: 1l.55, Spassky Tower (Moscow Kremlin) and Volga–Don canal.

343 "Unity"

1953. 3rd World Trades' Union Congress.
2314 **343** 55b. olive 50 20
2315 – 1l.25 red . . . . 1·30 45
DESIGN—VERT: 1l.25, Workers, flags and globe.

344 C. Porumbescu **345** Agricultural Machinery

1953. Birth Centenary of Porumbescu (composer).
2316 **344** 55b. lilac . . . . 5·25 25

1953. Agricultural designs.
2317 **345** 10b. olive 15 10
2318 – 35b. green 40 10
2319 – 2l.55 brown . . . . . . 2·75 65
DESIGNS: 35b. Tractor drawing disc harrows; 2l.55, Cows grazing.

346 Vlaicu and his Airplane No. 1 "Crazy Fly" **347** Lenin

1953. 40th Death Anniv of Vlaicu (pioneer aviator).
2320 **346** 50b. blue 85 25

1954. 30th Death Anniv of Lenin.
2321 **347** 55b. brown . . . . . . 1·10 25

348 Red Deer Stag **350** O. Bancila

349 Calimanesti

1954. Forestry Month.
2322 **348** 20b. brown on yellow . . 4·50 35
2323 – 55b. violet on yellow . . 2·30 35
2324 – 1l.75 blue on yellow . . 4·25 75
DESIGNS: 55b. Pioneers planting tree; 1l.75, Forest.

1954. Workers' Rest Homes.
2325 **349** 5b. black on yellow . . . 60 10
2326 – 1l.55 black on blue . . . 2·00 20
2327 – 2l. green on pink . . . . 4·50 25
2328 – 2l.35 brown on green . . 3·75 90
2329 – 2l.55 brown on green . . 4·25 1·10
DESIGNS: 1l.55, Siniai; 2l. Predeal; 2l.35, Tusnad; 2l.55, Govora.

1954. 10th Death Anniv of Bancila (painter).
2330 **350** 55b. green and brown . . 2·10 1·30

351 Child and Dove of Peace

353 Stephen the Great

352 Girl Pioneer feeding Calf

1954. International Children's Day.
2331 **351** 55b. brown 85 25

1954. 5th Anniv of Romanian Pioneer Organization.
2332 **352** 20b. black 40 15
2333 – 55b. blue 70 25
2334 – 1l.75 red . . . . 3·75 55
DESIGNS: 55b. Girl Pioneers harvesting; 1l.75, Young Pioneers examining globe.

1954. 450th Death Anniv of Stephen the Great.
2335 **353** 55b. brown . . . . . . 1·40 30

354 Miner operating Coal-cutter

355 Dr. V. Babes

1954. Miners' Day.
2336 **354** 1l.75 black . . . . . . 1·40 45

1954. Birth Centenary of Babes (pathologist).
2337 **355** 55b. red . . . . 1·20 25

356 Sailor, Flag and Destroyer "Regele Ferdinand"

357 Dedication Tablet

1954. Navy Day.
2338 **356** 55b. blue 95 25

1954. 5th Anniv of Mutual Aid Organization.
2339 – 20b. violet 55 10
2340 **357** 55b. brown 95 20
DESIGN: 20b. Man receiving money from counter clerk.

358 Liberation Monument

359 Recreation Centre

1954. 10th Anniv of Liberation.
2341 **358** 55b. violet and red . . . 1·10 25

1954. Liberation Anniv Celebrations.
2342 **359** 20b. blue 25 10
2343 – 38b. violet 85 25
2344 – 55b. purple 95 20
2345 – 1l.55 brown . . . . . 2·50 40
DESIGNS—38×22 mm: 55b. "Scanteia" offices. 24½×29½ mm: 38b. Opera House, Bucharest; 1l.55, Radio Station.

360 Pilot and Mikoyan Gurevich MiG-15 Jet Fighters

361 Chemical Plant and Oil Derricks

1954. Aviation Day.
2346 **360** 55b. blue . . . . 2·50 25

1954. International Chemical and Petroleum Workers Conference, Bucharest.
2347 **361** 55b. black . . . . 2·50 35

362 Dragon Pillar, Peking

363 T. Neculuta

1954. Chinese Culture Week.
2348 **362** 55b. black on yellow . . 2·40 35

1954. 50th Death Anniv of Dumitru Theodor Neculuta (poet).
2349 **363** 55b. violet . . . . . . 1·50 20

364 ARLUS Badge

365 Friendship

1954. 10th Anniv of "ARLUS" and Romanian–Russian Friendship.
2350 **364** 55b. red 50 20
2351 **365** 65b. purple 80 20

366 G. Tattarescu

367 B. Iscovescu

1954. 60th Death Anniv of Gheorghe Tattarescu (painter).
2352 **366** 55b. red . . . . 1·60 20

1954. Death Centenary of Barbu Iscovescu (painter).
2353 **367** 1l.75 brown . . . . . . 2·75 40

368 Teleprinter

369 Wild Boar

1954. Cent of Telecommunications in Romania.
2354 **368** 50b. lilac . . . . 1·00 20

1955. Forestry Month. Inscr "LUNA PADURII 1955".
2355 **369** 35b. brown . . . . . . 1·30 15
2356 – 65b. blue . . . . 1·40 25
2357 – 1l.20 red . . . . 4·25 50
DESIGNS: 65b. Tree planting; 1l.20, Logging.

370 Airman

371 Clasped Hands

1955. Occupations.
2358 – 3b. blue 15 10
2359 – 5b. violet 05 10
2360 **370** 10b. brown 15 10
2361 – 20b. mauve 05 10
2362 – 30b. blue . . . . 1·10 10
2363 – 35b. turquoise 30 10
2364 – 40b. blue . . . . 1·10 15
2365 – 55b. olive 75 10
2366 – 1l. violet . . . . 1·30 10
2367 – 1l.55 lake . . . . . . 2·10 10
2368 – 2l.35 buff . . . . . . 3·50 35
2369 – 2l.55 green . . . . . 4·00 30
DESIGNS: 3b. Scientist; 5b. Foundryman; 20b. Miner; 30b. Tractor driver; 35b. Schoolboy; 40b. Girl student; 55b. Bricklayer; 1l. Sailor; 1l.55, Mill girl; 2l.35, Soldier; 2l.55, Telegraph linesman.

1955. International Conference of Postal Municipal Workers, Vienna.
2370 **371** 25b. red 40 25

372 Lenin

373 Dove and Globe

1955. 85th Birth Anniv of Lenin. Portraits of Lenin.
2371 **372** 20b. brown and bistre 45 20
2372 – 55b. brown (full face) . . 1·10 20
2373 – 1l. lake and red (half length) . . . . 1·50 30

1955. Peace Congress, Helsinki.
2374 **373** 55b. blue 85 25

374 War Memorial, Berlin

375 Children and Dove

1955. 10th Anniv of Victory over Germany.
2375 **374** 55b. blue 85 25

1955. International Children's Day.
2376 **375** 55b. brown 85 25

376 "Service"

377 People's Art Museum

1955. European Volleyball Championships.
2377 – 55b. mauve and pink . . 4·25 1·40
2378 **376** 1l.75 mauve and yellow 9·50 1·60
DESIGN: 55b. Volleyball players.

1955. Bucharest Museums.
2379 – 20b. mauve 30 15
2380 – 55b. brown 55 15
2381 **377** 1l.20 black . . . . . . 1·30 50
2382 – 1l.75 green . . . . . . 1·40 50
2383 – 2l.55 purple . . . . . . 4·25 65
MUSEUMS—30×24½ mm: 20b. Theodor Aman; 2l.55, Simu. 34×23 mm: 55b. Lenin-Stalin; 1l.75, Republican Art.

378 Mother and Child

379 "Nature Study"

1955. 1st World Mothers' Congress, Lausanne.
2384 **378** 55b. blue 95 25

1955. 5th Anniv of Pioneer Headquarters, Bucharest.
2385 – 10b. blue . . . . 1·20 10
2386 **379** 20b. green . . . . . . 1·10 10
2387 – 55b. purple . . . . . . 2·75 10
DESIGNS: 10b. Model railway; 55b. Headquarters building.

380 Coxed Four

381 Anton Pann (folklorist)

1955. Women's European Rowing Championships, Snagov.
2388 **380** 55b. green . . . . . . 5·75 65
2389 – 1l. blue (Woman sculler) 10·00 1·10

1955. Romanian Writers.
2390 – 55b. blue 95 30
2391 – 55b. grey 95 30
2392 **381** 55b. olive 95 30
2393 – 55b. violet 95 30
2394 – 55b. purple 95 30
PORTRAITS—No. 2390, Dimitrie Cantemir (historian); 2391, Metropolitan Dosoftei (religious writer); 2393, Constantin Cantacuzino (historian); 2394, Ienachita Vacarescu (poet, grammarian and historian).

382 Marksman

383 Fire Engine

1955. European Sharpshooting Championships, Bucharest.
2395 **382** 1l. brown and light brown . . . . 3·25 45

1955. Firemen's Day.
2396 **383** 55b. red . . . . 1·40 40

384

385 Spraying Fruit Trees

1955. 10th Anniv of W.F.T.U.
2397 **384** 55b. olive 45 10
2398 – 1l. blue 80 20
DESIGN: 1l. Workers and flag.

1955. Fruit and Vegetable Cultivation.
2399 **385** 10b. green 40 15
2400 – 20b. red 70 30
2401 – 55b. blue . . . . 1·40 30
2402 – 1l. lake . . . . 4·25 90
DESIGNS: 20b. Fruit picking; 55b. Harvesting grapes; 1l. Gathering vegetables.

386

387 Michurin

1955. 4th ARLUS Congress.
2403 **386** 20b. blue and buff . . . 55 15

1955. Birth Cent of Ivan Michurin (Russian botanist).
2404 **387** 55b. blue 95 15

388 Cotton

389 Sheep and Shepherd blowing Bucium

1955.
2405 – 10b. purple (Sugar beet) 45 20
2406 **388** 20b. grey 70 20

2407 – 55b. blue (Linseed) 2·10 45
2408 – 1l.55 brown (Sunflower) 4·25 85

1955.
2409 **389** 5b. brown and green 1·10 15
2410 – 10b. violet and bistre 1·30 25
2411 – 35b. brown and salmon 2·75 55
2412 – 55b. brown and bistre 5·00 70
DESIGNS: 10b. Pigs and farm girl; 35b. Cows and dairy maid; 55b. Horses and groom.

390 Johann von Schiller (novelist)
391 Bank and Book

1955. Literary Anniversaries.
2413 – 20b. blue 40 10
2414 – 55b. blue 1·20 20
2415 **390** 1l. grey 1·80 20
2416 – 1l.55 brown 4·25 90
2417 – 1l.75 violet 4·50 90
2418 – 2l. lake 5·25 1·40
DESIGNS: 20b. Hans Christian Andersen (children's writer, 150th birth anniv); 55b. Adam Mickiewicz (poet, death centenary); 1l. Type **390** (150th death anniv); 1l.55, Baron de Montesquieu (philosopher, death bicentenary); 1l.75, Walt Whitman (centenary of publication of "Leaves of Grass"; 2l. Miguel de Cervantes (350th anniv of publication of "Don Quixote").

1955. Savings Bank.
2419 **391** 55b. blue 2·10 20
2420 55b. violet 5·50 3·50

392 Family
393 Brown Hare

1956. National Census.
2421 – 55b. orange 30 10
2422 **392** 1l.75 brown and green 1·50 55
DESIGNS: 55b. "21 FEBRUARIE 1956" in circle.

1956. Wild Life.
2423 **393** 20b. black and green 2·40 1·90
2424 – 20b. black and olive 3·00 1·90
2425 – 35b. black and blue 2·40 1·90
2426 – 50b. brown and blue 2·40 1·90
2427 – 55b. green and bistre 3·00 1·90
2428 – 55b. brown and turquoise 3·00 1·90
2429 – 1l. lake and green 5·50 4·25
2430 – 1l.55 lake and blue 5·75 4·25
2431 – 1l.75 brown and green 8·00 6·50
2432 – 2l. brown and blue 28·00 20·00
2433 – 3l.25 black and green 28·00 20·00
2434 – 4l.25 brown and salmon 28·00 20·00
DESIGNS—VERT: No. 2424, Great bustard; 35b. Brown trout; 1l.55, Eurasian red squirrel; 1l.75, Western capercaillie; 4l.25, Red deer. HORIZ: 50b. Wild boar; No. 2427, Common pheasant; No. 2428, Brown bear; 1l. Lynx; 2l. Chamois; 3l.25, Pintail.
See also Nos. 2474/85.

394 Insurgents
395 Boy and Globe

1956. 85th Anniv of Paris Commune.
2435 **394** 55b. red 95 40

1956. International Children's Day.
2436 **395** 55b. violet 1·20 35

396 Red Cross Nurse
397 Tree

1956. 2nd Romanian Red Cross Congress.
2437 **396** 55b. olive and red 1·70 35

1956. Forestry Month.
2438 **397** 20b. grey on green 65 20
2439 – 55b. black on green 5·00 30
DESIGN: 55b. Lumber train.

398 Woman Speaking
399 Academy Buildings

1956. International Women's Congress, Bucharest.
2440 **398** 55b. green 95 35

1956. 90th Anniv of Romanian People's Academy.
2441 **399** 55b. green and buff 95 25

400 Vuia, Biplane, Vuia No. 1 and Yakovlev Yak-25 Fighters

1956. 50th Anniv of 1st Flight by Traian Vuia (pioneer airman).
2442 **400** 55b. brown and olive 1·10 35

401 Georgescu and Statues
402 Farm Girl

1956. Birth Centenary of Ion Georgescu (sculptor).
2443 **401** 55b. brown and green 1·40 25

1956. Collective Farming. (a) Inscr "1951–1956".
2444 **402** 55b. plum 6·00 5·50

(b) Inscr "1949–56".
2445 **402** 55b. plum 85 25

403 Black-veined White
404 Striker

1956. Insect Pests.
2446 **403** 10b. cream, black and violet 6·50 40
2447 – 55b. orange and brown 8·00 65
2448 – 1l.75 lake and olive 12·00 7·50
2449 – 1l.75 brown and olive 15·00 1·30
PESTS: 55b. Colorado potato beetle; 1l.75 (2), May beetle.

1956. 50th Anniv of Dockers' Strike at Galatz.
2450 **404** 55b. brown on pink 95 25

405
406 Gorky

1956. 25th Anniv of "Scanteia" (Communist newspaper).
2451 **405** 55b. blue 85 25

1956. 20th Death Anniv of Maksim Gorky.
2452 **406** 55b. brown 1·40 35

407 T. Aman
408 Snowdrops and Polyanthus

1956. 125th Birth Anniv of Aman (painter).
2453 **407** 55b. grey 1·40 45

1956. Flowers. Designs multicoloured. Colours of backgrounds given.
2454 **408** 5b. blue 60 20
2455 – 55b. black 1·70 40
2456 – 1l.75 blue 4·50 55
2457 – 3l. green 8·75 95
FLOWERS: 55b. Daffodil and violets; 1l.75, Antirrhinums and campanulas; 3l. Poppies and lilies of the valley.

409 Janos Hunyadi
410 Olympic Flame

1956. 500th Death Anniv of Hunyadi.
2458 **409** 55b. violet 95 40

1956. Olympic Games.
2459 **410** 20b. red 70 20
2460 – 55b. blue 1·20 25
2461 – 1l. mauve 1·40 30
2462 – 1l.55 turquoise 2·20 35
2463 – 1l.75 violet 2·75 45
DESIGNS: 55b. Water-polo; 1l. Ice-skating; 1l.55, Canoeing; 1l.75, High-jumping.

411 George Bernard Shaw (dramatist)
412 Ilyushin Il-18 Airliner over City

1956. Cultural Anniversaries.
2464 – 20b. blue 45 10
2465 – 35b. red 55 15
2466 **411** 40b. brown 55 20
2467 – 50b. brown 70 50
2468 – 55b. olive 1·20 50
2469 – 1l. turquoise 1·30 20
2470 – 1l.55 violet 2·50 20
2471 – 1l.75 blue 3·25 20
2472 – 2l.55 purple 4·00 35
2473 – 3l.25 blue 4·50 70
DESIGNS: 20b. Benjamin Franklin (U.S. statesman and journalist, 250th birth anniv); 35b. Toyo Oda (painter, 450th death anniv); 40b. Type **411** (birth centenary); 50b. Ivan Franco (writer, birth centenary); 55b. Pierre Curie (physicist, 50th death anniv); 1l. Henrik Ibsen (dramatist, 50th death anniv); 1l.55, Fyodor Dostoevsky (novelist, 75th death anniv); 1l.75, Heinrich Heine (poet, death centenary); 2l.55, Wolfgang Amadeus Mozart (composer, birth bicentenary); 3l.25, Rembrandt (artist, 350th birth anniv).

1956. Wild Life. As Nos. 2423/34 but colours changed. Imperf.
2474 20b. brown and green 2·30 2·20
2475 20b. black and blue 3·75 3·50
2476 35b. black and blue 2·30 2·40
2477 50b. black and brown 2·30 2·40
2478 55b. black and violet 3·50 3·75
2479 55b. brown and green 2·30 2·40
2480 1l. brown and blue 2·30 2·40
2481 1l.55 brown and bistre 2·30 2·40
2482 1l.75 purple and green 3·25 3·50
2483 2l. black and blue 2·30 2·20
2484 3l.25 brown and green 6·50 7·25
2485 4l.25 brown and violet 3·50 3·25

1956. Air. Multicoloured.
2486 20b. Type **412** 50 40
2487 55b. Ilyushin Il-18 over mountains 75 40
2488 1l.75 Ilyushin Il-18 over cornfield 3·50 60
2489 2l.55 Ilyushin Il-18 over seashore 4·00 1·20

413 Georgi Enescu
414 "Rebels" (after Octav Bancila)

1956. 75th Birth Anniv of Enescu (musician).
2490 – 55b. blue 1·10 25
2491 **413** 1l.75 purple 1·70 35
DESIGN: 55b. Enescu when a child, holding violin.

1957. 50th Anniv of Peasant Revolt.
2492 **414** 55b. grey 85 25

415 Stephen the Great
416 Gheorghe Marinescu (neurologist) and Institute of Medicine

1957. 500th Anniv of Accession of Stephen the Great.
2493 **415** 55b. brown 50 35
2494 55b. olive 50 50

1957. National Congress of Medical Sciences, Bucharest, and Centenary of Medical and Pharmaceutical Teaching in Bucharest (1l.75).
2495 **416** 20b. green 25 20
2496 – 35b. brown 35 20
2497 – 55b. purple 1·00 30
2498 – 1l.75 red and blue 3·75 1·20
DESIGNS: As T **416**: 35b. Ioan Cantacuzino (bacteriologist) and Cantacuzino Institute; 55b. Victor Babes (pathologist and bacteriologist) and Babes Institute. 66 × 23 mm: 1l.75, Nicolae Kretzulescu and Carol Dairla (physicians) and Faculty of Medicine, Bucharest.

417 Gymnast and Spectator
418 Emblems of Atomic Energy

1957. 1st European Women's Gymnastic Championships, Bucharest.
2499 **417** 20b. green 35 10
2500 – 35b. red 65 20
2501 – 55b. blue 1·20 30
2502 – 1l.75 purple 3·50 65
DESIGNS—HORIZ: 35b. On asymmetric bars; 55b. Vaulting over horse. VERT: 1l.75, On beam.

1957. 2nd A.S.I.T. Congress.
2503 **418** 55b. brown 1·10 25
2504 55b. blue 1·30 25

419 Dove and Handlebars
420 Rhododendron

1957. 10th International Cycle Race.
2505 **419** 20b. blue 25 15
2506 – 55b. brown 1·00 25
DESIGN: 55b. Racing cyclist.

1957. Flowers of the Carpathian Mountains.
2513 **420** 5b. red and grey 25 10
2514 – 10b. green and grey 35 10
2515 – 20b. orange and grey 40 10
2516 – 35b. olive and grey 65 20
2517 – 55b. blue and grey 80 20
2518 – 1l. red and grey 1·90 50
2519 – 1l.55 yellow and grey 2·40 35
2520 – 1l.75 violet and grey 4·00 45
FLOWERS: 10b. Daphne; 20b. Lily; 35b. Edelweiss; 55b. Gentian; 1l. Dianthus; 1l.55, Primula; 1l.75, Anemone.

421 N. Grigorescu

1957. 50th Death Anniv of Nicolae Grigorescu (painter).
2521 – 20b. green 50 15
2522 **421** 55b. brown . . . . . . 1·00 25
2523 – 1l.75 blue . . . . 4·50 65
DESIGNS—HORIZ: 20b. "Ox-cart"; 1l.75, "Attack on Smirdan".

422 Festival Visitors 423 Festival Emblem

1957. 6th World Youth Festival, Moscow.
2524 **422** 20b. purple 25 10
2525 – 55b. green 75 10
2526 **423** 1l. orange . . . . . . 1·40 45
2527 – 1l.75 blue . . . . 1·80 25
DESIGNS: 55b. Girl with flags (22 × 38 mm); 1l.75, Dancers (49 × 20 mm).

424 Destroyer "Stalingrad" 425 "The Trumpeter" (after N. Grigorescu)

1957. Navy Day.
2528 **424** 1l.75 blue . . . . 1·80 25

1957. 80th Anniv of War of Independence.
2529 **425** 20b. violet 85 25

426 Soldiers Advancing 427 Child with Dove

1957. 40th Anniv of Battle of Marasesti.
2530 **426** 1l.75 brown . . . . . . 1·20 25

1957. Red Cross.
2531 **427** 55b. green and red . . . 85 25

428 Sprinter and Bird 429 Ovid

1957. Int Athletic Championships, Bucharest.
2532 **428** 20b. black and blue . . . 60 10
2533 – 55b. black and yellow . . 1·50 20
2534 – 1l.75 black and red . . . 4·00 45
DESIGNS: 55b. Javelin-thrower and bull; 1l.75, Runner and stag.

1957. Birth Bimillenary of Ovid (Latin poet).
2535 **429** 1l.75 blue . . . . 1·75 45

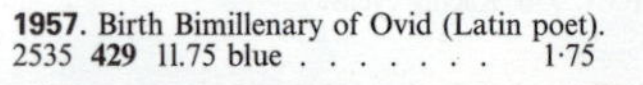

430 Congress Emblem 431 Oil Refinery, 1957

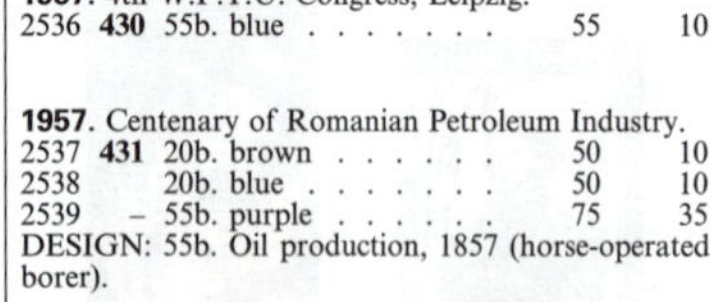

1957. 4th W.F.T.U. Congress, Leipzig.
2536 **430** 55b. blue 55 10

1957. Centenary of Romanian Petroleum Industry.
2537 **431** 20b. brown 50 10
2538 20b. blue 50 10
2539 – 55b. purple 75 35
DESIGN: 55b. Oil production, 1857 (horse-operated borer).

432 Lenin, Youth and Girl 433 Artificial Satellite encircling Globe

1957. 40th Anniv of Russian Revolution.
2540 **432** 10b. red 10 15
2541 – 35b. purple 40 15
2542 – 55b. brown 60 30
DESIGNS—HORIZ: 35b. Lenin and flags; 55b. Statue of Lenin.

1957. Air. Launching of Artificial Satellite by Russia.
2543 **433** 25b. blue 50 50
2545 25b. blue 50 35
2544 – 3l.75 green . . . . . . 4·50 95
2546 – 3l.75 blue . . . . 4·50 95
DESIGN: 3l.75 (2), Satellite's orbit around Globe.
See also Nos. 2593/6.

434 Peasant Soldiers 435 Endre Ady

1957. 520th Anniv of Bobilna Revolution.
2547 **434** 50b. purple 25 15
2548 – 55b. grey 35 20
DESIGN—VERT: 55b. Bobilna Memorial.

1957. 80th Birth Anniv of Endre Ady (Hungarian poet).
2549 **435** 55b. olive 70 25

436 Laika and "Sputnik 2" 437 Black-winged Stilt

1957. Space Flight of Laika (dog).
2550 **436** 1l.20 blue and brown . . 2·25 50
2551 1l.20 blue and brown . . 2·25 50

1957. Fauna of the Danube Delta.
2552 **437** 5b. grey & brown (postage) 30 10
2553 – 10b. orange and green 40 10
2554 – 20b. orange and red . . 45 10
2555 – 50b. orange and green 15 10
2556 – 55b. blue and purple . . 40 10
2557 – 1l.30 orange and violet 2·00 20
2558 – 3l.30 grey and blue (air) 3·00 75
2559 – 5l. orange and red . . . 5·00 1·10
DESIGNS—VERT: 10b. Great egret; 20b. White spoonbill; 50b. Stellate sturgeon. HORIZ: 55b. Stoat; 1l.30, Eastern white pelican; 3l.30, Black-headed gull; 5l. White-tailed sea eagle.

438 Emblem of Republic and Flags

1957. 10th Anniv of People's Republic.
2560 **438** 25b. buff, red and blue 15 10
2561 – 55b. yellow 65 20
2562 – 1l.20 red 75 35
DESIGNS: 55b. Emblem, Industry and Agriculture; 1l.20, Emblem, the Arts and Sports.

439 Republican Flag

1958. 25th Anniv of Strike at Grivitsa.
2563 **439** 1l. red and brown on buff 50 25
2564 1l. red and blue on buff 50 25

440 "Telecommunications"

1958. Socialist Countries' Postal Ministers Conference, Moscow.
2565 **440** 55b. violet 50 25
2566 – 1l.75 purple 85 25
DESIGN: 1l.75, Telegraph pole and pylons carrying lines.

441 Nicolae Balcescu (historian) 442 Fencer

1958. Romanian Writers.
2567 **441** 5b. blue 25 15
2568 – 10b. black 30 20
2569 – 35b. blue 45 20
2570 – 55b. brown 55 20
2571 – 1l.75 black . . . . . . 1·10 35
2572 – 2l. green . . . . 1·30 35
DESIGNS: 10b. Ion Creanga (folklorist); 35b. Alexandru Vlahuta (poet); 55b. Mihail Eminescu (poet); 1l.75, Vasile Alecsandri (poet and dramatist); 2l. Barbu Delavrancea (short-story writer and dramatist).

1958. World Youth Fencing Championships, Bucharest.
2573 **442** 1l.75 mauve 95 25

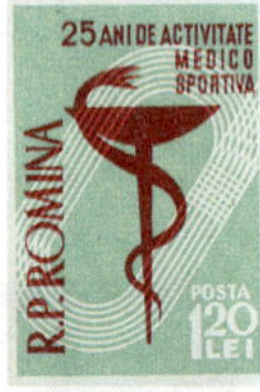

443 Symbols of Medicine and Sport 444

1958. 25th Anniv of Sports Doctors' Service.
2574 **443** 1l.20 red and green . . . 95 25

1958. 4th Int Congress of Democratic Women.
2575 **444** 55b. blue 55 25

445 Linnaeus (botanist) 446 Parasol Mushroom

1958. Cultural Anniversaries (1957).
2576 **445** 10b. blue 20 15
2577 – 20b. brown 30 15
2578 – 40b. mauve 40 20
2579 – 55b. blue 90 15
2580 – 1l. mauve 90 20
2581 – 1l.75 blue . . . . 1·50 30
2582 – 2l. brown . . . . 2·50 35
DESIGNS: 10b. Type **445** (250th birth anniv); 20b. Auguste Comte (philosopher, death centenary); 40b. William Blake (poet and artist, birth bicentenary); 55b. Mikhail Glinka (composer, death centenary); 1l. Henry Longfellow (poet, 150th birth anniv); 1l.75, Carlo Goldoni (dramatist, 250th birth anniv); 2l. John Komensky, Comenius (educationist, 300th death anniv).

1958. Mushrooms. As T **446**.
2583 **446** 5b. brown, lt brn & blue 20 15
2584 – 10b. brown, buff and bronze 20 15
2585 – 20b. red, yellow and grey 20 15
2586 – 30b. brown, orge & green 20 20
2587 – 35b. brown, lt brn & bl 30 15
2588 – 55b. brown, red and green 50 15
2589 – 1l. brown, buff and green . . . . 1·10 20
2590 – 1l.55 pink, drab and grey 1·90 25
2591 – 1l.75 brown, buff and green . . . . 2·25 35
2592 – 2l. yellow, brown and green . . . . 4·25 35
MUSHROOMS: 10b. "Clavaria aurea"; 20b. Caesar's mushroom; 30b. Saffron milk cap; 35b. Honey fungus; 55b. Shaggy ink cap; 1l. "Morchella conica"; 1l.55, Field mushroom; 1l.75, Cep; 2l. Chanterelle.

1958. Brussels International Exhibition. Nos. 2543/4 and 2545/6 optd **EXPOZITIA UNIVERSALA BRUXELLES 1958** and star or with star only.
2593 **433** 25b. green . . . . 2·50 1·80
2595 25b. blue . . . . 18·00 13·00
2594 – 3l.75 green . . . . . . 2·50 1·40
2596 – 3l.75 blue . . . . 17·00 13·00

448 Racovita and "Belgica" (Gerlache expedition, 1897)

1958. 10th Death Anniv (1957) of Emil Racovita (naturalist and explorer).
2597 **448** 55b. indigo and blue . . 2·25 25
2598 – 1l.20 violet and olive . . 1·40 20
DESIGN: 1l.20, Racovita and grotto.

449 Sputnik encircling Globe

1958. Air. Launching of Third Artificial Satellite by Russia.
2599 **449** 3l.25 buff and blue . . . 3·25 1·00

450 Servicemen's Statue

1958. Army Day.
2600 **450** 55b. brown (postage) . . 20 15
2601 – 75b. purple 30 15
2602 – 1l.75 blue 50 20
2603 – 3l.30 violet (air) . . . . 1·30 45
DESIGNS: 75b. Soldier guarding industrial plant; 1l.75, Sailor hoisting flag, and "Royal Ferdinand" destroyer; 3l.30, Pilot and Mikoyan Gurevich MiG-17 jet fighters.

451 Costume of Oltenia 452 Costume of Oltenia

1958. Provincial Costumes.
2604 **451** 35b. red, black and yellow (female) 20 25
2605 **452** 35b. red, black and yellow (male) 20 40
2606 – 40b. red, brown and light brown (female) 20 30
2607 – 40b. red, brown and light brown (male) . . 20 30
2608 – 50b. brown, red and lilac (female) 25 25
2609 – 50b. brown, red and lilac (male) 25 25
2610 – 55b. red, brown and drab (female) 35 25
2611 – 55b. red, brown and drab (male) 35 25
2612 – 1l. carmine, brown and red (female) 90 30
2613 – 1l. carmine, brown and red (male) 90 30
2614 – 1l.75 red, brown and blue (female) . . . . 1·20 50
2615 – 1l.75 red, brown and blue (male) . . . . . 1·20 50

PROVINCES: Nos. 2606/7, Tara Oasului; 2608/9, Transylvania; 2610/11, Muntenia; 2612/3, Banat; 2614/5, Moldova.

453 Stamp Printer **454** Runner

1958. Romanian Stamp Centenary. Inscr "1858 1958".

No.	Type	Description	Mint	Used
2617	**453**	35b. blue	20	15
2618	–	55b. brown	30	15
2619	–	1l.20 blue	60	30
2620	–	1l.30 plum	65	35
2621	–	1l.55 brown	90	20
2622	–	1l.75 red	1·25	25
2623	–	2l. violet	1·50	45
2624	–	3l.30 brown	2·10	55
MS2625		80 × 89 mm. 10l. blue on pale blue	40·00	30·00
MS2626		80 × 89 mm. 10l. red. Imperf	65·00	55·00

DESIGNS: 55b. Scissors and Moldavian stamps of 1858; 1l.20, Driver with whip and mail coach; 1l.30, Postman with horn and mounted courier; 1l.55 to 3l.30, Moldavian stamps of 1858 (Nos. 1/4).

1958. 3rd Youth Spartacist Games.

No.	Type	Description	Mint	Used
2627	**454**	1l. brown	65	25

455 Revolutionary Emblem **456** Boy Bugler

1958. 40th Anniv of Workers' Revolution.

No.	Type	Description	Mint	Used
2628	**455**	55b. red	40	25

1958. 10th Anniv of Education Reform.

No.	Type	Description	Mint	Used
2629	**456**	55b. red	40	25

457 Alexandru Cuza

1959. Centenary of Union of Romanian Provinces.

No.	Type	Description	Mint	Used
2630	**457**	1l.75 blue	85	20

458 First Cosmic Rocket

1959. Air. Launching of 1st Cosmic Rocket.

No.	Type	Description	Mint	Used
2631	**458**	3l.25 blue on salmon	8·00	1·20

1959. Air. 10th Anniv of State Philatelic Services. No. **MS**2625 optd **10 ANI DE COMERT FILATELIC DE STAT 1949–1959** in red.

No.	Type	Description	Mint	Used
MS2632		10l. blue on pale blue	£125	£120

459 Charles Darwin (naturalist) **460** Maize

1959. Cultural Anniversaries.

No.	Type	Description	Mint	Used
2633	**459**	55b. black (postage)	30	15
2634	–	55b. blue	30	15
2635	–	55b. red	30	15
2636	–	55b. purple	30	15
2637	–	55b. brown	30	5·75
2638	–	3l.25 blue (air)	3·00	50

DESIGNS—No. 2633, Type **459** (150th birth anniv); 2634, Robert Burns (poet, birth bicentenary); 2635, Aleksandr Popov (radio pioneer, birth centenary); 2636, Sholem Aleichem (writer, birth centenary); 2637, Frederick Handel (composer, death bicentenary); 2638, Frederic Joliot-Curie (nuclear physicist, 10th anniv of World Peace Council).

1959. 10th Anniv of Collective Farming in Romania.

No.	Type	Description	Mint	Used
2639	**460**	55b. green	30	20
2640	–	55b. orange	30	20
2641	–	55b. purple	30	20
2642	–	55b. olive	30	20
2643	–	55b. brown	30	20
2644	–	55b. bistre	30	20
2645	–	55b. blue	30	20
2646	–	55b. bistre	30	20
2647	–	5l. red	3·00	75

DESIGNS—VERT: No. 2640, Sunflower with bee; 2641, Sugar beet. HORIZ: No. 2642, Sheep; 2643, Cattle; 2644, Rooster and hens; 2645, Farm tractor; 2646, Farm wagon and horses; 2647 (38 × $26\frac{1}{2}$ mm), Farmer and wife, and wheatfield within figure "10".

461 Rock Thrush **462** Young Couple

1959. Air. Birds in natural colours. Inscriptions in grey. Colours of value tablets and backgrounds given.

No.	Type	Description	Mint	Used
2648	**461**	10b. grey on buff	15	10
2649	–	20b. grey on grey	15	10
2650	–	35b. grey on deep grey	15	10
2651	–	40b. red on pink	20	15
2652	–	55b. grey on green	30	10
2653	–	55b. grey on cream	30	10
2654	–	55b. green on azure	30	10
2655	–	1l. red on yellow	60	20
2656	–	1l.55 red on pink	1·10	20
2657	–	5l. grey on green	6·25	1·20

BIRDS—HORIZ: No. 2649, Golden oriole; 2656, Long-tailed tit; 2657, Wallcreeper. VERT: No. 2650, Northern lapwing; 2651, Barn swallow; 2652, Great spotted woodpecker; 2653, Eurasian goldfinch; 2654, Great tit; 2655, Northern bullfinch.

1959. 7th World Youth Festival, Vienna. Inscr "26 VII-4 VIII 1959".

No.	Type	Description	Mint	Used
2658	**462**	1l. blue	50	20
2659	–	1l.60 red	50	20

DESIGN: 1l.60, Folk-dancer in national costume.

463 Workers and Banners **(466)**

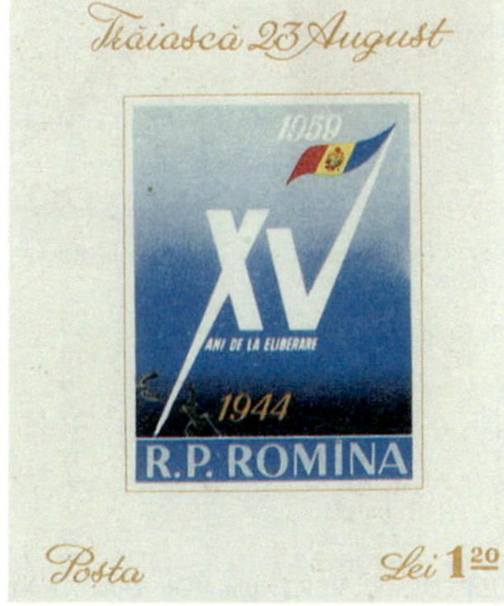

464

1959. 15th Anniv of Liberation.

No.	Type	Description	Mint	Used
2660	**463**	55b. multicoloured	40	25
MS2661	**464**	1l.20 multicoloured (39 × 72 mm). Imperf. No gum	2·00	90

1959. Air. Landing of Russian Rocket on the Moon. Surch **h. 00.02'.24" 14-IX-1959 PRIMA RACHETA COSMICA IN LUNA 5 LEI** and bars.

No.	Type	Description	Mint	Used
2662	**458**	5l. on 3l.25 blue on salmon	14·00	2·50

1959. 8th Balkan Games. Optd with T **466** in silver.

No.	Type	Description	Mint	Used
2663	**454**	1l. brown	14·00	12·50

467 Prince Vlad Tepes and Charter

1959. 500th Anniv of Bucharest.

No.	Type	Description	Mint	Used
2664	**467**	20b. black and blue	35	25
2665	–	40b. black and brown	1·20	25
2666	–	55b. black and bistre	90	30
2667	–	55b. black and purple	95	30
2668	–	1l.55 black and lilac	3·75	85
2669	–	1l.75 black and turquoise	3·25	1·10

DESIGNS—HORIZ: 40b. Peace Buildings, Bucharest; 55b. (No. 2666), Atheneum; 55b. (No 2667), "Scanteia" Printing House; 1l.55, Opera House; 1l.75, "23 August" Stadium.

468 Football **469** "Lenin"

1959. International Sport. Multicoloured.

No.	Type	Description	Mint	Used
2671		20b. Type **468** (postage)	15	10
2672		35b. Motor-cycle racing (horiz)	20	10
2673		40b. Ice-hockey (horiz)	30	20
2674		55b. Handball	30	10
2675		1l. Horse-jumping	45	10
2676		1l.50 Boxing	90	20
2677		1l.55 Rugby football (horiz)	1·00	10
2678		1l.60 Tennis (horiz)	1·20	25
2679		2l.80 Hydroplaning (horiz) (air)	1·75	75

1959. Launching of Atomic Ice-breaker "Lenin".

No.	Type	Description	Mint	Used
2680	**469**	1l.75 violet	1·50	35

STAMP DAY ISSUES. The annual issues for Stamp Day in November together with the stamp issued on 30 March 1963 for the Romanian Philatelists' Conference are now the only stamps which carry a premium which is expressed on se-tenant labels. This was for the Association of Romanian Philatelists. These labels were at first seperated by a vertical perforation but in the issues from 1963 to 1971 the label is an integral part of the stamp.

470 Stamp Album and Magnifier

1959. Stamp Day.

No.	Type	Description	Mint	Used
2681	**470**	1l.60(+40b.) blue	70	60

471 Foxglove **472** Cuza University

1959. Medicinal Flowers. Multicoloured.

No.	Type	Description	Mint	Used
2682		20b. Type **471**	15	10
2683		40b. Peppermint	20	20
2684		55b. False camomile	25	10
2685		55b. Cornflower	30	10
2686		1l. Meadow saffron	40	20
2687		1l.20 Monkshood	85	20
2688		1l.55 Common poppy	95	20
2689		1l.60 Silver lime	1·10	30
2690		1l.75 Dog rose	2·10	30
2691		3l.20 Yellow pheasant's-eye	1·50	45

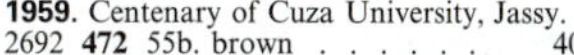

1959. Centenary of Cuza University, Jassy.

No.	Type	Description	Mint	Used
2692	**472**	55b. brown	40	25

473 Rocket, Dog and Rabbit **474** G. Cosbuc

1959. Air. Cosmic Rocket Flight.

No.	Type	Description	Mint	Used
2693	**473**	1l.55 blue	1·90	30
2694	–	1l.60 blue on cream	2·40	40
2695	–	1l.75 blue	2·40	40

DESIGNS—HORIZ: (52 × $29\frac{1}{2}$ mm): 1l.60, Picture of "invisible" side of the Moon, with lists of place-names in Romanian and Russian. VERT—(As Type **473**): 1l.75, Lunik 3's trajectory around the Moon.

1960. Romanian Authors.

No.	Type	Description	Mint	Used
2696	**474**	20b. blue	20	20
2697	–	40b. purple	55	20
2698	–	50b. brown	65	20
2699	–	55b. purple	65	20
2700	–	1l. violet	1·30	20
2701	–	1l.55 blue	2·20	35

PORTRAITS: 40b. I. L. Caragiale; 50b. G. Alexandrescu; 55b. A. Donici; 1l. C. Negruzzi; 1l.55, D. Bolintineanu.

475 Huchen **476** Woman and Dove

1960. Romanian Fauna.

No.	Type	Description	Mint	Used
2702	**475**	20b. blue (postage)	10	10
2703	–	55b. brown (Tortoise)	20	10
2704	–	1l.20 lilac (Common shelduck)	1·60	45
2705	–	1l.30 blue (Golden eagle) (air)	2·20	45
2706	–	1l.75 green (Black grouse)	2·20	45
2707	–	2l. red (Lammergeier)	2·30	65

1960. 50th Anniv of International Women's Day.

No.	Type	Description	Mint	Used
2708	**476**	55b. blue	60	30

477 Lenin (after painting by M. A. Gerasimov) **478** "Victory"

1960. 90th Birth Anniv of Lenin.

No.	Type	Description	Mint	Used
2709	**477**	40b. purple	35	15
2710	–	55b. blue	40	15
MS2711		65 × 75 mm. 1l.55 red	4·00	2·50

DESIGNS: 55b. Statue of Lenin by Boris Carogea; 1l.50 Lenin (sculpture by C. Baraschi).

1960. 15th Anniv of Victory.

No.	Type	Description	Mint	Used
2712	**478**	40b. blue	50	10
2714		40b. purple	2·30	2·50
2713	–	55b. blue	50	10
2715	–	55b. purple	2·30	2·50

DESIGN: 55b. Statue of soldier with flag.

479 Rocket Flight

1960. Air. Launching of Soviet Rocket.

No.	Type	Description	Mint	Used
2716	**479**	55b. blue	1·80	30

480 Diving **481** Gymnastics

1960. Olympic Games, Rome (1st issue). Mult.
2717 40b. Type **480** 70 95
2718 55b. Gymnastics . . . . . 90 1·00
2719 1l.20 High jumping . . . . 1·30 1·20
2720 1l.60 Boxing . . . . 2·00 1·30
2721 2l.45 Canoeing . . . . . . 2·10 1·40
2722 3l.70 Canoeing . . . . . . 4·50 3·25
Nos. 2717/9 and 2720/1 are arranged together in "brickwork" fashion, se-tenant, in sheets forming complete overall patterns of the Olympic rings.
No. 2722 is imperf.

1960. Olympic Games, Rome (2nd issue).
2723 – 20b. blue 15 10
2724 **481** 40b. purple 30 15
2725 – 55b. blue 55 10
2726 – 1l. red 70 10
2727 – 1l.60 purple . . . . . . 2·00 35
2728 – 2l. lilac . . . . 4·50 75
MS2729 90 × 69 mm. 5l. ultramarine 18·00 18·00
MS2730 90 × 69 mm. 6l. red. Imperf 30·00 30·00
DESIGNS: 20b. Diving; 55b. High-jumping; 1l. Boxing; 1l.60, Canoeing; 2l. Football; 5, 6l. Olympic flame and stadium.

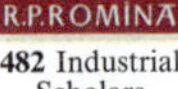

482 Industrial Scholars **483** Vlaicu and his Airplane No. 1 "Crazy Fly"

484 I.A.R. 817 Flying Ambulance

485 Pilot and Mikoyan Gurevich MiG-17 Jet Fighters

1960.
2731 **482** 3b. mauve (postage) . . 10 10
2732 – 5b. brown 30 10
2733 – 10b. purple 10 10
2734 – 20b. blue 10 10
2735 – 30b. red 15 10
2736 – 35b. red 15 10
2737 – 40b. bistre 25 10
2738 – 50b. violet 25 10
2739 – 55b. blue 30 10
2740 – 60b. green 30 10
2741 – 75b. olive 60 10
2742 – 1l. red 75 10
2743 – 1l.20 black 60 10
2744 – 1l.50 purple . . . . . 1·10 10
2745 – 1l.55 turquoise . . . . . 1·00 10
2746 – 1l.60 blue 90 10
2747 – 1l.75 brown . . . . . 1·10 10
2748 – 2l. brown . . . . . . 1·30 15
2749 – 2l.40 violet . . . . . 1·50 10
2750 – 3l. blue . . . . 2·00 15
2751 – 3l.20 blue (air) . . . . . 4·50 10
DESIGNS—VERT: 5b. Diesel train; 10b. Dam; 20b. Miner; 30b. Doctor; 35b. Textile worker; 50b. Children at play; 55b. Timber tractor; 1l. Atomic reactor; 1l.20, Petroleum refinery; 1l.50, Iron-works; 1l.75, Mason; 2l. Road-roller; 2l.40, Chemist; 3l. Radio communications and television. HORIZ: 40b. Grand piano and books; 60b. Combine harvester; 75b. Cattle-shed; 1l.55, Dock scene; 1l.60, Runner; 3l.20, Baneasa Airport, Bucharest.

1960. 50th Anniv of 1st Flight by A. Vlaicu and Aviation Day.
2752 **483** 10b. brown and yellow 15 10
2753 – 20b. brown and orange 20 10
2754 **484** 35b. red 30 10
2755 – 40b. violet 35 10
2756 **485** 55b. blue 50 10
2757 – 1l.60 multicoloured . . . 1·30 20
2758 – 1l.75 multicoloured . . . 1·70 35
DESIGNS—As T **483**: 20b. Vlaicu in flying helmet and his No. 2 airplane; 40b. Antonov An-2 biplane spraying crops. 59 × 22 mm: 1l.60, Ilyushin Il-18 airliner and Baneasa airport control tower; 1l.75, Parachute descents.

486 Worker and Emblem

1960. 3rd Workers' Party Congress.
2759 **486** 55b. orange and red . . 55 25

487 Leo Tolstoy (writer) **488** Tomis (Constantza)

1960. Cultural Anniversaries.
2760 **487** 10b. purple 10 10
2761 – 20b. brown 10 10
2762 – 35b. blue 15 10
2763 – 40b. green 20 10
2764 – 55b. brown 35 10
2765 – 1l. green 65 25
2766 – 1l.20 purple 75 10
2767 – 1l.55 grey . . . . . . 1·20 15
2768 – 1l.75 brown . . . . . 1·90 30
DESIGNS: 10b. Type **487** (50th death anniv); 20b. Mark Twain (writer, 50th death anniv); 35b. Katsushika Hokusai (painter, birth bicentenary); 40b. Alfred de Musset (poet, 150th birth anniv); 55b. Daniel Defoe (writer, 300th birth anniv); 1l. Janos Bolyai (mathematician, death centenary); 1l,20, Anton Chekhov (writer, birth centenary); 1l.55, Robert Koch (bacteriologist, 50th death anniv); 1l.75, Frederic Chopin (composer, 150th birth anniv).

1960. Black Sea Resorts. Multicoloured.
2769 20b. Type **488** (postage) . . 15 10
2770 35b. Constantza 30 10
2771 40b. Vasile Roaita 30 10
2772 55b. Mangalia 60 10
2773 1l. Eforie . . . . 1·00 25
2774 1l.60 Eforie (different) . . . 1·10 20
2775 2l. Mamaia (air) . . . . . 2·10 50

489 Globe and Flags **490** Viennese Emperor Moth

1960. International Puppet Theatre Festival, Bucharest. Designs (24 × 28½ mm, except 20b.) show puppets. Multicoloured.
2776 20b. Type **489** 20 10
2777 40b. Petrushka 25 10
2778 55b. Punch 30 10
2779 1l. Kaspar 45 10
2780 1l.20 Tindarica 55 10
2781 1l.75 Vasilache . . . . . . 1·00 20

1960. Air. Butterflies and Moths. Multicoloured.
2782 10b. Type **490** 25 10
2783 20b. Poplar admiral 25 10
2784 40b. Scarce copper 30 10
2785 55b. Swallowtail 55 15
2786 1l.60 Death's-head hawk moth . . . . 1·70 25
2787 1l.75 Purple emperor . . . 2·10 35
SIZES: TRIANGULAR—36½ × 21½ mm: 20, 40b. VERT—23½ × 34 mm: 55b., 1l.60. HORIZ—34 × 23½ mm: 1l.75.

491 Children tobogganing

1960. Village Children's Games. Multicoloured.
2788 20b. Type **491** 10 10
2789 35b. "Oina" (ball-game) (horiz) 15 10
2790 55b. Ice-skating (horiz) . . . 25 10
2791 1l. Running 50 10
2792 1l.75 Swimming (horiz) . . 1·40 15

492 Striker and Flag

1960. 40th Anniv of General Strike.
2793 **492** 55b. red and lake . . . 45 20

493 Compass Points and Ilyushin Il-18 Airliner

1960. Air. Stamp Day.
2794 **493** 55b.(+45b.) blue 60 35

494 "XV", Globe and "Peace" Banner **496** Woman tending Vine (Cotnari)

495 Black Sea Herrings

1960. 15th Anniv of World Democratic Youth Federation.
2795 **494** 55b. yellow and blue . . 45 15

1960. Fishes.
2796 – 10b. brown, yell & grn 15 10
2797 – 20b. multicoloured . . . 25 10
2798 – 40b. brn, lt brn & yell 40 10
2799 **495** 55b. grey, blue & orge 55 10
2800 – 1l. multicoloured . . . . 1·10 15
2801 – 1l.20 multicoloured . . . 1·40 20
2802 – 1l.60 multicoloured . . . 2·10 25
FISHES: 10b. Common carp; 20b. Zander; 40b. Black Sea turbot; 1l. Wels; 1l.20, Sterlet; 1l.60, Beluga.

1960. Romanian Vineyards. Multicoloured.
2803 20b. Dragasani 10 10
2804 30b. Dealul Mare (horiz) . . 25 10
2805 40b. Odobesti (horiz) . . . 35 10
2806 55b. Type **496** 55 10
2807 75b. Tirnave 75 20
2808 1l. Minis . . . . 1·30 25
2809 1l.20 Murfatlar . . . . . . 1·90 40
MS2810 95 × 115 mm. 5l. Antique wine jug. Imperf. No gum . . 4·00 2·25

497 "Furnaceman" (after I. Irimescu) **498** Slalom Racer

1961. Romanian Sculptures.
2811 **497** 5b. red 10 10
2812 – 10b. violet 10 10
2813 – 20b. black 20 10
2814 – 40b. bistre 25 10
2815 – 50b. brown 35 10
2816 – 55b. red 50 10
2817 – 1l. purple 85 15
2818 – 1l.55 blue . . . . . . 1·30 25
2819 – 1l.75 green . . . . . 1·70 25
SCULPTURES—VERT: 10b. "Gh. Doja" (I. Vlad); 20b. "Reunion" (B. Caragea); 40b. "Enescu" (G. Anghel); 50b. "Eminescu" (C. Baraschi); 1l. "Peace" (I. Jalea); 1l.55, "Constructive Socialism" (C. Medrea); 1l.75, "Birth of an Idea" (A. Szobotka). HORIZ: 55b. "Peasant Uprising, 1907" (M. Constantinescu).

1961. Air. 50th Anniv of Romanian Winter Sports. (a) Perf.
2820 – 10b. olive and grey . . . 20 15
2821 **498** 20b. red and grey . . . 20 15
2822 – 25b. turquoise and grey 35 15
2823 – 40b. violet and grey . . 40 15
2824 – 55b. blue and grey . . . 50 15
2825 – 1l. red and grey 70 20
2826 – 1l.55 brown and grey . . 1·70 30

(b) Imperf.
2827 – 10b. blue and grey . . . 10 10
2828 **498** 20b. brown and grey . . 20 10
2829 – 25b. olive and grey . . . 25 10
2830 – 40b. red and grey . . . 50 10
2831 – 55b. turquoise and grey 65 55
2832 – 1l. violet and grey . . . 1·00 90
2833 – 1l.55 red and grey . . . 1·70 1·80
DESIGNS—HORIZ: Skier: racing (10b.), jumping (55b.), walking (1l.55). VERT: 25b. Skiers climbing slope; 40b. Toboggan; 1l. Rock-climber.

499 Petru Poni (chemist) **500** Yuri Gagarin in Capsule

1961. Romanian Scientists. Inscr "1961". Portraits in sepia.
2834 **499** 10b. brown and pink . . 10 10
2835 – 20b. purple and yellow 25 10
2836 – 55b. red and blue . . . 40 15
2837 – 1l.55 violet and orange 1·20 35
PORTRAITS: 20b. Anghel Saligny (engineer) and Saligny Bridge, Cernavoda; 55b. Constantin Budeanu (electrical engineer); 1l.55, Gheorghe Titeica (mathematician).

1961. Air. World's First Manned Space Flight. Inscr "12 IV 1961". (a) Perf.
2838 – 1l.35 blue 55 20
2839 **500** 3l.20 blue . . . . 1·10 55

(b) Imperf.
2840 **500** 3l.20 red . . . . 5·50 2·10
DESIGN—VERT: 1l.35, Yuri Gagarin.

501 Freighter "Galati"

1961. Merchant Navy. Multicoloured.
2841 20b. Type **501** 35 10
2842 40b. "Oltenita" (Danube passenger vessel) 35 10
2843 55b. "Tomis" (hydrofoil) . . 55 10
2844 1l. "Arad" (freighter) . . . 80 10
2845 1l.55 "N. Cristea" (tug) . . 1·30 25
2846 1l.75 "Dobrogea" (freighter) 1·50 30

502 Red Flag with Marx, Engels and Lenin

1961. 40th Anniv of Romanian Communist Party.
2847 **502** 35b. multicoloured . . . 50 10
2848 – 55b. multicoloured . . . 85 10
MS2849 114 × 80 mm. 1l. multicoloured. Imperf. No gum 2·00 1·50
DESIGNS: 55b. Two bill-posters; 1l. "Industry and Agriculture" and party emblem.

503 Eclipse over Scanteia Building and Observatory **504** Roe Deer

1961. Air. Solar Eclipse.
2850 – 1l.60 blue . . . . 1·10 15
2851 **503** 1l.75 blue . . . . 1·30 15
DESIGN: 1l.60, Eclipse over Palace Square, Bucharest.

1961. Forest Animals. Inscr "1961". Multicoloured.
2852 10b. Type **504** 10 15
2853 20b. Lynx (horiz) 15 15
2854 35b. Wild boar (horiz) . . . 25 20
2855 40b. Brown bear (horiz) . . 45 20
2856 55b. Red deer 60 20
2857 75b. Red fox (horiz) 70 20
2858 1l. Chamois 95 20
2859 1l.55 Brown hare . . . . . 1·40 35
2860 1l.75 Eurasian badger . . . 1·70 30
2861 2l. Roe deer . . . . 2·40 55

505 George Enescu

1961. 2nd International George Enescu Festival.
2862 **505** 3l. lavender and brown . . . 1·40 30

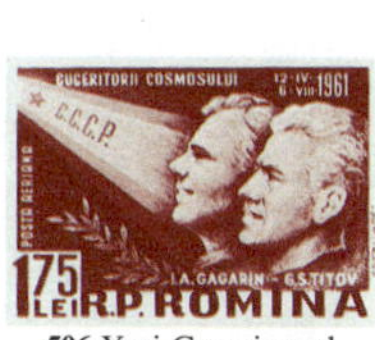

506 Yuri Gagarin and German Titov

507 Iris

1961. Air. 2nd Soviet Space Flight.
2863 – 55b. blue 35 10
2864 – 1l.35 violet 70 20
2865 **506** 1l.75 red . . . . 1·30 25
DESIGNS—VERT: 55b. "Vostok 2" in flight; 1l.35, G. S. Titov.

1961. Centenary of Bucharest Botanical Gardens. Flowers in natural colours. Background and inscription colours given. Perf or imperf.
2866 – 10b. yellow and brown . . . 10 10
2867 – 20b. green and red . . . 10 10
2868 – 25b. blue, green and red . . 15 10
2869 – 35b. lilac and grey . . . 25 10
2870 **507** 40b. yellow and violet . . 30 10
2871 – 55b. blue and ultramarine 45 10
2872 – 1l. orange and blue . . . 75 15
2873 – 1l.20 blue and brown . . 95 15
2874 – 1l.55 brown and lake . . 1·10 15
MS2875 125 × 92 mm. 1l.75 black, green and carmine . . . . . 5·00 3·50
FLOWERS—HORIZ: 10b. Primula; 35b. Opuntia; 1l. Hepatica. VERT: 20b. Dianthus; 25b. Peony; 55b. Ranunculus; 1l.20, Poppy; 1l.55, Gentian; C. Davila, D. Brindza and Botanical Gardens buildings.

508 Cobza Player

509 Heraclitus (Greek philosopher)

1961. Musicians. Multicoloured.
2876 10b. Pan piper 10 10
2877 20b. Alpenhorn player (horiz) 15 10
2878 40b. Flautist 30 10
2879 55b. Type **508** 50 10
2880 60b. Bagpiper 65 15
2881 1l. Cembalo player 85 25

1961. Cultural Anniversaries.
2882 **509** 10b. purple 30 20
2883 – 20b. brown 30 20
2884 – 40b. green 35 20
2885 – 55b. mauve 50 20
2886 – 1l.35 blue 85 25
2887 – 1l.75 violet . . . . . . 1·10 30
DESIGNS: 20b. Sir Francis Bacon (philosopher and statesman, 400th birth anniv); 40b. Rabindranath Tagore (poet and philosopher, birth centenary); 55b. Domingo Sarmiento (writer, 150th birth anniv; 1l.35, Heinrich von Kleist (dramatist, 150th death anniv); 1l.75, Mikhail Lomonosov (writer, 250th birth anniv).

510 Olympic Flame

512 Tower Building, Republic Palace Square, Bucharest

511 "Stamps Round the World"

1961. Olympic Games 1960. Gold Medal Awards. Inscr "MELBOURNE 1956" or "ROMA 1960". Perf or imperf.
2888 – 10b. turquoise and ochre . . 15 15
2889 **510** 20b. red 20 15
2890 – 20b. grey 20 15
2891 – 35b. brown and ochre . . . 30 15
2892 – 40b. purple and ochre . . . 30 15
2893 – 55b. blue 40 15
2894 – 55b. blue 40 15
2895 – 55b. red and ochre . . . 40 15
2896 – 1l.35 blue and ochre . . 1·10 25
2897 – 1l.75 red and ochre . . . 1·80 35
MS2898 109 × 86 mm. 4l. multicoloured. Imperf. No gum . . 8·50 7·00
DESIGNS (Medals)—DIAMOND: 10b. Boxing; 35b. Pistol-shooting; 40b. Rifle-shooting; 55b. (No. 2895), Wrestling; 1l.35, High-jumping. VERT: as Type **510**: 20b. (No. 2890), Diving; 55b. (No. 2893), Water-polo; 55b. (No. 2894), Women's high-jumping. HORIZ—45 × 33 mm: 1l.75, Canoeing. Larger — 4l. Gold medals of Melbourne and Rome.

1961. Air. Stamp Day.
2899 **511** 55b.(+45b.) blue, brown and red 95 40

1961. Air. Modern Romanian Architecture. Mult.
2900 20b. Type **512** 25 10
2901 40b. Constantza Railway Station (horiz) 90 15
2902 55b. Congress Hall, Republic Palace, Bucharest (horiz) 40 10
2903 75b. Rolling mill, Hunedoara (horiz) 45 10
2904 1l. Apartment blocks, Bucharest (horiz) 60 15
2905 1l.20 Circus Building, Bucharest (horiz) 65 35
2906 1l.75 Workers' Club, Mangalia (horiz) 60 20

513 U.N. Emblem

514 Workers with Flags

1961. 15th Anniv of U.N.O. Perf or imperf.
2907 – 20b. multicoloured . . . 15 10
2908 – 40b. multicoloured . . . 45 10
2909 **513** 55b. multicoloured . . . 65 15
DESIGNS (bearing U.N. emblem): 20b. Peace dove over Eastern Europe; 40b. Peace dove and youths of three races.

1961. 5th W.F.T.U. Congress, Moscow.
2910 **514** 55b. red 60 20

515 Cock and Savings Book

516 Footballer

1962. Savings Day. Inscr "1962". Multicoloured.
2911 40b. Type **515** 20 10
2912 55b. Savings Bank book, bee and "honeycombs" of agriculture, housing and industry 45 10

1962. European Junior Football Competition, Bucharest.
2913 **516** 55b. brown and green . . 95 25

517 Ear of Corn, Map and Tractor

518 Handball Player

1962. Completion of Agricultural Collectivisation Project. Inscr "1962".
2914 **517** 40b. red and orange . . 15 10
2915 – 55b. lake and yellow . . 20 10
2916 – 1l.55 yellow, red and blue 45 15
DESIGNS: 55b. Commemorative medal; 1l.55, Wheatsheaf, and hammer and sickle emblem.

1962. Women's World Handball Championships, Bucharest.
2917 **518** 55b. violet and yellow . . 95 20

519 Canoe Race

520 Jean Jacques Rousseau

1962. Boating and Sailing. Inscr "1962". (a) Perf.
2918 **519** 10b. blue and mauve . . 15 10
2919 – 20b. blue and brown . . 20 10
2920 – 40b. blue and brown . . 25 10
2921 – 55b. blue and ultramarine 35 15
2922 – 1l. blue and red 70 15
2923 – 1l.20 blue and purple . . 90 15
2924 – 1l.55 blue and red . . 1·10 15
2925 – 3l. blue and violet . . . 1·70 35

(b) Imperf. Colours changed.
2926 **519** 10b. blue and ultramarine 20 20
2927 – 20b. blue and mauve . . 30 20
2928 – 40b. blue and red . . . 45 30
2929 – 55b. blue and brown . . 50 40
2930 – 1l. blue and brown . . . 90 40
2931 – 1l.20 blue and violet . . 1·00 50
2932 – 1l.55 blue and red . . 1·00 55
2933 – 3l. blue and purple . . . 2·50 95
DESIGNS: 20b. Kayak; 40b. Racing "eight"; 55b. Sculling; 1l. "Star" yachts; 1l.20, Power boats; 1l.55, "Flying Dutchman" dinghy; 3l. Canoe slalom.

1962. Cultural Anniversaries (writers).
2934 **520** 40b. green 20 10
2935 – 55b. purple 25 15
2936 – 1l.75 blue 65 10
MS2937 91 × 122 mm. 3l.30 brown . . 5·50 4·50
DESIGNS: 40b. T **520** (250th birth anniv); 55b. Ion Caragiale (dramatist, 50th death anniv); 1l.75, Aleksandr Herzen (150th birth anniv). 32 × 55 mm—3l.30 Caragiale (full-length portrait).

521 Flags and Globes

1962. World Youth Festival, Helsinki.
2938 **521** 55b. multicoloured . . . 65 20

522 Traian Vuia (aviator)

523 Anglers by Pond

1962. Romanian Celebrities.
2939 **522** 15b. brown 15 10
2940 – 20b. red 20 10
2941 – 35b. purple 20 10
2942 – 40b. blue 30 15
2943 – 55b. blue 35 10
2944 – 1l. blue 55 10
2945 – 1l.20 red 70 25
2946 – 1l.35 turquoise 95 25
2947 – 1l.55 violet . . . . . . 1·10 15
PORTRAITS: 20b. Alexandru Davila (writer); 35b. Vasile Pirvan (archaeologist); 40b. Ion Negulici (painter); 55b. Grigore Cobilcescu (geologist); 1l. Dr. Gheorghe Marinescu (neurologist); 1l.20, Dr. Ion Cantacuzino (bacteriologist); 1l.35, Dr. Victor Babes (bacteriologist and pathologist; 1l.55, Dr. Constantin Levaditi (medical researcher).

1962. Fishing Sport. Multicoloured.
2948 10b. Rod-fishing in fishing punts 10 10
2949 25b. Line-fishing in mountain pool 15 10
2950 40b. Type **523** 25 10
2951 55b. Anglers on beach . . . 30 10
2952 75b. Line-fishing in mountain stream 45 10
2953 1l. Shore-fishing 50 20
2954 1l.75 Freshwater-fishing . . 85 20
2955 3l.25 Fishing in Danube delta . . . . 1·50 25

524 Dove and "Space" Stamps of 1957/58

527 "Vostok 3" and "4" in Orbit

1962. Air. Cosmic Flights.
2956 **524** 35b. brown 15 10
2957 – 55b. green 25 10
2958 – 1l.35 blue 60 15
2959 – 1l.75 red . . . . 1·00 35
MS2960 107 × 79 mm. Nos. 2956/9, but imperf and colours changed: 35b. blue, 55b. brown; 1l.35 red; 1l.75 green . . . . 3·25 2·25
DESIGNS—Dove and: 55b. "Space" stamps of 1959; 1l.35, "Space" stamps of 1957 ("Laika"), 1959 and 1960; 1l.75, "Spacemen" stamps of 1961.

1962. Romanian Victory in European Junior Football Competition, Bucharest. Surch **1962. Campioana Europeana 2 lei**.
2961 **516** 2l. on 55b. brown & grn . 1·90 1·80

1962. Romanian Victory in Women's World Handball Championships, Bucharest. Surch **Campioana Mondiala 5 lei**.
2962 **518** 5l. on 55b. vio & yell . . 4·00 2·40

1962. Air. 1st "Team" Manned Space Flight.
2963 – 55b. violet 35 10
2964 **527** 1l.60 blue 85 20
2965 – 1l.75 purple . . . . . . 1·20 25
DESIGNS: 55b. Andrian Nikolaev (cosmonaut); 1l.75, Pavel Popovich (cosmonaut).

528 Child and Butterfly

529 Pottery

1962. Children.
2966 **528** 20b. blue, brown and red . 15 10
2967 – 30b. yellow, blue and red . 20 10
2968 – 40b. blue, red & turquoise 25 10
2969 – 55b. olive, blue and red . 50 10
2970 – 1l.20 red, brown & blue . 1·00 20
2971 – 1l.55 ochre, blue and red . 1·30 25
DESIGNS—VERT: 30b. Girl feeding dove; 40b. Boy with model yacht; 1l.20, Boy violinist and girl pianist. HORIZ: 55b. Girl teaching boy to write; 1l.55, Pioneers around camp-fire.

1962. 4th Sample Fair, Bucharest. Inscr "AL IV-LEA PAVILION DE MOSTRE BUCURESTI 1962". Multicoloured.
2972 5b. Type **529** (postage) . . . 30 15
2973 10b. Preserved foodstuffs . . 30 15
2974 20b. Chemical products . . 30 15
2975 40b. Ceramics 40 10
2976 55b. Leather goods 50 10
2977 75b. Textiles . . . . 70 2·50
2978 1l. Furniture and fabrics . . 85 10
2979 1l.20 Office equipment . . . 1·20 10
2980 1l.55 Needlework . . . . . 1·40 10
2981 1l.60 Fair pavilion (horiz) (air) . . . . 2·00 20

530 Lenin and Red Flag

1962. 45th Anniv of Russian Revolution.
2982 **530** 55b. brown, red and blue 65 20

531 "The Coachmen" (after Szatmay)

1962. Air. Stamp Day and Centenary of 1st Romanian Stamps.
2983 **531** 55b.(+45b.) black and blue . . . . 1·00 30

532 Lamb

1962. Prime Farm Stock.
2984 **532** 20b. black and blue . . 15 10
2985 – 40b. brown, yellow & blue 15 10
2986 – 55b. green, buff and orange 25 10
2987 – 1l. brown, buff and grey 35 10
2988 – 1l.35 brown, black & green 50 15
2989 – 1l.55 brown, black & red 60 20
2990 – 1l.75 brown, cream & blue . . . . 1·00 35
DESIGNS—HORIZ: 40b. Ram; 1l.55, Heifer; 1l.75, Sows. VERT: 55b. Bull; 1l. Pig; 1l.35, Cow.

533 Arms, Industry and Agriculture

1962. 15th Anniv of People's Republic.
2991 **533** 1l.55 multicoloured . . . 95 25

534 Strikers

1963. 30th Anniv of Grivitsa Strike.
2992 **534** 1l.75 multicoloured . . . 1·30 25

535 Tractor-driver

1963. Freedom from Hunger.
2993 **535** 40b. blue 20 10
2994 – 55b. brown 30 10
2995 – 1l.55 red 65 10
2996 – 1l.75 green 75 20
DESIGNS (each with F.A.O. emblem): 55b. Girl harvester; 1l.55, Child with beaker of milk; 1l.75, Girl vintager.

1963. Air. Romanian Philatelists' Conference, Bucharest. No. 2983 optd **A.F.R.** surrounded by **CONFERINTA PE TARA BUCURESTI 30-III-1963** in diamond shape.
2997 **531** 55b.(+45b.) blk & bl . . 2·75 2·50
The opt is applied in the middle of the se-tenant pair—stamp and 45b. label.

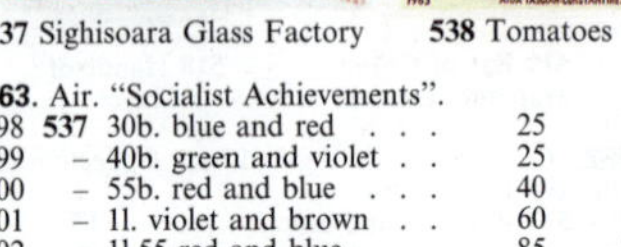

537 Sighisoara Glass Factory **538** Tomatoes

1963. Air. "Socialist Achievements".
2998 **537** 30b. blue and red . . . 25 10
2999 – 40b. green and violet . . 25 15
3000 – 55b. red and blue . . . 40 10
3001 – 1l. violet and brown . . 60 15
3002 – 1l.55 red and blue . . . 85 20
3003 – 1l.75 blue and purple . . 85 25
DESIGNS: 40b. Govora soda works; 55b. Tirgul-Jiu wood factory; 1l. Savinesti chemical works; 1l.55, Hunedoara metal works; 1l.75, Brazi thermic power station.

1963. Vegetable Culture. Multicoloured.
3004 35b. Type **538** 15 10
3005 40b. Hot peppers 25 10
3006 55b. Radishes 25 10
3007 75b. Aubergines 45 15
3008 1l.20 Mild peppers 65 20
3009 3l.25 Cucumbers (horiz) . . 1·30 30

539 Moon Rocket "Luna 4" **540** Chick

1963. Air. Launching of Soviet Moon Rocket "Luna 4". The 1l.75 is imperf.
3010 **539** 55b. red and blue . . . 20 15
3011 1l.75 red and violet . . . 95 15

1963. Domestic Poultry.
3012 **540** 20b. yellow and blue . . 20 10
3013 – 30b. red, blue and brown 25 10
3014 – 40b. blue, orange & brn 30 10
3015 – 55b. multicoloured . . . 35 10
3016 – 70b. blue, red and purple 40 10
3017 – 1l. red, grey and blue . . 45 15
3018 – 1l.35 red, blue and ochre 60 15
3019 – 3l.20 multicoloured . . . 1·20 35
POULTRY: 30b. Cockerel; 40b. Duck; 55b. White Leghorn; 70b. Goose; 1l. Rooster; 1l.35, Turkey (cock); 3l.20, Turkey (hen).

541 Diving **542** Congress Emblem

1963. Swimming. Bodies in drab.
3020 **541** 25b. green and brown . . 15 10
3021 – 30b. yellow and olive . . 20 10
3022 – 55b. red and turquoise 25 10
3023 – 1l. red and green 45 15
3024 – 1l.35 mauve and blue . . 50 15
3025 – 1l.55 orange and violet 90 20
3026 – 2l. yellow and mauve . . 90 50
DESIGNS—HORIZ: 30b. Crawl; 55b. Butterfly; 1l. Back stroke; 1l.35, Breast stroke. VERT: 1l.55, Swallow diving; 2l. Water polo.

1963. International Women's Congress, Moscow.
3027 **542** 55b. blue 45 20

543 Valery Bykovsky and Globe

1963. Air. 2nd "Team" Manned Space Flights.
3028 **543** 55b. blue 25 10
3029 – 1l.75 red . . . . 1·00 25
MS3030 118 × 80 mm. 1l.20, 1l.60 blue . . . . 3·00 1·25
DESIGNS: 1l.75 Valentina Tereshkova and globe; 25 × 41 mm—1l.20 Bykovsky; 1l.60 Tereshkova.
The stamps in No. **MS**3030 form a composite design.

544 Class 142 Steam Locomotive, 1936

1963. Air. Transport. Multicoloured.
3031 40b. Type **544** 50 15
3032 55b. Class 060-DA diesel-electric locomotive, 1959 50 15
3033 75b. Trolley bus 50 25
3034 1l.35 "Oltenita" (Danube passenger vessel) . . . . 1·30 30
3035 1l.75 Ilyushin Il-18 airplane 1·40 20

545 William Thackeray (novelist)

1963. Cultural Anniversaries. Inscr "MARILE ANNIVERSARI CULTURALE 1963".
3036 **545** 40b. black and lilac . . . 20 15
3037 – 50b. black and brown . . 30 15
3038 – 55b. black and olive . . 40 15
3039 – 1l.55 black and red . . . 80 15
3040 – 1l.75 black and blue . . 85 20
PORTRAITS: 40b. Type **545** (death centenary); 50b. Eugene Delacroix (painter, death centenary); 55b. Gheorghe Marinescu (neurologist, birth centenary); 1l.55, Giuseppe Verdi (composer, 150th birth anniv); 1l.75, Konstantin Stanislavsky (actor and stage director, birth centenary).

546 Walnuts **548** Volleyball

1963. Fruits and Nuts. Multicoloured.
3041 10b. Type **546** 25 10
3042 20b. Plums 25 10
3043 40b. Peaches 45 10
3044 55b. Strawberries 55 10
3045 1l. Grapes 60 10
3046 1l.55 Apples 80 15
3047 1l.60 Cherries . . . . 1·10 25
3048 1l.75 Pears . . . . 1·20 25

1963. Air. 50th Death Anniv of Aurel Vlaicu (aviation pioneer). No. 2752 surch **1913–1963 50 ani de la moarte 1,75 lei**.
3049 **483** 1l.75 on 10b. brn & yell 2·20 90

1963. European Volleyball Championships.
3050 **548** 5b. mauve and grey . . 20 10
3051 – 40b. blue and grey . . . 25 10
3052 – 55b. turquoise and grey 35 15
3053 – 1l.75 brown and grey . . 95 20
3054 – 3l.20 violet and grey . . 1·40 20
DESIGNS: 40b. to 1l.75, Various scenes of play at net; 3l.20, European Cup.

549 Romanian 1l.55 "Centenary" Stamp of 1958

1963. Air. Stamp Day and 15th U.P.U. Congress. Inscr "AL XV-LEA CONGRESS", etc.
3055 **549** 20b. brown and blue . . 15 10
3056 – 40b. blue and mauve . . 15 10
3057 – 55b. mauve and blue . . 20 10
3058 – 1l.20 violet and buff . . 40 15
3059 – 1l.55 green and red . . . 1·10 20
3060 – 1l.60+50b. mult . . . . 1·00 30
DESIGNS (Romanian stamps): 40b. (1l.20) "Laika", 1957 (blue); 55b. (3l.20) "Gagarin", 1961; 1l.20, (55b.) "Nikolaev" and (1l.75) "Popovich", 1962; 1l.55, (55b.) "Postwoman", 1953; 1l.60, U.P.U. Monument, Berne, globe, map of Romania and aircraft (76 × 27 mm).

551 Ski Jumping

1963. Winter Olympic Games, Innsbruck, 1964.
(a) Perf.
3061 **551** 10b. blue and red . . . 25 15
3062 – 20b. brown and blue . . 35 15
3063 – 40b. brown and green . . 40 10
3064 – 55b. brown and violet 50 15
3065 – 60b. blue and brown . . 75 20
3066 – 75b. blue and mauve . . 90 20
3067 – 1l. blue and ochre . . . 1·10 25
3068 – 1l.20 blue and turquoise 1·40 30

(b) Imperf. Colours changed.
3069 **551** 10b. brown and green . . 60 55
3070 – 20b. brown and violet 60 55
3071 – 40b. blue and red . . . 60 55
3072 – 55b. brown and blue . . 60 55
3073 – 60b. blue and turquoise 60 55
3074 – 75b. blue and ochre . . 60 55
3075 – 1l. blue and mauve . . . 60 55
3076 – 1l.20 blue and brown . . 60 55
MS3077 120 × 80 mm. 1l.50 ultramarine and red . . . . . 11·00 11·00
DESIGNS: 20b. Speed skating; 40b. Ice hockey; 55b. Figure skating; 60b. Slalom; 75b. Biathlon; 1l. Bobsleighing; 1l.20 Cross-country skiing. HORIZ: 1l.55 Stadium, Innsbruck.

552 Cone, Fern and Conifer **553** Silkworm Moth

1963. 18th Anniv of Reafforestation Campaign.
3078 **552** 55b. green 20 10
3079 – 1l.75 blue 40 15
DESIGN: 1l.75, Chestnut trees.

1963. Bee-keeping and Silkworm-breeding. Mult.
3080 10b. Type **553** 25 10
3081 20b. Moth emerging from chrysalis 35 10
3082 40b. Silkworm 45 10
3083 55b. Honey bee (horiz) . . . 55 10
3084 60b. Honey bee on flower 70 20
3085 1l.20 Honey bee approaching orange flowers (horiz) 90 25
3086 1l.35 Honey bee approaching pink flowers (horiz) . . . . 1·20 35
3087 1l.60 Honey bee and sunflowers (horiz) . . . . 1·40 35

554 Carved Pillar **556** George Stephanescu (composer)

555 Yuri Gagarin

1963. Village Museum, Bucharest.
3088 **554** 20b. purple 20 10
3089 – 40b. blue (horiz) 25 10
3090 – 55b. violet (horiz) . . . 30 10
3091 – 75b. green 40 10
3092 – 1l. red and brown . . . 60 10

3093 – 1l.20 green 70 15
3094 – 1l.75 blue and brown . . 1·20 15
DESIGNS: Various Romanian peasant houses.

1964. Air. "Space Navigation". Soviet flag, red and yellow; U.S. flag, red and blue; backgrounds, light blue; portrait and inscription colours below. (a) Perf.
3095 **555** 5b. blue 20 10
3096 – 10b. violet 25 10
3097 – 20b. bronze 30 10
3098 – 35b. grey 35 10
3099 – 40b. violet 40 15
3100 – 55b. violet 50 20
3101 – 60b. brown 50 20
3102 – 75b. blue 55 20
3103 – 1l. purple 75 25
3104 – 1l.40 purple . . . . . . 1·20 45

(b) Imperf. Colours changed.
3105 **555** 5b. violet 10 10
3106 – 10b. blue 10 10
3107 – 20b. grey 20 10
3108 – 35b. bronze 45 25
3109 – 40b. purple 60 30
3110 – 55b. purple 80 35
3111 – 60b. blue 80 50
3112 – 75b. brown . . . . . . 1·10 70
3113 – 1l. violet . . . . . . 1·30 85
3114 – 1l.40 violet . . . . . . 1·70 1·30
MS3115 120 × 80 mm. 2l. multicoloured . . . . 10·00 7·50
PORTRAITS (with flags of their countries)—As Type **555**: 10b. German Titov; 20b. John Glenn; 35b. Scott Carpenter; 60b. Walter Schirra; 75b. Gordon Cooper. 35½ × 33½ mm: 40b. Andrian Nikolaev; 55b. Pavel Popovich; 1l. Valery Bykovsky; 1l.40, Valentina Tereshkova. 59 × 43 mm—2l. Globe, orbits, laurel sprigs and commemorative dates.

1964. Romanian Opera Singers and their stage roles. Portraits in brown.
3116 **556** 10b. olive 25 10
3117 – 20b. blue 35 10
3118 – 35b. green 35 10
3119 – 40b. light blue 40 10
3120 – 55b. mauve 50 10
3121 – 75b. violet 50 10
3122 – 1l. blue 60 15
3123 – 1l.35 violet 65 15
3124 – 1l.55 red . . . . 1·10 25
DESIGNS: 20b. Elena Teodorini in "Carmen"; 35b. Ion Bajenaru in "Petru Rares"; 40b. Dimitrie Popovici-Bayreuth as Alberich in "Ring of the Nibelung"; 55b. Haricled Dardee in "Tosca"; 75b. George Folescu in "Boris Godunov"; 1l. Jean Athanasiu in "Rigoletto"; 1l.35, Traian Grosarescu as Duke in "Rigoletto"; 1l.55, Nicolae Leonard as Hoffmann in "Tales of Hoffmann".

557 Prof. G. M. Murgoci

558 "Ascalaphus macaronius" (owl-fly)

1964. 8th International Soil Congress, Bucharest.
3125 **557** 1l.60 indigo, ochre and blue 60 20

1964. Insects. Multicoloured.
3126 5b. Type **558** 15 10
3127 10b. "Ammophila sabulosa" (digger wasp) 20 10
3128 35b. "Scolia maculata" (dagger wasp) 20 10
3129 40b. Swamp tiger moth . . 35 10
3130 55b. Gypsy moth 40 10
3131 1l.20 Great banded grayling 60 20
3132 1l.55 "Carabus fabricii malachiticus" (ground beetle) 70 20
3133 1l.75 "Procerus gigas" (ground beetle) . . . . . 1·30 25

559 "Nicotiana alata"

560 Cross Country

1964. Romanian Flowers. Multicoloured.
3134 10b. Type **559** 15 15
3135 20b. "Pelargonium" 20 15
3136 40b. "Fuchsia gracilis" . . . 30 15
3137 55b. "Chrysanthemum indicum" 35 15
3138 75b. "Dahlia hybrida" . . . 40 15
3139 1l. "Lilium croceum" . . . 60 15
3140 1l.25 "Hosta ovata" 75 25
3141 1l.55 "Tagetes erectus" . . . 80 25

1964. Horsemanship.
3142 – 40b. multicoloured . . . 25 10
3143 **560** 55b. brown, red and lilac 30 10
3144 – 1l.35 brown, red & green 80 20
3145 – 1l.55 mauve, blue & bis 1·10 20
DESIGNS—HORIZ: 40b. Dressage; 1l.55, Horse race. VERT: 1l.35, Show jumping.

561 Brown Scorpionfish

562 M. Eminescu (poet)

1964. Constantza Aquarium. Fish designs. Mult.
3146 5b. Type **561** 10 10
3147 10b. Peacock blenny 10 10
3148 20b. Black Sea horse-mackerel 10 10
3149 40b. Russian sturgeon . . . 20 10
3150 50b. Short-snouted seahorse 30 15
3151 55b. Tub gurnard 35 15
3152 1l. Beluga 50 15
3153 3l.20 Common stingray . . 2·10 30

1964. Cultural Anniversaries. Portraits in brown.
3154 **562** 5b. green 15 10
3155 – 20b. red 15 10
3156 – 35b. red 20 10
3157 – 55b. bistre 65 10
3158 – 1l.20 blue . . . . 1·00 15
3159 – 1l.75 violet . . . . . . 2·00 40
DESIGNS: Type **562** (75th death anniv); 20b. Ion Creanga (folklorist, 75th death anniv); 35b. Emil Girleanu (writer, 50th death anniv); 55b. Michelangelo (artist, 400th death anniv); 1l.20, Galileo Galilei (astronomer, 400th birth anniv); 1l.75, William Shakespeare (dramatist, 400th birth anniv).

563 Cheile Bicazului (gorge)

564 High Jumping

1964. Mountain Resorts.
3160 **563** 40b. lake 20 10
3161 – 55b. blue 35 10
3162 – 1l. purple 45 10
3163 – 1l.35 brown 50 10
3164 – 1l.75 green 85 15
DESIGNS—VERT: 55b. Cabin on Lake Bilea; 1l. Poiana Brasov ski-lift; 1l.75, Alpine Hotel. HORIZ: 1l.35, Lake Bicaz.

1964. Balkan Games. Multicoloured.
3165 30b. Type **564** 15 10
3166 40b. Throwing the javelin 15 10
3167 55b. Running 25 10
3168 1l. Throwing the discus . . 50 10
3169 1l.20 Hurdling 50 15
3170 1l.55 Flags of competing countries (24 × 44 mm) . . 55 20

565 Arms and Flag

1964. 20th Anniv of Liberation. Multicoloured.
3171 55b. Type **565** 20 10
3172 60b. Industrial plant (horiz) 20 10
3173 75b. Harvest scene (horiz) 30 10
3174 1l.20 Apartment houses (horiz) 55 20
MS3175 131 × 94 mm. 2l. "Agriculture and Industry". Imperf. No gum . . . . . . 2·00 1·25

566 High Jumping

1964. Olympic Games, Tokyo. Multicoloured. (a) Perf.
3176 20b. Type **566** 25 10
3177 30b. Wrestling 35 10
3178 35b. Volleyball 35 10
3179 40b. Canoeing 40 15
3180 55b. Fencing 50 15
3181 1l.20 Gymnastics 85 25
3182 1l.35 Football . . . . . . 1·00 25
3183 1l.55 Rifle-shooting . . . . 1·20 30

(b) Imperf. Colours changed and new values.
3184 20b. Type **566** 20 10
3185 30b. Wrestling 25 10
3186 35b. Volleyball 45 10
3187 40b. Canoeing 45 15
3188 55b. Fencing 90 30
3189 1l.60 Gymnastics . . . . . 1·80 80
3190 2l. Football . . . . 1·90 1·00
3191 2l.40 Rifle-shooting . . . . 2·40 1·50
MS3192 80 × 110 mm. 3l.25 Runner (no gum) . . . . 12·50 7·50

567 George Enescu

568 Python

1964. 3rd International George Enescu Festival.
3193 **567** 10b. green 20 10
3194 – 55b. purple 30 10
3195 – 1l.60 purple 75 30
3196 – 1l.75 blue 95 20
DESIGNS (Portraits of Enescu): 55b. At piano; 1l.60, Medallion; 1l.75, When an old man.

1964. Bucharest Zoo. Multicoloured.
3197 5b. Type **568** 10 10
3198 10b. Black swans 45 10
3199 35b. Ostriches 75 10
3200 40b. Crowned cranes . . . 75 15
3201 55b. Tigers 35 10
3202 1l. Lions 55 10
3203 1l.55 Grevy's zebras 80 15
3204 2l. Bactrian camels . . . . 1·20 25

569 Brincoveanu, Cantacuzino, Lazar and Academy

570 Soldier

1964. Anniversaries. Multicoloured.
3205 20b. Type **569** 10 10
3206 40b. Cuza and seal 10 10
3207 55b. Emblems and the Arts (vert) 20 10
3208 75b. Laboratory workers and class 25 15
3209 1l. Savings Bank building 40 20
EVENTS, etc—HORIZ: 20b. 270th Anniv of Domneasca Academy; 40b., 75b. Bucharest University centenary; 1l. Savings Bank centenary. VERT: 55b. "Fine Arts" centenary (emblems are masks, curtain, piano keyboard, harp, palette and brushes).

1964. Centenary of Army Day.
3210 **570** 55b. blue and light blue 35 20

571 Post Office of 19th and 20th Centuries

1964. Air. Stamp Day.
3211 **571** 1l.60+40b. blue, red and yellow 95 25
No. 3211 is a two-part design, the two parts being arranged vert, imperf between.

572 Canoeing Medal (1956)

573 Strawberries

1964. Olympic Games—Romanian Gold Medal Awards. Medals in brown and bistre (Nos. 3218/19 and 3226/7 in sepia and gold). (a) Perf.
3212 **572** 20b. red and blue . . . 20 10
3213 – 30b. green and blue . . 35 15
3214 – 35b. turquoise and blue 45 15
3215 – 40b. lilac and blue . . . 55 25
3216 – 55b. orange and blue . . 60 20
3217 – 1l.20 green and blue . . 70 25
3218 – 1l.35 brown and blue . . 1·10 30
3219 – 1l.55 mauve and blue . . 2·40 30

(b) Imperf. Colours changed and new values.
3220 **572** 20b. orange and blue . . 10 15
3221 – 30b. turquoise and blue 30 20
3222 – 35b. green and blue . . 30 20
3223 – 40b. green and blue . . 35 30
3224 – 55b. red and blue . . . 40 30
3225 – 1l.60 lilac and blue . . . 1·30 1·00
3226 – 2l. mauve and blue . . . 2·00 1·30
3227 – 2l.40 brown and blue . . 2·50 1·70
MS3228 140 × 110 mm. 10l. gold, blue and blue (no gum) . . . . 10·50 8·00
MEDALS: 30b. Boxing (1956); 35b. Pistol-shooting (1956); 40b. High-jumping (1960); 55b. Wrestling (1960); 1l.20, 1l.60, Rifle-shooting (1960); 1l.35, 2l. High-jumping (1964); 1l.55, 2l.40, Throwing the javelin (1964). HORIZ: 10l. Tokyo gold medal and world map.

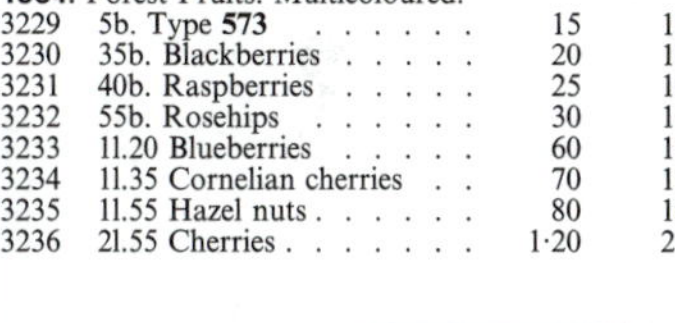

1964. Forest Fruits. Multicoloured.
3229 5b. Type **573** 15 10
3230 35b. Blackberries 20 10
3231 40b. Raspberries 25 10
3232 55b. Rosehips 30 10
3233 1l.20 Blueberries 60 15
3234 1l.35 Cornelian cherries . . 70 15
3235 1l.55 Hazel nuts 80 10
3236 2l.55 Cherries . . . . 1·20 25

574 "Syncom 3"

575 U.N. Headquarters, New York

1965. Space Navigation. Multicoloured.
3237 30b. Type **574** 15 10
3238 40b. "Syncom 3" (different) 20 10
3239 55b. "Ranger 7" (horiz) . . 35 10
3240 1l. "Ranger 7" (different) (horiz) 40 15
3241 1l.20 "Voskhod 1" (horiz) 70 10
3242 5l. Konstantin Feoktistov, Vladimir Komarov and Boris Yegorov (cosmonauts) and "Voskhod 1" (52 × 29 mm) . . . . . . 1·70 60

1965. 20th Anniv of U.N.O.
3243 **575** 55b. gold, blue and red 15 10
3244 – 1l.60 multicoloured . . . 55 25
DESIGN: 1l.60, Arms and U.N. emblem on Romanian flag.

576 Spur-thighed Tortoise

1965. Reptiles. Multicoloured.
3245 5b. Type **576** 10 10
3246 10b. Crimean lizard 15 10
3247 20b. Three-lined lizard . . . 15 10
3248 40b. Snake-eyed skink . . . 20 10
3249 55b. Slow worm 25 10
3250 60b. Sand viper 40 10
3251 1l. Arguta 45 15
3252 1l.20 Orsini's viper 55 15
3253 1l.35 European whip snake 70 15
3254 3l.25 Four-lined rat snake 2·30 35

577 Tabby Cat

1965. Domestic Cats. Multicoloured.

3255	5b. Type **577**	10	10
3256	10b. Ginger tomcat	10	10
3257	40b. White Persians (vert)	20	15
3258	55b. Kittens with shoe (vert)	30	10
3259	60b. Kitten with ball of wool (vert)	45	10
3260	75b. Cat and two kittens (vert)	60	10
3261	1l.35 Siamese (vert)	1·10	20
3262	3l.25 Heads of three cats (62 × 29 mm)	2·00	50

1965. Space Flight of "Ranger 9" (24.3.65). No. 3240 surch **RANGER 9 24-3-1965 5 Lei** and floral emblem over old value.

3263	5l. on 1l. multicoloured	17·00	17·00

579 Ion Bianu (philologist)

1965. Cultural Anniversaries. Portraits in sepia.

3264	**579**	40l. blue	15	10
3265	–	55b. ochre	15	10
3266	–	60b. purple	20	10
3267	–	1l. red	50	10
3268	–	1l.35 olive	45	15
3269	–	1l.75 red	70	25

PORTRAITS, etc: 40b. Type **579** (30th death anniv); 55b. Anton Bacalbasa (writer, birth cent); 60b. Vasile Conta (philosopher, 120th birth anniv); 1l. Jean Sibelius (composer, birth cent); 1l.35, Horace (Roman poet, birth bimillenary); 1l.75, Dante Alighieri (poet, 700th birth anniv).

580 I.T.U. Emblem and Symbols

1965. Centenary of I.T.U.

3270	**580**	1l.75 blue	70	20

581 Derdap Gorge (The Iron Gate)

1965. Inaug of Derdap Hydro-electric Project.

3271	**581**	30b. (25d.) green and grey	15	10
3272	–	55b. (50d.) red and grey	25	10
MS3273		103 × 80 mm. 80b., 1l.20, 100d., 150d. multicoloured (sold at 4l. or 500d.)	2·75	2·75

DESIGNS: 55b. Derap Dam; **MS**3273, Arms of Romania and Yugoslavia on alternate stamps with outline of dam superimposed over the four stamps.

582 Rifleman

583 "Fat-Frumos and the Beast"

1965. European Shooting Championships, Bucharest. Multicoloured. (a) Perf.

3274	20b. Type **582**	10	10
3275	40b. Prone rifleman	20	15
3276	55b. Pistol shooting	25	10
3277	1l. "Free" pistol shooting	45	15
3278	1l.60 Standing rifleman	65	15
3279	2l. Various marksmen	85	30

(b) Imperf. Colours changed and new values.

3280	40b. Prone rifleman	15	10
3281	55b. Pistol shooting	20	10
3282	1l. "Free" pistol shooting	35	15
3283	1l.60 Standing rifleman	50	15
3284	3l.25 Type **582**	1·00	35
3285	5l. Various marksmen	1·50	60

Apart from Type **582** the designs are horiz, the 2l. and 5l. being larger, $51\frac{1}{2} \times 28\frac{1}{2}$ mm.

1965. Romanian Fairy Tales. Multicoloured.

3286	20b. Type **583**	20	10
3287	40b. "Fat-Frumos and Ileana Cosinzeana"	20	10
3288	55b. "Harap Alb" (horseman and bear)	25	10
3289	1l. "The Moralist Wolf"	45	10
3290	1l.35 "The Ox and the Calf"	70	20
3291	2l. "The Bear and the Wolf" (drawing a sledge)	95	25

584 Honey Bee on Flowers

585 Pavel Belyaev, Aleksei Leonov, "Voskhod 2" and Leonov in Space

1965. 20th International Bee-keeping Association Federation ("Apimondia") Congress, Bucharest.

3292	**584**	55b. black, red and yellow	30	10
3293	–	1l.60 multicoloured	95	15

DESIGN—HORIZ: 1l.60, Congress Hall.

1965. Space Achievements. Multicoloured.

3294	5b. "Proton 1"	10	10
3295	10b. "Sonda 3" (horiz)	15	20
3296	15b. "Molnia 1"	20	20
3297	1l.75 Type **585**	60	10
3298	2l.40 "Early Bird" satellite	1·00	20
3299	3l.20 "Gemini 3" and astronauts in capsule	1·90	30
3300	3l.25 "Mariner 4"	2·00	30
3301	5l. "Gemini 5" (horiz)	3·00	75

586 Marx and Lenin

588 V. Alecsandri

587 Common Quail

1965. Socialist Countries' Postal Ministers' Congress, Peking.

3302	**586**	55b. multicoloured	35	20

1965. Migratory Birds. Multicoloured.

3303	5b. Type **587**	15	10
3304	10b. Eurasian woodcock	25	10
3305	20b. Common snipe	30	10
3306	40b. Turtle dove	30	10
3307	55b. Mallard	40	10
3308	60b. White fronted goose	50	10
3309	1l. Common crane	60	15
3310	1l.20 Glossy ibis	75	15
3311	1l.35 Mute swan	1·30	20
3312	3l.25 Eastern white pelican (32 × 73 mm)	3·75	55

1965. 75th Death Anniv of Vasile Alecsandri (poet).

3313	**588**	55b. multicoloured	35	20

589 Zanzibar Water-lily

1965. Cluj Botanical Gardens. Multicoloured.

3314	5b. Bird-of-paradise flower (vert)	10	10
3315	10b. "Stanhopea tigrina" (orchid) (vert)	15	10
3316	20b. "Paphiopedilum insigne" (orchid) (vert)	15	10
3317	30b. Type **589**	25	10
3318	40b. "Ferocactus glaucescens" (cactus)	30	10
3319	55b. Tree-cotton	30	10
3320	1l. "Hibiscus rosa sinensis"	40	15
3321	1l.35 "Gloxinia hibrida" (vert)	60	15
3322	1l.75 Amazon water-lily	1·20	20
3323	2l.30 Hibiscus, water-lily, bird-of-paradise flower and botanical building (52 × 30 mm)	1·40	30

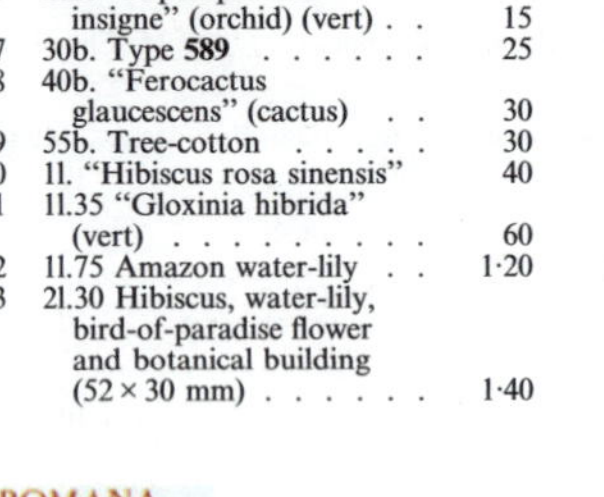

590 Running

592 Pigeon on TV Aerial

591 Pigeon and Horseman

1965. Spartacist Games. Multicoloured.

3324	55b. Type **590**	20	15
3325	1l.55 Football	55	20
3326	1l.75 Diving	60	20
3327	2l. Mountaineering (inscr "TURISM")	70	30
3328	5l. Canoeing (inscr "CAMPIONATELLE EUROPENE 1965") (horiz)	1·60	40

1965. Stamp Day.

3329	**591**	55b.+45b. blue & mve	35	10
3330	**592**	1l. brown and green	35	20
3331	–	1l.75 brown and green	80	20

DESIGN: As Type **592**: 1l.75, Pigeon in flight.

593 Chamois

1965. "Hunting Trophies".

3332	**593**	55b. brown, yell & mve	35	10
3333	–	1l. brown, green and red	60	10
3334	–	1l.60 brown, blue & orange	1·20	25
3335	–	1l.75 brown, red & green	1·60	25
3336	–	3l.20 multicoloured	2·00	50

DESIGNS—37 × 23 mm: 1l. Brown bear; 1l.60, Red deer stag; 1l.75, Wild boar. $49 \times 37\frac{1}{2}$ mm: 3l.20, Trophy and antlers of red deer.

594 Dachshund

1965. Hunting Dogs. Multicoloured.

3337	5b. Type **594**	10	20
3338	10b. Spaniel	10	20
3339	40b. Retriever with eurasian woodcock	55	20
3340	55b. Fox terrier	25	20
3341	60b. Red setter	35	20
3342	75b. White setter	60	20
3343	1l.55 Pointers	1·30	45
3344	3l.25 Duck-shooting with retriever	2·30	1·20

SIZES: DIAMOND—$47\frac{1}{2} \times 47\frac{1}{2}$ mm: 10b. to 75b. HORIZ—$43\frac{1}{2} \times 29$ mm: 1l.55, 3l.25.

595 Pawn and Globe

596 Tractor, Corn and Sun

1966. World Chess Championships, Cuba. Mult.

3345	20b. Type **595**	25	10
3346	40b. Jester and bishop	30	10
3347	55b. Knight and rook	50	10
3348	1l. As No. 3347	65	10
3349	1l.60 Type **595**	1·40	20
3350	3l.25 As No. 3346	2·75	1·00

1966. Co-operative Farming Union Congress.

3351	**596**	55b. green and yellow	25	20

597 G. Gheorghiu-Dej

598 Congress Emblem

1966. 1st Death Anniv of Gheorghe Gheorghiu-Dej (President 1961–65).

3352	**597**	55b. black and gold	25	20
MS3353		90 × 100 mm. 5l. Portrait as in Type **597**	4·50	4·50

1966. Communist Youth Union Congress.

3354	**598**	55b. red and yellow	25	20

599 Dance of Moldova

1966. Romanian Folk-dancing.

3355	**599**	30b. black and purple	20	10
3356	–	40b. black and red	35	25
3357	–	55b. black and turquoise	45	10
3358	–	1l. black and lake	55	10
3359	–	1l.60 black and blue	90	15
3360	–	2l. black and green	1·80	70

DANCES OF: 40b. Oltenia; 55b. Maramures; 1l. Muntenia; 1l.60, Banat; 2l. Transylvania.

600 Footballers

601 "Agriculture and Industry"

1966. World Cup Football Championship, England.

3361	**600**	5b. multicoloured	10	15
3362	–	10b. multicoloured	20	15
3363	–	15b. multicoloured	25	15
3364	–	55b. multicoloured	50	15
3365	–	1l.75 multicoloured	1·30	40
3366	–	4l. multicoloured	2·75	2·75
MS3367		85 × 100 mm. 10l. gold, black and blue	8·25	8·25

DESIGNS: 10b. to 1l.75, Various footballing scenes; 4l. Jules Rimet Cup. 33 × 46 mm—10l. As No. 3366.

1966. Trade Union Congress, Bucharest.

3368	**601**	55b. multicoloured	25	20

602 Red-breasted Flycatcher **603** "Venus 3"

1966. Song Birds. Multicoloured.
3369 5b. Type **602** 20 15
3370 10b. Red crossbill 35 15
3371 15b. Great reed warbler 55 15
3372 20b. Common redstart 60 15
3373 55b. European robin 90 15
3374 1l.20 Bluethroat 1·20 15
3375 1l.55 Yellow wagtail 1·70 30
3376 3l.20 Penduline tit 2·75 1·60

1966. Space Achievements. Multicoloured.
3377 10b. Type **603** 20 15
3378 20b. "FR 1" satellite 25 15
3379 1l.60 "Luna 9" 1·10 30
3380 5l. "Gemini 6" and "7" 2·50 1·00

604 Urechia Nestor (historian) **606** "Hottonia palustris"

605 "House" (after Petrascu)

1966. Cultural Anniversaries.
3381 – 5b. blue, black and green 10 10
3382 – 10b. green, black and red 10 10
3383 **604** 20b. purple, black & green 10 10
3384 – 40b. brown, black & blue 10 10
3385 – 55b. green, black & brn 15 10
3386 – 1l. violet, black and bistre 50 10
3387 – 1l.35 olive, black & blue 75 15
3388 – 1l.60 purple, blk & green 1·20 30
3389 – 1l.75 purple, blk & orge 80 15
3390 – 3l.25 lake, black and blue 1·50 30

PORTRAITS: 5b. George Cosbuc (poet, birth cent); 10b. Gheorghe Sincai (historian, 150th death anniv); 20b. Type **604** (birth cent); 40b. Aron Pumnul (linguist, death cent); 55b. Stefan Luchian (painter, 50th death anniv); 1l. Sun Yat-sen (Chinese statesman, birth cent); 1l.35, Gottfried Leibnitz (philosopher, 250th death anniv); 1l.60, Romain Rolland (writer, birth cent); 1l.75, Ion Ghica (revolutionary and diplomat, 150th birth anniv); 3l.25, Constantin Cantacuzino (historian, 250th death anniv).

1966. Paintings in National Gallery, Bucharest. Multicoloured.
3391 5b. Type **605** 15 15
3392 10b. "Peasant Girl" (Grigorescu) (vert) 20 15
3393 20b. "Midday Rest" (Rescu) 30 15
3394 55b. "Portrait of a Man" (Van Eyck) (vert) 75 20
3395 1l.55 "The 2nd Class Compartment" (Daumier) 3·75 55
3396 3l.25 "The Blessing" (El Greco) (vert) 4·25 3·75

1966. Aquatic Flora. Multicoloured.
3397 5b. Type **606** 10 10
3398 10b. "Ceratophyllum submersum" 10 10
3399 20b. "Aldrovanda vesiculosa" 10 10
3400 40b. "Callitriche verna" 30 10
3401 55b. "Vallisneria spiralis" 20 10
3402 1l. "Elodea canadensis" 30 10
3403 1l.55 "Hippuris vulgaris" 50 20
3404 3l.25 "Myriophyllum spicatum" (28 × 49½ mm) 2·75 1·10

607 Diagram showing one metre in relation to quadrant of Earth **608** Putna Monastery

1966. Centenary of Metric System in Romania.
3405 **607** 55b. blue and brown 15 10
3406 – 1l. violet and green 30 20
DESIGN: 1l. Metric abbreviations and globe.

1966. 500th Anniv of Putna Monastery.
3407 **608** 2l. multicoloured 75 30

609 "Medicine"

1966. Centenary of Romanian Academy.
3408 **609** 40b. multicoloured 15 10
3409 – 55b. multicoloured 20 10
3410 – 1l. brown, gold and blue 30 10
3411 – 3l. brown, gold & yellow 1·10 70
DESIGNS—As Type **609**: 55b. "Science" (formula). 22½ × 33½ mm: 1l. Gold medal. 67 × 27 mm: 3l. Ion Radulescu (writer), Mihail Kogalniceanu (historian) and Traian Savulescu (biologist).

610 Crayfish

1966. Crustaceans and Molluscs. Mult.
3412 5b. Type **610** 10 10
3413 10b. Netted nassa (vert) 15 10
3414 20b. Marbled rock crab 15 10
3415 40b. "Campylaea trizona" (snail) 25 10
3416 55b. Lucorum helix 40 10
3417 1l.35 Mediterranean blue mussel 95 20
3418 1l.75 Stagnant pond snail 1·20 20
3419 3l.25 Swan mussel 2·75 1·10

611 Bucharest and Mail Coach

1966. Stamp Day.
3420 **611** 55b.+45b. mult 65 30
No. 3420 is a two-part design arranged horiz, imperf between.

612 "Ursus spelaeus"

1966. Prehistoric Animals.
3421 **612** 5b. blue, brown and green 10 10
3422 – 10b. violet, bistre & green 10 10
3423 – 15b. brown, purple & green 10 10
3424 – 55b. violet, bistre & green 25 10
3425 – 1l.55 blue, brown & grn 1·40 20
3426 – 4l. mauve, bistre & green 2·75 50
ANIMALS: 10b. "Mamuthus trogontherii"; 15b. "Bison priscus"; 55b. "Archidiscodon"; 1l.55, "Megaceros eurycerus". (43 × 27 mm): 4l. "Deinotherium gigantissimum".

613 "Sputnik 1" orbiting Globe

1967. 10 Years of Space Achievements. Mult.
3427 10b. Type **613** (postage) 15 10
3428 20b. Yuri Gagarin and "Vostok 1" 15 10
3429 25b. Valentina Tereshkova ("Vostok 6") 20 10
3430 40b. Andrian Nikolaev and Pavel Popovich ("Vostok 3" and "4") 25 10
3431 55b. Aleksei Leonov in space ("Voskhod 2") 35 10
3432 1l.20 "Early Bird" (air) 75 20
3433 1l.55 Photo transmission ("Mariner 4") 1·00 20
3434 3l.25 Space rendezvous ("Gemini 6" and "7") 1·40 40
3435 5l. Space link up ("Gemini 8") 1·90 1·40

614 Barn Owl

1967. Birds of Prey. Multicoloured.
3442 10b. Type **614** 35 10
3443 20b. Eagle owl 55 10
3444 40b. Saker falcon 55 10
3445 55b. Egyptian vulture 65 10
3446 75b. Osprey 75 10
3447 1l. Griffon vulture 1·20 10
3448 1l.20 Lammergeier 2·20 20
3449 1l.75 Cinereous 2·50 95

615 "Washerwoman" (after I. Steriadi)

1967. Paintings.
3450 – 10b. blue, gold and red 15 10
3451 **615** 20b. green, gold & ochre 20 10
3452 – 40b. red, gold and blue 30 20
3453 – 1l.55 purple, gold & blue 50 25
3454 – 3l.20 brown, gold & brn 1·80 40
3455 – 5l. brown, gold & orange 2·20 1·50
PAINTINGS—VERT: 10b. "Model in Fancy Dress" (I. Andreescu); 40b. "Peasants Weaving" (S. Dimitrescu); 1l.55, "Venus and Cupid" (L. Cranach); 5l. "Haman beseeching Esther" (Rembrandt). HORIZ: 3l.20, "Hercules and the Lion" (Rubens).

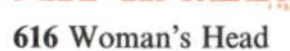

616 Woman's Head **618** "Infantryman" (Nicolae Grigorescu)

617 Copper and Silver Coins of 1867

1967. 10th Anniv of C. Brancusi (sculptor). Sculptures.
3456 **616** 5b. brown, yellow and red 10 10
3457 – 10b. black, green & violet 15 10
3458 – 20b. black, green and red 15 10
3459 – 40b. black, red & green 15 20
3460 – 55b. black, olive and blue 30 20
3461 – 1l.20 brown, violet and orange 65 25
3462 – 3l.25 black, green and mauve 3·25 95

DESIGNS—HORIZ: 10b. Sleeping muse; 40b. "The Kiss"; 3l.25, Gate of Kisses, Targujiu. VERT: 20b. "The Endless Column"; 55b. Seated woman; 1l.20, "Miss Pogany".

1967. Centenary of Romanian Monetary System.
3463 **617** 55b. multicoloured 20 20
3464 – 1l.20 multicoloured 40 50
DESIGN: 1l.20, Obverse and reverse of modern silver coin (1966).

1967. 90th Anniv of Independence.
3465 **618** 55b. multicoloured 70 75

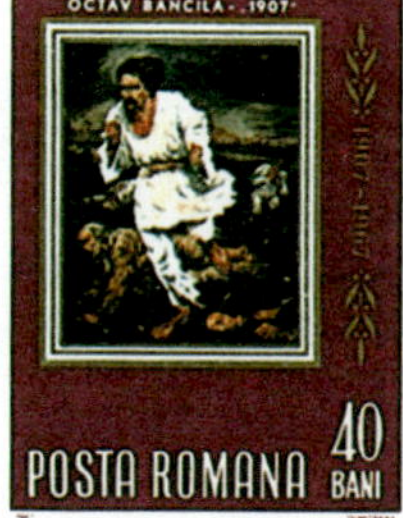

619 Peasants attacking (after Octav Bancila) **620** "Centaurca pinnatifida"

1967. 60th Anniv of Peasant Rising.
3466 **619** 40b. multicoloured 30 50
3467 – 1l.55 multicoloured 85 1·10
DESIGN—HORIZ: 1l.55, Peasants marching (after S. Luchian).

1967. Carpathian Flora. Multicoloured.
3468 20b. Type **620** 10 15
3469 40b. "Erysimum transsilvanicum" 15 15
3470 55b. "Aquilegia transsilvanica" 20 15
3471 1l.20 Alpine violet 55 20
3472 1l.75 Bellflower 95 25
3473 4l. Mountain avens (horiz) 2·20 1·30

621 Towers, Sibiu

1967. Historic Monuments and International Tourist Year. Multicoloured.
3474 20b. Type **621** 20 15
3475 40b. Castle at Cris 20 15
3476 55b. Wooden church, Plopis 40 15
3477 1l.60 Ruins, Neamtului 65 25
3478 1l.75 Mogosoaia Palace, Bucharest 90 25
3479 2l.25 Church, Voronet 1·30 1·30
MS3480 101 × 89 mm. **662** 5l. blue, black and light blue. Imperf 5·00 5·00
No. 3479 is horiz, 48½ × 36 mm.

623 "Battle of Marasesti" (E. Stoica)

1967. 50th Anniv of Battles of Marasesti, Marasti and Oituz.
3481 **623** 55b. brown, blue and grey 40 25

624 Dinu Lipatti (composer and pianist) **625** Wrestling

1967. Cultural Anniversaries.
3482 **624** 10b. violet, blue and black 10 10
3483 – 20b. blue, brown & black 10 10
3484 – 40b. brown, turq & blk 10 10
3485 – 55b. brown, red and black 15 10
3486 – 1l.20 brown, olive & black 25 15
3487 – 1l.75 green, blue & black 75 55

DESIGNS: 10b. Type **624** (50th birth anniv); 20b. Alexandru Orascu (architect, 150th birth anniv); 40b. Grigore Antipa (biologist, birth cent); 55b. Mihail Kogalniceanu (politician and historian, 150th birth anniv); 1l.20, Jonathan Swift (satirist, 300th birth anniv); 1l.75, Marie Curie (physicist, birth cent).

1967. World Wrestling Championships, Bucharest. Designs showing wrestlers and globes.

3488	**625**	10b. multicoloured	10	10
3489	–	20b. mult (horiz)	15	10
3490	–	55b. multicoloured	20	10
3491	–	1l.20 multicoloured	50	15
3492	–	2l. multicoloured (horiz)	90	60

626 Inscription on Globe

1967. International Linguists' Congress, Bucharest.

3493	**626**	1l.60 ultramarine, red and blue	60	20

627 Academy

1967. Centenary of Book Academy, Bucharest.

3494	**627**	55b. grey, brown and blue	40	20

628 Dancing on Ice

629 Curtea de Arges Monastery

1967. Winter Olympic Games, Grenoble. Mult.

3495		20b. Type **628**	10	10
3496		40b. Skiing	20	10
3497		55b. Bobsleighing	30	10
3498		1l. Downhill skiing	50	20
3499		1l.55 Ice hockey	80	20
3500		2l. Games emblem	1·10	40
3501		2l.30 Ski jumping	1·50	1·10
MS3502		80 × 100 mm. 5l. Bobsleighing. Imperf	5·00	5·00

1967. 450th Anniv of Curtea de Arges Monastery.

3503	**629**	55b. multicoloured	35	25

630 Karl Marx and Title Page

631 Lenin

1967. Centenary of Karl Marx's "Das Kapital".

3504	**630**	40b. black, yellow and red	25	20

1967. 50th Anniv of October Revolution.

3505	**631**	1l.20 black, gold and red	40	15

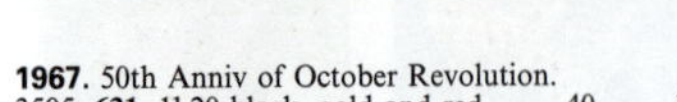

632 Arms of Romania

633 Telephone Dial and Map

1967. (a) T **632**.

3506	**632**	40b. blue	20	10
3507		55b. yellow	50	20
3508		1l.60 red	50	10

(b) T **633** and similar designs.

3509	–	5b. green	10	15
3510	–	10b. red	10	15
3511	–	20b. grey	35	15
3512	–	35b. blue	20	15
3513	–	40b. blue	10	15
3514	–	50b. orange	15	15
3515	–	55b. red	20	15
3516	–	60b. brown	35	15
3517	–	1l. green	35	15
3518	–	1l.20 violet	20	15
3519	–	1l.35 blue	70	15
3520	–	1l.50 red	35	15
3521	–	1l.55 brown	35	15
3522	–	1l.75 green	35	15
3523	–	2l. yellow	40	15
3524	–	2l.40 blue	40	15
3525	**633**	3l. turquoise	50	15
3526	–	3l.20 ochre	1·40	15
3527	–	3l.25 blue	1·60	15
3528	–	4l. mauve	2·00	15
3529	–	5l. violet	1·60	15

DESIGNS—23 × 17 mm: 5b. "Carpati" lorry; 20b. Railway Travelling Post Office coach; 35b. Zlin Z-226A Akrobat plane; 60b. Electric parcels truck. As Type **633**: 1l.20, Motorcoach; 1l.35, Mil Mi-4 helicopter; 1l.75, Lakeside highway; 2l. Postal van; 3l.20, Ilyushin Il-18 airliner; 4l. Electric train; 5l. Telex instrument and world map. 17 × 23 mm: 10b. Posthorn and telephone emblem; 40b. Power pylons; 50b. Telephone handset; 55b. Dam. As T **633** but vert: 1l. Diesel-electric train; 1l.50, Trolley-bus; 1l.55, Radio station; 2l.40, T.V. relay station; 3l.25, Liner "Transylvania".

No. 3525 also commemorates the 40th anniv of the automatic telephone service.

For Nos. 3517/29 in smaller format see Nos. 3842/57.

634 "Crossing the River Buzau" (lithograph by Raffet) (½-size illustration)

1967. Stamp Day.

3530	**634**	55b.+45b. blue and ochre	55	30

635 Monorail Train and Globe

636 Arms and Industrial Scene

1967. World Fair, Montreal. Multicoloured.

3531		55b. Type **635**	20	10
3532		1l. Expo emblem within atomic symbol	25	10
3533		1l.60 Gold cup and world map	35	10
3534		2l. Expo emblem	55	45

1967. 20th Anniv of Republic. Multicoloured.

3535		40b. Type **636**	15	10
3536		55b. Arms of Romania	15	10
3537		1l.60 Romanian flag (34 × 48 mm)	40	20
3538		1l.75 Arms and cultural emblems	65	60

637 I.A.R. 817 Flying Ambulance

1968. Air. Romanian Aviation.

3539	–	40b. multicoloured	10	10
3540	**637**	55b. multicoloured	25	10
3541	–	1l. multicoloured	30	10
3542	–	2l.40 multicoloured	80	40

DESIGNS—VERT: 40b. Antonov An-2 biplane spraying crops; 1l. "Aviasan" emblem and airliner; 2l.40, Mircea Zorileanu (pioneer aviator) and biplane.

638 "Angelica and Medor" (S. Ricci)

1968. Paintings in Romanian Galleries. Mult.

3543		40b. "Young Woman" (Misu Pop) (vert)	30	20
3544		55b. "Little Girl in Red Scarf" (N. Grigorescu) (vert)	40	20
3545		1l. "Old Nicholas, the Cobza-player" (S. Luchian) (vert)	65	25
3546		1l.60 "Man with Skull" (Dierick Bouts) (vert)	90	25
3547		2l.40 Type **638**	1·10	45
3548		3l.20 "Ecce Homo" (Titian) (vert)	2·50	2·75
MS3549		75 × 90 mm. 5l. As 3l.20. Imperf	12·50	12·50

See also Nos. 353/8, 3631/**MS**37, 3658/**MS**64, 3756/**MS**62 and 3779/**MS**85.

639 "Anemones" (Luchian)

1968. Birth Centenary of Stefan Luchian (painter). Sheet 90 × 100 mm. Imperf.

MS3550	**639**	10l. multicoloured	11·50	11·50

640 Human Rights Emblem

641 W.H.O. Emblem

1968. Human Rights Year.

3551	**640**	1l. multicoloured	55	20

1968. 20th Anniv of W.H.O.

3552	**641**	1l.60 multicoloured	70	20

642 "The Hunter" (after N. Grigorescu)

1968. Hunting Congress, Mamaia.

3553	**642**	1l.60 multicoloured	60	20

643 Pioneers and Liberation Monument

1968. Young Pioneers. Multicoloured.

3554		5b. Type **643**	10	10
3555		40b. Receiving scarves	15	10
3556		55b. With models	20	10
3557		1l. Operating radio sets	30	10
3558		1l.60 Folk-dancing	55	20
3559		2l.40 In camp	60	45

644 Prince Mircea

645 Ion Ionescu de la Brad (scholar)

1968. 550th Death Anniv of Prince Mircea (the Old).

3560	**644**	1l.60 multicoloured	70	20

1968. Cultural Anniversaries.

3561	**645**	40b. multicoloured	15	10
3562	–	55b. multicoloured	30	10

PORTRAITS AND ANNIVS: 40b. Type **645** (150th birth anniv); 55b. Emil Racovita (scientist, birth cent).

646 "Pelargonium zonale"

648 Throwing the Javelin

647 "Nicolae Balcescu" (Gheorghe Tattarescu)

1968. Garden Geraniums. Multicoloured.

3563		10b. Type **646**	10	10
3564		20b. "Pelargonium zonale" (orange)	10	10
3565		40b. "Pelargonium zonale" (red)	15	10
3566		55b. "Pelargonium zonale" (pink)	15	10
3567		60b. "Pelargonium grandiflorum" (red)	30	10
3568		1l.20 "Pelargonium peltatum" (red)	30	15
3569		1l.35 "Pelargonium peltatum" (pink)	40	15
3570		1l.60 "Pelargonium grandiflorum" (pink)	55	40

1968. 120th Anniv of 1848 Revolution. Paintings. Multicoloured.

3571		55b. Type **647**	20	10
3572		1l.20 "Avram Iancu" (B. Iscovescu)	40	10
3573		1l.60 "Vasile Alecsandri" (N. Livaditti)	80	50

1968. Olympic Games, Mexico. Multicoloured.

3574		10b. Type **648**	10	10
3575		20b. Diving	10	10
3576		40b. Volleyball	15	10
3577		55b. Boxing	20	10
3578		60b. Wrestling	20	10
3579		1l.20 Fencing	35	10
3580		1l.35 Punting	45	20
3581		1l.60 Football	85	35
MS3582		77 × 90 mm. 5l. running. Imperf	6·00	6·00

1968. Paintings in the Fine Arts Museum, Bucarest. Multicoloured.

3583		10b. "The Awakening of Romania" (G. Tattarescu) (28 × 49 mm)	10	10
3584		20b. "Composition" (Teodorescu Sionion)	10	10
3585		35b. "The Judgement of Paris" (H. van Balen)	20	10
3586		60b. "The Mystical Betrothal of St. Catherine" (L. Sustris)	35	10
3587		1l.75 "Mary with the Child Jesus" (J. van Bylert)	95	20
3588		3l. "The Summer" (J. Jordaens)	1·40	1·10

649 F.I.A.P. Emblem within "Lens"

650 Academy and Harp

1968. 20th Anniv of International Federation of Photographic Art (F.I.A.P.).
3589 **649** 1l.60 multicoloured . . . 60 20

1968. Centenary of Georgi Enescu Philharmonic Academy.
3590 **650** 55b. multicoloured . . . 40 15

651 Triumph of Trajan (Roman metope)

1968. Historic Monuments.
3591 **651** 10b. green, blue and red 10 10
3592 – 40b. blue, brown and red 15 10
3593 – 55b. violet, brown & green 20 10
3594 – 1l.20 purple, grey and ochre 35 20
3595 – 1l.55 blue, green & pur 50 20
3596 – 1l.75 brown, bistre and orange 60 40
DESIGNS—HORIZ: 40b. Monastery Church, Moldovita; 55b. Monastery. Church, Cozia; 1l.20, Tower and Church, Tirgoviste; 1l.55, Palace of Culture, Jassy; 1l.75, Corvinus Castle, Hunedoara.

652 Old Bucharest (18th-cent painting) (Illustration reduced. Actual size 76 × 28 mm)

1968. Stamp Day.
3597 **652** 55b.+45b. multicoloured 70 55

653 Mute Swan

655 Neamtz Costume (female)

654 "Entry of Michael the Brave into Alba Julia" (E. Stoica)

1968. Fauna of Nature Reservations. Multicoloured.
3598 10b. Type **653** 30 10
3599 20b. Black-winged stilt . . . 35 10
3600 40b. Common shelduck . . 45 10
3601 55b. Great egret 50 10
3602 60b. Golden eagle 65 10
3603 1l.20 Great bustard . . . . 1·30 20
3604 1l.35 Chamois 55 20
3605 1l.60 European bison . . . 70 30

1968. 50th Anniv of Union of Transylvania with Romania. Multicoloured.
3606 55b. Type **654** 15 15
3607 1l. "Union Dance" (T. Aman) 25 15
3608 1l.75 "Alba Julia Assembly" 55 35
MS3609 121 × 111 mm. Nos. 3606/8. Imperf. (Sold at 4l.) . . . . . 2·50 2·50

1968. Provincial Costumes (1st series). Mult.
3610 5b. Type **655** 10 10
3611 40b. Neamtz (male) 10 10
3612 55b. Hunedoara (female) . . 20 10
3613 1l. Hunedoara (male) . . . 35 10
3614 1l.60 Brasov (female) . . . 55 20
3615 2l.40 Brasov (male) 80 65
See also Nos. 3617/22.

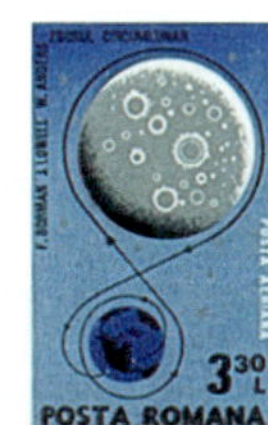

656 Earth, Moon and Orbital Track of "Apollo 8"

1969. Air. Flight of "Apollo 8" around the Moon.
3616 **656** 3l.30 black, silver & blue 1·20 1·10

1969. Provincial Costumes (2nd series). As T **655**. Multicoloured.
3617 5b. Doli (female) 10 10
3618 40b. Doli (male) 10 10
3619 55b. Arges (female) 20 10
3620 1l. Arges (male) 35 10
3621 1l.60 Timisoara (female) . . 60 20
3622 2l.40 Timisoara (male) . . . 90 65

657 Fencing

1969. Sports.
3623 **657** 10b. grey, black & brown 10 10
3624 – 20b. grey, black and violet 10 10
3625 – 40b. grey, black and blue 10 10
3626 – 55b. grey, black and red 20 10
3627 – 1l. grey, black and green 20 10
3628 – 1l.20 grey, black and blue 25 15
3629 – 1l.60 grey, black and red 35 20
3630 – 2l.40 grey, black & green 70 50
DESIGNS: 20b. Throwing the javelin; 40b. Canoeing; 55b. Boxing; 1l. Volleyball; 1l.20, Swimming; 1l.60, Wrestling; 2l.40, Football.

1969. Nude Paintings in the National Gallery. As T **638**. Multicoloured.
3631 10b. "Nude" (C. Tattarescu) 10 10
3632 20b. "Nude" (T. Pallady) 10 10
3633 35b. "Nude" (N. Tonitza) 10 10
3634 60b. "Venus and Cupid" (Flemish School) 30 15
3635 1l.75 "Diana and Endymion" (M. Liberi) 75 45
3636 3l. "The Three Graces" (J. H. von Achen) . . . . 1·70 1·10
MS3637 73 × 91 mm. 5l. Designs as 1l.75 . . . . 6·00 6·00
SIZES—36 × 49 mm: 10b., 35b., 60b., 1l.75. 27 × 49 mm: 3l. 49 × 36 mm: 20b.

1969. Air. Space Link-up of "Soyuz 4" and "Soyuz 5".
3638 **658** 3l.30 multicoloured . . . 1·70 1·50

658 "Soyuz 4" and "Soyuz 5"

659 I.L.O. Emblem

1969. 50th Anniv of International Labour Office.
3639 **659** 55b. multicoloured . . . 35 15

1969. Inter-European Cultural Economic Co-operation.
3640 **660** 55b. multicoloured . . . 30 40
3641 1l.50 multicoloured . . . 75 80

1969. Postal Ministers' Conference, Bucharest.
3642 **661** 55b. deep blue and blue 25 15

660 Stylized Head

662 Referee introducing Boxers

661 Posthorn

1969. European Boxing Championships, Bucharest. Multicoloured.
3643 35b. Type **662** 10 10
3644 40b. Sparring 15 10
3645 55b. Leading with punch . . 20 10
3646 1l.75 Declaring the winner 70 40

663 "Apollo 9" and Module over Earth

1969. Air. "Apollo" Moon Flights. Multicoloured.
3647 60b. Type **663** 15 10
3648 2l.40 "Apollo 10" and module approaching Moon (vert) 70 20

664 Lesser Purple Emperor

665 Astronaut and Module on Moon

1969. Butterflies and Moths. Multicoloured.
3649 5b. Type **664** 10 10
3650 10b. Willow-herb hawk moth 10 10
3651 20b. Eastern pale clouded yellow 10 10
3652 40b. Large tiger moth . . . 15 10
3653 55b. Pallas's fritillary . . . 20 10
3654 1l. Jersey tiger moth . . . 40 10
3655 1l.20 Orange-tip 55 20
3656 2l.40 Meleager's blue . . . 1·10 75

1969. Air. First Man on the Moon.
3657 **665** 3l.30 multicoloured . . . 1·20 1·20

1969. Paintings in the National Gallery, Bucharest. Multicoloured. As T **638**.
3658 10b. "Venetian Senator" (School of Tintoretto) . . 10 10
3659 20b. "Sofia Kretzulescu" (G. Tattarescu) 10 10
3660 35b. "Philip IV" (Velasquez) 15 10
3661 35b. "Man Reading" (Memling) 30 10
3662 1l.75 "Lady D'Aguesseau" (Vigee-Lebrun) 55 20
3663 3l. "Portrait of a Woman" (Rembrandt) . . . . . 1·40 80
MS3664 91 × 78 mm. 5l. "Return of the Prodigal Son" (Licino). Imperf . . . . 6·50 6·50

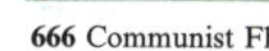
666 Communist Flag

667 Symbols of Learning

1969. 10th Romanian Communist Party Congress.
3665 **666** 55b. multicoloured . . . 30 15

1969. National "Economic Achievements" Exhibition, Bucharest. Multicoloured.
3666 35b. Type **667** 10 10
3667 40b. Symbols of Agriculture and Science 10 10
3668 1l.75 Symbols of Industry 60 15

668 Liberation Emblem

669 Juggling on Trick-cycle

1969. 25th Anniv of Liberation. Multicoloured.
3669 10b. Type **668** 10 10
3670 55b. Crane and trowel . . . 10 10
3671 60b. Flags on scaffolding . . 15 10

1969. Romanian State Circus. Multicoloured.
3672 10b. Type **669** 10 10
3673 20b. Clown 10 10
3674 35b. Trapeze artists 15 10
3675 60b. Equestrian act 20 10
3676 1l.75 High-wire act 45 15
3677 3l. Performing tiger . . . . 1·10 50

670 Forces' Memorial

1969. Army Day and 25th Anniv of People's Army.
3678 **670** 55b. black, gold and red 25 15

671 Electric Train (1965) and Steam Locomotive "Calugareni" (1869)

1969. Centenary of Romanian Railways.
3679 **671** 55b. multicoloured . . . 40 20

672 "Courtyard" (M. Bouquet) (⅔-size illustration)

1969. Stamp Day.
3680 **672** 55b.+45b. multicoloured 55 60

673 Branesti Mask

674 "Apollo 12" above Moon

1969. Folklore Masks. Multicoloured.
3681 40b. Type **673** 15 10
3682 55b. Tudora mask 15 10
3683 1l.55 Birsesti mask 40 20
3684 1l.75 Rudaria mask 55 30

1969. Moon Landing of "Apollo 12".
3685 **674** 1l.50 multicoloured . . . 40 60

675 "Three Kings" (Voronet Monastery)

1969. Frescoes from Northern Moldavian Monasteries (1st series). Multicoloured.
3686 10b. Type **675** 10 10
3687 20b. "Three Kings" (Sucevita) 10 10
3688 35b. "Holy Child in Manger" (Voronet) . . . 15 10
3689 60b. "Ship" (Sucevita) (vert) 25 10

3690 1l.75 "Walled City" (Moldovita) 55 25
3691 3l. "Pastoral Scene" (Voronet) (vert) . . . . . 1·20 70
See also Nos. 3736/42 and 3872/8.

676 "Old Mother Goose", Capra

678 Small Pasque Flower

677 Players and Emblem

1969. New Year. Children's Celebrations. Mult.
3692 40b. Type **676** 15 10
3693 55b. Decorated tree, Sorcova 55 10
3694 1l.50 Drummers, Buhaiul . . 40 10
3695 2l.40 Singer and bellringer, Plugusurol 65 40

1970. World Ice Hockey Championships (Groups B and C), Bucharest. Multicoloured.
3696 20b. Type **677** 10 10
3697 55b. Goalkeeper 15 10
3698 1l.20 Two players 25 10
3699 2l.40 Goalmouth melee . . 60 35

1970. Flowers. Multicoloured.
3700 5b. Type **678** 10 10
3701 10b. Yellow pheasant's-eye 10 10
3702 20b. Musk thistle 10 10
3703 40b. Dwarf almond 10 10
3704 55b. Dwarf bearded iris . . 10 10
3705 1l. Flax 20 10
3706 1l.20 Sage 30 15
3707 2l.40 Peony . . . . 1·40 65

679 Japanese Woodcut

681 Lenin

680 B.A.C. One Eleven Series 475 Jetliner and Silhouettes of Aircraft

1970. World Fair, Osaka, Japan. Expo 70. Mult.
3714 20b. Type **679** 15 15
3715 1l. Japanese pagoda (29 × 92 mm) 45 35
MS3716 182 × 120 mm. 5l. As design of 1l. . . . . 4·50 4·50
The design on 1l. and 5l. is vert, 29 × 92 mm. On No. **MS**3716 the face value appears on the sheet and not the stamp.

1970. 50th Anniv of Romanian Civil Aviation. Multicoloured.
3717 60b. Type **680** 25 10
3718 2l. Tail of B.A.C. One Eleven Series 475 and control tower at Otopeni Airport, Bucharest . . . 55 25

1970. Birth Centenary of Lenin.
3719 **681** 40b. multicoloured . . . 20 15

682 "Camille" (Monet) and Maximum Card

683 "Prince Alexander Cuza" (Szathmary)

1970. Maximafila Franco–Romanian Philatelic Exn, Bucharest.
3720 **682** 1l.50 multicoloured . . . 65 25

1970. 150th Birth Anniv of Prince Alexandru Cuza.
3721 **683** 55b. multicoloured . . . 35 20

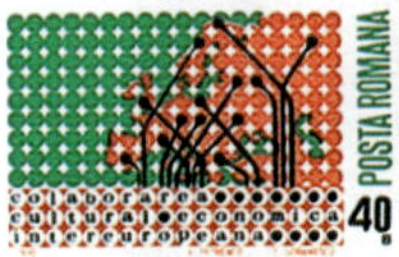

684 "Co-operation" Map

685 Victory Monument, Bucharest

1970. Inter-European Cultural and Economic Co-operation.
3722 **684** 40b. green, brown & black 35 40
3723 1l.50 blue, brown & blk 75 80

1970. 25th Anniv of Liberation.
3724 **685** 55b. multicoloured . . . 30 20

686 Greek Silver Drachma, 5th cent B.C.

1970. Ancient Coins.
3725 **686** 10b. black and blue . . 10 10
3726 – 20b. black and red 10 10
3727 – 35b. bronze and green 10 10
3728 – 60b. black and brown . . 15 10
3729 – 1l.75 black and blue . . 60 10
3730 – 3l. black and red . . . . 1·00 40
DESIGNS—HORIZ: 20b. Getic-Dacian silver didrachm, 2nd—1st-cent B.C.; 35b. Copper sestertius of Trajan, 106 A.D.; 60b. Mircea ducat, 1400; 1l.75, Silver groschen of Stephen the Great, 1460. VERT: 3l. Brasov klippe-thaler, 1601.

687 Footballers and Ball

1970. World Cup Football Championship, Mexico.
3731 **687** 40b. multicoloured . . . 10 10
3732 – 55b. multicoloured . . . 15 10
3733 – 1l.75 multicoloured . . . 40 20
3734 – 3l.30 multicoloured . . . 80 50
MS3735 110 × 110 mm. 6l. Four designs with face values 1l.20, 1l.50, 1l.55 and 1l.75 . . . . . 3·50 3·50
DESIGNS: Nos. 3732/4, various football scenes as Type **687**.

1970. Frescoes from Northern Moldavian Monasteries (2nd series). As T **675**. Mult.
3736 10b. "Prince Petru Rares and Family" (Moldovita) 10 10
3737 20b. "Metropolitan Grigore Rosca" (Voronet) (28 × 48 mm) 10 10
3738 40b. "Alexander the Good and Family" (Sucevita) 15 10
3739 55b. "The Last Judgement" (Voronet) (vert) 25 10
3740 1l.75 "The Last Judgement" (Voronet) (different) . . . 65 25
3741 3l. "St. Anthony" (Voronet) 1·40 70
MS3742 90 × 77 mm. 5l. "Byzantine Manor" (Arbore) . . . . 6·00 6·00

688 "Apollo 13" Spashdown

689 Engels

1970. Air. Space Flight of "Apollo 13".
3743 **688** 1l.50 multicoloured . . . 1·50 95

1970. 150th Birth Anniv of Friedrich Engels.
3744 **689** 1l.50 multicoloured . . . 50 15

690 Exhibition Hall

1970. National Events. Multicoloured.
3745 35b. "Iron Gates" Dam . . 10 10
3746 55b. Freighter and flag . . . 30 10
3747 1l.50 Type **690** 30 10
EVENTS: 35b. Danube navigation projects; 55b. 75th anniv of Romanian Merchant Marine; 1l.50, 1st International Fair, Bucharest.

691 New Headquarters Building

1970. New U.P.U. Headquarters Building, Berne.
3748 **691** 1l.50 blue and ultramarine 55 15

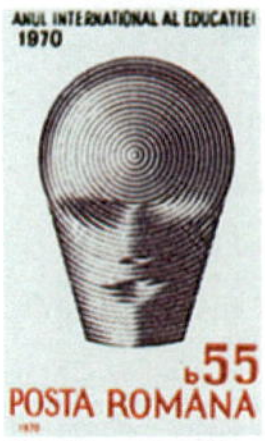

692 Education Year Emblem

693 "Iceberg"

1970. International Education Year.
3749 **692** 55b. plum, black and red 30 20

1970. Roses. Multicoloured.
3750 20b. Type **693** 10 10
3751 35b. "Wiener Charme" . . 10 10
3752 55b. "Pink Lustre" 15 10
3753 1l. "Piccadilly" 45 10
3754 1l.50 "Orange Delbard" . . 55 10
3755 2l.40 "Sibelius" 90 75

694 "Spaniel and Pheasant" (J. B. Oudry)

695 Refugee Woman and Child

1970. Paintings in Romanian Galleries. Mult.
3756 10b. "The Hunt" (D. Brandi) (38 × 50 mm) 10 10
3757 20b. Type **694** 10 10
3758 35b. "The Hunt" (Jan Fyt) (38 × 50 mm) 10 10
3759 60b. "After the Chase" (Jordaens) (As T **694**) . . 25 10
3760 1l.75 "The Game Dealer" (F. Snyders) (50 × 38 mm) 60 20
3761 3l. "The Hunt" (A. de Gryeff) (As T **694**) . . . 1·20 70
MS3762 90 × 78 mm. 5l. Design as 1l.75 . . . . 5·00 5·00

1970. Danube Flood Victims (1st issue).
3763 **695** 55b. black, blue and green (postage) . . . 15 10
3764 – 1l.50 multicoloured . . . 35 20
3765 – 1l.75 multicoloured . . . 75 70
3766 – 60b. black, drab and blue (air) 35 10
DESIGNS: 60b. Helicopter rescue; 1l.50, Red Cross post; 1l.75, Building reconstruction.
See also No. 3777.

696 U.N. Emblem

698 Beethoven

697 Arab Horse

1970. 25th Anniv of United Nations.
3767 **696** 1l.50 multicoloured . . . 35 20

1970. Horses. Multicoloured.
3768 20b. Type **697** 10 10
3769 35b. American trotter . . . 10 10
3770 55b. Ghidran 10 10
3771 1l. Hutul 30 10
3772 1l.50 Thoroughbred 45 20
3773 2l.40 Lippizaner . . . . . . 1·60 80

1970. Birth Bicentenary of Ludwig van Beethoven (composer).
3774 **698** 55b. multicoloured . . . 60 20

699 "Mail-cart in the Snow" (E. Volkers) (½-size illustration)

1970. Stamp Day.
3775 **699** 55b.+45b. mult 55 60

700 Henri Coanda's Model Airplane

1970. Air. 60th Anniv of First Experimental Turbine-powered Airplane.
3776 **700** 60b. multicoloured . . . 55 20

701 "The Flood" (abstract, Joan Miro)

1970. Danube Flood Victims (2nd issue).
3777 **701** 3l. multicoloured . . . . 1·60 1·60
MS3778 79 × 95 mm. **701** 5l. multicoloured. Imperf . . . . 5·50 5·50

702 "Sight" (G. Coques)

1970. Paintings from the Bruckenthal Museum, Sibiu. Multicoloured.
3779 10b. Type **702** 10 10
3780 20b. "Hearing" 10 10
3781 35b. "Smell" 10 10
3782 60b. "Taste" 20 10
3783 1l.75 "Touch" 40 15
3784 3l. Bruckenthal Museum . . 1·00 65
MS3785 90 × 78 mm. 5l. "View of Sibiu, 1808" (lithograph) (horiz) 5·00 5·00

Nos. 3779/83 show a series of pictures by Coques entitled "The Five Senses".

703 Vladimirescu (after Theodor Aman) **705** Alsatian

704 "Three Races"

1971. 150th Death Anniv of Tudor Vladimirescu (Wallachian revolutionary).
3786 **703** 1l.50 multicoloured . . . 50 20

1971. Racial Equality Year.
3787 **704** 1l.50 multicoloured . . . 55 20

1971. Dogs. Multicoloured.

3788	20b. Type **705**	10	10
3789	35b. Bulldog	10	10
3790	55b. Fox terrier	15	10
3791	1l. Setter	40	10
3792	1l.50 Cocker spaniel	60	20
3793	2l.40 Poodle	1·90	1·20

706 "Luna 16" leaving Moon **707** Proclamation of the Commune

1971. Air. Moon Missions of "Luna 16" and "Luna 17". Multicoloured.

3794	3l.30 Type **706**	1·70	95
3795	3l.30 "Lunokhod 1" on Moon	1·70	95

1971. Centenary of Paris Commune.
3796 **707** 40b. multicoloured . . . 30 15

708 Astronaut and Moon Trolley

1971. Air. Moon Mission of "Apollo 14".
3797 **708** 3l.30 multicoloured . . . 1·10 1·00

709 "Three Fists" Emblem and Flags **710** "Toadstool" Rocks, Babele

1971. Trade Union Congress, Bucharest.
3798 **709** 55b. multicoloured . . . 30 15

1971. Tourism. Multicoloured.

3799	10b. Gorge, Cheile Bicazului (vert)	10	10
3800	40b. Type **710**	10	10
3801	55b. Winter resort, Poiana Brasov	15	10
3802	1l. Fishing punt and tourist launch, Danube delta	40	10
3803	1l.50 Hotel, Baile Sovata	55	10
3804	2l.40 Venus, Jupiter and Neptune Hotels, Black Sea (77 × 29 mm)	85	55

711 "Arrows" **712** Museum Building

1971. Inter-European Cultural Economic Co-operation. Multicoloured.

3805	55b. Type **711**	85	90
3806	1l.75 Stylized map of Europe	1·30	1·30

1971. Historical Museum, Bucharest.
3807 **712** 55b. multicoloured . . . 20 15

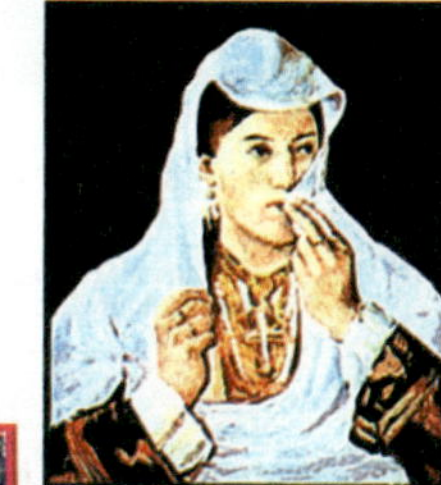

713 "The Secret Printing-press" (S. Szonyi) **714** "Motra Tone" (Kole Idromeno)

1971. 50th Anniv of Romanian Communist Party. Multicoloured.

3808	35b. Type **713**	10	10
3809	40b. Emblem and red flags (horiz)	10	10
3810	55b. "The Builders" (A. Anastasiu)	15	10

1971. "Balkanfila III". International Stamp Exhibition, Bucharest. Multicoloured.

3811	1l.20+60b. Type **714**	60	65
3812	1l.20+60b. "Maid" (Vladimir Dimitrov-Maistora)	60	65
3813	1l.20+60b. "Rosa Botzaris" (Joseph Stieler)	60	65
3814	1l.20+60b. "Portrait of a Lady" (Katarina Ivanovic)	60	65
3815	1l.20+60b. "Agreseanca" (C. Popp de Szathmary)	60	65
3816	1l.20+60b. "Woman in Modern Dress" (Calli Ibrahim)	60	65
MS3817	90 × 79 mm. 5l. "Dancing the Hora" (Theodor Aman) (horiz)	6·00	6·00

Each stamp has a premium-carrying "tab" as shown in Type **714**.

715 Pomegranate

1971. Flowers. Multicoloured.

3818	20b. Type **715**	10	10
3819	35b. "Calceolus speciosum"	10	10
3820	55b. "Life jagra"	10	10
3821	1l. Blood-drop emlets	30	10
3822	1l.50 Dwarf morning glory	45	20
3823	2l.40 "Phyllocactus phyllanthoides" (horiz)	1·00	30

716 "Nude" (J. Iser)

1971. Paintings of Nudes. Multicoloured.

3824	10b. Type **716**	10	10
3825	20b. "Nude" (C. Ressu) (29 × 50 mm)	10	10
3826	35b. "Nude" (N. Grigorescu)	10	10
3827	60b. "Odalisque" (Delacroix) (horiz)	10	10
3828	1l.75 "Nude in a Landscape" (Renoir)	60	25
3829	3l. "Venus and Cupid" (Il Vecchio) (horiz)	1·20	65
MS3830	90 × 78 mm. 5l. "Venus and Amour" (Il Bronzino) (horiz)	5·50	5·50

717 Cosmonauts Patsaev, Dobrovolsky and Volkov (B5)

1971. Air. "Soyuz 11" Commemoration. Sheet 101 × 81 mm.
MS3831 **717** 6l. black and blue 9·00 9·00

718 Astronauts and Lunar Rover on Moon

1971. Air. Moon Flight of "Apollo 15".
3833 **718** 1l.50 multicoloured (blue background) . . . . . 1·20 1·30

No. 3833 also exists imperforate, with background colour changed to green, from a restricted printing.

719 "Fishing Boats" (M. W. Arnold)

1971. Marine Paintings. Multicoloured.

3835	10b. "Coastal Storm" (B. Peters)	10	10
3836	20b. "Seascape" (I. Backhuysen)	10	10
3837	35b. "Boat in Stormy Seas" (A. van de Eertvelt)	10	10
3838	60b. Type **719**	20	10
3839	1l.75 "Seascape" (I. K. Aivazovsky)	50	20
3840	3l. "Fishing boats, Braila" (J. A. Steriadi)	1·20	50
MS3841	78 × 90 mm. 5l. "Venetian Fishing-boats" (N. Darascu) (vert)	4·75	4·75

1971. As Nos. 3517/29 and three new designs but in smaller format, 17 × 23 or 23 × 17 mm.

3842	1l. green	45	15
3843	1l.20 violet	25	15
3844	1l.35 blue	75	15
3845	1l.50 red	35	15
3846	1l.55 brown	35	15
3847	1l.75 green	35	15
3848	2l. yellow	40	15
3849	2l.40 blue	50	15
3850	3l. blue	60	15
3851	3l.20 brown	50	15
3852	3l.25 blue	75	15
3853	3l.60 blue	80	15
3854	4l. mauve	1·80	15
3855	4l.80 blue	1·00	15
3856	5l. violet	1·30	15
3857	6l. mauve	1·50	15

NEW DESIGNS—VERT: 3l.60, Clearing letter box; 4l.80, Postman on round; 6l. Postal Ministry, Bucharest.

720 "Neagoe Basarab" (fresco, Curtea de Arges) **721** "T. Pallady" (self-portrait)

1971. 450th Death Anniv of Prince Neagoe Basarab, Regent of Wallachia.
3858 **720** 60b. multicoloured . . . 25 15

1971. Artists' Anniversaries.

3859	**721**	40b. multicoloured	10	10
3860	–	55b. black, stone and gold	10	10
3861	–	1l.50 black, stone & gold	25	10
3862	–	2l.40 multicoloured	55	30

DESIGNS (self-portraits: 40b. Type **721** (birth centenary); 55b. Benevenuto Cellini (400th death anniv); 1l.50, Jean Watteau (250th death anniv); 2l.40, Albrecht Durer (500th birth anniv).

722 Persian Text and Seal **723** Figure Skating

1971. 2500th Anniv of Persian Empire.
3863 **722** 55b. multicoloured . . . 35 15

1971. Winter Olympic Games, Sapporo, Japan (1972). Multicoloured.

3864	10b. Type **723**	10	15
3865	20b. Ice-hockey	10	15
3866	40b. Biathlon	10	15
3867	55b. Bobsleighing	10	15
3868	1l.75 Downhill skiing	50	25
3869	3l. Games emblem	1·00	60
MS3870	78 × 90 mm. 5l. Symbolic flame (38 × 50 mm). Imperf	4·25	4·25

724 "Lady with Letter" (Sava Hentia)

1971. Stamp Day.
3871 **724** 1l.10+90b. mult 70 70

1971. Frescoes from Northern Moldavian Monasteries (3rd series). As T **675**. Multicoloured.

3872	10b. "St. George and The Dragon" (Moldovita) (vert)	10	10
3873	20b. "Three Kings and Angel" (Moldovita) (vert)	10	10
3874	40b. "The Crucifixion" (Moldovita) (vert)	10	10
3875	55b. "Trial" (Voronet) (vert)	10	10
3876	1l.75 "Death of a Martyr" (Voronet) (vert)	60	20
3877	3l. "King and Court" (Arborea)	1·20	85
MS3878	78 × 90 mm. 5l. Wall of frescoes, Voronet (vert)	4·75	4·75

725 Matei Millo (dramatist, 75th death anniv)

726 Magellan and Ships (450th death anniv)

1971. Famous Romanians. Multicoloured.

3879 55b. Type **725** 15 10
3880 1l. Nicolae Iorga (historian, birth cent) 20 10

1971. Scientific Anniversaries.

3881 **726** 40b. mauve, blue & green 35 10
3882 – 55b. blue, green and lilac 10 10
3883 – 1l. multicoloured 25 10
3884 – 1l.50 green, blue & brn 30 15

DESIGNS AND ANNIVERSARIES: 55b. Kepler and observatory (400th birth anniv); 1l. Gagarin, rocket and Globe (10th anniv of first manned space flight); 1l.50, Lord Rutherford and atomic symbol (birth cent).

727 Lynx Cubs

1972. Young Wild Animals. Multicoloured.

3885 20b. Type **727** 10 30
3886 35b. Red fox cubs 10 30
3887 55b. Roe deer fawns 20 30
3888 1l. Wild piglets 45 15
3889 1l.50 Wolf cubs 80 15
3890 2l.40 Brown bear cubs . . . 2·50 95

728 U.T.C. Emblem

730 Stylized Map of Europe

729 Wrestling

1972. 50th Anniv of Communist Youth Union (U.T.C.).

3891 **728** 55b. multicoloured . . . 25 15

1972. Olympic Games, Munich (1st issue). Mult.

3892 10b. Type **729** 10 10
3893 20b. Canoeing 10 10
3894 55b. Football 10 10
3895 1l.55 High-jumping 35 10
3896 2l.90 Boxing 60 10
3897 6l.70 Volleyball . . . . . . 1·60 85

MS3898 100 × 81 mm. 6l. Runner with Olympic Torch (air) . . . 11·50 11·50

See also Nos. 3914/**MS**3920 and 3926.

1972. Inter-European Cultural and Economic Co-operation.

3899 **730** 1l.75 gold, black & mve 1·10 85
3900 – 2l.90 gold, black & green 1·30 1·10

DESIGN: 2l.90, "Crossed arrows" symbol.

731 Astronauts in Lunar Rover

732 Modern Trains and Symbols

1972. Air. Moon Flight of "Apollo 16".

3901 **731** 3l. blue, green and pink 1·40 1·20

1972. 50th Anniv of International Railway Union.

3902 **732** 55b. multicoloured . . . 45 20

733 "Summer" (P. Brueghel)

1972. "Belgica 72" Stamp Exhibition, Brussels. Sheet 89 × 76 mm.

MS3903 **733** 6l. multicoloured . . 4·75 4·75

734 "Paeonia romanica"

1972. Scarce Romanian Flowers.

3904 **734** 20b. multicoloured . . . 10 10
3905 – 40b. purple, green & brown 10 10
3906 – 55b. brown and blue . . 20 10
3907 – 60b. red, green and light green 20 10
3908 – 1l.35 multicoloured . . . 45 10
3909 – 2l.90 multicoloured . . . 95 35

DESIGNS: 40b. "Dianthus callizonus"; 55b. Edelweiss; 60b. Vanilla orchid; 1l.35, "Narcissus stellaris"; 2l.90, Lady's slipper.

735 Saligny Bridge, Cernavoda

1972. Danube Bridges. Multicoloured.

3910 1l.35 Type **735** 50 10
3911 1l.75 Giurgeni Bridge, Vadul Oii 30 15
3912 2l.75 Friendship Bridge, Giurgiu–Ruse (Bulgaria) 2·50 25

736 North Railway Station, Bucharest, 1872

1972. Cent of North Railway Station, Bucharest.

3913 **736** 55b. multicoloured . . . 45 20

737 Water-polo

1972. Olympic Games, Munich (2nd issue). Mult.

3914 10b. Type **737** 10 10
3915 20b. Pistol-shooting 15 10
3916 55b. Throwing the discus . . 15 10
3917 1l.55 Gymnastics 35 10
3918 2l.75 Canoeing 85 20
3919 6l.40 Fencing . . . . 1·60 90

MS3920 90 × 78 mm. 6l. Football (air) . . . . 11·50 11·50

738 Rotary Stamp-printing Press

740 Runner with Torch

739 "E. Stoenescu" (Stefan Popescu)

1972. Centenary of State Stamp-printing Works.

3921 **738** 55b. multicoloured . . . 30 15

1972. Romanian Art. Portraits. Multicoloured.

3922 55b. Type **739** 10 10
3923 1l.75 Self-portrait (Octav Bancila) 20 10
3924 2l.90 Self-portrait (Gheorghe Petrascu) 40 10
3925 6l.50 Self-portrait (Ion Andreescu) 85 35

1972. Olympic Games, Munich (3rd issue). Olympic Flame.

3926 **740** 55b. purple & blue on silver 45 20

741 Aurel Vlaicu, his Airplane No. 1 "Crazy Fly" and Silhouette of Boeing 707 Jetliner

1972. Air. Romanian Aviation Pioneers. Mult.

3927 60b. Type **741** 15 10
3928 3l. Traian Vuia, Vuia No. 1 and silhouette of Boeing 707 jetliner 80 40

742 Cluj Cathedral

743 Satu Mare

1972.

3929 **742** 11.85 violet (postage) . . 25 10
3930 – 2l.75 grey 35 15
3931 – 3l.35 red 45 10
3932 – 3l.45 green 50 10
3933 – 5l.15 blue 70 10
3934 – 5l.60 blue 75 10
3935 – 6l.20 mauve 80 10
3936 – 6l.40 brown . . . . . . 1·00 10
3937 – 6l.80 red . . . . 1·00 10
3938 – 7l.05 black . . . . 1·10 10
3939 – 8l.45 red . . . . 1·10 10
3940 – 9l.05 green . . . . 1·30 10
3941 – 9l.10 blue . . . . 1·30 10
3942 – 9l.85 green . . . . 1·30 10
3943 – 10l. brown . . . . 1·50 10
3944 – 11l.90 blue . . . . 1·50 15
3945 – 12l.75 violet . . . . . . 1·80 15
3946 – 13l.30 red . . . . 2·00 15
3947 – 16l.20 green . . . . . . 2·50 15
3948 – 14l.60 blue (air) . . . . 3·00 30

DESIGNS—HORIZ: (As Type **742**): 2l.75, Sphinx Rock, Mt. Bucegi; 3l.45, Sinaia Castle; 5l.15, Hydro-electric power station, Arges; 6l.40, Hunidoara Castle; 6l.80, Bucharest Polytechnic complex; 9l.05, Coliseum, Sarmisegtetuza; 9l.10, Hydro-electric power station, Iron Gates. (29 × 21 mm): 11l.90, Palace of the Republic, Bucharest; 13l.30, City Gate, Alba Julia; 14l.60, Otopeni Airport, Bucharest. VERT: (As Type **742**): 3l.35, Heroes' Monument, Bucharest; 5l.60, Iasi-Biserica; 6l.20, Bran Castle; 7l.05, Black Church, Brasova; 8l.45, Atheneum, Bucharest; 9l.85, Decebal's statue, Cetatea Deva. (20 × 30 mm): 10l. City Hall Tower, Sibiu; 12l.75, T.V. Building, Bucharest; 16l.20, Clock Tower, Sighisoara.

1972. Millenium of Satu Mare.

3949 **743** 55b. multicoloured . . . 30 15

744 Davis Cup on Racquet

1972. Final of Davis Cup Men's Team Tennis Championship, Bucharest.

3950 **744** 2l.75 multicoloured . . . 85 35

745 "Venice" (Gheorghe Petrascu)

1972. UNESCO "Save Venice" Campaign. Paintings of Venice. Multicoloured.

3951 10b. Type **745** 10 15
3952 20b. Gondolas (N. Darascu) 10 15
3953 55b. Palace (Petrascu) . . . 15 15
3954 1l.55 Bridge (Marius Bunescu) 40 15
3955 2l.75 Palace (Darascu) (vert) 95 70
3956 6l.40 Canal (Bunesca) . . . 2·40 1·00

MS3957 91 × 79 mm. 6l. Old houses (Petrascu) . . . . 4·75 4·75

746 Fencing and Bronze Medal

748 Flags and "25"

747 "Travelling Romanies" (E. Volkers) (⅔-size illustration)

1972. Munich Olympic Games Medals. Mult.

3958 10b. Type **746** 10 15
3959 20b. Handball and Bronze Medal 10 10
3960 35b. Boxing and Silver Medal 15 10
3961 1l.45 Hurdling and Silver Medal 35 10
3962 2l.75 Shooting, Silver and Bronze Medals 70 25
3963 6l.20 Wrestling and two Gold Medals . . . . . . 1·80 80

MS3964 90 × 80 mm. 6l. Gold and Silver medals (horiz) (air) . . . 11·50 11·50

1972. Stamp Day.

3965 **747** 1l.10+90b. mult 80 60

1972. 25th Anniv of Proclamation of Republic. Multicoloured.

3966 55b. Type **748** 15 10
3967 1l.20 Arms and "25" . . . 20 15
3968 1l.75 Industrial scene and "25" 35 15

749 "Apollo 1", "2" and "3" **750** European Bee Eater

1972. "Apollo" Moon Flights. Multicoloured.
3969 10b. Type **749** 20 10
3970 35b. Grissom, Chaffee and White 20 10
3971 40b. "Apollo 4, 5, 6" . . . 30 10
3972 55b. "Apollo 7, 8" . . . 40 10
3973 1l. "Apollo 9, 10" 55 10
3974 1l.20 "Apollo 11, 12" . . . 75 10
3975 1l.85 "Apollo 13, 14" . . . 95 15
3976 2l.75 "Apollo 15, 16" . . . 1·70 15
3977 3l.60 "Apollo 17" . . . . . 2·40 55
MS3978 89 × 77 mm. 6l. Astronauts and Lunar Rover on Moon (horiz) (air) . . . . 11·50 11·50

1973. Protection of Nature. Multicoloured. (a) Birds.
3979 1l.40 Type **750** 70 15
3980 1l.85 Red-breasted goose . . 85 20
3981 2l.75 Peduline tit . . . . . 1·20 40

(b) Flowers.
3982 1l.40 Globe flower 25 10
3983 1l.85 Martagon lily 30 30
3984 2l.75 Gentian 40 30

751 Copernicus **752** Suceava Costume (female)

1973. 500th Birth Anniv of Copernicus (astronomer).
3985 **751** 2l.75 multicoloured . . . 80 35

1973. Regional Costumes. Multicoloured.
3986 10b. Type **752** 10 15
3987 40b. Suceava (male) 10 15
3988 55b. Harghila (female) . . . 10 15
3989 1l.75 Harghila (male) . . . 30 15
3990 2l.75 Gorj (female) 50 20
3991 6l.40 Gorj (male) . . . . . 1·00 70

753 Dimitrie Paciurea (sculptor) **754** Map of Europe

1973. Anniversaries. Multicoloured.
3992 10b. Type **753** (birth centenary) 10 10
3993 40b. Ioan Slavici (writer, 125th birth anniv) 10 10
3994 55b. Gheorghe Lazar (educationist, death cent) 10 10
3995 6l.40 Alexandru Flechtenmacher (composer, birth cent) . . 1·50 60

1973. Inter-European Cultural and Economic Co-operation.
3996 **754** 3l.35 gold, blue & purple 90 85
3997 – 3l.60 gold and purple . . 1·10 1·20
DESIGN: 3l.60, Emblem.

755 "The Rape of Proserpine" (Hans von Achen)

1973. "iBRA 73" Stamp Exhibition, Munich. Sheet 90 × 78 mm.
MS3998 **755** 12l. multicoloured 8·50 8·50

756 Hand with Hammer and Sickle **757** W.M.O. Emblem and Weather Satellite

1973. Anniversaries. Multicoloured.
3999 40b. Type **756** 15 20
4000 55b. Flags and bayonets . . 25 20
4001 1l.75 Prince Cuza 55 20
EVENTS: 40b. 25th anniv of Romanian Workers and Peasant Party; 55b. 40th anniv of National Anti-Fascist Committee; 1l.75, Death cent of Prince Alexandru Cuza.

1973. Centenary of W.M.O.
4002 **757** 2l. multicoloured 60 20

758 "Dimitri Ralet" (anon) **759** Prince Dimitri Cantemir

1973. "Socfilex III" Stamp Exhibition, Bucharest. Portrait Paintings. Multicoloured.
4003 40b. Type **758** 10 10
4004 60b. "Enacheta Vacarescu" (A. Chladek) 10 10
4005 1l.55 "Dimitri Aman" (C. Lecca) 20 10
4006 4l.+2l. "Barbat at his Desk" (B. Iscovescu) . . . . . . 1·20 60
MS4007 78 × 89 mm. 6l.+2l. "The Poet Alecsandri and his Family" (N. Livaditti) (38 × 51 mm) . . 5·75 5·75

1973. 300th Birth Anniv of Dimitri Cantemir, Prince of Moldavia (writer). Multicoloured.
4008 **759** 1l.75 multicoloured . . . 50 25
MS4009 77 × 90 mm. 6l. multicoloured . . . . 4·75 4·75
DESIGNS: (38 × 51 mm)—6l. Miniature of Cantemir.

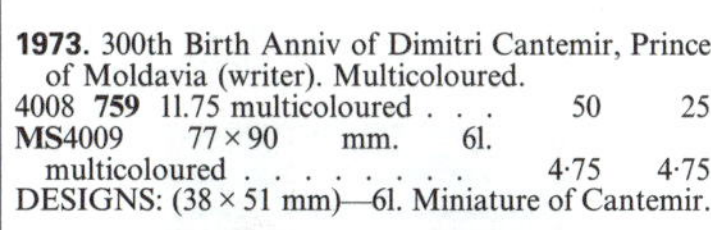

760 Fibular Brooches

1973. Treasures of Pietroasa. Multicoloured.
4010 10b. Type **760** 10 15
4011 20b. Golden figurine and bowl (horiz) 10 15
4012 55b. Gold oil flask 10 15
4013 1l.55 Brooch and bracelets (horiz) 45 15
4014 2l.75 Gold platter 65 20
4015 6l.80 Filgree cup holder (horiz) . . . . 1·40 70
MS4016 78 × 91 mm. 12l. Jewelled breast-plate . . . . 6·00 6·00

761 Map with Flower

1973. European Security and Co-operation Conference, Helsinki. Sheet 152 × 81 mm containing T **761** and similar horiz design. Multicoloured.
MS4017 2l.75 × 2 Type **761**; 5l. × 2 Europe "Tree" . . . . 6·50 6·50

762 Oboga Jar **763** "Postilion" (A. Verona)

1973. Romanian Ceramics. Multicoloured.
4018 10b. Type **762** 10 10
4019 20b. Vama dish and jug . . 10 10
4020 55b. Maginea bowl 10 10
4021 1l.55 Sibiu Saschiz jug and dish 35 10
4022 2l.75 Pisc pot and dish . . . 55 20
4023 6l.80 Oboga "bird" vessel 1·60 45

1973. Stamp Day.
4024 **763** 1l.10+90b. mult 60 65

764 "Textile Workers" (G. Saru) **765** Town Hall, Craiova

1973. Paintings showing Workers. Multicoloured.
4025 10b. Type **764** 10 10
4026 20b. "Construction Site" (M. Bunescu) (horiz) . . . 10 10
4027 55b. "Shipyard Workers" (H. Catargi) (horiz) . . . 10 10
4028 1l.55 "Working Man" (H. Catargi) 20 10
4029 2l.75 "Miners" (A. Phoebus) 40 15
4030 6l.80 "The Spinner" (N. Grigorescu) . . . . . 1·00 55
MS4031 90 × 77 mm. 12l. "Harvest Meal" (S. Popescu) (horiz) . . 4·75 4·75

1974. (a) Buidings.
4032 **765** 5b. red 10 10
4033 – 10b. blue 10 10
4034 – 20b. orange 10 10
4035 – 35b. green 10 10
4036 – 40b. violet 10 10
4037 – 50b. blue 10 10
4038 – 55b. brown 10 10
4039 – 60b. red 10 10
4040 – 1l. blue 10 10
4041 – 1l.20 green 10 10

(b) Ships.
4042 – 1l.35 black 25 10
4043 – 1l.45 blue 25 10
4044 – 1l.50 red 25 10
4045 – 1l.55 blue 35 10
4046 – 1l.75 green 40 10
4047 – 2l.20 blue 45 10
4048 – 3l.65 lilac 75 10
4049 – 4l.70 purple . . . . . . 1·20 15
DESIGNS—VERT: 10b. "Column of Infinity", Tirgu Jiu; 40b. Romanesque church, Densus; 50b. Reformed Church, Dej; 1l. Curtea de Arges Monastery. HORIZ: 20b. Heroes' Monument, Marasesti; 35b. Citadel, Risnov; 55b. Castle, Maldarasti; 60b. National Theatre, Jassy; 1l.20, Fortress and church, Tirgu Mures; 1l.35, Danube Tug "Impingator"; 1l.45, Freighter "Dimbovita"; 1l.50, Danube passenger vessel "Muntenia"; 1l.55, Cadet barque "Mircea"; 1l.75, Liner "Transylvania"; 2l.20, Bulk carrier "Oltul"; 3l.65, Trawler "Mures"; 4l.70, Tanker "Arges".

767 "Boats at Honfleur" (Monet)

1974. Impressionist Paintings. Multicoloured.
4056 20b. Type **767** 10 10
4057 40b. "Moret Church" (Sisley) (vert) 10 10
4058 55b. "Orchard in Blossom" (Pissarro) 10 10
4059 1l.75 "Jeanne" (Pissarro) (vert) 25 10
4060 2l.75 "Landscape" (Renoir) 45 20
4061 3l.60 "Portrait of a Girl" (Cezanne) (vert) . . . . . 1·10 35
MS4062 78 × 84 mm. 10l. "Women Bathing" (Renoir) (vert) . . . 4·75 4·75

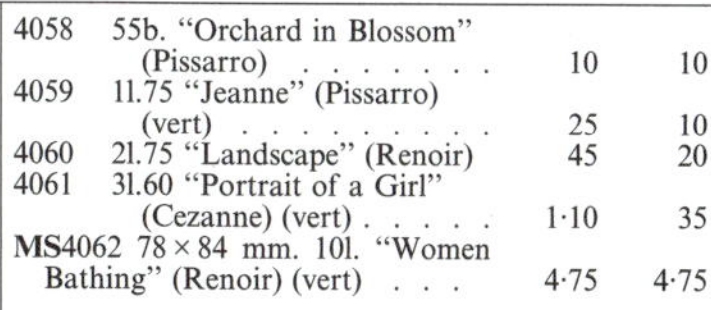

768 Trotting with Sulky **769** Nicolas Titulescu (Romanian League of Nations Delegate)

1974. Cent of Horse-racing in Romania. Mult.
4063 40b. Type **768** 10 10
4064 55b. Three horses racing . . 10 10
4065 60b. Horse galloping . . . 10 10
4066 1l.55 Two trotters racing . . 30 10
4067 2l.75 Three trotters racing 55 20
4068 3l.45 Two horses racing . . 85 30

1974. Interparliamentary Congress Session, Bucharest.
4069 **769** 1l.75 multicoloured . . . 35 20

770 Roman Monument

1974. 1850th Anniv of Cluj (Napoca). Sheet 78 × 91 mm.
MS4070 **770** 10l. black and brown 4·75 4·75

771 "Anniversary Parade" (Pepene Cornelia)

1974. 25th Anniv of Romanian Pioneers Organization.
4071 **771** 55b. multicoloured . . . 40 15

772 "Europe"

1974. Inter-European Cultural and Economic Co-operation. Multicoloured.
4072 2l.20 Type **772** . . . . . . 1·10 85
4073 3l.45 Satellite over Europe 1·30 1·10

1974. Romania's Victory in World Handball Championships. No. 3959 surch **ROMANIA CAMPIOANA MONDIALA 1974 175L**.
4074 1l.75 on 20b. multicoloured 2·00 1·80

774 Postal Motor Boat

1974. U.P.U. Centenary. Multicoloured.
4075 20b. Type **774** 10 15
4076 40b. Loading mail train . . 40 15
4077 55b. Loading Ilyushin Il-62M mail plane 10 15
4078 1l.75 Rural postman delivering letter 30 15

4079 2l.75 Town postman delivering letter 35 25
4080 3l.60 Young stamp collectors 60 25
MS4081 90 × 78 mm. 4l. Postman clearing postbox; 6l. Letters and GPO, Bucharest (each 28 × 22 mm) 5·00 5·00

775 Footballers

1974. World Cup Football Championship, West Germany.
4082 **775** 20b. multicoloured 10 10
4083 – 40b. multicoloured 10 10
4084 – 55b. multicoloured 10 10
4085 – 1l.75 multicoloured 20 10
4086 – 2l.75 multicoloured 50 15
4087 – 3l.60 multicoloured 65 25
MS4088 90 × 78 mm. 10l. Three footballers (horiz, 50 × 38 mm) 6·00 6·00
DESIGNS: Nos. 4083/7, Football scenes similar to Type **775**.

776 Anniversary Emblem
777 U.N. and World Population Emblems

1974. 25th Anniv of Council for Mutual Economic Aid.
4089 **776** 55b. multicoloured 25 20

1974. World Population Year Conference, Bucharest.
4090 **777** 2l. multicoloured 35 20

778 Emblem on Map of Europe

1974. "Euromax 1974" International Stamp Exhibition, Bucharest.
4091 **778** 4l.+3l. yellow, bl & red 1·10 35

779 Hand drawing Peace Dove
780 Prince John of Wallachia (400th birth anniv)

1974. 25th Anniv of World Peace Movement.
4092 **779** 2l. multicoloured 35 20

1974. Anniversaries.
4093 **780** 20b. blue 10 10
4094 – 55b. red 10 10
4095 – 1l. blue 10 10
4096 – 1l.10 brown 20 10
4097 – 1l.30 purple 30 10
4098 – 1l.40 violet 35 20
DESIGNS AND ANNIVERSARIES—VERT: 1l. Iron and Steel Works, Hunedoara (220th anniv); 1l.10, Avram Iancu (revolutionary, 150th anniv); 1l.30, Dr. C. I. Parhon (birth cent); 1l.40, Dosoftel (metropolitan) (350th birth anniv). HORIZ: 55b. Soldier guarding industrial installations (Romanian People's Army, 30th anniv).

781 Romanian and Soviet Flags as "XXX"
783 "Centaurea nervosa"

782 View of Stockholm

1974. 30th Anniv of Liberation. Multicoloured.
4099 40b. Type **781** 10 10
4100 55b. Citizens and flags (horiz) 10 20

1974. "Stockholmia 1974" International Stamp Exhibition. Sheet 91 × 78 mm.
MS4101 **782** 10l. multicoloured 4·50 4·50

1974. Nature Conservation. Wild Flowers. Mult.
4102 20b. Type **783** 10 10
4103 40b. "Fritillaria montana" 10 10
4104 55b. Yew 60 10
4105 1l.75 "Rhododendron kotschyi" 30 15
4106 2l.75 Alpine forget-me-not 40 20
4107 3l.60 Pink 65 30

784 Bust of Isis

1974. Romanian Archaeological Finds. Sculpture. Multicoloured.
4108 20b. Type **784** 10 10
4109 40b. Glykon serpent 10 10
4110 55b. Head of Emperor Decius 10 10
4111 1l.75 Romanian Woman 25 10
4112 2l.75 Mithras 40 25
4113 3l.60 Roman senator 65 30

785 Sibiu Market Place

1974. Stamp Day.
4114 **785** 2l.10+1l.90 mult 90 40

1974. "Nationala 74" Stamp Exhibition. No. 4114 optd **EXPOZITIA FILATELICA "NATIONALA '74" 15–24 noiembrie Bucuresti**.
4115 **786** 2l.10+1l.90 mult 1·50 1·50

787 Party Emblem

1974. 11th Romanian Communist Party Congress, Bucharest.
4116 **787** 55b. multicoloured 15 10
4117 – 1l. multicoloured 20 20
DESIGN: 1l. Similar to Type **787**, showing party emblem and curtain.

788 "The Discus-thrower" (Myron)

1974. 60th Anniv of Romanian Olympic Committee.
4118 **788** 2l. multicoloured 50 30

789 "Skylab"
790 Dr. Albert Schweitzer

1974. "Skylab" Space Laboratory Project.
4119 **789** 2l.50 multicoloured 2·20 80

1974. Birth Centenary of Dr. Albert Schweitzer (Nobel Peace Prize-winner).
4120 **790** 40b. brown 15 20

791 Handball
793 Torch and Inscription

792 "Rocks and Birches"

1975. World Universities Handball Championships, Romania.
4121 **791** 55b. multicoloured 10 10
4122 – 1l.75 multicoloured (vert) 20 10
4123 – 2l.20 multicoloured 40 30
DESIGNS: 1l.75, 2l.20, similar designs to Type **791**.

1975. Paintings by Ion Andreescu. Multicoloured.
4124 20b. Type **792** 10 10
4125 40b. "Peasant Woman with Green Kerchief" 10 10
4126 55b. "Winter in the Forest" 10 10
4127 1l.75 "Winter in Barbizon" (horiz) 25 15
4128 2l.75 Self-portrait 45 25
4129 3l.50 "Main Road" (horiz) 90 40

1975. 10th Anniv of Romanian Socialist Republic.
4130 **793** 40b. multicoloured 20 15

794 "Battle of the High Bridge" (O. Obedeanu)

1975. 500th Anniv of Victory over the Ottomans at High Bridge.
4131 **794** 55b. multicoloured 20 15

795 "Peasant Woman Spinning" (Nicolae Grigorescu)
796 "Self-portrait"

1975. International Women's Year.
4132 **795** 55b. multicoloured 20 15

1975. 500th Birth Anniv of Michelangelo.
4133 **796** 5l. multicoloured 85 50

797 Escorial Palace, Madrid

1975. "Espana 1975" International Stamp Exhibition, Madrid. Sheet 90 × 78 mm.
MS4134 **797** 10l. multicoloured 4·75 4·75

798 Mitsui Children's Science Pavilion, Okinawa

1975. International Exposition, Okinawa.
4135 **798** 4l. multicoloured 70 30

799 "Peonies" (Nicolae Tonitza)

1975. Inter-European Cultural and Economic Co-operation. Multicoloured.
4136 2l.20 Type **799** 80 80
4137 3l.45 "Chrysanthemums" (Stefan Luchian) 95 1·00

800 Dove with Coded Letter

1975. Introduction of Postal Coding.
4138 **800** 55b. multicoloured 15 15

801 Convention Emblem on "Globe"

1975. Centenary of International Metre Convention.
4139 **801** 1l.85 multicoloured 40 20

802 Mihail Eminescu and Museum

1975. 125th Birth Anniv of Mihail Eminescu (poet).
4140 **802** 55b. multicoloured . . . 15 15

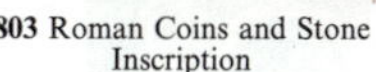

803 Roman Coins and Stone Inscription

805 Ana Ipatescu

804 "On the Banks of the Seine" (TH. Pallady)

1975. Bimillenary of Alba Julia.
4141 **803** 55b. multicoloured . . . 15 20

1975. "Arphila 1975" International Stamp Exhibition, Paris. Sheet 76 × 90 mm.
MS4142 **804** 10l. multicoloured 4·75 45

1975. Death Cent of Ana Ipatescu (revolutionary).
4143 **805** 55b. mauve 20 20

806 Turnu-Severin

1975. European Architectural Heritage Year. Roman Antiquities.

4144	–	55b. black and brown . .	10	10
4145	–	1l.20 black, lt bl & bl . .	15	15
4146	–	1l.55 black and green . .	40	15
4147	–	1l.75 black and red . . .	45	20
4148	**806**	2l. black and ochre . . .	55	20
4149	–	2l.25 black and blue . .	70	50

MS4150 79 × 91 mm. 10l. multicoloured . . . . 6·25 6·25

DESIGNS—VERT: 55b. Emperor Trajan; 1l.20, Trajan's Column, Rome; 1l.55, Decebalus (sculpture); 10l. Roman remains, Gradiste. HORIZ: 1l.75, Imperial monument, Adam Clissi; 2l.25, Trajan's Bridge.

807 "Apollo" and "Soyuz" Spacecraft

1975. Air. "Apollo"–"Soyuz" Space Link. Mult.
4151 1l.75 Type **807** . . . . . . 1·10 65
4152 3l.25 "Apollo" and "Soyuz" linked together . . . . . 1·50 85

808 "Michael the Brave" (Aegidius Sadeler)

1975. 375th Anniv of First Political Union of Romanian States. Multicoloured.
4153 55b. Type **808** 10 10
4154 1l.20 "Ottoman Envoys bringing gifts to Michael the Brave" (T. Aman) (horiz) 15 10
4155 2l.75 "Michael the Brave at Calugareni" (T. Aman) 45 15

809 Map of Europe

1975. European Security and Co-operation Conference, Helsinki. Sheet 111 × 81 mm containing T **809** and similar horiz designs. Multicoloured.
MS4156 2l.75 Type **809**; 5l. Open book; 5l. Children playing Postage; 2l.75 Peace doves (air) 4·75 4·75

810 Larkspur

812 Policeman using Walkie-talkie

1975. Flowers. Multicoloured.

4157	20b. Type **810**	10	10
4158	40b. Long-headed poppy . .	10	10
4159	55b. Common immortelle	10	10
4160	1l.75 Common rock-rose . .	25	15
4161	2l.75 Meadow clary	45	20
4162	3l.60 Chicory	60	30

1975. International Philatelic Fair, Riccione (Italy). Optd **Tîrg international de mărci postale Riccione – Italia 23-25 august 1975.**
4163 **796** 5l. multicoloured . . . . 2·40 2·20

1975. Road Safety.
4164 **812** 55b. blue 25 20

813 Text on Map of Pelendava

1975. 1750th Anniv of First Documentary Attestations of Daco-Getian Settlements of Pelendava and 500th Anniv of Craiova. Multicoloured.
4165 20b. Type **813** 15 15
4166 55b. Map of Pelendava showing location of Craiova (82 × 33 mm) . . 15 15
4167 1l. Text on map of Pelendava 20 15

Nos. 4165/7 were issued together, se-tenant, forming a composite design.

814 Muntenia Carpet

1975. Romanian Traditional Carpets. Mult.

4168	20b. Type **814**	10	10
4169	40b. Banat	10	10
4170	55b. Oltenia	10	10
4171	1l.75 Moldova	30	10
4172	2l.75 Oltenia (different) . .	45	25
4173	3l.60 Maramures	55	30

815 T.V. "12M" Minibus

1975. Romanian Motor Vehicles. Multicoloured.
4174 20b. Type **815** 10 10
4175 40b. L.K.W. "19 A.L.P." Oil tanker 10 10
4176 55b. A.R.O. "240" Field car 10 10
4177 1l.75 L.K.W. "R 8135 F" Truck 35 10
4178 2l.75 P.K.W. "Dacia 1300" Saloon car 50 25
4179 3l.60 L.K.W. "R 19215 D.F.K." Tipper truck . . 65 30

816 Postal Transit Centre, Bucharest

1975. Stamp Day. Multicoloured.
4180 1l.50+1l.50 Type **816** . . . 70 40
4181 2l.10+1l.90 Aerial view of P.T.C. . . . . 1·30 65

817 "Winter" (Peter Brueghel)

1975. "Themabelga 1975" International Stamp Exhibition, Brussels. Sheet 90 × 78 mm.
MS4182 **817** 10l. multicoloured 4·75 4·75

818 Tobogganing

1976. Winter Olympics Games, Innsbruck. Mult.
4183 20b. Type **818** 10 15
4184 40b. Rifle-shooting (biathlon) (vert) 10 15
4185 55b. Downhill skiing (slalom) 20 15
4186 1l.75 Ski jumping 35 20
4187 2l.75 Figure skating (women's) 50 30
4188 3l.60 Ice hockey 70 45
MS4189 91 × 78 mm. 10l. Bobsleighing . . . . 5·50 5·50

819 "Washington at Valley Forge" (W. Trego)

1976. Bicent of American Revolution. Mult.
4190 20b. Type **819** 10 10
4191 40b. "Washington at Trenton" (Trumbull) (vert) 10 10
4192 55b. "Washington crossing the Delaware" (Leutze) 15 10
4193 1l.75 "Capture of the Hessians" (Trumbull) . . 25 20
4194 2l.75 "Jefferson" (Sully) (vert) 45 25
4195 3l.60 "Surrender of Cornwallis at Yorktown" (Trumbull) 60 40
MS4196 91 × 78 mm. 10l. "Signing of Declaration of Independence" (J. Trumbull) . . . . 3·75 3·75

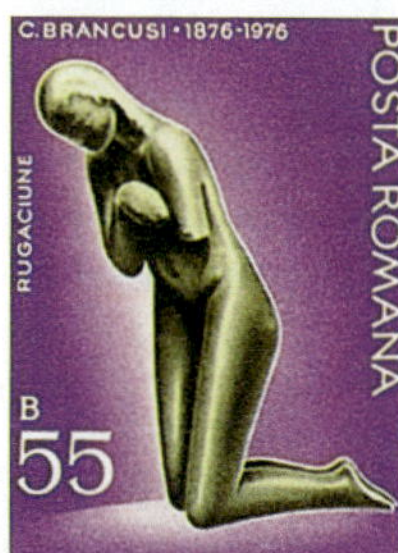

820 "Prayer"

1976. Birth Centenary of Constantin Brancusi (sculptor). Multicoloured.
4197 55b. Type **820** 10 15
4198 1l.75 Architectural Assembly, Tg. Jiu 25 20
4199 3l.60 C. Brancusi 65 20

821 Anton Davidoglu (mathematician) (birth cent)

823 Dr. Carol Davila

822 Inscribed Tablets, Tibiscum (Banat)

1976. Anniversaries. Multicoloured.
4200 40b. Type **821** 10 10
4201 55b. Prince Vlad Tepes (500th death anniv) . . . 10 10
4202 1l.20 Costache Negri (patriot—death centenary) 20 10
4203 1l.75 Gallery, Archives Museum (50th anniv) . . 25 10

1976. Daco-Roman Archaeological Finds. Mult.

4204	**822**	20b. multicoloured . . .	10	10
4205	–	40b. black, grey and red	10	10
4206	–	55b. multicoloured . . .	10	10
4207	–	1l.75 multicoloured . . .	40	10
4208	–	2l.75 black, grey and red	50	20
4209	–	3l.60 black, grey & green	70	35

MS4210 78 × 91 mm. 10l. multicoloured . . . . 4·75 4·75

DESIGNS: 40b. Sculptures (Banat); 55b. Inscribed tablet, coins and cup (Crisana); 1l.75, Pottery (Crisana); 2l.75, Altar and spears, Maramures (Banat); 3l.60, Vase and spears, Maramures.

1976. Centenary of Romanian Red Cross. Mult.
4211 55b. Type **823** (postage) . . 10 10
4212 1l.75 Nurse and patient . . 10 10
4213 2l.20 First aid 15 10
4214 3l.35 Blood donors (air) . . 55 20

824 King Decebalus Vase

825 Romanian Arms

1976. Inter-European Cultural and Economic Co-operation. Vases from Cluj-Napoca porcelain factory. Multicoloured.
4215 2l.20 Type **824** 50 40
4216 3l.45 Vase with portrait of King Michael the Brave 1·10 1·00

1976.
4217 **825** 1l.75 multicoloured . . . 45 20

826 De Havilland D.H.9C

1976. Air. 50th Anniv of Romanian Airline. Mult.

4218	20b. Type **826**	10	10
4219	40b. I.C.A.R. Comercial . .	15	10
4220	60b. Douglas DC-3	25	10
4221	1l.75 Antonov An-24 . . .	40	10
4222	2l.75 Ilyushin Il-62 jetliner	60	20
4223	3l.60 Boeing 707 jetliner . .	90	20

827 Gymnastics **828** Spiru Haret

1976. Olympic Games, Montreal. Multicoloured.
4224 20b. Type **827** 10 10
4225 40b. Boxing 10 10
4226 55b. Handball 20 10
4227 1l.75 Rowing (horiz) 35 15
4228 2l.75 Gymnastics (different) (horiz) 50 20
4229 3l.60 Canoeing (horiz) . . . 65 20
MS4230 91 × 78 mm. 10l. Gymnastics (55 × 42 mm) . . . 4·50 4·50

1976. 125th Birth Anniv of Spiru Haret (mathematician).
4231 **828** 20b. multicoloured . . . 20 20

829 Daco-Getian Sculpture on Map of Buzau

1976. 1600th Anniv of Buzau State.
4232 **829** 55b. multicoloured . . . 20 20

1976. Philatelic Exhibition, Bucharest. No. 4199 surch **EXPOZITIA FILATELICA BUCURESTI 12–19 IX 1976 1,80+**.
4233 3l.60+1l.80 multicoloured 4·00 3·50

831 Red Deer

1976. Endangered Animals. Multicoloured.
4234 20b. Type **831** 10 10
4235 40b. Brown bear 10 10
4236 55b. Chamois 15 10
4237 1l.75 Wild boar 25 10
4238 2l.75 Red fox 50 25
4239 3l.60 Lynx 65 35

832 Cathedral, Milan

1976. "Italia '76" International Philatelic Exhibition, Milan.
4240 **832** 4l.75 multicoloured . . . 80 20

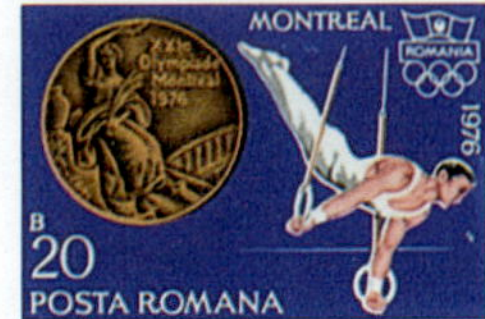

833 D. Grecu (gymnast) and Bronze Medal

1976. Olympic Games, Montreal. Romanian Medal Winners. Multicoloured.
4241 20b. Type **833** 10 10
4242 40b. Fencing (Bronze Medal) 10 10
4243 55b. Javelin (Bronze Medal) 15 10
4244 1l.75 Handball (Silver Medal) 25 10
4245 2l.75 Boxing (Silver and Bronze Medals) (horiz) . . 40 15
4246 3l.60 Wrestling (Silver and Bronze Medals) (horiz) . . 60 35
4247 5l.70 Nadia Comaneci (gymnastics – 3 Gold, 1 Silver and 1 Bronze Medals) (27 × 42 mm) . . 1·90 95
MS4248 90 × 78 mm. 10l. D. Vasile (canoeist) and gold and silver medals (42 × 54 mm) . . . . . 5·00 5·00

834 "Carnations and Oranges"

1976. Floral Paintings by Stefan Luchian. Mult.
4249 20b. Type **834** 10 10
4250 40b. "Flower Arrangement" . . 10 10
4251 55b. "Immortelles" 10 10
4252 1l.75 "Roses in Vase" . . . 20 10
4253 2l.75 "Cornflowers" 25 20
4254 3l.60 "Carnations in Vase" . . 60 25

835 "Elena Cuza" (T. Aman) **836** Arms of Alba

1976. Stamp Day.
4255 **835** 2l.10+1l.90 mult 85 80

1976. Romanian Districts' Coats of Arms (1st series). Multicoloured.
4256 55b. Type **836** 20 15
4257 55b. Arad 20 15
4258 55b. Arges 20 15
4259 55b. Bacau 20 15
4260 55b. Bihor 20 15
4261 55b. Bistrita Nasaud 20 15
4262 55b. Botosani 20 15
4263 55b. Brasov 20 15
4264 55b. Braila 20 15
4265 55b. Buzau 20 15
4266 55b. Caras-Severin 20 15
4267 55b. Cluj 20 15
4268 55b. Constanta 20 15
4269 55b. Covasna 20 15
4270 55b. Dimbovita 20 15
See also Nos. 4307/31, 4496/520 and 4542/63.

837 "Ox Cart"

1977. Paintings by Nicolae Grigorescu. Mult.
4271 55b. Type **837** 15 10
4272 1l. "Self-portrait" (vert) . . 15 10
4273 1l.50 "Shepherdess" 20 10
4274 2l.15 "Girl with Distaff" . . 30 10
4275 3l.40 "Shepherd" (vert) . . 35 20
4276 4l.80 "Halt at the Well" . . 55 25

838 Telecommunications Station, Cheia

1977.
4277 **838** 55b. multicoloured . . . 15 15

839 I.C.A.R.1

1977. Air. Romanian Gliders. Multicoloured.
4278 20b. Type **839** 10 10
4279 40b. IS-3d 10 10
4280 55b. RG-5 . . . . 10 10
4281 1l.50 IS-11 . . . . 25 10
4282 3l. IS-29D 50 20
4283 3l.40 IS-28B 90 35

840 Red Deer

1977. Protected Animals. Multicoloured.
4284 55b. Type **840** 10 10
4285 1l. Mute swan 30 10
4286 1l.50 Egyptian vulture . . . 45 10
4287 2l.15 European bison . . . 35 10
4288 3l.40 White-headed duck . . 85 20
4289 4l.80 River kingfisher . . . 1·00 45

841 "The Infantryman" (Oscar Obedeanu)

1977. Cent of Independence. Paintings. Mult.
4290 55b. Type **841** 10 10
4291 1l. "Artillery Battery at Calafat" (S. Hentia) (horiz) 10 10
4292 1l.50 "Soldiers Attacking" (Stefan Luchian) 15 10
4293 2l.15 "Battle of Plevna" (horiz) 30 10
4294 3l.40 "The Artillerymen" (Nicolae Grigorescu) (horiz) 40 20
4295 4l.80+2l. "Battle of Rahova" (horiz) 90 45
MS4296 90 × 78 mm. 10l. "Battle of Grivitza" . . . . 4·50 4·50

842 Sinaia, Carpathians **843** Petru Rares, Prince of Moldavia

1977. Inter-European Cultural and Economic Co-operation. Views. Multicoloured.
4297 2l. Type **842** 55 30
4298 2l.40 Auroa, Black Sea . . . 75 40

1977. Anniversaries. Multicoloured.
4299 40b. Type **843** (450th anniv of accession) 15 20
4300 55b. Ion Caragiale (dramatist, 125th birth anniv) 15 20

844 Nurse with Children and Emblems

1977. 23rd Int Red Cross Conference, Bucharest.
4301 **844** 1l.50 multicoloured . . . 30 20

845 Triumphal Arch, Bucharest

1977. 60th Anniv of Battles of Marasti, Marasesti and Oituz.
4302 **845** 2l.15 multicoloured . . . 50 20

846 Boeing 707 Jetliner over Bucharest Airport

1977. European Security and Co-operation Conference, Belgrade. Sheet 80 × 70 mm.
MS4303 **846** 10l. yellow, carmine and blue . . . . 4·00 4·00

847 Postwoman and Letters

1977. Air.
4304 20l. Type **847** . . . . . . 3·00 1·00
4305 30l. Douglas DC-10 jetliner and mail . . . . 4·50 1·70

848 Mount Titano Castle, San Marino

1977. Centenary of San Marino Postage Stamps.
4306 **848** 4l. multicoloured 85 15

1977. Romanian District Coats of Arms (2nd series). As T **836**. Multicoloured.
4307 55b. Dolj 15 10
4308 55b. Galati 15 10
4309 55b. Gorj 15 10
4310 55b. Harghita 15 10
4311 55b. Hunedoara 15 10
4312 55b. Ialomita 15 10
4313 55b. Iasi 15 10
4314 55b. Ilfov 15 10
4315 55b. Maramures 15 10
4316 55b. Mehedinti 15 10
4317 55b. Mures 15 10
4318 55b. Neamt 15 10
4319 55b. Olt 15 10
4320 55b. Prahova 15 10
4321 55b. Salaj 15 10
4322 55b. Satu Mare 15 10
4323 55b. Sibiu 15 10
4324 55b. Suceava 15 10
4325 55b. Teleorman 15 10
4326 55b. Timis 15 10
4327 55b. Tulcea 15 10
4328 55b. Vaslui 15 10
4329 55b. Vilcea 15 10
4330 55b. Vrancea 15 10
4331 55b. Romanian postal emblem 15 10

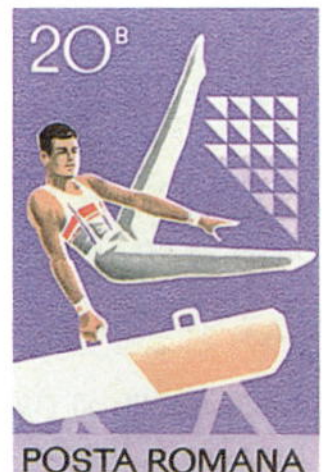

849 Gymnast on Vaulting Horse

850 Dispatch Rider and Army Officer

1977. Gymnastics. Multicoloured.
4332 20b. Type **849** 10 10
4333 40b. Floor exercise 10 10
4334 55b. Gymnast on parallel bars 10 10
4335 1l. Somersault on bar . . . 15 15
4336 2l.15 Gymnast on rings . . 30 25
4337 4l.80 Gymnastic exercise . . 1·10 65

1977. Stamp Day.
4338 **850** 2l.10+1l.90 mult 90 85

851 Two Dancers with Sticks

1977. Calusarii Folk Dance. Multicoloured.
4339 20b. Type **851** 10 10
4340 40b. Leaping dancer with stick 10 10
4341 55b. Two dancers 10 10
4342 1l. Dancer with stick . . . 15 10
4343 2l.15 Leaping dancers . . . 25 20
4344 4l.80 Leaping dancer . . . 95 50
MS4345 81 × 71 mm. 10l. Two children in costume . . . . . 3·50 3·50

852 "Carpati" at Cazane

1977. European Navigation on the Danube. Mult.
4346 55b. Type **852** 20 10
4347 1l. "Mircesti" near Orsova 25 10
4348 1l.50 "Oltenita" near Calafat 35 10
4349 2l.15 Hydrofoil at Giurgiu port 40 20
4350 3l. "Herculani" at Tulcea 50 25
4351 3l.40 "Muntenia" at Sulina 60 30
4352 4l.80 Map of Danube delta 1·40 80
MS4353 81 × 71 mm. 10l. River god Danubius (relief from Trajan's Column) (vert) . . . . 6·50 6·50

853 Arms and Flag of Romania

1977. 30th Anniv of Romanian Republic. Mult.
4354 55b. Type **853** 10 15
4355 1l.20 Romanian-built computers 20 20
4356 1l.75 National Theatre, Craiova 35 20

854 Firiza Dam

1978. Romanian Dams and Hydro-electric Installations. Multicoloured.
4357 20b. Type **854** 10 10
4358 40b. Negovanu dam 10 10
4359 55b. Piatra Neamt power station 15 10
4360 1l. Izvorul Montelui Bicaz dam 20 10
4361 2l.15 Vidraru dam 30 20
4362 4l.80 Danube barrage and navigation system, Iron Gates 65 40

855 LZ-1 over Lake Constance

1978. Air. Airships. Multicoloured.
4363 60b. Type **855** 10 10
4364 1l. Santos Dumont's "Ballon No. 6" over Paris 20 10
4365 1l.50 Beardmore R-34 over Manhattan Island 25 10
4366 2l.15 N.4 "Italia" at North Pole 35 10
4367 3l.40 "Graf Zeppelin" over Brasov 50 20
4368 4l.80 "Graf Zeppelin" over Sibiu 95 30
MS4369 80 × 70 mm. 10l. "Graf Zeppelin" over Bucharest (50 × 38 mm) . . . . 4·00 4·00

856 Footballers and Emblem

1978. World Cup Football Championship, Argentina.
4370 **856** 55b. blue 10 10
4371 – 1l. orange 10 10
4372 – 1l.50 yellow 20 10
4373 – 2l.15 red 30 10
4374 – 3l.40 green 50 20
4375 – 4l.80 mauve 75 30
MS4376 80 × 70 mm. 10l. blue (38 × 50 mm) . . . . 3·50 3·50
DESIGNS: 1l.50 to 10l., Footballers and emblem, similar to Type **856**.

857 King Decebalus of Dacia

858 Worker and Factory

1978. Inter-European Cultural and Economic Co-operation. Multicoloured.
4377 1l.30 Type **857** 55 50
4378 3l.40 Prince Mircea the Elder . . . . 1·50 1·50

1978. 30th Anniv of Nationalization of Industry.
4379 **858** 55b. multicoloured . . . 15 15

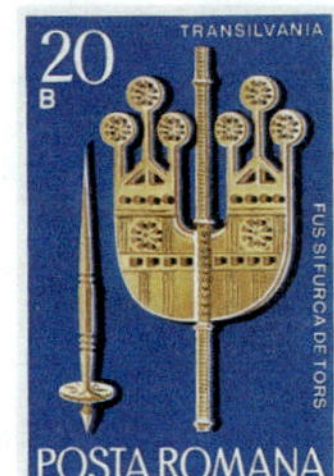

859 Spindle and Fork Handle, Transylvania

1978. Wood-carving. Multicoloured.
4380 20b. Type **859** 10 10
4381 40b. Cheese mould, Muntenia 10 10
4382 55b. Spoons, Oltenia . . . 10 10
4383 1l. Barrel, Moldavia 15 10
4384 2l.15 Ladle and mug, Transylvania 25 20
4385 4l.80 Water bucket, Oltenia 60 35

860 Danube Delta

1978. Tourism. Multicoloured.
4386 55b. Type **860** 65 30
4387 1l. Bran Castle (vert) . . . 10 10
4388 1l.50 Moldavian village . . 15 10
4389 2l.15 Muierii caves 20 10
4390 3l.40 Cable car at Boiana Brasov 40 10
4391 4l.80 Mangalia (Black Sea resort) 60 25
MS4392 80 × 70 mm. 10l. Strehaia Fortress and Monastery (37 × 49 mm) . . . . 3·25 3·50

861 MC-6 Electron Microscope

862 Polovraci Cave

1978. Romanian Industry. Multicoloured.
4393 20b. Type **861** 10 10
4394 40b. Hydraulic excavator . . 10 10
4395 55b. Power station control room 10 10
4396 1l.50 Oil drillheads 15 10
4397 3l. C-12 combine harvester (horiz) 35 15
4398 3l.40 Petro-chemical combine, Pitesti 40 15

1978. Caves and Caverns. Multicoloured.
4399 55b. Type **862** 10 10
4400 1l. Topolnita 15 10
4401 1l.50 Ponoare 15 10
4402 2l.15 Ratei 25 10
4403 3l.40 Closani 45 15
4404 4l.80 Epuran 65 25

863 Gymnastics

865 Symbols of Equality

864 Zoomorphic Gold Plate

1978. "Daciada" Romanian Games. Multicoloured.
4405 55b. Type **863** 10 10
4406 1l. Running 15 10
4407 1l.50 Skiing 20 10
4408 2l.15 Horse jumping 25 10
4409 3l.40 Football 40 15
4410 4l.80 Handball 65 25

1978. Daco-Roman Archaeology. Multicoloured.
4411 20b. Type **864** 10 10
4412 40b. Gold torque 10 10
4413 55b. Gold cameo ring . . . 10 10
4414 1l. Silver bowl 20 10
4415 2l.15 Bronze eagle (vert) . . 35 10
4416 4l.80 Silver armband 40 25
MS4417 74 × 89 mm. 10l. Gold helmet (38 × 50 mm). Imperf 12·50 12·50

1978. International Anti-Apartheid Year.
4418 **865** 3l.40 black, yellow & red 70 40

866 Romulus, Remus and Wolf

1978. International Stamp Exhibition, Essen. Sheet 75 × 90 mm.
MS4419 **866** 10l. multicoloured 1·40 1·25

867 Ptolemaic Map of Dacia (2000th anniv of first record of Ziridava)

1978. Anniversaries in the History of Arad. Mult.
4420 40b. Type **867** 10 10
4421 55b. Meeting place of National Council (60th anniv of unified Romania) 10 10
4422 1l.75 Ceramic pots (950th anniv of first documentary evidence of Arad) 20 15

868 Dacian Warrior

1978. Stamp Day.
4423 **868** 6l.+3l. multicoloured . . 95 80
No. 4423 was issued se-tenant with a premium-carrying tab as shown in Type **868**.

869 Assembly at Alba Julia

871 Dacian Warrior

870 Wright Brothers and Wright Type A

1979. 60th Anniv of National Unity. Mult.
4424 55b. Type **869** 10 10
4425 1l. Open book, flag and sculpture 15 10

1979. Air. Pioneers of Aviation. Multicoloured.
4426 55b. Type **870** 10 10
4427 1l. Louis Bleriot and Bleriot XI monoplane 15 10
4428 1l.50 Anthony Fokker and Fokker F.VIIa/3m "Josephine Ford" 20 10
4429 2l.15 Andrei Tupolev and Tupolev ANT-25 . . . . 30 10
4430 3l. Otto Lilienthal and Lilienthal monoplane glider 35 15
4431 3l.40 Traian Vuia and Vuia No. 1 . . . . 40 20
4432 4l.80 Aurel Vlaicu and No. 1 "Crazy Fly" . . . 50 30
MS4433 79 × 70 mm. 10l. Henri Coanda and turbine-powered model airplane . . . . 4·25 4·50

1979. 2050th Anniv of Independent Centralized Dacic State. Details from Trajan's Column. Multicoloured.
4434 5b. Type **871** 10 10
4435 1l.50 Dacian warrior on horseback 25 10

872 "The Heroes from Vaslui" **873** Championship Emblem

1979. International Year of the Child (1st issue). Children's Paintings. Multicoloured.
4436 55b. Type **872** 10 10
4437 1l. "Tica's Folk Music Band" 10 10
4438 1l.50 "Buildingsite" 10 10
4439 2l.15 "Industrial Landscape" (horiz) 20 10
4440 3l.40 "Winter Holiday" (horiz) 35 15
4441 4l.80 "Pioneers' Celebration" (horiz) . . . 55 20
See also Nos. 4453/6.

1979. European Junior Ice Hockey Championship, Miercurea-Ciuc, and World Championship, Galati. Multicoloured.
4442 1l.30 Type **873** 20 20
4443 3l.40 Championship emblem (different) 35 20

874 Dog's tooth Violet **876** Oil Derrick

875 Street with Mail Coach and Post-rider

1979. Protected Flowers. Multicoloured.
4444 55b. Type **874** 10 10
4445 1l. Alpine violet 10 10
4446 1l.50 "Linum borzaeanum" 15 10
4447 2l.15 "Convolvulus persicus" 20 10
4448 3l.40 Auricula 35 15
4449 4l.80 "Aquilegia transsylvanica" 45 25

1979. Inter-European Cultural and Economic Co-operation.
4450 1l.30 Type **875** (postage) . . 55 30
4451 3l.40 Boeing 707 and motorcycle postman (air) 65 35

1979. International Petroleum Congress, Bucharest.
4452 **876** 3l.40 multicoloured . . . 35 15

877 Children with Flowers **878** Young Pioneer

1979. International Year of the Child (2nd issue). Multicoloured.
4453 40b. Type **877** 10 20
4454 1l. Children at creative play 15 20
4455 2l. Children with hare . . . 30 20
4456 4l.60 Young pioneers . . . 65 50

1979. 30th Anniv of Romanian Young Pioneers.
4457 **878** 55b. multicoloured . . . 20 15

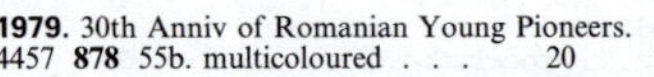

879 "Woman in Garden" **881** Stefan Gheorghiu

880 Brasov University

1979. Paintings by Gh. Tattarescu. Multicoloured.
4458 20b. Type **879** 10 10
4459 40b. "Muntenian Woman" 10 10
4460 55b. "Muntenian Man" . . 10 10
4461 1l. "General G. Magheru" 20 10
4462 2l.15 "The Artist's Daughter" 40 20
4463 4l.80 "Self-portrait" 75 25

1979. Contemporary Architecture. Multicoloured.
4464 20b. State Theatre, Tirgu Mures 10 10
4465 40b. Type **880** 10 10
4466 55b. Administration Centre, Baia Mare 10 10
4467 1l. Stefan Gheorghiu Academy, Bucharest . . . 15 10
4468 2l.15 Admnistration Centre, Botosani 30 20
4469 4l.80 House of Culture, Tirgoviste 65 25

1979. Anniversaries. Multicoloured.
4470 40b. Type **881** (birth cent) 10 10
4471 55b. Statue of Gheorghe Lazar (poet) (birth bicent) 10 10
4472 2l.15 Fallen Workers monument (Strike at Lupeni, 50th anniv) . . . 20 15

882 Moldavian and Wallachian Women and Monuments to Union **883** Party and National Flags

1979. 120th Anniv of Union of Moldavia and Wallachia.
4473 **882** 4l.60 multicoloured . . . 60 20

1979. 25th Anniv of Liberation. Multicoloured.
4474 55b. Type **883** 15 10
4475 1l. "Workers' Militia" (L. Suhar) (horiz) 20 10

884 Freighter "Galati" **885** "Snapdragons"

1979. Ships. Multicoloured.
4476 55b. Type **884** 15 10
4477 1l. Freighter "Buchuresti" 20 10
4478 1l.50 Bulk carrier "Resita" 25 10
4479 2l.15 Bulk carrier "Tomis" 35 30
4480 3l.40 Tanker "Dacia" . . . 50 15
4481 4l.80 Tanker "Independenta" 65 20

1979. "Socfilex 79" Stamp Exhibition, Bucharest. Flower Paintings by Stefan Luchian. Mult.
4482 40b. Type **885** 10 10
4483 60b. "Carnations" 15 10
4484 1l.55 "Flowers on a Stairway" 25 10
4485 4l.+2l. "Flowers of the Field" 75 70
MS4486 79 × 70 mm. 10l.+5l. "Roses" . . . . 4·25 4·50

886 Gymnast

1979. 4th European Sports Conference, Berchtesgaden. Sheet 90 × 75 mm.
MS4487 **886** 10l. multicoloured 25·00 25·00

887 Party and National Flags

1979. 12th Romanian Communist Party Congress. Sheet 70 × 80 mm.
MS4488 **887** 5l. multicoloured . . 1·40 1·40

888 Olympic Stadium, Melbourne (1956 Games)

1979. Olympic Games, Moscow (1980). Olympic Stadia. Multicoloured.
4489 55b. Type **888** 10 10
4490 1l. Rome (1960) 15 10
4491 1l.50 Tokyo (1964) 25 10
4492 2l.15 Mexico City (1968) . . 30 10
4493 3l.40 Munich (1972) 45 20
4494 4l.80 Montreal (1978) . . . 70 20
MS4495 79 × 69 mm. 10l. Moscow (1980) . . . . 4·50 5·00

1979. Municipal Coats of Arms. As T **836**. Mult.
4496 1l.20 Alba Julia 15 10
4497 1l.20 Arad 15 10
4498 1l.20 Bacau 15 10
4499 1l.20 Baia Mare 15 10
4500 1l.20 Birlad 15 10
4501 1l.20 Botosani 15 10
4502 1l.20 Brasov 15 10
4503 1l.20 Braila 15 10
4504 1l.20 Buzau 15 10
4505 1l.20 Calarasi 15 10
4506 1l.20 Cluj 15 10
4507 1l.20 Constanta 15 10
4508 1l.20 Craiova 15 10
4509 1l.20 Dej 15 10
4510 1l.20 Deva 15 10
4511 1l.20 Drobeta Turnu Severin 15 10
4512 1l.20 Focsani 15 10
4513 1l.20 Galati 15 10
4514 1l.20 Gheorghe Gheorghiu Dej 15 10
4515 1l.20 Giurgiu 15 10
4516 1l.20 Hunedoara 15 10
4517 1l.20 Iasi 15 10
4518 1l.20 Lugoj 15 10
4519 1l.20 Medias 15 10
4520 1l.20 Odorheiu Secuiesc . . 15 10

889 Costumes of Maramures (female) **891** Figure Skating

890 Post Coding Desks

1979. Costumes. Multicoloured.
4521 20b. Type **889** 10 10
4522 40b. Maramures (male) . . 10 10
4523 55b. Vrancea (female) . . . 10 10
4524 1l.50 Vrancea (male) 20 10
4525 3l. Padureni (female) 40 20
4526 3l.40 Padureni (male) . . . 45 30

1979. Stamp Day.
4527 **890** 2l.10+1l.90 mult 45 20

1979. Winter Olympic Games, Lake Placid (1980). Multicoloured.
4528 55b. Type **891** 10 10
4529 1l. Downhill skiing 10 10
4530 1l.50 Biathlon 20 10
4531 2l.15 Bobsleighing 25 10
4532 3l.40 Speed skating 45 20
4533 4l.80 Ice hockey 65 25
MS4534 70 × 78 mm. 10l. Ice hockey (different) (37 × 49 mm) . . . . 3·50 4·00

892 Locomotive "Calugareni", 1869 **893** Dacian Warrior

1979. International Transport Exhibition, Hamburg. Multicoloured.
4535 55b. Type **892** 10 10
4536 1l. Steam locomotive "Orleans" 20 10
4537 1l.50 Steam locomotive No. 1059 . . . . 20 10
4538 2l.15 Steam locomotive No. 150211 . . . . . . 30 10
4539 3l.40 Steam locomotive No. 231085 . . . . . . 45 20
4540 4l.80 Class 060-EA electric locomotive 20 10
MS4541 80 × 70 mm. 10l. Diesel locomotive (50 × 38 mm) . . . 3·75 1·50

1980. Arms (4th series). As T **836**. Multicoloured.
4542 1l.20 Oradea 20 10
4543 1l.20 Petrosani 20 10
4544 1l.20 Piatra Neamt 20 10
4545 1l.20 Pitesti 20 10
4546 1l.20 Ploiesti 20 10
4547 1l.20 Resita 20 10
4548 1l.20 Rimnicu Vilcea 20 10
4549 1l.20 Roman 20 10
4550 1l.20 Satu Mare 15 10
4551 1l.20 Sibiu 20 10
4552 1l.20 Sighetu Marmatiei . . 20 10
4553 1l.20 Sighisoara 20 10
4554 1l.20 Suceava 20 10
4555 1l.20 Tecuci 20 10
4556 1l.20 Timisoara 20 10
4557 1l.20 Tirgoviste 20 10
4558 1l.20 Tirgu Jiu 20 05
4559 1l.20 Tirgu-Mures 20 10
4560 1l.20 Tulcea 20 10
4561 1l.20 Turda 20 10
4562 1l.20 Turnu Magurele . . . 20 10
4563 1l.20 Bucharest 20 10

1980. 2050th Anniv of Independent Centralized Dacian State under Burebista.
4564 55b. Type **893** 10 10
4565 1l.50 Dacian fighters with flag 20 10

894 River Kingfisher

1980. European Nature Protection Year. Mult.
4566 55b. Type **894** 25 10
4567 1l. Great egret (vert) 40 10
4568 1l.50 Red-breasted goose . . 45 10
4569 2l.15 Red deer (vert) 35 10
4570 3l.40 Roe deer fawn 35 20
4571 4l.80 European bison (vert) 55 30
MS4572 90 × 78 mm. 10l. Eastern white pelicans ("Pelecanus onocrotallus") (38 × 50 mm) . . 5·00 5·00

895 Scarborough Lily **896** Tudor Vladimirescu

1980. Exotic Flowers from Bucharest Botanical Gardens. Multicoloured.

4573 55b. Type **895** 10 10
4574 1l. Floating water hyacinth 15 10
4575 1l.50 Jacobean lily 20 10
4576 2l.15 Rose of Sharon . . . 30 10
4577 3l.40 Camellia 35 20
4578 4l.80 Lotus 60 25

1980. Anniversaries. Multicoloured.

4579 40b. Type **896** (revolutionary leader) (birth bicent) 10 10
4580 55b. Mihail Sadoveanu (writer) (birth cent) . . . 10 10
4581 1l.50 Battle of Posada (650th anniv) 20 10
4582 2l.15 Tudor Arghezi (poet) (birth cent) 25 15
4583 3l. Horea (leader, Transylvanian uprising) (250th birth anniv) . . . 40 20

897 George Enescu playing Violin

1980. Inter-European Cultural and Economic Co-operation. Two sheets, each 107 × 81 mm containing horiz designs as T **897**.

MS4584 (a) 1l.30 × 4 emerald (Type **897**); red (Enescu conducting); violet (Enescu at piano); blue (Enescu composing). (b) 3l.40 × 4 emerald (Beethoven at piano); red (Beethoven conducting); violet (Beethoven at piano (different); blue (Beethoven composing) Set of 2 sheets . . 9·00 9·00

898 Dacian Fruit Dish

899 Throwing the Javelin

1980. Bimillenary of Dacian Fortress, Petrodava (now Piatra Neamt).

4585 **898** 1l. multicoloured 15 15

1980. Olympic Games, Moscow. Multicoloured.

4586 55b. Type **899** 10 10
4587 1l. Fencing 15 10
4588 1l.50 Pistol shooting 20 10
4589 2l.15 Single kayak 30 10
4590 3l.40 Wrestling 40 20
4591 4l.80 Single skiff 60 30

MS4592 90 × 78 mm. 10l. Handball (38 × 50 mm) . . . . 3·50 4·00

900 Postman handing Letter to Woman

1980. 2050th Anniv of Independent Centralized Dacic State National Stamp Exhibition. Sheet 78 × 90 mm.

MS4593 **900** 5l.+5l. multicoloured 2·50 2·50

901 Congress Emblem

902 Fireman carrying Child

1980. 15th International Congress of Historical Sciences.

4594 **901** 55b. deep blue and blue 15 15

1980. Firemen's Day.

4595 **902** 55b. multicoloured . . . 15 15

903 Chinese and Romanian Stamp Collectors

1980. Romanian–Chinese Stamp Exhibition, Bucharest.

4596 **903** 1l. multicoloured 15 15

904 National Assembly Building, Bucharest

1980. European Security and Co-operation Conference, Madrid. Sheet 78 × 90 mm.

MS4597 **904** 10l. multicoloured 3·00 3·00

905 Rooks and Chessboard

1980. 24th Chess Olympiad, Malta. Multicoloured.

4598 55b. Knights and chessboard 15 10
4599 1l. Type **905** 20 10
4600 2l.15 Male head and chessboard 40 10
4601 4l.80 Female head and chessboard 75 25

906 Dacian Warrior

1980. Military Uniforms. Multicoloured.

4602 20b. Type **906** 10 10
4603 40b. Moldavian soldier (15th century) 10 10
4604 55b. Wallachian horseman (17th century) 10 10
4605 1l. Standard bearer (19th century) 10 10
4606 1l.50 Infantryman (19th century) 15 10
4607 2l.15 Lancer (19th century) 25 15
4608 4l.80 Hussar (19th century) 65 30

907 Burebista (sculpture, P. Mercea)

908 George Oprescu

1980. Stamp Day and 2050th Anniv of Independent Centralized Dacic State.

4609 **907** 2l. multicoloured 25 15

1981. Celebrities' Birth Anniversaries. Mult.

4610 1l.50 Type **908** (historian and art critic, centenary) 20 10
4611 2l.15 Marius Bunescu (painter, centenary) . . . 25 10
4612 3l.40 Ion Georgescu (sculptor, 125th anniv) . . 35 20

909 St. Bernard

1981. Dogs. Multicoloured.

4613 40b. Mountain sheepdog (horiz) 10 15
4614 55b. Type **909** 10 15
4615 1l. Fox terrier (horiz) . . . 15 15
4616 1l.50 Alsatian (horiz) . . . 25 15
4617 2l.15 Boxer (horiz) 35 15
4618 3l.40 Dalmatian (horiz) . . 55 20
4619 4l.80 Poodle 70 30

910 Paddle-steamer "Stefan cel Mare"

1981. 125th Anniv of European Danube Commission. Multicoloured.

4620 55b. Type **910** 15 10
4621 1l. "Prince Ferdinand de Roumanie" steam launch 20 20
4622 1l.50 Paddle-steamer "Tudor Vladimirescu" 30 20
4623 2l.15 Dredger "Sulina" . . . 35 25
4624 3l.40 Paddle-steamer "Republica Populara Romana" 45 30
4625 4l.80 Freighter in Sulina Channel 80 65

MS4626 90 × 78 mm. 10l. "Moldova" (tourist ship) sailing past Galati (49 × 38 mm) . . . 3·50 3·50

911 Bare-neck Pigeon

912 Party Flag and Oak Leaves

1981. Pigeons. Multicoloured.

4627 40b. Type **911** 10 10
4628 55b. Orbetan pigeon 10 10
4629 1l. Craiova chestnut pigeon 15 10
4630 1l.50 Timisoara pigeon . . . 35 10
4631 2l.15 Homing pigeon . . . 55 20
4632 3l.40 Salonta giant pigeon 80 20

1981. 60th Anniv of Romanian Communist Party.

4633 **912** 1l. multicoloured 20 15

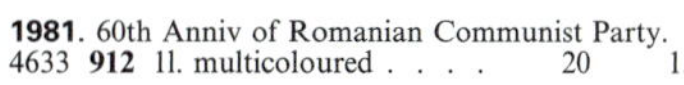

913 "Invirtita" Dance, Oas-Maramured

1981. Inter-European Cultural and Economic Co-operation. Two sheets, each 107 × 81 mm containing horiz designs as T **913**. Multicoloured.

MS4634 (a) 2l.50 × 4 Type **913**; "Hora" dance, Dobrogea; "Briuletul" dance, Oltenia; "Arderleana" dance, Crisana. (b) 2l.50 × 4 "Taraneasca" dance, Moldovia; "Invirtita Sibiana" dance, Transylvania; "Jocul de 2" dance, Banat; "Calusul" dance, Muntenia Set of 2 sheets . . . 7·50 7·50

914 "Soyuz 40"

1981. Air. Soviet–Romanian Space Flight. Mult.

4635 55b. Type **914** 15 10
4636 3l.40 "Soyuz"–"Salyut" link-up 40 10

MS4637 78 × 90 mm. 10l. Cosmonauts and space complex (49 × 38 mm) . . . . 3·50 3·50

915 Sun and Mercury

916 Industrial Symbols

1981. Air. The Planets. Multicoloured.

4638 55b. Type **915** 10 10
4639 1l. Venus, Earth and Mars 20 20
4640 1l.50 Jupiter 25 25
4641 2l.15 Saturn 35 30
4642 3l.40 Uranus 50 40
4643 4l.80 Neptune and Pluto . . 80 45

MS4644 90 × 77 mm. 10l. Earth seen from the Moon (38 × 49 mm) . . . . 4·00 4·00

1981. "Singing Romania" National Festival. Mult.

4645 55b. Type **916** 10 10
4646 1l.50 Technological symbols 25 10
4647 2l.15 Agricultural symbols 35 15
4648 3l.40 Cultural symbols . . . 70 30

917 Book and Flag

918 "Woman in an Interior"

1981. "Universiada" Games, Bucharest. Mult.

4649 1l. Type **917** 10 10
4650 2l.15 Games emblem 25 20
4651 4l.80 Stadium (horiz) . . . 55 65

1981. 150th Birth Anniv of Theodor Aman (painter). Multicoloured.

4652 40b. "Self-portrait" 10 10
4653 55b. "Battle of Giurgiu" (horiz) 10 10
4654 1l. "Family Picnic" (horiz) 15 10
4655 1l.50 "The Painter's Studio" (horiz) 20 10
4656 2l.15 Type **918** 30 10
4657 3l.10 Aman Museum, Bucharest (horiz) 50 10

919 "The Thinker of Cernavoda" (polished stone sculpture)

920 Blood Donation

1981. 16th International Congress of Historical Sciences.

4658 **919** 3l.40 multicoloured . . . 45 35

1981. Blood Donor Campaign.

4659 **920** 55b. multicoloured . . . 15 15

921 Central Military Hospital

1981. 150th Anniv of Central Military Hospital, Bucharest.
4660 **921** 55b. multicoloured . . . 15 15

922 Paul Constantinescu

923 Children at Stamp Exhibition

1981. Romanian Musicians and Composers. Mult.
4661 40b. George Enescu 10 10
4662 55b. Type **922** 10 10
4663 1l. Dinu Lipatti 15 10
4664 1l.50 Ionel Perlea 20 10
4665 2l.15 Ciprian Porumbescu . . 30 15
4666 3l.40 Mihail Jora 45 20

1981. Stamp Day.
4667 **923** 2l. multicoloured 25 20

924 Hopscotch

925 Football Players

1981. Children's Games and Activities. Mult.
4668 40b. Type **924** (postage) . . 10 10
4669 55b. Football 10 10
4670 1l. Children with balloons and hobby horse 15 15
4671 1l.50 Fishing 20 15
4672 2l.15 Dog looking through school window at child . . 30 25
4673 3l. Child on stilts 40 35
4674 4l. Child tending sick dog . . 55 45
4675 4l.80 Children with model gliders (air) 70 75
Nos. 4671/15 are from illustrations by Norman Rockwell.

1981. World Cup Football Championship, Spain (1982). Multicoloured.
4676 55b. Type **925** 10 10
4677 1l. Goalkeeper saving ball . . 15 10
4678 1l.50 Player heading ball . . 20 15
4679 2l.15 Player kicking ball over head 30 30
4680 3l.40 Goalkeeper catching ball 50 40
4681 4l.80 Player kicking ball . . 70 45
MS4682 90 × 78 mm. 10l. Goalkeeper catching ball headed by player (38 × 50 mm) . . . . 3·50 3·50

926 Alexander the Good, Prince of Moldavia

927 Entrance to Union Square Station

1982. Anniversaries. Multicoloured.
4683 1l. Type **926** (550th death anniv) 10 15
4684 1l.50 Bodgan P. Hasdeu (historian, 75th death anniv) 15 10
4685 2l.15 Nicolae Titulescu (diplomat and politician, birth centenary) 35 10

1982. Inauguration of Bucharest Underground Railway. Multicoloured.
4686 60b. Type **927** 10 10
4687 2l.40 Platforms and train at Heroes' Square station . . 35 15

928 Dog rescuing Child from Sea

1982. Dog, Friend of Mankind. Multicoloured.
4688 55b. Type **928** 10 20
4689 1l. Shepherd and sheepdog (vert) 10 15
4690 3l. Gundog (vert) 30 15
4691 3l.40 Huskies 40 15
4692 4l. Dog carrying woman's basket (vert) 45 30
4693 4l.80 Dog guiding blind person (vert) 55 30
4694 5l. Dalmatian and child with doll 60 40
4695 6l. St. Bernard 75 35

929 Dove, Banner and Crowd

1982. 60th Anniv of Communist Youth Union. Mult.
4696 1l. Type **929** 15 15
4697 1l.20 Construction worker . . 15 15
4698 1l.50 Farm workers 20 15
4699 2l. Laboratory worker and students 25 20
4700 2l.50 Labourers 40 20
4701 3l. Choir, musicians and dancers 45 15

930 Bran

1982. Inter-European Cultural and Economic Co-operation. Two sheets, each 108 × 80 mm containing horiz designs as T **930**. Multicoloured.
MS4702 2l.50 × 4 Type **930**; Hundedoara; Sinaia; Lasi. (b) 2l.50 × 4 Neuschwanstein; Stolzenfeis; Katz-Loreley; Linderhof Set of 2 sheets . . . 8·50 8·50

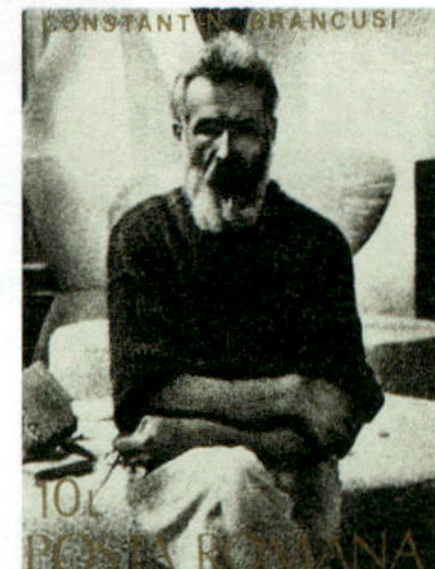

931 Constantin Brancusi (sculptor)

1982. "Philexfrance '82" International Stamp Exhibition, Paris. Sheet 71 × 81 mm.
MS4703 **931** 10l. multicoloured . . . 3·75 3·75

932 Harvesting Wheat

1982. 20th Anniv of Agricultural Co-operatives. Multicoloured.
4704 50b. Type **932** (postage) . . 10 10
4705 1l. Cows and milking equipment 15 10
4706 1l.50 Watering apple trees . . 20 10
4707 2l.50 Cultivator in vineyard . . 35 20
4708 3l. Watering vegetables . . . 40 25
4709 4l. Helicopter spraying cereal crop (air) 65 35
MS4710 68 × 80 mm. 10l. Aerial view of new village (50 × 37 mm) . . 3·75 3·75

933 Vladimir Nicolae's Standard 1 Hang-glider

1982. Air. Hang-gliders. Multicoloured.
4711 50b. Type **933** 10 10
4712 1l. Excelsior D 20 10
4713 1l.50 Dedal-1 . . . . 25 10
4714 2l.50 Entuziast 40 15
4715 4l. AK-22 . . . . 60 30
4716 5l. Grifrom 85 35

934 Baile Felix

936 Vlaicu Monument, Banesti-Prahova

935 "Legend"

1982. Spas and Health Resorts. Multicoloured.
4717 50b. Type **934** 10 10
4718 1l. Predeal (horiz) 10 10
4719 1l.50 Baile Herculane . . . 20 10
4720 2l.50 Eforie Nord (horiz) . . 40 10
4721 3l. Olimp (horiz) 50 10
4722 5l. Neptun (horiz) 70 20

1982. Paintings by Sabin Balasa. Multicoloured.
4723 1l. Type **935** 10 15
4724 1l.50 "Contrasts" 20 15
4725 2l.50 "Peace Relay" 50 25
4726 4l. "Genesis of the Romanian People" (vert) . . 55 35

1982. Air. Birth Centenary of Aurel Vlaicu (aviation pioneer). Multicoloured.
4727 50b. Vlaicu's glider, 1909 (horiz) 10 10
4728 1l. Type **936** 20 10
4729 2l.50 Air Heroes' Monument . 45 20
4730 3l. Vlaicu's No. 1 airplane "Crazy Fly", 1910 (horiz) . 50 15

937 "Cheerful Peasant Woman"

1982. 75th Death Anniv Nicolae Grigorescu (artist). Sheet 70 × 80 mm.
MS4731 **937** 10l. multicoloured . . . 3·75 3·75

938 Central Exhibition Pavilion

1982. "Tib '82" International Fair, Bucharest.
4732 **938** 2l. multicoloured 25 10

939 Young Pioneer with Savings Book and Books

940 Postwoman delivering Letters

1982. Savings Week. Multicoloured.
4733 1l. Type **939** 15 10
4734 2l. Savings Bank advertisement (Calin Popovici) 20 10

1982. Stamp Day. Multicoloured.
4735 1l. Type **940** 15 10
4736 2l. Postman 20 10

941 "Brave Young Man and the Golden Apples" (Petre Ispirescu)

942 Symbols of Industry, Party Emblem and Programme

1982. Fairy Tales. Multicoloured.
4737 50b. Type **941** 10 10
4738 1l. "Bear tricked by the Fox" (Ion Creanga) . . . 20 10
4739 1l.50 Warrior fighting bird ("Prince of Tears" (Mihai Eminescu)) 25 10
4740 2l.50 Hen with bag ("Bag with Two Coins" (Ion Creanga)) 35 10
4741 3l. Rider fighting three-headed dragon ("Ileana Simziana" (Petre Ispirescu)) 45 20
4742 5l. Man riding devil ("Danila Prepeleac" (Ion Creanga)) 75 30

1982. Romanian Communist Party National Conference, Bucharest. Multicoloured.
4743 1l. Type **942** 15 15
4744 2l. Wheat symbols of industry and Party emblem and open programme 25 15

943 Wooden Canteen from Suceava

944 Wheat, Cogwheel, Flask and Electricity Emblem

1982. Household Utensils.
4745 **943** 50b. red 10 10
4746 – 1l. blue 15 15
4747 – 1l.50 orange 20 10
4748 – 2l. blue 40 15
4749 – 3l. green 50 15
4750 – 3l.50 green 55 10
4751 – 4l. brown 70 15
4752 – 5l. blue 80 10
4753 – 6l. blue . . . . 1·00 15
4754 – 7l. purple . . . . . . 1·10 15
4755 – 7l.50 mauve . . . . . . 1·20 15
4756 – 8l. green . . . . 1·20 15
4757 – 10l. red . . . . 1·20 15
4758 – 20l. violet . . . . . . 2·50 15
4759 – 30l. blue . . . . 3·50 15
4760 – 50l. brown . . . . . . 7·25 25

DESIGNS: As T **943**—VERT: 1l. Ceramic plates from Radauti; 2l. Jug and plate from Vama-Maramures; 3l. Wooden churn and pail from North Moldavia; 4l. Wooden spoons and ceramic plate from Cluj; 5l. Ceramic bowl and pot from Marginea-Suceava. HORIZ: 1l.50, Wooden dipper from Valea Mare; 3l.50, Ceramic plates from Leheceni-Crisana. 29 × 23 mm: 10l. Wooden tubs from Hunedoara and Suceava; 30l. Wooden spoons from Alba. 23 × 29 mm: 6l. Ceramic pot and jug from Bihor; 7l. Distaff and spindle from Transylvania; 7l.50, Double wooden pail from Suceava; 8l. Pitcher and ceramic plate from Oboga and Horezu; 20l. Wooden canteen and six glasses from Horezu; 50l. Ceramic plates from Horezu.

1982. 35th Anniv of People's Republic. Mult.

4767	1l. Type **944**	15	10
4768	2l. National flag and oak leaves	20	10

945 H. Coanda and Diagram of Jet Engine

1983. Air. 25 Years of Space Exploration. Mult.

4769	50b. Type **945**	10	10
4770	1l. H. Oberth and diagram of rocket	10	10
4771	1l.50 "Sputnik 1", 1957 (first artificial satellite)	20	10
4772	2l.50 "Vostok 1", (first manned flight)	45	15
4773	4l. "Apollo 11, 1969 (first Moon landing)	65	20
4774	5l. Space shuttle "Columbia"	85	25
MS4775	93 × 80 mm. 10l. Earth (41 × 53 mm)	5·00	5·00

946 Rombac One Eleven 500 Jetliner **947** Matei Millo in "The Discontented" by Vasile Alecsandri

1983. Air. First Romanian-built Jetliner.

4776 **946**	11l. blue	2·00	50

1983. Romanian Actors.

4777 **947**	50b. red and black	10	15
4778 –	1l. green and black	10	10
4779 –	1l.50 violet and black	20	15
4780 –	2l. brown and black	30	15
4781 –	2l.50 green and black	40	10
4782 –	3l. blue and black	45	15
4783 –	4l. green and black	55	25
4784 –	5l. lilac and black	75	40

DESIGNS: 1l. Mihail Pascaly in "Director Millo" by Vasile Alecsandri; 1l.50, Aristizza Romanescu in "The Dogs" by H. Lecca; 2l. C. I. Nottara in "Blizzard" by B. S. Delavrancea; 2l.50, Grigore Manolescu in "Hamlet" by William Shakespeare; 3l. Agatha Birsescu in "Medea" by Lebouvet; 4l. Ion Brezeanu in "The Lost Letter" by I. L. Caragiale; 5l. Aristide Demetriad in "The Despotic Prince" by Vasile Alecsandri.

948 Hugo Grotius **949** Aro "10"

1983. 400th Birth Anniv of Hugo Grotius (Dutch jurist).

4785 **948**	2l. brown	30	10

1983. Romanian-built Vehicles. Multicoloured.

4786	50b. Type **949**	10	10
4787	1l. Dacia "1300" Break	20	10
4788	1l.50 Aro "242"	25	10
4789	2l.50 Aro "244"	45	10
4790	4l. Dacia "1310"	70	15
4791	5l. Oltcit "Club"	95	25

950 Johannes Kepler (astronomer)

1983. Inter-European Cultural and Economic Co-operation. Two sheets, each 110 × 80 mm containing horiz designs as T **950**. Multicoloured.

MS4792 (a) 3l. × 4 Type **950**; Alexander von Humboldt (explorer) and "Pizarro" J.W. von Goethe (writer); Richard Wagner (composer). (b) 3l. × 4 Ion Andreescu (artist); George Constantinescu (engineer); Tudor Arghezi (writer); C. I. Parhon (physician) Set of 2 sheets . . . 10·00 10·00

951 National and Communist Party Flags **953** Bluethroat

952 Loading Mail into Boeing 707

1983. 50th Anniv of 1933 Workers' Revolution.

4793 **951**	2l. multicoloured	30	10

1983. Air. World Communications Year.

4794 **952**	2l. multicoloured	50	10

1983. Birds of the Danube Delta. Multicoloured.

4795	50b. Type **953**	15	10
4796	1l. Rose-coloured starling	45	10
4797	1l.50 European roller	55	10
4798	2l.50 European bee eater	90	25
4799	4l. Reed bunting	1·60	30
4800	5l. Lesser grey shrike	2·00	40

954 Kayak

1983. Water Sports. Multicoloured.

4801	50b. Type **954**	10	15
4802	1l. Water polo	15	15
4803	1l.50 Canoeing	20	15
4804	2l.50 Diving	45	20
4805	4l. Rowing	70	25
4806	5l. Swimming (start of race)	95	40

955 Postman on Bicycle

1983. Stamp Day. Multicoloured.

4807	1l. Type **955**	15	10
4808	3l.50(+3l.) National flag as stamp	95	50
MS4809	90 × 79 mm. 10l. Unloading mail from Rombac One Eleven 500 at Bucharest airport (38 × 50 mm) (air)	4·50	4·50

No. 4808 was issued se-tenant with a premium-carrying tab showing the Philatelic Association emblem.

956 "Geum reptans"

1983. European Flora and Fauna. Multicoloured.

4810	1l. Type **956**	20	30
4811	1l. Long-headed poppy	20	15
4812	1l. Stemless carline thistle	20	30
4813	1l. "Paeonia peregrina"	20	30
4814	1l. "Gentiana excisa"	20	15
4815	1l. Eurasian red squirrel	20	30
4816	1l. "Grammia quenselii" (butterfly)	50	20
4817	1l. Middle-spotted woodpecker	50	45
4818	1l. Lynx	50	30
4819	1l. Wallcreeper	70	45

957 "Girl with Feather" **958** Flag and Oak Leaves

1983. Paintings by Corneliu Baba. Multicoloured.

4820	1l. Type **957**	20	15
4821	2l. "Congregation"	35	15
4822	3l. "Farm Workers"	65	20
4823	4l. "Rest in the Fields" (horiz)	85	30

1983. 65th Anniv of Union of Transylvania and Romania. Multicoloured.

4824	1l. Type **958**	15	15
4825	2l. National and Communist Party Flags and Parliament building, Bucharest	30	15

959 Postman and Post Office **961** Cross-country Skiing

960 "Orient Express" at Bucharest, 1883

1983. "Balkanfila IX '83" Stamp Exhibition, Bucharest. Multicoloured.

4826	1l. Type **959**	15	15
4827	2l. Postwoman and Athenaeum Concert Hall	30	15
MS4828	90 × 78 mm. 10l. Balkan flags and Athenaeum Concert Hall (37 × 50 mm)	4·00	4·00

1983. Centenary of "Orient Express". Sheet 90 × 78 mm.

MS4829 **960**	10l. multicoloured	5·50	5·50

1984. Winter Olympic Games, Sarajevo. Mult.

4830	50b. Type **961**	10	10
4831	1l. Biathlon	10	20
4832	1l.50 Ice skating	15	20
4833	2l. Speed skating	20	30
4834	3l. Ice hockey	30	35
4835	3l.50 Bobsleighing	40	15
4836	4l. Luge	45	55
4837	5l. Downhill skiing	55	65

962 Prince Cuza and Arms

1984. 125th Anniv of Union of Moldova and Wallachia. Sheet 90 × 78 mm.

MS4838 **962**	10l. multicoloured	3·50	3·50

963 Palace of Udriste Nasturel (Chancery official)

1984. Anniversaries.

4839	50b. green, pink and silver	10	10
4840	1l. violet, green and silver	20	10
4841	1l.50 multicoloured	30	15
4842	2l. brown, blue and silver	45	10
4843	3l.50 multicoloured	80	20
4844	4l. multicoloured	1·00	20

DESIGNS: 50b. Type **963** (325th death anniv); 1l. Miron Costin (poet, 350th birth anniv); 1l.50, Crisan (Giurgiu Marcu) (leader of peasant revolt, 250th birth anniv); 2l. Simion Barnutiu (scientist, 175th birth anniv); 3l.50, Diuliu Zamfirescu (writer, 125th birth anniv); 4l. Nicolae Milescu at Great Wall of China (explorer, 275th death anniv).

964 Chess Game

1984. 15th Balkan Chess Championships, Baile Herculane. Sheet 107 × 80 mm containing T **964** and similar horiz designs. Multicoloured.

MS4845	3l. × 4 various chess games	5·00	5·00

965 Orsova Bridge

1984. Inter-European Cultural and Economic Co-operation. Two sheets each 108 × 81 mm containing horiz designs as T **965**. Multicoloured.

MS4846 (a) 3l. × 4 Type **965**; Arges Bridge, Basarabi Bridge; Ohaba Bridge all in Rumania. (b) 3l. × 4 Kohlbrand Bridge, Hamburg; Bosphorus Bridge, Istanbul; Europa Bridge, Innsbruck; Tower Bridge, London Set of 2 sheets . . . 10·00 10·00

966 Sunflower

1984. Protection of Environment. Multicoloured.

4847	1l. Type **966**	15	10
4848	2l. Red deer	25	15
4849	3l. Carp	35	20
4850	4l. Jay	1·70	40

967 Flowering Rush

1984. Flowers of the Danube. Multicoloured.

4851	50b. Arrowhead	10	10
4852	1l. Yellow iris	10	10
4853	1l.50 Type **967**	20	10
4854	3l. White water lily	45	20
4855	4l. Fringed water lily (horiz)	65	20
4856	5l. Yellow water lily (horiz)	80	30

968 Crowd with Banners

970 Congress Emblem

969 High Jumping

1984. 45th Anniv of Anti-Fascist Demonstration.

4857 **968** 2l. multicoloured 35 30

1984. Olympic Games, Los Angeles (1st issue). Multicoloured.

4858 50b. Type **969** 10 10
4859 1l. Swimming 15 10
4860 1l.50 Running 20 15
4861 3l. Handball 50 35
4862 4l. Rowing 75 55
4863 5l. Canoeing 95 70

See also Nos. 4866/73.

1984. 25th Ear, Nose and Throat Association Congress, Bucharest.

4864 **970** 2l. multicoloured 30 15

971 Footballers and Romanian Flag

1984. European Cup Football Championship. Two sheets, each 109 × 81 mm containing horiz designs as T **971** showing footballers and national flag. Multicoloured.

MS4865 (a) 3l. × Type **971**; West Germany; Portugal; Spain. (b) 3l. × 4 France; Belgium; Yugoslavia; Denmark Set of 2 sheets . . . 10·00 10·00

1984. Olympic Games, Los Angeles (2nd issue). As T **969**. Multicoloured.

4866 50b. Boxing 10 10
4867 1l. Rowing 10 10
4868 1l. Handball 15 10
4869 2l. Judo 20 10
4870 3l. Wrestling 35 15
4871 3l.50 Fencing 45 20
4872 4l. Kayak 55 25
4873 5l. Swimming 65 35

972 Mihai Ciuca (bacteriologist, cent)

974 Flags, Flame and Power Station

973 Lockhead 14 Super Electra

1984. Birth Anniversaries. Dated "1983".

4874 **972** 1l. purple, blue and silver 15 15
4875 – 2l. brown and silver . . 30 15
4876 – 3l. green, brown and silver 45 25
4877 – 4l. violet, green and silver 65 40

DESIGNS: 2l. Petre S. Aurelian (agronomist, 150th anniv); 3l. Alexandru Vlahuta (writer, 125th anniv); 4l. Dimitrie Leonida (engineer, centenary).

1984. Air. 40th Anniv of International Civil Aviation Organization. Multicoloured.

4878 50b. Type **973** 15 10
4879 1l.50 Britten Norman Islander 30 10
4880 3l. Rombac One Eleven 500 jetliner 60 20
4881 6l. Boeing 707 jetliner . . . 1·10 30

1984. 40th Anniv of Liberation.

4882 **974** 2l. multicoloured 50 30

975 Lippizaner

1984. Horses. Multicoloured.

4883 50b. Type **975** 10 10
4884 1l. Hutul 15 10
4885 1l.50 Bukovina 20 10
4886 2l.50 Nonius 40 10
4887 4l. Arab 65 20
4888 5l. Romanian halfbreed . . 80 25

976 V. Racila (woman's singles sculls, gold)

1984. Romanian Olympic Games Medal Winners. Two sheets, each 125 × 129 mm containing four designs as T **976**. Multicoloured.

MS4889 (a) 3l. × 6 Type **976**; P. Becheru and N. Vlad (weightlifting, gold); D. Melinte (800m.) and M. Puica (3000m. women's running, gold); Men's canoeing (Canadian pairs, gold); Fencing (silver); Women's modern rhythmic gymnastics (silver). (b) 3l. × 6, Women's team gymnastics (gold); Women's kayak fours (gold); A. Stanciu (women's long jump, gold); I. Draica and V. Andrei (wrestling, gold); Judo (bronze); Pistol shooting (silver) Set of 2 sheets . . . . 16·00 16·00

977 Memorial, Alba Julia

978 "Portrait of a Child" (TH. Aman)

1984. Bicentenary of Horea, Closa and Crisan Uprisings.

4890 **977** 2l. multicoloured 30 15

1984. Paintings of Children. Multicoloured.

4891 50b. Type **978** 10 15
4892 1l. "The Little Shepherd" (N. Grigorescu) 10 10
4893 2l. "Lica with an Orange" (St. Luchian) 30 10
4894 3l. "Portrait of a Child" (N. Tonitza) 45 20
4895 4l. "Portrait of a Boy" (S. Popp) 65 25
4896 5l. "Portrait of Young Girl" (I. Tuculescu) 90 30

979 Stage Coach and Romanian Philatelic Association Emblem

1984. Stamp Day.

4897 **979** 2l.(+1l.) multicoloured 45 50

No. 4897 was issued with premium-carrying label as shown in T **979**.

980 Flags and Party Emblem

1984. 13th Romanian Communist Party Congress, Bucharest. Sheet 90 × 78 mm.

MS4898 **980** 10l. multicoloured 4·50 4·50

981 Dalmatian Pelicans

982 Dr. Petru Groza (former President)

1984. Protected Animals. Dalmatian Pelicans. Mult.

4899 50b. Type **981** 20 15
4900 1l. Pelican on nest 50 35
4901 1l. Pelicans on lake 50 35
4902 2l. Pelicans roosting . . . . 1·00 80

1984. Anniversaries. Multicoloured.

4903 50b. Type **982** (birth centenary) 25 15
4904 1l. Alexandru Odobescu (writer) (150th birth anniv) 55 10
4905 2l. Dr. Carol Davila (physician) (death centenary) 35 10
4906 3l. Dr. Nicolae Gh. Lupu (physician) (birth centenary) 55 15
4907 4l. Dr. Daniel Danielopolu (physician) (birth centenary) 65 25
4908 5l. Panait Istrati (writer) (birth centenary) 85 35

983 Generator

985 August Treboniu Laurian (linguist and historian)

984 Gounod and Paris Opera House

1984. Centenary of Power Station and Electric Street Lighting in Timisoara. Multicoloured.

4909 1l. Type **983** 15 15
4910 2l. Street lamp 35 10

1985. Inter-European Cultural and Economic Co-operation. Composers. Two sheets, each 110 × 80 mm containing horiz designs as T **984**.

MS4911 (a) 3l. × 4 green and violet (Type **984**); red and blue (Strauss and Munich Opera House); violet and green (Mozart and Vienna Opera House); blue and red (Verdi and La Scala, Milan). (b) 3l. × 4 violet and green (Tchaikovsky and Bolshoi Theatre, Moscow); blue and red (Enescu and Bucharest Opera House); green and violet (Wagner and Dresden Opera House); red and blue (Moniuszko and Warsaw Opera House) Set of 2 sheets . . . . 11·00 11·00

1985. Anniversaries. Multicoloured.

4912 50b. Type **985** (175th birth anniv) 10 15
4913 1l. Grigore Alexandrescu (writer) (death centenary) 20 15
4914 1l.50 Gheorghe Pop de Basesti (politician) (150th birth anniv) 30 15
4915 2l. Mateiu Caragiale (writer) (birth centenary) 35 10
4916 3l. Gheorghe Ionescu-Sisesti (scientist) (birth centenary) 55 20
4917 4l. Liviu Rebreanu (writer) (birth centenary) 85 25

986 Students in Science Laboratory

987 Racoon Dog

1985. International Youth Year. Multicoloured.

4918 1l. Type **986** 10 10
4919 2l. Students on construction site 35 10

MS4920 91 × 79 mm. 10l. Students with banner and dove (53 × 41 mm) . . . . 5·00 5·00

1985. Protected Animals. Multicoloured.

4921 50b. Type **987** 10 10
4922 1l. Grey partridge 40 10
4923 1l.50 Snowy owl . . . . . 1·00 15
4924 2l. Pine marten 20 10
4925 3l. Eurasian badger 30 10
4926 3l.50 Eurasian otter 30 20
4927 4l. Western Capercaillie . . 1·60 25
4928 5l. Great bustard . . . . . 2·20 35

988 Flags and Victory Monument, Bucharest

989 Union Emblem

1985. 40th Anniv of Victory in Europe Day.

4929 **988** 2l. multicoloured 50 25

1985. Communist Youth Union Congress.

4930 **989** 2l. multicoloured 40 15

990 Route Map and Canal

1985. Danube–Black Sea Canal. Multicoloured.

4931 1l. Type **990** 25 10
4932 2l. Canal and bridge, Cernavoda . . . . 1·10 25
4933 3l. Road over Canal, Medgidia 95 15
4934 4l. Canal control tower, Agigea . . . . 1·10 25

MS4935 90 × 79 mm. 10l. Opening ceremony (53 × 39 mm) . . . . 4·00 4·00

991 Brown Pelican
992 "Fire"

1985. Birth Bicentenary of John J. Audubon (ornithologist). Multicoloured.

4936 50b. American robin (horiz) 15 10
4937 1l. Type **991** 30 10
4938 1l.50 Yellow-crowned night heron 45 15
4939 2l. Northern oriole 65 15
4940 3l. Red-necked grebe 95 30
4941 4l. Mallard (horiz) 1·10 40

1985. Paintings by Ion Tuculescu. Multicoloured.

4942 1l. Type **992** 10 15
4943 2l. "Circulation" 35 15
4944 3l. "Interior of Peasant's Home" (horiz) 50 20
4945 4l. "Sunset" (horiz) 70 25

993 Peacock

1985. Butterflies and Moths. Multicoloured.

4946 50b. Type **993** 10 10
4947 1l. Swallowtail 25 10
4948 2l. Red admiral 40 15
4949 3l. Emperor moth 55 20
4950 4l. Hebe tiger moth 80 30
4951 5l. Eyed hawk moth 95 45

994 Transfagarasan Mountain Road

1985. 20th Anniv of Election of General Secretary Nicolae Ceausescu and 9th Communist Party Congress. Multicoloured.

4952 1l. Type **994** 20 15
4953 2l. Danube–Black Sea Canal 60 25
4954 3l. Bucharest underground railway 90 40
4955 4l. Irrigating fields 90 45

995 Romanian Crest, Symbols of Agriculture and "XX"
997 "Senecio glaberrimus"

996 Daimlers' Motor Cycle, 1885

1985. 20th Anniv of Romanian Socialist Republic. Multicoloured.

4956 1l. Type **995** 25 25
4957 2l. Crest, symbols of industry and "XX" 55 35

1985. Centenary of Motor Cycle. Sheet 91 × 79 mm.

MS4958 **996** 10l. multicoloured 4·00 4·00

1985. 50th Anniv of Retezat National Park. Mult.

4959 50b. Type **997** 10 10
4960 1l. Chamois 20 10
4961 2l. "Centaurea retezatensis" 40 20
4962 3l. Violet 55 20
4963 4l. Alpine marmot 80 30
4964 5l. Golden eagle 3·25 90
MS4965 91 × 80 mm. 10l. Lynx ("Lynx lynx") 4·00 4·00

998 Universal "530 DTC"

1985. Romanian Tractors. Multicoloured.

4966 50b. Type **998** 10 10
4967 1l. Universal "550 M HC" 25 10
4968 1l.50 Universal "650 Super" 35 10
4969 2l. Universal "850" 45 20
4970 3l. Universal "S 1801 IF" tracked front loader 65 20
4971 4l. Universal "A 3602 IF" front loader 95 30

999 Costume of Muscel (female)

1985. Costumes (1st series). Multicoloured.

4972 50b. Type **999** 10 10
4973 50b. Muscel (male) 10 10
4974 1l.50 Bistrita-Nasaud (female) 25 20
4975 1l.50 Bistrita-Nasaud (male) 25 20
4976 2l. Vrancea (female) 35 10
4977 2l. Vrancea (male) 35 10
4978 3l. Vilcea (female) 55 25
4979 3l. Vilcea (male) 55 25

See also Nos. 5143/5150.

1000 Footballer attacking Goal

1985. World Cup Football Championship, Mexico (1986) (1st issue). Multicoloured.

4980 50b. Type **1000** 10 15
4981 1l. Player capturing ball 20 15
4982 1l.50 Player heading ball 25 25
4983 2l. Player about to tackle 40 25
4984 3l. Player heading ball and goalkeeper 65 35
4985 4l. Player kicking ball over-head 1·00 45

See also Nos. 5038/43.

1001 U.N. Emblem and "40"
1002 Copper

1985. 40th Anniv of U.N.O. (4986) and 30th Anniv of Romanian Membership (4987).

4986 2l. Type **1001** 30 20
4987 2l. U.N. building, New York, U.N. emblem and Romanian crest 30 20

1985. Minerals. Multicoloured.

4988 50b. Quartz and calcite 10 15
4989 1l. Type **1002** 10 15
4990 2l. Gypsum 25 15
4991 3l. Quartz 40 20
4992 4l. Stibium 60 30
4993 5l. Tetrahedrite 90 40

1003 Posthorn

1985. Stamp Day.

4994 **1003** 2l.(+1l.) multicoloured 50 40

1004 Goofy as Hank waking to find himself at Camelot

1985. 150th Birth of Mark Twain (writer). Scenes from "A Connecticut Yankee in King Arthur's Court" (film). Multicoloured.

4995 50b. Type **1004** 2·40 1·60
4996 50b. Hank at the stake and Merlin (Mickey Mouse) 2·40 1·60
4997 50b. Hank being hoisted onto horseback in full armour 2·40 1·60
4998 50b. Pete as Sir Sagramoor on horseback 2·40 1·60
MS4999 122 × 96 mm. 5l. Hank at the tournament against Sir Sagramor 18·00 18·00

1985. Birth Bicentenaries of Grimm Brothers (folklorists). Scenes from "The Three Brothers". As T **1004**. Multicoloured.

5000 1l. Father (Donald Duck) bidding farewell to the brothers (Huey, Louie and Dewey) 3·00 2·75
5001 1l. Louie as fencing master brother 3·00 2·75
5002 1l. Louie keeping rain off his father with sword 3·00 2·75
5003 1l. Huey as blacksmith brother shoeing galloping horse 3·00 2·75
5004 1l. Dewey as barber brother shaving Brer Rabbit on the run 3·00 2·75
MS5005 120 × 95 mm. 5l. Brothers playing music 20·00 20·00

1005 Wright Brothers (aviation pioneers) and Wright Flyer 1

1985. Explorers and Pioneers. Multicoloured.

5006 1l. Type **1005** 15 10
5007 1l.50 Jacques Yves Cousteau (undersea explorer) and "Calypso" 45 10
5008 2l. Amelia Earhart (first woman trans-Atlantic flyer) and Fokker F.VIIb/3m seaplane "Friendship" 35 10
5009 3l. Charles Lindbergh (first solo trans-Atlantic flyer) and Ryan NYP Special "Spirit of St. Louis" 45 20
5010 3l.50 Sir Edmund Hillary (first man to reach summit of Everest) 45 25
5011 4l. Robert Peary and Emil Racovita (polar explorers) 50 25
5012 5l. Richard Byrd (polar explorer and aviator) and polar supply ship 1·20 40
5013 6l. Neil Armstrong (first man on Moon) and Moon 65 45

1006 Edmond Halley and Comet

1986. Air. Appearance of Halley's Comet.

5014 2l. Type **1006** 30 20
5015 4l. Comet, orbit and space probes 60 30

No. 5014 is wrongly inscr "Edmund".

1007 "Nina in Green"

1986. Paintings by Nicolae Tonitza. Multicoloured.

5016 1l. Type **1007** 10 15
5017 2l. "Irina" 30 20
5018 3l. "Forester's Daughter" 45 30
5019 4l. "Woman on Veranda" 70 30

1008 Wild Cat ("Felis silvestris")

1986. Inter-European Cultural and Economic Co-operation. Two sheets, each 110 × 81 mm containing horiz designs as T **1008**. Multicoloured.

MS5020 (a) 3l. × 4 Type **1008**; Stoat ("Mustela erminea"); Capercaillie ("Tetrao urogallus"); Brown bear ("Ursus arctos"). (b) 3l. × 4 "Dianthus callizonus"; Arolla pine ("Pinus cembra"); Willow ("Salix" sp.); "Rosa pendulina" Set of 2 sheets 11·00 9·75

1009 Goofy playing Clarinet

1986. 50th Anniv of Colour Animation. Scenes from "Band Concert" (cartoon film). Mult.

5021 50b. Type **1009** 2·40 1·70
5022 50b. Clarabelle playing flute 2·40 1·70
5023 50b. Mickey Mouse conducting 2·40 1·70
5024 50b. Paddy and Peter Pig playing euphonium and trumpet 2·40 1·70
5025 1l. Conductor Mickey and flautist Donald Duck 2·75 2·75
5026 1l. Donald caught in trombone slide 2·75 2·75
5027 1l. Horace playing drums 2·75 2·75
5028 1l. Donald selling ice cream 2·75 2·75
5029 1l. Mickey and euphonium caught in tornado 2·75 2·75
MS5030 120 × 95 mm. 5l. Instruments and musicians in tree 20·00 20·00

1010 Hotel Diana, Baile Herculane

1986. Spa Hotels. Multicoloured.

5031 50b. Type **1010** 10 10
5032 1l. Hotel Termal, Baile Felix 15 10
5033 2l. Hotels Delfin, Meduza and Steaua de Mare, North Eforie 35 10
5034 3l. Hotel Caciulata, Calimanesti-Caciulata 50 20
5035 4l. Villa Palas, Slanic Moldova 75 30
5036 5l. Hotel Bradet, Sovata 85 35

1011 Ceausescu and Red Flag

1986. 65th Anniv of Romanian Communist Party.
5037 **1011** 2l. multicoloured . . . 80 35

1012 Italy v. Bulgaria

1986. World Cup Football Championship, Mexico (2nd issue). Multicoloured.
5038 50b. Type **1012** 10 15
5039 1l. Mexico v. Belgium . . . 10 15
5040 2l. Canada v. France . . . 30 20
5041 3l. Brazil v. Spain 40 20
5042 4l. Uruguay v. W. Germany 60 35
5043 5l. Morocco v. Poland . . . 70 40

1013 Alexandru Papanas' Bucker Bu 133 Jungmeister Biplane (Aerobatics Champion, 1936)

1986. Air. "Ameripex" '86 International Stamp Exhibition, Chicago. Sheet 120 × 95 mm.
MS5044 **1013** 10l. multicoloured 4·00 3·50

1014 "Tulipa gesneriana"

1986. Garden Flowers. Multicoloured.
5045 50b. Type **1014** 10 15
5046 1l. "Iris hispanica" 10 15
5047 2l. "Rosa hybrida" 35 15
5048 3l. "Anemone coronaria" . . 50 20
5049 4l. "Freesia refracta" . . . 70 30
5050 5l. "Chrysanthemum indicum" 80 40

1015 Mircea the Great and Horsemen

1986. 600th Anniv of Mircea the Great's Accession.
5051 **1015** 2l. multicoloured . . . 30 25

1016 Thatched House with Veranda, Alba

1986. 50th Anniv of Museum of Historic Dwellings, Bucharest. Multicoloured.
5052 50b. Type **1016** 10 35
5053 1l. Stone-built house, Arges 10 35
5054 2l. House with veranda, Constanta 35 40
5055 3l. House with tiled roof and steps, Timis 50 40
5056 4l. House with ramp to veranda, Neamt 70 20
5057 5l. Two storey house with first floor veranda, Gorj 80 30

1017 Julius Popper (Tierra del Fuego, 1886–93)

1986. Polar Research. Multicoloured.
5058 50b. Type **1017** 15 10
5059 1l. Bazil Gh. Assan (Spitzbergen, 1896) . . . 35 10
5060 2l. Emil Racovita and "Belgica" (barque) (Antarctic, 1897–99) . . . 80 10
5061 3l. Constantin Dumbrava (Greenland, 1927–28) . . 60 20
5062 4l. Romanian participation in 17th Soviet Antarctic Expedition, 1971–72 . . . 1·60 25
5063 5l. 1977 "Sinoe" and 1979–80 "Tirnava" krill fishing expeditions . . . . 1·20 30

1018 Dove and map on Globe

1986. International Peace Year. Sheet 89 × 77 mm.
MS5064 **1018** 5l. multicoloured 1·75 1·75

1019 The Blusher **1020** Group of Cyclists

1986. Fungi. Multicoloured.
5065 50b. Type **1019** 15 10
5066 1l. Oak mushroom 20 10
5067 2l. Peppery milk cap 45 15
5068 3l. Shield fungus 70 35
5069 4l. The charcoal burner . . 1·00 40
5070 5l. "Tremiscus helvelloides" 1·10 55

1986. Cycle Tour of Romania. Multicoloured.
5071 1l. Type **1020** 10 15
5072 2l. Motor cycle following cyclist 30 15
5073 3l. Jeep following cyclists . . 40 25
5074 4l. Winner 65 25
MS5075 90 × 78 mm. 10l. Cyclist (38 × 51 mm) . . . . 4·25 4·25

1021 Emblem **1022** Petru Maior (historian) (225th birth anniv)

1986. 40th Anniv of UNESCO and 30th Anniv of Romanian Membership.
5076 **1021** 4l. multicoloured . . . 60 45

1986. Birth Anniversaries.
5077 **1022** 50b. purple, gold and green 10 10
5078 – 1b. green, gold and mauve 10 10
5079 – 2l. red, gold and blue 30 10
5080 – 3l. blue, gold and brown 55 20
DESIGNS: 1l. George Topirceanu (writer, centenary); 2l. Henri Coanda (engineer, centenary); 3l. Constantin Budeanu (engineer, centenary).

1023 Coach and Horses (½-size illustration)

1986. Stamp Day.
5081 **1023** 2l.(+1l.) multicoloured 50 40
No. 5081 includes the se-tenant premium-carrying tab shown in Type **1023**.

1024 F 300 Oil Drilling Rigs **1026** Tin Can and Motor Car ("Recycle metals")

1025 "Goat"

1986. Industry. Multicoloured.
5082 50b. Type **1024** 10 10
5083 1l. "Promex" excavator (horiz) 10 10
5084 2l. Petrochemical refinery, Pitesti 35 10
5085 3l. Tipper "110 t" (horiz) . . 50 20
5086 4l. "Coral" computer . . . 70 25
5087 5l. 350 m.w. turbine (horiz) 80 35

1986. New Year Folk Customs. Multicoloured.
5088 50b. Type **1025** 10 10
5089 1l. Sorcova 10 10
5090 2l. Plugusorul 35 10
5091 3l. Buhaiul 50 15
5092 4l. Caiutii 70 25
5093 5l. Uratorii 80 35

1986. "Save Waste Materials".
5094 **1026** 1l. red and orange . . . 15 10
5095 – 2l. light green and green 40 20
DESIGN: 2l. Trees and hand with newspaper ("Recycle waste paper").

1027 Flags and Young People **1028** Anniversary Emblem

1987. 65th Anniv of Communist Youth Union. Multicoloured.
5096 1l. Type **1027** 15 40
5097 2l. Anniversary emblem . . 45 55
5098 3l. Flags and young people (different) 65 70

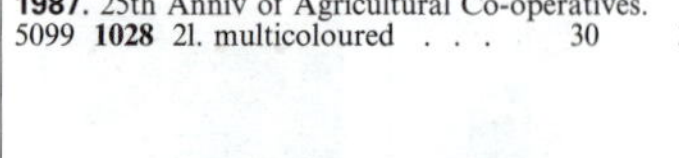

1987. 25th Anniv of Agricultural Co-operatives.
5099 **1028** 2l. multicoloured . . . 30 30

1029 Administrative Building, Satu Mare

1987. Inter-European Cultural and Economic Co-operation. Two sheets, each 110 × 80 mm containing horiz designs as T **1029**. Multicoloured.
MS5100 3l. × 4 (a) Type **1029**; House of Toung Pioneers, Bucharest; Valahia Hotel, Tirgoviste; Caciulata Hotel, Caciulata. (b) 3l. × 4 Exhibition Pavilion, Bucharest; Intercontinental Hotel, Bucharest; Europa Hotel, Eforie Nord; Polytechnic Institute, Bucharest
Set of 2 sheets . . . . 9·50 9·50

1030 "Birch Trees by Lake" (Ion Andreescu)

1987. Paintings. Multicoloured.
5101 50b. Type **1030** 10 15
5102 1l. "Young Peasant Girls spinning" (N. Grigorescu) 15 15
5103 2l. "Washerwoman" (St. Luchian) 30 15
5104 3l. "Interior" (St. Dimitrescu) 55 20
5105 4l. "Winter Landscape" (Al. Ciucurencu) 65 25
5106 5l. "Winter in Bucharest" (N. Tonitza) (vert) . . . 85 35

1031 "1907" and Peasants

1987. 80th Anniv of Peasant Uprising.
5107 **1031** 2l. multicoloured . . . 30 30

1032 Players **1033** 1 Leu Coin

1987. 10th Students World Men's Handball Championship.
5108 **1032** 50b. multicoloured . . 10 15
5109 – 1l. multicoloured (horiz) 45 15
5110 – 2l. multicoloured . . . 30 15
5111 – 3l. multicoloured (horiz) 55 25
5112 – 4l. multicoloured . . . 70 30
5113 – 5l. multicoloured (horiz) 85 40
DESIGNS: 1l. to 5l. Various match scenes.

1987. Currency. Multicoloured.
5114 1l. Type **1033** 20 15
MS5115 90 × 78 mm. 10l. 10lei banknote (53 × 41 mm) . . . . 3·50 3·50

1034 Eastern White Pelicans in the Danube Delta

1987. Tourism. Multicoloured.
5116 50b. Type **1034** 25 10
5117 1l. Cable car above Transfagarasan mountain road 25 10
5118 2l. Cheile Bicazului 45 10
5119 3l. Ceahlau mountains . . . 75 20
5120 4l. Lake Capra, Fagaras mountains 90 25
5121 5l. Borsa orchards . . . . . 1·10 35

1035 Henri August's Glider, 1909

1987. Air. Aircraft. Multicoloured.
5122 50b. Type **1035** 10 10
5123 1l. Sky diver jumping from IS-28 B2 glider 15 10
5124 2l. IS-29 D2 glider 25 15
5125 3l. IS-32 glider 50 15
5126 4l. I.A.R.35 light airplane 65 25
5127 5l. IS-28 M2 aircraft 90 30

1036 Youth on Winged Horse

1987. Fairy Tales by Petre Ispirescu. Multicoloured.
5128 50b. Type **1036** 10 15
5129 1l. King and princesses ("Salt in the Food") . . . 15 15
5130 2l. Girl on horse fighting lion ("Ileana Simziana") 25 15
5131 3l. Youth with bow and arrow aiming at bird ("The Youth and the Golden Apples") . . . 50 20
5132 4l. George and dead dragon ("George the Brave") . . 65 15
5133 5l. Girl looking at sleeping youth ("The Enchanted Pig") 90 20
MS5134 90 × 79 mm. 10l. Youth holding sun and moon ("Greuceanu") (41 × 53 mm) 3·50 3·50

1037 Class L 45H Diesel Shunter

1987. Railway Locomotives. Multicoloured.
5135 50b. Type **1037** 10 10
5136 1l. Class LDE 125 diesel goods locomotive 20 10
5137 2l. Class LDH 70 diesel goods locomotive 30 10
5138 3l. Class LDE 2100 diesel locomotive 50 20
5139 4l. Class LDE 3000 diesel locomotive 60 15
5140 5l. Class LE 5100 electric locomotive 80 20

1038 Alpine Columbine ("Aquelegia alpine")

1039 Bucharest Municipal Arms

1987. Nature Reserves in Europe. Two sheets, each 150 × 135 mm containing horiz designs as T **1038**. Multicoloured.
MS5141 Two sheets (a) 1l. × 12 Type **1038**; Pasque flower ("Pulsatilla vernalis"); Alpine aster ("Aster alpinus"); "Soldanell pusilla"; Ornage lily ("Lilium bulbiferum"); Alpine bearberry ("Arctostaphylos uva-ursi"); "Crocus vernus"; Golden hawksbeard ("Crepis aurea"); Lady's slipper ("Cypripedium calceolus"); "Centaurea nervosa"; Mountain avens ("Dryas octopetala"); "Gentiana excisa". (b) 1l. × 12 Pine martern ("Martes Martes"); Lynx ("Felis lynx"); Polar bear ("Ursus maritimus"); European otter ("Lutra lutra"); European bison ("Bison bonasus"); Red-breasted goose ("Branta ruficollis"); Greater flamingo ("Phoenicopterus rubber"); Great bustard ("Otis tarda"); Black grouse ("Lyrurus tetrix"); Lammergeier ("Gypaetus barbatus"); Marbled polecat ("Vormela peregusna"); White-headed duck ("Oxyura leucocephala") Set of 2 sheets 5·50 2·00

1987. "Philatelia '87" International Stamp Fair, Cologne. Sheet 79 × 109 mm containing T **1039** and similar design. Multicoloured.
MS5142 3l. Type **1039**; 3l. Cologne arms . . . . 4·00 2·00

1987. Costumes (2nd series). As T **999**. Mult.
5143 1l. Tirnave (female) 20 15
5144 1l. Tirnave (male) 20 15
5145 2l. Buzau (female) 35 15
5146 2l. Buzau (male) 35 15
5147 3l. Dobrogea (female) . . . 50 25
5148 3l. Dobrogea (male) 50 25
5149 4l. Ilfov (female) 65 25
5150 4l. Ilfov (male) 65 25

1040 Postal Services (½-size illustration)

1987. Stamp Day.
5151 **1040** 2l.(+1l.) multicoloured 50 30
No. 5151 includes the se-tenant premium-carrying tab shown in Type **1040**, the stamp and tab forming a composite design.

1041 Honey Bee on Flower

1987. Bee-keeping. Multicoloured.
5152 1l. Type **1041** 15 15
5153 2l. Honey bee, sunflowers and hives 45 15
5154 3l. Hives in Danube delta 50 25
5155 4l. Apiculture Complex, Bucharest 65 30

1042 Car behind Boy on Bicycle

1987. Road Safety. Multicoloured.
5156 50b. Type **1042** 10 15
5157 1l. Children using school crossing 10 15
5158 2l. Driver carelessly opening car door 15 15
5159 3l. Hand holding crossing sign and children using zebra crossing 55 25
5160 4l. Speedometer and crashed car 80 30
5161 5l. Child's face and speeding car . . . . 1·10 50

1043 Red Flag and Lenin

1987. 70th Anniv of Russian Revolution.
5162 **1043** 2l. multicoloured . . . 50 25

1044 Biathlon

1045 Crest and National Colours

1987. Winter Olympic Games, Calgary (1988). Multicoloured.
5163 50b. Type **1044** 10 15
5164 1l. Slalom 70 15
5165 1l.50 Ice hockey 15 15
5166 2l. Luge 15 15
5167 3l. Speed skating 30 15
5168 3l.50 Figure skating 55 25
5169 4l. Downhill skiing 60 30
5170 5l. Two-man bobsleigh . . . 75 40

1987. 40th Anniv of People's Republic.
5171 **1045** 2l. multicoloured . . . 40 35

1046 Pres. Ceausescu and Flags

1988. 70th Birthday and 55 Years of Revolutionary Activity of Pres. Ceausescu.
5172 **1046** 2l. multicoloured . . . 75 60

1047 Wide-necked Pot, Marginea

1988. Pottery. Multicoloured.
5173 50b. Type **1047** 10 10
5174 1l. Flask, Oboga 10 10
5175 2l. Jug and saucer, Horezu 20 10
5176 3l. Narrow-necked pot, Curtea de Arges 50 25
5177 4l. Jug, Birsa 70 25
5178 5l. Jug and plate, Vama . . 80 35

1048 "Santa Maria"

1988. Inter-European Cultural and Economic Co-operation. Two sheets, each 110 × 80 mm containing horiz designs as T **1048**. Multicoloured.
MS5179 Two sheets (a) 3l. × 4 Type **1048**; Dish aerials, Cheia earth station; Bucharest underground train; Airbus Industrie A320 jetliner. (b) 3l. × 4 Mail coach and horses; "ECS" satellite; Oltcit motor car; "ICE" express train Set of 2 sheets . . 10·50 10·50

1049 Ceramic Clock

1051 Constantin Brincoveanu

1050 West German Flag and Player kicking Ball into Net

1988. Clocks in Ploiesti Museum. Multicoloured.
5180 50b. Type **1049** 10 15
5181 1l.50 Gilt clock with sun at base 10 15
5182 2l. Clock with pastoral figure 20 15
5183 3l. Gilt clock surmounted by figure 50 15
5184 4l. Vase-shaped clock . . . 70 25
5185 5l. Clock surmounted by porcelain figures 80 40

1988. European Football Championship, West Germany. Two sheets each 110 × 80 mm containing horiz designs as T **1050**. Multicoloured.
MS5186 3l. × 4 Type **1050**; Goalkeeper diving to save ball and Spanish flag; Italian flag and player; Players and Danish flag. (b) 3l. × 4 English flag, referee and player; Players and Netherlands flag; Irish flag and players; Players and flag of U.S.S.R. Set of 2 sheets 10·50 10·50

1988. 300th Anniv of Election of Constantin Brincoveanu as Ruler of Wallachia.
5187 **1051** 2l. multicoloured . . . 35 25

1052 Gymnastics

1988. Olympic Games, Seoul (1st issue). Mult.
5188 50b. Type **1052** 10 15
5189 1l.50 Boxing 15 15
5190 2l. Lawn tennis 20 20
5191 3l. Judo 50 25
5192 4l. Running 70 35
5193 5l. Rowing 80 45
See also Nos. 5197/5204.

1053 Postal Emblems and Roses

1988. Romanian–Chinese Stamp Exhibition, Bucharest.
5194 **1053** 2l. multicoloured . . . 30 25

1054 Player and Wimbledon Centre Court

1988. "Grand Slam" Tennis Championships. Two sheets each 110 × 80 mm containing horiz designs as T **1054**. Multicoloured.
MS5195 (a) 3l. × 4 Type **1054**; Wimbledon match; Flushing Meadows match; Flushing Meadows centre courts, New York. (b) 3l. × 4 Melbourne centre court; Melbourne match; Roland Garros match; Roland Garros centre court, Paris Set of 2 sheets 10·50 10·50

1055 "Bowl of Flowers" (Stefan Luchian)

1988. "Praga '88" International Stamp Exhibition. Sheet 90 × 78 mm.
MS5196 **1055** 5l. multicoloured 2·50 2·50

1056 Running

1988. Olympic Games, Seoul (2nd issue). Mult.

5197	50b. Type **1056**	10	15
5198	1l. Canoeing	10	15
5199	1l.50 Gymnastics	10	15
5200	2l. Double kayak	15	15
5201	3l. Weightlifting	40	25
5202	3l.50 Swimming	45	25
5203	4l. Fencing	55	35
5204	5l. Double sculls	65	40

1057 "Oncidium lanceanum"

1988. Orchids. Two sheets, each 150 × 137 mm containing horiz designs as T **1057**. Multicoloured.
MS5205 (a) 1l. × 2 Type **1057**; "Cattleya trianae"; "Sophronitis cernua"; "Bulbophyllum lobbii"; "Lycaste cruenta"; "Mormolyce ringens"; "Phragmipedium schlimii"; "Angraecum atropurpurea"; "Dendrobium nobile"; "Oncidium splendidum". (b) 1l. × 12 "Brassavola perrinii"; "Paphiopedilum maudiae"; "Sophronitis coccinea"; "Vandopsis lissochiloides"; "Phalaenopsis lueddemanniana"; "Chysis bractescens"; "Cochleanthes discolor"; "Phalaenopsis amabilis"; "Pleione pricei"; "Sobralia macrantha"; "Aspasia lunata"; "Cattleya citrina" Set of 2 sheets 12·50 12·50

1058 Past and Present Postal Services (½-size illustration)

1988. Stamp Day.
5206 **1058** 2l.(+1l.) multicoloured 50 40
No. 5206 includes the se-tenant premium-carrying tab shown in T **1058**.

1059 Gymnastics and Three Gold Medals

1988. Seoul Olympic Games Romanian Medal Winners. Two sheets, each 110 × 80 mm containing horiz designs as T **1059**. Multicoloured.
MS5207 (a) 3l. × 4 Type **1059**; Pistol shooting and gold medal; Weightlifting and silver medal; Boxing and silver medal. (b) 3l. × 4 Athletics and silver medals; Swimming and silver medal; Wrestling and gold medal; Rowing and gold medal Set of 2 sheets 10·50 10·50

1060 State Arms

1988. 70th Anniv of Union of Transylvania and Romania.
5208 **1060** 2l. multicoloured 50 45

1061 Athenaeum Concert Hall, Bucharest (centenary)

1988. Romanian History. Multicoloured.

5209	50b. Type **1061**	10	15
5210	1l.50 Roman coin showing Drobeta Bridge	15	15
5211	2l. Ruins (600th anniv of Suceava as capital of Moldavian feudal state)	20	15
5212	3l. Scroll, arms and town (600th anniv of first documentary reference to Pitesti)	50	25
5213	4l. Dacian warriors from Trajan's Column	70	25
5214	5l. Thracian gold helmet from Cotofenesti-Prahova	80	35

1062 Zapodeni, 17th century

1989. Traditional House Architecture. Mult.

5215	50b. Type **1062**	10	15
5216	1l.50 Berbesti, 18th century	15	15
5217	2l. Voitinel, 18th century	20	15
5218	3l. Chiojdu Mic, 18th century	50	25
5219	4l. Cimpanii de Sus, 19th century	70	25
5220	5l. Naruja, 19th century	80	35

1063 Red Cross Worker

1989. Life-saving Services. Multicoloured.

5221	50b. Type **1063**	10	15
5222	1l. Red Cross orderlies giving first aid to girl (horiz)	10	15
5223	1l.50 Fireman carrying child	15	15
5224	2l. Rescuing child from earthquake damaged building	20	15
5225	3l. Mountain rescue team transporting casualty on sledge (horiz)	45	25
5226	3l.50 Rescuing climber from cliff face	55	25
5227	4l. Rescuing child from river	65	25
5228	5l. Lifeguard in rowing boat and children playing in sea (horiz)	75	35

1064 Tasca Bicaz Cement Factory

1989. Industrial Achievements. Multicoloured.

5229	50b. Type **1064**	15	10
5230	1l.50 New railway bridge, Cernavoda	35	10
5231	2l. Synchronous motor, Resita	35	15
5232	3l. Bucharest underground	40	20
5233	4l. Mangalia–Constanta train ferry	1·10	25
5234	5l. "Gloria" (oil drilling platform)	1·10	30

1065 Flags and Symbols of Industry and Agriculture

1988. 50th Anniv of Anti-Fascist Demonstration.
5235 2l. Type **1065** 60 40
MS5236 90 × 78 mm. 10l. Flag and demonstrators 3·50 3·50

1066 Roses

1989. "Bulgaria '89" International Stamp Exhibition, Sofia. Sheet 90 × 78 mm.
MS5237 **1066** 10l. multicoloured 3·50 3·50

1067 Girls playing with Dolls

1989. Inter-European Cultural and Economic Co-operation. Children. Two sheets, each 110 × 80 mm containing horiz designs as T **1067**.
MS5238 (a) 3l. × 4 Type **1067**; Playing football; On beach; Playing with toy cars. (b) 3l. × 4 Playing in sea; On slides; At playground; Flying kites Set of 2 sheets 10·50 10·50

1068 Ion Creanga (writer, death centenary)

1989. Anniversaries. Multicoloured.

5239	1l. Type **1068**	15	10
5240	2l. Mihai Eminescu (poet, death centenary)	25	10
5241	3l. Nicolae Teclu (scientist, 150th birth anniv)	60	10

1069 State and Communist Party Flags and Symbols of Industry and Agriculture

1989. 45th Anniv of Liberation.
5242 **1069** 2l. multicoloured 50 30

1070 "Pin-Pin"

1989. Romanian Cartoon Films. Multicoloured.

5243	50b. Type **1070**	10	15
5244	1l. "Maria"	10	15
5245	1l.50 "Gore and Grigore"	15	15
5246	2l. "Pisoiul, Balanel, Manole, Monk"	20	10
5247	3l. "Gruia lui Novac"	50	15
5248	3l.50 "Mihaela"	60	20
5249	4l. "Harap Alb"	65	25
5250	5l. "Homo Sapiens"	85	25

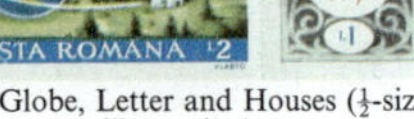

1071 Globe, Letter and Houses (½-size illustration)

1989. Stamp Day.
5251 **1071** 2l.(+1l.) multicoloured 45 20
No. 5251 includes the se-tenant premium-carrying tab as illustrated in T **1071**.

1072 Storming of the Bastille

1989. Bicentenary of French Revolution. Mult.

5252	50b. Type **1072**	10	10
5253	1l.50 Street boy and Marianne	15	10
5254	2l. Maximilien de Robespierre	20	10
5255	3l. Rouget de Lisle singing the "Marseillaise"	50	15
5256	4l. Denis Diderot (encyclopaedist)	70	20
5257	5l. Crowd with banner	85	25
MS5258	90 × 78 mm. 10l. "Philexfrance '89" International Stamp Exhibition emblem and Eiffel Tower (50 × 39 mm)	3·50	3·50

1073 Conrad Haas and Diagram

1989. Air. Space Pioneers. Multicoloured.

5259	50b. Type **1073**	10	10
5260	1l.50 Konstantin Tsiolkovski and diagram	20	10
5261	2l. Hermann Oberth and equation	30	10
5262	3l. Robert Goddard and diagram	45	10
5263	4l. Sergei Pavlovich Korolev, Earth and satellite	70	20
5264	5l. Wernher von Braun and landing module	85	25

1074 Horse-drawn Mail Coach

1989. Air. "World Stamp Expo '89" International Stamp Exhibition, Washington D.C. Sheet 90 × 77 mm.
MS5265 **1074** 5l. multicoloured 3·50 3·50

1075 State and Party Flags and Emblem

1989. 14th Communist Party Congress, Bucharest.
5266 **1075** 2l. multicoloured . . . 60 40
MS5267 77 × 89 mm. 10l. multicoloured . . . . 4·00 4·00
DESIGNS: 10l. Party emblem and "XIV".

1076 Date, Flag, Victory Sign and Candles

1990. Popular Uprising (1st issue).
5268 **1076** 2l. multicoloured . . . 35 10
See also Nos. 5294/5301.

1077 Flags and Footballers

1990. World Cup Football Championship, Italy (1st issue).
5269 **1077** 50b. multicoloured . . 10 15
5270 – 1l.50 multicoloured . . 20 15
5271 – 2l. multicoloured . . . 35 15
5272 – 3l. multicoloured . . . 50 25
5273 – 4l. multicoloured . . . 80 30
5274 – 5l. multicoloured . . . 1·00 40
DESIGNS: 1l.50 to 5l. Showing flags and footballers.
See also Nos. 5276/83.

1078 Penny Black and Moldavian 27p. Stamp

1990. "Stamp World London '90" International Stamp Exhibition. Sheet 90 × 78 mm.
MS5275 **1078** 10l. multicoloured 4·50 4·50

1079 Footballers

1990. World Cup Football Championship, Italy (2nd issue).
5276 **1079** 50b. multicoloured . . 10 15
5277 – 1l. multicoloured . . . 15 15
5278 – 1l.50 multicoloured . . 20 15
5279 – 2l. multicoloured . . . 30 15
5280 – 3l. multicoloured . . . 45 25
5281 – 3l.50 multicoloured . . 20 10
5282 – 4l. multicoloured . . . 30 10
5283 – 5l. multicoloured . . . 20 10
DESIGNS: 1l. to 5l. Different football scenes.

1080 German Shepherds

1990. International Dog Show, Brno. Mult.
5284 50b. Type **1080** 10 15
5285 1l. English setter 20 15
5286 1l.50 Boxers 25 15
5287 2l. Beagles 30 15
5288 3l. Dobermann pinschers . . 50 20
5289 3l.50 Great Danes 55 30
5290 4l. Afghan hounds 60 30
5291 5l. Yorkshire terriers 75 30

1081 Fountain, Brunnen

1990. "Riccione 90" International Stamp Fair.
5292 **1081** 2l. multicoloured . . . 30 15

1082 Athenaeum Concert Hall, Bucharest, and Chinese Temple

1990. Romanian–Chinese Stamp Exhibition, Bucharest.
5293 **1082** 2l. multicoloured . . . 30 15

1083 Soldiers and Crowd at Television Headquarters, Bucharest

1990. Popular Uprising (2nd issue). Multicoloured.
5294 50b.+50b. Republic Palace ablaze, Bucharest (horiz) 10 15
5295 1l.+1l. Crowd in Opera Square, Timisoara 15 15
5296 1l.50+1l. Soldiers joining crowd in Town Hall Square, Tirgu Mures (horiz) 20 15
5297 2l.+1l. Type **1083** 25 15
5298 3l.+1l. Mourners at funeral, Timisoara (horiz) 30 20
5299 3l.50+1l. Crowd celebrating, Brasov 40 20
5300 4l.+1l. Crowd with banners, Sibiu (horiz) 40 30
5301 5l.+2l. Cemetery, Bucharest (horiz) 60 35
MS5302 90 × 78 mm. 5l.+2l. Foreign aid (53 × 41 mm) . . . . . . 3·00 3·00

1084 "Nicolae Cobzarul" (Stefan Luchian)

1990. Paintings damaged during the Uprising. Mult.
5303 50b. Type **1084** 25 10
5304 1l.50 "Woman in White" (Ion Andreescu) 20 10
5305 2l. "Florist" (Luchian) . . . 25 10
5306 3l. "Vase of Flowers" (Jan Brueghel, the elder) . . . 40 20
5307 4l. "Spring" (Pieter Brueghel, the elder) (horiz) 55 25
5308 5l. "Madonna and Child" (G. B. Paggi) 65 30

1085 Flag Stamps encircling Globe (⅔-size illustration)

1990. Stamp Day.
5309 **1085** 2l.(+1l.) multicoloured 40 20
No. 5309 includes the se-tenant premium-carrying tab as shown in Type **1085**.

1086 Constantin Cantacuzino (historian, 350th birth anniv)

1087 Column of Infinity

1990. Anniversaries.
5310 **1086** 50b. brown and blue . . 10 10
5311 – 1l.50 green and mauve 20 10
5312 – 2l. red and blue 25 10
5313 – 3l. blue and brown . . 40 15
5314 – 4l. brown and blue . . 55 20
5315 – 5l. violet and green . . 70 25
DESIGNS: 1l.50, Ienachita Vacarescu (writer, 250th birth anniv); 2l. Titu Maiorescu (politician, 150th birth anniv); 3l. Nicolae Iorga (historian, 50th death anniv); 4l. Martha Bibescu (writer, birth centenary); 5l. Stefan Procupiu (scientist, birth centenary).

1990. National Day.
5316 **1087** 2l. multicoloured . . . 30 10

1990. 1st Anniv of Popular Uprising. No. 5268 surch **L4 UN AN DE LA VICTORIA REVOLUTIEI**.
5317 **1076** 4l. on 2l. multicoloured 60 20

1089 "Irises"

1991. Death Centenary of Vincent van Gogh (painter). Multicoloured.
5318 50b. Type **1089** 10 10
5319 2l. "The Artist's Room" . . 10 10
5320 3l. "Illuminated Coffee Terrace" (vert) 20 10
5321 3l.50 "Orchard in Blossom" 30 10
5322 5l. "Sunflowers" (vert) . . . 40 10

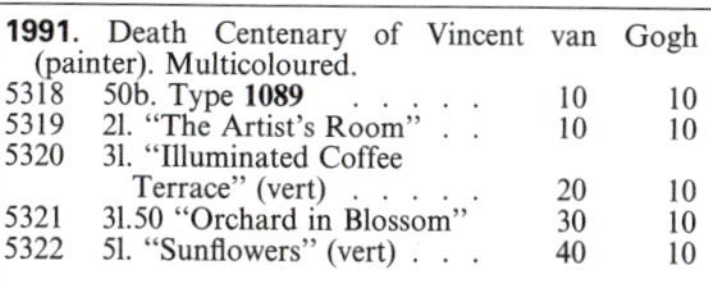

1090 Greater Black-backed Gull
1091 Crucifixion

1991. Water Birds.
5323 **1090** 50b. blue 10 10
5324 – 1l. green 10 10
5325 – 1l.50 bistre 10 10
5326 – 2l. blue 15 10
5327 – 3l. green 25 10
5328 – 3l.50 green 30 10
5329 – 4l. violet 35 10
5330 – 5l. brown 35 10
5331 – 6l. brown 50 10
5332 – 7l. blue 60 15
DESIGNS: 1l. Common tern; 1l.50, Pied avocet; 2l. Pomarine skua; 3l. Northern lapwings; 3l.50, Red-breasted merganser; 4l. Little egret; 5l. Dunlin; 6l. Black- tailed godwit; 7l. Whiskered tern.

1991. Easter.
5333 **1091** 4l. multicoloured . . . 20 10

1092 "Eutelsat 1" Communications Satellite

1991. Europa. Europe in Space.
5334 **1092** 4l.50 multicoloured . . 35 20

1093 Posthorn

1094 Rings Exercise

1991.
5335 **1093** 4l.50 blue 25 10

1991. Gymnastics. Multicoloured.
5336 1l. Type **1094** 10 15
5337 1l. Parallel bars 10 15
5338 4l.50 Vaulting 30 15
5339 4l.50 Asymmetric bars . . . 30 15
5340 8l. Floor exercises 45 25
5341 9l. Beam 55 30
For similar design to No. 5341, surcharged 90l. on 5l., see No. 5431.

1095 Curtea de Arges Monastery

1096 Hotel Continental, Timisoara

1991. Monasteries. Multicoloured.
5342 1l. Type **1095** 10 10
5343 1l. Putna 10 10
5344 4l.50 Varatec 30 10

5345	4l.50 Agapia (horiz)	30	10
5346	8l. Golia (horiz)	45	10
5347	9l. Sucevita (horiz)	55	10

1991. Hotels.

5349	**1096**	1l. blue	05	10
5350	–	2l. green	10	10
5351	–	4l. red	15	10
5352	–	5l. violet	30	10
5353	–	6l. brown	20	10
5354	–	8l. brown	15	10
5355	–	9l. red	50	10
5356	–	10l. green	55	10
5357	–	18l. red	65	10
5358	–	20l. orange	65	10
5359	–	25l. blue	90	10
5360	–	30l. purple	1·50	10
5361	–	45l. blue	1·00	10
5362	–	60l. brown	1·20	10
5363	–	80l. violet	1·50	10
5364b	–	120l. blue and grey	1·80	50
5365	–	160l. red and pink	2·30	40
5366	–	250l. blue and grey	2·75	50
5367	–	400l. brown and ochre	5·00	95
5368	–	500l. deep green & green	6·50	1·10
5369	–	800l. mauve and pink	9·00	1·80

DESIGNS—As T **1096**: HORIZ: 2l. Valea Caprei Chalet, Mt. Fagaras; 5l. Hotel Lebada, Crisan; 6l. Muntele Rosu Chalet, Mt. Ciucas; 8l. Trans-silvania Hotel, Cluj-Napoca; 9l. Hotel Orizont, Predeal; 20l. Alpin Hotel, Poiana Brasov; 25l. Constanta Casino; 30l. Miorita Chalet, Mt. Bucegi; 45l. Sura Dacilor Chalet, Poiana Brasov; 60l. Valea Draganului Tourist Complex; 80l. Hotel Florica, Venus. VERT: 4l. Intercontinental Hotel, Bucharest; 10l. Hotel Roman, Baile Herculcane; 18l. Rarau Chalet, Mt. Rarau. 26 × 40 mm: 120l. International Complex, Baile Felix; 160l. Hotel Egreta, Tulcea. 40 × 26 mm: 250l. Valea de Pesti Motel, Jiului Valley; 400l. Baisoara Tourist Complex; 500l. Bradul Hotel, Covasna; 800l. Gorj Hotel, Jiu.

Nos. 5362/9 have no frame.

1097 Gull and Sea Shore

1991. "Riccione 91" Stamp Exhibition, Riccione, Italy.

5381	**1097**	4l. multicoloured	20	10

1098 Vase decorated with Scarlet and Military Macaws

1099 Academy Emblem

1991. Romanian–Chinese Stamp Exhibition. Mult.

5382	5l. Type **1098**	40	10
5383	5l. Vase with peony decoration	40	10

1991. 125th Anniv of Romanian Academy.

5384	**1099**	1l. blue	15	10

1100 "Flowers" (Nicu Enea)

1101 Red-Billed Blue Magpie ("Casa erythorhynchai")

1991. "Balcanfila '91" Stamp Exhibition, Bacau. Multicoloured.

5385	4l. Type **1100**	20	10
5386	5l.(+2l.) "Peasant Girl of Vlasca" (Georghe Tattarescu)	35	10
MS5387	90 × 77 mm. 20l. Exhibition venue (53 × 41 mm)	1·50	1·50

1991. Birds. Two sheets, each 136 × 150 mm containing vert designs as T **1101**. Multicoloured.

MS5388 (a) 2l. × 12 Type **1101**; Grey-headed bush shrike ("Malaconotus blanchoti"); Eastern bluebird ("Sialia sialis"); Western meadowlark ("Sturnella neglecta"); Malabar trogon ("Harpactes fasciatus"); Hoopoe ("Upupa epops"); Blue wren ("Malurus cyaneus"); Scaly ground roller ("Brachypterus squamigera"); Blue vanga ("Leptopterus madagascariensis"); White-headed wood hoopoe ("Phoeniculus bollei"); Red-headed woodpecker ("Melanerpes erythrocephalus"); Scarlet minivet ("Pericrocotus flammeus"). (b) 2l. × 12 Golden-backed honeyeater ("Melithreptus laetior"); Kagu ("Rhynochetos jubata"); American robin ("Turdus migratorius"); Magpie robin ("Copsychus saularis"); Rock thrush ("Monticola saxatilis"); Yellow-headed blackbird ("Xanthocephalus xanthocephalus"); Pel's fishing owl ("Scotopelia peli"); Long-tailed silky flycatcher ("Ptilogonys caudatus"); Puerto Rican tody ("Todus mexicanus"); White-rumped shama ("Copsychus malabaricus"); Mangrove red-headed honeyeater ("Myzomela erythrocephala"); Montezuma oropendola ("Gymnostinops montezuma") Set of 2 sheets 3·25 2·10

1102 Map with House and People

1991. Population and Housing Census.

5389	**1102**	5l. multicoloured	25	10

1103 Bridge

1991. "Phila Nippon '91" International Stamp Exhibition, Tokyo.

5390	**1103**	10l. ochre, brown & red	45	15
5391	–	10l. multicoloured	45	15

DESIGN: No. 5391, Junk.

1104 Isabel ("Graellsia isabellae")

1991. Butterflies and Moths. Two sheets, each 155 × 36 mm containing horiz designs as T **1104**. Multicoloured.

MS5392 (a) 3l. × 12 Type **1104**; Orange-tip ("Antocharis cardamines"); Hebe tiger moth ("Ammobiota festiva"); Comma ("Polygonia c-album"); "Catocala promisa"; Purple tiger moth ("Phyparia purpurata"); "Arctica villica"; "Polyommatus daphnis"; Southern festoon ("Zerynthia polyxena"); Oleander hawk moth ("Daphnis nerii"); "Licaena dispar rutila"; "Parage roxelana". (b) 3l. × 12 Paradise birdwing ("Ornithoptera paradisea"); Bhutan glory ("Bhutanitis lidderdalii"); "Morpho Helena"; "Ornithoptera croesus"; Red-splashed sulphur ("Phoebis avellaneda"); Queen Victoria's birdwing ("Ornithoptera victoriae"); Kaiser-i-hind ("Teinopalpus imperialis"); "Hypolimnas dexithea"; "Dabasa payeni"; "Morpho achilleana"; "Heliconius melpomene"; "Agrias claudina sardanapalus" Set of 2 sheets 6·00 6·00

1105 Running

1106 Mihail Kogalniceanu (policitian and historian, death cent)

1991. World Athletics Championships, Tokyo. Multicoloured.

5393	1l. Type **1105**	10	10
5394	4l. Long jumping	20	10
5395	5l. High jumping	25	10
5396	5l. Athlete in starting blocks	25	10
5397	9l. Hurdling	45	20
5398	10l. Throwing the javelin	55	20

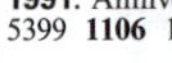

1991. Anniversaries.

5399	**1106**	1l. brown, blue & dp blue	10	10
5400	–	4l. green, lilac and violet	20	10
5401	–	5l. brown, blue & ultramarine	25	10
5402	–	5l. blue, brown and red	35	10
5403	–	9l. red, blue & deep blue	60	20
5404	–	10l. black, lt brn & brn	70	20

DESIGNS: No. 5400, Nicolae Titulescu (politician and diplomat, 50th death anniv); 5401, Andrei Mureseanu (poet, 175th birth anniv); 5402, Aron Pumnul (writer, 125th death anniv); 5403, George Bacovia (writer, 110th birth anniv); 5404, Perpessicius (literature critic, birth centenary).

1107 Library Building

1991. Centenary of Central University Library.

5405	**1107**	8l. brown	50	20

1108 Coach and Horses (⅔-size illustration)

1991. Stamp Day.

5406	**1108**	8l.(+2l.) multicoloured	45	30

No. 5406 includes the se-tenant premium-carrying label shown in Type **1108**.

1109 "Nativity" (17th-century icon)

1110 Biathlon

1991. Christmas.

5407	**1109**	8l. multicoloured	45	20

1992. Winter Olympic Games, Albertville. Mult.

5408	4l. Type **1110** (postage)	10	10
5409	5l. Downhill skiing	10	10
5410	8l. Cross-country skiing	15	10
5411	10l. Two-man luge	20	10
5412	20l. Speed skating	45	10
5413	25l. Ski-jumping	60	20

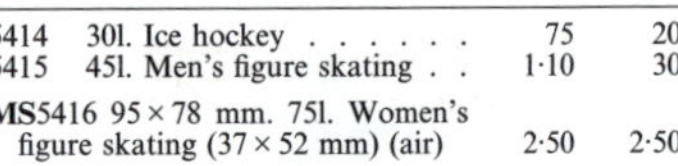

5414	30l. Ice hockey	75	20
5415	45l. Men's figure skating	1·10	30
MS5416	95 × 78 mm. 75l. Women's figure skating (37 × 52 mm) (air)	2·50	2·50

1112 Jug, Plate, Tray and Bowl

1992. Romanian Porcelain from Cluj Napoca. Multicoloured.

5419	4l. Type **1112**	10	15
5420	5l. Tea set	10	15
5421	8l. Jug and goblet (vert)	10	15
5422	30l. Tea set (different)	50	20
5423	45l. Vase (vert)	70	35

1113 Atlantic Mackerels

1992. Fishes. Multicoloured.

5424	4l. Type **1113**	10	15
5425	5l. Tench	10	15
5426	8l. Brook charr	10	15
5427	10l. Romanian bullhead perch	10	15
5428	30l. Nase	45	25
5429	45l. Black Sea red mullet	90	40

1114 Vase decorated with Scarlet and Military Macaws

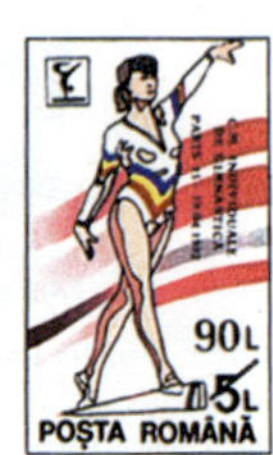

1115 Gymnast on Beam

1992. Apollo Art Gallery. Unissued stamp surch.

5430	**1114**	90l. on 5l. multicoloured	1·60	40

1992. Individual Gymnastic Championships, Paris. Unissued stamp surch.

5431	**1115**	90l. on 5l. multicoloured	1·20	40

For similar 9l. value, see No. 5341.

1116 Dressage

1118 "Descent into Hell" (icon)

1117 Columbus and "Santa Maria"

1992. Horses. Multicoloured.

5432	6l. Type **1116**	10	10
5433	7l. Racing (horiz)	10	10
5434	10l. Rearing	15	10
5435	25l. Jumping gate	35	10
5436	30l. Stamping foot (horiz)	40	20
5437	50l. Winged horse	75	25

1992. Europa. 500th Anniv of Discovery of America by Columbus. Sheet 130×88 mm containing T **1117** and similar horiz designs. Multicoloured.
MS5438 35l. Type **1117**; 35l. Columbus (hatless) and "Nina" at sea; 35l. Columbus (in hat) and "Pinta"; 35l. Columbus, "Santa Maria" and island . . . . . . 2·75 2·75

1992. Easter.
5439 **1118** 10l. multicoloured . . . 15 10

1119 Emblem

1992. "Granada '92" International Thematic Stamp Exhibition. Sheet 122×72 mm containing T **1119** and similar vert designs.
MS5440 10l. red, emerald and black; 25l. multicoloured; 30l. multicoloured . . . . 1·50 1·50
DESIGNS: 25l. Spanish 1850 6c. and Moldavian 1858 27p. stamps; 30l. Courtyard, Alhambra.

1120 Tower and Hand Pump

1992. Centenary of Bucharest Fire Tower.
5441 **1120** 10l. multicoloured . . . 20 10

1121 Filipino Vinta and Rook

1992. 30th Chess Olympiad, Manila, Philippines. Multicoloured.

5442	10l. Type **1121**	15	10
5443	10l. Exterior of venue and chessmen	15	10
MS5444	91×79 mm. 75l. Chessboard on beach (41×53 mm)	1·75	1·75

1122 Post Rider approaching Town

1992. Stamp Day.
5445 **1122** 10l.+4l. pink, violet and blue 15 10

1123 Pistol shooting **1124** Ion Bratianu

1992. Olympic Games, Barcelona. Multicoloured.

5446	6l. Type **1123**	10	10
5447	7l. Weightlifting	10	10
5448	9l. Two-man kayak (horiz)	10	10
5449	10l. Handball	10	10
5450	25l. Wrestling (horiz)	20	15
5451	30l. Fencing (horiz)	25	20
5452	50l. Running	45	30
5453	55l. Boxing (horiz)	50	30
MS5454	90×79 mm. 100l. Rowing (50×39 mm)	1·25	1·25

1992. 130th Anniv of Foreign Ministry. Designs showing former Ministers.

5455 **1124**	10l. violet, green and deep green	10	05
5456 –	25l. purple, blue & dp blue	20	10
5457 –	30l. blue, purple & brn	25	10

DESIGNS: 25l. Ion Duca; 30l. Grigore Gafencu.

1125 "The Thinker of Cernavoda" (sculpture)

1992. "Expo 92" World's Fair, Seville. "Era of Discovery". Multicoloured.

5458	6l. Type **1125**	10	10
5459	7l. Trajan's bridge, Turnu-Severin	10	10
5460	10l. House on stilts	10	10
5461	25l. Saligny Bridge, Cernavoda	35	10
5462	30l. Traian Vuia's No. 1 airplane	35	10
5463	55l. Hermann Oberth's rocket	25	15
MS5464	79×91 mm. 100l. "Kneeling Figure" (sculpture, Constantin Brancusi) (41×49 mm)	75	75

1126 Doves posting Letters in Globe

1992. World Post Day.
5465 **1126** 10l. multicoloured . . . 15 10

1127 "Santa Maria" and Bust of Columbus

1992. 500th Anniv of Discovery of America by Columbus. Multicoloured.

5466	6l. Type **1127**	15	10
5467	10l. "Nina"	15	10
5468	25l. "Pinta"	25	10
5469	55l. Columbus claiming New World	35	20
MS5470	91×79 mm. 100l. Columbus and "Santa Maria" (38×51 mm)	75	75

1128 Post Office Emblem

1992. 1st Anniv of Establishment of R.A. Posta Romana (postal organization).
5471 **1128** 10l. multicoloured . . . 15 10

1129 Jacob Negruzzi (writer, 150th birth anniv) **1130** American Bald Eagle

1992. Anniversaries.

5472 **1129**	6l. green and violet	10	10
5473 –	7l. mauve, purple and green	10	10
5474 –	9l. blue and mauve	10	10
5475 –	10l. light brown, brown and blue	10	10
5476 –	25l. blue and brown	20	15
5477 –	30l. green and blue	20	15

DESIGNS: 7l. Grigore Antipa (biologist, 125th birth anniv); 9l. Alexe Mateevici (poet, 75th death anniv); 10l. Cezar Petrescu (writer, birth centenary); 25l. Octav Onicescu (mathematician, birth centenary); 30l. Ecaterina Teodoroiu (First World War fighter, 75th death anniv).

1992. Animals. Multicoloured.

5478	6l. Type **1130**	10	15
5479	7l. Spotted owl	10	15
5480	9l. Brown bear	15	15
5481	10l. American black oystercatcher (horiz)	15	15
5482	25l. Wolf (horiz)	25	15
5483	30l. White-tailed deer (horiz)	25	15
5484	55l. Elk (horiz)	50	30
MS5485	91×80 mm. 100l. Killer whale ("Orcinus orca") (horiz)	75	75

1131 Arms **1133** Nativity

1132 Buildings and Street, Mogosoaiei

1992. New State Arms.
5486 **1131** 15l. multicoloured . . . 15 10

1992. Anniversaries. Multicoloured.

5487	7l. Type **1132** (300th anniv)	10	10
5488	9l. College building and statue, Roman (600th anniv)	10	10
5489	10l. Prince Basaral, monastery and Princess Despina (475th anniv of Curtea de Arges Monastery)	10	10
5490	25l. Bucharest School of Architecture (80th anniv)	20	10

1992. Christmas.
5491 **1133** 15l. multicoloured . . . 15 10

1134 Globe and Key-pad on Telephone

1992. New Telephone Number System.
5492 **1134** 15l. black, red and blue 15 10

1135 Woman's Gymnastics (two gold medals)

1992. Romanian Medals at Olympic Games, Barcelona. Two sheets, each 110×80 mm containing horiz designs as T **1135**. Multicoloured.
MS5493 (a) 35l. ×4 Type **1135**; Rowing (two gold medals); Fencing and bronze medal; High jumping and silver medal. (b) 35l. ×4 Shooting and bronze medal; Bronze medal and wrestling; Weightlifting and bronze medal; Bronze medal and boxing. Set of 2 sheets . . . . 3·00 3·00

1136 Mihai Voda Monastery

1993. Destroyed Bucharest Buildings. Mult.

5494	10l. Type **1136**	10	10
5495	15l. Vacaresti Monastery	10	10
5496	25l. Unirii Hall	20	10
5497	30l. Mina Minovici Medico-legal Institute	30	10

1137 Parseval Sigsfeld Kite-type Observation Balloon "Draken"

1993. Air. Balloons. Multicoloured.

5498	30l. Type **1137**	15	15
5499	90l. Caquot observation balloon, 1917	50	15

1138 Crucifixion **1139** Hawthorn

1993. Easter.
5500 **1138** 15l. multicoloured . . . 15 10

1993. Medicinal Plants. Multicoloured.

5501	10l. Type **1139**	10	10
5502	15l. Gentian	10	10
5503	25l. Sea buckthorn	10	10
5504	30l. Billberry	15	10
5505	50l. Arnica	25	20
5506	90l. Dog rose	45	30

1140 Stanescu **1141** Mounted Courier

1993. 60th Birth Anniv of Nichita Stanescu (poet).
5507 **1140** 15l. multicoloured . . . 15 10

1993. Stamp Day.
5508 **1141** 15l.+10l. multicoloured 15 10

1142 Exhibition Venue

1993. "Polska '93" International Stamp Exhibition, Poznan. Sheet 90 × 78 mm.

MS5509	**1142**	200l. multicoloured	1·10	1·10

1143 Black-billed Magpie

1993. Birds.

5510	**1143**	5l. black and green	15	10
5511	–	10l. black and red	15	10
5512	–	15l. black and red	15	10
5513	–	20l. black and brown	20	10
5514	–	25l. black and red	20	10
5515	–	50l. black and yellow	40	10
5516	–	65l. black and red	55	10
5517	–	90l. black and red	75	10
5518	–	160l. black and blue	1·30	15
5519	–	250l. black and mauve	2·10	25

DESIGNS—HORIZ: 10l. Golden eagle. VERT: 15l. Northern bullfinch; 20l. Hoopoe; 25l. Great spotted woodpecker; 50l. Golden oriole; 65l. White winged crossbill; 90l. Barn swallows; 160l. Azure tit; 250l. Rose-coloured starling.

1144 Long-hair

1145 "Lola Artists' Sister" (Pablo Picasso)

1993. Cats. Multicoloured.

5520	10l. Type **1144**		10	20
5521	15l. Tabby-point long-hair		10	20
5522	30l. Red long-hair		15	20
5523	90l. Blue Persian		35	30
5524	135l. Tabby		55	25
5525	160l. Long-haired white Persian		65	30

1993. Europa. Contemporary Art. Sheet 75 × 105 mm containing T **1145** and similar vert designs. Multicoloured.

MS5526	280l. Type **1145**; 280l. "World Inception" (sculpture, Constantin Brancusi); 280l. "Girl with Idol" (sculpture, Ion Irimescu); 280l. "Woman in Grey" (Alexandru Ciucurencu)	2·75	2·75

1146 Adder

1993. Protected Animals. Multicoloured.

5527	10l. Type **1146**	10	15
5528	15l. Lynx (vert)	10	15
5529	25l. Common shelduck	15	15
5530	75l. Huchen	25	15
5531	105l. Poplar admiral	35	20
5532	280l. Alpine longhorn beetle	95	70

1147 Pine Marten

1993. Mammals.

5533	**1147**	10l. black and yellow	20	10
5534	–	15l. black and brown	20	10
5535	–	20l. red and black	20	10
5536	–	25l. black and brown	25	10
5537	–	30l. black and red	25	10
5538	–	40l. black and red	25	10
5539	–	75l. black and yellow	55	10
5540	–	105l. black and brown	75	10
5541	–	150l. black and orange	1·10	10
5542	–	280l. black and yellow	1·80	25

DESIGNS—HORIZ: 15l. Common rabbit; 30l. Red fox; 150l. Stoat; 280l. Egyptian mongoose. VERT: 20l. Eurasian red squirrel; 25l. Chamois; 40l. Argali; 75l. Small spotted genet; 105l. Garden dormouse.

1148 Brontosaurus

1993. Prehistoric Animals. Multicoloured.

5543	29l. Type **1148**	10	15
5544	46l. Plesiosaurus	15	15
5545	85l. Triceratops	30	15
5546	171l. Stegosaurus	60	25
5547	216l. Tyannosaurus	80	30
5548	319l. Archaeopteryx	1·10	55

1149 "Woman selling Eggs" (Marcel Iancul)

1993. "Telafila 93" Israel–Romanian Stamp Exhibition, Tel Aviv. Sheet 90 × 78 mm.

MS5549	**1149**	535l. multicoloured	1·75	1·75

1150 St. Stefan the Great, Prince of Moldavia

1151 Mounted Officers

1993. Icons. Multicoloured.

5550	75l. Type **1150**	15	20
5551	171l. Prince Costantin Brancoveanu of Wallachia with his sons Constantin, Stefan, Radu and Matei and Adviser Ianache Vacarescu	15	20
5552	216l. St. Antim Ivireanul, Metropolitan of Wallachia	80	20

1993. Centenary of Rural Gendarmerie Law.

5553	**1151**	29l. multicoloured	15	10

1993. "Riccione 93" International Stamp Fair. No. 5292 surch **Riccione '93 3-5 septembrie 171L**.

5554	**1081**	171l. on 2l. multicoloured	60	40

1153 Temple Roof

1993. "Bangkok 1993" International Stamp Exhibition. Sheet 79 × 90 mm.

MS5555	**1153**	535l. multicoloured	1·75	1·75

1154 George Baritiu

1993. Anniversaries.

5556	**1154**	29l. flesh, black and lilac	10	15
5557	–	46l. flesh, black and blue	10	15
5558	–	85l. flesh, black & green	15	15
5559	–	171l. flesh, black & purple	25	25
5560	–	216l. flesh, black & blue	40	30
5561	–	319l. flesh, black and grey	75	40

DESIGNS: 29l. Type **1154** (politician and journalist, death centenary); 46l. Horia Creanga (architect, 50th death anniv); 85l. Armand Calinescu (leader of Peasant National Party, birth centenary); 171l. Dr. Dumitru Bagdasar (neuro-surgeon, birth centenary); 216l. Constantin Brailoiu (musician, birth centenary); 319l. Iuliu Maniu (Prime Minister, 1927–30 and 1932–33, 40th death anniv).

1993. 35th Annivs of Romanian Philatelic Association and Romanian Philatelic Federation. No. 5445 surch **35 ANI DE ACTIVITATE AFR-FFR 1958–1993 70L+45L**.

5562	**1122**	70l.+45l. on 10l.+4l. pink, violet and blue	50	40

1156 Map, National Flag and Council Emblem

1993. Admission to Council of Europe. Sheet 90 × 78 mm.

MS5563	**1156**	1590l. multicoloured	3·50	3·50

1157 Iancu Flondor (Bukovinan politician)

1993. 75th Anniv of Union of Bessarabia, Bukovina and Transylvania with Romania.

5564	**1157**	115l. brown, blue and black	15	10
5565	–	245l. violet, yellow and green	25	20
5566	–	255l. multicoloured	45	20
5567	–	325l. brown, pink and deep brown	80	25
MS5568		90 × 78 mm. 1060l. multicoloured (map in several shades of brown) (41 × 53 mm)	6·00	6·00

DESIGNS: 245l. Ionel Bratianu (Prime Minister 1918–19, 1922–26 and 1027; 255l. Iuliu Maniu (Prime Minister, 1927–30 and 1932–33); 325l. Pantelemon Halippa (Bessarabian politician); 1060l, King Ferdinand I and map.

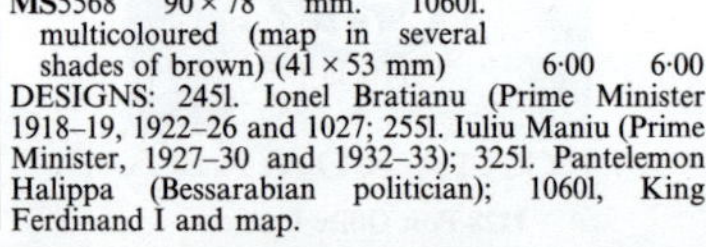

1158 Emblem

1159 "Nativity" (17th-century icon)

1993. Anniversaries. Multicoloured.

5569	115l. Type **1158** (75th anniv of General Association of Romanian Engineers)	15	20
5570	245l. Statue of Johannes Honterus (450th anniv of Romanian Humanist School)	25	25
5571	255l. Bridge, arms on book spine and seal (625th anniv of first documentary reference to Slatina)	40	25
5572	325l. Map and town arms (625th anniv of first documentary reference to Braila)	75	35

1993. Christmas.

5573	**1159**	45l. multicoloured	15	10

1160 "Clivina subterranea"

1993. Movile Cave Animals. Multicoloured.

5574	29l. Type **1160**	10	10
5575	46l. "Nepa anophthalma"	15	10
5576	85l. "Haemopis caeca"	20	15
5577	171l. "Lascona cristiani"	30	20
5578	216l. "Semisalsa dobrogica"	45	25
5579	319l. "Armadilidium tabacarui"	75	35
MS5580	90 × 78 mm. 535l. Diver exploring cave (41 × 53 mm)	1·50	1·50

1161 Prince Alexandru Ioan Cuza and Seal

1994. 130th Anniv of Court of Accounts.

5581	**1161**	45l. multicoloured	15	10

1162 Opera House

1994. Destroyed Buildings of Bucharest. Mult.

5582	115l. Type **1162**	10	15
5583	245l. Church of Vacaresti Monastery (vert)	30	25
5584	255l. St. Vineri's Church	35	25
5585	325l. Cloisters of Vacaresti Monastery	50	30

1164 Speed Skating

1165 Sarichioi Windmill, Tulcea

1994. Winter Olympic Games, Lillehammer, Norway. Multicoloured.
5588 70l. Type **1164** 10 10
5589 115l. Skiing 15 10
5590 125l. Bobsleighing 15 10
5591 245l. Cross-country skiing . . . 40 15
5592 255l. Ski jumping 45 15
5593 325l. Figure skating 60 20
MS5594 90 × 78 mm. 1590l. Single luge (41 × 53 mm) (air) . . . . 3·50 3·50

1994. Mills. Multicoloured.
5595 70l. Type **1165** 10 15
5596 115l. Nucarilor Valley windmill, Tulcea 10 15
5597 125l. Caraorman windmill, Tulcea 20 15
5598 245l. Romanii de Jos watermill, Valcea 40 25
5599 255l. Enisala windmill, Tulcea (horiz) 50 30
5600 325l. Nistoresti watermill, Vrancea 60 40

1166 Calin the Backward

1167 "Resurrection of Christ" (17th-century icon)

1994. Fairy Tales. Multicoloured.
5601 70l. Type **1166** 10 15
5602 115l. Ileana Cosanzeana flying 15 15
5603 125l. Ileana Cosanzeana seated 20 15
5604 245l. Ileana Cosanzeana and castle 40 25
5605 255l. Agheran the Brave . . 50 30
5606 325l. The Enchanted Wolf carrying Ileana Cosanzeana 60 35

1994. Easter.
5607 **1167** 60l. multicoloured . . . 15 10

1168 "Struthiosaurus transylvanicus"

1994. Prehistoric Animals. Multicoloured.
5608 90l. Type **1168** 10 15
5609 130l. Megalosaurus 15 15
5610 150l. Parasaurolophus . . . 30 15
5611 280l. Stenonychosaurus . . 30 20
5612 500l. Camarasaurus 55 40
5613 635l. Gallimimus 70 45

1169 Hermann Oberth (rocket designer)

1994. Europa. Inventions. Sheet 109 × 78 mm containing T **1169** and similar horiz design.
MS5614 240l. blue, indigo and black; 2100l. blue and black . . 2·75 2·75
DESIGN: 2100l. Henri Coanda (airplane designer).

1170 Silver Fir

1171 Players and Flags of U.S.A., Switzerland, Colombia and Romania

1994. Trees. Each green and black.
5615 15l. Type **1170** 10 10
5616 35l. Scots pine 10 10
5617 45l. White poplar 10 10
5618 60l. Pedunculate oak . . . 15 10
5619 70l. European larch 15 10
5620 125l. Beech 20 10
5621 350l. Sycamore 35 10
5622 940l. Ash . . . . 1·10 45
5623 1440l. Norway spruce . . . 1·50 70
5624 3095l. Large-leaved lime . . 2·75 1·50

1994. World Cup Football Championship, U.S.A. Designs showing various footballing scenes and flags of participating countries. Multicoloured.
5625 90l. Type **1171** 10 10
5626 130l. Brazil, Russia, Cameroun and Sweden (Group B) 10 10
5627 150l. Germany, Bolivia, Spain and South Korea (Group C) 15 10
5628 280l. Argentina, Greece, Nigeria and Bulgaria (Group D) 25 10
5629 500l. Italy, Ireland, Norway and Mexico (Group E) . . 55 30
5630 635l. Belgium, Morocco, Netherlands and Saudi Arabia (Group F) 70 35
MS5631 91 × 78 mm. 2075l. Goalkeeper stopping goal attempt (53 × 41 mm) . . . . 3·00 3·00

1172 Torch-bearer and Centenary Emblem

1994. Centenary of International Olympic Committee. Ancient Greek Athletes. Mult.
5632 150l. Type **1172** 15 10
5633 280l. Discus-thrower and International Sports Year emblem 30 10
5634 500l. Wrestlers and Olympic Peace emblem 60 15
5635 635l. Arbitrator and "Paris 1994" centenary congress emblem 75 20
MS5636 90 × 78 mm. 2075l. Athletes, National Olympic Committee emblem and wreath (80th anniv of Romanian membership of Olympic movement) (53 × 41 mm) 3·00 3·00

1173 National History Museum (former Postal Headquarters, Bucharest)

1174 Death Trumpet ("Craterellus cormucopoiodes")

1994. Stamp Day.
5637 **1173** 90l.+60l. multicoloured 25 15

1994. Edible (**MS**5638a) and Poisonous (**MS**5638b) Fungi. Two sheets, each 155 × 72 mm containing vert designs as T **1174**. Multicoloured.
MS5638 (a) 30l. Type **1174**; 60l. Wood blewit ("Lepista nuda"); 150l. Cep ("Boletus edulis"); 940l. Common puff-ball ("Lycoperdon perlatum"). (b) 90l. Satan's mushroom ("Boletus satanus"); 280l. Death cap ("Amanita phalloides"); 350l. Red-staining inocybe ("Inocybe patouillardii, wrongly inscr "patonillardi"); 500l. Fly agaric ("Amanita muscaria") Set of 2 sheets . . 3·00 3·00

1175 Traian Vuia's Airplane No. 1, 1906

1994. Air. 50th Anniv of I.C.A.O.
5639 **1175** 110l. brown, black & blue 15 30
5640 – 350l. multicoloured . . 45 30
5641 – 500l. multicoloured . . 70 30
5642 – 635l. black, ultramarine and blue 85 30
DESIGNS: 350l. Rombac One Eleven; 500l. Boeing 737-300; 635l. Airbus Industrie A310.

1176 Turning Fork

1994. "Philakorea 1994" International Stamp Exhibition, Seoul.
5643 **1176** 60l. black, orange and mauve 15 10
MS5644 78 × 91 mm. 2075l. multicoloured . . . . 3·00 3·00
DESIGN—38 × 52 mm. No. 5644, Korean drummer.

1177 Beluga

1994. Environmental Protection of Danube Delta. Multicoloured.
5645 150l. Type **1177** 20 10
5646 280l. Orsini's viper 35 15
5647 500l. White-tailed sea eagle 60 35
5648 635l. European mink . . . 80 45
MS5649 90 × 78 mm. 2075l. "Periploca gracca" (plant) (50 × 38 mm) . . . . 3·00 3·00

1994. Victory of Romanian Team in European Gymnastics Championships, Stockholm. Nos. 5338/9 surch **Echipa Romaniei Compioana Europeana Stockholm 1994** and value.
5650 150l. on 4l.50 multicoloured 20 25
5651 525l. on 4l.50 multicoloured 75 40

1179 Elephant

1994. The Circus. Multicoloured.
5652 90l. Type **1179** 10 15
5653 130l. Balancing bear (vert) 10 15
5654 150l. Cycling monkeys . . . 15 15
5655 280l. Tiger jumping through hoop 30 25
5656 500l. Clown on tightrope balancing dogs 60 35
5657 635l. Clown on horseback 80 45

1994. World Post Day. No. 5465 surch **150LEI 1994 Posta - cea mai buna alegere**.
5658 **1126** 150l. on 10l. mult . . . 25 20

1181 Emblem

1183 Snake

1182 Sterlet

1994. 20th International Fair, Bucharest.
5659 **1181** 525l. multicoloured . . 55 20

1994. Sturgeons.
5660 150l. Type **1182** 20 25
5661 280l. Russian sturgeon . . . 40 25
5662 500l. Stellate sturgeon . . . 65 45
5663 635l. Common sturgeon . . 85 55

1994. Romanian–Chinese Stamp Exhibition, Timisoara and Cluj-Napoca. Multicoloured.
5664 150l. Type **1183** 20 10
5665 1135l. Dragon . . . . . . 1·40 45

1184 Early Steam Train, Bucharest–Giurgii Line

1994. 125th Anniv of Romanian Railway Administration.
5666 **1184** 90l. multicoloured . . . 15 10

1185 Alexandru Orascu (architect and mathematician)

1994. Anniversaries. Multicoloured.
5667 30l. Type **1185** (death centenary) 10 15
5668 60l. Gheorghe Polizu (physician, 175th birth anniv) 10 15
5669 150l. Iulia Hasdeu (writer, 125th birth anniv) 20 15
5670 280l. S. Mehedinti (scientist, 125th birth anniv) 25 15
5671 350l. Camil Petrescu (writer, birth centenary) 35 25
5672 500l. N. Paulescu (physician, 125th birth anniv) 45 35
5673 940l. L. Grigorescu (painter, birth centenary) 95 50
See also No. 5684.

1186 Nativity

1994. Christmas.
5674 **1186** 60l. multicoloured . . . 15 10

1187 St. Mary's Church, Cleveland, U.S.A.

1994.
5675 **1187** 610l. multicoloured . . 65 15

1188 Anniversary Emblem

1994. 20th Anniv of World Tourism Organization.
5676 **1188** 525l. blue, orange & black 55 20

1189 Military Aviation Medal, 1938 **1190** Kittens

1994. Military Decorations. Sheet 73×104 mm containing T **1189** and similar vert designs. Multicoloured.
MS5677 30l. Type **1189**; 60l. "For Valour" Cross, Third Class, 1916; 150l. Military Medal, First Class, 1880; 940l. Rumanian Star, 1877 1·60 1·60

1994. Young Domestic Animals. Multicoloured.
5678 90l. Type **1190** 10 20
5679 130l. Puppies 15 20
5680 150l. Kid 25 20
5681 280l. Foal 50 20
5682 500l. Rabbit kittens 85 30
5683 635l. Lambs . . . . 1·10 50

1994. Death Centenary of Gheorghe Tattarescu (painter). As T **1185**. Multicoloured.
5684 90l. Tattarescu 15 10

1191 Emblem **1192** Tanar

1995. Save the Children Fund.
5685 **1191** 60l. blue 15 10

1995. Brasov Youth. Neighbourhood Group Leaders. Multicoloured.
5686 40l. Type **1192** 10 20
5687 60l. Batran 10 20
5688 150l. Curcan 15 20
5689 280l. Dorobant 25 20
5690 350l. Brasovechean 40 20
5691 500l. Rosior 50 30
5692 635l. Albior 75 50

1193 Hand and Barbed Wire

1995. 50th Anniv of Liberation of Concentration Camps.
5693 **1193** 960l. black and red . . 60 30

1194 Emblems of French and Romanian State Airlines

1995. Air. 75th Anniv of Founding of Franco-Romanian Air Company.
5694 **1194** 60l. blue and red . . . 55 10
5695 – 960l. blue and black . . 60 20
DESIGN: 960l. Potez IX biplane and Paris–Bucharest route map.

1195 Ear of Wheat

1995. 50th Anniversaries. Multicoloured.
5696 675l. Type **1195** (F.A.O.) . . 40 30
5697 960l. Anniversary emblem (U.N.O.) 60 35
5698 1615l. Hand holding pen showing members' flags (signing of U.N. Charter) 1·10 55

1196 "Resurrection" (icon)

1995. Easter.
5699 **1196** 60l. multicoloured . . . 15 10

1197 "Youth without Age and Life without Death"

1995. Fairy Tales. Multicoloured.
5700 90l. Type **1197** 10 20
5701 130l. "The Old Man's Servant and the Old Woman's Servant" (vert) 10 20
5702 150l. "The Prince with the Golden Hair" 10 20
5703 280l. "Son of the Red King" 15 20
5704 500l. "Praslea the Brave and the Golden Apples" (vert) 35 20
5705 635l. "King Dafin" (drawn by golden horses) 40 25

1198 Enescu

1995. 40th Death Anniv of George Enescu (composer).
5706 **1198** 960l. orange and black 60 15

1199 Dove with Section of Rainbow **1200** Blaga

1995. Europa. Peace and Freedom. Multicoloured.
5707 150l. Type **1199** 10 15
5708 4370l. Dove wings forming "EUROPA" around rainbow . . . . 3·25 2·30

1995. Birth Centenary of Lucian Blaga (poet).
5709 **1200** 150l. multicoloured . . 15 10
See also Nos. 5745/9.

1201 Bucharest Underground Railway, 1979

1995. Transport.
5712 **1201** 470l. yellow and black (postage) 45 10
5713 – 630l. red and blue . . . 35 10
5714 – 675l. red and black . . 40 10
5715 – 755l. blue and black . . 50 10
5716 – 1615l. green and black 1·00 15
5717 – 2300l. green and black 1·10 20
5718 – 2550l. black and red . . 1·60 25
5719 – 285l. green and black (air) 15 10
5720 – 715l. red and blue . . . 45 10
5721 – 965l. black and blue . . 55 10
5722 – 1575l. green and black 95 15
5723 – 3410l. blue and black 1·90 1·60
DESIGNS—HORIZ: 285l. I.A.R. 80 aircraft (70th anniv of Romanian aeronautical industry); 630l. "Masagerul" (post boat); 715l. I.A.R. 316 Red Cross helicopter; 755l. "Razboieni" (container ship); 965l. Sud Aviation SA 330 Puma helicopter; 1575l. I.A.R. 818H seaplane; 2300l. Trolleybus, 1904; 2550l. Steam train, 1869; 3410l. Boeing 737-300 (75th anniv of Romanian air transport). VERT: 675l. Cable-car, Brasov; 1615l. Electric tram, 1894.

1202 "Dacia" (liner) **1203** Fallow Deer

1995. Centenary of Romanian Maritime Service. Multicoloured.
5735 90l. Type **1202** 10 20
5736 130l. "Imparatul Traian" (Danube river steamer) (horiz) 10 20
5737 150l. "Romania" (Danube river steamer) (horiz) . . 10 20
5738 280l. "Costinesti" (tanker) (horiz) 20 20
5739 960l. "Caransebes" (container ship) (horiz) . . 60 30
5740 3410l. "Tutova" (car ferry) (horiz) . . . . 2·30 1·20

1995. European Nature Conservation Year. Mult.
5741 150l. Type **1203** 10 15
5742 280l. Great bustard 25 15
5743 960l. Lady's slipper 65 20
5744 1615l. Stalagmites . . . . . 1·00 45

1995. Anniversaries. As T **1200**. Multicoloured.
5745 90l. D. Rosca (birth centenary) 10 25
5746 130l. Vasile Conta (150th birth anniv) 10 25
5747 280l. Ion Barbu (birth centenary) 20 25
5748 960l. Iuliu Hatieganu (110th birth anniv) 60 35
5749 1650l. Dimitrie Brandza (botanist) (death centenary) 95 60

1204 Youths and Torch-bearer

1995. European Youth Olympic Days.
5750 **1204** 1650l. multicoloured . . 15 15

1205 Post Wagon (⅓-size illustration)

1995. Stamp Day. Centenary of Upper Rhine Local Post.
5751 **1205** 960l.(+715l.) mult . . . 75 60
No. 5751 includes the se-tenant premium-carrying tab shown in Type **1205**.

1206 Saligny Bridge

1995. Centenary of Saligny Bridge, Cernavoda.
5752 **1206** 675l. multicoloured . . 50 20

1207 Mallard **1208** General Dr. Victor Anastasiu

1995. Domestic Birds. Multicoloured.
5753 90l. Type **1207** 10 15
5754 130l. Red junglefowl (hen) 10 15
5755 150l. Helmeted guineafowl 10 15
5756 280l. Common turkey . . . 20 15
5757 960l. Greylag goose 60 25
5758 1650l. Red junglefowl (cock) 1·10 40

1995. 75th Anniv of Institute of Aeronautics Medicine.
5759 **1208** 960l. ultramarine, blue and red 50 10

1209 Battle Scene

1995. 400th Anniv of Battle of Calugareni.
5760 **1209** 100l. multicoloured . . 25 10

1210 Giurgiu Castle

1995. Anniversaries. Multicoloured.
5761 250l. Type **1210** (600th anniv) 15 15
5762 500l. Neamtului Castle (600th anniv) (vert) . . . 30 15
5763 960l. Sebes-Alba Mill (700th anniv) 50 25
5764 1615l. Dorohoi Church (500th anniv) (vert) . . . 85 40
5765 1650l. Military observatory, Bucharest (centenary) (vert) 85 40

1211 Moldovita Monastery **1212** Racket

1995. UNESCO World Heritage Sites. Mult.
5766 675l. Type **1211** 35 20
5767 960l. Hurez Monastery . . . 50 25
5768 1615l. Biertan Castle (horiz) 80 45

1995. 5th Open Tennis Championships, Bucharest.
5769 **1212** 1020l. multicoloured . . 50 15

1213 Ion Ionescu (editor)

1995. Centenary of Mathematics Gazette.
5770 **1213** 100l. pink and brown 15 10

1214 "Albizzia julibrissin"

1995. Plants from Bucharest Botanical Garden. Multicoloured.
5771 50l. Type **1214** 10 10
5772 100l. Yew 10 10
5773 150l. "Paulownia tomentosa" 10 10
5774 500l. Bird of Paradise flower 30 10
5775 960l. Amazon water-lily . . 55 15
5776 2300l. Azalea . . . . 1·50 45

1215 St. John's Church

1216 George Apostu (sculptor, 10th death (1996))

1995. 600th Anniv of First Documentary Reference to Piatra-Neamt.
5777 **1215** 250l. multicoloured . . 30 15

1995. Anniversaries.
5778 **1216** 150l. green and black 10 20
5779 – 250l. blue and black . . 15 20
5780 – 500l. light brown, brown and black . . 35 20
5781 – 960l. rose, purple and black 65 25
5782 – 1650l. brown and black 1·10 50
DESIGNS: 250l. Emil Cioran (philosopher, death in 1995); 500l. Eugen Ionescu (writer, 1st death anniv); 960l. Elena Vacarescu (poetess, 130th birth (1996)); 1650l. Mircea Eliade (philosopher, 10th death (1996)).

1217 Running

1995. Olympic Games, Atlanta (1996) (1st issue). Multicoloured.
5783 50l. Type **1217** 10 15
5784 100l. Gymnastics 10 15
5785 150l. Canoeing 10 15
5786 500l. Fencing 30 15
5787 960l. Rowing 60 25
5788 2300l. Boxing . . . . 1·40 60
MS5789 78 × 92 mm. 2610l. Gymnastics (different) (41 × 53 mm) . . . . 2·00 2·00
See also Nos. 5829/**MS**5834.

1218 Nativity

1995. Christmas.
5790 **1218** 100l. multicoloured . . 15 10

1219 Masked Person

1996. Folk Masks of Maramures (250l.) and Moldavia (others).
5791 **1219** 250l. multicoloured . . 10 20
5792 – 500l. multicoloured . . 15 20
5793 – 960l. mult (vert) . . . 25 20
5794 – 1650l. mult (vert) . . . 45 35
DESIGNS: 500l. to 1650l. Different masks.

1220 Tristan Tzara

1221 "Resurrection" (icon)

1996. Writers' Birth Anniversaries. Multicoloured.
5795 150l. Type **1220** (centenary) 10 20
5796 1500l. Anton Pann (bicentenary) 90 30

1996. Easter.
5797 **1221** 150l. multicoloured . . 15 10

1222 National History Museum

1996. "Romfilex '96" Romanian–Israeli Stamp Exhibition. Sheet 124 × 73 mm containing T **1222** and similar vert designs.
MS5798 150l. brown and black; 370l. multicoloured; 1500l. multicoloured . . . . 1·00 1·00
DESIGNS: 370l. "On The Terrace at Sinaia" (Theodor Aman); 1500l. "Old Jerusalem" (Reuven Rubin).

1223 "Chrysomela vigintipunctata" (leaf beetle)

1996. Beetles.
5799 **1223** 70l. yellow and black 10 10
5800 – 220l. red and black . . 10 10
5801 – 370l. brown and black 25 10
5802 – 650l. black, red & grey 35 10
5803 – 700l. red, black and green 40 10
5804 – 740l. black and yellow 30 10
5805 – 960l. black and red . . 40 10
5806 – 1000l. yellow and black 45 10
5807 – 1500l. black and brown 70 20
5808 – 2500l. red, black & green . . . . 1·00 25
DESIGNS: 220l. "Cerambyx cerdo" (longhorn beetle); 370l. "Entomoscelis adonidis"; 650l. Ladybird; 700l. Caterpillar-hunter; 740l. "Hedobia imperialis"; 960l. European rhinoceros beetle; 1000l. Bee chafer; 1500l. "Purpuricenus kaehleri" (longhorn beetle); 2500l. "Anthaxia salicis".

1224 Dumitru Prunariu (first Romanian cosmonaut)

1996. "Espamer" Spanish–Latin American and "Aviation and Space" Stamp Exhibitions, Seville, Spain. Sheet 91 × 78 mm.
MS5809 **1224** 2720l. multicoloured 1·25 1·25

1225 Arbore Church

1996. UNESCO World Heritage Sites. Mult.
5810 150l. Type **1225** 10 25
5811 1500l. Voronet Monastery 70 35
5812 2550l. Humor Monastery . . 1·00 60

1226 Ana Aslan (doctor)

1996. Europa. Famous Women. Multicoloured.
5813 370l. Type **1226** 25 25
5814 4140l. Lucia Bulandra (actress) . . . . 2·30 1·70

1227 "Mother and Children" (Oana Negoita)

1996. 50th Anniv of UNICEF. Prize-winning Children's Paintings. Multicoloured.
5815 370l. Type **1227** 15 25
5816 740l. "Winter Scene" (Badea Cosmin) 35 25
5817 1500l. "Children and Sun over House" (Nicoleta Georgescu) 75 40
5818 2550l. "House on Stilts" (Biborka Bartha) (vert) 1·20 70

1228 Goalkeeper with Ball

1996. European Football Championship, England. Multicoloured.
5819 220l. Type **1228** 10 10
5820 370l. Player with ball . . . 15 10
5821 740l. Two players with ball 35 10
5822 1500l. Three players with ball 70 15
5823 2550l. Player dribbling ball 1·10 25
MS5824 90 × 78 mm. 4050l. Balls and two players (41 × 53 mm) 2·00 2·00
Nos. 5819/23 were issued together, se-tenant, forming a composite design of the pitch and stadium.

1229 Metropolitan Toronto Convention Centre (venue)

1232 Boxing

1230 Factory

1996. "Capex '96" International Stamp Exhibition, Toronto, Canada. Multicoloured.
5825 150l. Type **1229** 15 10
MS5826 78 × 90 mm. 4050l. View of City (41 × 52 mm) . . . . . . 2·00 2·00

1996. 225th Anniv of Resita Works.
5827 **1230** 150l. brown 15 10

1996. 5th Anniv of Establishment of R.A. Posta Romana (postal organization). No. 5471 surch **1996 - 5 ANI DE LA INFIINTARE L150**.
5828 **1128** 150l. on 10l. multicoloured 50 60

1996. Centenary of Modern Olympic Games and Olympic Games, Atlanta (2nd issue). Mult.
5829 220l. Type **1232** 10 10
5830 370l. Running 15 10
5831 740l. Rowing 30 10
5832 1500l. Judo 75 15
5833 2550l. Gymnastics (asymmetrical bars) . . . 1·10 25
MS5834 90 × 78 mm. 4050l. Gymnastics (beam) (53 × 41 mm) (air) . . . . 2·00 2·00
No. **MS**5834 also commemorates "Olymphilex '96" sports stamp exhibition, Atlanta.

1233 Postman, Keyboard and Stamp under Magnifying Glass (⅔-size illustration)

1996. Stamp Day.
5835 **1233** 1500l.(+650l.) mult . . 95 50
No. 5835 includes the se-tenant premium-carrying tab shown in Type **1233**.

1234 White Spruce

1996. Coniferous Trees. Multicoloured.
5836 70l. Type **1234** 15 10
5837 150l. Serbian spruce 15 10
5838 220l. Blue Colorado spruce 15 10
5839 740l. Sitka spruce 40 10
5840 1500l. Scots pine 95 20
5841 3500l. Maritime pine . . . 2·10 45

1235 Grass Snake

1236 Madonna and Child

1996. Animals. Multicoloured.
5842 70l. Type **1235** 15 10
5843 150l. Hermann's tortoise . . 15 10
5844 220l. Eurasian sky lark (horiz) 15 10
5845 740l. Red fox (horiz) . . . 40 10

5846 1500l. Common porpoise . . 95 20
5847 3500l. Golden eagle (horiz) 2·10 45

1996. Christmas.
5848 **1236** 150l. multicoloured . . 15 10

1237 Stan Golestan (composer, 40th)

1996. Death Anniversaries.
5849 **1237** 100l. pink and black . . 30 30
5850 – 150l. purple and black 30 30
5851 – 370l. orange and black 65 30
5852 – 1500l. red and black . . 2·50 60
DESIGNS: 150l. Corneliu Coposu (politician, 1st); 370l. Horia Vintila (writer, 4th); 1500l. Alexandru Papana (test pilot, 50th).

1238 Ford "Spider", 1930

1996. Motor Cars. Two sheets containing horiz designs as T **1238**. Multicoloured.
MS5853 (a) 110 × 78 mm 70l. Type **1238**; 150l. Citroen (1932); 220l. Rolls Royce (1936); 280l. Mercedes Benz (1933). (b) 113 × 80 mm. 120l. Jaguar SS 100 (1937); 2500l. Bugatti Type 59 (1934); 2550l. Mercedes Benz 500K Roadster (1936); 2550l. Alfa Romeo 8C (1931) Set of 2 sheets 5·00 5·00

1239 Deng Xiaoping and Margaret Thatcher

1997. "Hong Kong '97" Stamp Exhibition. Sheet 92 × 78 mm.
MS5854 **1239** 1500l. multicoloured 35 35

1240 Stoat

1997. Fur-bearing Mammals. Multicoloured.
5855 70l. Type **1240** 20 40
5856 150l. Arctic fox 20 40
5857 220l. Racoon-dog 20 40
5858 740l. European otter 30 40
5859 1500l. Muskrat 65 40
5860 3500l. Pine marten . . . . 1·50 80

1241 Bow

1997. 26th Anniv of Greenpeace (environmental organization). The "Rainbow Warrior" (campaign ship). Multicoloured.
5861 150l. Type **1241** 20 25
5862 370l. Ship and ice 20 25
5863 1940l. Ship cruising past beach 90 25
5864 2500l. Rainbow and ship . . 1·10 25
MS5865 90 × 77 mm. 4050l. Ship carrying banner (49 × 38 mm) 90 90

1242 Thomas Edison (inventor)

1997. Birth Anniversaries. Multicoloured.
5866 200l. Type **1242** (150th anniv) 15 30
5867 400l. Franz Schubert (composer, bicentenary) 15 30
5868 3600l. Miguel de Cervantes Saavedra (writer, 450th anniv) . . . . 1·40 60

1243 Emblem **1244** Surdesti

1997. Inauguration of Mobile Telephone Network in Romania.
5869 **1243** 400l. multicoloured . . 20 10

1997. Churches. Each brown, agate and green.
5870 200l. Type **1244** 15 15
5871 400l. Plopis 15 15
5872 450l. Bogdan Voda 15 15
5873 850l. Rogoz 30 15
5874 3600l. Calinesti . . . . . . 1·30 30
5875 6000l. Birsana . . . . . . 2·30 50

1245 Al. Demetrescu Dan in "Hamlet", 1916 **1246** Vlad Tepes Dracula (Voivode of Wallachia)

1997. 2nd Shakespeare Festival, Craiova. Mult.
5876 200l. Type **1245** 15 45
5877 400l. Constantin Serghie in "Othello", 1855 . . . . . 15 45
5878 2400l. Gheorghe Cozorici in "Hamlet", 1957 . . . . . 90 45
5879 3600l. Ion Manolescu in "Hamlet", 1924 . . . . . 1·30 90

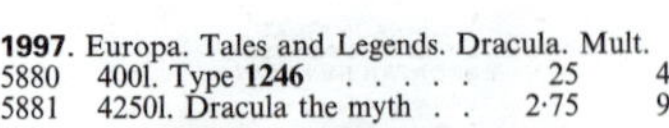

1997. Europa. Tales and Legends. Dracula. Mult.
5880 400l. Type **1246** 25 45
5881 4250l. Dracula the myth . . 2·75 90

1247 "Dolichothele uberiformis"

1997. Cacti. Multicoloured.
5882 100l. Type **1247** 15 30
5883 250l. "Rebutia" 15 30
5884 450l. "Echinofossulocactus lamellosus" 15 30
5885 500l. "Ferocactus glaucescens" 15 30
5886 650l. "Thelocactus" 25 30
5887 6150l. "Echinofossulocactus albatus" . . . . 2·40 90

1248 National Theatre, Cathedral and Statue of Mihai Viteazul

1997. "Balcanmax'97" Maximum Cards Exhibition, Cluj-Napoca.
5888 **1248** 450l. multicoloured . . 15 10

1249 19th-century Postal Transport (½-size illustration)

1997. Stamp Day.
5889 **1249** 3600l.(+1500l.) multicoloured . . . . 1·90 1·20
No. 5889 includes the se-tenant premium-carrying tab shown in Type **1249**.

1997. Nos. 5349/55 and 5357 surch.
5890 250l. on 1l. blue 20 20
5891 250l. on 2l. green 20 20
5892 250l. on 4l. red 20 20
5893 450l. on 5l. violet 20 20
5894 450l. on 6l. brown 20 20
5895 450l. on 18l. red 20 20
5896 950l. on 9l. red 40 20
5897 3600l. on 8l. brown . . . . 1·60 40

1251 Archway of Vlad Tepes Dracula's House **1252** Tourism Monument

1997. Sighisoara. Multicoloured.
5898 250l. Type **1251** 20 30
5899 650l. Town Hall clocktower 30 30
5900 3700l. Steps leading to fortress and clocktower 1·60 60

1997. Rusca Montana, Banat.
5901 **1252** 950l. multicoloured . . 35 20

1253 Printing Works **1254** Emil Racovita (biologist) and "Belgica" (polar barque)

1997. 125th Anniv of Stamp Printing Works.
5902 **1253** 450l. red, brown and blue 20 10

1997. Centenary of Belgian Antarctic Expedition.
5903 **1254** 450l. blue, grey and black 15 30
5904 – 650l. red, yellow and black 25 30
5905 – 1600l. green, pink and black 60 30
5906 – 3700l. brown, yellow and black . . . . . . 1·40 55
DESIGNS: 650l. Frederick Cook (anthropologist and photographer) and "Belgica" at sea; 1600l. Roald Amundsen and "Belgica" in port; 3700l. Adrien de Gerlache (expedition commander) and "Belgica" ice-bound.

1997. "Aeromfila '97" Stamp Exhibition, Brasov. No. 5334 surch **1050 L. AEROMFILA'97 Brasov** and airplane.
5907 **1292** 1050l. on 4l.50 mult . . 45 30

1256 Campsite **1258** Ion Mihalache (politician)

1997. Romanian Scout Association. Multicoloured.
5908 300l. Type **1256** 20 30
5909 700l. Romanian Scout Association emblem . . . 25 30
5910 1050l. Joined hands 40 30
5911 1750l. Carvings 65 30
5912 3700l. Scouts around campfire . . . . 1·50 60
Nos. 5908/12 were issued together, se-tenant, forming a composite design.

1997. 9th Romanian–Chinese Stamp Exhibition, Bucharest. No. 5293 surch **A IX-a editie a expozitiei filatelice romano-chineza 1997 500 L.**
5913 **1082** 500l. on 2l. mult . . . 30 20

1997. Anniversaries. Multicoloured.
5914 500l. Type **1258** (34th death anniv) 20 25
5915 1050l. King Carol I (131st anniv of accession) (black inscriptions and face value) 75 25
5916 1050l. As No. 5915 but mauve inscriptions and face value . . . . 1·00 25
5917 1050l. As No. 5915 but blue inscriptions and face value 1·00 25
5918 1050l. As No. 5915 but brown inscriptions and face value . . . . 1·00 25

1259 Rugby

1997. Sports. Multicoloured.
5919 500l. Type **1259** 20 35
5920 700l. American football (vert) 30 35
5921 1750l. Oina (Romanian bat and ball game) 65 35
5922 3700l. Mountaineering (vert) 1·60 75

1260 New Building

1998. 130th Anniv of Bucharest Chamber of Commerce and Industry.
5923 **1260** 700l. multicoloured . . 30 10

1261 Biathlon **1263** Four-leaved Clover (Good luck and Success)

1262 "Romania breaking the Chains on Libertatii Plain" (C. D. Rosenthal)

1998. Winter Olympic Games, Nagano, Japan. Mult.
5924 900l. Type **1261** 30 20
5925 3900l. Figure skating . . . 1·40 40

1998. National Tricolour Flag Day. Sheet 78 × 90 mm.
MS5926 **1262** 900l. multicoloured 10 55

1998. Europa. National Festivals.
5927 **1263** 900l. green and red . . 2·40 2·30
5928 – 3900l. red, orange and green . . . . 10·00 4·50
DESIGN: 3900l. Butterfly (youth and suaveness).

1264 Alfred Nobel **1265** Shrine, Cluj

1998. The 20th-century (1st series). Multicoloured.
5929 700l. Type **1264** (establishment of Nobel Foundation, 1901) 25 30
5930 900l. Guglielmo Marconi (first radio-telegraphic trans-Atlantic link, 1901) 35 30
5931 1500l. Albert Einstein (elaboration of Theory of Relativity, 1905) 55 30
5932 3900l. Traian Vuia (his first flight, 1906) . . . . . . 1·50 60
See also Nos. 5991/5, 6056/9, 6060/3, 6128/31, 6133/6, 6205/8 and 6230/3.

1998. Roadside Shrines. Multicoloured.
5933 700l. Type **1265** 30 10
5934 900l. Crucifixion, Prahovac 35 10
5935 1500l. Shrine, Arges 55 10

1998. "Israel '98" International Stamp Exhibition, Tel Aviv. No. **MS**5798 with each stamp surch **ISRAEL '98** and the old value cancelled by Menora emblem.
MS5936 700l. on 150l. brown and black; 900l. on 370l. multicoloured; 3900l. on 1500l. multicoloured . . . . 1·20 1·20

1267 Dr. Thoma Ionescu (founder) and Coltea Hospital, Bucharest

1998. Centenary of Romanian Surgery Society.
5937 **1267** 1050l. grey, brown and red 45 15

1998. Nos. 5350/1, 5353/4 and 5357 surch, the old value cancelled by a clover leaf.
5938 50l. on 2l. green 25 10
5939 100l. on 8l. brown 25 10
5940 200l. on 4l. red 25 10
5941 400l. on 6l. brown 25 10
5942 500l. on 18l. red 25 10

1269 Player **1272** Brown Kiwi

1998. World Cup Football Championship, France. Sheet 74 × 104 mm containing T **1269** and similar vert designs. Each ultramarine, brown and green.
MS5943 800l. Type **1269**; 1050l. Player in air; 1850l. Player bouncing ball on knee; 4150l. Player preparing to kick ball 1·75 1·75

1998. Nos. 5615/17 and 5620 surch, the old value cancelled by a hare.
5944 – 700l. on 125l. green and black 40 45
5945 – 800l. on 35l. green and black 40 45
5946 – 1050l. on 45l. green and black 40 45
5947 **1170** 4150l. on 15l. green and black . . . . 1·60 70

1998. Nos. 5352 and 5355 surch, the old value cancelled by a heart.
5948 1000l. on 9l. red 45 60
5949 1500l. on 5l. violet 70 60

1998. Nocturnal Birds. Multicoloured.
5950 700l. Type **1272** 25 25
5951 1500l. Barn owl 50 25
5952 1850l. Water rail 65 25
5953 2450l. European nightjar . . 80 25

1998. No. 5361 surch, the old value cancelled by a sign of the zodiac.
5954 250l. on 45l. blue (Aries) . . 20 25
5955 350l. on 45l. blue (Taurus) 20 25
5956 400l. on 45l. blue (Gemini) 20 25
5957 450l. on 45l. blue (Cancer) 20 25
5958 850l. on 45l. blue (Leo) . . 30 25
5959 900l. on 45l. blue (Aquarius) 40 25
5960 1000l. on 45l. blue (Libra) 40 25
5961 1600l. on 45l. blue (Scorpio) 60 25
5962 2500l. on 45l. blue (Sagittarius) 95 25

1274 81p. Stamp and Waslui Cancellation

1998. 140th Anniv of Bull's Head Issue of Moldavia. Multicoloured.
5963 700l. Type **1274** 30 25
5964 1050l. 27p. stamp and Jassy cancellation 40 25
MS5965 130 × 80 mm. 4150l.+850l. 54 and 108p. stamps and Galatz cancellation (53 × 41 mm) . . . 80 80

1275 Soldiers and Revolutionaries fighting

1998. 150th Anniv of the 1848 Revolutions.
5966 **1275** 1050l. black, yellow and red 40 30

1276 Nikolaus Lenau (poet) **1277** Diver and Marine Life

1998. German Personalities of Banat.
5967 **1276** 800l. orange, black and pink 50 30
5968 – 1850l. orange, black and green . . . . . 1·20 30
5969 – 4150l. orange, black and blue . . . . . . 2·75 45
DESIGNS: 1850l. Stefan Jager (artist); 4150l. Adam Muller-Guttenbrunn (writer).

1998. International Year of the Ocean.
5970 **1277** 1100l. multicoloured . . 40 30

1998. Nos. 5336/7 surch, the old value cancelled by a sporting emblem.
5971 **1094** 50l. on 1l. multicoloured (Figure skater) 40 45
5972 – 50l. on 1l. multicoloured (Trophy) 40 45

1279 "Tulipa gesneriana" **1281** "Proportions of Man" (Leonardo da Vinci)

1998. Flowers. Multicoloured.
5973 350l. Type **1279** 25 25
5974 850l. "Dahlia variabilis" "Rubin" 35 25
5975 1100l. Martagon lily 45 25
5976 4450l. "Rosa centifolia" . . 1·90 50
No. 5975 commemorates the 50th anniv of the Horticulture Institute, Bucharest.

1998. Various stamps surch. (a) Nos. 5399/5404, the old value cancelled by a transport emblem.
5977 **1106** 50l. on 1l. brown, blue and deep blue (Car) 15 15
5978 – 50l. on 4l. green, lilac and violet (Steam locomotive) 15 15
5979 – 50l. on 5l. brown, blue and ultramarine (Lorry) 15 15
5980 – 50l. on 5l. blue, brown and red (Helicopter) 15 15
5981 – 50l. on 9l. red, blue and deep blue (Airplane) 15 15
5982 – 50l. on 10l. black, light brown and brown (Ship) 15 15

(b) Nos. 5472/5 and 5477, the old value cancelled by a bird.
5983 **1129** 50l. on 6l. green and violet (Cockerel) . . 15 15
5984 – 50l. on 7l. mauve, purple and green (Duck) 15 15
5985 – 50l. on 9l. blue and mauve (Swan) . . . 15 15
5986 – 50l. on 10l. light brown, brown and blue (Dove) 15 15
5987 – 50l. on 30l. green and blue (Swallow) . . . 15 15

1998. 50th Anniv of Universal Declaration of Human Rights.
5988 **1281** 50l. multicoloured . . . 25 15

1282 Paciurea

1998. 125th Birth Anniv of Dimitrie Paciurea (sculptor).
5989 **1282** 850l. multicoloured . . 30 15

1283 Eclipse

1998. Total Eclipse of the Sun (1999) (1st issue).
5990 **1283** 1100l. multicoloured . . 70 20
See also No. 6050.

1284 Sinking of "Titanic" (liner), 1912

1998. The 20th century (2nd series).
5991 **1284** 350l. black, bl & red . . 30 30
5992 – 1100l. multicoloured . . 50 30
5993 – 1600l. multicoloured . . 65 30
5994 – 2000l. multicoloured . . 65 30
5995 – 2600l. blk, grey & red 95 30
DESIGNS: 1100l. Henri Coanda and his turbine-powered model airplane, 1910; 1600l. Louis Bleriot and his "Bleriot XI" airplane (first powered flight across English Channel, 1909); 2000l. Freighter in locks and map of American sea routes (opening of Panama Canal, 1914); 2600l. Prisoners in courtyard (Russian October revolution, 1917).

1998. Christmas. Nos. 5491 and 5674 surch with the old value cancelled by a Christmas emblem.
5996 **1133** 2000l. on 15l. multicoloured (Christmas tree) . . . 55 40
5997 **1186** 2600l. on 60l. multicoloured (Father Christmas) 85 40

1286 Gonovez Lighthouse

1998. Lighthouses. Multicoloured.
5998 900l. Type **1286** 20 30
5999 1000l. Constanta 20 30
6000 1100l. Sfantu Gheorghe . . 30 30
6001 2600l. Sulina 65 30

1287 Arnota Monastery

1999. Monasteries. Multicoloured.
6002 500l. Type **1287** 25 25
6003 700l. Bistrita 25 25
6004 1100l. Dintr'un Lemn . . . 35 25
6005 2100l. Govora 60 25
6006 4850l. Tismana . . . . . . 1·10 25

1999. No. 5492 surch with the old value cancelled by various fungi.
6007 **1134** 50l. on 15l. black, red and blue 20 25
6009 400l. on 15l. black, red and blue 20 25
6010 2300l. on 15l. black, red and blue 55 25
6011 3200l. on 15l. black, red and blue 75 25

1999. No. 5384 surch with the old value cancelled by a musical instrument.
6012 **1099** 100l. on 1l. blue (guitar) 20 25
6013 250l. on 1l. blue (saxophone) 20 25

1290 "Magnolia soulangiana"

1999. Shrubs. Multicoloured.
6014 350l. Type **1290** 30 25
6015 1000l. "Stewartia malacodendron" 30 25
6016 1100l. "Hibiscus rosa-sinensis" 45 25
6017 5350l. "Clematis patens" . . 1·80 25

1292 Easter Eggs

1999. Easter.
6023 **1292** 1100l. multicoloured . . 30 15

1999. No. 5799 surch with the old value cancelled by a dinosaur emblem.
6024 **1223** 100l. on 70l. yellow and black (Brontosaurus) 20 20
6025 200l. on 70l. yellow and black (Iguanodon) . . 20 20
6026 200l. on 70l. yellow and black (Allosaurus) . . 20 20
6027 1500l. on 70l. yellow and black (Diplodocus) 25 20
6028 1600l. on 70l. yellow and black (Tyrannosaurus) . . 35 20
6029 3200l. on 70l. yellow and black (Stegosaurus) 65 20
6030 6000l. on 70l. yellow and black (Plateosaurus) . . . 1·20 35

1294 Girdle of Keys (Padureni) **1295** Scarlet Macaw

1999. Jewellery. Multicoloured.
6031 1200l. Type **1294** 20 30
6032 2100l. Pendant of keys (Ilia, Hunedoara) 35 30
6033 2600l. Jewelled bib (Maramures) 40 30
6034 3200l. Necklace (Banat) (horiz) 50 30

1999. Birds. Multicoloured.
6035 1100l. Type **1295** 20 35
6036 2700l. White peafowl . . . 50 35
6037 3700l. Common peafowl . . 70 35
6038 5700l. Sulphur-crested cockatoo . . . . 1·10 55

1296 Council Flag and Headquarters, Strasbourg

1999. 50th Anniv of Council of Europe.
6039 **1296** 2300l. multicoloured . . 50 15

1297 St. Peter's Cathedral, Rome

1298 Northern Shoveler

1999. Papal Visit.
6040 **1297** 1300l. mauve and black 40 30
6041 – 1600l. mauve and black 50 30
6042 – 2300l. multicoloured . . 65 30
6043 – 6300l. multicoloured . . 1·70 50
DESIGNS: 1600l. Patriarchal Cathedral, Bucharest; 2300l. Father Teoctist (patriarch of Romanian Orthodox church); 6300l. Pope John Paul II (after Dina Bellotti).

1999. Europa. Parks and Gardens: the Danube Delta Nature Reserve. Multicoloured.
6044 1100l. Type **1298** 35 40
6045 5700l. Black stork . . . . . 1·40 60

1299 Gheorghe Cartan (historian, 150th birth anniv)

1999. Anniversaries.
6046 **1299** 600l. green, black & red 20 20
6047 – 1100l. purple, blk & red 25 20
6048 – 2600l. blue, black & red 50 20
6049 – 7300l. brown, blk & red 80 40
DESIGNS: 1100l. George Calinescu (critic and novelist, birth centenary); 2600l. Johann Wolfgang von Goethe (dramatist, 250th birth anniv); 7300l. Honore de Balzac (novelist, birth bicentenary).

1300 Moon eclipsing Sun

1999. Total Eclipse of the Sun (2nd issue).
6050 **1300** 1100l. multicoloured . . 35 20

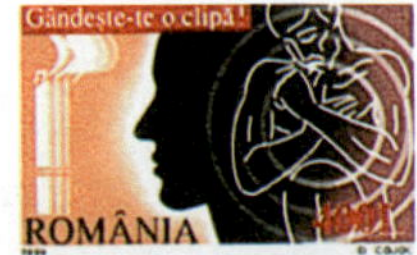

1301 Cigarette and Man with Arms Crossed

1999. Public Health Awareness Campaign. Mult.
6051 400l. Type **1301** (anti-smoking) 15 15
6052 800l. Bottles and man cradling glass and bottle (alcohol abuse) 15 15
6053 1300l. Cannabis leaf, pills and man injecting arm (drugs) 25 15
6054 2500l. Profiles and man on intravenous drip (HIV) . . 45 15

1302 Eclipse and Pavarotti (opera singer)

1999. Luciano Pavarotti's Concert on Day of Eclipse, Bucharest.
6055 **1302** 8100l. multicoloured . . 1·70 1·00

1303 Alexander Fleming (bacteriologist)

1999. The 20th century (3rd series). Multicoloured.
6056 800l. Type **1303** (discovery of penicillin, 1928) 20 30
6057 3000l. "Swords into Ploughshares" (sculpture) and map of Europe, Africa and Asia (foundation of League of Nations, 1920) 65 30
6058 7300l. Harold Clayton Urey (chemist) (discovery of heavy water, 1932) . . . 1·50 55
6059 17000l. Deep sea drilling (first oil platform, Beaumont, Texas, 1934) 2·75 1·10

1304 Karl Landsteiner (pathologist)

1999. The 20th-century (4th series).
6060 **1304** 1500l. orange, black and yellow 15 25
6061 – 3000l. ochre, black and brown 45 25
6062 – 7300l. multicoloured . . 55 55
6063 – 17000l. multicoloured 2·75 1·20
DESIGNS: 1500l. Type **1304** (discovery of blood groups, 1900–02); 3000l. Nicolae Paulescu (biochemist) (discovery of insulin, 1921); 7300l. Otto Hahn (radiochemist) (discovery of nuclear fission, 1938); 17000l. Ernst Ruska (electrical engineer) (designer of first electron microscope, 1931).

1305 Posthorn in Envelope and Berne

1306 Grigore Vasiliu Birlic

1999. 125th Anniv of Universal Postal Union.
6064 **1305** 3100l. multicoloured . . 60 30

1999. Comic Actors. Each purple, black and red.
6065 900l. Type **1306** 15 25
6066 1500l. Toma Caragiu 25 25
6067 3100l. Constantin Tanase . . 50 25
6068 7950l. Charlie Chaplin . . . 1·30 45
6069 8850l. Stan Laurel and Oliver Hardy (horiz) . . . 1·40 75

1307 Monastery

1999. 275th Anniv of Stavropoleos Church.
6070 **1307** 2100l. brown, stone and black 35 20

1308 Snowboarding

1309 Christmas Tree and Bell

1999. New Olympic Sports. Multicoloured.
6071 1600l. Type **1308** 35 35
6072 1700l. Softball 35 35
6073 7950l. Taekwondo . . . . . 1·40 70

1999. Christmas. Multicoloured.
6074 1500l. Type **1309** 25 25
6075 3100l. Father Christmas with presents 55 25

1310 Child as Flower (Antonela Vieriu)

1999. 10th Anniv of U.N. Convention on the Rights of the Child. Multicoloured.
6076 900l. Type **1310** 70 95
6077 3400l. Girl writing numbers (Ana-Maria Bulete) (vert) 55 35
6078 8850l. Group of people (Maria-Luiza Rogojeanu) 1·50 70

1311 Diana, Princess of Wales

1999. Diana, Princess of Wales Commemoration.
6079 **1311** 6000l. multicoloured . . 1·20 45

1312 Ferrari 365 GTB/4, 1968

1999. Birth Centenary (1998) of Enzo Ferrari (car designer). Multicoloured.
6080 1500l. Type **1312** 25 25
6081 1600l. Dino 246 GT, 1970 25 25
6082 1700l. 365 GT/4BB, 1973 . . 30 25
6083 7950l. Mondial 3.2, 1985 . . 1·40 50
6084 8850l. F 355, 1994 . . . . 1·50 75
6085 14500l. 456 MGT, 1998 . . 2·75 95

1313 Child with Romanian Flag

1999. 10th Anniv of Popular Uprising.
6086 **1313** 2100l. multicoloured . . 35 20

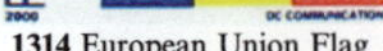

1314 European Union Flag

1316 Cupid

1315 Eminescu

2000. European Union Membership Negotiations.
6087 **1314** 6100l. multicoloured . . 95 70

2000. 150th Birth Anniv of Mihail Eminescu (poet). Sheet 120 × 92 mm containing T **1315** and similar horiz designs. Each grey, agate and black.
MS6088 3400l. Type **1315**; 3400l. Eminescu and people seated at table; 3400l. Eminescu and star shining over woman; 3400l. Eminescu and three men . . . 3·25 3·25

2000. St. Valentine's Day. Multicoloured.
6089 1500l. Type **1316** 25 50
6090 7950l. Couple . . . . 1·50 50

1317 Easter Eggs

2000. Easter.
6091 **1317** 1700l. blue, green and orange 35 20

2000. Nos. 5855 and 5842 surch, the old value cancelled by a different emblem.
6092 1700l. on 70l. multicoloured (crown) 30 20
6093 1700l. on 70l. multicoloured (snake) 30 20

1319 Greater Bird of Paradise

2000. Birds of Paradise. Multicoloured.
6094 1700l. Type **1319** 25 45
6095 2400l. Magnificent bird of paradise 35 45
6096 9050l. Superb bird of paradise . . . . 1·30 75
6097 10050l. King bird of paradise . . . . 1·50 1·00

2000. Nos. 5342/3 surch.
6098 1900l. on 1l. multicoloured 35 20
6099 2000l. on 1l. multicoloured 35 20

2000. Nos. 5310/14 surch, the old value cancelled by various book and quill emblems.
6100 1700l. on 50b. brown and black 30 20
6101 1700l. on 1l.50 green and mauve 30 20
6102 1700l. on 2l. red and blue 30 20
6103 1700l. on 3l. blue and brown 30 20
6104 1700l. on 4l. brown and blue 30 20

1322 Cineraria

1324 "Building Europe"

2000. Flowers. Multicoloured.
6105 1700l. Type **1322** 30 40
6106 3100l. Indoor lily 55 40
6107 5800l. Plumeria 95 40
6108 10050l. Fuchsia . . . . . . 1·60 85

2000. Nos. 5303/7 surch, the old value cancelled by an easel with palette emblem.
6109 1700l. on 50b. multicoloured 30 20
6110 1700l. on 11.50 multicoloured 30 20
6111 1700l. on 2l. multicoloured 30 20
6112 1700l. on 3l. multicoloured 30 20
6113 1700l. on 4l. multicoloured 30 20

2000. Europa.
6114 **1324** 10150l. multicoloured 1·70 1·00

2000. Death Centenary of Vincent van Gogh (artist). Nos. 5318 and 5321 surch, the old value cancelled by paint palette emblem.
6115 1700l. on 50b. multicoloured 30 20
6116 1700l. on 31.50 multicoloured 30 20

2000. No. 5642 surch, the old value cancelled by an airship.
6117 1700l. on 635l. black, ultramarine and blue . . 25 40
6118 2000l. on 635l. black, ultramarine and blue . . 25 40
6119 3900l. on 635l. black, ultramarine and blue . . 60 40
6120 9050l. on 635l. black, ultramarine and blue . . 1·30 60

1327 Mihai the Brave and Soldiers

2000. Anniversaries. Multicoloured.
6121 3800l. Type **1327** (400th anniv of first union of the Romanian provinces (Wallachia, Transylvania and Moldavia)) 55 45
6122 9050l. Printing press (550th anniv of the 42 line Bible (first Bible printed in Latin)) (36 × 23 mm) . . . 1·20 70

2000. No. 5801 surch, the old value cancelled by a flower.
6123 10000l. on 370l. brown and black . . . . 1·40 45
6124 19000l. on 370l. brown and black . . . . 2·50 95
6125 34000l. on 370l. brown and black . . . . 4·50 1·50

1329 Arnhem, Players and Flags of Romania and Portugal

2000. European Football Championship, The Netherlands and Belgium. Sheet 82 × 121 mm containing T **1329** and similar vert designs, each showing a map of Europe pinpointing the named town. Multicoloured.
MS6126 3800l. Type **1329**; 3800l. Players, Charleroi and English and Romanian flags; 10150l. Players, Liege and Romanian and German flags; 10150l. Goalkeeper and Rotterdam . . . . 6·25 6·25

1330 Ferdinand von Zeppelin and Airship

2000. Centenary of First Zeppelin Flight.
6127 **1330** 2100l. multicoloured . . 35 20

1331 Enrico Fermi (physicist) and Mathematical Equation

2000. The 20th Century (5th series).
6128 **1331** 2100l. black, grey and red 30 25
6129 – 2200l. black and grey 30 25
6130 – 2400l. red and black . . 35 25
6131 – 6000l. multicoloured . . 90 25
DESIGNS: 2100l. Type **1331** (construction of first nuclear reactor, 1942); 2200l. United Nations Charter (signing of charter, 1945); 2400l. Edith Piaf (singer) (release of *La Vie en Rose* (song), 1947); 6000l. Sir Edmund Percival Hillary (mountaineer) (conquest of Mt. Everest, 1953).

2000. No. 5365 surch, the old value cancelled by a bird.
6132 1700l. on 160l. red and pink 25 15

1333 Globe and "Sputnik 1" Satellite

2000. The Twentieth Century (6th series).
6133 **1333** 1700l. multicoloured . . 25 30
6134 – 3900l. multicoloured . . 50 30
6135 – 6400l. black and red . . 90 30
6136 – 11300l. multicoloured 1·50 50
DESIGNS: 1700l. Type **1333** (launch of first man-made satellite, 1957); 3900l. Yuri Gagarin (first manned space flight, 1961); 6400l. Surgeons operating (first heart transplant operation, 1967); 11300l. Edwin E. Aldrin and Moon (first manned landing on Moon, 1969).

1334 Boxing

2000. Olympic Games, Sydney. Multicoloured.
6137 1700l. Type **1334** 35 45
6138 2200l. High jump 35 45
6139 3900l. Weight lifting 65 45
6140 6200l. Gymnastics . . . . . 1·20 45
MS6141 89 × 78 mm. 11300l. Athletics (41 × 53 mm) . . . . 1·50 1·50

1335 Gabriela Szabo (athlete) and Emblem

1336 Palace of Agriculture Ministry

2000. "Olymphilex 2000" International Olympic Stamp Exhibition, Sydney. Sheet 81 × 60 mm.
MS6142 **1335** 14100l. multicoloured 65 65

2000. Bucharest Palaces.
6143 **1336** 1700l. black and grey 25 20
6144 – 2200l. black and stone (horiz) 25 20
6145 – 2400l. black and green (horiz) 25 20
6146 – 3900l. black and brown (horiz) 55 20
DESIGNS: 2200l. Cantacuzino Palace (now George Enescu Museum); 2400l. Grigore Ghica Palace; 3900l. Stirbei Palace (now Museum of Ceramics and Glass).

2000. No. 5836 surch, the old value cancelled by a house.
6147 300l. on 70l. multicoloured 15 10

2000. No. 5349 surch.
6148 300l. on 1l. blue 15 10

2000. Air. No. 5695 surch.
6149 2000l. on 960l. blue & black 25 50
6150 4200l. on 960l. blue & black 60 50
6151 4600l. on 960l. blue & black 65 50
6152 6500l. on 960l. blue & black 95 50

1340 Ilie Ilascu (political prisoner)

2000. 50th Anniv of United Nations Convention on Human Rights.
6153 **1340** 11300l. multicoloured 1·60 85

2000. No. 5700 surch, the old value cancelled by an inkwell and quill emblem.
6154 2000l. on 90l. multicoloured 25 15

2000. No. 5556 surch.
6155 2000l. on 29l. flesh, blk & lil 25 15

1343 Leopard

2000. Big Cats.
6156 **1343** 1200l. multicoloured . . 15 20
6157 – 2000l. blue and black 25 20
6158 – 2200l. multicoloured . . 25 20
6159 – 2300l. multicoloured . . 25 20
6160 – 4200l. brown, bl & blk 55 20
6161 – 6500l. multicoloured . . 90 20
MS6162 90 × 78 mm. 14100l. multicoloured 65 65
DESIGNS: 2000l. Snow Leopard; 2200l. Lion; 2300l. Bobcat; 4200l Mountain lion; 6500l Tiger; 53 × 41 mm—14100l. Lions.

1344 Camil Ressu

1345 Christmas Tree

2000. Self-portraits. Multicoloured.
6163 2000l. Type **1344** 25 30
6164 2400l. Jean Al Steriadi . . . 35 30
6165 4400l. Nicolae Tonitza . . . 55 30
6166 15000l. Nicolae Grigorescu 2·00 85

2000. Christmas.
6167 **1345** 4400l. multicoloured . . 65 35

1346 Jesus Christ and Angel

1349 Globe and Fireworks

2000. Birth Bimillenary of Jesus Christ. Mult.
6168 2000l. Type **1346** 25 25
6169 7000l. Jesus Christ and dove (22 × 38 mm) 95 40

2000. No. 5624 surch, the previous value cancelled by different animals.
6170 7000l. on 3095l. Large-leaved lime (Pig) 85 45
6171 10000l. on 3095l. Large-leaved lime (Bear) . . . . 1·20 60
6172 11500l. on 3095l. Large-leaved lime (Cow) . . . . 1·70 90

2001. New Millennium.
6176 **1349** 11500l. multicoloured 1·40 85

1350 Sculpture

1352 Ribbons forming Heart

2001. 125th Birth Anniv of Constantin Brancusi (sculptor). Multicoloured.
6177 4600l. Type **1350** 45 40
6178 7200l. Display of sculptures 65 40
Nos. 6177/8 were issued together, se-tenant, forming a composite design.

2001. No. 5542 surch, the previous value cancelled by different snakes.
6179 7400l. on 280l. black & yell 70 55
6180 13000l. on 280l. black & yell 1·30 90

2001. St. Valentine's Day. Each red and grey.
6181 2200l. Type **1352** 40 80
6182 11500l. Pierced heart . . . 1·80 80

2001. Nos. 5595/6 and 5598 surch, the previous value cancelled by an ear of corn.
6183 1300l. on 245l. mult 30 40
6184 2200l. on 115l. mult 30 40
6185 5000l. on 115l. mult 55 40
6186 16500l. on 70l. mult . . . . 2·00 60

1354 Hortensia Papadat-Bengescu

2001. Birth Anniversaries. Multicoloured.
6187 1300l. Type **1354** 30 05
6188 2200l. Eugen Lovinescu (writer, 120th anniv) . . . 30 05
6189 2400l. Ion Minulescu (poet, 120th anniv) 30 05
6190 4600l. Andre Malraux (writer, centenary) 45 05
6191 7200l. George H. Gallup (opinion pollster and journalist, centenary) . . 75 05
6192 35000l. Walt Disney (artist and film producer, centenary) . . . . 4·00 20

1355 Chick inside Egg

1356 Sloe (*Prunus spinosa*)

2001. Easter.
6193 **1355** 2200l. multicoloured . . 25 15

2001. Berries. Multicoloured.
6194 2200l. Type **1356** 10 10
6195 4600l. Red currant (*Ribes rubrum L.*) 20 10
6196 7400l. Gooseberry (*Ribes uva-crispa*) 30 10
6197 11500l. Mountain cranberry (*Vaccinium vitis-idaea L.*) 45 10

1357 Hagi

1358 Water Droplet and Globe surmounted by Tree

2001. Retirement of George Hagi (footballer).
6198 **1357** 2200l. multicoloured . . 10 10

2001. Europa. Water Resources.
6199 **1358** 13000l. multicoloured 50 15

1359 Collie

2001. Dogs. Multicoloured.
6200 1300l. Type **1359** 10 10
6201 5000l. Basset hound 20 10
6202 8000l. Siberian husky . . . 30 10
6203 13500l. Ciobanesc mioritic 50 15

1360 Goddess Europa

1362 George Palade (Nobel Prize winner for medicine, 1974)

2001. Romanian Presidency of Organization for Security and Co-operation in Europe.
6204 **1360** 11500l. multicoloured 40 10

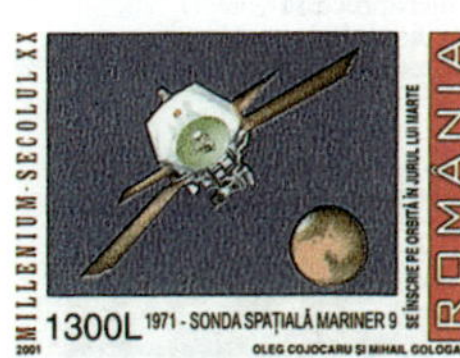

1361 Mariner 9 (spacecraft) and Mars

2001. The 20th Century (7th series). Multicoloured.
6205 1300l. Type **1361** (first orbit of Mars, 1979) 10 10
6206 2400l. Bull (discovery of Paleolithic cave paintings, Ardeche, 1994) 10 10

6207 5000l. Nadia Comaneci (gymnast) (first "10" for gymnastics, Olympic Games, Montreal, 1976) 20 10
6208 8000l. Wall (fall of the Berlin wall, 1989) 30 10

2001. 50th Anniv of United Nations High Commissioner for Refugees.
6209 **1362** 13500l. multicoloured 50 15

2001. Various stamps surch the previous values cancelled by various emblems as stated.
6210 **1100** 300l. on 4l. multicoloured (candlestick) 10 10
6211 **1110** 300l. on 4l. multicoloured (bobsled) 10 10
6212 **1132** 300l. on 7l. multicoloured (harp) 10 10
6213 – 300l. on 9l. multicoloured (No. 5488) (lyre) . . 10 10
6214 **1168** 300l. on 90l. multicoloured (lizard) 10 10
6215 **1190** 300l. on 90l. multicoloured (computer mouse) . . 10 10
6216 **1202** 300l. on 90l. multicoloured (fish) 10 10
6217 – 300l. on 90l. multicoloured (No. 5745) (chess knight) 10 10
6218 **1207** 300l. on 90l. multicoloured (fungi) 10 10
6219 **1157** 300l. on 115l. brown, blue and black (scroll) 10 10
6220 **1158** 300l. on 115l. multicoloured (train) 10 10
6221 **1162** 300l. on 115l. multicoloured (rectangle) 10 10
6222 – 300l. on 115l. multicoloured (No. 5602) (kite) . . 10 10

2001. Nos. 5715/16 and 5720 surch, the previous values cancelled by a sign of the zodiac.
6223 2500l. on 755l. blue and black (Pisces) (postage) 10 10
6224 2500l. on 1615l. green and black (Capricorn) 10 10
6225 2500l. on 715l. red and blue (Aquarius) (air) 10 10

1365 Trap Racing

2001. Equestrian Competitive Events. Mult.
6226 1500l. Type **1365** 10 10
6227 2500l. Dressage 10 10
6228 5300l. Show jumping . . . 20 10
6229 8300l. Flat racing 30 10

1366 Augustin Maior and Drawing

2001. The 20th Century (8th series). Multicoloured.
6230 1500l. Type **1366** (invention of multiple telephony, 1906) 10 10
6231 5300l. Pioneer 10 (satellite) (launched, 1972) 20 10
6232 13500l. Microchip (introduction of first microprocessor, 1971) . . 50 15
6233 15500l. Hubble space telescope (launched, 1990) 60 15

1367 Finger Coral (*Porites porites*)

2001. Corals and Sea Anemones (1st series). Multicoloured.
6234 2500l. Type **1367** 10 10
6235 8300l. Giant sea anemone (*Condylactis gigantia*) . . 30 10
6236 13500l. Northern red anemone (*Anemonia telia*) 50 15
6237 37500l. Common sea fan (*Gorgonia ventalina*) . . . 1·40 35
See also No. **MS**6260.

1368 Children encircling Globe

2001. United Nations Year of Dialogue among Civilizations.
6238 **1368** 8300l. multicoloured . . 30 10

1369 King, Bear and Cat

2001. Comics. Multicoloured.
6239 13500l. Type **1369** 50 15
6240 13500l. Fox beating drum and kicking cat 50 15
6241 13500l. King sleeping and fox beating drum 50 15
6242 13500l. Cat giving fox drum 50 15
6243 13500l. Drum exploding . . 50 15

1370 Top of Wreath with Baubles

2001. Christmas. Multicoloured.
6244 2500l. Type **1370** 10 10
6245 2500l. Bottom of wreath with stars 25 10
Nos. 6244/5 were issued together, se-tenant, forming a composite design of a wreath.

1371 Scorpio

2001. Signs of the Zodiac (1st series). Multicoloured.
6246 1500l. Type **1371** 10 10
6247 2500l. Libra 10 10
6248 5500l. Capricorn 20 10
6249 9000l. Pisces 35 10
6250 13500l. Aquarius 50 15
6251 16500l. Sagittarius 65 15
See also Nos. 6254/9.

1372 Building

2001. Centenary of Central Post Headquarters, Bucharest. Multicoloured.
6252 5500l. Type **1372** 20 10
6253 5500l. Obverse of medal showing building, 1901 (vert) 20 10

2002. Signs of the Zodiac (2nd series). As T **1371**. Multicoloured.
6254 1500l. Aries 10 10
6255 2500l. Taurus 10 10
6256 5500l. Gemini 20 10
6257 8700l. Cancer 30 10
6258 9000l. Leo 30 10
6259 23500l. Virgo 75 20

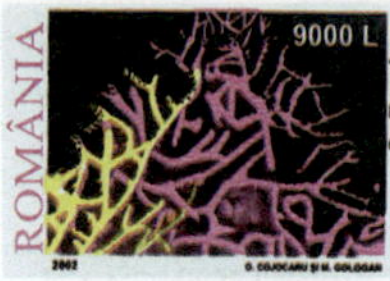

1373 Red Coral (*Corallum rubrum*)

2002. Corals and Sea Anemones (2nd series). Sheet 106 × 77 mm containing T **1373** and similar horiz designs. Multicoloured.
MS6260 9000l. Type **1373**; 9000l. Elkhorn coral (*Acropora palmate*); 16500l. Beadlet anemone (*Actinia equine*); 16500l. Pulmose anemone (*Metridium senile*) . . . . . . 1·70 1·70

1374 Emanuil Gojdu

2002. Birth Bicentenary of Emanuil Gojdu (nationalist).
6261 **1374** 2500l. black, blue and deep blue 10 10

1375 Mice

2002. St. Valentine's Day. Multicoloured.
6262 5500l. Type **1375** 20 10
6263 43500l. Elephants . . . . . 1·40 35

1376 Ion Mincu

2002. Birth Anniversaries.
6267 **1376** 1500l. green and black 10 10
6268 – 2500l. multicoloured . . 10 10
6269 – 5500l. multicoloured . . 20 10
6270 – 9000l. multicoloured . . 50 10
6271 – 16500l. multicoloured 55 10
6272 – 34000l. multicoloured 1·10 25
DESIGNS: Type **1376** (architect) (150th); 2500l. Costin Nenitescu (chemist) (centenary); 5500l. Alexander Dumas (writer) (bicentenary); 9000l. Serban Cioculescu (literary historian) (centenary); 16500l. Leonardo da Vinci (artist) (550th); 34000l. Victor Hugo (writer) (bicentenary).

1377 Flag and Statue of Liberty

2002. "United We Stand". Multicoloured.
6273 25500l. Type **1377** 80 20
6274 25500l. Flags and monument 80 20
Nos. 6273/4 were issued together, se-tenant, forming a composite design.

1378 Fortified Church and Tower, Saschiz

1379 Crucifixion

2002. Germanic Fortresses and Churches in Translyvania. Multicoloured.
6275 1500l. Type **1378** 10 10
6276 2500l. Church staircase, Darjiu 10 10
6277 6500l. Fortress, Viscri (horiz) 25 10
6278 10500l. Fortified church, Vorumloc (horiz) 35 10
6279 13500l. Tower gate, Calnic 45 10
6280 17500l. Fortified church, Prejmer 55 10

2002. Easter. Showing miniatures by Picu Patrut. Multicoloured.
6281 2500l. Type **1379** 10 10
6282 10500l. Resurrection 35 10

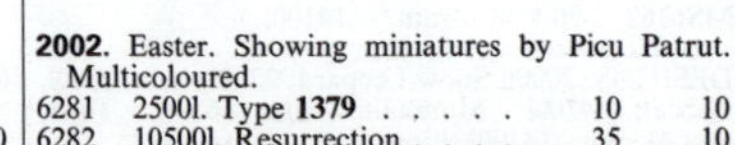

1380 Clown

1381 "Dorobantul" (Nicolae Grigorescu)

2002. Europa. Circus. Multicoloured.
6283 17500l. Type **1380** 55 10
6284 25500l. Clown (different) . . 80 20

2002. 125th Anniv of Independence. Sheet 77 × 91 mm.
MS6285 **1381** 25500l. multicoloured 80 80

1382 Post Mark

2002. 50th Anniv of International Federation Stamp Dealers' Association (IFSDA). Sheet 105 × 75 mm containing T **1382** and similar horiz designs. Multicoloured.
MS6286 10000l. Type **1382**; 10000l. IFSDA emblem; 27500l. World Trade Centre, Bucharest; 27500l. Philatelic shop, Bucharest . . . 2·40 2·40

1383 Mountains

2002. Year of Mountains (2000l.) and Year of Eco-tourism (3000l.). Multicoloured.
6287 2000l. Type **1383** 10 10
6288 3000l. Landscape and recycling symbol (32 × 24 mm) 10 10

1384 Cricket

2002. Sport. Multicoloured.
6289 7000l. Type **1384** 20 10
6290 11000l. Polo 35 10
6291 15500l. Golf 50 10
6292 19500l. Baseball 65 20

1385 Ion Luca Caragiale

2002. Anniversaries. Multicoloured.
6293 10000l. Type **1385** (playwright) (150th birth anniv) 30 10
6294 10000l. National Theatre, Bucharest (150th anniv) 30 10
Nos. 6293/4 were issued together, se-tenant, forming a composite design within the sheet.

1386 Financial Postal Service Emblem

2002. Postal Services.
6295 **1386** 2000l. multicoloured . . 10 10
6296 – 3000l. red, yellow and blue 10 10
6297 – 8000l. multicoloured . . 25 10

6298 – 10000l. purple and brown 30 10
6299 – 13000l. red, grey and black 40 10
6300 – 15500l. multicoloured 50 10
6301 – 20500l. mauve, blue and black 65 20
6302 – 27500l. multicoloured 90 20

DESIGNS: 2000l. Type **1386**; 3000l. Romania Post emblem; 8000l. Direct mailing centre emblem; 10000l. Post building (130th anniv); 13000l. Direct marketing emblem; 15500l. Rapid post emblem; 20500l. Priority post emblem; 27500l. Globe and stamp album (Romafilatelia).

1387 *Boloria pales carpathomeridionalis*

2002. Butterflies. Sheet 101 × 71 mm containing T **1387** and similar horiz designs. Multicoloured.
MS6310 44500l. Type **1387**; 44500l. *Erebia pharte romaniae*; 44500l. *Peridea korbl herculana*; 44500l. *Tomares nogelii dobrogensis* . . 2·75 2·75

1388 Locomotive 50115 (1930)

2002. Steam Locomotives. 130th Anniv of First Locomotive made at Machine Factory, Resita (**MS**6317). Multicoloured.
6311 4500l. Type **1388** 10 10
6312 6500l. 50025 (1921) 10 10
6313 7000l. 230128 (1933) 20 10
6314 11000l. 764493 (1956) . . . 35 10
6315 19500l. 142072 (1939) . . . 65 20
6316 44500l. 704209 (1909) . . . 1·40 35
MS6317 75 × 90 mm. 72500l. Steam locomotive (1872) (42 × 54 mm) 2·40 2·40

1389 Knight and Bishop
1390 Quince (*Cydonia oblonga*)

2002. 35th Chess Olympiad, Bled, Slovenia. Sheet 102 × 62 mm containing T **1389** and similar vert designs. Multicoloured.
MS6318 20500l. Type **1389**; 20500l. King and knight; 20500l. Queen and rook . . . . 1·00 1·00

2002. Fruit. Multicoloured.
6319 15500l. Type **1390** 50 10
6320 20500l. Apricot (*Armeniaca vulgaris*) 65 20
6321 44500l. Cherries (*Cerasus vulgaris*) . . . . 1·40 35
6322 73500l. Mulberry (*Morus nigra*) . . . . 2·40 60

1391 Father Christmas carrying Parcels

2002. Christmas. Multicoloured.
6323 3000l. Type **1391** 10 10
6324 15500l. Father Christmas and computer 50 10

1392 Eagle (Romanian emblem), Flags and NATO Emblem

2002. Romania Invitation to join North Atlantic Treaty Organization (NATO). Sheet 168 × 106 mm containing T **1392**.
MS6325 131000l. × 2, Type **1392** × 2 4·25 4·25
No. **MS**6325 contains a central label showing NATO emblem.

1393 “Braila Harbour” (Jean-Alexandru Steriadi)

2003. Art. Multicoloured.
6326 4500l. Type **1393** 20 10
6327 6500l. “Balcic” (Nicolae Darascu) 25 10
6328 30500l. “Conversation” (Nicolae Vermont) . . . 1·10 25
6329 34000l. “Dalmatia” (Nicolae Darascu) . . . . 1·30 30
6330 46500l. “Fishing Boats” (Jean-Alexandru Steriadi) 1·70 40
6331 53000l. “Nude” (Bogdan Pietris) . . . . 2·00 50
MS6332 75 × 91 mm. 83500l. “Woman on Seashore” (Nicolae Grigorescu) (42 × 54 mm) . . . 3·00 3·00

1394 Building Facade

2003. 80th Anniv of National Military Palace, Bucharest.
6333 **1394** 5000l. multicoloured . . 20 10

1395 Ladybird

2003. March Amulet (good luck). Multicoloured.
6334 3000l. Type **395** 10 10
6335 5000l. Chimney sweep (vert) 20 10

1396 “10”

2003. 10th Anniv of Romania signing European Agreement (precursor to joining EU).
6336 **1396** 142000l. multicoloured 5·25 1·30

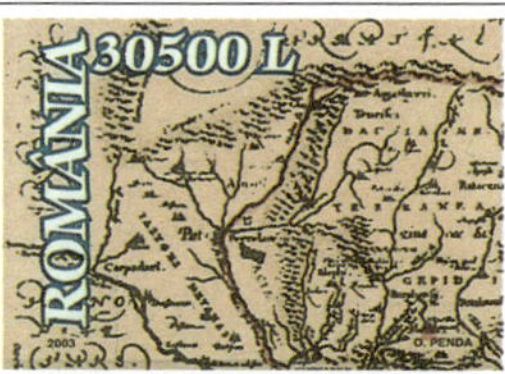

1399 Map (detail) (upper left quadrant)

2003. Pieter van den Keere (Petrus Kærius Cælavit) (cartographer) Commemoration. Two sheets containing T **1399** and similar multicoloured designs.
MS6348 (a) 120 × 90 mm. 30500l. × 4 “Vetus description Daciarum” (description of Dacia); (b) 76 × 91 mm. 46500l. National Map and Book Museum (42 × 54 mm) 4·00 4·00

1400 Rabbit carrying Egg and Envelope
1401 Eurasian Scops Owl (*Otus scops*)

2003. Easter.
6349 **1400** 3000l. multicoloured . . 10 10

2003. Owls. Multicoloured.
6350 5000l. Type **1401** 20 10
6351 8000l. Ural owl (*Strix uralensis*) 30 10
6352 10000l. Eurasian pygmy owl (*Glaucidium passerinum*) 40 10
6353 13000l. Short-eared owl (*Asio flammeus*) 50 10
6354 15500l. Long-eared owl (*Asio otus*) 60 15
6355 20500l. Tengmalm’s owl (*Aegolius funereus*) . . . 80 20

1402 Butterfly emerging from Cocoon

2003. Europa. Poster Art. Multicoloured.
6356 20500l. Type **1402** 80 20
6357 73500l. Figure holding Painting . . . . 2·70 65

1403 Dumltru Staniloae

2003. Birth Centenaries. Multicoloured.
6358 4500l. Type **1403** (theologian) 20 10
6359 8000l. Alexandru Ciucurencu (artist) . . . 30 10
6360 30500l. Ilarie Voronca (poet) 1·60 40
6361 46500l. Victor Brauner (artist) . . . . 1·70 40

1404 “Fantastic Animals”

2003. Birth Anniversaries. Multicoloured.
6337 6000l. Type **1397** (sculptor) (centenary) 20 10
6338 18000l. Hector Berlioz (composer) (bicentenary) 75 15
6339 20000l. Vincent van Gogh (artist) (150th) 75 15
6340 36000l. Groeges de Bellio (doctor and art collector) (175th) . . . . 1·70 40

1397 Ion Irimescu
1398 Post Palace

2003. Architecture. Multicoloured.
6341 4500l. Type **1398** 20 10
6342 5500l. Central Savings House 20 10
6343 10000l. National Bank (horiz) 40 10
6344 15500l. Stock Exchange . . 60 15
6345 20500l. Carol I University 80 20
6346 46500l. Athenium . . . . . 1·70 40
MS6347 76 × 91 mm. 73500l. Palace of Justice (42 × 54 mm) . . . . 2·70 2·70

2003. Birth Centenary of Victor Brauner (artist). Sheet 175 × 129 mm containing T **1404** and similar multicoloured designs showing paintings.
MS6362 10000l. × 12. Type **1404**; “Self Portrait” × 3 (24 × 33 mm); “Heron of Alexandria” (24 × 33 mm); “Surrealist Composition”; “Drobegea Landscape”; “Nude” (24 × 33 mm); “Drobegea Landscape” (different); “Courteous Passivity”; “Ion Minulescu Portrait” (abstract) (24 × 33 mm); “Dragon” . . . 4·75 4·75

1405 Nostradamus and Astrolabe

2003. 500th Birth Anniv of Nostradamus (prophet). Multicoloured.
6363 73500l. Type **1405** . . . . 2·70 65
6364 73500l. Astrolabe, diagram and Nostradamus . . . . 2·70 65

1406 Magnifying Glass, Building and Emblem

2003. Post Day. Centenary of Timisoara Philatelic Association.
6365 **1406** 5000l. multicoloured . . 20 10

1407 Yellow Stainer (*Agaricus xanthodermus*)
1408 Skydiving

2003. Fungi. Two sheets each 126 × 75 mm containing T **1407** and similar vert designs. Multicoloured.
MS6366 (a) 15500l. × 3 Type **1407**; Basket fungus (*Clathrus rubber*); Panther cap (*Amanita pantherina*); (b) 20500l. × 3 Red-capped scaber stalk (*Leccinum aurantiacum*); Chicken mushroom (*Laetiporus sulphurous*); *Russula xerampelina* 3·00 3·00

2003. Extreme Sports. Multicoloured.
6367 5000l. Type **1408** 20 10
6368 8000l. Windsurfing (horiz) 30 10
6369 10000l. Motor cycle racing (horiz) 40 10
6370 30500l. Skiing . . . . . . 1·20 30

1409 Green Lizard *Lacerta viridis*

2003. Amphibians. Sheet 125 × 105 mm containing T **1409** and similar vert designs.
MS6371 8000l. × 4 Type **1409**; Green tree frog (*Hyla arborea*); Snake-eyed skink (*Ablepharus kitaibelii*); Common frog (*Rana temporaria*) . . . . 1·20 1·20

1410 Cobza (stringed instrument)

2003. Traditional Instruments (1st series). Multicoloured.
6372 1000l. Type **1410** 10 10
6373 4000l. Bucium (wind) . . . 15 10
6374 6000l. Vioara cu Goarna (violin with horn) 20 10

1411 Map and Statue

2003. 125th Anniv of Berlin Treaty returning Dobrudja to Romania.
6375 **1411** 16000l. multicoloured 60 15

1412 Pope John Paul II and Teoctist, Romanian Patriarch

2003. 25th Anniv of Pontificate of Pope John Paul II. Multicoloured.
6376 16000l. Type **1412** 60 15
6377 16000l. Pope John Paul II and Teoctist (different) . . 60 15

1413 Father Christmas

1414 Woman wearing Suit and Cloche Hat (1921–1930)

2003. Christmas.
6378 **1413** 4000l. black, rosine and orange 15 10
6379 – 4000l. black and orange 15 10
DESIGN: No. 6379. Snowman.
Nos. 6378/9 were issued, together, se-tenant, forming a composite design.

2003. 20th-century Women's Fashion. Multicoloured.
6380 4000l. Type **1414** 15 10
6381 4000l. Wearing coat with fur collar (1931–1940) 15 10
6382 21000l. Wearing hat and carrying muff (1901–1910) 15 10
6383 21000l. Wearing caped coat and hat (1911–1920) . . . 15 10

1415 Early Woman Footballer

2003. Centenary of FIFA (Federation Internationale de Football Association). Multicoloured.
6384 3000l. Type **1415** 10 10
6385 4000l. Players and film camera 15 10
6386 6000l. Heads and newsprint 20 10
6387 10000l. Boots, pad and ball 40 10
6388 34000l. Rule book and pitch 1·30 30

1416 Grey Heron (*Ardea cinerea*)

2004. Water Birds. Sheet 94 × 96 mm containing T **1416** and similar vert designs. Multicoloured.
MS6389 16000l. × 4 Type **1416**; Mallard (*Anas platyrhynchos*); Great crested grebe (*Podiceps cristatus*); Eastern white pelican (*Pelecanus onocrotalus*) . . . . 2·40 2·40

1417 Globe, Satellite and Disc

2004. Information Technology. Sheet 93 × 69 mm containing T **1417** and similar horiz design. Multicoloured.
MS6390 20000l. × 4 Type **1417**; Computer screen; Satellite dish; Computer keyboard . . . . . 3·00 3·00

1418 Amerigo Vespucci

2004. 550th Birth Anniv of Amerigo Vespucci (explorer). Multicoloured.
6391 16000l. Type **1418** 60 15
6392 31000l. Sailing ship . . . . 1·20 30

1419 Couple

1421 Easter Egg and Rabbit holding Envelope

1420 UPU Emblem

2004. St. Valentine.
6393 **1419** 21000l. multicoloured 80 20

2004. Universal Postal Union Congress, Bucharest (1st. issues). Multicoloured.
6394 31000l. Type **1420** . . . . 1·20 30
6395 31000l. Bird holding envelope . . . . 1·20 30
Nos. 6394/5 were issued together, se-tenant, forming a composite design.
See also Nos. 6445/50.

2004. Easter.
6396 **1421** 4000l. multicoloured . . 15 10

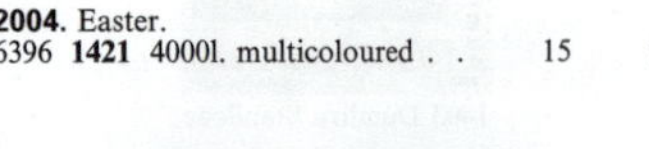

1422 Bullet Locomotive, Japan

2004. Modern Locomotives. Multicoloured.
6397 4000l. Type **1422** 15 10
6398 6000l. TGV, France 20 10
6399 10000l. KTX, South Korea 20 10
6400 16000l. AVE, Spain 60 15
6401 47000l. ICE, Germany . . . 1·80 45
6402 56000l. Eurostar, UK and France . . . . 2·10 50
MS6403 92 × 77 mm. 77000l. *Blue Arrow* (Sageti Albastre), Romania (54 × 42 mm) . . . . 3·00 3·00

1423 NATO Headquarters

2004. Romania's Accession to NATO.
6404 **1423** 40000l. multicoloured 15 15

1424 Pierre de Coubertin

1425 Marksman

2004. 90th Anniv of Romanian Olympic Committee. Sheet 120 × 86 mm containing T **1423** and similar multicoloured designs.
MS6405 16000l.+5000l. × 3, Type **1424** (founder of modern Olympics); Olympic stadium, Athens, 1896 (54 × 42 mm); George Bibescu (founder member) 60 60

2004. 20th-century Women's Fashion. Vert designs as T **1414** showing women's clothes. Mult.
6406 4000l. Calf length suit and hat (1941–1950) 15 10
6407 4000l. Knee length coat (1951–1960) 15 10
6408 21000l. Dress and jacket (1981–1990) 80 20
6409 21000l. Sleeveless dress (1991–2000) 80 20
6410 31000l. Mini skirted coat (1961–1970) . . . . . . 1·20 30
6411 31000l. Trouser suit (1971–1980) . . . . 1·20 30
Nos. 6406/7, 6408/9 and 6410/11, respectively, were issued together, se-tenant, each pair forming a composite design.

2004. 51st International Council for Game and Wildlife Conservation General Assembly. Multicoloured.
6412 16000l. Type **1425** 60 20
6413 16000l. Dog's head and pheasant 60 20
6414 16000l. Stag 60 20
6415 16000l. Ibex 60 20
6416 16000l. Bear 60 20
MS6417 99 × 87 mm. 16000l. Stag (54 × 42 mm) 60 60
Nos. 6412/16 were issued, together, se-tenant strips of five stamps, each strip forming a composite design.

1426 Sun and Shoreline

2004. Europa. Holidays. Multicoloured.
6418 21000l. Type **1426** 80 20
6419 77000l. Sun and snowy mountains . . . . 3·00 75

1427 Mihai Viteazul (Michael the Brave) (statue)

1429 Bram Stoker

1428 Facade

2004.
6420 **1427** 3000l. multicoloured . . 10 10

2004. National Philatelic Museum.
6421 **1428** 4000l. multicoloured . . 10 10

2004. "Dracula" (novel by Bram Stoker). Sheet 142 × 84 mm containing T **1429** and similar vert designs. Multicoloured.
MS6422 31000l. × 4, Type **1429**; Dracula and cross; Dracula carrying woman; Dracula in coffin 1·80 1·80

1430 Anghel Saligny

2004. Anniversaries. Multicoloured.
6423 4000l. Type **1430** (engineer) (150th birth) 10 10
6424 16000l. Gheorgi Anghel (sculptor) (birth centenary) 60 15
6425 21000l. George Sand (Aurore Dupin) (writer) (birth bicentenary) 80 20
6426 31000l. Oscar Wilde (writer) (150th birth) . . . . . . 1·20 30

1431 Roman Temple, Bucharest

2004.
6427 **1431** 10000l. olive and green 40 10

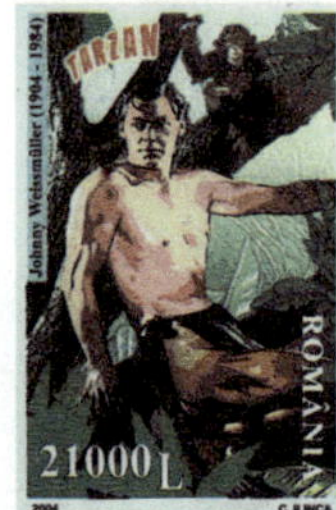

1432 Johnny Weissmuller

2004. Birth Centenary of Johnny Weissmuller (athlete and actor).
6428 **1432** 21000l. multicoloured 80 20

1433 Aircraft and Emblem

2004. 50th Anniv of TAROM Air Transport.
6429 **1433** 16000l. multicoloured 60 15

1434 Footballs and Anniversary Emblem

2004. Centenary of FIFA (Federation Internationale de Football Association).
6430 **1434** 31000l. multicoloured 1·20 30

1435 Stefan III (fresco), Dobrovat Monastery (¾-size illustration)

2004. 500th Death Anniv of Stefan III (Stefan cel Mare) (Moldavian ruler). Two sheets, each 173 × 62 mm, containing T **1435** and similar horiz designs. Multicoloured.

MS6431 (a) 10000l. × 3, Type **1435**; Ruins of Sucevei; Stefan III (embroidered panel). (b) 16000l. pale brown; 16000l. multicoloured; 16000l. pale brown . . . . . 3·00 3·00

DESIGN: **MS**6431b. 16000l. × 3, Putna monastery; Stefan III (painting); Neamt fortress.

1436 Alexandru Macedonski

2004. Anniversaries. Multicoloured.
6432 2000l. Type **1436** (writer) (150th birth) 10 10
6433 3000l. Victor Babes (scientist) (150th birth) . . 10 10
6434 6000l. Arthur Rimbaud (writer) (150th birth) . . . 20 10
6435 56000l. Salvador Dali (artist) (birth centenary) . . . . 2·10 50

1437 King Ferdinand and First Stamp Exhibition Poster

2004. Post Day. 80th Anniv of First National Stamp Exhibition. Sheet 134 × 112 mm.
MS6436 10000l. × 4, Type **1437** × 4. Perf and imperf . . . . 1·60 1·60

1438 Zeppelin LZ-127 and Buildings

2004. 75th Anniv of Zeppelin LZ-127's Flight over Brasov.
6437 **1438** 31000l. multicoloured 1·20 30

1439 Bank Building

2004. 140th Anniv of National Savings Bank (Casa de Economii si Consemnatiuni).
6438 **1439** 5000l. multicoloured . . 20 10

1440 Firemen and Engine

2004. 24th International CTIF (International Fire-fighters Association) Symposium, Brasov. Multicoloured.
6439 12000l. Type **1440** 45 10
6440 12000l. Firemen fighting fire 45 10

1441 Woman Rower

1443 "L'appel"

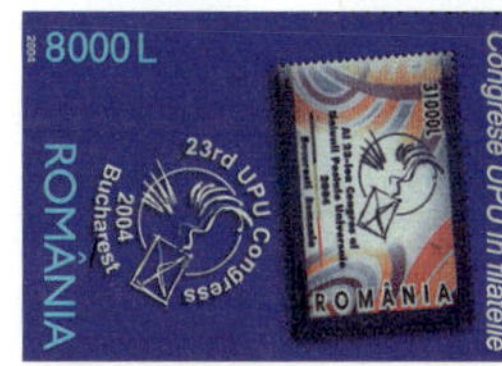

1442 23rd Conference Emblem and 2004 Romania Stamp

2004. Olympic Games, Athens. Multicoloured.
6441 7000l. Type **1441** 25 10
6442 12000l. Fencers 45 10
6443 21000l. Swimmer 80 20
6444 31000l.+9000l. Gymnast . . 1·50 35

2004. Universal Postal Union Congress, Bucharest (2nd issue). Showing emblem and stamps commemorating congresses. Multicoloured.
6445 8000l. Type **1442** 30 10
6446 10000l. 1974 Switzerland . . 40 10
6447 19000l. 1994 South Korea 70 15
6448 31000l. 1990 China . . . . 1·20 30
6449 47000l. 1989 USA . . . . 1·80 45
6450 77000l. 1979 Brasil . . . . 3·00 75

2004. 10th Death Anniv of Idel Ivanchelevici (sculptor). Statues. Multicoloured.
6451 21000l. Type **1443** 80 20
6452 31000l. "Perennis perdurat poeta" . . . . 1·20 30

Stamps of the same design were issued by Belgium.

1444 Bronze Age Cucuteni Pot

2004. Cultural Heritage. Multicoloured.
6453 5000l. Type **1444** 20 10
6454 5000l. Drum supported by phoenixes and tigers . . . 20 10

Stamps of the same design were issued by China.

1445 Gerard Kremer (Geradus Mercator) and Jodocus Hondius

2004. European Anniversaries. Sheet 158 × 144 mm containing T **1445** and similar horiz designs. Multicoloured.
MS6455 18000l. × 3, Type **1445** (cartographers) (450th anniv of Mercator's map of Europe and 400th anniv of Hondius—Mercator atlas); UPU monument, Berne (23rd UPU congress, Bucharest); Amerigo Vespucci (explorer) (550th birth anniv) 2·00 2·00

1446 Roman Riders and Foot Soldiers

2004. Fragments of Trajan's Column (Roman monument) (1st issue).
6456 **1446** 7000l. grey and ultramarine 25 10
6457 – 12000l. brown and ultramarine 40 10
6458 – 19000l. orange and ultramarine 70 20
6459 – 56000l. carmine and ultramarine . . . . . 2·00 50

DESIGNS: Type **1446**; 12000l. Neptune and soldiers embarking on ships; 19000l. Fortress and soldier holding cauldron in stream; 56000l. Chariot in moat and soldiers attacking fortress.

See also Nos. 6468/70.

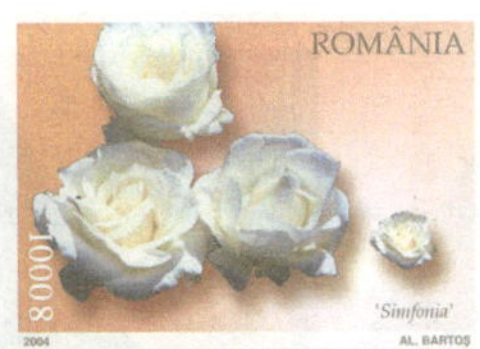

1447 "Simfonia" (Symphony) Rose

2004. Roses. Multicoloured.
6460 8000l. Type **1447** 30 10
6461 15000l. "Foc de Tabara" (Camp fire) 55 15
6462 25000l. "Golden Elegance" 90 20
6463 36000l. "Doamna in mov" (Lady in mauve) . . . . 1·30 35
MS6464 120 × 90 mm. Nos. 6460/3 3·00 3·00

1448 Ilie Nastase

2004. Ilie Nastase (tennis player). Multicoloured.
6465 10000l. Type **1448** 35 10
MS6466 Two sheets. (a) 110 × 200 mm. 72000l. Ilie Nastase (42 × 52 mm). (b) 91 × 110 mm. As No. **MS**6466a. Imperf . . . . 5·00 5·00

1449 Father Christmas

2004. Christmas.
6467 **1449** 5000l. multicoloured . . 20 10

2004. Fragments of Trajan's Column (Roman monument) (2nd issue). As T **1446**.
6468 21000l. green and ultramarine 65 15
6469 31000l. black and ultramarine . . . . 1·10 30
6470 145000l. vermilion and ultramarine . . . . 5·00 1·25

DESIGNS: 21000l. Ritual sacrifice; 31000l. Soldiers, trees, water and heads on posts; 145000l. Stone encampment.

1450 Scouts Emblem

2004. International Organizations. Showing emblems. Multicoloured.
6471 12000l. Type **1450** 40 10
6472 16000l. Lions International 60 15
6473 19000l. Red Cross and Red Crescent 70 20
MS6474 90 × 78 mm. 87000l. Dimitrie Cantemir (writer and linguist) (Freemasonry) (42 × 52 mm) . . . . 3·00 3·00

1451 Iolanda Balas-Soter

2004. Olympic Games, Athens. Women Athletes. Each black and gold.
6475 5000l. Type **1451** (high jump) 20 10
6476 33000l. Elsabeta Lipa (rowing) . . . . 1·20 30
6477 77000l. Ivan Patzaichin (kayaking) . . . . 2·70 70

1452 "Tristan Tzara" (M. H. Maxy)

2004. Modern Art. Two sheets, each 129 × 78 mm containing T **1452** and similar vert designs. Multicoloured.
MS6478 (a) 7000l. × 3, Type **1452**; "Baroneasa" (Merica Ramniceanu); "Portret de Femeie" (Jean David). (b) 12000l. × 3, "Compozitie" (Marcel Ianescu); "Femeie care viseaza II" (Victor Brauner); "Compozitie" (Hans Mattis-Teutsch) . . . . 2·00 2·00

1453 Gheorghe Magheru

2005. Anniversaries (1st issue). Multicoloured.
6479 15000l. Type **1453** (revolutionary leader) (125th death anniv) . . . 55 15
6480 25000l. Christian Dior (dress designer) (birth centenary) 85 20
6481 35000l. Henry Fonda (actor) (birth centenary) . . . . 1·20 30
6482 72000l. Greta Garbo (actress) (birth centenary) 2·50 65
6483 77000l. George Valentin Bibescu (aviation pioneer) (125th birth anniv) . . . 2·70 70

See also Nos. 6512/16.

1454 Emblem

2005. Centenary of Rotary International (charitable organization.).
6484 **1454** 21000l. multicoloured 75 20

1455 Wedding Pitcher (Oboga-Olt)

1457 *Carassius auratus*

1456 Elopteryx nopcsai

2005. Pottery (1st issue). Multicoloured.
6485 3000l. Type **1455** 10 10
6486 5000l. Jugs and pitchers (Sacel-Maramures) . . . 20 10
6487 12000l. Pitcher (Horezu-Valcea) 40 10
6488 16000l. Wedding pitcher (Corund-Harghita) . . . 55 15

See also Nos. 6498/6500 and 6591/7.

2005. Dinosaurs. Multicoloured.
6489 21000l. Type **1456** 75 20
6490 31000l. Telmatosaurus transylvanicus (inscr "transsylvanicus") . . . . 1·10 25

6491 35000l. Struthiosaurus transilvanicus . . . . . . 1·20 30
6492 47000l. Hatzegopteryx thambema . . . . 1·70 45
MS6493 125 × 120 mm. Nos. 6489/92 4·75 4·75

2005. Fish. Multicoloured.
6494 21000l. Type **1457** 75 20
6495 31000l. *Symphysodon discus* 1·10 25
6496 36000l. *Labidochromis* . . . 1·30 30
6497 47000l. *Betta splendens* . . . 1·70 45

2005. Pottery (2nd issue). As T **1455**. Multicoloured.
6498 7000l. Wedding pitchers (Romana-Olt) 25 10
6499 8000l. Jug (Vadul Crisului-Bihor) 30 10
6500 10000l. Jug (Tara Barsei-Brasov) 40 10

1458 "Castle of the Carpathians"

2005. Death Centenary of Jules Verne (writer). Multicoloured.
6501 19000l. Type **1458** 75 20
6502 21000l. "The Danube Pilot" 75 20
6503 47000l. "Claudius Bombarnac" . . . . . . 1·70 45
6504 56000l. "The Stubborn Keraban" . . . . 2·00 50
MS6505 120 × 116 mm. Nos. 6501/4 6·75 6·75

1459 Last Supper (icon) (Matei Purcariu)

2005. Easter. Multicoloured.
6506 5000l. Type **1459** 20 10
6507 5000l. Crucifixion 20 10
6508 5000l. Resurrection 20 10

1460 Pope John Paul II and Stylized Dove

2005. Pope John Paul II Commemoration. Multicoloured.
6509 5000l. Type **1460** 20 10
6510 21000l. Vatican 75 20
MS6511 106 × 78 mm Nos. 6509/10 each × 2 . . . . 1·90 1·90

2005. Anniversaries (2nd issue). As T **1453**. Multicoloured.
6512 3000l. Hans Christian Anderson (writer) (birth bicentenary) 10 10
6513 5000l. Jules Verne (writer) (death centenary) 20 10
6514 12000l. Albert Einstein (physicist) (50th death anniv) 40 10
6515 21000l. Dimitrie Gusti (sociologist and philosopher) (50th death anniv) 75 20
6516 22000l. George Enescu (musician) (50th death anniv) 80 20

1461 Map of Romania and European Stars

2005. Signing of Treaty of Accession to European Union. Multicoloured.
6517 5000l. Type **1461** 20 10
6518 5000l. As No. 6516 but map and vertical band silver 20 10

(1461a)

1463 Grasa de Cotnari Grapes

1462 Archer on Horseback and Casserole

2005. No. 5623 surch as T **1461a**.
6519 1500l. on 1440l. 10 10

2005. Europa. Gastronomy. Multicoloured.
6520 21000l. Type **1462** 75 20
6521 77000l. Retriever, fowl, vegetables and wine glass 2·75 70
MS6522 120 × 90 mm. Nos. 6520/1, each × 2 . . . . 7·00 7·00

2005. Viticulture. Showing grape varieties. Multicoloured.
6523 21000l. Type **1463** 75 20
6524 21000l. Feteasca neagra . . 75 20
6525 21000l. Feteasca alba . . . 75 20
6526 21000l. Victoria 75 20

1464 Fire Supervision

2005. Romania Scouts. Multicoloured.
6527 22000l. Type **1464** 80 20
6528 22000l. Orienteering 80 20
6529 22000l. Trail marking . . . 80 20
6530 22000l. Rock climbing . . . 80 20

On 1 July 2005 the currency of Romania was simplified so that now 1 new leu equals 10000 old leu.

New Currency

10000 leu (l.) = 1 leu (l.)

1465 1 bani Coin

2005. New Currency. Designs showing old and new currency. Multicoloured.
6531 30b. Type **1465** 15 10
6532 30b. As No. 6531 but design reversed 15 10
6533 50b. 1 leu bank note 20 10
6534 50b. As No. 6533 but design reversed 20 10
6535 70b. 5 bani coin 30 10
6536 70b. As No. 6535 but design reversed 30 10
6537 80b. 5 lei note 30 10
6538 80b. As No. 6537 but design reversed 30 10
6539 1l. 10 lei note 40 10
6540 1l. As No. 6539 but design reversed 40 10
6541 1l.20 50 lei note 45 10
6542 1l.20 As No. 6541 but design reversed 45 10
6543 1l.60 100 lei note 60 15
6544 1l.60 As No. 6543 but design reversed 60 15
6545 2l.10 10 bani 80 20
6546 2l.10 As No. 6545 but design reversed 80 20
6547 2l.20 500 lei note 85
6548 2l.20 As No. 6547 but design reversed 85 20
6549 3l.10 50 bani coin . . . . . 1·20 30
6550 3l.10 As No. 6549 but design reversed . . . . . 1·20 30

1466 *Constanta* (teaching ship)

2005. Stamp Day. Ships. Multicoloured.
6551 2l.20 Type **1466** 85 20
6552 2l.20 *Counter Admiral Horia Macellariu* (corvette) . . . 85 20
6553 2l.20 *Mihail Kogalniceanu* 85 20
6554 2l.20 *Marasesti* (frigate) . . 85 20

1467 Rainbow and Sphinx

2005. Floods—July 2005 (1st issue).
6555 **1467** 50b. multicoloured . . 20 10
See also Nos. 6563/6.

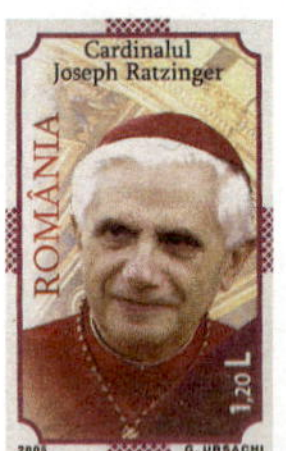

1468 Cardinal Joseph Ratzinger

1470 "The Forest Mailman" (Bianca Paul)

1469 Christopher Columbus

2005. Enthronement of Pontificate of Benedict XVI. Multicoloured.
6556 1l.20 Type **1468** 45 10
6557 2l.10 Pope Benedict XVI . . 80 20
MS6558 122 × 98 mm. Nos. 6556/7 1·40 1·40

2005. 50th Anniv of Europa Stamps. 500th Death Anniv of Christopher Columbus (2006). Multicoloured.
6559 4l.70 Type **1469** . . . . . 1·80 45
6560 4l.70 *Santa Maria* at left and Columbus . . . . . 1·80 45
6561 4l.70 *Santa Maria* at right and Columbus . . . . . 1·80 45
6562 4l.70 Christopher Columbus wearing wig and hat . . . 1·80 45

2005. Floods—July 2005 (2nd issue). Winning Entries in Children's Design a Stamp Competition. Multicoloured.
6563 30b. Type **1470** 15 10
6564 40b. "The Road to You" (Daniel Ciornei) 15 10
6565 60b. "A Messenger of Peace" (Stefan Ghiliman) (horiz) 25 10
6566 1l. "Good News for Everybody" (Adina Elena Mocanu) (horiz) 40 10

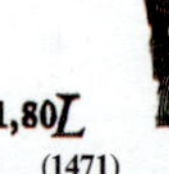

(1471)

1472 Jagd Terrier

2005. International Philatelic Exhibition, Bucharest. No. **MS**6455 optd as T **1471**.
MS6567 111.80 × 3 on 118000l. × 3, multicoloured . . . . 12·00 12·00

2005. Hunting Dogs. Multicoloured.
6568 2l.20 Type **1472** 45 10
6569 2l.20 Rhodesian ridgeback 45 10
6570 2l.20 Munsterlander 45 10
6571 2l.20 Bloodhound 45 10
6572 2l.20 Copoi ardelenesc (Transylvanian hound) . . 45 10
6573 2l.20 Pointer 45 10

1473 Bull's Head

2005. 1st Anniv of National Philatelic Museum.
6574 **1473** 40b. multicoloured . . 15 10

1474 Emblem

2005. World Information Society Summit, Tunis.
6575 **1474** 5l.60 multicoloured . . 2·20 55

1475 Members Flags, Dove and UN Emblem (50th anniv of Romania's membership)

2005. United Nations Anniversaries. Multicoloured.
6576 40b. Type **1475** 15 10
6577 1l.50 Council chamber (Romania's membership of Security Council, 2004—5 and Presidency, October 2005) 60 15
6578 2l.20 UN building and dove (60th anniv of UN) 85 20
MS6579 164 × 76 mm. Nos. 6576/8 1·60 1·60

1476 Birthplace and Society Emblem ($\frac{1}{2}$-size illustration)

2005. 160th Birth Anniv of Dimitrie Butculescu (1st president of Romanian Philatelic Society). Multicoloured.
6580 50b. Type **1476** 20 10
6581 50b. Romanian Philatelic Society gazette and Dimitrie Butculescu . . . 20 10
MS6582 114 × 82 mm. 9l. Dimitrie Butculescu. Imperf . . . . . . 3·50 3·50

1477 Library Building

2005. 110th Anniv of Central University Library (formerly Carol I University Foundation). Multicoloured.
6583 60b. Type **1477** 25 10
6584 60b. Horse and rider (statue) (21 × 30 mm) 25 10
MS6585 137 × 96 mm. Nos. 6583/4 50 50

1478 Gusat Englez (English Pouter)

2005. Domestic Pigeons. Multicoloured.
6586 2l.50 Type **1478** 1·00 25
6587 2l.50 Jucator pestrit (Parlour roller) 1·00 25
6588 2l.50 Calator tip standard (Standard carrier) 1·00 25
6589 2l.50 Zburator de Andaluzia (Andalusian) 1·00 25

1479 "Thinker of Hamangia"

2005. 60th Anniv of UNESCO.
6590 **1479** 2l.10 multicoloured 80 20

2005. Pottery (3rd issue). As T **1455**. Multicoloured.
6591 30b. Jug (Leheceni, Bihor) 15 10
6592 50b. Pitcher (Vladesti, Valcea) 20 10
6593 1l. Pitcher (Curtea de Arges, Arges) 40 10
6594 1l.20 Jug (Vama, Satu Mare) 45 10
6595 2l.20 Jug (Barsa, Arad) 85 20
6596 2l.50 Wide-necked pitcher (Corund, Harghita) 1·00 25
6597 14l.50 Wide-necked pitcher (Valea Izei, Maramures) 5·50

1480 The Annunciation

2005. Christmas. Designs showing icons. Mult.
6598 50b. Type **1480** 20 10
6599 50b. The Nativity (48 × 83 mm) 20 10
6600 50b. Madonna and Child 20 10

EXPRESS LETTER STAMPS

1919. Transylvania. Cluj Issue. No. E245 of Hungary optd as T **42**.
E784 **E 18** 2b. olive and red 30 45

1919. Transylvania. Oradea Issue. No. E245 of Hungary optd as T **42**.
E860 **E 18** 2b. olive and red 40 70

FRANK STAMPS

F 38

1913. Silistra Commemoration Committee.
F626 **F 38** (–) brown 4·25 5·25

F **108** Mail Coach and Biplane

1933. For free postage on book "75th Anniv of Introduction of Rumanian Postage Stamp".
F1286 **F 108** (–) green 1·50 2·10

1946. For Internees' Mail via Red Cross. Nos. T1589/95 optd **SCUTIT DE TAXA POSTALA SERVICIUL PRIZONIERILOR DE RAZBOI** and cross.
F1809 **T 171** (–) on 50t. orange 25
F1810 (–) on 1l. lilac 25
F1811 (–) on 2l. brown 25
F1812 (–) on 4l. blue 25
F1813 (–) on 5l. violet 25
F1814 (–) on 8l. green 25
F1815 (–) on 10l. brown 25

F **209** Queen Helen

1946. For Internees' Mail via Red Cross. Perf or imperf.
F1829 **F 209** (–) green and red 50
F1830 (–) purple and red 50
F1831 (–) red and carmine 50

F **227** King Michael F **228** Torch and Book

1947. King Michael's Fund. Perf or imperf.
(a) Postage.
F1904 **F 227** (–) purple 1·50 1·90
F1905 **F 228** (–) blue 1·50 1·90
F1906 – (–) brown 1·50 1·90

(b) Air. No. F1904 overprinted "**PRIN AVION**".
F1907 **F 227** (–) purple 1·80 3·25
DESIGN: As Type **227** but horiz—No. F1906, Man writing and couple reading.

NEWSPAPER STAMPS

1919. Transylvania. Cluj Issue. No. N136 of Hungary optd as T **42**.
N783 **N 9** 2b. orange 35 50

1919. Transylvania. Oradea Issue. No. 136 of Hungary optd as T **43**.
N859 **N 9** 2b. orange 50 70

OFFICIAL STAMPS

O **71** Rumanian Eagle and National Flag O **80**

1929.
O1115 **O 71** 25b. orange 20 15
O1116 50b. brown 20 15
O1117 1l. violet 15 10
O1118 2l. green 15 10
O1119 3l. red 30 10
O1120 4l. olive 25 15
O1221 6l. blue 1·20 20
O1222 10l. blue 35 25
O1223 25l. red 1·00 60
O1224 50l. violet 3·00 1·70

1930. Optd **8 IUNIE 1930**.
O1150 **O 71** 25b. orange 15 15
O1151 50b. brown 15 15
O1152 1l. violet 15 15
O1153 2l. green 15 15
O1159 3l. red 25 10
O1154 4l. olive 35 15
O1155 6l. blue 40 30
O1161 10l. blue 50 10
O1166 25l. red 25 10
O1157 50l. violet 3·00 1·90

1931.
O1243 **O 80** 25b. black 10 10
O1195 1l. purple 20 10
O1196 2l. green 35 20
O1197 3l. red 30 25
O1247 6l. red 85 40

PARCEL POST STAMPS

1895. As Type D **12** but inscr at top "TAXA DE FACTAGIU".
P353 25b. brown 4·50 50
P479 25b. red 4·50 80

1928. Surch **FACTAJ 5 LEI**.
P1078 **46** 5l. on 10b. green 85 25

POSTAGE DUE STAMPS
A. Ordinary Postage Due Stamps

D **12** D **38**

1881.
D152 **D 12** 2b. brown 2·75 1·30
D153 5b. brown 15·00 2·20
D200 10b. brown 7·00 50
D201 30b. brown 7·00 50
D156 50b. brown 12·00 3·00
D157 60b. brown 14·00 4·25

1887.
D448 **D 12** 2b. green 45 15
D449 5b. green 30 15
D450 10b. green 30 15
D451 30b. green 30 15
D371 50b. green 1·30 1·00
D458 60b. green 3·00 80

1911.
D617 **D 38** 2b. blue on yellow 15 15
D618 5b. blue on yellow 15 15
D619 10b. blue on yellow 15 15
D604 15b. blue on yellow 15 15
D621 20b. blue on yellow 15 15
D622 30b. blue on yellow 40 15
D623 50b. blue on yellow 55 15
D624 60b. blue on yellow 60 15
D609 2l. blue on yellow 80 40

1918. Optd **TAXA DE PLATA**.
D675 **37** 5b. green 80 35
D676 10b. red 80 35

1918. Re-issue of Type D **38**. On greenish or white paper.
D1001 **D 38** 5b. black 10 10
D 722 10b. black 10 10
D 995 20b. black 10 10
D 735 30b. black 15 15
D 736 50b. black 20 30
D 998 60b. black 15 10
D1007 1l. black 25 15
D1010 2l. black 35 10
D 991 3l. black 10 10
D 992 6l. black 25 10
D1547 50l. black 35 10
D1548 100l. black 35 15

1919. Transylvania. Cluj Issue. No. D190 etc of Hungary optd as T **42**.
D786 **D 9** 1b. red and green £225 £225
D787 2b. red and green 45 45
D788 5b. red and green 45 50·00
D789 10b. red and green 20 20
D790 15b. red and green 8·00 8·00
D791 20b. red and green 20 20
D792 30b. red and green 13·50 13·50
D793 50b. red and green 5·50 6·25

1919. Transylvania. Oradea Issue. No. D190, etc of Hungary optd as T **43**.
D861 **D 9** 1b. red and green 23·00 23·00
D862 2b. red and green 20 20
D863 5b. red and green 3·50 3·50
D864 6b. red and green 2·30 2·30
D865 10b. red and green 25 25
D866 12b. red and green 35 35
D867 15b. red and green 35 35
D868 20b. red and green 20 20
D869 30b. red and green 50 60

1930. Optd **8 IUNIE 1930**.
D1168 **D 38** 1l. black 40 15
D1169 2l. black 40 15
D1170 3l. black 50 25
D1171 6l. black 90 35

D **98** D **233**

1932.
D1249 **D 98** 1l. black 10 10
D1250 2l. black 10 10
D1251 3l. black 20 10
D1252 6l. black 20 10
D1835 20l. black 20 10
D1839 50l. black 25 25
D1840 80l. black 60 45
D1841 100l. black 55 30
D1842 200l. black 90 55
D1843 500l. black 1·40 90
D1844 5000l. black 1·70 1·10

1947. Type D **233** (without opts) perforated down centre.
D1919 2l. red 35
D1920 4l. blue 55
D1921 5l. black 90
D1922 10l. brown 1·80

The left half of Nos. D1919/22, showing Crown, served as a receipt and was stuck in the postman's book and so does not come postally used.

Prices for Nos. D1919/22 are for unused horizontal pairs.

1948. Nos. D1919/22, optd as in Type D **233**.
D1944 2l. red 35 20
D1945 4l. blue 55 25
D1946 5l. black 90 55
D1947 10l. brown 1·40 60

Prices for Nos. D1944 to D4055 are for unused and used horizontal pairs.

D **276** Badge and Postwoman

1950.
D2066 **D 276** 2l. red 90 90
D2067 4l. blue 90 90
D2068 5l. green 1·40 1·40
D2069 10l. brown 1·80 1·80

1952. Currency revalued. Nos. D2066/9 surch **4 Bani** on each half.
D2221 **D 276** 4b. on 2l. red 65 65
D2222 10b. on 4l. blue 65 65
D2223 20b. on 5l. green 1·40 1·40
D2224 50b. on 10l. brown 1·40 1·40

D **420** G.P.O., Bucharest and Posthorn

1957.
D2507 **D 420** 3b. black 20 10
D2508 5b. orange 20 10
D2509 10b. purple 20 10
D2510 20b. red 20 10
D2511 40b. green 65 25
D2512 1l. blue 1·80 45

D **614**

1967.
D3436 **D 614** 3b. green 10 10
D3437 5b. blue 10 10
D3438 10b. mauve 10 10
D3439 20b. red 10 10
D3440 40b. brown 20 10
D3441 1l. violet 55 20

D **766** Postal Emblems and Postman

1974.
D4050 **D 766** 5b. blue 10 10
D4051 10b. green 10 10
D4052 – 20b. red 10 10
D4053 – 40b. violet 20 10
D4054 – 50b. brown 35 10
D4055 – 1l. orange 55 10
DESIGNS: 20b., 40b. Dove with letter and Hermes with posthorn; 50b., 1l. G.P.O., Bucharest and emblem with mail van.

Prices for Nos. D4050/55 are for unused horizontal pairs.

1982. As Type D **766**.
D4761 – 25b. violet 10 10
D4762 **D 766** 50b. yellow 10 10
D4763 – 1l. red 25 10
D4764 – 2l. green 55 10
D4765 **D 766** 3l. brown 80 10
D4766 – 4l. blue 1·20 20
DESIGNS: 25b., 1l. Dove with letter and Hermes with posthorn; 2, 4l. G.P.O., Bucharest and emblem with mail van.

D **1111**

1992.
D5417 **D 1111** 4l. red 20 10
D5418 8l. blue 45 20

D **1163**

1994.
D5586 D **1163** 10l. brown 10 10
D5587 45l. orange 10 10

1999. Nos. D4762/4 and D4766 surch.
D6018 50l. on 50b. yellow . . . 10 10
D6019 50l. on 1l. red 10 10
D6020 100l. on 2l. green 10 10
D6021 700l. on 1l. red 10 10
D6022 1100l. on 4l. blue 20 20

2001. Nos. D5417 and D5587 surch on both stamps in the pair.
D6173 500l. on 4l. red 10 10
D6174 1000l. on 4l. red 10 10
D6175 2000l. on 45l. orange . . . 10 10

B. Postal Tax Due Stamps

1915. Optd **TIMBRU DE AJUTOR**.
TD643 D **38** 5b. blue on yellow 45 20
TD644 10b. blue on yellow 65 25

TD **42** TD **106**

1917. Green or white paper.
TD655 TD **42** 5b. brown 25 25
TD738 5b. red 45 25
TD654 10b. red 25 25
TD741 10b. brown 45 25

1918. Optd **TAXA DE PLATA**.
TD680 T **40** 5b. black 70 45
TD681 10b. brown 70 35

1922. As Type TD **42** but inscr "ASSISTENTA SOCIALA". On green or white paper.
TD1028 10b. brown 10 10
TD1029 20b. brown 10 10
TD1030 25b. brown 15 15
TD1031 50b. brown 10 10

1931. Aviation Fund. Optd **TIMBRUL AVIATIEI**.
TD1219 D **38** 1l. black 20 10
TD1220 2l. black 10 10

1932.
TD1278 TD **106** 3l. black . . . . 1·00 90

POSTAL TAX STAMPS

The following stamps were for compulsory use at certain times on inland mail to raise money for various funds. In some instances where the stamps were not applied the appropriate Postal Tax Postage Due stamps were applied.

Other denominations exist but these were purely for revenue purposes and were not applied to postal matter.

Soldiers' Families Fund

1915. Optd **TIMBRU DE AJUTOR**.
T638 **37** 5b. green 25 10
T639 10b. red 55 20

T **41** The Queen Weaving T **47** "Charity"

1916.
T649 T **41** 5b. black 25 20
T710 5b. green 90 20
T650 10b. brown 55 25
T711 10b. black 90 20
The 50b. and 1, 2, 5 and 50l. in similar designs were only used fiscally.

1918. Optd **1918.**
T671 **37** 5b. green (No. T638) 38·00 38·00
T667 T **41** 5b. black 90 65
T672 **37** 10b. red (No. T639) . . 38·00 38·00
T668 T **41** 10b. brown . . . . . 1·40 55

1921. Social Welfare.
T978 T **47** 10b. green 20 10
T979 25b. black 20 10

Aviation Fund

T **91** T **98**

1931.
T1216 T **91** 50b. green 65 10
T1217 1l. brown . . . . . . 1·10 10
T1218 2l. blue . . . . 1·10 25

1932.
T1253 T **98** 50b. green 40 10
T1254 1l. brown 65 10
T1255 2l. blue 75 10
Stamps as Type **98** but inscr "FONDUL AVIATIEI" were only for fiscal use. Nos. T1252/4 could only be used fiscally after 1937.

T **105** T **121** "Aviation"

1932. Cultural Fund.
T1276 T **105** 2l. blue 85 65
T1277 2l. brown 75 55
These were for compulsory use on postcards.

1936.
T1340 T **121** 50b. green 25 10
T1341 1l. brown 45 10
T1342 2l. blue 45 20
Other stamps inscr "FONDUL AVIATIEI" were only for fiscal use.

T **171** King Michael

1943.
T1589 T **171** 50b. orange 20 20
T1590 1l. lilac 20 20
T1591 2l. brown 20 20
T1592 4l. blue 20 20
T1593 5l. violet 20 20
T1594 8l. green 20 20
T1595 10l. brown 20 20

1947. Fiscal stamps (22 × 18½ mm), perf vert through centre surch **IOVR** and value.
T1923 1l. on 2l. red 20 20
T1924 5l. on 1l. green 80 80

1948. Vert designs (approx 18½ × 22 mm). Inscr "I.O.V.R.".
T1948 1l. red 25 45
T1949 1l. violet 65 45
T1950 2l. blue 90 65
T1951 5l. yellow . . . . 3·25 2·40

SAVINGS BANK STAMPS

1919. Transylvania. Cluj Issue. No. B199 of Hungary optd as T **42**.
B785 B **17** 10b. purple 50 70

1919. Transylvania. Oradea Issue. No. B199 of Hungary optd as T **43**.
B861 B **17** 10b. purple 50 70

ROMANIAN OCCUPATION OF HUNGARY Pt. 2

A. BANAT BACSKA

The following stamps were issued by the Temesvar postal authorities between the period of the Serbian evacuation and the Romanian occupation. This area was later divided, the Western part going to Yugoslavia and the Eastern part going to Romania.

100 filler = 1 korona.

1919. Stamps of Hungary optd **Banat Bacska 1919**.
(a) "Turul" Type.
1 **7** 50f. red on blue . . . . 11·50 11·50

(b) War Charity stamps of 1916.
2 **20** 10f.(+2f.) red 40 40
3 – 15f.(+2f.) violet 40 40
4 **22** 40f.(+2f.) red 40 40

(c) Harvesters and Parliament Types.
5 **18** 2f. brown 55 55
6 3f. purple 55 55
7 5f. green 55 55
8 6f. blue 55 55
9 15f. purple 55 55
10 35f. brown . . . . 11·50 11·50
11 **19** 50f. purple . . . . 11·50 11·50
12 75f. blue 55 55
13 80f. green 55 55
14 1k. red 55 55
15 2k. brown 55 55
16 2k. grey and violet . . . . 19·00 19·00
17 5k. light brown and brown 1·10 1·10
18 10k. mauve and brown . . . 2·30 2·30

(d) Charles and Zita stamps.
19 **27** 10f. pink 40 40
20 20f. brown 40 40
21 25f. blue 40 40
22 **28** 40f. green 40 40
23 50f. violet 40 40

(e) Harvesters Type inscr "MAGYAR POSTA".
24 **18** 10f. red . . . . 11·50 11·50
25 20f. brown . . . . 11·50 11·50
26 25f. blue . . . . 13·00 13·00

(f) Various Types optd **KOZTARSASAG**. (i) Harvesters and Parliament Types.
27 **18** 4f. grey 55 55
28 5f. green 55 55
29 6f. blue 55 55
30 10f. red . . . . 13·00 13·00
31 20f. brown . . . . 11·50 11·50
32 40f. green 25 25
33 **19** 1k. red 55 55
34 2k. brown . . . . 11·50 11·50
35 3k. grey and violet . . . . 11·50 11·50
36 5k. light brown and brown 11·50 11·50
37 10k. mauve and brown . . . 11·50 11·50

(iii) Charles portrait stamps.
38 **27** 15f. purple . . . . 11·50 11·50
39 25f. blue . . . . 2·30 2·30

(g) Serbian Occupation of Temesvar stamps.
40 **18** 10f. on 2f. brown 55 55
41 **20** 45f. on 10f.(+2f.) red . . . 75 75
42 **18** 1k.50 on 15f. purple . . . 2·30 2·30

EXPRESS LETTER STAMP

1919. No. E245 of Hungary optd **Banat Bacska 30 FILLER 1919**.
E44 E **18** 30f. on 2f. green and red 1·50 1·50

NEWSPAPER STAMP

1919. No. N136 of Hungary optd **Banat Bacska 1919**.
N43 N **9** (2f.) orange 55 55

POSTAGE DUE STAMPS

1919. Nos. D191 etc optd as above.
D46 D **9** 2f. red and green 55 55
D47 10f. red and green . . . 55 55
D48 15f. red and green . . . 11·50 11·50
D49 20f. red and green . . . 55 55
D50 30f. red and green . . . 9·25 9·25
D51 50f. black and green . . 13·00 13·00

SAVINGS BANK STAMP

1919. No. B199 of Hungary surch **Banat Bacska 50 FILLER 1919**.
B45 B **17** 50f. on 10f. purple . . . 1·50 1·50

B. DEBRECEN

This area was later returned to Hungary.

100 filler = 1 korona.

(1)

1919. Stamps of Hungary optd with **T1** or surch in addition. (a) "Turul" Type.
1 **7** 2f. yellow . . . . 22·00 14·00
2 3f. orange . . . . 28·00 28·00
3 6f. brown . . . . 4·50 4·50

(b) War Charity stamps of 1915.
4 **7** 2f.+2f. yellow (No. 171) . . . 27·00 27·00
5 3f.+2f. orange (No. 172) . . 27·00 27·00

(c) War Charity stamps of 1916.
6 **20** 10f.(+2f.) red 40 40
7 – 15f.(+2f.) lilac . . . . . . 1·90 1·90
8 **22** 40f.(+2f.) red 90 90

(d) Harvesters and Parliament Types.
9 **18** 2f. brown 15 15
10 3f. purple 10 10
11 5f. green 40 40
12 6f. blue 15 15
13 10f. red (No. 243) . . . . . 18·00 18·00
14 15f. violet (No. 244) . . . . 25·00 25·00
15 15f. purple 10 10
16 20f. brown . . . . 14·00 14·00
17 25f. blue 75 75
18 35f. brown . . . . 5·00 5·00
19 35f. on 3f. purple 25 25
20 40f. green 60 60
21 45f. on 2f. brown 25 25
22 **19** 50f. purple 60 60
23 75f. blue 15 15
24 80f. green 40 40
25 1k. red 40 40
26 2k. brown 15 15
27 3k. grey and violet . . . . 3·75 3·75
28 3k. on 75f. blue . . . . . 2·10 2·10
29 5k. light brown and brown 3·75 3·75
30 5k. on 75f. blue 75 75
31 10k. mauve and brown . . . 45·00 15·00
32 10k. on 80f. green . . . . 1·40 1·40

(e) Charles and Zita stamps.
33 **27** 10f. pink . . . . 4·50 4·25
34 15f. purple . . . . 16·00 16·00
35 20f. brown 75 75
36 25f. blue 50 50
37 **28** 40f. green 35 35
38 50f. purple . . . . 3·75 3·75

(f) Harvesters and Parliament Types inscr "MAGAR POSTA".
39 **18** 5f. green 10 10
40 6f. blue . . . . 2·50 2·50
41 10f. red 10 10
42 20f. brown 10 10
43 25f. blue 10 10
44 45f. orange . . . . 2·50 2·50
45 **19** 5k. brown 10 10

(g) Various Types optd **KOZTARSASAG**. (i) Harvesters and Parliament Types.
46 **18** 2f. brown 25 25
47 3f. purple . . . . 4·75 4·75
48 4f. grey 15 15
49 5f. green 10 10
50 10f. red . . . . 4·00 4·00
51 20f. brown 40 40
52 40f. green 25 25
53 **19** 1k. red 25 25
54 2k. brown . . . . 6·75 6·75
55 3k. grey and violet . . . . 1·40 1·40
56 5k. light brown and brown 60·00 60·00

(ii) War Charity stamps of 1916.
57 **20** 10f.(+2f.) red . . . . 4·75 4·75
58 – 15f.(+2f.) lilac . . . . . . 19·00 19·00
59 **22** 40f.(+2f.) red . . . . 1·40 1·40

(iii) Charles and Zita stamps.
60 **27** 10f. pink . . . . 4·25 4·25
61 15f. purple . . . . 7·50 7·50
62 20f. brown . . . . 1·10 1·10
63 25f. blue 50 50
64 **28** 50f. purple 70 70

2 **4**

1920. Types **2** and **4** and similar design, optd with inscr as T **1** but in circle.
65 **2** 2f. brown 15 15
66 3f. brown 15 15
67 4f. violet 15 15
68 5f. green 10 10
69 6f. grey 15 15
70 10f. red 10 10
71 15f. violet 25 25
72 20f. brown 10 10
73 – 25f. blue 80 80
74 – 30f. brown 80 80
75 – 35f. purple 80 80
76 – 40f. green 80 80
77 – 45f. red 80 80
78 – 50f. mauve 80 80
79 – 60f. green 80 80
80 – 75f. blue 80 80
81 **4** 80f. green 15 15
82 1k. red 25 25
83 1k.20 orange . . . . 4·25 4·25
84 2k. brown 75 75
85 3k. brown 75 75
86 5k. brown 75 75
87 10k. purple 75 75
DESIGN: Nos. 73/80, Horseman using lasso.

5

1920. War Charity. Type **5** with circular opt, and "Segely belyeg" at top.
88 **5** 20f. green 75 75
89 20f. green on blue 25 25
90 50f. brown . . . . 1·00 1·00
91 50f. brown on mauve 15 15
92 1k. green 80 80
93 1k. green on green 80 80
94 2k. green . . . . 1·10 1·10

EXPRESS LETTER STAMP

1919. No. E245 of Hungary optd with T **1**.
E66 E **18** 2f. green and red . . . 25 25

NEWSPAPER STAMP

1919. No. N136 of Hungary optd with T **1**.
N65 N **9** 2f. orange 20 20

POSTAGE DUE STAMPS

1919. (a) Nos. D190 etc of Hungary optd with T **1**.
D68 D **9** 1f. red and green . . . . 5·75 5·75
D69 2f. red and green 15 15
D70 5f. red and green . . . . 65·00 65·00
D71 6f. red and green . . . . 26·00 26·00
D72 10f. red and green 15 15
D73 12f. red and green . . . . 26·00 26·00
D74 15f. red and green . . . . 1·30 1·30
D75 20f. red and green . . . . 1·30 1·30
D76 30f. red and green . . . . 1·30 1·30

(b) With **KOZTARSASAG** opt.
D77 D **9** 2f. red and green . . . . 3·25 3·25
D78 3f. red and green . . . . 3·25 3·25
D79 10f. red and green . . . . 3·25 3·25
D80 20f. red and green . . . . 3·25 3·25
D81 40f. red and green . . . . 3·25 3·25
D82 50f. red and green . . . . 3·25 3·25

D 6

1920.

D95 D 6 5f. green 35 30
D96 10f. green 35 30
D97 20f. green 35 30
D98 30f. green 35 30
D99 40f. green 35 30

SAVINGS BANK STAMP

1919. No. B199 of Hungary optd with T **1**.
B67 B **17** 10f. purple . . . . . . 5·25 5·25

C. TEMESVAR

After being occupied by Serbia this area was then occupied by Romania. It later became part of Romania and was renamed Timisoara.

100 filler = 1 korona.

1919. Stamps of Hungary surch. (a) Harvesters Type.
6 **18** 30 on 2f. brown 15 15
7 1k. on 4f. grey (optd **KOZTARSASAG**) 15 15
8 150 on 3f. purple 10 10
9 150 on 5f. green 15 15

(b) Express Letter Stamp.
10 E **18** 3 KORONA on 2f. green and red 25 25

POSTAGE DUE STAMPS

1919. Charity stamp of Hungary surch **PORTO 40**.
D11 40 on 15+(2f.) lilac (No. 265) 30 30

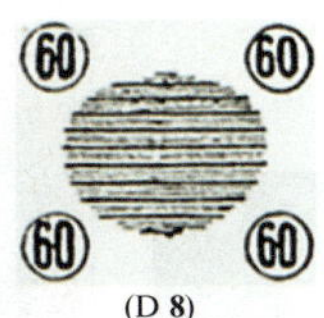

(D 8)

1919. Postage Due stamps of Hungary surch with Type D **8**.
D12 D **9** 60 on 2f. red and green 2·25 2·25
D13 60 on 10f. red and green 60 60

ROMANIAN POST OFFICES IN THE TURKISH EMPIRE Pt. 16

Romanian P.O.s in the Turkish Empire including Constantinople. Now closed.

I. GENERAL ISSUES

40 paras = 1 piastre.

1896. Stamps of Romania of 1893 surch in "PARAS".
9 10pa. on 5b. blue (No. 319) 11·00 11·00
10 20pa. on 10b. green (No. 320) 11·00 11·00
11 1pi. on 25b. mauve (No. 322) 11·00 11·00

II. CONSTANTINOPLE

100 bani = 1 leu.

(1)

1919. Stamps of Romania of 1893–1908 optd with T **1**.
18 **37** 5b. green 50 50
19 10b. red 60 60
20 15b. brown 75 75
30 – 25b. blue (No. 701) 80 80
31 – 40b. brown (No. 703) . . . 2·50 2·50

1919. 1916 Postal Tax stamp of Romania optd with T **1**.
33 T **41** 5b. green . . . . 1·60 1·80

ROSS DEPENDENCY Pt. 1

A dependency of New Zealand in the Antarctic on the Ross Sea.

The post office closed on 30 September 1987, but re-opened in November 1994.

1957. 12 pence = 1 shilling;
20 shillings = 1 pound.
1967. 100 cents = 1 dollar.

3 Map of Ross Dependency and New Zealand

4 Queen Elizabeth II

1957.

1 – 3d. blue . . . . 1·00 60
2 – 4d. red . . . . 1·00 60
3 **3** 8d. red and blue . . . . . . 1·00 60
4 **4** 1s.6d. purple . . . . 1·00 60

DESIGNS—HORIZ (As Type **3**): 3d. H.M.S. "Erebus"; 4d. Shackleton and Scott.

5 H.M.S. "Erebus"

1967. Nos. 1/4 with values inscr in decimal currency as T **5**.
5 **5** 2c. blue . . . . 7·00 5·50
6 – 3c. red . . . . 2·75 4·75
7 **3** 7c. red and blue . . . . . . 2·75 6·00
8 **4** 15c. purple . . . . 2·75 9·00

6 South Polar Skua

8 Adelie Penguins and South Polar Skua

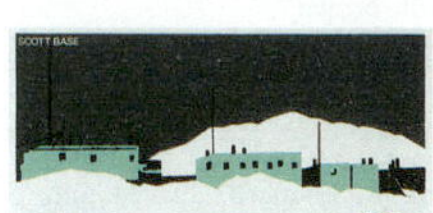

7 Scott Base

1972.

9a **6** 3c. black, grey and blue . . 70 1·60
10a – 4c. black, blue and violet . . 15 1·60
11a – 5c. black, grey and lilac . . 15 1·60
12a – 8c. black, grey and brown . . 15 1·60
13a **7** 10c. black, green and grey . . 15 1·60
14a – 18c. black, violet and light violet . . . . 15 1·60

DESIGNS—As Type **6**: 4c. Lockheed Hercules airplane at Williams Field; 5c. Shackleton's Hut; 8c. Supply ship H.M.N.Z.S. "Endeavour". As Type **7**: 18c. Tabular ice flow.

1982. Multicoloured.
15 5c. Type **8** . . . . 1·25 1·40
16 10c. Tracked vehicles . . . . 20 1·25
17 20c. Scott Base 20 75
18 30c. Field party 20 40
19 40c. Vanda Station 20 40
20 50c. Scott's hut, Cape Evans 20 40

9 South Polar Skua

1994. Wildlife. Multicoloured.
21 5c. Type **9** 10 10
22 10c. Snow petrel chick 10 10
23 20c. Black-browed albatross 15 20
24 40c. Emperor penguins . . . . 1·75 1·25
25 45c. As 40c. 35 40
26 50c. Bearded penguins ("Chinstrap Penguins") . . 35 40
27 70c. Adelie penguin 50 55
28 80c. Elephant seals 60 65
29 $1 Leopard seal 75 80
30 $2 Weddell seal . . . . 1·50 1·60
31 $3 Crabeater seal pup . . . . 2·20 2·30

10 Capt. James Cook with H.M.S. "Resolution" and H.M.S. "Adventure"

1995. Antarctic Explorers. Multicoloured.
32 40c. Type **10** 75 75
33 80c. James Clark Ross with H.M.S. "Erebus" and H.M.S. "Terror" . . . . . 1·25 1·25
34 $1 Roald Amundsen and "Fram" . . . . 1·40 1·40
35 $1.20 Robert Scott with "Terra Nova" . . . . . . 1·75 1·75
36 $1.50 Ernest Shackleton with "Endurance" . . . . 2·00 2·00
37 $1.80 Richard Byrd with Ford 4-AT-B Trimotor "Floyd Bennett" (airplane) . . . . 2·00 2·00

11 Inside Ice Cave

12 Snow Petrel

1996. Antarctic Landscapes. Multicoloured.
38 40c. Type **11** 50 35
39 80c. Base of glacier 80 65
40 $1 Glacier ice fall 95 80
41 $1.20 Climbers on crater rim (horiz) . . . . 1·25 95
42 $1.50 Pressure ridges (horiz) 1·40 1·25
43 $1.80 Fumarole ice tower (horiz) . . . . 1·60 1·40

1997. Antarctic Seabirds. Multicoloured. (a) With "WWF" panda emblem.
44 40c. Type **12** 80 60
45 80c. Pintado petrel ("Cape Petrel") . . . . 1·25 90
46 $1.20 Antarctic fulmar . . . . 1·60 1·25
47 $1.50 Antarctic petrel . . . . 1·60 1·25

(b) Without "WWF" panda emblem.
48 40c. Type **12** . . . . 1·10 80
49 80c. Pintado petrel ("Cape Petrel") . . . . 1·40 1·10
50 $1 Dove prion ("Antarctic Prion") . . . . 1·50 1·25
51 $1.20 Antarctic fulmar . . . . 1·50 1·40
52 $1.50 Antarctic petrel . . . . 1·50 1·40
53 $1.80 Antarctic tern . . . . . 1·60 1·50

Nos. 48/53 were printed together, se-tenant, with the backgrounds forming a composite design.

13 Sculptured Sea Ice

1997. Ice Formation. Multicoloured.
54 40c. Type **13** 50 35
55 80c. Glacial tongue 70 60
56 $1 Stranded tabular iceberg . . 90 80
57 $1.20 Autumn at Cape Evans 1·00 90
58 $1.50 Sea ice in summer thaw 1·25 1·10
59 $1.80 Sunset at tabular icebergs . . . . 1·40 1·40

14 Sea Smoke, McMurdo Sound

1999. Night Skies. Multicoloured.
60 40c. Type **14** 80 55
61 80c. Alpenglow, Mount Erebus 1·25 80
62 $1.10 Sunset, Black Island . . 1·40 1·10
63 $1.20 Pressure ridges, Ross Sea 1·60 1·25
64 $1.50 Evening light, Ross Island . . . . 1·90 1·50
65 $1.80 Mother of pearl clouds, Ross Island . . . . 2·25 1·60

15 R.N.Z.A.F. C130 Hercules

2000. Antarctic Transport. Multicoloured.
66 40c. Type **15** 80 50
67 80c. Hagglunds BV206 All Terrain carrier . . . . . . 1·00 75
68 $1.10 Tracked 4×4 motorbike 1·40 1·00
69 $1.20 ASV track truck . . . . 1·40 1·00
70 $1.50 Squirrel helicopter . . . 1·75 1·25
71 $1.80 Elan skidoo . . . . . . 1·75 1·25

2001. Penguins. As T **604** of New Zealand. Multicoloured.
72 40c. Two emperor penguins 65 60
73 80c. Two adelie penguins . . . 1·00 70
74 90c. Emperor penguin leaving water . . . . 1·10 80
75 $1.30 Adelie penguin in water 1·50 1·25
76 $1.50 Group of emperor penguins . . . . 1·75 1·40
77 $2 Group of adelie penguins 1·90 1·75

16 British Explorers by Sledge

2002. Antarctic Discovery Expedition, 1901–1904. Each black, grey and stone.
78 40c. Type **16** 75 60
79 80c. H.M.S. *Discovery*, at anchor . . . . 1·40 80
80 90c. H.M.S. *Discovery*, trapped in ice . . . . 1·40 90
81 $1.30 Sledges and tents on the ice . . . . 1·60 1·40
82 $1.50 Crew of H.M.S. *Discovery* . . . . 2·25 1·50
83 $2 Scott's base at Hut Point 2·40 1·60

17 *Odontaster validus* (red seastar)

2003. Marine Life. Multicoloured.
84 40c. Type **17** 75 55
85 90c. *Beroe cucumis* (comb jelly) 1·40 1·00
86 $1.30 *Macroptychaster accrescens* (giant seastar) . . 1·75 1·25
87 $1.50 *Sterechinus neumayeri* (sea urchin) . . . . 1·90 1·40
88 $2 *Perkinsiana littoralis* (fan worm) . . . . 2·25 1·90

18 Penguin and Chick

2004. Emperor Penguins. Multicoloured.
89 45c. Type **18** 80 55
90 90c. Penguin chick . . . . . 1·50 1·25
91 $1.35 Penguin feeding chick 1·75 1·50
92 $1.50 Two penguins and chick 1·90 1·75
93 $2 Group of penguins . . . . 2·25 2·25

19 Dry Valleys (Craig Potton)

2005. Photographs of Antarctica. Multicoloured.
94 45c. Type **19** 90 60
95 90c. Emperor penguins (Andris Apse) . . . . 1·75 1·50
96 $1.35 Antarctic fur seal (Mark Mitchell) . . . . 2·00 2·00
97 $1.50 Hut of Captain Robert F Scott (Colin Monteath) 2·25 2·50
98 $2 Antarctic minke whale (Kim Westerskov) . . . . . 2·50 2·75

ROUAD ISLAND (ARWAD) Pt. 6

An island in the E. Mediterranean off the coast of Syria. A French P.O. was established there during 1916.

25 centimes = 1 piastre.

1916. "Blanc" and "Mouchon" key-types inscr "LEVANT" and optd **ILE ROUAD** (vert).
1 A 5c. green £325 £160
2 B 10c. red £350 £190
3 1pi. on 25c. blue £350 £200

1916. "Blanc" "Mouchon" and "Merson" key-types inscr "LEVANT" and optd **ILE ROUAD** horiz.
4 A 1c. grey 35 4·75
5 2c. purple 35 3·50
6 3c. red 70 5·50
7 5c. green 1·30 4·50
8 B 10c. red 1·90 6·00
9 15c. red 1·40 5·75
10 20c. brown 3·50 7·00
11 1p. on 25c. blue 3·75 2·25
12 30c. lilac 3·00 7·50
13 C 40c. red and blue 4·25 11·50
14 2p. on 50c. brown & lav 6·50 14·00
15 4p. on 1f. red and yellow 12·50 25·00
16 30p. on 5f. blue and yellow 36·00 65·00

RUANDA-URUNDI Pt. 4

Part of German E. Africa, including Ruanda and Urundi, occupied by Belgian forces during the war of 1914–18 and a Trust Territory administered by Belgium until 1 July 1962. The territory then became two separate independent states, named Rwanda and Burundi.

100 centimes = 1 franc.

1916. Nos. 70/77 of Belgian Congo optd. (a) **RUANDA.**
1 **32** 5c. black and green 42·00
2 **33** 10c. black and red 42·00
3 **13** 15c. black and green 65·00
4 **34** 25c. black and blue 42·00
5 **14** 40c. black and red 42·00
6 – 50c. black and red 42·00
7 – 1f. black and brown £160
7a – 5f. black and orange £2000

(b) **URUNDI.**
8 **32** 5c. black and green 42·00
9 **33** 10c. black and red 42·00
10 **13** 15c. black and green 65·00
11 **34** 25c. black and blue 42·00
12 **14** 40c. black and red 42·00
13 – 50c. black and red 48·00
14 – 1f. black and brown £160
14a – 5f. black and orange £2000

1916. Stamps of Belgian Congo of 1915 optd **EST AFRICAIN ALLEMAND OCCUPATION BELGE. DUITSCH OOST AFRIKA BELGISCHE BEZETTING.**
15 **32** 5c. black and green 60 65
16 **33** 10c. black and red 70 70
17 **13** 15c. black and green 50 60
18 **34** 25c. black and blue 3·00 1·50
19 **14** 40c. black and lake 7·75 5·00
20 – 50c. black and lake 9·25 4·75
21 – 1f. black and olive 1·40 85
22 – 5f. black and orange 2·00 1·75

1918. Belgian Congo Red Cross stamps of 1918 optd **A. O.**
23 **32** 5c.+10c. blue and green 15 1·10
24 **33** 10c.+15c. blue and red 35 1·10
25 **13** 15c.+20c. blue and green 40 1·10
26 **34** 25c.+25c. blue 60 1·10
27 **14** 40c.+40c. blue and lake 60 1·40
28 – 50c.+50c. blue and lake 1·00 1·40
29 – 1f.+1f. blue and olive 1·75 3·00
30 – 5f.+5f. blue and orange 8·25 8·25
31 – 10f.+10f. blue and green 60·00 70·00

1922. Stamps of 1916 surch.
32 – 5c. on 50c. black and lake 1·10 3·25
33 **32** 10c. on 5c. black and green 45 85
34a **14** 25c. on 40c. black and lake 2·75 1·60
35 **33** 30c. on 10c. black and red 35 1·10
36 **34** 50c. on 25c. black and blue 80 1·00

1924. Belgian Congo stamps of 1923 optd **RUANDA URUNDI.**
37 A 5c. yellow 30 65
38 B 10c. green 20 65
39 C 15c. brown 15 40
40 D 20c. green 25 60
41 E 20c. green 15 55
42 F 25c. brown 25 20
43 **46** 30c. pink 20 55
44 30c. green 15 60
66 35c. green 35 65
45 D 40c. purple 30 70
46 G 50c. blue 20 30
47 50c. orange 25 70
48 E 75c. orange 25 30
49 75c. blue 30 25
67 **46** 75c. pink 45 80
50 H 1f. brown 35 60
51 1f. blue 60 35
68 1f. pink 85 60
69 D 1f.50 blue 1·10 1·40
71 1f.75 blue 1·25 90
52 I 3f. brown 2·50 3·50
53 J 5f. grey 4·50 5·75
54 K 10f. black 16·00 16·00

1925. Stamp of Belgian Congo optd **RUANDA-URUNDI.** Inscriptions in French or in Flemish.
61 **55** 25c.+25c. black and red 40 1·10

1925. Native cattle type of Belgian Congo optd **RUANDA-URUNDI.**
62 **56** 45c. purple 30 95
63 60c. red 35 60

1927. Belgian Congo stamps of 1923 optd **RUANDA URUNDI** in two lines, wide apart.
64 B 10c. green 25 1·00
65 C 15c. brown 1·25 2·25
66 **46** 35c. green 20 15
67 75c. red 30 25
68 H 1f. red 45 30
69 D 1f.25 blue 50 40
70 1f.50 blue 60 80
71 1f.75 blue 95 60

1927. No. 144 of Belgian Congo optd **RUANDA URUNDI.**
72 1f.75 on 1f.50 blue 40 1·00

1930. Native Fund stamps of Belgian Congo (Nos. 160/8), optd **RUANDA URUNDI.**
73 10c.+5c. red 40 1·10
74 20c.+10c. brown 90 1·50
75 35c.+15c. green 1·25 2·10
76 60c.+30c. purple 1·50 2·25
77 1f.+50c. red 2·10 3·25
78 1f.75+75c. blue 2·75 3·25
79 3f.50+1f.50 lake 5·50 7·25
80 5f.+2f.50 brown 4·00 5·75
81 10f.+5f. black 4·50 6·50

1931. Nos. 68 and 71 surch.
82 H 1f.25 on 1f. red 3·25 1·10
83 D 2f. on 1f.75 blue 4·00 2·25

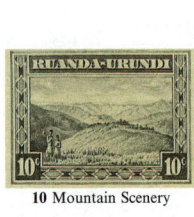

10 Mountain Scenery

11 King Albert I

1931.
84 – 5c. red 20 40
85 **10** 10c. grey 10 50
86 – 15c. red 20 60
87 – 25c. purple 25 50
88 – 40c. green 60 95
89 – 50c. violet 25 45
90 – 60c. red 25 75
91 – 75c. black 45 65
92 – 1f. red 40 45
93 – 1f.25 brown 30 30
94 – 1f.50 purple 30 60
95 – 2f. blue 60 1·00
96 – 2f.50 blue 45 65
97 – 3f.25 purple 40 1·00
98 – 4f. red 65 60
99 – 5f. grey 75 75
100 – 10f. purple 1·10 1·25
101 – 20f. brown 3·00 3·25
DESIGNS—HORIZ: 15c. Warrior; 25c. Chieftain's kraal; 50c. Head of African buffalo; 1f. Wives of Urundi chiefs; 1f.50, 2f. Wooden pot hewer; 2f.50, 3f.25, Workers making tissues from ficus bark; 4f. Hutu Potter. VERT: 5, 60c., Native porter; 40c. Two cowherds; 75c. Native greeting; 1f.25, Mother and child; 5f. Ruanda dancer; 10f. Warriors; 20f. Native prince of Urundi.

1934. King Albert Mourning Stamp.
102 **11** 1f.50 black 65 60

11a Queen Astrid and Children

14a "Belgium shall rise Again"

1936. Charity. Queen Astrid Fund.
103 **11a** 1f.25+5c. brown 75 1·00
104 1f.50+10c. red 55 1·25
105 2f.50+25c. blue 80 1·60

1941. Stamps of Belgian Congo optd **RUANDA URUNDI.**
106 **78** 10c. grey 9·00 9·00
107 1f.75 orange 4·00 5·25
108 2f.75 blue 4·75 6·25

1941. Ruanda-Urundi stamps of 1931 surch.
109 – 5c. on 40c. green 3·75 5·25
110 – 60c. on 50c. violet 5·25 6·25
111 – 2f.50 on 1f.50 purple 2·75 3·25
112 – 3f.25 on 2f. blue 11·00 11·00

1941. Stamps of Belgian Congo optd **RUANDA URUNDI** and surch also.
113 – 5c. on 1f.50 black and brown (No. 222) 20 65
114 – 75c. on 90c. brown and red (No. 221) 1·50 1·90
115 **78** 2f.50 on 10f. red 1·90 1·90

1942. War Relief.
116 **14a** 10f.+40f. red 2·40 3·50
117 10f.+40f. blue 2·40 3·50
On No. 116 the French slogan is above the Flemish, on No. 117 vice versa.

1942. Nos. 107/8 of Ruanda-Urundi surch.
118 **78** 75c. on 1f.75 orange 3·75 3·75
119 2f.50 on 2f.75 blue 6·00 6·25

15a Head of Warrior

17 Seated Figure

1942.
120 A 5c. red 10 45
121 10c. green 10 35
122 15c. brown 10 55
123 20c. blue 10 45
124 25c. purple 10 30
125 30c. blue 10 40
126 50c. green 20 20
127 60c. brown 10 35
128 **15a** 75c. black and lilac 30 25
129 1f. black and brown 35 30
130 1f.25 black and red 40 50
131 B 1f.75 brown 1·10 1·10
132 2f. orange 1·10 75
133 2f.50 red 80 15
134 C 3f.50 green 50 20
135 5f. orange 55 35
136 6f. blue 55 35
137 7f. black 50 45
138 10f. brown 90 65
139 – 20f. black and brown 1·75 1·10
140 – 50f. black and red 3·00 2·25
141 – 100f. black and green 5·25 6·00
DESIGNS—As Type **15a** (various frames): A, Oil palms; C, Askari sentry; 20f. Head of zebra. 35 × 24 mm: B, Leopard. 29 × 34 mm: 50f. Askari sentry; 100f. Head of warrior.

1944. Red Cross Fund. Nos. 126, 130, 131 and 134 surch **Au profit de la Croix Rouge Ten voordeele van het Roode Kruis** (50c., 1f.75) or with Flemish and French reversed (others) and premium.
147 50c.+50f. green 1·40 2·50
148 1f.25+100f. black and red 1·90 3·50
149 1f.75+100f. brown 1·75 2·50
150 3f.50+100f. green 1·75 3·50

1948. Native Carvings.
151 **17** 10c. orange 15 65
152 A 15c. blue 15 95
153 B 20c. blue 30 55
154 C 25c. red 50 25
155 D 40c. purple 30 60
156 **17** 50c. brown 30 10
157 A 70c. green 40 50
158 B 75c. purple 75 40
159 C 1f. purple and orange 75 10
160 D 1f.25 red and blue 95 40
161 E 1f.50 red and green 1·75 85
162 **17** 2f. red and vermilion 65 10
163 A 2f.50 green and brown 1·10 10
164 B 3f.50 green and blue 1·25 50
165 C 5f. red and bistre 1·60 15
166 D 6f. green and orange 1·75 15
167 E 10f. brown and violet 2·25 70
168 F 20f. brown and red 3·00 90
169 E 50f. black and brown 5·25 1·50
170 F 100f. black and red 9·00 3·25
DESIGNS: A, Seated figure (different); B, Kneeling figure; C, Double mask; D, Mask; E, Mask with tassels; F, Mask with horns.

1949. Surch.
171 3f. on 2f.50 (No. 163) 65 25
172 4f. on 6f. (No. 166) 1·00 20
173 6f.50 on 6f. (No. 166) 1·25 30

18a St. Francis Xavier

19 "Dissotis"

1953. 400th Death Anniv of St. Francis Xavier.
174 **18a** 1f.50 black and blue 60 70

1953. Flowers Multicoloured.
175 10c. Type **19** 20 40
176 15c. "Protea" 20 45
177 20c. "Vellozia" 20 10
178 25c. "Littonia" 20 40
179 40c. "Ipomoea" 20 45
180 50c. "Angraecum" 35 10
181 60c. "Euphorbia" 65 60
182 75c. "Ochna" 90 40
183 1f. "Hibiscus" 90 10
184 1f.25 "Protea" 1·75 1·25
185 1f.50 "Schizoglossum" 45 10
186 2f. "Ansellia" 3·50 45
187 3f. "Costus" 1·25 10
188 4f. "Nymphaea" 1·75 40
189 5f. "Thunbergia" 1·25 20
190 7f. "Gerbera" 1·75 45
191 8f. "Gloriosa" 2·25 55
192 10f. "Silene" 4·00 50
193 20f. "Aristolochia" 7·25 85

20 King Baudouin and Mountains

20a Mozart when a Child

1955.
194 **20** 1f.50 black and red 3·25 1·40
195 – 3f. black and green 3·25 85
196 – 4f.50 black and blue 3·25 75
197 – 6f.50 black and purple 3·75 90
DESIGNS: 3f. Forest; 4f.50, River; 6f.50, Grassland.

1956. Birth Bicentenary of Mozart.
198 **20a** 4f.50+1f.50 violet 1·90 2·25
199 – 6f.50+2f.50 purple 4·25 3·75
DESIGN—52 × 36 mm: 6f.50, Queen Elizabeth and Mozart sonata.

20b Nurse with Children

21 Gorilla

1957. Red Cross Fund.
200 **20b** 3f.+50c. blue 1·10 1·25
201 – 4f.50+50c. green 1·25 1·40
202 – 6f.50+50c. brown 1·25 1·60
DESIGNS: 4f.50, Doctor inoculating patient; 6f.50, Nurse in tropical kit bandaging patient.

1959. Fauna.
203 10c. black, red and brown 10 25
204 20c. black and green 10 20
205 40c. black, olive and mauve 10 50
206 50c. brown, yellow and green 10 55
207 1f. black, blue and brown 10 40
208 1f.50 black and orange 50 60
209 2f. black, brown and turquoise 50 45
210 3f. black, red and brown 60 40
211 5f. multicoloured 45 65
212 6f.50 brown, yellow and red 25 35
213 8f. black, mauve and blue 80 80
214 10f. multicoloured 80 75
DESIGNS—VERT: 10c., 1f. Type **21**: 40c., 2f. Eastern black and white colobus. HORIZ: 20c.1f.50, African buffaloes; 50c., 6f.50, Impala; 3, 8f. African elephants; 5, 10f. Eland and common zebras.

22 African Resources

1960. 10th Anniv of African Technical Co-operation Commission. Inscr in French or Flemish.
222 **22** 3f. salmon and blue 20 60

23 High Jumping

1960. Child Welfare Fund. Olympic Games, Rome.
223 50c.+25c. blue and red 20 85
224 1f.50+50c. lake and black 40 90
225 2f.+2f. black and red 50 95
226 3f.+1f.25 red and green 1·25 1·90
227 6f.50+3f.50 green and red 1·40 1·90
DESIGNS: 50c. Type **23**: 1f.50, Hurdling; 2f. Football; 3f. Throwing the javelin; 6f.50, Throwing the discus.

1960. No. 210 surch.
228 3f.50 on 3f. black, red and brown 45 60

25 Leopard

1961.

229	25	20f. multicoloured	60	1·00
230	–	50f. multicoloured	1·25	1·70

DESIGN: 50f. Lion and lioness.

26 Usumbura Cathedral

1961. Usumbura Cathedral Fund.

231	26	50c.+25c. brown and buff	35	75
232	–	1f.+50c. dp green & grn	30	65
233	–	1f.50+75c. multicoloured	20	75
234	26	3f.50+1f.50 blue & lt bl	35	65
235	–	5f.+2f. red and orange	20	95
236	–	6f.50+3f. multicoloured	30	1·00

DESIGNS: 1, 5f. Side view of Cathedral; 1f.50, 6f.50, Stained glass windows.

POSTAGE DUE STAMPS

1924. Postage Due stamps of Belgian Congo optd **RUANDA URUNDI**.

D55	D 54	5c. brown	10	35
D56a		10c. red	10	50
D57		15c. violet	15	35
D58		30c. green	30	60
D59a		50c. blue	40	65
D60		1f. grey	60	95

1943. Postage Due stamps of Belgian Congo optd **RUANDA URUNDI**.

D142	D 86	10c. olive	10	1·00
D143		20c. blue	15	80
D144		50c. green	30	1·00
D145		1f. brown	45	1·00
D146		2f. orange	45	1·25

1959. Postage Due stamps of Belgian Congo optd **RUANDA URUNDI**.

D215	D 99	10c. brown	40	55
D216		20c. purple	30	70
D217		50c. green	75	80
D218		1f. blue	90	80
D219		2f. red	1·00	1·10
D220		4f. violet	1·25	1·50
D221		6f. blue	1·25	1·75

For later issues see **BURUNDI** and **RWANDA**.

RUSSIA Pt. 10

A country in the E. of Europe and N. Asia. An empire until 1917 when the Russian Socialist Federal Soviet Republic was formed. In 1923 this became the Union of Soviet Socialist Republics (U.S.S.R.), eventually comprising 15 constituent republics.

In 1991 the U.S.S.R. was dissolved and subsequent issues were used in the Russian Federation only.

100 kopeks = 1 rouble.

1 5 8
9 10 11

1858. Imperf.

1	1	10k. blue and brown	£4000	£400

1858. Perf.

21	1	10k. blue and brown	32·00	25
22		20k. orange and blue	55·00	7·50
23		30k. green and red	75·00	25·00

1863.

8	5	5k. black and blue	20·00	£140

No. 8 was first issued as a local but was later authorised for general use.

1864.

18	9	1k. black and yellow	3·00	35
30		2k. black and red	6·50	60
19b		3k. black and green	4·00	45
20		5k. black and lilac	7·50	25

1875.

31	8	7k. red and grey	6·00	25
32		8k. red and grey	9·00	40
33		10k. blue and brown	25·00	3·00
34		20k. orange and blue	30·00	2·50

12 No thunderbolts

1883. Posthorns in design without thunderbolts, as T **12**.

38	9	1k. orange	3·00	45
39		2k. green	4·00	45
41		3k. red	4·25	30
42b		5k. purple	3·50	15
43b		7k. blue	3·75	15
44	10	14k. red and blue	9·00	35
45		35k. green and purple	20·00	4·00
46		70k. orange and brown	40·00	4·00
47	11	3r.50 grey and black	£425	£275
48		7r. yellow and black	£450	£375

14

15

13 With thunderbolts

1889. Posthorns in design with thunderbolts as T **13**. Perf.

50	9	1k. orange	25	10
51		2k. green	25	10
52		3k. red	30	10
53	14	4k. red	40	10
54	9	5k. purple	70	10
55		7k. blue	35	10
56	14	10k. blue	70	10
114A	10	14k. red and blue	10	10
100		15k. blue and purple	10	10
116A	14	20k. red and blue	10	10
102	10	25k. violet and green	10	10
103		35k. green and purple	10	10
119A	14	50k. green and purple	10	10
120A	10	70k. orange and brown	10	10
121A	15	1r. orange and brown	10	10
79	11	3r.50 grey and black	9·00	3·00
122A		3r.50 green and red	20	30
80		7r. yellow and black	8·50	5·00
124bA		7r. pink and green	20	50

For imperf stamps, see Nos. 107B/125aB.

16 Monument to Admiral Kornilov at Sevastopol

1905. War Orphans Fund (Russo-Japanese War).

88	16	3 (6) k. brown, red and green	2·75	2·00
82	–	5 (8) k. purple and yellow	2·75	2·50
83	–	7 (10) k. blue, lt blue & pink	3·50	3·00
87	–	10 (13) k. blue, lt bl & yell	5·00	3·75

DESIGNS: 5(8) k. Monument to Minin and Pozharsky, Moscow; 7(10) k. Statue of Peter the Great, St. Petersburg; 10(13) k. Moscow Kremlin.

22

23

20

1906.

107A	22	1k. orange	10	10
93		2k. green	10	10
94		3k. red	10	10
95	23	4k. red	10	10
96	22	5k. red	10	10
97		7k. blue	10	10
98a	23	10k. blue	10	10
123Aa	20	5r. blue and green	30	30
125Aa		10r. grey, red and yellow	60	65

For imperf stamps, see Nos. 107B/125aB.

25 Nicholas II

26 Elizabeth

27 The Kremlin

1913. Tercentenary of Romanov Dynasty. Views as T **27** and portraits as T **25/26**.

126		1k. orange (Peter I)	30	15
127		2k. green (Alexander II)	40	15
128		3k. red (Alexander III)	40	15
129		4k. red (Peter I)	40	15
130		7k. brown (Type **25**)	40	15
131		10k. blue (Nicholas II)	50	15
132		14k. green (Katherine II)	50	20
133		15k. brown (Nicholas I)	75	30
134		20k. olive (Alexander I)	1·10	30
135		25k. red (Alexis)	1·75	50
136		35k. green and violet (Paul I)	1·75	60
137		50k. grey and brown (T **26**)	3·50	60
138		70k. brown and green (Michael I, the first Russian tsar)	3·50	1·25
139		1r. green (Type **27**)	8·50	2·25
140		2r. brown	10·00	3·75
141		3r. violet	24·00	8·00
142		5r. brown	32·00	18·00

DESIGNS—As T **27**: 2r. The Winter Palace; 3r. Romanov House, Moscow (birthplace of first Romanov tsar). 23 × 29 mm: 5r. Nicholas II.

31 Russian hero, Ilya Murometz

1914. War Charity.

151	31	1 (2) k. green & red on yell	60	1·50
144	–	3 (4) k. green and red on red	50	1·25
145	–	7 (8) k. green and brown on buff	50	2·75
161	–	10 (11) k. brown and blue on blue	1·00	2·00

DESIGNS: 3k. Cossack shaking girl's hand; 7k. Symbolical of Russia surrounded by her children; 10k. St. George and Dragon.

1915. As last. Colours changed.

155	31	1 (2) k. grey and brown	1·00	2·00
156	–	3 (4) k. black and red	1·00	2·50
158	–	10 (11) k. brown and blue	1·00	2·00

35

39

41

45 Cutting the Fetters

1915. Nos. 131, 133 and 134 printed on card with inscriptions on back as T **35**. No gum.

165		10k. blue	1·50	5·00
166		15k. brown	1·50	5·00
167		20k. olive	1·50	5·00

1916. Various types surch.

168	–	10k. on 7k. brown (No. 130)	40	25
170	22	10k. on 7k. blue	40	15
169	–	20k. on 14k. green (No. 132)	40	20
171	10	20k. on 14k. red and blue	40	15

1917. Various earlier types, but imperf.

107B	22	1k. orange	10	10
108B		2k. green	10	10
109B		3k. red	10	10
110B	23	4k. red	15	25
111B	22	5k. lilac	10	10
113B	23	10k. blue	10·00	27·00
115B	10	15k. blue & pur (No. 100)	10	10
116B	14	20k. red and blue	15	30
117Bd	10	25k. vio & grn (No. 102)	50	1·00
118B		35k. grn & pur (No. 103)	15	25
119B	14	50k. green and purple	15	25
120B	10	70k. orange and brown (No. 120)	10	30
121B	15	1r. orange and brown	10	10
122B	11	3r.50 green and red	20	30
123Ba	20	5r. blue and green	30	60
124B	11	7r. pink and green	50	1·40
125B	20	10r. grey, red and yellow	22·00	30·00

1916. Types of 1913 printed on card with surch on back as T **39** or **41**, or optd with figure "**1**" or "**2**" in addition on front. No gum.

172	39	1k. orange (No. 126)	20·00	35·00
175		1 on 1k. orange (No. 126)	1·00	5·00
177	41	1 on 1k. orange (No. 126)	75	4·50
173	39	2k. green (No. 127)	40·00	45·00
176		2 on 2k. green (No. 127)	1·00	5·00
178	41	2 on 2k. green (No. 127)	75	4·75
174	39	3k. red (No. 128)	1·00	4·00
179	41	3k. red (No. 128)	75	4·50

1918.

187	45	35k. blue	1·50	4·00
188		70k. brown	1·50	5·00

46 Agriculture and Industry

47 Triumph of Revolution

48 Agriculture

49 Industry

55 Science and Arts

56

64 Industry

1921. Imperf.

195	48	1r. orange	1·25	7·50
196		2r. brown	1·25	7·50
197	49	5r. blue	1·50	7·50
198	46	20r. blue	2·50	4·00
199	47	40r. blue	2·50	4·00
214	48	100r. yellow	10	10
215		200r. brown	10	25
216	55	250r. purple	10	10
217	48	300r. green	20	40
218	49	500r. blue	25	45
219		1000r. red	10	10
256	64	5000r. violet	50	85
257	46	7500r. blue	30	30
259		7500r. blue on buff	50	35
258	64	10000r. blue	5·00	10·00
260		22500r. purple on buff	50	50

1921. 4th Anniv of October Revolution. Imperf.

227	56	100r. orange	50	2·00
228		250r. violet	50	2·00
229		1000r. purple	50	2·00

57 Famine Relief Work

58

Р. С. Ф. С. Р.
ГОЛОДАЮЩИМ
250 р.+250 р.
(62)

1921. Charity. Volga Famine. Imperf.

230	**57**	2250r. green	5·00	7·50
231		2250r. red	3·75	8·00
232		2250r. brown	7·50	11·00
233	**58**	2250r. blue	10·00	15·00

1922. Surch. Imperf.

239	**48**	5000r. on 1r. orange	1·00	2·00
240		5000r. on 2r. brown	1·00	2·00
236	**49**	5000r. on 5r. blue	1·00	2·50
242	**46**	5000r. on 20r. blue	2·00	2·75
243	**47**	10000r. on 40r. blue	1·50	3·00

1922. Famine Relief. Surch as T **62**. Perf.

245	**45**	100r.+100r. on 70k. brown	80	1·50
247		250r.+250r. on 25k. blue	80	1·75

(63)

1922. Surch as T **63**. Imperf.

250	**55**	7500r. on 250r. purple	20	15
251		100000r. on 250r. purple	15	30

65

1922. Obligatory Tax. Rostov-on-Don issue. Famine Relief. Various sizes. Without gum. Imperf.

261	**65**	2T. (2000r.) green	32·00	£200
262	–	2T. (2000r.) red	25·00	£200
263	–	4T. (4000r.) red	50·00	£200
264	–	6T. (6000r.) green	40·00	£200

DESIGNS: 2T. red, Worker and family (35 × 42 mm); 4T. Clasped hands (triangular, 57 mm each side); 6T. Sower (29 × 59 mm).

РСФСР
Филателия
– детям
19 - 8 - 22
(**70** "Philately for the children")

1922. Optd with T **70**. Perf or imperf.

273	**22**	1k. orange	£200	£300
274		2k. green	18·00	20·00
275		3k. red	10·00	12·00
276		5k. red	8·00	12·00
277	**23**	10k. blue	8·00	15·00

71

73

1922. 5th Anniv of October Revolution. Imperf.

279	**71**	5r. black and yellow	60	45
280		10r. black and brown	60	45
281		25r. black and purple	2·50	1·25
282		27r. black and red	6·00	5·50
283		45r. black and blue	4·00	5·00

1922. Air. Optd with airplane. Imperf.

284	**71**	45r. black and green	22·00	45·00

1922. Famine Relief. Imperf.

285	**73**	20r.+5r. lilac	60	2·00
286	–	20r.+5r. violet	60	2·00
287	–	20r.+5r. blue	1·00	2·50
288	–	20r.+5r. blue	3·50	15·00

DESIGNS—HORIZ: No. 286, Freighter; No. 287, Steam train. VERT: No. 288, Airplane.

(77)

78 Worker

79 Soldier

1922. Surch as T **77**. Imperf or perf.

289	**14**	5r. on 20k. red and blue	3·50	20·00
290	**10**	20r. on 15k. blue & purple	3·75	20·00
291		20r. on 70k. orange and brown	15	30
292a	**14**	30r. on 50k. green & pur	35	35
293	**10**	40r. on 15k. blue & pur	15	15
294		100r. on 15k. blue & pur	15	20
295		200r. on 15k. blue & pur	15	20

1922. Imperf or perf.

303	**78**	10r. blue	10	15
304	**79**	50r. brown	10	15
305		70r. purple	10	15
310		100r. red	15	15

1 мая
1923 г. Филателия —
Трудящимся,
1 р.+1 р.
(80)

1923. Charity. Surch as T **80**. Imperf.

315	**71**	1r.+1r. on 10r. black and brown	30·00	40·00
317	**55**	2r.+2r. on 250r. purple	30·00	40·00
318	**64**	4r.+4r. on 5000r. violet	45·00	55·00

83 Worker

84 Peasant

85 Soldier

1923. Perf.

320	**85**	3r. red	10	10
321	**83**	4r. brown	10	10
322	**84**	5r. blue	10	10
323	**85**	10r. grey	15	15
324		20r. purple	25	25

86 Reaper

88 Tractor

1923. Agricultural Exn, Moscow. Imperf or perf.

325	**86**	1r. brown and orange	2·00	6·00
326	–	2r. green and light green	2·00	6·00
327	**88**	5r. blue and light blue	2·00	6·00
328	–	7r. rose and pink	2·00	6·00

DESIGNS: As Type **86**: 2r. Sower; 7r. Exhibition buildings.

90 Worker

91 Peasant

92 Soldier

93

94

95

1923. Perf (some values also imperf).

335	**90**	1k. yellow	40	25
359	**91**	2k. green	30	15
360	**92**	3k. brown	35	15
361	**90**	4k. red	35	15
434		5k. purple	55	15
363	**91**	6k. blue	60	15
364	**92**	7k. brown	60	15
437	**90**	8k. olive	90	15
366	**91**	9k. red	90	40
341	**92**	10k. blue	55	15
385	**90**	14k. grey	1·00	20
386	**91**	15k. yellow	1·25	90
442	**92**	18k. violet	1·75	55
443	**90**	20k. green	2·00	30
444	**91**	30k. violet	2·75	40
445	**92**	40k. grey	4·00	60
343	**91**	50k. brown	4·50	60
447	**92**	1r. red and brown	4·75	80
375	**93**	2r. green and red	6·50	3·00
449	**94**	3r. green and brown	14·00	4·00
450	**95**	5r. brown and blue	17·00	5·00

96 Lenin

97 Fokker F.III Airplane

1924. Lenin Mourning. Imperf or perf.

413	**96**	3k. black and red	2·00	1·75
414		6k. black and red	2·00	1·75
411		12k. black and red	5·00	75
412		20k. black and red	2·75	85

1924. Air. Surch. Imperf.

417	**97**	5k. on 3r. blue	3·50	1·75
418		10k. on 5r. green	3·50	1·50
419		15k. on 1r. brown	2·00	1·50
420		20k. on 10r. red	2·50	1·25

С. С. С. Р.
пострадавшему
от наводнения
Ленинграду.
3 к. + 10 к.

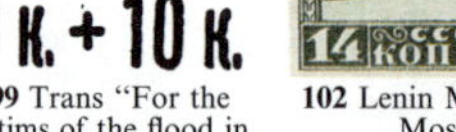

(**99** Trans "For the victims of the flood in Leningrad")

102 Lenin Mausoleum, Moscow

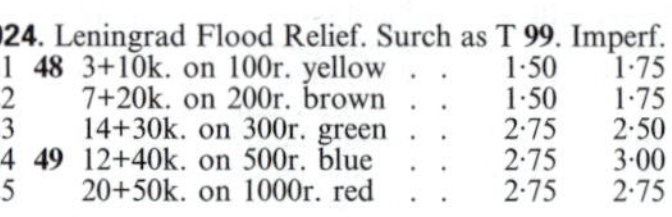

1924. Leningrad Flood Relief. Surch as T **99**. Imperf.

421	**48**	3+10k. on 100r. yellow	1·50	1·75
422		7+20k. on 200r. brown	1·50	1·75
423		14+30k. on 300r. green	2·75	2·50
424	**49**	12+40k. on 500r. blue	2·75	3·00
425		20+50k. on 1000r. red	2·75	2·75

1925. 1st Death Anniv of Lenin. Imperf or perf.

426	**102**	7k. blue	3·50	2·75
427		14k. olive	4·50	4·00
428		20k. red	5·00	4·00
429		40k. brown	7·50	4·00

104 Lenin

106 Prof. Lomonosov and Academy of Sciences, Leningrad

1925.

451	**104**	1r. brown	8·00	3·00
452		2r. brown	7·50	2·50
850		3r. green	2·25	75
851		5r. brown	3·50	1·50
852		10r. blue	7·50	5·00

1925. Bicentenary of Academy of Sciences.

456b	**106**	3k. brown	4·00	2·00
457		15k. olive	6·00	4·00

107 A. S. Popov

110 Moscow Barricade

1925. 30th Anniv of Popov's Radio Discoveries.

458	**107**	7k. blue	2·50	1·40
459		14k. green	4·00	2·25

1925. 20th Anniv of 1905 Rebellion. Imperf or perf.

463b	–	3k. green	3·00	1·75
464c	–	7k. brown	4·00	2·50
465a	**110**	14k. red	3·50	2·25

DESIGNS—VERT: 3k. Postal rioters; 7k. Orator and crowd.

111 "Decembrists in Exiles" (detail, A. Moravov)

112 Senate Square, St. Petersburg, 1825

1925. Centenary of Decembrist Rebellion. Imperf or perf.

466b	**111**	3k. green	2·50	2·25
467	**112**	7k. brown	4·00	3·25
468	–	14k. red	5·00	3·50

DESIGN—VERT: 14k. Medallion with heads of Pestel, Ryleev, Bestuzhev-Ryumin, Muravev-Apostol and Kakhovsky.

114

1926. 6th International Proletarian Esperanto Congress.

471	**114**	7k. red and green	5·00	3·00
472		14k. violet and green	5·00	1·75

115 Waifs

116 Lenin when a Child

1926. Child Welfare.

473	**115**	10k. brown	90	45
474	**116**	20k. blue	2·50	95

1927. Same type with new inscriptions.

475	**115**	8k.+2k. green	80	35
476	**116**	18k.+2k. red	1·75	65

ПОЧТОВАЯ
МАРКА
КОП. 8 КОП.
(117)

1927. Postage Due stamps surch with T **117**.

491	**D 104**	8k. on 1k. red	1·50	2·75
492		8k. on 2k. violet	1·50	2·75
493		8k. on 3k. blue	1·50	2·75
494		8k. on 7k. yellow	1·50	2·75
494c		8k. on 8k. green	1·00	2·25
494d		8k. on 10k. blue	1·50	2·75
494f		8k. on 14k. brown	1·50	2·75

1927. Various types of 7k. surch (some values imperf or perf).

495	**92**	8k. on 7k. brown	6·00	6·00
523	**107**	8k. on 7k. blue	3·00	3·25
524	–	8k. on 7k. brn (No. 464c)	6·00	5·00
527	**112**	8k. on 7k. brown	6·00	6·50
526	**114**	8k. on 7k. red and green	12·00	14·00

119 Dr. Zamenhof

1927. 40th Anniv of Publication of Zamenhof's "Langue Internationale" (Esperanto).

498	**119**	14k. green and brown	3·00	2·00

120 Tupolev ANT-3 Biplane and Map

1927. 1st Int Air Post Congress, The Hague.

499	**120**	10k. blue and brown	14·00	5·00
500		15k. red and olive	16·00	10·00

121 Worker, Soldier and Peasant

124 Sailor and Worker

122 Allegory of Revolution

1927. 10th Anniv of October Revolution.

No.	Type	Description	Unused	Used
501	**121**	3k. red	2·50	75
502	**122**	5k. brown	6·00	2·00
503	–	7k. green	8·00	2·50
504	**124**	8k. black and brown	4·25	85
505	–	14k. red and blue	6·00	1·25
506	–	18k. blue	4·00	1·00
507	–	28k. brown	13·00	8·00

DESIGNS—HORIZ: (As Type **122**): HORIZ: 7k. Smolny Institute; 14k. Map of Russia inscr "C.C.C.P."; 18k. Various Russian races; 28k. Worker, soldier and peasant.

128 Worker

129 Peasant

130 Lenin

1927.

No.	Type	Description	Unused	Used
508	**128**	1k. orange	90	50
509	**129**	2k. green	90	20
510	**128**	4k. blue	90	20
511	**129**	5k. brown	90	20
512		7k. red	4·50	1·00
513	**128**	8k. green	2·50	20
514		10k. brown	2·00	20
515	**130**	14k. green	2·25	45
516		18k. olive	3·00	40
517		18k. blue	5·00	70
518	**129**	20k. olive	2·75	35
519	**128**	40k. red	6·00	60
520	**129**	50k. blue	8·00	1·00
521	**128**	70k. olive	13·00	1·40
522	**129**	80k. orange	24·00	5·00

131 Infantryman, Lenin Mausoleum and Kremlin

1928. 10th Anniv of Red Army.

No.	Type	Description	Unused	Used
529	**131**	8k. brown	1·60	45
530	–	14k. blue	3·00	50
531	–	18k. red	3·00	1·75
532	–	28k. green	4·00	4·00

DESIGNS: 14k. Sailor and cruiser "Aurora"; 18k. Cavalryman; 28k. Airman.

135 Young Factory Workers

137 Trumpeter sounding the Assembly

1929. Child Welfare.

No.	Type	Description	Unused	Used
536	**135**	10k.+2k. brown & sepia	1·75	1·10
537	–	20k.+2k. blue & brown	2·75	2·75

DESIGN: 20k. Children in harvest field.

See also Nos. 567/8.

1929. 1st All-Union Gathering of Pioneers.

No.	Type	Description	Unused	Used
538	**137**	10k. brown	12·00	8·00
539		14k. blue	6·00	4·00

138 Worker (after I. Shadr)

139 Factory Girl

140 Peasant

141 Farm Girl

142 Guardsman

143 Worker, Soldier and Peasant (after I. Smirnov)

144 Lenin

242a Miner

242b Steel foundryman

242c Infantryman

242d Airman

242e Arms of U.S.S.R.

149 Central Telegraph Office, Moscow

150 Lenin Hydro-electric Power Station

743a Farm Girl

743b Architect

744 Furnaceman

1929. Perf, but some values exist imperf.

No.	Type	Description	Unused	Used
541	**138**	1k. yellow	50	15
542	**139**	2k. green	50	10
543	**140**	3k. blue	60	10
544	**141**	4k. mauve	90	15
545	**142**	5k. brown	90	10
847a	**242a**	5k. red	25	10
546	**143**	7k. red	2·00	60
547	**138**	10k. grey	1·40	10
727f	**139**	10k. blue	75	15
1214b		10k. black	65	15
554	**144**	14k. blue	1·50	60
548	**143**	15k. blue	2·00	10
847b	**242b**	15k. blue	1·75	30
847c	**242c**	15k. green	50	15
549	**140**	20k. green and blue	2·75	20
727h	**141**	20k. green	70	25
2252a	**743a**	20k. olive	80	30
2252b	**743b**	25k. brown	1·00	45
550	**139**	30k. violet and lilac	4·00	50
847d	**242d**	30k. blue	1·00	20
727l	**144**	40k. blue	1·50	40
727m	**141**	50k. brown and buff	1·25	40
847f	**242e**	60k. red	1·50	30
2253	**744**	60k. red	1·00	20
2253a		60k. blue	3·00	1·00
552	**142**	70k. red and pink	7·00	1·40
553	**140**	80k. brown and yellow	7·00	1·25
561	**149**	1r. blue	2·50	40
562	**150**	3r. brown and green	18·00	6·00

Nos. 727f, 1214b and 550 show the factory girl without factory in background. Nos. 549, 727m, 552, 553 have designs like those shown but with unshaded background.

151 Industry

153 "More metal more machines"

1929. Industrial Loan Propaganda.

No.	Type	Description	Unused	Used
563	**151**	5k. brown	2·00	1·25
564	–	10k. olive	2·50	2·00
565	**153**	20k. green	9·00	3·25
566	–	28k. violet	5·00	3·25

DESIGNS—HORIZ: 10k. Tractors. VERT: 28k. Blast furnace and graph of pig-iron output.

1930. Child Welfare.

No.	Type	Description	Unused	Used
567	**135**	10k.+2k. olive	1·50	1·75
568	–	20k.+2k. grn (as No. 537)	2·50	3·50

155 Cavalrymen (after M. Grekov)

1930. 10th Anniv of 1st Red Cavalry.

No.	Type	Description	Unused	Used
569	**155**	2k. green	2·50	1·40
570	–	5k. brown	2·50	1·40
571	–	10k. olive	5·00	3·00
572	–	14k. blue and red	2·50	2·50

DESIGNS: 5k. Cavalry attack (after Yu. Merkulov); 10k. Cavalry facing left (after M. Grekov); 14k. Cavalry charge (after Yu. Merkulov).

159 Group of Soviet Pupils

1930. Educational Exhibition, Leningrad.

No.	Type	Description	Unused	Used
573	**159**	10k. green	2·00	1·00

160

1930. Air. "Graf-Zeppelin" (airship) Flight to Moscow.

No.	Type	Description	Unused	Used
574	**160**	40k. blue	30·00	18·00
575		80k. red	35·00	13·00

162 Battleship "Potemkin"

1930. 25th Anniv of 1905 Rebellion. Imperf or perf.

No.	Type	Description	Unused	Used
576	**162**	3k. red	1·75	50
577	–	5k. blue	1·50	60
578	–	10k. red and green	2·75	1·10

DESIGNS—HORIZ: 5k. Barricade and rebels. VERT: 10k. Red flag at Presnya barricade.

165 From the Tundra (reindeer) to the Steppes (camel)

166 Above Dnieprostroi Dam

1931. Airship Construction Fund. Imperf or perf.

No.	Type	Description	Unused	Used
579c	**165**	10k. violet	4·00	2·50
580b	**166**	15k. blue	22·00	12·00
581c	–	20k. red	3·50	3·00
582b	–	50k. brown	3·50	3·00
583c	–	1r. green	5·50	5·00

DESIGNS—As Type **165**. VERT: 20k. Above Lenin's Mausoleum. HORIZ: 1r. Airship construction. As Type **166**: 50k. Above the North Pole.

See also No. E592.

170 "Graf Zeppelin" over Ice breaker "Malygin"

1931. Air. "Graf Zeppelin" (airship) North Pole Flight. Imperf or perf.

No.	Type	Description	Unused	Used
584	**170**	30k. purple	25·00	15·00
585b		35k. green	25·00	13·00
586		1r. black	25·00	15·00
587		2r. blue	25·00	15·00

172 Maksim Gorky

173 Storming the Winter Palace

1932. 40th Anniv of Publication of "Makar Chadra".

No.	Type	Description	Unused	Used
590	**172**	15k. brown	5·00	3·50
591		35k. blue	18·00	10·00

1932. Airship Construction Fund. Imperf or perf.

No.	Type	Description	Unused	Used
592	**166**	15k. black	3·50	1·50

1932. 15th Anniv of October Revolution.

No.	Type	Description	Unused	Used
593	–	3k. violet	1·25	50
594	**173**	5k. brown	1·25	50
595	–	10k. blue	3·25	1·25
596	–	15k. green	1·75	1·25
597	–	20k. red	7·25	1·75
598	–	30k. grey	9·00	1·90
599	–	35k. brown	60·00	45·00

DESIGNS—HORIZ: 10k. Dnieper Dam; 15k. Harvesting with combines; 20k. Industrial works, Magnitogorsk; 30k. Siberians listening to Moscow broadcast. VERT: 3k. Lenin's arrival in Petrograd; 35k. People of the World hailing Lenin.

175 "Liberation"

1932. 10th Anniv of International Revolutionaries' Relief Organization.

No.	Type	Description	Unused	Used
600	**175**	50k. red	14·00	6·00

176 Museum of Fine Arts

1932. 1st All-Union Philatelic Exn, Moscow.

No.	Type	Description	Unused	Used
601	**176**	15k. brown	24·00	13·00
602		35k. blue	40·00	20·00

177 Trier, Marx's Birthplace

1933. 50th Death Anniv of Marx.

No.	Type	Description	Unused	Used
603	**177**	3k. green	4·00	90
604	–	10k. brown	7·00	1·40
605	–	35k. purple	10·00	12·50

DESIGNS—VERT: 10k. Marx's grave, Highgate Cemetery; 35k. Marx.

1933. Leningrad Philatelic Exhibition. Surch **LENINGRAD 1933** in Russian characters and premium.

No.	Type	Description	Unused	Used
606	**176**	15k.+30k. black & brn	80·00	40·00
607		35k.+70k. blue	95·00	50·00

182

183

1933. Ethnographical Issue. Racial types.

No.	Type	Description	Unused	Used
608	–	1k. brown (Kazakhs)	1·75	40
609	**183**	2k. blue (Lesgins)	1·75	40
610	–	3k. green (Crimean Tatars)	1·75	40
611	–	4k. brown (Jews of Birobidzhan)	1·25	60
612	–	5k. red (Tungusians)	1·25	40
613	–	6k. blue (Buryats)	1·25	40
614	–	7k. brown (Chechens)	1·25	40
615	–	8k. red (Abkhazians)	1·75	55

616 – 9k. blue (Georgians) . . . 3·00 60
617 – 10k. brown (Samoyedes) 4·00 1·50
618 – 14k. green (Yakuts) . . . 3·50 40
619 – 15k. purple (Ukrainians) 4·00 1·25
620 – 15k. black (Uzbeks) . . . 4·00 80
621 – 15k. blue (Tadzhiks) . . . 4·00 75
622 – 15k. brown (Transcaucasians) . . . 4·00 75
623 – 15k. green (Byelorussians) 3·50 60
624 – 15k. orange (Great Russians) . . . . . . 3·50 80
625 – 15k. red (Turkmens) . . . 4·50 1·00
626 – 20k. blue (Koryaks) . . . 9·00 1·60
627 – 30k. red (Bashkirs) . . . 10·00 1·75
628 **182** 35k. brown (Chuvashes) 16·00 2·25
SIZES: Nos. 608, 610/11, 614/17, 626/7, As T **182**: Nos. 612/13, 618. As T **183**: Nos. 619/24, 48 × 22 mm. No. 625, 22 × 48 mm.

186 V. V. Vorovsky

1933. Communist Party Activists. Dated "1933", "1934" or "1935".
629 **186** 1k. green 65 50
718b – 2k. violet . . . . 4·50 25
630 – 3k. blue . . . . 1·40 60
719 – 4k. purple . . . . 5·00 4·00
631 – 5k. brown . . . . 3·00 1·90
632 – 10k. blue . . . . 16·00 6·00
633 – 15k. red . . . . 40·00 20·00
720 – 40k. brown . . . . . . 9·00 5·00
DESIGNS: 2k. M. Frunze; 3k. V. M. Volodarsky; 4k. N. E. Bauman; 5k. M. S. Uritsky; 10k. Iacov M. Sverdlov; 15k. Viktor P. Nogin; 40k. S. M. Kirov.

187 Stratosphere Balloon "U.S.S.R.-1" over Moscow

188 Massed Standard Bearers

1933. Air. Stratosphere record (19000 m).
634 **187** 5k. blue . . . . 80·00 19·00
635 10k. red . . . . 55·00 9·00
636 20k. violet . . . . 28·00 6·75

1933. 15th Anniv of Order of Red Banner.
637 **188** 20k. red, yellow and black 2·50 1·50

189 Commissar Shaumyan

190 Tupolev ANT-9 PS9 over Oilfield

1934. 15th Death Anniv of 26 Baku Commissars.
688 **189** 4k. brown . . . . 5·00 1·50
639 – 5k. black . . . . 5·00 1·50
640 – 20k. violet . . . . 3·00 85
641 – 35k. blue . . . . 18·00 4·00
642 – 40k. red . . . . 14·00 4·00
DESIGNS: 5k. Commissar Dzhaparidze. HORIZ: 20k. The 26 condemned commissars; 35k. Monument in Baku; 40k. Workman, peasant and soldier dipping flags in salute.

1934. Air. 10th Anniv of Soviet Civil Aviation and U.S.S.R. Airmail Service.
643 – 5k. blue . . . . 10·00 4·00
644 **190** 10k. green . . . . 10·00 4·00
645 – 20k. red . . . . 20·00 5·50
646 – 50k. blue . . . . 30·00 9·00
647 – 80k. violet . . . . 16·00 7·00
DESIGNS: Tupolev ANT-9 PS9 airplane over: 5k. Furnaces at Kuznetsk; 20k. Harvesters; 50k. Volga–Moscow Canal; 80k. Ice breaker "OB" in the Arctic.

191 New Lenin Mausoleum

1934. 10th Death Anniv of Lenin.
648 **191** 5k. brown . . . . 2·00 75
649 10k. blue . . . . 6·50 2·50
650 15k. red . . . . 6·00 2·00
651 20k. green . . . . 1·75 80
652 35k. brown . . . . 6·00 2·75

192 Fyodorov Monument, Moscow, and Hand and Rotary Presses

1934. 350th Death Anniv of Ivan Fyodorov (first Russian printer).
653 **192** 20k. red . . . . 8·00 3·75
654 40k. blue . . . . 8·00 3·00

194 Dmitri Mendeleev

1934. Birth Centenary of Dmitri Mendeleev (chemist).
655 – 5k. green . . . . 5·00 1·50
656 **194** 10k. brown . . . . 15·00 5·00
657 15k. red . . . . 13·00 4·50
658 – 20k. blue . . . . 7·50 2·50
DESIGN—VERT: 5k., 20k. Mendeleev seated.

195 A. V. Vasenko and "Osoaviakhim"

1934. Air. Stratosphere Balloon "Osoaviakhim" Disaster Victims.
659 – 5k. purple . . . . 22·00 5·00
660 **195** 10k. brown . . . . . . 55·00 6·00
661 – 20k. violet . . . . . . 60·00 8·00
1042 – 1r. green . . . . 8·50 3·00
1043 **195** 1r. green . . . . 8·50 3·00
1044 – 1r. blue . . . . 8·50 3·00
DESIGNS: 5k., 1r. (No. 1042). I. D. Usyskin; 20k., 1r. (No. 1044), P. F. Fedoseenko.
The 1r. values, issued in 1944, commemorated the 10th anniv of the disaster.

196 Airship "Pravda"

1934. Air. Airship Travel Propaganda.
662 **196** 5k. red . . . . 12·00 3·00
663 – 10k. lake . . . . 12·00 3·00
664 – 15k. brown . . . . 30·00 12·00
665 – 20k. black . . . . 16·00 7·50
666 – 30k. blue . . . . 55·00 26·00
DESIGNS—HORIZ: 10k. Airship landing; 15k. Airship "Voroshilov"; 30k. Airship "Lenin" and route map. VERT: 20k. Airship's gondolas and mooring mast.

199 Stalin and Marchers inspired by Lenin

1934. "Ten Years without Lenin". Portraits inscr "1924–1934".
667 – 1k. black and blue . . . 1·50 75
668 – 3k. black and blue . . . 1·50 80
669 – 5k. black and blue . . . 3·50 1·40
670 – 10k. black and blue . . . 4·25 2·50
671 – 20k. blue and orange . . 6·00 3·25
672 **199** 30k. red and orange . . 24·00 6·00
DESIGN—VERT: 1k. Lenin aged 3; 3k. Lenin as student; 5k. Lenin as man; 10k. Lenin as orator. HORIZ: 20k. Red demonstration, Lenin's Mausoleum.

200 "War Clouds"

1935. Anti-War. Inscr "1914–1934".
673 **200** 5k. black . . . . 4·50 90
674 – 10k. blue . . . . 7·50 3·75
675 – 15k. green . . . . 13·00 5·00
676 – 20k. brown . . . . 10·00 2·75
677 – 35k. red . . . . 22·00 13·00
DESIGNS: 10k. "Flight from a burning village"; 15k. "Before war and afterwards"; 20k. "Ploughing with the sword"; 35k. "Fraternization".

202 Capt. Voronin and Ice-breaker "Chelyuskin"

1935. Air. Rescue of "Chelyuskin" Expedition.
678 **202** 1k. orange . . . . 4·00 1·00
679 – 3k. red . . . . 4·75 1·40
680 – 5k. green . . . . 5·00 1·40
681 – 10k. brown . . . . 7·25 1·75
682 – 15k. black . . . . 9·25 2·50
683 – 20k. purple . . . . 14·50 2·50
684 – 25k. blue . . . . 42·00 11·00
685 – 30k. green . . . . 45·00 13·00
686 – 40k. violet . . . . . . 32·00 3·75
687 **202** 50k. blue . . . . 35·00 9·00
DESIGNS—HORIZ: 3k. Prof. Schmidt and Schmidt Camp; 50k. Schmidt Camp deserted. VERT: 5k. A. V. Lyapidevsky; 10k. S. A. Levanevsky; 15k. M. G. Slepnev; 20k. I. V. Doronin; 25k. M. V. Vodopyanov; 30k. V. S. Molokov; 40k. N. P. Kamanin.

205 Underground Station

1935. Opening of Moscow Underground.
688 – 5k. orange . . . . 8·50 3·25
689 – 10k. blue . . . . 10·00 3·25
690 **205** 15k. red . . . . 80·00 24·00
691 – 20k. green . . . . 17·00 9·00
DESIGNS—As Type **205**: 5k. Excavating tunnel; 10k. Section of tunnel, escalator and station. $48\frac{1}{2} \times 23$ mm: 20k. Train in station.

207 Rowing

1935. Spartacist Games.
692 – 1k. blue and orange . . . 2·75 80
693 – 2k. blue and black . . . 2·75 80
694 **207** 3k. brown and green . . . 5·50 1·50
695 – 4k. blue and red . . . . 3·00 90
696 – 5k. brown and violet . . 3·00 1·00
697 – 10k. purple and red . . . 14·00 3·00
698 – 15k. brown and black . . 30·00 8·00
699 – 20k. blue and brown . . . 22·00 3·25
700 – 35k. brown and blue . . . 30·00 13·00
701 – 40k. red and brown . . . 24·00 6·00
DESIGNS: 1k. Running; 2k. Diving; 4k. Football; 5k. Skiing; 10k. Cycling; 15k. Lawn tennis; 20k. Skating; 35k. Hurdling; 40k. Parade of athletes.

208 Friedrich Engels

Перелет
Москва—
Сан-Франциско
через Сев. полюс
1935
1 Р.

(209)

1935. 40th Death Anniv of F. Engels.
702 **208** 5k. red . . . . 6·00 60
703 10k. green . . . . 3·00 2·00
704 15k. blue . . . . 7·50 2·75
705 20k. black . . . . 5·00 3·00

1935. Air. Moscow–San Francisco via North Pole Flight. Surch with T **209**.
706 1r. on 10k. brown (No. 681) £300 £400

210 A "Lion Hunt" from a Sassanian Silver Plate

211 M. I. Kalinin

1935. 3rd International Congress of Persian Art and Archaeology, Leningrad.
707 **210** 5k. orange . . . . 7·00 1·00
708 10k. green . . . . 7·00 1·75
709 15k. purple . . . . 8·00 3·00
710 35k. brown . . . . 14·00 5·50

1935. Pres. Kalinin's 60th Birthday. Autographed portraits inscr "1875–1935".
711 – 3k. purple 75 20
712 – 5k. green . . . . 1·25 25
713 – 10k. blue . . . . 1·25 60
714 **211** 20k. brown . . . . . . 1·60 70
DESIGNS: 3k. Kalinin as machine worker; 5k. Harvester; 10k. Orator.
See also No. 1189.

212 Tolstoi

213 Pioneers securing Letter-box

1935. 25th Death Anniv of Tolstoi (writer).
715b – 3k. violet and black . . 75 25
716b **212** 10k. brown and blue . . 1·50 45
717b – 20k. brown and green 3·50 1·75
DESIGNS: 3k. Tolstoi in 1860; 20k. Monument in Moscow.

1936. Pioneer Movement.
721b **213** 1k. green . . . . 1·10 30
722 2k. red . . . . 1·00 70
723b – 3k. blue . . . . 1·25 1·60
724b – 5k. red . . . . 1·25 55
725b – 10k. blue . . . . 2·00 2·50
726 – 15k. brown . . . . . . 6·50 3·00
DESIGNS: 3, 5k. Pioneer preventing another from throwing stones; 10k. Pioneers disentangling kite line from telegraph wires; 15k. Girl pioneer saluting.

214 N. A. Dobrolyubov

215 Pushkin (after T. Paita)

1936. Birth Centenary of N. Dobrolyubov (author and critic).
727b **214** 10k. purple . . . . . . 5·00 1·00

1937. Death Centenary of A. S. Pushkin (poet).
728 **215** 10k. brown 55 30
729 20k. green 60 30
730 40k. red . . . . 1·25 50
731 – 50k. blue . . . . 2·75 75
732a – 80k. red . . . . 2·25 1·00
733a – 1r. green . . . . 4·50 1·00
DESIGN: 50k. to 1r. Pushkin's Monument, Moscow (A. Opekushin).

216 Pushkin Monument, Moscow (A. Operkushin)

218 F. E. Dzerzhinsky

217 Meyerhold Theatre

1937. Pushkin Exn, Moscow. Sheet 105 × 89 mm.
MS733c **215** 10k. brown; **216** 50k. brown . . . . 10·00 5·00

1937. 1st Soviet Architectural Congress.
734 **217** 3k. red . . . . 1·25 20
735 – 5k. lake . . . . 1·25 20
736 **217** 10k. brown . . . . 1·75 25
737 – 15k. black . . . . 2·00 25
738 – 20k. olive . . . . 1·10 40
739 – 30k. black . . . . 1·75 70
740 – 40k. violet . . . . 2·25 1·25
741 – 50k. brown . . . . 3·75 1·50
MS741a 120 × 93 mm. 40k. × 4 violet (as No. 740). Imperf . . . . . 15·00 45·00
DESIGNS—As T **217**: 5, 15k. G.P.O.; 20, 50k. Red Army Theatre. 45 × 27 mm: 30k. Hotel Moscow; 40k. Palace of Soviets.

1937. 10th Death Anniv of Feliks Dzerzhinsky.
742 **218** 10k. brown 40 20
743 20k. green 60 35
744 40k. red . . . . 1·75 55
745 80k. red . . . . 2·50 70

219 Yakovlev Ya-7 Air 7

1937. Air. Air Force Exhibition.
746 **219** 10k. black and brown . . 1·75 30
747 – 20k. black and green . . 1·75 30
748 – 30k. black and brown . . 2·75 40
749 – 40k. black and purple . . 5·00 90
750 – 50k. black and violet . . 6·50 1·50
751 – 80k. brown and blue . . . 7·50 2·00
752 – 1r. black, orange & brown 11·00 4·00
MS752b 165 × 90 mm. No. 752 × 4. Imperf . . . . 90·00 £180
DESIGNS—As T **219**: 20k. Tupolev ANT-9; 30k. Tupolev ANT-6 bomber; 40k. O.S.G.A. 101 flying boat; 50k. Tupolev ANT-4 TB-1 bomber. 60 × 26 mm: 80k. Tupolev ANT-20 "Maksim Gorki"; 1r. Tupolev ANT-14 "Pravda".

220 Arms of Ukraine

221 Arms of U.S.S.R.

1937. New U.S.S.R. Constitution. Arms of Constituent Republics.
753 – 20k. blue (Armenia) . . . 1·50 50
754 – 20k. purple (Azerbaijan) 1·50 50
755 – 20k. brown (Byelorussia) 1·50 50
756 – 20k. red (Georgia) . . . . 1·50 50
757 – 20k. green (Kazakhstan) 1·50 50
758 – 20k. red (Kirghizia) . . . 1·50 50
759 – 20k. red (Tadzhikistan) 1·50 50
760 – 20k. red (Turkmenistan) 1·50 50
761 **220** 20k. red (Ukraine) . . . 1·50 50
762 – 20k. orange (Uzbekistan) 1·50 50
763 – 20k. blue (R.S.F.S.R.) . . 1·50 50
764 **221** 40k. red (U.S.S.R.) . . . 5·00 1·50

222 "Worker and Collective Farmer" (sculpture, Vera Mukhina)

223 Russian Pavilion, Paris Exhibition

1938. Paris International Exhibition.
765 **222** 5k. red . . . . 1·00 40
766 **223** 20k. red . . . . 1·40 40
767 **222** 50k. blue . . . . 3·50 1·00

224 Shota Rustaveli

1938. 750th Anniv of Poem "Knight in Tiger Skin".
768 **224** 20k. green . . . . 1·50 40

225 Route of North Pole Flight

227 Infantryman

1938. North Pole Flight.
769 **225** 10k. black and brown . . 2·40 30
770 20k. black and grey . . . 3·75 40
771 – 40k. red and green . . . 8·50 1·40
772 – 80k. red and deep red . . 2·75 1·10
DESIGN: 40k., 80k. Soviet Flag at North Pole.

1938. 20th Anniv of Red Army.
773 **227** 10k. black and red . . . 50 20
774 – 20k. black and red . . . 85 25
775 – 30k. black, red and blue 1·25 25
776 – 40k. black, red and blue 1·75 75
777 – 50k. black and red . . . 2·25 75
778a – 80k. black and red . . . 4·75 75
779 – 1r. black and red . . . 2·75 75
DESIGNS—VERT: 20k. Tank driver; 30k. Sailor; 40k. Airman; 50k. Artilleryman. HORIZ: 80k. Stalin reviewing cavalry; 1r. Machine gunners.

229 G. Baidukov, V. Chkalov and A. Belyakov

230 M. Gromov, A. Yumashov and S. Danilin

1938. 1st Flight over North Pole.
780 **229** 10k. red and black . . . 2·00 50
781 20k. red and black . . . 2·25 70
782 40k. red and brown . . . 4·00 1·40
783 50k. red and purple . . . 7·25 1·75

1938. 2nd Flight over North Pole.
784 **230** 10k. purple . . . . 4·00 45
785 20k. black . . . . 4·00 90
786 50k. purple . . . . 7·75 1·25

231 Ice-breaker "Murman" approaching Survivors

1938. Rescue of Papanin's North Pole Meteorological Party.
787 **231** 10k. purple . . . . 4·00 60
788 20k. blue . . . . 4·00 70
789 – 30k. brown . . . . 7·00 1·25
790 – 50k. blue . . . . 8·00 2·50
DESIGNS—VERT: 30, 50k. Papanin survivors.

233 Nurse weighing Baby

234 Children visiting Statue of Lenin

1938. Soviet Union Children.
791 **233** 10k. blue . . . . 1·25 30
792 **234** 15k. blue . . . . 1·25 35
793 – 20k. purple . . . . 1·50 35
794 – 30k. red . . . . 1·90 45
795 – 40k. brown . . . . 2·40 55
796 – 50k. blue . . . . 6·00 1·50
797 – 80k. green . . . . 7·00 2·00
DESIGNS—HORIZ: 20, 40k. Biology class; 30k. Health camp; 50, 80k. Young inventors at play.

235 Crimean landscape

1938. Views of Crimea and Caucasus.
798 **235** 5k. black . . . . 1·10 40
799 A 5k. brown . . . . 1·10 40
800 B 10k. green . . . . 2·25 45
801 C 10k. brown . . . . 2·25 50
802 D 15k. black . . . . 3·75 60
803 A 15k. black . . . . 3·75 60
804 E 20k. brown . . . . 4·00 70
805 C 30k. black . . . . 4·00 75
806 F 40k. brown . . . . 4·75 90
807 G 50k. green . . . . 4·75 1·75
808 H 80k. brown . . . . 6·50 2·25
809 I 1r. green . . . . 9·00 6·00
DESIGNS—HORIZ: A, Yalta (two views); B, Georgian military road; E, Crimean resthouse; F, Alupka; H, Crimea; I, Swallows' Nest Castle. VERT: C, Crimea (two views); D, Swallows' Nest Castle; G, Gurzuf Park.

236 Schoolchildren and Model Tupolev ANT-6 Bomber

1938. Aviation.
810 **236** 5k. purple . . . . 1·75 75
811 – 10k. brown . . . . 1·75 75
812 – 15k. red . . . . 2·25 75
813 – 20k. blue . . . . 2·25 75
814 – 30k. red . . . . 4·00 1·25
815 – 40k. blue . . . . 7·00 1·25
816 – 50k. green . . . . 12·00 1·75
817 – 80k. brown . . . . 8·00 3·25
818 – 1r. green . . . . 14·00 3·25
DESIGNS—HORIZ: 10k. Glider in flight; 40k. Yakovlev VT-2 seaplane; 1r. Tupolev ANT-6 bomber. VERT: 15k. Captive observation balloon; 20k. Airship "Osoaviakhim" over Kremlin; 30k. Parachutists; 30k. Balloon in flight; 80k. Stratosphere balloon.

237 Underground Railway

1938. Moscow Underground Railway Extension.
819 – 10k. violet . . . . 2·40 85
820 – 15k. brown . . . . 3·00 85
821 – 20k. black . . . . 3·75 85
822 – 30k. violet . . . . 4·00 1·25
823 **237** 40k. black . . . . 6·00 1·40
824 – 50k. brown . . . . 5·50 2·25
DESIGNS—VERT: 10k. Mayakovskaya station; 15k. Sokol station; 20k. Kievsskaya station. HORIZ: 30k. Dynamo station; 50k. Revolutskaya station.

238 Miner and Pneumatic Drill

239 Diving

1938. 20th Anniv of Federation of Young Lenin Communists.
825 – 20k. blue 90 30
826 **238** 30k. purple . . . . 1·75 30
827 – 40k. purple . . . . 1·50 30
828 – 50k. red . . . . 1·90 90
829 – 80k. blue . . . . 6·00 1·25
DESIGNS—VERT: 20k. Girl parachutist; 50k. Students and university. HORIZ: 40k. Harvesting; 80k. Airman, sailor and battleship "Marat".

1938. Soviet Sports.
830 **239** 5k. red . . . . 2·00 30
831 – 10k. black . . . . 2·75 50
832 – 15k. brown . . . . 4·50 85
833 – 20k. green . . . . 4·50 80
834 – 30k. purple . . . . 9·00 1·25
835 – 40k. green . . . . 10·00 80
836 – 50k. blue . . . . 9·00 2·25
837 – 80k. blue . . . . 9·00 3·50
DESIGNS: 10k. Discus throwing; 15k. Tennis; 20k. Motor cycling; 30k. Skiing; 40k. Sprinting; 50k. Football; 80k. Athletic parade.

241 Council of People's Commissars Headquarters and Hotel Moscow

1939. New Moscow. Architectural designs as T **241**.
838 – 10k. brown . . . . 1·10 70
839 **241** 20k. green . . . . 1·40 70
840 – 30k. purple . . . . 1·90 1·00
841 – 40k. blue . . . . 2·75 1·00
842 – 50k. red . . . . 5·00 2·00
843 – 80k. olive . . . . 5·00 2·00
844 – 1r. blue . . . . 9·50 2·75
DESIGNS—HORIZ: 10k. Gorky Avenue; 30k. Lenin Library; 40k. Crimea suspension and 50k. Arched bridges over River Moskva; 80k. Khimki river station. VERT: 1r. Dynamo underground station.

242 Paulina Osipenko

243 Russian Pavilion, N.Y. World's Fair

1939. Women's Moscow–Far East Flight.
845 **242** 15k. green . . . . 2·25 80
846 – 30k. purple . . . . 2·25 1·00
847 – 60k. red . . . . 4·50 1·50
PORTRAITS: 30k. Marina Raskova; 60k. Valentina Grisodubova.

1939. New York World's Fair.
848 – 30k. red and black . . . 2·00 50
849 **243** 50k. brown and blue . . . 4·00 85
DESIGN—VERT: (26 × 41½ mm): 30k. Statue over Russian pavilion.

244 T. G. Shevchenko in early Manhood

245 Milkmaid

1939. 125th Birth Anniv of Shevchenko (Ukrainian poet and painter).
853 **244** 15k. black and brown . . 1·75 50
854 – 30k. black and red . . . 2·75 70
855 – 60k. brown and green . . 5·00 2·00
DESIGNS: 30k. Last portrait of Shevchenko; 60k. Monument to Shevchenko, Kharkov.

1939. All Union Agricultural Fair.
856 **245** 10k. red 75 25
857 – 15k. red 75 15
858a – 20k. grey . . . . 1·00 15
859 – 30k. orange 90 25
860 – 30k. violet 90 25
861 – 45k. green . . . . 1·75 35
862 – 50k. brown . . . . 2·50 40
863a – 60k. violet . . . . 3·00 60
864 – 80k. violet . . . . 3·00 60
865 – 1r. blue . . . . 5·00 1·25
DESIGNS—HORIZ: 15k. Harvesting; 20k. Sheep farming; 30k. (No. 860) Agricultural Fair Pavilion. VERT: 30k. (No. 859) Agricultural Fair Emblem; 45k. Gathering cotton; 50k. Thoroughbred horses; 60k. "Agricultural Wealth"; 80k. Girl with sugar beet; 1r. Trapper.

18 АВГУСТА
ДЕНЬ АВИАЦИИ СССР
(247)

1939. Aviation Day. As Nos. 811, 814/16 and 818 (colours changed) optd with T **247**.
866 10k. red . . . . 2·25 55
867 30k. blue . . . . 2·25 55
868 40k. green . . . . 3·50 55
869 50k. violet . . . . 4·50 1·25
870 1r. brown . . . . 8·00 4·00

1939. Surch.
871 **141** 30k. on 4k. mauve . . . 15·00 10·00

249 Saltykov-Shchedrin

250 Kislovodsk Sanatorium

1939. 50th Death Anniv of M. E. Saltykov-Shchedrin (writer and satirist).
872 **249** 15k. red 60 15
873 – 30k. green 80 20
874 **249** 45k. brown . . . . 1·00 35
875 – 60k. blue . . . . 1·50 70
DESIGN: 30, 60k. Saltykov-Shchedrin in later years.

1939. Caucasian Health Resorts.
876 **250** 5k. brown 30 15
877 – 10k. red 50 20
878 – 15k. green 55 30
879 – 20k. green . . . . 1·00 30
880 – 30k. blue . . . . 1·10 30
881 – 50k. black . . . . 2·00 35
882 – 60k. purple . . . . 2·50 90
883 – 80k. red . . . . 3·25 1·10
DESIGNS: 10, 15, 30, 50, 80k. Sochi Convalescent Homes; 20k. Abkhazia Sanatorium, Novyi Afon; 60k. Sukumi Rest Home.

251 M. I. Lermontov

252 N. G. Chernyshevsky

1939. 125th Birth Anniv of Lermontov (poet and novelist).
884 **251** 15k. brown and blue . . . 1·10 30
885 – 30k. black and green . . 2·75 55
886 – 45k. blue and red . . . . 3·00 95

1939. 50th Death Anniv of N. G. Chernyshevsky (writer and politician).
887b **252** 15k. green 50 30
888 30k. violet 90 40
889b 60k. green . . . . . . 2·00 70

253 A. P. Chekhov

254 Welcoming Soviet Troops

1940. 80th Birth Anniv of Chekhov (writer).
890 **253** 10k. green 40 15
891 15k. blue 40 15
892 – 20k. violet 80 30
893 – 30k. brown . . . . 2·00 55
DESIGN: 20, 30k. Chekhov with hat on.

1940. Occupation of Eastern Poland.
893a **254** 10k. red . . . . 1·00 35
894 – 30k. green . . . . 1·00 35
895 – 50k. black . . . . 1·50 55
896 – 60k. blue . . . . 2·00 1·00
897 – 1r. red . . . . 4·50 1·75
DESIGNS: 30k. Villagers welcoming tank crew; 50, 60k. Soldier distributing newspapers to crowd; 1r. People waving to column of tanks.

255 Ice-breaker "Georgy Sedov" and Badigin and Trofimov

1940. Polar Research.
898 – 15k. green . . . . 2·25 40
899 **255** 30k. violet . . . . 3·00 70
900 – 50k. brown . . . . 5·00 1·75
901 – 1r. blue . . . . 9·00 2·25
DESIGNS: 15k. Ice-breaker "Iosif Stalin" and portraits of Papanin and Belousov; 50k. Badgin and Papanin meeting. LARGER. (46 × 26 mm): 1r. Route of drift of "Georgy Sedov".

256 V. Mayakovsky

1940. 10th Death Anniv of Mayakovsky (poet).
902 **256** 15k. red 30 15
903 30k. brown 55 20
904 – 60k. violet . . . . 1·00 45
905 – 80k. blue 80 45
DESIGN—VERT: 60, 80k. Mayakovsky in profile wearing a cap.

257 Timiryazev

1940. 20th Death Anniv of K. A. Timiryazev (scientist).
906 – 10k. blue 50 20
907 – 15k. violet 50 25
908 **257** 30k. brown 80 30
909 – 60k. green . . . . 2·50 1·10
DESIGNS—HORIZ: 10k. Miniature of Timiryazev and Academy of Agricultural Sciences, Moscow; 15k. Timiryazev in laboratory. VERT: 60k. Timiryazev's statue (by S. Merkurov), Moscow.

258 Relay Runner

259 Tchaikovsky and Passage from his "Fourth Symphony"

1940. 2nd All Union Physical Culture Festival.
910 **258** 15k. red . . . . 1·10 35
911a – 30k. purple . . . . . . 2·00 30
912a – 50k. blue . . . . 3·00 55
913 – 60k. blue . . . . 4·50 60
914 – 1r. green . . . . 6·00 1·40
DESIGNS—HORIZ: 30k. Girls parade; 60k. Skiing; 1r. Grenade throwing. VERT: 50k. Children and sports badges.

1940. Birth Cent of Tchaikovsky (composer).
915 – 15k. green . . . . 1·50 20
916 **259** 20k. brown . . . . 1·50 20
917 30k. blue . . . . 1·75 35
918 – 50k. red . . . . 2·50 60
919 – 60k. red . . . . 2·75 85
DESIGNS: 15, 50k. Tchaikovsky's house at Klin; 60k. Tchaikovsky and excerpt from "Eugene Onegin".

260 Central Regions Pavilion

ПАВИЛЬОН «ПОВОЛЖЬЕ»
No. 920

ПАВИЛЬОН «ДАЛЬНИЙ ВОСТОК»
No. 921

ВОРТА ПАВИЛЬОНА „ЛЕНИНГРАД И СЕВЕРО-ВОСТОК РСФСР"
No. 922

ПАВИЛЬОН МОСКОВСКОЙ, РЯЗАНСКОЙ И ТУЛЬСКОЙ ОБЛ.
No. 923

ПАВИЛЬОН УКРАИНСКОЙ ССР
No. 924

ПАВИЛЬОН БЕЛОРУССКОЙ ССР
No. 925

ПАВИЛЬОН АЗЕРБАЙДЖАНСКОЙ ССР
No. 926

ПАВИЛЬОН ГРУЗИНСКОЙ ССР
No. 927

ПАВИЛЬОН АРМЯНСКОЙ ССР
No. 928

„У ВХОДА В ПАВИЛЬОН УЗБЕКСКОЙ ССР"
No. 929

ПАВИЛЬОН ТУРКМЕНСКОЙ ССР
No. 930

ПАВИЛЬОН ТАДЖИКСКОЙ ССР
No. 931

ПАВИЛЬОН КИРГИЗСКОЙ ССР
No. 932

ПАВИЛЬОН КАРЕЛО-ФИНСКОЙ ССР
No. 933

ПАВИЛЬОН КАЗАХСКОЙ ССР
No. 934

ГЛАВНЫЙ ПАВИЛЬОН
No. 935

ПАВИЛЬОН МЕХАНИЗАЦИИ
No. 936

1940. All Union Agricultural Fair, Coloured reproductions of Soviet Pavilions in green frames as T **260**. Inscriptions at foot as illustrated.
920 10k. Volga provinces (RSFSR) (horiz) . . . . . 2·50 90
921 15k. Far East . . . . 1·75 90
922 30k. Leningrad and North East RSFSR . . . . . . 1·90 90
923 30k. Three Central Regions (RSFSR) . . . . 1·90 90
924 30k. Ukrainian SSR . . . . 1·90 90
925 30k. Byelorussian SSR . . . 1·90 90
926 30k. Azerbaijan SSR . . . . 1·90 90
927 30k. Georgian SSR (horiz) . . 1·90 90
928 30k. Armenian SSR . . . . 1·90 90
929 30k. Uzbek SSR . . . . . . 1·90 90
930 30k. Turkmen SSR (horiz) . . 1·90 90
931 30k. Tadzhik SSR . . . . . 1·90 90
932 30k. Kirgiz SSR . . . . . . 1·90 90
933 30k. Karelo-Finnish SSR . . 3·25 90
934 30k. Kazakh SSR . . . . . 1·90 90
935 50k. Main Pavilion . . . . . 3·00 2·00
936 60k. Mechanization Pavilion and the statue of Stalin . . 4·00 2·25

261 Grenade Thrower

262 Railway Bridge and Moscow–Volga Canal, Khimka

1940. 20th Anniv of Wrangel's Defeat at Perekop (Crimea). Perf or imperf.
937b – 10k. green . . . . . . 1·40 30
938 **261** 15k. red 50 15
939 – 30k. brown and red . . 75 20
940b – 50k. purple 70 50
941 – 60k. blue . . . . 1·75 55
942 – 1r. black . . . . 4·00 1·40
DESIGNS—VERT: 10k. Red Army Heroes Monument; 30k. Map of Perekop and portrait of M. V. Frunze; 1r. Victorious soldier. HORIZ: 50k. Soldiers crossing R. Sivash; 60k. Army H.Q. at Stroganovka.

1941. Industrial and Agricultural Records.
943 – 10k. blue 30 15
944 – 15k. mauve 30 15
945 **262** 20k. blue . . . . 2·25 1·00
946 – 30k. brown . . . . 2·75 1·00
947 – 50k. brown 60 15
948 – 60k. brown . . . . 1·25 55
949 – 1r. green . . . . 1·60 80
DESIGNS—VERT: 10k. Coal-miners and pithead; 15k. Blast furnace; 1r. Derricks and petroleum refinery. HORIZ: 30k. Steam locomotives; 50k. Harvesting; 60k. Ball-bearing vehicles.

263 Red Army Ski Corps

264 N. E. Zhukovsky and Air Force Academy

1941. 23rd Anniv of Red Army. Designs with Hammer, Sickle and Star Symbol.
950a **263** 5k. violet . . . . 1·60 15
951 – 10k. blue . . . . 1·25 15
952 – 15k. green 45 15
953a – 20k. red 45 15
954a – 30k. brown 45 15
955a – 45k. green . . . . 1·90 70
956 – 50k. blue 70 75
957 – 1r. green . . . . 1·00 80
957b – 3r. green . . . . 6·50 3·00
DESIGNS—VERT: 10k. Sailor; 20k. Cavalry; 30k. Automatic Rifle Squad; 50k. Airman; 1, 3r. Marshal's star. HORIZ: 15k. Artillery; 45k. Clearing a hurdle.

1941. 20th Death Anniv of Zhukovsky (scientist).
958 – 15k. blue 65 20
959 **264** 30k. red . . . . 1·50 30
960 – 50k. red . . . . 2·00 55
DESIGNS—VERT: 15k. Zhukovsky; 50k. Zhukovsky lecturing.

265 Thoroughbred Horses

266 Arms of Karelo-Finnish S.S.R.

1941. 15th Anniv of Kirghiz S.S.R.
961 **265** 15k. brown . . . . . . 3·00 85
962a – 30k. violet . . . . . . 4·00 1·25
DESIGN: 30k. Coal miner and colliery.

1941. 1st Anniv of Karelo-Finnish Republic.
963 **266** 30k. red . . . . 1·00 45
964 45k. green . . . . 1·00 75

267 Marshal Suvorov

268 Spassky Tower, Kremlin

1941. 150th Anniv of Battle of Izmail.
965 – 10k. green 80 35
966 – 15k. red 80 45
967 **267** 30k. blue . . . . 1·90 40
968 1r. brown . . . . 2·75 1·25
DESIGN: 10, 15k. Storming of Izmail.

1941.
970 **268** 1r. red . . . . 2·00 55
971 – 2r. brown . . . . 4·50 1·10
DESIGN—HORIZ: 2r. Kremlin Palace.

269 "Razin on the Volga"

1941. 25th Death Anniv of Surikov (artist).
972 – 20k. black . . . . 1·50 1·00
973 **269** 30k. red . . . . 3·50 1·00
974 – 50k. purple . . . . 6·00 2·75
975 **269** 1r. green . . . . 9·00 4·00
976 – 2r. brown . . . . 16·00 5·00
DESIGNS—VERT: 20, 50k. "Suvorov's march through Alps, 1799"; 2r. Surikov.

270 Lenin Museum (interior)

271 M. Yu. Lermontov

1941. 5th Anniv of Lenin Museum.
977 **270** 15k. red . . . . 2·75 1·50
978 – 30k. violet on mauve . . 22·00 16·00
979 **270** 45k. green . . . . 3·50 2·50
980 – 1r. red on rose . . . . 16·00 12·00
DESIGN: 30k., 1r. Exterior of Lenin Museum.

1941. Death Centenary of M. Yu. Lermontov (poet and novelist).
981 **271** 15k. grey . . . . 4·50 3·75
982 30k. violet . . . . 8·00 6·00

272 Poster by L. Lisitsky

273 Mass Enlistment

1941. Mobilization.
983a **272** 30k. red . . . . 18·00 20·00

1941. National Defence.
984 **273** 30k. blue . . . . 55·00 50·00

274 Alishir Navoi **275** Lt. Talalikhin ramming Enemy Bomber

289a Five Heroes

1942. 5th Centenary of Uzbek poet Mir Ali Shir (Alishir Navoi).
985 **274** 30k. brown . . . . 14·00 8·50
986 1r. purple . . . . 16·00 18·00

1942. Russian Heroes (1st issue).
987 **275** 20k. blue 50 25
988 A 30k. grey 60 35
989 B 30k. black 60 30
990 C 30k. black 60 35
991 D 30k. black 60 40
1048c **275** 30k. green . . . . . 1·00 30
1048d A 30k. blue . . . . . 1·00 30
1048e C 30k. green . . . . . 1·00 30
1048f D 30k. purple . . . . . 1·00 30
1048g **289a** 30k. blue . . . . . 1·00 30
992 C 1r. green . . . . . . 5·00 3·25
993 D 2r. green . . . . . . 9·00 5·00
DESIGNS: A, Capt. Gastello and burning fighter plane diving into enemy petrol tanks; B, Maj-Gen. Dovator and Cossack cavalry in action; C, Shura Chekalin guerrilla fighting; D, Zoya Kosmodemyanskaya being led to death.
See also Nos. 1072/6.

276 Anti-tank Gun

1942. War Episodes (1st series).
994 **276** 20k. brown . . . . 1·75 75
995 – 30k. blue . . . . 1·75 75
996 – 30k. green . . . . . . 1·75 75
997 – 30k. red . . . . 1·75 75
998 – 60k. grey . . . . 2·50 1·75
999 – 1r. brown . . . . . . 5·00 4·50
DESIGNS—HORIZ: 30k. (No. 996), Guerrillas attacking train; 30k. (No. 997), Munition worker; 1r. Machine gunners. VERT: 30k. (No. 995), Signallers; 60k. Defenders of Leningrad.

277 Distributing Gifts to Soldiers

1942. War Episodes (2nd series).
1000 **277** 20k. blue . . . . 1·75 75
1001 – 20k. purple . . . . . . 1·75 75
1002 – 30k. purple . . . . . . 2·25 1·40
1003 – 45k. red . . . . 4·00 2·75
1004 – 45k. blue . . . . 5·00 3·75
DESIGNS—VERT: No. 1001, Bomber destroying tank; No. 1002, Food packers; No. 1003, Woman sewing; No. 1004, Anti-aircraft gun.
See also Nos. 1013/17.

278 Munition Worker

1943. 25th Anniv of Russian Revolution.
1005 **278** 5k. brown 55 25
1006 – 10k. brown 80 15
1007 – 15k. blue 65 20
1008 – 20k. blue 65 20
1009 – 30k. brown 85 20
1010 – 60k. brown . . . . . . 1·50 45
1011 – 1r. red . . . . 2·25 1·25
1012 – 2r. brown . . . . . . 4·00 1·50
DESIGNS: 10k. Lorry convoy; 15k. Troops supporting Lenin's banner; 20k. Leningrad seen through an archway; 30k. Spassky Tower, Lenin and Stalin; 60k. Tank parade; 1r. Lenin speaking; 2r. Star of Order of Lenin.

279 Nurses and Wounded Soldier

1943. War Episodes (3rd series).
1013 **279** 30k. green . . . . 1·50 1·00
1014 – 30k. green (Scouts) . . . 1·50 1·00
1015 – 30k. brown (Mine-thrower) . . . . . . 1·50 1·00
1016 – 60k. green (Anti-tank troops) . . . . 2·50 1·00
1017 – 60k. blue (Sniper) . . . 2·50 1·00

280 Routes of Bering's Voyages

1943. Death Bicent of Vitus Bering (explorer).
1018 – 30k. blue . . . . 1·60 30
1019 **280** 60k. grey . . . . 3·00 60
1020 – 1r. green . . . . 4·25 90
1021 **280** 2r. brown . . . . 7·75 1·75
DESIGN: 30k., 1r. Mt. St. Ilya.

281 Gorky

1943. 75th Birth Anniv of Maksim Gorky (novelist).
1022 **281** 30k. green . . . . 1·00 25
1023 60k. blue . . . . 1·50 25

282 Order of the Great Patriotic War (**a**) Order of Suvorov

1943. War Orders and Medals (1st series), Medals with ribbon attached.
1024 **282** 1r. black . . . . 2·75 2·00
1025 a 10r. olive . . . . 9·00 7·50
See also Nos. 1051/8, 1089/94, 1097/99a, 1172/86, 1197/1204 and 1776/80a.

283 Karl Marx **284** Naval Landing Party

1943. 125th Birth Anniv of Marx.
1026 **283** 30k. blue . . . . 1·50 40
1027 60k. green . . . . 2·50 60

1943. 25th Anniv of Red Army and Navy.
1028 **284** 20k. brown 30 20
1029 – 30k. green 40 15
1030 – 60k. green . . . . 1·25 40
1031 **284** 3r. blue . . . . 3·00 90
DESIGNS: 30k. Sailors and anti-aircraft gun; 60k. Tanks and infantry.

285 Ivan Turgenev **286** Loading a Gun

1943. 125th Birth Anniv of Ivan Turgenev (novelist).
1032 **285** 30k. green . . . . . . 12·00 10·00
1032a 60k. violet . . . . . . 18·00 16·00

1943. 25th Anniv of Young Communist League.
1033 **286** 15k. blue 60 15
1034 – 20k. orange 60 15
1035 – 30k. brown and red . . 75 15
1036a – 1r. green . . . . 1·25 35
1037 – 2r. green . . . . 2·50 75
DESIGNS—As T **286**: 20k. Tank and banner; 1r. Infantrymen; 2r. Grenade thrower. $22\frac{1}{2} \times 28\frac{1}{2}$ mm: 30k. Bayonet fighter and flag.

287 V. V. Mayakovsky **288** Memorial Tablet and Allied Flags

1943. 50th Birth Anniv of Mayakovsky (poet).
1038 **287** 30k. orange 65 20
1039 60k. blue . . . . 1·00 40

1943. Teheran Three Power Conference and 26th Anniv of Revolution.
1040 **288** 30k. black . . . . 1·10 50
1041 3r. blue . . . . 4·00 1·25

289 Defence of Odessa

1944. Liberation of Russian Towns.
1045 – 30k. brown and red . . 65 25
1046 – 30k. blue 65 25
1047 – 30k. green 65 25
1048 **289** 30k. green 65 25
MS1048b 139 × 105 mm. No. 1047 × 4. Imperf . . . . . 18·00 14·00
DESIGNS: No. 1045, Stalingrad; No. 1046, Sevastopol; No. 1047, Leningrad.

АВИАПОЧТА
1944 г.
1 РУБЛЬ
(**290**)

291 Order of Kutusov

(**b**) Order of Patriotic War (**c**) Order of Aleksandr Nevsky

(**d**) Order of Suvorov (**e**) Order of Kutusov

1944. Air. Surch with T **290**.
1049 **275** 1r. on 30k. grey . . . . 2·00 50
1050 A 1r. on 30k. blue (No. 1048d) . . . . . 2·00 50

1944. War Orders and Medals (2nd series). Various Stars without ribbons showing as Types **b** to **e**. Perf or imperf. (a) Frames as T **291**.
1051 b 15k. red 50 15
1052 c 20k. blue 50 15
1053 d 30k. green . . . . 1·00 25
1054 e 60k. red . . . . 1·50 40

(b) Frames as T **282**.
1055 b 1r. black 80 30
1056 c 3r. blue . . . . 3·25 60
1057 e 5r. green . . . . 4·00 1·00
1058 d 10r. red . . . . 4·00 1·50

293 Lenin Mausoleum and Red Square, Moscow

1944. "Twenty Years without Lenin". As Nos. 667/72, but inscr "1924–1944", and T **293**.
1059 – 30k. black and blue . . 50 20
1060 **199** 30k. red and orange . . 50 20
1061 – 45k. black and blue . . 65 25
1062 – 50k. black and blue . . 80 25
1063 – 60k. black and blue . . 1·75 50
1064 **293** 1r. brown and blue . . . 2·00 60
1065 **199** 3r. black and orange . . 4·00 1·75
DESIGNS—VERT: Lenin at 3 years of age (No. 1059): at school (45k.); as man (50k.); as orator (60k.).

294 Allied Flags **295** Rimsky-Korsakov and Bolshoi Theatre

1944. 14 June (Allied Nations' Day).
1066 **294** 60k. black, red and blue 1·50 45
1067 3r. blue and red . . . . 6·00 1·75

1944. Birth Centenary of Rimsky-Korsakov (composer). Imperf or perf.
1068 **295** 30k. grey 40 10
1069 60k. green 60 10
1070 1r. green . . . . 1·25 25
1071 3r. violet . . . . 2·50 50

296 Nuradilov and Machine-gun

297 Polivanova and Kovshova **298** S. A. Chaplygin

1944. War Heroes (3rd issue).
1072 **296** 30k. green 45 15
1073 – 60k. violet 85 15
1074 – 60k. blue 85 15
1075 **297** 60k. green . . . . 1·50 45
1076 – 60k. black . . . . 1·75 45
DESIGNS—HORIZ: No. 1073, Matrosov defending a snow-trench; 1074, Luzak hurling a hand grenade. VERT: No. 1076, B. Safonev, medals and aerial battle over the sea.

1944. 75th Birth Anniv of S. A. Chaplygin (scientist).
1077 **298** 30k. grey 30 20
1078 1r. brown . . . . 1·00 60

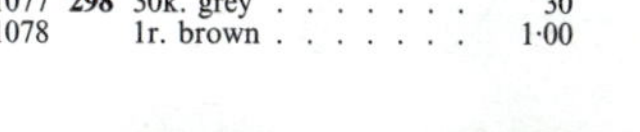

299 V. I. Chapaev **300** Repin (self-portrait)

301 "Reply of the Cossacks to Sultan Mahmoud IV" **302** I. A. Krylov

1944. Heroes of 1918 Civil War.
1079 **299** 30k. green . . . . 1·00 25
1080 – 30k. black (N. Shchors) 1·00 25
1081 – 30k. green (S. Lazo) . . 1·00 25
For 40k. stamp as Type **299**, see No. 1531.
See also Nos. 1349/51.

1944. Birth Centenary of Ilya Refimovich Repin (artist). Imperf or perf.
1082 **300** 30k. green 85 25
1083 **301** 50k. green 85 25
1084 60k. blue 85 25
1085 **300** 1r. brown . . . . 1·25 50
1086 **301** 2r. violet . . . . 2·75 1·00

1944. Death Centenary of Krylov (fabulist).
1087 **302** 30k. brown 60 15
1088 1r. blue . . . . 1·25 40

(f) Partisans' Medal — (g) Medal for Bravery — (h) Order of Bogdan Chmielnitsky

(j) Order of Victory — (k) Order of Ushakov — (l) Order of Nakhimov

1945. War Orders and Medals (3rd series). Frame as T **291** with various centres as Types **f** to **l**. Perf or imperf.

1089 f 15k. black 45 15
1090 g 30k. blue 85 20
1091 h 45k. blue 1·50 40
1092 j 60k. red 2·40 45
1093 k 1r. blue 3·25 1·00
1094 l 1r. green 3·25 1·00

303 Griboedov (after P. Karatygin) — **305** Soldier

1945. 150th Birth Anniv of Aleksander S. Griboedov (author).

1095 **303** 30k. green 1·50 20
1096 60k. brown 2·00 35

1945. War Orders and Medals (4th series). Frames as T **282**. Various centres.

1097 g 1r. black 1·60 65
1098 h 2r. black 7·50 1·75
1098a 2r. purple 42·00 14·00
1098b 2r. olive 6·00 2·00
1099 j 3r. red 4·25 1·25
1099a 3r. purple 6·25 3·00

1945. Relief of Stalingrad.

1100 **305** 60k. black and red 1·40 85
1101 3r. black and red 3·50 1·60
MS1101b 103 × 138 mm. No. 1101 × 4. Imperf 45·00 38·00

306 Standard Bearer — **308** Attack

1945. Red Army Victories.

1102 **306** 20k. green, red and black 40 15
1103 – 30k. black and red 40 15
1104 – 1r. green and red 2·25 1·40

DESIGN—HORIZ: 30k. Infantry v. Tank; 1r. Infantry charge.

1945. Liberation of Russian Soil.

1105 **308** 30k. blue 40 15
1106 – 60k. red 1·00 55
1107 – 1r. green 2·40 1·25

DESIGNS: 60k. Welcoming troops; 1r. Grenade thrower.

309 Badge and Guns — **310** Barricade

1945. Red Guards Commemoration.

1108 **309** 60k. red 2·75 1·00

1945. Battle of Moscow.

1109 – 30k. blue 40 20
1110 **310** 60k. black 80 45
1111 – 1r. black 1·50 60

DESIGNS: 30k. Tanks in Red Square, Moscow. 1r. Aerial battle and searchlights.

311 Prof. Lomonosov and Academy of Sciences, Leningrad  — **312** Popov

1945. 220th Anniv of Academy of Sciences.

1112 – 30k. blue 1·00 35
1113 **311** 2r. black 3·25 80

DESIGN—VERT: 30k. Moscow Academy, inscr "1725–1945".

1945. 50th Anniv of Popov's Radio Discoveries.

1114 **312** 30k. blue 70 30
1115 60k. red 1·25 40
1116 – 1r. brown (Popov) 1·90 65

314 Motherhood Medal — **315** Motherhood Medal

1945. Orders and Medals of Motherhood. Imperf or perf.

1117b **314** 20k. brown on blue 35 20
1118b – 30k. brown on green 60 20
1119b – 60k. red 1·40 20
1120 **315** 1r. black on green 1·75 20
1121 – 2r. blue 2·75 50
1122 – 3r. red on blue 4·00 90

DESIGNS: 30k., 2r. Order of Motherhood Glory; 60k., 3r. Order of Heroine-Mother.

316 Petlyakov Pe-2 Dive Bombers — **317** Ilyushin Il-2M3 Stormovik Fighters

318 Petlyakov Pe-8 TB-7 Bomber

1945. Air. Aviation Day.

1123 **316** 1r. brown 3·50 1·00
1124 **317** 1r. brown 3·50 1·00
1125 – 1r. red 3·50 1·00
1126 – 1r. black 3·50 1·00
1127 – 1r. blue 3·50 1·00
1128 – 1r. green 3·50 1·00
1129 **318** 1r. grey 3·50 1·00
1130 – 1r. brown 3·50 1·00
1131 – 1r. red 3·50 1·00

DESIGNS—As Type **317**: No. 1125, Lavochkin La-7 fighter shooting tail off enemy plane; 1126, Ilyushin Il-4 DB-3 bombers dropping bombs; 1127, Tupolev ANT-60 Tu-2 bombers in flight; 1128, Polikarpov Po-2 biplane. As Type **318**: No. 1130, Yakovlev Yak-3 fighter destroying Messerschmitt BF 109 fighter; 1131, Yakovlev Yak-9 fighter destroying Henschel Hs 129B fighter.

See also Nos. 1163/71.

ПРАЗДНИК ПОБЕДЫ

9 мая 1945 года

(**319**)

1945. VE Day. No. 1099 optd with T **319**.

1132 j 3r. red 4·00 1·50

320 Lenin — **321** Lenin

1945. 75th Birth Anniv of Lenin.

1133 **320** 30k. blue 40 20
1134 – 50k. brown 1·00 20
1135 – 60k. red 1·00 30
1136 **321** 1r. black 1·90 35
1137 – 3r. brown 3·75 1·75

DESIGNS—VERT: (inscr "1870–1945"). 50k. Lenin at desk; 60k. Lenin making a speech; 3r. Portrait of Lenin.

322 Kutuzov (after R. Volkov) — **323** A. I. Herzen

1945. Birth Bicentenary of Mikhail Kutuzov (military leader).

1138 **322** 30k. blue 1·00 25
1139 60k. brown 1·60 50

1945. 75th Death Anniv of Herzen (author and critic).

1140 **323** 30k. brown 85 20
1141 2r. black 1·90 55

324 I. I. Mechnikov — **325** Friedrich Engels

1945. Birth Centenary of Mechnikov (biologist).

1142 **324** 30k. brown 70 15
1143 1r. black 1·40 35

1945. 125th Birth Anniv of Engels.

1144 **325** 30k. brown 80 20
1145 60k. green 1·25 45

326 Observer and Guns

327 Heavy Guns

1945. Artillery Day.

1146 **326** 30k. brown 1·75 1·40
1147 **327** 60k. black 4·00 2·75

328 Tank Production

1945. Home Front.

1148 **328** 20k. blue and brown 2·25 50
1149 – 30k. black and brown 2·00 75
1150 – 60k. brown and green 3·25 1·40
1151 – 1r. blue and brown 4·75 1·50

DESIGNS: 30k. Harvesting; 60k. Designing aircraft; 1r. Firework display.

329 Victory Medal  — **330** Soldier with Victory Flag

1946. Victory Issue.

1152 **329** 30k. violet 30 15
1153 30k. brown 30 15
1154 60k. black 55 20
1155 60k. brown 55 20
1156 **330** 60k. black and red 1·75 85

331 Arms of U.S.S.R. — **332** Kremlin, Moscow

1946. Supreme Soviet Elections.

1157 **331** 30k. red 30 10
1158 **332** 45k. red 50 30
1159 **331** 60k. green 2·00 80

333 Tank Parade

334 Infantry Parade

1946. 28th Anniv of Red Army and Navy.

1160 **333** 60k. brown 1·00 15
1161 2r. violet 2·00 50
1162 **334** 3r. black and red 5·00 1·40

1946. Air. As Nos. 1123/31.

1163 – 5k. violet (as No. 1130) 65 60
1164 **316** 10k. red 65 60
1165 **317** 15k. red 70 65
1166 **318** 15k. green 70 65
1167 – 20k. black (as No. 1127) 70 65
1168 – 30k. violet (as No. 1127) 1·40 95
1169 – 30k. brown (as No. 1128) 1·40 95
1170 – 50k. blue (as No. 1125) 2·00 1·50
1171 – 60k. blue (as No. 1131) 4·00 1·75

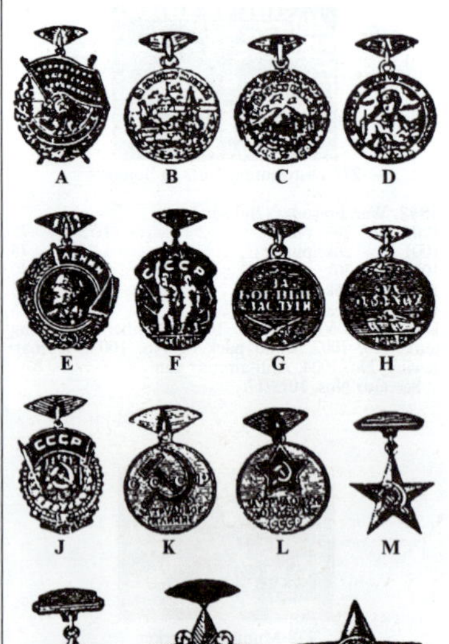

A B C D E F G H J K L M  N O P

1946. War Orders with Medals (5th series). Frames as T **291** with various centres as Types A to P.

1172 A 60k. red 1·60 1·25
1173 B 60k. red 1·60 1·25
1174 C 60k. green 1·60 1·25
1175 D 60k. green 1·60 1·25
1176 E 60k. green 1·60 1·25
1177 F 60k. blue 1·60 1·25
1178 G 60k. blue 1·60 1·25

1179 H 60k. violet . . . . 1·60 1·25
1180 J 60k. purple . . . . 1·60 1·25
1181 K 60k. brown . . . . 1·60 1·25
1182 L 60k. brown . . . . 1·60 1·25
1183 M 60k. purple . . . . 1·60 1·25
1184 N 60k. red . . . . 1·60 1·25
1185 O 60k. blue . . . . 1·60 1·25
1186 P 60k. purple . . . . 1·60 1·25

336 P. L. Chebyshev

337 Gorky

1946. 125th Birth Anniv of Chebyshev (mathematician).
1187 **336** 30k. brown 50 20
1188 60k. black 90 45

1946. Death of President Kalinin. As T **211**, but inscr "3-VI-1946".
1189 20k. black . . . . 1·90 75

1946. 10th Death Anniv of Maksim Gorky (novelist).
1190 **337** 30k. brown 55 15
1191 – 60k. green 80 20
DESIGN: 60k. Gorky and laurel leaves.

338 Gagry

340 Partisan Medal

339 Stalin and Parade of Athletes

1946. Health Resorts.
1192 – 15k. brown 40 15
1193 **338** 30k. green 60 25
1194 – 30k. green 70 25
1195 – 45k. brown . . . . . . 1·00 40
DESIGNS—HORIZ: 15k. Sukumi; 45k. Novy Afon. VERT: 30k. (No. 1194) Sochi.

1946. Sports Festival.
1196 **339** 30k. green . . . . 7·25 4·00

1946. War Medals (6th series). Frames as T **282** with various centres.
1197 **340** 1r. red . . . . 1·90 95
1198 B 1r. green . . . . 1·90 95
1199 C 1r. brown . . . . 1·90 95
1200 D 1r. blue . . . . 1·90 95
1201 G 1r. grey . . . . 1·90 95
1202 H 1r. red . . . . 1·90 95
1203 K 1r. purple . . . . 1·90 95
1204 L 1r. red . . . . 1·90 95

341 Moscow Opera House

342 Tanks in Red Square

1946. Moscow Buildings.
1205 – 5k. brown 40 15
1206 **341** 10k. grey 50 15
1207 – 15k. brown 40 15
1208 – 20k. brown 70 20
1209 – 45k. green 85 50
1210 – 50k. brown 95 75
1211 – 60k. violet . . . . . . 1·50 1·10
1212 – 1r. brown . . . . . . 2·25 1·75
DESIGNS—VERT: 5k. Church of Ivan the Great and Kremlin; 1r. Spassky Tower (larger). HORIZ: 15k. Hotel Moscow; 20k. Theatre and Sverdlov Square; 45k. As 5k. but horiz; 50k. Lenin Museum; 60k. St. Basil's Cathedral and Spassky Tower (larger).

1946. Heroes of Tank Engagements.
1213 **342** 30k. green . . . . 2·25 1·75
1214 60k. brown . . . . . . 3·50 2·25

343 "Iron"

345 Lenin and Stalin

344 Soviet Postage Stamps

1946. 4th Stalin "Five-Year Reconstruction Plan". Agriculture and Industry.
1215 – 5k. olive 30 10
1216 – 10k. green 40 10
1217 – 15k. brown 50 15
1218 – 20k. violet 80 20
1219 **343** 30k. brown . . . . . . 1·10 30
DESIGNS—HORIZ: 5k. "Agriculture"; 15k. "Coal". VERT: 10k. "Oil"; 20k. "Steel".

1946. 25th Anniv of Soviet Postal Services.
1220 – 15k. black and red . . . 1·75 40
1221 – 30k. brown and green . . 2·50 1·00
1222 **344** 60k. black and green . . 4·25 1·60
MS1222a 138 × 104 mm. 15k . . 65·00 55·00
MS1222b 132 × 104 mm. 30k . . 65·00 55·00
MS1222c 142 × 102 mm. 60k . . 75·00 60·00
DESIGNS: 15k. (48½ × 23 mm). Stamps on map of U.S.S.R.; 30k. (33 × 22½ mm). Reproduction of Type **47**.

1946. 29th Anniv of Russian Revolution. Imperf or Perf.
1223b **345** 30k. orange . . . . . 3·00 2·75
1224b 30k. green . . . . . . 3·00 2·75
MS1224c 101 × 134 mm. No. 1223 × 4. Imperf . . . . . 45·00 38·00

346 N. A. Nekrasov

347 Stalin Prize Medal

1946. 125th Birth Anniv of Nekrasov (poet).
1225 **346** 30k. black . . . . 1·10 25
1226 60k. brown . . . . . . 1·60 55

1946. Stalin Prize.
1227 **347** 30k. green . . . . 2·75 1·00

348 Dnieperprostroi Dam

1946. Restoration of Dnieperprostroi Hydro-electric Power Station.
1228 **348** 30k. black . . . . 1·75 65
1229 60k. blue . . . . 3·00 1·00

349 A. Karpinsky

350 N. E. Zhukovsky

1947. Birth Centenary of Karpinsky (geologist).
1230 **349** 30k. green . . . . 1·25 65
1231 50k. black . . . . 2·75 90

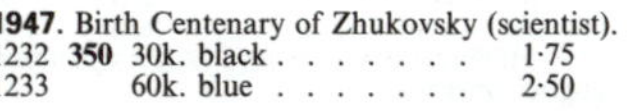

1947. Birth Centenary of Zhukovsky (scientist).
1232 **350** 30k. black . . . . 1·75 55
1233 60k. blue . . . . 2·50 85

351 Lenin Mausoleum

352 Lenin

1947. 23rd Death Anniv of Lenin.
1234 **351** 30k. green 90 50
1235 30k. blue 90 50
1236 **352** 50k. brown . . . . . . 3·25 1·00
For similar designs inscr "1924/1948" see Nos. 1334/6.

353 Nikolai M. Przhevalsky

354 Arms of R.S.F.S.R.

356 Arms of U.S.S.R.

1947. Centenary of Soviet Geographical Society.
1237 – 20k. brown . . . . . . 2·00 50
1238 – 20k. blue . . . . 2·00 50
1239 **353** 60k. olive . . . . 3·50 1·40
1240 – 60k. brown . . . . . . 3·50 1·40
DESIGN: 20k. Miniature portrait of F. P. Litke and full-rigged ship "Senyavin".

1947. Supreme Soviet Elections. Arms of Constituent Republics. As T **354**.
1241 **354** 30k. red (Russian Federation) 70 50
1242 – 30k. brown (Armenia) . . . 70 50
1243 – 30k. bistre (Azerbaijan) . . 70 50
1244 – 30k. green (Byelorussia) . . 70 50
1245 – 30k. grey (Estonia) . . . 70 50
1246 – 30k. brown (Georgia) . . 70 50
1247 – 30k. purple (Karelo-Finnish S.S.R.) . . . 70 50
1248 – 30k. orange (Kazakhstan) 70 50
1249 – 30k. purple (Kirgizia) . . 70 50
1250 – 30k. brown (Latvia) . . 70 50
1251 – 30k. green (Lithuania) . . 70 50
1252 – 30k. purple (Moldavia) . . 70 50
1253 – 30k. green (Tadzhikistan) . 70 50
1254 – 30k. black (Turkmenistan) . . . 70 50
1255 – 30k. blue (Ukraine) . . . 70 50
1256 – 30k. brown (Uzbekistan) . 70 50
1257 **356** 1r. multicoloured . . . . 2·75 85
A hammer and sickle in the centre of No. 1247 and at the base of No. 1249 should assist identification.

357 Russian Soldier

359 A. S. Pushkin

1947. 29th Anniv of Soviet Army. Perf or imperf.
1258b **357** 20k. black 60 20
1259b – 30k. blue 55 15
1260b – 30k. brown 65 20
DESIGNS—VERT: No. 1259, Military cadet. HORIZ: No. 1260, Soldier, sailor and airman.

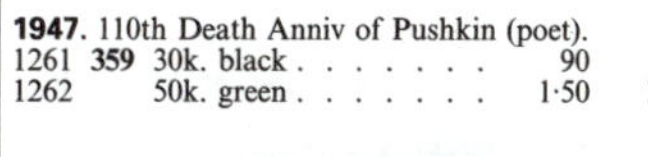

1947. 110th Death Anniv of Pushkin (poet).
1261 **359** 30k. black 90 45
1262 50k. green . . . . 1·50 1·00

360 Schoolroom

1947. International Women's Day.
1263 **360** 15k. blue . . . . 3·50 2·25
1264 – 30k. red . . . . 6·00 2·75

DESIGN—26½ × 39½ mm: 30k. Women students and banner.

362 Moscow Council Building

364 Yakovlev Yak-9 Fighter and Flag

363 May Day Procession

1947. 30th Anniv of Moscow Soviet. Perf or imperf.
1265b **362** 30k. red, blue and black . . . . 2·25 1·50

1947. May Day.
1266 **363** 30k. red . . . . 1·50 1·25
1267 1r. green . . . . 3·75 2·50

1947. Air Force Day.
1268 **364** 30k. violet 80 20
1269 1r. blue . . . . 2·25 55

365 Yakhromsky Lock

1947. 10th Anniv of Volga–Moscow Canal.
1270 – 30k. black 70 10
1271 **365** 30k. lake 70 10
1272 – 45k. red 90 25
1273 – 50k. blue . . . . 1·25 30
1274 – 60k. red . . . . 1·25 30
1275 – 1r. violet . . . . . . 2·50 60
DESIGNS—HORIZ: 30k. (No. 1270), Karamyshevsky Dam; 45k. Yakhromsky Pumping Station; 50k. Khimki Pier; 1r. Lock No. 8. VERT: 60k. Map of Volga–Moscow Canal.

800 лет Москвы
1147—1947 гг.
(366)

367 Izmailovskaya Station

1947. 800th Anniv of Moscow (1st issue). Optd as T **366**.
1276 20k. brown (No. 1208) . . . 55 15
1277 50k. brown (No. 1210) . . . 90 35
1278 60k. violet (No. 1211) . . . 1·50 60
1279 1r. brown (No. 1212) . . . 3·75 1·90
See also Nos. 1286/1300.

1947. Opening of New Moscow Underground Stations. Inscr "M".
1280 **367** 30k. blue 70 20
1281 – 30k. brown 70 20
1282 – 45k. brown . . . . . . 1·25 40
1283 – 45k. violet . . . . . . 1·25 40
1284 – 60k. green . . . . . . 2·50 65
1285 – 60k. red . . . . 2·50 65
DESIGNS—HORIZ: No. 1281, Power plant; No. 1282, Sokol underground station; No. 1283, Stalinskaya underground station; No. 1284, Kievskaya underground station. VERT: No. 1285, Maya Kovskaya underground station.

368 Crimea Bridge, Moscow

1947. 800th Anniv of Moscow (2nd issue).
1286 **368** 5k. brown and blue . . . 50 10
1287 – 10k. black and brown . . 30 10
1288 – 30k. grey . . . . 1·50 25
1289 – 30k. blue . . . . 1·50 25
1290 – 30k. brown 55 25
1291 – 30k. green 55 25
1292 – 30k. green 55 25

1293 – 50k. green 1·40 70
1294 – 60k. blue 2·00 55
1295 – 60k. black and brown 2·00 55
1296 – 1r. purple 3·25 80

Centre in yellow, red and blue.

1297 – 1r. blue 5·50 1·75
1298 – 2r. red 8·50 2·50
1299 – 3r. blue 13·50 3·50
1300 – 5r. blue 25·00 7·50
MS1300b 140 × 175 mm. No. 1299 55·00 38·00

DESIGNS—VERT: 10k. Gorky Street, Moscow; 30k. (No. 1292), Pushkin Place; 60k. (No. 1294), 2r. Kremlin; 1r. (No. 1296), "Old Moscow" after A. M. Vasnetsov; 1r. (No. 1279), St. Basil Cathedral. HORIZ: 30k. (No. 1288), Kiev railway station; 30k. (No. 1289), Kazan railway station; 30k. (No. 1290), Central Telegraph Offices; 30k. (No. 1291), Kaluga Street; 50k. Kremlin; 3r. Kremlin; 5r. Government Buildings. (54½ × 24½ mm): 60k. (No. 1295), Bridge and Kremlin.

369 "Ritz", Gagry

370 "Zapadugol", Sochi

1947. U.S.S.R. Health Resorts. (a) Vertical.

1301 **369** 30k. green 75 20
1302 – 30k. green (Sukhumi) 75 20

(b) Horizontal.

1303 **370** 30k. black 75 20
1304 – 30k. brown ("New Riviera", Sochi) 75 20
1305 – 30k. purple ("Voroshilov", Sochi) 75 20
1306 – 30k. violet ("Gulripsh", Sukhumi) 75 20
1307 – 30k. blue ("Kemeri", Riga) 75 20
1308 – 30k. brown ("Abkhazia", Novyi Afon) 75 20
1309 – 30k. bistre ("Krestyansky", Livadia) 75 20
1310 – 30k. blue ("Kirov", Kislovodsk) 75 20

371 1917 Revolution

1947. 30th Anniv of Revolution. Perf or imperf.

1311b **371** 30k. black and red 30 15
1312b – 50k. blue and red 1·60 20
1313b **371** 60k. black and red 1·00 30
1314b – 60k. brown and red 1·00 30
1315b – 1r. black and red 2·75 50
1316b – 2r. green and red 3·00 1·00

DESIGNS: 50k., 1r. "Industry"; 60k. (No. 1314), 2r. "Agriculture".

372 Metallurgical Works

373 Spassky Tower, Kremlin

1947. Post-War Five Year Plan. Horiz industrial designs. All dated "1947" except No. 1324. Perf or imperf.

1317 **372** 15k. brown 40 20
1318 – 20k. brown (Foundry) 50 30
1319 **372** 30k. purple 1·00 30
1320 – 30k. green (Harvesting machines) 75 50
1321 – 30k. brown (Tractor) 1·00 30
1322 – 30k. brown (Tractors) 75 30
1323 – 60k. bistre (Harvesting machines) 1·10 60
1324 – 60k. purple (Builders) 1·10 60
1325 – 1r. orange (Foundry) 2·25 1·25
1326 – 1r. red (Tractor) 3·75 1·75
1327 – 1r. violet (Tractors) 2·50 1·25

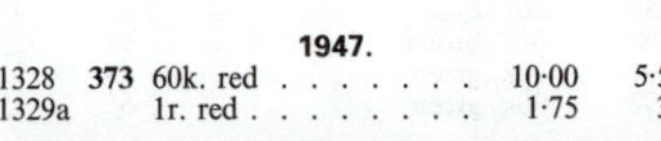

1947.

1328 **373** 60k. red 10·00 5·50
1329a 1r. red 1·75 35

374 Peter I Monument

376 Government Building, Kiev

1948. 4th Anniv of Relief of Leningrad.

1330 – 30k. violet 50 15
1331 **374** 50k. green 80 30
1332 – 60k. black 1·60 55
1333 – 1r. violet 2·10 1·10

DESIGNS—HORIZ: 30k. Winter Palace; 60k. Peter and Paul Fortress; 1r. Smolny Institute.

1948. 24th Death Anniv of Lenin. As issue of 1947, but dated "1924 1928".

1334 **351** 30k. red 85 50
1355 60k. blue 1·40 70
1336 **352** 60k. green 2·75 1·10

1948. 30th Anniv of Ukrainian S.S.R. Various designs inscr "XXX" and "1917–1947".

1337 **376** 30k. blue 55 15
1338 – 50k. violet 1·00 50
1339 – 60k. brown 1·25 75
1340 – 1r. brown 3·00 1·90

DESIGNS: 50k. Dnieper hydro-electric power station; 60k. Wheatfield and granary; 1r. Metallurgical works and colliery.

377 Vasily I. Surikov

378 Skiing

1948. Birth Centenary of Surikov (artist).

1341 **377** 30k. brown 1·60 65
1342 60k. green 2·40 1·40

1948. R.S.F.S.R. Games.

1343 **378** 15k. blue 2·25 25
1344 – 20k. blue 3·25 50

DESIGN—VERT: 20k. Motor cyclist crossing stream.

379 Artillery

381 Karl Marx and Friedrich Engels

380 Bulganin and Military School

1948. 30th Anniv of Founding of Soviet Defence Forces and of Civil War. (a) Various designs with arms and inscr "1918 XXX 1948".

1345 **379** 30k. brown 1·00 35
1346 – 30k. grey 1·25 35
1347 – 30k. blue 1·60 35
1348 **380** 60k. brown 2·50 70

DESIGNS—VERT: No. 1346, Navy. HORIZ: No. 1347, Air Force.

(b) Portraits of Civil War Heroes as Nos. 1079/81.

1349 **299** 60k. brown (Chapaev) 1·50 1·10
1350 – 60k. green (Shchors) 1·50 1·10
1351 – 60k. blue (Lazo) 1·50 1·10

1948. Centenary of Publication of "Communist Manifesto".

1352 **381** 30k. black 45 15
1353 50k. brown 65 25

382 Miner

384b Arms of U.S.S.R.

384d Spassky Tower, Kremlin

1948.

1354 **382** 5k. black 1·75 90
1355 – 10k. violet (Sailor) 1·75 90
1356 – 15k. blue (Airman) 5·50 2·50
1361i **382** 15k. black 20 10
1357 – 20k. brown (Farm girl) 5·50 2·50
1361j – 20k. green (Farm girl) 30 10
1361ka – 25k. blue (Airman) 50 10
1358 **384b** 30k. brown 7·00 3·75
1361l – 30k. brown (Scientist) 60 10
1361n **384b** 40k. red 2·50 10
1359 – 45k. violet (Scientist) 11·00 5·50
1361f **384d** 50k. blue 14·50 5·00
1361 – 60k. green (Soldier) 26·00 13·00

385 Parade of Workers

1948. May Day.

1362 **385** 30k. red 1·10 55
1363 60k. blue 1·90 1·10

386 Belinsky (after K. Gorbunov)

1948. Death Centenary of Vissarion Grigorievich Belinsky (literary critic and journalist).

1364 **386** 30k. brown 1·10 35
1365 50k. green 2·75 1·00
1366 60k. violet 2·25 1·10

387 Ostrovsky

388 Ostrovsky (after V. Perov)

1948. 125th Birth Anniv of Aleksandr Ostrovsky (dramatist).

1367 **387** 30k. green 1·25 50
1368 **388** 60k. brown 1·60 1·00
1369 1r. violet 3·25 1·75

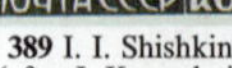
389 I. I. Shishkin (after I. Kramskoi)

391 Factories

390 "Rye Field"

1948. 50th Death Anniv of Shishkin (landscape painter).

1370 **389** 30k. brown and green 1·40 30
1371 **390** 50k. yellow, red and blue 3·00 55
1372 – 60k. multicoloured 4·50 75
1373 **389** 1r. blue and brown 5·00 1·75

DESIGN—HORIZ: 60k. "Morning in the Forest".

1948. Leningrad Workers' Four-Year Plan.

1374 **391** 15k. brown and red 2·50 1·00
1375 – 30k. black and red 2·25 1·50
1376 **391** 60k. brown and red 6·50 3·00

DESIGN—HORIZ (40 × 22 mm): 30k. Proclamation to Leningrad workers.

392 Arms and People of the U.S.S.R.

393 Caterpillar drawing Seed Drills

1948. 25th Anniv of U.S.S.R.

1377 **392** 30k. black and red 1·60 65
1378 60k. olive and red 2·75 1·40

1948. Five Year Agricultural Plan.

1379 **393** 30k. red 65 25
1380 30k. green 75 25
1381 – 45k. brown 1·40 60
1382 **393** 50k. black 2·10 1·00
1383 – 60k. green 1·60 40
1384 – 60k. green 1·60 40
1385 – 1r. violet 5·25 2·25

DESIGNS: 30k. (No. 1380), 1r. Harvesting sugar beet; 45, 60k. (No. 1383), Gathering cotton; 60k. (No. 1384), Harvesting machine.

(394)

395 Miners

396 A. Zhdanov

1948. Air Force Day. Optd with T **394**.

1386 **364** 30k. violet 4·50 2·50
1387 1r. blue 4·50 2·50

1948. Miners' Day.

1388 **395** 30k. blue 80 40
1389 – 60k. violet 1·50 65
1390 – 1r. green 3·50 1·00

DESIGNS: 60k. Inside a coal mine; 1r. Miner's emblem.

1948. Death of A. A. Zhdanov (statesman).

1391 **396** 40k. blue 2·75 1·10

397 Sailor

398 Football

1948. Navy Day.

1392 **397** 30k. green 2·25 1·10
1393 60k. blue 3·25 1·60

1948. Sports.

1394 – 15k. violet 1·25 15
1395a **398** 30k. brown 2·50 15
1396 – 45k. brown 2·75 35
1397a – 50k. blue 3·75 35

DESIGNS—VERT: 15k. Running; 50k. Diving. HORIZ: 45k. Power boat racing.

399 Tank and Drivers

1948. Tank Drivers' Day.

1398 **399** 30k. black 2·00 1·40
1399 – 1r. red 4·75 2·00

DESIGN: 1r. Parade of tanks.

400 Horses and Groom

1948. Five Year Livestock Development Plan.

1400 **400** 30k. black 2·00 1·40
1401 – 60k. green 3·25 1·90
1402 **400** 1r. brown 6·00 2·75

DESIGN: 60k. Dairy farming.

401 Steam and Electric Locomotives

1948. Five Year Transport Plan.
1403 **401** 30k. brown . . . . . . 4·00 1·25
1404 50k. green . . . . . . 6·75 4·00
1405 – 60k. blue . . . . . . 5·75 4·00
1406 – 1r. violet . . . . . . 9·00 5·00
DESIGNS: 60k. Road traffic; 1r. Liner "Vyacheslav Molotov".

402 Iron Pipe Manufacture

1948. Five Year Rolled Iron, Steel and Machine-building Plan.
1407 – 30k. violet . . . . . . 1·75 90
1408 – 30k. purple . . . . . . 1·75 90
1409 – 50k. brown . . . . . . 2·75 1·40
1410 – 50k. black . . . . . . 2·75 1·40
1411 – 60k. brown . . . . . . 3·75 2·50
1412 **402** 60k. red . . . . . . 3·75 2·50
1413 1r. blue . . . . 5·75 3·25
DESIGNS—HORIZ: Nos. 1407, 1410, Foundry; No. 1408/9, Pouring molten metal; No. 1411, Group of machines.

403 Abovyan 404 Miner

1948. Death Centenary of Khachatur Abovyan (writer).
1414 **403** 40k. purple . . . . . . 2·25 1·60
1415 50k. green . . . . . . 3·25 2·25

1948. Five Year Coal Mining and Oil Extraction Plan.
1416 **404** 30k. black . . . . . . 1·50 70
1417 60k. brown . . . . . . 3·00 1·60
1418 – 60k. brown . . . . . . 4·25 1·75
1419 – 1r. green . . . . . . 6·25 4·00
DESIGN: Nos. 1418/19, Oil wells and tanker train.

405 Farkhadsk Power Station 406 Flying Model Aircraft

1948. Five Year Electrification Plan.
1420 **405** 30k. green . . . . . . 1·40 1·10
1421 – 60k. red . . . . . . 3·00 2·25
1422 **405** 1r. red . . . . . . 5·00 2·50
DESIGN: 60k. Zuevsk Power Station.

1948. Government Care of School Children's Summer Vacation.
1423 **406** 30k. green . . . . . . 3·25 95
1424 – 45k. red . . . . . . 6·50 5·00
1425 – 45k. violet . . . . . . 3·25 2·00
1426 – 60k. blue . . . . . . 9·00 5·00
1427 – 1r. blue . . . . . . 17·00 6·00
DESIGNS—VERT: No. 1424, Boy and girl saluting; 60k. Boy trumpeter. HORIZ: No. 1425, Children marching; 1r. Children round camp fire.

407 Children in School 408 Flag of U.S.S.R.

1948. 30th Anniv of Lenin's Young Communist League.
1428 – 20k. purple . . . . . . 3·00 1·10
1429 – 25k. red . . . . . . 2·00 1·10
1430 – 40k. brown and red . . 4·75 2·00
1431 **407** 50k. green . . . . . . 4·75 2·50
1432 **408** 1r. multicoloured . . . . 15·00 10·00
1433 – 2r. violet . . . . . . 15·00 10·00
DESIGNS—HORIZ: 20k. Youth parade. VERT: 25k. Peasant girl; 40k. Young people and flag; 2r. Industrial worker.

409 Interior of Theatre 410 Searchlights over Moscow

1948. 50th Anniv of Moscow Arts Theatre.
1434 **409** 50k. blue . . . . . . 2·75 2·25
1435 – 1r. purple . . . . . . 5·00 4·00
DESIGN: 1r. Stanislavsky and Dantchenko.

1948. 31st Anniv of October Revolution.
1436 **410** 40k. red . . . . . . 2·25 1·60
1437 1r. green . . . . . . 5·00 3·25

411 Artillery Barrage

1948. Artillery Day.
1438 **411** 30k. blue . . . . . . 2·75 2·25
1439 1r. red . . . . . . 4·50 3·25

412 Trade Union Building (venue)

1948. 16th World Chess Championship, Moscow.
1440 **412** 30k. blue . . . . . . 4·00 65
1441 – 40k. violet . . . . . . 9·00 1·00
1442 **412** 50k. brown . . . . . . 9·00 1·75
DESIGN—VERT: 40k. Players' badge showing chessboard and rook.

413 Stasov and Building

1948. Death Centenary of Stasov (architect).
1443 – 40k. brown . . . . . . 1·40 1·25
1444 **413** 1r. black . . . . . . 3·25 3·00
DESIGN—VERT: 40k. Portrait of Stasov.

414 Yakovlev Yak-9 Fighters and Flag 415 Statue of Ya. M. Sverdlov

1948. Air Force Day.
1445a **414** 1r. blue . . . . . . 7·25 1·90

1948. 225th Anniv of Sverdlovsk City. Imperf or perf.
1446b **415** 30k. blue 65 15
1447b – 40k. purple . . . . . . 1·60 50
1448b **415** 1r. green . . . . . . 1·90 60
DESIGN: 40k. View of Sverdlovsk.

416 Sukhumi 417 State Emblem

1948. Views of Crimea and Caucasus.
1449 **416** 40k. green . . . . . . 1·00 30
1450 – 40k. violet . . . . . . 1·00 30
1451 – 40k. mauve . . . . . . 1·00 30
1452 – 40k. brown . . . . . . 1·00 30
1453 – 40k. purple . . . . . . 1·00 30
1454 – 40k. green . . . . . . 1·00 30
1455 – 40k. blue . . . . . . 1·00 30
1456 – 40k. green . . . . . . 1·00 30
DESIGNS—VERT: No. 1450, Gardens, Sochi; 1451, Eagle-topped monument, Pyatigorsk; 1452, Cliffs, Crimea. HORIZ: No. 1453, Terraced gardens, Sochi; 1454, Roadside garden, Sochi; 1455, Colonnade, Kislovodsk; 1456, Seascape, Gagry.

1949. 30th Anniv of Byelorussian Soviet Republic.
1457 **417** 40k. red . . . . . . 1·90 1·60
1458 1r. green . . . . . . 3·50 2·25

418 M. V. Lomonosov 419 Lenin Mausoleum

1949. Establishment of Lomonosov Museum of Academy of Sciences.
1459 **418** 40k. brown . . . . . . 1·60 1·10
1460 50k. green . . . . . . 1·90 1·10
1461 – 1r. blue . . . . . . 4·25 2·75
DESIGN—HORIZ: 1r. Museum.

1949. 25th Death Anniv of Lenin.
1462 **419** 40k. brown and green . . 5·50 5·00
1463 1r. brown & deep brown 10·50 9·50
MS1463a 175 × 132 mm. No. 1463 × 4 . . . . £170 £225

420 Dezhnev's Ship

1949. 300th Anniv of Dezhnev's Exploration of Bering Strait.
1464 – 40k. green . . . . . . 10·00 8·50
1465 **420** 1r. grey . . . . . . 20·00 12·50
DESIGN: 40k. Cape Dezhnev.

421 "Women in Industry" 422 Admiral S. O. Makarov

1949. International Women's Day.
1466 **421** 20k. violet 35 10
1467 – 25k. blue 40 10
1468 – 40k. red 55 15
1469 – 50k. grey . . . . . . 1·10 30
1470 – 50k. brown . . . . . . 1·10 30
1471 – 1r. green . . . . . . 3·50 50
1472 – 2r. red . . . . . . 5·25 80
DESIGNS—HORIZ: 25k. Kindergarten; 50k. grey, Woman teacher; 50k. brown, Women in field; 1r. Women sports champions. VERT: 40k., 2r. Woman broadcasting.

1949. Birth Centenary of Admiral S. O. Makarov (naval scientist).
1473 **422** 40k. blue . . . . . . 1·60 1·00
1474 1r. red . . . . . . 3·50 3·00

423 Soldier

1949. 31st Anniv of Soviet Army.
1475 **423** 40k. red . . . . . . 12·50 10·00

424 Kirov Military Medical Academy

1949. 150th Anniv of Kirov Military Medical Academy.
1476 **424** 40k. red . . . . . . 1·25 1·10
1477 – 50k. blue . . . . . . 1·75 1·60
1478 **424** 1r. green . . . . . . 4·25 3·00
DESIGN: 50k. Professors Botkin, Pirogov and Sechenov and Kirov Academy.

425 V. R. Williams 425a Three Russians with Flag

1949. Agricultural Reform.
1479 **425** 25k. green . . . . . . 3·25 2·25
1480 50k. brown . . . . . . 5·50 4·50

1949. Labour Day.
1481 **425a** 40k. red . . . . . . 1·75 1·25
1482 1r. green . . . . . . 3·25 2·00

426 Newspapers and Books 427 A. S. Popov and Radio Equipment

1949. Press Day. Inscr "5 MAR 1949".
1483 **426** 40k. red . . . . . . 3·00 4·75
1484 – 1r. violet . . . . . . 6·25 8·25
DESIGN: 1r. Man and boy reading newspaper.

1949. Radio Day.
1485 **427** 40k. violet . . . . . . 1·75 1·40
1486 – 50k. brown . . . . . . 3·25 2·50
1487 **427** 1r. green . . . . . . 5·50 4·25
DESIGN—HORIZ: 50k. Popov demonstrating receiver to Admiral Makarov.

428 A. S. Pushkin 429 "Pushkin reading Poems to Southern Society" (Dmitry Kardovsky)

1949. 150th Birth Anniv of Pushkin (poet).
1488 **428** 25k. black and grey . . 1·10 50
1489 – 40k. black and brown . . 1·75 1·50
1490 **429** 40k. purple and red . . 4·00 1·50
1491 – 1r. grey and brown . . . 5·25 5·00
1492 **429** 2r. blue and brown . . . 8·00 7·00
MS1492a 110 × 142 mm. Nos. 1488/9 (two of each). Imperf . . . . 42·00 32·00
DESIGNS—VERT: No. 1489, Pushkin portrait after Kiprensky. HORIZ: 1r. Pushkin museum, Boldino.

430 "Boksimi Typlokod" (tug) 431 I. V. Michurin

1949. Centenary of Krasnoe Sormovo Machine-building and Ship-building Plant, Gorky.
1493 **430** 40k. blue . . . . . . 6·75 5·25
1494 – 1r. brown . . . . . . 10·00 8·25
DESIGN: 1r. Freighter "Bolshaya Volga".

1949. Agricultural Reform.
1495 **431** 40k. blue . . . . . . 1·75 1·10
1496 1r. green . . . . . . 2·75 1·90

432 Yachting

1949. National Sports.
1497 **432** 20k. blue . . . . . . 1·25 10
1498 – 25k. green . . . . . . 1·25 15
1499 – 30k. violet . . . . . . 1·75 20
1500 – 40k. brown . . . . . . 2·25 40
1501 – 40k. green . . . . . . 2·25 40
1502 – 50k. grey . . . . . . 2·25 50
1503 – 1r. red . . . . . . 5·00 1·00
1504 – 2r. black . . . . . . 8·50 2·25

DESIGNS: 25k. Canoeing; 30k. Swimming; 40k. (No. 1500), Cycling; 40k. (No. 1501), Football; 50k. Mountaineering; 1r. Parachuting; 2r. High jumping.

433 V. V. Dokuchaev

1949. Soil Research.
1505 **433** 40k. brown . . . . . . 1·25 30
1506 1r. green . . . . 2·50 50

434 V. I. Bazhenov **435** A. N. Radischev

1949. 150th Death Anniv of V. I. Bazhenov (architect).
1507 **434** 40k. violet . . . . . . 1·40 45
1508 1r. brown . . . . 3·25 90

1949. Birth Bicent of A. N. Radischev (writer).
1509 **435** 40k. green . . . . 1·60 1·40
1510 1r. grey . . . . 2·75 2·25

436 Green Cape Sanatorium, Makhindzhauri

1949. State Sanatoria. Designs showing various buildings.
1511 **436** 40k. green 75 20
1512 – 40k. green 75 20
1513 – 40k. blue 75 20
1514 – 40k. violet 75 20
1515 – 40k. red 75 20
1516 – 40k. orange 75 20
1517 – 40k. brown 75 20
1518 – 40k. brown 75 20
1519 – 40k. black 75 20
1520 – 40k. black 75 20
DESIGNS—HORIZ: No. 1512, VTsSPS No. 41, Zheleznovodsk; No. 1513, Energetics, Hosta; No. 1514, VTsSPS No. 3, Kislovodsk; No. 1515, VTsSPS No. 3, Hosta; No. 1516, State Theatre, Sochi; No. 1517, Clinical, Tskhaltubo; No. 1518, Frunze, Sochi; No. 1519, VTsSPS No. 1, Kislovodsk; No. 1520, Communication, Hosta.

437 I. P. Pavlov

1949. Birth Centenary of I. P. Pavlov (scientist).
1521 **437** 40k. brown . . . . . . 1·00 20
1522 1r. black . . . . 2·25 60

438 Globe and Letters

1949. 75th Anniv of U.P.U. Perf or imperf.
1523b **438** 40k. blue and brown 2·25 25
1524b 50k. violet and blue . . 2·25 25

439 Tree Planting Machines

440 Map of S. W. Russia

1949. Forestry and Field Conservancy.
1525 **439** 25k. green 75 30
1526 – 40k. violet 90 30
1527 **440** 40k. green and black . . 90 60
1528 – 50k. blue . . . . 1·40 1·00
1529 **439** 1r. black . . . . 4·50 2·40
1530 – 2r. brown . . . . 7·25 4·75
DESIGNS—33×22½ mm: 40k. violet, Harvesters; 50k. River scene. 33×19½ mm: 2r. Old man and children.

1949. 30th Death Anniv of V. I. Chapaev (military strategist).
1531 **299** 40k. orange . . . . . . 10·50 10·00

442 I. S. Nikitin (after P. Borel) **443** Malyi Theatre, Moscow

1949. 125th Birth Anniv of Nikitin (poet).
1532 **442** 40k. brown . . . . . . 1·10 35
1533 1r. blue . . . . 2·25 60

1949. 125th Anniv of Malyi Theatre, Moscow.
1534 **443** 40k. green . . . . . . 1·25 25
1535 50k. orange . . . . . . 1·75 30
1536 – 1r. brown . . . . . . 4·00 80
DESIGN: 1r. Five portraits and theatre.

444 Crowd with Banner

1949. 32nd Anniv of October Revolution.
1537 **444** 40k. red . . . . 2·50 2·25
1538 1r. green . . . . 4·50 4·00

445 Sheep and Cows

1949. Cattle-breeding Collective Farm.
1539 **445** 40k. brown . . . . . . 1·25 40
1540 1r. violet . . . . 2·50 80

446 Lenin Hydro-electric Station, Caucasus **448** Ski Jumping

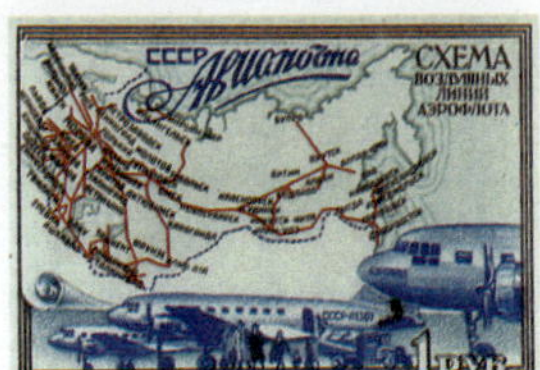

447 Ilyushin Il-12 Airliners and Map

1949. Air. Aerial views and map.
1541 **446** 50k. brown on yellow . 1·90 1·00
1542 – 60k. brown on buff . . . 2·00 1·50
1543 – 1r. orange on yellow . . 6·00 1·90
1544 – 1r. brown on buff . . . 5·50 1·90
1545 – 1r. blue on blue . . . . 5·50 1·90
1546 **447** 1r. blue, red and grey . . 10·00 5·50
1547 – 2r. red on blue . . . . 12·00 5·50
1548 – 3r. green on blue . . . . 23·00 13·50

DESIGNS—Ilyushin Il-12 airplane over: HORIZ: No. 1542, Farm; 1543, Sochi. VERT: 1544, Leningrad; 1545, Aleppo; 1547, Moscow; 1548, Arctic.

1949. National Sports.
1549 **448** 20k. green . . . . 1·00 15
1550 – 40k. orange . . . . . . 3·00 75
1551 – 50k. blue . . . . 2·75 60
1552 – 1r. red . . . . 5·25 60
1553 – 2r. violet . . . . 9·00 1·50
DESIGNS: 40k. Girl gymnast; 50k. Ice hockey; 1r. Weightlifting; 2r. Shooting wolves.

449 Diesel-electric Train **450** Arms of U.S.S.R.

1949. Modern Railway Development.
1554 – 25k. red . . . . 2·00 35
1555 **449** 40k. violet . . . . . . 2·50 45
1556 – 50k. brown . . . . . . 3·50 60
1557 **449** 1r. green . . . . 9·00 1·40
DESIGNS: 25k. Electric tram; 50k. Steam train.

1949. Constitution Day.
1558 **450** 40k. red . . . . 7·00 5·00

451 Government Buildings, Dushanbe **452** People with Flag

451a Stalin's Birthplace

1949. 20th Anniv of Republic of Tadzhikstan.
1559 – 20k. blue 70 10
1560 – 25k. green 80 10
1561 **451** 40k. red 90 30
1562 – 50k. violet . . . . . . 1·40 30
1563 **451** 1r. black . . . . 2·25 85
DESIGNS: 20k. Textile mills; 25k. Irrigation canal; 50k. Medical University.

1949. Stalin's 70th Birthday. Sheet 177×233 mm. Multicoloured.
MS1563a 40k. Type **451a**; 40k. Lenin and Stalin in Leningrad, 1917; 40k. Lenin and Stalin in Gorky; 40k. Marshal Stalin . . £130 £130

1949. 10th Anniv of Incorporation of West Ukraine and West Byelorussia in U.S.S.R.
1564 **452** 40k. red . . . . 9·00 9·00
1565 – 40k. orange . . . . . . 9·00 9·00
DESIGN—VERT: No. 1565, Ukrainians and flag.

453 Worker and Globe **454** Government Buildings, Tashkent

1949. Peace Propaganda.
1566 **453** 40k. red 85 25
1567 50k. blue . . . . 1·10 35

1950. 25th Anniv of Uzbek S.S.R.
1568 – 20k. blue 45 20
1569 – 25k. black 45 20
1570 **454** 40k. red . . . . 1·00 20
1571 – 40k. violet . . . . . . 1·40 40
1572 – 1r. green . . . . 2·75 75
1573 – 2r. brown . . . . 5·00 1·60
DESIGNS: 20k. Teachers' College; 25k. Opera and Ballet House, Tashkent; 40k. (violet) Navots Street, Tashkent; 1r. Map of Fergana Canal; 2r. Lock, Fergana Canal.

455 Dam **456** "Lenin at Rozliv" (sculpture, V. Pinchuk)

1950. 25th Anniv of Turkmen S.S.R.
1574 – 25k. black . . . . . . 3·25 3·25
1575 **455** 40k. brown . . . . . . 1·75 1·50
1576 – 50k. green . . . . . . 4·00 3·75
1577 **455** 1r. violet . . . . 8·75 6·00
DESIGNS: 25k. Textile factory, Ashkhabad; 50k. Carpet-making.

1950. 26th Death Anniv of Lenin.
1578 **456** 40k. brown and grey . . 85 25
1579 – 50k. red, brown and green . . . . 1·40 60
1580 – 1r. buff, green and brown . . . . 3·25 85
DESIGNS—HORIZ: 50k. Lenin's Office, Kremlin; 1r. Lenin Museum, Gorky.

457 Film Show **458** Voter

1950. 30th Anniv of Soviet Film Industry.
1581 **457** 25k. brown . . . . . . 16·00 13·50

1950. Supreme Soviet Elections. Inscr "12 MAPTA 1950".
1582 **458** 40k. green on yellow . . 3·75 2·75
1583 – 1r. red . . . . 5·50 4·50
DESIGN: 1r. Kremlin and flags.

459 Monument (I. Rabinovich) **460** Lenin Central Museum

1950. Unveiling of Monument in Moscow to Pavlik Morozov (model Soviet youth).
1584 **459** 40k. black and red . . . 4·00 3·25
1585 1r. green and red . . . . 6·50 5·00

1950. Moscow Museums. Buildings inscr "MOCKBA 1949".
1586 **460** 40k. olive . . . . 1·25 25
1587 – 40k. red . . . . 1·25 25
1588 – 40k. turquoise . . . . . 1·25 25
1589 – 40k. brown . . . . . . 1·25 25
1590 – 40k. mauve . . . . . . 1·25 25
1591 – 40k. blue (no tree) . . 1·25 25
1592 – 40k. brown . . . . . . 1·25 25
1593 – 40k. blue (with tree) . . 1·25 25
1594 – 40k. red . . . . 1·25 25
DESIGNS—HORIZ: (33½×23½ mm): No. 1587, Revolution Museum; 1588, Tretyakov Gallery; 1589, Timiryazev Biological Museum; No. 1591, Polytechnic Museum; 1593, Oriental Museum. (39½×26½ mm): No. 1590, Pushkin Pictorial Arts Museum. VERT: (22½×33½ mm): No. 1592, Historical Museum; 1594, Zoological Museum.

461 Hemispheres and Wireless Mast

1950. International Congress of P.T.T. and Radio Trade Unions, London.
1595 **461** 40k. green on blue . . . 3·25 2·75
1596 50k. blue on blue . . . 4·75 4·25

462 Three Workers

463 A. S. Shcherbakov

1950. Labour Day.
1597 **462** 40k. red and black 3·25 2·75
1598 – 1r. red and black 6·00 5·25
DESIGN—HORIZ: 1r. Four Russians and banner.

1950. 5th Death Anniv of Shcherbakov (statesman).
1599 **463** 40k. black 1·40 1·10
1600 1r. green on pink 3·00 2·75

464 Suvorov (after N. Utkin)

465 Statue

1950. 150th Death Anniv of Suvorov.
1601 **464** 40k. blue on pink 3·50 1·90
1602 – 50k. brown on pink 4·75 3·25
1603 – 60k. black on blue 4·75 3·25
1604 **464** 1r. brown on yellow 6·00 4·50
1605 – 2r. green 11·00 7·00
DESIGNS—32½ × 47 mm: 50k. "Suvorov crossing the Alps" (V. I. Surikov). 24½ × 39½ mm—60k. Order of Suvorov and military parade (after portrait by N. Smdyak). 19½ × 33½ mm—2r. "Suvorov in the Alps" (N. Abbakumov).

1950. 5th Anniv of Victory over Germany.
1606 **465** 40k. red and brown 4·00 2·75
1607 – 1r. red 6·50 4·00
DESIGN—22½ × 33 mm: 1r. Medal for the Victory over Germany (profile of Stalin and Order of Victory).

466 Sowing on Collective Farm

1950. Agricultural Workers.
1608 – 40k. green on blue 3·00 1·75
1609 **466** 40k. brown on pink 3·00 1·75
1610 1r. blue on yellow 4·75 3·75
DESIGNS: No. 1608, Collective farmers studying.

467 G. M. Dimitrov

468 State Opera and Ballet House, Baku

1950. 1st Death Anniv of Bulgarian Premier, Dimitrov.
1611 **467** 40k. black on yellow 1·75 1·40
1612 1r. black on orange 4·25 2·75

1950. 30th Anniv of Azerbaijan S.S.R.
1613 **468** 25k. green on yellow 1·60 1·40
1614 – 40k. brown on red 3·25 2·50
1615 – 1r. black on orange 5·50 4·50
DESIGNS: 40k. Science Academy; 1r. Stalin Avenue, Baku.

469 Lenin Street, Stalingrad

1950. Stalingrad Reconstruction.
1616 – 20k. blue 1·00 90
1617 **469** 40k. green 2·00 1·25
1618 – 50k. orange 4·25 3·25
1619 – 1r. black 5·00 4·00
DESIGNS—VERT: 20k. Pobeda Cinema. HORIZ: 50k. Gorky Theatre; 1r. Pavlov House and Tank Memorial.

470 Kaluzhskaya Station

472 Trade Union Building

471 National Flags and Civilians

1950. Underground Railway Stations.
1620 **470** 40k. green on buff 1·00 35
1621 A 40k. red 1·00 35
1622 B 40k. blue on buff 1·00 35
1623 C 1r. brown on yellow 3·00 1·10
1624 D 1r. violet on blue 3·00 1·10
1625 A 1r. green on yellow 3·00 1·10
1626 E 1r. black on orange 3·00 1·10
DESIGNS—HORIZ: (34 × 22½ mm): A, Culture Park; B, Taganskaya; C, Kurskaya; D, Paveletskaya. (34 × 18½ mm): E, Taganskaya.

1950. Unconquerable Democracy. Flags in red, blue and yellow.
1627 **471** 40k. black 1·10 20
1628 50k. brown 2·25 30
1629 1r. green 2·50 45

1950. 10th Anniv of Latvian S.S.R.
1630 **472** 25k. brown 90 60
1631 – 40k. red 1·40 90
1632 – 50k. green 2·10 1·40
1633 – 60k. blue 2·50 1·90
1634 – 1r. violet 4·50 3·00
1635 – 2r. brown 7·50 5·00
DESIGNS—VERT: 40k. Cabinet Council Offices; 50k. Monument to Jan Rainis (poet); 2r. Academy of Sciences. HORIZ: 60k. Theatre, Riga; 1r. State University, Riga.

473 Marite Melnikaite

474 Stalingrad Square, Tallinn

1950. 10th Anniv of Lithuanian S.S.R.
1636 – 25k. blue 1·25 70
1637 **473** 40k. brown 2·40 1·40
1638 – 1r. red 6·50 3·50
DESIGNS—HORIZ: 25k. Academy of Sciences; 1r. Cabinet Council Offices.

1950. 10th Anniv of Estonian S.S.R.
1639 **474** 25k. green 1·00 60
1640 – 40k. red 1·40 90
1641 – 50k. blue on yellow 2·25 1·60
1642 – 1r. brown on blue 7·00 5·50
DESIGNS—HORIZ: 40k. Government building; 50k. Opera and Ballet Theatre, Tallin. VERT: 1r. Viktor Kingisepp (revolutionary).

475 Signing Peace Appeal

1950. Peace Conference.
1643 **475** 40k. red on pink 1·60 1·10
1644 – 40k. black 1·60 1·10
1645 – 50k. red 3·50 3·00
1646 **475** 1r. brown on pink 5·50 4·75
DESIGNS—VERT: 40k. black, Children and teacher; 50k. Young people with banner.

476 Bellingshausan Lazarev and Globe

477 Frunze (after I. Brodsky)

1950. 130th Anniv of 1st Antarctic Expedition.
1647 **476** 40k. red on blue 18·00 11·00
1648 – 1r. violet on blue 32·00 15·00
DESIGN—VERT: 1r. "Mirnyi" and "Vostok" (ships) and map of Antarctica.

1950. 25th Death Anniv of M.V. Frunze (military strategist).
1649 **477** 40k. blue on pink 3·50 2·75
1650 1r. brown on blue 8·25 6·00

478 M. I. Kalinin

479 Picking Grapes

1950. 75th Birth Anniv of Kalinin (statesman).
1651 **478** 40k. green 1·25 85
1652 1r. brown 2·75 1·60
1653 5r. violet 7·25 6·50

1950. 30th Anniv of Armenian S.S.R.
1654 **479** 20k. blue on pink 1·50 1·10
1655 – 40k. orange on blue 2·75 1·60
1656 – 1r. black on yellow 5·75 3·75
DESIGNS—HORIZ: (33 × 16 mm): 40k. Government Offices. VERT: (21½ × 33 mm): 1r. G. M. Sundukian (dramatist).

480 Kotelnicheskaya Quay

481 Spassky Tower, Kremlin

1950. Moscow Building Projects.
1657 **480** 1r. brown on pink 35·00 25·00
1658 – 1r. black on pink 35·00 25·00
1659 – 1r. brown on blue 35·00 25·00
1660 – 1r. green on yellow 35·00 25·00
1661 – 1r. blue on pink 35·00 25·00
1662 – 1r. black 35·00 25·00
1663 – 1r. orange 35·00 25·00
1664 – 1r. green on blue 35·00 25·00
DESIGNS—HORIZ: No. 1659, Vosstaniya Square; 1660, Smolenskaya Square; 1662, Krasnye Vorota; 1664, Moscow University. VERT: No. 1658, Hotel Ukraine, Dorogomilovskaya Quay; 1661, Hotel Leningrad; 1663, Zaryade.

1950. 33rd Anniv of October Revolution.
1665 **481** 1r. red, yellow and green 16·00 9·00

482 "Golden Autumn"

1950. 50th Death Anniv of Levitan (painter).
1666 **482** 40k. multicoloured 4·00 85
1667 – 50k. brown 5·00 85
DESIGN: 50k. Portrait of Levitan by V. Serov.

483 Aivazovsky (after A. Tyranov)

484 Newspapers "Iskra" and "Pravda"

1950. 50th Death Anniv of Aivazovsky (painter). Multicoloured centres.
1668 – 40k. brown 3·00 40
1669 – 50k. brown 4·00 65
1670 **483** 1r. blue 7·75 1·40
PAINTINGS—HORIZ: 40k. "Black Sea"; 50k. "Ninth Wave".

1950. 50th Anniv of Newspaper "Iskra".
1671 – 40k. red and black 12·00 10·50
1672 **484** 1r. red and black 16·00 13·00
DESIGN: 40k. Newspapers and banners.

485 Government Offices

1950. 30th Anniv of Kazakh S.S.R.
1673 **485** 40k. black on blue 4·75 2·50
1674 – 1r. brown on yellow 6·25 3·50
DESIGN: 1r. Opera House, Alma-Ata.

486 Decembrists and "Decembrist Rising in Senate Square, St. Petersburg, 14 December 1825" (K. Kolman)

1950. 125th Anniv of Decembrist Rising.
1675 **486** 1r. brown on yellow 7·25 5·50

487 Govt Offices, Tirana

1951. Friendship with Albania.
1676 **487** 40k. green on blue 20·00 15·00

488 Greeting Soviet Troops

1951. Friendship with Bulgaria.
1677 **488** 25k. black on blue 2·25 1·90
1678 – 40k. orange on pink 6·00 3·25
1679 – 60k. brown on orange 6·75 4·25
DESIGNS: 40k. Lenin Square, Sofia; 60k. Monument to Soviet fighters, Kolarovgrad.

489 Lenin at Razliv

1951. 27th Death Anniv of Lenin. Multicoloured centres.
1680 **489** 40k. green 2·75 65
1681 – 1r. blue 5·50 1·00
DESIGN: 1r. Lenin talking to young Communists.

490 Horses

1951. 25th Anniv of Kirghiz S.S.R.
1682 **490** 25k. brown on blue 5·00 4·50
1683 – 40k. green on blue 7·25 6·75
DESIGN—33 × 22½ mm: 40k. Government Offices, Frunze.

490a Gathering Lemons

1951. 30th Anniv of Georgia S.S.R.
1683a – 20k. green on yellow 1·75 1·25
1683b **490a** 25k. orange and violet 2·75 2·00
1683c – 40k. brown on blue 4·50 3·00
1683d – 1r. green and brown 11·00 6·00
DESIGNS—VERT: 20k. State Opera and Ballet Theatre, Tbilisi. HORIZ: 40k. Rustaveli Avenue, Tbilisi; 1r. Plucking tea.

491 University, Ulan Bator

1951. Friendship with Mongolia.
1684 **491** 25k. violet on orange . . 1·75 75
1685 – 40k. orange on yellow 2·50 1·10
1686 – 1r. multicoloured . . . . 7·25 4·00
DESIGNS—HORIZ: (37 × 25 mm): 40k. State Theatre, Ulan Bator. VERT: (22 × 33 mm): 1r. State Emblem and Mongolian Flag.

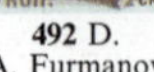

492 D. A. Furmanov

493 Soviet Soldiers Memorial, Berlin (E. Buchetich)

1951. 25th Death Anniv of D. A. Furmanov (writer).
1687 **492** 40k. brown on blue . . . 1·90 1·40
1688 – 1r. black on orange . . . 4·25 3·25
DESIGN—HORIZ: 1r. Furmanov writing.

1951. Stockholm Peace Appeal.
1689 **493** 40k. green and red . . . 4·25 3·25
1690 1r. black and red . . . . 9·00 7·50

494 Factories

1951. 150th Anniv of Kirov Machine-building Factory, Leningrad.
1691 **494** 40k. brown on yellow . . 6·75 5·00

495 Bolshoi State Theatre

1951. 175th Anniv of State Theatre.
1692 **495** 40k. multicoloured . . . . 5·00 55
1693 – 1r. multicoloured . . . . 7·25 1·40
DESIGN: 1r. Theatre and medallions of Glinka, Tchaikovsky, Moussorgsky, Rimsky-Korsakov, Borodin and theatre.

496 National Museum, Budapest

1951. Hungarian Peoples' Republic. Buildings in Budapest.
1694 – 25k. green . . . . 1·40 1·10
1695 – 40k. blue . . . . 1·50 90
1696 **496** 60k. black . . . . 2·50 1·25
1697 – 1r. black on pink . . . . 5·75 3·50
DESIGNS—HORIZ: 25k. Liberty Bridge; 40k. Parliament buildings. VERT: 1r. Liberation Monument.

497 Harvesting

1951. Agricultural Scenes.
1698 **497** 25k. green 90 50
1699 – 40k. green on blue . . 1·75 60
1700 – 1r. brown on yellow . . 3·00 2·75
1701 – 2r. green on pink . . . 5·25 4·75
DESIGNS: 40k. Apiary; 1r. Gathering citrus fruit; 2r. Harvesting cotton.

498 M. I. Kalinin

499 F. E. Dzerzhinsky

1951. 5th Death Anniv of Pres. Kalinin.
1702 – 20k. black, sepia & brown 75 35
1703 **498** 40k. brown, dp grn & grn . . . . 1·60 50
1704 – 1r. black, bl & ultram 3·25 90
DESIGNS—HORIZ: 20k. Kalinin Museum. VERT: 1r. Statue of Kalinin (G. Alekseev).

1951. 25th Death Anniv of Dzerzhinsky (founder of Cheka).
1705 **499** 40k. red . . . . 2·40 60
1706 – 1r. black (Portrait in uniform) . . . . . . 4·50 1·60

500 P. K. Kozlov

501 Kalinnikov

1951. Russian Scientists.
1707 **500** 40k. orange . . . . . . 1·50 25
1708 – 40k. orange on pink . . 1·50 25
1709 – 40k. orange on blue . . 4·50 1·10
1710 – 40k. brown . . . . . . 1·50 25
1711 – 40k. brown on pink (facing left) . . . . . 1·50 25
1712 – 40k. brown on pink (facing right) . . . . 1·50 25
1713 – 40k. grey . . . . 1·50 25
1714 – 40k. grey on pink . . . 1·50 25
1715 – 40k. grey on blue . . . 4·50 1·10
1716 – 40k. green . . . . . . 1·50 25
1717 – 40k. green on pink . . . 1·50 25
1718 – 40k. blue . . . . 1·50 25
1719 – 40k. blue on pink . . . 1·50 25
1720 – 40k. blue on blue . . . 1·50 25
1721 – 40k. violet . . . . . . 1·50 25
1722 – 40k. violet on pink . . . 1·50 25
PORTRAITS: No. 1708, N. N. Miklukho-Makai; 1709, A. M. Butlerov; 1710, N. I. Lobachevsky; 1711, K. A. Timiryazev; 1712, N. S. Kurnakov; 1713, P. N. Yablochkov; 1714, A. N. Severtsov; No. 1715, K. E. Tsiolkovsky; 1716, A. N. Lodygin; 1717, A. G. Stoletov; 1718, P. N. Lebedev; 1719, A. O. Kovalesky; 1720, D. I. Mendeleev; 1721, S. P. Krasheninnikov; 1722, S. V. Kovalevskaya.

1951. Russian Composers.
1723 **501** 40k. grey on pink . . . 10·00 8·25
1724 – 40k. brown on pink . . 10·00 8·25
PORTRAIT: No. 1724, A. Alyabev (after N. Andreev).

502 Aviation Society Badge

503 Vasnetsov (after I. Kramskoi)

1951. Aviation Developement.
1725 **502** 40k. multicoloured . . . 1·25 15
1726 – 60k. multicoloured . . . 2·00 20
1727 – 1r. multicoloured . . . 3·25 85
1728 – 2r. multicoloured . . . 6·25 1·50
DESIGNS—VERT: 60k. Boys and model gliders; 1r. Parachutists descending. HORIZ: (45 × 25 mm): 2r. Flight of Yakovlev Yak-18U trainers.

1951. 25th Death Anniv of Vasnetsov (painter).
1729 **503** 40k. brown, buff and blue . . . . 4·00 60
1730 – 1r. multicoloured . . . . 6·00 1·10
DESIGN (47 × 33 mm): 1r. "Three Heroes".

504 Lenin, Stalin and Dnieperprostroi Dam

1951. 34th Anniv of October Revolution.
1731 **504** 40k. blue and red . . . 6·00 3·25
1732 – 1r. brown and red . . . 8·00 5·50
DESIGN: 1r. Lenin, Stalin and Spassky Tower.

505 Volga–Don Canal

1951. Construction of Hydro-electric Power Stations.
1733 – 20k. multicoloured . . . 4·00 2·00
1734 **505** 30k. multicoloured . . . 4·50 3·50
1735 – 40k. multicoloured . . . 5·50 4·00
1736 – 60k. multicoloured . . . 8·50 4·50
1737 – 1r. multicoloured . . . . 13·00 8·00
DESIGNS—VERT: (32 × 47 mm): 20k. Khakhovsky power station. HORIZ: (47 × 32 mm); 40k. Stalingrad dam; 60k. Excavator and map of Turkmen canal; 1r. Kuibyshev power station.

506 Signing Peace Petition

507 M. V. Ostrogradsky

1951. 3rd U.S.S.R. Peace Conference.
1738 **506** 40k. red and brown . . 9·25 7·25

1951. 150th Birth Anniv of Ostrogradsky (mathematician).
1739 **507** 40k. brown on pink . . 7·25 4·50

508 Zhizka Monument, Prague (B. Kafka)

509 Volkhovsky Hydro-electric Station and Lenin Monument

1951. Friendship with Czechoslovakia.
1740 **508** 20k. blue on pink . . . 2·00 1·25
1741 – 25k. red on yellow . . . 4·50 1·75
1742 – 40k. orange on orange 2·25 1·50
1743 – 60k. grey on pink . . . 5·25 2·75
1744 – 1r. grey on cream . . . 8·00 5·00
DESIGNS—VERT: 25k. Soviet Army Monument, Ostrava; 40k. J. Fucik by M. Shvabinsky; 60k. Smetana Museum, Prague. HORIZ: 1r. Soviet Soldiers Monument, Prague.

1951. 25th Anniv of Lenin Volkhovsky Hydro-electric Station.
1745a **509** 40k. yellow, indigo and blue . . . . 1·10 35
1746 1r. yellow, indigo and violet . . . . 2·25 50

510 Lenin when a Student (after V. Prager)

511 P. P. Semenov-Tian-Shansky

1952. 28th Death Anniv of Lenin. Multicoloured centres.
1747 **510** 40k. green . . . . 2·25 75
1748 – 60k. blue . . . . 2·75 90
1749 – 1r. brown . . . . 3·25 1·40
DESIGNS—HORIZ: 60k. Lenin and children (after A. Varlamov); 1r. Lenin talking to peasants (after V. Serov).

1952. 125th Birth Anniv of Semenov-Tian-Shansky (scientist).
1750 **511** 1r. brown on blue . . . 3·75 2·50

512 Skaters

513 V. O. Kovalevsky

1952. Winter Sports.
1751 **512** 40k. multicoloured . . . 3·25 45
1752 – 60k. multicoloured (Skiers) . . . . 4·00 75

1952. Birth Centenary of Kovalevsky (scientist).
1753 **513** 40k. brown on yellow . . 6·25 5·00

514 Gogol (after F. Moller) and Character from "Taras Bulba"

1952. Death Centenary of Nikolai Gogol (writer).
1754 **514** 40k. black on blue . . . 1·00 20
1755 – 60k. orange and black 1·40 30
1756 – 1r. multicoloured . . . . 2·75 1·40
DESIGNS: 60k. Gogol and Belinsky (after B. Lebedev); 1r. Gogol and Ukrainian peasants.

515 G. K. Ordzhonikidze

516 Workers and Flag

1952. 15th Death Anniv of Ordzhonikidze (statesman).
1757 **515** 40k. green on pink . . . 5·50 3·25
1758 1r. black on blue . . . . 7·25 5·00

1952. 15th Anniv of Stalin Constitution.
1759 **516** 40k. red and black on cream . . . . 5·50 3·75
1760 – 40k. red and green on green . . . . 5·50 3·75
1761 – 40k. red and brown on blue . . . . 5·50 3·75
1762 – 40k. red and black . . . 5·50 3·75
DESIGNS—HORIZ: No. 1760, Chess players at recreation centre; 1761, Old people and banners. VERT: No. 1762, Schoolgirl and Spassky Tower, Kremlin.

517 Novikov-Priboy and Battleship "Orel"

1952. 75th Birth Anniv of Novikov-Priboy (writer).
1763 **517** 40k. grey, yellow & green . . . . 3·25 1·10

518 Victor Hugo

519 Yulaev (after T. Nechaevoi)

1952. 150th Birth Anniv of Victor Hugo (French writer).
1764 **518** 40k. black, blue & brown . . . . 1·75 50

1952. Birth Bicent of Yulaev (Bashkirian hero).
1765 **519** 40k. red on pink . . . . 1·75 55

520 G. Ya. Sedov

521 Arms and Flag of Rumania

1952. 75th Birth Anniv of Sedov (Arctic explorer).
1766 **520** 40k. brown, blue & green . . . . 10·50 8·00

1952. Friendship with Rumania.
1767 **521** 40k. multicoloured . . . 1·40 65
1768 – 60k. green on pink . . . 2·50 1·50
1769 – 1r. blue . . . . 3·00 2·25
DESIGNS—VERT: 60k. Soviet Soldiers' Monument, Bucharest. HORIZ: 1r. University Square, Bucharest.

522 Zhukovsky (after K. Bryullov)

523 Bryullov (after V. Tropilin)

1952. Death Centenary of V. Zhukovsky (poet).
1770 **522** 40k. black on blue . . . 1·10 55

1952. Death Centenary of K. Bryullov (artist).
1771 **523** 40k. green on blue . . . 1·10 55

524 Ogarev (after M. Lemmel)

525 Uspensky (after N. Yaroshenko)

1952. 75th Death Anniv of Ogarev (revolutionary writer).
1772 **524** 40k. green 65 35

1952. 50th Death Anniv of Uspensky (writer).
1773 **525** 40k. brown and blue . . 1·75 75

526 Nakhimov (after V. Timm)

527 Tartu University

1952. 150th Birth Anniv of Admiral Nakhimov.
1774 **526** 40k. multicoloured . . . 3·75 1·60

1952. 150th Anniv of Extension of Tartu University.
1775 **527** 40k. black on salmon . . 2·75 1·60

1952. War Orders and Medals (7th series). Frame as T **282** with various centres.
1776 F 1r. brown . . . . 12·00 9·00
1777 P 2r. red . . . . 1·90 1·00
1778 J 3r. violet 90 70
1779a A 5r. lake . . . . 1·25 85
1780 E 10r. red . . . . 1·75 1·00

528 Kayum Nasyri

529 A. N. Radishchev

1952. 50th Death Anniv of Nasyri (educationist).
1781 **528** 40k. brown on yellow . . 2·75 1·60

1952. 150th Death Anniv of Radishchev (writer).
1782 **529** 40k. black and red . . . 2·25 75

530 Entrance to Volga–Don Canal

531 P. A. Fedotov

1952. 35th Anniv of Russian Revolution.
1783 **530** 40k. multicoloured . . . 5·00 3·25
1784 – 1r. yellow, red and brown . . . . 7·25 5·00
DESIGN: 1r. Lenin, Stalin, Spassky Tower and flags.

1952. Death Centenary of Fedotov (painter).
1785 **531** 40k. brown and lake . . 2·25 65

532 Polenov (after I. Repin)

534 Odoevsky (after N. Bestuzhev)

533 "Moscow Courtyard" (painting)

1952. 25th Death Anniv of Polenov (painter).
1786 **532** 40k. lake and buff . . . 1·60 55
1787 **533** 1r. blue and grey . . . 3·75 1·25

1952. 150th Birth Anniv of A. I. Odoevsky (poet).
1788 **534** 40k. black and red . . . 1·75 50

535 Mamin-Sibiryak

536 V. M. Bekhterev

1952. Birth Centenary of D. N. Mamin-Sibiryak (writer).
1789 **535** 40k. green on yellow . . 1·10 25

1952. 25th Death Anniv of Bekhterev (psychiatrist).
1790 **536** 40k. black, grey and blue 1·40 55

537 Komsomolskaya Koltsevaya Station

1952. Underground Stations. Multicoloured centres.
1791 – 40k. violet . . . . . . 2·00 40
1792 – 40k. blue . . . . 2·00 40
1793 – 40k. grey . . . . 2·00 40
1794 **537** 40k. green . . . . 2·00 40
STATIONS: No. 1791, Belorussia Koltsevaya; 1792, Botanical Gardens; 1793, Novoslo-bodskaya.

538 U.S.S.R. Arms and Flags

1952. 30th Anniv of U.S.S.R.
1795 **538** 1r. brown, red and green 4·50 3·25

539 Lenin and Flags (after A. Gerasimov)

1953. 29th Death Anniv of Lenin.
1796 **539** 40k. multicoloured . . . 5·00 4·25

540 Peace Prize Medal

541 V. V. Kuibyshev

1953. Stalin Peace Prize.
1797 **540** 40k. yellow, blue & brown . . . . 5·50 5·00

1953. 65th Birth Anniv of Kuibyshev (statesman).
1798 **541** 40k. black and lake . . . 1·90 1·25

542 V. V. Mayakovsky

543 N. G. Chernyshevsky

1953. 60th Birth Anniv of Mayakovsky (poet).
1799 **542** 40k. black and red . . . 2·75 2·25

1953. 125th Birth Anniv of Chernyshevsky (writer).
1800 **543** 40k. brown and buff . . 2·75 2·25

544 R. Volga Lighthouse

1953. Volga–Don Canal. Multicoloured.
1801 40k. Type **544** . . . . . . 1·60 60
1802 40k. Lock No. 9 . . . . . 1·60 60
1803 40k. Lock No. 13 . . . . . 1·60 60
1804 40k. Lock No. 15 . . . . . 1·90 60
1805 40k. Tsimlyanskaya hydro-electric station . . . . . 1·60 60
1806 1r. "Iosif Stalin" (river vessel) . . . . 3·00 1·40

545 V. G. Korolenko

546 Tolstoi (after N. Ge)

1953. Birth Centenary of Korolenko (writer).
1807 **545** 40k. brown . . . . . . 1·10 25

1953. 125th Birth Anniv of Leo Tolstoi (writer).
1808 **546** 1r. brown . . . . 6·50 3·25

547 Lomonosov University and Students

548 Peoples of the U.S.S.R.

1953. 35th Anniv of "Komsomol" (Russian Youth Organization). Multicoloured.
1809 40k. Type **547** . . . . . . 2·25 1·40
1810 1r. Four medals and "Komsomol" badge . . . 4·50 2·75

1953. 36th Anniv of Russian Revolution. Mult.
1811 40k. Type **548** . . . . . . 7·25 5·50
1812 60k. Lenin and Stalin in Smolny Institute, 1917 . . 12·50 9·50

549 Lenin Medallion

550 Lenin Statue

551 Peter I Monument

1953. 50th Anniv of Communist Party.
1813 **549** 40k. multicoloured . . . 3·50 2·75

1953. Views of Leningrad as T **550/1**.
1814 **550** 40k. black on yellow . . 2·00 1·00
1815 40k. brown on pink . . 2·00 1·00
1816 – 40k. brown on yellow . . 1·25 45
1817 – 40k. black on buff . . . 1·75 85
1818 **551** 1r. brown on blue . . . 3·00 1·10
1819 1r. violet on yellow . . . 3·00 1·40
1820 – 1r. green on pink . . . 3·00 2·25
1821 – 1r. brown on blue . . . 3·50 2·40
DESIGNS: As Type **550**: Nos. 1816/17, Admiralty. As Type **551**: 1820/1, Smolny Institute.

552 Lenin and Book "What is to be Done?"

553 Pioneers and Moscow University Model

1953. 50th Anniv of 2nd Social Democratic Workers' Party Congress.
1822 **552** 1r. brown and red . . . 7·75 6·50

1953. Peace Propaganda.
1823 **553** 40k. black, olive and grey . . . . 3·75 2·75

554 Griboedov (after I. Kramskoi) **555** Kremlin

1954. 125th Death Anniv of A. S. Griboedov (author).
1824 **554** 40k. purple on buff . . 1·60 50
1825a 1r. black on green . . . 2·25 1·00

1954. General Election.
1826 **555** 40k. grey and red . . . 2·75 2·00

556 V. P. Chkalov **557** "Lenin in Smolny Institute" (after I. Brodsky)

1954. 50th Birthday of Chkalov (aviator).
1827 **556** 1r. multicoloured . . . . 4·00 1·60

1954. 30th Death Anniv of Lenin. Multicoloured.
1828 40k. Lenin (after M. Rundaltsov) (26 × 38 mm) . . . . . . 2·50 1·40
1829 40k. Type **557** . . . . . . 2·50 1·40
1830 40k. Cottage Museum, Ulyanovsk (after I. Sokolov) . . . . 2·50 1·40
1831 40k. "Lenin proclaims Soviet Regime" (V. Serov) (48 × 35 mm) . . . . . . 2·50 1·40
1832 40k. "Lenin at Kazan University" (A. Pushnin) (48 × 35 mm) . . . . . . 2·50 1·40

558 Stalin **559** Supreme Soviet Buildings in Kiev and Moscow

1954. 1st Death Anniv of Stalin.
1833 **558** 40k. brown . . . . . . 3·50 2·25

1954. Tercentenary of Reunion of Ukraine with Russia. Multicoloured. (a) Designs as T **559** inscr "1654–1954".
1834 40k. Type **559** . . . . . . 1·10 40
1835 40k. Shevchenko Memorial, Kharkhov (vert) . . . . 1·10 25
1836 40k. State Opera House, Kiev . . . . 1·10 25
1837 40k. Shevchenko University, Kiev . . . . 1·10 25
1838 40k. Academy of Sciences, Kiev . . . . 1·50 25
1839 60k. Bogdan Chmielnitsky Memorial, Kiev (vert) . . 1·60 25
1840 1r. Flags of R.S.F.S.R. and Ukrainian S.S.R. (vert) 3·50 55
1841 1r. Shevchenko Monument, Kanev (vert) . . . . . . 2·50 35
1842 1r. Pereyaslavskaya Rada 3·50 45

(b) No. 1098b optd with five lines of Cyrillic characters as inscr at top of T **559**.
1843 h 2r. green . . . . 7·50 1·75

561 Running

1954. Sports. Frames in brown.
1844 **561** 40k. black and stone . . 1·00 20
1845 – 40k. black and blue . . 1·25 20
1846 – 40k. brown and buff . . 1·00 20
1847 – 40k. black and blue . . 1·00 20
1848 – 40k. black . . . . 1·00 20
1849 – 1r. grey and blue . . . . 5·00 1·50
1850 – 1r. black and blue . . . 5·00 1·50
1851 – 1r. brown and drab . . 5·00 1·50
DESIGNS—HORIZ: No. 1845, "Soling" yachts; 1846, Cycling; 1847, Swimming; 1848, Hurdling; 1849, Mountaineering; 1850, Skiing. VERT: No. 1851, Basketball.

562 Cattle **563** A. P. Chekhov

1954. Agriculture.
1852 **562** 40k. blue, brown & cream . . . . 2·40 50
1853 – 40k. green, brown & buff 2·40 50
1854 – 40k. black, blue and green . . . . 2·40 50
DESIGNS: No. 1853, Potato cultivation; 1854, Collective farm hydro-electric station.

1954. 50th Death Anniv of Chekhov (writer).
1855 **563** 40k. brown and green . . 1·10 40

564 Bredikhin, Struve, Belopolsky and Observatory **565** M. I. Glinka

1954. Rebuilding of Pulkov Observatory.
1856 **564** 40k. black, blue and violet . . . . 8·00 1·60

1954. 150th Birth Anniv of Glinka (composer).
1857 **565** 40k. brown, pink and red . . . . 2·25 35
1858 – 60k. multicoloured . . . 3·25 65
DESIGN—HORIZ: (38 × 25½ mm): 60k. "Glinka playing piano for Pushkin and Zhukovsky" (V. Artamonov).

566 Exhibition Emblem **567** N. A. Ostrovsky

1954. Agricultural Exhibition. Multicoloured.
1859 40k. Type **566** 85 35
1860 40k. Agricultural Pavilion 85 35
1861 40k. Cattle breeding Pavilion 85 35
1862 40k. Mechanization Pavilion 85 35
1863 1r. Exhibition Entrance . . 3·00 1·40
1864 1r. Main Pavilion . . . . . 3·00 1·40
Nos. 1860/3 are horiz, 1860/1 being 41 × 30½ mm, 1862, 40 × 30 mm and 1863 41 × 33 mm. No. 1864 is vert, 29 × 41 mm.

1954. 50th Birth Anniv of Ostrovsky (writer).
1865 **567** 40k. multicoloured . . . 1·75 45

568 Monument **569** Marx, Engels, Lenin and Stalin

1954. Centenary of Defence of Sevastopol.
1866 **568** 40k. black, brown & grn 1·40 40
1867 – 60k. black, brown & buff 1·60 60
1868 – 1r. multicoloured . . . 3·50 1·00
DESIGNS—HORIZ: 60k. Heroes of Sevastopol (after V. Timm). VERT: 1r. Admiral Nakhimov (after V. Timm).

1954. 37th Anniv of October Revolution.
1869 **569** 1r. brown, red and orange . . . . 5·50 3·50

570 Kazan University

1954. 150th Anniv of Kazan University.
1870 **570** 40k. blue on blue . . . 1·00 45
1871 60k. red . . . . 1·75 55

571 Salomea Neris

1954. 50th Birth Anniv of Salomea Neris (poetess).
1872 **571** 40k. multicoloured . . . 1·25 35

572 Cultivating Vegetables **573** Stalin

1954. Agriculture. Multicoloured.
1873 40k. Type **572** . . . . . 1·50 30
1874 40k. Tractor and plough . . 1·50 30
1875 40k. Harvesting flax (49 × 25½ mm) . . . . . 1·50 30
1876 60k. Harvesting sunflowers (49 × 25½ mm) . . . . . 3·00 65

1954. 75th Birth Anniv of Stalin.
1877 **573** 40k. purple . . . . . . 1·50 50
1878 1r. blue . . . . 3·50 1·40

574 Rubinstein (after I. Repin)

1954. 125th Birth Anniv of Rubinstein (composer).
1879 **574** 40k. black and purple . . 2·00 40

575 V. M. Garshin **576** Ilyushin Il-12 over Landscape

1955. Birth Centenary of Garshin (writer).
1880 **575** 40k. black, brown & grn 1·10 35

1955. Air.
1881 – 1r. multicoloured . . . . 1·75 40
1882 **576** 2r. black and green . . . 3·75 60
DESIGN: 1r. Ilyushin Il-12 over coastline.

577 Savitsky (after N. Frandkovsky) and "Construction of Railway"

1955. 50th Death Anniv of K. Savitsky (painter).
1883 **577** 40k. brown . . . . . . 1·75 30
MS1883a 151 × 119 mm. No. 1883 × 4 . . . . 25·00 22·00
MS1883b Ditto brown inscriptions 25·00 22·00

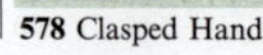

578 Clasped Hands **579** Pushkin and Mickiewicz

1955. International Conference of Postal and Municipal Workers, Vienna.
1884 **578** 50k. multicoloured . . . 1·10 30

1955. 10th Anniv of Russo–Polish Friendship Agreement.
1885 **579** 40k. multicoloured . . . 2·25 30
1886 – 40k. black . . . . 2·25 30
1887 – 1r. multicoloured . . . . 4·00 85
1888 – 1r. multicoloured . . . . 6·00 1·25
DESIGNS: No. 1886, "Brotherhood in Arms" Monument, Warsaw (26½ × 39 mm); No. 1887, Palace of Science, Warsaw (37½ × 25½ mm); No. 1888, Copernicus and Matejko (39 × 26½ mm).

580 Lenin at Shushenskoe (after V. Basov)

1955. 85th Birth Anniv of Lenin. Multicoloured centres.
1889 **580** 60k. red . . . . 2·00 30
1890 – 1r. red . . . . 4·00 60
1891 – 1r. red . . . . 4·00 60
DESIGNS: No. 1890, Lenin in secret printing house (after F. Golubkov) (26½ × 39 mm). As Type **580**: No. 1891, Lenin and Krupskaya at Gorky (after N. Sysoev).

581 Schiller **582** Ilyushin Il-12 over Globe

1955. 150th Death Anniv of Schiller (poet).
1892 **581** 40k. brown . . . . . . 1·50 65

1955. Air.
1893 **582** 2r. brown . . . . 6·75 1·25
1894 2r. blue . . . . 3·50 55

583 V. Mayakovsky

1955. 25th Death Anniv of Mayakovsky (poet).
1895 **583** 40k. multicoloured . . . 1·10 30

584 Tadzhik S.S.R. Pavilion

1955. Agricultural Exhibition. Soviet Pavilion. Multicoloured designs with green frames.
1896 40k. R.S.F.S.R. 80 25
1897 40k. Byelorussian S.S.R. . . 80 25
1898 40k. Type **584** 80 25
1899 40k. Azerbaijan S.S.R. . . . 80 25
1900 40k. Latvian S.S.R. 80 25
1901 40k. Lithuanian S.S.R. . . . 80 25
1902 40k. Karelo-Finnish S.S.R. 80 25
1903 40k. Estonian S.S.R. . . . 80 25
1904 40k. Armenian S.S.R. . . . 80 25
1905 40k. Ukrainian S.S.R. . . . 80 25
1906 40k. Georgian S.S.R. . . . 80 25
1907 40k. Kazakh S.S.R. 80 25
1908 40k. Turkmen S.S.R. . . . 80 25
1909 40k. Kirgiz S.S.R. 80 25
1910 40k. Uzbek S.S.R. 80 25
1911 40k. Moldavian S.S.R. . . . 80 25
MS1911a 156 × 104 mm. 40k. R.S.F.S.R . . . . 22·00 22·00
MS1911b 156 × 104 mm. 40k. Byelorussian S.S.R. . . . . . 22·00 22·00
MS1911c 156 × 104 mm. 40k. Ukrainian S.S.R. . . . . . . 22·00 22·00

585 M. V. Lomonosov and University

1955. Bicentenary of Lomonosov University. Multicoloured.
1912 40k. Type **585** . . . . . . 1·10 30
1913 1r. Lomonosov University 1·90 55
MS1913a 151 × 108 mm. 40k. Type **585** . . . . 12·00 10·00
MS1913c 151 × 109 mm. 1r. Lomonosov University . . . . 20·00 15·00

586 A. G. Venetsianov (self-portrait) and "The Labours of Spring"

1955. 175th Birth Anniv of Venetsianov (painter). Multicoloured centre.
1914 **586** 1r. black . . . . 2·75 55
MS1914a 151 × 115 mm. No. 1914 (block of four) . . . . 20·00 16·00

587 A. Lyadov

1955. Birth Centenary of Lyadov (composer).
1915 **587** 40k. multicoloured . . . 1·60 55

588 A. S. Popov  **589** Lenin

590 "Capture of Winter Palace" (detail, P. Sokolov-Skalya)

1955. 60th Anniv of Popov's Radio Discoveries. Multicoloured centres.
1916 **588** 40k. blue . . . . 1·50 20
1917 1r. brown . . . . 2·75 50

1955. 38th Anniv of Russian Revolution.
1918 **589** 40k. multicoloured . . . 2·25 1·10
1919 **590** 40k. multicoloured . . . 2·25 1·10
1920 – 1r. multicoloured . . . . 5·00 2·25
DESIGN: As T **590**: 1r. Lenin speaking to revolutionaries (after D. Nalbandyan).

„Сев. полюс"
— Москва
1955 г.
(591)

592 Magnitogorsk

1955. Air. Opening of North Pole Scientific Stations. Nos. 1881/2 optd with T **591**.
1921 – 1r. multicoloured . . . . 9·00 6·00
1922 **576** 2r. black and green . . . 13·50 6·50

1955. 25th Anniv of Magnitogorsk.
1923 **592** 40k. multicoloured . . . 1·60 35

593 Mil Mi-4 Helicopter over Station  **594** Shubin (self-portrait)

1955. North Pole Scientific Stations.
1924 **593** 40k. multicoloured . . . 3·25 30
1925 60k. multicoloured . . . 3·50 65
1926 – 1r. multicoloured . . . . 5·50 1·00
MS1926a 154 × 111 mm. No. 1926 (block of four) . . . . 38·00 20·00
DESIGN: 1r. Meteorologist taking observations.

1955. 150th Death Anniv of Shubin (sculptor).
1927 **594** 40k. multicoloured . . . 90 20
1928 1r. multicoloured . . . . 1·50 40

595 A. N. Krylov  **596** Racing

1956. 10th Death Anniv of Krylov (scientist).
1929 **595** 40k. multicoloured . . . 1·10 20

1956. International Horse Racing.
1930 **596** 40k. sepia and brown . . 1·25 25
1931 60k. blue and green . . . 1·50 30
1932 – 1r. purple and blue . . . 2·75 55
DESIGN—HORIZ: 1r. Trotting.

597 Badge and Stadium

1956. 5th Spartacist Games.
1933 **597** 1r. purple and green . . 1·75 45

598 Atomic Power Station

1956. Foundation of Atomic Power Station of Russian Academy of Sciences.
1934 **598** 25k. multicoloured . . . 85 20
1935 – 60k. yellow, turq & brn 2·00 35
1936 **598** 1r. yellow, red and blue 2·75 70
DESIGN: 60k. Top of atomic reactor.

599 Statue of Lenin (E. Buchetich)  **600** Kh. Abovyan

1956. 20th Communist Party Congress.
1937 **599** 40k. multicoloured . . . 90 35
1938 1r. multicoloured . . . . 1·75 55

1956. 150th Birth Anniv of Khatchatur Abovyan (Armenian writer).
1939 **600** 40k. black on blue . . . 1·10 20

601 Revolutionaries (after N. Tereshchenko)  **602**

1956. 50th Anniv of 1905 Revolution.
1940 **601** 40k. multicoloured . . . 4·25 1·60

ПАВИЛЬОН «УРАЛ»
No. 1941

ПАВИЛЬОН СЕВЕРО-ВОСТОЧНЫХ ОБЛАСТЕЙ
No. 1942

ПАВИЛЬОН ЦЕНТРАЛЬНЫХ ЧЕРНОЗЕМНЫХ ОБЛАСТЕЙ
No. 1943

ПАВИЛЬОН «ЛЕНИНГРАД • СЕВЕРО-ЗАПАД»
No. 1944

ПАВИЛЬОН МОСКОВСКОЙ, ТУЛЬСКОЙ, КАЛУЖСКОЙ, РЯЗАНСКОЙ И БРЯНСКОЙ ОБЛАСТЕЙ
No. 1945

ПАВИЛЬОН БАШКИРСКОЙ АССР
No. 1946

ПАВИЛЬОН ДАЛЬНЕГО ВОСТОКА
No. 1947

ПАВИЛЬОН ТАТАРСКОЙ АССР
No. 1948

ПАВИЛЬОН ЦЕНТРАЛЬНЫХ ОБЛАСТЕЙ
No. 1949

ПАВИЛЬОН ЮНЫХ НАТУРАЛИСТОВ
No. 1950

ПАВИЛЬОН СЕВЕРНОГО КАВКАЗА
No. 1951

ПАВИЛЬОН «СИБИРЬ»
No. 1952

ПАВИЛЬОН «ПОВОЛЖЬЕ»
No. 1953

Inscr at foot as shown above.

1956. Agricultural Exhibition. Multicoloured. Views of Pavilions of U.S.S.R. regions as T **602**. Inscr "BCXB".
1941 1r. Ural . . . . 1·50 40
1942 1r. North East . . . . . . 1·50 40
1943 1r. Central Black Soil Region . . . . 1·50 40
1944 1r. Leningrad . . . . 1·50 40
1945 1r. Moscow-Tula-Kaluga-Ryazan-Bryansk . . . . 1·50 40
1946 1r. Bashkir . . . . 1·50 40
1947 1r. Far East . . . . 1·50 40
1948 1r. Tatar . . . . 1·50 40
1949 1r. Central Regions . . . . 1·50 40
1950 1r. Young Naturalists . . . 1·50 40
1951 1r. North Caucasus . . . . 1·50 40
1952 1r. Siberia . . . . 1·50 40
1953 1r. Volga . . . . 1·50 40

603 N. A. Kasatkin (painter)

1956. Kasatkin Commemoration.
1954 **603** 40k. red 85 25

604 A. E. Arkhipov and Painting "On the Oka River"

1956. Arkhipov Commemoration.
1955 **604** 40k. multicoloured . . . 1·50 20
1956 1r. multicoloured . . . . 2·75 45

605 I. P. Kulibin

1956. 220th Birth Anniv of Kulibin (inventor).
1957 **605** 40k. multicoloured . . . 1·25 35

606 "Fowler" (after Perov)

1956. Perov Commemoration. Inscr "1956". Multicoloured centres.
1958 – 40k. green . . . . 1·75 25
1959 **606** 1r. brown . . . . 3·50 70
1960 – 1r. brown . . . . 3·50 70
DESIGNS—VERT: No. 1958, Self-portrait. HORIZ: No. 1960, "Hunters Resting".

607 Lenin (after P. Vasilev)  **608** N. I. Lobachevsky (after L. Kryukov)

1956. 86th Birth Anniv of Lenin.
1961 **607** 40k. multicoloured . . . 9·25 5·25

1956. Death Cent of Lobachevsky (mathematician).
1962 **608** 40k. brown 80 15

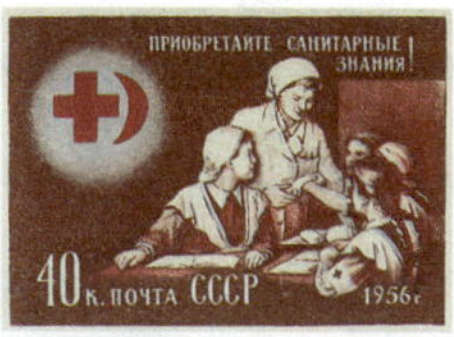

609 Student Nurses

1956. Red Cross.
1963 **609** 40k. red, blue and brown 1·00 30
1964 – 40k. red, olive & turquoise . . . . . 1·00 30
DESIGN—$37\frac{1}{2} \times 25\frac{1}{2}$ mm: No. 1964, Nurse and textile factory.

610 Scientific Station

1956. Air. Opening of North Pole Scientific Station No. 6.
1965 **610** 1r. multicoloured . . . . 4·25 1·40

611 Sechenov (after I. Repin)

1956. 50th Death Anniv (1995) of I. Sechenov (naturalist).
1966 **611** 40k. multicoloured . . . 1·60 35

612 Arsenev

1956. V. K. Arsenev (writer).
1967 **612** 40k. black, violet & pink 2·00 70

613 I. V. Michurin

1956. Birth Centenary of Michurin (naturalist). Multicoloured centres.
1968 **613** 25k. brown 45 15
1969 – 60k. green . . . . 1·10 25
1970 **613** 1r. blue . . . . 2·00 45
DESIGN—47½ × 26½ mm: 60k. Michurin and children.

614 Savrasov (after V. Perov) **615** N. K. Krupskaya (Lenin's wife)

1956. 125th Birth Anniv (1955) of A. K. Savrasov (painter).
1971 **614** 1r. brown and yellow . . 1·50 60

1956. Krupskaya Commemoration.
1972 **615** 40k. brown, black & blue . . . . 1·50 30

616 S. M. Kirov **617** A. A. Blok

1956. 70th Birth Anniv of Kirov (statesman).
1973 **616** 40k. multicoloured . . . 65 15

1956. Blok (poet) Commemoration.
1974 **617** 40k. brown, black & olive 95 15

618 N. S. Leskov

1956. 125th Birth Anniv of Leskov (writer).
1975 **618** 40k. multicoloured . . . 65 15
1976 1r. multicoloured . . . . 1·75 40

619 Factory Building

1956. 25th Anniv of Rostov Agricultural Machinery Works.
1977 **619** 40k. multicoloured . . . 90 25

620 G. N. Fedotova (actress)

1956. Fedotova Commemoration.
1978 **620** 40k. multicoloured . . . 80 25
For similar stamp see No. 2159.

621 P. M. Tretyakov (after I. Repin) and Art Gallery

1956. Centenary of Tretyakov Art Gallery, Moscow.
1979 **621** 40k. multicoloured . . . 2·25 60
1980 – 40k. multicoloured . . . 1·50 50
DESIGN—VERT: No. 1980, "Rooks have arrived" (painting by Savrasov).

622 Relay-race

1956. Spartacist Games.
1981 **622** 10k. red 30 10
1982 – 25k. brown 40 15
1983 – 25k. multicoloured . . . 40 15
1984 – 25k. blue 40 15
1985 – 40k. blue 65 15
1986 – 40k. green 65 15
1987 – 40k. brown and green . . 65 15
1988 – 40k. deep brown, brown and green 65 15
1989 – 40k. red, green and light green 65 15
1990 – 40k. brown 65 15
1991 – 40k. multicoloured . . . 65 15
1992 – 60k. violet . . . . . . 1·75 25
1993 – 60k. violet . . . . . . 1·75 25
1994 – 1r. brown . . . . 3·25 55
DESIGNS—VERT: No. 1982, Volleyball; 1983, Swimming; 1984, Rowing; 1985, Diving; 1989, Flag and stadium; 1990, Tennis; 1991, Medal; 1993, Boxing. HORIZ: No. 1986, Cycle racing; 1987, Fencing; 1988, Football; 1992, Gymnastics; 1994, Netball.

623 Parachutist Landing **624** Construction Work

1956. 3rd World Parachute-jumping Competition.
1995 **623** 40k. multicoloured . . . 1·00 25

1956. Builders' Day.
1996a **624** 40k. orange 65 25
1997 – 60k. brown 80 30
1998 – 1r. blue . . . . 2·50 50
DESIGNS: 60k. Plant construction; 1r. Dam construction.

625 Self-portrait and "Volga River Boatmen"

626 "Reply of the Cossacks to Sultan Mahmoud IV"

1956. 26th Death Anniv of I. E. Repin (artist).
1999 **625** 40k. multicoloured . . . 3·75 60
2000 **626** 1r. multicoloured . . . . 7·25 1·00

627 Robert Burns **628** Ivan Franko

1956. 160th Death Anniv of Burns (Scots poet).
2001 **627** 40k. brown . . . . . . 7·50 5·25
2002 40k. brown and blue . . 5·25 3·25

1956. Birth Cent of Franko (writer) (1st issue).
2003 **628** 40k. purple 85 40
2004 1r. blue . . . . 1·40 50
See also No. 2037.

1956. Lesya Ukrainka Commemoration. As T **615** but portrait of Ukrainka (author).
2005 40k. black, brown and green 85 50

629 M. Aivazov (farmer) **630** Statue of Nestor (M. Antokol)

1956. 148th Birthday of Aivazov. (a) Wrongly inscr "Muhamed" (7 characters).
2006 **629** 40k. green . . . . 23·00 21·00

(b) Corrected to "Makmud" (6 characters).
2006a **629** 40k. green . . . . . . 11·50 8·25

1956. 900th Birth Anniv of Nestor (historian).
2007 **630** 40k. multicoloured . . . 1·10 30
2008 1r. multicoloured . . . . 2·10 50

631 Ivanov (after S. Postnikov)

1956. 150th Birth Anniv of A. A. Ivanov (painter).
2009 **631** 40k. brown and grey . . 85 25

632 Feeding Poultry

1956. Agriculture. Multicoloured.
2010 10k. Type **632** 35 10
2011 10k. Harvesting 35 10
2012 25k. Gathering maize . . . 65 20
2013 40k. Maize field . . . . . 1·25 20
2014 40k. Tractor station . . . . 1·25 20
2015 40k. Cattle grazing . . . . 1·25 20
2016 40k. "Agriculture and Industry" . . . . . . 1·25 20
SIZES: Nos. 2010, 2014/15, 37 × 25½ mm. Nos. 2011/13, 37 × 28 mm. No. 2016, 37 × 21 mm.

633 Mozart **634** Mirnyi Base and Supply Ship "Lena"

1956. Cultural Anniversaries.
2017 40k. blue (Type **633**) . . . . 3·50 60
2018 40k. green (Curie) . . . . . 3·50 60
2019 40k. lilac (Heine) . . . . . 1·50 40
2020 40k. brown (Ibsen) . . . . 1·50 40
2021 40k. green (Dostoevsky) . . 1·50 40
2022 40k. brown (Franklin) . . . 1·50 40
2023 40k. black (Shaw) . . . . . 3·00 60
2024 40k. orange (Sessku-Toyo Oda) . . . . 1·50 40
2025 40k. black (Rembrandt) . . 1·50 40
Nos. 2022/5 are larger, 25 × 38 mm.

1956. Soviet Scientific Antarctic Expedition.
2026 **634** 40k. turquoise, red & grey . . . . 5·50 80

1956. Julia Zhemaite Commemoration. As T **615** but portrait of Zhemaite (author).
2027 40k. green, brown and sepia 1·00 35

635 F. A. Bredikhin **636** G. I. Kotovsky

1956. 125th Birth Anniv of Bredikhin (astronomer).
2028 **635** 40k. multicoloured . . . 5·00 1·25

1956. 75th Birth Anniv of Kotovsky (military leader).
2029a **636** 40k. mauve . . . . . . 1·60 65

637 Shatura Electric Power Station **638** Marshal Suvorov (after Utkin)

1956. 30th Anniv of Shatura Electric Power Station.
2030 **637** 40k. multicoloured . . . 90 35

1956. 225th Birth Anniv of Marshal Suvorov.
2031 **638** 40k. lake and orange . . 85 35
2032 1r. brown and olive . . 1·60 50
2033 3r. black and brown . . 4·25 1·10

639 Kryakutni's Ascent (after G. Savitsky)

1956. 225th Anniv of First Balloon Flight by Kryakutni.
2034 **639** 40k. multicoloured . . . 2·00 55

640 Vasnetsov (after S. Malyutin) and "Dawn at the Voskresenski Gate"

1956. 30th Death Anniv of A. M. Vasnetsov (artist).
2035 **640** 40k. multicoloured . . . 1·60 55

641 Y. M. Shokalsky (oceanographer) **642** Franko (after I. Trush)

1956. Birth Cent of Shokalsky.
2036 **641** 40k. brown and blue . . 2·25 50

1956. Birth Centenary of Franko (writer) (2nd issue).
2037 **642** 40k. green 75 25

643 Indian Temple and Books

644 F. G. Vokov (actor) (after A. Losenko) and State Theatre

1956. Kalidasa (Indian poet) Commemoration.
2038 **643** 40k. red 75 25

1956. Bicentenary of Leningrad State Theatre.
2039 **644** 40k. black, red and yellow 60 20

645 Lomonosov (after L. Miropolsky) at St. Petersburg University

1956. Russian Writers.
2040 **645** 40k. multicoloured . . . 1·00 25
2041 – 40k. multicoloured . . . 1·00 25
2042 – 40k. brown and blue . . 1·00 25
2043 – 40k. olive, brown & black . . . . 1·00 25
2044 – 40k. brown and turquoise . . . . 1·00 25
2045 – 40k. purple and brown 1·00 25
2046 – 40k. olive and blue . . . 1·00 25
DESIGNS: No. 2041, Gorky (after V. Efanov) and scene from "Mother" (novel); 2042, Pushkin and statue of Peter the Great, Leningrad (illustrating poem "Bronze Horseman"); 2043, Rustavely and episode from "The Knight in the Tiger Skin" (poem); 2044, Tolstoy and scene from "War and Peace" (novel); 2045, V. G. Belinsky and titles of literary works; 2046, M. Y. Lermontov and Daryal Pass.
See also Nos. 2076, 2089/90, 2256, 2316/22 and 2458.

646 Vitus Bering and Routes of his Voyages

647 Mendeleev

1956. 275th Birth Anniv of Bering (explorer).
2047 **646** 40k. multicoloured . . . 3·00 50

1957. 50th Death Anniv of Dmitri Mendeleev (chemist).
2048 **647** 40k. brown, grey & black . . . . 2·25 65

648 M. I. Glinka

649 Youth Festival Emblem

1957. Death Centenary of Glinka (composer). Mult.
2049a 40k. Type **648** . . . . . 1·40 25
2050a 1r. Scene from "Ivan Susanin" . . . . . . 2·50 55

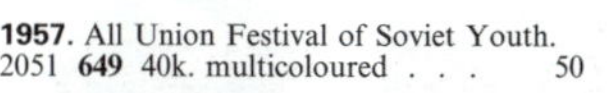

1957. All Union Festival of Soviet Youth.
2051 **649** 40k. multicoloured . . . 50 20

650 Ice Hockey Player

651 Youth Festival Emblem and Pigeon

1957. 23rd World and 35th European Ice Hockey Championships, Moscow.
2052a – 25k. violet 75 15
2053a **650** 40k. blue 90 15
2054a – 60k. green . . . . . . 1·00 30
DESIGNS: 25k. Championship emblem; 60k. Goalkeeper.

1957. 6th World Youth Festival, Moscow (1st issue). Perf or imperf.
2055 **651** 40k. multicoloured . . . 85 15
2056 60k. multicoloured . . . 1·40 30
See also Nos. 2084/7 and 2108/11.

652 Factory Plant

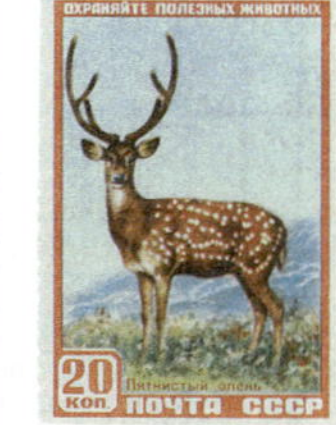
653 Sika Deer

1957. Cent of "Red Proletariat" Plant. Moscow.
2057 **652** 40k. multicoloured . . . 1·00 30

1957. Russian Wildlife. Multicoloured.
2057a 10k. Grey partridge . . . 80 25
2058 15k. Black grouse . . . . 1·00 10
2058a 15k. Polar bear 70 15
2059 20k. Type **653** 75 15
2059a 20k. Brown hare 60 25
2059b 25k. Tiger 75 25
2059c 25k. Wild horse 75 25
2060 30k. Mallard . . . . . . 1·25 25
2061 30k. European bison . . . 75 20
2062 40k. Elk . . . . 1·90 35
2063 40k. Sable . . . . 1·90 35
2063a 40k. Eurasian red squirrel 80 30
2063b 40k. Yellow-throated marten 80 30
2063c 60k. Hazel grouse . . . . 2·00 90
2063d 1r. Mute swan . . . . . . 2·50 1·75
Nos. 2058/a, 2059a/62, 2063a/b and 2063d are horiz.
See also Nos. 2534/6.

654 Vologda Lace-making

655 G. V. Plekhanov

1957. Regional Handicrafts. Multicoloured.
2064 40k. Moscow wood-carving 1·75 40
2065 40k. Woman engraving vase . . . . 1·75 40
2066 40k. Type **654** . . . . . 1·75 40
2067 40k. Northern bone-carving . . . . 1·75 40
2067a 40k. Wood-block engraving 1·25 45
2067b 40k. Turkmen carpet-weaving . . . . 1·25 45

1957. Birth Centenary of Plekhanov (politician).
2068 **655** 40k. plum . . . . 1·00 35

656 A. N. Bakh

657 L. Euler

1957. Birth Centenary of Bakh (biochemist).
2069a **656** 40k. multicoloured . . 1·10 25

1957. 250th Birth Anniv of Euler (mathematician).
2070a **657** 40k. black and purple 1·50 35

658 Lenin in Meditation

659 Dr. William Harvey

1957. 87th Birth Anniv of Lenin. Multicoloured.
2071 40k. Type **658** . . . . . . 1·00 20
2072 40k. Lenin carrying pole . . 1·00 20
2073 40k. Talking with soldier and sailor . . . . 1·00 20

1957. 300th Death Anniv of Dr. William Harvey (discoverer of circulation of blood).
2074 **659** 40k. brown 75 15

660 M. A. Balakirev

661 12th-century Narrator

1957. 120th Birth Anniv of Balakirev (composer).
2075 **660** 40k. black . . . . 1·25 20

1957. "The Tale of the Host of Igor".
2076 **661** 40k. multicoloured . . . 80 20

662 Agricultural Medal

663 A. I. Herzen (after N. Ge) and N. P. Ogarev (after M. Lemmel) (founders)

1957. Cultivation of Virgin Soil.
2077 **662** 40k. multicoloured . . . 1·10 30

1957. Centenary of Publication of Magazine "Kolokol".
2078 **663** 40k. brown, black & blue . . . . 1·00 30

664 Monument

250 лет Ленинграда
(665)

1957. 250th Anniv of Leningrad. Vert designs as T **664** and stamps as Nos. 1818 and 1820 optd as T **665**.
2079 **664** 40k. green 50 15
2080 – 40k. violet 50 15
2081 – 40k. brown 65 15
2082 **551** 1r. brown on green . . . 1·40 25
2083 – 1r. green on salmon . . 1·40 25
DESIGNS: No. 2080, Nevsky Prospect, Leningrad; No. 2081, Lenin Statue.

666 Youths with Banner

1957. 6th World Youth Festival, Moscow (2nd issue). Multicoloured. Perf or imperf.
2084 10k. Type **666** 30 10
2084c 20k. Sculptor with statue 50 15
2085 25k. Type **666** 80 25
2086 40k. Dancers 85 25
2087 1r. Festival emblem and fireworks over Moscow State University . . . . 1·10 50

667 A. M. Lyapunov

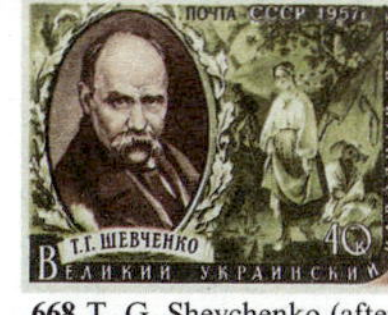
668 T. G. Shevchenko (after I. Repin) and Scene from "Katharina"

1957. Birth Centenary of Lyapunov (mathematician).
2088 **667** 40k. brown . . . . . . 5·50 2·75

1957. 19th-Century Writers. Multicoloured.
2089 40k. Type **668** 85 20
2090 40k. N. G. Chernyshevsky and scene from "What is to be Done?" 85 20

669 Henry Fielding

670 Racing Cyclists

1957. 250th Birth Anniv of Fielding (novelist).
2091 **669** 40k. multicoloured . . . 50 20

1957. 10th International Cycle Race.
2092 **670** 40k. multicoloured . . . 1·25 25

671 Interior of Observatory

1957. International Geophysical Year (1st issue).
2093 **671** 40k. brown, yellow and blue . . . . 1·75 45
2094 – 40k. indigo, yellow and blue . . . . 2·50 45
2095 – 40k. violet and lavender 2·25 45
2095a – 40k. blue . . . . . . 2·25 30
2095b – 40k. green . . . . . . 2·50 40
2095c – 40k. yellow and blue 2·25 30
DESIGNS—As T **671**: No. 2094, Meteor in sky; 2095a, Malakhit radar scanner and balloon (meteorology); 2095b, "Zarya" (non-magnetic research schooner) (geo-magnetism); 2095c, Northern Lights and C-180 camera. 15 × 21 mm: No. 2095, Rocket.
See also Nos. 2371/3a.

672 Gymnast

1957. 3rd International Youth Games.
2096 **672** 20k. brown and blue . . 30 15
2097 – 25k. red and green . . . 35 15
2098 – 40k. violet and red . . . 70 30
2099 – 40k. olive, red and green 70 30
2100 – 60k. brown and blue . . 1·60 50
DESIGNS—As Type **672**: No. 2097, Wrestlers; 2098, Young athletes; 2099, Moscow Stadium; 2100, Throwing the javelin.

673 Football

674 Yanka Kupala

1957. Russian Successes at Olympic Games, Melbourne.
2101 – 20k. brown, blue & black 35 15
2102 – 20k. red and green . . . 35 15
2103 – 25k. blue and orange . . 40 20
2104 **673** 40k. multicoloured . . . 75 20
2105 – 40k. brown and purple 75 20
2106 – 60k. brown and violet 1·00 50
DESIGNS—VERT: No. 2101, Throwing the javelin; 2102, Running; 2103, Gymnastics; 2105, Boxing; 2106, Weightlifting.

1957. 75th Birth Anniv of Kupala (poet).
2107 **674** 40k. brown . . . . . . 4·00 1·75

675 Moscow State University

1957. 6th World Youth Festival (3rd issue). Moscow Views.

2108 – 40k. black and brown . . 55 15
2109 – 40k. black and purple . . 55 15
2110 – 1r. black and blue . . . 1·25 30
2111 **675** 1r. black and red . . . . 1·25 30

DESIGNS—HORIZ: No. 2108, Kremlin; 2109, Stadium; 2110, Bolshoi State Theatre.

676 Lenin Library

1957. Int Philatelic Exn, Moscow. Perf or imperf.

2112 **676** 40k. turquoise 75 20
MS2112c 144 × 101 mm. **676** 40k. × 2 blue. Imperf . . . . 35·00 45·00

677 Dove of Peace encircling Globe

678 P. Beranger

1957. "Defence of Peace".

2113 **677** 40k. multicoloured . . . 1·10 40
2114 1r. multicoloured . . . . 2·25 95

1957. Birth Centenary of Clara Zetkin (German revolutionary). As T **615** but portrait of Zetkin.

2115 40k. multicoloured . . . . 1·10 35

1957. Death Centenary of Beranger (French poet).

2116 **678** 40k. green . . . . 1·10 30

679 Krengholm Factory, Narva

680 Factory Plant and Statue of Lenin (M. Kharlamev)

1957. Centenary of Krengholm Textile Factory, Narva, Estonia.

2117 **679** 40k. brown . . . . . . 1·10 30

1957. Centenary of Krasny Vyborzhetz Plant, Leningrad.

2118 **680** 40k. blue 50 25

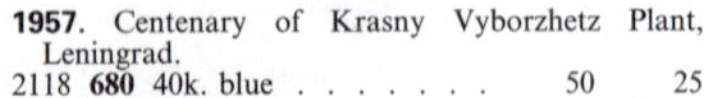

681 Stasov (after I. Repin)

682 Pigeon with Letter

1957. 50th Death Anniv of Stasov (art critic).

2119 **681** 40k. brown 55 15
2120 1r. blue . . . . . . 1·40 20

1957. International Correspondence Week.

2121 **682** 40k. blue 35 20
2122 60k. purple 55 25

683 K. E. Tsiolkovsky

1957. Birth Centenary of Tsiolkovsky (scientist).

2123 **683** 40k. multicoloured . . . 4·00 70

684 Congress Emblem

1957. 4th World T.U.C., Leipzig.

2124 **684** 40k. blue on blue . . . 45 20

685 Students

686 Workers and Emblem (Ukraine)

1957. 40th Anniv of Russian Revolution. (a) 1st issue. As T **685**. Multicoloured. Perf or imperf.

2125 10k. Type **685** 20 10
2126 40k. Railway worker (horiz) 70 20
2127 40k. Portrait of Lenin on banner 45 10
2128 40k. Lenin and workers with banners 45 10
2129 60k. Harvester (horiz) . . . 1·25 60

1957. 40th Anniv of Russian Revolution (2nd issue). Multicoloured.

2130 40k. Type **686** 65 30
2131 40k. Estonia 65 30
2132 40k. Uzbekistan 65 30
2133 40k. R.S.F.S.R. (horiz) . . . 1·10 30
2134 40k. Belorussia (horiz) . . . 65 30
2135 40k. Lithuania (horiz) . . . 65 30
2136 40k. Armenia (horiz) . . . 65 30
2137 40k. Azerbaijan (horiz) . . . 65 30
2138 40k. Georgia (horiz) 65 30
2139 40k. Kirghizia (horiz) . . . 65 30
2140 40k. Turkmenistan (horiz) 65 30
2141 40k. Tadzhikistan (horiz) . . 65 30
2142 40k. Kazakhstan (horiz) . . 65 30
2143 40k. Latvia (horiz) 65 30
2144 40k. Moldavia (horiz) . . . 65 30

687 Lenin (after G. Goldstein)

688 Satellite encircling Globe

1957. 40th Anniv of Russian Revolution (3rd issue). As T **687**.

2145 **687** 40k. blue . . . . 1·50 65
2146 – 60k. red . . . . 2·25 95

DESIGN—HORIZ: 60k. Lenin at desk.

1957. 40th Anniv of Russian Revolution (4th issue). Imperf.

MS2146a 145 × 99 mm. Nos. 2079/80 and 1816 . . . . 9·75 5·00
MS2146b 144 × 101 mm. Nos. 2126/7 and 2129 . . . . 9·75 5·00

1957. Launching of 1st Artifical Satellite.

2147 **688** 40k. indigo on blue . . . 3·25 85
2148 40k. blue . . . . 3·25 85

689 Meteor Falling

690 Kuibyshev Power Station Turbine

1957. Sikhote-Alin Meteor.

2149 **689** 40k. multicoloured . . . 2·75 1·10

1957. All Union Industrial Exhibition (1st issue).

2150 **690** 40k. brown 75 20

See also Nos. 2168.

4/X-57 г. Первый в мире искусств. спутник Земли

(691)

692 Soviet War Memorial, Berlin (after Ye. Bunchetich)

1957. 1st Artificial Satellite of the World. Optd with T **691**.

2151 **683** 40k. multicoloured . . . 35·00 22·00

1957. Bicentenary of Academy of Arts, Moscow.

2152 – 40k. black on salmon . . 40 10
2153 **692** 60k. black 80 15
2154 – 1r. black on pink . . . . 1·60 35

DESIGNS—25½ × 37½ mm: 40k. Academy and portraits of K. Bryullov, I. Repin and V. Surikov (after I. Repin). 21½ × 32 mm: 1r. "Worker and Collective Farmer", Moscow (sculpture, Vera Mukhina).

693 Arms of Ukraine

694 Garibaldi

1957. 40th Anniv of Ukraine S.S.R.

2155 **693** 40k. multicoloured . . . 85 15

1957. 150th Birth Anniv of Garibaldi.

2156 **694** 40k. purple, maroon and green 75 20

695 Edvard Grieg

696 Borovikovsky (after I. Bugaevsky-Blagodarny)

1957. 50th Death Anniv of Grieg (composer).

2157 **695** 40k. black on salmon . . 1·25 20

1957. Birth Bicent of Borovikovsky (painter).

2158 **696** 40k. brown 80 20

1967. M. N. Ermolova (actress) Commemoration. As T **620** but portrait of Ermolova.

2159 40k. brown and violet . . . 1·00 40

698 Kolas

699 Mitskyavichyus-Kapsukas

700 G. Z. Bashindzhagian

1957. 75th Birth Anniv of Yakyb Kolas (poet).

2160 **698** 40k. black . . . . . . 2·40 1·50

1957. 22nd Death Anniv of V. S. Mitskyavichyus-Kapsukas (Communist Party leader).

2161 **699** 40k. brown . . . . . . 2·25 1·10

1957. Bashindzhagian (artist) Commemoration.

2162 **700** 40k. brown . . . . . . 2·25 1·10

701 Kuibyshev Hydro-electric Station

702 "To the Stars" (Ye. Buchetich)

1957. 40th Anniv of Kuibyshev Hydro-electric Station.

2163 **701** 40k. blue on flesh . . . 1·10 25

1957. Launching of 2nd Artificial Satellite.

2164 **702** 20k. red and black . . . 1·00 10
2165 40k. green and black . . 1·50 15
2166 60k. brown and black . . 2·00 25
2167 1r. blue and black . . . 3·00 60

703 Allegory of Industry

704 Tsi Bai-shi

1958. All Union Industrial Exn (2nd issue).

2168 **703** 60k. red, black & lavender . . . . . . 1·00 30

1958. Rosa Luxemburg Commemoration. As T **615** but portrait of Luxemburg (German revolutionary).

2169 40k. brown and blue . . . . 1·00 35

1958. Tsi Bai-shi (Chinese artist) Commem.

2170 **704** 40k. violet 55 20

705 Linnaeus (Carl von Linne)

706 Tolstoi

1958. 250th Birth Anniv of Linnaeus.

2171 **705** 40k. brown . . . . . . 3·25 1·10

1958. 75th Birth Anniv of A. N. Tolstoi (writer).

2172 **706** 40k. bistre 65 20

707 Soldier, Sailor and Airman

708 E. Charents

1958. 40th Anniv of Red Army. Multicoloured.

2173 25k. Battle of Narva, 1918 40 15
2174 40k. Type **707** 60 20
2175 40k. Soldier and blast-furnaceman (vert) 60 20
2176 40k. Soldier and sailor (vert) 60 20
2177 60k. Storming the Reichstag, 1945 . . . . 1·75 60

1958. Charents (Armenian poet) Commemoration.

2178 **708** 40k. brown . . . . . . 2·40 1·40

709 Henry W. Longfellow

710 Blake

1958. 150th Birth Anniv of Longfellow.

2179 **709** 40k. black . . . . 2·40 1·40

1958. Birth Bicentenary of William Blake (poet).

2180 **710** 40k. black . . . . 2·50 1·40

711 Tchaikovsky

712 Admiral Rudnev and Cruiser "Varyag"

1958. Tchaikovsky International Music Competition, Moscow.

2181 **711** 40k. multicoloured . . 1·25 30
2182 – 40k. multicoloured . . 1·25 30
2183a – 1r. purple and green . . 3·50 75

DESIGNS—HORIZ: No. 2182, Scene from "Swan Lake" ballet. VERT: No. 2183, Pianist, violinist and inset portrait of Tchaikovsky.

1958. 45th Death Anniv of Admiral Rudnev.
2184 **712** 40k. multicoloured . . . 1·90 45

713 Gorky (after I. Brodsky)

714 Congress Emblem and Spassky Tower, Kremlin

1958. 90th Death Anniv of Maksim Gorky (writer).
2185 **713** 40k. multicoloured . . . 1·00 20

1958. 13th Young Communists' League Congress, Moscow.
2186 **714** 40k. violet on pink . . . 65 15
2187 60k. red on flesh . . . . 1·00 25

715 Russian Pavilion

716 J. A. Komensky ("Comenius")

1958. Brussels Int Exhibition. Perf or imperf.
2188 **715** 10k. multicoloured . . . 20 10
2189 40k. multicoloured . . . 65 15

1958. Komensky Commem.
2190 **716** 40k. green . . . . 3·25 1·10

717 Lenin

200 лет Академии художеств СССР. 1957
(**718**)

1958. Lenin Commemoration.
2191 **717** 40k. blue 60 10
2192 60k. red 85 15
2193 1r. brown . . . . 1·60 40

1958. Bicentenary of Russian Academy of Artists. Optd with T **718**.
2194 **557** 40k. multicoloured . . . 6·00 1·75

719 C. Goldoni

720 Lenin Prize Medal

1958. 250th Birth Anniv of C. Goldoni (Italian dramatist).
2195 **719** 40k. brown and blue . . 1·00 15

1958. Lenin Prize Medal.
2196 **720** 40k. red, yellow & brown 80 15

721 Karl Marx

1958. Karl Marx Commemoration.
2197 **721** 40k. brown 85 15
2198 60k. blue . . . . 1·00 25
2199 1r. red . . . . 2·10 35

722 Federation Emblem

723 Radio Beacon, Airliner and Freighter

1958. 4th International Women's Federation Congress.
2200 **722** 40k. blue and black . . 65 15
2201 60k. blue and black . . 1·00 20

1958. Radio Day.
2202 **723** 40k. green and red . . . 2·25 30

724 Chavchavadze (after G. Gabashvili)

725 Flags of Communist Countries

1958. Chavchavadze (Georgian poet) Commem.
2203 **724** 40k. black and blue . . 75 25

1958. Socialist Countries' Postal Ministers Conference, Moscow.
2204 **725** 40k. multicoloured (A) 17·00 6·25
2205 40k. multicoloured (B) 11·00 5·50
Central flag to left of inscription is in red, white and mauve. (A) has red at top and white at foot, (B) is vice versa.

726 Camp Bugler

727 Negro, European and Chinese Children

1958. "Pioneers" Day. Inscr "1958".
2206 **726** 10k. multicoloured . . . 35 10
2207 – 25k. multicoloured . . . 50 20
DESIGN: 25k. Pioneer with model airplane.

1958. International Children's Day. Inscr "1958".
2208 **727** 40k. multicoloured . . . 65 20
2209 – 40k. multicoloured . . . 65 20
DESIGN: No. 2209, Child with toys, and atomic bomb.

728 Fooballers and Globe

729 Rimsky-Korsakov

1958. World Cup Football Championship, Sweden. Perf or imperf.
2210 **728** 40k. multicoloured . . . 85 20
2211 60k. multicoloured . . . 1·40 40

1958. Rimsky-Korsakov (composer) Commem.
2212 **729** 40k. brown and blue . . 1·50 20

730 Athlete

1958. 14th World Gymnastic Championships, Moscow. Inscr "XIV". Multicoloured.
2213 40k. Type **730** 60 15
2214 40k. Gymnast 60 15

731 Young Construction Workers

1958. Russian Youth Day.
2215 **731** 40k. orange and blue . . 50 15
2216 60k. orange and green 60 20

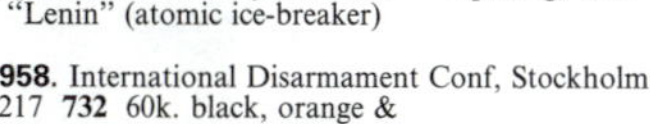
732 Atomic Bomb, Globe, Sputniks, Atomic Symbol and "Lenin" (atomic ice-breaker)

733 Kiev Arsenal Uprising, 1918

1958. International Disarmament Conf, Stockholm.
2217 **732** 60k. black, orange & blue . . . . 3·50 65

1958. 40th Anniv of Ukrainian Communist Party.
2218 **733** 40k. violet and red . . . 1·10 20

734 Silhouette of Moscow State University

1958. 5th Int Architects Union Congress, Moscow.
2219 **734** 40k. blue and red . . . 90 15
2220 – 60k. multicoloured . . . 1·40 25
MS2220a 105 × 143 mm. Nos. 2219/20. Imperf . . . . . 13·00 9·00
DESIGN—VERT: 60k. "U.I.A. Moscow 1958" in square panel of bricks and "V" in background.

735 Sadruddin Aini

1958. 80th Birth Anniv of Sadruddin Aini (Tadzhik writer).
2221 **735** 40k. red, black and buff 55 15

736 Third Artificial Satellite

737 Conference Emblem

1958. Launching of 3rd Artificial Satellite.
2222a **736** 40k. red, blue and green 1·60 50

1958. 1st World T.U. Young Workers' Conf, Prague.
2223 **737** 40k. blue and purple . . 40 20

738 Tupolev Tu-110 Jetliner

1958. Civil Aviation. Perf or imperf.
2224 – 20k. black, red and blue 50 10
2225 – 40k. black, red and green 75 15
2226 – 40k. black, red and blue 75 15
2227 – 60k. red, buff and blue 80 20
2228 **738** 60k. black and red . . . 80 20
2229 – 1r. black, red and orange 2·00 30
2230 – 2r. black, red and purple 2·75 45
DESIGNS—Russian aircraft flying across globe: No. 2224, Ilyushin Il-14M; 2225, Tupolev Tu-104; 2226, Tupolev Tu-114 Rossiya; 2229, Antonov An-10 Ukraina; 2230, Ilyushin Il-18B; No. 2227, Global air routes.

739 L. A. Kulik (scientist)

1958. 50th Anniv of Tunguz Meteor.
2231 **739** 40k. multicoloured . . . 2·25 40

740 Crimea Observatory

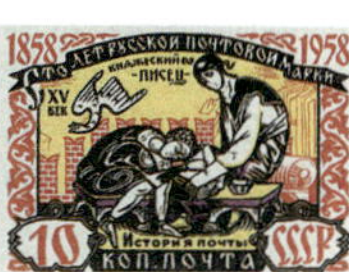
741 15th-century Scribe

1958. 10th International Astronomical Union Congress, Moscow.
2232 **740** 40k. turquoise and brown . . . . 1·25 20
2233 – 60k. yellow, violet & blue . . . . 1·60 30
2234 – 1r. brown and blue . . . 2·25 50
DESIGNS—HORIZ: 60k. Moscow University. VERT: 1r. Telescope of Moscow Observatory.

1958. Centenary of 1st Russian Postage Stamp.
2235 **741** 10k. multicoloured . . . 15 10
2236 – 10k. multicoloured . . . 15 10
2237 – 25k. blue, black and green 30 10
2238 – 25k. black and blue . . 30 10
2239 – 40k. brown, purple & sep 50 15
2240 – 40k. lake and brown . . 50 15
2241 – 40k. black, orange and red 50 15
2242 – 60k. turquoise, blk & vio 1·75 40
2243 – 60k. black, turquoise and purple . . . . . . 1·25 35
2244 – 1r. multicoloured . . . . 1·75 50
2245 – 1r. purple, black and orange . . . . 2·25 65
MS2245a Nos. 2235/8 and 2240. Imperf . . . . 7·50 5·00
MS2245b Nos. 2239 and 2242/3. Imperf . . . . 15·00 7·50
DESIGNS—HORIZ: No. 2236, 16th-century courier; 2237, Ordin-Nashchokin (17th-century postal administrator) (after Kh. Gusikov) and postal sleigh coach; 2238, 18th-century mail coach; 2239, Reproduction of Lenin portrait stamp of 1947; 2240, 19th-century postal troika (three-horse sleigh); 2241, Tupolev Tu-104 jetliner; 2242, Parcel post train; 2243, V. N. Podbelsky (postal administrator, 1918–20) and postal scenes; 2244, Parcel post Tupolev Tu-104; 2245, Globe and modern forms of mail transport.

741a Facade of Exhibition Building

742 Vladimir Gateway

1958. Stamp Cent Philatelic Exhibition, Leningrad.
2246 **741a** 40k. brown & lt brown 55 20

1958. 850th Anniv of Town of Vladimir. Mult.
2247 40k. Type **742** 50 15
2248 60k. Street scene in Vladimir 90 20

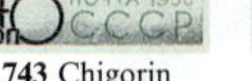
743 Chigorin

745 Red Cross Nurse and Patient

1958. 50th Death Anniv of Mikhail Ivanovich Chigorin (chess player).
2249 **743** 40k. green and black . . 1·75 20

1958. 40th Anniv of Red Cross and Crescent Societies.
2254 **745** 40k. multicoloured . . . 85 20
2255 – 40k. red, yellow and brown 85 20
DESIGN: No. 2255, Convalescent home.

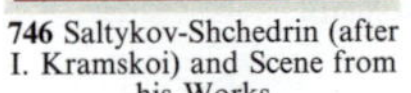

746 Saltykov-Shchedrin (after I. Kramskoi) and Scene from his Works

747 V. Kapnist (after A. Osipov)

1958. 69th Death Anniv of Mikhail Saltykov-Shchedrin (writer).
2256 **746** 40k. black and purple . . 70 20
For similar stamps see Nos. 2316/22 and 2458.

1958. Birth Bicentenary of V. Kapnist (poet).
2257 **747** 40k. black and blue . . 1·10 20

748 Yerevan, Armenia

1958. Republican Capitals.
2258 40k. brown (T **748**) 70 20
2259 40k. violet (Baku, Azerbaijan) 70 20
2260 40k. brown (Minsk, Byelorussia) 70 20
2261 40k. blue (Tbilisi, Georgia) 70 20
2262 40k. green (Tallin, Estonia) 70 20
2263 40k. green (Alma-Ata, Kazakhstan) 70 20
2264 40k. blue (Frunze, Kirgizia) 70 20
2265 40k. brown (Riga, Latvia) 70 20
2266 40k. red (Vilnius, Lithuania) 70 20
2267 40k. bistre (Kishinev, Moldavia) 70 20
2268 40k. violet (Moscow, R.S.F.S.R.) 70 20
2269 40k. blue (Stalinabad, Tadzhikistan) 70 20
2270 40k. green (Ashkhabad, Turkmenistan) 70 20
2271 40k. mauve (Kiev, Ukraine) 70 20
2272 40k. black (Tashkent, Uzbekistan) 70 20
See also No. 2940.

749 Open Book, Torch, Lyre and Flowers

750 Rudaki

1958. Asian-African Writers' Conference, Tashkent.
2273 **749** 40k. orange, black and olive . . . . 1·00 15

1958. 1100th Birth Anniv of Rudaki (Tadzhik poet and musician).
2274 **750** 40k. multicoloured . . . 60 15

751 Statue of Founder Vakhtang I Gorgasal (E. Amashukeli)

1958. 1500th Anniv of Founding of Tbilisi (Georgian capital).
2275 **751** 40k. multicoloured . . . 1·25 30

752 Chelyabinsk Tractor Plant

1958. 25th Anniv of Industrial Plants.
2276 **752** 40k. green and yellow . . 80 20
2277 – 40k. blue and light blue 55 20
2278 – 40k. lake and light orange 80 20
DESIGNS: No. 2277, Ural machine construction plant; No. 2278, Zaporozhe foundry plant.

753 Young Revolutionary

754 Marx and Lenin (bas-relief)

1958. 40th Anniv of Young Communists League. Multicoloured.
2279 10k. Type **753** 20 10
2280 20k. Riveters 30 10
2281 25k. Soldier 40 15
2282 40k. Harvester 60 15
2283 60k. Builder . . . . 1·00 20
2284 1r. Students . . . . 2·40 75

1958. 41st Anniv of October Revolution.
2285 **754** 40k. black, yellow and red 85 25
2286 – 1r. multicoloured . . . . 1·10 40
DESIGN—HORIZ: 1r. Lenin (after N. Andreev) with student, peasant and miner.

755 "Human Rights"

756 Yesenin

1958. 10th Anniv of Declaration of Human Rights.
2287 **755** 60k. blue, black and buff 70 20

1958. 30th Death Anniv of Sergei Yesenin (poet).
2288 **756** 40k. multicoloured . . . 55 20

757 Kuan Han-ching

758 Ordzhonikidze

1958. Kuan Han-ching (Chinese playwright) Commemoration.
2289 **757** 40k. black and blue . . 55 20

1958. 21st Death Anniv of G. K. Ordzhonikidze (statesman).
2290 **758** 40k. multicoloured . . . 70 15

759 John Milton

760 Lenin's Statue, Minsk (M. Manizes)

1958. 350th Birth Anniv of John Milton (poet).
2291 **759** 40k. brown . . . . . . 1·10 15

1958. 40th Anniv of Byelorussian Republic.
2292 **760** 40k. brown, grey and red 70 15

761 Fuzuli

762 Census Emblem

1958. Fuzuli (Azerbaijan poet). Commemoration.
2293 **761** 40k. bistre and turquoise 1·00 15

1958. All Union Census, 1959. Multicoloured.
2294 40k. Type **762** 35 15
2295 40k. Census official with worker's family 35 15

763 Eleonora Duse

764 Rule

1958. Birth Centenary of Eleonora Duse (Italian actress).
2296 **763** 40k. black, grey and green . . . . 1·00 20

1958. Death Centenary of K. F. Rule (naturalist).
2297 **764** 40k. black and blue . . 1·00 30

765 Atomic Ice-breaker "Lenin"

766 Moon Rocket and Sputniks

1958. All-Union Industrial Exhibition. Mult.
2298 40k. Type **765** . . . . . . 2·50 65
2299 60k. Class TE 3 diesel-electric frieght locomotive 4·75 75

1959. 21st Communist Party Congress, Moscow.
2300 – 40k. multicoloured . . . 55 25
2301 – 60k. multicoloured . . . 65 40
2302 **766** 1r. multicoloured . . . . 2·75 80
DESIGNS: 40k. Lenin (after N. Andreev), Red Banner and Kremlin view; 60k. Workers beside Lenin hydro-electric plant, Volga River.

767 E. Torricelli

768 Ice Skater

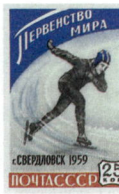

1959. 350th Birth Anniv of Torricelli (physicist).
2303 **767** 40k. black and green . . 1·00 20

1959. Women's World Ice Skating Championships, Sverdlovsk.
2304 **768** 25k. multicoloured . . . 50 10
2305 40k. black, blue and grey 85 20

769 Charles Darwin

770 N. Gamaleya

1959. 150th Birth Anniv of Charles Darwin (naturalist).
2306 **769** 40k. brown and blue . . 1·10 15

1959. Birth Centenary of Gamaleya (microbiologist).
2307 **770** 40k. black and red . . . 1·10 25

771 Sholem Aleichem

Победа баскетбольной команды СССР. Чили 1959 г.

(**772**)

1959. Birth Centenary of Aleichem (Jewish writer).
2308 **771** 40k. brown 90 20

1959. Russian (Unofficial) Victory in World Basketball Championships, Chile. No. 1851 optd with T **772**.
2309 1r. brown and drab . . . . 9·50 8·00

1959. Birth Bicent of Robert Burns. Optd **1759 1959**.
2310 **627** 40k. brown and blue . . 17·00 15·00

774 Selma Lagerlof

775 P. Cvirka

1959. Birth Centenary of Selma Lagerlof (Swedish writer).
2311 **774** 40k. black, brown and cream 95 20

1959. 50th Birth Anniv of Cvirka (Lithuanian poet).
2312 **775** 40k. black and red on yellow 55 15

776 F. Joliot-Curie (scientist)

777 Popov and Polar Rescue by Ice-breaker "Ermak"

1959. Joliot-Curie Commemoration.
2313 **776** 40k. black and turquoise 1·25 30

1959. Birth Centenary of A. S. Popov (radio pioneer).
2314 **777** 40k. brown, black & blue . . . . 1·00 40
2315 – 60k. multicoloured . . . 1·50 55
DESIGN: 60k. Popov and radio tower.

1959. Writers as T **746**. Inscr "1959".
2316 40k. grey, black and red . . 1·10 20
2317 40k. brown, sepia and yellow . . . . 1·10 20
2318 40k. brown and violet . . . 1·10 20
2319 40k. multicoloured . . . . 1·10 20
2320 40k. black, olive and yellow 1·10 20
2321 40k. multicoloured 90 90
2322 40k. slate and violet . . . . 1·10 20
PORTRAITS (with scene from works): No. 2316, Anton Chekhov; 2317, Ivan Krylov (after K. Bryullov); 2318, Aleksandr Ostrovsky; 2319, Aleksandr Griboedov (after I. Kramskoi); 2320, Nikolai Gogol (after F. Moller); 2321, Sergei Aksakov (after I. Kramskoi); 2322, Aleksei Koltsov (after K. Gorbunov).

778 Saadi (Persian poet)

1959. Saadi Commemoration.
2323 **778** 40k. black and blue . . 55 15

779 Orbeliani (Georgian writer)

780 "Hero riding Dolphin"

1959. Orbeliani Commemoration.
2324 **779** 40k. black and red . . . 55 15

1959. Birth Tercentenary of Ogata Korin (Japanese artist).
2325 **780** 40k. multicoloured . . . 2·50 2·00

781 "Rossiya" on Odessa-Batum Service

1959. Russian Liners. Multicoloured.
2326 10k. "Sovetsky Soyuz" on Vladivostok–Kamchatka service 30 15
2327 20k. "Feliks Dzerzhinsky" on Odessa–Latakia service 50 15
2328 40k. Type **781** 80 15
2329 40k. "Kooperatsiya" on Murmansk–Tyksi service 80 15

2330 60k. "Mikhail Kalinin" leaving Leningrad . . . . 1·10 20
2331 1r. "Baltika" on Leningrad–London service . . . . . 1·50 40

782 Trajectory of Moon Rocket

783 Lenin

1959. Launching of Moon Rocket. Inscr "2-1-1959".
2332 **782** 40k. brown and pink . . 1·00 30
2333 – 40k. blue and light blue 1·00 30
DESIGN: No. 2333, Preliminary route of moon rocket after launching.

1959. 89th Birth Anniv of Lenin.
2334 **783** 40k. brown . . . . . . 1·00 35

784 M. Cachin

785 Youths with Banner

1959. 90th Birth Anniv of Marcel Cachin (French communist leader).
2335 **784** 60k. brown 90 30

1959. 10th Anniv of World Peace Movement.
2336 **785** 40k. multicoloured . . . 65 30

786 A. von Humboldt

1959. Death Centenary of Alexander von Humboldt (German naturalist).
2337 **786** 40k. brown and violet 1·00 20

787 Haydn

788 Mountain Climbing

1959. 150th Death Anniv of Haydn (Austrian composer).
2338 **787** 40k. brown and blue . . 1·25 20

1959. Tourist Publicity. Multicoloured.
2339 40k. Type **788** 75 25
2340 40k. Map reading 75 25
2341 40k. Cross country skiing 75 25
2342 40k. Canoeing (horiz) . . . 75 25

789 Exhibition Emblem and New York Coliseum

790 Statue of I. Repin (painter), Moscow (M. Manizer)

1959. Russian Scientific, Technological and Cultural Exhibition, New York.
2343 **789** 20k. multicoloured . . . 35 15
2344 40k. multicoloured . . . 70 20
MS2344a 61 × 76 mm. As No. 2344 but larger. Imperf . . . . . . 6·50 4·50

1959. Cultural Celebrities. Inscr "1959". Statues in black.
2345 **790** 10k. ochre 15 10
2346 – 10k. red 15 10
2347 – 20k. lilac 40 10
2348 – 25k. turquoise 65 15
2349 – 60k. green 90 20
2350 – 1r. blue . . . . 1·40 50
STATUES: 10k. (No. 2346), Lenin, Ulanovsk (M. Manizer); 80k. V. Mayakosky (poet), Moscow (A. Kibalnikov); 25k Aleksandr Pushkin (writer), Leningrad, (M. Anikushin; 60k. Maksim Gorky (writer), Moscow (Vera Mukhina); 1r. Tchaikovsky (composer), Moscow (Vera Mukhina).

791 Russian Sturgeon

792 Louis Braille

1959. Fisheries Protection.
2350a – 20k. black and blue . . 40 10
2350b – 25k. brown and lilac . . 50 10
2351 **791** 40k. black and turquoise 70 20
2351a – 40k. purple and mauve 90 20
2352 – 60k. black and blue . . 1·40 40
DESIGNS: 20k. Zander; 25k. Northern fur seals; 40k. (No. 2351a), Common whitefish; 60k. Chum salmon and map.

1959. 150th Birth Anniv of Braille (inventor of Braille).
2353 **792** 60k. brown, yell & turq 70 25

793 Musa Djalil (Tatar poet)

794 Vaulting

1959. Djalil Commemoration.
2354 **793** 40k. black and violet . . 65 15

1959. 2nd Russian Spartakiad. Inscr "1959".
2355 **794** 15k. grey and purple . . 25 10
2356 – 25k. grey, brown & green 45 10
2357 – 30k. olive and red . . . 55 15
2358 – 60k. grey, blue and yellow 95 30
DESIGNS—HORIZ: 25k. Running; 60k. Water polo. VERT: 30k. Athletes supporting Spartakiad emblem.

795

796 Steel Worker

1959. 2nd International T.U. Conference, Leipzig.
2359 **795** 40k. red, blue and yellow 65 15

1959. Seven Year Plan.
2360 – 10k. red, blue and violet 10 10
2361 – 10k. lt red, dp red & yell 10 10
2362 – 15k. red, yellow & brn 15 10
2363 – 15k. brown, green & bis 15 10
2364 – 20k. red, yellow & green 25 10
2365 – 20k. multicoloured . . 25 10
2366 – 30k. red, flesh & purple 40 10
2366a – 30k. multicoloured . . 40 10
2367 **796** 40k. orange, yellow & bl 50 15
2368 – 40k. red, pink and blue 50 15
2369 – 60k. red, blue and yellow 95 35
2370 – 60k. red, buff and blue 95 35
DESIGNS: 2360, Chemist; 2361, Spassky Tower, hammer and sickle; 2362, Builder's labourer; 2363, Farm girl; 2364, Machine minder; No. 2365, Tractor driver; 2366, Oil technician; 2366a, Cloth production; . 2368, Coal miner; 2369, Iron moulder; 2370, Power station.

797 Glaciologist

798 Novgorod

1959. International Geophysical Year (2nd issue).
2371 **797** 10k. turquoise 60 15
2372 – 25k. red and blue . . . 1·25 15
2373 – 40k. red and blue . . . 2·75 20
2373a – 1r. blue and yellow . . 2·50 75
DESIGNS: 25k. Oceanographic survey ship "Vityaz"; 40k. Antarctic map, camp and emperor penguin; 1r. Observatory and rocket.

1959. 11th Centenary of Novgorod.
2374 **798** 40k. red, brown and blue 55 15

799 Schoolboys in Workshop

800 Exhibition Emblem

1959. Industrial Training Scheme for School-leavers. Inscr "1959".
2375 **799** 40k. violet 40 15
2376 – 1r. blue . . . . 1·00 30
DESIGN: 1r. Children at night-school.

1959. All Union Exhibition.
2377 **800** 40k. multicoloured . . . 55 20

801 Russian and Chinese Students

1959. 10th Anniv of Chinese Peoples' Republic.
2378 **801** 20k. multicoloured . . . 20 15
2379 – 40k. multicoloured . . . 65 20
DESIGN: 40k. Russian miner and Chinese foundryman.

802 Postwoman

803 Mahtumkuli (after A. Khadzhiev)

1959. International Correspondence Week.
2380 **802** 40k. multicoloured . . . 50 15
2381 60k. multicoloured . . . 75 20

1959. 225th Birth Anniv of Mahtumkuli (Turkestan writer).
2382 **803** 40k. brown 65 15

804 Arms and Workers of the German Democratic Republic

805 Lunik 3's Trajectory around the Moon

1959. 10th Anniv of German Democratic Republic.
2383 **804** 40k. multicoloured . . . 45 15
2384 – 60k. purple and cream 65 20
DESIGN—VERT: 60k. Town Hall, East Berlin.

1959. Launching of "Lunik 3" Rocket.
2385 **805** 40k. violet . . . . . . 1·90 30

806 Republican Arms and Emblem

807 Red Square, Moscow

1959. 30th Anniv of Tadzhikistan Republic.
2386 **806** 40k. multicoloured . . . 1·25 25

1959. 42nd Anniv of October Revolution.
2387 **807** 40k. red 65 15

808 Capitol, Washington and Kremlin, Moscow

1959. Visit of Russian Prime Minister to U.S.A.
2388 **808** 60k. blue and yellow . . 1·00 30

809 Mil Mi-1 Helicopter

1959. Military Sports.
2389 **809** 10k. red and violet . . . 30 10
2390 – 25k. brown and blue . . 55 10
2391 – 40k. blue and brown . . 60 15
2392 – 60k. bistre and blue . . 90 25
DESIGNS: 25k. Skin diver; 40k. Racing motor cyclist; 60k. Parachutist.

810 Track of Moon Rocket

811 Liberty Monument (Zs. Kisfaludy-Strobl), Budapest

1959. Landing of Russian Rocket on Moon. Inscr "14.IX.1959". Multicoloured.
2393 40k. Type **810** . . . . . . 1·00 25
2394 40k. Diagram of flight trajectory . . . . 1·00 25

1959. 15th Anniv of Hungarian Republic. Mult.
2395 20k. Sandor Petofi (Hungarian poet) (horiz) 35 15
2396 40k. Type **811** 70 20

812 Manolis Glezos (Greek Communist)

1959. Glezos Commemoration.
2397 **812** 40k. brown and blue . . 15·00 11·50

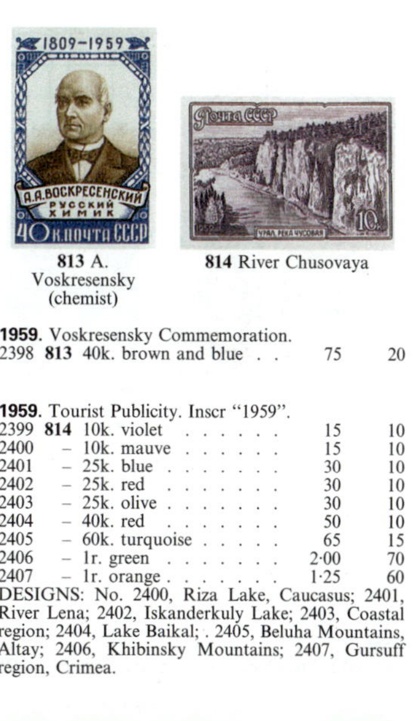

813 A. Voskresensky (chemist)

814 River Chusovaya

1959. Voskresensky Commemoration.
2398 **813** 40k. brown and blue . . 75 20

1959. Tourist Publicity. Inscr "1959".
2399 **814** 10k. violet 15 10
2400 – 10k. mauve 15 10
2401 – 25k. blue 30 10
2402 – 25k. red 30 10
2403 – 25k. olive 30 10
2404 – 40k. red 50 10
2405 – 60k. turquoise 65 15
2406 – 1r. green . . . . 2·00 70
2407 – 1r. orange . . . . 1·25 60
DESIGNS: No. 2400, Riza Lake, Caucasus; 2401, River Lena; 2402, Iskanderkuly Lake; 2403, Coastal region; 2404, Lake Baikal; . 2405, Beluha Mountains, Altay; 2406, Khibinsky Mountains; 2407, Gursuff region, Crimea.

815 "The Trumpeters of the First Horse Army" (M. Grekov)

1959. 40th Anniv of Russian Cavalry.
2408 **815** 40k. multicoloured . . . 85 20

816 A. P. Chekhov and Moscow Residence **817** M. V. Frunze

1960. Birth Centenary of Chekhov (writer).
2409 **816** 20k. red, brown & vio 35 15
2410 – 40k. brown, blue & sepia 75 25
DESIGN: 40k. Chekhov and Yalta residence.

1960. 75th Birth Anniv of M. V. Frunze (military leader).
2411 **817** 40k. brown 65 15

818 G. N. Gabrichevsky **819** Vera Komissarzhevskaya

1960. Birth Centenary of G. N. Gabrichevsky (microbiologist).
2412 **818** 40k. brown and violet 1·00 25

1960. 50th Death Anniv of V. F. Komissarzhevskaya (actress).
2413 **819** 40k. brown 65 15

820 Free-skating

1960. Winter Olympic Games.
2414 – 10k. blue and orange . . . 50 10
2415 – 25k. multicoloured . . . 75 10
2416 – 40k. orange, blue & pur 90 15
2417 **820** 60k. violet, brown & grn 1·40 20
2418 – 1r. blue, red and green 2·25 50
DESIGNS: 10k. Ice hockey; 25k. Ice skating; 40k. Skiing; 1r. Ski jumping.

821 Timur Frunze (fighter pilot) and Air Battle **822** Mil Mi-4 Helicopter over Kremlin

1960. War Heroes. Multicoloured.
2419 40k. Type **821** . . . . . . 1·75 55
2420 1r. Gen. Chernyakhovksy and battle scene . . . . . 1·40 40

1960. Air.
2421 **822** 60k. blue . . . . 1·25 25

823 Women of Various Races **824** "Swords into Ploughshares" (Ye. Buchetich)

1960. 50th Anniv of International Women's Day.
2422 **823** 40k. multicoloured . . . 85 25

1960. Presentation of Statue by Russia to U.N.
2423 **824** 40k. yellow, bistre and blue 65 15
MS2423a 78 × 115 mm. No. 2423 2·25 90

15 лет освобождения Венгрии
(825)

826 Lenin when a Child

1960. 15th Anniv of Liberation of Hungary. Optd with T **825**.
2424 **811** 40k. multicoloured . . . 5·00 3·25

1960. 90th Birth Anniv of Lenin. Portraits of Lenin. Multicoloured.
2425 **826** 10k. multicoloured . . . 10 10
2426 – 20k. multicoloured . . . 20 10
2427 – 30k. multicoloured . . . 40 15
2428 – 40k. multicoloured . . . 50 20
2429 – 60k. multicoloured . . . 1·40 35
2430 – 1r. brown, blue and red 1·60 50
DESIGNS: Lenin: 20k. holding child (after N. Zkukov); 30k. and revolutionary scenes; 40k. with party banners; 60k. and industrial scenes; 1r. with globe and rejoicing people (after A. Seral).

827 "Lunik 3" photographing Moon **828** Government House, Baku

1960. Flight of "Lunik 3". Inscr "7.X.1959".
2431 **827** 40k. yellow and blue . . 1·10 35
2432 – 60k. yellow, blue & indigo . . . . 1·10 35
DESIGN: 60k. Lunar map.

1960. 40th Anniv of Azerbaijan Republic.
2433 **828** 40k. brown, bistre & yell 65 15

829 "Fraternization" (K. Pokorny) **830** Furnaceman

1960. 15th Anniv of Czechoslovak Republic.
2434 **829** 40k. black and blue . . . 50 10
2435 – 60k. brown and yellow 85 15
DESIGN: 60k. Charles Bridge, Prague.

1960. Completion of First Year of Seven Year Plan.
2436 **830** 40k. brown and red . . 50 15

831 Popov Museum, Leningrad

1960. Radio Day.
2437 **831** 40k. multicoloured . . . 1·00 30

832 Robert Schumann **833** Sverdlov

1960. 150th Birth Anniv of Schumann (composer).
2438 **832** 40k. black and blue . . 1·00 20

1960. 75th Birth Anniv of Ya. M. Sverdlov (statesman).
2439 **833** 40k. sepia and brown . . 85 15

834 Magnifier and Stamp

1960. Philatelists' Day.
2440 **834** 60k. multicoloured . . . 1·10 30

835 Petrozavodsk (Karelian Republic)

1960. Capitals of Autonomous Republic (1st issue).
2441 **835** 40k. turquoise 80 20
2442 – 40k. blue 80 20
2443 – 40k. green 80 20
2444 – 40k. purple 80 20
2445 – 40k. red 80 20
2446 – 40k. blue 80 20
2447 – 40k. brown 80 20
2448 – 40k. brown 80 20
2449 – 40k. red 80 20
2450 – 40k. brown 80 20
CAPITALS: Nos. 2442, Batumi (Adzharian); 2443, Izhevsk (Udmurt); 2444, Grozny (Chechen-Ingush); 2445, Cheboksary (Chuvash); 2446, Yakutsk (Yakut); 2447, Ordzhonikidze (North Ossetian); 2448, Nukus (Kara-Kalpak); 2449, Makhachkala (Daghestan); 2450, Yoshkar-Ola (Mari).
See also Nos. 2586/92 and 2703/5.

836 Children of Different Races **838** Rocket

1960. International Children's Day. Multicoloured.
2451 10k. Type **836** 15 10
2452 20k. Children on farm (vert) 25 15
2453 25k. Children with snowman 40 15
2454 40k. Children in zoo gardens 65 20

1960. 40th Anniv of Karelian Autonomous Republic. Optd **40 лет КАССР 8.VI.1960.**
2455 **835** 40k. turquoise . . . . . 2·25 90

1960. Launching of Cosmic Rocket "Spacecraft 1" (first "Vostok" type spacecraft).
2456 **838** 40k. red and blue . . . 1·75 50

839 I.F.A.C. Emblem

1960. 1st International Automation Control Federation Congress, Moscow.
2457 **839** 60k. brown and yellow 1·90 40

1960. Birth Centenary (1959) of Kosta Khetagurov (poet). As T **746**. Inscr "1960".
2458 40k. brown and blue 80 15
DESIGN: 40k. Portrait of Khetagurov and scene from his works.

840 Cement Works, Belgorod

1960. 1st Plant Construction of Seven Year Plan.
2459 **840** 25k. black and blue . . 25 10
2460 – 40k. black and red . . . 50 10
DESIGN. 40k. Metal works, Novokrivorog.

841 Capstans and Cogwheel

1960. Industrial Mass-Production Plant.
2461 **841** 40k. turquoise 70 10
2462 – 40k. purple (Factory plant) 70 10

842 Vilnius (Lithuania)

1960. 20th Anniv of Soviet Baltic Republics. Multicoloured.
2463 40k. Type **842** 65 10
2464 40k. Riga (Latvia) 65 10
2465 40k. Tallin (Estonia) 65 10

843 Running

Международная ярмарка в Риччоне
(844)

1960. Olympic Games. Inscr "1960". Multicoloured.
2466 5k. Type **843** 15 10
2467 10k. Wrestling 20 10
2468 15k. Basketball 35 10
2469 20k. Weightlifting 35 10
2470 25k. Boxing 35 10
2471 40k. High diving 50 15
2472 40k. Fencing 50 15
2473 40k. Gymnastics 50 20
2474 60k. Canoeing 80 25
2475 1r. Horse jumping . . . . . 2·25 55

1960. 20th Anniv of Moldavian Republic. As T **842**.
2476 40k. multicoloured 65 10
DESIGN: 40k. Kishinev (capital).

1960. International Exhibition, Riccione. No. 2471 optd with T **844**.
2477 40k. multicoloured . . . . 16·00 11·00

845 "Agriculture and Industry" **846** G. H. Minkh

1960. 15th Anniv of Vietnam Democratic Republic.
2478 40k. Type **845** 55 15
2479 60k. Book Museum, Hanoi (vert) 85 20

1960. 125th Birth Anniv of G. H. Minkh (epidemiologist).
2480 **846** 60k. brown and bistre 70 15

847 "March" (after I. Levitan)

1960. Birth Centenary of I. Levitan (painter).
2481 **847** 40k. black and olive . . 95 15

848 "Forest" (after Shishkin)

1960. 5th World Forestry Congress, Seattle.
2482 **848** 1r. brown . . . . 2·40 70

849 Addressing Letter

1960. International Correspondence Week.
2483 **849** 40k. multicoloured . . . 40 10
2484 60k. multicoloured . . . 70 20

850 Kremlin, Dogs "Belka" and "Strelka" and Rocket Trajectory

1960. 2nd Cosmic Rocket Flight.
2485 **850** 40k. purple and yellow 1·10 20
2486 1r. blue and orange . . . 1·75 30

851 Globes **852** People of Kazakhstan

1960. 15th Anniv of W.F.T.U.
2487 **851** 60k. blue, drab and lilac 80 15

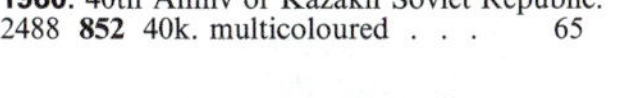

1960. 40th Anniv of Kazakh Soviet Republic.
2488 **852** 40k. multicoloured . . . 65 15

853 "Karl Marx"

1960. River Boats. Multicoloured.
2489 25k. Type **853** 40 10
2490 40k. "Lenin" 70 15
2491 60k. "Raketa" (hydrofoil) 1·40 25

854 A. N. Voronikhin and Leningrad Cathedral

1960. Birth Bicentenary of A. N. Voronikhin (architect).
2492 **854** 40k. black and grey . . 65 15

855 Motor Coach

1960. Russian Motor Industry.
2493 – 25k. black and blue . . 40 10
2494 – 40k. blue and olive . . 55 15
2495 – 60k. red and turquoise 1·10 20
2496 **855** 1r. multicoloured . . . 1·75 35
DESIGNS: 25k. Lorry; 40k. "Volga" car; 60k. "Moskvich" car.

856 J. S. Gogebashvily

1960. 120th Birth Anniv of J. S. Gogebashvily (Georgian teacher).
2497 **856** 40k. black and lake . . . 65 15

857 Industrial Plant and Power Plant **858** Federation Emblem

1960. 43rd Anniv of October Revolution.
2498 **857** 40k. multicoloured . . . 65 20

1960. 15th Anniv of International Federation of Democratic Women.
2499 **858** 60k. red and grey . . . 80 20

859 Youth of Three Races

40 лет Удмуртской АССР
4/XI 1960.
(**860**)

1960. 15th Anniv of World Democratic Youth Federation.
2500 **859** 60k. multicoloured . . . 80 20

1960. 40th Anniv of Udmurt Autonomous Republic. No. 2443 optd with T **860**.
2501 40k. green . . . . 2·75 1·10

861 Tolstoi and his Moscow Residence

1960. 50th Death Anniv of Leo Tolstoi (writer).
2502 **861** 20k. multicoloured . . . 30 15
2503 – 40k. brown, sepia & blue 55 15
2504 – 60k. multicoloured . . . 1·10 25
DESIGNS—HORIZ: 40k. Tolstoi and his country estate. VERT: 60k. Full face portrait.

862 Government House, Yerevan

1960. 40th Anniv of Armenian Republic.
2505 **862** 40k. multicoloured . . . 65 15

863 Students and University **864** Tulip

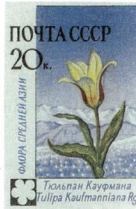

1960. Opening of Friendship University, Moscow.
2506 **863** 40k. purple 65 15

1960. Russian Flowers. Multicoloured.
2507 20k. Type **864** 30 10
2508 20k. Autumn crocus 30 10
2509 25k. Marsh marigold . . . 35 10
2510 40k. Tulip 45 10
2511 40k. Panax 45 10
2512 60k. Hypericum 90 25
2513 60k. Iris 90 25
2514 1r. Wild rose . . . . 1·60 45

865 Engels **867** N. Pirogov

866 Mark Twain

1960. 140th Birth Anniv of Engels.
2515 **865** 60k. grey . . . . 1·40 30

1960. 125th Birth Anniv of Mark Twain.
2516 **866** 40k. bistre and orange 2·75 1·75

1960. 150th Birth Anniv of N. Pirogov (surgeon).
2517 **867** 40k. brown and green . . 65 15

868 Chopin (after Eugene Delacroix) **869** North Korean Flag and Emblem

1960. 150th Birth Anniv of Chopin.
2518 **868** 40k. bistre and buff . . 1·50 20

1960. 15th Anniv of Korean Liberation.
2519 **869** 40k. multicoloured . . . 95 20

870 Lithuanian Costumes **871** A. Tseretely

1960. Provincial Costumes (1st issue). Inscr "1960". Multicoloured.
2520 10k. Type **870** 35 15
2521 60k. Uzbek costumes . . . 1·40 25
See also Nos. 2537/45, 2796 and 2835/8.

1960. 120th Birth Anniv of A. Tseretely (Georgian poet).
2522 **871** 40k. purple and lilac . . 1·00 20

Currency Revalued.
10 (old) Kopeks = 1 (new) Kopek.

872 Worker **873** "Ruslan and Lyudmila" (Pushkin)

1961. Inscr "1961".
2523 **872** 1k. bistre 70 10
2524 – 2k. green 25 10
2525 – 3k. violet . . . . . . 2·00 10
2526 – 4k. red 60 10
2526a – 4k. brown . . . . . . 3·00 1·40
2527 – 6k. red . . . . 4·50 45
2528 – 6k. claret . . . . . . 1·40 10
2529 – 10k. orange . . . . . 2·40 10
2533a – 12k. purple . . . . . 2·00 25
2530 – 16k. blue . . . . . . 3·50 70
DESIGNS: 2k. Combine harvester; 3k. Cosmic rocket; 4k. Soviet Arms and Flag; 6k. Spassky Tower and Kremlin; 10k. "Worker and Collective Farmer" (sculpture, Vera Mukhina); 12k. Monument to F. Minin and D. Pozharsky and Spassky Tower; 16k. Airliner over power station.

1961. Russian Wild Life. As T **653** but inscr "1961". Centres in natural colours. Frame colours given.
2534 1k. sepia (Brown bear) . . . 25 15
2535 6k. black (Eurasian beaver) 1·00 20
2536 10k. black (Roe deer) . . . 1·25 55
The 1k. is vert and the rest horiz.

1961. Provincial Costumes (2nd issue). As T **870** but inscr "1961".
2537 2k. red, brown and stone . . 25 10
2538 2k. multicoloured 25 10
2539 3k. multicoloured 50 10
2540 3k. multicoloured 50 10
2541 3k. multicoloured 50 10
2542 4k. multicoloured 60 15
2543 6k. multicoloured 70 20
2544 10k. multicoloured . . . . 1·40 30
2545 12k. multicoloured . . . . 2·25 35
COSTUMES: No. 2337, Moldavia; 2538, Georgia; 2539, Ukraine; 2540, Byelorussia; 2541, Kazakhs; 2542, Koryaks; 2543, Russia; 2544, Armenia; 2545, Estonia.

1961. Scenes from Russian Fairy Tales. Mult.
2546 1k. "Geese Swans" 25 10
2547 3k. "The Fox, the Hare and the Cock" 55 15
2548 4k. "The Little Humpbacked Horse" . . 75 15
2549 6k. "The Muzhik and the Bear" . . . . 1·10 20
2550 10k. Type **873** . . . . . . 1·60 40

874 Lenin, Map and Power Station

1961. 40th Anniv of State Electricity Plan.
2551 **874** 4k. brown, yellow & blue 60 15
2552 10k. black, purple and salmon . . . . 1·25 25

875 Tractor **876** Dobrolyubov (after P. Borel)

1961. Soviet Agricultural Achievements. Inscr "1961".
2553 – 3k. mauve and blue . . 40 15
2554 **875** 4k. black and green . . 45 10
2555 – 6k. brown and blue . . 55 25
2556 – 10k. purple and olive . . 1·10 15
DESIGNS: 3k. Dairy herd; 6k. Agricultural machinery; 10k. Fruit picking.

1961. 125th Birth Anniv of N. A. Dobrolyubov (writer).
2557 **876** 4k. buff, black and blue 55 20

877 N. D. Zelinsky

1961. Birth Centenary of N. D. Zelinsky (chemist).
2558 **877** 4k. purple and mauve . . 55 20

878 Georgian Republic Flag

1961. 40th Anniv of Georgian Republic.
2559 **878** 4k. multicoloured . . . 30 10

879 Sgt. Miroshnichenko and Battle

1961. War Hero.
2560 **879** 4k. blue and purple . . . 65 20
See also Nos. 2664/5.

880 Self-portrait and Birthplace **881** A. Rublev

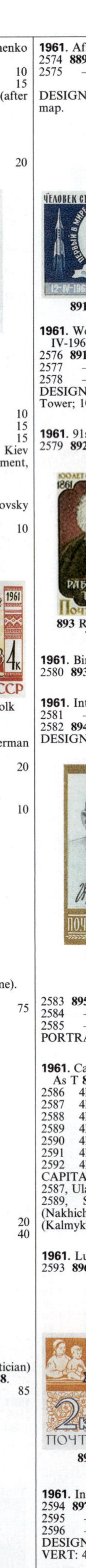

1961. Death Centenary of T. G. Shevchenko (Ukrainian poet and painter).
2561 **880** 3k. brown and violet . . 35 10
2562 – 6k. purple and green . . 65 15
DESIGN: 6k. Shevchenko in old age (after I. Kramskoi), pen, book and candle.
See also Nos. 2956/62.

1961. 600th Birth Anniv of Rublev (painter).
2563 **881** 4k. multicoloured . . . 60 20

882 Statue of Shevchenko (poet), Kharkov (M. Manizer)

883 N. V. Sklifosovsky

1961. Cultural Celebrities.
2564 – 2k. brown and blue . . . 25 10
2565 **882** 4k. brown and black . . 30 15
2566 – 4k. brown and purple . . 35 15
DESIGNS: 2k. Shchors Monument, Kiev (M. Lysenko); 4k. (No. 2566), Kotovsky Monument, Kishinev (L. Dubinovsky).

1961. 125th Birth Anniv of N. Y. Sklifosovsky (surgeon).
2567 **883** 4k. black and blue . . . 40 10

884 Robert Koch

885 Zither-player and Folk Dancers

1961. 50th Death Anniv of Robert Koch (German microbiologist).
2568 **884** 6k. brown 60 20

1961. 50th Anniv of Russian National Choir.
2569 **885** 4k. multicoloured . . . 35 10

886 "Popular Science"

1961. Cent of "Vokrug Sveta" (science magazine).
2570 **886** 6k. brown, blue and deep blue . . . . . . 1·10 75

887 Venus Rocket

1961. Launching of Venus Rocket.
2571 **887** 6k. orange and blue . . 1·40 20
2572 – 10k. blue and yellow . . 1·90 40
DESIGN: 10k. Capsule and flight route.

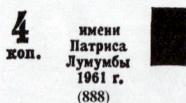

4 коп. имени Патриса Лумумбы 1961 г.

(888)

1961. Patrice Lumumba (Congolese politician) Commemoration (1st issue). Surch with T **888**.
2573 **863** 4k. on 40k. purple . . . 1·25 85
See also No. 2593.

889 African breaking Chains

1961. Africa Freedom Day. Inscr "1961".
2574 **889** 4k. multicoloured . . . 20 10
2575 – 6k. purple, orange and blue 45 20
DESIGN: 6k. Hands clasping Torch of Freedom, and map.

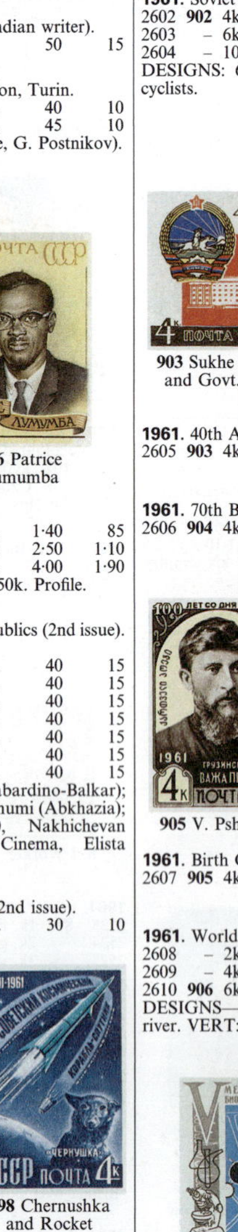

891 Yuri Gagarin

892 Lenin

1961. World's First Manned Space Flight. Inscr "12-IV-1961". Perf or imperf.
2576 **891** 3k. blue 45 10
2577 – 6k. blue, violet and red 65 20
2578 – 10k. red, green & brown 1·25 30
DESIGNS—37×26 mm: 6k. Rocket and Spassky Tower; 10k. Rocket, Gagarin and Kremlin.

1961. 91st Birth Anniv of Lenin.
2579 **892** 4k. blk, salmon and red 30 10

893 Rabindranath Tagore

894 Garibaldi

1961. Birth Centenary of Tagore (Indian writer).
2580 **893** 6k. black, bistre and red 50 15

1961. International Labour Exhibition, Turin.
2581 – 4k. salmon and red . . . 40 10
2582 **894** 6k. salmon and lilac . . 45 10
DESIGN: 4k. "To the Stars" (statue, G. Postnikov).

895 Lenin

896 Patrice Lumumba

1961.
2583 **895** 20k. green and brown . . 1·40 85
2584 – 30k. blue and brown . . 2·50 1·10
2585 – 50k. red and brown . . 4·00 1·90
PORTRAITS (Lenin): 30k. In cap; 50k. Profile.

1961. Capitals of Autonomous Republics (2nd issue). As T **835**.
2586 4k. deep violet 40 15
2587 4k. blue 40 15
2588 4k. orange 40 15
2589 4k. black 40 15
2590 4k. lake 40 15
2591 4k. green 40 15
2592 4k. deep purple 40 15
CAPITALS: No. 2586, Nalchik (Kabardino-Balkar); 2587, Ulan-Ude (Buryat); 2588, Sukhumi (Abkhazia); 2589, Syktyvkar (Komi); 2590, Nakhichevan (Nakhichevan); 2591, Rodina Cinema, Elista (Kalmyk); 2592, Ufa (Bashkir).

1961. Lumumba Commemoration (2nd issue).
2593 **896** 2k. multicoloured . . . 30 10

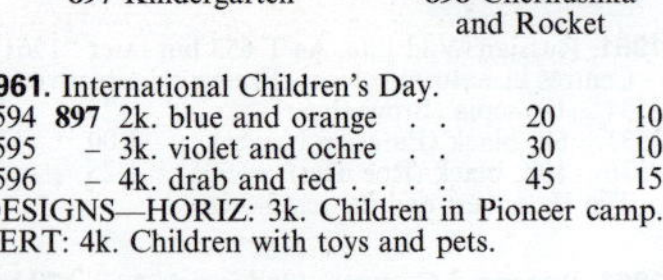

897 Kindergarten

898 Chernushka and Rocket

1961. International Children's Day.
2594 **897** 2k. blue and orange . . 20 10
2595 – 3k. violet and ochre . . 30 10
2596 – 4k. drab and red 45 15
DESIGNS—HORIZ: 3k. Children in Pioneer camp. VERT: 4k. Children with toys and pets.

1961. 4th and 5th "Spacecraft" Flights.
2597 – 2k. black, blue and violet 35 15
2598 **898** 4k. turquoise and blue 65 15
DESIGN—HORIZ: 2k. Dog "Zvezdochka", rocket and controller (inscr "25.III.1961").

899 Belinsky (after I. Astafev)

900

1961. 150th Birth Anniv of Vissarion Grigorievich Belinsky (literary critic and journalist).
2599 **899** 4k. black and red . . . 30 15

1961. 40th Anniv of Soviet Hydro-meteorological Service.
2600 **900** 6k. multicoloured . . . 90 25

901 D. M. Karbyshev

902 Glider

1961. Lieut-Gen. Karbyshev (war hero).
2601 **901** 4k. black, red and yellow 30 10

1961. Soviet Spartakiad.
2602 **902** 4k. red and grey 30 10
2603 – 6k. red and grey 55 15
2604 – 10k. red and grey . . . 90 35
DESIGNS: 6k. Inflatable motor boat; 10k. Motor cyclists.

903 Sukhe Bator Monument and Govt. Buildings, Ulan Bator

904 S. I. Vavilov

1961. 40th Anniv of Revolution in Mongolia.
2605 **903** 4k. multicoloured . . . 65 20

1961. 70th Birthday of Vavilov (scientist).
2606 **904** 4k. brown, bistre & green 30 15

905 V. Pshavela

906 "Youth Activities"

1961. Birth Cent of Pshavela (Georgian poet).
2607 **905** 4k. brown and cream . . 30 10

1961. World Youth Forum.
2608 – 2k. brown and orange 30 10
2609 – 4k. green and lilac . . . 35 10
2610 **906** 6k. blue and ochre . . . 65 20
DESIGNS—HORIZ: 2k. Youths pushing tank into river. VERT: 4k. "Youths and progress".

907

908

1961. 5th Int Biochemical Congress, Moscow.
2611 **907** 6k. multicoloured . . . 65 15

1961. Centenary of "Kalevipoeg" (Estonian Saga).
2612 **908** 4k. yellow, turq & blk 30 15

909 Javelin Thrower

1961. 7th Soviet Trade Union Sports.
2613 **909** 6k. red 55 20

910 A.D. Zakharov (after S. Shchukin)

1961. Birth Bicentenary of Zakharov (architect).
2614 **910** buff, brown and blue . . 80 25

911 Counter-attack (after P. Krivonogov)

1961. War of 1941–45 (1st issue). Inscr "1961".
2615 **911** 4k. multicoloured . . . 55 15
2616 – 4k. multicoloured . . . 55 15
2617 – 4k. indigo and brown . . 65 15
DESIGNS: No. 2616, Sailor with bayonet; No. 2617, Soldier with tommy gun.
See also Nos. 2717 and 2851/5.

912 Union Emblem

1961. 15th Anniv of International Union of Students.
2617a **912** 6k. violet and red . . . 45 10

913 Stamps commemorating Industry

1961. 40th Anniv of First Soviet Stamp. Centres multicoloured.
2618 **913** 2k. ochre and brown . . 30 15
2619 – 4k. blue and indigo . . 45 15
2620 – 6k. green and olive . . . 90 25
2621 – 10k. buff and brown . . 1·40 45
DESIGNS (stamps commemorating): 4k. Electrification; 8k. Peace; 10k. Atomic energy.

914 Titov and "Vostok 2"

1961. 2nd Manned Space Flight. Perf or imperf.
2622 – 4k. blue and purple . . . 70 20
2623 **914** 6k. orange, green & brn 1·00 30
DESIGN: 4k. Space pilot and globe.

915 Angara River Bridge

1961. Tercentenary of Irkutsk, Siberia.
2624 **915** 4k. black, lilac and bistre 55 15

916 Letters and Mail Transport

1961. International Correspondence Week.
2625 **916** 4k. black and mauve . . 55 10

917 Workers and Banners

1961. 22nd Communist Party Congress (1st issue).
2626 **917** 2k. brown, yellow and red 15 10
2627 – 3k. blue and orange . . 90 15
2628 – 4k. red, buff and purple 25 10
2629 – 4k. orange, black & mve 40 10
2630 – 4k. sepia, brown and red 25 10
DESIGNS: No. 2627, Moscow University and obelisk; 2628, Combine harvester; 2629, Workmen and machinery; 2630, Worker and slogan.
See also No. 2636.

918 Soviet Monument, Berlin

1961. 10th Anniv of International Federation of Resistance Fighters.
2631 **918** 4k. grey and red 35 10

919 Adult Education

1961. Communist Labour Teams.
2632 – 2k. purple & red on buff 20 10
2633 **919** 3k. brown & red on buff 20 10
2634 – 4k. blue and red on cream 35 15
DESIGNS: 2k. Worker at machine; 4k. Workers around piano.

920 Rocket and Globes

1961. Cosmic Flights. Aluminium-surfaced paper.
2635 **920** 1r. red and black on silver . . . . 22·00 22·00

XXII съезд
КПСС
(921)

1961. 22nd Communist Party Congress (2nd issue). Optd with T **921**.
2636 **920** 1r. red and black on silver . . . . 19·00 20·00

922 Imanov (after A. Kasteev)

923 Liszt, Piano and Music

1961. 42nd Death Anniv of Amangeldy Imanov (Kazakh Leader).
2637 **922** 4k. sepia, brown & green 35 10

1961. 150th Birth Anniv of Liszt.
2638 **923** 4k. brown, purple & yell 75 15

924 Flags, Rocket and Skyline

1961. 44th Anniv of October Revolution.
2639 **924** 4k. red, purple and yellow 70 15

925 Congress Emblem

926 Statue of Lomonosov (N. Tomsky) and Lomonosov University

1961. 5th W.F.T.U. Congress, Moscow. Inscr "MOCKBA 1961".
2640 **925** 2k. red and bistre . . . 25 10
2641 – 2k. violet and grey . . . 25 10
2642 – 4k. brown, purple & blue 50 15
2643 – 4k. red, blue and violet 50 15
2644 **925** 6k. red, bistre and green 75 20
2645 – 6k. blue, purple and bistre 75 20
DESIGNS—HORIZ: Nos. 2641, 2645, Negro breaking chains. VERT: No. 2642, Hand holding hammer; 2643, Hands holding globe.

1961. 250th Birth Anniv of Mikhail Lomonosov (scientist).
2646 **926** 4k. brown, green and blue 45 15
2647 – 6k. blue, buff and green 65 20
2648 – 10k. brown, blue & pur 1·40 40
DESIGNS—VERT: 6k. Lomonosov at desk (after M. Shreier). HORIZ: 10k. Lomonosov (after L. Miropolsky), his birthplace, and Leningrad Academy of Science.

927 Power Workers

928 Scene from "Romeo and Juliet" (Prokotiev)

1961. Young Builders of Seven Year Plan. Inscr "1961".
2649 **927** 3k. grey, brown and red 50 15
2650 – 4k. brown, blue and red 45 15
2651 – 6k. grey, brown and red 75 20
DESIGNS: 4k. Welders; 6k. Engineer with theodolite.

1961. Russian Ballet (1st issue). Multicoloured.
2652 6k. Type **928** . . . . . . 1·10 20
2653 10k. Scene from "Swan Lake" (Tchaikovsky) . . 1·50 45
See also Nos. 2666/7.

929 Hammer and Sickle

930 A. Pumpur

1961. 25th Anniv of Soviet Constitution.
2654 **929** 4k. lake, yellow and red 40 15

1961. 120th Birth Anniv of Pumpur (Lettish poet).
2655 **930** 4k. purple and grey . . . 25 10

1961. Air. Surch **1961 r. 6 kon.** and wavy lines.
2656 **822** 6k. on 60k. blue 90 20

932 "Bulgarian Achievements"

1961. 15th Anniv of Bulgarian Republic.
2657 **932** 4k. multicoloured . . . 35 10

933 Nansen and "Fram"

1961. Birth Centenary of Nansen (explorer).
2658 **933** 6k. brown, blue and black . . . . 1·75 15

934 M. Dolivo-Dobrovolsky

935 A. S. Pushkin (after O. Kiprensky)

1962. Birth Centenary of Dolivo-Dobrovolsky (electrical engineer).
2659 **934** 4k. blue and bistre . . . 35 10

1962. 125th Death Anniv of Pushkin (poet).
2660 **935** 4k. black, red and buff 30 10

936 Soviet Woman

1962. Soviet Women.
2661 **936** 4k. black, bistre & orange 35 10

937 People's Dancers

1962. 25th Anniv of Soviet People's Dance Ensemble.
2662 **937** 4k. brown and red . . . 35 10

938 Skaters

1962. Ice Skating Championships, Moscow.
2663 **938** 4k. blue and orange . . 40 10

1962. War Heroes. As T **879** but inscr "1962".
2664 4k. brown and blue 90 15
2665 6k. turquoise and brown . . 1·25 20
DESIGNS: 4k. Lieut. Shalandin, tanks and Yakovlev Yak-9T fighters; 6k. Capt. Gadzhiev, "K-3" submarine and sinking ship.

1962. Russian Ballet (2nd issue). As T **928** but inscr "1962".
2666 2k. multicoloured 60 15
2667 3k. multicoloured 65 15
DESIGNS: Scenes from—2k. "Red Flower" (Glier); 3k. "Paris Flame" (Asafev).

СОВЕТСКИЕ КОНЬКОБЕЖЦЫ—
ЧЕМПИОНЫ
МИРА
(939)

1962. Soviet Victory in Ice Skating Championships. Optd with T **939**.
2668 **938** 4k. blue and orange . . 2·75 1·50

940 Skiing

1962. 1st People's Winter Games, Sverdlovsk.
2669 **940** 4k. violet and red . . . 45 15
2670 – 6k. turquoise and purple 60 20
2671 – 10k. red, black and blue 1·25 30
DESIGN: 6k. Ice Hockey; 10k. Figure skating.

941 A. I. Herzen (after N. Ge)

942 Lenin on Banner

1962. 150th Birth Anniv of A. I. Herzen (writer).
2672 **941** 4k. flesh, black and blue 35 10

1962. 14th Leninist Young Communist League Congress. Inscr "1962".
2673 **942** 4k. red, yellow and purple 20 10
2674 – 6k. purple, orange & blue 35 10
DESIGN—HORIZ: 6k. Lenin (after A. Mylnikov) on flag.

943 Rocket and Globe

944 Tchaikovsky (after sculpture by Z. M. Vilensky)

1962. 1st Anniv of World's First Manned Space Flight. Perf or imperf.
2675 **943** 10k. multicoloured . . . 1·10 35

1962. 2nd Int Tchaikovsky Music Competition.
2676 **944** 4k. drab, black and blue 50 10

945 Youth of Three Races

1962. International Day of "Solidarity of Youth against Colonialism".
2677 **945** 6k. multicoloured . . . 45 10

946 The Ulyanov (Lenin's) Family

1962. 92nd Birth Anniv of Lenin.
2678 **946** 4k. brown, grey and red 40 15
2679 – 10k. purple, red and black . . . . 1·00 30
DESIGN: 10k. Bust of Lenin (N. Sokolov).

947 "Cosmos 3"

1962. Cosmic Research.
2680 **947** 6k. black, violet and blue 65 15

948 Charles Dickens

1962. 150th Birth Anniv of Charles Dickens.
2681 **948** 6k. purple, turq & brn 85 20

949 J. J. Rousseau

950 Karl Marx Monument, Moscow (L. Kerbel)

1962. 250th Birth Anniv of Rousseau.
2682 **949** 6k. bistre, purple and grey 70 20

1962. Karl Marx Commemoration.
2683 **950** 4k. grey and blue 35 10

951 Lenin reading "Pravda"

952 Mosquito and Campaign Emblem

1962. 50th Anniv of "Pravda" Newspaper.
2684 **951** 4k. purple, red and buff 30 15
2685 – 4k. multicoloured 30 15
2686 – 4k. multicoloured 30 15
DESIGNS—25×38 mm: No. 2685, Statuary and front page of first issue of "Pravda"; No. 2686, Lenin (after A. Mylnikov) and modern front page of "Pravda".

1962. Malaria Eradication. Perf (6k. also imperf).
2687 **952** 4k. black, turquoise & red 40 10
2688 6k. black, green and red 70 10

953 Model Rocket Construction

1962. 40th Anniv of All Union Lenin Pioneer Organization. Designs embody Pioneer badge. Multicoloured.
2689 2k. Lenin and Pioneers giving Oath 25 10
2690 3k. Lenya Golikov and Valya Kotik (pioneer heroes) 25 10
2691 4k. Type **953** 35 10
2692 4k. Hygiene education 40 15
2693 6k. Pioneers marching 90 25

1962. 25th Anniv of First Soviet Polar Drifting Station. No. **MS**1926*a* optd "1962" in red on each stamp and with commemorative inscription optd in margin below stamps.
MS2693a 154×111 mm. No. 1926×4 95·00 90·00

954 M. Mashtotz

955 Ski Jumping

1962. 1600th Birth Anniv of Mesrop Mashtotz (author of Armenian Alphabet).
2694 **954** 4k. brown and yellow 35 10

1962. F.I.S. International Ski Championships, Zakopane (Poland).
2695 **955** 2k. red, brown and blue 20 10
2696 – 10k. blue, black and red 90 35
DESIGN—VERT: 10k. Skier.

956 I. Goncharov (after I. Kramskoi)

957 Cycle Racing

1962. 150th Birth Anniv of I. Goncharov (writer).
2697 **956** 4k. brown and grey 35 10

1962. Summer Sports Championships.
2698 **957** 2k. black, red and brown 40 10
2699 – 4k. black, yellow & brn 75 20
2700 – 10k. black, lemon & blue 80 30
2701 – 12k. brown, yellow & bl 95 40
2702 – 16k. multicoloured 1·50 50
DESIGN—VERT: 4k. Volleyball; 10k. Rowing; 16k. Horse jumping. HORIZ: 12k. Football (goal keeper).

1962. Capitals of Autonomous Republics. 3rd issue. As T **835**.
2703 4k. black 50 15
2704 4k. purple 50 15
2705 4k. green 50 15
CAPITALS: No. 2703, Kazan (Tatar); No. 2704, Kyzyl (Tuva); No. 2705, Saransk (Mordovian).

958 Lenin Library, 1862

1962. Centenary of Lenin Library.
2706 **958** 4k. black and grey 35 15
2707 – 4k. black and grey 35 15
DESIGN: No. 2707, Modern library building.

959 Fur Bourse, Leningrad and Ermine

1962. Fur Bourse Commemoration.
2708 **959** 6k. multicoloured 65 30

960 Pasteur

961 Youth and Girl with Book

1962. Centenary of Pasteur's Sterilization Process.
2709 **960** 6k. brown and black 60 15

1962. Communist Party Programme. Mult.
2710 2k. Type **961** 20 10
2711 4k. Workers of three races and dove 35 10

962 Hands breaking Bomb

1962. World Peace Congress, Moscow.
2712 **962** 6k. bistre, black and blue 30 15

963 Ya. Kupala and Ya. Kolas

1962. Byelorussian Poets Commemoration.
2713 **963** 4k. brown and yellow 30 10

964 Sabir

965 Congress Emblem

1962. Birth Centenary of Sabir (Azerbaijan poet).
2714 **964** 4k. brown, buff and blue 30 10

1962. 8th Anti-cancer Congress, Moscow.
2715 **965** 6k. red, black and blue 45 15

966 N. N. Zinin

1962. 150th Birth Anniv of N. N. Zinin (chemist).
2716 **966** 4k. brown and violet 30 10

1962. War of 1941–45 (2nd issue). As T **911** inscr "1962".
2717 4k. multicoloured 55 15
DESIGN: Sailor throwing petrol bomb (Defence of Sevastopol, after A. Deinekin).

967 M. V. Nesterov (painter) (after P. Korin)

1962. Russian Artists Commemoration.
2718 **967** 4k. multicoloured 45 15
2719 – 4k. brown, purple & grey 45 15
2720 – 4k. black and brown 45 15
PORTRAITS—VERT: No. 2719, I. N. Kramskoi (painter) (after N. Yovoshenko). HORIZ: No. 2220, I. D. Shadr (sculptor).

968 "Vostok-2"

969 Nikolaev and "Vostok 3"

1962. 1st Anniv of Titov's Space Flight. Perf or imperf.
2721 **968** 10k. purple, black & blue 1·10 35
2722 10k. orange, black & blue 1·10 35

1962. 1st "Team" Manned Space Flight. Perf or imperf.
2723 **969** 4k. brown, red and blue 90 20
2724 – 4k. brown, red and blue 90 20
2725 – 6k. multicoloured 1·50 25
DESIGNS: No. 2724, As Type **969** but with Popovich and "Vostok-4"; No. 2725 (47×28½ mm), Cosmonauts in flight.

970 House of Friendship

1962. People's House of Friendship, Moscow.
2726 **970** 6k. grey and blue 30 10

971 Lomonosov University and Atomic Symbols

1962. "Atoms for Peace".
2727 **971** 4k. multicoloured 35 10
2728 – 6k. multicoloured 75 20
DESIGN: 6k. Map of Russia, Atomic symbol and "Peace" in ten languages.

972 Common Carp and Bream

973 F. E. Dzerzhinsky

1962. Fish Preservation Campaign.
2729 **972** 4k. yellow, violet and blue 50 10
2730 – 6k. blue, black and orange 75 20
DESIGN: 6k. Atlantic salmon.

1962. Birth Anniv of Feliks Dzerzhinsky (founder of Cheka).
2731 **973** 4k. blue and green 25 10

974 O. Henry

1962. Birth Cent of O. Henry (American writer).
2732 **974** 6k. black, brown & yell 45 10

975 Field Marshals Barclay de Tolly, Kutuzov and Bagration

1962. 150th Anniv of Patriotic War of 1812.
2733 **975** 3k. brown 40 10
2734 – 4k. blue 55 15
2735 – 6k. slate 65 20
2736 – 10k. violet 90 25
DESIGNS: 4k. D. V. Davydov and partisans; 6k. Battle of Borodino; 10k. Partisan Vasilisa Kozhina escorting French prisoners of war.

976 Lenin Street, Vinnitsa

1962. 600th Anniv of Vinnitsa.
2737 **976** 4k. black and bistre 30 10

977 Transport, "Stamp" and "Postmark"

978 Cedar

1962. International Correspondence Week.
2738 **977** 4k. black, purple & turq 30 10

1962. 150th Anniv of Nikitsky Botanical Gardens. Multicoloured.
2739 3k. Type **978** 35 10
2740 4k. "Vostok-2" canna (plant) 55 10
2741 6k. Strawberry tree (arbutus) 70 15
2742 10k. "Road to the Stars" (chrysanthemum) 95 25

979 Builder

981 Akhundov (after N. Ismailov)

980 "Sputnik 1"

1962. "The Russian People". Multicoloured.
2743 4k. Type **979** 30 15
2744 4k. Textile worker 30 15
2745 4k. Surgeon 30 15
2746 4k. Farm girl 30 15
2747 4k. P. T. instructor 30 15
2748 4k. Housewife 30 15
2749 4k. Rambler 30 15

1962. 5th Anniv of Launching of "Sputnik 1".
2750 **980** 10k. multicoloured . . . 1·10 30

1962. 150th Birth Anniv of Mirza Akhundov (poet).
2751 **981** 4k. brown and green . . 35 10

982 Harvester

983 N. N. Burdenko

1962. "Settlers on Virgin Lands". Multicoloured.
2752 4k. Type **982** 55 20
2753 4k. Surveyors, tractors and map 55 20
2754 4k. Pioneers with flag . . . 55 20

1962. Soviet Scientists. Inscr "1962". Multicoloured.
2755 4k. Type **983** 30 10
2756 4k. V. P. Filatov (wearing beret) 35 10

984 Lenin Mausoleum

1962. 92nd Birth Anniv of Lenin.
2757 **984** 4k. multicoloured . . . 30 10

985 Worker with Banner

986 "Into Space" (sculpture, G. Postnikov)

1962. 45th Anniv of October Revolution.
2758 **985** 4k. multicoloured . . . 30 10

1962. Space Flights Commem. Perf or imperf.
2759 **986** 6k. black, brown and blue 60 15
2760 10k. ultram, bis & vio 1·00 20

(987)

988 T. Moldo (Kirghiz poet)

1962. Launching of Rocket to Mars (1st issue). Optd with T **987**.
2761 **986** 10k. blue, bistre and violet . . . . 3·25 1·75
See also No. 2765.

1962. Poets' Anniversaries.
2762 **988** 4k. black and red . . . 40 10
2763 – 4k. black and blue . . . 40 10
DESIGN: No. 2763, Sayat-Nova (Armenian poet) with musical instrument (after G. Ruthkyan).

989 Hammer and Sickle

1962. 40th Anniv of U.S.S.R.
2764 **989** 4k. yellow, red and crimson 30 10

990 Mars Rocket in Space (¾-size illustration)

1962. Launching of Rocket to Mars (2nd issue).
2765 **990** 10k. violet and red . . . 1·10 30

991 Chemical Industry and Statistics

1962. 22nd Communist Party Congress. "Achievements of the People". Multicoloured.
2766 4k. Type **991** 55 20
2767 4k. Engineering (machinery and atomic symbol) . . . 55 20
2768 4k. Hydro-electric power . . 55 20
2769 4k. Agriculture (harvester) 55 20
2770 4k. Engineering (surveyor and welder) 55 20
2771 4k. Communications (telephone installation) . . 55 20
2772 4k. Heavy industry (furnace) 55 20
2773 4k. Transport (signalman, etc) 65 20
2774 4k. Dairy farming (milkmaid, etc) 55 20
All the designs show production targets relating to 1980.

992 Chessmen

994 V. K. Blucher (military commander)

993 Four Soviet Cosmonauts (½-size illustration)

1962. 30th Soviet Chess Championships, Yerevan.
2775 **992** 4k. black and ochre . . 75 20

1962. Soviet Cosmonauts Commem. Perf or imperf.
2776 **993** 1r. black and blue . . . 8·00 8·00

1962. V. K. Blucher Commemoration.
2777 **994** 4k. multicoloured . . . 40 10

995 V. N. Podbelsky

996 A. Gaidar

1962. 75th Birth Anniv of V. N. Podbelsky (postal administrator, 1918–20).
2778 **995** 4k. violet and brown . . 25 10

1962. Soviet Writers.
2779 **996** 4k. buff, black and blue 30 10
2780 – 4k. multicoloured . . . 30 10
DESIGN: No. 2780, A. S. Makharenko.

997 Dove and Christmas Tree

1962. New Year. Perf or imperf.
2781 **997** 4k. multicoloured . . . 35 10

998 D. N. Pryanishnikov (agricultural chemist)

999 Rose-coloured Starlings

1962. D. N. Pryanishnikov Commemoration.
2782 **998** 4k. multicoloured . . . 30 10

1962. Birds.
2783 **999** 3k. black, red and green 40 15
2784 – 4k. black, brown & orge 55 15
2785 – 6k. blue, black and red 65 20
2786 – 10k. blue, black and red 1·00 40
2787 – 16k. red, blue and black 1·50 65
BIRDS: 4k. Red-breasted geese; 6k. Snow geese; 10k. Great white cranes; 16k. Greater flamingos.

1000 F.I.R. Emblem and Handclasp

1001 Badge and Yakovlev Yak-9 Fighters

1962. 4th International Federation of Resistance Heroes Congress.
2788 **1000** 4k. violet and red . . . 30 10
2789 6k. turquoise and red 45 15

1962. 20th Anniv of French Air Force "Normandy-Niemen" Unit.
2790 **1001** 6k. red, green and buff 65 15

1002 Map and Savings Book

1962. 40th Anniv of Soviet Banks.
2791 **1002** 4k. multicoloured . . . 25 10
2792 – 6k. multicoloured . . . 45 15
DESIGN: 6k. Savings book and map containing savers.

1003 Fertilizer Plant, Rustavi, Georgia

1962. Heavy Industries.
2793 **1003** 4k. black, lt blue & blue 40 15
2794 – 4k. black, turquoise & grn 40 15
2795 – 4k. black, blue and grey 40 15
DESIGNS: No. 2794, Construction of Bratsk hydro-electric station; 2795, Volzhskaya hydro-electric station, Volgograd.

1962. Provincial Costumes (3rd issue). As T **870**. Inscr "1962".
2796 3k. red, brown and drab . . 40 15
COSTUME: 3k. Latvia.

1004 K. S. Stanislavsky

1005 A. S. Serafimovich

1963. Russian Stage Celebrities.
2797 **1004** 4k. green on pale green 35 10
2798 – 4k. brown 35 10
2799 – 4k. brown 35 10
PORTRAITS AND ANNIVERSARIES: No. 2797, Type **1004** (actor, birth cent); 2798, M. S. Shchepkin (actor, death cent); 2799, V. D. Durov (animal trainer and circus artiste, birth cent).

1963. Russian Writers and Poets.
2800 **1005** 4k. brown, sepia & mve 35 10
2801 – 4k. brown and purple 35 10
2802 – 4k. brown, red and buff 35 10
2803 – 4k. brown and green . . 35 10
2804 – 4k. brown, sepia & mve 35 10
2805 – 4k. multicoloured . . . 35 10
PORTRAITS AND ANNIVERSARIES: 2800, (birth cent); 2801, Demyan Bednyi (80th birth anniv); 2802, G. I. Uspensky (120th birth anniv); 2803, N. P. Ogarev (150th birth anniv); 2804, V. Ya. Bryusov (90th birth anniv); 2805, F. V. Gladkov (80th birth anniv).

1006 Children in Nursery

1007 Dolls and Toys

1963. Child Welfare.
2806 **1006** 4k. black and orange 30 10
2807 – 4k. purple, blue & orge 30 10
2808 – 4k. bistre, red and green 30 10
2809 – 4k. purple, red & orange 30 10
DESIGNS: No. 2807, Children with nurse; 2808, Young pioneers; 2809, Students at desk and trainee at lathe.

1963. Decorative Arts. Multicoloured.
2810 4k. Type **1007** 35 10
2811 6k. Pottery 45 15
2812 10k. Books 75 20
2813 12k. Porcelain . . . . . . 1·10 30

1008 Ilyushin Il-62 Jetliner

1962. 40th Anniv of "Aeroflot" Airline.
2814 **1008** 10k. black, brown & red 80 15
2815 – 12k. multicoloured . . 1·00 30
2816 – 16k. red, black and blue 1·40 60
DESIGNS: 12k. "Aeroflot" emblem; 16k. Tupolev Tu-124 airliner.

1009 M. N. Tukhachevsky

1010 M. A. Pavlov (scientist)

1963. 45th Anniv of Red Army and War Heroes.
2817 **1009** 4k. green and turquoise 30 10
2818 – 4k. black and brown . . 30 10
2819 – 4k. brown and blue . . 30 10
2820 – 4k. black and red . . . 30 10
2821 – 4k. violet and mauve 30 10
DESIGNS (Army heroes and battle scenes): 2817, Type **1009** (70th birth anniv); 2818, U. M. Avetisyan; 2819, A. M. Matrosov; 2820, I. V. Panfilov; 2821, Ya. F. Fabricius.

1963. Academy of Sciences Members.
2822 **1010** 4k. blue, grey and brown 30 10
2823 – 4k. brown and green . . 30 10
2824 – 4k. multicoloured . . . 30 10
2825 – 4k. brown, red and blue 30 10
2826 – 4k. multicoloured . . . 30 10

PORTRAITS: No. 2823, I. V. Kurchatov; No. 2824, V. I. Vernadsky. LARGER (23½ × 30 mm): No. 2825, A. Krylov; No. 2826, V. Obruchev. All commemorate birth centenaries except No. 2823 (60th anniv of birth).

1011 Games Emblem

Советские
хоккеисты-
чемпионы
мира
и Европы.
Стокгольм.
1963 г.

(1012)

1963. 5th Soviet T.U. Winter Sports.
2827 **1011** 4k. orange, black & blue 30 10

1963. Soviet Victory in Swedish Ice Hockey Championships. No. 2670 optd with T **1012**.
2828 6k. turquoise and purple . . 1·60 60

1013 V. Kingisepp

1014 R. M. Blauman

1963. 75th Birth Anniv of Victor Kingisepp (Estonian Communist Party Leader).
2829 **1013** 4k. brown and blue . . 25 10

1963. Birth Centenary of Rudolf Blauman (Latvian writer).
2830 **1014** 4k. purple and blue . . 25 10

1015 Globe and Flowers

1016 Lenin (after I. Brodsky)

1963. "World without Arms and Wars". Perf or imperf.
2831 **1015** 4k. green, blue and red 35 10
2832 – 6k. lilac, green and red 55 10
2833 – 10k. violet, blue and red . . . . 1·10 25
DESIGNS: 6k. Atomic emblem and pylon; 10k. Sun and rocket.

1963. 93rd Birth Anniv of Lenin.
2834 **1016** 4k. brown and red . . 3·75 1·40

1963. Provincial Costumes (4th issue). As T **870**. Inscr "1963". Multicoloured.
2835 3k. Tadzhikistan 40 15
2836 4k. Azerbaijan 55 15
2837 4k. Kirgizia 55 15
2838 4k. Turkmenistan 55 15

1017 "Luna 4" Rocket

1963. Launching of "Luna 4" Space Rocket. Perf or imperf.
2839 **1017** 6k. red, black and blue 70 20
See also No. 3250.

1018 Woman and Lido

1963. 5th Anniv of World Health Day. Mult.
2840 2k. Type **1018** 20 10
2841 4k. Man and stadium . . . 35 10
2842 10k. Child and school . . . 85 20

1019 Sputniks and Globe

1963. Cosmonautics Day.
2843 **1019** 10k. blue, black and purple (white figures of value) 75 20
2843b 10k. blue, black and purple (blue figures) 75 20
2844 – 10k. purple, black and blue (white figures) 75 20
2844a 10k. purple, black and blue (purple figures) 75 20
2845 – 10k. red, black and yellow (white figures) 75 20
2845a 10k. red, black and yellow (yellow figures) 75 20
DESIGNS: Nos. 2844/a, "Vostok 1" and Moon; Nos. 2845/a, Space rocket and Sun.

1021 Cuban Horsemen with Flag

1963. Cuban-Soviet Friendship.
2846 **1021** 4k. black, red and blue 40 10
2847 – 6k. black, blue and red 50 10
2848 – 10k. blue, red and black 65 20
DESIGNS: 6k. Hands, weapon, book and flag; 10k. Crane, hoisting tractor and flags.

1022 J. Hasek

1023 Karl Marx

1963. 40th Death Anniv of Jaroslav Hasek (writer).
2849 **1022** 4k. black 65 15

1963. 80th Death Anniv of Karl Marx.
2850 **1023** 4k. black and brown . . 30 10

1963. War of 1941–45 (3rd issue). As T **911** inscr "1963".
2851 4k. multicoloured 45 15
2852 4k. multicoloured 45 15
2853 4k. multicoloured 45 15
2854 4k. sepia and red 45 15
2855 6k. olive, black and red . . 70 20
DESIGNS: No. 2851, Woman making shells (Defence of Leningrad, 1942); 2852, Soldier in winter kit with tommy gun (20th anniv of Battle of the Volga); 2853, Soldiers attacking (Liberation of Kiev, 1943); 2854, Tanks and map indicating Battle of Kursk, 1943; 2855, Tank commander and tanks.

1024 International P.O. Building

1963. Opening of Int Post Office, Moscow.
2856 **1024** 6k. brown and blue . . 65 10

1025 Medal and Chessmen

1963. World Chess Championship, Moscow. Perf or imperf.
2857 **1025** 4k. multicoloured . . . 60 15
2858 – 6k. blue, mauve and ultramarine 70 20
2859 – 16k. black, mauve & pur . . . . 1·50 50
DESIGNS: 6k. Chessboard and pieces; 16k. Venue and pieces.

1026 Wagner

1027 Boxers on "Glove"

1963. 150th Birth Anniv of Wagner and Verdi (composers).
2860 **1026** 4k. black and red . . . 50 15
2861 – 4k. purple and red . . 50 15
DESIGN: No. 2861, Verdi.

1963. 15th European Boxing Championships, Moscow. Multicoloured.
2862 4k. Type **1027** 30 10
2863 6k. Referee and winning boxer on "glove" 55 15

1028 Bykovsky and "Vostok 5"

1963. Second "Team" Manned Space Flights (1st issue). Perf or imperf.
2864 **1028** 6k. brown and purple 55 20
2865 – 6k. red and green . . . 55 20
2866 – 10k. red and blue . . . 1·00 30
DESIGNS: No. 2865, Tereshkova and "Vostok 6"; No. 2866, Allegory—"Man and Woman in Space".
See also Nos. 2875/7.

Всемирный
конгресс
женщин.

(1029)

1030 Cycling

1963. International Women's Congress, Moscow. Optd with T **1029**.
2867 **1015** 4k. green, blue and red 55 30

1963. 3rd People's Spartakiad. Multicoloured. Perf or imperf.
2868b 3k. Type **1030** 25 10
2869b 4k. Athletics 30 15
2870b 6k. Swimming (horiz) . . . 45 15
2871b 12k. Basketball 85 35
2872b 16k. Football . . . . . . 1·25 50
MS2872a 152 × 105 mm. As Nos. 2868/9 and 2871/2 but colours changed. Imperf . . . 3·75 1·40

1031 Globe, Film and Camera

1032 V. V. Mayakovsky

1963. International Film Festival, Moscow.
2873 **1031** 4k. blue, black & brown 30 10

1963. 70th Birth Anniv of Mayakovsky (poet).
2874 **1032** 4k. brown 40 15

1033 Tereshkova

1034 Ice Hockey Player

1963. 2nd "Team" Manned Space Flights (2nd issue). Multicoloured.
2875 4k. Bykovsky (horiz) . . . 40 20
2876 4k. Tereshkova (horiz) . . . 40 20
2877 10k. Type **1033** . . . . . 1·60 35

1963. Russian Ice Hockey Championships.
2878 **1034** 6k. blue and red . . . 75 20

1035 Lenin

1037 Guibozo (polo)

1036 Freighter and Crate

1963. 60th Anniv of 2nd Socialist Party Congress.
2879 **1035** 4k. black and red . . . 30 10

1963. Red Cross Centenary.
2880 **1036** 6k. red and green . . . 60 15
2881 – 12k. red and blue . . . 1·25 30
DESIGN: 12k. Centenary emblem.

1963. Regional Sports.
2882 – 3k. multicoloured . . . 30 10
2883 **1037** 4k. black, red and ochre 40 10
2884 – 6k. red, brown & yellow 65 15
2885 – 10k. black, brn & olive 90 25
DESIGNS—HORIZ: 3k. Lapp reindeer racing; 6k. Buryat archery. VERT: 10k. Armenian wrestling.

1038 Aleksandr Mozhaisky and his Monoplane

1963. Aviation Celebrities.
2886 **1038** 6k. black and blue . . 60 10
2887 – 10k. black and blue . . 80 15
2888 – 16k. black and blue . . 1·25 35
DESIGNS: 10k. Pyotr Nesterov and "looping the loop"; 16k. N. E. Zhukovsky and "aerodynamics".

1039 S. S. Gulak-Artemovsky (composer, 150th birth anniv)

1040 Olga Kobilyanska (writer) (birth centenary)

1963. Celebrities.
2889 **1039** 4k. black and red . . . 40 15
2890 – 4k. brown and purple 40 15
2891 – 4k. brown and violet 40 15
2892 **1040** 4k. mauve and brown 40 15
2893 – 4k. mauve and green 40 15
DESIGNS AND ANNIVERSARIES: As Type **1039**: No. 2893, M. I. Petraskas (Lithuanian composer) and scene from one of his works (90th birth anniv). As Type **1040**: No. 2890, G. D. Eristavi (writer, death cent, 1964); No. 2891, A. S. Dargomizhsky (composer, 150th birth anniv).

1041 Antarctic Map and Supply Ship "Ob"

1043 E. O. Paton

1042 Letters and Transport

1963. Arctic and Antarctic Research. Mult.
2894 3k. Type **1041** . . . . . . 1·75 25
2895 4k. Convoy of snow tractors and map . . . . 1·00 30
2896 6k. Globe and aircraft at polar base . . . . 1·75 30
2897 12k. "Sovetskaya Ukraina" (whale factory ship), whale catcher and whale 4·00 50

1963. International Correspondence Week.
2898 **1042** 4k. violet, orange & blk 35 10

1963. 10th Death Anniv of Paton (engineer).
2899 **1043** 4k. black, red and blue 30 10

1045 D. Diderot 1046 "Peace"

1963. 250th Birth Anniv of Denis Diderot (French philosopher).
2900 **1045** 4k. brown, blue & bistre 30 10

1963. "Peace—Brotherhood—Liberty—Labour". All black, red and lake.
2901 4k. Type **1046** 35 15
2902 4k. Worker at desk and couple consulting plan ("Labour") 35 15
2903 4k. Artist and couple ("Liberty") 35 15
2904 4k. Voters ("Equality") . . 35 15
2905 4k. Man shaking hands with couple with banner ("Brotherhood") 35 15
2906 4k. Family group ("Happiness") 35 15

1047 Academy of Sciences, Frunze

1963. Centenary of Union of Kirgizia and Russia.
2907 **1047** 4k. blue, yellow and red 30 10

1049 Lenin and Congress Building 1050 Ilya Mechnikov

1963. 13th Soviet Trade Unions' Congress, Moscow.
2908 **1049** 4k. red and black . . . 25 10
2909 – 4k. red and black . . . 25 10
DESIGN: No. 2909, Lenin with man and woman workers.

1963. 75th Anniv of Pasteur Institute, Paris.
2910 **1050** 4k. green and bistre . . 35 10
2911 – 6k. violet and bistre . . 55 15
2912 – 12k. blue and bistre . . 1·25 30
PORTRAITS: 6k. Pasteur; 12k. Calmette.

1051 Cruiser "Aurora" and Rockets 1052 Gur Emi Mausoleum

1963. 46th Anniv of October Revolution.
2913 **1051** 4k. black, orange & lake 45 10
2914 4k. black, red and lake 65 30

1963. Ancient Samarkand Buildings. Mult.
2915 4k. Type **1052** 50 10
2916 4k. Shachi-Zinda Mosque 50 10
2917 6k. Registan Square (55 × 28½ mm) 65 20

1053 Inscription, Globe and Kremlin 1054 Pushkin Monument, Kiev (A. Kovalev)

1963. Signing of Nuclear Test-ban Treaty, Moscow.
2918 **1053** 6k. violet and pale blue 60 15

1963.
2919 **1054** 4k. brown 30 10

1056 Shukhov and Radio Tower, Moscow 1057 Ya. Steklov and "Izvestia"

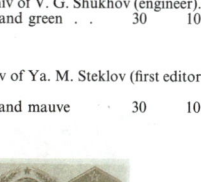

1963. 110th Birth Anniv of V. G. Shukhov (engineer).
2920 **1056** 4k. black and green . . 30 10

1963. 90th Birth Anniv of Ya. M. Steklov (first editor of "Izvestia").
2921 **1057** 4k. black and mauve 30 10

1058 Buildings and Emblems of Moscow (and U.S.S.R.) and Prague (and Czechoslovakia)

1963. 20th Anniv of Soviet-Czech Friendship Treaty.
2922 **1058** 6k. red, bistre and blue 45 10

1059 F. A. Poletaev (soldier) and Medals

1963. Poletaev Commemoration.
2923 **1059** 4k. multicoloured . . . 30 10

1062 J. Grimau (Spanish Communist) 1063 Rockets

1963. Grimau Commemoration.
2924 **1062** 6k. violet, red and cream 40 10

1963. New Year (1st issue).
2925 **1063** 6k. multicoloured . . . 50 10

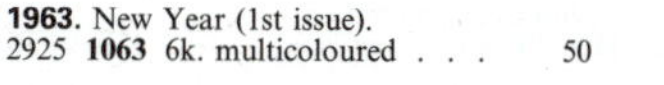

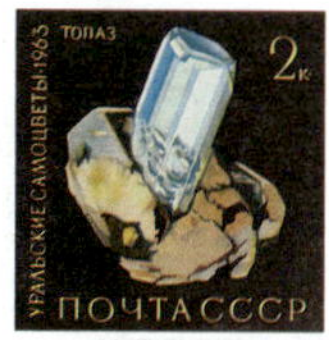

1064 "Happy New Year" 1067 Topaz

1963. New Year (2nd issue).
2926 **1064** 4k. red, blue and green 40 10
2927 6k. red, blue and green 55 10

1963. "Precious Stones of the Urals". Multicoloured.
2928 2k. Type **1067** 25 10
2929 4k. Jasper 50 10
2930 6k. Amethyst 70 15
2931 10k. Emerald 75 25
2932 12k. Ruby . . . . 1·00 45
2933 16k. Malachite . . . . . 1·25 55

1068 Sputnik 7 1071 Flame and Rainbow

1069 Dushanbe Putovsky Square

1963. "First in Space". Gold, vermilion and grey.
2934 10k. Type **1068** 90 30
2935 10k. Moon landing 90 30
2936 10k. Back of Moon 90 30
2937 10k. Vostok 7 . . . . . . 90 30
2938 10k. Twin flight 90 30
2939 10k. Seagull (first woman in space) 90 30

1963. Dushanbe, Capital of Tadzhikistan.
2940 **1069** 4k. blue 40 10

1963. 15th Anniv of Declaration of Human Rights.
2941 **1071** 6k. multicoloured . . . 45 10

1072 F. A, Sergeev ("Artem")

1963. 80th Birth Anniv of Sergeev (revolutionary).
2942 **1072** 4k. brown and red . . 30 10

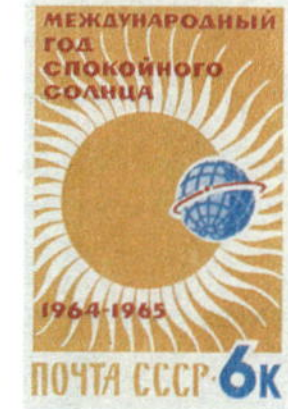

1073 Sun and Globe 1074 K. Donelaitis

1964. International Quiet Sun Year.
2943 – 4k. black, orange & mve 30 10
2944 **1073** 6k. blue, yellow and red 45 10
2945 – 10k. violet, red and blue 60 20
DESIGNS—HORIZ: 4k. Giant telescope and sun; 10k. Globe and Sun.

1964. 250th Birth Anniv of K. Donelaitis (Lithuanian poet).
2946 **1074** 4k. black and myrtle . . 30 10

1075 Speed Skating

1964. Winter Olympic Games, Innsbruck.
2947b **1075** 2k. black, mauve & bl 25 10
2948b – 4k. black, blue & mve 40 15
2949b – 6k. red, black and blue 60 20
2950b – 10k. black, mve & grn 85 25
2951b – 12k. black, grn & mve 1·00 35
DESIGNS: 4k. Skiing; 6k. Games emblem; 10k. Rifle shooting (biathlon); 12k. Figure skating (pairs).
See also Nos. 2969/73.

1076 Golubkina (after N. Ulyanov) and Statue, Tolstoi 1077 "Agriculture"

1964. Birth Cent of A. S. Golubkina (sculptress).
2952 **1076** 4k. sepia and grey . . . 30 10

1964. Heavy Chemical Industries. Multicoloured.
2953 4k. Type **1077** 40 10
2954 4k. "Textiles" 40 10
2955 4k. "Tyre Production" . . . 40 10

150 років з дня народження. 1964 р.

(1078)

1079 Shevchenko's Statue, Kiev (M. Manizer)

1964. 150th Birth Anniv of T. G. Shevchenko (Ukrainian poet and painter). No. 2561 optd with T **1078** and designs as T **1079**.
2956 **880** 3k. brown and violet 1·50 75
2959 **1079** 4k. green 25 10
2960 4k. red 25 10
2961 – 6k. blue 40 10
2962 – 6k. brown 40 10
2957 – 10k. violet and brown 80 20
2958 – 10k. brown and bistre 80 20
DESIGNS: Nos. 2957/8, Portrait of Shevchenko by I. Repin; Nos. 2961/2, Self-portrait.

1080 K. S. Zaslonov

1964. War Heroes.
2963 **1080** 4k. sepia and brown . . 55 15
2964 – 4k. purple and blue . . 35 15
2965 – 4k. blue and red . . . 35 15
2966 – 4k. brown and blue . . 35 15
PORTRAITS: No. 2964, N. A. Vilkov; 2965, Yu. V. Smirnov; 2966, V. Z. Khoruzhaya.

1081 Fyodorov printing the first Russian book, "Apostle"

1964. 400th Anniv of First Russian Printed Book. Multicoloured.
2967 4k. Type **1081** 30 10
2968 6k. Statue of Ivan Fyodorov, Moscow (S. Volnukin), books and newspapers 45 20

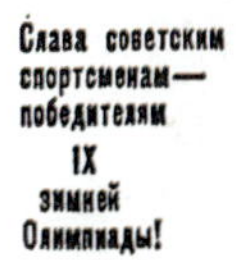

(1082)

1083 Ice Hockey Player

1964. Winter Olympic Games, Soviet Medal Winners. (a) Nos. 2947/51 optd with T **1082** or similarly.
2969 2k. black, mauve and blue 25 10
2970 4k. black, blue and mauve 40 10
2971 6k. red, black and blue . . 40 15

2972 10k. black, mauve and green 80 25
2973 12k. black, green and mauve 1·00 30

(b) New designs.
2974 **1083** 3k. red, black & turquoise 45 10
2975 – 16k. orange and brown 1·40 40
DESIGN: 16k. Gold medal and inscr "Triumph of Soviet Sport–11 Gold, 8 Silver, 6 Bronze medals".

1084 Militiaman and Factory Guard

1964. "Public Security".
2976 **1084** 4k. blue, red and black 30 10

1085 Lighthouse, Odessa and Sailor

1964. 20th Anniv of Liberation of Odessa and Leningrad. Multicoloured.
2977 4k. Type **1085** 35 10
2978 4k. Lenin Statue, Leningrad 35 10

1086 Sputniks

1087 N. I. Kibalchich

1964. "The Way to the Stars". Imperf or perf.
(a) Cosmonautics. As T **1086**.
2979 4k. green, black and red . . 50 10
2980 6k. black, blue and red . . 70 20
2981 12k. turquoise, brown & black . . . . 1·40 30
DESIGNS: 6k. "Mars I" space station; 12k. Gagarin and space capsule.

(b) Rocket Construction Pioneers. As T **1087**.
2982b 10k. black, green and violet . . . . 1·10 30
2983b 10k. black, turquoise and red . . . . 1·10 30
2984b 10k. black, turquoise and red . . . . 1·10 30
2985b 10k. black and blue . . . 1·00 30
DESIGNS: No. 2982, Type **1087**; 2983, F. A. Zander; 2984, K. E. Tsiolkovsky; 2985, Pioneers' medallion and Saransk memorial.

1088 Lenin

1964. 94th Birth Anniv of Lenin.
2986a **1088** 4k. black, blue & mve 3·25 2·50

1089 Shakespeare (400th Birth Anniv)

1964. Cultural Anniversaries.
2987 – 6k. yellow, brn & sepia 90 15
2988 **1089** 10k. brown and olive 1·40 25
2989 – 12k. green and brown 1·60 35
DESIGNS AND ANNIVERSARIES: 6k. Michelangelo (400th death anniv); 12k. Galileo (400th birth anniv).

1090 Crop-watering Machine and Produce

1964. "Irrigation".
2990 **1090** 4k. multicoloured . . . 30 10

1091 Gamarnik

1964. 70th Birth Anniv of Ya. B. Gamarnik (Soviet Army commander).
2991 **1091** 4k. brown, blue & black 30 10

1092 D. I. Gulia (Abhazian poet)

1094 Indian Elephant

1093 A. Gaidar

1964. Cultural Anniversaries.
2992 **1092** 4k. black, green and light green 30 15
2993 – 4k. black, verm & red 30 15
2994 – 4k. black, brown & bis 30 15
2995 – 4k. black, yellow & brn 30 15
2996 – 4k. multicoloured . . . 30 15
2997 – 4k. black, yellow & brn 30 15
DESIGNS: No. 2993, Nijazi (Uzbek writer, composer and painter); 2994, S. Seifullin (Kazakh poet); 2995, M. M. Kotsyubinsky (writer); 2996, S. Nazaryan (Armenian writer); 2997, T. Satylganov (Kirghiz poet).

1964. 60th Birth Annivs of Writers A. P. Gaidar and N. A. Ostrovsky.
2998 **1093** 4k. red and blue . . . 30 10
2999 – 4k. green and red . . . 35 10
DESIGN: No. 2999, N. Ostrovsky and battle scene.

1964. Centenary of Moscow Zoo. Multicoloured. Imperf or perf.
3000 1k. Type **1094** 10 10
3001 2k. Giant panda 20 10
3002 4k. Polar bear 45 10
3003 6k. Elk 55 10
3004 10k. Eastern white pelican 1·25 25
3005 12k. Tiger . . . . 2·00 30
3006 16k. Lammergeier . . . . . 1·50 40
The 2k. and 12k. are horiz; the 4k. and 10k. are "square", approx 26½ × 28 mm.

150 лет вхождения
в состав России
1964

4
коп.

(1095)

1964. 150th Anniv of Union of Azerbaijan and Russia. Surch with T **1095**.
3007 **328** 4k. on 40k. brown, bistre and yellow . . . . . 3·25 1·90

1096 Rumanian Woman and Emblems on Map

1097 Maize

1964. 20th. Anniv of Rumanian–Soviet Friendship Treaty.
3008 **1096** 6k. multicoloured . . . 50 15

1964. Agricultural Crops. Multicoloured. Imperf or perf.
3009b 2k. Type **1097** 15 10
3010b 3k. Wheat 20 10
3011b 4k. Potatoes 25 10
3012b 6k. Peas 35 20
3013b 10k. Sugar beet 70 25
3014b 12k. Cotton . . . . 1·00 30
3015b 16k. Flax . . . . 1·50 40

1098 Flag and Obelisk

1099 Leningrad G.P.O.

1964. 20th Anniv of Liberation of Byelorussia.
3016 **1098** 4k. multicoloured . . . 30 10

1964. 250th Anniv of Leningrad's Postal Service.
3017 **1099** 4k. black, bistre and red 30 10

1100 Map of Poland and Emblems

1964. 20th Anniv of Polish People's Republic.
3018 **1100** 6k. multicoloured . . . 45 10

1101 Horse-jumping

1102 M. Thorez (French Communist leader)

1964. Olympic Games, Tokyo. Imperf or perf.
3019b **1101** 3k. multicoloured . . 10 10
3020b – 4k. red, black & yellow 15 10
3021b – 6k. red, black and blue 25 15
3022b – 10k. red, black & turq 65 20
3023b – 12k. black and grey 80 25
3024b – 16k. violet, red and blue . . . . . . 1·40 30
MS3024a 90 × 71 mm. 1r. green background £225 £225
MS3024b 90 × 71 mm. 1r. red background . . . . 8·00 3·00
DESIGNS: 4k. Weightlifting; 6k. Pole vaulting; 10k. Canoeing; 12k Gymnastics; 16k. Fencing; 1r. Gymnast and stadium.

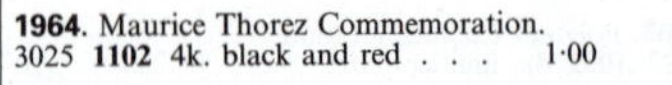

1964. Maurice Thorez Commemoration.
3025 **1102** 4k. black and red . . . 1·00 35

1103 Three Races

1104 Jawaharlal Nehru

1964. International Anthropologists and Ethnographers Congress, Moscow.
3026 **1103** 6k. black and yellow . . 40 15

1964. Nehru Commemoration.
3027 **1104** 4k. brown and grey . . 45 15

1104a

1964. World Orbit Flights. Sheet of six multicoloured stamps as T **1104a** making up composite design showing Earth, Moon, spacecraft etc.
MS3027a 140 × 110 mm. 10k. (× 6) 6·00 4·50

1105 Globe and Banner

1106 A. V. Vishnevsky (surgeon)

1964. Centenary of "First International".
3028 **1105** 4k. red, bistre and blue 30 10
3029 – 4k. red, olive and black 30 10
3030 – 4k. drab, red and lake 30 10
3031 – 4k. red, black and blue 30 10
3032 – 4k. multicoloured . . . 30 10
DESIGNS: No. 3029, Communist Party manifesto; 3030, Marx and Engels; 3031, Chain breaker; 3032, Lenin.

1964. "Outstanding Soviet Physicians".
3033 **1106** 4k. brown and purple 35 10
3034 – 4k. brown, red & yellow 35 10
3035 – 4k. brown, blue & bistre 35 10
DESIGNS: No. 3034, N. A. Semashko (public health pioneer). Both are 90th birth anniversaries. No. 3035, D. I. Ivanovsky and siphon (25 × 32 mm).

1107 Bulgarian Flag, Rose and Emblems

1108 P. Togliatti (Italian Communist leader)

1964. 20th Anniv of Bulgarian People's Republic.
3036 **1107** 6k. red, green and drab 45 15

1964. Togliatti Commemoration.
3037 **1108** 4k. black and red . . . 30 10

1110 Globe and Letters

1964. International Correspondence Week.
3038 **1110** 4k. mauve, blue & brn 30 10

1111 Soviet and Yugoslav Soldiers

1112 East German Arms, Industrial Plants, Freighter "Havel" and Electric Goods Train

1964. 20th Anniv of Liberation of Belgrade.
3039 **1111** 6k. multicoloured . . . 45 15

1964. 15th Anniv of German Democratic Republic.
3040 **1112** 6k. multicoloured . . . 45 15

1113 Woman holding Bowl of Produce (Moldavian Republic)

40 лет Советскому Таджикистану

1964 год

(1115)

1964. 40th Anniv of Soviet Republic. (a) As T **1113**.
3041 **1113** 4k. brown, green and red 30 10
3042 – 4k. multicoloured . . . 35 10
3043 – 4k. red, purple & yellow 35 10

(b) Optd with T **1115**.
3044 **1069** 4k. blue . . . . 1·10 60
DESIGNS—VERT: No. 3042, Woman holding Arms (Turkmenistan); 3043, Man and woman holding produce (Uzbekistan); 3044, commemorates the Tadzhikistan Republic.

1116 Yegorov

1964. Three-manned Space Flight. (a) Portraits in black, orange and turquoise.
3045 4k. Type **1116** 40 10
3046 4k. Feoktistov 40 10
3047 4k. Komarov 40 10
These can be identified by the close proximation of the Russian names on the stamps to the English versions.

(b) Designs $73\frac{1}{2} \times 22\frac{1}{2}$ mm.
3048 6k. purple and violet . . . 75 15
3049 10k. violet and blue . . . . 1·10 30
MS3049a 120 × 56 mm. 50k. violet, red and grey. Imperf . . . . . 6·75 3·25
DESIGNS: 6k. The three cosmonauts; 10k. Space ship "Voskhod 1".

1117 Soldier and Flags

1964. 20th Anniv of Liberation of Ukraine.
3050 **1117** 4k. multicoloured . . . 25 10

1119 Lermontov's Birthplace

1121 N. K. Krupskaya (Lenin's wife)

1120 Hammer and Sickle

1964. 150th Birth Anniv of M. Lermontov (poet).
3051 **1119** 4k. violet 30 10
3052 – 6k. black 45 10
3053 – 10k. brown and flesh 85 25
DESIGNS: 6k. Lermontov (after K. Gorbunov); 10k. Lermontov talking with V. Belinsky.

1964. 47th Anniv of October Revolution.
3054 **1120** 4k. multicoloured . . . 25 10

1964. 94th Anniv of Lenin. Sheet 144 × 101 mm, comprising pair of No. 2679.
MS3054a 10k. purple, lake and black . . . . 2·75 1·60

1964. Birth Anniversaries.
3055 **1121** 4k. multicoloured . . . 30 10
3056 – 4k. multicoloured . . . 30 10
DESIGNS: 3055 (95th anniv); 3056, A. I. Yelizarova-Ulyanova (Lenin's sister) (cent).

1122 Mongolian Woman and Lamb

1124 Butter Mushroom

1964. 40th Anniv of Mongolian People's Republic.
3057 **1122** 4k. multicoloured . . . 45 15

1964. Mushrooms. Multicoloured.
3058 2k. Type **1124** 30 10
3059 4k. Chanterelle 50 10
3060 6k. Ceps 65 15
3061 10k. Red-capped sacker stalk . . . . 1·10 40
3062 12k. Saffron milk cap . . . 1·40 50

1125 A. P. Dovzhenko

1126 Christmas Tree, Star and Globe

1964. 70th Birth Anniv of Dovzhenko (film producer).
3063 **1125** 4k. blue and grey . . . 30 10

1964. New Year.
3064 **1126** 4k. multicoloured . . . 75 25

1127 Struve

1128 Ivanov (after O. Braz) and "March of the Moscovites. 16th Century"

1964. Death Centenary of V. Ya. Struve (scientist).
3065 **1127** 4k. brown and blue . . 60 15

1964. Birth Centenary of S. V. Ivanov (painter).
3066 **1128** 4k. brown and black . . 65 15

1129 Scene from Film

1964. 30th Anniv of Film "Chapaev".
3067 **1129** 6k. black and green . . 50 15

1130 Test-tubes, Jar and Agricultural Scenes

1964. Chemistry for the National Economy.
3068 **1130** 4k. purple and olive . . 25 15
3069 – 6k. black and blue . . 45 10
DESIGN: 6k. Chemical plant.

1131 Cranberries

1132 Library

1964. Woodland Fruits. Multicoloured.
3070 1k. Type **1131** 15 10
3071 3k. Bilberries 20 10
3072 4k. Rowanberries 30 10
3073 10k. Blackberries 70 20
3074 16k. Red bilberries . . . . 1·10 40

1964. 250th Anniv of Academy of Sciences Library, Leningrad.
3075 **1132** 4k. black, green and red 40 10

1133 Congress Palace and Spassky Tower

1134 Mt Khan-Tengri

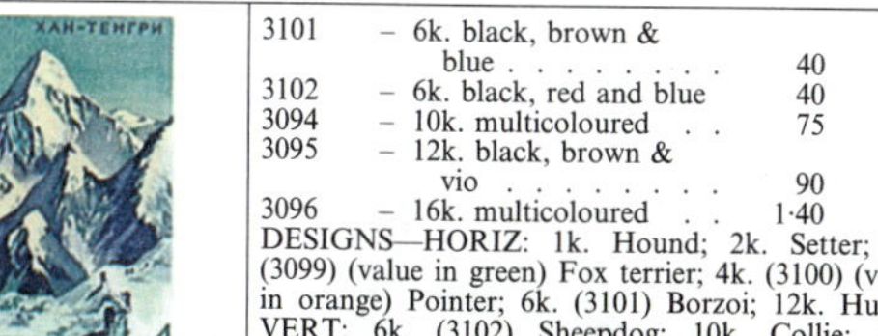

1964.
3076 **1133** 1r. blue . . . . 7·00 1·60

1964. Mountaineering. Multicoloured.
3077 4k. Type **1134** 30 10
3078 6k. Mt Kazbek (horiz) . . . 45 15
3079 12k. Mt Ushba 90 30

1136 Bowl

1964. Kremlin Treasures. Multicoloured.
3080 4k. Helmet 45 15
3081 6k. Quiver 65 20
3082 10k. Coronation headgear 1·00 35
3083 12k. Ladle . . . . 1·40 45
3084 16k. Type **1136** . . . . . 1·75 80

1137 I. M. Sivko

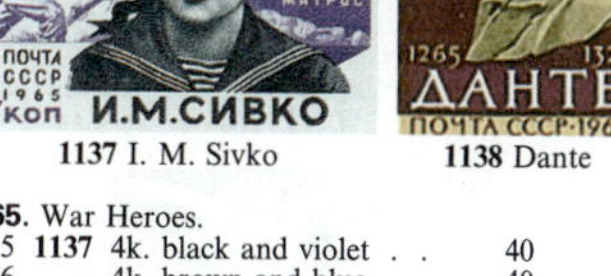

1138 Dante

1965. War Heroes.
3085 **1137** 4k. black and violet . . 40 15
3086 – 4k. brown and blue . . 40 15
DESIGN: No. 3086, General I. S. Polbin.

1965. 700th Birth Anniv of Dante.
3087 **1138** 4k. black, bistre and purple 60 15

1139 Blood Donor

1140 N. P. Kravkov

1965. Blood Donors. Multicoloured.
3088 4k. Type **1139** 35 15
3089 4k. Hand holding red carnation 35 15

1965. Birth Cent of N. Kravkov (pharmacologist).
3090 **1140** 4k. multicoloured . . . 35 10

1141 Figure Skaters

1142 Alsatian

1965. European Figure Skating Championships, Moscow.
3091 **1141** 6k. red, black and green 55 15
See also No. 3108.

1965. World Ice Hockey Championships, Moscow. Designs similar to T **1141** but depicting ice hockey players.
3092 4k. red, blue and bistre . . . 40 15

1965. Hunting and Service Dogs.
3093 – 1k. black, yellow and red 15 10
3097 – 2k. brown, blue & black 20 10
3098 **1142** 3k. black, red and yellow 20 10
3099 – 4k. black, brown & grn 30 10
3100 – 4k. black, orange & grn 30 10
3101 – 6k. black, brown & blue 40 20
3102 – 6k. black, red and blue 40 20
3094 – 10k. multicoloured . . 75 25
3095 – 12k. black, brown & vio 90 35
3096 – 16k. multicoloured . . 1·40 45
DESIGNS—HORIZ: 1k. Hound; 2k. Setter; 4k. (3099) (value in green) Fox terrier; 4k. (3100) (value in orange) Pointer; 6k. (3101) Borzoi; 12k. Husky. VERT: 6k. (3102) Sheepdog; 10k. Collie; 16k. Caucasian sheepdog.

1143 R. Sorge

1965. Richard Sorge (Soviet secret agent) Commem.
3103 **1143** 4k. black and red . . . 55 15

1144 I.T.U. Emblem and Telecommunications Symbol

1965. Centenary of I.T.U.
3104 **1144** 6k. violet and blue . . 65 15

1145 Leonov in Space ($\frac{1}{2}$-size illustration)

1965. Space Flight of "Voskhod 2" (1st issue). Imperf or perf.
3105 **1145** 10k. orange, black & bl 1·25 30
MS3106 1r. black, red and blue 7·75 2·75
See also Nos. 3138/9.

1965. Ice Hockey Championships. Optd **ТАМПЕРЕ 1965 г.**
3107 **1034** 6k. blue and red . . . 1·75 50

Советские фигуристы— чемпионы мира в парном катании

(1147)

1148 Soldier and Woman

1965. Soviet Victory in European Figure Skating Championships. Optd with T **1147**.
3108 **1141** 6k. red, black and green 1·75 50

1965. 20th Anniversaries.
3109 **1148** 6k. multicoloured . . . 40 15
3110 – 6k. multicoloured . . . 45 15
3111 – 6k. ochre and red . . . 40 15
3112 – 6k. multicoloured . . . 40 15
3113 – 6k. multicoloured . . . 40 15
DESIGNS: No. 3109, Type **1148** (Czech Liberation); 3110, Statue and emblems of development (Friendship with Hungary); 3111, Polish and Soviet arms (Polish–Soviet Friendship Treaty); 3112, Viennese buildings and Russian soldier (Freeing of Vienna); 3113, Liberation medal, Polish flag and building reconstruction (Freeing of Warsaw).
See also Nos. 3182 and 3232.

1149 Statue Rockets and Globe

1150 Rockets and Radio-telescope

1965. National Cosmonautics Day. Nos. 3117/18 on aluminium-surfaced paper.
3114 **1149** 4k. green, black and red 25 10
3115 – 12k. purple, red and blue 80 15
3116 – 16k. multicoloured . . 1·10 30
3117 **1150** 20k. red, black and green on silver . . . 7·00 5·00
3118 – 20k. red, black and blue on silver . . . . . . 7·00 5·00

DESIGNS: 12k. Statue and Globe; 16k. Rockets and Globe; No. 3118, Globe, satellite and cosomonauts.

1151 Lenin (after bas-relief by V. Sayapin)

1965. Lenin's 95th Birth Anniv.
3119 **1151** 10k. blue, black & brn 75 30

1152 Poppies

1153 Red Flag, Reichstag Building and Broken Swastika

1965. Flowers.
3120 **1152** 1k. red, lake and green 10 10
3121 – 3k. yellow, brown & grn 30 10
3122 – 4k. lilac, black and green 40 15
3123 – 6k. red, deep green and green 60 15
3124 – 10k. yellow, pur & grn 1·10 25
FLOWERS: 3k. Marguerite; 4k. Peony; 6k. Carnation; 10k. Tulips.

1965. 20th Anniv of Victory.
3125 **1153** 1k. black, gold and red 20 10
3126 – 2k. red, black and gold 25 15
3127 – 3k. blue and gold 40 15
3128 – 4k. violet and gold 55 15
3129 – 4k. green and gold 60 15
3130 – 6k. purple, green & gold 1·25 20
3131 – 10k. purple, brn & gold 1·75 25
3132 – 12k. black, red and gold 2·25 30
3133 – 16k. red and gold 2·50 40
3134 – 20k. black, red and gold 3·00 75
DESIGNS: 2k. Soviet mother holding manifesto (poster by I. Toidze); 3k. "The Battle for Moscow" (V. Bogatkin); 4k. (No. 3128), "Partisan Mother" (from S. Gerasimov's film); 4k. (No. 3129), "Red Army Soldiers and Partisans" (from Yu. Neprintsev's film); 6k. Soldiers and flag (poster by V. Ivanov); 10k. "Mourning the Fallen Hero" (from F. Bogorodsky's film); 12k. Soldier and worker holding bomb (poster by V. Korestsky); 16k. Victory celebrations, Red Square, Moscow (from K. Yuon's film); 20k. Soldier and machines of war.

1153a Popov's Radio Invention

1154 Marx and Lenin

1965. 70th Anniv of A. S. Popov's Radio Discoveries. Sheet 144 × 100 mm comprising six stamps without face value.
MS3135 1r. multicoloured 6·00 3·25
DESIGNS: T **1153a**: Transistor radio; TV screen; Radar; Radiotelescope; Telecommunications satellite. The value is printed on the sheet.

1965. Marxism and Leninism.
3136 **1154** 6k. black and red 40 10
No. 3136 is similar in design to those issued by China and Hungary for the Postal Ministers' Congress, Peking, but this event is not mentioned on the stamp or in the Soviet philatelic bulletins.

1155 Bolshoi Theatre

1965. International Theatre Day.
3137 **1155** 6k. ochre, black & turq 55 15

1156 Leonov

1157 Yakov Sverdlov (revolutionary)

1965. "Voskhod 2" Space Flight (2nd issue).
3138 **1156** 6k. violet and silver 45 15
3139 – 6k. purple and silver 45 15
DESIGN: No. 3139, Belyaev.

1965. 80th Birth Anniversaries.
3140 **1157** 4k. black and brown 35 10
3141 – 4k. black and violet 35 10
PORTRAIT: No. 3141, J. Akhunbabaev (statesman).

1158 Otto Grotewohl (1st death anniv)

1159 Telecommunications Satellite

1965. Annivs of Grotewohl and Thorez (Communist leaders).
3142 **1158** 4k. black and purple 35 10
3143 – 6k. brown and red 55 15
DESIGN: 6k. Maurice Thorez (65th birth anniv).

1965. International Co-operation Year. Mult.
3144 3k. Type **1159** 20 10
3145 6k. Star and sputnik 50 15
3146 6k. Foundry ladle, iron works and map of India 50 15
No. 3145 signifies peaceful uses of atomic energy and No. 3146 co-operation with India.

1160 Congress Emblem, Chemical Plant and Symbols

1965. 20th International Congress of Pure and Applied Chemistry, Moscow.
3147 **1160** 4k. red, black and blue 25 10

1161 V. A. Serov (after I. Repin)

1965. Birth Centenary of V. A. Serov (painter).
3148 **1161** 4k. black, brn & stone 95 20
3149 – 6k. black and drab 1·50 25
DESIGN: 6k. Full length portrait of Chaliapin (singer) by Serov.

1162 Vsevolod Ivanov and Armoured Train

1965. Famous Writers.
3150 **1162** 4k. black and purple 45 15
3151 – 4k. black and violet 40 15
3152 – 4k. black and blue 40 15
3153 – 4k. black and grey 40 15
3154 – 4k. black, red and green 40 15
3155 – 4k. black and brown 40 15
WRITERS AND ANNIVERSARIES: No. 3150, (70th birth anniv); 3151, A. Kunanbaev and military parade; 3152, J. Rainis (Lettish poet: 90th birth anniv); 3153, E. J. Vilde (Estonian author): 90th birth anniv); 3154, M. Ch. Abegjan (Armenian writer and critic: 90th birth anniv); 3155, M. L. Kropivnitsky and scene from play (Ukrainian playwright).

1163 Festival Emblem

1965. Film Festival, Moscow.
3156 **1163** 6k. black, gold and blue 50 15

1164 Concert Arena, Tallin

1165 Hand holding "Peace Flower"

1965. 25th Anniv of Incorporation of Estonia, Lithuania and Latvia in the U.S.S.R.
3157 **1164** 4k. multicoloured 40 10
3158 – 4k. brown and red 40 10
3159 – 4k. brown, red and blue 40 10
DESIGNS—VERT: No. 3158, Lithuanian girl and Arms. HORIZ: No. 3159, Latvian Flag and Arms.

1965. Peace Issue.
3160 **1165** 6k. yellow, black & blue 45 10

1167 "Potemkin" Sailors Monument (V. Bogdanov), Odessa

1965. 60th Anniv of 1905 Rebellion.
3161 **1167** 4k. blue and red 30 15
3162 – 4k. green, black and red 30 15
3163 – 4k. green, black and red 30 15
3164 – 4k. brown, black and red 30 15
DESIGNS: No. 3162, Demonstrator up lamp post; 3163, Defeated rebels; 3164, Troops at street barricade.

1168 G. Gheorghi-Dej (Rumanian Communist)

1169 Power Station

1965. G. Gheorgi-Dej Commemoration.
3165 **1168** 4k. black and red 25 10

1965. Industrial Progress.
3166 **1169** 1k. multicoloured 10 10
3167 – 2k. black, orange & yell 20 10
3168 – 3k. violet, yell & ochre 20 10
3169 – 4k. deep blue, blue and red 35 10
3170 – 6k. blue and bistre 45 10
3171 – 10k. brown, yellow and orange 70 20
3172 – 12k. turquoise and red 1·10 20
3173 – 16k. purple, blue & blk 1·40 40
DESIGNS: 2k. Steel works; 3k. Chemical works and formula; 4k. Machine tools production; 6k. Building construction; 10k. Agriculture; 12k. Communications and transport; 16k. Scientific research.

1170 Relay Racing

1171 Gymnastics

1965. Trade Unions Spartakiad. Multicoloured.
3174 4k. Type **1170** 35 15
3175 4k. Gymnastics 35 15
3176 4k. Cycling 35 15

1965. Schoolchildren's Spartakiad.
3177 **1171** 4k. red and blue 30 10
3178 – 6k. red, brown & turq 50 15
DESIGN: 6k. Cycle racing.

1172 Throwing the Javelin and Running

1173 Star, Palms and Lotus

1965. American–Soviet Athletic Meeting, Kiev.
3179 **1172** 4k. red, brown and lilac 20 10
3180 – 6k. red, brown and green 45 10
3181 – 10k. red, brown and grey 60 15
DESIGNS: 6k. High jumping and putting the shot; 10k. Throwing the hammer and hurdling.

1965. 20th Anniv of North Vietnamese People's Republic.
3182 **1173** 6k. multicoloured 40 15

1174 Worker with Hammer (World T.U. Federation)

1176 P. K. Sternberg (astonomer: birth cent)

1965. 20th Anniv of International Organizations.
3183 **1174** 6k. drab and plum 35 15
3184 – 6k. brown, red and blue 35 15
3185 – 6k. lt brown & turquoise 35 15
DESIGNS: No. 3184, Torch and heads of three races (World Democratic Youth Federation); No. 3185, Woman holding dove (International Democratic Women's Federation).

1965. Scientists' Anniversaries.
3186 **1176** 4k. brown and blue 50 15
3187 – 4k. black and purple 50 15
3188 – 4k. black, purple & yell 50 15
PORTRAITS: No. 3187, Ch. Valikhanov (scientific writer: death cent); 3188, V. A. Kistyakovsky (scientist: birth cent).

1177 "Battleship 'Potemkin'" (dir. Sergei Eisenshtein)

1965. Soviet Cinema Art. Designs showing scenes from films. Multicoloured.
3189 4k. Type **1177** 35 10
3190 6k. "Young Guard" (dir. S. Coesinov) 50 15
3191 12k. "A Soldier's Ballad" (dir. G. Chuthrai) 1·00 25

1178 Mounted Postman and Map

1965. History of the Russian Post Office.
3192 **1178** 1k. green, brown & vio 25 10
3193 – 1k. brown, ochre & grey 25 10
3194 – 2k. brown, blue and lilac 40 10
3195 – 4k. black, ochre & pur 45 10
3196 – 6k. black, green & brn 65 15
3197 – 12k. sepia, brown & blue 1·10 25
3198 – 16k. plum, red and grey 1·40 45
DESIGNS: No. 3193, Mail coach and map; 2k. Early steam train and medieval kogge; 4k. Mail lorry and map; 6k. Diesel-electric train and various transport; 12k. Moscow Post Office electronic facing sorting and cancelling machines; 16k. Airports and Lenin.

1179 "Vostok" and "Mirnyi" (Antarctic exploration vessels)

1965. Polar Research Annivs.
3199 – 4k. black, orange & blue 90 15
3200 – 4k. black, orange & blue 90 15
3201 – 6k. sepia and violet . . 75 25
3202 **1179** 10k. black, drab and red . . . . 1·75 35
3203 – 16k. black, violet & brn 1·25 65
DESIGNS—HORIZ: $37\frac{1}{2} \times 25\frac{1}{2}$ mm: No. 3199, Ice breakers "Taimyr" and "Vaigach" in Arctic (50th anniv); 3200, Atomic ice breaker "Lenin"; 3201, Dikson settlement (50th anniv); 3203, Vostok Antarctic station. SQUARE. No. 3202, (145th anniv of Lazarev–Bellingshausen Expedition).
Nos. 3199/200 were issued together, se-tenant, forming a composite design.

1180 Basketball Players and Map of Europe

1965. European Basketball Championships, Moscow. Sheet 65 × 90 mm.
MS3204 **1180** 1r. multicoloured 6·50 3·00

1181 Agricultural Academy

1965. Centenary of Academy of Agricultural Sciences, Moscow.
3205 **1181** 4k. violet, red and drab 30 15

1182 Lenin (after P. Vasilev)

1965. 48th Anniv of October Revolution. Sheet 64 × 95 mm.
MS3206 **1182** 10k. black, red and silver . . . . 3·25 2·25

1183 N. Poussin (self-portrait)

1184 Kremlin

1965. 300th Death Anniv of Nicolas Poussin (French painter).
3207 **1183** 4k. multicoloured . . . 50 10

1965. New Year.
3208 **1184** 4k. red, silver and black 40 10

1185 M. I. Kalinin

1966. 90th Birth Anniv of Kalinin (statesman).
3209 **1185** 4k. lake and red . . . 30 10

1186 Klyuchevski Volcano

1965. Soviet Volcanoes. Multicoloured.
3210 4k. Type **1186** 40 15
3211 12k. Karumski Volcano (vert) . . . . 1·00 30
3212 16k. Koryaski Volcano . . 1·10 45

1187 Oktyabrskaya Station, Moscow

1965. Soviet Metro Stations.
3213 **1187** 6k. blue 40 10
3214 – 6k. brown 40 10
3215 – 6k. brown 40 10
3216 – 6k. green 40 10
STATIONS: No. 3214, Leninksy Prospekt, Moscow; 3215, Moscow Gate, Leningrad; 3216, Bolshevik Factory, Kiev.

1188 Common Buzzard

1189 "Red Star" (medal) and Scenes of Odessa

1965. Birds of Prey. Birds in black.
3217 **1188** 1k. grey 30 10
3218 – 2k. brown 40 15
3219 – 3k. olive 45 15
3220 – 4k. drab 55 15
3221 – 10k. brown . . . . . . 1·10 30
3222 – 12k. blue . . . . 1·40 50
3223 – 14k. blue . . . . 1·50 65
3224 – 16k. purple . . . . . . 2·00 75
BIRDS—VERT: 2k. Common kestrel; 3k. Tawny eagle; 4k. Red kite; 10k. Peregrine falcon; 16k. Gyr falcon. HORIZ: 12k. Golden eagle; 14k. Lammergeier.

1965. Heroic Soviet Towns. Multicoloured.
3225 10k. Type **1189** 55 25
3226 10k. Leningrad 55 25
3227 10k. Kiev 55 25
3228 10k. Moscow 55 25
3229 10k. Brest-Litovsk 55 25
3230 10k. Volgograd 55 25
3231 10k. Sevastopol 55 25

1190 Flag, Map and Parliament Building, Belgrade

1965. 20th Anniv of Yugoslavia Republic.
3232 **1190** 6k. multicoloured . . . 45 15

1191 Tupolev Tu-134 Jetliner

1965. Soviet Civil Aviation. Multicoloured.
3233 6k. Type **1191** 55 10
3234 10k. Antonov An-24 . . . . 80 15
3235 12k. Mil Mi-10 helicopter 95 25
3236 16k. Beriev Be-10 flying boat . . . . 1·40 40
3237 20k. Antonov An-22 Anteus 1·90 45

1192 "The Proposal of Marriage" (P. Fedotov, 150th birth anniv)

1965. Soviet Painters' Annivs.
3238 – 12k. black and red . . 1·50 25
3239 **1192** 16k. blue and red . . . 2·40 40
DESIGN—VERT: 12k. "A Collective Farm Watchman" (S. Gerasimov, 80th birth anniv).

1193 Crystallography Congress Emblem

1966. International Congresses, Moscow.
3240 **1193** 6k. black, blue and bistre 35 15
3241 – 6k. black, red and blue 35 15
3242 – 6k. purple, grey & black 35 15
3243 – 6k. black and blue . . 35 15
3244 – 6k. black, red and yellow 35 15
CONGRESS EMBLEMS: No. 3241, Microbiology; 3242, Poultry-raising; 3243, Oceanography; 3244, Mathematics.

1194 Postman and Milkmaid (19th-century statuettes, des A. Venetsianov)

1966. Bicentenary of Dmitrov Ceramic Works. Multicoloured.
3245 6k. Type **1194** 30 15
3246 10k. Modern tea set 65 25

1195 Rolland (after A. Yar-Kravchenko)

1966. Birth Centenary of Romain Rolland (French writer) and 150th Birth Anniv of Eugene Potier (French poet).
3247 **1195** 4k. brown and blue . . 30 15
3248 – 4k. brown, red and black 30 15
DESIGN: No. 3248, Potier and revolutionary scene.

1196 Mongol Horseman

1966. 20th Anniv of Soviet–Mongolian Treaty.
3249 **1196** 4k. multicoloured . . . 30 10

„ЛУНА-9" — НА ЛУНЕ!
3.2.1966
(1197)

1966. Landing of "Luna 9" Rocket on Moon. Optd with T **1197**.
3250 **1017** 6k. red, black and blue 4·50 4·50

1198 Supply Ship "Ob"

1966. 10th Anniv of Soviet Antarctic Expedition.
3251 **1198** 10k. lake and silver . . 2·00 1·60
3252 – 10k. lake, silver and blue . . . . 2·25 50
3253 – 10k. lake, silver and blue . . . . 2·25 50
DESIGNS—TRIANGULAR: No. 3252, Snow vehicle. DIAMOND: No. 3253, Antarctic map. This stamp is partly perf across the centre.

1199 Mussa Dyalil and Scene from Poem

1966. Writers.
3254 **1199** 4k. black and brown . . 30 10
3255 – 4k. black and green . . 30 10
3256 – 4k. black and green . . 30 10
WRITERS: No. 3254 (Azerbaijan writer: 60th birth anniv); 3255, Akob Akopyan (Armenian poet: birth cent); 3256, Djalil Mamedkulizade (Azerbaijan writer: birth cent).

1200 Lenin (after bust by Kibalnikov)

1966. Lenin's 96th Birth Anniv.
3257 **1200** 10k. gold and green . . 1·10 65
3258 10k. silver and red . . 1·10 25

1201 N. Ilin

1202 Scene from "Alive and Dead" (dir. A. Stolper)

1966. War Heroes.
3259 **1201** 4k. violet and red . . . 30 15
3260 – 4k. lilac and blue . . . 30 15
3261 – 4k. brown and green . . 30 15
PORTRAITS: No. 3260, G. P. Kravchenko; 3261, A. Uglovsky.

1966. Soviet Cinema Art.
3262 **1202** 4k. black, green and red 25 10
3263 – 10k. black and blue . . 60 20
DESIGN: 10k. Scene from "Hamlet" (dir. G. Kozintsev).

1203 Kremlin and Inscription

Учредительная конференция
Всесоюзного общества
филателистов. 1966
(1204)

1966. 23rd Soviet Comunist Party Congress, Moscow (1st issue).
3264 **1203** 4k. gold, red and blue 30 10
See also Nos. 3337/41.

1966. Philatelists All-Union Society Conference. No. 3198 optd with T **1204**.
3265 16k. plum, red and grey . . 2·75 1·75

1205 Ice Skating

1966. 2nd People's Winter Spartakiad.
3266 **1205** 4k. blue, red and olive 30 15
3267 – 6k. red, lake and lilac 50 20
3268 – 10k. lake, red and blue 75 30
DESIGNS: Inscription emblem and 6k. Ice hockey; 10k. Skiing.
Nos. 3266/8 are each perf across the centre.

1206 Liner "Aleksandr Pushkin"

1966. Soviet Transport.
3269 – 4k. multicoloured . . . 55 10
3270 – 6k. multicoloured . . . 45 10
3271 – 10k. multicoloured . . 65 20
3272 **1206** 12k. multicoloured . . 1·00 20
3273 – 16k. multicoloured . . 1·00 25
DESIGNS—HORIZ: 4k. Electric train; 6k. Map of Lenin Volga–Baltic canal system; 16k. Silhouette of liner "Aleksandr Pushkin" on globe. VERT: 10k. Canal lock (Volga–Baltic canal).
Nos. 3271/3 commemorate the inauguration of Leningrad–Montreal Sea Service.

1207 Government Building, Frunze

1208 S. M. Kirov (80th Birth Anniv)

1966. 40th Anniv of Kirgizia.
3274 **1207** 4k. red 30 10

1966. Soviet Personalities.
3275 **1208** 4k. brown 30 10
3276 – 4k. green 30 10
3277 – 4k. violet 30 10
PORTRAITS: No. 3276, G. I. Ordzhonikidze (80th birth anniv); 3277, Ion Yakir (military commander, 70th birth anniv).

1209 Lenin

1210 A. Fersman (mineralogist)

1966. 23rd Soviet Communist Party Congress, Moscow (2nd issue). Sheet 119 × 80 mm.
MS3278 **1209** 50k. red, silver and lake . . . . 3·50 1·25

1966. Soviet Scientists. Multicoloured. Colours of name panels below.
3279 **1210** 4k. blue 60 15
3280 – 4k. brown 60 15
3281 – 4k. violet 60 15
3282 – 4k. brown and blue . . 60 15
PORTRAITS: No. 3280, D. K. Zabolotnyi (microbiologist); 3281, M. A. Shatelen (electrical engineer); 3282, O. Yu. Shmidt (arctic explorer).

„Луна-10"—XXIII съезду КПСС
(1211)

1966. Launching of "Luna 10". As No. 3284, but imperf, optd with T **1211**.
3283 **1212** 10k. multicoloured . . 3·75 3·00

1212 Arrowheads, "Luna 9" and Orbit

1966. Cosmonautics Day. Multicoloured.
3284 10k. Type **1212** 60 25
3285 12k. Rocket launching and different orbit 65 30

1213 "Molniya I" in Orbit

1214 Ernst Thalmann (80th birth anniv)

1966. Launching of "Molniya I" Telecommunications Satellite.
3286 **1213** 10k. multicoloured . . 55 20

1966. Prominent Leaders.
3287 **1214** 6k. red 45 10
3288 – 6k. violet 45 10
3289 – 6k. brown 45 10
PORTRAITS: No. 3288, Wilhelm Pieck (90th birth anniv); 3289, Sun Yat-sen (birth cent).

1216 Spaceman and Soldier

1966. 15th Young Communist League Congress.
3290 **1216** 4k. black and red . . . 30 10

1217 Ice Hockey Player

1966. Soviet Victory in World Ice Hockey Championships.
3291 **1217** 10k. multicoloured . . 60 25

1218 N. I. Kuznetsov

1219 Tchaikovsky

1966. War Heroes. Guerrilla Fighters.
3292 **1218** 4k. black and green . . 20 10
3293 – 4k. black and yellow . . 20 10
3294 – 4k. black and blue . . 20 10
3295 – 4k. black and purple . . 20 10
3296 – 4k. black and violet . . 20 10
PORTRAITS: No. 3293, I. Y. Sudmalis; 3294, A. A. Morozova; No. 3295, F. E. Strelets; 3296, T. P. Bumazhkov.

1966. 3rd International Tchaikovsky Music Competition, Moscow.
3297 – 4k. black, red and yellow 35 10
3298 **1219** 6k. black, red and yellow 55 10
3299 – 16k. black, red and blue 1·40 35
DESIGNS: 4k. Moscow State Conservatoire of Music; 16k. Tchaikovsky's house and museum, Klin.

1220 Running

1966. Sports Events.
3300 **1220** 4k. brown, olive & green 20 15
3301 – 6k. black, bistre & orge 45 15
3302 – 12k. black, bistre & blue 65 25
DESIGNS: 6k. Weightlifting; 12k. Wrestling.

1222 Gold Medal and Chess Pieces

1966. World Chess Championship, Moscow.
3303 **1222** 6k. multicoloured . . . 1·40 20

1223 Jules Rimet Cup and Football

1966. World Cup Football Championship (England) and World Fencing Championships (Moscow).
3304 **1223** 4k. black, gold and red 20 10
3305 – 6k. multicoloured . . 35 10
3306 – 12k. multicoloured . . 70 20
3307 – 16k. multicoloured . . 1·10 40
DESIGNS: 6k. Footballers; 12k. Fencers; 16k. Fencer and fencing emblems.

1224 Sable, Lake Baikal and Animals ($\frac{1}{2}$-size illustration)

1966. Barguzin Nature Reserve.
3308 **1224** 4k. black and blue . . 60 15
3309 – 6k. black and purple . . 90 25
DESIGN: 6k. Map of reserve, and brown bear.

1225 Lotus Plants

1226 "Venus 3" Medal, Globe and Flight Trajectory

1966. 125th Anniv of Sukhumi Botanical Gardens.
3310 **1225** 3k. red, yellow and green 25 10
3311 – 6k. bistre, brown & blue 45 10
3312 – 12k. red, green & turq 70 30
DESIGNS: 6k. Palms and cypresses; 12k. Water lilies.

1966. Space Achievements.
3313 **1226** 6k. black, silver and red 50 20
3314 – 6k. deep blue, blue and brown 50 20
3315 – 6k. ochre and blue . . 50 20
3316 – 6k. multicoloured . . . 60 20
3317 – 6k. pink, mauve & black 60 20
DESIGNS: No. 3314, Spacedogs, Ugolek and Veterok; 3315, "Luna 10"; 3316, "Molniya I"; 3317, "Luna 2's" pennant, Earth and Moon.

1227 Itkol

1966. Tourist Resorts. Multicoloured.
3318 1k. Type **1227** 10 10
3319 4k. Cruise ship on the Volga 30 10
3320 6k. Archway, Leningrad ($27\frac{1}{2} \times 28$mm) 35 10
3321 10k. Castle, Kislovodsk . . 55 15
3322 12k. Ismail Samani Mausoleum, Bokhara . . 80 20
3323 16k. Kavkaz Hotel, Sochi (Black Sea) . . . . 1·25 30

1229 Fencing

1966. World Sports Championships of 1966. Sheet 155 × 155 mm comprising four 10k. stamps as T **1229**.
MS3324 4 × 10k. multicoloured 8·00 3·25
DESIGNS: Type **1229**: Jules Rimet Cup (football); Chessmen; Ice Hockey.

1230 Congress Emblem

1231 Peace Dove and Japanese Crane

1966. 7th Consumers' Co-operative Societies Congress, Moscow.
3325 **1230** 4k. yellow and brown 40 10

1966. Soviet–Japanese Meeting, Khabarovsk.
3326 **1231** 6k. black and red . . . 50 20

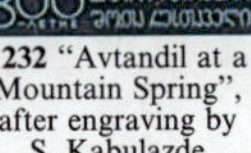

1232 "Avtandil at a Mountain Spring", after engraving by S. Kabulazde

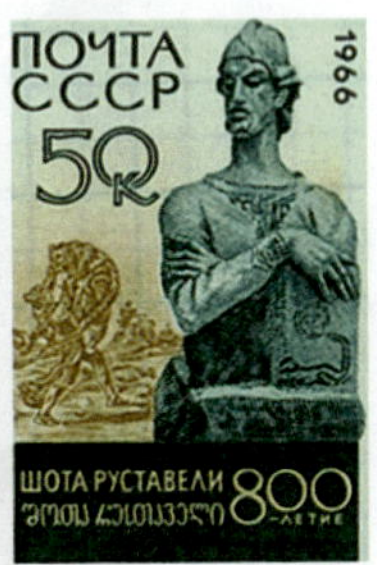

1233

1966. 800th Birth Anniv of Shota Rustaveli (Georgian poet).
3327 – 3k. black on green . . 35 10
3328 – 4k. brown on yellow . . 45 10
3329 **1232** 6k. black on blue . . . 55 15
MS3330 98 × 68 mm. **1233** 50k. green and bistre . . . . 5·50 1·75
DESIGNS: 3k. Scene from poem "The Knight in the Tiger's Skin" (after I. Toidze); 4k. Rustaveli, (after bas-relief by Ya. Nikoladze).

1234 Arms, Moscow Skyline and Fireworks

1235 Trawler, Net and Map of Lake Baikal

1966. 49th Anniv of October Revolution.
3331 **1234** 4k. multicoloured . . . 30 10

1966. Fish Resources of Lake Baikal. Mult.
3332 2k. Baikal grayling (horiz) 25 10
3333 4k. Baikal sturgeon (horiz) 30 10
3334 6k. Type **1235** 35 10
3335 10k. Omul (horiz) 70 20
3336 12k. Baikal whitefish (horiz) 85 25

1236 "Agriculture and Industry"

1966. 23rd Soviet Communist Party Congress, Moscow (3rd issue).
3337 **1236** 4k. silver and brown . . 20 10
3338 – 4k. silver and blue . . . 20 10
3339 – 4k. silver and red . . . 20 10
3340 – 4k. silver and red . . . 20 10
3341 – 4k. silver and green . . . 20 10
DESIGN (Map as Type **1236** with symbols of): No. 3338, "Communications and Transport"; 3339, "Education and Technology"; 3340, "Increased Productivity"; 3341, "Power Resources".

1237 Government Buildings, Kishinev

1966. 500th Anniv of Kishinev (Moldavian Republic).
3342 **1237** 4k. multicoloured . . . 30 10

1238 Clouds, Rain and Decade Emblem

1239 Nikitin Monument (S. Orlov and A. Zavalor), Kalinin

1966. International Hydrological Decade.
3343 **1238** 6k. multicoloured . . . 40 15

1966. 50th Anniv of Afanasy Nikitin's Voyage to India.
3344 **1239** 4k. black, green & yell 30 10

1240 Scene from "Nargiz" (Muslim Magomaev)

1966. Azerbaijan Operas.
3345 **1240** 4k. ochre and black . . 35 15
3346 – 4k. green and black . . 35 15
DESIGN: No. 3346, Scene from "Kehzoglu" (Uzeir Gadzhibekov).

1241 "Luna 9" and Moon

1242 Agricultural and Chemical Symbols

1966.
3347 – 1k. brown 10 10
3348 **1241** 2k. violet 10 10
3349 – 3k. purple 20 10
3350 – 4k. red 20 10
3351 – 6k. blue 60 10
3563 – 10k. olive 90 35
3353 – 12k. brown 70 10
3354 – 16k. blue 90 15
3355 – 20k. red, blue and drab 1·10 20
3566 – 20k. red . . . . 1·75 40
3356 **1242** 30k. green . . . . . . 1·75 40
3357 – 50k. ultram, blue & grey . . . . 3·00 50
3568 – 50k. blue . . . . 5·00 1·00
3358 – 1r. black and red . . . 5·25 1·50
3569 – 1r. brown and black . . 8·25 1·50
DESIGNS—As Type **1241**: 1k. Palace of Congresses, Kremlin; 3k. Youth, girl and Lenin emblem; 4k. Arms and hammer and sickle emblem; 6k. "Communications" (Antonov An-10A Ukrainia airplane and sputnik); 10k. Soldier and star emblem; 12k. Furnaceman; 16k. Girl with dove. As Type **1242**: 20k. Workers' demonstration and flower; 50k. "Postal communications"; 1r. Lenin and industrial emblems.

1243 "Presenting Arms"

1245 Campaign Meeting

1966. 25th Anniv of People's Voluntary Corps.
3359 **1243** 4k. brown and red . . 30 10

1966. "Hands off Vietnam".
3360 **1245** 6k. multicoloured . . . 30 10

1246 Servicemen

1966. 30th Anniv of Spanish Civil War.
3361 **1246** 6k. black, red and ochre 35 10

1247 Ostankino TV Tower, "Molniya I" (satellite) and "1967"

1249 Statue, Tank and Medal

1248 Flight Diagram

1966. New Year and "50th Year of October Revolution".
3362 **1247** 4k. multicoloured . . . 40 10

1966. Space Flight and Moon Landing of "Luna 9".
3363 **1248** 10k. black and silver . . 70 25
3364 – 10k. red and silver . . 70 25
3365 – 10k. black and silver . . 70 25
DESIGNS—SQUARE (25 × 25 mm): No. 3364, Arms of Russia and lunar pennant. HORIZ: No. 3365, "Lunar 9" on Moon's surface.

1966. 25th Anniv of Battle of Moscow.
3366 – 4k. brown 30 10
3367 **1249** 6k. ochre and sepia . . 30 15
3368 – 10k. yellow and brown 60 20
DESIGNS—HORIZ: (60 × 28 mm): 4k. Soviet troops advancing; 10k. "Moscow at peace"– Kremlin, Sun and "Defence of Moscow" medal.

1250 Cervantes and Don Quixote

1966. 350th Death Anniv of Cervantes.
3369 **1250** 6k. brown, green and deep green 40 15

1252 Bering's Ship "Sv. Pyotr" and Map of Komandor Islands

1966. Soviet Far Eastern Territories. Mult.
3370 1k. Type **1252** 40 10
3371 2k. Medny Island and map 45 10
3372 4k. Petropavlovsk Harbour, Kamchatka 65 10
3373 6k. Geyser, Kamchatka (vert) 80 10
3374 10k. Avatchinskaya Bay, Kamchatka . . . . 1·00 15
3375 12k. Northern fur seals, Bering Is . . . . 1·00 35
3376 16k. Common guillemot colony, Kurile Islands . . 1·50 75

1254 "The Lute Player" (Caravaggio)

1966. Art Treasures of the Hermitage Museum, Leningrad.
3377 – 4k. black on yellow . . 20 10
3378 – 6k. black on grey . . . 40 10
3379 – 10k. black on lilac . . . 65 15
3380 – 12k. black on green . . 85 20
3381 **1254** 16k. black on buff . . . 1·10 35
DESIGNS—HORIZ: 4k. "Golden Stag" (from Scythian battle shield (6th cent B.C.). VERT: 6k. Persian silver jug (5th cent A.D.; 10k. Statue of Voltaire (Houdon, 1781); 12k. Malachite vase (Urals, 1840).

1255 Sea-water Distilling Apparatus

1967. World Fair, Montreal.
3382 **1255** 4k. black, silver & green 20 10
3383 – 6k. multicoloured . . . 35 15
3384 – 10k. multicoloured . . 60 20
MS3385 127 × 76 mm. 30k. multicoloured . . . . 3·00 1·25
DESIGNS—VERT: 6k. "Atomic Energy" (explosion and symbol). HORIZ: 10k. Space station "Proton 1"; 30k. Soviet pavilion.

1256 Lieut. B. I. Sizov

1967. War Heroes.
3386 **1256** 4k. brown on yellow . . 30 10
3387 – 4k. brown on drab . . 30 10
DESIGN: No. 3387, Private V. V. Khodyrev.

1257 Woman's Face and Pavlov Shawl

1967. International Women's Day.
3388 **1257** 4k. red, violet and green 30 10

1258 Cine-camera and Film "Flower"

1967. 5th International Film Festival, Moscow.
3389 **1258** 6k. multicoloured . . . 40 10

1259 Factory Ship "Cheryashevsky"

1967. Soviet Fishing Industry. Multicoloured.
3390 6k. Type **1259** 45 15
3391 6k. Refrigerated trawler . . 45 15
3392 6k. Crab canning ship . . . 45 15
3393 6k. Trawler 45 15
3394 6k. Seine-fishing boat, Black Sea 45 15

1260 Newspaper Cuttings, Hammer and Sickle

1261 I.S.O. Congress Emblem

1967. 50th Anniv of Newspaper "Izvestiya".
3395 **1260** 4k. multicoloured . . . 30 10

1967. Moscow Congresses.
3396 6k. turquoise, black and blue 30 10
3397 6k. red, black and blue . . 30 10
DESIGNS: No. 3396, Type **1261** (7th Congress of Int Standards Assn "I.S.O."; 3397, "V" emblem of 5th Int Mining Congress.

1262 I.T.Y. Emblem

1967. International Tourist Year.
3398 **1262** 4k. black, silver and blue 30 10

Вена - 1967
(**1263**)

1265 "Lenin as Schoolboy" (V. Tsigal)

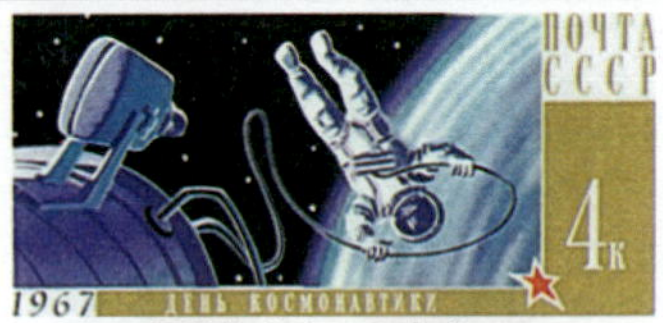

1264 A. A. Leonov in Space

1967. Victory in World Ice Hockey Championship. No. 3291 optd with T **1263**.
3399 **1217** 10k. multicoloured . . 2·75 1·40

1967. Cosmonautics Day. Multicoloured.
3400 4k. Type **1264** 35 10
3401 10k. Rocket and Earth . . . 80 15
3402 16k. "Luna 10" over Moon 1·00 35

1967. Lenin's 97th Birth Anniv.
3403 **1265** 2k. brown, yellow & grn 25 10
3404 – 3k. brown and lake . . 45 10
3405 – 4k. green, yellow and olive 60 15
3406 – 6k. silver, black and blue 90 20
3407 – 10k. blue, black & silver . . . . 2·10 45
3408 – 10k. black and gold . . 70 30
SCULPTURES—VERT: 3k. Lenin's monument, Ulyanovsk; 6k. Bust of Lenin (G. and Yu. Neroda); 10k. (both) "Lenin as Leader" (N. Andreev). HORIZ: 4k. "Lenin at Razliv" (V. Pinchuk).

1266 M. F. Shmyrev

1967. War Heroes.
3409 **1266** 4k. sepia and brown . . 20 10
3410 – 4k. brown and blue . . 20 10
3411 – 4k. brown and violet 20 10
DESIGNS: No. 3410, Major-General S. V. Rudnev; 3411, First Lieut. M. S. Kharchenko.

1267 Transport crossing Ice on Lake Ladoga

1967. Siege of Leningrad, 1941–42.
3412 **1267** 4k. grey, red and cream 20 10

1268 Marshal Biryuzov

1270 Red Cross and Tulip

1269 Minsk Old and New

1967. Biryuzov Commemoration.
3413 **1268** 4k. green and yellow . . 20 10

1967. 900th Anniv of Minsk.
3414 **1269** 4k. green and black . . 30 10

1967. Centenary of Russian Red Cross.
3415 **1270** 4k. red and ochre . . . 30 10

1271 Russian Stamps of 1918 and 1967

1967. 50th Anniv of U.S.S.R. Philatelic Exn, Moscow.
3416 **1271** 20k. green and blue . . 1·50 65
MS3417 92 × 75 mm. **1271** 20k. green (pair). Imperf . . . . . 5·50 1·40

1272 Komsomolsk-on-Amur and Map

1967. 35th Anniv of Komsomolsk-on-Amur.
3418 **1272** 4k. brown and red . . 50 10

1273 Motor Cyclist (International Motor Rally, Moscow)

1967. Sports and Pastimes. International Events.
3419 – 1k. brown, bistre & grn 20 10
3420 – 2k. brown 20 10
3421 – 3k. blue 20 10
3422 – 4k. turquoise 20 10
3423 – 6k. purple and bistre 30 10
3424 **1273** 10k. purple and lilac . . 75 30
DESIGNS AND EVENTS: 1k. Draughts board and players (World Draughts Championships); 2k. Throwing the javelin; 3k. Running; 4k. Long jumping (all preliminary events for Europa Cup Games); 6k. Gymnast (World Gymnastics Championships).

1274 "Sputnik 1" orbiting Globe (½-size illustration)

1967. 10th Anniv of First Earth Satellite. Sheet 105 × 132 mm.
MS3425 **1274** 30k. multicoloured 4·25 1·75

1275 G. D. Gai (soldier)

1276 Games Emblem and Cup

1967. Commander G. D. Gai Commemoration.
3426 **1275** 4k. black and red . . . 30 10

1967. All Union Schoolchildren's Spartakiad.
3427 **1276** 4k. red, black and silver 20 10

1277 Spartakiad Emblem and Cup

1967. 4th People's Spartakiad.
3428 4k. black, red and silver . . 25 10
3429 4k. black, red and silver . . 25 10
3430 4k. black, red and silver . . 25 10
3431 4k. black, red and silver . . 25 10
DESIGNS: Each with Cup. No. 3428, Type **1277**; No. 3429, Gymnastics; 3430, Diving; 3431, Cycling.

1278 V. G. Klochkov (Soviet hero)

1967. Klochkov Commemoration.
3432 **1278** 4k. black and red . . . 25 10

1279 Crest, Flag and Capital of Moldavia

АРМЯНСКАЯ ССР
ՀԱՅԿԱԿԱՆ ՍՍՀ
No. 3433

АЗЕРБАЙДЖАНСКАЯ ССР
АЗӘРБАЈҸАН ССР
No. 3434

БЕЛОРУССКАЯ ССР
БЕЛАРУСКАЯ ССР
No. 3435

ЭСТОНСКАЯ ССР
EESTI NSV
No. 3436

ГРУЗИНСКАЯ ССР
საქართველოს სსრ
No. 3437

КАЗАХСКАЯ ССР
ҚАЗАҚ ССР
No. 3438

КИРГИЗСКАЯ ССР
КЫРГЫЗ ССР
No. 3439

ЛАТВИЙСКАЯ ССР
LATVIJAS PSR
No. 3440

ЛИТОВСКАЯ ССР
LIETUVOS TSR
No. 3441

МОЛДАВСКАЯ ССР
РСС МОЛДОВЕНЯСКЭ
No. 3442

РОССИЙСКАЯ СОВЕТСКАЯ
ФЕДЕРАТИВНАЯ
СОЦИАЛИСТИЧЕСКАЯ РЕСПУБЛИКА
No. 3443

ТАДЖИКСКАЯ ССР
РСС ТОҶИКИСТОН
No. 3444

ТУРКМЕНСКАЯ ССР
ТҮРКМЕНИСТАН ССР
No. 3445

УКРАИНСКАЯ ССР
УКРАЇНСЬКА РСР
No. 3446

УЗБЕКСКАЯ ССР
ЎЗБЕКИСТОН ССР
No. 3447

Inscr at foot as shown above

1967. 50th Anniv of October Revolution (1st issue). Designs showing crests, flags and capitals of the Soviet Republics. Multicoloured.
3433 4k. Armenia 20 10
3434 4k. Azerbaijan 20 10
3435 4k. Belorussia 20 10
3436 4k. Estonia 20 10
3437 4k. Georgia 20 10
3438 4k. Kazakhstan 20 10
3439 4k. Kirgizia 20 10
3440 4k. Latvia 20 10
3441 4k. Lithuania 20 10
3442 4k. Type **1279** 20 10
3443 4k. Russia 20 10
3444 4k. Tadjikistan 20 10
3445 4k. Turkmenistan 20 10
3446 4k. Ukraine 20 10
3447 4k. Uzbekistan 20 10
3448 4k. Soviet Arms 20 10
No. 3448 is size 47 × 32 mm.
See also Nos. 3473/82.

1280 Telecommunications Symbols

1967. "Progress of Communism".
3449 **1280** 4k. red, purple and silver . . . . 3·25 1·40

1281 Manchurian Crane and Dove

1967. Soviet–Japanese Friendship.
3450 **1281** 16k. brown, black & red 90 35

1282 Karl Marx and Title Page

1967. Centenary of Karl Marx's "Das Kapital".
3451 **1282** 4k. brown and red . . 40 10

1283 Arctic Fox

1285 Krasnodon Memorial

1284 Ice Skating

1967. Fur-bearing Animals.
3452 **1283** 2k. blue, black & brown 20 10
3453 – 4k. blue, black and drab 30 10
3454 – 6k. ochre, black & green 45 10
3455 – 10k. brown, black & grn 60 15
3456 – 12k. black, ochre & vio 70 25
3457 – 16k. brown, black & yell 85 35
3458 – 20k. brown, black & turq . . . . 1·10 50
DESIGNS—VERT: 4k. Red fox; 12k. Stoat; 16k. Sable. HORIZ: 6k. Red fox; 10k. Muskrat; 20k. European mink.

1967. Winter Olympic Games, Grenoble (1968). Multicoloured.
3459 2k. Type **1284** 15 10
3460 3k. Ski jumping 25 10
3461 4k. Games emblem (vert) . . 30 10
3462 10k. Ice hockey 70 15
3463 12k. Skiing 90 30

1967. 25th Anniv of Krasnodon Defence.
3464 **1285** 4k. black, yellow & pur 20 10

1285a Map and Snow Leopard (½-size illustration)

1967. Cedar Valley Nature Reserve.
3465 **1285a** 10k. black and bistre 75 30

1286 Badge and Yakovlev Yak-9 Fighters

1288 Cosmonauts in Space

1287 Militiaman and Soviet Crest

1967. 25th Anniv of French "Normandie-Niemen" Fighter Squadron.
3466 **1286** 6k. red, blue and gold 40 15

1967. 50th Anniv of Soviet Militia.
3467 **1287** 4k. red and blue . . . 30 10

1967. Space Fantasies. Multicoloured.
3468 4k. Type **1288** 25 10
3469 6k. Men on the Moon (horiz) 40 10
3470 10k. Cosmic vehicle 65 15
3471 12k. Planetary landscape (horiz) 80 20
3472 16k. Imaginary spacecraft 90 30

1289 Red Star and Soviet Crest (⅔-size illustration)

1967. 50th Anniv of October Revolution (2nd issue). "50 Heroic Years". Designs showing paintings and Soviet Arms. Multicoloured.
3473 4k. Type **1289** 25 15
3474 4k. "Lenin addressing Congress" (Serov—1955) 25 15
3475 4k. "Lenin explaining the GOELRO map" (Schmatko—1957) 25 15
3476 4k. "The First Cavalry" (Grekov—1924) 25 15
3477 4k. "Students" (Yoganson—1928) 25 15
3478 4k. "People's Friendship" (Karpov—1924) 25 15
3479 4k. "Dawn of the Five Year Plan" (construction work, Romas—1934) 60 15
3480 4k. "Farmers' Holiday" (Gerasimov—1937) . . . 25 15
3481 4k. "Victory in World War II" (Korolev—1965) . . . 25 15
3482 4k. "Builders of Communism" (Merpert and Skripkov—1965) . . . 25 15
MS3483 93 × 141 mm. 40k. (2) in designs of Nos. 3474, 3482, but smaller (60 × 28 mm) and colours changed . . . . 5·50 2·25

1290 S. Katayama

1291 Hammer, Sickle and First Earth Satellite

1967. Katayama (founder of Japanese Communist Party) Commemoration.
3484 **1290** 6k. green 25 10

1967. 50th Anniv of October Revolution (3rd issue). "Conquest of Space". Sheet 129 × 80 mm.
MS3485 **1291** 1r. lake . . . . . 7·00 3·00

1292 T.V. Tower, Moscow

1967. Opening of Ostankino T.V. Tower, Moscow.
3486 **1292** 16k. black, silver & orge . . . . 1·00 20

1293 Narva-Joesuu (Estonia)

1967. Baltic Health Resorts. Multicoloured.
3487 4k. Yurmala (Latvia) . . . 20 10
3488 6k. Type **1293** 30 10
3489 10k. Druskininkai (Lithuania) 55 15
3490 12k. Zelenogradsk (Kaliningrad) (vert) . . . 70 20
3491 16k. Svetlogorsk (Kaliningrad) (vert) . . . 1·00 25

1294 K.G.B. Emblem

1295 Moscow View

1967. 50th Anniv of State Security Commission (K.G.B.).
3492 **1294** 4k. red, silver and blue 25 10

1967. New Year.
3493 **1295** 4k. brown, pink and silver 30 10

1296 Revolutionaries at Kharkov, and Monument

1967. 50th Anniv of Ukraine Republic.
3494 **1296** 4k. multicoloured . . . 20 10
3495 – 6k. multicoloured . . . 60 10
3496 – 10k. multicoloured . . 70 15
DESIGNS: 6k. Hammer and sickle and industrial and agricultural scenes; 10k. Unknown Soldier's monument, Kiev, and young Ukrainians with welcoming bread and salt.

1297 Armoury, Commandant and Trinity Towers

1299 Unknown Soldier's Tomb, Kremlin

1298 Moscow Badge, Lenin's Tomb and Rockets

1967. Kremlin Buildings.
3497 **1297** 4k. brown, purple & grn 20 10
3498 – 6k. brown, green & yell 30 10
3499 – 10k. brown and grey 55 15
3500 – 12k. green, violet and cream 80 30
3501 – 16k. brown, red and light brown 90 30
DESIGNS—HORIZ: 6k. Cathedral of the Annunciation. VERT: 10k. Konstantino-Yelenin, Alarm and Spassky Towers; 12k. Ivan the Great's bell tower; 16k. Kutafya and Trinity Towers.

1967. "50 Years of Communist Development".
3502 **1298** 4k. lake 25 10
3503 – 4k. brown 30 10
3504 – 4k. green 25 10
3505 – 4k. blue 25 10
3506 – 4k. blue 30 10
DESIGNS—HORIZ: No. 3503, Computer-tape cogwheel and industrial scene; 3504, Ear of wheat and grain silo; 3505, Microscope, radar antennae and Moscow University. VERT: No. 3506, T.V. Tower, "Aleksandr Pushkin" (liner), railway bridge and jet airliner.

1967. "Unknown Soldier" Commemoration.
3507 **1299** 4k. red 30 10

1300 "The Interrogation of Communists" (B. Ioganson)

1967. Paintings in the Tretyakov Gallery, Moscow. Multicoloured.
3508 3k. Type **1300** 20 10
3509 4k. "The Sea-shore" (I. Aivazovsky) 30 10
3510 4k. "The Lace Maker" (V. Tropinin) (vert) . . . 30 10
3511 6k. "The Bakery" (T. Yablonskaya) (60 × 34 mm) 40 10
3512 6k. "Aleksandr Nevsky" (part of triptych by P. Korin) (34 × 60 mm) 40 10
3513 6k. "Boyarynya Morozova" (V. Surikov) (60 × 34 mm) 40 10
3514 10k. "The Swan Maiden" (M. Vrubel) (vert) 80 20
3515 10k. "The Arrest of a Propagandist" (I. Repin) 80 20
3516 16k. "Moscow Suburb in February" (G. Nissky) . . 2·25 45

1301 Congress Emblem

1968. 14th Soviet Trade Unions Congress, Moscow.
3517 **1301** 6k. red and green . . . 30 10

1302 Lieut. S. G. Baikov

1968. War Heroes.
3518 **1302** 4k. black and blue . . 30 10
3519 – 4k. blue and green . . 20 10
3520 – 4k. black and red . . . 20 10
PORTRAITS: No. 3519, Lieut. P. L. Guchenko; No. 3520, A. A. Pokaltchuk.

1303 Racehorses

1304 M. Ulyanova

1968. Soviet Horse Breeding.
3521 **1303** 4k. black, purple & blue 25 10
3522 – 6k. black, blue and red 35 10
3523 – 10k. black, brn & turq 60 15
3524 – 12k. black, green & brn 65 20
3525 – 16k. black, red and green 90 30
DESIGNS (each with horse's head and horses "in the field"). VERT: 6k. Show horses; 12k. Show jumpers. HORIZ: 10k. Trotters; 16k. Hunters.

1968. 90th Birth Anniv of M. I. Ulyanova (Lenin's sister).
3526 **1304** 4k. blue and green . . 25 10

1305 Red Star and Forces' Flags

1968. 50th Anniv of Soviet Armed Forces. Multicoloured.
3527 4k. Type **1305** 25 10
3528 4k. Lenin addressing recruits (horiz) 25 10
3529 4k. Recruiting poster (D. Moor) and volunteers (horiz) 25 10
3530 4k. Red Army entering Vladivostok, 1922, and monument (L. Shervud) (horiz) 25 10
3531 4k. Dnieper Dam and statue "On Guard" (horiz) . . . 25 10
3532 4k. "Liberators" poster (V. Ivanov) and tanks in the Ukraine (horiz) . . . 25 10
3533 4k. "To the East" poster and retreating Germans fording river (horiz) . . . 25 10
3534 4k. Stalingrad battle monument and German prisoners-of-war 25 10
3535 4k. Victory parade, Red Square, Moscow, and monument, Treptow (Berlin) (horiz) 25 10
3536 4k. Rockets, tank, warships and Red Flag 25 10
MS3537 73 × 100 mm. 1r. Design as No. 3536 but smaller. Imperf 5·50 2·75

1306 Gorky (after Serov)

1307 Fireman and Appliances

1968. Birth Centenary of Maksim Gorky (writer).
3538 **1306** 4k. brown and drab . . 25 10

1968. 50th Anniv of Soviet Fire Services.
3539 **1307** 4k. black and red . . . 20 10

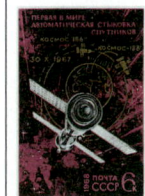

1308 Linked Satellites

1309 N. N. Popudrenko

1968. Space Link of "Cosmos" Satellites.
3540 **1308** 6k. black, gold & purple 30 10

1968. War Heroes.
3541 **1309** 4k. black and green . . 20 10
3542 – 4k. black and lilac . . . 20 10
DESIGN: No. 3542, P. P. Vershigora.

1310 Protective Hand

1968. "Solidarity with Vietnam".
3543 **1310** 6k. multicoloured . . . 25 10

1311 Leonov filming in Space

1968. Cosmonautics Day. Multicoloured.
3544 4k. Type **1311** 35 15
3545 6k. "Kosmos 186" and "Kosmos 188" linking in space 55 15
3546 10k. "Venera 4" space probe 1·00 15

1312 Lenin

1968. Lenin's 98th Birth Anniv.
3547 **1312** 4k. multicoloured . . . 85 15
3548 – 4k. black, red and gold 85 15
3549 – 4k. brown, red and gold 85 15
DESIGNS: No. 3548, Lenin speaking in Red Square; No. 3549, Lenin in peaked cap speaking from lorry during parade.

1313 Navoi (after V. Kaidalov)

1314 Karl Marx

1968. 525th Birth Anniv of Alisher Navoi (Uzbek poet).
3550 **1313** 4k. brown 25 10

1968. 150th Birth Anniv of Karl Marx.
3551 **1314** 4k. black and red . . . 30 10

1315 Frontier Guard

1316 Gem and Congress Emblem

1968. 50th Anniv of Soviet Frontier Guards. Multicoloured.
3552 4k. Type **1315** 25 10
3553 6k. Jubilee badge 40 10

1968. "International Congresses and Assemblies".
3554 **1316** 6k. deep blue, blue and green 25 15
3555 – 6k. gold, orange & brn 25 15
3556 – 6k. gold, black and red 25 15
3557 – 6k. orange, black & mve 25 15
DESIGNS: No. 3554, Type **1316** (8th Enriched Minerals Congress); 3555, Power stations, pylon and emblem (7th World Power Conference); 3556, "Carabus schaenherri" (ground beetle) and emblem (13th Entomological Congress); 3557, Roses and emblem (4th Congress on Volatile Oils).

1317 S. Aini

1319 "Kiev Uprising" (after V. Boroday)

1318 Congress Emblem and Postrider

1968. 90th Birth Anniv of Sadriddin Aini (Tadzhik writer).
3570 **1317** 4k. purple and bistre 30 10

1968. Meeting of U.P.U. Consultative Commission, Moscow.
3571 **1318** 6k. red and grey . . . 30 10
3572 – 6k. red and yellow . . 30 10
DESIGN: No. 3572, Emblem and transport.

1968. 50th Anniv of Ukraine Communist Party.
3573 **1319** 4k. red, purple and gold 20 10

1320 Athletes and "50"

1321 Handball

1968. Young Communist League's 50th Anniv Games.
3574 **1320** 4k. red, drab and yellow 25 10

1968. Various Sports Events.
3575 **1321** 2k. multicoloured . . . 20 10
3576 – 4k. multicoloured . . . 30 10
3577 – 6k. multicoloured . . . 40 10
3578 – 10k. red, black & bistre 45 20
3579 – 12k. multicoloured . . 80 25
DESIGNS AND EVENTS—VERT: Type **1321** (World Handball Games, Moscow); 6k. Yachting (20th Baltic Regatta); 10k. Football (70th anniv of Russian soccer). HORIZ: 4k. Table tennis (All European Juvenile Competitions); 12k. Underwater swimming (European Underwater Sports Championships, Alushta, Ukraine).

1322 Girl Gymnasts

1323 Gediminas Tower, Vilnius (Vilna)

1968. Olympic Games, Mexico. Backgrounds in gold.
3580 **1322** 4k. turquoise and blue 20 10
3581 – 6k. violet and red . . . 30 10
3582 – 10k. green and turquoise 55 10
3583 – 12k. brown and orange 70 15
3584 – 16k. blue and pink . . 1·00 30
MS3585 90 × 65 mm. 40k. multicoloured . . . . 2·25 1·25
DESIGNS: 6k. Weightlifting; 10k. Rowing; 12k. Women's hurdles; 16k. Fencing match; 40k. Running.

1968. 50th Anniv of Soviet Lithuania.
3586 **1323** 4k. red, drab and purple 30 10

1324 Tbilisi University

1325 "Death of Laocoon and his Sons" (from sculpture by Agesandre, Polidor and Asinodor)

1968. 50th Anniv of Tbilisi University.
3587 **1324** 4k. beige and green . . 25 10

1968. "Promote Solidarity with the Greek Democrats".
3588 **1325** 6k. drab, purple & brn 4·50 3·50

1326 Cavalryman

1968. 50th Anniv of Leninist Young Communist League (Komsomol) (1st issue). Multicoloured.
3589 2k. Type **1326** 10 10
3590 3k. Young workers 15 10
3591 4k. Army officer 20 10
3592 6k. Construction workers . . 25 10
3593 10k. Agricultural workers 40 20
MS3594 78 × 101 mm. 50k. Type **1326**. Imperf . . . . . . 3·75 1·50
See also No. 3654.

1327 Institute and Molecular Structure

1968. 50th Anniv of N. S. Kurnakov Institute of Chemistry.
3595 **1327** 4k. purple, black and blue 20 10

1328 Letter

1968. Int Correspondence Week and Stamp Day.
3596 **1328** 4k. brown, red and lake 20 10
3597 – 4k. blue, ochre and deep blue 20 10
DESIGN: No. 3597, Russian stamps.

1329 "The 26 Baku Commissars" (statue, S. Merkurov)

1330 T. Antikainen

1968. 50th Anniv of Execution of 26 Baku Commissars.
3598 **1329** 4k. multicoloured . . . 20 10

1968. 70th Birthday of Toivo Antikainen (Finnish Communist leader).
3599 **1330** 6k. brown and grey . . 25 10

1331 Liner "Ivan Franko"

1333 P. P. Postyshev (1887–1940)

1332 Order of the October Revolution

1968. Soviet Merchant Marine.
3600 **1331** 6k. red, dp blue & blue 35 10

1968. 51st Anniv of October Revolution.
3601 **1332** 4k. multicoloured . . . 20 10

1968. Soviet Personalities.
3602 **1333** 4k. black 15 10
3603 – 4k. black 15 10
3604 – 4k. black 15 10
DESIGNS: No. 3603, S. G. Shaumian (1878–1918); 3604, A. Ikramov (1898–1938).

1334 Statuette of Warrior and Ararat Mountains

1335 I. S. Turgenev

1968. 2,750th Anniv of Yerevan (Armenian capital).
3605 **1334** 4k. blk & brn on grey 25 10
3606 – 12k. brn & sepia on yell 60 25
DESIGN: 12k. David Sasunsky Monument (Ye. Kochar).

1968. 150th Birth Anniv of Ivan Turgenev (writer).
3607 **1335** 4k. green 25 10

1336 American Bison and Common Zebra

1968. Fauna. Soviet Wildlife Reservations. Mult.
3608 4k. Type **1336** 30 10
3609 4k. Purple swamphen and lotus 30 15
3610 6k. Great egrets (vert) . . . 35 15
3611 6k. Ostrich and golden pheasant (vert) 35 15
3612 10k. Eland and guanaco . . 55 25
3613 10k. Glossy ibis and white spoonbill 60 25

1337 Building and Equipment

1968. 50th Anniv of Lenin Radio-laboratory, Gorky.
3614 **1337** 4k. blue and ochre . . 20 10

1338 Prospecting for Minerals

1339 Djety-Oguz Kirgizia

1968. Geology Day. Multicoloured.
3615 4k. Type **1338** 30 10
3616 6k. "Tracking down" metals 30 20
3617 10k. Oil derrick 85 20

1968. Central Asian Spas. Multicoloured.
3618 4k. Type **1339** 20 10
3619 4k. Borovoe, Kazakhstan (horiz) 20 10

3620 6k. Issyk-kul, Kirgizia (horiz) 30 15
3621 6k. Borovoe, Kazakhstan . . 30 15

1340 Silver Medal, "Philatec", Paris 1964

1968. Awards to Soviet Post Office at Foreign Stamp Exhibitions.
3622 4k. black, silver and purple 20 10
3623 6k. black, gold and blue . . 25 10
3624 10k. black, gold and blue 55 15
3625 12k. black, silver & turquoise 45 15
3626 16k. black, gold and red . . 75 30
3627 20k. black, gold and blue 90 40
3628 30k. black, gold and brown 1·40 85
DESIGNS: 4k. Type **1340**; 6k. Plaque, "Debria", Berlin, 1959; 10k. Cup and medals, Riccione, 1952, 1968; 12k. Diploma and medal, "Thematic Biennale", Buenos Aires, 1965; 16k. Trophies and medals, Rome, 1952, 1954; 20k. Medals and plaques, "Wipa", Vienna, 1966; 30k. Glass trophies, Prague, 1950, 1955, 1962.

1341 V. K. Lebedinsky **1342** Soldier with Flag

1968. Birth Centenary of Lebedinsky (physicist).
3629 **1341** 4k. multicoloured . . . 30 10

1968. 50th Anniv of Estonian Workers' Commune.
3630 **1342** 4k. black and red . . . 20 10

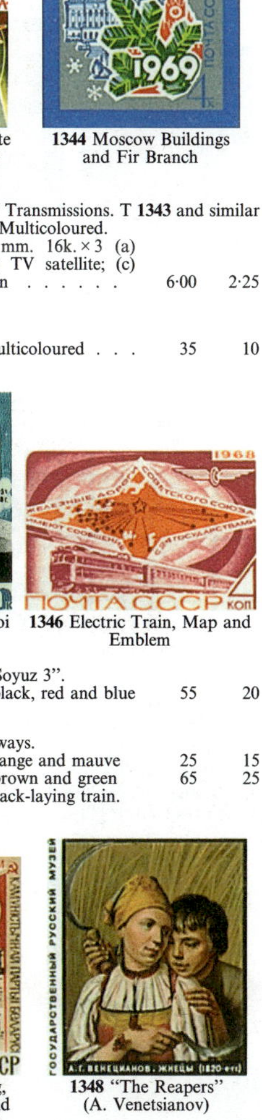

1343 TV Satellite and Receiving Stations **1344** Moscow Buildings and Fir Branch

1968. Satellite TV Transmissions. T **1343** and similar square designs. Multicoloured.
MS3631 96 × 76 mm. 16k. × 3 (a) Type **1343**; (b) TV satellite; (c) Receiving station . . . . . . 6·00 2·25

1968. New Year.
3632 **1344** 4k. multicoloured . . . 35 10

1345 G. Beregovoi (cosmonaut) **1346** Electric Train, Map and Emblem

1968. Flight of "Soyuz 3".
3633 **1345** 10k. black, red and blue 55 20

1968. Soviet Railways.
3634 **1346** 4k. orange and mauve 25 15
3635 – 10k. brown and green 65 25
DESIGN: 10k. Track-laying train.

1347 Red Flag, Newspapers and Monument at Minsk **1348** "The Reapers" (A. Venetsianov)

1968. 50th Anniv of Byelorussian Communist Party.
3636 **1347** 4k. black, brown and red 20 10

1968. Paintings in State Museum, Leningrad. Mult.
3637 1k. Type **1348** 15 10
3638 2k. "The Last Days of Pompeii" (K. Bryullov) (61 × 28 mm) 35 10
3639 3k. "A Knight at the Crossroads" (V. Vasentsov) (61 × 28 mm) 40 10
3640 4k. "Conquering a Town in Winter" (V. Surikov) (61 × 28 mm) 50 10
3641 6k. "The Lake" (I. Levitan) (61 × 28 mm) 70 10
3642 10k. "The Year 1919: Alarm" (K. Petrov-Vodkin) 85 15
3643 16k. "The Defence of Sevastopol" (A. Deineka) (61 × 28 mm) . . . . . . 1·00 20
3644 20k. "Homer's Bust (G. Korzhev) . . . . . . 1·25 25
3645 30k. "The Celebration in Uritsky Square" (B. Kustodiev) (61 × 28 mm) . . . . . . 1·40 30
3646 50k. "The Duel between Peresvet and Chelumbei" (M. Avilov) (61 × 28 mm) 2·00 80

1349 House, Onega Region

1968. Soviet Architecture.
3647 **1349** 3k. brown on buff . . . 20 10
3648 – 4k. green on yellow . . 35 10
3649 – 6k. violet on grey . . . 65 15
3650 – 10k. blue on green . . 95 35
3651 – 12k. red on drab . . . 1·10 60
3652 – 16k. black on yellow . . 1·60 80
DESIGNS: 4k. Farmhouse door, Gorky region; 6k. Wooden church, Kishi; 10k. Citadel, Rostov-Yaroslavl; 12k. Entrance gate, Tsaritzino; 16k. Master-builder Rossi's Street, Leningrad.

1968. 50th Death Anniv of N. G. Markin (1893–1918) (revolutionary). As T **1333**.
3653 4k. black 20 10

1350 Flags and Order of October Revolution

1968. 50th Anniv of Leninist Young Communist League (Komsomol) (2nd issue).
3654 **1350** 12k. multicoloured . . 55 15

1351 "Declaration of Republic"

1969. 50th Anniv of Belorussian Republic. Mult.
3655 2k. Type **1351** 10 10
3656 4k. Partisans at war, 1941–45 . . . . 20 10
3657 6k. Reconstruction workers 30 10

1352 Red Guard in Riga (statue) **1354** University Buildings

1353 Cosmonauts Shatalov, Volynov, Yeliseev and Khtunov

1969. 50th Anniv of Soviet Revolution in Latvia.
3658 **1352** 4k. red and orange . . 20 10

1969. Space Flights of "Soyuz 4" and "Soyuz 5". Sheet 95 × 68 mm.
MS3659 **1353** 50k. brown and ochre 5·50 2·75

1969. 150th Anniv of Leningrad University.
3660 **1354** 10k. black and lake . . 45 20

1355 Krylov (after K. Bryullov) **1356** N. D. Filchenkov

1969. Birth Bicent of Ivan Krylov (fabulist).
3661 **1355** 4k. multicoloured . . . 20 10

1969. War Heroes.
3662 **1356** 4k. brown and red . . 20 10
3663 – 4k. brown and green . . 20 10
DESIGN: No. 3663, A. A. Kosmodemiansky.

1357 "The Wheel Turns Round Again" (sculpture, Zs. Kisfaludi-Strobl)

1969. 50th Anniv of 1st Hungarian Soviet Republic.
3664 **1357** 6k. black, red and green 30 10

1358 Crest and Symbols of Petro-chemical Industry

1969. 50th Anniv of Bashkir Autonomous Soviet Socialist Republic.
3665 **1358** 4k. multicoloured . . . 20 10

1359 "Vostok 1" on Launching-pad

1969. Cosmonautics Day. Multicoloured.
3666 10k. Type **1359** 60 20
3667 10k. "Zond 5" in Lunar orbit (horiz) 60 20
3668 10k. Sergei Pavlovich Korolev (space scientist) (horiz) 60 20
MS3669 92 × 68 mm. 80k. "Soyuz 3" (horiz) . . . . 4·50 2·25

1360 Lenin University, Kazan

1969. Buildings connected with Lenin. Mult.
3670 4k. Type **1360** 20 10
3671 4k. Lenin Museum, Kuibyshev 20 10
3672 4k. Lenin Museum, Pskov 20 10
3673 4k. Lenin Museum, Shushenskaya 20 10
3674 4k. "Hay Hut", Razliv . . . 20 10
3675 4k. Lenin Museum, Gorky Park, Leningrad 20 10
3676 4k. Smolny Institute, Leningrad 20 10
3677 4k. Lenin's Office, Kremlin 20 10
3678 4k. Library, Ulyanovsk (wrongly inscr "Lenin Museum") 20 10
3679 4k. Lenin Museum, Ulyanovsk 20 10

1361 Telephone and Radio Set

1969. 50th Anniv of VEF Electrical Works, Riga.
3680 **1361** 10k. brown and red . . 50 15

1362 I.L.O. Emblem

1969. 50th Anniv of Int Labour Organization.
3681 **1362** 6k. gold and red . . . 30 10

1363 Otakar Jaros **1364** P. E. Dybenko

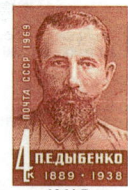

1969. Otakar Jaros (Czech war hero) Commem.
3682 **1363** 4k. black and blue . . 25 10

1969. Soviet Personalities. 80th Birth Annivs.
3683 **1364** 4k. red 20 10
3684 – 4k. blue 20 10
DESIGN: No. 3684, S. V. Kosior (1889–1939).

1365 Suleiman Stalsky

1969. Birth Centenary of Suleiman Stalsky (Dagestan poet).
3685 **1365** 4k. green and brown . . 30 10

1366 Rose "Clear Glade"

1969. Academy of Sciences Botanical Gardens, Moscow. Multicoloured.
3686 2k. Type **1366** 15 10
3687 4k. Lily "Slender" 20 10
3688 10k. "Cattleya hybr" (orchid) 50 15
3689 12k. Dahlia "Leaves Fall" 60 25
3690 14k. Gladiolus "Ural Girl" 90 40

1367 Scientific Centre

1969. 50th Anniv of Ukraine Academy of Sciences, Kiev.
3691 **1367** 4k. purple and yellow 30 10

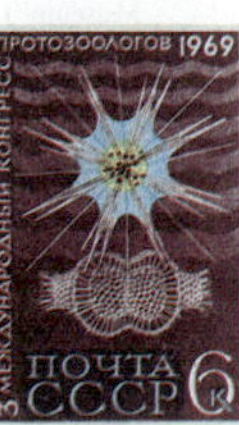

1368 Gold Medal within Film "Flower" **1369** Congress Emblem

1969. Cine and Ballet Events, Moscow. Mult.
3692 6k. Type **1368** (6th Int Cinema Festival) 30 15
3693 6k. Ballet dancers (1st Int Ballet Competitions) 30 15

1969. 3rd Int Protozoologists Congress, Leningrad.
3694 **1369** 6k. multicoloured 90 20

1370 Estonian Singer

1969. Centenary of Estonian Choir Festival.
3695 **1370** 4k. red and ochre 35 10

1371 Mendeleev (after N. Yarashenko) and Formula

1969. Centenary of Mendeleev's Periodic Law of Elements.
3696 **1371** 6k. brown and red 50 20
MS3697 76 × 104 mm. 30k. carmine 4·25 1·75
DESIGN: 30 × 41 mm. 30k. Dimtir Mendeleev (chemist).

1372 Peace Banner and World Landmarks **1373** Rocket on Laser Beam, and Moon

1969. 20th Anniv of World Peace Movement.
3698 **1372** 10k. multicoloured 40 15

1969. "50 Years of Soviet Inventions".
3699 **1373** 4k. red, black and silver 20 10

Стокгольм. 1969

1374 Kotlyarevsky **(1375)**

1969. Birth Bicentenary of Ivan Kotlyarevsky (Ukrainian writer).
3700 **1374** 4k. black, brown & grn 20 10

1969. Soviet Ice Hockey Victory in World Championships, Stockholm. No. 2828 further optd with **1375**.
3701 6k. turquoise and purple 3·25 2·00

1376 War Memorial in Minsk (A. Bembel) and Campaign Map **1377** Hands holding Torch, and Bulgarian Arms

1969. 25th Anniv of Belorussian Liberation.
3702 **1376** 4k. red, purple and olive 20 10

1969. 25th Anniv of Bulgarian and Polish Peoples' Republics.
3703 **1377** 6k. multicoloured 30 10
3704 – 6k. red and ochre 30 10
DESIGN: No. 3704, Polish map, flag and arms.

1378 Registan Square, Samarkand

1969. 2,500th Anniv of Samarkand. Mult.
3705 4k. Type **1378** 25 10
3706 6k. Intourist Hotel, Samarkand 40 15

1379 Liberation Monument, Nikolaev **1380** Volleyball (European Junior Championships)

1969. 25th Anniv of Liberation of Nikolaev.
3707 **1379** 4k. red, violet and black 25 10

1969. International Sporting Events.
3708 **1380** 4k. red, brown & orange 20 10
3709 – 6k. multicoloured 40 10
DESIGN: 6k. Canoeing (European Championships).

1381 M. Munkacsy and detail of painting, "Peasant Woman churning Butter" **1382** Miners' Statue, Donetsk

1969. 125th Birth Anniv of Mihaly Munkacsy (Hungarian painter).
3710 **1381** 6k. black, orange & brn 30 10

1969. Centenary of Donetsk.
3711 **1382** 4k. mauve and grey 20 10

1383 "Horse-drawn Machine-guns" (M. Grekov)

1969. 50th Anniv of 1st Cavalry Army.
3712 **1383** 4k. brown and red 40 15

1384 Ilya Repin (self-portrait) **1385** Running

1969. 125th Birth Anniv of Ilya Repin (painter). Multicoloured.
3713 4k. "Barge-haulers on the Volga" 25 10
3714 6k. "Unexpected" 35 15
3715 10k. Type **1384** 40 15
3716 12k. "The Refusal of Confession" 55 20
3717 16k. "Dnieper Cossacks" 75 30

1969. 9th Trade Unions' Games, Moscow.
3718 **1385** 4k. black, green and red 15 10
3719 – 10k. black, blue & green 35 10
MS3720 70 × 95 mm. **1385** 20k. black, bistre and red. Imperf 2·00 85
DESIGN: 10k. Gymnastics.

1386 V. L. Komarov **1387** O. Tumanyan and Landscape

1969. Birth Cent of V. L. Komarov (botanist).
3721 **1386** 4k. brown and olive 25 10

1969. Birth Cent of O. Tumanyan (Armenian poet).
3722 **1387** 10k. black and blue 50 15

1388 Turkoman Drinking- horn (2nd-cent B.C.) **1389** Mahatma Gandhi

1969. Oriental Art Treasures, State Museum of Oriental Art, Moscow. Multicoloured.
3723 4k. Type **1388** 25 10
3724 6k. Simurg vessel, Persia (13th-century) 35 10
3725 12k. Statuette, Korea (8th-century) 50 15
3726 16k. Bodhisatva statuette, Tibet (7th-century) 70 20
3727 20k. Ebisu statuette, Japan (17th-century) 1·00 50

1969. Birth Centenary of Mahatma Gandhi.
3728 **1389** 6k. brown 55 15

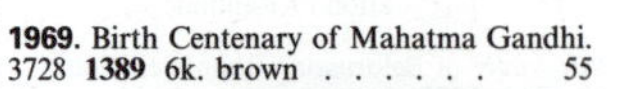

1390 Black Stork at Nest

1969. Belovezhskaya Pushcha Nature Reserve. Multicoloured.
3729 4k. Type **1390** 30 15
3730 6k. Red deer and fawn 45 15
3731 10k. European bison fighting 65 20
3732 12k. Lynx and cubs 75 20
3733 16k. Wild boar and young 90 35
No. 3731 is larger, 76 × 24 mm.

1391 "Komitas" and Rural Scene

1969. Birth Cent of "Komitas" (S. Sogomonyan, Armenian composer).
3734 **1391** 6k. black, flesh and grey 35 15

1392 Sergei Gritsevets (fighter-pilot) **1393** I. Pavlov (after portrait by A. Yar-Kravchenko)

1969. Soviet War Heroes.
3735 **1392** 4k. black and green 30 10
3736 – 4k. brown, red & yellow 20 10
3737 – 4k. brown and green 20 10
DESIGNS: As Type **1392**. No. 3737, Lisa Chaikina (partisan). (35½ × 24 mm); No. 3736, A. Cheponis, Y. Alexonis and G. Boris (Kaunas resistance fighters).

1969. 120th Birth Anniv of Ivan P. Pavlov (physiologist).
3738 **1393** 4k. multicoloured 25 10

1394 D.D.R. Arms and Berlin Landmarks **1395** A. V. Koltsov (from portrait by A. Yar-Kravchenko)

1969. 20th Anniv of German Democratic Republic.
3739 **1394** 6k. multicoloured 25 10

1969. 160th Birth Anniv of A. V. Koltsov (poet).
3740 **1395** 4k. brown and blue 25 10

1396 Arms of Ukraine and Memorial **1397** Kremlin, and Hammer and Sickle

1969. 25th Anniv of Ukraine Liberation.
3741 **1396** 4k. red and gold 30 15

1969. 52nd Anniv of October Revolution.
3742 **1397** 4k. multicoloured 25 10
MS3743 99 × 61 mm. 50k. gold, pink and red (40 × 30 mm) 3·25 1·10

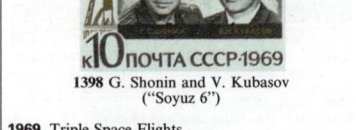

1398 G. Shonin and V. Kubasov ("Soyuz 6")

1969. Triple Space Flights.
3744 **1398** 10k. green and gold 55 15
3745 – 10k. green and gold 55 15
3746 – 10k. green and gold 55 15
DESIGNS: No. 3745, A. Filipchenko, V. Volkov and V. Gorbatko ("Soyuz 7"); No. 3746, V. Shatalov and A. Yeliseev ("Soyuz 8").

1399 Lenin when a Youth (after V. Tsigal) and Emblems **1400** Corps Emblem on Red Star

1969. U.S.S.R. Youth Philatelic Exhibition to commemorate Lenin's Birth Centenary, Kiev.
3747 **1399** 4k. lake and pink . . . 25 15

1969. 50th Anniv of Red Army Communications Corps.
3748 **1400** 4k. red, brown & bistre 25 15

1401 "Worker and Collective Farmer" (sculpture, Vera Mukhina) and Title-page

1969. 3rd Soviet Collective Farmers' Congress, Moscow.
3749 **1401** 4k. brown and gold . . 20 10

1402 "Vasilisa, the Beauty" (folk tale)

1969. Russian Fairy Tales. Multicoloured.
3750 4k. Type **1402** 35 30
3751 10k. "Maria Morevna" (folk tale) 85 60
3752 16k. "The Golden Cockerel" (Pushkin) (horiz) . . . . 1·25 75
3753 20k. "Finist, the Fine Fellow" (folk tale) . . . . 1·50 1·00
3754 50k. "Tale of the Tsar Saltan" (Pushkin) . . . . 2·75 2·00

1403 Venus Plaque and Radio-telescope

1969. Space Exploration.
3755 **1403** 4k. red, brown and black 35 10
3756 – 6k. purple, grey & black 45 15
3757 – 10k. multicoloured . . 70 20
MS3758 117 × 80 mm. 50k. (2) multicoloured. Imperf . . . . 5·75 2·75
DESIGNS: 6k. "Zond 7". Smaller (27 × 40 mm) 50k. (a) As 10k. (b) Close-up of Moon's surface taken by "Zond 6".

1404 Soviet and Afghan Flags

1405 Red Star and Arms

1969. 50th Anniv of U.S.S.R.–Afghanistan Diplomatic Relations.
3759 **1404** 6k. red, black and green 35 10

1969. Coil Stamp.
3760 **1405** 4k. red . . . . 1·75 80

1406 Mikoyan Gurevich MiG-3 and MiG-23 Fighters

1969. "30 Years of MiG Aircraft".
3761 **1406** 6k. black, grey and red 70 15

1407 Lenin

1969. New Year.
3762 **1407** 4k. multicoloured . . . 25 10

1408 Tupolev ANT-2

1969. Development of Soviet Civil Aviation.
3763 **1408** 2k. multicoloured . . . 20 10
3764 – 3k. multicoloured . . . 25 10
3765 – 4k. multicoloured . . . 25 10
3766 – 6k. black, red and purple 25 10
3767 – 10k. multicoloured . . 55 15
3768 – 12k. multicoloured . . 60 20
3769 – 16k. multicoloured . . 80 25
3770 – 20k. multicoloured . . 95 35
MS3771 92 × 66 mm. 50k. multicoloured . . . . 4·00 1·75
AIRCRAFT: 3k. Polikarpov Po-2; 4k. Tupolev ANT-9; 6k. TsAGI 1-EA helicopter; 10k. Tupolev ANT-20 "Maksim Gorky"; 12k. Tupolev Tu-104; 16k. Mil Mi-10 helicopter; 20k. Ilyushin Il-62; 50k. Tupolev Tu-144.

1409 Model Gliders

1969. Technical Sports.
3772 **1409** 3k. purple 15 10
3773 – 4k. green 20 10
3774 – 6k. brown 30 10
DESIGNS: 4k. Speed boat racing; 6k. Parachuting.

1410 Rumanian Arms and Soviet Memorial, Bucharest

1411 TV Tower, Ostankino

1969. 25th Anniv of Rumanian Liberation.
3775 **1410** 6k. red and brown . . 30 15

1969. Television Tower, Ostankino, Moscow.
3776 **1411** 10k. multicoloured . . 45 20

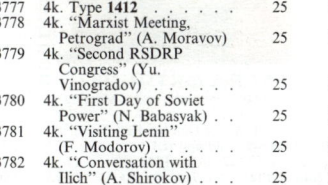

1412 "Lenin" (after N. Andreev)

1970. Birth Centenary of V. I. Lenin (1st issue). Multicoloured.
3777 4k. Type **1412** 25 10
3778 4k. "Marxist Meeting, Petrograd" (A. Moravov) 25 10
3779 4k. "Second RSDRP Congress" (Yu. Vinogradov) 25 10
3780 4k. "First Day of Soviet Power" (N. Babasyak) . . 25 10
3781 4k. "Visiting Lenin" (F. Modorov) 25 10
3782 4k. "Conversation with Ilich" (A. Shirokov) . . . 25 10
3783 4k. "May Day 1920" (I. Brodsky) 25 10
3784 4k. "With Lenin" (V. Serov) 25 10
3785 4k. "Conquerors of the Cosmos" (A. Deyineka) 25 10
3786 4k. "Communism Builders" (A. Korentsov, Ye. Merkulov, V. Burakov) 25 10
See also Nos. 3812/21.

1413 F. V. Sychkov and Painting "Tobogganing"

1970. Birth Centenary of F. V. Sychkov (artist).
3787 **1413** 4k. blue and brown . . 40 15

1414 "Vostok", "Mirnyi" and Antarctic Map

1415 V. I. Peshekhonov

1970. 150th Anniv of Antarctic Expedition by Bellinghausen and Lazarev.
3788 **1414** 4k. turquoise, mauve & bl . . . . 1·25 25
3789 – 16k. red, green & purple . . . . 2·50 55
DESIGN: 16k. Modern polar-station and map.

1970. Soviet War Heroes.
3790 **1415** 4k. purple and black . . 20 10
3791 – 4k. brown and olive . . 20 10
DESIGN: No. 3791, V. B. Borsoev (1906–1945).

1416 Geographical Society Emblem

1417 "The Torch of Peace" (A. Dumpe)

1970. 125th Anniv of Russian Geographical Society.
3792 **1416** 6k. multicoloured . . . 35 10

1970. 60th Anniv of Int Women's Solidarity Day.
3793 **1417** 6k. drab and turquoise 35 10

1418 Ivan Bazhov (folk hero) and Crafts

1419 Lenin

1970. World Fair "Expo 70", Osaka, Japan.
3794 **1418** 4k. black, red and green 15 10
3795 – 6k. silver, red and black 30 10
3796 – 10k. multicoloured . . 45 15
MS3797 72 × 97 mm. 50k. red . . 3·25 1·60
DESIGNS: 6k. U.S.S.R. Pavilion; 10k. Boy and model toys; 50k. Lenin in cap.

1970. Lenin Birth Centenary. All-Union Philatelic Exhibition, Moscow.
3798 **1419** 4k. black, gold and red 25 10
MS3799 73 × 92 mm. **1419** 20k. gold, red and black. Imperf . . . . 75·00 32·00

1420 Friendship Tree

1970. Friendship Tree, Sochi.
3800 **1420** 10k. multicoloured . . 45 20

1421 Ice Hockey Players

1970. World Ice Hockey Championships, Stockholm, Sweden.
3801 **1421** 6k. green and blue . . 60 15

1422 Hammer, Sickle and Azerbaijan Emblems

1970. 50th Anniv of Soviet Republics.
3802 **1422** 4k. red and gold . . . 20 10
3803 – 4k. brown and silver . . 20 10
3804 – 4k. purple and gold . . 20 10
DESIGNS: No. 3803, Woman and motifs of Armenia; 3804, Woman and emblem of Kazakh Republic.

1423 Worker and Book

1424 D. N. Medvedev

1970. UNESCO "Lenin Centenary" Symposium.
3805 **1423** 6k. ochre and lake . . 20 10

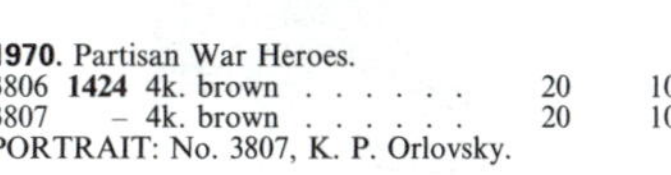

1970. Partisan War Heroes.
3806 **1424** 4k. brown 20 10
3807 – 4k. brown 20 10
PORTRAIT: No. 3807, K. P. Orlovsky.

(1425)

1426 Hungarian Arms and Budapest View

1970. Russian Victory in World Ice Hockey Championships, Stockholm. No. 3801 optd with T **1425**.
3808 **1421** 6k. green and blue . . 70 20

1970. 25th Anniv of Hungarian and Czech Liberation. Multicoloured.
3809 6k. Type **1426** 20 10
3810 6k. Czech Arms and Prague view 20 10

1427 Cosmonauts' Emblem

1428 Lenin, 1891

1970. Cosmonautics Day.
3811 **1427** 6k. multicoloured . . . 20 10

1970. Birth Centenary of Lenin (2nd issue).
3812 **1428** 2k. green 10 10
3813 – 2k. olive 10 10
3814 – 4k. blue 15 10
3815 – 4k. lake 15 10
3816 – 6k. brown 35 10
3817 – 6k. lake 35 10
3818 – 10k. purple 50 15
3819 – 10k. brown 50 15
3820 – 12k. black and silver . . 55 20
3821 – 12k. red and gold . . . 55 20
MS3822 66 × 102 mm. 20k. black and silver . . . . 3·75 1·60

PORTRAITS OF LENIN: No. 3813, In 1900; 3814, In 1914; 3815, In 1916; 3816, 3817, 3818, In 1918; 3819, In 1920; 3820, **MS**3822, Sculptured head by Yu. Kolesnikov; 3821, Sculptured head by N. Andreev.

1429 Order of Victory

1431 Lenin (sculpture, Yu. Kolesnikov)

1430 Komsomol Badge

1970. 25th Anniv of Victory in Second World War.

3823	**1429**	1k. gold, grey and purple	10	10
3824	–	2k. purple, brn & gold	10	10
3825	–	3k. red, black and gold	15	10
3826	–	4k. red, brown and gold	20	10
3827	–	10k. gold, red & purple	55	30
MS3828		67 × 97 mm. **1429** 30k. gold, grey and red. Imperf	2·50	1·00

DESIGNS: 2k. Eternal Flame; 3k. Treptow Monument, Berlin; 4k. Home Defence Order; 10k. Hero of the Soviet Union and Hero of Socialist Labour medals.

1970. 16th Congress of Leninist Young Communist League (Komsomol).
3829 **1430** 4k. multicoloured . . . 20 10

1970. World Youth Meeting for Lenin Birth Centenary.
3830 **1431** 6k. red 20 10

1432 "Young Workers" and Federation Emblem

1970. 25th Anniv of World Democratic Youth Federation.
3831 **1432** 6k. black and blue . . 35 10

1433 Arms and Government Building, Kazan

1970. 50th Anniv of Russian Federation Autonomous Soviet Socialist Republics.

3832	**1433**	4k. blue	30	10
3833	–	4k. green	30	10
3834	–	4k. red	30	10
3835	–	4k. brown	30	10
3836	–	4k. green	30	10
3837	–	4k. brown	30	10

DESIGNS: Arms and Government Buildings. No. 3832, (Tatar Republic); 3833, Petrozavodzk (Karelian Republic); 3834, Cheboksary (Chuvash Republic); 3835, Elista (Kalmyk Republic); 3836, Izhevsk (Udmurt Republic); 3837, Ioshkar-Ola (Mari Republic).

See also Nos. 3903/7, 4052/3, 4175, 4253, 4298, 4367 and 4955.

1434 Gymnast on Bar (World Championships, Yugoslavia)

1435 "Swords into Ploughshares" (sculpture by E. Vuchetich)

1970. International Sporting Events.

3838	**1434**	10k. red and drab	50	15
3839	–	16k. brown and green	80	30

DESIGN: 16k. Three footballers (World Cup Championship, Mexico).

1970. 25th Anniv of United Nations.
3840 **1435** 12k. purple and green 50 10

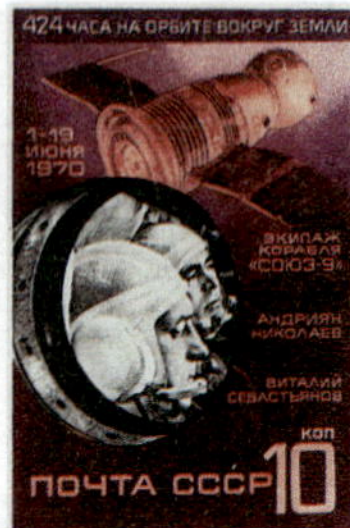
1436 Cosmonauts and "Soyuz 9"

1970. Space Flight by "Soyuz 9".
3841 **1436** 10k. black, red & purple 50 10

1437 Engels

1970. 150th Birth Anniv of Friedrich Engels.
3842 **1437** 4k. brown and red . . 20 10

1438 Cruiser "Aurora"

1970. Soviet Warships.

3843	**1438**	3k. pink, lilac and black	30	10
3844	–	4k. black and yellow	35	10
3845	–	10k. blue and mauve	85	20
3846	–	12k. brown and buff	1·10	25
3847	–	20k. purple, blue & turq	1·60	40

DESIGNS: 4k. Missile cruiser "Groznyi"; 10k. Cruiser "Oktyabrskaya Revolyutsiya"; 12k. Missile cruiser "Varyag"; 20k. Nuclear submarine "Leninsky Komsomol".

1439 Soviet and Polish Workers

1440 Allegory of the Sciences

1970. 25th Anniv of Soviet-Polish Friendship Treaty.
3848 **1439** 6k. red and blue . . . 20 10

1970. 13th Int Historical Sciences Congress, Moscow.
3849 **1440** 4k. multicoloured . . . 20 10

1441 Mandarins

1442 Magnifying Glass, "Stamp" and Covers

1970. Fauna of Sikhote-Alin Nature Reserve. Multicoloured.

3850	4k. Type **1441**	30	15
3851	6k. Yellow-throated marten	45	15
3852	10k. Asiatic black bear (vert)	60	15
3853	16k. Red deer	70	25
3854	20k. Tiger	1·00	35

1970. 2nd U.S.S.R. Philatelic Society Congress, Moscow.
3855 **1442** 4k. silver and red . . . 25 10

1443 V. I. Kikvidze

1444 University Building

1970. 75th Birth Anniv of V. J. Kikvidze (Civil War hero).
3856 **1443** 4k. brown 20 10

1970. 50th Anniv of Yerevan University.
3857 **1444** 4k. red and blue . . . 20 10

1445 Pioneer Badge

1446 Library Book-plate (A. Kuchas)

1970. Pioneer Organization.

3858	**1445**	1k. gold, red and grey	10	10
3859	–	2k. grey and brown	10	10
3860	–	4k. multicoloured	20	10

DESIGNS: 2k. "Lenin with Children" (sculpture, N. Scherbakov), 4k. Red Star and scarf.

1970. 400th Anniv of Vilnius (Vilna) University Library (Lithuania).
3861 **1446** 4k. black, grey and silver 20 10

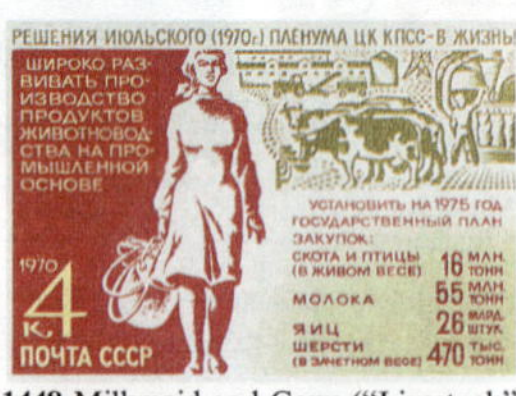
1447 Woman with Bouquet

1970. 25th Anniv of International Democratic Women's Federation.
3862 **1447** 6k. brown and blue . . 20 10

1448 Milkmaid and Cows ("Livestock")

1970. Soviet Agriculture. Multicoloured.

3863	4k. Type **1448**	20	10
3864	4k. Driver, tractor and harvester ("Mechanization")	20	10
3865	4k. Lock-operator and canal ("Irrigation and Chemical Research")	20	10

1449 Lenin addressing Meeting

1970. 53rd Anniv of October Revolution.

3866	**1449**	4k. gold and red	20	10
MS3867		107 × 82 mm. **1449** 30k. gold and red	2·75	1·00

50 лет
ленинскому плану
ГОЭЛРО • 1970
(**1450**)

1970. 50th Anniv of GOELRO Electrification Plan. No. 3475 optd with T **1450**.
3868 4k. multicoloured 85 40

1451 Spassky Tower, Kremlin

1452 A. A. Baikov

1970. New Year.
3869 **1451** 6k. multicoloured . . . 20 10

1970. Birth Centenary of A. A. Baikov (metallurgic scientist).
3870 **1452** 4k. black and brown . . 20 10

1453 Tsyurupa (after A. Yar-Kravchenko)

1454 St. Basil's Cathedral, Red Square, Moscow

1970. Birth Centenary of A. D. Tsyurupa (Vice-Chairman of Soviet People's Commissars).
3871 **1453** 4k. brown and yellow 20 10

1970. Tourism.

3872	**1454**	4k. multicoloured	20	10
3873	–	6k. blue, indigo & brown	35	10
3874	–	10k. brown and green	45	15
3875	–	12k. multicoloured	55	15
3876	–	14k. blue, red and brown	70	20
3877	–	16k. multicoloured	80	30

DESIGNS: 6k. Scene from ballet "Swan Lake" (Tchaikovsky); 10k. Sika deer; 12k. Souvenir handicrafts; 14k. "Swords into Ploughshares" (sculpture by Ye. Vuchetich); 16k. Tourist and camera.

1455 Camomile

1970. Flowers. Multicoloured.

3878	4k. Type **1455**	15	10
3879	6k. Dahlia	30	10
3880	10k. Phlox	45	10
3881	12k. Aster	1·00	20
3882	16k. Clematis	70	30

1456 African Woman and Child

1457 Beethoven

1970. 10th Anniv of U.N. Declaration on Colonial Independence.
3883 **1456** 10k. brown and blue . . 40 10

1970. Birth Bicentenary of Beethoven (composer).
3884 **1457** 10k. purple and pink 1·25 35

1458 "Luna 16" in Flight **1459** Speed Skating

1970. Flight of "Luna 16".
3885 **1458** 10k. green 50 15
3886 – 10k. purple 50 15
3887 – 10k. green 50 15
MS3888 100 × 76 mm. 20k. × 3 as Nos. 3885/7 but change of colours 5·00 1·00
DESIGNS: No. 3886, "Luna 16" on Moon's surface; 3887, Parachute descent.

1970. Trade Unions' Winter Games (1971).
3889 **1459** 4k. blue, red and grey 20 10
3890 – 10k. green, brn & grey 60 15
DESIGN: 10k. Cross-country skiing.

1460 "The Conestabile Madonna" (Raphael)

1970. Foreign Paintings in Soviet Galleries. Mult.
3891 3k. Type **1460** 20 10
3892 4k. "Saints Peter and Paul" (El Greco) 30 10
3893 10k. "Perseus and Andromeda" (Rubens) (horiz) 60 15
3894 12k. "The Return of the Prodigal Son" (Rembrandt) 70 15
3895 16k. "Family Portrait" (Van Dyck) 95 25
3896 20k. "The Actress Jeanne Samary" (Renoir) . . . . 1·10 35
3897 30k. "Woman with Fruit" (Gauguin) . . . . 1·50 85
MS3898 73 × 101 mm. 50k. "Madonna Litte" (Leonardo da Vinci). Imperf . . . . 5·25 1·90

1461 Harry Pollitt and Freighter "Jolly George"

1970. 80th Birth Anniv of H. Pollitt (British Communist).
3899 **1461** 10k. brown and purple 40 15

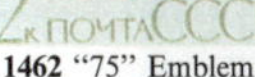

1462 "75" Emblem **1464** "50", State Emblem and Flag

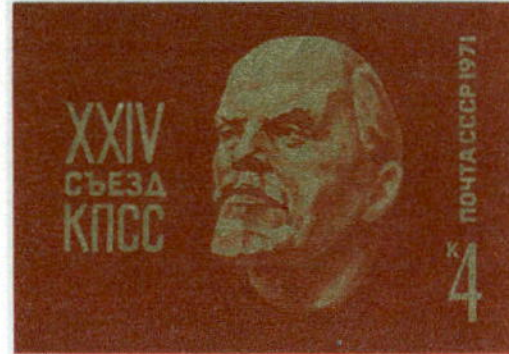

1463 Sculptured Head of Lenin (A. Belostotsky and E. Fridman)

1970. 75th Anniv of Int Co-operative Alliance.
3900 **1462** 12k. red and green . . 55 15

1971. 24th Soviet Union Communist Party Congress.
3901 **1463** 4k. red and gold . . . 20 10

1971. 50th Anniv of Georgian Soviet Republic.
3902 **1464** 4k. multicoloured . . . 20 10

1971. 50th Anniv of Autonomous Soviet Socialist Republics. Similar designs to T **1433**, but dated "1971".
3903 4k. turquoise 25 10
3904 4k. red 25 10
3905 4k. red 25 10
3906 4k. blue 25 10
3907 4k. green 25 10
DESIGNS: No. 3903, Russian Federation Arms and Supreme Soviet building (Dagestan Republic); 3904, National emblem and symbols of agriculture and industry (Abkhazian Republic); 3905, Arms, produce and industry (Adjarian Republic); 3906, Arms and State building (Kabardino-Balkar Republic); 3907, Arms, industrial products and Government building (Komi Republic).

1465 Genua Fortress and Cranes

1971. 2500th Anniv of Feodosia (Crimean city).
3908 **1465** 10k. multicoloured . . 50 15

1466 Palace of Culture, Kiev **1467** "Features of National Economy"

1971. 24th Ukraine Communist Party Congress, Kiev.
3909 **1466** 4k. multicoloured . . . 20 10

1971. 50th Anniv of Soviet State Planning Organization.
3910 **1467** 6k. red and brown . . 35 10

1468 N. Gubin, I. Chernykh and S. Kosinov (dive-bomber crew)

1971. Soviet Air Force Heroes.
3911 **1468** 4k. brown and green . . 20 10

1469 Gipsy Dance

1971. State Folk Dance Ensemble. Multicoloured.
3912 10k. Type **1469** 55 20
3913 10k. Russian "Summer" dance (women in circle) 55 20
3914 10k. Ukraine "Gopak" dance (dancer leaping) . . 55 20
3915 10k. Adjar "Khorumi" dance (with drummer) . . 55 20
3916 10k. "On the Ice" (ballet) 55 20

1470 L. Ukrainka **1472** Fighting at the Barricades

1471 "Luna 17" Module on Moon

1971. Birth Centenary of Lesya Ukrainka (Ukrainian writer).
3917 **1470** 4k. red and brown . . 20 10

1971. Soviet Moon Exploration.
3918 **1471** 10k. brown and violet 40 15
3919 – 12k. brown and blue . . 70 20
3920 – 12k. brown and blue . . 70 20
3921 – 16k. brown and violet 95 30
MS3922 91 × 69 mm. As Nos. 3918/21 but smaller 32½ × 21½ mm . . . . 4·00 1·60
DESIGNS: No. 3919, Control room and radio telescope; 3920, Moon trench; 3921, "Lunokhod 1" Moon-vehicle.

1971. Centenary of Paris Commune.
3923 **1472** 6k. black, brown and red 20 10

1473 Hammer, Sickle and Development Emblems **1475** E. Birznieks-Upitis

1474 Gagarin Medal, Spaceships and Planets

1971. 24th Soviet Communist Party Congress, Moscow.
3924 **1473** 6k. red, bistre & brown 20 10

1971. 10th Anniv of First Manned Space Flight (1st issue) and Cosmonautics Day.
3925 **1474** 10k. olive, yellow & brn 45 15
3926 – 12k. purple, blue & grey 60 20
DESIGN: 12k. Spaceship over Globe and economic symbols.
See also No. 3974.

1971. Birth Centenary of E. Birznieks-Upitis (Lithuanian writer).
3927 **1475** 4k. red and green . . . 20 10

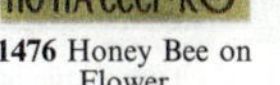

1476 Honey Bee on Flower **1477** "Vostok 1"

1971. 23rd Int Bee-keeping Congress, Moscow.
3928 **1476** 6k. multicoloured . . . 40 15

1971. 10th Anniv of First Manned Space Flight (2nd issue). Sheet 94 × 77 mm containing horiz designs as T **1477**.
MS3929 10k. purple, 12k. (2) green, 16k. purple . . . . 4·25 1·60

1478 Memorial Building

1971. Lenin Memorial Building, Ulyanovsk.
3930 **1478** 4k. olive and red . . . 20 10

1479 Lieut-Col. N. I. Vlasov **1480** Khafiz Shirazi

1971. 26th Anniv of Victory in 2nd World War.
3931 **1479** 4k. brown and green . . 20 10

1971. 650th Birth Anniv of Khafiz Shirazi (Tadzhik writer).
3932 **1480** 4k. multicoloured . . . 20 10

1481 "GAZ-66" Truck

1971. Soviet Motor Vehicles.
3933 **1481** 2k. multicoloured . . . 15 10
3934 – 3k. multicoloured . . . 15 10
3935 – 4k. blue, black and lilac 20 10
3936 – 4k. green, purple & drab 20 10
3937 – 10k. red, black and lilac 55 15
DESIGNS: 3k. "BelAZ-540" tipper truck; 4k. (3935) "Moskvitch-412" 4-door saloon; 4k. (3936) "Zaporozhets ZAZ-968" 2-door saloon; 10k. "Volga GAZ-24" saloon.

1482 Bogomolets (after A. Yar-Kravchenko) **1483** Commemorative Scroll

1971. 90th Birth Anniv of A. A. Bogomolets (medical scientist).
3938 **1482** 4k. black, pink & orange 20 10

1971. International Moscow Congresses.
3939 **1483** 6k. brown and green . . 35 10
3940 – 6k. multicoloured . . . 35 10
3941 – 6k. multicoloured . . . 25 10
DESIGNS AND EVENTS—HORIZ: No. 3939, (13th Science History Congress); 3940, Oil derrick and symbols (8th World Oil Congress). VERT: No. 3941, Satellite over globe (15th General Assembly of Geodesics and Geophysics Union).

1484 Sukhe Bator Statue, Ulan Bator

1971. 50th Anniv of Revolution in Mongolia.
3942 **1484** 6k. grey, gold and red 20 10

1485 Defence Monument (E. Guirbulis)

1486 Treaty Emblem

1971. 30th Anniv of Defence of Liepaja, Latvia.

3943 **1485** 4k. brown, black & grey 20 10

1971. 10th Anniv of Antarctic Treaty and 50th Anniv of Soviet Hydrometeorological Service.

3944 **1486** 6k. deep blue, black and blue 75 30
3945 – 10k. violet, black & red 1·00 35
DESIGN: 10k. Hydrometeorological map.

1487 "Motherland" (sculpture, Yu. Vuchetich)

1488 Throwing the Discus

1971. 20th Anniv of "Federation Internationale des Resistants".

3946 **1487** 6k. green and red . . . 20 10

1971. 5th Summer Spartakiad.

3947 **1488** 3k. blue on pink . . . 10 10
3948 – 4k. green on flesh . . . 15 10
3949 – 6k. brown on green . . . 30 10
3950 – 10k. purple on blue . . 55 20
3951 – 12k. brown on yellow 60 20
DESIGNS: 4k. Archery; 6k. Horse-riding (dressage); 10k. Basketball; 12k. Wrestling.

1489 "Benois Madonna" (Leonardo da Vinci)

1971. Foreign Paintings in Russian Museums. Multicoloured.

3952 2k. Type **1489** 10 10
3953 4k. "Mary Magdalene confesses her Sins" (Titian) 20 10
3954 10k. "The Washerwoman" (Chardin) (horiz) 40 15
3955 12k. "Young Man with Glove" (Hals) 50 20
3956 14k. "Tancred and Erminia" (Poussin) (horiz) 65 20
3957 16k. "Girl Fruit-seller" (Murillo) 80 35
3958 20k. "Child on Ball" (Picasso) . . . . 1·25 50

1490 Lenin Badge and Kazakh Flag

1971. 50th Anniv of Kazakh Communist Youth Assn.

3959 **1490** 4k. brown, red and blue 20 10

1491 Posthorn within Star

1971. International Correspondence Week.

3960 **1491** 4k. black, blue and green 20 10

1492 A. Spendiarov (Armenian composer) (after M. Saryan)

1971. Birth Anniversaries. Multicoloured.

3961 4k. Type **1492** (cent) 20 10
3962 4k. Nikolai Nekrasov (after I. Kramskoi) (poet, 150th anniv) 20 10
3963 10k. Fyodor Dostoevsky (after V. Perov) (writer, 150th anniv) 60 25

1493 Z. Paliashvili

1494 Emblem, Gorky Kremlin and Hydrofoil

1971. Birth Centenary of Z. Paliashvili (Georgian composer).

3964 **1493** 4k. brown 20 10

1971. 750th Anniv of Gorky (formerly Nizhni-Novgorod) (1st issue).

3965 **1494** 16k. multicoloured . . 65 20
See also No. 3974.

1495 Students and Globe

1971. 25th Anniv of Int Students Federation.

3966 **1495** 6k. blue, red and brown 20 10

1496 Atlantic White-sided Dolphins

1497 Star and Miners' Order

1971. Marine Fauna. Multicoloured.

3967 4k. Type **1496** 30 10
3968 6k. Sea otter 40 10
3969 10k. Narwhals 50 15
3970 12k. Walrus 75 20
3971 14k. Ribbon seals . . . . . 1·10 45

1971. 250th Anniv of Coal Discovery in Donetz Basin.

3972 **1497** 4k. red, brown and black 20 10

1498 Lord Rutherford and Atomic Formula

1499 Statue of Maksim Gorky (Vera Mukhina) and View

1971. Birth Cent of Lord Rutherford (physicist).

3973 **1498** 6k. brown and purple 35 15

1971. 750th Anniv of Gorky (formerly Nizhni-Novgorod) (2nd issue).

3974 **1499** 4k. multicoloured . . . 20 10

1500 Santa Claus in Troika

1971. New Year.

3975 **1500** 10k. red, gold and black 35 15

1501 Workers and Marx Books ("International Socialist Solidarity") (½-size illustration)

1971. 24th Soviet Union Communist Party Congress Resolutions.

3976 **1501** 4k. blue, ultram & red 25 10
3977 – 4k. red, yellow & brown 25 10
3978 – 4k. lilac, black and red 25 10
3979 – 4k. bistre, brown and red 25 10
3980 – 4k. red, green and yellow 25 10
MS3981 90 × 66 mm. 20k. vermilion, purple and green . . . . . . 2·25 75
DESIGNS: No. 3977, Farmworkers and wheatfield ("Agricultural Production"); 3978, Factory production line ("Increased Productivity"); 3979, Heavy industry ("Industrial Expansion"); 3980, Family in department store ("National Welfare"); (40 × 22 mm) 20k. Workers' demonstration.

1502 "Meeting" (V. Makovsky)

1503 V. V. Vorovsky

1971. Russian Paintings. Multicoloured.

3982 2k. Type **1502** 20 10
3983 4k. "Girl Student" (N. Yaroshenko) 25 10
3984 6k. "Woman Miner" (N. Kasatkin) 85 10
3985 10k. "Harvesters" (G. Myasoedov) (horiz) 55 15
3986 16k. "Country Road" (A. Savrasov) 80 30
3987 20k. "Pine Forest" (I. Shishkin) (horiz) . . . 1·25 40
MS3988 94 × 68 mm. 50k. "Self-portrait" (I. Kramskoi) (31 × 43 mm) . . . . 3·00 1·10
See also Nos. 4064/70.

1971. Birth Centenary of V. V. Vorovsky (diplomat).

3989 **1503** 4k. brown 20 10

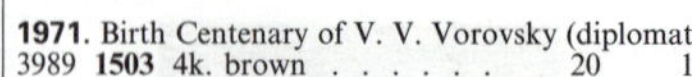
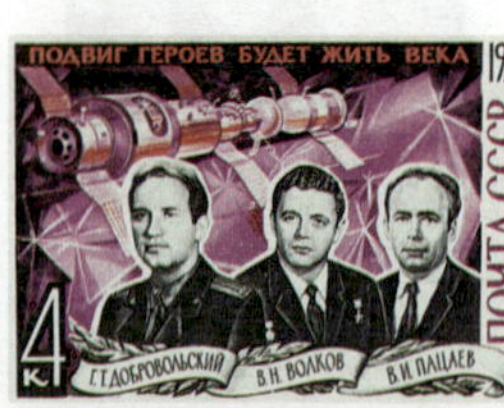

1504 Dobrovolsky, Volkov and Patsaev

1971. "Soyuz 11" Cosmonauts Commemoration.

3990 **1504** 4k. black, purple & orge 25 10

1505 Order of the Revolution and Building Construction

1971. 54th Anniv of October Revolution.

3991 **1505** 4k. multicoloured . . . 20 10

1506 E. Vakhtangov (founder) and characters from "Princess Turandot"

1507 "Dzhambul Dzhabaiev" (A. Yar-Kravchenko)

1971. 50th Anniv of Vakhtangov Theatre, Moscow.

3992 **1506** 10k. red and lake . . . 50 15
3993 – 10k. yellow and brown 50 15
3994 – 10k. orange and brown 50 15
DESIGNS—HORIZ: No. 3993, B. Shchukin (actor) and scene from "The Man with the Rifle"; 3994, R. Simonov (director) and scene from "Cyrano de Bergerac".

1971. 125th Anniv of Dzhambul Dzhabaiev (Kazakh poet).

3995 **1507** 4k. brown, yell & orge 20 10

1508 Pskov Kremlin

1971. Historical Buildings. Multicoloured.

3996 3k. Type **1508** 15 10
3997 4k. Novgorod kremlin . . . 20 10
3998 6k. Smolensk fortress and Liberation Monument . . 25 10
3999 10k. Kolomna kremlin . . . 40 15
MS4000 67 × 88 mm. 50k. Kremlin, Red Square, Moscow (22 × 32 mm) . . . . 2·75 1·00

1509 William Foster

1971. 90th Birth Anniv of Foster (American communist).

4001 **1509** 10k. black and brown 15·00 15·00
4002 10k. black and brown 50 15
No. 4001 shows the incorrect date of death "1964"; 4002 shows the correct date, "1961".

1510 Fadeev and Scene from "The Rout" (novel)

1971. 70th Birth Anniv of Aleksandr Fadeev (writer).

4003 **1510** 4k. orange and blue . . 20 10

1511 Sapphire Brooch

1971. Diamonds and Jewels. Multicoloured.

4004 10k. Type **1511** 60 15
4005 10k. "Shah" diamond . . . 60 15
4006 10k. "Narcissi" diamond brooch 60 15
4007 20k. Amethyst pendant . . 90 40
4008 20k. "Rose" platinum and diamond brooch 90 40
4009 30k. Pearl and diamond pendant . . . . 1·40 60

1512 Vanda Orchid

1514 Ice Hockey Players

1513 Peter the Great's Imperial Barge, 1723

1971. Tropical Flowers. Multicoloured.
4010 1k. Type **1512** 15 10
4011 2k. "Anthurium scherzerianum" 15 10
4012 4k. "Cactus epiphyllum" . . 30 10
4013 12k. Amaryllis 60 30
4014 14k. "Medinilla magnifica" 75 35
MS4015 81 × 97 mm. 10k. × 4 Designs as Nos. 4010 and 4012/14 but smaller (19 × 26 mm) and with white backgrounds . . . . . . 2·50 85

1971. History of the Russian Navy (1st series). Multicoloured.
4016 1k. Type **1513** 15 10
4017 4k. Galleon "Orel", 1668 (vert) 35 10
4018 10k. Ship of the line "Poltava", 1712 (vert) . . 75 15
4019 12k. Ship of the line "Ingermanland", 1715 (vert) . . . . 1·10 30
4020 16k. Steam frigate "Vladimir", 1848 . . . . 1·40 50
See also Nos. 4117/21, 4209/13 and 4303/6.

1971. 25th Anniv of Soviet Ice Hockey.
4021 **1514** 6k. multicoloured . . . 50 10

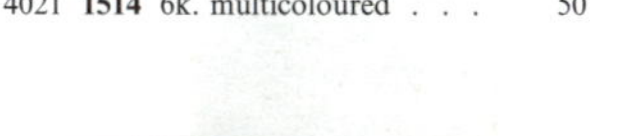

1515 Baku Oil Installations

1516 G. M. Krzhizhanovsky

1971. Baku Oil Industry.
4022 **1515** 4k. black, red and blue 30 10

1972. Birth Centenary of G. M. Krzhizhanovsky (scientist).
4023 **1516** 4k. brown 20 10

1517 Scriabin

1518 Red-faced Cormorant

1972. Birth Centenary of Aleksandr Scriabin (composer).
4024 **1517** 4k. blue and green . . 30 10

1972. Sea Birds. Multicoloured.
4025 4k. Type **1518** 40 15
4026 6k. Ross's gull (horiz) . . . 60 25
4027 10k. Pair of barnacle geese 75 35
4028 12k. Pair of spectacled eiders (horiz) . . . . . . 1·10 60
4029 16k. Mediterranean gull . . 1·25 75

1519 Speed Skating

1520 Heart Emblem

1972. Winter Olympic Games, Sapporo, Japan. Multicoloured.
4030 4k. Type **1519** 15 10
4031 6k. Figure skating 20 10
4032 10k. Ice hockey 50 15
4033 12k. Ski jumping 65 20
4034 16k. Cross-country skiing 75 30
MS4035 67½ × 92 mm. 50k. "Sapporo" emblem and Olympic rings . . . . 2·50 90

1972. World Heart Month.
4036 **1520** 4k. red and green . . . 20 10

1521 Fair Emblem

1522 Labour Emblems

1973. 50th Anniv of Soviet Participation in Leipzig Fair.
4037 **1521** 16k. gold and red . . . 85 30

1972. 15th Soviet Trade Unions Congress, Moscow.
4038 **1522** 4k. brown, red and pink 20 10

1523 "Aloe arborescens"

1524 Alexandra Kollontai (diplomat) (birth cent)

1972. Medicinal Plants. Multicoloured.
4039 1k. Type **1523** 10 10
4040 2k. Yellow horned poppy 10 10
4041 4k. Groundsel 20 10
4042 6k. Nephrite tea 30 10
4043 10k. Kangaroo apple . . . 55 15

1972. Birth Anniversaries.
4044 **1524** 4k. brown 20 10
4045 – 4k. lake 20 10
4046 – 4k. bistre 20 10
CELEBRITIES: No. 4045, G. Chicherin (Foreign Affairs Commissar) (birth cent); 4046, "Kamo" (S. A. Ter-Petrosyan—revolutionary) (90th birth anniv).

СОВЕТСКИЕ СПОРТСМЕНЫ
ЗАВОЕВАЛИ
8 ЗОЛОТЫХ
МЕДАЛЕЙ,
5 СЕРЕБРЯНЫХ,
3 БРОНЗОВЫХ.
(1525)

1972. Soviet Medals at Winter Olympic Games, Sapporo. No. **MS**4035 optd with T **1525** on the sheet.
MS4047 50k. multicoloured . . . 6·75 4·50

1526 "Salyut" Space-station and "Soyuz" Spacecraft

1972. Cosmonautics Day. Multicoloured.
4048 6k. Type **1526** 30 20
4049 6k. "Mars 2" approaching Mars 30 20
4050 16k. Capsule, "Mars 3" . . 75 30

1527 Factory and Products

1972. 250th Anniv of Izhora Factory.
4051 **1527** 4k. purple and silver . . 20 10

1972. 50th Anniv of Russian Federation Autonomous Soviet Socalist Republics. Designs similar to T **1433**, but dated "1972".
4052 4k. blue 35 10
4053 4k. mauve 25 10
DESIGNS: No. 4052, Arms, natural resources and industry (Yakut Republic); 4053, Arms, agriculture and industry (Checheno-Ingush Republic).

1528 L. Sobinov and scene from "Eugene Onegin"

1972. Birth Centenary of L. Sobinov (singer).
4054 **1528** 10k. brown 50 15

1529 Symbol of Knowledge and Children reading Books

1972. International Book Year.
4055 **1529** 6k. multicoloured . . . 30 10

1530 Pavlik Morosov Monument (I. Rabinovich) and Pioneers Saluting

1972. 50th Anniv of Pioneer Organization.
4056 **1530** 1k. multicoloured . . . 10 10
4057 – 2k. purple, red and green 10 10
4058 – 3k. blue, red and brown 20 10
4059 – 4k. red, blue and green 20 10
MS4060 103 × 82 mm. 30k. multicoloured . . . . 2·25 90
DESIGNS: Horiz 2k. Girl laboratory worker and Pioneers with book; 3k. Pioneer Place, Chukotka, and Pioneers at work; 4k. Pioneer parade. Vert (25 × 37 mm) 30k. Colour party (similar to 4k.).

1531 Pioneer Trumpeter

1972. "50th Anniv of Pioneer Organization" Youth Stamp Exhibition, Minsk.
4061 **1531** 4k. purple, red & yellow 20 10

1532 "World Security"

1972. European Security Conference, Brussels.
4062 **1532** 6k. blue, turquoise & gold 75 55

1533 M. S. Ordubady

1534 G. Dimitrov

1972. Birth Centenary of M. S. Ordubady (Azerbaijan writer).
4063 **1533** 4k. purple and orange 20 10

1972. Russian Paintings. As T **1502**, but dated "1972". Multicoloured.
4064 2k. "Cossack Hetman" (I. Nikitin) 10 10
4065 4k. "F. Volkov" (A. Lossenko) 20 10
4066 6k. "V. Majkov" (F. Rokotov) 25 10
4067 10k. "N. Novikov" (D. Levitsky) 40 10
4068 12k. "G. Derzhavin" (V. Borovikovsky) 55 15
4069 16k. "Peasants' Dinner" (M. Shibanov) (horiz) . . 75 25
4070 20k. "Moscow View" (F. Alexeiev) (horiz) . . . 1·10 45

1972. 90th Birth Anniv of Georgi Dimitrov (Bulgarian statesman).
4071 **1534** 6k. brown and bistre 20 10

1535 Congress Building and Emblem

1972. 9th Int Gerontology Congress, Kiev.
4072 **1535** 6k. brown and blue . . 20 10

1536 Fencing

1972. Olympic Games, Munich.
4073 **1536** 4k. purple and gold . . 25 10
4074 – 6k. green and gold . . 35 10
4075 – 10k. blue and gold . . 50 10
4076 – 14k. blue and gold . . 70 20
4077 – 16k. red and gold . . . 85 65
MS4078 67 × 87 mm. 50k. scarlet, gold and green . . . . 2·50 90
DESIGNS: 6k. Gymnastics; 10k. Canoeing; 14k. Boxing; 16k. Running; 50k. Weightlifting.

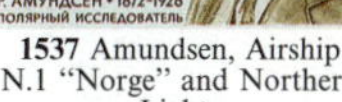
1537 Amundsen, Airship N.1 "Norge" and Northern Lights

1538 Market-place, Lvov (Lemberg)

1972. Birth Centenary of Roald Amundsen (Polar explorer).
4079 **1537** 6k. blue and brown . . 1·50 30

1972. Ukraine's Architectural Monuments. Mult.
4080 4k. Type **1538** 15 10
4081 6k. 17th-century house, Tchernigov (horiz) 30 15
4082 10k. Kovnirovsky building, Kiev (horiz) 45 20
4083 16k. Kamenetz-Podolsk Castle 75 30

1539 Indian Flag and Asokan Capital

1540 Liberation Monument, Vladivostok, and Cavalry

1972. 25th Anniv of India's Independence.
4084 **1539** 6k. red, blue and green . . . 30 10

1972. 50th Anniv of Liberation of Far Eastern Territories.
4085 **1540** 3k. grey, orange and red 15 10
4086 – 4k. grey, yellow & ochre 20 10
4087 – 6k. grey, pink and red . . . 30 15
DESIGNS: 4k. Labour Heroes Monument, Khabarovsk, and industrial scene; 6k. Naval statue, Vladivostok, "Vladivostok" (cruiser) and jet fighters.

1541 Miners' Day Emblem

1972. 25th Anniv of Miners' Day.
4088 **1541** 4k. red, black and violet 20 10

1542 "Boy with Dog" (Murillo)

1972. Paintings by Foreign Artists in Hermitage Gallery, Leningrad. Multicoloured.
4089 4k. "Breakfast" (Velazquez) (horiz) 20 10
4090 6k. "The Milk Seller's Family" (Le Nain) (horiz) 30 10
4091 10k. Type **1542** 55 20
4092 10k. "The Capricious Girl" (Watteau) 90 35
4093 20k. "Moroccan with Horse" (Delacroix) . . . 1·10 45
MS4094 75 × 100 mm. 50k. Van Dyck (self-portrait) . . . . . 3·75 1·40

1543 "Sputnik I"

1972. 15th Anniv of "Cosmic Era". Multicoloured.
4095 6k. Type **1543** 35 15
4096 6k. Launch of "Vostok I" . . 35 15
4097 6k. "Lunokhod" vehicle on Moon 35 15
4098 6k. Man in space 35 15
4099 6k. "Mars 3" module on Mars 35 15
4100 6k. Touch down of "Venera 7" on Venus 35 15

1544 Konstantin Mardzhanishvili

1545 Museum Emblem

1972. Birth Centenary of K. Mardzhanishvili (Georgian actor).
4101 **1544** 4k. green 20 10

1972. Centenary of Popov Central Communications Museum.
4102 **1545** 4k. blue, purple & green 20 10

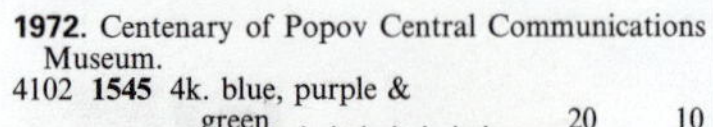

1546 Exhibition Labels

1972. "50th Anniv of U.S.S.R." Philatelic Exhibition.
4103 **1546** 4k. red & black on yell 20 10

1547 Lenin

1972. 55th Anniv of October Revolution.
4104 **1547** 4k. red and gold . . . 20 10

1548 Militia Badge and Soviet Flag

1549 Arms of U.S.S.R.

1972. 55th Anniv of Soviet Militia.
4105 **1548** 4k. gold, red and brown 20 10

1972. 50th Anniv of U.S.S.R.
4106 **1549** 4k. gold, purple and red 15 10
4107 – 4k. gold, red and brown 15 10
4108 – 4k. gold, purple & green 15 10
4109 – 4k. gold, purple and grey 15 10
4110 – 4k. gold, purple and grey 15 10
MS4111 127 × 102 mm. 30k. red and gold . . . . 1·75 65
DESIGNS: No. 4107, Lenin and banner; No. 4108, Arms and Kremlin; No. 4109, Arms and industrial scenes; No. 4110, Arms, worker and open book "U.S.S.R. Constitutions"; **MS**4111, Arms and Spassky Tower.

1550 Emblem of U.S.S.R.

1552 Savings Book

СЛАВА
СОВЕТСКИМ ОЛИМПИЙЦАМ,
ЗАВОЕВАВШИМ
50 ЗОЛОТЫХ, 27 СЕРЕБРЯНЫХ
И 22 БРОНЗОВЫЕ НАГРАДЫ!
(1551)

1972. U.S.S.R. Victories in Olympic Games, Munich. Multicoloured.
4112 20k. Type **1550** . . . . . 1·00 30
4113 30k. Olympic medals . . . 1·50 55
MS4114 Sheet No. **MS**4078 optd with T **1551** in red on margin 3·75 2·50

1972. "50 Years of Soviet Savings Bank".
4115 **1552** 4k. blue and purple . . 20 10

1553 Kremlin and Snowflakes

1555 Skovoroda (after P. Meshcheryakov)

1554 Battleship "Pyotr Veliky"

1972. New Year.
4116 **1553** 6k. multicoloured . . . 20 10

1972. History of the Russian Navy (2nd series). Multicoloured.
4117 2k. Type **1554** 25 10
4118 3k. Cruiser "Varyag" . . . 25 10
4119 4k. Battleship "Potemkin" 45 10
4120 6k. Cruiser "Ochakov" . . 55 15
4121 10k. Minelayer "Amur" . . 1·10 25

1972. 250th Birth Anniv of Grigory S. Skovoroda.
4122 **1555** 4k. blue 20 10

1556 "Pioneer Girl with Books" (N. A. Kasatkin)

1972. "History of Russian Painting". Mult.
4123 2k. "Meeting of Village Party Members" (E. M. Cheptsov) (horiz) 15 10
4124 4k. Type **1556** 20 15
4125 6k. "Party Delegate" (G. G. Ryazhsky) 25 15
4126 10k. "End of Winter—Midday" (K. F. Yuon) (horiz) 35 20
4127 16k. "Partisan Lunev" (N. I. Strunnikov) 70 35
4128 20k. "Self-portrait in Fur Coat" (I. E. Grabar) . . 1·10 50
MS4129 90 × 70 mm. 50k. "In Blue Space" (A. A. Rylov) (horiz) 4·50 1·00

1557 Child reading Safety Code

1558 Emblem of Technology

1972. Road Safety Campaign.
4130 **1557** 4k. black, blue and red 20 10

1972. Cent of Polytechnic Museum, Moscow.
4131 **1558** 4k. red, yellow and green 20 10

1559 "Venus 8" and Parachute

1972. Space Research.
4132 **1559** 6k. blue, black and purple 25 10
MS4133 90 × 70 mm. 50k. × 2 brown 21·00 14·00
DESIGNS—(40 × 20 mm): **MS**4133. (a) "Venera 8". (b) "Mars 3".

1560 Solidarity Emblem

1973. 15th Anniv of Asian and African People's Solidarity Organization.
4134 **1560** 10k. blue, red and brown 35 15

1561 Town and Gediminas Tower

1562 I. V. Babushkin

1973. 650th Anniv of Vilnius (Vilna).
4135 **1561** 10k. red, black and green 35 15

1973. Birth Cent of I. V. Babushkin (revolutionary).
4136 **1562** 4k. black 20 10

1563 Tupolev Tu-154 Jetliner

1973. 50th Anniv of Soviet Civil Aviation.
4137 **1563** 6k. multicoloured . . . 45 15

1564 "30" and Admiralty Spire, Leningrad

1565 Portrait and Masks (Mayakovsky Theatre)

1973. 30th Anniv of Relief of Leningrad.
4138 **1564** 4k. black, orange & brn 20 10

1973. 50th Anniv of Moscow Theatres.
4139 **1565** 10k. multicoloured . . 30 10
4140 – 10k. red and blue . . . 30 10
DESIGN: No. 4140, Commemorative panel (Mossoviet Theatre).

1566 Prishvin (after A. Kirillov)

1973. Birth Centenary of Mikhail Prishvin (writer).
4141 **1566** 4k. multicoloured . . . 30 10

1567 Heroes' Square, Volgograd

1973. 30th Anniv of Stalingrad Victory. Detail from Heroes' Memorial.
4142 – 3k. black, yellow & orge 20 10
4143 **1567** 4k. yellow and black . . 20 10
4144 – 10k. multicoloured . . 40 15
4145 – 12k. black, light red and red 60 20
MS4146 93 × 73 mm. 20k. × 2 multicoloured . . . . 2·75 1·10
DESIGNS—VERT (28 × 59 mm): 3k. Soldier and Allegory; 12k. Hand with torch; (18 × 40 mm)—Allegory, Mamai Barrow. HORIZ (59 × 28 mm)—Mourning mother; (40 × 18 mm) 20k. Mamai Barrow.

1568 Copernicus and Planetary Chart

1973. 500th Birth Anniv of Copernicus (astronomer).
4147 **1568** 10k. brown and blue . . 55 15

1569 Chaliapin (after K. Korovin)

1973. Birth Centenary of Fyodor Chaliapin (opera singer).
4148 **1569** 10k. multicoloured . . 45 15

1570 Ice Hockey Players **1571** Athletes

1973. World Ice Hockey Championships, Moscow.
4149 **1570** 10k. brown, blue & gold 60 15
MS4150 64 × 85 mm. 50k. sepia, green and gold (players) (21 × 32 mm) . . . . 2·50 1·00

1973. 50th Anniv of Central Red Army Sports Club.
4151 **1571** 4k. multicoloured . . . 20 10

1572 Red Star, Tank, and Map **1573** N. E. Bauman

1973. 30th Anniv of Battle of Kursk.
4152 **1572** 4k. black, red and grey 20 10

1973. Birth Centenary of Nikolai Bauman (revolutionary).
4153 **1573** 4k. brown 25 10

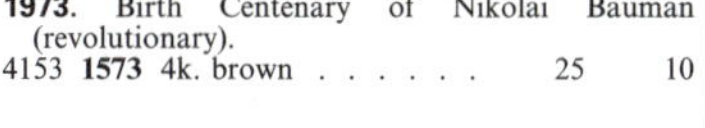

1574 Red Cross and Red Crescent

1973. International Co-operation.
4154 **1574** 4k. red, black and green 15 10
4155 – 6k. light blue, red and blue 20 10
4156 – 16k. green, red and mauve 80 25
DESIGNS AND EVENTS: 4k. (50th anniv of Soviet Red Cross and Red Crescent Societies Union); 6k. Mask, emblem and theatre curtain (15th Int Theatre Institution Congress); 16k. Floral emblem (10th World Festival of Youth, Berlin).

1575 Ostrovsky (after V. Perov) **1576** Satellites

1973. 150th Birth Anniv of Aleksandr Ostrovsky (writer).
4157 **1575** 4k. multicoloured . . . 20 10

1973. Cosmonautics Day. Multicoloured.
4158 6k. Type **1576** 20 10
4159 6k. "Lunokhod 2" 20 10
MS4160 75 × 100 mm. 20k. × 3, each 51 × 21 mm in lake, plum and gold 3·25 1·40
MS4161 As No. **MS**4160 but in green, purple and gold . . . . 3·25 1·40

1577 "Guitarist" (V. Tropinin) **1578** Athlete and Emblems

1973. "History of Russian Painting". Mult.
4162 2k. Type **1577** 15 10
4163 4k. "The Young Widow" (P. Fedotov) 20 10
4164 6k. "Self-portrait" (O. Kiprensky) 30 10
4165 10k. "An Afternoon in Italy" (K. Bryullov) . . . 45 20
4166 12k. "That's My Father's Dinner!" (boy with dog) (A. Venetsianov) 55 30
4167 16k. "Lower Gallery of Albano" (A. Ivanov) (horiz) 75 35
4168 20k. "Yermak conquering Siberia" (V. Surikov) (horiz) . . . . 1·00 50

1973. 50th Anniv of Dynamo Sports Club.
4169 **1578** 4k. multicoloured . . . 20 10

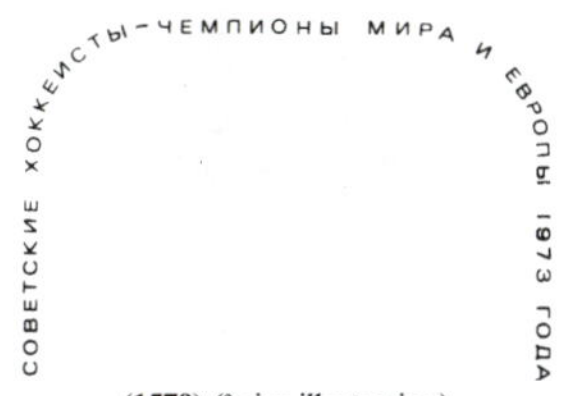

(**1579**) (⅔-size illustration)

1973. U.S.S.R.'s Victory in World Ice-Hockey Championships. No. **MS**4150 optd with T **1579** and frame at foot in green.
MS4170 67 × 86 mm. 50k. sepia, green and gold . . . . . . 7·50 5·00

1580 Liner "Mikhail Lermontov" **1582** Sports

1581 E. T. Krenkel and Polar Scenes

1973. Inauguration of Leningrad–New York Trans-Atlantic Service.
4171 **1580** 16k. multicoloured . . 70 30

1973. 70th Birth Anniv of E. T. Krenkel (Polar explorer).
4172 **1581** 4k. brown and blue . . 75 20

1973. "Sport for Everyone".
4173 **1582** 4k. multicoloured . . . 20 10

1583 Girls' Choir

1973. Centenary of Latvian Singing Festival.
4174 **1583** 10k. multicoloured . . 35 10

1973. 50th Anniv of Russian Federation Autonomous Soviet Socialist Republics. Design similar to T **1433**, but dated "1973".
4175 4k. blue 20 10
DESIGN: No. 4175, Arms and industries of Buryat Republic.

1584 Throwing the Hammer

1973. Universiade Games, Moscow. Mult.
4176 2k. Type **1584** 10 10
4177 3k. Gymnastics 10 10
4178 4k. Swimming 15 10
4179 16k. Fencing 85 25
MS4180 70 × 88 mm. 50k. Throwing the javelin . . . . 2·40 1·00

1585 Tereshkova

1973. 10th Anniv of Woman's First Space Flight by Valentina Nikolaieva-Tereshkova. Sheet 89 × 70 mm containing horiz designs as T **1585**. Multicoloured.
MS4181 20k. × 3 (a) Type **1585**; (b) Tereshkova with Indian and African women; (c) Holding her baby . . . . 3·25 1·50

1586 European Bison

1973. Caucasus and Voronezh Nature Reserves. Multicoloured.
4182 1k. Type **1586** 10 10
4183 3k. Ibex 15 10
4184 4k. Caucasian snowcocks . . 1·25 20
4185 6k. Eurasian beaver with young 35 10
4186 10k. Red deer with fawns 55 20

1587 Lenin, Banner and Membership Card

1973. 70th Anniv of 2nd Soviet Social Democratic Workers Party Congress.
4187 **1587** 4k. multicoloured . . . 20 10

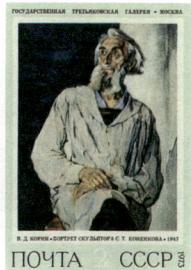

1588 A. R. al-Biruni (after M. Nabiev) **1590** "Portrait of the Sculptor S. T. Konenkov" (P. Korin)

1589 Schaumberg Palace, Bonn, and Spassky Tower, Moscow

1973. Millennium of Abu Reihan al-Biruni (astronomer and mathematician).
4188 **1588** 6k. brown 30 15

1973. General Secretary Leonid Brezhnev's Visits to West Germany, France and U.S.A. Multicoloured.
4189 **1589** 10k. mauve, brn & buff 40 15
4190 – 10k. brown, ochre and yellow 40 15
4191 – 10k. red, grey and brown 40 15
MS4192 134 × 139 mm. 4k. × 3 as Nos. 4189/91, each crimson, flesh and deep olive . . . . 3·25 1·75
DESIGNS: No. 4189, Type **1589**; Eiffel Tower, Paris and Spassky Tower; 4191, White House, Washington and Spassky Tower.
See also Nos. 4245 and 4257.

1973. "History of Russian Paintings". Mult.
4193 2k. Type **1590** 10 10
4194 4k. "Farm-workers' Supper" (A. Plastov) 15 10
4195 6k. "Letter from the Battle-front" (A. Laktionov) . . 25 15
4196 10k. "Mountain Landscape" (M. Saryan) 45 25
4197 16k. "Wedding on Tomorrow's Street" (Yu. Pimenov) 75 35
4198 20k. "Ice Hockey" (mosaic, A. Deineka) . . . . . 1·10 45
MS4199 72 × 92 mm. 50k. "Lenin making Speech" (B. Johanson) 2·75 1·90

1591 Lenin Museum **1592** Steklov

1973. Inaug of Lenin Museum, Tashkent.
4200 **1591** 4k. multicoloured . . . 20 10

1973. Birth Centenary of Y. Steklov (statesman).
4201 **1592** 4k. brown, red and pink 20 10

1593 "The Eternal Pen" **1594** "Oplopanax elatum"

1973. Afro-Asian Writers' Conference, Alma-Ata.
4202 **1593** 6k. multicoloured . . . 20 10

1973. Medicinal Plants. Multicoloured.
4203 1k. Type **1594** 10 10
4204 2k. Ginseng 15 10
4205 4k. Spotted orchid 20 10
4206 10k. Arnica 40 20
4207 12k. Lily of the valley . . . 55 25

1595 I. Nasimi (after M. Abdullaev)

1973. 600th Birth Anniv of Imadeddin Nasimi (Azerbaijan poet).
4208 **1595** 4k. brown 20 10

1596 Cruiser "Kirov"

1973. History of Russian Navy (3rd series). Multicoloured.
4209 3k. Type **1596** 20 10
4210 4k. Battleship "Oktyabrskaya Revolyutsiya" 25 10
4211 6k. Submarine "Krasnogvardeets" . . . 30 15
4212 10k. Destroyer "Soobrazitelnyi" 60 25
4213 16k. Cruiser "Krasnyi Kavkaz" . . . . 1·10 35

1597 Pugachev and Battle Scene

1973. Bicentenary of Peasant War.
4214 **1597** 4k. multicoloured . . . 20 10

1598 Red Flag encircling Globe

1973. 15th Anniv of Magazine "Problems of Peace and Socialism".
4215 **1598** 6k. red, gold and green 25 10

1599 Leningrad Mining Institute

1973. Bicentenary of Leningrad Mining Institute.
4216 **1599** 4k. multicoloured . . . 20 10

1600 Laurel and Hemispheres

1601 Elena Stasova

1973. World Congress of "Peaceful Forces", Moscow.
4217 **1600** 6k. multicoloured . . . 25 10

1973. Birth Centenary of Yelena Stasova (party official).
4218 **1601** 4k. mauve 20 10

1602 Order of People's Friendship

1603 Marshal Malinovsky

1973. Foundation of Order of People's Friendship.
4219 **1602** 4k. multicoloured . . . 20 10

1973. 75th Birth Anniv of Marshal R. Malinovsky.
4220 **1603** 4k. grey 20 10

1604 Workers and Red Guard

1605 D. Cantemir

1973. 250th Anniv of Sverdlovsk.
4221 **1604** 4k. black, gold and red 20 10

1973. 300th Birth Anniv of Dmitri Cantemir (Moldavian scientist and encyclopaedist).
4222 **1605** 4k. red 20 10

1606 Pres. Allende of Chile

1973. Allende Commemoration.
4223 **1606** 6k. black and brown . . 30 10

1607 Kremlin

1608 N. Narimanov

1973. New Year.
4224 **1607** 6k. multicoloured . . . 20 10

1973. Birth Centenary (1970) of Nariman Narimanov (Azerbaijan politician).
4225 **1608** 4k. green 20 10

1609 "Russobalt" Touring Car (1909)

1973. History of Soviet Motor Industry (1st series). Multicoloured.
4226 2k. Type **1609** 15 10
4227 3k. "AMO-F15" lorry (1924) 15 10
4228 4k. Spartak "NAMI-1" tourer (1927) 20 10
4229 12k. Yaroslavsky "Ya-6" bus (1929) 55 20
4230 16k. Gorkovsky "GAZ-A" tourer (1932) 75 40
See also Nos. 4293/7, 4397/401 and 4512/16.

1610 "Game and Lobster" (Sneiders)

1973. Foreign Paintings in Soviet Galleries. Mult.
4231 4k. Type **1610** 20 10
4232 6k. "Young Woman with Ear-rings" (Rembrandt) (vert) 20 10
4233 10k. "Sick Woman and Physician" (Steen) (vert) 35 15
4234 12k. "Attributes of Art" (Chardin) 45 20
4235 14k. "Lady in a Garden" (Monet) 50 25
4236 16k. "Village Lovers" (Bastien-Lepage) (vert) . . 60 30
4237 20k. "Girl with Fan" (Renoir) (vert) 75 40
MS4238 78 × 103 mm. 50k. "Flora" (Rembrandt) (vert) . . . . . . 2·25 1·25

1611 Great Sea Gate, Tallin

1612 Picasso

1973. Historical Buildings of Estonia, Latvia and Lithuania.
4239 **1611** 4k. black, red and green 20 10
4240 – 4k. brown, red and green 20 10
4241 – 4k. multicoloured . . . 20 10
4242 – 10k. multicoloured . . 50 20
DESIGNS: No. 4240, Organ pipes and Dome Cathedral, Riga; 4241, Traku Castle, Lithuania; 4242, Town Hall and weather-vane, Tallin.

1973. Pablo Picasso Commemoration.
4243 **1612** 6k. green, red and gold 30 10

1613 Petrovsky

1973. I. G. Petrovsky (mathematician and Rector of Moscow University) Commemoration.
4244 **1613** 4k. multicoloured . . . 20 10

1973. Brezhnev's Visit to India. As T **1589**, but showing Kremlin, Red Fort, Delhi and flags.
4245 4k. multicoloured 20 10

1614 Soviet Soldier and Title Page

1616 Oil Workers

1615 Siege Monument and Peter the Great Statue, Leningrad

1974. 50th Anniv of "Red Star" Newspaper.
4246 **1614** 4k. black, red and gold 20 10

1974. 30th Anniv of Soviet Victory in Battle for Leningrad.
4247 **1615** 4k. multicoloured . . . 30 10

1974. 10th Anniv of Tyumen Oil fields.
4248 **1616** 4k. black, red and blue 30 10

1617 "Comecon" Headquarters, Moscow

1618 Skaters and Stadium

1974. 25th Anniv of Council for Mutual Economic Aid.
4249 **1617** 16k. green, red & brown 45 20

1974. European Women's Ice Skating Championships, Medeo, Alma-Ata.
4250 **1618** 6k. red, blue and slate 20 10

1619 Kunstkammer Museum, Leningrad, Text and Academy

1620 L. A. Artsimovich

1974. 250th Anniv of Russian Academy of Sciences.
4251 **1619** 10k. multicoloured . . 25 10

1974. 1st Death Anniv of Academician L. A. Artsimovich (physicist).
4252 **1620** 4k. brown and green . . 20 10

1974. 50th Anniv of Autonomous Soviet Socialist Republics. Design similar to T **1433**, but dated "1974".
4253 4k. brown 20 10
DESIGN: No. 4253, Arms and industries of Nakhichevan ASSR (Azerbaijan).

1621 K. D. Ushinsky

1622 M. D. Millionshchikov

1974. 150th Birth Anniv of K. D. Ushinsky (educationalist).
4254 **1621** 4k. brown and green . . 20 10

1974. 1st Death Anniv of M. D. Millionshchikov (scientist).
4255 **1622** 4k. brown, pink & green 20 10

1623 Spartakiad Emblem

1624 Young Workers and Emblem

1974. 3rd Winter Spartakiad Games.
4256 **1623** 10k. multicoloured . . 25 15

1974. General Secretary Leonid Brezhnev's Visit to Cuba. As T **1589** but showing Kremlin, Revolution Square, Havana and Flags.
4257 4k. multicoloured 20 10

1974. Scientific and Technical Youth Work Review.
4258 **1624** 4k. multicoloured . . . 20 10

1625 Theatre Facade

1626 Globe and Meteorological Activities

1974. Cent of Azerbaijan Drama Theatre, Baku.
4259 **1625** 6k. brown, red & orange 20 10

1974. Cosmonautics Day.
4260 **1626** 6k. blue, red and violet 20 10
4261 – 10k. brown, red and blue 40 15
4262 – 10k. black, red & yellow 40 15
DESIGNS: No. 4261, V. G. Lazarev and O. G. Makarov, and launch of "Soyuz 12"; 4262, P. I. Klimuk and V. V. Lebedev, and "Soyuz 13".

1627 "Odessa by Moonlight" (Aivazovsky)

1974. Marine Paintings by Ivan Aivazovsky. Mult.
4263 2k. Type **1627** 10 10
4264 4k. "Battle of Chesme" (vert) 15 10
4265 6k. "St. George's Monastery" 20 10
4266 10k. "Storm at Sea" 35 15
4267 12k. "Rainbow" 65 20
4268 16k. "Shipwreck" 80 30
MS4269 68 × 91 mm. 50k. "Ivan Aivazovsky" (I. Kramskoi) (vert) 2·25 90

1628 Young Communists

1974. 17th Leninist Young Communist League (Komsomol) Congress (4270) and 50th Anniv of Naming League after Lenin (4271). Multicoloured.
4270 4k. Type **1628** 20 10
4271 4k. "Lenin" (from sculpture by V. Tsigal) 20 10

1629 "Lenin at the Telegraph" (I. E. Grabar)

1974. 104th Birth Anniv of Lenin. Sheet 108 × 82 mm.
MS4272 **1629** 50k. multicoloured 2·25 90

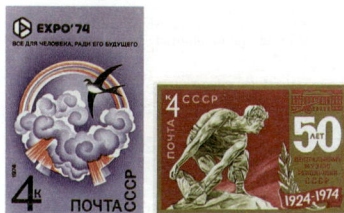

1630 Swallow ("Atmosphere")

1631 "Cobble-stone, Proletarian Weapon" (sculpture, I. Shadr)

1974. "EXPO 74" World Fair, Spokane, U.S.A. "Preserve the Environment".
4273 **1630** 4k. black, red and lilac 15 10
4274 – 6k. yellow, black & blue 20 10
4275 – 10k. black, violet and red 45 15
4276 – 16k. blue, green & black 65 20
4277 – 20k. black, brn & orge 90 40
MS4278 73 × 93 mm. 50k. multicoloured . . . . 2·25 90
DESIGNS: 6k. Fish and globe ("The Sea"); 10k. Crystals ("The Earth"); 16k. Rose bush ("Flora"); 20k. Young red deer ("Fauna"); (30 × 42 mm) 50k. Child and Sun ("Protest the Environment").

1974. 50th Anniv of Central Museum of the Revolution.
4279 **1631** 4k. green, red and gold 20 10

1632 Congress Emblem within Lucerne Grass

1634 Tchaikovsky and Competition Emblem

1633 Saiga

1974. 12th International Congress of Meadow Cultivation, Moscow.
4280 **1632** 4k. red, green & dp green 20 10

1974. 1st International Theriological Congress, Moscow. Fauna. Multicoloured.
4281 1k. Type **1633** 10 10
4282 3k. Asiatic wild ass 15 10
4283 4k. Russian desman 25 10
4284 6k. Northern fur seal . . . 35 15
4285 10k. Bowhead whale 75 25

1974. 5th Int Tchaikovsky Music Competition.
4286 **1634** 6k. black, violet & green 35 10

1635 "Puskin" (O. A. Kipernsky)

1974. 175th Birth Anniv of Aleksandr Pushkin (writer). Sheet 101 × 81 mm.
MS4287 **1635** 50k. multicoloured 2·25 70

1636 Marshal F. I. Tolbukhin

1638 Runner and Emblem

1637 K. Stanislavsky, V. Nemirovich-Danchenko and Theatre Curtain

1974. 80th Birth Anniv of Marshal F. I. Tolbukhin.
4288 **1636** 4k. green 20 10

1974. 75th Anniv of Moscow Arts Festival.
4289 **1637** 10k. multicoloured . . 35 15

1974. 13th Soviet Schools Spartakiad, Alma Ata.
4290 **1638** 4k. multicoloured . . . 25 10

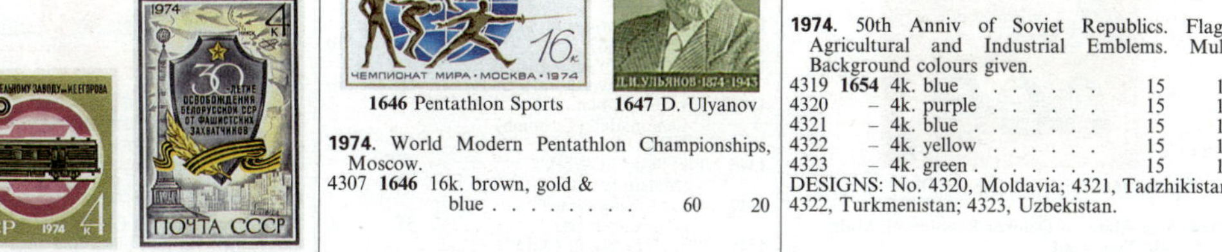

1639 Modern Passenger Coach

1640 Shield and Monument on Battle Map

1974. Centenary of Yegorov Railway Wagon Works, Leningrad.
4291 **1639** 4k. multicoloured . . . 30 10

1974. 30th Anniv of Liberation of Belorussia.
4292 **1640** 4k. multicoloured . . . 20 10
See also No. 4301.

1974. History of Soviet Motor Industry (2nd series). As T **1609**. Multicoloured.
4293 2k. Gorkovsky "GAZ-AA" lorry (1932) 15 10
4294 3k. Gorkovsky "GAZ-03-30" bus (1933) 15 10
4295 4k. Moscow Auto Works "ZIS-5" lorry (1933) . . . 20 10
4296 14k. Moscow Auto Works "ZIS-8" bus (1934) . . . 65 20
4297 16k. Moscow Auto Works "ZIS-101" saloon car (1936) 80 25

1974. 50th Anniv of Soviet Republics. As T **1433**, dated "1974".
4298 4k. red 20 10
DESIGN: 4k. Arms and industries of North Ossetian Republic.
No. 4298 also commemorates the 200th anniv of Ossetia's merger with Russia.

1641 Liberation Monument (E. Kuntsevich) and Skyline

1644 Admiral Isakov

1642 Flag and "Nike" Memorial, Warsaw

1974. 800th Anniv of Poltava.
4299 **1641** 4k. red and brown . . 20 10

1974. 30th Anniv of Polish People's Republic.
4300 **1642** 6k. brown and red . . 25 10

1974. 30th Anniv of Liberation of Ukraine. As T **1640**, but background details and colours changed.
4301 4k. multicoloured 20 10

1974. 80th Birth Anniv of Admiral I. S. Isakov.
4302 **1644** 4k. blue 20 10

1645 Minesweeper

1974. History of the Russian Navy (4th series). Modern Warships. Multicoloured.
4303 3k. Type **1645** 25 10
4304 4k. Aligator II tank landing ship 30 10
4305 6k. "Moskova" helicopter carrier 45 15
4306 16k. Destroyer "Otvazhny" 1·25 30

1646 Pentathlon Sports

1647 D. Ulyanov

1974. World Modern Pentathlon Championships, Moscow.
4307 **1646** 16k. brown, gold & blue 60 20

1974. Birth Centenary of D. Ulyanov (Lenin's brother).
4308 **1647** 4k. green 20 10

1648 V. Menzhinsky

1650 S. M. Budennyi

1649 "Lilac" (P. P. Konchalovsky)

1974. Birth Cent of V. Menzhinsky (statesman).
4309 **1648** 4k. maroon 20 10

1974. Soviet Paintings. Multicoloured.
4310 4k. Type **1649** 15 10
4311 6k. "Towards the Wind" (sailing) (E. Kalnins) . . . 25 15
4312 10k. "Spring" (young woman) (O. Zardaryan) 45 20
4313 16k. "Northern Harbour" (G. Nissky) 75 30
4314 20k. "Daughter of Soviet Kirgiz" (S. Chuikov) (vert) 90 35

1974. Marshal S. M. Budennyi Commemoration.
4315 **1650** 4k. green 20 10

1651 Page of First Russian Dictionary

1652 Flags and Soviet War Memorial, (K. Baraski), Bucharest

1974. 400th Anniv of First Russian Primer.
4316 **1651** 4k. red, black and gold 20 10

1974. 30th Anniv of Rumanian Liberation.
4317 **1652** 6k. blue, yellow and red 20 10

1653 Vitebsk

1974. Millenary of Vitebsk.
4318 **1653** 4k. red and green . . . 15 10

1654 Kirgizia

1655 Bulgarian Crest and Flags

1974. 50th Anniv of Soviet Republics. Flags, Agricultural and Industrial Emblems. Mult. Background colours given.
4319 **1654** 4k. blue 15 10
4320 – 4k. purple 15 10
4321 – 4k. blue 15 10
4322 – 4k. yellow 15 10
4323 – 4k. green 15 10
DESIGNS: No. 4320, Moldavia; 4321, Tadzhikistan; 4322, Turkmenistan; 4323, Uzbekistan.

1974. 30th Anniv of Bulgarian Revolution.
4324 **1655** 6k. multicoloured . . . 20 10

1656 G.D.R. Crest and Soviet War Memorial, Treptow, Berlin

1658 Theatre and Laurel Wreath

1657 Text and Stamp

1974. 25th Anniv of German Democratic Republic.
4325 **1656** 6k. multicoloured . . . 20 10

1974. 3rd Soviet Philatelic Society Congress, Moscow. Sheet 111 × 71 mm.
MS4326 **1657** 50k. bistre, black and claret . . . . 14·00 8·00

1974. 150th Anniv of Maly State Theatre, Moscow.
4327 **1658** 4k. gold, red and black 20 10

1659 "Guests from Overseas"

1974. Birth Centenary of Nikolai K. Rorich (painter).
4328 **1659** 6k. multicoloured . . . 25 10

1660 Soviet Crest and U.P.U. Monument, Berne

1974. Centenary of U.P.U. Multicoloured.
4329 10k. Type **1660** 45 15
4330 10k. Ukraine crest, U.P.U. Emblem and U.P.U. H.Q., Berne 45 15
4331 10k. Byelorussia crest, U.P.U. emblem and mail transport 45 15
MS4332 122 × 77 mm. 30k. Ilyushin Il-62M jetliner and U.P.U. emblem; 30k. Mail coach and U.P.U. emblem; 40k. U.P.U. emblem (each 31 × 43 mm) . . 16·00 10·00

1661 Order of Labour Glory

1974. 57th Anniv of October Revolution. Mult.
4333 4k. Type **1661** 25 10
4334 4k. Kamaz truck (vert) . . . 15 10
4335 4k. Hydro-electric power station, Nurek (vert) . . . 15 10

1662 Soviet "Space Stations" over Mars

1974. Soviet Space Exploration. Multicoloured.
4336 6k. Type **1662** 25 10
4337 10k. P. R. Popovich and Yu. P. Artyukhin ("Soyuz 14" cosomonauts) 45 15
4338 10k. I. V. Sarafanov and L. S. Demin ("Soyuz 15" cosmonauts) 45 15
SIZES—VERT: No. 4337, 28 × 40 mm. HORIZ: No. 4338, 40 × 28 mm.

1663 Mongolian Crest Flag

1664 Commemorative Inscription

1974. 50th Anniv of Mongolian People's Republic.
4339 **1663** 6k. multicoloured . . . 20 10

1974. 30th Anniv of Estonian Liberation.
4340 **1664** 4k. multicoloured . . . 20 10

1665 Liner "Aleksandr Pushkin", Freighter and Tanker

1974. 50th Anniv of Soviet Merchant Navy.
4341 **1665** 4k. multicoloured . . . 30 10

1666 Spassky Clock-tower, Kremlin, Moscow

1974. New Year.
4342 **1666** 4k. multicoloured . . . 20 10

1667 "The Market Place" (Beuckelaar)

1974. Foreign Paintings in Soviet Galleries. Mult.
4343 4k. Type **1667** 15 10
4344 6k. "Woman selling Fish" (Pieters) (vert) 25 10
4345 10k. "A Goblet of Lemonade" (Terborsh) (vert) 35 15
4346 14k. "Girl at Work" (Metsu) (vert) 50 25
4347 16k. "Saying Grace" (Chardin) (vert) 55 30
4348 20k. "The Spoilt Child" (Greuze) (vert) 80 35
MS4349 77 × 104 mm. 50k. "Self-portrait" (David) (vert) . . . . 2·50 90

1668 "Ostrowskia magnifica"

1669 Nikitin (after P. Borel)

1974. Flowers. Multicoloured.
4350 1k. Type **1668** 10 10
4351 2k. "Paeonia intermedia" . . 10 10
4352 4k. "Roemeria refracta" . . 20 10
4353 10k. "Tulipia dasystemon" 45 20
4354 12k. "Dianthus versicolor" 55 25

1974. 150th Birth Anniv of I. S. Nikitin (poet).
4355 **1669** 4k. black, green & olive 20 10

1670 Leningrad Mint Building

1974. 250th Anniv of Leningrad Mint.
4356 **1670** 6k. multicoloured . . . 35 10

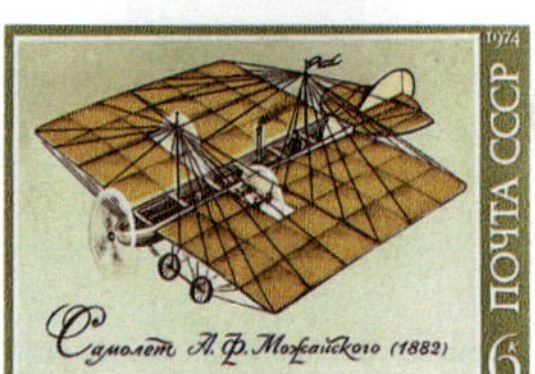

1671 Mozhaisky's Monoplane, 1884

1974. Early Russian Aircraft (1st series). Mult.
4357 6k. Type **1671** 30 15
4358 6k. Grizidubov No. 2 biplane, 1910 . . . . . . 30 15
4359 6k. Sikorsky "Russia A", 1910 . . . . 30 15
4360 6k. Sikorsky Russky Vityaz, 1913 . . . . 30 15
4361 6k. Grigorovich M-5 flying boat, 1914 . . . . . . 30 15
See also Nos. 4580/4, 4661/6 and 4791/6.

1672 Gymnastics and Army Sports Palace, Moscow

1974. Sports Buildings for Olympic Games, Moscow. Sheet 95 × 74 mm containing T **1672** and similar horiz designs in vermilion, brown and green.
MS4362 10k. Type **1672**; 10k. Running and Znamemsky Brothers' Athletics Hall, Sokolniki; 10k. Football and Lenin Central Stadium; 10k. Canoeing and Rowing Canal, Moscow . . . . 3·50 1·40

1673 Komsomol Emblem and Rotary Press ("Komsomolskaya Pravda")

1975. 50th Anniv of Children's Newspapers.
4363 **1673** 4k. red, black and blue 20 10
4364 – 4k. red, black and silver 20 10
DESIGN—VERT: No. 4364, Pioneer emblem and newspaper sheet ("Pioneerskaya Pravda").

1674 Emblem and Skiers (8th Trade Unions' Games)

1975. Winter Spartakiads.
4365 **1674** 4k. orange, black & blue 15 10
4366 – 16k. bistre, black & blue 55 20
DESIGN—HORIZ: 16k. Emblem, ice hockey player and skier (5th Friendly Forces Military Games).

1975. "50th Anniv of Automomous Soviet Socialist Republics. Designs similar to T **1433**, but dated "1975".
4367 4k. green 20 10
DESIGN: No. 4367, Arms, industries and produce of Karakalpak ASSR (Uzbekistan).

1675 "David"

1975. 500th Birth Anniv of Michelangelo.
4368 **1675** 4k. deep green and green 20 15
4369 – 6k. brown and ochre 25 15
4370 – 10k. deep green & green 35 15
4371 – 14k. brown and ochre 60 30
4372 – 20k. deep green & green 1·00 30
4373 – 30k. brown and ochre 1·50 30
MS4374 166 × 74 mm. 50k. multicoloured . . . . 3·25 1·40
DESIGNS—HORIZ: 6k. "Crouching Boy"; 10k. "Rebellious Slave"; 14k. "Creation of Adam" (detail, Sistine Chapel ceiling); 20k. Staircase of Laurentiana Library, Florence; 30k. Christ and the Virgins (detail of "The Last Judgement", Sistine Chapel). VERT: 50k. Self-portrait.

1676 Mozhaisky, his Monoplane (1884) and Tupolev Tu-144 Jetliner

1975. 150th Birth Anniv of Aleksandr Mozhaisky (aircraft designer).
4375 **1676** 6k. brown and blue . . 40 10

1677 Convention Emblem

1975. Cent of International Metre Convention.
4376 **1677** 6k. multicoloured . . . 20 10

1678 Games Emblem

1975. 6th Summer Spartakiad.
4377 **1678** 6k. multicoloured . . . 20 10

1679 Towers of Charles Bridge, Prague (Czechoslovakia)

1975. 30th Anniv of Liberation. Multicoloured.
4378 6k. Type **1679** 15 10
4379 6k. Liberation Monument and Parliament Buildings, Budapest (Hungary) . . . 15 10

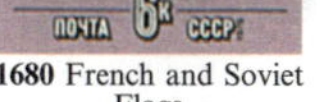

1680 French and Soviet Flags
1681 Yuri Gagarin (bust by L. Kerbel)

1975. 50th Anniv of Franco-Soviet Diplomatic Relations.
4380 **1680** 6k. multicoloured . . . 20 10

1975. Cosmonautics Day.
4381 **1681** 6k. red, silver and blue 20 10
4382 – 10k. red, black and blue 35 15
4383 – 16k. multicoloured . . . 55 20
DESIGNS—HORIZ: 10k. A. A. Gubarev, G. M. Grechko ("Soyuz 17") and "Salyut 4"; 16k. A. V. Filipchenko, N. N. Rukavishnikov and "Soyuz 16".

1682 Treaty Emblem
1684 Lenin

1683 Emblem and Exhibition Hall, Sokolniki, Moscow

1975. 20th Anniv of Warsaw Treaty.
4384 **1682** 6k. multicoloured . . . 20 10

1975. "Communication 75" International Exhibition, Moscow.
4385 **1683** 6k. red, silver and blue 20 10

1975. 30th Anniv of Victory in Second World War. Multicoloured.
4386 4k. Type **1684** 15 10
4387 4k. Eternal flame and Guard of Honour 15 10
4388 4k. Woman in ammunition factory 15 10
4389 4k. Partisans 15 10
4390 4k. "Destruction of the enemy" 15 10
4391 4k. Soviet forces 15 10
MS4392 111 × 57 mm. 50k. Order of the Patriotic War (33 × 49 mm). Imperf . . . . 6·00 5·00

1685 "Lenin" (V. G. Tsyplakov)
1686 Victory Emblems

1975. 105th Birth Anniv of Lenin.
4393 **1685** 4k. multicoloured . . . 20 10

1975. "Sozfilex 75" International Stamp Exhibition.
4394 **1686** 6k. multicoloured . . . 20 10
4395 6k. multicoloured . . . 20 10
MS4395 69 × 95 mm. **1686** 50k. multicoloured . . . . 1·90 80

1687 "Apollo"–"Soyuz" Space Link

1975. "Apollo"–"Soyuz" Space Project.
4396 **1687** 20k. multicoloured . . 75 25

1975. History of Soviet Motor Industry (3rd series). As T **1609**.
4397 2k. black, orange and blue 15 10
4398 3k. black, brown and green 15 10
4399 4k. black, blue and green . . 15 10
4400 12k. black, buff and purple 45 20
4401 16k. black, green and olive 60 30
DESIGNS: 2k. Gorkovsky "GAZ-M1" saloon, 1936; 3k. Yaroslavsky "YAG-6" truck, 1936; 4k. Moscow Auto Works "ZIS-16" bus, 1938; 12k. Moscow KIM Works "KIM-10" saloon, 1940; 16k. Gorkovsky "GAZ-67B" field car, 1943.

1688 Irrigation Canal and Emblem
1689 Flags and Crests of Poland and Soviet Union

1975. 9th Int Irrigation Congress, Moscow.
4402 **1688** 6k. multicoloured . . . 20 10

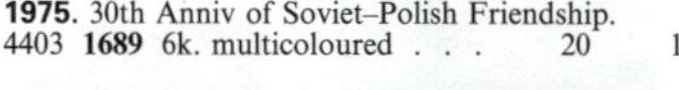

1975. 30th Anniv of Soviet–Polish Friendship.
4403 **1689** 6k. multicoloured . . . 20 10

1690 A. A. Leonov in Space
1691 Ya. M. Sverdlov

1975. 10th Anniv of First Space Walk by A. A. Leonov.
4404 **1690** 6k. multicoloured . . . 25 10

1975. 90th Birth Anniv of Ya. M. Sverdlov (statesman).
4405 **1691** 4k. brown, buff & silver 15 10

1692 Congress Emblem

1975. 8th Int Plant Conservation Congress, Moscow.
4406 **1692** 6k. multicoloured . . . 20 10

1693 Emblem and Plants

1975. 12th Int Botanical Congress, Leningrad.
4407 **1693** 6k. multicoloured . . . 60 15

1694 U.N.O. Emblem

1975. 30th Anniv of United Nations Organization. Sheet 67 × 78 mm.
MS4408 **1694** 50k. gold, blue and light blue . . . . 2·25 1·00

1695 Festival Emblem

1975. 9th International Film Festival, Moscow.
4409 **1695** 6k. multicoloured . . . 20 10

1696 Crews of "Apollo" and "Soyuz"

1975. "Apollo"–"Soyuz" Space Link. Mult.
4410 10k. Type **1696** 35 10
4411 12k. "Apollo" and "Soyuz 19" in docking procedure 55 20
4412 12k. "Apollo" and "Soyuz 19" linked together . . . 55 20
4413 16k. Launch of "Soyuz 19" (vert) 75 20
MS4414 83 × 120 mm. 50k. Mission Control Centre, Moscow (55 × 26 mm) . . . . 1·90 80

1697 Russian Sturgeon

1975. Int Exposition, Okinawa. Marine Life.
4415 **1697** 3k. bistre, black and blue 25 10
4416 – 4k. lilac, black and blue 30 10
4417 – 6k. purple, black & green 35 10
4418 – 10k. brown, black & bl 1·00 10
4419 – 16k. green, black & purple 70 25
4420 – 20k. blue, pur & stone 85 30
MS4421 83 × 120 mm. 30k. black, lilac and blue; 30k. black, lilac and blue . . . . 2·75 1·00
DESIGNS:—SQUARE: 4k. Thomas rapa whelk; 6k. European eel; 10k. Long-tailed duck; 16k. Crab; 20k. Grey damselfish. HORIZ: (56 × 26 mm)—30k. (2) Common dolphin (different).

1698 "Parade in Red Square, Moscow" (K. F. Yuon)

1975. Birth Centenaries of Soviet Painters. Mult.
4422 1k. Type **1698** 10 10
4423 2k. "Winter Morning in Industrial Moscow" (K. P. Yuon) 15 10
4424 6k. "Soldiers with Captured Guns" (E. E. Lansere) . . 25 10
4425 10k. "Excavating the Metro Tunnel" (E. E. Lansere) 75 20
4426 16k. "A. A. Pushkin and N. N. Pushkina at Palace Ball" (N. P. Ulyanov) (vert) 60 30
4427 20k. "Lauriston at Kutuzov's Headquarters" (N. P. Ulyanov) 80 40

1699 Conference Emblem
1700 Isaakjan (after M. Sargan)

1975. European Security and Co-operation Conf, Helsinki.
4428 **1699** 6k. black, gold and blue 30 10

1975. Birth Centenary of Avetic Isaakjan (Armenian poet).
4429 **1700** 4k. multicoloured . . . 20 10

1701 M. K. Ciurlionis
1702 J. Duclos

1975. Birth Centenary of M. K. Ciurlionis (Lithuanian composer).
4430 **1701** 4k. gold, green & yellow 20 10

1975. Jacques Duclos (French communist leader) Commemoration.
4431 **1702** 6k. purple and silver . . 20 10

1703 Al Farabi (after L. Leontev)
1704 Ruffs

1975. 1100th Birth Anniv of Al Farabi (Persian philosopher).
4432 **1703** 6k. multicoloured . . . 20 10

1975. 50th Anniv of Berezinsky and Stolby Nature Reserves. Multicoloured.
4433 1k. Type **1704** 20 10
4434 4k. Siberian musk deer . . . 30 10
4435 6k. Sable 30 10
4436 10k. Western capercaillie . . 60 30
4437 16k. Eurasian badger . . . 70 30

1705 Korean Crest with Soviet and Korean Flags
1707 Yesenin

1706 Cosmonauts, "Soyuz 18" and "Salyut 4" Linked

1975. 30th Anniversaries. Multicoloured.
4438 6k. Type **1705** (Korean liberation) 20 10
4439 6k. Vietnamese crest, Soviet and Vietnamese flags (Vietnam Democratic Republic) 20 10

1975. Space Flight of "Soyuz 18–Salyut 4" by Cosmonauts P. Klimuk and V. Sevastyanov.
4440 **1706** 10k. black, red and blue 30 10

1975. 80th Birth Anniv of Yesenin (poet).
4441 **1707** 6k. brown, yell & grey 20 10

1708 Standardization Emblems

1975. 50th Anniv of Soviet Communications Standardization Committee.
4442 **1708** 4k. multicoloured . . . 15 10

1709 Astrakhan Lamb

1710 M. P. Konchalovsky

1975. 3rd International Astrakhan Lamb Breeding Symposium, Samarkand.
4443 **1709** 6k. black, green & stone 20 10

1975. Birth Centenary of M. P. Konchalovsky (therapeutist).
4444 **1710** 4k. brown and red . . 15 10

1711 Exhibition Emblem

1712 I.W.Y. Emblem and Rose

1975. 3rd All-Union Philatelic Exhibition, Yerevan.
4445 **1711** 4k. red, brown and blue 15 10

1975. International Women's Year.
4446 **1712** 6k. red, blue & turquoise 20 10

1713 Parliament Buildings, Belgrade

1714 Title-page of 1938 Edition

1975. 30th Anniv of Yugoslav Republic.
4447 **1713** 6k. blue, red and gold 20 10

1975. 175th Anniv of Publication of "Tale of the Host of Igor".
4448 **1714** 4k. red, grey and bistre 15 10

1715 M. I. Kalinin (statesman)

1975. Celebrities' Birth Centenaries.
4449 **1715** 4k. brown 15 10
4450 – 4k. brown 15 10
DESIGN: No. 4450, A. V. Lunacharsky (politician).

1716 Torch and Inscription

1975. 70th Anniv of Russian 1905 Revolution.
4451 **1716** 4k. red and brown . . 15 10

1717 Track-laying Machine and Baikal-Amur Railway

1719 Star of Spassky Tower

1718 "Decembrists in Senate Square" (D. N. Kardovsky) ($\frac{2}{3}$-size illustration)

1975. 58th Anniv of October Revolution. Mult.
4452 4k. Type **1717** 35 10
4453 4k. Rolling mill, Novolipetsk steel plant (vert) 20 10
4454 4k. Formula and ammonia plant, Nevynomyssk chemical works (vert) . . 20 10

1975. 150th Anniv of Decembrist Rising.
4455 **1718** 4k. multicoloured . . . 20 10

1975. New Year.
4456 **1719** 4k. multicoloured . . . 15 10

1720 "Village Street"

1975. 125th Birth Anniv of F. A. Vasilev (painter). Multicoloured.
4457 2k. Type **1720** 10 10
4458 4k. "Forest Path" 15 10
4459 6k. "After the Thunderstorm" 25 10
4460 10k. "Forest Marsh" (horiz) 45 15
4461 12k. "In the Crimean Mountains" 65 20
4462 16k. "Wet Meadow" (horiz) 1·00 30
MS4463 63 × 94 mm. 50k. Vasilev (after I. Kramskoi) . . . . . . 2·25 85

1721 "Venus" Spacecraft

1975. Space Flights of "Venus 9" and "Venus 10".
4464 **1721** 10k. multicoloured . . 35 15

1722 G. Sundukyan

1975. 150th Birth Anniv of G. Sundukyan (Armenian playwright).
4465 **1722** 4k. multicoloured . . . 15 10

1723 Iceland Poppy

1724 A. L. Mints

1975. Flowers (1st series). Multicoloured.
4466 4k. Type **1723** 30 10
4467 6k. Globe flower 25 10
4468 10k. Yellow anemone . . . 35 15
4469 12k. Snowdrop windflower 40 20
4470 16k. "Eminium lehemannii" 50 30
See also Nos. 4585/9.

1975. A. L. Mints (scientist) Commemoration.
4471 **1724** 4k. brown and gold . . 15 10

1725 "Demon" (A. Kochupalov)

1726 Pieck

1975. Miniatures from Palekh Art Museum (1st series). Multicoloured.
4472 4k. Type **1725** 20 10
4473 6k. "Vasilisa the Beautiful" (I. Vakurov) 30 10
4474 10k. "The Snow Maiden" (T. Zubkova) 45 15
4475 16k. "Summer" (K. Kukulieva) 65 25
4476 20k. "Fisherman and Goldfish" (I. Vakurov) (horiz) 90 30
See also Nos. 4561/5.

1975. Birth Centenary of Wilhelm Pieck (President of German Democratic Republic).
4477 **1726** 6k. black 20 10

1727 Saltykov-Shchedrin (after I. Kramskoi)

1728 Congress Emblem

1976. 150th Birth Anniv of M. Saltykov-Shchedrin (writer).
4478 **1727** 4k. multicoloured . . . 15 10

1976. 25th Communist Party Congress, Moscow (1st issue).
4479 **1728** 4k. gold, brown and red 15 10
MS4480 106 × 74 mm. **1728** 50k. gold, lake and vermilion (27 × 37 mm) . . . . 2·25 80
See also Nos. 4489 and 4556/60.

1729 Lenin (statue, S. Merkurov), Kiev

1976. 25th Ukraine Communist Party Congress, Kiev.
4481 **1729** 4k. black, red and blue 15 10

1730 Ice Hockey

1976. Winter Olympic Games, Innsbruck (1st series). Multicoloured.
4482 2k. Type **1730** 15 10
4483 4k. Skiing 20 10
4484 6k. Figure skating 25 10
4485 10k. Speed skating 35 15
4486 20k. Tobogganing 75 35
MS4487 90 × 80 mm. 50k. red, yellow and blue (Games emblem) (vert) . . . . 2·25 85
See also No. **MS**4492.

1731 Marshal C. E. Voroshilov

1732 Congress Hall and Red Banner

1976. 95th Birth Anniv of Marshal C. E. Voroshilov.
4488 **1731** 4k. green 15 10

1976. 25th Communist Party Congress, Moscow (2nd issue).
4489 **1732** 20k. orange, red & green . . . . 3·50 2·25

1733 "Lenin on Red Square" (P. Vasilev)

1976. 106th Birth Anniv of Lenin.
4490 **1733** 4k. multicoloured . . . 20 10

1734 Atomic Symbol and Institute Emblem

1976. 20th Anniv of Joint Institute of Nuclear Research, Dubna.
4491 **1734** 6k. multicoloured . . . 20 10

СЛАВА
СОВЕТСКОМУ
СПОРТУ!
(1735a)

СПОРТСМЕНЫ СССР
ЗАВОЕВАЛИ
13 ЗОЛОТЫХ,
6 СЕРЕБРЯНЫХ,
8 БРОНЗОВЫХ
МЕДАЛЕЙ!
(1735b)

1976. Winter Olympic Games, Innsbruck (2nd issue). Dedicated to Soviet Medal Winners. No. **MS**4487 optd with Types **1735a** and **1735b** in red.
MS4492 90 × 80 mm. 50k. red, yellow and blue . . . . 9·00 7·25

1736 Bolshoi Theatre

1976. Bicentenary of Bolshoi Theatre.
4493 **1736** 10k. blue, brn & ochre 30 15

1737 "Back from the Fair"

1976. Birth Centenary of P. P. Konchalovsky (painter). Multicoloured.
4494 1k. Type **1737** 10 10
4495 2k. "The Green Glass" . . 10 10
4496 6k. "Peaches" 25 10
4497 16k. "Meat, Game and Vegetables by the Window" 70 30
4498 20k. Self-portrait (vert) . . . 95 40

1738 "Vostok", "Salyut" and "Soyuz" Spacecraft

1976. 15th Anniv of First Manned Space Flight by Yuri Gagarin.

4499 4k. Type **1738** 15 10
4500 6k. "Meteor" and "Molniya" satellites . . . 25 10
4501 10k. Cosmonauts on board "Salyut" space-station . . 45 15
4502 12k. "Interkosmos" satellite and "Apollo"–"Soyuz" space link 55 20
MS4503 65 × 100 mm. 50k. black (Yuri Gagarin) (37 × 52 mm) 15·00 10·00

1739 I. A. Dzhavakhishvili **1740** S. Vurgun

1976. Birth Centenary of I. A. Dzhavakhishvili (scientist).

4504 **1739** 4k. black, stone and green 15 10

1976. 70th Birth Anniv of Samed Vurgun (Azerbaijan poet).

4505 **1740** 4k. black, brown & green 15 10

1741 Festival Emblem **1742** F. I. P. Emblem

1976. 1st All-Union Amateur Art Festival.

4506 **1741** 4k. multicoloured . . . 15 10

1976. 50th Anniv of International Philatelic Federation.

4507 **1742** 6k. red and blue . . . 20 10

1744 Dnepropetrovsk Crest **1745** N. N. Burdenko

1976. Bicentenary of Dnepropetrovsk.

4509 **1744** 4k. multicoloured . . . 15 10

1976. Birth Centenary of N. N. Burdenko (neurologist).

4510 **1745** 4k. brown and red . . 15 10

1746 K. A. Trenev **1748** Electric Railway Train

1747 Canoeing

1976. Birth Centenary of K. A. Trenev (playwright).

4511 **1746** 4k. multicoloured . . . 15 10

1976. History of Soviet Motor Industry (4th series). As T **1609**.

4512 2k. black, red and green . . 10 10
4513 3k. black, orange and bistre 15 10
4514 4k. black, buff and blue . . 15 10
4515 12k. black, green and brown 45 20
4516 16k. black, red and yellow 65 30

DESIGNS: 2k. Moscow Auto Works "ZIS-110" saloon, 1945; 3k. Gorkovsky "GAZ-51" truck, 1946; 4k. Gorkovsky "GAZ-M20 (Pobeda)" saloon, 1946; 12k. Moscow Auto Works "ZIS-150" truck, 1947; 16k. Moscow Auto Works "ZIS-154" bus, 1947.

1976. Olympic Games, Montreal. Multicoloured.

4517 4k. Type **1747** 10 10
4518 6k. Basketball (vert) 20 10
4519 10k. Graeco-Roman wrestling 30 15
4520 14k. Discus throwing (vert) 45 15
4521 16k. Rifle-shooting 55 20
MS4522 67 × 88 mm. 50k. Obverse and reverse of Gold medal . . 2·75 1·10

See also No. **MS**4552.

1976. 50th Anniv of Soviet Railway Electrification.

4523 **1748** 4k. black, red and green 30 10

1749 L. M. Pavlichenko **1750** L. E. Rekabarren

1976. 60th Birth Anniv of L. M. Pavlichenko (war heroine).

4524 **1749** 4k. brown, yellow and silver 15 10

1976. Birth Centenary of Luis Rekabarren (founder of Chilean Communist Party).

4525 **1750** 6k. black, red and gold 15 10

1751 "Fresh Partner"

1976. Russian Art. Paintings by P. A. Fedotov. Multicoloured.

4526 2k. Type **1751** 10 10
4527 4k. "Fastidious Fiancee" (horiz) 15 10
4528 6k. "Aristocrat's Breakfast" 20 10
4529 10k. "The Gamblers" (horiz) 50 20
4530 16k. "The Outing" 70 30
MS4531 70 × 90 mm. 50k. Self-portrait . . . . 1·90 85

1752 S. S. Nemetkin **1753** Soviet Armed Forces Order

1754 Marx and Lenin (sculpture, Ye. Belostotsky and E. Fridman)

1976. Birth Centenary of Sergei S. Nemetkin (chemist).

4532 **1752** 4k. black, yellow & blue 15 10

1976. (a) As T **1753**. Size 14 × 21½ mm.

4533 1k. olive 15 10
4534 2k. magenta 20 10
4535 3k. scarlet 25 10
4536 4k. red 35 10
4537 6k. blue 45 10
4538 10k. green 50 10
4539 12k. ultramarine 55 10
4540 16k. green . . . . 1·00 15

(b) As T **1754**.

4541 20k. lake . . . . 1·40 35
4542 30k. vermillion . . . . . . 2·25 45
4543 50k. brown . . . . 3·50 70
4544 1r. blue . . . . 5·50 1·25

DESIGNS: 2k. Gold Star (military) and Hammer and Sickle (labour) decorations; 3k. "Worker and Collective Farmer" (sculpture, Vera Mukhina); 4k. Soviet crest; 6k. Globe and Tupolev Tu-154 jetliner (Soviet postal communications); 10k. Soviet Reputation for Work order; 12k. Yury Gagarin and rocket (space exploration); 16k. International Lenin Prize medal (international peace and security); 30k. Council for Mutual Economic Aid building; 50k. Lenin (after P. Zhukov); 1r. Satellites orbiting globe.

See also Nos. 4669/82.

1755 Cattle Egret

1976. Water Birds. Multicoloured.

4545 1k. Type **1755** 15 15
4546 3k. Black-throated diver . . 20 20
4547 4k. Black coot 45 40
4548 6k. Atlantic puffin 85 40
4549 10k. Slender-billed gull . . . 1·40 45

1756 Peace Dove with Laurel

1976. 2nd Stockholm World Peace Appeal.

4550 **1756** 4k. blue, yellow and gold 15 10

1757 Federation Emblem

1976. 25th Anniv of International Resistance Movement Federation.

4551 **1757** 6k. black, gold and blue 15 10

СПОРТСМЕНЫ
СССР
ЗАВОЕВАЛИ
47 ЗОЛОТЫХ,
43 СЕРЕБРЯНЫХ
И 35 БРОНЗОВЫХ
МЕДАЛЕЙ!

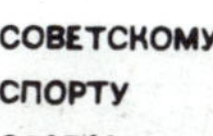

(1758)

1976. Olympic Games, Montreal (2nd issue). Dedicated to Soviet Medal Winners. No. **MS**4522 optd with T **1758**.

MS4552 67 × 88 mm. 50k. Obverse and reverse of Gold Medal . . 8·25 5·50

1759 Soviet and Indian Flags **1761** UNESCO Emblem

1760 B. V. Volynov and V. M. Zholobov

1976. Soviet–Indian Friendship.

4553 **1759** 4k. multicoloured . . . 15 10

1976. Space Flight of "Soyuz 21".

4554 **1760** 10k. black, blue & brn 30 15

1976. 30th Anniv of UNESCO.

4555 **1761** 16k. brown, bistre & blue 45 20

1762 "Industry"

1976. 25th Communist Party Congress (3rd issue).

4556 **1762** 4k. brown, red & yellow 15 10
4557 – 4k. green, red & orange 15 10
4558 – 4k. violet, red and pink 15 10
4559 – 4k. deep red, red and grey 20 10
4560 – 4k. violet, red and blue 15 10

DESIGNS: No. 4557, "Agriculture"; 4558, "Science and Technology"; 4559, "Transport and Communications"; 4560, "International Co-operation".

1763 "The Ploughman" (I. Golikov)

1976. Minatures from Palekh Art Museum (2nd series). Multicoloured.

4561 2k. Type **1763** 10 10
4562 4k. "The Search" (I. Markichev) (vert) . . . 15 10
4563 12k. "The Firebird" (A. Kotukhin) 40 20
4564 14k. "Folk Festival" (A. Vatagin) (vert) . . . 55 25
4565 20k. "Victory" (I. Vakurov) (vert) 90 35

1764 Shostakovich and Part of 7th Symphony **1765** G. K. Zhukov

1976. 70th Birth Anniv of Dmitri Shostakovich (composer).

4566 **1764** 6k. blue 30 10

1976. 80th Birth Anniversaries of Soviet Marshals.

4567 **1765** 4k. green 15 10
4568 – 4k. brown 15 10

DESIGN: No. 4568, K. K. Rokossovsky.

1766 "Interkosmos 14" Satellite   1767 V. I. Dal

1976. International Co-operation in Space Research.
4569 **1766** 6k. blue, gold and black . . 20 10
4570 – 10k. violet, gold & black 25 10
4571 – 12k. purple, gold & black 40 15
4572 – 16k. green, gold & black 50 20
4573 – 20k. mauve, gold & black 90 25
DESIGNS: 10k. "Aryabhata" (Indian satellite); 12k. "Apollo"–"Soyuz" space link; 16k. "Aureole" (French satellite); 20k. Globe and spacecraft.

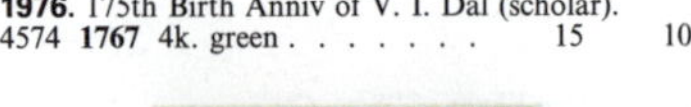

1976. 175th Birth Anniv of V. I. Dal (scholar).
4574 **1767** 4k. green 15 10

1768 Electric Power Station

1976. 59th Anniv of October Revolution. Mult.
4575 4k. Type **1768** 15 10
4576 4k. Balashovo fabrics factory 15 10
4577 4k. Irrigation ditch construction 15 10

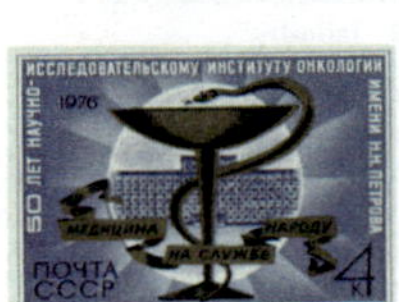

1769 Medicine Emblem   **1770** M. A. Novinsky (oncologist)

1976. 50th Anniv of Petrov Institute of Cancer Research.
4578 **1769** 4k. lilac, gold and blue 20 10

1976. Centenary of Cancer Research.
4579 **1770** 4k. brown, blue and buff 20 10

1771 Hakkel VII Biplane, 1911

1976. Early Russian Aircraft (2nd series). Mult.
4580 3k. Type **1771** 10 10
4581 6k. Hakkel IX monoplane, 1912 . . . . 20 10
4582 12k. Steglau No. 2, 1912 . . 35 15
4583 14k. Dybovsky Dolphin, 1913 . . . . 50 15
4584 16k. Sikorsky Ilya Mourometz, 1914 . . . . 55 25
See also Nos. 4661/6 and 4791/6.

1976. Flowers (2nd series). As T **1723**. Mult.
4585 1k. Safflower 10 10
4586 2k. Anemone 10 10
4587 3k. Gentian 10 10
4588 4k. Columbine 15 10
4589 6k. Fitillaria 25 15

1772 New Year Greeting

1976. New Year.
4590 **1772** 4k. multicoloured . . . 15 10

1773 "Parable of the Vineyard"

1976. 370th Birth Anniv of Rembrandt. Mult.
4591 4k. Type **1773** 15 10
4592 6k. "Danae" 25 10
4593 10k. "David and Jonathan" (vert) 35 15
4594 14k. "The Holy Family" (vert) 55 20
4595 20k. "Andrian" (vert) . . . 85 30
MS4596 125 × 66 mm. 50k. "Artaxeres, Hamann and Esther" 12·00 8·00

1774 "Luna 24" and Emblem

1976. "Luna 24" Unmanned Space Flight to Moon.
4597 **1774** 10k. brown, yellow & blue 30 15

1775 "Pailot'

1976. Russian Ice-breakers (1st series). Mult.
4598 4k. Type **1775** 40 10
4599 6k. "Ermak" (vert) 50 10
4600 10k. "Fyodor Litke" . . . 70 15
4601 16k. "Vladmir Ilich" (vert) 95 25
4602 20k. "Krassin" . . . . . . 1·25 50
See also Nos. 4654/60, 4843/8 and 5147.

1776 "Raduga" Experiment and Cosmonauts

1976. "Soyuz 22" Space Flight by V. F. Bykovsky and V. V. Aksenov.
4603 **1776** 10k. green, blue and red 30 15

1777 Olympic Torch

1976. Olympic Games, Moscow (1980).
4604 **1777** 4k.+2k. black, red and blue 30 10
4605 – 10k.+5k. black, blue and red 65 25
4606 – 16k.+6k. black, mauve and yellow . . . . . 1·25 40
MS4607 63 × 83 mm. 60k.+30k. black, gold and red . . . . . 8·75 5·00
DESIGNS: 30 × 42 mm—10, 16k. Games Emblem. 27 × 38 mm—6k. Kemlin.

1778 Society Emblem and "Red Star"   **1779** S. P. Korolev Memorial Medallion

1977. 50th Anniv of Red Banner Forces Voluntary Society.
4608 **1778** 4k. multicoloured . . . 15 10

1977. 70th Birth Anniv of S. P. Korolev (scientist and rocket pioneer).
4609 **1779** 4k. gold, black and blue 15 10

1780 Congress Emblem

1977. World Peace Congress, Moscow.
4610 **1780** 4k. gold, ultramarine and blue 15 10

1781 Sedov and "Sv. Foka"

1977. Birth Cent of G. Y. Sedov (polar explorer).
4611 **1781** 4k. multicoloured . . . 1·10 20

1782 Working Class Monument, Red Flag and Newspaper Cover   **1783** Ship on Globe

1977. 60th Anniv of Newspaper "Izvestiya".
4612 **1782** 4k. black, red and silver 15 10

1977. 24th International Navigation Congress, Leningrad.
4613 **1783** 6k. blue, black and gold 20 10

1784 Kremlin Palace of Congresses, Moscow   **1785** L. A. Govorov

1977. 16th Soviet Trade Unions Congress.
4614 **1784** 4k. gold, black and red 15 10

1977. 80th Birth Anniv of Marshal L. A. Govorov.
4615 **1785** 4k. brown 15 10

1786 Academy Emblem, Text and Building

1977. 150th Anniv of Grechko Naval Academy, Leningrad.
4616 **1786** 6k. multicoloured . . . 15 10

1787 J. Labourbe   **1788** Chess Pieces

1977. Birth Centenary of Jeanne Labourbe (French communist).
4617 **1787** 4k. black, blue and red 15 10

1977. 6th European Chess Team Championship, Moscow.
4618 **1788** 6k. multicoloured . . . 50 10

1789 "Soyuz 23" and Cosmonauts

1977. "Soyuz 23" Space Flight by V. D. Zudov and V. I. Rozhdestvensky.
4619 **1789** 10k. red, black & brown 35 15

1790 Novikov-Priboi   **1791** "Welcome" (N. M. Soloninkin)

1977. Birth Centenary of Aleksei Novikov-Priboi (writer).
4620 **1790** 4k. black, orange & blue 15 10

1977. Folk Paintings from Fedoskino Village. Multicoloured.
4621 4k. Type **1791** 15 10
4622 6k. "Along the Street" (V. D. Antonov) (horiz) 20 10
4623 10k. "Northern Song" (J. V. Karapaev) 40 15
4624 12k. "Fairy Tale about Tzar Sultan" (A. I. Kozlov) . . 40 15
4625 14k. "Summer Troika" (V. A. Nalimov) (horiz) 50 20
4626 16k. "Red Flower" (V. D. Lipitsky) 60 25

1792 Congress Emblem

1977. World Electronics Congress, Moscow.
4627 **1792** 6k. red, grey and blue 15 10

1793 "In Red Square" (K. V. Filatov)

1977. 107th Birth Anniv of Lenin.
4628 **1793** 4k. multicoloured . . . 15 10

1794 Yuri Gagarin and Spacecraft

1977. Cosmonautics Day.
4629 **1794** 6k. blue, lilac and purple 25 15

1795 N. I. Vavilov   **1796** F. E. Dzerzhinsky

1977. 90th Birth Anniv of N. I. Vavilov (biologist).
4630 **1795** 4k. black and brown . . 15 10

1977. Birth Centenary of Feliks Dzerzhinsky (founder of Cheka).
4631 **1796** 4k. black 15 10

1797 Mountain Saxifrage

1798 V. V. Gorbatko and Yu. N. Glazkov (cosmonauts)

1977. Flowers. Multicoloured.
4632 2k. Type **1797** 10 10
4633 3k. Pinks 10 10
4634 4k. "Novosieversia glacialis" 15 10
4635 6k. "Cerastium maximum" 20 25
4636 16k. "Rhododendron aureum" 65 30

1977. "Soyuz 24–Salyut 5" Space Project.
4637 **1798** 10k. black, red and blue 40 15

1799 I. S. Konev

1800 Festival Emblem

1977. 80th Birth Anniv of Soviet Marshals.
4638 **1799** 4k. green 15 10
4639 – 4k. black 15 10
4640 – 4k. brown 15 10
DESIGNS: No. 4639, V. D. Sokolovsky; 4640, K. A. Meretskov.

1977. 10th International Film Festival, Moscow.
4641 **1800** 6k. gold, red and lake 15 10

1801 Greco-Roman Wrestling

1977. Olympic Sports (1st series).
4642 **1801** 4k.+2k. black, ochre and gold 20 10
4643 – 6k.+3k. black, green and gold 30 10
4644 – 10k.+5k. black, mauve and gold 45 20
4645 – 16k.+6k. black, blue and gold 70 30
4646 – 20k.+10k. black, brown and gold 1·75 65
DESIGNS: 6k. Free-style wrestling; 10k. Judo; 16k. Boxing; 29k. Weightlifting.
See also Nos. 4684/9, 4749/53, 4820/4, 4870/4, 4896/4900, 4962/6 and 4973/7.

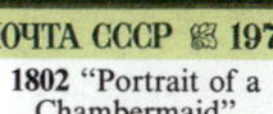

1802 "Portrait of a Chambermaid"

1804 Stamps and Emblem

1803 "Judith" (detail)

1977. 400th Birth Anniv of Rubens. Multicoloured.
4647 4k. Type **1802** 20 10
4648 6k. "The Lion Hunt" (horiz) 25 10
4649 10k. "Stone Carriers" (horiz) 35 10
4650 12k. "Water and Earth Alliance" 60 15
4651 20k. "Landscape with Rainbow" (horiz) 95 35
MS4652 104 × 74 mm. 50k. Rubens" (detail from "Portrait of Rubens and his Son") 2·25 85

1977. 500th Birth Anniv of Giorgione. Sheet 77 × 104 mm.
MS4653 **1803** 50k. multicoloured 2·25 85

1977. Soviet Ice-breakers (2nd series). As T **1775**. Multicoloured.
4654 4k. "Aleksandr Sibiryakov" 25 10
4655 6k. "Georgy Sedov" 30 10
4656 10k. "Sadko" 55 15
4657 12k. "Dezhnev" 65 15
4658 14k. "Sibur" 75 20
4659 16k. "Lena" 90 30
4660 20k. "Amguema" 1·10 40

1977. Air. Early Soviet Aircraft (3rd series). As T **1771** but dated 1977.
4661 4k. black, brown and blue 15 10
4662 6k. black, orange and green 25 10
4663 10k. black, mauve and blue 30 10
4664 12k. black, blue and red 35 15
4665 16k. multicoloured 50 15
4666 20k. black, green and blue 70 20
DESIGNS: 4k. Porokhovshchikov P-IV bis biplane trainer, 1917; 6k. Kalinin AK-1, 1924; 10k. Tupolev ANT-3 R-3, 1925; 12k. Tupolev ANT-4 TB-1 bomber, 1929; 16k. Polikarpov R-5 biplane, 1929; 20k. Shavrov Sh-2 flying boat, 1930.

1977. "60th Anniv of October Revolution" Philatelic Exhibition, Moscow.
4667 **1804** 4k. red, blue and brown 15 10

1805 Buildings and Arms, Stavropol

1807 Yuri Gagarin and "Vostok' Spacecraft

1806 "Arktika"

1977. Bicentenary of Stavropol.
4668 **1805** 6k. gold, red and green 20 10

1976. As Nos. 4533/44 and new value. (a) As T **1753**.
4669 1k. olive 10 10
4670 2k. mauve 10 10
4671 3k. red 10 10
4672 4k. red 15 10
4673 6k. blue 20 10
4674 10k. green 35 10
4675 12k. blue 40 10
4676 15k. blue 70 10
4677 16k. green 50 15

(b) As T **1754**.
4678 20k. red 55 10
4679 30k. red 85 20
4680 32k. blue 1·60 45
4681 50k. brown 1·40 40
4682 1r. blue 3·00 1·00
DESIGNS: 2k. Gold Star (military) and Hammer and Sickle (labour) decorations; 3k. "Worker and Collective Farmer" (sculpture, Vera Mukhina); 4k. Soviet crest; 6k. Globe and Tupolev Tu-154 jetliner (Soviet postal communications); 10k. Soviet Reputation for Work Order; 23k. Yuri Gagarin and rocket (space exploration); 15k. Ostankino T.V. tower and globe; 16k. International Lenin Prize medal (international peace and security); 30k. Council for Mutual Economic Aid building; 32k. Ilyushin Il-76 airplane and compass rose; 50k. Lenin (after P. Zhukov); 1r. Satellites orbiting globe.
The 6 and 32k. are airmail stamps.

1977. Journey to North Pole of "Arktika" (atomic ice-breaker). Sheet 107 × 80 mm.
MS4683 **1806** 50k. multicoloured 12·50 5·75

1977. Olympic Sports (2nd series). As T **1801**.
4684 4k.+2k. black, gold and red 20 10
4685 6k.+3k. black, gold & blue 45 15
4686 10k.+5k. black, gold & grn 75 20
4687 16k.+6k. black, gold & olive 1·00 30
4688 20k.+10k. black, gold & pur 1·75 65
MS4689 92 × 72 mm. 50k.+25k. black, gold and blue 9·50 6·75
DESIGNS—HORIZ: 4k. Cycling; 10k. Rifle-shooting; 16k. Horse-jumping; 20k. Fencing; 50k. horse-jumping and fencing (Modern pentathlon). VERT: 6k. Archery.

1977. 20th Anniv of Space Exploration.
4690 **1807** 10k. red, blue and brown 40 15
4691 – 10k. brown, blue & violet 40 15
4692 – 10k. red, purple & green 40 15
4693 – 20k. green, brown & red 70 25
4694 – 20k. purple, red and blue 70 25
4695 – 20k. red, blue and green 70 25
MS4696 66 × 86 mm. 50k. gold and lake (22 × 32 mm) 19·00 9·50
DESIGNS: No. 4691, Space walking; 4692, "Soyuz" spacecraft and "Salyut" space station linked; 4693, "Proton 4" satellite; 4694, "Luna Venus" and "Mars" space stations; 4695, "Intercosmos 10" satellite and "Apollo" and "Soyuz" spacecraft linked; **MS**4696, "Sputnik 1" satellite.

1808 Carving from St. Dmitri's Cathedral, Vladimir (12th-cent)

1977. Russian Art. Multicoloured.
4697 4k. Type **1808** 15 10
4698 6k. Bracelet, Ryazan (12th cent) 20 15
4699 10k. Detail of Golden Gate from Nativity Cathedral, Suzdal (13th-cent) 30 15
4700 12k. Detail from "Archangel Michael" (icon) (A. Rublev) (15th-cent) 40 15
4701 16k. Gold and marble chalice made by I. Fomin (15th-cent) 55 20
4702 20k. St. Basil's Cathedral, Moscow (16th-cent) 70 20

1809 "Snowflake and Fir Twig"

1810 Cruiser "Aurora"

1977. New Year.
4703 **1809** 4k. multicoloured 15 10

1977. 60th Anniv of October Revolution.
4704 **1810** 4k. multicoloured 15 10
4705 – 4k. black, red and gold 15 10
4706 – 4k. black, red and gold 15 10
4707 – 4k. multicoloured 15 10
MS4708 106 × 71 mm. 30k. black, vermilion and gold 1·25 55
DESIGNS: No. 4705, Statue of Lenin; 4706, Page of "Izvestiya", book by Brezhnev and crowd; 4707, Kremlin spire, star and fireworks. 26 × 38 mm—30k. Lenin medal.

1811 First Clause of U.S.S.R. Constitution

1977. New Constitution.
4709 **1811** 4k. yellow, red & brown 15 10
4710 – 4k. multicoloured 15 10
MS4711 112 × 82 mm. 50k. multicoloured 1·75 95
DESIGNS: 47 × 32 mm—No. 4710 People of U.S.S.R. welcoming new constitution. 69 × 47 mm—50k. Constitution as open book, and laurel branch.

1812 Leonid Brezhnev

1977. New Constitution (2nd issue). Sheet 143 × 74 mm.
MS4712 **1812** 50k. multicoloured 2·25 1·25

1813 Postwoman and Post Code

1977. Postal Communications. Multicoloured.
4713 4k. Type **1813** 15 10
4714 4k. Letter collection 15 10
4715 4k. "Map-O" automatic sorting machine 15 10
4716 4k. Mail transport 15 10
4717 4k. Delivering the mail 15 10

1814 Red Fort, Delhi and Asokan Capital

1815 Monument, Kharkov

1977. 30th Anniv of Indian Independence.
4718 **1814** 6k. gold, purple and red 20 10

1977. 60th Anniv of Establishment of Soviet Power in the Ukraine.
4719 **1815** 6k. multicoloured 15 10

1816 Adder

1977. Snakes and Protected Animals. Mult.
4720 1k. Type **1816** 10 10
4721 4k. Levantine viper 15 10
4722 6k. Saw-scaled viper 20 10
4723 10k. Central Asian viper 30 15
4724 12k. Central Asian cobra 30 15
4725 16k. Polar bear and cub 40 25
4726 20k. Walrus and young 50 25
4727 30k. Tiger and cub 85 30

1817 Olympic Emblem and Arms of Vladimir

1977. 1980 Olympics. "Tourism around the Golden Ring" (1st issue). Multicoloured.
4728 1r.+50k. Type **1817** 4·50 2·25
4729 1r.+50k. Vladimir Hotel 4·50 2·25
4730 1r.+50k. Arms of Suzdal 4·50 2·25
4731 1r.+50k. Pozharsky monument 4·50 2·25
4732 1r.+50k. Arms of Ivanovo and Frunze monument 4·50 2·25
4733 1r.+50k. Monument to Revolutionary Fighters 4·50 2·25
See also Nos. 4828/31, 4850/3, 4914/17, 4928/9, 4968/9, 4981/2 and 4990/5.

1818 Combine Harvester

1819 Kremlin Palace of Congresses

1978. 50th Anniv of "Gigant" Collective Farm, Rostov.
4734 **1818** 4k. brown, red & yellow 15 10

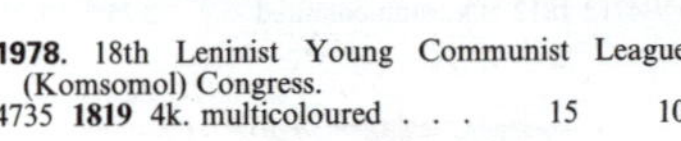

1978. 18th Leninist Young Communist League (Komsomol) Congress.
4735 **1819** 4k. multicoloured . . . 15 10

1820 Globe, Obelisk and Emblem

1978. 8th International Federation of Resistance Fighters Congress, Minsk.
4736 **1820** 6k. red, blue and black 15 10

1821 Red Army Detachment and Modern Sailor, Airman and Soldier

1978. 60th Anniv of Soviet Military Forces. Mult.
4737 4k. Type **1821** 15 10
4738 4k. Defenders of Moscow monument (detail), Lenin banner and Order of Patriotic War 15 10
4739 4k. Soviet soldier 15 10

1822 "Celebration in a Village" (½-size illustration)

1978. Birth Centenary of Boris M. Kustodiev (artist). Multicoloured.
4740 4k. Type **1822** 15 10
4741 6k. "Shrovetide" 20 10
4742 10k. "Morning" (50 × 36 mm) 30 15
4743 12k. "Merchant's Wife drinking Tea" (50 × 36 mm) 40 15
4744 20k. "Bolshevik" (50 × 36 mm) 55 25
MS4745 92 × 72 mm. 50k. "Self-portrait" (36 × 50 mm) . . . . 1·90 85

1823 Gubarev and Remek at Launch Pad

1824 "Soyuz" Capsules linked to "Salyut" Space Station

1978. Soviet–Czech Space Flight. Multicoloured.
4746 6k. Type **1823** 15 10
4747 15k. "Soyuz-28" docking with "Salyut-6" space station 45 15
4748 32k. Splashdown . . . . . 1·00 35

1978. Olympic Sports (3rd series). As T **1801**. Multicoloured.
4749 4k.+2k. Swimmer at start 20 10
4750 6k.+3k. Diving (vert) . . . 35 10
4751 10k.+5k. Water polo . . . 70 15
4752 10k.+6k. Canoeist . . . . . 1·00 20
4753 20k.+10k. Single sculls . . . 1·60 70
MS4754 92 × 71 mm. 50k.+25k. grey, black and green (Double sculls) . . . . 9·00 6·00

1978. Cosmonautics Day.
4755 **1824** 6k. gold, blue and deep blue 15 10

1825 Shield and Laurel Wreath

1826 E. A. and M. E. Cherepanov and their Locomotive, 1833

1978. 9th World Congress of Trade Unions.
4756 **1825** 6k. multicoloured . . . 15 10

1978. Russian Locomotives (1st series). Mult.
4757 1k. Type **1826** 20 10
4758 2k. Series D locomotive, 1845 . . . . 20 10
4759 3k. Series V locomotive (first passenger train, 1845) . . 20 10
4760 16k. Series Gv locomotive, 1863–67 . . . . 95 25
4761 20k. Series Bv locomotive, 1863–67 . . . . 1·25 30
Nos. 4758/61 are horizontal designs.
See also Nos. 4861/5.

1827 Lenin (after V. A. Servo)

1978. 108th Birth Anniv of Lenin. Sheet 73 × 96 mm.
MS4762 **1827** 50k. multicoloured 1·75 90

1828 "XI" and Laurel Branch

1830 I.M.C.O. Emblem

1829 Tulip "Bolshoi Theatre"

1978. 11th World Youth and Students Festival, Havana.
4763 **1828** 4k. multicoloured . . . 15 10

1978. Moscow Flowers. Multicoloured.
4764 1k. Type **1829** 10 10
4765 2k. Rose "Moscow Morning" 10 10
4766 4k. Dahlia "Red Star" . . . 10 10
4767 10k. Gladiolus "Moscovite" 40 15
4768 12k. Iris "To Il'ich's Anniversary" 45 20

1978. 20th Anniv of Intergovernment Maritime Consultative Organization, and World Maritime Day.
4769 **1830** 6k. multicoloured . . . 15 10

1831 "Salyut-6" Space Station performing Survey Work

1978. "Salyut-6" Space Station. Multicoloured.
4770 15k. Type **1831** 50 30
4771 15k. Yu. V. Romanenko and G. M. Grechko . . . 50 30
Nos. 4770/1 were issued in se-tenant pairs forming a composite design.

1832 "Space Meteorology"

1978. Space Research. Multicoloured.
4772 10k. Type **1832** 30 15
4773 10k. "Soyuz" orbiting globe ("Natural resources") . . 30 15
4774 10k. Radio waves, ground station and "Molniya" satellite ("Communication") . . . 30 15
4775 10k. Human figure, "Vostok" orbiting Earth ("Medicine and biology") 30 15
MS4776 102 × 77 mm. "Prognoz" satellite ("Physics") (36 × 51 mm) 1·90 85

1833 Transporting Rocket to Launch Site

1978. Soviet–Polish Space Flight. Multicoloured.
4777 6k. Type **1833** 15 10
4778 15k. Crystal (Sirena experiment) 50 15
4779 32k. Space station, map and scientific research ship "Kosmonavt Vladimir Komarov" . . . . 1·10 35

1834 Komsomol Awards

1835 M. V. Zakharov

1978. 60th Anniv of Leninist Young Communist League (Komsomol). Multicoloured.
4780 4k. Type **1834** 10 10
4781 4k. Products of agriculture and industry 30 10

1978. 80th Birth Anniv of Marshal M. V. Zakharov.
4782 **1835** 4k. brown 10 10

1836 N. G. Chernyshevsky

1978. 150th Birth Anniv of Nikolai G. Chernyshevsky (revolutionary).
4783 **1836** 4k. brown and yellow 10 10

1837 Snow Petrel

1978. Antarctic Fauna. Multicoloured.
4784 1k. Snares Island penguin (horiz) 60 15
4785 3k. Type **1837** 75 15
4786 4k. Emperor penguin . . . 95 15
4787 6k. Antarctic icefish . . . . 1·25 15
4788 10k. Southern elephant-seal (horiz) . . . . 1·25 15

1838 Torch and Flags

1839 William Harvey

1978. Construction of Orenburg–U.S.S.R. Western Frontier Gas Pipe-line.
4789 **1838** 4k. multicoloured . . . 15 10

1978. 400th Birth Anniv of William Harvey (discoverer of blood circulation).
4790 **1839** 6k. green, black and blue 15 10

1978. Air. Early Russian Aircraft (3rd series). As T **1771**.
4791 4k. green, brown and black 15 10
4792 6k. multicoloured 25 10
4793 10k. yellow, blue and black 45 15
4794 12k. orange, blue and black 55 15
4795 16k. blue, deep blue and black 70 15
4796 20k. multicoloured 90 20
DESIGNS: 4k. Polikarpov Po-2 biplane, 1928; 6k. Kalinin K-5, 1929; 10k. Tupolev ANT-6 TB-3 bomber, 1930; 12k. Putilov Stal-2, 1931; 16k. Beriev Be-2 MBR-2 reconnaissance seaplane, 1932; 20k. Polikarpov I-16 fighter, 1934.

1840 "Bathing of Red Horse"

1978. Birth Centenary of K. S. Petrov-Vodkin (painter). Multicoloured.
4797 4k. Type **1840** 10 10
4798 6k. "Petrograd, 1918" . . . 15 10
4799 10k. "Commissar's Death" 30 15
4800 12k. "Rose Still Life" . . . 40 15
4801 16k. "Morning Still Life" 60 15
MS4802 92 × 72 mm. 50k. "Self-portrait" (vert) . . . . . . 1·60 65

1841 Assembling "Soyuz 31"

1978. Soviet–East German Space Flight. Mult.
4803 6k. Type **1841** 15 10
4804 15k. Space photograph of Pamir mountains 55 15
4805 32k. Undocking from space station . . . . 1·10 35

1842 "Molniya 1" Satellite, "Orbita" Ground Station and Tupolev Tu-134 Jetliner

1978. "PRAGA 78" International Stamp Exhibition.
4806 **1842** 6k. multicoloured . . . 15 10

1843 Tolstoi

1978. 150th Birth Anniv of Leo Tolstoi (novelist).
4807 **1843** 4k. green . . . . 1·25 75

1844 Union Emblem

1845 Bronze Figure, Erebuni Fortress

1978. 14th General Assembly of International Union for the Protection of Nature and Natural Resources, Ashkhabad.
4808 **1844** 4k. multicoloured . . . 15 10

1978. Armenian Architecture. Multicoloured.
4809 4k. Type **1845** 10 10
4810 6k. Echmiadzin Cathedral 15 10
4811 10k. Khachkary (carved stones) 25 10
4812 12k. Matenadaran building (repository of manuscripts) (horiz) . . . 35 15
4813 16k. Lenin Square, Yerevan (horiz) 45 20

1846 Monument (P. Kufferge)

1847 Emblem, Ostankino TV Tower and Hammer and Sickle

1978. 70th Anniv of Russian Aid to Messina Earthquake Victims.
4814 **1846** 6k. multicoloured . . . 20 10

1978. 20th Anniv of Organization for Communications Co-operation.
4815 **1847** 4k. multicoloured . . . 10 10

1978. "60th Anniv of Komsomol" Philatelic Exhibition. Optd with T **1848**.
4816 **1834** 4k. multicoloured . . . 1·00 50

1849 "Diana" (detail)

1978. 450th Birth Anniv of Paolo Veronese (artist). Sheet 76 × 115 mm.
MS4817 **1849** 50k. multicoloured 1·75 85

1850 Kremlin

1978. 1st Anniv of New Constitution. Sheet 160 × 85 mm.
MS4818 **1850** 30k. multicoloured 1·10 50

1851 Shaumyan

1852 "Star" Yacht

1978. Birth Centenary of Stephan Georgievich Shaumyan (Commissar).
4819 **1851** 4k. green 10 10

1978. Olympic Sports (4th series). Sailing Regatta, Tallin. Multicoloured.
4820 4k.+2k. Type **1852** 20 10
4821 6k.+3k. "Soling" yacht . . . 30 10
4822 10k.+5k. "470" dinghy . . . 50 15
4823 16k.+6k. "Finn" dinghy . . 80 25
4824 20k.+10k. "Flying Dutchman" dinghy . . . 1·25 55
MS4825 71 × 94 mm. 50k.+25k. "Tornado" class catamaran (horiz) . . . . 9·00 5·00

1853 Industrial Structures and Flags

1854 Black Sea Ferry

1978. 61st Anniv of October Revolution.
4826 **1853** 4k. multicoloured . . . 10 10

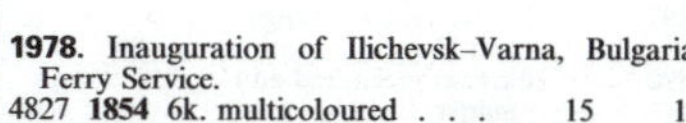

1978. Inauguration of Ilichevsk–Varna, Bulgaria, Ferry Service.
4827 **1854** 6k. multicoloured . . . 15 10

1855 Zagorsk

1978. 1980 Olympics. "Tourism around the Golden Ring" (2nd issue). Multicoloured.
4828 1r.+50k. Type **1855** . . . . 4·75 2·75
4829 1r.+50k. Palace of Culture, Zagorsk . . . . 4·75 2·75
4830 1r.+50k. Kremlin, Rostov-Veliki . . . . 4·75 2·75
4831 1r.+50k. View of Rostov-Veliki . . . . 4·75 2·75

1856 Church of the Intercession on River Nerl

1978. "Masterpieces of Old Russian Culture". Mult.
4832 6k. Golden crater (horiz) . . 15 10
4833 10k. Type **1856** 25 15
4834 12k. "St. George and the Dragon" (15th-century icon) 35 15
4835 16k. Tsar Cannon (horiz) 45 20

1857 Cup with Snake and Institute

1859 Spassky Tower, Kremlin

1858 Nestor Pechersky and "Chronicle of Past Days"

1978. 75th Anniv of Herzen Oncology Research Institute, Moscow.
4836 **1857** 4k. gold, purple & black 15 10

1978. History of the Russian Posts. Multicoloured.
4837 4k. Type **1858** 10 10
4838 6k. Birch-bark letter 15 10
4839 10k. Messenger with trumpet 30 15
4840 12k. Mail sledges 35 15
4841 16k. Interior of Prikaz Post Office 45 20

1978. New Year.
4842 **1859** 4k. multicoloured . . . 15 10

1978. Soviet Ice breakers (3rd series). As T **1775**. Multicoloured.
4843 4k. "Vasily Pronchishchev" 20 10
4844 6k. "Kapitan Belousov" (vert) 25 10
4845 10k. "Moskva" 30 15
4846 12k. "Admiral Makarov" 45 15
4847 16k. "Lenin" atomic ice-breaker (vert) 65 20
4848 20k. "Arktika" atomic ice-breaker 80 35

1860 V. Kovalenok and A. Ivanchenkov

1978. "140 Days in Space".
4849 **1860** 10k. multicoloured . . 30 15

1978. 1980 Olympics "Tourism around the Golden Ring" (3rd issue). As T **1855**. Multicoloured.
4850 1r.+50k. Alexander Nevsky Monument, Pereslavl-Zalessky . . . . 4·00 2·50
4851 1r.+50k. Peter I Monument, Pereslavl-Zalessky . . . . 4·00 2·50
4852 1r.+50k. Monastery of the Transfiguration, Yaroslavl 4·00 2·50
4853 1r.+50k. Ferry terminal and Eternal Glory Monument, Yaroslavl . . . . 4·00 2·50

1861 Globe and Newspaper Titles

1978. 60th Anniv of "Soyuzpechati" State Newspaper Distribution Service. Sheet 106 × 82 mm.
MS4854 **1861** 30k. multicoloured 1·10 50

1862 Cuban Flags

1863 Government Building, Minsk

1979. 20th Anniv of Cuban Revolution.
4855 **1862** 6k. multicoloured . . . 15 10

1979. 60th Anniv of Byelorussian Soviet Socialist Republic and Communist Party.
4856 **1863** 4k. multicoloured . . . 15 10

1864 Flags and Reunion Monument

1865 Old and New University Buildings

1979. 325th Anniv of Reunion of Ukraine with Russia.
4857 **1864** 4k. multicoloured . . . 15 10

1979. 400th Anniv of Vilnius University.
4858 **1865** 4k. black and pink . . 15 10

1866 Exhibition Hall and First Bulgarian Stamp

1979. "Philaserdica 79" International Stamp Exhibition, Sofia.
4859 **1866** 15k. multicoloured . . 50 15

1867 Satellites "Radio 1" and "Radio 2"

1979. Launching of "Radio" Satellites.
4860 **1867** 4k. multicoloured . . . 35 10

1868 Series A Locomotive, 1878

1979. Railway Locomotives (2nd series). Mult.
4861 2k. Type **1868** 15 10
4862 3k. Class Shch steam locomotive, 1912 . . . . 15 10
4863 4k. Class Lp steam locomotive, 1915 . . . . 25 10
4864 6k. Class Su steam locomotive, 1925 . . . . 45 15
4865 15k. Class L steam locomotive, 1947 . . . . 1·10 40

1869 Medal and Komsomol Pass

1979. 25th Anniv of Development of Virgin and Disused Land. Sheet 99 × 67 mm.
MS4866 **1869** 50k. multicoloured 1·90 70

1870 "Venera 12" over Venus

1871 Albert Einstein

1979. "Venera" Flights to Venus.
4867 **1870** 10k. red, lilac and purple 35 10

1979. Birth Centenary of Albert Einstein (physicist).
4868 **1871** 6k. multicoloured . . . 20 10

1872 Congress Emblem

1979. 21st World Veterinary Congress, Moscow.
4869 **1872** 6k. multicoloured . . . 15 10

1873 Free Exercise

1979. Olympic Sports (5th series). Gymnastics.
4870 **1873** 4k.+2k. brown, stone and orange 15 10
4871 – 6k.+3k. blue, grey and violet 20 10
4872 – 10k.+5k. red, stone and brown 30 15
4873 – 16k.+6k. mauve, grey and purple 75 40
4874 – 20k.+10k. red, stone and brown . . . . . 1·60 65
MS4875 91 × 71 mm. 50k.+25k. brown, stone and light brown 7·50 50
DESIGNS:—VERT: 6k. Parallel bars; 10k. Horizontal bar; 16k. Beam; 20k. Asymmetric bars. HORIZ: 50k. Rings.

1874 "To Arms" (poster by R. Beren)

1979. 60th Anniv of First Hungarian Socialist Republic.
4876 **1874** 4k. multicoloured . . . 10 10

1875 Cosmonauts at Yuri Gagarin Training Centre

1979. Soviet–Bulgarian Space Flight. Mult.
4877 6k. Type **1875** 20 10
4878 32k. Landing of cosmonauts 90 35

1876 "Intercosmos"

1979. Cosmonautics Day.
4879 **1876** 15k. multicoloured . . 50 15

1877 Ice Hockey

1979. World and European Ice Hockey Championship, Moscow. Sheet 85 × 65 mm.
MS4880 **1877** 50k. red, blue and maroon . . . . 1·90 85
See also **MS**4888.

1878 Exhibition Emblem

1979. U.S.S.R. Exhibition, London.
4881 **1878** 15k. multicoloured . . 40 15

1879 Lenin

1979. 109th Birth Anniv of Lenin. Sheet 89 × 71 mm.
MS4882 **1879** 50k. multicoloured 1·40 60

1880 Antonov An-28

1979. Air. Soviet Aircraft. Multicoloured.
4883 2k. Type **1880** 10 10
4884 3k. Yakovlev Yak-42 . . . 15 10
4885 10k. Tupolev Tu-154 . . . 40 15
4886 15k. Ilyushin Il-76 . . . . 60 20
4887 32k. Ilyushin Il-86 . . . . 1·00 40

СОВЕТСКИЕ ХОККЕИСТЫ—
ЧЕМПИОНЫ МИРА
И ЕВРОПЫ
(1881)

1979. Soviet Victory in European Ice Hockey Championship. No. **MS**4880 optd in margin with T **1881**.
MS4888 **1877** 50k. red, blue and maroon . . . . 5·25 2·75

1882 "Tent" Monument, Mining Institute, Pushkin Theatre and Blast Furnace

1883 Child and Apple Blossom

1979. 50th Anniv of Magnitogorsk City.
4889 **1882** 4k. multicoloured . . . 15 10

1979. International Year of the Child (1st issue).
4890 **1883** 4k. multicoloured . . . 15 10
See also Nos. 4918/21.

1884 Bogorodsk Wood-carvings

1979. Folk Crafts. Multicoloured.
4891 2k. Type **1884** 10 10
4892 3k. Khokhloma painted dish and jars 10 10
4893 4k. Zhostovo painted tray 15 10
4894 6k. Kholmogory bone-carvings 25 15
4895 15k. Vologda lace 50 35

1885 Football

1979. Olympic Sports (6th series). Multicoloured.
4896 **1885** 4k.+2k. blue, grey and orange 30 10
4897 – 6k.+3k. yellow, orange and blue 40 10
4898 – 10k.+5k. green, red and mauve 50 15

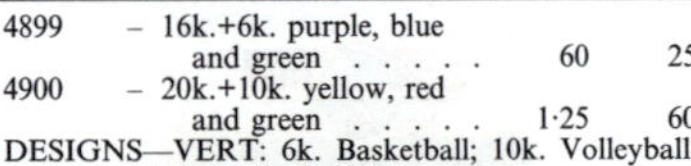
4899 – 16k.+6k. purple, blue and green 60 25
4900 – 20k.+10k. yellow, red and green . . . . . 1·25 60
DESIGNS—VERT: 6k. Basketball; 10k. Volleyball. HORIZ: 16k. Handball; 20k. Hockey.

1886 Lenin Square Underground Station

1979. Tashkent Underground Railway.
4901 **1886** 4k. multicoloured . . . 25 10

1887 V. A. Dzhanibekov and O. G. Makarov

1888 Council Building and Flags of Member Countries

1979. "Soyuz 27"–"Salyut 6"–"Soyuz 26" Orbital Complex.
4902 **1887** 4k. multicoloured . . . 20 10

1979. 30th Anniv of Council of Mutual Economic Aid.
4903 **1888** 16k. multicoloured . . 50 15

1889 Scene from "Battleship Potemkin"

1891 U.S.S.R. Philatelic Society Emblem

1979. 60th Anniv of Soviet Films (1st issue) and 11th International Film Festival, Moscow.
4904 **1889** 15k. multicoloured . . 50 15
See also No. 4907.

1979. 50th Anniv of First Five Year Plan. Sheet 66 × 87 mm.
MS4905 **1890** 30k. multicoloured 1·10 45

1979. 4th U.S.S.R. Philatelic Society Congress. Sheet 92 × 66 mm.
MS4906 **1891** 50k. rose and green 1·60 65

1892 Exhibition Hall and Film Still

1979. 60th Anniv of Soviet Films (2nd issue).
4907 **1892** 4k. multicoloured . . . 15 10

1893 "Lilac" (K. A. Korovin)

1894 John McClean

1979. Flower Paintings. Multicoloured.
4908 1k. "Flowers and Fruits" (I. F. Khrutsky) (horiz) 10 10
4909 2k. "Phloxes" (I. N. Kramskoi) 15 10
4910 3k. Type **1893** 20 10

4911 15k. "Bluebells" (S. V. Gerasimov) 50 20
4912 32k. "Roses" (P. P. Konchalovsky) (horiz) . . 95 40

1979. Birth Centenary of John McClean (first Soviet consul for Scotland).
4913 **1894** 4k. black and red . . . 15 10

1979. 1980 Olympics. "Tourism around the Golden Ring" (4th issue). As T **1855**. Multicoloured.
4914 1r.+50k. Narikaly Fortress, Tbilisi . . . . 4·00 2·50
4915 1r.+50k. Georgian Philharmonic Society Concert Hall and "Muse" (sculpture), Tbilisi . . . . 4·00 2·50
4916 1r.+50k. Chir-Dor Mosque, Samarkand . . . . 4·00 2·50
4917 1r.+50k. People's Friendship Museum and "Courage" monument, Tashkent . . 4·00 2·50

1895 "Friendship" (Lena Liberda)

1979. International Year of the Child (2nd issue). Children's Paintings. Multicoloured.
4918 2k. Type **1895** 10 10
4919 3k. "After Rain" (Daniya Akhmetshina) 10 10
4920 4k. "Dance of Friendship" (Liliya Elistratova) . . . 20 10
4921 15k. "On the Excursion" (Vika Smalyuk) 45 20

1896 Golden Oriole

1979. Birds. Multicoloured.
4922 2k. Type **1896** 15 10
4923 3k. Lesser spotted woodpecker 20 10
4924 4k. Crested tit 20 10
4925 10k. Barn owl 60 15
4926 15k. European nightjar . . 80 35

1897 Soviet Circus Emblem

1898 Marx, Engels, Lenin and View of Berlin

1979. 60th Anniv of Soviet Circus.
4927 **1897** 4k. multicoloured . . . 15 10

1979. 1980 Olympics. "Tourism around the Golden Ring" (5th issue). As T **1855**. Multicoloured.
4928 1r.+50k. Relics of Yerevan's origin . . . . 4·00 2·00
4929 1r.+50k. Armenian State Opera and Ballet Theatre, Yerevan . . . . 4·00 2·00

1979. 30th Anniv of German Democratic Republic.
4930 **1898** 6k. multicoloured . . . 15 10

1899 V. A. Lyakhov, V. V. Ryumin and "Salyut 6"

1979. Lyakhov and Ryumin's 175 Days in Space. Multicoloured.
4931 15k. Type **1899** 40 20
4932 15k. Radio telescope mounted on "Salyut 6" 40 20
Nos. 4931/2 were issued together, se-tenant, forming a composite design.

1900 Hammer and Sickle

1901 Communications Equipment and Signal Corps Emblem

1979. 62nd Anniv of October Revolution.
4933 **1900** 4k. multicoloured . . . 15 10

1979. 60th Anniv of Signal Corps.
4934 **1901** 4k. multicoloured . . . 15 10

1902 "Katherine" (T. G. Shevchenko)

1903 Shabolovka Radio Mast, Moscow

1979. Ukrainian Paintings. Multicoloured.
4935 2k. Type **1902** 10 10
4936 3k. "Into Service" (K. K. Kostandi) 25 10
4937 4k. "To Petrograd" (A. M. Lopukhov) 55 10
4938 10k. "Return" (V. N. Kostetsky) 30 15
4939 15k. "Working Morning" (M. G. Belsky) 40 25

1979. 50th Anniv of Radio Moscow.
4940 **1903** 32k. multicoloured . . 1·00 35

1904 Misha (Olympic mascot)

1905 "Peace" and Hammer and Sickle

1979. New Year.
4941 **1904** 4k. multicoloured . . . 25 10

1979. "Peace Programme in Action". Mult.
4942 4k. Type **1905** 15 10
4943 4k. Hand holding demand for peace 15 10
4944 4k. Hands supporting emblem of peace 15 10

1906 Traffic Policeman

1908 Skiers at North Pole

1907 "Vulkanolog"

1979. Road Safety. Multicoloured.
4945 3k. Type **1906** 10 10
4946 4k. Child playing in road . . 15 10
4947 6k. Speeding car out of control 25 10

1979. Soviet Scientific Research Ships. Mult.
4948 1k. Type **1907** 10 10
4949 2k. "Professor Bogorov" . . 10 10
4950 4k. "Ernst Krenkel" 15 10
4951 6k. "Kosmonavt Vladislav Volkov" 30 15
4952 10k. "Kosmonavt Yuri Gagarin" 60 25
4953 15k. "Akademik Kurchatov" 85 35

1979. Ski Expedition to North Pole. Sheet 66 × 85 mm.
MS4954 **1908** 50k. multicoloured 1·90 80

1909 Industrial Landscape

1980. 50th Anniv of Mordovian ASSR of Russian Federation.
4955 **1909** 4k. red 15 10

1910 Speed Skating

1912 N. I. Podvoisky

1911 Running

1980. Winter Olympic Games, Lake Placid.
4956 **1910** 4k. blue, lt blue & orange 15 10
4957 – 6k. violet, blue & orange 15 10
4958 – 10k. red, blue and gold 40 15
4959 – 15k. brown, blue & turquoise 50 15
4960 – 20k. turquoise, blue and red 60 25
MS4961 60 × 90 mm. 50k. multicoloured . . . . 2·25 1·25
DESIGNS—HORIZ: 6k. Figure skating (pairs); 10k. Ice hockey; 15k. Downhill skiing. VERT: 20k. Luge; 50k. Cross-country skiing.

1980. Olympic Sports (7th series). Athletics. Mult.
4962 4k.+2k. Type **1911** 20 10
4963 6k.+3k. Hurdling 25 10
4964 10k.+5k. Walking (vert) . . 50 20
4965 16k.+6k. High jumping . . 75 20
4966 20k.+10k. Long jumping . . 1·10 60

1980. Birth Centenary of Nikolai Ilich Podvoisky (revolutionary).
4967 **1912** 4k. brown 10 10

1980. 1980 Olympics. "Tourism around the Golden Ring" (6th issue). Moscow. As T **1855**. Mult.
4968 1r.+50k. Kremlin . . . . . 4·50 2·75
4969 1r.+50k. Kalinin Prospect 4·50 2·75

1913 "Rainbow" (A. K. Savrasov) (⅔-size illustration)

1980. Birth Annivs of Soviet Artists. Mult.
4970 6k. "Harvest Summer" (A. G. Venetsianov (bicent)) (vert) 20 10
4971 6k. Type **1913** (150th anniv) 20 10
4972 6k. "Old Yerevan" (M. S. Saryan) (centenary) . . . 20 10

1980. Olympic Sports (8th series). Athletics. As T **1911**. Multicoloured.
4973 4k.+2k. Pole vaulting . . . 20 10
4974 6k.+3k. Discus throwing . . 25 10
4975 10k.+5k. Javelin throwing 50 20
4976 16k.+6k. Hammer throwing 75 20
4977 20k.+10k. Putting the shot 1·10 60
MS4978 92 × 72 mm. 50k.+25k. Relay racing . . . . 7·75 5·50

1914 Aleksei Leonov

1980. 15th Anniv of First Space Walk in Space. Sheet 111 × 73 mm.
MS4979 **1914** 50k. multicoloured 1·90 85

1915 Georg Ots

1916 Order of Lenin

1980. 60th Birth Anniv of Georg K. Ots (artist).
4980 **1915** 4k. blue 10 10

1980. 1980 Olympics. "Tourism around the Golden Ring" (7th issue). As T **1855**. Multicoloured.
4981 1r.+50k. St. Isaac's Cathedral, Leningrad . . 4·50 2·75
4982 1r.+50k. Monument to the Defenders of Leningrad 4·50 2·75

1980. 50th Anniv of Order of Lenin.
4983 **1916** 4k. multicoloured . . . 10 10

1917 Cosmonauts, "Salyut", "Soyuz" Complex and Emblem

1980. Intercosmos Space Programme. Sheet 117 × 81 mm.
MS4984 **1917** 50k. multicoloured 1·90 85

1918 Lenin (after G. Nerod)

1980. 110th Birth Anniv of Lenin. Sheet 91 × 79 mm.
MS4985 **1918** 30k. brown, gold and vermilion . . . . 1·00 45

1919 "Motherland" (detail of Heroes Monument, Volgograd)

1920 Government House, Arms and Flag of Azerbaijan

1980. 35th Anniv of World War II Victory. Mult.
4986 4k. Type **1919** 15 10
4987 4k. Victory Monument, Treptow Park, Berlin . . 15 10
4988 4k. Victory Parade, Red Square, Moscow 15 10

1980. 60th Anniv of Azerbaijan Soviet Republic.
4989 **1920** 4k. multicoloured . . . 10 10

1980. 1980 Olympics. "Tourism around the Golden Ring" (8th issue). As T **1855**. Multicoloured.
4990 1r.+50k. Bogdan Khmelnitsky Monument and St. Sophia Monastery, Kiev . . . . 4·50 2·75
4991 1r.+50k. Underground bridge over River Dnieper, Kiev . . . . . 5·00 3·00
4992 1r.+50k. Sports Palace and War Memorial, Minsk . . 4·50 2·75
4993 1r.+50k. House of Cinematograhy, Minsk . . 4·50 2·75
4994 1r.+50k. Old City, Tallin . . 4·50 2·75
4995 1r.+50k. Hotel Viru, Tallin 4·50 2·75

1921 Monument, Ivanovo

1922 Shield and Industrial Complexes

1980. 75th Anniv of First Soviet of Workers Deputies, Ivanovo.
4996 **1921** 4k. multicoloured . . . 10 10

1980. 25th Anniv of Warsaw Treaty.
4997 **1922** 32k. multicoloured . . 1·25 65

1923 Yakovlev Yak-24 Helicopter, 1953

1980. Helicopters. Multicoloured.
4998 1k. Type **1923** 10 10
4999 2k. Mil Mi-8, 1962 . . . . 10 10
5000 3k. Kamov Ka-26, 1965 . . 20 10
5001 6k. Mil Mi-6, 1957 . . . . 30 15
5002 15k. Mil Mi-10K, 1965 . . 80 25
5003 32k. Mil Mi-V12, 1969 . . . 1·90 55

1924 Title Page of Book

1925 Medical Check-up of Cosmonauts

1980. 1500th Birth Anniv of David Anacht (Armenian philosopher).
5004 **1924** 4k. multicoloured . . . 10 10

1980. Soviet–Hungarian Space Flight. Mult.
5005 6k. Type **1925** 15 10
5006 15k. Crew meeting on "Salyut-6" space station 45 15
5007 32k. Press conference . . . 1·00 50

1926 Red Fox

1927 Kazan

1980. Fur-bearing Animals. Multicoloured.
5008 2k. Type **1926** 10 10
5009 4k. Artic fox (horiz) 15 10
5010 6k. European mink 25 10
5011 10k. Coypu 45 20
5012 15k. Sable (horiz) 60 30

1980. 60th Anniv of Tatar Republic.
5013 **1927** 4k. multicoloured . . . 10 10

1928 College and Emblem

1929 Ho Chi Minh

1980. 150th Anniv of Bauman Technical College, Moscow.
5014 **1928** 4k. multicoloured . . . 10 10

1980. 90th Birth Anniv of Ho Chi Minh (Vietnamese leader).
5015 **1929** 6k. multicoloured . . . 20 10

1930 Arms, Monument and Modern Buildings

1980. 40th Anniv of Soviet Socialist Republics of Lithuania, Latvia and Estonia. Multicoloured.
5016 **1930** 4k. Lithuania 10 10
5017 – 4k. Latvia 10 10
5018 – 4k. Estonia 10 10

1933 Crew of "Soyuz 27" at Launching Site

1934 Avicenna (after E. Sokdov and M. Gerasimov)

1980. Soviet–Vietnamese Space Flight. Mult.
5019 6k. Type **1933** 15 10
5020 15k. Cosmonauts at work in space 45 20
5021 32k. Cosmonauts returning to Earth . . . . 1·75 70

1980. Birth Millenary of Avicenna (Arab philosopher and physician).
5022 **1934** 4k. multicoloured . . . 10 10

1935 "Khadi-7" Gas turbine Car

1980. Racing cars designed by Kharkov Automobile and Road-building Institute. Mult.
5023 2k. Type **1935** 10 10
5024 6k. "Khadi-10" piston engined car 25 10
5025 15k. "Khadi-11 E" electric car 65 25
5026 32k. "Khadi-13 E" electric car . . . . 1·25 60

1936 Arms, Flags, Government House and Industrial Complex

1980. 60th Anniv of Kazakh Soviet Socialist Republic.
5027 **1936** 4k. multicoloured . . . 10 10

1937 "Self-portrait" and "The Spring"

1980. Birth Bicent of Jean Ingres (French painter).
5028 **1937** 32k. multicoloured . . 1·00 45

1938 "Morning on Kulikovo Field" (A. Bubnov)

1980. 600th Anniv of Battle of Kulikovo.
5029 **1938** 4k. multicoloured . . . 10 10

1939 Town Hall

1940 Yuri V. Malyshev and Valdimir V. Aksenov

1980. 950th Anniv of Tartu, Estonia.
5030 **1939** 4k. multicoloured . . . 10 10

1980. "Soyuz T-2" Space Flight.
5031 **1940** 10k. multicoloured . . 35 15

1941 Theoretical Training

1942 Crew Training

1980. 20th Anniv of Gagarin Cosmonaut Training Centre. Multicoloured.
5032 6k. Type **1941** 20 10
5033 15k. Practical training . . . 40 15
5034 32k. Physical endurance tests 95 50

1980. Soviet–Cuban Space Flight. Multicoloured.
5035 6k. Type **1942** 20 10
5036 15k. Physical exercise on board space complex . . 40 15
5037 32k. Returned cosmonauts and space capsule 95 50

1943 "Bargaining" (Nevrev) (⅔-size illustration)

1980. 150th Birth Anniv of N. V. Nevrev and K. D. Flavitsky (painters). Multicoloured.
5038 6k. Type **1943** 20 10
5039 6k. "Princess Tarakanova" (Flavitsky) 20 10

1944 Vasilevsky

1945 Banner

1980. 85th Birth Anniv of Marshal A. M. Vasilevsky.
5040 **1944** 4k. green 10 10

1980. 63rd Anniv of October Revolution.
5041 **1945** 4k. red, gold and purple 10 10

1946 Guramishvili

1947 Ioffe

1980. 275th Birth Anniv of David Guramishvili (Georgian poet).
5042 **1946** 4k. green, silver and black 10 10

1980. Birth Centenary of A. F. Ioffe (physicist).
5043 **1947** 4k. brown and buff . . 15 10

1948 Siberian Cedar

1980. Trees. Multicoloured.
5044 2k. Type **1948** 10 10
5045 4k. Pedunculate oak 10 10
5046 6k. Lime (vert) 20 10
5047 10k. Sea buckthorn 35 20
5048 15k. Ash 50 30

1949 Misha the Bear (Olympic mascot)

1980. Completion of Olympic Games, Moscow. Sheet 93 × 73 mm.
MS5049 **1949** 1r. multicoloured 15·00 10·00

1950 Suvorov (after N. Utkin)

1980. 250th Birth Anniv of Field Marshal A. V. Suvorov.

5050 **1950** 4k. blue 15 10

1951 State Emblem and Republican Government House

1952 Blok (after K. Somov)

1980. 60th Anniv of Armenian Soviet Socialist Republic.

5051 **1951** 4k. multicoloured . . . 10 10

1980. Birth Cent of Aleksandr Aleksandrovich Blok (poet).

5052 **1952** 4k. multicoloured . . . 10 10

1980. Soviet Scientific Research Ships (2nd series). As T **1907**. Multicoloured.

5053 2k. "Ayu-Dag" 10 10

5054 3k. "Valerian Uryvaev" . . 10 10

5055 4k. "Mikhail Somov" . . . 20 10

5056 6k. "Akademik Sergei Korolev" 25 10

5057 10k. "Otto Schmidt" . . . 40 20

5058 15k. "Akademik Mstislav Keldysh" 65 30

1953 Spassky Tower and Kremlin Palace of Congresses

1955 Sable in Cedar

1980. New Year.

5059 **1953** 4k. multicoloured . . . 15 10

1980. Perf or imperf (2r.), perf (others).

5060 – 3k. orange 10 10

5061 – 5k. blue 15 10

5063 **1955** 35k. olive . . . . . . 1·00 35

5064 – 45k. brown . . . . . 1·40 40

5066 – 50k. green . . . . . . 1·60 10

5067a – 2r. black 25 10

5068 – 3r. black . . . . . . 8·00 4·00

5069 – 3r. green . . . . . . 2·00 1·00

5071 – 5r. blue . . . . . . 3·25 1·60

DESIGNS—14 × 22 mm: 3k. State flag; 5k. Forms of transport. 22 × 33 mm: 45k. Spassky Tower; 50k. Vodovzodny Tower and Grand Palace, Moscow Kremlin; 2r. "Arklika" atomic ice-breaker; 3r. Globe, child and olive branch; 5r. Globe and feather ("Peace").

1957 Institute Building

1980. 50th Anniv of Institute for Advanced Training of Doctors.

5075 **1957** 4k. multicoloured . . . 15 10

1958 Lenin Monument, Leningrad, and Dneproges Hydro-electric Station

1959 Nesmeyanov

1980. 60th Anniv of GOELRO (electrification plan).

5076 **1958** 4k. multicoloured . . . 10 10

1980. Academician A. N. Nesmeyanov (organic chemist) Commemoration.

5077 **1959** 4k. multicoloured . . . 10 10

1960 Nagatinsky Bridge

1980. Moscow Bridges. Multicoloured.

5078 4k. Type **1960** 15 10

5079 6k. Luzhniki underground railway bridge 35 10

5080 15k. Kalininsky bridge . . . 45 20

1961 Timoshenko

1962 Indian and Russian Flags with Government House, New Delhi

1980. 10th Death Anniv of Marshal S. K. Timoshenko.

5081 **1961** 4k. purple 10 10

1980. President Brezhnev's Visit to India.

5082 **1962** 4k. multicoloured . . . 25 10

1963 Antarctic Research Station

1964 Arms and Symbols of Agriculture and Industry

1981. Antarctic Exploration. Multicoloured.

5083 4k. Type **1963** 15 10

5084 6k. Antennae, rocket, weather balloon and tracked vehicle (Meteorological research) 50 10

5085 15k. Map of Soviet bases and supply ship "Ob" . . 2·25 40

1981. 60th Anniv of Dagestan Autonomous Soviet Socialist Republic.

5086 **1964** 4k. multicoloured . . . 10 10

1965 Hockey Players and Emblem

1981. 12th World Hockey Championships, Khabarovsk.

5087 **1965** 6k. multicoloured . . . 20 10

1966 Banner and Star

1981. 26th Soviet Communist Party Congress. Multicoloured.

5088 4k. Type **1966** 10 10

5089 20k. Kremlin Palace of Congresses and Lenin (51 × 36 mm) . . . . . . 1·25 80

1967 Lenin and Congress Building

1968 Keldysh

1981. 26th Ukraine Communist Party Congress.

5090 **1967** 4k. multicoloured . . . 10 10

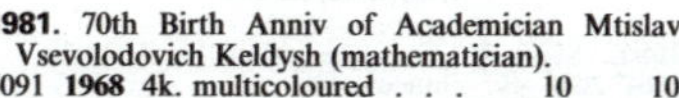

1981. 70th Birth Anniv of Academician Mtislav Vsevolodovich Keldysh (mathematician).

5091 **1968** 4k. multicoloured . . . 10 10

1969 Banner and Kremlin Palace of Congress

1981. 26th Soviet Communist Party Congress (2nd issue). Sheet 97 × 74 mm.

MS5092 **1969** 50k. multicoloured 1·90 90

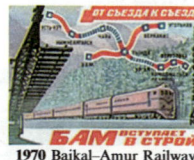

1970 Baikal–Amur Railway

1981. Construction Projects of the 10th Five Year Plan. Multicoloured.

5093 4k. Type **1970** 25 10

5094 4k. Urengoi gas field . . . 15 10

5095 4k. Sayano-Shushenakaya hydro-electric dam . . . 15 10

5096 4k. Atommash Volga–Don atomic reactor 15 10

5097 4k. Syktyvkar paper mill . . 15 10

5098 4k. Giant excavator, Ekibastuz 25 10

1971 Freighter and Russian and Indian Flags

1981. 25th Anniv of Soviet–Indian Shipping Line.

5099 **1971** 15k. multicoloured . . 55 20

1972 Arms, Monument and Building

1981. 60th Anniv of Georgian Soviet Socialist Republic.

5100 **1972** 4k. multicoloured . . . 10 10

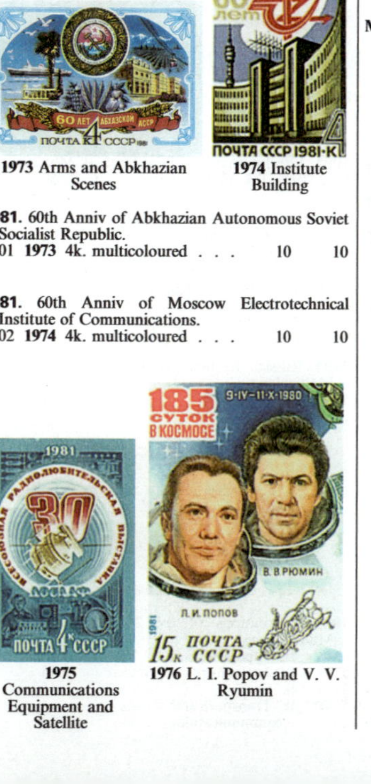

1973 Arms and Abkhazian Scenes

1974 Institute Building

1981. 60th Anniv of Abkhazian Autonomous Soviet Socialist Republic.

5101 **1973** 4k. multicoloured . . . 10 10

1981. 60th Anniv of Moscow Electrotechnical Institute of Communications.

5102 **1974** 4k. multicoloured . . . 10 10

1975 Communications Equipment and Satellite

1976 L. I. Popov and V. V. Ryumin

1981. 30th All-Union Amateur Radio Exhibition.

5103 **1975** 4k. multicoloured . . . 20 10

1981. 185 Days in Space of Cosmonauts Popov and Ryumin. Multicoloured.

5104 15k. Type **1976** 45 20

5105 15k. "Salyut 6"–"Soyuz" complex 45 20

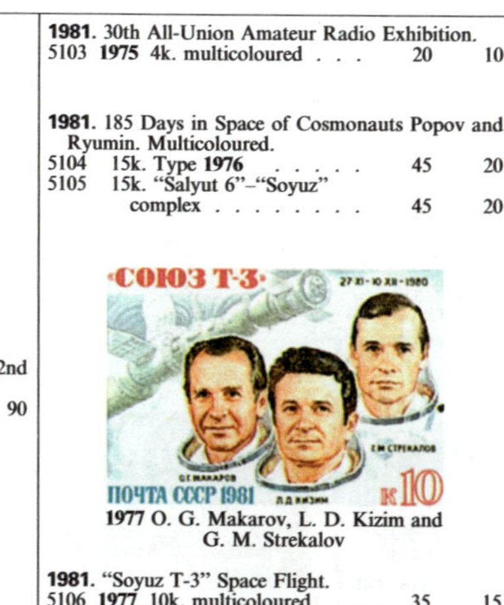

1977 O. G. Makarov, L. D. Kizim and G. M. Strekalov

1981. "Soyuz T-3" Space Flight.

5106 **1977** 10k. multicoloured . . 35 15

1978 Rocket Launch

1981. Soviet–Mongolian Space Flight. Mult.

5107 6k. Type **1978** 20 10

5108 15k. Mongolians watching space flight on television 40 15

5109 32k. Re-entry stages . . . . 1·00 40

1979 Bering

1980 Yuri Gagarin and Globe

1981. 300th Birth Anniv of Vitus Bering (navigator).

5110 **1979** 4k. blue 25 10

1981. 20th Anniv of First Manned Space Flight. Multicoloured.

5111 6k. Type **1980** 20 10

5112 15k. S. P. Korolev (spaceship designer) . . . 45 15

5113 32k. Statue of Gagarin and "Interkosmos" emblem 1·00 50

MS5114 102 × 62 mm. 50k. Head of Gagarin (51 × 36 mm) . . . . 7·75 5·00

1981 "Salyut" Orbital Space Station

1983 Prokofiev

1982 Lenin (after P. V. Vasilev)

1981. 10th Anniv of First Manned Space Station.
5115 **1981** 32k. multicoloured . . 1·25 50

1981. 111th Birth Anniv of Lenin. Sheet 93 × 91 mm.
MS5116 **1982** 50k. multicoloured 1·75 1·10

1981. 90th Birth Anniv of S. S. Prokofiev (composer).
5117 **1983** 4k. lilac 30 10

1984 New Hofburg Palace, Vienna

1985 Arms, Industrial Complex and Docks

1981. "WIPA 1981" International Stamp Exhibition, Vienna.
5118 **1984** 15k. multicoloured . . 50 20

1981. 60th Anniv of Adzharskian Autonomous Soviet Socialist Republic.
5119 **1985** 4k. multicoloured . . . 10 10

1986 N. N. Benardos

1987 Congress Emblem

1981. Centenary of Invention of Welding.
5120 **1986** 6k. multicoloured . . . 15 10

1981. 14th Congress of International Union of Architects, Warsaw.
5121 **1987** 15k. multicoloured . . 50 20

1988 "Albanian Girl in Doorway" (A. A. Ivanov)

1981. Paintings. Multicoloured.
5122 10k. Type **1988** 40 15
5123 10k. "Sunset over Sea at Livorno" (N. N. Ge) (horiz) 40 15
5124 10k. "Demon" (M. A. Vrubel) (horiz) 40 15
5125 10k. "Horseman" (F. A. Rubo) 40 15

1989 Flight Simulator

1981. Soviet–Rumanian Space Flight. Mult.
5126 6k. Type **1989** 20 10
5127 15k. "Salyut"–"Soyuz" space complex 45 15
5128 32k. Cosmonauts greeting journalists after return . . 1·00 50

1990 "Primula minima"

1981. Flowers of the Carpathians. Multicoloured.
5129 4k. Type **1990** 15 10
5130 6k. "Carlina acaulis" . . . 20 10
5131 10k. "Parageum montanum" . 35 15
5132 15k. "Atragene alpina" . . 55 20
5133 32k. "Rhododendron kotschyi" . . . . 1·25 50

1991 Gyandzhevi

1992 Longo

1981. 840th Birth Anniv of Nizami Gyandzhevi (poet and philosopher).
5134 **1991** 4k. brown, yellow & green 10 10

1981. Luigi Longo (Italian politician). Commem.
5135 **1992** 6k. multicoloured . . . 15 10

1993 Running

1994 Flag and Arms of Mongolia

1981. Sports. Multicoloured.
5136 4k. Type **1993** 15 10
5137 6k. Football 15 10
5138 10k. Throwing the discus . . 35 20
5139 15k. Boxing 60 25
5140 32k. Swimmer on block . . 1·25 60

1981. 60th Anniv of Revolution in Mongolia.
5141 **1994** 6k. multicoloured . . . 15 10

1995 Spassky Tower and Film encircling Globe

1996 "Lenin"

1981. 12th International Film Festival, Moscow.
5142 **1995** 15k. multicoloured . . 50 20

1981. River Ships. Multicoloured.
5143 4k. Type **1996** 20 10
5144 6k. "Kosmonavt Gagarin" (tourist ship) 25 10
5145 15k. "Valerian Kuibyshev" (tourist ship) 60 25
5146 32k. "Baltysky" (freighter) 1·40 55

1981. Russian Ice-breakers (4th issue). As T **1775**. Multicoloured.
5147 15k. "Malygin" 65 15

1997 Industry

1981. Resolutions of the 26th Party Congress. Multicoloured.
5148 4k. Type **1997** 20 10
5149 4k. Agriculture 15 10
5150 4k. Energy 15 10
5151 4k. Transport and communications 20 10
5152 4k. Arts and science 15 10
5153 4k. International co-operation 15 10

1998 Ulyanov

2000 Brushes, Palette and Gerasimov

1999 Facade of Theatre

1981. 150th Birth Anniv of I. N. Ulyanov (Lenin's father).
5154 **1998** 4k. brown, black & green 10 10

1981. 225th Anniv of Pushkin Drama Theatre, Leningrad.
5155 **1999** 6k. multicoloured . . . 15 10

1981. Birth Centenary of A. M. Gerasimov (artist).
5156 **2000** 4k. multicoloured . . . 10 10

2001 Institute Building

1981. 50th Anniv of Institute of Physical Chemistry, Academy of Sciences, Moscow.
5157 **2001** 4k. multicoloured . . . 10 10

2002 Severtzov's Tit Warbler

1981. Song Birds. Multicoloured.
5158 6k. Type **2002** 20 10
5159 10k. Asiatic paradise flycatcher (vert) 30 15
5160 15k. Jankowski's bunting . . 50 35
5161 20k. Vinous-throated parrotbill (vert) 65 45
5162 32k. Hodgson's bushchat (vert) . . . . 1·10 70

2003 Arms and Industrial Scenes

1981. 60th Anniv of Komi A.S.S.R.
5163 **2003** 4k. multicoloured . . . 30 10

2004 Orbiting Satellite and Exhibition Emblem

1981. "Svyaz 81" Communications Exhibition.
5164 **2004** 4k. multicoloured . . . 15 10

2005 Buildings, Arms and Monument

2006 Soviet Soldier (monument, Treptow Park, Berlin)

1981. 60th Anniv of Kabardino-Balkar A.S.S.R.
5165 **2005** 4k. multicoloured . . . 10 10

1981. 25th Anniv of Soviet War Veterans Committee.
5166 **2006** 4k. multicoloured . . . 10 10

2007 Four-masted Barque "Tovarishch"

1981. Cadet Sailing Ships. Multicoloured.
5167 4k. Type **2007** 15 10
5168 6k. Barquentine "Vega" . . 25 10
5169 10k. Schooner "Kodor" (vert) 35 15
5170 15k. Three-masted barque "Tovarishch" 55 20
5171 20k. Four-masted barque "Kruzenshtern" 85 40
5172 32k. Four-masted barque "Sedov" (vert) . . . . . 1·25 75

2008 Russian and Kazakh Citizens with Flags

2009 Lavrentev

1981. 250th Anniv of Unification of Russia and Kazakhstan.
5173 **2008** 4k. multicoloured . . . 10 10

1981. Academician Mikhail Alekseevich Lavrentev (mathematician) Commemoration.
5174 **2009** 4k. multicoloured . . . 10 10

2010 Kremlin Palace of Congresses, Moscow, and Arch of the General Staff, Leningrad

1981. 64th Anniv of October Revolution.
5175 **2010** 4k. multicoloured . . . 10 10

2011 Transmitter, Dish Aerial and "Ekran" Satellite

1981. "Ekran" Television Satellite.
5176 **2011** 4k. multicoloured . . . 10 10

2012 V. V. Kovalyonok and V. P. Savinykh

1981. "Soyuz T-4"–"Salyut 6" Space Complex. Multicoloured.
5177 10k. Type **2012** 30 15
5178 10k. Microscope slide, crystal and text 30 15

2013 Picasso

2014 Merkurov

1981. Birth Centenary of Pablo Picasso (artist). Sheet 101 × 71 mm.
MS5179 **2013** 50k. olive, sepia and blue . . . . 4·00 2·00

1981. Birth Centenary of Sergei Dmitrievich Merkurov (sculpture).
5180 **2014** 4k. brown, green & bis 10 10

2015 "Autumn" (Nino A. Piromanashvili)
2016 Arms and Saviour Tower, Moscow

1981. Paintings by Georgian Artists. Multicoloured.
5181 4k. Type **2015** 15 10
5182 6k. "Gurian Woman" (Sh. G. Kikodze) 15 10
5183 10k. "Travelling Companions" (U. M. Dzhaparidze) (horiz) . . . 35 15
5184 15k. "Shota Rustaveli" (S. S. Kobuladze) 60 35
5185 32k. "Tea Pickers" (V. D. Gudiashvili" (horiz)) . . . 1·25 55

1981. New Year.
5186 **2016** 4k. multicoloured . . . 10 10

2017 Horse-drawn Sleigh (19th century)

1981. Moscow Municipal Transport.
5187 **2017** 4k. brown and silver . . 15 10
5188 – 6k. green and silver . . 35 10
5189 – 10k. lilac and silver . . 30 15
5190 – 15k. black and silver . . 45 25
5191 – 20k. brown and silver 60 30
5192 – 32k. red and silver . . 1·25 50
DESIGNS: 6k. Horse tram (19th century); 10k. Horse-drawn cab (19th century); 15k. Taxi, 1926; 20k. British Leyland bus, 1926; 32k. Electric tram, 1912.

2018 Saviour Tower, Moscow and Rashtrapati Bhavan Palace, New Delhi

1981. Inauguration of Tropospheric Communications Link between U.S.S.R. and India. Sheet 123 × 67 mm.
MS5193 **2018** 50k. multicoloured 1·60 80

2019 Modern Kiev

1982. 1500th Anniv of Kiev.
5194 **2019** 10k. multicoloured . . 35 15

2020 S. P. Korolev

2021 Arms and Industrial Complex

1982. 75th Birth Anniv of Academician S. P. Korolev (spaceship designer).
5195 **2020** 4k. multicoloured . . . 15 10

1982. 60th Anniv of Checheno-Ingush A.S.S.R.
5196 **2021** 4k. multicoloured . . . 15 10

2022 Arms and Construction Sites

2023 Hikmet

1982. 60th Anniv of Yakut A.S.S.R.
5197 **2022** 4k. multicoloured . . . 15 10

1982. 80th Birth Anniv of Nazim Hikmet (Turkish poet).
5198 **2023** 6k. multicoloured . . . 15 10

2024 "The Oaks"

1982. 150th Birth Anniv of I. I. Shishkin (artist).
5199 **2024** 6k. multicoloured . . . 20 10

2025 Trade Unionists and World Map

1982. 10th World Trade Unions Congress, Havana.
5200 **2025** 15k. multicoloured . . 45 20

2026 Kremlin Palace of Congresses and Flag
2027 "Self-portrait"

1982. 17th Soviet Trade Unions Congress.
5201 **2026** 4k. multicoloured . . . 10 10

1982. 150th Birth Anniv of Edouard Manet (artist).
5202 **2027** 32k. multicoloured . . 1·10 40

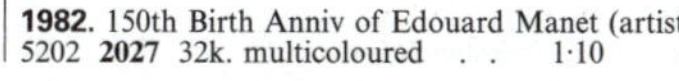

2028 Show Jumping

1982. Soviet Horse breeding. Multicoloured.
5203 4k. Type **2028** 30 10
5204 6k. Dressage 30 10
5205 15k. Racing 60 25

2029 Tito

2030 University, Book and Monument

1982. President Tito of Yugoslavia Commemoration.
5206 **2029** 6k. brown and black . . 15 10

1982. 350th Anniv of University of Tartu.
5207 **2030** 4k. multicoloured . . . 10 10

2031 Heart on Globe

1982. 9th Int Cardiologists Conference, Moscow.
5208 **2031** 15k. multicoloured . . 45 20

2032 Shooting and Skating

1982. 5th Winter Spartakiad. Sheet 93 × 66 mm.
MS5209 **2032** 50k. multicoloured 1·90 95

2033 Blackberry

1982. Wild Berries. Multicoloured.
5210 4k. Type **2033** 15 10
5211 6k. Blueberries 20 10
5212 10k. Cranberry 30 15
5213 15k. Cherry 60 25
5214 32k. Strawberry . . . . . . 1·25 55

2034 "Venera 13" and "14"

2035 "M. I. Lopukhina" (V. L. Borovikovsky)

1982. "Venera" Space Flights to Venus.
5215 **2034** 10k. multicoloured . . 30 15

1982. Paintings. Multicoloured.
5216 6k. Type **2035** 20 10
5217 6k. "E. V. Davydov" (O. A. Kiprensky) 20 10
5218 6k. "The Unequal Marriage" (V. V. Pukirev) 20 10

2036 Chukovsky

2038 Lenin (sculpture, N. V. Tomsky)

2037 Rocket, "Soyuz" Spaceship, Globe and Space Station

1982. Birth Cent of K. I. Chukovsky (author).
5219 **2036** 4k. black and grey . . 15 10

1982. Cosmonautics Day.
5220 **2037** 6k. multicoloured . . . 20 10

1982. 112th Birth Anniv of Lenin. Sheet 68 × 87 mm.
MS5221 **2038** 50k. multicoloured 1·60 85

2039 Solovev-Sedoi

1982. 75th Birth Anniv of V. P. Solovev-Sedoi (composer).
5222 **2039** 4k. brown 15 10

2040 Dimitrov
2041 Masthead

1982. Birth Centenary of Georgi Dimitrov (Bulgarian statesman).
5223 **2040** 6k. green 15 10

1982. 70th Anniv of "Pravda" (Communist Party Newspaper).
5224 **2041** 4k. multicoloured . . . 15 10

2042 Congress Emblem and Ribbons

2043 Globe and Hands holding Seedling

1982. 19th Congress of Leninist Young Communist League (Komsomol).
5225 **2042** 4k. multicoloured . . . 15 10

1982. 10th Anniv of U.N. Environment Programme.
5226 **2043** 6k. multicoloured . . . 15 10

2044 Pioneers

2045 I.T.U. Emblem, Satellite and Receiving Station

1982. 60th Anniv of Pioneer Organization.
5227 **2044** 4k. multicoloured . . . 10 10

1982. I.T.U. Delegates' Conference, Nairobi.
5228 **2045** 15k. multicoloured . . 50 25

2046 Class VL-80t Electric Locomotive

1982. Locomotives. Multicoloured.
5229 4k. Type **2046** 25 10
5230 6k. Class TEP-75 diesel . . 30 10
5231 10k. Class TEM-7 diesel . . 60 20
5232 15k. Class VL-82m electric 90 30
5233 32k. Class EP-200 electric 1·90 60

2047 Players with Trophy and Football

1982. World Cup Football Championship, Spain.
5234 **2047** 20k. lilac, yellow and brown 65 30

2048 Hooded Crane

1982. 18th International Ornithological Congress, Moscow. Multicoloured.
5235 2k. Type **2048** 10 10
5236 4k. Steller's sea eagle . . . 20 15
5237 6k. Spoon-billed sandpiper 25 15
5238 10k. Bar-headed goose . . . 45 25
5239 15k. Sociable plover 65 30
5240 32k. White stork . . . . . 1·50 65

2049 Buildings and Workers with Picks

2051 U.N. Flag

2050 "The Cart"

1982. 50th Anniv of Komsomolsk-on-Amur.
5241 **2049** 4k. multicoloured . . . 15 10

1982. Birth Centenary of M. B. Grekov (artist).
5242 **2050** 6k. multicoloured . . . 40 10

1982. Second U.N. Conference on the Exploration and Peaceful Uses of Outer Space, Vienna.
5243 **2051** 15k. multicoloured . . 50 20

2052 Scientific Research in Space

1982. Soviet–French Space Flight. Multicoloured.
5244 6k. Type **2052** 15 10
5245 20k. Rocket and trajectory 60 30
5246 45k. Satellites and globe . . 1·40 75
MS5247 96 × 68 mm. 50k. Flags, space station and emblems (41 × 29 mm) . . . . 2·00 85

2053 "Legend of the Golden Cockerel" (P. I. Sosin)

1982. Lacquerware Paintings. Multicoloured.
5248 6k. Type **2053** 20 10
5249 10k. "Minin's Appeal to Count Pozharsky" (I. A. Fomichev) 30 20
5250 15k. "Two Peasants" (A. F. Kotyagin) 45 25
5251 20k. "The Fisherman" (N. P. Klykov) 60 35
5252 32k. "Arrest of the Propagandists" (N. I. Shishakov) 95 55

2054 Early Telephone, Moscow, Leningrad, Odessa and Riga

2055 P. Schilling (inventor)

1982. Telephone Centenary.
5253 **2054** 4k. multicoloured . . . 15 10

1982. 150th Anniv of Electro-magnetic Telegraph in Russia.
5254 **2055** 6k. multicoloured . . . 15 10

2056 Gymnast and Television Screen

2058 Garibaldi

2057 Mastyazhart Glider, 1923

1982. Intervision Cup Gymnastics Contest.
5255 **2056** 15k. multicoloured . . 40 20

1982. Gliders (1st series). Multicoloured.
5256 4k. Type **2057** 20 10
5257 6k. Red Star, 1930 . . . . 20 10
5258 10k. TsAGI-2, 1934 . . . . 40 15
5259 20k. Stakhanovets, 1939 (60 × 27 mm) 90 35
5260 32k. GR-29, 1941 (60 × 27 mm) . . . . 1·40 55
See also Nos. 5301/5.

1982. 175th Birth Anniv of Giuseppe Garibaldi.
5261 **2058** 6k. multicoloured . . . 15 10

2059 Emblem

2060 F.I.D.E. Emblem, Chess Symbol for Queen and Equestrian Statue

1982. 25th Anniv of International Atomic Energy Agency.
5262 **2059** 20k. multicoloured . . 55 30

1982. World Chess Championship Interzone Tournaments for Women (Tbilisi) and Men (Moscow). Multicoloured.
5263 6k. Type **2060** 35 15
5264 6k. F.I.D.E. emblem, chess symbol for King and Kremlin tower 35 15

2061 Shaposhnikov

2062 Clenched Fist

1982. Birth Cent of Marshal B. M. Shaposhnikov.
5265 **2061** 4k. brown 15 10

1982. 70th Anniv of African National Congress.
5266 **2062** 6k. multicoloured . . . 15 10

2063 Botkin

2064 "Sputnik 1"

1982. 150th Birth Anniv of S. P. Botkin (therapeutist).
5267 **2063** 4k. green 15 10

1982. 25th Anniv of First Artificial Satellite. Sheet 92 × 62 mm.
MS5268 **2064** 50k. multicoloured 2·00 85

А. КАРПОВ — обладатель восьми „Шахматных Оскаров"

(2065)

2067 Flag and Arms

2066 Submarine "S-56"

1982. Anatoly Karpov's Victory in World Chess Championship. No. 5264 optd with T **2065**.
5269 6k. multicoloured 50 35

1982. Soviet Naval Ships. Multicoloured.
5270 4k. Type **2066** 20 10
5271 6k. Minelayer "Gremyashchy" 20 10
5272 15k. Minesweeper "Gafel" 65 25
5273 20k. Cruiser "Krasnyi Krim" 90 40
5274 45k. Battleship "Sevastopol" 1·90 85

1982. 65th Anniv of October Revolution.
5275 **2067** 4k. multicoloured . . . 10 10

2068 House of the Soviets, Moscow

1982. 60th Anniv of U.S.S.R. Multicoloured.
5276 10k. Type **2068** 30 20
5277 10k. Dnieper Dam and statue 30 20
5278 10k. Soviet war memorial and resistance poster . . 30 20
5279 10k. Newspaper, worker holding peace text, and sun illuminating city . . 30 20
5280 10k. Workers' Monument, Moscow, rocket, Ilyushin Il-86 jetliner and factories 30 20
5281 10k. Soviet arms and Kremlin tower 30 20
See also No. **MS**5290.

Всесоюзная филателистическая выставка

(2069)

1982. All-Union Stamp Exhibition, Moscow. No. 5280 optd with T **2069**.
5282 10k. multicoloured 60 30

2070 "Portrait of an Actor" (Domenico Fetti)

2072 Hammer and Sickle, Clock and Date

1982. Italian Paintings in the Hermitage Museum, Leningrad. Multicoloured.
5283 4k. Type **2070** 15 10
5284 10k. "St. Sebastian" (Pietro Perugino) 35 15
5285 20k. "Danae" (Titian) (horiz) 65 30
5286 45k. "Portrait of a Woman" (Correggio) . . . . . 1·40 75
5287 50k. "Portrait of a Young Man" (Capriolo) . . . . 1·60 85
MS5288 46 × 81 mm. 50k. × 2 "Portrait of a Young Woman" (Francesco Melzi) . . . . . . 5·50 2·25

1982. New Year.
5289 **2072** 4k. multicoloured . . . 10 10

2073 Lenin

2074 Camp and Route to Summit of Mt. Everest

1982. 60th Anniv of U.S.S.R. (2nd issue). Sheet 85 × 96 mm.
MS5290 **2073** 50k. green and gold 1·60 85

1982. Soviet Ascent of Mount Everest. Sheet 66 × 86 mm.
MS5291 **2074** 50k. multicoloured 2·50 95

2075 Kherson Lighthouse, Black Sea

2076 F. P. Tolstoi

1982. Lighthouses (1st series). Multicoloured.
5292 6k. Type **2075** 40 15
5293 6k. Vorontsov lighthouse, Odessa, Black Sea 40 15
5294 6k. Temryuk lighthouse, Sea of Azov 40 15
5295 6k. Novorossiisk lighthouse, Black Sea 40 15
5296 6k. Dneiper harbour light 40 15
See also Nos. 5362/6 and 5449/53.

1983. Birth Bicentenary of Fyodor Petrovich Tolstoi (artist).
5297 **2076** 4k. multicoloured . . . 15 10

2077 Masthead of "Iskra" **2078** Army Star and Flag

1983. 80th Anniv of 2nd Social Democratic Workers' Congress.
5298 **2077** 4k. multicoloured . . . 10 10

1983. 65th Anniv of U.S.S.R. Armed Forces.
5299 **2078** 4k. multicoloured . . . 15 10

2079 Ilyushin Il-86 Jetliner over Globe

1983. 60th Anniv of Aeroflot (state airline). Sheet 73 × 99 mm.
MS5300 **2079** 50k. multicoloured 1·60 75

1983. Gliders (2nd series). As T **2057**. Mult.
5301 2k. Antonov A-9, 1948 . . . 10 10
5302 4k. Sumonov KAU-12, 1957 15 10
5303 6k. Antonov A-15, 1960 . . 25 10
5304 20k. SA-7, 1970 . . . . . . 80 35
5305 45k. LAK-12, 1979 . . . . 1·75 80

2080 "The Holy Family" **2081** B. N. Petrov

1983. 500th Birth Anniv of Raphael (artist).
5306 **2080** 50k. multicoloured . . 1·50 75

1983. 70th Birth Anniv of Academician B. N. Petrov (chairman of Interkosmos).
5307 **2081** 4k. multicoloured . . . 10 10

2082 Tashkent Buildings

1983. 2000th Anniv of Tashkent.
5308 **2082** 4k. multicoloured . . . 25 10

2083 Popov, Serebrov and Savitskaya

1983. "Soyuz T-7"–"Salyut 7"–"Soyuz T-5" Space Flight.
5309 **2083** 10k. multicoloured . . 45 15

2084 Globe within Posthorn

1983. World Communications Year. Sheet 72 × 107 mm.
MS5310 **2084** 50k. multicoloured 1·75 80

2085 Aleksandrov and Bars of Music

1983. Birth Centenary of A. V. Aleksandrov (composer).
5311 **2085** 4k. multicoloured . . . 25 10

2086 "Portrait of an Old Woman"

1983. Rembrandt Paintings in Hermitage Museum, Leningrad. Multicoloured.
5312 4k. Type **2086** 20 10
5313 10k. "Portrait of a Learned Man" 40 15
5314 20k. "Old Warrior" 80 30
5315 45k. "Portrait of Mrs B. Martens Doomer" . . 1·50 75
5316 50k. "Sacrifice of Abraham" 1·75 1·00
MS5317 144 × 81 mm. 50k. × 2 "Portrait of an Old Man in Red" 5·50 2·25

2087 Space Complex

1983. Cosmonautics Day. Sheet 61 × 91 mm.
MS5318 **2087** 50k. multicoloured 1·60 85

2088 "Revolution is a Storm" (N. N. Zhukov)

1983. 13th Birth Aniv of Lenin. Sheet 73 × 91 mm.
MS5319 **2088** 50k. brown . . . . 1·60 85

2089 A. N. Berezovoi and V. V. Lebedev

1983. 211 Days in Space of Berezovoi and Lebedev. Multicoloured.
5320 10k. Type **2089** 40 20
5321 10k. "Salyut 7"–"Soyuz T" space complex 40 20

2090 Marx

1983. Death Centenary of Karl Marx.
5322 **2090** 4k. multicoloured . . . 15 10

2091 Memorial, Building and Hydrofoil

1983. Rostov-on-Don.
5323 **2091** 4k. multicoloured . . . 15 10

2092 Kirov Theatre

1983. Bicentenary of Kirov Opera and Ballet Theatre, Leningrad.
5324 **2092** 4k. black, blue and gold 20 10

2093 Arms, Communications and Industrial Complex

1983. 60th Anniv of Buryat A.S.S.R.
5325 **2093** 4k. multicoloured . . . 20 10

2094 Sports Vignettes

1983. 8th Summer Spartakiad.
5326 **2094** 6k. multicoloured . . . 15 10

2095 Khachaturyan

1983. 80th Birth Anniv of Aram I. Khachaturyan (composer).
5327 **2095** 4k. brown 30 10

2096 Tractor and Factory

1983. 50th Anniv of Lenin Tractor Factory, Chelyabinsk.
5328 **2096** 4k. multicoloured . . . 15 10

2097 Simon Bolivar

1983. Birth Bicentenary of Simon Bolivar.
5329 **2097** 6k. deep brown, brown and black 15 10

2098 18th-century Warship and modern Missile Cruiser "Groznyi"

1983. Bicentenary of Sevastopol.
5330 **2098** 5k. multicoloured . . . 40 15

2099 Snowdrops **2101** P. N. Pospelov

2100 "Vostok 6" and Tereshkova

1983. Spring Flowers. Multicoloured.
5331 4k. Type **2099** 15 10
5332 6k. Siberian squills 20 10
5333 10k. "Anemone hepatica" 45 15
5334 15k. Cyclamen 60 25
5335 20k. Yellow star of Bethlehem . . . . 1·10 45

1983. 20th Anniv of First Woman Cosmonaut Valentina V. Tereshkova's Space Flight.
5336 **2100** 10k. multicoloured . . 35 15

1983. 85th Birth Anniv of Pyotr Nicolaievich Pospelov (scientist).
5337 **2101** 4k. multicoloured . . . 10 10

2102 Congress Emblem **2103** Film around Globe and Festival Emblem

1983. 10th European Rheumatologists' Congress, Moscow.
5338 **2102** 4k. multicoloured . . . 20 10

1983. 13th International Film Festival, Moscow.
5339 **2103** 20k. multicoloured . . 55 25

2104 Vakhtangov

1983. Birth Centenary of Ye. B. Vakhtangov (producer and actor).
5340 **2104** 5k. multicoloured . . . 20 10

2105 Coastal Trawlers

1983. Fishing Vessels. Multicoloured.
5341 4k. Type **2105** 20 10
5342 6k. Refrigerated trawler . . 25 10
5343 10k. "Pulkovsky Meridian" (deep-sea trawler) 45 15
5344 15k. Refrigerated freighter 60 30
5345 20k. "50 Let SSR" (factory ship) . . . . 1·00 50

2106 "U.S.S.R.-1" 2107 Sockeye Salmon

1983. 50th Anniv of Stratosphere Balloon's Record Altitude Flight.
5346 **2106** 20k. multicoloured . . 85 30

1983. Fishes. Multicoloured.
5347 4k. Type **2107** 15 10
5348 6k. Zerro 25 10
5349 15k. Spotted wolffish . . . 60 20
5350 20k. Round goby 85 40
5351 45k. Starry flounder . . . . 1·75 90

2108 Exhibition Emblem 2110 S.W.A.P.O. Flag and Emblem

2109 Posthorns

1983. "Sozphilex 83" Stamp Exhibition, Moscow.
5352 **2108** 6k. multicoloured . . . 15 10
MS5353 90 × 69 mm. 50k. green 2·00 1·00
DESIGN: 36 × 22 mm—50k. Moskva River.

1983. 125th Anniv of First Russian Postage Stamp. Sheet 78 × 65 mm.
MS5354 **2109** 50k. stone and black 1·50 75

1983. Namibia Day.
5355 **2110** 5k. multicoloured . . . 15 10

2111 Palestinian with Flag 2112 Emblem and Ostankino TV Tower, Moscow

1983. Palestinian Solidarity.
5356 **2111** 5k. multicoloured . . . 30 10

1983. 1st European Radio-telegraphy Championship, Moscow.
5357 **2112** 6k. multicoloured . . . 20 10

2113 Council Session Emblem 2114 Mohammed al-Khorezmi

1983. 4th UNESCO International Communications Development Programme Council Session, Tashkent.
5358 **2113** 10k. blue, mauve & black 30 15

1983. 1200th Birth Anniv of Mohammed al-Khorezmi (astonomer and mathematician).
5359 **2114** 4k. multicoloured . . . 10 10

2115 Yegorov 2116 Treaty

1983. Birth Centenary of Marshal A. I. Yegorov.
5360 **2115** 4k. purple 10 10

1983. Bicentenary of First Russian–Georgian Friendship Treaty.
5361 **2116** 6k. multicoloured . . . 10 10

1983. Lighthouses (2nd series). As Type **2075**. Multicoloured.
5362 1k. Kipu lighthouse, Baltic Sea 10 10
5363 5k. Keri lighthouse, Gulf of Finland 25 10
5364 10k. Stirsudden lighthouse, Gulf of Finland 40 25
5365 12k. Takhkun lighthouse, Baltic Sea 55 30
5366 20k. Tallin lighthouse, Gulf of Finland 75 45

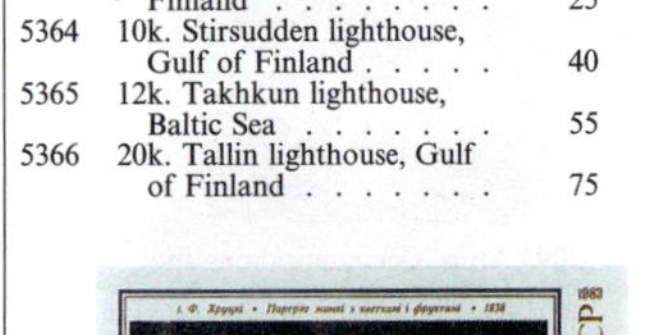

2117 "Wife's Portrait with Flowers" (I. F. Khrutsky)

1983. Byelorussian Paintings. Multicoloured.
5367 4k. Type **2117** 15 10
5368 6k. "Early spring" (V. K. Byalynitsky-Birulya) . . . 20 10
5369 15k. "Young Partisan" (E. A. Zaitsev) (vert) . . 50 20
5370 20k. "Partisan Madonna" (M. A. Savitsky) (vert) . . 70 30
5371 45k. "Corn Harvest" (V. K. Tsvirko) . . . . 1·50 70

2118 Steel Mill

1983. Centenary of Hammer and Sickle Steel Mill.
5372 **2118** 4k. multicoloured . . . 10 10

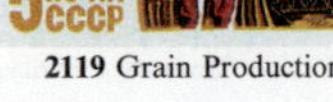

2119 Grain Production 2120 Banner and Symbols of Economic Growth

1983. Food Programme. Multicoloured.
5373 5k. Type **2119** 15 10
5374 5k. Cattle breeding 15 10
5375 5k. Fruit and vegetable production 15 10

1983. 66th Anniv of October Revolution.
5376 **2120** 4k. multicoloured . . . 10 10

2121 Ivan Fyodorov

1983. 400th Death Anniv of Ivan Fyodorov (printer) and 420th Anniv of Publication of "The Apostle" (first Russian printed book).
5377 **2121** 4k. black 15 10

2122 Pipeline Construction

1983. Inaug of Urengoi–Uzhgorod Gas Pipeline.
5378 **2122** 5k. multicoloured . . . 15 10

2123 Sidorenko 2124 Marchers pushing Nuclear Weapons off Globe

1983. Academician A. V. Sidorenko (geologist) Commemoration.
5379 **2123** 4k. multicoloured . . . 15 10

1983. Nuclear Disarmament.
5380 **2124** 5k. multicoloured . . . 15 10

2125 Makhtumkuli 2126 "Madonna and Child under Apple Tree" (Cranach the Elder)

1983. 250th Birth Anniv of Makhtumkuli (Turkmen poet).
5381 **2125** 5k. multicoloured . . . 15 10

1983. German Paintings in the Hermitage Museum. Multicoloured.
5382 4k. Type **2126** 15 10
5383 10k. "Self-portrait" (Anton Raphael Mengs) 35 15
5384 20k. "Self-portrait" (Jurgens Ovens) 70 30
5385 45k. "On Board a Sailing Vessel" (Caspar David Friedrich) . . . . 1·40 60
5386 50k. "Rape of the Sabine Women" (Johann Schonfeld) (horiz) . . . . 1·60 80
MS5387 144 × 79 mm. 50k. × 2 "Portrait of a Young Man" (Holbein) . . . . 5·50 2·00

2127 Sukhe Bator 2128 Globe and Hand holding Baby

1983. 90th Birth Anniv of Sukhe Bator (Mongolian statesman).
5388 **2127** 5k. multicoloured . . . 15 10

1983. International Association of Physicians against Nuclear War.
5389 **2128** 5k. multicoloured . . . 15 10

2129 Moscow Kremlin Tower Star

1983. New Year.
5390 **2129** 5k. multicoloured . . . 15 10

2130 Children's Music Theatre

1983. New Buildings in Moscow.
5391 **2130** 3k. green 10 10
5392 – 4k. blue 15 10
5393 – 6k. brown 15 10
5394 – 20k. green 60 30
5395 – 45k. green . . . . . . 1·40 70
DESIGNS—VERT: 4k. Hotel and Tourist Centre. HORIZ: 6k. Russian Federation Soviet (parliament building); 20k. Hotel Izmailovo; 45k. Novosti News and Press Agency.

2131 Mother and Child with Flowers

1983. Environmental Protection and Peace. Sheet 81 × 65 mm.
MS5396 **2131** 50k. multicoloured 2·25 75

2132 Cuban Flag 2133 Broadcasting Station

1984. 25th Anniv of Cuban Revolution.
5397 **2132** 5k. multicoloured . . . 15 10

1984. 50th Anniv of Moscow Broadcasting Network.
5398 **2133** 4k. multicoloured . . . 15 10

2134 Speed Skating

1984. Women's European Skating Championship, Alma-Ata.
5399 **2134** 5k. multicoloured . . . 20 10

2135 "T-34" Medium Tank

1984. World War II Armoured Vehicles. Mult.
5400 10k. Type **2135** 40 20
5401 10k. "KV" heavy tank . . . 40 20
5402 10k. "IS-2" heavy tank . . 40 20
5403 10k. "SU-100" self-propelled gun 40 20
5404 10k. "ISU-152" heavy self-propelled gun 40 20

2136 Biathlon

1984. Winter Olympic Games, Sarajevo. Mult.
5405 5k. Type **2136** 15 10
5406 10k. Speed skating 35 15
5407 20k. Ice hockey 65 30
5408 45k. Figure skating . . . . 1·25 60

2137 Mandrill

2139 Young Farmers

2138 Gagarin

1984. 120th Anniv of Moscow Zoo. Multicoloured.
5409 2k. Type **2137** 10 10
5410 3k. Blesbok 10 10
5411 4k. Snow leopard 15 10
5412 5k. South African crowned crane 20 15
5413 20k. Blue and yellow macaw 60 60

1984. 50th Birth Anniv of Yuri Alekseevich Gagarin (first man in Space).
5414 **2138** 15k. blue 45 20

1984. 30th Anniv of Development of Unused Land. Sheet 67 × 86 mm.
MS5415 **2139** 50k. multicoloured 1·60 65

2140 "E. K. Vorontsova" (George Hayter)

2141 Ilyushin

1984. English Paintings in Hermitage Museum, Leningrad. Multicoloured.
5416 4k. Type **2140** 15 10
5417 10k. "Portrait of Mrs. Harriet Greer" (George Romney) 35 15
5418 20k. "Approaching Storm" (George Morland) (horiz) 70 25
5419 45k. "Portrait of an Unknown Man" (Marcus Gheeraerts, the younger) 1·50 85
5420 50k. "Cupid untying the Robe of Venus" (Joshua Reynolds) . . . . 1·75 1·00
MS5421 144 × 80 mm. 50k. × 2 "Portrait of a Lady in Blue" (Thomas Gainsborough) . . . 5·50 2·00

1984. 90th Birth Anniv of Academician S. V. Ilyushin (aircraft designer).
5422 **2141** 5k. light brown, brown and black 15 10

2142 Bubnov

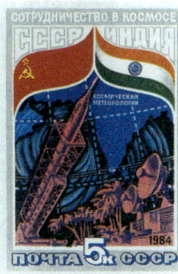

2143 Launching Site of "M-100" Meteorological Station

1984. Birth Centenary of Andrei Sergeevich Bubnov (Communist Party Leader).
5423 **2142** 5k. light brown, brown and black 15 10

1984. Soviet–Indian Space Co-operation. Mult.
5424 5k. Type **2143** 15 10
5425 20k. Satellite and observatory (space geodesy) 60 30
5426 45k. Rocket, satellites and dish aerials (Soviet–Indian space flight) . . . . . . 1·40 65
MS5427 66 × 86 mm. 50k. Cosmonauts abroad "Salyut 7" space station (25 × 36 mm) . . 1·60 65

2144 Globe and Cosmonaut

1984. Cosmonautics Day.
5428 **2144** 10k. multicoloured . . 30 15

2145 "Chelyuskin" (ice-breaker) and Route Map

1984. 50th Anniv of Murmansk–Vladivostok Voyage of "Chelyuskin". Multicoloured.
5429 6k. Type **2145** 25 10
5430 15k. Evacuation of sinking ship 60 25
5431 45k. Air rescue of crew . . 1·75 75

2146 Order of Hero of the Soviet Union

1984. 50th Anniv of Order of Hero of the Soviet Union. Sheet 105 × 70 mm.
MS5432 **2146** 50k. multicoloured 1·60 65

2147 Lenin (after Ye. N. Shirokov)

1984. 114th Birth Anniv of Lenin. Sheet 100 × 78 mm.
MS5433 **2147** 50k. multicoloured 1·60 65

2148 Lotus

2149 Globe and Peace March (left)

1984. Aquatic Flowers. Multicoloured.
5434 1k. Type **2148** 10 10
5435 2k. Euriala 10 10
5436 3k. Yellow water lilies (horiz) 15 10
5437 10k. White water lilies (horiz) 40 20
5438 20k. Marshflowers (horiz) 80 45

1984. Peace.
5439 **2149** 5k. multicoloured . . . 15 10
5440 – 5k. red, gold and black 15 10
5441 – 5k. multicoloured . . . 15 10
DESIGNS: No. 5440, Hammer and sickle and text; 5441, Globe and peace march (right).

2150 Welder

2151 Communications Emblem

1984. 50th Anniv of E. O. Paton Institute of Electric Welding, Kiev.
5442 **2150** 10k. multicoloured . . 25 15

1984. 25th Conference of Community for Mutual Economic Aid Electrical and Postal Communications Standing Committee, Cracow.
5443 **2151** 10k. multicoloured . . 25 15

2152 Emblem and Symbols of Match Venues

2153 Maurice Bishop

1984. European Youth Football Championship.
5444 **2152** 15k. multicoloured . . 50 20

1984. 40th Birth Anniv of Maurice Bishop (former Prime Minister of Grenada).
5445 **2153** 5k. brown 20 10

2154 Lenin and Museum

2155 Freighter, Monument and Aurora Borealis

1984. 60th Anniv of Lenin Central Museum, Moscow.
5446 **2154** 5k. multicoloured . . . 15 10

1984. 400th Anniv of Archangel.
5447 **2155** 5k. multicoloured . . . 15 10

2156 Headquarters and Spassky Tower, Moscow

2158 Liner

2157 Vladimir A. Lyakhov and Aleksandr Aleksandrov

1984. Council of Mutual Economic Aid Conference, Moscow.
5448 **2156** 5k. blue, red and black 15 10

1984. Lighthouses (3rd series). As T **2075**. Mult.
5449 1k. Petropavlovsk lighthouse, Kamchatka . . 10 10
5450 2k. Tokarev lighthouse, Sea of Japan 10 10
5451 4k. Basargin lighthouse, Sea of Japan 20 10
5452 5k. Kronotsky lighthouse, Kamchatka 20 10
5443 10k. Marekan lighthouse, Sea of Okhotsk 35 15

1984. 150 Days in Space of "Salyut 7"–"Soyuz T-9" Cosmonauts.
5454 **2157** 15k. multicoloured . . 45 20

1984. 60th Anniv of Morflot (Soviet merchant fleet).
5455 **2158** 10k. multicoloured . . 35 15

2159 Komsomol Badge and Banner

1984. 60th Anniv of Naming of Young Communist League (Komsomol) after Lenin.
5456 **2159** 5k. multicoloured . . . 15 10

2160 Memorial, Minsk

1984. 40th Anniv of Byelorussian Liberation.
5457 **2160** 5k. multicoloured . . . 15 10

2161 Congress Emblem

2162 Polish Arms and Flag

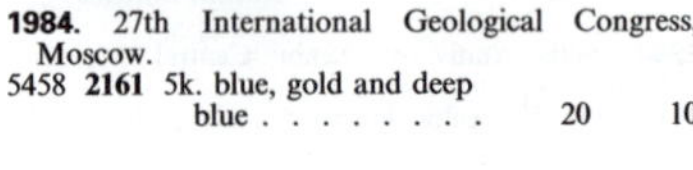

1984. 27th International Geological Congress, Moscow.
5458 **2161** 5k. blue, gold and deep blue 20 10

1984. 40th Anniv of Republic of Poland.
5459 **2162** 5k. multicoloured . . . 15 10

2163 Asafev

1984. Birth Centenary of Boris Vladimirovich Asafev (composer).
5460 **2163** 5k. green 20 10

2164 Russian and Mexican Flags and Scroll

1984. 60th Anniv of U.S.S.R.–Mexico Diplomatic Relations.
5461 **2164** 5k. multicoloured . . . 15 10

2165 Title Page of "The Princess-Frog"

1984. Folk Tales. Illustration by I. Bilibin. Mult.
5462 5k. Type **2165** 20 15
5463 5k. Hunter and frog in marshland 20 15
5464 5k. Old man and hunter in forest 20 15
5465 5k. Crowd and mute swans 20 20
5466 5k. Title page of "Ivan the Tsarevich, the Fire-bird and the Grey Wolf" . . . 20 15
5467 5k. Ivan and the Fire-bird 20 15
5468 5k. Grave and Ivan on horse 40 15
5469 5k. Ivan and princess . . . 20 15
5470 5k. Title page of "Vasilisa the Beautiful" 20 15
5471 5k. Knight on horse 20 15
5472 5k. Tree-man in forest . . . 40 15
5473 5k. Vasilisa and skulls . . . 40 15

2166 Basketball

1984. "Friendship 84" Sports Meetings. Mult.
5474 1k. Type **2166** 10 10
5475 5k. Gymnastics (vert) . . . 15 10
5476 10k. Weightlifting 30 10
5477 15k. Wrestling 50 20
5478 20k. High jumping 75 30

2167 Flag and Soviet Soldiers' Monument, Bucharest

2168 Emblem, Chess Symbol for Queen and Motherland Statue

1984. 40th Anniv of Rumania's Liberation.
5479 **2167** 5k. multicoloured . . . 15 10

1984. World Chess Championship Finals for Women (Volgograd) and Men (Moscow).
5480 **2168** 15k. gold, red and black 70 25
5481 – 15k. multicoloured . . 70 25
DESIGN: No. 5481, Emblem, chess symbol for king and Spassky tower, Moscow Kremlin.

2169 Party House and Soviet Army Monument, Sofia, and State Emblem

1984. 40th Anniv of Bulgarian Revolution.
5482 **2169** 5k. multicoloured . . . 15 10

2170 Arms and Flag

1984. 10th Anniv of Ethiopian Revolution.
5483 **2170** 5k. multicoloured . . . 15 10

2171 Excavator

1984. 50th Anniv of Lenin Machine-building Plant, Novokramatorsk.
5484 **2171** 5k. multicoloured . . . 15 10

2172 Arms and Symbols of Industry and Agriculture

1984. 60th Anniv of Nakhichevan A.S.S.R.
5485 **2172** 5k. multicoloured . . . 15 10

V СЪЕЗД ВОФ. МОСКВА. ОКТЯБРЬ 1984 г.
(**2173**) ($\frac{1}{2}$-size illustration)

1984. 5th Philatelic Congress, Moscow. No. **MS**5354 optd with T **2173**.
MS5486 **2109** 50k. stone and black 1·90 80

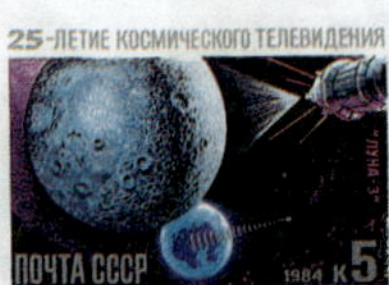

2174 "Luna 3" photographing Moon

1984. 25th Anniv of Photography in Space. Mult.
5487 5k. Type **2174** 15 10
5488 20k. "Venera-9" and control centre 60 25
5489 45k. "Meteor" meteorological satellite and Earth . . . . 1·40 60
MS5490 60 × 81 mm. 50k. V. Lyakhov installing solar battery on "Salyut 7" space station (21 × 32 mm) . . . . 1·60 65

2175 Arms and Flag

1984. 35th Anniv of German Democratic Republic.
5491 **2175** 5k. multicoloured . . . 15 10

2176 Arms and Motherland Statue, Kiev

1984. 40th Anniv of Liberation of the Ukraine.
5492 **2176** 5k. multicoloured . . . 15 10

2177 Town, Arms and Countryside

1984. 60th Anniv of Moldavian Soviet Socialist Republic.
5493 **2177** 5k. multicoloured . . . 15 10

2178 Arms, Power Station and Mountains

1984. 60th Anniv of Kirgizia Soviet Socialist Republic.
5494 **2178** 5k. multicoloured . . . 15 10

2179 Arms and Symbols of Industry and Agriculture

2180 Flags and Spassky Tower

1984. 60th Anniv of Tadzhikistan Soviet Socialist Republic.
5495 **2179** 5k. multicoloured . . . 15 10

1984. 67th Anniv of October Revolution.
5496 **2180** 5k. multicoloured . . . 15 10

2181 Arms, State Building and Dam

1984. 60th Anniv of Uzbekistan Soviet Socialist Republic.
5497 **2181** 5k. multicoloured . . . 15 10

2182 Arms, Flag and State Building

1984. 60th Anniv of Turkmenistan Soviet Socialist Republic.
5498 **2182** 5k. multicoloured . . . 15 10

2183 Medal, Workers, Diesel Train and Route Map

2184 Ilyushin Il-86 Jetliner, Rocket, "Soyuz"–"Salyut" Complex and Museum

1984. Completion of Baikal–Amur Railway.
5499 **2183** 5k. multicoloured . . . 30 10

1984. 60th Anniv of M. V. Frunze Central House of Aviation and Cosmonautics, Moscow.
5500 **2184** 5k. multicoloured . . . 15 10

2185 "Girl in Hat" (Jean-Louis Voile)

2186 Mongolian Arms and Flag

1984. French Paintings in Hermitage Museum, Leningrad. Multicoloured.
5501 4k. Type **2185** 15 10
5502 10k. "The Stolen Kiss" (Jean-Honore Fragonard) (horiz) 35 15
5503 20k. "Woman at her Toilette" (Edgar Degas) 70 30
5504 45k. "Pygmalion and Galatea" (Francois Boucher) (horiz) . . . . 1·50 60
5505 50k. "Landscape with Polyphemus" (Nicolas Poussin) (horiz) . . . . 1·75 85
MS5506 144 × 79 mm. 50k. × 2 "Child with Whip" (Pierre-Auguste Renoir) . . . . 5·50 2·00

1984. 60th Anniv of Mongolian People's Republic.
5507 **2186** 5k. multicoloured . . . 15 10

2187 Spassky Tower and Snowflakes

1984. New Year.
5508 **2187** 5k. multicoloured . . . 15 10

2188 Leaf and Urban Landscape

1984. Environmental Protection. Sheet 90 × 65 mm.
MS5509 **2188** 5k. multicoloured 2·10 1·00

2189 Horse-drawn Crew Wagon (19th-century)

1984. Fire Engines (1st series). Multicoloured.
5510 3k. Type **2189** 15 10
5511 5k. 19th-century horse-drawn steam pump . . . 25 10
5512 10k. "Freze" fire engine, 1904 . . . . 45 15
5513 15k. "Lessner" fire engine, 1904 . . . . 75 25
5514 20k. "Russo-Balt" fire engine, 1913 . . . . . . 1·00 35
See also Nos. 5608/12.

2190 Space Observatory and Flight Trajectory

1984. International Venus–Halley's Comet Space Project (1st issue).
5515 **2190** 15k. multicoloured . . 45 20
See also Nos. 5562 and 5630.

2191 Indira Gandhi

2192 Heroes of December Revolution Monument, Moscow

1984. Indira Gandhi (Indian Prime Minister) Commemoration.
5516 **2191** 5k. light brown & brown 30 10

1985. 80th Anniv of 1905 Revolution.
5517 **2192** 5k. multicoloured . . . 15 10

2193 Jubilee Emblem

2194 Frunze

1985. 25th Anniv of Patrice Lumumba University, Moscow.
5518 **2193** 5k. multicoloured . . . 15 10

1985. Birth Centenary of Mikhail Vasilievich Frunze (military strategist).
5519 **2194** 5k. stone, black and blue 15 10

2195 Arms and Industrial Landscape

2196 Ice Hockey Player

1985. 60th Anniv of Karakalpak A.S.S.R.
5520 **2195** 5k. multicoloured . . . 15 10

1985. 10th Friendly Armies Winter Spartakiad.
5521 **2196** 5k. multicoloured . . . 15 10

2197 Dulcimer Player and Title Page

2198 Pioneer Badge

1985. 150th Anniv of "Kalevala" (Karelian poems collected by Elino Lonnrot).
5522 **2197** 5k. brown, blue & black 20 10

1985. 60th Anniv of "Pionerskaya Pravda" (children's newspaper).
5523 **2198** 5k. multicoloured . . . 20 10

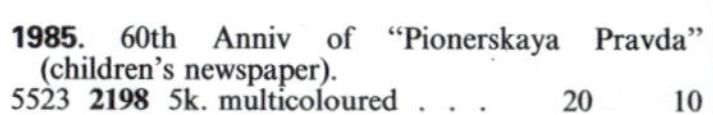

2199 Maria Aleksandrovna Ulyanova

2200 "Young Madonna Praying" (Francisco de Zurbaran)

1985. 150th Birth Anniv of Maria Aleksandrovna Ulyanova (Lenin's mother).
5524 **2199** 5k. black 20 10

1985. Spanish Paintings in Hermitage Museum, Leningrad. Multicoloured.
5525 4k. Type **2200** 15 10
5526 10k. "Still Life" (Antonio Pereda) (horiz) 30 15
5527 20k. "The Immaculate Conception" (Bartolome Esteban Murillo) 65 30
5528 45k. "The Grinder" (Antonio Puga) (horiz) . . 1·50 70
5529 50k. "Count Olivares" (Diego Velazquez) . . . . 1·75 85
MS5530 145 × 80 mm. 50k. × 2 "Antonia Zarate" (Francisco de Goya) . . . . 50 2·00

2201 Cosmonauts and Globe

2203 Hungarian Arms and Budapest

2202 Bach (after Hausman)

1985. "Expo 85" World's Fair, Tsukuba, Japan. Multicoloured.
5531 5k. Type **2201** 15 10
5532 10k. "Molniya-I" communications satellite . . 30 15
5533 20k. Energy sources of the future 65 30
5534 45k. Futuristic city . . . . 1·40 60
MS5535 64 × 85 mm. 50k. Soviet exhibition emblem, globe and tree (36 × 47 mm) . . . . 1·60 70

1985. 300th Birth Anniv of Johann Sebastian Bach (composer). Sheet 65 × 91 mm.
MS5536 **2202** 50k. black . . . . 1·90 70

1985. 40th Anniv of Hungary's Liberation.
5537 **2203** 5k. multicoloured . . . 20 10

2204 Emblem and Text

2206 Young People of Different Races

2205 Cosmonauts, "Soyuz T" Training Model and Gagarin

1985. 60th Anniv of Union of Soviet Societies of Friendship and Cultural Relations with Foreign Countries.
5538 **2204** 15k. multicoloured . . 45 20

1985. Cosmonautics Day. 25th Anniv of Yuri A. Gagarin Cosmonauts Training Centre.
5539 **2205** 15k. multicoloured . . 45 20

1985. 12th World Youth and Students' Festival, Moscow. Multicoloured.
5540 1k. Type **2206** 10 10
5541 3k. Girl with festival emblem in hair 10 10
5542 5k. Rainbow and girl 15 10
5543 20k. Youth holding camera 65 30
5544 45k. Festival emblem . . . 1·50 65

2207 Soviet Memorial, Berlin-Treptow

Всесоюзная филателистическая выставка
„40 лет Великой Победы"
(2209)

2208 Lenin and Paris Flat

1985. 40th Anniv of Victory in Second World War (1st issue). Multicoloured.
5545 5k. Type **2207** 20 15
5546 5k. Partisans 20 15
5547 5k. Lenin, soldier and Moscow Kremlin 20 15
5548 5k. Soldiers and military equipment 20 15
5549 5k. Woman worker, tank, tractor and assembly of Ilyushin Il-2M3 Stormovik fighter 20 15
MS5550 90 × 65 mm. 50k. Order of Patriotic War, Second Class (27 × 39 mm) . . . . 1·60 65

1985. 115th Birth Anniv of Lenin. Multicoloured.
5551 5k. Type **2208** 20 15
5552 5k. Lenin and Lenin Museum, Tampere, Finland 20 15
MS5553 65 × 89 mm. 30k. Lenin (26 × 38 mm) . . . . 1·00 60
See also No. 5555.

1985. "Second World War Victory" Philatelic Exhibition. No. 5545 optd with T **2209**.
5554 **2207** 5k. multicoloured . . . 25 20

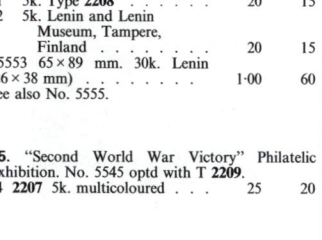

2210 Victory Order (½-size illustration)

1985. 40th Anniv of Victory in Second World War (2nd issue).
5555 **2210** 20k. multicoloured . . 65 35

2211 Czechoslovakian Arms and Prague Buildings

2212 Members' Flags on Shield

1985. 40th Anniv of Czechoslovakia's Liberation.
5556 **2211** 5k. multicoloured . . . 20 10

1985. 30th Anniv of Warsaw Pact Organization.
5557 **2212** 5k. multicoloured . . . 20 10

2213 Sholokhov and Books

2214 Sverdlov

1985. 80th Birth Anniv of Mikhail Aleksandrovich Sholokhov (writer).
5558 **2213** 5k. multicoloured . . . 20 10
5559 – 5k. multicoloured . . . 20 10
5560 – 5k. black, gold and brown 20 10
DESIGNS—As T **2213**. No. 5559, Sholokhov and books (different). 36 × 51 mm: No. 5560, Sholokhov.

1985. Birth Centenary of Ya. M. Sverdlov (Communist Party Leader).
5561 **2214** 5k. brown and red . . 15 10

1985. International Venus–Halley's Comet Space Project (2nd issue). As T **2190**. Multicoloured.
5562 15k. "Vega" space probe and Venus 55 30

2215 Battleship "Potemkin"

1985. 80th Anniv of Mutiny on Battleship "Potemkin".
5563 **2215** 5k. black, red and gold 20 10

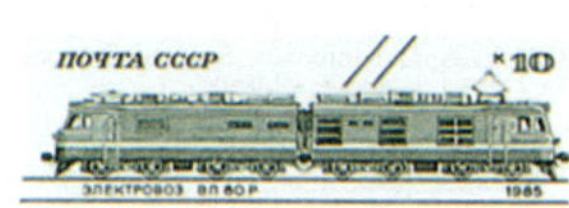
2216 Class VL-80R Electric Locomotive

1985. Locomotives and Rolling Stock.
5564 **2216** 10k. green 55 20
5565 – 10k. brown 55 20
5566 – 10k. blue 55 20
5567 – 10k. brown 55 20
5568 – 10k. blue 55 20
5569 – 10k. blue 55 20
5570 – 10k. brown 55 20
5571 – 10k. green 55 20
DESIGNS: No. 5565, Coal wagon; 5566, Oil tanker wagon; 5567, Goods wagon; 5568, Refrigerated wagon; 5569, Class TEM-2 diesel locomotive; 5570, Type SV passenger carriage; 5571, Mail van.

2217 Camp and Pioneer Badge

1985. 60th Anniv of Artek Pioneer Camp.
5572 **2217** 4k. multicoloured . . . 25 10

2218 Leonid Kizim, Vladimir Solovyov and Oleg Atkov

1985. "237 Days in Space".
5573 **2218** 15k. multicoloured . . 55 20

2219 Youths of different Races

2220 "Beating Swords into Ploughshares" (sculpture) and U.N. Emblem

1985. International Youth Year.
5574 **2219** 10k. multicoloured . . 30 15

1985. 40th Anniv of U.N.O. (1st issue).
5575 **2220** 45k. blue and gold . . 1·40 70
See also No. 5601.

2221 Festival Emblem

1985. 12th World Youth and Students' Festival, Moscow (2nd issue). Sheet 64 × 90 mm.
MS5576 **2221** 30k. multicoloured 1·25 60

2222 Larkspur

2224 Cecilienhof Palace and Flags

2223 V. A. Dzhanibekov, S. E. Savitskaya and I. P. Volk

1985. Plants of Siberia. Multicoloured.
5577 2k. Type **2222** 10 10
5578 3k. "Thermopsis lanceolata" 10 10
5579 5k. Rose 20 10
5580 20k. Cornflower 70 30
5581 45k. Bergenia . . . . 1·40 75

1985. 1st Anniv of First Space-walk by Woman Cosmonaut.
5582 **2223** 10k. multicoloured . . 35 15

1985. 40th Anniv of Potsdam Conference.
5583 **2224** 15k. multicoloured . . 40 20

2225 Finland Palace

2226 Russian and N. Korean Flags and Monument

1985. 10th Anniv of European Security and Co-operation Conference, Helsinki.
5584 **2225** 20k. multicoloured . . 75 25

1985. 40th Anniv of Liberation of Korea.
5585 **2226** 5k. multicoloured . . . 15 10

2227 Pamir Shrew

2228 A. G. Stakhanov and Industrial Scenes

1985. Protected Animals. Multicoloured.
5586 2k. Type **2227** 10 10
5587 3k. Satunin's jerboa (horiz) 10 10
5588 5k. Desert dormouse . . . 15 10
5589 20k. Caracal (47 × 32 mm) 65 30
5590 45k. Goitred gazelle (47 × 32 mm) . . . . . . 1·50 75
MS5591 90 × 65 mm. 50k. Leopard (horiz) . . . . 2·25 70

1985. 50th Anniv of Stakhanov Movement (for high labour productivity).
5592 **2228** 5k. yellow, red and black 15 10

2229 Cup, Football, F.I.F.A. Emblem and Kremlin Tower

2230 Chess Pieces

1985. World Junior Football Championship, Moscow.
5593 **2229** 5k. multicoloured . . . 20 10

1985. World Chess Championship Final between Anatoly Karpov and Gary Kasparov.
5594 **2230** 10k. multicoloured . . 55 20

2231 Vietnam State Emblem

2232 Immortality Monument and Buildings

1985. 40th Anniv of Vietnamese Independence.
5595 **2231** 5k. multicoloured . . . 15 10

1985. Millenary of Bryansk.
5596 **2232** 5k. multicoloured . . . 15 10

2233 Title Page

1985. 800th Anniv of "Song of Igor's Campaigns".
5597 **2233** 10k. multicoloured . . 35 15

2234 Lutsk Castle

2235 Gerasimov

1985. 900th Anniv of Lutsk.
5598 **2234** 5k. multicoloured . . . 15 10

1985. Birth Centenary of Sergei Vasilievich Gerasimov (artist).
5599 **2235** 5k. multicoloured . . . 15 10

2236 Globe, Cruiser "Aurora" and 1917

2237 Headquarters, New York, and Flag

1985. 68th Anniv of October Revolution.
5600 **2236** 5k. multicoloured . . . 20 10

1985. 40th Anniv of U.N.O. (2nd issue).
5601 **2237** 15k. green, blue and black 45 20

2238 Krisjanis Barons

1985. 150th Birth Anniv of Krisjanis Barons (writer).
5602 **2238** 5k. black and brown . . 15 10

2239 Lenin and Worker breaking Chains

1985. 90th Anniv of Petersburg Union of Struggle for Liberating the Working Class.
5603 **2239** 5k. multicoloured . . . 15 10

2240 Telescope

1985. 10th Anniv of World's Largest Telescope.
5604 **2240** 10k. blue 30 15

2241 Angolan Arms and Flag

2242 Yugoslav Arms, Flag and Parliament Building

1985. 10th Anniv of Independence of Angola.
5605 **2241** 5k. multicoloured . . . 15 10

1985. 40th Anniv of Federal People's Republic of Yugoslavia.
5606 **2242** 5k. multicoloured . . . 15 10

2243 Troitsky Tower and Palace of Congresses

2244 Samantha Smith

1985. New Year.
5607 **2243** 5k. multicoloured . . . 15 10

1985. Fire Engines (2nd series). As T **2189**. Mult.
5608 3k. "AMO-F15", 1926 . . . 15 10
5609 5k. "PMZ-1", 1933 . . . . 25 10
5610 10k. "ATs-40", 1977 . . . . 45 15
5611 20k. "AL-30" with automatic ladder, 1970 . . 80 30
5612 45k. "AA-60", 1978 . . . . 1·60 60

1985. Samantha Smith (American schoolgirl peace campaigner) Commemoration.
5613 **2244** 5k. brown, blue and red 35 10

2245 N. M. Emanuel

2246 Family and Places of Entertainment

1985. Academician N. M. Emanuel (chemist) Commemoration.
5614 **2245** 5k. multicoloured . . . 15 10

1985. Anti-alcoholism Campaign. Multicoloured.
5615 5k. Type **2246** 20 10
5616 5k. Sports centre and family 20 10

2247 Emblem

2248 Banners and Kremlin Palace of Congresses

1986. International Peace Year.
5617 **2247** 20k. blue, green & silver 55 25

1986. 27th Soviet Communist Party Congress.
5618 **2248** 5k. multicoloured . . . 15 10
5619 – 20k. multicoloured . . 55 25
MS5620 95 × 65 mm. 50k. red, gold and black . . . . 1·50 65
DESIGNS—36 × 51 mm: 20k. Palace of Congresses, Spassky Tower and Lenin. 27 × 39 mm—50k. Lenin (after sculpture by N. Andreev).

2249 1896 Olympics Medal

2250 Tulips

1986. 90th Anniv of First Modern Olympic Games.
5621 **2249** 15k. multicoloured . . 45 20

1986. Plants of Russian Steppes. Multicoloured.
5622 4k. Type **2250** 15 10
5623 5k. Grass (horiz) 20 10
5624 10k. Iris 35 15
5625 15k. Violets 55 25
5626 20k. Cornflower 70 30

2251 Voronezh and Arms

2252 Bela Kun

1986. 400th Anniv of Voronezh.
5627 **2251** 5k. multicoloured . . . 15 10

1986. Birth Centenary of Bela Kun (Hungarian Communist Party leader).
5628 **2252** 10k. blue 25 15

2253 Pozela

2255 Crimson-spotted Moth

2254 "Vega 1" and Halley's Comet

1986. 90th Birth Anniv of Karolis Pozela (founder of Lithuanian Communist Party).

5629 **2253** 5k. grey 15 10

1986. International Venus–Halley's Comet Space Project (3rd issue). As T **2190**. Multicoloured.

5630 15k. "Vega 1" and Halley's Comet 50 20
MS5631 65 × 91 mm. 50k. Type **2254** (different) . . . . 1·75 75

1986. Butterflies and Moths listed in U.S.S.R. Red Book (1st series). Multicoloured.

5632 4k. Type **2255** 15 10
5633 5k. Eastern festoon 20 10
5634 10k. Sooty orange-tip . . . 45 15
5635 15k. Dark crimson underwing 75 25
5636 20k. "Satyrus bischoffi" . . 95 40
See also Nos. 5726/30.

2256 Globe and Model of Space Complex

2257 Kirov

1986. "Expo '86" World's Fair, Vancouver.

5637 **2256** 20k. multicoloured . . 60 30

1986. Birth Centenary of S. M. Kirov (Communist Party Secretary).

5638 **2257** 5k. black 15 10

2258 Tsiolkovsky

1986. Cosmonautics Day. Multicoloured.

5639 5k. Type **2258** 15 10
5640 10k. Sergei Pavlovich Korolev (rocket designer) and "Vostok" rocket (vert) 30 15
5641 15k. Yuri Gagarin, "Vega", sputnik and globe (25th anniv of first man in space) 55 25

2259 Ice Hockey Player

2260 Thalmann

1986. World Ice Hockey Championship, Moscow.

5642 **2259** 15k. multicoloured . . 50 20

1986. Birth Centenary of Ernst Thalmann (German politician).

5643 **2260** 10k. brown 30 15

2261 Lenin Museum, Leipzig

1986. 116th Birth Anniv of Lenin.

5645 **2261** 5k. multicoloured . . . 15 10
5646 – 5k. olive, brown & black 15 10
5647 – 5k. multicoloured . . . 15 10

DESIGNS: No. 5646, Lenin (after P. Belousov) and Lenin Museum, Prague; 5647, Lenin Museum, Poronine, Poland.

2262 Tambov and Arms

1986. 350th Anniv of Tambov.

5648 **2262** 5k. multicoloured . . . 15 10

2263 Dove with Olive Branch and Globe

2264 Emblem and Cyclists

1986. 25th Anniv of Soviet Peace Fund.

5649 **2263** 10k. multicoloured . . 35 20

1986. 39th Peace Cycle Race.

5650 **2264** 10k. multicoloured . . 30 15

2265 Death Cap

2266 Globe and Wildlife

1986. Fungi. Multicoloured.

5651 4k. Type **2265** 15 10
5652 5k. Fly agaric 25 10
5653 10k. Panther cap 45 15
5654 15k. Bitter bolete 75 25
5655 20k. Clustered woodlover . . 95 45

1986. UNESCO Man and Biosphere Programme.

5656 **2266** 10k. multicoloured . . 35 15

2267 Torch and Runner

2268 Kuibyshev

1986. 9th People's Spartakiad.

5657 **2267** 10k. multicoloured . . 35 15

1986. 400th Anniv of Kuibyshev (formerly Samara).

5658 **2268** 5k. multicoloured 15 10

No. 5658 depicts the Lenin Museum, Eternal Glory and V. I. Chapaev monuments and Gorky State Theatre.

2269 Ostankino T.V. Tower

2270 Footballers

1986. "Communication 86" International Exhibition, Moscow.

5659 **2269** 5k. multicoloured . . . 15 10

1986. World Cup Football Championship, Mexico. Multicoloured.

5660 5k. Type **2270** 20 10
5661 10k. Footballers (different) 40 15
5662 15k. Championship medal 50 20

2271 "Lane in Albano" (M. I. Lebedev)

2272 Arms and City

1986. Russian Paintings in Tretyakov Gallery, Moscow. Multicoloured.

5663 4k. Type **2271** 15 10
5664 5k. "View of the Kremlin in foul Weather" (A. K. Savrasov) (horiz) 20 10
5665 10k. "Sunlit Pine Trees" (I. I. Shishkin) 30 15
5666 15k. "Journey Back" (A. E. Arkhipov) (69 × 33 mm) 50 25
5667 45k. "Wedding Procession in Moscow" (A. P. Ryabushkin) (69 × 33 mm) 1·50 70

1986. 300th Anniv of Irkutsk City Status.

5668 **2272** 5k. multicoloured . . . 15 10

2273 World Map, Stadium and Runners

2274 Globe, Punched Tape and Keyboard

1986. International Goodwill Games, Moscow.

5669 **2273** 10k. blue, brown & black 35 15

1986. UNESCO Programmes in U.S.S.R. Mult.

5671 5k. Type **2274** 20 10
5672 10k. Landscape and geological section (geological correlation) . . 35 15
5673 15k. Oceanographic research vessel, albatross and ocean (Inter-governmental Oceanographic Commission) 55 30
5674 35k. Fluvial drainage (International Hydrological Programme) 1·00 55

2275 Arms and Town Buildings

1986. 400th Anniv of Tyumen, Siberia.

5675 **2275** 5k. multicoloured . . . 15 10

2276 Olof Palme

2277 Hands, Ball and Basket

1986. Olof Palme (Swedish Prime Minister) Commemoration.

5676 **2276** 10k. blue, black & brn 35 15

1986. 10th Women's Basketball Championship.

5677 **2277** 15k. brown, black & red 45 20

2278 "Ural-375D"

1986. Lorries. Multicoloured.

5678 4k. Type **2278** 15 10
5679 5k. "GAZ-53A" 20 10
5680 10k. "KrAZ-256B" 35 15
5681 15k. "MAZ-515B" 55 25
5682 20k. "ZIL-133GYa" 70 35

2279 Lenin Peak

1986. U.S.S.R. Sports Committee's International Mountaineers' Camps (1st series). Multicoloured.

5683 4k. Type **2279** 15 10
5684 5k. E. Korzhenevskaya Peak 20 10
5685 10k. Belukha Peak 30 15
5686 15k. Communism Peak . . 55 25
5687 30k. Elbrus Peak 95 55
See also Nos. 5732/5.

2280 Globe and "Red Book"

1986. Environmental Protection. Sheet 60 × 90 mm.

MS5688 **2280** 50k. multicoloured 1·60 75

2281 Lenin Monument and Drama Theatre

2282 "Mukran", Maps and Flags

1986. 250th Anniv of Chelyabinsk City.

5689 **2281** 5k. multicoloured . . . 15 10

1986. Opening of Mukran (East Germany)–Klaipeda (U.S.S.R.) Railway Ferry.

5690 **2282** 15k. multicoloured . . 75 25

2283 Victory Monument and Buildings

2284 Lenin Monument and Moscow Kremlin

1986. 750th Anniv of Siauliai, Lithuania.

5691 **2283** 5k. buff, brown and red 15 10

1986. 69th Anniv of October Revolution.

5692 **2284** 5k. multicoloured . . . 30 15

2285 Ice-breaker "Vladivostok", Mil Mi-4 Helicopter, Satellite and Map

15.III–26.VII.1985
Дрейф во льдах Антарктики
(2286)

1986. Antarctic Drift of "Mikhail Somov" (research vessel). (a) As Type **2285**.
5693 5k. blue, black and red . . 25 10
5694 10k. multicoloured 50 20
MS5695 70 × 90 mm. 50k. ultramarine and black . . . . 2·00 1·60
(b) No. 5055 optd with T **2286**.
5696 4k. multicoloured 20 10
DESIGN—As T **2285**: 10k. Map and "Mikhail Somov". 51 × 36 mm—"Mikhail Somov" icebound.
Nos. 5693/4 were printed together, se-tenant, forming a composite design.

2287 Class Eu No. 684–37, Slavyansk

1986. Steam Locomotive as Monuments. Mult.
5697 4k. Type **2287** 20 10
5698 5k. Class FD No. 3000, Novosibirsk 20 10
5699 10k. Class Ov No. 5109, Volgograd 40 15
5700 20k. Class SO No. 17-1613, Dnepropetrovsk 75 30
5701 30k. Class FDp No. 20-578, Kiev . . . . 1·25 50

2288 G. K. Ordzhonikidze **2289** Novikov and Score

1986. Birth Centenary of Grigory Konstantinovich Ordzhonikidze (revolutionary).
5702 **2288** 5k. grey 15 10

1986. 90th Birth Anniv of Anatoli Novikov (composer).
5703 **2289** 5k. brown 20 10

2290 U.N. and UNESCO Emblem **2291** Sun Yat-sen

1986. 40th Anniv of UNESCO.
5704 **2290** 10k. silver and blue . . 35 15

1986. 120th Birth Anniv of Sun Yat-sen (first President of Chinese Republic).
5705 **2291** 5k. black and grey . . 15 10

2292 Lomonosov

1986. 275th Birth Anniv of Mikhail Vasilievich Lomonosov (scientist).
5706 **2292** 5k. brown 20 10

2293 Ya-1, 1927

1986. Sports Aircraft designed by Aleksandr Yakovlev. Multicoloured.
5707 4k. Type **2293** 15 10
5708 5k. VT-2 trainer, 1935 . . . 15 10
5709 10k. Yak-18, 1946 . . . . . 35 15
5710 20k. Yak-50, 1972 . . . . . 75 30
5711 30k. Yak-55, 1981 . . . . . 1·10 50

2294 Spassky, Senate and Nikolsky Towers, Kremlin **2295** Computer and Terminal

1986. New Year.
5712 **2294** 5k. multicoloured . . . 15 10

1986. Resolutions of 27th Communist Party Congress. Multicoloured.
5713 5k. Type **2295** (scientific and technical progress) 20 10
5714 5k. Construction engineer and building project . . . 20 10
5715 5k. City (welfare of people) 20 10
5716 5k. Peace demonstration at Council for Mutual Economic Aid building (peace) 20 10
5717 5k. Spassky Tower and Kremlin Palace, Moscow Kremlin (unity of party and people) 20 10

2296 Parkhomenko **2297** Machel

1986. Birth Centenary of Aleksandr Parkhomenko (revolutionary).
5718 **2296** 5k. black 15 10

1986. Samora Moizes Machel (President of Mozambique) Commemoration.
5719 **2297** 5k. brown and black . . 20 10

2298 Russian State Museum (Mikhailovsky Palace)

1986. Palace Museums of Leningrad.
5720 **2298** 5k. brown and green . . 20 15
5721 – 10k. green and blue . . 30 15
5722 – 15k. blue and green . . 50 20
5723 – 20k. green and brown 60 30
5724 – 50k. brown and blue . . 1·50 70
DESIGNS: 10k. Hermitage Museum (Winter Palace); 15k. Grand Palace Museum (Petrodvorets); 20k. Catherine Palace Museum (Pushkin); 50k. Palace Museum (Pavlovsk).

2299 Couple and Industrial Landscape **2300** Chinese Windmill

1987. 18th Soviet Trades Union Congress, Moscow.
5725 **2299** 5k. multicoloured . . . 15 10

1987. Butterflies listed in U.S.S.R. Red Book (2nd series). Multicoloured.
5726 4k. Type **2300** 20 10
5727 5k. Swallowtail 20 10
5728 10k. Southern swallowtail 35 15
5729 15k. "Papilio maackii" . . . 60 25
5730 30k. Scare swallowtail . . . 95 55

2301 Karlis Miesnieks **2302** Stasys Simkus

1987. Birth Centenary of Karlis Miesnieks (Latvian artist).
5731 **2301** 5k. multicoloured . . . 15 10

1987. U.S.S.R. Sports Committee's International Mountaineers' Camps (2nd series). As T **2279**. Multicoloured.
5732 4k. Chimbulak Gorge . . . 15 10
5733 10k. Shavla Gorge 30 15
5734 20k. Donguz-Orun and Nakra-Tau, Caucasus . . 70 30
5735 35k. Kazbek, Caucasus . . 1·25 60

1987. Birth Centenary of Stasys Simkus (Lithuanian composer).
5736 **2302** 5k. purple and yellow 20 10

2303 V. I. Chapaev **2304** Lenin

1987. Birth Cent of Vasily Ivanovich Chapaev (revolutionary).
5737 **2303** 5k. brown 15 10

1987. 20th Leninist Young Communist League (Komsomol) Congress, Moscow. Multicoloured.
5738 5k. Type **2304** 15 10
MS5739 60 × 85 mm. 50k. Emblem, laurel branch, banner and decoration ribbons (23 × 32 mm) 1·75 75

2305 Heino Eller **2306** Orbeli

1987. Birth Centenary of Heino Eller (Estonian composer).
5740 **2305** 5k. light brown & brown 20 10

1987. Birth Centenary of Academician Iosif Abgarovich Orbeli (first President of Armenian Academy of Sciences).
5741 **2306** 5k. brown and pink . . 15 10

2307 Bears in and out of Water

1987. Polar Bears. Multicoloured.
5742 5k. Type **2307** 20 10
5743 10k. Mother and cubs . . . 40 15
5744 20k. Mother and cubs (different) 75 30
5745 35k. Bears . . . . 1·25 55

2308 "Sputnik 1" and Globe **2309** Emblem and Headquarters, Bangkok

1987. Cosmonautics Day. Multicoloured.
5746 10k. Type **2308** (30th anniv of launching of first artificial satellite) 35 15
5747 10k. "Vostok-3", "Vostok-4" and globe (25th anniv of first group space flight) 35 15
5748 10k. "Mars-1" and globe (25th anniv of launching of automatic interplanetary station) . . 35 15

1987. 40th Anniv of U.N. Economic and Social Commission for Asia and the Pacific Ocean.
5749 **2309** 10k. multicoloured . . 35 15

2310 "Birthday" (N. A. Sysoev)

1987. 117th Birth Anniv of Lenin. Multicoloured.
5750 5k. Type **2310** 15 10
5751 5k. "V. I. Lenin with Delegates to the Third Congress of the Young Communist League" (P. P. Belousov) 15 10
MS5752 130 × 67 mm. 10k. "Lenin's Underground Activity" (D. A. Nalnabdyan) (39 × 27 mm); 20k. "Lenin" (N. Andreev) (39 × 55 mm); 10k. "We'll Show the Earth a New Way" (A. G. Lysenko) (39 × 27 mm); 10k. "Before the Assault" (S. P. Viktorov) (39 × 27 mm); 10k. "Lenin in Smolny, October 1917" (M. G. Sokolov) (39 × 27 mm) 1·75 75

2311 Gymnast on Rings **2312** Cyclists and "40"

1987. European Gymnastics Championships, Moscow.
5753 **2311** 10k. multicoloured . . 30 15

1987. 40th Peace Cycle Race.
5754 **2312** 10k. multicoloured . . 40 15

2313 Menzbir's Marmot **2315** "Portrait of a Woman" (Lucas Cranach the Elder)

2314 "Maksim Gorky"

1987. Mammals listed in U.S.S.R. Red Book. Multicoloured.
5755 5k. Type **2313** 20 10
5756 10k. Ratel (horiz) 35 15
5757 15k. Snow leopard (32 × 47 mm) 70 25

1987. River Tourist Ships. Multicoloured.
5758 5k. Type **2314** 25 10
5759 10k. "Aleksandr Pushkin" 40 15
5760 30k. "Sovetsky Soyuz" . . . 1·00 45

1987. West European Art in Hermitage Museum, Leningrad. Multicoloured.
5761 4k. Type **2315** 15 10
5762 5k. "St. Sebastian" (Titian) 15 10
5763 10k. "Justice" (drawing, Albrecht Durer) 30 15

5764 30k. "Adoration of the Magi" (Peter Breughel the younger) (horiz) . . . . . 1·00 45
5765 50k. "Statue of Ceres" (Peter Paul Rubens) . . . 1·75 80

2316 Car Production Line and Lenin Hydro-electric Power Station

2317 Pushkin (after T. Rait)

1987. 250th Anniv of Togliatti (formerly Stavropol).
5766 **2316** 5k. multicoloured . . . 15 10

1987. 150th Death Anniv of Aleksandr S. Pushkin (poet).
5767 **2317** 5k. deep brown, yellow and brown 15 10

2318 Kovpak

2319 Congress Emblem

1987. Birth Centenary of Major-General Sidor Artemevich Kovpak.
5768 **2318** 5k. black 15 10

1987. World Women's Congress, Moscow.
5769 **2319** 10k. multicoloured . . 35 15

2320 Arms, Kremlin, Docks, Drama Theatre and Yermak Monument

2321 Party Flag and Mozambican

1987. 400th Anniv of Tobolsk, Siberia.
5770 **2320** 5k. multicoloured . . . 15 10

1987. 25th Anniv of Mozambique Liberation Front (FRELIMO) (5771) and 10th Anniv of U.S.S.R.–Mozambique Friendship and Co-operation Treaty (5772). Multicoloured.
5771 5k. Type **2321** 15 10
5772 5k. Mozambique and U.S.S.R. flags 15 10

2322 "Scolopendrium vulgare"

2323 Moscow Kremlin and Indian Coin

1987. Ferns. Multicoloured.
5773 4k. Type **2322** 15 10
5774 5k. "Ceterach officinarum" 20 10
5775 10k. "Salvinia natans" (horiz) 35 15
5776 15k. "Matteuccia struthiopteris" 55 25
5777 50k. "Adiantum pedatum" 1·50 70

1987. Indian Festival in U.S.S.R. (5778) and U.S.S.R. Festival in India (5779). Multicoloured.
5778 5k. Type **2323** 15 10
5779 5k. Hammer, sickle, open book, satellite and Red Fort, Delhi 15 10

2324 Rossiya Hotel (venue), Globe and Film

2325 Cosmonauts training

1987. 15th International Film Festival, Moscow.
5780 **2324** 10k. multicoloured . . 35 15

1987. Soviet–Syrian Space Flight. Multicoloured.
5781 5k. Type **2325** 20 10
5782 10k. Moscow–Damascus satellite link and cosmonauts watching television screen 35 15
5783 15k. Cosmonauts at Gagarin monument, Zvezdny . . . 55 25
MS5784 90 × 62 mm. 50k. "Mir" space station (36 × 25 mm) 1·90 75

2326 Emblem and Vienna Headquarters

1987. 30th Anniv of Int Atomic Energy Agency.
5785 **2326** 20k. multicoloured . . 70 30

2327 14th–16th Century Messenger

1987. Russian Postal History.
5786 **2327** 4k. black and brown . . 15 10
5787 – 5k. black and brown . . 20 10
5788 – 10k. black and brown 35 15
5789 – 30k. black and brown 1·40 45
5790 – 35k. black and brown 3·00 50
MS5791 95 × 70 mm. 50k. black and yellow . . . . 1·90 75
DESIGNS: 5k. 17th–19th century horse-drawn sledge and 17th-century postman; 10k. 16th-century and 18th-century sailing packets; 30k. 19th-century railway mail vans; 35k. 1905 post car and 1926 "AMO-F-15" van; 50k. Mailvans in front of Moscow Head Post Office.

2328 "V. I. Lenin" (P. V. Vasilev)

1987. 70th Anniv of October Revolution. Mult.
5792 5k. Type **2328** 20 10
5793 5k. "V. I. Lenin proclaims Soviet Power" (V. A. Serov) 20 10
5794 5k. "Long Live the Socialist Revolution!" (V. V. Kuznetsov) 20 10
5795 5k. "Storming the Winter Palace" (V. A. Serov) (69 × 32 mm) 20 10
5796 5k. "On the Eve of the Storm" (portraying Lenin, Sverdlov and Podvoisky) (V. V. Pimenov) (69 × 32 mm) 20 10
MS5797 87 × 73 mm. 30k. (black and gold) "Lenin" (statue, V. V. Kozlov) (vert) . . . . 1·10 50

2329 Anniversary Emblem

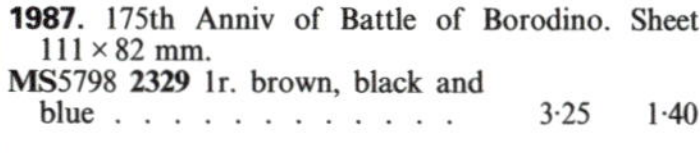

1987. 175th Anniv of Battle of Borodino. Sheet 111 × 82 mm.
MS5798 **2329** 1r. brown, black and blue . . . . 3·25 1·40

2330 Postyshev

2331 Yuri Dolgoruky (founder) Monument

1987. Birth Centenary of Pavel Petrovich Postyshev (revolutionary).
5799 **2330** 5k. blue 15 10

1987. 840th Anniv of Moscow.
5800 **2331** 5k. brown, yell & orge 15 10

2332 Ulugh Beg (astronomer and mathematician)

1987. Scientists.
5801 **2332** 5k. multicoloured . . . 20 15
5802 – 5k. black, green and blue 20 15
5803 – 5k. deep brown, brown and blue 20 15
DESIGNS: No. 5801, Type **2332** (550th anniv of "New Astronomical Tables"); 5802, Isaac Newton (300th anniv of "Principia Mathematica"); 5803, Marie Curie (120th birth anniv).

2333 KOSPAS Satellite

1987. 5th Anniv of KOSPAS–SARSAT (international satellite air/sea search system). Sheet 62 × 80 mm.
MS5804 **2333** 50k. multicoloured 1·90 1·00

Всесоюзная
филателистическая выставка
„70 лет Великого Октября"
(2334)

1987. "70th Anniv of October Revolution" All-Union Stamp Exhibition. No. 5795 optd with T **2334**.
5805 5k. multicoloured 25 20

2335 "There will be Cities in the Taiga" (A. A. Yakovlev)

2336 Reed

1987. Soviet Paintings of the 1980s. Multicoloured.
5806 4k. Type **2335** 15 10
5807 5k. "Mother" (V. V. Shcherbakov) 15 10
5808 10k. "My Quiet Homeland" (V. M. Sidorov) (horiz) 30 15
5809 30k. "In Yakutsk, Land of Pyotr Alekseev" (A. N. Osipov) (horiz) 90 40
5810 35k. "Ivan's Return" (V. I. Yerofeev) (horiz) . . . . 1·00 50
MS5811 92 × 78 mm. 50k. "Sun over Red Square" (P. P. Ossovsky) 1·75 75

1987. Birth Centenary of John Reed (American journalist and founder of U.S. Communist Party).
5812 **2336** 10k. brown, yell & blk 30 15

2337 Marshak

1987. Birth Centenary of Samuil Yakovlevich Marshak (poet).
5813 **2337** 5k. brown 15 10

2338 Chavchavadze

1987. 150th Anniv of Ilya Grigoryevich Chavchavadze (writer).
5814 **2338** 5k. blue 15 10

2339 Indira Gandhi

2340 Vadim N. Podbelsky (revolutionary)

1987. 70th Birth Anniv of Indira Gandhi (Indian Prime Minister, 1966–77 and 1980–84).
5815 **2339** 5k. brown and black . . 20 10

1987. Birth Centenaries.
5816 **2340** 5k. black 15 10
5817 – 5k. blue 15 10
DESIGN: No. 5817, Academician Nikolai Ivanovich Vavilov (geneticist).

2341 Tokamak Thermonuclear System

2342 Bagramyan

1987. Science.
5818 **2341** 5k. brown and grey . . 20 10
5819 – 10k. green, blue and black 35 15
5820 – 20k. black, stone and drab 60 30
DESIGNS: 10k. Kola borehole; 20k. "Ratan-600" radio telescope.

1987. 90th Birth Anniv of Marshal Ivan Khristoforovich Bagramyan.
5821 **2342** 5k. brown 15 10

2343 Moscow Kremlin

2344 Flags, Spassky Tower, Moscow, and Capitol, Washington

1987. New Year.
5822 **2343** 5k. multicoloured . . . 15 10

1987. Soviet–American Intermediate and Short-range Nuclear Weapons Treaty.
5823 **2344** 10k. multicoloured . . 30 15

2345 Grigori Andreevich Spiridov and "Tri Svyatitelya"

1987. Russian Naval Commanders (1st series).
5824 **2345** 4k. blue and deep blue 15 10
5825 – 5k. purple and blue . . 20 10
5826 – 10k. purple and blue . . 35 15
5827 – 25k. blue and deep blue 85 35
5828 – 30k. blue and deep blue 95 45
DESIGNS: 5k. Fyodor Fyodorovich Ushakov and "Sv. Pavel"; 10k. Dmitri Nikolaevich Senyavin, Battle of Afon and "Tverdyi" (battleship); 25k. Mikhail Petrovich Lazarev and "Azov"; 30k. Pavel Stepanovich Nakhimov and "Imperatritsa Maria".
See also Nos. 6091/6.

2346 Torch

2347 Biathlon

1987. 30th Anniv of Asia–Africa Solidarity Organization.
5829 **2346** 10k. multicoloured . . 25 15

1988. Winter Olympic Games, Calgary. Mult.
5830 5k. Type **2347** 20 10
5831 10k. Cross-country skiing 35 15
5832 15k. Slalom 45 25
5833 20k. Figure skating (pairs) 65 30
5834 30k. Ski jumping . . . . 1·10 45
MS5835 62 × 80 mm. 50k. Ice hockey (horiz) . . . . 1·90 75

2348 1918 Stamps

2349 Emblem

1988. 70th Anniv of First Soviet Postage Stamps.
5836 **2348** 10k. blue, brown and gold 35 15
5837 10k. brown, blue and gold 35 15
On No. 5836 the lower stamp depicted is the 35k. in blue, on No. 5837 the lower stamp is the 70k. in brown.

1988. 40th Anniv of W.H.O.
5838 **2349** 35k. gold, blue and black . . . . 1·00 40

2350 Byron

1988. Birth Bicentenary of Lord Byron (English poet).
5839 **2350** 15k. black, green and blue 45 25

2351 Exchange Activities and National Flags

2352 Lomov-Oppokov

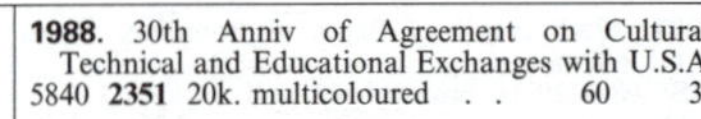
1988. 30th Anniv of Agreement on Cultural, Technical and Educational Exchanges with U.S.A.
5840 **2351** 20k. multicoloured . . 60 30

1988. Birth Centenary of Georgy Ippolitovich Lomov-Oppokov (Communist party official).
5841 **2352** 5k. black and brown . . 15 10

2353 "Little Humpbacked Horse" (dir. I. Ivanov-Vano, animated L. Milchin)

1988. Soviet Cartoon Films. Multicoloured.
5842 1k. Type **2353** 10 10
5843 3k. "Winnie the Pooh" (dir. F. Khitruk, animated V. Zuikov and E. Nazarov) 10 10
5844 4k. "Gena the Crocodile" (dir. R. Kachanov, animated L. Shartsmann) 15 10
5845 5k. "Just You Wait!" (dir. V. Kotyonochkin, animated S. Rusakov) . . 25 15
5846 10k. "Hedgehog in a Mist" (dir. Yu. Norshtein, animated F. Yarbusova) 45 25
MS5847 95 × 75 mm. 30k. Cover and stamps ("The Post" dir. M. Tsekhanovsky) . . . . . . 1·25 50

2354 Bonch-Bruevich

2355 Nurse and Emblems

1988. Birth Centenary of Mikhail Alexandrovich Bonch-Bruevich (radio engineer).
5848 **2354** 10k. black and brown 30 15

1988. 125th Anniv of International Red Cross and Red Crescent.
5849 **2355** 15k. black, blue and red 45 25

2356 Skater

1988. World Speed Skating Championships, Alma-Ata.
5850 **2356** 15k. blue, violet and black 45 25

2357 Makarenko

1988. Birth Centenary of Anton Semenovich Makarenko (educationist and writer).
5851 **2357** 10k. green 30 15

2358 Skorina

2359 Banners and Globe

1988. 500th Birth Anniv of Frantsisk Skorina (printer).
5852 **2358** 5k. black 15 10

1988. Labour Day.
5853 **2359** 5k. multicoloured . . . 15 10

2360 Kingisepp

2361 Track and Athlete

1988. Birth Centenary of Victor Eduardovich Kingisepp (revolutionary).
5854 **2360** 5k. green 15 10

1988. Centenary of Russian Athletics.
5855 **2361** 15k. multicoloured . . 45 25

2362 M. S. Shaginyan

1988. Birth Centenary of Marietta Sergeevna Shaginyan (writer).
5856 **2362** 10k. brown 30 10

2363 Palace of Congresses, Moscow, Finlandia Hall, Helsinki, and National Flags

2364 "Mir"–"Soyuz TM" Space Complex and "Progress" Spacecraft

1988. 40th Anniv of U.S.S.R.–Finland Friendship Treaty.
5857 **2363** 15k. multicoloured . . 45 25

1988. Cosmonautics Day.
5858 **2364** 15k. multicoloured . . 45 25

2365 Sochi

1988. 150th Anniv of Sochi.
5859 **2365** 5k. multicoloured . . . 25 10

2366 "Victory" (P. A. Krivonogov)

1988. V. E. Day.
5860 **2366** 5k. multicoloured . . . 15 10

2367 Lenin Museum, Moscow

1988. 118th Birth Anniv of Lenin. Designs showing branches of Lenin Central Museum.
5861 **2367** 5k. brown, deep brown and gold 15 10
5862 – 5k. red, purple and gold 15 10
5863 – 5k. ochre, brown & gold 15 10
5864 – 5k. yellow, green & gold 15 10
DESIGNS: No. 5862, Kiev; 5863, Leningrad; 5864, Krasnoyarsk.
See also Nos. 5990/2 and 6131/3.

2368 Akulov

2369 Soviet Display Emblem

1988. Birth Centenary of Ivan Alekseevich Akulov (Communist Party official).
5865 **2368** 5k. blue 15 10

1988. "Expo 88" World's Fair, Brisbane.
5866 **2369** 20k. multicoloured . . 60 30

2370 Marx

1988. 170th Birth Anniv of Karl Marx.
5867 **2370** 5k. brown 15 10

2371 Soldiers and Workers

1988. Perestroika (Reformation).
5868 **2371** 5k. multicoloured . . . 15 10
5869 – 5k. brown, red & orange 15 10
DESIGN: No. 5869, Banner, industrial scenes and worker.

Спортсмены СССР завоевали
11 золотых, 9 серебряных
и 9 бронзовых медалей!
(2372)

1988. Winter Olympic Games Soviet Medal Winners. No. **MS**5835 optd with T **2372**.
MS5870 62 × 80 mm. 50k. multicoloured . . . . 1·75 1·00

2373 Shvernik

1988. Birth Centenary of Nikolai Mikhailovich Shvernik (politician).
5871 **2373** 5k. black 15 10

2374 Russian Borzoi

1988. Hunting Dogs. Multicoloured.
5872 5k. Type **2374** 20 10
5873 10k. Kirgiz borzoi 30 25
5874 15k. Russian hound 45 25

5875 20k. Russian spaniel 60 30
5876 35k. East Siberian husky . . 1·25 50

2375 Flags, Spassky Tower and Handshake

2376 Kuibyshev

1988. Soviet–American Summit, Moscow.
5877 **2375** 5k. multicoloured . . . 15 10

1988. Birth Centenary of Valerian Vladimirovich Kuibyshev (politician).
5878 **2376** 5k. brown 15 10

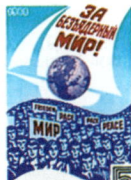

2377 Flags, "Mir" Space Station and "Soyuz TM" Spacecraft

2378 Crowd and Peace Banners

1988. Soviet–Bulgarian Space Flight.
5879 **2377** 15k. multicoloured . . 50 25

1988. "For a Nuclear-free World".
5880 **2378** 5k. multicoloured . . . 15 10

2379 Red Flag, Hammer and Sickle and Laurel Branch

2380 Flags, Skis and Globe

1988. 19th Soviet Communist Party Conference, Moscow (1st issue). Multicoloured.
5881 5k. Type **2379** 15 10
5882 5k. Lenin on red flag and interior of Palace of Congresses (35 × 23 mm) 15 10
MS5883 100 × 65 mm. 50k. Palace of Congresses and Spassky Tower, Moscow, Kremlin (50 × 36 mm) 1·60 1·00
See also Nos. 5960/2.

1988. Soviet–Canadian Transarctic Ski Expedition.
5884 **2380** 35k. multicoloured . . 1·25 50

2381 Hurdling

2382 Giant Bellflower

1988. Olympic Games, Seoul. Multicoloured.
5885 5k. Type **2381** 20 10
5886 10k. Long jumping 30 15
5887 15k. Basketball 45 25
5888 20k. Gymnastics 60 30
5889 30k. Swimming 95 45
MS5890 80 × 65 mm. 50k. Football 1·75 1·00

1988. Deciduous Forest Flowers. Multicoloured.
5891 5k. Type **2382** 20 10
5892 10k. Spring pea (horiz) . . . 30 15
5893 15k. Lungwort 45 25
5894 20k. Turk's cap lily 60 30
5895 35k. "Ficaria verna" . . . . 1·40 50

2383 Phobos and "Phobos" Space Probe

2384 Komsomol Badge

1988. Phobos (Mars Moon) International Space Project.
5896 **2383** 10k. multicoloured . . 30 15

1988. 70th Anniv of Leninist Young Communist League (Komsomol).
5897 **2384** 5k. multicoloured . . . 15 10

2385 Mandela

Филвыставка. Москва (2387)

2386 "Obeyan Serebryanyi, Light Grey Arab Stallion" (N. E. Sverchkov)

1988. 70th Birthday of Nelson Mandela (African nationalist).
5898 **2385** 10k. multicoloured . . 30 15

1988. Paintings in Moscow Horse Breeding Museum. Multicoloured.
5899 5k. Type **2386** 20 10
5900 10k. "Konvoets" (Kabardin breed) (M. A. Vrubel) (vert) 35 15
5901 15k. "Horsewoman on Orlov-Rastopchin Horse" (N. E. Sverchkov) 45 25
5902 20k. "Letuchy, Grey Stallion of Orlov Trotter Breed" (V. A. Serov) (vert) . . . 70 30
5903 30k. "Sardar, an Akhaltekin Stallion" (A. B. Villevalde) . . . . 1·10 45

1988. Stamp Exhibition, Moscow. No. 5897 optd with T **2387**.
5904 **2384** 5k. multicoloured . . . 20 10

2388 Voikov

2389 "Portrait of O. K. Lansere" (Z. E. Serebryakova)

1988. Birth Centenary of Pyotr Lazarevich Voikov (diplomat).
5905 **2388** 5k. black 15 10

1988. Soviet Culture Fund. Multicoloured.
5906 10k.+5k. Type **2389** 45 25
5907 15k.+7k. "Boyarynya (noblewoman) looking at Embroidery Design" (K. V. Lebedev) (horiz) 65 35
5908 30k.+15k. "Talent" (N. P. Bogdanov-Belsky) . . . . 1·40 70
MS5909 70 × 90 mm. 1r.+50k. "Holy Trinity" (icon, Novgorod School) 5·00 3·00

2390 Envelopes and U.P.U. Emblem

2391 "Mir" Space Station and "Soyuz-TM" Spacecraft

1988. International Correspondence Week.
5910 **2390** 5k. turquoise, blue & black 15 10

1988. Soviet–Afghan Space Flight.
5911 **2391** 15k. green, red and black 55 25

2392 Emblem and Open Book

2393 Kviring

1988. 30th Anniv of "Problems of Peace and Socialism" (magazine).
5912 **2392** 10k. multicoloured . . 30 15

1988. Birth Centenary of Emmanuil Ionovich Kviring (politician).
5913 **2393** 5k. black 15 10

2394 "Ilya Muromets" (Russia) (R. Smirnov)

2395 "Appeal of the Leader" (detail, I. M. Toidze)

1988. Epic Poems of Soviet Union (1st series). Illustrations by artists named. Multicoloured.
5914 10k. Type **2394** 30 15
5915 10k. "Cossack Golota" (Ukraine) (M. Deregus) (horiz) 30 15
5916 10k. "Musician-Magician" (Byelorussia) (N. Poplavskaya) 30 15
5917 10k. "Koblandy Batyr" (Kazakhstan) (I. Isabaev) (horiz) 30 15
5918 10k. "Alpamysh" (Uzbekistan) (R. Khalilov) 30 15
See also Nos. 6017/21 and 6139/43.

1988. 71st Anniv of October Revolution.
5919 **2395** 5k. multicoloured . . . 15 10

2396 Bolotov

2397 Tupolev

1988. 250th Birth Anniv of Andrei Timofeevich Bolotov (agriculturalist).
5920 **2396** 10k. brown 30 15

1988. Birth Centenary of Academician Andrei Nikolaevich Tupolev (aircraft designer).
5921 **2397** 10k. blue 30 15

2398 Bear

2399 "Sibir" (atomic ice-breaker)

1988. Zoo Relief Fund. Multicoloured.
5922 10k.+5k. Type **2398** 45 25
5923 10k.+5k. Wolf 45 25
5924 10k.+10k. Fox 95 45
5925 20k.+10k. Wild boar . . . 95 45
5926 20k.+10k. Lynx 95 45

1988. Soviet Arctic Expedition.
5927 **2399** 20k. multicoloured . . 90 60

2400 Ustinov

2401 National Initials

1988. 80th Birth Anniv of Marshal Dmitri Fyodorovich Ustinov.
5928 **2400** 5k. brown 15 10

1988. 10th Anniv of U.S.S.R.–Vietnam Friendship Treaty.
5929 **2401** 10k. multicoloured . . 30 15

2402 Building Facade

1988. 50th Anniv of State House of Broadcasting and Sound Recording.
5930 **2402** 10k. multicoloured . . 30 15

2403 Emblem

1988. 40th Anniv of Declaration of Human Rights.
5931 **2403** 10k. multicoloured . . 30 15

2404 Life Guard of Preobrazhensky Regt. with Peter I's New Year Decree

1988. New Year.
5932 **2404** 5k. multicoloured . . . 15 10

2405 Flags and Cosmonauts

1988. Soviet–French Space Flight.
5933 **2405** 15k. multicoloured . . 55 25

2406 "Skating Rink" (Olya Krutova)

1988. Lenin Soviet Children's Fund. Children's Paintings. Multicoloured.
5934 5k.+2k. Type **2406** 25 15
5935 5k.+2k. "Cock" (Nasta Shcheglova) 25 15
5936 5k.+2k. "May is flying over the Meadows, May is flying over the Fields" (Larisa Gaidash) 25 15

2407 Lacis

(2408)

1988. Birth Cent of Martins Lacis (revolutionary).
5937 **2407** 5k. green 15 10

1988. "Space Post". No. 4682 optd with T **2408**.
5938 1r. blue . . . . 5·50 3·50

(2409)

2410 Post Messenger

1988. Olympic Games Soviet Medal. No. **MS**5890 optd with T **2409**.
MS5939 80 × 65 mm. 50k. multicoloured . . . . 1·90 1·00

1988.
6072 **2410** 1k. brown 10 10
6073 – 2k. brown 10 10
6074 – 3k. green 10 10
6075 – 4k. blue 10 10
6076 – 5k. red 15 10
6077a – 7k. blue 20 10
6078 – 10k. brown 35 15
6079 – 12k. purple 40 20
6080 – 13k. violet 50 20
6081 – 15k. blue 50 25
6082 – 20k. brown 70 25
6083 – 25k. green 85 35
6084 – 30k. blue 80 60
6085 – 35k. brown . . . . . 1·00 50
6086 – 50k. blue . . . . . 1·25 95
6087 – 1r. blue . . . . . . 3·50 1·40
DESIGNS: 2k. Old mail transport (sailing packet, steam train and mail coach); 3k. "Aurora" (cruiser); 4k. Spassky Tower and Lenin's Tomb, Red Square, Moscow; 5k. State emblem and flag; 7k. Modern mail transport (Ilyushin Il-86 jetliner, Mil Mi-2 helicopter, "Aleksandr Pushkin" (liner), train and mail van); 10k. "The Worker and the Collective Farmer" (statue, Vera Mukhina); 12k. Rocket on launch pad; 13k. Satellite; 15k. "Orbit" dish aerial; 20k. Symbols of art and literature; 25k. "The Discus-thrower" (5th-century Greek statue by Miron); 30k. Map of Antarctica and emperor penguins; 35k. "Mercury" (statue, Giovanni da Bologna); 50k. Great white cranes; 1r. Universal Postal Union emblem.

2411 Great Cascade and Samson Fountain

2412 1st-cent B.C. Gold Coin of Tigran the Great

1988. Petrodvorets Fountains. Each green and grey.
5952 5k. Type **2411** 20 10
5953 10k. Adam fountain (D. Bonazza) 30 15
5954 15k. Golden Mountain cascade (Niccolo Michetti and Mikhail Zemtsov) . . 50 25
5955 30k. Roman fountains (Bartolomeo Rastrelli) . . 1·00 45
5965 50k. Oaklet trick fountain (Rastrelli) . . . . 1·60 1·00

1988. Armenian Earthquake Relief. Armenian History. Multicoloured.
5957 20k.+10k. Type **2412** . . . 95 45
5958 30k.+15k. Rispsime Church 1·25 65
5959 50k.+25k. "Madonna and Child" (18th-century fresco, Ovnat Ovnatanyan) . . . . . . 2·25 1·25

2413 Hammer and Sickle

1988. 19th Soviet Communist Party Conference, Moscow (2nd issue). Multicoloured.
5960 5k. Type **2413** 15 10
5961 5k. Hammer and sickle and building girders 15 10
5962 5k. Hammer and sickle and wheat 15 10

2414 "Buran"

1988. Launch of Space Shuttle Buran. Sheet 93 × 63 mm.
MS5963 **2414** 50k. multicoloured 2·00 1·10

2415 "Vostok" Rocket, "Lunar 1", Earth and Moon

2416 Virtanen

1989. 30th Anniv of First Russian Moon Flight.
5964 **2415** 15k. multicoloured . . 35 25

1989. Birth Centenary of Jalmari Virtanen (poet).
5965 **2416** 5k. brown and bistre 15 10

2417 Headquarters Building, Moscow

1989. 40th Anniv of Council for Mutual Economic Aid.
5966 **2417** 10k. multicoloured . . 30 15

2418 Forest Protection

2419 18th-century Samovar

1989. Nature Conservation. Multicoloured.
5967 5k. Type **2418** 50 20
5968 10k. Arctic preservation . . 35 15
5969 15k. Anti-desertification campaign 50 20

1989. Russian Samovars in State Museum, Leningrad. Multicoloured.
5970 5k. Type **2419** 20 10
5971 10k. 19th-century barrel samovar by Ivan Lisitsin of Tula 30 15
5972 20k. 1830s Kabachok travelling samovar by Sokolov Brothers factory, Tula 55 30
5973 30k. 1840s samovar by Nikolai Malikov factory, Tula 85 45

2420 Mussorgsky (after Repin) and Scene from "Boris Godunov"

2421 Dybenko

1989. 150th Birth Anniv of Modest Petrovich Mussorgsky (composer).
5974 **2420** 10k. purple and brown 30 15

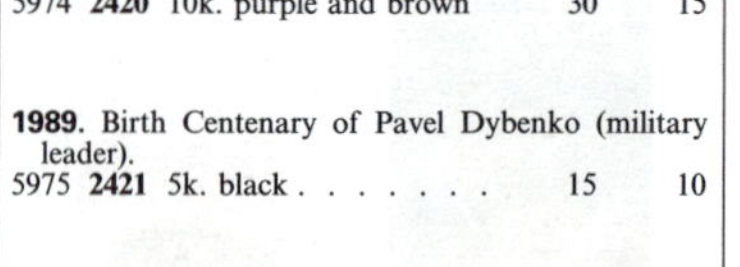

1989. Birth Centenary of Pavel Dybenko (military leader).
5975 **2421** 5k. black 15 10

2422 Shevchenko

2423 "Lilium speciosum"

1989. 175th Birth Anniv of Taras Shevchenko (Ukrainian poet and painter).
5976 **2422** 5k. brown, green & black 15 10

1989. Lilies. Multicoloured.
5977 5k. Type **2423** 20 10
5978 10k. "African Queen" . . . 35 15
5979 15k. "Eclat du Soir" . . . 45 20
5980 30k. "White Tiger" . . . . 1·10 45

2424 Marten

1989. Zoo Relief Fund. Multicoloured.
5981 10k.+5k. Type **2424** 45 20
5982 10k.+5k. Squirrel 45 20
5983 20k.+10k. Hare . . . . . . 1·00 45
5984 20k.+10k. Hedgehog . . . . 1·00 45
5985 20k.+10k. Badger . . . . . 1·00 45

2425 Red Flag, Rainbow and Globe

2426 "Victory Banner" (P. Loginov and V. Pamfilov)

1989. Centenary of "Second International" Declaration of 1 May as Labour Day. Sheet 105 × 75 mm.
MS5986 **2425** 30k. multicoloured 1·00 50

1989. Victory Day.
5987 **2426** 5k. multicoloured . . . 15 10

2427 "Mir" Space Station

1989. Cosmonautics Day.
5988 **2427** 15k. multicoloured . . 45 20

2428 Emblem and Flags

2430 Statue

2429 "Phobos"

1989. U.S.–Soviet Bering Bridge Expedition.
5989 **2428** 10k. multicoloured . . 35 15

1989. 119th Birth Anniv of Lenin. As T **2367**. Branches of Lenin Central Museum.
5990 5k. brown, ochre and gold 15 10
5991 5k. deep brown, brn & gold 15 10
5992 5k. multicoloured 15 10
DESIGNS: No. 5990, Frunze; 5991, Kazan; 5992, Kuibyshev.

1989. Launch of "Phobos" Space Probe to Mars. Sheet 89 × 65 mm.
MS5993 **2429** 50k. multicoloured 1·75 75

1989. 70th Anniv of First Hungarian Soviet Republic.
5994 **2430** 5k. multicoloured . . . 15 10

2431 "Motherland Statue"

2432 Drone

1989. 400th Anniv of Volgograd (formerly Tsaritsyn).
5995 **2431** 5k. multicoloured . . . 15 10

1989. Honey Bees. Multicoloured.
5996 5k. Type **2432** 20 10
5997 10k. Bees, flowers and hive 30 15
5998 20k. Bee on flower 60 30
5999 35k. Feeding queen bee . . 1·25 45

2433 Negative and Positive Images

2434 Map above Dove as Galley

1989. 150th Anniv of Photography.
6000 **2433** 5k. multicoloured . . . 15 10

1989. "Europe—Our Common Home". Mult.
6001 5k. Type **2434** 20 10
6002 10k. Laying foundations of Peace 30 15
6003 15k. White storks' nest . . . 65 55

2435 Mukhina modelling "God of Northern Wind" (after M. Nesterov)

2436 Racine

1989. Birth Centenary of Vera Mukhina (sculptress).
6004 **2435** 5k. blue 15 10

1989. 150th Birth Anniv of Jean Racine (dramatist).
6005 **2436** 15k. multicoloured . . 45 20

2437 Rabbit

1989. Lenin Soviet Children's Fund. Children's Paintings. Multicoloured.
6006 5k.+2k. Type **2437** 20 10
6007 5k.+2k. Cat 20 10
6008 5k.+2k. Nurse 20 10
See also Nos. 6162/4.

2438 Kuratov

1989. 150th Birth Anniv of Ivan Kuratov (writer).
6009 **2438** 5k. deep brown & brown 15 10

2439 Emblem **2440** Common Shelduck

1989. 13th World Youth and Students' Festival, Pyongyang.
6010 **2439** 10k. multicoloured . . 30 15

1989. Ducks (1st series). Multicoloured.
6011 5k. Type **2440** 15 10
6012 15k. Green-winged teal . . . 40 30
6013 20k. Ruddy shelduck . . . 55 35
See also Nos. 6159/61 and 6264/6.

2441 "Storming of Bastille" (Gelman after Monnet)

1989. Bicentenary of French Revolution.
6014 **2441** 5k. multicoloured . . . 20 10
6015 – 15k. blue, black and red 45 20
6016 – 20k. blue, black and red 60 25
DESIGNS: 15k. Jean-Paul Marat, Georges Danton and Maximilien Robespierre; 20k. "Marseillaise" (relief by F. Rude from Arc de Triomphe).

1989. Epic Poems of Soviet Union (2nd series). Illustrations by named artists. As T **2394**. Mult.
6017 10k. "Amirani" (Georgia) (V. Oniani) 35 15
6018 10k. "Koroglu" (Azerbaijan) (A. Gadzhiev) 35 15
6019 10k. "Fir, Queen of Grass Snakes" (Lithuania) (A. Makunaite) 35 15
6020 10k. "Mioritsa" (Moldavia) (I. Bogdesko) 35 15
6021 10k. "Lachplesis" (Lettish) (G. Wilks) 35 15

2442 Observatory **2443** Hemispheres, Roses in Envelope and Posthorn

1989. 150th Anniv of Pulkovo Observatory.
6022 **2442** 10k. multicoloured . . 30 15

1989. International Letter Week.
6023 **2443** 5k. multicoloured . . . 15 10

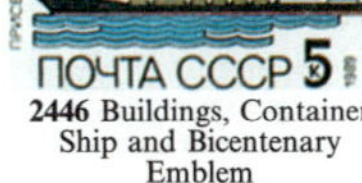

2444 Lynx **2446** Buildings, Container Ship and Bicentenary Emblem

2445 Ships and Peter I

1989. 50th Anniv of Tallin Zoo.
6024 **2444** 10k. multicoloured . . 30 15

1989. 275th Anniv of Battle of Hango Head. Sheet 95 × 65 mm.
MS6025 **2445** 50k. blue, black and brown . . . . 1·60 75

1989. Bicentenary of Nikolaev.
6026 **2446** 5k. multicoloured . . . 20 10

2447 Nkrumah **2448** 1921 40r. Stamp

1989. 80th Birth Anniv of Kwame Nkrumah (first Prime Minister and President of Ghana).
6027 **2447** 10k. multicoloured . . 30 15

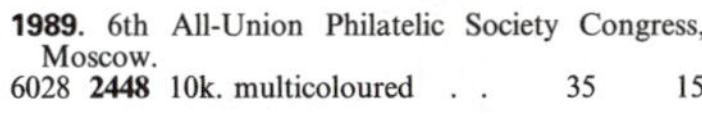

1989. 6th All-Union Philatelic Society Congress, Moscow.
6028 **2448** 10k. multicoloured . . 35 15

2449 Cooper

1989. Birth Bicentenary of James Fenimore Cooper (writer) (1st issue).
6029 **2449** 15k. multicoloured . . 45 20
See also Nos. 6055/9.

2450 V. L. Durov (trainer) and Sealions

1989. 70th Anniv of Soviet Circus. Multicoloured.
6030 1k. Type **2450** 10 10
6031 3k. M. N. Rumyantsev (clown "Karandash") with donkey 10 10
6032 4k. V. I. Filatov (founder of Bear Circus) and bears on motor cycles 15 10
6033 5k. E. T. Kio (illusionist) and act 25 10
6034 10k. V. E. Lazarenko (clown and acrobat) and act . . 45 20
MS6035 80 × 65 mm. 30k. Moscow Circus building, Tsvetnoi Boulevard (33 × 21½ mm) . . . 1·10 50

2451 Emblem on Glove **2452** Li Dazhao

1989. International Amateur Boxing Association Championship, Moscow.
6036 **2451** 15k. multicoloured . . 45 20

1989. Birth Centenary of Li Dazhao (co-founder of Chinese Communist Party).
6037 **2452** 5k. brown, stone & black 20 10

2453 Khetagurov

1989. 130th Birth Anniv of Kosta Khetagurov (Ossetian writer).
6038 **2453** 5k. brown 15 10

2454 "October Guardsmen" (M. M. Chepik)

1989. 72nd Anniv of October Revolution.
6039 **2454** 5k. multicoloured . . . 15 10

2455 Russian Spoons, Psaltery, Balalaika, Zhaleika and Accordion

1989. Traditional Musical Instruments (1st series). Multicoloured.
6040 10k. Type **2455** 35 15
6041 10k. Ukrainian bandura, trembita, drymba, svyril (pipes) and dulcimer . . . 35 15
6042 10k. Byelorussian tambourine, bastlya (fiddle), lera and dudka (pipe) 35 15
6043 10k. Uzbek nagors (drums), rubab, zang, karnai and gidzhak 35 15
See also Nos. 6183/6 and 6303/5.

2456 "Demonstration of First Radio Receiver, 1895" (N. A. Sysoev) **2457** National Flag and Provincial Arms

1989. 130th Birth Anniv of Aleksandr Stepanovich Popov (radio pioneer).
6044 **2456** 10k. multicoloured . . 30 15

1989. 40th Anniv of German Democratic Republic.
6045 **2457** 5k. multicoloured . . . 15 10

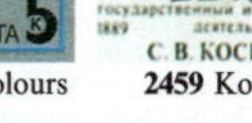

2458 Polish National Colours forming "45" **2459** Kosior

1989. 45th Anniv of Liberation of Poland.
6046 **2458** 5k. multicoloured . . . 15 10

1989. Birth Centenary of Stanislav Vikentievich Kosior (vice-chairman of Council of People's Commissars).
6047 **2459** 5k. black 15 10

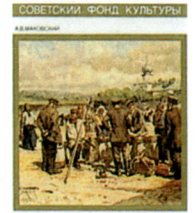

2460 Nehru **2461** "Village Market" (A. V. Makovsky)

1989. Birth Centenary of Jawaharlal Nehru (Indian statesman).
6048 **2460** 15k. brown 45 20

1989. Soviet Culture Fund. Multicoloured.
6049 4k.+2k. Type **2461** 20 10
6050 5k.+2k. "Lady in Hat" (E. L. Zelenin) 25 15
6051 10k.+5k. "Portrait of the Actress Bazhenova" (A. F. Sofronova) 50 20
6052 20k.+10k. "Two Women" (Hugo Shaiber) 85 65
6053 30k.+15k. 19th-century teapot and plates from Popov porcelain works . . 1·50 85

2462 Berzin **2463** "The Hunter"

1989. Birth Centenary of Yan Karlovich Berzin (head of Red Army Intelligence).
6054 **2462** 5k. black 15 10

1989. Birth Bicentenary of James Fenimore Cooper (writer) (2nd issue). Illustrations of his novels. Multicoloured.
6055 20k. Type **2463** 60 30
6056 20k. "Last of the Mohicans" 60 30
6057 20k. "The Pathfinder" . . . 60 30
6058 20k. "The Pioneers" 60 30
6059 20k. "The Prairie" 60 30
Nos. 6055/9 were printed together, se-tenant, forming a composite design.

2464 St. Basil's Cathedral and Minin and Pozharsky Statue, Moscow **2465** Dymkovo Toy

1989. Historical Monuments (1st series). Mult.
6060 15k. Type **2464** 45 25
6061 15k. Sts. Peter and Paul Cathedral and statue of Peter I. Leningrad 45 25
6062 15k. St. Sophia's Cathedral and statue of Bogdan Chmielnitsky, Kiev . . . 45 25
6063 15k. Khodzha Ahmed Yasavi mausoleum, Turkestan 45 25
6064 15k. Khazret Khyzr Mosque, Samarkand . . . 45 25
See also Nos. 6165/72 and 6231/3.

1989. New Year.
6065 **2465** 5k. multicoloured . . . 15 10

2466 Soviet Lunar Vehicle

2467 Barn Swallow

1989. "Expo 89" International Stamp Exhibition, Washington D.C. Multicoloured.
6066 25k. Type **2466** 90 45
6067 25k. Astronaut and landing module on Moon 90 45
6068 25k. Cosmonauts on Mars 90 45
6069 25k. Flag and shield on Mars 90 45
MS6070 104 × 84 mm. Nos. 6066/9 3·75 2·00

1989. Nature Preservation. Sheet 65 × 90 mm.
MS6071 **2467** 20k.+10k. multicoloured . . . . 1·25 75

1989. Russian Naval Commanders (2nd series). As T **2345**.
6091 5k. blue and brown 10 15
6092 10k. blue and brown 25 15
6093 15k. blue and deep blue . . 40 20
6094 20k. blue and deep blue . . 55 25
6095 30k. blue and brown 90 60
6096 35k. blue and brown . . . . 1·40 65
DESIGNS: 5k. V. A. Kornilov and "Vladimer" (steam frigate) and "Pervaz-Bakhric" (Turkish) steam frigate); 10k. V. I. Istomin and "Parizh"; 15k. G. I. Nevelskoi and "Baikal"; 20k. G. I. Butakov and iron-clad squadron; 30k. A. A. Popov, "Pyotr Veliky" and "Vitze Admiral Popov"; 35k. S. O. Makarov, "Intibah" (Turkish warship) and "Veliky Khyaz Konstantin".

2468 Acid Rain destroying Rose

1990. Nature Conservation. Multicoloured.
6097 10k. Type **2468** 30 15
6098 15k. Oil-smeared great black-headed gull perching on globe 40 30
6099 20k. Blade sawing down tree 65 25

2469 Ladya Monument and Golden Gates, Kiev (Ukraine)

2470 Flag and Hanoi Monument

1990. Republic Capitals. Multicoloured.
6100 5k. Lenin Palace of Culture, Government House and Academy of Sciences, Alma-Ata (Kazakhstan) 15 10
6101 5k. Library, Mollanepes Theatre and War Heroes Monument, Ashkhabad (Turkmenistan) 15 10
6102 5k. Maiden's Tower and Divan-Khane Palace, Baku (Azerbaijan) 15 10
6103 5k. Sadriddin Aini Theatre and Avicenna Monument, Dushanbe (Tadzhikistan) 15 10
6104 5k. Spendyarov Theatre and David Sasunsky Monument, Yerevan (Armenia) 15 10
6105 5k. Satylganov Philharmonic Society building and Manas Memorial, Frunze (Kirgizia) 15 10
6106 5k. Type **2469** 15 10
6107 5k. Cathedral and Victory Arch, Kishinev (Moldavia) 15 10
6108 5k. Government House and Liberation Monument, Minsk (Byelorussia) . . . 15 10
6109 5k. Konstantino-Yeleninsky Tower and Ivan the Great Bell Tower, Moscow (Russian Federation) . . 15 10
6110 5k. Cathedral, "Three Brothers" building and Freedom Monument, Riga (Latvia) 15 10
6111 5k. Herman the Long, Oliviste Church, Cathedral and Town hall towers and wall turret, Tallin (Estonia) 15 10
6112 5k. Kukeldash Medrese and University, Tashkent (Uzbekistan) 15 10
6113 5k. Metekh Temple and Vakhtang Gorgasal Monument, Tbilisi (Georgia) 15 10
6114 5k. Gediminas Tower and St. Anne's Church, Vilnius (Lithuania) . . . 15 10

1990. 60th Anniv of Vietnamese Communist Party.
6115 **2470** 5k. multicoloured . . . 15 10

2471 Ho Chi Minh

2472 Snowy Owl

1990. Birth Cent of Ho Chi Minh (Vietnamese leader).
6116 **2471** 10k. brown and black 30 15

1990. Owls. Multicoloured.
6117 10k. Type **2472** 20 15
6118 20k. Eagle owl (vert) . . . 35 25
6119 55k. Long-eared owl . . . . 1·00 60

2473 Paddle-steamer, Posthorn and Penny Black

1990. 150th Anniv of the Penny Black.
6120 **2473** 10k. multicoloured . . 30 15
6121 – 20k. black and gold . . 55 25
6122 – 20k. black and gold . . 55 25
6123 – 35k. multicoloured . . 1·25 65
6124 – 35k. multicoloured . . 1·25 65
MS6125 87 × 65 mm. 1r. black and green (36 × 25 mm) . . . . . 3·50 1·60
DESIGNS: No. 6121, Anniversary emblem and Penny Black (lettered "T P"); 6122, As No. 6121 but stamp lettered "T F"; 6123, "Stamp World London 90" International Stamp Exhibition emblem and Penny Black (lettered "V K"); 6124, As No. 6123 but stamp lettered "A H" ; 1r. Penny Black and anniversary emblem.

2474 Electric Cables

1990. 125th Anniv of I.T.U.
6126 **2474** 20k. multicoloured . . 55 30

2475 Flowers

1990. Labour Day.
6127 **2475** 5k. multicoloured . . . 15 10

2476 "Victory, 1945" (A. Lysenko)

1990. 45th Anniv of Victory in Second World War.
6128 **2476** 5k. multicoloured . . . 15 10

2477 "Mir" Space Complex and Cosmonaut

2478 Lenin

1990. Cosmonautics Day.
6129 **2477** 20k. multicoloured . . 45 25

1990. "Leniniana '90" All-Union Stamp Exhibition.
6130 **2478** 5k. brown 15 10

1990. 120th Birth Anniv of Lenin. Branches of Lenin Central Museum. As T **2367**.
6131 5k. red, lake and gold . . . 15 10
6132 5k. pink, purple and gold 15 10
6133 5k. multicoloured 15 10
DESIGNS: No. 6131, Ulyanovsk; 6132, Baku; 6133, Tashkent.

2479 Scene from "Iolanta" (opera) and Tchaikovsky

1990. 150th Birth Anniv of Pyotr Ilich Tchaikovsky (composer).
6134 **2479** 15k. black 60 30

2480 Golden Eagle

1990. Zoo Relief Fund. Multicoloured.
6135 10k.+5k. Type **2480** 35 25
6136 20k.+10k. Saker falcon ("Falco cherrug") 70 65
6137 20k.+10k. Common raven ("Corvus corax") 70 65

2481 Etching by G. A. Echeistov

2482 Goalkeeper and Players

1990. 550th Anniv of "Dzhangar" (Kalmuk folk epic).
6138 **2481** 10k. ochre, brown & black 30 15

1990. Epic Poems of Soviet Union (3rd series). Illustrations by named artists. As T **2394**. Mult.
6139 10k. "Manas" (Kirgizia) (T. Gertsen) (horiz) . . . 30 15
6140 10k. "Gurugli" (Tadzhikistan) (I. Martynov) (horiz) . . 30 15
6141 10k. "David Sasunsky" (Armenia) (M. Abegyan) 30 15
6142 10k. "Gerogly" (Turkmenistan) (I. Klychev) 30 15
6143 10k. "Kalevipoeg" (Estonia) (O. Kallis) 30 15

1990. World Cup Football Championship, Italy. Multicoloured.
6144 5k. Type **2482** 15 10
6145 10k. Players 35 15
6146 15k. Attempted tackle . . . 50 20
6147 25k. Referee and players . . 50 30
6148 35k. Goalkeeper saving ball 1·25 65

2483 Globe and Finlandia Hall, Helsinki

2484 Competitors and Target

1990. 15th Anniv of European Security and Co-operation Conference, Helsinki.
6149 **2483** 15k. multicoloured . .

1990. 45th World Shooting Championships, Moscow.
6150 **2484** 15k. multicoloured . . 45 20

2485 Glaciology Research

1990. Soviet–Australian Scientific Co-operation in Antarctica. Multicoloured.
6151 5k. Type **2485** 15 10
6152 50k. Krill (marine biology research) . . . . 1·50 90
MS6153 84 × 65 mm. Nos. 6151/2 1·75 80

2486 Emblem and Sports Pictograms

1990. Goodwill Games, Seattle.
6154 **2486** 10k. multicoloured . . 35 15

2487 Troops and Badge of order of Aleksandr Nevsky (B2)

1990. 750th Anniv of Battle of Neva. Sheet 94 × 65 mm.
MS6155 **2487** 50k. multicoloured 1·60 75

2488 Greylag Geese

1990. Poultry. Multicoloured.
6156 5k. Type **2488** 10 10
6157 10k. Adlers (chickens) . . . 35 15
6158 15k. Common turkeys . . . 40 40

2489 Mallards

1990. Ducks (2nd series). Multicoloured.
6159 5k. Type **2489** 10 10
6160 15k. Common goldeneyes 40 40
6161 20k. Red-crested pochards 50 50

1990. Lenin Soviet Children's Fund. Children's Paintings. As T **2437**. Multicoloured.
6162 5k.+2k. Clown 20 10
6163 5k.+2k. Ladies in crinolines 20 10
6164 5k.+2k. Children with banner 20 10

1990. Historical Monuments (2nd series). As T **2464**. Multicoloured.
6165 15k. St. Nshan's Church, Akhpat (Armenia) 45 20
6166 15k. Shirvanshah Palace, Baku (Azerbaijan) 45 20
6167 15k. Soroki Fortress and statue of Stefan III, Kishinev (Moldavia) . . . 45 20
6168 15k. Spaso-Efrosinevsky Cathedral, Polotsk (Byelorussia) 45 20
6169 15k. St. Peter's Church and 16th-century Riga (Latvia) 45 20
6170 15k. St. Nicholas's Church and carving of city arms, Tallin (Estonia) 45 20
6171 15k. Mtatsminda Pantheon and statue of Nikoloz Baratashvili, Tbilisi (Georgia) 45 20
6172 15k. Cathedral and bell tower, Vilnius (Lithuania) 45 20

2490 Sordes

1990. Prehistoric Animals. Multicoloured.
6173 1k. Type **2490** 10 10
6174 3k. Chalicotherium (vert) . . 10 10
6175 5k. Indricotherium (vert) . . 15 10
6176 10k. Saurolophus (vert) . . 25 15
6177 20k. Cephalaspid ostracoderm 65 30

2491 "St. Basil's Cathedral and Kremlin, Moscow" (Sanjay Adhikari)
2492 Pigeon Post

1990. Indo–Soviet Friendship. Children's Paintings. Multicoloured.
6178 10k. Type **2491** 30 10
6179 10k. "Life in India" (Tanya Vorontsova) 30 10

1990. Letter Writing Week.
6180 **2492** 5k. blue 15 10

2493 Traffic on Urban Roads
2495 Killer Whales

2494 Grey Heron

1990. Traffic Safety Week.
6181 **2493** 5k. multicoloured . . . 25 10

1990. Nature Conservation. Sheet 65 × 90 mm.
MS6182 **2494** 20k.+10k. multicoloured . . . . 1·00 55

1990. Traditional Musical Instruments (2nd series). As T **2455**. Multicoloured.
6183 10k. Azerbaijani balalian, shar and caz (stringed instruments), zurna and drum 40 15
6184 10k. Georgian bagpipes, tambourine, flute, pipes and chonguri (stringed instrument) 40 15
6185 10k. Kazakh flute, rattle, daubra and kobyz (stringed instruments) . . 40 15
6186 10k. Lithuanian bagpipes, horns and kankles 40 15

1990. Marine Mammals.
6187 25k. Type **2495** 75 40
6188 25k. Northern sealions . . . 75 40
6189 25k. Sea otter 75 40
6190 25k. Common dolphin . . . 75 40

2496 "Lenin among Delegates to Second Congress of Soviets" (S. V. Gerasimov)
2497 Ivan Bunin (1933)

1990. 73rd Anniv of October Revolution.
6191 **2496** 5k. multicoloured . . . 15 10

1990. Nobel Prize Winners for Literature.
6192 **2497** 15k. brown 45 20
6193 – 15k. brown 45 20
6194 – 15k. black 45 20
DESIGNS: No. 6193, Mikhail Sholokhov (1965); 6194, Boris Pasternak.

2498 "Sever 2"

1990. Research Submarines. Multicoloured.
6195 5k. Type **2498** 15 10
6196 10k. "Tinro 2" 30 15
6197 15k. "Argus" 50 20
6198 25k. "Paisis" 75 30
6199 35k. "Mir" . . . . 1·10 65

2499 "Motherland" Statue (E. Kocher), Screen and Emblem

Филателистическая выставка „Армения-90"	Восстановление, милосердие, помощь
(2500)	(2501)

1990. "Armenia '90" Stamp Exhibition, Yerevan. (a) Type **2499**.
6200 **2499** 10k. multicoloured . . 30 15

(b) Nos. 5957/9 optd with T **2500** (20k.) or as T **2501**.
6201 **2412** 20k.+10k. mult 75 40
6202 – 30k.+15k. mult . . . . 1·10 70
6203 – 50k.+25k. mult . . . . 2·00 1·10

2502 S. A. Vaupshasov
2503 Soviet and Japanese Flags above Earth

1990. Intelligence Agents.
6204 **2502** 5k. dp grn, grn and blk 20 10
6205 – 5k. dp brn, brn and blk 20 10
6206 – 5k. deep blue, blue and black 20 10
6207 – 5k. brown, buff & black 20 10
6208 – 5k. brown, bistre and black 20 10
DESIGNS: No. 6205, R. I. Abel; 6206, Kim Philby; 6207, I. D. Kudrya; 6208, Konon Molodyi (alias Gordon Lonsdale).

1990. Soviet–Japanese Space Flight.
6209 **2503** 20k. multicoloured . . 55 25

2504 Grandfather Frost and Toys

1990. New Year.
6210 **2504** 5k. multicoloured . . . 10 10

2505 "Unkrada"

1990. Soviet Culture Fund. Paintings by N. K. Rerikh. Multicoloured.
6211 10k.+5k. Type **2505** 15 10
6212 20k.+10k. "Pskovo-Pechorsky Monastery" . . 30 20

2506 "Joys to all those in Need" (detail of icon) and Fund Emblem

1990. Soviet Charity and Health Fund. Sheet 90 × 70 mm.
MS6213 **2506** 50k.+25k. multicoloured 90 55

2507 Globe, Eiffel Tower and Flags

1990. "Charter for New Europe". Signing of European Conventional Arms Treaty, Paris.
6214 **2507** 30k. multicoloured . . 35 15

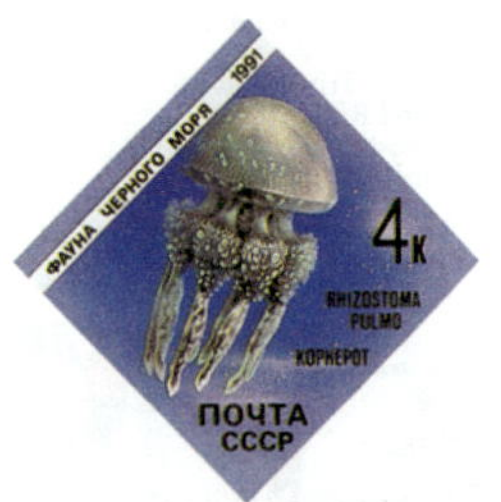

2508 Jellyfish

1991. Marine Animals. Multicoloured.
6215 4k. Type **2508** 10 10
6216 5k. Anemone 10 10
6217 10k. Spurdog 30 15
6218 15k. European anchovy . . 40 20
6219 20k. Bottle-nosed dolphin 45 25

2509 Keres

1991. 75th Birth Anniv of Paul Keres (chess player).
6220 **2509** 15k. brown 35 20

2510 Radioactive Particles killing Vegetation

1991. 5th Anniv of Chernobyl Nuclear Power Station Disaster.
6221 **2510** 15k. multicoloured . . 15 10

2511 "Sorrento Coast with View of Capri" (Shchedrin)

1991. Birth Bicentenary of Silvestr Shchedrin and 150th Birth Anniv of Arkhip Kuindzhi (painters). Multicoloured.
6222 10k. Type **2511** 15 10
6223 10k. "New Rome. View of St. Angelo's Castle" (Shchedrin) 15 10
6224 10k. "Evening in the Ukraine" (Kuindzhi) . . 15 10
6225 10k. "Birch Grove" (Kuindzhi) 15 10

2512 White Stork

1991. Zoo Relief Fund.
6226 **2512** 10k.+5k. mult 50 50

2513 Sturgeon and Bell Tower, Volga

1991. Environmental Protection. Multicoloured.
6227 10k. Type **2513** 20 10
6228 15k. Sable and Lake Baikal 15 10
6229 20k. Saiga and dried bed of Aral Sea 20 15

2514 Swallowtail on Flower

1991. 25th Anniv of All-Union Philatelic Society. Sheet 90 × 65 mm.
MS6230 **2514** 20k.+10k. multicoloured 65 40

1991. Historical Monuments (3rd series). As T **2464**. Multicoloured.
6231 15k. Minaret, Uzgen, Kirgizia 15 10
6232 15k. Mohammed Bashar Mausoleum, Tadzhikistan 15 10
6233 15k. Talkhatan-baba Mosque, Turkmenistan 15 10

2515 G. Shelikhov and Kodiak, 1784

1991. 500th Anniv of Discovery of America by Columbus. Russian Settlements.
6234 **2515** 20k. blue and black . . 20 10
6235 – 30k. bistre, brown & blk 35 15
6236 – 50k. orange, brown & blk 55 20
DESIGNS: 30k. Aleksandr Baranov and Sitka, 1804; 50k. I. Kuskov and Fort Ross, California, 1812.

2516 Satellite and Liner
2517 Yuri Gagarin in Uniform

1991. 10th Anniv of United Nations Transport and Communications in Asia and the Pacific Programme.
6237 **2516** 10k. multicoloured . . 20 10

1991. Cosmonautics Day. 30th Anniv of First Man in Space. Each brown.
6238 25k. Type **2517** 15 10
6239 25k. Gagarin wearing space suit 15 10
6240 25k. Gagarin in uniform with cap 15 10
6241 25k. Gagarin in civilian dress 15 10
MS6242 85 × 110 mm. Nos. 6238/41 50 40

МЕЖДУНАРОДНАЯ ВЫСТАВКА
«К ЗВЕЗДАМ-91»
КОСМОС НА СЛУЖБЕ МИРА И ПРОГРЕССА

(2518)

2519 "May 1945" (A. and S. Tkachev)

1991. "Ad Astra-91" International Stamp Exhibition, Moscow. No. **MS**6242 optd with T **2518**.
MS6243 85 × 119 mm. 4 × 25k. brown . . . . 1·00 75

1991. Victory Day.
6244 **2519** 5k. multicoloured . . . 10 10

2520 "Lenin working on Book 'Materialism and Empirical Criticism' in Geneva Library" (P. Belousov)

1991. 121st Birth Anniv of Lenin.
6245 **2520** 5k. multicoloured . . . 10 10

2521 Prokofiev

1991. Birth Centenary of Sergei Prokofiev (composer).
6246 **2521** 15k. brown 10 10

2522 Lady's Slipper

2523 Ilya I. Mechnikov (medicine, 1908)

1991. Orchids. Multicoloured.
6247 3k. Type **2522** 10 10
6248 5k. Lady orchid 10 10
6249 10k. Bee orchid 10 10
6250 20k. Calypso 15 10
6251 25k. Marsh helleborine . . . 20 15

1991. Nobel Prize Winners. Each black.
6252 15k. Type **2523** 10 10
6253 15k. Ivan P. Pavlov (medicine, 1904) 10 10
6254 15k. A. D. Sakharov (peace, 1975) 10 10

2524 Soviet and British Flags in Space

1991. Soviet–British Space Flight.
6255 **2524** 20k. multicoloured . . 15 10

2525 Saroyan

1991. 10th Death Anniv of William Saroyan (writer).
6256 **2525** 1r. multicoloured . . . 60 30

2526 "The Universe"

1991. Lenin Soviet Children's Fund. Paintings by V. Lukyanets. Multicoloured.
6257 10k.+5k. Type **2526** 10 10
6258 10k.+5k. "Another Planet" 10 10

2527 Miniature from "Ostromirov Gospel" (first book written in Cyrillic), 1056–57

1991. Culture of Medieval Russia. Multicoloured.
6259 10k. Type **2527** 10 10
6260 15k. Page from "Russian Truth" (code of laws), 11th–13th century 15 10
6261 20k. Portrait of Sergy Radonezhsky (embroidered book cover), 1424 . . . . 20 10
6262 25k. "The Trinity" (icon, Andrei Rublev), 1411 . . 20 10
6263 30k. Illustration from "Book of the Apostles", 1564 . . 20 15

2528 Pintails

2529 Emblem

1991. Ducks (3rd series). Multicoloured.
6264 5k. Type **2528** 10 10
6265 15k. Greater scaups 20 10
6266 20k. White-headed ducks . . 25 15

1991. European Conference on Security and Co-operation Session, Moscow.
6267 **2529** 10k. multicoloured . . 10 10

2530 Patroness

2531 Woman in Traditional Costume

1991. Soviet Charity and Health Fund.
6268 **2530** 20k.+10k. mult 25 15

1991. 1st Anniv of Declaration of Ukrainian Sovereignty.
6269 **2531** 30k. multicoloured . . 25 15

2532 "Albatros"

2534 Girl with Letter

2533 "Sv. Pyotr" and Route Map

1991. Airships. Multicoloured.
6270 1k. Type **2532** 10 10
6271 3k. GA-42 . . . . 15 10
6272 4k. "Norge" (horiz) 15 10
6273 5k. "Pobeda" (horiz) . . . 15 10
6274 20k. LZ-127 "Graf Zeppelin" (horiz) 55 30

1991. 250th Anniv of Vitus Bering's and A. Chirkov's Expedition. Multicoloured.
6275 30k. Type **2533** 25 15
6276 30k. Sighting land 25 15

1991. Letter Writing Week.
6277 **2534** 7k. brown 10 10

2535 Bell and Bell Towers

2536 Kayak Race and "Santa Maria"

1991. Soviet Culture Fund.
6278 **2535** 20k.+10k. mult 20 10
The belfries depicted are from Kuliga-Drakonovo, Church of the Assumption in Pskov, Ivan the Great in Moscow and Cathedral of the Assumption in Rostov.

1991. Olympic Games, Barcelona (1992) (1st issue). Multicoloured.
6279 10k. Type **2536** 20 10
6280 20k. Running and Church of the Holy Family . . . 15 10
6281 30k. Football and stadium 25 15
See also Nos. 6362/4.

2537 Rainbow, Globe and Flags

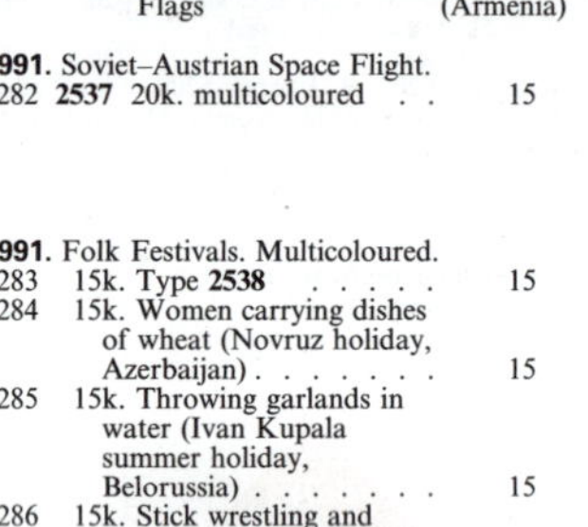

2538 Ascension Day (Armenia)

1991. Soviet–Austrian Space Flight.
6282 **2537** 20k. multicoloured . . 15 10

1991. Folk Festivals. Multicoloured.
6283 15k. Type **2538** 15 10
6284 15k. Women carrying dishes of wheat (Novruz holiday, Azerbaijan) 15 10
6285 15k. Throwing garlands in water (Ivan Kupala summer holiday, Belorussia) 15 10
6286 15k. Stick wrestling and dancing round decorated tree (New Year, Estonia) (horiz) 15 10
6287 15k. Masked dancers (Berikaoba spring holiday, Georgia) 15 10
6288 15k. Riders with goat skin (Kazakhstan) (horiz) . . . 15 10
6289 15k. Couple on horses (Kirgizia) (horiz) 15 10
6290 15k. Couple leaping over flames (Ligo (Ivan Kupala) holiday, Latvia) (horiz) 15 10
6291 15k. Family on way to church (Palm Sunday, Lithuania) (horiz) 15 10
6292 15k. Man in beribboned hat and musicians (Plugusorul (New Year) holiday, Moldova) 15 10
6293 15k. Sledge ride (Shrovetide, Russian Federation) . . . 15 10
6294 15k. Musicians on carpet and stilt-walkers (Novruz holiday, Tajikistan) . . . 15 10
6295 15k. Wrestlers (Harvest holiday, Turkmenistan) (horiz) 15 10
6296 15k. Dancers and couple with lute and tambourine (Christmas, Ukraine) (horiz) 15 10
6297 15k. Girls with tulips (Tulip holiday, Uzbekistan) . . . 15 10

2539 Dimitry Komar

2540 Federation Government House and Flag

1991. Defeat of Attempted Coup. Multicoloured.
6298 7k. Type **2539** 10 10
6299 7k. Ilya Krichevsky 10 10
6300 7k. Vladimir Usov 10 10
MS6301 90 × 64 mm. 50k. Barricades around Russian Federation Government House (51 × 33 mm) 40 30
Nos. 6298/6300 depict victims killed in opposing the attempted coup.

1991. Election of Boris Yeltsin as President of the Russian Federation.
6302 **2540** 7k. blue, gold and red 10 10

1991. Traditional Musical Instruments (3rd series). As T **2455**. Multicoloured.
6303 10k. Kirgiz flutes, komuzes and kyyak (string instruments) 10 10
6304 10k. Latvian ganurags and stabule (wind), tambourine, duga and kokle (string instruments) 10 10
6305 10k. Moldavian flute, bagpipes, nai (pipes), kobza and tsambal (string instruments) 10 10

2541 Decorations and Gifts

2542 Nikolai Mikhailovich Karamzin

1991. New Year.
6306 **2541** 7k. multicoloured . . . 10 10

1991. Historians' Birth Anniversaries. Mult.
6307 10k. Type **2542** (225th anniv) 10 10
6308 10k. V. O. Klyuchevsky (150th anniv) 10 10
6309 10k. Sergei M. Solovyov (171st anniv) 10 10
6310 10k. V. N. Tatishchev (after A. Osipov) (305th anniv) 10 10

RUSSIAN FEDERATION

2543 Cross-country Skiing and Ski Jumping

1992. Winter Olympic Games, Albertville, France. Multicoloured.
6311 14k. Type **2543** 10 10
6312 1r. Aerobatic skiing 20 10
6313 2r. Two and four-man bobsleighing 35 20

2544 Tiger Cubs

1992. Nature Conservation. Sheet 90 × 65 mm.
MS6314 **2544** 3r.+50k. multicoloured . . . . 1·25 85

2545 Battle Scene

1992. 750th Anniv of Battle of Lake Peipus. Sheet 95 × 65 mm.
MS6315 **2545** 50k. multicoloured 50 40

2546 Golden Gate, Vladimir

1992.
6316 **2546** 10k. orange 10 10
6317 – 15k. brown 10 10
6318 – 20k. red 10 10
6344 – 25k. red 10 10
6319 – 30k. black 10 10
6320 – 50k. blue 10 10
6321 – 55k. turquoise 10 10
6322 – 60k. green 10 10
6323 – 80k. purple 10 10
6324 – 1r. brown 10 10
6325 – 1r.50 green 10 10
6326 – 2r. blue 10 10
6327 – 3r. red 10 10
6328 – 4r. brown 10 10
6329 – 5r. brown 10 10
6330 – 6r. blue 10 10
6331 – 10r. blue 10 10
6332 – 15r. brown 10 10
6333 – 25r. purple 10 10
6334 – 45r. black 10 10
6335 – 50r. violet 10 10
6336 – 75r. brown 10 10
6337 – 100r. green 10 10
6338 **2546** 150r. blue 10 10
6339 – 250r. green 15 10
6340 – 300r. red 25 10
6341 – 500r. purple 30 10
6341a – 750r. green 25 10
6341b – 1000r. grey 35 15
6342 – 1500r. green 55 25
6342a – 2500r. bistre 85 40
6342b – 5000r. blue . . . . . 1·75 80
DESIGNS: 15k. Pskov kremlin; 20, 50k. St. George killing dragon; 25, 55k. Victory Arch, Moscow; 30, 80k. "Millennium of Russia" monument (M. Mikeshin), Novgorod; 60k., 300r. Statue of K. Minin and D. Pozharsky, Moscow; 1, 4r. Church, Kizhky; 1r.50, 6r. Statue of Peter I, St. Petersburg; 2r. St. Basil's Cathedral, Moscow; 3r. Tretyakov Gallery, Moscow; 5r. Europe House, Moscow; 10r. St. Isaac's Cathedral, St. Petersburg; 15, 45r. "The Horse-tamer" (statue), St. Petersburg; 25, 75r. Statue of Yuri Dolgoruky, Moscow; 50r. Rostov Kremlin; 100r. Moscow Kremlin; 250r. Church, Bogulyubovo; 500r. Moscow University; 750r. State Library, Moscow; 1000r. Peter and Paul Fortress, St. Petersburg; 1500r. Pushkin Museum, Moscow; 2500r. Admiralty, St. Petersburg; 5000r. Bolshoi Theatre, Moscow.

2547 "Victory" (N. Baskakov) **2548** Western Capercaillie, Oak and Pine

1992. Victory Day.
6350 **2547** 5k. multicoloured . . . 10 10

1992. Prioksko–Terrasnyi Nature Reserve.
6351 **2548** 50k. multicoloured . . 15 15

2549 "Mir" Space Station, Flags and Cosmonauts **2551** Pinocchio

2550 "Santa Maria" and Columbus

1992. Russian–German Joint Space Flight.
6352 **2549** 5r. multicoloured . . . 40 30

1992. 500th Anniv of Discovery of America by Columbus (1st issue). Sheet 88 × 65 mm.
MS6353 **2550** 3r. multicoloured 65 40
See also No. 6386.

1992. Characters from Children's Books (1st series). Multicoloured.
6354 25k. Type **2551** 10 10
6355 30k. Cipollino 10 10
6356 35k. Dunno 10 10
6357 50k. Karlson 15 10
See also Nos. 6391/5.

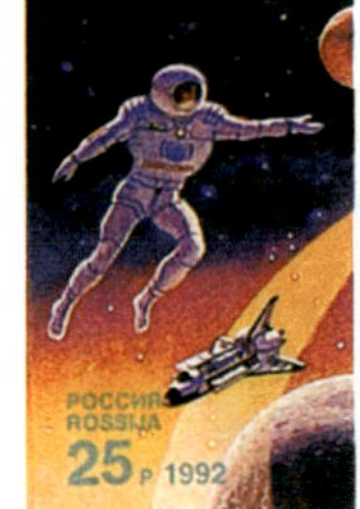

2552 Russian Cosmonaut and Space Shuttle **2553** Handball

1992. International Space Year. Multicoloured.
6358 25r. Type **2552** 15 10
6359 25r. American astronaut and "Mir" space station . . . 15 10
6360 25r. "Apollo" and "Vostok" spacecraft and sputnik . . 15 10
6361 25r. "Soyuz", "Mercury" and "Gemini" spacecraft 15 10
Nos. 6358/61 were issued together, se-tenant, forming a composite design.

1992. Olympic Games, Barcelona (2nd issue).
6362 **2553** 1r. multicoloured . . . 10 10
6363 – 2r. red, blue and black 10 10
6364 – 3r. red, green and black 15 10
DESIGNS—HORIZ: 2r. Fencing; 3r. Judo.

2554 L. A. Zagoskin and Yukon River, Alaska, 1842–44

1992. Expeditions. Multicoloured.
6365 55k. Type **2554** 10 10
6366 70k. N. N. Miklukho-Maklai in New Guinea, 1871–74 . . . . 10 10
6367 1r. G. I. Langsdorf and route map of expedition to Brazil, 1822–28 . . . . 10 10

2555 Garganeys

1992. Ducks. Multicoloured.
6368 1r. Type **2555** 15 10
6369 2r. Common pochards . . . 30 10
6370 3r. Falcated teals 40 20

2556 "Taj Mahal Mausoleum in Agra"

1992. 150th Birth Anniv of Vasily Vasilevich Vereshchagin (painter).
6371 1r.50 Type **2556** 15 10
6372 1r.50 "Don't Touch, Let Me Approach!" 15 10

2557 "The Saviour" (icon, Andrei Rublyov) **2558** Cathedral of the Assumption

1992.
6373 **2557** 1r. multicoloured . . . 10 10

1992. Moscow Kremlin Cathedrals. Multicoloured.
6374 1r. Type **2558** 10 10
6375 1r. Cathedral of the Annunciation (15th century) 10 10
6376 1r. Archangel Cathedral (16th century) 10 10
See also Nos. 6415/17 and 6440/2.

2559 Russian "Nutcracker" Puppets **2560** "Meeting of Joachim and Anna"

1992. Centenary of First Production of Tchaikovsky's Ballet "Nutcracker". Mult.
6377 10r. Type **2559** 10 10
6378 10r. German "Nutcracker" puppets 10 10
6379 25r. Pas de deux from ballet 30 20
6380 25r. Dance of the toys . . . 30 20

1992. Icons. Multicoloured.
6381 10r. Type **2560** 10 10
6382 10r. "Madonna and Child" 10 10
6383 10r. "Archangel Gabriel" (head) 10 10
6384 10r. "Saint Nicholas" (½-length portrait) 10 10

2561 Clockface and Festive Symbols **2562** "Discovery of America" Monument (Z. Tsereteli)

1992. New Year.
6385 **2561** 50k. multicoloured . . 10 10

1992. 500th Anniv of Discovery of America by Columbus.
6386 **2562** 15r. multicoloured . . . 20 10

2563 Petipa and Scene from "Paquita" **2564** Scrub 'n' Rub

1993. 175th Birth Anniv of Marius Petipa (choreographer). Multicoloured.
6387 25r. Type **2563** 10 10
6388 25r. "Sleeping Beauty", 1890 10 10
6389 25r. "Swan Lake", 1895 . . 10 10
6390 25r. "Raimunda", 1898 . . 10 10

1993. Characters from Children's Books (2nd series). Illustrations by Kornei Chukovsky. Mult.
6391 2r. Type **2564** 10 10
6392 3r. Big Cockroach 15 10
6393 10r. The Buzzer Fly 15 10
6394 15r. Doctor Doolittle . . . 15 10
6395 25r. Barmalei 20 10
Nos. 6391/5 were issued together, se-tenant, forming a composite design.

2565 Castle **2566** Part of Diorama in Belgorod Museum

1993. 700th Anniv of Vyborg.
6396 **2565** 10r. multicoloured . . . 10 10

1993. Victory Day. 50th Anniv of Battle of Kursk.
6397 **2566** 10r. multicoloured . . . 10 10

2567 African Violet **2568** "Molniya 3"

1993. Pot Plants. Multicoloured.
6398 10r. Type **2567** 10 10
6399 15r. "Hibiscus rosa-sinensis" 10 10
6400 25r. "Cyclamen persicum" 10 10
6401 50r. "Fuchsia hybrida" . . 15 10
6402 100r. "Begonia semperflorens" 35 25

1993. Communications Satellites. Multicoloured.
6403 25r. Type **2568** 10 10
6404 45r. "Ekran M" 10 10
6405 50r. "Gorizont" 10 10
6406 75r. "Luch" 15 10
6407 100r. "Ekspress" 20 15
MS6408 88 × 66 mm. 250r. Earth receiving station (horiz) 60 40

2569 Snuff Box (Dmitry Kolesnikov) and Tankard **2570** Map

1993. Silverware. Multicoloured.
6409 15r. Type **2569** 10 10
6410 25r. Teapot 10 10
6411 45r. Vase 10 10
6412 75r. Tray and candlestick 20 10
6413 100r. Cream jug, coffee pot and sugar basin (Aleksandr Kordes) . . . 25 15
MS6414 90 × 65 mm. 250r. Biscuit and sweet dishes (47 × 33 mm) 60 40

1993. Novgorod Kremlin. As T **2558**. Mult.
6415 25r. Kukui and Knyazhaya Towers (14th–17th century) 10 10
6416 25r. St. Sophia's Cathedral (11th century) 10 10
6417 25r. St. Sophia belfry (15th–18th century) 10 10
MS6418 70 × 93 mm. 250r. "Our Lady of the Apparition" (icon) (41 × 29 mm) 60 40

1993. Inauguration of Denmark–Russia Submarine Cable and 500th Anniv of Friendship Treaty.
6419 **2570** 90r. green & deep green 25 15

2571 Steller's Eider

1993. Ducks. Multicoloured.
6420 90r. Type **2571** 40 15
6421 100r. Eider 45 20
6422 250r. King eider . . . . . 1·10 55

2572 Ringed Seal

1993. Marine Animals. Multicoloured.
6423 50r. Type **2572** 20 10
6424 60r. "Paralithodes brevipes" (crab) 20 10
6425 90r. Japanese common squid 50 25
6426 100r. Cherry salmon 70 30
6427 250r. Fulmar . . . . 1·00 55

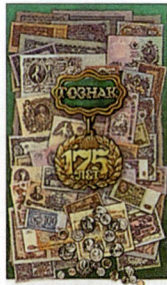

2573 Ceramic Candlestick, Skopino
2574 Banknotes and Coins

1993. Traditional Art. Multicoloured.
6428 50r. Type **2573** 10 10
6429 50r. Painted tray with picture "Summer Troika", Zhostovo (horiz) 10 10
6430 100r. Painted box, lid and distaff, Gorodets 15 10
6431 100r. Enamel icon of St. Dmitry of Solun, Rostov 15 10
6432 250r. "The Resurrection" (lacquer miniature), Fedoskino 35 20

1993. 175th Anniv of Goznak (State printing works and mint).
6433 **2574** 100r. multicoloured . . 15 10

2575 Peter I and "Goto Predestinatsiya"

1993. 300th Anniv of Russian Navy (1st issue). Multicoloured.
6434 100r. Type **2575** 15 10
6435 100r. K. A. Shilder and first all-metal submarine . . . 15 10
6436 100r. I. A. Amosov and "Arkhimed" (frigate) . . 15 10
6437 100r. I. G. Bubnov and "Bars" (submarine) . . . 15 10
6438 100r. B. M. Malinin and "Dekabrist" (submarine) 15 10
6439 100r. A. I. Maslov and "Kirov" (cruiser) 15 10

See also Nos. 6502/5, 6559/62 and 6612/18.

1993. Moscow Kremlin. As T **2558**. Mult.
6440 100r. Faceted Hall (15th century) 15 10
6441 100r. Church of the Deposition of the Virgin's Robe (15th century) . . . 15 10
6442 100r. Grand Palace (17th century) 15 10

2576 Tiger

1993. The Tiger. Multicoloured.
6443 50r. Type **2576** 10 10
6444 100r. Tiger in undergrowth 15 10
6445 250r. Two tiger cubs 30 15
6446 500r. Tiger in snow 60 30

2577 Splash of Blood on Figure
2579 Indian Elephant

2578 Seasonal Decorations

1993. Anti-AIDS Campaign.
6447 **2577** 90r. red, black and lilac 10 10

1993. New Year.
6448 **2578** 25r. multicoloured . . . 10 10

1993. Animals. Multicoloured.
6449 250r. Type **2579** 30 15
6450 250r. Japanese white-naped crane 40 20
6451 250r. Giant panda 30 15
6452 250r. American bald eagle 40 20
6453 250r. Dall's porpoise . . . 30 15
6454 250r. Koala 30 15
6455 250r. Hawaiian monk seal 30 15
6456 250r. Grey whale 30 15

2580 Rimsky-Korsakov and Scene from "Sadko"

1994. 150th Birth Anniv of Nikolai Rimsky-Korsakov (composer). Scenes from his operas. Multicoloured.
6457 250r. Type **2580** 25 15
6458 250r. "The Golden Cockerel" 25 15
6459 250r. "The Tsar's Bride" . . 25 15
6460 250r. "The Snow Maiden" 25 15

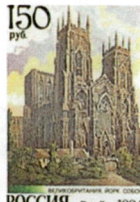

2581 "Epiphyllum peacockii"
2582 York Minster, Great Britain

1994. Cacti. Multicoloured.
6461 50r. Type **2581** 10 10
6462 100r. "Mammillaria swinglei" 10 10
6463 100r. "Lophophora williamsii" 10 10
6464 250r. "Opuntia basilaris" . . 30 15
6465 250r. "Selenicereus grandiflorus" 30 15

1994. Churches. Multicoloured.
6466 150r. Type **2582** 15 10
6467 150r. Small Metropolis church, Athens 15 10
6468 150r. Roskilde Cathedral, Denmark 15 10
6469 150r. Notre Dame Cathedral, Paris 15 10
6470 150r. St. Peter's, Vatican City 15 10
6471 150r. Cologne Cathedral, Germany 15 10
6472 150r. Seville Cathedral, Spain 15 10
6473 150r. St. Basil's Cathedral, Moscow 15 10
6474 150r. St. Patrick's Cathedral, New York 15 10

2583 "Soyuz" entering Earth's Atmosphere and "TsF-18" Centrifuge

1994. Yuri Gagarin Cosmonaut Training Centre. Multicoloured.
6475 100r. Type **2583** 10 10
6476 250r. "Soyuz"–"Mir" space complex and "Mir" simulator 15 10
6477 500r. Cosmonaut on space walk and hydrolaboratory 30 15

2584 Map and Rocket Launchers (Liberation of Russia)

1994. 50th Anniv of Liberation. Multicoloured.
6478 100r. Type **2584** 10 10
6479 100r. Map and airplanes (Ukraine) 10 10
6480 100r. Map, tank and soldiers (Belorussia) . . . 10 10

2585 Beautiful Gate, Moscow

1994. Architects' Birth Anniversaries.
6481 **2585** 50r. sepia, black and brown 10 10
6482 – 100r. brown, black and flesh 10 10
6483 – 150r. green, black and olive 15 10
6484 – 300r. violet, black and grey 35 15

DESIGNS: 50r. Type **2585** (D. V. Ukhtomsky, 250th anniv); 100r. Academy of Sciences, St. Petersburg (Giacomo Quarenghi, 250th anniv); 150r. Trinity Cathedral, St. Petersburg (V. P. Stasov, 225th anniv); 300r. Church of Christ the Saviour, Moscow (K. A. Ton, bicentenary).

2586 "Christ and the Sinner"

1994. 150th Birth Anniv of Vasily Dmitrievich Polenev (painter). Multicoloured.
6485 150r. Type **2586** 15 10
6486 150r. "Golden Autumn" . . 15 10

2587 European Wigeon
2588 Games Emblem and Runners

1994. Ducks. Multicoloured.
6487 150r. Type **2587** 15 10
6488 250r. Tufted duck 25 15
6489 300r. Baikal teal 50 30

1994. 3rd Goodwill Games, St. Petersburg.
6490 **2588** 100r. multicoloured . . 10 10

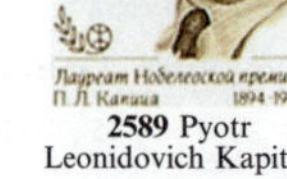
2589 Pyotr Leonidovich Kapitsa

2591 Design Motifs of First Russian Stamp

2590 Olympic Flag

1994. Physics Nobel Prize Winners. Each sepia.
6491 150r. Type **2589** (1978) . . . 15 10
6492 150r. Pavel Alekseevich Cherenkov (1958) 15 10

1994. Cent of International Olympic Committee.
6493 **2590** 250r. multicoloured . . 20 10

1994. Russian Stamp Day.
6494 **2591** 125r. multicoloured . . 10 10

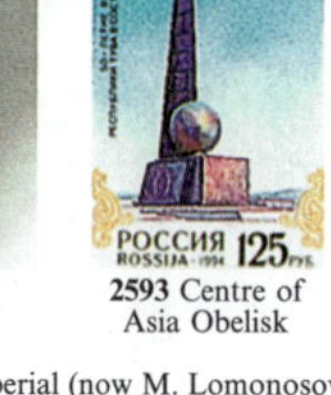
2592 Snuff Box (D. Vinogradov)
2593 Centre of Asia Obelisk

1994. 250th Anniv of Imperial (now M. Lomonosov) Porcelain Factory, St. Petersburg. Multicoloured.
6495 50r. Type **2592** 10 10
6496 100r. Candlestick 10 10
6497 150r. "Water-Carrier" (statuette, after S. Pimenov) 10 10
6498 250r. Sphinx vase 25 15
6499 300r. "Lady with Mask" (statuette, after K. Somov) 30 15
MS6500 60 × 90 mm. 500r. Dinner service (F. Solntsev) (36 × 36 mm) 60 30

1994. 50th Anniv of Incorporation of Tuva into Russian Socialist Federal Soviet Republic (R.S.F.S.R.).
6501 **2593** 125r. mulitcoloured . . 10 10

2594 Vice-Admiral V. M. Golovnin (Kurile Islands, 1811)

1994. 300th Anniv of Russian Navy (2nd issue). Explorations. Multicoloured.
6502 250r. Type **2594** 20 10
6503 250r. Admiral I. F. Kruzenshtern (first Russain round-the-world expedition, 1803–06) . . . 20 10
6504 250r. Admiral Ferdinand Petrovich Vrangel (Alaska, 1829–35) 20 10
6505 250r. Admiral F. P. Litke (Novaya Zemlya, 1821–24) 20 10

2595 Horses and Grandfather Frost

1994. New Year.
6506 **2595** 125r. blue, red and black 10 10

2596 Griboedov (after N. I. Utkin)

1995. Birth Bicentenary of Aleksandr Sergeevich Griboedov (dramatist and diplomat).
6507 **2596** 250r. brown, light brown and black . . 15 10

2597 "Sheherazade"

1995. 115th Birth Anniv of Mikhail Fokine (choreographer). Scenes from Ballets. Mult.
6508 500r. Type **2597** 25 15
6509 500r. "The Fire Bird" . . . 25 15
6510 500r. "Petrushka" 25 15

2598 Kutuzov (after J. Doe) and Sculptures from Monument, Moscow

1995. 250th Birth Anniv of Field-Marshal Mikhail Ilarionovich Kutuzov, Prince of Smolensk.
6511 **2598** 300r. multicoloured . . 15 10

2599 English Yard, Varvarka Street

2600 Syringes and Drugs around Addict

1995. 850th Anniv (1997) of Moscow (1st issue). Multicoloured.
6512 125r. Type **2599** 10 10
6513 250r. House of Averky Kirillov (scribe), Bersenevskaya Embankment 10 10
6514 300r. Volkov house, Bolshoi Kharitonevsky Lane . . . 15 10
See also Nos. 6600/5, **MS**6649 and 6666/75.

1995. U.N. Anti-drugs Decade.
6515 **2600** 150r. multicoloured . . 10 10

2601 Shoreline

1995. Endangered Animals. Multicoloured.
6516 250r. Type **2601** 15 10
6517 250r. Ringed seal 15 10
6518 250r. Lynx 15 10
6519 250r. Landscape 15 10
Nos. 6516/19 were issued together, se-tenant, Nos. 6516/17 and 6518/19 respectively forming composite designs.

2602 Tomb of the Unknown Soldier, Moscow

1995. 50th Anniv of End of Second World War. Multicoloured.
6520 250r. Sir Winston Churchill, U.S. Pres. Franklin Roosevelt and Iosif Stalin (Yalta Conference) (horiz) 15 10
6521 250r. Storming of the Reichstag, Berlin (horiz) 15 10
6522 250r. Flags, map of Germany and German banners (Potsdam Conference) 15 10
6523 250r. Bombers (operation against Japanese in Manchuria (horiz)) . . . 15 10
6524 250r. Urn with victims' ashes, Auschwitz, and memorial, Sachsenhausen (liberation of concentration camps) (horiz) 15 10
6525 250r. Type **2602** 15 10
6526 500r. Victory Parade, Moscow (36 × 47 mm) . . 40 20
MS6527 64 × 89 mm. No. 6526 40 30

2603 Aleksandr Popov (radio pioneer) and Radio-telegraph Equipment

2604 Spreading Bellflower

1995. Centenary of Radio.
6528 **2603** 250r. multicoloured . . 10 10

1995. Meadow Flowers. Multicoloured.
6529 250r. Type **2604** 15 10
6530 250r. Ox-eye daisy ("Leucanthemum vulgare") 15 10
6531 300r. Red clover ("Trifolium pratense") 15 10
6532 300r. Brown knapweed ("Centaurea jacea") . . . 15 10
6533 500r. Meadow cranesbill . . 25 15

2605 Eurasian Sky Lark ("Alauda arvensis")

2606 U.S. Space Shuttle "Atlantis"

1995. Songbirds. Multicoloured.
6534 250r. Type **2605** 15 10
6535 250r. Song thrush ("Turdus philomelos") 15 10
6536 500r. Eurasian goldfinch ("Carduelis carduelis") . . 30 15
6537 500r. Bluethroat ("Cyanosylvia svecica") 30 15
6538 750r. Thrush nightingale ("Luscinia luscinia") . . . 45 25

1995. Russian–American Space Co-operation. Mult.
6539 1500r. Type **2606** 55 25
6540 1500r. "Mir" space station 55 25
6541 1500r. "Apollo" spacecraft 55 25
6542 1500r. "Soyuz" spacecraft 55 25
Nos. 6539/42 were issued together, se-tenant, forming a composite design of the spacecraft over Earth.

2607 Cathedral of the Trinity, Jerusalem

2608 Kremlin Cathedrals

1995. Russian Orthodox Churches Abroad. Mult.
6543 300r. Type **2607** 15 10
6544 300r. Apostles Saints Peter and Paul Cathedral, Karlovy Vary, Czechoslovakia 15 10
6545 500r. St. Nicholas's Cathedral, Vienna 30 15
6546 500r. St. Nicholas's Cathedral, New York . . 30 15
6547 750r. St. Aleksei's Cathedral, Leipzig 45 20

1995. 900th Anniv of Ryazan.
6548 **2608** 250r. multicoloured . . 10 10

2609 Easter Egg with Model of "Shtandart" (yacht)

1995. Faberge Exhibits in Moscow Kremlin Museum. Multicoloured.
6549 150r. Type **2609** 10 10
6550 250r. Goblet 15 10
6551 300r. Cross pendant 20 10
6552 500r. Ladle 30 15
6553 750r. Easter egg with model of Alexander III monument 45 25
MS6554 65 × 90 mm. 1500r. "Moscow Kremlin" easter egg (36 × 51 mm) 90 60

2610 Harlequin Duck

1995. Ducks. Multicoloured.
6555 500r. Type **2610** 25 15
6556 750r. Baer's pochard 40 20
6557 1000r. Goosander 60 30

2611 City Buildings

1995. "Singapore '95" International Stamp Exhibition Sheet 90 × 65 mm.
MS6558 **2611** 2500r. multicoloured 1·10 75

2612 "The Battle of Grengam, July 27, 1720" (F. Perrault)

1995. 300th Anniv of Russian Navy (3rd issue). Paintings. Multicoloured.
6559 250r. Type **2612** 15 10
6560 300r. "Preparations for Attacking the Turkish Fleet in the Bay of Cesme, Night of June 26, 1770" (P. Hackert) . . . 20 10
6561 500r. "The Battle at the Revel Roadstead, May 2, 1790" (A. Bogolyubov) 35 20
6562 750r. "The Kronstadt Roadstead" (I. Aivazovsky) 45 25

2613 State Flag and Arms

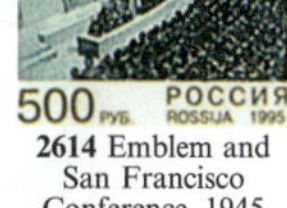

2614 Emblem and San Francisco Conference, 1945

1995. Constitution of the Russian Federation.
6563 **2613** 500r. multicoloured . . 25 10

1995. 50th Anniv of U.N.O.
6564 **2614** 500r. brown, blue and yellow 25 10

2615 White Storks in Nest

1995. Europa. Peace and Freedom. Multicoloured.
6565 1500r. Type **2615** 80 40
6566 1500r. Stork flying over landscape 80 40
Nos. 6565/6 were issued together, se-tenant, forming a composite design.

2616 "Birth of Christ" (icon, Assumption Cathedral, St. Cyril's Monastery, White Sea)

2618 Semyonov

2617 Yuri Dolgoruky (1090–1157), Kiev and Building of Moscow

1995. Christmas.
6567 **2616** 500r. multicoloured . . 20 10

1995. History of Russian State (1st series). Mult.
6568 1000r. Type **2617** 45 20
6569 1000r. Aleksandr Nevsky (1220–63), Battle of Lake Peipus and as Grand Duke of Vladimir 45 20
6570 1000r. Mikhail Yaroslavich (1271–1318), Tver and torture by the Golden Horde 45 20
6571 1000r. Dmitry Donskoi (1350–89), Moscow Kremlin and Battle of Kulikovo 45 20
6572 1000r. Ivan III (1440–1505), marriage to Sophia Paleologa and Battle of Ugra River 45 20
See also Nos. 6640/3.

1996. Birth Centenary of Nikolai Semyonov (Nobel Prize winner for chemistry, 1956).
6573 **2618** 750r. grey 30 15

2619 Pansies

2620 Tabbies

1996. Flowers. Multicoloured.
6574 500r. Type **2619** 20 10
6575 750r. Sweet-williams ("Dianthus barbatus") . . 35 15
6576 750r. Sweet peas ("Lathyrus odoratus") 35 15
6577 1000r. Crown imperial ("Fritillaria imperialis") 45 25
6578 1000r. Snapdragons ("Antirrhinum majus") . . 45 25

1996. Cats. Multicoloured.
6579 1000r. Type **2620** 40 20
6580 1000r. Russian blue 40 20
6581 1000r. White Persian . . . 40 20
6582 1000r. Sealpoint Siamese . . 40 20
6583 1000r. Siberian 40 20

2621 Torch Bearer

1996. Centenary of Modern Olympic Games. Sheet 64 × 85 mm.
MS6584 **2621** 5000r. multicoloured 1·90 1·00

2622 "Laying down of Banners" (A. Mikhailov)

1996. Victory Day.
6585 **2622** 1000r. multicoloured . . 40 20

2623 Tula Kremlin and Monument to Peter I

1996. 850th Anniv of Tula.
6586 **2623** 1500r. multicoloured . . 60 30

2624 Putilovsky Works Tramcar, 1896

1996. Centenary of First Russian Tramway, Nizhny Novgorod. Multicoloured.

6587 500r. Type **2624** 20 10
6588 750r. Sormovo tramcar, 1912 . . . . 35 15
6589 750r. 1928 Series X tramcar, 1928 . . . . 35 15
6590 1000r. 1931 Series KM tramcar, 1931 . . . . . . 40 20
6591 1000r. Type LM-57 tramcar, 1957 . . . . 40 20
6592 2500r. Model 71-608K tramcar, 1973 . . . . . . 75 45
MS6593 80 × 68 mm. No. 6592 75 55

50 лет ЮНИСЕФ
РОССИЯ 1000 руб

2625 Ye. Dashkova (President of Academy of Sciences)

2626 Children walking Hand in Hand

1996. Europa. Famous Women.
6594 **2625** 1500r. green and black 60 30
6595 – 1500r. purple and black 60 30
DESIGN: No. 6594, S. Kovalevskaya (mathematician).

1996. 50th Anniv of UNICEF.
6596 **2626** 1000r. multicoloured . . 40 20

2627 "Post Troika in Snowstorm" (P. Sokolov)

1996. Post Troikas in Paintings. Muliticoloured.
6597 1500r. Type **2627** 60 30
6598 1500r. "Post Troika in Summer" (P. Sokolov) . . 60 30
6599 1500r. "Post Troika" (P. Gruzinsky) 60 30

2628 "View of Bridge over Yauza and of Shapkin House in Moscow" (J. Delabarte)

1996. 850th Anniv (1997) of Moscow (2nd issue). Paintings. Multicoloured.
6600 500r. Type **2628** 20 10
6601 500r. "View of Moscow from Balcony of Kremlin Palace" (detail, J. Delabarte) 20 10
6602 750r. "View of Voskresenskie and Nikolskie Gates and Kamenny Bridge" (F. Ya. Alekseev) 35 20
6603 750r. "Moscow Yard near Volkhonka" (anon) . . . 35 20
6604 1000r. "Varvarka Street" (anon) 40 20
6605 1000r. "Sledge Races in Petrovsky Park" 40 20

2629 Traffic Policeman and Pedestrian Crossing

1996. 60th Anniv of Traffic Control Department. Sheet 120 × 150 mm containing T **2629** and similar horiz designs. Multicoloured.
MS6606 1500r. Type **2629**; 1500r. Children learning road safety; 1500r. Examiner and learner vehicle . . . . 1·60 1·25

2630 Basketball

2632 Gorsky and Scenes from "Gudula's Daughter" and "Salambo"

2631 "Yevstafy" (ship of the line), 1762

1996. Olympic Games, Atlanta, U.S.A. Mult.
6607 500r. Type **2630** 20 10
6608 1000r. Boxing 40 20
6609 1000r. Swimming 40 20
6610 1500r. Gymnastics 60 30
6611 1500r. Hurdling 60 30

1996. 300th Anniv of Russian Navy (4th issue).
(a) As T **2631**.
6612 **2631** 750r. brown and yellow 35 20
6613 – 1000r. deep blue, cobalt and blue 40 20
6614 – 1000r. purple, pink and rose 40 20
6615 – 1500r. multicoloured . . 60 30
6616 – 1500r. black, grey and stone 60 30
DESIGNS: No. 6613, "Petropavlovsk" (battleship); 6614, "Novik" (destroyer); 6615, "Tashkent" (destroyer); 6616, "S-13" (submarine).

(b) Size 35 x 24 mm. Each blue and black.
6617 1000r. "Principium" (galley) 40 20
6618 1000r. "Admiral Kuznetsov" (aircraft carrier) 40 20

Sheet size 130 × 65 mm containing as Nos. 6617/18 and similar horiz designs. Multicoloured (blue background).
MS6619 1000r. As No. 6617; 1000r. Nuclear-powered submarine; 1000r. "Azov" (ship of the line); 1000r. As No. 6618 . . . . . 1·60 1·25

1996. 125th Birth Anniv of Aleksandr Gorsky (ballet choreographer). Multicoloured.
6620 750r. Type **2632** 35 20
6621 750r. Scene from "La Bayadere" 35 20
6622 1500r. Scene from "Don Quixote" 60 30
6623 1500r. Scene from "Giselle" 60 30

2633 National Flags

1996. Formation of Community of Sovereign Republics (union of Russian Federation and Belarus).
6624 **2633** 1500r. multicoloured . . 60 30

2634 Chalice

1996. Objets d'Art. Multicoloured.
6625 1000r. Type **2634** 40 20
6626 1000r. Perfume bottles . . . 40 20
6627 1000r. Double inkwell . . . 40 20
6628 1500r. Coffee pot 60 30
6629 1500r. Pendent scent containers (one ladybird-shaped) 60 30
MS6630 70 × 90 mm. 5000r. "Our Lady of Kazan" (icon) (36 × 51 mm) . . . . 2·00 1·50

2635 Symbols of Science and Culture on Open Book

1996. 50th Anniv of UNESCO.
6631 **2635** 1000r. black, gold and blue 40 20

2636 "Madonna and Child" (icon), Moscow

2637 Clockface of Spassky Tower, Moscow Kremlin

1996. Orthodox Religion. Multicoloured.
6632 1500r. Type **2636** 60 30
6633 1500r. Stavrovouni Monastery, Cyprus . . . 60 30
6634 1500r. "St. Nicholas" (icon), Cyprus 60 30
6635 1500r. Voskresenkie ("Resurrection") Gate, Moscow 60 30

1996. New Year.
6636 **2637** 1000r. multicoloured . . 35 15

2638 First Match between U.S.S.R. and Canada, 1972

1996. 50th Anniv of Ice Hockey in Russia. Mult.
6637 1500r. Type **2638** 60 30
6638 1500r. Goalkeeper and players (first match between Moscow and Prague, 1948) 60 30
6639 1500r. Players and referee (Russia versus Sweden) 60 30

1996. History of Russian State (2nd series). As T **2617**. Multicoloured.
6640 1500r. Basil III (1479–1533), removal of bell from Pskov and Siege of Smolensk, 1514 . . . . . 60 30
6641 1500r. Ivan IV the Terrible (1530–84), coronation in Cathedral of the Assumption (Moscow Kremlin) and executions by the Oprichnina 60 30
6642 1500r. Fyodor I Ivanovich (1557–98), with Cossacks and Siberian Kings, and election of Iove (first Russian Patriarch) 60 30
6643 1500r. Boris Godunov (1551–1605), as Tsar in 1598 and food distribution during famine, 1601–03 . . . . 60 30

2639 Maule's Quince ("Chaenomeles japonica")

2640 Foundation Festival Emblem

1997. Shrubs. Multicoloured.
6644 500r. Type **2639** 20 10
6645 500r. Ornamental almond ("Amygdalus triloba") . . 20 10
6646 1000r. Broom ("Cytisus scoparius") 40 20
6647 1000r. Burnet rose ("Rosa pimpinellifolia") 40 20
6648 1000r. Mock orange ("Philadelphus coronarius") 40 20

1997. 850th Anniv of Moscow (3rd issue). Sheet 94 × 71 mm.
MS6649 **2640** 3000r. multicoloured 1·25 90

2641 Dmitri Shostakovich (composer) (from 90th birth anniv (1996) medal)

1997. "Shostakovich and World Musical Culture" International Music Festival.
6650 **2641** 1000r. multicoloured . . 35 15

2642 Russian Federation Arms

2643 Post Emblem

1997. 500th Anniv of Double Eagle as Russian State Emblem. Sheet 94 × 76 mm.
MS6651 **2642** 3000r. multicoloured 1·10 80

1997.
6652 **2643** 100r. brown and black 10 10
6653 – 150r. mauve and black 10 10
6654 – 250r. green and black 10 10
6655 – 300r. green and black 10 10
6656 – 500r. blue and black . . 15 10
6657 – 750r. brown and black 20 10
6658 – 1000r. red and blue . . 30 15
6659 – 1500r. blue and black 45 20
6660 – 2000r. green and black 60 30
6661 – 2500r. red and black . . 75 35
6662 – 3000r. violet and black 90 45
6663 – 5000r. brown and black 1·50 75
DESIGNS: 100r. Combine harvesters in field; 150r. Oil rigs; 250r. White storks; 300r. Radio mast; 750r. St. George killing dragon; 1000r. State flag and arms; 1500r. Electric pylon inside generating machinery; 2000r. Class VL65 electric railway locomotive; 2500r. Moscow Kremlin; 3000r. Space satellite; 5000r. Pianist and theatre.

For these designs in revised currency, see Nos. 6718/35.

2644 Ioan Zlatoust Church, Sofiiski Cathedral and Admiral Barsh's House

2645 "Volga Svyatoslavovich" (I. Bilibin)

1997. 850th Anniv of Vologda.
6664 **2644** 1000r. multicoloured . . 35 15

1997. Europa. Tales and Legends.
6665 **2645** 1500r. multicoloured . . 55 30

2646 Jesus Christ the Saviour Cathedral

1997. 850th Anniv of Moscow (3rd issue). Mult.
6666 1000r. Type **2646** 40 20
6667 1000r. Towers and walls of Kremlin 40 20
6668 1000r. Grand Palace and cathedrals, Kremlin . . . 40 20
6669 1000r. St. Basil's Cathedral, Spassky Tower and Trinity Church 40 20
6670 1000r. "St. George killing Dragon" (16th-century icon) 40 20

6671 1000r. First reference to Moscow in Ipatevsky Chronicle, 1147 . . . . . 40 20
6672 1000r. Prince Daniil Alexandrovich and Danilov Monastery . . . 40 20
6673 1000r. "Building Moscow Kremlin, 1366" (16th-century miniature) 40 20
6674 1000r. Kazan cap and "Coronation of Ivan IV" (miniature) 40 20
6675 1000r. 16th-century plan of Moscow 40 20

Nos. 6666/75 were issued together, se-tenant, Nos. 6666/70 forming a composite design of Moscow in late 19th century.

2647 Mil Mi-14 (float)

1997. Helicopters. Multicoloured.
6676 500r. Type **2647** 20 10
6677 1000r. Mil Mi-24 (gunship) 35 15
6678 1500r. Mil Mi-26 (transport) 55 30
6679 2000r. Mil Mi-28 (gunship) 70 35
6680 2500r. Mil Mi-34 (patrol) 90 45

2648 "The Priest and Balda"

1997. Birth Bicentenary (1999) of Aleksandr Sergeevich Pushkin (poet) (1st issue). Mult.
6681 500r. Type **2648** 15 10
6682 1000r. "Tsar Saltan" . . . 30 15
6683 1500r. "The Fisherman and the Golden Fish" 50 25
6684 2000r. "The Dead Princess and the Seven Knights" 60 30
6685 3000r. "The Golden Cockerel" 90 45

See also Nos. 6762/6 and 6827/9.

2649 Petrodvorets (St. Petersburg) National Flags and Marble Temple, Bangkok

1997. Centenary of Russia–Thailand Diplomatic Relations and of Visit of King Rama V to St. Petersburg.
6686 **2649** 1500r. multicoloured . . 45 20

2650 Siberian Flying Squirrel

1997. Wildlife. Multicoloured.
6687 500r. Type **2650** 20 10
6688 750r. Lynx 25 10
6689 1000r. Western capercaillie 35 15
6690 2000r. European otter . . . 70 35
6691 3000r. Western curlew . . . 1·25 65

2651 Arkhangel Province

1997. Regions of the Russian Federation (1st series). Multicoloured.
6692 1500r. Type **2651** 50 25
6693 1500r. Kaliningrad Province (vert) 50 25
6694 1500r. Kamchatka Province 50 25
6695 1500r. Krasnodar Territory 50 25
6696 1500r. Sakha Republic (Yakutiya) (vert) 50 25

See also Nos. 6784/8, 6831/5, 6920/5, 6980/4, 7062/6, 7153/8, 7229/33 and 7315/20.

2652 Klyopa flying with Balloons

1997. Klyopa (cartoon character). Multicoloured.
6697 500r. Type **2652** 15 10
6698 1000r. Klyopa hang-gliding over Red Square 30 15
6699 1500r. Klyopa in troika (45 × 33 mm) 45 20

2653 Emblem, Mascot and Russian Federation 1992 and 20k. Stamp

2654 Indian Flag and Asokan Capital

1997. "Moscow 97" International Stamp Exhbition. Multicoloured.
6700 1500r. Russian Empire 1858 10k. and R.S.F.S.R. 1918 35k. stamps, and Spassky Tower, Moscow Kremlin 50 25
6701 1500r. Type **2653** 50 25

1997. 50th Anniv of Independence of India.
6702 **2654** 500r. multicoloured . . 15 10

2655 Presentation of Standard

1997. 325th Birth Anniv of Tsar Peter I. Mult.
6703 2000r. Type **2655** (creation of regular army and navy) 60 30
6704 2000r. Sea battle (access to Baltic Sea) 60 30
6705 2000r. Peter I reviewing plans (construction of St. Petersburg) 60 30
6706 2000r. Council (administrative reforms) 60 30
6707 2000r. Boy before tutor (cultural and educational reforms) 60 30
MS6708 65 × 90 mm. 5000r. Peter I 1·60 1·25

2656 Pictograms of Five Events

1997. 50th Anniv of Modern Pentathlon in Russia.
6709 **2656** 1000r. multicoloured . . 30 15

2657 Match Scenes

1997. Centenary of Football in Russia.
6710 **2657** 2000r. multicoloured . . 60 30

2658 Radiation and Earth

2659 National Flag and Palace of Europe, Strasbourg

1997. World Ozone Layer Day. 10th Anniv of Montreal Protocol (on reduction of use of chlorofluorocarbons).
6711 **2658** 1000r. multicoloured . . 30 15

1997. Admission of Russian Federation to European Council.
6712 **2659** 1000r. multicoloured . . 30 15

2660 "Boris and Gleb" (14th-century icon)

2661 Sketch by Puskin of Himself and Onegin

1997. Centenary of Russian State Museum, St. Petersburg (1st issue). Multicoloured.
6713 500r. Type **2660** 15 10
6714 1000r. "Volga Boatmen" (I. Repin) (horiz) 30 15
6715 1500r. "Promenade" (Marc Chagall) 45 25
6716 2000r. "Merchant's Wife taking Tea" (B. Kustodiev) 60 30

See also Nos. 6753/**MS**6757.

1997. Translation into Hebrew by Abraham Shlonsky of Yevgeny Onegin (poem) by Aleksandr Pushkin. Sheet 76 × 60 mm.
MS6717 **2661** 3000r. black, magenta and yellow . . . . 1·00 75

1998. As Nos. 6652/63 but in reformed currency.
6718 10k. brown and black (as No. 6652) 10 10
6719 15k. mauve and black (as No. 6653) 10 10
6720 25k. green and black (as No. 6654) 10 10
6721 30k. green and black (as No. 6655) 10 10
6723 50k. blue and black (Type **2643**) 10 10
6726 1r. red and blue (as No. 6658) 15 10
6727 1r.50 blue and black (as No. 6659) 20 10
6728 2r. green and black (as No. 6660) 25 10
6729 2r.50 red and black (as No. 6661) 30 15
6730 3r. violet and black (as No. 6662) 35 20
6735 5r. brown and black (as No. 6663) 60 30

2662 "Menshikov in Beresovo" (detail, Surikov)

1998. 150th Birth Anniversaries of Vasily Ivanovich Surikov and V. M. Vasnetsov (artists). Multicoloured.
6741 1r.50 Type **2662** 20 10
6742 1r.50 "Morozov Boyar's Wife" (Surikov) 20 10
6743 1r.50 "Battle between Slavs and Nomads" (detail, Vasnetsov) (vert) 20 10
6744 1r.50 "Tsarevich Ivan on a Grey Wolf" (Vasnetsov) 20 10

2663 Cross-country Skiing

1998. Winter Olympic Games, Nagano, Japan. Mult.
6745 50k. Type **2663** 10 10
6746 1r. Figure skating (pairs) . . 15 10
6747 1r.50 Biathlon 20 10

2664 Red-tailed Black Labeo "Epalzeorhynchus bicolor"

1998. Fishes. Multicoloured.
6748 50k. Type **2664** 10 10
6749 50k. Jewel tetra ("Hyphessobrycon callistus") 10 10
6750 1r. Galina's catfish ("Synodontis galinae") . . 15 10
6751 1r.50 "Botia kristinae" . . . 20 10
6752 1r.50 "Cichlasoma labiatum" 20 10

2665 "The Last Day of Pompeii" (K. P. Bryullov)

1998. Centenary of State Russian Museum, St. Petersburg (2nd issue). Multicoloured.
6753 1r.50 Type **2665** 20 10
6754 1r.50 "The Ninth Wave" (I. K. Aivazovsky) . . . 20 10
6755 1r.50 "Pines for Masts" (I. I. Shishkin) 20 10
6756 1r.50 "Our Lady of Tenderness for Sick Hearts" (K. S. Petrov-Vodkin) 20 10
MS6757 91 × 70 mm. 3r. "The Milhailovsky Palace" (K.P. Beggrov) (51 × 36 mm) 40 20

2666 Saddleback Dolphins

1998. "Expo '98" World's Fair, Lisbon, Portugal. Sheet 91 × 71 mm.
MS6758 **2666** 3r. multicoloured 40 20

2667 Theatre and Characters

1998. Centenary of Moscow Art Theatre.
6759 **2667** 1r.50 multicoloured . . 20 10

2668 "End of Winter" (Shrove-tide)

1998. Europa. National Festivals.
6760 **2668** 1r.50 multicoloured . . 20 10

2669 War Memorial, Venets Hotel, History Museum and Goncharovsky Pavilion

2670 "The Lyceum"

1998. 350th Anniv of Ulyanovsk (formerly Simbirsk).
6761 **2669** 1r. multicoloured . . . 15 10

1998. Birth Bicentenary (1999) of Aleksandr Sergeevich Pushkin (poet) (2nd issue). Drawings by Pushkin.
6762 **2670** 1r.50 black and blue . . 20 10
6763 – 1r.50 brown, stone & blk 20 10
6764 – 1r.50 brown, stone & blk 20 10
6765 – 1r.50 brown, stone & blk 20 10
6766 – 1r.50 black and blue . . 20 10
DESIGNS: No. 6763, "A.N. Wolf"; 6764, Self-portrait; 6765, "Tatyana" (from "Vevgeny Onegin"); 6766, Knight in armour (manuscript cover from 1830).

2671 Local History Museum and Peter I Monument

2672 Games Emblem

1998. 300th Anniv of Taganrog.
6767 **2671** 1r. multicoloured . . . 15 10

1998. World Youth Games, Moscow. Sheet 70 × 90 mm.
MS6768 **2672** 3r. multicoloured 40 20

2673 Tsar Nicholas II

2674 Grapes

1998. 80th Death Anniv of Tsar Nicholas II.
6769 **2673** 3r. multicoloured . . . 35 20

1998. Berries. Multicoloured.
6770 50k. Type **2674** 10 10
6771 75k. Raspberry 10 10
6772 1r. Magnolia vine 15 10
6773 1r.50 Cowberrry 20 10
6774 2r. Arctic bramble 25 15

2675 Landmarks

2676 Leontina Cohen

1998. 275th Anniv of Yekaterinburg.
6775 **2675** 1r. multicoloured . . . 15 10

1998. Intelligence Agents.
6776 **2676** 1r. blue, indigo & blk 15 10
6777 – 1r. brown, yellow & blk 15 10
6778 – 1r. green, dp green & blk 15 10
6779 – 1r. purple, brown & blk 15 10
DESIGNS: No. 6777, Morris Cohen; 6778, L. R. Kvasnikov; 6779, A. A. Yatskov.

2677 Order of St. Andrew

1998. Russian Orders (1st series). Multicoloured.
6780 1r. Type **2677** 15 10
6781 1r.50 Order of St. Catherine 20 10
6782 2r. Order of St. Aleksandr Nevsky 25 15
6783 2r.50 Order of St. George 30 15
See also Nos. 6807/11 and 7242/7.

1998. Regions of the Russian Federation (2nd series). As T **2651**. Multicoloured.
6784 1r.50 Republic of Buryatiya (vert) 20 10
6785 1r.50 Republic of Kareliya (vert) 20 10
6786 1r.50 Khabarovsk Province 20 10
6787 1r.50 Murmansk Province 20 10
6788 1r.50 Primorsky Province . . 20 10

2678 Universal Postal Union Emblem

1998. World Post Day.
6789 **2678** 1r. multicoloured . . . 15 10

2679 Anniversary Emblem

1998. 50th Anniv of Universal Declaration of Human Rights.
6790 **2679** 1r.50 multicoloured . . 20 10

2680 Headquarters, Moscow

1998. 10th Anniv of Menatep Bank.
6791 **2680** 2r. multicoloured . . . 25 15

2681 Aviation

1998. Achievements of the Twentieth Century. Multicoloured.
6792 1r. Type **2681** 15 10
6793 1r. Computers 15 10
6794 1r. Genetics 15 10
6795 1r. Nuclear energy 15 10
6796 1r. Space exploration . . . 15 10
6797 1r. Television 15 10

2682 Koshkin

1998. Birth Centenary of Mikhail Ilich Koshkin (tank designer).
6798 **2682** 1r. multicoloured . . . 15 10

2683 Grandfather Frost

1998. New Year.
6799 **2683** 1r. multicoloured . . . 15 10

2684 Telephone and Switchboard Operators

1999. Centenary of First Long-distance Telephone Link in Russia (between Moscow and St. Petersburg).
6800 **2684** 1r. multicoloured . . . 15 10

2685 Western Capercaillie

1999. Hunting. Multicoloured.
6801 1r. Type **2685** 15 10
6802 1r.50 Shooting mallard ducks from rowing boat 20 10
6803 2r. Falconry (Gyr falcon) 25 15
6804 2r.50 Wolves 30 15
6805 3r. Bears 35 20

2686 Russian Ship of the Line off Corfu

1999. Bicentenary of Russian Naval Expedition to Mediterranean under Command of Admiral Fyodor Ushakov. Sheet 90 × 70 mm.
MS6806 **2686** 5r. multicoloured 60 45

1999. Russian Orders (2nd series). As T **2677**. Multicoloured.
6807 1r. Order of St. Vladimir . . 15 10
6808 1r.50 Order of St. Anne . . 20 10
6809 2r. Order of St. John of Jerusalem 25 15
6810 2r.50 Order of the White Eagle 30 15
6811 3r. Order of St. Stanislas . . 35 20

2687 18th-century Ship of the Line

1999. 300th Anniv of Adoption of St. Andrew's Flag by Tsar Peter I. Sheet 90 × 70 mm.
MS6812 **2687** 7r. multicoloured 75 75

2688 "Family at Tea" (Sofya Kondrashina)

1999. Russia in the 21st Century. Children's paintings. Multicoloured.
6813 1r.20 Type **2688** 15 10
6814 1r.20 "My Town" (Yuri Lapushkov) 15 10
6815 1r.20 "Fantasy City" (Aleksander Khudyshin) (vert) 15 10

2689 "Alpha" International Space Station

1999. Space Exploration Day. Sheet 120 × 68 mm.
MS6816 **2689** 7r. multicoloured 75 75

2690 Albrecht Durer's House

1999. "iBRA '99" International Stamp Exhibition, Nuremberg, Germany.
6817 **2690** 3r. multicoloured . . . 30 15

2691 Setting Weighted Lines

1999. Fishing. Multicoloured.
6818 1r. Type **2691** 10 10
6819 2r. Fishing by rod and line from bank and boat . . . 20 10
6820 2r. Fishing by rod and line from kayak 20 10
6821 3r. Fishing through holes in ice 30 15
6822 3r. Underwater fishing . . . 30 15

2692 Council Flag and Headquarters, Strasbourg, and Spassky Tower, Moscow

1999. 50th Anniv of Council of Europe.
6823 **2692** 3r. multicoloured . . . 30 15

2693 Oksky State Natural Biosphere Preserve

1999. Europa. Parks and Gardens.
6824 **2693** 5r. multicoloured . . . 55 30

2694 Stag

1999. Red Deer. Multicoloured.
6825 2r.50 Type **2694** 25 15
6826 2r.50 Doe and fawns . . . 25 15

2695 Pushkin, 1815 (after S. G. Chirikov)

2696 Rose "Carina" ("Happy Birthday")

1999. Birth Bicentenary of Aleksandr Sergeevich Pushkin (poet) (3rd issue). Multicoloured.
6827 1r. Type **2695** 10 10
6828 3r. Pushkin, 1826 (after I.-E. Viven) 30 15
6829 5r. Pushkin, 1836 (after Karl Bryullov) 55 25
MS6830 110 × 70 mm. 7r. Pushkin, 1827 (after V. A. Tropinin) (29 × 41 mm) 70 70

1999. Regions of the Russian Federation (3rd series). As T **2651**. Multicoloured.
6831 2r. Republic of North Osetia-Alaniya 20 10
6832 2r. Republic of Bashkortostan (vert) . . . 20 10
6833 2r. Kirov Province 20 10
6834 2r. Evenk Autonomous Region (vert) 20 10
6835 2r. Stavropol Region . . . 20 10

1999. Greetings stamps. Roses. Multicoloured.
6836 1r.20 Type **2696** 15 10
6837 1r.20 "Gloria Dei" ("From the bottom of my heart") 15 10
6838 2r. "Candia" ("Congratulations") . . . 20 10
6839 3r. "Confidence" ("Be happy") 30 15
6840 4r. "Ave Maria" ("With love") 40 20

1999. No. 6342b surch **1.20**.
6841 1r.20 on 5000r. blue 15 10

2698 River Station, City Arms and Nativity of the Virgin Cathedral

1999. 250th Anniv of Rostov-on-Don.
6842 **2698** 1r.20 multicoloured . . 15 10

2699 Automatic Post Sorting

1999. 125th Anniv of Universal Postal Union.
6843 **2699** 3r. multicoloured . . . 30 15

2700 "Horsewoman"

1999. Birth Bicentenary of Karl Bryullov (painter). Multicoloured.
6844 2r.50 Type **2700** 25 15
6845 2r.50 "Portrait of Yu. P. Samoilova and Amacilia Paccini" 25 15

2701 IZh-1 Motorcycle, 1929

1999. Russian Motor Cycles. Multicoloured.
6846 1r. Type **2701** 10 10
6847 1r.50 L-300, 1930 . . . . . 15 15
6848 2r. M-72, 1941 . . . . . . 20 10
6849 2r.50 M-1-A, 1945 . . . . 25 15
6850 5r. IZ–"Planeta-5", 1987 . . 55 25

2702 Suvorov's Vanguard passing Lake Klontal (after engraving by L. Hess)

1999. Bicentenary of General Aleksandr Suvorov's Crossing of the Alps. Multicoloured.
6851 2r.50 Type **2702** . . . . .
6852 2r.50 Schollenen Gorge Monument, Suvorov and soldiers . . . .

2703 Horse Racing

1999. Traditional Sports. Multicoloured.
6853 2r. Type **2703** 20 10
6854 2r. Wrestling 20 10
6855 2r. Gorodki (game with stick and blocks of wood) 20 10
6856 2r. Sleigh and deer team race 20 10
6857 2r. Weightlifting (vert) . . . 20 10

2704 Leonid Utesov

1999. Singers. Multicoloured.
6858 2r. Type **2704** 20 10
6859 2r. Lidiya Ruslanova (in costume) 20 10
6860 2r. Klavdiya Shulzhenko (with hands clasped) . . . 20 10
6861 2r. Mark Bernes (playing accordion) 20 10
6862 2r. Bulat Okudzhava (playing guitar in street scene) 20 10
6863 2r. Vladimir Vysotsky (with guitar and arms out wide) 20 10
6864 2r. Igor Talkov (with arm raised) 20 10
6865 2r. Victor Tsoi (playing guitar) 20 10

2705 Players chasing Ball and Club Badge

1999. Spartak-Alaniya, National Football Champions.
6877 **2705** 2r. multicoloured . . . 20 10

2706 Father Christmas and "2000"

1999. Christmas and New Year. Multicoloured.
6878 1r.20 Type **2706** 15 10
6879 1r.20 "2000", globe as pearl and shell 15 10

2707 "The Raising of the Daughter of Jairus" (V. D. Polenov)

2000. Bimillenary of Christianity. Religious Paintings. Multicoloured.
6880 3r. Type **2707** 30 15
6881 3r. "Christ in the Wilderness" (I. N. Kramskoy) 30 15
6882 3r. "Christ in the House of Mary and Martha" (G. I. Semiradsky) 30 15
6883 3r. "What is Truth?" (N. N. Ge) (vert) 30 15
MS6884 120 × 96 mm. 7r. "The Appearance of Christ to the People" (A. A. Ivanov) (51 × 36 mm) 75 75
See also Nos. **MS**6883 and **MS**6887.

2708 "The Virgin the Orans" (mosaic, St. Sophie's Cathedral, Kiev, Ukraine)

2000. Bimillenary of Christianity (2nd issue). Sheet 151 × 100 mm containing T **2708** and similar vert designs. Multicoloured.
MS6885 3r. Type **2708**; 3r. "Christ Pantocrator" (fresco, Spaso-Preobrazhenskaya Church, Polotsk, Belarus); 3r. "The Virgin of Vladimir" (icon, Tretyakov State Museum, Moscow) . . . 1·20 60

2709 Psurtsev and Central Telegraph Office, Moscow

2000. Birth Centenary of Nikolai D. Psurtsev (statesman).
6886 **2709** 2r.50 multicoloured . . 25 15

2710 Domes of Kremlin Cathedrals, Moscow

2000. Bimillenary of Christianity (3rd issue). Sheet 151 × 87 mm.
MS6887 **2710** 10r. multicoloured 1·30 65

2711 R. L. Samoilovich

2000. Polar Explorers. Multicoloured.
6888 2r. Type **2711** 20 10
6889 2r. V. Yu Vize and polar station 20 10
6890 2r. M. M. Somov and ship 20 10
6891 2r. P. A. Gordienko and airplane 20 10
6892 2r. A. F. Treshnikov and tracked vehicles 20 10

2712 N. A. Panin-Kolomenkin (first Russian Olympic Ice-skating Champion, 1908)

2000. The Twentieth Century (1st issue). Sport. Multicoloured.
6893 25k. Type **2712** 10 10
6894 30k. Wrestlers (Olympic Games, Stockholm, 1912) 10 10
6895 50k. Athlete crossing finishing line (All-Russian Olympiad, 1913 and 1914) 10 10
6896 1r. Cyclists (All-Union Spartacist Games, 1928) 10 10
6897 1r.35 Emblem and parade of athletes (Sports Association for Labour and Defence, 1931) . . . 15 10
6898 1r.50 Emblem and athletes ("Honoured Master of Sports", 1934) 20 10
6899 2r. Gymnasts and shot-putter (Olympic Games, Helsinki, 1952) 20 10
6900 2r.50 V. P. Kutz and athletes (Olympic Games, Melbourne, 1956) 25 15
6901 3r. Gold Medal, goalkeeper and player (Olympic Football Champion, Melbourne Olympic Games) 30 15
6902 4r. Mikhail Botvinnik (World Chess Champion, 1948–57, 1958–60 and 1961–63) 45 25
6903 5r. Soviet Union–Canada ice hockey match, 1972 . . . 55 30
6904 6r. Stadium and emblem (Olympic Games, Moscow, 1980) 65 35
See also Nos. 6926/37, 6950/61 and 6964/76.

2713 Emblem

2000. 50th Anniv of World Meteorological Society. Sheet 90 × 60 mm.
MS6905 **2713** 7r. multicoloured 75 75

2714 Soldier (L. F. Golovanov)

2000. 55th Anniv of End of Second World War. Posters by named artists. Multicoloured.
6906 1r.50 Type **2714** 20 10
6907 1r.50 Mother and son (N. N. Vatolina) 20 10
6908 1r.50 Soldiers celebrating (V. V. Suryaninov) . . . 20 10
6909 1r.50 Soldier and woman (V. I. Ladyagin) 20 10
6910 5r. Soldier and emblem (V. S. Klimashin) 55 30
MS6911 100 × 70 mm. No. 6910 55 55

2715 "Apollo"–"Soyuz" Space Link, 1975

2000. International Space Co-operation. Mult.
6912 2r. Type **2715** 20 10
6913 3r. Projected international space station and flags (horiz) 30 15
6914 5r. Rocket taking off from launch pad at sea 55 30

2716 Mother and Child crossing Road and Emblem

2717 Star of David, Doves and "Holocaust"

2000. World Road Safety Week.
6915 **2716** 1r.75 multicoloured . . 20 10

2000. Holocaust Victims' Commemoration.
6916 **2717** 2r. multicoloured . . . 20 10

2718 Spassky Tower and President's Flag

2719 "Building Europe"

2000. Election of President Vladimir Putin.
6917 **2718** 1r.75 multicoloured . . 20 10

2000. Europa.
6918 **2719** 7r. multicoloured . . . 75 40

2720 Globe, Shell, Cogs, Human Eye and Emblem

2000. "Expo 2000" International Stamp Exhibition, Hanover. Sheet 92 × 71 mm.
MS6919 **2720** 10r. multicoloured 1·30 65

2000. Regions of the Russian Federation (4th issue). As T **2651**. Multicoloured.
6920 3r. Republic of Kalmyk (vert) 30 15
6921 3r. Mari El Republic (vert) 30 15
6922 3r. Tatarstan Republic (vert) 30 15
6923 3r. Udmurt Republic (vert) 30 15

6924 3r. Chuvash Republic . . . 30 15
6925 3r. Autonomous Republic of Yamalo Nentsky 30 15

2721 V. K. Arkadjev (Observation of Ferromagnetic Resonance, 1913)

2000. The Twentieth Century (2nd issue). Science. Multicoloured.
6926 1r.30 Type **2721** (botanist and plant geneticist) . . . 15 10
6927 1r.30 Nikolai Ivanovich Vavilov (botanist and plant geneticist) and ears of corn (theory on plant divergence) 15 10
6928 1r.30 N. N. Luzin (founder of Moscow Mathematical School, 1920–30) 15 10
6929 1r.75 I. E. Tamm and chemical model (Phenoms Theory, 1929) 20 10
6930 1r.75 P. L. Kapitsa and diagram of experiment (discovery of liquid helium superfluidity, 1938) 20 10
6931 1r.75 Nikolai Nikolayevich Semenov (physical chemist) (chemical chain reactions theory, 1934) . . 20 10
6932 2r. V. I. Veksler and charged particles in accelerators, 1944–45 . . 20 10
6933 2r. Mayan text (decipherment of Mayan language by Yu V. Knorozov, 1950s) . . . 20 10
6934 2r. A. V. Ivanov (discovery of pogonophora, 1955–57) 20 10
6935 3r. Globe, Moon and Luna 3 (first photograph of Moon's dark side, 1959) 30 15
6936 3r. Scientific equipment (development of quantum electronics, 1960s) 30 15
6937 3r. N. J. Tolstoi (ethnolinguistic dictionary, 1995) 30 15

2722 Chihuahua

2723 Fencing

2000. Dogs. Multicoloured.
6938 1r. Type **2722** 10 10
6939 1r.50 Terrier 20 10
6940 2r. Poodle 20 10
6941 2r.50 French bulldog . . . 25 15
6942 3r. Japanese chin 30 15

2000. Olympic Games, Sydney. Multicoloured.
6943 2r. Type **2723** 20 10
6944 3r. Synchronized swimming 30 15
6945 5r. Volleyball 55 30

2724 Charoit

2000. Minerals. Multicoloured.
6946 1r. Type **2724** 10 10
6947 2r. Haematite 20 10
6948 3r. Rock crystal 30 15
6949 4r. Gold 45 25

2725 Ballerina and Actors

2000. The Twentieth Century (3rd series). Culture. Multicoloured.
6950 30k. Type **2725** (touring ballet and opera companies, 1908–14) . . . 10 10
6951 50k. "Black Square" (K. S. Malevich) 10 10
6952 1r. Sergi Mikhailovich Eisenstein (director) and scene from *Battleship Potemkin* (film, 1925) . . 10 10
6953 1r.30 Book and Aleksei Maksimovich Gorky (writer) 15 10
6954 1r.50 Sculptures and red star 20 10
6955 1r.75 Vladimir Vladimirovich Mayakovsky (poet and playwright) and propaganda posters, 1920s 20 10
6956 2r. V. E. Meierkhold and K. S. Stanislavsky (theatre producers) 20 10
6957 2r.50 Dmitri Dmitriyevich Shostakovich (composer) and musicians 25 15
6958 3r. Galina Sergeyevna Ulanova (ballerina) and dancers 30 15
6959 4r. A. T. Tvardovsky (poet) 45 25
6960 5r. Fountain and Great Palace, Petrodvorets (restoration of historical monuments) 55 30
6961 6r. D. S. Likhachev (literary critic) 65 35

2726 Zander (*Stizostedion lucioperca*) and Common Whitefish (*Coregonus lavaretus manaenoides*)

2000. Fish of Chudsko-Pskovskoye Lake. Mult.
6962 2r.50 Type **2726** 25 15
6963 2r.50 European smelt (*Osmerus eperlanus spirinchus*) and European cisco (*Coregonus albula*) 25 15

2727 Doctors Operating and Medical Equipment

2000. The Twentieth Century (4th series). Technology. Multicoloured.
6964 1r.50 Type **2727** 10 10
6965 1r.50 City skyline (construction) 10 10
6966 1r.50 Bus, car and truck (transport) 10 10
6967 2r. Dam, electricity pylons and generator (engineering) 15 10
6968 2r. Telephones, televisions and rocket and satellite (communication) 15 10
6970 2r. Space stations and rocket (space technology) 15 10
6971 3r. Civil and military airplanes (aviation) . . . 30 15
6972 3r. Steam, diesel and electric trains (rail transport) . . 30 15
6973 3r. Container ship, sailing ship and cruise liner (sea transport) 30 15
6974 4r. Furnace (metallurgy) . . 35 15
6975 4r. Oil refinery and truck (oil-refining industry) . . 35 15
6976 4r. Truck, conveyor and drill (mineral extraction) 35 15

2728 Moscow Kremlin, Pokrovsky Cathedral and Christmas Tree

2000. New Millennium.
6977 **2728** 2r. multicoloured . . . 15 10

2729 Emblem

2731 White Tulip ("Happy Birthday")

2730 Navigation School, Moscow and Mathematical Equipment

2000. 80th Anniv of Foreign Intelligence Service.
6978 **2729** 2r.50 multicoloured . . 25 15

2001. 300th Anniv of Russian Naval Education. Sheet 110 × 130 mm containing T **2710** and similar horiz designs. Multicoloured.
MS6979 1r.50 Type **2730**; 2r. Ship, chart of Antarctica and navigation equipment; 8r. St. Petersburg Naval Institute and statue . . 1·40 70

2001. Regions of the Russian Federation (5th issue). As T **2651**. Multicoloured.
6980 3r. Republic of Dagestan . . 30 15
6981 3r. Republic of Kabardino-Balkaskaya 30 15
6982 3r. Republic of Komi (vert) 30 15
6983 3r. Samara region 30 15
6984 3r. Chita region 30 15

2001. As Nos. 6718/35 but new designs and currency expressed as "P".
6985 10p. mauve and black . . . 90 45
6986 25p. brown and black . . . 2·25 1·10
6987 50p. blue and black . . . . 4·50 2·25
6988 100p. mauve and black . . 9·00 4·50
DESIGNS: 10p. Ballet dancer; 25p. Gymnast; 50p. Globe and computer; 100p. Universal Postal Union emblem.

2001. Greetings Stamps. Tulips. Multicoloured.
7000 2r. Type **2731** 15 10
7001 2r. Deep pink tulips ("With Love") 15 10
7002 2r. Orange tulip ("Good Luck") 15 10
7003 2r. Yellow tulip ("Congratulations") . . . 15 10
7004 2r. Magenta and white tulip ("Be Happy") 15 10

2732 I. A. Galitsin

2001. 300th Birth Anniv of Andrei Matveeich Matveev (artist) (Nos. 7005/6) and 225th Birth Anniv of Vasily Andreevich Tropinin (artist) (Nos. 7007/8). Multicoloured.
7005 3r. Type **2732** 30 15
7006 3r. A. P. Galitsina 30 15
7007 3r. P. A. Bulakhov 30 15
7008 3r. E. I. Karzinkina 30 15

2733 "Senate Square and St. Peter the Great Monument" (B. Patersen)

2001. 300th Anniv of St. Petersburg. Paintings. Multicoloured.
7009 1r. Type **2733** 10 10
7010 2r. "English embankment near Senate" (B. Patersen) 15 10
7011 3r. "Mikhailovsky Castle from Fontanka Embankment" (B. Patersen) 30 15
7012 4r. "River Moika near Stable Department" (A. E. Martynov) 35 15
7013 5r. "Neva from Peter and Paul Fortress" (K. P. Beggrov) 45 20

2734 *Pyrrhosoma numphula* (damselfly)

2001. Damselflies and Dragonflies. Multicoloured.
7014 1r. Type **2734** 10 10
7015 1r.50 *Epitheca bimaculata* (dragonfly) 10 10
7016 2r. Brown aeshna (*Aeschna grandis*) 15 10
7017 3r. *Libellula depressa* (dragonfly) 30 15
7018 5r. *Coenagrion hastulatum* (damselfly) 45 20

2735 Yuri Gagarin, S. P. Korolev (spaceship designer) and Baikonur Launch Site

2001. 40th Anniv of First Manned Space Flight. Multicoloured.
7019 3r. Type **2735** 30 15
7020 3r. Gagarin in uniform . . . 30 15
Nos. 7019/20 were issued together, se-tenant, forming a composite design.

2736 Baikal Lake

2001. Europa. Water Resources.
7021 **2736** 8r. multicoloured . . . 70 35

2737 Emblem

2001. 75th Anniv of International Philatelic Federation.
7022 **2737** 2r.50 multicoloured . . 25 10

2738 Russian Flag

2001. State Emblems. Multicoloured.
7023 2r.50 Type **2738** 20 10
7024 2r.50 Russian Federation national anthem 20 10
7025 5r. State Arms 40 20
MS7026 Sheet 150 × 00 mm. 2r.50 Type **2738**; 2r.50 As No. 7024; 100r. State Arms . . . . . 10·00 10·00
The 100r. stamp in No. **MS**7026 has the arms embossed in gold foil.

2739 Map of Russian Federation and State Arms

2001. 11th Anniv of Declaration of State Sovereignty.
7027 **2739** 5r. multicoloured . . . 40 20

2740 Cathedral of the Assumption, Vladimir (1189)

2001. Religious Architecture. Multicoloured.
7028 2r.50 Type **2740** 20 10
7029 2r.50 Cathedral of the Nativity of the Virgin, Zvenigorod (1405) 20 10
7030 2r.50 Cathedral of the Intercession of the Virgin of the Old Belief Community of Rogozhsk, Moscow (1792) 20 10
7031 2r.50 Roman Catholic Church of the Immaculate Conception of the Blessed Virgin Mary, Moscow (1911) 20 10
7032 2r.50 Lutheran Church of St. Peter, St. Petersburg (1838) 20 10
7033 2r.50 Prayer House of the Evangelical Christians (Pentecostal), Lesosibirsk (1999) 20 10
7034 2r.50 Revival Church of Evangelical Christians (Baptist), Bezhitsk, Bryansk (1996) 20 10
7035 2r.50 Church of Seventh Day Adventists, Ryazan (1996) 20 10
7036 2r.50 Armenian Cathedral Surb Khach, Rostov-on-Don (1792) and Monastery of St. Daniel, Moscow (13th-century) . . 20 10
7037 2r.50 First Mosque, Ufa (1830) 20 10
7038 2r.50 Hay Market Mosque, Kazan (1849) 20 10
7039 2r.50 Choral Synagogue, Moscow (1891) 20 10
7040 2r.50 Large Choral Synagogue, St. Petersburg (1893) 20 10
7041 2r.50 Buddhist Soskshin-Dugan, Ivolginsk Datsan (1976) 20 10

2741 "Sokol" (high speed passenger train)

2001. 150th Anniv of St. Petersburg–Moscow Railway. Sheet 90 × 80 mm.
MS7042 **2741** 12r. multicoloured 1·00 50

2742 G. S. Titov (cosmonaut)

2001. 40th Anniv of First Manned Space Flight.
7043 **2742** 3r. multicoloured . . . 25 10

2743 Faina G. Ranevskaya in Cinderella

2001. Cinema Actors. Showing scenes from their films. Multicoloured.
7044 2r.50 Type **2743** 20 10
7045 2r.50 Mikhail I. Zharov in *Peter I* 20 10
7046 2r.50 Lubov P. Orlova in *Circus* 20 10
7047 2r.50 Nikolai A. Kryuchkov in *Tractor Drivers* 20 10
7048 2r.50 Yury V. Nikulin in *Diamond Arm* 20 10
7049 2r.50 Anatoly D. Papanov in *Alive and Dead* 20 10
7050 2r.50 Evgeny P. Leonov in *Stripy Voyage* 20 10
7051 2r.50 Nikolai N. Rybnikov in *Height* 20 10
7052 2r.50 Andrei A. Mironov in *Twelve Chairs* 20 10

2744 Lazarian and Institute

2001. Death Bicentenary of Horhannes Lazarian (founder of Oriental Languages Institute, Moscow).
7053 **2744** 2r.50 multicoloured . . 20 10
A stamp in a similar design was issued by Armenia.

2745 Arkadi Raikin

РОССИЯ 5.00
2746 Children encircling Globe

2001. 90th Birth Anniv of Arkadi I. Raikin (actor).
7054 **2745** 2r. agate and black . . 15 10

2001. United Nations Year of Dialogue among Civilizations.
7055 **2746** 5r. multicoloured . . . 45 25

2747 Vladimir Dal

2001. Birth Bicentenary of Vladimir I. Dal (writer and lexicographer). Sheet 70 × 100 mm.
MS7056 **2747** 10r. multicoloured 1·00 1·00

2748 Court Tower

2001. 10th Anniv of Russian Federation Constitutional Court.
7057 **2748** 3r. multicoloured . . . 30 15

СБЕРБАНКУ РОССИИ 160 ЛЕТ
РОССИЯ 2001 ROSSIJA 2.20

2749 Tsar Nicholas I, St. Petersburg Winter Palace and Coin

2001. 160th Anniv of Savings Bank.
7058 **2749** 2r.20 multicoloured . . 25 15

2750 Soldiers, Map and Red Square

2001. 60th Anniv of Battle for Moscow. Sheet 100 × 76 mm.
MS7059 **2750** 10r. multicoloured 1·00 1·00

2751 Union Emblem

2001. 10th Anniv of Union of Independent States.
7060 **2751** 2r. multicoloured . . . 25 10

2752 Father Christmas driving Troika with Three White Horses

2001. "Happy New Year".
7061 **2752** 2r.50 multicoloured . . 30 15

2002. Regions of the Russian Federation (6th issue). As T **2651**. Multicoloured.
7062 3r. Amur region 30 15
7063 3r. Republic of Karachaevo-Cherkeskaya 30 15
7064 3r. Republic of Altai (vert) 30 15
7065 3r. Sakhalin region 30 15
7066 3r. Republic of Khakassiya 30 15

2753 Skiing

2002. Winter Olympic Games, Salt Lake City. Multicoloured.
7067 3r. Type **2753** 30 15
7068 4r. Figure skating 45 20
7069 5r. Ski-jumping 50 25

2754 Dove, Rainbow and Globe

12.00 РОССИЯ ROSSIJA • 2002
2755 Locomotive emerging from Tunnel

2002. "World Unity against Terrorism".
7070 **2754** 5r. multicoloured . . . 55 30

2002. Centenary of Trans-Siberian Railway. Sheet 92 × 73 mm.
MS7071 **2755** 12r. multicoloured 1·30 1·30

2756 "Courtesan" (Hendrick Golzius)

2002. 150th Anniv of New Hermitage Museum, St. Petersburg. Multicoloured.
7072 2r.50 Type **2756** 25 15
7073 2r.50 "Ecco Homo" (Peter Paul Rubens) 25 15
7074 5r. 16th-century Italian Burgonet (helmet) 45 25
7075 5r. The Gonzaga Cameo . . 45 25
MS7076 76 × 106 mm. 12r. "New Hermitage" (Luigi Premazzi) (51 × 48 mm) (horiz) . . . . . 1·30 1·30

2757 Cinnabar Lily ("Congratulations")

2002. Greetings Stamps. Lilies. Multicoloured.
7077 2r.50 Type **2757** 25 15
7078 2r.50 Orange lily ("Happy Birthday") 25 15
7079 2r.50 Pink lily ("Happiness") 25 15
7080 2r.50 Gilded lily ("From our Hearts") 25 15
7081 2r.50 Regal lily ("Love and Joy") 25 15

2758 Cane-Corso

2002. Dogs. Multicoloured.
7082 1r. Type **2758** 15 10
7083 2r. Shar pei 20 10
7084 3r. Bull mastiff 30 15
7085 4r. Brazilian mastiff (*Fila Brasileiro*) 45 25
7086 5r. Neapolitan mastiff . . . 60 30
MS7087 151 × 152 mm. Nos. 7082 × 2, 7083 × 4 and 7085/6 1·60 1·60

2759 Cathedral of Our Lady of Kazan and Marshal Barclay de Tolli Monument

2002. 300th Anniv of St. Petersburg. Multicoloured.
7088 5r. Type **2759** 45 25
7089 5r. St. Isaak Cathedral . . . 45 25
7090 25r. River Neva, St. Peter and Paul Fortress and gilded angel (vert) . . . . 2·20 2·20
7091 25r. Griboedov Canal, Cathedral of the Resurrection and gilded griffin . . . . 2·20 2·20
7092 25r. Gilded ship and Admiralty building . . . 2·20 2·20

2760 Artur Artuzov

2002. Intelligence Agents. Sheet 141 × 91 mm containing T **2760** and similar horiz designs.
MS7093 2r. × 6, Type **2760**; Nikolai Demidenko; Jan Olsky; Sergei Putzitsky; Vladimir Styrne; Grigory Syroezhkin . . . . . 1·40 1·40

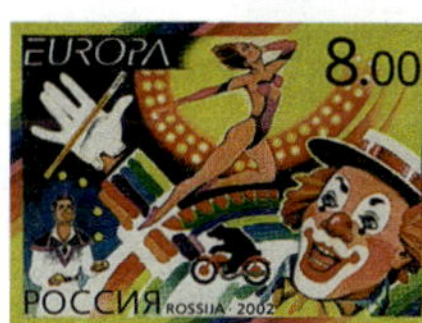

2761 Juggler, Trapeze Artist and Clown

2002. Europa. Circus.
7094 **2761** 8r. multicoloured . . . 90 45

2762 Pavel Nakhimov

2002. Birth Bicentenary of Pavel S. Nakhimov (naval commander).
7095 **2762** 2r. multicoloured . . . 25 15

2763 Congress Emblem

2002. 5th Eurosai (European Organization of Supreme Audit Institutions) Congress, Moscow.
7096 **2763** 2r. multicoloured . . . 25 15

2764 Geysers

2002. Volcanoes of Kamchatka Region. Multicoloured.

7097	1r. Type **2764**	10	10
7098	2r. Caldera, Uzon volcano	25	15
7099	3r. Karymsky volcano	70	35
7100	5r. Troitsky acid lake, Maly Semyachic volcano	45	25

2765 Russian Carriage (c. 1640)

2002. Horse-drawn Carriages. Multicoloured.

7101	2r.50 Type **2765**	25	15
7102	2r.50 Enclosed sleigh, Moscow (1732)	25	15
7103	5r. Coupe carriage, Berlin (1746)	45	25
7104	5r. English carriage (c. 1770)	45	25
7105	5r. St. Petersburg Berline type carriage (1769)	45	25
MS7106	151 × 71 mm. 25r. × 3 Nos. 7103/5	1·80	1·80

2766 Helicopter KA-10

2002. Birth Centenary of Nikolai Kamov (helicopter designer and manufacturer). Multicoloured.

7107	1r. Type **2766**	10	10
7108	1r.50 KA-22	15	10
7109	2r. KA-26	25	15
7110	2r.50 Navy helicopter KA-27	25	15
7111	5r. Army helicopter KA-50 Black Shark	45	25

2767 Anatoli Sobchak

2768 Demoiselle Crane (*Anthropoides virgo*)

2002. 65th Birth Anniv of Anatoli Sobchak (reformer and mayor of St. Petersburg).

7112	**2767** 3r.25 multicoloured	30	15

2002. Endangered Species. Birds. Multicoloured.

7113	2r.50 Type **2768**	30	15
7114	2r.50 Great black-headed gull (Pallas' Gull) (*Larus ichthyaetus Pallas*)	30	15

Stamps of the same design were issued by Kazakhstan.

2769 City and Emblem

2002. 850th Anniv of Kostroma.

7115	**2769** 2r. multicoloured	25	15

2770 Ministry of Internal Affairs

2002. Bicentenary of Government Ministries. Multicoloured.

7116	3r. Type **2770**	30	15
7117	3r. Palace Square, Alexander column, St. Petersburg and Ministry of Foreign Affairs building, Moscow	30	15
7118	3r. Church, Ministry of Defence building and state emblem (foreground)	30	15
7119	3r. Educational symbols and Moscow State University building	30	15
7120	3r. State emblem (centre) and Ministry of Finance building	30	15
7121	3r. Justice (statue), column, flag and state emblem (right) (Ministry of Justice)	30	15

2771 Census Emblem surrounded by People

2772 Russian Millenary Monument, Novgorod

2002. National Census. Multicoloured. (a) Self-adhesive.

7122	3r. Type **2771**	25	10

(b) Ordinary gum.

7123	4r. Census emblem	30	15

2002. 1140th Anniv of Russian State.

7124	**2772** 3r. multicoloured	30	15

2773 Custom House, Archangelsk (19th-century engraving)

2002. Custom and Excise Service. Sheet 117 × 137 mm containing T **2773** and similar horiz designs. Multicoloured.

MS7125	2r. Type **2773**; 3r. Custom officers on horseback, St. Petersburg; 5r. Customs warehouse, Kalanchovsky Square	1·00	1·00

2774 The Motherland (statue)

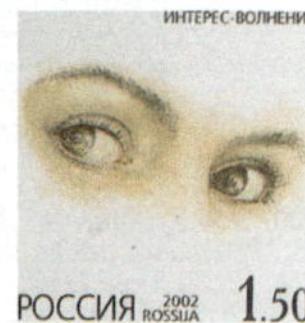

2775 Eyes

2002. 60th Anniv of Battle for Stalingrad. Sheet 101 × 75 mm.

MS7126	**2774** 10r. multicoloured	95	95

2002. Eyes. Sheet 181 × 107 mm containing T **2775** and similar square designs. Multicoloured.

MS7127	1r.50 × 10 Ten different stamps showing eye	1·50	1·50

2776 Emperor Alexander I, Neva River and St. Peter and Paul Cathedral

2778 Snowman on Skis

2777 Saint Daniel Monastery, Moscow (1282)

2002. History of Russian State. Alexander I. Multicoloured.

7128	4r. Type **2776**	40	20
7129	4r. N. M. Karamzin (author, History of State) and Alexander I	40	20
7130	7r. M. Speransky handing plan for Code of Law to Alexander I	70	35
7131	7r. Alexander I entering Paris, 1814	70	35
MS7132	66 × 91 mm. 10r. Alexander I	95	95

2002. Monasteries (1st series). Multicoloured.

7133	5r. Type **2777**	55	25
7134	5r. Holy Trinity Monastery, Sergiev Posad (1337)	55	25
7135	5r. Transfiguration of Our Saviour Monastery, Valaam (14th-century)	55	25
7136	5r. Rev. Savva of Storozha Monastery, Zvenigorod (1398)	55	25
7137	5r. Monastery of the Holy Assumption, Pechory (1470)	55	25

See also Nos. 7168/73.

2002. "Happy New Year".

7138	**2778** 3r.50 multicoloured	35	15

2779 *Artemis with Deer* (sculpture) and Palace, Arkhangelkoe

2002. Palaces and Parks. Multicoloured. Self-adhesive.

7138a	1r. Oatankino Palace and Appollo Belvedere statue, Moscow	10	10
7138b	1r.50 Gatchina Palace and Paul II monument, St. Petersburg	15	10
7139	2r. Type **2779**	25	10
7140	2r.50 *Omphala* (sculpture) Chinese Palace, Oranienbaum	35	15
7141	3r. *Gryphon* (sculpture) and mansion, Marfino	40	20
7142	4r. *Erminia* (sculpture) and palace, Pavlovsk	45	25
7143	5r. Scamander river (allegorical sculpture) and palace, Kuskovo	55	30
7144	6r. Peter's Palace and fountain, Peterhoff, St. Petersburg	80	40
7149	10r. Catherine Palace and Aphrodite statue, Tsarskoye, St. Petersburg	1·10	60

2780 I. V. Kurchatov and Nuclear Reactor

2003. Physicists' Birth Centenaries. Multicoloured.

7150	2r.50 Type **2780**	30	15
7151	2r.50 A. P. Alexandrov, reactor and *Arktica* (nuclear-powered ice-breaker)	30	15

2781 Map, Lake Contours and Ice Cores

2003. International Antarctic Lake Survey. Sheet 90 × 65 mm containing T **2781** and similar horiz design. Multicoloured.

MS7152	5r. Type **2781**; 5r. Vostok polar station and drilling rig	1·00	1·00

2003. Regions of the Russian Federation (7th issue). As T **2651**. Multicoloured.

7153	3r. Kemerovo region	30	15
7154	3r. Kurgan region	30	15
7155	3r. Astrakhan region (vert)	30	15
7156	3r. Magadan region	30	15
7157	3r. Perm region	30	15
7158	3r. Ulijanovsk region	30	15

2782 Organization Emblem

2003. 10th Anniv of Intergovernmental Communications Courier Service.

7159	**2782** 3r. multicoloured	25	10

2783 Russian Tennis Fans

2003. Russia, Winner of Davis Cup, 2002. Multicoloured.

7160	4r. Type **2783**	30	15
7161	8r. Flags, net and ball	55	25
MS7162	125 × 91 mm. 50r. Davis Cup	3·50	3·50

2784 Building Yaroslavl Fortress, Yaroslav the Wise and Crowd

2003. History of Russian State. Princes. Multicoloured.

7163	8r. Type **2784**	75	40
7164	8r. Entering Kiev, Vladimir Monomach and Vladimir giving "Admonition"	75	40
7165	8r. Riding with army, Daniel of Moscow and founding St. Daniel monastery	75	40
7166	8r. Inauguration, Ivan Ivanovich of Moscow and Golden Horde	75	40

2785 Alexander Nevsky Cathedral, Peter I (statue) and Karelia Postal Building

2003. 300th Anniv of Petrozavodsk City.

7167	**2785** 3r. multicoloured	35	25

2003. Monasteries (2nd series). As T **2777**. Multicoloured.

7168	5r. Yuriev Monastery, Novgorod (1030)	55	30
7169	5r. Tolgsky Nunnery (1314)	55	30
7170	5r. Kozelsk Optina Pustyn Monastery (14th–15th century)	55	30
7171	5r. Solovetsky Zosima and Savvatii Monastery, Zvenigorod (14th century)	55	30
7172	5r. Novodevichy Nunnery, Smolensk (1524)	55	30
7173	5r. Seraphim Nunnery, Diveeyevo, Nizhny Novgorod (1780)	55	30

2786 State Theatre, Youth Theatre, Statue and Novosibirsk Science Academy Emblem

2003. Centenary of Novosibirsk City.

7174	**2786** 3r. multicoloured	35	25

2787 "Capture of Swedish Ships Gedan and Astrild, Neva Delta, May 7, 1703" (painting, L. Blinov)

2003. 300th Anniv of Baltic Fleet. Sheet 90 × 129 mm.

MS7175 **2787** 12r. multicoloured . . . 1·20 1·20

2788 Aram Khachaturyan and *Spartacus* (ballet)

2003. Birth Centenary of Aram I. Katchaturyan (composer).

7176 **2788** 2r.50 multicoloured . . 25 15

2789 "My first Steps for Einem Biscuits"

2003. Europa. Poster Art.

7177 **2789** 8r. multicoloured . . . 75 35

2790 Bells of St. Rumbold's Cathedral, Maline

2003. 150th Anniv of Belgium–Russia Diplomatic Relations. Multicoloured.

7178 5r. Type **2790** 55 30

7179 5r. Bells of St. Peter and Paul's Cathedral, St. Petersburg 55 30

Nos. 7178/9 were issued together, se-tenant, forming a composite design.

Stamps of the same design were issued by Belgium.

2791 Anichkov Bridge over Fontanka River

2003. 300th Anniv of St. Petersburg. Multicoloured.

7180 5r. Type **2791** 55 30

7181 5r. Raised bridge on Neva river 55 30

7182 5r. Central Naval Museum, Vasilievsky Island 55 30

7183 5r. Palace Square 55 30

7184 5r. Winter Palace 55 30

7185 5r. Summer Gardens . . . 55 30

MS7186 3 sheets, each 165 × 70 mm. (a) 50r. The Bronze Horseman (statue, E. Falkonet) (38 × 51 mm); (b) 75r. As **MS**7186a (38 × 51 mm) (23.5); (c) 100r. As **MS**7186a (38 × 51 mm) . . . . 4·25 4·25

2792 Earth, Vostok Flight Paths and Valentina Tereshkova

2003. 40th Anniv of First Female Cosmonaut (Valentina V. Tereshkova).

7187 **2792** 3r. multicoloured . . . 35 25

2793 Globe and Emblem

2003. 2nd International "21st-century without Drugs" Conference, Moscow.

7188 **2793** 3r. multicoloured . . . 35 25

2794 Pskov Kremlin and Mirozhsky Monastery Cathedral

2003. 1100th Anniv of Pskov City.

7189 **2794** 3r. multicoloured . . . 35 25

2795 Town Arms and Andrey Dubensky Monument

2003. 375th Anniv of Krasnoyarsk City.

7190 **2795** 4r. multicoloured . . . 40 20

2796 5r. Coin and Industrial Scene

2003. Transparent Economy Legislation.

7191 **2796** 5r. multicoloured . . . 45 25

2797 Belfry, Prokhorovka and Triumphal Arch, Kursk

2003. 60th Anniv of Battle for Kursk. Sheet 100 × 75 mm.

MS7192 **2797** 10r. multicoloured . . . 95 50

2798 Stone Pillars, Manpupuner Mountains

2003. UNESCO World Heritage Sites. Komi Virgin Forest. Multicoloured.

7193 2r. Type **2798** 25 15

7194 3r. Kozhim river 35 25

7195 5r. Pechora river 45 25

2799 Tsar Peter I receiving Letter from Count Aspraksin, Voronezh

2003. 300th Anniv of St. Petersburg Post. Sheet 103 × 95 mm.

MS7196 **2799** 12r. multicoloured . . . 1·20 1·20

2800 Stag Beetle (*Lucanus cervus*)

2003. Beetles. Multicoloured.

7197 1r. Type **2800** 10 10

7198 2r. Caterpillar hunter (*Calosoma sycophanta*) . . 20 15

7199 3r. *Carabus lopatini* 35 25

7200 4r. *Carabus costricticollis* . . 35 25

7201 5r. *Carabus caucasicus* . . . 45 25

2801 Association Emblem

2003. 10th Anniv of International Association of Science Academies.

7202 **2801** 2r.50 multicoloured . . 20 15

2802 Archangel Mikhail Church, Transbaikalia Rail Building, Shumovs Palace and Post Building

2003. 350th Anniv of Chita, Eastern Siberia.

7203 **2802** 3r. multicoloured . . . 35 25

2803 Icebergs and Climate Zones Map

2003. World Climate Change Conference, Moscow.

7204 **2803** 4r. multicoloured . . . 40 20

2804 Satan's Bolete (*Boletus satanas*) (poisonous) and Oak Mushroom (*Boletus luridus*) (edible)

2003. Fungi. Edible and poisonous fungi. Multicoloured.

7205 2r. Type **2804** 20 15

7206 2r.50 Death cap (*Amanita phalloides*) (poisonous) and Field mushroom (*Agricus campestris*) (edible) 20 15

7207 3r. The panther (*Amanita pantherina*) (poisonous) and The blusher (*Amanita rubescens*) (edible) 35 25

7208 4r. *Amanita porphyria* (poisonous) and Grisette (*Amanita vaginata*) (edible) 40 20

7209 5r. Bitter bolete (*Tylopilus fellus*) (poisonous) and edible mushroom (*Boletus edulis*) (edible) 45 25

2805 Pineapple

2003. Fruits. Multicoloured.

7210 5r. Type **2805** 45 25

7211 5r. Strawberries 45 25

7212 5r. Apples 45 25

7213 5r. Pear 45 25

7214 5r. Melon 45 25

Nos. 7210/14 were each perforated in a circle within an outer perforated square and impregnated with the scent of the fruit pictured.

2806 Caspian Seal (*Phoca caspia*)

2003. Preservation of the Caspian Sea. Multicoloured.

7215 2r.50 Type **2806** 20 15

7216 2r.50 Beluga (*Huso huso*) . . 20 15

Stamps of a similar design were issued by Iran.

2807 18th-century Printing Works and *Vedomosti* (newspaper)

2003. 300th Anniv of Russian Journalism. Sheet 90 × 65 mm.

MS7217 **2807** 10r. multicoloured . . . 95 50

2808 Russo-Balt K 12/20 (1911)

2003. Russian Cars. Multicoloured.

7218 3r. Type **2808** 35 25

7219 4r. Nami 1 (1929) 40 20

7220 4r. Gaz M1 (1939) 40 20

7221 5r. Gaz 67b (1946) 45 25

7222 5r. Gaz M20 "Pobeda" (1954) 45 25

2809 Spassky Tower, Constitution Title Page and Kremlin

2003. 10th Anniv of Russian Federation Constitution.

7223 **2809** 3r. multicoloured . . . 20 10

2810 Airship Count Zeppelin, Icebreaker *Malygin*, Call Sign and Ernst Krenkel

2003. Birth Centenary of Ernst Krenkel (polar radio operator and explorer).

7224 **2810** 4r. multicoloured . . . 20 10

2811 "The Battle of Sinop" (A. P. Bogolyubov)

2003. 150th Anniv of Battle of Sinop (Crimea war). Sheet 121 × 84 mm.

MS7225 **2811** 12r. multicoloured . . . 70 35

2812 Grandfather Frost

2003. "Happy New Year".
7226 **2812** 7r. multicoloured . . . 40 20

2813 Federation Council Building and Interior

2003. 10th Anniv of Federation Council and Stat Duma (parliament). Multicoloured.
7227 2r.50 Type **2813** 15 10
7228 2r.50 Stat Duma building and interior 15 10

2004. Regions of the Russian Federation (8th issue). As T **2651**. Multicoloured.
7229 5r. Belgorod region 30 15
7230 5r. Ivanov region 30 15
7231 5r. Lipetsk region 30 15
7232 5r. Nenetsky autonomous region 30 15
7233 5r. Nizhny Novogorod region 30 15

2814 Unknown Warrior (statue)

2004. 60th Anniv of World War II Offensive. Sheet 130 × 95 mm.
MS7234 **2814** 10r. multicoloured 60 30

2815 Valery Chkalov

2004. Birth Centenary of Valery Chkalov (test pilot).
7235 **2815** 3r. multicoloured . . . 20 10

2816 The Stone Flower

2004. 125th Birth Anniv of Pavel Bazhov (writer). Showing scenes from his books. Multicoloured.
7236 2r. Type **2816** 15 10
7237 4r. The Malachite Box . . . 20 10
7238 6r. Golden Hair 35 20
MS7239 131 × 143 mm. Nos. 7236/8, each × 2 . . . . 1·40 1·40

2817 Yuli Khariton

2004. Birth Centenary of Yuli Khariton (physicist).
7240 **2817** 3r. multicoloured . . . 20 10

2818 Yuri Gagarin

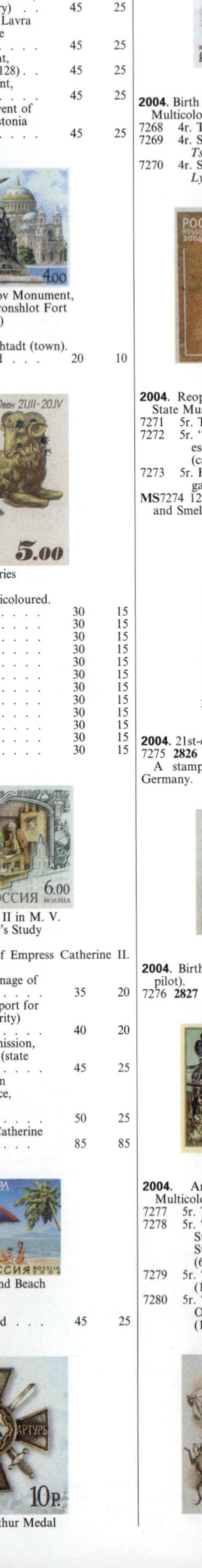

2004. 70th Birth Anniv of Yuri Gagarin (first astronaut).
7241 **2818** 3r. multicoloured . . . 20 10

2004. Monasteries (3rd series). As T **2777**. Multicoloured.
7242 8r. St. Panteleimon Monastery, Mount Athos, Greece (11th-century) . . 45 25
7243 8r. Kiev-Pecherskaya Lavra Monastery, Ukraine (1051) 45 25
7244 8r. Evfrosinia Convent, Polotsk, Belarus (1128) . . 45 25
7245 8r. Gornensky Convent, Israel (1886) 45 25
7246 8r. Pyukhtinsky Convent of the Assumption, Estonia (1891) 45 25

2819 S. O. Makarov Monument, Cathedral and Kronshlot Fort (1704)

2004. 300th Anniv of Kronshtadt (town).
7248 **2819** 4r. multicoloured . . . 20 10

2820 Aries

2004. Western Zodiac. Multicoloured.
7249 5r. Type **2820** 30 15
7250 5r. Leo 30 15
7251 5r. Sagittarius 30 15
7252 5r. Pisces 30 15
7253 5r. Cancer 30 15
7254 5r. Scorpio 30 15
7255 5r. Capricorn 30 15
7256 5r. Taurus 30 15
7257 5r. Virgo 30 15
7258 5r. Gemini 30 15
7259 5r. Aquarius 30 15
7260 5r. Libra 30 15

2821 Catherine II in M. V. Lomonosov's Study

2004. 275th Birth Anniv of Empress Catherine II. Multicoloured.
7261 6r. Type **2821** (patronage of arts and sciences) 35 20
7262 7r. Giving alms (support for education and charity) (vert) 40 20
7263 8r. Legislative Commission, Kremlin, Moscow (state reform) (vert) 45 25
7264 9r. Viewing fleet from Inkermansky Palace, Crimea (border expansion) 50 25
MS7265 73 × 91 mm. 15r. Catherine II (37 × 52 mm) 85 85

2822 City and Beach

2004. Europa. Holidays.
7266 **2822** 8r. multicoloured . . . 45 25

2823 Port Arthur Medal

2004. Centenary of Battle of Port Arthur (Sino-Russian war, 1905–5). Sheet 75 × 95 mm.
MS7267 **2823** 10r. multicoloured 55 30

2824 Mikhail Glinka

2004. Birth Centenary of Mikhail Glinka (composer). Multicoloured.
7268 4r. Type **2824** 20 10
7269 4r. Scene from *Life for the Tsar* (opera) 20 10
7270 4r. Scene from *Ruslan and Lyudmila* 20 10

2825 Crown (carved relief)

2004. Reopening of Amber Room, Tsarskoe Selo State Museum (2003). Multicoloured.
7271 5r. Type **2825** 30 15
7272 5r. "Moses and Pharaon escaping from Serpents" (cameo) (vert) 30 15
7273 5r. Head surrounded by garland (carved relief) . . 30 15
MS7274 125 × 91 mm. 25r. "Touch and Smell" (mosaic) (52 × 40 mm) 1·40 1·40

2826 National Flags as Heart-shaped Kite

2004. 21st-century German—Russian Youth Forum.
7275 **2826** 8r. multicoloured . . . 45 25
A stamp of the same design was issued by Germany.

2827 Vladimir Kokkinaki

2004. Birth Centenary of Vladimir Kokkinaki (test pilot).
7276 **2827** 3r. multicoloured . . . 20 10

2828 "Victory"

2004. Art. Paintings by Sergey Prisekin. Multicoloured.
7277 5r. Type **2828** 30 15
7278 5r. "Whosoever lives by the Sword shall perish by the Sword" (1983) (65 × 32 mm) 30 15
7279 5r. "Marshal Zhukov" (1980) 30 15
7280 5r. "We have honoured the Oath of Allegiance" (1991) (65 × 32 mm) . . . 30 15

2829 Riding Habit

2004. Women's Costumes. Multicoloured.
7281 4r. Type **2829** 20 10
7282 4r. Two women, wearing riding habit and hat with brim and wearing walking dress, bonnet and shawl 40 10
7283 4r. Two women, wearing riding habit and hat with veil and wearing open-fronted dress with sash . . 20 10

2830 Runner

2004. Olympic Games, Athens. Multicoloured.
7284 3r. Type **2830** 20 10
7285 3r. Wrestlers 20 10

2831 Launch of Saratov Class Tanker

2004. 300th Anniv of Admiralty Wharfs (shipbuilding company). Sheet 76 × 96 mm.
MS7286 **2831** 12r. multicoloured 70 35

2832 Ducks using Pedestrian Crossing

2004. Children's Road Safety Campaign. Sheet 101 × 106 mm containing T **2832** and similar horiz designs.
MS7287 4r. × 5, Type **2832**; Crossing at traffic lights; Road closed by garden; Motor cycle stopping suddenly for girl playing ball; Car smash between teddy bears and chicken . . . . . . 2·00 2·00

2833 Wolverine

2004. Wolverine (*Gulo gulo*). Multicoloured.
7288 8r. Type **2833** 45 25
7289 8r. With prey 45 25
7290 8r. Standing on branch . . 45 25
7291 8r. Mother and cubs 45 25

2834 Buildings

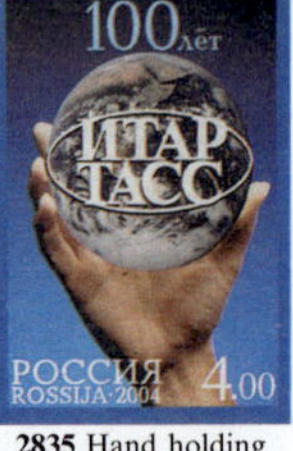

2835 Hand holding Globe

2004. 400th Anniv of Tomsk (town).
7292 **2834** 4r. multicoloured . . . 20 10

2004. Centenary of *ITAR TASS* (news agency).
7293 **2835** 4r. multicoloured . . . 20 10

2836 N. L. Duhov **2837** Paul I

2004. Birth Centenaries. Multicoloured.
7294 5r. Type **2836** (military designer) 30 15
7295 5r. B. G. Muzrukov (manufacturer) 30 15

2004. 250th Birth Anniv of Emperor Paul I. Multicoloured.
7296 10r. Type **2837** 55 30
7297 10r. Wearing crown and robes 55 30
MS7298 90 × 75 mm. 20r. Wearing tri-corn hat . . . . 1·10 1·10

2838 Svyatoslav Rerikh

2004. Birth Centenary of Svyatoslav Nikolayevich Rerikh (artist).
7299 **2838** 4r. multicoloured . . . 20 10

2839 Vsevolod the Big Nest (½-size illustration)

2004. History of Russian State. 850th Birth Anniv of Vsevolod III Yuryevich (Vsevolod the Big Nest).
7300 **2839** 12r. multicoloured . . . 60 30

2840 University Building

2004. Bicentenary of Kazan State University.
7301 **2840** 5r. multicoloured . . . 25 15

2841 Bowl (c. 1880—90)

2004. Silverware. Multicoloured.
7302 4r.70 Type **2841** 25 15
7304 4r.70 Ladle (c.1910) 25 15
7305 4r.70 Jug (c. 1900) 25 15
7306 4r.70 Vase (c. 1900—08) (vert) 25 15

2842 Tree

2004. Happy New Year. Self-adhesive.
7307 **2842** 5r. multicoloured . . . 25 15

2843 Belukha Mountain

2004. Altai Mountain Range. Multicoloured.
7308 2r. Type **2843** 10 10
7309 3r. Katun River 15 10
7310 5r. Teletskoye Lake 25 15

2844 R-7 Intercontinental Missile

2004. 50th Anniv of Baikonur Cosmodrome. Multicoloured.
7311 2r.50 Type **2844** 15 10
7312 3r.50 Proton rocket 20 10
7313 4r. Soyuz rocket 20 10
7314 6r. Zenit rocket 30 15

2005. Regions of the Russian Federation (9th issue). As T **2651**. Multicoloured.
7315 5r. Koyrak region 25 15
7316 5r. Mordovia Republic . . . 25 15
7317 5r. Smolensk region 25 15
7318 5r. Taimyr autonomous region 25 15
7319 5r. Tver region 25 15
7320 5r. Chukotski autonomous region 25 15

2845 University Building

2005. 250th Anniv of Lomonosov State University, Moscow.
7321 **2845** 5r. multicoloured . . . 25 15

2846 Tree and Emblem

2005. EXPO 2005 World Exposition, Aichi, Japan. Sheet 91 × 71 mm.
MS7322 **2846** 15r. multicoloured 75 75

2847 Drinking Horn with Bull-shaped Base

2005. Sarmat (early tribe) Artefacts from Filippov Burial Ground. Multicoloured.
7323 5r. Type **2847** 25 15
7324 5r. Bear-shaped bowl . . . 25 15
7325 7r. Camels on gold hemisphere 35 20
7326 7r. Deer-shaped ornament (vert) 35 20

2848 Type M Submarine VI-bis Series

2005. Submarines. Multicoloured.
7327 2r. Type **2848** 10 10
7328 3r. Type S submarine IX-bis series 15 10
7329 5r. Type Sch submarine X-bis series 25 15
7330 8r. Type K submarine . . . 40 20

2849 Suyumbike Tower

2005. Kazan Millenary. Multicoloured.
7331 5r. Type **2849** 25 15
7332 5r. Kul Sharif Mosque . . . 25 15
7333 7r. Cathedral of the Annunciation 35 20

2850 Alexander with W. Schukowskij

2005. 150th Anniv of Coronation of Emperor Alexander II.
7334 10r. Type **2850** 50 25
7335 10r. Coronation in Uspenski Cathedral in the Kremlin 50 25
7336 10r. In his study 50 25
7337 10r. Mounted during Turkish—Russian war . . 50 25
MS7338 92 × 77 mm. 25r. Alexander II . . . . 1·20 1·20

2851 Russian Soldier signing Column (Berlin, 1945)

2005. 60th Anniv of End of World War II. Multicoloured.
7339 2r. Type **2851** 10 10
7340 2r. Soldiers celebrating (Berlin, 1945) 10 10
7341 3r. Soldier feeding pigeons (Kalinsky front, 1943) . . 15 10
7342 3r. Soldiers holding flowers (Moscow, 1945) 15 10
7343 5r. Russian soldiers with captured German banners (Kremlin, 1945) 25 15
MS7344 71 × 101 mm. 10r. Two soldiers with weapons raised 50 50

2852 City Hall

2005. 60th Anniv of Liberation of Vienna.
7345 **2852** 6r. multicoloured . . . 30 15

2853 Greater Spotted Eagle (*Aquila clanga*)

2005. Fauna. Sheet 133 × 68 mm containing T **2853** and similar horiz designs. Multicoloured.
MS7346 5r. × 4, Type **2853**; *Catocala sponsa*; Beaver (*Castor fiber*); Badger (*Meles meles*) . . . . . 1·00 1·00

The stamps and margin of No. **MS**7346 form a composite design.

Stamps of the same design were issued by Belarus.

2854 Train and Map of First Route

2005. 70th Anniv of Moscow Metro. Sheet 91 × 71 mm containing T **2854** and similar horiz design. Multicoloured.
MS7347 5r. Type **2854**; 10r. Modern routes 75 75

2855 Emblem

2005. Moscow's Bid for Olympic Games—2012.
7348 **2855** 4r. multicoloured . . . 20 10

2856 Blinis, Caviar and Samovar **2857** M.A. Sholokhov

2005. Europa. Gastronomy.
7349 **2856** 8r. multicoloured . . . 40 20

2005. Birth Centenary of Mikhail Aleksandrovich Sholokhov (writer).
7350 **2857** 5r. black and brown . . 25 15

2858 Sable (*Martes zibellina*)

2005. Fauna. Multicoloured.
7351 8r. Type **2858** 40 20
7352 8r. Siberian tiger (*Panthera tigris altaica*) 40 20

Stamps of a similar design were issued by People's Democratic Republic of Korea.

2859 *Bombus armeniacus*

2860 Monuments, Gate and Towers

2005. Bees. Multicoloured.

7353	3r. Type **2859**		15	10
7354	4r. *Bombus fragrans*		20	10
7355	5r. *Bombus anachoreta*		25	15
7356	6r. *Bombus unicus*		30	15
7357	7r. *Bombus czerskii*		35	20

2005. 750th Anniv of Kaliningrad (Koenigsberg).

7358	**2860**	5r. multicoloured	25	15

2861 University Facade

2005. 175th Anniv of Moscow Technical University.

7359	**2861**	5r. multicoloured	25	15

2862 Mudyugsky Lighthouse

2005. Lighthouses. Multicoloured.

7360	5r. Type **2862**		25	15
7361	6r. Solovetsky lighthouse		30	15
7362	8r. Svyatonossky lighthouse		40	20

2863 MiG-3 Fighter Aircraft

2005. Birth Centenary of Artem Ivanovich Mikoyan (aircraft designer). Multicoloured.

7363	5r. Type **2863**		25	15
7364	5r. MiG-15		25	15
7365	5r. MiG-21		25	15
7366	5r. MiG-25		25	15
7367	5r. MiG-29		25	15

2864 Priest blessing Troops

2005. 625th Anniv of Kulikovo Battle (Russian victory against the Mongols). Sheet 97 × 65 mm.

MS7368	**2864**	15r. multicoloured	75	75

2865 Hands

2005. Earth. Sheet 147 × 105 mm containing T **2865** and similar horiz designs. Multicoloured.

MS7369	3r. Type **2865**; 3r.50 Water droplets on leaf; 3r.50 Surf; 4r. Snow-topped mountain; 4r.50 Waterfall; 5r. Water droplets	80	80

2866 Alexander Suvorov

2005. 275th Birth Anniv of Alexander Vasilievich Suvorov (military commander).

7370	**2866**	4r. multicoloured	20	10

2867 Early Sea Infantry

2005. 300th Anniv of Sea Infantry. Multicoloured.

7371	2r. Type **2867**	10	10
7372	3r. Fighting in Crimea	15	10
7373	4r. Fighting during World War II	20	10
7374	5r. Modern Sea Infantry	25	15

2868 Ded Moroz (Father Christmas)

2005.

7375	**2868**	5r. multicoloured	25	15

2869 Emblem

2005. 60th Anniv of UNESCO.

7376	**2869**	5r.60 multicoloured	30	15

2870 Trees

2005. Christmas and New Year.

7377	**2870**	5r.60 multicoloured	30	15

2871 AH-12

2006. Birth Centenary of Oleg Konstantinovich Antonov (aircraft designer). Multicoloured.

7378	5r.60 Type **2871**	30	15
7379	5r.60 AH-24	30	15
7380	5r.60 AH-124	30	15
7381	5r.60 AH-74	30	15
7382	5r.60 AH-3T	30	15

2872 Speed Skating

2006. Winter Olympic Games, Turin. Multicoloured.

7383	4r. Type **2872**	20	10
7384	4r. Luge	20	10
7385	4r. Snowboarding	20	10

2873 Armenian and Russian Flags and Arms

2006. Year of Armenia in Russia.

7386	**2873**	10r. multicoloured	50	25

EXPRESS STAMPS

E 171 Motor Cyclist

1932. Inscr "EXPRES".

E588	**E 171**	5k. sepia	5·00	2·25
E589	–	10k. purple	8·50	3·50
E590	–	80k. green	35·00	14·00

DESIGNS—HORIZ: 10k. Express motor van; 80k. Class Ta steam locomotive.

E 173 Polar Region and Kalinin K-4 Airplane over Ice-breaker "Taimyr"

1932. Air Express. 2nd Int Polar Year and Franz Joseph's Land to Archangel Flight.

E591	**E 173**	50k. red	42·00	18·00
E592		1r. green	60·00	20·00

POSTAGE DUE STAMPS

Доплата
1 коп.
золотом.
(D 96)

ДОПЛАТА
1 коп.
(D 99)

1924. Surch as Type **D 96**.

D401b	**45**	1k. on 35k. blue	20	30
D402b		3k. on 35k. blue	20	30
D403b		5k. on 35k. blue	20	30
D404		8k. on 35k. blue	50	50
D405b		10k. on 35k. blue	30	60
D406b		12k. on 70k. brown	20	40
D407c		14k. on 35k. blue	20	40
D408b		32k. on 35k. blue	90	90
D409c		40k. on 35k. blue	1·00	90

1924. Optd with Type **D 99**.

D421	**48**	1k. on 100r. yellow	4·50	10·00

D 104

1925.

D464	**D 104**	1k. red	25	30
D465		2k. mauve	25	30
D466		3k. blue	25	30
D467		7k. yellow	35	30
D468		8k. green	35	30
D469		10k. blue	40	50
D470		14k. brown	60	70

RUSSIAN POST OFFICES IN CHINA Pt. 17

Russian Post Offices were opened in various towns in Manchuria and China from 1870 onwards.

1899. 100 kopeks = 1 rouble.
1917. 100 cents = 1 dollar (Chinese).

(1)

1899. Arms types (with thunderbolts) of Russia optd with T **1**.

1	**9**	1k. orange	40	40
2		2k. green	50	40
3		3k. red	50	35
9	**14**	4k. red	3·00	1·50
4	**9**	5k. purple	65	50
5		7k. blue	70	50
6	**14**	10k. blue	75	50
30	**10**	14k. red and blue	75	1·75
31		15k. blue and brown	45	1·00
32	**14**	20k. red and blue	40	1·25
33	**10**	25k. violet and green	65	2·25
34		35k. green and purple	70	1·25
35	**14**	50k. green and purple	85	1·25
36	**10**	70k. orange and brown	60	1·50
37	**15**	1r. orange and brown	1·50	1·50
20	**11**	3r.50 grey and black	9·00	10·00
21	**20**	5r. blue and green on green	6·75	6·50
22	**11**	7r. yellow and black	12·00	11·00
23	**20**	10r. grey and red on yellow	55·00	55·00

1910. Arms types of Russia optd with T **1**.

24	**22**	1k. orange	35	60
25		2k. green	40	60
26		3k. red	30	35
27	**23**	4k. red	25	50
28	**22**	7k. blue	35	65
29	**23**	10k. blue	35	50

1917. Arms types of Russia surch in "cents" and "dollars" diagonally in one line.

42	**22**	1c. on 1k. orange	50	3·50
43		2c. on 2k. green	50	3·50
44		3c. on 3k. red	60	3·50
45	**23**	4c. on 4k. red	50	3·25
46	**22**	5c. on 5k. lilac	90	3·00
47	**23**	10c. on 10k. blue	60	3·00
48	**10**	14c. on 14k. red and blue	2·00	5·00
49		15c. on 15k. blue and purple	1·50	3·75
50	**14**	20c. on 20k. red and blue	1·75	3·50
51	**10**	25c. on 25k. violet and green	1·75	5·00
52		35c. on 35k. green & purple	1·75	6·50
53	**14**	50c. on 50k. green & purple	1·50	5·50
54	**10**	70c. on 70k. orange & brn	1·50	6·50
55	**15**	1d. on 1r. orge & brn on brn	1·50	7·00
39	**10**	3d.50 on 3r.50 grey & blk	10·00	14·00
40	**20**	5d. on 5r. bl & dp bl on grn	7·50	16·00
41	**11**	7d. on 7r. yellow and black	5·00	13·00
57	**20**	10d. on 10r. grey and red on yellow	38·00	55·00

1920. Arms types of Russia surch in "cents" in two lines. Perf or imperf.

65	**22**	1c. on 1k. orange	16·00	25·00
59		2c. on 2k. green	6·00	15·00
60		3c. on 3k. red	6·00	15·00
61	**23**	4c. on 4k. red	16·00	22·00
62	**22**	5c. on 5k. lilac	18·00	28·00
63	**23**	10c. on 10k. blue	60·00	60·00
64	**22**	10c. on 10k. on 7k. blue	60·00	65·00

RUSSIAN POST OFFICES IN CRETE Pt. 3

(RETHYMNON PROVINCE)

The Russian Postal Service operated from 1 May to 29 July 1899.

4 metallik = 1 grosion (Turkish piastre).

These issues were optd with circular control marks as shown on Types **R 3/4**. Prices are for stamps with these marks, but unused examples without them are known.

R 1

R 2

1899. Imperf.

R1	**R 1**	1m. blue	45·00	12·00
R2	**R 2**	1m. green	5·00	3·50
R3		2m. red	£150	£120
R4		2m. green	5·00	3·50

R 3

R 4

1899. Without stars in oval.

R 5	**R 3**	1m. pink	55·00	35·00
R 6		2m. pink	55·00	35·00
R 7		1g. pink	55·00	35·00
R 8		1m. blue	55·00	35·00
R 9		2m. blue	55·00	35·00
R10		1g. blue	55·00	35·00
R11		1m. green	55·00	35·00
R12		2m. green	55·00	35·00

R13 1g. green 55·00 35·00
R14 1m. red 55·00 35·00
R15 2m. red 55·00 35·00
R16 1g. red 55·00 35·00
R17 1m. orange 55·00 35·00
R18 2m. orange 55·00 35·00
R19 1g. orange 55·00 35·00
R20 1m. yellow 55·00 35·00
R21 2m. yellow 55·00 35·00
R22 1g. yellow 55·00 35·00
R23 1m. black £550 £550
R24 2m. black £550 £550
R25 1g. black £475 £475

1899. Starred at each side.
R26 **R 4** 1m. pink 35·00 25·00
R27 2m. pink 11·00 3·25
R28 1g. pink 4·00 4·25
R29 1m. blue 18·00 10·00
R30 2m. blue 5·00 3·25
R31 1g. blue 4·00 4·25
R32 1m. green 14·00 10·00
R33 2m. green 5·00 3·25
R34 1g. green 4·00 4·25
R35 1m. red 14·00 10·00
R36 2m. red 5·00 3·25
R37 1g. red 4·00 2·25

RUSSIAN POST OFFICES IN TURKISH EMPIRE Pt. 16

General issues for Russian P.O.s in the Turkish Empire and stamps specially overprinted for use at particular offices.

1863. 100 kopeks = 1 rouble.
1900. 40 paras = 1 piastre.

1 Inscription = "Dispatch under Wrapper to the East"

1863. Imperf.
2a **1** 6k. blue £190 £1100

2

3

1865. Imperf.
4 **2** (10pa.) brown and blue £500 £400
5 **3** (2pi.) blue and red £700 £450

4

5

1865. Imperf.
6 **4** (10pa.) red and blue 24·00 38·00
7 **5** (2pi.) blue and red 35·00 45·00
The values of 4/7 were 10pa. (or 2k.) and 2pi. (or 20k.).

6 Inscription = "Eastern Correspondence"

12

1868. Perf.
14 **6** 1k. brown 8·00 4·50
11 3k. green 22·00 13·00
16 5k. blue 5·50 3·25
17a 10k. red and green 4·00 3·25
See also Nos. 26/35.

1876. Surch with large figures of value.
24 **6** 7k. on 10k. red and green 65·00 50·00
22 8k. on 10k. red and green 65·00 60·00

1879.
26 **6** 1k. black and yellow 2·25 1·25
32 1k. orange 50 35
27 2k. black and red 3·00 1·75
33 2k. green 50 35
34 5k. purple 1·25 1·00
28 7k. red and grey 4·50 1·10
35 7k. blue 85 35

1900. Arms types of Russia surch in "PARA" or "PIASTRES".
37 **9** 4pa. on 1k. orange 15 10
50 **22** 5pa. on 1k. orange 10 15
38 **9** 10pa. on 2k. green 40 25
51 **22** 10pa. on 2k. green 10 15
201 15pa. on 3k. red 20 5·00
41 **14** 20pa. on 4k. red 40 40
52 **23** 20pa. on 4k. red 10 15
42 **9** 20pa. on 5k. purple 40 40
181 **22** 20pa. on 5k. purple 10 15
43 **14** 1pi. on 10k. blue 20 20
53 **23** 1pi. on 10k. blue 10 15
182 **10** 1½pi. on 15k. blue & purple 15 20
183 **14** 2pi. on 20k. red and blue 15 20
184 **10** 2½pi. on 25k. violet & green 15 20
185 3½pi. on 35k. green & pur 20 30
54 **14** 5pi. on 50k. green and lilac 50 75
55 **10** 7pi. on 70k. orange & brn 70 90
56 **15** 10pi. on 1r. orange and brown on brown 80 1·10
48 **11** 35pi. on 3r.50 grey & blk 6·00 6·00
202 **20** 50pi. on 5r. blue on green 3·25 80·00
49 **11** 70pi. on 7r. yellow & black 9·00 9·00
203 **20** 100pi. on 10r. grey and red on yellow 14·00 £275

1909. As T **14**, **15**, and **11** of Russia, but ship and date in centre as T **12**, and surch in "paras" or "piastres".
57 **14** 5pa. on 1k. orange 20 30
58 10pa. on 2k. green 30 40
59 20pa. on 4k. red 60 75
60 1pi. on 10k. blue 70 1·10
61 5pi. on 50k. green & purple 1·25 2·50
62 7pi. on 70k. orange & brn 2·50 3·75
63 **15** 10pi. on 1r. orange & brown 3·75 6·50
64 **11** 35pi. on 3r.50 green & pur 9·00 35·00
65 70pi. on 7r. pink and green 26·00 55·00
The above stamps exist overprinted for Constantinople, Jaffa, Jerusalem, Kerassunde, Mount Athos, Salonika, Smyrna, Trebizonde, Beyrouth, Dardanelles, Mytilene and Rizeh. For full list see Part 10 (Russia) of the Stanley Gibbons Catalogue.

1913. Nos. 126/42 (Romanov types) of Russia surch.
186 5pa. on 1k. orange 40 40
187 10pa. on 3k. green 40 40
188 15pa. on 3k. red 40 40
189 20pa. on 4k. red 40 40
190 1pi. on 10k. blue 40 40
191 1½pi. on 15k. brown 60 60
192 2pi. on 20k. green 70 70
193 2½pi. on 25k. purple 1·00 1·00
194 3½pi. on 35k. green and violet 2·00 2·00
195 5pi. on 50k. grey and brown 2·25 2·25
196 7pi. on 70k. brown and green 7·00 17·00
197 10pi. on 1r. green 8·00 17·00
198 20pi. on 2r. brown 3·25 5·50
199 30pi. on 3r. violet 4·50 £170
200 50pi. on 5r. brown 90·00 £475

RWANDA Pt. 14

An independent republic established in July 1962, formerly part of Ruanda-Urundi.

100 centimes = 1 franc.

1 Pres. Kayibanda and Map

1962. Independence.
1 **1** 10c. sepia and green 10 10
2 – 40c. sepia and purple 10 10
3 **1** 1f. sepia and blue 70 35
4 – 1f.50 sepia and brown 10 10
5 **1** 3f.50 sepia and orange 10 10
6 – 6f.50 sepia and blue 15 10
7 **1** 10f. sepia and olive 30 15
8 – 20f. sepia and red 60 30
DESIGN: Nos. 2, 4, 6, 8 are as Type **1** but with halo around Rwanda on map in place of "R".

1963. Admission to U.N. No. 204 of Ruanda-Urundi with coloured frame obliterating old inscr (colours below), and surch **Admission a l'O.N.U. 18-9-1962 REPUBLIQUE RWANDAISE** and new value.
9 3f.50 on 3f. grey 10 10
10 6f.50 on 3f. pink 1·10 90
11 10f. on 3f. blue 25 25
12 20f. on 3f. silver 40 40

1963. Flowers issue of Ruanda-Urundi (Nos. 178 etc) optd **REPUBLIQUE RWANDAISE** or surch also in various coloured panels over old inscription and values. Flowers in natural colours.
13 25c. orange and green 20 20
14 40c. salmon and green 20 20
15 60c. purple and green 20 20
16 1f.25 blue and green 90 90
17 1f.50 green and violet 90 90
18 2f. on 1f.50 green and violet 1·40 1·10
19 4f. on 1f.50 green and violet 1·40 1·10
20 5f. green and purple 1·40 1·10
21 7f. brown and green 1·40 1·10
22 10f. olive and purple 1·75 1·50
The coloured panels are in various shades of silver except No. 19 which is in blue.

4 Ears of Wheat and Native Implements

1963. Freedom from Hunger.
23 **4** 2f. brown and green 10 10
24 4f. mauve and blue 10 10
25 7f. red and grey 20 10
26 10f. green and yellow 75 55

5 Coffee

6 Postal Services Emblem

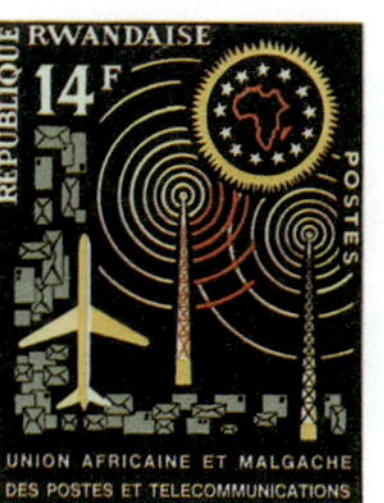

5a "Post and Telecommunications"

1963. 1st Anniv of Independence.
27 **5** 10c. brown and blue 10 10
28 – 20c. yellow and blue 10 10
29 – 30c. green and orange 10 10
30 **5** 40c. brown and turquoise 10 10
31 – 1f. yellow and purple 10 10
32 – 2f. green and blue 80 45
33 **5** 4f. brown and red 10 10
34 – 7f. yellow and green 20 15
35 – 10f. green and violet 35 30
DESIGNS: 20c., 1, 7f. Bananas; 30c., 2, 10f. Tea.

1963. 2nd Anniv of African and Malagasy Posts and Telcommunications Union.
36 **5a** 14f. multicoloured 1·10 90

1963. Admission of Rwanda to U.P.U.
37 **6** 50c. blue and pink 10 10
38 1f.50 brown and blue 65 45
39 3f. purple and grey 10 10
40 20f. green and yellow 45 20

7 Emblem

8 Child Care

1963. 15th Anniv of Declaration of Human Rights.
41 **7** 5f. red 15 10
42 6f. violet 50 35
43 10f. blue 35 15

1963. Red Cross Centenary.
44 **8** 10c. multicoloured 10 10
45 – 20c. multicoloured 10 10
46 – 30c. multicoloured 10 10
47 – 40c. brown, red and violet 10 10
48 **8** 2f. multicoloured 80 60
49 – 7f. multicoloured 15 10
50 – 10f. brown, red and brown 20 15
51 – 20f. brown, red and orange 60 35
DESIGNS—HORIZ: 20c., 7f. Patient having blood test; 40, 20c. Stretcher party. VERT: 30c., 10f. Doctor examining child.

9 Map and Hydraulic Pump

10 Boy with Crutch

1964. World Meteorological Day.
52 **9** 3f. sepia, blue and green 10 10
53 7f. sepia, blue and red 35 20
54 10f. sepia, blue and orange 50 35

1964. Stamps of Ruanda-Urundi optd **REPUBLIQUE RWANDAISE** or surch also in black over coloured metallic panels obliterating old inscription or value.
55 10c. on 20c. (No. 204) 10 10
56 20c. (No. 204) 10 10
57 30c. on 1f.50 (No. 208) 10 10
58 40c. (No. 205) 10 10
59 50c. (No. 206) 10 10
60 1f. (No. 207) 10 10
61 2f. (No. 209) 10 10
62 3f. (No. 210) 10 10
63 4f. on 3f.50 on 3f. (No. 228) 20 10
64 5f. (No. 211) 20 10
65 7f.50 on 6f.50 (No. 212) 45 15
66 8f. (No. 213) 4·50 2·25
67 10f. (No. 214) 65 20
68 20f. (No. 229) 1·10 45
69 50f. (No. 230) 2·10 85

1964. Gatagara Re-education Centre.
70 **10** 10c. sepia and violet 10 10
71 – 40c. sepia and blue 10 10
72 – 4f. sepia and brown 10 10
73 **10** 7f.50 sepia and green 45 15
74 – 8f. sepia and bistre 1·40 95
75 – 10f. sepia and purple 45 20
DESIGNS—HORIZ: 40c., 8f. Children operating sewing machines. VERT: 4, 10f. Crippled child on crutches.

11 Running

1964. Olympic Games, Tokyo. Sportsmen in slate.
76 **11** 10c. blue 10 10
77 – 20c. red 10 10
78 – 30c. turquoise 10 10
79 – 40c. brown 10 10
80 **11** 4f. blue 10 10
81 – 5f. green 1·40 1·25
82 – 20f. purple 35 35
83 – 50f. grey 1·10 90
DESIGNS—VERT: 20c., 5f. Basketball; 40c., 50f. Football. HORIZ: 20f. High-jumping.

12 Faculties of "Letters" and "Sciences"

13 Abraham Lincoln

1965. National University. Multicoloured.
84 10c. Type **12** 10 10
85 20c. Student with microscope and building ("Medicine") (horiz) 10 10
86 30c. Scales of Justice, Hand of Law ("Social Sciences" and "Normal High School") 10 10
87 40c. University buildings (horiz) 10 10
88 5f. Type **12** 10 10
89 7f. As 20c. 15 10
90 10f. As 30c. 1·00 85
91 12f. As 40c. 30 15

1965. Death Centenary of Abraham Lincoln.
92 **13** 10c. green and red 10 10
93 20c. brown and blue 10 10
94 30c. violet and red 10 10
95 40c. blue and brown 10 10
96 9f. brown and purple 20 15
97 40f. purple and green 1·90 70

14 Marabou Storks

15 "Telstar" Satellite

1965. Kagera National Park. Multicoloured.
98 10c. Type **14** 30 15
99 20c. Common zebras 10 10
100 30c. Impalas 10 10
101 40c. Crowned cranes, hippopotami and cattle egrets 30 15
102 1f. African buffaloes 10 10
103 3f. Hunting dogs 10 10
104 5f. Yellow baboons . . . . . 4·25 1·10
105 10f. African elephant and map 20 15
106 40f. Reed cormorants and African darters . . . . . 1·75 50
107 100f. Lions . . . . 2·25 50
SIZES—As Type **14**: VERT: 30c., 2, 5f. HORIZ: 20, 40c., 3, 10f. LARGER (45 × 25½ mm); 40, 100f.

1965. Centenary of I.T.U. Multicoloured.
108 10c. Type **15** 10 10
109 40c. "Syncom" satellite . . . 10 10
110 4f.50 Type **15** . . . . 1·40 50
111 50f. "Syncom" satellite . . . 90 35

16 "Colotis aurigineus"

17 Cattle and I.C.Y. Emblem

1965. Rwanda Butterflies. Multicoloured.
112 10c. "Papilio bromius" . . . 15 20
113 15c. "Papilio hesperus" . . . 15 20
114 20c. Type **16** 15 20
115 30c. "Amphicallia pactolicus" 15 20
116 35c. "Lobobunaea phaedusa" 15 20
117 40c. "Papilio jacksoni ruandana" 15 20
118 1f.50 "Papilio dardanus" . . 15 20
119 3f. "Amaurina elliotti" . . . 4·25 1·25
120 4f. "Colias electo pseudohecate" . . . . . . 2·75 1·00
121 10f. "Bunaea alcinoe" . . . 55 30
122 50f. "Athletes gigas" . . . . 1·75 85
123 100f. "Charaxes ansorgei R" 3·50 1·25
The 10, 30, 35c., 3, 4 and 100f. are vert.

1965. International Co-operation Year.
124 **17** 10c. green and yellow . . . 10 10
125 – 40c. brown, blue and green 10 10
126 – 4f.50 green, brown & yell 1·10 50
127 – 45f. purple and brown . . 90 40
DESIGNS: 40c. Crater lake and giant plants; 4f.50, Gazelle and candelabra tree; 45f. Mt. Ruwenzori. Each with I.C.Y. emblem.

18 Pres. Kennedy, Globe and Satellites

19 Madonna and Child

1965. 2nd Anniv of Pres. Kennedy's Death.
128 **18** 10c. brown and green . . . 10 10
129 40c. brown and red . . . 10 10
130 50c. brown and blue . . . 10 10
131 1f. brown and olive . . . 10 10
132 8f. brown and violet . . . 1·75 1·10
133 50f. brown and grey . . . 1·10 90

1965. Christmas.
134 **19** 10c. green and gold 10 10
135 40c. brown and gold . . . 10 10
136 50c. blue and gold 10 10
137 4f. black and gold 70 65
138 6f. violet and gold 15 10
139 30f. brown and gold . . . 65 45

20 Father Damien

1966. World Leprosy Day.
140 **20** 10c. blue and brown . . . 10 10
141 – 40c. red and blue 10 10
142 **20** 4f.50 slate and green . . . 20 15
143 – 45f. brown and red . . . . 1·75 1·25
DESIGNS: 40c., 45f. Dr. Schweitzer.

21 Pope Paul, Rome and New York

1966. Pope Paul's Visit to U.N. Organization.
144 **21** 10c. blue and brown . . . 10 10
145 – 40c. indigo and blue . . . 10 10
146 **21** 4f.50 blue and purple . . . 1·60 1·00
147 – 50f. blue and green . . . 1·00 55
DESIGN: 40c., 50f. Pope Paul, Arms and U.N. emblem.

22 "Echinops amplexicaulis" and "E. bequaertii"

1966. Flowers. Multicoloured.
148 10c. Type **22** 10 10
149 20c. "Haemanthus multiflorus" (vert) 10 10
150 30c. "Helichrysum erici-rosenii" 10 10
151 40c. "Carissa edulis" (vert) 10 10
152 1f. "Spathodea campanulata" (vert) 10 10
153 3f. "Habenaria praestans" (vert) 10 10
154 5f. "Aloe lateritia" (vert) . . 4·50 2·25
155 10f. "Ammocharis tinneana" (vert) 30 20
156 40f. "Erythrina abyssinica" 1·10 75
157 100f. "Capparis tomentosa" 2·75 1·40

23 W.H.O. Building

1966. Inaug of W.H.O. Headquarters, Geneva.
159 **23** 2f. olive 10 10
160 3f. red 20 20
161 5f. blue 10 10

24 Football

25 Mother and Child within Flames

1966. "Youth and Sports".
162 **24** 10c. black, blue and green 10 10
163 – 20c. black, green and red 10 10
164 – 30c. black, purple and blue 10 10
165 **24** 40c. black, green and bistre 10 10
166 – 9f. black, purple and grey 20 10
167 – 50f. black, blue and purple 1·10 1·00
DESIGNS: 20c., 9f. Basketball; 30c., 50f. Volleyball.

1966. Nuclear Disarmament.
168 **25** 20c. brown, red and mauve 10 10
169 30c. brown, red and green 10 10
170 50c. brown, red and blue 10 10
171 6f. brown, red and yellow 10 10
172 15f. brown, red & turquoise 65 30
173 18f. brown, red and lavender 65 40

26 Football

27 Yellow-crested Helmet Shrike and Mikeno Volcano

1966. World Cup Football Championship.
174 **26** 20c. blue and turquoise . . 10 10
175 30c. blue and violet 10 10
176 50c. blue and green 10 10
177 6f. blue and mauve 20 10
178 12f. blue and brown . . . 1·10 35
179 25f. indigo and blue . . . 2·25 60

1966. Rwanda Scenery.
180 **27** 10c. green 30 10
181 – 40c. lake 10 10
182 – 4f.50 blue 50 40
183 – 55f. purple 60 45
DESIGNS—VERT: 40c. Nyamiranga Falls (inscr "Nyamilanga"); 55f. Rusumo Falls (inscr "Rusumu"). HORIZ: 4f.50, Gahinga and Mahubura Volcanoes, and giant plants.

28 UNESCO and Cultural Emblems

1966. 20th Anniv of UNESCO.
184 **28** 20c. mauve and blue . . . 10 10
185 – 30c. turquoise and black 10 10
186 – 50c. brown and black . . . 10 10
187 – 1f. violet and black . . . 10 10
188 **28** 5f. green and brown . . . 10 10
189 – 10f. brown and black . . . 15 10
190 – 15f. purple and blue . . . 55 35
191 – 50f. blue and black . . . 65 50
DESIGNS: 30c., 10f. "Animal" primer; 50c., 15f. Atomic symbol and drill operator; 1, 50f. Nubian monument partly submerged in the Nile.

29 "Bitis gabonica"

1967. Snakes. Multicoloured.
192 20c. Head of mamba 20 15
193 30c. Python (vert) 20 15
194 50c. Type **29** 20 15
195 1f. "Naja melanoleuca" (vert) 20 15
196 3f. Head of python 20 15
197 5f. "Psammophis sibilans" (vert) 45 15
198 20f. "Dendroaspis jamesoni kaimosae" . . . . 1·25 50
199 70f. "Dasypeltis scabra" (vert) . . . . 1·50 70

30 Girders and Tea Flower

1967. Ntaruka Hydro-electric Project.
200 **30** 20c. blue and purple . . . 10 10
201 – 30c. brown and black . . . 10 10
202 – 50c. violet and brown . . . 10 10
203 **30** 4f. purple and green . . . 10 10
204 – 25f. green and violet . . . 50 50
205 – 50f. brown and blue . . . 1·00 1·00
DESIGNS: 30c., 25f. Power conductors and pyrethrum flower; 50c., 50f. Barrage and coffee beans.

33 "St. Martin" (Van Dyck)

1967. Paintings.
208 **33** 20c. black, gold and violet 10 10
209 – 40c. black, gold and green 10 10
210 – 60c. black, gold and red . . 10 10
211 – 80c. black, gold and blue 10 10
212 **33** 9f. black, gold and brown 90 50
213 – 15f. black, gold and red . . 35 20
214 – 18f. black, gold and bronze 35 20
215 – 26f. black, gold and lake 45 45
PAINTINGS—HORIZ: 40c., 15f. "Rebecca and Eliezer" (Murillo); 80c., 26f. "Job and his Friends" (attributed to Il Calabrese). VERT: 60c., 18f. "St. Christopher" (D. Bouts).

34 Rwanda "Round Table" Emblem and Common Zebra's Head

1967. Rwanda "Round Table" Fund for Charitable Works. Each with "Round Table" Emblem. Mult.
216 20c. Type **34** 10 10
217 40c. African elephant's head 10 10
218 60c. African buffalo's head 10 10
219 80c. Impala's head 10 10
220 18f. Ear of wheat 35 15
221 100f. Palm . . . . 1·60 90

35 "Africa Place" and Dancers

1967. World Fair, Montreal.
222 **35** 20c. blue and sepia 10 10
223 – 30c. purple and sepia . . . 10 10
224 – 50c. orange and sepia . . . 10 10
225 – 1f. green and sepia 10 10
226 – 3f. violet and sepia 10 10
227 **35** 15f. green and sepia . . . 15 15
228 – 34f. red and sepia 50 40
229 – 40f. turquoise and sepia . . 70 55
DESIGNS: "Africa Place" (two different views used alternately in order of value) and 30c., 3f. Drum and handicrafts; 50c., 40f. Dancers leaping; 1f., 34f. Spears, shields and weapons.

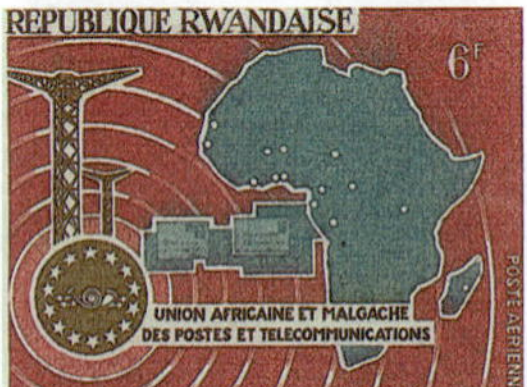

35a Map of Africa, Letters and Pylons

1967. Air. 5th Anniv of U.A.M.P.T.
230 **35a** 6f. slate, brown and lake 20 10
231 18f. purple and brown . . 65 35
232 30f. red, green and blue 1·10 65

36 Common Zebra's Head and Lion's Emblem

37 Red Bishop

1967. 50th Anniv of Lions International.
233 **36** 20c. black, blue and violet 10 10
234 80c. black, blue and green 10 10
235 1f. black, blue and red 10 10
236 8f. black, blue and brown 20 10
237 10f. black, blue and ultramarine 30 20
238 50f. black, blue and green 1·40 95

1967. Birds of Rwanda. Multicoloured.
239 20c. Type **37** 10 30
240 40c. Woodland kingfisher (horiz) 10 30
241 60c. Red-billed quelea 10 30
242 80c. Double-toothed barbet (horiz) 10 30
243 2f. Pin-tailed whydah 25 30
244 3f. Red-chested cuckoo (horiz) 35 30
245 18f. Green wood hoopoe 1·40 55
246 25f. Cinnamon-chested bee eater (horiz) 2·00 90
247 80f. Regal sunbird 4·50 2·50
248 100f. Fan-tailed whydah (horiz) 6·50 3·00

39 Running, and Mexican Antiquities

1968. Olympic Games, Mexico (1st issue). Mult.
250 20c. Type **39** 35 10
251 40c. Hammer-throwing 35 10
252 60c. Hurdling 35 10
253 80c. Javelin-throwing 35 10
254 8f. Football (vert) 45 10
255 10f. Mexican horseman and cacti (vert) 45 10
256 12f. Hockey (vert) 55 10
257 18f. Cathedral (vert) 70 15
258 20f. Boxing (vert) 90 55
259 30f. Mexico City (vert) 1·10 65
The 20c. to 80c. include Mexican antiquities in their designs.

41 "Diaphananthe fragrantissima"

1968. Flowers. Multicoloured.
261 20c. Type **41** 10 10
262 40c. "Phaeomeria speciosa" 10 10
263 60c. "Ravenala madagascariensis" 10 10
264 80c. "Costus afer" 10 10
265 2f. Banana flowers 10 10
266 3f. Flowers and young fruit of pawpaw 10 10
267 18f. "Clerodendron sp." 35 15
268 25f. Sweet potato flowers 45 30
269 80f. Baobab flower 1·90 80
270 100f. Passion flower 2·25 1·25

42 Horse-jumping

43 Tuareg (Algeria)

1968. Olympic Games, Mexico (2nd issue).
271 **42** 20c. brown and orange 10 10
272 – 40c. brown and turquoise 10 10
273 – 60c. brown and purple 10 10
274 – 80c. brown and blue 10 10
275 – 38f. brown and red 50 40
276 – 60f. brown and green 1·10 65
SPORTS: 40c. Judo; 60c. Fencing; 80c. High-jumping; 38f. High-diving; 60f. Weightlifting. Each design also represents the location of previous Olympics as at left in Type **42**.

1968. African National Costumes (1st series). Mult.
277 30c. Type **43** 10 10
278 40c. Upper Volta 10 10
279 60c. Senegal 10 10
280 70c. Rwanda 10 10
281 8f. Morocco 10 10
282 20f. Nigeria 35 20
283 40f. Zambia 80 35
284 50f. Kenya 1·10 55
See also Nos. 345/52.

44a "Alexandre Lenoir" (J. L. David)

1968. Air. "Philexafrique" Stamp Exhibition, Abidjan (Ivory Coast, 1969) (1st issue).
286 **44a** 100f. multicoloured 2·50 1·60

45 Rwanda Scene and Stamp of Ruanda-Urundi (1953)

1969. Air. "Philexafrique" Stamp Exn (2nd issue).
287 **45** 50f. multicoloured 1·90 1·25

46 "The Musical Angels" (Van Eyck)

47 Tuareg Tribesmen

1969. "Paintings and Music". Multicoloured.
288 20c. Type **46** (postage) 10 10
289 40c. "The Angels' Concert" (M. Grunewald) 10 10
290 60c. "The Singing Boy" (Frans Hals) 10 10
291 80c. "The Lute player" (G. Terborch) 10 10
292 2f. "The Fifer" (Manet) 10 10
293 6f. "Young Girls at the Piano" (Renoir) 15 10
294 50f. "The Music Lesson" (Fragonard) (air) 1·40 85
295 100f. "Angels playing their Musical Instruments" (Memling) (horiz) 2·75 1·60

1969. African Headdresses (1st series). Mult.
297 20c. Type **47** 10 10
298 40c. Young Ovambo woman 10 10
299 60c. Ancient Guinean and Middle Congo festival headdresses 10 10
300 80c. Guinean "Dagger" dancer 10 10
301 8f. Nigerian Muslims 10 10
302 20f. Luba dancer, Kabondo (Congo) 40 20
303 40f. Senegalese and Gambian women 85 45
304 80f. Rwanda dancer 1·25 1·00
See also Nos. 408/15.

48 "The Moneylender and his Wife" (Quentin Metsys)

1969. 5th Anniv of African Development Bank.
305 **48** 30f. multicoloured on silver 55 50
306 – 70f. multicoloured on gold 1·60 1·40
DESIGN: 70f. "The Moneylender and his Wife" (Van Reymerswaele).

50 Pyrethrum

51 Revolutionary

1969. Medicinal Plants. Multicoloured.
308 20c. Type **50** 10 10
309 40c. Aloes 10 10
310 60c. Cola 10 10
311 80c. Coca 10 10
312 3f. Hagenia 10 10
313 75f. Cassia 1·40 80
314 80f. Cinchona 2·25 90
315 100f. Tephrosia 2·50 1·10

1969. 10th Anniv of Revolution.
316 **51** 6f. multicoloured 15 10
317 18f. multicoloured 50 45
318 40f. multicoloured 1·00 95

53 "Napoleon on Horseback" (David)

1969. Birth Bicent of Napoleon Bonaparte. Mult. Portraits of Napoleon. Artist's name given.
320 20c. Type **53** 10 10
321 40c. Debret 10 10
322 60c. Gautherot 10 10
323 80c. Ingres 10 10
324 8f. Pajou 20 15
325 20f. Gros 55 40
326 40f. Gros 1·00 55
327 80f. David 2·25 1·25

54 "The Quarryman" (O. Bonnevalle)

1969. 50th Anniv of I.L.O. Multicoloured.
328 20c. Type **54** 10 10
329 40c. "Ploughing" (detail Brueghel's "Descent of Icarus") 10 10
330 60c. "The Fisherman" (C. Meunier) 10 10
331 80c. "Ostend Slipway" (J. van Noten) 10 10
332 8f. "The Cook" (P. Aertsen) 20 10
333 10f. "Vulcan's Blacksmiths" (Velazquez) 35 15
334 50f. "Hiercheuse" (C. Meunier) 1·25 60
335 70f. "The Miner" (P. Paulus) 1·60 80
Nos. 330, 332 and 334/5 are vert.

55 "The Derby at Epsom" (Gericault)

1970. Paintings of Horses. Multicoloured.
336 20c. Type **55** 10 10
337 40c. "Horses leaving the Sea" (Delacroix) 10 10
338 60c. "Charles V at Muhlberg" (Titian) (vert) 10 10
339 80c. "To the Races, Amateur Jockeys" (Degas) 10 10
340 8f. "Horsemen at Rest" (Wouwermans) 20 10
341 20f. "Officer of the Imperial Guard" (Gericault) (vert) 60 30
342 40f. "Horse and Dromedary" (Bonnevalle) 1·50 45
343 80f. "The Prodigal Child" (Rubens) 2·00 80

1970. African National Costumes (2nd series). As T **43**. Multicoloured.
345 20c. Tharaka Meru woman 10 10
346 30c. Niger flautist 10 10
347 50c. Tunisian water-carrier 10 10
348 1f. Kano ceremonial (Nigeria) 10 10
349 3f. Mali troubador 10 10
350 5f. Quipongo, Angola women 10 10
351 50f. Mauritanian at prayer 95 55
352 90f. Sinehatiali dancers, Ivory Coast 2·00 1·00

58 Footballer attacking Goal

1970. World Cup Football Championship, Mexico.
353 **58** 20c. multicoloured 10 10
354 – 30c. multicoloured 10 10
355 – 50c. multicoloured 10 10
356 – 1f. multicoloured 10 10
357 – 6f. multicoloured 10 10
358 – 18f. multicoloured 45 30
359 – 30f. multicoloured 85 45
360 – 90f. multicoloured 2·00 95
Nos. 354/60 show footballers in various positions, similar to Type **58**.

59 Flowers and Green Peafowl

1970. "EXPO 70", World Fair, Osaka, Japan. Mult.
361 20c. Type **59** 60 10
362 30c. Torii gate and "Hibiscus" (Yashuda) 10 10
363 50c. Dancer and "Musician" (Katayama) 10 10
364 1f. Sun Tower and "Warrior" 10 10
365 3f. House and "Seated Buddha" 10 10
366 5f. Pagoda and "Head of Girl" (Yamakawa) 10 10
367 20f. Greeting and "Imperial Palace" 55 35
368 70f. Expo emblem and "Horseman" 1·60 90

60 Two Young Gorillas

1970. Gorillas of the Mountains.
369 **60** 20c. black and green 35 35
370 – 40c. black, brown & purple 35 35
371 – 60c. black, blue and brown 35 35
372 – 80c. black, orange & brown 35 35
373 – 1f. black and mauve 35 35
374 – 2f. multicoloured 35 35
375 – 15f. black and sepia 70 45
376 – 100f. black, brown and blue 3·75 2·25
GORILLA—VERT: 40c. Squatting; 80c. Beating chest; 2f. Eating banana; 100f. With young. HORIZ: 60c. Walking; 1f. With family; 15f. Heads.

61 Cinchona Bark

1970. 150th Anniv of Discovery of Quinine. Mult.
377 20c. Type **61** 10 10
378 80c. Pharmaceutical equipment 10 10
379 1f. Anopheles mosquito 10 10
380 3f. Malaria patient and nurse 10 10
381 25f. "Attack" on mosquito 55 35
382 70f. Pelletier and Caventou (discoverers of quinine) 1·50 80

62 Rocket in Flight

65 Pope Paul VI

63 F. D. Roosevelt and "Brasscattleya olympia alba"

1970. Moon Missions. Multicoloured.

No.	Description	Unused	Used
383	20c. Type **62**	10	10
384	30c. Separation during orbit	10	10
385	50c. Spaceship above the moon	10	10
386	1f. Module and astonauts on moon	10	10
387	3f. Take-off from the moon	10	10
388	5f. Return journey to earth	15	10
389	10f. Final separation before landing	30	15
390	80f. Splashdown	2·25	1·40

1970. 25th Death Anniv of F. D. Roosevelt. Portraits and Orchids.

No.	Description	Unused	Used
391 **63**	20c. brown, blue and black	10	10
392 –	30c. brown, red and black	10	10
393 –	50c. brown, orange & black	10	10
394 –	1f. brown, green and black	10	10
395 –	2f. green, brown and black	10	10
396 –	6f. green, purple and black	20	15
397 –	30f. green, blue and black	1·25	40
398 –	60f. green, red and black	2·00	70

ORCHIDS: 30c. "Laeliocattleya callistoglossa"; 50c. "Chondrorrhyncha chestertoni"; 1f. "Paphiopedilum"; 2f. "Cymbidium hybride"; 6f. "Cattleya labiata"; 30f. "Dendrobium nobile"; 60f. "Laelia gouldiana".

1970. Centenary of 1st Vatican Council.

No.	Description	Unused	Used
400 **65**	10c. brown and gold	10	10
401 –	20c. green and gold	10	10
402 –	30c. lake and gold	10	10
403 –	40c. blue and gold	10	10
404 –	1f. violet and gold	10	10
405 –	18f. purple and gold	50	20
406 –	20f. orange and gold	60	20
407 –	60f. brown and gold	1·60	70

POPES: 20c. John XXIII; 30c. Pius XII; 40c. Pius XI; 1f. Benedict XV; 18f. Pius X; 20f. Leo XIII; 60f. Pius IX.

1971. African Headdresses (2nd series). Mult. As T **47**.

No.	Description	Unused	Used
408	20c. Rendille woman	10	10
409	30c. Chad woman	10	10
410	50c. Bororo man (Niger)	10	10
411	1f. Masai man (Kenya)	10	10
412	5f. Air girl (Niger)	10	10
413	18f. Rwanda woman	35	20
414	25f. Mauritania man	65	35
415	50f. Rwanda girls	1·50	65

68 "Beethoven" (C. Horneman)

1971. Birth Cent (1970) of Beethoven. Portraits and funeral scene by various artists. Mult.

No.	Description	Unused	Used
418	20c. Type **68**	10	10
419	30c. K. Stieler	10	10
420	50c. F. Schimon	10	10
421	3f. H. Best	10	10
422	6f. W. Fassbender	30	10
423	90f. "Beethoven's Burial" (Stober)	2·10	2·00

69 Horse-jumping

1971. Olympic Games, Munich (1972) (1st issue).

No.	Description	Unused	Used
424 **69**	20c. gold and black	10	10
425 –	30c. gold and purple	10	10
426 –	50c. gold and violet	10	10
427 –	1f. gold and green	10	10
428 –	8f. gold and red	20	10
429 –	10f. gold and violet	30	15
430 –	20f. gold and brown	50	30
431 –	60f. gold and green	1·40	65

DESIGNS: 30c. Running (start); 50c. Basketball; 1f. High-jumping; 8f. Boxing; 10f. Pole-vaulting; 20f. Wrestling; 60f. Gymnastics.

See also Nos. 490/7.

70 U.A.M.P.T. H.Q. and Rwandaise Woman and Child

1971. Air. 10th Anniv of U.A.M.P.T.

No.	Description	Unused	Used
432 **70**	100f. multicoloured	2·10	2·00

72 "Durer" (self-portrait)

1971. 500th Birth Anniv of Durer. Paintings. Multicoloured.

No.	Description	Unused	Used
434	20c. "Adam"	10	10
435	30c. "Eve"	10	10
436	50c. "Portrait of H. Holzschuher"	10	10
437	1f. "Mourning the Dead Christ"	10	10
438	3f. "Madonna and Child"	10	10
439	5f. "St. Eustace"	10	10
440	20f. "St. Paul and St. Mark"	45	30
441	70f. Type **72**	1·60	1·00

73 Astronauts in Moon Rover

1972. Moon Mission of "Apollo 15".

No.	Description	Unused	Used
442 **73**	600f. gold	95·00	

74 Participation in Sport

1972. National Guard. Multicoloured.

No.	Description	Unused	Used
443	4f. Type **74**	10	10
444	6f. Transport of emergency supplies	15	10
445	15f. Helicopter transport for the sick	40	20
446	25f. Participation in health service	65	35
447	50f. Guard, map and emblem (vert)	1·25	1·10

75 Ice Hockey

1972. Winter Olympic Games, Sapporo, Japan. Multicoloured.

No.	Description	Unused	Used
448	20c. Type **75**	10	10
449	30c. Speed-skating	10	10
450	50c. Ski-jumping	10	10
451	1f. Figure skating	10	10
452	6f. Cross-country skiing	10	10
453	12f. Slalom	15	15
454	20f. Tobogganing	45	20
455	60f. Downhill skiing	1·40	1·10

76 Savanna Monkey and Impala

1972. Akagera National Park. Multicoloured.

No.	Description	Unused	Used
456	20c. Type **76**	15	10
457	30c. African buffalo	15	10
458	50c. Common zebra	15	10
459	1f. White rhinoceros	40	40
460	2f. Warthogs	15	10
461	6f. Hippopotamus	20	10
462	18f. Spotted hyenas	40	20
463	32f. Helmeted guineafowl	2·25	95
464	60f. Waterbucks	2·00	1·10
465	80f. Lion and lioness	2·75	1·75

77 Family supporting Flag

78 Variable Sunbirds

1972. 10th Anniv of Referendum.

No.	Description	Unused	Used
466 **77**	6f. multicoloured	10	10
467	18f. multicoloured	45	35
468	60f. multicoloured	1·25	1·10

1972. Rwanda Birds. Multicoloured.

No.	Description	Unused	Used
469	20c. Common waxbills	10	10
470	30c. Collared sunbird	15	10
471	50c. Type **78**	20	10
472	1f. Greater double-collared sunbird	30	10
473	4f. Ruwenzori puff-back flycatcher	35	15
474	6f. Red-billed fire finch	40	20
475	10f. Scarlet-chested sunbird	70	20
476	18f. Red-headed quelea	1·50	40
477	60f. Black-headed gonolek	4·75	1·50
478	100f. African golden oriole	8·00	2·40

79 King Baudouin and Queen Fabiola with President and Mrs. Kayibanda in Rwanda

1972. "Belgica 72" Stamp Exhibition, Brussels.

No.	Description	Unused	Used
479 –	18f. multicoloured	70	70
480 –	22f. multicoloured	90	90
481 **79**	40f. blue, black and gold	1·75	1·75

DESIGNS: 18f. Rwanda village; 22f. View of Bruges.
Nos. 479/80 are smaller, size 39 × 36 mm.

80 Announcement of Independence

1972. 10th Anniv of Independence.

No.	Description	Unused	Used
482 **80**	20c. green and gold	10	10
483 –	30c. purple and gold	10	10
484 –	50c. sepia and gold	10	10
485 –	6f. blue and gold	10	10
486 –	10f. purple and gold	15	10
487 –	15f. blue and gold	35	20
488 –	18f. brown and gold	45	30
489 –	50f. green and gold	1·10	70

DESIGNS—HORIZ: 30c. Promotion ceremony, officers of the National Guard; 50c. Pres. Kayibanda, wife and family; 6f. Pres. Kayibanda casting vote in legislative elections; 10f. Pres. and Mrs. Kayibanda at "Festival of Justice"; 15f. President and members of National Assembly; 18f. Investiture of Pres. Kayibanda. VERT: 50f. President Kayibanda.

81 Horse-jumping

1972. Olympic Games, Munich (2nd issue).

No.	Description	Unused	Used
490 **81**	20c. green and gold	10	10
491 –	30c. violet and gold	10	10
492 –	50c. green and gold	10	10
493 –	1f. purple and gold	10	10
494 –	6f. black and gold	10	10
495 –	18f. brown and gold	35	30
496 –	30f. violet and gold	80	55
497 –	44f. blue and gold	1·10	65

DESIGNS: 30c. Hockey; 50c. Football; 1f. Long-jumping; 6f. Cycling; 18f. Yachting; 30f. Hurdling; 44f. Gymnastics.

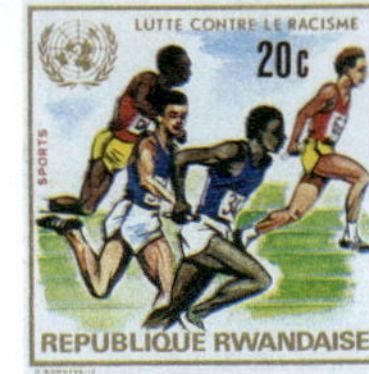

82 Runners

1972. Racial Equality Year. "Working Together". Multicoloured.

No.	Description	Unused	Used
498	20c. Type **82**	10	10
499	30c. Musicians	10	10
500	50c. Ballet dancers	10	10
501	1f. Medical team in operating theatre	10	10
502	6f. Weaver and painter	10	10
503	18f. Children in class	35	20
504	24f. Laboratory technicians	55	35
505	50f. U.N. emblem and hands of four races	1·00	65

84 "Phymateus brunneri"

1973. Rwanda Insects. Multicoloured.

No.	Description	Unused	Used
507	20c. Type **84**	10	10
508	30c. "Diopsis fumipennis" (vert)	10	10
509	50c. "Kitoko alberti"	10	10
510	1f. "Archibracon fasciatus" (vert)	10	10
511	2f. "Ornithacris cyanea imperialis"	10	10
512	6f. "Clitodaca fenestralis" (vert)	15	10
513	18f. "Senaspis oesacus"	40	20
514	22f. "Phonoctonus grandis" (vert)	55	35
515	70f. "Loba leopardina"	2·25	2·40
516	100f. "Ceratocoris distortus" (vert)	4·00	3·10

85 "Emile Zola" (Manet)

86 Longombe

1973. International Book Year. "Readers and Writers". Paintings and portraits. Multicoloured.

No.	Description	Unused	Used
518	20c. Type **85**	10	10
519	30c. "Rembrandt's Mother" (Rembrandt)	10	10
520	50c. "St. Jerome removing Thorn from Lion's paw" (Colantonio)	10	10
521	1f. "St. Peter and St. Paul" (El Greco)	10	10
522	2f. "Virgin and Child" (Van der Weyden)	10	10
523	6f. "St. Jerome in his Cell" (Antonella de Messina)	15	10

524 40f. "St. Barbara" (Master of Flemalle) . . . . 1·00 60
525 100f. "Don Quixote" (O. Bonnevalle) . . . . . 2·40 1·90

1973. Musical Instruments. Multicoloured.
527 20c. Type **86** 10 10
528 30c. Horn 10 10
529 50c. "Xylophone" 10 10
530 1f. "Harp" 10 10
531 4f. Alur horns 10 10
532 6f. Horn, bells and drum . . 10 10
533 18f. Drums 40 40
534 90f. Gourds . . . . 2·00 1·40

87 "Rubens and Isabelle Brandt" (Rubens)

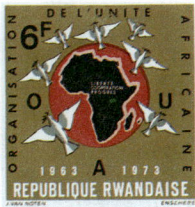

88 Map of Africa and Doves

1973. "IBRA" Stamp Exhibition, Munich. Famous Paintings. Multicoloured.
535 20c. Type **87** 10 10
536 30c. "Portrait of a Lady" (Cranach the Younger) . . 10 10
537 50c. "Woman peeling Turnips" (Chardin) 10 10
538 1f. "Abduction of the Daughters of Leucippe" (Rubens) 10 10
539 2f. "Virgin and Child" (Lippi) 10 10
540 6f. "Boys eating Fruit" (Murillo) 20 10
541 40f. "The Sickness of Love" (Steen) 90 45
542 100f. "Jesus divested of His Garments" (El Greco) . . 2·25 1·40

1973. 10th Anniv of O.A.U. Multicoloured.
544 6f. Type **88** 20 10
545 94f. Map of Africa and hands 2·25 1·90

1973. Pan-African Drought Relief. Nos. 308/13 and 315 optd **SECHERESSE SOLIDARITE AFRICAINE** and No. 315 additionally surch.
546 **50** 20c. multicoloured 10 10
547 – 40c. multicoloured 10 10
548 – 60c. multicoloured 10 10
549 – 80c. multicoloured 10 10
550 – 3f. multicoloured 10 10
551 – 75f. multicoloured . . . . 1·60 1·40
552 – 100f.+50f. multicoloured 5·00 4·00

90 Six-banded Distichodus

1973. Fishes. Multicoloured.
553 20c. Type **90** 10 10
554 30c. Lesser tigerfish 10 10
555 50c. Angel squeaker 10 10
556 1f. Nile mouthbrooder . . . 10 10
557 2f. African lungfish 15 10
558 6f. Mandeville's catfish . . . 35 10
559 40f. Congo tetra . . . . . . 1·90 95
560 150f. Golden julie . . . . . 6·25 3·50

91 Crane with Letter and Telecommunications Emblem

1973. 12th Anniv of U.A.M.P.T.
562 **91** 100f. blue, brown and mauve . . . . 2·50 1·90

1973. African Fortnight, Brussels. Nos. 408/15 optd **QUINZAINE AFRICAINE BRUXELLES 15/30 SEPT. 1973** and globe.
563 20c. multicoloured 10 10
564 30c. multicoloured 10 10
565 50c. multicoloured 10 10
566 1f. multicoloured 10 10
567 5f. multicoloured 10 10
568 18f. multicoloured 40 20
569 25f. multicoloured 50 45
570 50f. multicoloured . . . . . 1·40 85

1973. Air. Congress of French-speaking Nations, Liege. No. 432 optd **LIEGE ACCUEILLE LES PAYS DE LANGUE FRANCAISE 1973** (No. 562) or congress emblem (No. 563).
571 100f. multicoloured . . . . . 4·00 2·75
572 100f. multicoloured . . . . . 4·00 2·75

1973. 25th Anniv of Declaration of Human Rights. Nos. 443/7 optd with Human Rights emblem.
574 **74** 4f. multicoloured 10 10
575 – 6f. multicoloured 10 10
576 – 15f. multicoloured 30 15
577 – 25f. multicoloured 60 40
578 – 50f. multicoloured . . . . 1·40 95

96 Copernicus and Astrolabe

97 Pres. Habyarimana

1973. 500th Birth Anniv of Copernicus. Mult.
580 20c. Type **96** 10 10
581 30c. Copernicus 10 10
582 50c. Copernicus and heliocentric system 10 10
583 1f. Type **96** 10 10
584 18f. As 30c. 65 60
585 80f. As 50c. . . . . 2·40 2·00

1974. "New Regime".
587 **97** 1f. brown, black and buff 10 10
588 2f. brown, black and blue 10 10
589 5f. brown, black and red 10 10
590 6f. brown, black and blue 10 10
591 26f. brown, black and lilac 55 45
592 60f. brown, black and green . . . . 1·25 1·00

99 Yugoslavia v Zaire

101 "Diane de Poiters" (Fontainebleau School)

100 Marconi's Steam Yacht "Elettra"

1974. World Cup Football Championship, West Germany. Players represent specified teams. Mult.
594 20c. Type **99** 10 10
595 40c. Netherlands v Sweden 10 10
596 60c. West Germany v Australia 10 10
597 80c. Haiti v Argentina . . . 10 10
598 2f. Brazil v Scotland 10 10
599 6f. Bulgaria v Uruguay . . . 10 10
600 40f. Italy v Poland 80 65
601 50f. Chile v East Germany 1·40 1·00

1974. Birth Centenary of Guglielmo Marconi (radio pioneer). Multicoloured.
602 20c. Type **100** 20 10
603 30c. Cruiser "Carlo Alberto" 20 10
604 50c. Marconi's telegraph equipment 10 10
605 4f. "Global Telecommunications" . . . 10 10
606 35f. Early radio receiver . . . 85 45
607 60f. Marconi and Poldhu radio station . . . . . . 1·50 1·10

1974. International Stamp Exhibitions "Stockholmia" and "Internaba". Paintings from Stockholm and Basle. Multicoloured.
609 20c. Type **101** 10 10
610 30c. "The Flute-player" (J. Leyster) 10 10
611 50c. "Virgin Mary and Child" (G. David) 10 10
612 1f. "The Triumph of Venus" (F. Boucher) 10 10
613 10f. "Harlequin Seated" (P. Picasso) 15 10
614 18f. "Virgin and Child" (15th-century) 35 15
615 20f. "The Beheading of St. John" (H. Fries) . . . 45 35
616 50f. "The Daughter of Andersdotter" (J. Hockert) 1·40 1·00

102 Monastic Messenger

105 Head of Uganda Kob

1974. Centenary of U.P.U. Multicoloured.
619 20c. Type **102** 10 10
620 30c. Inca messenger 10 10
621 50c. Moroccan postman . . . 10 10
622 1f. Indian postman 10 10
623 18f. Polynesian postman . . 55 40
624 80f. Early Rwanda messenger with horn and drum . . . 2·00 1·40

1974. 15th Anniv of Revolution. Nos. 316/18 optd **1974 15e ANNIVERSAIRE.**
625 **51** 6f. multicoloured . . . .
626 18f. multicoloured . . . .
627 40f. multicoloured . . . .
Set of 3 . . . . 11·00 9·50

1974. 10th Anniv of African Development Bank. Nos. 305/6 optd **1974 10e ANNIVERSAIRE.**
629 **48** 30f. multicoloured 85 65
630 – 70f. multicoloured . . . . 1·90 1·40

1975. Antelopes. Multicoloured.
631 20c. Type **105** 15 10
632 30c. Bongo with calf (horiz) 15 10
633 50c. Roan antelope and sable antelope heads 15 10
634 1f. Young sitatungas (horiz) 15 10
635 4f. Great kudu 15 10
636 10f. Impala family (horiz) . . 80 10
637 34f. Waterbuck head . . . . 2·00 70
638 100f. Giant eland (horiz) . . 5·75 2·50

108 Pyrethrum Daisies

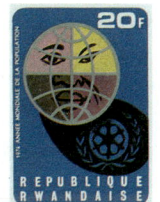

111 Globe and Emblem

110 Eastern White Pelicans

1975. Agricultural Labour Year. Multicoloured.
642 20c. Type **108** 10 10
643 30c. Tea plant 10 10
644 50c. Coffee berries 10 10
645 4f. Bananas 10 10
646 10f. Maize 20 10
647 12f. Sorghum 35 15
648 26f. Rice 80 45
649 47f. Coffee cultivation . . . 1·60 90

1975. Holy Year. Nos. 400/7 optd **1975 ANNEE SAINTE.**
652 **65** 10c. brown and gold . . . 10 10
653 – 20c. green and gold . . . 10 10
654 – 30c. lake and gold 10 10
655 – 40c. blue and gold 10 10
656 – 1f. violet and gold 10 10
657 – 18f. purple and gold . . . 40 20
658 – 20f. orange and gold . . . 45 20
659 – 60f. brown and gold . . . 1·90 1·25

1975. Aquatic Birds. Multicoloured.
660 20c. Type **110** 10 10
661 30c. Malachite kingfisher . . 10 10
662 50c. Goliath herons 10 10
663 1f. Saddle-bill stork 10 10
664 4f. African jacana 40 15
665 10f. African darter 85 35
666 34f. Sacred ibis . . . . . . 2·40 1·00
667 80f. Hartlaub's duck . . . . 6·50 2·75

1975. World Population Year (1974). Mult.
669 20f. Type **111** 45 30
670 26f. Population graph 65 35
671 34f. Symbolic doorway . . . 95 50

112 "La Toilette" (M. Cassatt)

113 "Arts"

1975. International Women's Year. Multicoloured.
672 20c. Type **112** 10 10
673 30c. "Mother and Child" (G. Melchers) 10 10
674 50c. "The Milk Jug" (Vermeer) 10 10
675 1f. "The Water-carrier" (Goya) 10 10
676 8f. Coffee picking 20 10
677 12f. Laboratory technician . . 35 20
678 18f. Rwandaise mother and child 55 20
679 60f. Woman carrying water jug . . . . 1·50 1·25

1975. 10th Anniv of National University. The Faculties. Multicoloured.
681 20c. Type **113** 10 10
682 30c. "Medicine" 10 10
683 1f.50 "Jurisprudence" 10 10
684 18f. "Science" 40 20
685 26f. "Commerce" 45 30
686 34f. University Building, Kigali 85 55

114 Cattle at Pool, and "Impatiens stuhlmannii"

1975. Protection of Nature. Multicoloured.
688 20c. Type **114** 10 10
689 30c. Euphorbis "candelabra" and savannah bush 10 10
690 50c. Bush fire and "Tapinanthus prunifolius" 10 10
691 5f. Lake Bulera and "Nymphaea lotus" 10 10
692 8f. Soil erosion and "Protea madiensis" 15 10
693 10f. Protected marshland and "Melanthera brownei" . . 20 15
694 26f. Giant lobelias and groundsel 55 40
695 100f. Sabyinyo volcano and "Polystachya kermesina" 2·50 2·25

1975. Pan-African Drought Relief. Nos. 345/52 optd or surch **SECHERESSE SOLIDARITE 1975** (both words share same initial letter).
696 20c. multicoloured 10 10
697 30c. multicoloured 10 10
698 50c. multicoloured 10 10
699 1f. multicoloured 10 10
700 3f. multicoloured 10 10
701 5f. multicoloured 15 10
702 50f.+25f. multicoloured . . . 1·60 1·25
703 90f.+25f. multicoloured . . . 2·40 2·00

116 Loading Douglas DC-8F Jet Trader

1975. Year of Increased Production. Multicoloured.
704 20c. Type **116** 10 10
705 30c. Coffee-picking plant . . 10 10
706 50c. Lathe operator 10 10
707 10f. Farmer with hoe (vert) 15 10
708 35f. Coffee-picking (vert) . . 60 55
709 54f. Mechanical plough . . . 1·10 95

117 African Woman with Basket on Head

1975. "Themabelga" Stamp Exhibition, Brussels. African Costumes.
710 117 20c. multicoloured 10 10
711 – 30c. multicoloured 10 10
712 – 50c. multicoloured 10 10
713 – 1f. multicoloured 10 10
714 – 5f. multicoloured 10 10
715 – 7f. multicoloured 15 10
716 – 35f. multicoloured 70 60
717 – 51f. multicoloured . . . . 1·40 95
DESIGNS: 30c. to 51f. Various Rwanda costumes.

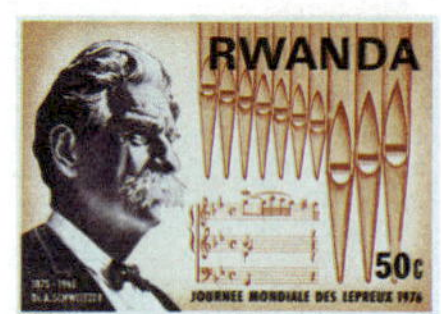
118 Dr. Schweitzer, Organ Pipes and Music Score

1976. World Leprosy Day.
719 – 20c. lilac, brown and black 10 10
720 – 30c. lilac, green and black 10 10
721 118 50c. lilac, brown and black 10 10
722 – 1f. lilac, purple and black 10 10
723 – 3f. lilac, blue and black 10 10
724 – 5f. lilac, brown and black 10 10
725 118 10f. lilac, blue and black 30 10
726 – 80f. lilac, red and black 1·90 1·40
DESIGNS: Dr. Schweitzer and: 20c. Piano keyboard and music; 30c. Lambarene Hospital; 1f. Lambarene residence; 3f. as 20c.; 5f. as 30 c; 80f. as 1f.

119 "Surrender at Yorktown"

1976. Bicentenary of American Revolution. Mult.
727 20c. Type 119 . . . . 10 10
728 30c. "The Sergeant-Instructor at Valley Forge" 10 10
729 50c. "Presentation of Captured Yorktown Flags to Congress" 10 10
730 1f. "Washington at Fort Lee" 10 10
731 18f. "Washington boarding a British warship" 45 30
732 26f. "Washington studying Battle plans" 55 40
733 34f. "Washington firing a Cannon" 90 55
734 40f. "Crossing the Delaware" 1·00 85

120 Sister Yohana

121 Yachting

1976. 75th Anniv of Catholic Church in Rwanda. Multicoloured.
736 20c. Type 120 . . . . 10 10
737 30c. Abdon Sabakati 10 10
738 50c. Father Alphonse Brard 10 10
739 4f. Abbe Balthazar Gafuku 10 10
740 10f. Monseigneur Bigirumwami 20 10
741 25f. Save Catholic Church (horiz) 60 45
742 60f. Kabgayi Catholic Cathedral (horiz) . . . . . 1·25 80

1976. Olympic Games, Montreal (1st issue).
743 121 20c. brown and green . . 10 10
744 – 30c. blue and green . . . 10 10
745 – 50c. black and green . . 10 10
746 – 1f. violet and green . . . 10 10
747 – 10f. blue and green . . . 20 10
748 – 18f. brown and green . . 35 30
749 – 29f. purple and green . . 80 60
750 – 51f. deep green and green 1·00 80
DESIGNS: 30c. Horse-jumping; 50c. Long jumping; 1f. Hockey; 10f. Swimming; 18f. Football; 29f. Boxing; 51f. Gymnastics.
See also Nos. 767/74.

122 Bell's Experimental Telephone and Manual Switchboard

1976. Telephone Centenary.
751 122 20c. brown and blue . . . 10 10
752 – 30c. blue and violet . . . 10 10
753 – 50c. brown and blue . . . 10 10
754 – 1f. orange and blue . . . 10 10
755 – 4f. mauve and blue . . . 10 10
756 – 8f. green and blue . . . . 2·50 35
757 – 26f. red and blue 70 55
758 – 60f. lilac and blue . . . . 1·40 1·00
DESIGNS: 30c. Early telephone and man making call; 50c. Early telephone and woman making call; 1f. Early telephone and exchange building; 4f. Alexander Graham Bell and "candlestick" telephone; 8f. Rwanda subscriber and dial telephone; 26f. Dish aerial, satellite and modern handset; 60f. Rwanda PTT building, operator and push-button telephone.

1976. Bicentenary of Declaration of American Independence. Nos. 727/34 optd **INDEPENDENCE DAY** and Bicentennial Emblem.
759 119 20c. multicoloured 10 10
760 – 30c. multicoloured 10 10
761 – 50c. multicoloured 10 10
762 – 1f. multicoloured 10 10
763 – 18f. multicoloured 35 20
764 – 26f. multicoloured 65 45
765 – 34f. multicoloured 80 55
766 – 40f. multicoloured . . . . 1·10 80

124 Football

1976. Olympic Games, Montreal (2nd issue). Mult.
767 20c. Type 124 . . . . 10 10
768 30c. Rifle-shooting 10 10
769 50c. Canoeing 10 10
770 1f. Gymnastics 10 10
771 10f. Weightlifting 15 10
772 12f. Diving 30 20
773 26f. Horse-riding 55 40
774 50f. Throwing the hammer 1·40 90

125 "Apollo" and "Soyuz" Launches and ASTP Badge

1976. "Apollo"–"Soyuz" Test Project. Mult.
776 20c. Type 125 . . . . 10 10
777 30c. "Soyuz" rocket 10 10
778 50c. "Apollo" rocket 10 10
779 1f. "Apollo" after separation 10 10
780 2f. Approach to link-up . . . 10 10
781 12f. Spacecraft docked . . . 35 15
782 30f. Sectional view of interiors . . . . 1·10 55
783 54f. "Apollo" splashdown . . 2·25 1·25

126 "Eulophia cucullata"

128 Hands embracing "Cultural Collaboration"

1976. Rwandaise Orchids. Multicoloured.
784 20c. Type 126 . . . . 10 10
785 30c. "Eulophia streptopetala" 10 10
786 50c. "Disa stairsii" 10 10
787 1f. "Aerangis kotschyana" . . 10 10
788 10f. "Eulophia abyssinica" . 20 10
789 12f. "Bonatea steudneri" . . 30 15
790 26f. "Ansellia gigantea" . . . 1·10 45
791 50f. "Eulophia angolensis" 2·00 1·25

1977. World Leprosy Day. Nos. 719/26 optd with **JOURNEE MONDIALE 1977.**
793 – 20c. lilac, brown and black 10 10
794 – 30c. lilac, green and black 10 10
795 118 50c. lilac, brown and black 10 10
796 – 1f. lilac, purple and black 10 10
797 – 3f. lilac, blue and black 10 10
798 – 5f. lilac, brown and black 20 10
799 118 10f. lilac, brown and black 35 20
800 – 80f. lilac, red and black 1·60 1·60

1977. 10th OCAM Summit Meeting, Kigali. Mult.
801 10f. Type 128 . . . . 30 10
802 26f. Hands embracing "Technical Collaboration" 70 40
803 64f. Hands embracing "Economic Collaboration" 1·25 90

1977. World Water Conference. Nos. 688/95 optd **CONFERENCE MONDIALE DE L'EAU.**
805 114 20c. multicoloured 10 10
806 – 30c. multicoloured 10 10
807 – 50c. multicoloured 10 10
808 – 5f. multicoloured 15 10
809 – 8f. multicoloured 20 10
810 – 10f. multicoloured 40 15
811 – 26f. multicoloured . . . . 1·40 75
812 – 100f. multicoloured . . . 3·50 3·25

131 Roman Signal Post and African Tam-Tam

1977. World Telecommunications Day. Mult.
813 20c. Type 131 . . . . 10 10
814 30c. Chappe's semaphore and post-rider 10 10
815 50c. Morse code 10 10
816 1f. "Goliath" laying Channel cable 10 10
817 4f. Telephone, radio and television 10 10
818 18f. "Kingsport" and maritime communications satellite 75 40
819 26f. Telecommunications satellite and aerial 50 40
820 50f. "Mariner 2" satellite . . 1·40 90

132 "The Ascent to Calvary" (detail)

135 Long-crested Eagle

133 Chateau Sassenage, Grenoble

1977. 400th Birth Anniv of Peter Paul Rubens. Multicoloured.
823 20c. Type 132 . . . . 10 10
824 30c. "The Judgement of Paris" (horiz) 10 10
825 50c. "Marie de Medici, Queen of France" 10 10
826 1f. "Heads of Negroes" (horiz) 10 10
827 4f. "St. Idelfonse Triptych" (detail) 10 10
828 8f. "Helene Fourment with her Children" (horiz) . . . 15 10
829 26f. "St. Idelfonse Triptych" (different detail) 80 65
830 60f. "Helene Fourment" . . 2·50 1·75

1977. Air. 10th Anniv of International French Language Council.
831 133 50f. multicoloured . . . . 1·60 1·10

1977. Birds of Prey. Multicoloured.
833 20c. Type 135 . . . . 10 10
834 30c. African harrier hawk . . 10 10
835 50c. African fish eagle . . . 15 10
836 1f. Hooded vulture 15 15
837 3f. Augur buzzard 20 15
838 5f. Black kite 30 15
839 20f. Black-shouldered kite . . 1·50 70
840 100f. Bateleur . . . . 5·75 3·25

1912. Dr. Wernher von Braun Commemoration. Nos. 776/83 optd with **in memoriam WERNHER VON BRAUN 1912 - 1977.**
841 20c. Type 125 . . . . 10 10
842 30c. "Soyuz" rocket 10 10
843 50c. "Apollo" rocket 10 10
844 1f. "Apollo" after separation 10 10
845 2f. Approach to link up . . . 10 10
846 12f. Spacecraft docked . . . 40 20
847 30f. Sectional view of interiors . . . . 1·40 50
848 54f. "Apollo" after splashdown . . . . 2·50 1·50

138 Scout playing Whistle

139 Chimpanzees

1978. 10th Anniv of Rwanda Scout Association. Multicoloured.
851 20c. Type 138 . . . . 10 10
852 30c. Camp fire 10 10
853 50c. Scouts constructing a platform 10 10
854 1f. Two scouts 10 10
855 10f. Scouts on look-out . . . 20 10
856 18f. Scouts in canoe 45 35
857 26f. Cooking at camp fire . . 80 60
858 44f. Lord Baden-Powell . . . 1·50 1·25

1978. Apes. Multicoloured.
859 20c. Type 139 . . . . 10 10
860 30c. Gorilla 10 10
861 50c. Eastern black-and-white colobus 10 10
862 3f. Eastern needle-clawed bushbaby 10 10
863 10f. Mona monkey 30 10
864 26f. Potto 65 65
865 60f. Savanna monkey . . . . 1·90 1·90
866 150f. Olive baboon . . . . . 3·75 3·75

140 "Euporus strangulatus"

1978. Beetles. Multicoloured.
867 20c. Type 140 . . . . 10 10
868 30c. "Rhina afzelii" (vert) . . 10 10
869 50c. "Pentalobus palini" . . 10 10
870 3f. "Corynodes dejeani" (vert) 10 10
871 10f. "Mecynorhina torquata" 20 10
872 15f. "Mecocerus rhombeus" (vert) 55 10
873 20f. "Macrotoma serripes" 75 20
874 25f. "Neptunides stanleyi" (vert) 90 40
875 26f. "Petrognatha gigas" . . 90 40
876 100f. "Eudicella gralli" (vert) 3·25 2·50

141 Poling Boat across River of Poverty

1978. National Revolutionary Development Movement. Multicoloured.
877 4f. Type 141 . . . . 10 10
878 10f. Poling boat to right . . 15 10
879 26f. Type 141 . . . . 60 40
880 60f. As 10f. . . . . 1·10 85

142 Footballers, Cup and Flags of Netherlands and Peru

1978. World Cup Football Championship, Argentina. Multicoloured.
881 20c. Type 142 . . . . 10 10
882 30c. Flags of FIFA, Sweden and Spain 10 10
883 50c. Mascot and flags of Scotland and Iran 10 10

884 2f. Emblem and flags of West Germany and Tunisia . . . 10 10
885 3f. Cup and flags of Italy and Hungary 10 10
886 10f. Flags of FIFA, Brazil and Austria 20 10
887 34f. Mascot and flags of Poland and Mexico 85 70
888 100f. Emblem and flags of Argentina and France . . 2·50 2·00
No. 883 shows the Union Jack.

143 Wright Brothers and Wright Flyer I, 1903

1978. Aviation History. Multicoloured.
889 20c. Type **143** 10 10
890 30c. Alberto Santos-Dumont and biplane "14 bis", 1906 10 10
891 50c. Henri Farman and Farman Voisin No. 1 bis, 1908 . . . . 10 10
892 1f. Jan Olieslagers and Bleriot XI 10 10
893 3f. General Italo Balbo and Savoia S-17 flying boat, 1919 . . . . 10 10
894 10f. Charles Lindbergh and "Spirit of St. Louis", 1927 15 10
895 55f. Hugo Junkers and Junkers Ju 52/3m, 1932 . . 1·10 55
896 60f. Igor Sikorsky and Vought-Sikorsky VS-300 helicopter prototype . . . 1·60 85

143a Great Spotted Woodpecker and Oldenburg 1852⅓sgr. Stamp

1978. Air. "Philexafrique" Stamp Exhibition, Libreville, Gabon and Int Stamp Fair, Essen, West Germany. Multicoloured.
898 30f. Type **143a** . . . . . . 1·40 90
899 30f. Greater kudu and Rwanda 1967 20c. stamp 1·40 90

1978. 15th Anniv of Organization of African Unity. Nos. 544/5 optd **1963 1978**.
901 **88** 6f. multicoloured 30 10
902 – 94f. multicoloured . . . . 1·90 1·10

146 Spur-winged Goose and Mallard **147** "Papilio demodocus"

1978. Stock Rearing Year. Multicoloured.
903 20c. Type **146** 20 10
904 30c. Goats (horiz) 10 10
905 50c. Chickens 10 10
906 4f. Rabbits (horiz) 20 10
907 5f. Pigs 20 10
908 15f. Common turkey (horiz) 90 30
909 50f. Sheep and cattle . . . . 1·50 50
910 75f. Bull (horiz) . . . . . . 1·90 70

1979. Butterflies. Multicoloured.
911 20c. Type **147** 10 10
912 30c. "Precis octavia" 10 10
913 50c. "Charaxes smaragdalis caerulea" 10 10
914 4f. "Charaxes guderiana" . . 15 10
915 15f. "Colotis evippe" 20 10
916 30f. "Danaus limniace petiverana" 55 30
917 50f. "Byblia acheloia" . . . 1·50 55
918 150f. "Utetheisa pulchella" . 3·75 1·40

148 "Euphorbia grantii" and Women weaving

1979. "Philexafrique" Exhibition, Libreville. Mult.
919 40f. Type **148** . . . . 1·40 85
920 60f. Drummers and "Intelsat" satellite . . . . 2·25 1·10

149 "Polyscias fulva" **150** European Girl

1979. Trees. Multicoloured.
921 20c. Type **149** 10 10
922 30c. "Entandrophragma excelsum" (horiz) 10 10
923 50c. "Ilex mitis" 10 10
924 4f. "Kigelia africana" (horiz) 15 10
925 15f. "Ficus thonningi" . . . 35 10
926 20f. "Acacia senegal" (horiz) 50 20
927 50f. "Symphonia globulifera" 1·25 45
928 110f. "Acacia sieberana" (horiz) . . . . 2·50 1·25

1979. International Year of the Child. Each brown, gold and stone.
929 26f. Type **150** 65 60
930 26f. Asian 65 60
931 26f. Eskimo 65 60
932 26f. Asian boy 65 60
933 26f. African 65 60
934 26f. South American Indian 65 60
935 26f. Polynesian 65 60
936 26f. European girl (different) 65 60
937 42f. European and African (horiz) . . . . 2·00 65

151 Basket Weaving

1979. Handicrafts. Multicoloured.
939 50c. Type **151** 10 10
940 1f.50 Wood-carving (vert) . . 10 10
941 2f. Metal working 10 10
942 10f. Basket work (vert) . . . 35 10
943 20f. Basket weaving (different) 50 20
944 26f. Mural painting (vert) . . 65 55
945 40f. Pottery 95 65
946 100f. Smelting (vert) . . . . 2·50 1·75

153 Rowland Hill and 40c. Ruanda Stamp of 1916

1979. Death Centenary of Sir Rowland Hill. Multicoloured.
948 20c. Type **153** 10 10
949 30c. 1916 Occupation stamp 10 10
950 50c. 1918 "A.O." overprint 10 10
951 3f. 1925 overprinted 60c. stamp 10 10
952 10f. 1931 50c. African buffalo stamp 30 10
953 26f. 1942 20f. Common zebra stamp 65 15
954 60f. 1953 25f. Protea stamp 1·40 60
955 100f. 1960 Olympic stamp . . 2·75 1·10

154 Strange Weaver **156** Butare Rotary Club Banner, Globe and Chicago Club Emblem of 1905

155 Armstrong's first Step on Moon

1980. Birds. Multicoloured.
956 20c. Type **154** 15 10
957 30c. Regal sunbird (vert) . . 15 15
958 50c. White-spotted crake . . 15 15
959 3f. Black-casqued hornbill . . 30 15
960 10f. Ituri owl (vert) 70 25
961 26f. African emerald cuckoo 1·60 65
962 60f. Black-crowned waxbill (vert) . . . . 3·00 1·50
963 100f. Crowned eagle (vert) . . 5·50 2·50

1980. 10th Anniv of "Apollo 11" Moon Landing. Multicoloured.
964 50c. Type **155** 10 10
965 1f.50 Aldrin descending to Moon's surface 10 10
966 8f. Planting the American flag 55 10
967 30f. Placing seismometer . . . 95 60
968 50f. Taking samples . . . . 1·75 70
969 60f. Setting-up experiment . . 2·50 90

1980. 75th Anniv of Rotary International. Mult.
971 20c. Type **156** 10 10
972 30c. Kigali Rotary Club banner 10 10
973 50c. Type **156** 10 10
974 4f. As No. 972 . . . . 15 10
975 15f. Type **156** 35 10
976 20f. As No. 972 . . . . . . 45 20
977 50f. Type **156** 95 45
978 60f. As No. 972 . . . . . . 1·10 65

157 Gymnastics

1980. Olympic Games, Moscow.
979 **157** 20c. yellow and black . . 10 10
980 – 30c. green and black . . . 10 10
981 – 50c. red and black 10 10
982 – 3f. blue and black 15 10
983 – 20f. orange and black . . 45 20
984 – 26f. purple and black . . 50 25
985 – 50f. turquoise and black 1·10 45
986 – 100f. brown and black . . 2·50 1·10
DESIGNS: 30c. Basketball; 50c. Cycling; 3f. Boxing; 20f. Archery; 26f. Weightlifting; 50f. Javelin; 100f. Fencing.

159 "Geaster"

1980. Mushrooms. Multicoloured.
988 20c. Type **159** 10 10
989 30c. "Lentinus atrobrunneus" 10 10
990 50c. "Gomphus stereoides" . 10 10
991 4f. "Cantharellus cibarius" . 30 10
992 10f. "Stilbothamnium dybowskii" 65 20
993 15f. "Xeromphalina tenuipes" 90 20
994 70f. "Podoscypha elegans" . 3·75 80
995 100f. "Mycena" . . . . . . 7·50 1·60

160 "At the Theatre" (Toulouse-Lautrec)

1980. Impressionist Paintings. Multicoloured.
996 20c. "Still Life" (horiz) (Renoir) 10 10
997 30c. Type **160** 10 10
998 50c. "Seaside Garden" (Monet) (horiz) 10 10
999 4f. "Mother and Child" (Mary Cassatt) 10 10
1000 5f. "Starry Night" (Van Gogh) (horiz) 20 10
1001 10f. "Three Dancers at their Toilette" (Degas) 35 10
1002 50f. "The Card Players" (Cezanne) (horiz) . . . . 1·10 45
1003 70f. "Tahitian Girls" (Gauguin) . . . . 1·75 65
1004 100f. "La Grande Jatte" (Seurat) (horiz) . . . . . 2·75 90

162 Revolutionary Scene

1980. 150th Anniv of Belgian Independence. Scenes of the Independence War from contemporary engravings.
1007 **162** 20c. green and brown . . 10 10
1008 – 30c. buff and brown . . 10 10
1009 – 50c. blue and brown . . 10 10
1010 – 9f. orange and brown . . 20 10
1011 – 10f. mauve and brown . 30 10
1012 – 20f. green and brown . . 45 20
1013 – 70f. pink and brown . . 1·50 65
1014 – 90f. yellow and brown . 1·90 1·00

163 Draining the Marshes

1980. Soil Protection and Conservation Year. Mult.
1015 20c. Type **163** 25 10
1016 30c. Bullock in pen (mixed farming and land fertilization) 10 10
1017 1f.50 Land irrigation and rice 10 10
1018 8f. Soil erosion and planting trees 20 10
1019 10f. Terrace 30 15
1020 40f. Crop fields . . . . . . 1·00 40
1021 90f. Bean crop . . . . . . 2·10 85
1022 100f. Picking tea . . . . . 2·25 1·10

164 "Pavetta rwandensis"

1981. Flowers. Multicoloured.
1023 20c. Type **164** 10 10
1024 30c. "Cyrtorchis praetermissa" 10 10
1025 50c. "Pavonia urens" . . . 10 10
1026 4f. "Cynorkis kassnerana" . 10 10
1027 5f. "Gardenia ternifolia" . . 15 10
1028 10f. "Leptactina platyphylla" 20 10
1029 20f. "Lobelia petiolata" . . 50 15
1030 40f. "Tapinanthus brunneus" . . . . 1·25 50
1031 70f. "Impatiens niamniamensis" . . . . . 1·60 95
1032 150f. "Dissotis rwandensis" 4·00 1·60

165 Mother and Child **166** Carol Singers

1981. SOS Children's Village. Multicoloured.
1033 20c. Type **165** 10 10
1034 30c. Child with pots 10 10
1035 50c. Children drawing . . . 10 10
1036 1f. Girl sewing 10 10
1037 8f. Children playing 20 10
1038 10f. Girl knitting 20 10
1039 70f. Children making models 1·50 70
1040 150f. Mother and children . 3·25 1·60

1981. Paintings by Norman Rockwell. Mult.
1041 20c. Type **166** 10 10
1042 30c. People of different races 10 10
1043 50c. Father Christmas . . . 10 10
1044 1f. Coachman 10 10
1045 8f. Man at piano 15 10
1046 20f. "Springtime" 50 20
1047 50f. Man making donation to girl "nurse" . . . . . 1·25 70
1048 70f. Clown . . . . 1·75 1·10

167 Serval

1981. Carnivorous Animals. Multicoloured.
1049 20c. Type **167** 10 10
1050 30c. Black-backed jackal . . 10 10
1051 2f. Servaline genet 10 10
1052 2f.50 Banded mongoose . . 10 10
1053 10f. Zorilla 20 10
1054 15f. Zaire clawless otter . . 55 10
1055 70f. African golden cat . . . 1·75 1·25
1056 200f. Hunting dog (vert) . . 5·75 4·25

168 Drummer

1981. Telecommunications and Health. Mult.
1057 20c. Type **168** 10 10
1058 30c. Telephone receiver and world map 10 10
1059 2f. Airliner and radar screen 10 10
1060 2f.50 Satellite and computer tape 10 10
1061 10f. Satellite orbit and dish aerial 20 10
1062 15f. Tanker and radar equipment 35 25
1063 70f. Red Cross helicopter . . 1·90 70
1064 200f. Satellite . . . . 4·25 2·25

169 "St. Benedict leaving His Parents"

1981. 1500th Birth Anniv of St. Benedict. Mult.
1065 20c. Type **169** 10 10
1066 30c. Portrait (10th century) (vert) 10 10
1067 50c. Portrait (detail from "The Virgin of the Misericord" polyptich) (vert) 10 10
1068 4f. "St. Benedict presenting the Rules of His Order" 10 10
1069 5f. "St. Benedict and His Monks at their Meal" . . 15 10
1070 20f. Portrait (13th century) (vert) 45 40
1071 70f. St. Benedict at prayer (detail from "Our Lady in Glory with Sts. Gregory and Benedict") (vert) . . 1·75 1·40
1072 100f. "Priest bringing the Easter Meal to St. Benedict" (Jan van Coninxlo) . . . . . . 2·75 1·75

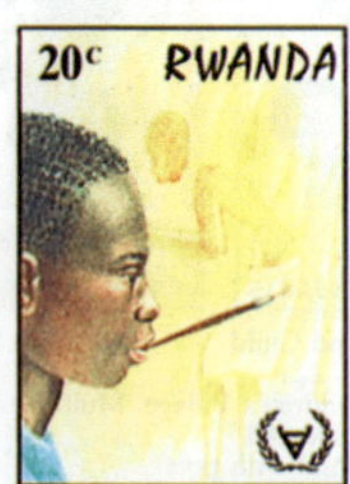

170 Disabled Child painting with Mouth

1981. International Year of Disabled Persons. Mult.
1073 20c. Type **170** 10 10
1074 30c. Boys on crutches playing football 10 10
1075 4f.50 Disabled girl knitting 10 10
1076 5f. Disabled child painting pot 15 10
1077 10f. Boy in wheelchair using saw 20 10
1078 60f. Child using sign language . . . . 1·25 60
1079 70f. Child in wheelchair playing with puzzle . . . 1·60 70
1080 100f. Disabled child . . . . 2·00 1·10

172 Kob drinking at Pool

1981. Rural Water Supplies. Multicoloured.
1082 20c. Type **172** 10 10
1083 30c. Women collecting water (vert) 10 10
1084 50c. Constructing a pipeline 10 10
1085 10f. Woman collecting water from pipe (vert) 20 10
1086 10f. Man drinking 45 20
1087 70f. Woman collecting water (vert) . . . . 1·50 70
1088 100f. Floating pump (vert) 2·50 1·10

173 Cattle

1982. World Food Day. Multicoloured.
1089 20c. Type **173** 10 10
1090 30c. Bee keeping 10 10
1091 50c. Fishes 10 10
1092 1f. Avocado 10 10
1093 8f. Boy eating banana . . . 10 10
1094 20f. Sorghum 45 15
1095 70f. Vegetables . . . . . 1·50 65
1096 100f. Three generations and balanced diet . . . . . . 3·00 1·10

174 "Hibiscus berberidfolius"

1982. Flowers. Multicoloured.
1097 20c. Type **174** 10 10
1098 30c. "Hypericum lanceolatum" (vert) . . . 10 10
1099 50c. "Canarina eminii" . . 10 10
1100 4f. "Polygala ruwenzoriensis" 10 10
1101 10f. "Kniphofia grantii" (vert) 15 10
1102 35f. "Euphorbia candelabrum" (vert) . . . 90 60
1103 70f. "Disa erubescens" (vert) 1·75 80
1104 80f. "Gloriosa simplex" . . 2·40 1·10

175 Pres. Habyarimana and Flags

1982. 20th Anniv of Independence. Multicoloured.
1105 10f. Type **175** 20 10
1106 20f. Hands releasing doves (Peace) 35 20
1107 30f. Clasped hands and flag (Unity) 65 35
1108 50f. Building (Development) 1·00 50

176 Football

1982. World Cup Football Championship, Spain.
1109 **176** 20c. multicoloured . . . 10 10
1110 – 30c. multicoloured . . . 10 10
1111 – 1f.50 multicoloured . . . 10 10
1112 – 8f. multicoloured 15 10
1113 – 10f. multicoloured . . . 20 10
1114 – 20f. multicoloured . . . 40 15
1115 – 70f. multicoloured . . . 1·60 65
1116 – 90f. multicoloured . . . 2·25 85
DESIGNS: 30c. to 90f. Designs show different players.

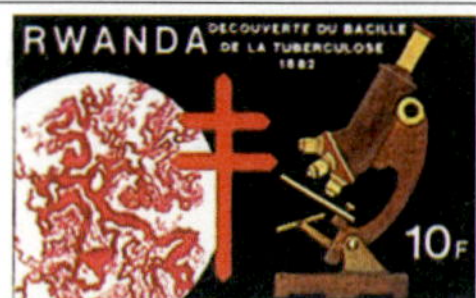

177 Microscope and Slide

1982. Centenary of Discovery of Tubercle Bacillus. Multicoloured.
1117 10f. Type **177** 15 10
1118 20f. Hand with test tube and slide 40 15
1119 70f. Lungs and slide . . . . 1·60 65
1120 100f. Dr. Robert Koch . . . 2·25 95

180 African Elephants

1982. 10th Anniv of United Nations Environment Programme. Multicoloured.
1123 20c. Type **180** 10 10
1124 30c. Lion hunting impala . . 10 10
1125 50c. Flower 10 10
1126 4f. African buffalo 10 10
1127 5f. Impala 10 10
1128 10f. Flower (different) . . . 20 10
1129 20f. Common zebra 45 15
1130 40f. Crowned cranes . . . . 1·50 35
1131 50f. African fish eagle . . . 1·75 55
1132 70f. Woman with basket of fruit . . . . 1·60 80

181 Scout tending Injured Kob

1982. 75th Anniv of Scout Movement. Mult.
1133 20c. Type **181** 10 10
1134 30c. Tents and northern doubled-collared sunbird 35 10
1135 1f.50 Campfire 10 10
1136 8f. Scout 15 10
1137 10f. Knot 20 10
1138 20f. Tent and campfire . . . 40 15
1139 70f. Scout cutting stake . . 1·90 80
1140 90f. Scout salute . . . . . 2·40 1·00

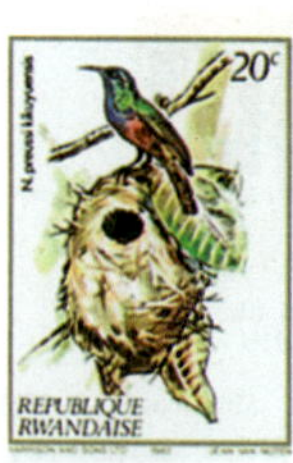

182 Northern Double-collared Sunbird

183 Driving Cattle

1983. Nectar-sucking Birds. Multicoloured.
1141 20c. Type **182** 10 10
1142 30c. Regal sunbird (horiz) 10 10
1143 50c. Red-tufted malachite sunbird 10 10
1144 4f. Bronze sunbird (horiz) 25 10
1145 5f. Collared sunbird 35 10
1146 10f. Blue-headed sunbird (horiz) 70 20
1147 20f. Purple-breasted sunbird 1·40 50
1148 40f. Coppery sunbird (horiz) 3·00 95
1149 50f. Olive-bellied sunbird . . 3·25 1·25
1150 70f. Red-chested sunbird (horiz) . . . . 4·50 2·00

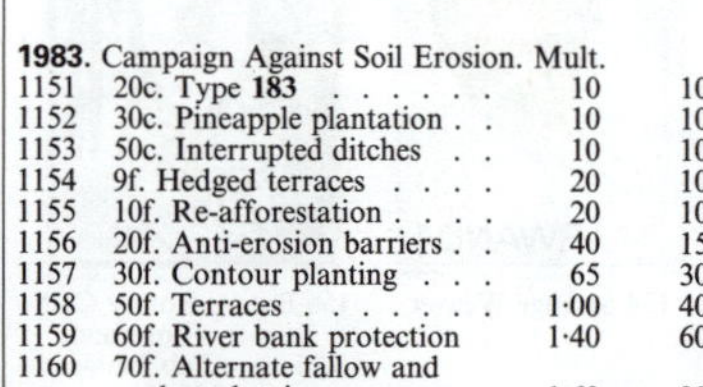

1983. Campaign Against Soil Erosion. Mult.
1151 20c. Type **183** 10 10
1152 30c. Pineapple plantation . . 10 10
1153 50c. Interrupted ditches . . 10 10
1154 9f. Hedged terraces 20 10
1155 10f. Re-afforestation 20 10
1156 20f. Anti-erosion barriers . . 40 15
1157 30f. Contour planting 65 30
1158 50f. Terraces . . . . 1·00 40
1159 60f. River bank protection 1·40 60
1160 70f. Alternate fallow and planted strips . . . . . . 1·60 80

184 Feeding Ducks

1983. Birth Cent of Cardinal Cardijan (founder of Young Catholic Workers Movement). Mult.
1161 20c. Type **184** 10 10
1162 30c. Harvesting bananas . . 10 10
1163 50c. Carrying melons . . . 10 10
1164 10f. Wood-carving 20 10
1165 19f. Making shoes 35 15
1166 20f. Children in field of millet 45 15
1167 70f. Embroidering . . . . . 1·40 60
1168 80f. Cardinal Cardijan . . . 1·60 65

185 Young Gorillas

1983. Mountain Gorillas. Multicoloured.
1169 20c. Type **185** 10 10
1170 30c. Gorilla family 10 10
1171 9f.50 Young and adult . . . 45 30
1172 10f. Mother with young . . 45 30
1173 20f. Heads 65 45
1174 30f. Adult and head 90 50
1175 60f. Adult (vert) . . . . . 2·00 1·40
1176 70f. Close-up of adult (vert) 2·40 1·50

187 "Hagenia abyssinica"

1984. Trees. Multicoloured.
1178 20c. Type **187** 10 10
1179 30c. "Dracaena steudneri" 10 10
1180 50c. "Phoenix reclinata" . . 10 10
1181 10f. "Podocarpus milanjianus" 15 10
1182 19f. "Entada abyssinica" . . 40 15
1183 70f. "Parinari excelsa" . . . 1·60 65
1184 100f. "Newtonia buchananii" . . . . . . 2·00 95
1185 200f. "Acacia gerrardi" (vert) . . . . 4·50 1·60

188 "Hikari" Express Train, Japan

189 "Le Martial", 1783

1984. World Communications Year. Multicoloured.
1186 20c. Type **188** 20 10
1187 30c. Liner and radar 15 10
1188 4f.50 Radio and transmitter 15 10
1189 10f. Telephone dial and cable 20 10
1190 15f. Letters and newspaper 35 10
1191 50f. Airliner and control tower . . . . 1·10 45
1192 70f. Television and antenna 1·60 65
1193 100f. Satellite and computer tape . . . . 2·50 90

1984. Bicentenary of Manned Flight. Mult.
1194 20c. Type **189** 10 10
1195 30c. De Rozier and Marquis d'Arlandes flight, 1783 . . 10 10
1196 50c. Charles and Robert (1783) and Blanchard (1784) flights 10 10
1197 9f. M. and Mme. Blanchard 20 10
1198 10f. Blanchard and Jeffries, 1785 . . . . 20 10
1199 50f. Demuyter (1937) and Piccard and Kipfer (1931) flights . . . . 1·10 40
1200 80f. Modern hot-air balloons . . . . 2·75 1·90
1201 200f. Trans-Atlantic flight, 1978 . . . . 3·50 2·50

190 Equestrian

1984. Olympic Games, Los Angeles. Multicoloured.

1202 20c. Type **190** 10 10
1203 30c. Windsurfing 15 10
1204 50c. Football 10 10
1205 9f. Swimming 20 10
1206 10f. Hockey 20 10
1207 40f. Fencing 1·25 70
1208 80f. Running 2·00 1·75
1209 200f. Boxing 5·00 4·00

191 Mare and Foal

1984. Common Zebras and African Buffaloes. Mult.

1210 20c. Type **191** 10 10
1211 30c. Buffalo and calf (vert) 10 10
1212 50c. Pair of zebras (vert) 10 10
1213 9f. Zebras fighting 20 10
1214 10f. Close-up of buffalo (vert) 30 10
1215 80f. Herd of zebras 1·90 1·40
1216 100f. Close-up of zebras (vert) 2·50 1·75
1217 200f. Buffalo charging 4·75 3·50

193 Gorillas at Water-hole

1985. Gorillas. Multicoloured.

1219 10f. Type **193** 1·90 80
1220 15f. Two gorillas in tree 2·75 85
1221 25f. Gorilla family 3·75 2·10
1222 30f. Three adults 4·75 3·00

194 Man feeding Fowl

1985. Food Production Year. Multicoloured.

1224 20c. Type **194** 20 10
1225 30c. Men carrying pineapples 15 10
1226 50c. Farm animals 10 10
1227 9f. Men filling sacks with produce 20 10
1228 10f. Agricultural instruction 30 10
1229 50f. Sowing seeds 1·00 45
1230 80f. Storing produce 1·60 65
1231 100f. Working in banana plantation 2·10 80

195 Emblem

1985. 10th Anniv of National Revolutionary Redevelopment Movement.

1232 **195** 10f. multicoloured 20 10
1233 30f. multicoloured 65 30
1234 70f. multicoloured 1·60 70

196 U.N. Emblem within "40"

1985. 40th Anniv of U.N.O.

1235 **196** 50f. multicoloured 1·10 90
1236 100f. multicoloured 2·50 2·10

197 Barn Owls

1985. Birth Bicentenary of John J. Audubon (ornithologist). Multicoloured.

1237 10f. Type **197** 75 30
1238 20f. White-faced scops owls 1·60 60
1239 40f. Ruby-throated humming birds 3·00 1·10
1240 80f. Eastern meadowlarks 6·75 2·40

198 "Participation, Development and Peace"

1985. International Youth Year. Multicoloured.

1241 7f. Type **198** 15 10
1242 9f. Cycling 30 10
1243 44f. Youths carrying articles on head (teamwork) 1·10 45
1244 80f. Education 1·75 80

1985. 75th Anniv of Girl Guide Movement. Nos. 1133/40 optd **1910/1985** and guide emblem.

1245 20c. Type **181** 10 10
1246 30c. Tents 30 10
1247 1f.50 Campfire 10 10
1248 8f. Scout 20 10
1249 10f. Knot 20 10
1250 20f. Tent and campfire 45 10
1251 70f. Scout cutting stake 1·60 65
1252 90f. Scout salute 2·50 90

201 Container Lorry (Transport)

1986. Transport and Communications. Mult.

1254 10f. Type **201** 35 10
1255 30f. Handstamping cover (posts) 80 35
1256 40f. Kigali Earth Station (telecommunication) 1·10 45
1257 80f. Kigali airport (aviation) (48 × 31 mm) 1·75 1·25

1986. Intensified Agriculture Year. Nos. 1152/60 optd **ANNEE 1986 INTENSIFICATION AGRICOLE** or surch also.

1258 9f. Hedged terraces 20 10
1259 10f. Re-afforestation 20 10
1260 10f. on 30c. Pineapple plantation 20 10
1261 10f. on 50c. Interrupted ditches 20 10
1262 20f. Anti-erosion barriers 45 20
1263 30f. Contour planning 65 35
1264 50f. Terraces 1·10 50
1265 60f. River bank protection 1·40 55
1266 70f. Alternate fallow and planted strips 1·60 70

203 Morocco v England

1986. World Cup Football Championship, Mexico. Multicoloured.

1267 2f. Type **203** 10 10
1268 4f. Paraguay v Iraq 10 10
1269 5f. Brazil v Spain 10 10
1270 10f. Italy v Argentina 55 35
1271 40f. Mexico v Belgium 1·60 85
1272 45f. France v Russia 1·75 1·00

204 Roan Antelopes

1986. Akagera National Park. Multicoloured.

1273 4f. Type **204** 15 10
1274 7f. Whale-headed storks 45 20
1275 9f. Cape eland 20 10
1276 10f. Giraffe 40 10
1277 80f. African elephant 2·50 85
1278 90f. Crocodile 3·00 1·00
1279 100f. Heuglin's masked weavers 5·00 2·75
1280 100f. Zebras and eastern white pelican 5·00 2·75

205 People of Different Races on Globe

1986. Christmas. International Peace Year. Mult.

1281 10f. Type **205** 35 15
1282 15f. Dove and globe 45 15
1283 30f. Type **205** 80 35
1284 70f. As No. 1282 1·75 1·00

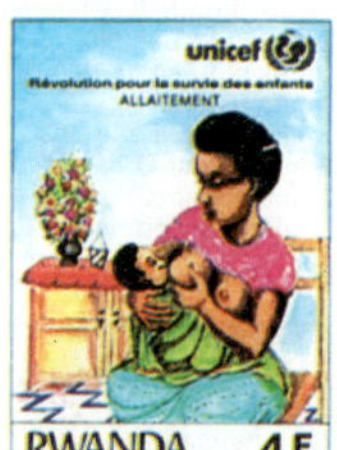

206 Mother breast-feeding Baby

1987. UNICEF Child Survival Campaign. Multicoloured.

1285 4f. Type **206** 15 15
1286 6f. Mother giving oral rehydration therapy to baby 20 15
1287 10f. Nurse immunizing baby 35 25
1288 70f. Nurse weighing baby and graph 1·75 1·60

207 Couple packing Baskets with Food

1987. Food Self-sufficiency Year. Multicoloured.

1289 5f. Type **207** 10 10
1290 7f. Woman and baskets of food 15 10
1291 40f. Man with baskets of fish and fruits 1·75 45
1292 60f. Fruits and vegetables 2·25 80

208 Pres. Habyarimana and Soldiers

1987. 25th Anniv of Independence. Multicoloured.

1293 10f. Type **208** 20 10
1294 40f. President at meeting 90 45
1295 70f. President with Pope John Paul II 2·50 85
1296 100f. Pres. Habyarimana (vert) 2·50 1·10

209 Bananas

1987. Fruits. Multicoloured.

1297 10f. Type **209** 20 10
1298 40f. Pineapples (horiz) 90 45
1299 80f. Papaya (horiz) 2·25 90
1300 90f. Avocados (horiz) 2·50 1·00
1301 100f. Strawberries 2·50 1·10

210 Mother carrying cub

1987. The Leopard. Multicoloured.

1302 50f. Type **210** 2·00 1·10
1303 50f. Leopards fighting 2·00 1·10
1304 50f. Leopards with prey 2·00 1·10
1305 50f. Leopard with prey in tree 2·00 1·10
1306 50f. Leopard leaping from tree 2·00 1·10

211 Village Activities

1987. International Volunteers Day. Mult.

1307 5f. Type **211** 10 10
1308 12f. Pupils in schoolroom 35 10
1309 20f. View of village 55 30
1310 60f. Woman tending oxen 1·75 85

213 Carpenter's Shop

1988. Rural Incomes Protection Year. Mult.

1312 10f. Type **213** 20 10
1313 40f. Dairy farm 95 95
1314 60f. Workers in field 1·50 55
1315 80f. Selling baskets of eggs 2·10 1·50

214 Chimpanzees

1988. Primates of Nyungwe Forest. Multicoloured.

1316 2f. Type **214** 25 15
1317 3f. Black and white colobus 25 15
1318 10f. Lesser bushbabies 85 50
1319 90f. Monkeys 6·00 3·00

215 Boxing

1988. Olympic Games, Seoul. Multicoloured.

1320 5f. Type **215** 10 10
1321 7f. Relay race 15 10
1322 8f. Table tennis 20 10
1323 10f. Running 35 15
1324 90f. Hurdling 2·25 1·00

216 "25" on Map of Africa

1988. 25th Anniv of Organization of African Unity. Multicoloured.

1325	5f. Type **216**	15	10
1326	7f. Hands clasped across map	20	10
1327	8f. Building on map	20	10
1328	90f. Words forming map	2·75	2·25

218 Newspaper Fragment and Refugees in Boat

1988. 125th Anniv of Red Cross Movement. Mult.

1330	10f. Type **218**	20	10
1331	30f. Red Cross workers and patient	80	35
1332	40f. Red Cross worker and elderly lady (vert)	95	40
1333	100f. Red Cross worker and family (vert)	2·75	1·25

219 "Plectranthus barbatus"

1989. Plants. Multicoloured.

1334	5f. Type **219**	15	20
1335	10f. "Tetradenia riparia"	50	20
1336	20f. "Hygrophila auriculata	1·00	45
1337	40f. "Datura stramonium	2·10	1·00
1338	50f. "Pavetta ternifolia"	2·75	1·40

220 Emblem, Dates and Sunburst

1989. Centenary of Interparliamentary Union. Mult.

1339	10f. Type **220**	30	10
1340	30f. Lake	85	65
1341	70f. River	1·60	1·40
1342	90f. Sun's rays	2·25	1·75

222 Throwing Clay and Finished Pots

1989. Rural Self-help Year. Multicoloured.

1344	10f. Type **222**	30	10
1345	70f. Carrying baskets of produce (vert)	1·60	1·40
1346	90f. Firing clay pots	2·50	2·00
1347	200f. Clearing roadway	5·00	3·50

223 "Triumph of Marat" (Boilly)

1990. Bicentenary of French Revolution. Mult.

1348	10f. Type **223**	30	10
1349	60f. "Rouget de Lisle singing La Marseillaise" (Pils)	1·60	1·50
1350	70f. "Oath of the Tennis Court" (Jacques Louis David)	2·00	1·75
1351	100f. "Trial of Louis XVI" (Joseph Court)	3·00	2·75

224 Old and New Lifestyles

1990. 30th Anniv of Revolution. Multicoloured.

1352	10f. Type **224**	30	10
1353	60f. Couple holding farming implements (vert)	1·60	1·40
1354	70f. Modernization	1·75	1·40
1355	100f. Flag, map and warrior	2·50	2·50

225 Construction

1990. 25th Anniv (1989) of African Development Bank. Multicoloured.

1356	10f. Type **225**	30	10
1357	20f. Tea picking	55	35
1358	40f. Road building	1·10	95
1359	90f. Tea pickers and modern housing	2·50	2·10

1990. World Cup Football Championship, Italy. Nos. 1267/72 optd **ITALIA 90.**

1361	**203** 2f. multicoloured	35	35
1362	– 4f. multicoloured	35	35
1363	– 5f. multicoloured	40	40
1364	– 10f. multicoloured	65	65
1365	– 40f. multicoloured	2·50	2·50
1366	– 45f. multicoloured	2·75	2·75

228 Pope John Paul II

1990. Papal Visits. Multicoloured.

1367	10f. Type **228**	75	75
1368	70f. Pope giving blessing	8·25	8·25

229 Adults learning Alphabet at School

1991. International Literacy Year (1990). Mult.

1370	10f. Type **229**	15	10
1371	20f. Children reading at school	35	20
1372	50f. Lowland villagers learning alphabet in field	90	80
1373	90f. Highland villagers learning alphabet outdoors	1·40	1·10

230 Tool-making

1991. Self-help Organizations. Multicoloured.

1374	10f. Type **230**	15	10
1375	20f. Rearing livestock	35	20
1376	50f. Textile manufacture	1·40	1·10
1377	90f. Construction	2·00	1·50

231 Statue of Madonna

1992. Death Centenary of Cardinal Lavigerie (founder of Orders of White Fathers and Sisters).

1378	**231** 5f. multicoloured	95	1·00
1379	– 15f. multicoloured	2·50	2·50
1380	– 70f. black and mauve	12·00	12·00
1381	– 110f. black and blue	18·00	20·00

DESIGNS—VERT: 15f. White Sister; 110f. Cardinal Lavigerie. HORIZ: 70f. White Fathers in Uganda, 1908.

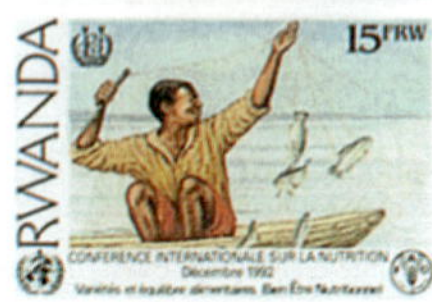

232 Fisherman

1992. Int Nutrition Conference, Rome. Mult.

1382	15f. Type **232**	80	45
1383	50f. Market fruit stall	1·60	1·40
1384	100f. Man milking cow	3·25	2·75
1385	500f. Woman breastfeeding	17·00	14·50

233 Running

1993. Olympic Games, Barcelona (1992). Mult.

1386	20f. Type **233**	2·50	2·50
1387	30f. Swimming	4·00	4·50
1388	90f. Football	12·00	10·00

234 Toad

1998. Animals. Multicoloured.

1390	15f. Type **234**	20	30
1391	100f. Snail	80	85
1392	150f. Porcupine	1·25	1·25
1393	300f. Chameleon	2·50	2·75

235 "Opuntia"

1998. Plants. Multicoloured.

1395	15f. Type **235**	20	30
1396	100f. "Gloriosa superba"	80	85
1397	150f. "Markhamia lutea"	1·25	1·25
1398	300f. "Hagenia abyssinica" (horiz)	2·50	2·75

RYUKYU ISLANDS Pt. 18

Group of islands between Japan and Taiwan, formerly Japanese until occupied by U.S. forces in 1945. After a period of military rule they became semi-autonomous under U.S. administration. The Amami Oshima group reverted to Japan in December 1953. The remaining islands were returned to Japan on 15 May 1972. Japanese stamps are now in use.

1948. 100 sen = 1 yen.
1958. 100 cents = 1 dollar (U.S.).

1 Cycad Palm

3 Tribute Junk

1948.

1	**1** 5s. purple	3·00	1·75
2	– 10s. green	3·50	2·25
3	**1** 20s. green	3·50	2·25
4	**3** 30s. red	3·50	2·25
5	– 40s. purple	3·00	1·75
6	**3** 50s. blue	3·50	2·50
7	– 1y. blue	3·50	2·50

DESIGNS: 10s., 40s. Easter lily; 1y. Farmer with hoe.

6 Shi-Shi Roof Tiles

12 Dove over Map of Ryukyus

1950.

8	**6** 50s. red	25	25
10	– 1y. blue	2·75	1·25
11	– 2y. purple	12·00	3·00
12	– 3y. pink	20·00	8·00
13	– 4y. grey	8·00	3·00
14	– 5y. green	10·00	4·50

DESIGNS: 1y. Shuri woman; 2y. Former Okinawa Palace, Shuri; 3y. Dragon's head; 4y. Okinawa women; 5y. Common spider and strawberry conches and radula scallop.

1950. Air.

15	**12** 8y. blue	65·00	20·00
16	12y. green	42·00	16·00
17	16y. red	18·00	12·00

14 University and Shuri Castle

15 Pine Tree

1951. Inauguration of Ryukyu University.

19	**14** 3y. brown	45·00	18·00

1951. Afforestation Week.

20	**15** 3y. green	45·00	18·00

16 Flying Goddess (17)

1951. Air.

21	**16** 13y. blue	2·00	40
22	18y. green	2·50	3·00
23	30y. mauve	4·00	1·25
24	40y. purple	6·00	2·25
25	50y. orange	7·50	3·25

1952. Surch as T **17**.

27	**6** 10y. on 50s. red	10·00	5·50
29	– 100y. on 2y. purple (No. 11)	£2000	£850

18 Dove and Bean Seedling

19 Madanbashi Bridge

1952. Establishment of Ryukyuan Government.

30	**18** 3y. red	£100	20·00

1952.

31	**19** 1y. red	25	25
32	– 2y. green	30	25
33	– 3y. turquoise	60	25
34	– 6y. blue	4·00	3·25
35	– 10y. red	1·75	50
36	– 30y. green	4·75	2·50
37	– 50y. purple	6·00	2·00
38	– 100y. purple	12·00	1·50

DESIGNS: 2y. Presence Chamber, Shuri Palace; 3y. Shuri Gate; 6y. Sogenji Temple Wall; 10y. Bensaitendo Temple; 30y. Sonohyamutake Gate; 50y. Tamaudum Mausoleum, Shuri; 100y. Hosho-chai Bridge.

27 Reception at Shuri Castle

28 Perry and American Fleet at Naha Harbour 29 Chofu Ota and Matrix

1953. Centenary of Commodore Perry's Visit to Okinawa.
39 **27** 3y. purple . . . . 12·00 4·00
40 **28** 6y. blue . . . . 2·25 2·40

1953. 3rd Press Week.
41 **29** 4y. brown . . . . 12·00 5·00

30 Wine Flask to fit around Waist 33 Shigo Toma and Pen-nib

1954.
42 **30** 4y. brown 50 35
43 – 15y. red . . . . 2·25 1·75
44 – 20y. orange . . . . 3·25 2·25
DESIGNS: 15y. Tung Dar Bon (lacquer bowl); 20y. Kasuri (textile pattern).

1954. 4th Press Week.
45 **33** 4y. blue . . . . 10·00 3·50

34 Noguni Shrine and Sweet Potatoes 35 Stylized Trees

1955. 350th Anniv of Introduction of Sweet Potato Plant.
46 **34** 4y. blue . . . . 10·00 4·00

1956. Afforestation Week.
47 **35** 4y. green . . . . 8·00 3·00

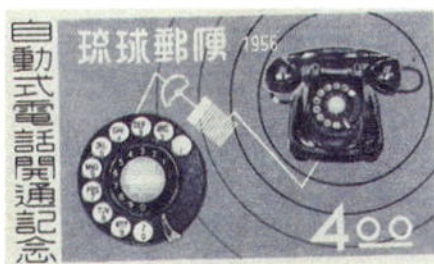

38 Nidotekito Dance 39 Telephone and Dial

1956. National Dances.
48 – 5y. purple . . . . 1·10 60
49 – 8y. violet . . . . 1·40 1·25
50 **38** 14y. brown . . . . 2·25 2·25
DESIGNS: 5y. Willow dance; 8y. Straw-hat dance.

1956. Inauguration of Telephone Dialling System.
51 **39** 4y. violet . . . . 12·00 8·00

40 Floral Garland 41 Flying Goddess

1956. New Year.
52 **40** 2y. multicoloured . . . . . 2·00 1·40

1957. Air.
53 **41** 15y. green . . . . 2·00 40
54 20y. red . . . . 4·50 3·00
55 35y. green . . . . 10·00 4·00
56 45y. brown . . . . 16·00 6·00
57 60y. grey . . . . 22·00 8·50

42 "Rocket" Pencils 43 Phoenix

1957. 7th Press Week.
58 **42** 4y. blue 55 55

1957. New Year.
59 **43** 2y. multicoloured 40 20

44 Various Ryukyuan Postage Stamps

1958. 10th Anniv of First Postage Stamps of Ryukyu Islands.
60 **44** 4y. multicoloured . . . . . 1·00 60

45 Stylized Dollar Sign over Yen Symbol

1958. With or without gum (Nos. 68/69), no gum (others).
61 **45** $\frac{1}{2}$c. yellow 25 20
62 1c. green 25 20
63 2c. blue 25 25
64 3c. red 20 15
65 4c. green 60 45
66 5c. brown . . . . 2·00 50
67 10c. blue . . . . 3·25 50
68 25c. blue . . . . 3·50 80
69 50c. grey . . . . 7·00 1·00
70 $1 purple . . . . 10·00 1·25

46 Gateway of Courtesy

1958. Restoration of Shuri Gateway.
71 **46** 3c. multicoloured . . . . . 1·25 50

47 Lion Dance 48 Trees

1958. New Year.
72 **47** 1$\frac{1}{2}$c. multicoloured 30 25

1959. Afforestation Week.
73 **48** 3c. multicoloured . . . . . 1·50 1·25

49 Atlas Moth 50 Hibiscus

1959. Japanese Biological Teachers' Conference, Okinawa.
74 **49** 3c. multicoloured . . . . . 2·00 1·25

1959. Multicoloured. (a) Inscr as in T **50**.
75 $\frac{1}{2}$c. Type **50** 30 20
76 3c. Moorish idol . . . . . . 1·10 25
77 8c. Zebra moon, banded bonnet and textile cone (shells) . . . . 8·00 2·00
78 13c. Leaf butterfly (value at left) . . . . 2·00 1·50
79 17c. Jellyfish . . . . 22·00 5·50
(b) Inscr smaller and 13c. with value at right.
87 $\frac{1}{2}$c. Type **50** 30 15
88 3c. As No. 76 . . . . 2·00 20
89 8c. As No. 77 . . . . 2·50 1·00
90 13c. As No. 78 . . . . 1·75 1·00
91 17c. As No. 79 . . . . 8·00 3·25

改訂 9¢

55 Yakazi (Ryukyuan toy) (56)

1959. New Year.
80 **55** 1$\frac{1}{2}$c. multicoloured 80 40

1959. Air. Surch as T **56**.
81 **41** 9c. on 15y. green . . . . . 2·00 40
82 14c. on 20y. red . . . . . . 3·50 3·00
83 19c. on 35y. green . . . . . 5·00 4·00
84 27c. on 45y. brown . . . . 10·00 6·00
85 35c. on 60y. grey . . . . . 14·00 8·00

57 University Badge 60 "Munjuru"

1960. 10th Anniv of University of the Ryukyus.
86 **57** 3c. multicoloured . . . . . 1·25 60

1960. Air. Surch.
92 **30** 9c. on 4y. brown . . . . . 5·00 60
93 – 14c. on 5y. purple (No. 48) 3·00 2·00
94 – 19c. on 15y. red (No. 43) . . 5·00 2·75
95 **38** 27c. on 14y. brown . . . . 6·00 4·25
96 – 35c. on 20y. orange (No. 44) 7·00 5·25

1960. Ryukyuan Dances. Mult. (a) Inscr as in T **60**.
97 1c. Type **60** . . . . 2·00 1·00
98 2$\frac{1}{2}$c. "Inohabushi" . . . . . 1·75 1·00
99 5c. "Hatomabushi" . . . . . 1·00 1·00
100 10c. "Hanafu" . . . . 1·50 1·00
(b) As T **60** but additionally inscr "RYUKYUS".
107 1c. Type **60** 15 15
108 2$\frac{1}{2}$c. As No. 98 . . . . . . 15 15
109 4c. As No. 98 . . . . 20 15
110 5c. As No. 99 . . . . 30 25
111 10c. As No. 100 . . . . . . 50 15
112 20c. "Shudun" . . . . 1·25 35
113 25c. "Haodori" . . . . . . 1·25 60
114 50c. "Nobori Kuduchi" . . . 1·75 60
115 $1 "Koteibushi" . . . . . . 2·25 70

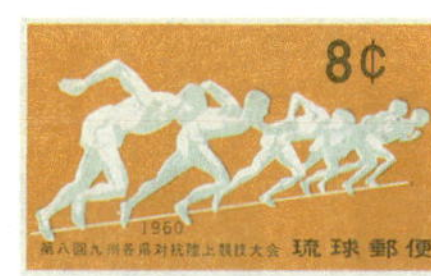

65 Start of Race

1960. 8th Kyushu Athletic Meeting.
101 – 3c. red, green and blue . . 5·00 1·50
102 **65** 8c. green and orange . . . 1·75 1·00
DESIGN: 3c. Torch and coastal scene.

66 Little Egret and Rising Sun

1960. National Census.
103 **66** 3c. brown . . . . 6·25 2·50

67 Bull Fight

1960. New Year.
104 **67** 1$\frac{1}{2}$c. brown, buff and blue 1·00 60

68 Native Pine Tree

1961. Afforestation Week.
105 **68** 3c. deep green, red & green 1·75 90

69 Naha, Junk, Liner and City Seal

1961. 40th Anniv of Naha City.
106 **69** 3c. turquoise . . . . . . 2·50 1·25

74 Flying Goddess 79 White Silver Temple

1961. Air.
116 **74** 9c. multicoloured 50 15
117 – 14c. multicoloured 70 60
118 – 19c. multicoloured . . . . 1·25 75
119 – 27c. multicoloured . . . . 1·50 75
120 – 35c. multicoloured . . . . 2·00 75
DESIGNS: 14c. Flying goddess playing flute; 19c. Wind god; 27c. Wind god (different); 35c. Flying goddess over trees.

1961. Unification of Itoman District and Takamine, Kanegushiku and Miwa Villages.
121 **79** 3c. brown . . . . 1·25 75

80 Books and Bird 81 Sunrise and Eagles

1961. 10th Anniv of Ryukyu Book Week.
122 **80** 3c. multicoloured . . . . . 1·25 75

1961. New Year.
123 **81** 1$\frac{1}{2}$c. red, black and gold . . 3·25 1·00

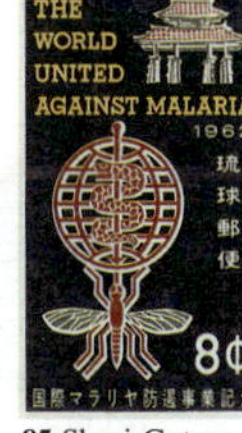

82 Govt Building, Steps and Trees 85 Shuri Gate and Campaign Emblem

1962. 10th Anniv of Ryukyu Government. Mult.
124 1$\frac{1}{2}$c. Type **82** 60 60
125 3c. Government building . . 90 75

1962. Malaria Eradication. Multicoloured.
126 3c. "Anopheles hyrcanus sinensis" (mosquito) . . . 70 60
127 8c. Type **85** . . . . 1·25 1·75

86 Windmill, Dolls and Horse 87 "Hibiscus lilaceus"

1962. Children's Day.
128 **86** 3c. multicoloured . . . . . 2·00 1·25

1962. Ryukyu Flowers. Multicoloured.
129 $\frac{1}{2}$c. Type **87** 20 15
142 1$\frac{1}{2}$c. "Etithyllum strictum" . . 30 20
130 2c. "Ixora chinensis" 20 25
131 3c. "Erythrina indica" . . . 50 20
132 3c. "Caesalpinia pulcherrima" 20 20
133 8c. "Schima mertensiana" . . 75 25
134 13c. "Impatiens balsamina" . . 1·00 50
135 15c. "Hamaomoto" (herb) . . 1·25 55
136 17c. "Alpinia speciosa" . . . 1·00 30
No. 142 is smaller, 18$\frac{3}{4}$ × 22$\frac{1}{2}$ mm.

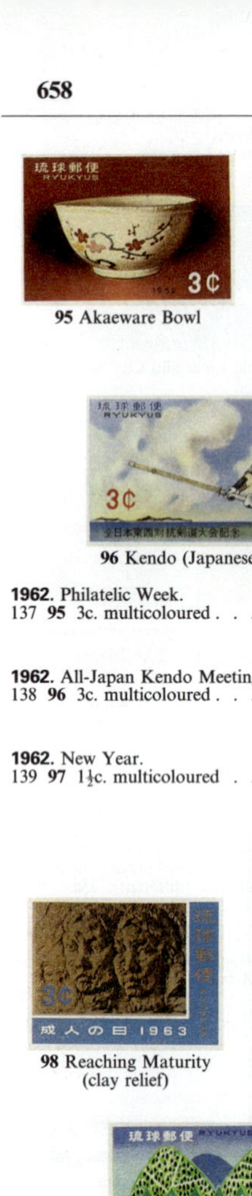

95 Akaewarc Bowl

97 "Hare and Water" (textile design)

96 Kendo (Japanese Fencing)

1962. Philatelic Week.
137 **95** 3c. multicoloured . . . . . 5·00 2·25

1962. All-Japan Kendo Meeting.
138 **96** 3c. multicoloured . . . . . 5·00 2·50

1962. New Year.
139 **97** 1½c. multicoloured . . . . 2·50 1·00

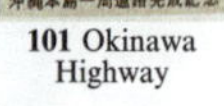

98 Reaching Maturity (clay relief)

101 Okinawa Highway

99 Trees and Wooded Hills

1963. Adults' Day.
140 **98** 3c. gold, black and blue . . 80 50

1963. Afforestation Week.
141 **99** 3c. multicoloured 80 50

1963. Opening of Okinawa Highway.
143 **101** 3c. multicoloured . . . . 1·00 60

102 Black Kites over Islands

1963. Bird Week.
144 **102** 3c. multicoloured . . . . 1·25 1·00

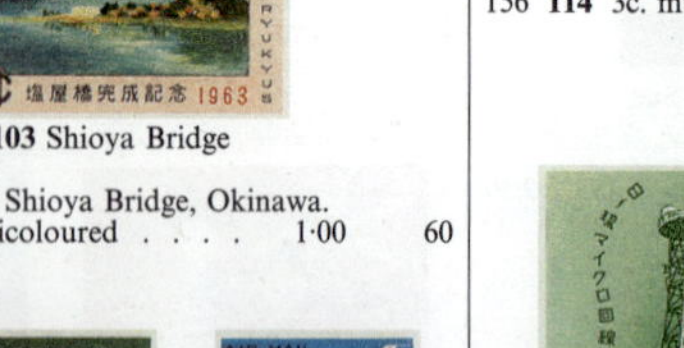

103 Shioya Bridge

1963. Opening of Shioya Bridge, Okinawa.
145 **103** 3c. multicoloured . . . . 1·00 60

104 Lacquerware Bowl

105 Convair 880 Jetliner and Shuri Gate

1963. Philatelic Week.
146 **104** 3c. multicoloured . . . . 3·25 1·50

1963. Air.
147 **105** 5½c. multicoloured 25 20
148 – 7c. black, red and blue . . 35 30
DESIGN: 7c. Convair 880 jetliner over sea.

107 Map and Emblem

1963. Meeting of Junior Int Chamber, Naha.
149 **107** 3c. multicoloured 60 50

108 Nakagusuku Castle Ruins

1963. Ancient Buildings Protection Week.
150 **108** 3c. multicoloured 90 50

109 Flame

110 Bingata "dragon" (textile design)

1963. 15th Anniv of Declaration of Human Rights.
151 **109** 3c. multicoloured 70 40

1963. New Year.
152 **110** 1½c. multicoloured 40 30

111 Carnation

112 Pineapples and Sugar-cane

1964. Mothers' Day.
153 **111** 3c. multicoloured 60 30

1964. Agricultural Census.
154 **112** 3c. multicoloured 45 30

113 Hand-woven Sash

114 Girl Scout and Emblem

1964. Philatelic Week.
155 **113** 3c. brown, blue and pink 60 30

1964. 10th Anniv of Ryukyu Girl Scouts.
156 **114** 3c. multicoloured 40 25

115 Transmitting Tower

117 Shuri Gate and Olympic Torch

1964. Inauguration of Ryukyu–Jap'an Microwave Link.
157 **115** 3c. green and black . . . 1·00 85
158 – 8c. blue and black . . . . 1·40 1·00
DESIGN: 8c. "Bowl" receiving aerial.
Both stamps have "1963" cancelled by bars and "1964" inserted in black.

1964. Passage of Olympic Torch through Okinawa.
159 **117** 3c. multicoloured 40 30

118 "Naihanchi" (Karate stance)

1964. Karate ("self-defence"). Multicoloured.
160 3c. Type **118** 65 40
161 3c. "Makiwara" (karate training) 60 50
162 3c. "Kumite" exercise 55 50

121 "Miyara Dunchi" (old Ryukyuan Residence)

1964. Ancient Buildings Protection Week.
163 **121** 3c. multicoloured 40 30

122 Bingata "snake" (textile design)

123 Boy Scouts, Badge and Shuri Gate

1964. New Year.
164 **122** 1½c. multicoloured 45 35

1965. 10th Anniv of Ryukyuan Boy Scouts.
165 **123** 3c. multicoloured 50 40

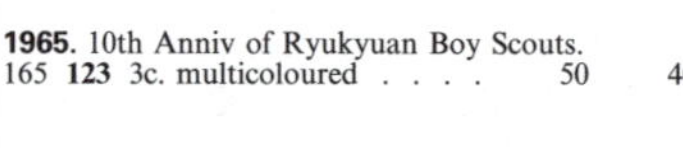
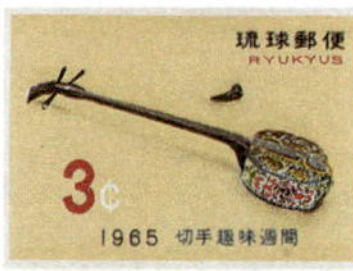

124 "Samisen" (musical instrument)

1965. Philatelic Week.
166 **124** 3c. multicoloured 50 40

125 Stadium

1965. Completion of Onoyama Sports Ground.
167 **125** 3c. multicoloured 30 25

126 Kin Power Station

127 I.C.Y. Emblem and "Globe"

1965. Completion of Kin Power Plant.
168 **126** 3c. multicoloured 30 25

1965. International Co-operation Year and 20th Anniv of United Nations.
169 **127** 3c. multicoloured 30 25

128 City Hall, Naha

1965. Completion of Naha City Hall.
170 **128** 3c. multicoloured 30 25

129 Semaruhakogame Turtle

1965. Ryukyuan Turtles. Multicoloured.
171 3c. Type **129** 80 35
172 3c. Taimai or hawksbill turtle 65 35
173 3c. Yamagame or hill tortoise 65 35

132 Bingata "horse" (textile design)

133 Pryer's Woodpecker

1965. New Year.
174 **132** 1½c. multicoloured 30 25

1966. "Natural Monument" (Wildlife). Mult.
175 3c. Type **133** 60 30
176 3c. Sika deer 50 25
177 3c. Dugong 50 25

136 Pacific Swallow

137 Lilies and Ruins

1966. Bird Week.
178 **136** 3c. multicoloured 45 25

1966. Memorial Day (Battle of Okinawa).
179 **137** 3c. multicoloured 30 25

138 University of the Ryukyus

139 Lacquer Box

1966. Transfer of University of the Ryukyus to Government Administration.
180 **138** 3c. multicoloured 30 25

1966. Philatelic Week.
181 **139** 3c. multicoloured 30 25

140 Ryukyuan Tiled House

141 "GRI" Museum, Shuri

1966. 20th Anniv of UNESCO.
182 **140** 3c. multicoloured 30 25

1966. Completion of Government Museum, Shuri.
183 **141** 3c. multicoloured 30 25

142 Nakasone-Tuimya Tomb

143 Bingata "ram" (textile design)

1966. Ancient Buildings Protection Week.
184 **142** 3c. multicoloured 30 25

1966. New Year.
185 **143** 1½c. multicoloured 30 25

144 Tomato Anemonefish **149** Tsuboya Urn

1966. Tropical Fish. Multicoloured.
186 3c. Type **144** 50 30
187 3c. Blue-spotted boxfish . . . 50 30
188 3c. Long-nosed butterflyfish 50 30
189 3c. Clown triggerfish 50 30
190 3c. Saddle butterflyfish . . . 50 30

1967. Philatelic Week.
191 **149** 3c. multicoloured 40 25

150 Episcopal Mitre **155** Roof Tiles and Emblem

1967. Sea Shells. Multicoloured.
192 3c. Type **150** 40 25
193 3c. Venus comb murex ("Murex (Aranea) triremus") 40 25
194 3c. Chiragra spider conch ("Lambis (Harpago) chiragra") 60 40
195 3c. Great green turban ("Turbo (Olearia) marmoratus") 60 40
196 3c. Bubble conch ("Euprotomus bulla") . . 80 40

1967. International Tourist Year.
197 **155** 3c. multicoloured 30 25

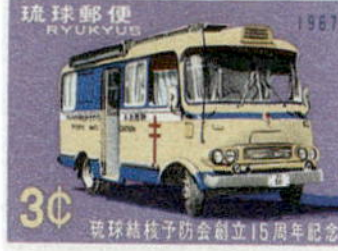

156 Mobile Clinic

1967. 15th Anniv of Anti-T.B. Association.
198 **156** 3c. multicoloured 35 20

157 Hojo Bridge, Enkaku

1967. Ancient Buildings Protection Week.
199 **157** 3c. multicoloured 30 25

158 Bingata "monkey" (textile design) **159** T.V. Tower and Map

1967. New Year.
200 **158** 1½c. multicoloured 30 25

1967. Opening of T.V. Broadcasting Stations in Miyako and Yaeyama.
201 **159** 3c. multicoloured 30 25

160 Dr. Nakachi and Assistant **161** Medicine Case (after Sokei Dana)

1968. 120th Anniv of 1st Ryukyu Vaccination (by Dr. Kijin Nakachi).
202 **160** 3c. multicoloured 30 25

1968. Philatelic Week.
203 **161** 3c. multicoloured 50 30

162 Young Man, Book, Map and Library

1968. Library Week.
204 **162** 3c. multicoloured 45 30

163 Postmen with Ryukyu Stamp of 1948

1968. 20th Anniv of 1st Ryukyu Islands Stamps.
205 **163** 3c. multicoloured 40 30

164 Temple Gate **165** Old Man Dancing

1968. Restoration of Enkaku Temple Gate.
206 **164** 3c. multicoloured 40 30

1968. Old People's Day.
207 **165** 3c. multicoloured 40 30

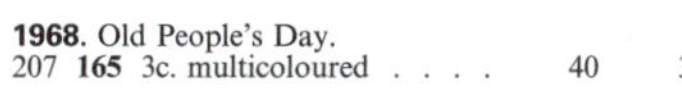

166 "Mictyris longicarpus"

1968. Crabs. Multicoloured.
208 3c. Type **166** 80 60
209 3c. "Uca dubia" 80 60
210 3c. "Baptozius vinosus" . . . 80 60
211 3c. "Cardisoma carnifex" . . 80 60
212 3c. "Ocypode ceratophthalma" 80 60

171 Saraswati Pavilion **172** Player

1968. Ancient Buildings Protection Week.
213 **171** 3c. multicoloured 35 25

1968. 35th All-Japan East v West Men's Softball Tennis Tournament, Onoyama.
214 **172** 3c. multicoloured 40 25

173 Bingata "cock" (textile design) **174** Boxer

1968. New Year.
215 **173** 1½c. multicoloured 30 20

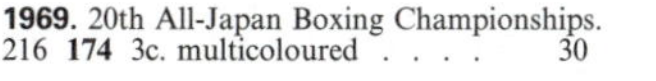

1969. 20th All-Japan Boxing Championships.
216 **174** 3c. multicoloured 30 25

175 Inkwell Screen **176** UHF Antennae and Map

1969. Philatelic Week.
217 **175** 3c. multicoloured 35 25

1969. Inauguration of Okinawa–Sakishima U.H.F. Radio Service.
218 **176** 3c. multicoloured 30 25

177 Gate of Courtesy **178** "Tug of War" Festival

1969. 22nd All-Japan Formative Education Study Conference, Naha.
219 **177** 3c. multicoloured 30 25

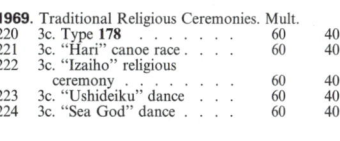

1969. Traditional Religious Ceremonies. Mult.
220 3c. Type **178** 60 40
221 3c. "Hari" canoe race 60 40
222 3c. "Izaiho" religious ceremony 60 40
223 3c. "Ushideiku" dance . . . 60 40
224 3c. "Sea God" dance 60 40

1969. No. 131 surch.
225 ½c. on 3c. multicoloured . . . 15 25

184 Nakamura-Ke

1969. Ancient Buildings Protection Week.
226 **184** 3c. multicoloured 25 20

185 Kyuzo Toyama and Map **186** Bingata "dog and flowers" (textile design)

1969. 70th Anniv of Toyama's Ryukyu–Hawaii Emigration Project.
227 **185** 3c. multicoloured 40 35
No. 227 has "1970" cancelled by bars and "1969" inserted in black.

1969. New Year.
228 **186** 1½c. multicoloured 20 20

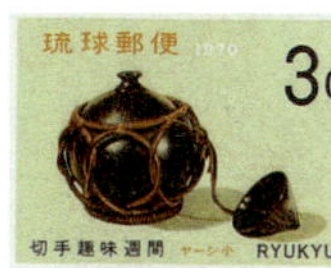

187 Sake Flask

1970. Philatelic Week.
229 **187** 3c. multicoloured 35 20

188 "Shushin-Kaneiri"

189 "Chu-nusudu"

190 "Mekarushi"

191 "Nidotichiuchi"

192 "Kokonomaki"

1970. "Kumi-Odori" Ryukyu Theatre. Mult.
230 **188** 3c. multicoloured 70 55
231 **189** 3c. multicoloured 70 55
232 **190** 3c. multicoloured 70 55
233 **191** 3c. multicoloured 70 55
234 **192** 3c. multicoloured 70 55

193 Observatory **194** Noboru Jahana (politician)

1970. Completion of Underwater Observatory, Busena-Misaki, Nago.
240 **193** 3c. multicoloured 30 25

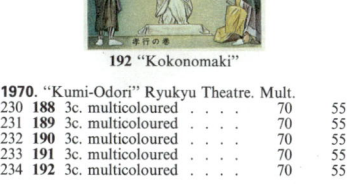

1970. Famous Ryukyuans.
241 **194** 3c. purple 60 60
242 – 3c. green 70 60
243 – 3c. black 60 60
PORTRAITS: No. 242, Saion Gushichan Bunjaku (statesman); 243, Choho Giwan (Regent).

197 "Population **198** "Great Cycad of Une"

1970. Population Census.
244 **197** 3c. multicoloured 25 25

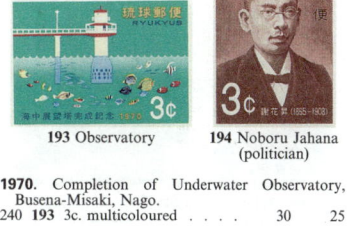

1970. Ancient Buildings Protection Week.
245 **198** 3c. multicoloured 40 25

199 Ryukyu Islands, Flag and Japan Diet **200** "Wild Boar" (Bingata textile design)

1970. Election of Ryukyu Representatives to the Japanese Diet.
246 **199** 3c. multicoloured 85 60

1970. New Year.
247 **200** 1½c. multicoloured 30 25

201 "Jibata" (hand-loom)

202 "Filature" (spinning-wheel)

203 Farm-worker wearing "Shurunnu" Coat and "Kubagasa" Hat

204 Woman using "Shiri-Ushi" (rice huller)

205 Fisherman's "Umi-Fujo" (box) and "Yutui" (bailer)

1971. Ryukyu Handicrafts.

248	**201**	3c. multicoloured	40	30
249	**202**	3c. multicoloured	40	30
250	**203**	3c. multicoloured	40	30
251	**204**	3c. multicoloured	40	30
252	**205**	3c. multicoloured	40	30

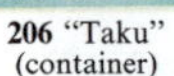

206 "Taku" (container)

208 Restored Battlefield, Okinawa

207 Civic Emblem with Old and New City Views

1971. Philatelic Week.

253	**206**	3c. multicoloured	35	25

1971. 50th Anniv of Naha's City Status.

254	**207**	3c. multicoloured	30	25

1971. Government Parks. Multicoloured.

255	3c. Type **208**	30	30
256	3c. Haneji Inland Sea	30	30
257	4c. Yabuchi Island	30	30

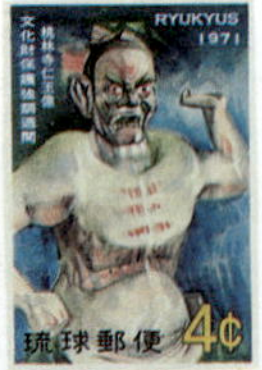

211 Deva King, Torinji Temple

212 "Rat" (Bingata textile pattern)

1971. Anicent Buildings Protection Week.

258	**211**	4c. multicoloured	25	25

1971. New Year.

259	**212**	2c. multicoloured	30	20

213 Student-nurse and Candle

214 Islands and Sunset

1971. 25th Anniv of Nurses' Training Scheme.

260	**213**	4c. multicoloured	25	25

1972. Maritime Scenery. Multicoloured.

261	5c. Type **214**	30	70
262	5c. Coral reef (horiz)	30	70
263	5c. Island and short-tailed albatrosses	95	45

217 Dove and Flags of Japan and U.S.A

218 "Yushibin" (ceremonial sake container)

1972. Ratification of Treaty for Return of Ryukyu Islands to Japan.

264	**217**	5c. multicoloured	40	1·00

1972. Philatelic Week.

265	**218**	5c. multicoloured	50	1·00

SPECIAL DELIVERY STAMP

E **13** Sea-horse

1951.

E18	E **13**	5y. blue	30·00	15·00

INDEX

COLLECT

STAMPS OF THE WORLD

Priority order form

Four easy ways to order

Phone:
020 7836 8444
Overseas: +44 (0)20 7836 8444

Fax:
020 7557 4499
Overseas: +44 (0)20 7557 4499

Email:
stampsales@stanleygibbons.com

Post:
Stamp Mail Order Department
Stanley Gibbons Ltd, 399 Strand
London, WC2R 0LX, England

Customer details

Account Number ______________________________

Name ______________________________

Address ______________________________

____________________ Postcode __________

Country ____________________ Email __________

Tel no ____________________ Fax no __________

Payment details

Registered Postage & Packing £3.60

I enclose my cheque/postal order for £............ in full payment. Please make cheques/postal orders payable to Stanley Gibbons Ltd. Cheques must be in £ sterling and drawn on a UK bank

Please debit my credit card for £............. in full payment. I have completed the Credit Card section below.

Card Number

□□□□□□□□□□□□□□□□

Start Date (Switch & Amex) □□□□

Expiry Date □□□□

Issue No (switch) □□

Signature ____________________ Date ____________________

COLLECT

STAMPS OF THE WORLD

Condition (mint/UM/used)	Country	SG No.	Description	Price	Office use only

POSTAGE & PACKAGING	£3.60
GRAND TOTAL	£

Please complete payment, name and address details overleaf